Peterson's
Two-Year
Colleges
2005

THOMSON

PETERSON'S

Australia • Canada • Mexico • Singapore • Spain • United Kingdom • United States

About Thomson Peterson's

Thomson Peterson's (www.petersons.com) is a leading provider of education information and advice, with books and online resources focusing on education search, test preparation, and financial aid. Its Web site offers searchable databases and interactive tools for contacting educational institutions, online practice tests and instruction, and planning tools for securing financial aid. Thomson Peterson's serves 110 million education consumers annually.

For more information, contact Thomson Peterson's, 2000 Lenox Drive, Lawrenceville, NJ 08648; 800-338-3282; or find us on the World Wide Web at www.petersons.com/about.

Editor: Fern A. Oram; Production Editor: Linda Seghers; Copy Editors: Bret Bollmann, Jim Colbert, Michele N. Firestone, Michael Haines, Sally Ross, Jill C. Schwartz, Pam Sullivan, and Valerie Bolus Vaughan; Research Project Manager: Daniel Margolin; Research Associates: Mary Meyer-Penniston, Jared A. Stein, and Amy L. Weber; Programmers: Phyllis Johnson and Alex Lin; Manufacturing Manager: Ivona Skibicki; Composition Manager: Linda M. Williams; Cover Design: Allison Sullivan; Client Service Representatives: Mimi Kaufman, Lois Regina Milton, Mary Ann Murphy, Jim Swinarski, and Eric Wallace; Contributing Editors: Kitty M. Villa and Richard Woodland.

ISSN 0894-9328
ISBN 0-7689-1380-2

Printed in the United States of America

10 9 8 7 6 5 4 3 2 1   06 05 04

Thirty-fifth Edition

Contents

APPENDIX

INDEXES

A Note from the Peterson's Editors

For more than 35 years, Peterson's has given students and parents the most comprehensive, up-to-date information on undergraduate institutions in the United States. Peterson's researches the data published in *Peterson's Two-Year Colleges* each year. The information is furnished by the colleges and is accurate at the time of publishing.

This guide also features advice and tips on the college search and selection process, such as how to decide if a two-year college is right for you, how to approach transferring between colleges, and what's in store for adults returning to college. If you seem to be getting more, not less, anxious about choosing and getting into the right college, *Peterson's Two-Year Colleges* provides just the right help, giving you the information you need to make important college decisions and ace the admission process.

Opportunities abound for students, and this guide can help you find what you want in a number of ways:

- In "What You Need to Know About Two-Year Colleges," David R. Pierce, former President of the American Association of Community Colleges, outlines the basic features and advantages of two-year colleges. "Surviving Standardized Tests" gives an overview of the common examinations students take prior to attending college. "Who's Paying for This? Financial Aid Basics" provides guidelines for financing your college education. "Frequently Asked Questions About Transferring" takes a look at the two-year college scene from the perspective of a student who is looking toward the day when he or she may pursue additional education at a four-year institution. "Returning to School: Advice for Adult Students" is an analysis of the pros and cons (mostly pros) of returning to college after already having begun a professional career. "What International Students Need to Know About Admission to U.S. Colleges" is an article designed particularly for students overseas who are considering a U.S. college education. "Searching for Two-Year Colleges Online" outlines why you'll want to visit Petersons.com for even more college search and selection resources. Finally, "How to Use This Guide" gives details on the data in this guide: what terms mean and why they're here.

- If you already have specifics in mind, such as a particular institution or major, turn to the easy-to-use **Quick-Reference Chart** or **Indexes.** You can look up a particular feature—location and programs offered—or use the alphabetical index and immediately find the colleges that meet your criteria.

- For information about particular colleges, turn to the **Profiles of Two-Year Colleges** section. Here our comprehensive college descriptions are arranged alphabetically by state. They provide a complete picture of need-to-know information about every accredited two-year college—from admission to graduation, including expenses, financial aid, majors, computerization, and campus safety. All the information you need to apply is placed together at the conclusion of each college profile. In addition, for nearly 100 colleges, two-page narrative descriptions appear in the **In-Depth Descriptions of Two-Year Colleges** section, in the back of the book. These descriptions are paid for and written by admissions deans and provide great detail about each college. They are edited to provide a consistent format across entries for your ease of comparison.

Peterson's publishes a full line of resources to help you and your family with any information you need to guide you through the admissions process. Peterson's publications can be found at your local bookstore, library, and high school guidance office—or visit us on the Web at www.petersons.com.

Colleges will be pleased to know that Peterson's helped you in your selection. Admissions staff members are more than happy to answer questions, address specific problems and help in any way they can. The editors at Peterson's wish you great success in your college search.

The College Admissions Process:

An overview

What You Need to Know About Two-Year Colleges

David R. Pierce

Two-year colleges—better known as community colleges—are often called "the people's colleges." With their open-door policies (admission is open to individuals with a high school diploma or its equivalent), community colleges provide access to higher education for millions of Americans who might otherwise be excluded from higher education. Community college students are diverse, of all ages, races, and economic backgrounds. While many community college students enroll full-time, an equally large number attend on a part-time basis so they can fulfill employment and family commitments as they advance their education.

Today, there are more than 1,900 community colleges in the United States. They enroll more than 5.6 million students, who represent 45 percent of all undergraduates in the United States. Nearly 55 percent of all first-time freshmen begin their higher education in a community college.

Community colleges can also be referred to as either technical or junior colleges, and they may either be under public or independent control. What unites these two-year colleges is that they are regionally accredited, postsecondary institutions, whose highest credential awarded is the associate degree. With few exceptions, community colleges offer a comprehensive curriculum, which includes transfer, technical, and continuing education programs.

IMPORTANT FACTORS IN A COMMUNITY COLLEGE EDUCATION

The student who attends a community college can count on receiving high-quality instruction in a supportive learning community. This setting frees the student to pursue his or her own goals, nurture special talents, explore new fields of learning, and develop the capacity for lifelong learning.

From the student's perspective, four characteristics capture the essence of community colleges:

- They are community-based institutions that work in close partnership with high schools, community groups, and employers in extending high-quality programs at convenient times and places.

- Community colleges are cost effective. Annual tuition and fees at public community colleges average approximately half those at public four-year colleges and less than 15 percent of private four-year institutions. In addition, since most community colleges are generally close to their students' homes, these students can also save a significant amount of money on the room, board, and transportation expenses traditionally associated with a college education.

- They provide a caring environment, with faculty members who are expert instructors, known for excellent teaching and for meeting students at the point of their individual needs, regardless of age, sex, race, current job status, or previous academic preparation. Community colleges join a strong curriculum with a broad range of counseling and career services that are intended to assist students in making the most of their educational opportunities.

- Many offer comprehensive programs, including transfer curricula in such liberal arts programs as chemistry, psychology, and business management, that lead directly to a baccalaureate degree and career programs that prepare students for employment or assist those already employed in upgrading their skills. For those students who need to strengthen their academic skills, community colleges also offer a wide range of developmental programs in mathematics, languages, and learning skills, designed to prepare the student for success in college studies.

GETTING TO KNOW YOUR TWO-YEAR COLLEGE

The first step in determining the quality of a community college is to check the status of its accreditation. Once you have established that a community college is appropriately accredited, find out as much as you can about the programs and services it has to offer. Much of that information can be found in materials the college provides. However, the best way to learn about a college is to visit in person.

During a campus visit, be prepared to ask a lot of questions. Talk to students, faculty members, administrators, and counselors about the college and its programs, particularly those in which you have a special interest. Ask about available certificates and associate degrees. Don't be shy. Do what you can to dig below the surface. Ask college officials about the transfer rate to four-year colleges. If a college emphasizes student services, find out what particular assistance is offered, such as educational or career guidance. Colleges are eager to provide you with the information you need to make informed decisions.

COMMUNITY COLLEGES CAN SAVE YOU MONEY

If you are able to live at home while you attend college, you will certainly save money on room and board, but it does cost something to commute. Many two-year colleges can now offer you instruction in your own home through cable television or public broadcast stations or through home study courses that can save both time and money. Look into all the options, and be sure to add up all the costs of attending various colleges before deciding which is best for you.

FINANCIAL AID

Many students who attend community colleges are eligible for a range of financial aid programs, including Federal Pell Grants, Perkins and Stafford Loans, state aid, and on-campus jobs. Your high school counselor or the financial aid officer at a community college will also be able to help you. It is in your interest to apply for financial aid months in advance of the date you intend to start your college program, so find out early what assistance is available to you. While many community colleges are able to help students who make a last-minute decision to attend college, either through short-term loans or emergency grants, if you are considering entering college and think you might need financial aid, it is best to find out as much as you can as early as you can.

WORKING AND GOING TO SCHOOL

Many two-year college students maintain full-time or part-time employment while they earn their degrees. Over the years, a steadily growing number of students have chosen to attend community colleges while they fulfill family and employment responsibilities. To enable these students to balance the demands of home, work, and school, most community colleges offer classes at night and on weekends.

For the full-time student, the usual length of time it takes to obtain an associate degree is two years. However, your length of study will depend on the course load you take: the fewer credits you earn each term, the longer it will take you to earn a degree. To assist you in moving more quickly to your degree, many community colleges now award credit through examination or for equivalent

knowledge gained through relevant life experiences. Be certain to find out the credit options that are available to you at the college in which you are interested. You may discover that it will take less time to earn a degree than you first thought.

PREPARATION FOR TRANSFER

Studies have repeatedly shown that students who first attend a community college and then transfer to a four-year college or university do at least as well academically as the students who entered the four-year institutions as freshmen. Most community colleges have agreements with nearby four-year institutions to make transfer of credits easier. If you are thinking of transferring, be sure to meet with a counselor or faculty adviser before choosing your courses. You will want to map out a course of study with transfer in mind. Make sure you also find out the credit-transfer requirements of the four-year institution you might want to attend.

ATTENDING A TWO-YEAR COLLEGE IN ANOTHER REGION

Although many community colleges serve a specific county or district, they are committed (to the extent of their ability) to the goal of equal educational opportunity without regard to economic status, race, creed, color, sex, or national origin. Independent two-year colleges recruit from a much broader geographical area—throughout the United States and, increasingly, around the world.

Although some community colleges do provide on-campus housing for their students, most do not. However, even if on-campus housing is not available, most colleges do have housing referral services.

NEW CAREER OPPORTUNITIES

Community colleges realize that many entering students are not sure about the field in which they want to focus their studies or the career they would like to pursue. Often, students discover fields and careers they never knew existed. Community colleges have the resources to help students identify areas of career interest and to set challenging occupational goals.

Once a career goal is set, you can be confident that a community college will provide job-relevant, technical education. About half of the students who take courses for credit at community colleges do so to prepare for employment or to acquire or upgrade skills for their current job. Especially helpful in charting a career path is the assistance of a counselor or a faculty adviser, who can discuss job opportunities in your chosen field and help you map out your course of study.

In addition, since community colleges have close ties to their communities, they are in constant contact with leaders in business, industry, organized labor, and public life. Community colleges work with these individuals and their organizations to prepare students for direct entry into the world of work. For example, some community colleges have established partnerships with local businesses and industries to provide specialized training programs. Some also provide the academic portion of apprenticeship training, while others offer extensive job-shadowing and cooperative education opportunities. Be sure to examine all of the career-preparation opportunities offered by the community colleges in which you are interested.

David R. Pierce is the former President of the American Association of Community Colleges.

Surviving Standardized Tests

WHAT ARE STANDARDIZED TESTS?

Colleges and universities in the United States use tests to help evaluate applicants' readiness for admission or to place them in appropriate courses. The tests that are most frequently used by colleges are the ACT Assessment of American College Testing, Inc., and the College Board's SAT. In addition, the Educational Testing Service (ETS) offers the TOEFL test, which evaluates the English-language proficiency of nonnative speakers. The tests are offered at designated testing centers located at high schools and colleges throughout the United States and U.S. territories and at testing centers in various countries throughout the world. The ACT Assessment test and the SAT tests are each taken by more than a million students each year. The TOEFL test is taken by more than 700,000 students each year.

Upon request, special accommodations for students with documented visual, hearing, physical, or learning disabilities are available. Examples of special accommodations include tests in Braille or large print and such aids as a reader, recorder, magnifying glass, or sign language interpreter. Additional testing time may be allowed in some instances. Contact the appropriate testing program or your guidance counselor for details on how to request special accommodations.

College Board SAT Program

Currently, the SAT Program consists of the SAT I Reasoning Test and the SAT II Subject Tests. The SAT I is a 3-hour test made up of seven sections, primarily multiple-choice, that measures verbal and mathematical abilities. The three verbal sections test vocabulary, verbal reasoning, and critical reading skills. Emphasis is placed on reading passages, which are 400–850 words in length. Some reading passages are paired; the second opposes, supports, or in some way complements the point of view expressed in the first. The three mathematics sections test a student's ability to solve problems involving arithmetic, algebra, and geometry. They include questions that require students to produce their own responses, in addition to questions that students can choose from four or five answer choices. Calculators may be used on the SAT I mathematics sections. Beginning in the spring of 2005, the SAT will be a 3-hour-and-35-minute test that focuses on college success skills of writing, critical reading, and mathematics. The new writing component will measure grammar and usage and include a short, student-written essay.

The SAT II Subject Tests are 1-hour tests, primarily multiple-choice, in specific subjects that measure students' knowledge of these subjects and their ability to apply that knowledge. Some colleges may require or recommend these tests for placement, or even admission. The Subject Tests measure a student's academic achievement in high school and may indicate readiness for certain college programs. Tests offered include Writing, Literature, U.S. History, World History, Mathematics Level IC, Mathematics Level IIC, Biology E/M (Ecological/Molecular), Chemistry, Physics, French, German, Modern Hebrew, Italian, Latin, and Spanish, as well as Foreign Language Tests with Listening in Chinese, French, German, Japanese, Korean, Spanish, and English Language Proficiency (ELPT). The Mathematics Level IC and IIC tests require the use of a scientific calculator.

SAT scores are automatically sent to each student who has taken the test. On average, they are mailed about three weeks after the test. Students may request that the scores be reported to their high schools or to the colleges to which they are applying.

ACT Assessment Program

The ACT Assessment Program is a comprehensive data collection, processing, and reporting service designed to assist in educational and career planning. The ACT Assessment instrument consists of four academic tests, taken under timed conditions, and a Student Profile Section and Interest Inventory, completed when students register for the ACT Assessment.

The academic tests cover four areas—English, mathematics, reading, and science reasoning. The ACT Assessment consists of 215 multiple-choice questions and takes approximately 3 hours and 30 minutes to complete with breaks (testing time is actually 2 hours and 55 minutes). They are designed to assess the student's educational development and readiness to handle college-level work. The minimum standard score is 1, the maximum is 36, and the national

---

DON'T FORGET TO . . .

- Take the SAT or ACT Assessment before application deadlines.
- Note that test registration deadlines precede test dates by about six weeks.
- Register to take the TOEFL test if English is not your native language and you are planning on studying at a North American college.
- Practice your test-taking skills with **Peterson's Ultimate SAT Tool Kit, Peterson's Ultimate ACT Tool Kit,** and **Peterson's TOEFL Success** (all available with software).
- Contact the College Board or American College Testing, Inc., in advance if you need special accommodations when taking tests.

average is 21. Students should note that beginning in February 2005, an optional writing test will be offered.

The Student Profile Section requests information about each student's admission and enrollment plans, academic and out-of-class high school achievements and aspirations, and high school course work. The student is also asked to supply biographical data and self-reported high school grades in the four subject-matter areas covered by the academic tests.

The ACT Assessment has a number of career planning services, including the ACT Assessment Interest Inventory, which is designed to measure six major dimensions of student interests—business contact, business operations, technical, science, arts, and social service. Results are used to compare the student's interests with those of college-bound students who later majored in each of a wide variety of areas. Inventory results are also used to help students compare their work-activity preferences with work activities that characterize twenty-three "job families."

Because the information resulting from the ACT Assessment Program is used in a variety of educational settings, American College Testing, Inc., prepares three reports for each student: the Student Report, the High School Report, and the College Report. The Student Report normally is sent to the student's high school, except after the June test date, when it is sent directly to the student's home address. The College Report is sent to the colleges the student designates.

Early in the school year, American College Testing, Inc., sends registration packets to high schools across the country that contain all the information a student needs to register for the ACT Assessment. High school guidance offices also receive a supply of *Preparing for the ACT Assessment,* a booklet that contains a complete practice test, an answer key, and general information about preparing for the test.

Test of English as a Foreign Language (TOEFL)

The TOEFL test is used by various organizations, such as colleges and universities, to determine English proficiency. The test is mainly offered in a computer-based format (TOEFL CBT), although the paper-based test is still offered in some areas. Eventually, the TOEFL will be completely computer based.

The TOEFL tests students in the areas of listening, structure, reading comprehension, and writing. Score requirements are set by individual institutions. For more information on TOEFL, and to obtain a copy of the Information Bulletin, contact the Educational Testing Service.

Peterson's *TOEFL CBT Success* can help you prepare for the exam. The CD version of the book includes a TOEFL practice test and adaptive English skill building exercise. An online CBT test can also be taken for a small fee at Petersons.com.

Contact your secondary school counselor for full information about the SAT and ACT Assessment programs and the TOEFL test.

2004–05 ACT ASSESSMENT AND SAT TEST DATES

ACT Assessment
September 25, 2004*
October 23, 2004
December 11, 2004
February 12, 2005**
April 9, 2005
June 11, 2005

All test dates fall on a Saturday. Tests are also given on the Sundays following the Saturday test dates for students who cannot take the test on Saturday because of religious reasons. The basic ACT Assessment registration fee for 2003–04 was $26 ($29 in Florida and $42 outside of the U.S.).

*The September test is available only in Arizona, California, Florida, Georgia, Illinois, Indiana, Maryland, Nevada, North Carolina, Pennsylvania, South Carolina, Texas, and Washington.

**The February test date is not available in New York.

SAT
October 9, 2004 (SAT I and SAT II)
November 6, 2004 (SAT I, SAT II, and Language Tests with Listening, including ELPT*)
December 4, 2004 (SAT I and SAT II)
January 22, 2005 (SAT I, SAT II, and ELPT)
March 12, 2005 (SAT I only)** NEW SAT
May 7, 2005 (SAT I and SAT II) NEW SAT
June 4, 2005 (SAT I and SAT II) NEW SAT

For the 2003–04 academic year, the basic fee for the SAT I Reasoning Test was $28.50, which included the $16 basic registration and reporting fee. The basic fee for the SAT II Subject Tests was $16 for the Writing Test, $13 for the Language Tests with Listening, and $8 each for all other Subject Tests. Students can take up to three SAT II Subject Tests on a single date, and a $16 basic registration and reporting fee should be added for each test date. Tests are also given on the Sundays following the Saturday test dates for students who cannot take the test on Saturday because of religious reasons. Fee waivers are available to juniors and seniors who cannot afford test fees.

*Language Tests with Listening (including the English Language Proficiency Test, or ELPT) are only offered on November 6; the ELPT is offered on November 6 and January 22 at some test centers. See the Registration Bulletin for details.

**The March 12 test date is only available in the U.S. and its territories.

Who's Paying for This? Financial Aid Basics

A college education can be expensive—costing more than $100,000 for four years at some of the higher-priced private colleges and universities. Even at the lower-cost state colleges and universities, the cost of a four-year education can approach $50,000. Determining how you and your family will come up with the necessary funds to pay for your education requires planning, perseverance, and learning as much as you can about the options that are available to you.

Paying for college should not be looked on as a four-year financial commitment. For most families, paying the total cost of a student's college education out of current savings is usually not realistic. For families that have planned ahead and have financial savings established for higher education, the burden is a lot easier. But for most, meeting the cost of college requires the pooling of current income and assets and investing in longer-term loan options. These family resources, together with possible financial assistance from the state, federal, and institutional resources enable millions of students each year to attend the institution of their choice.

HOW NEED-BASED FINANCIAL AID IS AWARDED

When you apply for aid, your family's financial situation is analyzed using a government-approved formula called the Federal Methodology. This formula looks at five items:

1. Demographic information of the family.
2. Income of the parents.
3. Assets of the parents.
4. Income of the student.
5. Assets of the student.

This analysis determines the amount you and your family are expected to contribute toward your college expenses, called your Expected Family Contribution or EFC. If the EFC is equal to or more than the cost at a particular college, then you do not demonstrate financial need. However, even if you don't have financial need, you may still qualify for aid, as there are grants, scholarships, and loan programs that are not need-based.

If the cost of your education is greater than your EFC, then you do demonstrate financial need and qualify for assistance. The amount of your financial need that can be met varies from school to school. Some are able to meet your full need, while others can only cover a certain percentage of need. Here's the formula:

$$\begin{aligned} &\text{Cost of Attendance} \\ -\ &\text{Expected Family Contribution} \\ \hline = \ &\text{Financial Need} \end{aligned}$$

The EFC remains constant, but your need will vary according to the costs of attendance at a particular college. In general, the higher the tuition and fees at a particular college, the higher the cost of attendance will be. Expenses for books and supplies, room and board, and other miscellaneous costs are included in the overall cost of attendance. It is important to remember that you do not have to be "needy" to qualify for financial aid. Many middle- and upper-middle-income families qualify for need-based financial aid.

SOURCES OF FINANCIAL AID

The largest single source of aid is the federal government, which awards almost $84 billion to more than 8.9 million students each year.

The next largest source of financial aid is found in the college and university community. Institutions award an estimated $20 billion to students each year. Most of this aid is awarded to students who have a demonstrated need based on the Federal Methodology. Some institutions use a different formula, the Institutional Methodology, to award their own funds in conjunction with other forms of aid. Institutional aid may be either need-based or non-need based. Aid that is not based on need is usually awarded for a student's academic performance (merit awards), specific talents or abilities, or to attract the type of students a college seeks to enroll.

Another source of financial aid is from state government, awarding more than $5.6 billion per year. All states offer grant and/or scholarship aid, most of which is need-based. However, more and more states are offering substantial merit-based aid programs. Most state programs award aid only to students attending college in their home state.

Other sources of financial aid include:

- Private agencies
- Foundations
- Corporations

- Clubs
- Fraternal and service organizations
- Civic associations
- Unions
- Religious groups that award grants, scholarships, and low-interest loans
- Employers that provide tuition reimbursement benefits for employees and their children

More information about these different sources of aid is available from high school guidance offices, public libraries, college financial aid offices, directly from the sponsoring organizations and on the Web at www.finaid. org.

APPLYING FOR FINANCIAL AID

Every student must complete the Free Application for Federal Student Aid (FAFSA) to be considered for financial aid. The FAFSA is available from your high school guidance office, many public libraries, colleges in your area, or directly from the U.S. Department of Education.

Students also can apply for federal student aid over the Internet using the interactive FAFSA on the Web. FAFSA on the Web can be accessed at www.fafsa.ed.gov. Both the student and at least one parent must apply for a federal pin number at www.pin.ed.gov. The pin number serves as your electronic signature when applying for aid on the Web.

To award their own funds, some colleges require an additional application, the Financial Aid PROFILE® form. The PROFILE asks supplemental questions that some colleges and awarding agencies feel provide a more accurate assessment of the family's ability to pay for college. It is up to the college to decide whether it will use only the FAFSA or both the FAFSA and the PROFILE. PROFILE applications are available from the high school guidance office and on the Web. Both the paper application and the Web site list those colleges and programs that require the PROFILE application.

If Every College You're Applying to for Fall 2005 Requires Just the FAFSA

. . . then it's pretty simple: Complete the FAFSA after January 1, 2005, being certain to send it in before any college-imposed deadlines. (You are not permitted to send in the 2005-06 FAFSA before January 1, 2005.) Most college FAFSA application deadlines are in February or early March. It is easier if you have all your financial records for the previous year available, but if that is not possible, you are strongly encouraged to use estimated figures.

After you send in your FAFSA, either with the paper application or electronically, you'll receive a Student Aid Report (SAR) that includes all of the information you reported and shows your EFC. If you provided an e-mail address, the SAR is sent to you electronically; otherwise, you will receive a paper copy in the mail. Be sure to review the SAR, checking to see if the information you reported is accurate. If you used estimated numbers to complete the

FAFSA, you may have to resubmit the SAR with any corrections to the data. The college(s) you have designated on the FAFSA will receive the information you reported and will use that data to make their decision. In many instances, the colleges you've applied to will ask you to send copies of your and your parents' federal income tax returns for 2004, plus any other documents needed to verify the information you reported.

If a College Requires the PROFILE

Step 1: Register for the Financial Aid PROFILE in the fall of your senior year in high school.

Registering for the Financial Aid PROFILE begins the financial aid process. You can register by calling the College Scholarship Service at 1-800-778-6888 and providing basic demographic information, a list of colleges to which you are applying, and your credit card number to pay for the service. You can also apply for the PROFILE online at http://profileonline.collegeboard.com/index.jsp. Registration packets with a list of the colleges that require the PROFILE are available in most high school guidance offices. There is a fee for using the Financial Aid PROFILE application ($23 for the first college and $18 for each additional college). You must pay for the service by credit card when you register. If you do not have a credit card, you will be billed.

Step 2: Fill out your customized Financial Aid PROFILE.

A few weeks after you register, you'll receive in the mail a customized financial aid application that you can use to apply for institutional aid at the colleges you've designated, as well as from some private scholarship programs, like the National Merit Scholarship. (Note: If you've waited until winter and a college's financial aid application deadline is approaching, you can get overnight delivery by paying an extra fee.) The PROFILE contains all the questions necessary to calculate your "institutional" EFC, plus any additional questions that the colleges and organizations you've designated require you to answer. Your individualized packet will also contain a customized cover letter instructing you what to do and informing you about deadlines and requirements for the colleges and programs you designated when you registered for the PROFILE, codes that indicate which colleges wanted which additional questions, and supplemental forms (if any of the colleges to which you are applying require them—e.g. the Business/Farm Supplement for students whose parents own a business or farm or the Divorced/ Separated Parents' Statement).

Make sure you submit your PROFILE by the earliest deadline listed. Two to four weeks after you do so, you will receive an acknowledgment and a report estimating your "institutional" EFC based on the data elements you provided on your PROFILE. Remember, this is a different formula from the federal system that uses the FAFSA.

FINANCIAL AID PROGRAMS
There are three types of financial aid:

1. Gift-aid—Scholarships and grants are funds that do not have to be repaid.
2. Loans—Loans must be repaid, usually after graduation; the amount you have to pay back is the total you've borrowed plus any accrued interest. This is considered a source of self-help aid.
3. Student employment—Student employment is a job arranged for you by the financial aid office. This is another source of self-help aid.

The federal government has two major grant programs—the Federal Pell Grant and the Federal Supplemental Educational Opportunity Grant. These grants are targeted to low-to-moderate income families with significant financial need. The federal government also sponsors a student employment program called Federal Work-Study, which offers jobs both on and off campus; and several loan programs, including those for students and for parents of undergraduate students.

There are two types of student loan programs, subsidized and unsubsidized. The Subsidized Stafford Loan and the Federal Perkins Loan are need-based, government-subsidized loans. Students who borrow through these programs do not have to pay interest on the loan until after they graduate or leave school. The Unsubsidized Stafford Loan and the Parent Loan Programs are not based on need, and borrowers are responsible for the interest while the student is in school. There are different methods on how these loans are administered. Once you choose your college, the financial aid office will guide you through this process.

After you've submitted your financial aid application and you've been accepted for admission, each college will send you a letter describing your financial aid award. Most award letters show estimated college costs, how much you and your family are expected to contribute, and the amount and types of aid you have been awarded. Most students are awarded aid from a combination of sources and programs. Hence, your award is often called a financial aid "package."

IF YOU DON'T QUALIFY FOR NEED-BASED AID
If you are not eligible for need-based aid, you can still find ways to lessen the burden on your parents.

Here are some suggestions:

- Search for merit scholarships. You can start at the initial stages of your application process. College merit awards are becoming increasingly important as more

and more colleges award these grants to students they especially want to attract. As a result, applying to a college at which your qualifications put you at the top of the entering class may give you a larger merit award. Another source of aid to look for is private scholarships that are given for special skills and talents. Additional information can be found at petersons.com and at www.finaid.org.

- Seek employment during the summer and the academic year. The student employment office at your college can help you locate a school-year job. Many colleges and local businesses have vacancies remaining after they have hired students who are receiving Federal Work-Study financial aid.
- Borrow through the Unsubsidized Stafford Loan programs. These are open to all students. The terms and conditions are similar to the subsidized loans. The biggest difference is that the borrower is responsible for the interest while still in college, although most lenders permit students to delay paying the interest right away and add the accrued interest to the total amount owed. You must file the FAFSA to be considered.
- After you've secured what you can through scholarships, working, and borrowing, your parents will be expected to meet their share of the college bill (the Expected Family Contribution). Many colleges offer monthly payment plans that spread the cost over the academic year. If the monthly payments are too high, parents can borrow through the Federal Parent Loan for Undergraduate Students (PLUS program), through one of the many private education loan programs available, or through home equity loans and lines of credit. Families seeking assistance in financing college expenses should inquire at the financial aid office about what programs are available at the college. Some families seek the advice of professional financial advisers and tax consultants.

HOW IS YOUR FAMILY CONTRIBUTION CALCULATED?
The chart on the next page makes the following assumptions:

- two parent family where age of older parent is 45
- lower income families will file the 1040A or 1040EZ tax form
- student income is less than $2300
- there are no student assets
- there is only one family member in college

All figures are estimates and may vary when the complete FAFSA or PROFILE application is submitted.

Approximate Expected Family Contribution

ASSETS	FAMILY SIZE	$20,000	30,000	40,000	50,000	60,000	70,000	80,000	90,000	100,000
					INCOME BEFORE TAXES					
$ 20,000	3	$ 0	870	2,450	4,350	7,000	9,800	12,600	15,500	18,000
	4	0	80	1,670	3,350	5,600	8,300	11,000	14,000	17,100
	5	0	0	930	2,500	4,500	7,000	9,700	12,600	15,600
	6	0	0	100	1,700	3,350	5,500	8,100	11,000	14,000
$ 30,000	3	$ 0	870	2,450	4,350	7,000	9,800	12,600	15,500	18,000
	4	0	80	1,670	3,350	5,600	8,300	11,000	14,000	17,100
	5	0	0	930	2,500	4,500	7,000	9,700	12,600	15,600
	6	0	0	100	1,700	3,350	5,500	8,100	11,000	14,000
$ 40,000	3	$ 0	870	2,450	4,350	7,000	9,800	12,600	15,500	18,000
	4	0	80	1,670	3,350	5,600	8,300	11,000	14,000	17,100
	5	0	0	930	2,500	4,500	7,000	9,700	12,600	15,600
	6	0	0	100	1,700	3,350	5,500	8,100	11,000	14,000
$ 50,000	3	$ 0	870	2,450	4,350	7,500	10,300	13,000	16,000	19,000
	4	0	80	1,670	3,350	6,000	8,800	11,500	14,400	17,500
	5	0	0	930	2,500	4,700	7,400	10,100	13,000	16,100
	6	0	0	100	1,700	3,600	5,900	8,500	11,400	14,500
$ 60,000	3	$ 0	870	2,450	5,100	8,050	10,800	13,600	16,500	19,600
	4	0	80	1,670	3,950	6,550	9,300	12,200	15,000	18,100
	5	0	0	930	3,000	5,300	7,900	10,800	13,600	16,700
	6	0	0	100	2,150	4,000	6,300	9,100	12,000	15,000
$ 80,000	3	$ 0	870	2,450	6,000	9,200	12,000	14,800	17,600	20,700
	4	0	80	1,670	4,700	7,600	10,500	13,200	16,100	19,200
	5	0	0	930	3,700	6,100	9,000	11,800	14,700	17,800
	6	0	0	100	2,700	4,700	7,400	10,200	13,100	16,200
$ 100,000	3	$ 0	870	2,450	7,000	10,300	13,000	15,900	18,800	21,850
	4	0	80	1,670	5,600	8,700	11,500	14,300	17,200	20,300
	5	0	0	930	4,400	7,100	10,200	12,900	15,800	18,900
	6	0	0	100	3,300	5,500	8,500	11,300	14,200	17,300
$ 120,000	3	$ 0	870	2,450	8,100	11,400	14,200	17,000	19,900	23,000
	4	0	80	1,670	6,600	9,800	12,600	15,500	18,400	21,500
	5	0	0	930	5,300	8,200	11,300	14,100	17,000	20,000
	6	0	0	100	4,000	6,500	9,700	12,500	15,300	18,400
$ 140,000	3	$ 0	870	2,450	9,300	12,600	15,400	18,200	21,000	24,100
	4	0	80	1,670	7,600	11,000	13,900	16,700	19,500	22,600
	5	0	0	930	6,100	9,500	12,500	15,200	18,100	21,200
	6	0	0	100	4,700	7,600	10,800	13,600	16,500	19,600

Frequently Asked Questions About Transferring

Muriel M. Shishkoff

Among the students attending two-year colleges are a large number who began their higher education knowing they would eventually transfer to a four-year school to obtain their bachelor's degree. There are many reasons why students are going this route. Upon graduating from high school, some simply do not have definite career goals. Although they don't want to put their education on hold, they prefer not to pay exorbitant amounts in tuition while trying to "find themselves." As the cost of a university education escalates—even in public institutions—the option of spending the freshman and sophomore years at a two-year college looks attractive to many students. Others attend a two-year college because they are unable to meet the initial entrance standards—a specified grade point average (GPA), standardized test scores, or knowledge of specific academic subjects—required by the four-year school of their choice. Many such students praise the community college system for giving them the chance to be, academically speaking, "born again." In addition, students from other countries often find that they can adapt more easily to language and cultural changes at a two-year school before transferring to a larger, more diverse four-year college.

If your plan is to attend a two-year college with the ultimate goal of transferring to a four-year school, you will be pleased to know that the increased importance of the community college route to a bachelor's degree is recognized by all segments of higher education. As a result, many two-year schools have revised their course outlines and established new courses in order to comply with the programs and curricular offerings of the universities. Institutional improvements to make transferring easier have also proliferated at both the two- and four-year levels. The generous transfer policies of the Pennsylvania, New York, and Florida state university systems, among others, reflect this attitude; these systems accept *all* credits from students who have graduated from accredited community colleges.

If you are interested in moving from a two-year college to a four-year school, the sooner you make up your mind that you are going to make the switch, the better position you will be in to transfer successfully (that is, without having wasted valuable time and credits). The ideal point at which to make such a decision is *before* you register for classes at your two-year school; a counselor can help you plan your course work with an eye toward fulfilling the requirements needed for your major course of study.

Naturally, it is not always possible to plan your transferring strategy that far in advance, but keep in mind that the key to a successful transfer is *preparation,* and preparation takes time—time to think through your objectives and time to plan the right classes to take at that school.

As students face the prospect of transferring from a two-year to a four-year school, many thoughts and concerns about this complicated and often frustrating process race through their minds. Here are answers to the questions that are most frequently asked by transferring students.

Q Does every college and university accept transfer students?

A Most four-year institutions accept transfer students, but some do so more enthusiastically than others. Graduating from a community college is an advantage at, for example, Arizona State University and the University of Massachusetts Boston; both accept more community college transfer students than traditional freshmen. At the State University of New York at Albany, graduates of two-year transfer programs within the State University of New York System are given priority for upper-division (i.e., junior- and senior-level) vacancies.

Schools offering undergraduate work at the upper division only, such as Metropolitan State University in St. Paul, Minnesota, are especially receptive to transfer applications. On the other hand, some schools accept only a few transfer students; others refuse entrance to sophomores or those in their final year. Princeton University requires an "excellent academic record and particularly compelling reasons to transfer." Check the catalogs of several colleges for their transfer requirements before you make your final choice.

13

Frequently Asked Questions About Transferring

Q Do students who go directly from high school to a four-year college do better academically than transfer students from community colleges?

A On the contrary: some institutions report that transfers from two-year schools who persevere until graduation do *better* than those who started as freshmen.

Q Why is it so important that my two-year college be accredited?

A Four-year colleges and universities accept transfer credit only from schools formally recognized by a regional, national, or professional educational agency. This accreditation signifies that an institution or program of study meets or exceeds a minimum level of educational quality necessary for meeting stated educational objectives.

Q After enrolling at a four-year school, may I still make up necessary courses at a community college?

A Some institutions restrict credit after transfer to their own facilities. Others allow students to take a limited number of transfer courses after matriculation, depending on the subject matter. A few provide opportunities for cross-registration or dual enrollment, which means taking classes on more than one campus.

Q What do I need to do to transfer?

A First, send for your high school and college transcripts. Having chosen the school you wish to transfer to, check its admission requirements against your transcripts. If you find that you are admissible, file an application as early as possible before the deadline. Part of the process will be asking your former schools to send *official transcripts* to the admission office, i.e., not the copies you used in determining your admissibility.

Plan your transfer program with the head of your new department as soon as you have decided to transfer. Determine the recommended general education pattern and necessary preparation for your major. At your present school, take the courses you will need to meet transfer requirements for the new one.

Q What qualifies me for admission as a transfer student?

A Admission requirements for most four-year institutions vary. Depending on the reputation or popularity of the school and program you wish to enter, requirements may be quite selective and competitive. Usually, you will need to show satisfactory test scores, an academic record up to a certain standard, and completion of specific subject matter.

Transfer students can be eligible to enter a four-year school in a number of ways: by having been eligible for admission directly upon graduation from high school, by making up shortcomings in grades (or in subject matter not covered in high school) at a community college, or by satisfactory completion of necessary courses or credit hours at another postsecondary institution. Ordinarily, students coming from a community college or from another four-year institution must meet or exceed the receiving institution's standards for freshmen and show appropriate college-level course work taken since high school. Students who did not graduate from high school can present proof of proficiency through results on the General Educational Development (GED) test.

Q Are exceptions ever made for students who don't meet all the requirements for transfer?

A Extenuating circumstances, such as disability, low family income, refugee or veteran status, or athletic talent, may permit the special enrollment of students who would not otherwise be eligible but who demonstrate the potential for academic success. Consult the appropriate office—the Educational Opportunity Program, the disabled students' office, the athletic department, or the academic dean—to see whether an exception can be made in your case.

Q How far in advance do I need to apply for transfer?

A Some schools have a rolling admission policy, which means that they process transfer applications as they are received, all year long. With other schools, you must apply during the priority filing period, which can be up to a year before you wish to enter. Check the date with the admission office at your prospective campus.

Q Is it possible to transfer courses from several different institutions?

A Institutions ordinarily accept the courses that they consider transferable, regardless of the number of accredited schools involved. However, there is the danger of exceeding the maximum number of credit hours that can be transferred from all other schools or earned through credit by examination, extension courses, or correspondence courses. The limit placed on transfer credits varies from school to school, so read the catalog carefully to avoid taking courses you won't be able to use. To avoid duplicating courses, keep attendance at different campuses to a minimum.

Q What is involved in transferring from a semester system to a quarter or trimester system?

A In the semester system, the academic calendar is divided into two equal parts. The quarter system is more aptly named trimester, since the academic calendar is divided into three equal terms (not counting a summer session). To convert semester units into quarter units or credit hours, simply multiply the semester units by one and a half. Conversely, multiply quarter units by two thirds to come up with semester units. If you are used to a semester system of fifteen- to sixteen-week courses, the ten-week courses of the quarter system may seem to fly by.

Q Why might a course be approved for transfer credit by one four-year school but not by another?

A The beauty of postsecondary education in the United States lies in its variety. Entrance policies and graduation requirements are designed to reflect and serve each institution's mission. Because institutional policies vary so widely, schools may interpret the subject matter of a course from quite different points of view. Given that the granting of transfer credit indicates that a course is viewed as being, in effect, parallel to one offered by the receiving institution, it is easy to see how this might be the case at one university and not another.

Q Must I take a foreign language to transfer?

A Foreign language proficiency is often required for admission to a four-year institution; such proficiency also often figures in certain majors or in the general education pattern. At Princeton University, for example, where foreign language proficiency is a

graduation requirement, all students must demonstrate it by the end of their junior year.

However, at the University of Southern California and other schools, the foreign language competence necessary for admission can be certified before entrance. Often, two or three years of a single language in high school will do the trick. Find out if scores received on Advanced Placement examinations, placement examinations given by the foreign language department, or SAT II Subject Tests will be accepted in lieu of college course work.

Q Will the school to which I'm transferring accept pass/no pass, pass/fail, or credit/no credit grades in lieu of letter grades?

A Usually, a limit is placed on the number of these courses you can transfer, and there may be other restrictions as well. If you want to use other-than-letter grades for the fulfillment of general education requirements or lower-division (freshman and sophomore) preparation for the major, check with the receiving institution.

Q Which is more important for transfer—my grade point average or my course completion pattern?

A Some schools believe that your past grades indicate academic potential and overshadow prior preparation for a specific degree program. Others require completion of certain introductory courses before transfer to prepare you for upper-division work in your major. In any case, appropriate course selection will cut down the time to graduation and increase your chances of making a successful transfer.

Q What happens to my credits if I change majors?

A If you change majors after admission, your transferable course credit should remain fairly intact. However, because you may need extra or different preparation for your new major, some of the courses you've taken may now be useful only as electives. The need for additional lower-level preparation may mean you're staying longer at your new school than you originally planned. On the other hand, you may already have taken courses that count toward your new major as part of the university's general education pattern.

Excerpted from *Transferring Made Easy: A Guide to Changing Colleges Successfully*, by Muriel M. Shishkoff, © 1991 by Muriel M. Shishkoff (published by Peterson's).

Returning to School: Advice for Adult Students

Sandra Cook, Ph.D.
Director, University Advising Center, San Diego State University

Many adults think about returning to school for a long time without taking any action. One purpose of this article is to help the "thinkers" finally make some decisions by examining what is keeping them from action. Another purpose is to describe not only some of the difficulties and obstacles that adult students may face when returning to school but also tactics for coping with them.

If you have been thinking about going back to college, and believing that you are the only person your age contemplating college, you should know that approximately 7 million adult students are currently enrolled in higher education institutions. This number represents 50 percent of total higher education enrollments. The majority of adult students are enrolled at two-year colleges.

There are many reasons why adult students choose to attend a two-year college. Studies have shown that the three most important criteria that adult students consider when choosing a college are location, cost, and availability of the major or program desired. Most two-year colleges are public institutions that serve a geographic district, making them readily accessible to the community. Costs at most two-year colleges are far less than at other types of higher education institutions. For many students who plan to pursue a bachelor's degree, completing their first two years of college at a community college is an affordable means to that end. If you are interested in an academic program that will transfer to a four-year institution, most two-year colleges offer the "general education" courses that comprise most freshman and sophomore years. If you are interested in a vocational or technical program, two-year colleges excel in providing this type of training.

UNCERTAINTY, CHOICE, AND SUPPORT

There are three different "stages" in the process of adults returning to school. The first stage is uncertainty. Do I really want to go back to school? What will my friends or family think? Can I compete with those 18-year-old whiz kids? Am I too old? The second stage is choice. Once the decision to return has been made, you must choose where you will attend. There are many criteria to use in making this decision. The third stage is support. You have just added another role to your already-too-busy life. There are, however, strategies that will help you accomplish your goals—perhaps not without struggle, but with grace and humor. Let's look at each of these stages.

UNCERTAINTY

Why are you thinking about returning to school? Is it to:

- fulfill a dream that had to be delayed?
- become more educationally well-rounded?
- fill an intellectual void in your life?

These reasons focus on *personal growth*.

If you are returning to school to:

- meet people and make friends
- attain and enjoy higher social status and prestige among friends, relatives, and associates
- understand/study a cultural heritage, or
- have a medium in which to exchange ideas,

you are interested in *social and cultural opportunities*.

If you are like most adult students, you want to:

- qualify for a new occupation
- enter or reenter the job market
- increase earnings potential, or
- qualify for a more challenging position in the same field of work.

You are seeking *career growth*.

Understanding the reasons why you want to go back to school is an important step in setting your educational goals and will help you to establish some criteria for selecting a college. However, don't delay your decision because you have not been able to clearly define your motives. Many times, these aren't clear until you have already begun the process, and they may change as you move through your college experience.

Assuming that you agree that additional education will be of benefit to you, what is it that keeps you from returning to school? You may have a litany of excuses running through your mind:

- I don't have time.
- I can't afford it.
- I'm too old to learn.
- My friends will think I'm crazy.
- The teachers will be younger than I.
- My family can't survive without me to take care of them every minute.
- I'll be X years old when I finish.
- I'm afraid.
- I don't know what to expect.

And that is just what these are—excuses. You can make school, like anything else in your life, a priority or not. If you really want to return, you can. The more you understand your motivation for returning to school and the more you understand what excuses are keeping you from taking action, the easier your task will be.

If you think you don't have time: The best way to decide how attending class and studying can fit into your schedule is to keep track of what you do with your time each day for several weeks. Completing a standard time-management grid (each day is plotted out by the half hour) is helpful for visualizing how your time is spent. For each 3-credit-hour class you take, you will need to find 3 hours for class plus 6 to 9 hours for reading-studying-library time. This study time should be spaced evenly throughout the week, not loaded up on one day. It is not possible to learn or retain the material that way. When you examine your grid, see where there are activities that could be replaced with school and study time. You may decide to give up your bowling league or some time in front of the TV. Try not to give up sleeping, and don't cut out every moment of free time. Here are some suggestions that have come from adults who have returned to school:

- Enroll in a time-management workshop. It helps you rethink how you use your time.
- Don't think you have to take more than one course at a time. You may eventually want to work up to taking more, but consider starting with one. (It is more than you are taking now!)
- If you have a family, start assigning those household chores that you usually do to them—and don't redo what they do.
- Use your lunch hour or commuting time for reading.

If you think you can not afford it: As mentioned earlier, two-year colleges are extremely affordable. If you cannot afford the tuition, look into the various financial aid options. Most federal and state funds are available to full- and part-time students. Loans are also available. While many people prefer not to accumulate a debt for school, these same people will think nothing of taking out a loan to buy a car. After five or six years, which is the better investment? Adult students who work should look into whether their company has a tuition-reimbursement policy. There are also an increasing number of private scholarships, available through foundations, service organizations, and clubs, that are focused on adult learners. Your public library and a college financial aid adviser are two excellent sources for reference materials regarding financial aid.

If you think you are too old to learn: This is pure myth. A number of studies have shown that adult learners perform as well as or better than traditional-age students.

If you are afraid your friends will think you're crazy: Who cares? Maybe they will, maybe they won't. Usually, they will admire your courage and be just a little jealous of your ambition (although they'll never tell you that). Follow your dreams, not theirs.

If you are concerned because the teachers or students will be younger than you: Don't be. The age differences that may be apparent in other settings evaporate in the classroom. If anything, an adult in the classroom strikes fear into the hearts of some 18-year-olds because adults have been known to be prepared, ask questions, be truly motivated, and be there to learn!

If you think your family will have a difficult time surviving while you are in school: If you have done everything for them up to now, they might struggle. Consider this an opportunity to help them become independent and self-sufficient. Your family can only make you feel guilty if you let them. You are not abandoning them; you are becoming an educational role model. When you are happy and working toward your goals, everyone benefits. Admittedly, it sometimes takes time for them to realize this. For single parents, there are schools that have begun to offer support groups, child care, and cooperative babysitting.

If you're appalled at the thought of being X years old when you graduate in Y years: How old will you be in Y years if you don't go back to school?

If you are afraid or don't know what to expect: Know that these are natural feelings when one encounters any new situation. Adult students find that their fears usually dissipate once they begin classes. Fear of trying is usually the biggest roadblock to the reentry process.

No doubt you have dreamed up a few more reasons for not making the decision to return to school. Keep in mind that what you are doing is making up excuses, and you are using these excuses to release you from the obligation to make a decision about your life. The thought of returning to college can be scary. Anytime anyone ventures into unknown territory, there is a risk, but taking risks is a necessary component of personal and professional growth. It is your life, and you alone are responsible for making the decisions that determine its course. Education is an investment in your future.

CHOICE

Once you have decided to go back to school, your next task is to decide where to go. If your educational goals are well defined (e.g., you want to pursue a degree in order to change careers), then your task is a bit easier. But even if your educational goals are still evolving, do not deter your return. Many students who enter higher education with a specific major in mind change that major at least once.

Most students who attend a public two-year college choose the community college in the district in which they live. This is generally the closest and least expensive option if the school offers the programs you want. If you are planning to begin your education at a two-year college and then transfer to a four-year school, there are distinct advantages to choosing your four-year school early. Many community and four-year colleges have "articulation" agreements that designate what credits from the two-year school will transfer to the four-year college and how. Some four-year institutions accept an associate degree as equivalent to the freshman and sophomore years, regardless of the courses you have taken. Some four-year schools accept two-year college work only on a course-by-course basis. If you can identify which school you will transfer to, you can know in advance exactly how your two-year credits will apply, preventing an unexpected loss of credit or time.

Each institution of higher education is distinctive. Your goal in choosing a college is to come up with the best student-institution fit—matching your needs with the offerings and characteristics of the school. The first step in choosing a college is to determine what criteria are most important to you in attaining your educational goals. Location, cost, and program availability are the three main factors that influence an adult student's college choice. In considering location, don't forget that some colleges have conveniently located branch campuses. In considering cost, remember to explore your financial aid options before ruling out an institution because of its tuition. Program availability should include not only the major in which you are interested, but also whether or not classes in that major are available when you can take them.

Some additional considerations beyond location, cost, and programs are:

- Does the school have a commitment to adult students and offer appropriate services, such as child care, tutoring, and advising?
- Are classes offered at times when you can take them?
- Are there academic options for adults, such as credit for life or work experience, credit by examination (including CLEP and PEP), credit for military service, or accelerated programs?
- Is the faculty sensitive to the needs of adult learners?

Once you determine which criteria are vital in your choice of an institution, you can begin to narrow your choices. There are myriad ways for you to locate the information you desire. Many urban newspapers publish a "School Guide" several times a year in which colleges and universities advertise to an adult student market. In addition, schools themselves publish catalogs, class schedules, and promotional materials that contain much of the information you need, and they are yours for the asking. Many colleges sponsor information sessions and open houses that allow you to visit the campus and ask questions. An appointment with an adviser is a good way to assess the fit between you and the institution. Be sure to bring your questions with you to your interview.

SUPPORT

Once you have made the decision to return to school and have chosen the institution that best meets your needs, take some additional steps to ensure your success during your crucial first semester. Take advantage of institutional support and build some social support systems of your own. Here are some ways of doing just that:

- Plan to participate in any orientation programs. These serve the threefold purpose of providing you with a great deal of important information, familiarizing you with the campus and its facilities, and giving you the opportunity to meet and begin networking with other students.
- Take steps to deal with any academic weaknesses. Take mathematics and writing placement tests if you have reason to believe you may need some extra help in these areas. It is not uncommon for adult students to need a math refresher course or a program to help alleviate math anxiety. Ignoring a weakness won't make it go away.
- Look into adult reentry programs. Many institutions offer adults workshops focusing on ways to improve study skills, textbook reading, test-taking, and time-management skills.
- Build new support networks by joining an adult student organization, making a point of meeting other adult students through workshops, or actively seeking out a "study buddy" in each class—that invaluable friend who shares and understands your experience.
- You can incorporate your new status as "student" into your family life. Doing your homework with your children at a designated "homework time" is a valuable family activity and reinforces the importance of education.
- Make sure you take a reasonable course load in your first semester. It is far better to have some extra time on your hands and to succeed magnificently than to spend the entire semester on the brink of a breakdown. Also, whenever possible, try to focus your first courses not only on requirements, but also in areas of personal interest.

■ Faculty members, advisers, and student affairs personnel are there to help you during difficult times—let them assist you as often as necessary.

After completing your first semester, you will probably look back in wonder at why you thought going back to school was so imposing. Certainly, it's not without its occasional exasperations. But, as with life, keeping things in perspective and maintaining your sense of humor make the difference between just coping and succeeding brilliantly.

What International Students Need to Know About Admission to U.S. Colleges

Kitty M. Villa

Assistant Director, International Office, University of Texas at Austin

Selecting an institution and securing admission require a significant investment of time and effort.

There are two principles to remember about admission to a college in the United States. First, applying is almost never a one-time request for admission but an ongoing process that may involve several exchanges of information between applicant and institution. "Admission process" or "application process" means that a "yes" or "no" is usually not immediate, and requests for additional information are to be expected. To successfully manage this process, you must be prepared to send additional information when requested and then wait for replies. You need a thoughtful balance of persistence to communicate regularly and effectively with your selected colleges and patience to endure what can be a very long process.

The second principle involves a marketplace analogy. The most successful applicants are alert to opportunities to create a positive impression that sets them apart from other applicants. They are able to market themselves to their target institution. Institutions are also trying to attract the highest-quality student that they can. The admissions process presents you with the opportunity to analyze your strengths and weaknesses as a student and to look for ways to present yourself in the most marketable manner.

FIRST STEP—SELECTING INSTITUTIONS

With thousands of institutions of higher education in the U.S., how do you begin to narrow your choices down to the institutions that are best for you? There are many factors to consider, and you must ultimately decide which factors are most important to you.

Location

You may spend several years studying in the U.S. Do you prefer an urban or rural campus? Large or small metropolitan area? If you need to live on campus, will you be unhappy at a college where most students commute from off-campus housing? How do you feel about extremely hot summers or cold winters? Eliminating institutions that do not match your preferences in terms of location will narrow your choices.

Recommendations from Friends, Professors, or Others

There are valid academic reasons to consider the recommendations of people who know you well and have first-hand knowledge about particular institutions. Friends and contacts may be able to provide you with "inside information" about the campus or its academic programs to which published sources have no access. You should carefully balance anecdotal information with your own research and your own impressions. However, current and former students, professors, and others may provide excellent information during the application process.

Your Own Academic and Career Goals

Consideration of your academic goals is more complex than it may seem at first glance. All institutions do not offer the same academic programs. The application form usually provides a definitive listing of the academic programs offered by an institution. A course catalog describes the degree program and all the courses offered. In addition to printed sources, there is a tremendous amount of institutional information available through the Internet. Program descriptions, even course descriptions and course syllabi, are often available to peruse via computer.

You may be interested in the rankings of either the college or of a program of study. Keep in mind, however, that rankings usually assume that quality is quantifiable. Rankings are usually based on presumptions about how data relate to quality that are likely to be unproven. It is important to carefully consider the source and the criteria of any ranking information before believing and acting upon it.

Your Own Educational Background

You may be concerned about the interpretation of your educational credentials, since your country's degree nomenclature and the grading scale may differ from those in the U.S. Colleges use reference books about the educational systems of other countries to help them understand specific educational credentials. Generally, these credentials are interpreted by each institution; there is not a single interpretation that applies to every institution. The lack of uniformity is good news for most students, since it means that students from a wide variety of educational backgrounds can find a U.S. college that is appropriate to their needs.

To choose an appropriate institution, you can and should do an informal self-evaluation of your educational background. This self-analysis involves three important questions:

How Many Years of Study Have You Completed?

Completion of secondary school with at least twelve total years of education usually qualifies students to apply for undergraduate degree programs. Completion of a college degree program that involves at least sixteen years of total education qualifies one to apply for admission to graduate (master's) degree programs in the U.S.

Does the Education That You Have Completed in Your Country Provide Access to Further Study in the U.S.?

Consider the kind of institution where you completed your previous studies. If educational opportunities in your country are limited, it may be necessary to investigate many U.S. institutions and programs in order to find a match.

Are Your Previous Marks or Grades Excellent, Average, or Poor?

Your educational record influences your choice of U.S. institutions. If your grades are average or poor, it may be advisable to apply to several institutions with minimally difficult or noncompetitive entrance levels.

YOU are one of the best sources of information about the level and quality of your previous studies. Awareness of your educational assets and liabilities will serve you well throughout the application process.

SECOND STEP—PLANNING AND ASSEMBLING THE APPLICATION

Planning and assembling a college application can be compared to the construction of a building. First, you must start with a solid foundation, which is the application form itself. The application, often available online as well as in paper form, usually contains a wealth of useful information, such as deadlines, fees, and degree programs available at that institution. To build a solid application, it is best to begin well in advance of the application deadline.

How to Obtain the Application Form

Application forms and links to institutional Web sites may also be available at a U.S. educational advising center associated with the American Embassy or Consulate in your country. These centers are excellent resources for international students and provide information about standardized test administration, scholarships, and other matters to students who are interested in studying in the U.S. Your local U.S. Embassy or Consulate can guide you to the nearest educational advising center.

Completing the Application Form

Whether sent by mail or electronically, the application form must be neat and thoroughly filled out. Parts of the application may not seem to apply to you or your situation. Do your best to answer all the questions.

Remember that this is a process. You provide information, and your proposed college then requests clarification and further information. If you have questions, it is better to initiate the entire process by submitting the application form rather than asking questions before you apply. The college will be better able to respond to you after it has your application. Always complete as much as you can. Do not permit uncertainty about the completion of the application form to cause unnecessary delays.

What Are the Key Components of a Complete Application?

Institutional requirements vary, but the standard components of a complete application include:

- Transcript
- Required standardized examination scores
- Evidence of financial support
- Letters of recommendation
- Application fee

Transcript

A complete academic record or transcript includes all courses completed, grades earned, and degrees awarded. Most colleges require an official transcript to be sent directly from the school or university. In many other countries, however, the practice is to issue official transcripts and degree certificates directly to the student. If you have only one official copy of your transcript, it may be a challenge to get additional certified copies that are acceptable to U.S. colleges. Some institutions will issue additional official copies for application purposes.

If your institution does not provide this service, you may have to seek an alternate source of certification. As a last resort, you may send a photocopy of your official transcript, explain that you have only one original, and ask the college for advice on how to deal with this situation.

Required Standardized Examination Scores

Arranging to take standardized examinations and earning the required scores seem to cause the most anxiety for international students.

The college application form usually indicates which examinations are required. The standardized examination required most often for undergraduate admission is the Test of English as a Foreign Language (TOEFL). In most countries, TOEFL has changed from a paper-and-pencil test to a computer-based test. Institutions may also require the SAT I of undergraduate applicants. Some institutions also require the Test of Spoken English (TSE). These standardized examinations are administered by the Educational Testing Service (ETS). Please note: In September 2005, ETS will introduce a new TOEFL CBT, which will include a speaking section.

These examinations are offered in almost every country of the world. It is advisable to begin planning for standardized examinations at least six months prior to the application deadline of your desired institutions. Test centers fill up quickly, so it is important to register as soon as possible. Information about the examinations is available at U.S. educational advising centers associated with embassies or consulates.

FOR MORE INFORMATION

Questions about test formats, locations, dates, and registration may be addressed to:

TOEFL/TSE Services
P.O. Box 6151
Princeton, New Jersey 08541-6151
Web sites: http://www.ets.org
　　　　　http://www.toefl.org
E-mail: toefl@ets.org
Telephone: 609-771-7100
Fax: 609-771-7500

Most universities require that the original test scores, not a student copy, be sent directly by the testing service. When you register for the test, be sure to indicate that the testing service should send the test scores directly to your proposed colleges.

You should usually begin your application process before you receive your test scores. Delaying submission of your application until the test scores arrive may cause

you to miss deadlines and negatively effect the outcome of your application. If you want to know your scores in order to assess your chances of admission to an institution with rigorous admission standards, you should take the tests early.

Many colleges in the U.S. set minimum required scores on the TOEFL or on other standardized examinations. Test scores are an important factor, but most institutions also look at a number of other factors in their consideration of a candidate for admission.

Evidence of Financial Support

Evidence of financial support is required to issue immigration documents to admitted students. This is part of a complete application package but usually plays no role in determining admission. Most institutions make admissions decisions without regard to the source and amount of financial support.

Letters of Recommendation

Most institutions require one or more letters of recommendation. The best letters are written by former professors, employers, or others who can comment on your academic achievements or professional potential.

Some colleges provide a special form for the letters of recommendation. If possible, use the forms provided. If you are applying to a large number of colleges, however, or if your recommenders are not available to complete several forms, it may be necessary for you to duplicate a general recommendation letter.

Application Fee

Most colleges also require an application fee, ranging from $25 to $100, which must be paid to initiate consideration of the application.

THIRD STEP—DISTINGUISH YOUR APPLICATION

To distinguish your application—to market yourself successfully—is ultimately the most important part of the application process. As you select your prospective colleges, you begin to analyze your strengths and weaknesses as a prospective student. As you complete your application, you should strive to create a positive impression and set yourself apart from other applicants, to highlight your assets and bring these qualities to the attention of the appropriate college administrators and professors. Applying early is a very easy way to distinguish your application.

Deadline or Guideline?

The application deadline is the last date that an application for a given semester will be accepted. Often, the application will specify that all required documents and information be submitted before the deadline date. To meet the deadlines, start the application process early. This also gives you more time to take—and perhaps retake and improve—the required standardized tests.

Admissions deliberations may take several weeks or months. In the meantime, most institutions accept additional information, including improved test scores, after the posted deadline.

Even if your application is initially rejected, you may be able to provide additional information to change the decision. You can request reconsideration based on additional information, such as improved test scores, strong letters of recommendation, or information about your class rank. Applying early allows more time to improve your application. Also, some students may decide not to accept their offers of admission, leaving room for offers to students on a waiting list. Reconsideration of the admission decisions can occur well beyond the application deadline.

Think of the deadline as a guideline rather than an impermeable barrier. Many factors—the strength of the application, your research interests, the number of spaces available at the proposed institution—can override the enforcement of an application deadline. So, if you lack a test score or transcript by the official deadline, you may still be able to apply and be accepted.

Statement of Purpose

The statement of purpose is your first and perhaps best opportunity to present yourself as an excellent candidate for admission. Whether or not a personal history essay or statement of purpose is required, always include a carefully written statement of purpose with your applications. A compelling statement of purpose does not have to be lengthy, but it should include some basic components:

- Part One—Introduce yourself and describe your previous educational background. This is your opportunity to describe any facet of your educational experience that you wish to emphasize. Perhaps you attended a highly ranked secondary school or college in your home country. Mention the name and any noteworthy characteristics of the secondary school or college from which you graduated. Explain the grading scale used at your school. Do not forget to mention your rank in your graduating class and any honors you may have received. This is not the time to be modest.

- Part Two—Describe your current academic interests and goals. It is very important to describe in some detail your specific study or career interests. Think about how these will fit into those of the institution to which you are applying, and mention the reasons why you have selected that institution.

- Part Three—Describe your long-term goals. When you finish your program of study, what do you plan to do next? If you already have a job offer or a career plan, describe it. Give some thought to how you'll demonstrate that studying in the U.S. will ultimately benefit others.

Use Personal Contacts When Possible

Appropriate and judicious use of your own network of contacts can be very helpful. Friends, former professors, former students of your selected institutions, and others may be willing to advise you during the application process and provide you with introductions to key administrators or professors. If suggested, you may wish to contact certain professors or administrators by mail, telephone, or e-mail. A personal visit to discuss your interest in the institution may be appropriate. Whatever your choice of communication, try to make the encounter pleasant and personal. Your goal is to make a positive impression, not to rush the admission decision.

There is no single right way to be admitted to U.S. colleges. The same characteristics that make the educational choice in the U.S. so difficult—the number of institutions and the variety of programs of study—are the same attributes that allow so many international students to find the institution that's right for them.

Searching for Two-Year Colleges Online

The Internet can be a great tool for gathering information about two-year colleges. There are many worthwhile sites that are ready to help guide you through the various aspects of the selection process, including Peterson's Undergraduate Channel at www.petersons.com/ugchannel.

HOW PETERSON'S UNDERGRADUATE CHANNEL CAN HELP

Choosing a college involves a serious commitment of time and resources. Therefore, it is important to have the most up-to-date information about prospective schools at your fingertips. That is why Peterson's Undergraduate Channel is a great place to start your college search and selection process.

Find a College

Peterson's Undergraduate Channel is a comprehensive information resource that will help you make sense of the college admissions process. Peterson's Undergraduate Channel offers visitors enhanced search criteria and an easily navigable interface. The Channel is organized into various sections that make finding a program easy and fun. You can search for colleges based on name or location for starters, or do a detailed search on the following criteria:

- *Location*
- *Major*
- *Tuition*
- *Size*
- *Student/faculty ratio*
- *Average GPA*
- *Type of college*
- *Sports*
- *Religion*

Once you have found the school of your choice, simply click on it to get information about the institution, including majors, off-campus programs, costs, faculty, admission requirements, location, academic programs, academic facilities, athletics, student life, financial aid, student government, and application information and contacts.

E-mail the School

If, after looking at the information provided on Peterson's Undergraduate Channel, you still have questions, you can send an e-mail directly to the admissions department of the school. Just click on the "E-mail the School" button and send your message. In most instances, if you keep your questions short and to the point, you will receive an answer in no time at all.

School Web Site

For institutions that have provided information about their Web sites, simply click on the "School Web Site" button and you will be taken directly to that institution's Web page. Once you arrive at the school's Web site, look around and get a feel for the place. Often, schools offer virtual tours of the campus, complete with photos and commentary. If you have specific questions about the school, a visit to a school's Web site will often yield an answer.

Detailed Description

If the schools you are interested in have provided Peterson's with an **In-Depth Description,** you can do a keyword search on that description. Here, schools are given the opportunity to communicate unique features of their programs to prospective students.

Microsite

Several educational institutions provide students access to microsites, where more information about the types of resources and services offered can be found. In addition, students can take campus tours, apply for admissions, and explore academic majors.

Apply

The Apply link gives you the ability to directly apply to the school online.

Add to My List

The My List feature is designed to help you with your college planning. Here you can save the list of schools you're interested in, which you can then revisit at any time, access all the features of the site, and be reminded of important dates. You'll also be notified when new features are added to the site.

Get Recruited

Here's your chance to stop looking for colleges and let them find you with CollegesWantYou^{SM} (www.collegeswantyou.com), the new approach to the search and selection process. Unlike other college search and selection tools, CollegesWantYou^{SM} allows you to enter information on your preferences, test scores, and extracurricular activities into the online form, and before you know it, colleges that meet your specifications will be in touch with you. Registration is free, and all you need to do is complete a short profile indicating your preferences and then sit back and wait as colleges contact you directly!

Write Admissions Essays

This year, 500,000 college applicants will write 500,000 different admissions essays. Half will be rejected by their first-choice school, while only an 11 eleven percent will gain admission to the nation's most selective colleges. With acceptance rates at all-time lows, setting yourself apart requires more than just blockbuster SAT scores and impeccable transcripts—it requires the perfect application essay. Named "the world's premier application essay editing service" by the New York Times Learning Network and "one of the best essay services on the Internet" by the *Washington Post,* EssayEdge (www.essayedge.com)

has helped more applicants write successful personal statements than any other company in the world. Learn more about EssayEdge and how it can give you an edge over hundreds of applicants with comparable academic credentials.

Practice for Your Test

At Peterson's, we understand that the college admissions process can be very stressful. With the stakes so high and the competition getting tighter every year, it's easy to feel like the process is out of your control. Fortunately, preparing for college admissions tests like the SAT, ACT, and PSAT helps you exert some control over the options you will have available to you. You can visit Peterson's Test Prep Channel (www.petersonstestprep.com) to learn more about how Peterson's can help you maximize your scores—and your options.

Use the Tools to Your Advantage

Choosing a college is an involved and complicated process. The tools available to you on www.petersons.com/ ugchannel can help you to be more productive in this process. So, what are you waiting for? Fire up your computer; your future alma mater may be just a click away!

How to Use This Guide

Peterson's Two-Year Colleges 2005 contains a wealth of information for anyone interested in colleges offering associate degrees. This section details the criteria that institutions must meet to be included in this guide and provides information about research procedures used by Peterson's.

QUICK-REFERENCE CHART

The Two-Year Colleges At-a-Glance chart is a geographically arranged table that lists colleges by name and city within the state, territory, or country in which they are located. Areas are listed in the following order: United States, U.S. territories, and other countries; the institutions in these countries are included because they are accredited by recognized U.S. accrediting bodies (see **Criteria for Inclusion** section).

The At-a-Glance chart contains basic information that will enable you to compare institutions quickly according to broad characteristics such as enrollment, application requirements, types of financial aid available, and numbers of sports and majors offered. An asterisk (*) after an institution's name denotes that a **Special Message** is included in the college's profile, and a dagger (†) indicates that an institution has one or more entries in the **In-Depth Descriptions of Two-Year Colleges** section.

Column 1 (Degrees Awarded)

C = *college transfer associate degree:* the degree awarded after a "university-parallel" program, equivalent to the first two years of a bachelor's degree.

T = *terminal associate degree:* the degree resulting from a one- to three-year program providing training for a specific occupation.

B = *bachelor's degree (baccalaureate):* the degree resulting from a liberal arts, science, professional, or preprofessional program normally lasting four years, although in some cases an accelerated program can be completed in three years.

M = *master's degree:* the first graduate (postbaccalaureate) degree in the liberal arts and sciences and certain professional fields, usually requiring one to two years of full-time study.

D = *doctoral degree (doctorate):* the highest degree awarded in research-oriented academic disciplines, usually requiring from three to six years of full-time study beyond the baccalaureate and intended as preparation for university-level teaching and research.

F = *first professional degree:* the degree required to be academically qualified to practice in certain professions, such as law and medicine, having as a prerequisite at least two years of college credit and usually requiring a total of at least six years of study including prior college-level work.

Column 2 (Institutional Control)

Private institutions are designated as one of the following:

Ind = *independent* (nonprofit)

I-R = *independent-religious:* nonprofit; sponsored by or affiliated with a particular religious group or having a nondenominational or interdenominational religious orientation.

Prop = *proprietary* (profit-making)

Public institutions are designated by the source of funding, as follows:

Fed = *federal*

St = *state*

Comm = *commonwealth* (Puerto Rico)

Terr = *territory* (U.S. territories)

Cou = *county*

Dist = *district:* an administrative unit of public education, often having boundaries different from units of local government.

City = *city*

St-L = *state and local:* "local" may refer to county, district, or city.

St-R = *state-related:* funded primarily by the state but administratively autonomous.

Column 3 (Student Body)

M = *men only* (100% of student body)

PM = *coed, primarily men*

W = *women only* (100% of student body)

PW = *coed, primarily women*

M/W = *coeducational*

Column 4 (Undergraduate Enrollment)

The figure shown represents the number of full-time and part-time students enrolled in undergraduate degree programs as of fall 2003.

Columns 5–7 (Enrollment Percentages)

Figures are shown for the percentages of the fall 2003 undergraduate enrollment made up of students attending part-time (column 5) and students 25 years of age or older (column 6). Also listed is the percentage of students in the last graduating class who completed a college-transfer associate program and went directly on to four-year colleges (column 7).

For columns 8 through 15, the following letter codes are used: Y = yes; N = no; R = recommended; S = for some.

Columns 8–10 (Admission Policies)

The information in these columns shows whether the college has an open admission policy (column 8) whereby virtually all applicants are accepted without regard to standardized test scores, grade average, or class rank; whether a high school equivalency certificate is accepted in place of a high school diploma for admission consideration (column 9); and whether a high school transcript (column 10) is required as part of the application process. In column 10, the combination of the codes R and S indicates that a high school transcript is recommended for all applicants and required for some.

Columns 11–12 (Financial Aid)

These columns show which colleges offer the following types of financial aid: need-based aid (column 11) and part-time jobs (column 12), including those offered through the federal government's Federal Work-Study Program.

Columns 13–15 (Services and Facilities)

These columns show which colleges offer the following: career counseling (column 13) on either an individual or group basis, job placement services (column 14) for individual students, and college-owned or -operated housing facilities (column 16) for noncommuting students.

Column 16 (Sports)

This figure indicates the number of sports that a college offers at the intramural and/or intercollegiate levels.

Column 17 (Majors)

This figure indicates the number of major fields of study in which a college offers degree programs.

PROFILES OF TWO-YEAR COLLEGES AND SPECIAL MESSAGES

The **Profiles of Two-Year Colleges** contain basic data in capsule form for quick review and comparison. The follow-ing outline of the profile format shows the section headings and the items that each section covers. Any item that does not apply to a particular college or for which no information was supplied is omitted from that college's profile. **Special Messages,** which appear in the profiles just below the bulleted highlights, have been written by those colleges that wished to supplement the profile data with additional information.

Bulleted Highlights

The bulleted highlights feature important information for quick reference and comparison. The number of *possible* bulleted highlights that an ideal profile would have if all questions were answered in a timely manner are represented below. However, not every institution provides all of the information necessary to fill out every bulleted line. In such instances, the line will not appear.

First bullet

Institutional control: Private institutions are designated as independent (nonprofit), proprietary (profit-making), or independent, with a specific religious denomination or affiliation. Nondenominational or interdenominational religious orientation is possible and would be indicated. Public institutions are designated by the source of funding. Designations include federal, state, province, commonwealth (Puerto Rico), territory (U.S. territories), county, district (an educational administrative unit often having boundaries different from units of local government), city, state and local (local may refer to county, district, or city), or state-related (funded primarily by the state but administratively autonomous).

Religious affiliation is also noted here.

Institutional type: Each institution is classified as one of the following:

Primarily two-year college: Awards baccalaureate degrees, but the vast majority of students are enrolled in two-year programs.

Four-year college: Awards baccalaureate degrees; may also award associate degrees; does not award graduate (postbaccalaureate) degrees.

Five-year college: Awards a five-year baccalaureate in a professional field such as architecture or pharmacy; does not award graduate degrees.

Upper-level institution: Awards baccalaureate degrees, but entering students must have at least two years of previous college-level credit; may also offer graduate degrees.

Comprehensive institution: Awards baccalaureate degrees; may also award associate degrees; offers graduate degree programs, primarily at the master's, specialist's, or professional level, although one or two doctoral programs may be offered.

University: Offers four years of undergraduate work plus graduate degrees through the doctorate in more than two academic or professional fields.

Founding date: If the year an institution was chartered differs from the year when instruction actually began, the earlier date is given.

System or administrative affiliation: Any coordinate institutions or system affiliations are indicated. An institution that has separate colleges or campuses for men and women but shares facilities and courses it is termed a coordinate institution. A formal administrative grouping of institutions, either private or public, of which the college is a part, or the name of a single institution with which the college is administratively affiliated is a system.

Second bullet

Calendar: Most colleges indicate one of the following: *4-1-4, 4-4-1,* or a similar arrangement (two terms of equal length plus an abbreviated winter or spring term, with the numbers referring to months); *semesters; trimesters; quarters; 3-3* (three courses for each of three terms); *modular* (the academic year is divided into small blocks of time; course of varying lengths are assembled according to individual programs); or *standard year* (for most Canadian institutions).

Third bullet

Degree: This names the full range of levels of certificates, diplomas, and degrees, including prebaccalaureate, graduate, and professional, that are offered by this institution.

Associate degree: Normally requires at least two but fewer than four years of full-time college work or its equivalent.

Bachelor's degree (baccalaureate): Requires at least four years but not more than five years of full-time college-level work or its equivalent. This includes all bachelor's degrees in which the normal four years of work are completed in three years and bachelor's degrees conferred in a five-year cooperative (work-study plan) program. A cooperative plan provides for alternate class attendance and employment in business, industry, or government. This allows students to combine actual work experience with their college studies.

Master's degree: Requires the successful completion of a program of study of at least the full-time equivalent of one but not more than two years of work beyond the bachelor's degree.

Doctoral degree (doctorate): The highest degree in graduate study. The doctoral degree classification includes Doctor of Education, Doctor of Juridical Science, Doctor of Public Health, and the Doctor of Philosophy in any nonprofessional field.

First professional degree: The first postbaccalaureate degree in one of the following fields: chiropractic (DC, DCM), dentistry (DDS, DMD), medicine (MD), optometry (OD), osteopathic medicine (DO), rabbinical and Talmudic studies (MHL, Rav), pharmacy (BPharm, PharmD), podiatry (PodD, DP, DPM), veterinary medicine (DVM), law (JD), or divinity/ministry (BD, MDiv).

First professional certificate (postdegree): Requires completion of an organized program of study after completion of the first professional degree. Examples are refresher courses or additional units of study in a specialty or subspecialty.

Post-master's certificate: Requires completion of an organized program of study of 24 credit hours beyond the master's degree but does not meet the requirements of academic degrees at the doctoral level.

Fourth bullet

Setting: Schools are designated as *urban* (located within a major city), *suburban* (a residential area within commuting distance of a major city), *small-town* (a small but compactly settled area not within commuting distance of a major city), or *rural* (a remote and sparsely populated area). The phrase *easy access to . . .* indicates that the campus is within an hour's drive of the nearest major metropolitan area that has a population greater than 500,000.

Fifth bullet

Endowment: The total dollar value of donations to the institution or the multicampus educational system of which the institution is a part.

Sixth bullet

Student body: An institution is coed (coeducational—admits men and women), primarily (80 percent or more) women, primarily men, women only, or men only.

Undergraduate students: Represents the number of full-time and part-time students enrolled in undergraduate degree programs as of fall 2003. The percentage of full-time undergraduates and the percentages of men and women are given.

Special Messages

These messages have been written by those colleges that wished to supplement the profile data with additional timely and important information.

Category Overviews

Undergraduates

For fall 2003, the number of full- and part-time undergraduate students is listed. This list provides the number of states and U.S. territories, including the District of Columbia and Puerto Rico and other countries from which undergraduates come. Percentages are given of undergraduates who are from out of state; Native American, African American, and Asian American or Pacific Islander; international students; transfer students; and living on campus

Retention: The percentage of 2002 freshmen who returned for the fall 2003 term.

Freshmen

Admission: Figures are given for the number of students who applied for fall 2003 admission, the number of those who were admitted, and the number who enrolled. Freshman statistics include the average high school GPA; the percentage of freshmen who took the SAT I and received verbal and math scores above 500, above 600, and above 700, as well as the percentage of freshmen taking the ACT Assessment who received a composite score of 18 or higher.

Faculty

Total: The total number of faculty members; the percentage of full-time faculty members as of fall 2003; and the percentage of full-time faculty members who hold doctoral/first professional/terminal degrees.

Student-faculty ratio: The school's estimate of the ratio of matriculated undergraduate students to faculty members teaching undergraduate courses.

Majors

This section lists the major fields of study offered by the college.

Academic Programs

Details are given here on study options available at each college.

Accelerated degree program: Students may earn a bachelor's degree in three academic years.

Academic remediation for entering students: Instructional courses designed for students deficient in the general competencies necessary for a regular postsecondary curriculum and educational setting.

Adult/continuing education programs: Courses offered for nontraditional students who are currently working or are returning to formal education.

Advanced placement: Credit toward a degree awarded for acceptable scores on College Board Advanced Placement tests.

Cooperative (co-op) education programs: Formal arrangements with off-campus employers allowing students to combine work and study in order to gain degree-related experience, usually extending the time required to complete a degree.

Distance learning: For-credit courses that can be accessed off campus via cable television, the Internet, satellite, videotapes, correspondence course, or other media.

Double major: A program of study in which a student concurrently completes the requirements of two majors.

English as a second language (ESL): A course of study designed specifically for students whose native language is not English.

External degree programs: A program of study in which students earn credits toward a degree through a combination of independent study, college courses, proficiency examinations, and personal experience. External degree programs require minimal or no classroom attendance.

Freshmen honors college: A separate academic program for talented freshmen.

Honors programs: Any special program for very able students offering the opportunity for educational enrichment, independent study, acceleration, or some combination of these.

Independent study: Academic work, usually undertaken outside the regular classroom structure, chosen or designed by the student with the departmental approval and instructor supervision.

Internships: Any short-term, supervised work experience usually related to a student's major field, for which the student earns academic credit. The work can be full- or part-time, on or off campus, paid or unpaid.

Off-campus study: A formal arrangement with one or more domestic institutions under which students may take courses at the other institution(s) for credit.

Part-time degree program: Students may earn a degree through part-time enrollment in regular session (daytime) classes or evening, weekend, or summer classes.

Self-designed major: Program of study based on individual interests, designed by the student with the assistance of an adviser.

Services for LD students: Special help for learning-disabled students with resolvable difficulties, such as dyslexia.

Study abroad: An arrangement by which a student completes part of the academic program studying in another country. A college may operate a campus abroad or it may have a cooperative agreement with other U.S. institutions or institutions in other countries.

Summer session for credit: Summer courses through which students may make up degree work or accelerate their program.

Tutorials: Undergraduates can arrange for special in-depth academic assignments (not for remediation) working with faculty one-on-one or in small groups.

ROTC: Army, Naval, or Air Force Reserve Officers' Training Corps programs offered either on campus or at a cooperating host institution [designated by (C)].

Unusual degree programs: Nontraditional programs such as a 3-2 degree program, in which 3 years of liberal arts study is followed by two years of study in a professional field at another institution (or in a professional division of the same institution), resulting in two bachelor's degrees or a bachelor's and a master's degree.

Library

This section lists the name of the main library; the number of other libraries on campus; numbers of books, microform titles, serials, commercial online services, and audiovisual materials.

Computers on Campus

This paragraph includes the number of on-campus computer terminals and PCs available for general student use and their locations; computer purchase or lease plans; PC requirements for entering students; and campuswide computer network, e-mail, and access to computer labs, the Internet, and software.

Student Life

Housing options: The institution's policy about whether students are permitted to live off campus or are required to live on campus for a specified period; whether freshmen-only, coed, single-sex, cooperative, and disabled student housing options are available; whether campus housing is leased by the school and/or provided by a third party; whether freshman applicants are given priority for college housing. The phrase *college housing not available* indicates that no college-owned or -operated housing facilities are provided for undergraduates and that noncommuting students must arrange for their own accommodations.

Activities and organizations: Lists information on drama-theater groups, choral groups, marching bands, student-run campus newspapers, student-run radio stations and social organizations (sororities, fraternities, eating clubs, etc.) and how many are represented on campus.

Campus security: Campus safety measures including 24-hour emergency response devices (telephones and alarms) and patrols by trained security personnel, student patrols, late-night transport-escort service, and controlled dormitory access (key, security card, etc.).

Student services: Information provided indicates services offered to students by the college, such as legal services, health clinics, personal-psychological counseling and women's centers.

Athletics

Membership in one or more of the following athletic associations is indicated by initials.

NCAA: National Collegiate Athletic Association

NAIA: National Association of Intercollegiate Athletics

NCCAA: National Christian College Athletic Association

NSCAA: National Small College Athletic Association

NJCAA: National Junior College Athletic Association

CIS: Canadian Interuniversity Sports

The overall NCAA division in which all or most intercollegiate teams compete is designated by a roman numeral I, II, or III. All teams that do not compete in this division are listed as exceptions.

Sports offered by the college are divided into two groups: intercollegiate (**M** or **W** following the name of each sport indicates that it is offered for men or women) and intramural. An **s** in parentheses following an **M** or **W** for an intercollegiate sport indicates that athletic scholarships (or grants-in-aid) are offered for men or women in that sport, and a **c** indicates a club team as opposed to a varsity team.

Standardized Tests

The most commonly required standardized tests are ACT Assessment, SAT I, and SAT II Subject Tests, including the SAT II: Writing. These and other standardized tests may be used for selective admission, as a basis for counseling or course placement, or for both purposes. This section notes if a test is used for admission or placement and whether it is required, required for some, or recommended.

In addition to the ACT Assessment and SAT I, the following standardized entrance and placement examinations are referred to by their initials:

ABLE: Adult Basic Learning Examination

ACT ASSET: ACT Assessment of Skills for Successful Entry and Transfer

ACT PEP: ACT Proficiency Examination Program

CAT: California Achievement Tests

CELT: Comprehensive English Language Test

CPAt: Career Programs Assessment

CPT: Computerized Placement Test

DAT: Differential Aptitude Test

LSAT: Law School Admission Test

MAPS: Multiple Assessment Program Service

MCAT: Medical College Admission Test

MMPI: Minnesota Multiphasic Personality Inventory

OAT: Optometry Admission Test

PAA: Prueba de Aptitud Académica (Spanish-language version of the SAT I)

PCAT: Pharmacy College Admission Test

PSAT: Preliminary SAT

SCAT: Scholastic College Aptitude Test

SRA: Scientific Research Association (administers verbal, arithmetical, and achievement tests)

TABE: Test of Adult Basic Education

TASP: Texas Academic Skills Program

TOEFL: Test of English as a Foreign Language (for international students whose native language is not English)

WPCT: Washington Pre-College Test

Costs

Costs are given for the 2004–05 academic year or for the 2003–04 academic year if 2004–05 figures were not yet available. Annual expenses may be expressed as a comprehensive fee (including full-time tuition, mandatory fees, and college room and board) or as separate figures for full-time tuition, fees, room and board, or room only. For public institutions where tuition differs according to residence, separate figures are given for area or state residents and for nonresidents. Part-time tuition is expressed in terms of a per-unit rate (per credit, per semester hour, etc.) as specified by the institution.

The tuition structure at some institutions is complex in that freshmen and sophomores may be charged a different rate from that for juniors and seniors, a professional or vocational division may have a different fee structure from the liberal arts division of the same institution, or part-time tuition may be prorated on a sliding scale according to the number of credit hours taken. Tuition and fees may vary according to academic program, campus/location, class time (day, evening, weekend), course/credit load, course level, degree level, reciprocity agreements, and student level. Room and board charges are reported as an average for one academic year and may vary according to the board plan selected, campus/location, type of housing facility, or student level. If no college-owned or -operated housing facilities are offered, the phrase *college housing not available* will appear in the Housing section of the Student Life paragraph.

Tuition payment plans that may be offered to undergraduates include tuition prepayment, installment payments, and deferred payment. A tuition prepayment plan gives a student the option of locking in the current tuition rate for the entire term of enrollment by paying the full amount in advance rather than year by year. Colleges that offer such a prepayment plan may also help the student to arrange financing.

The availability of full or partial undergraduate tuition waivers to minority students, children of alumni, employees or their children, adult students, and senior citizens may be listed.

Financial Aid

Financial aid information presented represents aid awarded to undergraduates for the 2003–04 academic year. Figures are given for the number of undergraduates who applied for aid, the number who were judged to have need, and the number who had their need met. The number of Federal Work-Study and/or part-time jobs and average earnings are listed, as well as the number of non-need based awards that were made. Non-need based awards are college-administered scholarships for which the college determines the recipient and amount of each award. These scholarships are awarded to full-time undergraduates on the basis of merit or personal attributes without regard to need, although they many certainly be given to students who also happen to need aid. The average percent of need met, the average financial aid package awarded to undergraduates (the amount of scholarships, grants, work-study payments, or loans in the institutionally administered financial aid package divided by the number of students who received any financial aid—amounts used to pay the officially designated Expected Family Contribution (EFC), such as PLUS or other alternative loans, are excluded from the amounts reported), the average amount of need-based gift aid, and the average amount of non-need based aid are given. Average indebtedness, which is the average per-borrower indebtedness of the last graduating undergraduate class from amounts borrowed at this institution through any loan programs, excluding parent loans, is listed last.

Applying

Application and admission options include the following:

Early admission: Highly qualified students may matriculate before graduating from high school.

Early action plan: An admission plan that allows students to apply and be notified of an admission decision well in advance of the regular notification dates. If accepted, the candidate is not committed to enroll; students may reply to the offer under the college's regular reply policy.

Early decision plan: A plan that permits students to apply and be notified of an admission decision (and financial aid offer, if applicable) well in advance of the regular notification date. Applicants agree to accept an offer of admission and to withdraw their applications from other colleges. Candidates who are not accepted under early decision are automatically considered with the regular applicant pool, without prejudice.

Deferred entrance: The practice of permitting accepted students to postpone enrollment, usually for a period of one academic term or year.

Application fee: The fee required with an application is noted. This is typically nonrefundable, although under certain specified conditions it may be waived or returned.

Requirements: Other application requirements are grouped into three categories: required for all, required for some, and recommended. They may include an essay, standardized test scores, a high school transcript, a minimum high school grade point average (expressed as a number on a scale of 0 to 4.0, where 4.0 equals A, 3.0 equals B, etc.), letters of recommendation, an interview on campus or with local alumni, and, for certain types of schools or programs, special requirements such as a musical audition or an art portfolio.

Application deadlines and notification dates:
Admission application deadlines and dates for notification of acceptance or rejection are given either as specific dates or as *rolling* and *continuous*. Rolling means that applications are processed as they are received, and qualified students are accepted as long as there are openings. Continuous means that applicants are notified of acceptance or rejection as applications are processed up until the date indicated or the actual beginning of classes. The application deadline and the notification date for transfers are given if they differ from the dates for freshmen. Early decision and early action application deadlines and notification dates are also indicated when relevant.

Freshmen Application Contact

The name, title, and telephone number of the person to contact for application information are given at the end of the profile. The admission office address is listed. Toll-free telephone numbers may also be included. The admission office fax number and e-mail address, if available, are listed, provided the school wanted them printed for use by prospective students.

Additional Information

Each college that has an *In-Depth Description* in the guide will have a cross-reference appended to the profile, referring you directly to that In-Depth Description.

IN-DEPTH DESCRIPTIONS OF TWO-YEAR COLLEGES

Nearly 100 two-page narrative descriptions appear here. This section shifts the focus to a variety of other factors, some of them intangible, which should also be considered in the college decision-making equation. The descriptions are prepared exclusively by college officials and are designed to help give students a better sense of the individuality of each institution, in terms that include campus environment, student activities, and lifestyle. Such quality-of-life intangibles can be the deciding factors in the college selection process. The absence from this section of any college does not constitute an editorial decision on the part of Peterson's. In essence, this section is an open forum for colleges, on a voluntary basis, to communicate their particular messages to prospective students. The colleges included have paid a fee to Peterson's to provide this information to you. The descriptions are arranged alphabetically by the official name of the institution and are edited to provide a consistent format across entries for your ease of comparison.

INDEXES

Associate Degree Programs at Two- and Four-Year Colleges

These indexes present hundreds of undergraduate fields of study that are currently offered most widely according to the colleges' responses on *Thomson Peterson's Annual Survey of Undergraduate Institutions*. The majors appear in alphabetical order, each followed by an alphabetical list of the schools that offer an associate-level program in that field. Liberal Arts and Studies indicates a general program with no specified major. The terms used for the majors are those of the U.S. Department of Education Classification of Instructional Programs (CIPs). Many institutions, however, use different terms. Readers should visit www.petersons.com in order to contact a college and ask for its catalog or refer to the **In-Depth Description** in this book for the school's exact terminology. In addition, although the term "major" is used in this guide, some colleges may use other terms, such as "concentration," "program of study," or "field."

DATA COLLECTION PROCEDURES

The data contained in the **Profiles of Two-Year Colleges** and **Indexes** were researched between fall 2003 and spring 2004 through *Thomson Peterson's Annual Survey of Undergraduate Institutions*. Questionnaires were sent to the more than 1,700 colleges that meet the outlined inclusion criteria. All data included in this edition have been submitted by officials (usually admission and financial aid officers, registrars, or institutional research personnel) at the colleges themselves. In addition, the great majority of institutions that submitted data were contacted directly by Peterson's research staff to verify unusual figures, resolve discrepancies, and obtain additional data. All usable information received in time for publication has been included. The omission of any particular item from the **Profiles of Two-Year Colleges** and **Indexes** listing signifies either that the item is not applicable to that institution or that data were not available. Because of the comprehensive editorial review that takes place in our offices and because all material comes directly from college officials, Peterson's has every reason to believe that the information presented in this guide is accurate at the time of printing. However, students should check with a specific college or university at the time of application to verify such figures as tuition and fees, which may have changed since the publication of this volume.

CRITERIA FOR INCLUSION IN THIS BOOK

Peterson's Two-Year Colleges 2005 covers accredited institutions in the United States, U.S. territories, and other countries that award the associate degree as their most popular undergraduate offering (a few also offer bachelor's, master's, or doctoral degrees). The term two-year college is the commonly used designation for institutions that grant the associate degree, since two years is the normal duration of the traditional associate degree program. However, some programs may be completed in one year, others require three years, and, of course, part-time programs may take a considerably longer period. Therefore, "two-year college" should be understood as a conventional term that accurately describes most of the institutions included in this guide but which should not be taken literally in all cases. Also included are some non-degree-granting institutions, usually branch campuses of a multicampus system, which offer the equivalent of the first two years of a bachelor's degree, transferable to a bachelor's degree–granting institution. To be included in this guide, an institution must have full accreditation or be a candidate for accreditation (preaccreditation) status by an institutional or specialized accrediting body recognized by the U.S. Department of Education or the Council for Higher Education Accreditation (CHEA). Institutional accrediting bodies, which review each institution as a whole, include the six regional associations of schools and colleges (Middle States, New England, North Central, Northwest, Southern, and Western), each of which is responsible for a specified portion of the United States and its territories. Other institutional accrediting bodies are national in scope and accredit specific kinds of institutions (e.g., Bible colleges, independent colleges, and rabbinical and Talmudic schools). Program registration by the New York State Board of Regents is considered to be the equivalent of institutional accreditation, since the board requires that all programs offered by an institution meet its standards before recognition is granted. This guide also includes institutions outside the United States that are accredited by these U.S. accrediting bodies. There are recognized specialized or professional accrediting bodies in more than forty different fields, each of which is authorized to accredit institutions or specific programs in its particular field. For specialized institutions that offer programs in one field only, we designate this to be the equivalent of institutional accreditation. A full explanation of the accrediting process and complete information on recognized, institutional (regional and national) and specialized accrediting bodies can be found online at www.chea.org or at www.ed.gov//admins/finaid/accred/index.html.

Quick-Reference CHART

Two-Year Colleges At-a-Glance

This chart includes the names and locations of accredited two-year colleges in the United States and U.S. territories and shows institutions' responses to the *Thomson Peterson's Survey of Undergraduate Institutions*. If an institution submitted incomplete data, one or more columns opposite the institution's name is blank.
An asterisk after the school name denotes a *Special Message* following the college's profile, and a dagger indicates that the institution has one or more entries in the *In-Depth Descriptions of Two-Year Colleges* section. If a school does not appear, it did not report any of the information.

Y—Yes; N—No; R—Recommended; S—For Some

Degrees Awarded: College Transfer Associate (C); Terminal Associate (T); Bachelor's (B); Master's (M); Doctoral (D); First Professional (F)

Institutional Control: County, District, City, State and Local, State-Related; Federal, State, Commonwealth, Territory; Independent, Independent-Religious, Proprietary

Student Body: Men, Primarily Men, Women, Primarily Women, Coed

College	Location	Degrees Awarded	Institutional Control	Student Body	Undergrad Enrollment Fall 2003	% Attending Part-Time	% 25 Years of Age or Older	% of Grads Going on to Four-Year Colleges	HS Equivalency Certificate Accepted	Open Admissions	HS Transcript Required	Need-Based Aid Available	Part-Time Jobs Available	Career Counseling Available	Job Placement Services Available	College Housing Available	Number of Majors Offered	Number of Sports Offered
U.S. AND U.S. TERRITORIES																		
Alabama																		
Bevill State Community College	Sumiton	C,T	St	M/W	4,327	43												
Bishop State Community College	Mobile	C,T	St	M/W	4,439	44												
Calhoun Community College	Decatur	C,T	St	M/W	8,923	60	38		Y	Y	S	Y	Y			N	1	46
Central Alabama Community College	Alexander City	C,T	St	M/W	1,790		52	33	Y	Y	S	Y	Y	Y	Y	N	5	11
Chattahoochee Valley Community College	Phenix City	C,T	St	M/W	613	18												
Community College of the Air Force	Maxwell Air Force Base	T	Fed	PM				63	Y		Y				Y	Y	15	51
Enterprise-Ozark Community College	Enterprise	C,T	St	M/W	1,590	46												
Gadsden State Community College	Gadsden	C,T	St	M/W	5,868				Y	Y	Y	Y	Y	Y	Y	Y	7	21
Herzing College	Birmingham	C,T,B	Prop	M/W	600	34												
ITT Technical Institute	Birmingham	T,B	Prop	M/W	415				N	Y	Y	Y	Y	Y	Y	N		14
James H. Faulkner State Community College*	Bay Minette	C,T	St	M/W	3,067	37	39		Y	Y	Y	Y	Y	Y	Y	Y	6	16
Jefferson Davis Community College	Brewton	C,T	St	M/W	1,442	37	30		Y	Y	Y	Y	Y	Y	Y		1	19
Jefferson State Community College	Birmingham	C,T	St	M/W	7,183	61	39		Y	Y	S	Y	Y	Y	Y	N	8	22
J. F. Drake State Technical College	Huntsville	C	St	M/W	796	42	55		Y		Y			Y	Y	N		7
Lawson State Community College	Birmingham	C,T	St	M/W	2,168	35	33	1	Y	Y	Y	Y	Y	Y	Y	N	11	44
Lurleen B. Wallace Community College	Andalusia	C,T	St	M/W	1,490	27			Y	Y	Y	Y	Y	Y	Y	N	4	3
Northeast Alabama Community College	Rainsville	C,T	St	M/W	2,072	50	32	30	Y	Y			Y	Y	Y	N		18
Northwest-Shoals Community College	Muscle Shoals	C,T	St	M/W	4,663	42	40		Y	Y	Y	Y	Y	Y	Y	Y	9	35
Prince Institute of Professional Studies	Montgomery	T	Ind	PW	94	40	50			Y	Y	Y				N		1
Reid State Technical College	Evergreen	T	St	M/W	806	41	55		Y		Y	Y	Y	Y	Y	N		2
Remington College–Mobile Campus	Mobile	C,T,B	Prop	M/W	454		49			Y	Y	Y	Y	Y	Y	N		7
Shelton State Community College	Tuscaloosa	C,T	St	M/W	5,931		12		Y	Y	Y	Y	Y	Y	Y	N	6	32
Snead State Community College	Boaz	C,T	St	M/W	1,787	37	26	53	Y	Y	Y	Y	Y	Y	Y	Y	6	10
Trenholm State Technical College	Montgomery	T	St	M/W	1,615	46	55		Y	Y	Y	Y	Y			N		30
Wallace State Community College	Hanceville	C,T	St	M/W	6,028													
Alaska																		
U of Alaska Anchorage, Kenai Peninsula College	Soldotna	C,T	St	M/W	1,923		82		Y	Y	Y	Y	Y	Y		N		7
U of Alaska Anchorage, Kodiak College	Kodiak	C,T	St	M/W	786													
U of Alaska Anchorage, Matanuska-Susitna College	Palmer	C,T	St	M/W	1,431	73	82		Y	Y	Y	Y	Y	Y		N		8
U of Alaska Southeast, Ketchikan Campus	Ketchikan	C,T	St-L	M/W	692		46		Y	Y	Y	Y		Y	Y			4
Arizona																		
Arizona Automotive Institute	Glendale	T	Prop		600													
Arizona Western College	Yuma	C,T	St-L	M/W	6,454	74	40		Y	Y			Y	Y	Y	Y	9	43
The Bryman School	Phoenix	T	Prop	PW	1,100													
Central Arizona College	Coolidge	C,T	Cou	M/W	5,745	71	71		Y				Y	Y	Y	Y	8	26
Chandler-Gilbert Community College	Chandler	C,T	St-L	M/W	7,513													
Chaparral College	Tucson	C,T,B	Prop	M/W	400		70		Y	Y	Y	Y		Y	Y	N		5
Cochise College	Douglas	C,T	St-L	M/W	5,782													
Cochise College	Sierra Vista	C,T	St-L	M/W	4,446	72												
Diné College	Tsaile	C,T	Fed	M/W	1,836													
Eastern Arizona College	Thatcher	C,T	St-L	M/W	3,925	59	19		Y		R	Y	Y	Y	Y	Y	10	49
Estrella Mountain Community College	Avondale	C,T	St-L	M/W	5,410	79			Y				Y	Y				2
Everest College	Phoenix	C,T	Prop	M/W	590	27	95	2	N	Y	Y	Y		Y	Y	N		4
GateWay Community College	Phoenix	C,T	St-L	M/W	9,377	90												
Glendale Community College	Glendale	C,T	St-L	M/W	20,692	71	44		Y		S		Y	Y	Y	N	11	28
High-Tech Institute	Phoenix	T,B	Prop	M/W	1,544				Y	Y	Y	Y	Y			N		4
International Institute of the Americas	Phoenix	C,T,B	Ind	M/W	1,386		76		Y	Y			Y	Y		N		9
ITT Technical Institute	Phoenix	T,B	Prop	M/W	447													
ITT Technical Institute	Tucson	T,B	Prop	M/W	375				N	Y	Y	Y	Y	Y	Y	N		12
Mesa Community College	Mesa	C,T	St-L	M/W	28,000													
Mohave Community College	Kingman	C,T	St	M/W	6,695	69			Y		S	Y	Y	Y	Y	Y		23
Northland Pioneer College	Holbrook	C,T	St-L	M/W	4,928	80	76		Y			Y	Y	Y	Y			58
Paradise Valley Community College	Phoenix	C,T	St-L	M/W	7,709													
Phoenix College	Phoenix	C,T	St-L	M/W	13,150				Y	Y	Y	Y	Y			N	12	40
Pima Community College	Tucson	C,T	St-L	M/W	31,216	70	46	15	Y			Y	Y	Y	Y	N	18	59
Pima Medical Institute	Mesa	T	Prop						N							N		2

This chart includes the names and locations of accredited two-year colleges in the United States and U.S. territories and shows institutions' responses to the *Thomson Peterson's Survey of Undergraduate Institutions.* If an institution submitted incomplete data, one or more columns opposite the institution's name is blank.

An asterisk after the school name denotes a *Special Message* following the college's profile, and a dagger indicates that the institution has one or more entries in the *In-Depth Descriptions of Two-Year Colleges* section. If a school does not appear, it did not report any of the information.

Y—Yes; N—No; R—Recommended; S—For Some

Column headers (diagonal): Degrees Awarded [College Transfer Associate (C), Terminal Associate (T), Bachelor's (B), Master's (M), Doctoral (D), First Professional (P)] | Institutional Control | Student Body | Undergraduate Enrollment Fall 2003 | Percent Attending Part-Time | Percent 25 Years of Age or Older | Percent of Grads Going on to Four-Year Colleges | High School Equivalency Certificate Accepted | Open Admissions | High School Transcript Required | Need-Based Aid Available | Part-Time Jobs Available | Career Counseling Available | Job Placement Services Available | College Housing Available | Number of Sports Offered | Number of Majors Offered

Institution	Location	Deg	Ctrl	Body	Enroll	PT%	25+%	Grad%	HSEq	Open	HSTr	NeedAid	PTjob	Career	JobPl	Hous	Sports	Majors
Pima Medical Institute	Tucson	T	Prop	M/W	350							N					N	1	2
The Refrigeration School	Phoenix	T	Prop	M/W	350									Y			N		1
Rio Salado College	Tempe	C,T	St-L	M/W	6,000		43		Y				Y	Y	Y	N	14	25
Scottsdale Community College	Scottsdale	C,T	St-L	M/W			43		Y				Y	Y	Y	N	14	25
Scottsdale Culinary Institute	Scottsdale	T	Prop	M/W	1,200														
South Mountain Community College	Phoenix	C,T	St-L	M/W	3,933														
Yavapai College	Prescott	C,T	St-L	M/W	8,188	84	70	80	Y	Y	Y	Y	Y	Y	Y	Y	5	25
Arkansas																		
Arkansas Northeastern College	Blytheville	C,T	St	M/W	2,067	38	41	5	Y	Y	R	Y	Y	Y	Y	N		14
Arkansas State University–Beebe	Beebe	C,T	St	M/W	3,192	44	38		Y	Y	Y	Y	Y	Y	Y	N	12	22
Arkansas State University–Mountain Home	Mountain Home	C,T	St	M/W	1,347		43		Y	Y	Y	Y				N		11
Arkansas State University–Newport	Newport	C	St	M/W	896													
Black River Technical College	Pocahontas	C,T	St	M/W	1,243	48												
Cossatot Community College of the University of Arkansas	De Queen	C,T	St	M/W	944	61			Y	Y	R	Y	Y	Y	Y			12
Crowley's Ridge College	Paragould	C,T	I-R	M/W	183				Y	Y	Y	Y	Y			Y	4	2
East Arkansas Community College	Forrest City	C,T	St	M/W	1,415		47		Y	Y	Y	Y	Y	Y	Y	N		7
ITT Technical Institute	Little Rock	T,B	Prop	M/W	352				N	Y	Y	Y	Y	Y	Y	N		11
Mid-South Community College	West Memphis	C,T	St	M/W	1,159	71	45		Y	Y	Y	Y	Y	Y		N		5
National Park Community College	Hot Springs	C,T	St-L	M/W	2,996	59												
North Arkansas College	Harrison	C,T	St-L	M/W	2,120	43	40		Y	Y	S	Y	Y	Y	Y	N	11	11
Ouachita Technical College	Malvern	C,T	St	M/W	1,291	56	45		Y	Y	Y	Y	Y	Y	Y	N		16
Ozarka College	Melbourne	C,T	St	M/W	756	25	43	52	Y	Y	Y	Y	Y	Y	Y	N		10
Phillips Comm Coll of the U of Arkansas	Helena	C,T	St-L	M/W	2,322													
Pulaski Technical College	North Little Rock	C,T	St	M/W	6,128		55		Y	Y	Y	Y	Y	Y	Y	N		6
Rich Mountain Community College	Mena	C,T	St-L	M/W	1,078			75	Y	Y	Y	Y	Y	Y	Y	N		2
South Arkansas Community College	El Dorado	C,T	St	M/W	1,087	64	43		Y			Y	Y	Y	Y	N	4	10
Southeast Arkansas College	Pine Bluff	C,T	St	M/W	2,197	54	58		Y	Y	Y	Y	Y	Y	Y	N	1	14
Southern Arkansas University Tech	Camden	C,T	St	M/W	1,223	62	54		Y	Y	R,S	Y				Y	6	18
University of Arkansas Community College at Batesville	Batesville	C,T	St	M/W	1,317	40	40		Y	Y		Y						13
University of Arkansas Community College at Hope	Hope	C,T	St	M/W	1,160	41	38		Y			Y	Y	Y	Y	N		10
University of Arkansas Community College at Morrilton	Morrilton	C,T	St	M/W	1,511													
California																		
Allan Hancock College	Santa Maria	C,T	St-L	M/W	10,000													1
American Academy of Dramatic Arts/Hollywood†	Hollywood	C	Ind	M/W	177	15			N	Y	Y	Y	Y	Y	Y	N		1
American River College	Sacramento	C,T	Dist	M/W	30,000		19		Y				Y	Y	Y	N	10	67
Antelope Valley College	Lancaster	C,T	St-L	M/W	12,073													
Barstow College	Barstow	C,T	St-L	M/W	3,000													
Butte College	Oroville	C,T	Dist	M/W	14,251	53			Y		S		Y	Y	Y	N	11	55
Cabrillo College	Aptos	C,T	Dist	M/W	13,905	50			Y		S		Y	Y	Y	N	17	38
California Culinary Academy	San Francisco	T	Prop	M/W	822	62				Y		Y	Y	Y	Y	Y		2
Cañada College	Redwood City	C,T	St-L	M/W	6,421	65			Y	Y			Y	Y	Y	N	5	49
Cerritos College	Norwalk	C,T	St-L	M/W	24,000													
Chabot College	Hayward	C,T	St	M/W	15,075		47		Y	Y		Y	Y	Y	Y	N	21	90
Chaffey College	Rancho Cucamonga	C,T	Dist	M/W	17,930													
Citrus College	Glendora	C,T	St-L	M/W	11,703													
City College of San Francisco	San Francisco	C,T	St-L	M/W	106,480													
Coastline Community College	Fountain Valley	C	St-L	M/W	8,559	94	75		Y			R	Y	Y	Y	N		1
Coleman College	San Marcos	T	Ind	M/W	203													
College of Alameda	Alameda	C,T	St-L	M/W	5,500													
College of Marin	Kentfield	C,T	St-L	M/W	6,516													
College of Oceaneering	Wilmington	C	Prop	PM	272		40		N	Y	Y	Y	Y	Y	Y	N		3
College of the Canyons	Santa Clarita	C,T	St-L	M/W	15,053		35		Y		R	Y	Y	Y	Y	N	11	46
College of the Desert	Palm Desert	C,T	St-L	M/W	9,946		40		Y	Y			Y	Y	Y	N	15	64
College of the Redwoods	Eureka	C,T	St-L	M/W	7,708													
College of the Sequoias	Visalia	C,T	St-L	M/W	11,169	60	46		Y			Y	Y	Y	Y	N	12	75
College of the Siskiyous*	Weed	C,T	St-L	M/W	3,002													
Columbia College	Sonora	C,T	St-L	M/W	3,572	74	68	91	Y	Y	S	Y	Y	Y	Y		3	32
Contra Costa College	San Pablo	C,T	St-L	M/W	8,834	55	54		Y				Y	Y	Y	N	7	46
Copper Mountain College	Joshua Tree	C,T	St	M/W	1,800											N		
Cosumnes River College	Sacramento	C,T	Dist	M/W	19,284													
Crafton Hills College	Yucaipa	C,T	St-L	M/W	5,300													
Crestmont College	Rancho Palos Verdes	C,T,B	I-R	M/W	213	14	100		N	Y	Y					Y		1
Cuesta College	San Luis Obispo	C,T	Dist	M/W	10,771		33		Y			Y	Y	Y	Y	N	11	50
Cuyamaca College	El Cajon	C,T	St	M/W	7,690		37		Y			Y	Y	Y	Y	N	6	33
De Anza College	Cupertino	C,T	St-L	M/W	25,177													
Deep Springs College	Deep Springs	C	Ind	M	25													
Diablo Valley College	Pleasant Hill	C,T	St-L	M/W	21,097		38		Y			R	Y	Y	Y	N	10	1
East Los Angeles College	Monterey Park	C,T	St-L	M/W	24,015	76	51	15	N			R	Y	Y	Y	N	9	60

This chart includes the names and locations of accredited two-year colleges in the United States and U.S. territories and shows institutions' responses to the *Thomson Peterson's Survey of Undergraduate Institutions.* If an institution submitted incomplete data, one or more columns opposite the institution's name is blank. An asterisk after the school name denotes a *Special Message* following the college's profile, and a dagger indicates that the institution has one or more entries in the *In-Depth Descriptions of Two-Year Colleges* section. If a school does not appear, it did not report any of the information.

Column key (diagonal headers): College Transfer Associate (C); County District City, Federal, State and Local, State-Related; Independent, Independent-Religious, Proprietary; Men, Primarily Men, Women, Primarily Women, Coed; Bachelor's (B), Master's (M), Terminal Associate (T), Doctoral (D), First Professional (F) — **Degrees Awarded**; **Institutional Control**; **Student Body**

Y—Yes; N—No; R—Recommended; S—For Some

Name	Location	Degrees Awarded	Institutional Control	Student Body	Undergrad Enrollment Fall 2003	% Attending Part-Time	% 25 Years or Older	% Grads to Four-Year Colleges	HS Equiv Cert Accepted	HS Transcript Accepted	Open Admissions	Need-Based Aid Required	Part-Time Jobs Available	Career Counseling Available	Job Placement Services Available	College Housing Available	No. Sports Offered	No. Majors Offered
El Camino College	Torrance	C	St	M/W	27,039		42	19	Y		Y		Y	Y	Y	N	16	73
Empire College	Santa Rosa	T	Prop	M/W	834													
Fashion Careers of California College	San Diego	C,T	Prop	PW	106	9	0		N	Y	Y	Y	Y	Y	Y	N		2
Fashion Inst of Design & Merchandising, LA Campus†	Los Angeles	C	Prop	M/W	3,254	22	22		N	Y	Y	Y	Y	Y	Y	N		8
Fashion Inst of Design & Merchandising, SD Campus	San Diego	C	Prop	M/W	262	9	13	18	N	Y	Y	Y	Y	Y	Y	N		7
Fashion Inst of Design & Merchandising, SF Campus	San Francisco	C	Prop	PW	837	22	20		N	Y	Y		Y	Y	Y	N		8
Feather River Community College District	Quincy	C,T	St-L	M/W	1,547	69	31		Y				Y	Y	Y	Y	9	19
Foothill College	Los Altos Hills	C,T	St-L	M/W	18,328	67	31		Y		R		Y	Y	Y	N	9	66
Foundation College	San Diego	C,T	Ind	M/W					N	Y				Y		N		6
Fresno City College	Fresno	C,T	Dist	M/W	22,812													
Gavilan College	Gilroy	C,T	St-L	M/W	5,060		58		Y	Y				Y	Y	N	9	40
Glendale Community College	Glendale	C,T	St-L	M/W	14,911													
Golden West College	Huntington Beach	C,T	St-L	M/W	13,091													
Grossmont College	El Cajon	C,T	St-L	M/W	18,241													
Hartnell College	Salinas	C,T	Dist	M/W	10,074													
Heald College-Concord	Concord	T	Ind	M/W														
Heald College-Fresno	Fresno	T	Ind	M/W														
Heald College-Hayward	Hayward		Ind	M/W														
Heald College-Rancho Cordova	Rancho Cordova	C,T	Ind	M/W														
Heald College-Roseville	Roseville	T	Ind	M/W														
Heald College-Salinas	Salinas	T	Ind	M/W														
Heald College-San Francisco	San Francisco	T	Ind	M/W														
Heald College-San Jose	Milpitas	T	Ind	M/W														
Heald College-Stockton	Stockton	C,T	Ind	M/W														
Imperial Valley College	Imperial	C,T	St-L	M/W	7,413													
ITT Technical Institute	Anaheim	T,B	Prop	M/W	642				N	Y	Y	Y	Y	Y	Y	N		15
ITT Technical Institute	Lathrop	T,B	Prop	M/W	428													
ITT Technical Institute	Oxnard	C,T,B	Prop	M/W	569													
ITT Technical Institute	Rancho Cordova	T,B	Prop	M/W	518				N	Y	Y	Y	Y	Y	Y	N		16
ITT Technical Institute	San Bernardino	T,B	Prop	M/W	920				N	Y	Y	Y	Y	Y	Y	N		13
ITT Technical Institute	San Diego	T,B	Prop	M/W	990				N	Y	Y	Y	Y	Y	Y	N		15
ITT Technical Institute	Sylmar	T,B	Prop	M/W	755				N	Y	Y	Y	Y	Y	Y	N		15
ITT Technical Institute	Torrance	T,B	Prop	M/W	708				N	Y	Y	Y	Y	Y	Y	N		15
ITT Technical Institute	West Covina	T,B	Prop	M/W	816				N	Y	Y	Y	Y	Y	Y	N		16
Laney College	Oakland	C,T	St-L	M/W	13,463	82												
Long Beach City College	Long Beach	C,T	St	M/W	25,142	72												
Los Angeles City College	Los Angeles	C,T	Dist	M/W	25,000													
Los Angeles Harbor College	Wilmington	C,T	St-L	M/W	9,469	76	49	18	Y			S	Y	Y	Y	N	7	23
Los Angeles Pierce College	Woodland Hills	C,T	St-L	M/W	16,255		48		Y				Y	Y	Y	N	16	34
Los Angeles Trade-Technical College	Los Angeles	C,T	St-L	M/W	13,194	68	47		Y			R	Y	Y	Y	N	5	34
Los Angeles Valley College	Van Nuys	C,T	St-L	M/W	18,761	73	43		Y			R	Y	Y	Y	N	16	62
Los Medanos College	Pittsburg	C,T	Dist	M/W	7,152													
Maric College	Modesto	T	Prop	PW	289											N		
Maric College	Sacramento	C,T	Prop		360													
Maric College	San Diego	C,T	Prop	M/W	298		60		Y	Y			Y	Y	Y	N		1
Mendocino College	Ukiah	C,T	St-L	M/W	5,400													
Merced College	Merced	C,T	St-L	M/W	8,200													
Merritt College	Oakland	C,T	St-L	M/W	7,984	85	55		Y	Y				Y	Y	N	7	33
MiraCosta College*	Oceanside	C,T	St	M/W	10,166		33	80	Y				Y	Y	Y	N	4	54
Mission College	Santa Clara	C,T	St-L	M/W	10,500	62												
Modesto Junior College	Modesto	C,T	St-L	M/W	16,560		53		Y			R	Y	Y	Y	N	15	87
Monterey Peninsula College	Monterey	C,T	St	M/W	14,074													
Moorpark College	Moorpark	C,T	Cou	M/W	15,266													
Mt. San Antonio College	Walnut	C,T	Dist	M/W	26,440	70			Y			S	Y	Y	Y	N	14	72
Mt. San Jacinto College	San Jacinto	C,T	St-L	M/W	12,592		60		Y			R	Y	Y	Y	N	7	29
MTI College of Business and Technology	Sacramento	C,T	Prop	M/W	850													
Napa Valley College	Napa	C,T	St-L	M/W	7,053	72	44		Y			S	Y	Y	Y	N	20	37
Ohlone College	Fremont	C,T	St-L	M/W	11,500													
Orange Coast College	Costa Mesa	C,T	St-L	M/W	25,628	62	34		Y				Y	Y	Y	N	14	102
Oxnard College	Oxnard	C	St	M/W	7,233		44		Y	Y			Y	Y	Y	N	6	44
Palomar College	San Marcos	C	St-L	M/W	28,597		3		Y				Y	Y	Y	N	15	78
Palo Verde College	Blythe	C,T	St-L	M/W	3,200													
Pasadena City College	Pasadena	C,T	St-L	M/W	30,417		41		Y				Y	Y	Y	N	11	104
Pima Medical Institute	Chula Vista	T	Prop	M/W	550													
Platt College	Cerritos	C,T	Prop	M/W	320													
Platt College†	Newport Beach	C,B	Ind	M/W	270				N	Y	Y			Y	Y	N		7
Platt College†	Ontario	C,T	Ind	M/W	385													
Platt College—Los Angeles, Inc†	Los Angeles	C,T	Prop	M/W	179													
Platt College San Diego*	San Diego	C,B	Prop	M/W	335		70	90	N	Y	Y					N		22
Porterville College	Porterville	C,T	St	M/W	5,024													

Two-Year Colleges At-a-Glance

Y—Yes; N—No; R—Recommended; S—For Some

Name	City	Degrees Awarded	Institutional Control	Student Body	Undergraduate Enrollment Fall 2003	Percent Attending Part-Time	Percent 25 Years of Age or Older	Percent of Grads Going on to Four-Year Colleges	High School Equivalency Certificate Accepted	High School Transcript Required	Open Admissions	Need-Based Aid Available	Part-Time Jobs Available	Career Counseling Available	Job Placement Services Available	College Housing Available	Number of Sports Offered	Number of Majors Offered
Professional Golfers Career College	Temecula	T	Ind	PM	220													
Queen of the Holy Rosary College	Mission San Jose	C	I-R	PW	195													
Riverside Community College	Riverside	T	St-L	M/W	2,476	53	40		Y		Y	Y	Y	Y	Y	N	16	65
San Bernardino Valley College	San Bernardino	C,T	St-L	M/W	1,540													
San Diego City College	San Diego	C	St-L	M/W	15,925	79	63		Y		S	Y	Y	Y	Y	N	16	68
San Diego Mesa College	San Diego	C,T	St-L	M/W	22,573													
San Joaquin Delta College	Stockton	C,T	Dist	M/W	17,131	61	40		Y			Y	Y	Y	Y	N	18	82
San Joaquin Valley College	Visalia	T	Ind	M/W	2,450													
San Jose City College	San Jose	C,T	Dist	M/W	9,819		56		Y			Y	Y	Y	Y	N	8	27
Santa Ana College	Santa Ana	C,T	St	M/W	22,189													
Santa Barbara City College	Santa Barbara	T	St-L	M/W	15,156	60	28		Y	Y	R	Y	Y	Y	Y	N	10	79
Santa Monica College†	Santa Monica	C,T	St-L	M/W	24,497	64	25		Y	Y	Y	Y	Y	Y	Y	N	10	64
Santa Rosa Junior College	Santa Rosa	C,T	St-L	M/W	34,535													
Santiago Canyon College	Orange	C,T	St	M/W	10,214													
Sequoia Institute	Fremont	T	Prop	PM	1,076													
Shasta College	Redding	C,T	St-L	M/W	10,240	58												
Sierra College	Rocklin	C,T	St	M/W	19,416	72	32		Y			Y	Y	Y	Y	Y	16	51
Silicon Valley College	Emeryville	C,B	Prop	M/W	375													
Silicon Valley College	Fremont	T,B	Prop	M/W	460													
Silicon Valley College	San Jose	T,B	Prop	M/W	478													
Silicon Valley College	Walnut Creek	T,B	Prop	M/W	472		49					Y		Y	Y	N		21
Solano Community College	Suisun City	C,T	St-L	M/W	12,027													
Sonoma College	Petaluma	T	Prop	M/W	118													
Southern California Institute of Technology	Anaheim	T,B,M	Prop		664													
Southwestern College	Chula Vista	C,T	St-L	M/W	18,799	70	26		Y		S	Y	Y	Y	Y	N	10	73
Taft College	Taft	C,T	St-L	M/W	8,230	90												
Ventura College	Ventura	C,T	St-L	M/W	12,096	66	47		Y	Y	Y	Y	Y	Y	Y	N	12	42
Victor Valley College	Victorville	C,T	St	M/W	10,580	65			Y			Y	Y	Y	Y	N	12	41
Vista Community College	Berkeley	C,T	St-L	M/W	4,500		65	90	Y		R	Y	Y	Y		N		21
West Hills Community College	Coalinga	C,T	St	M/W	4,344	58	48	22	Y		R	Y	Y	Y	Y	Y	7	29
West Valley College	Saratoga	C,T	St-L	M/W	11,000													
Westwood College–Anaheim†	Anaheim	T,B	Prop	M/W	674	15	23							Y	Y			11
Westwood College–Inland Empire†	Upland	T,B	Prop	M/W	803	19	31							Y	Y			19
Westwood College–Los Angeles†	Los Angeles	T,B	Prop	M/W	679	15	25							Y	Y			13
Westwood College–Long Beach†	Long Beach	T,B	Prop	M/W	154		50						Y	Y	Y	N	2	4
Yuba College	Marysville	C	St-L	M/W	9,165		48		Y	Y	Y	Y	Y	Y	Y	Y	9	58
Colorado																		
Aims Community College	Greeley	C,T	Dist	M/W	5,098	56												
Arapahoe Community College	Littleton	C,T	St	M/W	7,080				Y			Y	Y	Y	Y	N	8	50
Bel–Rea Institute of Animal Technology	Denver	T	Prop	M/W	615													
Blair College	Colorado Springs	C,T	Prop	M/W	600													
CollegeAmerica–Fort Collins	Fort Collins	T,B	Prop	M/W	232		70		Y	Y	Y			Y	Y	N	1	10
Colorado Mountn Coll, Alpine Cmps	Steamboat Springs	C,T	Dist	M/W	1,196		21		Y	Y	Y	Y	Y	Y	Y	Y	7	20
Colorado Mountn Coll*†	Glenwood Springs	C,T	Dist	M/W	716		23		Y	Y	Y	Y	Y	Y	Y	Y	7	25
Colorado Mountn Coll, Timberline Cmps	Leadville	C,T	Dist	M/W	1,241		33		Y	Y	Y	Y	Y	Y	Y	Y	6	24
Colorado Northwestern Community College*	Rangely	C,T	St	M/W	2,242	78	12		Y	Y	Y	Y	Y	Y	Y	Y	12	40
Colorado School of Trades	Lakewood	T	Prop	M/W	115										Y			
Community College of Aurora	Aurora	C,T	St	M/W	5,525	73	59	20	Y			Y	Y	Y	Y			17
Community College of Denver	Denver	C,T	St	M/W	9,008	73	51		Y			Y	Y	Y	Y	N	23	29
Denver Automotive and Diesel College	Denver	T	Prop	PM	368													
Front Range Community College	Westminster	C,T	St	M/W	15,301	66	19		Y			Y	Y	Y	Y	N		30
Institute of Business & Medical Careers	Fort Collins	T	Priv	PW	302		20	10				Y	Y		Y			9
IntelliTec College	Colorado Springs	T	Prop	M/W	427				Y	Y	Y			Y	Y	N		4
IntelliTec College	Grand Junction	C	Prop	M/W	255									Y	Y			11
ITT Technical Institute	Thornton	T,B	Prop	M/W	491				N	Y	Y	Y	Y	Y	Y	N		15
Lamar Community College	Lamar	C,T	St	M/W	1,021													
Morgan Community College	Fort Morgan	C,T	St	M/W	1,564	78	52		Y			Y	Y	Y	Y	N		10
Northeastern Junior College	Sterling	C,T	St	M/W	3,633	75												
Otero Junior College	La Junta	C,T	St	M/W	1,650	45	51	36	Y	Y	R	Y	Y	Y	Y	Y	5	27
Pikes Peak Community College	Colorado Springs	C,T	St	M/W	10,581	65	50		Y		S	Y	Y	Y	Y	N	3	31
Pueblo Community College	Pueblo	C,T	St	M/W	5,747	62												
Red Rocks Community College	Lakewood	C,T	St	M/W	7,693	71	53		Y			Y	Y	Y	Y	N	2	40
Trinidad State Junior College	Trinidad	C,T	St	M/W	2,022	53	59		Y	Y	Y	Y	Y	Y	Y	Y	13	50
Westwood College–Denver South†	Denver	T,B	Prop	M/W	429	31	49							Y	Y			15
Westwood College–Denver†	Broomfield	T	Prop	M/W	951		42				Y			Y	Y	Y	N		3
Westwood College–Denver North†	Denver	T,B	Prop	M/W	1,368	26	31					N	Y	Y	Y	Y	N		23
Connecticut																		
Asnuntuck Community College	Enfield	T	St	M/W	1,476	69	50		Y		Y	Y	Y	Y	Y	N	1	15

This chart includes the names and locations of accredited two-year colleges in the United States and U.S. territories and shows institutions' responses to the *Thomson Peterson's Survey of Undergraduate Institutions*. If an institution submitted incomplete data, one or more columns opposite the institution's name is blank.

An asterisk after the school name denotes a *Special Message* following the college's profile, and a dagger indicates that the institution has one or more entries in the *In-Depth Descriptions of Two-Year Colleges* section. If a school does not appear, it did not report any of the information.

Y—Yes; N—No; R—Recommended; S—For Some

Column headers (left to right): Degrees Awarded [College Transfer Associate (C); Terminal Associate (T); Bachelor's (B); Master's (M); Doctoral (D); First Professional (P)] | Institutional Control | Student Body | Undergraduate Enrollment Fall 2003 | Percent Attending Part-Time | Percent 25 Years of Age or Older | Percent of Grads Going on to Four-Year Colleges | Open Admissions | High School Equivalency Certificate Accepted | High School Transcript Required | Need-Based Aid Available | Part-Time Jobs Available | Career Counseling Available | Job Placement Services Available | College Housing Available | Number of Sports Offered | Number of Majors Offered

Institution	Location	Degrees	Control	Student Body	Enroll	%PT	%25+	%→4yr	OpenAdm	HSEquiv	HSTrans	NeedAid	PTJobs	CareerCns	JobPlace	Housing	Sports	Majors
Briarwood College†	Southington	C,T	Prop	M/W	588	34	38	7	N	Y		Y	Y	Y	Y	Y	4	22
Capital Community College	Hartford	C,T	St	M/W	3,317	74	56		Y	Y		R	Y	Y	Y	Y	N	1	20
Gateway Community College	New Haven	C,T	St	M/W	5,326	71													
Gibbs College	Norwalk	T	Prop	M/W	770													
Goodwin College	East Hartford	C,T	Prop	M/W	667	58	59		Y	Y		Y	Y	Y	Y	Y	N		12
Housatonic Community College	Bridgeport	C,T	St	M/W	4,343													
International College of Hospitality Management, *César Ritz**†	Washington	C,T,B	Prop	M/W	116													
Manchester Community College	Manchester	C,T	St	M/W	5,717	61	40		Y	Y		Y	Y	Y	Y	Y	N	4	31
Middlesex Community College	Middletown	C,T	St	M/W	2,400	69	64		Y	Y	Y	Y	Y	Y	Y	N		25
Naugatuck Valley Community College	Waterbury	C,T	St	M/W	5,155		51		Y	Y	Y	Y	Y	Y	Y	N	3	50
Northwestern Connecticut Community-Technical Coll	Winsted	C,T	St	M/W	1,543	67	37	30	Y	Y		Y	Y	Y	Y	N		35
Norwalk Community College	Norwalk	C,T	St	M/W	5,800													
Quinebaug Valley Community College	Danielson	C,T	St	M/W	1,571	68	50		Y	Y	R,S	Y	Y	Y		N	2	18
St. Vincent's College	Bridgeport	C	I-R	M/W	413		64	12	N	Y	Y	Y	Y	Y		N		4
Three Rivers Community College	Norwich	C,T	St	M/W	3,624													
Tunxis Community College	Farmington	C,T	St	M/W	4,035	69												
Delaware																		
Delaware Tech & Comm Coll, Jack F Owens Cmps	Georgetown	T	St	M/W	3,565	58												
Delaware Tech & Comm Coll, Stanton/Wilmington Cmps	Newark	T	St	M/W	6,892	60												
Delaware Tech & Comm Coll, Terry Cmps	Dover	T	St	M/W	2,304		57		Y		Y	Y	Y	Y	Y	N		25
Florida																		
ATI Career Training Center	Fort Lauderdale	T	Prop	M/W	350													
ATI Career Training Center	Miami		Prop		325													
Brevard Community College	Cocoa	C,T	St	M/W	14,806	65	39	42	Y	Y	Y	Y	Y	Y	Y	N	5	37
Central Florida Community College	Ocala	C,T	St-L	M/W	6,298	60	41	33	Y	Y	Y	Y	Y	Y	Y	N	5	31
Central Florida Institute	Palm Harbor	T	Prop	M/W	346													
Chipola College	Marianna	C,T,B	St	M/W	2,249	54		45	Y	Y	Y	Y	Y	Y	N	3	19
Daytona Beach Community College	Daytona Beach	C,T	St	M/W	12,361	61	44		Y	Y	Y	Y	Y	Y	N	11	95
Edison Community College	Fort Myers	C,T	St-L	M/W	10,642		70	66	Y	Y	Y	Y	Y	Y	N		29
Florida Career College	Miami	T	Prop	M/W	2,131	19	75		Y	Y	Y	Y	Y	Y	N		5
Florida Culinary Institute	West Palm Beach	T	Prop		600								Y	Y			3
Florida Hospital College of Health Sciences	Orlando	T,B	Ind	M/W	1,403	57	53		Y	Y	S	Y		Y	Y		6
Florida National College†	Hialeah	C,T	Prop	M/W	1,345	9	61		Y	Y	Y	Y	Y	Y	N		34
The Florida School of Midwifery	Gainesville	T	Ind	W	25												2
Florida Technical College	Orlando	T	Prop	M/W													
Full Sail Real World Education	Winter Park	T,B	Prop	PM	4,300		19										6
Gulf Coast Community College	Panama City	C,T	St	M/W	6,058	63	41	60	Y	Y	Y	Y	Y	Y	Y	N	5	45
Herzing College	Winter Park	T	Prop	M/W	307	21												
Hillsborough Community College	Tampa	C,T	St	M/W	22,149	68	37		Y	Y	Y	Y	Y	Y	N	5	63
Indian River Community College	Fort Pierce	C,T	St	M/W	38,464													
ITT Technical Institute	Fort Lauderdale	T,B	Prop	M/W	588				N	Y	Y	Y	Y	Y	N		15
ITT Technical Institute	Jacksonville	T,B	Prop	M/W	568				N	Y	Y	Y	Y	Y	N		12
ITT Technical Institute	Maitland	T,B	Prop	M/W	447													
ITT Technical Institute	Miami	T,B	Prop	M/W	450				N	Y	Y	Y	Y	Y	N		11
ITT Technical Institute	Tampa	T,B	Prop	M/W	573				N	Y	Y	Y	Y	N	N		12
Keiser College	Miami	C,T	Prop	M/W	393	55	12			Y					N		9
Key College	Fort Lauderdale	C,T	Prop	PW	147													
Lake City Community College	Lake City	C,T	St	M/W	2,695		52		Y	Y	S	Y	Y	Y	Y	9	19
Lake-Sumter Community College	Leesburg	C,T	St-L	M/W	3,222	67	40		Y	Y	Y	Y	Y	Y	N	5	14
Manatee Community College	Bradenton	C,T	St	M/W	9,172	62	41		Y	Y	Y	Y	Y	Y	N	5	96
Miami Dade College*†	Miami	C,T,B	St-L	M/W	58,490	64	43	78	Y	Y	Y	Y	Y		Y	N	10	142
National School of Technology, Inc.	Miami	T	Prop	M/W	700													
National School of Technology, Inc.	North Miami Beach	T	Prop	M/W	608													4
New England Inst of Tech & Florida Culinary Inst	West Palm Beach	C,T	Prop	M/W	1,200		40		Y	Y	Y	Y	Y	Y	N		9
North Florida Community College	Madison	C,T	St	M/W	1,297	54	31		Y	Y	Y	Y	Y		N	3	9
Okaloosa-Walton Community College	Niceville	C,T	St-L	M/W	8,647													
Palm Beach Community College	Lake Worth	C,T	St	M/W	25,022	71	18	90		Y	Y	Y	Y	Y	N	9	67
Pasco-Hernando Community College	New Port Richey	C,T	St	M/W	6,914	68	42		Y	Y	Y	Y	Y	Y	N	5	17
Pensacola Junior College	Pensacola	C,T	St	M/W	11,000		50		Y	Y	Y	Y	Y	Y	N	17	64
Polk Community College	Winter Haven	C,T	St	M/W	7,109	72	38		Y	Y	Y	Y	Y	Y	N	5	22
Education America–Tampa Tech Inst Campus	Tampa	C,B	Prop	M/W	863													
St. Johns River Community College	Palatka	C,T	St	M/W	3,459		43		Y	Y	Y	Y	Y	Y	N	4	21
St. Petersburg College	St. Petersburg	C,T,B	St-L	M/W	24,146		46		Y	Y	Y	Y	Y		N	5	46
Santa Fe Community College	Gainesville	C,T	St-L	M/W	13,806	52												
Seminole Community College	Sanford	C,T	St-L	M/W	12,108	62	45										6	50
South Florida Community College	Avon Park	C,T	St	M/W	2,076	61												
South University	West Palm Beach	T,B	Prop	M/W	450		38	3	N	Y	Y	Y	Y	Y	N		14
Southwest Florida College	Fort Myers	T	Ind	M/W	1,263													

Two-Year Colleges At-a-Glance

This chart includes the names and locations of accredited two-year colleges in the United States and U.S. territories and shows institutions' responses to the *Thomson Peterson's Survey of Undergraduate Institutions*. If an institution submitted incomplete data, one or more columns opposite the institution's name is blank.

An asterisk after the school name denotes a *Special Message* following the college's profile, and a dagger indicates that the institution has one or more entries in the *In-Depth Descriptions of Two-Year Colleges* section. If a school does not appear, it did not report any of the information.

Y—Yes; N—No; R—Recommended; S—For Some

Name	Location	Degrees Awarded	Institutional Control	Student Body	Undergrad Enrollment Fall 2003	% Attending Part-Time	% 25 Years or Older	% Grads Going on to Four-Year Colleges	HS Equivalency Cert. Accepted	Open Admissions	HS Transcript Required	Need-Based Aid Available	Part-Time Jobs Available	Career Counseling Available	Job Placement Services Available	College Housing Available	No. of Sports Offered	No. of Majors Offered
Summit Institute	West Palm Beach	T	Prop	M/W	200													
Tallahassee Community College	Tallahassee	C,T	St-L	M/W	11,966	54												
Valencia Community College	Orlando	C,T	St	M/W	29,447													
Webster College	Holiday	T,B	Prop	M/W	220													
Webster College	Tampa	T	Priv	PW	152													
Georgia																		
Abraham Baldwin Agricultural College	Tifton	C,T	St	M/W	3,407	42	29		Y	Y	Y	Y		Y	Y	Y	10	57
Albany Technical College	Albany		St	M/W	3,000													11
Andrew College†	Cuthbert	C	I-R	M/W	331	1	2	96	N	Y	Y	Y		Y	Y		Y	21	39
Asher School of Business	Norcross	C	Prop	M/W	222													
Ashworth College	Norcross	C,T	Prop	M/W														
Atlanta Metropolitan College	Atlanta	C,T	St	M/W	1,907	56			N	Y	Y	Y			Y	N	2	32
Augusta Technical College	Augusta	T	St	M/W	4,438		49		N	Y	Y	Y	Y	Y	Y	N	1	10
Bainbridge College	Bainbridge	C,T	St	M/W	2,279	44	30		Y	Y	S	Y	Y	Y	Y	N	2	34
Bauder College	Atlanta	C	Prop	PW	715													
Central Georgia Technical College	Macon	T	St	M/W	5,727	53	55		Y		Y	Y		Y	Y	N		10
Chattahoochee Technical College	Marietta	T	St	M/W	5,963													
Coastal Georgia Community College	Brunswick	C,T	St	M/W	2,210		50			Y	Y	Y		Y	Y	N	6	35
Columbus Technical College	Columbus	T	St	M/W	4,144													
Darton College	Albany	C,T	St	M/W	3,811	54	38	75	N	Y	Y	Y		Y	Y	N	10	60
DeKalb Technical College	Clarkston	C,T	St	M/W	5,303	63	60		Y	Y	Y	Y		Y	Y	N		19
East Central Technical Institute	Fitzgerald		St	M/W	1,566													
East Georgia College	Swainsboro	C	St	M/W	1,420													
Emory University, Oxford College	Oxford	C	I-R	M/W	554													
Floyd College	Rome	C,T	St	M/W	2,863													
Georgia Military College	Milledgeville	C,T	St-L	M/W	4,062	39												
Georgia Perimeter College	Decatur	C,T	St	M/W	18,986	55	36		N	N	Y	Y		Y	Y	N	5	37
Gordon College	Barnesville	C,T	St	M/W	3,413	35		50	Y	Y	Y	Y		Y	Y	Y	13	25
Griffin Technical College	Griffin	C,T	St	M/W	4,225													
Gupton-Jones College of Funeral Service	Decatur	T	Ind	M/W	198		35		Y	Y	Y	Y		Y	Y	N		1
Gwinnett Technical College	Lawrenceville	T	St	M/W	4,476	61	80		N	Y	Y	Y	Y			N		25
Heart of Georgia Technical College	Dublin	T	St	M/W	1,500						Y							4
ITT Technical Institute	Duluth	T,B	Prop	M/W	101				N	Y	Y	Y		Y	Y	N		10
Lanier Technical College	Oakwood	T	St	M/W														16
Middle Georgia College*	Cochran	C,T	St	M/W	2,517	38	26		N	Y	Y	Y		Y	Y	Y	9	15
Middle Georgia Technical College	Warner Robbins	T	St	M/W														
Northwestern Technical College	Rock Springs	T	St	M/W	2,224										N			
Ogeechee Technical College	Statesboro	T	St	M/W	2,200													9
Okefenokee Technical College	Waycross	T	St	M/W	2,000													9
Southeastern Technical College	Vidalia		St	M/W														9
South Georgia College	Douglas	C,T	St	M/W	1,431													
Southwest Georgia Technical College	Thomasville	T	St	M/W	796	54												
Truett-McConnell College	Cleveland	C,T,B	I-R	M/W	390	11	4		N	Y	Y	Y	Y	Y		Y	7	6
Valdosta Technical College	Valdosta		St	M/W	2,553	43												
Waycross College	Waycross	C,T	St	M/W	1,026	68	43			Y	Y	Y	Y	Y	Y	N	2	41
West Central Technical College	Waco	T	St	M/W	2,800													
West Georgia Technical College	LaGrange	T	St	M/W	1,234													
Westwood College–Atlanta Campus	Atlanta	T,B	Prop	M/W														12
Young Harris College	Young Harris	C	I-R	M/W	622													
Hawaii																		
Hawaii Business College	Honolulu	C,T	Ind	M/W	426													
Hawaii Community College	Hilo	C,T	St	M/W	2,409	57	40		Y					Y		Y		17
Hawaii Tokai International College	Honolulu	C	Ind	M/W	50		17	88	N	Y	Y	Y		Y	Y			1
Heald College-Honolulu	Honolulu	T	Ind	M/W														
Honolulu Community College	Honolulu	C,T	St	M/W	4,238	61	41		Y				Y	Y	Y	N		22
Kapiolani Community College	Honolulu	C,T	St	M/W	7,582		40		Y				Y	Y	Y	N	2	17
Kauai Community College	Lihue	C	St	M/W	1,210				Y		R,S	Y	Y	Y	Y	N	3	11
Leeward Community College	Pearl City	C,T	St	M/W	6,000													
Idaho																		
American Institute of Health Technology, Inc.	Boise	C,T	Prop	PW	269	9												
Brigham Young University –Idaho	Rexburg	C,T	I-R	M/W	10,100													
College of Southern Idaho	Twin Falls	C,T	St-L	M/W	7,018		57		Y	Y	Y	Y	Y	Y	Y	Y	14	73
Eastern Idaho Technical College	Idaho Falls	T	St	M/W	860	54	47		Y	Y	Y	Y	Y	Y	Y	N		11
ITT Technical Institute	Boise	T,B	Prop	M/W	389				N	Y	Y	Y	Y	Y	Y	N		15
North Idaho College	Coeur d'Alene	C,T	St-L	M/W	4,452		36		N	Y	S	Y	Y	Y	Y	Y	18	68

This chart includes the names and locations of accredited two-year colleges in the United States and U.S. territories and shows institutions' responses to the *Thomson Peterson's Survey of Undergraduate Institutions.* If an institution submitted incomplete data, one or more columns opposite the institution's name is blank.

An asterisk after the school name denotes a *Special Message* following the college's profile, and a dagger indicates that the institution has one or more entries in the *In-Depth Descriptions of Two-Year Colleges* section. If a school does not appear, it did not report any of the information.

Y—Yes; N—No; R—Recommended; S—For Some

Name	Location	Degrees Awarded	Institutional Control	Student Body	Undergraduate Enrollment Fall 2003	Percent Attending Part-Time	Percent 25 Years of Age or Older	Percent of Grads Going on to Four-Year Colleges	High School Equivalency Certificate Accepted	High School Transcript Required	Open Admissions	Need-Based Aid Available	Part-Time Jobs Available	Career Counseling Available	Job Placement Services Available	College Housing Available	Number of Sports Offered	Number of Majors Offered
Illinois																		
Black Hawk College	Moline	C,T	St-L	M/W	6,266	51												
Carl Sandburg College	Galesburg	C,T	St-L	M/W	5,000			63	Y		Y	Y	Y	Y	Y	N	3	21
City Colls of Chicago, Kennedy-King Coll	Chicago	C,T	St-L	M/W	3,054													
City Colls of Chicago, Malcolm X Coll	Chicago	C,T	St-L	M/W	8,024	49	55	38	Y	Y	Y	Y	Y	Y	Y	N	3	26
City Colls of Chicago, Olive-Harvey Coll	Chicago	C,T	St-L	M/W	3,015													
City Colls of Chicago, Richard J Daley Coll	Chicago	C,T	St-L	M/W	10,654	67												
City Colls of Chicago, Wilbur Wright Coll	Chicago	C,T	St-L	M/W	7,128		43	33	Y	Y		Y	Y	Y	Y	N	8	30
College of DuPage	Glen Ellyn	C,T	St-L	M/W	30,378	66	53	76	Y			Y	Y	Y	Y	N	16	85
College of Lake County	Grayslake	C,T	Dist	M/W	15,768	74	43		Y		S	Y	Y	Y	Y	N	9	40
The Cooking and Hospitality Institute of Chicago†	Chicago	C,T	Prop	M/W	950		65	10	Y	Y	R	Y	Y	Y	Y	N		2
Elgin Community College	Elgin	C,T	St-L	M/W	18,242		51	72	Y		S		Y	Y	Y	N	8	49
Gem City College	Quincy	T	Prop	M/W	150		40		Y	Y		Y			Y			11
Heartland Community College	Normal	C,T	St-L	M/W	4,566	60	38	94	Y	Y	R	Y	Y	Y	Y	N		37
Highland Community College	Freeport	C,T	St-L	M/W	3,600													
Illinois Eastern Comm Colls, Frontier Comm Coll	Fairfield	C,T	St-L	M/W	1,907	89	48		Y	Y	Y	Y	Y	Y	N		8
Illinois Eastern Comm Colls, Lincoln Trail Coll	Robinson	C,T	St-L	M/W	1,357	67	52		Y	Y	Y	Y	Y	Y	Y	N	4	14
Illinois Eastern Comm Colls, Olney Central Coll	Olney	C,T	St-L	M/W	1,707	50	39		Y	Y	Y	Y	Y	Y	Y	N	4	19
Illinois Eastern Comm Colls, Wabash Valley Coll	Mount Carmel	C,T	St-L	M/W	4,098	84	71		Y	Y	Y	Y	Y	Y	Y	N	6	18
Illinois Valley Community College	Oglesby	C,T	Dist	M/W	4,315													
ITT Technical Institute	Burr Ridge	T	Prop	M/W	355				N	Y	Y	Y	Y	Y	N		7
ITT Technical Institute	Matteson	T	Prop	M/W	430				N	Y	Y	Y	Y	Y	N		7
ITT Technical Institute	Mount Prospect	T,B	Prop	M/W	590				N	Y	Y	Y	Y	Y	N		9
John A. Logan College	Carterville	C	St-L	M/W	5,314		54		Y	Y	Y	Y	Y	Y	N	5	49
John Wood Community College	Quincy	C,T	Dist	M/W	2,374	49	33		Y	Y	Y	Y	Y	Y	N	5	35
Joliet Junior College	Joliet	C,T	St-L	M/W	13,245													
Kankakee Community College	Kankakee	C,T	St-L	M/W	3,475													
Kaskaskia College	Centralia	C,T	St-L	M/W	4,636	54	41		Y	Y	Y	Y	Y	Y	N	5	21
Kishwaukee College	Malta	C,T	St-L	M/W	4,076	86	33	72	Y	Y	Y	Y	Y	Y	N	7	29
Lake Land College	Mattoon	C,T	St-L	M/W	7,256		36		Y		R	Y	Y	Y	Y	N	8	37
Lewis and Clark Community College	Godfrey	C,T	Dist	M/W	7,352		29		Y		R	Y	Y	Y	Y	N	7	25
Lincoln College†	Lincoln	C	Ind	M/W	758	8	3	89	N	Y	Y	Y	Y	Y	Y	20	72
Lincoln College†	Normal	C,T,B	Ind	M/W	520	33												
Lincoln Land Community College	Springfield	C,T	Dist	M/W	7,115	62	39		Y		R	Y	Y	Y	Y	N	6	29
MacCormac College	Chicago	C,T	Ind	PW	377	58	20	20	N	Y	Y	Y	Y	Y	N		15
McHenry County College	Crystal Lake	C,T	St-L	M/W	5,940	66	39	51	Y		Y	Y	Y	Y	N	8	23
Moraine Valley Community College	Palos Hills	C,T	St-L	M/W	15,780	61	38	85	Y		Y	Y	Y	Y	N	9	28
Morrison Institute of Technology†	Morrison	C,T	Ind	PM	143	1	8	20	Y	Y	Y	Y	Y	Y	5	6
Morton College	Cicero	C,T	St-L	M/W	5,244		53		Y	Y	Y	Y	Y	N	7	20
Northwestern Business College†	Chicago	C,T	Prop	M/W	2,000													
Oakton Community College	Des Plaines	C,T	Dist	M/W	9,893		45	60	Y	Y	R	Y	Y	Y	N	11	44
Parkland College	Champaign	C,T	Dist	M/W	9,245	49	31		Y	Y	R	Y	Y	Y	N	7	53
Prairie State College	Chicago Heights	C,T	St-L	M/W	4,697													
Rend Lake College	Ina	C,T	St	M/W	5,142		70		Y	Y	Y	Y	Y	Y	N	7	62
Richland Community College	Decatur	C,T	Dist	M/W	3,568													
Rockford Business College	Rockford	T	Ind	PW	428	43												
Rock Valley College	Rockford	C,T	Dist	M/W	9,016	65												
Sauk Valley Community College	Dixon	C,T	Dist	M/W	3,161		50		Y		R	Y	Y	Y	Y	N	5	52
Shawnee Community College	Ullin	C,T	St-L	M/W	3,400													
Southeastern Illinois College	Harrisburg	C,T	St	M/W	3,373													
South Suburban College	South Holland	C,T	St-L	M/W	6,672		49	43	Y	Y	Y	Y	Y	Y	Y	N	7	40
Southwestern Illinois College	Belleville	C,T	Dist	M/W	16,425		45		Y	Y	Y	Y	Y	Y	Y	N	7	43
Spoon River College	Canton	C,T	St	M/W	2,600		36		Y	Y	Y	Y	Y	Y	N	5	41
Springfield College in Illinois	Springfield	C	I-R	M/W	400													
Triton College	River Grove	C,T	St	M/W	10,464		45		Y	Y	Y	Y	Y	Y	N	7	90
Waubonsee Community College	Sugar Grove	C,T	Dist	M/W	8,373	71	32	85	Y			Y	Y	Y	N	11	42
Westwood College–Chicago Du Page†	Woodridge	T,B	Prop	M/W	470	11	21					Y	Y					19
Westwood College–Chicago O'Hare Airport†	Schiller Park	T,B	Prop	M/W	425	26	24					Y	Y					18
Westwood College–Chicago River Oaks†	Calumet City	T,B	Prop	M/W	650	9	37					Y	Y					15
Westwood College–Chicago Loop Campus†	Chicago	T,B	Prop	M/W	106	1	21					Y	Y					14
William Rainey Harper College	Palatine	C,T	St-L	M/W	14,991													
Worsham College of Mortuary Science	Wheeling	T	Ind	M/W	115									Y				1
Indiana																		
Ancilla College	Donaldson	C,T	I-R	M/W	602	37	40	59	Y	Y	Y	Y	Y	Y	Y	N	5	15
College of Court Reporting	Hobart	C,T	Prop	PW	156	43												
Commonwealth Business College	Merrillville	T	Prop	M/W	450		40		Y	Y	Y	Y	Y	Y	N		6
Commonwealth Business College	Michigan City	C,T	Prop	M/W	200		44		Y	Y	Y	Y	Y	N		7
Holy Cross College†	Notre Dame	C,B	I-R	M/W	492	4	2	85	N	Y	Y	Y	Y	Y	Y	4	1
Indiana Business College	Anderson	T	Prop	M/W	216				Y	Y	Y		Y	Y			6

Two-Year Colleges At-a-Glance

Y—Yes; N—No; R—Recommended; S—For Some

Degrees Awarded: College Transfer Associate (C), Terminal Associate (T), Master's (M), Doctoral (D), First Professional (F), Bachelor's (B)

Institution	Location	Degrees Awarded	Institutional Control	Student Body	Undergraduate Enrollment Fall 2003	Percent 25 Years of Age or Older	Percent Attending Part-Time	Percent of Grads Going on to Four-Year Colleges	High School Equivalency Certificate Accepted	Open Admissions	High School Transcript Required	Need-Based Aid Available	Part-Time Jobs Available	Career Counseling Available	Job Placement Services Available	College Housing Available	Number of Sports Offered	Number of Majors Offered
Indiana Business College	Columbus	T	Prop	M/W	296				Y	Y	Y	Y	Y	Y	Y			9
Indiana Business College	Evansville	C,T	Prop	M/W	271				Y		Y	Y	Y	Y	Y			7
Indiana Business College	Fort Wayne	C,T	Prop	M/W	268				Y	Y	Y	Y	Y	Y	Y			5
Indiana Business College†	Indianapolis	T	Prop	M/W	768				Y	Y	Y	Y	Y	Y	Y	N		12
Indiana Business College	Lafayette	C,T	Prop	M/W	240				Y	Y	Y	Y	Y		Y	Y		7
Indiana Business College	Marion	T	Prop	M/W	184				Y	Y	Y				Y	Y		4
Indiana Business College	Muncie	T	Prop	M/W	335			0	Y	Y	Y	Y	Y	Y	Y	N		10
Indiana Business College	Terre Haute	C,T	Prop	M/W	279				Y	Y	Y				Y	Y		10
Indiana Business College-Medical	Indianapolis	T	Prop	M/W	624				Y	Y	Y				Y	Y		4
International Business College	Fort Wayne	T,B	Prop	PW	800	14												
International Business College	Indianapolis	T	Prop	M/W	326													
ITT Technical Institute	Fort Wayne	T,B	Prop	M/W	468				N	Y	Y	Y	Y	Y	Y	N		16
ITT Technical Institute	Indianapolis	T,B	Prop	M/W	899				N	Y	Y	Y	Y	Y	Y	N		16
ITT Technical Institute	Newburgh	T,B	Prop	M/W	400				N	Y	Y	Y	Y	Y	Y	N		13
Ivy Tech State College–Bloomington	Bloomington	C,T	St	M/W	2,858	58	49		Y		Y	Y	Y					21
Ivy Tech State College–Central Indiana	Indianapolis	C,T	St	M/W	8,833	65	56		Y		Y	Y	Y	Y	Y	N		35
Ivy Tech State College–Columbus	Columbus	C,T	St	M/W	1,614	68	60		Y		Y	Y	Y	Y	Y	N		26
Ivy Tech State College–Eastcentral	Muncie	C,T	St	M/W	5,443	55	55		Y		Y	Y	Y	Y	Y	N		31
Ivy Tech State College–Kokomo	Kokomo	C,T	St	M/W	2,522	67	58		Y		Y	Y	Y	Y	Y	N		24
Ivy Tech State College–Lafayette	Lafayette	C,T	St	M/W	4,905	57	52		Y		Y	Y	Y	Y	Y	N		32
Ivy Tech State College–North Central	South Bend	C,T	St	M/W	4,366	71	62		Y		Y	Y	Y	Y	Y	N		33
Ivy Tech State College–Northeast	Fort Wayne	C,T	St	M/W	5,005	65	61		Y		Y	Y	Y	Y	Y	N		29
Ivy Tech State College–Northwest	Gary	C,T	St	M/W	5,229	66	61		Y		Y	Y	Y	Y	Y	N		30
Ivy Tech State College–Southcentral	Sellersburg	C,T	St	M/W	2,917	72	64		Y		Y	Y	Y	Y	Y	N		26
Ivy Tech State College–Southeast	Madison	C,T	St	M/W	1,581	65	56		Y		Y	Y	Y	Y	Y	N	1	12
Ivy Tech State College–Southwest	Evansville	C,T	St	M/W	4,328	68	53		Y		Y	Y	Y	Y	Y	N		35
Ivy Tech State College–Wabash Valley	Terre Haute	C,T	St	M/W	4,347	59	52		Y		Y	Y	Y	Y	Y	N	2	37
Ivy Tech State College–Whitewater	Richmond	C,T	St	M/W	1,541	72	61		Y		Y	Y	Y	Y	Y	N	1	23
Lincoln Technical Institute	Indianapolis	T	Prop	M/W	650													
Michiana College	Fort Wayne	T	Prop	M/W	483													
Michiana College	South Bend	C,T	Prop	PW	513		65		N	Y	Y	Y		Y	Y	N		13
Mid-America College of Funeral Service	Jeffersonville	T,B	Ind	PM	120													
Sawyer College	Hammond	C,T	Prop	M/W	261									Y				7
Sawyer College	Merrillville	C,T	Prop	M/W	395													
Vincennes University†	Vincennes	C,T	St	M/W	5,175		22		Y	Y	Y	Y	Y	Y	Y	Y	19	156
Vincennes University Jasper Campus	Jasper	C,T	St	M/W	835													
Iowa																		
AIB College of Business	Des Moines	T	Ind	M/W	938	20	24		N	Y	Y	Y	Y	Y	Y	Y	9	18
Clinton Community College	Clinton	C,T	St-L	M/W	1,328													
Des Moines Area Community College	Ankeny	C,T	St-L	M/W	13,719	56	30	72	Y		S	Y	Y	Y	Y	N	7	52
Hamilton College	Cedar Rapids	C,T,B	Prop	M/W	511	14												
Hawkeye Community College	Waterloo	C,T	St-L	M/W	5,310	36	26	62	Y		Y	Y	Y	Y	Y	N	7	60
Indian Hills Community College	Ottumwa	C,T	St-L	M/W	2,867	29	40	45	Y		S	Y	Y			Y	10	25
Iowa Central Community College	Fort Dodge	C,T	St-L	M/W	4,567													
Iowa Lakes Community College	Estherville	C,T	St-L	M/W	2,993	54	35	60	Y	Y	Y	Y	Y	Y	Y	Y	16	195
Iowa Western Community College	Council Bluffs	C,T	Dist	M/W	4,299													
Kaplan College	Davenport	C,T,B	Prop	M/W	9,194	82	92		N	Y	Y	Y	Y	Y	Y	N		13
Kirkwood Community College	Cedar Rapids	C,T	St-L	M/W	15,032	45	29		Y	Y	Y	Y	Y	Y	Y	N	10	108
Marshalltown Community College	Marshalltown	C,T	Dist	M/W	1,421	36	35	80	Y	Y	Y	Y	Y	Y	Y	Y	13	21
Muscatine Community College	Muscatine	C,T	St	M/W	1,195													
Northeast Iowa Community College	Calmar	C,T	St-L	M/W	4,724		36		Y	Y	R	Y		Y	Y	N	9	13
North Iowa Area Community College	Mason City	C,T	St-L	M/W	2,837	37	30	70	Y	Y	R,S	Y	Y	Y	Y	Y	14	29
Northwest Iowa Community College	Sheldon	C,T	St	M/W	1,079	51	20	62	Y	Y	Y	Y	Y	Y	Y	Y	4	22
St. Luke's College	Sioux City	T	Ind	PW	147	35	21	61	N	Y	Y	Y			Y			3
Scott Community College	Bettendorf	C,T	St-L	M/W	4,595													
Southeastern Community College, North Campus	West Burlington	C,T	St-L	M/W	2,045													
Southeastern Community College, South Campus	Keokuk	C,T	St-L	M/W	548													
Southwestern Community College	Creston	C,T	St	M/W	1,301													
Vatterott College	Des Moines		Prop	M/W	131													
Western Iowa Tech Community College	Sioux City	C	St	M/W	5,238	61	30		Y	Y	Y	Y	Y	Y	Y	Y	8	26
Kansas																		
Allen County Community College	Iola	C,T	St-L	M/W	2,256	63												
Barton County Community College	Great Bend	C,T	St-L	M/W	3,032	72	45		Y	Y	R	Y	Y	Y	Y	Y	16	84
The Brown Mackie College	Salina	C,T	Prop	M/W	386													
The Brown Mackie College–Lenexa Campus	Lenexa	T	Prop	M/W	230		60		Y	Y	Y	Y	Y	Y	Y	N		16
Butler County Community College	El Dorado	C,T	St-L	M/W	8,631	60	42	95	Y	Y	Y	Y	Y	Y	Y	Y	12	41
Cloud County Community College	Concordia	C,T	St-L	M/W	3,521													
Coffeyville Community College	Coffeyville	C,T	St-L	M/W	1,766	62	43	70	Y		Y	Y	Y	Y		Y	14	69

This chart includes the names and locations of accredited two-year colleges in the United States and U.S. territories and shows institutions' responses to the *Thomson Peterson's Survey of Undergraduate Institutions.* If an institution submitted incomplete data, one or more columns opposite the institution's name is blank.

An asterisk after the school name denotes a *Special Message* following the college's profile, and a dagger indicates that the institution has one or more entries in the *In-Depth Descriptions of Two-Year Colleges* section. If a school does not appear, it did not report any of the information.

Column key (diagonal headers): College Transfer Associate (C); Terminal Associate (T); Bachelor's (B), Master's (M), First Professional (P), Doctoral (D) — **Degrees Awarded** · County, District, City, State and Local, State-Related, Independent, Federal, Independent-Religious, Proprietary, State, Commonwealth, Territory — **Institutional Control** · Men, Primarily Men, Women, Primarily Women, Coed — **Student Body** · Undergraduate Enrollment Fall 2003 · Percent Attending Part-Time · Percent 25 Years of Age or Older · Percent of Grads Going on to Four-Year Colleges · High School Equivalency Certificate Accepted · Open Admissions · High School Transcript Required · Need-Based Aid Available · Part-Time Jobs Available · Career Counseling Available · Job Placement Services Available · College Housing Available · Number of Sports Available · Number of Majors Offered

Y—Yes; N—No; R—Recommended; S—For Some

Institution	City	Degrees	Control	Body	Enroll	%PT	%25+	%→4yr	HS Equiv	Open Adm	HS Transcript	Need Aid	PT Jobs	Career Couns	Job Place	Housing	Sports	Majors
Colby Community College*	Colby	C,T	St-L	M/W	1,951	59	24	60	Y	Y		Y		Y	Y	Y		9	58
Cowley County Comm Coll and Voc-Tech School	Arkansas City	C,T	St-L	M/W	4,656													
Dodge City Community College	Dodge City	C,T	St-L	M/W	1,956													
Donnelly College	Kansas City	C,T	I-R	M/W	398	50	85	90	Y	Y	R	Y		Y	Y	Y			22
Fort Scott Community College	Fort Scott	C,T	St-L	M/W	1,923				Y	Y		Y		Y	Y	Y		10	36
Garden City Community College	Garden City	C,T	Cou	M/W	2,176	58	39	60	Y	Y	Y	Y	Y	Y	Y	Y		14	64
Hesston College	Hesston	C,T	I-R	M/W	446	12	15		Y	Y	Y	Y	Y	Y	Y	Y		7	7
Highland Community College	Highland	C,T	St-L	M/W	3,040													
Hutchinson Comm Coll and Area Vocational School	Hutchinson	C,T	St-L	M/W	4,312	52	32	70	Y	Y	R	Y		Y	Y	Y		14	40
Independence Community College	Independence	C,T	St	M/W	1,100													
Johnson County Community College	Overland Park	C,T	St-L	M/W	18,432	67	43		Y	Y	S	Y	Y	Y	Y	N		8	36
Kansas City Kansas Community College	Kansas City	C,T	St-L	M/W	5,642	67	48		Y	Y	Y	Y	Y	Y	Y	N		8	22
Labette Community College	Parsons	C,T	St-L	M/W	1,401	67												
Manhattan Area Technical College	Manhattan	T	St-L	M/W	350	5												12
Neosho County Community College	Chanute	C,T	St-L	M/W	1,826	66												
Pratt Comm Coll and Area Vocational School	Pratt	C,T	St-L	M/W	1,685	61			Y	Y	Y	Y	Y			Y		12	65
Seward County Community College	Liberal	C,T	St-L	M/W	2,325		67	67	Y	Y	Y	Y	Y	Y	Y	Y		4	45
Wichita Area Technical College	Wichita	C,T	Dist	M/W	2,052	73												16
Kentucky																		
AEC Southern Ohio College, Northern Kentucky Campus	Fort Mitchell	C,T	Prop	M/W	357		42		Y	Y	Y	Y	Y	Y	Y	N		5
Ashland Community and Technical College	Ashland	C,T	St	M/W	2,565													
Beckfield College	Florence	T	Prop	M/W	320		60		Y	Y		Y		Y	Y			4
Big Sandy Community and Technical College	Prestonsburg	C,T	St	M/W	4,406		44	36	Y	Y	Y	Y	Y	Y		N	5	12
Daymar College	Louisville	T	Prop	M/W	227							Y						5
Daymar College	Owensboro	C	Prop	M/W	446	25												5
Draughons Junior College	Bowling Green	C	Prop	PW	368	53	27	0.06	Y	Y	Y	Y	Y	Y	Y	N		8
Elizabethtown Community College	Elizabethtown	C,T	St	M/W	3,615	54	50		Y	Y	Y	Y	Y	Y	Y	N	7	12
Gateway Community and Technical College	Covington	C	St	M/W	2,597													
Hazard Community and Technical College	Hazard	C,T	St	M/W	3,500													
Henderson Community College	Henderson	C,T	St	M/W	2,241		57		Y	Y	Y	Y	Y	Y	Y	N	5	19
Hopkinsville Community College	Hopkinsville	C,T	St	M/W	3,116	60	55		Y	Y	S	Y	Y	Y	Y	N	5	18
ITT Technical Institute	Louisville	T,B	Prop	M/W	476				N	Y	Y	Y	Y	Y	Y	N		15
Jefferson Community College	Louisville	C,T	St	M/W	9,665	62	41		Y			Y	Y	Y	Y	N	1	17
Jefferson Technical College	Louisville	T	St	M/W	3,778	84												
Louisville Technical Institute	Louisville	T	Prop	M/W	667	6	32		N	Y	Y	Y		Y	Y	Y		47
Madisonville Community College	Madisonville	C,T	St	M/W	3,500													
Maysville Community College	Maysville	C,T	St	M/W	1,917	60	40		Y	Y	Y	Y	Y	Y	Y	N		9
National College of Business & Technology	Danville	T	Prop	M/W	232				Y	Y	Y	Y	Y	Y	Y	N		5
National College of Business & Technology	Florence	T	Prop	M/W	163				Y	Y	S	Y	Y	Y	Y	N		5
National College of Business & Technology	Lexington	T	Prop	M/W	307				Y	Y	Y	Y	Y	Y	Y	N		5
National College of Business & Technology	Louisville	T	Prop	M/W	566				Y	Y	S	Y	Y	Y	Y	N		6
National College of Business & Technology	Pikeville	T	Prop	M/W	222				Y	Y	S	Y	Y	Y	Y	N		5
National College of Business & Technology	Richmond	T	Prop	M/W	233				Y	Y	S	Y	Y	Y	Y	N		5
Owensboro Community and Technical College	Owensboro	C,T	St	M/W	3,664	50	28	26	Y	Y		Y	Y	Y	Y	N	2	17
RETS Medical and Business Institute	Hopkinsville	C	Prop	PW	130									Y	Y			
Rowan Technical College	Morehead	T	St	M/W	842	65												
St. Catharine College	St. Catharine	C,T	I-R	M/W	737													
Somerset Community College	Somerset	C,T	St	M/W	5,751		47		Y	Y	Y	Y	Y	Y	Y	N	4	27
Southeast Community College	Cumberland	C,T	St	M/W	4,364				Y	Y	Y	Y	Y	Y	Y		5	14
Spencerian College	Louisville	C,T	Prop	M/W	1,326		50					Y	Y			Y		3
U of Kentucky, Lexington Community College	Lexington	C,T	St	M/W	8,639	38	20		Y	Y	Y	Y	Y	Y	Y	Y	11	15
West Kentucky Community and Technical College	Paducah	C,T	St	M/W	3,545		41		Y	Y	S	Y	Y	Y	Y	N	4	10
Louisiana																		
Bossier Parish Community College	Bossier City	C,T	St	M/W	4,121													
Delgado Community College	New Orleans	C,T	St	M/W	16,501	55	42		Y	Y	R,S	Y	Y	Y	Y	N	8	44
Delta College of Arts and Technology	Baton Rouge	T	Prop	PW	434													2
Elaine P. Nunez Community College	Chalmette	C,T	St	M/W	2,363	49	53	31	Y		S	Y	Y	Y	Y	N	4	21
ITI Technical College	Baton Rouge	T	Prop	M/W	361													5
ITT Technical Institute	St. Rose	T,B	Prop	M/W	541				N	Y	Y	Y	Y	Y	Y	N		11
Louisiana State University at Alexandria	Alexandria	C,T,B	St	M/W	3,061													
Louisiana Technical College–Acadian Campus	Crowley		St		260									Y				
Louisiana Technical College–Alexandria Campus	Alexandria		St		449									Y	Y			
Louisiana Technical College–Ascension Campus	Sorrento		St		216									Y	Y			
Louisiana Technical College–Avoyelles Campus	Cottonport		St		470									Y	Y			
Louisiana Technical College–Bastrop Campus	Bastrop		St		254				Y	Y			Y	Y	Y	Y		1
Louisiana Technical College–Baton Rouge Campus	Baton Rouge		St		1,080									Y	Y			
Louisiana Technical College–Charles B. Coreil Campus	Ville Platte		St		239									Y	Y			
Louisiana Technical College–Delta Ouachita Campus	West Monroe	C,T	St	M/W	410	21								Y	Y			10

This chart includes the names and locations of accredited two-year colleges in the United States and U.S. territories and shows institutions' responses to the *Thomson Peterson's Survey of Undergraduate Institutions.* If an institution submitted incomplete data, one or more columns opposite the institution's name is blank. An asterisk after the school name denotes a *Special Message* following the college's profile, and a dagger indicates that institution has one or more entries in the *In-Depth Descriptions of Two-Year Colleges* section. If a school does not appear, it did not report any of the information.

Y—Yes; N—No; R—Recommended; S—For Some

Institution	Location	Degrees Awarded	Institutional Control	Student Body	Undergraduate Enrollment Fall 2003	Percent Attending Part-Time	Percent 25 Years of Age or Older	Percent of Grads Going on to Four-Year Colleges	High School Equivalency Certificate Accepted	Open Admissions	High School Transcript Required	Need-Based Aid Available	Part-Time Jobs Available	Career Counseling Available	Job Placement Services Available	College Housing Available	Number of Sports Offered	Number of Majors Offered
Louisiana Technical College–Evangeline Campus	St. Martinville	T	St		275									Y	Y			2
Louisiana Technical College–Florida Parishes Campus	Greensburg	T	St	M/W	414	88	40	2	Y	Y	S	S	Y	Y	Y	N		8
Louisiana Technical College–Folkes Campus	Jackson	T	St	M/W	164		87		Y	Y	S	S	Y	Y	Y			3
Louisiana Technical College–Gulf Area Campus	Abbeville	C,T	St		355		39					S	S	Y	Y			3
Louisiana Technical College–Hammond Campus	Hammond	C,T	St	M/W	247									Y	Y			
Louisiana Technical College–Huey P. Long Campus	Winnfield		St		247									Y	Y			
Louisiana Technical College–Jefferson Campus	Metairie		St		320									Y				
Louisiana Technical College–Jumonville Campus	New Roads		St	M/W	365									Y	Y			
Louisiana Technical College–Lafayette Campus	Lafayette		St		735									Y	Y			
Louisiana Technical College–LaFourche Campus	Thibodaux		St		334									Y	Y			
Louisiana Technical College–Lamar Salter Campus	Leesville	T	St	M/W	289									Y	Y			2
Louisiana Technical College–Mansfield Campus	Mansfield	C,T	St	M/W	119		75							Y	Y	N		4
Louisiana Technical College–Morgan Smith Campus	Jennings		St		179									Y	Y			
Louisiana Technical College–Natchitoches Campus	Natchitoches	C	St	M/W	456									Y	Y			3
Louisiana Technical College–North Central Campus	Farmerville	T	St	M/W	170		71					S		Y	Y	N		3
Louisiana Technical College–Northeast Louisiana Campus	Winnsboro		St		310									Y	Y			
Louisiana Technical College–Northwest Louisiana Campus	Minden	T	St		810		40							Y	Y			5
Louisiana Technical College–Oakdale Campus	Oakdale		St		251									Y	Y			
Louisiana Technical College–River Parishes Campus	Reserve		St		325									Y	Y			
Louisiana Technical College–Ruston Campus	Ruston		St	M/W	116									Y	Y			
Louisiana Technical College–Sabine Valley Campus	Many	T	St	M/W	135									Y	Y			2
Louisiana Technical College–Shelby M. Jackson Campus	Ferriday		St		195									Y	Y			
Louisiana Technical College–Shreveport-Bossier Campus	Shreveport		St		818									Y				
Louisiana Technical College–Sidney N. Collier Campus	New Orleans	T	St		399									Y	Y			2
Louisiana Technical College–Slidell Campus	Slidell		St		366									Y	Y			
Louisiana Technical College–Sullivan Campus	Bogalusa		St		717									Y	Y			
Louisiana Technical College–Tallulah Campus	Tallulah		St		449									Y	Y			
Louisiana Technical College–Teche Area Campus	New Iberia		St		443									Y	Y			
Louisiana Technical College–T.H. Harris Campus	Opelousas		St		598									Y	Y			
Louisiana Technical College–West Jefferson Campus	Harvey		St		284									Y	Y			
Louisiana Technical College–Young Memorial Campus	Morgan City	T	St	M/W	734									Y	Y			2
Remington College–Lafayette Campus	Lafayette	T	Prop	M/W	452		40		N	Y	Y	Y			Y	N		11
Remington College–New Orleans Campus	Metairie	T	Prop	M/W	650													
Maine																		
Andover College*	Portland	T	Prop	M/W	564		65		Y	Y	Y	Y	Y	Y	Y	N		16
Beal College	Bangor	T	Prop	M/W	345	35												
Central Maine Community College	Auburn	C,T	St	M/W	1,850													
Central Maine Medical Center School of Nursing	Lewiston	T	Ind	PW	130	81	74		N	Y	Y	Y			Y			1
Eastern Maine Community College	Bangor	C,T	St	M/W	1,790	58	26		N	Y	Y	Y	Y	Y	Y	Y	10	19
Kennebec Valley Community College	Fairfield	C,T	St	M/W	1,501	70												
Northern Maine Community College	Presque Isle	T	St-R	M/W	1,013	37	45		Y	Y	Y	Y	Y	Y	Y	Y	12	22
Southern Maine Community College	South Portland	C,T	St	M/W	3,505	51	48		N	Y	Y	Y	Y	Y	Y	Y	7	46
Washington County Community College	Calais	C,T	St	M/W	350													
York County Community College	Wells	C,T	St	M/W	990					Y	Y	Y	Y	Y	Y	N		11
Maryland																		
Allegany College of Maryland	Cumberland	C,T	St-L	M/W	3,631		35	80	Y	Y	Y	Y		Y	Y	N	8	26
Anne Arundel Community College	Arnold	C,T	St-L	M/W	14,290	67	43		Y					Y	Y	N	8	69
Baltimore City Community College	Baltimore	C,T	St	M/W	7,095													
Baltimore International College†	Baltimore	C,T,B	Ind	M/W	571	7	34		N	Y	Y	Y			Y	Y	1	4
Carroll Community College	Westminster	C,T	St-L	M/W	2,765	55												
Cecil Community College	North East	C	Cou	M/W	1,797	67	38		Y	Y	R			Y	Y	N	9	34
Chesapeake College	Wye Mills	C,T	St-L	M/W	2,354	69	45	45	Y	Y	Y	Y		Y	Y	N	6	29
College of Southern Maryland	La Plata	C,T	St-L	M/W	7,367	66	42		Y		R			Y	Y	N	7	14
The Community College of Baltimore County	Baltimore	C,T	Cou	M/W	20,025													
Frederick Community College	Frederick	C,T	St-L	M/W	4,736		60		Y					Y	Y	N	6	41
Garrett College	McHenry	C,T	St-L	M/W	614	39	22		Y			Y		Y	Y	Y	6	24
Hagerstown Business College	Hagerstown	T	Prop	M/W	932													
Hagerstown Community College	Hagerstown	C,T	St-L	M/W	3,206	65	39		Y			S		Y	Y	N	12	19
Harford Community College	Bel Air	C,T	St-L	M/W	5,525	60	36	23	Y					Y	Y	N	8	29
Howard Community College	Columbia	C,T	St-L	M/W	6,435		43	76			S			Y	Y	N	8	55
Montgomery College	Rockville	C,T	St-L	M/W	21,805	64	41		Y					Y	Y	N	12	31
Prince George's Community College	Largo	C,T	Cou	M/W	12,564	73	51		Y		R			Y	Y	N		30
Wor-Wic Community College	Salisbury	C,T	St-L	M/W	3,007	70	47											18
Massachusetts																		
Bay State College†	Boston	C,T	Ind	M/W	757		12		N	Y	Y	Y	Y	Y	Y	Y		17
Benjamin Franklin Institute of Technology†	Boston	C,T,B	Ind	PM	388													
Berkshire Community College	Pittsfield	C,T	St	M/W	2,272	59	39	47	Y	Y	Y	Y	Y	Y	Y	N		18

This chart includes the names and locations of accredited two-year colleges in the United States and U.S. territories and shows institutions' responses to the *Thomson Peterson's Survey of Undergraduate Institutions*. If an institution submitted incomplete data, one or more columns opposite the institution's name is blank. An asterisk after the school name denotes a *Special Message* following the college's profile, and a dagger indicates that the institution has one or more entries in the *In-Depth Descriptions of Two-Year Colleges* section. If a school does not appear, it did not report any of the information.

Y—Yes; N—No; R—Recommended; S—For Some

Column headers (angled): Degrees Awarded — Bachelor's (B), Associate (C), Terminal Associate (T), Master's (M), Doctoral (D), First Professional (F); College Transfer Associate (C); Institutional Control — County, District City, State and Local, State-Related; Federal, State, Commonwealth, Territory; Independent; Independent-Religious; Proprietary; Student Body — Primarily Men, Primarily Women, Coed; Undergraduate Enrollment Fall 2003; Percent Attending Part-Time; Percent 25 Years of Age or Older; Percent of Grads Going on to Four-Year Colleges; High School Equivalency Certificate Accepted; High School Transcript Required; Open Admissions; Need-Based Aid Available; Part-Time Jobs Available; Career Counseling Available; Job Placement Services Available; College Housing Available; Number of Sports Offered; Number of Majors Offered

College	City	Degrees	Control	Student Body	Enroll. Fall 2003	% Part-Time	% 25+	% to 4-Yr	HS Equiv Accepted	HS Transcript Req	Open Adm	Need-Based Aid	Part-Time Jobs	Career Counsel	Job Placement	College Housing	Sports	Majors
Boston Baptist College ✓	Boston	C,T,B	I-R	M/W	25													
Bristol Community College ✓	Fall River	C,T	St	M/W	6,639	56	35	43	Y	Y	Y	Y	Y	Y	Y	N		71
Bunker Hill Community College†	Boston	C,T	St	M/W	7,397	65	51	35	Y	Y	Y	Y	Y	Y	Y	N	6	40
Cape Cod Community College	West Barnstable	C,T	St	M/W	4,243	65	58	67	Y	Y	Y	Y	Y	Y	Y	N	12	41
Dean College*†	Franklin	C,T,B	Ind	M/W	1,303		3	90	N	Y		Y	Y	Y	Y	Y	11	15
Fisher College†	Boston	C,B	Ind	M/W	556		47	50	N	Y		Y	Y	Y	Y	Y	3	13
Greenfield Community College	Greenfield	C,T	St	M/W	2,368	58	46		Y	Y	S	Y	Y	Y	Y	N		29
Holyoke Community College	Holyoke	C,T	St	M/W	6,000		35		Y	Y	Y	Y	Y	Y	Y	N	7	40
ITT Technical Institute	Norwood	T	Prop	M/W	272				N	Y		Y	Y	Y	Y	N		6
ITT Technical Institute	Woburn	T	Prop	M/W	285				Y	Y		Y	Y	Y	Y	N		6
Labouré College*	Boston	C,T	I-R	M/W	432		72	25	N	Y		Y	Y	Y	Y	N		5
Massachusetts Bay Community College†	Wellesley Hills	C,T	St	M/W	4,994													
Massasoit Community College	Brockton	C,T	St	M/W	6,808	53	35	32	Y			Y	Y	Y	Y	N	4	39
Middlesex Community College	Bedford	C,T	St	M/W	8,016		39		Y		S	Y	Y	Y	Y	N	3	39
Mount Wachusett Community College*	Gardner	C,T	St	M/W	4,118	57	42	61	Y	Y	Y	Y	Y	Y	Y			28
New England College of Finance	Boston	T,B	Ind	PW	1,748													
Northern Essex Community College*	Haverhill	C,T	St	M/W	6,301		51	40	Y			Y	Y	Y	Y	N	11	59
North Shore Community College	Danvers	C,T	St	M/W	6,612	61	38	57	Y	Y	S	Y	Y	Y	Y	N		42
Quincy College	Quincy	C,T	City	M/W	4,500													
Quinsigamond Community College ✓	Worcester	C,T	St	M/W	6,591	57	45	40	Y	Y	Y	Y	Y	Y	Y	N	10	28
Springfield Technical Community College ✓	Springfield	C,T	St	M/W	6,157	54	33		Y	Y	Y	Y	Y	Y	Y	N	11	57
Urban College of Boston	Boston	T	Ind	PW	609	98	100	50		Y			Y			N		3
Michigan																		
Alpena Community College	Alpena	C,T	St-L	M/W	1,937	49	40	42	Y		Y	Y	Y	Y	Y	Y	7	29
Bay de Noc Community College	Escanaba	C,T	Cou	M/W	2,549													
Bay Mills Community College	Brimley	C	Dist	M/W	489													
Delta College	University Center	C,T	Dist	M/W	10,450	64			Y		R	Y	Y	Y	Y	N	8	115
Glen Oaks Community College	Centreville	C,T	St-L	M/W	1,710	61	53		Y			Y	Y	Y	Y	N	5	5
Gogebic Community College	Ironwood	C,T	St-L	M/W	1,058	46	46		Y	Y	Y	Y	Y	Y	Y	N	11	43
Grand Rapids Community College	Grand Rapids	C,T	Dist	M/W	14,039	57	27	78	Y	Y	Y	Y	Y	Y	Y	N	14	30
ITT Technical Institute	Canton	T	Prop	M/W	327				N	Y		Y	Y	Y	Y	N		6
ITT Technical Institute	Grand Rapids	T	Prop	M/W	616				N	Y		Y	Y	Y	Y	N		6
ITT Technical Institute	Troy	T	Prop	M/W	658				N	Y		Y	Y	Y	Y	N		6
Jackson Community College	Jackson	C,T	Cou	M/W	5,899	65	44		Y			Y	Y	Y	Y	N		26
Kalamazoo Valley Community College	Kalamazoo	C,T	St-L	M/W	10,438	64	50		Y			Y	Y	Y	Y	N	6	29
Kellogg Community College	Battle Creek	C,T	St-L	M/W	5,523	67	47		Y		S	Y	Y	Y	Y	N	5	73
Kirtland Community College	Roscommon	C,T	Dist	M/W	1,918	68	52		Y			Y	Y	Y	Y	N		20
Lake Michigan College	Benton Harbor	C,T	Dist	M/W	3,586													
Lansing Community College	Lansing	C,T	St-L	M/W	18,575	69	53		Y		S	Y	Y	Y	Y	N	9	104
Lewis College of Business	Detroit	C,T	Ind	M/W	324													
Macomb Community College	Warren	C,T	Dist	M/W	22,245	72	45		Y			Y	Y	Y	Y	N	11	73
Mid Michigan Community College	Harrison	C,T	St-L	M/W	3,064	55	32	15	Y	Y	R	Y	Y	Y	Y	N		52
Monroe County Community College	Monroe	C,T	Cou	M/W	3,943	62	45		Y	Y	Y		Y	Y	Y			43
Montcalm Community College	Sidney	C,T	St-L	M/W	1,802	70	45		Y	Y	R	Y	Y	Y	Y	N	1	22
Mott Community College	Flint	C,T	Dist	M/W	10,188	66	44		Y		Y	Y	Y	Y	Y	N	6	51
North Central Michigan College	Petoskey	C,T	Cou	M/W	2,738													
Northwestern Michigan College	Traverse City	C,T	St-L	M/W	4,471	60	37		Y		S	Y	Y	Y	Y	Y	8	44
Oakland Community College	Bloomfield Hills	C,T	St-L	M/W	24,145	70	46		Y		R	Y	Y	Y	Y	N	8	90
St. Clair County Community College	Port Huron	C,T	St-L	M/W	4,523		38		Y	Y	Y	Y	Y	Y	Y		6	36
Schoolcraft College	Livonia	C,T	Dist	M/W	10,159	66	61		Y	Y	R,S	Y	Y	Y	Y	N	5	36
Southwestern Michigan College	Dowagiac	C,T	St-L	M/W	2,948	63	43		Y	Y	Y	Y	Y	Y	Y	N	17	27
Washtenaw Community College	Ann Arbor	C,T	St-L	M/W	12,070	72	48	89	Y	Y	S	Y	Y	Y	Y	N	7	58
Wayne County Community College District†	Detroit	C,T	St-L	M/W	11,673													
West Shore Community College	Scottville	C,T	Dist	M/W	1,372													
Minnesota																		
Academy College	Minneapolis	C,T,B	Prop	M/W	320	29			Y	Y		Y	Y	Y	Y			25
Alexandria Technical College	Alexandria	C,T	St	M/W	2,164		23		Y	Y	Y	Y	Y	Y	Y	N	5	52
Anoka-Ramsey Community College*	Coon Rapids	C,T	St	M/W	5,797													
Anoka Technical College	Anoka	C,T	St	M/W	2,371	55	53		Y	Y	Y	Y	Y	Y	Y	N		24
The Art Institutes International Minnesota	Minneapolis	T,B	Prop	M/W	1,162		33	3	N	Y		Y	Y	Y	Y	Y		11
Brown College	Mendota Heights	C,T,B	Prop	M/W	2,250													
Central Lakes College	Brainerd	C,T	St	M/W	2,947		33		Y		Y	Y	Y	Y	Y	N	8	10
Century College	White Bear Lake	C,T	St	M/W	8,490	52			Y		Y	Y	Y	Y	Y	N	5	36
Dakota County Technical College	Rosemount	C,T	St	M/W	6,069	51	55		Y	Y	S	Y	Y	Y	Y	N	3	59
Duluth Business University	Duluth	T	Prop	PW	325													9
Dunwoody College of Technology	Minneapolis	T	Ind	PM	1,611	23	28		N	Y		Y	Y	Y	Y			15
Fond du Lac Tribal and Community College	Cloquet	C,T	St	M/W	1,735													
Globe College	Oakdale	T,B,M	Priv	M/W	997		48		Y	Y		Y		Y	Y			20

This chart includes the names and locations of accredited two-year colleges in the United States and U.S. territories and shows institutions' responses to the *Thomson Peterson's Survey of Undergraduate Institutions.* If an institution submitted incomplete data, one or more columns opposite the institution's name is blank. An asterisk after the school name denotes a *Special Message* following the college's profile, and a dagger indicates that the institution has one or more entries in the *In-Depth Descriptions of Two-Year Colleges* section. If a school does not appear, it did not report any of the information.

Y—Yes; N—No; R—Recommended; S—For Some

College	City	Degrees Awarded	Institutional Control	Student Body	Undergrad Enrollment Fall 2003	Percent Attending Part-Time	Percent 25 Years of Age or Older	Percent of Grads Going on to Four-Year Colleges	High School Equivalency Certificate Accepted	High School Transcript Required	Open Admissions	Need-Based Aid Available	Part-Time Jobs Available	Career Counseling Available	Job Placement Services Available	College Housing Available	Number of Sports Available	Number of Majors Offered
Hennepin Technical College	Brooklyn Park	C,T	St	M/W	8,623													
Herzing College, Minneapolis Drafting School Division	Minneapolis	T,B	Prop	PW	346	41	43		Y	Y	Y				Y	Y	N		8
Hibbing Community College	Hibbing	C,T	St	M/W	1,832		55		Y	Y	Y	Y		Y	Y	Y	N	11	19
Inver Hills Community College	Inver Grove Heights	C,T	St	M/W	4,325													
Itasca Community College	Grand Rapids	C,T	St	M/W	1,131		31	75	Y	Y	Y	Y	Y	Y		Y		9	29
ITT Technical Institute	Eden Prairie		Prop	M/W														12
Lake Superior College	Duluth	C,T	St	M/W	4,215		30		Y		S	Y	Y	Y	Y	N	3	34
Mesabi Range Community and Technical College	Virginia	C,T	St	M/W	1,509		32	80	Y	Y		Y	Y	Y	Y	Y	13	16
Minneapolis Business College	Roseville	C,T	Prop	PW	300		1									Y		4
Minneapolis Community and Technical College	Minneapolis	C,T	St	M/W	7,446		43		Y		Y	Y	Y	Y	Y	N	3	25
Minnesota School of Business–Brooklyn Center	Brooklyn Center	T,B,M	Prop	M/W	809													19
Minnesota School of Business-Plymouth	Minneapolis	T,B,M	Prop	M/W	500													20
Minnesota School of Business-Richfield	Richfield	T,B,M	Prop	M/W	944		40		Y	Y	Y		Y	Y	Y	N		20
Minnesota State College–Southeast Technical	Winona	C,T	St	M/W	1,875	47	46		Y	Y	Y	Y	Y	Y	Y	N		28
Minnesota State Community and Technical College–Fergus Falls	Fergus Falls	C,T	St	M/W	1,739	46	20	81	Y	Y	Y	Y	Y	Y	Y	Y	13	13
Minnesota West Comm & Tech Coll-Pipestone Cmps	Pipestone	C,T	St	M/W	3,175	54	32		Y	Y	Y	Y	Y	Y	Y	N	6	5
Musictech College	Saint Paul	C,T	Prop	M/W	405	16	10		Y	Y	Y		Y	Y	Y	N		2
Normandale Community College	Bloomington	C,T	St	M/W	7,811		34	70	Y	Y	S	Y	Y	Y	Y	N	13	28
North Hennepin Community College	Brooklyn Park	C,T	St	M/W	7,787	63	43		Y		S	Y	Y	Y	Y	N	7	26
Northland Community and Technical College–Thief River Falls	Thief River Falls	C,T	St	M/W	2,152													
Northwest Technical Institute	Eden Prairie	C,T	Prop	M/W	108		10		Y	Y	Y		Y	Y	Y	N		2
Pine Technical College	Pine City	C,T	St	M/W	770	66												
Rainy River Community College	International Falls	C,T	St	M/W	384		54	62	Y	Y	Y	Y	Y	Y	Y	Y	11	6
Rasmussen College Mankato	Mankato	T	Prop	PW	330		40		N	Y	Y	Y	Y	Y	Y	N		32
Rasmussen College Minnetonka	Minnetonka	T	Prop	PW	325	42	80		N	Y	Y		Y	Y	Y			8
Rasmussen College St. Cloud	St. Cloud	C,T	Prop	PW	454	33	47		N	Y	Y	Y	Y	Y	Y			9
Ridgewater College	Willmar	C,T	St	M/W	3,578													
Riverland Community College	Austin	C,T	St	M/W	4,000		42	68	Y	Y	Y	Y	Y	Y	Y	N	5	28
Rochester Community and Technical College	Rochester	C,T,B	St	M/W	5,862		34		Y	Y	Y	Y	Y	Y	Y	N	10	25
St. Cloud Technical College	St. Cloud	T	St	M/W	3,205	32	29		Y	Y	Y	Y	Y	Y	Y	N	4	56
Saint Paul College–A Community & Technical College	St. Paul	C,T	St-R	M/W	5,552	72	60		Y	Y	S	Y	Y	Y	Y	N		13
South Central Technical College	North Mankato	T	St	M/W	2,350				Y					Y				17
Vermilion Community College	Ely	C,T	St	M/W	1,191		10		Y	Y	Y	Y	Y	Y	Y	Y	14	77
Mississippi																		
Antonelli College	Jackson	C,T	Prop	M/W	214													
Coahoma Community College	Clarksdale	C,T	St-L	M/W	1,400													
Copiah-Lincoln Community College	Wesson	C,T	St-L	M/W	2,161	34	22		Y	Y	Y	Y	Y	Y	Y	Y	9	45
Copiah-Lincoln Community College–Natchez Campus	Natchez	C,T	St-L	M/W	900	38	50		Y	Y	Y	Y	Y	Y	Y			11
East Mississippi Community College	Scooba	C,T	St-L	M/W	3,417		30		Y	Y	Y	Y	Y	Y	Y	Y	9	36
Hinds Community College	Raymond	C,T	St-L	M/W	9,961	28	40		Y	Y	Y	Y	Y	Y	Y	Y	10	75
Holmes Community College	Goodman	C,T	St-L	M/W	1,046	26		80	Y	Y	Y	Y	Y	Y	Y	Y	9	29
Jones County Junior College	Ellisville	C,T	St-L	M/W	5,640													
Meridian Community College	Meridian	C,T	St-L	M/W	3,635		30	75	Y	Y	Y	Y	Y	Y	Y	Y	11	21
Mississippi Delta Community College	Moorhead	C,T	Dist	M/W	4,000													
Mississippi Gulf Coast Community College	Perkinston	C,T	Dist	M/W	10,231		0		Y	Y	Y	Y	Y	Y	Y	Y	9	46
Northeast Mississippi Community College	Booneville	C,T	St	M/W	3,224	14	20		Y	Y			Y	Y	Y	Y	10	102
Northwest Mississippi Community College	Senatobia	C,T	St-L	M/W	6,300													
Pearl River Community College	Poplarville	C,T	St-L	M/W	3,700													
Southwest Mississippi Community College	Summit	C,T	St-L	M/W	2,268		31		Y	Y	Y	Y	Y	Y	Y	Y	6	38
Virginia College at Jackson	Jackson	T	Prop	M/W	1,108								Y	Y	Y		N		9
Missouri																		
Blue River Community College	Blue Springs	C,T	St-L	M/W	2,323	56	33		Y	Y		Y	Y	Y	N		9
Cottey College	Nevada	C	Ind	W	298													
Crowder College	Neosho	C,T	St-L	M/W	2,616	47	23		Y	Y	Y	Y	Y	Y	Y	Y	3	35
East Central College	Union	C,T	Dist	M/W	3,320	57												
Hickey College*	St. Louis	T,B	Prop	M/W	500				Y	Y					Y			7
IHM Health Studies Center	St. Louis	T	Ind	M/W	136													1
ITT Technical Institute	Arnold	T,B	Prop	M/W	483				N	Y	Y	Y	Y	Y	Y	N		15
ITT Technical Institute	Earth City	T,B	Prop	M/W	603				N	Y	Y	Y	Y	Y	Y	N		15
Jefferson College	Hillsboro	C,T	St	M/W	4,065	46	17		Y	Y	Y	Y	Y	Y	Y	Y	3	63
Linn State Technical College	Linn	T	St	PM	872	10	16			Y	Y	Y	Y		Y		6	20
Longview Community College	Lee's Summit	C,T	St-L	M/W	5,713	59	32		Y	Y		Y	Y	Y	N	4	28
Maple Woods Community College	Kansas City	C,T	St-L	M/W	4,747	57	29		Y	Y		Y	Y	Y	Y	N	3	24
Metro Business College	Cape Girardeau	T,B	Prop	M/W	118													
Metropolitan Community College-Business & Technology College	Kansas City	C,T	St-L	PM	401	73	73									N		43
Mineral Area College	Park Hills	C,T	Dist	M/W	2,946	44	36		Y		Y	Y	Y	Y	Y		3	34
Missouri College	St. Louis	T	Prop	PW	560													

This chart includes the names and locations of accredited two-year colleges in the United States and U.S. territories, and shows institutions' responses to the *Thomson Peterson's Survey of Undergraduate Institutions.* If an institution submitted incomplete data, one or more columns opposite the institution's name is blank.

An asterisk after the school name denotes a *Special Message* following the college's profile, and a dagger indicates that the institution has one or more entries in the *In-Depth Descriptions of Two-Year Colleges* section. If a school does not appear, it did not report any of the information.

Legend: Y—Yes; N—No; R—Recommended; S—For Some

Degrees Awarded: College Transfer Associate (C), Bachelor's (B), Master's (M), Doctoral (D), First Professional (F), Terminal Associate (T)

Institution	City	Degrees	Control	Student Body	Enrollment Fall 2003	% Part-Time	% 25+	% Grads to 4-Yr	Open Admissions	HS Equiv Cert Accepted	HS Transcript Required	Part-Time Jobs Available	Career Counseling	Job Placement	College Housing	Sports	Majors
Moberly Area Community College	Moberly	C,T	St-L	M/W	3,588	51	26		Y	Y	Y	Y	Y	Y	Y	3	14
North Central Missouri College	Trenton	C,T	Dist	M/W	1,319	53	25		Y	Y	Y	Y	Y	Y	Y	3	17
Ozarks Technical Community College	Springfield	C,T	Dist	M/W	8,130	55											
Patricia Stevens College	St. Louis	C,T	Prop	PW	212		37			Y	Y	Y		Y	Y		7
Penn Valley Community College	Kansas City	C,T	St-L	M/W	4,559	66	55		Y	Y	Y	Y	Y	Y	N	1	38
Pinnacle Career Institute	Kansas City	C	Prop	M/W	170												
Ranken Technical College	St. Louis	C,T,B	Ind	PM	1,423	48	40	5	N	Y	Y	Y	Y	Y	Y		11
Saint Charles Community College	St. Peters	C,T	St	M/W	6,696	53	52		Y	Y	R,S	Y	Y	Y	N	6	22
St. Louis Community College at Florissant Valley	St. Louis	C,T	Dist	M/W			53		Y	Y	Y	Y	Y	Y	N	7	48
St. Louis Community College at Forest Park	St. Louis	C,T	Dist	M/W	7,610												
St. Louis Community College at Meramec	Kirkwood	C,T	Dist	M/W	12,607												
Sanford-Brown College	Fenton	T,B	Prop	M/W	440	10											
Sanford-Brown College	Hazelwood	C,T	Prop	M/W	600				N	Y	Y	Y	Y	Y	Y	1	7
Southwest Missouri State University–West Plains	West Plains	C,T	St	M/W	1,701		10		Y	Y	S	Y	Y	Y	Y	2	8
State Fair Community College	Sedalia	C,T	Dist	M/W	3,391	50											
Three Rivers Community College	Poplar Bluff	C,T	St-L	M/W	3,235	49	49	40	Y	Y	Y	Y	Y	Y	Y	5	24
Vatterott College	Springfield	T	Prop	M/W										Y	N		5
Vatterott College	St. Ann	T,B	Prop	M/W	580				N			Y	Y	Y	Y		9
Vatterott College	St. Joseph	T	Prop	M/W													4
Vatterott College	Sunset Hills	T,B	Prop	M/W	600												
Wentworth Military Academy and Junior College	Lexington	C	Ind	M/W	290												
Montana																	
Blackfeet Community College	Browning	C,T	Ind	M/W	503	16	61		Y	Y	Y	Y	Y	Y	N	1	16
Dawson Community College	Glendive	C,T	St-L	M/W	475	31	31		Y	Y	Y	Y	Y	Y	Y	10	10
Flathead Valley Community College*	Kalispell	C,T	St-L	M/W	2,267	50											
Fort Belknap College	Harlem	C	Fed	M/W	158	26											
Little Big Horn College	Crow Agency	C,T	Ind	M/W	317												
Miles Community College	Miles City	C,T	St-L	M/W	474	24	19		Y	Y	Y	Y	Y	Y	Y	10	23
Montana State U Coll of Tech-Great Falls	Great Falls	C,T	St	M/W	1,463	51	54		Y	Y	Y	Y	Y	Y	N	1	27
Salish Kootenai College	Pablo	C,T,B	Ind	M/W	1,088	46											
Helena Coll of Tech of The U of Montana	Helena	C,T	St	M/W	850												
Nebraska																	
Central Community College–Columbus Campus	Columbus	C,T	St-L	M/W	1,937	75	48		Y	Y	Y	Y	Y	Y	Y	5	22
Central Community College–Grand Island Campus	Grand Island	C,T	St-L	M/W	2,771	82	53		Y	Y	Y	Y	Y	Y	N	3	22
Central Community College–Hastings Campus	Hastings	C,T	St-L	M/W	2,400	61	35		Y	Y	Y	Y	Y	Y	Y	6	36
The Creative Center	Omaha	T	Prop	M/W	131	1											3
Hamilton College	Omaha	T,B	Prop	M/W	700		60		N	Y	Y	Y	Y	Y	Y		9
Hamilton College-Lincoln	Lincoln	C,T	Prop	M/W	1,000												
ITT Technical Institute	Omaha	T,B	Prop	M/W	382				N	Y		Y	Y	Y	N		10
Little Priest Tribal College	Winnebago	C,T	Ind	M/W	130	48							Y	Y			
Metropolitan Community College*	Omaha	C,T	St-L	M/W	12,838	64	48		Y		R	Y	Y	Y	N		33
Mid-Plains Community College	North Platte	C,T	Dist	M/W	3,084	65	67	80	Y	Y	Y			Y	Y	5	18
Nebraska Indian Community College	Macy	C,T	Fed	M/W	190	49	66		Y	Y	Y	Y	Y		N		12
Northeast Community College	Norfolk	C,T	St-L	M/W	4,858	61	39	21	Y	Y	R	Y	Y	Y	Y	8	76
Southeast Community College, Beatrice Campus	Beatrice	C,T	Dist	M/W	1,220	40		80	Y	Y	Y	Y	Y	Y	Y	6	24
Southeast Community College, Lincoln Campus	Lincoln	C,T	Dist	M/W	7,547	50	35		Y	Y	Y	Y	Y	Y	N	5	20
Southeast Community College, Milford Campus	Milford	T	Dist	PM	936	2											
Vatterott College	Omaha		Prop														
Vatterott College	Omaha	C	Prop	M/W	414		58		N			Y	Y	Y	Y		
Western Nebraska Community College	Sidney	C,T	St-L	M/W	3,151												
Nevada																	
The Art Institute of Las Vegas	Henderson	C,B	Prop	M/W	678	5											
Career College of Northern Nevada	Reno	T	Prop	M/W	389				Y	Y	Y	Y	Y	Y	N		6
Great Basin College	Elko	C,T,B	St	M/W	2,731		60		Y		Y	Y	Y	Y	Y	4	25
ITT Technical Institute	Henderson	T,B	Prop	M/W	536				N	Y	Y	Y	Y	Y	N		12
Las Vegas College	Las Vegas	T	Prop	M/W	651	37											
Western Nevada Community College	Carson City	C,T	St	M/W	4,714		68		Y	Y	S	Y	Y	Y	N		42
New Hampshire																	
Hesser College†	Manchester	C,T,B	Prop	M/W	2,860	34	25	65	N	Y	Y	Y	Y	Y	Y	8	33
McIntosh College†	Dover	C,T	Prop	M/W	1,386	13	65		Y	Y	Y	Y	Y	Y	Y	1	19
New Hampshire Comm Tech Coll, Berlin/Laconia	Berlin	C,T	St	M/W	2,080	66			N	Y	Y	Y	Y	Y	N	6	19
New Hampshire Comm Tech Coll, Manchester/Stratham	Manchester	C,T	St	M/W	2,309			9	N	Y	Y	Y	Y	Y	N	8	23
New Hampshire Comm Tech Coll, Nashua/Claremont	Nashua	C,T	St	M/W	2,299												
New Hampshire Technical Institute	Concord	C	St	M/W	3,650		50	18	Y	Y	Y	Y	Y	Y	Y	5	30

Two-Year Colleges At-a-Glance

This chart includes the names and locations of accredited two-year colleges in the United States and U.S. territories and shows institutions' responses to the *Thomson Peterson's Survey of Undergraduate Institutions*. If an institution submitted incomplete data, one or more columns opposite the institution's name is blank.

An asterisk after the school name denotes a *Special Message* following the college's profile, and a dagger indicates that the institution has one or more entries in the *In-Depth Descriptions of Two-Year Colleges* section. If a school does not appear, it did not report any of the information.

Y—Yes; N—No; R—Recommended; S—For Some

Institution	Location	Degrees Awarded	Institutional Control	Student Body	Undergraduate Enrollment Fall 2003	Percent 25 Years of Age or Older	Percent Attending Part-Time	Percent of Grads Going on to Four-Year Colleges	High School Equivalency Certificate Accepted	High School Transcript Required	Open Admissions	Need-Based Aid Available	Part-Time Jobs Available	Career Counseling Available	Job Placement Services Available	College Housing Available	Number of Sports Available	Number of Majors Offered
New Jersey																		
Assumption College for Sisters	Mendham	C	I-R	W	30	47	66	100		Y	Y	Y		Y		Y		2
Atlantic Cape Community College†	Mays Landing	C,T	Cou	M/W	6,177		68	14	Y		R	Y	Y	Y	Y	N	10	34
Bergen Community College*	Paramus	C,T	Cou	M/W	13,991	51	31	80	Y	Y		Y	Y	Y	Y	N	9	56
Berkeley College†	West Paterson	C,T,B	Prop	M/W	2,198		26		N	Y	Y	Y	Y	Y	Y	N	5	11
Brookdale Community College	Lincroft	C,T	Cou	M/W	12,724	48	28		Y	Y	Y	Y	Y	Y	Y	N	8	57
Burlington County College	Pemberton	C,T	Cou	M/W	7,519	55	39	60	Y	Y	Y	Y	Y	Y	Y	N	5	49
Camden County College*	Blackwood	C,T	St-L	M/W	14,829		39		Y	Y	S	Y	Y	Y	Y	N	4	53
County College of Morris	Randolph	C,T	Cou	M/W	8,496		27	76	Y		Y	Y	Y	Y	Y	N	12	28
Cumberland County College	Vineland	C,T	St-L	M/W	3,112		50		Y		Y	Y	Y	Y	Y	N	6	39
Essex County College	Newark	C,T	Cou	M/W	9,274	48	50	65	Y		Y	Y	Y	Y	Y	N	6	51
Gloucester County College	Sewell	C,T	Cou	M/W	5,610	47			Y		Y	Y	Y	Y	Y	N	9	43
Hudson County Community College	Jersey City	C,T	St-L	M/W	6,087	34	42	13	Y		Y	Y	Y	Y	Y	N		16
Middlesex County College†	Edison	C,T	Cou	M/W	11,276		44		Y	Y	Y	Y	Y	Y	Y	N	11	68
Ocean County College	Toms River	C,T	Cou	M/W	8,436				Y		S	Y	Y	Y	Y	N	9	27
Passaic County Community College	Paterson	C,T	Cou	M/W	6,308													
Raritan Valley Community College	Somerville	C,T	Cou	M/W	6,470	61	33		Y		Y	Y	Y	Y	Y	N	4	46
Salem Community College	Carneys Point	C,T	Cou	M/W	301	31	52		Y		Y	Y	Y	Y	Y	N	4	30
Somerset Christian College	Zarephath	C	I-R	M/W	142													
Sussex County Community College	Newton	C,T	St-L	M/W	2,924	54	41		Y			Y	Y	Y	Y	N	6	20
Union County College	Cranford	C,T	St-L	M/W	10,399	48	5		Y	Y	Y	Y	Y	Y	Y	N	8	35
Warren County Community College	Washington	C,T	St-L	M/W	705	51												
New Mexico																		
Albuquerque Technical Vocational Institute	Albuquerque	C,T	St	M/W	22,077	70	53		Y		R	Y	Y	Y	Y	N		35
Clovis Community College	Clovis	C,T	St	M/W	3,093	64	52		Y		R	Y	Y	Y	Y	N	5	39
Doña Ana Branch Community College	Las Cruces	T	St-L	M/W	5,872	44			Y		Y	Y	Y	Y	Y	Y		22
Eastern New Mexico University–Roswell	Roswell	C,T	St	M/W	3,522													
International Institute of the Americas	Albuquerque	T,B	Ind	M/W	163													
ITT Technical Institute	Albuquerque	T,B	Prop	M/W	487				N	Y	Y	Y	Y	Y	Y	N		15
Luna Community College	Las Vegas	C,T	St	M/W	1,815	79							Y	Y				13
Mesalands Community College	Tucumcari	C,T	St	M/W	563		52					Y				N		14
New Mexico Junior College	Hobbs	C,T	St-L	M/W	3,222													
New Mexico Military Institute*†	Roswell	C	St	PM	423													
New Mexico State University–Carlsbad	Carlsbad	C,T	St	M/W	1,228		70		Y		Y	Y	Y	Y	Y	N		17
New Mexico State University–Grants	Grants	C,T	St	M/W	636	63			Y		Y	Y	Y	Y	Y	N		8
Northern New Mexico Community College	Española	C,T	St	M/W	2,272													
Pima Medical Institute	Albuquerque	T	Prop	M/W	400													
San Juan College	Farmington	C,T	St	M/W	5,114	51			Y	Y	Y	Y	Y	Y	Y	N	14	52
Santa Fe Community College	Santa Fe	C,T	St-L	M/W	5,452	83	64	50	Y		Y	Y	Y	Y	Y	N	1	33
University of New Mexico–Gallup	Gallup	C,T,B	St	M/W	2,858													
University of New Mexico–Los Alamos Branch	Los Alamos	C,T	St	M/W	890													
New York																		
Adirondack Community College	Queensbury	C,T	St-L	M/W	3,200													
American Acad McAllister Inst of Funeral Service	New York	T	Ind	M/W	130													
American Academy of Dramatic Arts†	New York	T	Ind	M/W	224		14		N	Y	R,S	Y	Y	Y	Y	N	1	1
The Art Institute of New York City	New York	C,T	Prop	M/W	1,484			1	Y	Y	Y	Y	Y	Y	Y	N		5
Berkeley College-New York City Campus†	New York	C,T,B	Prop	M/W	1,807	12	31		N	Y	Y	Y	Y	Y	Y	N		8
Berkeley College-Westchester Campus†	White Plains	C,T,B	Prop	M/W	629	13	20		N	Y	Y	Y	Y	Y	Y	Y		8
Borough of Manhattan Comm Coll of City U of NY	New York	C,T	St-L	M/W	17,629	37	42	57	Y	Y	Y	Y	Y	Y	Y	N	4	17
Bramson ORT College	Forest Hills	T	Ind	M/W	600													
Bronx Comm Coll of City U of NY	Bronx	C,T	St-L	M/W	7,952	41	48		Y	Y		Y	Y	Y		N	6	27
Broome Community College	Binghamton	C,T	St-L	M/W	6,542	37	35	56	Y	Y	Y	Y	Y	Y	Y	N	11	35
Bryant & Stratton Business Inst	Albany	T	Prop	M/W	398													
Bryant & Stratton Business Inst	Buffalo	T	Prop	M/W	567	9	67		N	Y	Y	Y	Y	Y	Y	N		5
Bryant & Stratton Business Inst	Lackawanna	T	Prop	M/W	285	18	63	4	N	Y	Y	Y	Y	Y	Y	N		5
Bryant & Stratton Business Inst	Rochester	T	Prop	M/W	180	26												
Bryant & Stratton Business Inst	Rochester	T	Prop	M/W	362	20												
Bryant & Stratton Business Inst	Syracuse	T	Prop	M/W	570	17	26		N	Y	Y	Y	Y	Y	Y	Y	1	12
Bryant & Stratton Business Inst, Amherst Cmps	Clarence	T	Prop	M/W	317	38	61		N	Y	Y	Y	Y	Y	Y	N		7
Bryant & Stratton Business Inst	Liverpool	T	Prop	M/W	357	9												
Cayuga County Community College	Auburn	C,T	St-L	M/W	2,835													
Clinton Community College	Plattsburgh	C,T	St-L	M/W	2,192	43	31		Y	Y	Y	Y	Y	Y	Y	Y	6	17
Cochran School of Nursing	Yonkers	T	Ind	PW	157	36	76		N	Y	Y	Y				N		1
The College of Westchester†	White Plains	C,T	Prop	M/W	973	6	48		N	Y	Y	Y	Y	Y	Y	N	1	26
Columbia-Greene Community College	Hudson	C,T	St-L	M/W	1,715	45	41		Y		Y	Y	Y	Y	Y	N	11	23
Corning Community College	Corning	C,T	St-L	M/W	4,443	47	41	74	Y	Y	Y	Y	Y	Y	Y	N	12	44
Crouse Hospital School of Nursing	Syracuse	C	Ind	PW	222	43	55		N	Y	Y	Y	Y				Y		1

This chart includes the names and locations of accredited two-year colleges in the United States and U.S. territories and shows institutions' responses to the *Thomson Peterson's Survey of Undergraduate Institutions*. If an institution submitted incomplete data, one or more columns opposite the institution's name is blank.
An asterisk after the school name denotes a *Special Message* following the college's profile, and a dagger indicates that the institution has one or more entries in the *In-Depth Descriptions of Two-Year Colleges* section. If a school does not appear, it did not report any of the information.

Y—Yes; N—No; R—Recommended; S—For Some

Name	Location	Degrees Awarded	Institutional Control	Student Body	Undergraduate Enrollment Fall 2003	% Attending Part-Time	% 25 Years or Older	% Grads to Four-Year Colleges	HS Equivalency Cert. Accepted	HS Transcript Required	Open Admissions	Need-Based Aid Available	Part-Time Jobs Available	Career Counseling Available	Job Placement Services Available	College Housing Available	No. of Sports Offered	No. of Majors Offered
Dorothea Hopfer School of Nursing at The Mount Vernon Hospital	Mount Vernon		Ind		120													
Dutchess Community College	Poughkeepsie	C,T	St-L	M/W	7,810	48	56		Y	Y	Y	Y	Y	Y	Y	N	10	44
Elmira Business Institute	Elmira	C,T	Priv	PW	340	70			Y	Y	Y	Y		Y	Y	N		5
Erie Community College	Buffalo	C,T	St-L	M/W	12,284	34	35	29	Y	Y	Y	Y	Y	Y	Y	N	13	17
Eugenio María de Hostos Comm Coll of City U of NY	Bronx	C,T	St-L	M/W	3,705	28	57	25	Y	Y	Y	Y	Y	Y	Y	N	5	17
Finger Lakes Community College	Canandaigua	C,T	St-L	M/W	4,955	32			Y	Y	Y	Y	Y	Y	Y	Y	8	49
Fiorello H LaGuardia Comm Coll of City U of NY*	Long Island City	C,T	St-L	M/W	12,875	52	40	50	Y	Y	Y	Y	Y	Y	Y	N	6	33
Fulton-Montgomery Community College	Johnstown	C,T	St-L	M/W	1,956	30	34		Y			Y	Y	Y	Y	N	9	44
Genesee Community College	Batavia	C,T	St-L	M/W	5,204	52												
Herkimer County Community College	Herkimer	C,T	St-L	M/W	3,074													
Hudson Valley Community College	Troy	C,T	St-L	M/W	11,405													
Institute of Design and Construction	Brooklyn	C	Ind	PM	246													
Interboro Institute	New York	T	Prop	M/W	1,891													
Island Drafting and Technical Institute	Amityville	C,T	Prop	PM	222	56			Y	Y	R	Y		Y	Y	N		8
ITT Technical Institute	Albany	T	Prop	M/W	390				N	Y	Y	Y	Y	Y	Y	N		5
ITT Technical Institute	Getzville	T	Prop	M/W	643				N	Y	Y	Y	Y	Y	Y	N		6
ITT Technical Institute	Liverpool	T	Prop	M/W	334				N	Y	Y	Y	Y	Y	Y	N		5
Jamestown Business College	Jamestown	T	Prop	M/W	327	55			N	Y	Y	Y		Y	Y	N	10	7
Jamestown Community College	Jamestown	C,T	St-L	M/W	3,598	31	32		Y	Y	Y	Y	Y	Y	Y	Y	14	24
Jefferson Community College	Watertown	C,T	St-L	M/W	3,481	46	37	61	N	Y	Y	Y	Y	Y	Y	N	9	29
Katharine Gibbs School	Melville	C,T	Prop	PW	897													
Kingsborough Comm Coll of City U of NY	Brooklyn	C,T	St-L	M/W	14,944	50	31	75	Y	Y	Y	Y	Y	Y	Y	N	8	38
Long Island Business Institute	Commack	C	Prop	PW	169	95	0		Y	Y	Y	Y			Y	N		4
Maria College*†	Albany	C,T	Ind	M/W	689	64												
Mildred Elley	Latham	C,T	Priv		394	64								Y	Y	N		5
Mohawk Valley Community College†	Utica	C,T	St-L	M/W	5,842	34	28	71	Y	Y	Y	Y			Y	Y	17	53
Monroe College*	Bronx	C,T,B	Prop	M/W	4,028	46	26		N		Y	Y	Y	Y	Y	Y	4	8
Monroe College	New Rochelle	C,T,B	Prop	M/W	1,433	17	54	26	N		Y	Y	Y	Y	Y	Y	4	7
Monroe Community College	Rochester	C,T	St-L	M/W	16,596	43												
Nassau Community College	Garden City	C,T	St-L	M/W	20,984	38	17	65		Y		Y	Y		Y	N	19	55
New York City Tech Coll of the City U of NY	Brooklyn	C,T,B	St-L	M/W	11,380	38												
New York Col Health Professions†	Syosset	T,B,M	Ind	M/W					N	Y	Y	Y			Y	N		2
Niagara County Community College	Sanborn	C,T	St-L	M/W	5,252	36	31	62	Y	Y	Y	Y	Y	Y	Y	N	10	35
North Country Community College	Saranac Lake	C,T	St-L	M/W	1,357	29	36	34	Y	Y	Y	Y	Y	Y	Y	Y	12	14
Olean Business Institute	Olean	T	Prop	M/W	138													
Orange County Community College	Middletown	C,T	St-L	M/W	6,109	50	31	62	Y	Y	Y	Y	Y	Y	Y	N	10	41
Phillips Beth Israel School of Nursing	New York	C,T	Ind	PW	133	80	65	10	N	Y	Y	Y				N		1
Queensborough Comm Coll of City U of NY	Bayside	C,T	St-L	M/W	11,704	48	32		Y	Y	Y	Y	Y	Y	Y	N	14	21
Rochester Business Institute	Rochester	T	Prop	M/W	1,223	16	57		N	Y	Y	Y	Y	Y	Y	N	2	5
Rockland Community College	Suffern	C,T	St-L	M/W	6,549	44												
Saint Joseph's Hospital Health Center School of Nursing	Syracuse	T	Ind	PW	293	39	51		Y		Y	Y			Y	Y		1
Cath Med Ctr of Brooklyn & Queens Sch of Nursing	Fresh Meadows	T	Ind	M/W	93	70			N	Y	Y	Y		Y	Y	N		1
Schenectady County Community College	Schenectady	C,T	St-L	M/W	4,140	50	47	74	Y	Y	Y	Y	Y	Y	Y	N	7	33
Simmons Institute of Funeral Service	Syracuse	C,T	Prop	M/W	60	38												
State U of NY Coll of A&T at Morrisville	Morrisville	C,T,B	St	M/W	3,269	14	22	44	N	Y	Y	Y		Y	Y	Y	19	61
State U of NY Coll of Environ Sci & For Ranger Sch†	Wanakena	C,T	St	PM	43	20	38		N	N	Y	Y	Y	Y	Y	Y	7	2
State U of NY Coll of Technology at Alfred	Alfred	C,T,B	St	M/W	3,471	23		83	N	Y	Y	Y	Y	Y	Y	Y	20	59
State U of NY Coll of Technology at Canton	Canton	C,T,B	St	M/W	2,538	16	21		N	Y	Y	Y	Y	Y	Y	Y	12	36
State U of NY Coll of Technology at Delhi	Delhi	C,T,B	St	M/W	2,281	10	19	81	N	Y	Y	Y	Y	Y	Y	Y	18	40
Suffolk County Community College	Selden	C,T	St-L	M/W	20,820	46												
Sullivan County Community College	Loch Sheldrake	C,T	St-L	M/W	1,902	38	31		Y	Y	Y	Y	Y	Y	Y	N	14	31
TCI-The College of Technology	New York	C,T	Prop	M/W	3,842													
Tompkins Cortland Community College	Dryden	C,T	St-L	M/W	3,227	34	37		Y		Y	Y	Y	Y	Y	Y	17	45
Trocaire College	Buffalo	C,T	Ind	PW	780													
Ulster County Community College	Stone Ridge	C,T	St-L	M/W	3,105													
Utica School of Commerce	Utica	C,T	Prop	PW	400													
Villa Maria College of Buffalo	Buffalo	C,T	I-R	M/W	459	27	38	59	N	Y	Y	Y	Y	Y	Y	N		13
Westchester Community College	Valhalla	C,T	St-L	M/W	11,981	56												
Wood Tobe–Coburn School	New York	T	Prop	PW	400													
North Carolina																		
Alamance Community College	Graham	C,T	St	M/W	4,627	66	47	1	Y	Y	Y	Y	Y	Y	Y	N	4	33
The Art Institute of Charlotte	Charlotte	T	Prop	M/W	697	33												
Asheville-Buncombe Technical Community College	Asheville	C,T	St	M/W	5,627	64	47		Y	Y	Y	Y		Y	Y	N	3	27
Beaufort County Community College	Washington	C,T	St	M/W	1,756		58	75	Y	Y	Y	Y	Y	Y	Y	N		21
Bladen Community College	Dublin	C,T	St-L	M/W	1,407	40	62	81	Y	Y	Y	Y	Y	Y	Y	N		15
Blue Ridge Community College	Flat Rock	C	St-L	M/W	2,083	53	69		Y	Y	Y	Y	Y	Y	Y	N	1	22
Brunswick Community College	Supply	C,T	St	M/W	1,109	51	41		Y	Y		Y	Y	Y	Y	N	4	17
Cabarrus College of Health Sciences	Concord	T,B	Ind	PW	242	24	59		N	Y	Y	Y	Y	Y		N		6

This chart includes the names and locations of accredited two-year colleges in the United States and U.S. territories and shows institutions' responses to the *Thomson Peterson's Survey of Undergraduate Institutions.* If an institution submitted incomplete data, one or more columns opposite the institution's name is blank. An asterisk after the school name denotes a *Special Message* following the college's profile, and a dagger indicates that that institution has one or more entries in the *In-Depth Descriptions of Two-Year Colleges* section. If a school does not appear, it did not report any of the information.

Y—Yes; N—No; R—Recommended; S—For Some

	Location	Degrees Awarded	Institutional Control	Student Body	Undergraduate Enrollment Fall 2003	Percent Attending Part-Time	Percent of Grads Going on to Four-Year Colleges	Percent 25 Years of Age or Older	High School Equivalency Certificate Accepted	High School Transcript Required	Open Admissions	Need-Based Aid Available	Part-Time Jobs Available	Career Counseling Available	Job Placement Services Available	College Housing Available	Number of Sports Offered	Number of Majors Offered
Caldwell Comm Coll and Tech Inst	Hudson	C,T	St	M/W	3,636	56	44		Y	Y	Y	Y	Y	Y	Y	N	3	25
Cape Fear Community College	Wilmington	C,T	St	M/W	7,010	48	14	85	Y	Y	Y	Y	Y	Y	Y	N	7	31
Carolinas College of Health Sciences	Charlotte	T	Ind	PW	405	69	53	5	N	Y	Y	Y	Y	Y	Y	N		3
Carteret Community College	Morehead City	C,T	St	M/W	1,732		53		Y	Y	Y	Y	Y	Y	Y	N	2	18
Central Carolina Community College	Sanford	C,T	St-L	M/W	4,857	62												
Central Piedmont Community College	Charlotte	C,T	St-L	M/W	16,245	65	49	46	Y	Y	S	Y	Y	Y	Y	N	1	69
Cleveland Community College	Shelby	C,T	St	M/W	2,793	61	49	50	Y	Y	Y	Y	Y	Y	Y	N		31
Coastal Carolina Community College	Jacksonville	C,T	St-L	M/W	4,231	51	45		Y	Y	Y	Y	Y	Y	Y	N		19
College of The Albemarle	Elizabeth City	C,T	St	M/W	2,071	59												
Durham Technical Community College	Durham	C,T	St	M/W	5,642	74	63	45	Y	Y	Y	Y	Y	Y		N		37
ECPI Technical College	Raleigh	T	Prop	M/W	350													
Edgecombe Community College	Tarboro	C,T	St-L	M/W	2,498	59	47	90	Y	Y	Y	Y	Y	Y	Y	N	1	25
Fayetteville Technical Community College	Fayetteville	C,T	St	M/W	10,141	56	59		Y	Y	S	Y	Y	Y	Y	N	3	79
Forsyth Technical Community College	Winston-Salem	C,T	St	M/W	7,157	51			Y	Y	Y	Y	Y	Y	Y	N	4	38
Gaston College	Dallas	C,T	St-L	M/W	5,025	67	52	42	Y	Y	S	Y	Y	Y	Y	N		22
Guilford Technical Community College	Jamestown	C,T	St-L	M/W	9,380	52	44		Y	Y	Y	Y	Y	Y	Y	N		52
Halifax Community College	Weldon	C,T	St-L	M/W	1,580													
Haywood Community College	Clyde	C,T	St-L	M/W	1,988	56												
Isothermal Community College	Spindale	C,T	St	M/W	2,005	51	49		Y	Y	Y	Y	Y	Y	Y	N	3	34
James Sprunt Community College	Kenansville	C,T	St	M/W	1,405	46	54	68	Y	Y	Y	Y	Y	Y	Y	N	2	13
Johnston Community College	Smithfield	C,T	St	M/W	3,806	56	43			Y	Y	Y	Y	Y	Y	N	4	19
Lenoir Community College	Kinston	C,T	St	M/W	2,607					Y	Y	Y	Y	Y	Y	N	4	44
Louisburg College	Louisburg	C	I-R	M/W	502	2												
Martin Community College	Williamston	C,T	St	M/W	834	66												
Mayland Community College	Spruce Pine	C,T	St-L	M/W	1,494		48		Y	Y	Y	Y	Y	Y	Y	N		18
Mitchell Community College	Statesville	C,T	St	M/W	2,243		57		Y	Y	Y	Y	Y	Y	Y	N		24
Montgomery Community College	Troy	C,T	St	M/W	843	52												
Nash Community College	Rocky Mount	C,T	St	M/W	2,567	65	43	90	Y	Y	Y	Y	Y	Y	Y	N		16
Pamlico Community College	Grantsboro	C,T	St	M/W	300													
Piedmont Community College	Roxboro	C,T	St	M/W	2,189	62												
Pitt Community College	Greenville	C,T	St-L	M/W	5,980	46	44		Y	Y	Y	Y	Y	Y	Y	N	5	35
Randolph Community College	Asheboro	C,T	St	M/W	2,291													
Richmond Community College	Hamlet	C,T	St	M/W	1,690	47	57		Y	Y	Y	Y	Y	Y	Y	N		16
Roanoke-Chowan Community College	Ahoskie	C,T	St	M/W	989	49	48		Y	Y		Y	Y	Y	Y	N	2	16
Robeson Community College	Lumberton	C,T	St	M/W	2,449													
Rockingham Community College	Wentworth	C,T	St	M/W	2,060	49			Y	Y			Y	Y	Y	N	8	32
Rowan-Cabarrus Community College	Salisbury	C,T	St	M/W	5,200	57	55	95	Y	Y	Y	Y	Y	Y	Y	N	1	16
Sampson Community College	Clinton	C,T	St-L	M/W	1,579	57												
Sandhills Community College	Pinehurst	C,T	St	M/W	3,502													
South College-Asheville	Asheville	T	Prop	M/W	112	21	64		Y	Y	Y	Y	Y	Y		N		6
Southeastern Community College	Whiteville	C,T	St	M/W	2,460		45		Y	Y	Y	Y	Y	Y	Y	N	4	20
Southwestern Community College	Sylva	C,T	St	M/W	1,939	54	36	75	Y	Y	Y	Y	Y	Y	Y	N		32
Stanly Community College	Albemarle	C,T	St	M/W	2,000		48		Y	Y	Y	Y	Y	Y	Y	N	1	31
Surry Community College	Dobson	C,T	St	M/W	3,600													
Tri-County Community College	Murphy	C,T	St	M/W	1,234	65	40		Y	Y	Y	Y	Y	Y	Y	N		11
Vance-Granville Community College	Henderson	C,T	St	M/W	4,315	55	53		Y	Y	Y	Y	Y	Y	Y	N	2	30
Wake Technical Community College	Raleigh	C,T	St-L	M/W	10,971													
Wayne Community College	Goldsboro	C,T	St-L	M/W	3,181													
Western Piedmont Community College	Morganton	C,T	St	M/W	2,897													
Wilkes Community College	Wilkesboro	C,T	St	M/W	2,741	44												
Wilson Technical Community College	Wilson	C,T	St	M/W	2,103		57	80	Y	Y	Y	Y	Y	Y	Y	N		19
North Dakota																		
Bismarck State College	Bismarck	C,T	St	M/W	3,430	33	32		Y	Y	Y	Y	Y	Y	Y	Y	6	23
Lake Region State College	Devils Lake	C,T	St	M/W	1,473	73	21		Y	Y	Y	Y	Y	Y	Y	Y	8	35
Minot State University–Bottineau Campus	Bottineau	C,T	St	M/W	620	38	14	60	Y	Y	Y	Y	Y	Y	Y	Y	9	32
North Dakota State College of Science	Wahpeton	B,M,D,F	St	M/W	2,398		18	81	Y	Y	Y	Y	Y	Y	Y	Y	5	31
Sitting Bull College	Fort Yates	C,T	Ind	M/W	214													
United Tribes Technical College ✓	Bismarck	C,T	Fed	M/W	678				Y	Y	Y	Y	Y	Y	Y	Y	3	23
Williston State College	Williston	C,T	St	M/W	871	31	28	80	Y	Y	Y	Y	Y	Y	Y		4	15
Northern Mariana Islands																		
Northern Marianas College	Saipan	C,T,B	Terr	M/W	1,299	40												
Ohio																		
AEC Southern Ohio College	North Canton	T	Prop	M/W	700				N	Y					Y	Y	N		11
AEC Southern Ohio College, Akron Campus	Akron	T	Prop	M/W	425													
AEC Southern Ohio College, Cincinnati Campus	Cincinnati	T	Prop	M/W	971													
AEC Southern Ohio College, Findlay Campus	Findlay	T	Prop	M/W	430													
Antonelli College	Cincinnati	T	Prop	M/W	387		30		Y	Y	Y	Y	Y	Y	Y	N		8

This chart includes the names and locations of accredited two-year colleges in the United States and U.S. territories and shows institutions' responses to the *Thomson Peterson's Survey of Undergraduate Institutions*. If an institution submitted incomplete data, one or more columns opposite the institution's name is blank.
An asterisk after the school name denotes a *Special Message* following the college's profile, and a dagger indicates that the institution has one or more entries in the *In-Depth Descriptions of Two-Year Colleges* section. If a school does not appear, it did not report any of the information.

Key: Y—Yes; N—No; R—Recommended; S—For Some

Institution	Location	Degrees Awarded	Institutional Control	Student Body	Undergraduate Enrollment Fall 2003	Percent Attending Part-Time	Percent 25 Years of Age or Older	Percent of Grads Going on to Four-Year Colleges	High School Equivalency Certificate Accepted	Open Admissions	High School Transcript Required	Need-Based Aid Available	Part-Time Jobs Available	Career Counseling Available	Job Placement Services Available	College Housing Available	Number of Sports Offered	Number of Majors Offered
The Art Institute of Cincinnati	Cincinnati	C	Prop	M/W	85													
Belmont Technical College	St. Clairsville	T	St	M/W	1,658	34												
Bowling Green State University-Firelands Coll ✓	Huron	C,T	St	M/W	1,738	48	45	33	Y	Y	Y	Y	Y	Y	Y	N	6	28
Bradford School	Columbus	C,T	Prop	M/W	312		8		N	Y	Y	Y		Y	Y	Y	1	9
Bryant and Stratton Coll	Parma	T	Prop	M/W	225	45	51	2	N	Y	Y	Y	Y	Y	Y	N		6
Central Ohio Technical College	Newark	T	St	M/W	2,225	60												
Chatfield College	St. Martin	C,T	I-R	PW	230		50	39	Y	Y	Y	Y	Y			N		4
Cincinnati College of Mortuary Science	Cincinnati	T,B	Ind	M/W	121		55		N	Y	Y	Y		Y	Y	N	4	1
Cincinnati State Technical and Community College	Cincinnati	C,T	St	M/W	7,722	62	44	31	Y	Y	Y	Y		Y	Y	N	4	65
Clark State Community College	Springfield	C,T	St	M/W	3,309	59			Y		Y	Y	Y	Y	Y	N	4	37
Cleveland Institute of Electronics	Cleveland	T	Prop	PM	2,612		85		Y	Y	Y					N		1
Columbus State Community College	Columbus	C,T	St	M/W	23,297	61	47	31	Y		R	Y	Y	Y	Y	N	9	75
Cuyahoga Community College	Cleveland	C,T	St-L	M/W	23,808	61	39		Y		S	Y	Y	Y	Y	N	8	32
Davis College	Toledo	T	Prop	M/W	417	55	70		N	Y	Y	Y	Y	Y	Y	N		14
Edison State Community College	Piqua	C,T	St	M/W	3,000	66	49		Y	Y	Y		Y	Y	Y	N	2	38
Gallipolis Career College	Gallipolis	T	Ind	PW	161	4			N	Y	Y			Y	Y	N		9
Hocking College	Nelsonville	C,T	St	M/W	5,250													
Hondros College	Westerville	C,T	Prop	M/W	100													
International College of Broadcasting	Dayton	C,T	Priv	M/W	87									Y				2
ITT Technical Institute	Dayton	T	Prop	M/W	483				N	Y	Y	Y	Y	Y	Y	N		6
ITT Technical Institute	Hillard	T	Prop	M/W	26													9
ITT Technical Institute	Norwood	C	Prop	M/W	593				N	Y	Y	Y	Y	Y	Y	N		4
ITT Technical Institute	Strongsville	T	Prop	M/W	709				N	Y	Y	Y	Y	Y	Y	N		9
ITT Technical Institute	Youngstown	T	Prop	M/W	518				N	Y	Y	Y	Y	Y	Y	N		6
James A. Rhodes State College	Lima	C,T	St	M/W	2,842	50	48	12	Y	Y	Y	Y	Y	Y	Y	N	7	33
Jefferson Community College	Steubenville	C,T	St-L	M/W	1,604	47	43		Y	Y	S	Y	Y	Y	Y	N	5	25
Kent State University, Ashtabula Campus	Ashtabula	C,T,B	St	M/W	1,371													
Kent State University, East Liverpool Campus	East Liverpool	C,T	St	M/W	657													
Kent State University, Geauga Campus	Burton	C,B,M	St	M/W	884													
Kent State University, Salem Campus	Salem	C,T,B	St	M/W	1,320		55		Y	Y	Y	Y	Y	Y	Y	N	5	22
Kent State University, Stark Campus	Canton	C,B	St	M/W	3,736		30		Y	Y	Y	Y	Y	Y	Y	N		6
Kent State University, Trumbull Campus	Warren	C,T	St	M/W	2,270		54		Y	Y	Y	Y	Y	Y	Y	N	4	16
Kent State University, Tuscarawas Campus	New Philadelphia	C,T,B,M	St	M/W	2,008		29		Y	Y	Y	Y	Y	Y	Y	N	3	16
Kettering College of Medical Arts	Kettering	C,T,B	I-R	PW	653		51		N	Y	Y	Y		Y	Y	Y	3	7
Lakeland Community College	Kirtland	C,T	St-L	M/W	8,635	64	43		Y	Y	Y	Y	Y	Y	Y	N	9	37
Lorain County Community College	Elyria	C,T	St-L	M/W	9,409	64	45	80	Y	Y	S	Y	Y	Y	Y	N	6	74
Marion Technical College	Marion	C,T	St	M/W	2,121	54	51	24	Y		Y	Y	Y	Y	Y	N	14	27
Mercy College of Northwest Ohio	Toledo	C,T,B	I-R	PW	565	50	48		Y		Y	Y	Y	Y	Y	Y		6
Miami–Jacobs College	Dayton	T	Prop	M/W	317													
Miami University Hamilton ✓	Hamilton	C,T,B,M	St	M/W	3,322	57	24		Y	Y	Y	Y	Y	Y	Y	N	11	99
Miami University–Middletown Campus	Middletown	C,T,B	St	M/W	2,660													
North Central State College	Mansfield	T	St	M/W	3,249		49		Y	Y	S	Y	Y	Y	Y	N	7	26
Northwest State Community College	Archbold	C,T	St	M/W	3,347	67	49		Y	Y	Y	Y	Y	Y	Y	N	4	32
Ohio Business College	Lorain	T	Prop	PW	258	10												
Ohio Business College	Sandusky	C	Prop	M/W	198													8
Ohio Institute of Photography and Technology	Dayton	T	Prop	M/W	581		33	5	N	Y	Y	Y	Y	Y	Y	N		4
Ohio State U Agricultural Technical Institute	Wooster	C,T	St	M/W	830	12	10		Y	Y	Y	Y	Y	Y	Y	Y	5	37
Ohio Valley College of Technology	East Liverpool	T	Prop	PW	126	4	69			Y	Y		Y	Y	Y	N		7
Owens Community College	Findlay	C,T	St	M/W	2,623	57	47		Y		Y	Y	Y	Y	Y	N	11	19
Owens Community College	Toledo	C,T	St	M/W	16,992	66	50		Y		Y	Y	Y	Y	Y	N	11	24
Remington College–Cleveland Campus	Cleveland	C	Prop	M/W	750													
RETS Tech Center	Centerville	C,T	Prop	M/W	464		55	0	N	Y	Y		Y	Y	Y	N		6
School of Advertising Art	Kettering	C,T	Prop	M/W	125	3	1					S				N		1
Sinclair Community College	Dayton	C,T	St-L	M/W	19,860	62	45	53	Y		S	S	Y	Y	Y	N	5	89
Southeastern Business College	Chillicothe	T	Prop	M/W	100													
Southern State Community College	Hillsboro	C,T	St	M/W	2,234				Y	Y	R	Y	Y	Y	Y	N	5	14
Southwestern College of Business	Dayton	T	Prop	M/W	214													
Stark State College of Technology	Canton	C,T	St-L	M/W	5,667	67	55		Y	Y	Y	Y	Y	Y	Y	N		49
Stautzenberger College	Toledo	T	Prop	M/W	792									Y	Y			8
Terra State Community College ✓	Fremont	C,T	St	M/W	2,549	58	41		Y	Y	Y	Y	Y	Y	Y	N	7	37
Trumbull Business College	Warren	T	Prop	PW	411	16	51				Y	Y	Y			N		7
The University of Akron–Wayne College	Orrville	C,T	St	M/W	1,884	44	40	75	Y	Y	S	Y	Y	Y	Y	N	4	21
University of Cincinnati Clermont College	Batavia	C,T	St	M/W	2,408													
University of Northwestern Ohio*	Lima	C,B	Ind	M/W	2,665	11	18	40									3	16
Washington State Community College	Marietta	C,T	St	M/W	2,086	44												
Zane State College	Zanesville	C,T	St-L	M/W	1,915													
Oklahoma																		
Connors State College	Warner	C,T	St	M/W	2,335		38		Y		S	Y	Y	Y		Y	7	21
Eastern Oklahoma State College	Wilburton	C,T	St	M/W	2,639		31	80	Y	Y	Y	Y	Y	Y	Y	Y	12	52

Two-Year Colleges At-a-Glance

This chart includes the names and locations of accredited two-year colleges in the United States and U.S. territories and shows institutions' responses to the *Thomson Peterson's Survey of Undergraduate Institutions*. If an institution submitted incomplete data, one or more columns opposite the institution's name is blank. An asterisk after the school name denotes a *Special Message* following the college's profile, and a dagger indicates that the institution has one or more entries in the *In-Depth Descriptions of Two-Year Colleges* section. If a school does not appear, it did not report any of the information.

Y—Yes; N—No; R—Recommended; S—For Some

Institution	City	Degrees Awarded	Institutional Control	Student Body	Undergraduate Enrollment Fall 2003	Percent Attending Part-Time	Percent 25 Years of Age or Older	Percent of Grads Going on to Four-Year Colleges	High School Equivalency Certificate Accepted	High School Transcript Required	Open Admissions	Need-Based Aid	Part-Time Jobs Available	Career Counseling Services Available	Job Placement Services Available	College Housing Available	Number of Sports Available	Number of Majors Offered
Murray State College	Tishomingo	C,T	St	M/W	1,958													
Northeastern Oklahoma A&M College	Miami	C,T	St	M/W	2,102	30	35	70	Y	Y	Y	Y	Y			Y	7	58
Oklahoma City Community College	Oklahoma City	C,T	St	M/W	12,048	60		27	Y			Y	Y	Y	Y	Y	N	6	44
Oklahoma State U, Oklahoma City	Oklahoma City	C,T	St	M/W	5,654		51	30	Y	Y		Y	Y	Y	Y	N	2	29
Redlands Community College	El Reno	C,T	St	M/W	2,323	75												
Rose State College	Midwest City	C,T	St-L	M/W	7,000													
Seminole State College	Seminole	C,T	St	M/W	2,250													
Southwestern Oklahoma State University at Sayre	Sayre	C,T	St-L	M/W	552													
Spartan School of Aeronautics	Tulsa	T,B	Prop	PM	1,500													
Tulsa Community College	Tulsa	C,T	St	M/W	22,866													
Tulsa Welding School	Tulsa	C	Prop	PM	362	37										N		1
Vatterott College	Oklahoma City	T,F	Prop	M/W	191													5
Vatterott College	Tulsa	T	Prop	PW	80													5
Western Oklahoma State College	Altus	C,T	St	M/W	2,047													
Oregon																		
Blue Mountain Community College	Pendleton	C,T	St-L	M/W	1,878	54												
Central Oregon Community College*	Bend	C,T	Dist	M/W	4,076	65	42	50	Y	Y	R,S	Y	Y	Y		Y	14	38
Chemeketa Community College	Salem	C,T	St-L	M/W	14,454	75	45		Y		S	Y	Y	Y	Y	N	5	48
Clackamas Community College	Oregon City	C,T	Dist	M/W	6,866	58												
Clatsop Community College	Astoria	C,T	Cou	M/W	1,824	76												
Heald College-Portland	Portland	T	Ind	M/W														
ITT Technical Institute	Portland	T,B	Prop	M/W	525				N	Y	Y	Y	Y	Y	Y	N		13
Linn-Benton Community College	Albany	C,T	St-L	M/W	5,453	45	47		Y		S	Y	Y	Y	Y	N	6	61
Pioneer Pacific College	Wilsonville	C,B	Prop	M/W	760	67			Y	Y	Y	Y		Y	Y	N		10
Portland Community College*	Portland	C,T	St-L	M/W	96,764	55			Y			Y	Y	Y	Y	N	19	53
Rogue Community College	Grants Pass	C,T	St-L	M/W	4,383	59	56		Y			Y	Y	Y	Y	N	5	25
Southwestern Oregon Community College	Coos Bay	C,T	St-L	M/W	2,068	58	40		Y		S	Y	Y	Y		Y	8	26
Tillamook Bay Community College	Tillamook	C,T	Dist	M/W	250	88	46									N		14
Treasure Valley Community College	Ontario	C,T	St-L	M/W	1,869	41												
Umpqua Community College	Roseburg	C,T	St-L	M/W	2,141		60	35	Y		R	Y	Y	Y	Y	N	2	53
Pennsylvania																		
Academy of Medical Arts and Business	Harrisburg	C,T	Prop	PW	491	70			Y	Y	Y	Y	Y	Y		N		14
Allentown Business School†	Center Valley	T	Prop	M/W	1,511	11	55	0	Y	Y	Y	Y	Y	Y		N		14
Antonelli Institute	Erdenheim	T	Prop	M/W	191		8	0	Y	Y	Y	Y	Y	Y	Y			2
The Art Institute of Philadelphia*†	Philadelphia	T,B	Prop	M/W	3,007	32	20		N	Y	Y	Y	Y	Y	Y	Y	2	15
The Art Institute of Pittsburgh†	Pittsburgh	C,T,B	Prop	M/W	3,405	38			N	Y	Y	Y	Y	Y	Y	Y		36
Berean Institute	Philadelphia	C,T	Ind	M/W	208	18	25	10	Y	Y	Y		Y	Y	Y	N	1	7
Bradley Academy for the Visual Arts†	York	T	Prop	M/W	407	7												
Bucks County Community College	Newtown	C,T	Cou	M/W	10,096	60	39		Y	Y	Y	Y	Y			N	12	57
Business Institute of Pennsylvania	Sharon	T	Prop	M/W	146													
Cambria County Area Community College	Johnstown	C,T	St-L	M/W	1,327	55	66		Y		R	Y	Y	Y	Y			22
Cambria-Rowe Business College	Indiana	C,T	Prop	PW	118	6												
Cambria-Rowe Business College	Johnstown	C,T	Prop	PW	230		51	3	N	Y	Y	Y		Y	Y	N		5
Central Pennsylvania College*	Summerdale	T,B	Prop	M/W	822	17	14	6	Y	Y	Y	Y	Y	Y	Y	Y	4	22
CHI Institute	Southampton	C,T	Prop	M/W	700		50		N	Y	Y	Y		Y	Y	N		16
Churchman Business School	Easton	C,T	Prop	M/W	113													
Commonwealth Technical Institute	Johnstown	T	St	M/W	231				Y	Y			Y			Y		7
Community College of Allegheny County†	Pittsburgh	C,T	Cou	M/W	18,964	59	48	39	Y		R	Y	Y	Y	Y	N	15	116
Consolidated School of Business	Lancaster	T	Prop	PW	178													
Consolidated School of Business	York	T	Prop	PW	202		41		Y	Y	Y		Y	Y	Y	N		7
Dean Institute of Technology	Pittsburgh	T	Prop	M/W	228		15		Y	Y		Y		Y	Y	N		2
Delaware County Community College	Media	C,T	St-L	M/W	10,608	60	42	69	Y	Y	Y	Y	Y	Y	Y	N	8	49
Douglas Education Center	Monessen	C,T	Prop	M/W	140													
DuBois Business College	DuBois	T	Prop	PW	240													
Duff's Business Institute	Pittsburgh	C	Prop	PW	1,251													
Education Direct Center for Degree Studies†	Scranton	T	Prop	M/W	18,058	100	76		Y	Y	Y					N		13
Electronic Institute	Middletown	C,T	Ind	PM	51	25												
Erie Business Center, Main	Erie	T	Prop	M/W	385													
Erie Business Center South	New Castle	C,T	Prop	PW	64				N	Y	Y	Y		Y	Y	N	4	10
Erie Institute of Technology	Erie	T	Prop	M/W	173				N	Y		Y	Y					1
Harcum College†	Bryn Mawr	C,T	Ind	PW	542	32	40		Y	Y	Y	Y	Y	Y	Y	Y	6	21
Harrisburg Area Community College	Harrisburg	C,T	St-L	M/W	14,918	61	45	67	Y		Y	Y	Y	Y	Y	N	11	87
Hussian School of Art	Philadelphia	C,T	Prop	M/W	138		2		N	Y	Y	Y	Y	Y		N		2
Johnson College†	Scranton	T	Ind	M/W	377													
Keystone College†	La Plume	C,T,B	Ind	M/W	1,445	31	29	71	N	Y	Y	Y	Y	Y	Y	Y	16	71
Lackawanna College	Scranton	C,T	Ind	M/W	1,108	42	41	57	Y	Y	Y	Y	Y	Y	Y	Y	7	23
Laurel Business Institute	Uniontown	C,T	Prop	M/W	378													
Lehigh Carbon Community College	Schnecksville	C,T	St-L	M/W	6,353	63	46	57	Y		S	Y	Y	Y	Y	N	18	71

This chart includes the names and locations of accredited two-year colleges in the United States and U.S. territories and shows institutions' responses to the *Thomson Peterson's Survey of Undergraduate Institutions*. If an institution submitted incomplete data, one or more columns opposite the institution's name is blank.
An asterisk after the school name denotes a *Special Message* following the college's profile, and a dagger indicates that the institution has one or more entries in the *In-Depth Descriptions of Two-Year Colleges* section. If a school does not appear, it did not report any of the information.

Y—Yes; N—No; R—Recommended; S—For Some

Name	Location	Degrees Awarded	Institutional Control	Student Body	Undergraduate Enrollment Fall 2003	Percent 25 Years of Age or Older	Percent Attending Part-Time	Percent of Grads Going on to Four-Year Colleges	High School Equivalency Certificate Accepted	High School Transcript Required	Open Admissions	Need-Based Aid Available	Part-Time Jobs Available	Career Counseling Available	Job Placement Services Available	College Housing Available	Number of Sports Offered	Number of Majors Offered
Lincoln Technical Institute	Allentown	T	Prop	M/W	500														
Luzerne County Community College	Nanticoke	C,T	Cou	M/W	6,170	52	43		Y	Y	R	Y	Y	Y	Y	N	11	75
Manor College*†	Jenkintown	C,T	I-R	M/W	865	50													
McCann School of Business & Technology	Pottsville	C,T	Prop	M/W	841	36													
Median School of Allied Health Careers	Pittsburgh	T	Prop	M/W	287														
Montgomery County Community College	Blue Bell	C,T	Cou	M/W	10,622	58	42	74	Y	Y	S	Y	Y	Y	Y	N	13	53
New Castle School of Trades	Pulaski	C	Ind	PM	451		35	1		Y	Y					N		5
Newport Business Institute	Lower Burrell	T	Prop	M/W	89		40	4	Y	Y		Y	Y			Y	N		13
Newport Business Institute	Williamsport	T	Prop	PW	112	2	54	0	N	Y	Y	Y		Y	Y	N		4
Northampton County Area Community College	Bethlehem	C,T	St-L	M/W	7,621	57	42	68	Y	Y	Y	Y	Y	Y	Y	N	12	50
Oakbridge Academy of Arts	Lower Burrell	C,T	Prop	M/W	103	1	28		N	Y	Y	Y		Y	Y	N		3
Orleans Technical Institute-Center City Campus	Philadelphia	C,T	Prop	PW	207	42	73		Y	Y	Y	Y	Y	Y	Y	N		
Pace Institute	Reading	C,T	Priv	M/W	274														
Penn Commercial Business and Technical School	Washington	C,T	Prop	M/W	304														
Pennsylvania College of Technology†	Williamsport	C,T,B	St-R	M/W	6,255	17	21		Y	Y	Y	Y	Y	Y	Y	Y	17	108
Pennsylvania Culinary Institute	Pittsburgh	T	Prop	M/W	991		16		N	Y	Y	Y		Y	Y			2
Pennsylvania Institute of Technology	Media	C,T	Ind	M/W	282	40	51			Y	Y	Y	Y	Y	Y	N	2	9
Penn State U Beaver Campus of the Commonwealth Coll	Monaca	C,T,B	St-R	M/W	735	12	9		N		Y	Y	Y	Y	Y	Y	10	120
Penn State U Delaware County Campus of the Commonwealth Coll	Media	T,B	St-R	M/W	1,733	17	8		N	Y		Y	Y	Y	Y	Y	10	118
Penn State U DuBois Campus of the Commonwealth Coll	DuBois	C,T,B	St-R	M/W	919	25	30		N		Y	Y	Y	Y	Y	N	7	127
Penn State U Fayette Campus of the Commonwealth Coll	Uniontown	C,T,B	St-R	M/W	1,156	25	28		N	Y	Y	Y	Y	Y	Y	N	11	125
Penn State U Hazleton Campus of the Commonwealth Coll	Hazleton	C,T,B	St-R	M/W	1,214	6	6		N	Y	Y	Y	Y	Y	Y	Y	8	126
Penn State U McKeesport Campus of the Commonwealth Coll	McKeesport	T,B	St-R	M/W	826	9	8		N	Y	Y	Y	Y	Y	Y	Y	12	118
Penn State U Mont Alto Campus of the Commonwealth Coll	Mont Alto	T,B	St-R	M/W	1,098	31	21		N	Y	Y	Y	Y	Y	Y	Y	10	121
Penn State U New Kensington Campus of the Commonwealth Coll	New Kensington	C,T,B	St-R	M/W	1,082	27	18		N	Y	Y	Y	Y	Y	Y	N	13	125
Penn State U Shenango Campus of the Commonwealth Coll	Sharon	C,T,B	St-R	M/W	904	42	35		N	Y	Y	Y	Y	Y	Y	N	7	123
Penn State U Wilkes-Barre Campus of the Commonwealth Coll	Lehman	C,T,B	St-R	M/W	782	25	11		N	Y	Y	Y	Y	Y	Y	N	11	123
Penn State U Worthington Scranton Cmps Commonwealth Coll	Dunmore	T,B	St-R	M/W	1,338	24	22		N	Y	Y	Y	Y	Y	Y	N	10	120
Penn State U York Campus of the Commonwealth Coll	York	C,T,B	St-R	M/W	1,730	42	22		N	Y	Y	Y	Y	Y	Y	N	10	124
Pittsburgh Institute of Aeronautics	Pittsburgh	C	Ind	PM	571														
Pittsburgh Institute of Mortuary Science, Inc	Pittsburgh	C,T	Ind	M/W	132	8													
Pittsburgh Technical Institute	Oakdale		Prop	M/W	1,975														
Reading Area Community College	Reading	C,T	Cou	M/W	4,158	62	56		Y	Y		Y	Y	Y	Y	N	4	53
The Restaurant School at Walnut Hill College†	Philadelphia	T,B	Prop	M/W	585		21		Y	Y	Y		Y	Y	Y			2
Rosedale Technical Institute	Pittsburgh	T	Ind	PW	205														2
Schuylkill Institute of Business and Technology	Pottsville	C,T	Prop	M/W	135		45		Y	Y	Y		Y	Y	N			8
South Hills School of Business & Technology	Altoona	C,T	Prop	M/W	148	4													
South Hills School of Business & Technology	State College	C,T	Prop	M/W	754	7	43	2	N	Y	Y		Y	Y				12
Thaddeus Stevens College of Technology	Lancaster	C,T	St	PM	660														
Thompson Institute	Harrisburg	T,B	Prop	M/W	485		60		Y	Y	Y	Y	Y	Y	Y			9
Triangle Tech, Inc.	Pittsburgh	C,T	Prop	PM	394		35		N	Y	Y	Y	Y	Y	N			6
Triangle Tech, Inc.–DuBois School	DuBois	T	Prop	PM	291		40		N	Y	Y		Y	Y	Y			
Triangle Tech, Inc.–Erie School	Erie	C,T	Prop	PM	83														
Triangle Tech, Inc.–Greensburg Center	Greensburg	T	Prop	PM	283		49		N	Y	Y		Y	Y				8
University of Pittsburgh at Titusville	Titusville	C,T	St-R	M/W	516	24		100	N	Y	Y	Y	Y	Y	Y	Y	11	5
Valley Forge Military College*†	Wayne	C	Ind	M	240			98	N	Y	Y	Y	Y			Y	14	5
Western School of Health and Business Careers	Pittsburgh	T	Prop	M/W	600														
Westmoreland County Community College	Youngwood	C,T	Cou	M/W	6,257	59	47		Y	Y		Y	Y	Y	Y	N	12	53
The Williamson Free School of Mechanical Trades	Media	T	Ind	M	253	0	19		N	Y	Y		Y	Y	Y		14	8
York Technical Institute	York	T	Priv	M/W	1,296		15		Y	Y	Y	Y	Y	Y	Y		1	9
Yorktowne Business Institute	York	C,T	Prop	M/W	320														
Rhode Island																		
Community College of Rhode Island	Warwick	C,T	St	M/W	16,223	65	43		Y			Y	Y	Y	Y	N	10	43
New England Institute of Technology	Warwick	C,T,B	Ind	M/W	2,839														
South Carolina																		
Central Carolina Technical College	Sumter	C,T	St	M/W	3,191	68	55	11	Y	Y	Y	Y	Y	Y	Y	N		17
Denmark Technical College	Denmark	C,T	St	M/W	1,404														
Florence-Darlington Technical College	Florence	C,T	St	M/W	4,041	47													
Forrest Junior College	Anderson	C,T	Prop	PW	207		20	2		Y	Y	Y	Y	Y	Y	N		1
Greenville Technical College	Greenville	C,T	St	M/W	13,000														
Horry-Georgetown Technical College	Conway	C,T	St-L	M/W	5,128														
ITT Technical Institute	Greenville	T,B	Prop	M/W	338				N	Y	Y	Y	Y	Y	Y	N		12
Midlands Technical College	Columbia	C,T	St-L	M/W	10,925	56	41		Y	Y	R	Y	Y	Y	Y	N	4	38
Miller-Motte Technical College	Charleston		Prop	M/W															
Northeastern Technical College	Cheraw	C,T	St-L	M/W	1,098	48	45		Y	Y	Y	Y	Y	Y	Y			11

Two-Year Colleges At-a-Glance

This chart includes the names and locations of accredited two-year colleges in the United States and U.S. territories and shows institutions' responses to the *Thomson Peterson's Survey of Undergraduate Institutions*. If an institution submitted incomplete data, one or more columns opposite the institution's name is blank.

An asterisk after the school name denotes a *Special Message* following the college's profile, and a dagger indicates that the institution has one or more entries in the *In-Depth Descriptions of Two-Year Colleges* section. If a school does not appear, it did not report any of the information.

Y—Yes; N—No; R—Recommended; S—For Some

Name	Location	Degrees Awarded	Institutional Control	Student Body	Undergrad Enrollment Fall 2003	% Attending Part-Time	% 25 Years or Older	% Grads to Four-Year	HS Equivalency Accepted	Open Admissions	HS Transcript Required	Need-Based Aid Available	Part-Time Jobs Available	Career Counseling Available	Job Placement Services	College Housing Available	Number of Sports	Number of Majors
Orangeburg-Calhoun Technical College	Orangeburg	C,T	St-L	M/W	2,491	45	35		Y	Y	Y	Y		Y	Y	Y	N		16
South University	Columbia	T,B	Prop	M/W	318	20	51		N	Y	Y	Y		Y	Y	Y	N		6
Spartanburg Methodist College*†	Spartanburg	C,T	I-R	M/W	732	5	4	93	N	Y	Y	Y	Y	Y	Y	Y	Y	13	4
Spartanburg Technical College	Spartanburg	C,T	St	M/W	4,123		39		Y			Y	Y	Y	Y	N			24
Tri-County Technical College	Pendleton	C,T	St	M/W	4,100														
Trident Technical College	Charleston	C,T	St-L	M/W	11,791	56	47		Y	Y	S	Y	Y	Y	Y		N		40
U of South Carolina Salkehatchie	Allendale	C	St	M/W	777		27	60	Y	Y	Y	Y	Y	Y			N	6	3
U of South Carolina at Sumter	Sumter	C	St	M/W	1,184	52	76		N	Y	Y	Y		Y	Y		N	11	2
U of South Carolina at Union	Union	C	St	M/W	313		35		N	Y	Y	Y		Y			N		2
Williamsburg Technical College	Kingstree	C,T	St	PW	595		49	30	Y	Y	Y	Y	Y	Y	Y		N		9
York Technical College	Rock Hill	C,T	St	M/W	4,171	51	39		Y		S	Y	Y	Y	Y		N		24
South Dakota																		
Kilian Community College	Sioux Falls	C,T	Ind	M/W	444		52		Y		Y	Y	Y	Y	Y		N		13
Lake Area Technical Institute	Watertown	T	St	M/W	1,057				N	Y	Y	Y	Y	Y	Y	N	3	27
Mitchell Technical Institute	Mitchell	C,T	Dist	M/W	832		24	2	Y	Y	Y	Y	Y	Y	Y	N	5	38
Sisseton-Wahpeton Community College	Sisseton	C,T	Fed	M/W	287	43	48		Y	Y	Y	Y		Y	Y	Y	N		12
Southeast Technical Institute	Sioux Falls	T	St	M/W	2,123	18													
Western Dakota Technical Institute	Rapid City	T	St	M/W	1,057	29	33		Y		Y	Y	Y	Y	Y	N	1	16
Tennessee																		
American Academy of Nutrition, Coll of Nutrition	Knoxville	C,T	Prop	M/W	241		90		Y					S					1
Chattanooga State Technical Community College	Chattanooga	C,T	St	M/W	8,120														
Cleveland State Community College	Cleveland	C,T	St	M/W	3,161	45	43	40	Y	Y	Y	Y	Y	Y	Y	N	10	11
Columbia State Community College	Columbia	C,T	St	M/W	4,613	47	28		Y	Y	Y	Y	Y	Y	Y	N	5	33
Draughons Junior College	Clarksville	T	Prop	M/W	340														
Draughons Junior College	Nashville	C,T	Prop	M/W	600														
Dyersburg State Community College	Dyersburg	C,T	St	M/W	2,362	42													
Electronic Computer Programming College	Chattanooga	C	Prop		178														
Fountainhead College of Technology	Knoxville	C,T,B	Prop	M/W	120		20		Y	Y	R	Y		Y	Y	N		4
Hiwassee College	Madisonville	C,T	I-R	M/W	398	12	8	72	N	Y	Y	Y	Y	Y		Y	10	45
ITT Technical Institute	Knoxville	T,B	Prop	M/W	575				N	Y	Y	Y	Y	Y	Y	N		10
ITT Technical Institute	Memphis	T,B	Prop	M/W	520				N	Y	Y	Y	Y	Y	Y	N		12
ITT Technical Institute	Nashville	T,B	Prop	M/W	713				N	Y	Y	Y	Y	Y	Y	N		12
Jackson State Community College	Jackson	C,T	St	M/W	4,004	45	39	67	Y	Y	S	Y	Y	Y	Y	N	8	15
John A. Gupton College	Nashville	C	Ind	M/W	97	6													
Mid-America Baptist Theological Seminary	Germantown	T,M,D,F	I-R	PM	43	33			Y	Y	Y	Y		Y	Y	Y		1
Motlow State Community College	Tullahoma	C,T	St	M/W	3,478	43	32	69	Y	Y	Y	Y	Y	Y	Y	N	9	5
Nashville Auto Diesel College	Nashville	T	Prop	PM	1,306		5		N	Y	Y	Y	Y	Y	Y	N		3
Nashville State Technical Community College	Nashville	C,T	St	M/W	6,766	68	61		Y		Y	Y	Y	Y	Y	N	2	19
National College of Business & Technology	Knoxville	T	Prop	M/W	209														4
National College of Business & Technology	Nashville	T	Prop	M/W	434				Y	Y			Y	Y	Y	N		4
North Central Institute	Clarksville	T	Prop	PM	107	51	50		Y	Y			Y	Y	Y	N		2
Northeast State Technical Community College	Blountville	C,T	St	M/W	4,836	48	47	90	Y	Y	Y	Y	Y	Y	Y	N	3	22
Pellissippi State Technical Community College	Knoxville	C,T	St	M/W	7,563		40		Y		Y	Y	Y	Y	Y	N	6	39
Roane State Community College	Harriman	C,T	St	M/W	5,385	45	45		Y		Y	Y	Y	Y	Y	N	9	39
South College	Knoxville	T,B	Prop	PW	443		50		N	Y	Y	Y	Y	Y	Y	N		15
Southwest Tennessee Community College	Memphis	T	St	PW	11,039	54													
Volunteer State Community College	Gallatin	C,T	St	M/W	6,991	52	40		Y		Y	Y	Y	Y	Y	N	3	11
Walters State Community College	Morristown	C,T	St	M/W	6,214	48	36		Y		Y	Y	Y	Y	Y	N	4	20
Texas																		
Alvin Community College	Alvin	C,T	St-L	M/W	3,902	60	41		Y	Y	S	Y	Y	Y	Y	N	4	33
Amarillo College	Amarillo	C,T	St-L	M/W	9,348		43	52	Y			Y	Y	Y	Y	N	3	83
Angelina College	Lufkin	C,T	St-L	M/W	4,976														
The Art Institute of Dallas	Dallas	T	Prop	M/W	1,532	24													
The Art Institute of Houston	Houston	T,B	Prop	M/W	1,651	36	31		N	Y	Y	Y	Y	Y	Y	Y	4	8
Austin Community College	Austin	C,T	Dist	M/W	35,576		39		Y	Y			Y	Y	Y	N	6	75
Blinn College	Brenham	C,T	St-L	M/W	14,057														
Border Institute of Technology	El Paso	C,T	Prop	PM	250		40							Y	Y			
Brazosport College	Lake Jackson	C,T	St-L	M/W	3,587	73													
Cedar Valley College	Lancaster	C,T	St	M/W	4,405		40		Y	Y	R	Y	Y	Y	Y	N	5	16
Central Texas College†	Killeen	C,T	St-L	M/W	17,255	83													
Cisco Junior College	Cisco	C,T	St-L	M/W	3,250														
Clarendon College	Clarendon	C,T	St-L	M/W	963	60	28		Y		Y	Y	Y	Y	Y	Y	6	36
Coastal Bend College	Beeville	C,T	Cou	M/W	3,660	53	42		Y	Y	Y	Y	Y	Y	Y	Y	13	67
College of the Mainland	Texas City	C,T	St-L	M/W	3,919														
Collin County Community College District	Plano	C,T	St-L	M/W	16,574	60	37		Y			Y	Y	Y	Y	N	3	31
Commonwealth Institute of Funeral Service	Houston	T	Ind	M/W	152	5	48		N	Y	Y	Y		Y	Y	N		1
Computer Career Center	El Paso	C,T	Prop	M/W	300														

This chart includes the names and locations of accredited two-year colleges in the United States and U.S. territories and shows institutions' responses to the *Thomson Peterson's Survey of Undergraduate Institutions*. If an institution submitted incomplete data, one or more columns opposite the institution's name is blank.

An asterisk after the school name denotes a *Special Message* following the college's profile, and a dagger indicates that the institution has one or more entries in the *In-Depth Descriptions of Two-Year Colleges* section. If a school does not appear, it did not report any of the information.

Y—Yes; N—No; R—Recommended; S—For Some

Institution	City	Degrees Awarded	Institutional Control	Student Body	Undergraduate Enrollment Fall 2003	Percent Attending Part-Time	Percent 25 Years or Older	Percent of Grads Going on to Four-Year Colleges	HS Equivalency Certificate Accepted	Open Admissions	HS Transcript Required	Need-Based Aid Available	Part-Time Jobs Available	Career Counseling Available	Job Placement Services Available	College Housing Available	Number of Sports Offered	Number of Majors Offered
Court Reporting Institute of Dallas	Dallas	C,T	Prop	PW	526		68							Y	Y				1
Cy-Fair College	Houston	C,T	St-L	M/W	6,900				Y	Y				Y	Y			
Dallas Institute of Funeral Service	Dallas	C,T	Ind	M/W	221		52		Y	Y	Y	Y				N		1
Del Mar College	Corpus Christi	C,T	St-L	M/W	11,338		41		Y	Y	Y	Y	Y	Y	Y	N	14	102
Eastfield College	Mesquite	C,T	St-L	M/W	11,708	72	35	60	Y	Y	R	Y	Y	Y	Y	N	7	29
El Centro College	Dallas	C,T	Cou	M/W	5,884	73	51	30	Y	Y	S	Y	Y	Y	Y	N	4	46
Galveston College	Galveston	C,T	St-L	M/W	2,214	63	45		Y	Y	S	Y	Y	Y	Y	N	5	33
Grayson County College	Denison	C,T	St-L	M/W	3,344													
Hallmark Institute of Technology	San Antonio	T	Prop	M/W	462													
Hill College of the Hill Junior College District	Hillsboro	C,T	Dist	M/W	3,236	52	20	40	Y		Y	Y	Y	Y	Y		5	86
Houston Community College System	Houston	C,T	St-L	M/W	37,846	68	54	25	Y		S	Y	Y	Y	Y	N		65
Howard College	Big Spring	C,T	St-L	M/W	2,659	58	35		Y		Y	Y	Y	Y	Y	Y	7	31
ITT Technical Institute	Arlington	T	Prop	M/W	458				N	Y	Y	Y	Y	Y	Y	N		7
ITT Technical Institute	Austin	T	Prop	M/W	725				N	Y	Y	Y	Y	Y	Y	N		6
ITT Technical Institute	Houston	T	Prop	M/W	478				N	Y	Y	Y	Y	Y	Y	N		6
ITT Technical Institute	Houston	T	Prop	M/W	612				N	Y	Y	Y	Y	Y	Y	N		6
ITT Technical Institute	Houston	T	Prop	M/W	585				N	Y	Y	Y	Y	Y	Y	N		6
ITT Technical Institute	Richardson	T	Prop	M/W	715				N	Y	Y	Y	Y	Y	Y	N		6
ITT Technical Institute	San Antonio	T	Prop	M/W	788				N	Y	Y	Y	Y	Y	Y	N		6
Jacksonville College	Jacksonville	C,T	I-R	M/W	323	26	12		Y	Y				Y	Y	Y	4	2
KD Studio	Dallas	T	Prop	M/W	129		20	5	Y	Y	Y	Y				N		1
Kilgore College	Kilgore	C,T	St-L	M/W	4,578	46												
Kingwood College	Kingwood	C,T	St-L	M/W	6,056	76	34		Y			Y	Y	Y	Y	N	1	17
Lamar State College–Orange	Orange	C,T	St	M/W	1,853	50	38		Y			Y	Y	Y	Y	N	4	16
Lamar State College–Port Arthur	Port Arthur	C,T	St	M/W	2,429		41		Y			Y	Y	Y	Y	N		31
Laredo Community College	Laredo	C,T	St-L	M/W	8,297	63	35		Y			Y	Y	Y	Y	Y	7	29
Lon Morris College	Jacksonville	C,T	I-R	M/W	432	9	1				Y	Y	Y	Y	Y	Y		49
McLennan Community College	Waco	C,T	Cou	M/W	7,052	56	42		Y		Y	Y	Y	Y	Y	N	7	26
Midland College	Midland	C,T	St-L	M/W	5,405	62	24		Y		Y	Y	Y	Y	Y	Y	11	58
Mountain View College	Dallas	C,T	St-L	M/W	6,410		41		Y		Y	Y	Y	Y	Y	N	4	16
MTI College of Business and Technology	Houston		Prop		718		59							Y	Y		N		6
MTI College of Business and Technology	Houston	T	Prop	M/W	287		53		N	Y	Y	Y	Y			N		4
North Central Texas College	Gainesville	C,T	Cou	M/W	6,183													
Northeast Texas Community College	Mount Pleasant	C,T	St-L	M/W	2,512	46	36		Y	Y		Y	Y	Y	Y	Y	6	22
North Harris College	Houston	C,T	St-L	M/W	10,591		41		Y	Y	S	Y	Y	Y			15	41
Odessa College	Odessa	C,T	St-L	M/W	4,858		40	42	Y	Y		Y	Y	Y	Y		10	60
Palo Alto College	San Antonio	C,T	St-L	M/W	7,727		35		Y	Y	Y	Y	Y	Y		N	4	38
Panola College	Carthage	C,T	St-L	M/W	1,682	48	28		Y	Y	R,S	Y	Y	Y			6	5
Paris Junior College	Paris	C,T	St-L	M/W	3,862	63	41		Y	Y		Y	Y	Y	Y		8	24
Remington College–Houston Campus	Houston	T	Prop	M/W	250													
Richland College	Dallas	C,T	St-L	M/W	14,128													
St. Philip's College	San Antonio	C,T	Dist	M/W	9,490	56	48		Y	Y	Y	Y	Y	Y	Y	N	6	72
San Antonio College	San Antonio	C,T	St-L	M/W	22,190													
South Plains College	Levelland	C,T	St-L	M/W	9,636	53	39	90	Y	Y	Y	Y	Y	Y		Y	10	59
South Texas Community College	McAllen	C,T	Dist	M/W	15,334	54	35		Y	Y	Y	Y	Y			N	10	26
Southwest Institute of Technology	Austin	C,T	Prop	PM	63									Y	Y			
Southwest Texas Junior College	Uvalde	C,T	St-L	M/W	4,350													
Tarrant County College District	Fort Worth	C,T	Cou	M/W	31,250	63												
Temple College	Temple	C,T	Dist	M/W	3,934	62	33		Y	Y	S	Y	Y	Y	Y		8	20
Texarkana College	Texarkana	C,T	St-L	M/W	3,895	60												
Texas Culinary Academy	Austin	C,T	Ind	M/W	200									Y	Y			1
Texas State Tech Coll–Harlingen	Harlingen	C,T	St	M/W	4,028	57	31		Y	Y		Y	Y	Y	Y	Y	14	43
Texas State Tech Coll–Waco/Marshall Campus	Waco	C,T	St	M/W	4,129		18		Y	Y	Y	Y	Y	Y	Y	Y	7	44
Texas State Tech Coll	Sweetwater	T	St	M/W	1,628													
Tomball College	Tomball	C,T	St-L	M/W	7,620	74												
Trinity Valley Community College	Athens	C,T	St-L	M/W	5,213													
Tyler Junior College	Tyler	C,T	St-L	M/W	9,591													
Victoria College	Victoria	C,T	Cou	M/W	4,244													
Wade College†	Dallas	C,T	Prop	PW	87													
Weatherford College	Weatherford	C,T	St-L	M/W	3,999						Y	Y	Y	Y	Y	N	4	15
Western Texas College	Snyder	C,T	St-L	M/W	1,685													
Westwood College–Dallas†	Dallas	T	Prop	M/W	404	2	32											4
Westwood College–Fort Worth†	Euless	T	Prop	M/W	472	21	33								Y	Y		6
Westwood College–Houston South Campus†	Houston	T	Prop	M/W	16		50											4
Wharton County Junior College	Wharton	C,T	St-L	M/W	5,892													
Utah																		
College of Eastern Utah	Price	C,T	St	M/W	2,692	46	26	60	Y	Y	R	Y	Y	Y	Y	Y	7	15
Dixie State College of Utah	St. George	C,T,B	St	M/W	7,490	54												
ITT Technical Institute	Murray	T,B	Prop	M/W	494				N	Y	Y	Y	Y	Y	Y	N		16

Two-Year Colleges At-a-Glance

This chart includes the names and locations of accredited two-year colleges in the United States and U.S. territories and shows institutions' responses to the *Thomson Peterson's Survey of Undergraduate Institutions.* If an institution submitted incomplete data, one or more columns opposite the institution's name is blank.

An asterisk after the school name denotes a *Special Message* following the college's profile, and a dagger indicates that the institution has one or more entries in the *In-Depth Descriptions of Two-Year Colleges* section. If a school does not appear, it did not report any of the information.

Y—Yes; N—No; R—Recommended; S—For Some

Degrees Awarded: College Transfer Associate (C), Terminal Associate (T), Bachelor's (B), Master's (M), Doctoral (D), First Professional (F)

Name	Location	Degrees Awarded	Institutional Control	Student Body	Undergrad Enrollment Fall 2003	% Attending Part-Time	% 25 or Older	% Grads to 4-Yr Colleges	HS Equiv. Accepted	Open Admissions	HS Transcript Required	Need-Based Aid Available	Part-Time Jobs Available	Career Counseling Available	Job Placement Available	College Housing Available	Sports Offered	Majors Offered
LDS Business College	Salt Lake City	C,T	I-R	M/W	1,282	25	29		Y	Y	Y	Y	Y	Y	Y	N		20
Mountain West College	West Valley City	C,T	Prop	M/W	773		42		N	Y	Y	Y	Y	Y	Y	N		8
Salt Lake Community College	Salt Lake City	C,T	St	M/W	23,154													
Snow College	Ephraim	C,T	St	M/W	2,990	18			Y	Y	Y	Y	Y	Y		Y	12	66
Stevens-Henager College	Ogden	T,B	Prop	M/W	479													
Utah Career College	West Jordan	C	Prop	M/W	482		53						Y	Y		N		7
Utah Valley State College	Orem	C,T,B	St	M/W	23,803	48	34		Y		R	Y	Y	Y	Y	N	17	82
Vermont																		
Community College of Vermont	Waterbury	C,T	St	M/W	5,801													
Landmark College†	Putney	C,T	Ind	M/W	336	33	6	90	N	Y	Y	Y	Y	Y	Y	Y	12	1
New England Culinary Institute	Montpelier	T,B	Prop	M/W	606		32	14	N	Y	Y	Y	Y	Y	Y	Y		4
Virginia																		
Blue Ridge Community College	Weyers Cave	C,T	St	M/W	3,552	64												
Bryant and Stratton College, Virginia Beach	Virginia Beach	T,B	Prop	PW	340	30												
Dabney S. Lancaster Community College	Clifton Forge	C,T	St	M/W	1,443													
Danville Community College	Danville	C,T	St	M/W	4,089	67	58		Y	Y	Y	Y	Y	Y	Y	N	7	9
Eastern Shore Community College	Melfa	C,T	St	M/W	807		45	50	Y	Y	Y	Y	Y	Y	Y	N		9
ECPI College of Technology	Newport News	T	Prop		493		64		N	Y	Y	Y	Y	Y	Y	N		17
ECPI College of Technology	Virginia Beach	T	Prop	M/W	3,223	7	50		N	Y	Y	Y	Y	Y	Y	Y		20
ECPI Technical College	Glen Allen	T	Prop	M/W	360		48						Y			N		6
ECPI Technical College	Richmond	T	Prop	M/W	448		46		N	Y	Y	Y	Y	Y	Y	N		25
ECPI Technical College	Roanoke	T	Prop	M/W	356		47		N	Y	Y	Y	Y	Y	Y	N		21
Germanna Community College	Locust Grove	C,T	St	M/W	4,520	71	53		Y		S	Y	Y	Y	Y	N	7	11
ITT Technical Institute	Chantilly	T	Prop	M/W	147				N	Y	Y	Y	Y	Y	Y	N		10
ITT Technical Institute	Norfolk	T,B	Prop	M/W	443				N	Y	Y	Y	Y	Y	Y	N		13
ITT Technical Institute	Richmond	T,B	Prop	M/W	297				N	Y	Y	Y	Y	Y	Y	N		11
ITT Technical Institute	Springfield	T,B	Prop	M/W	339				N	Y	Y	Y	Y	Y	Y	N		10
John Tyler Community College	Chester	C,T	St	M/W	6,054	76	51		Y		R	Y	Y	Y		N	4	14
J. Sargeant Reynolds Community College	Richmond	C,T	St	M/W	11,132	45	32		Y		Y	Y	Y	Y	Y	N	7	39
Lord Fairfax Community College	Middletown	C,T	St	M/W	5,500	49			Y		R	Y	Y	Y		N		21
Mountain Empire Community College	Big Stone Gap	C,T	St	M/W	2,885		30	90	Y	Y		Y	Y	Y	Y	N	5	34
National College of Business & Technology	Bluefield	T	Prop	M/W	216				Y	Y			Y	Y	Y	N		5
National College of Business & Technology	Bristol	T	Prop	M/W	267				Y	Y		Y	Y	Y	Y	Y		5
National College of Business & Technology	Charlottesville	T	Prop	M/W	144				Y	Y		S	Y	Y	Y	Y		5
National College of Business & Technology	Harrisonburg	T	Prop	M/W	193				Y	Y		S	Y	Y	N			5
National College of Business & Technology	Lynchburg	T	Prop	M/W	312		24		Y	Y		S	Y	Y	Y	N		5
National College of Business & Technology	Martinsville	T	Prop	M/W	302				Y	Y		S	Y	Y	Y	N		4
National College of Business & Technology	Salem	C,T,B	Prop	M/W	756				Y	Y		Y	Y	Y	Y	Y		12
New River Community College	Dublin	C,T	St	M/W	4,345	54	40		Y		S	Y	Y	Y		N	10	30
Northern Virginia Community College	Annandale	C,T	St	M/W	39,353													
Parks College	Arlington	T	Prop	M/W														
Patrick Henry Community College	Martinsville	C,T	St	M/W	3,456													
Paul D. Camp Community College	Franklin	C,T	St	M/W	1,636	76	55	45	Y	Y	Y	Y	Y	Y	Y	N		6
Piedmont Virginia Community College	Charlottesville	C,T	St	M/W	4,343	74	47	23	Y	Y	S	Y	Y	Y	Y	N	11	18
Rappahannock Community College	Glenns	C,T	St-R	M/W	2,824													
Richard Bland Coll of the Coll of William and Mary	Petersburg	C	St	M/W	1,342	42	18	68	N	Y	Y	Y		Y		N	5	1
Southside Virginia Community College	Alberta	C,T	St	M/W	4,894	70	48		Y	Y	Y	Y	Y	Y	Y	N	5	14
Southwest Virginia Community College	Richlands	C,T	St	M/W	4,093	56												
Thomas Nelson Community College	Hampton	C,T	St	M/W	7,889	64			Y			Y	Y	Y		N	5	23
Tidewater Community College	Norfolk	C,T	St	M/W	23,029		53		Y				Y	Y		N	7	21
Virginia Highlands Community College	Abingdon	C,T	St	M/W	3,867													
Virginia Western Community College	Roanoke	C,T	St	M/W	8,124	74	46		Y	Y	Y	Y	Y	Y	Y	N	2	25
Wytheville Community College	Wytheville	C,T	St	M/W	2,450													
Washington																		
The Art Institute of Seattle†	Seattle	T,B	Prop	M/W	2,520	46	49			Y	Y	Y	Y	Y	Y	Y	1	11
Bates Technical College	Tacoma	T	St	M/W	16,162									Y	Y		N		38
Bellevue Community College	Bellevue	C,T	St	M/W	13,716		68		Y				Y	Y	Y	N	11	19
Bellingham Technical College	Bellingham	T	St		4,159													
Big Bend Community College	Moses Lake	C,T	St	M/W	2,090	38	30		Y		S	Y	Y	Y	Y	Y	4	14
Cascadia Community College	Bothell	C,T	St	M/W	1,964	45										N		3
Centralia College	Centralia	C,T	St	M/W	4,097		55		Y	Y	Y	Y	Y	Y	Y	N	5	66
Clark College	Vancouver	C,T	St	M/W	10,043	56	38	67	Y		S	Y	Y	Y	Y	N	9	28
Clover Park Technical College	Lakewood	T	St	M/W	7,342	74	61		Y	Y	S	Y	Y	Y	Y	N		30
Crown College	Tacoma	T,B	Prop	M/W	316		59				Y	Y	Y	Y	Y	N		4
Edmonds Community College	Lynnwood	C,T	St-L	M/W	8,385		11	25	Y			Y	Y	Y		N	10	32
Everett Community College	Everett	C,T	St	M/W	7,188	55	46		Y		R	Y	Y	Y	Y	N	12	72
Grays Harbor College	Aberdeen	C,T	St	M/W	2,181	47												

This chart includes the names and locations of accredited two-year colleges in the United States and U.S. territories and shows institutions' responses to the *Thomson Peterson's Survey of Undergraduate Institutions*. If an institution submitted incomplete data, one or more columns opposite the institution's name is blank. An asterisk after the school name denotes a *Special Message* following the college's profile, and a dagger indicates that the institution has one or more entries in the *In-Depth Descriptions of Two-Year Colleges* section. If a school does not appear, it did not report any of the information.

Y—Yes; N—No; R—Recommended; S—For Some

College	Location	Degrees Awarded	Institutional Control	Student Body	Undergrad Enrollment Fall 2003	Percent Attending Part-Time	Percent 25 Years of Age or Older	Percent of Grads Going on to Four-Year Colleges	Open Admissions	High School Equivalency Certificate Accepted	High School Transcript Required	Need-Based Aid Available	Part-Time Jobs Available	Career Counseling Available	Job Placement Services Available	College Housing Available	Number of Sports Available	Number of Majors Offered
Green River Community College	Auburn	C,T	St	M/W	6,621	41	31		Y	Y	S	Y	Y	Y	Y	N	10	24
Highline Community College*	Des Moines	C,T	St	M/W	6,372	49												
ITT Technical Institute	Bothell	T,B	Prop	M/W	263				N	Y	Y	Y	Y	Y	Y	N		15
ITT Technical Institute	Seattle	T,B	Prop	M/W	422				N	Y	Y	Y	Y	Y	Y	N		15
ITT Technical Institute	Spokane	T,B	Prop	M/W	455				N	Y	Y	Y	Y	Y	Y	N		11
Lake Washington Technical College	Kirkland	C,T	Dist	M/W	4,860	58	70		Y		S	Y	Y	Y		N		19
Lower Columbia College	Longview	C,T	St	M/W	3,320	46	36		Y		R	Y	Y	Y		N	5	79
North Seattle Community College	Seattle	C,T	St	M/W	6,465	50	55	40	Y			Y	Y	Y		N	1	26
Northwest Indian College	Bellingham	C,T	Fed	M/W	1,189													
Olympic College	Bremerton	C,T	St	M/W	7,102		49	31	Y		S	Y	Y	Y	Y	N	9	46
Peninsula College	Port Angeles	C,T	St	M/W	4,591	65	66		Y		S	Y	Y	Y	Y	Y	12	19
Pierce College	Puyallup	C,T	St	M/W	13,294													
Pima Medical Institute	Seattle	T	Prop	PW	292				N					Y			N	1
Seattle Central Community College	Seattle	C,T	St	M/W	10,721													
Shoreline Community College	Shoreline	C	St	M/W	8,591													
Skagit Valley College	Mount Vernon	C,T	St	M/W	6,858													
South Puget Sound Community College	Olympia	C,T	St	M/W	6,351		49		Y			Y	Y	Y	Y	N	3	30
Spokane Community College	Spokane	C,T	St	M/W	7,258		40		Y	Y	R	Y	Y	Y	Y	N	12	53
Spokane Falls Community College	Spokane	C,T	St	M/W	5,734		28		Y	Y	R	Y	Y	Y	Y	N	11	31
Tacoma Community College	Tacoma	C,T	St	M/W	6,056													
Walla Walla Community College	Walla Walla	C,T	St	M/W	4,440	51												
Wenatchee Valley College	Wenatchee	C,T	St-L	M/W	4,046													
Western Business College	Vancouver	T	Prop	M/W	555													
Whatcom Community College	Bellingham	C,T	St	M/W	4,209	46												
Yakima Valley Community College	Yakima	C,T	St	M/W	7,133		43		Y		R,S	Y	Y	Y	Y	Y	8	38
West Virginia																		
Eastern West Virginia Community and Technical College	Moorefield	C,T	St	M/W	405	88											1	
Fairmont State Community & Technical College†	Fairmont	C,T	St	M/W	3,355	44	15		Y	Y	R					Y		18
Huntington Junior College	Huntington	T	Prop	M/W	700													
Mountain State College	Parkersburg	T	Prop	PW	150		55		N	Y		Y	Y	Y	Y	N		6
National Institute of Technology	Cross Lanes	C	Prop	M/W	520		30		N	Y	Y	Y	Y	Y	Y	N		2
Southern West Virginia Comm and Tech Coll	Mount Gay	C,T	St	M/W	2,042	34	38		Y	Y	Y	Y	Y	Y	Y	N		16
Valley College of Technology	Martinsburg	T	Prop	PW	47													1
West Virginia Business College	Wheeling	T	Prop	PW	56	7	50							Y				4
West Virginia Junior College	Morgantown	T	Prop	PW														
West Virginia Northern Community College	Wheeling	C,T	St	M/W	2,879	57	94	33	Y	Y	S	Y	Y	Y	Y	N	4	18
West Virginia University at Parkersburg	Parkersburg	C,T,B	St	M/W	3,370	44												
Wisconsin																		
Blackhawk Technical College	Janesville	C,T	Dist	M/W	2,627	61	60		Y	Y	Y	Y	Y	Y	Y	N		17
Bryant and Stratton College	Milwaukee	T,B	Prop	M/W	656			9	N	Y	Y	Y	Y	Y	Y	N		7
Chippewa Valley Technical College	Eau Claire	T	Dist	M/W	16,100													
College of Menominee Nation	Keshena	C,T	Ind	M/W	499													
Fox Valley Technical College	Appleton	C,T	St-L	M/W	7,261	76												
Gateway Technical College	Kenosha	T	St-L	M/W	6,816	81												
Herzing College	Madison	C,B	Prop	PM	650													
ITT Technical Institute	Green Bay	T,B	Prop	M/W	419				N	Y	Y	Y	Y	Y	Y	N		12
ITT Technical Institute	Greenfield	T,B	Prop	M/W	548				N	Y	Y	Y	Y	Y	Y	N		12
Lac Courte Oreilles Ojibwa Community College	Hayward	C,T	Fed	M/W	561	43	75	15	Y	Y	Y	Y	Y	Y	Y	N	4	9
Lakeshore Technical College	Cleveland	C,T	St-L	M/W	3,069	74	55		Y	Y	S	Y	Y	Y	Y			21
Madison Area Technical College	Madison	C,T	Dist	M/W	13,479													
Mid-State Technical College	Wisconsin Rapids	C,T	St-L	M/W	10,737													
Milwaukee Area Technical College	Milwaukee	C,T	Dist	M/W	56,862				Y	Y	Y	Y	Y	Y	Y	N	12	98
Moraine Park Technical College	Fond du Lac	C,T	St-L	M/W	7,277	81	51		Y		R	Y	Y	Y	Y	N	2	27
Nicolet Area Technical College	Rhinelander	C,T	St-L	M/W	1,945													
Northcentral Technical College	Wausau	C,T	Dist	M/W	3,734	66	65	5	Y	Y	Y	Y	Y	Y	Y	N	8	26
Northeast Wisconsin Technical College	Green Bay	T	St-L	M/W	8,760	66	55		N	Y	S	Y	Y	Y	Y	N	2	84
Southwest Wisconsin Technical College	Fennimore	T	St-L	M/W	1,861	58												
U of Wisconsin Center–Baraboo/ Sauk County	Baraboo	C,T	St	M/W	566		22	80	N	Y	Y	Y	Y			N	11	1
U of Wisconsin Center–Barron County	Rice Lake	C	St	M/W	644		21		N	Y	Y	Y	Y			N	7	1
U of Wisconsin Center–Fox Valley	Menasha	C	St	M/W	1,797													
U of Wisconsin Center–Manitowoc	Manitowoc	C	St	M/W	635		23	90	N	Y	Y	Y	Y			N	4	1
U of Wisconsin Center–Marathon County	Wausau	C	St	M/W	1,295		21	96	N			Y	Y			Y	19	1
U of Wisconsin Center–Marinette	Marinette	C	St	M/W	560													
U of Wisconsin Center–Marshfield/ Wood County	Marshfield	C	St	M/W	643													
U of Wisconsin Center–Richland	Richland Center	C	St	M/W	517	35	16					Y	Y			Y	10	2
U of Wisconsin Center–Rock County	Janesville	C	St	M/W	945													
U of Wisconsin Center–Washington County	West Bend	C	St	M/W	968		16		N	Y	Y	Y	Y	Y		N	8	1
U of Wisconsin Center–Waukesha County	Waukesha	C	St	M/W	2,214		16	95	N	Y	Y	Y	Y	Y		N	9	1

This chart includes the names and locations of accredited two-year colleges in the United States and U.S. territories and shows institutions' responses to the *Thomson Peterson's Survey of Undergraduate Institutions.* If an institution submitted incomplete data, one or more columns opposite the institution's name is blank.

An asterisk after the school name denotes a *Special Message* following the college's profile, and a dagger indicates that the institution has one or more entries in the *In-Depth Descriptions of Two-Year Colleges* section. If a school does not appear, it did not report any of the information.

Y—Yes; N—No; R—Recommended; S—For Some

Institution	Location	Degrees Awarded	Institutional Control	Student Body	Undergraduate Enrollment Fall 2003	Percent Attending Part-Time	Percent 25 Years of Age or Older	Percent of Grads Going on to Four-Year Colleges	High School Equivalency Certificate Accepted	Open Admissions	High School Transcript Accepted	Need-Based Aid Required	Part-Time Jobs Available	Career Counseling Available	Job Placement Services Available	College Housing Available	Number of Sports Offered	Number of Majors Offered
Waukesha County Technical College	Pewaukee	T	St-L	M/W	27,052													
Western Wisconsin Technical College	La Crosse	T	Dist	M/W	5,286	61	16		Y	Y	Y	Y	Y	Y	Y	Y	4	44
Wisconsin Indianhead Technical College	Shell Lake	T	Dist	M/W	3,606		45											25
Wyoming																		
Casper College	Casper	C,T	Dist	M/W	4,158	51	45		Y	Y	Y	Y	Y	Y	Y	Y	18	85
Central Wyoming College	Riverton	C,T	St-L	M/W	1,808	55	46		Y	Y	R	Y	Y	Y	Y	Y	12	37
Eastern Wyoming College	Torrington	C,T	St-L	M/W	1,448	64	32		Y	Y	R	Y	Y	Y	Y	Y	12	46
Laramie County Community College	Cheyenne	C,T	St	M/W	4,485	66	47	46	Y	Y	Y	Y	Y	Y	Y	Y	4	79
Northwest College	Powell	C,T	St-L	M/W	1,711	34	23		Y	Y	Y	Y	Y	Y	Y	Y	21	70
Sheridan College	Sheridan	C,T	St-L	M/W	2,665	64	38		Y	Y	R,S	Y	Y	Y	Y	Y	7	42
Western Wyoming Community College*	Rock Springs	C,T	St-L	M/W	2,315	55	54	35	Y	Y	Y	Y	Y	Y	Y	Y	14	86
WyoTech	Laramie	T	Prop	PM	2,011													
INTERNATIONAL																		
Palau																		
Palau Community College	Koror	C,T	Terr	M/W	668	30												
Switzerland																		
Schiller International University	Engelberg	C,T	Ind	M/W	58			5	N	Y	Y			Y	Y	Y	11	3

Profiles of Two-Year
COLLEGES

U.S. AND U.S. TERRITORIES

ALABAMA

ALABAMA SOUTHERN COMMUNITY COLLEGE
Monroeville, Alabama

Admissions Contact Ms. Jana S. Horton, Registrar, Alabama Southern Community College, PO Box 2000, Monroeville, AL 36461. *Phone:* 251-575-3156 Ext. 252. *E-mail:* jhorton@ascc.edu.

BESSEMER STATE TECHNICAL COLLEGE
Bessemer, Alabama

Admissions Contact Director of Admissions, Bessemer State Technical College, PO Box 308, Bessemer, AL 35021-0308. *Phone:* 205-428-6391. *Toll-free phone:* 800-235-5368.

BEVILL STATE COMMUNITY COLLEGE
Sumiton, Alabama

- **State-supported** 2-year, founded 1969, part of Alabama College System
- **Calendar** semesters
- **Degree** certificates and associate
- **Rural** 23-acre campus with easy access to Birmingham
- **Coed**

Faculty *Student/faculty ratio:* 16:1.
Athletics Member NJCAA.
Standardized Tests *Required:* ACT ASSET (for placement). *Required for some:* ACT (for placement).
Costs (2003–04) *Tuition:* state resident $2718 full-time, $68 per credit hour part-time; nonresident $4894 full-time, $136 per credit hour part-time. *Required fees:* $510 full-time, $111 per credit hour part-time. *Room and board:* $5535; room only: $1350.
Financial Aid Of all full-time matriculated undergraduates who enrolled, 91 Federal Work-Study jobs (averaging $1618).
Applying *Options:* early admission, deferred entrance. *Required:* high school transcript.
Admissions Contact Ms. Melissa Stowe, Enrollment Supervisor, Bevill State Community College, PO Box 800, Sumiton, AL 35148. *Phone:* 205-932-3221 Ext. 5101.

BISHOP STATE COMMUNITY COLLEGE
Mobile, Alabama

- **State-supported** 2-year, founded 1965, part of Alabama College System
- **Calendar** semesters
- **Degree** certificates and associate
- **Urban** 9-acre campus
- **Coed**

Faculty *Student/faculty ratio:* 14:1.
Student Life *Campus security:* 24-hour emergency response devices and patrols.
Athletics Member NJCAA.
Standardized Tests *Required for some:* ACT ASSET.
Costs (2003–04) *Tuition:* state resident $2016 full-time, $68 per credit part-time; nonresident $4032 full-time, $136 per credit part-time. *Required fees:* $192 full-time.
Financial Aid Of all full-time matriculated undergraduates who enrolled, 299 Federal Work-Study jobs (averaging $2400).
Applying *Options:* common application, early admission, deferred entrance. *Required:* high school transcript.
Admissions Contact Dr. Terry Hazzard, Dean of Students, Bishop State Community College, 351 North Broad Street, Mobile, AL 36603-5898. *Phone:* 251-690-6419. *Fax:* 251-438-5403. *E-mail:* info@bishop.edu.

CALHOUN COMMUNITY COLLEGE
Decatur, Alabama

- **State-supported** 2-year, founded 1965, part of Alabama College System
- **Calendar** semesters
- **Degree** certificates and associate
- **Suburban** campus
- **Coed,** 8,923 undergraduate students, 40% full-time, 58% women, 42% men

Undergraduates 3,569 full-time, 5,354 part-time. Students come from 9 states and territories, 16 other countries, 1% are from out of state, 19% African American, 1% Asian American or Pacific Islander, 2% Hispanic American, 2% Native American, 0.2% international, 3% transferred in.
Freshmen *Admission:* 5,014 applied, 4,301 admitted, 1,726 enrolled. *Test scores:* SAT verbal scores over 500: 22%; SAT math scores over 500: 28%; ACT scores over 18: 63%; SAT math scores over 600: 6%; ACT scores over 24: 12%; ACT scores over 30: 1%.
Faculty *Total:* 418, 29% full-time, 13% with terminal degrees. *Student/faculty ratio:* 21:1.
Majors Accounting; aeronautical/aerospace engineering technology; agriculture; biology/biological sciences; business administration and management; child care and support services management; computer and information sciences; computer graphics; criminal justice/police science; dental assisting; drafting and design technology; dramatic/theatre arts; education; electrical and power transmission installation related; electrical, electronic and communications engineering technology; electromechanical and instrumentation and maintenance technologies related; elementary education; emergency medical technology (EMT paramedic); English; entrepreneurship; family resource management; fire services administration; general studies; graphic design; heating, air conditioning and refrigeration technology; heating, air conditioning, ventilation and refrigeration maintenance technology; industrial mechanics and maintenance technology; legal assistant/paralegal; liberal arts and sciences/liberal studies; machine tool technology; mathematics; military technologies; music; nursing (registered nurse training); office management; photographic and film/video technology; pre-dentistry studies; pre-law studies; pre-medical studies; pre-pharmacy studies; pre-veterinary studies; real estate; secondary education; special education (early childhood); transportation management; visual and performing arts.
Academic Programs *Special study options:* academic remediation for entering students, accelerated degree program, adult/continuing education programs, advanced placement credit, cooperative education, distance learning, English as a second language, independent study, part-time degree program, services for LD students, summer session for credit. *ROTC:* Army (c).
Library Brewer Library plus 2 others with 36,699 titles, 202 serial subscriptions, 23,948 audiovisual materials, an OPAC, a Web page.
Computers on Campus 160 computers available on campus for general student use. A campuswide network can be accessed.
Student Life *Housing:* college housing not available. *Activities and Organizations:* drama/theater group, student-run newspaper, television station, choral group, Student Government Association, Black Students Alliance, Phi Theta Kappa, BACCHUS/SADD, VICA. *Campus security:* 24-hour patrols. *Student services:* personal/psychological counseling.
Standardized Tests *Required for some:* SAT I or ACT (for admission).
Costs (2004–05) *Tuition:* state resident $2160 full-time, $72 per semester hour part-time; nonresident $4320 full-time, $144 per semester hour part-time. *Required fees:* $540 full-time, $18 per semester hour part-time. *Waivers:* senior citizens and employees or children of employees.
Financial Aid Of all full-time matriculated undergraduates who enrolled, 50 Federal Work-Study jobs (averaging $3000).
Applying *Required for some:* high school transcript. *Application deadline:* rolling (freshmen), rolling (transfers). *Notification:* continuous (freshmen), continuous (transfers).
Admissions Contact Ms. Patricia Landers, Admissions Receptionist, Calhoun Community College, PO Box 2216, 6250 Highway 31 North, Decatur, AL 35609-2216. *Phone:* 256-306-2593. *Toll-free phone:* 800-626-3628 Ext. 2594. *Fax:* 256-306-2941. *E-mail:* pml@calhoun.cc.al.us.

CENTRAL ALABAMA COMMUNITY COLLEGE
Alexander City, Alabama

- **State-supported** 2-year, founded 1965, part of Alabama College System
- **Calendar** semesters
- **Degree** certificates and associate
- **Small-town** 100-acre campus
- **Coed,** 1,790 undergraduate students

Undergraduates Students come from 6 states and territories, 25% African American, 0.4% Asian American or Pacific Islander, 0.7% Hispanic American, 0.2% Native American.
Faculty *Total:* 193, 27% full-time. *Student/faculty ratio:* 15:1.
Majors Administrative assistant and secretarial science; business administration and management; clothing/textiles; computer programming; computer science; drafting and design technology; electrical, electronic and communications engineering technology; environmental engineering technology; information science/studies; liberal arts and sciences/liberal studies; nursing (registered nurse training).

Academic Programs *Special study options:* academic remediation for entering students, adult/continuing education programs, advanced placement credit, cooperative education, distance learning, internships, part-time degree program, services for LD students, summer session for credit.

Library Thomas D. Russell Library with 35,000 titles, 455 serial subscriptions.

Computers on Campus 70 computers available on campus for general student use. A campuswide network can be accessed from off campus. Internet access, at least one staffed computer lab available.

Student Life *Housing:* college housing not available. *Activities and Organizations:* drama/theater group, student-run radio station, choral group, Cultural Unity, Baptist Campus Ministry, Student Government Association, Phi Theta Kappa. *Campus security:* evening security. *Student services:* personal/psychological counseling.

Athletics Member NJCAA. *Intercollegiate sports:* baseball M(s), golf M(s), softball W(s), tennis M(s)/W(s), volleyball W(s).

Standardized Tests *Required for some:* SAT I or ACT (for admission).

Costs (2003–04) *Tuition:* state resident $2448 full-time, $68 per hour part-time; nonresident $4896 full-time, $136 per hour part-time. *Required fees:* $576 full-time. *Waivers:* senior citizens and employees or children of employees.

Applying *Options:* common application, early admission. *Required:* high school transcript. *Required for some:* 3 letters of recommendation, interview. *Application deadlines:* 9/9 (freshmen), 9/9 (transfers).

Admissions Contact Ms. Bettie Macmillan, Admission, Central Alabama Community College, PO Box 699, Alexander City, AL 35011-0699. *Phone:* 256-234-6346 Ext. 6232. *Toll-free phone:* 800-643-2657 Ext. 6232. *Fax:* 256-234-0384.

CHATTAHOOCHEE VALLEY COMMUNITY COLLEGE
Phenix City, Alabama

- **State-supported** 2-year, founded 1974
- **Calendar** semesters
- **Degree** certificates and associate
- **Small-town** 103-acre campus
- **Endowment** $42,791
- **Coed**

Faculty *Student/faculty ratio:* 18:1.

Student Life *Campus security:* 24-hour emergency response devices and patrols.

Athletics Member NJCAA.

Standardized Tests *Required for some:* SAT I or ACT (for placement).

Costs (2003–04) *Tuition:* state resident $2100 full-time, $60 per semester hour part-time; nonresident $3900 full-time, $120 per semester hour part-time. *Required fees:* $10 per semester hour part-time.

Financial Aid Of all full-time matriculated undergraduates who enrolled, 40 Federal Work-Study jobs (averaging $2000). 10 state and other part-time jobs (averaging $2000).

Applying *Options:* common application, early admission. *Required:* high school transcript.

Admissions Contact Ms. Rita Cherry, Admissions Clerk, Chattahoochee Valley Community College, PO Box 1000, Phenix City, AL 36869. *Phone:* 334-291-4995. *Toll-free phone:* 800-842-2822. *Fax:* 334-291-4994. *E-mail:* information@cv.edu.

COMMUNITY COLLEGE OF THE AIR FORCE
Maxwell Air Force Base, Alabama

- **Federally supported** 2-year, founded 1972
- **Calendar** continuous
- **Degrees** certificates and associate (courses conducted at 125 branch locations worldwide for members of the U.S. Air Force)
- **Suburban** campus
- **Coed, primarily men**

Undergraduates 16% African American, 2% Asian American or Pacific Islander, 5% Hispanic American, 0.5% Native American.

Freshmen *Admission:* 42,967 applied, 42,967 admitted.

Faculty *Total:* 7,393, 100% full-time. *Student/faculty ratio:* 50:1.

Majors Aeronautics/aviation/aerospace science and technology; airframe mechanics and aircraft maintenance technology; air traffic control; apparel and textile marketing management; atmospheric sciences and meteorology; automobile/automotive mechanics technology; avionics maintenance technology; biomedical technology; cardiovascular technology; clinical/medical laboratory technology; commercial and advertising art; communications technology; construction engineering technology; criminal justice/law enforcement administration; dental assisting; dental laboratory technology; dietetics; educational/instructional media design; educational leadership and administration; electrical, electronic and communications engineering technology; environmental health; environmental studies; finance; fire science; health/health care administration; hematology technology; hotel/motel administration; human resources management; industrial technology; legal assistant/paralegal; logistics and materials management; management information systems; medical physiology; medical radiologic technology; mental health/rehabilitation; metallurgical technology; military technologies; music performance; nuclear medical technology; occupational safety and health technology; office management; ophthalmic laboratory technology; parks, recreation and leisure; pharmacy technician; physical therapist assistant; public relations/image management; purchasing, procurement/acquisitions and contracts management; security and loss prevention; social work; surgical technology; vehicle/equipment operation.

Academic Programs *Special study options:* academic remediation for entering students, adult/continuing education programs, advanced placement credit, distance learning, independent study, internships.

Library Air Force Library Service with 5.0 million titles, 56,654 serial subscriptions, an OPAC, a Web page.

Computers on Campus Internet access available.

Student Life *Housing:* on-campus residence required for freshman year. *Options:* coed. Campus housing is university owned, leased by the school and is provided by a third party. Freshman applicants given priority for college housing. *Campus security:* 24-hour emergency response devices and patrols. *Student services:* health clinic, personal/psychological counseling, legal services.

Athletics *Intramural sports:* badminton M/W, baseball M, basketball M/W, bowling M/W, cross-country running M/W, football M, golf M/W, racquetball M/W, softball M/W, squash M/W, table tennis M/W, tennis M/W, track and field M/W, volleyball M/W, weight lifting M/W.

Standardized Tests *Required:* Armed Services Vocational Aptitude Battery (for admission).

Costs (2003–04) *Tuition:* Tuition, room and board, and medical and dental care are provided by the U.S. government. Each student receives a salary from which to pay for uniforms, supplies, and personal expenses. *Waivers:* minority students and adult students.

Applying *Options:* electronic application. *Required:* high school transcript, interview. *Application deadline:* rolling (freshmen), rolling (transfers). *Notification:* continuous (freshmen), continuous (transfers).

Admissions Contact C.M. Sgt. Robert McAlexander, Director of Admissions/Registrar, Community College of the Air Force, 130 West Maxwell Boulevard, Building 836, Maxwell Air Force Base, Maxwell AFB, AL 36112-6613. *Phone:* 334-953-6436. *E-mail:* ronald.hall@maxwell.af.mil.

ENTERPRISE-OZARK COMMUNITY COLLEGE
Enterprise, Alabama

- **State-supported** 2-year, founded 1965, part of Alabama College System
- **Calendar** semesters
- **Degree** certificates and associate
- **Small-town** 100-acre campus
- **Coed**

Student Life *Campus security:* security personnel.

Athletics Member NJCAA.

Standardized Tests *Recommended:* SAT I or ACT (for placement).

Costs (2003–04) *Tuition:* state resident $2040 full-time; nonresident $4080 full-time. *Required fees:* $480 full-time.

Financial Aid Of all full-time matriculated undergraduates who enrolled, 99 Federal Work-Study jobs (averaging $2000).

Applying *Options:* early admission, deferred entrance. *Required:* high school transcript.

Admissions Contact Ms. Robin Wyatt, Director of Admissions, Enterprise-Ozark Community College, PO Box 1300, Enterprise, AL 36331. *Phone:* 334-347-2623 Ext. 2273.

GADSDEN STATE COMMUNITY COLLEGE
Gadsden, Alabama

- **State-supported** 2-year, founded 1965, part of Alabama College System
- **Calendar** semesters
- **Degree** certificates and associate
- **Small-town** 275-acre campus with easy access to Birmingham
- **Endowment** $1.3 million
- **Coed,** 5,868 undergraduate students

Undergraduates Students come from 10 states and territories, 19% African American, 0.3% Asian American or Pacific Islander, 1% Hispanic American, 0.5% Native American, 3% international.

Gadsden State Community College (continued)

Freshmen *Admission:* 1,476 applied, 1,476 admitted.

Faculty *Total:* 333, 51% full-time, 3% with terminal degrees.

Majors Administrative assistant and secretarial science; child care and support services management; civil engineering technology; clinical/medical laboratory technology; computer and information sciences; court reporting; criminal justice/police science; emergency medical technology (EMT paramedic); general retailing/wholesaling; general studies; heating, air conditioning and refrigeration technology; legal assistant/paralegal; liberal arts and sciences/liberal studies; mechanical engineering/mechanical technology; medical radiologic technology; nursing (registered nurse training); physical education teaching and coaching; radio and television broadcasting technology; substance abuse/addiction counseling; telecommunications; tool and die technology.

Academic Programs *Special study options:* academic remediation for entering students, adult/continuing education programs, advanced placement credit, cooperative education, English as a second language, external degree program, part-time degree program, services for LD students, summer session for credit.

Library Meadows Library with 72,915 titles, 303 serial subscriptions.

Computers on Campus 200 computers available on campus for general student use. A campuswide network can be accessed. Internet access, at least one staffed computer lab available.

Student Life *Housing Options:* coed. *Activities and Organizations:* drama/theater group, student-run newspaper, radio station, choral group, Science, Math, and Engineering Club, Student Government Association, Circle K, Phi Beta Lambda, VICA. *Campus security:* 24-hour patrols. *Student services:* women's center.

Athletics Member NJCAA. *Intercollegiate sports:* baseball M(s), basketball M(s)/W(s), cross-country running W(s), golf M(s), softball W(s), tennis M(s), volleyball W(s). *Intramural sports:* basketball M/W, volleyball M/W.

Costs (2003–04) *Tuition:* state resident $3192 full-time, $84 per credit hour part-time; nonresident $5776 full-time, $152 per credit hour part-time. *Room and board:* $2800.

Financial Aid Of all full-time matriculated undergraduates who enrolled, 95 Federal Work-Study jobs (averaging $1364).

Applying *Options:* early admission, deferred entrance. *Required:* high school transcript. *Application deadline:* rolling (freshmen), rolling (transfers).

Admissions Contact Ms. Teresa Rhea, Admissions and Records, Gadsden State Community College, Admissions, Allen Hall. *Phone:* 256-549-8263. *Toll-free phone:* 800-226-5563. *Fax:* 256-549-8205. *E-mail:* info@gadsdenstate.edu.

GADSDEN STATE COMMUNITY COLLEGE-AYERS CAMPUS
Anniston, Alabama

Admissions Contact Mrs. Michele Conger, Director of Admissions and Records, Gadsden State Community College-Ayers Campus, 1801 Coleman Road, Anniston, AL 36207. *Phone:* 256-835-5400. *Fax:* 256-835-5479. *E-mail:* mlonger@ayers.cc.al.us.

GEORGE CORLEY WALLACE STATE COMMUNITY COLLEGE
Selma, Alabama

Admissions Contact Ms. Sunette Newman, Registrar, George Corley Wallace State Community College, 3000 Earl Goodwin Parkway, Selma, AL 36702-2530. *Phone:* 334-876-9305. *Fax:* 334-876-9300.

GEORGE C. WALLACE COMMUNITY COLLEGE
Dothan, Alabama

Admissions Contact Mrs. Brenda Barnes, Assistant Dean of Student Affairs, George C. Wallace Community College, 1141 Wallace Drive, Dothan, AL 36303-9234. *Phone:* 334-983-3521 Ext. 283. *Toll-free phone:* 800-543-2426.

HERZING COLLEGE
Birmingham, Alabama

- **Proprietary** primarily 2-year, founded 1965, part of Herzing Institutes, Inc.
- **Calendar** semesters
- **Degrees** diplomas, associate, and bachelor's
- **Urban** 4-acre campus
- **Coed**

Faculty *Student/faculty ratio:* 20:1.

Student Life *Campus security:* 24-hour emergency response devices, late-night transport/escort service, security guard.

Standardized Tests *Required:* (for admission).

Costs (2003–04) *Tuition:* $24,300 full-time, $270 per credit hour part-time. Full-time tuition and fees vary according to program.

Applying *Options:* early admission, deferred entrance.

Admissions Contact Ms. Tess Anderson, Admissions Coordinator, Herzing College, 280 West Valley Avenue, Birmingham, AL 35209. *Phone:* 205-916-2800. *Fax:* 205-916-2807.

ITT TECHNICAL INSTITUTE
Birmingham, Alabama

- **Proprietary** primarily 2-year, founded 1994, part of ITT Educational Services, Inc.
- **Calendar** quarters
- **Degrees** associate and bachelor's
- **Suburban** campus
- **Coed**

Student Life *Campus security:* 24-hour emergency response devices.

Standardized Tests *Required:* Wonderlic aptitude test (for admission).

Costs (2003–04) *Tuition:* Total Program Cost varies depending on course of study. Consult school catalog.

Applying *Options:* deferred entrance. *Application fee:* $100. *Required:* high school transcript, interview. *Recommended:* letters of recommendation.

Admissions Contact Jesse L. Johnson, Director of Recruitment, ITT Technical Institute, 500 Riverhills Business Park, Birmingham, AL 35242. *Phone:* 205-991-5410. *Toll-free phone:* 800-488-7033. *Fax:* 205-991-5025.

JAMES H. FAULKNER STATE COMMUNITY COLLEGE
Bay Minette, Alabama

- **State-supported** 2-year, founded 1965, part of Alabama College System
- **Calendar** semesters
- **Degree** certificates and associate
- **Small-town** 105-acre campus
- **Coed,** 3,067 undergraduate students, 63% full-time, 61% women, 39% men

Faulkner State Community College (FSCC), accredited by the Southern Association of Colleges and Schools, offers both transfer and certificate programs. The main campus is located in Bay Minette, Alabama, with branches in Fairhope and Gulf Shores, Alabama. FSCC serves the entire Gulf Coast area. For information, call 800-231-3752 (toll-free).

Undergraduates 1,925 full-time, 1,142 part-time. 3% are from out of state, 13% African American, 0.5% Asian American or Pacific Islander, 0.6% Hispanic American, 1% Native American, 9% live on campus.

Freshmen *Admission:* 853 enrolled.

Faculty *Total:* 158, 39% full-time. *Student/faculty ratio:* 15:1.

Majors Administrative assistant and secretarial science; business administration and management; commercial and advertising art; computer and information sciences; court reporting; dental assisting; environmental engineering technology; general studies; hospitality administration; landscaping and groundskeeping; legal assistant/paralegal; liberal arts and sciences/liberal studies; nursing (licensed practical/vocational nurse training); nursing (registered nurse training); parks, recreation and leisure facilities management; surgical technology.

Academic Programs *Special study options:* academic remediation for entering students, adult/continuing education programs, advanced placement credit, cooperative education, honors programs, internships, part-time degree program, services for LD students.

Library Austin R. Meadows Library with 53,100 titles, 200 serial subscriptions, 2,513 audiovisual materials, an OPAC.

Computers on Campus 208 computers available on campus for general student use. A campuswide network can be accessed. Internet access, at least one staffed computer lab available.

Student Life *Housing Options:* men-only, women-only. *Activities and Organizations:* drama/theater group, student-run newspaper, choral group, Student Government Association, Pow-Wow Leadership Society, Phi Theta Kappa, Association of Computational Machinery, Phi Beta Lambda, national fraternities. *Campus security:* 24-hour patrols, controlled dormitory access. *Student services:* personal/psychological counseling.

Athletics Member NJCAA. *Intercollegiate sports:* baseball M(s), basketball M(s)/W(s), golf M(s), softball W(s), tennis M(s)/W(s), volleyball W(s). *Intramural sports:* basketball M, tennis M/W, volleyball M/W.

Standardized Tests *Required for some:* ACT ASSET, ACT COMPASS. *Recommended:* ACT ASSET, ACT COMPASS.

Costs (2004–05) *Tuition:* state resident $2232 full-time; nonresident $3936 full-time. *Room and board:* $2931. *Payment plan:* deferred payment. *Waivers:* employees or children of employees.

Applying *Options:* early admission, deferred entrance. *Required:* high school transcript. *Application deadline:* rolling (freshmen), rolling (transfers). *Notification:* continuous until 8/18 (freshmen), continuous until 8/18 (transfers).

Admissions Contact Ms. Peggy Duck, Director of High School Relations/Student Activities, James H. Faulkner State Community College, 1900 Highway 31 South, Bay Minette, AL 36507. *Phone:* 251-580-2152. *Toll-free phone:* 800-231-3752 Ext. 2111. *Fax:* 251-580-2285. *E-mail:* crobinson@faulkner.cc.al.us.

JEFFERSON DAVIS COMMUNITY COLLEGE
Brewton, Alabama

- **State-supported** 2-year, founded 1965
- **Calendar** semesters
- **Degree** certificates and associate
- **Small-town** 100-acre campus
- **Coed,** 1,442 undergraduate students, 63% full-time, 58% women, 42% men

Undergraduates 908 full-time, 534 part-time. Students come from 8 states and territories, 13% are from out of state, 30% African American, 0.5% Asian American or Pacific Islander, 0.7% Hispanic American, 3% Native American.

Freshmen *Admission:* 407 enrolled.

Faculty *Total:* 122, 38% full-time, 3% with terminal degrees. *Student/faculty ratio:* 11:1.

Majors Administrative assistant and secretarial science; applied art; biological and physical sciences; biology/biological sciences; business administration and management; criminal justice/police science; dramatic/theatre arts; education; elementary education; finance; history; liberal arts and sciences/liberal studies; marketing/marketing management; medical/clinical assistant; music; nursing (registered nurse training); parks, recreation and leisure; physical education teaching and coaching; political science and government.

Academic Programs *Special study options:* academic remediation for entering students, adult/continuing education programs, advanced placement credit, honors programs, part-time degree program, services for LD students, summer session for credit.

Library 926 titles, 330 serial subscriptions.

Computers on Campus 40 computers available on campus for general student use.

Student Life *Activities and Organizations:* drama/theater group. *Student services:* personal/psychological counseling.

Standardized Tests *Required:* ACT COMPASS (for placement).

Costs (2004–05) *Tuition:* state resident $2160 full-time, $72 per credit hour part-time; nonresident $4290 full-time, $143 per credit hour part-time. *Required fees:* $548 full-time, $18 per credit hour part-time, $4 per term part-time. *Room and board:* Room and board charges vary according to housing facility. *Waivers:* senior citizens and employees or children of employees.

Financial Aid Of all full-time matriculated undergraduates who enrolled, 50 Federal Work-Study jobs (averaging $2700).

Applying *Options:* early admission. *Required:* high school transcript. *Application deadline:* rolling (freshmen), rolling (transfers).

Admissions Contact Ms. Robin Sessions, Coordinator of Admissions and Records, Jefferson Davis Community College, PO Box 958, Brewton, AL 36427. *Phone:* 251-867-4832. *Fax:* 251-809-1596.

JEFFERSON STATE COMMUNITY COLLEGE
Birmingham, Alabama

- **State-supported** 2-year, founded 1965, part of Alabama College System
- **Calendar** semesters
- **Degree** certificates and associate
- **Suburban** 234-acre campus
- **Endowment** $1.5 million
- **Coed,** 7,183 undergraduate students, 39% full-time, 61% women, 39% men

Undergraduates 2,813 full-time, 4,370 part-time. Students come from 21 states and territories, 51 other countries, 1% are from out of state, 20% African American, 1% Asian American or Pacific Islander, 1% Hispanic American, 0.3% Native American, 3% international, 8% transferred in.

Freshmen *Admission:* 1,234 enrolled. *Average high school GPA:* 2.72.

Faculty *Total:* 381, 28% full-time, 13% with terminal degrees. *Student/faculty ratio:* 22:1.

Majors Accounting technology and bookkeeping; administrative assistant and secretarial science; agricultural business and management; banking and financial support services; biomedical technology; business/commerce; child care and support services management; clinical/medical laboratory technology; computer and information sciences; construction engineering technology; criminal justice/police science; fire services administration; funeral service and mortuary science; general studies; home furnishings and equipment installation; hospitality administration; liberal arts and sciences/liberal studies; medical radiologic technology; nursing (registered nurse training); physical therapist assistant; radio and television broadcasting technology; robotics technology.

Academic Programs *Special study options:* academic remediation for entering students, adult/continuing education programs, advanced placement credit, distance learning, honors programs, independent study, internships, part-time degree program, services for LD students, summer session for credit. *ROTC:* Army (c), Air Force (c).

Library James B. Allen Library plus 1 other with 77,015 titles, 242 serial subscriptions, 3,349 audiovisual materials, an OPAC.

Computers on Campus A campuswide network can be accessed from off campus. Internet access, online (class) registration, at least one staffed computer lab available.

Student Life *Housing:* college housing not available. *Activities and Organizations:* drama/theater group, student-run newspaper, radio station, choral group, Student Government Association, Phi Theta Kappa, Baptist Campus Ministries, Jefferson State Ambassadors, Students in Free Enterprise (SIFE). *Campus security:* 24-hour patrols. *Student services:* women's center.

Athletics Member NJCAA. *Intercollegiate sports:* baseball M(s), softball W(s). *Intramural sports:* badminton M/W, basketball M/W, bowling M/W, soccer M/W, softball M/W, tennis M/W, volleyball M/W.

Standardized Tests *Required for some:* ACT ASSET, ACT COMPASS. *Recommended:* SAT I or ACT (for placement).

Costs (2003–04) *Tuition:* state resident $2040 full-time, $68 per semester hour part-time; nonresident $4080 full-time, $136 per semester hour part-time. *Required fees:* $480 full-time, $16 per semester hour part-time. *Waivers:* senior citizens and employees or children of employees.

Financial Aid Of all full-time matriculated undergraduates who enrolled, 189 Federal Work-Study jobs (averaging $1926).

Applying *Options:* common application, electronic application, early admission, deferred entrance. *Required for some:* high school transcript. *Application deadline:* rolling (freshmen). *Notification:* continuous (freshmen), continuous (transfers).

Admissions Contact Mr. Michael Hobbs, Director of Admissions, Advising, and Records, Jefferson State Community College, 2601 Carson Road, Birmingham, AL 35215-3098. *Phone:* 205-853-1200 Ext. 7991. *Toll-free phone:* 800-239-5900. *Fax:* 205-856-6070.

J. F. DRAKE STATE TECHNICAL COLLEGE
Huntsville, Alabama

- **State-supported** 2-year, founded 1961, part of State of Alabama Department of Postsecondary Education
- **Calendar** semesters
- **Degree** certificates, diplomas, and associate
- **Urban** 6-acre campus with easy access to Huntsville
- **Coed,** 796 undergraduate students, 58% full-time, 54% women, 46% men

Undergraduates 461 full-time, 335 part-time. Students come from 1 other state, 4% are from out of state, 57% African American, 0.8% Asian American or Pacific Islander, 0.5% Hispanic American, 0.1% Native American.

Freshmen *Admission:* 645 applied, 565 admitted, 215 enrolled.

Faculty *Total:* 62, 34% full-time, 3% with terminal degrees. *Student/faculty ratio:* 20:1.

Majors Accounting; administrative assistant and secretarial science; commercial and advertising art; drafting and design technology; electrical, electronic and communications engineering technology; information science/studies; machine tool technology.

Academic Programs *Special study options:* academic remediation for entering students, cooperative education, internships, part-time degree program, services for LD students.

Computers on Campus 380 computers available on campus for general student use. At least one staffed computer lab available.

Student Life *Housing:* college housing not available. *Activities and Organizations:* student-run newspaper, Phi Beta Lambda, Vocational Industrial Clubs of America. *Campus security:* 24-hour patrols.

Standardized Tests *Required:* ACT COMPASS (for placement).

Costs (2003–04) *Tuition:* state resident $2184 full-time, $68 per semester hour part-time; nonresident $4368 full-time, $136 per semester hour part-time. *Required fees:* $96 full-time, $24 per semester hour part-time. *Waivers:* employees or children of employees.

J. F. Drake State Technical College (continued)

Applying *Options:* deferred entrance. *Required:* high school transcript. *Application deadline:* rolling (freshmen).

Admissions Contact Mrs. Shirley Clemons, Registrar, J. F. Drake State Technical College, 3421 Meridian Street, Huntsville, AL 35811. *Phone:* 256-551-3109 Ext. 109. *Toll-free phone:* 888-413-7253. *Fax:* 256-551-3142. *E-mail:* clemons@drakestate.edu.

LAWSON STATE COMMUNITY COLLEGE
Birmingham, Alabama

- **State-supported** 2-year, founded 1949, part of Alabama College System
- **Calendar** semesters
- **Degree** certificates and associate
- **Urban** 30-acre campus
- **Coed,** 2,168 undergraduate students, 65% full-time, 69% women, 31% men

Undergraduates 1,411 full-time, 757 part-time. Students come from 2 states and territories, 1% are from out of state, 98% African American, 0.1% Native American, 3% transferred in. *Retention:* 68% of 2002 full-time freshmen returned.
Freshmen *Admission:* 1,124 applied, 551 admitted, 527 enrolled.
Faculty *Total:* 137, 42% full-time. *Student/faculty ratio:* 16:1.
Majors Accounting; administrative assistant and secretarial science; art; biology/biological sciences; business administration and management; business teacher education; carpentry; chemistry; clinical laboratory science/medical technology; clothing/textiles; computer and information sciences related; cosmetology; crafts, folk art and artisanry; criminal justice/law enforcement administration; criminal justice/police science; dietetics; drafting and design technology; education; electrical, electronic and communications engineering technology; English; fire science; health and physical education; heavy equipment maintenance technology; history; hydrology and water resources science; information science/studies; legal administrative assistant/secretary; liberal arts and sciences/liberal studies; library science; mathematics; music; nursing (registered nurse training); parks, recreation and leisure; physical sciences; physical therapy; political science and government; pre-engineering; pre-law studies; psychology; radio and television; social sciences; social work; sociology; urban studies/affairs.
Academic Programs *Special study options:* academic remediation for entering students, adult/continuing education programs, cooperative education, distance learning, freshman honors college, honors programs, internships, part-time degree program, summer session for credit.
Library Lawson State Library with 31,998 titles, 170 serial subscriptions, 506 audiovisual materials, an OPAC.
Computers on Campus 140 computers available on campus for general student use. A campuswide network can be accessed. Internet access, online (class) registration, at least one staffed computer lab available.
Student Life *Housing:* college housing not available. *Activities and Organizations:* choral group. *Campus security:* 24-hour emergency response devices and patrols, student patrols. *Student services:* health clinic.
Athletics Member NJCAA. *Intercollegiate sports:* basketball M/W, cross-country running M(s), equestrian sports M, volleyball W(s). *Intramural sports:* basketball M/W, softball M/W, swimming M/W, table tennis M/W, tennis M/W, track and field M/W, volleyball W, weight lifting M.
Standardized Tests *Recommended:* ACT (for placement).
Costs (2004–05) *Tuition:* state resident $2016 full-time, $68 per credit part-time; nonresident $4032 full-time, $136 per credit part-time. *Required fees:* $384 full-time, $8 per credit part-time, $10 per term part-time. *Waivers:* senior citizens and employees or children of employees.
Financial Aid Of all full-time matriculated undergraduates who enrolled, 91 Federal Work-Study jobs (averaging $3000).
Applying *Options:* common application, early admission, deferred entrance. *Required:* high school transcript. *Application deadline:* rolling (freshmen), rolling (transfers). *Notification:* continuous (freshmen), continuous (transfers).
Admissions Contact Mr. Darren C. Allen, Director of Admissions and Records, Lawson State Community College, 3060 Wilson Road, SW, Birmingham, AL 35221-1798. *Phone:* 205-929-6361. *Fax:* 205-923-7106. *E-mail:* dallen@lawsonstate.edu.

LURLEEN B. WALLACE COMMUNITY COLLEGE
Andalusia, Alabama

- **State-supported** 2-year, founded 1969, part of Alabama College System
- **Calendar** semesters
- **Degree** certificates and associate
- **Small-town** 200-acre campus
- **Coed,** 1,490 undergraduate students

Undergraduates Students come from 6 states and territories, 5% are from out of state, 18% African American, 0.5% Asian American or Pacific Islander, 1% Hispanic American, 0.3% Native American.
Freshmen *Admission:* 588 admitted.
Faculty *Total:* 165, 66% full-time.
Majors Emergency medical technology (EMT paramedic); forestry technology; liberal arts and sciences/liberal studies.
Academic Programs *Special study options:* academic remediation for entering students, advanced placement credit, cooperative education, freshman honors college, part-time degree program, services for LD students, summer session for credit.
Library Lurleen B. Wallace Library with 35,278 titles, 133 serial subscriptions.
Computers on Campus 45 computers available on campus for general student use. Internet access, at least one staffed computer lab available.
Student Life *Housing:* college housing not available. *Activities and Organizations:* drama/theater group, student-run newspaper, Student Government Association, College Ambassadors, Phi Theta Kappa, Mu Alpha Theta, Christian Student Union. *Campus security:* 24-hour emergency response devices. *Student services:* personal/psychological counseling.
Athletics Member NJCAA. *Intercollegiate sports:* baseball M(s), basketball M(s)/W(s), cross-country running M(s)/W(s), softball W(s).
Standardized Tests *Recommended:* ACT (for placement).
Costs (2004–05) *Tuition:* state resident $2160 full-time.
Applying *Options:* early admission, deferred entrance. *Required:* high school transcript. *Application deadline:* rolling (freshmen), rolling (transfers). *Notification:* continuous until 9/15 (freshmen), continuous until 9/15 (transfers).
Admissions Contact Mrs. Judy Hall, Director of Student Services, Lurleen B. Wallace Community College, PO Box 1418, Andalusia, AL 36420. *Phone:* 334-222-6591 Ext. 271.

MARION MILITARY INSTITUTE
Marion, Alabama

Admissions Contact Dan Sumlin, Director of Admissions, Marion Military Institute, 1101 Washington Street, Marion, AL 36756. *Phone:* 800-664-1842 Ext. 306. *Toll-free phone:* 800-664-1842 Ext. 307. *Fax:* 334-683-2383. *E-mail:* marionmilitary@zebra.net.

NORTHEAST ALABAMA COMMUNITY COLLEGE
Rainsville, Alabama

- **State-supported** 2-year, founded 1963, part of Alabama College System
- **Calendar** quarters
- **Degree** certificates and associate
- **Rural** 100-acre campus
- **Coed,** 2,072 undergraduate students, 50% full-time, 64% women, 36% men

Undergraduates 1,035 full-time, 1,037 part-time. Students come from 3 states and territories, 2% are from out of state, 1% African American, 0.4% Asian American or Pacific Islander, 0.7% Hispanic American, 6% Native American. *Retention:* 62% of 2002 full-time freshmen returned.
Freshmen *Admission:* 409 applied, 409 admitted, 397 enrolled.
Faculty *Total:* 136, 22% full-time, 10% with terminal degrees. *Student/faculty ratio:* 32:1.
Majors Administrative assistant and secretarial science; biological and physical sciences; business administration and management; computer graphics; computer science; computer typography and composition equipment operation; electrical, electronic and communications engineering technology; emergency medical technology (EMT paramedic); finance; hydrology and water resources science; information science/studies; legal administrative assistant/secretary; legal assistant/paralegal; liberal arts and sciences/liberal studies; medical administrative assistant and medical secretary; nursing (registered nurse training); pre-engineering; real estate.
Academic Programs *Special study options:* academic remediation for entering students, accelerated degree program, adult/continuing education programs, advanced placement credit, honors programs, part-time degree program, services for LD students, summer session for credit.
Library 45,000 titles, 142 serial subscriptions, an OPAC.
Computers on Campus 50 computers available on campus for general student use. At least one staffed computer lab available.
Student Life *Housing:* college housing not available. *Activities and Organizations:* drama/theater group, choral group, Baptist Campus Ministry, theater, SGA, Spectrum Art Club, choral group. *Campus security:* 24-hour emergency response devices and patrols, late-night transport/escort service. *Student services:* personal/psychological counseling.

Standardized Tests *Required:* ACT ASSET, ACT COMPASS (for placement).

Costs (2003–04) *Tuition:* state resident $2280 full-time, $76 per credit hour part-time; nonresident $4560 full-time, $152 per credit hour part-time. *Waivers:* senior citizens and employees or children of employees.

Financial Aid Of all full-time matriculated undergraduates who enrolled, 40 Federal Work-Study jobs (averaging $2500).

Applying *Options:* early admission, deferred entrance. *Application deadline:* rolling (freshmen), rolling (transfers). *Notification:* continuous (freshmen), continuous (transfers).

Admissions Contact Dr. Joe Burke, Director of Admissions, Northeast Alabama Community College, PO Box 159, Rainsville, AL 35986. *Phone:* 256-228-6001.

NORTHWEST-SHOALS COMMUNITY COLLEGE
Muscle Shoals, Alabama

- **State-supported** 2-year, founded 1963, part of State of Alabama Department of Postsecondary Education
- **Calendar** semesters
- **Degree** certificates, diplomas, and associate
- **Small-town** 205-acre campus
- **Coed,** 4,663 undergraduate students, 58% full-time, 64% women, 36% men

Undergraduates 2,698 full-time, 1,965 part-time. Students come from 8 states and territories, 5 other countries, 2% are from out of state, 14% African American, 0.3% Asian American or Pacific Islander, 0.5% Hispanic American, 1% Native American, 0.1% international, 2% live on campus.

Freshmen *Admission:* 2,658 admitted, 1,286 enrolled.

Faculty *Total:* 270, 28% full-time, 6% with terminal degrees. *Student/faculty ratio:* 23:1.

Majors Accounting; administrative assistant and secretarial science; agricultural teacher education; art; business administration and management; child development; clinical laboratory science/medical technology; computer and information sciences; computer engineering technology; computer programming; computer science; computer typography and composition equipment operation; criminal justice/law enforcement administration; criminal justice/police science; drafting and design technology; education; electrical, electronic and communications engineering technology; elementary education; fire science; forestry; general studies; industrial electronics technology; industrial mechanics and maintenance technology; information science/studies; liberal arts and sciences/liberal studies; medical laboratory technology; multi-/interdisciplinary studies related; music; nursing (licensed practical/vocational nurse training); nursing (registered nurse training); pharmacy; pre-engineering; secondary education; veterinary sciences; water quality and wastewater treatment management and recycling technology.

Academic Programs *Special study options:* academic remediation for entering students, accelerated degree program, adult/continuing education programs, advanced placement credit, cooperative education, honors programs, internships, part-time degree program, summer session for credit. *ROTC:* Army (b).

Library Larry W. McCoy Learning Resource Center and James Glasgow Library with 57,827 titles, 268 serial subscriptions, 1,428 audiovisual materials.

Computers on Campus 620 computers available on campus for general student use. A campuswide network can be accessed from off campus. Internet access, at least one staffed computer lab available.

Student Life *Housing Options:* coed. *Activities and Organizations:* choral group, Student Government Association, Science Club, Phi Theta Kappa, Baptist Campus Ministry, Northwest-Shoals Singers. *Campus security:* 24-hour emergency response devices and patrols. *Student services:* personal/psychological counseling.

Athletics Member NJCAA. *Intercollegiate sports:* baseball M(s), basketball M(s)/W(s), cheerleading M(s)/W(s), cross-country running M(s), golf M(s), softball W(s), tennis W(s), volleyball W(s). *Intramural sports:* basketball M/W, softball M/W, table tennis M/W, tennis M/W, volleyball M/W.

Standardized Tests *Required:* ACT, ACT ASSET, or ACT COMPASS (for placement).

Costs (2004–05) *Tuition:* state resident $2176 full-time, $68 per credit hour part-time; nonresident $4352 full-time, $136 per credit hour part-time. *Required fees:* $512 full-time, $16 per credit hour part-time. *Room and board:* room only: $1600. *Waivers:* senior citizens and employees or children of employees.

Financial Aid *Financial aid deadline:* 6/1.

Applying *Options:* common application. *Required:* high school transcript. *Application deadline:* rolling (freshmen), rolling (transfers). *Notification:* continuous (transfers).

Admissions Contact Dr. Karen Berryhill, Vice President of Student Development Services, Northwest-Shoals Community College, PO Box 2545, Muscle Shoals, AL 35662. *Phone:* 256-331-5261. *Toll-free phone:* 800-645-8967. *Fax:* 256-331-5366.

PRINCE INSTITUTE OF PROFESSIONAL STUDIES
Montgomery, Alabama

- **Independent** 2-year
- **Calendar** quarters
- **Degree** certificates and associate
- **Suburban** campus
- **Endowment** $6040
- **Coed, primarily women,** 94 undergraduate students, 60% full-time, 100% women

Undergraduates 56 full-time, 38 part-time. 1% are from out of state, 17% African American.

Freshmen *Admission:* 9 applied, 9 admitted, 4 enrolled.

Faculty *Total:* 7, 71% full-time, 29% with terminal degrees. *Student/faculty ratio:* 15:1.

Majors Court reporting.

Student Life *Housing:* college housing not available. *Student services:* personal/psychological counseling.

Costs (2004–05) *Tuition:* $5826 full-time, $1992 per term part-time. *Required fees:* $150 full-time, $50 per term part-time. *Payment plan:* installment.

Applying *Application fee:* $90. *Required:* high school transcript, interview. *Application deadline:* 10/1 (freshmen).

Admissions Contact Ms. Candace Reed, Director of Admissions, Prince Institute of Professional Studies, 7735 Atlanta Highway, Montgomery, AL 36117. *Phone:* 334-271-1670. *Toll-free phone:* 877-853-5569. *Fax:* 334-271-1671. *E-mail:* enterpips@aol.com.

REID STATE TECHNICAL COLLEGE
Evergreen, Alabama

- **State-supported** 2-year, founded 1966, part of Alabama College System
- **Calendar** semesters
- **Degree** certificates, diplomas, and associate
- **Rural** 26-acre campus
- **Coed,** 806 undergraduate students, 59% full-time, 61% women, 39% men

Undergraduates 477 full-time, 329 part-time. Students come from 2 states and territories, 1% are from out of state, 58% African American, 0.1% Asian American or Pacific Islander, 0.5% Hispanic American, 1% Native American.

Freshmen *Admission:* 176 applied, 176 admitted, 176 enrolled.

Faculty *Total:* 44, 55% full-time, 59% with terminal degrees. *Student/faculty ratio:* 16:1.

Majors Administrative assistant and secretarial science; electrical, electronic and communications engineering technology.

Academic Programs *Special study options:* academic remediation for entering students, adult/continuing education programs, double majors, independent study, internships, part-time degree program, services for LD students, summer session for credit.

Library an OPAC, a Web page.

Computers on Campus 70 computers available on campus for general student use. A campuswide network can be accessed from off campus. Internet access, at least one staffed computer lab available.

Student Life *Housing:* college housing not available. *Activities and Organizations:* student-run newspaper, Student Government Association. *Campus security:* 24-hour emergency response devices, day and evening security guard. *Student services:* personal/psychological counseling.

Standardized Tests *Required:* ACT ASSET, Ability-To-Benefit Admissions Test (for placement).

Costs (2003–04) *Tuition:* state resident $2448 full-time, $68 per credit hour part-time; nonresident $4896 full-time, $136 per credit hour part-time. *Required fees:* $360 full-time.

Financial Aid Of all full-time matriculated undergraduates who enrolled, 35 Federal Work-Study jobs (averaging $1500).

Applying *Options:* common application, early admission. *Required:* high school transcript. *Application deadline:* rolling (freshmen), rolling (transfers).

Admissions Contact Ms. Alesia Stuart, Public Relations/Marketing, Reid State Technical College, PO Box 588, Intersection of I-95 and Highway 83, Evergreen, AL 36401-0588. *Phone:* 251-578-1313 Ext. 108. *Fax:* 251-578-5355.

REMINGTON COLLEGE-MOBILE CAMPUS
Mobile, Alabama

- **Proprietary** primarily 2-year, part of Education America
- **Calendar** quarters
- **Degrees** diplomas, associate, and bachelor's

Remington College-Mobile Campus (continued)
■ **Suburban** 5-acre campus
■ **Coed,** 454 undergraduate students, 100% full-time, 39% women, 61% men

Undergraduates 454 full-time. Students come from 3 states and territories, 4% are from out of state, 45% African American, 0.9% Asian American or Pacific Islander, 0.7% Hispanic American, 1% Native American. *Retention:* 90% of 2002 full-time freshmen returned.
Freshmen *Admission:* 117 applied, 117 admitted.
Faculty *Total:* 41, 76% full-time, 10% with terminal degrees. *Student/faculty ratio:* 16:1.
Majors Computer and information sciences; computer engineering technology; computer systems networking and telecommunications; drafting and design technology; information science/studies; operations management; web/multimedia management and webmaster.
Academic Programs *Special study options:* adult/continuing education programs, cooperative education, services for LD students.
Library SCT plus 1 other.
Computers on Campus Internet access available.
Student Life *Housing:* college housing not available. *Activities and Organizations:* Association of Information Technology Professionals, Instrumentation Technology Association.
Standardized Tests *Required:* Wonderlic aptitude test (for admission).
Costs (2004–05) *Tuition:* $30,480 full-time, $318 per credit hour part-time. Full-time tuition and fees vary according to class time, course level, course load, degree level, location, program, reciprocity agreements, and student level. No tuition increase for student's term of enrollment. *Payment plan:* installment. *Waivers:* employees or children of employees.
Financial Aid Of all full-time matriculated undergraduates who enrolled, 500 applied for aid, 500 were judged to have need. 15 Federal Work-Study jobs (averaging $5500). *Average percent of need met:* 45%. *Average financial aid package:* $7043. *Average need-based loan:* $3000. *Average need-based gift aid:* $7043. *Average indebtedness upon graduation:* $14,000.
Applying *Application fee:* $50. *Required:* high school transcript, interview.
Admissions Contact Mr. Chris Jones, Director of Recruitment, Remington College-Mobile Campus, 828 Downtowner Loop West, Mobile, AL 36609. *Phone:* 251-343-8200 Ext. 208. *Toll-free phone:* 800-866-0850. *Fax:* 251-343-0577.

SHELTON STATE COMMUNITY COLLEGE
Tuscaloosa, Alabama

■ **State-supported** 2-year, founded 1979, part of Alabama College System
■ **Calendar** semesters
■ **Degree** certificates, diplomas, and associate
■ **Small-town** 30-acre campus with easy access to Birmingham
■ **Coed,** 5,931 undergraduate students

Undergraduates Students come from 13 states and territories, 2% are from out of state.
Freshmen *Admission:* 2,073 applied, 1,908 admitted.
Faculty *Total:* 278, 29% full-time, 7% with terminal degrees. *Student/faculty ratio:* 19:1.
Majors Administrative assistant and secretarial science; art teacher education; automobile/automotive mechanics technology; biology/biological sciences; business administration and management; business teacher education; chemistry; clinical/medical laboratory technology; computer science; cosmetology; data processing and data processing technology; drafting and design technology; education; electrical, electronic and communications engineering technology; elementary education; emergency medical technology (EMT paramedic); family and consumer sciences/human sciences; health information/medical records administration; heating, air conditioning, ventilation and refrigeration maintenance technology; kindergarten/preschool education; liberal arts and sciences/liberal studies; medical administrative assistant and medical secretary; medical/clinical assistant; music; music teacher education; nursing (licensed practical/vocational nurse training); nursing (registered nurse training); pharmacy; physical education teaching and coaching; respiratory care therapy; tourism and travel services management; welding technology.
Academic Programs *Special study options:* academic remediation for entering students, accelerated degree program, adult/continuing education programs, advanced placement credit, distance learning, honors programs, part-time degree program, services for LD students, summer session for credit. *ROTC:* Army (b), Air Force (b).
Library Brooks-Cork Library plus 1 other with 43,151 titles, 312 serial subscriptions, 3,446 audiovisual materials, an OPAC, a Web page.
Computers on Campus 150 computers available on campus for general student use. A campuswide network can be accessed from off campus. Internet access, online (class) registration, at least one staffed computer lab available.
Student Life *Housing:* college housing not available. *Activities and Organizations:* drama/theater group, student-run newspaper, choral group, PTK, Student Government Association, African American Cultural Association. *Campus security:* 24-hour emergency response devices and patrols.
Athletics Member NJCAA. *Intercollegiate sports:* baseball M(s), basketball M(s)/W(s), cheerleading M/W, soccer W(s), softball W(s). *Intramural sports:* fencing M/W.
Standardized Tests *Required:* ACT COMPASS (for placement).
Costs (2004–05) *Tuition:* state resident $2040 full-time, $68 per credit hour part-time; nonresident $4080 full-time, $136 per credit hour part-time. *Required fees:* $480 full-time, $16 per credit hour part-time. *Payment plan:* deferred payment. *Waivers:* senior citizens and employees or children of employees.
Financial Aid Of all full-time matriculated undergraduates who enrolled, 97 Federal Work-Study jobs.
Applying *Required:* high school transcript. *Application deadline:* rolling (freshmen), rolling (transfers).
Admissions Contact Ms. Loretta Jones, Assistant to the Dean of Students, Shelton State Community College, Shelton State Community College, 9500 Old Greensboro Road, Tuscaloosa, AL 35405. *Phone:* 205-391-2236.

SNEAD STATE COMMUNITY COLLEGE
Boaz, Alabama

■ **State-supported** 2-year, founded 1898, part of Alabama College System
■ **Calendar** semesters
■ **Degree** certificates and associate
■ **Small-town** 42-acre campus with easy access to Birmingham
■ **Endowment** $1.6 million
■ **Coed,** 1,787 undergraduate students, 63% full-time, 61% women, 39% men

Undergraduates 1,133 full-time, 654 part-time. Students come from 6 states and territories, 1% are from out of state, 2% African American, 0.6% Asian American or Pacific Islander, 2% Hispanic American, 1% Native American, 8% transferred in, 2% live on campus.
Freshmen *Admission:* 499 enrolled.
Faculty *Total:* 90, 32% full-time. *Student/faculty ratio:* 28:1.
Majors Business administration and management; child care and support services management; computer and information sciences; data processing and data processing technology; engineering technology; general studies; liberal arts and sciences/liberal studies; multi-/interdisciplinary studies related; veterinary/animal health technology.
Academic Programs *Special study options:* academic remediation for entering students, accelerated degree program, adult/continuing education programs, advanced placement credit, distance learning, independent study, internships, part-time degree program, services for LD students, student-designed majors, summer session for credit.
Library McCain Learning Resource Center with 40,690 titles, 223 serial subscriptions, 1,699 audiovisual materials, an OPAC, a Web page.
Computers on Campus 250 computers available on campus for general student use. A campuswide network can be accessed from off campus. Internet access, online (class) registration, at least one staffed computer lab available.
Student Life *Housing Options:* coed. Campus housing is university owned. *Activities and Organizations:* drama/theater group, student-run newspaper, choral group, Phi Theta Kappa, Snead Agricultural Organization, North American Veterinary Technician Association, Ambassadors, Baptist Campus Ministry. *Campus security:* 24-hour patrols, student patrols. *Student services:* personal/psychological counseling.
Athletics Member NJCAA. *Intercollegiate sports:* baseball M(s), basketball M(s)/W(s), softball W(s), tennis W(s). *Intramural sports:* basketball M/W, softball M/W, volleyball M/W.
Standardized Tests *Required for some:* SAT I or ACT (for placement), ACT ASSET, ACT COMPASS.
Costs (2003–04) *Tuition:* state resident $2176 full-time, $68 per semester hour part-time; nonresident $4352 full-time, $136 per semester hour part-time. *Required fees:* $512 full-time, $16 per semester hour part-time. *Room and board:* $1724; room only: $600. *Waivers:* senior citizens and employees or children of employees.
Financial Aid Of all full-time matriculated undergraduates who enrolled, 40 Federal Work-Study jobs.
Applying *Options:* early admission, deferred entrance. *Required:* high school transcript. *Required for some:* interview. *Application deadlines:* 8/20 (freshmen), 8/20 (transfers). *Notification:* 8/20 (freshmen), 8/20 (transfers).
Admissions Contact Ms. Martha Buchanan, Director of Admissions and Records, Snead State Community College, PO Box 734, Boaz, AL 35957-0734. *Phone:* 256-593-5120 Ext. 207. *Fax:* 256-593-7180. *E-mail:* mbuchanan@snead.edu.

SOUTHERN UNION STATE COMMUNITY COLLEGE
Wadley, Alabama

Admissions Contact Mrs. Susan Salatto, Director of Student Development, Southern Union State Community College, PO Box 1000, Roberts Street, Wadley, AL 36276. *Phone:* 256-395-2211. *Fax:* 256-395-2215.

TRENHOLM STATE TECHNICAL COLLEGE
Montgomery, Alabama

- **State-supported** 2-year, founded 1962, part of Alabama Department of Post Secondary Education
- **Calendar** semesters
- **Degree** certificates, diplomas, and associate
- **Urban** 78-acre campus
- **Coed**, 1,615 undergraduate students, 54% full-time, 52% women, 48% men

Undergraduates 877 full-time, 738 part-time. Students come from 1 other state, 64% African American, 0.9% Asian American or Pacific Islander, 0.6% Hispanic American, 0.2% Native American.
Freshmen *Admission:* 767 applied, 465 admitted, 378 enrolled.
Faculty *Total:* 127, 54% full-time. *Student/faculty ratio:* 14:1.
Majors Accounting technology and bookkeeping; administrative assistant and secretarial science; automobile/automotive mechanics technology; automotive engineering technology; carpentry; child care and support services management; clothing/textiles; computer and information sciences; construction engineering technology; cosmetology; culinary arts; dental assisting; dental laboratory technology; drafting and design technology; electrical, electronic and communications engineering technology; electrician; emergency medical technology (EMT paramedic); graphic and printing equipment operation/production; graphic communications related; heating, air conditioning, ventilation and refrigeration maintenance technology; heavy equipment maintenance technology; industrial electronics technology; industrial mechanics and maintenance technology; information science/studies; instrumentation technology; machine tool technology; medical/clinical assistant; pipefitting and sprinkler fitting; tool and die technology; welding technology.
Academic Programs *Special study options:* academic remediation for entering students, adult/continuing education programs, advanced placement credit, cooperative education, internships, part-time degree program, services for LD students, summer session for credit.
Library Main Library plus 1 other with 2,945 titles, 80 serial subscriptions, 206 audiovisual materials, an OPAC, a Web page.
Computers on Campus 443 computers available on campus for general student use. A campuswide network can be accessed. Internet access, at least one staffed computer lab available.
Student Life *Housing:* college housing not available. *Campus security:* 24-hour emergency response devices and patrols.
Standardized Tests *Required for some:* ACT COMPASS. *Recommended:* ACT (for placement).
Costs (2004–05) *Tuition:* state resident $3060 full-time, $68 per credit hour part-time; nonresident $6120 full-time, $136 per credit hour part-time. *Required fees:* $720 full-time, $16 per credit hour part-time. *Waivers:* employees or children of employees.
Applying *Options:* early admission. *Required:* high school transcript. *Application deadline:* rolling (freshmen), rolling (transfers).
Admissions Contact Ms. Tennie McBryde, Registrar, Trenholm State Technical College, 1225 Air Base Boulevard, Montgomery, AL 36108. *Phone:* 334-420-4306. *Fax:* 334-420-4201. *E-mail:* tmcbryde@trenholmtech.cc.al.us.

VIRGINIA COLLEGE AT HUNTSVILLE
Huntsville, Alabama

Admissions Contact Ms. Pat Foster, Director of Admissions, Virginia College at Huntsville, 2800-A Bob Wallace Avenue, Huntsville, AL 35805. *Phone:* 205-533-7387.

VIRGINIA COLLEGE-TECHNICAL
Pelham, Alabama

Admissions Contact 2790 Pelham Parkway, Pelham, AL 35124. *Toll-free phone:* 877-5-VCTECH.

WALLACE STATE COMMUNITY COLLEGE
Hanceville, Alabama

- **State-supported** 2-year, founded 1966
- **Calendar** semesters
- **Degree** diplomas and associate
- **Rural** 216-acre campus with easy access to Birmingham
- **Coed**

Faculty *Student/faculty ratio:* 30:1.
Athletics Member NJCAA.
Standardized Tests *Required for some:* ACT (for placement), nursing exam. *Recommended:* ACT (for placement).
Costs (2003–04) *Tuition:* state resident $2040 full-time; nonresident $4080 full-time. *Required fees:* $480 full-time. *Room and board:* room only: $1450.
Financial Aid Of all full-time matriculated undergraduates who enrolled, 70 Federal Work-Study jobs. *Financial aid deadline:* 5/1.
Applying *Options:* early admission, deferred entrance. *Required:* high school transcript.
Admissions Contact Ms. Linda Sperling, Director of Admissions, Wallace State Community College, PO Box 2000, Hanceville, AL 35077-2000. *Phone:* 256-352-8278. *Fax:* 256-352-8228.

ALASKA

CHARTER COLLEGE
Anchorage, Alaska

Admissions Contact Ms. Lily Sirianni, Vice President, Charter College, 2221 East Northern Lights Boulevard, Suite 120, Anchorage, AK 99508-4157. *Phone:* 907-277-1000. *Toll-free phone:* 800-279-1008. *Fax:* 907-274-3342. *E-mail:* contact@chartercollege.org.

ILISAGVIK COLLEGE
Barrow, Alaska

Admissions Contact Dr. Edna Ahgeak MacLean, President, Ilisagvik College, UIC/Narl, Barrow, AK 99723. *Phone:* 907-852-1820. *Toll-free phone:* 800-478-7337.

UNIVERSITY OF ALASKA ANCHORAGE, KENAI PENINSULA COLLEGE
Soldotna, Alaska

- **State-supported** 2-year, founded 1964, part of University of Alaska System
- **Calendar** semesters
- **Degree** certificates and associate
- **Rural** 360-acre campus
- **Endowment** $950,000
- **Coed**, 1,923 undergraduate students

Freshmen *Admission:* 91 applied, 91 admitted.
Faculty *Total:* 150, 20% full-time. *Student/faculty ratio:* 15:1.
Majors Administrative assistant and secretarial science; business administration and management; electrical, electronic and communications engineering technology; instrumentation technology; liberal arts and sciences/liberal studies; machine tool technology; petroleum technology.
Academic Programs *Special study options:* academic remediation for entering students, adult/continuing education programs, advanced placement credit, English as a second language, part-time degree program, services for LD students.
Library Kenai Peninsula College Library with 25,000 titles, 95 serial subscriptions.
Computers on Campus 45 computers available on campus for general student use. A campuswide network can be accessed. At least one staffed computer lab available.
Student Life *Housing:* college housing not available. *Activities and Organizations:* drama/theater group, student-run newspaper. *Campus security:* 24-hour emergency response devices. *Student services:* personal/psychological counseling.
Standardized Tests *Required:* ACT ASSET (for placement).
Costs (2004–05) *Tuition:* state resident $2970 full-time, $99 per credit hour part-time; nonresident $10,290 full-time, $343 per credit hour part-time. Part-

University of Alaska Anchorage, Kenai Peninsula College (continued)
time tuition and fees vary according to course level and course load. *Required fees:* $44 full-time, $4 per credit hour part-time. *Payment plans:* tuition prepayment, installment, deferred payment. *Waivers:* employees or children of employees.

Financial Aid Of all full-time matriculated undergraduates who enrolled, 50 Federal Work-Study jobs (averaging $3000). 50 state and other part-time jobs (averaging $3000).

Applying *Options:* common application. *Application fee:* $40. *Required:* high school transcript. *Required for some:* interview. *Application deadline:* rolling (freshmen), rolling (transfers).

Admissions Contact Ms. Shelly Love, Admission and Registration Coordinator, University of Alaska Anchorage, Kenai Peninsula College, 34820 College Drive, Soldotna, AK 99669-9798. *Phone:* 907-262-0311.

UNIVERSITY OF ALASKA ANCHORAGE, KODIAK COLLEGE
Kodiak, Alaska

- **State-supported** 2-year, founded 1968, part of University of Alaska System
- **Calendar** semesters
- **Degree** certificates and associate
- **Rural** 68-acre campus
- **Coed**

Faculty *Student/faculty ratio:* 19:1.
Standardized Tests *Required:* ACT ASSET (for placement).
Costs (2003–04) *Tuition:* state resident $2340 full-time, $78 per credit part-time; nonresident $7740 full-time, $269 per credit part-time. *Required fees:* $10 full-time, $5 per term part-time.
Applying *Application fee:* $35. *Recommended:* high school transcript.
Admissions Contact Ms. Karen Hamer, Registrar, University of Alaska Anchorage, Kodiak College, 117 Benny Benson Drive, Kodiak, AK 99615. *Phone:* 907-486-1235. *Fax:* 907-486-1264.

UNIVERSITY OF ALASKA ANCHORAGE, MATANUSKA-SUSITNA COLLEGE
Palmer, Alaska

- **State-supported** 2-year, founded 1958, part of University of Alaska System
- **Calendar** semesters
- **Degree** certificates and associate
- **Small-town** 950-acre campus with easy access to Anchorage
- **Coed**, 1,431 undergraduate students, 27% full-time, 66% women, 34% men

Undergraduates 390 full-time, 1,041 part-time. Students come from 10 other countries, 1% African American, 1% Asian American or Pacific Islander, 2% Hispanic American, 8% Native American, 0.2% international. *Retention:* 67% of 2002 full-time freshmen returned.
Freshmen *Admission:* 126 applied, 109 admitted, 90 enrolled.
Faculty *Total:* 108, 19% full-time, 19% with terminal degrees. *Student/faculty ratio:* 16:1.
Majors Accounting; administrative assistant and secretarial science; business administration and management; electrical, electronic and communications engineering technology; fire science; heating, air conditioning, ventilation and refrigeration maintenance technology; human services; liberal arts and sciences/liberal studies.
Academic Programs *Special study options:* academic remediation for entering students, adult/continuing education programs, advanced placement credit, cooperative education, distance learning, double majors, independent study, internships, off-campus study, part-time degree program, summer session for credit.
Library Al Okeson Library with 50,000 titles, 280 serial subscriptions, 1,400 audiovisual materials, an OPAC, a Web page.
Computers on Campus 207 computers available on campus for general student use. A campuswide network can be accessed from off campus. Internet access, at least one staffed computer lab available.
Student Life *Housing:* college housing not available. *Activities and Organizations:* student-run newspaper, choral group, student government, Math Club. *Campus security:* 24-hour patrols.
Standardized Tests *Recommended:* SAT I or ACT (for placement), ACT COMPASS.
Costs (2004–05) *Tuition:* area resident $2376 full-time, $99 per credit part-time; nonresident $7920 full-time, $330 per credit part-time. Full-time tuition and fees vary according to course level and course load. Part-time tuition and fees vary according to course level and course load. *Required fees:* $200

full-time, $5 per credit part-time, $40 per term part-time. *Payment plan:* installment. *Waivers:* children of alumni, senior citizens, and employees or children of employees.
Financial Aid Of all full-time matriculated undergraduates who enrolled, 8 Federal Work-Study jobs (averaging $3000).
Applying *Application fee:* $35. *Required:* high school transcript. *Recommended:* minimum 2.0 GPA. *Application deadline:* rolling (freshmen), rolling (transfers).
Admissions Contact Ms. Sandra Gravley, Student Services Manager, University of Alaska Anchorage, Matanuska-Susitna College, PO Box 2889, Palmer, AK 99645-2889. *Phone:* 907-745-9712. *Fax:* 907-745-9747. *E-mail:* info@matsu.alaska.edu.

UNIVERSITY OF ALASKA, PRINCE WILLIAM SOUND COMMUNITY COLLEGE
Valdez, Alaska

Admissions Contact Mr. Nathan J. Platt, Director of Student Services, University of Alaska, Prince William Sound Community College, PO Box 97, Valdez, AK 99686-0097. *Phone:* 907-834-1631. *Toll-free phone:* 800-478-8800 Ext. 1600. *Fax:* 907-834-1627. *E-mail:* vnnjp@uaa.alaska.edu.

UNIVERSITY OF ALASKA SOUTHEAST, KETCHIKAN CAMPUS
Ketchikan, Alaska

- **State and locally supported** 2-year, founded 1954, part of University of Alaska System
- **Calendar** semesters
- **Degree** associate
- **Small-town** 51-acre campus
- **Endowment** $2.6 million
- **Coed**, 692 undergraduate students

Undergraduates Students come from 5 states and territories, 2 other countries.
Faculty *Total:* 12, 100% full-time. *Student/faculty ratio:* 15:1.
Majors Administrative assistant and secretarial science; business administration and management; liberal arts and sciences/liberal studies; tourism and travel services management.
Academic Programs *Special study options:* academic remediation for entering students, adult/continuing education programs, distance learning, English as a second language, independent study, internships, off-campus study, part-time degree program, services for LD students, student-designed majors.
Library Ketchikan Campus Library with 54,000 titles, 175 serial subscriptions, an OPAC.
Computers on Campus 40 computers available on campus for general student use. Internet access, at least one staffed computer lab available.
Student Life *Activities and Organizations:* student council. *Campus security:* 24-hour emergency response devices. *Student services:* personal/psychological counseling.
Standardized Tests *Required for some:* ACT ASSET. *Recommended:* SAT I or ACT (for placement).
Costs (2004–05) *Tuition:* state resident $2376 full-time. *Required fees:* $166 full-time. *Room and board:* $8370; room only: $5940. *Payment plan:* deferred payment. *Waivers:* senior citizens and employees or children of employees.
Applying *Options:* early admission. *Application fee:* $35. *Required:* high school transcript. *Required for some:* essay or personal statement. *Application deadline:* rolling (freshmen).
Admissions Contact Mrs. Gail Klein, Student Services Coordinator, University of Alaska Southeast, Ketchikan Campus, 2600 7th Avenue, Ketchikan, AK 99901-5798. *Phone:* 907-228-4508. *Fax:* 907-225-3624. *E-mail:* gail.klein@uas.alaska.edu.

UNIVERSITY OF ALASKA SOUTHEAST, SITKA CAMPUS
Sitka, Alaska

Admissions Contact Mr. Tim Schroeder, Coordinator of Admissions, University of Alaska Southeast, Sitka Campus, 1332 Seward Avenue, Sitka, AK 99835-9418. *Phone:* 907-747-7703. *Toll-free phone:* 800-478-6653. *Fax:* 907-747-7747. *E-mail:* tnkmn@acadl.alaska.edu.

ARIZONA

APOLLO COLLEGE-PHOENIX, INC.
Phoenix, Arizona

Admissions Contact Mr. Randy Utley, Campus Director, Apollo College-Phoenix, Inc., 2701 West Bethany Home Road, Phoenix, AZ 85051. *Phone:* 602-864-1571. *Toll-free phone:* 800-36-TRAIN.

APOLLO COLLEGE-TRI-CITY, INC.
Mesa, Arizona

Admissions Contact Mr. James Norris Miller, Campus Director, Apollo College-Tri-City, Inc., 630 West Southern Avenue, Mesa, AZ 85210-5004. *Phone:* 480-831-6585. *Toll-free phone:* 800-36-TRAIN.

APOLLO COLLEGE-TUCSON, INC.
Tucson, Arizona

Admissions Contact Ms. Jenell McKinney, Campus Director, Apollo College-Tucson, Inc., 3870 North Oracle Road, Tucson, AZ 85705-3227. *Phone:* 520-888-5885. *Toll-free phone:* 800-36-TRAIN.

APOLLO COLLEGE-WESTSIDE, INC.
Phoenix, Arizona

Admissions Contact Ms. Cindy Nestor, Vice President, Apollo College-Westside, Inc., 2701 West Bethany Home Road, Phoenix, AZ 85017. *Phone:* 602-433-1222 Ext. 251. *Toll-free phone:* 800-36-TRAIN.

ARIZONA AUTOMOTIVE INSTITUTE
Glendale, Arizona

- **Proprietary** 2-year
- **Degree** diplomas and associate
- 600 undergraduate students

Costs (2003–04) *Tuition:* $13,995 full-time. *Required fees:* $100 full-time.
Applying *Required:* high school transcript.
Admissions Contact Mr. Mark LaCara, Director of Admissions, Arizona Automotive Institute, 6829 North 46th Avenue, Glendale, AZ 85301-3597. *Phone:* 623-934-7273 Ext. 211.

ARIZONA COLLEGE OF ALLIED HEALTH
Glendale, Arizona

Admissions Contact 4425 West Olive Avenue, Suite 300, Glendale, AZ 85302-3843.

ARIZONA WESTERN COLLEGE
Yuma, Arizona

- **State and locally supported** 2-year, founded 1962, part of Arizona State Community College System
- **Calendar** semesters
- **Degree** certificates and associate
- **Rural** 640-acre campus
- **Coed,** 6,454 undergraduate students, 26% full-time, 60% women, 40% men

Undergraduates 1,664 full-time, 4,790 part-time. Students come from 17 states and territories, 12% are from out of state, 3% African American, 1% Asian American or Pacific Islander, 65% Hispanic American, 2% Native American, 0.2% international, 7% live on campus. *Retention:* 50% of 2002 full-time freshmen returned.
Freshmen *Admission:* 843 enrolled.
Faculty *Total:* 417, 25% full-time, 6% with terminal degrees. *Student/faculty ratio:* 15:1.
Majors Administrative assistant and secretarial science; agricultural business and management; agriculture; art; automobile/automotive mechanics technology; biological and physical sciences; biology/biological sciences; broadcast journalism; business administration and management; chemistry; computer science; criminal justice/law enforcement administration; criminal justice/police science; developmental and child psychology; drafting and design technology; dramatic/theatre arts; education; electrical, electronic and communications engi-neering technology; engineering technology; English; environmental studies; family and consumer economics related; finance; fire science; geology/earth science; health science; heating, air conditioning, ventilation and refrigeration maintenance technology; hospitality administration; human services; information science/studies; liberal arts and sciences/liberal studies; mathematics; music; nursing (licensed practical/vocational nurse training); nursing (registered nurse training); oceanography (chemical and physical); personal and culinary services related; physical education teaching and coaching; physics; pre-engineering; social sciences; Spanish; welding technology.
Academic Programs *Special study options:* academic remediation for entering students, adult/continuing education programs, advanced placement credit, cooperative education, distance learning, English as a second language, honors programs, independent study, part-time degree program, summer session for credit.
Library Arizona Western College Library with 698 serial subscriptions, 10,800 audiovisual materials, an OPAC, a Web page.
Computers on Campus 120 computers available on campus for general student use. A campuswide network can be accessed from off campus. Internet access, at least one staffed computer lab available.
Student Life *Housing Options:* coed. Campus housing is university owned. *Activities and Organizations:* drama/theater group, student-run newspaper, radio and television station, choral group, Associated Students Governing Board, MECHA, Umoja, Honors Club, UVU. *Campus security:* 24-hour emergency response devices and patrols, student patrols, late-night transport/escort service. *Student services:* health clinic, personal/psychological counseling.
Athletics Member NJCAA. *Intercollegiate sports:* baseball M(s), basketball M(s), football M(s), soccer M(s), softball W(s), volleyball W(s). *Intramural sports:* badminton M/W, basketball M/W, football M, soccer M, softball M/W, swimming M/W, table tennis M/W, volleyball M/W.
Costs (2004–05) *Tuition:* state resident $1110 full-time; nonresident $5670 full-time.
Financial Aid Of all full-time matriculated undergraduates who enrolled, 350 Federal Work-Study jobs (averaging $1500). 100 state and other part-time jobs (averaging $1800).
Applying *Options:* common application, early admission, deferred entrance. *Required for some:* minimum 3.0 GPA. *Application deadline:* rolling (freshmen), rolling (transfers).
Admissions Contact Mr. Bryan Doak, Registrar, Arizona Western College, PO Box 929, Yuma, AZ 85366. *Phone:* 928-317-7617. *Toll-free phone:* 888-293-0392. *Fax:* 928-344-7730. *E-mail:* bryan.doak@azwestern.edu.

THE BRYMAN SCHOOL
Phoenix, Arizona

- **Proprietary** 2-year, founded 1964
- **Calendar** continuous
- **Degree** diplomas and associate
- **Urban** campus
- **Coed, primarily women**

Faculty *Student/faculty ratio:* 18:1.
Student Life *Campus security:* late-night transport/escort service.
Standardized Tests *Required:* The Health Occupations Basic Entrance Test (for admission).
Applying *Required:* high school transcript, interview.
Admissions Contact Ms. Vicki Maurer, Admission Manager, The Bryman School, 4343 North 16th Street, Phoenix, AZ 85016-5338. *Phone:* 602-274-4300. *Toll-free phone:* 800-729-4819. *Fax:* 602-248-9087.

CENTRAL ARIZONA COLLEGE
Coolidge, Arizona

- **County-supported** 2-year, founded 1961
- **Calendar** semesters
- **Degree** certificates and associate
- **Rural** 709-acre campus with easy access to Phoenix
- **Coed,** 5,745 undergraduate students, 29% full-time, 57% women, 43% men

Undergraduates 1,646 full-time, 4,099 part-time. Students come from 6 other countries, 4% African American, 0.8% Asian American or Pacific Islander, 29% Hispanic American, 6% Native American, 0.4% international.
Freshmen *Admission:* 5,745 enrolled.
Faculty *Total:* 95. *Student/faculty ratio:* 15:1.
Majors Accounting; administrative assistant and secretarial science; agriculture; automobile/automotive mechanics technology; business administration and management; child development; civil engineering technology; computer and information sciences; computer science; corrections; criminal justice/law enforcement administration; dietetics; emergency medical technology (EMT para-

Central Arizona College (continued)

medic); engineering; health aide; hotel/motel administration; industrial technology; kindergarten/preschool education; legal administrative assistant/secretary; liberal arts and sciences/liberal studies; marketing/marketing management; materials science; medical administrative assistant and medical secretary; medical transcription; nursing (licensed practical/vocational nurse training); nursing (registered nurse training).

Academic Programs *Special study options:* academic remediation for entering students, adult/continuing education programs, distance learning, honors programs, independent study, part-time degree program, services for LD students, student-designed majors, summer session for credit.

Library Learning Resource Center with 99,480 titles, 494 serial subscriptions.

Computers on Campus Internet access, at least one staffed computer lab available.

Student Life *Activities and Organizations:* drama/theater group, student-run newspaper, choral group. *Campus security:* 24-hour emergency response devices and patrols. *Student services:* personal/psychological counseling.

Athletics Member NJCAA. *Intercollegiate sports:* baseball M(s), basketball M(s)/W(s), cross-country running M(s)/W(s), equestrian sports M(s)/W(s), golf M(s), softball W(s), track and field M(s)/W(s). *Intramural sports:* rock climbing M/W.

Standardized Tests *Required:* ACT ASSET or ACT COMPASS (for placement).

Costs (2004–05) *Tuition:* state resident $1320 full-time, $44 per credit part-time; nonresident $5328 full-time, $88 per credit part-time. *Required fees:* $16 full-time, $800 per semester hour part-time. *Room and board:* $3840.

Financial Aid Of all full-time matriculated undergraduates who enrolled, 68 Federal Work-Study jobs (averaging $1310).

Applying *Options:* common application, early admission, deferred entrance. *Application deadline:* rolling (freshmen), rolling (transfers). *Notification:* continuous (freshmen), continuous (transfers).

Admissions Contact Doris Helmich, Interim Dean of Enrollment and Student Services, Central Arizona College, 8470 North Overfield Road, Coolidge, AZ 85228. *Phone:* 520-426-4406. *Toll-free phone:* 800-237-9814. *Fax:* 520-426-4271. *E-mail:* leonor_verduzco@centralaz.edu.

CHANDLER-GILBERT COMMUNITY COLLEGE
Chandler, Arizona

- **State and locally supported** 2-year, founded 1985, part of Maricopa County Community College District System
- **Calendar** semesters
- **Degree** certificates, diplomas, and associate
- **Rural** 80-acre campus with easy access to Phoenix
- **Coed**

Faculty *Student/faculty ratio:* 20:1.

Student Life *Campus security:* 24-hour emergency response devices and patrols, late-night transport/escort service.

Standardized Tests *Required for some:* ACT ASSET.

Costs (2003–04) *Tuition:* area resident $1380 full-time, $46 per credit hour part-time; state resident $6210 full-time, $207 per credit hour part-time; nonresident $6330 full-time, $211 per credit hour part-time. *Required fees:* $10 full-time, $5 per term part-time.

Applying *Options:* common application, electronic application, early admission.

Admissions Contact Ms. Irene Pearl, Supervisor of Admissions and Records, Chandler-Gilbert Community College, 2626 East Pecos Road, Chandler, AZ 85225-2479. *Phone:* 480-732-7307.

CHAPARRAL COLLEGE
Tucson, Arizona

- **Proprietary** primarily 2-year, founded 1972
- **Calendar** 5 five-week modules
- **Degrees** certificates, diplomas, associate, and bachelor's (bachelor's degree in business administration only)
- **Suburban** campus with easy access to Phoenix
- **Coed,** 400 undergraduate students

Undergraduates Students come from 1 other state, 3 other countries.

Faculty *Total:* 38, 37% full-time, 58% with terminal degrees. *Student/faculty ratio:* 20:1.

Majors Accounting; administrative assistant and secretarial science; business administration and management; computer systems networking and telecommunications; criminal justice/safety.

Academic Programs *Special study options:* academic remediation for entering students, internships, summer session for credit.

Library 6,000 titles, 65 serial subscriptions, 500 audiovisual materials, a Web page.

Computers on Campus 150 computers available on campus for general student use. A campuswide network can be accessed. Internet access, at least one staffed computer lab available.

Student Life *Housing:* college housing not available. *Activities and Organizations:* student-run newspaper. *Campus security:* 24-hour emergency response devices. *Student services:* personal/psychological counseling.

Standardized Tests *Required:* CPAt (for admission).

Applying *Options:* common application. *Application fee:* $35. *Required:* high school transcript, interview. *Required for some:* letters of recommendation, entrance test. *Application deadline:* rolling (freshmen), rolling (transfers).

Admissions Contact Chaparral College, 4585 East Speedway No. 204, Tucson, AZ 85712. *Phone:* 520-327-6866. *Fax:* 520-325-0108. *E-mail:* admissions@chap-col.edu.

COCHISE COLLEGE
Douglas, Arizona

- **State and locally supported** 2-year, founded 1962, part of Cochise College
- **Calendar** semesters
- **Degree** certificates and associate
- **Rural** 500-acre campus
- **Coed**

Student Life *Campus security:* 24-hour emergency response devices and patrols, controlled dormitory access.

Athletics Member NJCAA.

Standardized Tests *Recommended:* SAT I or ACT (for placement).

Costs (2003–04) *Tuition:* state resident $1140 full-time. *Required fees:* $60 full-time. *Room and board:* $3452.

Financial Aid Of all full-time matriculated undergraduates who enrolled, 137 Federal Work-Study jobs (averaging $1070).

Applying *Options:* early admission, deferred entrance. *Recommended:* high school transcript.

Admissions Contact Ms. Pati Mapp, Admissions Counselor, Cochise College, 4190 West Highway 80, Douglas, AZ 85607-9724. *Phone:* 520-364-0336. *Toll-free phone:* 800-966-7946. *Fax:* 520-364-0236. *E-mail:* mappp@cochise.cc.az.us.

COCHISE COLLEGE
Sierra Vista, Arizona

- **State and locally supported** 2-year, founded 1977, part of Cochise College
- **Calendar** semesters
- **Degree** certificates and associate
- **Small-town** 200-acre campus with easy access to Tucson
- **Coed**

Faculty *Student/faculty ratio:* 14:1.

Student Life *Campus security:* 24-hour emergency response devices and patrols.

Athletics Member NJCAA.

Standardized Tests *Required for some:* ACCUPLACER. *Recommended:* SAT I (for admission), ACT (for admission), SAT I or ACT (for admission), SAT I and SAT II or ACT (for admission), SAT II: Subject Tests (for admission), SAT II: Writing Test (for admission), SAT I or ACT (for placement).

Costs (2003–04) *Tuition:* state resident $912 full-time, $38 per credit part-time; nonresident $5184 full-time, $48 per credit part-time. Part-time tuition and fees vary according to course load. *Required fees:* $60 full-time. *Room and board:* $3502; room only: $1310. Room and board charges vary according to board plan.

Applying *Options:* common application, electronic application, early admission, deferred entrance. *Recommended:* high school transcript.

Admissions Contact Ms. Debbie Quick, Admissions Officer, Cochise College, 901 North Columbo, Sierra Vista, AZ 85635-2317. *Phone:* 520-515-5412. *Toll-free phone:* 800-593-9567. *Fax:* 520-515-4006. *E-mail:* quickd@cochise.cc.az.us.

COCONINO COMMUNITY COLLEGE
Flagstaff, Arizona

Admissions Contact Mr. Steve Miller, Director of Admissions/Registrar, Coconino Community College, 3000 North Fourth Street, Flagstaff, AZ 86003. *Phone:* 928-527-1222. *Toll-free phone:* 800-350-7122. *Fax:* 520-526-1821. *E-mail:* smiller@coco.cc.az.us.

COLLEGEAMERICA-FLAGSTAFF
Flagstaff, Arizona

Admissions Contact Mr. Pescal Berlioux, Executive Director, CollegeAmerica-Flagstaff, 5200 East Cortland Boulevard, Suite A-19, Flagstaff, AZ 86004. *Phone:* 800-977-5455.

DINE COLLEGE
Tsaile, Arizona

- **Federally supported** 2-year, founded 1968
- **Calendar** semesters
- **Degree** certificates and associate
- **Rural** 1200-acre campus
- **Endowment** $3.5 million
- **Coed**

Student Life *Campus security:* 24-hour emergency response devices and patrols, student patrols, late-night transport/escort service.
Athletics Member NSCAA, NJCAA.
Standardized Tests *Recommended:* SAT I and SAT II or ACT (for placement), SAT II: Writing Test (for placement).
Costs (2003–04) *Tuition:* $25 per credit hour part-time; state resident $600 full-time, $25 per credit hour part-time; nonresident $600 full-time. *Required fees:* $50 full-time. *Room and board:* $3040; room only: $1120.
Financial Aid Of all full-time matriculated undergraduates who enrolled, 100 Federal Work-Study jobs (averaging $650).
Applying *Options:* common application, early admission. *Required:* high school transcript, certificate of Indian Blood form for Native American Students. *Recommended:* minimum 2.0 GPA.
Admissions Contact Mrs. Louise Litzin, Registrar, Dine College, PO Box 67, Tsaile, AZ 86556. *Phone:* 928-724-6633. *Fax:* 928-724-3349. *E-mail:* louise@dinecollege.edu.

EASTERN ARIZONA COLLEGE
Thatcher, Arizona

- **State and locally supported** 2-year, founded 1888, part of Arizona State Community College System
- **Calendar** semesters
- **Degree** certificates and associate
- **Small-town** campus
- **Endowment** $612,810
- **Coed**, 3,925 undergraduate students, 41% full-time, 55% women, 45% men

Undergraduates 1,618 full-time, 2,307 part-time. Students come from 29 states and territories, 5% are from out of state, 3% African American, 0.9% Asian American or Pacific Islander, 20% Hispanic American, 5% Native American, 0.5% international, 5% live on campus. *Retention:* 71% of 2002 full-time freshmen returned.
Freshmen *Admission:* 546 enrolled.
Faculty *Total:* 167, 41% full-time. *Student/faculty ratio:* 24:1.
Majors Agribusiness; agriculture; anthropology; art; art teacher education; automobile/automotive mechanics technology; biology/biological sciences; business administration and management; business, management, and marketing related; business operations support and secretarial services related; business teacher education; chemistry; child care provision; civil engineering technology; commercial and advertising art; corrections; criminal justice/law enforcement administration; criminal justice/police science; data entry/microcomputer applications; drafting and design technology; dramatic/theatre arts; elementary education; emergency medical technology (EMT paramedic); English; entrepreneurship; foreign languages and literatures; forestry; geology/earth science; health and physical education; health/medical preparatory programs related; history; information science/studies; liberal arts and sciences/liberal studies; machine shop technology; mathematics; mining technology; music; nursing (registered nurse training); physics; political science and government; pre-law studies; pre-medical studies; pre-pharmacy studies; psychology; secondary education; sociology; technology/industrial arts teacher education; welding technology; wildlife biology.
Academic Programs *Special study options:* academic remediation for entering students, adult/continuing education programs, advanced placement credit, cooperative education, double majors, independent study, part-time degree program, services for LD students, study abroad, summer session for credit.
Library Alumni Library plus 1 other with an OPAC, a Web page.
Computers on Campus 458 computers available on campus for general student use. A campuswide network can be accessed from student residence rooms and from off campus. Internet access, online (class) registration, at least one staffed computer lab available.

Student Life *Housing Options:* men-only, women-only. Campus housing is university owned. *Activities and Organizations:* drama/theater group, choral group, marching band, Latter-Day Saints Student Association, Criminal Justice Student Association, Multicultural Council, Phi Theta Kappa, Mark Allen Dorm Club. *Campus security:* late-night transport/escort service, controlled dormitory access, 20-hour patrols by trained security personnel. *Student services:* personal/psychological counseling.
Athletics Member NJCAA. *Intercollegiate sports:* baseball M(s), basketball M(s)/W(s), football M(s), softball W(s), volleyball W(s). *Intramural sports:* basketball M/W, cheerleading W, racquetball M/W, swimming M/W, table tennis M/W, tennis M/W, volleyball M/W.
Standardized Tests *Recommended:* SAT I or ACT (for placement).
Costs (2004–05) *Tuition:* state resident $1008 full-time, $42 per credit part-time; nonresident $5988 full-time, $87 per credit part-time. Full-time tuition and fees vary according to course load. Part-time tuition and fees vary according to course load. *Room and board:* $3800; room only: $1895. Room and board charges vary according to board plan and housing facility. *Payment plan:* deferred payment. *Waivers:* senior citizens and employees or children of employees.
Financial Aid Of all full-time matriculated undergraduates who enrolled, 287 Federal Work-Study jobs (averaging $1346). 453 state and other part-time jobs (averaging $1257).
Applying *Options:* electronic application, early admission, deferred entrance. *Recommended:* high school transcript. *Application deadline:* rolling (freshmen), rolling (transfers). *Notification:* continuous (freshmen).
Admissions Contact Mr. Jeff Savage, Coordinator of Recruitment, Eastern Arizona College, 615 North Stadium Avenue, Thatcher, AZ 85552-0769. *Phone:* 928-428-8247. *Toll-free phone:* 800-678-3808. *Fax:* 928-428-8462. *E-mail:* admissions@eac.edu.

ESTRELLA MOUNTAIN COMMUNITY COLLEGE
Avondale, Arizona

- **State and locally supported** 2-year, part of Maricopa County Community College District System
- **Calendar** semesters
- **Degree** certificates and associate
- **Urban** campus with easy access to Phoenix
- **Coed**, 5,410 undergraduate students, 21% full-time, 62% women, 38% men

Undergraduates 1,140 full-time, 4,270 part-time. 6% African American, 3% Asian American or Pacific Islander, 31% Hispanic American, 2% Native American.
Freshmen *Admission:* 5,200 applied, 5,200 admitted, 366 enrolled.
Faculty *Total:* 267, 20% full-time. *Student/faculty ratio:* 20:1.
Majors General studies; liberal arts and sciences/liberal studies.
Costs (2004–05) *Tuition:* state resident $1320 full-time, $55 per credit hour part-time; nonresident $5040 full-time, $80 per credit hour part-time. *Required fees:* $10 full-time, $5 per term part-time.
Financial Aid Of all full-time matriculated undergraduates who enrolled, 50 Federal Work-Study jobs (averaging $3000).
Admissions Contact Dr. Ernesto Laura, Dean of Student Services, Estrella Mountain Community College, 3000 North Dysart Road, Avondale, AZ 85323-1000. *Phone:* 623-935-8808.

EVEREST COLLEGE
Phoenix, Arizona

- **Proprietary** 2-year, founded 1982
- **Calendar** 6 or 12 week terms
- **Degree** diplomas and associate
- **Urban** campus
- **Coed**, 590 undergraduate students, 73% full-time, 74% women, 26% men

Undergraduates 429 full-time, 161 part-time. Students come from 2 states and territories, 2 other countries, 2% are from out of state, 13% African American, 1% Asian American or Pacific Islander, 27% Hispanic American, 5% Native American, 0.7% international.
Freshmen *Admission:* 95 applied, 65 admitted, 29 enrolled.
Faculty *Total:* 30, 33% full-time, 20% with terminal degrees. *Student/faculty ratio:* 21:1.
Majors Accounting; administrative assistant and secretarial science; computer engineering technology; legal assistant/paralegal.
Academic Programs *Special study options:* adult/continuing education programs, distance learning, double majors, internships, summer session for credit.
Library Academy of Business College Library with 57 serial subscriptions, a Web page.

Everest College (continued)

Computers on Campus 50 computers available on campus for general student use. Internet access, at least one staffed computer lab available.

Student Life *Housing:* college housing not available. *Activities and Organizations:* Collegiate Secretaries International, Toastmasters. *Campus security:* 24-hour emergency response devices and patrols. *Student services:* personal/psychological counseling.

Standardized Tests *Required:* Wonderlic aptitude test, Nelson Denny Reading Test (for admission).

Costs (2003–04) *Tuition:* $220 per quarter hour part-time. *Required fees:* $25 per term part-time.

Applying *Options:* deferred entrance. *Application fee:* $25. *Required:* high school transcript, minimum 2.0 GPA, interview. *Required for some:* essay or personal statement. *Application deadline:* rolling (freshmen). *Notification:* continuous (freshmen).

Admissions Contact Mr. Jack Rose, Director of Admissions, Everest College, 2525 West Beryl Avenue, Phoenix, AZ 85021. *Phone:* 602-942-4141. *Fax:* 602-943-0960.

GATEWAY COMMUNITY COLLEGE
Phoenix, Arizona

- **State and locally supported** 2-year, founded 1968, part of Maricopa County Community College District System
- **Calendar** semesters
- **Degree** certificates and associate
- **Urban** 20-acre campus
- **Coed**

Faculty *Student/faculty ratio:* 25:1.

Student Life *Campus security:* 24-hour emergency response devices and patrols, student patrols, late-night transport/escort service.

Athletics Member NJCAA.

Standardized Tests *Required:* ACT ASSET or ACT COMPASS (for placement).

Costs (2003–04) *Tuition:* area resident $1530 full-time, $51 per credit part-time; state resident $5280 full-time, $176 per credit part-time; nonresident $176 per credit part-time. Part-time tuition and fees vary according to course load. *Required fees:* $1224 full-time. *Payment plans:* installment, deferred payment.

Applying *Options:* common application, electronic application, early admission, deferred entrance. *Required for some:* high school transcript.

Admissions Contact Ms. Cathy Gibson, Director of Admissions and Records, GateWay Community College, 108 North 40th Street, Phoenix, AZ 85034. *Phone:* 602-286-8052. *Fax:* 602-286-8200. *E-mail:* cathy.gibson@gwmail.maricopa.edu.

GLENDALE COMMUNITY COLLEGE
Glendale, Arizona

- **State and locally supported** 2-year, founded 1965, part of Maricopa County Community College District System
- **Calendar** semesters
- **Degree** certificates and associate
- **Suburban** 160-acre campus with easy access to Phoenix
- **Endowment** $191,151
- **Coed**, 20,692 undergraduate students, 29% full-time, 57% women, 43% men

Undergraduates 6,071 full-time, 14,621 part-time. Students come from 50 states and territories, 63 other countries, 2% are from out of state, 7% African American, 4% Asian American or Pacific Islander, 21% Hispanic American, 3% Native American, 0.8% international, 27% transferred in.

Freshmen *Admission:* 1,114 enrolled.

Faculty *Total:* 838, 31% full-time, 65% with terminal degrees. *Student/faculty ratio:* 24:1.

Majors Accounting technology and bookkeeping; administrative assistant and secretarial science; agribusiness; applied horticulture; architectural drafting and CAD/CADD; automobile/automotive mechanics technology; business administration and management; business/commerce; cinematography and film/video production; commercial and advertising art; computer systems networking and telecommunications; consumer merchandising/retailing management; criminal justice/law enforcement administration; criminal justice/police science; electrical, electronic and communications engineering technology; emergency medical technology (EMT paramedic); engineering technology; fire science; human services; industrial technology; kindergarten/preschool education; landscaping and groundskeeping; liberal arts and sciences/liberal studies; management information systems; nursing assistant/aide and patient care assistant; nursing (registered nurse training); public relations/image management; real estate.

Academic Programs *Special study options:* academic remediation for entering students, adult/continuing education programs, advanced placement credit, cooperative education, distance learning, double majors, English as a second language, freshman honors college, honors programs, internships, off-campus study, part-time degree program, services for LD students, summer session for credit. *ROTC:* Army (c), Air Force (c).

Library Library/Media Center plus 1 other with 79,006 titles, 406 serial subscriptions, 3,807 audiovisual materials, an OPAC, a Web page.

Computers on Campus 1500 computers available on campus for general student use. A campuswide network can be accessed from off campus. Internet access, online (class) registration, at least one staffed computer lab available.

Student Life *Housing:* college housing not available. *Activities and Organizations:* drama/theater group, student-run newspaper, choral group, marching band, LDS Student Association, Phi Theta Kappa International Honor Society, band, Glendale Association of Student Nurses, Inter-Varsity Christian Fellowship. *Campus security:* 24-hour patrols, student patrols, late-night transport/escort service. *Student services:* personal/psychological counseling, legal services.

Athletics Member NJCAA. *Intercollegiate sports:* baseball M(s), basketball M(s)/W(s), cross-country running M(s)/W(s), football M(s), golf M(s), soccer M(s)/W(s), softball W(s), tennis M(s)/W(s), track and field M(s)/W(s), volleyball W(s). *Intramural sports:* golf M, racquetball M/W, softball W, tennis M/W, volleyball W.

Standardized Tests *Required for some:* ACT ASSET.

Costs (2004–05) *Tuition:* area resident $1320 full-time, $55 per credit hour part-time; nonresident $5280 full-time, $220 per credit hour part-time. *Required fees:* $10 full-time, $5 per term part-time.

Financial Aid Of all full-time matriculated undergraduates who enrolled, 350 Federal Work-Study jobs (averaging $1700).

Applying *Options:* common application, electronic application. *Required for some:* high school transcript. *Application deadlines:* 8/23 (freshmen), 8/23 (transfers). *Notification:* continuous until 8/23 (freshmen), continuous until 8/23 (transfers).

Admissions Contact Mrs. Mary Lou Massal, Senior Associate Dean of Student Services, Glendale Community College, 6000 West Olive Avenue, Glendale, AZ 85302. *Phone:* 623-435-3305. *Toll-free phone:* 623-845-3000. *Fax:* 623-845-3303. *E-mail:* info@gc.maricopa.edu.

HIGH-TECH INSTITUTE
Phoenix, Arizona

- **Proprietary** primarily 2-year
- **Calendar** semesters
- **Degrees** diplomas, associate, and bachelor's
- **Urban** 4-acre campus
- **Coed**, 1,544 undergraduate students, 100% full-time, 28% women, 72% men

Undergraduates 1,544 full-time. 12% African American, 2% Asian American or Pacific Islander, 35% Hispanic American, 5% Native American.

Freshmen *Admission:* 768 enrolled.

Faculty *Total:* 60, 92% full-time, 2% with terminal degrees. *Student/faculty ratio:* 27:1.

Majors Computer engineering technology; computer systems networking and telecommunications; computer technology/computer systems technology; drafting and design technology.

Student Life *Housing:* college housing not available. *Activities and Organizations:* Alpha Beta Kappa, American Design Drafting Association, American Institute of Architects, American Institute of Building Designers, American Institute for Design and Drafting.

Costs (2003–04) *Tuition:* $12,351 full-time. *Required fees:* $461 full-time.

Financial Aid Of all full-time matriculated undergraduates who enrolled, 29 Federal Work-Study jobs (averaging $2500).

Applying *Required:* high school transcript. *Application deadline:* rolling (freshmen), rolling (transfers).

Admissions Contact Mr. Glen Husband, Vice President of Admissions, High-Tech Institute, 1515 East Indian School Road, Phoenix, AZ 85014-4901. *Phone:* 602-279-9700. *Fax:* 602-279-2999.

INTERNATIONAL INSTITUTE OF THE AMERICAS
Mesa, Arizona

Admissions Contact 925 South Gilbert Road, Suite 201, Mesa, AZ 85204-4448. *Toll-free phone:* 888-886-2428.

INTERNATIONAL INSTITUTE OF THE AMERICAS
Phoenix, Arizona

Admissions Contact Dr. Lynda K. Angel, Vice President, International Institute of the Americas, 4136 North 75th Avenue, Suite 211, Phoenix, AZ 85033-3196. *Phone:* 602-242-6265. *Toll-free phone:* 888-884-2428.

INTERNATIONAL INSTITUTE OF THE AMERICAS
Phoenix, Arizona

- **Independent** primarily 2-year, founded 1979
- **Calendar** semesters
- **Degrees** certificates, diplomas, associate, and bachelor's
- **Urban** campus
- **Coed,** 1,386 undergraduate students, 100% full-time, 69% women, 31% men

Undergraduates 1,386 full-time. Students come from 7 states and territories, 2% are from out of state, 11% African American, 5% Asian American or Pacific Islander, 35% Hispanic American, 12% Native American.
Faculty *Total:* 130, 40% full-time, 33% with terminal degrees. *Student/faculty ratio:* 17:1.
Majors Accounting related; business administration and management; computer/information technology services administration related; criminal justice/law enforcement administration; health professions related; information technology; management information systems and services related; medical/clinical assistant; medical transcription.
Academic Programs *Special study options:* accelerated degree program, adult/continuing education programs, cooperative education, distance learning, internships, summer session for credit.
Library Learning Resource Center with 1,974 titles, 1,750 serial subscriptions, 120 audiovisual materials, an OPAC, a Web page.
Computers on Campus 421 computers available on campus for general student use. A campuswide network can be accessed. Internet access, online (class) registration, at least one staffed computer lab available.
Student Life *Housing:* college housing not available. *Campus security:* 24-hour emergency response devices.
Costs (2003–04) *Tuition:* $8500 full-time, $283 per credit part-time. Full-time tuition and fees vary according to program. No tuition increase for student's term of enrollment. *Required fees:* $350 full-time. *Payment plan:* tuition prepayment. *Waivers:* employees or children of employees.
Applying *Options:* electronic application, early admission, deferred entrance. *Required:* interview. *Application deadline:* rolling (freshmen). *Notification:* continuous (freshmen).
Admissions Contact International Institute of the Americas, 6049 North 43 Avenue, Phoenix, AZ 85019. *Phone:* 800-793-2428. *Toll-free phone:* 800-793-2428. *Fax:* 602-973-2572. *E-mail:* info@aibt.edu.

INTERNATIONAL INSTITUTE OF THE AMERICAS
Tucson, Arizona

Admissions Contact Mrs. Leigh Anne Pechota, Director, International Institute of the Americas, 5441 East 22nd Street, Suite 125, Tucson, AZ 85711-5444. *Phone:* 520-748-9799. *Toll-free phone:* 888-292-2428.

ITT TECHNICAL INSTITUTE
Phoenix, Arizona

- **Proprietary** primarily 2-year, founded 1972, part of ITT Educational Services, Inc.
- **Calendar** quarters
- **Degrees** associate and bachelor's
- **Urban** 2-acre campus
- **Coed**

Standardized Tests *Required:* Wonderlic aptitude test (for admission).
Costs (2003–04) *Tuition:* $347 per credit hour part-time.
Financial Aid Of all full-time matriculated undergraduates who enrolled, 10 Federal Work-Study jobs (averaging $4000).
Applying *Options:* deferred entrance. *Application fee:* $100. *Required:* high school transcript, interview. *Recommended:* letters of recommendation.
Admissions Contact Mr. Gene McWhorter, Director of Recruitment, ITT Technical Institute, 4837 East McDowell Road, Phoenix, AZ 85008. *Phone:* 602-252-2331. *Toll-free phone:* 800-879-4881. *Fax:* 602-267-8727.

ITT TECHNICAL INSTITUTE
Tucson, Arizona

- **Proprietary** primarily 2-year, founded 1984, part of ITT Educational Services, Inc.
- **Calendar** quarters
- **Degrees** associate and bachelor's
- **Urban** 3-acre campus
- **Coed**

Standardized Tests *Required:* Wonderlic aptitude test (for admission).
Applying *Options:* deferred entrance. *Application fee:* $100. *Required:* high school transcript, interview. *Recommended:* letters of recommendation.
Admissions Contact Ms. Linda Lemken, Director of Recruitment, ITT Technical Institute, 1455 West River Road, Tucson, AZ 85704. *Phone:* 520-408-7488. *Toll-free phone:* 800-870-9730. *Fax:* 520-292-9899.

LAMSON COLLEGE
Tempe, Arizona

Admissions Contact Mr. Chico Chavez, Director of Admissions, Lamson College, 1126 North Scottsdale Road, Suite 17, Tempe, AZ 85281. *Phone:* 480-898-7000. *Toll-free phone:* 800-898-7017.

LONG TECHNICAL COLLEGE
Phoenix, Arizona

Admissions Contact Mr. Michael S. Savely, Executive Director, Long Technical College, 13450 North Black Canyon Highway, Suite 104, Phoenix, AZ 85029. *Phone:* 602-548-1955. *Toll-free phone:* 877-548-1955.

MESA COMMUNITY COLLEGE
Mesa, Arizona

- **State and locally supported** 2-year, founded 1965, part of Maricopa County Community College District System
- **Calendar** semesters
- **Degree** certificates and associate
- **Urban** 160-acre campus with easy access to Phoenix
- **Coed**

Student Life *Campus security:* 24-hour emergency response devices and patrols, student patrols.
Athletics Member NJCAA.
Standardized Tests *Required:* ACT ASSET (for placement).
Costs (2003–04) *Tuition:* area resident $1530 full-time, $51 per credit part-time; state resident $2280 full-time, $76 per credit part-time; nonresident $6480 full-time, $216 per credit part-time.
Applying *Options:* electronic application, early admission, deferred entrance.
Admissions Contact Ms. Carol Petersen, Director, Admissions and Records, Mesa Community College, 1833 West Southern Avenue, Mesa, AZ 85202-4866. *Phone:* 480-461-7478. *Fax:* 480-461-7805. *E-mail:* admissions@mc.maricopa.edu.

MOHAVE COMMUNITY COLLEGE
Kingman, Arizona

- **State-supported** 2-year, founded 1971
- **Calendar** semesters
- **Degree** certificates and associate
- **Small-town** 160-acre campus
- **Coed,** 6,695 undergraduate students

Undergraduates Students come from 8 states and territories, 8% are from out of state, 0.4% African American, 2% Asian American or Pacific Islander, 13% Hispanic American, 2% Native American.
Faculty *Total:* 460, 12% full-time.
Majors Accounting; art; automobile/automotive mechanics technology; business administration and management; ceramic arts and ceramics; computer and information sciences related; computer programming (specific applications); computer science; criminal justice/police science; English; fire science; health science; history; information technology; liberal arts and sciences/liberal studies; marketing/marketing management; mathematics; metal and jewelry arts; music; nursing (registered nurse training); psychology; sociology; word processing.
Academic Programs *Special study options:* academic remediation for entering students, adult/continuing education programs, distance learning, English as a second language, independent study, part-time degree program, summer session for credit.

Mohave Community College (continued)

Library Mohave Community College Library with 45,849 titles, 476 serial subscriptions.

Computers on Campus 120 computers available on campus for general student use. At least one staffed computer lab available.

Student Life *Housing:* college housing not available. *Activities and Organizations:* drama/theater group, student-run newspaper, choral group, Art Club, Pottery Club, Astronomy Club, Phi Theta Kappa, national fraternities, national sororities. *Campus security:* 24-hour emergency response devices, late-night transport/escort service.

Standardized Tests *Recommended:* SAT I and SAT II or ACT (for placement).

Costs (2003–04) *Tuition:* state resident $1140 full-time, $38 per credit hour part-time; nonresident $3420 full-time, $114 per credit hour part-time. Full-time tuition and fees vary according to reciprocity agreements. Part-time tuition and fees vary according to course load and reciprocity agreements. *Waivers:* employees or children of employees.

Applying *Options:* early admission, deferred entrance. *Required for some:* high school transcript, interview. *Recommended:* minimum 2.0 GPA. *Application deadline:* rolling (freshmen), rolling (transfers). *Notification:* continuous (freshmen), continuous (transfers).

Admissions Contact Mr. John Wilson, Registrar/Director of Enrollment Services, Mohave Community College, 1971 Jagerson Avenue, Kingman, AZ 86401. *Phone:* 928-757-0847. *Toll-free phone:* 888-664-2832. *Fax:* 928-757-0808. *E-mail:* thinkmcc@mohave.edu.

NORTHLAND PIONEER COLLEGE
Holbrook, Arizona

- **State and locally supported** 2-year, founded 1974, part of Arizona State Community College System
- **Calendar** semesters
- **Degree** certificates and associate
- **Rural** 50-acre campus
- **Coed,** 4,928 undergraduate students, 20% full-time, 67% women, 33% men

Undergraduates 971 full-time, 3,957 part-time. Students come from 13 states and territories, 5 other countries, 1% African American, 0.7% Asian American or Pacific Islander, 7% Hispanic American, 42% Native American, 9% transferred in, 1% live on campus. *Retention:* 2% of 2002 full-time freshmen returned.

Freshmen *Admission:* 364 admitted, 267 enrolled.

Faculty *Total:* 363, 18% full-time. *Student/faculty ratio:* 14:1.

Majors Accounting technology and bookkeeping; administrative assistant and secretarial science; agriculture; biological and physical sciences; building/property maintenance and management; business administration and management; business and personal/financial services marketing; business automation/technology/data entry; business/commerce; carpentry; child care and support services management; child care provision; child development; child guidance; clothing/textiles; computer and information sciences; computer graphics; computer installation and repair technology; computer systems networking and telecommunications; corrections; cosmetology; court reporting; data modeling/warehousing and database administration; drafting and design technology; early childhood education; electrical, electronic and communications engineering technology; electrician; elementary education; emergency medical technology (EMT paramedic); entrepreneurial and small business related; fire science; general studies; health information/medical records administration; industrial mechanics and maintenance technology; industrial technology; information science/studies; kindergarten/preschool education; legal administrative assistant/secretary; legal assistant/paralegal; legal professions and studies related; liberal arts and sciences/liberal studies; library assistant; management information systems; management information systems and services related; massage therapy; medical transcription; museum studies; nursing (licensed practical/vocational nurse training); nursing (registered nurse training); parks, recreation and leisure facilities management; photography; restaurant, culinary, and catering management; small business administration; special education (early childhood); teacher assistant/aide; teaching assistants/aides related; turf and turfgrass management; welding technology.

Academic Programs *Special study options:* academic remediation for entering students, advanced placement credit, cooperative education, distance learning, double majors, English as a second language, freshman honors college, honors programs, independent study, internships, part-time degree program, services for LD students, summer session for credit.

Library Northland Pioneer College Library with 60,000 titles, 240 serial subscriptions, an OPAC.

Computers on Campus 200 computers available on campus for general student use. At least one staffed computer lab available.

Student Life *Housing Options:* coed. Campus housing is university owned. *Activities and Organizations:* drama/theater group, choral group, Hiking/Skiing Club. *Campus security:* evening security.

Costs (2004–05) *Tuition:* state resident $912 full-time, $38 per credit part-time; nonresident $6000 full-time, $65 per credit part-time. *Room and board:* room only: $1500. *Payment plan:* deferred payment. *Waivers:* senior citizens and employees or children of employees.

Financial Aid Of all full-time matriculated undergraduates who enrolled, 80 Federal Work-Study jobs (averaging $4000).

Applying *Options:* early admission. *Application deadline:* rolling (freshmen). *Notification:* continuous (transfers).

Admissions Contact Ms. Dawn Edgmon, Coordinator of Admissions, Northland Pioneer College, PO Box 610, Holbrook, AZ 86025-0610. *Phone:* 928-536-6257. *Toll-free phone:* 800-266-7845. *Fax:* 928-536-6211.

PARADISE VALLEY COMMUNITY COLLEGE
Phoenix, Arizona

- **State and locally supported** 2-year, founded 1985, part of Maricopa County Community College District System
- **Calendar** semesters
- **Degree** certificates and associate
- **Urban** campus
- **Coed**

Student Life *Campus security:* 24-hour emergency response devices, late-night transport/escort service.

Athletics Member NJCAA.

Costs (2003–04) *Tuition:* area resident $1530 full-time, $51 per hour part-time; nonresident $6480 full-time, $216 per hour part-time.

Financial Aid Of all full-time matriculated undergraduates who enrolled, 50 Federal Work-Study jobs (averaging $2500).

Applying *Options:* early admission.

Admissions Contact Dr. Shirley Green, Associate Dean of Student Services, Paradise Valley Community College, 18401 North 32nd Street, Phoenix, AZ 85032. *Phone:* 602-787-7020. *Fax:* 602-787-7025.

THE PARALEGAL INSTITUTE, INC.
Phoenix, Arizona

Admissions Contact Mr. John W. Morrison, President, The Paralegal Institute, Inc., 2933 West Indian School Road, Drawer 11408, Phoenix, AZ 85061-1408. *Phone:* 602-212-6501. *Toll-free phone:* 800-354-1254. *E-mail:* paralegalinst@mindspring.com.

PHOENIX COLLEGE
Phoenix, Arizona

- **State and locally supported** 2-year, founded 1920, part of Maricopa County Community College District System
- **Calendar** semesters
- **Degree** certificates, diplomas, and associate
- **Urban** 52-acre campus
- **Coed,** 13,150 undergraduate students

Undergraduates Students come from 42 states and territories, 2% are from out of state, 7% African American, 2% Asian American or Pacific Islander, 30% Hispanic American, 3% Native American.

Faculty *Total:* 104, 100% full-time.

Majors Accounting; administrative assistant and secretarial science; architectural engineering technology; art; behavioral sciences; business administration and management; civil engineering technology; clinical laboratory science/medical technology; clinical/medical laboratory technology; computer and information sciences; computer graphics; construction engineering technology; corrections; criminal justice/police science; criminal justice/safety; data processing and data processing technology; dental hygiene; drafting and design technology; emergency medical technology (EMT paramedic); family and consumer sciences/human sciences; fashion/apparel design; finance; fire science; health information/medical records administration; information science/studies; interior design; legal administrative assistant/secretary; legal assistant/paralegal; liberal arts and sciences/liberal studies; management science; marketing/marketing management; mass communication/media; mechanical design technology; medical administrative assistant and medical secretary; medical/clinical assistant; medical laboratory technology; nursing (registered nurse training); real estate; special products marketing; tourism and travel services management.

Academic Programs *Special study options:* academic remediation for entering students, adult/continuing education programs, advanced placement credit, cooperative education, English as a second language, freshman honors college, honors programs, internships, part-time degree program, services for LD students, study abroad, summer session for credit. *ROTC:* Army (c), Air Force (c).

Library Fannin Library with 83,000 titles, 394 serial subscriptions.
Computers on Campus 250 computers available on campus for general student use. A campuswide network can be accessed from off campus. Internet access, at least one staffed computer lab available.
Student Life *Housing:* college housing not available. *Activities and Organizations:* drama/theater group, student-run newspaper, choral group, Black Student Union, NASA (Native American Club), Asian American Club, MECHA (Mexican Club). *Campus security:* 24-hour emergency response devices, student patrols, late-night transport/escort service. *Student services:* personal/psychological counseling, women's center, legal services.
Athletics Member NJCAA. *Intercollegiate sports:* baseball M(s), basketball M(s)/W(s), cross-country running M(s)/W(s), football M(s), golf M(s)/W(s), soccer M/W, softball W(s), tennis M(s)/W(s), track and field M(s)/W(s), volleyball W(s). *Intramural sports:* skiing (cross-country) M(c)/W(c), skiing (downhill) M(c)/W(c).
Standardized Tests *Required:* ACT ASSET (for placement).
Costs (2003–04) *Tuition:* area resident $1224 full-time, $51 per credit hour part-time; state resident $5040 full-time, $76 per credit hour part-time; nonresident $5184 full-time, $76 per credit hour part-time. *Required fees:* $10 full-time, $5 per term part-time.
Financial Aid Of all full-time matriculated undergraduates who enrolled, 350 Federal Work-Study jobs (averaging $2800).
Applying *Options:* common application, electronic application, early admission, deferred entrance. *Application deadline:* rolling (freshmen), rolling (transfers). *Notification:* continuous (freshmen), continuous (transfers).
Admissions Contact Ms. Donna Fischer, Supervisor of Admissions and Records, Phoenix College, Phoenix, AZ 85013. *Phone:* 602-285-7500. *Fax:* 602-285-7813.

PIMA COMMUNITY COLLEGE
Tucson, Arizona

- **State and locally supported** 2-year, founded 1966, part of Arizona State Community College System
- **Calendar** semesters
- **Degrees** certificates, associate, and postbachelor's certificates
- **Urban** 483-acre campus
- **Coed**, 31,216 undergraduate students, 30% full-time, 57% women, 43% men

Undergraduates 9,405 full-time, 21,811 part-time. Students come from 44 states and territories, 66 other countries, 3% are from out of state, 5% African American, 3% Asian American or Pacific Islander, 32% Hispanic American, 4% Native American, 1% international, 5% transferred in.
Freshmen *Admission:* 5,088 applied, 5,088 admitted, 5,088 enrolled. *Test scores:* ACT scores over 18: 52%; ACT scores over 24: 14%; ACT scores over 30: 2%.
Faculty *Total:* 1,623, 18% full-time. *Student/faculty ratio:* 23:1.
Majors Accounting; administrative assistant and secretarial science; aircraft powerplant technology; American Indian/Native American studies; anthropology; archeology; architectural drafting and CAD/CADD; art; Asian studies; automobile/automotive mechanics technology; banking and financial support services; building/construction finishing, management, and inspection related; building/property maintenance and management; business administration and management; child care and support services management; child care provision; commercial and advertising art; computer and information sciences; computer systems analysis; computer systems networking and telecommunications; computer technology/computer systems technology; construction engineering technology; criminal justice/police science; criminal justice/safety; dental hygiene; dental laboratory technology; design and visual communications; dramatic/theatre arts; electrical, electronic and communications engineering technology; emergency medical technology (EMT paramedic); environmental engineering technology; fire science; general studies; gerontology; hospitality administration; hotel/motel administration; industrial engineering; international business/trade/commerce; journalism; legal assistant/paralegal; liberal arts and sciences/liberal studies; machine shop technology; medical administrative assistant and medical secretary; medical radiologic technology; music; nursing (registered nurse training); pharmacy technician; political science and government; radio and television; real estate; respiratory care therapy; restaurant, culinary, and catering management; security and protective services related; sign language interpretation and translation; sociology; speech and rhetoric; tourism and travel services management; veterinary/animal health technology; welding technology.
Academic Programs *Special study options:* academic remediation for entering students, accelerated degree program, adult/continuing education programs, advanced placement credit, cooperative education, distance learning, double majors, English as a second language, freshman honors college, honors programs, independent study, internships, part-time degree program, services for LD students, student-designed majors, summer session for credit. *ROTC:* Army (c), Navy (c), Air Force (c).
Library Pima College Library with 160,492 titles, 1,340 serial subscriptions, 17,940 audiovisual materials, an OPAC, a Web page.

Computers on Campus 2500 computers available on campus for general student use. A campuswide network can be accessed from off campus. Internet access, online (class) registration, at least one staffed computer lab available.
Student Life *Housing:* college housing not available. *Activities and Organizations:* drama/theater group, student-run newspaper, choral group. *Campus security:* 24-hour emergency response devices and patrols, late-night transport/escort service. *Student services:* personal/psychological counseling, women's center.
Athletics Member NJCAA. *Intercollegiate sports:* baseball M(s), basketball M(s)/W(s), cheerleading W, cross-country running M(s)/W(s), football M(s), golf M(s)/W(s), soccer M(s)/W(s), softball W(s), tennis M(s)/W(s), track and field M(s)/W(s), volleyball W(s). *Intramural sports:* badminton M/W, basketball M/W, cross-country running M/W, equestrian sports M(c)/W(c), football M, golf M/W, ice hockey M(c), racquetball M/W, tennis M/W, track and field M/W, volleyball M/W, wrestling M(c).
Standardized Tests *Recommended:* SAT I or ACT (for placement).
Costs (2004–05) *Tuition:* state resident $1092 full-time, $42 per credit part-time; nonresident $5486 full-time, $72 per credit part-time. *Required fees:* $75 full-time, $3 per credit part-time, $5 per term part-time.
Applying *Options:* common application, early admission. *Application fee:* $5. *Application deadline:* rolling (freshmen), rolling (transfers).
Admissions Contact Dr. Wendy Kilgore, Director of Enrollment Services and Registration, Pima Community College, 4905B East Broadway Boulevard, Tucson, AZ 85709-1120. *Phone:* 520-206-4640. *Fax:* 520-206-4790.

PIMA MEDICAL INSTITUTE
Mesa, Arizona

- **Proprietary** 2-year, founded 1985, part of Vocational Training Institutes, Inc
- **Calendar** modular
- **Degree** certificates and associate
- **Urban** campus

Majors Radiologic technology/science; respiratory care therapy.
Student Life *Housing:* college housing not available.
Standardized Tests *Required:* (for admission).
Admissions Contact Mr. Dave Brown, Associate Director of Admissions, Pima Medical Institute, 957 South Dobson Road, Mesa, AZ 85202. *Phone:* 602-345-7777.

PIMA MEDICAL INSTITUTE
Tucson, Arizona

- **Proprietary** 2-year, founded 1972, part of Vocational Training Institutes, Inc
- **Calendar** modular
- **Degree** certificates and associate
- **Urban** campus
- **Coed**, 350 undergraduate students

Faculty *Student/faculty ratio:* 20:1.
Majors Radiologic technology/science; respiratory care therapy.
Student Life *Housing:* college housing not available.
Standardized Tests *Required:* (for admission).
Admissions Contact Mr. Carlos Flores, Admissions Director, Pima Medical Institute, 3350 East Grant Road, Tucson, AZ 85716-2800. *Phone:* 520-326-1600 Ext. 5112.

THE REFRIGERATION SCHOOL
Phoenix, Arizona

- **Proprietary** 2-year
- **Calendar** continuous
- **Degree** certificates, diplomas, and associate
- **Urban** campus
- **Coed**, 350 undergraduate students

Faculty *Total:* 19, 53% full-time. *Student/faculty ratio:* 38:1.
Majors Mechanical engineering/mechanical technology.
Student Life *Housing:* college housing not available.
Costs (2003–04) *Tuition:* $9500 full-time. Full-time tuition and fees vary according to program.
Admissions Contact Ms. Mary Simmons, Admissions Director, The Refrigeration School, 4210 East Washington Street, Phoenix, AZ 85034-1816. *Phone:* 602-275-7133. *Fax:* 602-267-4805. *E-mail:* Admissions@rsiaz.org.

RIO SALADO COLLEGE
Tempe, Arizona

- **State and locally supported** 2-year, founded 1978, part of Maricopa County Community College District System
- **Calendar** semesters
- **Degree** certificates and associate
- **Urban** campus
- **Coed**

Faculty *Student/faculty ratio:* 25:1.

Student Life *Campus security:* 24-hour emergency response devices, late-night transport/escort service.

Standardized Tests *Required for some:* ACT ASSET.

Costs (2003–04) *Tuition:* area resident $1224 full-time, $51 per credit hour part-time; state resident $5184 full-time, $76 per credit hour part-time; nonresident $3240 full-time, $135 per credit hour part-time. *Required fees:* $10 full-time, $5 per term part-time.

Applying *Options:* electronic application, early admission, deferred entrance.

Admissions Contact Mrs. Deborah Lain, Supervisor of Admissions and Records, Rio Salado College, Tampe, AZ 85281. *Phone:* 480-517-8152. *Toll-free phone:* 800-729-1197. *Fax:* 480-517-8199. *E-mail:* admission@email.rio.maricopa.

SCOTTSDALE COMMUNITY COLLEGE
Scottsdale, Arizona

- **State and locally supported** 2-year, founded 1969, part of Maricopa County Community College District System
- **Calendar** semesters
- **Degree** certificates, diplomas, and associate
- **Urban** 160-acre campus with easy access to Phoenix
- **Coed**, 11,465 undergraduate students, 30% full-time, 56% women, 44% men

Undergraduates 3,455 full-time, 8,010 part-time. Students come from 49 other countries, 3% are from out of state, 3% African American, 2% Asian American or Pacific Islander, 7% Hispanic American, 4% Native American, 6% international.

Faculty *Total:* 631, 24% full-time, 12% with terminal degrees. *Student/faculty ratio:* 20:1.

Majors Accounting; administrative assistant and secretarial science; business administration and management; criminal justice/law enforcement administration; culinary arts; dramatic/theatre arts; electrical, electronic and communications engineering technology; emergency medical technology (EMT paramedic); environmental design/architecture; equestrian studies; fashion merchandising; finance; fire science; hospitality administration; hotel/motel administration; information science/studies; interior design; kindergarten/preschool education; mathematics; medical administrative assistant and medical secretary; nursing (registered nurse training); photography; public administration; real estate; special products marketing.

Academic Programs *Special study options:* academic remediation for entering students, adult/continuing education programs, advanced placement credit, cooperative education, English as a second language, honors programs, off-campus study, part-time degree program, services for LD students, student-designed majors, summer session for credit.

Library an OPAC, a Web page.

Computers on Campus 75 computers available on campus for general student use. A campuswide network can be accessed. Internet access, online (class) registration, at least one staffed computer lab available.

Student Life *Housing:* college housing not available. *Activities and Organizations:* drama/theater group, student-run newspaper, choral group. *Campus security:* 24-hour emergency response devices and patrols, student patrols, late-night transport/escort service, 24-hour automatic surveillance cameras. *Student services:* personal/psychological counseling, women's center, legal services.

Athletics Member NJCAA. *Intercollegiate sports:* baseball M, basketball M/W, cross-country running M/W, football M, golf M/W, soccer M/W, softball W, tennis M/W, track and field M/W, volleyball W. *Intramural sports:* archery M/W, badminton M/W, basketball M/W, bowling M/W, racquetball M/W, track and field M/W, volleyball M/W.

Standardized Tests *Required for some:* ACT ASSET. *Recommended:* ACT ASSET.

Costs (2004–05) *Tuition:* area resident $1650 full-time, $55 per credit hour part-time; state resident $6420 full-time, $214 per credit hour part-time; nonresident $6600 full-time, $220 per credit hour part-time. *Required fees:* $10 full-time.

Financial Aid Of all full-time matriculated undergraduates who enrolled, 75 Federal Work-Study jobs (averaging $2000). *Financial aid deadline:* 7/15.

Applying *Options:* early admission. *Application deadline:* rolling (freshmen). *Notification:* continuous (freshmen).

Admissions Contact Ms. Fran Watkins, Supervisor of Admissions and Records, Scottsdale Community College, 9000 East Chaparral Road, Scottsdale, AZ 85256. *Phone:* 602-423-6128. *Fax:* 480-423-6200. *E-mail:* fran.watkins@sccmail.maricopa.edu.

SCOTTSDALE CULINARY INSTITUTE
Scottsdale, Arizona

- **Proprietary** 2-year, founded 1986
- **Calendar** semesters
- **Degree** certificates and associate
- **Coed**

Faculty *Student/faculty ratio:* 16:1.

Costs (2004–05) *Comprehensive fee:* $39,913 includes full-time tuition ($35,000) and room and board ($4913).

Admissions Contact Mr. Jon Alberts, President, Scottsdale Culinary Institute, 8100 East Camelback Road, Suite 1001, Scottsdale, AZ 85251-3940. *Phone:* 800-848-2433. *Toll-free phone:* 800-848-2433.

SOUTH MOUNTAIN COMMUNITY COLLEGE
Phoenix, Arizona

- **State and locally supported** 2-year, founded 1979, part of Maricopa County Community College District System
- **Calendar** semesters
- **Degree** certificates and associate
- **Suburban** 108-acre campus
- **Coed**

Student Life *Campus security:* late-night transport/escort service, 18-hour patrols, campus lockdown.

Athletics Member NJCAA.

Costs (2003–04) *Tuition:* area resident $1224 full-time; state resident $5040 full-time; nonresident $5184 full-time. *Required fees:* $10 full-time.

Financial Aid Of all full-time matriculated undergraduates who enrolled, 36 Federal Work-Study jobs (averaging $2000).

Admissions Contact Mr. Tony Bracamonte, Senior Associate Dean of Enrollment Services, South Mountain Community College, 7050 South 24th Street, Phoenix, AZ 85042. *Phone:* 602-243-8120. *Fax:* 602-243-8329. *E-mail:* bracamonte@smc.maricopa.edu.

SOUTHWEST INSTITUTE OF HEALING ARTS
Tempe, Arizona

Admissions Contact Joann Lassell, Student Advisor, Southwest Institute of Healing Arts, 1100 East Apache Boulevard, Tempe, AZ 85281. *Phone:* 480-994-9244. *Toll-free phone:* 888-504-9106.

TOHONO O'ODHAM COMMUNITY COLLEGE
Sells, Arizona

Admissions Contact PO Box 3129, Sells, AZ 85634.

UNIVERSAL TECHNICAL INSTITUTE
Phoenix, Arizona

Admissions Contact 3121 West Weldon Avenue, Phoenix, AZ 85017-4599. *Toll-free phone:* 800-859-1202.

YAVAPAI COLLEGE
Prescott, Arizona

- **State and locally supported** 2-year, founded 1966, part of Arizona State Community College System
- **Calendar** semesters
- **Degree** certificates and associate
- **Small-town** 100-acre campus
- **Endowment** $1.2 million

■ **Coed,** 8,188 undergraduate students, 16% full-time, 63% women, 37% men

Undergraduates 1,335 full-time, 6,853 part-time. 5% are from out of state, 1% African American, 1% Asian American or Pacific Islander, 7% Hispanic American, 4% Native American, 5% live on campus.

Freshmen *Admission:* 834 enrolled.

Faculty *Total:* 429, 21% full-time. *Student/faculty ratio:* 13:1.

Majors Accounting; administrative assistant and secretarial science; agribusiness; agricultural business and management; agriculture; aquaculture; architectural drafting and CAD/CADD; automobile/automotive mechanics technology; business administration and management; commercial and advertising art; construction engineering technology; criminal justice/police science; education related; equestrian studies; film/cinema studies; fine arts related; fire science; graphic design; gunsmithing; horse husbandry/equine science and management; information science/studies; legal administrative assistant/secretary; legal assistant/paralegal; liberal arts and sciences/liberal studies; nursing (registered nurse training).

Academic Programs *Special study options:* academic remediation for entering students, adult/continuing education programs, advanced placement credit, cooperative education, distance learning, English as a second language, honors programs, independent study, internships, off-campus study, part-time degree program, services for LD students, summer session for credit. *ROTC:* Army (c), Air Force (c).

Library Yavapai College Library with 81,144 titles, 1,091 serial subscriptions, an OPAC, a Web page.

Computers on Campus 150 computers available on campus for general student use. A campuswide network can be accessed from off campus. Internet access, at least one staffed computer lab available.

Student Life *Housing Options:* coed. Campus housing is university owned. *Activities and Organizations:* drama/theater group, student-run newspaper, choral group, Re-Entry Club, Student Nurses Association, Native American Club, International Club, VICA. *Campus security:* 24-hour emergency response devices and patrols, student patrols, late-night transport/escort service, controlled dormitory access. *Student services:* health clinic, personal/psychological counseling, women's center.

Athletics Member NJCAA. *Intercollegiate sports:* baseball M(s), basketball M(s)/W(s), cross-country running W(s), soccer M(s), volleyball W(s).

Standardized Tests *Recommended:* SAT I or ACT (for placement).

Costs (2004–05) *Tuition:* state resident $912 full-time, $38 per credit part-time; nonresident $6312 full-time, $48 per credit part-time. Full-time tuition and fees vary according to program. *Room and board:* $4340. Room and board charges vary according to board plan. *Waivers:* employees or children of employees.

Applying *Options:* early admission, deferred entrance. *Required:* high school transcript. *Required for some:* essay or personal statement, letters of recommendation. *Application deadline:* rolling (freshmen), rolling (transfers).

Admissions Contact Mr. David Vanness, Admissions, Registration, and Records Manager, Yavapai College, 1100 East Sheldon Street, Prescott, AZ 86301-3297. *Phone:* 928-776-2188. *Toll-free phone:* 800-922-6787. *Fax:* 520-776-2151. *E-mail:* registration@yc.edu.

ARKANSAS

ARKANSAS NORTHEASTERN COLLEGE
Blytheville, Arkansas

■ **State-supported** 2-year, founded 1975
■ **Calendar** semesters
■ **Degree** certificates and associate
■ **Rural** 80-acre campus with easy access to Memphis
■ **Coed,** 2,067 undergraduate students, 62% full-time, 72% women, 28% men

Undergraduates 1,283 full-time, 784 part-time. Students come from 3 states and territories, 18% are from out of state, 37% African American, 1% Asian American or Pacific Islander, 1% Hispanic American, 0.1% Native American, 5% transferred in. *Retention:* 50% of 2002 full-time freshmen returned.

Freshmen *Admission:* 529 applied, 529 admitted, 379 enrolled.

Faculty *Total:* 180, 43% full-time, 2% with terminal degrees. *Student/faculty ratio:* 16:1.

Majors Agriculture; applied horticulture; business/commerce; child care and support services management; criminal justice/police science; drafting; general studies; industrial mechanics and maintenance technology; industrial production technologies related; industrial technology; metallurgical technology; middle school education; nursing (registered nurse training); welding technology.

Academic Programs *Special study options:* academic remediation for entering students, adult/continuing education programs, advanced placement credit, distance learning, double majors, part-time degree program, summer session for credit.

Library Adams/Vines Library with 14,132 titles, 165 serial subscriptions, 709 audiovisual materials, an OPAC.

Computers on Campus 280 computers available on campus for general student use. A campuswide network can be accessed. Internet access, at least one staffed computer lab available.

Student Life *Housing:* college housing not available. *Activities and Organizations:* choral group, Gamma Beta Phi, Association of Childhood Education International, Nursing Club, Cultural Diversity, Adult Student Association. *Campus security:* 24-hour patrols.

Standardized Tests *Required:* ACT ASSET (for placement). *Recommended:* ACT (for placement).

Costs (2003–04) *Tuition:* area resident $1080 full-time, $45 per semester hour part-time; state resident $1320 full-time, $55 per semester hour part-time; nonresident $2520 full-time, $105 per semester hour part-time. *Required fees:* $116 full-time, $4 per semester hour part-time, $10 per term part-time. *Payment plans:* installment, deferred payment. *Waivers:* senior citizens and employees or children of employees.

Financial Aid Of all full-time matriculated undergraduates who enrolled, 42 Federal Work-Study jobs (averaging $2500).

Applying *Options:* deferred entrance. *Recommended:* high school transcript. *Application deadline:* rolling (freshmen), rolling (transfers). *Notification:* continuous (freshmen), continuous (transfers).

Admissions Contact Mrs. Leslie Wells, Admissions Counselor, Arkansas Northeastern College, PO Box 1109, Blytheville, AR 72316. *Phone:* 870-762-1020 Ext. 1118. *Fax:* 870-763-1654. *E-mail:* goff@anc.edu.

ARKANSAS STATE UNIVERSITY-BEEBE
Beebe, Arkansas

■ **State-supported** 2-year, founded 1927, part of Arkansas State University System
■ **Calendar** semesters
■ **Degree** certificates and associate
■ **Small-town** 320-acre campus with easy access to Memphis
■ **Coed,** 3,192 undergraduate students, 56% full-time, 60% women, 40% men

Undergraduates 1,798 full-time, 1,394 part-time. Students come from 25 states and territories, 7% African American, 1% Asian American or Pacific Islander, 2% Hispanic American, 1% Native American, 0.2% international, 2% transferred in, 12% live on campus.

Freshmen *Admission:* 677 enrolled. *Average high school GPA:* 2.75.

Faculty *Total:* 97, 65% full-time, 22% with terminal degrees. *Student/faculty ratio:* 30:1.

Majors Agriculture; animal sciences; artificial intelligence and robotics; biology/biological sciences; business administration and management; clinical/medical laboratory technology; computer engineering related; computer engineering technology; computer graphics; computer programming (vendor/product certification); computer systems networking and telecommunications; drafting and design technology; electrical, electronic and communications engineering technology; information science/studies; information technology; liberal arts and sciences/liberal studies; mathematics; nursing (registered nurse training); physical sciences; quality control technology; social sciences; speech and rhetoric.

Academic Programs *Special study options:* academic remediation for entering students, adult/continuing education programs, advanced placement credit, distance learning, honors programs, part-time degree program, summer session for credit.

Library Abington Library with 90,000 titles, 500 serial subscriptions, 10 audiovisual materials.

Computers on Campus 375 computers available on campus for general student use. A campuswide network can be accessed from off campus. Internet access, at least one staffed computer lab available.

Student Life *Housing Options:* men-only, women-only. Campus housing is university owned. *Activities and Organizations:* drama/theater group, choral group, Student Arkansas Education Association, Art Club, Agri Club, Social Science Club, Leadership Council. *Campus security:* 24-hour emergency response devices and patrols. *Student services:* personal/psychological counseling.

Athletics *Intramural sports:* archery M/W, badminton M/W, basketball M/W, football M/W, golf M/W, racquetball M/W, softball M/W, squash M/W, table tennis M/W, tennis M/W, track and field M/W, volleyball M/W.

Standardized Tests *Recommended:* ACT (for placement).

Costs (2004–05) *Tuition:* state resident $60 per credit hour part-time; nonresident $110 per credit hour part-time. Full-time tuition and fees vary according to course load. *Required fees:* $8 per credit hour part-time. *Waivers:* senior citizens.

Financial Aid Of all full-time matriculated undergraduates who enrolled, 36 Federal Work-Study jobs (averaging $1800). 112 state and other part-time jobs (averaging $750).

Arkansas

Arkansas State University-Beebe (continued)

Applying *Options:* common application, deferred entrance. *Required:* high school transcript. *Application deadline:* rolling (freshmen). *Notification:* continuous (freshmen).

Admissions Contact Mr. James Washburn, Director of Admissions, Arkansas State University-Beebe, PO Box 1000, Beebe, AR 72012-1000. *Phone:* 501-882-8280. *Toll-free phone:* 800-632-9985. *Fax:* 501-882-8370. *E-mail:* rahayes@asub.arknet.edu.

ARKANSAS STATE UNIVERSITY-MOUNTAIN HOME
Mountain Home, Arkansas

- **State-supported** 2-year, part of Arkansas State University
- **Calendar** semesters
- **Degree** certificates and associate
- **Small-town** 136-acre campus
- **Endowment** $2.1 million
- **Coed,** 1,347 undergraduate students

Undergraduates Students come from 13 states and territories, 0.1% African American, 1% Asian American or Pacific Islander, 1% Hispanic American, 0.7% Native American.

Freshmen *Admission:* 434 applied, 311 admitted.

Faculty *Total:* 67, 54% full-time, 22% with terminal degrees. *Student/faculty ratio:* 20:1.

Majors Audiology and hearing sciences; business automation/technology/data entry; criminal justice/law enforcement administration; criminal justice/safety; emergency medical technology (EMT paramedic); forensic science and technology; funeral service and mortuary science; information science/studies; liberal arts and sciences/liberal studies; middle school education; opticianry.

Academic Programs *Special study options:* academic remediation for entering students, advanced placement credit, cooperative education, distance learning, independent study, part-time degree program, services for LD students, summer session for credit.

Library Norma Wood Library with 13,329 titles, 220 serial subscriptions, 1,328 audiovisual materials, an OPAC.

Computers on Campus 60 computers available on campus for general student use. A campuswide network can be accessed from off campus. Internet access, online (class) registration, at least one staffed computer lab available.

Student Life *Housing:* college housing not available. *Activities and Organizations:* drama/theater group, choral group, Phi Theta Kappa, Circle K, Criminal Justice Club, Mortuary Science Club, Student Ambassadors.

Standardized Tests *Required:* SAT I and SAT II or ACT (for placement), ACT ASSET or ACT COMPASS (for placement).

Costs (2004–05) *Tuition:* state resident $1920 full-time, $60 per credit part-time; nonresident $3090 full-time, $102 per credit part-time. Full-time tuition and fees vary according to course load. Part-time tuition and fees vary according to course load. *Required fees:* $240 full-time, $8 per credit part-time. *Room and board:* Room and board charges vary according to housing facility. *Payment plan:* installment. *Waivers:* children of alumni, senior citizens, and employees or children of employees.

Applying *Required:* high school transcript. *Recommended:* placement scores. *Notification:* continuous (freshmen).

Admissions Contact Ms. Marla Strecker, Admissions Counselor, Arkansas State University-Mountain Home, 1600 South College Street, Mountain Home, AR 72653. *Phone:* 870-508-6262. *Fax:* 870-508-6287. *E-mail:* mstrecker@asumh.edu.

ARKANSAS STATE UNIVERSITY-NEWPORT
Newport, Arkansas

- **State-supported** 2-year, part of Arkansas State University
- **Calendar** semesters
- **Degree** certificates, diplomas, and associate
- **Coed**

Faculty *Student/faculty ratio:* 12:1.

Standardized Tests *Required:* ACT (for admission).

Applying *Options:* common application. *Required:* interview.

Admissions Contact Ms. Tara Byrd, Registrar, Director of Admissions, Arkansas State University-Newport, 7648 Victory Boulevard, Newport, AR 72112. *Phone:* 870-512-7800. *Toll-free phone:* 800-976-1676. *Fax:* 870-512-7825. *E-mail:* tlbryd@asun.arknet.edu.

BLACK RIVER TECHNICAL COLLEGE
Pocahontas, Arkansas

- **State-supported** 2-year, founded 1972
- **Calendar** semesters
- **Degree** associate
- **Small-town** 55-acre campus
- **Coed**

Faculty *Student/faculty ratio:* 16:1.

Student Life *Campus security:* night patrol.

Standardized Tests *Required for some:* ACT, ACT ASSET, or SAT I.

Costs (2003–04) *Tuition:* area resident $1560 full-time, $52 per credit hour part-time; state resident $1980 full-time, $66 per credit hour part-time; nonresident $5340 full-time, $178 per credit hour part-time. *Required fees:* $90 full-time, $3 per credit hour part-time.

Applying *Options:* common application. *Required for some:* high school transcript, interview.

Admissions Contact Mr. Jim Ulmer, Director of Admissions, Black River Technical College, Highway 304 East, PO Box 468, Pocahontas, AR 72455. *Phone:* 870-892-4565. *Toll-free phone:* 800-919-3086. *Fax:* 870-892-3546.

COSSATOT COMMUNITY COLLEGE OF THE UNIVERSITY OF ARKANSAS
De Queen, Arkansas

- **State-supported** 2-year, founded 1991, part of University of Arkansas System
- **Calendar** semesters
- **Degree** certificates, diplomas, and associate
- **Rural** campus
- **Coed,** 944 undergraduate students, 39% full-time, 71% women, 29% men

Undergraduates 368 full-time, 576 part-time. 12% African American, 0.3% Asian American or Pacific Islander, 6% Hispanic American, 2% Native American.

Freshmen *Admission:* 361 applied, 301 admitted, 115 enrolled.

Faculty *Total:* 74, 46% full-time, 3% with terminal degrees. *Student/faculty ratio:* 12:1.

Majors Automobile/automotive mechanics technology; business administration and management; carpentry; computer management; emergency medical technology (EMT paramedic); environmental studies; industrial technology; liberal arts and sciences/liberal studies; medical/clinical assistant; occupational safety and health technology; welding technology; wood science and wood products/pulp and paper technology.

Academic Programs *Special study options:* academic remediation for entering students, adult/continuing education programs, advanced placement credit, cooperative education, distance learning, double majors, English as a second language, external degree program, independent study, internships, off-campus study, part-time degree program, services for LD students, summer session for credit.

Library Kimbell Library.

Computers on Campus Internet access, online (class) registration available.

Standardized Tests *Required for some:* SAT I or ACT (for placement).

Costs (2003–04) *Tuition:* area resident $960 full-time, $40 per credit hour part-time; state resident $1128 full-time, $47 per credit hour part-time; nonresident $3432 full-time, $143 per credit hour part-time. *Required fees:* $588 full-time, $15 per course part-time, $68 per term part-time.

Financial Aid Of all full-time matriculated undergraduates who enrolled, 10 Federal Work-Study jobs (averaging $2500).

Applying *Options:* common application, electronic application. *Recommended:* high school transcript.

Admissions Contact Ms. Nancy Cowling, Admissions Advisor, Cossatot Community College of the University of Arkansas, P.O. Box 960, DeQueen, AR 71832. *Phone:* 870-584-4471. *Toll-free phone:* 800-844-4471. *Fax:* 870-642-8766. *E-mail:* ncowling@cccua.edu.

CROWLEY'S RIDGE COLLEGE
Paragould, Arkansas

- **Independent** 2-year, affiliated with Church of Christ
- **Calendar** semesters
- **Degree** associate
- **Small-town** 112-acre campus
- **Endowment** $1.0 million
- **Coed,** 183 undergraduate students

Undergraduates 2% African American, 1% Asian American or Pacific Islander, 1% international.

Faculty *Total:* 16, 38% full-time. *Student/faculty ratio:* 16:1.

Majors Biblical studies; general studies.

Academic Programs *Special study options:* academic remediation for entering students, double majors, honors programs, independent study, part-time degree program, summer session for credit.

Library Learning Center with an OPAC, a Web page.

Computers on Campus 9 computers available on campus for general student use. A campuswide network can be accessed from student residence rooms. Internet access, at least one staffed computer lab available.

Student Life *Housing:* on-campus residence required through sophomore year. *Options:* men-only, women-only. Campus housing is university owned. *Activities and Organizations:* drama/theater group, student-run newspaper, choral group.

Athletics Member NSCAA. *Intercollegiate sports:* baseball M, basketball M/W, cheerleading W(s), volleyball W.

Standardized Tests *Required:* ACT, ACT ASSET (for placement).

Costs (2004–05) *Comprehensive fee:* $9270 includes full-time tuition ($5970), mandatory fees ($800), and room and board ($2500). Part-time tuition: $199 per semester hour. *Required fees:* $20 per credit part-time. *Room and board:* college room only: $1500. *Payment plan:* installment. *Waivers:* employees or children of employees.

Financial Aid Of all full-time matriculated undergraduates who enrolled, 78 Federal Work-Study jobs (averaging $500).

Applying *Options:* common application, electronic application. *Required:* high school transcript, recommendation form filled out by high school. *Required for some:* interview. *Application deadline:* rolling (freshmen).

Admissions Contact Mrs. Nancy Joneshill, Director of Admissions, Crowley's Ridge College, 100 College Drive, Paragould, AR 72450. *Phone:* 870-236-6901 Ext. 14. *Toll-free phone:* 800-264-1096. *Fax:* 870-236-7748. *E-mail:* njoneshi@crc.pioneer.paragould.ar.us.

EAST ARKANSAS COMMUNITY COLLEGE
Forrest City, Arkansas

- **State-supported** 2-year, founded 1974
- **Calendar** semesters
- **Degree** certificates and associate
- **Small-town** 40-acre campus with easy access to Memphis
- **Endowment** $28,661
- **Coed,** 1,415 undergraduate students

Undergraduates Students come from 4 states and territories.

Faculty *Total:* 100.

Majors Business administration and management; computer engineering technology; criminal justice/law enforcement administration; criminal justice/police science; drafting and design technology; liberal arts and sciences/liberal studies; nursing (licensed practical/vocational nurse training).

Academic Programs *Special study options:* academic remediation for entering students, adult/continuing education programs, advanced placement credit, honors programs, part-time degree program, services for LD students, summer session for credit.

Library Learning Resource Center plus 1 other with 21,908 titles, 109 serial subscriptions.

Computers on Campus 26 computers available on campus for general student use. At least one staffed computer lab available.

Student Life *Housing:* college housing not available. *Activities and Organizations:* drama/theater group, choral group, Gamma Beta Phi, Baptist Student Union, Student Activities Committee, Lambda Alpha Epsilon. *Campus security:* 24-hour emergency response devices, 16-hour patrols by trained security personnel. *Student services:* personal/psychological counseling.

Standardized Tests *Required:* ACT ASSET (for placement). *Recommended:* ACT (for placement).

Costs (2003–04) *Tuition:* area resident $1290 full-time; state resident $1530 full-time; nonresident $1860 full-time. *Required fees:* $150 full-time.

Financial Aid Of all full-time matriculated undergraduates who enrolled, 74 Federal Work-Study jobs (averaging $1104).

Applying *Options:* early admission, deferred entrance. *Required:* high school transcript. *Application deadline:* rolling (freshmen), rolling (transfers). *Notification:* continuous (freshmen), continuous (transfers).

Admissions Contact Mrs. Sarah C. Buford, Director of Enrollment Management/Registrar, East Arkansas Community College, 1700 Newcastle Road, Forrest City, AR 72335-2204. *Phone:* 870-633-4480 Ext. 219. *Toll-free phone:* 877-797-3222.

ITT TECHNICAL INSTITUTE
Little Rock, Arkansas

- **Proprietary** primarily 2-year, founded 1993, part of ITT Educational Services, Inc

- **Calendar** quarters
- **Degrees** associate and bachelor's
- **Urban** campus
- **Coed**

Standardized Tests *Required:* Wonderlic aptitude test (for admission).

Costs (2003–04) *Tuition:* Total Program Cost varies depending on course of study. Consult school catalog.

Applying *Options:* deferred entrance. *Application fee:* $100. *Required:* high school transcript, interview. *Recommended:* letters of recommendation.

Admissions Contact Mr. Reed W. Thompson, Director of Recruitment, ITT Technical Institute, 4520 South University Avenue, Little Rock, AR 72204. *Phone:* 501-565-5550. *Toll-free phone:* 800-359-4429. *Fax:* 501-565-4747.

MID-SOUTH COMMUNITY COLLEGE
West Memphis, Arkansas

- **State-supported** 2-year, founded 1993
- **Calendar** semesters
- **Degree** certificates and associate
- **Suburban** 80-acre campus with easy access to Memphis
- **Coed,** 1,159 undergraduate students, 29% full-time, 67% women, 33% men

Undergraduates 332 full-time, 827 part-time. Students come from 5 states and territories, 3 other countries, 3% are from out of state, 57% African American, 0.6% Asian American or Pacific Islander, 0.6% Hispanic American, 0.5% Native American, 0.8% international, 8% transferred in. *Retention:* 44% of 2002 full-time freshmen returned.

Freshmen *Admission:* 377 applied, 377 admitted, 277 enrolled.

Faculty *Total:* 87, 33% full-time. *Student/faculty ratio:* 13:1.

Majors Computer and information sciences; liberal arts and sciences/liberal studies; management information systems and services related; multi-/interdisciplinary studies related; web/multimedia management and webmaster.

Academic Programs *Special study options:* academic remediation for entering students, adult/continuing education programs, distance learning, independent study, internships, part-time degree program, summer session for credit.

Library Mid-South Community College Library/Media Center with 7,565 titles, 92 serial subscriptions, 1,321 audiovisual materials, an OPAC, a Web page.

Computers on Campus 280 computers available on campus for general student use. A campuswide network can be accessed from off campus. Internet access, at least one staffed computer lab available.

Student Life *Housing:* college housing not available. *Activities and Organizations:* choral group, Phi Theta Kappa, Baptist Collegiate Ministry, Campus Ministry International, Student Ambassador, Skills-USA-Vica. *Campus security:* 24-hour emergency response devices, security during class hours.

Standardized Tests *Required:* ACT ASSET, ACT COMPASS (for placement). *Recommended:* ACT (for placement).

Costs (2004–05) *Tuition:* area resident $1200 full-time, $40 per credit part-time; state resident $1500 full-time, $50 per credit part-time; nonresident $1800 full-time, $60 per credit part-time. Full-time tuition and fees vary according to course load and reciprocity agreements. Part-time tuition and fees vary according to course load and reciprocity agreements. *Required fees:* $90 full-time, $3 per credit part-time. *Payment plan:* installment. *Waivers:* senior citizens and employees or children of employees.

Financial Aid Of all full-time matriculated undergraduates who enrolled, 29 Federal Work-Study jobs (averaging $1914).

Applying *Options:* early admission. *Required:* high school transcript. *Required for some:* 2 letters of recommendation. *Application deadline:* rolling (freshmen), rolling (transfers). *Notification:* continuous (freshmen), continuous (transfers).

Admissions Contact Ms. Leslie Anderson, Registrar, Mid-South Community College, 2000 West Broadway, West Memphis, AR 72301. *Phone:* 870-733-6732. *Fax:* 870-733-6719. *E-mail:* landerson@midsouthcc.edu.

NATIONAL PARK COMMUNITY COLLEGE
Hot Springs, Arkansas

- **State and locally supported** 2-year, founded 1973, part of Arkansas Department of Higher Education
- **Calendar** semesters
- **Degree** certificates, diplomas, and associate
- **Suburban** 50-acre campus with easy access to Little Rock
- **Endowment** $11.3 million
- **Coed**

Faculty *Student/faculty ratio:* 21:1.

Student Life *Campus security:* 24-hour emergency response devices and patrols.

Standardized Tests *Required:* SAT I and SAT II or ACT (for admission). *Recommended:* ACT ASSET.

National Park Community College (continued)

Costs (2003–04) *Tuition:* area resident $1056 full-time, $44 per credit hour part-time; state resident $1128 full-time, $47 per credit hour part-time; nonresident $2760 full-time, $115 per credit hour part-time. *Required fees:* $30 full-time, $15 per semester part-time.

Applying *Options:* common application, early admission, deferred entrance. *Required:* high school transcript.

Admissions Contact Dr. Allen B. Moody, Director of Institutional Services/ Registrar, National Park Community College, 101 College Drive, Hot Springs, AR 71913. *Phone:* 501-760-4222. *Fax:* 501-760-4100. *E-mail:* admissions@ gccc.cc.ar.us.

NORTH ARKANSAS COLLEGE
Harrison, Arkansas

- **State and locally supported** 2-year, founded 1974
- **Calendar** semesters
- **Degree** certificates and associate
- **Small-town** 40-acre campus
- **Endowment** $103,275
- **Coed,** 2,120 undergraduate students, 58% full-time, 62% women, 38% men

Undergraduates 1,219 full-time, 901 part-time. Students come from 14 states and territories, 5% are from out of state, 0.5% African American, 0.2% Asian American or Pacific Islander, 2% Hispanic American, 0.8% Native American, 5% transferred in. *Retention:* 48% of 2002 full-time freshmen returned.

Freshmen *Admission:* 673 applied, 673 admitted, 495 enrolled. *Test scores:* ACT scores over 18: 78%; ACT scores over 24: 24%; ACT scores over 30: 1%.

Faculty *Total:* 152, 43% full-time, 7% with terminal degrees. *Student/faculty ratio:* 17:1.

Majors Administrative assistant and secretarial science; agriculture; business administration and management; clinical/medical laboratory technology; electromechanical technology; emergency medical technology (EMT paramedic); general studies; liberal arts and sciences/liberal studies; medical radiologic technology; nursing (registered nurse training); surgical technology.

Academic Programs *Special study options:* academic remediation for entering students, adult/continuing education programs, advanced placement credit, distance learning, freshman honors college, honors programs, independent study, part-time degree program, services for LD students, summer session for credit.

Library North Arkansas College Library plus 1 other with 29,969 titles, 340 serial subscriptions, 2,879 audiovisual materials, an OPAC, a Web page.

Computers on Campus 200 computers available on campus for general student use. A campuswide network can be accessed from off campus. Internet access, at least one staffed computer lab available.

Student Life *Housing:* college housing not available. *Activities and Organizations:* drama/theater group, choral group, Phi Beta Lambda, Phi Theta Kappa, Student Nurses Association, Vocational Industrial Clubs, Baptist Student Union. *Campus security:* 24-hour patrols. *Student services:* personal/psychological counseling.

Athletics Member NJCAA. *Intercollegiate sports:* baseball M, basketball M(s)/W(s), softball W. *Intramural sports:* archery M/W, badminton M/W, baseball M/W, football M/W, golf M/W, racquetball M/W, softball W, table tennis M/W, tennis M/W, volleyball M/W.

Standardized Tests *Required:* ACT (for placement), ACT ASSET, ACT COMPASS (for placement).

Costs (2004–05) *Tuition:* area resident $1320 full-time, $44 per credit hour part-time; state resident $1650 full-time, $55 per credit hour part-time; nonresident $3390 full-time, $113 per credit hour part-time. Full-time tuition and fees vary according to location and reciprocity agreements. Part-time tuition and fees vary according to location and reciprocity agreements. *Required fees:* $150 full-time, $5 per credit hour part-time, $75 per term part-time. *Payment plan:* installment. *Waivers:* employees or children of employees.

Financial Aid Of all full-time matriculated undergraduates who enrolled, 107 Federal Work-Study jobs (averaging $1103).

Applying *Options:* deferred entrance. *Required for some:* high school transcript. *Application deadline:* rolling (freshmen), rolling (transfers). *Notification:* continuous (freshmen), continuous (transfers).

Admissions Contact Ms. Charla McDonald Jennings, Director of Admissions, North Arkansas College, 1515 Pioneer Drive, Harrison, AR 72601. *Phone:* 870-391-3221. *Toll-free phone:* 800-679-6622. *Fax:* 870-391-3339. *E-mail:* charlam@northark.edu.

NORTHWEST ARKANSAS COMMUNITY COLLEGE
Bentonville, Arkansas

Admissions Contact Dr. Charles Mullins, Director of Admissions, NorthWest Arkansas Community College, One College Drive, Bentonville, AR 72712.

Phone: 479-636-9222 Ext. 4231. *Toll-free phone:* 800-995-6922. *Fax:* 479-619-4116. *E-mail:* asknewstudentadmissions@nwacc.edu.

OUACHITA TECHNICAL COLLEGE
Malvern, Arkansas

- **State-supported** 2-year, founded 1972
- **Calendar** semesters
- **Degree** certificates and associate
- **Small-town** 11-acre campus
- **Coed,** 1,291 undergraduate students, 44% full-time, 52% women, 48% men

Undergraduates 566 full-time, 725 part-time. Students come from 2 states and territories, 2 other countries, 0.8% are from out of state, 12% African American, 0.3% Asian American or Pacific Islander, 1% Hispanic American, 0.9% Native American, 0.1% international, 8% transferred in.

Freshmen *Admission:* 376 applied, 376 admitted, 236 enrolled. *Test scores:* ACT scores over 18: 73%; ACT scores over 24: 3%.

Faculty *Total:* 95, 36% full-time, 7% with terminal degrees. *Student/faculty ratio:* 13:1.

Majors Accounting; administrative assistant and secretarial science; automobile/ automotive mechanics technology; business administration and management; child care and support services management; computer and information sciences; industrial arts; industrial technology; legal administrative assistant/secretary; legal assistant/paralegal; liberal arts and sciences/liberal studies; machine tool technology; management information systems; marketing/marketing management; medical administrative assistant and medical secretary; nursing (licensed practical/vocational nurse training).

Academic Programs *Special study options:* academic remediation for entering students, accelerated degree program, advanced placement credit, cooperative education, distance learning, double majors, independent study, internships, part-time degree program, services for LD students, summer session for credit.

Library Ouachita Technical College Library/Learning Resource Center with 8,000 titles, 100 serial subscriptions, 1,200 audiovisual materials, an OPAC, a Web page.

Computers on Campus 125 computers available on campus for general student use. A campuswide network can be accessed from off campus. Internet access, at least one staffed computer lab available.

Student Life *Housing:* college housing not available. *Activities and Organizations:* student-run newspaper. *Campus security:* 24-hour patrols. *Student services:* personal/psychological counseling.

Standardized Tests *Required for some:* SAT I or ACT (for placement), ACT ASSET, ACT COMPASS.

Costs (2004–05) *Tuition:* state resident $1470 full-time, $49 per credit hour part-time; nonresident $4410 full-time, $147 per credit hour part-time. Full-time tuition and fees vary according to program. Part-time tuition and fees vary according to program. No tuition increase for student's term of enrollment. *Required fees:* $390 full-time, $13 per credit hour part-time. *Payment plan:* installment. *Waivers:* senior citizens and employees or children of employees.

Financial Aid Of all full-time matriculated undergraduates who enrolled, 18 Federal Work-Study jobs (averaging $2400).

Applying *Options:* electronic application, early admission, deferred entrance. *Application fee:* $20. *Required:* high school transcript. *Application deadline:* rolling (freshmen), rolling (transfers).

Admissions Contact Mr. Vaughn Kesterson, Counselor, Ouachita Technical College, One College Circle, Malvern, AR 72104. *Phone:* 501-337-5000 Ext. 1117. *Toll-free phone:* 800-337-0266. *Fax:* 501-337-9382. *E-mail:* lindaj@ otcweb.edu.

OZARKA COLLEGE
Melbourne, Arkansas

- **State-supported** 2-year, founded 1973
- **Calendar** semesters
- **Degree** certificates and associate
- **Rural** 40-acre campus
- **Coed,** 756 undergraduate students, 75% full-time, 71% women, 29% men

Undergraduates 569 full-time, 187 part-time. 1% are from out of state, 0.3% African American, 0.8% Hispanic American, 0.7% Native American.

Freshmen *Admission:* 157 applied, 157 admitted, 157 enrolled.

Faculty *Total:* 71, 44% full-time, 4% with terminal degrees. *Student/faculty ratio:* 20:1.

Majors Administrative assistant and secretarial science; automobile/automotive mechanics technology; banking and financial support services; business administration and management; criminal justice/law enforcement administration; culinary arts; health information/medical records technology; information science/ studies; liberal arts and sciences/liberal studies; middle school education.

Academic Programs *Special study options:* academic remediation for entering students, advanced placement credit, distance learning, external degree program, internships, part-time degree program, services for LD students, summer session for credit.

Library Ozarka College Library with 10,500 titles, 4,000 serial subscriptions, 1,500 audiovisual materials, an OPAC.

Computers on Campus 114 computers available on campus for general student use. A campuswide network can be accessed from off campus that provide access to check on grades—midterm and final. Internet access, online (class) registration, at least one staffed computer lab available.

Student Life *Housing:* college housing not available. *Activities and Organizations:* drama/theater group, VICA, Phi Beta Lambda, Drama Club, HOSA, Phi Theta Kappa. *Campus security:* security patrols 7 a.m. to 11 p.m. *Student services:* personal/psychological counseling.

Standardized Tests *Required:* ACT (for placement), ACT ASSET (for placement).

Costs (2004–05) *Tuition:* state resident $1800 full-time; nonresident $5040 full-time. *Required fees:* $180 full-time.

Financial Aid Of all full-time matriculated undergraduates who enrolled, 50 Federal Work-Study jobs, 40 state and other part-time jobs.

Applying *Options:* deferred entrance. *Required:* high school transcript. *Required for some:* essay or personal statement, letters of recommendation, interview. *Recommended:* minimum 2.0 GPA. *Application deadlines:* 8/19 (freshmen), 8/15 (transfers).

Admissions Contact Mr. Randy Scaggs, Counselor and Recruiter, Ozarka College, PO Box 12, 218 College Drive, Melbourne, AR 72556. *Phone:* 870-368-7371 Ext. 2028. *Toll-free phone:* 800-821-4335. *Fax:* 870-368-4733. *E-mail:* rscaggs@ozarka.edu.

PHILLIPS COMMUNITY COLLEGE OF THE UNIVERSITY OF ARKANSAS
Helena, Arkansas

- **State and locally supported** 2-year, founded 1965, part of University of Arkansas System
- **Calendar** semesters
- **Degree** certificates and associate
- **Small-town** 80-acre campus with easy access to Memphis
- **Coed**

Student Life *Campus security:* 24-hour patrols.

Standardized Tests *Required:* ACT (for placement), ACT ASSET (for placement).

Costs (2003–04) *Tuition:* state resident $790 full-time, $52 per credit hour part-time; nonresident $1495 full-time, $99 per credit hour part-time.

Applying *Options:* early admission.

Admissions Contact Mr. Lynn Boone, Registrar, Phillips Community College of the University of Arkansas, PO Box 785, Helena, AR 72342-0785. *Phone:* 870-338-6474.

PULASKI TECHNICAL COLLEGE
North Little Rock, Arkansas

- **State-supported** 2-year, founded 1945
- **Calendar** semesters
- **Degree** certificates and associate
- **Urban** 40-acre campus with easy access to Little Rock
- **Coed**, 6,128 undergraduate students

Undergraduates Students come from 1 other state, 42% African American.

Freshmen *Admission:* 3,150 applied, 3,150 admitted.

Faculty *Total:* 319, 26% full-time. *Student/faculty ratio:* 20:1.

Majors Administrative assistant and secretarial science; computer engineering technology; drafting and design technology; electromechanical technology; industrial technology; information science/studies.

Academic Programs *Special study options:* academic remediation for entering students, advanced placement credit, distance learning, part-time degree program, services for LD students, summer session for credit.

Library Library Resource Center with an OPAC.

Computers on Campus 75 computers available on campus for general student use. A campuswide network can be accessed. Internet access, at least one staffed computer lab available.

Student Life *Housing:* college housing not available. *Campus security:* security personnel 7 a.m. to 11 p.m.

Standardized Tests *Required:* ACT, ACT ASSET, or ACT COMPASS (for placement).

Costs (2004–05) *Tuition:* state resident $64 per credit hour part-time. Full-time tuition and fees vary according to course load. *Required fees:* $8 per credit hour part-time. *Payment plan:* deferred payment. *Waivers:* senior citizens and employees or children of employees.

Applying *Options:* common application. *Required:* high school transcript. *Application deadline:* rolling (freshmen).

Admissions Contact Ms. Janice Hurd, Director of Admissions and Records, Pulaski Technical College, 3000 West Scenic Drive, North Little Rock, AR 72118. *Phone:* 501-812-2232. *Fax:* 501-812-2316.

REMINGTON COLLEGE-LITTLE ROCK CAMPUS
Little Rock, Arkansas

Admissions Contact Mr. David Caldwell, Campus President, Remington College-Little Rock Campus, 8901 Kanis Road, Little Rock, AR 72205. *Phone:* 501-312-0007.

RICH MOUNTAIN COMMUNITY COLLEGE
Mena, Arkansas

- **State and locally supported** 2-year, founded 1983
- **Calendar** semesters
- **Degree** certificates and associate
- **Small-town** 40-acre campus
- **Endowment** $301,360
- **Coed**, 1,078 undergraduate students, 42% full-time, 74% women, 26% men

Undergraduates 452 full-time, 626 part-time. Students come from 2 states and territories, 2 other countries, 2% are from out of state, 0.1% African American, 0.9% Asian American or Pacific Islander, 0.7% Hispanic American, 2% Native American.

Freshmen *Average high school GPA:* 2.81.

Faculty *Total:* 55, 35% full-time, 4% with terminal degrees. *Student/faculty ratio:* 18:1.

Majors Administrative assistant and secretarial science; liberal arts and sciences/liberal studies.

Academic Programs *Special study options:* academic remediation for entering students, adult/continuing education programs, advanced placement credit, distance learning, double majors, English as a second language, part-time degree program, services for LD students, summer session for credit.

Library St. John Library with 13,299 titles, 81 serial subscriptions, 674 audiovisual materials, an OPAC.

Computers on Campus 88 computers available on campus for general student use. A campuswide network can be accessed from off campus. Internet access, at least one staffed computer lab available.

Student Life *Housing:* college housing not available. *Activities and Organizations:* student-run television station, SGA, Baptist Student Union, Phi Theta Kappa, Golf Club, TV and Video Club. *Campus security:* administrator on night duty. *Student services:* personal/psychological counseling.

Costs (2003–04) *Tuition:* area resident $888 full-time, $37 per semester hour part-time; state resident $1104 full-time, $46 per semester hour part-time; nonresident $3312 full-time, $138 per semester hour part-time. *Required fees:* $48 full-time, $2 per semester hour part-time. *Payment plan:* installment. *Waivers:* senior citizens and employees or children of employees.

Financial Aid Of all full-time matriculated undergraduates who enrolled, 12 Federal Work-Study jobs (averaging $1500).

Applying *Options:* common application, early admission. *Required:* high school transcript. *Application deadlines:* 8/25 (freshmen), 8/25 (transfers). *Notification:* continuous until 8/25 (freshmen), continuous until 8/25 (transfers).

Admissions Contact Dr. Steve Rook, Dean of Students, Rich Mountain Community College, 1100 College Drive, Mena, AR 71953. *Phone:* 479-394-7622 Ext. 1400.

SOUTH ARKANSAS COMMUNITY COLLEGE
El Dorado, Arkansas

- **State-supported** 2-year, founded 1975, part of Arkansas Department of Higher Education
- **Calendar** semesters
- **Degree** certificates and associate
- **Small-town** 4-acre campus
- **Coed**, 1,087 undergraduate students, 36% full-time, 64% women, 36% men

Arkansas

South Arkansas Community College (continued)

Undergraduates 391 full-time, 696 part-time. Students come from 2 states and territories, 3% are from out of state, 28% African American, 0.4% Asian American or Pacific Islander, 1% Hispanic American, 0.6% Native American.
Freshmen *Admission:* 313 enrolled.
Faculty *Total:* 88, 58% full-time. *Student/faculty ratio:* 13:1.
Majors Administrative assistant and secretarial science; business/commerce; clinical/medical laboratory technology; criminal justice/police science; emergency medical technology (EMT paramedic); general studies; industrial technology; management information systems; medical radiologic technology; physical therapist assistant.
Academic Programs *Special study options:* academic remediation for entering students, adult/continuing education programs, advanced placement credit, internships, part-time degree program, services for LD students, summer session for credit.
Library South Arkansas Community College Library with 22,652 titles, 223 serial subscriptions.
Computers on Campus 75 computers available on campus for general student use. A campuswide network can be accessed. Internet access, at least one staffed computer lab available.
Student Life *Housing:* college housing not available. *Activities and Organizations:* choral group. *Campus security:* security guard. *Student services:* personal/psychological counseling.
Athletics *Intramural sports:* badminton M/W, basketball M/W, tennis M/W, volleyball M/W.
Standardized Tests *Required:* ACT ASSET (for placement). *Recommended:* SAT I or ACT (for placement).
Costs (2003–04) *Tuition:* area resident $1620 full-time; state resident $1950 full-time; nonresident $3600 full-time. *Required fees:* $95 full-time. *Payment plan:* installment. *Waivers:* senior citizens.
Financial Aid Of all full-time matriculated undergraduates who enrolled, 45 Federal Work-Study jobs (averaging $1300).
Applying *Options:* early admission, deferred entrance. *Application deadline:* 8/25 (freshmen), rolling (transfers).
Admissions Contact Mr. Dean Inman, Director of Enrollment Services, South Arkansas Community College, PO Box 7010, El Dorado, AR 71731-7010. *Phone:* 870-864-7142. *Toll-free phone:* 800-955-2289 Ext. 142. *Fax:* 870-864-7109. *E-mail:* dinman@southark.edu.

SOUTHEAST ARKANSAS COLLEGE
Pine Bluff, Arkansas

- **State-supported** 2-year, founded 1991
- **Calendar** semesters
- **Degree** certificates and associate
- **Coed,** 2,197 undergraduate students, 46% full-time, 70% women, 30% men

Undergraduates 1,017 full-time, 1,180 part-time. Students come from 3 states and territories, 48% African American, 0.7% Asian American or Pacific Islander, 1% Hispanic American, 0.5% Native American, 0.1% international.
Freshmen *Admission:* 446 enrolled.
Faculty *Total:* 129, 38% full-time. *Student/faculty ratio:* 18:1.
Majors Automobile/automotive mechanics technology; biology/biotechnology laboratory technician; business administration and management; business/commerce; criminology; drafting and design technology; electrical, electronic and communications engineering technology; emergency medical technology (EMT paramedic); general studies; industrial technology; legal assistant/paralegal; radiologic technology/science; science, technology and society; surgical technology.
Academic Programs *Special study options:* academic remediation for entering students, accelerated degree program, advanced placement credit, cooperative education, distance learning, double majors, honors programs, independent study, internships, part-time degree program, services for LD students, summer session for credit.
Library Southeast Arkansas Technical College Library with 5,000 titles, 75 serial subscriptions.
Computers on Campus 62 computers available on campus for general student use. Internet access, at least one staffed computer lab available.
Student Life *Housing:* college housing not available. *Activities and Organizations:* choral group, Phi Beta Lambda, HOSA, Phi Theta Kappa, Student Senate. *Campus security:* student patrols. *Student services:* personal/psychological counseling.
Standardized Tests *Required:* SAT I or ACT (for placement), ACT ASSET (for placement).
Costs (2003–04) *Tuition:* state resident $1500 full-time, $50 per credit part-time; nonresident $3000 full-time, $100 per credit part-time. *Required fees:* $100 full-time, $3 per credit hour part-time, $5 per term part-time.
Financial Aid Of all full-time matriculated undergraduates who enrolled, 60 Federal Work-Study jobs (averaging $3000).

Applying *Options:* common application, early admission. *Required:* high school transcript. *Application deadline:* 8/21 (transfers). *Notification:* continuous (freshmen), continuous (transfers).
Admissions Contact Ms. Barbara Dunn, Coordinator of Admissions and Enrollment Management, Southeast Arkansas College, 1900 Hazel Street, Pine Bluff, AR 71603. *Phone:* 870-543-5957. *Toll-free phone:* 888-SEARK TC. *E-mail:* main@seark.edu.

SOUTHERN ARKANSAS UNIVERSITY TECH
Camden, Arkansas

- **State-supported** 2-year, founded 1967, part of Arkansas Department of Higher Education
- **Calendar** semesters
- **Degree** certificates and associate
- **Rural** 96-acre campus
- **Coed,** 1,223 undergraduate students, 38% full-time, 50% women, 50% men

Undergraduates 464 full-time, 759 part-time. Students come from 6 states and territories, 1% are from out of state, 36% African American, 0.3% Asian American or Pacific Islander, 0.6% Hispanic American, 0.3% Native American, 3% transferred in.
Freshmen *Admission:* 202 applied, 202 admitted, 128 enrolled. *Average high school GPA:* 2.70. *Test scores:* ACT scores over 18: 50%; ACT scores over 24: 3%.
Faculty *Total:* 51, 55% full-time, 8% with terminal degrees. *Student/faculty ratio:* 20:1.
Majors Aircraft powerplant technology; business administration and management; child care provision; commercial and advertising art; computer and information sciences and support services related; computer programming; computer science; computer technology/computer systems technology; drafting and design technology; educational/instructional media design; emergency medical technology (EMT paramedic); engineering technologies related; environmental engineering technology; fire science; general studies; industrial mechanics and maintenance technology; industrial technology; office management.
Academic Programs *Special study options:* academic remediation for entering students, adult/continuing education programs, advanced placement credit, distance learning, double majors, honors programs, independent study, internships, off-campus study, part-time degree program, summer session for credit.
Library Southern Arkansas University Tech Learning Resource Center with 17,389 titles, 115 serial subscriptions, 960 audiovisual materials, an OPAC.
Computers on Campus 200 computers available on campus for general student use. A campuswide network can be accessed. Internet access, at least one staffed computer lab available.
Student Life *Housing Options:* Campus housing is university owned. *Activities and Organizations:* Phi Beta Lambda, SAU Tech Ambassadors, Allied Health Student Club, Computer Club, Phi Theta Kappa. *Campus security:* 24-hour emergency response devices, patrols by trained security personnel. *Student services:* personal/psychological counseling.
Athletics *Intramural sports:* basketball M/W, football M/W, soccer M/W, softball M/W, table tennis M/W, volleyball M/W.
Standardized Tests *Required:* SAT I or ACT (for placement), ACT ASSET (for placement).
Costs (2003–04) *Tuition:* $60 per credit hour part-time; state resident $1440 full-time, $60 per credit hour part-time; nonresident $1920 full-time, $80 per credit hour part-time. Part-time tuition and fees vary according to course level. *Required fees:* $480 full-time. *Waivers:* senior citizens and employees or children of employees.
Financial Aid Of all full-time matriculated undergraduates who enrolled, 26 Federal Work-Study jobs (averaging $1023).
Applying *Options:* deferred entrance. *Required for some:* high school transcript. *Recommended:* high school transcript, minimum 2.0 GPA. *Application deadline:* 8/15 (freshmen), rolling (transfers). *Notification:* continuous (freshmen), continuous (transfers).
Admissions Contact Mr. Scott Raney, Admissions Director, Southern Arkansas University Tech, PO Box 3499, East Camden, AR 71711. *Phone:* 870-574-4558. *Fax:* 870-574-4478. *E-mail:* sraney@sautech.edu.

UNIVERSITY OF ARKANSAS COMMUNITY COLLEGE AT BATESVILLE
Batesville, Arkansas

- **State-supported** 2-year, part of University of Arkansas System
- **Calendar** semesters

- **Degree** certificates and associate
- **Small-town** campus
- **Coed,** 1,317 undergraduate students, 60% full-time, 69% women, 31% men

Undergraduates 784 full-time, 533 part-time. 3% African American, 0.5% Asian American or Pacific Islander, 1% Hispanic American, 0.5% Native American, 0.1% international, 9% transferred in. *Retention:* 57% of 2002 full-time freshmen returned.

Freshmen *Admission:* 225 enrolled.

Faculty *Total:* 96, 40% full-time. *Student/faculty ratio:* 13:1.

Majors Business/commerce; computer systems networking and telecommunications; criminal justice/safety; data entry/microcomputer applications; education; emergency medical technology (EMT paramedic); industrial technology; information technology; kindergarten/preschool education; medical office management; nursing (registered nurse training); system administration; web page, digital/multimedia and information resources design.

Academic Programs *Special study options:* academic remediation for entering students, adult/continuing education programs, advanced placement credit, cooperative education, distance learning, double majors, English as a second language, external degree program, independent study, internships, off-campus study, part-time degree program, services for LD students, student-designed majors, summer session for credit.

Library University of Arkansas Community College at Batesville Library with 8,000 titles, 149 serial subscriptions, 1,500 audiovisual materials, an OPAC.

Computers on Campus 25 computers available on campus for general student use. A campuswide network can be accessed. Internet access, at least one staffed computer lab available.

Student Life *Campus security:* security cameras. *Student services:* personal/psychological counseling.

Standardized Tests *Required:* SAT I and SAT II or ACT (for placement).

Costs (2003–04) *Tuition:* area resident $1008 full-time, $42 per credit part-time; state resident $1272 full-time, $53 per credit part-time; nonresident $2496 full-time, $107 per credit part-time. Full-time tuition and fees vary according to program. Part-time tuition and fees vary according to program. *Required fees:* $250 full-time, $10 per credit part-time. *Waivers:* senior citizens.

Financial Aid Of all full-time matriculated undergraduates who enrolled, 32 Federal Work-Study jobs (averaging $781).

Applying *Options:* common application. *Application deadline:* rolling (freshmen). *Notification:* continuous (freshmen).

Admissions Contact Mr. Andy Thomas, Director of Admissions, University of Arkansas Community College at Batesville, PO Box 3350, Batesville, AR 72503. *Phone:* 870-612-2010. *Toll-free phone:* 800-508-7878. *Fax:* 870-612-2129. *E-mail:* athomas@uaccb.edu.

UNIVERSITY OF ARKANSAS COMMUNITY COLLEGE AT HOPE
Hope, Arkansas

- **State-supported** 2-year, founded 1966, part of University of Arkansas System
- **Calendar** semesters
- **Degree** certificates, diplomas, and associate
- **Rural** 60-acre campus
- **Coed,** 1,160 undergraduate students, 59% full-time, 69% women, 31% men

Undergraduates 687 full-time, 473 part-time. Students come from 4 states and territories, 33% African American, 0.3% Asian American or Pacific Islander, 2% Hispanic American, 0.3% Native American.

Freshmen *Admission:* 296 applied, 296 admitted, 296 enrolled.

Faculty *Total:* 84, 49% full-time, 6% with terminal degrees.

Majors Business administration and management; child care provision; criminal justice/law enforcement administration; funeral service and mortuary science; human services; industrial mechanics and maintenance technology; liberal arts and sciences/liberal studies; machine shop technology; respiratory care therapy; trade and industrial teacher education.

Academic Programs *Special study options:* academic remediation for entering students, accelerated degree program, English as a second language, internships, part-time degree program, summer session for credit.

Library University of Arkansas Community College at Hope Library with 5,150 titles, 250 serial subscriptions, 524 audiovisual materials, an OPAC, a Web page.

Computers on Campus Internet access, at least one staffed computer lab available.

Student Life *Housing:* college housing not available. *Activities and Organizations:* Student Government Association, Phi Theta Kappa, Phi Beta Lambda, Circle K. *Campus security:* on-campus security during class hours.

Standardized Tests *Required for some:* ACT ASSET. *Recommended:* ACT (for placement), ACT ASSET.

Costs (2003–04) *Tuition:* area resident $1248 full-time, $52 per credit hour part-time; state resident $1368 full-time, $57 per credit hour part-time; nonresi-

dent $2664 full-time, $111 per credit hour part-time. Part-time tuition and fees vary according to course load. *Required fees:* $150 full-time, $5 per credit hour part-time. *Payment plan:* installment. *Waivers:* senior citizens and employees or children of employees.

Financial Aid Of all full-time matriculated undergraduates who enrolled, 60 Federal Work-Study jobs (averaging $3000).

Applying *Options:* early admission. *Required:* high school transcript. *Application deadline:* rolling (freshmen), rolling (transfers).

Admissions Contact Ms. Danita Ormand, Director of Enrollment Services, University of Arkansas Community College at Hope, 71802-0140. *Phone:* 870-777-5722 Ext. 1267. *Fax:* 870-722-6630.

UNIVERSITY OF ARKANSAS COMMUNITY COLLEGE AT MORRILTON
Morrilton, Arkansas

- **State-supported** 2-year, founded 1961, part of University of Arkansas System
- **Calendar** semesters
- **Degree** certificates and associate
- **Rural** 63-acre campus
- **Coed**

Faculty *Student/faculty ratio:* 19:1.

Student Life *Campus security:* 24-hour emergency response devices.

Standardized Tests *Required:* ACT (for placement), ACT ASSET or ACT COMPASS (for placement).

Costs (2004–05) *Tuition:* area resident $1920 full-time, $64 per credit hour part-time; state resident $2100 full-time, $70 per credit hour part-time; nonresident $3060 full-time, $102 per credit hour part-time. *Required fees:* $130 full-time, $65 per term part-time.

Financial Aid Of all full-time matriculated undergraduates who enrolled, 20 Federal Work-Study jobs (averaging $1000). *Financial aid deadline:* 7/23.

Applying *Options:* common application, early admission, deferred entrance. *Required:* high school transcript. *Required for some:* immunization records.

Admissions Contact Dr. Gary Gaston, Vice Chancellor for Student Services, University of Arkansas Community College at Morrilton, One Bruce Street, Morrilton, AR 72110. *Phone:* 501-977-2014. *Toll-free phone:* 800-264-1094. *Fax:* 501-354-9948.

CALIFORNIA

ALLAN HANCOCK COLLEGE
Santa Maria, California

- **State and locally supported** 2-year, founded 1920
- **Calendar** semesters
- **Degree** certificates and associate
- **Small-town** 120-acre campus
- **Endowment** $1.1 million
- **Coed**

Student Life *Campus security:* 24-hour emergency response devices and patrols, student patrols, late-night transport/escort service.

Standardized Tests *Required for some:* Assessment and Placement Services for Community Colleges.

Financial Aid Of all full-time matriculated undergraduates who enrolled, 250 Federal Work-Study jobs (averaging $3000).

Applying *Options:* early admission. *Required:* high school transcript.

Admissions Contact Ms. Norma Razo, Director of Admissions and Records, Allan Hancock College, 800 South College Drive, Santa Maria, CA 93454-6399. *Phone:* 805-922-6966 Ext. 3272. *Toll-free phone:* 866-342-5242. *Fax:* 805-922-3477. *E-mail:* nrazo@ahc.sbceo.k12.ca.us.

AMERICAN ACADEMY OF DRAMATIC ARTS/HOLLYWOOD
Hollywood, California

- **Independent** 2-year, founded 1974
- **Calendar** continuous
- **Degree** certificates, diplomas, and associate
- **Suburban** 4-acre campus with easy access to Los Angeles
- **Coed,** 177 undergraduate students, 100% full-time, 58% women, 42% men

American Academy of Dramatic Arts / Hollywood (continued)

Undergraduates 177 full-time. Students come from 21 states and territories, 3 other countries, 40% are from out of state, 6% African American, 5% Asian American or Pacific Islander, 12% Hispanic American, 0.6% Native American, 8% international.

Freshmen *Admission:* 507 applied, 176 admitted, 45 enrolled. *Average high school GPA:* 2.98.

Faculty *Total:* 28, 29% with terminal degrees. *Student/faculty ratio:* 15:1.

Majors Dramatic/theatre arts.

Library Bryn Morgan Library with 7,700 titles, 24 serial subscriptions, 320 audiovisual materials.

Student Life *Housing:* college housing not available. *Campus security:* 24-hour emergency response devices, 8-hour patrols by trained security personnel.

Costs (2004–05) *Tuition:* $14,900 full-time. *Required fees:* $450 full-time. *Payment plan:* installment.

Financial Aid Of all full-time matriculated undergraduates who enrolled, 15 Federal Work-Study jobs (averaging $2000).

Applying *Options:* deferred entrance. *Application fee:* $50. *Required:* essay or personal statement, high school transcript, 2 letters of recommendation, interview, audition. *Recommended:* minimum 2.0 GPA. *Application deadline:* rolling (freshmen), rolling (transfers). *Notification:* continuous (freshmen), continuous (transfers).

Admissions Contact Mr. Dan Justin, Director of Admissions, American Academy of Dramatic Arts/Hollywood, 1336 North LaBrea Avenue, Hollywood, CA 90028. *Phone:* 800-222-2867 Ext. 103. *Toll-free phone:* 800-222-2867. *E-mail:* admissions-ca@aada.org.

▶ **See page 496 for a narrative description.**

AMERICAN RIVER COLLEGE
Sacramento, California

- **District-supported** 2-year, founded 1955, part of Los Rios Community College District System
- **Calendar** semesters
- **Degree** certificates and associate
- **Suburban** 153-acre campus
- **Coed**, 30,000 undergraduate students

Undergraduates 0.2% are from out of state.

Freshmen *Admission:* 2,471 applied, 2,471 admitted.

Faculty *Total:* 1,200. *Student/faculty ratio:* 34:1.

Majors Accounting; administrative assistant and secretarial science; advertising; art; automobile/automotive mechanics technology; biological and physical sciences; business administration and management; carpentry; child development; computer and information sciences related; computer and information systems security; computer engineering technology; computer graphics; computer programming; computer programming related; computer programming (specific applications); computer programming (vendor/product certification); computer software and media applications related; computer systems networking and telecommunications; computer/technical support; construction engineering technology; consumer merchandising/retailing management; culinary arts; data entry/microcomputer applications; data processing and data processing technology; drafting and design technology; dramatic/theatre arts; electrical, electronic and communications engineering technology; engineering technology; family and consumer sciences/home economics teacher education; fashion/apparel design; fashion merchandising; finance; fire science; forestry technology; gerontology; horticultural science; hospitality and recreation marketing; hotel/motel administration; human services; industrial arts; interior design; journalism; kindergarten/preschool education; landscape architecture; legal administrative assistant/secretary; legal assistant/paralegal; liberal arts and sciences/liberal studies; marketing/marketing management; mathematics; medical administrative assistant and medical secretary; music; music management and merchandising; natural resources management and policy; nursing (registered nurse training); parks, recreation and leisure; physical sciences; pre-engineering; real estate; respiratory care therapy; sign language interpretation and translation; social sciences; special products marketing; system administration; web/multimedia management and webmaster; web page, digital/multimedia and information resources design; welding technology.

Academic Programs *Special study options:* academic remediation for entering students, adult/continuing education programs, advanced placement credit, cooperative education, English as a second language, part-time degree program, services for LD students, summer session for credit.

Library 78,400 titles, 75 serial subscriptions.

Computers on Campus At least one staffed computer lab available.

Student Life *Housing:* college housing not available. *Activities and Organizations:* drama/theater group, student-run newspaper. *Campus security:* 24-hour

emergency response devices and patrols, student patrols, late-night transport/escort service. *Student services:* health clinic, personal/psychological counseling, women's center.

Athletics *Intercollegiate sports:* basketball M/W, cheerleading W(s), cross-country running M/W, football M, golf M/W, soccer M/W, swimming M/W, tennis M/W, track and field M/W, volleyball M/W. *Intramural sports:* basketball M/W.

Standardized Tests *Required for some:* nursing exam. *Recommended:* SAT I or ACT (for placement).

Costs (2003–04) *Tuition:* nonresident $5010 full-time, $167 per unit part-time. *Required fees:* $542 full-time, $18 per unit part-time, $1 per term part-time.

Financial Aid Of all full-time matriculated undergraduates who enrolled, 300 Federal Work-Study jobs (averaging $1500). 100 state and other part-time jobs (averaging $2000).

Applying *Options:* common application, early admission, deferred entrance. *Application deadline:* rolling (freshmen), rolling (transfers).

Admissions Contact Ms. Celia Esposito, Dean of Enrollment Services, American River College, 4700 College Oak Drive, Sacramento, CA 95841-4286. *Phone:* 916-484-8171. *E-mail:* recadmiss@mail.arc.losrios.cc.ca.us.

ANTELOPE VALLEY COLLEGE
Lancaster, California

- **State and locally supported** 2-year, founded 1929, part of California Community College System
- **Calendar** semesters
- **Degree** certificates and associate
- **Suburban** 160-acre campus with easy access to Los Angeles
- **Endowment** $299,569
- **Coed**

Student Life *Campus security:* 24-hour emergency response devices and patrols, late-night transport/escort service.

Costs (2003–04) *Tuition:* state resident $0 full-time; nonresident $3576 full-time, $149 per unit part-time. *Required fees:* $432 full-time, $18 per unit part-time.

Applying *Options:* common application, early admission. *Required:* high school transcript.

Admissions Contact Office of Admissions, Antelope Valley College, 3041 West Avenue K, Lancaster, CA 93536-5426. *Phone:* 661-722-6300. *E-mail:* info@avc.edu.

AVIATION & ELECTRONIC SCHOOLS OF AMERICA
Colfax, California

Admissions Contact 210 South Railroad Street, PO Box 1810, Colfax, CA 95713-1810. *Toll-free phone:* 800-345-2742.

BAKERSFIELD COLLEGE
Bakersfield, California

Admissions Contact Ms. Sue Vaughn, Director of Enrollment Services, Bakersfield College, 1801 Panorama Drive, Bakersfield, CA 93305-1299. *Phone:* 661-395-4301. *E-mail:* svaughn@bc.cc.ca.us.

BARSTOW COLLEGE
Barstow, California

- **State and locally supported** 2-year, founded 1959, part of California Community College System
- **Calendar** semesters
- **Degree** associate
- **Small-town** 50-acre campus
- **Coed**

Faculty *Student/faculty ratio:* 20:1.

Student Life *Campus security:* evening security personnel.

Athletics Member NJCAA.

Standardized Tests *Required:* assessment test approved by the Chancellor's office (for placement).

Applying *Options:* common application, early admission, deferred entrance. *Recommended:* high school transcript.

Admissions Contact Mr. Don Low, Interim Vice President, Barstow College, 2700 Barstow Road, Barstow, CA 92311-6699. *Fax:* 760-252-1875.

BROOKS COLLEGE
Long Beach, California

Admissions Contact Ms. Christina Varon, Director of Admissions, Brooks College, 4825 East Pacific Coast Highway, Long Beach, CA 90804-3291. *Phone:* 562-498-2441 Ext. 265. *Toll-free phone:* 800-421-3775. *Fax:* 562-597-7412. *E-mail:* info@brookscollege.edu.

BROOKS COLLEGE
Sunnyvale, California

Admissions Contact 1120 Kifer Road, Sunnyvale, CA 94086.

BRYMAN COLLEGE
Ontario, California

Admissions Contact 520 North Euclid Avenue, Ontario, CA 91762-3591.

BRYMAN COLLEGE
Whittier, California

Admissions Contact 12449 Putnam Street, Whittier, CA 90602.

BUTTE COLLEGE
Oroville, California

- **District-supported** 2-year, founded 1966, part of California Community College System
- **Calendar** semesters
- **Degree** certificates and associate
- **Rural** 900-acre campus
- **Coed,** 14,251 undergraduate students

Undergraduates Students come from 19 states and territories, 25 other countries, 2% African American, 5% Asian American or Pacific Islander, 11% Hispanic American, 2% Native American, 1% international.
Freshmen *Admission:* 1,102 applied, 1,102 admitted.
Faculty *Total:* 625, 28% full-time. *Student/faculty ratio:* 24:1.
Majors Accounting; administrative assistant and secretarial science; agricultural business and management; agricultural economics; agriculture; agronomy and crop science; animal sciences; applied art; art; automobile/automotive mechanics technology; biology/biological sciences; business teacher education; civil engineering technology; clinical laboratory science/medical technology; commercial and advertising art; construction engineering technology; cosmetology; court reporting; criminal justice/law enforcement administration; criminal justice/police science; data processing and data processing technology; drafting and design technology; electrical, electronic and communications engineering technology; family and consumer economics related; family and consumer sciences/human sciences; fashion/apparel design; fashion merchandising; finance; fire science; health science; horticultural science; kindergarten/preschool education; landscape architecture; legal administrative assistant/secretary; liberal arts and sciences/liberal studies; marketing/marketing management; mathematics; medical administrative assistant and medical secretary; music; natural resources management and policy; nursing (licensed practical/vocational nurse training); nursing (registered nurse training); ornamental horticulture; parks, recreation and leisure facilities management; photography; physical education teaching and coaching; physical sciences; political science and government; psychology; real estate; respiratory care therapy; social sciences; telecommunications; tourism and travel services management; welding technology.
Academic Programs *Special study options:* academic remediation for entering students, accelerated degree program, adult/continuing education programs, advanced placement credit, cooperative education, English as a second language, honors programs, internships, part-time degree program, services for LD students, study abroad, summer session for credit.
Library 50,000 titles, 300 serial subscriptions, an OPAC.
Computers on Campus 65 computers available on campus for general student use. A campuswide network can be accessed from off campus. At least one staffed computer lab available.
Student Life *Housing:* college housing not available. *Activities and Organizations:* drama/theater group, student-run newspaper, television station. *Campus security:* 24-hour emergency response devices and patrols, student patrols. *Student services:* health clinic, personal/psychological counseling, legal services.
Athletics *Intercollegiate sports:* baseball M, basketball M/W, cross-country running M/W, football M, golf M/W, soccer W, softball W, tennis M/W, track and field M/W, volleyball W. *Intramural sports:* equestrian sports M/W.

Costs (2004–05) *Tuition:* state resident $0 full-time; nonresident $4200 full-time, $175 per unit part-time. Part-time tuition and fees vary according to course load. *Required fees:* $596 full-time, $18 per unit part-time.
Applying *Options:* early admission, deferred entrance. *Required for some:* high school transcript. *Application deadline:* rolling (freshmen), rolling (transfers).
Admissions Contact Ms. Nancy Jenson, Registrar, Butte College, 3536 Butte Campus Drive, Oroville, CA 95965. *Phone:* 530-895-2361. *E-mail:* admissions@butte.cc.ca.us.

CABRILLO COLLEGE
Aptos, California

- **District-supported** 2-year, founded 1959, part of California Community College System
- **Calendar** semesters
- **Degree** certificates and associate
- **Small-town** 120-acre campus with easy access to San Jose
- **Coed,** 13,905 undergraduate students, 29% full-time, 58% women, 42% men

Undergraduates 4,041 full-time, 9,864 part-time. Students come from 21 states and territories, 63 other countries, 3% are from out of state, 2% African American, 5% Asian American or Pacific Islander, 23% Hispanic American, 1% Native American, 2% international.
Faculty *Total:* 651, 18% full-time, 29% with terminal degrees.
Majors Accounting; biological and physical sciences; business administration and management; business machine repair; cartography; ceramic arts and ceramics; child development; computer programming; computer science; construction management; consumer merchandising/retailing management; data processing and data processing technology; dental hygiene; drafting and design technology; electrical, electronic and communications engineering technology; energy management and systems technology; fire science; food science; food services technology; health information/medical records administration; health science; horticultural science; industrial design; kindergarten/preschool education; liberal arts and sciences/liberal studies; medical administrative assistant and medical secretary; natural sciences; nursing (registered nurse training); parks, recreation and leisure; physical education teaching and coaching; pre-engineering; real estate; solar energy technology; Spanish; special products marketing; welding technology; wildlife and wildlands science and management; women's studies.
Academic Programs *Special study options:* academic remediation for entering students, adult/continuing education programs, advanced placement credit, cooperative education, distance learning, double majors, English as a second language, honors programs, independent study, internships, part-time degree program, services for LD students, study abroad, summer session for credit.
Library 60,000 titles, 300 serial subscriptions, an OPAC, a Web page.
Computers on Campus 500 computers available on campus for general student use. A campuswide network can be accessed. Internet access, online (class) registration, at least one staffed computer lab available.
Student Life *Housing:* college housing not available. *Activities and Organizations:* drama/theater group, student-run newspaper. *Student services:* health clinic, personal/psychological counseling, women's center.
Athletics *Intercollegiate sports:* baseball M, basketball M/W, cross-country running M/W, football M, golf M/W, soccer M/W, softball W, swimming M/W, tennis M/W, track and field M/W, volleyball M/W, water polo M/W, wrestling M. *Intramural sports:* basketball M/W, cheerleading W, sailing M/W, skiing (cross-country) M/W, skiing (downhill) M/W, volleyball W.
Costs (2003–04) *Tuition:* state resident $0 full-time; nonresident $4452 full-time, $159 per unit part-time. Full-time tuition and fees vary according to course load. Part-time tuition and fees vary according to course load. *Required fees:* $36 full-time, $18 per unit part-time, $18 per term part-time.
Financial Aid Of all full-time matriculated undergraduates who enrolled, 50 Federal Work-Study jobs (averaging $4000).
Applying *Options:* early admission. *Required for some:* high school transcript. *Application deadline:* rolling (freshmen), rolling (transfers).
Admissions Contact Ms. Gloria Garing, Director of Admissions and Records, Cabrillo College, 6500 Soquel Drive, Aptos, CA 95003. *Phone:* 831-479-6201. *Fax:* 831-479-5782. *E-mail:* ar-mail@cabrillo.edu.

CALIFORNIA CULINARY ACADEMY
San Francisco, California

- **Proprietary** 2-year, founded 1977
- **Calendar** continuous
- **Degree** certificates and associate
- **Urban** campus
- **Coed,** 822 undergraduate students, 100% full-time, 45% women, 55% men

Undergraduates 822 full-time. Students come from 40 states and territories, 12 other countries, 30% are from out of state, 7% African American, 12% Asian American or Pacific Islander, 13% Hispanic American, 1% Native American, 7% international, 39% live on campus.

California Culinary Academy (continued)
Freshmen *Admission:* 822 enrolled.
Faculty *Total:* 72, 97% full-time. *Student/faculty ratio:* 16:1.
Majors Baking and pastry arts; culinary arts; restaurant, culinary, and catering management.
Academic Programs *Special study options:* cooperative education, services for LD students.
Library Academy Library plus 1 other with 3,000 titles, 70 serial subscriptions.
Computers on Campus 50 computers available on campus for general student use. Internet access, at least one staffed computer lab available.
Student Life *Housing Options:* coed. Campus housing is leased by the school and is provided by a third party. *Activities and Organizations:* Student Council. *Campus security:* 24-hour emergency response devices and patrols, controlled dormitory access.
Costs (2003–04) *Tuition:* Full-time tuition and fees vary according to program. The tuition is $22,680—$42,395 and the fees are $68—$127 depending on program selected. *Room and board:* room only: $7200.
Financial Aid Of all full-time matriculated undergraduates who enrolled, 45 Federal Work-Study jobs (averaging $3000).
Applying *Options:* common application, electronic application. *Application fee:* $65. *Required:* high school transcript, interview. *Application deadline:* rolling (freshmen). *Notification:* continuous (freshmen), continuous (transfers).
Admissions Contact Ms. Nancy Seyfert, Vice President of Admissions, California Culinary Academy, 625 Polk Street, San Francisco, CA 94102-3368. *Phone:* 800-229-2433 Ext. 275. *Toll-free phone:* 800-229-2433 (in-state); 800-BAYCHEF (out-of-state). *Fax:* 415-771-2194. *E-mail:* admissions@baychef.com.

CALIFORNIA DESIGN COLLEGE
Los Angeles, California

Admissions Contact Mr. Allan S. Gueco, Director of Admissions, California Design College, 3440 Wilshire Boulevard, Seventh Floor, Los Angeles, CA 90010. *Phone:* 213-251-3636 Ext. 120. *Fax:* 213-385-3545. *E-mail:* sk@cdc.edu.

CANADA COLLEGE
Redwood City, California

- **State and locally supported** 2-year, founded 1968, part of San Mateo County Community College District System
- **Calendar** semesters
- **Degree** certificates and associate
- **Suburban** 131-acre campus with easy access to San Francisco and San Jose
- **Coed,** 6,421 undergraduate students

Undergraduates Students come from 32 other countries, 4% African American, 8% Asian American or Pacific Islander, 42% Hispanic American, 0.4% Native American. *Retention:* 65% of 2002 full-time freshmen returned.
Freshmen *Admission:* 1,020 applied, 1,020 admitted.
Faculty *Total:* 250.
Majors Accounting; administrative assistant and secretarial science; anatomy; anthropology; art; art history, criticism and conservation; biological and physical sciences; biology/biological sciences; business administration and management; business machine repair; chemistry; computer engineering technology; computer programming; computer science; dance; data processing and data processing technology; dramatic/theatre arts; drawing; economics; engineering; English; environmental studies; fashion/apparel design; French; geography; geology/earth science; German; health science; health teacher education; history; humanities; industrial radiologic technology; information science/studies; interior design; journalism; kindergarten/preschool education; kinesiology and exercise science; legal assistant/paralegal; liberal arts and sciences/liberal studies; mathematics; music; philosophy; physical education teaching and coaching; political science and government; psychology; sociology; Spanish; speech and rhetoric; tourism and travel services management.
Academic Programs *Special study options:* academic remediation for entering students, accelerated degree program, adult/continuing education programs, advanced placement credit, cooperative education, English as a second language, internships, part-time degree program, services for LD students, study abroad, summer session for credit.
Library 53,417 titles, 414 serial subscriptions, an OPAC.
Computers on Campus 55 computers available on campus for general student use. At least one staffed computer lab available.
Student Life *Housing:* college housing not available. *Activities and Organizations:* drama/theater group, choral group, Latin-American Club, student government, Environmental Club, athletics, Interior Design Club. *Campus security:* 12-hour patrols by trained security personnel. *Student services:* health clinic, personal/psychological counseling.

Athletics *Intercollegiate sports:* baseball M. *Intramural sports:* basketball M/W, soccer M, tennis M/W, volleyball M/W.
Costs (2003–04) *Tuition:* state resident $0 full-time; nonresident $4176 full-time, $174 per unit part-time. *Required fees:* $458 full-time, $11 per unit part-time, $18 per term part-time.
Financial Aid Of all full-time matriculated undergraduates who enrolled, 25 Federal Work-Study jobs (averaging $4000).
Applying *Options:* early admission. *Application deadline:* rolling (freshmen), rolling (transfers).
Admissions Contact Mr. Jose Romero, Lead Records Clerk, Canada College, 4200 Farm Hill Boulevard, Redwood City, CA 94061. *Phone:* 650-306-3395. *Fax:* 650-306-3113.

CERRITOS COLLEGE
Norwalk, California

- **State and locally supported** 2-year, founded 1956, part of California Community College System
- **Calendar** semesters
- **Degree** associate
- **Suburban** 140-acre campus with easy access to Los Angeles
- **Coed**

Athletics Member NJCAA.
Standardized Tests *Recommended:* CEPT, Nelson Denny Reading Test.
Costs (2003–04) *Tuition:* nonresident $149 per unit part-time. *Required fees:* $18 per unit part-time, $23 per term part-time.
Financial Aid Of all full-time matriculated undergraduates who enrolled, 180 Federal Work-Study jobs (averaging $3000). 89 state and other part-time jobs (averaging $2734).
Applying *Options:* early admission, deferred entrance.
Admissions Contact Ms. Stephanie Murguia, Director of Admissions and Records, Cerritos College, 11110 Alondra Boulevard, Norwalk, CA 90650-6298. *Phone:* 562-860-2451. *E-mail:* rbell@cerritos.edu.

CERRO COSO COMMUNITY COLLEGE
Ridgecrest, California

Admissions Contact Ms. Lois Bozarth, Director of Admissions and Records, Cerro Coso Community College, 3000 College Heights Boulevard, Ridgecrest, CA 93555. *Phone:* 760-384-6100. *Fax:* 760-375-4776.

CHABOT COLLEGE
Hayward, California

- **State-supported** 2-year, founded 1961, part of California Community College System
- **Calendar** semesters
- **Degree** certificates and associate
- **Suburban** 245-acre campus with easy access to San Francisco
- **Coed,** 15,075 undergraduate students

Undergraduates Students come from 78 other countries, 2% are from out of state, 13% African American, 30% Asian American or Pacific Islander, 22% Hispanic American, 0.8% Native American. *Retention:* 66% of 2002 full-time freshmen returned.
Freshmen *Admission:* 1,248 applied, 1,248 admitted.
Faculty *Total:* 512, 36% full-time. *Student/faculty ratio:* 24:1.
Majors Accounting; administrative assistant and secretarial science; advertising; animal physiology; applied mathematics; architectural engineering technology; art; automobile/automotive mechanics technology; behavioral sciences; biological and physical sciences; biology/biological sciences; broadcast journalism; business administration and management; business machine repair; business/managerial economics; business teacher education; chemistry; civil engineering technology; commercial and advertising art; computer and information sciences related; computer engineering technology; computer programming (specific applications); computer science; computer typography and composition equipment operation; consumer merchandising/retailing management; corrections; criminal justice/law enforcement administration; criminal justice/police science; data processing and data processing technology; dental hygiene; drawing; ecology; economics; education; electrical, electronic and communications engineering technology; electromechanical technology; emergency medical technology (EMT paramedic); engineering; engineering technology; English; fashion/apparel design; fashion merchandising; finance; fine/studio arts; fire science; health information/medical records administration; health teacher education; history; horticultural science; humanities; human services; industrial arts; industrial technology; information science/studies; instrumentation technology; interdisciplinary studies; Italian; journalism; kindergarten/preschool education;

landscaping and groundskeeping; legal administrative assistant/secretary; liberal arts and sciences/liberal studies; literature; mass communication/media; mathematics; medical/clinical assistant; music; natural sciences; nursing (registered nurse training); ornamental horticulture; parks, recreation and leisure; photography; physical education teaching and coaching; physics; political science and government; pre-engineering; psychology; radio and television; real estate; social sciences; sociology; solar energy technology; Spanish; statistics; survey technology; teacher assistant/aide; tourism and travel services management; welding technology; women's studies; zoology/animal biology.

Academic Programs *Special study options:* academic remediation for entering students, adult/continuing education programs, advanced placement credit, distance learning, double majors, English as a second language, internships, off-campus study, part-time degree program, services for LD students, student-designed majors, study abroad, summer session for credit. *ROTC:* Army (c), Air Force (c).

Library Chabot Library with 100,000 titles, 160 serial subscriptions.

Computers on Campus 100 computers available on campus for general student use. A campuswide network can be accessed from off campus. Internet access, online (class) registration, at least one staffed computer lab available.

Student Life *Housing:* college housing not available. *Activities and Organizations:* drama/theater group, student-run newspaper, radio and television station, choral group, Chinese Club, International Club, MECHA, ASCC, SCTA (Student California Teachers Association). *Campus security:* 24-hour emergency response devices, late-night transport/escort service. *Student services:* personal/psychological counseling, legal services.

Athletics *Intercollegiate sports:* baseball M, basketball M/W, cross-country running M/W, football M, golf M, soccer M/W, softball W, swimming M/W, tennis M/W, track and field M/W, wrestling M. *Intramural sports:* archery M/W, badminton M/W, basketball M/W, bowling M/W, football M, golf M/W, gymnastics M/W, racquetball M/W, skiing (cross-country) M/W, skiing (downhill) M/W, soccer M/W, softball M/W, swimming M/W, table tennis M/W, tennis M/W, track and field M/W, volleyball M/W, weight lifting M/W.

Costs (2003–04) *Tuition:* state resident $0 full-time; nonresident $3576 full-time, $149 per unit part-time. *Required fees:* $264 full-time, $18 per unit part-time.

Financial Aid Of all full-time matriculated undergraduates who enrolled, 75 Federal Work-Study jobs (averaging $3000).

Applying *Options:* electronic application. *Required:* high school transcript. *Notification:* continuous (freshmen), continuous (transfers).

Admissions Contact Ms. Judy Young, Director of Admissions and Records, Chabot College, 25555 Hesperian Boulevard, Hayward, CA 94545. *Phone:* 510-723-6700. *Fax:* 510-723-7510.

CHAFFEY COLLEGE
Rancho Cucamonga, California

- **District-supported** 2-year, founded 1883, part of California Community College System
- **Calendar** semesters
- **Degree** certificates and associate
- **Suburban** 200-acre campus with easy access to Los Angeles
- **Coed**

Student Life *Campus security:* 24-hour emergency response devices, late-night transport/escort service.

Athletics Member NJCAA.

Costs (2003–04) *Tuition:* state resident $0 full-time. *Required fees:* $18 per unit part-time.

Financial Aid Of all full-time matriculated undergraduates who enrolled, 1,200 Federal Work-Study jobs (averaging $2000).

Applying *Options:* early admission.

Admissions Contact Ms. Cecilia Carerra, Director of Admissions, Registration, and Records, Chaffey College, 5885 Haven Avenue, Rancho Cucamonga, CA 91737-3002. *Phone:* 909-941-2631.

CITRUS COLLEGE
Glendora, California

- **State and locally supported** 2-year, founded 1915, part of California Community College System
- **Calendar** semesters
- **Degree** certificates, diplomas, and associate
- **Small-town** 104-acre campus with easy access to Los Angeles
- **Coed**

Student Life *Campus security:* 24-hour patrols, student patrols, late-night transport/escort service.

Standardized Tests *Required for some:* ACT ASSET.

Costs (2003–04) *Tuition:* state resident $0 full-time; nonresident $4886 full-time, $150 per unit part-time. Full-time tuition and fees vary according to course load. Part-time tuition and fees vary according to course load. *Required fees:* $386 full-time, $11 per unit part-time.

Financial Aid Of all full-time matriculated undergraduates who enrolled, 141 Federal Work-Study jobs (averaging $5500).

Applying *Required:* high school transcript.

Admissions Contact Admissions and Records, Citrus College, 1000 West Foothill Boulevard, Glendora, CA 91741-1899. *Phone:* 626-914-8511. *Fax:* 626-914-8613. *E-mail:* admissions@citruscollege.edu.

CITY COLLEGE OF SAN FRANCISCO
San Francisco, California

- **State and locally supported** 2-year, founded 1935, part of California Community College System
- **Calendar** semesters
- **Degree** certificates, diplomas, and associate
- **Urban** 56-acre campus
- **Coed**

Student Life *Campus security:* 24-hour patrols.

Financial Aid Of all full-time matriculated undergraduates who enrolled, 3,000 Federal Work-Study jobs (averaging $3000). *Financial aid deadline:* 6/11.

Applying *Options:* early admission.

Admissions Contact Mr. Robert Balesteri, Dean of Admissions and Records, City College of San Francisco, 50 Phelan Avenue, San Francisco, CA 94112-1821. *Phone:* 415-239-3291. *Fax:* 415-239-3936.

COASTLINE COMMUNITY COLLEGE
Fountain Valley, California

- **State and locally supported** 2-year, founded 1976, part of Coast Community College District System
- **Calendar** semesters
- **Degree** certificates and associate
- **Urban** campus with easy access to Los Angeles
- **Coed**, 8,559 undergraduate students, 6% full-time, 60% women, 40% men

Undergraduates 493 full-time, 8,066 part-time. Students come from 1 other state, 6% African American, 29% Asian American or Pacific Islander, 14% Hispanic American, 1% Native American, 1% international, 48% transferred in.

Freshmen *Admission:* 409 enrolled.

Faculty *Total:* 349, 14% full-time. *Student/faculty ratio:* 24:1.

Majors Liberal arts and sciences/liberal studies.

Academic Programs *Special study options:* academic remediation for entering students, adult/continuing education programs, advanced placement credit, cooperative education, distance learning, English as a second language, external degree program, internships, part-time degree program, services for LD students, summer session for credit.

Computers on Campus Internet access available.

Student Life *Housing:* college housing not available. *Campus security:* 24-hour emergency response devices. *Student services:* health clinic.

Costs (2003–04) *Tuition:* state resident $0 full-time; nonresident $4500 full-time. *Required fees:* $563 full-time.

Financial Aid Of all full-time matriculated undergraduates who enrolled, 20 Federal Work-Study jobs (averaging $4500).

Applying *Options:* common application, early admission. *Recommended:* high school transcript. *Application deadline:* rolling (freshmen), rolling (transfers).

Admissions Contact Jennifer McDonald, Director of Admissions and Records, Coastline Community College, 11460 Warner Avenue, Fountain Valley, CA 92708. *Phone:* 714-241-6163. *Fax:* 714-241-6288.

COLEMAN COLLEGE
San Marcos, California

- **Independent** 2-year, founded 1967
- **Calendar** quarters
- **Degree** certificates and associate
- **Suburban** campus
- **Coed**, 203 undergraduate students, 100% full-time, 27% women, 73% men

Undergraduates 203 full-time. 8% African American, 9% Asian American or Pacific Islander, 16% Hispanic American.

Freshmen *Admission:* 138 enrolled.

Admissions Contact Mr. James Warner, Senior Admissions Officer, Coleman College, 1284 West San Marcos Boulevard, San Marcos, CA 92069. *Phone:* 760-747-3990.

COLLEGE OF ALAMEDA
Alameda, California

- **State and locally supported** 2-year, founded 1970, part of Peralta Community College District System
- **Calendar** semesters
- **Degree** certificates and associate
- **Urban** 62-acre campus with easy access to San Francisco
- **Coed**

Standardized Tests *Recommended:* SAT I or ACT (for placement).
Financial Aid Of all full-time matriculated undergraduates who enrolled, 90 Federal Work-Study jobs (averaging $2500).
Admissions Contact Ms. Barbara Simmons, District Admissions Officer, College of Alameda, 555 Atlantic Avenue, Alameda, CA 94501-2109. *Phone:* 510-466-7370. *E-mail:* hperdue@peralta.cc.ca.us.

COLLEGE OF MARIN
Kentfield, California

- **State and locally supported** 2-year, founded 1926, part of California Community College System
- **Calendar** semesters
- **Degree** associate
- **Small-town** 410-acre campus with easy access to San Francisco
- **Coed**

Student Life *Campus security:* 24-hour patrols.
Costs (2003–04) *Tuition:* state resident $0 full-time; nonresident $3816 full-time, $159 per unit part-time. *Required fees:* $432 full-time, $18 per unit part-time.
Financial Aid Of all full-time matriculated undergraduates who enrolled, 100 Federal Work-Study jobs (averaging $2500).
Applying *Options:* early admission.
Admissions Contact Ms. Gina Longo, Secretary to the Dean of Enrollment Services, College of Marin, 835 College Avenue, Kentfield, CA 94904. *Phone:* 415-485-9417.

COLLEGE OF OCEANEERING
Wilmington, California

- **Proprietary** 2-year
- **Calendar** continuous
- **Degree** certificates and associate
- **Suburban** 5-acre campus with easy access to Los Angeles
- **Coed, primarily men,** 272 undergraduate students

Undergraduates Students come from 52 states and territories, 5 other countries, 50% are from out of state.
Freshmen *Admission:* 598 applied, 352 admitted.
Faculty *Total:* 14, 100% full-time. *Student/faculty ratio:* 15:1.
Majors Emergency medical technology (EMT paramedic); marine technology; welding technology.
Academic Programs *Special study options:* advanced placement credit, cooperative education, double majors, internships, off-campus study.
Computers on Campus 3 computers available on campus for general student use. A campuswide network can be accessed. Internet access, online (class) registration available.
Student Life *Housing:* college housing not available. *Campus security:* 24-hour emergency response devices. *Student services:* personal/psychological counseling.
Costs (2003–04) *Tuition:* $16,100 full-time.
Financial Aid Of all full-time matriculated undergraduates who enrolled, 22 Federal Work-Study jobs (averaging $4000).
Applying *Options:* common application, electronic application, deferred entrance. *Application fee:* $50. *Required:* essay or personal statement, high school transcript, interview, physical examination. *Application deadline:* rolling (freshmen), rolling (transfers). *Notification:* continuous (freshmen), continuous (transfers).
Admissions Contact Ms. Deborah Montgomery, Director of Admissions, College of Oceaneering, 272 South Fries Avenue, Wilmington, CA 90744-6399. *Phone:* 310-834-2501 Ext. 237. *Toll-free phone:* 800-432-DIVE Ext. 237. *Fax:* 310-834-7132. *E-mail:* sestep@diveco.com.

COLLEGE OF SAN MATEO
San Mateo, California

Admissions Contact Mr. Henry Villareal, Dean of Admissions and Records, College of San Mateo, 1700 West Hillsdale Boulevard, San Mateo, CA 94402-3784. *Phone:* 650-574-6594. *E-mail:* csmadmission@smcccd.cc.ca.us.

COLLEGE OF THE CANYONS
Santa Clarita, California

- **State and locally supported** 2-year, founded 1969, part of California Community College System
- **Calendar** semesters
- **Degree** certificates and associate
- **Suburban** 158-acre campus with easy access to Los Angeles
- **Coed,** 15,053 undergraduate students

Undergraduates Students come from 15 states and territories, 3% are from out of state, 4% African American, 6% Asian American or Pacific Islander, 20% Hispanic American, 0.7% Native American. *Retention:* 51% of 2002 full-time freshmen returned.
Faculty *Total:* 562, 29% full-time. *Student/faculty ratio:* 28:1.
Majors Accounting; administrative assistant and secretarial science; art; biological and physical sciences; biology/biological sciences; business administration and management; chemistry; child development; cinematography and film/video production; computer and information sciences related; computer engineering related; computer science; criminal justice/law enforcement administration; criminal justice/police science; developmental and child psychology; drafting and design technology; electrical, electronic and communications engineering technology; English; French; geography; geology/earth science; German; health science; history; hotel/motel administration; humanities; hydrology and water resources science; information science/studies; interior design; journalism; kindergarten/preschool education; liberal arts and sciences/liberal studies; mathematics; natural sciences; nursing (licensed practical/vocational nurse training); nursing (registered nurse training); physical education teaching and coaching; physical sciences; political science and government; pre-engineering; psychology; quality control technology; real estate; social sciences; Spanish; welding technology.
Academic Programs *Special study options:* academic remediation for entering students, adult/continuing education programs, advanced placement credit, cooperative education, distance learning, double majors, English as a second language, honors programs, independent study, internships, off-campus study, part-time degree program, services for LD students, study abroad, summer session for credit.
Library College of the Canyons Library with 40,646 titles, 233 serial subscriptions, 29,955 audiovisual materials, an OPAC, a Web page.
Computers on Campus 650 computers available on campus for general student use. A campuswide network can be accessed. Internet access, at least one staffed computer lab available.
Student Life *Housing:* college housing not available. *Activities and Organizations:* drama/theater group, student-run newspaper, choral group, HITE, Phi Theta Kappa, Alpha Gamma Sigma, MECHA, Biology Club. *Campus security:* student patrols, late-night transport/escort service. *Student services:* health clinic, personal/psychological counseling.
Athletics *Intercollegiate sports:* baseball M, basketball M/W, cross-country running M/W, football M, golf M, soccer W, softball W, swimming M/W, track and field M/W, volleyball W, water polo M.
Standardized Tests *Recommended:* SAT I or ACT (for placement).
Costs (2004–05) *Tuition:* state resident $0 full-time; nonresident $4600 full-time. *Required fees:* $562 full-time.
Applying *Options:* electronic application, early admission. *Recommended:* high school transcript. *Application deadlines:* 8/22 (freshmen), 8/22 (transfers). *Notification:* continuous until 8/22 (freshmen), continuous until 8/22 (transfers).
Admissions Contact Ms. Deborah Rio, Director, Admissions and Records and Online Services, College of the Canyons, 26455 Rockwell Canyon Road, Santa Clara, CA 91355. *Phone:* 661-362-3280. *Toll-free phone:* 888-206-7827. *Fax:* 661-254-7996.

COLLEGE OF THE DESERT
Palm Desert, California

- **State and locally supported** 2-year, founded 1959, part of California Community College System
- **Calendar** semesters
- **Degree** certificates, diplomas, and associate
- **Small-town** 160-acre campus
- **Coed,** 9,946 undergraduate students

Undergraduates Students come from 23 states and territories, 1% are from out of state, 3% African American, 6% Asian American or Pacific Islander, 52% Hispanic American, 0.6% Native American.

Freshmen *Average high school GPA:* 2.72.

Faculty *Total:* 338, 30% full-time.

Majors Administrative assistant and secretarial science; agricultural business and management; anthropology; architectural engineering technology; art; automobile/automotive mechanics technology; biology/biological sciences; business administration and management; business/managerial economics; chemistry; computer and information sciences related; computer graphics; computer programming related; computer science; computer/technical support; computer typography and composition equipment operation; construction management; criminal justice/law enforcement administration; criminal justice/police science; culinary arts; drafting and design technology; dramatic/theatre arts; economics; education; engineering technology; English; environmental studies; fire science; French; geography; geology/earth science; heating, air conditioning, ventilation and refrigeration maintenance technology; history; horticultural science; interior design; Italian; journalism; kindergarten/preschool education; liberal arts and sciences/liberal studies; marketing/marketing management; mass communication/media; mathematics; medical/clinical assistant; music; natural resources management and policy; nursing (registered nurse training); ornamental horticulture; parks, recreation and leisure; parks, recreation and leisure facilities management; philosophy; physical education teaching and coaching; physics; political science and government; pre-engineering; psychology; real estate; respiratory care therapy; Romance languages; social sciences; sociology; speech and rhetoric; teacher assistant/aide; welding technology; word processing.

Academic Programs *Special study options:* academic remediation for entering students, adult/continuing education programs, English as a second language, honors programs, part-time degree program, services for LD students, summer session for credit.

Library College of the Desert Library with 58,000 titles, 260 serial subscriptions.

Computers on Campus 43 computers available on campus for general student use. A campuswide network can be accessed from off campus. At least one staffed computer lab available.

Student Life *Housing:* college housing not available. *Activities and Organizations:* drama/theater group, student-run newspaper, choral group, student association, International Club, African-Americans for College Education. *Campus security:* 24-hour emergency response devices, late-night transport/escort service. *Student services:* health clinic, personal/psychological counseling.

Athletics *Intercollegiate sports:* baseball M, basketball M/W, cross-country running M/W, football M, golf M/W, soccer M, softball W, tennis M/W, track and field M/W, volleyball W. *Intramural sports:* badminton M/W, basketball M/W, fencing M/W, golf M/W, rock climbing W, soccer M, softball M/W, swimming M/W, table tennis M/W, tennis M/W, volleyball M/W.

Financial Aid Of all full-time matriculated undergraduates who enrolled, 125 Federal Work-Study jobs (averaging $750). 50 state and other part-time jobs (averaging $750).

Applying *Options:* early admission. *Application deadline:* rolling (freshmen), rolling (transfers). *Notification:* continuous (freshmen), continuous (transfers).

Admissions Contact Ms. Kathi Westerfield, Registrar, College of the Desert, 43-500 Monterey Avenue, Palm Desert, CA 92260-9305. *Phone:* 760-773-2519. *Toll-free phone:* 760-773-2516.

COLLEGE OF THE REDWOODS
Eureka, California

- **State and locally supported** 2-year, founded 1964, part of California Community College System
- **Calendar** semesters
- **Degree** certificates and associate
- **Small-town** 322-acre campus
- **Endowment** $1.8 million
- **Coed**

Faculty *Student/faculty ratio:* 21:1.

Student Life *Campus security:* 24-hour emergency response devices and patrols, late-night transport/escort service.

Financial Aid Of all full-time matriculated undergraduates who enrolled, 50 Federal Work-Study jobs (averaging $4000). 20 state and other part-time jobs (averaging $4000).

Applying *Options:* common application, early admission.

Admissions Contact Ms. Sue Bailey, Director of Enrollment Management, College of the Redwoods, 7351 Tompkins Hill Road, Eureka, CA 95501-9300. *Phone:* 707-476-4168. *Toll-free phone:* 800-641-0400. *Fax:* 707-476-4406. *E-mail:* admissions@redwoods.edu.

COLLEGE OF THE SEQUOIAS
Visalia, California

- **State and locally supported** 2-year, founded 1925, part of California Community College System
- **Calendar** semesters
- **Degree** certificates and associate
- **Suburban** 215-acre campus
- **Endowment** $1.2 million
- **Coed,** 11,169 undergraduate students, 40% full-time, 60% women, 40% men

Undergraduates 4,427 full-time, 6,742 part-time. Students come from 23 states and territories, 4% African American, 5% Asian American or Pacific Islander, 44% Hispanic American, 1% Native American, 0.2% international, 45% transferred in.

Freshmen *Admission:* 2,171 applied, 2,171 admitted, 2,071 enrolled.

Faculty *Total:* 174. *Student/faculty ratio:* 26:1.

Majors Accounting; administrative assistant and secretarial science; agricultural business and management; agricultural mechanization; agricultural teacher education; agriculture; animal sciences; architectural engineering technology; art; athletic training; automobile/automotive mechanics technology; biological and physical sciences; biology/biological sciences; business administration and management; carpentry; chemistry; commercial and advertising art; community organization and advocacy; computer engineering technology; computer graphics; computer programming; computer science; computer software and media applications related; computer typography and composition equipment operation; construction engineering technology; corrections; cosmetology; criminal justice/law enforcement administration; criminal justice/police science; culinary arts; cultural studies; dairy science; data modeling/warehousing and database administration; developmental and child psychology; drafting and design technology; dramatic/theatre arts; electrical, electronic and communications engineering technology; engineering; English; family and consumer sciences/home economics teacher education; family and consumer sciences/human sciences; fashion/apparel design; fashion merchandising; fire science; French; health teacher education; heating, air conditioning, ventilation and refrigeration maintenance technology; history; horticultural science; humanities; industrial arts; information science/studies; interior design; journalism; kindergarten/preschool education; legal assistant/paralegal; liberal arts and sciences/liberal studies; marketing/marketing management; mass communication/media; mathematics; modern languages; music; nursing (registered nurse training); ornamental horticulture; physical education teaching and coaching; pre-engineering; real estate; sign language interpretation and translation; social sciences; sociology; Spanish; speech and rhetoric; web page, digital/multimedia and information resources design; welding technology; word processing.

Academic Programs *Special study options:* academic remediation for entering students, accelerated degree program, adult/continuing education programs, advanced placement credit, cooperative education, English as a second language, freshman honors college, honors programs, internships, part-time degree program, services for LD students, study abroad, summer session for credit. *ROTC:* Air Force (c).

Library College of the Sequoias Library with 73,557 titles, 430 serial subscriptions, an OPAC, a Web page.

Computers on Campus 190 computers available on campus for general student use. A campuswide network can be accessed from off campus. At least one staffed computer lab available.

Student Life *Housing:* college housing not available. *Activities and Organizations:* drama/theater group, student-run newspaper, choral group, MECHA, Ag Club, Alpha Gamma Sigma, Paralegal Association, Sports Medicine Club. *Campus security:* 24-hour emergency response devices and patrols, student patrols, late-night transport/escort service, 18 hour patrols by trained security personnel. *Student services:* health clinic, personal/psychological counseling, women's center.

Athletics Member NJCAA. *Intercollegiate sports:* baseball M, basketball M/W, cross-country running M/W, football M, golf M, soccer W, softball W, swimming M/W, tennis M/W, track and field M/W, volleyball W, water polo M.

Costs (2003–04) *Tuition:* state resident $0 full-time; nonresident $4650 full-time. Part-time tuition and fees vary according to course load. *Required fees:* $560 full-time.

Applying *Options:* early admission. *Required:* high school transcript. *Application deadlines:* 8/15 (freshmen), 8/15 (transfers). *Notification:* continuous (freshmen), continuous (transfers).

Admissions Contact Mr. Don Mast, Associate Dean of Admissions/Registrar, College of the Sequoias, 915 South Mooney Boulevard, Visalia, CA 93277-2234. *Phone:* 559-737-4844. *Fax:* 559-737-4820.

COLLEGE OF THE SISKIYOUS
Weed, California

- **State and locally supported** 2-year, founded 1957, part of California Community College System

College of the Siskiyous (continued)
- **Calendar** semesters
- **Degree** certificates and associate
- **Rural** 260-acre campus
- **Coed**

COS is located at the base of Mt. Shasta in northern California, 60 miles south of the Oregon border, and provides many recreational opportunities. COS offers excellent transfer and vocational programs, support services, on-campus residence halls, and athletic programs. Small class sizes and individualized instruction provide a supportive environment that encourages learning.

Faculty *Student/faculty ratio:* 21:1.

Student Life *Campus security:* 24-hour emergency response devices, controlled dormitory access.

Athletics Member NJCAA.

Costs (2003–04) *Tuition:* state resident $0 full-time; nonresident $5514 full-time. *Required fees:* $564 full-time. *Room and board:* $5506.

Financial Aid Of all full-time matriculated undergraduates who enrolled, 51 Federal Work-Study jobs (averaging $1897). 30 state and other part-time jobs (averaging $2000).

Applying *Options:* early admission, deferred entrance.

Admissions Contact Ms. Christina Bruck, Recruitment and Outreach Coordinator, College of the Siskiyous, 800 College Avenue, Weed, CA 96094. *Phone:* 530-938-5847. *Toll-free phone:* 888-397-4339 Ext. 5847. *Fax:* 530-938-5367. *E-mail:* info@siskiyous.edu.

COLUMBIA COLLEGE
Sonora, California

- **State and locally supported** 2-year, founded 1968, part of Yosemite Community College District System
- **Calendar** semesters
- **Degree** certificates and associate
- **Rural** 200-acre campus
- **Coed,** 3,572 undergraduate students, 26% full-time, 54% women, 46% men

Undergraduates 914 full-time, 2,658 part-time. Students come from 7 states and territories, 5% are from out of state, 0.8% African American, 2% Asian American or Pacific Islander, 7% Hispanic American, 2% Native American, 0.1% international.

Freshmen *Admission:* 312 applied, 312 admitted, 312 enrolled.

Faculty *Total:* 150, 41% full-time. *Student/faculty ratio:* 12:1.

Majors Administrative assistant and secretarial science; anthropology; art; automobile/automotive mechanics technology; biology/biological sciences; business administration and management; chemistry; computer science; culinary arts; developmental and child psychology; dramatic/theatre arts; English; environmental studies; fire science; food services technology; forestry technology; geology/earth science; health teacher education; history; hotel/motel administration; humanities; liberal arts and sciences/liberal studies; mathematics; music; natural resources management and policy; photography; physical education teaching and coaching; physical sciences; physics; psychology; sociology; special products marketing.

Academic Programs *Special study options:* academic remediation for entering students, adult/continuing education programs, advanced placement credit, cooperative education, distance learning, double majors, English as a second language, independent study, internships, part-time degree program, services for LD students, summer session for credit.

Library Columbia College Library with 34,892 titles, 320 serial subscriptions, 4,852 audiovisual materials, an OPAC, a Web page.

Computers on Campus 85 computers available on campus for general student use. Internet access, at least one staffed computer lab available.

Student Life *Activities and Organizations:* drama/theater group, choral group, International Club, Jazz Club, Ecology Action Club, Christian Club. *Campus security:* 24-hour emergency response devices and patrols, late-night transport/escort service. *Student services:* health clinic.

Athletics Member NJCAA. *Intercollegiate sports:* basketball M, tennis M/W, volleyball W.

Standardized Tests *Required:* CPT, ACCUPLACER (for placement).

Costs (2004–05) *Tuition:* state resident $0 full-time; nonresident $3576 full-time, $149 per unit part-time. *Required fees:* $432 full-time, $18 per unit part-time.

Financial Aid Of all full-time matriculated undergraduates who enrolled, 42 Federal Work-Study jobs (averaging $2350).

Applying *Options:* common application, electronic application, early admission. *Required for some:* high school transcript. *Application deadline:* rolling (freshmen), rolling (transfers). *Notification:* continuous (freshmen), continuous (transfers).

Admissions Contact Dr. Kathleen Smith, Director Student Success/ Matriculation, Columbia College, Columbia College, 11600 Columbia College Drive, Sonora, CA 95370. *Phone:* 209-588-5231. *Fax:* 209-588-5337. *E-mail:* chavezc@yosemite.cc.ca.us.

COMPTON COMMUNITY COLLEGE
Compton, California

Admissions Contact Dr. Essie French-Preston, Vice President of Student Affairs, Compton Community College, 1111 East Artesia Boulevard, Compton, CA 90221-5393. *Phone:* 310-637-2660 Ext. 2024.

CONCORDE CAREER INSTITUTE
North Hollywood, California

Admissions Contact Concorde Career Institute, 12412 Victory Boulevard, North Hollywood, CA 91606.

CONTRA COSTA COLLEGE
San Pablo, California

- **State and locally supported** 2-year, founded 1948, part of Contra Costa Community College District and California Community College System
- **Calendar** semesters
- **Degree** certificates and associate
- **Small-town** 83-acre campus with easy access to San Francisco
- **Coed,** 8,834 undergraduate students, 45% full-time, 62% women, 38% men

Undergraduates 3,973 full-time, 4,861 part-time. Students come from 5 states and territories, 16 other countries, 28% African American, 15% Asian American or Pacific Islander, 28% Hispanic American, 0.6% Native American, 2% international.

Freshmen *Admission:* 5,794 applied, 4,126 enrolled.

Faculty *Total:* 415, 28% full-time, 22% with terminal degrees.

Majors Administrative assistant and secretarial science; African-American/ Black studies; anthropology; art; automobile/automotive mechanics technology; biology/biological sciences; biology/biotechnology laboratory technician; business administration and management; chemistry; computer programming; computer science; criminal justice/law enforcement administration; criminal justice/ police science; culinary arts; dental hygiene; drafting and design technology; electrical, electronic and communications engineering technology; emergency medical technology (EMT paramedic); engineering; English; family and consumer sciences/human sciences; French; geography; geology/earth science; German; Hispanic-American, Puerto Rican, and Mexican-American/Chicano studies; history; humanities; industrial arts; Italian; journalism; kindergarten/ preschool education; liberal arts and sciences/liberal studies; materials science; mathematics; music; nursing (licensed practical/vocational nurse training); nursing (registered nurse training); philosophy; physics; political science and government; quality control technology; real estate; sociology; Spanish; welding technology.

Academic Programs *Special study options:* academic remediation for entering students, adult/continuing education programs, cooperative education, English as a second language, honors programs, off-campus study, part-time degree program, services for LD students, study abroad, summer session for credit. *ROTC:* Army (c), Air Force (c).

Library Contra Costa College Library with 57,017 titles, 333 serial subscriptions, 1,860 audiovisual materials, a Web page.

Computers on Campus 180 computers available on campus for general student use. Online (class) registration, at least one staffed computer lab available.

Student Life *Housing:* college housing not available. *Activities and Organizations:* drama/theater group, student-run newspaper. *Campus security:* 24-hour patrols. *Student services:* personal/psychological counseling, women's center.

Athletics *Intercollegiate sports:* baseball M, basketball M/W, cross-country running M/W, football M, softball W, track and field M/W, volleyball W.

Standardized Tests *Recommended:* SAT I or ACT (for placement).

Costs (2003–04) *Tuition:* state resident $0 full-time; nonresident $4350 full-time, $145 per unit part-time. Full-time tuition and fees vary according to course load. Part-time tuition and fees vary according to course load. *Required fees:* $540 full-time, $18 per unit part-time.

Financial Aid Of all full-time matriculated undergraduates who enrolled, 100 Federal Work-Study jobs (averaging $3000).

Applying *Options:* common application, early admission. *Application deadline:* rolling (freshmen).

Admissions Contact Mrs. Linda Ames, Admissions and Records Supervisor, Contra Costa College, 2600 Mission Bell Drive, San Pablo, CA 94806-3195. *Phone:* 510-235-7800 Ext. 4211.

COPPER MOUNTAIN COLLEGE
Joshua Tree, California

- **State-supported** 2-year, founded 1966
- **Calendar** semesters
- **Degree** certificates and associate
- **Coed**

Admissions Contact Dr. Laraine Turk, Associate Dean of Student Services, Copper Mountain College, 6162 Rotary Way, Joshua Tree, CA 92252. *Phone:* 760-366-5290.

COSUMNES RIVER COLLEGE
Sacramento, California

- **District-supported** 2-year, founded 1970, part of Los Rios Community College District System
- **Calendar** semesters
- **Degree** certificates and associate
- **Rural** 180-acre campus
- **Coed**

Student Life *Campus security:* 24-hour emergency response devices and patrols, student patrols, late-night transport/escort service.
Standardized Tests *Recommended:* SAT I or ACT (for placement).
Costs (2003–04) *Tuition:* state resident $0 full-time; nonresident $4008 full-time, $167 per unit part-time. *Required fees:* $434 full-time, $18 per unit part-time, $1 per term part-time.
Financial Aid Of all full-time matriculated undergraduates who enrolled, 139 Federal Work-Study jobs (averaging $2000).
Applying *Options:* early admission.
Admissions Contact Ms. Dianna L. Moore, Supervisor of Admissions Records, Cosumnes River College, 8401 Center Parkway, Sacramento, CA 95823-5799. *Phone:* 916-688-7423. *Fax:* 916-688-7467.

CRAFTON HILLS COLLEGE
Yucaipa, California

- **State and locally supported** 2-year, founded 1972, part of California Community College System
- **Calendar** semesters
- **Degree** certificates and associate
- **Small-town** 526-acre campus with easy access to Los Angeles
- **Coed**

Student Life *Campus security:* 24-hour patrols, late-night transport/escort service.
Standardized Tests *Required for some:* ACT, SAT, SCAT, CGP, ACT ASSET, Nelson Denny Reading Test, or ACCUPLACER.
Costs (2003–04) *Tuition:* state resident $0 full-time; nonresident $3576 full-time, $149 per unit part-time. *Required fees:* $432 full-time, $18 per unit part-time.
Financial Aid Of all full-time matriculated undergraduates who enrolled, 42 Federal Work-Study jobs (averaging $3000).
Applying *Options:* common application, early admission, deferred entrance. *Required for some:* high school transcript.
Admissions Contact Mr. Marco Cota, Interim Director of Admissions, Crafton Hills College, 11711 Sand Canyon Road, Yucaipa, CA 92399. *Phone:* 909-389-3355. *Fax:* 909-389-9141. *E-mail:* admissions@craftonhills.edu.

CRESTMONT COLLEGE
Rancho Palos Verdes, California

- **Independent religious** primarily 2-year, founded 1878
- **Calendar** quarters
- **Degrees** associate and bachelor's
- **Suburban** 44-acre campus with easy access to Los Angeles
- **Endowment** $81.0 million
- **Coed,** 213 undergraduate students, 86% full-time, 56% women, 44% men

Undergraduates 183 full-time, 30 part-time. Students come from 14 states and territories, 1 other country, 49% are from out of state, 4% African American, 7% Asian American or Pacific Islander, 15% Hispanic American, 0.5% Native American, 2% international, 100% live on campus. *Retention:* 98% of 2002 full-time freshmen returned.
Freshmen *Admission:* 26 applied, 17 admitted, 4 enrolled.
Faculty *Total:* 63, 51% full-time, 62% with terminal degrees. *Student/faculty ratio:* 5:1.

Majors Divinity/ministry.
Academic Programs *Special study options:* academic remediation for entering students, accelerated degree program, cooperative education, distance learning, English as a second language, external degree program, independent study, internships, off-campus study, student-designed majors.
Library The Salvation Army Elfman Memorial Library with 35,700 titles, 125 serial subscriptions, an OPAC.
Computers on Campus 65 computers available on campus for general student use. A campuswide network can be accessed from student residence rooms and from off campus. Internet access, at least one staffed computer lab available. Computer purchase or lease plan available.
Student Life *Housing:* on-campus residence required through sophomore year. *Options:* Campus housing is university owned. Freshman campus housing is guaranteed. *Activities and Organizations:* drama/theater group, choral group. *Campus security:* 24-hour emergency response devices and patrols. *Student services:* health clinic, personal/psychological counseling.
Costs (2004–05) *Comprehensive fee:* $10,600 includes full-time tuition ($1500), mandatory fees ($850), and room and board ($8250). Part-time tuition: $100 per quarter hour. *Required fees:* $850 per year part-time.
Applying *Application fee:* $15. *Required:* essay or personal statement, high school transcript, letters of recommendation, interview. *Application deadline:* 6/1 (freshmen).
Admissions Contact Maj. Donna Jackson, Director of Records and Admissions, Crestmont College, 30840 Hawthorne Boulevard, Rancho Palos Verdes, CA 90275. *Phone:* 310-544-6440. *Toll-free phone:* 310-544-6440. *Fax:* 310-265-6520.

CUESTA COLLEGE
San Luis Obispo, California

- **District-supported** 2-year, founded 1964
- **Calendar** semesters
- **Degree** certificates and associate
- **Rural** 129-acre campus
- **Coed,** 10,771 undergraduate students

Undergraduates Students come from 19 other countries, 10% are from out of state, 1% African American, 4% Asian American or Pacific Islander, 15% Hispanic American, 1% Native American.
Faculty *Total:* 417, 32% full-time, 10% with terminal degrees.
Majors Administrative assistant and secretarial science; agricultural mechanization; applied art; art; artificial intelligence and robotics; arts management; automobile/automotive mechanics technology; biology/biological sciences; business administration and management; chemistry; child development; computer engineering technology; computer hardware engineering; computer science; computer systems networking and telecommunications; computer/technical support; construction engineering technology; data processing and data processing technology; electrical, electronic and communications engineering technology; engineering; family and consumer economics related; fashion merchandising; foods, nutrition, and wellness; geology/earth science; human development and family studies; human services; industrial technology; information technology; interior design; journalism; kindergarten/preschool education; liberal arts and sciences/liberal studies; library science; marketing/marketing management; mass communication/media; mathematics; medical/clinical assistant; nursing (registered nurse training); parks, recreation and leisure facilities management; physical education teaching and coaching; physics; pre-engineering; psychology; radio and television; real estate; system administration; telecommunications; therapeutic recreation; web page, digital/multimedia and information resources design; welding technology.
Academic Programs *Special study options:* academic remediation for entering students, adult/continuing education programs, advanced placement credit, cooperative education, distance learning, double majors, English as a second language, honors programs, independent study, internships, off-campus study, part-time degree program, services for LD students, study abroad, summer session for credit. *ROTC:* Army (c).
Library Cuesta College Library with 64,814 titles, 584 serial subscriptions, an OPAC, a Web page.
Computers on Campus 400 computers available on campus for general student use. A campuswide network can be accessed from off campus. At least one staffed computer lab available.
Student Life *Housing:* college housing not available. *Activities and Organizations:* drama/theater group, student-run newspaper, radio station, choral group, Associated Students of Cuesta College, Alpha Gamma Sigma, Student Nurses Association, Latina Leadership Network, MECHA. *Campus security:* 24-hour emergency response devices and patrols, late-night transport/escort service. *Student services:* health clinic, personal/psychological counseling, legal services.
Athletics *Intercollegiate sports:* baseball M, basketball M/W, cross-country running M/W, soccer W, softball W, swimming M/W, tennis W, track and field M/W, volleyball W, water polo M/W, wrestling M.

Cuesta College (continued)

Standardized Tests *Recommended:* Assessment and Placement Services for Community Colleges.

Costs (2004–05) *Tuition:* nonresident $4704 full-time. *Required fees:* $504 full-time.

Applying *Options:* common application, electronic application, early admission, deferred entrance. *Required:* high school transcript. *Recommended:* essay or personal statement. *Application deadline:* rolling (freshmen), rolling (transfers). *Notification:* continuous (freshmen), continuous (transfers).

Admissions Contact Ms. Juileta Siu, Admissions Clerk, Cuesta College, PO Box 8106, Highway 1, San Luis Obispo, CA 93403-8106. *Phone:* 805-546-3140. *Fax:* 805-546-3975. *E-mail:* admit@cuesta.edu.

CUYAMACA COLLEGE
El Cajon, California

- **State-supported** 2-year, founded 1978, part of Grossmont-Cuyamaca Community College District
- **Calendar** semesters
- **Degree** certificates, diplomas, and associate
- **Suburban** 165-acre campus with easy access to San Diego
- **Coed,** 7,690 undergraduate students

Undergraduates Students come from 8 other countries, 1% are from out of state, 8% African American, 6% Asian American or Pacific Islander, 20% Hispanic American, 2% Native American, 2% international.

Faculty *Total:* 280, 24% full-time, 14% with terminal degrees.

Majors Accounting; accounting technology and bookkeeping; automobile/automotive mechanics technology; biological and physical sciences; business administration and management; business/commerce; chemistry; child guidance; commercial and advertising art; drafting and design technology; drawing; elementary education; English; entrepreneurship; environmental engineering technology; general studies; history; information science/studies; landscaping and groundskeeping; legal assistant/paralegal; liberal arts and sciences/liberal studies; mechanical design technology; occupational safety and health technology; office management; ornamental horticulture; painting; physics; plant nursery management; real estate; special products marketing; speech and rhetoric; survey technology; turf and turfgrass management.

Academic Programs *Special study options:* academic remediation for entering students, adult/continuing education programs, advanced placement credit, cooperative education, distance learning, English as a second language, part-time degree program, services for LD students, student-designed majors, study abroad, summer session for credit. *ROTC:* Army (c), Air Force (c).

Library Library plus 1 other with 32,129 titles, 130 serial subscriptions, 2,588 audiovisual materials, an OPAC, a Web page.

Computers on Campus 396 computers available on campus for general student use. A campuswide network can be accessed from off campus. Internet access, online (class) registration, at least one staffed computer lab available.

Student Life *Housing:* college housing not available. *Activities and Organizations:* student-run newspaper. *Student services:* health clinic, personal/psychological counseling.

Athletics *Intercollegiate sports:* basketball M/W, cross-country running M/W, soccer M/W, tennis W, track and field M/W, volleyball W.

Standardized Tests *Required:* ACT ASSET (for placement).

Costs (2003–04) *Tuition:* state resident $0 full-time; nonresident $4756 full-time, $164 per unit part-time. Full-time tuition and fees vary according to course load. Part-time tuition and fees vary according to course load. *Required fees:* $546 full-time, $18 per unit part-time, $12 per term part-time.

Financial Aid Of all full-time matriculated undergraduates who enrolled, 81 Federal Work-Study jobs (averaging $1600). 39 state and other part-time jobs (averaging $900).

Applying *Options:* common application, electronic application, early admission. *Application deadline:* rolling (freshmen), rolling (transfers).

Admissions Contact Dr. Beth Appenzeller, Dean of Admissions and Records, Cuyamaca College, 900 Rancho San Diego Parkway, El Cajon, CA 92019-4304. *Phone:* 619-660-4302. *Fax:* 610-660-4575.

CYPRESS COLLEGE
Cypress, California

Admissions Contact Cypress College, 9200 Valley View, Cypress, CA 90630. *Phone:* 714-484-7435. *Fax:* 714-484-7446. *E-mail:* info@cypress.cc.ca.us.

DE ANZA COLLEGE
Cupertino, California

- **State and locally supported** 2-year, founded 1967, part of California Community College System

- **Calendar** quarters
- **Degree** certificates, diplomas, and associate
- **Small-town** 112-acre campus with easy access to San Francisco and San Jose
- **Coed**

Student Life *Campus security:* 24-hour emergency response devices, student patrols, late-night transport/escort service.

Standardized Tests *Required for some:* SAT I (for placement), CPT, DTLS, DTMS.

Costs (2003–04) *Tuition:* state resident $0 full-time; nonresident $3600 full-time, $100 per unit part-time. *Required fees:* $590 full-time, $12 per unit part-time.

Applying *Options:* common application, early admission. *Application fee:* $22.

Admissions Contact Ms. Kathleen Kayne, Director of Records and Admissions, De Anza College, 21250 Stevens Creek Boulevard, Cupertino, CA 95014. *Phone:* 408-864-8292. *Fax:* 408-864-8329. *E-mail:* webregda@fhda.edu.

DEEP SPRINGS COLLEGE
Deep Springs, California

- **Independent** 2-year, founded 1917
- **Calendar** 6 seven-week terms
- **Degree** associate
- **Rural** 3000-acre campus
- **Endowment** $11.1 million
- **Men only**

Faculty *Student/faculty ratio:* 3:1.

Standardized Tests *Required:* SAT I and SAT II or ACT (for admission).

Applying *Options:* common application. *Required:* essay or personal statement, high school transcript, letters of recommendation, interview.

Admissions Contact Dr. L. Jackson Newell, President, Deep Springs College, HC 72, Box 45001, Dyer, NV 89010-9803. *Phone:* 760-872-2000. *E-mail:* apcom@deepsprings.edu.

DIABLO VALLEY COLLEGE
Pleasant Hill, California

- **State and locally supported** 2-year, founded 1949, part of Contra Costa Community College District, part of California Community Colleges
- **Calendar** semesters
- **Degree** certificates and associate
- **Suburban** 100-acre campus with easy access to San Francisco
- **Coed,** 21,097 undergraduate students, 32% full-time, 54% women, 46% men

Undergraduates 6,751 full-time, 14,346 part-time. Students come from 16 states and territories, 5% African American, 19% Asian American or Pacific Islander, 12% Hispanic American, 0.7% Native American.

Faculty *Total:* 831, 31% full-time.

Majors Liberal arts and sciences/liberal studies.

Academic Programs *Special study options:* academic remediation for entering students, adult/continuing education programs, advanced placement credit, cooperative education, part-time degree program, services for LD students, student-designed majors, study abroad, summer session for credit. *ROTC:* Air Force (c).

Library 88,286 titles, 298 serial subscriptions.

Computers on Campus 450 computers available on campus for general student use. A campuswide network can be accessed from off campus. Internet access, online (class) registration, at least one staffed computer lab available.

Student Life *Housing:* college housing not available. *Activities and Organizations:* drama/theater group, student-run newspaper. *Campus security:* 24-hour emergency response devices and patrols, student patrols. *Student services:* women's center.

Athletics *Intercollegiate sports:* basketball M/W, cross-country running M/W, football M, soccer W, softball W, swimming M/W, tennis M/W, track and field M/W, volleyball W, water polo M/W.

Costs (2003–04) *Tuition:* nonresident $3912 full-time, $163 per credit part-time. *Required fees:* $460 full-time, $18 per credit part-time, $19 per term part-time.

Financial Aid Of all full-time matriculated undergraduates who enrolled, 67 Federal Work-Study jobs (averaging $3000). *Financial aid deadline:* 5/23.

Applying *Options:* early admission. *Recommended:* high school transcript. *Application deadline:* 8/15 (freshmen), rolling (transfers).

Admissions Contact Catherine Fites-Chavis, Supervisor of Admissions and Records, Diablo Valley College, 321 Golf Club Road, Pleasant Hill, CA 94523-1529. *Phone:* 925-685-1230 Ext. 2330.

DON BOSCO COLLEGE OF SCIENCE AND TECHNOLOGY
Rosemead, California

Admissions Contact Mr. Tom Bauman, Director of College Admissions, Don Bosco College of Science and Technology, 1151 San Gabriel Boulevard, Rosemead, CA 91770-4299. *Phone:* 626-940-2036.

D-Q UNIVERSITY
Davis, California

Admissions Contact Ms. Irma Hernandez, Director of Admissions and Records, D-Q University, PO Box 409, Davis, CA 95617-0409. *Phone:* 530-758-0470 Ext. 1016. *Fax:* 530-758-4891.

EAST LOS ANGELES COLLEGE
Monterey Park, California

- **State and locally supported** 2-year, founded 1945, part of Los Angeles Community College District
- **Calendar** semesters
- **Degree** certificates and associate
- **Urban** 84-acre campus with easy access to Los Angeles
- **Coed,** 24,015 undergraduate students, 24% full-time, 60% women, 40% men

Undergraduates 5,773 full-time, 18,242 part-time. 3% African American, 19% Asian American or Pacific Islander, 70% Hispanic American, 0.2% Native American.
Freshmen *Admission:* 5,348 applied, 5,348 admitted, 1,630 enrolled.
Faculty *Total:* 619, 40% full-time, 6% with terminal degrees. *Student/faculty ratio:* 34:1.
Majors Accounting; administrative assistant and secretarial science; anthropology; architectural engineering technology; art; Asian studies; automobile/automotive mechanics technology; biology/biological sciences; business administration and management; chemistry; child development; civil engineering technology; computer engineering technology; computer programming; counselor education/school counseling and guidance; criminal justice/law enforcement administration; criminal justice/police science; data processing and data processing technology; developmental and child psychology; drafting and design technology; dramatic/theatre arts; electrical, electronic and communications engineering technology; emergency medical technology (EMT paramedic); engineering; English; environmental studies; family and consumer sciences/human sciences; fashion/apparel design; finance; fire science; French; geography; geology/earth science; health information/medical records administration; Hispanic-American, Puerto Rican, and Mexican-American/Chicano studies; history; Japanese; journalism; legal administrative assistant/secretary; liberal arts and sciences/liberal studies; marketing/marketing management; mathematics; medical administrative assistant and medical secretary; medical/clinical assistant; music; nursing (registered nurse training); philosophy; photography; physical education teaching and coaching; political science and government; pre-engineering; psychology; public administration; real estate; respiratory care therapy; social work; sociology; Spanish; speech and rhetoric; trade and industrial teacher education.
Academic Programs *Special study options:* academic remediation for entering students, adult/continuing education programs, advanced placement credit, cooperative education, distance learning, English as a second language, honors programs, independent study, part-time degree program, services for LD students, student-designed majors.
Library ELAC Helen Miller Bailey Library plus 2 others with 102,000 titles, 228 serial subscriptions, an OPAC, a Web page.
Computers on Campus 350 computers available on campus for general student use. A campuswide network can be accessed from off campus that provide access to student email, tutorials. Internet access, online (class) registration, at least one staffed computer lab available.
Student Life *Housing:* college housing not available. *Activities and Organizations:* drama/theater group, student-run newspaper, radio station, choral group, marching band, Asian Club, Spanish Club, Chicanos for Creative Medicine. *Campus security:* 24-hour emergency response devices and patrols, late-night transport/escort service. *Student services:* health clinic, personal/psychological counseling.
Athletics *Intercollegiate sports:* baseball M, basketball M, football M, golf M, soccer M, softball W, swimming W, track and field M/W, wrestling M.
Costs (2003–04) *Tuition:* state resident $0 full-time; nonresident $4008 full-time, $167 per unit part-time. *Required fees:* $468 full-time, $18 per unit part-time.
Financial Aid Of all full-time matriculated undergraduates who enrolled, 189 Federal Work-Study jobs (averaging $3000).

Applying *Options:* common application, early admission. *Recommended:* high school transcript, English and mathematics placement test. *Application deadline:* 9/12 (freshmen). *Notification:* continuous until 9/12 (freshmen).
Admissions Contact Mr. Jeremy Allred, Associate Dean of Admissions, East Los Angeles College, 1301 Avenida Cesar Chavez, Monterey Park, CA 91754-6001. *Phone:* 323-265-8801. *Fax:* 323-265-8688.

EL CAMINO COLLEGE
Torrance, California

- **State-supported** 2-year, founded 1947, part of California Community College System
- **Calendar** semesters
- **Degree** certificates, diplomas, and associate
- **Urban** 115-acre campus with easy access to Los Angeles
- **Coed,** 27,039 undergraduate students

Undergraduates 18% African American, 19% Asian American or Pacific Islander, 29% Hispanic American, 0.4% Native American. *Retention:* 81% of 2002 full-time freshmen returned.
Faculty *Total:* 533, 62% full-time.
Majors Accounting; administrative assistant and secretarial science; advertising; African-American/Black studies; American studies; anthropology; architectural engineering technology; art; art history, criticism and conservation; Asian studies; astronomy; automobile/automotive mechanics technology; biology/biological sciences; botany/plant biology; business administration and management; chemistry; construction engineering technology; cosmetology; criminal justice/police science; culinary arts; data processing and data processing technology; drafting and design technology; dramatic/theatre arts; economics; electrical, electronic and communications engineering technology; engineering; English; family and consumer sciences/human sciences; fashion/apparel design; finance; fire science; forestry technology; geography; geology/earth science; German; gerontology; heating, air conditioning, ventilation and refrigeration maintenance technology; history; horticultural science; industrial arts; interior design; Italian; Japanese; journalism; kindergarten/preschool education; labor and industrial relations; legal assistant/paralegal; liberal arts and sciences/liberal studies; marketing/marketing management; mathematics; medical/clinical assistant; music; nursing (licensed practical/vocational nurse training); nursing (registered nurse training); ornamental horticulture; philosophy; photography; physical education teaching and coaching; physical sciences; physics; political science and government; psychology; real estate; respiratory care therapy; Russian; social work; sociology; Spanish; special products marketing; speech and rhetoric; technical and business writing; welding technology; zoology/animal biology.
Academic Programs *Special study options:* academic remediation for entering students, advanced placement credit, cooperative education, English as a second language, honors programs, part-time degree program, services for LD students, student-designed majors, summer session for credit.
Library 116,051 titles, 864 serial subscriptions.
Computers on Campus 151 computers available on campus for general student use.
Student Life *Housing:* college housing not available. *Activities and Organizations:* drama/theater group, student-run newspaper. *Student services:* health clinic, personal/psychological counseling, women's center.
Athletics *Intercollegiate sports:* baseball M, basketball M/W, cross-country running M/W, football M, golf M, gymnastics W, soccer M, swimming M/W, tennis M/W, track and field M/W, volleyball M/W, water polo M, wrestling M. *Intramural sports:* archery M/W, badminton M/W, bowling M/W.
Costs (2003–04) *Tuition:* state resident $0 full-time; nonresident $3600 full-time, $150 per unit part-time. *Required fees:* $432 full-time, $18 per unit part-time.
Applying *Options:* early admission. *Required:* high school transcript. *Application deadline:* rolling (freshmen), rolling (transfers). *Notification:* continuous (freshmen), continuous (transfers).
Admissions Contact Mr. William Robinson, Director of Admissions, El Camino College, 16007 Crenshaw Boulevard, Torrance, CA 90506. *Phone:* 310-660-3418. *Toll-free phone:* 866-ELCAMINO. *Fax:* 310-660-3818.

EMPIRE COLLEGE
Santa Rosa, California

- **Proprietary** 2-year, founded 1961
- **Calendar** continuous
- **Degree** certificates, diplomas, and associate
- **Suburban** campus with easy access to San Francisco
- **Coed**

Faculty *Student/faculty ratio:* 20:1.
Student Life *Campus security:* 24-hour emergency response devices.
Standardized Tests *Required:* Wonderlic aptitude test (for admission).

Empire College (continued)

Costs (2003–04) *Comprehensive fee:* $8283 includes full-time tuition ($7350), mandatory fees ($75), and room and board ($858).

Financial Aid Of all full-time matriculated undergraduates who enrolled, 15 Federal Work-Study jobs (averaging $1500).

Applying *Application fee:* $75. *Required:* high school transcript, interview. *Required for some:* essay or personal statement.

Admissions Contact Ms. Dahnja Barker, Admissions Officer, Empire College, 3035 Cleveland Avenue, Santa Rosa, CA 95403. *Phone:* 707-546-4000. *Fax:* 707-546-4058. *E-mail:* rhurd@empcol.com.

EVEREST COLLEGE
Rancho Cucamonga, California

Admissions Contact Everest College, 9616 Archibald Avenue, Suite 100, Rancho Cucamonga, CA 91730.

EVERGREEN VALLEY COLLEGE
San Jose, California

Admissions Contact Ms. Kathleen Moberg, Director of Admissions and Records, Evergreen Valley College, 3095 Yerba Buena Road, San Jose, CA 95135-1598. *Phone:* 408-270-6423. *Fax:* 408-223-9351.

FASHION CAREERS OF CALIFORNIA COLLEGE
San Diego, California

- **Proprietary** 2-year, founded 1979
- **Calendar** quarters
- **Degree** certificates and associate
- **Urban** campus
- **Coed, primarily women,** 106 undergraduate students, 100% full-time, 92% women, 8% men

Undergraduates 106 full-time. Students come from 18 states and territories, 3 other countries, 27% are from out of state, 10% African American, 6% Asian American or Pacific Islander, 35% Hispanic American, 4% international. *Retention:* 75% of 2002 full-time freshmen returned.

Freshmen *Admission:* 33 enrolled.

Faculty *Total:* 11. *Student/faculty ratio:* 20:1.

Majors Fashion/apparel design; fashion merchandising.

Academic Programs *Special study options:* adult/continuing education programs, cooperative education, double majors, internships.

Library Fashion Careers of California Library with 800 titles, 14 serial subscriptions, 175 audiovisual materials.

Computers on Campus 36 computers available on campus for general student use. Internet access, at least one staffed computer lab available.

Student Life *Housing:* college housing not available. *Campus security:* 24-hour emergency response devices.

Standardized Tests *Required:* Wonderlic aptitude test (for admission).

Costs (2004–05) *One-time required fee:* $300. *Tuition:* $14,900 full-time, $350 per credit part-time. Full-time tuition and fees vary according to program. No tuition increase for student's term of enrollment. *Required fees:* $25 full-time. *Payment plans:* installment, deferred payment. *Waivers:* employees or children of employees.

Financial Aid Of all full-time matriculated undergraduates who enrolled, 10 Federal Work-Study jobs (averaging $1200).

Applying *Options:* common application, electronic application. *Application fee:* $25. *Required:* essay or personal statement, high school transcript, interview. *Application deadline:* rolling (freshmen), rolling (transfers).

Admissions Contact Ms. Leslie Phillips, Admissions Representative, Fashion Careers of California College, 1923 Morena Boulevard, San Diego, CA 92110. *Phone:* 619-275-4700 Ext. 309. *Toll-free phone:* 888-FCCC999. *Fax:* 619-275-0635. *E-mail:* leslie@fashioncollege.com.

FASHION INSTITUTE OF DESIGN AND MERCHANDISING, LOS ANGELES CAMPUS
Los Angeles, California

- **Proprietary** 2-year, founded 1969, part of Fashion Institute of Design and Merchandising
- **Calendar** quarters
- **Degrees** associate (also includes Costa Mesa campus)
- **Urban** campus
- **Coed,** 3,254 undergraduate students, 78% full-time, 91% women, 9% men

Undergraduates 2,528 full-time, 726 part-time. Students come from 40 states and territories, 30 other countries, 28% are from out of state, 5% African American, 17% Asian American or Pacific Islander, 20% Hispanic American, 0.4% Native American, 9% international.

Freshmen *Admission:* 1,837 admitted, 915 enrolled.

Faculty *Total:* 169, 27% full-time. *Student/faculty ratio:* 19:1.

Majors Apparel and accessories marketing; apparel and textiles; commercial and advertising art; consumer merchandising/retailing management; design and visual communications; fashion/apparel design; fashion merchandising; interior design.

Academic Programs *Special study options:* academic remediation for entering students, adult/continuing education programs, advanced placement credit, cooperative education, English as a second language, internships, part-time degree program, study abroad, summer session for credit.

Library Resource and Research Center with 234 serial subscriptions, 5,899 audiovisual materials, a Web page.

Computers on Campus 74 computers available on campus for general student use. Internet access, at least one staffed computer lab available.

Student Life *Housing:* college housing not available. *Activities and Organizations:* student-run newspaper, ASID (student chapter), International Club, DECA, Association of Manufacturing Students, Honor Society. *Campus security:* 24-hour emergency response devices and patrols, late-night transport/escort service. *Student services:* personal/psychological counseling.

Standardized Tests *Required:* (for admission).

Costs (2003–04) *Tuition:* $15,500 full-time. No tuition increase for student's term of enrollment. *Required fees:* $500 full-time. *Payment plan:* tuition prepayment.

Financial Aid Of all full-time matriculated undergraduates who enrolled, 88 Federal Work-Study jobs (averaging $2935).

Applying *Options:* common application, electronic application, deferred entrance. *Application fee:* $25. *Required:* essay or personal statement, high school transcript, 3 letters of recommendation. *Required for some:* interview, major-determined project. *Recommended:* minimum 2.0 GPA. *Application deadline:* rolling (freshmen), rolling (transfers).

Admissions Contact Ms. Susan Aronson, Director of Admissions FIDM/The Fashion Institute of Design and Merchandise, Fashion Institute of Design and Merchandising, Los Angeles Campus, 90015. *Phone:* 213-624-1200 Ext. 5400. *Toll-free phone:* 800-624-1200. *Fax:* 213-624-4799. *E-mail:* info@fidm.com.

▶ **See page 542 for a narrative description.**

FASHION INSTITUTE OF DESIGN AND MERCHANDISING, ORANGE COUNTY
Irvine, California

Admissions Contact Admissions, Fashion Institute of Design and Merchandising, Orange County, 17590 Gillette Avenue, Irvine, CA 92614-5610. *Phone:* 949-851-6200. *Toll-free phone:* 888-974-3436. *Fax:* 949-851-6808.

FASHION INSTITUTE OF DESIGN AND MERCHANDISING, SAN DIEGO CAMPUS
San Diego, California

- **Proprietary** 2-year, founded 1985, part of Fashion Institute of Design and Merchandising
- **Calendar** quarters
- **Degree** associate
- **Urban** campus
- **Coed,** 262 undergraduate students, 91% full-time, 95% women, 5% men

Undergraduates 238 full-time, 24 part-time. Students come from 15 states and territories, 15% are from out of state, 7% African American, 13% Asian American or Pacific Islander, 24% Hispanic American, 1% Native American, 0.4% international.

Freshmen *Admission:* 297 admitted, 157 enrolled.

Faculty *Total:* 24, 8% full-time. *Student/faculty ratio:* 11:1.

Majors Apparel and accessories marketing; commercial and advertising art; consumer merchandising/retailing management; design and visual communications; fashion/apparel design; fashion merchandising; interior design.

Academic Programs *Special study options:* academic remediation for entering students, adult/continuing education programs, advanced placement credit, cooperative education, internships, part-time degree program, study abroad, summer session for credit.

Library Resource and Research Center with 2,000 titles, 100 serial subscriptions, a Web page.

Computers on Campus 9 computers available on campus for general student use. At least one staffed computer lab available.

Student Life *Housing:* college housing not available. *Options:* Campus housing is provided by a third party. *Activities and Organizations:* ASID (student chapter), DECA, Honor Society, Phi Theta Kappa. *Campus security:* 24-hour emergency response devices and patrols. *Student services:* personal/psychological counseling.

Costs (2004–05) *Tuition:* $15,500 full-time. No tuition increase for student's term of enrollment. *Payment plan:* tuition prepayment.

Applying *Options:* common application, electronic application, deferred entrance. *Application fee:* $25. *Required:* essay or personal statement, high school transcript, 3 letters of recommendation. *Required for some:* interview, major-determined project. *Recommended:* minimum 2.5 GPA. *Application deadline:* rolling (freshmen), rolling (transfers).

Admissions Contact Ms. Susan Aronson, Director of Admissions, Fashion Institute of Design and Merchandising, San Diego Campus, 1010 Second Avenue, Suite 200, San Diego, CA 92101-4903. *Phone:* 213-624-1200 Ext. 5400. *Toll-free phone:* 800-243-3436. *Fax:* 619-232-4322. *E-mail:* info@fidm.com.

FASHION INSTITUTE OF DESIGN AND MERCHANDISING, SAN FRANCISCO CAMPUS
San Francisco, California

- **Proprietary** 2-year, founded 1973, part of Fashion Institute of Design and Merchandising
- **Calendar** quarters
- **Degree** associate
- **Urban** campus
- **Coed, primarily women,** 837 undergraduate students, 78% full-time, 93% women, 7% men

Undergraduates 654 full-time, 183 part-time. Students come from 20 other countries, 6% African American, 18% Asian American or Pacific Islander, 17% Hispanic American, 0.2% Native American, 3% international, 2% transferred in.

Freshmen *Admission:* 266 enrolled.

Faculty *Total:* 57, 16% full-time. *Student/faculty ratio:* 15:1.

Majors Apparel and accessories marketing; apparel and textiles; commercial and advertising art; consumer merchandising/retailing management; design and visual communications; fashion/apparel design; fashion merchandising; interior design.

Academic Programs *Special study options:* academic remediation for entering students, adult/continuing education programs, English as a second language, honors programs, internships, off-campus study, part-time degree program, study abroad, summer session for credit.

Library Resource and Research Center with 4,168 titles, 148 serial subscriptions, a Web page.

Computers on Campus 26 computers available on campus for general student use. At least one staffed computer lab available.

Student Life *Housing:* college housing not available. *Activities and Organizations:* ASID (student chapter), DECA, Visual Design Form, Honor Society. *Campus security:* 24-hour emergency response devices and patrols. *Student services:* personal/psychological counseling.

Standardized Tests *Required:* Wonderlic aptitude test (for admission).

Costs (2004–05) *Tuition:* $15,500 full-time. *Required fees:* $500 full-time.

Applying *Options:* common application, electronic application, deferred entrance. *Application fee:* $25. *Required:* essay or personal statement, high school transcript, 3 letters of recommendation. *Required for some:* interview, major-determined project. *Recommended:* minimum 2.0 GPA. *Application deadline:* rolling (freshmen), rolling (transfers).

Admissions Contact Ms. Sheryl Bada Lamenti, Director of Admissions, Fashion Institute of Design and Merchandising, San Francisco Campus, 55 Stockton Street, San Francisco, CA 94108. *Phone:* 415-433-6691 Ext. 200. *Toll-free phone:* 800-711-7175. *Fax:* 415-296-7299. *E-mail:* info@fidm.com.

FEATHER RIVER COMMUNITY COLLEGE DISTRICT
Quincy, California

- **State and locally supported** 2-year, founded 1968, part of California Community College System
- **Calendar** semesters
- **Degree** certificates, diplomas, and associate
- **Rural** 150-acre campus
- **Endowment** $2296
- **Coed,** 1,547 undergraduate students, 31% full-time, 56% women, 44% men

Undergraduates 479 full-time, 1,068 part-time. Students come from 13 states and territories, 1 other country, 23% are from out of state, 10% African American, 2% Asian American or Pacific Islander, 6% Hispanic American, 3% Native American, 3% transferred in, 24% live on campus. *Retention:* 62% of 2002 full-time freshmen returned.

Freshmen *Admission:* 162 applied, 162 admitted, 117 enrolled.

Faculty *Total:* 75, 37% full-time.

Majors Administrative assistant and secretarial science; animal/livestock husbandry and production; biology/biological sciences; business/commerce; child care and support services management; child care/guidance; construction engineering technology; criminal justice/law enforcement administration; English; forestry; history; liberal arts and sciences/liberal studies; mathematics; natural resources management; nursing (licensed practical/vocational nurse training); parks, recreation and leisure facilities management; parks, recreation, and leisure related; physical sciences; social sciences.

Academic Programs *Special study options:* academic remediation for entering students, adult/continuing education programs, advanced placement credit, cooperative education, distance learning, double majors, freshman honors college, honors programs, independent study, internships, part-time degree program, services for LD students, summer session for credit.

Library Feather River Library plus 1 other with 19,744 titles, 118 serial subscriptions, 1,762 audiovisual materials, an OPAC.

Computers on Campus 125 computers available on campus for general student use. A campuswide network can be accessed. Internet access, at least one staffed computer lab available.

Student Life *Housing Options:* coed. Campus housing is university owned. *Activities and Organizations:* drama/theater group, choral group, Mountain Ultimate Disc (MUD), Varsity Club, Feather River Outings Group, SIFE, Chess Club. *Campus security:* student patrols.

Athletics *Intercollegiate sports:* baseball M, basketball M/W, football M, soccer M/W, softball W. *Intramural sports:* cheerleading W(c), ultimate Frisbee M(c)/W(c).

Costs (2003–04) *Tuition:* state resident $0 full-time; nonresident $5250 full-time, $175 per unit part-time. *Required fees:* $564 full-time, $18 per unit part-time. *Room and board:* room only: $3753. Room and board charges vary according to housing facility. *Payment plan:* deferred payment.

Financial Aid Of all full-time matriculated undergraduates who enrolled, 22 Federal Work-Study jobs (averaging $750). 103 state and other part-time jobs (averaging $1504).

Applying *Options:* common application, electronic application, early admission.

Admissions Contact Ms. Michelle Jaureguito, College Outreach and Recruitment, Feather River Community College District, 570 Golden Eagle Avenue, Quincy, CA 95971. *Phone:* 530-283-0202 Ext. 276. *Toll-free phone:* 800-442-9799 Ext. 286. *Fax:* 530-283-9961. *E-mail:* info@frc.edu.

FOOTHILL COLLEGE
Los Altos Hills, California

- **State and locally supported** 2-year, founded 1958, part of Foothill/DeAnza Community College District System
- **Calendar** quarters
- **Degree** certificates and associate
- **Suburban** 122-acre campus with easy access to San Jose
- **Coed,** 18,328 undergraduate students, 23% full-time, 52% women, 48% men

Undergraduates 4,215 full-time, 14,113 part-time. Students come from 51 states and territories, 101 other countries, 3% African American, 23% Asian American or Pacific Islander, 12% Hispanic American, 0.5% Native American, 5% international.

Freshmen *Admission:* 1,178 applied, 1,178 admitted.

Faculty *Total:* 812, 25% full-time.

Majors Accounting; American studies; anthropology; art; art history, criticism and conservation; athletic training; avionics maintenance technology; biology/biological sciences; biology/biotechnology laboratory technician; business administration and management; chemistry; child development; classics and languages, literatures and linguistics; commercial and advertising art; communication/speech communication and rhetoric; computer engineering technology; computer science; creative writing; cultural studies; dental assisting; dental hygiene; diagnostic medical sonography and ultrasound technology; dramatic/theatre arts; economics; electrical, electronic and communications engineering technology; emergency medical technology (EMT paramedic); engineering; English; fine/studio arts; French; geography; geology/earth science; German; history; humanities; international business/trade/commerce; Japanese; landscape architecture; legal studies; liberal arts and sciences/liberal studies; library science; linguistics; literature; mathematics; medical radiologic technology; music; ornamental hor-

California

Foothill College (continued)

ticulture; philosophy; photography; physical education teaching and coaching; physician assistant; physics; plant nursery management; political science and government; psychology; radio and television; radiologic technology/science; real estate; respiratory care therapy; social sciences; sociology; Spanish; speech and rhetoric; tourism and travel services management; veterinary technology; women's studies.

Academic Programs *Special study options:* academic remediation for entering students, accelerated degree program, adult/continuing education programs, advanced placement credit, cooperative education, distance learning, English as a second language, honors programs, independent study, internships, off-campus study, part-time degree program, services for LD students, student-designed majors, study abroad, summer session for credit. *ROTC:* Army (c), Air Force (c).

Library Hubert H. Semans Library with 70,000 titles, 450 serial subscriptions, an OPAC, a Web page.

Computers on Campus 200 computers available on campus for general student use. A campuswide network can be accessed from off campus. Internet access, online (class) registration, at least one staffed computer lab available.

Student Life *Housing:* college housing not available. *Activities and Organizations:* drama/theater group, student-run newspaper, radio station, choral group, Alpha Gamma Sigma, student government. *Campus security:* 24-hour emergency response devices and patrols, late-night transport/escort service. *Student services:* health clinic, personal/psychological counseling, legal services.

Athletics Member NJCAA. *Intercollegiate sports:* basketball M/W, football M, golf M/W, soccer M/W, softball W, swimming M/W, tennis M, volleyball W, water polo M/W.

Costs (2003–04) *Tuition:* state resident $0 full-time; nonresident $4995 full-time, $111 per unit part-time. *Required fees:* $626 full-time, $12 per unit part-time, $29 per term part-time.

Financial Aid Of all full-time matriculated undergraduates who enrolled, 80 Federal Work-Study jobs (averaging $1300). 210 state and other part-time jobs.

Applying *Options:* electronic application. *Recommended:* high school transcript. *Application deadline:* 9/15 (freshmen), rolling (transfers). *Notification:* continuous (freshmen), continuous (transfers).

Admissions Contact Ms. Penny Johnson, Dean, Counseling and Student Services, Foothill College, Admissions and Records, 12345 El Monte Road, Los Altos Hills, CA 94022. *Phone:* 650-949-7326. *Fax:* 650-949-7375.

FOUNDATION COLLEGE
San Diego, California

■ **Independent** 2-year
■ **Calendar** continuous
■ **Degree** certificates and associate
■ **Urban** campus
■ **Coed**

Freshmen *Admission:* 0 applied, 0 admitted.
Faculty *Total:* 13, 77% full-time.
Majors Computer engineering technology; computer programming; computer science; computer systems networking and telecommunications; computer technology/computer systems technology; data processing and data processing technology.
Student Life *Housing:* college housing not available.
Costs (2004–05) *Tuition:* $260 per credit part-time.
Applying *Application deadline:* rolling (freshmen), rolling (transfers). *Notification:* continuous (freshmen), continuous (transfers).
Admissions Contact Peggy Aplin, Admissions Manager, Foundation College, 5353 Mission Center Road, Suite 100, San Diego, CA 92108-1306. *Phone:* 619-683-3273 Ext. 105. *Toll-free phone:* 888-707-3273. *E-mail:* jdurb@foundationcollege.com.

FRESNO CITY COLLEGE
Fresno, California

■ **District-supported** 2-year, founded 1910, part of California Community College System
■ **Calendar** semesters
■ **Degree** certificates and associate
■ **Urban** 103-acre campus
■ **Endowment** $853,060
■ **Coed**

Faculty *Student/faculty ratio:* 16:1.
Student Life *Campus security:* 24-hour emergency response devices and patrols, late-night transport/escort service.
Athletics Member NJCAA.
Standardized Tests *Required:* ACCUPLACER (for placement).

Costs (2003–04) *Tuition:* state resident $0 full-time; nonresident $3120 full-time, $130 per unit part-time. *Required fees:* $456 full-time, $18 per unit part-time, $12 per term part-time.
Financial Aid Of all full-time matriculated undergraduates who enrolled, 350 Federal Work-Study jobs (averaging $3000).
Applying *Options:* common application, early admission, deferred entrance. *Required:* high school transcript.
Admissions Contact Ms. Stephanie Pauhi, Office Assistant, Fresno City College, 1101 East University Avenue, Fresno, CA 93741. *Phone:* 559-442-8225. *Fax:* 559-237-4232.

FULLERTON COLLEGE
Fullerton, California

Admissions Contact Mr. Peter Fong, Dean of Admissions and Records, Fullerton College, 321 East Chapman Avenue, Fullerton, CA 92832-2095. *Phone:* 714-992-7582. *E-mail:* pfong@fullcoll.edu.

GAVILAN COLLEGE
Gilroy, California

■ **State and locally supported** 2-year, founded 1919, part of California Community College System
■ **Calendar** semesters
■ **Degree** certificates, diplomas, and associate
■ **Rural** 150-acre campus with easy access to San Jose
■ **Coed**, 5,060 undergraduate students

Undergraduates Students come from 6 states and territories, 11 other countries, 20% are from out of state, 2% African American, 5% Asian American or Pacific Islander, 45% Hispanic American, 0.7% Native American.
Freshmen *Admission:* 1,926 admitted.
Faculty *Total:* 164, 45% full-time.
Majors Accounting; administrative assistant and secretarial science; art; automobile/automotive mechanics technology; avionics maintenance technology; biological and physical sciences; biology/biological sciences; business administration and management; chemistry; child development; computer and information sciences related; computer graphics; computer programming; computer science; corrections; cosmetology; criminal justice/law enforcement administration; criminal justice/police science; developmental and child psychology; drafting and design technology; English; history; information science/studies; information technology; journalism; kindergarten/preschool education; legal administrative assistant/secretary; liberal arts and sciences/liberal studies; mathematics; music; natural sciences; nursing (licensed practical/vocational nurse training); nursing (registered nurse training); physical education teaching and coaching; political science and government; pre-engineering; psychology; social sciences; sociology; Spanish.
Academic Programs *Special study options:* academic remediation for entering students, adult/continuing education programs, advanced placement credit, cooperative education, distance learning, English as a second language, honors programs, independent study, internships, part-time degree program, services for LD students, study abroad, summer session for credit.
Library 55,440 titles, 205 serial subscriptions.
Computers on Campus 31 computers available on campus for general student use. A campuswide network can be accessed. Internet access, at least one staffed computer lab available.
Student Life *Housing:* college housing not available. *Activities and Organizations:* drama/theater group, student-run newspaper, Student Government. *Campus security:* 24-hour emergency response devices and patrols, late-night transport/escort service. *Student services:* health clinic, personal/psychological counseling.
Athletics *Intercollegiate sports:* baseball W, basketball M/W, football M, golf M, soccer M/W, softball W, tennis M, volleyball W, wrestling M.
Standardized Tests *Required for some:* ACT ASSET.
Costs (2003–04) *Tuition:* state resident $0 full-time; nonresident $3888 full-time, $162 per unit part-time. *Required fees:* $300 full-time, $11 per unit part-time, $12 per term part-time.
Financial Aid Of all full-time matriculated undergraduates who enrolled, 50 Federal Work-Study jobs (averaging $2000). *Financial aid deadline:* 6/30.
Applying *Application deadline:* rolling (freshmen), rolling (transfers). *Notification:* continuous (freshmen), continuous (transfers).
Admissions Contact Ms. Joy Parker, Director of Admissions, Gavilan College, 5055 Santa Teresa Boulevard, Gilroy, CA 95020. *Phone:* 408-848-4735. *Fax:* 408-846-4910.

GLENDALE COMMUNITY COLLEGE
Glendale, California

- **State and locally supported** 2-year, founded 1927, part of California Community College System
- **Calendar** semesters
- **Degree** certificates and associate
- **Urban** 119-acre campus with easy access to Los Angeles
- **Endowment** $4.3 million
- **Coed**

Student Life *Campus security:* student patrols, late-night transport/escort service.

Costs (2003–04) *Tuition:* state resident $0 full-time; nonresident $3678 full-time, $140 per unit part-time. Full-time tuition and fees vary according to course load. Part-time tuition and fees vary according to course load. *Required fees:* $372 full-time, $18 per unit part-time.

Financial Aid Of all full-time matriculated undergraduates who enrolled, 300 Federal Work-Study jobs (averaging $2500).

Applying *Options:* common application, electronic application, early admission, deferred entrance. *Recommended:* high school transcript.

Admissions Contact Ms. Sharon Combs, Dean, Admissions and Records, Glendale Community College, 1500 North Verdugo Road, Glendale, CA 91208. *Phone:* 818-551-5115. *Fax:* 818-551-5255. *E-mail:* info@glendale.edu.

GOLDEN WEST COLLEGE
Huntington Beach, California

- **State and locally supported** 2-year, founded 1966, part of Coast Community College District System
- **Calendar** semesters (summer session)
- **Degree** certificates and associate
- **Suburban** 122-acre campus with easy access to Los Angeles
- **Endowment** $880,684
- **Coed**

Faculty *Student/faculty ratio:* 32:1.

Student Life *Campus security:* 24-hour emergency response devices and patrols, late-night transport/escort service.

Athletics Member NJCAA.

Standardized Tests *Required for some:* ACT COMPASS. *Recommended:* ACT COMPASS.

Costs (2003–04) *Tuition:* state resident $0 full-time; nonresident $3600 full-time, $150 per unit part-time. *Required fees:* $480 full-time, $18 per unit part-time, $24 per term part-time.

Applying *Options:* early admission. *Required for some:* essay or personal statement. *Recommended:* high school transcript.

Admissions Contact Ms. Shirley Donnelly, Director of Enrollment Services, Golden West College, 15744 Golden West Street, Huntington Beach, CA 92647. *Phone:* 714-892-7711 Ext. 58196.

GROSSMONT COLLEGE
El Cajon, California

- **State and locally supported** 2-year, founded 1961, part of California Community College System
- **Calendar** semesters
- **Degree** certificates and associate
- **Suburban** 135-acre campus with easy access to San Diego
- **Coed**

Faculty *Student/faculty ratio:* 17:1.

Student Life *Campus security:* 24-hour emergency response devices, student patrols, late-night transport/escort service.

Athletics Member NJCAA.

Standardized Tests *Recommended:* Assessment and Placement Services for Community Colleges.

Costs (2003–04) *Tuition:* state resident $0 full-time; nonresident $4380 full-time, $146 per unit part-time. *Required fees:* $364 full-time, $11 per unit part-time.

Financial Aid Of all full-time matriculated undergraduates who enrolled, 289 Federal Work-Study jobs (averaging $1802).

Applying *Options:* common application, early admission.

Admissions Contact Ms. Sharon Clark, Registrar, Grossmont College, El Cajon, CA 92020-1799. *Phone:* 619-644-7170. *Fax:* 619-644-7922.

HARTNELL COLLEGE
Salinas, California

- **District-supported** 2-year, founded 1920, part of California Community College System
- **Calendar** semesters
- **Degree** certificates and associate
- **Small-town** 50-acre campus with easy access to San Jose
- **Coed**

Student Life *Campus security:* 24-hour emergency response devices, student patrols, late-night transport/escort service.

Costs (2003–04) *Tuition:* state resident $0 full-time; nonresident $4470 full-time, $149 per unit part-time. *Required fees:* $548 full-time, $18 per unit part-time, $4 per term part-time.

Financial Aid Of all full-time matriculated undergraduates who enrolled, 100 Federal Work-Study jobs (averaging $6000). 29 state and other part-time jobs (averaging $3000).

Applying *Options:* early admission, deferred entrance. *Required for some:* high school transcript.

Admissions Contact Ms. Mary Dominguez, Director of Admissions, Hartnell College, 156 Homestead Avenue, Salinas, CA 93901-1697. *Phone:* 831-755-6711. *Fax:* 331-759-6014.

HEALD COLLEGE-CONCORD
Concord, California

- **Independent** 2-year, founded 1863
- **Calendar** quarters
- **Degree** certificates, diplomas, and associate
- **Small-town** 5-acre campus with easy access to San Francisco
- **Coed**

Student Life *Campus security:* 24-hour emergency response devices.

Standardized Tests *Required:* (for admission).

Applying *Options:* electronic application, early admission, deferred entrance. *Application fee:* $100. *Required:* high school transcript, interview.

Admissions Contact Director of Admissions, Heald College-Concord, 5130 Commercial Circle, Concord, CA 94520. *Phone:* 925-288-5800. *Toll-free phone:* 800-755-3550. *E-mail:* info@heald.edu.

HEALD COLLEGE-FRESNO
Fresno, California

- **Independent** 2-year, founded 1863
- **Calendar** quarters
- **Degree** certificates, diplomas, and associate
- **Suburban** 3-acre campus
- **Coed**

Standardized Tests *Required:* (for admission).

Applying *Options:* electronic application, early admission, deferred entrance. *Application fee:* $100. *Required:* high school transcript, interview.

Admissions Contact Director of Admissions, Heald College-Fresno, 255 West Bullard Avenue, Fresno, CA 93704-1706. *Phone:* 559-438-4222. *Toll-free phone:* 800-755-3550. *E-mail:* info@heald.edu.

HEALD COLLEGE-HAYWARD
Hayward, California

- **Independent** 2-year, founded 1863
- **Calendar** quarters
- **Degree** certificates, diplomas, and associate
- **Urban** campus with easy access to San Francisco
- **Coed**

Student Life *Campus security:* 24-hour emergency response devices and patrols.

Standardized Tests *Required:* CPAt (for admission).

Applying *Options:* electronic application, early admission, deferred entrance. *Application fee:* $100. *Required:* high school transcript, interview.

Admissions Contact Director of Admissions, Heald College-Hayward, 25500 Industrial Boulevard, Hayward, CA 94545. *Phone:* 510-783-2100. *Toll-free phone:* 800-755-3550. *E-mail:* info@heald.edu.

HEALD COLLEGE-RANCHO CORDOVA
Rancho Cordova, California

- **Independent** 2-year, founded 1863
- **Calendar** quarters

Heald College-Rancho Cordova (continued)
- **Degree** certificates, diplomas, and associate
- **Suburban** 1-acre campus with easy access to Sacramento
- **Coed**

Student Life *Campus security:* late-night transport/escort service.
Standardized Tests *Required:* (for admission).
Applying *Options:* electronic application, early admission, deferred entrance. *Application fee:* $100. *Required:* high school transcript, interview.
Admissions Contact Director of Admissions, Heald College-Rancho Cordova, 2910 Prospect Park Drive, Rancho Cordova, CA 95670-6005. *Phone:* 916-638-1616. *Toll-free phone:* 800-755-3550. *E-mail:* info@heald.edu.

HEALD COLLEGE-ROSEVILLE
Roseville, California

- **Independent** 2-year, founded 1863
- **Calendar** quarters
- **Degree** certificates, diplomas, and associate
- **Urban** 5-acre campus
- **Coed**

Student Life *Campus security:* 24-hour emergency response devices, evening security guard.
Standardized Tests *Required:* (for admission).
Financial Aid Of all full-time matriculated undergraduates who enrolled, 35 Federal Work-Study jobs.
Applying *Options:* electronic application, early admission, deferred entrance. *Application fee:* $100. *Required:* high school transcript, interview.
Admissions Contact Director of Admissions, Heald College-Roseville, 7 Sierra Gate Plaza, Roseville, CA 95678. *Phone:* 916-789-8600. *Toll-free phone:* 800-755-3550. *E-mail:* info@heald.edu.

HEALD COLLEGE-SALINAS
Salinas, California

- **Independent** 2-year, founded 1863
- **Calendar** quarters
- **Degree** certificates, diplomas, and associate
- **Small-town** campus with easy access to San Jose
- **Coed**

Student Life *Campus security:* 24-hour emergency response devices, evening security personnel.
Standardized Tests *Required:* (for admission).
Applying *Options:* electronic application, early admission, deferred entrance. *Application fee:* $100. *Required:* high school transcript, interview.
Admissions Contact Director of Admissions, Heald College-Salinas, 1450 North Main Street, Salinas, CA 93906. *Phone:* 831-443-1700. *Toll-free phone:* 800-755-3550. *E-mail:* info@heald.edu.

HEALD COLLEGE-SAN FRANCISCO
San Francisco, California

- **Independent** 2-year, founded 1863
- **Calendar** quarters
- **Degree** certificates, diplomas, and associate
- **Urban** campus
- **Coed**

Standardized Tests *Required:* (for admission).
Applying *Options:* electronic application, early admission, deferred entrance. *Application fee:* $100. *Required:* high school transcript, interview.
Admissions Contact Director of Admissions, Heald College-San Francisco, 350 Mission Street, San Francisco, CA 94105. *Phone:* 415-808-3000. *Toll-free phone:* 800-755-3550. *E-mail:* info@heald.edu.

HEALD COLLEGE-SAN JOSE
Milpitas, California

- **Independent** 2-year, founded 1863
- **Calendar** quarters
- **Degree** certificates, diplomas, and associate
- **Small-town** 5-acre campus with easy access to San Jose
- **Coed**

Standardized Tests *Required:* (for admission).

Financial Aid Of all full-time matriculated undergraduates who enrolled, 20 Federal Work-Study jobs.
Applying *Options:* electronic application, early admission, deferred entrance. *Application fee:* $100. *Required:* high school transcript, interview.
Admissions Contact Heald College-San Jose, 341 Great Mall Parkway, Milpitas, CA 95035. *Phone:* 408-934-4900. *Toll-free phone:* 800-755-3550. *E-mail:* info@heald.edu.

HEALD COLLEGE-STOCKTON
Stockton, California

- **Independent** 2-year, founded 1863
- **Calendar** quarters
- **Degree** certificates, diplomas, and associate
- **Coed**

Standardized Tests *Required:* (for admission).
Applying *Options:* electronic application, early admission, deferred entrance. *Application fee:* $100. *Required:* high school transcript, interview.
Admissions Contact Director of Admissions, Heald College-Stockton, 1605 East March Lane, Stockton, CA 95210. *Phone:* 209-473-5200. *Toll-free phone:* 800-755-3550. *E-mail:* info@heald.edu.

HIGH-TECH INSTITUTE
Sacramento, California

Admissions Contact Mr. Richard Dyer, School Director, High-Tech Institute, 1111 Howe Avenue, #250, Sacramento, CA 95825. *Phone:* 916-929-9700. *Toll-free phone:* 800-987-0110.

IMPERIAL VALLEY COLLEGE
Imperial, California

- **State and locally supported** 2-year, founded 1922, part of California Community College System
- **Calendar** semesters
- **Degree** certificates and associate
- **Rural** 160-acre campus
- **Endowment** $832,061
- **Coed**

Student Life *Campus security:* student patrols.
Costs (2003–04) *Tuition:* state resident $0 full-time; nonresident $4470 full-time. *Required fees:* $540 full-time.
Financial Aid Of all full-time matriculated undergraduates who enrolled, 389 Federal Work-Study jobs (averaging $1500). 250 state and other part-time jobs (averaging $1900).
Applying *Required for some:* high school transcript. *Recommended:* high school transcript.
Admissions Contact Mrs. Sandra Standiford, Dean of Admissions, Imperial Valley College, PO Box 158, Imperial, CA 92251. *Phone:* 760-352-8320 Ext. 200.

IRVINE VALLEY COLLEGE
Irvine, California

Admissions Contact Mr. Jess Craig, Dean of Students, Irvine Valley College, 5500 Irvine Center Drive, Irvine, CA 92618. *Phone:* 949-451-5410.

ITT TECHNICAL INSTITUTE
Anaheim, California

- **Proprietary** primarily 2-year, founded 1982, part of ITT Educational Services, Inc.
- **Calendar** quarters
- **Degrees** associate and bachelor's
- **Suburban** 5-acre campus with easy access to Los Angeles
- **Coed**

Standardized Tests *Required:* Wonderlic aptitude test (for admission).
Costs (2003–04) *Tuition:* Total Program Cost varies depending on course of study. Consult school catalog.
Financial Aid Of all full-time matriculated undergraduates who enrolled, 20 Federal Work-Study jobs (averaging $5000).
Applying *Options:* deferred entrance. *Application fee:* $100. *Required:* high school transcript, interview. *Recommended:* letters of recommendation.

Admissions Contact Mr. Albert A. Naranjo, Director of Recruitment, ITT Technical Institute, 525 North Muller Avenue, Anaheim, CA 92801. *Phone:* 714-535-3700. *Fax:* 714-535-1802.

ITT TECHNICAL INSTITUTE
Lathrop, California

- **Proprietary** primarily 2-year, part of ITT Educational Services
- **Calendar** quarters
- **Degrees** associate and bachelor's
- **Coed**

Standardized Tests *Required:* Wonderlic aptitude test (for admission).
Costs (2003–04) *Tuition:* $347 per credit hour part-time.
Applying *Options:* deferred entrance. *Application fee:* $100. *Required:* high school transcript, interview. *Recommended:* letters of recommendation.
Admissions Contact Mr. Donald Fraser, Director of Recruitment, ITT Technical Institute, 16916 South Harlan Road, Lathrop, CA 95330. *Phone:* 209-858-0077. *Toll-free phone:* 800-346-1786. *Fax:* 209-858-0277.

ITT TECHNICAL INSTITUTE
Oxnard, California

- **Proprietary** primarily 2-year, founded 1993, part of ITT Educational Services, Inc.
- **Calendar** quarters
- **Degrees** associate and bachelor's
- **Urban** campus with easy access to Los Angeles
- **Coed**

Student Life *Campus security:* 24-hour emergency response devices and patrols.
Standardized Tests *Required:* Wonderlic aptitude test (for admission).
Costs (2003–04) *Tuition:* $347 per credit hour part-time.
Applying *Options:* deferred entrance. *Application fee:* $100. *Required:* high school transcript, interview. *Recommended:* letters of recommendation.
Admissions Contact Mr. Dean K. Dunbar, Director of Recruitment, ITT Technical Institute, 2051 Solar Drive, Building B, Oxnard, CA 93036. *Phone:* 805-988-0143. *Toll-free phone:* 800-530-1582. *Fax:* 805-988-1813.

ITT TECHNICAL INSTITUTE
San Diego, California

- **Proprietary** primarily 2-year, founded 1981, part of ITT Educational Services, Inc.
- **Calendar** quarters
- **Degrees** associate and bachelor's
- **Suburban** campus
- **Coed**

Standardized Tests *Required:* Wonderlic aptitude test (for admission).
Costs (2003–04) *Tuition:* Total Program Cost varies depending on course of study. Consult school catalog.
Applying *Options:* deferred entrance. *Application fee:* $100. *Required:* high school transcript, interview. *Recommended:* letters of recommendation.
Admissions Contact Ms. Sheryl Schulgen, Director of Recruitment, ITT Technical Institute, 9680 Granite Ridge Drive, San Diego, CA 92123. *Phone:* 858-571-8500. *Toll-free phone:* 800-883-0380. *Fax:* 858-571-1277.

ITT TECHNICAL INSTITUTE
Sylmar, California

- **Proprietary** primarily 2-year, founded 1982, part of ITT Educational Services, Inc.
- **Calendar** quarters
- **Degrees** associate and bachelor's
- **Urban** campus with easy access to Los Angeles
- **Coed**

Standardized Tests *Required:* Wonderlic aptitude test (for admission).
Costs (2003–04) *Tuition:* Total Program Cost varies depending on course of study. Consult school catalog.
Applying *Options:* deferred entrance. *Application fee:* $100. *Required:* high school transcript, interview. *Recommended:* letters of recommendation.
Admissions Contact Mr. Dominick Miciotta, Director of Recruitment, ITT Technical Institute, 12669 Encinitas Avenue, Sylmar, CA 91342. *Phone:* 818-364-5151. *Toll-free phone:* 800-363-2086. *Fax:* 818-364-5150.

ITT TECHNICAL INSTITUTE
West Covina, California

- **Proprietary** primarily 2-year, founded 1982, part of ITT Educational Services, Inc.
- **Calendar** quarters
- **Degrees** associate and bachelor's
- **Suburban** 4-acre campus with easy access to Los Angeles
- **Coed**

Standardized Tests *Required:* Wonderlic aptitude test (for admission).
Costs (2003–04) *Tuition:* Total Program Cost varies depending on course of study. Consult school catalog.
Financial Aid Of all full-time matriculated undergraduates who enrolled, 20 Federal Work-Study jobs (averaging $4500).
Applying *Options:* deferred entrance. *Application fee:* $100. *Required:* high school transcript, interview. *Recommended:* letters of recommendation.
Admissions Contact Mr. Michael Snyder, Director of Recruitment, ITT Technical Institute, 1530 West Cameron Avenue, West Covina, CA 91790. *Phone:* 626-960-8681. *Toll-free phone:* 800-414-6522. *Fax:* 626-337-5271.

ITT TECHNICAL INSTITUTE
Rancho Cordova, California

- **Proprietary** primarily 2-year, founded 1954, part of ITT Educational Services, Inc.
- **Calendar** quarters
- **Degrees** associate and bachelor's
- **Urban** 5-acre campus
- **Coed**

Standardized Tests *Required:* Wonderlic aptitude test (for admission).
Applying *Options:* deferred entrance. *Application fee:* $100. *Required:* high school transcript, interview. *Recommended:* letters of recommendation.
Admissions Contact Mr. Robert Menszer, Director of Recruitment, ITT Technical Institute, 10863 Gold Center Drive, Rancho Cordova, CA 95670. *Phone:* 916-851-3900. *Toll-free phone:* 800-488-8466. *Fax:* 916-851-9225.

ITT TECHNICAL INSTITUTE
Torrance, California

- **Proprietary** primarily 2-year, founded 1987, part of ITT Educational Services, Inc.
- **Calendar** quarters
- **Degrees** associate and bachelor's
- **Urban** campus with easy access to Los Angeles
- **Coed**

Standardized Tests *Required:* Wonderlic aptitude test (for admission).
Costs (2003–04) *Tuition:* Total Program Cost varies depending on course of study. Consult school catalog.
Financial Aid Of all full-time matriculated undergraduates who enrolled, 6 Federal Work-Study jobs (averaging $4000).
Applying *Options:* deferred entrance. *Application fee:* $100. *Required:* high school transcript, interview. *Recommended:* letters of recommendation.
Admissions Contact Mr. Freddie Polk, Director of Recruitment, ITT Technical Institute, 20050 South Vermont Avenue, Torrance, CA 90502. *Phone:* 310-380-1555. *Fax:* 310-380-1557.

ITT TECHNICAL INSTITUTE
San Bernardino, California

- **Proprietary** primarily 2-year, founded 1987, part of ITT Educational Services, Inc.
- **Calendar** quarters
- **Degrees** associate and bachelor's
- **Urban** campus with easy access to Los Angeles
- **Coed**

Standardized Tests *Required:* Wonderlic aptitude test (for admission).
Costs (2003–04) *Tuition:* Total Program Cost varies depending on course of study. Consult school catalog.
Applying *Options:* deferred entrance. *Application fee:* $100. *Required:* high school transcript, interview. *Recommended:* letters of recommendation.
Admissions Contact Ms. Maria Alamat, Director of Recruitment, ITT Technical Institute, 630 East Brier Drive, Suite 150, San Bernardino, CA 92408. *Phone:* 909-889-3800 Ext. 11. *Toll-free phone:* 800-888-3801. *Fax:* 909-888-6970.

LAKE TAHOE COMMUNITY COLLEGE
South Lake Tahoe, California

Admissions Contact Ms. Linda M. Stevenson, Director of Admissions and Records, Lake Tahoe Community College, One College Drive, South Lake Tahoe, CA 96150-4524. *Phone:* 530-541-4660 Ext. 282. *Fax:* 530-541-7852.

LANEY COLLEGE
Oakland, California

- **State and locally supported** 2-year, founded 1953, part of Peralta Community College District System
- **Calendar** semesters
- **Degree** certificates and associate
- **Urban** campus with easy access to San Francisco
- **Coed**

Costs (2003–04) *Tuition:* $18 per unit part-time; state resident $18 per unit part-time; nonresident $5408 full-time, $175 per unit part-time. *Required fees:* $508 full-time.
Financial Aid Of all full-time matriculated undergraduates who enrolled, 120 Federal Work-Study jobs (averaging $2500).
Applying *Options:* early admission.
Admissions Contact Mrs. Barbara Simmons, District Admissions Officer, Laney College, 900 Fallon Street, Oakland, CA 94607-4893. *Phone:* 510-466-7369.

LAS POSITAS COLLEGE
Livermore, California

Admissions Contact Mrs. Sylvia R. Rodriguez, Director of Admissions and Records, Las Positas College, 3033 Collier Canyon Road, Livermore, CA 94551-7650. *Phone:* 925-373-4942.

LASSEN COMMUNITY COLLEGE DISTRICT
Susanville, California

Admissions Contact Mr. Chris J. Alberico, Registrar, Lassen Community College District, Highway 139, PO Box 3000, Susanville, CA 96130. *Phone:* 530-257-6181 Ext. 132.

LONG BEACH CITY COLLEGE
Long Beach, California

- **State-supported** 2-year, founded 1927, part of California Community College System
- **Calendar** semesters
- **Degree** certificates and associate
- **Urban** 40-acre campus with easy access to Los Angeles
- **Coed**

Faculty *Student/faculty ratio:* 33:1.
Student Life *Campus security:* 24-hour emergency response devices and patrols, student patrols, late-night transport/escort service.
Athletics Member NJCAA.
Costs (2003–04) *Tuition:* state resident $0 full-time; nonresident $4470 full-time. *Required fees:* $330 full-time.
Financial Aid Of all full-time matriculated undergraduates who enrolled, 275 Federal Work-Study jobs (averaging $4400). 225 state and other part-time jobs (averaging $4400).
Applying *Options:* early admission. *Recommended:* high school transcript.
Admissions Contact Mr. Ross Miyashiro, Dean of Admissions and Records, Long Beach City College, 4901 East Carson Boulevard, Long Beach, CA 90808. *Phone:* 562-938-4130. *Fax:* 562-938-4858.

LOS ANGELES CITY COLLEGE
Los Angeles, California

- **District-supported** 2-year, founded 1929, part of Los Angeles Community College District System
- **Calendar** semesters
- **Degree** certificates, diplomas, and associate
- **Urban** 42-acre campus
- **Coed**

Student Life *Campus security:* 24-hour emergency response devices and patrols, student patrols, late-night transport/escort service.
Costs (2003–04) *Tuition:* state resident $0 full-time; nonresident $5364 full-time. *Required fees:* $688 full-time.
Admissions Contact Elaine Geismar, Director of Student Assistance Center, Los Angeles City College, 855 North Vermont Avenue, Los Angeles, CA 90029. *Phone:* 323-953-4340. *Fax:* 323-953-4536.

LOS ANGELES COUNTY COLLEGE OF NURSING AND ALLIED HEALTH
Los Angeles, California

Admissions Contact Ms. Maria Caballero, Manager, Admissions, Los Angeles County College of Nursing and Allied Health, 1237 North Mission Road, Los Angeles, CA 90033. *Phone:* 323-226-4911. *Fax:* 323-226-6343.

LOS ANGELES HARBOR COLLEGE
Wilmington, California

- **State and locally supported** 2-year, founded 1949, part of Los Angeles Community College District System
- **Calendar** semesters
- **Degree** certificates and associate
- **Suburban** 80-acre campus
- **Coed**, 9,469 undergraduate students, 24% full-time, 61% women, 39% men

Undergraduates 2,311 full-time, 7,158 part-time. Students come from 14 states and territories, 15% African American, 17% Asian American or Pacific Islander, 43% Hispanic American.
Freshmen *Admission:* 1,970 applied, 1,970 admitted, 1,970 enrolled. *Average high school GPA:* 2.50.
Faculty *Total:* 270, 41% full-time. *Student/faculty ratio:* 40:1.
Majors Accounting; administrative assistant and secretarial science; architectural engineering technology; automobile/automotive mechanics technology; biology/biological sciences; business administration and management; computer engineering technology; criminal justice/police science; data processing and data processing technology; developmental and child psychology; drafting and design technology; electrical, electronic and communications engineering technology; electromechanical technology; engineering technology; fire science; information science/studies; legal administrative assistant/secretary; liberal arts and sciences/liberal studies; medical administrative assistant and medical secretary; nursing (registered nurse training); physics; pre-engineering; real estate.
Academic Programs *Special study options:* academic remediation for entering students, adult/continuing education programs, advanced placement credit, cooperative education, distance learning, double majors, English as a second language, external degree program, freshman honors college, honors programs, independent study, off-campus study, part-time degree program, services for LD students, study abroad, summer session for credit.
Library Harbor College Library with 82,790 titles, 302 serial subscriptions, an OPAC, a Web page.
Computers on Campus 250 computers available on campus for general student use. A campuswide network can be accessed from off campus. Internet access, online (class) registration, at least one staffed computer lab available.
Student Life *Housing:* college housing not available. *Activities and Organizations:* drama/theater group, student-run radio and television station, choral group, Alpha Gamma Sigma, Abilities Unlimited, Students in Free Enterprise, Association of Future Firefighters. *Campus security:* 24-hour emergency response devices and patrols. *Student services:* health clinic, personal/psychological counseling, legal services.
Athletics *Intercollegiate sports:* baseball M, basketball M/W, football M, golf M, soccer M, tennis W, volleyball W.
Costs (2003–04) *Tuition:* state resident $0 full-time; nonresident $3216 full-time, $134 per unit part-time. *Required fees:* $280 full-time, $11 per unit part-time, $16 per year part-time. *Waivers:* employees or children of employees.
Financial Aid Of all full-time matriculated undergraduates who enrolled, 122 Federal Work-Study jobs (averaging $1800).
Applying *Options:* early admission, deferred entrance. *Required for some:* essay or personal statement, high school transcript. *Application deadlines:* 9/3 (freshmen), 9/3 (transfers).
Admissions Contact Mr. David Ching, Dean of Admissions and Records, Los Angeles Harbor College, 1111 Figueroa Place, Wilmington, CA 90744-2397. *Phone:* 310-233-4091. *Fax:* 310-834-1882.

LOS ANGELES MISSION COLLEGE
Sylmar, California

Admissions Contact Ms. Angela Merrill, Admissions Supervisor, Los Angeles Mission College, 13356 Eldridge Avenue, Sylmar, CA 91342-3245. *Phone:* 818-364-7658.

LOS ANGELES PIERCE COLLEGE
Woodland Hills, California

- **State and locally supported** 2-year, founded 1947, part of Los Angeles Community College District System
- **Calendar** semesters
- **Degree** certificates and associate
- **Suburban** 425-acre campus with easy access to Los Angeles
- **Coed,** 16,255 undergraduate students

Undergraduates Students come from 2 states and territories, 48 other countries.
Freshmen *Admission:* 26,070 applied, 26,070 admitted.
Faculty *Total:* 558.
Majors Accounting; agriculture; animal sciences; architectural engineering technology; art; automobile/automotive mechanics technology; computer engineering technology; computer programming; computer science; construction engineering technology; data processing and data processing technology; drafting and design technology; dramatic/theatre arts; electrical, electronic and communications engineering technology; equestrian studies; horticultural science; industrial arts; industrial technology; journalism; landscape architecture; landscaping and groundskeeping; liberal arts and sciences/liberal studies; machine tool technology; music; nursing (registered nurse training); ornamental horticulture; photography; plant protection and integrated pest management; pre-engineering; quality control technology; real estate; sign language interpretation and translation; veterinary technology; welding technology.
Academic Programs *Special study options:* academic remediation for entering students, adult/continuing education programs, advanced placement credit, cooperative education, distance learning, English as a second language, honors programs, independent study, internships, part-time degree program, services for LD students, study abroad, summer session for credit.
Library Pierce College Library plus 1 other with 106,122 titles, 395 serial subscriptions.
Computers on Campus 60 computers available on campus for general student use. A campuswide network can be accessed. At least one staffed computer lab available.
Student Life *Housing:* college housing not available. *Activities and Organizations:* drama/theater group, student-run newspaper, choral group, Alpha Gamma Sigma, Club Latino United for Education, United African-American Student Association, Hillel Club, Filipino Club. *Campus security:* 24-hour patrols, late-night transport/escort service. *Student services:* health clinic, personal/psychological counseling, women's center.
Athletics Member NJCAA. *Intercollegiate sports:* baseball M, basketball W, football M, softball W, swimming M/W, tennis M/W, volleyball M/W, water polo M. *Intramural sports:* cross-country running M/W, equestrian sports M/W, fencing M/W, golf M/W, racquetball M/W, skiing (downhill) M/W, soccer M/W, swimming M/W, tennis M/W, volleyball M/W, weight lifting M/W.
Costs (2004–05) *Tuition:* state resident $0 full-time; nonresident $3696 full-time, $154 per unit part-time. *Required fees:* $456 full-time, $18 per unit part-time, $12 per term part-time.
Financial Aid Of all full-time matriculated undergraduates who enrolled, 124 Federal Work-Study jobs (averaging $3000). 28 state and other part-time jobs (averaging $3000).
Applying *Options:* common application, electronic application, early admission. *Application deadline:* 8/20 (freshmen).
Admissions Contact Ms. Shelley L. Gerstl, Dean of Admissions and Records, Los Angeles Pierce College, 6201 Winnetka Avenue, Woodland Hills, CA 91371-0001. *Phone:* 818-719-6448.

LOS ANGELES SOUTHWEST COLLEGE
Los Angeles, California

Admissions Contact Dr. Lawrence Jarmon, Vice President of Student Services, Los Angeles Southwest College, 1600 West Imperial Highway, Los Angeles, CA 90047-4810. *Phone:* 323-241-5279.

LOS ANGELES TRADE-TECHNICAL COLLEGE
Los Angeles, California

- **State and locally supported** 2-year, founded 1925, part of Los Angeles Community College District System
- **Calendar** semesters
- **Degree** certificates, diplomas, and associate
- **Urban** 25-acre campus
- **Coed,** 13,194 undergraduate students, 32% full-time, 51% women, 49% men

Undergraduates 4,160 full-time, 9,034 part-time. Students come from 25 states and territories, 20 other countries, 35% African American, 9% Asian American or Pacific Islander, 47% Hispanic American, 0.3% Native American, 0.8% international.
Freshmen *Admission:* 342 enrolled.
Faculty *Total:* 443, 45% full-time.
Majors Accounting; architectural engineering technology; automobile/automotive mechanics technology; business administration and management; carpentry; chemical engineering; commercial and advertising art; computer engineering technology; computer programming; construction engineering technology; cosmetology; culinary arts; data processing and data processing technology; drafting and design technology; electrical, electronic and communications engineering technology; engineering; fashion/apparel design; fashion merchandising; graphic and printing equipment operation/production; heating, air conditioning, ventilation and refrigeration maintenance technology; heavy equipment maintenance technology; hydrology and water resources science; industrial technology; information science/studies; journalism; labor and industrial relations; liberal arts and sciences/liberal studies; mechanical engineering/mechanical technology; nursing (registered nurse training); photography; pipefitting and sprinkler fitting; real estate; transportation technology; welding technology.
Academic Programs *Special study options:* academic remediation for entering students, adult/continuing education programs, advanced placement credit, cooperative education, English as a second language, part-time degree program, services for LD students, summer session for credit.
Library 98,000 titles, 367 serial subscriptions.
Computers on Campus 200 computers available on campus for general student use. A campuswide network can be accessed. At least one staffed computer lab available.
Student Life *Housing:* college housing not available. *Activities and Organizations:* choral group. *Campus security:* 24-hour patrols, student patrols, late-night transport/escort service. *Student services:* health clinic, personal/psychological counseling, women's center.
Athletics *Intercollegiate sports:* basketball M/W, cross-country running M/W, tennis M, track and field M/W.
Costs (2004–05) *Tuition:* state resident $0 full-time; nonresident $4152 full-time, $154 per unit part-time. *Required fees:* $456 full-time, $18 per unit part-time.
Applying *Options:* early admission, deferred entrance. *Recommended:* high school transcript. *Application deadline:* 9/7 (freshmen).
Admissions Contact Mrs. Rosemary Royal, Dean of Enrollment Management, Los Angeles Trade-Technical College, 400 West Washington Boulevard, Los Angeles, CA 90015. *Phone:* 213-763-5301.

LOS ANGELES VALLEY COLLEGE
Van Nuys, California

- **State and locally supported** 2-year, founded 1949, part of Los Angeles Community College District System
- **Calendar** semesters
- **Degree** certificates and associate
- **Suburban** 105-acre campus
- **Endowment** $120,000
- **Coed,** 18,761 undergraduate students, 27% full-time, 60% women, 40% men

Undergraduates 5,021 full-time, 13,740 part-time. Students come from 43 other countries, 4% are from out of state, 27% transferred in.
Freshmen *Admission:* 992 enrolled.
Faculty *Total:* 525, 45% full-time.
Majors Accounting; administrative assistant and secretarial science; advertising; African-American/Black studies; art; biology/biological sciences; broadcast journalism; business administration and management; business machine repair; ceramic arts and ceramics; child development; civil engineering technology; commercial and advertising art; computer and information sciences related; computer programming; consumer merchandising/retailing management; criminal justice/law enforcement administration; criminal justice/police science; data processing and data processing technology; developmental and child psychology; drafting and design technology; dramatic/theatre arts; economics; electrical, electronic and communications engineering technology; engineering related; family and consumer economics related; family and consumer sciences/human sciences; film/cinema studies; fire science; French; geography; geology/earth science; Hebrew; history; hotel/motel administration; information science/studies; interior design; Italian; journalism; kindergarten/preschool education; liberal arts and sciences/liberal studies; library science; machine tool technology; marketing/marketing management; mass communication/media; mathematics; mechanical design technology; mechanical engineering/mechanical technology; music; nursing (licensed practical/vocational nurse training); nursing (registered nurse training); photography; physical education teaching and coaching; pre-engineering; psychology; radio and television; real estate; respiratory care therapy; sociology; Spanish; speech and rhetoric; word processing.

Los Angeles Valley College (continued)

Academic Programs *Special study options:* academic remediation for entering students, adult/continuing education programs, cooperative education, distance learning, double majors, English as a second language, honors programs, independent study, internships, part-time degree program, services for LD students, student-designed majors, summer session for credit.

Library Los Angeles Valley Library with 124,000 titles, 400 serial subscriptions, an OPAC, a Web page.

Computers on Campus 200 computers available on campus for general student use. A campuswide network can be accessed from off campus that provide access to student records access, catalog, e-mail. Internet access, online (class) registration, at least one staffed computer lab available.

Student Life *Housing:* college housing not available. *Activities and Organizations:* drama/theater group, student-run newspaper, radio station, choral group. *Campus security:* 24-hour emergency response devices and patrols, student patrols, late-night transport/escort service. *Student services:* health clinic, personal/psychological counseling, women's center, legal services.

Athletics Member NJCAA. *Intercollegiate sports:* basketball M/W, cross-country running M/W, fencing M/W, football M, gymnastics M/W, swimming M/W, tennis M/W, track and field M/W, volleyball M/W, water polo M, wrestling M. *Intramural sports:* badminton M/W, basketball M/W, cross-country running M/W, fencing M/W, football M, golf M/W, gymnastics M/W, skiing (cross-country) M/W, skiing (downhill) M/W, soccer M/W, swimming M/W, tennis M/W, track and field M/W, volleyball M/W, water polo M/W, wrestling M.

Standardized Tests *Required:* ACT (for placement).

Costs (2004–05) *Tuition:* state resident $0 full-time; nonresident $3696 full-time, $154 per unit part-time. *Required fees:* $450 full-time, $18 per unit part-time.

Financial Aid Of all full-time matriculated undergraduates who enrolled, 100 Federal Work-Study jobs (averaging $4000).

Applying *Options:* common application, electronic application, early admission. *Recommended:* high school transcript. *Application deadline:* rolling (freshmen), rolling (transfers).

Admissions Contact Mr. Florentino Manzano, Associate Dean, Los Angeles Valley College, 5800 Fulton Avenue, Valley Glen, CA 91401. *Phone:* 818-947-2353. *Fax:* 818-947-2501.

LOS MEDANOS COLLEGE
Pittsburg, California

- **District-supported** 2-year, founded 1974, part of California Community College System
- **Calendar** semesters
- **Degree** certificates and associate
- **Suburban** 120-acre campus with easy access to San Francisco
- **Coed**

Student Life *Campus security:* 24-hour patrols, student patrols, late-night transport/escort service.

Standardized Tests *Required for some:* Assessment and Placement Services for Community Colleges.

Financial Aid Of all full-time matriculated undergraduates who enrolled, 150 Federal Work-Study jobs (averaging $800).

Applying *Options:* common application. *Required for some:* high school transcript.

Admissions Contact Ms. Gail Newman, Director of Admissions and Records, Los Medanos College, 2700 East Leland Road, Pittsburg, CA 94565-5197. *Phone:* 925-439-2181 Ext. 7500.

MARIC COLLEGE
Anaheim, California

Admissions Contact 1360 South Anaheim Boulevard, Anaheim, CA 92805. *Toll-free phone:* 800-206-0095.

MARIC COLLEGE
Modesto, California

- **Proprietary** 2-year
- **Calendar** semesters
- **Degree** diplomas and associate
- **Coed, primarily women,** 289 undergraduate students, 100% full-time, 94% women, 6% men

Undergraduates 289 full-time. 13% African American, 13% Asian American or Pacific Islander, 38% Hispanic American.

Freshmen *Admission:* 16 applied, 16 admitted, 16 enrolled. *Average high school GPA:* 2.75.

Faculty *Total:* 5, 20% full-time, 60% with terminal degrees. *Student/faculty ratio:* 8:1.

Student Life *Housing:* college housing not available.

Costs (2004–05) *Tuition:* $8995 full-time. *Required fees:* $98 full-time.

Admissions Contact Mrs. Linda Stovall, Chief Admission Officer, Maric College, 5172 Kiernan Court, Modesto, CA 95368. *Phone:* 209-543-7000.

MARIC COLLEGE
North Hollywood, California

Admissions Contact Mr. Mark Newman, Executive Director, Maric College, 6180 Laurel Canyon Boulevard, Suite 101, North Hollywood, CA 91606. *Phone:* 818-763-2563 Ext. 240. *Toll-free phone:* 800-404-9729.

MARIC COLLEGE
Panorama City, California

Admissions Contact 14355 Roscoe Boulevard, Panorama City, CA 91402. *Toll-free phone:* 800-206-0095.

MARIC COLLEGE
Sacramento, California

- **Proprietary** 2-year
- **Calendar** semesters
- **Degree** associate
- 360 undergraduate students

Standardized Tests *Required:* CPAt (for admission).

Admissions Contact Mr. Charles Reese, Director of Admissions, Maric College, 4330 Watt Avenue, Suite 400, Sacramento, CA 95660. *Phone:* 916-649-8168. *Toll-free phone:* 800-955-8168.

MARIC COLLEGE
San Diego, California

- **Proprietary** 2-year, founded 1976
- **Calendar** semesters
- **Degrees** certificates and associate (also includes Vista campus)
- **Urban** 4-acre campus
- **Coed,** 298 undergraduate students, 100% full-time, 90% women, 10% men

Undergraduates 298 full-time. 9% African American, 3% Asian American or Pacific Islander, 40% Hispanic American, 4% Native American.

Freshmen *Admission:* 5 enrolled.

Faculty *Total:* 65, 69% full-time.

Majors Nursing (registered nurse training).

Academic Programs *Special study options:* academic remediation for entering students, adult/continuing education programs, internships, summer session for credit.

Library Student Resource Center.

Computers on Campus 100 computers available on campus for general student use. At least one staffed computer lab available.

Student Life *Housing:* college housing not available. *Campus security:* 24-hour patrols.

Costs (2003–04) *Tuition:* $9000 full-time. *Required fees:* $136 full-time.

Applying *Options:* common application. *Required:* essay or personal statement, high school transcript, interview. *Notification:* continuous (freshmen).

Admissions Contact Admissions, Maric College, 3666 Kearny Villa Road, Suite 100, San Diego, CA 92123-1995. *Phone:* 858-654-3601. *Toll-free phone:* 800-400-8232.

MARYMOUNT COLLEGE, PALOS VERDES, CALIFORNIA
Rancho Palos Verdes, California

Admissions Contact Ms. Nina Lococo, Dean of Admission and School Relations, Marymount College, Palos Verdes, California, 30800 Palos Verdes Drive East, Rancho Palos Verdes, CA 90815. *Phone:* 310-377-5501 Ext. 182. *Fax:* 310-265-0962. *E-mail:* admissions@marymountpv.edu.

MENDOCINO COLLEGE
Ukiah, California

- **State and locally supported** 2-year, founded 1973, part of California Community College System

- **Calendar** semesters
- **Degree** certificates and associate
- **Rural** 127-acre campus
- **Coed**

Faculty *Student/faculty ratio:* 12:1.

Student Life *Campus security:* late-night transport/escort service, security patrols 6 p.m. to 10 p.m.

Standardized Tests *Required for some:* CPT. *Recommended:* SAT I or ACT (for placement).

Costs (2003–04) *Tuition:* state resident $0 full-time; nonresident $4650 full-time, $155 per unit part-time. *Required fees:* $344 full-time, $11 per unit part-time, $14 per year part-time.

Financial Aid *Financial aid deadline:* 5/20.

Applying *Options:* early admission, deferred entrance.

Admissions Contact Ms. Kristie A. Taylor, Director of Admissions and Records, Mendocino College, 1000 Hensley Creek Road, Ukiah, CA 95482-0300. *Phone:* 707-468-3103. *Fax:* 707-468-3430. *E-mail:* ktaylor@mendocino.cc.ca.us.

MERCED COLLEGE

Merced, California

- **State and locally supported** 2-year, founded 1962, part of California Community College System
- **Calendar** semesters
- **Degree** associate
- **Small-town** 168-acre campus
- **Endowment** $1.0 million
- **Coed**

Student Life *Campus security:* 24-hour patrols, late-night transport/escort service.

Standardized Tests *Recommended:* SAT I or ACT (for placement).

Costs (2003–04) *Tuition:* state resident $0 full-time; nonresident $3384 full-time, $167 per unit part-time. *Required fees:* $307 full-time, $18 per unit part-time.

Financial Aid Of all full-time matriculated undergraduates who enrolled, 329 Federal Work-Study jobs (averaging $3545). 231 state and other part-time jobs (averaging $3545).

Applying *Options:* common application, early admission.

Admissions Contact Ms. Helen Torres, Admissions Clerk, Merced College, 3600 M Street, Merced, CA 95348-2898. *Phone:* 209-384-6187.

MERRITT COLLEGE

Oakland, California

- **State and locally supported** 2-year, founded 1953, part of Peralta Community College District System
- **Calendar** semesters
- **Degree** certificates and associate
- **Urban** 130-acre campus with easy access to San Francisco
- **Coed**, 7,984 undergraduate students, 15% full-time, 70% women, 30% men

Undergraduates 1,195 full-time, 6,789 part-time. Students come from 12 other countries, 47% African American, 19% Asian American or Pacific Islander, 13% Hispanic American, 0.5% Native American.

Freshmen *Admission:* 82 admitted, 82 enrolled.

Faculty *Total:* 201, 47% full-time.

Majors Accounting; administrative assistant and secretarial science; African-American/Black studies; biological and physical sciences; business administration and management; business teacher education; child development; community organization and advocacy; computer engineering technology; computer programming; computer typography and composition equipment operation; economics; French; general studies; health science; horticultural science; humanities; industrial radiologic technology; information science/studies; kindergarten/preschool education; landscape architecture; landscaping and groundskeeping; land use planning and management; legal assistant/paralegal; liberal arts and sciences/liberal studies; mathematics; nursing (licensed practical/vocational nurse training); nursing (registered nurse training); parks, recreation and leisure; reading teacher education; real estate; social sciences; Spanish.

Academic Programs *Special study options:* academic remediation for entering students, adult/continuing education programs, cooperative education, English as a second language, off-campus study, part-time degree program, services for LD students, summer session for credit.

Library Merritt College Library with 80,000 titles, 200 serial subscriptions.

Computers on Campus 20 computers available on campus for general student use. At least one staffed computer lab available.

Student Life *Housing:* college housing not available. *Activities and Organizations:* student-run newspaper. *Student services:* women's center.

Athletics *Intercollegiate sports:* basketball M, cross-country running M, fencing M, gymnastics M/W, soccer M, tennis M/W, track and field M.

Standardized Tests *Recommended:* SAT I or ACT (for placement).

Costs (2003–04) *Tuition:* nonresident $5408 full-time, $175 per unit part-time. *Required fees:* $508 full-time, $18 per unit part-time.

Applying *Options:* early admission, deferred entrance. *Application deadline:* 8/28 (freshmen). *Notification:* continuous (freshmen), continuous (transfers).

Admissions Contact Ms. Barbara Simmons, District Admissions Officer, Merritt College, 12500 Campus Drive, Oakland, CA 94619-3196. *Phone:* 510-466-7369. *E-mail:* hperdue@peralta.cc.ca.us.

MIRACOSTA COLLEGE

Oceanside, California

- **State-supported** 2-year, founded 1934, part of California Community College System
- **Calendar** semesters
- **Degree** certificates, diplomas, and associate
- **Suburban** 131-acre campus with easy access to San Diego
- **Endowment** $894,495
- **Coed,** 10,166 undergraduate students

MiraCosta's campuses in Oceanside and Cardiff are minutes from the beach. MiraCosta offers a strong university transfer program, including transfer admission guarantees. Courses of special interest include music technology, multimedia, horticulture, and computer science. Facilities include technology hubs at both campuses and a wellness center at the Oceanside campus.

Undergraduates Students come from 37 states and territories, 44 other countries, 2% are from out of state, 5% African American, 9% Asian American or Pacific Islander, 18% Hispanic American, 0.8% Native American, 2% international.

Faculty *Total:* 393, 27% full-time. *Student/faculty ratio:* 23:1.

Majors Accounting; administrative assistant and secretarial science; African studies; architectural engineering technology; art; automobile/automotive mechanics technology; behavioral sciences; biology/biological sciences; business administration and management; chemistry; child care and support services management; computer engineering technology; consumer/homemaking education; cosmetology; criminal justice/law enforcement administration; criminal justice/police science; dance; developmental and child psychology; drafting and design technology; dramatic/theatre arts; economics; English; French; general studies; history; horticultural science; hotel/motel administration; humanities; industrial technology; information science/studies; institutional food workers; Japanese; journalism; kindergarten/preschool education; landscaping and groundskeeping; liberal arts and sciences/liberal studies; machine tool technology; marketing/marketing management; mathematics; music; nursing (licensed practical/vocational nurse training); ornamental horticulture; philosophy; physical sciences; physics; political science and government; psychology; real estate; social sciences; sociology; Spanish; speech and rhetoric; teacher assistant/aide; tourism and travel services management.

Academic Programs *Special study options:* academic remediation for entering students, accelerated degree program, adult/continuing education programs, advanced placement credit, cooperative education, distance learning, double majors, English as a second language, freshman honors college, honors programs, independent study, internships, part-time degree program, services for LD students, student-designed majors, study abroad, summer session for credit.

Library MiraCosta College Library with 113,810 titles, 272 serial subscriptions, 5,340 audiovisual materials, an OPAC, a Web page.

Computers on Campus 753 computers available on campus for general student use. A campuswide network can be accessed from off campus that provide access to course listing. Internet access, at least one staffed computer lab available.

Student Life *Housing:* college housing not available. *Activities and Organizations:* drama/theater group, student-run newspaper, choral group, African-American Student Alliance, Spanish Club, Cultural Exchange Program, Phi Theta Kappa, Friends of EOPS. *Campus security:* 24-hour emergency response devices, student patrols, late-night transport/escort service, trained security personnel during class hours. *Student services:* health clinic, personal/psychological counseling, women's center.

Athletics Member NJCAA. *Intercollegiate sports:* basketball M, cross-country running M/W, soccer W, track and field W. *Intramural sports:* soccer M/W.

Costs (2003–04) *Tuition:* state resident $0 full-time; nonresident $4470 full-time, $149 per unit part-time. Part-time tuition and fees vary according to course load. *Required fees:* $364 full-time, $11 per unit part-time, $17 per term part-time. *Payment plan:* deferred payment.

Financial Aid Of all full-time matriculated undergraduates who enrolled, 83 Federal Work-Study jobs (averaging $1315).

MiraCosta College (continued)

Applying *Options:* early admission, deferred entrance. *Application deadline:* rolling (freshmen), rolling (transfers).

Admissions Contact Admissions and Records Assistant, MiraCosta College, One Barnard Drive, Oceanside, CA 92056. *Phone:* 760-795-6620. *Toll-free phone:* 888-201-8480. *Fax:* 760-795-6626.

MISSION COLLEGE
Santa Clara, California

- **State and locally supported** 2-year, founded 1977, part of California Community College System
- **Calendar** semesters
- **Degree** certificates, diplomas, and associate
- **Urban** 167-acre campus with easy access to San Francisco and San Jose
- **Coed**

Faculty *Student/faculty ratio:* 26:1.

Student Life *Campus security:* 24-hour emergency response devices, late-night transport/escort service.

Standardized Tests *Recommended:* SAT I (for placement).

Costs (2003–04) *Tuition:* state resident $0 full-time; nonresident $4710 full-time. *Required fees:* $557 full-time.

Financial Aid Of all full-time matriculated undergraduates who enrolled, 75 Federal Work-Study jobs (averaging $2000). *Financial aid deadline:* 5/15.

Applying *Options:* common application, electronic application, early admission.

Admissions Contact Dr. Sam Bersolo, Interim Vice President of Student Services, Mission College, 3000 Mission College Boulevard, Santa Clara, CA 95054-1897. *Phone:* 408-855-5195. *Fax:* 408-855-5467.

MODESTO JUNIOR COLLEGE
Modesto, California

- **State and locally supported** 2-year, founded 1921, part of Yosemite Community College District System
- **Calendar** semesters
- **Degree** certificates and associate
- **Urban** 229-acre campus
- **Endowment** $817,811
- **Coed,** 16,560 undergraduate students, 100% full-time, 60% women, 40% men

Undergraduates 16,560 full-time. 3% African American, 9% Asian American or Pacific Islander, 29% Hispanic American.

Freshmen *Admission:* 10,451 applied, 10,451 admitted.

Faculty *Total:* 806, 39% full-time. *Student/faculty ratio:* 40:1.

Majors Accounting; administrative assistant and secretarial science; agricultural business and management; agricultural mechanization; agricultural production; agriculture; agronomy and crop science; animal sciences; apparel and textiles; architectural engineering technology; art; autobody/collision and repair technology; automobile/automotive mechanics technology; banking and financial support services; behavioral sciences; biology/biological sciences; building/home/construction inspection; business administration and management; child care and support services management; child care provision; child development; commercial and advertising art; communications systems installation and repair technology; computer graphics; computer/information technology services administration related; computer installation and repair technology; computer science; construction management; corrections; criminal justice/law enforcement administration; criminal justice/police science; dairy science; data entry/microcomputer applications; dental assisting; drafting and design technology; dramatic/theatre arts; electrical, electronic and communications engineering technology; electrical/electronics equipment installation and repair; emergency medical technology (EMT paramedic); engineering; English; family and consumer economics related; fashion merchandising; finance; fire science; food science; food services technology; foreign languages and literatures; forestry; forestry technology; general studies; graphic and printing equipment operation/production; heating, air conditioning, ventilation and refrigeration maintenance technology; housing and human environments; humanities; human services; industrial arts; industrial electronics technology; interior design; kindergarten/preschool education; landscape architecture; machine shop technology; machine tool technology; management information systems; marketing/marketing management; mass communication/media; mathematics; medical/clinical assistant; music; nursing assistant/aide and patient care assistant; nursing (registered nurse training); office management; office occupations and clerical services; ornamental horticulture; parks, recreation and leisure facilities management; photography; physical education teaching and coaching; plant nursery management; poultry science; radio and television; real estate; respiratory care therapy; social sciences; special products marketing; speech and rhetoric; welding technology; word processing.

Academic Programs *Special study options:* academic remediation for entering students, adult/continuing education programs, advanced placement credit,

cooperative education, distance learning, English as a second language, honors programs, independent study, part-time degree program, services for LD students, study abroad, summer session for credit.

Library Modesto Junior College Library with 69,865 titles, 4,161 audiovisual materials, an OPAC, a Web page.

Computers on Campus 95 computers available on campus for general student use. A campuswide network can be accessed from off campus. Internet access, at least one staffed computer lab available.

Student Life *Housing:* college housing not available. *Activities and Organizations:* drama/theater group, student-run newspaper, radio and television station, choral group, Young Farmers, Red Nations, Psychology Club, Alpha Gamma Sigma, MECHA. *Campus security:* 24-hour emergency response devices and patrols, late-night transport/escort service. *Student services:* health clinic, personal/psychological counseling.

Athletics *Intercollegiate sports:* baseball M, basketball M/W, cross-country running M/W, football M, golf M, gymnastics W, soccer M/W, softball W, swimming M/W, tennis M/W, track and field M/W, volleyball W, water polo M/W, wrestling M. *Intramural sports:* basketball M/W, football M, softball W, table tennis M/W, tennis M/W, volleyball M/W.

Costs (2004–05) *Tuition:* nonresident $4696 full-time, $167 per unit part-time. *Required fees:* $524 full-time, $18 per unit part-time.

Financial Aid Of all full-time matriculated undergraduates who enrolled, 152 Federal Work-Study jobs (averaging $2732). 62 state and other part-time jobs (averaging $1655).

Applying *Options:* electronic application. *Recommended:* high school transcript, interview. *Application deadline:* rolling (freshmen), rolling (transfers). *Notification:* continuous (freshmen), continuous (transfers).

Admissions Contact Ms. Susie Agostini, Dean of Matriculation, Admissions, and Records, Modesto Junior College, 435 College Avenue, Modesto, CA 95350. *Phone:* 209-575-6470. *Fax:* 209-575-6859. *E-mail:* mjcinfo@mail.yosemite.cc.ca.us.

MONTEREY PENINSULA COLLEGE
Monterey, California

- **State-supported** 2-year, founded 1947, part of California Community College System
- **Calendar** semesters
- **Degree** certificates and associate
- **Small-town** 87-acre campus
- **Coed**

Student Life *Campus security:* 24-hour emergency response devices, late-night transport/escort service.

Costs (2003–04) *Tuition:* state resident $0 full-time; nonresident $3576 full-time, $149 per unit part-time. *Required fees:* $476 full-time, $18 per unit part-time.

Financial Aid Of all full-time matriculated undergraduates who enrolled, 167 Federal Work-Study jobs.

Applying *Options:* early admission.

Admissions Contact Dr. Elizabeth L. Cipres, Dean of Enrollment Services, Monterey Peninsula College, 980 Fremont Street, Monterey, CA 93940. *Phone:* 831-645-1372. *Fax:* 831-646-4015. *E-mail:* rmontori@mpc.edu.

MOORPARK COLLEGE
Moorpark, California

- **County-supported** 2-year, founded 1967, part of Ventura County Community College District System
- **Calendar** semesters
- **Degree** certificates and associate
- **Small-town** 121-acre campus with easy access to Los Angeles
- **Coed**

Faculty *Student/faculty ratio:* 30:1.

Student Life *Campus security:* 24-hour patrols.

Costs (2003–04) *Tuition:* state resident $0 full-time; nonresident $3576 full-time, $149 per unit part-time. *Required fees:* $18 per unit part-time.

Financial Aid Of all full-time matriculated undergraduates who enrolled, 70 Federal Work-Study jobs (averaging $2000).

Applying *Options:* electronic application, early admission, deferred entrance. *Required for some:* high school transcript. *Recommended:* high school transcript.

Admissions Contact Ms. Kathy Colborn, Registrar, Moorpark College, 7075 Campus Road, Moorpark, CA 93021-2899. *Phone:* 805-378-1415. *Fax:* 805-378-1583. *E-mail:* mcadmissions@vcccd.net.

MT. SAN ANTONIO COLLEGE
Walnut, California

- **District-supported** 2-year, founded 1946, part of California Community College System

- **Calendar** semesters
- **Degree** certificates, diplomas, and associate
- **Suburban** 421-acre campus with easy access to Los Angeles
- **Coed,** 26,440 undergraduate students, 30% full-time, 57% women, 43% men

Undergraduates 7,971 full-time, 18,469 part-time. Students come from 51 states and territories, 6% African American, 24% Asian American or Pacific Islander, 39% Hispanic American, 0.5% Native American, 2% international.
Freshmen *Admission:* 2,404 enrolled.
Faculty *Total:* 1,114, 33% full-time.
Majors Accounting; administrative assistant and secretarial science; advertising; agricultural business and management; agricultural mechanization; agriculture; agronomy and crop science; airframe mechanics and aircraft maintenance technology; airline pilot and flight crew; air traffic control; animal sciences; apparel and textiles; architectural engineering technology; avionics maintenance technology; business administration and management; business teacher education; child development; civil engineering technology; commercial and advertising art; computer engineering technology; computer graphics; computer science; construction management; corrections; criminal justice/police science; dairy science; data processing and data processing technology; drafting and design technology; electrical, electronic and communications engineering technology; emergency medical technology (EMT paramedic); engineering technology; family and consumer sciences/human sciences; fashion merchandising; finance; fire science; forestry technology; heating, air conditioning, ventilation and refrigeration maintenance technology; horticultural science; hotel/motel administration; industrial arts; industrial design; industrial radiologic technology; interior design; journalism; kindergarten/preschool education; landscape architecture; legal administrative assistant/secretary; legal assistant/paralegal; liberal arts and sciences/liberal studies; machine tool technology; marketing/marketing management; materials science; mechanical design technology; medical administrative assistant and medical secretary; mental health/rehabilitation; nursing (registered nurse training); occupational safety and health technology; ornamental horticulture; parks, recreation and leisure; parks, recreation and leisure facilities management; photography; physical sciences related; pre-engineering; quality control technology; radio and television; real estate; respiratory care therapy; sign language interpretation and translation; survey technology; transportation technology; welding technology; wildlife and wildlands science and management.
Academic Programs *Special study options:* academic remediation for entering students, adult/continuing education programs, cooperative education, distance learning, English as a second language, honors programs, part-time degree program, services for LD students, study abroad, summer session for credit.
Library Learning Resources Center with 64,291 titles, 753 serial subscriptions, 6,494 audiovisual materials, an OPAC, a Web page.
Computers on Campus 1200 computers available on campus for general student use. A campuswide network can be accessed from off campus. Internet access, at least one staffed computer lab available.
Student Life *Activities and Organizations:* drama/theater group, student-run radio station, choral group, Alpha Gamma Sigma, Muslim Student Association, student government, Asian Student Association, Kasama-Filipino Student Organization. *Campus security:* 24-hour emergency response devices and patrols, late-night transport/escort service. *Student services:* health clinic, personal/psychological counseling, women's center, legal services.
Athletics *Intercollegiate sports:* badminton W, baseball M, basketball M/W, cross-country running M/W, football M, golf M/W, soccer M/W, softball W, swimming M/W, tennis M/W, track and field M/W, volleyball M/W, water polo M/W, wrestling M.
Costs (2003–04) *Tuition:* state resident $0 full-time; nonresident $3600 full-time, $150 per unit part-time. *Required fees:* $480 full-time, $18 per unit part-time, $24 per term part-time.
Financial Aid Of all full-time matriculated undergraduates who enrolled, 250 Federal Work-Study jobs (averaging $2898).
Applying *Options:* early admission, deferred entrance. *Required for some:* high school transcript. *Application deadline:* 8/22 (freshmen). *Notification:* continuous (freshmen), continuous (transfers).
Admissions Contact Ms. Patricia Montoya, Acting Director of Admissions and Records, Mt. San Antonio College, 1100 North Grand Avenue, Walnut, CA 91789. *Phone:* 909-594-5611 Ext. 4415. *Toll-free phone:* 800-672-2463 Ext. 4415. *E-mail:* admissions@mtsac.edu.

MT. SAN JACINTO COLLEGE
San Jacinto, California

- **State and locally supported** 2-year, founded 1963, part of California Community College System
- **Calendar** semesters
- **Degree** certificates, diplomas, and associate
- **Suburban** 180-acre campus with easy access to San Diego
- **Endowment** $2.0 million
- **Coed,** 12,592 undergraduate students, 28% full-time, 64% women, 36% men

Undergraduates 3,506 full-time, 9,086 part-time. Students come from 11 states and territories, 1% are from out of state.
Faculty *Total:* 421, 25% full-time. *Student/faculty ratio:* 24:1.
Majors Administrative assistant and secretarial science; art; audio engineering; automobile/automotive mechanics technology; behavioral sciences; biological and physical sciences; business administration and management; computer science; computer software engineering; criminal justice/police science; dance; engineering; fire science; gerontology; home health aide/home attendant; humanities; interdisciplinary studies; kindergarten/preschool education; legal assistant/paralegal; mathematics; music; nursing (registered nurse training); photography; physical education teaching and coaching; public administration; real estate; social sciences; substance abuse/addiction counseling; visual and performing arts.
Academic Programs *Special study options:* academic remediation for entering students, adult/continuing education programs, advanced placement credit, distance learning, double majors, English as a second language, honors programs, off-campus study, part-time degree program, services for LD students, study abroad, summer session for credit.
Library Milo P. Johnson Library plus 1 other with 28,000 titles, 330 serial subscriptions.
Computers on Campus 35 computers available on campus for general student use. Internet access, online (class) registration, at least one staffed computer lab available.
Student Life *Housing:* college housing not available. *Activities and Organizations:* drama/theater group. *Campus security:* part-time trained security personnel. *Student services:* personal/psychological counseling.
Athletics *Intercollegiate sports:* baseball M, basketball M/W, football M, golf M, soccer W, tennis M/W, volleyball W.
Standardized Tests *Required:* Assessment and Placement Services for Community Colleges (for placement).
Costs (2004–05) *Tuition:* state resident $0 full-time; nonresident $5305 full-time, $175 per unit part-time. *Required fees:* $1615 full-time, $26 per unit part-time.
Financial Aid Of all full-time matriculated undergraduates who enrolled, 109 Federal Work-Study jobs (averaging $1114). 125 state and other part-time jobs (averaging $1000).
Applying *Options:* early admission. *Recommended:* high school transcript. *Application deadline:* rolling (freshmen), rolling (transfers).
Admissions Contact Ms. Susan Loomis, Supervisor, Enrollment Services, Mt. San Jacinto College, 1499 North State Street, San Jacinto, CA 92583-2399. *Phone:* 909-672-6752 Ext. 2401. *Toll-free phone:* 800-624-5561 Ext. 1410. *Fax:* 909-654-6738. *E-mail:* egonzale@msjc.edu.

MTI COLLEGE OF BUSINESS AND TECHNOLOGY
Sacramento, California

- **Proprietary** 2-year, founded 1965
- **Calendar** continuous
- **Degree** diplomas and associate
- **Coed**

Costs (2003–04) *Tuition:* $9000 full-time. *Required fees:* $75 full-time.
Financial Aid Of all full-time matriculated undergraduates who enrolled, 35 Federal Work-Study jobs (averaging $1722).
Applying *Application fee:* $75.
Admissions Contact Ms. Monica Burden, Director of Admissions, MTI College of Business and Technology, 5221 Madison Avenue, Sacramento, CA 95841. *Phone:* 916-339-1500.

NAPA VALLEY COLLEGE
Napa, California

- **State and locally supported** 2-year, founded 1942, part of California Community College System
- **Calendar** semesters
- **Degree** certificates and associate
- **Suburban** 188-acre campus with easy access to San Francisco
- **Coed,** 7,053 undergraduate students, 28% full-time, 61% women, 39% men

Undergraduates 2,004 full-time, 5,049 part-time. Students come from 12 states and territories, 8% African American, 18% Asian American or Pacific Islander, 20% Hispanic American, 1% Native American. *Retention:* 66% of 2002 full-time freshmen returned.
Freshmen *Admission:* 3,300 applied, 3,300 admitted, 588 enrolled.
Faculty *Total:* 306, 33% full-time. *Student/faculty ratio:* 23:1.
Majors Accounting; administrative assistant and secretarial science; agriculture; art; behavioral sciences; biological and physical sciences; biomedical

California

Napa Valley College (continued)

technology; business administration and management; child development; communications technology; computer science; corrections; cosmetology; criminal justice/law enforcement administration; criminal justice/police science; data processing and data processing technology; drafting and design technology; electrical, electronic and communications engineering technology; emergency medical technology (EMT paramedic); engineering; environmental engineering technology; environmental studies; humanities; kindergarten/preschool education; legal administrative assistant/secretary; legal assistant/paralegal; machine tool technology; management information systems; marketing/marketing management; music; nursing (registered nurse training); photography; radio and television; real estate; respiratory care therapy; telecommunications; welding technology.

Academic Programs *Special study options:* academic remediation for entering students, advanced placement credit, cooperative education, English as a second language, part-time degree program, services for LD students, study abroad, summer session for credit.

Library Napa Valley College Library plus 1 other with 42,000 titles, 250 serial subscriptions, an OPAC, a Web page.

Computers on Campus 90 computers available on campus for general student use. Internet access, at least one staffed computer lab available.

Student Life *Housing:* college housing not available. *Activities and Organizations:* drama/theater group, student-run newspaper, choral group, Hispano-Americano Club, African-American Club, Environmental Action Coalition, International Student Club, Phi Theta Kappa. *Campus security:* late-night transport/escort service. *Student services:* personal/psychological counseling, women's center.

Athletics Member NJCAA. *Intercollegiate sports:* baseball M, basketball M/W, cross-country running M/W, soccer M, softball W, swimming M/W, tennis M/W, volleyball M, wrestling M. *Intramural sports:* archery M/W, badminton M/W, basketball M/W, bowling M/W, fencing M/W, gymnastics M/W, racquetball M/W, rugby M, skiing (cross-country) M/W, skiing (downhill) M/W, soccer M/W, swimming M/W, tennis M/W, volleyball M/W, water polo M/W, weight lifting M/W, wrestling M.

Standardized Tests *Required for some:* SAT I or ACT (for placement).

Costs (2003–04) *Tuition:* state resident $0 full-time; nonresident $3432 full-time, $143 per unit part-time. *Required fees:* $432 full-time, $18 per unit part-time.

Financial Aid *Financial aid deadline:* 3/2.

Applying *Options:* early admission, deferred entrance. *Required for some:* high school transcript. *Application deadline:* rolling (freshmen), rolling (transfers). *Notification:* continuous (freshmen), continuous (transfers).

Admissions Contact Dr. Edward Shenk, Vice President of Student Services-Advisor, Napa Valley College, 2277 Napa-Vallejo Highway, Napa, CA 94558-6236. *Phone:* 707-253-3000. *Fax:* 707-253-3064. *E-mail:* snelson@admin.nvc.cc.ca.us.

NORTHROP RICE AVIATION INSTITUTE OF TECHNOLOGY
Inglewood, California

Admissions Contact Mr. James Michael Rice, Chief Administrative Officer, Northrop Rice Aviation Institute of Technology, 1155 West Arbor Vitae Street, Suite 115, Inglewood, CA 90301-2904. *Phone:* 310-568-8541.

NORTHWESTERN TECHNICAL COLLEGE
Sacramento, California

Admissions Contact Mr. Robert Naylor, Director of Admissions, Northwestern Technical College, 1825 Bell Street, #100, Sacramento, CA 95825. *Phone:* 916-649-2400. *Toll-free phone:* 866-649-2400.

OHLONE COLLEGE
Fremont, California

- **State and locally supported** 2-year, founded 1967, part of California Community College System
- **Calendar** semesters
- **Degree** associate
- **Suburban** 530-acre campus with easy access to San Francisco
- **Coed**

Student Life *Campus security:* 24-hour emergency response devices and patrols, late-night transport/escort service.

Athletics Member NJCAA.

Standardized Tests *Required for some:* ACT ASSET.

Costs (2003–04) *Tuition:* state resident $0 full-time; nonresident $4470 full-time. *Required fees:* $574 full-time.

Financial Aid Of all full-time matriculated undergraduates who enrolled, 35 Federal Work-Study jobs (averaging $1800).

Applying *Options:* early admission. *Required:* high school transcript.

Admissions Contact Ms. Allison Hill, Director, Admissions and Records, Ohlone College, 43600 Mission Boulevard, Fremont, CA 94539-5884. *Phone:* 510-659-6108.

ORANGE COAST COLLEGE
Costa Mesa, California

- **State and locally supported** 2-year, founded 1947, part of Coast Community College District System
- **Calendar** semesters plus summer session
- **Degree** certificates and associate
- **Suburban** 200-acre campus with easy access to Los Angeles
- **Endowment** $5.1 million
- **Coed,** 25,628 undergraduate students, 38% full-time, 51% women, 49% men

Undergraduates 9,654 full-time, 15,974 part-time. Students come from 52 states and territories, 76 other countries, 2% are from out of state, 2% African American, 25% Asian American or Pacific Islander, 17% Hispanic American, 0.7% Native American, 3% international, 8% transferred in. *Retention:* 79% of 2002 full-time freshmen returned.

Freshmen *Admission:* 3,659 enrolled.

Faculty *Total:* 940, 32% full-time. *Student/faculty ratio:* 20:1.

Majors Accounting; administrative assistant and secretarial science; aeronautics/aviation/aerospace science and technology; airline pilot and flight crew; anthropology; architectural engineering technology; art; athletic training; avionics maintenance technology; behavioral sciences; biology/biological sciences; building/home/construction inspection; business administration and management; cardiovascular technology; chemistry; child care and support services management; child care provision; cinematography and film/video production; clinical laboratory science/medical technology; commercial and advertising art; communications technology; computer engineering technology; computer graphics; computer programming; computer programming (specific applications); computer typography and composition equipment operation; construction engineering technology; culinary arts; cultural studies; dance; data entry/microcomputer applications related; data processing and data processing technology; dental hygiene; dietetics; drafting and design technology; dramatic/theatre arts; economics; electrical and power transmission installation; electrical, electronic and communications engineering technology; electrical/electronics equipment installation and repair; emergency medical technology (EMT paramedic); engineering; English; family and consumer economics related; family and consumer sciences/human sciences; fashion merchandising; film/cinema studies; food science; food services technology; foods, nutrition, and wellness; French; general retailing/wholesaling; geography; geology/earth science; German; health science; heating, air conditioning, ventilation and refrigeration maintenance technology; history; horticultural science; hotel/motel administration; housing and human environments; human development and family studies; humanities; industrial design; industrial radiologic technology; information science/studies; interior design; journalism; kindergarten/preschool education; kinesiology and exercise science; legal administrative assistant/secretary; liberal arts and sciences/liberal studies; machine shop technology; machine tool technology; marine technology; marketing/marketing management; mass communication/media; mathematics; medical administrative assistant and medical secretary; medical/clinical assistant; music; musical instrument fabrication and repair; music management and merchandising; natural sciences; nuclear medical technology; ornamental horticulture; philosophy; photography; physical education teaching and coaching; physics; political science and government; religious studies; respiratory care therapy; restaurant, culinary, and catering management; retailing; selling skills and sales; social sciences; sociology; Spanish; special products marketing; welding technology; word processing.

Academic Programs *Special study options:* academic remediation for entering students, adult/continuing education programs, advanced placement credit, cooperative education, distance learning, double majors, English as a second language, external degree program, freshman honors college, honors programs, internships, off-campus study, part-time degree program, services for LD students, student-designed majors, study abroad, summer session for credit. *ROTC:* Army (c), Air Force (c).

Library Norman E. Watson Library with 84,447 titles, 420 serial subscriptions, 2,510 audiovisual materials, an OPAC, a Web page.

Computers on Campus 1515 computers available on campus for general student use. A campuswide network can be accessed from off campus. Internet access, at least one staffed computer lab available.

Student Life *Housing:* college housing not available. *Activities and Organizations:* drama/theater group, student-run newspaper, choral group, Vietnamese Student Association, International Club, Adventurist Souls, Muslim Student Association. *Campus security:* 24-hour emergency response devices and patrols, student patrols, late-night transport/escort service. *Student services:* health clinic, personal/psychological counseling, legal services.

Athletics *Intercollegiate sports:* baseball M, basketball M/W, bowling M(c)/W(c), crew M/W, cross-country running M/W, football M, golf M/W, soccer M/W, softball W, swimming M/W, tennis M/W, track and field M/W, volleyball M/W, water polo M/W.

Costs (2003–04) *Tuition:* state resident $0 full-time; nonresident $5040 full-time, $161 per unit part-time. *Required fees:* $572 full-time, $18 per unit part-time, $32 per year part-time.

Financial Aid Of all full-time matriculated undergraduates who enrolled, 108 Federal Work-Study jobs (averaging $3000). *Financial aid deadline:* 5/28.

Applying *Options:* common application. *Application deadline:* rolling (freshmen), rolling (transfers). *Notification:* continuous (freshmen), continuous (transfers).

Admissions Contact Ms. Nancy Kidder, Administrative Dean of Admissions and Records, Orange Coast College, 2701 Fairview Road, Costa Mesa, CA 92626. *Phone:* 714-432-5788. *Fax:* 714-432-5072. *E-mail:* nkidder@cccd.edu.

OXNARD COLLEGE
Oxnard, California

- **State-supported** 2-year, founded 1975, part of Ventura County Community College District System
- **Calendar** semesters
- **Degree** certificates, diplomas, and associate
- **Urban** 119-acre campus
- **Coed,** 7,233 undergraduate students

Undergraduates Students come from 10 states and territories, 30 other countries, 5% African American, 10% Asian American or Pacific Islander, 61% Hispanic American, 0.8% Native American.

Freshmen *Admission:* 1,367 applied, 1,367 admitted.

Faculty *Total:* 369, 24% full-time. *Student/faculty ratio:* 25:1.

Majors Accounting; administrative assistant and secretarial science; agricultural business and management; agricultural mechanization; anthropology; art teacher education; automobile/automotive mechanics technology; behavioral sciences; biology/biological sciences; business administration and management; child development; culinary arts; dental assisting; dental hygiene; dramatic/theatre arts; economics; electrical, electronic and communications engineering technology; English; family and community services; family and consumer sciences/human sciences; fashion merchandising; fire science; heating, air conditioning, ventilation and refrigeration maintenance technology; history; hotel/motel administration; information science/studies; journalism; kindergarten/preschool education; legal studies; liberal arts and sciences/liberal studies; library science; machine tool technology; marketing/marketing management; mathematics; mental health/rehabilitation; philosophy; physical education teaching and coaching; radio and television; real estate; sociology; Spanish; telecommunications; transportation technology; welding technology.

Academic Programs *Special study options:* academic remediation for entering students, accelerated degree program, adult/continuing education programs, advanced placement credit, distance learning, double majors, English as a second language, honors programs, independent study, part-time degree program, services for LD students, summer session for credit.

Library Oxnard College Library with 31,500 titles, 107 serial subscriptions, an OPAC, a Web page.

Computers on Campus 116 computers available on campus for general student use. A campuswide network can be accessed. Internet access, online (class) registration, at least one staffed computer lab available. Computer purchase or lease plan available.

Student Life *Housing:* college housing not available. *Activities and Organizations:* drama/theater group, student-run newspaper, television station, choral group. *Campus security:* 24-hour patrols. *Student services:* health clinic, personal/psychological counseling, women's center.

Athletics *Intercollegiate sports:* baseball M, basketball M/W, cross-country running M/W, soccer M/W, track and field M/W, volleyball W.

Costs (2004–05) *Tuition:* state resident $0 full-time; nonresident $3912 full-time, $163 per unit part-time. Full-time tuition and fees vary according to course load. Part-time tuition and fees vary according to course load. *Required fees:* $624 full-time, $26 per unit part-time. *Payment plan:* installment.

Financial Aid Of all full-time matriculated undergraduates who enrolled, 80 Federal Work-Study jobs (averaging $3000).

Applying *Options:* common application, electronic application, early admission. *Application deadline:* rolling (freshmen), rolling (transfers). *Notification:* continuous (freshmen), continuous (transfers).

Admissions Contact Ms. Susan O. Brent, Registrar, Oxnard College, 4000 South Rose Avenue, Oxnard, CA 93033-6699. *Phone:* 805-986-5843. *Fax:* 805-986-5943.

PALOMAR COLLEGE
San Marcos, California

- **State and locally supported** 2-year, founded 1946, part of California Community College System
- **Calendar** semesters
- **Degree** certificates and associate
- **Suburban** 156-acre campus with easy access to San Diego
- **Coed,** 28,597 undergraduate students, 26% full-time, 53% women, 47% men

Undergraduates 7,499 full-time, 21,098 part-time. 3% African American, 8% Asian American or Pacific Islander, 24% Hispanic American, 1% Native American.

Freshmen *Admission:* 5,569 applied, 5,569 admitted.

Faculty *Total:* 1,089, 25% full-time. *Student/faculty ratio:* 24:1.

Majors Accounting; administrative assistant and secretarial science; advertising; anthropology; applied art; archeology; art; arts management; art teacher education; astronomy; automobile/automotive mechanics technology; aviation/airway management; avionics maintenance technology; biology/biological sciences; business administration and management; business machine repair; business teacher education; carpentry; ceramic arts and ceramics; chemistry; commercial and advertising art; computer science; construction engineering technology; criminal justice/law enforcement administration; criminal justice/police science; dance; dental hygiene; developmental and child psychology; drafting and design technology; dramatic/theatre arts; drawing; economics; electrical, electronic and communications engineering technology; emergency medical technology (EMT paramedic); engineering; family and consumer economics related; fashion/apparel design; fashion merchandising; film/cinema studies; fire science; food services technology; geology/earth science; graphic and printing equipment operation/production; hydrology and water resources science; information science/studies; interior design; international business/trade/commerce; journalism; kindergarten/preschool education; legal administrative assistant/secretary; legal assistant/paralegal; liberal arts and sciences/liberal studies; library science; marketing/marketing management; mathematics; medical administrative assistant and medical secretary; medical/clinical assistant; metal and jewelry arts; music; nursing (registered nurse training); parks, recreation and leisure; parks, recreation and leisure facilities management; photography; physical education teaching and coaching; pipefitting and sprinkler fitting; public administration; radio and television; real estate; sanitation technology; sign language interpretation and translation; special products marketing; speech and rhetoric; survey technology; telecommunications; tourism and travel services management; welding technology; women's studies; zoology/animal biology.

Academic Programs *Special study options:* academic remediation for entering students, advanced placement credit, cooperative education, distance learning, English as a second language, internships, part-time degree program, services for LD students, study abroad, summer session for credit.

Library Palomar Library with 108,000 titles, an OPAC, a Web page.

Computers on Campus 922 computers available on campus for general student use. A campuswide network can be accessed. Internet access, at least one staffed computer lab available.

Student Life *Housing:* college housing not available. *Activities and Organizations:* drama/theater group, student-run newspaper, radio station, choral group, Bible clubs. *Campus security:* 24-hour patrols, student patrols, late-night transport/escort service. *Student services:* health clinic, personal/psychological counseling.

Athletics *Intercollegiate sports:* basketball M/W, football M, soccer M, swimming M/W, tennis M/W, volleyball W, water polo M, wrestling M. *Intramural sports:* basketball M/W, bowling M, golf M, skiing (downhill) M/W, soccer M, softball W, tennis M, volleyball M, water polo M, wrestling M.

Standardized Tests *Required for some:* ACT ASSET.

Costs (2003–04) *Tuition:* state resident $0 full-time; nonresident $4170 full-time, $139 per unit part-time. *Required fees:* $364 full-time, $11 per unit part-time, $10 per year part-time. *Payment plan:* deferred payment.

Applying *Options:* electronic application. *Application deadline:* rolling (freshmen), rolling (transfers). *Notification:* continuous (freshmen), continuous (transfers).

Admissions Contact Mr. Herman Lee, Director of Enrollment Services, Palomar College, 1140 West Mission Road, San Marcos, CA 92069-1487. *Phone:* 760-744-1150 Ext. 2171. *Fax:* 760-744-2932. *E-mail:* admissions@palomar.edu.

PALO VERDE COLLEGE
Blythe, California

- **State and locally supported** 2-year, founded 1947, part of California Community College System
- **Calendar** semesters
- **Degree** associate
- **Small-town** 10-acre campus
- **Coed**

Palo Verde College (continued)

Faculty *Student/faculty ratio:* 20:1.

Student Life *Campus security:* student patrols, security personnel during open hours.

Financial Aid Of all full-time matriculated undergraduates who enrolled, 30 Federal Work-Study jobs (averaging $1000).

Applying *Options:* early admission. *Recommended:* high school transcript.

Admissions Contact Ms. Sally Rivera, Vice President of Student Services, Palo Verde College, 1 College Drive, Blythe, CA 92225. *Phone:* 760-921-5409. *Fax:* 760-921-3608.

PASADENA CITY COLLEGE
Pasadena, California

- **State and locally supported** 2-year, founded 1924, part of California Community College System
- **Calendar** semesters
- **Degree** certificates and associate
- **Urban** 55-acre campus with easy access to Los Angeles
- **Coed,** 30,417 undergraduate students, 100% full-time, 57% women, 43% men

Undergraduates 30,417 full-time. Students come from 15 states and territories, 6% African American, 34% Asian American or Pacific Islander, 31% Hispanic American, 0.6% Native American.

Faculty *Total:* 1,296, 29% full-time. *Student/faculty ratio:* 20:1.

Majors Accounting; administrative assistant and secretarial science; advertising; African-American/Black studies; African studies; airline pilot and flight crew; anthropology; architectural engineering technology; art; art history, criticism and conservation; astronomy; automobile/automotive mechanics technology; aviation/airway management; avionics maintenance technology; biological and physical sciences; biology/biological sciences; broadcast journalism; business administration and management; business teacher education; carpentry; ceramic arts and ceramics; ceramic sciences and engineering; chemistry; civil engineering technology; communications technology; computer engineering technology; computer programming; computer science; computer typography and composition equipment operation; construction engineering technology; cosmetology; criminal justice/law enforcement administration; cultural studies; data processing and data processing technology; dental hygiene; developmental and child psychology; drafting and design technology; dramatic/theatre arts; drawing; economics; electrical, electronic and communications engineering technology; engineering; engineering technology; English; fashion merchandising; fiber, textile and weaving arts; finance; fire science; forestry technology; French; geography; geology/earth science; German; Hispanic-American, Puerto Rican, and Mexican-American/Chicano studies; history; human services; industrial radiologic technology; information science/studies; interdisciplinary studies; interior design; journalism; kindergarten/preschool education; landscape architecture; Latin American studies; legal administrative assistant/secretary; legal studies; liberal arts and sciences/liberal studies; library science; machine tool technology; marketing/marketing management; mass communication/media; mathematics; mechanical engineering/mechanical technology; medical/clinical assistant; metal and jewelry arts; modern languages; music; music therapy; nursing (licensed practical/vocational nurse training); nursing (registered nurse training); occupational therapy; parks, recreation and leisure; pharmacy; philosophy; photography; physical education teaching and coaching; physical sciences; physics; political science and government; psychology; radio and television; real estate; religious studies; sign language interpretation and translation; social sciences; sociology; Spanish; speech and rhetoric; statistics; teacher assistant/aide; telecommunications; tourism and travel services management; veterinary sciences; welding technology.

Academic Programs *Special study options:* academic remediation for entering students, adult/continuing education programs, advanced placement credit, English as a second language, honors programs, part-time degree program, services for LD students, student-designed majors, study abroad, summer session for credit.

Library Pasadena City College Library plus 1 other with 117,660 titles, 300 serial subscriptions, an OPAC.

Computers on Campus 300 computers available on campus for general student use. At least one staffed computer lab available.

Student Life *Housing:* college housing not available. *Activities and Organizations:* drama/theater group, student-run newspaper, radio station, choral group, marching band. *Campus security:* 24-hour emergency response devices and patrols, late-night transport/escort service, cadet patrols. *Student services:* health clinic, personal/psychological counseling, women's center.

Athletics *Intercollegiate sports:* baseball M, basketball M/W, cross-country running M/W, football M, soccer M/W, softball W, swimming M/W, tennis M/W, track and field M/W, volleyball W, water polo M.

Costs (2004–05) *Tuition:* nonresident $157 per unit part-time. *Required fees:* $26 per unit part-time.

Applying *Options:* early admission, deferred entrance. *Application deadline:* rolling (freshmen), rolling (transfers). *Notification:* continuous (freshmen), continuous (transfers).

Admissions Contact Ms. Carol Kaser, Supervisor of Admissions and Records, Pasadena City College, 1570 East. Colorado Boulevard, Pasadena, CA 91106. *Phone:* 626-585-7397. *Fax:* 626-585-7915.

PIMA MEDICAL INSTITUTE
Chula Vista, California

- **Proprietary** 2-year
- **Degree** certificates and associate
- 550 undergraduate students

Faculty *Student/faculty ratio:* 14:1.

Admissions Contact Ms. Marie DeFede, Admissions Director, Pima Medical Institute, 780 Bay Boulevard, Suite 101, Chula Vista, CA 91910. *Phone:* 619-425-3200.

PLATT COLLEGE
Cerritos, California

- **Proprietary** 2-year, founded 1879
- **Calendar** continuous
- **Degree** certificates, diplomas, and associate
- **Urban** campus with easy access to Los Angeles
- **Coed**

Faculty *Student/faculty ratio:* 12:1.

Standardized Tests *Required:* Wonderlic aptitude test (for admission).

Admissions Contact Ms. Ilene Holt, Dean of Student Services, Platt College, 10900 East 183rd Street, Suite 290, Cerritos, CA 90703-5342. *Phone:* 562-809-5100. *Toll-free phone:* 800-807-5288.

PLATT COLLEGE
Newport Beach, California

- **Independent** primarily 2-year, founded 1985
- **Calendar** continuous
- **Degrees** certificates, diplomas, associate, and bachelor's
- **Urban** campus
- **Coed,** 270 undergraduate students, 100% full-time, 33% women, 67% men

Undergraduates 270 full-time. Students come from 12 states and territories, 5 other countries.

Freshmen *Admission:* 50 applied, 40 admitted.

Faculty *Total:* 24, 33% full-time. *Student/faculty ratio:* 16:1.

Majors Commercial and advertising art; computer graphics; design and applied arts related; information science/studies; information technology; intermedia/multimedia; legal assistant/paralegal.

Academic Programs *Special study options:* accelerated degree program, adult/continuing education programs, summer session for credit.

Library Platt Library with 1,100 titles, 15 serial subscriptions, 100 audiovisual materials.

Computers on Campus 10 computers available on campus for general student use. Internet access, at least one staffed computer lab available.

Student Life *Housing:* college housing not available. *Campus security:* 24-hour emergency response devices.

Standardized Tests *Required:* CPAt (for admission).

Costs (2003–04) *Tuition:* $24,000 full-time. Full-time tuition and fees vary according to program. No tuition increase for student's term of enrollment. *Payment plans:* tuition prepayment, installment. *Waivers:* employees or children of employees.

Applying *Application fee:* $75. *Required:* essay or personal statement, high school transcript, interview. *Application deadline:* rolling (freshmen). *Notification:* continuous (freshmen).

Admissions Contact Ms. Lisa Rhodes, President, Platt College, 3901 MacArthur Boulevard, Suite 101, Newport Beach, CA 92660. *Phone:* 949-833-2300 Ext. 222. *Toll-free phone:* 888-866-6697 Ext. 230. *Fax:* 949-833-0269. *E-mail:* lrhodes@plattcollege.edu.

▶ **See page 594 for a narrative description.**

PLATT COLLEGE
Ontario, California

- **Independent** 2-year
- **Calendar** continuous

- **Degree** certificates, diplomas, and associate
- **Coed**

Standardized Tests *Required:* CPAt (for admission).
Costs (2003–04) *Tuition:* $24,000 full-time.
Applying *Application fee:* $75. *Required:* essay or personal statement, interview.
Admissions Contact Ms. Jennifer Abandonato, Director of Admissions, Platt College, 3700 Inland Empire Boulevard, Ontario, CA 91764. *Phone:* 909-941-9410. *Toll-free phone:* 888-866-6697.

▶ **See page 596 for a narrative description.**

PLATT COLLEGE–LOS ANGELES, INC
Los Angeles, California

- **Proprietary** 2-year, founded 1987
- **Calendar** continuous
- **Degree** certificates, diplomas, and associate
- **Suburban** campus
- **Coed**

Student Life *Campus security:* parking lot security.
Standardized Tests *Required:* CPAt (for admission).
Costs (2003–04) *Tuition:* $24,000 full-time. Full-time tuition and fees vary according to program. *Payment plans:* installment, deferred payment.
Applying *Options:* common application. *Application fee:* $75. *Required:* interview. *Required for some:* essay or personal statement.
Admissions Contact Mr. Detroit Whiteside, Director of Admissions, Platt College-Los Angeles, Inc, 7470 North Figueroa Street, Los Angeles, CA 90041-1717. *Phone:* 323-258-8050. *Toll-free phone:* 888-866-6697. *Fax:* 323-258-8532. *E-mail:* ademitroff@plattcollege.edu.

▶ **See page 592 for a narrative description.**

PLATT COLLEGE SAN DIEGO
San Diego, California

- **Proprietary** primarily 2-year, founded 1879
- **Calendar** continuous
- **Degrees** certificates, diplomas, associate, and bachelor's
- **Suburban** campus with easy access to San Diego
- **Coed,** 335 undergraduate students, 100% full-time, 27% women, 73% men

Students' investment in themselves should not take a lifetime to repay. Platt offers the BS degree in media arts (2½ years); AAS degrees in multimedia design and graphic design (15 months); specialized diplomas in DV production, 3-D animation, and Web design; and diplomas in multimedia and graphic design. For further information, students should call 866-PLATT-COLLEGE (toll-free) or visit the College's Web site (http://www.platt.edu).

Undergraduates 335 full-time. Students come from 4 states and territories, 2 other countries, 5% are from out of state, 8% African American, 13% Asian American or Pacific Islander, 21% Hispanic American, 1% Native American. *Retention:* 42% of 2002 full-time freshmen returned.
Freshmen *Admission:* 259 admitted, 109 enrolled.
Faculty *Total:* 21, 33% full-time, 5% with terminal degrees. *Student/faculty ratio:* 20:1.
Majors Animation, interactive technology, video graphics and special effects; art; cinematography and film/video production; commercial and advertising art; communication and media related; computer graphics; computer software and media applications related; computer typography and composition equipment operation; design and applied arts related; design and visual communications; desktop publishing and digital imaging design; digital communication and media/multimedia; general studies; graphic communications; graphic communications related; graphic design; intermedia/multimedia; liberal arts and sciences and humanities related; mathematics; photographic and film/video technology; web/multimedia management and webmaster; web page, digital/multimedia and information resources design.
Student Life *Housing:* college housing not available. *Campus security:* 24-hour emergency response devices, video camera. *Student services:* personal/psychological counseling.
Costs (2003–04) *Tuition:* $13,952 full-time. Full-time tuition and fees vary according to program. *Required fees:* $75 full-time. *Payment plans:* tuition prepayment, installment. *Waivers:* employees or children of employees.
Applying *Application fee:* $75. *Required:* high school transcript, interview.
Admissions Contact Carly Westerfield, Coordinator, Platt College San Diego, 6250 El Cajon Boulevard, San Diego, CA 92115-3919. *Phone:* 619-265-0107. *Toll-free phone:* 800-255-0613. *Fax:* 619-265-8655. *E-mail:* info@platt.edu.

PORTERVILLE COLLEGE
Porterville, California

- **State-supported** 2-year, founded 1927, part of Kern Community College District System
- **Calendar** semesters
- **Degree** certificates and associate
- **Rural** 60-acre campus
- **Endowment** $1.3 million
- **Coed**

Student Life *Campus security:* 24-hour emergency response devices, student patrols.
Costs (2003–04) *Tuition:* state resident $0 full-time; nonresident $3576 full-time. *Required fees:* $456 full-time.
Applying *Options:* electronic application, early admission. *Required:* high school transcript.
Admissions Contact Ms. Judy Pope, Director of Admissions and Records/Registrar, Porterville College, 100 East College Avenue, Porterville, CA 93257-6058. *Phone:* 559-791-2222. *Fax:* 559-791-2349.

PROFESSIONAL GOLFERS CAREER COLLEGE
Temecula, California

- **Independent** 2-year
- **Calendar** semesters
- **Degree** associate
- **Coed, primarily men**

Faculty *Student/faculty ratio:* 30:1.
Costs (2004–05) *Tuition:* $4790 full-time. *Required fees:* $120 full-time. *Room only:* $5000.
Admissions Contact Ms. Sandi Somerville, Director of Admissions, Professional Golfers Career College, PO Box 892319, Temecula, CA 92589. *Phone:* 909-693-2963 Ext. 17. *Toll-free phone:* 800-877-4380.

QUEEN OF THE HOLY ROSARY COLLEGE
Mission San Jose, California

- **Independent Roman Catholic** 2-year, founded 1930
- **Calendar** semesters
- **Degree** associate
- **Suburban** 37-acre campus with easy access to San Jose
- **Coed, primarily women**

Faculty *Student/faculty ratio:* 5:1.
Student Life *Campus security:* 24-hour emergency response devices.
Standardized Tests *Recommended:* SAT I (for admission).
Costs (2003–04) *One-time required fee:* $15. *Tuition:* $2500 full-time, $100 per credit part-time. *Required fees:* $30 full-time.
Applying *Application fee:* $15. *Required:* essay or personal statement, high school transcript, minimum 2.0 GPA. *Recommended:* minimum 3.0 GPA, interview.
Admissions Contact Sr. Mary Paul Mehegan, Dean of the College, Queen of the Holy Rosary College, 43326 Mission Boulevard, PO Box 3908, Mission San Jose, CA 94539. *Phone:* 510-657-2468 Ext. 322. *Fax:* 510-657-1734.

REEDLEY COLLEGE
Reedley, California

Admissions Contact Ms. Leticia Alvarez, Admissions and Records Manager, Reedley College, 995 North Reed Avenue, Reedley, CA 93654. *Phone:* 559-638-0323 Ext. 3624.

RIO HONDO COLLEGE
Whittier, California

Admissions Contact Ms. Mary Becerril, Supervisor, Records/Admissions, Rio Hondo College, 3600 Workman Mill Road, Whittier, CA 90601-1699. *Phone:* 562-692-0921 Ext. 3153. *Fax:* 562-692-9318.

RIVERSIDE COMMUNITY COLLEGE
Riverside, California

■ **State and locally supported** 2-year, founded 1916, part of California Community College System
■ **Calendar** semesters
■ **Degree** certificates and associate
■ **Suburban** 108-acre campus with easy access to Los Angeles
■ **Coed,** 30,945 undergraduate students, 4% full-time, 5% women, 3% men

Undergraduates 1,155 full-time, 1,321 part-time. Students come from 23 states and territories, 60 other countries, 14% African American, 9% Asian American or Pacific Islander, 32% Hispanic American, 0.7% Native American, 46% transferred in.
Freshmen *Admission:* 2,656 applied, 2,656 admitted, 2,476 enrolled.
Faculty *Total:* 1,288, 25% full-time. *Student/faculty ratio:* 24:1.
Majors Accounting; agricultural business and management; anatomy; anthropology; architecture; art; astronomy; biological and physical sciences; botany/plant biology; business administration and management; chemistry; child development; clinical/medical laboratory assistant; computer and information sciences; computer graphics; computer programming; computer programming related; computer systems networking and telecommunications; computer/technical support; criminal justice/law enforcement administration; culinary arts; cultural studies; dental hygiene; dietetics; dramatic/theatre arts; economics; education; engineering; English; environmental studies; family and consumer sciences/human sciences; forestry; French; geography; geology/earth science; German; health and physical education; health science; history; humanities; journalism; kindergarten/preschool education; landscape architecture; liberal arts and sciences/liberal studies; library science; marketing research; mathematics; medical microbiology and bacteriology; music; nursing (registered nurse training); oceanography (chemical and physical); pharmacy; philosophy; physical sciences; physical therapy; political science and government; pre-law studies; psychology; sign language interpretation and translation; social sciences; Spanish; speech and rhetoric; theology; urban studies/affairs; word processing.
Academic Programs *Special study options:* academic remediation for entering students, adult/continuing education programs, advanced placement credit, distance learning, double majors, English as a second language, internships, part-time degree program, services for LD students, study abroad, summer session for credit. *ROTC:* Army (c), Air Force (c).
Library Martin Luther King Jr. Library with 101,243 titles, 911 serial subscriptions, 5,417 audiovisual materials, an OPAC, a Web page.
Computers on Campus 200 computers available on campus for general student use. A campuswide network can be accessed from off campus. Internet access, at least one staffed computer lab available.
Student Life *Housing:* college housing not available. *Activities and Organizations:* drama/theater group, student-run newspaper, radio station, choral group, marching band, Marching Tigers Band, Wind Ensemble, Student Nurses Organization, Gospel Singers, Alpha Gamma Sigma. *Campus security:* 24-hour patrols, late-night transport/escort service. *Student services:* health clinic, personal/psychological counseling.
Athletics *Intercollegiate sports:* baseball M, basketball M/W, cross-country running M/W, football M, golf M, soccer M/W, softball W, swimming M/W, tennis M/W, track and field M/W, volleyball W, water polo M/W. *Intramural sports:* badminton M/W, basketball M/W, bowling M/W, football M, golf M/W, racquetball M/W, soccer M/W, tennis M/W, volleyball M/W, weight lifting M/W.
Standardized Tests *Required:* Assessment and Placement Services for Community Colleges (for placement).
Costs (2004–05) *Tuition:* state resident $0 full-time; nonresident $4470 full-time, $167 per unit part-time. *Required fees:* $560 full-time, $18 per unit part-time, $10 per unit part-time.
Applying *Required:* high school transcript. *Application deadline:* rolling (freshmen), rolling (transfers). *Notification:* continuous (freshmen), continuous (transfers).
Admissions Contact Ms. Lorraine Anderson, Dean of Admissions and Records, Riverside Community College, 4800 Magnolia Avenue, Riverside, CA 92506. *Phone:* 909-222-8615. *Fax:* 909-222-8037.

SACRAMENTO CITY COLLEGE
Sacramento, California

Admissions Contact Mr. Sam T. Sandusky, Dean, Student Services, Sacramento City College, 3835 Freeport Boulevard, Sacramento, CA 95822-1386. *Phone:* 916-558-2438. *Fax:* 916-558-2190.

SADDLEBACK COLLEGE
Mission Viejo, California

Admissions Contact Admissions Office, Saddleback College, 28000 Marguerite Parkway, Mission Viejo, CA 92692-3635. *Phone:* 949-582-4555. *E-mail:* earaiza@saddleback.cc.ca.us.

SAGE COLLEGE
Moreno Valley, California

Admissions Contact 12125 Day Street, Building L, Moreno Valley, CA 92557-6720.

SAN BERNARDINO VALLEY COLLEGE
San Bernardino, California

■ **State and locally supported** 2-year, founded 1926, part of San Bernardino Community College District System
■ **Calendar** semesters
■ **Degree** certificates, diplomas, and associate
■ 82-acre campus with easy access to Los Angeles
■ **Coed**

Standardized Tests *Required:* CGP (for placement).
Costs (2003–04) *Tuition:* state resident $0 full-time; nonresident $3480 full-time. *Required fees:* $468 full-time.
Financial Aid Of all full-time matriculated undergraduates who enrolled, 100 Federal Work-Study jobs (averaging $3000).
Admissions Contact Mr. Joe Cobrales, Director of Admissions and Records, San Bernardino Valley College, 701 South Mt Vernon Avenue, San Bernardino, CA 92410-2748. *Phone:* 909-888-6511.

SAN DIEGO CITY COLLEGE
San Diego, California

■ **State and locally supported** 2-year, founded 1914, part of San Diego Community College District System
■ **Calendar** semesters
■ **Degree** certificates and associate
■ **Urban** 56-acre campus
■ **Coed,** 15,925 undergraduate students, 21% full-time, 54% women, 46% men

Undergraduates 3,303 full-time, 12,622 part-time. 16% African American, 12% Asian American or Pacific Islander, 27% Hispanic American, 1% Native American, 0.8% international.
Freshmen *Admission:* 5,937 admitted, 1,109 enrolled.
Faculty *Total:* 485, 33% full-time, 26% with terminal degrees. *Student/faculty ratio:* 35:1.
Majors Accounting; administrative assistant and secretarial science; African-American/Black studies; anthropology; art; artificial intelligence and robotics; automobile/automotive mechanics technology; behavioral sciences; biology/biological sciences; business administration and management; carpentry; commercial and advertising art; computer engineering technology; consumer services and advocacy; cosmetology; court reporting; data processing and data processing technology; developmental and child psychology; drafting and design technology; dramatic/theatre arts; electrical, electronic and communications engineering technology; emergency medical technology (EMT paramedic); engineering technology; English; environmental engineering technology; fashion merchandising; finance; graphic and printing equipment operation/production; Hispanic-American, Puerto Rican, and Mexican-American/Chicano studies; hospitality administration; industrial arts; industrial technology; insurance; interior design; journalism; labor and industrial relations; Latin American studies; legal administrative assistant/secretary; legal assistant/paralegal; liberal arts and sciences/liberal studies; machine tool technology; marketing/marketing management; mathematics; modern languages; music; nursing (licensed practical/vocational nurse training); nursing (registered nurse training); occupational safety and health technology; parks, recreation and leisure; photography; physical education teaching and coaching; physical sciences; political science and government; postal management; pre-engineering; psychology; radio and television; real estate; social sciences; social work; sociology; special products marketing; speech and rhetoric; teacher assistant/aide; telecommunications; tourism and travel services management; transportation technology; welding technology.
Academic Programs *Special study options:* academic remediation for entering students, adult/continuing education programs, cooperative education, distance learning, English as a second language, external degree program, honors programs, independent study, off-campus study, part-time degree program, services for LD students, student-designed majors, summer session for credit. *ROTC:* Air Force (c).
Library San Diego City College Library with 73,000 titles, 337 serial subscriptions, an OPAC.
Computers on Campus 396 computers available on campus for general student use. A campuswide network can be accessed. At least one staffed computer lab available.
Student Life *Housing:* college housing not available. *Activities and Organizations:* drama/theater group, student-run newspaper, radio station, choral group, Alpha Gamma Sigma, Association of United Latin American Students, MECHA,

Afrikan Student Union, Student Nurses Association. *Campus security:* 24-hour emergency response devices and patrols, late-night transport/escort service. *Student services:* health clinic, personal/psychological counseling.

Athletics Member NJCAA. *Intercollegiate sports:* baseball M, basketball M/W, cross-country running M/W, football M, golf M/W, soccer M/W, softball W, tennis M/W, track and field M/W, volleyball M/W. *Intramural sports:* archery M/W, badminton M/W, baseball M, basketball M/W, bowling M/W, racquetball M/W, soccer M/W, softball W, swimming M/W, tennis M/W, track and field M/W, volleyball M/W, weight lifting M/W.

Costs (2004–05) *Tuition:* state resident $0 full-time; nonresident $5340 full-time. Full-time tuition and fees vary according to course load. Part-time tuition and fees vary according to course load. *Required fees:* $540 full-time.

Financial Aid Of all full-time matriculated undergraduates who enrolled, 100 Federal Work-Study jobs (averaging $4000).

Applying *Options:* common application, early admission. *Required for some:* high school transcript. *Application deadline:* rolling (freshmen), rolling (transfers).

Admissions Contact Ms. Lou Humphries, Supervisor of Admissions and Records, San Diego City College, 1313 Twelfth Avenue, San Diego, CA 92101-4787. *Phone:* 619-388-3474. *Fax:* 619-388-3135. *E-mail:* lhumphr@sdccd.net.

SAN DIEGO GOLF ACADEMY
Vista, California

Admissions Contact Ms. Deborah Wells, Admissions Coordinator, San Diego Golf Academy, 1910 Shadowridge Drive, Suite 111, Vista, CA 92083. *Phone:* 760-414-1501. *Toll-free phone:* 800-342-7342. *Fax:* 760-918-8949. *E-mail:* sdga@sdgagolf.com.

SAN DIEGO MESA COLLEGE
San Diego, California

- **State and locally supported** 2-year, founded 1964, part of San Diego Community College District System
- **Calendar** semesters
- **Degree** certificates, diplomas, and associate
- **Suburban** 104-acre campus
- **Coed**

Student Life *Campus security:* 24-hour emergency response devices and patrols, late-night transport/escort service.

Standardized Tests *Recommended:* ACT (for placement).

Costs (2003–04) *Tuition:* state resident $0 full-time; nonresident $4008 full-time, $167 per unit part-time. *Required fees:* $18 per unit part-time, $12 per term part-time.

Financial Aid Of all full-time matriculated undergraduates who enrolled, 180 Federal Work-Study jobs (averaging $4000). *Financial aid deadline:* 6/30.

Applying *Options:* early admission.

Admissions Contact Ms. Ivonne Alvarez, Director of Admissions and Records, San Diego Mesa College, 7250 Mesa College Drive, San Diego, CA 92111. *Phone:* 619-388-2689. *Fax:* 619-388-3960. *E-mail:* csawyer@sdccd.cc.ca.us.

SAN DIEGO MIRAMAR COLLEGE
San Diego, California

Admissions Contact Ms. Dana Andras, Admissions Supervisor, San Diego Miramar College, 10440 Black Mountain Road, San Diego, CA 92126-2999. *Phone:* 619-536-7854. *Fax:* 619-693-1899. *E-mail:* dandras@sdccd.cc.ca.us.

SAN JOAQUIN DELTA COLLEGE
Stockton, California

- **District-supported** 2-year, founded 1935, part of California Community College System
- **Calendar** semesters
- **Degree** certificates and associate
- **Urban** 165-acre campus with easy access to Sacramento
- **Coed,** 17,131 undergraduate students, 39% full-time, 59% women, 41% men

Undergraduates 6,668 full-time, 10,463 part-time. Students come from 15 states and territories, 9% African American, 20% Asian American or Pacific Islander, 24% Hispanic American, 1% Native American, 0.7% international. *Retention:* 25% of 2002 full-time freshmen returned.

Freshmen *Admission:* 9,162 applied, 9,162 admitted, 1,762 enrolled.

Faculty *Total:* 565, 39% full-time. *Student/faculty ratio:* 33:1.

Majors Accounting; agricultural business and management; agricultural mechanization; agriculture; animal sciences; anthropology; art; automobile/automotive mechanics technology; behavioral sciences; biology/biological sciences; botany/plant biology; broadcast journalism; business administration and management; business/managerial economics; carpentry; chemistry; child development; civil engineering technology; commercial and advertising art; computer engineering technology; computer programming; computer science; construction engineering technology; corrections; criminal justice/police science; culinary arts; dance; developmental and child psychology; drafting and design technology; dramatic/theatre arts; drawing; economics; electrical, electronic and communications engineering technology; emergency medical technology (EMT paramedic); engineering; engineering related; engineering technology; English; family and consumer sciences/human sciences; fashion merchandising; fire science; food services technology; French; geology/earth science; German; graphic and printing equipment operation/production; health science; heating, air conditioning, ventilation and refrigeration maintenance technology; history; humanities; industrial radiologic technology; interior design; Italian; Japanese; journalism; kindergarten/preschool education; liberal arts and sciences/liberal studies; literature; machine tool technology; marketing/marketing management; mathematics; mechanical engineering/mechanical technology; music; natural resources management and policy; natural sciences; nursing (licensed practical/vocational nurse training); nursing (registered nurse training); ornamental horticulture; philosophy; photography; physical education teaching and coaching; physical sciences; political science and government; psychiatric/mental health services technology; psychology; public administration; religious studies; social sciences; sociology; Spanish; special products marketing; speech and rhetoric.

Academic Programs *Special study options:* academic remediation for entering students, adult/continuing education programs, advanced placement credit, cooperative education, distance learning, English as a second language, honors programs, independent study, part-time degree program, services for LD students, summer session for credit.

Library Goleman Library plus 1 other with 92,398 titles, 605 serial subscriptions, an OPAC, a Web page.

Computers on Campus 400 computers available on campus for general student use. A campuswide network can be accessed from off campus. Internet access, online (class) registration, at least one staffed computer lab available.

Student Life *Housing:* college housing not available. *Activities and Organizations:* drama/theater group, student-run newspaper, radio station, choral group, Alpha Gamma Sigma, Fashion Club, International Club, Badminton Club. *Campus security:* 24-hour emergency response devices and patrols, late-night transport/escort service. *Student services:* personal/psychological counseling, legal services.

Athletics Member NJCAA. *Intercollegiate sports:* baseball M, basketball M/W, cross-country running M/W, fencing M/W, football M, golf M/W, soccer M/W, softball W, swimming M/W, tennis M/W, track and field M/W, volleyball W, water polo M/W, wrestling M. *Intramural sports:* badminton M/W, basketball M/W, bowling M/W, soccer M/W, swimming M/W, tennis M/W, ultimate Frisbee M/W, volleyball M/W, weight lifting M/W.

Standardized Tests *Recommended:* Michigan Test of English Language Proficiency.

Costs (2003–04) *Tuition:* state resident $0 full-time; nonresident $4500 full-time, $150 per unit part-time. *Required fees:* $540 full-time, $26 per unit part-time. *Payment plan:* installment. *Waivers:* employees or children of employees.

Financial Aid Of all full-time matriculated undergraduates who enrolled, 315 Federal Work-Study jobs (averaging $3100). 210 state and other part-time jobs (averaging $1172).

Applying *Options:* common application, electronic application, early admission. *Application deadline:* rolling (freshmen), rolling (transfers). *Notification:* continuous (freshmen), continuous (transfers).

Admissions Contact Ms. Catherine Mooney, Registrar, San Joaquin Delta College, 5151 Pacific Avenue, Stockton, CA 95207. *Phone:* 209-954-5635. *Fax:* 209-954-5769. *E-mail:* admissions@deltacollege.edu.

SAN JOAQUIN VALLEY COLLEGE
Visalia, California

- **Independent** 2-year, founded 1977
- **Calendar** continuous
- **Degree** associate
- **Small-town** campus
- **Coed**

Faculty *Student/faculty ratio:* 14:1.

Student Life *Campus security:* late-night transport/escort service, full-time security personnel.

Costs (2004–05) *Tuition:* $10,440 full-time. *Required fees:* $100 full-time.

Applying *Required:* high school transcript. *Required for some:* essay or personal statement, interview.

San Joaquin Valley College (continued)
Admissions Contact Mr. Joseph Holt, Director of Marketing and Admissions, San Joaquin Valley College, 8400 West Mineral King Avenue, Visalia, CA 93291. *Phone:* 559-651-2500.

SAN JOSE CITY COLLEGE
San Jose, California

- **District-supported** 2-year, founded 1921, part of San Jose/Evergreen Community College District System
- **Calendar** semesters
- **Degree** associate
- **Urban** 58-acre campus
- **Coed,** 9,819 undergraduate students, 77% full-time, 56% women, 44% men

Undergraduates 7,578 full-time, 2,241 part-time. Students come from 33 other countries, 7% African American, 34% Asian American or Pacific Islander, 30% Hispanic American, 0.8% Native American.

Faculty *Total:* 338, 36% full-time.

Majors Accounting; administrative assistant and secretarial science; business administration and management; child development; computer engineering technology; computer science; construction engineering technology; cosmetology; criminal justice/law enforcement administration; data processing and data processing technology; dental hygiene; drafting and design technology; electrical, electronic and communications engineering technology; engineering; family and community services; heating, air conditioning, ventilation and refrigeration maintenance technology; history; human services; kindergarten/preschool education; labor and industrial relations; liberal arts and sciences/liberal studies; machine tool technology; marketing/marketing management; public administration; real estate; solar energy technology; teacher assistant/aide.

Academic Programs *Special study options:* academic remediation for entering students, adult/continuing education programs, advanced placement credit, cooperative education, English as a second language, part-time degree program, services for LD students, student-designed majors, summer session for credit. *ROTC:* Army (c), Air Force (c).

Library San Jose City College Library with 54,075 titles, 345 serial subscriptions.

Computers on Campus 48 computers available on campus for general student use. At least one staffed computer lab available.

Student Life *Housing:* college housing not available. *Activities and Organizations:* drama/theater group, student-run newspaper, radio station. *Student services:* health clinic.

Athletics *Intercollegiate sports:* baseball M, basketball M/W, cross-country running M/W, football M, golf M, softball W, track and field M/W, volleyball W.

Costs (2003–04) *Tuition:* state resident $0 full-time; nonresident $5034 full-time. *Required fees:* $564 full-time.

Financial Aid Of all full-time matriculated undergraduates who enrolled, 105 Federal Work-Study jobs (averaging $2500).

Applying *Options:* early admission, deferred entrance. *Application deadline:* rolling (freshmen), rolling (transfers).

Admissions Contact Mr. Carlo Santos, Director of Admissions/Registrar, San Jose City College, 2100 Moorpark Avenue, San Jose, CA 95128-2799. *Phone:* 408-288-3707.

SANTA ANA COLLEGE
Santa Ana, California

- **State-supported** 2-year, founded 1915, part of California Community College System
- **Calendar** semesters
- **Degree** certificates and associate
- **Urban** 58-acre campus with easy access to Los Angeles
- **Coed**

Faculty *Student/faculty ratio:* 20:1.

Student Life *Campus security:* late-night transport/escort service.

Costs (2004–05) *Tuition:* state resident $0 full-time; nonresident $3768 full-time, $157 per unit part-time. *Required fees:* $458 full-time, $18 per unit part-time, $13 per term part-time.

Financial Aid Of all full-time matriculated undergraduates who enrolled, 259 Federal Work-Study jobs (averaging $1600).

Applying *Options:* early admission.

Admissions Contact Mrs. Christie Steward, Admissions Clerk, Santa Ana College, 1530 West 17th Street, Santa Ana, CA 92704. *Phone:* 714-564-6053. *Fax:* 714-564-4379.

SANTA BARBARA CITY COLLEGE
Santa Barbara, California

- **State and locally supported** 2-year, founded 1908, part of California Community College System
- **Calendar** semesters
- **Degree** certificates and associate
- **Small-town** 65-acre campus
- **Coed,** 15,156 undergraduate students, 40% full-time, 52% women, 48% men

Undergraduates 6,127 full-time, 9,029 part-time. Students come from 49 states and territories, 63 other countries, 4% are from out of state, 2% African American, 5% Asian American or Pacific Islander, 23% Hispanic American, 1% Native American, 5% international, 6% transferred in.

Freshmen *Admission:* 2,365 applied, 2,365 admitted, 1,547 enrolled.

Faculty *Total:* 707, 34% full-time. *Student/faculty ratio:* 23:1.

Majors Accounting; acting; administrative assistant and secretarial science; African-American/Black studies; American Indian/Native American studies; anthropology; applied horticulture; art history, criticism and conservation; athletic training; automobile/automotive mechanics technology; biology/biological sciences; biomedical technology; biotechnology; business administration and management; chemistry; child care and support services management; commercial and advertising art; communication/speech communication and rhetoric; computer engineering; computer science; cosmetology; criminal justice/law enforcement administration; culinary arts related; cultural studies; drafting and design technology; dramatic/theatre arts; economics; electrical, electronic and communications engineering technology; electrical/electronics equipment installation and repair; engineering; engineering technology; English; environmental/environmental health engineering; environmental studies; film/cinema studies; finance; fine/studio arts; foodservice systems administration; French; geography; geology/earth science; health information/medical records technology; Hispanic-American, Puerto Rican, and Mexican-American/Chicano studies; history; hotel/motel administration; industrial engineering; industrial technology; information science/studies; information technology; institutional food workers; interior design; international relations and affairs; kindergarten/preschool education; kinesiology and exercise science; landscaping and groundskeeping; legal studies; liberal arts and sciences/liberal studies; marine technology; marketing/marketing management; mathematics; medical radiologic technology; music; nursing (licensed practical/vocational nurse training); nursing (registered nurse training); ornamental horticulture; parks, recreation and leisure; philosophy; physical education teaching and coaching; physics; political science and government; psychology; real estate; sales, distribution and marketing; selling skills and sales; sociology; Spanish; system administration; theatre design and technology; therapeutic recreation.

Academic Programs *Special study options:* academic remediation for entering students, adult/continuing education programs, advanced placement credit, cooperative education, distance learning, double majors, English as a second language, honors programs, independent study, internships, part-time degree program, services for LD students, study abroad, summer session for credit. *ROTC:* Army (c).

Library Eli Luria Library with 119,478 titles, 3,433 serial subscriptions, 17,760 audiovisual materials, an OPAC, a Web page.

Computers on Campus 980 computers available on campus for general student use. A campuswide network can be accessed from off campus. Internet access, at least one staffed computer lab available.

Student Life *Housing:* college housing not available. *Activities and Organizations:* drama/theater group, student-run newspaper, choral group, MECHA, International-Cultural Exchange Club, Geology Club, Computer Club, Future Teachers Club. *Campus security:* 24-hour emergency response devices and patrols, late-night transport/escort service. *Student services:* health clinic, personal/psychological counseling.

Athletics *Intercollegiate sports:* baseball M, basketball M/W, cross-country running M/W, football M, golf M/W, soccer M/W, softball W, tennis M/W, track and field M/W, volleyball M/W.

Standardized Tests *Recommended:* SAT I (for placement), SAT II: Subject Tests (for placement), SAT II: Writing Test (for placement), California State University EPT, UC Subject A Exam.

Costs (2003–04) *Tuition:* state resident $0 full-time; nonresident $5010 full-time, $149 per unit part-time. Full-time tuition and fees vary according to course load. Part-time tuition and fees vary according to course load. *Required fees:* $605 full-time, $18 per unit part-time, $65 per term part-time. *Waivers:* employees or children of employees.

Applying *Options:* early admission. *Recommended:* high school transcript. *Application deadlines:* 8/18 (freshmen), 8/18 (transfers). *Notification:* continuous (freshmen), continuous (transfers).

Admissions Contact Ms. Allison Curtis, Director of Admissions and Records, Santa Barbara City College, 721 Cliff Drive, Santa Barbara, CA 93109. *Phone:* 805-965-0581 Ext. 2352. *Fax:* 805-962-0497 Ext. 2200. *E-mail:* admissions@sbcc.edu.

SANTA MONICA COLLEGE
Santa Monica, California

- **State and locally supported** 2-year, founded 1929, part of California Community College System
- **Calendar** semester plus optional winter and summer terms
- **Degree** certificates and associate
- **Urban** 40-acre campus with easy access to Los Angeles
- **Endowment** $4.6 million
- **Coed,** 24,497 undergraduate students, 36% full-time, 54% women, 46% men

Undergraduates 8,902 full-time, 15,595 part-time. Students come from 50 states and territories, 101 other countries, 4% are from out of state, 10% African American, 16% Asian American or Pacific Islander, 29% Hispanic American, 0.5% Native American, 14% international, 56% transferred in.
Freshmen *Admission:* 6,393 applied, 2,358 enrolled. *Average high school GPA:* 2.61.
Faculty *Total:* 1,238, 27% full-time. *Student/faculty ratio:* 26:1.
Majors Accounting; administrative assistant and secretarial science; anthropology; architectural engineering technology; art; astronomy; athletic training; automobile/automotive mechanics technology; biology/biological sciences; broadcast journalism; business administration and management; chemistry; commercial and advertising art; computer and information sciences related; computer programming; computer programming (specific applications); construction engineering technology; cosmetology; criminal justice/law enforcement administration; criminal justice/police science; cultural studies; dance; data processing and data processing technology; dental hygiene; developmental and child psychology; drafting and design technology; dramatic/theatre arts; economics; electrical, electronic and communications engineering technology; English; environmental studies; family and consumer sciences/human sciences; fashion merchandising; fire science; French; geography; geology/earth science; German; graphic and printing equipment operation/production; history; industrial arts; information science/studies; interior design; journalism; kindergarten/preschool education; liberal arts and sciences/liberal studies; mass communication/media; mathematics; music; nursing (registered nurse training); parks, recreation and leisure; philosophy; photography; physical education teaching and coaching; physics; political science and government; pre-engineering; psychology; radio and television; real estate; respiratory care therapy; sociology; urban studies/affairs; welding technology.
Academic Programs *Special study options:* academic remediation for entering students, adult/continuing education programs, advanced placement credit, cooperative education, distance learning, English as a second language, honors programs, independent study, internships, part-time degree program, services for LD students, study abroad, summer session for credit. *ROTC:* Army (c).
Library Santa Monica College Library with 101,317 titles, 389 serial subscriptions, an OPAC, a Web page.
Computers on Campus 600 computers available on campus for general student use. A campuswide network can be accessed from off campus. Internet access, online (class) registration, at least one staffed computer lab available.
Student Life *Housing:* college housing not available. *Activities and Organizations:* drama/theater group, student-run newspaper, choral group, Club Latino United for Education, African Student Union, Gay and Lesbian Union, Alpha Gamma Sigma, International Speakers Club. *Campus security:* 24-hour emergency response devices and patrols, student patrols, late-night transport/escort service. *Student services:* health clinic, personal/psychological counseling, women's center, legal services.
Athletics Member NJCAA. *Intercollegiate sports:* basketball M/W, cross-country running M/W, football M, soccer W, softball W, swimming M/W, tennis W, track and field M/W, volleyball M/W, water polo M/W.
Standardized Tests *Required for some:* ACT, ACT COMPASS, ACCUPLACER.
Costs (2003–04) *Tuition:* state resident $0 full-time; nonresident $4470 full-time, $171 per unit part-time. *Required fees:* $570 full-time, $18 per unit part-time, $29 per term part-time.
Financial Aid Of all full-time matriculated undergraduates who enrolled, 450 Federal Work-Study jobs (averaging $3000).
Applying *Options:* early admission. *Required:* high school transcript. *Application deadlines:* 8/30 (freshmen), 8/30 (transfers). *Notification:* continuous until 8/30 (freshmen), continuous until 8/30 (transfers).
Admissions Contact Ms. Teresita Rodriguez, Dean of Enrollment Services, Santa Monica College, 1900 Pico Boulevard, Santa Monica, CA 90405-1628. *Phone:* 310-434-4880 Ext. 4774.

▶ **See page 600 for a narrative description.**

SANTA ROSA JUNIOR COLLEGE
Santa Rosa, California

- **State and locally supported** 2-year, founded 1918, part of California Community College System
- **Calendar** semesters
- **Degree** certificates and associate
- **Urban** 93-acre campus with easy access to San Francisco
- **Endowment** $19.2 million
- **Coed**

Faculty *Student/faculty ratio:* 17:1.
Student Life *Campus security:* 24-hour emergency response devices and patrols.
Athletics Member NJCAA.
Standardized Tests *Required for some:* Assessment and Placement Services for Community Colleges.
Costs (2003–04) *Tuition:* state resident $0 full-time; nonresident $4104 full-time, $189 per unit part-time. *Required fees:* $458 full-time, $18 per unit part-time.
Financial Aid Of all full-time matriculated undergraduates who enrolled, 228 Federal Work-Study jobs (averaging $3500).
Applying *Options:* electronic application, early admission.
Admissions Contact Ms. Renee LoPilato, Dean of Admissions, Santa Rosa Junior College, 1501 Mendocino Avenue, Santa Rosa, CA 95401-4395. *Phone:* 707-527-4510. *Fax:* 707-527-4798. *E-mail:* admininfo@santarosa.edu.

SANTIAGO CANYON COLLEGE
Orange, California

- **State-supported** 2-year, founded 2000, part of California Community College System
- **Calendar** semesters
- **Degree** certificates and associate
- **Coed**

Faculty *Student/faculty ratio:* 23:1.
Costs (2003–04) *Tuition:* state resident $0 full-time; nonresident $3960 full-time, $165 per unit part-time. *Required fees:* $264 full-time, $11 per unit part-time, $12 per term part-time.
Applying *Options:* early admission.
Admissions Contact Denise Pennock, Admissions and Records, Santiago Canyon College, 8045 East Chapman, Orange, CA 92669. *Phone:* 714-564-4000. *Fax:* 714-564-4379.

SEQUOIA INSTITUTE
Fremont, California

- **Proprietary** 2-year, founded 1966
- **Degree** certificates, diplomas, and associate
- **Coed, primarily men**

Faculty *Student/faculty ratio:* 32:1.
Costs (2003–04) *Tuition:* $9646 full-time. *Required fees:* $399 full-time.
Admissions Contact Mr. Joseph Files, Vice President of Marketing and Admissions, Sequoia Institute, 200 Whitney Place, Fremont, CA 94539-7663. *Phone:* 510-580-5440. *Toll-free phone:* 800-248-8585.

SHASTA COLLEGE
Redding, California

- **State and locally supported** 2-year, founded 1948, part of California Community College System
- **Calendar** semesters
- **Degree** certificates and associate
- **Rural** 336-acre campus
- **Endowment** $1.3 million
- **Coed**

Student Life *Campus security:* 24-hour emergency response devices, student patrols, late-night transport/escort service, 16-hour patrols by trained security personnel.
Standardized Tests *Required:* Assessment and Placement Services for Community Colleges (for placement). *Recommended:* SAT I or ACT (for placement).
Costs (2003–04) *Tuition:* state resident $0 full-time; nonresident $3912 full-time. *Required fees:* $456 full-time.
Financial Aid Of all full-time matriculated undergraduates who enrolled, 1,000 Federal Work-Study jobs (averaging $2500).
Applying *Options:* common application, early admission. *Required:* high school transcript.
Admissions Contact Ms. Cassandra Ryan, Admissions and Records Office Director, Shasta College, PO Box 496006, Redding, CA 96049-6006. *Phone:* 530-225-4841.

SIERRA COLLEGE
Rocklin, California

- **State-supported** 2-year, founded 1936, part of California Community College System
- **Calendar** semesters
- **Degree** certificates and associate
- **Suburban** 327-acre campus with easy access to Sacramento
- **Coed**, 19,416 undergraduate students, 28% full-time, 57% women, 43% men

Undergraduates 5,355 full-time, 14,061 part-time. 1% are from out of state, 2% African American, 2% Asian American or Pacific Islander, 8% Hispanic American, 2% Native American, 1% international, 4% transferred in, 1% live on campus.

Freshmen *Admission:* 24,000 applied, 24,000 admitted, 2,112 enrolled.

Faculty *Total:* 870, 18% full-time. *Student/faculty ratio:* 25:1.

Majors Accounting; administrative assistant and secretarial science; agricultural mechanization; agronomy and crop science; animal sciences; art; automobile/automotive mechanics technology; biology/biological sciences; business administration and management; carpentry; chemistry; computer engineering technology; computer science; construction engineering technology; construction management; corrections; criminal justice/law enforcement administration; criminal justice/police science; drafting and design technology; electrical, electronic and communications engineering technology; engineering; equestrian studies; family and consumer sciences/human sciences; fashion merchandising; fire science; food services technology; forestry; forestry technology; geology/earth science; horticultural science; industrial arts; industrial technology; information science/studies; interior design; journalism; kindergarten/preschool education; legal administrative assistant/secretary; liberal arts and sciences/liberal studies; marketing/marketing management; mass communication/media; medical administrative assistant and medical secretary; metallurgical technology; mining technology; nursing (licensed practical/vocational nurse training); nursing (registered nurse training); ornamental horticulture; photography; real estate; survey technology; teacher assistant/aide; welding technology.

Academic Programs *Special study options:* academic remediation for entering students, accelerated degree program, advanced placement credit, distance learning, double majors, English as a second language, independent study, internships, off-campus study, part-time degree program, services for LD students, study abroad, summer session for credit.

Library Leary Resource Center plus 1 other with 69,879 titles, 189 serial subscriptions, an OPAC.

Computers on Campus 430 computers available on campus for general student use. A campuswide network can be accessed from off campus. Internet access, online (class) registration, at least one staffed computer lab available.

Student Life *Housing Options:* coed. Campus housing is university owned. *Activities and Organizations:* drama/theater group, student-run newspaper, choral group, Drama Club, student government, Art Club, band, Aggie Club. *Campus security:* 24-hour emergency response devices and patrols, late-night transport/escort service. *Student services:* health clinic, personal/psychological counseling.

Athletics *Intercollegiate sports:* baseball M, basketball M/W, cross-country running M/W, football M, golf M/W, skiing (cross-country) M/W, skiing (downhill) M/W, softball W, swimming M/W, tennis M/W, track and field M/W, volleyball W, water polo M/W, wrestling M. *Intramural sports:* archery M/W, badminton M/W, basketball M/W, tennis M/W, volleyball M/W.

Standardized Tests *Required:* APS (for placement). *Recommended:* ACT (for placement).

Costs (2003–04) *Tuition:* state resident $0 full-time; nonresident $3576 full-time. Full-time tuition and fees vary according to course load and location. Part-time tuition and fees vary according to course load and location. *Required fees:* $466 full-time.

Financial Aid Of all full-time matriculated undergraduates who enrolled, 150 Federal Work-Study jobs (averaging $2340).

Applying *Options:* common application, electronic application, early admission. *Application deadline:* rolling (freshmen). *Notification:* continuous (freshmen), continuous (transfers).

Admissions Contact Ms. Carla Epting-Davis, Associate Dean of Student Services, Sierra College, 5000 Rocklin Road, Rocklin, CA 93677-3397. *Phone:* 916-789-2939. *E-mail:* jradford-harris@sierracollege.edu.

SILICON VALLEY COLLEGE
Emeryville, California

- **Proprietary** primarily 2-year, founded 2001
- **Calendar** semesters
- **Degrees** certificates, diplomas, associate, and bachelor's
- **Coed**

Faculty *Student/faculty ratio:* 18:1.

Standardized Tests *Required:* ACT (for admission).

Applying *Options:* common application. *Application fee:* $125. *Required:* interview. *Required for some:* high school transcript.

Admissions Contact Ms. Marianne Dulay, Admissions Representative, Silicon Valley College, 1400 65th Street, Suite 200, Emeryville, CA 94608. *Phone:* 510-601-0133 Ext. 14. *Toll-free phone:* 800-750-5627. *E-mail:* mdulay@svcollege.com.

SILICON VALLEY COLLEGE
Fremont, California

- **Proprietary** primarily 2-year, founded 1989
- **Calendar** semesters
- **Degrees** certificates, diplomas, associate, and bachelor's
- **Coed**

Faculty *Student/faculty ratio:* 18:1.

Standardized Tests *Required:* ACT (for admission).

Costs (2003–04) *Tuition:* $9450 full-time. Full-time tuition and fees vary according to program. *Required fees:* $625 full-time.

Applying *Options:* common application. *Application fee:* $125. *Required:* interview. *Required for some:* high school transcript.

Admissions Contact Mr. Anton Croos, Admissions Director, Silicon Valley College, 41350 Christy Street, Fremont, CA 94538. *Phone:* 510-623-9966 Ext. 212. *Toll-free phone:* 800-750-5627. *Fax:* 510-623-9822. *E-mail:* acroos@svcollege.com.

SILICON VALLEY COLLEGE
San Jose, California

- **Proprietary** primarily 2-year, founded 1999
- **Calendar** semesters
- **Degrees** certificates, diplomas, associate, and bachelor's
- **Coed**

Faculty *Student/faculty ratio:* 20:1.

Standardized Tests *Required:* ACT (for admission).

Costs (2003–04) *Tuition:* $9450 full-time. Full-time tuition and fees vary according to program. *Required fees:* $625 full-time.

Applying *Options:* common application. *Application fee:* $125. *Required:* interview. *Required for some:* high school transcript.

Admissions Contact Ms. Patricia Fraser, Admissions Director, Silicon Valley College, 6201 San Ignacio Avenue, San Jose, CA 95119. *Phone:* 408-360-0840 Ext. 247. *Toll-free phone:* 800-750-5627. *E-mail:* pfraser@svcollege.com.

SILICON VALLEY COLLEGE
Walnut Creek, California

- **Proprietary** primarily 2-year, founded 1997
- **Calendar** continuous
- **Degrees** certificates, diplomas, associate, and bachelor's
- **Coed**, 472 undergraduate students, 100% full-time, 65% women, 35% men

Undergraduates 472 full-time. Students come from 4 states and territories, 16% African American, 10% Asian American or Pacific Islander, 9% Hispanic American, 4% Native American, 0.4% international.

Faculty *Total:* 17, 71% full-time, 18% with terminal degrees.

Majors Animation, interactive technology, video graphics and special effects; architectural drafting and CAD/CADD; architectural technology; architecture; architecture related; CAD/CADD drafting/design technology; design and visual communications; desktop publishing and digital imaging design; drafting and design technology; graphic and printing equipment operation/production; graphic communications; health and medical administrative services related; information technology; mechanical drafting and CAD/CADD; medical administrative assistant and medical secretary; medical office assistant; pharmacology and toxicology; pharmacology and toxicology related; pharmacy technician; system administration; system, networking, and LAN/wan management.

Academic Programs *Special study options:* accelerated degree program, cooperative education.

Library Silicon Valley College plus 1 other with 1,000 titles, 50 audiovisual materials.

Computers on Campus Internet access, at least one staffed computer lab available.

Student Life *Housing:* college housing not available. *Campus security:* 24-hour emergency response devices.

Standardized Tests *Required:* CPAt (for admission).

Costs (2004–05) *Tuition:* $12,000 full-time. Full-time tuition and fees vary according to degree level. No tuition increase for student's term of enrollment. *Waivers:* employees or children of employees.

Applying *Application fee:* $125. *Required:* high school transcript, interview, entrance exam. *Required for some:* essay or personal statement. *Notification:* continuous (freshmen), continuous (transfers).
Admissions Contact Mr. Mark Millen, Admissions Director, Silicon Valley College, 2800 Mitchell Drive, Walnut Creek, CA 94598. *Phone:* 925-280-0235 Ext. 37. *Toll-free phone:* 800-750-5627. *E-mail:* mmillen@svcollege.com.

SKYLINE COLLEGE
San Bruno, California

Admissions Contact Supervisor, Admissions Office, Skyline College, 3300 College Drive, San Bruno, CA 94066-1698. *Phone:* 650-738-4251. *E-mail:* skyadmissions@smccd.net.

SOLANO COMMUNITY COLLEGE
Suisun City, California

- **State and locally supported** 2-year, founded 1945, part of California Community College System
- **Calendar** semesters
- **Degree** certificates, diplomas, and associate
- **Rural** 192-acre campus with easy access to Sacramento and San Francisco
- **Coed**

Faculty *Student/faculty ratio:* 27:1.
Student Life *Campus security:* 24-hour patrols, student patrols, late-night transport/escort service.
Standardized Tests *Recommended:* SAT I and SAT II or ACT (for placement).
Costs (2003–04) *Tuition:* state resident $0 full-time; nonresident $4290 full-time. *Required fees:* $572 full-time.
Financial Aid Of all full-time matriculated undergraduates who enrolled, 125 Federal Work-Study jobs (averaging $2000). 30 state and other part-time jobs (averaging $2000).
Applying *Options:* electronic application, early admission, deferred entrance.
Admissions Contact Mr. Gerald Fisher, Dean of Admissions and Records, Solano Community College, 4000 Suisun Valley Road, Fairfield, CA 94534. *Phone:* 707-864-7113. *Fax:* 707-864-7175. *E-mail:* admissions@solano.cc.ca.us.

SONOMA COLLEGE
Petaluma, California

- **Proprietary** 2-year, founded 1993
- **Calendar** semesters
- **Degree** certificates and associate
- **Suburban** campus with easy access to San Francisco
- **Coed**

Faculty *Student/faculty ratio:* 8:1.
Student Life *Campus security:* 24-hour emergency response devices and patrols.
Financial Aid Of all full-time matriculated undergraduates who enrolled, 19 Federal Work-Study jobs (averaging $1000).
Applying *Application fee:* $100. *Required:* essay or personal statement, high school transcript, minimum 2.0 GPA, 2 letters of recommendation, interview.
Admissions Contact Ms. Delores Ford, Chief Operating Officer/Campus Director, Sonoma College, 130 Avram Avenue, Rhonert Park, CA 94928. *Phone:* 707-664-9267 Ext. 12. *Toll-free phone:* 800-437-9474. *E-mail:* info@westerni.org.

SONOMA COLLEGE
San Francisco, California

Admissions Contact 78 First Street, San Francisco, CA 94105. *Toll-free phone:* 888-649-7801.

SOUTH COAST COLLEGE
Orange, California

Admissions Contact 2011 West Chapman Avenue, Orange, CA 92868. *Toll-free phone:* 800-337-8366.

SOUTHERN CALIFORNIA INSTITUTE OF TECHNOLOGY
Anaheim, California

- **Proprietary** primarily 2-year
- **Degrees** associate, bachelor's, and master's

- 664 undergraduate students, 100% full-time

Faculty *Student/faculty ratio:* 24:1.
Financial Aid Of all full-time matriculated undergraduates who enrolled, 8 Federal Work-Study jobs (averaging $2800).
Admissions Contact Ms. Flor Rojas, Director of Admissions, Southern California Institute of Technology, 1900 West Crescent Avenue, Building B, Anaheim, CA 92801. *Phone:* 714-520-5552.

SOUTHWESTERN COLLEGE
Chula Vista, California

- **State and locally supported** 2-year, founded 1961, part of California Community College System
- **Calendar** semesters
- **Degree** certificates and associate
- **Suburban** 158-acre campus with easy access to San Diego
- **Endowment** $320,596
- **Coed,** 18,799 undergraduate students, 30% full-time, 56% women, 44% men

Undergraduates 5,609 full-time, 13,190 part-time. 2% are from out of state, 5% African American, 17% Asian American or Pacific Islander, 58% Hispanic American, 0.5% Native American, 56% transferred in.
Freshmen *Admission:* 2,117 applied, 5,210 enrolled.
Faculty *Total:* 806, 24% full-time, 3% with terminal degrees. *Student/faculty ratio:* 22:1.
Majors Accounting; administrative assistant and secretarial science; African-American/Black studies; African studies; anthropology; architectural engineering technology; art; Asian-American studies; astronomy; automobile/automotive mechanics technology; biological and physical sciences; biology/biological sciences; business administration and management; chemistry; commercial and advertising art; computer and information sciences related; computer and information systems security; computer graphics; computer programming; computer science; construction engineering technology; corrections; criminal justice/law enforcement administration; dance; dental hygiene; dramatic/theatre arts; economics; electrical, electronic and communications engineering technology; elementary education; emergency medical technology (EMT paramedic); engineering; English; finance; fire science; French; general studies; geography; geology/earth science; Hispanic-American, Puerto Rican, and Mexican-American/Chicano studies; history; information science/studies; information technology; journalism; kindergarten/preschool education; landscape architecture; landscaping and groundskeeping; legal administrative assistant/secretary; liberal arts and sciences/liberal studies; literature; marketing/marketing management; mathematics; music; nursing (registered nurse training); parks, recreation and leisure facilities management; philosophy; photography; physical sciences; physics; political science and government; pre-engineering; psychology; public administration; real estate; small engine mechanics and repair technology; social work; sociology; Spanish; surgical technology; telecommunications; tourism and travel services management; web/multimedia management and webmaster; web page, digital/multimedia and information resources design; women's studies.
Academic Programs *Special study options:* academic remediation for entering students, adult/continuing education programs, advanced placement credit, cooperative education, English as a second language, external degree program, freshman honors college, honors programs, independent study, internships, part-time degree program, services for LD students, summer session for credit.
Library Southwestern College Library with 85,003 titles, 6,983 audiovisual materials, an OPAC, a Web page.
Computers on Campus 1300 computers available on campus for general student use. A campuswide network can be accessed from off campus. At least one staffed computer lab available.
Student Life *Housing:* college housing not available. *Activities and Organizations:* drama/theater group, student-run newspaper, choral group, MECHA, Business Club, Alpha Phi Epsilon, ABLE (disabled club), Society of Hispanic Engineers, national fraternities. *Campus security:* 24-hour emergency response devices, student patrols, late-night transport/escort service. *Student services:* health clinic, personal/psychological counseling, women's center.
Athletics *Intercollegiate sports:* baseball M, basketball M/W, cross-country running M/W, football M, golf M, soccer M, softball W, swimming M/W, tennis M/W, track and field M/W.
Costs (2004–05) *Tuition:* nonresident $4172 full-time, $167 per unit part-time. *Required fees:* $598 full-time, $18 per unit part-time. *Payment plan:* deferred payment.
Applying *Options:* early admission. *Required for some:* high school transcript. *Application deadline:* rolling (freshmen), rolling (transfers). *Notification:* continuous (freshmen), continuous (transfers).
Admissions Contact Ms. Georgia A. Copeland, Director of Admissions and Records, Southwestern College, 900 Otay Lakes Road, Chula Vista, CA 91910. *Phone:* 619-482-6550.

TAFT COLLEGE
Taft, California

- **State and locally supported** 2-year, founded 1922, part of California Community College System
- **Calendar** semesters
- **Degree** certificates and associate
- **Small-town** 15-acre campus
- **Endowment** $16,000
- **Coed**

Faculty *Student/faculty ratio:* 18:1.

Student Life *Campus security:* controlled dormitory access, parking lot security.

Costs (2004–05) *Tuition:* nonresident $167 per unit part-time. Full-time tuition and fees vary according to course load. Part-time tuition and fees vary according to course load. *Required fees:* $18 per unit part-time.

Financial Aid Of all full-time matriculated undergraduates who enrolled, 64 Federal Work-Study jobs (averaging $2295). 201 state and other part-time jobs (averaging $2295).

Applying *Options:* electronic application. *Required for some:* high school transcript.

Admissions Contact Ms. Gayle Roberts, Director of Financial Aid and Admissions, Taft College, 29 Emmons Park Drive, Taft, CA 93268. *Phone:* 661-763-7763. *Fax:* 661-763-7758. *E-mail:* cdeclue@taft.org.

VENTURA COLLEGE
Ventura, California

- **State and locally supported** 2-year, founded 1925, part of California Community College System
- **Calendar** semesters
- **Degree** certificates, diplomas, and associate
- **Suburban** 103-acre campus with easy access to Los Angeles
- **Coed**, 12,096 undergraduate students, 34% full-time, 57% women, 43% men

Undergraduates 4,112 full-time, 7,984 part-time. Students come from 25 states and territories, 11% are from out of state, 2% African American, 6% Asian American or Pacific Islander, 34% Hispanic American, 1% Native American, 1% international, 20% transferred in.

Freshmen *Admission:* 2,652 applied, 738 enrolled.

Faculty *Total:* 506, 24% full-time. *Student/faculty ratio:* 22:1.

Majors Accounting; administrative assistant and secretarial science; agricultural business and management; agronomy and crop science; animal sciences; architectural engineering technology; art; automobile/automotive mechanics technology; biology/biological sciences; business administration and management; ceramic arts and ceramics; commercial and advertising art; communication/speech communication and rhetoric; computer and information sciences; construction engineering technology; criminal justice/law enforcement administration; cultural studies; drafting and design technology; dramatic/theatre arts; education; engineering; family and consumer sciences/human sciences; fashion/apparel design; food services technology; horticultural science; hydrology and water resources science; information science/studies; journalism; kindergarten/preschool education; landscape architecture; liberal arts and sciences/liberal studies; machine tool technology; medical/clinical assistant; music; natural resources management and policy; nursing (registered nurse training); ornamental horticulture; parks, recreation and leisure; photography; physical sciences; real estate; welding technology.

Academic Programs *Special study options:* academic remediation for entering students, adult/continuing education programs, advanced placement credit, English as a second language, independent study, internships, part-time degree program, services for LD students, summer session for credit.

Library Ventura College Library with 63,529 titles, 341 serial subscriptions, an OPAC, a Web page.

Computers on Campus 40 computers available on campus for general student use. Internet access, online (class) registration, at least one staffed computer lab available.

Student Life *Housing:* college housing not available. *Activities and Organizations:* drama/theater group, student-run newspaper, choral group, Pan American Student Union, MECHA, Automotive Technology Club, Campus Christian Fellowship, Asian-American Club. *Campus security:* 24-hour emergency response devices and patrols, student patrols. *Student services:* health clinic, personal/psychological counseling, women's center.

Athletics *Intercollegiate sports:* baseball M, basketball M/W, cross-country running M/W, football M, golf M, soccer M/W, softball W, swimming M/W, tennis M/W, track and field M/W, volleyball W, water polo M/W.

Costs (2004–05) *Tuition:* state resident $0 full-time; nonresident $4890 full-time, $163 per unit part-time. *Required fees:* $576 full-time, $18 per unit part-time, $23 per term part-time.

Financial Aid Of all full-time matriculated undergraduates who enrolled, 70 Federal Work-Study jobs.

Applying *Required:* high school transcript.

Admissions Contact Ms. Susan Bricker, Registrar, Ventura College, 4667 Telegraph Road, Ventura, CA 93003-3899. *Phone:* 805-654-6456. *Fax:* 805-654-6466. *E-mail:* sbricker@server.vcccd.cc.ca.us.

VICTOR VALLEY COLLEGE
Victorville, California

- **State-supported** 2-year, founded 1961, part of California Community College System
- **Calendar** semesters
- **Degree** certificates and associate
- **Small-town** 253-acre campus with easy access to Los Angeles
- **Coed**, 10,580 undergraduate students, 35% full-time, 62% women, 38% men

Undergraduates 3,663 full-time, 6,917 part-time. 10% African American, 4% Asian American or Pacific Islander, 24% Hispanic American, 1% Native American.

Freshmen *Admission:* 1,226 enrolled.

Faculty *Total:* 460, 30% full-time.

Majors Administrative assistant and secretarial science; agricultural teacher education; art; automobile/automotive mechanics technology; biological and physical sciences; biology/biological sciences; business administration and management; business/commerce; child care and support services management; child development; computer and information sciences; computer programming (specific applications); computer science; construction engineering technology; construction management; criminal justice/police science; dramatic/theatre arts; electrical, electronic and communications engineering technology; fire protection and safety technology; fire science; food services technology; horticultural science; humanities; information science/studies; kindergarten/preschool education; liberal arts and sciences/liberal studies; management information systems; mathematics; music; natural sciences; nursing (registered nurse training); ornamental horticulture; physical sciences; real estate; respiratory care therapy; science technologies related; social sciences; teacher assistant/aide; trade and industrial teacher education; vehicle maintenance and repair technologies related; welding technology.

Academic Programs *Special study options:* academic remediation for entering students, advanced placement credit, cooperative education, distance learning, English as a second language, honors programs, off-campus study, part-time degree program, services for LD students, study abroad, summer session for credit.

Library Learning Resource Center with 41,789 titles, 534 serial subscriptions, an OPAC, a Web page.

Computers on Campus 260 computers available on campus for general student use. A campuswide network can be accessed. Internet access, online (class) registration, at least one staffed computer lab available.

Student Life *Housing:* college housing not available. *Activities and Organizations:* drama/theater group, student-run newspaper, choral group, Black Student Union, Drama Club, rugby, Phi Theta Kappa. *Campus security:* 24-hour emergency response devices and patrols, late-night transport/escort service, part-time trained security personnel. *Student services:* health clinic, personal/psychological counseling.

Athletics Member NCAA, NJCAA. *Intercollegiate sports:* baseball M, basketball M/W, cross-country running M/W, football M, golf M, soccer M/W, softball W, tennis M/W, track and field M/W, volleyball W, wrestling M. *Intramural sports:* rock climbing M/W.

Standardized Tests *Recommended:* ACCUPLACER.

Costs (2003–04) *Tuition:* state resident $0 full-time; nonresident $3576 full-time, $149 per unit part-time. *Required fees:* $432 full-time, $18 per unit part-time.

Financial Aid Of all full-time matriculated undergraduates who enrolled, 300 Federal Work-Study jobs (averaging $5000). 50 state and other part-time jobs (averaging $5000).

Applying *Options:* early admission. *Application deadline:* rolling (freshmen). *Notification:* continuous (freshmen), continuous (transfers).

Admissions Contact Ms. Becky Millen, Director of Admissions and Records, Victor Valley College, 18422 Bear Valley Road, Victorville, CA 92392. *Phone:* 760-245-4271 Ext. 2668. *Fax:* 760-245-9745. *E-mail:* millenb@vvc.edu.

VISTA COMMUNITY COLLEGE
Berkeley, California

- **State and locally supported** 2-year, founded 1974
- **Calendar** semesters
- **Degree** certificates and associate
- **Urban** campus with easy access to San Francisco
- **Coed**, 4,500 undergraduate students

Undergraduates 1% are from out of state.

Faculty *Total:* 164, 21% full-time. *Student/faculty ratio:* 25:1.

Majors Accounting; art; biology/biotechnology laboratory technician; business administration and management; business/commerce; computer and information sciences; computer and information sciences related; computer and information systems security; computer graphics; computer software and media applications related; creative writing; data entry/microcomputer applications related; English; English composition; fine/studio arts; general studies; liberal arts and sciences/liberal studies; medical administrative assistant and medical secretary; office management; Spanish; web page, digital/multimedia and information resources design.

Academic Programs *Special study options:* academic remediation for entering students, adult/continuing education programs, English as a second language, independent study, internships, off-campus study, part-time degree program, services for LD students, student-designed majors, study abroad, summer session for credit.

Library Vista Community College Library with a Web page.

Computers on Campus 50 computers available on campus for general student use. A campuswide network can be accessed. Internet access, online (class) registration, at least one staffed computer lab available.

Student Life *Housing:* college housing not available.

Costs (2003–04) *Tuition:* state resident $0 full-time; nonresident $4392 full-time, $175 per unit part-time. *Required fees:* $432 full-time, $18 per unit part-time.

Financial Aid Of all full-time matriculated undergraduates who enrolled, 50 Federal Work-Study jobs (averaging $3000).

Applying *Options:* common application, electronic application, early admission, deferred entrance. *Recommended:* high school transcript. *Application deadline:* rolling (freshmen).

Admissions Contact Dr. Mario Rivas, Vice President of Student Services, Vista Community College, 2020 Milvia Street, Berkeley, CA 94704. *Phone:* 510-981-2820. *Fax:* 510-841-7333. *E-mail:* sfogarino@peralta.cc.ca.us.

WESTERN CAREER COLLEGE
Pleasant Hill, California

Admissions Contact 380 Civic Drive, Pleasant Hill, CA 94523. *Toll-free phone:* 800-584-4520.

WESTERN CAREER COLLEGE
Sacramento, California

Admissions Contact 8909 Folsom Boulevard, Sacramento, CA 95826. *Toll-free phone:* 800-321-2386.

WESTERN CAREER COLLEGE
San Leandro, California

Admissions Contact 170 Bay Fair Mall, San Leandro, CA 94578. *Toll-free phone:* 800-584-4553.

WEST HILLS COMMUNITY COLLEGE
Coalinga, California

- **State-supported** 2-year, founded 1932, part of California Community College System
- **Calendar** semesters
- **Degree** certificates, diplomas, and associate
- **Small-town** 193-acre campus
- **Coed,** 4,344 undergraduate students, 42% full-time, 63% women, 37% men

Undergraduates 1,828 full-time, 2,516 part-time. Students come from 25 states and territories, 5 other countries, 6% African American, 6% Asian American or Pacific Islander, 45% Hispanic American, 1% Native American, 0.5% international.

Freshmen *Admission:* 2,034 applied, 2,034 admitted, 627 enrolled.

Faculty *Total:* 180, 44% full-time. *Student/faculty ratio:* 20:1.

Majors Accounting; administrative assistant and secretarial science; agricultural business and management; agricultural mechanization; agronomy and crop science; animal sciences; art; automobile/automotive mechanics technology; biology/biological sciences; business administration and management; chemistry; child development; criminal justice/law enforcement administration; equestrian studies; geography; geology/earth science; health science; humanities; information science/studies; kindergarten/preschool education; liberal arts and sciences/liberal studies; mathematics; physical education teaching and coaching; physics; pre-engineering; psychology; social sciences; transportation technology; welding technology.

Academic Programs *Special study options:* academic remediation for entering students, adult/continuing education programs, advanced placement credit, cooperative education, distance learning, English as a second language, independent study, off-campus study, part-time degree program, services for LD students, study abroad, summer session for credit.

Library West Hills Community College Library with 32,000 titles, 210 serial subscriptions.

Computers on Campus 82 computers available on campus for general student use. A campuswide network can be accessed from student residence rooms and from off campus. Internet access, at least one staffed computer lab available.

Student Life *Housing Options:* men-only, women-only. *Activities and Organizations:* drama/theater group. *Student services:* personal/psychological counseling.

Athletics *Intercollegiate sports:* baseball M, basketball M, equestrian sports M/W, football M, softball W, tennis W, volleyball W.

Standardized Tests *Recommended:* SAT I or ACT (for placement).

Costs (2003–04) *Tuition:* state resident $0 full-time; nonresident $3576 full-time, $148 per unit part-time. *Required fees:* $432 full-time, $18 per unit part-time. *Room and board:* $5000.

Financial Aid Of all full-time matriculated undergraduates who enrolled, 253 Federal Work-Study jobs (averaging $1351). 42 state and other part-time jobs (averaging $1669).

Applying *Options:* early admission. *Recommended:* high school transcript. *Application deadline:* rolling (freshmen), rolling (transfers). *Notification:* continuous (freshmen), continuous (transfers).

Admissions Contact West Hills Community College, 300 Cherry Lane, Coalinga, CA 93210-1399. *Phone:* 559-934-3204. *Toll-free phone:* 800-266-1114. *E-mail:* darlenegeorgatos@westhillcollege.com.

WEST LOS ANGELES COLLEGE
Culver City, California

Admissions Contact Mr. Len Isaksen, Director of Admissions, West Los Angeles College, 4800 Freshman Drive, Culver City, CA 90230-3519. *Phone:* 310-287-4255.

WEST VALLEY COLLEGE
Saratoga, California

- **State and locally supported** 2-year, founded 1963, part of California Community College System
- **Calendar** semesters
- **Degree** certificates and associate
- **Small-town** 143-acre campus with easy access to San Francisco and San Jose
- **Coed**

Costs (2003–04) *Tuition:* state resident $0 full-time; nonresident $3120 full-time. *Required fees:* $470 full-time.

Financial Aid Of all full-time matriculated undergraduates who enrolled, 125 Federal Work-Study jobs (averaging $2000).

Applying *Options:* common application, early admission.

Admissions Contact Mr. Albert Moore, Admissions and Records Supervisor, West Valley College, 14000 Fruitvale Avenue, Saratoga, CA 95070-5698. *Phone:* 408-741-2533.

WESTWOOD COLLEGE-ANAHEIM
Anaheim, California

- **Proprietary** primarily 2-year
- **Calendar** continuous
- **Degrees** associate and bachelor's
- **Suburban** campus with easy access to Los Angeles
- **Coed,** 674 undergraduate students, 85% full-time, 23% women, 77% men

Undergraduates 570 full-time, 104 part-time. 2% African American, 11% Asian American or Pacific Islander, 41% Hispanic American, 0.4% Native American, 0.1% international.

Freshmen *Admission:* 811 applied, 303 admitted, 278 enrolled.

Faculty *Total:* 52.

Majors Accounting and business/management; architectural drafting and CAD/CADD; computer systems networking and telecommunications; corrections and criminal justice related; design and applied arts related; design and visual communications; e-commerce; graphic design; interior design; intermedia/multimedia; marketing/marketing management.

Applying *Required:* interview, HS diploma or GED and passing scores on SAT/ACT or Accuplacer test.

Westwood College-Anaheim (continued)

Admissions Contact Mr. Paul Sallenbach, Director of Admissions, Westwood College-Anaheim, 2461 West La Palma Avenue, Anaheim, CA 92801-2610. *Phone:* 714-226-9990. *Toll-free phone:* 877-650-6050. *Fax:* 714-826-7398. *E-mail:* info@westwood.edu.

▶ **See page 614 for a narrative description.**

WESTWOOD COLLEGE-INLAND EMPIRE
Upland, California

- **Proprietary** primarily 2-year
- **Calendar** continuous
- **Degrees** associate and bachelor's
- **Suburban** campus with easy access to Los Angeles
- **Coed,** 803 undergraduate students, 81% full-time, 27% women, 73% men

Undergraduates 647 full-time, 156 part-time. 7% African American, 4% Asian American or Pacific Islander, 50% Hispanic American, 1% Native American.

Freshmen *Admission:* 801 enrolled.

Faculty *Total:* 41.

Majors Accounting; accounting and business/management; architectural drafting and CAD/CADD; commercial and advertising art; computer and information systems security; computer programming; computer programming (specific applications); computer software and media applications related; computer systems networking and telecommunications; corrections and criminal justice related; design and applied arts related; design and visual communications; graphic design; interior design; intermedia/multimedia; marketing/marketing management; system, networking, and LAN/wan management; web/multimedia management and webmaster; web page, digital/multimedia and information resources design.

Applying *Required:* interview, H.S. diploma or GED, pass entrance exam (or provide acceptable SAT/ACT scores).

Admissions Contact Mr. Lyle Seavers, Director of Admissions, Westwood College-Inland Empire, 20 West 7th Street, Upland, CA 91786-7148. *Phone:* 909-931-7550. *Toll-free phone:* 866-288-9488. *Fax:* 909-931-9195. *E-mail:* info@westwood.edu.

▶ **See page 634 for a narrative description.**

WESTWOOD COLLEGE-LONG BEACH
Long Beach, California

- **Proprietary** primarily 2-year, founded 2002
- **Calendar** continuous
- **Degrees** associate and bachelor's
- **Urban** 1-acre campus with easy access to Los Angeles
- **Coed,** 154 undergraduate students, 100% full-time, 31% women, 69% men

Undergraduates 154 full-time. Students come from 4 states and territories, 2% are from out of state, 15% African American, 10% Asian American or Pacific Islander, 46% Hispanic American, 0.6% Native American.

Freshmen *Admission:* 45 applied, 28 admitted.

Faculty *Total:* 19, 11% full-time, 11% with terminal degrees. *Student/faculty ratio:* 15:1.

Majors CAD/CADD drafting/design technology; computer hardware engineering; design and visual communications; graphic design.

Student Life *Housing:* college housing not available. *Activities and Organizations:* Westwood Expo, Mentorship Program, Director's Advisory Board. *Campus security:* 24-hour emergency response devices and patrols, late-night transport/escort service. *Student services:* personal/psychological counseling.

Athletics *Intramural sports:* basketball M/W, ultimate Frisbee M/W.

Standardized Tests *Required:* ACCUPLACER (for admission). *Recommended:* SAT I or ACT (for admission).

Costs (2004–05) *Tuition:* $18,645 full-time. Full-time tuition and fees vary according to course load and program. Part-time tuition and fees vary according to course load and program. *Required fees:* $2726 full-time. *Payment plans:* tuition prepayment, installment. *Waivers:* employees or children of employees.

Applying *Application fee:* $100. *Required:* high school transcript, interview. *Application deadline:* 10/4 (transfers). *Notification:* continuous (transfers).

Admissions Contact Mr. Craig McVey, Director of Admissions, Westwood College of Technology-Long Beach, 3901 Via Oro Avenue, Suite 103, Long Beach, CA 90810. *Phone:* 310-522-2088 Ext. 100. *Toll-free phone:* 888-403-3308. *Fax:* 310-522-2098. *E-mail:* cmcvey@westwood.edu.

▶ **See page 636 for a narrative description.**

WESTWOOD COLLEGE-LOS ANGELES
Los Angeles, California

- **Proprietary** primarily 2-year
- **Calendar** continuous
- **Degrees** associate and bachelor's
- **Urban** campus with easy access to Los Angeles
- **Coed,** 679 undergraduate students, 85% full-time, 26% women, 74% men

Undergraduates 577 full-time, 102 part-time. 13% African American, 10% Asian American or Pacific Islander, 66% Hispanic American.

Freshmen *Admission:* 630 applied, 341 enrolled.

Faculty *Total:* 52.

Majors Accounting and business/management; architectural drafting and CAD/CADD; computer and information systems security; computer programming; computer systems networking and telecommunications; corrections and criminal justice related; design and visual communications; e-commerce; graphic design; interior design; intermedia/multimedia; marketing/marketing management; web/multimedia management and webmaster.

Applying *Application fee:* $100. *Required:* interview, HS diploma/GED and passing scores on ACT/SAT or Accuplacer.

Admissions Contact Mr. Ron Milman, Director of Admissions, Westwood College-Los Angeles, 3460 Wilshire Boulevard, Suite 700, Los Angeles, CA 90010-2210. *Phone:* 213-739-9999. *Toll-free phone:* 877-377-4600. *Fax:* 213-382-2468. *E-mail:* info@westwood.edu.

▶ **See page 638 for a narrative description.**

WYOTECH
West Sacramento, California

Admissions Contact 980 Riverside Parkway, West Sacramento, CA 95605-1507.

YUBA COLLEGE
Marysville, California

- **State and locally supported** 2-year, founded 1927, part of California Community College System
- **Calendar** semesters
- **Degree** certificates and associate
- **Rural** 160-acre campus with easy access to Sacramento
- **Endowment** $3.7 million
- **Coed,** 9,165 undergraduate students, 35% full-time, 66% women, 34% men

Undergraduates 3,216 full-time, 5,949 part-time. 4% African American, 11% Asian American or Pacific Islander, 28% Hispanic American, 2% Native American.

Faculty *Total:* 830, 14% full-time, 5% with terminal degrees.

Majors Accounting; administrative assistant and secretarial science; advertising; African-American/Black studies; agricultural business and management; agricultural mechanization; agriculture; agronomy and crop science; animal sciences; art; automobile/automotive mechanics technology; biological and physical sciences; biology/biological sciences; business administration and management; chemistry; child development; communication/speech communication and rhetoric; computer and information sciences related; computer science; corrections; cosmetology; criminal justice/law enforcement administration; criminal justice/police science; cultural studies; dramatic/theatre arts; education; electrical, electronic and communications engineering technology; elementary education; English; family and consumer economics related; family and consumer sciences/human sciences; fire science; health teacher education; Hispanic-American, Puerto Rican, and Mexican-American/Chicano studies; history; human services; industrial radiologic technology; industrial technology; kindergarten/preschool education; machine tool technology; mass communication/media; mathematics; music; nursing (licensed practical/vocational nurse training); nursing (registered nurse training); philosophy; photography; physical education teaching and coaching; pre-engineering; psychiatric/mental health services technology; psychology; robotics technology; social sciences; substance abuse/addiction counseling; veterinary technology; welding technology; women's studies; word processing.

Academic Programs *Special study options:* academic remediation for entering students, advanced placement credit, distance learning, double majors, English as a second language, part-time degree program, services for LD students, summer session for credit.

Library Learning Resource Center and Library plus 1 other with 65,000 titles, 1,300 serial subscriptions, 9,419 audiovisual materials, an OPAC.

Computers on Campus 200 computers available on campus for general student use. A campuswide network can be accessed from student residence rooms and from off campus. Internet access, online (class) registration, at least one staffed computer lab available.

Student Life *Housing Options:* coed. Campus housing is university owned. *Activities and Organizations:* drama/theater group, choral group. *Campus security:* 24-hour patrols, student patrols. *Student services:* health clinic, personal/psychological counseling, women's center.

Athletics Member NCAA. *Intercollegiate sports:* baseball M(s), basketball M/W, cross-country running M/W, football M, soccer M/W, softball W, tennis M/W, track and field M/W, volleyball W.

Costs (2003–04) *Tuition:* state resident $0 full-time; nonresident $4920 full-time, $146 per unit part-time. No tuition increase for student's term of enrollment. *Required fees:* $540 full-time, $18 per unit part-time. *Room and board:* $5974.

Financial Aid Of all full-time matriculated undergraduates who enrolled, 290 Federal Work-Study jobs (averaging $2400). 50 state and other part-time jobs (averaging $1000).

Applying *Options:* common application, electronic application. *Required:* high school transcript.

Admissions Contact Yuba College, 2088 North Beale Road, Marysville, CA 95901. *Phone:* 530-741-6720.

COLORADO

AIMS COMMUNITY COLLEGE
Greeley, Colorado

- **District-supported** 2-year, founded 1967
- **Calendar** semesters
- **Degree** certificates, diplomas, and associate
- **Urban** 185-acre campus with easy access to Denver
- **Endowment** $71,813
- **Coed**

Faculty *Student/faculty ratio:* 16:1.
Student Life *Campus security:* 24-hour emergency response devices, day and evening patrols by trained security personnel.
Standardized Tests *Required:* CPT (for placement).
Costs (2004–05) *Tuition:* area resident $1500 full-time, $50 per credit hour part-time; state resident $2580 full-time, $86 per credit hour part-time; nonresident $9000 full-time, $300 per credit hour part-time. *Required fees:* $390 full-time, $12 per credit hour part-time, $15 per term part-time.
Financial Aid Of all full-time matriculated undergraduates who enrolled, 26 Federal Work-Study jobs (averaging $1800). 185 state and other part-time jobs (averaging $1800).
Applying *Options:* early admission, deferred entrance.
Admissions Contact Ms. Susie Gallardo, Admissions Technician, Aims Community College, Box 69, Greeley, CO 80632-0069. *Phone:* 970-330-8008 Ext. 6624. *Fax:* 970-339-6682. *E-mail:* wgreen@aims.edu.

ARAPAHOE COMMUNITY COLLEGE
Littleton, Colorado

- **State-supported** 2-year, founded 1965, part of Community Colleges of Colorado
- **Calendar** semesters
- **Degree** certificates, diplomas, and associate
- **Suburban** 52-acre campus with easy access to Denver
- **Coed**, 7,080 undergraduate students, 50% full-time, 59% women, 41% men

Undergraduates 3,540 full-time, 3,540 part-time. Students come from 42 states and territories, 35 other countries, 2% African American, 3% Asian American or Pacific Islander, 7% Hispanic American, 1% Native American, 2% international.
Freshmen *Admission:* 3,540 applied, 3,540 admitted.
Faculty *Total:* 414, 28% full-time. *Student/faculty ratio:* 19:1.
Majors Accounting; administrative assistant and secretarial science; architectural engineering technology; automobile/automotive mechanics technology; biological and physical sciences; building/home/construction inspection; business administration and management; child care and support services management; child care provision; clinical laboratory science/medical technology; clinical/medical laboratory technology; commercial and advertising art; communications systems installation and repair technology; communications technology; computer graphics; computer/information technology services administration related; computer programming; computer programming related; computer programming (specific applications); computer science; computer software and media applications related; computer systems networking and telecommunica-

tions; computer/technical support; construction management; consumer merchandising/retailing management; criminal justice/law enforcement administration; criminal justice/police science; data modeling/warehousing and database administration; drafting and design technology; electrical, electronic and communications engineering technology; emergency medical technology (EMT paramedic); engineering; environmental engineering technology; finance; food services technology; funeral service and mortuary science; health information/medical records administration; information science/studies; legal administrative assistant/secretary; legal assistant/paralegal; liberal arts and sciences/liberal studies; management information systems; marketing/marketing management; mechanical design technology; medical/clinical assistant; nursing (registered nurse training); pharmacy; physical therapy; tourism and travel services management; web page, digital/multimedia and information resources design.

Academic Programs *Special study options:* academic remediation for entering students, accelerated degree program, adult/continuing education programs, advanced placement credit, cooperative education, distance learning, double majors, English as a second language, honors programs, independent study, internships, off-campus study, part-time degree program, services for LD students, student-designed majors, study abroad, summer session for credit. *ROTC:* Army (c), Air Force (c).
Library Weber Center for Learning Resources plus 1 other with 45,000 titles, 441 serial subscriptions, an OPAC, a Web page.
Computers on Campus 200 computers available on campus for general student use. A campuswide network can be accessed from off campus. Internet access, at least one staffed computer lab available.
Student Life *Housing:* college housing not available. *Activities and Organizations:* drama/theater group, student-run newspaper, choral group. *Campus security:* 24-hour emergency response devices and patrols, late-night transport/escort service. *Student services:* personal/psychological counseling.
Athletics Member NJCAA. *Intercollegiate sports:* baseball M(s), soccer M(c), softball W(s), volleyball M(c)/W(c). *Intramural sports:* skiing (cross-country) M/W, skiing (downhill) M/W, soccer M/W, swimming M/W, tennis M/W, volleyball M/W.
Standardized Tests *Required:* CPT (for placement). *Recommended:* SAT II: Writing Test (for placement).
Costs (2003–04) *Tuition:* state resident $1585 full-time; nonresident $8284 full-time. Full-time tuition and fees vary according to course load, location, and program. Part-time tuition and fees vary according to course load, location, and program. *Required fees:* $141 full-time. *Payment plans:* installment, deferred payment. *Waivers:* employees or children of employees.
Financial Aid Of all full-time matriculated undergraduates who enrolled, 100 Federal Work-Study jobs (averaging $4200). 200 state and other part-time jobs (averaging $4200).
Applying *Options:* common application, electronic application, early admission, deferred entrance. *Application deadline:* rolling (freshmen), rolling (transfers).
Admissions Contact Mr. Howard Fukaye, Admissions Specialist, Arapahoe Community College, 5900 South Santa Fe Drive, PO Box 9002, Littleton, CO 80160-9002. *Phone:* 303-797-5622. *Fax:* 303-797-5970. *E-mail:* hfukaye@arapahoe.edu.

BEL-REA INSTITUTE OF ANIMAL TECHNOLOGY
Denver, Colorado

- **Proprietary** 2-year, founded 1971
- **Calendar** quarters
- **Degree** associate
- **Suburban** 4-acre campus
- **Endowment** $17,500
- **Coed**

Faculty *Student/faculty ratio:* 25:1.
Costs (2003–04) *Tuition:* $9000 full-time.
Applying *Options:* common application. *Application fee:* $100. *Required:* high school transcript, minimum 2.5 GPA. *Recommended:* interview.
Admissions Contact Ms. Paulette Kaufman, Director, Bel-Rea Institute of Animal Technology, 1681 South Dayton Street, Denver, CO 80247. *Phone:* 303-751-8700. *Toll-free phone:* 800-950-8001.

BLAIR COLLEGE
Colorado Springs, Colorado

- **Proprietary** 2-year, founded 1897, part of Corinthian Colleges, Inc
- **Calendar** quarters
- **Degree** diplomas and associate
- **Suburban** 5-acre campus with easy access to Denver
- **Coed**

Blair College (continued)

Faculty *Student/faculty ratio:* 13:1.

Student Life *Campus security:* 24-hour emergency response devices.

Standardized Tests *Required:* CPAt (for admission).

Applying *Application fee:* $25. *Required:* high school transcript.

Admissions Contact Ms. Dawn Collins, Director of Admissions, Blair College, 1815 Jet Wing Drive, Colorado Springs, CO 80916. *Phone:* 719-630-6580. *Toll-free phone:* 888-741-4271.

BOULDER COLLEGE OF MASSAGE THERAPY
Boulder, Colorado

Admissions Contact 6255 Longbow Drive, Boulder, CO 80301. *Toll-free phone:* 800-442-5131.

CAMBRIDGE COLLEGE
Aurora, Colorado

Admissions Contact Cambridge College, 12500 East Iliff Avenue, # 100, Aurora, CO 80014.

COLLEGEAMERICA-COLORADO SPRINGS
Colorado Spring, Colorado

Admissions Contact 3645 Citadel Drive South, Colorado Spring, CO 80909.

COLLEGEAMERICA-DENVER
Denver, Colorado

Admissions Contact Barbara W. Thomas, President, CollegeAmerica-Denver, 1385 South Colorado Boulevard, Denver, CO 80222-1912. *Phone:* 303-691-9756. *Toll-free phone:* 800-97-SKILLS.

COLLEGEAMERICA-FORT COLLINS
Fort Collins, Colorado

- **Proprietary** primarily 2-year, founded 1962
- **Calendar** continuous
- **Degrees** associate and bachelor's
- **Suburban** campus
- **Coed,** 232 undergraduate students

Undergraduates Students come from 3 states and territories.

Freshmen *Average high school GPA:* 2.69.

Faculty *Total:* 33, 33% full-time. *Student/faculty ratio:* 22:1.

Majors Accounting; business administration and management; computer and information sciences; computer graphics; computer installation and repair technology; computer programming; computer programming (specific applications); computer systems networking and telecommunications; medical/clinical assistant; web page, digital/multimedia and information resources design.

Academic Programs *Special study options:* independent study, internships.

Library Library with 12 serial subscriptions, 30 audiovisual materials.

Computers on Campus 86 computers available on campus for general student use. A campuswide network can be accessed. Internet access, at least one staffed computer lab available.

Student Life *Housing:* college housing not available.

Costs (2004–05) *Comprehensive fee:* $14,325. Full-time tuition and fees vary according to program. Part-time tuition: $275 per credit. No tuition increase for student's term of enrollment. *Payment plans:* tuition prepayment, installment, deferred payment. *Waivers:* employees or children of employees.

Applying *Required:* essay or personal statement, high school transcript, interview. *Required for some:* letters of recommendation. *Recommended:* minimum 2.0 GPA. *Notification:* continuous (freshmen), continuous (transfers).

Admissions Contact Ms. Anna DiTorrice-Mull, Director of Admissions, CollegeAmerica-Fort Collins, 4601 South Mason Street, Fort Collins, CO 80525. *Phone:* 970-223-6060 Ext. 8002. *Toll-free phone:* 800-97-SKILLS. *Fax:* 970-225-6059. *E-mail:* anna@collegeamerica.edu.

COLORADO MOUNTAIN COLLEGE, ALPINE CAMPUS
Steamboat Springs, Colorado

- **District-supported** 2-year, founded 1965, part of Colorado Mountain College District System
- **Calendar** semesters
- **Degree** certificates and associate
- **Rural** 10-acre campus
- **Coed,** 1,196 undergraduate students, 42% full-time, 38% women, 62% men

Undergraduates 508 full-time, 688 part-time. Students come from 49 states and territories, 40% are from out of state, 44% live on campus.

Freshmen *Admission:* 453 applied, 453 admitted. *Average high school GPA:* 2.40.

Faculty *Total:* 19. *Student/faculty ratio:* 15:1.

Majors Accounting; behavioral sciences; biological and physical sciences; biology/biological sciences; business administration and management; computer engineering technology; consumer merchandising/retailing management; data entry/microcomputer applications related; English; fine/studio arts; geology/earth science; hospitality administration; hotel/motel administration; humanities; liberal arts and sciences/liberal studies; marketing/marketing management; mathematics; parks, recreation and leisure facilities management; physical sciences; social sciences.

Academic Programs *Special study options:* academic remediation for entering students, adult/continuing education programs, advanced placement credit, cooperative education, distance learning, honors programs, independent study, internships, part-time degree program, services for LD students, study abroad, summer session for credit.

Library 17,000 titles, 192 serial subscriptions, an OPAC, a Web page.

Computers on Campus 60 computers available on campus for general student use. A campuswide network can be accessed from student residence rooms. Internet access, at least one staffed computer lab available.

Student Life *Housing:* on-campus residence required for freshman year. *Options:* coed. *Activities and Organizations:* student-run newspaper, student government, Forensics Team, Ski Club, International Club, Phi Theta Kappa. *Campus security:* 24-hour emergency response devices, controlled dormitory access. *Student services:* health clinic, personal/psychological counseling.

Athletics *Intercollegiate sports:* skiing (cross-country) M(s)/W(s), skiing (downhill) M(s)/W(s). *Intramural sports:* basketball M/W, rock climbing M/W, skiing (cross-country) M/W, skiing (downhill) M/W, soccer M/W, ultimate Frisbee M/W, volleyball M/W.

Standardized Tests *Recommended:* SAT I or ACT (for placement).

Costs (2004–05) *Tuition:* area resident $948 full-time, $41 per credit part-time; state resident $1656 full-time, $69 per credit part-time; nonresident $5280 full-time, $220 per credit part-time. Full-time tuition and fees vary according to course load. Part-time tuition and fees vary according to course load. *Required fees:* $180 full-time. *Room and board:* $6280; room only: $3192. Room and board charges vary according to board plan and housing facility. *Waivers:* employees or children of employees.

Applying *Options:* early admission, deferred entrance. *Required:* high school transcript. *Application deadline:* rolling (freshmen), rolling (transfers).

Admissions Contact Ms. Janice Bell, Admissions Assistant, Colorado Mountain College, Alpine Campus, PO Box 10001, Department PG, Glenwood Springs, CO 81602. *Phone:* 970-870-4417. *Toll-free phone:* 800-621-8559. *E-mail:* joinus@coloradomtn.edu.

COLORADO MOUNTAIN COLLEGE, SPRING VALLEY CAMPUS
Glenwood Springs, Colorado

- **District-supported** 2-year, founded 1965, part of Colorado Mountain College District System
- **Calendar** semesters
- **Degree** certificates and associate
- **Rural** 680-acre campus
- **Coed,** 716 undergraduate students, 56% full-time, 60% women, 40% men

Colorado Mountain College (CMC) offers high-quality education programs in a variety of occupational and transfer-degree options. CMC's Associate of Arts and Associate of Science degrees are part of the State Transfer Guarantee to any 4-year public college/university in Colorado. CMC also offers specialized occupational programs in the ski industry, natural resources, culinary, outdoor leadership, photography, graphic design, and veterinary technology.

Undergraduates 399 full-time, 317 part-time. Students come from 48 states and territories, 45% are from out of state, 44% live on campus.

Freshmen *Admission:* 421 applied, 421 admitted. *Average high school GPA:* 2.40.

Faculty *Total:* 22. *Student/faculty ratio:* 15:1.

Majors Accounting; art; behavioral sciences; biological and physical sciences; biology/biological sciences; business administration and management; commercial and advertising art; computer engineering technology; computer systems networking and telecommunications; computer/technical support; criminal justice/law enforcement administration; data entry/microcomputer applications related;

dramatic/theatre arts; English; humanities; liberal arts and sciences/liberal studies; mathematics; natural sciences; nursing (licensed practical/vocational nurse training); nursing (registered nurse training); photography; psychology; social sciences; therapeutic recreation; veterinary technology.

Academic Programs *Special study options:* academic remediation for entering students, adult/continuing education programs, advanced placement credit, cooperative education, distance learning, honors programs, independent study, internships, part-time degree program, services for LD students, study abroad, summer session for credit.

Library 36,000 titles, 186 serial subscriptions, an OPAC, a Web page.

Computers on Campus 65 computers available on campus for general student use. A campuswide network can be accessed from student residence rooms. Internet access, at least one staffed computer lab available.

Student Life *Housing Options:* coed. *Activities and Organizations:* drama/theater group, student-run newspaper, student government, outdoor activities, World Awareness Society, Peer Mentors, Student Activities Board. *Campus security:* 24-hour emergency response devices, controlled dormitory access. *Student services:* personal/psychological counseling.

Athletics *Intramural sports:* basketball M/W, cheerleading M/W, skiing (cross-country) M/W, skiing (downhill) M/W, soccer M/W, ultimate Frisbee M/W, volleyball M/W.

Standardized Tests *Recommended:* SAT I or ACT (for placement).

Costs (2004–05) *Tuition:* area resident $948 full-time, $41 per credit part-time; state resident $1656 full-time, $69 per credit part-time; nonresident $5280 full-time, $220 per credit part-time. Full-time tuition and fees vary according to course load. Part-time tuition and fees vary according to course load. *Required fees:* $180 full-time. *Room and board:* $6280; room only: $3192. Room and board charges vary according to board plan and housing facility. *Payment plan:* installment. *Waivers:* senior citizens and employees or children of employees.

Applying *Options:* early admission, deferred entrance. *Required:* high school transcript. *Application deadline:* rolling (freshmen), rolling (transfers).

Admissions Contact Ms. Deb Markiecki, Admissions Assistant, Colorado Mountain College, Spring Valley Campus, PO Box 10001, Department PG, Glenwood Springs, CO 81601. *Phone:* 970-947-8276. *Toll-free phone:* 800-621-8559. *E-mail:* joinus@coloradomtn.edu.

▶ **See page 530 for a narrative description.**

COLORADO MOUNTAIN COLLEGE, TIMBERLINE CAMPUS
Leadville, Colorado

- **District-supported** 2-year, founded 1965, part of Colorado Mountain College District System
- **Calendar** semesters
- **Degree** certificates and associate
- **Rural** 200-acre campus
- **Coed,** 1,241 undergraduate students, 18% full-time, 54% women, 46% men

Undergraduates 226 full-time, 1,015 part-time. Students come from 48 states and territories, 76% are from out of state, 30% live on campus.

Freshmen *Admission:* 453 applied, 261 admitted. *Average high school GPA:* 2.40.

Faculty *Total:* 14. *Student/faculty ratio:* 15:1.

Majors Accounting; art; behavioral sciences; biological and physical sciences; biology/biological sciences; business administration and management; child development; computer engineering technology; data entry/microcomputer applications; data entry/microcomputer applications related; ecology; English; environmental education; environmental studies; humanities; hydrology and water resources science; kindergarten/preschool education; land use planning and management; liberal arts and sciences/liberal studies; mathematics; parks, recreation and leisure; parks, recreation and leisure facilities management; psychology; social sciences.

Academic Programs *Special study options:* academic remediation for entering students, adult/continuing education programs, advanced placement credit, cooperative education, distance learning, English as a second language, honors programs, independent study, internships, part-time degree program, services for LD students, study abroad, summer session for credit.

Library 25,000 titles, 185 serial subscriptions.

Computers on Campus 30 computers available on campus for general student use. A campuswide network can be accessed from student residence rooms. Internet access, at least one staffed computer lab available.

Student Life *Housing Options:* coed. *Activities and Organizations:* Environmental Club, Outdoor Club, Student Activities Board. *Campus security:* 24-hour emergency response devices, controlled dormitory access. *Student services:* personal/psychological counseling.

Athletics *Intramural sports:* basketball M, rock climbing M/W, skiing (cross-country) M/W, skiing (downhill) M/W, soccer M/W, volleyball M/W.

Standardized Tests *Recommended:* SAT I or ACT (for placement).

Costs (2004–05) *Tuition:* area resident $948 full-time, $41 per credit part-time; state resident $1656 full-time, $69 per credit part-time; nonresident $5280 full-time, $220 per credit part-time. Full-time tuition and fees vary according to course load. Part-time tuition and fees vary according to course load. *Required fees:* $180 full-time. *Room and board:* $6280; room only: $3192. Room and board charges vary according to board plan and housing facility. *Payment plans:* installment, deferred payment. *Waivers:* senior citizens and employees or children of employees.

Applying *Options:* early admission, deferred entrance. *Required:* high school transcript. *Application deadline:* rolling (freshmen), rolling (transfers).

Admissions Contact Ms. Virginia Espinoza, Admissions Assistant, Colorado Mountain College, Timberline Campus, PO Box 10001, Department PG, Glenwood Springs, CO 81602. *Phone:* 719-486-4291. *Toll-free phone:* 800-621-8559. *E-mail:* joinus@coloradomtn.edu.

COLORADO NORTHWESTERN COMMUNITY COLLEGE
Rangely, Colorado

- **State-supported** 2-year, founded 1962, part of Colorado Community College and Occupational Education System
- **Calendar** semesters
- **Degree** certificates and associate
- **Rural** 150-acre campus
- **Endowment** $27,000
- **Coed,** 2,242 undergraduate students, 22% full-time, 51% women, 49% men

Colorado Northwestern Community College provides a residential campus in Rangely, with varsity athletics and outdoor recreation opportunities. Both the Rangely and Craig campuses offer 2-year AA and AS degrees, together with various vocational programs. Students should visit http://www.cncc.edu or call 800-562-1105 (toll-free) for more information or to arrange a campus tour.

Undergraduates 499 full-time, 1,743 part-time. Students come from 28 states and territories, 3 other countries, 5% are from out of state, 0.8% African American, 0.6% Asian American or Pacific Islander, 5% Hispanic American, 1% Native American, 0.3% international, 7% transferred in, 62% live on campus. *Retention:* 55% of 2002 full-time freshmen returned.

Freshmen *Admission:* 171 applied, 171 admitted, 171 enrolled.

Faculty *Total:* 277, 15% full-time, 6% with terminal degrees. *Student/faculty ratio:* 9:1.

Majors Accounting; aesthetician/esthetician and skin care; aircraft powerplant technology; airframe mechanics and aircraft maintenance technology; airline pilot and flight crew; art; business administration and management; child care and support services management; criminal justice/law enforcement administration; dental hygiene; early childhood education; e-commerce; education; emergency medical technology (EMT paramedic); English; entrepreneurship; environmental science; fine arts related; fire science; general studies; geology/earth science; hair styling and hair design; health services/allied health/health sciences; history; human services; instrumentation technology; legal assistant/paralegal; liberal arts and sciences/liberal studies; marine biology and biological oceanography; music; nail technician and manicurist; natural resources/conservation; nursing assistant/aide and patient care assistant; nursing (registered nurse training); parks, recreation and leisure; physical sciences; political science and government; psychology; teacher assistant/aide; wildlife biology.

Academic Programs *Special study options:* academic remediation for entering students, adult/continuing education programs, advanced placement credit, distance learning, double majors, independent study, internships, part-time degree program, services for LD students, student-designed majors, summer session for credit.

Library Colorado Northwestern Community College Library plus 1 other with 20,063 titles, 230 serial subscriptions, 3,559 audiovisual materials, an OPAC.

Computers on Campus 83 computers available on campus for general student use. A campuswide network can be accessed from student residence rooms and from off campus. Internet access, online (class) registration, at least one staffed computer lab available.

Student Life *Housing:* on-campus residence required for freshman year. *Options:* coed. Campus housing is university owned. Freshman applicants given priority for college housing. *Activities and Organizations:* drama/theater group, student-run newspaper, choral group, Campus Activities Board, SADHA, Aero Club, Criminal Justice Club, Spartan Times Newspaper Club. *Campus security:* student patrols, late-night transport/escort service. *Student services:* personal/psychological counseling.

Athletics Member NJCAA. *Intercollegiate sports:* baseball M(s), basketball M(s)/W(s), cross-country running W, softball W(s). *Intramural sports:* basketball M/W, football M/W, golf M/W, racquetball M/W, skiing (cross-country) M/W, skiing (downhill) M/W, softball M/W, table tennis M/W, tennis M/W, volleyball M/W.

Standardized Tests *Recommended:* ACT (for placement).

Colorado

Colorado Northwestern Community College (continued)

Costs (2003–04) *Tuition:* state resident $1982 full-time, $66 per semester hour part-time; nonresident $8283 full-time, $270 per semester hour part-time. Full-time tuition and fees vary according to reciprocity agreements. *Required fees:* $183 full-time, $56 per semester hour part-time, $10 per term part-time. *Room and board:* $5040; room only: $1990. Room and board charges vary according to housing facility. *Payment plan:* installment. *Waivers:* senior citizens.

Financial Aid Of all full-time matriculated undergraduates who enrolled, 35 Federal Work-Study jobs (averaging $1000). 80 state and other part-time jobs (averaging $1600).

Applying *Options:* early admission, deferred entrance. *Required:* high school transcript. *Required for some:* essay or personal statement, 3 letters of recommendation, interview. *Application deadline:* rolling (freshmen), rolling (transfers).

Admissions Contact Mr. Gene Bilodeau, Registrar, Colorado Northwestern Community College, 500 Kennedy Drive, Rangely, CO 81648. *Phone:* 970-824-1103. *Toll-free phone:* 970-675-3221 Ext. 218 (in-state); 800-562-1105 Ext. 218 (out-of-state). *Fax:* 970-675-3343. *E-mail:* merrie.byers@cncc.edu.

COLORADO SCHOOL OF HEALING ARTS
Lakewood, Colorado

Admissions Contact Victoria Steere, Director, Colorado School of Healing Arts, 7655 West Mississippi Avenue, Suite 100, Lakewood, CO 80226. *Phone:* 303-986-2320.

COLORADO SCHOOL OF TRADES
Lakewood, Colorado

- **Proprietary** 2-year
- **Degree** associate
- **Coed,** 115 undergraduate students

Costs (2003–04) *Tuition:* $8100 full-time.

Admissions Contact Mr. Robert Martin, Director, Colorado School of Trades, 1575 Hoyt Street, Lakewood, CO 80215-2996. *Phone:* 800-234-4594. *Toll-free phone:* 800-234-4594.

COMMUNITY COLLEGE OF AURORA
Aurora, Colorado

- **State-supported** 2-year, founded 1983
- **Calendar** semesters
- **Degree** certificates and associate
- **Suburban** campus with easy access to Denver
- **Coed,** 5,525 undergraduate students, 27% full-time, 61% women, 39% men

Undergraduates 1,502 full-time, 4,023 part-time. 20% African American, 7% Asian American or Pacific Islander, 11% Hispanic American, 1% Native American, 1% transferred in.

Freshmen *Admission:* 2,726 enrolled.

Faculty *Total:* 325, 10% full-time, 11% with terminal degrees. *Student/faculty ratio:* 16:1.

Majors Accounting; administrative assistant and secretarial science; automobile/automotive mechanics technology; biological and physical sciences; business administration and management; carpentry; commercial and advertising art; criminal justice/law enforcement administration; finance; information science/studies; kindergarten/preschool education; legal assistant/paralegal; liberal arts and sciences/liberal studies; marketing/marketing management; medical administrative assistant and medical secretary; medical/clinical assistant; ophthalmic laboratory technology.

Academic Programs *Special study options:* academic remediation for entering students, adult/continuing education programs, distance learning, English as a second language, external degree program, independent study, internships, off-campus study, part-time degree program, services for LD students, summer session for credit.

Library 7,440 titles, 126 serial subscriptions, an OPAC, a Web page.

Computers on Campus 160 computers available on campus for general student use. A campuswide network can be accessed. Internet access, at least one staffed computer lab available.

Student Life *Housing Options:* Campus housing is leased by the school. *Activities and Organizations:* drama/theater group, student-run newspaper. *Campus security:* late-night transport/escort service. *Student services:* women's center.

Standardized Tests *Recommended:* SAT I or ACT (for placement).

Costs (2004–05) *Tuition:* state resident $2004 full-time, $67 per credit hour part-time; nonresident $10,468 full-time, $345 per credit hour part-time. *Required*

fees: $125 full-time, $3 per credit hour part-time, $21 per term part-time. *Room and board:* $5274; room only: $3416.

Financial Aid Of all full-time matriculated undergraduates who enrolled, 61 Federal Work-Study jobs (averaging $2357). 91 state and other part-time jobs (averaging $2431).

Applying *Options:* early admission. *Application deadline:* rolling (freshmen), rolling (transfers). *Notification:* continuous (freshmen), continuous (transfers).

Admissions Contact Ms. Connie Simpson, Director of Registrations, Records, and Admission, Community College of Aurora, 16000 East CentreTech Parkway, Aurora, CO 80011-9036. *Phone:* 303-360-4700. *Fax:* 303-361-7432. *E-mail:* connie.simpson@ccaurora.edu.

COMMUNITY COLLEGE OF DENVER
Denver, Colorado

- **State-supported** 2-year, founded 1970, part of Community Colleges of Colorado
- **Calendar** semesters
- **Degree** certificates and associate
- **Urban** 171-acre campus
- **Endowment** $599,331
- **Coed,** 9,008 undergraduate students, 27% full-time, 64% women, 36% men

Undergraduates 2,463 full-time, 6,545 part-time. Students come from 34 states and territories, 1% are from out of state, 15% African American, 5% Asian American or Pacific Islander, 28% Hispanic American, 2% Native American, 6% international, 2% transferred in.

Freshmen *Admission:* 1,469 enrolled.

Faculty *Total:* 416, 20% full-time.

Majors Accounting; administrative assistant and secretarial science; business administration and management; commercial and advertising art; computer programming; computer typography and composition equipment operation; construction trades related; dental hygiene; drafting and design technology; electrical, electronic and communications engineering technology; environmental engineering technology; graphic and printing equipment operation/production; heating, air conditioning, ventilation and refrigeration maintenance technology; human services; industrial radiologic technology; information science/studies; intermedia/multimedia; kindergarten/preschool education; legal administrative assistant/secretary; legal assistant/paralegal; liberal arts and sciences/liberal studies; medical administrative assistant and medical secretary; nursing (registered nurse training); parks, recreation and leisure; photography; postal management; radiologic technology/science; tourism and travel services management; veterinary technology.

Academic Programs *Special study options:* academic remediation for entering students, adult/continuing education programs, advanced placement credit, cooperative education, distance learning, English as a second language, honors programs, independent study, internships, off-campus study, part-time degree program, services for LD students, study abroad, summer session for credit. *ROTC:* Army (c).

Library Auraria Library plus 1 other with 460,518 titles, 3,233 serial subscriptions, an OPAC, a Web page.

Computers on Campus 1142 computers available on campus for general student use. A campuswide network can be accessed from off campus. Internet access, at least one staffed computer lab available.

Student Life *Housing:* college housing not available. *Activities and Organizations:* student-run newspaper, Trio Advocates for Multicultural Students, Student Alliance for Human Services, Ad Hoc Nursing, Black Men on Campus, Auraria Fine Arts, national fraternities. *Campus security:* 24-hour emergency response devices and patrols, late-night transport/escort service. *Student services:* health clinic, personal/psychological counseling, women's center, legal services.

Athletics *Intramural sports:* archery M/W, badminton M/W, basketball M/W, bowling M/W, cross-country running M/W, equestrian sports M/W, fencing M/W, field hockey M/W, football M/W, golf M/W, gymnastics M/W, racquetball M/W, riflery M/W, rugby M/W, skiing (cross-country) M/W, skiing (downhill) M/W, soccer M/W, swimming M/W, table tennis M/W, tennis M/W, track and field M/W, volleyball M/W, weight lifting M/W.

Standardized Tests *Recommended:* SAT I or ACT (for placement).

Costs (2003–04) *Tuition:* state resident $1585 full-time, $66 per credit part-time; nonresident $8284 full-time, $345 per credit part-time. Full-time tuition and fees vary according to location and program. Part-time tuition and fees vary according to location and program. *Required fees:* $304 full-time, $152 per term part-time. *Payment plan:* deferred payment. *Waivers:* senior citizens.

Financial Aid Of all full-time matriculated undergraduates who enrolled, 95 Federal Work-Study jobs (averaging $2442). 305 state and other part-time jobs (averaging $2156).

Applying *Options:* electronic application, early admission, deferred entrance. *Recommended:* interview. *Application deadline:* rolling (freshmen), rolling (transfers).

Admissions Contact Ms. Emita Samuels, Director of Registration and Records, Community College of Denver, PO Box 173363, 1111 West Colfax Avenue, Denver, CO 80217-3363. *Phone:* 303-556-2430. *E-mail:* emita.samuels@ccd.cccoes.edu.

DENVER ACADEMY OF COURT REPORTING
Westminster, Colorado

Admissions Contact Mr. Howard Brookner, Director of Admissions, Denver Academy of Court Reporting, 7290 Samuel Drive, Suite 200, Denver, CO 80221-2792. *Phone:* 303-427-5292 Ext. 14. *Toll-free phone:* 800-574-2087. *Fax:* 303-427-5383.

DENVER AUTOMOTIVE AND DIESEL COLLEGE
Denver, Colorado

- **Proprietary** 2-year, founded 1963
- **Calendar** 8 six-week terms
- **Degree** diplomas and associate
- **Urban** campus
- **Coed, primarily men**

Student Life *Campus security:* 24-hour emergency response devices and patrols.
Applying *Options:* common application. *Application fee:* $150.
Admissions Contact Mr. John Chalupa, Director of Admissions, Denver Automotive and Diesel College, 460 South Lipan Street, Denver, CO 80223-2025. *Phone:* 303-722-5724. *Toll-free phone:* 800-347-3232. *Fax:* 303-778-8264. *E-mail:* dad@mho.net.

FRONT RANGE COMMUNITY COLLEGE
Westminster, Colorado

- **State-supported** 2-year, founded 1968, part of Community Colleges of Colorado System
- **Calendar** semesters
- **Degree** certificates and associate
- **Suburban** 90-acre campus with easy access to Denver
- **Coed,** 15,301 undergraduate students, 34% full-time, 60% women, 40% men

Undergraduates 5,154 full-time, 10,147 part-time. Students come from 40 states and territories, 104 other countries, 0.7% are from out of state, 1% African American, 4% Asian American or Pacific Islander, 10% Hispanic American, 1% Native American, 1% international.
Freshmen *Admission:* 7,202 applied, 7,202 admitted, 3,381 enrolled.
Faculty *Total:* 997, 17% full-time. *Student/faculty ratio:* 15:1.
Majors Accounting technology and bookkeeping; administrative assistant and secretarial science; animal sciences related; applied horticulture; architectural engineering technology; athletic training; automobile/automotive mechanics technology; business administration and management; business automation/technology/data entry; child care and support services management; design and visual communications; dietitian assistant; drafting and design technology; electrical, electronic and communications engineering technology; entrepreneurship; environmental engineering technology; foods and nutrition related; general studies; heating, air conditioning and refrigeration technology; industrial technology; laser and optical technology; liberal arts and sciences/liberal studies; machine shop technology; management information systems; nursing (registered nurse training); respiratory care therapy; science technologies related; sign language interpretation and translation; welding technology; wildlife and wildlands science and management.
Academic Programs *Special study options:* academic remediation for entering students, adult/continuing education programs, advanced placement credit, cooperative education, distance learning, double majors, English as a second language, external degree program, freshman honors college, honors programs, internships, off-campus study, part-time degree program, services for LD students, student-designed majors, study abroad, summer session for credit. *ROTC:* Army (c), Air Force (c).
Library College Hill Library with an OPAC, a Web page.
Computers on Campus 62 computers available on campus for general student use. A campuswide network can be accessed from off campus that provide access to online courses. Internet access, online (class) registration, at least one staffed computer lab available.
Student Life *Housing:* college housing not available. *Activities and Organizations:* drama/theater group, student-run newspaper, Student Government Association, Student Colorado Registry of Interpreters for the Deaf, Alpha Mu Psi,

Alpha Tau Kappa, Hispanic Club. *Campus security:* 24-hour patrols, late-night transport/escort service. *Student services:* personal/psychological counseling, women's center.
Costs (2004–05) *Tuition:* state resident $1982 full-time, $66 per credit part-time; nonresident $10,355 full-time, $345 per credit part-time.
Financial Aid Of all full-time matriculated undergraduates who enrolled, 165 Federal Work-Study jobs (averaging $1316). 277 state and other part-time jobs (averaging $1635).
Applying *Options:* common application, electronic application, early admission, deferred entrance. *Application deadline:* rolling (freshmen), rolling (transfers).
Admissions Contact Ms. Darcy Clodio, Director of Enrollment Services, Front Range Community College, 3645 West 112th Avenue, Westminster, CO 80031. *Phone:* 303-404-5471. *Fax:* 303-439-2614. *E-mail:* darcy.clodio@frontrange.edu.

HERITAGE COLLEGE
Denver, Colorado

Admissions Contact Heritage College, 12 Lakeside Lane, Denver, CO 80212-7413.

INSTITUTE OF BUSINESS & MEDICAL CAREERS
Fort Collins, Colorado

- **Private** 2-year, founded 1987
- **Calendar** continuous
- **Degree** certificates, diplomas, and associate
- **Suburban** campus with easy access to Denver
- **Coed, primarily women,** 302 undergraduate students, 100% full-time, 89% women, 11% men

Undergraduates 302 full-time. Students come from 1 other state, 2% are from out of state, 1% African American, 6% Asian American or Pacific Islander, 22% Hispanic American, 0.3% Native American. *Retention:* 69% of 2002 full-time freshmen returned.
Freshmen *Admission:* 366 applied, 366 admitted, 302 enrolled.
Faculty *Total:* 34, 32% full-time. *Student/faculty ratio:* 14:1.
Majors Accounting technology and bookkeeping; business administration and management; legal administrative assistant/secretary; legal assistant/paralegal; massage therapy; medical administrative assistant and medical secretary; medical/clinical assistant; office occupations and clerical services; pharmacy technician.
Student Life *Activities and Organizations:* student-run newspaper, Alpha Beta Kappa.
Costs (2004–05) *Tuition:* $13,800 full-time. No tuition increase for student's term of enrollment. *Required fees:* $75 full-time. *Payment plan:* installment.
Applying *Application fee:* $75. *Required:* high school transcript. *Application deadline:* rolling (freshmen).
Admissions Contact Mr. Steve Steele, Vice President of Operations, Institute of Business & Medical Careers, 1609 Oakridge Drive, Fort Collins, CO 80525. *Phone:* 970-223-2669 Ext. 102. *Toll-free phone:* 800-495-2669. *Fax:* 970-223-2796. *E-mail:* info@ibmcedu.com.

INTELLITEC COLLEGE
Colorado Springs, Colorado

- **Proprietary** 2-year, founded 1965, part of Technical Trades Institute, Inc
- **Calendar** 6-week terms
- **Degree** certificates, diplomas, and associate
- **Urban** 2-acre campus with easy access to Denver
- **Coed,** 427 undergraduate students, 100% full-time, 15% women, 85% men

Undergraduates 427 full-time. Students come from 3 states and territories, 5% are from out of state, 19% African American, 2% Asian American or Pacific Islander, 15% Hispanic American, 0.7% Native American.
Faculty *Total:* 28, 46% full-time. *Student/faculty ratio:* 18:1.
Majors Drafting and design technology; electrical, electronic and communications engineering technology; environmental engineering technology; interior design.
Academic Programs *Special study options:* advanced placement credit, double majors.
Library 274 titles, 28 serial subscriptions.
Computers on Campus 45 computers available on campus for general student use. Internet access, at least one staffed computer lab available.

IntelliTec College (continued)

Student Life *Housing:* college housing not available. *Campus security:* 24-hour emergency response devices.

Costs (2003–04) *Tuition:* $12,595 full-time. *Required fees:* $1330 full-time.

Financial Aid Of all full-time matriculated undergraduates who enrolled, 10 Federal Work-Study jobs (averaging $6500).

Applying *Options:* common application. *Required:* high school transcript, interview. *Application deadline:* rolling (freshmen), rolling (transfers).

Admissions Contact Ms. Ellen Pitrone, Director of Admissions, IntelliTec College, 2315 East Pikes Peak Avenue, Colorado Springs, CO 80909-6030. *Phone:* 719-632-7626. *Toll-free phone:* 800-748-2282. *Fax:* 719-632-7451.

INTELLITEC COLLEGE
Grand Junction, Colorado

- **Proprietary** 2-year
- **Calendar** continuous
- **Degree** certificates, diplomas, and associate
- **Small-town** campus
- **Coed,** 255 undergraduate students, 100% full-time, 69% women, 31% men

Undergraduates 255 full-time.

Freshmen *Admission:* 177 applied, 177 admitted, 177 enrolled.

Faculty *Total:* 24, 71% full-time.

Majors Architectural drafting; clinical/medical laboratory assistant; computer and information sciences; computer systems networking and telecommunications; data entry/microcomputer applications; electrical, electronic and communications engineering technology; heating, air conditioning, ventilation and refrigeration maintenance technology; massage therapy; mechanical drafting; medical administrative assistant and medical secretary; system administration.

Costs (2003–04) *Tuition:* $150 per credit hour part-time.

Admissions Contact Ms. Lisa Watson, Director of Admissions, IntelliTec College, 772 Horizon Drive, Grand Junction, CO 81506. *Phone:* 970-245-8101.

INTELLITEC MEDICAL INSTITUTE
Colorado Springs, Colorado

Admissions Contact Michelle Squibb, Admissions Representative, IntelliTec Medical Institute, 2345 North Academy Boulevard, Colorado Springs, CO 80909. *Phone:* 719-596-7400. *E-mail:* adm@intellitecmedicalinstitute.com.

ITT TECHNICAL INSTITUTE
Thornton, Colorado

- **Proprietary** primarily 2-year, founded 1984, part of ITT Educational Services, Inc.
- **Calendar** quarters
- **Degrees** associate and bachelor's
- **Suburban** 2-acre campus with easy access to Denver
- **Coed**

Standardized Tests *Required:* Wonderlic aptitude test (for admission).

Costs (2003–04) *Tuition:* Total Program Cost varies depending on course of study. Consult school catalog.

Applying *Options:* deferred entrance. *Application fee:* $100. *Required:* high school transcript, interview. *Recommended:* letters of recommendation.

Admissions Contact Niki Donahue, Director of Recruitment, ITT Technical Institute, 500 East 84th Avenue, Suite B12, Thornton, CO 80229. *Phone:* 303-288-4488. *Toll-free phone:* 800-395-4488. *Fax:* 303-288-8166.

LAMAR COMMUNITY COLLEGE
Lamar, Colorado

- **State-supported** 2-year, founded 1937, part of Colorado Community College and Occupational Education System
- **Calendar** semesters
- **Degree** certificates, diplomas, and associate
- **Small-town** 125-acre campus
- **Endowment** $200,000
- **Coed**

Student Life *Campus security:* 24-hour emergency response devices and patrols, student patrols, late-night transport/escort service, controlled dormitory access.

Athletics Member NJCAA.

Standardized Tests *Recommended:* SAT I or ACT (for placement).

Financial Aid Of all full-time matriculated undergraduates who enrolled, 32 Federal Work-Study jobs (averaging $1000). 89 state and other part-time jobs (averaging $1000).

Applying *Options:* common application, early admission.

Admissions Contact Director of Admissions, Lamar Community College, 2401 South Main Street, Lamar, CO 81052-3999. *Phone:* 719-336-1590. *Toll-free phone:* 800-968-6920. *Fax:* 719-336-2400. *E-mail:* admissions@lamarcc.edu.

MORGAN COMMUNITY COLLEGE
Fort Morgan, Colorado

- **State-supported** 2-year, founded 1967, part of Colorado Community College and Occupational Education System
- **Calendar** semesters
- **Degree** certificates and associate
- **Rural** 20-acre campus with easy access to Denver
- **Coed,** 1,564 undergraduate students, 22% full-time, 65% women, 35% men

Undergraduates 351 full-time, 1,213 part-time. Students come from 3 states and territories, 2% are from out of state, 0.2% African American, 0.6% Asian American or Pacific Islander, 11% Hispanic American, 1% Native American, 0.2% international, 3% transferred in.

Freshmen *Admission:* 177 applied, 177 admitted, 177 enrolled.

Faculty *Total:* 221, 16% full-time. *Student/faculty ratio:* 10:1.

Majors Accounting; administrative assistant and secretarial science; automobile/automotive mechanics technology; biological and physical sciences; business administration and management; business/managerial economics; business teacher education; liberal arts and sciences/liberal studies; occupational therapy; physical therapy.

Academic Programs *Special study options:* academic remediation for entering students, adult/continuing education programs, advanced placement credit, internships, part-time degree program, services for LD students, summer session for credit.

Library Learning Resource Center with 13,800 titles, 80 serial subscriptions, 1,096 audiovisual materials, an OPAC, a Web page.

Computers on Campus 60 computers available on campus for general student use. A campuswide network can be accessed from off campus. Internet access, online (class) registration, at least one staffed computer lab available.

Student Life *Housing:* college housing not available. *Activities and Organizations:* student-run newspaper.

Standardized Tests *Required for some:* ACT (for placement).

Costs (2004–05) *Tuition:* state resident $2004 full-time, $67 per credit hour part-time; nonresident $349 per credit hour part-time. *Required fees:* $160 full-time.

Financial Aid Of all full-time matriculated undergraduates who enrolled, 20 Federal Work-Study jobs (averaging $1700). 50 state and other part-time jobs (averaging $2000).

Applying *Options:* early admission, deferred entrance. *Required:* high school transcript. *Application deadline:* rolling (freshmen), rolling (transfers).

Admissions Contact Ms. Jody Brown, Student Services, Morgan Community College, Student Services, 17800 Road 20, Fort Morgan, CO 80701. *Phone:* 970-542-3156. *Toll-free phone:* 800-622-0216. *Fax:* 970-867-6608. *E-mail:* jody.brown@mcc.cccoes.edu.

NORTHEASTERN JUNIOR COLLEGE
Sterling, Colorado

- **State-supported** 2-year, founded 1941, part of Colorado Community College and Occupational Education System
- **Calendar** semesters
- **Degree** certificates and associate
- **Small-town** 65-acre campus
- **Endowment** $800,000
- **Coed**

Faculty *Student/faculty ratio:* 4:1.

Student Life *Campus security:* 24-hour emergency response devices, controlled dormitory access, night patrols by trained security personnel.

Athletics Member NJCAA.

Standardized Tests *Required for some:* SAT I or ACT (for placement). *Recommended:* ACT (for placement).

Costs (2003–04) *Tuition:* state resident $66 per credit hour part-time; nonresident $276 per credit hour part-time. *Required fees:* $7 per credit hour part-time.

Applying *Options:* common application, electronic application, early admission, deferred entrance. *Required:* high school transcript.

Admissions Contact Ms. Tina Joyce, Director of Admissions, Northeastern Junior College, 100 College Avenue, Sterling, CO 80751. *Phone:* 970-521-7000. *Toll-free phone:* 800-626-4637. *Fax:* 970-521-6801. *E-mail:* tina.joyce@njc.edu.

OTERO JUNIOR COLLEGE
La Junta, Colorado

- **State-supported** 2-year, founded 1941, part of Colorado Community College and Occupational Education System
- **Calendar** semesters
- **Degree** certificates and associate
- **Rural** 50-acre campus
- **Coed,** 1,650 undergraduate students, 55% full-time, 62% women, 38% men

Undergraduates 905 full-time, 745 part-time. Students come from 10 states and territories, 10 other countries, 2% are from out of state, 2% African American, 0.8% Asian American or Pacific Islander, 30% Hispanic American, 1% Native American, 15% transferred in, 13% live on campus.
Freshmen *Admission:* 428 enrolled.
Faculty *Total:* 73, 42% full-time.
Majors Administrative assistant and secretarial science; agricultural business and management; automobile/automotive mechanics technology; biological and physical sciences; biology/biological sciences; business administration and management; child development; computer management; data processing and data processing technology; dramatic/theatre arts; education; elementary education; history; humanities; kindergarten/preschool education; legal administrative assistant/secretary; liberal arts and sciences/liberal studies; literature; mathematics; medical administrative assistant and medical secretary; modern languages; nursing (registered nurse training); physical sciences; political science and government; pre-engineering; psychology; social sciences.
Academic Programs *Special study options:* academic remediation for entering students, adult/continuing education programs, advanced placement credit, distance learning, external degree program, internships, part-time degree program, summer session for credit.
Library Wheeler Library with 35,638 titles, 300 serial subscriptions, an OPAC.
Computers on Campus 100 computers available on campus for general student use. A campuswide network can be accessed from student residence rooms. Internet access, at least one staffed computer lab available.
Student Life *Housing:* on-campus residence required for freshman year. *Options:* coed. Campus housing is university owned. *Activities and Organizations:* drama/theater group, student-run newspaper, choral group. *Campus security:* 24-hour patrols, late-night transport/escort service. *Student services:* personal/psychological counseling.
Athletics Member NJCAA. *Intercollegiate sports:* baseball M(s), basketball M(s)/W(s), golf M(s)/W(s), softball W(s), volleyball W(s). *Intramural sports:* basketball M, volleyball M/W.
Standardized Tests *Recommended:* SAT I or ACT (for placement).
Costs (2004–05) *Tuition:* state resident $1603 full-time; nonresident $6626 full-time. Full-time tuition and fees vary according to reciprocity agreements. Part-time tuition and fees vary according to reciprocity agreements. *Required fees:* $184 full-time. *Room and board:* $4200. Room and board charges vary according to board plan. *Payment plan:* installment.
Financial Aid Of all full-time matriculated undergraduates who enrolled, 30 Federal Work-Study jobs (averaging $2000). 100 state and other part-time jobs (averaging $2000).
Applying *Options:* electronic application, early admission. *Recommended:* high school transcript. *Application deadlines:* 8/30 (freshmen), 8/30 (transfers). *Notification:* continuous (freshmen), continuous (transfers).
Admissions Contact Mr. Brad Franz, Vice President for Student Services, Otero Junior College, 1802 Colorado Avenue, La Junta, CO 81050-3415. *Phone:* 719-384-6833. *Fax:* 719-384-6933. *E-mail:* j_schiro@ojc.cccoes.edu.

PARKS COLLEGE
Aurora, Colorado

Admissions Contact Mr. Rick Harding, Director of Admissions, Parks College, 14280 East Jewell Avenue, Suite 100, Aurora, CO 80014. *Phone:* 303-745-6244.

PARKS COLLEGE
Denver, Colorado

Admissions Contact Ms. JoAnn Q. Navarro, Director of Admissions, Parks College, 9065 Grant Street, Denver, CO 80229-4339. *Phone:* 303-457-2757.

PIKES PEAK COMMUNITY COLLEGE
Colorado Springs, Colorado

- **State-supported** 2-year, founded 1968, part of Colorado Community College System
- **Calendar** semesters
- **Degree** certificates and associate
- **Urban** 287-acre campus with easy access to Denver
- **Endowment** $1.4 million
- **Coed,** 10,581 undergraduate students, 35% full-time, 58% women, 42% men

Undergraduates 3,658 full-time, 6,923 part-time. Students come from 48 states and territories, 90 other countries, 12% are from out of state, 11% African American, 4% Asian American or Pacific Islander, 12% Hispanic American, 2% Native American, 0.8% international, 6% transferred in.
Freshmen *Admission:* 2,455 applied, 2,455 admitted, 2,286 enrolled.
Faculty *Total:* 673, 22% full-time. *Student/faculty ratio:* 18:1.
Majors Accounting technology and bookkeeping; architectural engineering technology; autobody/collision and repair technology; automobile/automotive mechanics technology; building/property maintenance and management; business administration and management; child development; construction management; cooking and related culinary arts; criminal justice/law enforcement administration; dental assisting; electrical, electronic and communications engineering technology; emergency medical technology (EMT paramedic); fire protection and safety technology; general studies; graphic communications; interior design; landscaping and groundskeeping; legal assistant/paralegal; liberal arts and sciences and humanities related; liberal arts and sciences/liberal studies; machine shop technology; management information systems; medical office management; natural resources management and policy; nursing (registered nurse training); psychiatric/mental health services technology; robotics technology; sign language interpretation and translation; system, networking, and LAN/wan management; welding technology.
Academic Programs *Special study options:* academic remediation for entering students, adult/continuing education programs, advanced placement credit, cooperative education, distance learning, double majors, English as a second language, independent study, internships, part-time degree program, services for LD students, summer session for credit. *ROTC:* Army (c).
Library PPCC Library plus 1 other with 34,332 titles, 311 serial subscriptions, 3,832 audiovisual materials, an OPAC.
Computers on Campus 180 computers available on campus for general student use. A campuswide network can be accessed from off campus. Internet access, online (class) registration, at least one staffed computer lab available.
Student Life *Housing:* college housing not available. *Activities and Organizations:* drama/theater group, student-run newspaper. *Campus security:* 24-hour emergency response devices and patrols, late-night transport/escort service. *Student services:* women's center.
Athletics *Intercollegiate sports:* basketball M, soccer M, volleyball W.
Standardized Tests *Recommended:* SAT I or ACT (for placement).
Costs (2004–05) *Tuition:* state resident $2004 full-time, $67 per credit hour part-time; nonresident $10,469 full-time, $349 per credit hour part-time. Full-time tuition and fees vary according to course load. Part-time tuition and fees vary according to course load. *Required fees:* $151 full-time, $39 per term part-time. *Payment plan:* deferred payment. *Waivers:* senior citizens and employees or children of employees.
Financial Aid Of all full-time matriculated undergraduates who enrolled, 146 Federal Work-Study jobs (averaging $1960). 275 state and other part-time jobs (averaging $2045).
Applying *Required for some:* high school transcript. *Application deadline:* rolling (freshmen), rolling (transfers).
Admissions Contact Mr. Troy Nelson, Associate Director, Enrollment Services, Admissions, Pikes Peak Community College, 5675 South Academy Boulevard, Colorado Springs, CO 80906-5498. *Phone:* 719-540-7041. *Toll-free phone:* 866-411-7722. *Fax:* 719-540-7092. *E-mail:* admissions@ppcc.edu.

PIMA MEDICAL INSTITUTE
Colorado Springs, Colorado

Admissions Contact Ms. Karen McGrath, Campus Director, Pima Medical Institute, 370 Printer Parkway, Colorado Springs, CO 80910. *Phone:* 719-482-7462.

PIMA MEDICAL INSTITUTE
Denver, Colorado

Admissions Contact Ms. Susan J. Anderson, Campus Director, Pima Medical Institute, 1701 West 72nd Avenue, Suite 130, Denver, CO 80221. *Phone:* 303-426-1800.

PLATT COLLEGE
Aurora, Colorado

Admissions Contact Admissions Office, Platt College, 3100 South Parker Road, Suite 200, Aurora, CO 80014-3141. *Phone:* 303-369-5151. *E-mail:* admissions@plattcolo.com.

PUEBLO COMMUNITY COLLEGE
Pueblo, Colorado

- **State-supported** 2-year, founded 1933, part of Colorado Community College and Occupational Education System
- **Calendar** semesters
- **Degree** certificates and associate
- **Urban** 35-acre campus
- **Endowment** $5.4 million
- **Coed**

Faculty *Student/faculty ratio:* 19:1.

Student Life *Campus security:* 24-hour emergency response devices, late-night transport/escort service.

Standardized Tests *Required for some:* ACT (for placement).

Costs (2004–05) *Tuition:* state resident $1982 full-time, $66 per credit hour part-time; nonresident $10,355 full-time, $345 per credit hour part-time. *Required fees:* $283 full-time, $19 per credit hour part-time.

Financial Aid Of all full-time matriculated undergraduates who enrolled, 116 Federal Work-Study jobs (averaging $1450). 207 state and other part-time jobs (averaging $2235).

Applying *Options:* electronic application, early admission, deferred entrance.

Admissions Contact Pueblo Community College, 900 West Orman Avenue, Pueblo, CO 81004. *Phone:* 719-549-3010. *Fax:* 719-549-3012. *E-mail:* mary.santoro@pueblocc.edu.

RED ROCKS COMMUNITY COLLEGE
Lakewood, Colorado

- **State-supported** 2-year, founded 1969, part of Colorado Community College and Occupational Education System
- **Calendar** semesters
- **Degree** certificates and associate
- **Urban** 120-acre campus with easy access to Denver
- **Coed**, 7,693 undergraduate students, 29% full-time, 48% women, 52% men

Undergraduates 2,264 full-time, 5,429 part-time. Students come from 27 states and territories, 1% African American, 2% Asian American or Pacific Islander, 11% Hispanic American, 2% Native American, 2% international.

Freshmen *Admission:* 4,499 applied, 4,499 admitted, 1,335 enrolled.

Faculty *Total:* 424, 17% full-time. *Student/faculty ratio:* 9:1.

Majors Accounting; administrative assistant and secretarial science; art; biological and physical sciences; biology/biological sciences; business administration and management; carpentry; chemistry; computer engineering technology; computer programming; computer science; criminal justice/law enforcement administration; drafting and design technology; economics; electrical, electronic and communications engineering technology; English; fire science; French; geology/earth science; German; heavy equipment maintenance technology; history; humanities; hydrology and water resources science; liberal arts and sciences/liberal studies; marketing/marketing management; mass communication/media; mathematics; mechanical engineering/mechanical technology; physics; political science and government; psychology; public administration; real estate; sanitation technology; sociology; solar energy technology; Spanish; survey technology; welding technology.

Academic Programs *Special study options:* academic remediation for entering students, adult/continuing education programs, cooperative education, English as a second language, off-campus study, part-time degree program, study abroad, summer session for credit. *ROTC:* Army (c).

Library Marvin Buckels Library with 55,188 titles, 350 serial subscriptions, 4,497 audiovisual materials, an OPAC, a Web page.

Computers on Campus 580 computers available on campus for general student use. Internet access, online (class) registration, at least one staffed computer lab available.

Student Life *Housing:* college housing not available. *Activities and Organizations:* drama/theater group, student-run newspaper. *Campus security:* 24-hour emergency response devices and patrols. *Student services:* personal/psychological counseling, women's center.

Athletics *Intramural sports:* rock climbing M/W, volleyball M/W.

Costs (2003–04) *Tuition:* $84 per credit part-time. *Payment plan:* deferred payment.

Financial Aid Of all full-time matriculated undergraduates who enrolled, 21 Federal Work-Study jobs (averaging $2600). 65 state and other part-time jobs (averaging $3600).

Applying *Options:* early admission. *Application deadline:* rolling (freshmen), rolling (transfers). *Notification:* continuous (freshmen), continuous (transfers).

Admissions Contact Ms. Judy Beckmann, Director of Student Recruitment, Red Rocks Community College, 13300 West 6th Avenue Box 5, Lakewood, CO 80228-1255. *Phone:* 303-914-6234. *Fax:* 303-969-6919.

TRINIDAD STATE JUNIOR COLLEGE
Trinidad, Colorado

- **State-supported** 2-year, founded 1925, part of Colorado Community College and Occupational Education System
- **Calendar** semesters
- **Degree** certificates, diplomas, and associate
- **Small-town** 17-acre campus
- **Endowment** $3.2 million
- **Coed**, 2,022 undergraduate students, 47% full-time, 59% women, 41% men

Undergraduates 948 full-time, 1,074 part-time. Students come from 33 states and territories, 11 other countries, 3% African American, 0.5% Asian American or Pacific Islander, 42% Hispanic American, 3% Native American, 0.5% international, 2% transferred in, 30% live on campus. *Retention:* 60% of 2002 full-time freshmen returned.

Freshmen *Admission:* 1,017 applied, 1,017 admitted, 583 enrolled.

Faculty *Student/faculty ratio:* 20:1.

Majors Accounting; administrative assistant and secretarial science; art teacher education; automobile/automotive mechanics technology; biological and physical sciences; biology/biological sciences; business administration and management; carpentry; chemistry; civil engineering technology; commercial and advertising art; computer and information sciences related; computer science; computer systems networking and telecommunications; construction engineering technology; corrections; cosmetology; criminal justice/police science; data processing and data processing technology; design and visual communications; drafting and design technology; dramatic/theatre arts; education; electrical, electronic and communications engineering technology; engineering; English; farm and ranch management; forestry; heavy equipment maintenance technology; industrial technology; information science/studies; information technology; journalism; kindergarten/preschool education; landscape architecture; liberal arts and sciences/liberal studies; management information systems; marketing/marketing management; mining technology; music; natural resources management and policy; nursing assistant/aide and patient care assistant; nursing (licensed practical/vocational nurse training); nursing (registered nurse training); occupational safety and health technology; physical education teaching and coaching; pre-engineering; psychology; soil conservation; water quality and wastewater treatment management and recycling technology.

Academic Programs *Special study options:* academic remediation for entering students, accelerated degree program, adult/continuing education programs, advanced placement credit, cooperative education, distance learning, double majors, English as a second language, honors programs, independent study, internships, part-time degree program, services for LD students, student-designed majors, summer session for credit.

Library Frendenthal Library plus 1 other with 49,033 titles, 123 serial subscriptions, an OPAC.

Computers on Campus 125 computers available on campus for general student use. A campuswide network can be accessed from student residence rooms and from off campus. Internet access, online (class) registration, at least one staffed computer lab available.

Student Life *Housing Options:* coed, men-only, women-only. Campus housing is university owned. *Activities and Organizations:* drama/theater group, student-run newspaper, choral group, student association, International Club, Gunsmithing Club, Nursing Club, Cosmetology Club. *Campus security:* 24-hour emergency response devices and patrols, late-night transport/escort service.

Athletics Member NJCAA. *Intercollegiate sports:* baseball M(s), basketball M(s), softball W, volleyball W(s). *Intramural sports:* badminton M/W, basketball M, bowling M/W, football M/W, riflery M/W, skiing (cross-country) M/W, skiing (downhill) M/W, softball M/W, table tennis M/W, tennis M/W, volleyball M/W, weight lifting M/W.

Standardized Tests *Required for some:* ACT (for placement), ACT ASSET, ACCUPLACER. *Recommended:* SAT I and SAT II or ACT (for placement).

Costs (2003–04) *Tuition:* state resident $1982 full-time, $66 per credit part-time; nonresident $8284 full-time, $276 per credit part-time. *Required fees:* $143 full-time, $9 per credit part-time. *Room and board:* $4316. Room and board charges vary according to board plan. *Payment plan:* installment. *Waivers:* senior citizens and employees or children of employees.

Financial Aid Of all full-time matriculated undergraduates who enrolled, 30 Federal Work-Study jobs (averaging $2040). 40 state and other part-time jobs (averaging $2040).

Applying   *Options:* common application, electronic application, deferred entrance. *Required:* high school transcript. *Application deadline:* rolling (freshmen), rolling (transfers). *Notification:* continuous (freshmen), continuous (transfers).

Admissions Contact   Maria de la Cruz, Director, Trinidad State Junior College, 600 Prospect, Trinidad, CO 81082-2396. *Phone:* 719-846-5623. *Toll-free phone:* 800-621-8752. *Fax:* 719-846-5667.

WESTWOOD COLLEGE-DENVER SOUTH
Denver, Colorado

- **Proprietary** primarily 2-year
- **Calendar** continuous
- **Degrees** associate and bachelor's
- **Urban** campus with easy access to Denver, CO
- **Coed,** 429 undergraduate students, 69% full-time, 31% women, 69% men

Undergraduates   294 full-time, 135 part-time. 4% African American, 4% Asian American or Pacific Islander, 17% Hispanic American.

Freshmen   *Admission:* 303 applied, 177 admitted, 47 enrolled.

Faculty   *Total:* 38.

Majors   Accounting and business/management; commercial and advertising art; computer and information systems security; computer programming; computer programming (specific applications); computer systems networking and telecommunications; design and visual communications; e-commerce; electrical, electronic and communications engineering technology; graphic design; interior design; intermedia/multimedia; marketing/marketing management; system, networking, and LAN/wan management; web/multimedia management and webmaster.

Applying   *Required:* interview, HS diploma or GED and entrance exam (SAT/ACT or Accuplacer).

Admissions Contact   Mr. Ron DeJong, Director of Admissions, Westwood College-Denver South, 3150 South Sheridan Boulevard, Denver, CO 80227-5548. *Phone:* 303-934-2790. *Fax:* 303-934-2583. *E-mail:* info@westwood.edu.

▶ **See page 628 for a narrative description.**

WESTWOOD COLLEGE OF AVIATION TECHNOLOGY-DENVER
Broomfield, Colorado

- **Proprietary** 2-year, founded 1965
- **Calendar** continuous
- **Degree** certificates and associate
- **Suburban** 4-acre campus with easy access to Denver
- **Coed,** 951 undergraduate students, 100% full-time, 9% women, 91% men

Undergraduates   951 full-time. Students come from 47 states and territories, 59% are from out of state, 6% African American, 2% Asian American or Pacific Islander, 10% Hispanic American, 0.9% Native American, 1% international.

Freshmen   *Admission:* 951 enrolled.

Faculty   *Total:* 32.

Majors   Aircraft powerplant technology; airframe mechanics and aircraft maintenance technology; avionics maintenance technology.

Library   Resource Center.

Computers on Campus   A campuswide network can be accessed. At least one staffed computer lab available.

Student Life   *Housing:* college housing not available.

Financial Aid   Of all full-time matriculated undergraduates who enrolled, 20 Federal Work-Study jobs.

Applying   *Options:* electronic application. *Required:* interview, references, student profile. *Application deadline:* rolling (freshmen), rolling (transfers). *Notification:* continuous (freshmen), continuous (transfers).

Admissions Contact   Mr. Robert Lee, Director of Admissions, Westwood College of Aviation Technology-Denver, 10851 West 120th Avenue, Broomfield, CO 80021. *Phone:* 303-466-1714. *Toll-free phone:* 800-888-3995. *Fax:* 303-469-3797. *E-mail:* info@westwood.edu.

▶ **See page 640 for a narrative description.**

WESTWOOD COLLEGE-DENVER NORTH
Denver, Colorado

- **Proprietary** primarily 2-year, founded 1953
- **Calendar** 5 terms
- **Degrees** diplomas, associate, and bachelor's
- **Suburban** 11-acre campus
- **Coed,** 1,368 undergraduate students, 74% full-time, 29% women, 71% men

Undergraduates   1,010 full-time, 358 part-time. Students come from 31 states and territories, 3 other countries, 12% are from out of state, 4% African American, 4% Asian American or Pacific Islander, 18% Hispanic American, 3% Native American, 0.2% international, 0.5% transferred in. *Retention:* 28% of 2002 full-time freshmen returned.

Freshmen   *Admission:* 2,143 applied, 1,031 admitted, 254 enrolled.

Faculty   *Total:* 101, 41% full-time, 4% with terminal degrees. *Student/faculty ratio:* 16:1.

Majors   Accounting and business/management; animation, interactive technology, video graphics and special effects; architectural drafting and CAD/CADD; automobile/automotive mechanics technology; business/commerce; computer and information systems security; computer engineering technology; computer/information technology services administration related; computer programming; computer software technology; computer systems networking and telecommunications; design and visual communications; electrical, electronic and communications engineering technology; graphic design; heating, air conditioning, ventilation and refrigeration maintenance technology; interior architecture; interior design; marketing/marketing management; mechanical drafting and CAD/CADD; medical/clinical assistant; medical transcription; survey technology; web page, digital/multimedia and information resources design.

Academic Programs   *Special study options:* academic remediation for entering students, accelerated degree program, advanced placement credit, distance learning, independent study, internships, part-time degree program, services for LD students, summer session for credit.

Library   Westwood DNN Library with 2,500 titles, 160 serial subscriptions, 40 audiovisual materials, an OPAC.

Computers on Campus   30 computers available on campus for general student use. A campuswide network can be accessed. Internet access available.

Student Life   *Housing:* college housing not available. *Activities and Organizations:* American Institute of Graphic Arts, Social Club, Gaming Club. *Campus security:* 24-hour emergency response devices.

Standardized Tests   *Required for some:* ACCUPLACER. *Recommended:* SAT I and SAT II or ACT (for admission), SAT II: Writing Test (for admission).

Costs (2004-05)   *Tuition:* $18,645 full-time, $2654 per term part-time. Full-time tuition and fees vary according to course load and program. Part-time tuition and fees vary according to course load and program. *Required fees:* $950 full-time, $404 per credit part-time. *Payment plan:* installment. *Waivers:* employees or children of employees.

Applying   *Options:* deferred entrance. *Application fee:* $100. *Required:* high school transcript. *Recommended:* interview. *Application deadline:* rolling (freshmen), rolling (transfers). *Notification:* continuous (freshmen), continuous (transfers).

Admissions Contact   Ms. Nicole Blaschko, New Student Coordinator, Westwood College of Technology-Denver North, 7350 North Broadway, Denver, CO 80221-3653. *Phone:* 303-650-5050 Ext. 329. *Toll-free phone:* 800-992-5050.

▶ **See page 626 for a narrative description.**

CONNECTICUT

ASNUNTUCK COMMUNITY COLLEGE
Enfield, Connecticut

- **State-supported** 2-year, founded 1972, part of Connecticut Community College System
- **Calendar** semesters
- **Degree** certificates and associate
- **Suburban** 4-acre campus
- **Coed,** 1,476 undergraduate students, 31% full-time, 59% women, 41% men

Undergraduates   456 full-time, 1,020 part-time. Students come from 3 states and territories, 3% are from out of state, 6% African American, 2% Asian American or Pacific Islander, 3% Hispanic American, 0.1% Native American, 3% transferred in. *Retention:* 54% of 2002 full-time freshmen returned.

Freshmen   *Admission:* 521 applied, 521 admitted, 188 enrolled.

Faculty   *Total:* 122, 18% full-time. *Student/faculty ratio:* 9:1.

Majors   Accounting; administrative assistant and secretarial science; art; business administration and management; commercial and advertising art; computer science; criminal justice/safety; engineering science; general studies; human services; kindergarten/preschool education; liberal arts and sciences/liberal studies; mass communication/media; special products marketing; substance abuse/addiction counseling.

Connecticut

Asnuntuck Community College (continued)

Academic Programs *Special study options:* academic remediation for entering students, adult/continuing education programs, advanced placement credit, distance learning, double majors, English as a second language, independent study, internships, part-time degree program, services for LD students, student-designed majors, study abroad, summer session for credit.

Library ACTC Learning Resource Center with 31,700 titles, 257 serial subscriptions, 2,570 audiovisual materials, an OPAC.

Computers on Campus 90 computers available on campus for general student use. A campuswide network can be accessed from off campus. Internet access, at least one staffed computer lab available.

Student Life *Housing:* college housing not available. *Activities and Organizations:* drama/theater group, student-run newspaper, Phi Theta Kappa, Drama Club, Outdoor Club, Poetry Club, Ski Club. *Campus security:* 24-hour patrols, late-night transport/escort service. *Student services:* women's center.

Standardized Tests *Required for some:* SAT I (for placement).

Costs (2004–05) *Tuition:* state resident $2112 full-time, $88 per credit part-time; nonresident $6336 full-time, $264 per credit part-time. *Required fees:* $294 full-time, $53 per credit part-time.

Financial Aid Of all full-time matriculated undergraduates who enrolled, 20 Federal Work-Study jobs (averaging $3000). 5 state and other part-time jobs (averaging $3000).

Applying *Options:* deferred entrance. *Application fee:* $20. *Required:* high school transcript. *Application deadline:* rolling (freshmen), rolling (transfers). *Notification:* continuous (freshmen), continuous (transfers).

Admissions Contact Ms. Donna Shaw, Director of Admissions and Marketing, Asnuntuck Community College, 170 Elm Street, Enfield, CT 06082-3800. *Phone:* 860-253-3018. *Toll-free phone:* 800-501-3967. *Fax:* 860-253-3014.

BRIARWOOD COLLEGE
Southington, Connecticut

- **Proprietary** 2-year, founded 1966
- **Calendar** semesters
- **Degree** certificates, diplomas, and associate
- **Small-town** 32-acre campus with easy access to Boston and Hartford
- **Endowment** $27,595
- **Coed,** 588 undergraduate students, 66% full-time, 74% women, 26% men

Undergraduates 389 full-time, 199 part-time. Students come from 11 states and territories, 7% are from out of state, 20% African American, 1% Asian American or Pacific Islander, 10% Hispanic American, 0.7% Native American, 0.5% international, 14% transferred in, 21% live on campus.

Freshmen *Admission:* 772 applied, 510 admitted, 197 enrolled. *Test scores:* SAT verbal scores over 500: 16%; SAT math scores over 500: 19%; SAT verbal scores over 600: 3%; SAT math scores over 600: 16%; SAT verbal scores over 700: 3%; SAT math scores over 700: 16%.

Faculty *Total:* 91, 27% full-time.

Majors Accounting; administrative assistant and secretarial science; biotechnology; business administration and management; child development; communication/speech communication and rhetoric; criminal justice/law enforcement administration; dental assisting; dietetics; fashion merchandising; funeral service and mortuary science; general studies; health information/medical records administration; hotel/motel administration; legal administrative assistant/secretary; legal assistant/paralegal; medical administrative assistant and medical secretary; medical/clinical assistant; medical office management; occupational therapist assistant; radio and television broadcasting technology; tourism and travel services management.

Academic Programs *Special study options:* academic remediation for entering students, adult/continuing education programs, double majors, English as a second language, independent study, internships, part-time degree program, services for LD students, summer session for credit.

Library Pupillo Library with 11,500 titles, 154 serial subscriptions, 130 audiovisual materials, a Web page.

Computers on Campus 54 computers available on campus for general student use. Internet access, online (class) registration, at least one staffed computer lab available.

Student Life *Housing Options:* coed. *Activities and Organizations:* student-run radio station, student government, Yearbook Committee, Student Ambassador Club, F.A.M.E. (Fashion Merchandising Club). *Campus security:* 24-hour patrols, late-night transport/escort service. *Student services:* personal/psychological counseling.

Athletics *Intramural sports:* basketball M, softball M/W, tennis M/W, volleyball M/W.

Standardized Tests *Required:* College Board Diagnostic Tests (for placement).

Costs (2004–05) *Tuition:* $14,625 full-time, $485 per credit part-time. Part-time tuition and fees vary according to course load and program. *Required*

fees: $220 full-time, $125 per term part-time. *Room only:* $3200. *Payment plan:* installment. *Waivers:* employees or children of employees.

Financial Aid Of all full-time matriculated undergraduates who enrolled, 33 Federal Work-Study jobs (averaging $600). 30 state and other part-time jobs.

Applying *Options:* common application, electronic application. *Application fee:* $25. *Required:* high school transcript. *Required for some:* essay or personal statement, letters of recommendation, interview. *Application deadline:* rolling (freshmen), rolling (transfers).

Admissions Contact Ms. Donna Yamanis, Director of Enrollment Management, Briarwood College, 2279 Mount Vernon Road, Southington, CT 06489. *Phone:* 860-628-4751 Ext. 133. *Toll-free phone:* 800-952-2444. *Fax:* 860-628-6444.

► See page 522 for a narrative description.

CAPITAL COMMUNITY COLLEGE
Hartford, Connecticut

- **State-supported** 2-year, founded 1946, part of Connecticut Community College System
- **Calendar** semesters
- **Degree** certificates and associate
- **Urban** 10-acre campus
- **Coed,** 3,317 undergraduate students, 26% full-time, 71% women, 29% men

Undergraduates 848 full-time, 2,469 part-time. Students come from 3 states and territories, 37% African American, 3% Asian American or Pacific Islander, 26% Hispanic American, 0.2% Native American, 0.4% international.

Freshmen *Admission:* 665 enrolled.

Faculty *Total:* 223, 23% full-time, 6% with terminal degrees.

Majors Accounting; administrative assistant and secretarial science; business administration and management; computer and information sciences; computer and information sciences related; computer engineering technology; data entry/microcomputer applications related; electrical, electronic and communications engineering technology; emergency medical technology (EMT paramedic); fire protection and safety technology; fire services administration; information technology; kindergarten/preschool education; liberal arts and sciences/liberal studies; medical/clinical assistant; medical radiologic technology; nursing (registered nurse training); physical therapist assistant; social work; web page, digital/multimedia and information resources design.

Academic Programs *Special study options:* academic remediation for entering students, accelerated degree program, adult/continuing education programs, advanced placement credit, distance learning, double majors, English as a second language, independent study, internships, part-time degree program, services for LD students, summer session for credit.

Library Arthur C. Banks, Jr. Library plus 1 other with 46,760 titles, 359 serial subscriptions, 2,409 audiovisual materials, an OPAC, a Web page.

Computers on Campus 180 computers available on campus for general student use. A campuswide network can be accessed from off campus. Internet access, at least one staffed computer lab available.

Student Life *Housing:* college housing not available. *Activities and Organizations:* drama/theater group, choral group, Latin American Student Association, Student Senate, Senior Renewal Club, Early Childhood Club, Pre-Professional Club. *Campus security:* late-night transport/escort service, security staff during hours of operation, emergency telephones 7 a.m.—11 p.m. *Student services:* personal/psychological counseling.

Standardized Tests *Required for some:* SAT I (for placement).

Costs (2003–04) *Tuition:* state resident $2028 full-time, $85 per credit hour part-time; nonresident $6084 full-time, $254 per credit hour part-time. Part-time tuition and fees vary according to course load. *Required fees:* $282 full-time. *Waivers:* employees or children of employees.

Financial Aid Of all full-time matriculated undergraduates who enrolled, 74 Federal Work-Study jobs, 190 state and other part-time jobs.

Applying *Application fee:* $20. *Recommended:* high school transcript. *Application deadline:* rolling (freshmen), rolling (transfers). *Notification:* continuous until 9/1 (freshmen), continuous until 9/1 (transfers).

Admissions Contact Ms. Jackie Phillips, Director of the Welcome and Advising Center, Capital Community College, 950 Main Street, Hartford, CT 06103. *Phone:* 860-906-5078. *Toll-free phone:* 800-894-6126. *E-mail:* mball-davis@ccc.commnet.edu.

GATEWAY COMMUNITY COLLEGE
New Haven, Connecticut

- **State-supported** 2-year, founded 1992, part of Connecticut Community College System
- **Calendar** semesters
- **Degree** certificates and associate

- **Urban** 5-acre campus with easy access to New York City
- **Coed**

Faculty *Student/faculty ratio:* 20:1.
Student Life *Campus security:* late-night transport/escort service.
Athletics Member NJCAA.
Financial Aid Of all full-time matriculated undergraduates who enrolled, 60 Federal Work-Study jobs (averaging $6000).
Applying *Options:* early admission, deferred entrance. *Application fee:* $20. *Required:* high school transcript. *Required for some:* essay or personal statement, interview.
Admissions Contact Ms. Catherine Surface, Director of Admissions, Gateway Community College, 60 Sargent Drive, New Haven, CT 06511. *Phone:* 203-789-7043. *Toll-free phone:* 800-390-7723. *Fax:* 203-285-2018. *E-mail:* gateway_ctc@commnet.edu.

GIBBS COLLEGE
Norwalk, Connecticut

- **Proprietary** 2-year, founded 1975, part of Career Education Corporation
- **Calendar** quarters
- **Degree** certificates and associate
- **Suburban** 2-acre campus with easy access to New York City
- **Coed**

Faculty *Student/faculty ratio:* 20:1.
Student Life *Campus security:* 24-hour emergency response devices.
Costs (2003–04) *Tuition:* $13,488 full-time. No tuition increase for student's term of enrollment. *Required fees:* $100 full-time. *Payment plans:* tuition prepayment, installment, deferred payment.
Applying *Options:* common application, electronic application, deferred entrance. *Application fee:* $50. *Required:* high school transcript, interview. *Recommended:* essay or personal statement.
Admissions Contact Mr. Ted Havelka, Vice President of Admissions/Marketing, Gibbs College, 148 East Avenue, Norwalk, CT 06851. *Phone:* 203-633-2311. *Toll-free phone:* 800-845-5333. *Fax:* 203-899-0788. *E-mail:* norwalkadmissions@gibbsnorwalk.com.

GOODWIN COLLEGE
East Hartford, Connecticut

- **Proprietary** 2-year
- **Calendar** semesters
- **Degree** certificates, diplomas, and associate
- **Urban** campus with easy access to Hartford
- **Endowment** $1.0 million
- **Coed,** 667 undergraduate students, 42% full-time, 81% women, 19% men

Undergraduates 282 full-time, 385 part-time. Students come from 1 other state, 33% African American, 2% Asian American or Pacific Islander, 17% Hispanic American, 0.3% Native American, 17% transferred in.
Freshmen *Admission:* 470 applied, 392 admitted, 392 enrolled. *Average high school GPA:* 2.8.
Faculty *Total:* 62, 29% full-time, 3% with terminal degrees. *Student/faculty ratio:* 7:1.
Majors Accounting technology and bookkeeping; administrative assistant and secretarial science; business/commerce; computer and information sciences; computer/technical support; entrepreneurship; medical administrative assistant and medical secretary; medical/clinical assistant; medical insurance coding; non-profit management; nursing (registered nurse training); operations management.
Academic Programs *Special study options:* academic remediation for entering students, accelerated degree program, adult/continuing education programs, advanced placement credit, cooperative education, distance learning, double majors, English as a second language, external degree program, honors programs, independent study, internships, off-campus study, part-time degree program, services for LD students, summer session for credit.
Library Goodwin College Library with 6,000 titles, 1,300 serial subscriptions, 506 audiovisual materials, an OPAC.
Computers on Campus 220 computers available on campus for general student use. A campuswide network can be accessed from off campus. Internet access, at least one staffed computer lab available.
Student Life *Housing:* college housing not available. *Campus security:* evening security patrolman.
Standardized Tests *Required:* ACCUPLACER (for placement). *Recommended:* SAT I and SAT II or ACT (for placement), SAT II: Writing Test (for placement).
Costs (2003–04) *Tuition:* $11,600 full-time, $350 per credit part-time. Full-time tuition and fees vary according to course load, program, and student level.

Part-time tuition and fees vary according to course load, program, and student level. *Required fees:* $250 full-time. *Payment plans:* installment, deferred payment. *Waivers:* employees or children of employees.
Applying *Options:* common application, electronic application, deferred entrance. *Application fee:* $25. *Required:* essay or personal statement, high school transcript, minimum 2.0 GPA, medical exam. *Recommended:* 2 letters of recommendation, interview. *Notification:* continuous until 8/1 (freshmen), continuous until 8/1 (transfers).
Admissions Contact Daniel P. Noonan, Director of Enrollment and Student Services, Goodwin College, 745 Burnside Avenue, East Hartford, CT 06108. *Phone:* 860-528-4111 Ext. 230. *Toll-free phone:* 800-889-3282. *Fax:* 860-291-9550. *E-mail:* dnoonan@goodwin.edu.

HOUSATONIC COMMUNITY COLLEGE
Bridgeport, Connecticut

- **State-supported** 2-year, founded 1965, part of Connecticut Community-Technical College System
- **Calendar** semesters
- **Degree** certificates and associate
- **Urban** 4-acre campus with easy access to New York City
- **Coed**

Faculty *Student/faculty ratio:* 17:1.
Student Life *Campus security:* 24-hour emergency response devices, late-night transport/escort service.
Standardized Tests *Required for some:* ACCUPLACER.
Costs (2003–04) *Tuition:* state resident $2028 full-time, $85 per credit hour part-time; nonresident $6084 full-time, $254 per credit hour part-time. Part-time tuition and fees vary according to course load. *Required fees:* $262 full-time.
Financial Aid Of all full-time matriculated undergraduates who enrolled, 70 Federal Work-Study jobs (averaging $2850).
Applying *Options:* common application, deferred entrance. *Application fee:* $20. *Required:* high school transcript. *Required for some:* letters of recommendation, interview.
Admissions Contact Ms. Delores Y. Curtis, Director of Admissions, Housatonic Community College, 900 Lafayette Boulevard, Bridgeport, CT 06604-4704. *Phone:* 203-332-5102.

INTERNATIONAL COLLEGE OF HOSPITALITY MANAGEMENT, CÉSAR RITZ
Washington, Connecticut

- **Proprietary** primarily 2-year, founded 1992
- **Calendar** continuous
- **Degrees** certificates, associate, and bachelor's
- **Small-town** 27-acre campus with easy access to New York City
- **Coed**

The International College of Hospitality Management, César Ritz, is the only Swiss college of hospitality management in the United States. The Swiss tradition of *hôtellerie*, combined with practical experience obtained on paid internships in the best American hospitality properties, prepares students for managerial positions in the fastest-growing industry in the world.

Faculty *Student/faculty ratio:* 6:1.
Student Life *Campus security:* 24-hour emergency response devices, student patrols, late-night transport/escort service, controlled dormitory access, weekend patrols by trained security personnel.
Standardized Tests *Recommended:* SAT I (for admission).
Applying *Options:* common application, electronic application, deferred entrance. *Application fee:* $25. *Required:* high school transcript, 2 letters of recommendation. *Required for some:* essay or personal statement, interview. *Recommended:* interview.
Admissions Contact Ms. Jacqueline Ocholla, Enrollment Coordinator, International College of Hospitality Management, *César Ritz*, 101 Wykeham Road, Washington, CT 06793-1310. *Phone:* 860-868-9555 Ext. 126. *Toll-free phone:* 800-955-0809. *Fax:* 860-868-2114. *E-mail:* admissions@ichm.cc.ct.us.

▶ See page 556 for a narrative description.

MANCHESTER COMMUNITY COLLEGE
Manchester, Connecticut

- **State-supported** 2-year, founded 1963, part of Connecticut Community College System
- **Calendar** semesters

Manchester Community College (continued)
- **Degree** certificates and associate
- **Small-town** 160-acre campus with easy access to Hartford
- **Coed,** 5,717 undergraduate students, 39% full-time, 56% women, 44% men

Undergraduates 2,238 full-time, 3,479 part-time. Students come from 5 states and territories, 1% are from out of state, 13% African American, 3% Asian American or Pacific Islander, 10% Hispanic American, 0.5% Native American, 0.8% international, 10% transferred in.

Freshmen *Admission:* 1,995 applied, 1,995 admitted, 695 enrolled.

Faculty *Total:* 301, 28% full-time. *Student/faculty ratio:* 22:1.

Majors Accounting; administrative assistant and secretarial science; business administration and management; clinical/medical laboratory technology; commercial and advertising art; communication/speech communication and rhetoric; criminal justice/law enforcement administration; dramatic/theatre arts; engineering science; fine/studio arts; general studies; hotel/motel administration; human services; industrial engineering; industrial technology; information science/studies; journalism; kindergarten/preschool education; legal administrative assistant/secretary; legal assistant/paralegal; liberal arts and sciences/liberal studies; management information systems; marketing/marketing management; medical administrative assistant and medical secretary; music; occupational therapist assistant; physical therapist assistant; respiratory care therapy; social work; surgical technology; teacher assistant/aide.

Academic Programs *Special study options:* academic remediation for entering students, adult/continuing education programs, cooperative education, distance learning, double majors, English as a second language, honors programs, independent study, internships, off-campus study, part-time degree program, services for LD students, student-designed majors, summer session for credit. *ROTC:* Army (c).

Library 45,265 titles, 493 serial subscriptions, 2,481 audiovisual materials.

Student Life *Housing:* college housing not available. *Activities and Organizations:* drama/theater group, student-run newspaper, choral group. *Student services:* women's center.

Athletics Member NJCAA. *Intercollegiate sports:* baseball M, basketball M/W, soccer M/W, softball W.

Costs (2003–04) *Tuition:* state resident $2028 full-time, $84 per credit hour part-time; nonresident $6084 full-time, $253 per credit hour part-time. *Required fees:* $282 full-time.

Financial Aid Of all full-time matriculated undergraduates who enrolled, 100 Federal Work-Study jobs (averaging $2000). 25 state and other part-time jobs (averaging $2000).

Applying *Options:* electronic application, deferred entrance. *Application fee:* $20. *Required:* high school transcript. *Application deadline:* rolling (freshmen). *Notification:* continuous (freshmen), continuous (transfers).

Admissions Contact Mr. Peter Harris, Director of Admissions, Manchester Community College, PO Box 1046, MS #12, Manchester, CT 06045-1046. *Phone:* 860-512-3210. *Fax:* 860-512-3221.

MIDDLESEX COMMUNITY COLLEGE
Middletown, Connecticut

- **State-supported** 2-year, founded 1966, part of Connecticut Community College System
- **Calendar** semesters
- **Degree** certificates and associate
- **Suburban** 38-acre campus with easy access to Hartford
- **Coed,** 2,400 undergraduate students, 31% full-time, 62% women, 38% men

Undergraduates 752 full-time, 1,648 part-time. Students come from 4 states and territories, 1% are from out of state, 7% African American, 3% Asian American or Pacific Islander, 8% Hispanic American, 0.3% Native American, 0.5% international. *Retention:* 44% of 2002 full-time freshmen returned.

Freshmen *Admission:* 1,163 applied, 1,163 admitted, 349 enrolled.

Faculty *Total:* 120, 33% full-time.

Majors Accounting; administrative assistant and secretarial science; biological and physical sciences; biology/biotechnology laboratory technician; broadcast journalism; business administration and management; commercial and advertising art; computer programming; engineering science; engineering technology; environmental studies; fine/studio arts; human services; industrial radiologic technology; intermedia/multimedia; legal administrative assistant/secretary; liberal arts and sciences/liberal studies; marketing/marketing management; mass communication/media; medical administrative assistant and medical secretary; mental health/rehabilitation; ophthalmic laboratory technology; pre-engineering; radio and television; substance abuse/addiction counseling.

Academic Programs *Special study options:* academic remediation for entering students, advanced placement credit, cooperative education, distance learning, double majors, English as a second language, honors programs, independent study, internships, off-campus study, part-time degree program, services for LD students, summer session for credit. *ROTC:* Army (b).

Library Jean Burr Smith Library with 45,000 titles, 180 serial subscriptions, an OPAC, a Web page.

Computers on Campus 50 computers available on campus for general student use. A campuswide network can be accessed from off campus. Internet access, at least one staffed computer lab available.

Student Life *Housing:* college housing not available. *Activities and Organizations:* student-run radio station, Collegiate Secretaries International, Minority Opportunities in Education, Radio Club. *Campus security:* 24-hour patrols. *Student services:* personal/psychological counseling, women's center.

Standardized Tests *Required:* ACCUPLACER (for placement).

Costs (2004–05) *Tuition:* state resident $2028 full-time, $74 per semester hour part-time; nonresident $6084 full-time, $220 per semester hour part-time. *Required fees:* $282 full-time, $47 per semester part-time.

Financial Aid Of all full-time matriculated undergraduates who enrolled, 50 Federal Work-Study jobs (averaging $5000). 2 state and other part-time jobs (averaging $5000).

Applying *Options:* early admission, deferred entrance. *Application fee:* $20. *Required:* high school transcript, CPT. *Application deadline:* rolling (freshmen), rolling (transfers).

Admissions Contact Dr. Walter Clark MSW, JD, Director of Admissions, Middlesex Community College, 100 Training Hill Road, Middletown, CT 06457-4889. *Phone:* 860-343-5897. *Fax:* 860-344-7488.

NAUGATUCK VALLEY COMMUNITY COLLEGE
Waterbury, Connecticut

- **State-supported** 2-year, founded 1992, part of Connecticut Community-Technical College System
- **Calendar** semesters
- **Degree** certificates and associate
- **Urban** 110-acre campus
- **Coed,** 5,155 undergraduate students

Undergraduates 8% African American, 3% Asian American or Pacific Islander, 10% Hispanic American, 0.4% Native American, 1% international.

Freshmen *Admission:* 2,858 applied, 1,313 admitted.

Faculty *Total:* 210. *Student/faculty ratio:* 5:1.

Majors Accounting; administrative assistant and secretarial science; American studies; automobile/automotive mechanics technology; biological and physical sciences; business administration and management; chemical engineering; computer/information technology services administration related; computer programming; computer programming (specific applications); criminal justice/law enforcement administration; drafting and design technology; electrical, electronic and communications engineering technology; engineering technology; environmental studies; finance; fire science; gerontology; history; horticultural science; hospitality administration; hotel/motel administration; human services; industrial radiologic technology; industrial technology; information science/studies; information technology; international relations and affairs; kindergarten/preschool education; kinesiology and exercise science; legal administrative assistant/secretary; legal assistant/paralegal; liberal arts and sciences/liberal studies; marketing/marketing management; mathematics; mechanical engineering/mechanical technology; medical administrative assistant and medical secretary; mental health/rehabilitation; music; natural sciences; nursing (registered nurse training); physical sciences; physical therapist assistant; pre-engineering; quality control technology; social work; special products marketing; substance abuse/addiction counseling; system administration; word processing.

Academic Programs *Special study options:* academic remediation for entering students, accelerated degree program, adult/continuing education programs, advanced placement credit, cooperative education, English as a second language, external degree program, independent study, internships, off-campus study, part-time degree program, services for LD students, student-designed majors, study abroad, summer session for credit.

Library Max R. Traurig Learning Resource Center with 35,000 titles, 520 serial subscriptions, an OPAC, a Web page.

Computers on Campus 450 computers available on campus for general student use. A campuswide network can be accessed. Internet access, at least one staffed computer lab available.

Student Life *Housing:* college housing not available. *Activities and Organizations:* drama/theater group, student-run newspaper, choral group, Student Senate, Choral Society, Automotive Technician Club, Human Service Club, Legal Assistant Club. *Campus security:* 24-hour emergency response devices and patrols, late-night transport/escort service, security escort service. *Student services:* health clinic, personal/psychological counseling.

Athletics Member NJCAA. *Intercollegiate sports:* baseball M, basketball M/W, softball W.

Standardized Tests *Required:* ACCUPLACER (for placement). *Required for some:* SAT I (for placement).

Costs (2004–05) *Tuition:* state resident $2406 full-time; nonresident $7178 full-time. Full-time tuition and fees vary according to course level.

Financial Aid Of all full-time matriculated undergraduates who enrolled, 70 Federal Work-Study jobs (averaging $1942). 16 state and other part-time jobs (averaging $1660).

Applying *Options:* deferred entrance. *Application fee:* $20. *Required:* high school transcript. *Required for some:* interview. *Application deadline:* rolling (freshmen), rolling (transfers). *Notification:* continuous (freshmen), continuous (transfers).

Admissions Contact Ms. Lucretia Sveda, Director of Enrollment Services, Naugatuck Valley Community College, Waterbury, CT 06708. *Phone:* 203-575-8016. *Fax:* 203-596-8766. *E-mail:* nv_admissions@commnet.edu.

NORTHWESTERN CONNECTICUT COMMUNITY COLLEGE
Winsted, Connecticut

- **State-supported** 2-year, founded 1965, part of Connecticut Community-Technical College System
- **Calendar** semesters
- **Degree** certificates and associate
- **Small-town** 5-acre campus with easy access to Hartford
- **Coed,** 1,543 undergraduate students, 33% full-time, 65% women, 35% men

Undergraduates 510 full-time, 1,033 part-time. Students come from 6 states and territories, 1% are from out of state, 3% African American, 2% Asian American or Pacific Islander, 3% Hispanic American, 0.3% Native American, 0.2% international, 7% transferred in. *Retention:* 60% of 2002 full-time freshmen returned.

Freshmen *Admission:* 361 applied, 361 admitted, 252 enrolled.

Faculty *Total:* 87, 32% full-time. *Student/faculty ratio:* 18:1.

Majors Accounting; administrative assistant and secretarial science; art; behavioral sciences; biology/biological sciences; business administration and management; child development; commercial and advertising art; communications technology; computer engineering technology; computer graphics; computer programming; computer science; criminal justice/law enforcement administration; criminal justice/police science; electrical, electronic and communications engineering technology; engineering; English; health science; human services; information science/studies; kindergarten/preschool education; legal assistant/paralegal; liberal arts and sciences/liberal studies; mathematics; medical/clinical assistant; parks, recreation and leisure; parks, recreation and leisure facilities management; physical sciences; pre-engineering; sign language interpretation and translation; social sciences; substance abuse/addiction counseling; therapeutic recreation; veterinary technology.

Academic Programs *Special study options:* academic remediation for entering students, adult/continuing education programs, advanced placement credit, cooperative education, distance learning, double majors, English as a second language, independent study, internships, part-time degree program, services for LD students, summer session for credit.

Library Northwestern Connecticut Community-Technical College Learning Center with 37,666 titles, 267 serial subscriptions, 1,599 audiovisual materials, an OPAC.

Computers on Campus 90 computers available on campus for general student use. A campuswide network can be accessed from off campus. Internet access, at least one staffed computer lab available.

Student Life *Housing:* college housing not available. *Activities and Organizations:* student-run newspaper, Ski Club, Student Senate, Deaf Club, Recreation Club, Early Childhood Educational Club. *Campus security:* evening security patrols.

Standardized Tests *Required:* ACCUPLACER (for placement).

Costs (2004–05) *Tuition:* state resident $2406 full-time, $141 per semester hour part-time; nonresident $7178 full-time, $414 per semester hour part-time.

Applying *Options:* deferred entrance. *Application fee:* $20. *Application deadline:* rolling (freshmen). *Notification:* continuous (freshmen), continuous (transfers).

Admissions Contact Ms. Beverly Chrzan, Director of Admissions, Northwestern Connecticut Community College, Park Place East, Winsted, CT 06098. *Phone:* 860-738-6329. *Fax:* 860-738-6437. *E-mail:* bschott@nwcc.commnet.edu.

NORWALK COMMUNITY COLLEGE
Norwalk, Connecticut

- **State-supported** 2-year, founded 1961, part of Connecticut Community College System
- **Calendar** semesters
- **Degree** certificates and associate
- **Urban** 30-acre campus with easy access to New York City
- **Coed**

Faculty *Student/faculty ratio:* 16:1.

Student Life *Campus security:* 24-hour emergency response devices and patrols, student patrols, late-night transport/escort service, patrols by security.

Costs (2003–04) *Tuition:* state resident $2028 full-time, $85 per semester hour part-time; nonresident $6084 full-time, $254 per semester hour part-time. *Required fees:* $282 full-time, $78 per term part-time.

Financial Aid Of all full-time matriculated undergraduates who enrolled, 42 Federal Work-Study jobs (averaging $2581). 60 state and other part-time jobs (averaging $2046).

Applying *Options:* deferred entrance. *Application fee:* $20. *Required:* high school transcript.

Admissions Contact Ms. Danita Brown, Admissions Counselor, Norwalk Community College, 188 Richards Avenue, Norwalk, CT 06854-1655. *Phone:* 203-857-7060. *Toll-free phone:* 888-462-6282. *Fax:* 203-857-3335. *E-mail:* nccadmit@commnet.edu.

QUINEBAUG VALLEY COMMUNITY COLLEGE
Danielson, Connecticut

- **State-supported** 2-year, founded 1971, part of Connecticut Community College System
- **Calendar** semesters
- **Degree** certificates and associate
- **Rural** 60-acre campus
- **Coed,** 1,571 undergraduate students, 32% full-time, 68% women, 32% men

Undergraduates 510 full-time, 1,061 part-time. Students come from 3 states and territories, 1 other country, 1% are from out of state, 2% African American, 1% Asian American or Pacific Islander, 8% Hispanic American, 0.6% Native American, 0.2% international, 10% transferred in.

Freshmen *Admission:* 509 applied, 508 admitted, 357 enrolled.

Faculty *Total:* 126, 13% full-time. *Student/faculty ratio:* 16:1.

Majors Accounting; administrative assistant and secretarial science; art; avionics maintenance technology; business administration and management; computer and information sciences related; computer graphics; computer systems networking and telecommunications; data entry/microcomputer applications; engineering technology; human services; liberal arts and sciences/liberal studies; medical/clinical assistant; plastics engineering technology; pre-engineering; substance abuse/addiction counseling; system administration; word processing.

Academic Programs *Special study options:* academic remediation for entering students, adult/continuing education programs, advanced placement credit, distance learning, English as a second language, external degree program, internships, part-time degree program, services for LD students, summer session for credit.

Library Audrey Beck Library with 26,000 titles, 300 serial subscriptions, an OPAC.

Computers on Campus 80 computers available on campus for general student use. A campuswide network can be accessed. Internet access, at least one staffed computer lab available.

Student Life *Housing:* college housing not available. *Activities and Organizations:* student-run newspaper. *Campus security:* evening security guard.

Athletics *Intramural sports:* basketball M/W, volleyball M/W.

Costs (2004–05) *Tuition:* state resident $2112 full-time, $88 per credit part-time; nonresident $6336 full-time, $264 per credit part-time. Full-time tuition and fees vary according to reciprocity agreements. Part-time tuition and fees vary according to reciprocity agreements. *Required fees:* $294 full-time, $58 per term part-time. *Payment plans:* installment, deferred payment. *Waivers:* employees or children of employees.

Financial Aid Of all full-time matriculated undergraduates who enrolled, 38 Federal Work-Study jobs (averaging $1400). 24 state and other part-time jobs (averaging $1350).

Applying *Options:* common application, electronic application, early admission, deferred entrance. *Application fee:* $20. *Required for some:* high school transcript. *Recommended:* high school transcript. *Application deadlines:* 9/1 (freshmen), 9/1 (transfers). *Notification:* continuous until 9/1 (freshmen), continuous until 9/1 (transfers).

Admissions Contact Dr. Toni Moumouris, Director of Admissions, Quinebaug Valley Community College, 742 Upper Maple Street, Danielson, CT 06239. *Phone:* 860-774-1130 Ext. 318. *Fax:* 860-774-7768. *E-mail:* qu_lsd@commnet.edu.

ST. VINCENT'S COLLEGE
Bridgeport, Connecticut

- **Independent** 2-year, founded 1991, affiliated with Roman Catholic Church
- **Calendar** semesters

St. Vincent's College (continued)
- **Degree** certificates and associate
- **Urban** campus with easy access to New York City
- **Coed,** 413 undergraduate students

Undergraduates   Students come from 1 other state.
Freshmen   *Admission:* 661 applied, 182 admitted.
Faculty   *Total:* 19, 53% full-time. *Student/faculty ratio:* 23:1.
Majors   Health/health care administration; medical/clinical assistant; medical radiologic technology; nursing (registered nurse training).
Academic Programs   *Special study options:* academic remediation for entering students, advanced placement credit, part-time degree program, summer session for credit.
Library   Daniel T. Banks Health Science Library with 9,428 titles, 332 serial subscriptions.
Computers on Campus   17 computers available on campus for general student use. At least one staffed computer lab available.
Student Life   *Housing:* college housing not available. *Activities and Organizations:* student-run newspaper, choral group, community service, Student Congress, Mentors, yearbook, Heartbeat. *Campus security:* 24-hour patrols, late-night transport/escort service. *Student services:* health clinic, personal/psychological counseling.
Standardized Tests   *Required for some:* SAT I or ACT (for placement).
Costs (2003–04)   *Tuition:* $9610 full-time, $322 per credit hour part-time. *Required fees:* $450 full-time, $205 per term part-time.
Financial Aid   Of all full-time matriculated undergraduates who enrolled, 15 Federal Work-Study jobs (averaging $1000).
Applying   *Options:* deferred entrance. *Application fee:* $30. *Required:* essay or personal statement, high school transcript, letters of recommendation. *Required for some:* interview. *Recommended:* minimum 3.0 GPA. *Application deadline:* rolling (freshmen), rolling (transfers).
Admissions Contact   Mr. Joseph Marrone, Director of Admissions and Recruitment Marketing, St. Vincent's College, 2800 Main Street, Bridgeport, CT 06606-4292. *Phone:* 203-576-5515.

THREE RIVERS COMMUNITY COLLEGE
Norwich, Connecticut

- **State-supported** 2-year, founded 1963, part of Connecticut Community-Technical College System
- **Calendar** semesters
- **Degrees** certificates and associate (engineering technology programs are offered on the Thames Valley Campus; liberal arts, transfer and career programs are offered on the Mohegan Campus)
- **Small-town** 40-acre campus with easy access to Hartford
- **Coed**

Student Life   *Campus security:* late-night transport/escort service, 14 hour patrols by trained security personnel.
Standardized Tests   *Required:* ACCUPLACER (for placement).
Costs (2003–04)   *Tuition:* state resident $2028 full-time, $85 per credit hour part-time; nonresident $6588 full-time, $254 per credit hour part-time. *Required fees:* $282 full-time.
Financial Aid   Of all full-time matriculated undergraduates who enrolled, 40 Federal Work-Study jobs (averaging $3000). 80 state and other part-time jobs (averaging $3000).
Applying   *Options:* early admission, deferred entrance. *Application fee:* $20. *Required for some:* minimum 3.0 GPA. *Recommended:* high school transcript.
Admissions Contact   Ms. Aida Garcia, Admissions and Recruitment Counselor, Mohegan Campus, Three Rivers Community College, Mahan Drive, Norwich, CT 06360. *Phone:* 860-892-5762. *Fax:* 860-886-0691. *E-mail:* info3rivers@trcc.commnet.edu.

TUNXIS COMMUNITY COLLEGE
Farmington, Connecticut

- **State-supported** 2-year, founded 1969, part of Connecticut Community College System
- **Calendar** semesters
- **Degree** certificates and associate
- **Suburban** 12-acre campus with easy access to Hartford
- **Coed**

Faculty   *Student/faculty ratio:* 20:1.
Student Life   *Campus security:* 24-hour patrols.
Costs (2003–04)   *Tuition:* state resident $2028 full-time, $85 per credit hour part-time; nonresident $6890 full-time, $254 per credit hour part-time. Full-time tuition and fees vary according to reciprocity agreements. Part-time tuition and fees vary according to course load and reciprocity agreements. *Required fees:* $282 full-time.
Applying   *Options:* common application, deferred entrance. *Application fee:* $20. *Required:* high school transcript.
Admissions Contact   Mr. Peter McCloskey, Director of Admissions, Tunxis Community College, 271 Scott Swamp Road, Farmington, CT 06032. *Phone:* 860-677-7701 Ext. 152. *Fax:* 860-676-8906.

DELAWARE

DELAWARE COLLEGE OF ART AND DESIGN
Wilmington, Delaware

Admissions Contact   Chantel Vanderhost, Assistant Director of Admissions, Delaware College of Art and Design, 600 North Market Street, Wilmington, DE 19801. *Phone:* 302-622-8867. *Fax:* 302-622-8870.

DELAWARE TECHNICAL & COMMUNITY COLLEGE, JACK F. OWENS CAMPUS
Georgetown, Delaware

- **State-supported** 2-year, founded 1967, part of Delaware Technical and Community College System
- **Calendar** semesters
- **Degree** certificates, diplomas, and associate
- **Small-town** 120-acre campus
- **Coed**

Student Life   *Campus security:* 24-hour patrols, late-night transport/escort service.
Athletics   Member NJCAA.
Standardized Tests   *Required:* CPT (for placement). *Recommended:* SAT I or ACT (for placement).
Costs (2003–04)   *Tuition:* state resident $1752 full-time; nonresident $4380 full-time. *Required fees:* $180 full-time.
Financial Aid   Of all full-time matriculated undergraduates who enrolled, 250 Federal Work-Study jobs (averaging $2000).
Applying   *Options:* early admission. *Application fee:* $10. *Required:* high school transcript.
Admissions Contact   Ms. Claire McDonald, Admissions Counselor, Delaware Technical & Community College, Jack F. Owens Campus, PO Box 610, Georgetown, DE 19947. *Phone:* 302-856-5400.

DELAWARE TECHNICAL & COMMUNITY COLLEGE, STANTON/WILMINGTON CAMPUS
Newark, Delaware

- **State-supported** 2-year, founded 1968, part of Delaware Technical and Community College System
- **Calendar** semesters
- **Degree** certificates, diplomas, and associate
- **Coed**

Faculty   *Student/faculty ratio:* 16:1.
Student Life   *Campus security:* 24-hour patrols, late-night transport/escort service.
Athletics   Member NJCAA.
Standardized Tests   *Required:* CPT (for placement).
Costs (2003–04)   *Tuition:* state resident $1752 full-time; nonresident $4380 full-time. Part-time tuition and fees vary according to course load. *Required fees:* $180 full-time.
Applying   *Options:* early admission. *Application fee:* $10. *Required:* high school transcript.
Admissions Contact   Ms. Rebecca Bailey, Admissions Coordinator, Wilmington, Delaware Technical & Community College, Stanton/Wilmington Campus, 333 Shipley Street, Wilmington, DE 19713. *Phone:* 302-571-5366.

DELAWARE TECHNICAL & COMMUNITY COLLEGE, TERRY CAMPUS
Dover, Delaware

- **State-supported** 2-year, founded 1972, part of Delaware Technical and Community College System
- **Calendar** semesters
- **Degree** certificates, diplomas, and associate
- **Small-town** 70-acre campus with easy access to Philadelphia
- **Coed,** 2,304 undergraduate students

Undergraduates Students come from 10 states and territories, 10 other countries, 3% are from out of state, 23% African American, 3% Asian American or Pacific Islander, 3% Hispanic American, 0.7% Native American, 2% international.

Freshmen *Admission:* 977 applied, 782 admitted.

Faculty *Total:* 158, 37% full-time. *Student/faculty ratio:* 14:1.

Majors Accounting; administrative assistant and secretarial science; aeronautics/aviation/aerospace science and technology; architectural engineering technology; aviation/airway management; avionics maintenance technology; business administration and management; civil engineering technology; computer engineering technology; computer programming; construction engineering technology; construction management; corrections; criminal justice/law enforcement administration; data processing and data processing technology; drafting and design technology; electrical, electronic and communications engineering technology; electromechanical technology; engineering technology; human services; industrial technology; kindergarten/preschool education; nursing (licensed practical/vocational nurse training); nursing (registered nurse training); survey technology.

Academic Programs *Special study options:* academic remediation for entering students, adult/continuing education programs, cooperative education, English as a second language, internships, part-time degree program, services for LD students, summer session for credit.

Library 9,663 titles, 245 serial subscriptions, an OPAC.

Computers on Campus 125 computers available on campus for general student use. A campuswide network can be accessed. At least one staffed computer lab available.

Student Life *Housing:* college housing not available. *Activities and Organizations:* Students of Kolor, Human Services Organization, Phi Theta Kappa, Alpha Beta Gamma. *Campus security:* late-night transport/escort service.

Standardized Tests *Required:* CPT (for placement).

Costs (2003–04) *Tuition:* state resident $1752 full-time; nonresident $4380 full-time. Full-time tuition and fees vary according to course load. Part-time tuition and fees vary according to course load. *Required fees:* $180 full-time. *Payment plans:* installment, deferred payment. *Waivers:* employees or children of employees.

Financial Aid Of all full-time matriculated undergraduates who enrolled, 50 Federal Work-Study jobs (averaging $1500).

Applying *Options:* early admission. *Application fee:* $10. *Required:* high school transcript. *Application deadline:* rolling (freshmen), rolling (transfers). *Notification:* continuous (freshmen).

Admissions Contact Mrs. Maria Harris, Admissions Officer, Delaware Technical & Community College, Terry Campus, 100 Campus Drive, Dover, DE 19904. *Phone:* 302-857-1020. *Fax:* 302-857-1020. *E-mail:* mharris@outland.dtcc.edu.

FLORIDA

ATI CAREER TRAINING CENTER
Fort Lauderdale, Florida

- **Proprietary** 2-year
- **Calendar** quarters
- **Degree** associate
- **Suburban** campus
- **Coed**

Admissions Contact Ms. Wendy Hopkins Goffinet, Director of Admissions, ATI Career Training Center, 2880 NW 62nd Street, Fort Lauderdale, FL 33309-9731. *Phone:* 954-973-4760. *Fax:* 954-973-6422.

ATI CAREER TRAINING CENTER
Miami, Florida

- **Proprietary** 2-year

- 325 undergraduate students

Admissions Contact Ms. Mary Fernandez, Director of Admissions, ATI Career Training Center, 1 NE 19th Street, Miami, FL 33132. *Phone:* 305-573-1600.

ATI CAREER TRAINING CENTER
Oakland Park, Florida

Admissions Contact 3501 NW 9th Avenue, Oakland Park, FL 33309-9612.

ATI HEALTH EDUCATION CENTER
Miami, Florida

Admissions Contact Mrs. Barbara Woosley, Director, ATI Health Education Center, 1395 NW 167th Street, Suite 200, Miami, FL 33169-5742. *Phone:* 305-628-1000.

BREVARD COMMUNITY COLLEGE
Cocoa, Florida

- **State-supported** 2-year, founded 1960, part of Florida Community College System
- **Calendar** semesters
- **Degree** certificates and associate
- **Suburban** 100-acre campus with easy access to Orlando
- **Endowment** $6.8 million
- **Coed,** 14,806 undergraduate students, 35% full-time, 59% women, 41% men

Undergraduates 5,242 full-time, 9,564 part-time. Students come from 46 states and territories, 61 other countries, 5% are from out of state, 8% African American, 3% Asian American or Pacific Islander, 6% Hispanic American, 0.6% Native American, 1% international. *Retention:* 65% of 2002 full-time freshmen returned.

Freshmen *Admission:* 4,327 applied, 4,327 admitted, 3,315 enrolled.

Faculty *Total:* 856, 22% full-time, 89% with terminal degrees. *Student/faculty ratio:* 19:1.

Majors Accounting; business administration and management; chemical engineering; clinical/medical laboratory technology; computer engineering technology; computer/information technology services administration related; computer programming; computer programming (specific applications); computer software and media applications related; computer systems analysis; computer systems networking and telecommunications; corrections; criminal justice/law enforcement administration; criminal justice/police science; culinary arts; dental hygiene; digital communication and media/multimedia; drafting and design technology; early childhood education; electrical, electronic and communications engineering technology; electrical/electronics drafting and CAD/CADD; emergency medical technology (EMT paramedic); fire science; international business/trade/commerce; legal assistant/paralegal; liberal arts and sciences/liberal studies; manufacturing technology; medical administrative assistant and medical secretary; medical/clinical assistant; nursing (registered nurse training); radio and television; radiologic technology/science; surgical technology; system administration; system, networking, and LAN/wan management; veterinary technology; web page, digital/multimedia and information resources design.

Academic Programs *Special study options:* academic remediation for entering students, accelerated degree program, adult/continuing education programs, advanced placement credit, cooperative education, distance learning, double majors, English as a second language, external degree program, honors programs, independent study, internships, part-time degree program, services for LD students, study abroad, summer session for credit. *ROTC:* Army (b), Air Force (b).

Library UCF Library with 146,776 titles, 877 serial subscriptions, 23,713 audiovisual materials, an OPAC, a Web page.

Computers on Campus 125 computers available on campus for general student use. A campuswide network can be accessed from off campus. Online (class) registration, at least one staffed computer lab available.

Student Life *Housing:* college housing not available. *Activities and Organizations:* drama/theater group, student-run newspaper, television station, choral group, Phi Theta Kappa, ROTORACT, African-American Student Union, Student Government Association, Psi Beta. *Campus security:* 24-hour emergency response devices and patrols, late-night transport/escort service. *Student services:* women's center.

Athletics Member NJCAA. *Intercollegiate sports:* baseball M(s), basketball M(s)/W(s), golf M(s)/W(s), softball W(s), volleyball W(s).

Standardized Tests *Required:* SAT I, ACT, or CPT (for placement).

Costs (2003–04) *Tuition:* state resident $1356 full-time, $57 per credit hour part-time; nonresident $5046 full-time, $210 per credit hour part-time. *Waivers:* senior citizens and employees or children of employees.

Brevard Community College (continued)

Financial Aid Of all full-time matriculated undergraduates who enrolled, 200 Federal Work-Study jobs (averaging $2244). 200 state and other part-time jobs (averaging $2000).

Applying *Options:* common application, electronic application, early admission, deferred entrance. *Application fee:* $20. *Required:* high school transcript. *Application deadline:* rolling (freshmen), rolling (transfers). *Notification:* continuous (freshmen), continuous (transfers).

Admissions Contact Ms. Stephanie Burnette, Supervisor of Admissions, Brevard Community College, 1519 Clearlake Road, Cocoa, FL 32922-6597. *Phone:* 321-433-7271. *Fax:* 321-633-4565.

BROWARD COMMUNITY COLLEGE
Fort Lauderdale, Florida

Admissions Contact Ms. Barbara Bryan, Associate Vice President for Student Affairs/College Registrar, Broward Community College, 225 East Las Olas Boulevard, Fort Lauderdale, FL 33301-2298. *Phone:* 954-761-7465.

CENTRAL FLORIDA COLLEGE
Winter Park, Florida

Admissions Contact 1573 West Fairbanks Avenue, Suite 1-A, Winter Park, FL 32789.

CENTRAL FLORIDA COMMUNITY COLLEGE
Ocala, Florida

- **State and locally supported** 2-year, founded 1957, part of Florida Community College System
- **Calendar** semesters
- **Degree** certificates and associate
- **Small-town** 139-acre campus
- **Endowment** $12.0 million
- **Coed,** 6,298 undergraduate students, 40% full-time, 64% women, 36% men

Undergraduates 2,497 full-time, 3,801 part-time. Students come from 20 states and territories, 11% African American, 1% Asian American or Pacific Islander, 6% Hispanic American, 0.6% Native American, 0.6% international.

Freshmen *Admission:* 724 admitted, 724 enrolled.

Faculty *Total:* 477, 22% full-time. *Student/faculty ratio:* 17:1.

Majors Accounting technology and bookkeeping; airline pilot and flight crew; applied horticulture/horticultural business services related; automotive engineering technology; business administration and management; child care and support services management; child care provision; computer hardware technology; computer programming; computer systems analysis; criminal justice/law enforcement administration; electrical, electronic and communications engineering technology; emergency medical technology (EMT paramedic); environmental control technologies related; executive assistant/executive secretary; fire protection and safety technology; health information/medical records administration; hospitality administration; industrial radiologic technology; legal administrative assistant/secretary; legal assistant/paralegal; liberal arts and sciences/liberal studies; management information systems and services related; marketing/marketing management; nuclear/nuclear power technology; nursing (registered nurse training); ornamental horticulture; physical therapist assistant; psychiatric/mental health services technology; restaurant, culinary, and catering management; veterinary/animal health technology.

Academic Programs *Special study options:* academic remediation for entering students, adult/continuing education programs, advanced placement credit, cooperative education, distance learning, English as a second language, freshman honors college, honors programs, part-time degree program, services for LD students, study abroad, summer session for credit.

Library Central Florida Community College Library plus 1 other with 54,491 titles, 367 serial subscriptions, an OPAC, a Web page.

Computers on Campus 737 computers available on campus for general student use. A campuswide network can be accessed from off campus. Internet access, at least one staffed computer lab available.

Student Life *Housing Options:* Campus housing is provided by a third party. *Activities and Organizations:* drama/theater group, student-run newspaper, choral group, Student Activities Board, African-American Student Union, ROC (Realizing Our Cause), Gay Straight Alliance, Musagettas. *Campus security:* 24-hour emergency response devices and patrols, student patrols, late-night transport/escort service. *Student services:* personal/psychological counseling, women's center.

Athletics Member NJCAA. *Intercollegiate sports:* baseball M(s), basketball M(s)/W(s), softball W(s), tennis W(s). *Intramural sports:* cheerleading W.

Standardized Tests *Required:* SAT I, ACT, or CPT (for placement).

Costs (2003–04) *Tuition:* state resident $1381 full-time, $49 per credit hour part-time; nonresident $5123 full-time, $197 per credit hour part-time. *Required fees:* $201 full-time, $8 per credit hour part-time.

Financial Aid Of all full-time matriculated undergraduates who enrolled, 103 Federal Work-Study jobs (averaging $1500).

Applying *Options:* early admission. *Application fee:* $20. *Required:* high school transcript. *Application deadlines:* 8/3 (freshmen), 8/3 (transfers). *Notification:* continuous (freshmen), continuous (transfers).

Admissions Contact Ms. Sheryl Graham, Executive Director, Student Records and Financial Aid, Central Florida Community College, PO Box 1388, 3001 SW College Road, Ocala, FL 34474-1388. *Phone:* 352-237-2111 Ext. 1340. *Fax:* 352-873-5882. *E-mail:* grahams@cf.edu.

CENTRAL FLORIDA INSTITUTE
Palm Harbor, Florida

- **Proprietary** 2-year
- **Calendar** continuous
- **Degree** certificates, diplomas, and associate
- **Urban** campus
- **Coed,** 346 undergraduate students, 100% full-time, 83% women, 17% men

Undergraduates 346 full-time. 12% African American, 2% Asian American or Pacific Islander, 10% Hispanic American, 0.9% Native American.

Freshmen *Admission:* 123 applied, 200 enrolled.

Faculty *Total:* 23, 96% full-time. *Student/faculty ratio:* 7:1.

Costs (2004–05) *Tuition:* $8479 full-time.

Admissions Contact Carol Bruno, Director of Admissions, Central Florida Institute, 60522 US Highway 19 North, Suite 200, Palm Harbor, FL 34684. *Phone:* 727-786-4707.

CHIPOLA COLLEGE
Marianna, Florida

- **State-supported** primarily 2-year, founded 1947
- **Calendar** semesters
- **Degrees** certificates, associate, and bachelor's
- **Rural** 105-acre campus
- **Coed,** 2,249 undergraduate students, 46% full-time, 62% women, 38% men

Undergraduates 1,030 full-time, 1,219 part-time. Students come from 13 states and territories, 3% are from out of state, 19% African American, 0.9% Asian American or Pacific Islander, 2% Hispanic American, 0.7% Native American.

Freshmen *Admission:* 798 applied, 755 admitted, 285 enrolled.

Faculty *Total:* 69, 78% full-time, 12% with terminal degrees. *Student/faculty ratio:* 24:1.

Majors Accounting; agriculture; agronomy and crop science; art; biological and physical sciences; business administration and management; clinical laboratory science/medical technology; computer and information sciences related; computer science; education; finance; liberal arts and sciences/liberal studies; mass communication/media; mathematics teacher education; nursing (registered nurse training); pre-engineering; science teacher education; secondary education; social work.

Academic Programs *Special study options:* academic remediation for entering students, adult/continuing education programs, advanced placement credit, distance learning, honors programs, independent study, part-time degree program, services for LD students, summer session for credit.

Library Chipola Library with 37,740 titles, 226 serial subscriptions.

Computers on Campus 80 computers available on campus for general student use. A campuswide network can be accessed from off campus. Internet access, at least one staffed computer lab available.

Student Life *Housing:* college housing not available. *Activities and Organizations:* drama/theater group, student-run newspaper, choral group, Drama/Theater Group. *Campus security:* night security personnel.

Athletics Member NJCAA. *Intercollegiate sports:* baseball M(s), basketball M(s)/W(s), softball W(s).

Standardized Tests *Required:* SAT I or ACT (for placement).

Costs (2003–04) *Tuition:* state resident $57 per semester hour part-time; nonresident $176 per semester hour part-time.

Applying *Options:* early admission. *Required:* high school transcript. *Application deadline:* rolling (freshmen), rolling (transfers). *Notification:* continuous (freshmen), continuous (transfers).

Admissions Contact Mrs. Annette Widner, Registrar and Admissions Director, Chipola College, Marianna, FL 32446. *Phone:* 850-526-2761 Ext. 2292. *Fax:* 850-718-2287.

CITY COLLEGE
Casselberry, Florida

Admissions Contact Ms. Yvonne C. Hunter, Director of Admissions, City College, 853 Semoran Boulevard, Suite 200, Casselberry, FL 32707-5342. *Phone:* 407-831-9816.

CITY COLLEGE
Fort Lauderdale, Florida

Admissions Contact Mr. Michael Beauregard, Vice President, City College, 1401 West Cypress Creek Road, Fort Lauderdale, FL 33309. *Phone:* 954-492-5353. *Fax:* 954-491-1695. *E-mail:* info@citycollege.edu.

CITY COLLEGE
Gainesville, Florida

Admissions Contact City College, 2400 Southwest 13th Street, Gainesville, FL 32608.

CITY COLLEGE
Miami, Florida

Admissions Contact City College, 9300 South Dadeland Boulevard, Miami, FL 33156.

COLLEGE OF BUSINESS AND TECHNOLOGY
Miami, Florida

Admissions Contact 8991 SW 107th Avenue, Suite 200, Miami, FL 33176.

COOPER CAREER INSTITUTE
West Palm Beach, Florida

Admissions Contact Mr. Joseph D. Jaap, President and CEO, Cooper Career Institute, 2247 Palm Beach Lakes Boulevard, Suite 110, West Palm Beach, FL 33409. *Phone:* 561-640-6999. *Toll-free phone:* 800-588-4401.

DAYTONA BEACH COMMUNITY COLLEGE
Daytona Beach, Florida

- **State-supported** 2-year, founded 1958, part of Florida Community College System
- **Calendar** semesters
- **Degree** certificates and associate
- **Suburban** 100-acre campus with easy access to Orlando
- **Endowment** $3.5 million
- **Coed,** 12,361 undergraduate students, 39% full-time, 62% women, 38% men

Undergraduates 4,768 full-time, 7,593 part-time. Students come from 54 states and territories, 69 other countries, 5% are from out of state, 12% African American, 2% Asian American or Pacific Islander, 7% Hispanic American, 0.4% Native American, 1% international, 6% transferred in.

Freshmen *Admission:* 3,098 applied, 3,098 admitted, 1,791 enrolled.

Faculty *Total:* 893, 27% full-time, 13% with terminal degrees. *Student/faculty ratio:* 21:1.

Majors Accounting; administrative assistant and secretarial science; advertising; agriculture; anthropology; architectural engineering technology; art; astronomy; atmospheric sciences and meteorology; automobile/automotive mechanics technology; behavioral sciences; biological and physical sciences; biology/biological sciences; business administration and management; chemistry; child development; cinematography and film/video production; civil engineering technology; commercial and advertising art; computer and information sciences related; computer engineering related; computer graphics; computer/information technology services administration related; computer programming; computer programming (specific applications); computer science; computer systems networking and telecommunications; computer typography and composition equipment operation; construction engineering technology; corrections; cosmetology; court reporting; criminal justice/law enforcement administration; criminal justice/police science; criminology; culinary arts; dance; drafting and design technology; dramatic/theatre arts; economics; education; electrical, electronic and communications engineering technology; emergency medical technology (EMT paramedic); engineering; English; fashion/apparel design; finance; fire science; foods, nutrition, and wellness; forestry; geology/earth science;

health information/medical records administration; health science; health teacher education; heating, air conditioning, ventilation and refrigeration maintenance technology; history; hospitality administration; hotel/motel administration; humanities; human services; industrial radiologic technology; information science/studies; information technology; insurance; interior design; journalism; kindergarten/preschool education; legal administrative assistant/secretary; legal assistant/paralegal; liberal arts and sciences/liberal studies; marine biology and biological oceanography; marketing/marketing management; mass communication/media; mathematics; medical administrative assistant and medical secretary; music; nursing (licensed practical/vocational nurse training); nursing (registered nurse training); occupational therapy; philosophy; photography; physical education teaching and coaching; physical therapy; physics; postal management; psychology; radio and television; respiratory care therapy; social sciences; sociology; special products marketing; statistics; telecommunications; tourism and travel services management; zoology/animal biology.

Academic Programs *Special study options:* academic remediation for entering students, adult/continuing education programs, advanced placement credit, cooperative education, English as a second language, honors programs, internships, part-time degree program, services for LD students, study abroad, summer session for credit. *ROTC:* Army (c), Air Force (c).

Library Mary Karl Memorial Library with 66,312 titles, 699 serial subscriptions, 3,862 audiovisual materials.

Computers on Campus 752 computers available on campus for general student use. A campuswide network can be accessed. Internet access, at least one staffed computer lab available.

Student Life *Housing:* college housing not available. *Activities and Organizations:* drama/theater group, student-run newspaper, choral group, Florida Student Nursing Association, International Club, SGA, History Club, Drama Club. *Campus security:* 24-hour patrols, late-night transport/escort service. *Student services:* personal/psychological counseling, women's center.

Athletics Member NJCAA. *Intercollegiate sports:* basketball M(s), softball W(s). *Intramural sports:* basketball M/W, bowling M/W, fencing M/W, football M, golf M, racquetball M/W, soccer M/W, table tennis M/W, tennis M/W, volleyball M/W.

Standardized Tests *Required:* ACT ASSET, CPT (for placement). *Recommended:* SAT I and SAT II or ACT (for placement).

Costs (2003–04) *Tuition:* state resident $1739 full-time, $58 per credit hour part-time; nonresident $6530 full-time, $218 per credit hour part-time. *Required fees:* $314 full-time. *Waivers:* employees or children of employees.

Financial Aid Of all full-time matriculated undergraduates who enrolled, 161 Federal Work-Study jobs (averaging $1722).

Applying *Options:* common application, early admission, deferred entrance. *Required:* high school transcript. *Application deadline:* rolling (freshmen), rolling (transfers).

Admissions Contact Mr. Joseph Roof, Dean of Enrollment Development, Daytona Beach Community College, PO Box 2811, Daytona Beach, FL 32120-2811. *Phone:* 386-254-4414. *E-mail:* levys@dbcc.cc.fl.us.

EDISON COMMUNITY COLLEGE
Fort Myers, Florida

- **State and locally supported** 2-year, founded 1962, part of Florida Community College System
- **Calendar** semesters
- **Degree** certificates and associate
- **Urban** 80-acre campus
- **Coed,** 10,642 undergraduate students

Undergraduates Students come from 21 states and territories, 45 other countries, 3% are from out of state, 9% African American, 2% Asian American or Pacific Islander, 10% Hispanic American, 0.3% Native American, 3% international.

Freshmen *Admission:* 1,034 admitted.

Faculty *Total:* 417, 22% full-time.

Majors Accounting; applied art; art; business administration and management; clinical laboratory science/medical technology; computer programming; computer programming (specific applications); computer science; criminal justice/law enforcement administration; dental hygiene; drafting and design technology; electrical, electronic and communications engineering technology; emergency medical technology (EMT paramedic); engineering; engineering technology; finance; fire science; horticultural science; hospitality administration; human services; information technology; legal studies; liberal arts and sciences/liberal studies; music; nursing (registered nurse training); radiologic technology/science; respiratory care therapy; social sciences; system administration.

Academic Programs *Special study options:* academic remediation for entering students, accelerated degree program, adult/continuing education programs, advanced placement credit, cooperative education, distance learning, English as a second language, honors programs, independent study, internships, part-time degree program, services for LD students, summer session for credit.

Edison Community College (continued)

Library Learning Resources Center with 181,085 titles, 10,297 audiovisual materials.

Computers on Campus 160 computers available on campus for general student use. A campuswide network can be accessed from off campus. Internet access, at least one staffed computer lab available.

Student Life *Housing:* college housing not available. *Activities and Organizations:* drama/theater group, choral group, Student Government Association, Phi Theta Kappa, African-American Student Association, Latin-American Student Association, national fraternities, national sororities. *Campus security:* 24-hour emergency response devices and patrols, student patrols, late-night transport/escort service.

Standardized Tests *Required:* SAT I, ACT, or CPT (for placement).

Costs (2003–04) *Tuition:* state resident $1747 full-time, $58 per credit hour part-time; nonresident $6513 full-time, $217 per credit hour part-time. *Required fees:* $20 full-time, $5 per term part-time.

Applying *Options:* early admission, deferred entrance. *Application fee:* $20. *Required:* high school transcript. *Application deadlines:* 8/18 (freshmen), 8/18 (transfers). *Notification:* continuous (freshmen), continuous (transfers).

Admissions Contact Ms. Pat Armstrong, Admissions Specialist, Edison Community College, PO Box 60210, Fort Myers, FL 33906-6210. *Phone:* 941-489-9121. *Toll-free phone:* 800-749-2ECC. *Fax:* 941-489-9094.

FLORIDA CAREER COLLEGE
Miami, Florida

- **Proprietary** 2-year, founded 1982
- **Calendar** quarters
- **Degree** certificates, diplomas, and associate
- **Urban** campus
- **Coed,** 2,131 undergraduate students, 81% full-time, 41% women, 59% men

Undergraduates 1,717 full-time, 414 part-time. Students come from 2 states and territories, 3 other countries, 32% African American, 2% Asian American or Pacific Islander, 49% Hispanic American, 0.1% Native American, 1% international.

Freshmen *Admission:* 1,707 enrolled.

Faculty *Total:* 82, 52% full-time, 33% with terminal degrees. *Student/faculty ratio:* 15:1.

Majors Computer engineering related; computer programming; computer programming (specific applications); computer science; web/multimedia management and webmaster.

Academic Programs *Special study options:* academic remediation for entering students, independent study, part-time degree program, summer session for credit.

Library Resource Center plus 1 other with 1,200 titles, 200 serial subscriptions.

Computers on Campus 288 computers available on campus for general student use. A campuswide network can be accessed from off campus that provide access to online student information, grades, schedules. Internet access, at least one staffed computer lab available.

Student Life *Housing:* college housing not available. *Campus security:* 24-hour emergency response devices.

Costs (2004–05) *Tuition:* $9900 full-time, $275 per credit part-time. *Required fees:* $200 full-time, $50 per term part-time.

Applying *Options:* common application, deferred entrance. *Application fee:* $100. *Required:* high school transcript, interview. *Application deadline:* rolling (freshmen), rolling (transfers). *Notification:* continuous (freshmen), continuous (transfers).

Admissions Contact Mr. David Knobel, President, Florida Career College, 1321 Southwest 107 Avenue, Miami, FL 33174. *Phone:* 305-553-6065. *Fax:* 305-225-0128.

FLORIDA COLLEGE OF NATURAL HEALTH
Altamonte Springs, Florida

Admissions Contact Mr. Steve Richards, Campus Director, Florida College of Natural Health, 887 East Altamonte Drive, Altamonte Springs, FL 32701. *Phone:* 407-261-0319. *Toll-free phone:* 800-393-7337.

FLORIDA COLLEGE OF NATURAL HEALTH
Miami, Florida

Admissions Contact Ms. Lissette Vidal, Admissions Coordinator, Florida College of Natural Health, 7925 Northwest 12th Street, Suite 201, Miami, FL 33126. *Phone:* 305-597-9599. *Toll-free phone:* 800-599-9599.

FLORIDA COLLEGE OF NATURAL HEALTH
Pompano Beach, Florida

Admissions Contact Mr. Darren Teigue, Campus Director, Florida College of Natural Health, 2001 West Sample Road, Suite 100, Pompano Beach, FL 33064. *Phone:* 954-975-6400. *Toll-free phone:* 800-541-9299.

FLORIDA COLLEGE OF NATURAL HEALTH
Sarasota, Florida

Admissions Contact Ms. Karen Curry, Director, Florida College of Natural Health, 1751 Mound Street, Suite G100, Sarasota, FL 34236. *Phone:* 941-954-8999. *Toll-free phone:* 800-966-7117.

FLORIDA COMMUNITY COLLEGE AT JACKSONVILLE
Jacksonville, Florida

Admissions Contact Mr. Peter J. Biegel, District Director of Enrollment Services and Registrar, Florida Community College at Jacksonville, 501 West State Street, Jacksonville, FL 32202. *Phone:* 904-632-3131. *Fax:* 904-632-5105. *E-mail:* admissions@fccj.org.

FLORIDA CULINARY INSTITUTE
West Palm Beach, Florida

- **Proprietary** 2-year
- **Degrees** associate (degree in science only (18 or 24 month program))
- 600 undergraduate students, 100% full-time

Undergraduates 600 full-time.

Faculty *Total:* 19.

Majors Baking and pastry arts; culinary arts; restaurant, culinary, and catering management.

Costs (2003–04) *Tuition:* $12,000 full-time. *Required fees:* $1200 full-time.

Financial Aid Of all full-time matriculated undergraduates who enrolled, 28 Federal Work-Study jobs (averaging $4160).

Admissions Contact Mr. David Conway, Associate Director of Admissions, Florida Culinary Institute, 2400 Metrocentre Boulevard, West Palm Beach, FL 33407. *Phone:* 561-842-8324 Ext. 202. *Toll-free phone:* 800-826-9986. *E-mail:* info@floridaculinary.com.

FLORIDA HOSPITAL COLLEGE OF HEALTH SCIENCES
Orlando, Florida

- **Independent** primarily 2-year
- **Calendar** semesters
- **Degrees** certificates, associate, and bachelor's
- **Urban** 9-acre campus
- **Endowment** $906,128
- **Coed,** 1,403 undergraduate students, 43% full-time, 75% women, 25% men

Undergraduates 609 full-time, 794 part-time. Students come from 7 states and territories, 14% African American, 9% Asian American or Pacific Islander, 15% Hispanic American, 0.7% Native American, 8% live on campus.

Freshmen *Admission:* 617 applied, 569 admitted, 138 enrolled. *Average high school GPA:* 2.60. *Test scores:* ACT scores over 18: 68%; ACT scores over 24: 12%.

Faculty *Total:* 71, 52% full-time, 37% with terminal degrees. *Student/faculty ratio:* 24:1.

Majors Diagnostic medical sonography and ultrasound technology; general studies; nuclear medical technology; nursing (registered nurse training); occupational therapist assistant; radiologic technology/science.

Academic Programs *Special study options:* academic remediation for entering students, advanced placement credit, distance learning, independent study, services for LD students. *ROTC:* Air Force (c).

Library Robert Arthur Williams Library with 18,181 titles, 168 serial subscriptions, 1,121 audiovisual materials, an OPAC.

Computers on Campus 45 computers available on campus for general student use. A campuswide network can be accessed. Internet access, at least one staffed computer lab available.

Student Life *Housing Options:* coed. Campus housing is leased by the school. *Activities and Organizations:* drama/theater group, student-run newspaper. *Campus security:* 24-hour emergency response devices and patrols, late-night transport/ escort service, controlled dormitory access. *Student services:* personal/ psychological counseling.

Standardized Tests *Required for some:* SAT I or ACT (for admission).

Costs (2004–05) *Tuition:* $5280 full-time, $220 per credit part-time. *Required fees:* $250 full-time, $125 per term part-time. *Room only:* $1680. Room and board charges vary according to housing facility. *Payment plan:* installment. *Waivers:* employees or children of employees.

Applying *Options:* common application, electronic application. *Application fee:* $20. *Required:* minimum 2.7 GPA. *Required for some:* essay or personal statement, high school transcript, 3 letters of recommendation.

Admissions Contact Ms. Fiona Ghosn, Director of Admissions, Florida Hospital College of Health Sciences, 800 Lake Estelle Drive, Orlando, FL 32803. *Phone:* 407-303-9798 Ext. 5548. *Toll-free phone:* 800-500-7747. *Fax:* 407-303-9408. *E-mail:* fiona.ghosn@fhchs.edu.

FLORIDA KEYS COMMUNITY COLLEGE
Key West, Florida

Admissions Contact Ms. Cheryl A. Malsheimer, Director of Admissions and Records, Florida Keys Community College, 5901 College Road, Key West, FL 33040. *Phone:* 305-296-9081 Ext. 201. *Fax:* 305-292-5163. *E-mail:* dubois_d@popmail.firn.edu.

FLORIDA METROPOLITAN UNIVERSITY-ORANGE PARK CAMPUS
Orange Park, Florida

Admissions Contact 805 Wells Road, Orange Park, FL 32073.

FLORIDA NATIONAL COLLEGE
Hialeah, Florida

- **Proprietary** 2-year, founded 1982
- **Calendar** semesters
- **Degree** certificates, diplomas, and associate
- **Urban** campus with easy access to Miami
- **Coed,** 1,345 undergraduate students, 91% full-time, 68% women, 32% men

Undergraduates 1,219 full-time, 126 part-time. Students come from 1 other state, 7% African American, 0.4% Asian American or Pacific Islander, 80% Hispanic American, 0.7% Native American, 4% international.

Freshmen *Admission:* 583 applied, 441 admitted, 303 enrolled.

Faculty *Total:* 44, 73% full-time, 32% with terminal degrees. *Student/faculty ratio:* 14:1.

Majors Accounting; administrative assistant and secretarial science; allied health and medical assisting services related; business administration and management; computer and information systems security; computer graphics; computer programming; computer programming related; computer programming (specific applications); computer science; computer systems networking and telecommunications; computer/technical support; data entry/microcomputer applications; data entry/microcomputer applications related; data processing and data processing technology; dental hygiene; diagnostic medical sonography and ultrasound technology; education; health services/allied health/health sciences; hospitality administration; legal administrative assistant/secretary; legal assistant/paralegal; legal professions and studies related; legal studies; liberal arts and sciences/liberal studies; medical administrative assistant and medical secretary; medical/clinical assistant; radiologic technology/science; system administration; technical and business writing; tourism and travel services management; tourism promotion; web page, digital/multimedia and information resources design; word processing.

Academic Programs *Special study options:* academic remediation for entering students, adult/continuing education programs, cooperative education, English as a second language, services for LD students, student-designed majors, summer session for credit.

Library Hialeah Campus Library with 24,351 titles, 112 serial subscriptions, 1,430 audiovisual materials, an OPAC, a Web page.

Computers on Campus 136 computers available on campus for general student use. A campuswide network can be accessed from off campus. Internet access available.

Student Life *Housing:* college housing not available. *Activities and Organizations:* Student Government Association. *Campus security:* 24-hour emergency response devices.

Standardized Tests *Required:* TABE (for placement).

Costs (2003–04) *Tuition:* $8990 full-time. *Required fees:* $420 full-time.

Financial Aid Of all full-time matriculated undergraduates who enrolled, 18 Federal Work-Study jobs (averaging $7800).

Applying *Options:* common application, deferred entrance. *Required:* high school transcript. *Application deadline:* rolling (freshmen), rolling (transfers). *Notification:* continuous (freshmen).

Admissions Contact Ms. Maria C. Reguerio, Vice President, Florida National College, 4425 West 20 Avenue, Hialeah, FL 33012. *Phone:* 305-821-3333 Ext. 1002. *Fax:* 305-362-0595. *E-mail:* admissions@fnc.edu.

▶ See page 546 for a narrative description.

THE FLORIDA SCHOOL OF MIDWIFERY
Gainseville, Florida

- **Independent** 2-year, founded 1993
- **Calendar** quarters
- **Degree** associate
- **Women only,** 25 undergraduate students

Faculty *Total:* 40. *Student/faculty ratio:* 10:1.

Majors Direct entry midwifery; nursing midwifery.

Costs (2003–04) *Tuition:* $6000 full-time. *Required fees:* $150 full-time.

Admissions Contact Ms. Gloria Huffman, Director of Finance, The Florida School of Midwifery, PO Box 5505, Gainesville, FL 32627-5505. *Phone:* 352-338-0766.

FLORIDA TECHNICAL COLLEGE
Auburndale, Florida

Admissions Contact Mr. Charles Owens, Admissions Office, Florida Technical College, 298 Havendale Boulevard, Auburndale, FL 33823. *Phone:* 863-967-8822.

FLORIDA TECHNICAL COLLEGE
DeLand, Florida

Admissions Contact Mr. Bill Atkinson, Director, Florida Technical College, 1450 South Woodland Boulevard, 3rd Floor, DeLand, FL 32720. *Phone:* 386-734-3303.

FLORIDA TECHNICAL COLLEGE
Jacksonville, Florida

Admissions Contact Mr. Bryan Gulebiam, Director of Admissions, Florida Technical College, 8711 Lone Star Road, Jacksonville, FL 32211. *Phone:* 407-678-5600.

FLORIDA TECHNICAL COLLEGE
Orlando, Florida

- **Proprietary** 2-year, founded 1982, part of Forefront Education
- **Calendar** quarters
- **Degree** certificates, diplomas, and associate
- **Urban** 1-acre campus
- **Endowment** $14,000
- **Coed**

Applying *Options:* common application. *Required:* high school transcript, interview. *Recommended:* essay or personal statement.

Admissions Contact Ms. Jeanette E. Muschlitz, Director of Admissions, Florida Technical College, 1819 North Semoran Boulevard, Orlando, FL 32807-3546. *Phone:* 407-678-5600. *Fax:* 407-678-1149.

FULL SAIL REAL WORLD EDUCATION
Winter Park, Florida

- **Proprietary** primarily 2-year, founded 1979
- **Calendar** modular
- **Degrees** associate and bachelor's
- **Suburban** campus with easy access to Orlando
- **Coed, primarily men,** 4,300 undergraduate students, 100% full-time, 17% women, 83% men

Undergraduates 4,300 full-time. Students come from 44 states and territories, 9 other countries, 9% African American, 3% Asian American or Pacific Islander, 10% Hispanic American, 0.6% Native American, 2% international.

Florida

Full Sail Real World Education (continued)

Freshmen *Admission:* 1,954 admitted.

Faculty *Total:* 550. *Student/faculty ratio:* 6:1.

Majors Audio engineering; cinematography and film/video production; commercial and advertising art; computer graphics; intermedia/multimedia; music management and merchandising.

Academic Programs *Special study options:* academic remediation for entering students, adult/continuing education programs, cooperative education, internships, part-time degree program, services for LD students, summer session for credit.

Library Full Sail Library with 610 titles, 31 serial subscriptions.

Computers on Campus 32 computers available on campus for general student use. A campuswide network can be accessed from off campus. Internet access, at least one staffed computer lab available.

Student Life *Housing:* college housing not available. *Activities and Organizations:* Student Chapter of Audio Engineering Society. *Campus security:* 24-hour patrols. *Student services:* personal/psychological counseling.

Financial Aid Of all full-time matriculated undergraduates who enrolled, 212 Federal Work-Study jobs (averaging $561).

Applying *Options:* common application, early admission, deferred entrance. *Application fee:* $150. *Required:* high school transcript. *Application deadline:* rolling (freshmen), rolling (transfers).

Admissions Contact Ms. Mary Beth Plank, Director of Admissions, Full Sail Real World Education, 3300 University Boulevard, Winter Park, FL 32792. *Phone:* 407-679-6333 Ext. 2141. *Toll-free phone:* 800-226-7625. *E-mail:* admissions@fullsail.com.

GULF COAST COMMUNITY COLLEGE
Panama City, Florida

- **State-supported** 2-year, founded 1957
- **Calendar** semesters
- **Degree** certificates and associate
- **Suburban** 80-acre campus
- **Endowment** $13.9 million
- **Coed,** 6,058 undergraduate students, 37% full-time, 60% women, 40% men

Undergraduates 2,248 full-time, 3,810 part-time. Students come from 28 states and territories, 8 other countries, 12% African American, 2% Asian American or Pacific Islander, 3% Hispanic American, 0.7% Native American, 0.7% international.

Freshmen *Admission:* 553 enrolled.

Faculty *Total:* 494, 25% full-time. *Student/faculty ratio:* 14:1.

Majors Accounting; administrative assistant and secretarial science; anthropology; art; biology/biological sciences; business administration and management; child care provision; child guidance; civil engineering technology; computer engineering technology; computer programming; computer programming (specific applications); construction engineering technology; criminal justice/law enforcement administration; culinary arts; dental hygiene; drafting and design technology; economics; electrical, electronic and communications engineering technology; electromechanical and instrumentation and maintenance technologies related; elementary education; emergency medical technology (EMT paramedic); engineering technology; English; fire science; foreign languages and literatures; history; hospitality administration; human services; industrial radiologic technology; legal assistant/paralegal; liberal arts and sciences/liberal studies; mathematics; music; nursing (registered nurse training); physical therapist assistant; political science and government; pre-law studies; psychology; radio and television; respiratory care therapy; secondary education; sociology; theatre/theatre arts management.

Academic Programs *Special study options:* academic remediation for entering students, accelerated degree program, adult/continuing education programs, advanced placement credit, cooperative education, distance learning, double majors, English as a second language, external degree program, honors programs, independent study, off-campus study, part-time degree program, services for LD students, summer session for credit.

Library Gulf Coast Community College Library with 80,000 titles, 521 serial subscriptions, 32,041 audiovisual materials, an OPAC, a Web page.

Computers on Campus 850 computers available on campus for general student use. A campuswide network can be accessed from off campus. Internet access, at least one staffed computer lab available.

Student Life *Housing:* college housing not available. *Activities and Organizations:* drama/theater group, student-run newspaper, radio station, choral group, Student Activities Board, Baptist Campus Ministry, Theater Club, Phi Theta Kappa, Muslim Student Association. *Campus security:* patrols by trained security personnel during campus hours. *Student services:* personal/psychological counseling.

Athletics Member NJCAA. *Intercollegiate sports:* baseball M(s), basketball M(s)/W(s), cheerleading M(s)/W(s), softball W(s), volleyball W(s). *Intramural sports:* basketball M/W, volleyball M/W.

Standardized Tests *Required:* CPT (for placement). *Recommended:* SAT I and SAT II or ACT (for placement).

Costs (2003–04) *Tuition:* state resident $1374 full-time, $46 per credit part-time; nonresident $5553 full-time, $185 per credit part-time. *Required fees:* $298 full-time, $10 per credit part-time.

Financial Aid Of all full-time matriculated undergraduates who enrolled, 145 Federal Work-Study jobs (averaging $3200). 60 state and other part-time jobs (averaging $2600).

Applying *Options:* electronic application, early admission, deferred entrance. *Required:* high school transcript. *Application deadline:* rolling (freshmen), rolling (transfers). *Notification:* continuous (freshmen).

Admissions Contact Mrs. Jackie Kuczenski, Administrative Secretary of Admissions, Gulf Coast Community College, 5230 West Highway 98, Panama City, FL 32401. *Phone:* 850-769-1551 Ext. 4892. *Toll-free phone:* 800-311-3628. *Fax:* 850-913-3308.

HERZING COLLEGE
Winter Park, Florida

- **Proprietary** 2-year, founded 1989
- **Calendar** semesters
- **Degree** certificates, diplomas, and associate
- **Coed**

Faculty *Student/faculty ratio:* 21:1.

Costs (2003–04) *Tuition:* $12,000 full-time. *Required fees:* $100 full-time.

Admissions Contact Ms. Karen Mohamad, Director of Admissions, Herzing College, 1595 South Semoran Boulevard, Suite 1501, Winter Park, FL 32792-5509. *Phone:* 407-478-0500.

HILLSBOROUGH COMMUNITY COLLEGE
Tampa, Florida

- **State-supported** 2-year, founded 1968, part of Florida Community College System
- **Calendar** semesters
- **Degree** certificates and associate
- **Urban** campus
- **Endowment** $1.6 million
- **Coed,** 22,149 undergraduate students, 32% full-time, 59% women, 41% men

Undergraduates 7,009 full-time, 15,140 part-time. Students come from 40 states and territories, 100 other countries, 4% are from out of state, 19% African American, 4% Asian American or Pacific Islander, 19% Hispanic American, 0.4% Native American, 0.8% international, 19% transferred in. *Retention:* 57% of 2002 full-time freshmen returned.

Freshmen *Admission:* 4,223 applied, 4,223 admitted, 3,791 enrolled.

Faculty *Total:* 774, 30% full-time, 10% with terminal degrees. *Student/faculty ratio:* 28:1.

Majors Accounting; administrative assistant and secretarial science; agricultural production; aquaculture; architectural engineering technology; art; biomedical technology; business administration and management; business operations support and secretarial services related; child development; commercial and advertising art; computer engineering technology; computer programming; computer systems networking and telecommunications; construction engineering technology; corrections; criminal justice/law enforcement administration; criminal justice/police science; culinary arts; culinary arts related; dance; dental hygiene; diagnostic medical sonography and ultrasound technology; digital communication and media/multimedia; dramatic/theatre arts; education; electrical, electronic and communications engineering technology; elementary education; emergency medical technology (EMT paramedic); engineering; environmental studies; finance; fire science; hospitality administration; hotel/motel administration; human services; industrial radiologic technology; information science/studies; interior design; intermedia/multimedia; legal administrative assistant/secretary; legal studies; liberal arts and sciences/liberal studies; marketing/marketing management; mass communication/media; medical administrative assistant and medical secretary; music; nuclear medical technology; nursing (registered nurse training); occupational therapy; office occupations and clerical services; ophthalmic laboratory technology; ornamental horticulture; pharmacy technician; physical education teaching and coaching; physical therapy; radio and television; radio and television broadcasting technology; radiologic technology/science; radio, television, and digital communication related; respiratory care therapy; restaurant, culinary, and catering management; sign language interpretation and translation.

Academic Programs *Special study options:* academic remediation for entering students, adult/continuing education programs, advanced placement credit, cooperative education, distance learning, English as a second language, honors programs, off-campus study, part-time degree program, services for LD students, summer session for credit. *ROTC:* Army (c), Air Force (c).

Library Main Library plus 4 others with 170,615 titles, 1,283 serial subscriptions, 50,000 audiovisual materials, an OPAC, a Web page.
Computers on Campus 600 computers available on campus for general student use. Internet access, online (class) registration, at least one staffed computer lab available.
Student Life *Housing:* college housing not available. *Activities and Organizations:* drama/theater group, student-run newspaper, radio station, Student Government Association, Student Nursing Association, Phi Theta Kappa, Disabled Students Association, Radiography Club, national fraternities. *Campus security:* 24-hour emergency response devices and patrols. *Student services:* personal/psychological counseling.
Athletics Member NJCAA. *Intercollegiate sports:* baseball M(s), basketball M(s)/W(s), softball W(s), tennis W(s), volleyball W(s).
Standardized Tests *Required for some:* CPT.
Costs (2003–04) *Tuition:* state resident $1627 full-time, $54 per credit hour part-time; nonresident $6065 full-time, $202 per credit hour part-time. *Waivers:* senior citizens and employees or children of employees.
Applying *Options:* common application, early admission. *Application fee:* $20. *Required:* high school transcript. *Application deadline:* rolling (freshmen), rolling (transfers).
Admissions Contact Ms. Kathy G. Cecil, Admissions, Registration, and Records Officer, Hillsborough Community College, PO Box 31127, Tampa, FL 33631-3127. *Phone:* 813-253-7027.

INDIAN RIVER COMMUNITY COLLEGE
Fort Pierce, Florida

- **State-supported** 2-year, founded 1960, part of Florida Community College System
- **Calendar** semesters
- **Degree** certificates, diplomas, and associate
- **Small-town** 133-acre campus
- **Coed**

Student Life *Campus security:* 24-hour patrols.
Athletics Member NJCAA.
Standardized Tests *Required:* SAT I, ACT, or CPT (for placement).
Costs (2003–04) *Tuition:* state resident $1656 full-time, $55 per credit part-time; nonresident $6240 full-time, $208 per credit part-time.
Financial Aid Of all full-time matriculated undergraduates who enrolled, 110 Federal Work-Study jobs (averaging $1500).
Applying *Options:* early admission, deferred entrance. *Required:* high school transcript.
Admissions Contact Mrs. Linda Hays, Dean of Educational Services, Indian River Community College, 3209 Virginia Avenue, Fort Pierce, FL 34981-5596. *Phone:* 772-462-4740.

ITT TECHNICAL INSTITUTE
Maitland, Florida

- **Proprietary** primarily 2-year, founded 1989, part of ITT Educational Services, Inc.
- **Calendar** quarters
- **Degrees** associate and bachelor's
- **Suburban** 1-acre campus with easy access to Orlando
- **Coed**

Standardized Tests *Required:* Wonderlic aptitude test (for admission).
Costs (2003–04) *Tuition:* $347 per credit hour part-time.
Applying *Options:* deferred entrance. *Application fee:* $100. *Required:* high school transcript, interview. *Recommended:* letters of recommendation.
Admissions Contact Mr. Larry Johnson, Director of Recruitment, ITT Technical Institute, 2600 Lake Lucien Drive, Suite 140, Maitland, FL 32751. *Phone:* 407-660-2900. *Fax:* 407-660-2566.

ITT TECHNICAL INSTITUTE
Miami, Florida

- **Proprietary** primarily 2-year, founded 1996, part of ITT Educational Services, Inc.
- **Calendar** quarters
- **Degrees** associate and bachelor's
- **Coed**

Standardized Tests *Required:* Wonderlic aptitude test (for admission).
Costs (2003–04) *Tuition:* Total Program Cost varies depending on course of study. Consult school catalog.

Applying *Options:* deferred entrance. *Application fee:* $100. *Required:* high school transcript, interview. *Recommended:* letters of recommendation.
Admissions Contact Mrs. Rosa Sacarello Daratany, Director of Recruitment, ITT Technical Institute, 7955 NW 12th Street, Suite 119, Miami, FL 33126. *Phone:* 305-477-3080. *Fax:* 305-477-7561.

ITT TECHNICAL INSTITUTE
Tampa, Florida

- **Proprietary** primarily 2-year, founded 1981, part of ITT Educational Services, Inc.
- **Calendar** quarters
- **Degrees** associate and bachelor's
- **Suburban** campus with easy access to St. Petersburg
- **Coed**

Standardized Tests *Required:* Wonderlic aptitude test (for admission).
Costs (2003–04) *Tuition:* Total Program Cost varies depending on course of study. Consult school catalog.
Applying *Options:* deferred entrance. *Application fee:* $100. *Required:* high school transcript, interview. *Recommended:* letters of recommendation.
Admissions Contact Mr. Joseph E. Rostkowski, Director of Recruitment, ITT Technical Institute, 4809 Memorial Highway, Tampa, FL 33634. *Phone:* 813-885-2244. *Toll-free phone:* 800-825-2831. *Fax:* 813-888-8451.

ITT TECHNICAL INSTITUTE
Fort Lauderdale, Florida

- **Proprietary** primarily 2-year, founded 1991, part of ITT Educational Services, Inc.
- **Calendar** quarters
- **Degrees** associate and bachelor's
- **Suburban** campus with easy access to Miami
- **Coed**

Standardized Tests *Required:* Wonderlic aptitude test (for admission).
Costs (2003–04) *Tuition:* Total Program Cost varies depending on course of study. Consult school catalog.
Applying *Options:* deferred entrance. *Application fee:* $100. *Required:* high school transcript, interview. *Recommended:* letters of recommendation.
Admissions Contact Mr. Bob Bixler, Director of Recruitment, ITT Technical Institute, 3401 South University Drive, Fort Lauderdale, FL 33328. *Phone:* 954-476-9300. *Toll-free phone:* 800-488-7797. *Fax:* 954-476-6889.

ITT TECHNICAL INSTITUTE
Jacksonville, Florida

- **Proprietary** primarily 2-year, founded 1991, part of ITT Educational Services, Inc.
- **Calendar** quarters
- **Degrees** associate and bachelor's
- **Urban** 1-acre campus
- **Coed**

Standardized Tests *Required:* Wonderlic aptitude test (for admission).
Costs (2003–04) *Tuition:* Total Program Cost varies depending on course of study. Consult school catalog.
Financial Aid Of all full-time matriculated undergraduates who enrolled, 5 Federal Work-Study jobs.
Applying *Options:* deferred entrance. *Application fee:* $100. *Required:* high school transcript, interview. *Recommended:* letters of recommendation.
Admissions Contact Mr. Jorge Torres, Director of Recruitment, ITT Technical Institute, 6600-10 Youngerman Circle, Jacksonville, FL 32244. *Phone:* 904-573-9100. *Toll-free phone:* 800-318-1264. *Fax:* 904-573-0512.

KEISER CAREER COLLEGE
Pembroke Pines, Florida

Admissions Contact 12520 Pines Boulevard, Pembroke Pines, FL 33027.

KEISER CAREER COLLEGE
Port St. Lucie, Florida

Admissions Contact 9468 South US Highway 1, Port St. Lucie, FL 34952.

KEISER CAREER COLLEGE
West Palm Beach, Florida

Admissions Contact 2085 Vista Parkway, West Palm Beach, FL 33411.

KEISER COLLEGE
Daytona Beach, Florida

Admissions Contact Mr. Jim Wallis, Director of Admissions, Keiser College, 1800 West International Speedway, Building 3, Daytona Beach, FL 32114. *Phone:* 904-255-1707. *Toll-free phone:* 800-749-4456. *Fax:* 904-239-0955.

KEISER COLLEGE
Fort Lauderdale, Florida

Admissions Contact Mr. Brian Woods, Vice President of Enrollment Management, Keiser College, 1500 Northwest 49th Street, Fort Lauderdale, FL 33309. *Phone:* 954-776-4476. *Toll-free phone:* 800-749-4456. *Fax:* 954-351-4030. *E-mail:* admissions@keisercollege.edu.

KEISER COLLEGE
Lakeland, Florida

Admissions Contact 3515 Aviation Drive, Lakeland, FL 33811.

KEISER COLLEGE
Melbourne, Florida

Admissions Contact Ms. Susan Zeigelhofer, Director of Admissions, Keiser College, 900 South Babcock Street, Melbourne, FL 32901-1461. *Phone:* 954-776-4456. *Toll-free phone:* 800-749-4456. *E-mail:* susanz@keisercollege.cc.fl.us.

KEISER COLLEGE
Miami, Florida

- **Proprietary** 2-year
- **Calendar** 3 semesters per year
- **Degree** associate
- **Coed,** 393 undergraduate students, 100% full-time, 71% women, 29% men

Undergraduates 393 full-time. Students come from 3 states and territories, 24% African American, 3% Asian American or Pacific Islander, 65% Hispanic American, 0.3% Native American, 0.5% international.
Faculty *Total:* 18, 28% full-time, 22% with terminal degrees. *Student/faculty ratio:* 18:1.
Majors Business administration and management; computer systems networking and telecommunications; criminal justice/law enforcement administration; health and medical administrative services related; health services/allied health/health sciences; legal assistant/paralegal; medical office assistant; nursing (registered nurse training); radiologic technology/science.
Student Life *Housing:* college housing not available. *Activities and Organizations:* student-run newspaper, Student Ambassador Program. *Campus security:* 24-hour patrols.
Standardized Tests *Recommended:* SAT I or ACT (for admission).
Costs (2003–04) *Tuition:* $5060 per term part-time. *Required fees:* $400 per term part-time. *Payment plan:* installment.
Applying *Required:* high school transcript, interview.
Admissions Contact Mr. Ted Weiner, Director of Admissions, Keiser College, 8505 Mills Drive, Miami, FL 33183. *Phone:* 305-596-2226. *E-mail:* tedw@keisercollege.edu.

KEISER COLLEGE
Orlando, Florida

Admissions Contact 5600 Lake Underhill Road, Orlando, FL 32807.

KEISER COLLEGE
Sarasota, Florida

Admissions Contact Mr. Roger Buck, Executive Director, Keiser College, 332 Sarasota Quay, Sarasota, FL 34236. *Phone:* 941-954-0954.

KEISER COLLEGE
Tallahassee, Florida

Admissions Contact Guy Peirce, Director of Admissions, Keiser College, 1700 Halstead Boulevard, Tallahassee, FL 32308. *Phone:* 850-906-9494. *Toll-free phone:* 800-749-4456. *Fax:* 850-906-9497.

KEY COLLEGE
Fort Lauderdale, Florida

- **Proprietary** 2-year, founded 1881
- **Calendar** quarters
- **Degree** certificates, diplomas, and associate
- **Suburban** campus with easy access to Miami
- **Coed, primarily women**

Faculty *Student/faculty ratio:* 12:1.
Student Life *Campus security:* 24-hour emergency response devices.
Standardized Tests *Required for some:* CPAt, SAT I, or ACT.
Costs (2003–04) *Tuition:* $6885 full-time, $135 per quarter hour part-time. Full-time tuition and fees vary according to program. No tuition increase for student's term of enrollment. *Required fees:* $95 full-time. *Payment plans:* tuition prepayment, installment, deferred payment.
Applying *Options:* common application, electronic application, deferred entrance. *Application fee:* $95. *Required:* high school transcript, interview.
Admissions Contact Mr. Ronald H. Dooley, President and Director of Admissions, Key College, 5225 West Broward Boulevard, Ft. Lauderdale, FL 33317. *Phone:* 954-581-2223 Ext. 23. *Toll-free phone:* 800-581-8292. *Fax:* 954-583-9458. *E-mail:* rhd114@aol.com.

LAKE CITY COMMUNITY COLLEGE
Lake City, Florida

- **State-supported** 2-year, founded 1962, part of Florida Community College System
- **Calendar** semesters
- **Degree** certificates and associate
- **Small-town** 132-acre campus with easy access to Jacksonville
- **Endowment** $3.3 million
- **Coed,** 2,695 undergraduate students

Undergraduates Students come from 18 states and territories, 7 other countries, 11% African American, 1% Asian American or Pacific Islander, 3% Hispanic American, 0.3% Native American, 2% live on campus.
Freshmen *Admission:* 439 applied, 270 admitted. *Test scores:* SAT verbal scores over 500: 13%; SAT math scores over 500: 15%; ACT scores over 18: 72%; SAT verbal scores over 600: 7%; SAT math scores over 600: 10%; ACT scores over 24: 16%; SAT verbal scores over 700: 2%; SAT math scores over 700: 2%.
Faculty *Total:* 204, 27% full-time, 21% with terminal degrees. *Student/faculty ratio:* 19:1.
Majors Administrative assistant and secretarial science; business administration and management; clinical/medical laboratory technology; computer hardware engineering; computer programming; computer programming (specific applications); computer programming (vendor/product certification); computer software engineering; criminal justice/law enforcement administration; electrical, electronic and communications engineering technology; emergency medical technology (EMT paramedic); forest/forest resources management; forestry technology; landscaping and groundskeeping; liberal arts and sciences/liberal studies; nursing (registered nurse training); physical therapist assistant; turf and turfgrass management; web page, digital/multimedia and information resources design.
Academic Programs *Special study options:* academic remediation for entering students, adult/continuing education programs, advanced placement credit, cooperative education, distance learning, English as a second language, independent study, internships, part-time degree program, services for LD students, study abroad, summer session for credit.
Library Learning Resources Center with 42,000 titles, 180 serial subscriptions, an OPAC.
Computers on Campus 150 computers available on campus for general student use. A campuswide network can be accessed. Internet access, at least one staffed computer lab available.
Student Life *Housing Options:* coed. *Activities and Organizations:* drama/theater group, choral group, student government, Florida Turf Grass Association, Florida Student Nurses Association, Phi Theta Kappa, Multicultural Student Union. *Campus security:* 24-hour patrols.
Athletics Member NJCAA. *Intercollegiate sports:* baseball M(s), golf W(s), softball W(s). *Intramural sports:* basketball M, racquetball M/W, softball M/W, table tennis M/W, tennis M/W, volleyball M/W, weight lifting M/W.

Standardized Tests *Required:* SAT I, ACT, or CPT (for placement). *Recommended:* SAT I or ACT (for placement).

Costs (2004–05) *Tuition:* $56 per semester hour part-time; state resident $65 per semester hour part-time; nonresident $211 per semester hour part-time. Full-time tuition and fees vary according to program. Part-time tuition and fees vary according to program. *Room and board:* Room and board charges vary according to board plan.

Financial Aid Of all full-time matriculated undergraduates who enrolled, 58 Federal Work-Study jobs (averaging $975).

Applying *Options:* early admission, deferred entrance. *Application fee:* $15. *Required for some:* high school transcript. *Application deadline:* rolling (freshmen), rolling (transfers). *Notification:* continuous (freshmen), continuous (transfers).

Admissions Contact Vince C. Rice, Director of Postsecondary Transition, Lake City Community College, Route 19, Box 1030, Lake City, FL 32025-8703. *Phone:* 386-754-4288. *Fax:* 386-755-1521. *E-mail:* admissions@mail.lakecity.cc.fl.us.

LAKE-SUMTER COMMUNITY COLLEGE
Leesburg, Florida

- **State and locally supported** 2-year, founded 1962, part of Florida Department of Education
- **Calendar** semesters
- **Degree** certificates, diplomas, and associate
- **Suburban** 110-acre campus with easy access to Orlando
- **Endowment** $2.2 million
- **Coed,** 3,222 undergraduate students, 33% full-time, 67% women, 33% men

Undergraduates 1,077 full-time, 2,145 part-time. Students come from 8 states and territories, 6 other countries, 2% are from out of state, 9% African American, 2% Asian American or Pacific Islander, 6% Hispanic American, 0.5% Native American, 0.3% international, 33% transferred in.

Freshmen *Admission:* 1,757 applied, 1,200 admitted, 479 enrolled.

Faculty *Total:* 154, 34% full-time, 7% with terminal degrees. *Student/faculty ratio:* 20:1.

Majors Business administration and management; commercial and advertising art; computer and information sciences related; computer science; criminal justice/law enforcement administration; emergency medical technology (EMT paramedic); fire science; health information/medical records administration; legal assistant/paralegal; liberal arts and sciences/liberal studies; nursing (registered nurse training); office management; sport and fitness administration; theatre design and technology.

Academic Programs *Special study options:* academic remediation for entering students, adult/continuing education programs, advanced placement credit, cooperative education, distance learning, double majors, off-campus study, part-time degree program, services for LD students, summer session for credit. *ROTC:* Air Force (c).

Library Lake-Sumter Community College Library with 67,683 titles, 364 serial subscriptions, 1,522 audiovisual materials, an OPAC, a Web page.

Computers on Campus 552 computers available on campus for general student use. A campuswide network can be accessed from off campus. Internet access, at least one staffed computer lab available.

Student Life *Housing:* college housing not available. *Activities and Organizations:* drama/theater group, student-run newspaper, television station, choral group, Phi Theta Kappa, Baptist Collegiate Ministry, Environmental Society, Nursing Students' Association. *Campus security:* 24-hour emergency response devices. *Student services:* women's center.

Athletics Member NJCAA. *Intercollegiate sports:* baseball M(s), softball W(s), volleyball W(s). *Intramural sports:* basketball M/W, golf M/W, softball M/W, volleyball M/W.

Standardized Tests *Required:* SAT I, ACT, or CPT (for placement).

Costs (2003–04) *Tuition:* state resident $1731 full-time, $57 per credit part-time; nonresident $5715 full-time, $212 per credit part-time. Full-time tuition and fees vary according to course load. Part-time tuition and fees vary according to course load. *Required fees:* $273 full-time, $1 per credit part-time. *Waivers:* employees or children of employees.

Applying *Options:* early admission, deferred entrance. *Application fee:* $25. *Required:* high school transcript. *Application deadline:* rolling (freshmen), rolling (transfers). *Notification:* continuous (freshmen), continuous (transfers).

Admissions Contact Ms. Amy Prancl, Enrollment Specialist, Lake-Sumter Community College, 9501 US Highway 441, Leesburg, FL 34788-8751. *Phone:* 352-365-3561. *Fax:* 352-365-3573. *E-mail:* prancla@lscc.edu.

MANATEE COMMUNITY COLLEGE
Bradenton, Florida

- **State-supported** 2-year, founded 1957, part of Florida Community College System

- **Calendar** semesters
- **Degree** certificates and associate
- **Suburban** 100-acre campus with easy access to Tampa-St. Petersburg
- **Coed,** 9,172 undergraduate students, 38% full-time, 64% women, 36% men

Undergraduates 3,506 full-time, 5,666 part-time. Students come from 47 states and territories, 86 other countries, 3% are from out of state, 10% African American, 2% Asian American or Pacific Islander, 6% Hispanic American, 0.3% Native American, 2% international, 6% transferred in. *Retention:* 64% of 2002 full-time freshmen returned.

Freshmen *Admission:* 1,905 enrolled. *Test scores:* SAT verbal scores over 500: 43%; SAT math scores over 500: 47%; ACT scores over 18: 42%; SAT verbal scores over 600: 10%; SAT math scores over 600: 11%; ACT scores over 24: 10%; SAT math scores over 700: 1%; ACT scores over 30: 1%.

Faculty *Total:* 461, 25% full-time, 10% with terminal degrees. *Student/faculty ratio:* 23:1.

Majors Accounting; administrative assistant and secretarial science; advertising; African-American/Black studies; American government and politics; American studies; art; art history, criticism and conservation; Asian studies; astronomy; biology/biological sciences; biology teacher education; business administration and management; business/commerce; business/managerial economics; chemistry; chemistry teacher education; child guidance; civil engineering technology; commercial and advertising art; community health services counseling; computer and information sciences; computer and information sciences related; computer engineering technology; computer graphics; computer programming; computer programming related; construction engineering technology; criminal justice/safety; dietetics; drafting and design technology; dramatic/theatre arts; economics; electrical, electronic and communications engineering technology; engineering; English; English/language arts teacher education; European studies (Central and Eastern); family and consumer sciences/home economics teacher education; finance; fine/studio arts; fire science; foreign language teacher education; French; German; health/health care administration; health teacher education; history; hospital and health care facilities administration; humanities; information science/studies; jazz/jazz studies; Jewish/Judaic studies; journalism; kindergarten/preschool education; Latin American studies; legal assistant/paralegal; liberal arts and sciences/liberal studies; mass communication/media; mathematics teacher education; medical radiologic technology; music; music performance; music teacher education; music theory and composition; nursing (registered nurse training); occupational therapist assistant; occupational therapy; philosophy; physical education teaching and coaching; physical therapist assistant; physical therapy; physician assistant; physics; physics teacher education; pre-pharmacy studies; psychology; public administration; radio and television; radio and television broadcasting technology; radiologic technology/science; religious studies; respiratory care therapy; Russian studies; science teacher education; social psychology; social sciences; social studies teacher education; social work; Spanish; speech and rhetoric; statistics; technology/industrial arts teacher education; trade and industrial teacher education; vocational rehabilitation counseling; women's studies.

Academic Programs *Special study options:* academic remediation for entering students, advanced placement credit, cooperative education, distance learning, English as a second language, honors programs, independent study, part-time degree program, services for LD students, summer session for credit.

Library Sara Harlee Library plus 1 other with 65,386 titles, 378 serial subscriptions, 14,617 audiovisual materials, an OPAC, a Web page.

Computers on Campus 1000 computers available on campus for general student use. A campuswide network can be accessed from off campus. Internet access, online (class) registration, at least one staffed computer lab available.

Student Life *Housing:* college housing not available. *Activities and Organizations:* drama/theater group, student-run newspaper, choral group, Student Government Association, Phi Theta Kappa, American Chemical Society Student Affiliate, Campus Ministry, Medical Community Club. *Campus security:* 24-hour emergency response devices and patrols, late-night transport/escort service.

Athletics Member NJCAA. *Intercollegiate sports:* baseball M(s), basketball M(s), softball W(s), volleyball W(s). *Intramural sports:* basketball M/W, softball M/W, volleyball M/W, weight lifting M/W.

Standardized Tests *Required:* SAT I or ACT (for placement), Florida College Entry-Level Placement Test (for placement).

Costs (2004–05) *Tuition:* state resident $1833 full-time, $61 per credit part-time; nonresident $6852 full-time, $228 per credit part-time.

Financial Aid Of all full-time matriculated undergraduates who enrolled, 82 Federal Work-Study jobs (averaging $2800). *Financial aid deadline:* 8/15.

Applying *Options:* early admission. *Application fee:* $20. *Required:* high school transcript. *Application deadlines:* 8/20 (freshmen), 8/20 (transfers). *Notification:* continuous (freshmen), continuous (transfers).

Admissions Contact Ms. MariLynn Paro, Registrar, Manatee Community College, PO Box 1849, Bradenton, FL 34206. *Phone:* 941-752-5031. *Fax:* 941-727-6380.

MEDVANCE INSTITUTE
Atlantis, Florida

Admissions Contact Ms. Brenda Cortez, Campus Director, MedVance Institute, 170 JFK Drive, Atlantis, FL 33462. *Phone:* 561-304-3466. *Toll-free phone:* 888-86-GO-MED.

MIAMI DADE COLLEGE
Miami, Florida

- **State and locally supported** primarily 2-year, founded 1960, part of Florida Community College System
- **Calendar** 16-16-6-6
- **Degrees** certificates, associate, and bachelor's
- **Urban** campus
- **Endowment** $106.5 million
- **Coed,** 58,490 undergraduate students, 36% full-time, 62% women, 38% men

Miami Dade College offers undergraduate study in more than 200 academic areas and professions. The College is internationally recognized as an educational leader in undergraduate programs that are innovative and diverse within a multicultural, multiethnic environment. Annually, more than 155,000 credit and noncredit students are enrolled at 6 major campuses and numerous outreach centers.

Undergraduates 21,009 full-time, 37,481 part-time. Students come from 37 states and territories, 155 other countries, 1% are from out of state, 22% African American, 1% Asian American or Pacific Islander, 65% Hispanic American, 3% international, 2% transferred in.

Freshmen *Admission:* 16,216 applied, 16,216 admitted, 8,623 enrolled. *Test scores:* SAT verbal scores over 500: 18%; SAT math scores over 500: 16%; ACT scores over 18: 36%; SAT verbal scores over 600: 2%; SAT math scores over 600: 2%; ACT scores over 24: 2%.

Faculty *Total:* 2,081, 34% full-time, 15% with terminal degrees. *Student/faculty ratio:* 29:1.

Majors Accounting technology and bookkeeping; administrative assistant and secretarial science; aeronautics/aviation/aerospace science and technology; agriculture; airline pilot and flight crew; air traffic control; American studies; anthropology; architectural drafting and CAD/CADD; architectural engineering technology; art; art teacher education; Asian studies; aviation/airway management; behavioral sciences; biology/biological sciences; biology teacher education; biomedical technology; business administration and management; chemistry; chemistry teacher education; child development; cinematography and film/video production; civil engineering technology; clinical/medical laboratory technology; commercial and advertising art; computer engineering technology; computer graphics; computer programming; computer science; computer software technology; computer technology/computer systems technology; construction engineering technology; court reporting; criminal justice/law enforcement administration; criminal justice/police science; dance; data processing and data processing technology; dental hygiene; diagnostic medical sonography and ultrasound technology; dietetics; dietetic technician; drafting and design technology; dramatic/theatre arts; economics; education; education (specific subject areas) related; electrical and electronic engineering technologies related; electrical, electronic and communications engineering technology; elementary education; emergency medical technology (EMT paramedic); engineering; engineering related; engineering technology; English; environmental engineering technology; finance; fire science; food science; forestry; French; funeral service and mortuary science; general studies; geology/earth science; German; health information/medical records administration; heating, air conditioning and refrigeration technology; heating, air conditioning, ventilation and refrigeration maintenance technology; histologic technician; history; horticultural science; hospitality administration; humanities; human services; industrial technology; information science/studies; interior design; international relations and affairs; Italian; journalism; kindergarten/preschool education; landscaping and groundskeeping; Latin American studies; legal administrative assistant/secretary; legal assistant/paralegal; literature; management information systems; marketing/marketing management; mass communication/media; mathematics; mathematics teacher education; medical/clinical assistant; middle school education; music; music performance; music teacher education; natural sciences; non-profit management; nuclear medical technology; nursing midwifery; nursing (registered nurse training); ophthalmic technology; ornamental horticulture; parks, recreation and leisure; philosophy; photographic and film/video technology; photography; physical education teaching and coaching; physical sciences; physical therapist assistant; physical therapy; physics; physics teacher education; plant nursery management; political science and government; Portuguese; pre-dentistry studies; pre-engineering; pre-medical studies; pre-nursing studies; pre-pharmacy studies; pre-veterinary studies; psychology; public administration; radio and television; radio and television broadcasting technology; radiologic technology/science; recording arts technology; respiratory care therapy; respiratory therapy technician; science teacher education; sign language interpretation and translation; social sciences; social work; sociology; Spanish; special education; substance abuse/addiction counseling; teacher assistant/aide; telecommunications technology; tourism and travel services management; veterinary sciences.

Academic Programs *Special study options:* academic remediation for entering students, adult/continuing education programs, advanced placement credit, cooperative education, distance learning, English as a second language, honors programs, independent study, internships, part-time degree program, services for LD students, study abroad, summer session for credit. *ROTC:* Army (c), Air Force (c).

Library Main Library plus 8 others with 347,302 titles, 3,586 serial subscriptions, 17,186 audiovisual materials, an OPAC, a Web page.

Computers on Campus 6136 computers available on campus for general student use. A campuswide network can be accessed from off campus. Internet access, online (class) registration, at least one staffed computer lab available.

Student Life *Housing:* college housing not available. *Activities and Organizations:* drama/theater group, student-run newspaper, radio station, choral group, Welcome Back, Hispanic Heritage Month, Black History Month, Paella Festival. *Campus security:* 24-hour patrols. *Student services:* personal/psychological counseling, women's center.

Athletics Member NJCAA. *Intercollegiate sports:* baseball M(s), basketball M(s)/W(s), softball W(s), volleyball W(s). *Intramural sports:* basketball M/W, racquetball M/W, soccer M/W, softball M/W, swimming M/W, tennis M/W, track and field M/W, volleyball M/W, weight lifting M/W.

Standardized Tests *Required:* (for placement). *Recommended:* SAT I and SAT II or ACT (for placement), SAT II: Subject Tests (for placement), SAT II: Writing Test (for placement).

Costs (2003–04) *Tuition:* state resident $1419 full-time, $47 per credit part-time; nonresident $5286 full-time, $176 per credit part-time. Full-time tuition and fees vary according to degree level. Part-time tuition and fees vary according to degree level. *Required fees:* $276 full-time, $9 per credit part-time. *Waivers:* employees or children of employees.

Financial Aid Of all full-time matriculated undergraduates who enrolled, 800 Federal Work-Study jobs (averaging $5000). 125 state and other part-time jobs (averaging $5000).

Applying *Options:* electronic application, early admission. *Application fee:* $20. *Required:* high school transcript. *Application deadline:* rolling (freshmen). *Notification:* continuous (freshmen), continuous (transfers).

Admissions Contact Mr. Steven Kelly, College Registrar, Miami Dade College, 11011 SW 104th Street, Miami, FL 33176. *Phone:* 305-237-0633. *Fax:* 305-237-2964. *E-mail:* jstewart@mdcc.edu.

▶ **See page 576 for a narrative description.**

NATIONAL SCHOOL OF TECHNOLOGY, INC.
Fort Lauderdale, Florida

Admissions Contact Ashly Miller, Director of Admissions, National School of Technology, Inc., 1040 Bayview Drive, Fort Lauderdale, FL 33304. *Phone:* 954-630-0066.

NATIONAL SCHOOL OF TECHNOLOGY, INC.
Hialeah, Florida

Admissions Contact Mr. Daniel Alonso, Director of Admissions, National School of Technology, Inc., 4410 West 16th Avenue, Suite 52, Hialeah, FL 33012. *Phone:* 305-558-9500.

NATIONAL SCHOOL OF TECHNOLOGY, INC.
Miami, Florida

- **Proprietary** 2-year
- **Calendar** continuous
- **Degree** diplomas and associate
- **Coed**

Faculty *Student/faculty ratio:* 20:1.

Admissions Contact Ms. Amber Stenbeck, Director of Admissions, National School of Technology, Inc., 9020 Southwest 137th Avenue, Miami, FL 33186. *Phone:* 305-386-9900.

NATIONAL SCHOOL OF TECHNOLOGY, INC.
North Miami Beach, Florida

- **Proprietary** 2-year, founded 1977
- **Calendar** continuous

- **Degree** diplomas and associate
- **Urban** campus
- **Coed,** 608 undergraduate students, 100% full-time, 67% women, 33% men

Undergraduates 608 full-time. 70% African American, 13% Hispanic American, 0.3% Native American.
Freshmen *Admission:* 370 applied, 440 enrolled.
Faculty *Total:* 50, 70% full-time. *Student/faculty ratio:* 12:1.
Majors Massage therapy; medical/clinical assistant; medical insurance coding; pharmacy technician; surgical technology.
Costs (2004–05) *Tuition:* $10,200 full-time.
Admissions Contact Mr. Walter McQuade, Director of Admissions, National School of Technology, Inc., 16150 Northeast 17th Avenue, North Miami Beach, FL 33162-4744. *Phone:* 305-949-9500.

NEW ENGLAND INSTITUTE OF TECHNOLOGY AT PALM BEACH
West Palm Beach, Florida

- **Proprietary** 2-year, founded 1983
- **Calendar** quarters
- **Degree** certificates, diplomas, and associate
- **Urban** 7-acre campus with easy access to Miami
- **Coed,** 1,200 undergraduate students

Freshmen *Admission:* 450 applied, 450 admitted.
Faculty *Total:* 46, 100% full-time. *Student/faculty ratio:* 25:1.
Majors Architectural drafting and CAD/CADD; automobile/automotive mechanics technology; computer systems networking and telecommunications; cosmetology; dental assisting; drafting and design technology; electrical, electronic and communications engineering technology; heating, air conditioning, ventilation and refrigeration maintenance technology; hospitality and recreation marketing; industrial electronics technology; legal assistant/paralegal; medical/clinical assistant; office management.
Academic Programs *Special study options:* academic remediation for entering students, internships.
Computers on Campus 58 computers available on campus for general student use.
Student Life *Housing:* college housing not available. *Student services:* personal/psychological counseling.
Costs (2003–04) *Tuition:* $12,000 full-time, $19,500 per degree program part-time. *Required fees:* $1200 full-time.
Applying *Options:* early admission. *Application fee:* $150. *Required:* high school transcript. *Application deadline:* rolling (freshmen), rolling (transfers). *Notification:* continuous (freshmen), continuous (transfers).
Admissions Contact Mr. Kevin Cassidy, Director of Admissions, New England Institute of Technology at Palm Beach, 1126 53rd Court, West Palm Beach, FL 33407-2384. *Phone:* 561-842-8324 Ext. 117. *Toll-free phone:* 800-826-9986.

NORTH FLORIDA COMMUNITY COLLEGE
Madison, Florida

- **State-supported** 2-year, founded 1958
- **Calendar** semesters
- **Degree** certificates and associate
- **Small-town** 109-acre campus
- **Coed,** 1,297 undergraduate students, 46% full-time, 65% women, 35% men

Undergraduates 593 full-time, 704 part-time. Students come from 1 other state, 24% African American, 1% Asian American or Pacific Islander, 1% Hispanic American.
Freshmen *Admission:* 142 enrolled. *Average high school GPA:* 2.60. *Test scores:* SAT verbal scores over 500: 48%; SAT math scores over 500: 42%; ACT scores over 18: 37%; SAT verbal scores over 600: 13%; SAT math scores over 600: 7%; ACT scores over 24: 9%; SAT verbal scores over 700: 3%.
Faculty *Total:* 44, 57% full-time. *Student/faculty ratio:* 18:1.
Majors Accounting technology and bookkeeping; architectural drafting and CAD/CADD; business administration and management; business and personal/financial services marketing; criminal justice/safety; industrial technology; liberal arts and sciences/liberal studies; mechanical drafting and CAD/CADD; special education (hearing impaired).
Academic Programs *Special study options:* academic remediation for entering students, accelerated degree program, adult/continuing education programs, advanced placement credit, distance learning, honors programs, part-time degree program, services for LD students, summer session for credit.
Library Dr. Marshall Hamilton Library with 30,137 titles, 125 serial subscriptions, an OPAC, a Web page.

Computers on Campus 60 computers available on campus for general student use. A campuswide network can be accessed. Internet access, at least one staffed computer lab available.
Student Life *Housing:* college housing not available. *Activities and Organizations:* drama/theater group, student-run newspaper, choral group, Student Government Association, Sentinel Ambassadors, Phi Theta Kappa, African-American Student Union, Fellowship of Christian Athletes. *Campus security:* 24-hour emergency response devices. *Student services:* women's center.
Athletics Member NJCAA. *Intercollegiate sports:* baseball M, basketball W, softball W. *Intramural sports:* baseball M, basketball W.
Standardized Tests *Required for some:* SAT I or ACT (for placement).
Costs (2004–05) *Tuition:* state resident $1671 full-time; nonresident $6141 full-time.
Applying *Options:* common application, early admission. *Application fee:* $20. *Required:* high school transcript, minimum 2.0 GPA. *Application deadline:* rolling (freshmen), rolling (transfers).
Admissions Contact Mrs. Betty Starling, Admissions Assistant, North Florida Community College, 1000 Turner Davis Drive, Madison, FL 32340-1602. *Phone:* 850-973-1622. *Fax:* 850-973-1697.

OKALOOSA-WALTON COMMUNITY COLLEGE
Niceville, Florida

- **State and locally supported** 2-year, founded 1963, part of Florida Community College System
- **Calendar** semesters plus summer sessions
- **Degree** certificates and associate
- **Small-town** 264-acre campus
- **Endowment** $18.4 million
- **Coed**

Faculty *Student/faculty ratio:* 20:1.
Student Life *Campus security:* 24-hour patrols.
Athletics Member NJCAA.
Standardized Tests *Required:* ACT, SAT I, ACT ASSET, MAPS, or Florida College Entry Placement Test (for admission).
Costs (2003–04) *Tuition:* state resident $1454 full-time, $48 per semester hour part-time; nonresident $5607 full-time, $194 per semester hour part-time. *Payment plans:* installment, deferred payment.
Financial Aid Of all full-time matriculated undergraduates who enrolled, 81 Federal Work-Study jobs (averaging $1500). 11 state and other part-time jobs (averaging $1460).
Applying *Options:* early admission, deferred entrance. *Required:* high school transcript.
Admissions Contact Ms. Christine Bishop, Registrar/Division Director Enrollment Services, Okaloosa-Walton Community College, 100 College Boulevard, Niceville, FL 32578. *Phone:* 850-729-5373. *Toll-free phone:* 850-729-5373. *Fax:* 850-729-5323. *E-mail:* registrar@owcc.net.

ORLANDO CULINARY ACADEMY
Orlando, Florida

Admissions Contact 8511 Commodity Circle, Suite 100, Orlando, FL 32819. *Toll-free phone:* 866-OCA-CHEF.

PALM BEACH COMMUNITY COLLEGE
Lake Worth, Florida

- **State-supported** 2-year, founded 1933, part of Florida Community College System
- **Calendar** semesters
- **Degree** certificates and associate
- **Urban** 150-acre campus with easy access to West Palm Beach
- **Endowment** $9.0 million
- **Coed,** 25,022 undergraduate students, 29% full-time, 60% women, 40% men

Undergraduates 7,219 full-time, 17,803 part-time. Students come from 45 states and territories, 141 other countries, 9% are from out of state, 22% African American, 3% Asian American or Pacific Islander, 14% Hispanic American, 0.3% Native American, 3% international, 9% transferred in, 2% live on campus.
Freshmen *Admission:* 3,125 applied, 3,125 admitted, 2,366 enrolled.
Faculty *Total:* 1,296, 17% full-time. *Student/faculty ratio:* 22:1.
Majors Accounting; administrative assistant and secretarial science; airline pilot and flight crew; art; art history, criticism and conservation; biology/biological sciences; botany/plant biology; business administration and manage-

Palm Beach Community College (continued)

ment; ceramic arts and ceramics; chemistry; clothing/textiles; commercial and advertising art; computer programming; computer programming (specific applications); computer science; computer/technical support; construction management; criminal justice/law enforcement administration; criminal justice/police science; data processing and data processing technology; dental hygiene; drafting and design technology; dramatic/theatre arts; economics; education; electrical, electronic and communications engineering technology; elementary education; English; family and consumer sciences/human sciences; fashion/apparel design; fashion merchandising; finance; fire science; foods, nutrition, and wellness; health teacher education; history; hotel/motel administration; industrial radiologic technology; interior design; journalism; kindergarten/preschool education; legal administrative assistant/secretary; liberal arts and sciences/liberal studies; literature; marketing/marketing management; mass communication/media; mathematics; music; nursing (registered nurse training); occupational therapy; philosophy; photography; physical education teaching and coaching; physical sciences; physical therapy; political science and government; pre-engineering; psychology; religious studies; social sciences; social work; special products marketing; survey technology; system administration; web page, digital/multimedia and information resources design; word processing; zoology/animal biology.

Academic Programs *Special study options:* academic remediation for entering students, adult/continuing education programs, advanced placement credit, cooperative education, distance learning, double majors, English as a second language, freshman honors college, honors programs, independent study, internships, off-campus study, part-time degree program, services for LD students, student-designed majors, study abroad, summer session for credit.

Library Harold C. Manor Library plus 3 others with 151,000 titles, 1,474 serial subscriptions, 9,700 audiovisual materials, an OPAC, a Web page.

Computers on Campus 2300 computers available on campus for general student use. A campuswide network can be accessed from off campus. Internet access, online (class) registration, at least one staffed computer lab available.

Student Life *Housing Options:* coed, disabled students. *Activities and Organizations:* drama/theater group, student-run newspaper, choral group, student government, Phi Theta Kappa, Students for International Understanding, Black Student Union, Drama Club, national fraternities. *Campus security:* 24-hour emergency response devices and patrols. *Student services:* health clinic, women's center.

Athletics Member NJCAA. *Intercollegiate sports:* baseball M(s), basketball M(s)/W(s), softball W(s), volleyball M(s)/W(s). *Intramural sports:* basketball M/W, bowling M/W, football M/W, racquetball M/W, soccer M, tennis M/W, volleyball M/W.

Standardized Tests *Required:* SAT I, ACT, or CPT (for placement).

Costs (2004–05) *Tuition:* state resident $1650 full-time, $55 per credit part-time; nonresident $6240 full-time, $208 per credit part-time. *Required fees:* $250 full-time, $10 per term part-time. *Room and board:* room only: $6000. *Payment plan:* tuition prepayment. *Waivers:* minority students, senior citizens, and employees or children of employees.

Applying *Options:* electronic application, early admission, deferred entrance. *Application fee:* $20. *Application deadlines:* 8/20 (freshmen), 8/20 (transfers). *Notification:* continuous until 8/20 (freshmen), continuous until 8/20 (transfers).

Admissions Contact Ms. Annaleah Morrow, College Registrar, Palm Beach Community College, 4200 Congress Avenue, Lake Worth, FL 33461. *Phone:* 561-868-3032. *Fax:* 561-868-3584.

PASCO-HERNANDO COMMUNITY COLLEGE
New Port Richey, Florida

- **State-supported** 2-year, founded 1972, part of Florida Community College System
- **Calendar** semesters
- **Degree** certificates, diplomas, and associate
- **Small-town** 142-acre campus with easy access to Tampa
- **Endowment** $20.3 million
- **Coed,** 6,914 undergraduate students, 32% full-time, 68% women, 32% men

Undergraduates 2,217 full-time, 4,697 part-time. Students come from 11 states and territories, 10 other countries, 1% are from out of state, 4% African American, 2% Asian American or Pacific Islander, 6% Hispanic American, 0.7% Native American, 0.5% international, 6% transferred in.

Freshmen *Admission:* 2,568 applied, 2,541 admitted, 1,580 enrolled.

Faculty *Total:* 270, 34% full-time, 14% with terminal degrees. *Student/faculty ratio:* 25:1.

Majors Business administration and management; computer programming related; computer programming (specific applications); computer systems networking and telecommunications; criminal justice/law enforcement administration; dental hygiene; drafting and design technology; emergency medical technology (EMT paramedic); human services; information technology; legal assistant/paralegal; liberal arts and sciences/liberal studies; marketing/marketing

management; nursing (registered nurse training); physical therapist assistant; radiologic technology/science; web page, digital/multimedia and information resources design.

Academic Programs *Special study options:* academic remediation for entering students, accelerated degree program, adult/continuing education programs, advanced placement credit, cooperative education, distance learning, double majors, honors programs, independent study, internships, off-campus study, part-time degree program, services for LD students, summer session for credit. *ROTC:* Army (c).

Library Pottberg Library plus 2 others with 67,852 titles, 351 serial subscriptions, 4,357 audiovisual materials, an OPAC, a Web page.

Computers on Campus 974 computers available on campus for general student use. A campuswide network can be accessed. Online (class) registration, at least one staffed computer lab available. Computer purchase or lease plan available.

Student Life *Housing:* college housing not available. *Activities and Organizations:* drama/theater group, choral group, Student Government Association, Phi Theta Kappa, Phi Beta Lambda, Human Services, PHCC Cares. *Campus security:* 24-hour patrols.

Athletics Member NJCAA. *Intercollegiate sports:* baseball M(s), basketball M(s), softball W(s), tennis W(s), volleyball W(s).

Standardized Tests *Required:* CPT (preferred), SAT I, or ACT (for placement).

Costs (2003–04) *Tuition:* state resident $1644 full-time, $55 per credit part-time; nonresident $6086 full-time, $203 per credit part-time.

Financial Aid Of all full-time matriculated undergraduates who enrolled, 45 Federal Work-Study jobs (averaging $2133).

Applying *Options:* electronic application. *Application fee:* $20. *Required:* high school transcript. *Application deadline:* rolling (freshmen), rolling (transfers). *Notification:* continuous (freshmen), continuous (transfers).

Admissions Contact Mr. Michael Malizia, Director of Admissions and Student Records, Pasco-Hernando Community College, 10230 Ridge Road, New Port Richey, FL 34654-5199. *Phone:* 727-816-3261. *Fax:* 727-816-3389. *E-mail:* malizim@phcc.edu.

PENSACOLA JUNIOR COLLEGE
Pensacola, Florida

- **State-supported** 2-year, founded 1948, part of Florida Community College System
- **Calendar** semesters
- **Degree** certificates, diplomas, and associate
- **Urban** 160-acre campus
- **Coed,** 11,000 undergraduate students

Undergraduates Students come from 37 states and territories, 21 other countries, 2% are from out of state.

Faculty *Total:* 747, 28% full-time.

Majors Accounting; administrative assistant and secretarial science; agriculture; art; art teacher education; automobile/automotive mechanics technology; biology/biological sciences; business administration and management; business/commerce; chemical technology; chemistry; child development; civil engineering technology; clinical laboratory science/medical technology; commercial and advertising art; computer science; construction engineering technology; court reporting; criminal justice/safety; criminology; culinary arts; dental hygiene; design and visual communications; dietetics; drafting and design technology; dramatic/theatre arts; education; electrical, electronic and communications engineering technology; emergency medical technology (EMT paramedic); environmental studies; fire science; forestry technology; general studies; geology/earth science; health and physical education; health/health care administration; health information/medical records administration; history; horticultural science; hotel/motel administration; industrial technology; information science/studies; journalism; kindergarten/preschool education; landscaping and groundskeeping; legal assistant/paralegal; liberal arts and sciences/liberal studies; mathematics; medical administrative assistant and medical secretary; music; music teacher education; natural resources/conservation; nursing (registered nurse training); ornamental horticulture; philosophy; physical therapist assistant; physical therapy; physics; pre-engineering; psychology; radiologic technology/science; religious studies; respiratory care therapy; zoology/animal biology.

Academic Programs *Special study options:* academic remediation for entering students, adult/continuing education programs, advanced placement credit, cooperative education, distance learning, double majors, external degree program, honors programs, independent study, part-time degree program, services for LD students, summer session for credit. *ROTC:* Army (b).

Library Learning Resource Center plus 2 others.

Computers on Campus 1200 computers available on campus for general student use. A campuswide network can be accessed. Internet access, at least one staffed computer lab available.

Student Life *Housing:* college housing not available. *Activities and Organizations:* drama/theater group, student-run newspaper, choral group, Baptist

Student Union, Campus Activities Board, Students for a Multicultural Society, International Council, Engineering Club, national fraternities, national sororities. *Campus security:* 24-hour emergency response devices and patrols, student patrols, late-night transport/escort service. *Student services:* health clinic, personal/ psychological counseling.

Athletics Member NJCAA. *Intercollegiate sports:* baseball M(s), basketball M(s)/W(s), golf M/W, softball W(s), swimming M/W. *Intramural sports:* archery M/W, badminton M/W, basketball M/W, bowling M/W, cross-country running M/W, gymnastics M/W, racquetball M/W, sailing M/W, swimming M/W, tennis M/W, track and field M/W, volleyball M/W, weight lifting M/W, wrestling M.

Standardized Tests *Required:* SAT I, ACT, or CPT (for placement).

Costs (2003–04) *Tuition:* state resident $1337 full-time, $56 per credit hour part-time; nonresident $4985 full-time, $208 per credit hour part-time.

Financial Aid Of all full-time matriculated undergraduates who enrolled, 120 Federal Work-Study jobs (averaging $3000).

Applying *Options:* early admission. *Application fee:* $30. *Required:* high school transcript. *Application deadlines:* 8/30 (freshmen), 8/30 (transfers). *Notification:* continuous until 8/30 (freshmen), continuous until 8/30 (transfers).

Admissions Contact Pensacola Junior College, 1000 College Boulevard, Pensacola, FL 32504-8998. *Phone:* 850-484-1600. *Fax:* 850-484-1829.

POLK COMMUNITY COLLEGE
Winter Haven, Florida

- **State-supported** 2-year, founded 1964, part of Florida Community College System
- **Calendar** semesters 16-16-6-6
- **Degree** certificates and associate
- **Suburban** 98-acre campus with easy access to Orlando and Tampa
- **Endowment** $5.9 million
- **Coed,** 7,109 undergraduate students, 28% full-time, 65% women, 35% men

Undergraduates 2,010 full-time, 5,099 part-time. Students come from 25 states and territories, 73 other countries, 10% are from out of state, 14% African American, 1% Asian American or Pacific Islander, 7% Hispanic American, 0.5% Native American, 4% international.

Freshmen *Admission:* 1,097 applied, 1,097 admitted, 1,097 enrolled.

Faculty *Total:* 444, 25% full-time, 10% with terminal degrees. *Student/faculty ratio:* 25:1.

Majors Accounting technology and bookkeeping; business administration and management; child development; corrections; criminal justice/law enforcement administration; criminal justice/police science; data processing and data processing technology; emergency medical technology (EMT paramedic); finance; fire science; health information/medical records administration; information science/studies; legal administrative assistant/secretary; liberal arts and sciences/liberal studies; marketing/marketing management; medical administrative assistant and medical secretary; nursing (registered nurse training); occupational therapist assistant; physical therapist assistant; pre-engineering; radiologic technology/science; surgical technology.

Academic Programs *Special study options:* academic remediation for entering students, accelerated degree program, adult/continuing education programs, advanced placement credit, cooperative education, distance learning, double majors, English as a second language, independent study, part-time degree program, services for LD students, student-designed majors, summer session for credit. *ROTC:* Army (c).

Library Polk Community College Library with 181,000 titles, 325 serial subscriptions, 4,527 audiovisual materials, an OPAC, a Web page.

Computers on Campus 171 computers available on campus for general student use. A campuswide network can be accessed. Internet access, online (class) registration, at least one staffed computer lab available.

Student Life *Housing:* college housing not available. *Activities and Organizations:* drama/theater group, student-run newspaper, choral group. *Campus security:* 24-hour emergency response devices and patrols.

Athletics Member NJCAA. *Intercollegiate sports:* baseball M(s), basketball M(s), soccer W(s), softball W(s), volleyball W(s).

Standardized Tests *Required:* CPT (for placement).

Costs (2003–04) *Tuition:* state resident $1673 full-time, $56 per credit hour part-time; nonresident $6234 full-time, $208 per credit hour part-time.

Financial Aid Of all full-time matriculated undergraduates who enrolled, 16 Federal Work-Study jobs (averaging $400).

Applying *Options:* early admission, deferred entrance. *Application fee:* $20. *Required:* high school transcript. *Application deadline:* rolling (freshmen), rolling (transfers). *Notification:* continuous (freshmen), continuous (transfers).

Admissions Contact Ms. Barbara Guthrie, Registrar, Polk Community College, 999 Avenue H North East, Winter Haven, FL 33881. *Phone:* 863-297-1010 Ext. 5016. *Toll-free phone:* 863-297-1000 Ext. 5016. *Fax:* 863-297-1010.

REMINGTON COLLEGE-JACKSONVILLE CAMPUS
Jacksonville, Florida

Admissions Contact Mr. Tony Galang, Campus President, Remington College-Jacksonville Campus, 7011 A.C. Skinner Parkway, Jacksonville, FL 32256. *Phone:* 904-296-3435 Ext. 218.

REMINGTON COLLEGE-PINELLAS CAMPUS
Largo, Florida

Admissions Contact Ms. Edna Higgins, Campus President, Remington College-Pinellas Campus, 8550 Ulmerton Road, Largo, FL 33771. *Phone:* 727-532-1999. *Toll-free phone:* 888-900-2343.

REMINGTON COLLEGE-TAMPA CAMPUS
Tampa, Florida

- **Proprietary** primarily 2-year, founded 1948
- **Calendar** quarters
- **Degrees** diplomas, associate, and bachelor's
- **Urban** 10-acre campus
- **Coed**

Student Life *Campus security:* late-night transport/escort service.

Standardized Tests *Required:* Wonderlic aptitude test (for admission).

Costs (2003–04) *Tuition:* $281 per credit hour part-time.

Financial Aid Of all full-time matriculated undergraduates who enrolled, 12 Federal Work-Study jobs (averaging $8000).

Applying *Options:* common application, deferred entrance. *Application fee:* $50. *Required:* high school transcript, interview.

Admissions Contact Ms. Kathy Miller, Director of Admissions, Remington College-Tampa Campus, 2410 East Busch Boulevard, Tampa, FL 33612. *Phone:* 813-935-5700 Ext. 211. *Toll-free phone:* 800-992-4850.

ST. JOHNS RIVER COMMUNITY COLLEGE
Palatka, Florida

- **State-supported** 2-year, founded 1958
- **Calendar** semesters
- **Degree** certificates, diplomas, and associate
- **Small-town** 105-acre campus with easy access to Jacksonville
- **Coed,** 3,459 undergraduate students

Freshmen *Admission:* 1,200 applied, 1,200 admitted.

Faculty *Total:* 157, 39% full-time.

Majors Accounting technology and bookkeeping; administrative assistant and secretarial science; applied art; art; business administration and management; chemical technology; commercial and advertising art; computer and information sciences; computer engineering technology; computer programming; computer typography and composition equipment operation; criminal justice/law enforcement administration; dance; dramatic/theatre arts; electrical, electronic and communications engineering technology; emergency medical technology (EMT paramedic); fire science; health information/medical records administration; liberal arts and sciences/liberal studies; marketing/marketing management; nursing (registered nurse training).

Academic Programs *Special study options:* academic remediation for entering students, accelerated degree program, adult/continuing education programs, advanced placement credit, distance learning, part-time degree program, services for LD students, summer session for credit.

Library 56,925 titles, 7,015 audiovisual materials, an OPAC, a Web page.

Computers on Campus 203 computers available on campus for general student use. At least one staffed computer lab available.

Student Life *Housing:* college housing not available. *Activities and Organizations:* student-run newspaper, choral group. *Campus security:* 24-hour patrols.

Athletics Member NJCAA. *Intercollegiate sports:* baseball M(s), basketball M(s), softball W(s), volleyball W(s).

Standardized Tests *Recommended:* SAT I and SAT II or ACT (for placement).

Costs (2003–04) *Tuition:* state resident $1694 full-time; nonresident $6348 full-time.

Financial Aid Of all full-time matriculated undergraduates who enrolled, 38 Federal Work-Study jobs (averaging $1070). 33 state and other part-time jobs (averaging $1250).

St. Johns River Community College (continued)

Applying *Options:* common application, early admission. *Required:* high school transcript. *Application deadline:* rolling (freshmen), rolling (transfers). *Notification:* continuous (freshmen), continuous (transfers).

Admissions Contact Mr. O'Neal Williams, Dean of Admissions and Records, St. Johns River Community College, 5001 Saint Johns Avenue, Palatka, FL 32177-3897. *Phone:* 386-312-4032.

ST. PETERSBURG COLLEGE
St. Petersburg, Florida

- **State and locally supported** primarily 2-year, founded 1927
- **Calendar** semesters
- **Degrees** certificates, diplomas, associate, and bachelor's
- **Suburban** campus
- **Endowment** $12.0 million
- **Coed,** 24,146 undergraduate students

Undergraduates Students come from 45 states and territories, 30 other countries, 4% are from out of state, 11% African American, 3% Asian American or Pacific Islander, 6% Hispanic American, 0.7% Native American, 1% international.

Freshmen *Admission:* 3,832 applied, 3,832 admitted. *Test scores:* SAT verbal scores over 500: 42%; SAT math scores over 500: 41%; ACT scores over 18: 73%; SAT verbal scores over 600: 10%; SAT math scores over 600: 9%; ACT scores over 24: 26%; SAT verbal scores over 700: 1%; SAT math scores over 700: 1%; ACT scores over 30: 2%.

Faculty *Total:* 1,678, 17% full-time.

Majors Accounting technology and bookkeeping; architectural engineering technology; business administration and management; clinical/medical laboratory technology; commercial and advertising art; computer engineering technology; computer programming; computer systems networking and telecommunications; construction engineering technology; corrections; criminal justice/police science; dental hygiene; drafting and design technology; education; electrical, electronic and communications engineering technology; emergency medical technology (EMT paramedic); engineering/industrial management; fire science; funeral service and mortuary science; health/health care administration; health information/medical records administration; hospitality administration; human services; hydrology and water resources science; industrial radiologic technology; industrial technology; information science/studies; kindergarten/preschool education; landscaping and groundskeeping; legal administrative assistant/secretary; legal assistant/paralegal; liberal arts and sciences/liberal studies; marketing/marketing management; natural resources management; nursing (registered nurse training); physical therapist assistant; plastics engineering technology; quality control technology; radiologic technology/science; respiratory care therapy; sign language interpretation and translation; substance abuse/addiction counseling; telecommunications; tourism and travel services management; veterinary technology; web/multimedia management and webmaster.

Academic Programs *Special study options:* academic remediation for entering students, adult/continuing education programs, advanced placement credit, cooperative education, distance learning, English as a second language, freshman honors college, honors programs, internships, part-time degree program, services for LD students, summer session for credit.

Library M. M. Bennett Library plus 5 others with 222,990 titles, 1,393 serial subscriptions, 16,543 audiovisual materials, an OPAC, a Web page.

Computers on Campus 2951 computers available on campus for general student use. A campuswide network can be accessed from off campus. Internet access, online (class) registration, at least one staffed computer lab available. Computer purchase or lease plan available.

Student Life *Housing:* college housing not available. *Activities and Organizations:* drama/theater group, student-run newspaper. *Campus security:* late-night transport/escort service. *Student services:* women's center.

Athletics Member NJCAA. *Intercollegiate sports:* baseball M(s), basketball M(s)/W(s), softball W(s), volleyball W(s). *Intramural sports:* basketball M, bowling M/W, volleyball M/W.

Standardized Tests *Required for some:* SAT I and SAT II or ACT (for placement), SAT II: Writing Test (for placement), CPT.

Costs (2003–04) *Tuition:* state resident $1493 full-time, $50 per credit part-time; nonresident $5975 full-time, $199 per credit part-time. Full-time tuition and fees vary according to degree level and program. Part-time tuition and fees vary according to degree level and program. *Required fees:* $254 full-time, $8 per credit part-time. *Payment plan:* deferred payment. *Waivers:* senior citizens and employees or children of employees.

Financial Aid Of all full-time matriculated undergraduates who enrolled, 350 Federal Work-Study jobs (averaging $2500).

Applying *Options:* common application, electronic application, early admission, deferred entrance. *Application fee:* $35. *Required:* high school transcript. *Application deadline:* rolling (freshmen). *Notification:* continuous (freshmen).

Admissions Contact St. Petersburg College, PO Box 13489, St. Petersburg, FL 33733-3489. *Phone:* 727-712-5892. *Fax:* 727-712-5872. *E-mail:* information@spcollege.edu.

SANTA FE COMMUNITY COLLEGE
Gainesville, Florida

- **State and locally supported** 2-year, founded 1966, part of Florida Community College System
- **Calendar** semesters
- **Degrees** certificates and associate (offers bachelor's degrees in conjunction with Saint Leo College)
- **Suburban** 175-acre campus with easy access to Jacksonville
- **Coed**

Student Life *Campus security:* 24-hour emergency response devices and patrols.

Athletics Member NJCAA.

Standardized Tests *Required:* SAT I, ACT, or CPT (for placement).

Costs (2003–04) *Tuition:* state resident $1557 full-time, $52 per credit hour part-time; nonresident $5803 full-time, $193 per credit hour part-time.

Financial Aid Of all full-time matriculated undergraduates who enrolled, 190 Federal Work-Study jobs.

Applying *Options:* early admission. *Application fee:* $30. *Required:* high school transcript.

Admissions Contact Ms. Margaret Karrh, Registrar, Santa Fe Community College, 3000 Northwest 83rd Street, Gainesville, FL 32606-6200. *Phone:* 352-395-5857. *Fax:* 352-395-4118. *E-mail:* information@sfcc.edu.

SEMINOLE COMMUNITY COLLEGE
Sanford, Florida

- **State and locally supported** 2-year, founded 1966
- **Calendar** semesters
- **Degree** certificates, diplomas, and associate
- **Small-town** 200-acre campus with easy access to Orlando
- **Endowment** $3.5 million
- **Coed,** 12,108 undergraduate students, 38% full-time, 60% women, 40% men

Undergraduates 4,616 full-time, 7,492 part-time. Students come from 18 states and territories, 3% are from out of state, 13% African American, 3% Asian American or Pacific Islander, 12% Hispanic American, 0.4% Native American, 5% international, 20% transferred in.

Freshmen *Admission:* 2,464 applied, 2,464 admitted, 2,464 enrolled.

Faculty *Total:* 928, 20% full-time, 8% with terminal degrees. *Student/faculty ratio:* 23:1.

Majors Accounting; administrative assistant and secretarial science; architectural engineering technology; automobile/automotive mechanics technology; banking and financial support services; business administration and management; child development; civil engineering technology; computer and information sciences related; computer and information systems security; computer engineering related; computer engineering technology; computer graphics; computer hardware engineering; computer/information technology services administration related; computer programming; computer programming related; computer programming (specific applications); computer programming (vendor/product certification); computer software and media applications related; computer software engineering; computer systems networking and telecommunications; computer/technical support; construction engineering technology; construction management; criminal justice/law enforcement administration; data entry/microcomputer applications; data entry/microcomputer applications related; data modeling/warehousing and database administration; data processing and data processing technology; drafting and design technology; electrical, electronic and communications engineering technology; emergency medical technology (EMT paramedic); finance; fire science; industrial technology; information science/studies; information technology; interior design; legal assistant/paralegal; liberal arts and sciences/liberal studies; marketing/marketing management; nursing (registered nurse training); physical therapy; respiratory care therapy; system administration; telecommunications; web/multimedia management and webmaster; web page, digital/multimedia and information resources design; word processing.

Academic Programs *Special study options:* academic remediation for entering students, accelerated degree program, adult/continuing education programs, advanced placement credit, cooperative education, distance learning, double majors, English as a second language, honors programs, independent study, internships, part-time degree program, services for LD students, study abroad, summer session for credit. *ROTC:* Army (b).

Library Seminole Community College Library plus 1 other with 151,617 titles, 425 serial subscriptions, 7,189 audiovisual materials, an OPAC, a Web page.

Computers on Campus 56 computers available on campus for general student use. A campuswide network can be accessed from off campus. Internet access, online (class) registration, at least one staffed computer lab available.

Student Life *Activities and Organizations:* drama/theater group, student-run newspaper, choral group, Phi Beta Lambda, Phi Theta Kappa, Student Government Association, International Student Organization. *Campus security:* 24-hour emergency response devices and patrols. *Student services:* personal/psychological counseling.
Athletics Member NJCAA. *Intercollegiate sports:* baseball M(s), basketball M(s)/W(s), softball W(s). *Intramural sports:* basketball M/W, golf M, tennis M/W, volleyball M/W.
Standardized Tests *Required:* SAT I, ACT and Enhanced ACT, ACT ASSET, MARS and New MAPS, or CPT (for placement).
Costs (2003–04) *Tuition:* state resident $1439 full-time, $48 per credit hour part-time; nonresident $6205 full-time, $194 per credit hour part-time. *Required fees:* $10 per credit hour part-time. *Room and board:* $308.
Applying *Options:* early admission, deferred entrance. *Required:* high school transcript, minimum 2.0 GPA. *Application deadline:* rolling (freshmen), rolling (transfers). *Notification:* continuous (freshmen), continuous (transfers).
Admissions Contact Ms. Pamela Palaez, Director of Admissions, Seminole Community College, 100 Weldon Boulevard, Sanford, FL 32773-6199. *Phone:* 407-328-2041. *Fax:* 407-328-2395. *E-mail:* admissions@scc-fl.edu.

SOUTH FLORIDA COMMUNITY COLLEGE
Avon Park, Florida

- **State-supported** 2-year, founded 1965, part of Florida Community College System
- **Calendar** semesters
- **Degree** certificates, diplomas, and associate
- **Rural** 80-acre campus with easy access to Tampa-St. Petersburg and Orlando
- **Endowment** $3.3 million
- **Coed**

Faculty *Student/faculty ratio:* 15:1.
Student Life *Campus security:* 24-hour patrols.
Athletics Member NJCAA.
Standardized Tests *Required:* SAT I, ACT or Florida College Entry-Level Placement Test, CPT (for placement).
Costs (2003–04) *Tuition:* state resident $1600 full-time, $53 per credit hour part-time; nonresident $6000 full-time, $197 per credit hour part-time. *Required fees:* $550 full-time. *Room and board:* $900.
Applying *Options:* early admission, deferred entrance. *Required:* high school transcript.
Admissions Contact Ms. Annie Alexander-Harvey, Dean of Student Services, South Florida Community College, 600 West College Drive, Avon Park, FL 33825-9356. *Phone:* 863-453-6661 Ext. 7107.

SOUTH UNIVERSITY
West Palm Beach, Florida

- **Proprietary** primarily 2-year, founded 1899
- **Calendar** quarters
- **Degrees** associate and bachelor's
- **Suburban** 1-acre campus with easy access to Miami
- **Coed,** 450 undergraduate students

Undergraduates Students come from 1 other state.
Faculty *Total:* 60. *Student/faculty ratio:* 8:1.
Majors Accounting; administrative assistant and secretarial science; business administration and management; health services/allied health/health sciences; information science/studies; information technology; legal administrative assistant/secretary; legal assistant/paralegal; legal studies; medical/clinical assistant; nursing (registered nurse training); physical therapist assistant; pre-nursing studies.
Academic Programs *Special study options:* academic remediation for entering students, adult/continuing education programs, advanced placement credit, double majors, internships, part-time degree program.
Library South College Library plus 1 other with 8,400 titles, 67 serial subscriptions.
Computers on Campus 53 computers available on campus for general student use. A campuswide network can be accessed. Internet access, at least one staffed computer lab available.
Student Life *Housing:* college housing not available. *Activities and Organizations:* student-run newspaper, Pro Bono Club. *Campus security:* evening security personnel. *Student services:* personal/psychological counseling.
Standardized Tests *Required:* SAT I or ACT (for admission).
Costs (2003–04) *Tuition:* $10,185 full-time, $2995 per term part-time. *Waivers:* employees or children of employees.
Financial Aid Of all full-time matriculated undergraduates who enrolled, 14 Federal Work-Study jobs (averaging $1530).

Applying *Options:* common application, electronic application, early admission, deferred entrance. *Application fee:* $25. *Required:* high school transcript. *Required for some:* letters of recommendation, interview. *Application deadline:* rolling (freshmen), rolling (transfers). *Notification:* continuous (transfers).
Admissions Contact Mr. Peter Grosfeld, Director of Admissions, South University, 1760 North Congress Avenue, West Palm Beach, FL 33409-5178. *Phone:* 561-697-9200. *Toll-free phone:* 866-629-2902 (in-state); 866-629-9200 (out-of-state). *Fax:* 561-697-9944. *E-mail:* wpbadmiss@southuniversity.edu.

SOUTHWEST FLORIDA COLLEGE
Fort Myers, Florida

- **Independent** 2-year, founded 1940
- **Calendar** quarters
- **Degree** diplomas and associate
- **Urban** campus
- **Coed**

Student Life *Campus security:* day and evening security guards.
Standardized Tests *Required:* CPAt (for placement).
Costs (2003–04) *Tuition:* $7200 full-time, $200 per credit hour part-time. *Required fees:* $590 full-time, $590 per year part-time.
Financial Aid Of all full-time matriculated undergraduates who enrolled, 10 Federal Work-Study jobs (averaging $5000).
Applying *Options:* common application. *Recommended:* high school transcript.
Admissions Contact Ms. Carmen King, Director of Admissions, Southwest Florida College, 1685 Medical Lane, Fort Myers, FL 33907. *Phone:* 239-939-4766. *Toll-free phone:* 866-SWFC-NOW.

SUMMIT INSTITUTE
West Palm Beach, Florida

- **Proprietary** 2-year, founded 1975
- **Calendar** quarters
- **Degree** diplomas and associate
- **Suburban** campus
- **Coed**

Applying *Options:* common application. *Application fee:* $50. *Required:* high school transcript, interview.
Admissions Contact Mr. Mark Proefrock, Vice President, Summit Institute, 1750 45th Street, West Palm Beach, FL 33407-2192. *Phone:* 561-881-0220.

TALLAHASSEE COMMUNITY COLLEGE
Tallahassee, Florida

- **State and locally supported** 2-year, founded 1966, part of Florida Community College System
- **Calendar** semesters
- **Degree** certificates and associate
- **Suburban** 191-acre campus
- **Coed**

Faculty *Student/faculty ratio:* 30:1.
Student Life *Campus security:* 24-hour emergency response devices, late-night transport/escort service.
Athletics Member NJCAA.
Standardized Tests *Required:* Florida College Entry-Level Placement Test (for placement). *Recommended:* SAT I or ACT (for placement).
Financial Aid Of all full-time matriculated undergraduates who enrolled, 226 Federal Work-Study jobs (averaging $2000).
Applying *Options:* electronic application, early admission, deferred entrance. *Required:* high school transcript.
Admissions Contact Ms. Sharon Jefferson, Director of Enrollment Services, Tallahassee Community College, 444 Appleyard Drive, Tallahassee, FL 32304-2895. *Phone:* 850-201-8555. *Fax:* 850-201-8474. *E-mail:* enroll@tcc.fl.edu.

ULTRASOUND DIAGNOSTIC SCHOOL
Jacksonville, Florida

Admissions Contact 10255 Fortune Parkway, Suite 501, Jacksonville, FL 32256.

ULTRASOUND DIAGNOSTIC SCHOOL
Lauderdale Lakes, Florida

Admissions Contact 2760 East Atlantic Boulevard, Lauderdale Lakes, FL 33319.

ULTRASOUND DIAGNOSTIC SCHOOL
Tampa, Florida

Admissions Contact 5701 Hillsborough Avenue, Tampa, FL 33617.

VALENCIA COMMUNITY COLLEGE
Orlando, Florida

- **State-supported** 2-year, founded 1967, part of Florida Community College System
- **Calendar** semesters
- **Degree** certificates and associate
- **Urban** campus
- **Endowment** $14.4 million
- **Coed**

Faculty *Student/faculty ratio:* 21:1.
Student Life *Campus security:* 24-hour emergency response devices and patrols, student patrols, late-night transport/escort service.
Standardized Tests *Required:* SAT I, ACT, or CPT (for placement).
Costs (2003–04) *Tuition:* state resident $1383 full-time, $58 per credit hour part-time; nonresident $5195 full-time, $216 per credit hour part-time.
Financial Aid Of all full-time matriculated undergraduates who enrolled, 293 Federal Work-Study jobs (averaging $2714).
Applying *Options:* early admission. *Application fee:* $25. *Required:* high school transcript.
Admissions Contact Dr. Renee K. Simpson, Director of Admissions and Records, Valencia Community College, PO Box 3028, Orlando, FL 32802-3028. *Phone:* 407-582-1511.

WEBSTER COLLEGE
Holiday, Florida

- **Proprietary** primarily 2-year
- **Degrees** diplomas, associate, and bachelor's
- 209 undergraduate students

Faculty *Student/faculty ratio:* 12:1.
Standardized Tests *Required:* Wonderlic aptitude test (for admission).
Financial Aid Of all full-time matriculated undergraduates who enrolled, 6 Federal Work-Study jobs.
Applying *Required:* high school transcript, minimum 2.0 GPA, interview. *Required for some:* essay or personal statement.
Admissions Contact Ms. Claire L. Walker, Senior Admissions Representative, Webster College, 2127 Grand Boulevard, Holiday, FL 34690. *Phone:* 727-942-0069. *Toll-free phone:* 888-729-7247. *Fax:* 813-938-5709.

WEBSTER COLLEGE
Ocala, Florida

Admissions Contact Admissions Office, Webster College, 1530 SW Third Avenue, Ocala, FL 34474. *Phone:* 352-629-1941.

WEBSTER COLLEGE
Tampa, Florida

- **Private** 2-year, founded 1978
- **Calendar** quarters
- **Degree** diplomas and associate
- **Urban** 2-acre campus
- **Coed, primarily women**

Faculty *Student/faculty ratio:* 12:1.
Student Life *Campus security:* 24-hour emergency response devices, evening security guard.
Financial Aid Of all full-time matriculated undergraduates who enrolled, 5 Federal Work-Study jobs.
Applying *Options:* electronic application. *Required:* interview.
Admissions Contact Mr. Todd A. Matthews Sr., Regional Vice President, Webster College, 3910 US Hwy 301 North, Suite 200, Tampa, FL 33619. *Phone:* 813-620-1446. *Toll-free phone:* 888-729-7247. *E-mail:* admissions@websterinstitute.com.

GEORGIA

ABRAHAM BALDWIN AGRICULTURAL COLLEGE
Tifton, Georgia

- **State-supported** 2-year, founded 1933, part of University System of Georgia
- **Calendar** semesters
- **Degree** certificates and associate
- **Small-town** 390-acre campus
- **Coed,** 3,407 undergraduate students, 58% full-time, 57% women, 43% men

Undergraduates 1,969 full-time, 1,438 part-time. Students come from 10 states and territories, 18% African American, 0.4% Asian American or Pacific Islander, 3% Hispanic American, 0.2% Native American, 1% international, 28% live on campus.
Freshmen *Admission:* 999 enrolled. *Average high school GPA:* 2.8.
Faculty *Total:* 115, 80% full-time. *Student/faculty ratio:* 25:1.
Majors Accounting; administrative assistant and secretarial science; agricultural business and management; agricultural economics; agricultural mechanization; agriculture; animal sciences; art; biological and physical sciences; biology/biological sciences; business administration and management; chemistry; child development; computer engineering technology; computer programming; computer science; computer typography and composition equipment operation; criminal justice/law enforcement administration; criminal justice/police science; data processing and data processing technology; ecology; education; elementary education; English; environmental design/architecture; family and consumer sciences/human sciences; farm and ranch management; fashion merchandising; fish/game management; forestry; forestry technology; history; horticultural science; hospitality administration; humanities; journalism; kindergarten/preschool education; landscaping and groundskeeping; liberal arts and sciences/liberal studies; marketing/marketing management; mathematics; music; nursing (registered nurse training); ornamental horticulture; parks, recreation and leisure facilities management; pharmacy; physical education teaching and coaching; physical sciences; political science and government; poultry science; pre-engineering; psychology; social sciences; social work; sociology; speech and rhetoric; wildlife and wildlands science and management.
Academic Programs *Special study options:* academic remediation for entering students, adult/continuing education programs, advanced placement credit, English as a second language, honors programs, internships, off-campus study, part-time degree program, services for LD students, summer session for credit.
Library Baldwin Library with 69,986 titles, 431 serial subscriptions.
Computers on Campus 158 computers available on campus for general student use. Internet access, at least one staffed computer lab available.
Student Life *Housing:* on-campus residence required for freshman year. *Options:* coed. *Activities and Organizations:* drama/theater group, student-run newspaper, radio station, choral group, Rodeo Club, Baptist Student Union, Forestry/Wildlife Club. *Campus security:* 24-hour emergency response devices and patrols, late-night transport/escort service. *Student services:* health clinic, personal/psychological counseling.
Athletics Member NJCAA. *Intercollegiate sports:* baseball M(s), basketball M(s), softball W(s), tennis M(s)/W(s). *Intramural sports:* basketball M/W, bowling M/W, cheerleading M/W, football M/W, golf M/W, soccer M/W, softball M/W, tennis M/W, volleyball M/W.
Standardized Tests *Required:* SAT I or ACT (for placement).
Costs (2004–05) *Tuition:* state resident $1468 full-time, $59 per credit hour part-time; nonresident $5872 full-time, $233 per credit hour part-time. Part-time tuition and fees vary according to course load. *Required fees:* $454 full-time, $27 per credit hour part-time. *Room and board:* room only: $4140. Room and board charges vary according to board plan and housing facility. *Waivers:* senior citizens and employees or children of employees.
Financial Aid Of all full-time matriculated undergraduates who enrolled, 158 Federal Work-Study jobs (averaging $1675).
Applying *Options:* common application, early admission, deferred entrance. *Application fee:* $5. *Required:* high school transcript. *Application deadline:* 9/24 (freshmen).
Admissions Contact Dr. Donna E. Miller, Director of Institutional Research, Abraham Baldwin Agricultural College, 2802 Moore Highway, Tifton, GA 31793. *Phone:* 229-386-7231. *Toll-free phone:* 800-733-3653. *Fax:* 912-386-7006.

ALBANY TECHNICAL COLLEGE
Albany, Georgia

- **State-supported** 2-year, founded 1961
- **Calendar** quarters
- **Coed,** 3,000 undergraduate students

Majors Child care and guidance related; computer and information sciences; corrections and criminal justice related; culinary arts; drafting and design technology; early childhood education; electrical and electronic engineering technologies related; forestry technology; industrial technology; manufacturing technology; pharmacy technician.

Costs (2004–05) *Tuition:* state resident $1110 full-time, $27 per credit hour part-time; nonresident $2220 full-time, $54 per credit hour part-time.

Admissions Contact Ms. Suzann Culpepper, Director of Admissions, Albany Technical College, 1704 South Slappey Boulevard, Albany, GA 31701-3514. *Phone:* 229-430-3520.

ALTAMAHA TECHNICAL COLLEGE
Jesup, Georgia

Admissions Contact 1777 West Cherry Street, Jesup, GA 31545.

ANDREW COLLEGE
Cuthbert, Georgia

- **Independent United Methodist** 2-year, founded 1854
- **Calendar** semesters
- **Degree** certificates and associate
- **Small-town** 40-acre campus
- **Endowment** $7.0 million
- **Coed,** 331 undergraduate students, 99% full-time, 48% women, 52% men

Undergraduates 328 full-time, 3 part-time. Students come from 11 states and territories, 10 other countries, 16% are from out of state, 45% African American, 0.9% Asian American or Pacific Islander, 4% Hispanic American, 6% international, 6% transferred in, 90% live on campus.

Freshmen *Admission:* 578 applied, 554 admitted, 147 enrolled. *Average high school GPA:* 2.60.

Faculty *Total:* 41, 85% full-time. *Student/faculty ratio:* 12:1.

Majors Agriculture; art; athletic training; biological and physical sciences; biology/biological sciences; business administration and management; chemistry; clinical laboratory science/medical technology; computer and information sciences; dental hygiene; divinity/ministry; dramatic/theatre arts; education; English; forestry; history; humanities; journalism; literature; mass communication/media; mathematics; music; natural sciences; nursing (registered nurse training); occupational therapy; parks, recreation and leisure facilities management; philosophy; physical education teaching and coaching; physical therapy; physics; pre-engineering; pre-pharmacy studies; psychology; religious studies; respiratory care therapy; social sciences; social work; sociology; speech and rhetoric.

Academic Programs *Special study options:* academic remediation for entering students, advanced placement credit, English as a second language, honors programs, part-time degree program, services for LD students, summer session for credit.

Library Pitts Library with 40,000 titles, 100 serial subscriptions.

Computers on Campus 50 computers available on campus for general student use. A campuswide network can be accessed from student residence rooms and from off campus. Internet access, online (class) registration, at least one staffed computer lab available.

Student Life *Housing:* on-campus residence required through sophomore year. *Options:* coed, men-only, women-only. Campus housing is university owned. Freshman campus housing is guaranteed. *Activities and Organizations:* drama/theater group, student-run newspaper, choral group, Drama Club, Outdoor Club, International Club, BSU. *Campus security:* 24-hour patrols, controlled dormitory access, night patrols by trained security personnel. *Student services:* health clinic, personal/psychological counseling.

Athletics Member NJCAA. *Intercollegiate sports:* baseball M(s), golf M(s), soccer M(s)/W(s), softball W(s). *Intramural sports:* archery M/W, badminton M/W, basketball M/W, equestrian sports M/W, fencing M/W, football M, golf M, racquetball M/W, rock climbing M/W, skiing (downhill) M/W, soccer M/W, softball M/W, swimming M/W, table tennis M/W, tennis M/W, ultimate Frisbee M/W, volleyball M/W, weight lifting M/W, wrestling M.

Costs (2004–05) *Comprehensive fee:* $13,935 includes full-time tuition ($8550) and room and board ($5385). Part-time tuition: $350 per credit hour. *Payment plan:* installment. *Waivers:* employees or children of employees.

Financial Aid Of all full-time matriculated undergraduates who enrolled, 72 Federal Work-Study jobs (averaging $772).

Applying *Options:* electronic application, early admission, deferred entrance. *Application fee:* $20. *Required:* high school transcript. *Required for some:* essay or personal statement, 1 letter of recommendation, interview. *Recommended:* minimum 2.0 GPA. *Application deadlines:* 8/6 (freshmen), 8/6 (transfers).

Admissions Contact E. Dean Sims, Director of Admission, Andrew College, 413 College Street, Cuthbert, GA 39840. *Phone:* 229-732-5934. *Toll-free phone:* 800-664-9250. *Fax:* 229-732-2176. *E-mail:* admissions@andrewcollege.edu.

▶ **See page 498 for a narrative description.**

APPALACHIAN TECHNICAL COLLEGE
Jasper, Georgia

Admissions Contact 100 Campus Drive, Jasper, GA 30143.

ASHER SCHOOL OF BUSINESS
Norcross, Georgia

- **Proprietary** 2-year
- **Degree** diplomas and associate
- **Coed**

Faculty *Student/faculty ratio:* 18:1.

Admissions Contact Mr. Darrell Woodrum, Director, Asher School of Business, 4975 Jimmy Carter Boulevard, Suite 600, Norcross, GA 30093. *Phone:* 770-638-0121.

ASHWORTH COLLEGE
Norcross, Georgia

- **Proprietary** 2-year
- **Calendar** semesters
- **Degree** associate
- **Coed**

Costs (2003–04) *Tuition:* Full-time tuition and fees vary according to program. Part-time tuition and fees vary according to program. Contact college as tuition and fees varies by program. *Payment plans:* tuition prepayment, installment.

Applying *Options:* common application, electronic application. *Required:* high school transcript.

Admissions Contact Mr. John Graves, Dean of Undergraduate Studies, Ashworth College, 430 Technology Parkway, Norcross, GA 30092. *Toll-free phone:* 800-223-4542. *E-mail:* info@ashworthcollege.com.

ATHENS TECHNICAL COLLEGE
Athens, Georgia

Admissions Contact Mr. Lenzy Reid, Director of Admissions, Athens Technical College, 800 US Highway 29 North, Athens, GA 30601-1500. *Phone:* 706-355-5008. *Fax:* 706-369-5753.

ATLANTA METROPOLITAN COLLEGE
Atlanta, Georgia

- **State-supported** 2-year, founded 1974, part of University System of Georgia
- **Calendar** semesters
- **Degree** certificates and associate
- **Urban** 68-acre campus
- **Coed,** 1,907 undergraduate students, 44% full-time, 67% women, 33% men

Undergraduates 831 full-time, 1,076 part-time. Students come from 22 states and territories, 33 other countries, 8% are from out of state, 94% African American, 1% Asian American or Pacific Islander, 0.6% Hispanic American, 0.1% Native American, 4% international, 9% transferred in.

Freshmen *Admission:* 1,172 applied, 1,112 admitted, 420 enrolled. *Test scores:* SAT verbal scores over 500: 15%; SAT math scores over 500: 12%; SAT verbal scores over 600: 2%; SAT math scores over 600: 2%.

Faculty *Total:* 76, 62% full-time, 42% with terminal degrees. *Student/faculty ratio:* 26:1.

Majors African-American/Black studies; art; biology/biological sciences; business administration and management; chemistry; child development; communication/speech communication and rhetoric; computer and information sciences; computer/information technology services administration related; computer science; criminal justice/law enforcement administration; education (multiple levels); engineering technology; English; foreign languages and literatures; general studies; health and physical education; health services/allied health/health sciences; history; human services; information science/studies; information technology; mathematics; music; nursing (licensed practical/vocational nurse training); operations management; physics; political science and government; psychology; social work; speech and rhetoric.

Academic Programs *Special study options:* academic remediation for entering students, adult/continuing education programs, cooperative education, part-time degree program, services for LD students, study abroad, summer session for credit.

Library Atlanta Metropolitan College Library with an OPAC, a Web page.

Computers on Campus 576 computers available on campus for general student use. A campuswide network can be accessed from off campus. Internet access, at least one staffed computer lab available.

Atlanta Metropolitan College (continued)

Student Life *Housing:* college housing not available. *Activities and Organizations:* drama/theater group, student-run newspaper, choral group, International Students Organization, Drama Club, choir, Criminal Justice Club, Study Abroad Club. *Campus security:* 24-hour emergency response devices and patrols. *Student services:* personal/psychological counseling.

Athletics Member NJCAA. *Intercollegiate sports:* basketball M(s)/W(s), cheerleading M/W.

Standardized Tests *Required:* SAT I or ACT (for admission). *Required for some:* SAT I or ACT (for admission).

Costs (2004–05) *Tuition:* state resident $1398 full-time, $59 per credit hour part-time; nonresident $5592 full-time, $233 per credit hour part-time. *Required fees:* $200 full-time, $100 per term part-time.

Applying *Options:* common application. *Application fee:* $20. *Required:* high school transcript, minimum 1.9 GPA, Must meet the University System of Georgia's freshman index. *Application deadlines:* 7/25 (freshmen), 7/25 (transfers). *Notification:* continuous until 8/20 (freshmen), continuous until 8/20 (transfers).

Admissions Contact Ms. Joanne Crump, Director, Office of Admissions, Atlanta Metropolitan College, 1630 Metropolitan Parkway, SW, Atlanta, GA 30310-4498. *Phone:* 404-756-4004. *Fax:* 404-756-4407. *E-mail:* admissions@atlm.edu.

ATLANTA TECHNICAL COLLEGE
Atlanta, Georgia

Admissions Contact Atlanta Technical College, 1560 Metropolitan Parkway, Atlanta, GA 30310.

AUGUSTA TECHNICAL COLLEGE
Augusta, Georgia

- **State-supported** 2-year, founded 1961, part of Georgia Department of Technical and Adult Education
- **Calendar** quarters
- **Degree** certificates, diplomas, and associate
- **Urban** 70-acre campus
- **Coed,** 4,438 undergraduate students

Undergraduates Students come from 2 states and territories, 54% African American, 2% Asian American or Pacific Islander, 2% Hispanic American, 0.3% Native American, 0.5% international.

Faculty *Total:* 549, 46% full-time.

Majors Accounting; administrative assistant and secretarial science; child development; computer programming; electrical, electronic and communications engineering technology; emergency medical technology (EMT paramedic); information science/studies; marketing/marketing management; mechanical engineering/mechanical technology; respiratory care therapy.

Academic Programs *Special study options:* academic remediation for entering students, advanced placement credit, cooperative education, distance learning, double majors, English as a second language, internships, part-time degree program, services for LD students, summer session for credit.

Library Information Technology Center with 75,816 titles, 3,445 serial subscriptions, 2,733 audiovisual materials, an OPAC, a Web page.

Computers on Campus 339 computers available on campus for general student use. A campuswide network can be accessed from off campus. Internet access, at least one staffed computer lab available.

Student Life *Housing:* college housing not available. *Activities and Organizations:* VICA, professional organizations. *Campus security:* 24-hour emergency response devices, 12-hour patrols by trained security personnel.

Athletics *Intercollegiate sports:* golf M.

Standardized Tests *Required:* ACT ASSET (for placement).

Costs (2004–05) *Tuition:* state resident $1008 full-time, $28 per quarter hour part-time; nonresident $2016 full-time, $56 per quarter hour part-time. Full-time tuition and fees vary according to course load. Part-time tuition and fees vary according to course load. *Required fees:* $150 full-time, $50 per term part-time. *Waivers:* senior citizens and employees or children of employees.

Applying *Options:* early admission, deferred entrance. *Application fee:* $15. *Required:* high school transcript. *Application deadline:* rolling (freshmen), rolling (transfers). *Notification:* continuous (freshmen), continuous (transfers).

Admissions Contact Mr. Brian Roberts, Director of Admissions and Counseling, Augusta Technical College, 3200 Augusta Tech Drive, Augusta, GA 30906. *Phone:* 706-771-4031. *Fax:* 706-771-4034. *E-mail:* bcrobert@augusta.tec.ga.us.

BAINBRIDGE COLLEGE
Bainbridge, Georgia

- **State-supported** 2-year, founded 1972, part of University System of Georgia
- **Calendar** semesters
- **Degree** certificates and associate
- **Small-town** 160-acre campus
- **Coed,** 2,279 undergraduate students, 34% full-time, 66% women, 34% men

Undergraduates 786 full-time, 1,493 part-time. Students come from 3 states and territories, 1% are from out of state, 43% African American, 0.7% Asian American or Pacific Islander, 0.8% Hispanic American, 0.1% Native American.

Freshmen *Admission:* 1,322 applied, 1,089 admitted.

Faculty *Total:* 106, 40% full-time, 18% with terminal degrees.

Majors Accounting; administrative assistant and secretarial science; agriculture; art; automobile/automotive mechanics technology; biology/biological sciences; business administration and management; business teacher education; chemistry; criminal justice/law enforcement administration; data processing and data processing technology; drafting and design technology; dramatic/theatre arts; education; electrical, electronic and communications engineering technology; elementary education; English; family and consumer sciences/human sciences; forestry; health teacher education; history; information science/studies; journalism; kindergarten/preschool education; liberal arts and sciences/liberal studies; marketing/marketing management; mathematics; nursing (licensed practical/vocational nurse training); nursing (registered nurse training); political science and government; psychology; sociology; speech and rhetoric; welding technology.

Academic Programs *Special study options:* academic remediation for entering students, adult/continuing education programs, advanced placement credit, distance learning, double majors, independent study, part-time degree program, services for LD students, study abroad, summer session for credit.

Library Bainbridge College Library with 35,959 titles, 299 serial subscriptions, 1,679 audiovisual materials, an OPAC.

Computers on Campus 250 computers available on campus for general student use. A campuswide network can be accessed. Internet access, online (class) registration, at least one staffed computer lab available.

Student Life *Housing:* college housing not available. *Activities and Organizations:* drama/theater group, Phi Theta Kappa, Alpha Beta Gamma, Drama Club, Delta Club, Sigma Kappa Delta. *Campus security:* 24-hour patrols.

Athletics *Intramural sports:* table tennis M/W, volleyball M/W.

Standardized Tests *Required for some:* SAT I or ACT (for admission), ACT COMPASS.

Costs (2003–04) *Tuition:* state resident $1522 full-time; nonresident $5716 full-time. *Required fees:* $62 full-time.

Applying *Options:* electronic application, early admission. *Required for some:* high school transcript, minimum 1.8 GPA, 3 letters of recommendation, interview. *Application deadlines:* 8/1 (freshmen), 8/1 (transfers). *Notification:* continuous (freshmen), continuous (transfers).

Admissions Contact Mrs. Connie Snyder, Director of Admissions and Records, Bainbridge College, 2500 East Shotwell Street, Bainbridge, GA 39819. *Phone:* 229-248-2504. *Fax:* 229-248-2525. *E-mail:* csnyder@bainbridge.edu.

BAUDER COLLEGE
Atlanta, Georgia

- **Proprietary** 2-year, founded 1964
- **Calendar** quarters
- **Degree** associate
- **Suburban** campus
- **Coed, primarily women**

Student Life *Campus security:* 24-hour emergency response devices and patrols.

Applying *Options:* electronic application. *Required:* essay or personal statement, high school transcript, 2 letters of recommendation, interview.

Admissions Contact Ms. Lillie Lanier, Admissions Representative, Bauder College, Phipps Plaza, 3500 Peachtree Road NE, Atlanta, GA 30326. *Phone:* 404-237-7573. *Toll-free phone:* 404-237-7573 (in-state); 800-241-3797 (out-of-state). *Fax:* 404-237-1642. *E-mail:* admissions@bauder.edu.

CENTRAL GEORGIA TECHNICAL COLLEGE
Macon, Georgia

- **State-supported** 2-year, founded 1966, part of Georgia Department of Technical and Adult Education
- **Calendar** quarters
- **Degree** certificates, diplomas, and associate

- **Suburban** 152-acre campus
- **Coed,** 5,727 undergraduate students, 47% full-time, 63% women, 37% men

Undergraduates 2,682 full-time, 3,045 part-time. Students come from 1 other state, 61% African American, 0.5% Asian American or Pacific Islander, 0.5% Hispanic American, 0.4% Native American, 24% transferred in.
Freshmen *Admission:* 2,136 applied, 2,032 admitted, 1,598 enrolled. *Average high school GPA:* 2.50.
Faculty *Total:* 511, 22% full-time, 2% with terminal degrees. *Student/faculty ratio:* 12:1.
Majors Accounting; accounting technology and bookkeeping; business administration and management; child care and support services management; clinical/medical laboratory technology; computer management; developmental and child psychology; human resources management; industrial technology; information science/studies.
Academic Programs *Special study options:* academic remediation for entering students, cooperative education, distance learning, external degree program, internships, off-campus study, part-time degree program, services for LD students.
Computers on Campus Internet access, at least one staffed computer lab available.
Student Life *Housing:* college housing not available. *Activities and Organizations:* Skills USA-VICA, student government. *Campus security:* 24-hour patrols.
Standardized Tests *Required:* ACT ASSET (for admission).
Costs (2004–05) *Tuition:* state resident $972 full-time, $27 per credit part-time; nonresident $1944 full-time, $54 per credit part-time. Full-time tuition and fees vary according to program. Part-time tuition and fees vary according to program. *Required fees:* $138 full-time, $15 per term part-time. *Waivers:* senior citizens.
Financial Aid Of all full-time matriculated undergraduates who enrolled, 100 Federal Work-Study jobs. *Financial aid deadline:* 9/1.
Applying *Application fee:* $15. *Required:* high school transcript. *Application deadline:* 9/10 (freshmen).
Admissions Contact Office of Admissions, Central Georgia Technical College, 3300 Macon Tech Drive, Macon, GA 31206-3628. *Phone:* 478-757-3403. *Fax:* 478-757-3454. *E-mail:* info@cgtcollege.org.

CHATTAHOOCHEE TECHNICAL COLLEGE
Marietta, Georgia

- **State-supported** 2-year, founded 1961, part of Georgia Department of Technical and Adult Education
- **Calendar** quarters
- **Degree** certificates, diplomas, and associate
- **Suburban** campus with easy access to Atlanta
- **Coed**

Faculty *Student/faculty ratio:* 19:1.
Student Life *Campus security:* full-time day and evening security.
Standardized Tests *Required for some:* ACT ASSET.
Financial Aid Of all full-time matriculated undergraduates who enrolled, 50 Federal Work-Study jobs (averaging $1500).
Applying *Options:* early admission, deferred entrance. *Application fee:* $15. *Recommended:* high school transcript.
Admissions Contact Ms. Nichole Kennedy, Director of the Access Center, Chattahoochee Technical College, 980 South Cobb Drive, Marietta, GA 30060. *Phone:* 770-528-4581. *Fax:* 770-528-4578.

COASTAL GEORGIA COMMUNITY COLLEGE
Brunswick, Georgia

- **State-supported** 2-year, founded 1961, part of University System of Georgia
- **Calendar** semesters
- **Degree** certificates and associate
- **Small-town** 193-acre campus with easy access to Jacksonville
- **Endowment** $78,366
- **Coed,** 2,210 undergraduate students

Undergraduates Students come from 8 states and territories, 14% are from out of state, 23% African American, 1% Asian American or Pacific Islander, 2% Hispanic American, 0.4% Native American.
Freshmen *Admission:* 644 applied, 494 admitted. *Average high school GPA:* 2.30.
Faculty *Total:* 94, 66% full-time.
Majors Agricultural business and management; art; biology/biological sciences; business administration and management; chemistry; clinical/medical

laboratory technology; computer science; criminal justice/law enforcement administration; dental hygiene; education (multiple levels); English; foreign languages and literatures; forestry; geology/earth science; health and physical education; history; liberal arts and sciences/liberal studies; mathematics; medical radiologic technology; nursing (registered nurse training); occupational therapy; parks, recreation and leisure facilities management; philosophy; physical therapy; physician assistant; physics; political science and government; pre-dentistry studies; pre-engineering; pre-medical studies; pre-pharmacy studies; pre-veterinary studies; psychology; respiratory care therapy; sociology.
Academic Programs *Special study options:* academic remediation for entering students, adult/continuing education programs, advanced placement credit, distance learning, double majors, part-time degree program, services for LD students, study abroad, summer session for credit.
Library Clara Wood Gould Memorial Library with 535 serial subscriptions, 1,151 audiovisual materials, an OPAC.
Computers on Campus 250 computers available on campus for general student use. A campuswide network can be accessed from off campus. Internet access, at least one staffed computer lab available.
Student Life *Housing:* college housing not available. *Activities and Organizations:* student-run newspaper, Association of Nursing Students, Minority Advisement and Social Development Association, Student Government Association, Baptist Student Union, Phi Theta Kappa. *Campus security:* 24-hour patrols, late-night transport/escort service. *Student services:* personal/psychological counseling.
Athletics Member NJCAA. *Intercollegiate sports:* basketball M(s), softball W(s). *Intramural sports:* basketball M/W, soccer M/W, swimming M/W, tennis M/W, volleyball M/W.
Standardized Tests *Required for some:* SAT I and SAT II or ACT (for admission), SAT II: Writing Test (for admission).
Costs (2004–05) *Tuition:* state resident $1468 full-time, $62 per credit hour part-time; nonresident $5872 full-time, $245 per credit hour part-time. *Required fees:* $212 full-time, $52 per term part-time. *Waivers:* senior citizens.
Financial Aid Of all full-time matriculated undergraduates who enrolled, 80 Federal Work-Study jobs (averaging $1500).
Applying *Options:* common application, electronic application, deferred entrance. *Application fee:* $20. *Required:* high school transcript, minimum 2.0 GPA, immunization records. *Application deadlines:* 8/19 (freshmen), 8/19 (transfers). *Notification:* continuous (freshmen), continuous (transfers).
Admissions Contact Dr. Mollie DeHart, Director of Admissions/Registrar, Coastal Georgia Community College, 3700 Altama Avenue, Brunswick, GA 31525. *Phone:* 912-264-7253. *Toll-free phone:* 800-675-7235. *Fax:* 912-262-3072. *E-mail:* admiss@cgcc.edu.

COLUMBUS TECHNICAL COLLEGE
Columbus, Georgia

- **State-supported** 2-year, founded 1961, part of Georgia Department of Technical and Adult Education
- **Calendar** quarters
- **Degree** certificates, diplomas, and associate
- **Urban** campus with easy access to Atlanta
- **Coed**

Student Life *Campus security:* security patrols during class hours.
Standardized Tests *Required:* SAT I or ACT (for admission).
Financial Aid Of all full-time matriculated undergraduates who enrolled, 6 Federal Work-Study jobs (averaging $2000).
Applying *Options:* common application, early admission. *Application fee:* $15. *Required:* high school transcript. *Required for some:* letters of recommendation, interview.
Admissions Contact Dr. Pamela Robinson, Registrar, Columbus Technical College, 928 Manchester Expressway, Columbus, GA 31904. *Phone:* 706-649-1858. *E-mail:* bvincent@columbustech.org.

COOSA VALLEY TECHNICAL COLLEGE
Rome, Georgia

Admissions Contact Coosa Valley Technical College, One Maurice Culberson Drive, Rome, GA 30161. *Toll-free phone:* 888-331-CVTC.

DARTON COLLEGE
Albany, Georgia

- **State-supported** 2-year, founded 1965, part of University System of Georgia
- **Calendar** semesters
- **Degrees** certificates, associate, and postbachelor's certificates
- **Suburban** 185-acre campus

Darton College (continued)

■ **Coed,** 3,811 undergraduate students, 46% full-time, 71% women, 29% men

Undergraduates 1,767 full-time, 2,044 part-time. Students come from 6 other countries, 4% are from out of state, 42% African American, 0.9% Asian American or Pacific Islander, 1% Hispanic American, 0.2% Native American, 0.7% international, 6% transferred in. *Retention:* 72% of 2002 full-time freshmen returned.

Freshmen *Admission:* 1,238 applied, 999 admitted, 960 enrolled. *Average high school GPA:* 2.70. *Test scores:* SAT verbal scores over 500: 24%; SAT math scores over 500: 21%; ACT scores over 18: 31%; SAT verbal scores over 600: 5%; SAT math scores over 600: 3%; ACT scores over 24: 2%; SAT verbal scores over 700: 2%.

Faculty *Total:* 207, 41% full-time. *Student/faculty ratio:* 19:1.

Majors Accounting; administrative assistant and secretarial science; agriculture; anthropology; art; biology/biological sciences; business administration and management; business teacher education; cardiovascular technology; chemistry; clinical laboratory science/medical technology; computer and information sciences; computer management; computer programming; computer science; criminal justice/law enforcement administration; diagnostic medical sonography and ultrasound technology; dramatic/theatre arts; economics; education; engineering technology; English; environmental science; foreign languages and literatures; forensic science and technology; forestry; general studies; geography; health and physical education; health information/medical records administration; health information/medical records technology; histologic technician; history; journalism; mathematics; music; nuclear medical technology; nursing (licensed practical/vocational nurse training); nursing (registered nurse training); occupational therapist assistant; office occupations and clerical services; optometric technician; pharmacy technician; philosophy; physical therapist assistant; physician assistant; physics; political science and government; pre-dentistry studies; pre-engineering; pre-law; pre-medical studies; pre-pharmacy studies; pre-veterinary studies; psychiatric/mental health services technology; psychology; respiratory care therapy; social work; sociology; speech and rhetoric.

Academic Programs *Special study options:* academic remediation for entering students, accelerated degree program, adult/continuing education programs, advanced placement credit, cooperative education, distance learning, double majors, English as a second language, honors programs, independent study, part-time degree program, services for LD students, student-designed majors, study abroad, summer session for credit. *ROTC:* Army (c).

Library Weatherbee Learning Resources Center with 67,507 titles, an OPAC, a Web page.

Computers on Campus A campuswide network can be accessed from off campus. Internet access, online (class) registration, at least one staffed computer lab available.

Student Life *Housing:* college housing not available. *Activities and Organizations:* drama/theater group, student-run newspaper, choral group, Students in Free Enterprise (SIFE), Darton Ambassadors, Alpha Beta Gamma, Darton Association of Nursing Students (DANS), Delta Psi Omega. *Campus security:* 24-hour patrols, student patrols, late-night transport/escort service. *Student services:* personal/psychological counseling, women's center.

Athletics Member NJCAA. *Intercollegiate sports:* baseball M, basketball W, golf M/W, softball W, swimming M/W, tennis M/W. *Intramural sports:* badminton M/W, basketball M/W, bowling M/W, football M, volleyball M/W.

Standardized Tests *Required for some:* SAT I or ACT (for admission), SAT II: Subject Tests (for admission).

Costs (2004–05) *Tuition:* state resident $1398 full-time, $59 per credit hour part-time; nonresident $5592 full-time, $236 per credit hour part-time. Full-time tuition and fees vary according to course load. Part-time tuition and fees vary according to course load. *Required fees:* $264 full-time, $132 per term part-time. *Payment plan:* deferred payment. *Waivers:* senior citizens and employees or children of employees.

Financial Aid Of all full-time matriculated undergraduates who enrolled, 60 Federal Work-Study jobs.

Applying *Options:* common application, electronic application, early admission. *Application fee:* $20. *Required:* high school transcript, minimum 1.8 GPA, proof of immunization. *Application deadlines:* 7/20 (freshmen), 7/20 (transfers). *Notification:* continuous until 7/27 (freshmen), continuous until 7/27 (transfers).

Admissions Contact Assistant Director, Admissions, Darton College, 2400 Gillionville Road, Albany, GA 31707. *Phone:* 229-430-6740. *Fax:* 229-430-2926. *E-mail:* darton@mail.dartnet.peachnet.edu.

DEKALB TECHNICAL COLLEGE
Clarkston, Georgia

■ **State-supported** 2-year, founded 1961, part of Georgia Department of Technical and Adult Education
■ **Calendar** quarters
■ **Degree** certificates, diplomas, and associate
■ **Suburban** 17-acre campus with easy access to Atlanta
■ **Coed,** 5,303 undergraduate students, 37% full-time, 61% women, 39% men

Undergraduates 1,975 full-time, 3,328 part-time. Students come from 15 states and territories, 8% are from out of state, 70% African American, 4% Asian American or Pacific Islander, 2% Hispanic American, 0.3% Native American.

Freshmen *Admission:* 5,303 applied, 5,303 admitted.

Faculty *Total:* 400, 25% full-time. *Student/faculty ratio:* 15:1.

Majors Accounting; administrative assistant and secretarial science; automobile/automotive mechanics technology; business/commerce; clinical/medical laboratory technology; computer engineering technology; computer programming; electrical, electronic and communications engineering technology; electromechanical technology; engineering technology; heating, air conditioning and refrigeration technology; instrumentation technology; legal administrative assistant/secretary; marketing/marketing management; medical/clinical assistant; operations management; ophthalmic laboratory technology; surgical technology; telecommunications.

Academic Programs *Special study options:* academic remediation for entering students, adult/continuing education programs, English as a second language, internships, part-time degree program, services for LD students, summer session for credit.

Library an OPAC, a Web page.

Computers on Campus 500 computers available on campus for general student use. A campuswide network can be accessed. Internet access, at least one staffed computer lab available.

Student Life *Housing:* college housing not available. *Activities and Organizations:* Student Government Association, Phi Beta Lambda, National Vocational-Technical Honor Society, Collegiate Secretaries International, Epsilon Delta Phi. *Campus security:* security during class hours.

Standardized Tests *Required:* ACT ASSET (for admission). *Recommended:* SAT I or ACT (for admission).

Costs (2004–05) *Tuition:* state resident $1215 full-time, $27 per credit hour part-time; nonresident $2430 full-time, $54 per credit hour part-time. *Required fees:* $186 full-time, $62 per term part-time.

Financial Aid Of all full-time matriculated undergraduates who enrolled, 50 Federal Work-Study jobs (averaging $4000).

Applying *Options:* common application, early admission. *Application fee:* $15. *Required:* high school transcript. *Application deadline:* rolling (freshmen), rolling (transfers).

Admissions Contact Ms. Tracey Axelberd, Recruiter/Admissions Specialist, DeKalb Technical College, 495 North Indian Creek Drive, Clarkston, GA 30021-2397. *Phone:* 404-297-9522 Ext. 1602. *Fax:* 404-294-4234. *E-mail:* admissionsclark@dekalbtech.org.

EAST CENTRAL TECHNICAL INSTITUTE
Fitzgerald, Georgia

■ **State-supported** 2-year, founded 1968
■ **Calendar** quarters
■ **Degree** certificates and diplomas
■ **Rural** 30-acre campus
■ **Coed,** 1,566 undergraduate students

Undergraduates 38% African American, 0.3% Asian American or Pacific Islander, 0.9% Hispanic American, 0.1% Native American.

Costs (2004–05) *Tuition:* $27 per credit hour part-time; nonresident $54 per credit hour part-time.

Admissions Contact Ms. Connie Coffey, Vice President of Student Services, East Central Technical Institute, 667 Perry House Road, Fitzgerald, GA 31750. *Phone:* 229-468-2033. *E-mail:* admissions@eastcentraltech.edu.

EAST GEORGIA COLLEGE
Swainsboro, Georgia

■ **State-supported** 2-year, founded 1973, part of University System of Georgia
■ **Calendar** semesters
■ **Degree** associate
■ **Rural** 207-acre campus
■ **Endowment** $32,500
■ **Coed**

Faculty *Student/faculty ratio:* 23:1.

Student Life *Campus security:* 24-hour patrols.

Standardized Tests *Required:* SAT I or ACT (for admission).

Costs (2004–05) *Tuition:* state resident $1468 full-time, $62 per credit hour part-time; nonresident $5872 full-time, $245 per credit hour part-time. *Required fees:* $132 full-time, $38 per term part-time.

Financial Aid Of all full-time matriculated undergraduates who enrolled, 34 Federal Work-Study jobs (averaging $1410).

Applying *Options:* early admission, deferred entrance. *Application fee:* $20. *Required:* high school transcript.

Admissions Contact Ms. Linda Connelly, Admissions Specialist, East Georgia College, 131 College Circle, Swainsboro, GA 30401. *Phone:* 478-289-2019. *Fax:* 478-289-2038.

EMORY UNIVERSITY, OXFORD COLLEGE
Oxford, Georgia

- **Independent Methodist** 2-year, founded 1836, part of Emory University
- **Calendar** semesters
- **Degree** associate
- **Small-town** 150-acre campus with easy access to Atlanta
- **Endowment** $26.0 million
- **Coed**

Faculty *Student/faculty ratio:* 10:1.
Student Life *Campus security:* 24-hour emergency response devices and patrols, student patrols, late-night transport/escort service, controlled dormitory access.
Athletics Member NJCAA.
Standardized Tests *Required:* SAT I or ACT (for admission). *Required for some:* SAT II: Subject Tests (for admission).
Costs (2003–04) *Comprehensive fee:* $27,156 includes full-time tuition ($20,620), mandatory fees ($220), and room and board ($6316). Part-time tuition: $859 per credit hour. *Room and board:* college room only: $4162. Room and board charges vary according to housing facility. *Payment plans:* tuition prepayment, installment.
Financial Aid Of all full-time matriculated undergraduates who enrolled, 225 Federal Work-Study jobs (averaging $1600).
Applying *Options:* common application, electronic application, early admission, early action, deferred entrance. *Application fee:* $40. *Required:* essay or personal statement, high school transcript, 1 letter of recommendation, level of interest. *Required for some:* interview. *Recommended:* minimum 3.0 GPA, 2 letters of recommendation.
Admissions Contact Ms. Jennifer B. Taylor, Associate Dean of Admission and Financial Aid, Emory University, Oxford College, 100 Hamill Street, PO Box 1418, Oxford, GA 30054. *Phone:* 770-784-8328. *Toll-free phone:* 800-723-8328. *Fax:* 770-784-8359.

FLINT RIVER TECHNICAL COLLEGE
Thomaston, Georgia

Admissions Contact Mr. Gary Williams, Vice President of Student Services, Flint River Technical College, 1533 Highway 19 South, Thomaston, GA 30286-4752. *Phone:* 706-646-6148. *Toll-free phone:* 800-752-9681.

FLOYD COLLEGE
Rome, Georgia

- **State-supported** 2-year, founded 1970, part of University System of Georgia
- **Calendar** semesters
- **Degree** certificates, diplomas, and associate
- **Small-town** 226-acre campus with easy access to Atlanta
- **Coed**

Faculty *Student/faculty ratio:* 30:1.
Student Life *Campus security:* 24-hour patrols.
Standardized Tests *Required:* SAT I or ACT (for admission).
Financial Aid Of all full-time matriculated undergraduates who enrolled, 50 Federal Work-Study jobs (averaging $3500).
Applying *Options:* common application, electronic application, early admission, deferred entrance. *Application fee:* $20. *Required:* high school transcript, minimum 1.8 GPA.
Admissions Contact Ms. Renee L. Tumblin, Recruitment Coordinator, Floyd College, PO Box 1864, Rome, GA 30162-1864. *Phone:* 706-295-6339. *Toll-free phone:* 706-295-6339 (in-state); 800-332-2406 Ext. 6339 (out-of-state). *Fax:* 706-295-6610. *E-mail:* admitme@mail.fc.peachnet.edu.

GAINESVILLE COLLEGE
Oakwood, Georgia

Admissions Contact Tim Buchanan, Director of Admissions, Gainesville College, PO Box 1358, Gainesville, GA 30503-1358. *Phone:* 770-718-3641. *Fax:* 770-718-3859.

GEORGIA AVIATION & TECHNICAL COLLEGE
Eastman, Georgia

Admissions Contact 71 Airport Road, Heart of Georgia Regional Airport, Eastman, GA 31023.

GEORGIA MEDICAL INSTITUTE-DEKALB
Atlanta, Georgia

Admissions Contact Ms. Trish Sherwood, Director of Admissions, Georgia Medical Institute-DeKalb, 1706 Northeast Expressway, Atlanta, GA 30329. *Phone:* 404-327-8787.

GEORGIA MILITARY COLLEGE
Milledgeville, Georgia

- **State and locally supported** 2-year, founded 1879
- **Calendar** quarters
- **Degree** associate
- **Small-town** 40-acre campus
- **Coed**

Faculty *Student/faculty ratio:* 20:1.
Student Life *Campus security:* 24-hour emergency response devices and patrols.
Athletics Member NSCAA.
Standardized Tests *Required for some:* SAT I or ACT (for admission). *Recommended:* SAT I or ACT (for admission).
Financial Aid Of all full-time matriculated undergraduates who enrolled, 51 Federal Work-Study jobs (averaging $1218).
Applying *Options:* early admission, deferred entrance. *Application fee:* $25. *Required:* high school transcript.
Admissions Contact Mrs. Donna W. Findley, Director of Admissions, Georgia Military College, 201 East Greene Street, Milledgeville, GA 31061-3398. *Phone:* 478-445-2751. *Toll-free phone:* 800-342-0413.

GEORGIA PERIMETER COLLEGE
Decatur, Georgia

- **State-supported** 2-year, founded 1964, part of University System of Georgia
- **Calendar** semesters
- **Degree** certificates and associate
- **Suburban** 100-acre campus with easy access to Atlanta
- **Endowment** $136,686
- **Coed**, 18,986 undergraduate students, 45% full-time, 63% women, 37% men

Undergraduates 8,548 full-time, 10,438 part-time. Students come from 40 states and territories, 125 other countries, 7% are from out of state, 37% African American, 9% Asian American or Pacific Islander, 4% Hispanic American, 0.3% Native American, 5% international, 5% transferred in.
Freshmen *Admission:* 3,247 enrolled. *Average high school GPA:* 2.88.
Faculty *Total:* 1,653, 20% full-time, 20% with terminal degrees. *Student/faculty ratio:* 21:1.
Majors Anthropology; art; biological and physical sciences; biology/biological sciences; business administration and management; chemistry; computer/information technology services administration related; computer science; dental hygiene; dramatic/theatre arts; education; education (multiple levels); elementary education; English; fire science; foreign languages and literatures; foreign languages related; general studies; geology/earth science; health and physical education; history; journalism; marketing/marketing management; mathematics; music; nursing (registered nurse training); philosophy; physical education teaching and coaching; physics; political science and government related; pre-dentistry studies; pre-engineering; pre-medical studies; pre-pharmacy studies; psychology; sign language interpretation and translation; sociology.
Academic Programs *Special study options:* academic remediation for entering students, adult/continuing education programs, advanced placement credit, distance learning, English as a second language, honors programs, part-time degree program, services for LD students, study abroad, summer session for credit. *ROTC:* Army (c).
Library Georgia Perimeter College Library with 369,969 titles, 2,032 serial subscriptions, 15,500 audiovisual materials, an OPAC.
Computers on Campus A campuswide network can be accessed from off campus. At least one staffed computer lab available.
Student Life *Housing:* college housing not available. *Activities and Organizations:* drama/theater group, student-run newspaper, choral group. *Campus*

Georgia Perimeter College (continued)

security: 24-hour emergency response devices and patrols, late-night transport/escort service. *Student services:* personal/psychological counseling.

Athletics Member NJCAA. *Intercollegiate sports:* baseball M(s), basketball M(s)/W(s), soccer M(s)/W(s), softball W(s), tennis M(s)/W(s).

Standardized Tests *Required:* SAT I or ACT (for admission).

Costs (2003–04) *Tuition:* state resident $1398 full-time, $59 per credit hour part-time; nonresident $5592 full-time, $233 per credit hour part-time. Full-time tuition and fees vary according to course load. Part-time tuition and fees vary according to course load. *Required fees:* $244 full-time, $122 per term part-time. *Waivers:* senior citizens.

Financial Aid Of all full-time matriculated undergraduates who enrolled, 218 Federal Work-Study jobs (averaging $3000).

Applying *Options:* early admission. *Application fee:* $20. *Required:* high school transcript. *Application deadlines:* 7/1 (freshmen), 7/1 (transfers). *Notification:* continuous (freshmen), continuous (transfers).

Admissions Contact Ms. Erin Hart, Director of Enrollment Management, Georgia Perimeter College, 555 North Indian Creek Drive, Clarkston, GA 30021-2396. *Phone:* 404-299-4551. *Toll-free phone:* 888-696-2780. *Fax:* 404-299-4574.

GORDON COLLEGE
Barnesville, Georgia

- **State-supported** 2-year, founded 1852, part of University System of Georgia
- **Calendar** semesters
- **Degree** certificates and associate
- **Small-town** 125-acre campus with easy access to Atlanta
- **Endowment** $4.5 million
- **Coed,** 3,413 undergraduate students, 65% full-time, 65% women, 35% men

Undergraduates 2,227 full-time, 1,186 part-time. Students come from 12 other countries, 1% are from out of state, 23% African American, 2% Asian American or Pacific Islander, 2% Hispanic American, 0.4% Native American, 100% transferred in, 20% live on campus.

Freshmen *Admission:* 1,674 applied, 1,447 admitted, 1,127 enrolled. *Average high school GPA:* 2.55. *Test scores:* SAT verbal scores over 500: 33%; SAT math scores over 500: 30%; SAT verbal scores over 600: 6%; SAT math scores over 600: 6%; SAT verbal scores over 700: 1%; SAT math scores over 700: 1%.

Faculty *Total:* 141, 62% full-time, 61% with terminal degrees. *Student/faculty ratio:* 25:1.

Majors Administrative assistant and secretarial science; agriculture; art; behavioral sciences; biological and physical sciences; biology/biological sciences; business administration and management; computer and information sciences related; computer science; dramatic/theatre arts; education; English; general studies; history; information technology; journalism; mathematics; nursing (licensed practical/vocational nurse training); nursing (registered nurse training); parks, recreation and leisure; physical sciences; political science and government; psychology; sociology; Spanish.

Academic Programs *Special study options:* academic remediation for entering students, accelerated degree program, adult/continuing education programs, advanced placement credit, cooperative education, honors programs, off-campus study, part-time degree program, services for LD students, summer session for credit.

Library Hightower Library with 118,000 titles, 98 serial subscriptions, an OPAC, a Web page.

Computers on Campus 142 computers available on campus for general student use. A campuswide network can be accessed from student residence rooms and from off campus. At least one staffed computer lab available.

Student Life *Housing Options:* coed, men-only, women-only. Campus housing is university owned. *Activities and Organizations:* drama/theater group, student-run newspaper, choral group, Explorers, Minority Advisement Program, Georgia Association of Nursing Students, Baptist Student Union, Phi Beta Lambda. *Campus security:* 24-hour patrols, late-night transport/escort service. *Student services:* personal/psychological counseling.

Athletics Member NJCAA. *Intercollegiate sports:* baseball M(s), soccer M(s)/W(s), softball W(s), tennis W(s). *Intramural sports:* badminton M/W, basketball M/W, cheerleading W, football M/W, golf M/W, racquetball M/W, table tennis M/W, volleyball M/W, wrestling M.

Standardized Tests *Required:* SAT I or ACT (for admission).

Costs (2003–04) *Tuition:* state resident $1512 full-time, $56 per credit part-time; nonresident $5508 full-time, $222 per credit part-time. *Required fees:* $90 full-time, $90 per semester part-time. *Room and board:* $2992; room only: $1280. Room and board charges vary according to board plan. *Waivers:* employees or children of employees.

Financial Aid Of all full-time matriculated undergraduates who enrolled, 75 Federal Work-Study jobs (averaging $1850).

Applying *Options:* electronic application, early admission, deferred entrance. *Application fee:* $20. *Required:* high school transcript, minimum 1.8 GPA. *Application deadline:* rolling (freshmen), rolling (transfers).

Admissions Contact Mr. Brian Gipson, Director of Admissions, Gordon College, 419 College Drive, Barnesville, GA 30204. *Phone:* 770-358-5023. *Toll-free phone:* 800-282-6504. *Fax:* 770-358-3031. *E-mail:* gordon@gdn.edu.

GRIFFIN TECHNICAL COLLEGE
Griffin, Georgia

- **State-supported** 2-year, founded 1965, part of Georgia Department of Technical and Adult Education
- **Calendar** quarters
- **Degree** certificates and associate
- **Small-town** 10-acre campus with easy access to Atlanta
- **Coed**

Faculty *Student/faculty ratio:* 28:1.

Costs (2003–04) *Tuition:* state resident $936 full-time, $26 per credit hour part-time; nonresident $1872 full-time, $52 per credit hour part-time. Full-time tuition and fees vary according to course load and program. Part-time tuition and fees vary according to course load and program. *Required fees:* $150 full-time, $50 per term part-time.

Applying *Options:* early admission. *Required:* high school transcript.

Admissions Contact Ms. Christine James-Brown, Vice President of Student Services, Griffin Technical College, 501 Varsity Road, Griffin, GA 30223. *Phone:* 770-228-7371. *Fax:* 770-229-3227. *E-mail:* admissions@griftec.org.

GUPTON-JONES COLLEGE OF FUNERAL SERVICE
Decatur, Georgia

- **Independent** 2-year, founded 1920, part of Pierce Mortuary Colleges, Inc
- **Calendar** quarters
- **Degree** associate
- **Suburban** 3-acre campus with easy access to Atlanta
- **Coed,** 198 undergraduate students, 100% full-time, 49% women, 51% men

Undergraduates 198 full-time. Students come from 12 states and territories, 30% are from out of state, 74% African American.

Freshmen *Admission:* 122 enrolled.

Faculty *Total:* 9, 100% full-time. *Student/faculty ratio:* 25:1.

Majors Funeral service and mortuary science.

Academic Programs *Special study options:* academic remediation for entering students, distance learning, summer session for credit.

Library Russell Millison Library with 3,500 titles, 15 serial subscriptions, an OPAC.

Computers on Campus 20 computers available on campus for general student use. Internet access, at least one staffed computer lab available.

Student Life *Housing:* college housing not available. *Activities and Organizations:* national fraternities.

Costs (2004–05) *Tuition:* $7500 full-time. No tuition increase for student's term of enrollment. *Payment plan:* installment.

Applying *Options:* common application, electronic application. *Application fee:* $25. *Required:* high school transcript, health certificate. *Recommended:* minimum 3.0 GPA. *Application deadline:* rolling (freshmen).

Admissions Contact Ms. Beverly Wheaton, Registrar, Gupton-Jones College of Funeral Service, 5141 Snapfinger Woods Drive, Decatur, GA 30035. *Phone:* 770-593-2257. *Toll-free phone:* 800-848-5352. *Fax:* 770-593-1891. *E-mail:* gjcfs@mindspring.com.

GWINNETT TECHNICAL COLLEGE
Lawrenceville, Georgia

- **State-supported** 2-year, founded 1984
- **Calendar** quarters
- **Degree** certificates, diplomas, and associate
- **Suburban** 93-acre campus with easy access to Atlanta
- **Coed,** 4,476 undergraduate students, 39% full-time, 51% women, 49% men

Undergraduates 1,751 full-time, 2,725 part-time. 22% African American, 7% Asian American or Pacific Islander, 5% Hispanic American, 0.2% Native American, 0.3% international. *Retention:* 48% of 2002 full-time freshmen returned.

Freshmen *Admission:* 1,517 enrolled. *Average high school GPA:* 3.20. *Test scores:* SAT verbal scores over 500: 28%; SAT math scores over 500: 29%; SAT verbal scores over 600: 4%; SAT math scores over 600: 4%.

Faculty *Total:* 212, 35% full-time, 11% with terminal degrees. *Student/faculty ratio:* 22:1.

Majors Accounting; administrative assistant and secretarial science; automobile/automotive mechanics technology; computer programming; computer science;

construction management; dental hygiene; drafting and design technology; electrical, electronic and communications engineering technology; emergency medical technology (EMT paramedic); fashion merchandising; horticultural science; hotel/motel administration; industrial radiologic technology; interior design; machine tool technology; management information systems; marketing/marketing management; medical/clinical assistant; ornamental horticulture; photography; physical therapy; respiratory care therapy; telecommunications; tourism and travel services management.

Academic Programs *Special study options:* academic remediation for entering students, adult/continuing education programs, advanced placement credit, English as a second language, part-time degree program, services for LD students, summer session for credit.

Library Gwinnett Technical Institute Media Center with 16,800 titles, 269 serial subscriptions.

Computers on Campus 264 computers available on campus for general student use. Internet access, at least one staffed computer lab available.

Student Life *Housing:* college housing not available. *Campus security:* patrols by campus police. *Student services:* personal/psychological counseling.

Standardized Tests *Required:* ACT ASSET (for admission). *Recommended:* SAT I or ACT (for admission).

Costs (2003–04) *Tuition:* state resident $1164 full-time; nonresident $2136 full-time. *Required fees:* $192 full-time.

Financial Aid Of all full-time matriculated undergraduates who enrolled, 20 Federal Work-Study jobs (averaging $2100).

Applying *Required:* high school transcript. *Application deadline:* 8/1 (freshmen). *Notification:* continuous (freshmen).

Admissions Contact Ms. Sandra Causey, Director of Admissions and Records, Gwinnett Technical College, PO Box 1505, Lawrenceville, GA 30046-1505. *Phone:* 770-962-7580 Ext. 246.

HEART OF GEORGIA TECHNICAL COLLEGE
Dublin, Georgia

- **State-supported** 2-year, founded 1984
- **Calendar** quarters
- **Degree** certificates, diplomas, and associate
- **Small-town** campus with easy access to Atlanta
- **Coed,** 1,500 undergraduate students

Majors Business, management, and marketing related; corrections and criminal justice related; early childhood education; respiratory therapy technician.

Costs (2003–04) *Tuition:* state resident $972 full-time, $27 per credit hour part-time; nonresident $1944 full-time, $54 per credit hour part-time. *Required fees:* $150 full-time, $40 per term part-time.

Applying *Application fee:* $15. *Required:* high school transcript.

Admissions Contact Ms. Lisa Kelly, Director of Admissions, Heart of Georgia Technical College, 560 Pinehill Road, Dublin, GA 31021. *Phone:* 478-274-7837.

HERZING COLLEGE
Atlanta, Georgia

Admissions Contact Stacy Johnston, Director of Admissions, Herzing College, 3355 Lenox Road, Suite 100, Atlanta, GA 30326. *Phone:* 404-816-4533. *Toll-free phone:* 800-573-4533. *Fax:* 404-816-5576. *E-mail:* leec@atl.herzing.edu.

HIGH-TECH INSTITUTE
Marietta, Georgia

Admissions Contact Frank Webster, Office Manager, High-Tech Institute, 1090 Northchase Parkway, Suite 150, Marietta, GA 30067. *Phone:* 770-988-9877. *Toll-free phone:* 800-987-0110.

INTERACTIVE COLLEGE OF TECHNOLOGY
Chamblee, Georgia

Admissions Contact Ms. Diana Mamas, Associate Dean of Admissions, Interactive College of Technology, 5303 New Peachtree Road, Chamblee, GA 30341. *Phone:* 770-216-2960. *Toll-free phone:* 800-550-3475.

ITT TECHNICAL INSTITUTE
Duluth, Georgia

- **Proprietary** primarily 2-year, founded 2003, part of ITT Educational Services, Inc.

- **Calendar** quarters
- **Degrees** associate and bachelor's
- **Coed**

Standardized Tests *Required:* (for admission).

Costs (2003–04) *Tuition:* Total Program Cost varies depending on course of study. Consult school catalog.

Applying *Options:* deferred entrance. *Application fee:* $100. *Required:* high school transcript, interview. *Recommended:* letters of recommendation.

Admissions Contact Mr. Chip Hinton, Director of Recruitment, ITT Technical Institute, 10700 Abbotts Bridge Road, Suite 190, Duluth, GA 30097. *Phone:* 678-957-8510. *Toll-free phone:* 866-489-8818.

LANIER TECHNICAL COLLEGE
Oakwood, Georgia

- **State-supported** 2-year, founded 1964
- **Calendar** quarters
- **Degree** certificates, diplomas, and associate
- **Coed**

Majors Accounting; banking and financial support services; business administration, management and operations related; business, management, and marketing related; computer science; computer systems networking and telecommunications; corrections and criminal justice related; data modeling/warehousing and database administration; early childhood education; electrical, electronic and communications engineering technology; fire science; health professions related; industrial technology; occupational safety and health technology; office occupations and clerical services; surgical technology.

Costs (2003–04) *Tuition:* state resident $972 full-time, $27 per credit hour part-time; nonresident $1944 full-time, $54 per credit hour part-time. *Required fees:* $165 full-time, $55 per term part-time.

Admissions Contact 2990 Landrun Education Drive, PO Box 58, Oakwood, GA 30566.

MIDDLE GEORGIA COLLEGE
Cochran, Georgia

- **State-supported** 2-year, founded 1884, part of University System of Georgia
- **Calendar** semesters
- **Degree** certificates and associate
- **Small-town** 165-acre campus
- **Endowment** $1.0 million
- **Coed,** 2,517 undergraduate students, 62% full-time, 60% women, 40% men

Middle Georgia College is a 2-year residential public college with a student population of approximately 2,400. Transfer programs are offered in more than 100 academic disciplines, including engineering, nursing, business, and education. Numerous clubs and organizations, as well as intercollegiate athletics for men and women, enrich student life.

Undergraduates 1,572 full-time, 945 part-time. Students come from 31 states and territories, 26 other countries, 4% are from out of state, 32% African American, 0.9% Asian American or Pacific Islander, 0.9% Hispanic American, 0.1% Native American, 0.6% international, 13% transferred in, 32% live on campus.

Freshmen *Admission:* 1,661 applied, 1,018 admitted, 862 enrolled. *Average high school GPA:* 2.75. *Test scores:* SAT verbal scores over 500: 32%; SAT math scores over 500: 33%; ACT scores over 18: 44%; SAT verbal scores over 600: 8%; SAT math scores over 600: 9%; ACT scores over 24: 8%; SAT verbal scores over 700: 1%; SAT math scores over 700: 1%.

Faculty *Total:* 129, 55% full-time, 26% with terminal degrees. *Student/faculty ratio:* 21:1.

Majors Business administration and management; computer and information sciences related; computer engineering related; computer/information technology services administration related; computer science; criminal justice/police science; data processing and data processing technology; fashion merchandising; information science/studies; liberal arts and sciences/liberal studies; nursing (registered nurse training); occupational therapist assistant; physical therapist assistant; public administration; survey technology.

Academic Programs *Special study options:* academic remediation for entering students, accelerated degree program, adult/continuing education programs, advanced placement credit, cooperative education, distance learning, honors programs, part-time degree program, services for LD students, study abroad, summer session for credit.

Library Roberts Memorial Library with 110,000 titles, 147 serial subscriptions, 5,119 audiovisual materials, an OPAC, a Web page.

Computers on Campus 360 computers available on campus for general student use. A campuswide network can be accessed from student residence

Middle Georgia College (continued)

rooms and from off campus. Internet access, online (class) registration, at least one staffed computer lab available.

Student Life *Housing:* on-campus residence required through sophomore year. *Options:* men-only, women-only. Campus housing is university owned. Freshman campus housing is guaranteed. *Activities and Organizations:* drama/theater group, student-run newspaper, choral group, marching band, Baptist Student Union, Student Government Association, MGC Ambassadors, Encore Productions, United Voices of Praise. *Campus security:* 24-hour emergency response devices and patrols, student patrols, late-night transport/escort service, controlled dormitory access, patrols by police officers. *Student services:* health clinic, personal/psychological counseling.

Athletics Member NJCAA. *Intercollegiate sports:* baseball M(s), basketball M(s)/W(s), cheerleading W, softball W(s), tennis W(s). *Intramural sports:* badminton M/W, basketball M/W, football M, golf M, softball M/W, swimming M/W, tennis M/W.

Standardized Tests *Required:* SAT I or ACT (for admission). *Required for some:* SAT II: Subject Tests (for admission).

Costs (2003–04) *Tuition:* state resident $1398 full-time, $59 per credit hour part-time; nonresident $5592 full-time, $233 per credit hour part-time. *Required fees:* $434 full-time, $385 per year part-time. *Room and board:* $3960; room only: $1750.

Financial Aid Of all full-time matriculated undergraduates who enrolled, 100 Federal Work-Study jobs (averaging $451).

Applying *Options:* common application, electronic application, early admission, deferred entrance. *Application fee:* $20. *Required:* high school transcript, minimum 2.0 GPA. *Required for some:* essay or personal statement, minimum 3.5 GPA, letters of recommendation, interview. *Application deadline:* rolling (freshmen), rolling (transfers). *Notification:* continuous (freshmen), continuous (transfers).

Admissions Contact Ms. Jennifer Brannon, Assistant Director of Admissions for Operations, Middle Georgia College, 1100 2nd Street, SE, Cochran, GA 31014. *Phone:* 478-934-3138. *Fax:* 478-934-3049. *E-mail:* admissions@mgc.edu.

MIDDLE GEORGIA TECHNICAL COLLEGE
Warner Robbins, Georgia

- **State-supported** 2-year, founded 1973
- **Calendar** quarters
- **Degree** certificates, diplomas, and associate
- **Coed**

Costs (2003–04) *Tuition:* state resident $624 full-time. *Required fees:* $101 full-time.

Admissions Contact Mr. Howard Gregory, Director of Admissions, Middle Georgia Technical College, 80 Cohen Walker Drive, Warner Robbins, GA 31088. *Phone:* 478-988-6843. *Toll-free phone:* 800-474-1031.

MOULTRIE TECHNICAL COLLEGE
Moultrie, Georgia

Admissions Contact 361 Industrial Drive, Moultrie, GA 31768.

NORTH GEORGIA TECHNICAL COLLEGE
Clarkesville, Georgia

Admissions Contact Georgia Highway 197, North, PO Box 65, Clarkesville, GA 30523.

NORTH METRO TECHNICAL COLLEGE
Acworth, Georgia

Admissions Contact 5198 Ross Road, Acworth, GA 30102.

NORTHWESTERN TECHNICAL COLLEGE
Rock Springs, Georgia

- **State-supported** 2-year, founded 1966, part of Georgia Department of Technical and Adult Education
- **Calendar** quarters
- **Degree** certificates, diplomas, and associate
- **Rural** campus
- **Coed**

Faculty *Student/faculty ratio:* 15:1.

Standardized Tests *Required:* ACT ASSET, SAT I, or ACT (for placement).

Financial Aid Of all full-time matriculated undergraduates who enrolled, 30 Federal Work-Study jobs (averaging $4800).

Applying *Application fee:* $15. *Required for some:* essay or personal statement, high school transcript, letters of recommendation, interview.

Admissions Contact Mrs. Carolyn Solmon, Director of Admissions and Career Planning, Northwestern Technical College, PO Box 569, Rock Springs, GA 30739. *Phone:* 706-764-3511. *Toll-free phone:* 800-735-5726. *E-mail:* csolmon@northwestern.tec.ga.us.

OGEECHEE TECHNICAL COLLEGE
Statesboro, Georgia

- **State-supported** 2-year, founded 1989
- **Calendar** quarters
- **Degree** certificates, diplomas, and associate
- **Small-town** campus
- **Coed,** 2,200 undergraduate students

Faculty *Total:* 123, 54% full-time. *Student/faculty ratio:* 17:1.

Student Life *Housing:* college housing not available.

Costs (2003–04) *Tuition:* state resident $972 full-time, $27 per credit hour part-time; nonresident $1944 full-time, $54 per credit hour part-time. *Required fees:* $153 full-time.

Admissions Contact Mr. Steve Miller, Director of Admissions, Ogeechee Technical College, One Joe Kennedy Boulevard, Statesboro, GA 30458. *Phone:* 912-871-1600. *Toll-free phone:* 800-646-1316.

OKEFENOKEE TECHNICAL COLLEGE
Waycross, Georgia

- **State-supported** 2-year
- **Calendar** quarters
- **Degree** certificates, diplomas, and associate
- **Small-town** campus
- **Coed,** 2,000 undergraduate students

Faculty *Total:* 180, 56% full-time. *Student/faculty ratio:* 20:1.

Majors Clinical/medical laboratory technology; computer technology/computer systems technology; criminal justice/police science; early childhood education; forestry technology; occupational safety and health technology; office occupations and clerical services; respiratory therapy technician; surgical technology.

Standardized Tests *Required:* ACT COMPASS (for placement).

Costs (2003–04) *Tuition:* state resident $1104 full-time, $27 per credit hour part-time; nonresident $2208 full-time, $54 per credit hour part-time.

Applying *Application fee:* $15.

Admissions Contact Ms. Carol Shugart, Director of Admissions, Okefenokee Technical College, 1701 Carswell Avenue, Waycross, GA 31503. *Phone:* 912-287-5809.

SANDERSVILLE TECHNICAL COLLEGE
Sandersville, Georgia

Admissions Contact 1189 Deepstep Road, Sandersville, GA 31082.

SAVANNAH TECHNICAL COLLEGE
Savannah, Georgia

Admissions Contact Ms. Shevon Carr, Vice President of Student Services, Savannah Technical College, 5717 White Bluff Road, Savannah, GA 31405. *Phone:* 912-303-1775. *Toll-free phone:* 800-769-6362. *Fax:* 912-303-1781. *E-mail:* vlampley@savtec.org.

SOUTHEASTERN TECHNICAL COLLEGE
Vidalia, Georgia

- **State-supported** 2-year, founded 1989
- **Calendar** quarters
- **Degree** certificates
- **Coed**

Majors Accounting; business administration and management; corrections and criminal justice related; data entry/microcomputer applications; early childhood education; electrical, electronic and communications engineering technology; marketing/marketing management; system, networking, and LAN/wan management; web page, digital/multimedia and information resources design.

Costs (2004–05) *Tuition:* state resident $1008 full-time. *Required fees:* $138 full-time.
Admissions Contact 3001 East First Street, Vidalia, GA 30474.

SOUTH GEORGIA COLLEGE
Douglas, Georgia

- **State-supported** 2-year, founded 1906, part of University System of Georgia
- **Calendar** semesters
- **Degree** certificates and associate
- **Small-town** 250-acre campus
- **Endowment** $150,321
- **Coed**

Faculty *Student/faculty ratio:* 24:1.
Student Life *Campus security:* 24-hour emergency response devices and patrols, controlled dormitory access.
Athletics Member NJCAA.
Standardized Tests *Required:* SAT I or ACT (for placement). *Required for some:* SAT II: Subject Tests (for placement).
Costs (2003–04) *Tuition:* state resident $1332 full-time; nonresident $5324 full-time. *Required fees:* $160 full-time. *Room and board:* room only: $1990.
Applying *Options:* electronic application, early admission, deferred entrance. *Required:* high school transcript.
Admissions Contact Dr. Randy L. Braswell, Director of Admissions, Records, and Research, South Georgia College, 100 West College Park Drive, Douglas, GA 31533-5098. *Phone:* 912-389-4200. *Toll-free phone:* 800-342-6364. *Fax:* 912-389-4392. *E-mail:* admissions@sga.edu.

SOUTH GEORGIA TECHNICAL COLLEGE
Americus, Georgia

Admissions Contact 1583 Southerfield Road, Americus, GA 31709.

SOUTHWEST GEORGIA TECHNICAL COLLEGE
Thomasville, Georgia

- **State-supported** 2-year, founded 1963, part of Georgia Department of Technical and Adult Education
- **Calendar** quarters
- **Degree** certificates, diplomas, and associate
- **Coed**

Faculty *Student/faculty ratio:* 18:1.
Standardized Tests *Required:* SAT I, ACT, ACT ASSET, or ACT COMPASS (for placement).
Costs (2003–04) *Tuition:* area resident $972 full-time; nonresident $1994 full-time. Full-time tuition and fees vary according to course load. Part-time tuition and fees vary according to course load. *Required fees:* $138 full-time.
Applying *Options:* electronic application. *Application fee:* $15. *Required:* high school transcript.
Admissions Contact Ms. Lorette M. Hoover, Vice President, Southwest Georgia Technical College, 15689 US Highway 19N, Thomasville, GA 31792. *Phone:* 229-225-5077. *Fax:* 229-225-4330. *E-mail:* lhoover@swgte.net.

SWAINSBORO TECHNICAL COLLEGE
Swainsboro, Georgia

Admissions Contact 346 Kite Road, Swainsboro, GA 30401.

TRUETT-MCCONNELL COLLEGE
Cleveland, Georgia

- **Independent Baptist** primarily 2-year, founded 1946
- **Calendar** semesters
- **Degrees** certificates, associate, and bachelor's
- **Rural** 310-acre campus with easy access to Atlanta
- **Endowment** $6.7 million
- **Coed,** 390 undergraduate students, 89% full-time, 46% women, 54% men

Undergraduates 346 full-time, 44 part-time. Students come from 4 states and territories, 2% are from out of state, 12% African American, 0.3% Asian American or Pacific Islander, 2% Hispanic American, 0.3% international, 8% transferred in, 71% live on campus. *Retention:* 21% of 2002 full-time freshmen returned.

Freshmen *Admission:* 250 applied, 200 admitted, 164 enrolled. *Average high school GPA:* 2.78. *Test scores:* SAT verbal scores over 500: 29%; SAT math scores over 500: 28%; ACT scores over 18: 50%; SAT verbal scores over 600: 5%; SAT math scores over 600: 3%; ACT scores over 24: 4%.
Faculty *Total:* 51, 51% full-time. *Student/faculty ratio:* 11:1.
Majors Business/commerce; Christian studies; education; general studies; liberal arts and sciences/liberal studies; music.
Academic Programs *Special study options:* academic remediation for entering students, accelerated degree program, advanced placement credit, double majors, honors programs, part-time degree program, services for LD students, study abroad, summer session for credit.
Library Cofer Library with 36,562 titles, 343 serial subscriptions, 2,716 audiovisual materials, an OPAC.
Computers on Campus 124 computers available on campus for general student use. A campuswide network can be accessed. Internet access, at least one staffed computer lab available.
Student Life *Housing Options:* men-only, women-only. Campus housing is university owned. *Activities and Organizations:* choral group, intramurals, Baptist Student Union, College Choir, Student Government Association, Fellowship of Christian Athletes (FCA). *Campus security:* 24-hour weekday patrols, 10-hour weekend patrols by trained security personnel. *Student services:* personal/psychological counseling.
Athletics Member NJCAA. *Intercollegiate sports:* baseball M(s), basketball M(s)/W(s), cross-country running M(s)/W(s), soccer M(s)/W(s). *Intramural sports:* basketball M/W, football M/W, ultimate Frisbee M/W, volleyball M/W.
Standardized Tests *Required:* SAT I or ACT (for admission).
Costs (2003–04) *Comprehensive fee:* $14,028 includes full-time tuition ($9828) and room and board ($4200). Part-time tuition: $330 per credit hour. *Room and board:* college room only: $2000. *Waivers:* employees or children of employees.
Applying *Options:* early admission, deferred entrance. *Required:* high school transcript, minimum 2.0 GPA, minimum SAT score of 720 or ACT score of 15. *Required for some:* interview. *Application deadlines:* 8/1 (freshmen), 8/1 (transfers). *Notification:* continuous (freshmen), continuous (transfers).
Admissions Contact Mr. Alan Coker, Dean for Admissions, Truett-McConnell College, 100 Alumni Drive, Cleveland, GA 30528-9799. *Phone:* 706-865-2134 Ext. 129. *Toll-free phone:* 800-226-8621. *Fax:* 706-865-7615. *E-mail:* admissions@ truett.edu.

VALDOSTA TECHNICAL COLLEGE
Valdosta, Georgia

- **State-supported** 2-year, founded 1963
- **Calendar** quarters
- **Degree** certificates and diplomas
- **Suburban** 18-acre campus
- **Coed,** 2,553 undergraduate students, 57% full-time, 50% women, 50% men

Undergraduates 1,447 full-time, 1,106 part-time.
Freshmen *Admission:* 553 applied, 353 admitted, 353 enrolled.
Faculty *Total:* 276, 33% full-time, 2% with terminal degrees. *Student/faculty ratio:* 12:1.
Admissions Contact 4089 Val Tech Road, PO Box 928, Valdosta, GA 31603-0928.

WAYCROSS COLLEGE
Waycross, Georgia

- **State-supported** 2-year, founded 1976, part of University System of Georgia
- **Calendar** semesters
- **Degree** certificates and associate
- **Small-town** 150-acre campus
- **Endowment** $85,583
- **Coed,** 1,026 undergraduate students, 32% full-time, 68% women, 32% men

Undergraduates 326 full-time, 700 part-time. Students come from 9 states and territories, 1 other country, 1% are from out of state, 20% African American, 1% Asian American or Pacific Islander, 0.8% Hispanic American, 0.2% Native American, 0.2% international.
Freshmen *Admission:* 231 applied, 231 admitted, 231 enrolled. *Average high school GPA:* 2.90.
Faculty *Total:* 47, 43% full-time, 26% with terminal degrees. *Student/faculty ratio:* 22:1.
Majors Accounting; administrative assistant and secretarial science; agriculture; automobile/automotive mechanics technology; biology/biological sciences; business administration and management; business teacher education; chemistry; clinical laboratory science/medical technology; clinical/medical labo-

Waycross College (continued)

ratory technology; computer and information sciences; computer science; cosmetology; criminal justice/law enforcement administration; developmental and child psychology; drafting and design technology; education; electrical, electronic and communications engineering technology; elementary education; emergency medical technology (EMT paramedic); engineering technology; English; forestry; forestry technology; health teacher education; heavy equipment maintenance technology; history; liberal arts and sciences/liberal studies; machine tool technology; mathematics; medical radiologic technology; nursing (registered nurse training); physical education teaching and coaching; physical therapy; political science and government; psychology; radiologic technology/science; respiratory care therapy; sociology; surgical technology; welding technology.

Academic Programs *Special study options:* academic remediation for entering students, adult/continuing education programs, advanced placement credit, off-campus study, part-time degree program, services for LD students, study abroad, summer session for credit.

Library Waycross College Library with 32,461 titles, 251 serial subscriptions.

Computers on Campus 56 computers available on campus for general student use. Internet access, online (class) registration, at least one staffed computer lab available.

Student Life *Housing:* college housing not available. *Activities and Organizations:* drama/theater group, student-run newspaper, choral group, Black Student Alliance, Georgia Association of Nursing Students, Baptist Student Union, Sigma Club, Student Government Association. *Campus security:* late-night transport/escort service, security guards. *Student services:* personal/psychological counseling.

Athletics *Intramural sports:* football M/W, softball M/W.

Standardized Tests *Required:* SAT I or ACT (for admission).

Costs (2004–05) *Tuition:* state resident $1468 full-time, $62 per semester hour part-time; nonresident $5872 full-time. *Required fees:* $154 full-time.

Financial Aid Of all full-time matriculated undergraduates who enrolled, 20 Federal Work-Study jobs (averaging $2000).

Applying *Options:* electronic application, early admission, deferred entrance. *Application fee:* $20. *Required:* high school transcript. *Application deadline:* rolling (freshmen), rolling (transfers). *Notification:* continuous (freshmen), continuous (transfers).

Admissions Contact Mrs. Susan Dukes, Assistant Director for Admissions, Waycross College, 2001 South Georgia Parkway, Waycross, GA 31503. *Phone:* 912-285-6133. *Fax:* 912-285-6158. *E-mail:* admiss@waycross.edu.

WEST CENTRAL TECHNICAL COLLEGE
Waco, Georgia

- **State-supported** 2-year, founded 1968, part of Georgia Department of Technical and Adult Education
- **Calendar** quarters
- **Degree** certificates, diplomas, and associate
- **Coed**

Standardized Tests *Required:* ACT ASSET or ACT COMPASS (for admission).

Costs (2003–04) *Tuition:* state resident $972 full-time, $27 per quarter hour part-time; nonresident $1944 full-time, $54 per quarter hour part-time. Full-time tuition and fees vary according to program. *Required fees:* $150 full-time, $50 per term part-time.

Financial Aid Of all full-time matriculated undergraduates who enrolled, 40 Federal Work-Study jobs (averaging $1000).

Applying *Options:* electronic application. *Application fee:* $15. *Required:* high school transcript. *Required for some:* interview.

Admissions Contact Mrs. Mary Aderhold, Director of Student Services, West Central Technical College, 176 Murphy Campus Boulevard, Waco, GA 30182. *Phone:* 770-537-6000. *Fax:* 770-836-6814.

WEST GEORGIA TECHNICAL COLLEGE
LaGrange, Georgia

- **State-supported** 2-year, founded 1966, part of Georgia Department of Technical and Adult Education
- **Calendar** quarters
- **Degree** certificates, diplomas, and associate
- **Endowment** $58,000
- **Coed**

Faculty *Student/faculty ratio:* 12:1.

Student Life *Campus security:* 24-hour emergency response devices.

Standardized Tests *Required:* SAT I, ACT, or ACT ASSET (for admission).

Costs (2003–04) *Tuition:* state resident $1296 full-time; nonresident $2592 full-time. Full-time tuition and fees vary according to program. Part-time tuition and fees vary according to program. *Required fees:* $184 full-time.

Financial Aid Of all full-time matriculated undergraduates who enrolled, 68 Federal Work-Study jobs (averaging $800).

Applying *Application fee:* $15. *Required:* high school transcript.

Admissions Contact Ms. Tina Jackson, Admissions Coordinator/Assistant Registrar, West Georgia Technical College, 303 Fort Drive, LaGrange, GA 30240. *Phone:* 706-845-4323 Ext. 5711. *Fax:* 706-845-4340. *E-mail:* tjackson@westga.tec.ga.us.

WESTWOOD COLLEGE-ATLANTA CAMPUS
Atlanta, Georgia

- **Proprietary** primarily 2-year, founded 2003
- **Calendar** continuous
- **Degrees** associate and bachelor's
- **Coed**

Majors Accounting and business/management; architectural drafting and CAD/CADD; computer and information systems security; computer programming; computer systems networking and telecommunications; design and visual communications; graphic design; intermedia/multimedia; marketing/marketing management; system, networking, and LAN/wan management; web/multimedia management and webmaster; web page, digital/multimedia and information resources design.

Applying *Required:* interview, HS diploma or GE, and passing scores on ACT/SAT or Accuplacer exam.

Admissions Contact Rory Laney, Director of Admissions, Westwood College-Atlanta Campus, 1100 Spring Street, Ste. 101A, Atlanta, GA 30309. *Phone:* 404-745-9862. *E-mail:* info@westwood.edu.

YOUNG HARRIS COLLEGE
Young Harris, Georgia

- **Independent United Methodist** 2-year, founded 1886
- **Calendar** semesters
- **Degree** associate
- **Rural** campus
- **Endowment** $96.5 million
- **Coed**

Faculty *Student/faculty ratio:* 15:1.

Student Life *Campus security:* 24-hour emergency response devices and patrols.

Athletics Member NJCAA.

Standardized Tests *Required:* SAT I or ACT (for admission).

Costs (2004–05) *Comprehensive fee:* $17,694 includes full-time tuition ($13,200) and room and board ($4494). Part-time tuition and fees vary according to course load. No tuition increase for student's term of enrollment.

Financial Aid Of all full-time matriculated undergraduates who enrolled, 89 Federal Work-Study jobs (averaging $1000). 242 state and other part-time jobs (averaging $1000).

Applying *Options:* electronic application, early admission, deferred entrance. *Application fee:* $30. *Required:* high school transcript, minimum 2.5 GPA. *Required for some:* letters of recommendation. *Recommended:* interview.

Admissions Contact Mr. Clinton G. Hobbs, Director of Admissions, Young Harris College, PO Box 116, Young Harris, GA 30582-0098. *Phone:* 706-379-3111 Ext. 5147. *Toll-free phone:* 800-241-3754. *Fax:* 706-379-3108. *E-mail:* admissions@yhc.edu.

HAWAII

HAWAII BUSINESS COLLEGE
Honolulu, Hawaii

- **Independent** 2-year, founded 1973
- **Calendar** quarters
- **Degree** certificates, diplomas, and associate
- **Urban** campus
- **Coed**

Faculty *Student/faculty ratio:* 15:1.

Standardized Tests *Required:* Wonderlic Basic Skills Test (for placement).

Applying *Options:* deferred entrance. *Application fee:* $30. *Required:* high school transcript. *Required for some:* essay or personal statement, interview.

Admissions Contact Ms. Michell Basilio, Director of Admissions, Hawaii Business College, 33 South King Street, Fourth Floor, Honolulu, HI 96813. *Phone:* 808-524-4014. *Fax:* 808-524-0284. *E-mail:* admin@hbc.edu.

HAWAII COMMUNITY COLLEGE
Hilo, Hawaii

- **State-supported** 2-year, founded 1954, part of University of Hawaii System
- **Calendar** semesters
- **Degree** certificates, diplomas, and associate
- **Small-town** campus
- **Coed,** 2,409 undergraduate students, 43% full-time, 64% women, 36% men

Undergraduates 1,025 full-time, 1,384 part-time. Students come from 12 states and territories, 32 other countries, 0.6% African American, 57% Asian American or Pacific Islander, 2% Hispanic American, 0.7% Native American, 3% international.
Freshmen *Admission:* 1,163 applied, 1,156 admitted, 685 enrolled.
Faculty *Total:* 260, 50% full-time.
Majors Accounting; administrative assistant and secretarial science; agriculture; automobile/automotive mechanics technology; carpentry; criminal justice/law enforcement administration; drafting and design technology; electrical, electronic and communications engineering technology; fire science; food services technology; hotel/motel administration; kindergarten/preschool education; liberal arts and sciences/liberal studies; mechanical engineering/mechanical technology; nursing (licensed practical/vocational nurse training); nursing (registered nurse training); welding technology.
Academic Programs *Special study options:* advanced placement credit, cooperative education, English as a second language, honors programs, part-time degree program, services for LD students, summer session for credit.
Library Edwin H. Mookini Library plus 1 other.
Computers on Campus 100 computers available on campus for general student use. A campuswide network can be accessed from off campus. Internet access, at least one staffed computer lab available.
Student Life *Housing Options:* coed. *Campus security:* 24-hour patrols.
Costs (2003–04) *Tuition:* state resident $1080 full-time, $45 per credit part-time; nonresident $5808 full-time, $242 per credit part-time. *Required fees:* $50 full-time, $25 per term part-time.
Applying *Options:* common application, early admission. *Application deadline:* 8/1 (freshmen).
Admissions Contact Mrs. Tammy M. Tanaka, Admissions Specialist, Hawaii Community College, 200 West Kawili Street, Hilo, HI 96720-4091. *Phone:* 808-974-7661. *E-mail:* loeding@hawaii.edu.

HAWAII TOKAI INTERNATIONAL COLLEGE
Honolulu, Hawaii

- **Independent** 2-year, founded 1992, part of Tokai University Educational System (Japan)
- **Calendar** quarters
- **Degree** certificates and associate
- **Urban** campus
- **Coed,** 50 undergraduate students, 100% full-time, 62% women, 38% men

Undergraduates 50 full-time. Students come from 1 other state, 3 other countries, 100% Asian American or Pacific Islander, 60% live on campus. *Retention:* 83% of 2002 full-time freshmen returned.
Freshmen *Admission:* 9 applied, 9 admitted, 6 enrolled.
Faculty *Total:* 21, 33% full-time, 19% with terminal degrees. *Student/faculty ratio:* 12:1.
Majors Liberal arts and sciences/liberal studies.
Academic Programs *Special study options:* English as a second language, summer session for credit.
Library The Learning Center with 7,000 titles, 100 serial subscriptions, 500 audiovisual materials, an OPAC, a Web page.
Computers on Campus 45 computers available on campus for general student use. A campuswide network can be accessed from student residence rooms and from off campus. Internet access, at least one staffed computer lab available.
Student Life *Housing:* on-campus residence required for freshman year. *Options:* coed. *Activities and Organizations:* student-run newspaper, Basketball Club, Hula Club, Martial Arts Club, Chinese and Japanese Culture Club, fishing. *Campus security:* 24-hour patrols.
Costs (2003–04) *Comprehensive fee:* $10,775 includes full-time tuition ($8700), mandatory fees ($75), and room and board ($2000). Part-time tuition: $375 per credit. Part-time tuition and fees vary according to course load.

Required fees: $25 per term part-time. *Room and board:* college room only: $1000. Room and board charges vary according to board plan. *Waivers:* employees or children of employees.
Applying *Options:* deferred entrance. *Application fee:* $50. *Required:* essay or personal statement, high school transcript, interview. *Application deadline:* 9/1 (freshmen). *Notification:* continuous (freshmen).
Admissions Contact Ms. Terry Lee McCandliss, Admissions Officer, Hawaii Tokai International College, 2241 Kapiolani Boulevard, Honolulu, HI 96826. *Phone:* 808-983-4154. *E-mail:* htic@tokai.edu.

HEALD COLLEGE-HONOLULU
Honolulu, Hawaii

- **Independent** 2-year, founded 1863
- **Calendar** quarters
- **Degree** certificates, diplomas, and associate
- **Urban** campus
- **Coed**

Standardized Tests *Required:* (for admission).
Applying *Options:* electronic application, early admission, deferred entrance. *Application fee:* $100. *Required:* high school transcript, interview.
Admissions Contact Director of Admissions, Heald College-Honolulu, 1500 Kapiolani Boulevard, Suite 201, Honolulu, HI 96814. *Phone:* 808-955-1500. *Toll-free phone:* 800-755-3550. *E-mail:* info@heald.edu.

HONOLULU COMMUNITY COLLEGE
Honolulu, Hawaii

- **State-supported** 2-year, founded 1920, part of University of Hawaii System
- **Calendar** semesters
- **Degree** certificates and associate
- **Urban** 20-acre campus
- **Endowment** $472,659
- **Coed,** 4,238 undergraduate students, 39% full-time, 47% women, 53% men

Undergraduates 1,672 full-time, 2,566 part-time. Students come from 36 states and territories, 39 other countries, 2% African American, 78% Asian American or Pacific Islander, 2% Hispanic American, 0.2% Native American, 0.6% international, 29% transferred in.
Freshmen *Admission:* 1,467 applied, 1,223 admitted, 636 enrolled.
Faculty *Total:* 183, 61% full-time, 8% with terminal degrees. *Student/faculty ratio:* 23:1.
Majors Architectural engineering technology; automobile/automotive mechanics technology; avionics maintenance technology; carpentry; commercial and advertising art; community organization and advocacy; cosmetology; criminal justice/police science; drafting and design technology; electrical, electronic and communications engineering technology; engineering technology; fashion/apparel design; fire science; food services technology; heating, air conditioning, ventilation and refrigeration maintenance technology; human services; industrial arts; kindergarten/preschool education; liberal arts and sciences/liberal studies; marine technology; occupational safety and health technology; welding technology.
Academic Programs *Special study options:* academic remediation for entering students, accelerated degree program, advanced placement credit, cooperative education, distance learning, English as a second language, internships, part-time degree program, services for LD students, student-designed majors, summer session for credit. *ROTC:* Army (c), Air Force (c).
Library Honolulu Community College Library with 54,902 titles, 1,280 serial subscriptions, 858 audiovisual materials, an OPAC, a Web page.
Computers on Campus 120 computers available on campus for general student use. A campuswide network can be accessed from off campus. At least one staffed computer lab available.
Student Life *Housing:* college housing not available. *Activities and Organizations:* student-run newspaper. *Campus security:* 24-hour emergency response devices. *Student services:* health clinic.
Costs (2004–05) *Tuition:* state resident $1350 full-time, $45 per credit part-time; nonresident $7260 full-time, $242 per credit part-time. *Required fees:* $30 full-time. *Waivers:* employees or children of employees.
Financial Aid Of all full-time matriculated undergraduates who enrolled, 43 Federal Work-Study jobs (averaging $1600).
Applying *Options:* common application, early admission. *Application deadlines:* 8/15 (freshmen), 8/15 (transfers). *Notification:* continuous until 8/15 (freshmen), continuous until 8/15 (transfers).
Admissions Contact Admissions Office, Honolulu Community College, 874 Dillingham Boulevard, Honolulu, HI 96817. *Phone:* 808-845-9129. *E-mail:* admission@hcc.hawaii.edu.

KAPIOLANI COMMUNITY COLLEGE
Honolulu, Hawaii

- **State-supported** 2-year, founded 1957, part of University of Hawaii System
- **Calendar** semesters
- **Degree** certificates and associate
- **Urban** 52-acre campus
- **Coed,** 7,582 undergraduate students

Undergraduates Students come from 27 states and territories, 59 other countries.
Freshmen *Admission:* 2,161 applied, 1,939 admitted.
Faculty *Total:* 251, 94% full-time.
Majors Accounting; clinical/medical laboratory technology; culinary arts; data processing and data processing technology; hotel/motel administration; industrial radiologic technology; legal administrative assistant/secretary; legal assistant/paralegal; liberal arts and sciences/liberal studies; marketing/marketing management; medical/clinical assistant; nursing (registered nurse training); occupational therapy; physical therapy; respiratory care therapy; special products marketing; tourism and travel services management.
Academic Programs *Special study options:* academic remediation for entering students, adult/continuing education programs, advanced placement credit, cooperative education, distance learning, English as a second language, honors programs, internships, off-campus study, part-time degree program, services for LD students, student-designed majors, summer session for credit. *ROTC:* Army (c), Air Force (c).
Library Lama Library with 50,000 titles, 600 serial subscriptions.
Computers on Campus 175 computers available on campus for general student use. A campuswide network can be accessed from off campus. Internet access, at least one staffed computer lab available.
Student Life *Housing:* college housing not available. *Activities and Organizations:* student-run newspaper, choral group, Hawaiian Club, Phi Theta Kappa, Chinese Club, Hospitality Industry, Bayanihan. *Campus security:* 24-hour patrols.
Athletics *Intramural sports:* bowling M/W, volleyball M/W.
Costs (2003–04) *Tuition:* state resident $1032 full-time; nonresident $5808 full-time. *Required fees:* $60 full-time.
Financial Aid Of all full-time matriculated undergraduates who enrolled, 30 Federal Work-Study jobs (averaging $2275). 440 state and other part-time jobs (averaging $1762).
Applying *Options:* early admission. *Application deadlines:* 7/1 (freshmen), 7/1 (transfers). *Notification:* continuous until 8/15 (freshmen), continuous until 8/15 (transfers).
Admissions Contact Ms. Cynthia Suzuki, Chief Admissions Officer, Kapiolani Community College, 4303 Diamond Head Road, Honolulu, HI 96816-4421. *Phone:* 808-734-9897. *E-mail:* cio@leahi.kcc.hawaii.edu.

KAUAI COMMUNITY COLLEGE
Lihue, Hawaii

- **State-supported** 2-year, founded 1965, part of University of Hawaii System
- **Calendar** semesters
- **Degree** certificates and associate
- **Small-town** 100-acre campus
- **Coed,** 1,210 undergraduate students

Majors Accounting; administrative assistant and secretarial science; autobody/collision and repair technology; automobile/automotive mechanics technology; carpentry; culinary arts; electrical, electronic and communications engineering technology; hospitality administration; kindergarten/preschool education; liberal arts and sciences/liberal studies; nursing (registered nurse training).
Academic Programs *Special study options:* accelerated degree program, advanced placement credit, cooperative education, distance learning, English as a second language, internships, part-time degree program, services for LD students, summer session for credit.
Library S. W. Wilcox II Learning Resource Center plus 1 other with 51,875 titles, 165 serial subscriptions, 1,248 audiovisual materials, an OPAC, a Web page.
Computers on Campus 173 computers available on campus for general student use. A campuswide network can be accessed. Internet access, at least one staffed computer lab available.
Student Life *Housing:* college housing not available. *Activities and Organizations:* student-run newspaper, choral group, Food Service Club, Hui O Hana Po'okela (Hoper Club), Nursing Club, Phi Theta Kappa, Pamantasan Club. *Campus security:* student patrols, 6-hour evening patrols by trained security personnel. *Student services:* health clinic, personal/psychological counseling.
Athletics *Intramural sports:* basketball M/W, golf M/W, tennis M/W.
Standardized Tests *Recommended:* ACT COMPASS.
Costs (2004–05) *Tuition:* state resident $1128 full-time, $47 per credit part-time; nonresident $5808 full-time, $242 per credit part-time. Full-time tuition and fees vary according to course load. Part-time tuition and fees vary

according to course load. *Required fees:* $15 full-time, $1 per credit part-time. *Waivers:* minority students, senior citizens, and employees or children of employees.
Financial Aid Of all full-time matriculated undergraduates who enrolled, 10 Federal Work-Study jobs (averaging $3000). 30 state and other part-time jobs (averaging $3000).
Applying *Options:* common application, early admission. *Required for some:* high school transcript. *Recommended:* high school transcript. *Application deadlines:* 8/1 (freshmen), 8/1 (transfers). *Notification:* continuous until 8/1 (freshmen), continuous until 8/1 (transfers).
Admissions Contact Mr. Leighton Oride, Admissions Officer and Registrar, Kauai Community College, 3-1901 Kaumualii Highway, Lihue, HI 96766. *Phone:* 808-245-8226. *Fax:* 808-245-8297. *E-mail:* adrec@mail.kauaicc.hawaii.edu.

LEEWARD COMMUNITY COLLEGE
Pearl City, Hawaii

- **State-supported** 2-year, founded 1968, part of University of Hawaii System
- **Calendar** semesters
- **Degree** associate
- **Suburban** 49-acre campus with easy access to Honolulu
- **Coed**

Student Life *Campus security:* 24-hour patrols, late-night transport/escort service.
Costs (2003–04) *Tuition:* state resident $1080 full-time; nonresident $5808 full-time. *Required fees:* $25 full-time.
Financial Aid Of all full-time matriculated undergraduates who enrolled, 40 Federal Work-Study jobs (averaging $2000).
Applying *Options:* early admission. *Application fee:* $25. *Required for some:* high school transcript, letters of recommendation.
Admissions Contact Ms. Veda Tokashiki, Clerk, Leeward Community College, 96-045 Ala Ike, Pearl City, HI 96782-3393. *Phone:* 808-455-0217.

MAUI COMMUNITY COLLEGE
Kahului, Hawaii

Admissions Contact Mr. Stephen Kameda, Director of Admissions and Records, Maui Community College, 310 Kaahumanu Avenue, Kahului, HI 96732. *Phone:* 808-984-3267. *Toll-free phone:* 800-479-6692. *Fax:* 808-242-9618.

TRANSPACIFIC HAWAII COLLEGE
Honolulu, Hawaii

Admissions Contact Ms. Loreen Toji, Assistant to the President, TransPacific Hawaii College, 5257 Kalanianaole Highway, Honolulu, HI 96821. *Phone:* 808-377-5402 Ext. 309. *Fax:* 808-373-4754. *E-mail:* admissions@transpacific.org.

WINDWARD COMMUNITY COLLEGE
Kaneohe, Hawaii

Admissions Contact Mr. Russell Chan, Registrar, Windward Community College, 45-720 Keaahala Road, Kaneohe, HI 96744. *Phone:* 808-235-7400. *E-mail:* wccinfo@hawaii.edu.

IDAHO

AMERICAN INSTITUTE OF HEALTH TECHNOLOGY, INC.
Boise, Idaho

- **Proprietary** 2-year, founded 1980
- **Calendar** semesters
- **Degree** certificates, diplomas, and associate
- **Coed, primarily women**

Faculty *Student/faculty ratio:* 10:1.
Student Life *Campus security:* 24-hour patrols.
Standardized Tests *Required:* Wonderlic aptitude test (for admission).

Costs (2003–04) *Tuition:* $33,480 per degree program part-time. *Required fees:* $150 full-time.
Applying *Application fee:* $30. *Required:* high school transcript, 3 letters of recommendation, interview.
Admissions Contact Ms. Susanna Hancock, Associate Director, American Institute of Health Technology, Inc., 1200 North Liberty, Boise, ID 83607. *Phone:* 208-377-8080 Ext. 21. *Toll-free phone:* 800-473-4365 Ext. 21. *Fax:* 208-322-7658. *E-mail:* receptionist@aiht.com.

BRIGHAM YOUNG UNIVERSITY -IDAHO
Rexburg, Idaho

- **Independent** 2-year, founded 1888, affiliated with The Church of Jesus Christ of Latter-day Saints
- **Calendar** semesters
- **Degree** associate
- **Small-town** 255-acre campus
- **Coed**

Faculty *Student/faculty ratio:* 25:1.
Student Life *Campus security:* 24-hour emergency response devices and patrols, late-night transport/escort service.
Athletics Member NJCAA.
Standardized Tests *Required:* SAT I or ACT (for admission).
Costs (2003–04) *Comprehensive fee:* $5950 includes full-time tuition ($2554) and room and board ($3396). *Room and board:* college room only: $2998.
Financial Aid Of all full-time matriculated undergraduates who enrolled, 2,400 state and other part-time jobs.
Applying *Options:* electronic application. *Application fee:* $30. *Required:* essay or personal statement, high school transcript, interview.
Admissions Contact Mr. Steven Davis, Assistant Director of Admissions, Brigham Young University -Idaho, 120 Kimball, Rexburg, ID 83460-1615. *Phone:* 208-356-1026. *Fax:* 208-356-1220. *E-mail:* harrisk@ricks.edu.

COLLEGE OF SOUTHERN IDAHO
Twin Falls, Idaho

- **State and locally supported** 2-year, founded 1964
- **Calendar** semesters
- **Degree** certificates, diplomas, and associate
- **Small-town** 287-acre campus
- **Endowment** $15.0 million
- **Coed,** 7,018 undergraduate students

Undergraduates Students come from 20 states and territories, 5% are from out of state, 0.5% African American, 1% Asian American or Pacific Islander, 8% Hispanic American, 0.9% Native American, 10% live on campus.
Faculty *Total:* 197, 77% full-time. *Student/faculty ratio:* 26:1.
Majors Accounting; agricultural business and management; agriculture; anthropology; art; autobody/collision and repair technology; automobile/automotive mechanics technology; biology/biological sciences; botany/plant biology; business administration and management; business/commerce; cabinetmaking and millwork; chemistry; child development; clinical laboratory science/medical technology; commercial and advertising art; communication/speech communication and rhetoric; computer science; criminal justice/law enforcement administration; criminal justice/police science; culinary arts; dental assisting; dental hygiene; diesel mechanics technology; dietetics; drafting and design technology; dramatic/theatre arts; education; electrical, electronic and communications engineering technology; elementary education; engineering; English; environmental studies; equestrian studies; finance; fish/game management; foreign languages and literatures; forestry; geography; geology/earth science; health/health care administration; heating, air conditioning, ventilation and refrigeration maintenance technology; history; hotel/motel administration; human services; hydrology and water resources science; liberal arts and sciences/liberal studies; library science; marketing/marketing management; mathematics; medical radiologic technology; music; natural sciences; nursing (registered nurse training); occupational therapy; photography; physical education teaching and coaching; physical therapy; physician assistant; physics; political science and government; prepharmacy studies; psychology; public health education and promotion; range science and management; real estate; respiratory care therapy; sociology; surgical technology; veterinary technology; welding technology; woodworking; zoology/animal biology.
Academic Programs *Special study options:* academic remediation for entering students, adult/continuing education programs, advanced placement credit, cooperative education, distance learning, English as a second language, honors programs, internships, part-time degree program, services for LD students, summer session for credit.
Library College of Southern Idaho Library with 57,443 titles, 306 serial subscriptions, 3,177 audiovisual materials, an OPAC, a Web page.

Computers on Campus 350 computers available on campus for general student use. A campuswide network can be accessed from off campus. Internet access, online (class) registration, at least one staffed computer lab available. Computer purchase or lease plan available.
Student Life *Housing Options:* coed. Campus housing is university owned. *Activities and Organizations:* drama/theater group, student-run newspaper, radio station, choral group, BPA, Dex, Chi Alpha (Christian Group), Vet Tech, Equine Club. *Campus security:* 24-hour emergency response devices and patrols, controlled dormitory access. *Student services:* health clinic, personal/psychological counseling, women's center, legal services.
Athletics Member NJCAA. *Intercollegiate sports:* baseball M(s), basketball M(s)/W(s), cheerleading M(s)/W(s), equestrian sports M(s)/W(s), volleyball W(s). *Intramural sports:* basketball M/W, football M/W, golf M/W, racquetball M/W, rock climbing M/W, skiing (downhill) M/W, soccer M/W, softball M/W, tennis M/W, ultimate Frisbee M/W, volleyball M/W.
Standardized Tests *Required:* ACT COMPASS (for admission). *Required for some:* ACT (for admission).
Costs (2004–05) *Tuition:* state resident $1800 full-time, $90 per credit part-time; nonresident $5000 full-time, $250 per credit part-time. *Room and board:* $3960. Room and board charges vary according to board plan. *Payment plan:* installment. *Waivers:* senior citizens and employees or children of employees.
Financial Aid Of all full-time matriculated undergraduates who enrolled, 250 Federal Work-Study jobs (averaging $2000). 100 state and other part-time jobs (averaging $2000).
Applying *Options:* common application. *Required:* high school transcript. *Required for some:* letters of recommendation, interview. *Application deadline:* rolling (freshmen), rolling (transfers).
Admissions Contact Dr. John S. Martin, Director of Admissions, Registration, and Records, College of Southern Idaho, PO Box 1238, 315 Falls Avenue, Twin Falls, ID 83303. *Phone:* 208-732-6232. *Toll-free phone:* 800-680-0274. *Fax:* 208-736-3014.

EASTERN IDAHO TECHNICAL COLLEGE
Idaho Falls, Idaho

- **State-supported** 2-year, founded 1970
- **Calendar** semesters
- **Degree** certificates and associate
- **Small-town** 40-acre campus
- **Endowment** $1.6 million
- **Coed,** 860 undergraduate students, 46% full-time, 73% women, 27% men

Undergraduates 397 full-time, 463 part-time. Students come from 7 states and territories, 0.3% African American, 0.7% Asian American or Pacific Islander, 6% Hispanic American, 2% Native American, 10% transferred in. *Retention:* 50% of 2002 full-time freshmen returned.
Freshmen *Admission:* 144 admitted, 144 enrolled.
Faculty *Total:* 67, 58% full-time, 3% with terminal degrees. *Student/faculty ratio:* 11:1.
Majors Accounting; administrative assistant and secretarial science; automobile/automotive mechanics technology; computer systems networking and telecommunications; diesel mechanics technology; electrical, electronic and communications engineering technology; legal assistant/paralegal; marketing/marketing management; medical/clinical assistant; surgical technology; welding technology.
Academic Programs *Special study options:* academic remediation for entering students, adult/continuing education programs, cooperative education, distance learning, internships, part-time degree program, services for LD students, summer session for credit.
Library Eastern Idaho Technical College Library plus 1 other with 7,500 titles, 50 serial subscriptions, 100 audiovisual materials, an OPAC, a Web page.
Computers on Campus 105 computers available on campus for general student use. A campuswide network can be accessed. Internet access, at least one staffed computer lab available.
Student Life *Housing:* college housing not available. *Campus security:* 24-hour patrols. *Student services:* personal/psychological counseling.
Standardized Tests *Required:* ACT COMPASS (for placement).
Costs (2004–05) *Tuition:* state resident $1488 full-time, $74 per credit part-time; nonresident $5454 full-time, $148 per credit part-time. Full-time tuition and fees vary according to course load and reciprocity agreements. Part-time tuition and fees vary according to class time and reciprocity agreements. *Required fees:* $106 full-time. *Waivers:* employees or children of employees.
Financial Aid Of all full-time matriculated undergraduates who enrolled, 37 Federal Work-Study jobs (averaging $1176). 11 state and other part-time jobs (averaging $1619).

Eastern Idaho Technical College (continued)

Applying *Options:* deferred entrance. *Application fee:* $10. *Required:* high school transcript, interview. *Required for some:* essay or personal statement. *Recommended:* letters of recommendation. *Application deadline:* 8/20 (freshmen).

Admissions Contact Dr. Steve Albiston, Dean of Students, Eastern Idaho Technical College, 1600 South 25th E., Idaho Falls, ID 83404. *Phone:* 208-524-3000 Ext. 3366. *Toll-free phone:* 800-662-0261 Ext. 3371. *Fax:* 208-525-7026. *E-mail:* salbisto@eitc.edu.

ITT TECHNICAL INSTITUTE
Boise, Idaho

- **Proprietary** primarily 2-year, founded 1906, part of ITT Educational Services, Inc.
- **Calendar** quarters
- **Degrees** associate and bachelor's
- **Urban** 1-acre campus
- **Coed**

Standardized Tests *Required:* Wonderlic aptitude test (for admission).

Costs (2003–04) *Tuition:* Total Program Cost varies depending on course of study. Consult school catalog.

Financial Aid Of all full-time matriculated undergraduates who enrolled, 9 Federal Work-Study jobs (averaging $5500).

Applying *Options:* deferred entrance. *Application fee:* $100. *Required:* high school transcript, interview. *Recommended:* letters of recommendation.

Admissions Contact Terry G. Lowder, Director of Recruitment, ITT Technical Institute, 12302 West Explorer Drive, Boise, ID 83713. *Phone:* 208-322-8844. *Toll-free phone:* 800-666-4888. *Fax:* 208-322-0173.

NORTH IDAHO COLLEGE
Coeur d'Alene, Idaho

- **State and locally supported** 2-year, founded 1933
- **Calendar** semesters
- **Degree** certificates and associate
- **Small-town** 42-acre campus
- **Endowment** $4.9 million
- **Coed**, 4,452 undergraduate students

Undergraduates Students come from 27 states and territories, 16 other countries, 8% are from out of state, 0.2% African American, 0.8% Asian American or Pacific Islander, 2% Hispanic American, 2% Native American, 0.5% international.

Freshmen *Admission:* 2,069 applied, 2,069 admitted. *Average high school GPA:* 2.81.

Faculty *Total:* 280, 51% full-time. *Student/faculty ratio:* 17:1.

Majors Administrative assistant and secretarial science; agriculture; American Indian/Native American studies; anthropology; art; astronomy; athletic training; automobile/automotive mechanics technology; biological and physical sciences; biology/biological sciences; botany/plant biology; business administration and management; business teacher education; carpentry; chemistry; clinical laboratory science/medical technology; commercial and advertising art; computer and information sciences related; computer programming; computer science; computer/technical support; criminal justice/law enforcement administration; criminal justice/police science; culinary arts; developmental and child psychology; drafting and design technology; dramatic/theatre arts; education; electrical, electronic and communications engineering technology; elementary education; engineering; English; environmental health; fish/game management; forestry; French; geology/earth science; German; health/health care administration; heating, air conditioning, ventilation and refrigeration maintenance technology; heavy equipment maintenance technology; history; hospitality administration; human services; journalism; legal administrative assistant/secretary; legal assistant/paralegal; liberal arts and sciences/liberal studies; machine tool technology; marine technology; mass communication/media; mathematics; medical administrative assistant and medical secretary; music; music teacher education; nursing (licensed practical/vocational nurse training); nursing (registered nurse training); physical sciences; physics; political science and government; psychology; social sciences; sociology; Spanish; welding technology; wildlife and wildlands science and management; wildlife biology; zoology/animal biology.

Academic Programs *Special study options:* academic remediation for entering students, adult/continuing education programs, advanced placement credit, cooperative education, distance learning, English as a second language, independent study, internships, off-campus study, part-time degree program, services for LD students, summer session for credit.

Library Molstead Library Computer Center with 60,893 titles, 751 serial subscriptions, an OPAC, a Web page.

Computers on Campus 145 computers available on campus for general student use. A campuswide network can be accessed. Internet access, at least one staffed computer lab available.

Student Life *Housing Options:* Campus housing is university owned. *Activities and Organizations:* drama/theater group, student-run newspaper, choral group, Ski Club, Fusion, Baptist student ministries, Journalism Club, Phi Theta Kappa. *Campus security:* 24-hour emergency response devices and patrols, late-night transport/escort service. *Student services:* health clinic, personal/psychological counseling, women's center, legal services.

Athletics Member NJCAA. *Intercollegiate sports:* basketball M(s)/W(s), cheerleading M(s)/W(s), soccer M(s)/W(s), softball W(s), volleyball W(s), wrestling M(s). *Intramural sports:* basketball M/W, bowling M/W, cheerleading M/W, crew M(c)/W(c), cross-country running M(c)/W(c), football M/W, golf M/W, racquetball M/W, sailing M(c)/W(c), skiing (cross-country) M(c)/W(c), skiing (downhill) M(c)/W(c), soccer M(c)/W(c), softball M/W, table tennis M/W, tennis M/W, track and field M(c)/W(c), volleyball M/W.

Standardized Tests *Required for some:* ACT ASSET, ACT COMPASS. *Recommended:* SAT I or ACT (for placement), ACT ASSET, ACT COMPASS.

Costs (2003–04) *Tuition:* area resident $1696 full-time, $105 per credit part-time; state resident $2696 full-time, $168 per credit part-time; nonresident $5788 full-time, $361 per credit part-time. *Required fees:* $10 per term part-time. *Room and board:* $5400.

Financial Aid Of all full-time matriculated undergraduates who enrolled, 142 Federal Work-Study jobs (averaging $1425). 106 state and other part-time jobs (averaging $1327).

Applying *Options:* electronic application, early admission, deferred entrance. *Application fee:* $25. *Required for some:* essay or personal statement, high school transcript, minimum 2.0 GPA, county residency certificate. *Application deadlines:* 8/20 (freshmen), 8/20 (transfers).

Admissions Contact Ms. Maxine Gish, Director of Admissions, North Idaho College, 1000 West Garden Avenue, Coeur d'Alene, ID 83814-2199. *Phone:* 208-769-3303. *Toll-free phone:* 877-404-4536 Ext. 3311. *Fax:* 208-769-3399 Ext. 3311. *E-mail:* admit@nic.edu.

ILLINOIS

BLACK HAWK COLLEGE
Moline, Illinois

- **State and locally supported** 2-year, founded 1946, part of Black Hawk College District System
- **Calendar** semesters
- **Degree** certificates and associate
- **Urban** 161-acre campus
- **Coed**

Faculty *Student/faculty ratio:* 14:1.

Student Life *Campus security:* 24-hour patrols.

Athletics Member NJCAA.

Standardized Tests *Required for some:* ACT (for placement), ACT ASSET.

Costs (2004–05) *Tuition:* area resident $1710 full-time, $57 per credit hour part-time; state resident $4200 full-time, $140 per credit hour part-time; nonresident $7770 full-time, $259 per credit hour part-time. *Required fees:* $210 full-time, $7 per credit hour part-time. *Payment plans:* installment, deferred payment.

Financial Aid Of all full-time matriculated undergraduates who enrolled, 183 Federal Work-Study jobs (averaging $1281). 202 state and other part-time jobs (averaging $1098).

Applying *Options:* early admission, deferred entrance. *Required:* high school transcript.

Admissions Contact Ms. Rose Hernandez, Coordinator of Recruitment, Black Hawk College, 6600 34th Avenue, Moline, IL 61265. *Phone:* 309-796-5342. *Fax:* 309-792-5976.

CAREER COLLEGES OF CHICAGO
Chicago, Illinois

Admissions Contact Ms. Rosa Alvarado, Admissions Assistant, Career Colleges of Chicago, 11 East Adams Street, Chicago, IL 60603. *Phone:* 312-895-6306. *Fax:* 312-895-6301. *E-mail:* icoburn@careerchi.com.

CARL SANDBURG COLLEGE
Galesburg, Illinois

- **State and locally supported** 2-year, founded 1967, part of Illinois Community College Board
- **Calendar** semesters

- **Degree** certificates and associate
- **Small-town** 105-acre campus with easy access to Peoria
- **Coed,** 5,000 undergraduate students

Undergraduates Students come from 5 states and territories, 2 other countries, 4% African American, 0.5% Asian American or Pacific Islander, 2% Hispanic American, 0.3% Native American, 0.4% international.
Faculty *Total:* 208, 28% full-time. *Student/faculty ratio:* 17:1.
Majors Accounting; administrative assistant and secretarial science; agricultural business and management; agricultural mechanization; automobile/automotive mechanics technology; business administration and management; cosmetology; criminal justice/law enforcement administration; criminal justice/police science; data processing and data processing technology; developmental and child psychology; drafting and design technology; electrical, electronic and communications engineering technology; fashion merchandising; funeral service and mortuary science; industrial radiologic technology; liberal arts and sciences/liberal studies; marketing/marketing management; nursing (licensed practical/vocational nurse training); nursing (registered nurse training); real estate.
Academic Programs *Special study options:* academic remediation for entering students, adult/continuing education programs, advanced placement credit, cooperative education, English as a second language, internships, part-time degree program, services for LD students, student-designed majors, summer session for credit. *ROTC:* Army (c).
Library Learning Resource Center plus 1 other with 39,900 titles, 290 serial subscriptions.
Computers on Campus 110 computers available on campus for general student use. At least one staffed computer lab available.
Student Life *Housing:* college housing not available. *Activities and Organizations:* drama/theater group, choral group. *Campus security:* 24-hour emergency response devices and patrols. *Student services:* personal/psychological counseling.
Athletics Member NJCAA. *Intercollegiate sports:* baseball M(s), basketball M(s)/W(s), volleyball W(s).
Standardized Tests *Required:* ACT ASSET (for placement).
Costs (2003–04) *Tuition:* $62 per semester hour part-time; state resident $2445 full-time, $81 per semester hour part-time; nonresident $221 per semester hour part-time. *Required fees:* $9 per semester hour part-time. *Payment plan:* deferred payment. *Waivers:* senior citizens and employees or children of employees.
Financial Aid Of all full-time matriculated undergraduates who enrolled, 80 Federal Work-Study jobs (averaging $3000).
Applying *Options:* early admission, deferred entrance. *Required:* high school transcript. *Application deadline:* rolling (freshmen), rolling (transfers).
Admissions Contact Ms. Carol Kreider, Director of Admissions and Records, Carl Sandburg College, 2400 Tom L. Wilson Boulevard, Galesburg, IL 61401-9576. *Phone:* 309-341-5234.

CITY COLLEGES OF CHICAGO, HAROLD WASHINGTON COLLEGE
Chicago, Illinois

Admissions Contact Mr. Terry Pendleton, Admissions Coordinator, City Colleges of Chicago, Harold Washington College, 30 East Lake Street, Chicago, IL 60601-2449. *Phone:* 312-553-6006. *Fax:* 312-553-6077.

CITY COLLEGES OF CHICAGO, HARRY S. TRUMAN COLLEGE
Chicago, Illinois

Admissions Contact Mrs. Kelly O'Malley, Assistant Dean, Student Services, City Colleges of Chicago, Harry S. Truman College, 1145 West Wilson Avenue, Chicago, IL 60640-5616. *Phone:* 773-907-4720. *Fax:* 773-989-6135.

CITY COLLEGES OF CHICAGO, KENNEDY-KING COLLEGE
Chicago, Illinois

- **State and locally supported** 2-year, founded 1935, part of City Colleges of Chicago
- **Calendar** semesters
- **Degree** certificates and associate
- **Urban** 18-acre campus
- **Endowment** $14.1 million
- **Coed**

Student Life *Campus security:* late-night transport/escort service.

Athletics Member NJCAA.
Standardized Tests *Recommended:* SAT I or ACT (for placement).
Costs (2003–04) *Tuition:* area resident $1560 full-time, $52 per credit hour part-time; state resident $5235 full-time, $175 per credit hour part-time; nonresident $7416 full-time, $247 per credit hour part-time. Full-time tuition and fees vary according to course load. Part-time tuition and fees vary according to course load. *Required fees:* $150 full-time, $52 per credit hour part-time.
Financial Aid Of all full-time matriculated undergraduates who enrolled, 148 Federal Work-Study jobs (averaging $1539).
Applying *Options:* electronic application. *Required:* high school transcript.
Admissions Contact Ms. Joyce Collins, Clerical Supervisor for Admissions and Records, City Colleges of Chicago, Kennedy-King College, 6800 South Wentworth Avenue, Chicago, IL 60621. *Phone:* 773-602-5000 Ext. 5055. *Fax:* 773-602-5247. *E-mail:* w.murphy@ccc.edu.

CITY COLLEGES OF CHICAGO, MALCOLM X COLLEGE
Chicago, Illinois

- **State and locally supported** 2-year, founded 1911, part of City Colleges of Chicago
- **Calendar** semesters
- **Degree** certificates and associate
- **Urban** 20-acre campus
- **Coed,** 8,024 undergraduate students, 51% full-time, 66% women, 34% men

Undergraduates 4,069 full-time, 3,955 part-time. Students come from 1 other state, 79% African American, 4% Asian American or Pacific Islander, 12% Hispanic American, 0.8% Native American.
Freshmen *Admission:* 861 applied, 861 admitted, 861 enrolled.
Faculty *Total:* 194, 30% full-time. *Student/faculty ratio:* 22:1.
Majors Accounting; administrative assistant and secretarial science; art; child care provision; clinical/medical laboratory technology; computer programming (specific applications); dietitian assistant; elementary education; emergency medical technology (EMT paramedic); funeral service and mortuary science; general studies; hospital and health care facilities administration; liberal arts and sciences/liberal studies; medical/clinical assistant; medical radiologic technology; music; nursing (registered nurse training); physical education teaching and coaching; physician assistant; pre-medical studies; pre-pharmacy studies; respiratory care therapy; restaurant, culinary, and catering management; secondary education; surgical technology; teacher assistant/aide.
Academic Programs *Special study options:* academic remediation for entering students, adult/continuing education programs, advanced placement credit, cooperative education, distance learning, English as a second language, part-time degree program, services for LD students, summer session for credit.
Library The Carter G. Woodson Library with 50,000 titles, 250 serial subscriptions, 300 audiovisual materials, an OPAC, a Web page.
Computers on Campus 275 computers available on campus for general student use. A campuswide network can be accessed. Internet access, at least one staffed computer lab available.
Student Life *Housing:* college housing not available. *Activities and Organizations:* student-run newspaper, Student Government Association, Phi Theta Kappa Honor Society, Phi Beta Lambda business organization, Chess Club, Latino Leadership Council. *Campus security:* 24-hour emergency response devices and patrols. *Student services:* personal/psychological counseling.
Athletics Member NJCAA. *Intercollegiate sports:* basketball M/W, cross-country running M. *Intramural sports:* basketball M/W, weight lifting M/W.
Standardized Tests *Required for some:* SAT I and SAT II or ACT (for placement).
Costs (2004–05) *Tuition:* area resident $1860 full-time, $62 per credit part-time; state resident $6876 full-time, $229 per credit part-time; nonresident $9449 full-time, $315 per credit part-time. Part-time tuition and fees vary according to course load. *Required fees:* $375 full-time, $75 per term part-time. *Payment plan:* deferred payment. *Waivers:* employees or children of employees.
Financial Aid Of all full-time matriculated undergraduates who enrolled, 200 Federal Work-Study jobs (averaging $2500).
Applying *Options:* common application, early admission, deferred entrance. *Required:* high school transcript, minimum 2.0 GPA. *Required for some:* essay or personal statement, interview. *Application deadline:* rolling (freshmen), rolling (transfers). *Notification:* continuous (freshmen).
Admissions Contact Mr. Ghingo Brooks, Vice President of Enrollment Management and Student Services, City Colleges of Chicago, Malcolm X College, 1900 West Van Buren Street, Chicago, IL 60612. *Phone:* 312-850-7120. *Fax:* 312-850-7092. *E-mail:* gbrooks@ccc.edu.

Illinois

CITY COLLEGES OF CHICAGO, OLIVE-HARVEY COLLEGE
Chicago, Illinois

- **State and locally supported** 2-year, founded 1970, part of City Colleges of Chicago
- **Calendar** semesters
- **Degree** certificates and associate
- **Urban** 67-acre campus
- **Coed**

Student Life *Campus security:* 24-hour emergency response devices and patrols.

Athletics Member NJCAA.

Standardized Tests *Recommended:* SAT I or ACT (for placement).

Costs (2003–04) *Tuition:* area resident $1248 full-time; state resident $3990 full-time; nonresident $5833 full-time. *Required fees:* $250 full-time.

Financial Aid Of all full-time matriculated undergraduates who enrolled, 150 Federal Work-Study jobs (averaging $3900).

Applying *Options:* common application, early admission, deferred entrance.

Admissions Contact Ms. Ernestine Taylor, Director of Admissions, City Colleges of Chicago, Olive-Harvey College, 10001 South Woodlawn, Chicago, IL 60628-1696. *Phone:* 773-291-6359. *Fax:* 773-291-6304.

CITY COLLEGES OF CHICAGO, RICHARD J. DALEY COLLEGE
Chicago, Illinois

- **State and locally supported** 2-year, founded 1960, part of City Colleges of Chicago
- **Calendar** semesters
- **Degree** certificates and associate
- **Urban** 25-acre campus
- **Coed**

Student Life *Campus security:* 24-hour patrols.

Standardized Tests *Required for some:* ACT (for placement). *Recommended:* ACT (for placement).

Costs (2003–04) *Tuition:* area resident $1560 full-time; state resident $5235 full-time; nonresident $7628 full-time. *Required fees:* $250 full-time.

Financial Aid Of all full-time matriculated undergraduates who enrolled, 250 Federal Work-Study jobs (averaging $2500).

Applying *Options:* common application, early admission, deferred entrance. *Required:* high school transcript. *Required for some:* essay or personal statement, letters of recommendation. *Recommended:* interview.

Admissions Contact Ms. Karla Reynolds, Registrar, City Colleges of Chicago, Richard J. Daley College, 7500 South Pulaski Road, Chicago, IL 60652-1242. *Phone:* 773-838-7599. *E-mail:* kreynolds@ccc.edu.

CITY COLLEGES OF CHICAGO, WILBUR WRIGHT COLLEGE
Chicago, Illinois

- **State and locally supported** 2-year, founded 1934, part of City Colleges of Chicago
- **Calendar** semesters
- **Degree** certificates and associate
- **Urban** 20-acre campus with easy access to Chicago, Illinois
- **Coed,** 7,128 undergraduate students, 32% full-time, 60% women, 40% men

Undergraduates 2,273 full-time, 4,855 part-time. 10% African American, 11% Asian American or Pacific Islander, 37% Hispanic American, 0.6% Native American.

Freshmen *Admission:* 2,700 applied, 2,700 admitted. *Average high school GPA:* 2.5.

Faculty *Total:* 246, 39% full-time. *Student/faculty ratio:* 22:1.

Majors Accounting; architectural engineering technology; architectural technology; art; biological and physical sciences; business administration and management; computer and information sciences; computer and information systems security; criminal justice/police science; data processing and data processing technology; elementary education; engineering; English; environmental engineering technology; environmental science; general studies; gerontology; Hispanic-American, Puerto Rican, and Mexican-American/Chicano studies; journalism; liberal arts and sciences/liberal studies; library science; machine tool technology; marketing/marketing management; medical radiologic technology; modern languages; music; occupational therapy; physical sciences; pre-engineering; speech and rhetoric.

Academic Programs *Special study options:* academic remediation for entering students, accelerated degree program, adult/continuing education programs, distance learning, English as a second language, part-time degree program, summer session for credit.

Library Learning Resource Center plus 1 other with 60,000 titles, 350 serial subscriptions.

Computers on Campus 600 computers available on campus for general student use. A campuswide network can be accessed. Internet access, at least one staffed computer lab available.

Student Life *Housing:* college housing not available. *Activities and Organizations:* drama/theater group, student-run newspaper, choral group, student government, Circle K, Phi Theta Kappa, Black Student Union. *Campus security:* 24-hour emergency response devices and patrols, student patrols, late-night transport/escort service. *Student services:* legal services.

Athletics Member NJCAA. *Intercollegiate sports:* basketball M(s)/W(s), wrestling M(s). *Intramural sports:* basketball M, cross-country running M/W, golf M/W, swimming M/W, tennis M, volleyball M/W, weight lifting M/W, wrestling M/W.

Standardized Tests *Required:* ACT (for placement).

Costs (2004–05) *Tuition:* area resident $2040 full-time, $62 per credit hour part-time; state resident $6282 full-time, $185 per credit hour part-time; nonresident $9082 full-time, $262 per credit hour part-time. Full-time tuition and fees vary according to course load. Part-time tuition and fees vary according to course load. *Required fees:* $250 full-time. *Payment plan:* installment. *Waivers:* senior citizens and employees or children of employees.

Financial Aid Of all full-time matriculated undergraduates who enrolled, 67 Federal Work-Study jobs (averaging $1000).

Applying *Options:* common application, early admission, deferred entrance. *Application deadline:* rolling (freshmen), rolling (transfers). *Notification:* continuous (freshmen), continuous (transfers).

Admissions Contact Ms. Amy Aiello, Assistant Dean of Student Services, City Colleges of Chicago, Wilbur Wright College, 4300 North Narragansett, Chicago, IL 60634. *Phone:* 773-481-8207.

COLLEGE OF DUPAGE
Glen Ellyn, Illinois

- **State and locally supported** 2-year, founded 1967, part of Illinois Community College Board
- **Calendar** quarters
- **Degree** certificates and associate
- **Suburban** 297-acre campus with easy access to Chicago
- **Endowment** $10.5 million
- **Coed,** 30,378 undergraduate students, 34% full-time, 57% women, 43% men

Undergraduates 10,322 full-time, 20,056 part-time. Students come from 6 states and territories, 5% African American, 11% Asian American or Pacific Islander, 7% Hispanic American, 0.2% Native American, 6% transferred in. *Retention:* 65% of 2002 full-time freshmen returned.

Freshmen *Admission:* 3,844 admitted, 3,844 enrolled.

Faculty *Total:* 1,697, 18% full-time, 13% with terminal degrees. *Student/faculty ratio:* 21:1.

Majors Accounting; administrative assistant and secretarial science; automobile/automotive mechanics technology; baking and pastry arts; biological and physical sciences; building/property maintenance and management; business administration and management; child care and support services management; child care provision; child development; cinematography and film/video production; commercial and advertising art; communications systems installation and repair technology; communications technology; computer installation and repair technology; computer programming (specific applications); computer typography and composition equipment operation; corrections; criminal justice/law enforcement administration; criminal justice/police science; culinary arts; data entry/microcomputer applications related; dental hygiene; design and visual communications; desktop publishing and digital imaging design; drafting and design technology; electrical, electronic and communications engineering technology; electrical/electronics equipment installation and repair; electromechanical technology; emergency medical technology (EMT paramedic); engineering; fashion and fabric consulting; fashion/apparel design; fashion merchandising; fire science; graphic and printing equipment operation/production; health/health care administration; health information/medical records administration; health information/medical records technology; heating, air conditioning, ventilation and refrigeration maintenance technology; hospital and health care facilities administration; hospitality administration; hotel/motel administration; human services; industrial electronics technology; industrial technology; interior design; landscaping and groundskeeping; legal administrative assistant/secretary; liberal arts and sciences/liberal studies; library assistant; library science; machine tool technology; manufacturing technology; marketing/marketing management; massage therapy; mechanical design technology; medical radiologic technology; merchandising; nuclear medical technology; nursing (registered nurse training); occupational therapist assistant; occupational therapy; office management; ornamental horticulture; photography; physical therapist assistant; plastics engineering technology; precision production trades; real estate; respiratory care therapy; restaurant, culinary, and catering management; retailing; robotics technology; sales, distribution and marketing; selling skills and sales; speech-language pathology; substance abuse/addiction counseling; surgical technology; tourism and travel services management; tourism and travel services marketing; tourism promotion; transportation technology; welding technology.

Academic Programs *Special study options:* academic remediation for entering students, accelerated degree program, adult/continuing education programs, advanced placement credit, cooperative education, distance learning, double majors, English as a second language, external degree program, honors programs, independent study, internships, off-campus study, part-time degree program, services for LD students, student-designed majors, study abroad, summer session for credit.

Library College of DuPage Library with 203,300 titles, 6,005 serial subscriptions, 33,600 audiovisual materials, an OPAC, a Web page.

Computers on Campus 2403 computers available on campus for general student use. A campuswide network can be accessed from off campus. Internet access, online (class) registration, at least one staffed computer lab available. Computer purchase or lease plan available.

Student Life *Housing:* college housing not available. *Activities and Organizations:* drama/theater group, student-run newspaper, choral group, Latino Ethnic Awareness Association, The Christian Group, Phi Theta Kappa, International Students Organization, Muslim Student Association. *Campus security:* 24-hour emergency response devices and patrols, student patrols, late-night transport/escort service. *Student services:* health clinic, personal/psychological counseling.

Athletics Member NJCAA. *Intercollegiate sports:* baseball M, basketball M/W, cheerleading M/W, cross-country running M/W, football M, golf M, soccer M/W, softball W, swimming M/W, tennis M/W, track and field M/W, volleyball W. *Intramural sports:* basketball M/W, bowling M/W, golf M/W, ice hockey M(c), racquetball M/W, soccer M/W, softball M/W, swimming M/W, tennis M/W, volleyball M/W, weight lifting M/W.

Standardized Tests *Recommended:* ACT (for placement).

Costs (2004–05) *Tuition:* area resident $2400 full-time, $50 per quarter hour part-time; state resident $6480 full-time, $135 per quarter hour part-time; nonresident $8688 full-time, $181 per quarter hour part-time. *Required fees:* $322 full-time.

Applying *Options:* early admission, deferred entrance. *Application fee:* $10. *Application deadline:* rolling (freshmen), rolling (transfers). *Notification:* continuous (freshmen), continuous (transfers).

Admissions Contact Mrs. Christine A. Legner, Coordinator of Admission Services, College of DuPage, SRC 2046, 425 Fawell Boulevard, Glen Ellyn, IL 60137-6599. *Phone:* 630-942-2442. *Fax:* 630-790-2686. *E-mail:* protis@cdnet.cod.edu.

COLLEGE OF LAKE COUNTY
Grayslake, Illinois

- **District-supported** 2-year, founded 1967, part of Illinois Community College Board
- **Calendar** semesters
- **Degree** certificates and associate
- **Suburban** 226-acre campus with easy access to Chicago and Milwaukee
- **Endowment** $530,495
- **Coed,** 15,768 undergraduate students, 26% full-time, 58% women, 42% men

Undergraduates 4,086 full-time, 11,682 part-time. Students come from 15 states and territories, 42 other countries, 2% are from out of state, 10% African American, 6% Asian American or Pacific Islander, 18% Hispanic American, 0.4% Native American, 2% international, 1% transferred in. *Retention:* 60% of 2002 full-time freshmen returned.

Freshmen *Admission:* 2,183 applied, 2,183 admitted, 1,847 enrolled.

Faculty *Total:* 809, 22% full-time, 8% with terminal degrees. *Student/faculty ratio:* 21:1.

Majors Accounting technology and bookkeeping; administrative assistant and secretarial science; architectural drafting; art; automobile/automotive mechanics technology; biological and physical sciences; business administration and management; business automation/technology/data entry; business computer programming; business systems networking/ telecommunications; chemical technology; child care provider; civil engineering technology; computer installation and repair technology; construction engineering technology; criminal justice/police science; dental hygiene; electrical, electronic and communications engineering technology; electrician; engineering; fire protection and safety technology; heating, air conditioning, ventilation and refrigeration maintenance technology; industrial mechanics and maintenance technology; landscaping and grounds-keeping; liberal arts and sciences/liberal studies; machine shop technology; mechanical engineering/mechanical technology; medical office management; medical radiologic technology; music; music teacher education; natural resources management and policy; nursing (registered nurse training); ornamental horti-

culture; restaurant, culinary, and catering management; sales operations; social work; substance abuse/addiction counseling; technical and business writing; turf and turfgrass management.

Academic Programs *Special study options:* academic remediation for entering students, adult/continuing education programs, advanced placement credit, cooperative education, distance learning, double majors, English as a second language, honors programs, independent study, internships, off-campus study, part-time degree program, services for LD students, student-designed majors, study abroad, summer session for credit.

Library College of Lake County Library plus 1 other with 120,642 titles, 904 serial subscriptions, 8,028 audiovisual materials, an OPAC, a Web page.

Computers on Campus 1000 computers available on campus for general student use. A campuswide network can be accessed from off campus. Internet access, at least one staffed computer lab available.

Student Life *Housing:* college housing not available. *Activities and Organizations:* drama/theater group, student-run newspaper, radio station, choral group, Latino Alliance, Asian Student Alliance, Black Student Union, International Student Council, Phi Theta Kappa. *Campus security:* 24-hour emergency response devices and patrols, late-night transport/escort service. *Student services:* health clinic, personal/psychological counseling, women's center.

Athletics Member NJCAA. *Intercollegiate sports:* baseball M(s), basketball M(s)/W(s), cross-country running M(s)/W(s), golf M(s), soccer M(s)/W(s), softball W(s), tennis M(s)/W(s), volleyball W(s), wrestling M(s). *Intramural sports:* golf M/W.

Standardized Tests *Recommended:* SAT I or ACT (for placement).

Costs (2004–05) *Tuition:* area resident $1724 full-time, $57 per credit hour part-time; state resident $5474 full-time, $182 per credit hour part-time; nonresident $7064 full-time, $253 per credit hour part-time. *Required fees:* $197 full-time, $7 per credit hour part-time. *Payment plan:* installment. *Waivers:* employees or children of employees.

Financial Aid Of all full-time matriculated undergraduates who enrolled, 68 Federal Work-Study jobs (averaging $1856). 178 state and other part-time jobs (averaging $1937).

Applying *Options:* common application, electronic application, early admission, deferred entrance. *Required for some:* high school transcript, interview. *Application deadline:* rolling (freshmen), rolling (transfers). *Notification:* continuous (freshmen), continuous (transfers).

Admissions Contact Terry Spets, Director-Student Recruitment, College of Lake County, 19351 West Washington Street, Grayslake, IL 60030-1198. *Phone:* 847-543-2383. *Fax:* 847-223-1017. *E-mail:* terryspets@clcillinois.edu.

THE COLLEGE OF OFFICE TECHNOLOGY
Chicago, Illinois

Admissions Contact Mr. William Bolton, Director of Admissions, The College of Office Technology, 1514-20 West Division Street, Second Floor, Chicago, IL 60622. *Phone:* 773-278-0042.

THE COOKING AND HOSPITALITY INSTITUTE OF CHICAGO
Chicago, Illinois

- **Proprietary** 2-year, founded 1983, part of Career Education Corporation
- **Calendar** continuous
- **Degree** associate
- **Urban** campus
- **Endowment** $35,000
- **Coed,** 950 undergraduate students, 100% full-time, 51% women, 49% men

Undergraduates 950 full-time. Students come from 25 states and territories, 15 other countries, 25% are from out of state.

Freshmen *Test scores:* ACT scores over 18: 75%; ACT scores over 24: 15%.

Faculty *Student/faculty ratio:* 16:1.

Majors Baking and pastry arts; culinary arts.

Academic Programs *Special study options:* academic remediation for entering students, accelerated degree program, adult/continuing education programs, advanced placement credit, cooperative education, double majors, services for LD students, summer session for credit.

Library Learning Resource Center plus 1 other with 5,000 titles, 100 serial subscriptions, 200 audiovisual materials.

Computers on Campus 25 computers available on campus for general student use. A campuswide network can be accessed from off campus. Internet access, at least one staffed computer lab available.

Student Life *Housing:* college housing not available. *Activities and Organizations:* student-run newspaper, The Student Board, Culinary Competition Club, Recipe Development Association, The Cellar Club, Pastry Display Club.

Standardized Tests *Recommended:* SAT I or ACT (for placement).

The Cooking and Hospitality Institute of Chicago *(continued)*

Costs (2003–04) *Tuition:* $36,750 full-time. No tuition increase for student's term of enrollment. *Payment plans:* tuition prepayment, installment.

Financial Aid Of all full-time matriculated undergraduates who enrolled, 10 Federal Work-Study jobs.

Applying *Options:* common application, electronic application, deferred entrance. *Application fee:* $150. *Recommended:* essay or personal statement, high school transcript, interview.

Admissions Contact The Cooking and Hospitality Institute of Chicago, 361 West Chestnut, Chicago, IL 60610. *Phone:* 312-873-2064. *Toll-free phone:* 877-828-7772. *Fax:* 312-944-8557. *E-mail:* chic@chicnet.org.

▶ **See page 534 for a narrative description.**

DANVILLE AREA COMMUNITY COLLEGE
Danville, Illinois

Admissions Contact Ms. Stacy L. Ehmen, Director of Admissions of Records/Registrar, Danville Area Community College, 2000 East Main Street, Danville, IL 61832-5199. *Phone:* 217-443-8800. *Fax:* 217-443-8560. *E-mail:* sehmen@dacc.cc.il.us.

ELGIN COMMUNITY COLLEGE
Elgin, Illinois

- **State and locally supported** 2-year, founded 1949, part of Illinois Community College Board
- **Calendar** semesters
- **Degree** certificates, diplomas, and associate
- **Suburban** 145-acre campus with easy access to Chicago
- **Coed**, 18,242 undergraduate students

Undergraduates Students come from 4 states and territories, 22 other countries, 1% are from out of state, 5% African American, 6% Asian American or Pacific Islander, 13% Hispanic American, 0.2% Native American, 0.4% international.

Freshmen *Admission:* 10,573 applied, 10,573 admitted.

Faculty *Total:* 413, 24% full-time. *Student/faculty ratio:* 18:1.

Majors Accounting; accounting technology and bookkeeping; administrative assistant and secretarial science; art; automobile/automotive mechanics technology; biological and physical sciences; business administration and management; clinical/medical laboratory technology; commercial and advertising art; computer graphics; computer programming (specific applications); computer typography and composition equipment operation; consumer merchandising/retailing management; corrections; criminal justice/law enforcement administration; criminal justice/police science; culinary arts; design and visual communications; drafting and design technology; electrical, electronic and communications engineering technology; emergency medical technology (EMT paramedic); executive assistant/executive secretary; fire protection and safety technology; fire science; general retailing/wholesaling; gerontology; health information/medical records administration; heating, air conditioning, ventilation and refrigeration maintenance technology; hotel/motel administration; human services; industrial technology; information science/studies; kindergarten/preschool education; legal administrative assistant/secretary; legal assistant/paralegal; liberal arts and sciences/liberal studies; machine tool technology; marketing/marketing management; medical administrative assistant and medical secretary; medical transcription; mental health/rehabilitation; metallurgical technology; nursing (licensed practical/vocational nurse training); nursing (registered nurse training); pre-engineering; social work; substance abuse/addiction counseling; tourism and travel services management; welding technology.

Academic Programs *Special study options:* academic remediation for entering students, accelerated degree program, adult/continuing education programs, advanced placement credit, cooperative education, distance learning, double majors, English as a second language, honors programs, independent study, internships, off-campus study, part-time degree program, services for LD students, student-designed majors, summer session for credit.

Library Renner Learning Resource Center with 58,413 titles, 458 serial subscriptions, 7,394 audiovisual materials, an OPAC, a Web page.

Computers on Campus 1011 computers available on campus for general student use. A campuswide network can be accessed. Internet access, at least one staffed computer lab available. Computer purchase or lease plan available.

Student Life *Housing:* college housing not available. *Activities and Organizations:* drama/theater group, student-run newspaper, choral group, Phi Theta Kappa, United Students of All Cultures, Organization of Latin American Students, Black Student Association, Office Administration Association. *Campus security:* 24-hour patrols. *Student services:* personal/psychological counseling, legal services.

Athletics Member NJCAA. *Intercollegiate sports:* baseball M(s)/W, basketball M(s)/W(s), cheerleading W(s), cross-country running M/W, golf M(s), softball W, tennis W(s), volleyball W(s).

Standardized Tests *Recommended:* ACT (for placement).

Costs (2003–04) *Tuition:* area resident $1875 full-time, $62 per credit hour part-time; state resident $7874 full-time, $262 per credit hour part-time; nonresident $9476 full-time, $315 per credit hour part-time. Full-time tuition and fees vary according to program. Part-time tuition and fees vary according to program. *Required fees:* $20 full-time, $1 per credit hour part-time. *Payment plan:* installment. *Waivers:* senior citizens and employees or children of employees.

Applying *Options:* early admission. *Application fee:* $15. *Required for some:* high school transcript. *Application deadline:* rolling (freshmen), rolling (transfers). *Notification:* continuous (freshmen), continuous (transfers).

Admissions Contact Ms. Kelly Sinclair, Admissions, Recruitment, and Student Life, Elgin Community College, 1700 Spartan Drive, Elgin, IL 60123-7193. *Phone:* 847-214-7914. *E-mail:* admissions@mail.elgin.cc.il.us.

FOX COLLEGE
Oak Lawn, Illinois

Admissions Contact Ms. Susan Szala, Director of Admissions, Fox College, 4201 West 93rd Street, Oak Lawn, IL 60453. *Phone:* 708-636-7700. *Toll-free phone:* 866-636-7711.

GEM CITY COLLEGE
Quincy, Illinois

- **Proprietary** 2-year, founded 1870
- **Calendar** quarters
- **Degree** diplomas and associate
- **Small-town** campus
- **Coed**, 150 undergraduate students

Undergraduates Students come from 10 states and territories, 1 other country.

Freshmen *Admission:* 65 applied, 65 admitted.

Faculty *Total:* 7, 71% full-time.

Majors Accounting; administrative assistant and secretarial science; business administration and management; computer science; cosmetology; information science/studies; legal administrative assistant/secretary; legal assistant/paralegal; medical administrative assistant and medical secretary; medical/clinical assistant; metal and jewelry arts.

Academic Programs *Special study options:* academic remediation for entering students, adult/continuing education programs, internships, part-time degree program, summer session for credit.

Library 2,700 titles, 40 serial subscriptions.

Computers on Campus 40 computers available on campus for general student use. At least one staffed computer lab available.

Student Life *Housing:* college housing not available. *Student services:* personal/psychological counseling.

Applying *Options:* early admission, deferred entrance. *Application fee:* $25. *Application deadline:* rolling (freshmen), rolling (transfers).

Admissions Contact Admissions Director, Gem City College, PO Box 179, Quincy, IL 62306-0179. *Phone:* 217-222-0391.

HEARTLAND COMMUNITY COLLEGE
Normal, Illinois

- **State and locally supported** 2-year, founded 1990, part of Illinois Community College Board
- **Calendar** semesters
- **Degree** certificates and associate
- **Urban** campus
- **Coed**, 4,566 undergraduate students, 40% full-time, 56% women, 44% men

Undergraduates 1,811 full-time, 2,755 part-time. Students come from 5 states and territories, 2 other countries, 1% are from out of state, 7% African American, 1% Asian American or Pacific Islander, 2% Hispanic American, 0.4% Native American, 0.1% international, 15% transferred in. *Retention:* 55% of 2002 full-time freshmen returned.

Freshmen *Admission:* 1,051 admitted, 1,051 enrolled.

Faculty *Total:* 270, 23% full-time, 11% with terminal degrees. *Student/faculty ratio:* 21:1.

Majors Administrative assistant and secretarial science; biological and physical sciences; business administration and management; business and personal/financial services marketing; child care provision; child development; computer and information sciences; computer and information sciences related; computer engineering technology; computer programming; computer programming (specific applications); computer programming (vendor/product certification); computer science; computer systems networking and telecommunications; computer/technical support; corrections; data entry/microcomputer applications; data entry/microcomputer applications related; drafting and design technology; electrical, electronic and communications engineering technology; engineering; heating, air conditioning, ventilation and refrigeration maintenance technology; industrial mechanics and maintenance technology; industrial technology; information science/studies; information technology; kindergarten/preschool education; liberal arts and sciences/liberal studies; machine tool technology; management information systems; mechanical design technology; nursing (licensed practical/vocational nurse training); nursing (registered nurse training); quality control technology; system administration; web page, digital/multimedia and information resources design; welding technology.

Academic Programs *Special study options:* academic remediation for entering students, adult/continuing education programs, advanced placement credit, cooperative education, distance learning, double majors, English as a second language, independent study, internships, part-time degree program, services for LD students, study abroad, summer session for credit. *ROTC:* Army (c).

Library Heartland Community College Library with 5,000 titles, 188 serial subscriptions, 4,000 audiovisual materials, an OPAC, a Web page.

Computers on Campus 400 computers available on campus for general student use. A campuswide network can be accessed. Internet access, at least one staffed computer lab available.

Student Life *Housing:* college housing not available. *Activities and Organizations:* drama/theater group, student-run newspaper, choral group, Environmental Club, Early Childhood Club, student government, Nursing Club, Phi Theta Kappa. *Campus security:* 24-hour emergency response devices and patrols. *Student services:* personal/psychological counseling.

Standardized Tests *Required for some:* ACT COMPASS. *Recommended:* SAT I (for placement), ACT (for placement).

Costs (2003–04) *Tuition:* area resident $1650 full-time; state resident $3300 full-time; nonresident $4950 full-time.

Financial Aid Of all full-time matriculated undergraduates who enrolled, 65 Federal Work-Study jobs (averaging $1500).

Applying *Recommended:* high school transcript. *Application deadline:* rolling (freshmen), rolling (transfers). *Notification:* continuous (freshmen).

Admissions Contact Ms. Christine Riley, Director of Advisement and Enrollment Services, Heartland Community College, 1500 West Raab Road, Normal, IL 61761. *Phone:* 309-268-8000. *Fax:* 309-268-7992. *E-mail:* angie.robinson@heartland.edu.

HIGHLAND COMMUNITY COLLEGE
Freeport, Illinois

- **State and locally supported** 2-year, founded 1962, part of Illinois Community College Board
- **Calendar** semesters
- **Degree** certificates and associate
- **Rural** 240-acre campus
- **Endowment** $6.8 million
- **Coed**

Faculty *Student/faculty ratio:* 19:1.

Student Life *Campus security:* 24-hour patrols.

Athletics Member NJCAA.

Standardized Tests *Required for some:* ACT (for placement). *Recommended:* ACT (for placement).

Costs (2003–04) *Tuition:* area resident $1368 full-time, $57 per semester hour part-time; state resident $1944 full-time, $81 per semester hour part-time; nonresident $2285 full-time, $95 per semester hour part-time. Full-time tuition and fees vary according to course load and reciprocity agreements. Part-time tuition and fees vary according to course load and reciprocity agreements.

Financial Aid Of all full-time matriculated undergraduates who enrolled, 50 Federal Work-Study jobs (averaging $2000). 50 state and other part-time jobs (averaging $2000).

Applying *Options:* early admission, deferred entrance. *Required for some:* high school transcript.

Admissions Contact Mr. Karl Richards, Dean of Enrollment Services, Highland Community College, 2998 West Pearl City Road, Freeport, IL 61032. *Phone:* 815-235-6121 Ext. 3486. *Fax:* 815-235-6130.

ILLINOIS CENTRAL COLLEGE
East Peoria, Illinois

Admissions Contact Mr. John Avendano, Vice President of Academic Affairs and Student Development, Illinois Central College, One College Drive, East Peoria, IL 61635-0001. *Phone:* 309-694-5784. *Toll-free phone:* 800-422-2293. *Fax:* 309-694-5450.

ILLINOIS EASTERN COMMUNITY COLLEGES, FRONTIER COMMUNITY COLLEGE
Fairfield, Illinois

- **State and locally supported** 2-year, founded 1976, part of Illinois Eastern Community College System
- **Calendar** semesters
- **Degree** certificates and associate
- **Rural** 8-acre campus
- **Coed,** 1,907 undergraduate students, 11% full-time, 63% women, 37% men

Undergraduates 209 full-time, 1,698 part-time. 0.3% African American, 1% Asian American or Pacific Islander, 0.5% Hispanic American, 0.1% Native American.

Freshmen *Admission:* 104 enrolled.

Faculty *Total:* 150, 3% full-time.

Majors Administrative assistant and secretarial science; biological and physical sciences; business automation/technology/data entry; corrections; general studies; liberal arts and sciences/liberal studies; nursing (registered nurse training); quality control technology.

Academic Programs *Special study options:* academic remediation for entering students, adult/continuing education programs, advanced placement credit, cooperative education, distance learning, double majors, English as a second language, external degree program, independent study, part-time degree program, services for LD students, student-designed majors, summer session for credit.

Library 17,347 titles, 99 serial subscriptions, 1,972 audiovisual materials.

Computers on Campus 42 computers available on campus for general student use. At least one staffed computer lab available.

Student Life *Housing:* college housing not available.

Standardized Tests *Required:* SAT I or ACT (for placement), ACT ASSET (for placement).

Costs (2004–05) *Tuition:* area resident $1440 full-time; state resident $6341 full-time; nonresident $7496 full-time. *Required fees:* $106 full-time.

Applying *Options:* early admission, deferred entrance. *Application fee:* $10. *Required:* high school transcript. *Application deadline:* rolling (freshmen), rolling (transfers). *Notification:* continuous (freshmen), continuous (transfers).

Admissions Contact Mrs. Suzanne Brooks, Coordinator of Registration and Records, Illinois Eastern Community Colleges, Frontier Community College, 2 Frontier Drive, Fairfield, IL 62837. *Phone:* 618-842-3711 Ext. 4111.

ILLINOIS EASTERN COMMUNITY COLLEGES, LINCOLN TRAIL COLLEGE
Robinson, Illinois

- **State and locally supported** 2-year, founded 1969, part of Illinois Eastern Community College System
- **Calendar** semesters
- **Degree** certificates and associate
- **Rural** 120-acre campus
- **Coed,** 1,357 undergraduate students, 33% full-time, 46% women, 54% men

Undergraduates 443 full-time, 914 part-time. 15% African American, 2% Asian American or Pacific Islander, 4% Hispanic American, 0.4% Native American, 0.1% international.

Freshmen *Admission:* 322 enrolled.

Faculty *Total:* 61, 49% full-time.

Majors Biological and physical sciences; building/property maintenance and management; business automation/technology/data entry; corrections; culinary arts; general studies; heating, air conditioning, ventilation and refrigeration maintenance technology; liberal arts and sciences/liberal studies; mechanical engineering/mechanical technology; music; music teacher education; quality control technology; teacher assistant/aide; telecommunications.

Academic Programs *Special study options:* academic remediation for entering students, adult/continuing education programs, advanced placement credit, cooperative education, distance learning, double majors, English as a second language, external degree program, independent study, internships, part-time degree program, services for LD students, student-designed majors, summer session for credit.

Library Eagleton Learning Resource Center with 21,278 titles, 83 serial subscriptions, 1,318 audiovisual materials.

Computers on Campus 96 computers available on campus for general student use. At least one staffed computer lab available.

Student Life *Housing:* college housing not available. *Activities and Organizations:* drama/theater group, choral group, national fraternities. *Student services:* personal/psychological counseling.

Illinois Eastern Community Colleges, Lincoln Trail College (continued)

Athletics Member NJCAA. *Intercollegiate sports:* baseball M(s), basketball M(s)/W(s), softball W(s), volleyball W(s). *Intramural sports:* baseball M, basketball M, softball W, volleyball M/W.

Standardized Tests *Required:* SAT I or ACT (for placement), ACT ASSET (for placement).

Costs (2003–04) *Tuition:* area resident $1440 full-time, $45 per credit hour part-time; state resident $6341 full-time, $198 per credit hour part-time; nonresident $7496 full-time, $243 per credit hour part-time. *Required fees:* $106 full-time, $3 per credit hour part-time.

Applying *Options:* early admission, deferred entrance. *Application fee:* $10. *Required:* high school transcript. *Application deadline:* rolling (freshmen), rolling (transfers). *Notification:* continuous (freshmen), continuous (transfers).

Admissions Contact Ms. Becky Mikeworth, Director of Admissions, Illinois Eastern Community Colleges, Lincoln Trail College, 11220 State Highway 1, Robinson, IL 62454. *Phone:* 618-544-8657 Ext. 1137.

ILLINOIS EASTERN COMMUNITY COLLEGES, OLNEY CENTRAL COLLEGE
Olney, Illinois

- **State and locally supported** 2-year, founded 1962, part of Illinois Eastern Community College System
- **Calendar** semesters
- **Degree** certificates and associate
- **Rural** 128-acre campus
- **Coed,** 1,707 undergraduate students, 50% full-time, 58% women, 42% men

Undergraduates 845 full-time, 862 part-time. 0.7% African American, 0.9% Asian American or Pacific Islander, 0.2% Hispanic American, 0.5% international.

Freshmen *Admission:* 186 enrolled.

Faculty *Total:* 83, 52% full-time.

Majors Accounting; administrative assistant and secretarial science; autobody/collision and repair technology; automobile/automotive mechanics technology; biological and physical sciences; business automation/technology/data entry; cabinetmaking and millwork; corrections; criminal justice/police science; general studies; heavy equipment maintenance technology; industrial mechanics and maintenance technology; liberal arts and sciences/liberal studies; medical administrative assistant and medical secretary; medical radiologic technology; music; music teacher education; nursing (licensed practical/vocational nurse training); nursing (registered nurse training).

Academic Programs *Special study options:* academic remediation for entering students, adult/continuing education programs, advanced placement credit, cooperative education, distance learning, double majors, English as a second language, external degree program, independent study, internships, part-time degree program, services for LD students, student-designed majors, summer session for credit.

Library Anderson Learning Resources Center with 24,191 titles, 925 serial subscriptions, 194 audiovisual materials.

Computers on Campus 125 computers available on campus for general student use. At least one staffed computer lab available.

Student Life *Housing:* college housing not available. *Activities and Organizations:* drama/theater group, student-run newspaper, choral group. *Student services:* personal/psychological counseling, women's center.

Athletics Member NJCAA. *Intercollegiate sports:* baseball M(s), basketball M(s)/W(s), softball W(s), volleyball W(s). *Intramural sports:* baseball M, basketball M/W, softball W.

Standardized Tests *Required:* SAT I or ACT (for placement), ACT ASSET (for placement).

Costs (2003–04) *Tuition:* area resident $1440 full-time, $45 per credit hour part-time; state resident $6341 full-time, $198 per credit hour part-time; nonresident $7496 full-time, $243 per credit hour part-time. *Required fees:* $106 full-time, $3 per credit hour part-time. *Waivers:* employees or children of employees.

Applying *Options:* early admission, deferred entrance. *Application fee:* $10. *Required:* high school transcript. *Application deadline:* rolling (freshmen), rolling (transfers). *Notification:* continuous (freshmen), continuous (transfers).

Admissions Contact Ms. Chris Webber, Assistant Dean for Student Services, Illinois Eastern Community Colleges, Olney Central College, 305 North West Street, Olney, IL 62450. *Phone:* 618-395-7777 Ext. 2005.

ILLINOIS EASTERN COMMUNITY COLLEGES, WABASH VALLEY COLLEGE
Mount Carmel, Illinois

- **State and locally supported** 2-year, founded 1960, part of Illinois Eastern Community College System
- **Calendar** semesters
- **Degree** certificates and associate
- **Rural** 40-acre campus
- **Coed,** 4,098 undergraduate students, 16% full-time, 53% women, 47% men

Undergraduates 653 full-time, 3,445 part-time. 2% African American, 1% Asian American or Pacific Islander, 0.8% Hispanic American, 0.1% Native American.

Freshmen *Admission:* 382 enrolled.

Faculty *Total:* 102, 37% full-time.

Majors Administrative assistant and secretarial science; agricultural business and management; agricultural production; biological and physical sciences; business administration and management; business automation/technology/data entry; child development; corrections; court reporting; diesel mechanics technology; electrical, electronic and communications engineering technology; general studies; industrial technology; liberal arts and sciences/liberal studies; machine shop technology; mining technology; radio and television; social work.

Academic Programs *Special study options:* academic remediation for entering students, adult/continuing education programs, advanced placement credit, cooperative education, distance learning, double majors, English as a second language, external degree program, independent study, internships, part-time degree program, services for LD students, student-designed majors, summer session for credit.

Library Bauer Media Center with 32,755 titles, 103 serial subscriptions, 1,628 audiovisual materials.

Computers on Campus 100 computers available on campus for general student use. At least one staffed computer lab available.

Student Life *Housing:* college housing not available. *Activities and Organizations:* drama/theater group, student-run newspaper, radio and television station, choral group.

Athletics Member NJCAA. *Intercollegiate sports:* baseball M(s), basketball M(s)/W(s), softball W(s), tennis M, volleyball W(s). *Intramural sports:* baseball M, basketball M/W, cross-country running M/W, softball W, volleyball M/W.

Standardized Tests *Required:* SAT I or ACT (for placement), ACT ASSET (for placement).

Costs (2003–04) *Tuition:* area resident $1440 full-time, $45 per credit hour part-time; state resident $6341 full-time, $198 per credit hour part-time; nonresident $7496 full-time, $243 per credit hour part-time. *Required fees:* $106 full-time, $3 per credit hour part-time.

Applying *Options:* early admission, deferred entrance. *Application fee:* $10. *Required:* high school transcript. *Application deadline:* rolling (freshmen), rolling (transfers). *Notification:* continuous (freshmen), continuous (transfers).

Admissions Contact Mrs. Diana Spear, Assistant Dean for Student Services, Illinois Eastern Community Colleges, Wabash Valley College, 2200 College Drive, Mt. Carmel, IL 62863. *Phone:* 618-262-8641 Ext. 3101.

ILLINOIS VALLEY COMMUNITY COLLEGE
Oglesby, Illinois

- **District-supported** 2-year, founded 1924, part of Illinois Community College Board
- **Calendar** semesters
- **Degree** associate
- **Rural** 410-acre campus with easy access to Chicago
- **Coed**

Student Life *Campus security:* 24-hour patrols.

Standardized Tests *Recommended:* ACT (for placement).

Costs (2003–04) *Tuition:* area resident $1620 full-time; state resident $4532 full-time; nonresident $5919 full-time. *Required fees:* $218 full-time.

Financial Aid Of all full-time matriculated undergraduates who enrolled, 81 Federal Work-Study jobs (averaging $955).

Applying *Options:* early admission, deferred entrance. *Required:* high school transcript.

Admissions Contact Ms. Kelly Conrad, Director of Admissions and Records, Illinois Valley Community College, 815 North Orlando Smith Avenue, Oglesby, IL 61348. *Phone:* 815-224-0437. *Fax:* 815-224-3033. *E-mail:* kathy-sramek@ivcc.edu.

ITT TECHNICAL INSTITUTE
Burr Ridge, Illinois

- **Proprietary** 2-year, part of ITT Educational Services, Inc
- **Calendar** quarters
- **Degree** associate
- **Coed**

Standardized Tests *Required:* Wonderlic aptitude test (for admission).

Costs (2003–04) *Tuition:* Total Program Cost varies depending on course of study. Consult school catalog.
Applying *Options:* deferred entrance. *Application fee:* $100. *Required:* high school transcript, interview. *Recommended:* letters of recommendation.
Admissions Contact Mr. Leo Rodriguez, Director of Recruitment, ITT Technical Institute, 7040 High Grove Boulevard, Burr Ridge, IL 60527. *Phone:* 630-455-6470. *Toll-free phone:* 877-488-0001. *Fax:* 630-455-6476.

ITT TECHNICAL INSTITUTE
Matteson, Illinois

- **Proprietary** 2-year, founded 1993, part of ITT Educational Services, Inc
- **Calendar** quarters
- **Degree** associate
- **Suburban** campus with easy access to Chicago
- **Coed**

Standardized Tests *Required:* Wonderlic aptitude test (for admission).
Costs (2003–04) *Tuition:* Total Program Cost varies depending on course of study. Consult school catalog.
Financial Aid Of all full-time matriculated undergraduates who enrolled, 6 Federal Work-Study jobs (averaging $4000).
Applying *Options:* deferred entrance. *Application fee:* $100. *Required:* high school transcript, interview. *Recommended:* letters of recommendation.
Admissions Contact Ms. Lillian Williams-McClain, Director, ITT Technical Institute, 600 Holiday Plaza Drive, Matteson, IL 60443. *Phone:* 708-747-2571. *Fax:* 708-747-0023.

ITT TECHNICAL INSTITUTE
Mount Prospect, Illinois

- **Proprietary** primarily 2-year, founded 1986, part of ITT Educational Services, Inc.
- **Calendar** quarters
- **Degrees** associate and bachelor's
- **Suburban** 1-acre campus with easy access to Chicago
- **Coed**

Standardized Tests *Required:* Wonderlic aptitude test (for admission).
Costs (2003–04) *Tuition:* Total Program Cost varies depending on course of study. Consult school catalog.
Applying *Options:* deferred entrance. *Application fee:* $100. *Required:* high school transcript, interview. *Recommended:* letters of recommendation.
Admissions Contact Mr. Ernest Lloyd, Director of Recruitment, ITT Technical Institute, 1401 Feehanville Drive, Mount Prospect, IL 60056. *Phone:* 847-375-8800. *Fax:* 847-375-9022.

JOHN A. LOGAN COLLEGE
Carterville, Illinois

- **State and locally supported** 2-year, founded 1967, part of Illinois Community College Board
- **Calendar** semesters
- **Degree** certificates and associate
- **Rural** 160-acre campus
- **Endowment** $19,000
- **Coed,** 5,314 undergraduate students

Undergraduates Students come from 2 states and territories.
Faculty *Total:* 43, 53% full-time, 2% with terminal degrees.
Majors Accounting; agriculture; art; art teacher education; automobile/automotive mechanics technology; biology/biological sciences; business administration and management; business teacher education; chemistry; clinical/medical laboratory technology; computer science; consumer merchandising/retailing management; cosmetology; criminal justice/law enforcement administration; data processing and data processing technology; dental hygiene; drafting and design technology; education; electrical, electronic and communications engineering technology; elementary education; emergency medical technology (EMT paramedic); English; fashion merchandising; finance; health information/medical records administration; heating, air conditioning, ventilation and refrigeration maintenance technology; history; humanities; information science/studies; journalism; kindergarten/preschool education; legal administrative assistant/secretary; liberal arts and sciences/liberal studies; machine tool technology; marketing/marketing management; mathematics; nursing (licensed practical/vocational nurse training); nursing (registered nurse training); occupational therapy; physical education teaching and coaching; physics; political science and government; pre-engineering; psychology; sign language interpretation and translation; social work; teacher assistant/aide; tourism and travel services management; welding technology.

Academic Programs *Special study options:* academic remediation for entering students, adult/continuing education programs, advanced placement credit, cooperative education, distance learning, internships, off-campus study, part-time degree program, services for LD students, study abroad, summer session for credit. *ROTC:* Army (c), Air Force (c).
Library Learning Resource Center with 33,306 titles, 298 serial subscriptions, a Web page.
Computers on Campus 150 computers available on campus for general student use. Internet access, at least one staffed computer lab available.
Student Life *Housing:* college housing not available. *Activities and Organizations:* drama/theater group, student-run newspaper, choral group. *Campus security:* 24-hour emergency response devices and patrols.
Athletics Member NJCAA. *Intercollegiate sports:* baseball M, basketball M/W, golf M/W, softball W, volleyball W.
Standardized Tests *Required:* ACT ASSET (for placement). *Recommended:* SAT I or ACT (for placement).
Costs (2003–04) *Tuition:* area resident $1500 full-time, $54 per semester hour part-time; state resident $4500 full-time, $165 per semester hour part-time; nonresident $7000 full-time, $240 per semester hour part-time.
Applying *Options:* electronic application, early admission. *Required:* high school transcript. *Application deadlines:* 8/25 (freshmen), 8/25 (transfers). *Notification:* continuous (freshmen), continuous (transfers).
Admissions Contact Mr. Terry Crain, Associate Dean of Student Services, John A. Logan College, 700 Logan College Road, Carterville, IL 62918-9900. *Phone:* 618-985-3741 Ext. 8382. *Fax:* 618-985-4433. *E-mail:* terry.crain@jal.cc.il.us.

JOHN WOOD COMMUNITY COLLEGE
Quincy, Illinois

- **District-supported** 2-year, founded 1974, part of Illinois Community College Board
- **Calendar** semesters
- **Degree** certificates and associate
- **Small-town** campus
- **Coed,** 2,374 undergraduate students, 51% full-time, 63% women, 37% men

Undergraduates 1,211 full-time, 1,163 part-time. Students come from 4 states and territories, 3 other countries, 11% are from out of state, 4% African American, 0.7% Asian American or Pacific Islander, 0.7% Hispanic American, 0.2% Native American, 0.2% international, 4% transferred in.
Freshmen *Admission:* 564 enrolled. *Test scores:* ACT scores over 18: 59%; ACT scores over 24: 12%; ACT scores over 30: 1%.
Faculty *Total:* 211, 24% full-time, 4% with terminal degrees. *Student/faculty ratio:* 15:1.
Majors Accounting; accounting technology and bookkeeping; administrative assistant and secretarial science; agricultural business and management; agricultural production; animal/livestock husbandry and production; applied horticulture; biological and physical sciences; business administration and management; business/commerce; child guidance; clinical/medical laboratory technology; computer programming (specific applications); criminal justice/police science; early childhood education; electrical, electronic and communications engineering technology; electrician; emergency medical technology (EMT paramedic); executive assistant/executive secretary; fire protection and safety technology; general studies; health and physical education; hotel/motel administration; industrial electronics technology; industrial mechanics and maintenance technology; legal administrative assistant/secretary; liberal arts and sciences/liberal studies; mechanical drafting and CAD/CADD; medical administrative assistant and medical secretary; medical radiologic technology; nursing (registered nurse training); psychology; restaurant, culinary, and catering management; sales, distribution and marketing; sociology.
Academic Programs *Special study options:* academic remediation for entering students, adult/continuing education programs, advanced placement credit, cooperative education, distance learning, English as a second language, external degree program, independent study, internships, off-campus study, part-time degree program, services for LD students, student-designed majors, study abroad, summer session for credit.
Library 18,000 titles, 160 serial subscriptions, 2,200 audiovisual materials, an OPAC, a Web page.
Computers on Campus 250 computers available on campus for general student use. A campuswide network can be accessed. Internet access, at least one staffed computer lab available.
Student Life *Housing:* college housing not available. *Activities and Organizations:* choral group. *Campus security:* 24-hour emergency response devices, late-night transport/escort service.
Athletics Member NJCAA. *Intercollegiate sports:* baseball M(s), basketball M(s)/W(s), golf M(s), softball W(s), volleyball W(s). *Intramural sports:* basketball M/W, volleyball M/W.
Standardized Tests *Required:* ACT ASSET, ACT COMPASS (for placement). *Recommended:* SAT I or ACT (for placement).

John Wood Community College (continued)

Costs (2003–04) *Tuition:* area resident $1980 full-time, $66 per credit hour part-time; state resident $4980 full-time, $166 per credit hour part-time; nonresident $166 per credit hour part-time. *Required fees:* $150 full-time, $15 per credit hour part-time. *Payment plan:* installment. *Waivers:* senior citizens and employees or children of employees.

Financial Aid Of all full-time matriculated undergraduates who enrolled, 440 Federal Work-Study jobs (averaging $494).

Applying *Options:* common application, early admission. *Required:* high school transcript. *Application deadline:* rolling (freshmen), rolling (transfers). *Notification:* continuous (freshmen), continuous (transfers).

Admissions Contact Mr. Mark C. McNett, Director of Admissions, John Wood Community College, 1301 South 48th Street, Quincy, IL 62305-8736. *Phone:* 217-641-4339. *Fax:* 217-224-4208. *E-mail:* admissions@jwcc.edu.

JOLIET JUNIOR COLLEGE
Joliet, Illinois

- **State and locally supported** 2-year, founded 1901, part of Illinois Community College Board
- **Calendar** semesters
- **Degree** certificates, diplomas, and associate
- **Suburban** campus with easy access to Chicago
- **Coed**

Faculty *Student/faculty ratio:* 12:1.

Student Life *Campus security:* 24-hour emergency response devices and patrols, student patrols, late-night transport/escort service.

Athletics Member NJCAA.

Standardized Tests *Required for some:* ACT (for placement). *Recommended:* SAT I or ACT (for placement).

Costs (2003–04) *Tuition:* $51 per hour part-time; state resident $194 per hour part-time; nonresident $280 per hour part-time. *Required fees:* $10 per hour part-time.

Financial Aid Of all full-time matriculated undergraduates who enrolled, 96 Federal Work-Study jobs (averaging $1168). 254 state and other part-time jobs (averaging $1778).

Applying *Options:* early admission, deferred entrance. *Required:* high school transcript.

Admissions Contact Dr. Denis Wright, Vice President of Academic Affairs, Joliet Junior College, 1215 Houbolt Road, Joliet, IL 60431. *Phone:* 815-280-2239.

KANKAKEE COMMUNITY COLLEGE
Kankakee, Illinois

- **State and locally supported** 2-year, founded 1966, part of Illinois Community College Board
- **Calendar** semesters
- **Degrees** certificates, diplomas, and associate (also offers continuing education program with significant enrollment not reflected in profile)
- **Small-town** 178-acre campus with easy access to Chicago
- **Coed**

Student Life *Campus security:* 24-hour patrols.

Athletics Member NJCAA.

Standardized Tests *Required for some:* ACT (for placement), ACT ASSET or ACT COMPASS. *Recommended:* ACT ASSET or ACT COMPASS.

Costs (2003–04) *Tuition:* area resident $1800 full-time, $60 per semester hour part-time; state resident $4112 full-time, $137 per semester hour part-time; nonresident $10,224 full-time, $341 per semester hour part-time.

Financial Aid Of all full-time matriculated undergraduates who enrolled, 70 Federal Work-Study jobs (averaging $1100). *Financial aid deadline:* 10/1.

Applying *Options:* early admission. *Required:* high school transcript.

Admissions Contact Ms. Michelle Driscoll, Kankakee Community College, Box 888, Kankakee, IL 60901. *Phone:* 815-802-8520.

KASKASKIA COLLEGE
Centralia, Illinois

- **State and locally supported** 2-year, founded 1966, part of Illinois Community College Board
- **Calendar** semesters
- **Degree** certificates and associate
- **Rural** 195-acre campus with easy access to St. Louis
- **Endowment** $417,874
- **Coed,** 4,636 undergraduate students, 46% full-time, 61% women, 39% men

Undergraduates 2,135 full-time, 2,501 part-time. Students come from 9 states and territories, 4 other countries, 7% transferred in.

Freshmen *Admission:* 923 applied, 923 admitted, 923 enrolled.

Faculty *Total:* 249, 27% full-time, 6% with terminal degrees. *Student/faculty ratio:* 25:1.

Majors Agricultural business and management; applied horticulture; architectural drafting and CAD/CADD; autobody/collision and repair technology; automobile/automotive mechanics technology; biological and physical sciences; business administration and management; business automation/technology/data entry; carpentry; computer programming (specific applications); criminal justice/police science; culinary arts; electrical, electronic and communications engineering technology; executive assistant/executive secretary; general studies; industrial mechanics and maintenance technology; liberal arts and sciences/liberal studies; medical radiologic technology; nursing (registered nurse training); physical therapist assistant; respiratory care therapy.

Academic Programs *Special study options:* academic remediation for entering students, adult/continuing education programs, cooperative education, distance learning, double majors, English as a second language, honors programs, independent study, internships, off-campus study, part-time degree program, services for LD students, study abroad, summer session for credit.

Library Kaskaskia College Library with 22,646 titles, 145 serial subscriptions, 522 audiovisual materials, an OPAC, a Web page.

Computers on Campus 350 computers available on campus for general student use. Internet access, at least one staffed computer lab available.

Student Life *Housing:* college housing not available. *Activities and Organizations:* drama/theater group, student-run newspaper, choral group, Phi Theta Kappa, Administration of Justice, Student Radiology Club, Cosmetology Club, Vocal Music Club. *Campus security:* 24-hour patrols, late-night transport/escort service. *Student services:* personal/psychological counseling.

Athletics Member NJCAA. *Intercollegiate sports:* baseball M(s), basketball M(s)/W(s), golf M, softball W(s), volleyball W(s).

Standardized Tests *Required for some:* ACT (for placement). *Recommended:* ACT (for admission), ACT (for placement).

Costs (2004–05) *Tuition:* area resident $1600 full-time, $50 per credit hour part-time; state resident $2801 full-time, $88 per credit hour part-time; nonresident $8184 full-time, $255 per credit hour part-time. Full-time tuition and fees vary according to location. Part-time tuition and fees vary according to location. *Required fees:* $224 full-time. *Payment plan:* installment. *Waivers:* senior citizens and employees or children of employees.

Applying *Options:* common application, early admission, deferred entrance. *Required:* high school transcript. *Required for some:* interview. *Application deadline:* rolling (freshmen), rolling (transfers). *Notification:* continuous (freshmen), continuous (transfers).

Admissions Contact Daniel Herbst, Dean of Enrollment Services, Kaskaskia College, 27210 College Road, Centralia, IL 62801. *Phone:* 618-545-3066. *Toll-free phone:* 800-642-0859. *Fax:* 618-532-1135.

KISHWAUKEE COLLEGE
Malta, Illinois

- **State and locally supported** 2-year, founded 1967, part of Illinois Community College Board
- **Calendar** semesters
- **Degree** certificates and associate
- **Rural** 120-acre campus with easy access to Chicago
- **Endowment** $1.3 million
- **Coed,** 4,076 undergraduate students, 14% full-time, 56% women, 44% men

Undergraduates 578 full-time, 3,499 part-time. Students come from 25 states and territories, 14 other countries, 11% African American, 4% Asian American or Pacific Islander, 11% Hispanic American, 0.2% Native American, 0.2% international, 15% transferred in.

Freshmen *Admission:* 417 applied, 417 admitted, 867 enrolled.

Faculty *Total:* 231, 35% full-time, 8% with terminal degrees. *Student/faculty ratio:* 15:1.

Majors Administrative assistant and secretarial science; agricultural business and management; agricultural mechanization; agricultural production; applied horticulture; art; art teacher education; autobody/collision and repair technology; automobile/automotive mechanics technology; business administration and management; child care and support services management; computer and information sciences related; computer programming related; computer programming (specific applications); criminal justice/police science; emergency medical technology (EMT paramedic); engineering; greenhouse management; industrial design; landscaping and groundskeeping; liberal arts and sciences/liberal studies; medical radiologic technology; nursing (registered nurse training); operations management; ornamental horticulture; quality control technology; tool and die technology; turf and turfgrass management; word processing.

Academic Programs *Special study options:* academic remediation for entering students, adult/continuing education programs, advanced placement credit, cooperative education, distance learning, double majors, English as a second language, external degree program, independent study, internships, off-campus study, part-time degree program, services for LD students, study abroad, summer session for credit.

Library Learning Resource Center with 52,075 titles, 248 serial subscriptions, 3,500 audiovisual materials, an OPAC, a Web page.

Computers on Campus 565 computers available on campus for general student use. A campuswide network can be accessed. Internet access, online (class) registration, at least one staffed computer lab available.

Student Life *Housing:* college housing not available. *Activities and Organizations:* drama/theater group, student-run newspaper, choral group, student association, Black Student Union, Horticulture Club, Student Nurses Association, International Club. *Campus security:* 24-hour patrols. *Student services:* health clinic, personal/psychological counseling.

Athletics Member NJCAA. *Intercollegiate sports:* baseball M(s), basketball M(s)/W(s), golf M(s), soccer M(s), softball W(s), tennis W(s), volleyball W(s). *Intramural sports:* basketball M/W, volleyball W.

Standardized Tests *Required for some:* ACT, SAT I, or in-house placement test.

Costs (2003–04) *Tuition:* area resident $1624 full-time, $58 per credit part-time; state resident $5808 full-time, $207 per credit part-time; nonresident $7010 full-time, $250 per credit part-time. *Required fees:* $244 full-time, $7 per credit part-time, $30 per term part-time. *Payment plan:* deferred payment. *Waivers:* employees or children of employees.

Financial Aid Of all full-time matriculated undergraduates who enrolled, 107 Federal Work-Study jobs (averaging $1285). 45 state and other part-time jobs (averaging $1100).

Applying *Options:* common application, early admission, deferred entrance. *Required:* high school transcript, transcripts from all other colleges or universities previously attended. *Required for some:* minimum 2.0 GPA. *Recommended:* minimum 2.0 GPA. *Application deadline:* rolling (freshmen), rolling (transfers). *Notification:* continuous (freshmen), continuous (transfers).

Admissions Contact Ms. Sally Misciasci, Admission Analyst, Kishwaukee College, 21193 Malta Road, Malta, IL 60150-9699. *Phone:* 815-825-2086 Ext. 400. *Fax:* 815-825-2306.

LAKE LAND COLLEGE
Mattoon, Illinois

- **State and locally supported** 2-year, founded 1966, part of Illinois Community College Board
- **Calendar** semesters
- **Degree** certificates and associate
- **Rural** 304-acre campus
- **Endowment** $2.6 million
- **Coed,** 7,256 undergraduate students, 45% full-time, 48% women, 52% men

Undergraduates 3,255 full-time, 4,001 part-time. Students come from 23 other countries, 9% African American, 0.3% Asian American or Pacific Islander, 3% Hispanic American, 0.2% Native American, 0.6% international.

Freshmen *Admission:* 1,882 applied, 1,882 admitted.

Faculty *Total:* 191, 61% full-time, 5% with terminal degrees. *Student/faculty ratio:* 21:1.

Majors Accounting technology and bookkeeping; administrative assistant and secretarial science; agricultural business and management; agricultural mechanization; agricultural production; architectural engineering technology; automobile/automotive mechanics technology; biological and physical sciences; business administration and management; child care and support services management; civil engineering technology; computer programming (specific applications); computer systems networking and telecommunications; corrections; criminal justice/police science; dental hygiene; desktop publishing and digital imaging design; drafting and design technology; electrical, electronic and communications engineering technology; electromechanical technology; executive assistant/ executive secretary; general studies; graphic and printing equipment operation/ production; human services; industrial technology; information technology; legal administrative assistant/secretary; liberal arts and sciences/liberal studies; marketing/marketing management; medical administrative assistant and medical secretary; nursing (registered nurse training); office management; physical therapist assistant; printing press operation; radio and television; social work; telecommunications.

Academic Programs *Special study options:* academic remediation for entering students, accelerated degree program, adult/continuing education programs, cooperative education, distance learning, English as a second language, external degree program, honors programs, internships, part-time degree program, services for LD students, summer session for credit.

Library Virgil H. Judge Learning Resource Center with 36,912 titles, 193 serial subscriptions, 1,446 audiovisual materials, an OPAC.

Computers on Campus 100 computers available on campus for general student use. A campuswide network can be accessed. Internet access, online (class) registration, at least one staffed computer lab available.

Student Life *Housing:* college housing not available. *Activities and Organizations:* student-run newspaper, radio station, choral group, Agriculture Production and Management Club, Cosmetology Club, Agriculture Transfer Club, Phi Theta Kappa, Civil Engineering Technology Club. *Campus security:* 24-hour patrols. *Student services:* personal/psychological counseling.

Athletics Member NJCAA. *Intercollegiate sports:* baseball M(s), basketball M(s)/W(s), cheerleading W, softball W(s), tennis M(s)/W, volleyball W(s). *Intramural sports:* basketball M/W, bowling M/W, golf M/W, softball M/W, volleyball M/W.

Standardized Tests *Required for some:* ACT (for placement). *Recommended:* ACT (for placement).

Costs (2003–04) *Tuition:* area resident $1440 full-time, $48 per credit hour part-time; state resident $3148 full-time, $105 per credit hour part-time; nonresident $6997 full-time, $233 per credit hour part-time. *Required fees:* $344 full-time, $11 per credit hour part-time.

Financial Aid Of all full-time matriculated undergraduates who enrolled, 120 Federal Work-Study jobs (averaging $1400).

Applying *Options:* common application, electronic application, early admission. *Required for some:* letters of recommendation. *Recommended:* high school transcript. *Application deadline:* rolling (freshmen), rolling (transfers). *Notification:* continuous (freshmen), continuous (transfers).

Admissions Contact Mr. Jon VanDyke, Dean of Admission Services, Lake Land College, Mattoon, IL 61938-9366. *Phone:* 217-234-5378. *Toll-free phone:* 800-252-4121.

LEWIS AND CLARK COMMUNITY COLLEGE
Godfrey, Illinois

- **District-supported** 2-year, founded 1970, part of Illinois Community College Board
- **Calendar** semesters
- **Degree** certificates and associate
- **Small-town** 275-acre campus with easy access to St. Louis
- **Coed,** 7,352 undergraduate students, 31% full-time, 58% women, 42% men

Undergraduates 2,304 full-time, 5,048 part-time. Students come from 3 states and territories, 4 other countries, 1% are from out of state, 6% African American, 0.5% Asian American or Pacific Islander, 1% Hispanic American, 0.4% Native American, 0.5% international.

Faculty *Total:* 309, 28% full-time.

Majors Accounting; administrative assistant and secretarial science; art; automobile/automotive mechanics technology; biological and physical sciences; biology/biological sciences; business administration and management; child development; computer programming; criminal justice/law enforcement administration; data processing and data processing technology; dental hygiene; drafting and design technology; fire science; kindergarten/preschool education; legal administrative assistant/secretary; liberal arts and sciences/liberal studies; machine tool technology; medical administrative assistant and medical secretary; music; nursing (registered nurse training); occupational therapist assistant; pre-engineering; radio and television; teacher assistant/aide.

Academic Programs *Special study options:* academic remediation for entering students, adult/continuing education programs, advanced placement credit, cooperative education, distance learning, double majors, English as a second language, independent study, internships, off-campus study, part-time degree program, services for LD students, summer session for credit. *ROTC:* Army (b).

Library Reid Memorial with 30,000 titles, 300 serial subscriptions, 500 audiovisual materials, an OPAC, a Web page.

Computers on Campus 350 computers available on campus for general student use. Internet access, at least one staffed computer lab available.

Student Life *Housing:* college housing not available. *Activities and Organizations:* student-run newspaper, radio station, choral group, Phi Beta Lambda, Data Processing Club, Nursing Club, Clinical Laboratory Technicians Club, Music Club. *Campus security:* 24-hour emergency response devices and patrols. *Student services:* health clinic, personal/psychological counseling.

Athletics Member NJCAA. *Intercollegiate sports:* baseball M, basketball M/W(s), golf M, soccer M(s)/W, softball W(s), tennis M(s)/W(s), volleyball W(s).

Costs (2004–05) *Tuition:* area resident $1800 full-time, $60 per credit part-time; state resident $5400 full-time, $180 per credit part-time; nonresident $7200 full-time, $247 per credit part-time. *Required fees:* $210 full-time, $7 per credit part-time. *Payment plans:* installment, deferred payment. *Waivers:* senior citizens and employees or children of employees.

Applying *Options:* early admission, deferred entrance. *Required for some:* interview. *Recommended:* high school transcript. *Application deadline:* rolling (freshmen), rolling (transfers). *Notification:* continuous (freshmen), continuous (transfers).

Admissions Contact Ms. Peggy Hudson, Director of Enrollment Center for Admissions Services, Lewis and Clark Community College, Enrollment Center,

Peterson's Two-Year Colleges 2005   *www.petersons.com* **173**

Illinois

Lewis and Clark Community College (continued)
5800 Godfrey Road, Godfrey, IL 62035. *Phone:* 618-468-5100. *Toll-free phone:* 800-500-LCCC. *Fax:* 618-467-2310.

LINCOLN COLLEGE
Lincoln, Illinois

■ **Independent** 2-year, founded 1865
■ **Calendar** semesters
■ **Degree** associate
■ **Small-town** 42-acre campus
■ **Endowment** $14.0 million
■ **Coed,** 758 undergraduate students, 92% full-time, 46% women, 54% men

Undergraduates 700 full-time, 58 part-time. Students come from 15 states and territories, 9% are from out of state, 2% transferred in, 90% live on campus.
Freshmen *Admission:* 835 applied, 544 admitted, 380 enrolled. *Average high school GPA:* 2.59. *Test scores:* ACT scores over 18: 48%; ACT scores over 24: 8%.
Faculty *Total:* 53, 64% full-time. *Student/faculty ratio:* 15:1.
Majors Accounting; applied art; applied mathematics; art history, criticism and conservation; art teacher education; behavioral sciences; biological and physical sciences; biology/biological sciences; botany/plant biology; broadcast journalism; business administration and management; business/managerial economics; business teacher education; ceramic arts and ceramics; chemistry; commercial and advertising art; computer programming; computer science; computer typography and composition equipment operation; corrections; cosmetology; creative writing; criminal justice/law enforcement administration; criminal justice/police science; criminology; dance; data processing and data processing technology; developmental and child psychology; dramatic/theatre arts; drawing; economics; education; elementary education; English; fine/studio arts; foods, nutrition, and wellness; geography; geology/earth science; history; human development and family studies; humanities; jazz/jazz studies; journalism; kindergarten/preschool education; liberal arts and sciences/liberal studies; marine biology and biological oceanography; marketing/marketing management; mass communication/media; mathematics; middle school education; music; music history, literature, and theory; music management and merchandising; nursing (licensed practical/vocational nurse training); nursing (registered nurse training); painting; philosophy; photography; physical education teaching and coaching; physical sciences; piano and organ; political science and government; psychology; radio and television; religious education; sociology; Spanish; statistics; tourism and travel services management; voice and opera; western civilization; zoology/animal biology.
Academic Programs *Special study options:* academic remediation for entering students, accelerated degree program, freshman honors college, honors programs, independent study, part-time degree program, summer session for credit.
Library McKinstry Library with 42,500 titles, 380 serial subscriptions, an OPAC, a Web page.
Computers on Campus 72 computers available on campus for general student use. Internet access, at least one staffed computer lab available.
Student Life *Housing:* on-campus residence required through sophomore year. *Options:* men-only, women-only. Campus housing is university owned. *Activities and Organizations:* drama/theater group, student-run newspaper, radio station, choral group, Admissions Ambassadors, Phi Beta Kappa, Connections, SHOS, Spanish Club. *Campus security:* 24-hour emergency response devices and patrols, controlled dormitory access. *Student services:* health clinic.
Athletics Member NJCAA. *Intercollegiate sports:* baseball M(s), basketball M(s)/W(s), golf M(s)/W(s), soccer M(s)/W(s), softball W(s), swimming M(s)/W(s), tennis M/W, volleyball W(s), wrestling M(s). *Intramural sports:* basketball M/W, bowling M/W, equestrian sports M/W, football M, golf M/W, racquetball M/W, soccer M, softball M/W, swimming M/W, table tennis M/W, track and field M/W, volleyball M/W, water polo M/W, weight lifting M/W, wrestling M.
Standardized Tests *Required:* SAT I or ACT (for admission).
Costs (2004–05) *Comprehensive fee:* $19,960 includes full-time tuition ($13,600), mandatory fees ($960), and room and board ($5400). No tuition increase for student's term of enrollment. *Room and board:* Room and board charges vary according to housing facility. *Payment plans:* installment, deferred payment. *Waivers:* employees or children of employees.
Financial Aid Of all full-time matriculated undergraduates who enrolled, 200 Federal Work-Study jobs (averaging $900).
Applying *Options:* early admission, deferred entrance. *Application fee:* $25. *Required:* high school transcript. *Required for some:* 1 letter of recommendation. *Recommended:* interview. *Application deadline:* rolling (freshmen), rolling (transfers).
Admissions Contact Mr. Tony Schilling, Director of Admissions, Lincoln College, 300 Keokuk Street, Lincoln, IL 62656-1699. *Phone:* 800-569-0556 Ext. 254. *Toll-free phone:* 800-569-0556. *Fax:* 217-732-7715. *E-mail:* information@lincolncollege.com.

▶ **See page 564 for a narrative description.**

LINCOLN COLLEGE
Normal, Illinois

■ **Independent** primarily 2-year, founded 1865
■ **Calendar** semesters
■ **Degrees** certificates, associate, and bachelor's
■ **Suburban** 10-acre campus
■ **Endowment** $14.0 million
■ **Coed**

Faculty *Student/faculty ratio:* 14:1.
Student Life *Campus security:* 24-hour emergency response devices and patrols, student patrols, late-night transport/escort service, controlled dormitory access.
Athletics Member NJCAA.
Standardized Tests *Required for some:* SAT I or ACT (for admission).
Costs (2004–05) *Comprehensive fee:* $19,170 includes full-time tuition ($13,600), mandatory fees ($570), and room and board ($5000). Full-time tuition and fees vary according to program. Part-time tuition: $453 per credit hour. Part-time tuition and fees vary according to course load. No tuition increase for student's term of enrollment. *Required fees:* $25 per term part-time. *Room and board:* college room only: $3200. Room and board charges vary according to board plan.
Applying *Options:* common application, electronic application, deferred entrance. *Application fee:* $25. *Required:* high school transcript, interview. *Required for some:* 2 letters of recommendation.
Admissions Contact Mr. Joe Hendrix, Director of Admissions, Lincoln College, 715 West Raab Road, Normal, IL 61761. *Phone:* 309-452-0500. *Toll-free phone:* 800-569-0558. *Fax:* 309-454-5652. *E-mail:* admissions@lincoln.mclean.il.us.

▶ **See page 566 for a narrative description.**

LINCOLN LAND COMMUNITY COLLEGE
Springfield, Illinois

■ **District-supported** 2-year, founded 1967, part of Illinois Community College Board
■ **Calendar** semesters
■ **Degree** certificates and associate
■ **Suburban** 441-acre campus with easy access to St. Louis
■ **Endowment** $1.5 million
■ **Coed,** 7,115 undergraduate students, 38% full-time, 58% women, 42% men

Undergraduates 2,720 full-time, 4,395 part-time. Students come from 3 states and territories, 2 other countries, 7% African American, 0.9% Asian American or Pacific Islander, 1% Hispanic American, 0.2% Native American, 0.4% international, 5% transferred in. *Retention:* 47% of 2002 full-time freshmen returned.
Freshmen *Admission:* 1,088 applied, 1,088 admitted, 1,088 enrolled. *Test scores:* ACT scores over 18: 61%; ACT scores over 24: 13%; ACT scores over 30: 1%.
Faculty *Total:* 342, 35% full-time, 31% with terminal degrees. *Student/faculty ratio:* 21:1.
Majors Administrative assistant and secretarial science; agricultural production; architectural drafting and CAD/CADD; art; automobile/automotive mechanics technology; biological and physical sciences; business administration and management; business automation/technology/data entry; child care provision; child guidance; computer programming (specific applications); computer systems networking and telecommunications; criminal justice/police science; electrical, electronic and communications engineering technology; fire protection and safety technology; general studies; hotel/motel administration; landscaping and groundskeeping; legal administrative assistant/secretary; liberal arts and sciences/liberal studies; literature; medical radiologic technology; music; nursing (registered nurse training); occupational therapist assistant; physical therapist assistant; pre-engineering; respiratory care therapy; selling skills and sales.
Academic Programs *Special study options:* academic remediation for entering students, accelerated degree program, adult/continuing education programs, advanced placement credit, distance learning, English as a second language, external degree program, honors programs, independent study, internships, off-campus study, part-time degree program, services for LD students, study abroad, summer session for credit.
Library Learning Resource Center plus 1 other with 72,956 titles, 438 serial subscriptions, an OPAC.
Computers on Campus 130 computers available on campus for general student use. Internet access, at least one staffed computer lab available.
Student Life *Housing:* college housing not available. *Activities and Organizations:* drama/theater group, student-run newspaper, choral group, Student Senate, Phi Theta Kappa, Model Illinois Government, student newspaper, Madrigals. *Campus security:* 24-hour emergency response devices and patrols, late-night transport/escort service. *Student services:* health clinic, personal/psychological counseling, women's center.

174 *www.petersons.com*

Peterson's Two-Year Colleges 2005

Athletics Member NJCAA. *Intercollegiate sports:* baseball M(s), basketball M(s)/W(s), soccer M(s), softball W(s), volleyball W(s). *Intramural sports:* basketball M/W, tennis M/W.

Costs (2003–04) *Tuition:* area resident $1410 full-time, $47 per credit hour part-time; state resident $6420 full-time; nonresident $8550 full-time. Full-time tuition and fees vary according to course load. Part-time tuition and fees vary according to course load. *Required fees:* $165 full-time, $6 per credit hour part-time. *Payment plan:* installment. *Waivers:* senior citizens and employees or children of employees.

Applying *Options:* common application, early admission, deferred entrance. *Recommended:* high school transcript. *Application deadline:* rolling (freshmen), rolling (transfers). *Notification:* continuous (freshmen), continuous (transfers).

Admissions Contact Mr. Ron Gregoire, Executive Director of Admissions and Records, Lincoln Land Community College, 5250 Shepherd Road, PO Box 19256, Springfield, IL 62794-9256. *Phone:* 217-786-2243. *Toll-free phone:* 800-727-4161 Ext. 298. *Fax:* 217-786-2492. *E-mail:* rgregoir@llcc.edu.

MacCormac College
Chicago, Illinois

- **Independent** 2-year, founded 1904
- **Calendar** semesters
- **Degree** certificates, diplomas, and associate
- **Urban** campus
- **Coed, primarily women,** 377 undergraduate students, 42% full-time, 87% women, 13% men

Undergraduates 159 full-time, 218 part-time. Students come from 7 states and territories, 8 other countries, 1% are from out of state, 42% African American, 0.5% Asian American or Pacific Islander, 27% Hispanic American.

Freshmen *Admission:* 227 enrolled.

Faculty *Total:* 34, 12% full-time, 12% with terminal degrees. *Student/faculty ratio:* 15:1.

Majors Accounting; administrative assistant and secretarial science; business administration and management; computer and information sciences; computer typography and composition equipment operation; consumer merchandising/retailing management; court reporting; hotel/motel administration; international business/trade/commerce; legal administrative assistant/secretary; legal assistant/paralegal; legal studies; marketing/marketing management; medical administrative assistant and medical secretary; tourism and travel services management.

Academic Programs *Special study options:* academic remediation for entering students, adult/continuing education programs, advanced placement credit, English as a second language, honors programs, internships, part-time degree program, summer session for credit.

Library MacCormac College Library with 11,000 titles, 140 serial subscriptions.

Computers on Campus 180 computers available on campus for general student use. A campuswide network can be accessed. Internet access available.

Student Life *Housing:* college housing not available. *Campus security:* late-night transport/escort service.

Standardized Tests *Required:* ACT (for admission). *Recommended:* SAT I (for admission).

Costs (2004–05) *Tuition:* $9960 full-time, $350 per credit part-time. *Required fees:* $200 full-time, $10 per credit part-time.

Financial Aid Of all full-time matriculated undergraduates who enrolled, 16 Federal Work-Study jobs.

Applying *Options:* common application, deferred entrance. *Application fee:* $20. *Required:* high school transcript. *Recommended:* interview. *Application deadline:* rolling (freshmen), rolling (transfers). *Notification:* continuous (freshmen), continuous (transfers).

Admissions Contact Ms. Rosa Medina, Coordinator of Admissions, MacCormac College, 506 South Wabash Avenue, Chicago, IL 60605-1667. *Phone:* 312-922-1884 Ext. 106. *Fax:* 630-941-0937.

McHenry County College
Crystal Lake, Illinois

- **State and locally supported** 2-year, founded 1967, part of Illinois Community College Board
- **Calendar** semesters
- **Degree** certificates and associate
- **Suburban** 109-acre campus with easy access to Chicago
- **Coed,** 5,940 undergraduate students, 34% full-time, 58% women, 42% men

Undergraduates 2,048 full-time, 3,892 part-time. Students come from 6 states and territories, 17 other countries, 1% are from out of state, 0.6% African American, 2% Asian American or Pacific Islander, 5% Hispanic American, 0.3% Native American, 0.5% international, 6% transferred in.

Freshmen *Admission:* 869 enrolled. *Average high school GPA:* 2.67. *Test scores:* ACT scores over 18: 69%; ACT scores over 24: 19%.

Faculty *Total:* 295, 30% full-time, 11% with terminal degrees. *Student/faculty ratio:* 20:1.

Majors Accounting technology and bookkeeping; administrative assistant and secretarial science; applied horticulture; art; automobile/automotive mechanics technology; biological and physical sciences; building/home/construction inspection; business administration and management; child care and support services management; child care provision; computer programming (specific applications); criminal justice/police science; electrical, electronic and communications engineering technology; emergency medical technology (EMT paramedic); engineering; fire science; general studies; liberal arts and sciences/liberal studies; mechanical engineering/mechanical technology; music; operations management; real estate; selling skills and sales.

Academic Programs *Special study options:* academic remediation for entering students, accelerated degree program, adult/continuing education programs, advanced placement credit, cooperative education, distance learning, English as a second language, honors programs, independent study, internships, part-time degree program, services for LD students, study abroad, summer session for credit.

Library McHenry County College Library with 40,000 titles, 330 serial subscriptions, 6,000 audiovisual materials, an OPAC, a Web page.

Computers on Campus 100 computers available on campus for general student use. A campuswide network can be accessed. Internet access, at least one staffed computer lab available.

Student Life *Housing:* college housing not available. *Activities and Organizations:* drama/theater group, student-run newspaper, choral group, Phi Theta Kappa, Tallywackers, Latinos Unidos, Campus Activities Board, Student Trustee. *Campus security:* 24-hour emergency response devices and patrols, late-night transport/escort service. *Student services:* personal/psychological counseling.

Athletics Member NJCAA. *Intercollegiate sports:* baseball M(s), basketball M(s)/W(s), soccer M(s), softball W(s), tennis M(s)/W(s), volleyball W(s). *Intramural sports:* bowling M/W, rock climbing M/W.

Standardized Tests *Recommended:* ACT (for placement).

Costs (2003–04) *Tuition:* area resident $1590 full-time, $53 per credit part-time; state resident $7333 full-time, $244 per credit part-time; nonresident $8601 full-time, $287 per credit part-time. *Required fees:* $284 full-time, $9 per credit part-time, $7 per term part-time. *Payment plans:* installment, deferred payment. *Waivers:* senior citizens and employees or children of employees.

Financial Aid Of all full-time matriculated undergraduates who enrolled, 200 Federal Work-Study jobs (averaging $3700). 130 state and other part-time jobs (averaging $2000).

Applying *Options:* early admission, deferred entrance. *Required:* high school transcript. *Application deadline:* rolling (freshmen), rolling (transfers). *Notification:* continuous (freshmen), continuous (transfers).

Admissions Contact Ms. Sue Grenwis, Admissions Specialist, McHenry County College, 8900 US Highway 14, Crystal Lake, IL 60012. *Phone:* 815-455-8530. *Toll-free phone:* 815-455-8530. *Fax:* 815-455-8530. *E-mail:* admissions@mchenry.edu.

Midstate College
Peoria, Illinois

- **Proprietary** primarily 2-year, founded 1888
- **Calendar** quarters
- **Degrees** diplomas, associate, and bachelor's
- **Urban** 1-acre campus
- **Coed, primarily women**

Faculty *Student/faculty ratio:* 13:1.

Student Life *Campus security:* late-night transport/escort service.

Standardized Tests *Required:* Wonderlic aptitude test (for admission).

Costs (2003–04) *Tuition:* $11,600 full-time, $775 per course part-time.

Financial Aid Of all full-time matriculated undergraduates who enrolled, 20 Federal Work-Study jobs (averaging $618).

Applying *Options:* common application, early admission, deferred entrance. *Application fee:* $25. *Required:* high school transcript. *Recommended:* interview.

Admissions Contact Ms. Jessica Auer, Director of Admissions, Midstate College, 411 West Northmoor Road, Peoria, IL 61614. *Phone:* 309-692-4092. *Fax:* 309-692-3893.

Moraine Valley Community College
Palos Hills, Illinois

- **State and locally supported** 2-year, founded 1967, part of Illinois Community College Board

Moraine Valley Community College (continued)
- **Calendar** semesters
- **Degree** certificates and associate
- **Suburban** 294-acre campus with easy access to Chicago
- **Endowment** $11.9 million
- **Coed**, 15,780 undergraduate students, 39% full-time, 59% women, 41% men

Undergraduates 6,230 full-time, 9,550 part-time. Students come from 5 states and territories, 35 other countries, 7% African American or Pacific Islander, 8% Hispanic American, 0.2% Native American, 2% international, 1% transferred in. *Retention:* 73% of 2002 full-time freshmen returned.

Freshmen *Admission:* 3,507 applied, 3,507 admitted, 3,478 enrolled. *Test scores:* ACT scores over 18: 74%; ACT scores over 24: 18%; ACT scores over 30: 1%.

Faculty *Total:* 891, 19% full-time. *Student/faculty ratio:* 23:1.

Majors Administrative assistant and secretarial science; automobile/automotive mechanics technology; biological and physical sciences; business administration and management; business/commerce; child care provision; computer programming (specific applications); computer systems networking and telecommunications; corrections; criminal justice/police science; design and visual communications; entrepreneurship; fire protection and safety technology; health information/medical records technology; human resources management; instrumentation technology; liberal arts and sciences/liberal studies; mechanical engineering/mechanical technology; medical radiologic technology; nursing (registered nurse training); parks, recreation and leisure facilities management; respiratory care therapy; restaurant, culinary, and catering management; retailing; selling skills and sales; therapeutic recreation; tourism and travel services marketing; visual and performing arts.

Academic Programs *Special study options:* academic remediation for entering students, accelerated degree program, adult/continuing education programs, advanced placement credit, cooperative education, distance learning, double majors, English as a second language, independent study, internships, off-campus study, part-time degree program, services for LD students, study abroad, summer session for credit.

Library Robert E. Turner Learning Resources Center/Library plus 1 other with 65,163 titles, 632 serial subscriptions, 22,928 audiovisual materials, an OPAC, a Web page.

Computers on Campus 775 computers available on campus for general student use. A campuswide network can be accessed from off campus. Internet access, online (class) registration, at least one staffed computer lab available.

Student Life *Housing:* college housing not available. *Activities and Organizations:* drama/theater group, student-run newspaper, choral group, student newspaper, Speech Team, Alliance of Latin American Students, Phi Theta Kappa, Arab Student Union. *Campus security:* 24-hour emergency response devices and patrols, late-night transport/escort service, safety and security programs. *Student services:* personal/psychological counseling, women's center.

Athletics Member NJCAA. *Intercollegiate sports:* baseball M(s), basketball M(s)/W(s), cross-country running M(s)/W(s), golf M(s), soccer M(s)/W(s), softball W(s), tennis W(s), volleyball W(s). *Intramural sports:* badminton M/W, basketball M/W, softball W, volleyball M/W.

Standardized Tests *Required:* ACT COMPASS (for placement). *Required for some:* ACT (for placement). *Recommended:* ACT (for placement).

Costs (2003–04) *Tuition:* area resident $1590 full-time, $53 per credit hour part-time; state resident $5970 full-time, $199 per credit hour part-time; nonresident $7260 full-time, $242 per credit hour part-time. *Required fees:* $150 full-time, $5 per credit hour part-time. *Payment plan:* installment. *Waivers:* senior citizens and employees or children of employees.

Financial Aid Of all full-time matriculated undergraduates who enrolled, 84 Federal Work-Study jobs (averaging $1900). 150 state and other part-time jobs (averaging $800).

Applying *Options:* electronic application, early admission, deferred entrance. *Required:* high school transcript. *Required for some:* minimum 2.0 GPA. *Recommended:* minimum 2.0 GPA. *Application deadline:* rolling (freshmen), rolling (transfers). *Notification:* continuous (freshmen), continuous (transfers).

Admissions Contact Ms. Claudia Roselli, Director, Admissions and Recruitment, Moraine Valley Community College, 10900 South 88th Avenue, Palos Hills, IL 60465-0937. *Phone:* 708-974-5357. *Fax:* 708-974-0681. *E-mail:* roselli@morainevalley.edu.

MORRISON INSTITUTE OF TECHNOLOGY
Morrison, Illinois

- **Independent** 2-year, founded 1973
- **Calendar** semesters
- **Degree** associate
- **Small-town** 17-acre campus
- **Endowment** $76,000
- **Coed, primarily men,** 143 undergraduate students, 99% full-time, 15% women, 85% men

Undergraduates 141 full-time, 2 part-time. Students come from 5 states and territories, 6% are from out of state, 2% African American, 4% Hispanic American, 0.7% Native American, 8% transferred in, 69% live on campus.

Freshmen *Admission:* 78 applied, 74 admitted, 62 enrolled. *Average high school GPA:* 2.3. *Test scores:* ACT scores over 18: 72%; ACT scores over 24: 10%; ACT scores over 30: 2%.

Faculty *Total:* 10, 90% full-time. *Student/faculty ratio:* 14:1.

Majors CAD/CADD drafting/design technology; construction engineering technology; drafting and design technology; engineering technology; mechanical drafting and CAD/CADD; survey technology.

Academic Programs *Special study options:* academic remediation for entering students, double majors, internships, part-time degree program.

Library Milikan Library with 7,946 titles, 39 serial subscriptions.

Computers on Campus 60 computers available on campus for general student use. A campuswide network can be accessed from student residence rooms. Internet access, at least one staffed computer lab available. Computer purchase or lease plan available.

Student Life *Housing:* on-campus residence required for freshman year. *Options:* coed. Freshman applicants given priority for college housing. *Campus security:* late-night transport/escort service, controlled dormitory access.

Athletics *Intramural sports:* basketball M, bowling M/W, softball M/W, table tennis M/W, volleyball M/W.

Standardized Tests *Recommended:* SAT I or ACT (for admission).

Costs (2004–05) *Tuition:* $11,000 full-time, $458 per credit part-time. *Required fees:* $250 full-time, $250 per year part-time. *Room only:* $2200.

Financial Aid Of all full-time matriculated undergraduates who enrolled, 25 Federal Work-Study jobs (averaging $2000).

Applying *Options:* common application, deferred entrance. *Application fee:* $100. *Required:* high school transcript, proof of immunization. *Application deadline:* rolling (freshmen). *Notification:* continuous until 9/1 (freshmen), continuous (transfers).

Admissions Contact Mrs. Tammy Pruis, Admission Secretary, Morrison Institute of Technology, 701 Portland Avenue, Morrison, IL 61270. *Phone:* 815-772-7218. *Fax:* 815-772-7584. *E-mail:* admissions@morrison.tec.il.us.

▶ **See page 582 for a narrative description.**

MORTON COLLEGE
Cicero, Illinois

- **State and locally supported** 2-year, founded 1924, part of Illinois Community College Board
- **Calendar** semesters
- **Degree** certificates and associate
- **Suburban** 25-acre campus with easy access to Chicago
- **Coed,** 5,244 undergraduate students, 100% full-time, 61% women, 39% men

Undergraduates 5,244 full-time. Students come from 2 states and territories, 3% African American, 2% Asian American or Pacific Islander, 68% Hispanic American, 0.1% Native American.

Faculty *Total:* 191, 25% full-time.

Majors Accounting; administrative assistant and secretarial science; art; automobile/automotive mechanics technology; biological and physical sciences; business administration and management; criminal justice/police science; data processing and data processing technology; drafting and design technology; finance; fine/studio arts; heating, air conditioning, ventilation and refrigeration maintenance technology; legal administrative assistant/secretary; liberal arts and sciences/liberal studies; marketing/marketing management; medical administrative assistant and medical secretary; music; nursing (registered nurse training); physical therapy; real estate.

Academic Programs *Special study options:* academic remediation for entering students, adult/continuing education programs, advanced placement credit, English as a second language, internships, part-time degree program, services for LD students, student-designed majors, summer session for credit.

Library Learning Resource Center with 40,972 titles, 327 serial subscriptions.

Computers on Campus 150 computers available on campus for general student use. At least one staffed computer lab available.

Student Life *Housing:* college housing not available. *Activities and Organizations:* drama/theater group, student-run newspaper, choral group, Hispanic Heritage Club, Program Board, Student Senate, Law Enforcement Association, Nursing Club. *Campus security:* 24-hour patrols, security cameras.

Athletics Member NJCAA. *Intercollegiate sports:* baseball M(s), basketball M(s)/W(s), cross-country running M(s)/W(s), soccer M, softball W(s), volleyball W(s). *Intramural sports:* basketball M/W, cross-country running M/W, volleyball M/W, weight lifting M/W.

Costs (2003–04) *Tuition:* area resident $1416 full-time, $55 per credit part-time; state resident $4056 full-time, $165 per credit part-time; nonresident $5376 full-time, $220 per credit part-time. *Required fees:* $4 per credit part-time. *Payment plan:* deferred payment. *Waivers:* employees or children of employees.

Financial Aid Of all full-time matriculated undergraduates who enrolled, 15 Federal Work-Study jobs (averaging $2000).

Applying *Application fee:* $10. *Required:* high school transcript. *Application deadline:* rolling (freshmen), rolling (transfers).

Admissions Contact Ms. Jill Caccamo-Beer, Director of Enrollment Management, Morton College, 3801 South Central Avenue, Cicero, IL 60804. *Phone:* 708-656-8000 Ext. 400. *Fax:* 708-656-9592. *E-mail:* enroll@morton.cc.il.us.

NORTHWESTERN BUSINESS COLLEGE
Chicago, Illinois

- **Proprietary** 2-year, founded 1902
- **Calendar** quarters
- **Degree** certificates and associate
- **Urban** 3-acre campus
- **Coed**

Faculty *Student/faculty ratio:* 18:1.

Standardized Tests *Required:* SAT I or ACT (for admission).

Costs (2003–04) *Tuition:* $275 per credit hour part-time.

Applying *Application fee:* $25. *Required:* high school transcript.

Admissions Contact Mr. Mark Sliz, Director of Admissions, Northwestern Business College, 4839 North Milwaukee Avenue, Chicago, IL 60630. *Phone:* 773-481-3730. *Toll-free phone:* 800-396-5613. *Fax:* 773-481-3738.

► See page 588 for a narrative description.

OAKTON COMMUNITY COLLEGE
Des Plaines, Illinois

- **District-supported** 2-year, founded 1969, part of Illinois Community College Board
- **Calendar** semesters
- **Degree** certificates and associate
- **Suburban** 193-acre campus with easy access to Chicago
- **Coed,** 9,893 undergraduate students

Undergraduates Students come from 50 other countries, 7% are from out of state, 5% African American, 17% Asian American or Pacific Islander, 7% Hispanic American, 0.2% Native American, 2% international.

Faculty *Total:* 662, 23% full-time, 16% with terminal degrees. *Student/faculty ratio:* 25:1.

Majors Accounting; administrative assistant and secretarial science; architectural engineering technology; art; automobile/automotive mechanics technology; biological and physical sciences; business administration and management; CAD/CADD drafting/design technology; clinical/medical laboratory technology; computer and information sciences; computer and information sciences related; computer graphics; computer programming; computer programming (specific applications); computer science; computer/technical support; construction management; criminal justice/police science; early childhood education; electrical, electronic and communications engineering technology; engineering; finance; fire science; health information/medical records administration; heating, air conditioning and refrigeration technology; information science/studies; international business/trade/commerce; kindergarten/preschool education; liberal arts and sciences and humanities related; liberal arts and sciences/liberal studies; machine tool technology; management science; marketing/marketing management; mathematics; mechanical design technology; mechanical drafting and CAD/CADD; music; nursing (licensed practical/vocational nurse training); nursing (registered nurse training); physical therapist assistant; physical therapy; pre-engineering; real estate; special products marketing.

Academic Programs *Special study options:* academic remediation for entering students, adult/continuing education programs, advanced placement credit, distance learning, English as a second language, honors programs, independent study, part-time degree program, services for LD students, study abroad, summer session for credit.

Library Oakton Community College Library plus 1 other with 92,000 titles, 586 serial subscriptions, 10,500 audiovisual materials, an OPAC, a Web page.

Computers on Campus 750 computers available on campus for general student use. A campuswide network can be accessed from off campus. At least one staffed computer lab available.

Student Life *Housing:* college housing not available. *Activities and Organizations:* drama/theater group, student-run newspaper, choral group, Board of Student Affairs, College Program Board, Phi Theta Kappa, honors student organization, Occurrence (student newspaper). *Campus security:* 24-hour emergency response devices and patrols, student patrols, late-night transport/escort service. *Student services:* health clinic, personal/psychological counseling.

Athletics Member NJCAA. *Intercollegiate sports:* baseball M, basketball M/W, cross-country running M/W, golf M, soccer M/W, softball W, tennis M/W, track and field M/W, volleyball W. *Intramural sports:* basketball M/W, cheerleading W, soccer M, table tennis M/W, volleyball M/W.

Costs (2004–05) *Tuition:* $62 per credit part-time; state resident $183 per credit part-time; nonresident $247 per credit part-time. *Required fees:* $3 per credit part-time, $15 per term part-time. *Payment plan:* installment. *Waivers:* senior citizens and employees or children of employees.

Financial Aid Of all full-time matriculated undergraduates who enrolled, 15 Federal Work-Study jobs (averaging $3500). 200 state and other part-time jobs (averaging $3200).

Applying *Application fee:* $25. *Required for some:* letters of recommendation, interview. *Recommended:* high school transcript. *Application deadline:* rolling (freshmen), rolling (transfers). *Notification:* continuous (freshmen), continuous (transfers).

Admissions Contact Mr. Dale Cohen, Admissions Specialist, Oakton Community College, 1600 East Golf Road, Des Plaines, IL 60016. *Phone:* 847-635-1703. *Fax:* 847-635-1890. *E-mail:* admiss@oakton.edu.

PARKLAND COLLEGE
Champaign, Illinois

- **District-supported** 2-year, founded 1967, part of Illinois Community College Board
- **Calendar** semesters
- **Degree** certificates and associate
- **Suburban** 233-acre campus
- **Coed,** 9,245 undergraduate students, 51% full-time, 56% women, 44% men

Undergraduates 4,679 full-time, 4,566 part-time. Students come from 30 states and territories, 14 other countries, 1% are from out of state, 13% African American, 3% Asian American or Pacific Islander, 3% Hispanic American, 0.5% Native American, 4% international, 7% transferred in.

Freshmen *Admission:* 3,194 applied, 2,799 admitted, 1,393 enrolled. *Test scores:* ACT scores over 18: 61%; ACT scores over 24: 14%; ACT scores over 30: 1%.

Faculty *Total:* 547, 32% full-time, 12% with terminal degrees. *Student/faculty ratio:* 17:1.

Majors Accounting technology and bookkeeping; administrative assistant and secretarial science; advertising; agricultural business and management; agricultural mechanization; art; art teacher education; autobody/collision and repair technology; automobile/automotive mechanics technology; biological and physical sciences; biomedical technology; business administration and management; business automation/technology/data entry; child care provision; computer and information sciences; computer graphics; computer/information technology services administration related; computer programming; computer programming (specific applications); computer programming (vendor/product certification); computer science; computer software and media applications related; computer systems networking and telecommunications; computer/technical support; construction management; consumer merchandising/retailing management; criminal justice/safety; data entry/microcomputer applications; dental hygiene; design and visual communications; desktop publishing and digital imaging design; electroneurodiagnostic/electroencephalographic technology; engineering science; equestrian studies; general studies; human services; industrial technology; information science/studies; landscaping and groundskeeping; liberal arts and sciences/liberal studies; medical radiologic technology; music performance; music teacher education; nursing (registered nurse training); occupational therapist assistant; radio and television; radio and television broadcasting technology; respiratory care therapy; sales and marketing/marketing and distribution teacher education; speech-language pathology; system administration; veterinary/animal health technology; web page, digital/multimedia and information resources design.

Academic Programs *Special study options:* academic remediation for entering students, adult/continuing education programs, advanced placement credit, cooperative education, distance learning, double majors, English as a second language, honors programs, independent study, internships, off-campus study, part-time degree program, services for LD students, study abroad, summer session for credit. *ROTC:* Army (c), Navy (c), Air Force (c).

Library Parkland College Library with 122,676 titles, 300 serial subscriptions, 8,115 audiovisual materials, an OPAC, a Web page.

Computers on Campus 800 computers available on campus for general student use. A campuswide network can be accessed. Internet access, online (class) registration, at least one staffed computer lab available.

Student Life *Housing:* college housing not available. *Activities and Organizations:* drama/theater group, student-run newspaper, radio and television station, choral group. *Campus security:* 24-hour emergency response devices and patrols, late-night transport/escort service. *Student services:* personal/psychological counseling, women's center.

Athletics Member NJCAA. *Intercollegiate sports:* baseball M(s), basketball M(s)/W(s), golf M(s), soccer M(s)/W(s), softball W(s), volleyball W(s). *Intramural sports:* basketball M/W, bowling M/W, softball M/W, volleyball M/W.

Standardized Tests *Required for some:* ACT (for placement).

Costs (2004–05) *Tuition:* area resident $2010 full-time, $67 per credit hour part-time; state resident $6510 full-time, $217 per credit hour part-time; nonresident $8340 full-time, $278 per credit hour part-time.

Parkland College (continued)

Financial Aid Of all full-time matriculated undergraduates who enrolled, 100 Federal Work-Study jobs (averaging $2000).

Applying *Recommended:* high school transcript. *Application deadline:* rolling (freshmen), rolling (transfers). *Notification:* continuous (freshmen), continuous (transfers).

Admissions Contact Admissions Representative, Parkland College, 2400 West Bradley Avenue, Champaign, IL 61821. *Phone:* 217-351-2482. *Toll-free phone:* 800-346-8089. *Fax:* 217-351-7640. *E-mail:* mhenry@parkland.edu.

PRAIRIE STATE COLLEGE
Chicago Heights, Illinois

- **State and locally supported** 2-year, founded 1958, part of Illinois Community College Board
- **Calendar** semesters
- **Degree** certificates and associate
- **Suburban** 68-acre campus with easy access to Chicago
- **Endowment** $750,000
- **Coed**

Faculty *Student/faculty ratio:* 17:1.

Student Life *Campus security:* 24-hour emergency response devices and patrols, student patrols, late-night transport/escort service.

Athletics Member NJCAA.

Standardized Tests *Required for some:* ACT COMPASS.

Costs (2004–05) *Tuition:* area resident $1608 full-time, $67 per credit hour part-time; state resident $5064 full-time, $211 per credit hour part-time; nonresident $6984 full-time, $291 per credit hour part-time. *Required fees:* $236 full-time, $9 per credit hour part-time, $10 per term part-time.

Financial Aid Of all full-time matriculated undergraduates who enrolled, 60 Federal Work-Study jobs.

Applying *Options:* common application, deferred entrance. *Application fee:* $10. *Required:* high school transcript.

Admissions Contact Ms. Mary Welsh, Director of Admissions, Records and Registration, Prairie State College, 202 South Halsted Street, Chicago Heights, IL 60411. *Phone:* 708-709-3513. *Toll-free phone:* 708-709-3516. *E-mail:* webmaster@prairiestate.edu.

REND LAKE COLLEGE
Ina, Illinois

- **State-supported** 2-year, founded 1967, part of Illinois Community College Board
- **Calendar** semesters
- **Degree** certificates and associate
- **Rural** 350-acre campus
- **Endowment** $1.7 million
- **Coed**, 5,142 undergraduate students, 29% full-time, 50% women, 50% men

Undergraduates 1,499 full-time, 3,643 part-time. Students come from 2 states and territories, 2 other countries, 1% are from out of state, 3% African American, 0.7% Asian American or Pacific Islander, 0.6% Hispanic American, 0.2% Native American, 0.1% international.

Faculty *Total:* 224, 27% full-time, 2% with terminal degrees.

Majors Administrative assistant and secretarial science; agricultural business and management; agricultural mechanization; agricultural production; agriculture; applied horticulture; architectural technology; art; automobile/automotive mechanics technology; automotive engineering technology; biological and physical sciences; business administration and management; chemistry; child development; clinical/medical laboratory technology; commercial and advertising art; computer and information sciences; computer engineering technology; computer programming (specific applications); computer science; corrections; criminal justice/police science; culinary arts; diesel mechanics technology; early childhood education; electrician; elementary education; emergency medical technology (EMT paramedic); engineering; engineering physics; engineering science; engineering technology; English; health information/medical records technology; health services/allied health/health sciences; heavy equipment maintenance technology; history; hospitality administration; industrial electronics technology; industrial mechanics and maintenance technology; industrial technology; manufacturing technology; mathematics; medical administrative assistant and medical secretary; nursing (registered nurse training); occupational therapist assistant; parks, recreation and leisure; plant sciences; political science and government; pre-dentistry studies; pre-law studies; pre-medical studies; pre-pharmacy studies; pre-veterinary studies; psychology; secondary education; social work; sociology; special education; speech and rhetoric; survey technology; welding technology.

Academic Programs *Special study options:* academic remediation for entering students, adult/continuing education programs, advanced placement credit, cooperative education, distance learning, honors programs, independent study, internships, off-campus study, part-time degree program, services for LD students, summer session for credit.

Library Learning Resource Center with 35,426 titles, 265 serial subscriptions, 3,770 audiovisual materials, an OPAC, a Web page.

Computers on Campus 451 computers available on campus for general student use. A campuswide network can be accessed from off campus that provide access to online registration for online courses. Internet access, at least one staffed computer lab available. Computer purchase or lease plan available.

Student Life *Housing:* college housing not available. *Activities and Organizations:* drama/theater group, student-run newspaper, choral group, Student Senate, Psi Beta, Phi Theta Kappa, Student Ambassadors. *Campus security:* 24-hour emergency response devices and patrols, late-night transport/escort service.

Athletics Member NJCAA. *Intercollegiate sports:* baseball M(s), basketball M(s)/W(s), cross-country running M(s), golf M(s)/W(s), softball W(s), tennis W(s), volleyball W(s).

Standardized Tests *Required:* SAT I or ACT (for placement), ACT ASSET, ACT COMPASS (for placement).

Costs (2004–05) *Tuition:* area resident $1824 full-time, $57 per credit hour part-time; state resident $2592 full-time, $81 per credit hour part-time; nonresident $4800 full-time, $150 per credit hour part-time. *Payment plan:* installment. *Waivers:* senior citizens and employees or children of employees.

Financial Aid Of all full-time matriculated undergraduates who enrolled, 133 Federal Work-Study jobs (averaging $1000). 174 state and other part-time jobs (averaging $940).

Applying *Options:* electronic application, deferred entrance. *Required:* high school transcript. *Application deadlines:* 8/18 (freshmen), 8/18 (transfers).

Admissions Contact Ms. Lisa Price, Director, Counseling, Rend Lake College, 468 North Ken Gray Parkway, Ina, IL 62846-9801. *Phone:* 618-437-5321 Ext. 205. *Toll-free phone:* 618-437-5321 Ext. 230. *Fax:* 618-437-5677. *E-mail:* admiss@rlc.edu.

RICHLAND COMMUNITY COLLEGE
Decatur, Illinois

- **District-supported** 2-year, founded 1971, part of Illinois Community College Board
- **Calendar** semesters
- **Degree** certificates and associate
- **Small-town** 117-acre campus
- **Endowment** $3.8 million
- **Coed**

Faculty *Student/faculty ratio:* 14:1.

Student Life *Campus security:* 24-hour emergency response devices and patrols.

Standardized Tests *Required for some:* ACT (for placement).

Costs (2003–04) *Tuition:* area resident $1655 full-time; state resident $5750 full-time; nonresident $9600 full-time.

Financial Aid Of all full-time matriculated undergraduates who enrolled, 43 Federal Work-Study jobs (averaging $1339). 129 state and other part-time jobs (averaging $578).

Applying *Options:* early admission. *Required:* high school transcript.

Admissions Contact Ms. Nancy A. Cooper, Dean of Enrollment Services, Richland Community College, One College Park, Decatur, IL 62521. *Phone:* 217-875-7200 Ext. 246. *Fax:* 217-875-7783.

ROCKFORD BUSINESS COLLEGE
Rockford, Illinois

- **Independent** 2-year, founded 1862
- **Calendar** quarters
- **Degree** certificates, diplomas, and associate
- **Urban** campus with easy access to Chicago
- **Coed, primarily women**

Faculty *Student/faculty ratio:* 15:1.

Student Life *Campus security:* 24-hour patrols, late-night transport/escort service.

Applying *Options:* common application, electronic application, early admission. *Application fee:* $50. *Required:* high school transcript, interview. *Required for some:* essay or personal statement.

Admissions Contact Ms. Barbara Holliman, Director of Admissions, Rockford Business College, 730 North Church Street, Rockford, IL 61103. *Phone:* 815-965-8616 Ext. 16. *Fax:* 815-965-0360.

ROCK VALLEY COLLEGE
Rockford, Illinois

- **District-supported** 2-year, founded 1964, part of Illinois Community College Board
- **Calendar** semesters
- **Degree** certificates and associate
- **Suburban** 217-acre campus with easy access to Chicago
- **Coed**

Faculty *Student/faculty ratio:* 22:1.
Student Life *Campus security:* 24-hour emergency response devices and patrols, late-night transport/escort service.
Athletics Member NJCAA.
Standardized Tests *Required for some:* ACT (for placement). *Recommended:* ACT (for placement).
Costs (2003–04) *Tuition:* area resident $1500 full-time, $45 per credit part-time; state resident $4800 full-time, $189 per credit part-time; nonresident $7000 full-time, $284 per credit part-time. *Required fees:* $224 full-time, $7 per credit part-time, $3 per term part-time.
Financial Aid Of all full-time matriculated undergraduates who enrolled, 120 Federal Work-Study jobs (averaging $1800).
Applying *Options:* early admission. *Required:* high school transcript.
Admissions Contact Ms. Lisa Allman, Coordinator of Admissions and Records, Rock Valley College, 3301 North Mulford Road, Rockford, IL 61114-5699. *Phone:* 815-654-5527. *Toll-free phone:* 800-973-7821. *Fax:* 815-654-5568.

SAUK VALLEY COMMUNITY COLLEGE
Dixon, Illinois

- **District-supported** 2-year, founded 1965, part of Illinois Community College Board
- **Calendar** semesters
- **Degree** certificates and associate
- **Rural** 165-acre campus
- **Coed**, 3,161 undergraduate students

Undergraduates 1% African American, 1% Asian American or Pacific Islander, 7% Hispanic American, 0.4% Native American.
Freshmen *Admission:* 1,400 applied, 1,400 admitted.
Faculty *Total:* 152, 39% full-time. *Student/faculty ratio:* 18:1.
Majors Accounting; administrative assistant and secretarial science; architecture; art; athletic training; biology/biological sciences; business administration and management; chemistry; chiropractic assistant; communication/speech communication and rhetoric; computer and information sciences related; corrections; criminal justice/law enforcement administration; criminal justice/police science; dramatic/theatre arts; early childhood education; economics; education; electrical, electronic and communications engineering technology; elementary education; English; French; heating, air conditioning, ventilation and refrigeration maintenance technology; history; human services; industrial radiologic technology; legal administrative assistant; liberal arts and sciences/liberal studies; marketing/marketing management; mathematics; mechanical engineering/mechanical technology; medical office assistant; music; nursing (registered nurse training); occupational therapy; optometric technician; physical education teaching and coaching; physical therapy; physics; political science and government; pre-dentistry studies; pre-medical studies; pre-pharmacy studies; pre-veterinary studies; psychology; public administration and social service professions related; secondary education; social work; sociology; Spanish; special education; speech and rhetoric.
Academic Programs *Special study options:* academic remediation for entering students, accelerated degree program, adult/continuing education programs, cooperative education, distance learning, English as a second language, honors programs, independent study, internships, off-campus study, part-time degree program, services for LD students, student-designed majors.
Library Learning Resource Center plus 1 other with 55,000 titles, 268 serial subscriptions.
Computers on Campus 100 computers available on campus for general student use. A campuswide network can be accessed. Internet access, at least one staffed computer lab available.
Student Life *Housing:* college housing not available. *Activities and Organizations:* drama/theater group, choral group. *Campus security:* 24-hour emergency response devices and patrols, late-night transport/escort service. *Student services:* personal/psychological counseling.
Athletics Member NJCAA. *Intercollegiate sports:* baseball M(s), basketball M(s)/W(s), softball W, tennis M(s)/W(s), volleyball W(s). *Intramural sports:* basketball M/W.
Standardized Tests *Required:* ACT ASSET, Nelson Denny Reading Test (for placement).

Costs (2003–04) *Tuition:* area resident $1800 full-time; state resident $5970 full-time; nonresident $7530 full-time. *Payment plan:* deferred payment. *Waivers:* employees or children of employees.
Financial Aid Of all full-time matriculated undergraduates who enrolled, 150 Federal Work-Study jobs (averaging $3000).
Applying *Options:* early admission, deferred entrance. *Recommended:* high school transcript. *Application deadline:* rolling (freshmen), rolling (transfers). *Notification:* continuous (freshmen), continuous (transfers).
Admissions Contact Ms. Pamela Clodfelter, Director of Admissions, Records, and Placement, Sauk Valley Community College, 173 Illinois Route 2, Dixon, IL 61021. *Phone:* 815-288-5511 Ext. 310. *Fax:* 815-288-3190. *E-mail:* skyhawk@svcc.edu.

SHAWNEE COMMUNITY COLLEGE
Ullin, Illinois

- **State and locally supported** 2-year, founded 1967, part of Illinois Community College Board
- **Calendar** semesters
- **Degree** certificates and associate
- **Rural** 163-acre campus
- **Coed**

Student Life *Campus security:* student patrols.
Athletics Member NJCAA.
Standardized Tests *Required:* ACT ASSET (for placement). *Required for some:* ACT (for placement). *Recommended:* ACT (for placement).
Costs (2004–05) *Tuition:* $48 per credit hour part-time; state resident $82 per credit hour part-time; nonresident $82 per credit hour part-time.
Financial Aid Of all full-time matriculated undergraduates who enrolled, 60 Federal Work-Study jobs (averaging $2000). 50 state and other part-time jobs (averaging $2000).
Applying *Options:* common application, early admission, deferred entrance. *Required:* high school transcript.
Admissions Contact Ms. Dee Blakely, Director of Admissions, Shawnee Community College, 8364 Shawnee College Road, Ullin, IL 62992-2206. *Phone:* 618-634-3200 Ext. 3247. *Toll-free phone:* 800-481-2242. *Fax:* 618-634-9028.

SOUTHEASTERN ILLINOIS COLLEGE
Harrisburg, Illinois

- **State-supported** 2-year, founded 1960, part of Illinois Community College Board
- **Calendar** semesters
- **Degree** certificates and associate
- **Rural** 140-acre campus
- **Coed**

Faculty *Student/faculty ratio:* 26:1.
Student Life *Campus security:* student patrols, evening security guard.
Athletics Member NJCAA.
Standardized Tests *Required:* ACT ASSET (for placement). *Recommended:* ACT (for placement).
Costs (2003–04) *Tuition:* area resident $1560 full-time; state resident $2250 full-time; nonresident $2610 full-time.
Financial Aid Of all full-time matriculated undergraduates who enrolled, 34 Federal Work-Study jobs (averaging $1300). 41 state and other part-time jobs (averaging $1300).
Applying *Options:* electronic application, early admission, deferred entrance. *Required:* high school transcript.
Admissions Contact Ms. Tyra Taylor, Registrar, Southeastern Illinois College, 3575 College Road, Harrisburg, IL 62946-4925. *Phone:* 618-252-5400 Ext. 2440. *Toll-free phone:* 866-338-2742.

SOUTH SUBURBAN COLLEGE
South Holland, Illinois

- **State and locally supported** 2-year, founded 1927, part of Illinois Community College Board
- **Calendar** semesters
- **Degree** certificates and associate
- **Suburban** campus with easy access to Chicago
- **Coed**, 6,672 undergraduate students

Undergraduates Students come from 1 other state, 60% African American, 1% Asian American or Pacific Islander, 8% Hispanic American, 0.4% Native American, 0.4% international.

South Suburban College (continued)

Freshmen *Admission:* 851 applied, 851 admitted. *Average high school GPA:* 2.33.

Faculty *Total:* 354, 36% full-time. *Student/faculty ratio:* 18:1.

Majors Accounting; administrative assistant and secretarial science; advertising; architectural engineering technology; biomedical technology; chemistry; child development; commercial and advertising art; construction engineering technology; consumer merchandising/retailing management; court reporting; criminal justice/law enforcement administration; criminal justice/police science; data processing and data processing technology; drafting and design technology; electrical, electronic and communications engineering technology; elementary education; fashion merchandising; finance; fine/studio arts; fire science; graphic and printing equipment operation/production; human services; industrial radiologic technology; industrial technology; information science/studies; kindergarten/preschool education; legal assistant/paralegal; liberal arts and sciences/liberal studies; machine tool technology; management information systems; marketing/marketing management; mathematics; mechanical design technology; mental health/rehabilitation; nursing (registered nurse training); occupational therapist assistant; pre-engineering; sales, distribution and marketing; teacher assistant/aide.

Academic Programs *Special study options:* academic remediation for entering students, adult/continuing education programs, advanced placement credit, cooperative education, double majors, English as a second language, honors programs, independent study, internships, off-campus study, part-time degree program, services for LD students, study abroad, summer session for credit.

Library South Suburban College Library plus 2 others with 38,845 titles, 403 serial subscriptions, an OPAC, a Web page.

Computers on Campus 250 computers available on campus for general student use. A campuswide network can be accessed from off campus. Internet access, online (class) registration, at least one staffed computer lab available.

Student Life *Housing:* college housing not available. *Activities and Organizations:* drama/theater group, student-run newspaper, choral group, Returning Adult Organization, Business Professionals, Disabled Students Organization, O.T. Organization, PAC Rats. *Campus security:* 24-hour emergency response devices and patrols. *Student services:* personal/psychological counseling.

Athletics Member NJCAA. *Intercollegiate sports:* baseball M, basketball M/W, cross-country running M/W, softball W, volleyball W. *Intramural sports:* baseball M, basketball M/W, bowling M/W, cross-country running M/W, soccer M, softball W, volleyball W.

Standardized Tests *Required:* ACT ASSET (for placement).

Costs (2004–05) *Tuition:* area resident $1874 full-time, $69 per credit hour part-time. Part-time tuition and fees vary according to course load. *Required fees:* $210 full-time, $9 per credit hour part-time.

Financial Aid Of all full-time matriculated undergraduates who enrolled, 121 Federal Work-Study jobs (averaging $1750).

Applying *Options:* early admission, deferred entrance. *Application fee:* $20. *Required:* high school transcript. *Required for some:* essay or personal statement, interview. *Recommended:* minimum 2.0 GPA. *Application deadline:* rolling (freshmen), rolling (transfers). *Notification:* continuous (freshmen), continuous (transfers).

Admissions Contact Ms. Jazaer Farrar, Director of New Student Services, South Suburban College, 15800 South State Street, South Holland, IL 60473-1270. *Phone:* 708-596-2000 Ext. 2291.

SOUTHWESTERN ILLINOIS COLLEGE
Belleville, Illinois

- **District-supported** 2-year, founded 1946, part of Illinois Community College Board
- **Calendar** semesters
- **Degree** certificates, diplomas, and associate
- **Suburban** 150-acre campus with easy access to St. Louis
- **Endowment** $3.1 million
- **Coed,** 16,425 undergraduate students

Undergraduates Students come from 6 states and territories, 19 other countries, 17% African American, 2% Asian American or Pacific Islander, 3% Hispanic American, 0.5% Native American.

Freshmen *Admission:* 913 admitted.

Faculty *Total:* 791, 17% full-time. *Student/faculty ratio:* 16:1.

Majors Accounting; administrative assistant and secretarial science; airframe mechanics and aircraft maintenance technology; autobody/collision and repair technology; avionics maintenance technology; banking and financial support services; business administration and management; carpentry; child development; clinical/medical laboratory technology; construction engineering technology; construction management; criminal justice/law enforcement administration; data processing and data processing technology; desktop publishing and digital imaging design; drafting and design technology; electrical, electronic and communications engineering technology; elementary education; engineering technology; fine/studio arts; fire science; health information/medical records

administration; heating, air conditioning, ventilation and refrigeration maintenance technology; horticultural science; hospitality administration; industrial radiologic technology; information science/studies; instrumentation technology; legal administrative assistant/secretary; legal assistant/paralegal; liberal arts and sciences/liberal studies; machine tool technology; marketing/marketing management; medical administrative assistant and medical secretary; medical/clinical assistant; metallurgical technology; nursing (registered nurse training); physical education teaching and coaching; physical therapist assistant; pre-pharmacy studies; real estate; sign language interpretation and translation; welding technology.

Academic Programs *Special study options:* academic remediation for entering students, accelerated degree program, adult/continuing education programs, advanced placement credit, cooperative education, distance learning, double majors, English as a second language, internships, off-campus study, part-time degree program, services for LD students, study abroad, summer session for credit. *ROTC:* Army (c), Air Force (c).

Library Belleville Area College Library with 82,537 titles, 638 serial subscriptions, 2,688 audiovisual materials, an OPAC, a Web page.

Computers on Campus 348 computers available on campus for general student use. A campuswide network can be accessed. Internet access, at least one staffed computer lab available.

Student Life *Housing:* college housing not available. *Activities and Organizations:* drama/theater group, student-run newspaper, choral group, College Activities Board, Phi Theta Kappa, Student Nurses Association, Horticulture Club, Data Processing Management Association. *Campus security:* 24-hour emergency response devices and patrols, student patrols, late-night transport/escort service. *Student services:* personal/psychological counseling, women's center.

Athletics Member NJCAA. *Intercollegiate sports:* baseball M(s), basketball M(s)/W(s), soccer M(s), softball W(s), tennis M(s)/W(s), volleyball W(s). *Intramural sports:* basketball M/W, bowling M/W, softball M/W, tennis M/W, volleyball M/W.

Standardized Tests *Required for some:* ACT ASSET or ACT COMPASS, ACT ASSET or ACT COMPASS.

Costs (2004–05) *Tuition:* area resident $1650 full-time; state resident $4680 full-time; nonresident $7410 full-time.

Financial Aid Of all full-time matriculated undergraduates who enrolled, 170 Federal Work-Study jobs (averaging $1537). 179 state and other part-time jobs (averaging $1004).

Applying *Options:* early admission, deferred entrance. *Application fee:* $10. *Required:* high school transcript. *Application deadline:* rolling (freshmen), rolling (transfers).

Admissions Contact Ms. Michelle Birk, Director of Admission, Southwestern Illinois College, 2500 Carlyle Road, Belleville, IL 62221-5899. *Phone:* 618-235-2700 Ext. 5400. *Toll-free phone:* 800-222-5131. *Fax:* 618-277-0631.

SPOON RIVER COLLEGE
Canton, Illinois

- **State-supported** 2-year, founded 1959, part of Illinois Community College Board
- **Calendar** semesters
- **Degree** certificates and associate
- **Rural** 160-acre campus
- **Endowment** $267,036
- **Coed,** 2,600 undergraduate students, 39% full-time, 55% women, 58% men

Undergraduates 1,006 full-time, 1,921 part-time. Students come from 6 states and territories, 1% are from out of state.

Freshmen *Test scores:* ACT scores over 18: 64%; ACT scores over 24: 12%.

Faculty *Total:* 147, 24% full-time, 7% with terminal degrees. *Student/faculty ratio:* 14:1.

Majors Accounting; administrative assistant and secretarial science; agricultural mechanization; agricultural teacher education; art; automobile/automotive mechanics technology; biological and physical sciences; biology/biological sciences; botany/plant biology; business administration and management; business teacher education; chemistry; child development; criminal justice/law enforcement administration; criminal justice/police science; dramatic/theatre arts; education; electrical, electronic and communications engineering technology; English; finance; health science; history; industrial technology; information science/studies; kindergarten/preschool education; legal administrative assistant/secretary; liberal arts and sciences/liberal studies; mass communication/media; mathematics; medical administrative assistant and medical secretary; nursing (registered nurse training); physical education teaching and coaching; physical sciences; physics; political science and government; pre-engineering; psychology; social sciences; sociology; speech and rhetoric; zoology/animal biology.

Academic Programs *Special study options:* accelerated degree program, adult/continuing education programs, advanced placement credit, distance learning, English as a second language, freshman honors college, honors programs, internships, part-time degree program, services for LD students, summer session for credit. *ROTC:* Army (b).

Library Learning Resource Center with 34,799 titles, 121 serial subscriptions, 3,213 audiovisual materials, an OPAC.

Computers on Campus 34 computers available on campus for general student use. A campuswide network can be accessed. At least one staffed computer lab available.

Student Life *Housing:* college housing not available. *Activities and Organizations:* drama/theater group, Student Senate, PEACE, Peer Ambassadors. *Campus security:* 24-hour emergency response devices. *Student services:* personal/psychological counseling.

Athletics Member NJCAA. *Intercollegiate sports:* baseball M(s), basketball M(s)/W(s), softball W(s), track and field M(s)/W(s), volleyball W(s).

Standardized Tests *Required for some:* nursing exam, ACT ASSET. *Recommended:* SAT I or ACT (for placement).

Costs (2004–05) *Tuition:* area resident $1710 full-time, $57 per credit hour part-time; state resident $2565 full-time, $86 per credit hour part-time; nonresident $4275 full-time, $143 per credit hour part-time. Full-time tuition and fees vary according to course load. Part-time tuition and fees vary according to course load. *Required fees:* $255 full-time, $9 per credit hour part-time. *Payment plan:* installment. *Waivers:* senior citizens and employees or children of employees.

Applying *Options:* early admission. *Required:* high school transcript. *Application deadline:* rolling (freshmen), rolling (transfers).

Admissions Contact Dr. Sharon Wrenn, Dean of Student Services, Spoon River College, 23235 North County 22, Canton, IL 61520-9801. *Phone:* 309-649-6305. *Toll-free phone:* 800-334-7337. *Fax:* 309-649-6235. *E-mail:* info@src.cc.il.us.

SPRINGFIELD COLLEGE IN ILLINOIS
Springfield, Illinois

- **Independent** 2-year, founded 1929, affiliated with Roman Catholic Church
- **Calendar** semesters
- **Degree** associate
- **Urban** 8-acre campus
- **Endowment** $519,554
- **Coed**

Faculty *Student/faculty ratio:* 10:1.

Student Life *Campus security:* 24-hour emergency response devices.

Athletics Member NJCAA.

Standardized Tests *Required:* ACT (for admission).

Costs (2003–04) *Tuition:* $7272 full-time. *Required fees:* $112 full-time. *Room only:* $2244.

Financial Aid Of all full-time matriculated undergraduates who enrolled, 30 Federal Work-Study jobs (averaging $1700).

Applying *Options:* common application. *Application fee:* $15. *Required:* high school transcript. *Required for some:* interview. *Recommended:* minimum 2.0 GPA.

Admissions Contact Ms. Kim Fontana, Director of Admissions, Springfield College in Illinois, 1500 North Fifth Street, Springfield, IL 62702-2694. *Phone:* 217-525-1420 Ext. 241. *Toll-free phone:* 800-635-7289. *Fax:* 217-525-1497.

TAYLOR BUSINESS INSTITUTE
Chicago, Illinois

Admissions Contact Mr. Rashed Jahangir, Taylor Business Institute, 200 North Michigan Avenue, Suite 301, Chicago, IL 60601.

TRITON COLLEGE
River Grove, Illinois

- **State-supported** 2-year, founded 1964, part of Illinois Community College Board
- **Calendar** semesters
- **Degree** certificates and associate
- **Suburban** 100-acre campus with easy access to Chicago
- **Coed,** 10,464 undergraduate students, 33% full-time, 57% women, 43% men

Undergraduates 3,495 full-time, 6,969 part-time. Students come from 26 other countries, 1% are from out of state, 20% African American, 4% Asian American or Pacific Islander, 16% Hispanic American, 0.2% Native American, 0.1% international.

Freshmen *Admission:* 2,214 applied, 2,214 admitted.

Faculty *Total:* 572, 20% full-time. *Student/faculty ratio:* 20:1.

Majors Accounting; administrative assistant and secretarial science; anthropology; architectural engineering technology; art; automobile/automotive mechan-

ics technology; baking and pastry arts; biological and physical sciences; biology/biological sciences; business administration and management; chemistry; child care provision; commercial and advertising art; computer and information systems security; computer engineering technology; computer graphics; computer programming related; computer science; computer software and media applications related; computer systems networking and telecommunications; computer/technical support; computer typography and composition equipment operation; construction engineering technology; construction management; consumer merchandising/retailing management; court reporting; criminal justice/law enforcement administration; criminal justice/police science; culinary arts; data processing and data processing technology; drafting and design technology; dramatic/theatre arts; economics; education; electrical, electronic and communications engineering technology; engineering related; engineering technology; English; fashion merchandising; fire science; French; geography; geology/earth science; graphic and printing equipment operation/production; heating, air conditioning, ventilation and refrigeration maintenance technology; history; hospitality administration; hotel/motel administration; industrial technology; information science/studies; interdisciplinary studies; interior design; international business/trade/commerce; Italian; journalism; kindergarten/preschool education; landscape architecture; landscaping and groundskeeping; legal administrative assistant/secretary; liberal arts and sciences/liberal studies; machine tool technology; management information systems; marketing/marketing management; mass communication/media; mathematics; music; nuclear medical technology; nursing (licensed practical/vocational nurse training); nursing (registered nurse training); ophthalmic laboratory technology; ophthalmic technology; opticianry; ornamental horticulture; philosophy; physics; political science and government; psychology; radiologic technology/science; real estate; respiratory care therapy; social sciences; Spanish; speech and rhetoric; substance abuse/addiction counseling; system administration; transportation technology; web/multimedia management and webmaster; web page, digital/multimedia and information resources design; welding technology.

Academic Programs *Special study options:* academic remediation for entering students, adult/continuing education programs, advanced placement credit, cooperative education, distance learning, English as a second language, freshman honors college, honors programs, internships, part-time degree program, student-designed majors, summer session for credit.

Library Learning Resource Center with 70,859 titles, 1,247 serial subscriptions.

Computers on Campus 350 computers available on campus for general student use. At least one staffed computer lab available.

Student Life *Housing:* college housing not available. *Activities and Organizations:* drama/theater group, student-run newspaper, radio station, choral group, student government, Program Board. *Campus security:* 24-hour emergency response devices and patrols. *Student services:* health clinic, personal/psychological counseling.

Athletics Member NJCAA. *Intercollegiate sports:* baseball M, basketball M/W, soccer M, softball W, swimming W, volleyball W, wrestling M.

Standardized Tests *Recommended:* SAT I or ACT (for placement).

Costs (2003–04) *Tuition:* area resident $1680 full-time, $56 per credit hour part-time; state resident $5244 full-time, $175 per credit hour part-time; nonresident $6670 full-time, $222 per credit hour part-time. Full-time tuition and fees vary according to course load. Part-time tuition and fees vary according to course load. *Required fees:* $240 full-time. *Payment plan:* installment. *Waivers:* senior citizens and employees or children of employees.

Financial Aid Of all full-time matriculated undergraduates who enrolled, 250 Federal Work-Study jobs (averaging $2000).

Applying *Options:* deferred entrance. *Required:* high school transcript. *Application deadline:* rolling (freshmen), rolling (transfers).

Admissions Contact Mr. Doug Olson, Dean of Student Services, Triton College, 2000 Fifth Avenue, River Grove, IL 60171. *Phone:* 708-456-0300 Ext. 3230. *Toll-free phone:* 800-942-7404. *E-mail:* gfuller@triton.cc.il.us.

WAUBONSEE COMMUNITY COLLEGE
Sugar Grove, Illinois

- **District-supported** 2-year, founded 1966, part of Illinois Community College Board
- **Calendar** semesters
- **Degree** certificates and associate
- **Rural** 243-acre campus with easy access to Chicago
- **Coed,** 8,373 undergraduate students, 29% full-time, 57% women, 43% men

Undergraduates 2,391 full-time, 5,982 part-time. Students come from 1 other state, 2 other countries, 6% African American, 2% Asian American or Pacific Islander, 16% Hispanic American, 0.6% Native American, 2% transferred in.

Freshmen *Admission:* 1,257 enrolled.

Faculty *Total:* 517, 16% full-time, 12% with terminal degrees. *Student/faculty ratio:* 16:1.

Majors Accounting technology and bookkeeping; administrative assistant and secretarial science; art; art teacher education; autobody/collision and repair

Waubonsee Community College (continued)

technology; automobile/automotive mechanics technology; banking and financial support services; biological and physical sciences; business administration and management; business automation/technology/data entry; child care provision; communication/speech communication and rhetoric; computer and information sciences; computer programming (specific applications); criminal justice/police science; design and visual communications; electrical, electronic and communications engineering technology; engineering; entrepreneurship; executive assistant/executive secretary; fire protection and safety technology; general studies; heating, air conditioning, ventilation and refrigeration maintenance technology; industrial mechanics and maintenance technology; industrial technology; kindergarten/preschool education; liberal arts and sciences/liberal studies; logistics and materials management; massage therapy; mass communication/media; medical/clinical assistant; music; music teacher education; nursing assistant/aide and patient care assistant; nursing (registered nurse training); operations management; quality control technology; retailing; robotics technology; sign language interpretation and translation; social work; tourism and travel services marketing.

Academic Programs *Special study options:* academic remediation for entering students, accelerated degree program, advanced placement credit, distance learning, honors programs, independent study, part-time degree program, services for LD students, study abroad, summer session for credit. *ROTC:* Army (c).

Library Todd Library with 62,984 titles, 649 serial subscriptions, 5,900 audiovisual materials, an OPAC, a Web page.

Computers on Campus 160 computers available on campus for general student use. A campuswide network can be accessed from off campus. Internet access, online (class) registration, at least one staffed computer lab available.

Student Life *Housing:* college housing not available. *Activities and Organizations:* drama/theater group, student-run newspaper, television station, choral group, Phi Theta Kappa, VICA, Alpha Sigma Lamda, Latinos Unidos, Christian Fellowship. *Campus security:* 24-hour emergency response devices and patrols, late-night transport/escort service.

Athletics Member NJCAA. *Intercollegiate sports:* baseball M(s), basketball M(s)/W(s), cross-country running M(s)/W(s), golf M(s), soccer M(s), softball W(s), tennis M(s), volleyball W(s), wrestling M(s). *Intramural sports:* basketball M/W, bowling M/W, golf M/W, table tennis M/W, volleyball M/W.

Costs (2004–05) *Tuition:* area resident $1620 full-time, $54 per semester hour part-time; state resident $5914 full-time, $197 per semester hour part-time; nonresident $6840 full-time, $228 per semester hour part-time. *Required fees:* $36 full-time, $1 per credit hour part-time, $3 per term part-time.

Financial Aid Of all full-time matriculated undergraduates who enrolled, 23 Federal Work-Study jobs (averaging $2000).

Applying *Application fee:* $10. *Application deadline:* rolling (freshmen), rolling (transfers).

Admissions Contact Ms. Faith LaShure, Recruitment and Retention Manager, Waubonsee Community College, Route 47 at Waubonsee Drive, Sugar Grove, IL 60554. *Phone:* 630-466-7900 Ext. 2938. *Fax:* 630-466-4964. *E-mail:* recruitment@waubonsee.edu.

WESTWOOD COLLEGE-CHICAGO DU PAGE
Woodridge, Illinois

- **Proprietary** primarily 2-year
- **Calendar** continuous
- **Degrees** associate and bachelor's
- **Suburban** campus with easy access to Chicago, IL
- **Coed,** 470 undergraduate students, 89% full-time, 24% women, 76% men

Undergraduates 420 full-time, 50 part-time. 10% are from out of state, 12% African American, 3% Asian American or Pacific Islander, 12% Hispanic American, 0.2% Native American, 0.4% international.

Freshmen *Admission:* 881 applied, 354 admitted, 227 enrolled.

Faculty *Total:* 46, 2% with terminal degrees.

Majors Accounting; accounting and business/management; architectural drafting and CAD/CADD; commercial and advertising art; computer and information systems security; computer programming; computer programming (specific applications); computer software engineering; computer systems networking and telecommunications; corrections and criminal justice related; design and applied arts related; design and visual communications; e-commerce; graphic design; interior design; intermedia/multimedia; marketing/marketing management; system, networking, and LAN/wan management; web/multimedia management and webmaster.

Applying *Required:* interview, entrance exam (SAT, ACT or Accuplacer) and H.S. diploma or GED.

Admissions Contact Mr. Scott Kawall, Director of Admissions, Westwood College-Chicago Du Page, 7155 James Avenue, Woodridge, IL 60517-2321.

Phone: 630-434-8244. *Toll-free phone:* 888-721-7646. *Fax:* 630-434-8255. *E-mail:* info@westwood.edu.

▶ **See page 616 for a narrative description.**

WESTWOOD COLLEGE-CHICAGO O'HARE AIRPORT
Schiller Park, Illinois

- **Proprietary** primarily 2-year
- **Calendar** continuous
- **Degrees** associate and bachelor's
- **Urban** campus with easy access to Chicago
- **Coed,** 425 undergraduate students, 74% full-time, 28% women, 72% men

Undergraduates 315 full-time, 110 part-time. 10% are from out of state, 12% African American, 8% Asian American or Pacific Islander, 28% Hispanic American, 0.5% Native American.

Freshmen *Admission:* 399 applied, 367 enrolled.

Faculty *Total:* 32.

Majors Accounting; accounting and business/management; architectural drafting and CAD/CADD; commercial and advertising art; computer and information systems security; computer programming; computer software engineering; computer systems networking and telecommunications; corrections and criminal justice related; design and applied arts related; design and visual communications; e-commerce; graphic design; interior design; intermedia/multimedia; marketing/marketing management; system, networking, and LAN/wan management; web/multimedia management and webmaster.

Applying *Required:* essay or personal statement, interview, entrance exam (SAT, ACT or ACCUPLACER) and H.S. diploma/GED.

Admissions Contact Mr. David Traub, Director of Admissions, Westwood College-Chicago O'Hare Airport, 4825 North Scott Street, Suite 100, Schiller Park, IL 60176-1209. *Phone:* 847-928-0200 Ext. 100. *Toll-free phone:* 877-877-8857. *E-mail:* info@westwood.edu.

▶ **See page 620 for a narrative description.**

WESTWOOD COLLEGE-CHICAGO RIVER OAKS
Calumet City, Illinois

- **Proprietary** primarily 2-year
- **Calendar** continuous
- **Degrees** associate and bachelor's
- **Suburban** campus with easy access to Chicago
- **Coed,** 650 undergraduate students, 91% full-time, 38% women, 62% men

Undergraduates 592 full-time, 58 part-time. 62% African American, 15% Hispanic American, 0.2% Native American.

Freshmen *Admission:* 574 applied, 316 admitted, 92 enrolled.

Faculty *Total:* 77.

Majors Accounting and business/management; architectural drafting and CAD/CADD; computer and information systems security; computer programming; computer programming (specific applications); computer systems networking and telecommunications; corrections and criminal justice related; design and visual communications; e-commerce; graphic design; interior design; intermedia/multimedia; marketing/marketing management; system, networking, and LAN/wan management; web/multimedia management and webmaster.

Applying *Required:* interview, HS diploma or GED and passing scores on entrance exam (ACT/SAT or Accuplacer).

Admissions Contact Tash Uray, Director of Admissions, Westwood College-Chicago River Oaks, 80 River Oaks Drive, Suite D-49, Calumet City, IL 60409-5820. *Phone:* 708-832-1988. *Toll-free phone:* 888-549-6873. *Fax:* 708-832-9617. *E-mail:* info@westwood.edu.

▶ **See page 622 for a narrative description.**

WESTWOOD COLLEGE-CHICAGO LOOP CAMPUS
Chicago, Illinois

- **Proprietary** primarily 2-year, founded 2002
- **Degrees** associate and bachelor's
- **Coed,** 106 undergraduate students, 99% full-time, 46% women, 54% men

Undergraduates 105 full-time, 1 part-time. 66% African American, 0.9% Asian American or Pacific Islander, 24% Hispanic American.

Freshmen *Admission:* 163 applied, 111 admitted, 106 enrolled.

Faculty *Total:* 15, 7% with terminal degrees.

Majors Accounting and business/management; architectural drafting and CAD/CADD; computer and information systems security; computer programming; computer programming (specific applications); computer software and media applications related; computer systems networking and telecommunications; design and visual communications; graphic design; interior design; intermedia/multimedia; marketing/marketing management; web/multimedia management and webmaster; web page, digital/multimedia and information resources design.

Applying *Required:* interview, HS diploma or GED, and passing SAT/ACT or Accuplacer scores.

Admissions Contact Gus Pyrolis, Acting Director of Admissions, Westwood College of Technology-Chicago Loop Campus, 17 North State Street, Suite 1500, Chicago, IL 60602. *Phone:* 312-739-0850. *E-mail:* info@westwood.edu.

▶ **See page 618 for a narrative description.**

WILLIAM RAINEY HARPER COLLEGE
Palatine, Illinois

- **State and locally supported** 2-year, founded 1965, part of Illinois Community College Board
- **Calendar** semesters
- **Degree** certificates and associate
- **Suburban** 200-acre campus with easy access to Chicago
- **Endowment** $2.5 million
- **Coed**

Faculty *Student/faculty ratio:* 5:1.

Student Life *Campus security:* 24-hour emergency response devices and patrols, late-night transport/escort service.

Athletics Member NJCAA.

Standardized Tests *Required for some:* SAT I or ACT (for placement).

Costs (2004–05) *Tuition:* $71 per credit hour part-time; state resident $281 per credit hour part-time; nonresident $348 per credit hour part-time.

Financial Aid Of all full-time matriculated undergraduates who enrolled, 85 Federal Work-Study jobs (averaging $1210).

Applying *Options:* electronic application, early admission, deferred entrance. *Application fee:* $25. *Required:* high school transcript. *Required for some:* minimum 2.0 GPA.

Admissions Contact William Rainey Harper College, 1200 West Algonquin Road, Palatine, IL 60067. *Phone:* 847-925-6206. *Fax:* 847-925-6044.

WORSHAM COLLEGE OF MORTUARY SCIENCE
Wheeling, Illinois

- **Independent** 2-year
- **Calendar** quarters
- **Degree** associate
- **Coed,** 115 undergraduate students

Undergraduates 20% African American, 10% Asian American or Pacific Islander, 10% Hispanic American.

Freshmen *Admission:* 70 applied, 70 admitted.

Faculty *Total:* 12. *Student/faculty ratio:* 10:1.

Majors Funeral service and mortuary science.

Costs (2003–04) *Tuition:* $13,300 full-time. *Required fees:* $275 full-time.

Admissions Contact Ms. Stephanie Kann, President, Worsham College of Mortuary Science, 495 Northgate Parkway, Wheeling, IL 60090-2646. *Phone:* 847-808-8444.

INDIANA

AMERICAN TRANS AIR AVIATION TRAINING ACADEMY
Indianapolis, Indiana

Admissions Contact American Trans Air Aviation Training Academy, 7251 West McCarty Street, Indianapolis, IN 46241. *Toll-free phone:* 800-241-9699.

ANCILLA COLLEGE
Donaldson, Indiana

- **Independent Roman Catholic** 2-year, founded 1937
- **Calendar** semesters
- **Degree** certificates and associate
- **Rural** 63-acre campus with easy access to Chicago
- **Endowment** $96,559
- **Coed,** 602 undergraduate students, 63% full-time, 69% women, 31% men

Undergraduates 382 full-time, 220 part-time. Students come from 2 states and territories, 4 other countries, 1% are from out of state, 4% African American, 0.3% Asian American or Pacific Islander, 4% Hispanic American, 1% Native American, 0.5% international, 7% transferred in. *Retention:* 55% of 2002 full-time freshmen returned.

Freshmen *Admission:* 396 applied, 274 admitted, 179 enrolled. *Average high school GPA:* 2.50. *Test scores:* SAT verbal scores over 500: 27%; SAT math scores over 500: 23%; ACT scores over 18: 32%; SAT verbal scores over 600: 4%; SAT math scores over 600: 6%; ACT scores over 24: 15%; SAT math scores over 700: 1%.

Faculty *Total:* 53, 32% full-time, 11% with terminal degrees. *Student/faculty ratio:* 15:1.

Majors Biology/biological sciences; business administration and management; business operations support and secretarial services related; chemistry; computer programming; computer software and media applications related; computer systems networking and telecommunications; criminal justice/law enforcement administration; elementary education; fine arts related; health/medical preparatory programs related; humanities; liberal arts and sciences/liberal studies; mathematics; social sciences.

Academic Programs *Special study options:* academic remediation for entering students, adult/continuing education programs, advanced placement credit, cooperative education, double majors, independent study, part-time degree program, services for LD students, summer session for credit.

Library Ball Library with 28,199 titles, 179 serial subscriptions, 1,426 audiovisual materials, an OPAC, a Web page.

Computers on Campus 82 computers available on campus for general student use. A campuswide network can be accessed. Internet access, at least one staffed computer lab available. Computer purchase or lease plan available.

Student Life *Housing:* college housing not available. *Activities and Organizations:* student-run newspaper, Student Senate, Scripta Literary Magazine, Ancilla student ambassadors. *Campus security:* 24-hour patrols, late-night transport/escort service. *Student services:* personal/psychological counseling.

Athletics Member NJCAA. *Intercollegiate sports:* baseball M(s), basketball M(s)/W(s), golf M(s), softball W(s), tennis M(s)/W(s).

Costs (2004–05) *Tuition:* $8700 full-time, $290 per credit hour part-time. *Required fees:* $200 full-time, $50 per term part-time.

Financial Aid Of all full-time matriculated undergraduates who enrolled, 28 Federal Work-Study jobs (averaging $1820). 16 state and other part-time jobs (averaging $1000). *Financial aid deadline:* 3/1.

Applying *Options:* common application, electronic application. *Application fee:* $25. *Required:* high school transcript. *Recommended:* interview. *Application deadline:* rolling (freshmen), rolling (transfers).

Admissions Contact Mr. Jim Bastis, Executive Director of Enrollment Management, Ancilla College, 9601 Union Road, Donaldson, IN 46513. *Phone:* 574-936-8898 Ext. 350. *Toll-free phone:* 866-262-4552 Ext. 350. *Fax:* 574-935-1773. *E-mail:* admissions@ancilla.edu.

COLLEGE OF COURT REPORTING
Hobart, Indiana

- **Proprietary** 2-year
- **Degree** certificates, diplomas, and associate
- **Coed, primarily women**

Faculty *Student/faculty ratio:* 8:1.

Costs (2003–04) *One-time required fee:* $50. *Tuition:* $215 per credit hour part-time. *Required fees:* $375 per term part-time.

Admissions Contact Ms. Stacy Drohosky, Director of Admissions, College of Court Reporting, 111 West Tenth Street, Suite 111, Hobart, IN 46342. *Phone:* 219-942-1459 Ext. 226. *Fax:* 219-942-1631. *E-mail:* dmiller@ccredu.com.

COMMONWEALTH BUSINESS COLLEGE
Merrillville, Indiana

- **Proprietary** 2-year, founded 1890, part of American Education Centers
- **Calendar** quarters
- **Degree** certificates and associate
- **Small-town** 2-acre campus with easy access to Chicago

Indiana

Commonwealth Business College (continued)
■ **Coed,** 450 undergraduate students

Freshmen *Admission:* 477 admitted.
Faculty *Total:* 12, 25% full-time.
Majors Accounting; business administration and management; information science/studies; legal assistant/paralegal; management information systems; medical/clinical assistant.
Academic Programs *Special study options:* internships, student-designed majors, summer session for credit.
Computers on Campus 150 computers available on campus for general student use. At least one staffed computer lab available.
Student Life *Housing:* college housing not available. *Campus security:* 24-hour emergency response devices.
Standardized Tests *Required:* ACT ASSET (for placement).
Costs (2004–05) *Tuition:* $159 per credit hour part-time.
Financial Aid Of all full-time matriculated undergraduates who enrolled, 2 Federal Work-Study jobs.
Applying *Options:* common application, early admission, deferred entrance. *Application fee:* $20. *Required:* high school transcript. *Application deadline:* rolling (freshmen), rolling (transfers). *Notification:* continuous (freshmen), continuous (transfers).
Admissions Contact Ms. Sheryl Elston, Director of Admissions, Commonwealth Business College, 1000 East 80th Place, Suite 101, N, Merrillville, IN 46410. *Phone:* 219-769-3321. *Fax:* 219-738-1076.

COMMONWEALTH BUSINESS COLLEGE
Michigan City, Indiana

■ **Proprietary** 2-year, founded 1890, part of Commonwealth Business College, Inc
■ **Calendar** quarters
■ **Degree** certificates, diplomas, and associate
■ **Rural** 2-acre campus with easy access to Chicago
■ **Coed,** 200 undergraduate students

Undergraduates Students come from 2 states and territories.
Faculty *Total:* 11, 27% full-time.
Majors Accounting; administrative assistant and secretarial science; business administration and management; computer typography and composition equipment operation; legal administrative assistant/secretary; medical administrative assistant and medical secretary; medical/clinical assistant.
Academic Programs *Special study options:* adult/continuing education programs, advanced placement credit, internships, part-time degree program, student-designed majors, summer session for credit.
Computers on Campus 24 computers available on campus for general student use. At least one staffed computer lab available.
Student Life *Housing:* college housing not available. *Activities and Organizations:* student-run newspaper. *Campus security:* 24-hour emergency response devices.
Standardized Tests *Required:* ABLE, Wonderlic aptitude test (for placement).
Costs (2004–05) *Tuition:* $159 per credit hour part-time.
Applying *Options:* early admission, deferred entrance. *Application fee:* $25. *Required:* high school transcript. *Application deadline:* rolling (freshmen), rolling (transfers). *Notification:* continuous (freshmen), continuous (transfers).
Admissions Contact Ms. Sheryl Elston, Director of Admissions, Commonwealth Business College, 325 East US Highway 20, Michigan City, IN 46360. *Phone:* 219-877-3100.

DAVENPORT UNIVERSITY
Granger, Indiana

Admissions Contact Davenport University, 7121 Grape Road, Granger, IN 46530. *Toll-free phone:* 800-277-8447.

DAVENPORT UNIVERSITY
Hammond, Indiana

Admissions Contact 5727 Solh Avenue, Hammond, IN 46320. *Toll-free phone:* 800-994-2894.

DAVENPORT UNIVERSITY
Merrillville, Indiana

Admissions Contact 8200 Georgia Street, Merrillville, IN 46410. *Toll-free phone:* 800-748-7880.

HOLY CROSS COLLEGE
Notre Dame, Indiana

■ **Independent Roman Catholic** primarily 2-year, founded 1966
■ **Calendar** semesters
■ **Degrees** associate and bachelor's
■ **Urban** 150-acre campus
■ **Coed,** 492 undergraduate students, 96% full-time, 37% women, 63% men

Undergraduates 471 full-time, 21 part-time. Students come from 12 other countries, 46% are from out of state, 7% transferred in, 50% live on campus.
Freshmen *Admission:* 459 applied, 238 enrolled. *Average high school GPA:* 3.00.
Faculty *Total:* 42, 60% full-time, 29% with terminal degrees. *Student/faculty ratio:* 17:1.
Majors Liberal arts and sciences/liberal studies.
Academic Programs *Special study options:* academic remediation for entering students, advanced placement credit, English as a second language, off-campus study, part-time degree program, summer session for credit. *ROTC:* Army (c), Air Force (c).
Library Holy Cross Library with 15,000 titles, 160 serial subscriptions, an OPAC.
Computers on Campus 60 computers available on campus for general student use. A campuswide network can be accessed from student residence rooms and from off campus. Internet access, at least one staffed computer lab available.
Student Life *Housing Options:* coed. *Activities and Organizations:* drama/theater group, student-run newspaper, choral group, Student Advisory Committee, Campus Ministry, Volunteers in Support of Admissions, intramural athletics. *Campus security:* 24-hour emergency response devices, 24-hour patrols by trained personnel on certain days. *Student services:* personal/psychological counseling.
Athletics *Intramural sports:* basketball M/W, football M/W, golf M/W, volleyball M/W.
Standardized Tests *Required:* SAT I or ACT (for admission).
Costs (2004–05) *Comprehensive fee:* $18,000 includes full-time tuition ($10,500), mandatory fees ($400), and room and board ($7100). Part-time tuition: $345 per semester hour.
Financial Aid Of all full-time matriculated undergraduates who enrolled, 54 Federal Work-Study jobs (averaging $857).
Applying *Options:* common application, electronic application, deferred entrance. *Application fee:* $50. *Required:* essay or personal statement, high school transcript, minimum 2.0 GPA. *Recommended:* interview. *Application deadline:* rolling (freshmen), rolling (transfers).
Admissions Contact Office of Admissions, Holy Cross College, PO Box 308, Notre Dame, IN 46556. *Phone:* 574-239-8400. *Fax:* 574-233-7427. *E-mail:* vduke@hcc-nd.edu.

► See page 552 for a narrative description.

INDIANA BUSINESS COLLEGE
Anderson, Indiana

■ **Proprietary** 2-year, founded 1902
■ **Calendar** quarters
■ **Degree** certificates, diplomas, and associate
■ **Coed,** 216 undergraduate students

Faculty *Student/faculty ratio:* 20:1.
Majors Accounting; administrative assistant and secretarial science; business administration and management; business administration, management and operations related; health information/medical records technology; medical/clinical assistant.
Academic Programs *Special study options:* adult/continuing education programs, cooperative education, distance learning, double majors, internships, part-time degree program.
Computers on Campus Internet access, online (class) registration available.
Costs (2003–04) *Tuition:* Full and part-time tuition varies by program.
Applying *Options:* electronic application, early admission. *Application fee:* $30. *Required:* high school transcript, interview. *Application deadline:* rolling (freshmen), rolling (transfers). *Notification:* continuous (freshmen), continuous (transfers).
Admissions Contact Ms. Charlene Stacy, Executive Director, Indiana Business College, 140 East 53rd Street, Anderson, IN 46013. *Phone:* 765-644-7514. *Toll-free phone:* 800-IBC-GRAD. *Fax:* 765-644-5724.

184 *www.petersons.com*

Peterson's Two-Year Colleges 2005

INDIANA BUSINESS COLLEGE
Columbus, Indiana

- **Proprietary** 2-year
- **Calendar** quarters
- **Degree** certificates, diplomas, and associate
- **Coed**, 296 undergraduate students

Undergraduates Students come from 4 states and territories.
Faculty *Student/faculty ratio:* 20:1.
Majors Accounting; administrative assistant and secretarial science; business administration and management; business administration, management and operations related; computer and information sciences and support services related; health professions related; information technology; management information systems and services related; medical/clinical assistant.
Academic Programs *Special study options:* adult/continuing education programs, cooperative education, distance learning, double majors, internships, part-time degree program.
Computers on Campus Internet access, online (class) registration available.
Costs (2003–04) *Tuition:* Full and part-time tuition varies by program.
Applying *Options:* electronic application. *Application fee:* $30. *Required:* high school transcript, interview. *Application deadline:* rolling (freshmen), rolling (transfers). *Notification:* continuous (freshmen), continuous (transfers).
Admissions Contact Mr. Gary McGee, Regional Director, Indiana Business College, 2222 Poshard Drive, Columbus, IN 47203. *Phone:* 812-379-9000. *Toll-free phone:* 800-IBC-GRAD. *Fax:* 812-375-0414.

INDIANA BUSINESS COLLEGE
Evansville, Indiana

- **Proprietary** 2-year
- **Calendar** quarters
- **Degree** certificates and associate
- **Coed**, 271 undergraduate students

Undergraduates Students come from 4 states and territories.
Faculty *Student/faculty ratio:* 20:1.
Majors Accounting; administrative assistant and secretarial science; business administration and management; computer programming (specific applications); health information/medical records administration; information technology; medical/clinical assistant.
Academic Programs *Special study options:* adult/continuing education programs, cooperative education, distance learning, double majors, internships, part-time degree program.
Computers on Campus Internet access, online (class) registration available.
Costs (2003–04) *Tuition:* Full and part-time tuition varies by program.
Applying *Options:* electronic application. *Application fee:* $30. *Required:* high school transcript, interview. *Application deadline:* rolling (freshmen), rolling (transfers). *Notification:* continuous (freshmen), continuous (transfers).
Admissions Contact Mr. Steve Hardin, Executive Director, Indiana Business College, 4601 Theater Drive, Evansville, IN 47715. *Phone:* 812-476-6000. *Toll-free phone:* 800-IBC-GRAD. *Fax:* 812-471-8576.

INDIANA BUSINESS COLLEGE
Fort Wayne, Indiana

- **Proprietary** 2-year
- **Calendar** quarters
- **Degree** certificates and associate
- **Coed**, 268 undergraduate students

Faculty *Student/faculty ratio:* 20:1.
Majors Accounting; administrative assistant and secretarial science; business administration and management; health professions related; medical/clinical assistant.
Academic Programs *Special study options:* adult/continuing education programs, cooperative education, distance learning, double majors, internships, part-time degree program.
Computers on Campus Internet access, online (class) registration available.
Costs (2003–04) *Tuition:* Full-time tuition and fees vary according to program. Part-time tuition and fees vary according to program. Full and part-time tuition varies by program.
Applying *Options:* electronic application. *Application fee:* $30. *Required:* high school transcript, interview. *Application deadline:* rolling (freshmen), rolling (transfers). *Notification:* continuous (freshmen), continuous (transfers).
Admissions Contact Ms. Janet Hein, Executive Director, Indiana Business College, 6413 North Clinton Street, Fort Wayne, IN 46825. *Phone:* 219-471-7667. *Toll-free phone:* 800-IBC-GRAD. *Fax:* 219-471-6918.

INDIANA BUSINESS COLLEGE
Indianapolis, Indiana

- **Proprietary** 2-year, founded 1902
- **Calendar** quarters
- **Degree** certificates, diplomas, and associate
- **Urban** 1-acre campus
- **Coed**, 768 undergraduate students

Undergraduates Students come from 4 states and territories.
Faculty *Student/faculty ratio:* 20:1.
Majors Accounting; administrative assistant and secretarial science; business administration and management; business administration, management and operations related; computer and information sciences; computer and information sciences and support services related; computer programming; computer programming (specific applications); fashion merchandising; information technology; legal administrative assistant/secretary; management information systems and services related.
Academic Programs *Special study options:* adult/continuing education programs, cooperative education, distance learning, double majors, internships, part-time degree program, summer session for credit.
Computers on Campus Internet access, online (class) registration available.
Student Life *Housing:* college housing not available. *Activities and Organizations:* Student Advisory Board, Student Ambassadors, Phi Beta Lambda. *Campus security:* 24-hour patrols.
Costs (2003–04) *Tuition:* Full and part-time tuition varies by program.
Applying *Options:* electronic application. *Application fee:* $30. *Required:* high school transcript, interview. *Application deadline:* rolling (freshmen), rolling (transfers). *Notification:* continuous (freshmen), continuous (transfers).
Admissions Contact Ms. Donna Reed, Regional Director, Indiana Business College, 550 East Washington Street, Indianapolis, IN 46204. *Phone:* 317-264-5656. *Toll-free phone:* 800-IBC-GRAD. *Fax:* 317-264-5650.

▶ **See page 554 for a narrative description.**

INDIANA BUSINESS COLLEGE
Lafayette, Indiana

- **Proprietary** 2-year
- **Calendar** quarters
- **Degree** certificates and associate
- **Coed**, 240 undergraduate students

Faculty *Student/faculty ratio:* 20:1.
Majors Accounting; administrative assistant and secretarial science; business administration and management; business administration, management and operations related; computer and information sciences and support services related; information technology; management information systems and services related.
Academic Programs *Special study options:* adult/continuing education programs, cooperative education, distance learning, double majors, internships, part-time degree program.
Computers on Campus Internet access, online (class) registration available.
Costs (2003–04) *Tuition:* Full and part-time tuition varies by program.
Applying *Options:* electronic application. *Application fee:* $30. *Required:* high school transcript, interview. *Application deadline:* rolling (freshmen), rolling (transfers). *Notification:* continuous (freshmen), continuous (transfers).
Admissions Contact Mr. Greg Reger, Executive Director, Indiana Business College, 2 Executive Drive, Lafayette, IN 47905. *Phone:* 765-447-9550. *Toll-free phone:* 800-IBC-GRAD. *Fax:* 765-447-0868.

INDIANA BUSINESS COLLEGE
Marion, Indiana

- **Proprietary** 2-year
- **Calendar** quarters
- **Degree** certificates, diplomas, and associate
- **Coed**, 184 undergraduate students

Undergraduates Students come from 4 states and territories.
Faculty *Student/faculty ratio:* 20:1.
Majors Accounting; administrative assistant and secretarial science; business administration and management; health and medical administrative services related.
Academic Programs *Special study options:* adult/continuing education programs, cooperative education, distance learning, double majors, internships, part-time degree program.
Computers on Campus Internet access, online (class) registration available.
Costs (2003–04) *Tuition:* Full and part-time tuition varies by program.

Indiana

Indiana Business College (continued)

Applying *Options:* electronic application. *Application fee:* $30. *Required:* high school transcript, minimum 2.0 GPA, interview. *Application deadline:* rolling (freshmen), rolling (transfers). *Notification:* continuous (freshmen), continuous (transfers).

Admissions Contact Mr. Richard Herman, Executive Director, Indiana Business College, 830 North Miller Avenue, Marion, IN 46952. *Phone:* 765-662-7497. *Toll-free phone:* 800-IBC-GRAD. *Fax:* 765-651-6421.

INDIANA BUSINESS COLLEGE
Muncie, Indiana

- **Proprietary** 2-year
- **Calendar** quarters
- **Degree** certificates, diplomas, and associate
- **Coed,** 335 undergraduate students

Undergraduates Students come from 4 states and territories.
Faculty *Student/faculty ratio:* 20:1.
Majors Accounting; administrative assistant and secretarial science; business administration and management; business administration, management and operations related; computer and information sciences and support services related; computer programming (specific applications); health information/medical records technology; information technology; management information systems and services related; medical office assistant.
Academic Programs *Special study options:* cooperative education, distance learning, double majors, internships, part-time degree program.
Computers on Campus Internet access, online (class) registration available.
Student Life *Housing:* college housing not available. *Activities and Organizations:* Phi Beta Lambda.
Costs (2003–04) *Tuition:* Full and part-time tuition varies by program.
Applying *Options:* electronic application. *Application fee:* $30. *Required:* high school transcript, interview. *Application deadline:* rolling (freshmen), rolling (transfers). *Notification:* continuous (freshmen), continuous (transfers).
Admissions Contact Mr. Gregory Bond, Executive Director, Indiana Business College, 411 West Riggin Road, Muncie, IN 47303. *Phone:* 765-288-8681. *Toll-free phone:* 800-IBC-GRAD. *Fax:* 765-288-8797.

INDIANA BUSINESS COLLEGE
Terre Haute, Indiana

- **Proprietary** 2-year, founded 1902
- **Calendar** quarters
- **Degree** certificates, diplomas, and associate
- **Coed,** 279 undergraduate students

Faculty *Student/faculty ratio:* 20:1.
Majors Accounting; administrative assistant and secretarial science; business administration and management; business administration, management and operations related; computer and information sciences and support services related; computer programming (specific applications); health professions related; information technology; management information systems and services related; medical/clinical assistant.
Academic Programs *Special study options:* adult/continuing education programs, cooperative education, distance learning, double majors, internships, part-time degree program.
Computers on Campus Internet access, online (class) registration available.
Costs (2003–04) *Tuition:* Full and part-time tuition varies by program.
Applying *Options:* electronic application. *Application fee:* $30. *Required:* high school transcript, interview. *Application deadline:* rolling (freshmen), rolling (transfers). *Notification:* continuous (freshmen), continuous (transfers).
Admissions Contact Ms. Laura Hale, Executive Director, Indiana Business College, 3175 South Third Place, Terre Haute, IN 47802. *Phone:* 812-234-2361. *Toll-free phone:* 800-IBC-GRAD. *Fax:* 812-234-2361.

INDIANA BUSINESS COLLEGE-MEDICAL
Indianapolis, Indiana

- **Proprietary** 2-year
- **Calendar** quarters
- **Degree** certificates, diplomas, and associate
- **Coed,** 624 undergraduate students

Undergraduates Students come from 4 states and territories.
Faculty *Student/faculty ratio:* 20:1.
Majors Health and physical education related; health professions related; massage therapy; medical/clinical assistant.

Academic Programs *Special study options:* adult/continuing education programs, cooperative education, distance learning, double majors, internships, part-time degree program.
Computers on Campus Internet access, online (class) registration available.
Costs (2003–04) *Tuition:* Full and part-time tuition varies by program.
Applying *Options:* electronic application. *Application fee:* $30. *Required:* high school transcript, interview. *Application deadline:* rolling (freshmen), rolling (transfers). *Notification:* continuous (freshmen), continuous (transfers).
Admissions Contact Ms. Pam Soladine-Davis, Regional Director, Indiana Business College-Medical, 8150 Brookville Road, Indianapolis, IN 46239. *Phone:* 317-375-8000. *Toll-free phone:* 800-IBC-6611. *Fax:* 317-351-1871.

INTERNATIONAL BUSINESS COLLEGE
Fort Wayne, Indiana

- **Proprietary** primarily 2-year, founded 1889, part of Bradford Schools, Inc.
- **Calendar** semesters
- **Degrees** diplomas, associate, and bachelor's
- **Suburban** 2-acre campus
- **Coed, primarily women**

Faculty *Student/faculty ratio:* 24:1.
Student Life *Campus security:* controlled dormitory access.
Costs (2003–04) *Tuition:* $10,100 full-time. *Room only:* $4600.
Applying *Options:* deferred entrance. *Application fee:* $50. *Required:* high school transcript.
Admissions Contact Mr. Steve Kinzer, School Director, International Business College, 5699 Coventry Lane, Fort Wayne, IN 46804. *Phone:* 219-459-4513. *Toll-free phone:* 800-589-6363. *Fax:* 219-436-1896.

INTERNATIONAL BUSINESS COLLEGE
Indianapolis, Indiana

- **Proprietary** 2-year
- **Calendar** semesters
- **Degree** diplomas and associate
- **Coed**

Faculty *Student/faculty ratio:* 20:1.
Costs (2004–05) *Tuition:* $10,800 full-time. *Required fees:* $300 full-time. *Room only:* $5000.
Applying *Options:* common application, electronic application. *Required:* high school transcript.
Admissions Contact Ms. Kathy Chiudioni, Director of Admissions, International Business College, 7205 Shadeland Station, Indianapolis, IN 46256. *Phone:* 317-213-2320. *E-mail:* info@intlbusinesscollege.com.

ITT TECHNICAL INSTITUTE
Fort Wayne, Indiana

- **Proprietary** primarily 2-year, founded 1967, part of ITT Educational Services, Inc.
- **Calendar** quarters
- **Degrees** associate and bachelor's
- **Coed**

Standardized Tests *Required:* Wonderlic aptitude test (for admission).
Costs (2003–04) *Tuition:* Total Program Cost varies depending on course of study. Consult school catalog.
Applying *Options:* deferred entrance. *Application fee:* $100. *Required:* high school transcript, interview. *Recommended:* letters of recommendation.
Admissions Contact Mr. Michael D. Frantom, ITT Technical Institute, 4919 Coldwater Road, Fort Wayne, IN 46825. *Phone:* 260-484-4107. *Toll-free phone:* 800-866-4488. *Fax:* 260-484-0860.

ITT TECHNICAL INSTITUTE
Newburgh, Indiana

- **Proprietary** primarily 2-year, founded 1966, part of ITT Educational Services, Inc.
- **Calendar** quarters
- **Degrees** associate and bachelor's
- **Coed**

Standardized Tests *Required:* Wonderlic aptitude test (for admission).
Costs (2003–04) *Tuition:* Total Program Cost varies depending on course of study. Consult school catalog.

Applying *Options:* deferred entrance. *Application fee:* $100. *Required:* high school transcript, interview. *Recommended:* letters of recommendation.

Admissions Contact Mr. Jim Smolinski, Director of Recruitment, ITT Technical Institute, 10999 Stahl Road, Newburgh, IN 47630. *Phone:* 812-858-1600. *Toll-free phone:* 800-832-4488. *Fax:* 812-858-0646.

ITT TECHNICAL INSTITUTE
Indianapolis, Indiana

- **Proprietary** founded 1966, part of ITT Educational Services, Inc.
- **Calendar** quarters
- **Degrees** diplomas, associate, and bachelor's
- **Suburban** 10-acre campus
- **Coed**

Standardized Tests *Required:* Wonderlic aptitude test (for admission).

Costs (2003–04) *Tuition:* Total Program Cost varies depending on course of study. Consult school catalog.

Applying *Options:* deferred entrance. *Application fee:* $100. *Required:* high school transcript, interview. *Recommended:* letters of recommendation.

Admissions Contact Ms. Martha Watson, ITT Technical Institute, 9511 Angola Court, Indianapolis, IN 46268. *Phone:* 317-875-8640. *Toll-free phone:* 800-937-4488. *Fax:* 317-875-8641.

IVY TECH STATE COLLEGE-BLOOMINGTON
Bloomington, Indiana

- **State-supported** 2-year, founded 2001, part of Ivy Tech State College System
- **Calendar** semesters
- **Degree** associate
- **Endowment** $11.2 million
- **Coed,** 2,858 undergraduate students, 42% full-time, 60% women, 40% men

Undergraduates 1,194 full-time, 1,664 part-time. 2% African American, 1% Asian American or Pacific Islander, 1% Hispanic American, 0.5% Native American, 0.5% international, 7% transferred in.

Freshmen *Admission:* 682 applied, 682 admitted, 396 enrolled.

Faculty *Total:* 226, 17% full-time.

Majors Accounting technology and bookkeeping; building/property maintenance and management; business administration and management; cabinetmaking and millwork; child care and support services management; computer and information sciences; criminal justice/safety; electrical, electronic and communications engineering technology; electrician; emergency medical technology (EMT paramedic); executive assistant/executive secretary; heating, air conditioning, ventilation and refrigeration maintenance technology; industrial technology; legal assistant/paralegal; liberal arts and sciences/liberal studies; machine tool technology; mechanics and repair; nursing (registered nurse training); pipefitting and sprinkler fitting; psychiatric/mental health services technology; tool and die technology.

Academic Programs *Special study options:* academic remediation for entering students, adult/continuing education programs, advanced placement credit, distance learning, external degree program, internships, part-time degree program, services for LD students, summer session for credit.

Library an OPAC, a Web page.

Computers on Campus 201 computers available on campus for general student use. Internet access, online (class) registration available.

Student Life *Activities and Organizations:* Student Government, Phi Theta Kappa. *Campus security:* late-night transport/escort service.

Standardized Tests *Required:* ACT ASSET (for placement).

Costs (2003–04) *Tuition:* state resident $2318 full-time, $77 per credit part-time; nonresident $4686 full-time, $156 per credit part-time. Full-time tuition and fees vary according to course load and reciprocity agreements. Part-time tuition and fees vary according to course load and reciprocity agreements. *Required fees:* $60 full-time, $30 per term part-time. *Payment plan:* installment. *Waivers:* employees or children of employees.

Financial Aid Of all full-time matriculated undergraduates who enrolled, 51 Federal Work-Study jobs (averaging $3259).

Applying *Options:* deferred entrance. *Required:* high school transcript. *Required for some:* interview. *Application deadline:* rolling (freshmen), rolling (transfers). *Notification:* continuous (freshmen), continuous (transfers).

Admissions Contact Mr. Neil Frederick, Assistant Director of Admissions, Ivy Tech State College-Bloomington, 200 Daniels Way, Bloomington, IN 47404-1511. *Phone:* 812-332-1559 Ext. 4118. *Fax:* 812-332-8147. *E-mail:* nfrederi@ivytech.edu.

IVY TECH STATE COLLEGE-CENTRAL INDIANA
Indianapolis, Indiana

- **State-supported** 2-year, founded 1963, part of Ivy Tech State College System
- **Calendar** semesters
- **Degree** associate
- **Urban** 10-acre campus
- **Endowment** $11.2 million
- **Coed,** 8,833 undergraduate students, 35% full-time, 63% women, 37% men

Undergraduates 3,129 full-time, 5,704 part-time. 24% African American, 1% Asian American or Pacific Islander, 1% Hispanic American, 0.3% Native American, 0.3% international, 8% transferred in.

Freshmen *Admission:* 2,972 applied, 2,972 admitted, 1,538 enrolled.

Faculty *Total:* 631, 19% full-time.

Majors Accounting technology and bookkeeping; automobile/automotive mechanics technology; building/property maintenance and management; business administration and management; cabinetmaking and millwork; carpentry; child care and support services management; child guidance; computer and information sciences; criminal justice/safety; design and visual communications; drafting and design technology; electrical, electronic and communications engineering technology; electrician; executive assistant/executive secretary; heating, air conditioning, ventilation and refrigeration maintenance technology; industrial technology; legal assistant/paralegal; liberal arts and sciences/liberal studies; machine shop technology; machine tool technology; masonry; mechanics and repair; medical/clinical assistant; medical radiologic technology; nursing (registered nurse training); occupational safety and health technology; occupational therapist assistant; painting and wall covering; pipefitting and sprinkler fitting; psychiatric/mental health services technology; respiratory care therapy; sheet metal technology; surgical technology; tool and die technology.

Academic Programs *Special study options:* academic remediation for entering students, adult/continuing education programs, advanced placement credit, cooperative education, distance learning, English as a second language, internships, off-campus study, part-time degree program, services for LD students, summer session for credit.

Library 19,444 titles, 300 serial subscriptions, 11,164 audiovisual materials, an OPAC, a Web page.

Computers on Campus 370 computers available on campus for general student use. Internet access, online (class) registration, at least one staffed computer lab available.

Student Life *Housing:* college housing not available. *Activities and Organizations:* student-run newspaper, Student Government, Phi Theta Kappa, Human Services Club, Administrative Office Assistants Club, Radiology Club. *Campus security:* 24-hour emergency response devices and patrols, late-night transport/escort service. *Student services:* personal/psychological counseling.

Standardized Tests *Required:* ACT ASSET (for placement).

Costs (2003–04) *Tuition:* state resident $2318 full-time, $77 per credit part-time; nonresident $4686 full-time, $156 per credit part-time. Full-time tuition and fees vary according to course load. Part-time tuition and fees vary according to course load. *Required fees:* $60 full-time, $30 per term part-time. *Payment plan:* installment. *Waivers:* senior citizens and employees or children of employees.

Financial Aid Of all full-time matriculated undergraduates who enrolled, 92 Federal Work-Study jobs (averaging $3766).

Applying *Options:* early admission, deferred entrance. *Required:* high school transcript. *Required for some:* interview. *Application deadline:* rolling (freshmen), rolling (transfers). *Notification:* continuous (freshmen), continuous (transfers).

Admissions Contact Ms. Sonia Dickerson, Director of Admissions, Ivy Tech State College-Central Indiana, One West 26th Street, Indianapolis, IN 46208-4777. *Phone:* 317-921-4882 Ext. 4612. *Toll-free phone:* 800-732-1470. *Fax:* 317-921-4753. *E-mail:* sdickers@ivytech.edu.

IVY TECH STATE COLLEGE-COLUMBUS
Columbus, Indiana

- **State-supported** 2-year, founded 1963, part of Ivy Tech State College System
- **Calendar** semesters
- **Degree** associate
- **Small-town** campus with easy access to Indianapolis
- **Endowment** $11.2 million
- **Coed,** 1,614 undergraduate students, 32% full-time, 71% women, 29% men

Undergraduates 523 full-time, 1,091 part-time. 1% African American, 0.6% Asian American or Pacific Islander, 0.7% Hispanic American, 0.7% Native American, 0.3% international, 5% transferred in.

Freshmen *Admission:* 315 applied, 315 admitted, 165 enrolled.

Faculty *Total:* 150, 21% full-time.

Ivy Tech State College-Columbus (continued)

Majors Accounting technology and bookkeeping; automobile/automotive mechanics technology; building/property maintenance and management; business administration and management; cabinetmaking and millwork; child care and support services management; computer and information sciences; design and visual communications; drafting and design technology; electrical and power transmission installation; electrical, electronic and communications engineering technology; executive assistant/executive secretary; heating, air conditioning, ventilation and refrigeration maintenance technology; industrial technology; legal assistant/paralegal; liberal arts and sciences/liberal studies; machine tool technology; masonry; mechanics and repair; medical/clinical assistant; medical radiologic technology; pipefitting and sprinkler fitting; psychiatric/mental health services technology; robotics technology; surgical technology; tool and die technology.

Academic Programs *Special study options:* academic remediation for entering students, adult/continuing education programs, advanced placement credit, distance learning, internships, part-time degree program, services for LD students, summer session for credit.

Library 216 serial subscriptions, 781 audiovisual materials, an OPAC, a Web page.

Computers on Campus 168 computers available on campus for general student use. Internet access, online (class) registration, at least one staffed computer lab available.

Student Life *Housing:* college housing not available. *Activities and Organizations:* Student Government, Phi Theta Kappa, LPN Club. *Campus security:* late-night transport/escort service, trained evening security personnel, escort service.

Standardized Tests *Required:* ACT ASSET (for placement).

Costs (2003–04) *Tuition:* state resident $2318 full-time, $77 per credit part-time; nonresident $4686 full-time, $156 per credit part-time. *Required fees:* $60 full-time, $30 per term part-time.

Financial Aid Of all full-time matriculated undergraduates who enrolled, 26 Federal Work-Study jobs (averaging $1694).

Applying *Options:* early admission, deferred entrance. *Required:* high school transcript. *Required for some:* interview. *Application deadline:* rolling (freshmen), rolling (transfers). *Notification:* continuous (freshmen), continuous (transfers).

Admissions Contact Mr. William Gardner, Director of Admissions, Ivy Tech State College-Columbus, 4475 Central Avenue, Columbus, IN 47203-1868. *Phone:* 812-372-9925 Ext. 129. *Toll-free phone:* 800-922-4838. *Fax:* 812-372-0311. *E-mail:* wgardner@ivytech.edu.

IVY TECH STATE COLLEGE-EASTCENTRAL

Muncie, Indiana

- **State-supported** 2-year, founded 1968, part of Ivy Tech State College System
- **Calendar** semesters
- **Degree** associate
- **Suburban** 15-acre campus with easy access to Indianapolis
- **Endowment** $11.2 million
- **Coed,** 5,443 undergraduate students, 45% full-time, 64% women, 36% men

Undergraduates 2,468 full-time, 2,975 part-time. 7% African American, 0.3% Asian American or Pacific Islander, 1% Hispanic American, 0.4% Native American, 0.1% international, 2% transferred in.

Freshmen *Admission:* 1,572 applied, 1,572 admitted, 1,220 enrolled.

Faculty *Total:* 405, 19% full-time.

Majors Accounting technology and bookkeeping; automobile/automotive mechanics technology; building/property maintenance and management; business administration and management; cabinetmaking and millwork; carpentry; child care and support services management; computer and information sciences; construction trades; criminal justice/safety; drafting and design technology; electrical, electronic and communications engineering technology; electrician; executive assistant/executive secretary; heating, air conditioning, ventilation and refrigeration maintenance technology; hospitality administration; industrial mechanics and maintenance technology; industrial technology; legal assistant/paralegal; liberal arts and sciences/liberal studies; machine tool technology; masonry; medical/clinical assistant; medical radiologic technology; nursing (registered nurse training); painting and wall covering; physical therapist assistant; pipefitting and sprinkler fitting; psychiatric/mental health services technology; surgical technology; tool and die technology.

Academic Programs *Special study options:* academic remediation for entering students, adult/continuing education programs, advanced placement credit, distance learning, internships, part-time degree program, services for LD students.

Library 5,314 titles, 250 serial subscriptions, 5,307 audiovisual materials, an OPAC, a Web page.

Computers on Campus 245 computers available on campus for general student use. A campuswide network can be accessed from off campus. Internet access, online (class) registration, at least one staffed computer lab available.

Student Life *Housing:* college housing not available. *Activities and Organizations:* Business Professionals of America, Skills USA-VICA, Student Government, Phi Theta Kappa, Human Services Club.

Standardized Tests *Required:* ACT ASSET (for placement).

Costs (2003–04) *Tuition:* state resident $2318 full-time, $77 per credit part-time; nonresident $4686 full-time, $156 per credit part-time. Full-time tuition and fees vary according to course load. Part-time tuition and fees vary according to course load. *Required fees:* $60 full-time, $30 per term part-time. *Payment plan:* installment. *Waivers:* senior citizens and employees or children of employees.

Financial Aid Of all full-time matriculated undergraduates who enrolled, 65 Federal Work-Study jobs (averaging $2666).

Applying *Options:* early admission, deferred entrance. *Required:* high school transcript. *Required for some:* interview. *Application deadline:* rolling (freshmen), rolling (transfers). *Notification:* continuous (freshmen), continuous (transfers).

Admissions Contact Corey Sharp, Recruitment/Outreach Specialist, Ivy Tech State College-Eastcentral, 4301 S Cowan Road, Muncie, IN 47302-9448. *Phone:* 765-289-2291. *Toll-free phone:* 800-589-8324. *Fax:* 765-289-2292. *E-mail:* csharp@ivytech.edu.

IVY TECH STATE COLLEGE-KOKOMO

Kokomo, Indiana

- **State-supported** 2-year, founded 1968, part of Ivy Tech State College System
- **Calendar** semesters
- **Degree** associate
- **Small-town** 20-acre campus with easy access to Indianapolis
- **Endowment** $11.2 million
- **Coed,** 2,522 undergraduate students, 33% full-time, 63% women, 37% men

Undergraduates 842 full-time, 1,680 part-time. 4% African American, 0.3% Asian American or Pacific Islander, 0.9% Hispanic American, 1% Native American, 3% transferred in.

Freshmen *Admission:* 627 applied, 627 admitted, 362 enrolled.

Faculty *Total:* 233, 33% full-time.

Majors Accounting technology and bookkeeping; automobile/automotive mechanics technology; building/property maintenance and management; business administration and management; cabinetmaking and millwork; child care and support services management; computer and information sciences; criminal justice/safety; drafting and design technology; electrical, electronic and communications engineering technology; electrician; emergency medical technology (EMT paramedic); executive assistant/executive secretary; heating, air conditioning, ventilation and refrigeration maintenance technology; industrial technology; legal assistant/paralegal; liberal arts and sciences/liberal studies; machine tool technology; mechanics and repair; medical/clinical assistant; pipefitting and sprinkler fitting; psychiatric/mental health services technology; surgical technology; tool and die technology.

Academic Programs *Special study options:* academic remediation for entering students, adult/continuing education programs, advanced placement credit, distance learning, internships, part-time degree program, services for LD students, summer session for credit.

Library 5,177 titles, 99 serial subscriptions, 772 audiovisual materials, an OPAC, a Web page.

Computers on Campus 290 computers available on campus for general student use. A campuswide network can be accessed from off campus. Internet access, online (class) registration, at least one staffed computer lab available.

Student Life *Housing:* college housing not available. *Activities and Organizations:* Student Government, Collegiate Secretaries International, Licensed Practical Nursing Club, Phi Theta Kappa. *Campus security:* 24-hour emergency response devices, late-night transport/escort service. *Student services:* personal/psychological counseling.

Standardized Tests *Required:* ACT ASSET (for placement).

Costs (2003–04) *Tuition:* state resident $2318 full-time, $77 per credit part-time; nonresident $4686 full-time, $156 per credit part-time. Full-time tuition and fees vary according to course load. Part-time tuition and fees vary according to course load. *Required fees:* $60 full-time, $30 per term part-time. *Payment plan:* installment. *Waivers:* senior citizens and employees or children of employees.

Financial Aid Of all full-time matriculated undergraduates who enrolled, 45 Federal Work-Study jobs (averaging $1829).

Applying *Options:* early admission. *Required:* high school transcript. *Required for some:* interview. *Application deadline:* rolling (freshmen), rolling (transfers). *Notification:* continuous (freshmen), continuous (transfers).

Admissions Contact Alayne Cook, Assistant Director of Admissions, Ivy Tech State College-Kokomo, 1815 E. Morgan Street, Kokomo, IN 46903-1373.

Phone: 765-459-0561 Ext. 318. *Toll-free phone:* 800-459-0561. *Fax:* 765-454-5111. *E-mail:* acook@ivytech.edu.

IVY TECH STATE COLLEGE-LAFAYETTE
Lafayette, Indiana

- **State-supported** 2-year, founded 1968, part of Ivy Tech State College System
- **Calendar** semesters
- **Degree** certificates and associate
- **Suburban** campus with easy access to Indianapolis
- **Endowment** $11.2 million
- **Coed**, 4,905 undergraduate students, 43% full-time, 51% women, 49% men

Undergraduates 2,103 full-time, 2,802 part-time. 3% African American, 0.9% Asian American or Pacific Islander, 3% Hispanic American, 0.5% Native American, 0.4% international, 6% transferred in.
Freshmen *Admission:* 1,003 applied, 1,003 admitted, 581 enrolled.
Faculty *Total:* 279, 21% full-time.
Majors Accounting; accounting technology and bookkeeping; automobile/automotive mechanics technology; building/property maintenance and management; business administration and management; cabinetmaking and millwork; carpentry; child care and support services management; computer and information sciences; drafting and design technology; electrical, electronic and communications engineering technology; electrician; executive assistant/executive secretary; heating, air conditioning, ventilation and refrigeration maintenance technology; industrial technology; ironworking; legal assistant/paralegal; liberal arts and sciences/liberal studies; lineworker; machine tool technology; masonry; mechanics and repair; medical/clinical assistant; nursing (registered nurse training); painting and wall covering; pipefitting and sprinkler fitting; psychiatric/mental health services technology; quality control technology; respiratory care therapy; sheet metal technology; surgical technology; tool and die technology.
Academic Programs *Special study options:* academic remediation for entering students, advanced placement credit, distance learning, internships, part-time degree program, services for LD students, summer session for credit.
Library 8,347 titles, 217 serial subscriptions, 1,946 audiovisual materials, an OPAC, a Web page.
Computers on Campus 243 computers available on campus for general student use. A campuswide network can be accessed. Internet access, online (class) registration, at least one staffed computer lab available.
Student Life *Housing:* college housing not available. *Activities and Organizations:* student-run newspaper, Student Government, Phi Theta Kappa, LPN Club, Accounting Club, Student Computer Technology Association. *Student services:* personal/psychological counseling.
Standardized Tests *Required:* ACT ASSET (for placement).
Costs (2003–04) *Tuition:* state resident $2318 full-time, $77 per credit part-time; nonresident $4686 full-time, $156 per credit part-time. Full-time tuition and fees vary according to course load. Part-time tuition and fees vary according to course load. *Required fees:* $60 full-time, $30 per term part-time. *Payment plan:* installment. *Waivers:* senior citizens and employees or children of employees.
Financial Aid Of all full-time matriculated undergraduates who enrolled, 65 Federal Work-Study jobs (averaging $2222). 1 state and other part-time job (averaging $2436).
Applying *Required:* high school transcript. *Required for some:* interview. *Application deadline:* rolling (freshmen), rolling (transfers). *Notification:* continuous (freshmen), continuous (transfers).
Admissions Contact Ms. Judy Dopplefeld, Director of Admissions, Ivy Tech State College-Lafayette, 3101 South Creagy Lane, PO Box 6299, Lafayette, IN 47903. *Phone:* 765-772-9116. *Toll-free phone:* 800-669-4882. *Fax:* 765-772-9107. *E-mail:* jdopplef@ivytech.edu.

IVY TECH STATE COLLEGE-NORTH CENTRAL
South Bend, Indiana

- **State-supported** 2-year, founded 1968, part of Ivy Tech State College System
- **Calendar** semesters
- **Degree** certificates and associate
- **Suburban** 4-acre campus
- **Endowment** $11.2 million
- **Coed**, 4,366 undergraduate students, 29% full-time, 60% women, 40% men

Undergraduates 1,250 full-time, 3,116 part-time. 1% are from out of state, 15% African American, 0.5% Asian American or Pacific Islander, 4% Hispanic American, 0.8% Native American, 0.5% international, 2% transferred in.
Freshmen *Admission:* 1,025 applied, 1,025 admitted, 567 enrolled.
Faculty *Total:* 303, 21% full-time.
Majors Accounting technology and bookkeeping; automobile/automotive mechanics technology; building/property maintenance and management; busi-

ness administration and management; cabinetmaking and millwork; carpentry; child care and support services management; clinical/medical laboratory technology; computer and information sciences; criminal justice/safety; design and visual communications; drafting and design technology; educational/instructional media design; electrical, electronic and communications engineering technology; electrician; emergency medical technology (EMT paramedic); executive assistant/executive secretary; heating, air conditioning, ventilation and refrigeration maintenance technology; hospitality administration; industrial technology; interior design; ironworking; legal assistant/paralegal; liberal arts and sciences/liberal studies; machine tool technology; masonry; mechanics and repair; medical/clinical assistant; nursing (registered nurse training); painting and wall covering; pipefitting and sprinkler fitting; sheet metal technology; tool and die technology.
Academic Programs *Special study options:* academic remediation for entering students, adult/continuing education programs, advanced placement credit, distance learning, English as a second language, internships, off-campus study, part-time degree program, services for LD students, summer session for credit.
Library 6,200 titles, 80 serial subscriptions, 737 audiovisual materials, an OPAC, a Web page.
Computers on Campus 394 computers available on campus for general student use. Internet access, online (class) registration, at least one staffed computer lab available.
Student Life *Housing:* college housing not available. *Activities and Organizations:* Phi Theta Kappa, Student Government, LPN Club. *Campus security:* 24-hour emergency response devices and patrols, late-night transport/escort service, security during open hours. *Student services:* personal/psychological counseling, women's center.
Standardized Tests *Required:* ACT ASSET (for placement).
Costs (2003–04) *Tuition:* state resident $2318 full-time, $77 per credit part-time; nonresident $4686 full-time, $156 per credit part-time. Full-time tuition and fees vary according to course load. Part-time tuition and fees vary according to course load. *Required fees:* $60 full-time, $30 per term part-time. *Payment plan:* installment. *Waivers:* senior citizens and employees or children of employees.
Financial Aid Of all full-time matriculated undergraduates who enrolled, 100 Federal Work-Study jobs (averaging $1538).
Applying *Options:* early admission, deferred entrance. *Required:* high school transcript. *Required for some:* interview. *Application deadline:* rolling (freshmen), rolling (transfers). *Notification:* continuous (freshmen), continuous (transfers).
Admissions Contact Ms. Pam Decker, Director of Admissions, Ivy Tech State College-North Central, 220 Dean Johnson Boulevard, South Bend, IN 46601-3415. *Phone:* 574-289-7001 Ext. 423. *Toll-free phone:* 888-489-5463. *Fax:* 219-236-7177. *E-mail:* pdecker@ivytech.edu.

IVY TECH STATE COLLEGE-NORTHEAST
Fort Wayne, Indiana

- **State-supported** 2-year, founded 1969, part of Ivy Tech State College System
- **Calendar** semesters
- **Degree** certificates and associate
- **Urban** 22-acre campus
- **Endowment** $11.2 million
- **Coed**, 5,005 undergraduate students, 35% full-time, 58% women, 42% men

Undergraduates 1,745 full-time, 3,260 part-time. 1% are from out of state, 14% African American, 0.9% Asian American or Pacific Islander, 2% Hispanic American, 0.5% Native American, 0.8% international, 3% transferred in.
Freshmen *Admission:* 1,572 applied, 1,572 admitted, 454 enrolled.
Faculty *Total:* 395, 20% full-time.
Majors Accounting technology and bookkeeping; automobile/automotive mechanics technology; building/property maintenance and management; business administration and management; cabinetmaking and millwork; child care and support services management; computer and information sciences; construction trades; drafting and design technology; electrical, electronic and communications engineering technology; electrician; executive assistant/executive secretary; heating, air conditioning, ventilation and refrigeration maintenance technology; hospitality administration; industrial technology; ironworking; legal assistant/paralegal; liberal arts and sciences/liberal studies; machine tool technology; masonry; mechanics and repair; medical/clinical assistant; occupational safety and health technology; painting and wall covering; pipefitting and sprinkler fitting; psychiatric/mental health services technology; respiratory care therapy; sheet metal technology; tool and die technology.
Academic Programs *Special study options:* academic remediation for entering students, adult/continuing education programs, advanced placement credit, distance learning, English as a second language, internships, part-time degree program, services for LD students, summer session for credit.
Library 14,905 titles, 140 serial subscriptions, 3,550 audiovisual materials, an OPAC, a Web page.

Ivy Tech State College-Northeast (continued)

Computers on Campus 347 computers available on campus for general student use. Internet access, online (class) registration, at least one staffed computer lab available.

Student Life *Housing:* college housing not available. *Activities and Organizations:* Student Government, LPN Club, Phi Theta Kappa. *Campus security:* 24-hour emergency response devices and patrols, late-night transport/escort service.

Standardized Tests *Required:* ACT ASSET (for placement).

Costs (2003–04) *Tuition:* state resident $2318 full-time, $77 per credit part-time; nonresident $4686 full-time, $156 per credit part-time. Full-time tuition and fees vary according to course load. Part-time tuition and fees vary according to course load. *Required fees:* $60 full-time, $30 per term part-time. *Payment plan:* installment. *Waivers:* senior citizens and employees or children of employees.

Financial Aid Of all full-time matriculated undergraduates who enrolled, 40 Federal Work-Study jobs (averaging $4041).

Applying *Options:* early admission. *Required:* high school transcript. *Required for some:* interview. *Application deadline:* rolling (freshmen), rolling (transfers). *Notification:* continuous (freshmen), continuous (transfers).

Admissions Contact Mr. Steve Scheer, Director of Admissions, Ivy Tech State College-Northeast, 3800 N. Anthony Boulevard, Ft. Wayne, IN 46805-1489. *Phone:* 260-480-4221. *Toll-free phone:* 800-859-4882. *Fax:* 260-480-4177. *E-mail:* sscheer@ivytech.edu.

IVY TECH STATE COLLEGE-NORTHWEST
Gary, Indiana

- **State-supported** 2-year, founded 1963, part of Ivy Tech State College System
- **Calendar** semesters
- **Degree** certificates and associate
- **Urban** 13-acre campus with easy access to Chicago
- **Endowment** $11.8 million
- **Coed,** 5,229 undergraduate students, 34% full-time, 58% women, 42% men

Undergraduates 1,781 full-time, 3,448 part-time. 29% African American, 0.4% Asian American or Pacific Islander, 8% Hispanic American, 0.3% Native American, 0.3% international, 5% transferred in.

Freshmen *Admission:* 1,139 applied, 1,139 admitted, 664 enrolled.

Faculty *Total:* 426, 21% full-time.

Majors Accounting technology and bookkeeping; automobile/automotive mechanics technology; building/property maintenance and management; business administration and management; cabinetmaking and millwork; carpentry; child care and support services management; computer and information sciences; construction trades; criminal justice/safety; drafting and design technology; electrical, electronic and communications engineering technology; electrician; executive assistant/executive secretary; heating, air conditioning, ventilation and refrigeration maintenance technology; ironworking; legal assistant/paralegal; machine tool technology; masonry; mechanics and repair; medical/clinical assistant; nursing (registered nurse training); occupational safety and health technology; painting and wall covering; pipefitting and sprinkler fitting; psychiatric/mental health services technology; respiratory care therapy; sheet metal technology; surgical technology; tool and die technology.

Academic Programs *Special study options:* academic remediation for entering students, adult/continuing education programs, advanced placement credit, distance learning, internships, part-time degree program, services for LD students, summer session for credit.

Library 11,407 titles, 265 serial subscriptions, 3,984 audiovisual materials, an OPAC, a Web page.

Computers on Campus 243 computers available on campus for general student use. Internet access, online (class) registration, at least one staffed computer lab available.

Student Life *Housing:* college housing not available. *Activities and Organizations:* Phi Theta Kappa, LPN Club, Computer Club, Student Government, Business Club. *Campus security:* 24-hour emergency response devices, late-night transport/escort service.

Standardized Tests *Required:* ACT ASSET (for placement).

Costs (2003–04) *Tuition:* state resident $2318 full-time, $77 per credit part-time; nonresident $4686 full-time, $156 per credit part-time. Full-time tuition and fees vary according to course load. Part-time tuition and fees vary according to course load. *Required fees:* $60 full-time, $30 per term part-time. *Payment plan:* installment. *Waivers:* senior citizens and employees or children of employees.

Financial Aid Of all full-time matriculated undergraduates who enrolled, 74 Federal Work-Study jobs (averaging $2131).

Applying *Options:* deferred entrance. *Required:* high school transcript. *Required for some:* interview. *Application deadline:* rolling (freshmen), rolling (transfers). *Notification:* continuous (freshmen), continuous (transfers).

Admissions Contact Ms. Twilla Lewis, Associate Dean of Student Affairs, Ivy Tech State College-Northwest, 1440 East 35th Avenue, Gary, IN 46409-1499. *Phone:* 219-981-1111 Ext. 273. *Toll-free phone:* 800-843-4882. *Fax:* 219-981-4415. *E-mail:* tlewis@ivytech.edu.

IVY TECH STATE COLLEGE-SOUTHCENTRAL
Sellersburg, Indiana

- **State-supported** 2-year, founded 1968, part of Ivy Tech State College System
- **Calendar** semesters
- **Degree** associate
- **Small-town** 63-acre campus with easy access to Louisville
- **Endowment** $11.2 million
- **Coed,** 2,917 undergraduate students, 28% full-time, 50% women, 50% men

Undergraduates 819 full-time, 2,098 part-time. 30% are from out of state, 4% African American, 0.5% Asian American or Pacific Islander, 0.6% Hispanic American, 0.7% Native American, 6% transferred in.

Freshmen *Admission:* 773 applied, 773 admitted, 438 enrolled.

Faculty *Total:* 144, 28% full-time.

Majors Accounting technology and bookkeeping; automobile/automotive mechanics technology; building/property maintenance and management; business administration and management; cabinetmaking and millwork; carpentry; child care and support services management; computer and information sciences; design and visual communications; electrical, electronic and communications engineering technology; electrician; executive assistant/executive secretary; heating, air conditioning, ventilation and refrigeration maintenance technology; industrial technology; legal assistant/paralegal; liberal arts and sciences/liberal studies; machine tool technology; masonry; mechanics and repair; medical/clinical assistant; nursing (registered nurse training); pipefitting and sprinkler fitting; psychiatric/mental health services technology; respiratory care therapy; sheet metal technology; tool and die technology.

Academic Programs *Special study options:* academic remediation for entering students, adult/continuing education programs, advanced placement credit, cooperative education, distance learning, internships, part-time degree program, services for LD students, summer session for credit.

Library 5,116 titles, 128 serial subscriptions, 4,970 audiovisual materials, an OPAC, a Web page.

Computers on Campus 170 computers available on campus for general student use. A campuswide network can be accessed. Internet access, online (class) registration, at least one staffed computer lab available.

Student Life *Housing:* college housing not available. *Activities and Organizations:* Phi Theta Kappa, Practical Nursing Club, Medical Assistant Club, Accounting Club, Student Government. *Campus security:* late-night transport/escort service.

Standardized Tests *Required:* ACT ASSET (for placement).

Costs (2003–04) *Tuition:* state resident $2318 full-time, $77 per credit part-time; nonresident $4686 full-time, $156 per credit part-time. Full-time tuition and fees vary according to course load and reciprocity agreements. Part-time tuition and fees vary according to course load and reciprocity agreements. *Required fees:* $60 full-time, $30 per term part-time. *Payment plan:* installment. *Waivers:* senior citizens and employees or children of employees.

Financial Aid Of all full-time matriculated undergraduates who enrolled, 20 Federal Work-Study jobs (averaging $5007). 1 state and other part-time job (averaging $6080).

Applying *Options:* early admission, deferred entrance. *Required:* high school transcript. *Required for some:* interview. *Application deadline:* rolling (freshmen), rolling (transfers). *Notification:* continuous (freshmen), continuous (transfers).

Admissions Contact Mindy Steinberg, Director of Admissions, Ivy Tech State College-Southcentral, 8204 Highway 311, Sellersburg, IN 47172-1897. *Phone:* 812-246-3301 Ext. 4137. *Toll-free phone:* 800-321-9021. *Fax:* 812-246-9905. *E-mail:* msteinbe@ivytech.edu.

IVY TECH STATE COLLEGE-SOUTHEAST
Madison, Indiana

- **State-supported** 2-year, founded 1963, part of Ivy Tech State College System
- **Calendar** semesters
- **Degree** associate
- **Small-town** 5-acre campus with easy access to Louisville
- **Endowment** $11.2 million
- **Coed,** 1,581 undergraduate students, 35% full-time, 74% women, 26% men

Undergraduates 553 full-time, 1,028 part-time. 2% are from out of state, 1% African American, 0.5% Asian American or Pacific Islander, 0.3% Hispanic American, 0.2% Native American, 0.1% international, 1% transferred in.

Freshmen *Admission:* 354 applied, 354 admitted, 232 enrolled.

Faculty *Total:* 139, 23% full-time.

Majors Accounting technology and bookkeeping; business administration and management; child care and support services management; computer and information sciences; electrical, electronic and communications engineering technology; executive assistant/executive secretary; industrial technology; legal assistant/paralegal; liberal arts and sciences/liberal studies; medical/clinical assistant; nursing (registered nurse training); psychiatric/mental health services technology.

Academic Programs *Special study options:* academic remediation for entering students, advanced placement credit, distance learning, internships, part-time degree program, services for LD students, summer session for credit.

Library 6,321 titles, 154 serial subscriptions, 775 audiovisual materials, an OPAC, a Web page.

Computers on Campus 112 computers available on campus for general student use. A campuswide network can be accessed. Internet access, online (class) registration, at least one staffed computer lab available.

Student Life *Housing:* college housing not available. *Activities and Organizations:* Student Government, Phi Theta Kappa, LPN Club. *Campus security:* 24-hour emergency response devices.

Athletics *Intramural sports:* basketball M.

Standardized Tests *Required:* ACT ASSET (for placement).

Costs (2003–04) *Tuition:* state resident $2318 full-time, $77 per credit part-time; nonresident $4686 full-time, $156 per credit part-time. Full-time tuition and fees vary according to course load and reciprocity agreements. Part-time tuition and fees vary according to course load and reciprocity agreements. *Required fees:* $60 full-time, $30 per term part-time. *Payment plan:* installment. *Waivers:* senior citizens and employees or children of employees.

Financial Aid Of all full-time matriculated undergraduates who enrolled, 26 Federal Work-Study jobs (averaging $1696).

Applying *Required:* high school transcript. *Required for some:* interview. *Application deadline:* rolling (freshmen), rolling (transfers). *Notification:* continuous (freshmen), continuous (transfers).

Admissions Contact Ms. Cindy Hutcherson, Assistant Director of Admission/Career Counselor, Ivy Tech State College-Southeast, 590 Ivy Tech Drive, Madison, IN 47250-1881. *Phone:* 812-265-2580 Ext. 4142. *Toll-free phone:* 800-403-2190. *Fax:* 812-265-4028. *E-mail:* chutcher@ivytech.edu.

IVY TECH STATE COLLEGE-SOUTHWEST
Evansville, Indiana

- **State-supported** 2-year, founded 1963, part of Ivy Tech State College System
- **Calendar** semesters
- **Degree** associate
- **Suburban** 15-acre campus
- **Endowment** $11.2 million
- **Coed,** 4,328 undergraduate students, 32% full-time, 52% women, 48% men

Undergraduates 1,385 full-time, 2,943 part-time. 2% are from out of state, 7% African American, 0.4% Asian American or Pacific Islander, 0.6% Hispanic American, 0.5% Native American, 0.1% international, 5% transferred in.

Freshmen *Admission:* 1,163 applied, 1,163 admitted, 622 enrolled.

Faculty *Total:* 294, 22% full-time.

Majors Accounting technology and bookkeeping; automobile/automotive mechanics technology; boilermaking; building/property maintenance and management; business administration and management; cabinetmaking and millwork; carpentry; child care and support services management; computer and information sciences; construction/heavy equipment/earthmoving equipment operation; criminal justice/safety; design and visual communications; electrical, electronic and communications engineering technology; electrician; emergency medical technology (EMT paramedic); executive assistant/executive secretary; graphic design; heating, air conditioning, ventilation and refrigeration maintenance technology; industrial technology; interior design; ironworking; legal assistant/paralegal; liberal arts and sciences/liberal studies; machine tool technology; masonry; mechanics and repair; medical/clinical assistant; nursing (registered nurse training); painting and wall covering; pipefitting and sprinkler fitting; psychiatric/mental health services technology; robotics technology; sheet metal technology; surgical technology; tool and die technology.

Academic Programs *Special study options:* academic remediation for entering students, advanced placement credit, cooperative education, distance learning, independent study, internships, part-time degree program, services for LD students, summer session for credit.

Library 5,419 titles, 102 serial subscriptions, 785 audiovisual materials, an OPAC, a Web page.

Computers on Campus 329 computers available on campus for general student use. Internet access, online (class) registration, at least one staffed computer lab available.

Student Life *Housing:* college housing not available. *Activities and Organizations:* Student Government, Phi Theta Kappa, LPN Club, National Association of Industrial Technology, Design Club. *Campus security:* late-night transport/escort service.

Standardized Tests *Required:* ACT ASSET (for placement).

Costs (2003–04) *Tuition:* state resident $2318 full-time, $77 per credit part-time; nonresident $4686 full-time, $156 per credit part-time. Full-time tuition and fees vary according to course load and reciprocity agreements. Part-time tuition and fees vary according to course load and reciprocity agreements. *Required fees:* $60 full-time, $30 per term part-time. *Payment plan:* installment. *Waivers:* senior citizens and employees or children of employees.

Financial Aid Of all full-time matriculated undergraduates who enrolled, 65 Federal Work-Study jobs (averaging $2264).

Applying *Options:* early admission, deferred entrance. *Required:* high school transcript. *Required for some:* interview. *Application deadline:* rolling (freshmen), rolling (transfers). *Notification:* continuous (freshmen), continuous (transfers).

Admissions Contact Ms. Denise Johnson-Kincaid, Director of Admissions, Ivy Tech State College-Southwest, 3501 First Avenue, Evansville, IN 47710-3398. *Phone:* 812-429-1430. *Fax:* 812-429-1483. *E-mail:* ajohnson@ivytech.edu.

IVY TECH STATE COLLEGE-WABASH VALLEY
Terre Haute, Indiana

- **State-supported** 2-year, founded 1966, part of Ivy Tech State College System
- **Calendar** semesters
- **Degree** associate
- **Suburban** 55-acre campus with easy access to Indianapolis
- **Endowment** $11.2 million
- **Coed,** 4,347 undergraduate students, 41% full-time, 55% women, 45% men

Undergraduates 1,779 full-time, 2,568 part-time. 2% are from out of state, 3% African American, 0.2% Asian American or Pacific Islander, 0.6% Hispanic American, 0.5% Native American, 0.2% international, 3% transferred in.

Freshmen *Admission:* 1,179 applied, 1,179 admitted, 632 enrolled.

Faculty *Total:* 253, 28% full-time.

Majors Accounting technology and bookkeeping; airframe mechanics and aircraft maintenance technology; automobile/automotive mechanics technology; building/property maintenance and management; business administration and management; cabinetmaking and millwork; carpentry; child care and support services management; clinical/medical laboratory technology; computer and information sciences; construction/heavy equipment/earthmoving equipment operation; criminal justice/safety; design and visual communications; drafting and design technology; electrical, electronic and communications engineering technology; electrician; emergency medical technology (EMT paramedic); executive assistant/executive secretary; heating, air conditioning, ventilation and refrigeration maintenance technology; industrial technology; ironworking; legal assistant/paralegal; liberal arts and sciences/liberal studies; machine tool technology; masonry; mechanics and repair; medical/clinical assistant; medical radiologic technology; nursing (registered nurse training); occupational safety and health technology; painting and wall covering; pipefitting and sprinkler fitting; psychiatric/mental health services technology; robotics technology; sheet metal technology; surgical technology; tool and die technology.

Academic Programs *Special study options:* academic remediation for entering students, adult/continuing education programs, advanced placement credit, distance learning, internships, part-time degree program, services for LD students, summer session for credit.

Library 4,034 titles, 75 serial subscriptions, 316 audiovisual materials, an OPAC, a Web page.

Computers on Campus 287 computers available on campus for general student use. A campuswide network can be accessed. Internet access, online (class) registration, at least one staffed computer lab available.

Student Life *Housing:* college housing not available. *Activities and Organizations:* Student Government, Phi Theta Kappa, LPN Club, National Association of Industrial Technology. *Campus security:* 24-hour emergency response devices. *Student services:* personal/psychological counseling, women's center.

Athletics *Intramural sports:* basketball M/W, volleyball M/W.

Standardized Tests *Required:* ACT ASSET (for placement).

Costs (2003–04) *Tuition:* state resident $2318 full-time, $77 per credit part-time; nonresident $4686 full-time, $156 per credit part-time. Full-time tuition and fees vary according to course load. Part-time tuition and fees vary according to course load. *Required fees:* $60 full-time, $30 per term part-time. *Payment plan:* installment. *Waivers:* senior citizens and employees or children of employees.

Financial Aid Of all full-time matriculated undergraduates who enrolled, 51 Federal Work-Study jobs (averaging $2110). 1 state and other part-time job (averaging $2963).

Applying *Options:* early admission, deferred entrance. *Required:* high school transcript. *Required for some:* interview. *Application deadline:* rolling (freshmen), rolling (transfers). *Notification:* continuous (freshmen), continuous (transfers).

Indiana

Ivy Tech State College-Wabash Valley (continued)

Admissions Contact Mr. Michael Fisher, Director of Admissions, Ivy Tech State College-Wabash Valley, 7999 U.S. Highway 41 South, Terre Haute, IN 47802-4898. *Phone:* 812-298-2300. *Toll-free phone:* 800-377-4882. *Fax:* 812-299-5723. *E-mail:* mfisher@ivytech.edu.

IVY TECH STATE COLLEGE-WHITEWATER
Richmond, Indiana

- **State-supported** 2-year, founded 1963, part of Ivy Tech State College System
- **Calendar** semesters
- **Degree** associate
- **Small-town** 23-acre campus with easy access to Indianapolis
- **Endowment** $11.2 million
- **Coed,** 1,541 undergraduate students, 28% full-time, 72% women, 28% men

Undergraduates 425 full-time, 1,116 part-time. 3% are from out of state, 3% African American, 0.4% Asian American or Pacific Islander, 0.5% Hispanic American, 0.2% Native American, 0.1% international, 0.8% transferred in.
Freshmen *Admission:* 350 applied, 350 admitted, 210 enrolled.
Faculty *Total:* 141, 17% full-time.
Majors Accounting technology and bookkeeping; automobile/automotive mechanics technology; building/property maintenance and management; business administration and management; cabinetmaking and millwork; child care and support services management; computer and information sciences; construction trades; electrical, electronic and communications engineering technology; electrician; executive assistant/executive secretary; heating, air conditioning, ventilation and refrigeration maintenance technology; industrial technology; legal assistant/paralegal; liberal arts and sciences/liberal studies; machine tool technology; mechanics and repair; medical/clinical assistant; nursing (registered nurse training); pipefitting and sprinkler fitting; psychiatric/mental health services technology; robotics technology; tool and die technology.
Academic Programs *Special study options:* academic remediation for entering students, adult/continuing education programs, advanced placement credit, distance learning, independent study, internships, off-campus study, part-time degree program, services for LD students, summer session for credit.
Library 332 audiovisual materials.
Computers on Campus 154 computers available on campus for general student use. A campuswide network can be accessed. Internet access, online (class) registration, at least one staffed computer lab available.
Student Life *Housing:* college housing not available. *Activities and Organizations:* Student Government, Phi Theta Kappa, LPN Club, CATS 2000, Business Professionals of America. *Campus security:* 24-hour emergency response devices, late-night transport/escort service. *Student services:* personal/psychological counseling.
Athletics *Intramural sports:* softball M/W.
Standardized Tests *Required:* ACT ASSET (for placement).
Costs (2003–04) *Tuition:* state resident $2318 full-time, $77 per credit part-time; nonresident $4686 full-time, $156 per credit part-time. Full-time tuition and fees vary according to course load. Part-time tuition and fees vary according to course load. *Required fees:* $60 full-time, $30 per term part-time. *Payment plan:* installment. *Waivers:* senior citizens and employees or children of employees.
Financial Aid Of all full-time matriculated undergraduates who enrolled, 14 Federal Work-Study jobs (averaging $3106). 1 state and other part-time job (averaging $3380).
Applying *Options:* early admission. *Required:* high school transcript. *Required for some:* interview. *Application deadline:* rolling (freshmen), rolling (transfers). *Notification:* continuous (freshmen), continuous (transfers).
Admissions Contact Mr. Jeff Plasterer, Director of Admissions, Ivy Tech State College-Whitewater, 2325 Chester Boulevard, Richmond, IN 47374-1298. *Phone:* 765-966-2656 Ext. 335. *Toll-free phone:* 800-659-4562. *Fax:* 765-962-8741. *E-mail:* jplaster@ivytech.edu.

LINCOLN TECHNICAL INSTITUTE
Indianapolis, Indiana

- **Proprietary** 2-year, founded 1946, part of Lincoln Technical Institute, Inc
- **Calendar** modular
- **Degree** certificates and associate
- **Urban** campus
- **Coed**

Applying *Required:* high school transcript, interview.
Admissions Contact Ms. Cindy Ryan, Director of Admissions, Lincoln Technical Institute, 1201 Stadium Drive, Indianapolis, IN 46202-2194. *Phone:* 317-632-5553. *Toll-free phone:* 800-554-4465.

MICHIANA COLLEGE
Fort Wayne, Indiana

- **Proprietary** 2-year
- **Calendar** quarters
- **Degree** certificates, diplomas, and associate
- **Coed**

Costs (2003–04) *Tuition:* $3744 full-time, $156 per credit hour part-time.
Applying *Application fee:* $20.
Admissions Contact 4422 East State Boulevard, Fort Wayne, IN 46815.

MICHIANA COLLEGE
South Bend, Indiana

- **Proprietary** 2-year, founded 1882, part of American Education Centers
- **Calendar** quarters
- **Degree** certificates and associate
- **Urban** 5-acre campus with easy access to Chicago
- **Coed, primarily women,** 513 undergraduate students, 100% full-time, 83% women, 17% men

Undergraduates 513 full-time. Students come from 2 states and territories, 7% are from out of state, 24% African American, 0.2% Asian American or Pacific Islander, 4% Hispanic American, 0.2% Native American, 6% transferred in.
Freshmen *Admission:* 27 applied, 27 admitted, 27 enrolled. *Average high school GPA:* 2.0.
Faculty *Total:* 21, 43% full-time. *Student/faculty ratio:* 16:1.
Majors Accounting; business administration and management; business automation/technology/data entry; computer management; computer programming; computer systems networking and telecommunications; corrections administration; drafting and design technology; electrical, electronics and communications engineering; legal assistant/paralegal; medical/clinical assistant; occupational therapist assistant; physical therapist assistant.
Academic Programs *Special study options:* academic remediation for entering students, accelerated degree program, adult/continuing education programs, double majors, summer session for credit.
Library Michiana College Library with 1,409 titles, 65 serial subscriptions, 65 audiovisual materials.
Computers on Campus 8 computers available on campus for general student use. Internet access available.
Student Life *Housing:* college housing not available. *Activities and Organizations:* Business Club, Medical Assisting Club, Legal Club, Physical Therapy Assistant Club, Occupational Therapy Assistant Club. *Campus security:* 24-hour emergency response devices. *Student services:* personal/psychological counseling.
Costs (2003–04) *Tuition:* $5976 full-time, $156 per credit hour part-time. Full-time tuition and fees vary according to course load. *Required fees:* $360 full-time, $10 per credit hour part-time. *Payment plan:* installment. *Waivers:* employees or children of employees.
Applying *Options:* common application, deferred entrance. *Application fee:* $20. *Required:* essay or personal statement, high school transcript, interview. *Required for some:* minimum 2.0 GPA, 2 letters of recommendation. *Application deadline:* rolling (freshmen), rolling (transfers). *Notification:* continuous (transfers).
Admissions Contact Ms. Rita Harvey, Admissions Representative; High School, Michiana College, 1030 East Jefferson Boulevard, South Bend, IN 46617-3123. *Phone:* 574-237-0774. *Toll-free phone:* 800-743-2447. *Fax:* 574-237-3585. *E-mail:* mcsb@michianacollege.com.

MID-AMERICA COLLEGE OF FUNERAL SERVICE
Jeffersonville, Indiana

- **Independent** primarily 2-year, founded 1905
- **Calendar** quarters
- **Degrees** associate and bachelor's
- **Small-town** 3-acre campus with easy access to Louisville
- **Coed, primarily men**

Faculty *Student/faculty ratio:* 13:1.
Applying *Options:* deferred entrance. *Application fee:* $25. *Required:* high school transcript.
Admissions Contact Mr. Richard Nelson, Dean of Students, Mid-America College of Funeral Service, 3111 Hamburg Pike, Jeffersonville, IN 47130-9630. *Phone:* 812-288-8878. *Toll-free phone:* 800-221-6158. *E-mail:* macfs@mindspring.com.

PROFESSIONAL CAREERS INSTITUTE
Indianapolis, Indiana

Admissions Contact Ms. Paulette M. Clay, Director of Admissions, Professional Careers Institute, 7302 Woodland Drive, Indianapolis, IN 46217. *Phone:* 317-299-6001 Ext. 320. *E-mail:* lilgeneral9@hotmail.com.

SAWYER COLLEGE
Hammond, Indiana

- **Proprietary** 2-year, founded 1962
- **Calendar** quarters
- **Degree** associate
- **Suburban** 3-acre campus
- **Coed,** 261 undergraduate students

Majors Accounting and business/management; computer programming; legal assistant/paralegal; massage therapy; medical office assistant; system, networking, and LAN/wan management; web/multimedia management and webmaster.
Standardized Tests *Required:* Wonderlic aptitude test (for admission).
Admissions Contact Director, Sawyer College, 6040 Hohman Avenue, Hammond, IN 46320. *Phone:* 219-844-0100. *E-mail:* info@sawyercollege.com.

SAWYER COLLEGE
Merrillville, Indiana

- **Proprietary** 2-year, founded 1968
- **Degree** associate
- **Coed**

Standardized Tests *Required:* Wonderlic aptitude test (for admission).
Admissions Contact 3803 East Lincoln Highway, Merrillville, IN 46410. *E-mail:* info@sawyercollege.com.

VINCENNES UNIVERSITY
Vincennes, Indiana

- **State-supported** 2-year, founded 1801
- **Calendar** semesters
- **Degree** certificates and associate
- **Small-town** 100-acre campus
- **Endowment** $25.6 million
- **Coed,** 5,175 undergraduate students, 86% full-time, 40% women, 60% men

Undergraduates 4,467 full-time, 708 part-time. Students come from 22 states and territories, 31 other countries, 7% are from out of state, 8% African American, 0.4% Asian American or Pacific Islander, 1% Hispanic American, 0.3% Native American, 2% international, 50% live on campus.
Freshmen *Admission:* 4,553 applied, 4,300 admitted. *Average high school GPA:* 2.50. *Test scores:* SAT verbal scores over 500: 20%; SAT math scores over 500: 20%; ACT scores over 18: 55%; SAT verbal scores over 600: 10%; SAT math scores over 600: 10%; ACT scores over 24: 15%.
Faculty *Total:* 812, 36% full-time. *Student/faculty ratio:* 15:1.
Majors Accounting; administrative assistant and secretarial science; advertising; agricultural and extension education; agricultural business and management; agricultural mechanization; airframe mechanics and aircraft maintenance technology; airline pilot and flight crew; anthropology; architectural engineering technology; art; artificial intelligence and robotics; art teacher education; athletic training; automobile/automotive mechanics technology; avionics maintenance technology; baking and pastry arts; behavioral sciences; biology/biological sciences; broadcast journalism; building/home/construction inspection; business administration and management; business teacher education; chemistry; child care and support services management; child care provision; child development; civil engineering technology; clinical laboratory science/medical technology; clinical/medical laboratory technology; commercial and advertising art; communication/speech communication and rhetoric; communications technology; computer and information sciences related; computer engineering related; computer engineering technology; computer graphics; computer hardware engineering; computer/information technology services administration related; computer programming; computer programming related; computer programming (specific applications); computer programming (vendor/product certification); computer science; computer software and media applications related; computer software engineering; computer systems networking and telecommunications; computer/technical support; construction engineering technology; corrections; cosmetology; criminal justice/law enforcement administration; criminal justice/police science; culinary arts; data entry/microcomputer applications; data entry/microcomputer applications related; dental hygiene; dietetics; drafting and design technology; dramatic/theatre arts; education; education (K-12); electrical, electronic and communications engineering technology; elementary education; engineering; engineering tech-

nology; English; environmental health; environmental studies; family and consumer economics related; family and consumer sciences/human sciences; family and consumer sciences/human sciences communication; fashion/apparel design; fashion merchandising; fire science; food science; forestry; French; funeral service and mortuary science; geography; geology/earth science; German; graphic and printing equipment operation/production; health information/medical records administration; heavy equipment maintenance technology; history; horticultural science; hospitality and recreation marketing; hotel/motel administration; housing and human environments; industrial design; industrial electronics technology; industrial mechanics and maintenance technology; information science/studies; information technology; interior design; international business/trade/commerce; journalism; kindergarten/preschool education; kinesiology and exercise science; landscape architecture; laser and optical technology; legal administrative assistant/secretary; legal assistant/paralegal; liberal arts and sciences/liberal studies; machine shop technology; machine tool technology; management information systems; marketing/marketing management; mass communication/media; mathematics; mechanical engineering/mechanical technology; medical administrative assistant and medical secretary; medical/clinical assistant; medical laboratory technology; middle school education; music; music teacher education; natural resources/conservation; natural resources management and policy; nuclear medical technology; nursing (licensed practical/vocational nurse training); nursing (registered nurse training); occupational therapy; parks, recreation and leisure; pharmacy; physical education teaching and coaching; physical therapy; physics; political science and government; pre-engineering; psychology; public administration; public relations/image management; radio and television; respiratory care therapy; restaurant, culinary, and catering management; sales, distribution and marketing; science teacher education; sign language interpretation and translation; social sciences; social work; sociology; Spanish; speech/theater education; sport and fitness administration; substance abuse/addiction counseling; survey technology; system administration; therapeutic recreation; veterinary sciences; web/multimedia management and webmaster; web page, digital/multimedia and information resources design; welding technology; word processing.
Academic Programs *Special study options:* academic remediation for entering students, adult/continuing education programs, advanced placement credit, cooperative education, distance learning, English as a second language, external degree program, freshman honors college, honors programs, independent study, internships, off-campus study, part-time degree program, services for LD students, student-designed majors, summer session for credit. *ROTC:* Army (c), Air Force (c).
Library Shake Learning Resource Center plus 1 other with 103,000 titles, 557 serial subscriptions, 5,260 audiovisual materials, an OPAC, a Web page.
Computers on Campus 600 computers available on campus for general student use. A campuswide network can be accessed from student residence rooms and from off campus. Internet access, at least one staffed computer lab available.
Student Life *Housing:* on-campus residence required for freshman year. *Options:* coed, men-only, women-only, disabled students. Campus housing is university owned. Freshman campus housing is guaranteed. *Activities and Organizations:* drama/theater group, student-run newspaper, radio and television station, choral group, Student Senate, Student Alumni Corporation, Intramurals, Law Enforcement Association, Campus Christian Fellowship, national fraternities, national sororities. *Campus security:* 24-hour emergency response devices and patrols, student patrols, late-night transport/escort service, controlled dormitory access, surveillance cameras. *Student services:* health clinic, personal/psychological counseling.
Athletics Member NJCAA. *Intercollegiate sports:* baseball M(s), basketball M(s)/W(s), bowling M(s)/W(s), cheerleading M(s)/W(s), cross-country running M(s)/W(s), golf M(s), soccer M/W, swimming M(s)/W(s), tennis M(s), track and field M(s)/W(s), volleyball W(s). *Intramural sports:* archery M/W, badminton M/W, basketball M/W, bowling M/W, cross-country running M/W, gymnastics M/W, racquetball M/W, skiing (downhill) M/W, soccer M/W, softball M/W, swimming M/W, tennis M/W, track and field M/W, volleyball M/W, weight lifting M/W, wrestling M.
Standardized Tests *Required for some:* SAT I or ACT (for admission). *Recommended:* SAT I or ACT (for admission).
Costs (2004–05) *Tuition:* state resident $3048 full-time, $101 per credit hour part-time; nonresident $7609 full-time, $254 per credit hour part-time. Full-time tuition and fees vary according to course load. Part-time tuition and fees vary according to course load. *Required fees:* $350 full-time. *Room and board:* $5700. Room and board charges vary according to board plan and housing facility. *Payment plan:* installment. *Waivers:* senior citizens and employees or children of employees.
Financial Aid Of all full-time matriculated undergraduates who enrolled, 213 Federal Work-Study jobs (averaging $2400). *Financial aid deadline:* 3/10.
Applying *Options:* common application, electronic application, early admission, deferred entrance. *Application fee:* $20. *Required:* high school transcript. *Required for some:* interview. *Application deadline:* rolling (freshmen), rolling (transfers). *Notification:* continuous until 8/1 (freshmen), continuous (transfers).

Vincennes University (continued)

Admissions Contact Mr. Chris M. Crews, Director of Admissions, Vincennes University, 1002 North First Street, Vincennes, IN 47591. *Phone:* 812-888-4313. *Toll-free phone:* 800-742-9198. *Fax:* 812-888-5707. *E-mail:* vuadmit@indian.vinu.edu.

▶ **See page 608 for a narrative description.**

VINCENNES UNIVERSITY JASPER CAMPUS

Jasper, Indiana

- **State-supported** 2-year, founded 1970, part of Vincennes University
- **Calendar** semesters
- **Degree** certificates and associate
- **Small-town** 120-acre campus
- **Coed**

Faculty *Student/faculty ratio:* 16:1.
Standardized Tests *Required for some:* SAT I or ACT (for placement). *Recommended:* SAT I or ACT (for placement).
Costs (2003–04) *Tuition:* state resident $2876 full-time; nonresident $7178 full-time. *Required fees:* $285 full-time.
Financial Aid Of all full-time matriculated undergraduates who enrolled, 3 Federal Work-Study jobs (averaging $3200).
Applying *Application fee:* $20. *Required:* high school transcript.
Admissions Contact Ms. LouAnn Gilbert, Director, Vincennes University Jasper Campus, Jasper, IN 47546. *Phone:* 812-482-3030. *Toll-free phone:* 800-809-VUJC. *Fax:* 812-481-5960. *E-mail:* lgilbert@indian.vinu.edu.

IOWA

AIB COLLEGE OF BUSINESS

Des Moines, Iowa

- **Independent** 2-year, founded 1921
- **Calendar** continuous
- **Degree** diplomas and associate
- **Urban** 20-acre campus
- **Coed**, 938 undergraduate students, 80% full-time, 69% women, 31% men

Undergraduates 750 full-time, 188 part-time. Students come from 5 states and territories, 5% are from out of state, 2% African American, 2% Asian American or Pacific Islander, 1% Hispanic American, 0.2% Native American, 21% transferred in, 48% live on campus.
Freshmen *Admission:* 546 applied, 405 admitted, 250 enrolled. *Average high school GPA:* 3.34.
Faculty *Total:* 67, 39% full-time, 7% with terminal degrees. *Student/faculty ratio:* 21:1.
Majors Accounting; administrative assistant and secretarial science; business administration and management; computer management; computer programming (specific applications); computer software and media applications related; computer systems networking and telecommunications; court reporting; data entry/microcomputer applications related; finance; hospitality and recreation marketing; legal administrative assistant/secretary; marketing/marketing management; medical administrative assistant and medical secretary; system administration; tourism and travel services management; tourism and travel services marketing; tourism promotion.
Academic Programs *Special study options:* academic remediation for entering students, accelerated degree program, adult/continuing education programs, double majors, internships, part-time degree program, summer session for credit.
Library 5,400 titles, 185 serial subscriptions.
Computers on Campus 188 computers available on campus for general student use. A campuswide network can be accessed from student residence rooms and from off campus. Internet access, at least one staffed computer lab available.
Student Life *Housing:* on-campus residence required through sophomore year. *Options:* coed. *Activities and Organizations:* Business Management Association, Institute of Management Accountants, International Association of Administrative Professionals, Association of Information Technology Professionals, Student Court Reporters Association, national fraternities, national sororities. *Campus security:* 24-hour emergency response devices, late-night transport/escort service, controlled dormitory access, video security. *Student services:* personal/psychological counseling.
Athletics *Intramural sports:* badminton M/W, basketball M/W, bowling M/W, football M/W, golf M/W, rock climbing M/W, softball M/W, table tennis M/W, volleyball M/W.

Standardized Tests *Recommended:* ACT (for admission).
Costs (2004–05) *Tuition:* $8820 full-time, $245 per credit hour part-time. *Required fees:* $240 full-time, $240 per year part-time. *Room only:* $2775.
Financial Aid Of all full-time matriculated undergraduates who enrolled, 104 Federal Work-Study jobs (averaging $1135).
Applying *Options:* electronic application. *Application fee:* $25. *Required:* high school transcript. *Recommended:* interview. *Application deadline:* rolling (freshmen), rolling (transfers).
Admissions Contact Ms. Gail Cline, Director of Admissions, AIB College of Business, Keith Fenton Administration Building, 2500 Fleur Drive, Des Moines, IA 50321-1799. *Phone:* 515-244-4221 Ext. 5634. *Toll-free phone:* 800-444-1921. *Fax:* 515-244-6773. *E-mail:* clineg@aib.edu.

CLINTON COMMUNITY COLLEGE

Clinton, Iowa

- **State and locally supported** 2-year, founded 1946, part of Eastern Iowa Community College District
- **Calendar** semesters
- **Degree** certificates, diplomas, and associate
- **Small-town** 20-acre campus
- **Coed**

Athletics Member NJCAA.
Standardized Tests *Required:* DTMS and DTLS or ACT (for placement).
Costs (2003–04) *Tuition:* area resident $2400 full-time, $80 per semester hour part-time; nonresident $3600 full-time, $120 per semester hour part-time.
Financial Aid Of all full-time matriculated undergraduates who enrolled, 44 Federal Work-Study jobs (averaging $3000).
Applying *Options:* early admission, deferred entrance. *Required:* high school transcript.
Admissions Contact Mr. Neil Mandsager, Executive Director of Enrollment Management and Marketing, Clinton Community College, 1000 Lincoln Boulevard, Clinton, IA 52732-6299. *Phone:* 563-244-7007.

DES MOINES AREA COMMUNITY COLLEGE

Ankeny, Iowa

- **State and locally supported** 2-year, founded 1966, part of Iowa Area Community Colleges System
- **Calendar** semesters
- **Degrees** certificates, diplomas, and associate (profile also includes information from the Boone, Carroll, Des Moines, and Newton campuses)
- **Small-town** 362-acre campus
- **Endowment** $1.8 million
- **Coed**, 13,719 undergraduate students, 44% full-time, 56% women, 44% men

Undergraduates 6,002 full-time, 7,717 part-time. Students come from 31 states and territories, 53 other countries, 1% are from out of state, 4% African American, 3% Asian American or Pacific Islander, 2% Hispanic American, 0.3% Native American, 2% international, 3% transferred in.
Freshmen *Admission:* 4,174 enrolled. *Test scores:* ACT scores over 18: 76%; ACT scores over 24: 17%; ACT scores over 30: 1%.
Faculty *Total:* 272, 98% full-time. *Student/faculty ratio:* 50:1.
Majors Accounting; administrative assistant and secretarial science; agricultural business and management; artificial intelligence and robotics; automobile/automotive mechanics technology; biology/biotechnology laboratory technician; business administration and management; carpentry; child development; civil engineering technology; clinical/medical laboratory technology; commercial and advertising art; computer engineering technology; computer programming; computer programming (specific applications); consumer merchandising/retailing management; corrections; criminal justice/law enforcement administration; criminal justice/police science; culinary arts; data processing and data processing technology; dental hygiene; drafting and design technology; education; electrical, electronic and communications engineering technology; fashion merchandising; fire science; graphic and printing equipment operation/production; health/health care administration; heating, air conditioning, ventilation and refrigeration maintenance technology; heavy equipment maintenance technology; horticultural science; hospitality administration; hotel/motel administration; human services; legal administrative assistant/secretary; legal assistant/paralegal; liberal arts and sciences/liberal studies; machine tool technology; marketing/marketing management; medical administrative assistant and medical secretary; medical/clinical assistant; nursing (licensed practical/vocational nurse training); nursing (registered nurse training); quality control technology; respiratory care therapy; safety/security technology; social work; special products marketing; teacher assistant/aide; telecommunications; welding technology.
Academic Programs *Special study options:* academic remediation for entering students, adult/continuing education programs, advanced placement credit,

cooperative education, distance learning, English as a second language, honors programs, off-campus study, part-time degree program, services for LD students, student-designed majors, summer session for credit.

Library DMACC District Library plus 4 others with 62,986 titles, 3,784 serial subscriptions, 7,224 audiovisual materials, an OPAC, a Web page.

Computers on Campus 700 computers available on campus for general student use. A campuswide network can be accessed from off campus. Internet access, online (class) registration, at least one staffed computer lab available. Computer purchase or lease plan available.

Student Life *Housing:* college housing not available. *Activities and Organizations:* drama/theater group, student-run newspaper, choral group, Agri-Business Club, Horticulture Club, Hospitality Arts Club, Iowa Delta Epsilon Chi, Dental Hygienist Club. *Campus security:* 24-hour emergency response devices and patrols, late-night transport/escort service. *Student services:* health clinic, personal/psychological counseling.

Athletics Member NJCAA. *Intercollegiate sports:* basketball M(s)/W(s), golf M/W, softball W. *Intramural sports:* badminton M/W, basketball M/W, football M/W, golf M/W, soccer M/W, volleyball M/W.

Standardized Tests *Required:* ACT COMPASS (for placement). *Recommended:* ACT (for placement).

Costs (2003–04) *Tuition:* state resident $2442 full-time, $81 per hour part-time; nonresident $4884 full-time, $163 per hour part-time. *Payment plan:* installment. *Waivers:* senior citizens and employees or children of employees.

Financial Aid Of all full-time matriculated undergraduates who enrolled, 377 Federal Work-Study jobs (averaging $1055).

Applying *Options:* electronic application, early admission, deferred entrance. *Required for some:* high school transcript, interview. *Application deadline:* rolling (freshmen), rolling (transfers).

Admissions Contact Mr. Keith Knowles, Director of Admissions and Assessment, Des Moines Area Community College, Building 1, 2006 South Ankeny Boulevard, Ankeny, IA 50021. *Phone:* 515-964-6216. *Toll-free phone:* 800-362-2127.

ELLSWORTH COMMUNITY COLLEGE
Iowa Falls, Iowa

Admissions Contact Mr. Philip Rusley, Director of Admissions/Registrar, Ellsworth Community College, 1100 College Avenue, Iowa Falls, IA 50126-1199. *Phone:* 641-648-4611. *Toll-free phone:* 800-ECC-9235.

HAMILTON COLLEGE
Cedar Rapids, Iowa

- **Proprietary** primarily 2-year, founded 1900
- **Calendar** quarters
- **Degrees** certificates, diplomas, associate, and bachelor's (branch locations in Des Moines, Mason City, and Cedar Falls with significant enrollment reflected in profile)
- **Suburban** 4-acre campus
- **Coed**

Faculty *Student/faculty ratio:* 25:1.

Student Life *Campus security:* 24-hour emergency response devices.

Standardized Tests *Required:* CPAt (for admission).

Costs (2003–04) *Tuition:* $14,160 full-time. *Payment plans:* tuition prepayment, installment.

Financial Aid Of all full-time matriculated undergraduates who enrolled, 10 Federal Work-Study jobs (averaging $889). 3 state and other part-time jobs (averaging $1885).

Applying *Options:* common application, early admission, deferred entrance. *Application fee:* $25. *Required:* high school transcript, minimum 2.0 GPA, interview.

Admissions Contact Mr. Brad Knudson, Director of Admissions, Hamilton College, 1924 D Street SW, Cedar Rapids, IA 52404. *Phone:* 319-363-0481. *Toll-free phone:* 800-728-0481. *Fax:* 319-363-3812.

HAWKEYE COMMUNITY COLLEGE
Waterloo, Iowa

- **State and locally supported** 2-year, founded 1966
- **Calendar** semesters
- **Degree** certificates, diplomas, and associate
- **Rural** 320-acre campus
- **Coed,** 5,310 undergraduate students, 64% full-time, 57% women, 43% men

Undergraduates 3,402 full-time, 1,908 part-time. Students come from 26 states and territories, 10 other countries, 1% are from out of state, 9% African

American, 0.8% Asian American or Pacific Islander, 1% Hispanic American, 0.3% Native American, 0.7% international, 12% transferred in.

Freshmen *Admission:* 1,803 enrolled. *Average high school GPA:* 2.73. *Test scores:* ACT scores over 18: 46%; ACT scores over 24: 11%; ACT scores over 30: 1%.

Faculty *Total:* 271, 44% full-time, 6% with terminal degrees. *Student/faculty ratio:* 24:1.

Majors Accounting; administrative assistant and secretarial science; agricultural business and management; agricultural mechanization; agronomy and crop science; airframe mechanics and aircraft maintenance technology; animal sciences; architectural engineering technology; autobody/collision and repair technology; automobile/automotive mechanics technology; avionics maintenance technology; biology/biological sciences; business administration and management; business/commerce; child development; civil engineering technology; clinical/medical laboratory technology; commercial and advertising art; computer engineering technology; computer/information technology services administration related; computer systems networking and telecommunications; computer/technical support; corrections; criminal justice/law enforcement administration; criminal justice/police science; data entry/microcomputer applications related; dental hygiene; drafting and design technology; education; emergency medical technology (EMT paramedic); engineering technology; farm and ranch management; fire science; food science; heating, air conditioning, ventilation and refrigeration maintenance technology; heavy equipment maintenance technology; horticultural science; information technology; interdisciplinary studies; interior design; liberal arts and sciences/liberal studies; machine tool technology; marketing/marketing management; mechanical design technology; mechanical engineering/mechanical technology; medical administrative assistant and medical secretary; natural resources management and policy; nursing (licensed practical/vocational nurse training); nursing (registered nurse training); ornamental horticulture; parks, recreation and leisure facilities management; photography; respiratory care therapy; survey technology; system administration; tool and die technology; web/multimedia management and webmaster; web page, digital/multimedia and information resources design; welding technology; word processing.

Academic Programs *Special study options:* academic remediation for entering students, adult/continuing education programs, advanced placement credit, cooperative education, distance learning, English as a second language, external degree program, part-time degree program, services for LD students, summer session for credit. *ROTC:* Army (c).

Library Hawkeye Community College Library with 31,883 titles, 491 serial subscriptions, 1,843 audiovisual materials, an OPAC, a Web page.

Computers on Campus 276 computers available on campus for general student use. A campuswide network can be accessed. Internet access, online (class) registration, at least one staffed computer lab available.

Student Life *Housing:* college housing not available. *Activities and Organizations:* Student Senate, Phi Theta Kappa, Environmental Conservation Club/Ag Club, Law Enforcement/Criminal Justice, Fashion Merchandising. *Campus security:* 24-hour patrols. *Student services:* personal/psychological counseling, women's center.

Athletics *Intercollegiate sports:* cheerleading M(s)/W(s). *Intramural sports:* basketball M/W, bowling M/W, golf M/W, softball M/W, ultimate Frisbee M, volleyball M/W.

Standardized Tests *Required:* ACT ASSET, ACT COMPASS (for placement). *Required for some:* SAT I or ACT (for placement). *Recommended:* SAT I or ACT (for placement).

Costs (2003–04) *Tuition:* state resident $2610 full-time, $87 per credit part-time; nonresident $5220 full-time, $174 per credit part-time. Full-time tuition and fees vary according to course load. Part-time tuition and fees vary according to course load. *Required fees:* $300 full-time, $10 per credit part-time. *Payment plan:* installment. *Waivers:* employees or children of employees.

Applying *Options:* electronic application, deferred entrance. *Required:* high school transcript. *Application deadline:* rolling (freshmen), rolling (transfers). *Notification:* continuous (freshmen), continuous (transfers).

Admissions Contact Holly Grimm, Admissions Coordinator, Hawkeye Community College, PO Box 8015, Waterloo, IA 50704-8015. *Phone:* 319-296-4277. *Toll-free phone:* 800-670-4769. *Fax:* 319-296-2505. *E-mail:* admission@hawkeyecollege.edu.

INDIAN HILLS COMMUNITY COLLEGE
Ottumwa, Iowa

- **State and locally supported** 2-year, founded 1966, part of Iowa Area Community Colleges System
- **Calendar** quarters
- **Degree** certificates, diplomas, and associate
- **Small-town** 400-acre campus
- **Coed,** 2,867 undergraduate students, 71% full-time, 59% women, 41% men

Undergraduates 2,046 full-time, 821 part-time. Students come from 16 states and territories, 7% are from out of state, 0.4% transferred in, 15% live on campus.

Indian Hills Community College (continued)

Freshmen *Admission:* 2,477 applied, 2,477 admitted, 1,069 enrolled.

Faculty *Total:* 148, 86% full-time.

Majors Agricultural mechanization; airline pilot and flight crew; artificial intelligence and robotics; automobile/automotive mechanics technology; avionics maintenance technology; biology/biotechnology laboratory technician; business administration and management; child development; computer engineering technology; computer programming; criminal justice/law enforcement administration; drafting and design technology; electrical, electronic and communications engineering technology; food services technology; health/health care administration; health information/medical records administration; heavy equipment maintenance technology; horticultural science; industrial radiologic technology; laser and optical technology; liberal arts and sciences/liberal studies; machine tool technology; nursing (licensed practical/vocational nurse training); nursing (registered nurse training); physical therapy.

Academic Programs *Special study options:* academic remediation for entering students, adult/continuing education programs, cooperative education, English as a second language, honors programs, internships, part-time degree program, services for LD students, student-designed majors, summer session for credit.

Library Indian Hills Community College Library plus 2 others with 53,073 titles, 350 serial subscriptions, an OPAC, a Web page.

Computers on Campus 150 computers available on campus for general student use. A campuswide network can be accessed. At least one staffed computer lab available.

Student Life *Housing Options:* coed. Campus housing is university owned. *Activities and Organizations:* drama/theater group, Student Senate, Warriors Club. *Campus security:* 24-hour emergency response devices and patrols. *Student services:* personal/psychological counseling, women's center.

Athletics Member NJCAA. *Intercollegiate sports:* baseball M(s), basketball M(s), golf M(s), softball W(s), volleyball W(s). *Intramural sports:* basketball M/W, fencing M/W, football M/W, racquetball M/W, riflery M/W, tennis M/W, volleyball M/W.

Standardized Tests *Required:* ACT ASSET (for placement). *Required for some:* ACT (for placement).

Costs (2003–04) *Tuition:* state resident $2370 full-time; nonresident $3570 full-time. *Required fees:* $60 full-time. *Room and board:* $3888; room only: $1650. Room and board charges vary according to board plan and housing facility.

Financial Aid Of all full-time matriculated undergraduates who enrolled, 123 Federal Work-Study jobs (averaging $742). 62 state and other part-time jobs (averaging $823).

Applying *Options:* common application, early admission. *Required for some:* high school transcript. *Application deadline:* rolling (freshmen), rolling (transfers).

Admissions Contact Mrs. Jane Sapp, Admissions Officer, Indian Hills Community College, 525 Grandview Avenue, Building #1, Ottumwa, IA 52501-1398. *Phone:* 641-683-5155. *Toll-free phone:* 800-726-2585.

IOWA CENTRAL COMMUNITY COLLEGE
Fort Dodge, Iowa

- **State and locally supported** 2-year, founded 1966, part of Iowa Department of Education Division of Community Colleges
- **Calendar** semesters
- **Degree** certificates, diplomas, and associate
- **Small-town** 110-acre campus
- **Coed**

Faculty *Student/faculty ratio:* 18:1.

Student Life *Campus security:* 24-hour emergency response devices and patrols, student patrols, late-night transport/escort service, controlled dormitory access.

Athletics Member NJCAA.

Standardized Tests *Required:* SAT I or ACT (for placement), ACT ASSET or ACT COMPASS (for placement).

Costs (2003–04) *Tuition:* state resident $2250 full-time; nonresident $3652 full-time. *Required fees:* $278 full-time.

Applying *Options:* early admission, deferred entrance. *Required:* high school transcript.

Admissions Contact Mr. Brian K. Dioguardi, Director of Admissions, Iowa Central Community College, 330 Avenue M, Ft. Dodge, IA 50501. *Phone:* 515-576-0099 Ext. 2471. *Toll-free phone:* 800-362-2793. *Fax:* 515-576-7724. *E-mail:* admis@duke.iccc.cc.ia.us.

IOWA LAKES COMMUNITY COLLEGE
Estherville, Iowa

- **State and locally supported** 2-year, founded 1967, part of Iowa Area Community Colleges System

- **Calendar** semesters
- **Degree** certificates, diplomas, and associate
- **Small-town** 20-acre campus
- **Endowment** $63,000
- **Coed,** 2,993 undergraduate students, 46% full-time, 55% women, 45% men

Undergraduates 1,371 full-time, 1,622 part-time. Students come from 12 states and territories, 2 other countries, 13% are from out of state, 0.5% African American, 0.3% Asian American or Pacific Islander, 0.7% Hispanic American, 0.3% Native American, 0.4% international, 4% transferred in, 10% live on campus.

Freshmen *Admission:* 1,897 applied, 1,541 admitted, 917 enrolled. *Test scores:* ACT scores over 18: 67%; ACT scores over 24: 12%; ACT scores over 30: 1%.

Faculty *Total:* 153, 53% full-time. *Student/faculty ratio:* 19:1.

Majors Accounting; accounting technology and bookkeeping; administrative assistant and secretarial science; agribusiness; agricultural business and management; agricultural business and management related; agricultural business technology; agricultural economics; agricultural/farm supplies retailing and wholesaling; agricultural mechanics and equipment technology; agricultural mechanization; agricultural power machinery operation; agricultural production; agricultural production related; agricultural teacher education; agriculture; agronomy and crop science; airline pilot and flight crew; animal/livestock husbandry and production; animal sciences; applied art; art; art history, criticism and conservation; art teacher education; astronomy; athletic training; autobody/collision and repair technology; automobile/automotive mechanics technology; aviation/airway management; behavioral sciences; biological and physical sciences; biology/biological sciences; botany/plant biology; broadcast journalism; business administration and management; business automation/technology/data entry; business machine repair; business teacher education; carpentry; ceramic arts and ceramics; chemistry; child care provision; child development; chiropractic assistant; commercial and advertising art; communication and journalism related; computer and information sciences related; computer graphics; computer/information technology services administration related; computer programming; computer science; computer software technology; computer systems networking and telecommunications; construction engineering technology; construction management; construction trades; consumer merchandising/retailing management; cooking and related culinary arts; corrections; criminal justice/law enforcement administration; criminal justice/police science; crop production; culinary arts related; data entry/microcomputer applications; data processing and data processing technology; desktop publishing and digital imaging design; developmental and child psychology; drafting and design technology; drawing; early childhood education; ecology; economics; education; elementary education; emergency care attendant (EMT ambulance); emergency medical technology (EMT paramedic); energy management and systems technology; engineering; English; environmental design/architecture; environmental education; environmental engineering technology; environmental studies; family and consumer sciences/human sciences; farm and ranch management; fashion merchandising; finance; fine/studio arts; fish/game management; fishing and fisheries sciences and management; flight instruction; food preparation; foods and nutrition related; food service and dining room management; foreign languages and literatures; forestry; general studies; geology/earth science; graphic and printing equipment operation/production; graphic communications; graphic design; health and physical education; health/health care administration; history; hospitality administration; hotel/motel administration; humanities; human resources management and services related; hydrology and water resources science; information technology; institutional food workers; jazz/jazz studies; journalism; kindergarten/preschool education; landscaping and groundskeeping; legal administrative assistant/secretary; legal assistant/paralegal; legal studies; liberal arts and sciences and humanities related; liberal arts and sciences/liberal studies; literature; marine maintenance and ship repair technology; marketing/marketing management; massage therapy; mass communication/media; mathematics; medical administrative assistant and medical secretary; medical/clinical assistant; medical laboratory technology; medical office assistant; medical office computer specialist; medical reception; medical transcription; merchandising, sales, and marketing operations related (general); motorcycle maintenance and repair technology; music; music teacher education; natural resources/conservation; natural sciences; nursing (registered nurse training); office management; office occupations and clerical services; parks, recreation and leisure; pharmacy; philosophy; photography; physical education teaching and coaching; physical sciences; piano and organ; political science and government; pre-dentistry studies; pre-engineering; pre-law studies; pre-medical studies; pre-nursing studies; pre-pharmacy studies; pre-veterinary studies; printing press operation; psychology; radio and television; radio and television broadcasting technology; real estate; receptionist; rehabilitation therapy; restaurant, culinary, and catering management; restaurant/food services management; retailing; sales, distribution and marketing; science teacher education; selling skills and sales; small business administration; small engine mechanics and repair technology; social sciences; social work; sociology; soil science and agronomy; Spanish; speech and rhetoric; sport and fitness administration; surgical technology; system administration; system, networking, and LAN/wan management; technology/industrial arts teacher education; tourism and travel services management; tourism and travel services marketing; tourism promotion; trade and industrial teacher education;

turf and turfgrass management; voice and opera; water, wetlands, and marine resources management; welding technology; wildlife and wildlands science and management; wildlife biology; wind/percussion instruments; word processing.

Academic Programs *Special study options:* academic remediation for entering students, accelerated degree program, adult/continuing education programs, advanced placement credit, cooperative education, distance learning, honors programs, independent study, internships, part-time degree program, services for LD students, study abroad, summer session for credit.

Library Iowa Lakes Community College Library plus 2 others with 36,881 titles, 353 serial subscriptions, 1,133 audiovisual materials, an OPAC.

Computers on Campus 1000 computers available on campus for general student use. A campuswide network can be accessed. Internet access, online (class) registration, at least one staffed computer lab available.

Student Life *Housing Options:* coed. Campus housing is university owned. Freshman campus housing is guaranteed. *Activities and Organizations:* drama/theater group, student-run newspaper, radio and television station, choral group, Criminal Justice Club, Ecology Club, Nursing Club, Student Senate, BPA. *Campus security:* 24-hour emergency response devices, student patrols. *Student services:* personal/psychological counseling, women's center.

Athletics Member NJCAA. *Intercollegiate sports:* baseball M(s), basketball M(s)/W(s), cross-country running M/W, golf M(s)/W(s), softball W(s), volleyball W(s), weight lifting M/W. *Intramural sports:* basketball M/W, football M/W, golf M/W, racquetball M/W, skiing (cross-country) M/W, skiing (downhill) M/W, soccer M/W, softball M/W, swimming M/W, table tennis M/W, tennis M/W, volleyball M/W, weight lifting M/W, wrestling M.

Standardized Tests *Required for some:* ACT (for placement), ACT ASSET, ACT COMPASS.

Costs (2003–04) *Tuition:* state resident $2880 full-time, $90 per semester hour part-time; nonresident $2944 full-time, $92 per semester hour part-time. Full-time tuition and fees vary according to course load and program. Part-time tuition and fees vary according to course load and program. *Required fees:* $436 full-time, $9 per semester hour part-time. *Room and board:* $3700. *Payment plan:* installment. *Waivers:* employees or children of employees.

Financial Aid Of all full-time matriculated undergraduates who enrolled, 210 Federal Work-Study jobs (averaging $800).

Applying *Options:* deferred entrance. *Required:* high school transcript. *Required for some:* letters of recommendation, interview. *Application deadline:* rolling (freshmen), rolling (transfers).

Admissions Contact Ms. Anne Stansbury, Assistant Director Admissions, Iowa Lakes Community College, 300 South 18th Street, Estherville, IA 51334. *Phone:* 712-852-5254. *Toll-free phone:* 800-521-5054. *Fax:* 712-362-3969. *E-mail:* info@ilcc.cc.ia.us.

IOWA WESTERN COMMUNITY COLLEGE
Council Bluffs, Iowa

- **District-supported** 2-year, founded 1966, part of Iowa Department of Education Division of Community Colleges
- **Calendar** semesters
- **Degree** certificates, diplomas, and associate
- **Suburban** 282-acre campus with easy access to Omaha
- **Coed**

Student Life *Campus security:* 24-hour patrols, late-night transport/escort service.

Athletics Member NJCAA.

Standardized Tests *Required:* SAT I (for placement), ACT (for placement), ACT ASSET or ACT COMPASS (for placement).

Costs (2003–04) *One-time required fee:* $25. *Tuition:* state resident $2730 full-time; nonresident $4095 full-time. *Required fees:* $320 full-time. *Room and board:* $4050.

Applying *Options:* early admission, deferred entrance. *Required:* high school transcript.

Admissions Contact Mrs. Tammy Young, Director of Admissions, Iowa Western Community College, 2700 College Road, Box 4-C, Council Bluffs, IA 51502. *Phone:* 712-325-3288. *Toll-free phone:* 800-432-5852. *Fax:* 712-325-3720. *E-mail:* tyoung@iwcc.cc.ia.us.

KAPLAN COLLEGE
Davenport, Iowa

- **Proprietary** primarily 2-year, founded 1937, part of Kaplan Higher Education
- **Calendar** quarters
- **Degrees** certificates, diplomas, associate, and bachelor's (profile includes both traditional and on-line students)
- **Suburban** campus
- **Coed**, 9,194 undergraduate students, 18% full-time, 72% women, 28% men

Undergraduates 1,648 full-time, 7,546 part-time. Students come from 2 states and territories, 91% are from out of state, 1% African American, 0.1% Asian American or Pacific Islander, 0.4% Hispanic American, 16% transferred in.

Freshmen *Admission:* 5,017 applied, 4,695 admitted, 4,635 enrolled.

Faculty *Total:* 411, 14% full-time, 23% with terminal degrees. *Student/faculty ratio:* 11:1.

Majors Accounting; business administration and management; business/commerce; computer and information sciences; court reporting; criminal justice/safety; information technology; legal assistant/paralegal; management information systems; medical/clinical assistant; medical transcription; multi-/interdisciplinary studies related; tourism and travel services management.

Academic Programs *Special study options:* academic remediation for entering students, adult/continuing education programs, cooperative education, distance learning, double majors, independent study, internships, part-time degree program, summer session for credit.

Library Academic Resource Center with 7,000 titles, 120 serial subscriptions, 504 audiovisual materials, an OPAC.

Computers on Campus 120 computers available on campus for general student use. A campuswide network can be accessed. Internet access, at least one staffed computer lab available.

Student Life *Housing:* college housing not available. *Activities and Organizations:* academic department clubs. *Student services:* personal/psychological counseling.

Costs (2003–04) *Tuition:* $10,620 full-time, $236 per credit part-time. *Waivers:* employees or children of employees.

Applying *Options:* early admission, deferred entrance. *Application fee:* $25. *Required:* high school transcript, interview. *Application deadline:* rolling (freshmen), rolling (transfers).

Admissions Contact Mr. Robert Hoffmann, Director of Admissions, Kaplan College, 1801 East Kimberly Road, Suite 1, Davenport, IA 52807. *Phone:* 563-441-2496. *Toll-free phone:* 800-747-1035. *Fax:* 563-355-1320. *E-mail:* infoke@kaplancollege.edu.

KIRKWOOD COMMUNITY COLLEGE
Cedar Rapids, Iowa

- **State and locally supported** 2-year, founded 1966, part of Iowa Department of Education Division of Community Colleges
- **Calendar** semesters
- **Degree** certificates, diplomas, and associate
- **Suburban** 630-acre campus
- **Endowment** $4.4 million
- **Coed**, 15,032 undergraduate students, 55% full-time, 54% women, 46% men

Undergraduates 8,319 full-time, 6,713 part-time. Students come from 15 states and territories, 85 other countries, 2% are from out of state, 4% African American, 1% Asian American or Pacific Islander, 2% Hispanic American, 1% Native American, 2% international, 9% transferred in.

Freshmen *Admission:* 3,049 enrolled. *Test scores:* ACT scores over 18: 71%; ACT scores over 24: 16%; ACT scores over 30: 1%.

Faculty *Total:* 737, 35% full-time. *Student/faculty ratio:* 23:1.

Majors Accounting; administrative assistant and secretarial science; agricultural business and management; agricultural teacher education; agriculture; agronomy and crop science; animal sciences; applied art; art; artificial intelligence and robotics; art teacher education; automobile/automotive mechanics technology; biological and physical sciences; biology/biological sciences; biology/biotechnology laboratory technician; broadcast journalism; business administration and management; business teacher education; ceramic arts and ceramics; child development; communications technology; computer programming; computer science; construction engineering technology; consumer merchandising/retailing management; corrections; criminal justice/law enforcement administration; criminal justice/police science; culinary arts; data processing and data processing technology; developmental and child psychology; drafting and design technology; dramatic/theatre arts; education; electrical, electronic and communications engineering technology; electromechanical technology; elementary education; engineering; English; equestrian studies; farm and ranch management; fashion/apparel design; fashion merchandising; finance; fire science; fish/game management; food services technology; forestry; French; graphic and printing equipment operation/production; health information/medical records administration; heating, air conditioning, ventilation and refrigeration maintenance technology; history; horticultural science; hospitality and recreation marketing; hotel/motel administration; humanities; human services; hydrology and water resources science; industrial technology; interior design; international business/trade/commerce; jazz/jazz studies; journalism; kindergarten/preschool education; landscape architecture; legal administrative assistant/secretary; legal assistant/paralegal; legal studies; liberal arts and sciences/liberal studies; management information systems; marketing/marketing management; mass communication/media; mathematics; mechanical design technology; mechanical engineering/mechanical technology; medical administrative assistant and medical secretary; medical/clinical assistant; music; natural resources/conservation; nursing (licensed

Kirkwood Community College (continued)

practical/vocational nurse training); nursing (registered nurse training); occupational therapy; ornamental horticulture; parks, recreation and leisure; parks, recreation and leisure facilities management; physical education teaching and coaching; political science and government; pre-engineering; psychology; public relations/image management; radio and television; respiratory care therapy; sanitation technology; social sciences; social work; sociology; Spanish; special products marketing; teacher assistant/aide; telecommunications; veterinary sciences; veterinary technology; voice and opera; welding technology; wildlife and wildlands science and management; wildlife biology; wind/percussion instruments.

Academic Programs *Special study options:* academic remediation for entering students, accelerated degree program, adult/continuing education programs, advanced placement credit, cooperative education, distance learning, English as a second language, external degree program, honors programs, internships, off-campus study, part-time degree program, services for LD students, student-designed majors, summer session for credit.

Library Library with 60,622 titles, 565 serial subscriptions, 3,677 audiovisual materials, an OPAC.

Computers on Campus 1000 computers available on campus for general student use. A campuswide network can be accessed. Internet access, online (class) registration, at least one staffed computer lab available.

Student Life *Housing:* college housing not available. *Activities and Organizations:* drama/theater group, student-run newspaper, choral group. *Campus security:* 24-hour patrols. *Student services:* health clinic, personal/psychological counseling, legal services.

Athletics Member NJCAA. *Intercollegiate sports:* baseball M(s), basketball M(s)/W(s), golf M(s), soccer M/W, softball W(s), volleyball W(s). *Intramural sports:* basketball M/W, football M/W, golf M/W, racquetball M/W, soccer M/W, softball W, tennis M/W, volleyball M/W, weight lifting M/W.

Standardized Tests *Required:* ACT (for placement), ACT COMPASS (for placement).

Costs (2003–04) *Tuition:* state resident $2490 full-time; nonresident $4980 full-time.

Applying *Options:* electronic application, early admission. *Required:* high school transcript. *Application deadline:* rolling (freshmen), rolling (transfers). *Notification:* continuous (freshmen), continuous (transfers).

Admissions Contact Mr. Doug Bannon, Director of Admissions, Kirkwood Community College, PO Box 2068, Cedar Rapids, IA 52406-2068. *Phone:* 319-398-5517. *Toll-free phone:* 800-332-2055. *E-mail:* dbannon@kirkwood.cc.ia.us.

MARSHALLTOWN COMMUNITY COLLEGE
Marshalltown, Iowa

- **District-supported** 2-year, founded 1927, part of Iowa Valley Community College District System
- **Calendar** semesters
- **Degree** certificates, diplomas, and associate
- **Small-town** 200-acre campus
- **Endowment** $1.7 million
- **Coed**, 1,421 undergraduate students, 64% full-time, 61% women, 39% men

Undergraduates 903 full-time, 518 part-time. Students come from 3 states and territories, 10 other countries, 1% are from out of state, 3% African American, 1% Asian American or Pacific Islander, 4% Hispanic American, 3% Native American, 2% international, 100% transferred in, 8% live on campus.

Freshmen *Admission:* 495 enrolled. *Average high school GPA:* 1.88.

Faculty *Total:* 109, 38% full-time. *Student/faculty ratio:* 29:1.

Majors Accounting; administrative assistant and secretarial science; biological and physical sciences; business administration and management; child development; community organization and advocacy; computer science; dental assisting; drafting and design technology; economics; electrical, electronic and communications engineering technology; heavy equipment maintenance technology; industrial radiologic technology; liberal arts and sciences/liberal studies; machine tool technology; marketing/marketing management; mental health/rehabilitation; nursing (licensed practical/vocational nurse training); nursing (registered nurse training); political science and government; pre-engineering.

Academic Programs *Special study options:* academic remediation for entering students, adult/continuing education programs, advanced placement credit, cooperative education, distance learning, English as a second language, freshman honors college, honors programs, independent study, internships, part-time degree program, services for LD students, student-designed majors, study abroad, summer session for credit. *ROTC:* Air Force (c).

Library Learning Resource Center with 39,348 titles, 216 serial subscriptions, a Web page.

Computers on Campus 250 computers available on campus for general student use. A campuswide network can be accessed from student residence rooms. Internet access, online (class) registration, at least one staffed computer lab available.

Student Life *Housing Options:* coed. Campus housing is university owned. *Activities and Organizations:* drama/theater group, student-run newspaper, radio and television station, choral group, Student Activities Council, Student Senate, College Community Connection, SAMS, International Student Association. *Student services:* personal/psychological counseling.

Athletics Member NJCAA. *Intercollegiate sports:* baseball M(s), basketball M(s)/W(s), cheerleading M(s)/W(s), golf M(s)/W(s), soccer M(s)/W, softball W(s), volleyball W(s). *Intramural sports:* bowling M/W, racquetball M/W, table tennis M/W, tennis M/W, ultimate Frisbee M/W, volleyball W, weight lifting M/W.

Standardized Tests *Required:* ACT COMPASS (for admission). *Recommended:* ACT (for admission).

Costs (2003–04) *Tuition:* state resident $2430 full-time, $89 per credit part-time; nonresident $2460 full-time. Full-time tuition and fees vary according to course load and program. Part-time tuition and fees vary according to course load and program. *Required fees:* $645 full-time, $22 per credit part-time. *Room and board:* $4400; room only: $2600. *Payment plan:* installment. *Waivers:* senior citizens and employees or children of employees.

Financial Aid Of all full-time matriculated undergraduates who enrolled, 28 Federal Work-Study jobs (averaging $1800).

Applying *Options:* common application, electronic application, early admission. *Required:* high school transcript. *Required for some:* letters of recommendation, interview. *Application deadline:* rolling (freshmen), rolling (transfers). *Notification:* continuous (freshmen), continuous (transfers).

Admissions Contact Ms. Deana Trawny, Director of Admissions, Marshalltown Community College, 3700 South Center Street, Marshalltown, IA 50158. *Phone:* 641-752-7106 Ext. 391. *Toll-free phone:* 866-622-4748. *Fax:* 641-752-8149.

MUSCATINE COMMUNITY COLLEGE
Muscatine, Iowa

- **State-supported** 2-year, founded 1929, part of Eastern Iowa Community College District
- **Calendar** semesters
- **Degree** certificates, diplomas, and associate
- **Small-town** 25-acre campus
- **Coed**

Athletics Member NJCAA.

Standardized Tests *Required:* ACT or DTLS, DTMS (for placement).

Costs (2003–04) *Tuition:* area resident $2400 full-time, $80 per semester hour part-time; nonresident $3600 full-time, $120 per semester hour part-time. *Room and board:* room only: $3655.

Financial Aid Of all full-time matriculated undergraduates who enrolled, 48 Federal Work-Study jobs (averaging $3000).

Applying *Options:* early admission, deferred entrance. *Required:* high school transcript.

Admissions Contact Neil Mandsager, Executive Director of Enrollment Management and Marketing, Muscatine Community College, 152 Colorado Street, Muscatine, IA 52761-5396. *Phone:* 563-288-6012. *Toll-free phone:* 800-351-4669.

NORTHEAST IOWA COMMUNITY COLLEGE
Calmar, Iowa

- **State and locally supported** 2-year, founded 1966, part of Iowa Area Community Colleges System
- **Calendar** semesters
- **Degree** certificates, diplomas, and associate
- **Small-town** 210-acre campus
- **Coed**, 4,724 undergraduate students

Undergraduates Students come from 5 states and territories, 3% are from out of state, 1% African American, 0.5% Asian American or Pacific Islander, 0.5% Hispanic American, 0.5% Native American.

Faculty *Total:* 174, 67% full-time, 11% with terminal degrees. *Student/faculty ratio:* 16:1.

Majors Accounting; agricultural business and management; clinical/medical laboratory technology; computer engineering technology; construction engineering technology; dairy science; electrical, electronic and communications engineering technology; health information/medical records administration; liberal arts and sciences/liberal studies; marketing/marketing management; mechanical design technology; nursing (registered nurse training); trade and industrial teacher education.

Academic Programs *Special study options:* academic remediation for entering students, adult/continuing education programs, cooperative education, distance learning, double majors, English as a second language, independent study, internships, off-campus study, services for LD students, student-designed majors, study abroad, summer session for credit.

Library Wilder Resource Center plus 1 other with 18,634 titles, 302 serial subscriptions, an OPAC.

Computers on Campus 4000 computers available on campus for general student use. A campuswide network can be accessed from off campus. Internet access, at least one staffed computer lab available.

Student Life *Housing:* college housing not available. *Campus security:* security personnel on week nights. *Student services:* personal/psychological counseling.

Athletics *Intramural sports:* basketball M/W, bowling M/W, football M/W, golf M/W, skiing (cross-country) M/W, skiing (downhill) M/W, swimming M/W, tennis M/W, volleyball M/W.

Standardized Tests *Required:* ACT ASSET (for placement). *Required for some:* ACT (for placement).

Costs (2003–04) *Tuition:* state resident $2976 full-time, $93 per credit part-time. *Required fees:* $384 full-time, $12 per credit part-time. *Payment plan:* deferred payment. *Waivers:* senior citizens and employees or children of employees.

Financial Aid Of all full-time matriculated undergraduates who enrolled, 154 Federal Work-Study jobs (averaging $1248). 45 state and other part-time jobs (averaging $980).

Applying *Recommended:* high school transcript. *Application deadline:* rolling (freshmen), rolling (transfers). *Notification:* continuous (freshmen), continuous (transfers).

Admissions Contact Ms. Martha Keune, Admissions Representative, Northeast Iowa Community College, PO Box 400, Calmar, IA 52132. *Phone:* 563-562-3263 Ext. 307. *Toll-free phone:* 800-728-CALMAR. *E-mail:* keunem@nicc.edu.

NORTH IOWA AREA COMMUNITY COLLEGE
Mason City, Iowa

- **State and locally supported** 2-year, founded 1918, part of Iowa Community Colleges System
- **Calendar** semesters
- **Degree** certificates, diplomas, and associate
- **Rural** 320-acre campus
- **Coed,** 2,837 undergraduate students, 63% full-time, 55% women, 45% men

Undergraduates 1,776 full-time, 1,061 part-time. Students come from 24 states and territories, 21 other countries, 3% are from out of state, 4% African American, 0.9% Asian American or Pacific Islander, 3% Hispanic American, 0.2% Native American, 0.8% international, 15% live on campus. *Retention:* 58% of 2002 full-time freshmen returned.

Freshmen *Admission:* 3,133 applied, 3,133 admitted, 742 enrolled. *Average high school GPA:* 2.62. *Test scores:* ACT scores over 18: 78%; ACT scores over 24: 21%; ACT scores over 30: 1%.

Faculty *Total:* 157, 54% full-time, 6% with terminal degrees. *Student/faculty ratio:* 13:1.

Majors Accounting; accounting technology and bookkeeping; administrative assistant and secretarial science; agricultural business technology; agricultural economics; agricultural production; automobile/automotive mechanics technology; business administration and management; carpentry; clinical/medical laboratory technology; computer and information sciences; criminal justice/police science; electrical, electronic and communications engineering technology; emergency medical technology (EMT paramedic); entrepreneurship; fire services administration; heating, air conditioning, ventilation and refrigeration maintenance technology; industrial electronics technology; liberal arts and sciences/liberal studies; machine shop technology; machine tool technology; medical/clinical assistant; nursing assistant/aide and patient care assistant; nursing (licensed practical/vocational nurse training); nursing (registered nurse training); physical therapist assistant; sport and fitness administration; tool and die technology; welding technology.

Academic Programs *Special study options:* academic remediation for entering students, advanced placement credit, cooperative education, distance learning, double majors, English as a second language, external degree program, honors programs, independent study, internships, off-campus study, part-time degree program, services for LD students, student-designed majors, summer session for credit.

Library North Iowa Area Community College Library with 49,287 titles, 377 serial subscriptions, 14,548 audiovisual materials, an OPAC, a Web page.

Computers on Campus 365 computers available on campus for general student use. A campuswide network can be accessed from off campus. Internet access, at least one staffed computer lab available.

Student Life *Housing:* on-campus residence required for freshman year. *Options:* coed. Campus housing is provided by a third party. Freshman applicants given priority for college housing. *Activities and Organizations:* student-run

newspaper, choral group, Student Senate, school newspaper, intramurals, choral groups, band/orchestra. *Campus security:* 24-hour emergency response devices, controlled dormitory access. *Student services:* health clinic, personal/psychological counseling.

Athletics Member NJCAA. *Intercollegiate sports:* baseball M(s), basketball M(s)/W(s), cross-country running W(s), football M(s), golf M(s)/W(s), soccer M(s)/W(s), softball W(s), volleyball W(s). *Intramural sports:* basketball M/W, bowling M/W, cheerleading W, football M, skiing (downhill) M/W, soccer M/W, softball W, table tennis M/W, tennis M/W, volleyball M/W, weight lifting M/W.

Standardized Tests *Required for some:* ACT (for placement). *Recommended:* ACT (for placement), ACT COMPASS.

Costs (2003–04) *Tuition:* state resident $2490 full-time, $83 per semester hour part-time; nonresident $3735 full-time, $125 per semester hour part-time. *Required fees:* $314 full-time, $10 per semester hour part-time. *Room and board:* $3660. Room and board charges vary according to board plan. *Payment plan:* installment.

Financial Aid Of all full-time matriculated undergraduates who enrolled, 125 Federal Work-Study jobs (averaging $2000).

Applying *Options:* common application, electronic application. *Required for some:* high school transcript. *Recommended:* high school transcript. *Application deadline:* rolling (freshmen), rolling (transfers). *Notification:* continuous (freshmen), continuous (transfers).

Admissions Contact Ms. Rachel McGuire, Director of Admissions, North Iowa Area Community College, 500 College Drive, Mason City, IA 50401. *Phone:* 641-422-4104. *Toll-free phone:* 888-GO NIACC Ext. 4245. *Fax:* 641-422-4385. *E-mail:* request@niacc.edu.

NORTHWEST IOWA COMMUNITY COLLEGE
Sheldon, Iowa

- **State-supported** 2-year, founded 1966, part of Iowa Department of Education Division of Community Colleges
- **Calendar** semesters
- **Degree** certificates, diplomas, and associate
- **Small-town** 263-acre campus with easy access to Sioux City, IA; Sioux Falls, SD
- **Coed,** 1,079 undergraduate students, 49% full-time, 55% women, 45% men

Undergraduates 533 full-time, 546 part-time. Students come from 10 states and territories, 4% are from out of state, 0.3% African American, 1% Asian American or Pacific Islander, 0.7% Hispanic American, 0.2% Native American, 5% live on campus. *Retention:* 56% of 2002 full-time freshmen returned.

Freshmen *Admission:* 1,113 applied, 1,106 admitted, 304 enrolled.

Faculty *Total:* 80, 48% full-time, 8% with terminal degrees. *Student/faculty ratio:* 15:1.

Majors Accounting; administrative assistant and secretarial science; autobody/collision and repair technology; automobile/automotive mechanics technology; business administration and management; computer programming; computer programming related; computer systems networking and telecommunications; construction/heavy equipment/earthmoving equipment operation; diesel mechanics technology; electrical, electronic and communications engineering technology; emergency medical technology (EMT paramedic); health information/medical records technology; industrial electronics technology; liberal arts and sciences/liberal studies; lineworker; machine shop technology; mechanical design technology; nursing (licensed practical/vocational nurse training); nursing (registered nurse training); tool and die technology; welding technology.

Academic Programs *Special study options:* academic remediation for entering students, adult/continuing education programs, cooperative education, distance learning, part-time degree program, services for LD students, summer session for credit.

Library Northwest Iowa Community College Library plus 1 other with 12,500 titles, 340 serial subscriptions, 2,500 audiovisual materials, an OPAC, a Web page.

Computers on Campus 142 computers available on campus for general student use. A campuswide network can be accessed. Internet access, at least one staffed computer lab available.

Student Life *Housing Options:* coed. Campus housing is university owned. *Activities and Organizations:* student-run newspaper. *Campus security:* 24-hour emergency response devices. *Student services:* personal/psychological counseling.

Athletics *Intramural sports:* basketball M/W, bowling M/W, football M, volleyball M/W.

Standardized Tests *Required:* ACT COMPASS (for placement). *Required for some:* ACT COMPASS.

Costs (2004–05) *Tuition:* state resident $3496 full-time, $92 per credit part-time; nonresident $4788 full-time, $126 per credit part-time. Full-time tuition and fees vary according to course load. Part-time tuition and fees vary according to course load. *Required fees:* $700 full-time, $15 per credit part-time. *Room and board:* room only: $1900. *Payment plan:* deferred payment.

Northwest Iowa Community College (continued)

Financial Aid Of all full-time matriculated undergraduates who enrolled, 60 Federal Work-Study jobs (averaging $900).

Applying *Options:* common application, electronic application. *Application fee:* $10. *Required:* high school transcript. *Required for some:* 2.0 letters of recommendation. *Application deadline:* rolling (freshmen), rolling (transfers). *Notification:* continuous (freshmen), continuous (transfers).

Admissions Contact Ms. Lisa Story, Director of Enrollment Management, Northwest Iowa Community College, 603 West Park Street, Sheldon, IA 51201-1046. *Phone:* 712-324-5061 Ext. 115. *Toll-free phone:* 800-352-4907. *Fax:* 712-324-4136.

ST. LUKE'S COLLEGE
Sioux City, Iowa

- **Independent** 2-year, part of St. Luke's Regional Medical Center
- **Calendar** semesters
- **Degree** certificates and associate
- **Rural** campus
- **Endowment** $424,225
- **Coed, primarily women,** 147 undergraduate students, 65% full-time, 91% women, 9% men

Undergraduates 96 full-time, 51 part-time. Students come from 8 states and territories, 1 other country, 25% are from out of state, 0.7% African American, 1% Hispanic American, 0.7% international, 6% transferred in, 34% live on campus. *Retention:* 82% of 2002 full-time freshmen returned.

Freshmen *Admission:* 60 applied, 33 admitted, 27 enrolled. *Average high school GPA:* 3.12. *Test scores:* ACT scores over 18: 100%; ACT scores over 24: 13%.

Faculty *Total:* 16, 63% full-time, 31% with terminal degrees. *Student/faculty ratio:* 7:1.

Majors Nursing (registered nurse training); radiologic technology/science; respiratory care therapy.

Academic Programs *Special study options:* advanced placement credit, cooperative education, part-time degree program, summer session for credit.

Library St. Luke's Media Services Library plus 1 other with 115 serial subscriptions, 1,800 audiovisual materials, an OPAC, a Web page.

Computers on Campus 10 computers available on campus for general student use. A campuswide network can be accessed. Internet access, at least one staffed computer lab available.

Student Life *Housing Options:* coed. Campus housing is university owned. *Campus security:* 24-hour emergency response devices and patrols, late-night transport/escort service. *Student services:* health clinic, personal/psychological counseling.

Standardized Tests *Required:* ACT (for admission).

Costs (2004–05) *Comprehensive fee:* $14,780 includes full-time tuition ($11,088), mandatory fees ($570), and room and board ($3122). Full-time tuition and fees vary according to course load and program. Part-time tuition: $308 per credit hour. Part-time tuition and fees vary according to course load and program. *Room and board:* college room only: $2622. Room and board charges vary according to board plan. *Payment plan:* installment. *Waivers:* employees or children of employees.

Financial Aid Of all full-time matriculated undergraduates who enrolled, 12 Federal Work-Study jobs (averaging $935).

Applying *Application fee:* $100. *Required:* essay or personal statement, high school transcript, minimum 2.50 GPA, minimum ACT score of 19. *Application deadline:* 8/1 (freshmen). *Notification:* 8/1 (freshmen), continuous (transfers).

Admissions Contact Ms. Sherry McCarthy, Admissions Coordinator, St. Luke's College, 2720 Stone Park Boulevard, Sioux City, IA 51104. *Phone:* 712-279-3149. *Toll-free phone:* 800-352-4660 Ext. 3149. *Fax:* 712-233-8017. *E-mail:* mccartsj@stlukes.org.

SCOTT COMMUNITY COLLEGE
Bettendorf, Iowa

- **State and locally supported** 2-year, founded 1966, part of Eastern Iowa Community College District
- **Calendar** semesters
- **Degree** certificates, diplomas, and associate
- **Urban** campus
- **Coed**

Faculty *Student/faculty ratio:* 20:1.

Student Life *Campus security:* 24-hour emergency response devices.

Athletics Member NJCAA.

Standardized Tests *Required:* ACT (for placement), College Board Diagnostic Tests (for placement).

Costs (2003–04) *Tuition:* area resident $2400 full-time, $80 per semester hour part-time; nonresident $3600 full-time, $120 per semester hour part-time.

Financial Aid Of all full-time matriculated undergraduates who enrolled, 67 Federal Work-Study jobs (averaging $3000).

Applying *Options:* early admission, deferred entrance. *Required:* high school transcript.

Admissions Contact Mr. Neil Mandsager, Executive Director of Enrollment Management and Marketing, Scott Community College, 500 Belmont Road, Bettendorf, IA 52722-6804. *Phone:* 563-441-4007. *Toll-free phone:* 800-895-0811.

SOUTHEASTERN COMMUNITY COLLEGE, NORTH CAMPUS
West Burlington, Iowa

- **State and locally supported** 2-year, founded 1968, part of Iowa Department of Education Division of Community Colleges
- **Calendar** semesters
- **Degree** diplomas and associate
- **Small-town** 160-acre campus
- **Coed**

Student Life *Campus security:* controlled dormitory access, night patrols by trained security personnel.

Athletics Member NJCAA.

Standardized Tests *Required:* ACT ASSET (for placement). *Recommended:* ACT (for placement).

Costs (2003–04) *Tuition:* state resident $2040 full-time, $85 per credit hour part-time; nonresident $2208 full-time, $92 per credit hour part-time.

Applying *Options:* early admission, deferred entrance.

Admissions Contact Ms. Stacy White, Admissions, Southeastern Community College, North Campus, 1015 South Gear Avenue, PO Box 180, West Burlington, IA 52655-0180. *Phone:* 319-752-2731 Ext. 8137. *Toll-free phone:* 866-722-4692. *E-mail:* admoff@secc.cc.ia.us.

SOUTHEASTERN COMMUNITY COLLEGE, SOUTH CAMPUS
Keokuk, Iowa

- **State and locally supported** 2-year, founded 1967, part of Iowa Department of Education Division of Community Colleges
- **Calendar** semesters
- **Degree** certificates, diplomas, and associate
- **Small-town** 3-acre campus
- **Coed**

Standardized Tests *Required:* ACT ASSET (for placement).

Costs (2003–04) *Tuition:* state resident $2040 full-time, $85 per credit hour part-time; nonresident $2208 full-time, $92 per credit hour part-time.

Applying *Options:* electronic application, early admission, deferred entrance. *Recommended:* high school transcript.

Admissions Contact Ms. Kari Bevans, Admissions Coordinator, Southeastern Community College, South Campus, PO Box 6007, 335 Messenger Road, Keokuk, IA 52632. *Phone:* 319-752-2731. *Toll-free phone:* 866-722-4692 Ext. 8416. *Fax:* 319-524-8621. *E-mail:* kbevans@secc.cc.ia.us.

SOUTHWESTERN COMMUNITY COLLEGE
Creston, Iowa

- **State-supported** 2-year, founded 1966, part of Iowa Department of Education Division of Community Colleges
- **Calendar** semesters
- **Degree** diplomas and associate
- **Rural** 420-acre campus
- **Endowment** $318,170
- **Coed**

Faculty *Student/faculty ratio:* 14:1.

Student Life *Campus security:* 24-hour emergency response devices and patrols, controlled dormitory access.

Athletics Member NJCAA.

Standardized Tests *Required:* ACT (for placement), ACT ASSET (for placement).

Costs (2003–04) *Tuition:* state resident $2910 full-time, $85 per credit part-time; nonresident $4185 full-time, $128 per credit part-time. *Required fees:* $384 full-time, $12 per hour part-time. *Room and board:* $3400.

Financial Aid Of all full-time matriculated undergraduates who enrolled, 95 Federal Work-Study jobs (averaging $1800). 50 state and other part-time jobs (averaging $1000).

Applying *Options:* common application, early admission. *Required:* high school transcript.

Admissions Contact Ms. Lisa Carstens, Admissions Coordinator, Southwestern Community College, 1501 West Townline Street, Creston, IA 50801. *Phone:* 641-782-7081. *Toll-free phone:* 800-247-4023. *Fax:* 641-782-3312. *E-mail:* admissions@swcc.cc.ia.us.

VATTEROTT COLLEGE
Des Moines, Iowa

- **Proprietary** 2-year
- **Calendar** semesters
- **Degree** certificates and first professional certificates
- **Urban** 25-acre campus
- **Coed,** 131 undergraduate students, 100% full-time, 15% women, 85% men

Undergraduates 131 full-time. 6% African American, 3% Asian American or Pacific Islander, 3% Hispanic American.
Freshmen *Admission:* 131 enrolled.
Faculty *Total:* 9, 78% full-time. *Student/faculty ratio:* 15:1.
Costs (2004–05) *Tuition:* $8650 full-time. *Required fees:* $525 full-time.
Admissions Contact Mr. Henry Franken, Co-Director, Vatterott College, 6100 Thornton Avenue, Suite 290, Des Moines, IA 50321. *Phone:* 515-309-9000. *Toll-free phone:* 800-353-7264.

WESTERN IOWA TECH COMMUNITY COLLEGE
Sioux City, Iowa

- **State-supported** 2-year, founded 1966, part of Iowa Department of Education Division of Community Colleges
- **Calendar** semesters
- **Degree** certificates, diplomas, and associate
- **Urban** 143-acre campus
- **Endowment** $337,763
- **Coed,** 5,238 undergraduate students, 39% full-time, 54% women, 46% men

Undergraduates 2,063 full-time, 3,175 part-time. Students come from 11 states and territories, 11% are from out of state, 3% African American, 2% Asian American or Pacific Islander, 5% Hispanic American, 2% Native American, 4% transferred in, 3% live on campus.
Freshmen *Admission:* 2,041 applied, 2,041 admitted, 410 enrolled. *Average high school GPA:* 2.50.
Faculty *Total:* 257, 34% full-time, 7% with terminal degrees. *Student/faculty ratio:* 23:1.
Majors Agricultural/farm supplies retailing and wholesaling; architectural engineering technology; autobody/collision and repair technology; automobile/automotive mechanics technology; biomedical technology; business administration and management; child care and support services management; clinical/medical laboratory technology; computer programming (specific applications); computer typography and composition equipment operation; criminal justice/law enforcement administration; diesel mechanics technology; electrical, electronic and communications engineering technology; emergency medical technology (EMT paramedic); executive assistant/executive secretary; heating, air conditioning, ventilation and refrigeration maintenance technology; legal administrative assistant/secretary; liberal arts and sciences/liberal studies; machine tool technology; medical administrative assistant and medical secretary; nursing assistant/aide and patient care assistant; nursing (registered nurse training); occupational therapist assistant; physical therapist assistant; tool and die technology; turf and turfgrass management.
Academic Programs *Special study options:* academic remediation for entering students, accelerated degree program, adult/continuing education programs, cooperative education, distance learning, double majors, English as a second language, honors programs, independent study, internships, part-time degree program, services for LD students, summer session for credit.
Library Western Iowa Tech Community College Library Services with 25,696 titles, 1,886 serial subscriptions, 3,456 audiovisual materials, an OPAC.
Computers on Campus 640 computers available on campus for general student use. A campuswide network can be accessed from student residence rooms and from off campus. Internet access, at least one staffed computer lab available.
Student Life *Housing Options:* coed. *Activities and Organizations:* Student Senate. *Campus security:* 24-hour emergency response devices and patrols. *Student services:* health clinic, personal/psychological counseling.

Athletics *Intramural sports:* basketball M/W, bowling M/W, football M/W, golf M/W, skiing (downhill) M/W, softball W, volleyball M/W, weight lifting M/W.
Standardized Tests *Required:* CPT (for placement).
Costs (2003–04) *Tuition:* state resident $2520 full-time; nonresident $3990 full-time. *Required fees:* $390 full-time. *Room and board:* room only: $1890.
Applying *Options:* common application, early admission, deferred entrance. *Application fee:* $10. *Required:* high school transcript. *Application deadline:* rolling (freshmen), rolling (transfers). *Notification:* continuous (freshmen), continuous (transfers).
Admissions Contact Lora Vanderzwaag, Director of Admissions, Western Iowa Tech Community College, 4647 Stone Avenue, Sioux City, IA 51102-5199. *Phone:* 712-274-6400. *Toll-free phone:* 800-352-4649 Ext. 6403. *Fax:* 712-274-6441.

KANSAS

ALLEN COUNTY COMMUNITY COLLEGE
Iola, Kansas

- **State and locally supported** 2-year, founded 1923, part of Kansas State Board of Regents
- **Calendar** semesters
- **Degree** certificates and associate
- **Small-town** 88-acre campus
- **Endowment** $2.7 million
- **Coed**

Faculty *Student/faculty ratio:* 17:1.
Student Life *Campus security:* controlled dormitory access.
Athletics Member NJCAA.
Standardized Tests *Recommended:* ACT (for placement).
Costs (2003–04) *Tuition:* area resident $1024 full-time, $32 per credit hour part-time; state resident $1120 full-time, $35 per credit hour part-time. *Required fees:* $768 full-time, $24 per credit hour part-time. *Room and board:* $3456; room only: $2450. Room and board charges vary according to housing facility.
Financial Aid Of all full-time matriculated undergraduates who enrolled, 25 Federal Work-Study jobs (averaging $1650). 80 state and other part-time jobs (averaging $1650).
Applying *Options:* common application, early admission, deferred entrance. *Required:* high school transcript.
Admissions Contact Ms. Tina Rockhotel, Director of Admissions, Allen County Community College, 1801 North Cottonwood, Iola, KS 66749. *Phone:* 620-365-5116 Ext. 267. *E-mail:* kegler@allencc.net.

BARTON COUNTY COMMUNITY COLLEGE
Great Bend, Kansas

- **State and locally supported** 2-year, founded 1969, part of Kansas Board of Regents
- **Calendar** semesters
- **Degree** certificates and associate
- **Rural** 140-acre campus
- **Endowment** $4.2 million
- **Coed,** 3,032 undergraduate students, 28% full-time, 61% women, 39% men

Undergraduates 851 full-time, 2,181 part-time. Students come from 40 states and territories, 18 other countries, 7% are from out of state, 15% African American, 2% Asian American or Pacific Islander, 7% Hispanic American, 0.7% Native American, 2% international, 16% transferred in, 8% live on campus.
Freshmen *Admission:* 754 applied, 754 admitted, 743 enrolled.
Faculty *Total:* 201, 34% full-time, 4% with terminal degrees. *Student/faculty ratio:* 14:1.
Majors Accounting; administrative assistant and secretarial science; agricultural business and management; agriculture; anthropology; architecture; art; athletic training; automobile/automotive mechanics technology; banking and financial support services; biology/biological sciences; business administration and management; business computer programming; chemistry; child care and support services management; chiropractic assistant; clinical/medical laboratory technology; communication/speech communication and rhetoric; computer/information technology services administration related; computer science; computer systems networking and telecommunications; criminal justice/police science; crop production; cytotechnology; dance; dental hygiene; dietitian assistant; dramatic/theatre arts; early childhood education; economics; elementary educa-

Barton County Community College (continued)

tion; emergency medical technology (EMT paramedic); engineering technology; English; fire science; forestry; funeral service and mortuary science; general studies; geology/earth science; graphic design; hazardous materials management and waste technology; health information/medical records administration; history; home health aide; human resources management and services related; information science/studies; journalism; kinesiology and exercise science; liberal arts and sciences/liberal studies; livestock management; marketing/marketing management; mathematics; medical administrative assistant and medical secretary; military studies; modern languages; music; nursing (registered nurse training); occupational therapy; optometric technician; pharmacy; philosophy; physical education teaching and coaching; physical sciences; physical therapist assistant; physical therapy; physician assistant; physics; political science and government; pre-dentistry studies; pre-engineering; pre-law; pre-medical studies; pre-veterinary studies; psychology; public administration; radiologic technology/science; religious studies; respiratory care therapy; secondary education; social work; sociology; sport and fitness administration; wildlife and wildlands science and management.

Academic Programs *Special study options:* academic remediation for entering students, accelerated degree program, adult/continuing education programs, advanced placement credit, cooperative education, distance learning, English as a second language, external degree program, honors programs, independent study, internships, part-time degree program, services for LD students, student-designed majors, summer session for credit.

Library Barton County Community College Library with 30,429 titles, 186 serial subscriptions, 712 audiovisual materials, an OPAC, a Web page.

Computers on Campus 350 computers available on campus for general student use. A campuswide network can be accessed from student residence rooms and from off campus. Internet access, online (class) registration, at least one staffed computer lab available.

Student Life *Housing:* on-campus residence required for freshman year. *Options:* coed, disabled students. Campus housing is university owned. Freshman campus housing is guaranteed. *Activities and Organizations:* drama/theater group, student-run newspaper, choral group, Danceline, Business Professionals, Psychology Club, Agriculture Club, Cougarettes. *Campus security:* 24-hour emergency response devices and patrols. *Student services:* health clinic, personal/psychological counseling.

Athletics Member NJCAA. *Intercollegiate sports:* baseball M(s), basketball M(s)/W(s), cheerleading M(s)/W, cross-country running M(s)/W(s), golf M(s), soccer M(s)/W(s), softball W(s), tennis M(s)/W(s), track and field M(s)/W(s), volleyball W(s). *Intramural sports:* basketball M/W, bowling M/W, football M/W, golf M/W, swimming M/W, table tennis M/W, tennis M/W, track and field M/W, volleyball M/W.

Standardized Tests *Required:* ACT ASSET (for placement). *Recommended:* ACT (for placement).

Costs (2004–05) *Tuition:* state resident $1440 full-time, $45 per credit hour part-time; nonresident $2176 full-time, $68 per credit hour part-time. *Required fees:* $576 full-time, $18 per credit hour part-time. *Room and board:* $3191. Room and board charges vary according to board plan. *Payment plans:* installment, deferred payment. *Waivers:* senior citizens and employees or children of employees.

Financial Aid Of all full-time matriculated undergraduates who enrolled, 102 Federal Work-Study jobs (averaging $2400).

Applying *Options:* common application, electronic application, early admission. *Recommended:* high school transcript. *Application deadline:* rolling (freshmen), rolling (transfers).

Admissions Contact Mrs. Cari Ringwald, Director of Marketing, Barton County Community College, 245 Northeast 30th Road, Great Bend, KS 67530. *Phone:* 620-792-9241. *Toll-free phone:* 800-722-6842. *Fax:* 620-786-1160. *E-mail:* ringwaldc@barton.ccc.edu.

THE BROWN MACKIE COLLEGE
Salina, Kansas

- **Proprietary** 2-year, founded 1892
- **Calendar** modular
- **Degree** certificates, diplomas, and associate
- **Small-town** 10-acre campus with easy access to Wichita
- **Coed**

Faculty *Student/faculty ratio:* 15:1.

Athletics Member NJCAA.

Standardized Tests *Required:* ACT ASSET (for placement).

Costs (2003–04) *Tuition:* $179 per quarter hour part-time. Full-time tuition and fees vary according to course load.

Financial Aid Of all full-time matriculated undergraduates who enrolled, 10 Federal Work-Study jobs (averaging $1500).

Applying *Options:* common application, deferred entrance. *Application fee:* $20. *Required:* high school transcript, interview.

Admissions Contact Ms. Diann Heath, Director of Admissions, The Brown Mackie College, 2106 South 9th Street, Salina, KS 67401. *Phone:* 785-825-5422 Ext. 17. *Toll-free phone:* 800-365-0433. *Fax:* 785-827-7623.

THE BROWN MACKIE COLLEGE-LENEXA CAMPUS
Lenexa, Kansas

- **Proprietary** 2-year, founded 1892, part of The Brown Mackie College
- **Calendar** quarters
- **Degree** certificates, diplomas, and associate
- **Suburban** 3-acre campus with easy access to Kansas City
- **Coed,** 230 undergraduate students, 100% full-time, 77% women, 23% men

Undergraduates 230 full-time. Students come from 2 states and territories, 35% are from out of state, 23% African American, 2% Asian American or Pacific Islander, 8% Hispanic American, 0.9% Native American.

Freshmen *Admission:* 121 enrolled.

Faculty *Total:* 13, 31% full-time, 15% with terminal degrees. *Student/faculty ratio:* 14:1.

Majors Accounting; business administration and management; computer programming related; computer/technical support; computer typography and composition equipment operation; data entry/microcomputer applications; data entry/microcomputer applications related; dental hygiene; health information/medical records administration; health unit coordinator/ward clerk; health unit management/ward supervision; information technology; legal assistant/paralegal; medical administrative assistant and medical secretary; medical/clinical assistant; system administration.

Academic Programs *Special study options:* academic remediation for entering students, adult/continuing education programs, summer session for credit.

Library The Brown Mackie College Library plus 1 other with 48 serial subscriptions, an OPAC, a Web page.

Computers on Campus 185 computers available on campus for general student use. A campuswide network can be accessed from off campus. Internet access, at least one staffed computer lab available.

Student Life *Housing:* college housing not available. *Activities and Organizations:* Coffee Club (service and social organization). *Campus security:* 24-hour emergency response devices. *Student services:* personal/psychological counseling.

Standardized Tests *Required:* ACT ASSET (for placement). *Recommended:* SAT I or ACT (for placement).

Costs (2004–05) *Tuition:* $6444 full-time. *Required fees:* $452 full-time.

Applying *Options:* deferred entrance. *Application fee:* $20. *Required:* high school transcript, interview. *Recommended:* essay or personal statement, minimum 2.0 GPA. *Application deadline:* rolling (freshmen), rolling (transfers). *Notification:* continuous (freshmen), continuous (transfers).

Admissions Contact Ms. Julia M. Denniston, Director of Admissions, The Brown Mackie College-Lenexa Campus, 9705 Lenexa Drive, Lenexa, KS 66215. *Phone:* 913-768-1900 Ext. 14. *Toll-free phone:* 800-635-9101. *Fax:* 913-495-9555. *E-mail:* jjohnson@amedcts.com.

BUTLER COUNTY COMMUNITY COLLEGE
El Dorado, Kansas

- **State and locally supported** 2-year, founded 1927, part of Kansas Board of Regents
- **Calendar** semesters
- **Degree** certificates and associate
- **Small-town** 80-acre campus
- **Coed,** 8,631 undergraduate students, 40% full-time, 60% women, 40% men

Undergraduates 3,466 full-time, 5,165 part-time. Students come from 28 states and territories, 21 other countries, 5% are from out of state, 10% African American, 2% Asian American or Pacific Islander, 5% Hispanic American, 2% Native American, 4% international, 5% transferred in. *Retention:* 43% of 2002 full-time freshmen returned.

Freshmen *Admission:* 1,102 enrolled.

Faculty *Total:* 555, 25% full-time, 2% with terminal degrees. *Student/faculty ratio:* 19:1.

Majors Accounting; administrative assistant and secretarial science; agricultural business and management; art; automobile/automotive mechanics technology; biology/biological sciences; business administration and management; chemistry; child development; computer and information sciences; computer science; criminal justice/police science; data processing and data processing technology; drafting and design technology; dramatic/theatre arts; electrical, electronic and communications engineering technology; English; farm and ranch management; fire science; health information/medical records administration; history; hotel/motel administration; journalism; kindergarten/preschool education; liberal arts and sciences/liberal studies; marketing/marketing management; mass communication/media; mathematics; medical administrative assistant and medical secretary; music; music performance; nursing (registered nurse training); physical education teaching and coaching; physical therapy; physics; political science and government; pre-engineering; psychology; sociology; substance abuse/addiction counseling; welding technology.

Academic Programs *Special study options:* academic remediation for entering students, accelerated degree program, adult/continuing education programs, advanced placement credit, cooperative education, distance learning, double majors, English as a second language, honors programs, independent study, part-time degree program, services for LD students, student-designed majors, summer session for credit.

Library L.W. Nixon Library with 38,000 titles, 220 serial subscriptions, 914 audiovisual materials, an OPAC, a Web page.

Computers on Campus 90 computers available on campus for general student use. Internet access, at least one staffed computer lab available.

Student Life *Housing Options:* coed, men-only, women-only. Campus housing is university owned. *Activities and Organizations:* drama/theater group, student-run newspaper, radio and television station, choral group, Agriculture Club, Art Club, Campus Crusade for Christ, Grizzly Ambassadors, intramurals. *Campus security:* 24-hour emergency response devices and patrols, controlled dormitory access, video cameras at dormitory entrances and parking lot. *Student services:* personal/psychological counseling.

Athletics Member NJCAA. *Intercollegiate sports:* baseball M(s), basketball M(s)/W(s), cross-country running M(s)/W(s), football M(s), soccer W(s), softball W(s), tennis M(s)/W(s), track and field M(s)/W(s), volleyball W(s). *Intramural sports:* basketball M/W, bowling M/W, cheerleading M/W, football M, soccer W, softball W, table tennis M/W, tennis M/W, track and field M/W, volleyball W.

Standardized Tests *Required for some:* ACT ASSET. *Recommended:* ACT (for placement).

Costs (2003–04) *Tuition:* state resident $1608 full-time, $50 per credit hour part-time; nonresident $2952 full-time, $92 per credit hour part-time. *Required fees:* $424 full-time, $13 per credit hour part-time. *Room and board:* $4235; room only: $2901. Room and board charges vary according to housing facility. *Payment plan:* installment. *Waivers:* employees or children of employees.

Financial Aid Of all full-time matriculated undergraduates who enrolled, 180 Federal Work-Study jobs (averaging $1305).

Applying *Options:* early admission, deferred entrance. *Required:* high school transcript. *Application deadlines:* 8/19 (freshmen), 8/20 (transfers). *Notification:* continuous (freshmen), continuous (transfers).

Admissions Contact Mr. Paul Kyle, Director of Enrollment Management, Butler County Community College, 901 South Haverhill Road, El Dorado, KS 67042. *Phone:* 316-321-2222 Ext. 163. *E-mail:* admissions@butlercc.edu.

CLOUD COUNTY COMMUNITY COLLEGE
Concordia, Kansas

- **State and locally supported** 2-year, founded 1965, part of Kansas Community College System
- **Calendar** semesters
- **Degree** certificates, diplomas, and associate
- **Rural** 35-acre campus
- **Coed**

Student Life *Campus security:* 24-hour emergency response devices.
Athletics Member NJCAA.
Standardized Tests *Required:* ACT ASSET (for placement). *Recommended:* ACT (for placement).
Costs (2004–05) *Tuition:* state resident $1410 full-time, $47 per credit hour part-time; nonresident $2010 full-time, $67 per credit hour part-time. *Required fees:* $540 full-time, $18 per credit hour part-time. *Room and board:* $3600.
Financial Aid Of all full-time matriculated undergraduates who enrolled, 122 Federal Work-Study jobs (averaging $800).
Applying *Options:* common application, early admission, deferred entrance. *Required:* high school transcript.
Admissions Contact Mr. Heath Martin, Director of Admissions, Cloud County Community College, 2221 Campus Drive, PO Box 1002, Concordia, KS 66901-1002. *Phone:* 785-243-1435 Ext. 209. *Toll-free phone:* 800-729-5101. *E-mail:* thayer@mg.cloudccc.cc.ks.us.

COFFEYVILLE COMMUNITY COLLEGE
Coffeyville, Kansas

- **State and locally supported** 2-year, founded 1923, part of Kansas Board of Regents
- **Calendar** semesters
- **Degree** certificates and associate
- **Small-town** 39-acre campus with easy access to Tulsa

- **Endowment** $2.8 million
- **Coed**, 1,766 undergraduate students, 38% full-time, 54% women, 46% men

Undergraduates 665 full-time, 1,101 part-time. Students come from 19 states and territories, 4 other countries, 8% are from out of state, 12% African American, 0.3% Asian American or Pacific Islander, 2% Hispanic American, 2% Native American, 1% international, 38% transferred in, 27% live on campus.
Freshmen *Admission:* 1,499 applied, 1,499 admitted, 371 enrolled. *Test scores:* ACT scores over 18: 54%; ACT scores over 24: 13%; ACT scores over 30: 1%.
Faculty *Total:* 85, 60% full-time, 5% with terminal degrees. *Student/faculty ratio:* 20:1.
Majors Accounting; administrative assistant and secretarial science; agricultural business and management; agricultural economics; agricultural mechanization; agricultural teacher education; agriculture; animal sciences; applied art; art; athletic training; automobile/automotive mechanics technology; behavioral sciences; biological and physical sciences; biology/biological sciences; botany/plant biology; broadcast journalism; business administration and management; business machine repair; business teacher education; carpentry; chemistry; communications technology; computer and information sciences; computer programming; computer science; construction engineering technology; consumer merchandising/retailing management; drafting and design technology; dramatic/theatre arts; drawing; economics; education; elementary education; emergency medical technology (EMT paramedic); engineering; English; family and consumer sciences/human sciences; history; horticultural science; humanities; industrial technology; information science/studies; journalism; legal administrative assistant/secretary; liberal arts and sciences/liberal studies; machine tool technology; marketing/marketing management; mass communication/media; mathematics; mechanical engineering/mechanical technology; medical administrative assistant and medical secretary; music; music teacher education; nursing (licensed practical/vocational nurse training); nursing (registered nurse training); occupational therapy; physical education teaching and coaching; political science and government; pre-engineering; psychology; radio and television; social sciences; social work; sociology; telecommunications; voice and opera; welding technology; wind/percussion instruments.

Academic Programs *Special study options:* academic remediation for entering students, adult/continuing education programs, advanced placement credit, cooperative education, distance learning, double majors, English as a second language, honors programs, internships, part-time degree program, services for LD students, student-designed majors, summer session for credit.

Library Russell H. Graham Learning Resource Center plus 1 other with 27,482 titles, 238 serial subscriptions, 1,415 audiovisual materials, an OPAC, a Web page.

Computers on Campus 90 computers available on campus for general student use. A campuswide network can be accessed from off campus. Internet access, at least one staffed computer lab available.

Student Life *Housing Options:* coed. Campus housing is university owned. *Activities and Organizations:* drama/theater group, student-run television station, choral group, marching band, Student Government Association, Phi Theta Kappa, Delta Psi Omega, Agriculture Club. *Campus security:* 24-hour patrols, late-night transport/escort service. *Student services:* health clinic, personal/psychological counseling, women's center.

Athletics Member NJCAA. *Intercollegiate sports:* baseball M(s), basketball M(s)/W(s), cheerleading M/W, cross-country running M(s)/W(s), football M(s), golf M(s), softball W(s), track and field M(s)/W(s), volleyball W(s). *Intramural sports:* basketball M/W, bowling M/W, soccer M/W, table tennis M/W, tennis M/W, volleyball M/W, weight lifting M.

Standardized Tests *Required:* ACT (for placement), ACT COMPASS (for placement).

Costs (2003–04) *Tuition:* state resident $768 full-time, $37 per credit hour part-time; nonresident $1920 full-time, $87 per credit hour part-time. Full-time tuition and fees vary according to reciprocity agreements. Part-time tuition and fees vary according to reciprocity agreements. *Required fees:* $576 full-time, $18 per credit hour part-time. *Room and board:* $3280. Room and board charges vary according to board plan. *Payment plan:* installment. *Waivers:* senior citizens and employees or children of employees.

Financial Aid Of all full-time matriculated undergraduates who enrolled, 120 Federal Work-Study jobs (averaging $1000).

Applying *Options:* common application, early admission, deferred entrance. *Required:* high school transcript. *Application deadline:* rolling (freshmen), rolling (transfers). *Notification:* continuous (freshmen), continuous (transfers).

Admissions Contact Ms. Kim Lay, Coordinator/Advisor of Enrollment Services, Coffeyville Community College, 400 West 11th, Coffeyville, KS 67337. *Phone:* 620-252-7155. *Fax:* 620-252-7098.

COLBY COMMUNITY COLLEGE
Colby, Kansas

- **State and locally supported** 2-year, founded 1964
- **Calendar** semesters
- **Degree** certificates, diplomas, and associate

Kansas

Colby Community College (continued)
- **Small-town** 80-acre campus
- **Endowment** $1.4 million
- **Coed,** 1,951 undergraduate students, 41% full-time, 65% women, 35% men

Colby Community College offers 2-year career programs in veterinary technology, beef and equine production, criminal justice, physical therapist assistant studies, nursing, office technology, midmanagement, dental hygiene, and radio/television; transfer curricula in health, education, arts and letters, behavioral science, business, mass communications, and math/science; preprofessional options in law, engineering, and medicine; and a College-owned farm operated by agriculture students.

Undergraduates 795 full-time, 1,156 part-time. Students come from 16 states and territories, 4 other countries, 10% are from out of state, 1% African American, 0.5% Asian American or Pacific Islander, 2% Hispanic American, 0.4% Native American, 2% international, 8% transferred in, 30% live on campus.
Freshmen *Admission:* 694 applied, 694 admitted, 463 enrolled. *Average high school GPA:* 3.40.
Faculty *Total:* 60, 92% full-time, 25% with terminal degrees. *Student/faculty ratio:* 21:1.
Majors Accounting; agricultural business and management; agricultural economics; agricultural teacher education; agriculture; agronomy and crop science; animal sciences; behavioral sciences; biological and physical sciences; biology/biological sciences; broadcast journalism; business administration and management; business/managerial economics; business teacher education; chemistry; child development; commercial and advertising art; computer and information sciences related; computer science; criminal justice/law enforcement administration; dental hygiene; dramatic/theatre arts; education; English; family and consumer sciences/human sciences; farm and ranch management; foods, nutrition, and wellness; forestry; geology/earth science; history; humanities; journalism; kindergarten/preschool education; liberal arts and sciences/liberal studies; library science; marketing/marketing management; mass communication/media; mathematics; music; music teacher education; nursing (licensed practical/vocational nurse training); nursing (registered nurse training); pharmacy; physical education teaching and coaching; physical therapist assistant; physical therapy; political science and government; pre-engineering; psychology; radio and television; range science and management; science teacher education; social work; sociology; veterinary sciences; veterinary technology; wildlife biology; zoology/animal biology.
Academic Programs *Special study options:* academic remediation for entering students, adult/continuing education programs, advanced placement credit, cooperative education, distance learning, internships, part-time degree program, services for LD students, student-designed majors, summer session for credit.
Library Davis Library with 32,000 titles, 350 serial subscriptions, an OPAC.
Computers on Campus 110 computers available on campus for general student use. A campuswide network can be accessed. Internet access, at least one staffed computer lab available.
Student Life *Housing Options:* men-only, women-only. Campus housing is university owned. *Activities and Organizations:* drama/theater group, student-run newspaper, radio and television station, choral group, KSNEA, Physical Therapist Assistants Club, Block and Bridle, SVTA, COPNS. *Campus security:* 24-hour emergency response devices and patrols. *Student services:* health clinic, personal/psychological counseling.
Athletics Member NJCAA. *Intercollegiate sports:* baseball M(s), basketball M(s)/W(s), cheerleading W(s), cross-country running M(s)/W(s), equestrian sports M/W, softball W(s), track and field M(s)/W(s), volleyball W(s), wrestling M(s). *Intramural sports:* basketball M/W, softball M/W, volleyball M/W.
Standardized Tests *Required:* ACT ASSET or ACT COMPASS (for placement).
Costs (2004–05) *Tuition:* state resident $1280 full-time, $56 per credit hour part-time; nonresident $2528 full-time, $95 per credit hour part-time. *Required fees:* $512 full-time. *Room and board:* $3314. *Waivers:* employees or children of employees.
Financial Aid Of all full-time matriculated undergraduates who enrolled, 95 Federal Work-Study jobs (averaging $1500). 30 state and other part-time jobs (averaging $2000).
Applying *Options:* early admission, deferred entrance. *Required:* high school transcript. *Application deadline:* rolling (freshmen), rolling (transfers). *Notification:* continuous (freshmen), continuous (transfers).
Admissions Contact Mr. Skip Sharp, Dean of Students, Colby Community College, 1255 South Range, Colby, KS 67701-4099. *Phone:* 785-462-4690 Ext. 200. *Toll-free phone:* 888-634-9350 Ext. 690. *Fax:* 785-462-4691. *E-mail:* leasa@colbycc.edu.

COWLEY COUNTY COMMUNITY COLLEGE AND AREA VOCATIONAL-TECHNICAL SCHOOL
Arkansas City, Kansas

- **State and locally supported** 2-year, founded 1922, part of Kansas State Board of Education
- **Calendar** semesters
- **Degree** certificates, diplomas, and associate
- **Small-town** 19-acre campus
- **Endowment** $1.2 million
- **Coed**

Student Life *Campus security:* student patrols, late-night transport/escort service, residence hall entrances are locked at night.
Athletics Member NJCAA.
Standardized Tests *Required for some:* ACT ASSET, ACCUPLACER. *Recommended:* ACT (for placement).
Costs (2003–04) *Tuition:* state resident $1440 full-time; nonresident $3168 full-time. *Required fees:* $576 full-time. *Room and board:* $3120.
Financial Aid Of all full-time matriculated undergraduates who enrolled, 50 Federal Work-Study jobs (averaging $1500). 75 state and other part-time jobs (averaging $2000).
Applying *Options:* early admission, deferred entrance. *Required:* high school transcript.
Admissions Contact Ms. Sue Saia, Associate Dean of Admissions, Cowley County Community College and Area Vocational-Technical School, 125 South Second, PO Box 1147, Arkansas City, KS 67005-1147. *Phone:* 620-441-5245. *Toll-free phone:* 800-593-CCCC. *Fax:* 620-441-5264. *E-mail:* admissions@cowley.cc.ks.us.

DODGE CITY COMMUNITY COLLEGE
Dodge City, Kansas

- **State and locally supported** 2-year, founded 1935, part of Kansas State Board of Education
- **Calendar** semesters
- **Degree** certificates and associate
- **Small-town** 143-acre campus
- **Coed**

Athletics Member NJCAA.
Standardized Tests *Required:* ACT ASSET (for placement). *Recommended:* SAT I and SAT II or ACT (for placement).
Costs (2003–04) *Tuition:* state resident $792 full-time, $33 per credit hour part-time; nonresident $960 full-time, $40 per credit hour part-time. *Required fees:* $418 full-time, $17 per credit hour part-time. *Room and board:* $3560.
Applying *Options:* common application, early admission, deferred entrance. *Required:* high school transcript.
Admissions Contact Corbin Strobel, Director of Admissions, Placement, Testing and Student Services Marketing, Dodge City Community College, 2501 North 14th Avenue, Dodge City, KS 67801-2399. *Phone:* 316-225-1321. *Toll-free phone:* 800-742-9519. *Fax:* 316-225-0918. *E-mail:* admin@dccc.dodge-city.cc.ks.us.

DONNELLY COLLEGE
Kansas City, Kansas

- **Independent Roman Catholic** 2-year, founded 1949
- **Calendar** semesters
- **Degree** certificates and associate
- **Urban** 4-acre campus
- **Endowment** $4.0 million
- **Coed,** 398 undergraduate students, 50% full-time, 70% women, 30% men

Undergraduates 198 full-time, 200 part-time. Students come from 15 states and territories, 12% are from out of state, 54% African American, 3% Asian American or Pacific Islander, 22% Hispanic American, 0.8% Native American, 4% international, 109% transferred in.
Freshmen *Admission:* 327 applied, 327 admitted, 262 enrolled.
Faculty *Total:* 46, 28% full-time, 15% with terminal degrees. *Student/faculty ratio:* 10:1.
Majors Accounting; biological and physical sciences; business administration and management; computer and information sciences related; computer programming related; computer science; data entry/microcomputer applications related; data processing and data processing technology; drafting and design technology; education; engineering; English; health teacher education; history; kindergarten/

preschool education; liberal arts and sciences/liberal studies; mathematics; nursing (registered nurse training); philosophy; physical therapy; political science and government; psychology.

Academic Programs *Special study options:* academic remediation for entering students, advanced placement credit, double majors, English as a second language, external degree program, independent study, internships, part-time degree program, services for LD students, summer session for credit.

Library Trant Memorial Library with 33,752 titles, 114 serial subscriptions, 1,020 audiovisual materials, an OPAC, a Web page.

Computers on Campus 51 computers available on campus for general student use. A campuswide network can be accessed from off campus. Internet access, at least one staffed computer lab available.

Student Life *Housing Options:* Campus housing is provided by a third party. *Campus security:* 24-hour emergency response devices. *Student services:* personal/psychological counseling.

Costs (2003–04) *Tuition:* $3780 full-time, $145 per credit part-time. Full-time tuition and fees vary according to course load. Part-time tuition and fees vary according to course load. *Required fees:* $40 full-time. *Waivers:* senior citizens and employees or children of employees.

Applying *Options:* early admission, deferred entrance. *Recommended:* high school transcript. *Application deadline:* rolling (freshmen), rolling (transfers).

Admissions Contact Mr. Kevin Kelley, Vice President of Enrollment Management, Donnelly College, 608 North 18th Street, Kansas City, KS 66102. *Phone:* 913-621-8769. *Fax:* 913-621-0354. *E-mail:* bernetta@donnelly.edu.

FLINT HILLS TECHNICAL COLLEGE
Emporia, Kansas

Admissions Contact 3301 West 18th Avenue, Emporia, KS 66801. *Toll-free phone:* 800-711-6947.

FORT SCOTT COMMUNITY COLLEGE
Fort Scott, Kansas

- **State and locally supported** 2-year, founded 1919
- **Calendar** semesters
- **Degree** certificates and associate
- **Small-town** 147-acre campus
- **Coed,** 1,923 undergraduate students

Undergraduates Students come from 24 states and territories, 6% African American, 0.5% Asian American or Pacific Islander, 1% Hispanic American, 1% Native American, 0.3% international, 9% live on campus.

Freshmen *Admission:* 662 applied.

Faculty *Total:* 105, 33% full-time. *Student/faculty ratio:* 26:1.

Majors Accounting; administrative assistant and secretarial science; agricultural business and management; agricultural economics; agricultural mechanization; agricultural teacher education; agriculture; agronomy and crop science; animal sciences; architectural engineering technology; athletic training; business administration and management; clinical laboratory science/medical technology; commercial and advertising art; computer science; consumer merchandising/retailing management; cosmetology; criminal justice/law enforcement administration; drafting and design technology; education; electrical, electronic and communications engineering technology; emergency medical technology (EMT paramedic); hydrology and water resources science; industrial arts; legal administrative assistant/secretary; liberal arts and sciences/liberal studies; medical administrative assistant and medical secretary; music; nursing (registered nurse training); photography; physical sciences; public policy analysis; quality control technology; teacher assistant/aide; transportation technology; welding technology.

Academic Programs *Special study options:* academic remediation for entering students, adult/continuing education programs, advanced placement credit, cooperative education, distance learning, English as a second language, external degree program, independent study, internships, part-time degree program, services for LD students, student-designed majors, study abroad, summer session for credit. *ROTC:* Army (c).

Library Learning Resource Center with 25,308 titles, 124 serial subscriptions, an OPAC.

Computers on Campus 95 computers available on campus for general student use. Internet access, at least one staffed computer lab available.

Student Life *Housing Options:* coed. *Activities and Organizations:* drama/theater group, choral group, marching band, Aggie Club, Student Nurses Association, student government, Soccer Club, Phi Theta Kappa. *Campus security:* controlled dormitory access, evening security from 9 pm to 6am. *Student services:* personal/psychological counseling.

Athletics Member NJCAA. *Intercollegiate sports:* baseball M(s), basketball M(s)/W(s), football M(s), softball W(s), volleyball W(s). *Intramural sports:* basketball M/W, racquetball M/W, soccer M/W, softball M/W, table tennis M/W, tennis M/W, volleyball M/W, weight lifting M/W.

Standardized Tests *Required:* ACT ASSET (for placement). *Required for some:* ACT (for placement).

Costs (2004–05) *Tuition:* $56 per credit hour part-time; state resident $1680 full-time; nonresident $3360 full-time, $112 per credit hour part-time.

Applying *Options:* early admission, deferred entrance. *Application deadlines:* 8/15 (freshmen), 8/15 (transfers).

Admissions Contact Mrs. Mert Barrows, Director of Admissions, Fort Scott Community College, 2108 South Horton, Fort Scott, KS 66701. *Phone:* 316-223-2700 Ext. 353. *Toll-free phone:* 800-874-3722 Ext. 87 (in-state); 800-874-3722 (out-of-state).

GARDEN CITY COMMUNITY COLLEGE
Garden City, Kansas

- **County-supported** 2-year, founded 1919, part of Kansas Board of Regents
- **Calendar** semesters
- **Degree** certificates and associate
- **Rural** 63-acre campus
- **Endowment** $4.3 million
- **Coed,** 2,176 undergraduate students, 42% full-time, 57% women, 43% men

Undergraduates 911 full-time, 1,265 part-time. Students come from 31 states and territories, 7% are from out of state, 12% live on campus. *Retention:* 78% of 2002 full-time freshmen returned.

Freshmen *Admission:* 886 applied, 886 admitted, 401 enrolled. *Average high school GPA:* 3.07. *Test scores:* ACT scores over 18: 64%; ACT scores over 24: 12%.

Faculty *Total:* 180, 39% full-time, 3% with terminal degrees. *Student/faculty ratio:* 17:1.

Majors Accounting; administrative assistant and secretarial science; agricultural business and management; agricultural economics; agricultural mechanization; agricultural mechanization related; agriculture; athletic training; automobile/automotive mechanics technology; biological and physical sciences; business administration and management; ceramic arts and ceramics; child development; commercial and advertising art; computer engineering technology; computer graphics; computer programming; computer science; computer systems networking and telecommunications; consumer merchandising/retailing management; cosmetology; criminal justice/law enforcement administration; criminal justice/police science; developmental and child psychology; drafting and design technology; dramatic/theatre arts; education; electrical, electronic and communications engineering technology; elementary education; emergency medical technology (EMT paramedic); engineering; engineering technology; English; family and community services; family and consumer sciences/human sciences; farm and ranch management; fashion/apparel design; fashion merchandising; fine/studio arts; health and physical education related; humanities; industrial arts; industrial technology; information science/studies; interior design; journalism; legal administrative assistant/secretary; liberal arts and sciences/liberal studies; marketing/marketing management; mathematics; mechanical design technology; mechanical engineering/mechanical technology; metal and jewelry arts; music; nursing (registered nurse training); physical education teaching and coaching; pre-engineering; retailing; social sciences; sociology; speech and rhetoric; teacher assistant/aide; trade and industrial teacher education; welding technology.

Academic Programs *Special study options:* academic remediation for entering students, adult/continuing education programs, advanced placement credit, distance learning, English as a second language, external degree program, part-time degree program, services for LD students, student-designed majors, summer session for credit.

Library Saffell Library with 43,987 titles, 116 serial subscriptions, 303 audiovisual materials, an OPAC, a Web page.

Computers on Campus 150 computers available on campus for general student use. A campuswide network can be accessed from student residence rooms. Internet access, at least one staffed computer lab available.

Student Life *Housing Options:* coed. Campus housing is university owned. *Activities and Organizations:* drama/theater group, student-run newspaper, choral group, student government, Hispanic American Leadership Organization, Business Professionals of America, Criminal Justice Organization, Phi Theta Kappa. *Campus security:* 24-hour emergency response devices and patrols, student patrols, late-night transport/escort service, controlled dormitory access. *Student services:* health clinic, personal/psychological counseling.

Athletics Member NJCAA. *Intercollegiate sports:* baseball M(s), basketball M(s)/W(s), cheerleading M(s)/W(s), cross-country running M(s)/W(s), football M(s), softball W(s), track and field M(s)/W(s), volleyball W(s). *Intramural sports:* archery M/W, basketball M/W, bowling M/W, football M/W, golf M/W, racquetball M/W, table tennis M/W, tennis M/W, track and field M/W, volleyball M/W.

Standardized Tests *Required:* ACT COMPASS (for placement).

Costs (2004–05) *Tuition:* state resident $1184 full-time, $37 per credit hour part-time; nonresident $2080 full-time, $65 per credit hour part-time. Full-time tuition and fees vary according to course load. Part-time tuition and fees vary according to course load. *Required fees:* $672 full-time, $21 per credit hour

Garden City Community College (continued)
part-time. *Room and board:* $4100. Room and board charges vary according to housing facility. *Payment plans:* installment, deferred payment. *Waivers:* senior citizens and employees or children of employees.

Financial Aid Of all full-time matriculated undergraduates who enrolled, 90 Federal Work-Study jobs (averaging $1000). 100 state and other part-time jobs (averaging $900).

Applying *Options:* deferred entrance. *Required:* high school transcript. *Application deadline:* rolling (freshmen), rolling (transfers).

Admissions Contact Ms. Nikki Geier, Director of Admissions, Garden City Community College, 801 Campus Drive, Garden City, KS 67846. *Phone:* 620-276-7611 Ext. 531. *E-mail:* nikki.geier@gcccks.edu.

HESSTON COLLEGE
Hesston, Kansas

- **Independent Mennonite** 2-year, founded 1909
- **Calendar** semesters
- **Degree** associate
- **Small-town** 50-acre campus with easy access to Wichita
- **Coed,** 446 undergraduate students, 88% full-time, 55% women, 45% men

Undergraduates 394 full-time, 52 part-time. Students come from 30 states and territories, 12 other countries, 57% are from out of state, 2% African American, 0.9% Asian American or Pacific Islander, 2% Hispanic American, 11% international, 12% transferred in, 71% live on campus. *Retention:* 76% of 2002 full-time freshmen returned.

Freshmen *Admission:* 496 applied, 496 admitted, 174 enrolled. *Average high school GPA:* 3.07. *Test scores:* SAT verbal scores over 500: 62%; SAT math scores over 500: 72%; ACT scores over 18: 82%; SAT verbal scores over 600: 23%; SAT math scores over 600: 27%; ACT scores over 24: 37%; SAT verbal scores over 700: 6%; SAT math scores over 700: 3%; ACT scores over 30: 6%.

Faculty *Total:* 43, 65% full-time, 23% with terminal degrees. *Student/faculty ratio:* 12:1.

Majors Biblical studies; business administration and management; computer/information technology services administration related; kindergarten/preschool education; liberal arts and sciences/liberal studies; nursing (registered nurse training); pastoral studies/counseling.

Academic Programs *Special study options:* academic remediation for entering students, advanced placement credit, cooperative education, double majors, English as a second language, independent study, internships, part-time degree program, services for LD students, summer session for credit.

Library Mary Miller Library with 35,000 titles, 234 serial subscriptions, 2,409 audiovisual materials, an OPAC, a Web page.

Computers on Campus 67 computers available on campus for general student use. A campuswide network can be accessed from student residence rooms and from off campus. Internet access, at least one staffed computer lab available.

Student Life *Housing:* on-campus residence required through sophomore year. *Options:* men-only, women-only. Campus housing is university owned. Freshman campus housing is guaranteed. *Activities and Organizations:* drama/theater group, student-run newspaper, choral group. *Campus security:* 24-hour emergency response devices. *Student services:* personal/psychological counseling.

Athletics Member NJCAA. *Intercollegiate sports:* baseball M(s), basketball M(s)/W(s), soccer M(s), softball W(s), tennis M/W, volleyball W(s). *Intramural sports:* basketball M/W, golf M(c)/W(c), soccer M/W, softball W, tennis M/W, volleyball M/W.

Standardized Tests *Recommended:* SAT I or ACT (for placement).

Costs (2004–05) *Comprehensive fee:* $19,998 includes full-time tuition ($14,378), mandatory fees ($220), and room and board ($5400). Part-time tuition: $600 per hour. Part-time tuition and fees vary according to course load. *Required fees:* $55 per term part-time. *Payment plan:* installment. *Waivers:* senior citizens and employees or children of employees.

Financial Aid Of all full-time matriculated undergraduates who enrolled, 120 Federal Work-Study jobs (averaging $800).

Applying *Options:* electronic application, early admission, deferred entrance. *Application fee:* $15. *Required:* high school transcript, letters of recommendation. *Required for some:* interview. *Application deadline:* rolling (freshmen), rolling (transfers).

Admissions Contact Mr. Clark Roth, Vice President for Admissions, Hesston College, Box 3000, Hesston, KS 67062. *Phone:* 620-327-8222. *Toll-free phone:* 800-995-2757. *Fax:* 620-327-8300. *E-mail:* admissions@hesston.edu.

HIGHLAND COMMUNITY COLLEGE
Highland, Kansas

- **State and locally supported** 2-year, founded 1858, part of Kansas Community College System

- **Calendar** semesters
- **Degree** certificates and associate
- **Rural** 20-acre campus
- **Coed**

Athletics Member NJCAA.

Standardized Tests *Required:* ACT ASSET (for placement). *Recommended:* ACT (for placement).

Costs (2003–04) *Tuition:* area resident $792 full-time, $33 per credit hour part-time; state resident $960 full-time, $40 per credit hour part-time; nonresident $2160 full-time, $90 per credit hour part-time. *Required fees:* $744 full-time, $31 per credit hour part-time. *Room and board:* $3714.

Financial Aid Of all full-time matriculated undergraduates who enrolled, 75 Federal Work-Study jobs (averaging $1200). 25 state and other part-time jobs (averaging $1000).

Applying *Options:* early admission. *Required:* high school transcript.

Admissions Contact Ms. Cheryl Rasmussen, Vice President of Student Services, Highland Community College, 606 West Main Street, Highland, KS 66035-4165. *Phone:* 785-442-6020. *Fax:* 785-442-6100.

HUTCHINSON COMMUNITY COLLEGE AND AREA VOCATIONAL SCHOOL
Hutchinson, Kansas

- **State and locally supported** 2-year, founded 1928, part of Kansas Board of Regents
- **Calendar** semesters
- **Degree** certificates and associate
- **Small-town** 47-acre campus
- **Endowment** $3.5 million
- **Coed,** 4,312 undergraduate students, 48% full-time, 57% women, 43% men

Undergraduates 2,086 full-time, 2,226 part-time. Students come from 34 states and territories, 18 other countries, 5% are from out of state, 4% African American, 0.8% Asian American or Pacific Islander, 5% Hispanic American, 2% Native American, 1% international, 11% transferred in, 11% live on campus. *Retention:* 63% of 2002 full-time freshmen returned.

Freshmen *Admission:* 2,823 applied, 2,823 admitted, 1,236 enrolled. *Average high school GPA:* 2.84. *Test scores:* ACT scores over 18: 73%; ACT scores over 24: 20%; ACT scores over 30: 1%.

Faculty *Total:* 313, 35% full-time, 6% with terminal degrees. *Student/faculty ratio:* 15:1.

Majors Administrative assistant and secretarial science; agricultural mechanization; agriculture; autobody/collision and repair technology; automobile/automotive mechanics technology; biology/biological sciences; business and personal/financial services marketing; business/commerce; carpentry; child care and support services management; communication/speech communication and rhetoric; communications technology; computer and information sciences; criminal justice/police science; drafting and design technology; education; educational/instructional media design; electrical/electronics equipment installation and repair; emergency medical technology (EMT paramedic); engineering; English; family and consumer sciences/human sciences; farm and ranch management; fire science; foreign languages and literatures; health information/medical records technology; legal assistant/paralegal; liberal arts and sciences/liberal studies; machine tool technology; management information systems; manufacturing technology; mathematics; medical radiologic technology; nursing (registered nurse training); physical sciences; psychology; retailing; social sciences; visual and performing arts; welding technology.

Academic Programs *Special study options:* academic remediation for entering students, adult/continuing education programs, advanced placement credit, cooperative education, distance learning, double majors, English as a second language, honors programs, independent study, internships, part-time degree program, services for LD students, student-designed majors, summer session for credit. *ROTC:* Army (c).

Library John F. Kennedy Library plus 1 other with 41,812 titles, 245 serial subscriptions, 3,039 audiovisual materials, an OPAC, a Web page.

Computers on Campus 475 computers available on campus for general student use. A campuswide network can be accessed from off campus. Internet access, at least one staffed computer lab available.

Student Life *Housing Options:* men-only, women-only. Campus housing is university owned. *Activities and Organizations:* drama/theater group, student-run newspaper, choral group, Student Government Association, Black Cultural Society, Hispanic-American Leadership Organization, Hutchinson Christian Fellowship, Campus Crusade for Christ. *Campus security:* 24-hour emergency response devices and patrols, student patrols, late-night transport/escort service, controlled dormitory access. *Student services:* health clinic, personal/psychological counseling.

Athletics Member NJCAA. *Intercollegiate sports:* baseball M(s), basketball M(s)/W(s), cheerleading W(s), cross-country running M(s)/W(s), football M(s), golf M(s), softball W(s), tennis M(s)/W(s), track and field M(s)/W(s), volleyball

W(s). *Intramural sports:* badminton M/W, basketball M/W, bowling M/W, football M/W, racquetball M/W, soccer M/W, tennis M/W, track and field M/W, volleyball M/W.

Standardized Tests *Required for some:* ACT (for placement), ACT ASSET, ACT COMPASS, ACCUPLACER. *Recommended:* ACT (for placement).

Costs (2003–04) *Tuition:* state resident $1504 full-time, $47 per hour part-time; nonresident $2752 full-time, $86 per hour part-time. *Required fees:* $448 full-time, $14 per hour part-time. *Room and board:* $3664. Room and board charges vary according to board plan. *Payment plan:* installment.

Applying *Options:* electronic application, early admission, deferred entrance. *Required for some:* interview. *Recommended:* high school transcript. *Application deadline:* rolling (freshmen), rolling (transfers).

Admissions Contact Ms. Lori Bair, Director of Admissions, Hutchinson Community College and Area Vocational School, 1300 North Plum, Hutchinson, KS 67501. *Phone:* 620-665-3536. *Toll-free phone:* 800-289-3501 Ext. 3536. *Fax:* 620-665-3301. *E-mail:* bairl@hutchcc.edu.

INDEPENDENCE COMMUNITY COLLEGE
Independence, Kansas

- **State-supported** 2-year, founded 1925, part of Kansas State Board of Education
- **Calendar** semesters
- **Degree** certificates and associate
- **Small-town** 68-acre campus
- **Coed**

Student Life *Campus security:* night patrol.

Athletics Member NJCAA.

Standardized Tests *Recommended:* SAT I or ACT (for placement).

Costs (2004–05) *Tuition:* $56 per credit hour part-time; state resident $61 per credit hour part-time; nonresident $61 per credit hour part-time. *Room and board:* $4100.

Financial Aid Of all full-time matriculated undergraduates who enrolled, 85 Federal Work-Study jobs (averaging $900).

Applying *Options:* common application, early admission. *Required:* high school transcript.

Admissions Contact Mr. Richard Carvajal, Dean of Student Services, Independence Community College, PO Box 708, Independence, KS 67301. *Phone:* 620-331-4100. *Toll-free phone:* 800-842-6063. *Fax:* 620-331-5344. *E-mail:* admissions@indycc.edu.

JOHNSON COUNTY COMMUNITY COLLEGE
Overland Park, Kansas

- **State and locally supported** 2-year, founded 1967, part of Kansas State Board of Education
- **Calendar** semesters
- **Degree** certificates and associate
- **Suburban** 220-acre campus with easy access to Kansas City
- **Endowment** $4.4 million
- **Coed**, 18,432 undergraduate students, 33% full-time, 56% women, 44% men

Undergraduates 6,143 full-time, 12,289 part-time. Students come from 26 states and territories, 36 other countries, 5% are from out of state, 4% African American, 4% Asian American or Pacific Islander, 3% Hispanic American, 0.8% Native American, 1% international, 1% transferred in.

Freshmen *Admission:* 2,095 enrolled.

Faculty *Total:* 826, 36% full-time. *Student/faculty ratio:* 19:1.

Majors Accounting technology and bookkeeping; administrative assistant and secretarial science; airframe mechanics and aircraft maintenance technology; automobile/automotive mechanics technology; business administration and management; chemical technology; civil engineering technology; commercial and advertising art; computer programming (specific applications); computer systems networking and telecommunications; cosmetology; criminal justice/police science; dental hygiene; drafting and design technology; education; electrical and power transmission installation; emergency medical technology (EMT paramedic); fire services administration; health information/medical records technology; heating, air conditioning and refrigeration technology; hospitality administration; hotel/motel administration; legal assistant/paralegal; liberal arts and sciences/liberal studies; machine tool technology; nursing assistant/aide and patient care assistant; nursing (licensed practical/vocational nurse training); nursing (registered nurse training); occupational therapist assistant; physical therapist assistant; respiratory care therapy; retailing; sales, distribution and marketing; sign language interpretation and translation; tourism and travel services management; veterinary technology.

Academic Programs *Special study options:* academic remediation for entering students, adult/continuing education programs, advanced placement credit,

cooperative education, distance learning, double majors, English as a second language, honors programs, independent study, internships, off-campus study, part-time degree program, services for LD students, student-designed majors, summer session for credit.

Library Johnson County Community College Library with 89,400 titles, 708 serial subscriptions, 4,770 audiovisual materials, an OPAC, a Web page.

Computers on Campus 800 computers available on campus for general student use. A campuswide network can be accessed from off campus. Internet access, online (class) registration, at least one staffed computer lab available.

Student Life *Housing:* college housing not available. *Activities and Organizations:* drama/theater group, student-run newspaper. *Campus security:* 24-hour emergency response devices and patrols, late-night transport/escort service.

Athletics Member NJCAA. *Intercollegiate sports:* baseball M(s), basketball M(s)/W(s), cross-country running M(s)/W(s), soccer M(s), softball W(s), tennis M(s)/W(s), track and field M(s)/W(s), volleyball W(s). *Intramural sports:* basketball M/W, soccer M, tennis M/W, volleyball M/W.

Standardized Tests *Required for some:* ACT (for placement), ACT ASSET.

Costs (2004–05) *Tuition:* $62 per credit hour part-time; state resident $77 per credit hour part-time; nonresident $139 per credit hour part-time.

Financial Aid Of all full-time matriculated undergraduates who enrolled, 85 Federal Work-Study jobs (averaging $4000).

Applying *Options:* early admission. *Application fee:* $10. *Required for some:* high school transcript. *Application deadline:* rolling (freshmen), rolling (transfers). *Notification:* continuous (freshmen), continuous (transfers).

Admissions Contact Dr. Charles J. Carlsen, President, Johnson County Community College, 12345 College Boulevard, Overland Park, KS 66210-1299. *Phone:* 913-469-8500 Ext. 3806.

KANSAS CITY KANSAS COMMUNITY COLLEGE
Kansas City, Kansas

- **State and locally supported** 2-year, founded 1923
- **Calendar** semesters
- **Degree** certificates, diplomas, and associate
- **Urban** 148-acre campus
- **Coed,** 5,642 undergraduate students, 33% full-time, 63% women, 37% men

Undergraduates 1,843 full-time, 3,799 part-time. Students come from 27 states and territories, 22 other countries, 5% are from out of state, 27% African American, 2% Asian American or Pacific Islander, 6% Hispanic American, 0.9% Native American, 1% international, 8% transferred in. *Retention:* 58% of 2002 full-time freshmen returned.

Freshmen *Admission:* 722 admitted, 722 enrolled.

Faculty *Total:* 362, 30% full-time. *Student/faculty ratio:* 14:1.

Majors Administrative assistant and secretarial science; business administration and management; child care and support services management; computer engineering technology; criminal justice/police science; data processing and data processing technology; drafting and design technology; emergency medical technology (EMT paramedic); fire science; funeral service and mortuary science; hazardous materials management and waste technology; international business/trade/commerce; legal assistant/paralegal; liberal arts and sciences and humanities related; liberal arts and sciences/liberal studies; nursing (registered nurse training); physical therapist assistant; recording arts technology; respiratory care therapy; respiratory therapy technician; substance abuse/addiction counseling; web page, digital/multimedia and information resources design.

Academic Programs *Special study options:* academic remediation for entering students, accelerated degree program, adult/continuing education programs, advanced placement credit, cooperative education, distance learning, double majors, English as a second language, external degree program, freshman honors college, honors programs, independent study, internships, part-time degree program, services for LD students, summer session for credit.

Library Kansas City Kansas Community College Library with 55,000 titles, 400 serial subscriptions, 12,000 audiovisual materials, an OPAC, a Web page.

Computers on Campus 750 computers available on campus for general student use. A campuswide network can be accessed from off campus. Internet access, online (class) registration, at least one staffed computer lab available.

Student Life *Housing:* college housing not available. *Activities and Organizations:* drama/theater group, student-run newspaper, television station, choral group, Student Senate, Phi Theta Kappa, Drama Club, The African American Student Union, Christian Student Union. *Campus security:* 24-hour emergency response devices and patrols, student patrols, late-night transport/escort service. *Student services:* health clinic, personal/psychological counseling, women's center.

Athletics Member NJCAA. *Intercollegiate sports:* baseball M(s), basketball M(s)/W(s), cross-country running M(s)/W(s), golf M(s), soccer M(s), softball W(s), track and field M(s)/W(s), volleyball W(s).

Standardized Tests *Required:* ACCUPLACER (for placement).

Kansas City Kansas Community College (continued)

Costs (2004–05) *Tuition:* state resident $1344 full-time, $48 per credit hour part-time; nonresident $4032 full-time, $144 per credit hour part-time. Full-time tuition and fees vary according to course load. Part-time tuition and fees vary according to course load. *Required fees:* $280 full-time, $10 per credit hour part-time. *Payment plan:* installment. *Waivers:* employees or children of employees.

Financial Aid Of all full-time matriculated undergraduates who enrolled, 125 Federal Work-Study jobs (averaging $3000).

Applying *Options:* common application, electronic application, early admission, deferred entrance. *Required:* high school transcript. *Application deadline:* rolling (freshmen), rolling (transfers). *Notification:* continuous (freshmen), continuous (transfers).

Admissions Contact Ms. Sherri Neff, Assistant Director of Admissions, Kansas City Kansas Community College, 7250 State Avenue, Kansas City, KS 66112. *Phone:* 913-288-7201. *Fax:* 913-288-7646. *E-mail:* admiss@toto.net.

LABETTE COMMUNITY COLLEGE
Parsons, Kansas

- **State and locally supported** 2-year, founded 1923, part of Kansas State Board of Education
- **Calendar** semesters
- **Degree** certificates and associate
- **Small-town** 4-acre campus
- **Coed**

Athletics Member NJCAA.
Standardized Tests *Required:* ACT COMPASS (for placement). *Recommended:* ACT (for placement).
Costs (2003–04) *Tuition:* state resident $1200 full-time, $40 per hour part-time; nonresident $2850 full-time, $95 per hour part-time. *Required fees:* $480 full-time, $16 per hour part-time. *Room and board:* $3040.
Financial Aid Of all full-time matriculated undergraduates who enrolled, 17 Federal Work-Study jobs (averaging $1172).
Applying *Options:* early admission. *Required for some:* letters of recommendation, interview. *Recommended:* high school transcript.
Admissions Contact Mr. Jeff Almond, Director of Admission, Labette Community College, 200 South 14th Street, Parsons, KS 67357. *Phone:* 620-421-6700 Ext. 1228. *Toll-free phone:* 888-LABETTE. *E-mail:* jeffa@labette.edu.

MANHATTAN AREA TECHNICAL COLLEGE
Manhattan, Kansas

- **State and locally supported** 2-year, founded 1965
- **Calendar** semesters
- **Degree** certificates, diplomas, and associate
- **Suburban** 19-acre campus
- **Coed,** 350 undergraduate students, 95% full-time, 41% women, 59% men

Undergraduates 331 full-time, 19 part-time. 6% African American, 0.3% Asian American or Pacific Islander, 3% Hispanic American, 1% Native American.
Freshmen *Admission:* 109 enrolled.
Faculty *Total:* 31, 94% full-time. *Student/faculty ratio:* 20:1.
Majors Autobody/collision and repair technology; automobile/automotive mechanics technology; building/construction finishing, management, and inspection related; computer systems networking and telecommunications; computer technology/computer systems technology; drafting and design technology; electrical and power transmission installation related; heating, air conditioning and refrigeration technology; management information systems; nursing (licensed practical/vocational nurse training); nursing (registered nurse training); welding technology.
Costs (2004–05) *Tuition:* state resident $1870 full-time, $55 per credit hour part-time. *Required fees:* $85 full-time, $5 per credit hour part-time.
Admissions Contact Mr. Rick Smith, Coordinator of Admissions and Recruitment, Manhattan Area Technical College, 3136 Dickens Avenue, Manhattan, KS 66503-2499. *Phone:* 785-587-2800 Ext. 104. *Toll-free phone:* 800-352-7575.

NEOSHO COUNTY COMMUNITY COLLEGE
Chanute, Kansas

- **State and locally supported** 2-year, founded 1936, part of Kansas State Board of Education
- **Calendar** semesters
- **Degree** certificates, diplomas, and associate
- **Small-town** 50-acre campus
- **Endowment** $370,000
- **Coed**

Student Life *Campus security:* controlled dormitory access.
Athletics Member NJCAA.
Standardized Tests *Required:* ACT (for placement).
Costs (2003–04) *Tuition:* $35 per credit hour part-time; state resident $1120 full-time, $45 per credit hour part-time; nonresident $1600 full-time, $60 per credit hour part-time. *Required fees:* $640 full-time, $20 per credit hour part-time. *Room and board:* $3750.
Financial Aid Of all full-time matriculated undergraduates who enrolled, 73 Federal Work-Study jobs (averaging $800).
Applying *Options:* common application, early admission. *Required:* high school transcript.
Admissions Contact Ms. Lisa Last, Director of Admission/Registrar, Neosho County Community College, 800 West 14th Street, Chanute, KS 66720-2699. *Phone:* 620-431-2820 Ext. 213. *Toll-free phone:* 800-729-6222. *Fax:* 620-431-6222.

NORTH CENTRAL KANSAS TECHNICAL COLLEGE
Beloit, Kansas

Admissions Contact Ms. Judy Heidrick, Director of Admissions, North Central Kansas Technical College, PO Box 507, Beloit, KS 67420. *Phone:* 800-658-4655. *Toll-free phone:* 800-658-4655.

NORTHEAST KANSAS TECHNICAL COLLEGE
Atchison, Kansas

Admissions Contact 1501 West Riley Street, Atchison, KS 66002. *Toll-free phone:* 800-567-4890.

NORTHWEST KANSAS TECHNICAL COLLEGE
Goodland, Kansas

Admissions Contact PO Box 668, 1209 Harrison Street, Goodland, KS 67735. *Toll-free phone:* 800-316-4127.

PRATT COMMUNITY COLLEGE
Pratt, Kansas

- **State and locally supported** 2-year, founded 1938, part of Kansas Board of Regents
- **Calendar** semesters
- **Degree** certificates and associate
- **Rural** 80-acre campus with easy access to Wichita
- **Coed,** 1,685 undergraduate students, 39% full-time, 50% women, 50% men

Undergraduates 655 full-time, 1,030 part-time. Students come from 17 states and territories, 3 other countries, 4% African American, 0.6% Asian American or Pacific Islander, 3% Hispanic American, 0.9% Native American, 0.8% international. *Retention:* 51% of 2002 full-time freshmen returned.
Freshmen *Admission:* 817 applied, 817 admitted, 211 enrolled.
Faculty *Total:* 92, 46% full-time, 9% with terminal degrees. *Student/faculty ratio:* 13:1.
Majors Accounting; administrative assistant and secretarial science; agricultural business and management; agricultural economics; agricultural mechanization; agricultural teacher education; agriculture; animal/livestock husbandry and production; animal sciences; applied art; art; art teacher education; athletic training; automobile/automotive mechanics technology; biological and physical sciences; biology/biological sciences; broadcast journalism; business administration and management; business teacher education; chemistry; child development; commercial and advertising art; computer systems networking and telecommunications; computer/technical support; computer typography and composition equipment operation; counselor education/school counseling and guidance; data entry/microcomputer applications; data entry/microcomputer applications related; education; education (K-12); elementary education; energy management and systems technology; English; family and consumer sciences/human sciences; farm and ranch management; fine/studio arts; fish/game man-

agement; health teacher education; history; humanities; human services; industrial arts; kindergarten/preschool education; liberal arts and sciences/liberal studies; literature; marketing/marketing management; mass communication/media; mathematics; music; nursing (registered nurse training); physical education teaching and coaching; physical sciences; pre-engineering; professional studies; psychology; social sciences; social work; sociology; speech and rhetoric; speech/theater education; trade and industrial teacher education; welding technology; wildlife and wildlands science and management; wildlife biology; word processing.

Academic Programs *Special study options:* academic remediation for entering students, adult/continuing education programs, advanced placement credit, cooperative education, internships, part-time degree program, summer session for credit.

Library 26,000 titles, 250 serial subscriptions, a Web page.

Computers on Campus 100 computers available on campus for general student use. A campuswide network can be accessed from off campus. Internet access, at least one staffed computer lab available.

Student Life *Housing:* on-campus residence required through sophomore year. *Options:* coed, men-only, women-only. *Activities and Organizations:* drama/theater group, student-run newspaper, choral group, Phi Theta Kappa, Student Senate, Baptist Student Union, Block and Bridle, Business Professionals Club. *Campus security:* 24-hour patrols, late-night transport/escort service, controlled dormitory access. *Student services:* health clinic, personal/psychological counseling.

Athletics Member NJCAA. *Intercollegiate sports:* baseball M(s), basketball M(s)/W(s), cross-country running M(s)/W(s), golf M(s)/W(s), softball W(s), tennis M(s)/W(s), track and field M(s)/W(s), volleyball W(s). *Intramural sports:* badminton M/W, basketball M/W, bowling M/W, softball M/W, table tennis M/W, volleyball M/W, weight lifting M/W.

Standardized Tests *Recommended:* ACT (for placement).

Costs (2004–05) *Tuition:* state resident $1216 full-time, $38 per credit hour part-time; nonresident $1216 full-time, $38 per credit hour part-time. Full-time tuition and fees vary according to course load. Part-time tuition and fees vary according to course load. *Required fees:* $832 full-time, $26 per credit hour part-time. *Room and board:* $3558. Room and board charges vary according to board plan and housing facility. *Waivers:* employees or children of employees.

Financial Aid Of all full-time matriculated undergraduates who enrolled, 77 Federal Work-Study jobs (averaging $800). 13 state and other part-time jobs (averaging $800). *Financial aid deadline:* 8/1.

Applying *Options:* common application, early admission. *Required:* high school transcript. *Application deadline:* rolling (freshmen), rolling (transfers).

Admissions Contact Ms. Mary Bolyard, Administrative Assistant, Pratt Community College, 348 Northeast State Road, Pratt, KS 67124. *Phone:* 620-672-5641 Ext. 217. *Toll-free phone:* 800-794-3091. *Fax:* 620-672-5288. *E-mail:* lynnp@prattcc.edu.

SEWARD COUNTY COMMUNITY COLLEGE
Liberal, Kansas

- **State and locally supported** 2-year, founded 1969, part of Kansas State Board of Regents
- **Calendar** semesters
- **Degree** certificates, diplomas, and associate
- **Rural** 120-acre campus
- **Endowment** $8.5 million
- **Coed,** 2,325 undergraduate students, 23% full-time, 58% women, 42% men

Undergraduates 538 full-time, 1,787 part-time. Students come from 8 states and territories, 7 other countries, 11% are from out of state, 21% live on campus.

Faculty *Total:* 208, 4% with terminal degrees. *Student/faculty ratio:* 18:1.

Majors Accounting; administrative assistant and secretarial science; agriculture; art; athletic training; biological and physical sciences; biology/biological sciences; business administration and management; chemistry; child development; clinical/medical laboratory technology; computer programming; computer science; criminal justice/police science; data processing and data processing technology; dramatic/theatre arts; drawing; economics; education; elementary education; English; farm and ranch management; finance; fish/game management; history; journalism; liberal arts and sciences/liberal studies; literature; marketing/marketing management; mass communication/media; mathematics; music; natural sciences; nursing (licensed practical/vocational nurse training); nursing (registered nurse training); physical education teaching and coaching; physical sciences; pre-engineering; psychology; respiratory care therapy; social work; sociology; speech and rhetoric; surgical technology; wildlife and wildlands science and management.

Academic Programs *Special study options:* academic remediation for entering students, adult/continuing education programs, cooperative education, distance learning, English as a second language, external degree program, internships, part-time degree program, student-designed majors, summer session for credit.

Library Learning Resource Center plus 1 other with 32,926 titles, 318 serial subscriptions.

Computers on Campus 102 computers available on campus for general student use. Internet access, at least one staffed computer lab available.

Student Life *Housing Options:* coed. *Activities and Organizations:* drama/theater group, student-run newspaper, choral group, HALO, ATLAS, Block and Bridle, DECA, Sigma Chi Chi. *Campus security:* 24-hour patrols, late-night transport/escort service.

Athletics Member NJCAA. *Intercollegiate sports:* baseball M(s), basketball M(s)/W(s), tennis M(s)/W(s), volleyball W(s).

Standardized Tests *Recommended:* SAT I or ACT (for placement).

Costs (2003–04) *Tuition:* $38 per credit hour part-time; state resident $1440 full-time, $48 per credit hour part-time; nonresident $1830 full-time, $61 per credit hour part-time. *Required fees:* $570 full-time, $19 per credit hour part-time.

Financial Aid Of all full-time matriculated undergraduates who enrolled, 60 Federal Work-Study jobs (averaging $1854). 173 state and other part-time jobs (averaging $1854).

Applying *Options:* early admission, deferred entrance. *Required:* high school transcript. *Required for some:* minimum 2.0 GPA, 1 letter of recommendation, interview. *Application deadlines:* 8/15 (freshmen), 8/15 (transfers). *Notification:* continuous (freshmen), continuous (transfers).

Admissions Contact Dr. Gerald Harris, Dean of Student Services, Seward County Community College, PO Box 1137, Liberal, KS 67905-1137. *Phone:* 620-624-1951 Ext. 617. *Toll-free phone:* 800-373-9951 Ext. 710. *Fax:* 316-629-2725. *E-mail:* admit@sccc.cc.ks.us.

WICHITA AREA TECHNICAL COLLEGE
Wichita, Kansas

- **District-supported** 2-year, founded 1963
- **Calendar** semesters
- **Degree** certificates, diplomas, and associate
- **Urban** campus
- **Coed,** 2,052 undergraduate students, 27% full-time, 43% women, 57% men

Undergraduates 547 full-time, 1,505 part-time. 14% African American, 4% Asian American or Pacific Islander, 7% Hispanic American, 2% Native American.

Freshmen *Admission:* 855 enrolled.

Faculty *Total:* 65, 89% full-time. *Student/faculty ratio:* 17:1.

Majors Allied health and medical assisting services related; autobody/collision and repair technology; automobile/automotive mechanics technology; carpentry; clinical/medical laboratory technology; dental assisting; diesel mechanics technology; dietetics; gerontological services; machine shop technology; mechanical engineering/mechanical technology; nursing (licensed practical/vocational nurse training); pharmacy technician; surgical technology; truck and bus driver/commercial vehicle operation; welding technology.

Costs (2004–05) *Tuition:* state resident $2700 full-time, $75 per credit hour part-time; nonresident $12,600 full-time, $394 per credit hour part-time. *Required fees:* $90 full-time, $3 per credit hour part-time. *Room and board:* $5877.

Applying *Application fee:* $3. *Application deadline:* rolling (freshmen), rolling (transfers).

Admissions Contact Mrs. Shirley Antes, Facilitator for Accreditation and Institutional Advancement, Wichita Area Technical College, 301 South Grove Street, Wichita, KS 67211. *Phone:* 316-677-9559.

KENTUCKY

AEC SOUTHERN OHIO COLLEGE, NORTHERN KENTUCKY CAMPUS
Fort Mitchell, Kentucky

- **Proprietary** 2-year, founded 1927, part of American Education Centers, Inc
- **Calendar** quarters
- **Degree** certificates, diplomas, and associate
- **Suburban** 5-acre campus with easy access to Cincinnati
- **Coed,** 357 undergraduate students, 100% full-time, 60% women, 40% men

Undergraduates 357 full-time. Students come from 3 states and territories, 1 other country, 13% African American, 0.3% Asian American or Pacific Islander, 0.8% Hispanic American.

Freshmen *Admission:* 271 enrolled.

Majors Accounting technology and bookkeeping; business administration and management; computer science; information science/studies; medical/clinical assistant.

AEC Southern Ohio College, Northern Kentucky Campus (continued)

Academic Programs *Special study options:* academic remediation for entering students, adult/continuing education programs, internships, part-time degree program, summer session for credit.

Library 1,500 titles, 50 serial subscriptions.

Computers on Campus 50 computers available on campus for general student use. Internet access, at least one staffed computer lab available.

Student Life *Housing:* college housing not available. *Campus security:* 24-hour emergency response devices, late-night transport/escort service. *Student services:* personal/psychological counseling.

Applying *Options:* common application, early admission, deferred entrance. *Application fee:* $50. *Required:* high school transcript, interview. *Application deadline:* rolling (freshmen), rolling (transfers).

Admissions Contact Ms. Joanne Dellefield, Director of Admissions, AEC Southern Ohio College, Northern Kentucky Campus, 309 Buttermilk Pike, Fort Mitchell, KY 41017-2191. *Phone:* 859-341-5627.

ASHLAND COMMUNITY AND TECHNICAL COLLEGE
Ashland, Kentucky

- **State-supported** 2-year, founded 1937, part of Kentucky Community and Technical College System
- **Calendar** semesters
- **Degree** certificates, diplomas, and associate
- **Small-town** 47-acre campus
- **Endowment** $870,926
- **Coed**

Faculty *Student/faculty ratio:* 19:1.

Student Life *Campus security:* 24-hour emergency response devices and patrols, late-night transport/escort service, electronic surveillance of bookstore and business office.

Standardized Tests *Required:* ACT COMPASS (for placement). *Recommended:* ACT (for placement).

Costs (2003–04) *Tuition:* state resident $2370 full-time, $79 per credit hour part-time; nonresident $7110 full-time, $237 per credit hour part-time.

Financial Aid Of all full-time matriculated undergraduates who enrolled, 12 Federal Work-Study jobs (averaging $2500). 1 state and other part-time job (averaging $1000).

Applying *Options:* common application, early admission, deferred entrance. *Required:* high school transcript.

Admissions Contact Mr. Steven D. Flouhouse, Dean of Students, Ashland Community and Technical College, 1400 College Drive, Ashland, KY 41101. *Phone:* 606-326-2068 Ext. 2. *Toll-free phone:* 800-370-7191. *Fax:* 606-326-2192. *E-mail:* willie.mccullough@kctcs.net.

BECKFIELD COLLEGE
Florence, Kentucky

- **Proprietary** 2-year
- **Calendar** quarters
- **Degree** certificates, diplomas, and associate
- **Suburban** campus
- **Coed**, 480 undergraduate students, 100% full-time, 50% women, 50% men

Undergraduates 480 full-time.

Freshmen *Admission:* 87 applied, 320 enrolled.

Faculty *Total:* 26, 15% full-time. *Student/faculty ratio:* 17:1.

Majors Computer systems networking and telecommunications; computer technology/computer systems technology; legal assistant/paralegal; medical staff services technology.

Computers on Campus Computer purchase or lease plan available.

Costs (2003–04) *Tuition:* $10,000 full-time.

Admissions Contact Mr. Ken Leeds, Director of Admissions, Beckfield College, 16 Spiral Drive, Florence, KY 41022-0143. *Phone:* 859-371-9393.

BIG SANDY COMMUNITY AND TECHNICAL COLLEGE
Prestonsburg, Kentucky

- **State-supported** 2-year, founded 1964, part of Kentucky Community and Technical College System
- **Calendar** semesters
- **Degree** associate
- **Rural** 50-acre campus
- **Endowment** $700,000
- **Coed**, 4,406 undergraduate students

Undergraduates Students come from 1 other state, 0.8% African American, 0.2% Asian American or Pacific Islander, 0.2% Hispanic American, 0.1% Native American.

Faculty *Total:* 114, 61% full-time.

Majors Accounting; business administration and management; criminal justice/law enforcement administration; dental hygiene; human services; information technology; liberal arts and sciences/liberal studies; management information systems; nursing (registered nurse training); nursing related; office occupations and clerical services; real estate.

Academic Programs *Special study options:* academic remediation for entering students, adult/continuing education programs, advanced placement credit, cooperative education, distance learning, independent study, off-campus study, part-time degree program, services for LD students, summer session for credit.

Library Magoffin Learning Resource Center with 34,668 titles, 259 serial subscriptions, an OPAC.

Computers on Campus 200 computers available on campus for general student use. Internet access, at least one staffed computer lab available.

Student Life *Housing:* college housing not available. *Activities and Organizations:* choral group, Phi Theta Kappa, Baptist Student Union, Student Government Association, Phi Beta Lambda, Kentucky Association of Nursing Students. *Campus security:* 24-hour emergency response devices. *Student services:* health clinic, personal/psychological counseling.

Athletics *Intramural sports:* archery M/W, bowling M/W, golf M/W, table tennis M/W, volleyball M/W.

Standardized Tests *Required:* ACT (for placement). *Recommended:* ACT ASSET.

Costs (2004–05) *Tuition:* state resident $2760 full-time, $92 per credit part-time; nonresident $8280 full-time, $276 per credit part-time.

Financial Aid Of all full-time matriculated undergraduates who enrolled, 112 Federal Work-Study jobs (averaging $1749).

Applying *Options:* common application, early admission, deferred entrance. *Required:* high school transcript. *Application deadline:* rolling (freshmen), rolling (transfers).

Admissions Contact Mr. Jim Glover, Director of Admissions, Big Sandy Community and Technical College, One Bert T. Combs Drive, Prestonsburg, KY 41653-1815. *Phone:* 606-886-3863 Ext. 220. *Toll-free phone:* 888-641-4132. *Fax:* 606-886-6943. *E-mail:* jim.glover@kctcs.edu.

BOWLING GREEN TECHNICAL COLLEGE
Bowling Green, Kentucky

Admissions Contact 1845 Loop Drive, Bowling Green, KY 42101.

CENTRAL KENTUCKY TECHNICAL COLLEGE
Lexington, Kentucky

Admissions Contact 308 Vo Tech Road, Lexington, KY 40511.

DAYMAR COLLEGE
Louisville, Kentucky

- **Proprietary** 2-year, founded 2001
- **Calendar** quarters
- **Degree** diplomas and associate
- **Coed**, 227 undergraduate students

Majors Computer installation and repair technology; computer programming; computer systems networking and telecommunications; legal assistant/paralegal; medical office assistant.

Applying *Required:* high school transcript, interview.

Admissions Contact Mr. Patrick Carney, Director of Admissions, Daymar College, 4400 Breckenridge Lane, Suite 415, Louisville, KY 40218.

DAYMAR COLLEGE
Owensboro, Kentucky

- **Proprietary** 2-year, founded 1963
- **Calendar** quarters
- **Degree** certificates, diplomas, and associate
- **Small-town** 1-acre campus
- **Coed**

Faculty *Student/faculty ratio:* 9:1.
Student Life *Campus security:* 24-hour emergency response devices.
Standardized Tests *Required:* Wonderlic aptitude test (for admission). *Required for some:* SAT I or ACT (for admission).
Costs (2004–05) *Tuition:* $7020 full-time, $195 per credit hour part-time. *Required fees:* $730 full-time, $65 per course part-time.
Financial Aid Of all full-time matriculated undergraduates who enrolled, 12 Federal Work-Study jobs (averaging $6500).
Applying *Options:* deferred entrance. *Application fee:* $20. *Required:* high school transcript, interview.
Admissions Contact Ms. Vickie McDougal, Director of Admissions, Daymar College, 3361 Buckland Square, PO Box 22150, Owensboro, KY 42303. *Phone:* 270-926-4040. *Toll-free phone:* 800-960-4090. *Fax:* 270-685-4090. *E-mail:* info@daymarcollege.edu.

DRAUGHONS JUNIOR COLLEGE
Bowling Green, Kentucky

- **Proprietary** 2-year, founded 1989
- **Calendar** semesters
- **Degree** diplomas and associate
- **Suburban** campus with easy access to Nashville
- **Coed, primarily women,** 368 undergraduate students, 47% full-time, 86% women, 14% men

Undergraduates 172 full-time, 196 part-time. Students come from 2 states and territories, 1% are from out of state, 10% African American, 1% Hispanic American, 11% transferred in. *Retention:* 78% of 2002 full-time freshmen returned.
Freshmen *Admission:* 120 applied, 120 admitted, 120 enrolled. *Average high school GPA:* 3.00.
Faculty *Total:* 27, 37% full-time, 4% with terminal degrees. *Student/faculty ratio:* 13:1.
Majors Accounting; administrative assistant and secretarial science; business administration and management; health information/medical records administration; information science/studies; information technology; legal administrative assistant/secretary; medical/clinical assistant.
Academic Programs *Special study options:* adult/continuing education programs, internships, part-time degree program.
Library Draughons Junior College Library with 5,000 titles, 30 serial subscriptions, 75 audiovisual materials, a Web page.
Computers on Campus 52 computers available on campus for general student use. A campuswide network can be accessed. Internet access, online (class) registration, at least one staffed computer lab available.
Student Life *Housing:* college housing not available. *Activities and Organizations:* student-run newspaper, Student Council. *Campus security:* 24-hour emergency response devices. *Student services:* personal/psychological counseling.
Standardized Tests *Recommended:* SAT I or ACT (for placement).
Costs (2004–05) *Tuition:* $11,600 full-time, $300 per credit part-time. Full-time tuition and fees vary according to program. Part-time tuition and fees vary according to program. *Required fees:* $1000 full-time, $75 per course part-time. *Payment plan:* installment.
Financial Aid Of all full-time matriculated undergraduates who enrolled, 2 Federal Work-Study jobs (averaging $4950).
Applying *Options:* common application. *Application fee:* $20. *Required:* high school transcript.
Admissions Contact Amye Melton, Admissions Director, Draughons Junior College, 2421 Fitzgerald Industrial Drive, Bowling Green, KY 42101. *Phone:* 270-843-6750. *Fax:* 270-843-6976.

ELIZABETHTOWN COMMUNITY COLLEGE
Elizabethtown, Kentucky

- **State-supported** 2-year, founded 1964, part of Kentucky Community and Technical College System
- **Calendar** semesters
- **Degree** certificates, diplomas, and associate
- **Small-town** 40-acre campus with easy access to Louisville
- **Coed,** 3,615 undergraduate students, 46% full-time, 68% women, 32% men

Undergraduates 1,645 full-time, 1,970 part-time. Students come from 10 states and territories, 11% African American, 2% Asian American or Pacific Islander, 3% Hispanic American, 0.6% Native American.
Freshmen *Admission:* 737 enrolled.
Majors Administrative assistant and secretarial science; biological and physical sciences; business administration and management; child guidance; criminal justice/police science; dental hygiene; finance; information science/studies;

liberal arts and sciences/liberal studies; nursing (registered nurse training); quality control technology; real estate.
Academic Programs *Special study options:* academic remediation for entering students, adult/continuing education programs, advanced placement credit, cooperative education, external degree program, internships, off-campus study, part-time degree program, services for LD students, summer session for credit.
Library Elizabethtown Community College Media Center with 35,175 titles, 240 serial subscriptions, an OPAC.
Computers on Campus 70 computers available on campus for general student use. Internet access, at least one staffed computer lab available.
Student Life *Housing:* college housing not available. *Activities and Organizations:* drama/theater group, student-run newspaper, choral group, Baptist Student Union, Kentucky Association of Nursing Students. *Campus security:* late night security.
Athletics *Intramural sports:* basketball M/W, football M, golf M, soccer M, table tennis M/W, tennis M/W, volleyball M/W.
Standardized Tests *Required:* ACT ASSET (for admission). *Required for some:* ACT (for admission).
Costs (2003–04) *Tuition:* state resident $1896 full-time, $79 per credit hour part-time; nonresident $5688 full-time, $237 per credit hour part-time. *Payment plan:* deferred payment. *Waivers:* senior citizens and employees or children of employees.
Financial Aid Of all full-time matriculated undergraduates who enrolled, 20 Federal Work-Study jobs (averaging $2000).
Applying *Options:* common application, early admission. *Required:* essay or personal statement, high school transcript. *Application deadline:* rolling (freshmen), rolling (transfers). *Notification:* continuous (freshmen), continuous (transfers).
Admissions Contact Dr. Dale Buckles, Dean of Student Affairs, Elizabethtown Community College, Elizabethtown Community College, 600 College Street Road, Elizabethtown, KY 42701. *Phone:* 270-769-2371 Ext. 4231. *Toll-free phone:* 877-246-2322 Ext. 4308.

ELIZABETHTOWN TECHNICAL COLLEGE
Elizabethtown, Kentucky

Admissions Contact 620 College Street Road, Elizabethtown, KY 42701.

GATEWAY COMMUNITY AND TECHNICAL COLLEGE
Covington, Kentucky

- **State-supported** 2-year, founded 1961
- **Calendar** semesters
- **Degree** certificates, diplomas, and associate
- **Coed**

Standardized Tests *Required:* ACT or ACT COMPASS (for admission).
Costs (2003–04) *Tuition:* state resident $2370 full-time, $79 per credit hour part-time; nonresident $7110 full-time, $237 per credit hour part-time.
Admissions Contact Mr. Paul Brinkman, Dean of Student Affairs, Gateway Community and Technical College, 1025 Amsterdam Road, Covington, KY 41011.

HAZARD COMMUNITY AND TECHNICAL COLLEGE
Hazard, Kentucky

- **State-supported** 2-year, founded 1968, part of Kentucky Community and Technical College System
- **Calendar** semesters
- **Degree** certificates, diplomas, and associate
- **Rural** 34-acre campus
- **Coed**

Student Life *Campus security:* late-night transport/escort service.
Standardized Tests *Required:* ACT (for placement).
Costs (2003–04) *Tuition:* state resident $1896 full-time, $79 per credit hour part-time; nonresident $5688 full-time, $237 per credit hour part-time. Part-time tuition and fees vary according to course load.
Applying *Options:* common application, early admission. *Required:* high school transcript.
Admissions Contact Mr. Steve Jones, Director of Admissions, Hazard Community and Technical College, 1 Community College Drive, Hazard, KY 41701-2403. *Phone:* 606-436-5721 Ext. 8076. *Toll-free phone:* 800-246-7521.

HENDERSON COMMUNITY COLLEGE
Henderson, Kentucky

- **State-supported** 2-year, founded 1963, part of Kentucky Community and Technical College System
- **Calendar** semesters
- **Degree** associate
- **Small-town** 120-acre campus
- **Coed,** 2,241 undergraduate students, 31% full-time, 63% women, 37% men

Undergraduates 690 full-time, 1,551 part-time. Students come from 12 states and territories, 1% are from out of state, 5% African American, 0.3% Asian American or Pacific Islander, 0.6% Hispanic American, 0.8% Native American.

Freshmen *Admission:* 1,923 applied, 1,923 admitted.

Faculty *Total:* 101, 48% full-time. *Student/faculty ratio:* 13:1.

Majors Administrative assistant and secretarial science; business administration and management; clinical laboratory science/medical technology; computer and information sciences related; computer/information technology services administration related; computer programming related; computer programming (specific applications); computer programming (vendor/product certification); computer systems networking and telecommunications; data entry/microcomputer applications; data entry/microcomputer applications related; data processing and data processing technology; electrical, electronic and communications engineering technology; engineering technology; human services; information technology; mass communication/media; nursing (registered nurse training); word processing.

Academic Programs *Special study options:* academic remediation for entering students, accelerated degree program, adult/continuing education programs, advanced placement credit, cooperative education, distance learning, double majors, English as a second language, external degree program, independent study, internships, off-campus study, part-time degree program, summer session for credit.

Library Hartfield Learning Resource Center plus 1 other with 30,206 titles, 231 serial subscriptions, 1,053 audiovisual materials, an OPAC, a Web page.

Computers on Campus 200 computers available on campus for general student use. Internet access available.

Student Life *Housing:* college housing not available. *Activities and Organizations:* drama/theater group, student-run radio station. *Campus security:* 24-hour emergency response devices. *Student services:* personal/psychological counseling.

Athletics *Intramural sports:* basketball M, football M, golf M, softball M/W, table tennis M/W.

Standardized Tests *Required:* ACT (for admission), ACT COMPASS (for admission).

Costs (2003–04) *Tuition:* area resident $2370 full-time, $79 per credit hour part-time; state resident $2850 full-time, $95 per credit hour part-time; nonresident $7110 full-time, $237 per credit hour part-time. *Payment plan:* deferred payment. *Waivers:* senior citizens.

Applying *Options:* common application. *Required:* high school transcript. *Required for some:* essay or personal statement, letters of recommendation, interview. *Application deadlines:* 9/1 (freshmen), 9/1 (transfers).

Admissions Contact Ms. Teresa Hamiton, Admissions Counselor, Henderson Community College, 2660 South Green Street, Henderson, KY 42420-4623. *Phone:* 270-827-1867 Ext. 354.

HOPKINSVILLE COMMUNITY COLLEGE
Hopkinsville, Kentucky

- **State-supported** 2-year, founded 1965, part of Kentucky Community and Technical College System
- **Calendar** semesters
- **Degree** certificates, diplomas, and associate
- **Small-town** 70-acre campus with easy access to Nashville
- **Endowment** $2.4 million
- **Coed,** 3,116 undergraduate students, 40% full-time, 73% women, 27% men

Undergraduates 1,255 full-time, 1,861 part-time. Students come from 3 states and territories, 23% are from out of state, 22% African American, 1% Asian American or Pacific Islander, 3% Hispanic American, 0.4% Native American, 60% transferred in. *Retention:* 55% of 2002 full-time freshmen returned.

Freshmen *Admission:* 1,669 enrolled. *Test scores:* ACT scores over 18: 69%; ACT scores over 24: 6%.

Faculty *Total:* 173, 40% full-time, 5% with terminal degrees. *Student/faculty ratio:* 27:1.

Majors Administrative assistant and secretarial science; animal/livestock husbandry and production; business administration and management; child care and support services management; criminal justice/police science; early childhood education; electrical, electronic and communications engineering technology; finance; human services; industrial technology; kindergarten/preschool education; liberal arts and sciences/liberal studies; management information systems;

manufacturing technology; mental health/rehabilitation; nursing (licensed practical/vocational nurse training); nursing (registered nurse training).

Academic Programs *Special study options:* academic remediation for entering students, adult/continuing education programs, advanced placement credit, distance learning, honors programs, independent study, part-time degree program, summer session for credit.

Library HCC Library plus 1 other with 45,640 titles, 152 serial subscriptions, 2,720 audiovisual materials, an OPAC, a Web page.

Computers on Campus 350 computers available on campus for general student use. A campuswide network can be accessed from off campus. Internet access, at least one staffed computer lab available.

Student Life *Housing:* college housing not available. *Activities and Organizations:* student-run newspaper, television station, Baptist Student Union, Circle K, Minority Student Union, Donovan Scholars, Nursing Club. *Campus security:* 24-hour emergency response devices, late-night transport/escort service.

Athletics *Intramural sports:* basketball M, football M, golf M, table tennis M/W, volleyball M/W.

Standardized Tests *Required:* ACT (for placement), ACT COMPASS (for placement).

Costs (2003–04) *Tuition:* state resident $2370 full-time, $79 per credit hour part-time; nonresident $7110 full-time, $237 per credit hour part-time. *Payment plan:* installment. *Waivers:* employees or children of employees.

Financial Aid Of all full-time matriculated undergraduates who enrolled, 30 Federal Work-Study jobs (averaging $1500). *Financial aid deadline:* 6/30.

Applying *Options:* common application, early admission, deferred entrance. *Required for some:* high school transcript, interview. *Application deadline:* rolling (freshmen), rolling (transfers). *Notification:* continuous (freshmen), continuous (transfers).

Admissions Contact Ms. Ruth Ann Rettie, Registrar, Hopkinsville Community College, North Drive, PO Box 2100, Hopkinsville, KY 42241-2100. *Phone:* 270-886-3921 Ext. 6197. *Fax:* 270-886-0237. *E-mail:* admit.record@kctcs.net.

ITT TECHNICAL INSTITUTE
Louisville, Kentucky

- **Proprietary** primarily 2-year, founded 1993, part of ITT Educational Services, Inc.
- **Calendar** quarters
- **Degrees** associate and bachelor's
- **Suburban** campus
- **Coed**

Standardized Tests *Required:* Wonderlic aptitude test (for admission).

Costs (2003–04) *Tuition:* Total Program Cost varies depending on course of study. Consult school catalog.

Applying *Options:* deferred entrance. *Application fee:* $100. *Required:* high school transcript, interview. *Recommended:* letters of recommendation.

Admissions Contact Mr. Chuck Taylor, Director of Recruitment, ITT Technical Institute, 10509 Timberwood Circle, Louisville, KY 40223. *Phone:* 502-327-7424. *Fax:* 502-327-7624.

JEFFERSON COMMUNITY COLLEGE
Louisville, Kentucky

- **State-supported** 2-year, founded 1968, part of Kentucky Community and Technical College System
- **Calendar** semesters
- **Degree** certificates and associate
- **Urban** 10-acre campus
- **Endowment** $1.1 million
- **Coed,** 9,665 undergraduate students, 38% full-time, 61% women, 39% men

Undergraduates 3,657 full-time, 6,008 part-time. Students come from 11 states and territories, 3% are from out of state, 17% African American, 2% Asian American or Pacific Islander, 2% Hispanic American, 0.3% Native American, 16% transferred in.

Freshmen *Admission:* 2,104 applied, 1,371 admitted, 1,371 enrolled.

Faculty *Total:* 417, 61% full-time. *Student/faculty ratio:* 18:1.

Majors Accounting; business administration and management; child development; commercial and advertising art; culinary arts; data processing and data processing technology; electrical, electronic and communications engineering technology; health information/medical records technology; liberal arts and sciences/liberal studies; mechanical engineering/mechanical technology; medical radiologic technology; nuclear medical technology; nursing (registered nurse training); physical therapy; real estate; respiratory care therapy; social work.

Academic Programs *Special study options:* academic remediation for entering students, adult/continuing education programs, advanced placement credit, cooperative education, distance learning, English as a second language, external degree program, honors programs, independent study, internships, off-campus study, part-time degree program, services for LD students, summer session for credit. *ROTC:* Army (c).

Library John T. Smith Learning Resource Center plus 2 others with 76,578 titles, 391 serial subscriptions, 15,103 audiovisual materials, an OPAC, a Web page.

Computers on Campus 895 computers available on campus for general student use. A campuswide network can be accessed from off campus. Internet access, at least one staffed computer lab available.

Student Life *Housing:* college housing not available. *Activities and Organizations:* drama/theater group, student-run newspaper. *Campus security:* 24-hour emergency response devices and patrols, late-night transport/escort service. *Student services:* personal/psychological counseling.

Standardized Tests *Required:* ACT COMPASS (for placement).

Costs (2003–04) *Tuition:* state resident $2370 full-time, $79 per credit hour part-time; nonresident $7110 full-time, $237 per credit hour part-time. *Required fees:* $25 full-time, $25 per term part-time. *Payment plans:* installment, deferred payment. *Waivers:* senior citizens and employees or children of employees.

Financial Aid Of all full-time matriculated undergraduates who enrolled, 50 Federal Work-Study jobs (averaging $4000).

Applying *Options:* early admission. *Application deadline:* rolling (freshmen), rolling (transfers). *Notification:* continuous (freshmen), continuous (transfers).

Admissions Contact Dr. Maryetta Fisher, Dean of Student Affairs, Jefferson Community College, 109 East Broadway, Louisville, KY 40202. *Phone:* 502-213-2136. *Fax:* 502-213-2540.

JEFFERSON TECHNICAL COLLEGE
Louisville, Kentucky

- **State-supported** 2-year, founded 1967
- **Calendar** semesters
- **Degree** certificates, diplomas, and associate
- **Urban** campus
- **Coed,** 3,778 undergraduate students, 16% full-time, 34% women, 66% men

Undergraduates 601 full-time, 3,177 part-time. 17% African American, 0.8% Asian American or Pacific Islander, 0.7% Hispanic American, 0.6% Native American.

Freshmen *Admission:* 364 enrolled.

Faculty *Total:* 156, 53% full-time. *Student/faculty ratio:* 15:1.

Costs (2004–05) *Tuition:* state resident $92 full-time, $92 per credit hour part-time; nonresident $276 full-time, $276 per credit hour part-time. *Required fees:* $50 full-time, $25 per term part-time.

Admissions Contact Maryetta Fisher, Dean of Students, Jefferson Technical College, 727 West Chestnut Street, Louisville, KY 40203. *Phone:* 502-213-2136.

LOUISVILLE TECHNICAL INSTITUTE
Louisville, Kentucky

- **Proprietary** 2-year, founded 1961, part of Sullivan University System
- **Calendar** quarters
- **Degree** certificates, diplomas, and associate
- **Suburban** 10-acre campus
- **Coed,** 667 undergraduate students, 94% full-time, 35% women, 65% men

Undergraduates 626 full-time, 41 part-time. Students come from 6 states and territories, 17% are from out of state, 11% African American, 1% Asian American or Pacific Islander, 2% Hispanic American, 1% Native American, 11% transferred in, 6% live on campus. *Retention:* 68% of 2002 full-time freshmen returned.

Freshmen *Admission:* 182 applied, 140 admitted, 130 enrolled. *Average high school GPA:* 3.17.

Faculty *Total:* 59, 51% full-time. *Student/faculty ratio:* 9:1.

Majors Animation, interactive technology, video graphics and special effects; architectural drafting and CAD/CADD; architectural engineering technology; architecture related; artificial intelligence and robotics; CAD/CADD drafting/design technology; computer and information sciences; computer and information sciences and support services related; computer and information systems security; computer engineering technology; computer graphics; computer hardware engineering; computer hardware technology; computer installation and repair technology; computer programming (vendor/product certification); computer systems networking and telecommunications; computer/technical support; computer technology/computer systems technology; desktop publishing and digital imaging design; digital communication and media/multimedia; drafting and design technology; drafting/design engineering technologies related; electrical and electronic engineering technologies related; electrical, electronic and communications engineering technology; electrical/electronics equipment installation and repair; electrical/electronics maintenance and repair technology related; electromechanical and instrumentation and maintenance technologies related;

engineering technologies related; engineering technology; graphic and printing equipment operation/production; graphic communications; graphic communications related; graphic design; housing and human environments; industrial electronics technology; industrial mechanics and maintenance technology; information technology; interior design; marine technology; mechanical design technology; mechanical drafting and CAD/CADD; mechanical engineering/mechanical technology; robotics technology; small engine mechanics and repair technology; system administration; web page, digital/multimedia and information resources design.

Academic Programs *Special study options:* academic remediation for entering students, accelerated degree program, adult/continuing education programs, cooperative education, internships, part-time degree program, services for LD students, summer session for credit.

Library Louisville Tech Library plus 1 other with 3,463 titles, 96 serial subscriptions, 242 audiovisual materials, an OPAC.

Computers on Campus 193 computers available on campus for general student use. A campuswide network can be accessed from off campus. Internet access, at least one staffed computer lab available.

Student Life *Housing Options:* coed. Campus housing is leased by the school. *Activities and Organizations:* student-run newspaper, ASID, IIDA, ADDA, Robotics International. *Campus security:* late-night transport/escort service.

Standardized Tests *Required:* ACT, SAT or CPAt (for admission).

Costs (2004–05) *Tuition:* $12,480 full-time, $260 per credit hour part-time. Full-time tuition and fees vary according to program. Part-time tuition and fees vary according to program. No tuition increase for student's term of enrollment. *Required fees:* $415 full-time, $25 per course part-time. *Room only:* $3690. *Payment plans:* tuition prepayment, installment. *Waivers:* employees or children of employees.

Applying *Options:* deferred entrance. *Application fee:* $90. *Required:* high school transcript, minimum 2.0 GPA, interview. *Application deadline:* rolling (freshmen).

Admissions Contact Mr. David Ritz, Director of Admissions, Louisville Technical Institute, 3901 Atkinson Square Drive, Louisville, KY 40218. *Phone:* 502-456-6509. *Toll-free phone:* 800-884-6528. *E-mail:* dritz@louisvilletech.com.

MADISONVILLE COMMUNITY COLLEGE
Madisonville, Kentucky

- **State-supported** 2-year, founded 1968, part of Kentucky Community and Technical College System
- **Calendar** semesters
- **Degree** certificates, diplomas, and associate
- **Small-town** 150-acre campus
- **Endowment** $2.4 million
- **Coed**

Student Life *Campus security:* 24-hour emergency response devices, late-night transport/escort service, evening patrols.

Standardized Tests *Required:* ACT (for placement), ACT ASSET (for placement).

Costs (2003–04) *Tuition:* state resident $2370 full-time; nonresident $7110 full-time. Full-time tuition and fees vary according to course load. Part-time tuition and fees vary according to course load. *Payment plans:* tuition prepayment, installment, deferred payment.

Financial Aid Of all full-time matriculated undergraduates who enrolled, 50 Federal Work-Study jobs (averaging $2100). 15 state and other part-time jobs (averaging $1600).

Applying *Options:* electronic application, early admission, deferred entrance. *Required:* high school transcript.

Admissions Contact Mr. Jay Parent, Registrar, Madisonville Community College, 2000 College Drive, Madisonville, KY 42431. *Phone:* 270-821-2250. *Fax:* 502-821-1555. *E-mail:* dmcox@pop.uky.edu.

MAYSVILLE COMMUNITY COLLEGE
Maysville, Kentucky

- **State-supported** 2-year, founded 1967, part of Kentucky Community and Technical College System
- **Calendar** semesters
- **Degree** certificates, diplomas, and associate
- **Rural** 12-acre campus
- **Coed,** 1,917 undergraduate students, 40% full-time, 68% women, 32% men

Undergraduates 776 full-time, 1,141 part-time. Students come from 2 states and territories, 7% are from out of state, 2% African American, 0.2% Asian American or Pacific Islander, 0.1% Hispanic American, 0.1% Native American, 1% transferred in.

Freshmen *Admission:* 727 admitted, 197 enrolled.

Maysville Community College (continued)

Faculty *Total:* 121, 44% full-time, 10% with terminal degrees.

Majors Accounting; administrative assistant and secretarial science; business administration and management; electrical, electronic and communications engineering technology; electromechanical technology; liberal arts and sciences/liberal studies; marketing/marketing management; nursing (registered nurse training); respiratory care therapy.

Academic Programs *Special study options:* academic remediation for entering students, adult/continuing education programs, advanced placement credit, cooperative education, distance learning, English as a second language, external degree program, honors programs, independent study, internships, off-campus study, part-time degree program, services for LD students, summer session for credit.

Library Finch Library with 36,600 titles, 288 serial subscriptions, an OPAC, a Web page.

Computers on Campus 250 computers available on campus for general student use. A campuswide network can be accessed from off campus. Internet access, at least one staffed computer lab available.

Student Life *Housing:* college housing not available. *Activities and Organizations:* student-run television station, Student Government Association, Math and Science Club, Retail Marketing Club, Student Education Association. *Campus security:* student patrols, evening parking lot security. *Student services:* personal/psychological counseling.

Standardized Tests *Required for some:* ACT (for placement).

Costs (2004–05) *Tuition:* $92 per credit part-time; state resident $92 per credit part-time; nonresident $276 per credit part-time. *Payment plans:* installment, deferred payment.

Financial Aid Of all full-time matriculated undergraduates who enrolled, 30 Federal Work-Study jobs (averaging $1960).

Applying *Options:* early admission. *Required:* high school transcript. *Application deadline:* rolling (freshmen), rolling (transfers). *Notification:* continuous (freshmen), continuous (transfers).

Admissions Contact Ms. Patee Massie, Registrar, Maysville Community College, 1755 US 68, Maysville, KY 41056. *Phone:* 606-759-7141 Ext. 6184. *Fax:* 606-759-5818. *E-mail:* patee.massie@kctcs.net.

NATIONAL COLLEGE OF BUSINESS & TECHNOLOGY
Danville, Kentucky

- **Proprietary** 2-year, founded 1962, part of National College of Business and Technology
- **Calendar** quarters
- **Degree** diplomas and associate
- **Coed,** 232 undergraduate students

Faculty *Total:* 24. *Student/faculty ratio:* 10:1.

Majors Accounting; administrative assistant and secretarial science; business administration and management; computer and information sciences related; medical/clinical assistant.

Academic Programs *Special study options:* advanced placement credit, double majors, honors programs, internships, part-time degree program, services for LD students, summer session for credit.

Computers on Campus 30 computers available on campus for general student use. A campuswide network can be accessed. Internet access, at least one staffed computer lab available.

Student Life *Housing:* college housing not available.

Costs (2004–05) *Tuition:* $6120 full-time, $170 per credit hour part-time. *Required fees:* $75 full-time. *Payment plans:* installment, deferred payment. *Waivers:* employees or children of employees.

Financial Aid Of all full-time matriculated undergraduates who enrolled, 1 Federal Work-Study job.

Applying *Options:* common application, electronic application. *Application fee:* $30. *Required:* high school transcript. *Application deadline:* rolling (freshmen), rolling (transfers). *Notification:* continuous (freshmen).

Admissions Contact Ms. Stacie Catlett, Campus Director, National College of Business & Technology, 115 East Lexington Avenue, Danville, KY 40422. *Phone:* 859-236-6991. *Toll-free phone:* 800-664-1886. *Fax:* 859-236-1063. *E-mail:* adm@educorp.edu.

NATIONAL COLLEGE OF BUSINESS & TECHNOLOGY
Florence, Kentucky

- **Proprietary** 2-year, founded 1941, part of National College of Business and Technology
- **Calendar** quarters
- **Degree** diplomas and associate
- **Suburban** campus
- **Coed,** 163 undergraduate students

Faculty *Total:* 16, 13% full-time. *Student/faculty ratio:* 10:1.

Majors Accounting; administrative assistant and secretarial science; business administration and management; computer and information sciences related; medical/clinical assistant.

Academic Programs *Special study options:* advanced placement credit, double majors, honors programs, internships, part-time degree program, services for LD students, summer session for credit.

Computers on Campus 30 computers available on campus for general student use. Internet access, at least one staffed computer lab available.

Student Life *Housing:* college housing not available. *Campus security:* 24-hour emergency response devices.

Costs (2004–05) *Tuition:* $6120 full-time, $170 per credit hour part-time. *Required fees:* $75 full-time.

Financial Aid Of all full-time matriculated undergraduates who enrolled, 3 Federal Work-Study jobs.

Applying *Options:* electronic application. *Application fee:* $30. *Required for some:* high school transcript. *Recommended:* interview. *Application deadline:* rolling (freshmen), rolling (transfers). *Notification:* continuous (freshmen).

Admissions Contact Mr. Kerry Tarvin, Campus Director, National College of Business & Technology, 7627 Ewing Boulevard, Florence, KY 41042. *Phone:* 859-525-6510. *Toll-free phone:* 800-664-1886. *Fax:* 859-525-8961. *E-mail:* adm@educorp.edu.

NATIONAL COLLEGE OF BUSINESS & TECHNOLOGY
Lexington, Kentucky

- **Proprietary** 2-year, founded 1947, part of National College of Business and Technology
- **Calendar** quarters
- **Degree** diplomas and associate
- **Urban** campus
- **Coed,** 307 undergraduate students

Faculty *Total:* 24, 4% full-time. *Student/faculty ratio:* 10:1.

Majors Accounting; administrative assistant and secretarial science; business administration and management; computer and information sciences related; radio and television.

Academic Programs *Special study options:* advanced placement credit, double majors, honors programs, internships, part-time degree program, summer session for credit.

Computers on Campus 30 computers available on campus for general student use. Internet access, at least one staffed computer lab available.

Student Life *Housing:* college housing not available. *Student services:* personal/psychological counseling.

Costs (2004–05) *Tuition:* $6120 full-time, $170 per credit hour part-time. Full-time tuition and fees vary according to course load. Part-time tuition and fees vary according to course load. *Required fees:* $75 full-time. *Payment plans:* installment, deferred payment. *Waivers:* employees or children of employees.

Financial Aid Of all full-time matriculated undergraduates who enrolled, 6 Federal Work-Study jobs.

Applying *Options:* electronic application. *Application fee:* $30. *Required:* high school transcript. *Application deadline:* rolling (freshmen), rolling (transfers). *Notification:* continuous (freshmen).

Admissions Contact Ms. Carolyn Howard, Campus Director, National College of Business & Technology, 628 East Main Street, Lexington, KY 40508-2312. *Phone:* 859-266-0401. *Toll-free phone:* 800-664-1886. *Fax:* 859-233-3054. *E-mail:* market@educorp.edu.

NATIONAL COLLEGE OF BUSINESS & TECHNOLOGY
Louisville, Kentucky

- **Proprietary** 2-year, founded 1990, part of National College of Business and Technology
- **Calendar** quarters
- **Degree** diplomas and associate
- **Coed,** 566 undergraduate students

Faculty *Total:* 22, 45% full-time. *Student/faculty ratio:* 10:1.

Majors Accounting; administrative assistant and secretarial science; business administration and management; computer and information sciences related; health/health care administration; medical/clinical assistant.

Academic Programs *Special study options:* advanced placement credit, double majors, honors programs, internships, part-time degree program, services for LD students, summer session for credit.
Computers on Campus 55 computers available on campus for general student use. Internet access, at least one staffed computer lab available.
Student Life *Housing:* college housing not available.
Costs (2004–05) *Tuition:* $6120 full-time, $170 per credit hour part-time. Full-time tuition and fees vary according to course load. Part-time tuition and fees vary according to course load. *Required fees:* $75 full-time. *Payment plans:* installment, deferred payment. *Waivers:* employees or children of employees.
Financial Aid Of all full-time matriculated undergraduates who enrolled, 2 Federal Work-Study jobs.
Applying *Options:* electronic application. *Application fee:* $30. *Required for some:* high school transcript. *Recommended:* interview. *Application deadline:* rolling (freshmen), rolling (transfers). *Notification:* continuous (freshmen), continuous (transfers).
Admissions Contact Mike Fiore, Campus Director, National College of Business & Technology, 3950 Dixie Highway, Louisville, KY 40216. *Phone:* 502-447-7634. *Toll-free phone:* 800-664-1886. *Fax:* 502-447-7665. *E-mail:* adm@educorp.edu.

NATIONAL COLLEGE OF BUSINESS & TECHNOLOGY
Pikeville, Kentucky

- **Proprietary** 2-year, founded 1976, part of National College of Business and Technology
- **Calendar** quarters
- **Degree** diplomas and associate
- **Rural** campus
- **Coed,** 222 undergraduate students

Faculty *Total:* 12, 17% full-time. *Student/faculty ratio:* 10:1.
Majors Accounting; administrative assistant and secretarial science; business administration and management; computer and information sciences related; medical/clinical assistant.
Academic Programs *Special study options:* advanced placement credit, double majors, honors programs, internships, part-time degree program, services for LD students, summer session for credit.
Computers on Campus 24 computers available on campus for general student use. Internet access, at least one staffed computer lab available.
Student Life *Housing:* college housing not available.
Costs (2004–05) *Tuition:* $6120 full-time, $170 per credit hour part-time. Full-time tuition and fees vary according to course load. Part-time tuition and fees vary according to course load. *Required fees:* $75 full-time. *Payment plans:* installment, deferred payment. *Waivers:* employees or children of employees.
Financial Aid Of all full-time matriculated undergraduates who enrolled, 4 Federal Work-Study jobs.
Applying *Application fee:* $30. *Required for some:* high school transcript. *Recommended:* interview. *Application deadline:* rolling (freshmen), rolling (transfers). *Notification:* continuous (freshmen).
Admissions Contact Mr. Jerry Lafferty, Campus Director, National College of Business & Technology, 288 South Mayo Trail, Suite 2, Pikeville, KY 41501. *Phone:* 540-986-1800. *Toll-free phone:* 800-664-1886. *Fax:* 606-437-4952. *E-mail:* adm@educorp.edu.

NATIONAL COLLEGE OF BUSINESS & TECHNOLOGY
Richmond, Kentucky

- **Proprietary** 2-year, founded 1951, part of National College of Business and Technology
- **Calendar** quarters
- **Degree** diplomas and associate
- **Suburban** campus
- **Coed,** 233 undergraduate students

Faculty *Total:* 15, 20% full-time. *Student/faculty ratio:* 10:1.
Majors Accounting; administrative assistant and secretarial science; business administration and management; computer and information sciences related; medical/clinical assistant.
Academic Programs *Special study options:* advanced placement credit, double majors, honors programs, internships, part-time degree program, summer session for credit.
Computers on Campus 20 computers available on campus for general student use. Internet access, at least one staffed computer lab available.
Student Life *Housing:* college housing not available.

Costs (2004–05) *Tuition:* $6120 full-time, $170 per credit hour part-time. Full-time tuition and fees vary according to course load. Part-time tuition and fees vary according to course load. *Required fees:* $75 full-time. *Payment plans:* installment, deferred payment. *Waivers:* employees or children of employees.
Financial Aid Of all full-time matriculated undergraduates who enrolled, 1 Federal Work-Study job.
Applying *Options:* electronic application. *Application fee:* $30. *Required for some:* high school transcript. *Recommended:* interview. *Application deadline:* rolling (freshmen), rolling (transfers). *Notification:* continuous (freshmen).
Admissions Contact Ms. Keeley Gadd, Campus Director, National College of Business & Technology, 139 Killarney Lane, Richmond, KY 40475. *Phone:* 859-623-8956. *Toll-free phone:* 800-664-1886. *Fax:* 606-624-5544. *E-mail:* adm@educorp.edu.

OWENSBORO COMMUNITY AND TECHNICAL COLLEGE
Owensboro, Kentucky

- **State-supported** 2-year, founded 1986, part of Kentucky Community and Technical College System
- **Calendar** semesters
- **Degree** certificates and associate
- **Suburban** 102-acre campus
- **Coed,** 3,664 undergraduate students, 50% full-time, 60% women, 40% men

Undergraduates 1,848 full-time, 1,816 part-time. Students come from 6 states and territories, 2 other countries, 5% are from out of state, 3% African American, 0.5% Asian American or Pacific Islander, 0.3% Hispanic American, 0.2% Native American, 2% transferred in.
Freshmen *Admission:* 789 applied, 789 admitted, 700 enrolled. *Test scores:* ACT scores over 18: 72%; ACT scores over 24: 17%; ACT scores over 30: 1%.
Faculty *Total:* 203, 47% full-time. *Student/faculty ratio:* 21:1.
Majors Agriculture; business administration and management; computer and information sciences; computer/information technology services administration related; criminal justice/police science; data entry/microcomputer applications; electrical, electronic and communications engineering technology; executive assistant/executive secretary; human services; information technology; kindergarten/preschool education; liberal arts and sciences/liberal studies; medical radiologic technology; nursing (registered nurse training); social work; system administration; word processing.
Academic Programs *Special study options:* academic remediation for entering students, adult/continuing education programs, advanced placement credit, cooperative education, distance learning, double majors, external degree program, honors programs, internships, off-campus study, part-time degree program, study abroad, summer session for credit.
Library Learning Resource Center with 18,200 titles, 80 serial subscriptions, an OPAC, a Web page.
Computers on Campus 90 computers available on campus for general student use. A campuswide network can be accessed. Internet access, at least one staffed computer lab available.
Student Life *Housing:* college housing not available. *Activities and Organizations:* drama/theater group, student-run newspaper, radio and television station, choral group, student government, Psychology Club, Nursing Club. *Campus security:* 24-hour emergency response devices, late-night transport/escort service.
Athletics *Intramural sports:* basketball M, softball M/W.
Standardized Tests *Required:* ACT (for placement). *Required for some:* ACT COMPASS.
Costs (2003–04) *Tuition:* state resident $2370 full-time, $79 per credit hour part-time; nonresident $7110 full-time, $237 per credit hour part-time. *Payment plan:* installment. *Waivers:* senior citizens and employees or children of employees.
Financial Aid Of all full-time matriculated undergraduates who enrolled, 50 Federal Work-Study jobs (averaging $2478). *Financial aid deadline:* 4/1.
Applying *Required:* high school transcript. *Application deadline:* rolling (freshmen), rolling (transfers). *Notification:* continuous (freshmen), continuous (transfers).
Admissions Contact Ms. Barbara Tipmore, Admissions Counselor, Owensboro Community and Technical College, 4800 New Hartford Road, Owensboro, KY 42303. *Phone:* 270-686-4527. *Toll-free phone:* 866-755-6282.

PADUCAH TECHNICAL COLLEGE
Paducah, Kentucky

Admissions Contact Mr. Arnold Harris, Director of Admissions, Paducah Technical College, 509 South 30th Street, PO Box 8252, Paducah, KY 42001. *Phone:* 502-444-9676. *Toll-free phone:* 800-995-4438.

RETS Institute of Technology
Louisville, Kentucky

Admissions Contact Mr. Dan Squires, Director of Admissions, RETS Institute of Technology, 300 Highrise Drive, Louisville, KY 40213. *Phone:* 502-968-7191. *Toll-free phone:* 800-999-7387. *Fax:* 502-968-1727.

RETS Medical and Business Institute
Hopkinsville, Kentucky

- **Proprietary** 2-year
- **Calendar** quarters
- **Degree** diplomas and associate
- **Small-town** campus
- **Coed, primarily women,** 130 undergraduate students, 100% full-time, 96% women, 4% men

Undergraduates 130 full-time. 46% African American, 2% Asian American or Pacific Islander, 2% Hispanic American.
Freshmen *Admission:* 150 applied, 150 admitted, 73 enrolled.
Faculty *Total:* 7, 43% full-time, 43% with terminal degrees. *Student/faculty ratio:* 16:1.
Majors Business administration and management; medical/clinical assistant; medical office management; office management.
Costs (2004–05) *Tuition:* $149 per credit hour part-time. *Required fees:* $10 per credit hour part-time.
Financial Aid Of all full-time matriculated undergraduates who enrolled, 12 Federal Work-Study jobs.
Admissions Contact Jody Gray, Admissions Coordinator, RETS Medical and Business Institute, 4001 Fort Campbell Boulevard, Hopkinsville, KY 42240-4962. *Phone:* 270-886-1302. *Toll-free phone:* 800-359-4753.

Rowan Technical College
Morehead, Kentucky

- **State-supported** 2-year, founded 1984
- **Calendar** semesters
- **Degree** certificates, diplomas, and associate
- **Coed,** 842 undergraduate students, 35% full-time, 29% women, 71% men

Undergraduates 294 full-time, 548 part-time. 3% African American, 0.2% Asian American or Pacific Islander, 0.1% Hispanic American.
Freshmen *Admission:* 217 admitted, 140 enrolled.
Faculty *Total:* 28, 79% full-time.
Costs (2004–05) *Tuition:* $92 per credit part-time; state resident $92 per credit part-time; nonresident $276 per credit part-time.
Admissions Contact Patee Massie, Registrar, Rowan Technical College, 609 Viking Drive, Morehead, KY 40351. *Phone:* 606-759-7141 Ext. 66184.

St. Catharine College
St. Catharine, Kentucky

- **Independent Roman Catholic** 2-year, founded 1931
- **Calendar** semesters
- **Degree** certificates and associate
- **Rural** 643-acre campus with easy access to Louisville
- **Endowment** $300,000
- **Coed**

Faculty *Student/faculty ratio:* 15:1.
Student Life *Campus security:* 24-hour emergency response devices, night security guard.
Athletics Member NJCAA.
Standardized Tests *Required:* ACT (for admission).
Costs (2003–04) *Comprehensive fee:* $14,000 includes full-time tuition ($9000) and room and board ($5000). Full-time tuition and fees vary according to program. Part-time tuition: $340 per credit hour.
Financial Aid Of all full-time matriculated undergraduates who enrolled, 45 Federal Work-Study jobs (averaging $1000).
Applying *Options:* common application, electronic application, early admission. *Application fee:* $15. *Required:* minimum ACT score of 12. *Required for some:* high school transcript.
Admissions Contact Ms. Amy C. Carrico, Director of Admissions, St. Catharine College, 2735 Bardstown Road, St. Catharine, KY 40061. *Phone:* 859-336-5082. *Toll-free phone:* 800-599-2000 Ext. 1227. *Fax:* 859-336-5031. *E-mail:* admissions@secky.edu.

Somerset Community College
Somerset, Kentucky

- **State-supported** 2-year, founded 1965, part of Kentucky Community and Technical College System
- **Calendar** semesters
- **Degree** certificates, diplomas, and associate
- **Small-town** 70-acre campus
- **Coed,** 5,751 undergraduate students, 52% full-time, 57% women, 43% men

Undergraduates 2,992 full-time, 2,759 part-time. Students come from 5 states and territories, 0.9% African American, 0.2% Asian American or Pacific Islander, 0.2% Hispanic American, 0.3% Native American. *Retention:* 60% of 2002 full-time freshmen returned.
Freshmen *Admission:* 846 applied, 846 admitted. *Test scores:* ACT scores over 18: 54%; ACT scores over 24: 7%.
Faculty *Total:* 323, 42% full-time. *Student/faculty ratio:* 19:1.
Majors Autobody/collision and repair technology; automobile/automotive mechanics technology; avionics maintenance technology; business/commerce; CAD/CADD drafting/design technology; carpentry; clinical/medical laboratory assistant; communication and media related; cosmetology; criminal justice/police science; diesel mechanics technology; early childhood education; electrical, electronic and communications engineering technology; heating, air conditioning, ventilation and refrigeration maintenance technology; industrial technology; information technology; machine tool technology; masonry; medical/clinical assistant; nail technician and manicurist; nursing (registered nurse training); nursing related; physical therapy; radiologic technology/science; respiratory care therapy; surgical technology; welding technology.
Academic Programs *Special study options:* academic remediation for entering students, adult/continuing education programs, advanced placement credit, cooperative education, distance learning, double majors, independent study, internships, part-time degree program, services for LD students, summer session for credit.
Library Somerset Community College Library with 54,107 titles, 233 serial subscriptions, 3,575 audiovisual materials, an OPAC, a Web page.
Computers on Campus 897 computers available on campus for general student use. A campuswide network can be accessed from off campus. Internet access, at least one staffed computer lab available.
Student Life *Housing:* college housing not available. *Activities and Organizations:* drama/theater group, student-run newspaper, choral group, Student Government Association, Students in Free Enterprise, Phi Beta Lambda, Phi Theta Kappa.
Athletics *Intercollegiate sports:* cheerleading M(s)/W(s). *Intramural sports:* basketball M/W, football M/W, softball M/W.
Standardized Tests *Required:* ACT (for admission). *Required for some:* ACT COMPASS.
Costs (2004–05) *Tuition:* state resident $2760 full-time, $92 per credit hour part-time; nonresident $8280 full-time, $276 per credit hour part-time.
Financial Aid Of all full-time matriculated undergraduates who enrolled, 40 Federal Work-Study jobs (averaging $2500). 25 state and other part-time jobs (averaging $2500).
Applying *Options:* common application, early admission. *Required:* high school transcript. *Application deadlines:* 8/22 (freshmen), 8/31 (transfers). *Notification:* continuous (freshmen), continuous (transfers).
Admissions Contact Mr. Sean Ayers, Recruiter, Somerset Community College, 808 Monticello Street, Somerset, KY 42501. *Phone:* 606-677-4049 Ext. 156. *Toll-free phone:* 877-629-9722.

Southeast Community College
Cumberland, Kentucky

- **State-supported** 2-year, founded 1960, part of Kentucky Community and Technical College System
- **Calendar** semesters
- **Degree** certificates, diplomas, and associate
- **Small-town** 150-acre campus
- **Endowment** $1.8 million
- **Coed,** 4,364 undergraduate students

Undergraduates 1% African American, 0.2% Asian American or Pacific Islander, 0.3% Hispanic American, 0.2% Native American.
Freshmen *Admission:* 531 applied, 531 admitted.
Faculty *Total:* 119, 56% full-time, 12% with terminal degrees. *Student/faculty ratio:* 20:1.
Majors Administrative assistant and secretarial science; business administration and management; clinical/medical laboratory technology; computer engi-

neering technology; computer/information technology services administration related; criminal justice/police science; data processing and data processing technology; information technology; liberal arts and sciences/liberal studies; management information systems; medical radiologic technology; nursing (registered nurse training); physical therapist assistant; respiratory care therapy.

Academic Programs *Special study options:* academic remediation for entering students, accelerated degree program, adult/continuing education programs, advanced placement credit, distance learning, internships, part-time degree program, summer session for credit.

Library Gertrude Dale Library with 25,921 titles, 200 serial subscriptions, an OPAC, a Web page.

Computers on Campus 46 computers available on campus for general student use. A campuswide network can be accessed from off campus that provide access to online admissions. Internet access, at least one staffed computer lab available.

Student Life *Activities and Organizations:* drama/theater group, student-run newspaper, choral group, Professional Business Leaders, Student Government Association, Phi Theta Kappa, Black Student Union, Nursing Club.

Athletics *Intramural sports:* basketball M/W, football M/W, golf M/W, table tennis M/W, volleyball M/W.

Costs (2004–05) *Tuition:* state resident $2760 full-time, $92 per credit hour part-time; nonresident $8280 full-time, $276 per credit hour part-time. *Required fees:* $164 full-time.

Financial Aid Of all full-time matriculated undergraduates who enrolled, 90 Federal Work-Study jobs (averaging $635).

Applying *Required:* high school transcript. *Application deadline:* 8/20 (freshmen). *Notification:* continuous until 9/3 (freshmen), continuous until 9/3 (transfers).

Admissions Contact Cookie Baker, Director of Admissions, Southeast Community College, 700 College Road, Cumberland, KY 40823-1099. *Phone:* 606-589-2145 Ext. 2108. *Toll-free phone:* 888-274-SECC Ext. 2108. *Fax:* 606-589-5435. *E-mail:* red.sellars@kctcs.net.

SOUTHWESTERN COLLEGE OF BUSINESS
Florence, Kentucky

Admissions Contact Mr. Bruce Budesheim, Director, Southwestern College of Business, 8095 Connector Drive, Florence, KY 41042. *Phone:* 859-341-6633. *Fax:* 859-341-6749.

SPENCERIAN COLLEGE
Louisville, Kentucky

■ **Proprietary** 2-year, founded 1892
■ **Calendar** quarters
■ **Degree** certificates, diplomas, and associate
■ **Urban** 10-acre campus
■ **Coed,** 1,326 undergraduate students, 100% full-time, 91% women, 9% men

Undergraduates 1,326 full-time. Students come from 2 states and territories, 13% are from out of state, 25% African American, 0.7% Asian American or Pacific Islander, 0.3% Hispanic American, 0.6% Native American.

Freshmen *Admission:* 391 admitted.

Faculty *Total:* 73, 23% full-time, 4% with terminal degrees. *Student/faculty ratio:* 14:1.

Majors Accounting; business administration and management; medical office management.

Student Life *Housing Options:* coed. Campus housing is leased by the school and is provided by a third party. *Activities and Organizations:* student-run newspaper, Spencerian Business Leaders. *Campus security:* 24-hour emergency response devices. *Student services:* personal/psychological counseling.

Costs (2003–04) *Tuition:* $11,085 full-time, $185 per credit hour part-time. *Required fees:* $555 full-time, $50 per term part-time. *Room only:* $3555.

Applying *Application fee:* $80. *Required:* high school transcript. *Required for some:* essay or personal statement, interview.

Admissions Contact Terri D. Thomas, Director of Admissions, Spencerian College, 4627 Dixie Highway, Louisville, KY 40299. *Phone:* 502-447-1000 Ext. 7808. *Toll-free phone:* 800-264-1799.

SPENCERIAN COLLEGE-LEXINGTON
Lexington, Kentucky

Admissions Contact Ms. Georgia Mullins, Admissions Representative, Spencerian College-Lexington, 2355 Harrodsburg Road, Lexington, KY 40504. *Phone:* 800-456-3253 Ext. 8010. *Toll-free phone:* 800-456-3253. *Fax:* 859-224-7744. *E-mail:* admissions@spencerian.edu.

UNIVERSITY OF KENTUCKY, LEXINGTON COMMUNITY COLLEGE
Lexington, Kentucky

■ **State-supported** 2-year, founded 1965, part of Kentucky Community and Technical College System
■ **Calendar** semesters
■ **Degree** associate
■ **Urban** 10-acre campus
■ **Endowment** $750,000
■ **Coed,** 8,639 undergraduate students, 62% full-time, 56% women, 44% men

Undergraduates 5,354 full-time, 3,285 part-time. Students come from 35 states and territories, 5% are from out of state, 11% African American, 2% Asian American or Pacific Islander, 1% Hispanic American, 0.6% Native American, 9% transferred in, 5% live on campus.

Freshmen *Admission:* 5,828 applied, 5,828 admitted, 2,181 enrolled. *Test scores:* ACT scores over 18: 60%; ACT scores over 24: 10%; ACT scores over 30: 1%.

Faculty *Total:* 446, 35% full-time. *Student/faculty ratio:* 19:1.

Majors Accounting; architectural drafting and CAD/CADD; architectural engineering technology; business administration and management; civil engineering technology; computer systems networking and telecommunications; dental hygiene; dental laboratory technology; electrical, electronic and communications engineering technology; information science/studies; liberal arts and sciences/liberal studies; medical radiologic technology; nuclear medical technology; nursing (registered nurse training); respiratory care therapy.

Academic Programs *Special study options:* academic remediation for entering students, accelerated degree program, adult/continuing education programs, advanced placement credit, cooperative education, distance learning, part-time degree program, services for LD students, summer session for credit. *ROTC:* Army (c), Air Force (c).

Library Lexington Community College Library with 27,000 titles, 250 serial subscriptions, an OPAC, a Web page.

Computers on Campus 80 computers available on campus for general student use. A campuswide network can be accessed. Internet access, online (class) registration, at least one staffed computer lab available.

Student Life *Housing Options:* Campus housing is university owned. Freshman applicants given priority for college housing. *Activities and Organizations:* student-run newspaper, Baptist Student Union, Unity, KANS, Veterans Union, Athena. *Campus security:* 24-hour emergency response devices and patrols, late-night transport/escort service. *Student services:* health clinic, personal/psychological counseling.

Athletics *Intramural sports:* basketball M/W, football M/W, golf M/W, racquetball M/W, soccer M/W, swimming M/W, tennis M/W, track and field M/W, volleyball M/W, water polo M/W, wrestling M.

Standardized Tests *Required for some:* SAT I or ACT (for placement).

Costs (2004–05) *Tuition:* state resident $1220 full-time, $93 per credit part-time; nonresident $3757 full-time, $305 per credit part-time. Part-time tuition and fees vary according to course load. *Required fees:* $545 full-time, $14 per term part-time. *Room and board:* $4285; room only: $2785. Room and board charges vary according to board plan. *Payment plan:* installment. *Waivers:* senior citizens and employees or children of employees.

Applying *Options:* early admission. *Application fee:* $20. *Required:* high school transcript. *Application deadlines:* 8/2 (freshmen), 8/2 (transfers).

Admissions Contact Mrs. Shelbie Hugle, Director of Admission Services, University of Kentucky, Lexington Community College, 200 Oswald Building, Cooper Drive, Lexington, KY 40506-0235. *Phone:* 859-257-4872 Ext. 4197. *Toll-free phone:* 866-744-4872 Ext. 5111. *E-mail:* shugl@uky.edu.

WEST KENTUCKY COMMUNITY AND TECHNICAL COLLEGE
Paducah, Kentucky

■ **State-supported** 2-year, founded 1932, part of University of Kentucky Community College System
■ **Calendar** semesters
■ **Degree** certificates, diplomas, and associate
■ **Small-town** 117-acre campus
■ **Coed,** 3,545 undergraduate students, 41% full-time, 59% women, 41% men

Undergraduates 1,455 full-time, 2,090 part-time. Students come from 12 states and territories, 6% African American, 0.4% Asian American or Pacific Islander, 0.6% Hispanic American, 0.4% Native American.

Freshmen *Average high school GPA:* 2.35.

Faculty *Total:* 153, 50% full-time. *Student/faculty ratio:* 15:1.

Majors Accounting; administrative assistant and secretarial science; business administration and management; consumer merchandising/retailing manage-

West Kentucky Community and Technical College (continued)

ment; electrical, electronic and communications engineering technology; industrial radiologic technology; information science/studies; mass communication/media; nursing (registered nurse training); physical therapy.

Academic Programs *Special study options:* academic remediation for entering students, adult/continuing education programs, cooperative education, honors programs, internships, part-time degree program, services for LD students, summer session for credit.

Library Paducah Community College Library with 31,339 titles, 152 serial subscriptions, an OPAC, a Web page.

Computers on Campus 160 computers available on campus for general student use. At least one staffed computer lab available.

Student Life *Housing:* college housing not available. *Activities and Organizations:* drama/theater group, student-run newspaper, choral group. *Campus security:* 14-hour patrols by trained security personnel. *Student services:* women's center.

Athletics *Intramural sports:* basketball M/W, golf M/W, soccer M/W, volleyball M/W.

Standardized Tests *Required for some:* ACT (for placement).

Costs (2003–04) *Tuition:* state resident $2370 full-time; nonresident $7110 full-time. Part-time tuition and fees vary according to course load. *Payment plan:* deferred payment. *Waivers:* senior citizens and employees or children of employees.

Financial Aid Of all full-time matriculated undergraduates who enrolled, 50 Federal Work-Study jobs (averaging $1650).

Applying *Options:* early admission. *Required for some:* high school transcript. *Application deadline:* rolling (freshmen), rolling (transfers).

Admissions Contact Mr. Jerry Anderson, Admissions Counselor, West Kentucky Community and Technical College, PO Box 7380, Paducah, KY 42002-7380. *Phone:* 270-554-9200.

LOUISIANA

BATON ROUGE COMMUNITY COLLEGE
Baton Rouge, Louisiana

Admissions Contact 5310 Florida Boulevard, Baton Rouge, LA 70806.

BATON ROUGE SCHOOL OF COMPUTERS
Baton Rouge, Louisiana

Admissions Contact 10425 Plaza Americana, Baton Rouge, LA 70816.

BOSSIER PARISH COMMUNITY COLLEGE
Bossier City, Louisiana

- **State-supported** 2-year, founded 1967, part of University of Louisiana System
- **Calendar** semesters
- **Degree** certificates, diplomas, and associate
- **Urban** 64-acre campus
- **Coed**

Student Life *Campus security:* student patrols.

Athletics Member NJCAA.

Standardized Tests *Required:* ACT (for placement).

Costs (2003–04) *Tuition:* state resident $1596 full-time; nonresident $3736 full-time.

Financial Aid Of all full-time matriculated undergraduates who enrolled, 53 Federal Work-Study jobs.

Applying *Options:* early admission. *Application fee:* $15. *Required:* high school transcript.

Admissions Contact Ms. Ann Jempole, Director of Admissions, Bossier Parish Community College, 2719 Airline Drive North, Bossier City, LA 71111-5801. *Phone:* 318-746-9851 Ext. 215. *Fax:* 318-742-8664.

BRYMAN COLLEGE
New Orleans, Louisiana

Admissions Contact 2322 Canal Street, New Orleans, LA 70119.

CAMELOT COLLEGE
Baton Rouge, Louisiana

Admissions Contact Rev. Ronny L. Williams, President, Camelot College, 2618 Wooddale Boulevard, Suite A, Baton Rouge, LA 70805. *Phone:* 225-928-3005. *Toll-free phone:* 800-470-3320.

CAMERON COLLEGE
New Orleans, Louisiana

Admissions Contact 2740 Canal Street, New Orleans, LA 70119.

CAREER TECHNICAL COLLEGE
Monroe, Louisiana

Admissions Contact 2319 Louisville Avenue, Monroe, LA 71201. *Toll-free phone:* 800-234-6766.

DELGADO COMMUNITY COLLEGE
New Orleans, Louisiana

- **State-supported** 2-year, founded 1921, part of Louisiana Community and Technical college System
- **Calendar** semesters
- **Degree** certificates and associate
- **Urban** 57-acre campus
- **Endowment** $1.0 million
- **Coed**, 16,501 undergraduate students, 45% full-time, 70% women, 30% men

Undergraduates 7,376 full-time, 9,125 part-time. Students come from 33 states and territories, 3 other countries, 0.3% are from out of state, 43% African American, 2% Asian American or Pacific Islander, 4% Hispanic American, 0.7% Native American. *Retention:* 53% of 2002 full-time freshmen returned.

Freshmen *Admission:* 2,657 applied, 2,657 enrolled.

Faculty *Total:* 833, 43% full-time. *Student/faculty ratio:* 20:1.

Majors Accounting; administrative assistant and secretarial science; applied horticulture; architectural engineering technology; automobile/automotive mechanics technology; biological and physical sciences; biomedical technology; building/property maintenance and management; business administration and management; civil engineering technology; clinical/medical laboratory technology; commercial and advertising art; communication and journalism related; computer engineering technology; computer installation and repair technology; construction management; criminal justice/police science; data processing and data processing technology; dental hygiene; dental laboratory technology; dietetics; drafting and design technology; electrical, electronic and communications engineering technology; electrical/electronics equipment installation and repair; emergency medical technology (EMT paramedic); fine/studio arts; fire protection and safety technology; funeral service and mortuary science; general studies; health information/medical records technology; hospitality administration; institutional food workers; interior architecture; kindergarten/preschool education; machine shop technology; machine tool technology; medical radiologic technology; music; nursing (registered nurse training); occupational safety and health technology; occupational therapist assistant; physical therapist assistant; respiratory care therapy; sign language interpretation and translation.

Academic Programs *Special study options:* academic remediation for entering students, advanced placement credit, cooperative education, distance learning, English as a second language, honors programs, off-campus study, part-time degree program, services for LD students, student-designed majors, summer session for credit. *ROTC:* Army (c), Air Force (c).

Library Moss Memorial Library with 110,000 titles, 1,299 serial subscriptions, an OPAC, a Web page.

Computers on Campus 950 computers available on campus for general student use. A campuswide network can be accessed from off campus. Internet access, at least one staffed computer lab available.

Student Life *Housing:* college housing not available. *Activities and Organizations:* drama/theater group, student-run newspaper, choral group, student government, Circle K, International Club, Phi Theta Kappa, Lambda Phi Nu. *Campus security:* 24-hour patrols, student patrols. *Student services:* health clinic, personal/psychological counseling.

Athletics Member NJCAA. *Intercollegiate sports:* baseball M(s), basketball M(s)/W(s), track and field W. *Intramural sports:* football M, golf M, soccer M, tennis M/W, volleyball M/W.

Standardized Tests *Required for some:* ACT (for placement). *Recommended:* ACT (for placement).

Costs (2004–05) *Tuition:* state resident $1482 full-time, $420 per term part-time; nonresident $4462 full-time, $1275 per term part-time. Part-time tuition and fees vary according to course load. *Required fees:* $174 full-time, $5 per credit part-time, $10 per term part-time. *Payment plan:* deferred payment. *Waivers:* children of alumni, senior citizens, and employees or children of employees.

Financial Aid Of all full-time matriculated undergraduates who enrolled, 308 Federal Work-Study jobs (averaging $1375).

Applying *Application fee:* $15. *Required for some:* high school transcript. *Recommended:* high school transcript, proof of immunization. *Application deadline:* rolling (freshmen), rolling (transfers).

Admissions Contact Ms. Gwen Boute, Director of Admissions, Delgado Community College, 615 City Park Avenue, New Orleans, LA 70119. *Phone:* 504-483-4004. *Fax:* 504-483-1895. *E-mail:* enroll@dcc.edu.

DELTA COLLEGE OF ARTS AND TECHNOLOGY
Baton Rouge, Louisiana

- **Proprietary** 2-year
- **Calendar** continuous (for most programs)
- **Degree** certificates, diplomas, and associate
- **Urban** 3-acre campus
- **Coed, primarily women,** 434 undergraduate students

Faculty *Total:* 35, 86% full-time.

Majors Commercial and advertising art; nursing (licensed practical/vocational nurse training).

Costs (2003–04) *Tuition:* $14,500 per degree program part-time.

Applying *Application fee:* $100.

Admissions Contact Ms. Beulah Laverghe-Brown, Admissions Director, Delta College of Arts and Technology, 7380 Exchange Place, Baton Rouge, LA 70806. *Phone:* 225-928-7770. *Fax:* 225-927-9096. *E-mail:* dcat@deltacollege.com.

DELTA SCHOOL OF BUSINESS & TECHNOLOGY
Lake Charles, Louisiana

Admissions Contact Mr. Gary J. Holt, President, Delta School of Business & Technology, 517 Broad Street, Lake Charles, LA 70601. *Phone:* 337-439-5765.

ELAINE P. NUNEZ COMMUNITY COLLEGE
Chalmette, Louisiana

- **State-supported** 2-year, founded 1992, part of Louisiana Community and Technical Colleges System
- **Calendar** semesters
- **Degree** certificates and associate
- **Suburban** 20-acre campus with easy access to New Orleans
- **Endowment** $770,000
- **Coed,** 2,363 undergraduate students, 51% full-time, 69% women, 31% men

Undergraduates 1,213 full-time, 1,150 part-time. Students come from 3 states and territories, 28% African American, 2% Asian American or Pacific Islander, 3% Hispanic American, 1% Native American, 0.8% international, 19% transferred in.

Freshmen *Admission:* 423 applied, 423 admitted, 423 enrolled.

Faculty *Total:* 155, 37% full-time, 5% with terminal degrees. *Student/faculty ratio:* 18:1.

Majors Accounting; administrative assistant and secretarial science; computer and information sciences related; computer engineering technology; computer/information technology services administration related; computer science; computer/technical support; drafting and design technology; electrical, electronic and communications engineering technology; emergency medical technology (EMT paramedic); environmental engineering technology; health information/medical records administration; heating, air conditioning, ventilation and refrigeration maintenance technology; information science/studies; institutional food workers; kindergarten/preschool education; laser and optical technology; legal assistant/paralegal; liberal arts and sciences/liberal studies; nursing (licensed practical/vocational nurse training); plastics engineering technology.

Academic Programs *Special study options:* academic remediation for entering students, adult/continuing education programs, advanced placement credit, cooperative education, distance learning, double majors, English as a second language, independent study, internships, off-campus study, part-time degree program, services for LD students, student-designed majors, summer session for credit.

Library Nunez Community College Library with 37,626 titles, 1,391 audiovisual materials, an OPAC, a Web page.

Computers on Campus 200 computers available on campus for general student use. A campuswide network can be accessed from student residence rooms. Internet access, at least one staffed computer lab available.

Student Life *Housing:* college housing not available. *Activities and Organizations:* drama/theater group, student-run newspaper, choral group, Nunez Environmental Team, national fraternities. *Campus security:* 24-hour emergency response devices, late-night transport/escort service. *Student services:* personal/psychological counseling.

Athletics *Intramural sports:* basketball M, football M/W, softball M/W, volleyball M/W.

Standardized Tests *Required for some:* ACT ASSET or ACT COMPASS. *Recommended:* ACT (for placement).

Costs (2004–05) *Tuition:* state resident $1740 full-time, $145 per credit hour part-time; nonresident $3822 full-time, $319 per credit hour part-time. *Required fees:* $325 full-time, $20 per credit hour part-time. *Payment plan:* deferred payment. *Waivers:* senior citizens and employees or children of employees.

Financial Aid Of all full-time matriculated undergraduates who enrolled, 68 Federal Work-Study jobs (averaging $1545).

Applying *Options:* deferred entrance. *Application fee:* $10. *Required for some:* high school transcript. *Recommended:* minimum 2.0 GPA. *Application deadlines:* 8/1 (freshmen), 8/1 (transfers).

Admissions Contact Ms. Donna Clark, Dean of Student Affairs, Elaine P. Nunez Community College, 3710 Paris Road, Chalmette, LA 70043. *Phone:* 504-680-2457. *Fax:* 504-278-7353.

GRETNA CAREER COLLEGE
Gretna, Louisiana

Admissions Contact 1415 Whitney Avenue, Gretna, LA 70053-5835.

HERZING COLLEGE
Kenner, Louisiana

Admissions Contact Genny Bordelon, Director of Admissions, Herzing College, 2400 Veterans Boulevard, Kenner, LA 70062. *Phone:* 504-733-0074.

ITI TECHNICAL COLLEGE
Baton Rouge, Louisiana

- **Proprietary** 2-year, founded 1973
- **Calendar** continuous
- **Degree** certificates and associate
- **Suburban** 10-acre campus
- **Coed,** 361 undergraduate students

Freshmen *Admission:* 435 applied, 361 admitted.

Faculty *Total:* 27, 81% full-time. *Student/faculty ratio:* 20:1.

Majors Computer technology/computer systems technology; drafting and design technology; electrical, electronic and communications engineering technology; information technology; instrumentation technology.

Costs (2004–05) *Tuition:* $10,000 full-time.

Admissions Contact Mr. Joe Martin III, President, ITI Technical College, 13944 Airline Highway, Baton Rouge, LA 70817. *Phone:* 225-752-4230 Ext. 213. *Toll-free phone:* 800-467-4484.

ITT TECHNICAL INSTITUTE
St. Rose, Louisiana

- **Proprietary** primarily 2-year, part of ITT Educational Services, Inc.
- **Calendar** quarters
- **Degrees** associate and bachelor's
- **Coed**

Standardized Tests *Required:* Wonderlic aptitude test (for admission).

Costs (2003–04) *Tuition:* Total Program Cost varies depending on course of study. Consult school catalog.

Applying *Options:* deferred entrance. *Application fee:* $100. *Required:* high school transcript, interview. *Recommended:* letters of recommendation.

Admissions Contact Mr. Richard Beard, Director of Recruitment, ITT Technical Institute, 140 James Drive East, Saint Rose, LA 70087. *Phone:* 504-463-0338. *Toll-free phone:* 866-463-0338. *Fax:* 504-463-0979.

Louisiana

LOUISIANA STATE UNIVERSITY AT ALEXANDRIA

Alexandria, Louisiana

- **State-supported** primarily 2-year, founded 1960, part of Louisiana State University System
- **Calendar** semesters
- **Degrees** certificates, associate, and bachelor's
- **Rural** 3114-acre campus
- **Endowment** $508,942
- **Coed**

Faculty *Student/faculty ratio:* 21:1.
Student Life *Campus security:* 24-hour patrols.
Standardized Tests *Recommended:* ACT (for placement).
Costs (2004–05) *Tuition:* area resident $2817 full-time; nonresident $5277 full-time. *Required fees:* $390 full-time.
Financial Aid Of all full-time matriculated undergraduates who enrolled, 53 Federal Work-Study jobs (averaging $1226). 76 state and other part-time jobs (averaging $1261).
Applying *Options:* early admission. *Application fee:* $20. *Required:* high school transcript. *Required for some:* essay or personal statement, 3 letters of recommendation, interview.
Admissions Contact Ms. Shelly Kieffer, Recruiter/Admissions Counselor, Louisiana State University at Alexandria, 8100 Highway 71 South, Alexandria, LA 71302-9121. *Phone:* 318-473-6508. *Toll-free phone:* 888-473-6417. *Fax:* 318-473-6418. *E-mail:* skieffer@lsua.edu.

LOUISIANA STATE UNIVERSITY AT EUNICE

Eunice, Louisiana

Admissions Contact Ms. Gracie Guillory, Director of Financial Aid, Louisiana State University at Eunice, PO Box 1129, Eunice, LA 70535-1129. *Phone:* 337-550-1282. *Toll-free phone:* 888-367-5783. *Fax:* 337-550-1306.

LOUISIANA TECHNICAL COLLEGE-ACADIAN CAMPUS

Crowley, Louisiana

- **State-supported** 2-year, founded 1938
- **Calendar** semesters
- 260 undergraduate students

Faculty *Total:* 24, 79% full-time.
Costs (2003–04) *Tuition:* state resident $488 full-time, $21 per credit hour part-time; nonresident $976 full-time, $42 per credit hour part-time. *Required fees:* $178 full-time, $7 per credit hour part-time, $5 per term part-time.
Applying *Application fee:* $5.
Admissions Contact Admissions Office, Louisiana Technical College-Acadian Campus, 1933 West Hutchinson Avenue, Crowley, LA 70526-3215. *Phone:* 337-788-7521. *Toll-free phone:* 800-265-6229. *Fax:* 337-788-7642.

LOUISIANA TECHNICAL COLLEGE-ALEXANDRIA CAMPUS

Alexandria, Louisiana

- **State-supported** 2-year
- **Calendar** semesters
- 449 undergraduate students

Faculty *Total:* 56, 46% full-time.
Costs (2003–04) *Tuition:* state resident $488 full-time, $21 per credit hour part-time; nonresident $976 full-time, $42 per credit hour part-time. *Required fees:* $178 full-time, $7 per credit hour part-time, $5 per term part-time.
Applying *Application fee:* $5.
Admissions Contact Admissions Office, Louisiana Technical College-Alexandria Campus, 4311 South MacArthur Drive, P.O. Box 5698, Alexandria, LA 71307-5698. *Phone:* 318-487-5439. *Fax:* 318-487-5970.

LOUISIANA TECHNICAL COLLEGE-ASCENSION CAMPUS

Sorrento, Louisiana

- **State-supported** 2-year
- **Calendar** semesters

- 216 undergraduate students

Faculty *Total:* 38, 29% full-time.
Costs (2003–04) *Tuition:* state resident $488 full-time, $21 per credit hour part-time; nonresident $976 full-time, $42 per credit hour part-time. *Required fees:* $178 full-time, $7 per credit hour part-time, $5 per term part-time.
Applying *Application fee:* $5.
Admissions Contact Admissions Office, Louisiana Technical College-Ascension Campus, 9697 Airline Highway, Sorrento, LA 70778-3007. *Phone:* 225-675-5398. *Fax:* 225-675-6007.

LOUISIANA TECHNICAL COLLEGE-AVOYELLES CAMPUS

Cottonport, Louisiana

- **State-supported** 2-year
- **Calendar** semesters
- 470 undergraduate students

Faculty *Total:* 37, 51% full-time.
Costs (2003–04) *Tuition:* state resident $488 full-time, $21 per credit hour part-time; nonresident $976 full-time, $42 per credit hour part-time. *Required fees:* $178 full-time, $7 per credit hour part-time, $5 per term part-time.
Applying *Application fee:* $5.
Admissions Contact Admissions Office, Louisiana Technical College-Avoyelles Campus, 508 Choupique Street, Cottonport, LA 71327. *Phone:* 318-876-2401. *Fax:* 318-876-2634.

LOUISIANA TECHNICAL COLLEGE-BASTROP CAMPUS

Bastrop, Louisiana

- **State-supported** 2-year, part of Louisiana Community and Technical College System
- **Calendar** semesters
- **Degree** certificates and diplomas
- 254 undergraduate students

Freshmen *Admission:* 340 applied, 241 admitted.
Faculty *Total:* 21, 52% full-time. *Student/faculty ratio:* 15:1.
Majors Administrative assistant and secretarial science.
Academic Programs *Special study options:* part-time degree program.
Costs (2003–04) *Tuition:* state resident $488 full-time, $21 per credit hour part-time; nonresident $976 full-time, $42 per credit hour part-time. *Required fees:* $178 full-time, $7 per credit hour part-time, $5 per term part-time.
Applying *Application fee:* $5. *Notification:* continuous (freshmen).
Admissions Contact Ms. Vickye Branton, Admissions Office, Louisiana Technical College-Bastrop Campus, P.O. Box 1120, Kammell Street, Bastrop, LA 71221-1120. *Phone:* 318-283-0836. *Fax:* 318-283-0871. *E-mail:* vbranton@lctcs.state.la.us.

LOUISIANA TECHNICAL COLLEGE-BATON ROUGE CAMPUS

Baton Rouge, Louisiana

- **State-supported** 2-year
- **Calendar** semesters
- 1,080 undergraduate students

Faculty *Total:* 144, 31% full-time.
Costs (2003–04) *Tuition:* state resident $488 full-time, $21 per credit hour part-time; nonresident $976 full-time, $42 per credit hour part-time. *Required fees:* $178 full-time, $7 per credit hour part-time, $5 per term part-time.
Applying *Application fee:* $5.
Admissions Contact Admissions Office, Louisiana Technical College-Baton Rouge Campus, 3250 North Acadian Thruway East, Baton Rouge, LA 70805. *Phone:* 225-359-9201. *Fax:* 225-359-9296.

LOUISIANA TECHNICAL COLLEGE-CHARLES B. COREIL CAMPUS

Ville Platte, Louisiana

- **State-supported** 2-year
- **Calendar** semesters

■ 239 undergraduate students

Faculty *Total:* 15, 80% full-time.
Costs (2003–04) *Tuition:* state resident $488 full-time, $21 per credit hour part-time; nonresident $976 full-time, $42 per credit hour part-time. *Required fees:* $178 full-time, $7 per credit hour part-time, $5 per term part-time.
Applying *Application fee:* $5.
Admissions Contact Admissions Office, Louisiana Technical College-Charles B. Coreil Campus, P.O. Box 296, 1124 Vocational Drive-Ward 1, Industrial Park, Ville Platte, LA 70586-0296. *Phone:* 318-363-2197. *Fax:* 318-363-7984.

LOUISIANA TECHNICAL COLLEGE-DELTA OUACHITA CAMPUS
West Monroe, Louisiana

■ **State-supported** 2-year, founded 1941
■ **Calendar** semesters
■ **Degree** certificates, diplomas, and associate
■ **Coed,** 410 undergraduate students, 79% full-time, 40% women, 60% men

Undergraduates 322 full-time, 88 part-time. 28% African American, 0.5% Asian American or Pacific Islander, 0.7% Hispanic American, 0.7% Native American.
Freshmen *Admission:* 87 enrolled.
Faculty *Total:* 48, 40% full-time. *Student/faculty ratio:* 12:1.
Majors Accounting technology and bookkeeping; autobody/collision and repair technology; automobile/automotive mechanics technology; computer science; culinary arts; diesel mechanics technology; drafting and design technology; heating, air conditioning, ventilation and refrigeration maintenance technology; machine tool technology; welding technology.
Student Life *Activities and Organizations:* National Vocational Technical Honor Society. *Campus security:* 24-hour emergency response devices.
Costs (2004–05) *Tuition:* state resident $526 full-time, $22 per credit hour part-time; nonresident $1152 full-time, $44 per credit hour part-time. *Required fees:* $576 full-time, $104 per year part-time.
Applying *Application fee:* $5.
Admissions Contact Admissions Office, Louisiana Technical College-Delta Ouachita Campus, 609 Vocational Parkway, West Ouachita Industrial Park, West Monroe, LA 71292-9064. *Phone:* 318-397-6100. *Fax:* 318-397-6106.

LOUISIANA TECHNICAL COLLEGE-EVANGELINE CAMPUS
St. Martinville, Louisiana

■ **State-supported** 2-year
■ **Calendar** semesters
■ **Degree** diplomas and associate
■ 275 undergraduate students

Undergraduates 54% African American, 8% Asian American or Pacific Islander, 0.3% Hispanic American, 0.7% Native American.
Faculty *Total:* 36, 56% full-time.
Majors Accounting technology and bookkeeping; management information systems.
Costs (2003–04) *Tuition:* state resident $488 full-time, $21 per credit hour part-time; nonresident $976 full-time, $42 per credit hour part-time. *Required fees:* $178 full-time, $7 per credit hour part-time, $5 per term part-time.
Applying *Application fee:* $5.
Admissions Contact Mr. Joe Reiser, Admissions Office, Louisiana Technical College-Evangeline Campus, P.O. Box 68, 600 South Martin Luther King, Jr. Drive, St. Martinville, LA 70582. *Phone:* 337-394-6466. *Fax:* 337-394-3965.

LOUISIANA TECHNICAL COLLEGE-FLORIDA PARISHES CAMPUS
Greensburg, Louisiana

■ **State-supported** 2-year, part of Louisiana Community and Technical College System
■ **Calendar** semesters
■ **Degree** certificates, diplomas, and associate
■ **Coed,** 414 undergraduate students, 12% full-time, 25% women, 75% men

Undergraduates 51 full-time, 363 part-time. Students come from 1 other state, 39% African American, 1% Hispanic American, 0.2% Native American.
Freshmen *Admission:* 288 enrolled.

Faculty *Total:* 17, 47% full-time, 47% with terminal degrees. *Student/faculty ratio:* 15:1.
Majors Accounting; business operations support and secretarial services related; computer software and media applications related; early childhood education; information science/studies; nursing (licensed practical/vocational nurse training); teaching assistants/aides related; word processing.
Academic Programs *Special study options:* academic remediation for entering students, adult/continuing education programs, advanced placement credit, cooperative education, distance learning, internships, services for LD students.
Computers on Campus 20 computers available on campus for general student use. At least one staffed computer lab available.
Student Life *Housing:* college housing not available. *Activities and Organizations:* Student Government Association, Skills USA. *Campus security:* 24-hour emergency response devices. *Student services:* personal/psychological counseling.
Standardized Tests *Required:* ACT COMPASS (for admission).
Costs (2004–05) *Tuition:* state resident $333 full-time, $21 per credit hour part-time; nonresident $577 full-time, $42 per credit hour part-time. Full-time tuition and fees vary according to course load. Part-time tuition and fees vary according to course load. *Required fees:* $90 full-time, $30 per semester part-time.
Applying *Options:* early action. *Application fee:* $5. *Required:* high school transcript, ACT COMPASS. *Required for some:* essay or personal statement, letters of recommendation, interview. *Notification:* continuous (freshmen), continuous (transfers).
Admissions Contact Mrs. Sharon G. Hornsby, Campus Dean, Louisiana Technical College-Florida Parishes Campus, Student Services, PO Box 1300, 100 College Street, Greensburg, LA 70441. *Phone:* 225-222-4251. *Toll-free phone:* 800-827-9750. *Fax:* 225-222-6064. *E-mail:* shornsby@lctcs.state.la.us.

LOUISIANA TECHNICAL COLLEGE-FOLKES CAMPUS
Jackson, Louisiana

■ **State-supported** 2-year, part of Louisiana Community and Technical College System (LCTCS)
■ **Calendar** semesters
■ **Degree** certificates, diplomas, and associate
■ **Coed,** 164 undergraduate students

Undergraduates Students come from 1 other state.
Faculty *Total:* 16, 81% full-time, 13% with terminal degrees. *Student/faculty ratio:* 7:1.
Majors Automobile/automotive mechanics technology; business administration and management; emergency medical technology (EMT paramedic); nursing (licensed practical/vocational nurse training); welding technology.
Academic Programs *Special study options:* academic remediation for entering students, adult/continuing education programs, advanced placement credit, cooperative education, internships, services for LD students.
Computers on Campus 5 computers available on campus for general student use. At least one staffed computer lab available.
Student Life *Housing:* college housing not available. *Student services:* personal/psychological counseling.
Standardized Tests *Required:* TABE (for admission).
Costs (2003–04) *Tuition:* state resident $488 full-time, $21 per credit hour part-time; nonresident $976 full-time, $42 per credit hour part-time. *Required fees:* $178 full-time, $7 per credit hour part-time, $5 per term part-time.
Applying *Application fee:* $5. *Required for some:* high school transcript. *Recommended:* interview.
Admissions Contact Ms. Dildred S. Womack, Student Personnel Officer, Louisiana Technical College-Folkes Campus, P.O. Box 808, 3337 Highway 10, Jackson, LA 70748. *Phone:* 225-634-2636. *Fax:* 225-634-4225. *E-mail:* dwomack@lctcs.state.la.us.

LOUISIANA TECHNICAL COLLEGE-GULF AREA CAMPUS
Abbeville, Louisiana

■ **State-supported** 2-year
■ **Calendar** semesters
■ **Degree** certificates, diplomas, and associate
■ 355 undergraduate students

Undergraduates Students come from 1 other state.
Freshmen *Admission:* 480 applied, 450 admitted. *Average high school GPA:* 2.00.

Louisiana

Louisiana Technical College-Gulf Area Campus (continued)
Faculty *Total:* 32, 59% full-time. *Student/faculty ratio:* 24:1.
Majors Business/commerce; computer engineering technology; electrical, electronic and communications engineering technology.
Costs (2003–04) *Tuition:* state resident $488 full-time, $21 per credit hour part-time; nonresident $976 full-time, $42 per credit hour part-time. *Required fees:* $178 full-time, $7 per credit hour part-time, $5 per term part-time.
Applying *Application fee:* $5. *Required for some:* high school transcript.
Admissions Contact Mr. Ray E. Lavergne, Admissions Office, Louisiana Technical College-Gulf Area Campus, P.O. Box 878, 1115 Clover Street, Abbeville, LA 70510. *Phone:* 337-893-4984. *Fax:* 337-893-4991.

LOUISIANA TECHNICAL COLLEGE-HAMMOND CAMPUS
Hammond, Louisiana

- **State-supported** 2-year, founded 1964
- **Calendar** semesters
- **Degree** certificates, diplomas, and associate
- **Coed,** 247 undergraduate students

Faculty *Total:* 22, 55% full-time.
Costs (2003–04) *Tuition:* state resident $488 full-time, $21 per credit hour part-time; nonresident $976 full-time, $42 per credit hour part-time. *Required fees:* $178 full-time, $7 per credit hour part-time, $5 per term part-time.
Applying *Application fee:* $5.
Admissions Contact Admissions Office, Louisiana Technical College-Hammond Campus, P.O. Box 489, Hammond, LA 70404-0489. *Phone:* 985-543-4123. *Toll-free phone:* 800-469-0238. *Fax:* 985-543-4119.

LOUISIANA TECHNICAL COLLEGE-HUEY P. LONG CAMPUS
Winnfield, Louisiana

- **State-supported** 2-year, founded 1939
- **Calendar** semesters
- 247 undergraduate students

Faculty *Total:* 24, 54% full-time.
Costs (2003–04) *Tuition:* state resident $488 full-time, $21 per credit hour part-time; nonresident $976 full-time, $42 per credit hour part-time. *Required fees:* $178 full-time, $7 per credit hour part-time, $5 per term part-time.
Applying *Application fee:* $5.
Admissions Contact Admissions Office, Louisiana Technical College-Huey P. Long Campus, 303 South Jones Street, Winnfield, LA 71483. *Phone:* 318-628-4342. *Fax:* 318-628-7768.

LOUISIANA TECHNICAL COLLEGE-JEFFERSON CAMPUS
Metairie, Louisiana

- **State-supported** 2-year, founded 1949
- **Calendar** semesters
- 320 undergraduate students

Faculty *Total:* 74, 26% full-time.
Costs (2003–04) *Tuition:* state resident $488 full-time, $21 per credit hour part-time; nonresident $976 full-time, $42 per credit hour part-time. *Required fees:* $178 full-time, $7 per credit hour part-time, $5 per term part-time.
Applying *Application fee:* $5.
Admissions Contact Admissions Office, Louisiana Technical College-Jefferson Campus, 5200 Blair Drive, Metairie, LA 70001. *Phone:* 504-736-7072. *Fax:* 504-736-7120.

LOUISIANA TECHNICAL COLLEGE-JUMONVILLE CAMPUS
New Roads, Louisiana

- **State-supported** 2-year, founded 1952
- **Calendar** semesters
- **Coed,** 365 undergraduate students

Faculty *Total:* 23, 91% full-time.
Costs (2003–04) *Tuition:* state resident $488 full-time, $21 per credit hour part-time; nonresident $976 full-time, $42 per credit hour part-time. *Required fees:* $178 full-time, $7 per credit hour part-time, $5 per term part-time.
Applying *Application fee:* $5.
Admissions Contact Admissions Office, Louisiana Technical College-Jumonville Campus, P.O. Box 725, 605 Hospital Road, New Roads, LA 70760. *Phone:* 225-638-8613. *Fax:* 225-342-4516.

LOUISIANA TECHNICAL COLLEGE-LAFAYETTE CAMPUS
Lafayette, Louisiana

- **State-supported** 2-year, founded 1978
- **Calendar** semesters
- 735 undergraduate students

Faculty *Total:* 92, 54% full-time.
Costs (2003–04) *Tuition:* state resident $488 full-time, $21 per credit hour part-time; nonresident $976 full-time, $42 per credit hour part-time. *Required fees:* $178 full-time, $7 per credit hour part-time, $5 per term part-time.
Applying *Application fee:* $5.
Admissions Contact Admissions Office, Louisiana Technical College-Lafayette Campus, 1101 Bertrand Drive, P.O. Box 4909, Lafayette, LA 70502-4909. *Phone:* 337-262-1251. *Fax:* 337-262-1782.

LOUISIANA TECHNICAL COLLEGE-LAFOURCHE CAMPUS
Thibodaux, Louisiana

- **State-supported** 2-year
- **Calendar** semesters
- 334 undergraduate students

Faculty *Total:* 32, 50% full-time.
Costs (2003–04) *Tuition:* state resident $488 full-time, $21 per credit hour part-time; nonresident $976 full-time, $42 per credit hour part-time. *Required fees:* $178 full-time, $7 per credit hour part-time, $5 per term part-time.
Applying *Application fee:* $5.
Admissions Contact Admissions Office, Louisiana Technical College-LaFourche Campus, P.O. Box 1831, 1425 Tiger Drive, Thibodaux, LA 70302-1831. *Phone:* 985-447-0926. *Fax:* 985-447-0927.

LOUISIANA TECHNICAL COLLEGE-LAMAR SALTER CAMPUS
Leesville, Louisiana

- **State-supported** 2-year
- **Calendar** semesters
- **Degree** certificates, diplomas, and associate
- **Coed,** 289 undergraduate students

Faculty *Total:* 29, 52% full-time.
Majors Accounting technology and bookkeeping; data processing and data processing technology.
Costs (2003–04) *Tuition:* state resident $488 full-time, $21 per credit hour part-time; nonresident $976 full-time, $42 per credit hour part-time. *Required fees:* $178 full-time, $7 per credit hour part-time, $5 per term part-time.
Applying *Application fee:* $5.
Admissions Contact Mr. Alan Dunbar, Admissions Office, Louisiana Technical College-Lamar Salter Campus, 15014 Lake Charles Highway, Leesville, LA 71446. *Phone:* 337-537-3135. *Fax:* 337-537-5571. *E-mail:* adunbar@lctcs.state.la.us.

LOUISIANA TECHNICAL COLLEGE-MANSFIELD CAMPUS
Mansfield, Louisiana

- **State-supported** 2-year, part of Louisiana Community Technical College System
- **Calendar** semesters
- **Degree** certificates, diplomas, and associate
- **Coed,** 119 undergraduate students

Undergraduates Students come from 1 other state.
Freshmen *Admission:* 30 admitted.
Faculty *Total:* 10, 100% full-time. *Student/faculty ratio:* 10:1.
Majors Heating, air conditioning, ventilation and refrigeration maintenance technology; nursing assistant/aide and patient care assistant; nursing (licensed practical/vocational nurse training); welding technology.

Academic Programs *Special study options:* academic remediation for entering students, cooperative education, internships, services for LD students.
Computers on Campus 100 computers available on campus for general student use. A campuswide network can be accessed. Internet access, at least one staffed computer lab available.
Student Life *Housing:* college housing not available.
Costs (2003–04) *Tuition:* state resident $488 full-time, $21 per credit hour part-time; nonresident $976 full-time, $42 per credit hour part-time. *Required fees:* $178 full-time, $7 per credit hour part-time, $5 per term part-time.
Applying *Application fee:* $5.
Admissions Contact Ms. Hilda Rives, Student Personnel Services Officer, Louisiana Technical College-Mansfield Campus, 943 Oxford Road, PO Box 1236, Mansfield, LA 71052. *Phone:* 318-872-2243. *Fax:* 318-872-4249.

LOUISIANA TECHNICAL COLLEGE- MORGAN SMITH CAMPUS
Jennings, Louisiana

- **State-supported** 2-year
- **Calendar** semesters
- 179 undergraduate students

Faculty *Total:* 13, 54% full-time.
Costs (2003–04) *Tuition:* state resident $488 full-time, $21 per credit hour part-time; nonresident $976 full-time, $42 per credit hour part-time. *Required fees:* $178 full-time, $7 per credit hour part-time, $5 per term part-time.
Applying *Application fee:* $5.
Admissions Contact Admissions Office, Louisiana Technical College-Morgan Smith Campus, P.O. Box 1327, 1230 North Main Street, Jennings, LA 70546-1327. *Phone:* 337-824-4811. *Fax:* 337-824-5653.

LOUISIANA TECHNICAL COLLEGE- NATCHITOCHES CAMPUS
Natchitoches, Louisiana

- **State-supported** 2-year, founded 1938
- **Calendar** semesters
- **Degree** certificates, diplomas, and associate
- **Coed,** 456 undergraduate students

Faculty *Total:* 70, 29% full-time, 14% with terminal degrees. *Student/faculty ratio:* 15:1.
Majors Accounting technology and bookkeeping; kindergarten/preschool education; management information systems.
Costs (2003–04) *Tuition:* state resident $488 full-time, $21 per credit hour part-time; nonresident $976 full-time, $42 per credit hour part-time. *Required fees:* $178 full-time, $7 per credit hour part-time, $5 per term part-time.
Applying *Application fee:* $5.
Admissions Contact Ms. Carol Hebert, Admissions Office, Louisiana Technical College-Natchitoches Campus, P.O. Box 657, 6587 Highway 1 Bypass, Natchitoches, LA 71457. *Phone:* 318-357-3162. *Fax:* 318-352-2248.

LOUISIANA TECHNICAL COLLEGE- NORTH CENTRAL CAMPUS
Farmerville, Louisiana

- **State-supported** 2-year, founded 1952
- **Calendar** semesters
- **Degree** certificates, diplomas, and associate
- **Coed,** 170 undergraduate students

Undergraduates Students come from 2 states and territories.
Faculty *Total:* 6, 100% full-time. *Student/faculty ratio:* 15:1.
Majors Accounting technology and bookkeeping; administrative assistant and secretarial science; data processing and data processing technology.
Student Life *Housing:* college housing not available. *Student services:* personal/psychological counseling.
Standardized Tests *Required:* ABLE (for admission).
Costs (2003–04) *Tuition:* state resident $488 full-time; nonresident $1154 full-time. *Required fees:* $178 full-time.
Applying *Application fee:* $5. *Required for some:* high school transcript. *Recommended:* interview.
Admissions Contact Ms. Donna C. Sewell, Admissions Office, Louisiana Technical College-North Central Campus, PO Box 548, 605 West Boundary, Farmerville, LA 71241. *Phone:* 318-368-3179. *Fax:* 318-368-9180. *E-mail:* dsewell@theltc.net.

LOUISIANA TECHNICAL COLLEGE- NORTHEAST LOUISIANA CAMPUS
Winnsboro, Louisiana

- **State-supported** 2-year
- **Calendar** semesters
- 310 undergraduate students

Faculty *Total:* 18, 50% full-time.
Costs (2003–04) *Tuition:* state resident $488 full-time, $21 per credit hour part-time; nonresident $976 full-time, $42 per credit hour part-time. *Required fees:* $178 full-time, $7 per credit hour part-time, $5 per term part-time.
Financial Aid Of all full-time matriculated undergraduates who enrolled, 3 state and other part-time jobs.
Applying *Application fee:* $5.
Admissions Contact Admissions Office, Louisiana Technical College-Northeast Louisiana Campus, 1710 Warren Street, Winnsboro, LA 71295. *Phone:* 318-435-2163. *Toll-free phone:* 800-320-6133. *Fax:* 318-435-2166.

LOUISIANA TECHNICAL COLLEGE- NORTHWEST LOUISIANA CAMPUS
Minden, Louisiana

- **State-supported** 2-year, founded 1952
- **Calendar** semesters
- **Degree** certificates, diplomas, and associate
- 810 undergraduate students

Faculty *Total:* 82, 41% full-time.
Majors Accounting technology and bookkeeping; computer science; hotel/motel administration; instrumentation technology; management information systems.
Costs (2003–04) *Tuition:* state resident $488 full-time, $21 per credit hour part-time; nonresident $976 full-time, $42 per credit hour part-time. *Required fees:* $178 full-time, $7 per credit hour part-time, $5 per term part-time.
Applying *Application fee:* $5.
Admissions Contact Ms. Helen Deville, Admissions Office, Louisiana Technical College-Northwest Louisiana Campus, P.O. Box 835, 814 Constable Street, Minden, LA 71058-0835. *Phone:* 318-371-3035. *Toll-free phone:* 800-529-1387. *Fax:* 318-371-3055.

LOUISIANA TECHNICAL COLLEGE- OAKDALE CAMPUS
Oakdale, Louisiana

- **State-supported** 2-year
- **Calendar** semesters
- 251 undergraduate students

Faculty *Total:* 20, 75% full-time.
Costs (2003–04) *Tuition:* state resident $488 full-time, $21 per credit hour part-time; nonresident $976 full-time, $42 per credit hour part-time. *Required fees:* $178 full-time, $7 per credit hour part-time, $5 per term part-time.
Applying *Application fee:* $5.
Admissions Contact Admissions Office, Louisiana Technical College-Oakdale Campus, P.O. Drawer EM, 117 Highway 1152, Oakdale, LA 71463. *Phone:* 318-335-3944. *Fax:* 318-335-3347.

LOUISIANA TECHNICAL COLLEGE-RIVER PARISHES CAMPUS
Reserve, Louisiana

- **State-supported** 2-year
- **Calendar** semesters
- 325 undergraduate students

Faculty *Total:* 68, 16% full-time.
Costs (2003–04) *Tuition:* state resident $488 full-time, $21 per credit hour part-time; nonresident $976 full-time, $42 per credit hour part-time. *Required fees:* $178 full-time, $7 per credit hour part-time, $5 per term part-time.
Applying *Application fee:* $5.
Admissions Contact Admissions Office, Louisiana Technical College-River Parishes Campus, P.O. Drawer AQ, 181 Regala Park Road, Reserve, LA 70084. *Phone:* 985-536-4418. *Toll-free phone:* 800-590-9773. *Fax:* 985-536-7697.

LOUISIANA TECHNICAL COLLEGE-RUSTON CAMPUS

Ruston, Louisiana

- **State-supported** 2-year
- **Calendar** semesters
- **Coed,** 116 undergraduate students

Faculty *Total:* 19, 68% full-time.
Costs (2003–04) *Tuition:* state resident $488 full-time, $21 per credit hour part-time; nonresident $976 full-time, $42 per credit hour part-time. *Required fees:* $178 full-time, $7 per credit hour part-time, $5 per term part-time.
Applying *Application fee:* $5.
Admissions Contact Admissions Office, Louisiana Technical College-Ruston Campus, P.O. Box 1070, 1010 James Street, Ruston, LA 71273-1070. *Phone:* 318-251-4145. *Fax:* 318-251-4159.

LOUISIANA TECHNICAL COLLEGE-SABINE VALLEY CAMPUS

Many, Louisiana

- **State-supported** 2-year
- **Calendar** semesters
- **Degree** certificates, diplomas, and associate
- **Coed,** 135 undergraduate students

Faculty *Total:* 17, 53% full-time.
Majors Accounting technology and bookkeeping; computer science.
Costs (2003–04) *Tuition:* state resident $488 full-time, $21 per credit hour part-time; nonresident $976 full-time, $42 per credit hour part-time. *Required fees:* $178 full-time, $7 per credit hour part-time, $5 per term part-time.
Applying *Application fee:* $5.
Admissions Contact Mr. Barry Goss, Admissions Office, Louisiana Technical College-Sabine Valley Campus, PO Box 790, 1255 Fisher Road, Many, LA 71449. *Phone:* 318-256-4101. *Fax:* 318-256-4134.

LOUISIANA TECHNICAL COLLEGE-SHELBY M. JACKSON CAMPUS

Ferriday, Louisiana

- **State-supported** 2-year
- **Calendar** semesters
- 195 undergraduate students

Faculty *Total:* 24, 67% full-time.
Costs (2003–04) *Tuition:* state resident $488 full-time, $21 per credit hour part-time; nonresident $976 full-time, $42 per credit hour part-time. *Required fees:* $178 full-time, $7 per credit hour part-time, $5 per term part-time.
Applying *Application fee:* $5.
Admissions Contact Admissions Office, Louisiana Technical College-Shelby M. Jackson Campus, PO Box 1465, 2100 E.E. Wallace Boulevard, Ferriday, LA 71334. *Phone:* 318-757-7638. *Fax:* 318-757-8659.

LOUISIANA TECHNICAL COLLEGE-SHREVEPORT-BOSSIER CAMPUS

Shreveport, Louisiana

- **State-supported** 2-year
- **Calendar** semesters
- 818 undergraduate students

Faculty *Total:* 127, 26% full-time.
Costs (2003–04) *Tuition:* state resident $488 full-time, $21 per credit hour part-time; nonresident $976 full-time, $42 per credit hour part-time. *Required fees:* $178 full-time, $7 per credit hour part-time, $5 per term part-time.
Applying *Application fee:* $5.
Admissions Contact Admissions Office, Louisiana Technical College-Shreveport-Bossier Campus, PO Box 78527, 2010 North Market Street, Shreveport, LA 71137-8527. *Phone:* 318-676-7811. *Fax:* 318-676-7805.

LOUISIANA TECHNICAL COLLEGE-SIDNEY N. COLLIER CAMPUS

New Orleans, Louisiana

- **State-supported** 2-year
- **Calendar** semesters

- **Degree** certificates, diplomas, and associate
- 399 undergraduate students

Faculty *Total:* 56, 52% full-time.
Majors Accounting technology and bookkeeping; management information systems.
Costs (2003–04) *Tuition:* state resident $488 full-time, $21 per credit hour part-time; nonresident $976 full-time, $42 per credit hour part-time. *Required fees:* $178 full-time, $7 per credit hour part-time, $5 per term part-time.
Applying *Application fee:* $5.
Admissions Contact Ms. Linda Eubanks, Admissions Office, Louisiana Technical College-Sidney N. Collier Campus, 3727 Louisa Street, New Orleans, LA 70126. *Phone:* 504-942-8333 Ext. 137. *Fax:* 504-942-8337.

LOUISIANA TECHNICAL COLLEGE-SLIDELL CAMPUS

Slidell, Louisiana

- **State-supported** 2-year, founded 1972
- **Calendar** semesters
- 366 undergraduate students

Faculty *Total:* 45, 40% full-time.
Costs (2003–04) *Tuition:* state resident $488 full-time, $21 per credit hour part-time; nonresident $976 full-time, $42 per credit hour part-time. *Required fees:* $178 full-time, $7 per credit hour part-time, $5 per term part-time.
Applying *Application fee:* $5.
Admissions Contact Admissions Office, Louisiana Technical College-Slidell Campus, P.O. Box 827, 1000 Canulette Road, Slidell, LA 70459-0827. *Phone:* 985-646-6431. *Fax:* 985-646-6442.

LOUISIANA TECHNICAL COLLEGE-SULLIVAN CAMPUS

Bogalusa, Louisiana

- **State-supported** 2-year
- **Calendar** semesters
- 717 undergraduate students

Faculty *Total:* 80, 51% full-time.
Costs (2003–04) *Tuition:* state resident $488 full-time, $21 per credit hour part-time; nonresident $976 full-time, $42 per credit hour part-time. *Required fees:* $178 full-time, $7 per credit hour part-time, $5 per term part-time.
Applying *Application fee:* $5.
Admissions Contact Admissions Office, Louisiana Technical College-Sullivan Campus, 1710 Sullivan Drive, Bogalusa, LA 70427. *Phone:* 985-732-6640. *Fax:* 985-732-6603.

LOUISIANA TECHNICAL COLLEGE-TALLULAH CAMPUS

Tallulah, Louisiana

- **State-supported** 2-year
- **Calendar** semesters
- 449 undergraduate students

Faculty *Total:* 39, 56% full-time.
Costs (2003–04) *Tuition:* state resident $488 full-time, $21 per credit hour part-time; nonresident $976 full-time, $42 per credit hour part-time. *Required fees:* $178 full-time, $7 per credit hour part-time, $5 per term part-time.
Applying *Application fee:* $5.
Admissions Contact Admissions Office, Louisiana Technical College-Tallulah Campus, P.O. Drawer 1740, Old Highway 65 South, Tallulah, LA 71284-1740. *Phone:* 318-574-4820. *Toll-free phone:* 800-215-3905. *Fax:* 318-574-1868.

LOUISIANA TECHNICAL COLLEGE-TECHE AREA CAMPUS

New Iberia, Louisiana

- **State-supported** 2-year
- **Calendar** semesters
- 443 undergraduate students

Faculty *Total:* 38, 58% full-time.

Costs (2003–04) *Tuition:* state resident $488 full-time, $21 per credit hour part-time; nonresident $976 full-time, $42 per credit hour part-time. *Required fees:* $178 full-time, $7 per credit hour part-time, $5 per term part-time.
Applying *Application fee:* $5.
Admissions Contact Admissions Office, Louisiana Technical College-Teche Area Campus, P.O. Box 11057, 609 Ember Drive, New Iberia, LA 70562-1057. *Phone:* 337-373-0011. *Fax:* 337-373-0039.

LOUISIANA TECHNICAL COLLEGE-T.H. HARRIS CAMPUS
Opelousas, Louisiana

- **State-supported** 2-year
- **Calendar** semesters
- 598 undergraduate students

Faculty *Total:* 40, 95% full-time.
Costs (2003–04) *Tuition:* state resident $488 full-time, $21 per credit hour part-time; nonresident $976 full-time, $42 per credit hour part-time. *Required fees:* $178 full-time, $7 per credit hour part-time, $5 per term part-time.
Applying *Application fee:* $5.
Admissions Contact Admissions Office, Louisiana Technical College-T.H. Harris Campus, 322 East South Street, Opelousas, LA 70570-6114. *Phone:* 337-948-0239. *Fax:* 337-948-0243.

LOUISIANA TECHNICAL COLLEGE-WEST JEFFERSON CAMPUS
Harvey, Louisiana

- **State-supported** 2-year
- **Calendar** semesters
- 284 undergraduate students

Faculty *Total:* 45, 51% full-time.
Costs (2003–04) *Tuition:* state resident $488 full-time, $21 per credit hour part-time; nonresident $976 full-time, $42 per credit hour part-time. *Required fees:* $178 full-time, $7 per credit hour part-time, $5 per term part-time.
Applying *Application fee:* $5.
Admissions Contact Admissions Office, Louisiana Technical College-West Jefferson Campus, 475 Manhattan Boulevard, Harvey, LA 70058. *Phone:* 504-361-6464. *Fax:* 504-361-6465.

LOUISIANA TECHNICAL COLLEGE-YOUNG MEMORIAL CAMPUS
Morgan City, Louisiana

- **State-supported** 2-year
- **Calendar** semesters
- **Degree** certificates, diplomas, and associate
- **Coed,** 734 undergraduate students

Faculty *Total:* 63, 62% full-time.
Majors Accounting technology and bookkeeping; management information systems.
Costs (2003–04) *Tuition:* state resident $488 full-time, $21 per credit hour part-time; nonresident $976 full-time, $42 per credit hour part-time. *Required fees:* $178 full-time, $7 per credit hour part-time, $5 per term part-time.
Applying *Application fee:* $5.
Admissions Contact Ms. Melanie Henry, Admissions Office, Louisiana Technical College-Young Memorial Campus, P.O. Drawer 2148, 900 Youngs Road, Morgan City, LA 70381. *Phone:* 504-380-2436. *Fax:* 985-380-2440.

MEDVANCE INSTITUTE
Baton Rouge, Louisiana

Admissions Contact Ms. Sheri Kirley, Associate Director of Admissions, MedVance Institute, 4173 Government Street, Baton Rouge, LA 70806. *Phone:* 225-248-1015. *Fax:* 225-343-5426.

METROPOLITAN COMMUNITY COLLEGE
Gretna, Louisiana

Admissions Contact 1500 Lafayette Street, Gretna, LA 70053.

REMINGTON COLLEGE-BATON ROUGE CAMPUS
Baton Rouge, Louisiana

Admissions Contact Mr. Gregg Falcon, Campus President, Remington College-Baton Rouge Campus, 1900 North Lobdell, Baton Rouge, LA 70806. *Phone:* 225-922-3990.

REMINGTON COLLEGE-LAFAYETTE CAMPUS
Lafayette, Louisiana

- **Proprietary** 2-year, founded 1940, part of Education America Inc
- **Calendar** continuous
- **Degree** diplomas and associate
- **Urban** 4-acre campus
- **Coed,** 452 undergraduate students, 100% full-time, 66% women, 34% men

Undergraduates 452 full-time. 44% African American, 2% Asian American or Pacific Islander, 2% Hispanic American, 0.9% Native American.
Faculty *Total:* 24, 58% full-time. *Student/faculty ratio:* 15:1.
Majors Business administration and management; computer programming; computer programming related; computer systems analysis; computer systems networking and telecommunications; computer/technical support; data entry/microcomputer applications related; electrical, electronic and communications engineering technology; legal assistant/paralegal; medical/clinical assistant; web page, digital/multimedia and information resources design.
Academic Programs *Special study options:* honors programs, independent study.
Library Remington College Library with 15,435 titles, 85 serial subscriptions, 182 audiovisual materials, an OPAC.
Computers on Campus 120 computers available on campus for general student use. A campuswide network can be accessed from off campus. Internet access, at least one staffed computer lab available.
Student Life *Housing:* college housing not available. *Campus security:* 24-hour emergency response devices.
Costs (2003–04) *Tuition:* $10,900 full-time.
Applying *Options:* early admission, deferred entrance. *Application fee:* $50. *Required:* high school transcript, interview.
Admissions Contact Mr. William Duncan, Director of Recruiting, Remington College-Lafayette Campus, 303 Rue Louis XIV, Lafayette, LA 70508. *Phone:* 337-981-9010. *Toll-free phone:* 800-736-2687. *Fax:* 337-983-7130.

REMINGTON COLLEGE-NEW ORLEANS CAMPUS
Metairie, Louisiana

- **Proprietary** 2-year
- **Calendar** quarters
- **Degree** associate
- **Coed**

Costs (2003–04) *Tuition:* Contact Remington College, New Orleans directly for full and part-time tuition and fees.
Applying *Application fee:* $50.
Admissions Contact Mr. Roy Kimble, Director of Recruitment, Remington College-New Orleans Campus, 321 Veterans Memorial Boulevard, Metairie, LA 70005. *Phone:* 504-831-8889. *Fax:* 504-831-6803.

RIVER PARISHES COMMUNITY COLLEGE
Sorrento, Louisiana

Admissions Contact PO Box 310, Sorrento, LA 70778.

SCHOOL OF URBAN MISSIONS-NEW ORLEANS
New Orleans, Louisiana

Admissions Contact PO Box 53344, New Orleans, LA 70153. *Toll-free phone:* 800-385-6364.

SOUTHERN UNIVERSITY AT SHREVEPORT
Shreveport, Louisiana

Admissions Contact Ms. Juanita Johnson, Acting Admissions Records Technician, Southern University at Shreveport, 3050 Martin Luther King, Jr. Drive, Shreveport, LA 71107. *Phone:* 318-674-3342. *Toll-free phone:* 800-458-1472 Ext. 342.

MAINE

ANDOVER COLLEGE
Portland, Maine

- **Proprietary** 2-year, founded 1966
- **Calendar** modular
- **Degree** certificates and associate
- **Urban** 2-acre campus
- **Coed,** 564 undergraduate students, 98% full-time, 79% women, 21% men

Associate degrees offered in 16 to 24 months in accounting, business administration, computer technology, criminal justice, early childhood education, legal studies, medical assisting, office administration, and travel and tourism. Certificates include early childhood education, hospitality operations, legal studies, medical transcription, office administration, and travel and tourism. Facilities and services include 4 computer labs, Internet access, an Academic Assistance Center, internships, and lifetime placement services.

Undergraduates 550 full-time, 14 part-time. Students come from 5 states and territories, 3 other countries.
Freshmen *Admission:* 99 applied, 99 admitted.
Faculty *Total:* 38, 37% full-time. *Student/faculty ratio:* 18:1.
Majors Accounting; administrative assistant and secretarial science; business administration and management; computer/information technology services administration related; computer management; computer programming; computer science; criminal justice/law enforcement administration; health information/medical records administration; kindergarten/preschool education; legal administrative assistant/secretary; legal assistant/paralegal; medical administrative assistant and medical secretary; medical/clinical assistant; system administration; web/multimedia management and webmaster.
Academic Programs *Special study options:* academic remediation for entering students, adult/continuing education programs, cooperative education, independent study, internships, part-time degree program, summer session for credit.
Library Andover Library with 6,000 titles, 106 serial subscriptions, 59 audiovisual materials.
Computers on Campus 100 computers available on campus for general student use. Internet access, at least one staffed computer lab available.
Student Life *Housing:* college housing not available. *Activities and Organizations:* Student Advisors, Andover Computer, Student Advisors Group, Andover Student Medical Assistants, C.O.P.S. *Campus security:* 24-hour emergency response devices. *Student services:* personal/psychological counseling.
Costs (2003–04) *Tuition:* $5940 full-time, $495 per course part-time. *Required fees:* $1000 full-time, $80 per term part-time. *Waivers:* employees or children of employees.
Financial Aid Of all full-time matriculated undergraduates who enrolled, 25 Federal Work-Study jobs (averaging $3000).
Applying *Options:* common application, early admission, deferred entrance. *Application fee:* $25. *Required:* high school transcript. *Recommended:* interview. *Application deadline:* rolling (freshmen), rolling (transfers).
Admissions Contact Mr. David Blessing, Director of Enrollment Management, Andover College, 901 Washington Avenue, Portland, ME 04103-2791. *Phone:* 207-774-6126 Ext. 261. *Toll-free phone:* 800-639-3110 Ext. 240 (in-state); 800-639-3110 Ext. 242 (out-of-state). *Fax:* 207-774-1715 Ext. 243. *E-mail:* enroll@andovercollege.com.

BEAL COLLEGE
Bangor, Maine

- **Proprietary** 2-year, founded 1891
- **Calendar** modular
- **Degree** certificates, diplomas, and associate
- **Small-town** 4-acre campus
- **Coed**

Faculty *Student/faculty ratio:* 16:1.

Costs (2003–04) *Tuition:* $5040 full-time, $420 per term part-time. *Required fees:* $485 full-time.
Applying *Options:* deferred entrance. *Application fee:* $25. *Required:* high school transcript. *Recommended:* interview.
Admissions Contact Ms. Susan Palmer, Admissions Assistant, Beal College, 629 Main Street, Bangor, ME 04401. *Phone:* 207-947-4591. *Toll-free phone:* 800-660-7351. *Fax:* 207-947-0208.

CENTRAL MAINE COMMUNITY COLLEGE
Auburn, Maine

- **State-supported** 2-year, founded 1964, part of Maine Technical College System
- **Calendar** semesters
- **Degree** certificates, diplomas, and associate
- **Small-town** 135-acre campus
- **Coed**

Faculty *Student/faculty ratio:* 15:1.
Student Life *Campus security:* 24-hour emergency response devices, controlled dormitory access, night patrols by police.
Athletics Member NSCAA.
Standardized Tests *Required for some:* ACCUPLACER. *Recommended:* SAT I (for placement).
Costs (2004–05) *Tuition:* area resident $2176 full-time, $68 per credit hour part-time; state resident $3264 full-time, $102 per credit hour part-time; nonresident $4768 full-time, $149 per credit hour part-time. *Required fees:* $690 full-time, $25 per credit part-time. *Room and board:* $5600.
Financial Aid Of all full-time matriculated undergraduates who enrolled, 170 Federal Work-Study jobs (averaging $1200).
Applying *Options:* deferred entrance. *Application fee:* $20. *Required:* essay or personal statement, high school transcript. *Required for some:* 2 letters of recommendation, interview. *Recommended:* minimum 2.0 GPA.
Admissions Contact Ms. Elizabeth Oken, Director of Admissions, Central Maine Community College, 1250 Turner Street, Auburn, ME 04210-6498. *Phone:* 207-755-5334 Ext. 334. *Toll-free phone:* 800-891-2002. *Fax:* 207-755-5493. *E-mail:* enroll@cmtc.net.

CENTRAL MAINE MEDICAL CENTER SCHOOL OF NURSING
Lewiston, Maine

- **Independent** 2-year, founded 1891
- **Calendar** semesters
- **Degree** certificates and associate
- **Urban** campus
- **Coed, primarily women,** 130 undergraduate students, 19% full-time, 86% women, 14% men

Undergraduates 25 full-time, 105 part-time. Students come from 2 states and territories, 1% are from out of state.
Freshmen *Admission:* 4 enrolled. *Average high school GPA:* 3.70. *Test scores:* SAT verbal scores over 500: 25%; SAT math scores over 500: 50%; SAT verbal scores over 600: 25%; SAT math scores over 600: 25%.
Faculty *Total:* 11, 82% full-time, 9% with terminal degrees. *Student/faculty ratio:* 8:1.
Majors Nursing (registered nurse training).
Academic Programs *Special study options:* advanced placement credit, off-campus study.
Library Gerrish True Health Sciences Library with 1,975 titles, 339 serial subscriptions, an OPAC, a Web page.
Computers on Campus 10 computers available on campus for general student use. Internet access, at least one staffed computer lab available.
Student Life *Housing Options:* coed. Campus housing is university owned. *Activities and Organizations:* Student Communication Council, student government, Student Nurses Association. *Campus security:* 24-hour emergency response devices and patrols, late-night transport/escort service, controlled dormitory access. *Student services:* health clinic, personal/psychological counseling.
Standardized Tests *Required:* SAT I (for admission).
Costs (2004–05) *Tuition:* $2730 full-time, $130 per credit part-time. *Required fees:* $1085 full-time, $20 per term part-time. *Room only:* $1500.
Applying *Application fee:* $40. *Required:* essay or personal statement, high school transcript, 2 letters of recommendation, SAT I or 12 college credits. *Application deadline:* 6/1 (freshmen).
Admissions Contact Mrs. Kathleen C. Jacques, Registrar, Central Maine Medical Center School of Nursing, 70 Middle Street, Lewiston, ME 04240-0305. *Phone:* 207-795-2858. *Fax:* 207-795-2849. *E-mail:* jacqueka@cmhc.org.

EASTERN MAINE COMMUNITY COLLEGE
Bangor, Maine

- **State-supported** 2-year, founded 1966, part of Maine Community College System
- **Calendar** semesters
- **Degree** certificates, diplomas, and associate
- **Small-town** 72-acre campus
- **Endowment** $1.5 million
- **Coed**, 1,790 undergraduate students, 42% full-time, 52% women, 48% men

Undergraduates 744 full-time, 1,046 part-time. Students come from 2 states and territories, 1% are from out of state, 0.1% African American, 0.3% Asian American or Pacific Islander, 0.1% Hispanic American, 1% Native American, 20% live on campus.

Freshmen *Admission:* 1,407 applied, 705 admitted, 410 enrolled.

Faculty *Total:* 142, 38% full-time, 8% with terminal degrees. *Student/faculty ratio:* 11:1.

Majors Administrative assistant and secretarial science; automobile/automotive mechanics technology; banking and financial support services; business administration and management; carpentry; computer technology/computer systems technology; construction engineering technology; culinary arts; drafting and design technology; electrical, electronic and communications engineering technology; heating, air conditioning, ventilation and refrigeration maintenance technology; heavy equipment maintenance technology; kindergarten/preschool education; liberal arts and sciences/liberal studies; machine tool technology; nursing (licensed practical/vocational nurse training); nursing (registered nurse training); radiologic technology/science; welding technology.

Academic Programs *Special study options:* academic remediation for entering students, adult/continuing education programs, advanced placement credit, part-time degree program, summer session for credit.

Library Eastern Maine Technical College Library plus 1 other with 17,554 titles, 159 serial subscriptions, an OPAC, a Web page.

Computers on Campus 85 computers available on campus for general student use. A campuswide network can be accessed from off campus. Internet access, at least one staffed computer lab available.

Student Life *Housing Options:* coed. Campus housing is university owned. *Activities and Organizations:* student-run newspaper, Student Senate, Phi Theta Kappa, Senior Council, Resident's Council, Associated General Contractors Student Chapter. *Campus security:* late-night transport/escort service, controlled dormitory access. *Student services:* health clinic, personal/psychological counseling.

Athletics Member NSCAA. *Intercollegiate sports:* basketball M, soccer M/W. *Intramural sports:* badminton M/W, basketball M/W, bowling M/W, ice hockey M(c)/W(c), skiing (cross-country) M/W, skiing (downhill) M/W, soccer M/W, table tennis M/W, volleyball M/W, weight lifting M/W.

Standardized Tests *Required:* ACCUPLACER (for admission). *Required for some:* SAT I (for admission).

Costs (2003–04) *Tuition:* state resident $2448 full-time, $68 per credit part-time; nonresident $5364 full-time, $149 per credit part-time. Full-time tuition and fees vary according to program. Part-time tuition and fees vary according to program. *Required fees:* $1122 full-time. *Room and board:* $4052. Room and board charges vary according to board plan. *Waivers:* senior citizens and employees or children of employees.

Financial Aid Of all full-time matriculated undergraduates who enrolled, 100 Federal Work-Study jobs (averaging $1000).

Applying *Options:* deferred entrance. *Application fee:* $20. *Required:* essay or personal statement, high school transcript, letters of recommendation. *Required for some:* interview. *Recommended:* minimum 2.0 GPA. *Application deadline:* rolling (freshmen). *Notification:* continuous (freshmen).

Admissions Contact Ms. Veronica Delcort, Director of Admissions, Eastern Maine Community College, 354 Hogan Road, Bangor, ME 04401. *Phone:* 207-974-4680. *Toll-free phone:* 800-286-9357. *Fax:* 207-974-4683. *E-mail:* admissions@emcc.edu.

KENNEBEC VALLEY COMMUNITY COLLEGE
Fairfield, Maine

- **State-supported** 2-year, founded 1970, part of Maine Community College System
- **Calendar** semesters
- **Degree** certificates, diplomas, and associate
- **Small-town** 58-acre campus
- **Endowment** $215,503
- **Coed**

Faculty *Student/faculty ratio:* 28:1.

Student Life *Campus security:* Evening security patrol.

Standardized Tests *Required for some:* nursing exam, HOBET, ASSET.

Costs (2003–04) *Tuition:* state resident $2040 full-time, $68 per credit hour part-time; nonresident $4470 full-time, $149 per credit hour part-time. *Required fees:* $450 full-time.

Financial Aid Of all full-time matriculated undergraduates who enrolled, 34 Federal Work-Study jobs (averaging $1207).

Applying *Options:* electronic application, deferred entrance. *Application fee:* $20. *Required:* essay or personal statement, high school transcript. *Required for some:* letters of recommendation, interview.

Admissions Contact Mr. Jim Bourgoin, Director of Recruitment, Kennebec Valley Community College, 92 Western Avenue, Fairfield, ME 04937-1367. *Phone:* 207-453-5035. *Toll-free phone:* 800-528-5882 Ext. 5035. *Fax:* 207-453-5011. *E-mail:* admissions@kvcc.me.edu.

NORTHERN MAINE COMMUNITY COLLEGE
Presque Isle, Maine

- **State-related** 2-year, founded 1963, part of Maine Technical College System
- **Calendar** semesters
- **Degree** certificates, diplomas, and associate
- **Small-town** 86-acre campus
- **Coed**, 1,013 undergraduate students, 63% full-time, 54% women, 46% men

Undergraduates 641 full-time, 372 part-time. Students come from 5 states and territories, 1 other country, 0.8% African American, 0.1% Asian American or Pacific Islander, 0.8% Hispanic American, 3% Native American, 5% international, 28% live on campus.

Freshmen *Admission:* 656 applied, 551 admitted, 258 enrolled.

Faculty *Total:* 76, 59% full-time.

Majors Accounting; administrative assistant and secretarial science; agricultural business and management; automobile/automotive mechanics technology; business administration and management; carpentry; computer engineering technology; computer programming; data processing and data processing technology; drafting and design technology; electrical, electronic and communications engineering technology; emergency medical technology (EMT paramedic); heating, air conditioning, ventilation and refrigeration maintenance technology; heavy equipment maintenance technology; industrial arts; instrumentation technology; kindergarten/preschool education; legal administrative assistant/secretary; medical administrative assistant and medical secretary; nursing (licensed practical/vocational nurse training); nursing (registered nurse training); pipefitting and sprinkler fitting.

Academic Programs *Special study options:* academic remediation for entering students, adult/continuing education programs, advanced placement credit, cooperative education, double majors, independent study, internships, off-campus study, part-time degree program, services for LD students, summer session for credit.

Library Northern Maine Technical College Library with 11,200 titles, 233 serial subscriptions, 250 audiovisual materials, an OPAC, a Web page.

Computers on Campus A campuswide network can be accessed from student residence rooms and from off campus. Internet access, at least one staffed computer lab available.

Student Life *Housing Options:* coed. *Campus security:* 24-hour patrols. *Student services:* health clinic, personal/psychological counseling.

Athletics Member NSCAA. *Intercollegiate sports:* basketball M/W, golf M/W, ice hockey M/W, soccer M/W. *Intramural sports:* archery M/W, basketball M/W, football M/W, golf M, racquetball M/W, soccer M, softball M/W, table tennis M/W, tennis M/W, volleyball M/W, weight lifting M/W.

Standardized Tests *Required:* Assessment and Placement Services for Community Colleges (for placement).

Costs (2004–05) *Tuition:* state resident $1632 full-time, $68 per credit part-time; nonresident $3576 full-time, $149 per credit part-time. *Required fees:* $229 full-time. *Room and board:* $4460; room only: $1680.

Financial Aid Of all full-time matriculated undergraduates who enrolled, 55 Federal Work-Study jobs (averaging $3000).

Applying *Options:* common application, electronic application, early admission. *Application fee:* $20. *Required:* high school transcript. *Required for some:* letters of recommendation. *Recommended:* essay or personal statement, minimum 2.0 GPA. *Application deadline:* rolling (freshmen). *Notification:* continuous (freshmen).

Admissions Contact Ms. Nancy Gagnon, Admissions Secretary, Northern Maine Community College, 33 Edgemont Drive, Presque Isle, ME 04769-2016. *Phone:* 207-768-2785. *Toll-free phone:* 800-535-6682. *Fax:* 207-768-2831. *E-mail:* wcasavant@nmtc.net.

SOUTHERN MAINE COMMUNITY COLLEGE
South Portland, Maine

- **State-supported** 2-year, founded 1946, part of Maine Community College System
- **Calendar** semesters
- **Degree** certificates, diplomas, and associate
- **Small-town** 65-acre campus
- **Endowment** $513,726
- **Coed,** 3,505 undergraduate students, 49% full-time, 51% women, 49% men

Undergraduates 1,720 full-time, 1,785 part-time. Students come from 9 states and territories, 6% are from out of state, 2% African American, 1% Asian American or Pacific Islander, 1% Hispanic American, 1% Native American, 1% international, 10% live on campus.

Freshmen *Admission:* 1,193 applied, 1,119 admitted, 777 enrolled.

Faculty *Total:* 259, 34% full-time. *Student/faculty ratio:* 18:1.

Majors Agronomy and crop science; architectural engineering technology; automobile/automotive mechanics technology; botany/plant biology; business administration and management; business machine repair; cardiovascular technology; carpentry; child development; cinematography and film/video production; communications technology; computer engineering technology; computer management; construction engineering technology; criminal justice/law enforcement administration; criminal justice/police science; culinary arts; dietetics; drafting and design technology; electrical, electronic and communications engineering technology; engineering related; environmental engineering technology; fire science; food services technology; general studies; heating, air conditioning, ventilation and refrigeration maintenance technology; horticultural science; hospitality administration; hotel/motel administration; industrial radiologic technology; information science/studies; kindergarten/preschool education; landscaping and groundskeeping; liberal arts and sciences/liberal studies; machine tool technology; management information systems; marine biology and biological oceanography; medical/clinical assistant; nursing (licensed practical/vocational nurse training); nursing (registered nurse training); oceanography (chemical and physical); pipefitting and sprinkler fitting; radiologic technology/science; respiratory care therapy; special products marketing; surgical technology.

Academic Programs *Special study options:* academic remediation for entering students, advanced placement credit, cooperative education, distance learning, double majors, English as a second language, internships, off-campus study, part-time degree program, services for LD students, study abroad, summer session for credit.

Library Southern Maine Community College Library with 15,000 titles, 350 serial subscriptions, an OPAC, a Web page.

Computers on Campus 200 computers available on campus for general student use. A campuswide network can be accessed from student residence rooms and from off campus. Internet access, at least one staffed computer lab available.

Student Life *Housing Options:* coed. *Activities and Organizations:* drama/theater group, student-run newspaper, choral group, SEA Club, student government, Phi Theta Kappa, VICA. *Campus security:* 24-hour emergency response devices, student patrols, late-night transport/escort service. *Student services:* health clinic, personal/psychological counseling, women's center.

Athletics Member NSCAA. *Intercollegiate sports:* baseball M, basketball M, golf M/W, soccer M/W, softball W, volleyball M/W. *Intramural sports:* basketball M/W, football M/W, golf M/W, soccer M/W, volleyball M/W.

Standardized Tests *Required for some:* ACCUPLACER. *Recommended:* SAT I (for placement).

Costs (2004–05) *Tuition:* state resident $2040 full-time, $68 per credit part-time; nonresident $4470 full-time, $149 per credit part-time. *Required fees:* $570 full-time, $19 per credit part-time, $50 per term part-time. *Room and board:* $6300; room only: $2781.

Financial Aid Of all full-time matriculated undergraduates who enrolled, 130 Federal Work-Study jobs (averaging $1500).

Applying *Options:* electronic application. *Application fee:* $20. *Required:* high school transcript. *Application deadline:* rolling (freshmen), rolling (transfers). *Notification:* continuous (freshmen), continuous (transfers).

Admissions Contact Linda Gabrielson, Interim Assistant Dean for Enrollment Services, Southern Maine Community College, Admissions, 2 Fort Road, South Portland, ME 04106. *Phone:* 207-741-5520. *Toll-free phone:* 877-282-2182. *Fax:* 207-741-5671. *E-mail:* admissions@smccme.edu.

WASHINGTON COUNTY COMMUNITY COLLEGE
Calais, Maine

- **State-supported** 2-year, founded 1969, part of Maine Technical College System
- **Calendar** semesters
- **Degree** certificates, diplomas, and associate
- **Rural** 40-acre campus
- **Coed**

Faculty *Student/faculty ratio:* 9:1.

Student Life *Campus security:* 24-hour emergency response devices.

Standardized Tests *Required:* ACT ASSET (for placement).

Costs (2003–04) *Tuition:* state resident $1632 full-time, $68 per credit hour part-time; nonresident $3576 full-time, $149 per credit hour part-time. *Required fees:* $448 full-time, $19 per credit hour part-time. *Room and board:* room only: $1856.

Financial Aid Of all full-time matriculated undergraduates who enrolled, 42 Federal Work-Study jobs (averaging $562).

Applying *Options:* deferred entrance. *Application fee:* $20. *Required:* essay or personal statement, high school transcript, interview. *Recommended:* minimum 2.0 GPA, letters of recommendation.

Admissions Contact Mr. Kent Lyons, Admissions Counselor, Washington County Community College, RR#1, Box 22C River Road, Calais, ME 04619. *Phone:* 207-454-1000. *Toll-free phone:* 800-210-6932 Ext. 41049. *Fax:* 207-454-1026.

YORK COUNTY COMMUNITY COLLEGE
Wells, Maine

- **State-supported** 2-year, founded 1994, part of Maine Technical College System
- **Calendar** semesters
- **Degree** certificates and associate
- **Small-town** 84-acre campus with easy access to Boston
- **Coed,** 990 undergraduate students

Undergraduates Students come from 3 states and territories, 1% are from out of state.

Freshmen *Admission:* 216 applied, 195 admitted.

Faculty *Total:* 67, 10% full-time, 7% with terminal degrees. *Student/faculty ratio:* 13:1.

Majors Accounting; business administration and management; computer engineering technology; computer/information technology services administration related; computer systems networking and telecommunications; culinary arts; drafting and design technology; general studies; hotel/motel administration; kindergarten/preschool education; web page, digital/multimedia and information resources design.

Academic Programs *Special study options:* accelerated degree program, cooperative education, distance learning, double majors, independent study, internships, part-time degree program, summer session for credit.

Library Library and Learning Resource Center plus 1 other with 4,000 titles, 75 serial subscriptions, 200 audiovisual materials, an OPAC, a Web page.

Computers on Campus 35 computers available on campus for general student use. A campuswide network can be accessed. Internet access, at least one staffed computer lab available.

Student Life *Housing:* college housing not available. *Activities and Organizations:* student-run newspaper, Student Senate, Veteran's Club, Early Childhood Education Club, Skills-USA Club. *Campus security:* 24-hour emergency response devices.

Standardized Tests *Recommended:* SAT I (for placement).

Costs (2004–05) *Tuition:* state resident $2040 full-time, $68 per credit part-time; nonresident $4470 full-time, $149 per credit part-time. Full-time tuition and fees vary according to course load and program. Part-time tuition and fees vary according to course load and program. *Required fees:* $710 full-time, $24 per credit part-time. *Payment plan:* installment. *Waivers:* minority students and employees or children of employees.

Financial Aid Of all full-time matriculated undergraduates who enrolled, 20 Federal Work-Study jobs (averaging $1200).

Applying *Application fee:* $20. *Required:* essay or personal statement, high school transcript. *Application deadline:* rolling (freshmen), rolling (transfers).

Admissions Contact Ms. Leisa Collins, Director of Admissions, York County Community College, 112 College Drive, Wells, ME 04090. *Phone:* 207-646-9282 Ext. 305. *Toll-free phone:* 800-580-3820. *Fax:* 207-641-0837. *E-mail:* admissions@yctc.net.

MARYLAND

ALLEGANY COLLEGE OF MARYLAND
Cumberland, Maryland

- **State and locally supported** 2-year, founded 1961, part of Maryland State Community Colleges System

- **Calendar** semesters
- **Degree** certificates and associate
- **Small-town** 311-acre campus
- **Endowment** $5.3 million
- **Coed,** 3,631 undergraduate students, 57% full-time, 67% women, 33% men

Undergraduates 2,055 full-time, 1,576 part-time. Students come from 21 states and territories, 3 other countries, 50% are from out of state, 6% African American, 0.4% Asian American or Pacific Islander, 0.8% Hispanic American, 0.4% Native American.

Freshmen *Admission:* 2,058 applied, 2,040 admitted. *Average high school GPA:* 2.84. *Test scores:* ACT scores over 18: 62%; ACT scores over 24: 9%.

Faculty *Total:* 227, 47% full-time. *Student/faculty ratio:* 16:1.

Majors Accounting technology and bookkeeping; administrative assistant and secretarial science; automobile/automotive mechanics technology; business administration and management; clinical/medical laboratory assistant; clinical/medical laboratory technology; communications technology; computer engineering technology; cosmetology and personal grooming arts related; criminal justice/police science; culinary arts; dental hygiene; forest/forest resources management; health professions related; hospitality administration; legal assistant/paralegal; liberal arts and sciences/liberal studies; management information systems; marketing/marketing management; medical radiologic technology; nursing (registered nurse training); occupational therapist assistant; occupational therapy; physical therapist assistant; psychiatric/mental health services technology; respiratory care therapy.

Academic Programs *Special study options:* academic remediation for entering students, adult/continuing education programs, advanced placement credit, distance learning, double majors, honors programs, independent study, internships, part-time degree program, summer session for credit. *ROTC:* Army (c).

Library Allegany College of Maryland Library with 51,999 titles, 404 serial subscriptions, 4,209 audiovisual materials, an OPAC, a Web page.

Computers on Campus 700 computers available on campus for general student use. A campuswide network can be accessed from off campus. Internet access, online (class) registration, at least one staffed computer lab available.

Student Life *Housing:* college housing not available. *Activities and Organizations:* choral group, SAHDA, Honors Club, EMT Club, Forestry Club. *Campus security:* 24-hour emergency response devices and patrols, late-night transport/escort service. *Student services:* personal/psychological counseling, women's center.

Athletics Member NJCAA. *Intercollegiate sports:* baseball M, basketball M/W, soccer M/W, tennis M/W, volleyball W. *Intramural sports:* archery M/W, badminton M/W, baseball M/W, basketball M/W, bowling M/W, tennis M/W, volleyball M/W.

Standardized Tests *Required for some:* ACT (for admission).

Costs (2003–04) *Tuition:* area resident $2550 full-time, $85 per credit part-time; state resident $5010 full-time, $167 per credit part-time; nonresident $5910 full-time, $197 per credit part-time. Full-time tuition and fees vary according to course load and location. Part-time tuition and fees vary according to course load and location. *Required fees:* $170 full-time, $5 per credit part-time, $30 per term part-time. *Waivers:* employees or children of employees.

Applying *Options:* electronic application, early admission. *Required:* high school transcript. *Application deadline:* rolling (freshmen), rolling (transfers). *Notification:* continuous (transfers).

Admissions Contact Ms. Cathy Nolan, Director of Admissions and Registration, Allegany College of Maryland, 12401 Willowbrook Road, SE, Cumberland, MD 21502. *Phone:* 301-784-5000 Ext. 5202. *Fax:* 301-784-5220. *E-mail:* cnolan@allegany.edu.

ANNE ARUNDEL COMMUNITY COLLEGE
Arnold, Maryland

- **State and locally supported** 2-year, founded 1961
- **Calendar** semesters
- **Degree** certificates and associate
- **Suburban** 230-acre campus with easy access to Baltimore and Washington, DC
- **Endowment** $2.4 million
- **Coed,** 14,290 undergraduate students, 33% full-time, 62% women, 38% men

Undergraduates 4,780 full-time, 9,510 part-time. Students come from 12 states and territories, 19 other countries, 0.8% are from out of state, 12% African American, 3% Asian American or Pacific Islander, 2% Hispanic American, 0.6% Native American, 0.7% international, 19% transferred in. *Retention:* 58% of 2002 full-time freshmen returned.

Freshmen *Admission:* 3,228 admitted, 2,737 enrolled.

Faculty *Total:* 827, 29% full-time, 9% with terminal degrees. *Student/faculty ratio:* 18:1.

Majors Accounting; administrative assistant and secretarial science; American studies; applied art; architectural engineering technology; art; astronomy; behavioral sciences; biological and physical sciences; biology/biological sciences;

botany/plant biology; broadcast journalism; business administration and management; business/managerial economics; chemistry; cinematography and film/video production; clinical laboratory science/medical technology; communications technology; computer and information sciences related; computer engineering technology; computer management; computer programming; computer science; computer/technical support; consumer merchandising/retailing management; corrections; criminal justice/law enforcement administration; criminal justice/police science; data entry/microcomputer applications; data processing and data processing technology; economics; education; electrical, electronic and communications engineering technology; elementary education; emergency medical technology (EMT paramedic); engineering technology; English; environmental studies; European studies; food services technology; health teacher education; horticultural science; hotel/motel administration; humanities; human services; industrial radiologic technology; industrial technology; information science/studies; kindergarten/preschool education; landscape architecture; legal assistant/paralegal; liberal arts and sciences/liberal studies; marine science/merchant marine officer; marketing/marketing management; mass communication/media; mathematics; mechanical engineering/mechanical technology; medical/clinical assistant; mental health/rehabilitation; music; nursing (registered nurse training); photography; physical education teaching and coaching; public administration; public policy analysis; real estate; social sciences; system administration; telecommunications.

Academic Programs *Special study options:* academic remediation for entering students, accelerated degree program, adult/continuing education programs, advanced placement credit, cooperative education, distance learning, English as a second language, freshman honors college, honors programs, independent study, internships, part-time degree program, services for LD students, summer session for credit. *ROTC:* Army (c), Air Force (c).

Library Andrew G. Truxal Library with 144,694 titles, 403 serial subscriptions, 8,060 audiovisual materials, an OPAC, a Web page.

Computers on Campus 250 computers available on campus for general student use. A campuswide network can be accessed from off campus. Internet access, online (class) registration, at least one staffed computer lab available.

Student Life *Housing:* college housing not available. *Activities and Organizations:* drama/theater group, student-run newspaper, choral group, Drama Club, student association, Black Student Union, International Student Association, Chemistry Club. *Campus security:* 24-hour emergency response devices and patrols, student patrols, late-night transport/escort service. *Student services:* health clinic, personal/psychological counseling.

Athletics Member NJCAA. *Intercollegiate sports:* baseball M(s), basketball M/W, cross-country running M(s)/W(s), golf M, lacrosse M(s), soccer M(s)/W(s), softball W(s), volleyball W. *Intramural sports:* lacrosse W.

Standardized Tests *Recommended:* SAT I or ACT (for placement).

Costs (2004–05) *Tuition:* $85 per credit hour part-time; state resident $159 per credit hour part-time; nonresident $282 per credit hour part-time. *Required fees:* $5 per credit hour part-time, $20 per term part-time. *Waivers:* employees or children of employees.

Financial Aid Of all full-time matriculated undergraduates who enrolled, 104 Federal Work-Study jobs (averaging $1900). 55 state and other part-time jobs (averaging $1740).

Applying *Options:* early admission, deferred entrance. *Application deadline:* rolling (freshmen), rolling (transfers).

Admissions Contact Mr. Thomas McGinn, Director of Enrollment Development and Admissions, Anne Arundel Community College, 101 College Parkway, Arnold, MD 21012-1895. *Phone:* 410-777-2240. *Fax:* 410-777-2246. *E-mail:* 4info@aacc.edu.

BALTIMORE CITY COMMUNITY COLLEGE
Baltimore, Maryland

- **State-supported** 2-year, founded 1947
- **Calendar** semesters
- **Degree** certificates and associate
- **Urban** 19-acre campus
- **Endowment** $139,215
- **Coed**

Faculty *Student/faculty ratio:* 17:1.

Standardized Tests *Recommended:* SAT I and SAT II or ACT (for placement), SAT II: Subject Tests (for placement), SAT II: Writing Test (for placement).

Costs (2003–04) *Tuition:* $69 per credit hour part-time; state resident $2070 full-time, $159 per credit hour part-time; nonresident $4770 full-time. *Required fees:* $120 full-time, $4 per credit hour part-time.

Financial Aid Of all full-time matriculated undergraduates who enrolled, 331 Federal Work-Study jobs (averaging $1879).

Applying *Options:* common application, early admission, deferred entrance. *Application fee:* $10. *Required:* high school transcript. *Recommended:* interview.

Baltimore City Community College (continued)

Admissions Contact Mrs. Scheherazade Forman, Admissions Coordinator, Baltimore City Community College, 2901 Liberty Heights Avenue, Baltimore, MD 21215. *Phone:* 410-462-8300. *Toll-free phone:* 888-203-1261 Ext. 8300. *Fax:* 410-462-7677. *E-mail:* sforman@bccc.state.md.us.

BALTIMORE INTERNATIONAL COLLEGE
Baltimore, Maryland

- **Independent** primarily 2-year, founded 1972
- **Calendar** semesters
- **Degrees** certificates, associate, and bachelor's
- **Urban** 6-acre campus with easy access to Washington, DC
- **Endowment** $94,812
- **Coed,** 571 undergraduate students, 93% full-time, 52% women, 48% men

Undergraduates 531 full-time, 40 part-time. Students come from 17 states and territories, 4 other countries, 47% African American, 4% Asian American or Pacific Islander, 2% Hispanic American, 0.4% Native American, 0.9% international, 5% transferred in, 24% live on campus. *Retention:* 50% of 2002 full-time freshmen returned.

Freshmen *Admission:* 825 applied, 233 admitted, 144 enrolled.

Faculty *Total:* 32, 41% full-time, 75% with terminal degrees. *Student/faculty ratio:* 9:1.

Majors Business administration and management; culinary arts; hospitality administration; hotel/motel administration.

Academic Programs *Special study options:* academic remediation for entering students, accelerated degree program, adult/continuing education programs, advanced placement credit, cooperative education, double majors, honors programs, internships, off-campus study, study abroad.

Library George A. Piendak Library with 13,000 titles, 200 serial subscriptions, 1,000 audiovisual materials.

Computers on Campus 35 computers available on campus for general student use. A campuswide network can be accessed from off campus. Internet access, at least one staffed computer lab available.

Student Life *Housing:* on-campus residence required for freshman year. *Options:* coed. Campus housing is university owned. Freshman campus housing is guaranteed. *Activities and Organizations:* student-run newspaper, American Culinary Federation, Beta Iota Kappa. *Campus security:* late-night transport/escort service, controlled dormitory access. *Student services:* health clinic, personal/psychological counseling.

Standardized Tests *Required for some:* SAT I or ACT (for admission).

Costs (2004–05) *Comprehensive fee:* $20,057 includes full-time tuition ($14,049), mandatory fees ($102), and room and board ($5906). *Room and board:* Room and board charges vary according to housing facility. *Payment plans:* tuition prepayment, installment. *Waivers:* employees or children of employees.

Applying *Options:* common application, electronic application, deferred entrance. *Application fee:* $35. *Required:* high school transcript. *Required for some:* essay or personal statement. *Recommended:* interview. *Application deadline:* rolling (freshmen), rolling (transfers). *Notification:* continuous until 8/15 (freshmen), continuous until 8/15 (transfers).

Admissions Contact Ms. Lori Makowski, Director of Admissions, Baltimore International College, Commerce Exchange, 17 Commerce Street, Baltimore, MD 21202-3230. *Phone:* 410-752-4710 Ext. 124. *Toll-free phone:* 800-624-9926 Ext. 120. *Fax:* 410-752-3730. *E-mail:* admissions@bic.edu.

▶ **See page 510 for a narrative description.**

CARROLL COMMUNITY COLLEGE
Westminster, Maryland

- **State and locally supported** 2-year, founded 1993, part of Maryland Higher Education Commission
- **Calendar** semesters plus winter session
- **Degree** certificates and associate
- **Small-town** 80-acre campus with easy access to Baltimore
- **Coed**

Faculty *Student/faculty ratio:* 18:1.

Student Life *Campus security:* late-night transport/escort service.

Standardized Tests *Recommended:* SAT I or ACT (for placement).

Costs (2003–04) *Tuition:* area resident $2889 full-time; state resident $4476 full-time; nonresident $6788 full-time.

Financial Aid Of all full-time matriculated undergraduates who enrolled, 27 Federal Work-Study jobs (averaging $965).

Applying *Options:* early admission. *Required:* high school transcript.

Admissions Contact Ms. Edie Hemingway, Coordinator of Admissions, Carroll Community College, 1601 Washington Road, Westminster, MD 21157.

Phone: 410-386-8430. *Toll-free phone:* 888-221-9748. *Fax:* 410-386-8446. *E-mail:* ehemingway@carrollcc.edu.

CECIL COMMUNITY COLLEGE
North East, Maryland

- **County-supported** 2-year, founded 1968
- **Calendar** semesters
- **Degree** certificates and associate
- **Small-town** 100-acre campus with easy access to Baltimore
- **Coed,** 1,797 undergraduate students, 33% full-time, 67% women, 33% men

Undergraduates 596 full-time, 1,201 part-time. Students come from 4 states and territories, 3 other countries, 10% are from out of state, 8% African American, 2% Asian American or Pacific Islander, 1% Hispanic American, 0.5% Native American, 1% international, 3% transferred in.

Freshmen *Admission:* 780 applied, 780 admitted, 413 enrolled.

Faculty *Total:* 177, 23% full-time, 8% with terminal degrees. *Student/faculty ratio:* 10:1.

Majors Accounting; administrative assistant and secretarial science; air traffic control; art; artificial intelligence and robotics; biology/biological sciences; business administration and management; carpentry; computer engineering technology; computer graphics; computer programming; construction engineering technology; criminal justice/law enforcement administration; data processing and data processing technology; education; education (K-12); electrical, electronic and communications engineering technology; elementary education; general studies; hydrology and water resources science; information science/studies; information technology; kindergarten/preschool education; liberal arts and sciences/liberal studies; marketing/marketing management; mathematics; medical laboratory technology; nursing (registered nurse training); photography; physical sciences; physics; pipefitting and sprinkler fitting; transportation and materials moving related; welding technology.

Academic Programs *Special study options:* academic remediation for entering students, adult/continuing education programs, advanced placement credit, cooperative education, distance learning, double majors, English as a second language, independent study, internships, part-time degree program, services for LD students, summer session for credit.

Library Cecil County Veteran's Memorial Library with 33,881 titles, 183 serial subscriptions, 1,093 audiovisual materials, an OPAC, a Web page.

Computers on Campus 66 computers available on campus for general student use. A campuswide network can be accessed from off campus. Internet access, online (class) registration, at least one staffed computer lab available.

Student Life *Housing:* college housing not available. *Activities and Organizations:* drama/theater group, student-run newspaper, student government, Non-traditional Student Organization, Student Nurses Association, student newspaper, national fraternities. *Campus security:* 24-hour emergency response devices, late-night transport/escort service. *Student services:* personal/psychological counseling, women's center.

Athletics Member NJCAA. *Intercollegiate sports:* baseball M, basketball M(s)/W(s), cheerleading W, field hockey W, softball W, volleyball W(s). *Intramural sports:* basketball M/W, bowling M/W, soccer M, tennis M/W, volleyball M/W.

Costs (2003–04) *Tuition:* area resident $2250 full-time, $75 per credit part-time; state resident $4950 full-time, $165 per credit part-time; nonresident $6300 full-time, $210 per credit part-time. Full-time tuition and fees vary according to reciprocity agreements. *Required fees:* $205 full-time, $10 per credit part-time, $30 per term part-time. *Payment plan:* installment. *Waivers:* children of alumni and employees or children of employees.

Financial Aid Of all full-time matriculated undergraduates who enrolled, 59 Federal Work-Study jobs (averaging $1421).

Applying *Options:* common application, early admission, deferred entrance. *Application fee:* $25. *Recommended:* high school transcript. *Application deadline:* rolling (freshmen), rolling (transfers). *Notification:* continuous (freshmen), continuous (transfers).

Admissions Contact Ms. Sandra S. Rajaski, Registrar, Cecil Community College, One Seahawk Drive, North East, MD 21901. *Phone:* 410-287-1004 Ext. 567. *Fax:* 410-287-1026. *E-mail:* srajaski@cecilcc.edu.

CHESAPEAKE COLLEGE
Wye Mills, Maryland

- **State and locally supported** 2-year, founded 1965
- **Calendar** semesters
- **Degree** certificates and associate
- **Rural** 170-acre campus with easy access to Baltimore and Washington, DC
- **Coed,** 2,354 undergraduate students, 31% full-time, 71% women, 29% men

Undergraduates 724 full-time, 1,630 part-time. Students come from 2 states and territories, 1% are from out of state, 21% African American, 0.9% Asian American or Pacific Islander, 1% Hispanic American, 0.2% Native American, 0.1% international, 30% transferred in.

Freshmen *Admission:* 403 enrolled.

Faculty *Total:* 137, 34% full-time, 17% with terminal degrees. *Student/faculty ratio:* 16:1.

Majors Accounting; administrative assistant and secretarial science; architectural engineering technology; art; biological and physical sciences; business administration and management; computer engineering technology; computer programming; computer science; corrections; criminal justice/law enforcement administration; data processing and data processing technology; electrical, electronic and communications engineering technology; elementary education; health teacher education; humanities; human services; kindergarten/preschool education; legal administrative assistant/secretary; liberal arts and sciences/liberal studies; mathematics; medical administrative assistant and medical secretary; medical radiologic technology; music; parks, recreation and leisure; physical education teaching and coaching; physical sciences; social sciences; sociology.

Academic Programs *Special study options:* academic remediation for entering students, adult/continuing education programs, advanced placement credit, cooperative education, distance learning, English as a second language, honors programs, independent study, internships, part-time degree program, services for LD students, student-designed majors, summer session for credit.

Library Learning Resource Center plus 1 other with 44,049 titles, 132 serial subscriptions, 1,600 audiovisual materials, an OPAC, a Web page.

Computers on Campus A campuswide network can be accessed from off campus. Internet access, online (class) registration, at least one staffed computer lab available.

Student Life *Housing:* college housing not available. *Activities and Organizations:* drama/theater group, choral group, student government action teams, Phi Theta Kappa, UHURU, Chesapeake Players. *Campus security:* 24-hour patrols. *Student services:* personal/psychological counseling, women's center.

Athletics Member NJCAA. *Intercollegiate sports:* baseball M, basketball M/W, soccer M/W, softball W, tennis M/W, volleyball W. *Intramural sports:* soccer M/W, volleyball M/W.

Costs (2003–04) *Tuition:* area resident $1800 full-time, $75 per credit hour part-time; state resident $2808 full-time, $117 per credit hour part-time; nonresident $4056 full-time, $169 per credit hour part-time. *Required fees:* $274 full-time, $10 per credit part-time, $22 per credit part-time.

Financial Aid Of all full-time matriculated undergraduates who enrolled, 40 Federal Work-Study jobs (averaging $1161).

Applying *Options:* early admission, deferred entrance. *Required:* high school transcript. *Application deadline:* rolling (freshmen), rolling (transfers). *Notification:* continuous (freshmen), continuous (transfers).

Admissions Contact Ms. Kathy Petrichenko, Director of Admissions, Chesapeake College, PO Box 8, Wye Mills, MD 21679. *Phone:* 410-822-5400 Ext. 257. *Fax:* 410-827-9466.

COLLEGE OF SOUTHERN MARYLAND
La Plata, Maryland

- **State and locally supported** 2-year, founded 1958
- **Calendar** semesters
- **Degree** certificates and associate
- **Rural** 175-acre campus with easy access to Washington, DC
- **Coed,** 7,367 undergraduate students, 34% full-time, 66% women, 34% men

Undergraduates 2,493 full-time, 4,874 part-time. Students come from 3 states and territories, 1% are from out of state, 18% African American, 3% Asian American or Pacific Islander, 3% Hispanic American, 1% Native American, 0.4% international.

Freshmen *Admission:* 2,584 applied, 2,584 admitted, 1,379 enrolled. *Average high school GPA:* 2.92.

Faculty *Total:* 435, 25% full-time, 13% with terminal degrees. *Student/faculty ratio:* 19:1.

Majors Accounting; business administration and management; computer programming; education; electrical, electronic and communications engineering technology; elementary education; engineering; human services; information science/studies; kindergarten/preschool education; legal assistant/paralegal; liberal arts and sciences/liberal studies; nursing (licensed practical/vocational nurse training); nursing (registered nurse training).

Academic Programs *Special study options:* academic remediation for entering students, accelerated degree program, adult/continuing education programs, advanced placement credit, cooperative education, distance learning, honors programs, internships, part-time degree program, services for LD students, study abroad, summer session for credit.

Library Charles County Community College Library with 34,157 titles, 238 serial subscriptions, 14,187 audiovisual materials.

Computers on Campus 130 computers available on campus for general student use. A campuswide network can be accessed. Internet access, at least one staffed computer lab available.

Student Life *Housing:* college housing not available. *Activities and Organizations:* drama/theater group, student-run newspaper, choral group, Spanish Club, Nursing Student Association, Science Club, Black Student Union, BACCHUS. *Campus security:* 24-hour emergency response devices and patrols. *Student services:* personal/psychological counseling, women's center.

Athletics Member NJCAA. *Intercollegiate sports:* baseball M, basketball M, golf M/W, soccer M/W, softball W, tennis M/W, volleyball W.

Costs (2004–05) *Tuition:* area resident $2700 full-time, $87 per credit part-time; state resident $5220 full-time, $100 per credit part-time; nonresident $6948 full-time, $200 per credit part-time.

Financial Aid Of all full-time matriculated undergraduates who enrolled, 25 Federal Work-Study jobs (averaging $1200).

Applying *Options:* early admission, deferred entrance. *Recommended:* high school transcript. *Application deadline:* rolling (freshmen), rolling (transfers). *Notification:* continuous (freshmen), continuous (transfers).

Admissions Contact Ms. Charlotte Hill, Admissions Coordinator, College of Southern Maryland, PO Box 910, La Plata, MD 20646-0910. *Phone:* 301-934-2251 Ext. 7044. *Toll-free phone:* 800-933-9177. *Fax:* 301-934-7698. *E-mail:* info@csmd.edu.

THE COMMUNITY COLLEGE OF BALTIMORE COUNTY
Baltimore, Maryland

- **County-supported** 2-year, founded 1957
- **Calendar** semesters
- **Degree** certificates and associate
- **Suburban** 350-acre campus
- **Coed,** 20,025 undergraduate students

Undergraduates 28% African American, 4% Asian American or Pacific Islander, 2% Hispanic American, 0.4% Native American, 2% international.

Faculty *Total:* 1,006, 35% full-time, 10% with terminal degrees. *Student/faculty ratio:* 20:1.

Costs (2003–04) *Tuition:* area resident $2610 full-time, $87 per hour part-time; state resident $4500 full-time, $150 per hour part-time; nonresident $6150 full-time, $205 per hour part-time. *Required fees:* $310 full-time, $310 per term part-time.

Admissions Contact Diane Drake, Director of Admissions, The Community College of Baltimore County, 800 South Rolling Road, Baltimore, MD 21228-5381. *Phone:* 410-455-4392.

FREDERICK COMMUNITY COLLEGE
Frederick, Maryland

- **State and locally supported** 2-year, founded 1957
- **Calendar** semesters
- **Degree** certificates and associate
- **Small-town** 125-acre campus with easy access to Baltimore and Washington, DC
- **Endowment** $4.0 million
- **Coed,** 4,736 undergraduate students, 38% full-time, 63% women, 37% men

Undergraduates 1,791 full-time, 2,945 part-time. Students come from 9 states and territories, 1% are from out of state, 7% African American, 2% Asian American or Pacific Islander, 2% Hispanic American, 0.5% Native American.

Freshmen *Admission:* 917 applied, 917 admitted.

Faculty *Total:* 326, 24% full-time.

Majors Accounting; administrative assistant and secretarial science; agricultural business and management; agriculture; art; avionics maintenance technology; biology/biological sciences; business administration and management; chemistry; child development; computer engineering technology; construction management; criminal justice/law enforcement administration; data processing and data processing technology; drafting and design technology; education; electrical, electronic and communications engineering technology; elementary education; engineering; English; finance; human services; international business/trade/commerce; kindergarten/preschool education; legal administrative assistant/secretary; legal assistant/paralegal; liberal arts and sciences/liberal studies; marketing/marketing management; mass communication/media; mathematics; medical administrative assistant and medical secretary; medical laboratory technology; music teacher education; nursing (registered nurse training); parks, recreation and leisure; parks, recreation and leisure facilities management; physical education teaching and coaching; physical sciences; psychology; respiratory care therapy; wildlife and wildlands science and management.

Academic Programs *Special study options:* academic remediation for entering students, adult/continuing education programs, advanced placement credit,

Frederick Community College (continued)
cooperative education, distance learning, external degree program, honors programs, independent study, off-campus study, part-time degree program, services for LD students, study abroad, summer session for credit. *ROTC:* Army (c).

Library FCC Library with 40,000 titles, 5,150 serial subscriptions, 1,400 audiovisual materials, an OPAC, a Web page.

Computers on Campus A campuswide network can be accessed from off campus. Internet access, online (class) registration, at least one staffed computer lab available.

Student Life *Housing:* college housing not available. *Activities and Organizations:* drama/theater group, student-run newspaper. *Campus security:* 24-hour emergency response devices and patrols. *Student services:* personal/psychological counseling.

Athletics Member NJCAA. *Intercollegiate sports:* baseball M, basketball M/W, golf M/W, soccer M/W, softball W, volleyball W.

Standardized Tests *Recommended:* SAT I or ACT (for placement).

Costs (2004–05) *Tuition:* area resident $1968 full-time, $82 per credit hour part-time; state resident $4320 full-time, $180 per credit hour part-time; nonresident $5952 full-time, $248 per credit hour part-time. *Required fees:* $278 full-time, $10 per credit part-time, $18 per term part-time. *Payment plan:* deferred payment. *Waivers:* senior citizens and employees or children of employees.

Financial Aid Of all full-time matriculated undergraduates who enrolled, 25 Federal Work-Study jobs (averaging $1368). 14 state and other part-time jobs (averaging $2715).

Applying *Options:* early admission, deferred entrance. *Application deadlines:* 9/1 (freshmen), 9/1 (transfers). *Notification:* continuous (freshmen), continuous (transfers).

Admissions Contact Ms. Kathy Frawley, Associate Vice President, Registrar, Frederick Community College, Welcome and Registration Center, 7932 Opossumtown Pike. *Phone:* 301-846-2432. *Fax:* 301-624-2799.

GARRETT COLLEGE
McHenry, Maryland

- **State and locally supported** 2-year, founded 1966
- **Calendar** semesters
- **Degree** certificates and associate
- **Rural** 62-acre campus
- **Coed,** 614 undergraduate students, 61% full-time, 55% women, 45% men

Undergraduates 377 full-time, 237 part-time. Students come from 12 states and territories, 1 other country, 20% are from out of state, 7% African American, 0.4% Asian American or Pacific Islander, 0.8% Hispanic American, 0.4% Native American, 1% international, 48% transferred in, 8% live on campus.

Freshmen *Admission:* 213 enrolled.

Faculty *Total:* 50, 32% full-time, 12% with terminal degrees. *Student/faculty ratio:* 12:1.

Majors Administrative assistant and secretarial science; agricultural mechanization; art; behavioral sciences; biology/biological sciences; business administration and management; criminal justice/safety; education; elementary education; fish/game management; general studies; hotel/motel administration; liberal arts and sciences/liberal studies; mathematics; music; natural resources management and policy; parks, recreation and leisure; parks, recreation and leisure facilities management; physical education teaching and coaching; psychology; social sciences; sociology; wildlife and wildlands science and management; wildlife biology.

Academic Programs *Special study options:* academic remediation for entering students, adult/continuing education programs, advanced placement credit, distance learning, double majors, external degree program, honors programs, independent study, internships, part-time degree program, services for LD students, summer session for credit.

Library Learning Resource Center with 24,230 titles, 87 serial subscriptions, 2,151 audiovisual materials, an OPAC, a Web page.

Computers on Campus 60 computers available on campus for general student use. A campuswide network can be accessed. Internet access, at least one staffed computer lab available. Computer purchase or lease plan available.

Student Life *Housing Options:* coed. Campus housing is provided by a third party. *Activities and Organizations:* drama/theater group, student-run newspaper, Wildlife Club, Raiders of the Lost Arts, student government, national fraternities. *Student services:* personal/psychological counseling.

Athletics Member NJCAA. *Intercollegiate sports:* baseball M(s), basketball M(s)/W(s), golf M, skiing (downhill) M(c)/W(c), volleyball W(s). *Intramural sports:* softball W.

Standardized Tests *Recommended:* SAT I or ACT (for placement).

Costs (2004–05) *Tuition:* area resident $2280 full-time, $76 per credit hour part-time; state resident $5160 full-time, $172 per credit hour part-time; nonresident $6450 full-time, $215 per credit hour part-time. Full-time tuition and fees vary according to course load. Part-time tuition and fees vary according to course

load. *Required fees:* $570 full-time, $18 per credit hour part-time. *Room and board:* $4935; room only: $2510. Room and board charges vary according to board plan and housing facility. *Payment plan:* deferred payment. *Waivers:* senior citizens and employees or children of employees.

Financial Aid Of all full-time matriculated undergraduates who enrolled, 55 Federal Work-Study jobs (averaging $1018). 75 state and other part-time jobs (averaging $954).

Applying *Options:* common application, early admission, deferred entrance. *Required:* high school transcript, interview. *Application deadline:* rolling (freshmen), rolling (transfers). *Notification:* continuous (freshmen), continuous (transfers).

Admissions Contact Robin Swearengen, Coordinator of Student Assistance Center, Garrett College, 687 Mosser Road, McHenry, MD 21541. *Phone:* 301-387-3044. *Fax:* 301-387-3038. *E-mail:* admissions@garrettcollege.edu.

HAGERSTOWN BUSINESS COLLEGE
Hagerstown, Maryland

- **Proprietary** 2-year, founded 1938, part of Kaplan Higher Education Corporation
- **Calendar** trimesters
- **Degree** certificates and associate
- **Small-town** 8-acre campus with easy access to Baltimore and Washington, DC
- **Coed**

Faculty *Student/faculty ratio:* 13:1.

Student Life *Campus security:* 24-hour emergency response devices.

Costs (2003–04) *Tuition:* Contact college for current tuition, fees, and room and board expenses.

Financial Aid Of all full-time matriculated undergraduates who enrolled, 21 Federal Work-Study jobs (averaging $1343).

Applying *Options:* early admission, deferred entrance. *Application fee:* $35. *Required:* high school transcript, interview.

Admissions Contact Hagerstown Business College, 18617 Crestwood Drive, Hagerstown, MD 21742-2797. *Phone:* 301-739-2670. *Toll-free phone:* 800-422-2670. *Fax:* 301-791-7661. *E-mail:* info@hagerstownbusinesscol.org.

HAGERSTOWN COMMUNITY COLLEGE
Hagerstown, Maryland

- **State and locally supported** 2-year, founded 1946
- **Calendar** semesters
- **Degree** certificates and associate
- **Suburban** 187-acre campus with easy access to Baltimore and Washington, DC
- **Endowment** $5.0 million
- **Coed,** 3,206 undergraduate students, 35% full-time, 61% women, 39% men

Undergraduates 1,132 full-time, 2,074 part-time. Students come from 9 states and territories, 2 other countries, 22% are from out of state, 7% African American, 1% Asian American or Pacific Islander, 2% Hispanic American, 0.5% Native American, 0.1% international, 6% transferred in. *Retention:* 63% of 2002 full-time freshmen returned.

Freshmen *Admission:* 1,415 applied, 677 admitted, 677 enrolled.

Faculty *Total:* 201, 31% full-time. *Student/faculty ratio:* 16:1.

Majors Accounting technology and bookkeeping; business administration and management; business/commerce; child care and support services management; commercial and advertising art; computer and information sciences; criminal justice/police science; education; electromechanical technology; elementary education; emergency medical technology (EMT paramedic); engineering; liberal arts and sciences and humanities related; liberal arts and sciences/liberal studies; management information systems; mechanical engineering/mechanical technology; medical radiologic technology; nursing (registered nurse training); psychiatric/mental health services technology.

Academic Programs *Special study options:* academic remediation for entering students, accelerated degree program, adult/continuing education programs, advanced placement credit, cooperative education, distance learning, honors programs, independent study, internships, off-campus study, part-time degree program, services for LD students, student-designed majors, summer session for credit.

Library William Brish Library with 45,705 titles, 228 serial subscriptions, 1,585 audiovisual materials, an OPAC, a Web page.

Computers on Campus 500 computers available on campus for general student use. A campuswide network can be accessed from off campus. Internet access, online (class) registration, at least one staffed computer lab available. Computer purchase or lease plan available.

Student Life *Housing:* college housing not available. *Activities and Organizations:* drama/theater group, student-run newspaper, choral group, Phi Theta

Kappa, Robinwood Players, Association of Nursing Students, Theta Lambda Upsilon, Art Club. *Campus security:* 24-hour patrols. *Student services:* health clinic, personal/psychological counseling.
Athletics Member NJCAA. *Intercollegiate sports:* baseball M(s), basketball M(s)/W(s), cross-country running M(s)/W(s), golf M/W, soccer M(s)/W(s), softball W(s), track and field M(s)/W(s), volleyball W(s). *Intramural sports:* cheerleading M/W, golf M/W, lacrosse M/W, table tennis M/W, tennis M/W.
Standardized Tests *Required for some:* ACT (for admission).
Costs (2003–04) *Tuition:* area resident $2430 full-time, $81 per credit hour part-time; state resident $3900 full-time, $130 per credit hour part-time; nonresident $5130 full-time, $171 per credit hour part-time. Full-time tuition and fees vary according to course load. Part-time tuition and fees vary according to course load. *Required fees:* $220 full-time, $7 per credit hour part-time. *Payment plan:* installment. *Waivers:* senior citizens and employees or children of employees.
Financial Aid Of all full-time matriculated undergraduates who enrolled, 27 Federal Work-Study jobs (averaging $2955).
Applying *Options:* common application, early admission, deferred entrance. *Required for some:* high school transcript, minimum 2.0 GPA, ACT composite score of 21, 1 lab chemistry and algebra for admission into nursing and radiography programs. *Application deadline:* rolling (freshmen), rolling (transfers). *Notification:* continuous (freshmen), continuous (transfers).
Admissions Contact Dr. Daniel Bock, Assistant Director, Admissions, Records and Registration, Hagerstown Community College, 11400 Robinwood Drive, Hagerstown, MD 21742-6590. *Phone:* 301-790-2800 Ext. 335. *Fax:* 301-791-4165. *E-mail:* mattosk@hagerstowncc.edu.

HARFORD COMMUNITY COLLEGE
Bel Air, Maryland

- **State and locally supported** 2-year, founded 1957
- **Calendar** semesters
- **Degree** certificates, diplomas, and associate
- **Small-town** 331-acre campus with easy access to Baltimore
- **Endowment** $3.2 million
- **Coed,** 5,525 undergraduate students, 40% full-time, 62% women, 38% men

Undergraduates 2,222 full-time, 3,303 part-time. Students come from 6 states and territories, 14 other countries, 1% are from out of state, 11% African American, 2% Asian American or Pacific Islander, 3% Hispanic American, 0.5% Native American, 1% international, 44% transferred in. *Retention:* 66% of 2002 full-time freshmen returned.
Freshmen *Admission:* 1,080 enrolled.
Faculty *Total:* 295, 30% full-time. *Student/faculty ratio:* 21:1.
Majors Accounting technology and bookkeeping; administrative assistant and secretarial science; audio engineering; business administration and management; business/commerce; child care and support services management; commercial and advertising art; communications technologies and support services related; computer and information sciences; education; electroneurodiagnostic/electroencephalographic technology; elementary education; engineering; engineering technologies related; environmental engineering technology; interior design; legal assistant/paralegal; liberal arts and sciences and humanities related; liberal arts and sciences/liberal studies; management information systems; mechanical engineering/mechanical technology; medical laboratory technology; multi-/interdisciplinary studies related; nursing (registered nurse training); philosophy; political science and government; psychology; science technologies related; security and loss prevention.
Academic Programs *Special study options:* academic remediation for entering students, adult/continuing education programs, advanced placement credit, cooperative education, English as a second language, internships, part-time degree program, services for LD students, student-designed majors, summer session for credit.
Library Learning Resources Center with 74,731 titles, 422 serial subscriptions, 6,700 audiovisual materials, an OPAC, a Web page.
Computers on Campus 267 computers available on campus for general student use. A campuswide network can be accessed from off campus. Internet access, at least one staffed computer lab available.
Student Life *Housing:* college housing not available. *Activities and Organizations:* drama/theater group, student-run newspaper, radio station, choral group, Student Association, Paralegal Club, Multi-National Students Association, Student Nurses Association, Video Club. *Campus security:* 24-hour patrols, late-night transport/escort service. *Student services:* personal/psychological counseling.
Athletics Member NJCAA. *Intercollegiate sports:* baseball M(s), basketball M/W(s), field hockey W(s), lacrosse M/W(s), soccer M/W, softball W(s), tennis M/W(s), volleyball M/W. *Intramural sports:* lacrosse W(c).
Costs (2003–04) *Tuition:* area resident $2250 full-time, $75 per credit part-time; state resident $4500 full-time, $150 per credit part-time; nonresident $6750 full-time, $225 per credit part-time. Full-time tuition and fees vary according to course load. *Required fees:* $225 full-time, $8 per credit part-time. *Payment plan:* installment. *Waivers:* employees or children of employees.

Financial Aid Of all full-time matriculated undergraduates who enrolled, 55 Federal Work-Study jobs (averaging $1800).
Applying *Options:* early admission, deferred entrance. *Application deadline:* rolling (freshmen), rolling (transfers). *Notification:* continuous (transfers).
Admissions Contact Ms. Donna Strasavich, Enrollment Specialist, Harford Community College, 401 Thomas Run Road, Bel Air, MD 21015-1698. *Phone:* 410-836-4311. *Fax:* 410-836-4169. *E-mail:* sendinfo@harford.edu.

HOWARD COMMUNITY COLLEGE
Columbia, Maryland

- **State and locally supported** 2-year, founded 1966
- **Calendar** semesters
- **Degree** certificates and associate
- **Suburban** 122-acre campus with easy access to Baltimore and Washington, DC
- **Endowment** $2.0 million
- **Coed,** 6,435 undergraduate students

Undergraduates Students come from 4 states and territories, 1% are from out of state, 20% African American, 9% Asian American or Pacific Islander, 4% Hispanic American, 0.4% Native American.
Faculty *Total:* 369, 25% full-time, 10% with terminal degrees. *Student/faculty ratio:* 16:1.
Majors Accounting; administrative assistant and secretarial science; applied art; architecture; art; biological and physical sciences; biomedical technology; biotechnology; business administration and management; cardiovascular technology; child development; clinical laboratory science/medical technology; computer and information sciences related; computer graphics; computer/information technology services administration related; computer science; computer systems networking and telecommunications; consumer merchandising/retailing management; criminal justice/law enforcement administration; data entry/microcomputer applications; dramatic/theatre arts; electrical, electronic and communications engineering technology; elementary education; emergency medical technology (EMT paramedic); engineering; environmental studies; fashion merchandising; financial planning and services; general studies; health teacher education; information science/studies; information technology; kindergarten/preschool education; legal administrative assistant/secretary; liberal arts and sciences/liberal studies; medical administrative assistant and medical secretary; music; nuclear medical technology; nursing (licensed practical/vocational nurse training); nursing (registered nurse training); office management; ophthalmic/optometric services; photography; physical sciences; pre-dentistry studies; pre-medical studies; pre-pharmacy studies; pre-veterinary studies; psychology; secondary education; social sciences; sport and fitness administration; substance abuse/addiction counseling; telecommunications; theatre design and technology.
Academic Programs *Special study options:* academic remediation for entering students, adult/continuing education programs, advanced placement credit, cooperative education, distance learning, double majors, English as a second language, honors programs, off-campus study, part-time degree program, services for LD students, summer session for credit.
Library Howard Community College Library with 40,380 titles, 1,201 serial subscriptions, 6,253 audiovisual materials, an OPAC, a Web page.
Computers on Campus 750 computers available on campus for general student use. Internet access, online (class) registration, at least one staffed computer lab available.
Student Life *Housing:* college housing not available. *Activities and Organizations:* drama/theater group, student-run newspaper, choral group, Secretarial Club, Nursing Club, Black Leadership Organization, student newspaper, Student Government Association. *Campus security:* 24-hour emergency response devices and patrols, late-night transport/escort service. *Student services:* personal/psychological counseling.
Athletics Member NJCAA. *Intercollegiate sports:* basketball M/W, cross-country running M/W, lacrosse M, soccer M/W, tennis M/W, track and field M/W, volleyball W. *Intramural sports:* basketball M/W, lacrosse M, softball W.
Standardized Tests *Required for some:* SAT I or ACT (for admission).
Costs (2004–05) *Tuition:* area resident $3000 full-time, $100 per credit part-time; state resident $5490 full-time, $183 per credit part-time; nonresident $6840 full-time, $228 per credit part-time. *Required fees:* $408 full-time, $14 per credit part-time.
Applying *Options:* electronic application, early admission, deferred entrance. *Application fee:* $15. *Required for some:* essay or personal statement, high school transcript, minimum 3.0 GPA, 2 letters of recommendation, interview. *Application deadline:* rolling (freshmen), rolling (transfers). *Notification:* continuous (freshmen), continuous (transfers).
Admissions Contact Mr. John Kvach, Assistant Director of Admissions, Howard Community College, 10901 Little Patuxent Parkway, Columbia, MD 21044-3197. *Phone:* 410-772-4856. *Fax:* 410-772-4589. *E-mail:* mamiller@howardcc.edu.

MONTGOMERY COLLEGE
Rockville, Maryland

- **State and locally supported** 2-year
- **Calendar** semesters
- **Degree** certificates and associate
- **Suburban** campus with easy access to Washington D.C.
- **Coed,** 21,805 undergraduate students, 36% full-time, 57% women, 43% men

Undergraduates 7,748 full-time, 14,057 part-time. Students come from 169 other countries, 3% are from out of state, 27% African American, 13% Asian American or Pacific Islander, 14% Hispanic American, 0.2% Native American, 8% international, 40% transferred in.
Freshmen *Admission:* 2,368 enrolled.
Faculty *Total:* 1,308, 33% full-time, 25% with terminal degrees. *Student/faculty ratio:* 20:1.
Majors Accounting technology and bookkeeping; applied horticulture; architectural drafting and CAD/CADD; automobile/automotive mechanics technology; business administration and management; business/commerce; child care and support services management; civil engineering technology; commercial and advertising art; commercial photography; computer and information sciences; computer technology/computer systems technology; construction management; criminal justice/police science; diagnostic medical sonography and ultrasound technology; education; electrical, electronic and communications engineering technology; electromechanical technology; engineering; fire protection and safety technology; general studies; graphic and printing equipment operation/production; health information/medical records technology; hotel/motel administration; legal assistant/paralegal; liberal arts and sciences/liberal studies; management information systems; medical radiologic technology; nursing (registered nurse training); physical therapist assistant; psychiatric/mental health services technology.
Student Life *Housing:* college housing not available. *Activities and Organizations:* drama/theater group, student-run newspaper, radio station, choral group. *Campus security:* 24-hour emergency response devices and patrols, late-night transport/escort service. *Student services:* personal/psychological counseling, women's center.
Athletics Member NJCAA. *Intercollegiate sports:* baseball M/W, basketball M/W, cross-country running M/W, golf M, soccer M/W, swimming M/W, tennis M/W, track and field M/W, volleyball W. *Intramural sports:* baseball M/W, basketball M/W, bowling M/W, cross-country running M/W, fencing M/W, football M/W, golf M/W, soccer M/W, swimming M/W, tennis M/W, volleyball M/W.
Costs (2003–04) *Tuition:* area resident $2580 full-time, $86 per credit part-time; state resident $5310 full-time, $177 per credit part-time; nonresident $7080 full-time, $236 per credit part-time. *Required fees:* $756 full-time, $8 per credit part-time. *Payment plan:* installment. *Waivers:* children of alumni, senior citizens, and employees or children of employees.
Financial Aid Of all full-time matriculated undergraduates who enrolled, 216 Federal Work-Study jobs (averaging $3050). 250 state and other part-time jobs (averaging $2000).
Applying *Options:* common application. *Application fee:* $25. *Application deadline:* rolling (freshmen), rolling (transfers). *Notification:* continuous (freshmen), continuous (transfers).
Admissions Contact Mr. Sherman Helberg, Acting Director of Admissions and Enrollment, Montgomery College, 51 Mannakee Street, Rockville, MD 20850. *Phone:* 301-279-5034.

PRINCE GEORGE'S COMMUNITY COLLEGE
Largo, Maryland

- **County-supported** 2-year, founded 1958
- **Calendar** semesters plus 2 summer sessions
- **Degree** certificates and associate
- **Suburban** 150-acre campus with easy access to Washington, DC
- **Coed,** 12,564 undergraduate students, 27% full-time, 66% women, 34% men

Undergraduates 3,352 full-time, 9,212 part-time. Students come from 20 states and territories, 98 other countries, 4% are from out of state, 76% African American, 4% Asian American or Pacific Islander, 3% Hispanic American, 0.5% Native American, 3% international, 13% transferred in. *Retention:* 58% of 2002 full-time freshmen returned.
Freshmen *Admission:* 4,570 applied, 4,570 admitted, 2,193 enrolled.
Faculty *Total:* 639, 39% full-time, 23% with terminal degrees. *Student/faculty ratio:* 18:1.
Majors Accounting; aerospace, aeronautical and astronautical engineering; business administration and management; business teacher education; computer engineering technology; computer management; computer programming; computer science; computer typography and composition equipment operation;

criminal justice/law enforcement administration; drafting and design technology; education; electrical, electronic and communications engineering technology; elementary education; emergency medical technology (EMT paramedic); engineering; forensic science and technology; health information/medical records administration; health teacher education; information science/studies; kindergarten/preschool education; legal assistant/paralegal; liberal arts and sciences/liberal studies; marketing/marketing management; medical office management; nuclear medical technology; nursing (registered nurse training); physical education teaching and coaching; radiologic technology/science; respiratory care therapy.
Academic Programs *Special study options:* academic remediation for entering students, adult/continuing education programs, advanced placement credit, cooperative education, distance learning, English as a second language, external degree program, honors programs, part-time degree program, services for LD students, summer session for credit. *ROTC:* Army (c).
Library Accokeek Hall with 242,519 titles, 750 serial subscriptions, 16,645 audiovisual materials, an OPAC.
Computers on Campus 450 computers available on campus for general student use. A campuswide network can be accessed from off campus. Internet access, online (class) registration, at least one staffed computer lab available.
Student Life *Housing:* college housing not available. *Activities and Organizations:* drama/theater group, student-run newspaper, choral group, Crusaders for Christ, Student Program Board, Union of Black Scholars, International Student Groups. *Campus security:* 24-hour emergency response devices and patrols, late-night transport/escort service. *Student services:* health clinic, personal/psychological counseling.
Athletics Member NJCAA. *Intercollegiate sports:* baseball M, basketball M/W, bowling M/W, golf M, soccer M/W, softball W, tennis M/W, volleyball W. *Intramural sports:* basketball M/W, tennis M/W, volleyball W.
Standardized Tests *Required for some:* ACCUPLACER.
Costs (2004–05) *Tuition:* area resident $2808 full-time, $90 per hour part-time; state resident $4464 full-time, $159 per credit part-time; nonresident $6528 full-time, $245 per credit part-time. *Required fees:* $74 full-time, $1 per hour part-time, $25 per semester part-time.
Financial Aid Of all full-time matriculated undergraduates who enrolled, 99 Federal Work-Study jobs (averaging $2000).
Applying *Options:* early admission. *Application fee:* $25. *Required for some:* high school transcript. *Recommended:* minimum 2.0 GPA. *Application deadline:* rolling (freshmen), rolling (transfers). *Notification:* continuous (freshmen), continuous (transfers).
Admissions Contact Ms. Vera Bagley, Director of Admissions and Records, Prince George's Community College, 301 Largo Road, Largo, MD 20774-2199. *Phone:* 301-322-0801. *Fax:* 301-322-0119.

TESST COLLEGE OF TECHNOLOGY
Baltimore, Maryland

Admissions Contact Ms. Susan Sherwood, Director, TESST College of Technology, 1520 South Caton Avenue, Baltimore, MD 21227-1063. *Phone:* 410-644-6400.

TESST COLLEGE OF TECHNOLOGY
Beltsville, Maryland

Admissions Contact Mr. Reginald M. Morton, Executive Director, TESST College of Technology, 4600 Powder Mill Road, Beltsville, MD 20705. *Phone:* 301-937-8448.

TESST COLLEGE OF TECHNOLOGY
Towson, Maryland

Admissions Contact Mr. Ray Joll, Executive Director, TESST College of Technology, 803 Glen Eagles Court, Towson, MD 21286-2201. *Phone:* 410-296-5350.

WOR-WIC COMMUNITY COLLEGE
Salisbury, Maryland

- **State and locally supported** 2-year, founded 1976, part of Maryland State Community Colleges System
- **Calendar** semesters
- **Degree** certificates and associate
- **Small-town** 202-acre campus
- **Endowment** $2.3 million
- **Coed,** 3,007 undergraduate students, 30% full-time, 69% women, 31% men

Undergraduates 899 full-time, 2,108 part-time. Students come from 12 states and territories, 3% are from out of state, 23% African American, 1% Asian American or Pacific Islander, 1% Hispanic American, 0.6% Native American, 7% transferred in.

Freshmen *Admission:* 959 applied, 959 admitted, 614 enrolled.
Faculty *Total:* 186, 28% full-time, 11% with terminal degrees. *Student/faculty ratio:* 20:1.
Majors Accounting technology and bookkeeping; administrative assistant and secretarial science; business administration and management; business/commerce; child care and support services management; computer and information sciences; computer systems analysis; criminal justice/police science; education; electrical, electronic and communications engineering technology; elementary education; emergency medical technology (EMT paramedic); engineering technologies related; hospitality administration; liberal arts and sciences and humanities related; medical radiologic technology; nursing (registered nurse training); substance abuse/addiction counseling.
Academic Programs *Special study options:* academic remediation for entering students, accelerated degree program, adult/continuing education programs, advanced placement credit, distance learning, double majors, English as a second language, honors programs, independent study, internships, part-time degree program, services for LD students, summer session for credit.
Library Electronic Media Center plus 2 others with 9 titles, 272 audiovisual materials, a Web page.
Computers on Campus 450 computers available on campus for general student use. A campuswide network can be accessed from off campus. Internet access, at least one staffed computer lab available.
Student Life *Housing:* college housing not available. *Activities and Organizations:* drama/theater group, student-run newspaper, choral group, Student Government Association, Arts Club, Bioneer Club, Future Educators of America Club, student newspaper. *Campus security:* 24-hour emergency response devices, late-night transport/escort service, patrols by trained security personnel 9 a.m. to midnight. *Student services:* personal/psychological counseling.
Standardized Tests *Required for some:* ACT (for admission).
Costs (2004–05) *Tuition:* area resident $1680 full-time, $70 per credit hour part-time; state resident $4224 full-time, $176 per credit hour part-time; nonresident $4944 full-time, $206 per credit hour part-time. *Required fees:* $50 full-time, $1 per credit hour part-time, $13 per term part-time. *Payment plan:* deferred payment. *Waivers:* senior citizens and employees or children of employees.
Applying *Options:* early admission. *Recommended:* high school transcript. *Application deadline:* rolling (freshmen), rolling (transfers).
Admissions Contact Mr. Richard Webster, Director of Admissions, Wor-Wic Community College, 32000 Campus Drive, Salisbury, MD 21804. *Phone:* 410-334-2895. *Fax:* 410-334-2954. *E-mail:* admissions@worwic.edu.

MASSACHUSETTS

BAY STATE COLLEGE
Boston, Massachusetts

- **Independent** 2-year, founded 1946
- **Calendar** semesters
- **Degree** associate
- **Urban** campus
- **Coed,** 757 undergraduate students, 69% full-time, 78% women, 22% men

Undergraduates 522 full-time, 235 part-time. Students come from 11 states and territories, 11 other countries, 11% are from out of state, 18% African American, 8% Asian American or Pacific Islander, 10% Hispanic American, 0.9% international, 21% live on campus. *Retention:* 50% of 2002 full-time freshmen returned.
Freshmen *Admission:* 1,405 applied, 1,119 admitted. *Average high school GPA:* 2.00.
Faculty *Total:* 66, 29% full-time. *Student/faculty ratio:* 12:1.
Majors Accounting; administrative assistant and secretarial science; business administration and management; consumer merchandising/retailing management; fashion/apparel design; fashion merchandising; hospitality administration; hotel/motel administration; kindergarten/preschool education; legal administrative assistant/secretary; legal studies; liberal arts and sciences/liberal studies; medical administrative assistant and medical secretary; medical/clinical assistant; occupational therapy; physical therapy; tourism and travel services management.
Academic Programs *Special study options:* academic remediation for entering students, adult/continuing education programs, advanced placement credit, cooperative education, English as a second language, independent study, internships, part-time degree program.
Library Bay State College Library with 4,490 titles, 262 serial subscriptions, 471 audiovisual materials, an OPAC.
Computers on Campus 55 computers available on campus for general student use. A campuswide network can be accessed. At least one staffed computer lab available.

Student Life *Housing Options:* coed, women-only. Campus housing is provided by a third party. *Activities and Organizations:* Activities Club, Hospitality Travel Association, Fashion Club, Early Childhood Education Club, Student Medical Assisting Society. *Campus security:* late-night transport/escort service, controlled dormitory access, 14-hour patrols by trained security personnel. *Student services:* personal/psychological counseling.
Costs (2004–05) *Comprehensive fee:* $24,750 includes full-time tuition ($14,900), mandatory fees ($350), and room and board ($9500). Part-time tuition: $220 per credit.
Financial Aid Of all full-time matriculated undergraduates who enrolled, 20 Federal Work-Study jobs (averaging $2600).
Applying *Options:* common application, early admission. *Application fee:* $25. *Required:* essay or personal statement, high school transcript. *Recommended:* minimum 2.0 GPA, interview. *Application deadline:* rolling (freshmen), rolling (transfers).
Admissions Contact Ms. Pam Notemyer-Rogers, Director of Admissions, Bay State College, 122 Commonwealth Avenue, Boston, MA 02116. *Phone:* 617-236-8006. *Toll-free phone:* 800-81-LEARN. *Fax:* 617-536-1735. *E-mail:* admissions@baystate.edu.

▶ See page 512 for a narrative description.

BENJAMIN FRANKLIN INSTITUTE OF TECHNOLOGY
Boston, Massachusetts

- **Independent** primarily 2-year, founded 1908
- **Calendar** semesters
- **Degrees** certificates, associate, and bachelor's
- **Urban** 3-acre campus
- **Endowment** $8.0 million
- **Coed, primarily men**

Faculty *Student/faculty ratio:* 11:1.
Student Life *Campus security:* 24-hour emergency response devices, student patrols.
Standardized Tests *Recommended:* SAT I or ACT (for admission).
Costs (2003–04) *Tuition:* $11,950 full-time, $498 per credit part-time. *Required fees:* $339 full-time. *Room only:* Room and board charges vary according to board plan and housing facility.
Applying *Options:* common application, electronic application, deferred entrance. *Application fee:* $20. *Required:* high school transcript. *Recommended:* essay or personal statement, minimum 2.0 GPA, letters of recommendation, interview.
Admissions Contact Mr. Will Arvelo, Dean of Enrollment Services, Benjamin Franklin Institute of Technology, 41 Berkeley Street, Boston, MA 02116-6296. *Phone:* 617-423-4630 Ext. 122. *Fax:* 617-482-3706. *E-mail:* fibadm@fib.edu.

▶ See page 514 for a narrative description.

BERKSHIRE COMMUNITY COLLEGE
Pittsfield, Massachusetts

- **State-supported** 2-year, founded 1960, part of Massachusetts Public Higher Education System
- **Calendar** semesters
- **Degree** certificates and associate
- **Suburban** 100-acre campus
- **Endowment** $56,429
- **Coed,** 2,272 undergraduate students, 41% full-time, 64% women, 36% men

Undergraduates 929 full-time, 1,343 part-time. Students come from 6 states and territories, 20 other countries, 4% are from out of state, 4% African American, 1% Asian American or Pacific Islander, 3% Hispanic American, 0.5% Native American, 3% international, 6% transferred in.
Freshmen *Admission:* 414 applied, 414 admitted, 414 enrolled.
Faculty *Total:* 160, 34% full-time, 74% with terminal degrees. *Student/faculty ratio:* 13:1.
Majors Administrative assistant and secretarial science; business administration and management; business automation/technology/data entry; business/commerce; community organization and advocacy; computer and information sciences; criminal justice/safety; electrical, electronic and communications engineering technology; engineering; environmental science; fire science; health professions related; hospitality administration; liberal arts and sciences/liberal studies; nursing (registered nurse training); physical therapist assistant; respiratory care therapy; visual and performing arts.
Academic Programs *Special study options:* academic remediation for entering students, adult/continuing education programs, advanced placement credit, distance learning, double majors, English as a second language, honors pro-

Berkshire Community College (continued)

grams, independent study, internships, off-campus study, part-time degree program, services for LD students, summer session for credit.

Library Jonathan Edwards Library plus 1 other with 72,319 titles, 329 serial subscriptions, 3,247 audiovisual materials, an OPAC, a Web page.

Computers on Campus 417 computers available on campus for general student use. A campuswide network can be accessed from off campus. Internet access, at least one staffed computer lab available. Computer purchase or lease plan available.

Student Life *Housing:* college housing not available. *Activities and Organizations:* drama/theater group, choral group, Mass PIRG, Student Nurse Organization, Student Senate, Diversity Club, LPN Organization. *Campus security:* 24-hour emergency response devices and patrols. *Student services:* personal/psychological counseling.

Athletics Member NJCAA.

Standardized Tests *Required:* ACCUPLACER (for placement).

Costs (2003–04) *Tuition:* state resident $780 full-time, $26 per credit part-time; nonresident $7800 full-time, $260 per credit part-time. Full-time tuition and fees vary according to course load. Part-time tuition and fees vary according to course load. *Required fees:* $2610 full-time, $87 per credit part-time. *Payment plan:* installment. *Waivers:* employees or children of employees.

Financial Aid Of all full-time matriculated undergraduates who enrolled, 72 Federal Work-Study jobs (averaging $1600).

Applying *Options:* common application, early admission, deferred entrance. *Application fee:* $10. *Required:* high school transcript. *Recommended:* interview. *Application deadline:* rolling (freshmen), rolling (transfers). *Notification:* continuous (freshmen), continuous (transfers).

Admissions Contact Ms. Margo J. Handschu, Admissions Counselor, Berkshire Community College, 1350 West Street, Pittsfield, MA 01201-5786. *Phone:* 413-499-4660 Ext. 425. *Toll-free phone:* 800-816-1233 Ext. 242. *Fax:* 413-496-9511. *E-mail:* admissions@berkshirecc.edu.

BOSTON BAPTIST COLLEGE

Boston, Massachusetts

- **Independent Baptist** primarily 2-year, founded 1976
- **Calendar** semesters
- **Degrees** certificates, diplomas, associate, and bachelor's
- **Suburban** 8-acre campus with easy access to Providence
- **Coed**

Student Life *Campus security:* 24-hour emergency response devices, student patrols.

Standardized Tests *Required:* SAT I or ACT (for admission).

Costs (2003–04) *Comprehensive fee:* $9970 includes full-time tuition ($3850), mandatory fees ($1480), and room and board ($4640). Part-time tuition: $150 per credit hour. *Required fees:* $715 per term part-time. *Room and board:* college room only: $2760.

Applying *Options:* common application. *Application fee:* $25. *Required:* essay or personal statement, high school transcript, letters of recommendation. *Recommended:* interview.

Admissions Contact Mr. James Thomasson, Director of Admissions and Records, Boston Baptist College, 950 Metropolitan Avenue, Boston, MA 02136. *Phone:* 617-364-3510 Ext. 215. *Toll-free phone:* 888-235-2014. *Fax:* 617-364-0723.

BRISTOL COMMUNITY COLLEGE

Fall River, Massachusetts

- **State-supported** 2-year, founded 1965
- **Calendar** semesters
- **Degree** certificates and associate
- **Urban** 105-acre campus with easy access to Boston
- **Coed**, 6,639 undergraduate students, 44% full-time, 63% women, 37% men

Undergraduates 2,901 full-time, 3,738 part-time. Students come from 7 states and territories, 25 other countries, 9% are from out of state, 5% African American, 2% Asian American or Pacific Islander, 3% Hispanic American, 0.5% Native American, 0.8% international, 5% transferred in. *Retention:* 67% of 2002 full-time freshmen returned.

Freshmen *Admission:* 4,172 applied, 3,280 admitted, 1,451 enrolled.

Faculty *Total:* 432, 24% full-time. *Student/faculty ratio:* 19:1.

Majors Accounting; applied art; banking and financial support services; business administration and management; business automation/technology/data entry; business, management, and marketing related; business operations support and secretarial services related; business teacher education; child care/guidance; civil engineering related; civil engineering technology; clinical/medical laboratory technology; communication disorders sciences and services related; communication/speech communication and rhetoric; communications systems

installation and repair technology; computer and information sciences; computer and information sciences related; computer programming; computer programming (specific applications); computer science; computer typography and composition equipment operation; cosmetology and personal grooming arts related; criminal justice/safety; data processing and data processing technology; dental hygiene; design and visual communications; dramatic/theatre arts and stagecraft related; early childhood education; electrical, electronic and communications engineering technology; electrical/electronics equipment installation and repair; elementary education; engineering; engineering related; engineering science; engineering technologies related; entrepreneurship; environmental engineering technology; environmental/environmental health engineering; environmental science; environmental studies; finance and financial management services related; fine/studio arts; fire science; fishing and fisheries sciences and management; general studies; graphic design; health information/medical records technology; humanities; human services; information science/studies; information technology; intermedia/multimedia; legal administrative assistant/secretary; liberal arts and sciences/liberal studies; management information systems; manufacturing engineering; marketing/marketing management; mathematics and statistics related; mechanical engineering; medical administrative assistant and medical secretary; nursing (registered nurse training); occupational therapist assistant; occupational therapy; real estate; receptionist; social sciences; social work; structural engineering; visual and performing arts; water quality and wastewater treatment management and recycling technology; water resources engineering.

Academic Programs *Special study options:* academic remediation for entering students, adult/continuing education programs, cooperative education, distance learning, English as a second language, honors programs, independent study, internships, off-campus study, part-time degree program, services for LD students, student-designed majors, summer session for credit.

Library Learning Resources Center with 65,000 titles, 380 serial subscriptions, an OPAC, a Web page.

Computers on Campus 150 computers available on campus for general student use. A campuswide network can be accessed from off campus. Internet access, at least one staffed computer lab available.

Student Life *Housing:* college housing not available. *Activities and Organizations:* drama/theater group, student-run newspaper, International Club, MASS/PIRG WaterWatch, Criminal Justice Society, Society for Students in Free Enterprise, Portuguese Club. *Campus security:* 24-hour emergency response devices and patrols, student patrols, late-night transport/escort service. *Student services:* health clinic, personal/psychological counseling, women's center.

Standardized Tests *Required for some:* SAT I (for admission).

Costs (2004–05) *Tuition:* state resident $576 full-time, $24 per credit part-time; nonresident $7656 full-time, $230 per credit part-time. Full-time tuition and fees vary according to course load. Part-time tuition and fees vary according to course load. *Required fees:* $2136 full-time, $82 per credit part-time, $30 per term part-time. *Payment plan:* installment. *Waivers:* senior citizens and employees or children of employees.

Financial Aid Of all full-time matriculated undergraduates who enrolled, 205 Federal Work-Study jobs (averaging $1627). 65 state and other part-time jobs (averaging $1478).

Applying *Options:* common application. *Application fee:* $10. *Required:* high school transcript. *Notification:* continuous (freshmen), continuous (transfers).

Admissions Contact Mr. Rodney S. Clark, Director of Admissions, Bristol Community College, 777 Elsbree Street, Hudnall Administration Building, Fall River, MA 02720. *Phone:* 508-678-2811 Ext. 2516. *Fax:* 508-730-3265. *E-mail:* rclark@bristol.mass.edu.

BUNKER HILL COMMUNITY COLLEGE

Boston, Massachusetts

- **State-supported** 2-year, founded 1973
- **Calendar** semesters
- **Degree** certificates and associate
- **Urban** 21-acre campus
- **Endowment** $1.3 million
- **Coed**, 7,397 undergraduate students, 35% full-time, 60% women, 40% men

Undergraduates 2,577 full-time, 4,820 part-time. Students come from 11 states and territories, 92 other countries, 1% are from out of state, 26% African American, 14% Asian American or Pacific Islander, 14% Hispanic American, 0.5% Native American, 9% international, 3% transferred in.

Freshmen *Admission:* 3,746 applied, 2,434 admitted, 1,237 enrolled.

Faculty *Total:* 345, 33% full-time. *Student/faculty ratio:* 17:1.

Majors Accounting; art; business administration and management; cardiovascular technology; chemistry; communication/speech communication and rhetoric; computer and information sciences and support services related; computer programming; computer programming (specific applications); computer science; computer systems networking and telecommunications; criminal justice/law enforcement administration; culinary arts; data entry/microcomputer applications; design and visual communications; dramatic/theatre arts; early childhood education; education; electrical/electronics maintenance and repair technology related; English; finance; fire protection and safety technology; general studies; health information/medical records administration; history; hospitality administration; hotel/motel administration; human services; international business/trade/commerce; mass communication/media; mathematics; medical radiologic technology; nursing (registered nurse training); operations management; physics; psychology; sociology; tourism and travel services management; web page, digital/multimedia and information resources design.

Academic Programs *Special study options:* academic remediation for entering students, advanced placement credit, cooperative education, distance learning, English as a second language, external degree program, honors programs, independent study, internships, part-time degree program, services for LD students, study abroad, summer session for credit.

Library Bunker Hill Community College Library with 59,946 titles, 253 serial subscriptions, 339 audiovisual materials, an OPAC, a Web page.

Computers on Campus 555 computers available on campus for general student use. A campuswide network can be accessed from off campus. Internet access, online (class) registration, at least one staffed computer lab available.

Student Life *Housing:* college housing not available. *Activities and Organizations:* drama/theater group, student-run newspaper, radio station, African-American Cultural Society, Asian-Pacific Students Association, Arab Students Association, Hospitality Club, Rradio statation. *Campus security:* 24-hour emergency response devices and patrols, late-night transport/escort service. *Student services:* health clinic, personal/psychological counseling.

Athletics Member NJCAA. *Intercollegiate sports:* baseball M, basketball M/W, soccer M/W, softball W. *Intramural sports:* basketball M/W, table tennis M/W, tennis M/W.

Standardized Tests *Required for some:* nursing exam.

Costs (2003–04) *Tuition:* state resident $576 full-time, $24 per credit part-time; nonresident $5520 full-time, $230 per credit part-time. *Required fees:* $1824 full-time, $76 per credit part-time. *Payment plan:* installment. *Waivers:* minority students, senior citizens, and employees or children of employees.

Financial Aid Of all full-time matriculated undergraduates who enrolled, 116 Federal Work-Study jobs (averaging $1500).

Applying *Options:* common application, deferred entrance. *Application fee:* $10. *Required:* high school transcript. *Application deadline:* rolling (freshmen), rolling (transfers). *Notification:* continuous (freshmen), continuous (transfers).

Admissions Contact Ms. Debra Boyer, Registrar/Director of Enrollment Service, Bunker Hill Community College, BHCC Enrollment Services Center, 250 New Rutherford Avenue, Boston, MA 02129. *Phone:* 617-228-2420. *Fax:* 617-228-2082.

▶ See page 524 for a narrative description.

CAPE COD COMMUNITY COLLEGE
West Barnstable, Massachusetts

- **State-supported** 2-year, founded 1961, part of Massachusetts Public Higher Education System
- **Calendar** semesters
- **Degree** certificates and associate
- **Rural** 120-acre campus with easy access to Boston
- **Endowment** $3.8 million
- **Coed,** 4,243 undergraduate students, 35% full-time, 65% women, 35% men

Undergraduates 1,470 full-time, 2,773 part-time. Students come from 24 states and territories, 5 other countries, 1% are from out of state, 4% African American, 0.9% Asian American or Pacific Islander, 2% Hispanic American, 1% Native American, 0.9% international, 10% transferred in.

Freshmen *Admission:* 1,179 applied, 1,151 admitted, 730 enrolled.

Faculty *Total:* 331, 24% full-time, 24% with terminal degrees. *Student/faculty ratio:* 18:1.

Majors Accounting; administrative assistant and secretarial science; art; biological and physical sciences; business administration and management; computer and information sciences related; computer graphics; computer science; computer systems networking and telecommunications; criminal justice/law enforcement administration; dental hygiene; dramatic/theatre arts; education; environmental engineering technology; environmental studies; executive assistant/executive secretary; fire science; history; hotel/motel administration; information science/studies; information technology; kindergarten/preschool education; legal administrative assistant/secretary; legal assistant/paralegal; liberal arts and sciences/liberal studies; management science; mass communication/media; mathematics; medical administrative assistant and medical secretary; modern languages; music; nursing (registered nurse training); parks, recreation and leisure; philosophy; physical education teaching and coaching; physical therapist assistant; pre-engineering; psychology; system administration; web/multimedia management and webmaster; web page, digital/multimedia and information resources design.

Academic Programs *Special study options:* academic remediation for entering students, adult/continuing education programs, advanced placement credit, cooperative education, distance learning, English as a second language, fresh-

man honors college, honors programs, independent study, internships, off-campus study, part-time degree program, services for LD students, study abroad, summer session for credit.

Library Cape Cod Community College Learning Resource Center with 54,342 titles, 705 serial subscriptions, 6,107 audiovisual materials, an OPAC.

Computers on Campus 240 computers available on campus for general student use. A campuswide network can be accessed from off campus. Internet access, at least one staffed computer lab available.

Student Life *Housing:* college housing not available. *Activities and Organizations:* drama/theater group, student-run newspaper, radio station, choral group, Innkeepers Club, Phi Theta Kappa, Student Senate, Learning Disabilities Support Group, Ethnic Diversity. *Campus security:* 24-hour patrols. *Student services:* health clinic, personal/psychological counseling, women's center.

Athletics *Intramural sports:* badminton M/W, baseball M, basketball M/W, crew M/W, racquetball M/W, sailing M/W, skiing (downhill) M/W, soccer M, softball M/W, tennis M/W, volleyball M/W, weight lifting M/W.

Costs (2003–04) *Tuition:* state resident $720 full-time; nonresident $6900 full-time. *Required fees:* $2460 full-time. *Payment plan:* deferred payment. *Waivers:* senior citizens and employees or children of employees.

Financial Aid Of all full-time matriculated undergraduates who enrolled, 56 Federal Work-Study jobs (averaging $1250).

Applying *Options:* deferred entrance. *Application fee:* $10. *Required:* high school transcript. *Required for some:* essay or personal statement, letters of recommendation. *Application deadlines:* 8/10 (freshmen), 8/10 (transfers). *Notification:* continuous (freshmen), continuous (transfers).

Admissions Contact Ms. Susan Kline-Symington, Director of Admissions, Cape Cod Community College, 2240 Lyanough Road, West Barnstable, MA 02668-1599. *Phone:* 508-362-2131 Ext. 4311. *Toll-free phone:* 877-846-3672. *Fax:* 508-375-4089. *E-mail:* info@capecod.mass.edu.

DEAN COLLEGE
Franklin, Massachusetts

- **Independent** primarily 2-year, founded 1865
- **Calendar** semesters
- **Degrees** certificates, associate, and bachelor's
- **Small-town** 100-acre campus with easy access to Boston and Providence
- **Endowment** $15.5 million
- **Coed,** 1,303 undergraduate students, 67% full-time, 52% women, 48% men

Dean College offers a Bachelor of Arts (BA) degree in dance. The program includes the disciplines of tap, ballet, modern, and modern jazz dance within a broad liberal arts environment. The BA program is appropriate for students interested in teaching, arts management, movement therapy, dance journalism, and performance.

Undergraduates 868 full-time, 435 part-time. Students come from 25 states and territories, 14 other countries, 42% are from out of state, 4% African American, 0.5% Asian American or Pacific Islander, 2% Hispanic American, 0.2% Native American, 6% international, 90% live on campus.

Freshmen *Admission:* 1,532 applied, 1,137 admitted. *Average high school GPA:* 2.20. *Test scores:* SAT verbal scores over 500: 22%; SAT math scores over 500: 20%; ACT scores over 18: 74%; SAT verbal scores over 600: 4%; SAT math scores over 600: 3%; ACT scores over 24: 10%; SAT verbal scores over 700: 1%.

Faculty *Total:* 88, 30% full-time, 10% with terminal degrees. *Student/faculty ratio:* 22:1.

Majors Athletic training; business administration and management; child development; communication/speech communication and rhetoric; criminal justice/law enforcement administration; criminal justice/police science; dance; dramatic/theatre arts; health and physical education; humanities; liberal arts and sciences/liberal studies; mathematics and computer science; physical education teaching and coaching; social sciences; sport and fitness administration.

Academic Programs *Special study options:* academic remediation for entering students, accelerated degree program, adult/continuing education programs, advanced placement credit, English as a second language, freshman honors college, honors programs, independent study, internships, off-campus study, part-time degree program, services for LD students, student-designed majors, summer session for credit.

Library E. Ross Anderson Library with 46,226 titles, 185 serial subscriptions.

Computers on Campus 150 computers available on campus for general student use. A campuswide network can be accessed from student residence rooms. At least one staffed computer lab available.

Student Life *Housing:* on-campus residence required through sophomore year. *Options:* coed. Campus housing is university owned. Freshman campus housing is guaranteed. *Activities and Organizations:* drama/theater group, student-run radio station, choral group, Emerging Leaders, College Success Staff, Student Ambassadors, student government, Phi Theta Kappa. *Campus security:* 24-hour emergency response devices and patrols, late-night transport/escort service, controlled dormitory access. *Student services:* health clinic, personal/psychological counseling.

Dean College *(continued)*

Athletics Member NJCAA. *Intercollegiate sports:* baseball M(s), basketball M(s)/W(s), football M(s), golf M, lacrosse M(s)/W(s), soccer M(s)/W(s), softball W(s), volleyball W(s). *Intramural sports:* basketball M, football M, golf M, lacrosse M, skiing (cross-country) M/W, skiing (downhill) M/W, tennis M/W, volleyball M/W.

Standardized Tests *Required:* SAT I or ACT (for admission).

Costs (2004–05) *Comprehensive fee:* $30,680 includes full-time tuition ($19,420), mandatory fees ($1960), and room and board ($9300). Full-time tuition and fees vary according to program. Part-time tuition and fees vary according to program. *Room and board:* college room only: $5880. *Payment plan:* installment. *Waivers:* senior citizens and employees or children of employees.

Applying *Options:* common application, electronic application, deferred entrance. *Application fee:* $35. *Required:* essay or personal statement, high school transcript, letters of recommendation. *Recommended:* minimum 2.0 GPA, interview. *Application deadline:* rolling (freshmen), rolling (transfers). *Notification:* continuous (freshmen), continuous (transfers).

Admissions Contact Mr. Jay Leiendecker, Vice President for Enrollment Services, Dean College, 99 Main Street, Franklin, MA 02038. *Phone:* 508-541-1508. *Toll-free phone:* 877-TRY-DEAN. *Fax:* 508-541-8726. *E-mail:* admissions@dean.edu.

▶ **See page 536 for a narrative description.**

FINE MORTUARY COLLEGE
Westwood, Massachusetts

Admissions Contact FINE Mortuary College, 77 University Avenue, Westwood, MA 02090.

FISHER COLLEGE
Boston, Massachusetts

- **Independent** primarily 2-year, founded 1903
- **Calendar** semesters
- **Degrees** associate and bachelor's
- **Urban** campus
- **Endowment** $12.9 million
- **Coed,** 556 undergraduate students, 100% full-time, 69% women, 31% men

Undergraduates 556 full-time. Students come from 14 states and territories, 21 other countries, 21% are from out of state, 20% African American, 6% Asian American or Pacific Islander, 15% Hispanic American, 0.4% Native American, 10% international, 17% transferred in, 50% live on campus.

Freshmen *Admission:* 1,534 applied, 1,006 admitted, 314 enrolled. *Average high school GPA:* 2.52.

Faculty *Total:* 48, 50% full-time, 21% with terminal degrees.

Majors Accounting; business administration and management; data processing and data processing technology; fashion/apparel design; fashion merchandising; hospitality administration; humanities; kindergarten/preschool education; legal assistant/paralegal; liberal arts and sciences/liberal studies; office management; psychology; tourism and travel services management.

Academic Programs *Special study options:* academic remediation for entering students, adult/continuing education programs, advanced placement credit, English as a second language, internships, off-campus study, part-time degree program, summer session for credit.

Library Fisher College Library plus 1 other with 30,000 titles, 160 serial subscriptions, an OPAC.

Computers on Campus 112 computers available on campus for general student use. A campuswide network can be accessed from off campus. Internet access, at least one staffed computer lab available.

Student Life *Housing Options:* coed, women-only. *Activities and Organizations:* drama/theater group, choral group, Drama Club, student government, Student Activity Club, Inter-Cultural Club. *Campus security:* 24-hour emergency response devices and patrols, controlled dormitory access. *Student services:* health clinic, personal/psychological counseling, women's center.

Athletics Member NAIA. *Intercollegiate sports:* baseball M, basketball M/W, softball W.

Costs (2004–05) *Comprehensive fee:* $27,550 includes full-time tuition ($15,975), mandatory fees ($1600), and room and board ($9975). Part-time tuition: $200 per credit. Part-time tuition and fees vary according to class time, course load, and program. *Payment plan:* installment. *Waivers:* employees or children of employees.

Applying *Options:* deferred entrance. *Application fee:* $25. *Required:* high school transcript. *Required for some:* essay or personal statement, letters of recommendation, interview. *Recommended:* minimum 2.0 GPA. *Application deadline:* rolling (freshmen), rolling (transfers). *Notification:* continuous (freshmen), continuous (transfers).

Admissions Contact Mr. William Graceffa, Director Admissions, Fisher College, 118 Beacon Street, Boston, MA 02116. *Phone:* 617-236-8800 Ext. 8822. *Toll-free phone:* 800-821-3050 (in-state); 800-446-1226 (out-of-state). *Fax:* 617-236-5473. *E-mail:* admissions@fisher.edu.

▶ **See page 544 for a narrative description.**

GIBBS COLLEGE
Boston, Massachusetts

Admissions Contact Mr. Robert A. Andriola, Director of Admissions, Gibbs College, 126 Newbury Street, Boston, MA 02116-2904. *Phone:* 617-578-7150. *Toll-free phone:* 800-6SKILLS. *Fax:* 617-262-2610.

GREENFIELD COMMUNITY COLLEGE
Greenfield, Massachusetts

- **State-supported** 2-year, founded 1962
- **Calendar** semesters
- **Degree** certificates and associate
- **Small-town** 120-acre campus
- **Coed,** 2,368 undergraduate students, 42% full-time, 62% women, 38% men

Undergraduates 997 full-time, 1,371 part-time. Students come from 8 states and territories, 7 other countries, 3% African American, 3% Asian American or Pacific Islander, 3% Hispanic American, 0.6% Native American, 0.1% international, 7% transferred in. *Retention:* 55% of 2002 full-time freshmen returned.

Freshmen *Admission:* 712 applied, 711 admitted, 425 enrolled.

Faculty *Total:* 182, 30% full-time. *Student/faculty ratio:* 18:1.

Majors Accounting; administrative assistant and secretarial science; American studies; art; behavioral sciences; biological and physical sciences; business administration and management; commercial and advertising art; computer programming; criminal justice/law enforcement administration; education; engineering science; fire science; food science; human ecology; humanities; human services; industrial technology; information science/studies; kindergarten/preschool education; liberal arts and sciences/liberal studies; marketing/marketing management; mass communication/media; mathematics; natural resources management and policy; nursing (registered nurse training); parks, recreation and leisure; photography; pre-engineering.

Academic Programs *Special study options:* academic remediation for entering students, adult/continuing education programs, advanced placement credit, cooperative education, distance learning, English as a second language, honors programs, independent study, part-time degree program, services for LD students, summer session for credit.

Library Greenfield Community College Library with 52,690 titles, 356 serial subscriptions.

Computers on Campus 115 computers available on campus for general student use. A campuswide network can be accessed. Internet access, at least one staffed computer lab available.

Student Life *Housing:* college housing not available. *Activities and Organizations:* drama/theater group, choral group. *Campus security:* 24-hour emergency response devices and patrols, late-night transport/escort service. *Student services:* health clinic, personal/psychological counseling, women's center.

Standardized Tests *Required for some:* Psychological Corporation Practical Nursing Entrance Examination.

Costs (2003–04) *Tuition:* state resident $624 full-time; nonresident $6744 full-time. *Required fees:* $2054 full-time.

Applying *Options:* early admission. *Application fee:* $10. *Required for some:* high school transcript, interview. *Application deadline:* rolling (freshmen), rolling (transfers).

Admissions Contact Mr. Herbert Hentz, Assistant Director of Admission, Greenfield Community College, 1 College Drive, Greenfield, MA 01301-9739. *Phone:* 413-775-1000. *E-mail:* admission@gcc.mass.edu.

HOLYOKE COMMUNITY COLLEGE
Holyoke, Massachusetts

- **State-supported** 2-year, founded 1946, part of Massachusetts Public Higher Education System
- **Calendar** semesters
- **Degree** certificates and associate
- **Suburban** 135-acre campus
- **Coed,** 6,000 undergraduate students

Undergraduates Students come from 7 states and territories, 11 other countries, 5% African American, 2% Asian American or Pacific Islander, 13% Hispanic American, 0.6% Native American, 0.2% international.

Faculty *Total:* 116. *Student/faculty ratio:* 18:1.

Majors Accounting; administrative assistant and secretarial science; American studies; biology/biological sciences; business administration and management; business teacher education; chemistry; cinematography and film/video production; clinical laboratory science/medical technology; commercial and advertising art; computer typography and composition equipment operation; consumer merchandising/retailing management; criminal justice/police science; dramatic/theatre arts; elementary education; engineering science; environmental studies; family and consumer sciences/human sciences; fine/studio arts; foods, nutrition, and wellness; health information/medical records administration; hospitality administration; hotel/motel administration; human services; information science/studies; kindergarten/preschool education; legal administrative assistant/secretary; liberal arts and sciences/liberal studies; mass communication/media; music; nursing (registered nurse training); photography; physics; pre-engineering; radiologic technology/science; sport and fitness administration; tourism and travel services management; veterinary sciences; veterinary technology; visual and performing arts.

Academic Programs *Special study options:* academic remediation for entering students, adult/continuing education programs, advanced placement credit, cooperative education, English as a second language, honors programs, internships, off-campus study, part-time degree program, services for LD students, student-designed majors, study abroad, summer session for credit. *ROTC:* Army (c), Air Force (c).

Library Elaine Marieb Library with 68,965 titles, 459 serial subscriptions.

Computers on Campus 275 computers available on campus for general student use. A campuswide network can be accessed. Internet access, at least one staffed computer lab available.

Student Life *Housing:* college housing not available. *Activities and Organizations:* drama/theater group, student-run newspaper, radio station, choral group, Drama Club, Music Club, Student Advisory Board. *Campus security:* 24-hour emergency response devices and patrols, student patrols, late-night transport/escort service. *Student services:* health clinic, personal/psychological counseling, women's center.

Athletics Member NJCAA. *Intercollegiate sports:* baseball M, basketball M, skiing (downhill) M(c)/W(c), soccer M/W, softball W, tennis M/W. *Intramural sports:* rock climbing M/W.

Standardized Tests *Required for some:* Assessment and Placement Services for Community Colleges, Health Occupations Exam.

Costs (2004–05) *Tuition:* $100 per credit part-time; state resident $3096 full-time; nonresident $306 per credit part-time.

Applying *Options:* early admission, deferred entrance. *Application fee:* $10. *Required:* high school transcript. *Recommended:* interview. *Application deadline:* rolling (freshmen), rolling (transfers). *Notification:* continuous (freshmen), continuous (transfers).

Admissions Contact Dr. Joan Mikalson, Director of Admissions and Transfer Affairs, Holyoke Community College, 303 Homestead Avenue, Holyoke, MA 01040-1099. *Phone:* 413-552-2850.

ITT TECHNICAL INSTITUTE
Woburn, Massachusetts

- **Proprietary** 2-year, part of ITT Educational Services, Inc.
- **Calendar** quarters
- **Degree** associate
- **Coed**

Standardized Tests *Required:* Wonderlic aptitude test (for admission).

Costs (2003–04) *Tuition:* Total Program Cost varies depending on course of study. Consult school catalog.

Applying *Options:* deferred entrance. *Application fee:* $100. *Required:* high school transcript, interview. *Recommended:* letters of recommendation.

Admissions Contact Mr. David Lundgren, ITT Technical Institute, 10 Forbes Road, Woburn, MA 01801. *Phone:* 781-937-8324. *Toll-free phone:* 800-430-5097. *Fax:* 781-937-3402.

ITT TECHNICAL INSTITUTE
Norwood, Massachusetts

- **Proprietary** 2-year, founded 1990, part of ITT Educational Services, Inc
- **Calendar** quarters
- **Degree** associate
- **Suburban** campus with easy access to Boston
- **Coed**

Standardized Tests *Required:* Wonderlic aptitude test (for admission).

Costs (2003–04) *Tuition:* Total Program Cost varies depending on course of study. Consult school catalog.

Applying *Options:* deferred entrance. *Application fee:* $100. *Required:* high school transcript, interview. *Recommended:* letters of recommendation.

Admissions Contact Mr. Thomas F. Ryan III, Director of Recruitment, ITT Technical Institute, 333 Providence Highway, Norwood, MA 02062. *Phone:* 781-278-7200. *Toll-free phone:* 800-879-8324. *Fax:* 781-278-0766.

LABOURÉ COLLEGE
Boston, Massachusetts

- **Independent Roman Catholic** 2-year, founded 1971
- **Calendar** semesters
- **Degree** certificates and associate
- **Urban** campus
- **Endowment** $951,296
- **Coed,** 432 undergraduate students

Labouré's programs in health care are supported by its affiliations with more than 75 Boston-area health-care institutions. Each program offers career education and general education courses. The student-faculty ratio is 8:1. Opportunities for full- and part-time study, day or evening, and certificate programs are available. In 2003, all graduates who elected to work found employment in their respective fields upon graduation.

Undergraduates Students come from 3 states and territories, 4 other countries, 1% are from out of state, 31% African American, 4% Asian American or Pacific Islander, 6% Hispanic American. *Retention:* 65% of 2002 full-time freshmen returned.

Freshmen *Admission:* 88 applied, 19 admitted.

Faculty *Total:* 39, 64% full-time, 13% with terminal degrees. *Student/faculty ratio:* 8:1.

Majors Clinical laboratory science/medical technology; dietetics; health information/medical records administration; industrial radiologic technology; nursing (registered nurse training).

Academic Programs *Special study options:* academic remediation for entering students, accelerated degree program, adult/continuing education programs, independent study, part-time degree program, services for LD students, summer session for credit.

Library Helen Stubblefield Law Library with 10,975 titles, 155 serial subscriptions, 650 audiovisual materials, an OPAC.

Computers on Campus 20 computers available on campus for general student use. At least one staffed computer lab available.

Student Life *Housing:* college housing not available. *Activities and Organizations:* student-run newspaper, Student Government Association, college yearbook, peer advisors. *Campus security:* 24-hour emergency response devices. *Student services:* health clinic, personal/psychological counseling.

Costs (2004–05) *Tuition:* $375 per credit part-time.

Financial Aid Of all full-time matriculated undergraduates who enrolled, 18 Federal Work-Study jobs (averaging $1000).

Applying *Options:* deferred entrance. *Application fee:* $25. *Required:* high school transcript, letters of recommendation. *Application deadline:* rolling (freshmen), rolling (transfers).

Admissions Contact Labouré College, 2120 Dorchester Avenue, Boston, MA 02124. *Phone:* 617-296-8300. *Fax:* 617-296-7947. *E-mail:* admit@laboure.edu.

MARIAN COURT COLLEGE
Swampscott, Massachusetts

Admissions Contact Mrs. Lisa Emerson Parker, Director of Admissions, Marian Court College, 35 Little's Point Road, Swampscott, MA 01907-2840. *Phone:* 781-595-6768 Ext. 139. *Fax:* 781-595-3560. *E-mail:* marianct@shore.net.

MASSACHUSETTS BAY COMMUNITY COLLEGE
Wellesley Hills, Massachusetts

- **State-supported** 2-year, founded 1961
- **Calendar** semesters
- **Degree** certificates and associate
- **Suburban** 84-acre campus with easy access to Boston
- **Coed**

Faculty *Student/faculty ratio:* 21:1.

Student Life *Campus security:* 24-hour emergency response devices and patrols.

Athletics Member NJCAA.

Costs (2003–04) *Tuition:* state resident $720 full-time, $104 per credit part-time; nonresident $6900 full-time, $310 per credit part-time. Full-time tuition and fees vary according to program and reciprocity agreements. Part-time tuition and fees vary according to class time, program, and reciprocity agreements. *Required fees:* $2100 full-time.

Massachusetts Bay Community College (continued)

Financial Aid Of all full-time matriculated undergraduates who enrolled, 25 Federal Work-Study jobs (averaging $2000).

Applying *Options:* common application, electronic application, early admission.

Admissions Contact Ms. Donna Raposa, Director for Admissions, Massachusetts Bay Community College, 50 Oakland Street, Wellesley Hills, MA 02481. *Phone:* 781-239-2501. *Fax:* 781-239-1047. *E-mail:* info@massbay.edu.

▶ **See page 572 for a narrative description.**

MASSASOIT COMMUNITY COLLEGE
Brockton, Massachusetts

- **State-supported** 2-year, founded 1966
- **Calendar** semesters
- **Degree** certificates and associate
- **Suburban** campus with easy access to Boston
- **Coed,** 6,808 undergraduate students, 47% full-time, 59% women, 41% men

Undergraduates 3,178 full-time, 3,630 part-time. Students come from 4 states and territories, 3 other countries, 1% are from out of state, 15% African American, 1% Asian American or Pacific Islander, 2% Hispanic American, 1% Native American, 0.4% international, 5% transferred in.

Freshmen *Admission:* 1,488 admitted, 1,488 enrolled.

Faculty *Total:* 490, 27% full-time.

Majors Accounting; administrative assistant and secretarial science; architectural engineering technology; business administration and management; business administration, management and operations related; child care and support services management; child care provision; computer and information sciences; computer and information sciences and support services related; computer and information sciences related; computer programming; computer/technical support; criminal justice/police science; culinary arts; dental assisting; diesel mechanics technology; dramatic/theatre arts; electrical and electronic engineering technologies related; electrical, electronic and communications engineering technology; engineering technologies related; fine/studio arts; fire science; graphic design; heating, air conditioning and refrigeration technology; hotel/motel administration; human services; liberal arts and sciences and humanities related; liberal arts and sciences/liberal studies; marketing/marketing management; medical/clinical assistant; nursing (registered nurse training); operations management; radiologic technology/science; respiratory care therapy; respiratory therapy technician; restaurant/food services management; tourism and travel services management; vehicle maintenance and repair technologies related.

Academic Programs *Special study options:* academic remediation for entering students, accelerated degree program, adult/continuing education programs, cooperative education, distance learning, English as a second language, internships, off-campus study, part-time degree program, services for LD students, summer session for credit.

Library 75,000 titles, 396 serial subscriptions.

Computers on Campus 350 computers available on campus for general student use. At least one staffed computer lab available.

Student Life *Housing:* college housing not available. *Activities and Organizations:* drama/theater group, student-run newspaper, radio station, Drama Club, student newspaper, Phi Theta Kappa, International Student Association, Student Senate. *Campus security:* 24-hour patrols. *Student services:* health clinic, personal/psychological counseling, women's center.

Athletics Member NJCAA. *Intercollegiate sports:* baseball M, basketball M(s)/W, soccer M(s)/W, softball W(s). *Intramural sports:* basketball M/W.

Costs (2003–04) *Tuition:* state resident $576 full-time, $24 per credit part-time; nonresident $5520 full-time, $230 per credit part-time. *Required fees:* $2088 full-time, $87 per credit part-time. *Payment plan:* installment. *Waivers:* senior citizens and employees or children of employees.

Financial Aid Of all full-time matriculated undergraduates who enrolled, 45 Federal Work-Study jobs (averaging $3200).

Applying *Application deadline:* rolling (freshmen), rolling (transfers). *Notification:* continuous (freshmen), continuous (transfers).

Admissions Contact Ms. Michelle Hughes, Director of Admissions, Massasoit Community College, 1 Massasoit Boulevard, Brockton, MA 02302-3996. *Phone:* 508-588-9100 Ext. 1412. *Toll-free phone:* 800-CAREERS.

MIDDLESEX COMMUNITY COLLEGE
Bedford, Massachusetts

- **State-supported** 2-year, founded 1970, part of Massachusetts Public Higher Education System
- **Calendar** semesters
- **Degree** certificates and associate
- **Suburban** 200-acre campus with easy access to Boston
- **Endowment** $1.1 million
- **Coed,** 8,016 undergraduate students

Undergraduates Students come from 5 states and territories, 5% are from out of state.

Faculty *Total:* 468, 27% full-time.

Majors Accounting; art; automobile/automotive mechanics technology; biomedical technology; business administration and management; business/corporate communications; commercial and advertising art; computer engineering technology; computer science; computer software technology; consumer merchandising/retailing management; criminal justice/law enforcement administration; culinary arts; data modeling/warehousing and database administration; dental assisting; dental hygiene; dental laboratory technology; diagnostic medical sonography and ultrasound technology; drafting and design technology; dramatic/theatre arts; electrical, electronic and communications engineering technology; elementary education; fashion merchandising; fire science; general studies; hospitality/recreation marketing; hotel/motel administration; human services; kindergarten/preschool education; legal assistant/paralegal; liberal arts and sciences/liberal studies; marketing/marketing management; mass communication/media; medical/clinical assistant; nursing (registered nurse training); office management; pre-engineering; radiologic technology/science; telecommunications.

Academic Programs *Special study options:* academic remediation for entering students, accelerated degree program, adult/continuing education programs, advanced placement credit, cooperative education, distance learning, English as a second language, honors programs, independent study, internships, off-campus study, part-time degree program, services for LD students, study abroad, summer session for credit. *ROTC:* Air Force (c).

Library Main Library plus 1 other with 52,960 titles, 538 serial subscriptions, an OPAC, a Web page.

Computers on Campus 325 computers available on campus for general student use. A campuswide network can be accessed from off campus that provide access to word processing; graphics programs. Internet access, online (class) registration, at least one staffed computer lab available.

Student Life *Housing:* college housing not available. *Activities and Organizations:* drama/theater group, student-run newspaper, Mental Health Club, International Club, Early Childhood Education Club, Student Union Government Association, Student Activities Board. *Campus security:* 24-hour emergency response devices and patrols. *Student services:* health clinic, personal/psychological counseling, legal services.

Athletics *Intramural sports:* basketball M/W, table tennis M/W, volleyball M/W.

Standardized Tests *Required for some:* CPT.

Costs (2003–04) *Tuition:* state resident $3330 full-time; nonresident $9510 full-time. *Required fees:* $300 full-time.

Financial Aid Of all full-time matriculated undergraduates who enrolled, 52 Federal Work-Study jobs (averaging $1802).

Applying *Options:* common application, electronic application, early admission. *Required for some:* essay or personal statement, high school transcript, 3 letters of recommendation, interview. *Application deadline:* rolling (freshmen), rolling (transfers). *Notification:* continuous (freshmen), continuous (transfers).

Admissions Contact Ms. Laurie Dimitrov, Director, Admissions and Recruitment, Middlesex Community College, 33 Kearney Square, Lowell, MA 01852. *Phone:* 978-656-3207. *Toll-free phone:* 800-818-3434. *Fax:* 978-656-3322. *E-mail:* middlesex@middlesex.mass.edu.

MOUNT WACHUSETT COMMUNITY COLLEGE
Gardner, Massachusetts

- **State-supported** 2-year, founded 1963, part of Massachusetts Public Higher Education System
- **Calendar** semesters
- **Degree** certificates and associate
- **Small-town** 270-acre campus with easy access to Boston
- **Endowment** $1.0 million
- **Coed,** 4,118 undergraduate students, 43% full-time, 65% women, 35% men

MWCC is a 2-year public community college that offers more than 40 associate degree and certificate programs and noncredit and professional development courses. At MWCC, students gain education and training to build new skills, start a career, or transfer to a 4-year public or private college or university. Students may visit the College's Web site at http://www.mwcc.edu.

Undergraduates 1,773 full-time, 2,345 part-time. Students come from 9 states and territories, 18 other countries, 5% are from out of state, 4% African American, 3% Asian American or Pacific Islander, 7% Hispanic American, 0.2% Native American, 4% international, 10% transferred in.

Freshmen *Admission:* 3,494 applied, 2,828 admitted, 920 enrolled.

Faculty *Total:* 206, 36% full-time. *Student/faculty ratio:* 15:1.

Majors Accounting; art; automobile/automotive mechanics technology; broadcast journalism; business administration and management; computer graphics;

computer technology/computer systems technology; criminal justice/law enforcement administration; electrical, electronic and communications engineering technology; environmental studies; fine/studio arts; fire science; general studies; human services; industrial engineering; industrial technology; information science/studies; kinesiology and exercise science; legal assistant/paralegal; liberal arts and sciences/liberal studies; management information systems; medical/clinical assistant; nursing (registered nurse training); physical therapy; plastics engineering technology; sign language interpretation and translation; speech therapy; telecommunications.

Academic Programs *Special study options:* academic remediation for entering students, adult/continuing education programs, advanced placement credit, cooperative education, distance learning, English as a second language, honors programs, independent study, internships, part-time degree program, services for LD students, summer session for credit. *ROTC:* Army (c), Navy (c), Air Force (c).

Library Mount Wachusett Community College Library with 56,344 titles, 535 serial subscriptions, 2,612 audiovisual materials, an OPAC, a Web page.

Computers on Campus 340 computers available on campus for general student use. A campuswide network can be accessed. Internet access, at least one staffed computer lab available.

Student Life *Activities and Organizations:* drama/theater group, choral group, Sophomore Nursing Club, Freshman Nursing Club, Alpha Beta Gamma, Physical Therapist Assistant Club, Multicultural Club. *Campus security:* 24-hour emergency response devices and patrols. *Student services:* health clinic, personal/psychological counseling, women's center.

Costs (2004–05) *Tuition:* state resident $750 full-time, $25 per credit part-time; nonresident $6900 full-time, $230 per credit part-time. *Required fees:* $3330 full-time, $106 per credit part-time, $55 per term part-time. *Payment plan:* installment. *Waivers:* employees or children of employees.

Financial Aid Of all full-time matriculated undergraduates who enrolled, 75 Federal Work-Study jobs (averaging $1500).

Applying *Options:* common application, early admission. *Application fee:* $10. *Required:* high school transcript. *Required for some:* essay or personal statement, 2 letters of recommendation. *Application deadline:* rolling (freshmen), rolling (transfers). *Notification:* continuous (freshmen), continuous (transfers).

Admissions Contact Mr. Richard Pastor, Associate Vice President of Student Services, Mount Wachusett Community College, 444 Green Street, Gardner, MA 01440-1000. *Phone:* 978-630-9110. *Fax:* 978-630-9554. *E-mail:* admissions@mwcc.mass.edu.

NEW ENGLAND COLLEGE OF FINANCE
Boston, Massachusetts

- **Independent** primarily 2-year, founded 1909
- **Calendar** semesters
- **Degrees** certificates, associate, and bachelor's (offers primarily part-time evening degree programs; bachelor's degree offered jointly with Bentley College, Assumption College, Providence College, University of Hartford, and University System College for Lifelong Learning)
- **Urban** campus
- **Coed, primarily women**

Student Life *Campus security:* reception desk in lobby of building.

Costs (2004–05) *Tuition:* $230 per credit hour part-time.

Applying *Options:* common application. *Required:* essay or personal statement, high school transcript, 1 letter of recommendation, interview.

Admissions Contact Ms. Diane Monaghan, Vice President for Academic Affairs, New England College of Finance, 1 Lincoln Plaza, Boston, MA 02111-2645. *Phone:* 617-951-2350 Ext. 227. *Toll-free phone:* 888-696-NECF. *Fax:* 617-951-2533.

NORTHERN ESSEX COMMUNITY COLLEGE
Haverhill, Massachusetts

- **State-supported** 2-year, founded 1960
- **Calendar** semesters
- **Degree** certificates and associate
- **Suburban** 106-acre campus with easy access to Boston
- **Endowment** $1.6 million
- **Coed,** 6,301 undergraduate students, 36% full-time, 66% women, 34% men

Two-year public community college with an open and rolling admission process, offering more than 70 degree and certificate programs in arts and sciences, business, computer information sciences, electronic technology and engineering science, health, human services, and paralegal studies. Students can prepare for a career or begin a bachelor's degree through the Joint Admissions Program or transfer agreements with 4-year colleges and universities.

Undergraduates 2,257 full-time, 4,044 part-time. Students come from 3 states and territories, 16% are from out of state, 4% African American, 2% Asian American or Pacific Islander, 21% Hispanic American, 0.2% Native American, 0.9% international. *Retention:* 54% of 2002 full-time freshmen returned.

Freshmen *Admission:* 3,600 applied, 3,400 admitted.

Faculty *Total:* 486, 19% full-time. *Student/faculty ratio:* 21:1.

Majors Accounting; administrative assistant and secretarial science; biological and physical sciences; business administration and management; business teacher education; civil engineering technology; commercial and advertising art; computer and information sciences; computer engineering technology; computer graphics; computer programming; computer programming related; computer programming (specific applications); computer science; computer systems networking and telecommunications; computer typography and composition equipment operation; criminal justice/law enforcement administration; dance; data processing and data processing technology; dental assisting; dramatic/theatre arts; education; electrical, electronic and communications engineering technology; elementary education; engineering science; finance; general studies; health information/medical records administration; history; hotel/motel administration; human services; industrial radiologic technology; international relations and affairs; journalism; kindergarten/preschool education; legal assistant/paralegal; liberal arts and sciences/liberal studies; machine tool technology; marketing/marketing management; materials science; medical administrative assistant and medical secretary; medical transcription; mental health/rehabilitation; music; nursing (registered nurse training); parks, recreation and leisure; physical education teaching and coaching; political science and government; radiologic technology/science; real estate; respiratory care therapy; respiratory therapy technician; sign language interpretation and translation; telecommunications technology; tourism and travel services management; web/multimedia management and webmaster; web page, digital/multimedia and information resources design; women's studies; word processing.

Academic Programs *Special study options:* academic remediation for entering students, adult/continuing education programs, advanced placement credit, cooperative education, distance learning, double majors, English as a second language, freshman honors college, honors programs, independent study, internships, off-campus study, part-time degree program, services for LD students, study abroad, summer session for credit. *ROTC:* Air Force (c).

Library Bentley Library with 61,120 titles, 598 serial subscriptions, an OPAC.

Computers on Campus 250 computers available on campus for general student use. A campuswide network can be accessed from off campus. At least one staffed computer lab available.

Student Life *Housing:* college housing not available. *Activities and Organizations:* drama/theater group, student-run newspaper. *Campus security:* 24-hour emergency response devices and patrols. *Student services:* health clinic, personal/psychological counseling, women's center.

Athletics Member NJCAA. *Intercollegiate sports:* baseball M, basketball M/W, golf M/W, soccer M/W, softball W. *Intramural sports:* basketball M/W, cross-country running M/W, golf M/W, racquetball M/W, skiing (cross-country) M/W, skiing (downhill) M/W, weight lifting M/W.

Standardized Tests *Required:* Psychological Corporation Aptitude Test for Practical Nursing (for admission).

Costs (2003–04) *Tuition:* state resident $2670 full-time, $99 per credit part-time; nonresident $10,200 full-time, $340 per credit part-time. Full-time tuition and fees vary according to degree level. Part-time tuition and fees vary according to degree level. *Waivers:* employees or children of employees.

Financial Aid Of all full-time matriculated undergraduates who enrolled, 159 Federal Work-Study jobs (averaging $2010).

Applying *Options:* early admission. *Required:* high school transcript. *Application deadline:* rolling (freshmen), rolling (transfers). *Notification:* continuous (freshmen), continuous (transfers).

Admissions Contact Northern Essex Community College, 100 Elliott Street, Haverhill,, MA 01830. *Phone:* 978-556-3616. *Toll-free phone:* 800-NECC-123. *Fax:* 978-556-3155. *E-mail:* ssullivan@necc.mass.edu.

NORTH SHORE COMMUNITY COLLEGE
Danvers, Massachusetts

- **State-supported** 2-year, founded 1965
- **Calendar** semesters
- **Degree** certificates and associate
- **Suburban** campus with easy access to Boston
- **Endowment** $3.2 million
- **Coed,** 6,612 undergraduate students, 39% full-time, 63% women, 37% men

Undergraduates 2,598 full-time, 4,014 part-time. Students come from 5 states and territories, 1% are from out of state, 9% African American, 3% Asian American or Pacific Islander, 12% Hispanic American, 0.4% Native American, 0.2% international, 7% transferred in.

Freshmen *Admission:* 1,344 applied, 1,253 admitted, 1,402 enrolled.

Faculty *Total:* 402, 32% full-time. *Student/faculty ratio:* 25:1.

North Shore Community College (continued)

Majors Accounting; administrative assistant and secretarial science; airline pilot and flight crew; applied horticulture; biology/biotechnology laboratory technician; business administration and management; child development; computer and information sciences related; computer engineering technology; computer graphics; computer programming; computer programming (specific applications); computer science; criminal justice/law enforcement administration; culinary arts; data entry/microcomputer applications; engineering science; fire science; foods, nutrition, and wellness; forestry; gerontology; health science; hospitality administration; information science/studies; interdisciplinary studies; kindergarten/preschool education; landscaping and groundskeeping; legal administrative assistant/secretary; legal assistant/paralegal; liberal arts and sciences/liberal studies; marketing/marketing management; medical administrative assistant and medical secretary; medical radiologic technology; mental health/rehabilitation; nursing (registered nurse training); occupational therapy; physical therapist assistant; pre-engineering; respiratory care therapy; substance abuse/addiction counseling; tourism and travel services management; veterinary technology.

Academic Programs *Special study options:* academic remediation for entering students, adult/continuing education programs, advanced placement credit, cooperative education, distance learning, English as a second language, honors programs, independent study, internships, part-time degree program, services for LD students, summer session for credit.

Library Learning Resource Center plus 2 others with 75,000 titles, 606 serial subscriptions, 4,890 audiovisual materials, an OPAC.

Computers on Campus 300 computers available on campus for general student use. A campuswide network can be accessed. Internet access, online (class) registration, at least one staffed computer lab available.

Student Life *Housing:* college housing not available. *Activities and Organizations:* drama/theater group, student-run newspaper, Program Council, student government, performing arts, student newspaper, Phi Theta Kappa. *Campus security:* 24-hour emergency response devices and patrols, late-night transport/escort service. *Student services:* health clinic, personal/psychological counseling, women's center.

Standardized Tests *Required for some:* nursing exam.

Costs (2004–05) *Tuition:* state resident $600 full-time, $25 per credit part-time; nonresident $6168 full-time, $257 per credit part-time. *Required fees:* $2112 full-time, $88 per credit part-time. *Payment plans:* installment, deferred payment. *Waivers:* senior citizens and employees or children of employees.

Financial Aid Of all full-time matriculated undergraduates who enrolled, 62 Federal Work-Study jobs (averaging $2385).

Applying *Options:* early admission. *Required for some:* high school transcript, minimum 2.0 GPA, interview. *Application deadline:* rolling (freshmen), rolling (transfers). *Notification:* continuous (freshmen), continuous (transfers).

Admissions Contact Dr. Joanne Light, Director of Admissions, North Shore Community College, PO Box 3340, Danvers, MA 01923. *Phone:* 978-762-4000 Ext. 4337. *Fax:* 978-762-4015. *E-mail:* info@northshore.edu.

QUINCY COLLEGE
Quincy, Massachusetts

- **City-supported** 2-year, founded 1958
- **Calendar** semesters
- **Degree** certificates and associate
- **Suburban** 2-acre campus with easy access to Boston
- **Endowment** $112,021
- **Coed**

Student Life *Campus security:* 24-hour emergency response devices and patrols.

Standardized Tests *Required:* CPT (for placement).

Costs (2003–04) *Tuition:* state resident $3780 full-time.

Applying *Options:* common application, early admission, deferred entrance. *Application fee:* $20. *Required:* high school transcript.

Admissions Contact Ms. Kristen Caputo, Assistant Director of Admissions, Quincy College, 34 Coddington Street, Quincy, MA 02169. *Phone:* 617-984-1704. *Toll-free phone:* 800-698-1700. *Fax:* 617-984-1669. *E-mail:* kcaputo@quincycollege.com.

QUINSIGAMOND COMMUNITY COLLEGE
Worcester, Massachusetts

- **State-supported** 2-year, founded 1963
- **Calendar** semesters
- **Degree** certificates and associate
- **Urban** 57-acre campus with easy access to Boston
- **Coed,** 6,591 undergraduate students, 43% full-time, 61% women, 39% men

Undergraduates 2,852 full-time, 3,739 part-time. Students come from 3 states and territories, 13 other countries, 8% African American, 4% Asian American or Pacific Islander, 10% Hispanic American, 0.6% Native American, 1% international, 4% transferred in.

Freshmen *Admission:* 1,285 enrolled.

Faculty *Total:* 370, 29% full-time.

Majors Accounting; administrative assistant and secretarial science; art; automobile/automotive mechanics technology; business administration and management; commercial and advertising art; computer programming; computer technology/computer systems technology; consumer merchandising/retailing management; criminal justice/law enforcement administration; data processing and data processing technology; dental hygiene; electrical, electronic and communications engineering technology; emergency medical technology (EMT paramedic); fire science; general studies; hotel/motel administration; human services; information science/studies; kindergarten/preschool education; liberal arts and sciences/liberal studies; medical radiologic technology; nursing (registered nurse training); occupational therapist assistant; occupational therapy; pre-engineering; respiratory care therapy; tourism and travel services management.

Academic Programs *Special study options:* academic remediation for entering students, accelerated degree program, adult/continuing education programs, advanced placement credit, cooperative education, double majors, English as a second language, internships, off-campus study, part-time degree program, services for LD students, summer session for credit. *ROTC:* Army (c).

Library Quinsigamond Library plus 1 other with 54,000 titles, 310 serial subscriptions, 230 audiovisual materials, an OPAC.

Computers on Campus 200 computers available on campus for general student use. A campuswide network can be accessed from off campus. At least one staffed computer lab available.

Student Life *Housing:* college housing not available. *Activities and Organizations:* student-run newspaper, Phi Theta Kappa, Nursing Club, Rad Tech Club, Gay Straight Alliance, Criminal Justice Club. *Campus security:* 24-hour emergency response devices and patrols, late-night transport/escort service. *Student services:* health clinic, personal/psychological counseling, women's center.

Athletics Member NJCAA. *Intercollegiate sports:* baseball M, basketball M/W. *Intramural sports:* archery M/W, badminton M/W, basketball M/W, cross-country running M/W, skiing (cross-country) M/W, skiing (downhill) M/W, swimming M/W, tennis M/W, volleyball M/W.

Costs (2004–05) *Tuition:* state resident $576 full-time, $24 per credit part-time; nonresident $5520 full-time, $230 per credit part-time. *Required fees:* $2359 full-time, $91 per credit part-time, $75 per term part-time. *Payment plan:* installment. *Waivers:* senior citizens and employees or children of employees.

Financial Aid Of all full-time matriculated undergraduates who enrolled, 70 Federal Work-Study jobs (averaging $2500).

Applying *Options:* common application. *Application fee:* $10. *Required:* high school transcript. *Required for some:* interview. *Application deadline:* rolling (freshmen), rolling (transfers). *Notification:* continuous until 8/15 (freshmen), continuous until 8/15 (transfers).

Admissions Contact Mr. Ronald C. Smith, Director of Admissions, Quinsigamond Community College, 670 West Boylston Street, Worcester, MA 01606-2092. *Phone:* 508-854-4262. *Fax:* 508-854-4357. *E-mail:* qccadm@qcc.mass.edu.

ROXBURY COMMUNITY COLLEGE
Roxbury Crossing, Massachusetts

Admissions Contact Milton Samuels, Director/Admissions, Roxbury Community College, 1234 Columbus Avenue, Roxbury Crossing, MA 02120-3400. *Phone:* 617-541-5310. *Fax:* 617-427-5316.

SPRINGFIELD TECHNICAL COMMUNITY COLLEGE
Springfield, Massachusetts

- **State-supported** 2-year, founded 1967
- **Calendar** semesters
- **Degree** certificates and associate
- **Urban** 34-acre campus
- **Endowment** $2.1 million
- **Coed,** 6,157 undergraduate students, 46% full-time, 55% women, 45% men

Undergraduates 2,843 full-time, 3,314 part-time. Students come from 10 states and territories, 15% African American, 2% Asian American or Pacific Islander, 12% Hispanic American, 0.5% Native American, 1% international.

Freshmen *Admission:* 2,616 applied, 1,816 admitted, 987 enrolled.

Faculty *Total:* 449, 35% full-time. *Student/faculty ratio:* 22:1.

Majors Accounting; administrative assistant and secretarial science; architectural engineering technology; automotive engineering technology; biology/

biological sciences; biotechnology; business administration and management; business/commerce; CAD/CADD drafting/design technology; chemistry; civil engineering technology; clinical/medical laboratory technology; commercial and advertising art; communications technologies and support services related; computer and information sciences and support services related; computer engineering technology; computer science; cosmetology; criminal justice/police science; dental hygiene; desktop publishing and digital imaging design; diagnostic medical sonography and ultrasound technology; electrical and electronic engineering technologies related; electrical, electronic and communications engineering technology; electromechanical technology; elementary education; engineering; entrepreneurship; finance; fine/studio arts; fire science; general studies; graphic design; health aide; heating, air conditioning and refrigeration technology; kindergarten/preschool education; landscaping and groundskeeping; laser and optical technology; liberal arts and sciences/liberal studies; logistics and materials management; marketing/marketing management; massage therapy; mathematics; mechanical engineering/mechanical technology; medical administrative assistant and medical secretary; medical/clinical assistant; medical insurance coding; medical radiologic technology; nuclear medical technology; nursing (registered nurse training); occupational therapist assistant; physical therapist assistant; quality control technology; rehabilitation and therapeutic professions related; respiratory care therapy; surgical technology; web/multimedia management and webmaster.

Academic Programs *Special study options:* academic remediation for entering students, adult/continuing education programs, advanced placement credit, cooperative education, distance learning, English as a second language, honors programs, independent study, internships, off-campus study, part-time degree program, services for LD students, summer session for credit.

Library Springfield Technical Community College Library with 62,509 titles, 359 serial subscriptions, 16,677 audiovisual materials, an OPAC, a Web page.

Computers on Campus 1068 computers available on campus for general student use. A campuswide network can be accessed from off campus. Internet access, at least one staffed computer lab available.

Student Life *Housing:* college housing not available. *Activities and Organizations:* drama/theater group, student-run television station, Phi Theta Kappa Honor Society, Landscape Club, Dental Hygiene Club, Clinical Lab Club, Physical Therapist Assistant Club. *Campus security:* 24-hour emergency response devices and patrols, late-night transport/escort service. *Student services:* health clinic, personal/psychological counseling.

Athletics Member NJCAA. *Intercollegiate sports:* baseball M, basketball M/W, golf M/W, soccer M/W, softball W, tennis M/W, wrestling M. *Intramural sports:* basketball M/W, cross-country running M/W, golf M/W, skiing (cross-country) M/W, softball M/W, volleyball M/W, weight lifting M/W.

Standardized Tests *Required for some:* SAT I (for admission).

Costs (2003–04) *Tuition:* state resident $750 full-time, $25 per credit part-time; nonresident $7260 full-time, $242 per credit part-time. *Required fees:* $2340 full-time.

Financial Aid Of all full-time matriculated undergraduates who enrolled, 124 Federal Work-Study jobs (averaging $2400).

Applying *Application fee:* $10. *Required:* high school transcript. *Required for some:* interview. *Application deadline:* rolling (freshmen), rolling (transfers).

Admissions Contact Ms. Andrea Lucy-Allen, Director of Admissions, Springfield Technical Community College, One Armory Square, Springfield, MA 01105. *Phone:* 413-781-7822 Ext. 4380. *E-mail:* admissions@stccadm.stcc.mass.edu.

URBAN COLLEGE OF BOSTON
Boston, Massachusetts

- **Independent** 2-year, founded 1993
- **Calendar** semesters
- **Degree** certificates and associate
- **Urban** campus
- **Coed, primarily women,** 609 undergraduate students, 2% full-time, 95% women, 5% men

Undergraduates 12 full-time, 597 part-time. Students come from 1 other state, 31% African American, 17% Asian American or Pacific Islander, 38% Hispanic American.

Freshmen *Admission:* 10 applied, 10 admitted, 10 enrolled.

Faculty *Total:* 24, 13% full-time, 25% with terminal degrees. *Student/faculty ratio:* 20:1.

Majors Human services; kindergarten/preschool education; liberal arts and sciences/liberal studies.

Academic Programs *Special study options:* part-time degree program.

Student Life *Housing:* college housing not available.

Costs (2003–04) *Tuition:* $2400 full-time, $100 per credit part-time. *Required fees:* $20 full-time, $10 per term part-time.

Applying *Application fee:* $10.

Admissions Contact Dr. Henry J. Johnson, Director of Enrollment Services/Registrar, Urban College of Boston, 178 Tremont Street, Boston, MA 02111-1093. *Phone:* 617-292-4723 Ext. 6357. *Fax:* 617-423-4758.

MICHIGAN

ALPENA COMMUNITY COLLEGE
Alpena, Michigan

- **State and locally supported** 2-year, founded 1952
- **Calendar** semesters
- **Degree** certificates and associate
- **Small-town** 700-acre campus
- **Endowment** $3.3 million
- **Coed,** 1,937 undergraduate students, 51% full-time, 58% women, 42% men

Undergraduates 984 full-time, 953 part-time. Students come from 4 states and territories, 0.8% African American, 0.5% Asian American or Pacific Islander, 0.2% Hispanic American, 0.4% Native American, 2% transferred in, 2% live on campus. *Retention:* 55% of 2002 full-time freshmen returned.

Freshmen *Admission:* 1,163 applied, 1,163 admitted, 423 enrolled. *Average high school GPA:* 2.67.

Faculty *Total:* 121, 42% full-time, 2% with terminal degrees. *Student/faculty ratio:* 17:1.

Majors Accounting; administrative assistant and secretarial science; automobile/automotive mechanics technology; biology/biological sciences; business administration and management; business automation/technology/data entry; chemical engineering; chemistry; computer and information sciences; computer/information technology services administration related; computer systems networking and telecommunications; corrections; criminal justice/police science; data processing and data processing technology; drafting and design technology; elementary education; English; general studies; information science/studies; liberal arts and sciences/liberal studies; manufacturing technology; mathematics; medical office assistant; nursing (licensed practical/vocational nurse training); nursing (registered nurse training); office management; operations management; pre-engineering; secondary education.

Academic Programs *Special study options:* academic remediation for entering students, advanced placement credit, distance learning, double majors, internships, part-time degree program, services for LD students, summer session for credit.

Library Stephen Fletcher Library with 29,000 titles, 183 serial subscriptions, an OPAC, a Web page.

Computers on Campus 75 computers available on campus for general student use. A campuswide network can be accessed from off campus. Internet access, at least one staffed computer lab available.

Student Life *Housing Options:* coed, men-only, women-only. Campus housing is provided by a third party. *Activities and Organizations:* drama/theater group, student-run newspaper, choral group, Nursing Association, Student Senate, Phi Theta Kappa, Lumberjack Newspaper, Law Enforcement Club. *Campus security:* 24-hour emergency response devices. *Student services:* personal/psychological counseling, women's center.

Athletics Member NJCAA. *Intercollegiate sports:* basketball M(s)/W(s), golf M, softball W(s), volleyball W(s). *Intramural sports:* basketball M/W, bowling M/W, football M, soccer M, softball M/W, volleyball M/W.

Standardized Tests *Required:* ACT COMPASS (for placement). *Recommended:* ACT (for placement).

Costs (2003–04) *Tuition:* area resident $2480 full-time, $66 per contact hour part-time; state resident $3470 full-time, $99 per contact hour part-time; nonresident $4460 full-time, $132 per contact hour part-time. Full-time tuition and fees vary according to course load. Part-time tuition and fees vary according to course load. *Required fees:* $500 full-time, $16 per contact hour part-time, $10 per term part-time. *Room and board:* room only: $2700. *Waivers:* senior citizens and employees or children of employees.

Financial Aid Of all full-time matriculated undergraduates who enrolled, 80 Federal Work-Study jobs (averaging $1200). 20 state and other part-time jobs (averaging $800).

Applying *Options:* electronic application, early admission, deferred entrance. *Required:* high school transcript. *Application deadline:* rolling (freshmen), rolling (transfers). *Notification:* continuous (freshmen), continuous (transfers).

Admissions Contact Mr. Mike Kollien, Admissions Technician, Alpena Community College, 666 Johnson Street, Alpena, MI 49707-1495. *Phone:* 989-358-7339. *Toll-free phone:* 888-468-6222. *Fax:* 989-358-7561.

BAY DE NOC COMMUNITY COLLEGE
Escanaba, Michigan

- **County-supported** 2-year, founded 1963, part of Michigan Department of Education

Bay de Noc Community College (continued)
■ **Calendar** semesters
■ **Degree** certificates and associate
■ **Rural** 150-acre campus
■ **Endowment** $2.1 million
■ **Coed**

Student Life *Campus security:* evening housing security personnel.
Standardized Tests *Required:* ACT COMPASS (for placement).
Costs (2003–04) *Tuition:* $60 per contact hour part-time; state resident $84 per contact hour part-time; nonresident $132 per contact hour part-time. *Required fees:* $8 per contact hour part-time, $25 per term part-time.
Financial Aid Of all full-time matriculated undergraduates who enrolled, 80 Federal Work-Study jobs (averaging $2500). 40 state and other part-time jobs (averaging $2500).
Applying *Options:* early admission. *Required:* high school transcript.
Admissions Contact Ms. Cynthia Aird, Director of Admissions, Bay de Noc Community College, Student Center, 2001 North Lincoln Road, Escanaba, MI 49829-2511. *Phone:* 906-786-5802 Ext. 1276. *Toll-free phone:* 800-221-2001 Ext. 1276. *Fax:* 906-786-8515. *E-mail:* wallbern@baydenoc.cc.mi.us.

BAY MILLS COMMUNITY COLLEGE
Brimley, Michigan

■ **District-supported** 2-year, founded 1984
■ **Calendar** semesters
■ **Degree** certificates, diplomas, and associate
■ **Rural** campus
■ **Coed**

Faculty *Student/faculty ratio:* 10:1.
Student Life *Campus security:* 24-hour emergency response devices.
Standardized Tests *Required:* ACT ASSET (for placement).
Costs (2003–04) *Tuition:* state resident $6700 full-time, $210 per credit hour part-time. *Required fees:* $500 full-time. *Room and board:* $3526; room only: $1300.
Financial Aid Of all full-time matriculated undergraduates who enrolled, 7 Federal Work-Study jobs (averaging $2466). 6 state and other part-time jobs (averaging $2634).
Applying *Options:* common application, early admission. *Required:* high school transcript.
Admissions Contact Ms. Elaine Lehre, Admissions Officer, Bay Mills Community College, 12214 West Lakeshore Drive, Brimley, MI 49715. *Phone:* 906-248-3354. *Toll-free phone:* 800-844-BMCC. *Fax:* 906-248-3351.

DAVENPORT UNIVERSITY
Alma, Michigan

Admissions Contact 1500 North Pine Street, Alma, MI 48801.

DAVENPORT UNIVERSITY
Bad Axe, Michigan

Admissions Contact 150 Nugent Road, Bad Axe, MI 48413. *Toll-free phone:* 800-968-5894.

DAVENPORT UNIVERSITY
Bay City, Michigan

Admissions Contact Ms. Angelia Pierson, Registration Specialist, Davenport University, 3930 Traxler Court, Bay City, MI 48706. *Phone:* 989-686-1572. *Toll-free phone:* 800-968-4416.

DAVENPORT UNIVERSITY
Caro, Michigan

Admissions Contact 1231 Cleaver Road, Caro, MI 48723. *Toll-free phone:* 800-968-9710.

DAVENPORT UNIVERSITY
Midland, Michigan

Admissions Contact Davenport University, 3555 East Patrick Road, Midland, MI 48642. *Toll-free phone:* 800-968-4860. *Fax:* 517-752-3453.

DAVENPORT UNIVERSITY
Romeo, Michigan

Admissions Contact 71180 Van Dyke Road, Romeo, MI 48065.

DAVENPORT UNIVERSITY
Saginaw, Michigan

Admissions Contact 5300 Bay Road, Saginaw, MI 48604. *Toll-free phone:* 800-968-8133.

DELTA COLLEGE
University Center, Michigan

■ **District-supported** 2-year, founded 1961
■ **Calendar** semesters
■ **Degree** certificates and associate
■ **Rural** 640-acre campus
■ **Endowment** $6.6 million
■ **Coed,** 10,450 undergraduate students, 36% full-time, 58% women, 42% men

Undergraduates 3,797 full-time, 6,653 part-time. Students come from 22 other countries, 8% African American, 0.9% Asian American or Pacific Islander, 4% Hispanic American, 0.6% Native American, 0.7% international, 5% transferred in.
Freshmen *Admission:* 3,677 applied, 3,341 enrolled.
Faculty *Total:* 465, 44% full-time, 9% with terminal degrees. *Student/faculty ratio:* 21:1.
Majors Accounting; administrative assistant and secretarial science; agricultural business and management; agricultural mechanization; agriculture; apparel and textile marketing management; applied art; architectural engineering technology; art teacher education; automobile/automotive mechanics technology; avionics maintenance technology; biology/biological sciences; broadcast journalism; business administration and management; business automation/technology/data entry; business teacher education; carpentry; chemical engineering; chemistry; child development; computer and information sciences; computer and information sciences related; computer graphics; computer management; computer programming; computer programming related; computer programming (specific applications); computer science; computer software and media applications related; construction engineering technology; construction management; construction trades; consumer merchandising/retailing management; corrections; corrections and criminal justice related; cosmetology; criminal justice/law enforcement administration; criminal justice/police science; data entry/microcomputer applications; data entry/microcomputer applications related; data processing and data processing technology; dental assisting; dental hygiene; dietetics; drafting and design technology; dramatic/theatre arts; education; electrician; elementary education; emergency medical technology (EMT paramedic); engineering; engineering technology; English; environmental science; environmental studies; executive assistant/executive secretary; family and consumer sciences/human sciences; fashion merchandising; finance; fire science; forestry; funeral service and mortuary science; funeral service and mortuary science related; geology/earth science; graphic and printing equipment operation/production; heating, air conditioning and refrigeration technology; heating, air conditioning, ventilation and refrigeration maintenance technology; hydrology and water resources science; industrial arts; industrial radiologic technology; information science/studies; information technology; interior design; journalism; legal administrative assistant/secretary; legal assistant/paralegal; legal studies; liberal arts and sciences/liberal studies; machine tool technology; marketing/marketing management; mathematics; mechanical design technology; mechanical engineering; mechanical engineering/mechanical technology; medical administrative assistant and medical secretary; medical/clinical assistant; mortuary science and embalming; music; music teacher education; natural resources/conservation; natural resources management and policy; nursing (licensed practical/vocational nurse training); nursing (registered nurse training); office management; office occupations and clerical services; physical therapist assistant; physical therapy; physician assistant; pipefitting and sprinkler fitting; pre-engineering; pre-pharmacy studies; psychology; quality control technology; radio and television; radiologic technology/science; real estate; respiratory care therapy; social work; surgical technology; teacher assistant/aide; water quality and wastewater treatment management and recycling technology; web/multimedia management and webmaster; web page, digital/multimedia and information resources design; welding technology; word processing.
Academic Programs *Special study options:* academic remediation for entering students, adult/continuing education programs, advanced placement credit, cooperative education, distance learning, double majors, English as a second language, external degree program, freshman honors college, honors programs, independent study, internships, off-campus study, part-time degree program, services for LD students, student-designed majors, summer session for credit.
Library Library Learning Information Center with 93,167 titles, 400 serial subscriptions, 4,200 audiovisual materials, an OPAC, a Web page.

Computers on Campus 550 computers available on campus for general student use. A campuswide network can be accessed from off campus. Internet access, online (class) registration, at least one staffed computer lab available.

Student Life *Housing:* college housing not available. *Activities and Organizations:* student-run newspaper, radio and television station, intramural activities, Student Senate, Phi Theta Kappa, Inter-Varsity Christian Fellowship, DECA. *Campus security:* 24-hour emergency response devices and patrols, student patrols, late-night transport/escort service. *Student services:* personal/psychological counseling.

Athletics Member NJCAA. *Intercollegiate sports:* basketball M(s)/W(s), golf M(s), soccer M(s), softball W(s), volleyball W(s). *Intramural sports:* baseball M, basketball M/W, football M, golf M/W, racquetball M/W, soccer M/W, softball M/W, volleyball M/W.

Standardized Tests *Required:* ACT ASSET or ACT COMPASS (for placement). *Recommended:* ACT (for placement).

Costs (2003–04) *Tuition:* area resident $2430 full-time, $68 per credit part-time; state resident $3366 full-time, $94 per credit part-time; nonresident $4806 full-time, $114 per credit part-time. *Required fees:* $60 full-time, $30 per term part-time. *Waivers:* senior citizens and employees or children of employees.

Financial Aid Of all full-time matriculated undergraduates who enrolled, 156 Federal Work-Study jobs (averaging $1640). 386 state and other part-time jobs (averaging $1722).

Applying *Options:* common application, early admission, deferred entrance. *Application fee:* $20. *Required for some:* essay or personal statement. *Recommended:* high school transcript. *Application deadline:* rolling (freshmen), rolling (transfers).

Admissions Contact Mr. Duff Zube, Director of Admissions, Delta College, 1961 Delta Road, University Center, MI 48710. *Phone:* 989-686-9449. *Fax:* 989-667-2202. *E-mail:* admit@alpha.delta.edu.

Glen Oaks Community College
Centreville, Michigan

- **State and locally supported** 2-year, founded 1965, part of Michigan Department of Career Development
- **Calendar** semesters
- **Degree** certificates and associate
- **Rural** 300-acre campus
- **Endowment** $1.4 million
- **Coed,** 1,710 undergraduate students, 39% full-time, 61% women, 39% men

Undergraduates 659 full-time, 1,051 part-time. Students come from 3 states and territories, 1 other country, 2% African American, 0.8% Asian American or Pacific Islander, 2% Hispanic American, 0.9% Native American, 0.1% international.

Freshmen *Admission:* 227 admitted, 214 enrolled.

Faculty *Total:* 108, 26% full-time. *Student/faculty ratio:* 16:1.

Majors Automobile/automotive mechanics technology; biological and physical sciences; business administration and management; liberal arts and sciences/liberal studies; nursing (registered nurse training).

Academic Programs *Special study options:* academic remediation for entering students, adult/continuing education programs, advanced placement credit, distance learning, internships, part-time degree program, services for LD students, summer session for credit.

Library E. J. Shaheen Library with 37,087 titles, 347 serial subscriptions, an OPAC.

Computers on Campus 50 computers available on campus for general student use. A campuswide network can be accessed. Internet access, at least one staffed computer lab available.

Student Life *Housing:* college housing not available. *Activities and Organizations:* student government, choir, band, Phi Theta Kappa. *Campus security:* 24-hour emergency response devices. *Student services:* personal/psychological counseling.

Athletics Member NJCAA. *Intercollegiate sports:* baseball M(s), basketball M(s)/W(s), tennis W(s), volleyball W(s). *Intramural sports:* baseball M, basketball M/W, table tennis M/W, tennis W.

Standardized Tests *Required:* ACT ASSET (for placement).

Costs (2004–05) *Tuition:* area resident $2040 full-time; state resident $3026 full-time; nonresident $3876 full-time. *Required fees:* $310 full-time.

Financial Aid Of all full-time matriculated undergraduates who enrolled, 70 Federal Work-Study jobs (averaging $1100). 38 state and other part-time jobs (averaging $1200).

Applying *Application deadline:* rolling (freshmen), rolling (transfers).

Admissions Contact Ms. Beverly M. Andrews, Director of Admissions/Registrar, Glen Oaks Community College, 62249 Shimmel Road, Centreville, MI 49032-9719. *Phone:* 269-467-9945 Ext. 248. *Toll-free phone:* 888-994-7818. *Fax:* 269-467-9068. *E-mail:* webmaster@glenoaks.cc.mi.us.

Gogebic Community College
Ironwood, Michigan

- **State and locally supported** 2-year, founded 1932, part of Michigan Department of Education
- **Calendar** semesters
- **Degree** certificates and associate
- **Small-town** 195-acre campus
- **Endowment** $675,000
- **Coed,** 1,058 undergraduate students, 54% full-time, 64% women, 36% men

Undergraduates 573 full-time, 485 part-time. Students come from 7 states and territories, 5 other countries, 22% are from out of state, 0.3% African American, 0.3% Asian American or Pacific Islander, 0.8% Hispanic American, 3% Native American, 1% international, 3% transferred in.

Freshmen *Admission:* 299 admitted, 282 enrolled.

Faculty *Total:* 90, 33% full-time. *Student/faculty ratio:* 13:1.

Majors Accounting; administrative assistant and secretarial science; automobile/automotive mechanics technology; biology/biological sciences; business administration and management; business automation/technology/data entry; carpentry; child care and support services management; child development; commercial and advertising art; computer engineering technology; computer graphics; computer/information technology services administration related; computer programming (specific applications); computer science; computer typography and composition equipment operation; construction engineering technology; construction management; corrections; criminal justice/law enforcement administration; data processing and data processing technology; drafting and design technology; education; engineering; forest sciences and biology; graphic and printing equipment operation/production; health information/medical records administration; humanities; information technology; kindergarten/preschool education; legal administrative assistant/secretary; liberal arts and sciences/liberal studies; mathematics; medical administrative assistant and medical secretary; nursing (licensed practical/vocational nurse training); nursing (registered nurse training); office management; psychology; social sciences; social work; sociology; system administration; word processing.

Academic Programs *Special study options:* academic remediation for entering students, adult/continuing education programs, advanced placement credit, cooperative education, distance learning, honors programs, internships, part-time degree program, services for LD students, summer session for credit.

Library Alex D. Chisholm Learning Resources Center with 22,000 titles, 220 serial subscriptions, an OPAC, a Web page.

Computers on Campus 210 computers available on campus for general student use. A campuswide network can be accessed. Internet access, online (class) registration, at least one staffed computer lab available.

Student Life *Housing:* college housing not available. *Activities and Organizations:* drama/theater group, choral group, Drama Club, Student Senate, Phi Theta Kappa, intramural sports. *Student services:* personal/psychological counseling.

Athletics Member NJCAA. *Intercollegiate sports:* basketball M(s)/W(s), cheerleading M/W. *Intramural sports:* basketball M/W, bowling M/W, football M/W, golf M/W, skiing (cross-country) M/W, skiing (downhill) M/W, softball M/W, tennis M/W, track and field M/W, volleyball M/W.

Standardized Tests *Required for some:* nurse entrance exam.

Costs (2003–04) *Tuition:* area resident $1984 full-time, $64 per credit part-time; state resident $2542 full-time, $82 per credit part-time; nonresident $3317 full-time, $107 per credit part-time. *Required fees:* $348 full-time, $5 per credit part-time. *Waivers:* senior citizens and employees or children of employees.

Financial Aid Of all full-time matriculated undergraduates who enrolled, 75 Federal Work-Study jobs (averaging $1800). 50 state and other part-time jobs (averaging $1800).

Applying *Options:* electronic application, early admission, deferred entrance. *Application fee:* $10. *Required:* high school transcript. *Application deadlines:* rolling (freshmen), 8/15 (out-of-state freshmen), 8/15 (transfers). *Notification:* continuous (freshmen).

Admissions Contact Ms. Jeanne Graham, Director of Admissions, Gogebic Community College, E-4946 Jackson Road, Ironwood, MI 49938. *Phone:* 906-932-4231 Ext. 306. *Toll-free phone:* 800-682-5910 Ext. 207. *Fax:* 906-932-0229. *E-mail:* nancyg@gogebic.edu.

Grand Rapids Community College
Grand Rapids, Michigan

- **District-supported** 2-year, founded 1914, part of Michigan Department of Education
- **Calendar** semesters
- **Degree** certificates and associate
- **Urban** 35-acre campus
- **Endowment** $11.0 million
- **Coed,** 14,039 undergraduate students, 43% full-time, 51% women, 49% men

Grand Rapids Community College (continued)

Undergraduates 6,011 full-time, 8,028 part-time. Students come from 9 states and territories, 35 other countries, 2% are from out of state, 11% African American, 3% Asian American or Pacific Islander, 5% Hispanic American, 0.9% Native American, 1% international, 42% transferred in. *Retention:* 55% of 2002 full-time freshmen returned.

Freshmen *Admission:* 5,894 applied, 4,858 admitted, 3,183 enrolled. *Average high school GPA:* 2.72.

Faculty *Total:* 628, 39% full-time, 7% with terminal degrees. *Student/faculty ratio:* 22:1.

Majors Administrative assistant and secretarial science; architectural engineering technology; art; automobile/automotive mechanics technology; business administration and management; computer engineering technology; computer programming; computer science; corrections; criminal justice/law enforcement administration; criminal justice/police science; culinary arts; dental hygiene; drafting and design technology; electrical, electronic and communications engineering technology; fashion merchandising; forestry; geology/earth science; heating, air conditioning, ventilation and refrigeration maintenance technology; industrial technology; legal administrative assistant/secretary; liberal arts and sciences/liberal studies; mass communication/media; medical administrative assistant and medical secretary; music; nursing (licensed practical/vocational nurse training); nursing (registered nurse training); plastics engineering technology; quality control technology; welding technology.

Academic Programs *Special study options:* academic remediation for entering students, adult/continuing education programs, advanced placement credit, cooperative education, distance learning, English as a second language, off-campus study, part-time degree program, services for LD students, study abroad, summer session for credit.

Library Arthur Andrews Memorial Library plus 1 other with 56,250 titles, 620 serial subscriptions, an OPAC, a Web page.

Computers on Campus 1022 computers available on campus for general student use. A campuswide network can be accessed from off campus. Internet access, at least one staffed computer lab available.

Student Life *Housing:* college housing not available. *Activities and Organizations:* drama/theater group, student-run newspaper, choral group, Student Congress, Phi Theta Kappa, Hispanic Student Organization, Asian Student Organization, Service Learning Advisory Board, national fraternities, national sororities. *Campus security:* 24-hour emergency response devices, late-night transport/escort service. *Student services:* personal/psychological counseling.

Athletics Member NJCAA. *Intercollegiate sports:* baseball M/W(s), basketball M(s)/W(s), football M(s), golf M(s), softball W(s), swimming M(s)/W(s), tennis M(s)/W(s), track and field M(s), volleyball W(s), wrestling M(s). *Intramural sports:* badminton M/W, basketball M/W, skiing (cross-country) M/W, skiing (downhill) M/W, soccer M/W, swimming M/W, tennis M/W, volleyball M/W.

Standardized Tests *Required for some:* ACT ASSET. *Recommended:* SAT I or ACT (for admission).

Costs (2003–04) *Tuition:* area resident $1950 full-time, $65 per credit hour part-time; state resident $3000 full-time, $100 per credit hour part-time; nonresident $3900 full-time, $130 per credit hour part-time. Full-time tuition and fees vary according to course load. Part-time tuition and fees vary according to course load. *Required fees:* $80 full-time, $40 per term part-time. *Payment plan:* installment. *Waivers:* employees or children of employees.

Financial Aid Of all full-time matriculated undergraduates who enrolled, 250 Federal Work-Study jobs (averaging $1500). 75 state and other part-time jobs (averaging $1000).

Applying *Options:* early admission, deferred entrance. *Application fee:* $20. *Required:* high school transcript. *Application deadline:* 8/30 (freshmen). *Notification:* continuous (freshmen), continuous (transfers).

Admissions Contact Ms. Diane Patrick, Director of Admissions, Grand Rapids Community College, 143 Bostwick Avenue, NE, Grand Rapids, MI 49503-3201. *Phone:* 616-234-4100. *Fax:* 616-234-4005. *E-mail:* dpatrick@grcc.edu.

HENRY FORD COMMUNITY COLLEGE
Dearborn, Michigan

Admissions Contact Ms. Dorothy A. Murphy, Coordinator of Recruitment, Henry Ford Community College, 5101 Evergreen Road, Dearborn, MI 48128-1495. *Phone:* 313-845-9766. *E-mail:* dorothy@mail.henryford.cc.mi.us.

ITT TECHNICAL INSTITUTE
Grand Rapids, Michigan

- **Proprietary** 2-year, part of ITT Educational Services, Inc
- **Calendar** quarters
- **Degree** associate
- **Coed**

Standardized Tests *Required:* Wonderlic aptitude test (for admission).

Costs (2003–04) *Tuition:* Total Program Cost varies depending on course of study. Consult school catalog.

Applying *Options:* deferred entrance. *Application fee:* $100. *Required:* high school transcript, interview. *Recommended:* letters of recommendation.

Admissions Contact Director of Recruitment, ITT Technical Institute, 4020 Sparks Drive SE, Grand Rapids, MI 49546. *Phone:* 616-956-1060. *Toll-free phone:* 800-632-4676. *Fax:* 616-956-5606.

ITT TECHNICAL INSTITUTE
Canton, Michigan

- **Proprietary** 2-year, founded 2002, part of ITT Educational Services, Inc
- **Calendar** quarters
- **Degree** associate
- **Coed**

Standardized Tests *Required:* (for admission).

Costs (2003–04) *Tuition:* Total Program Cost varies depending on course of study. Consult school catalog.

Applying *Options:* deferred entrance. *Application fee:* $100. *Required:* high school transcript, interview. *Recommended:* letters of recommendation.

Admissions Contact Mr. Dudley Layfield III, Director of Recruitment, ITT Technical Institute, 1905 South Haggerty Road, Canton, MI 48188. *Phone:* 784-397-7800. *Toll-free phone:* 800-247-4477. *Fax:* 734-397-1945.

ITT TECHNICAL INSTITUTE
Troy, Michigan

- **Proprietary** 2-year, founded 1987, part of ITT Educational Services, Inc
- **Calendar** quarters
- **Degree** associate
- **Coed**

Standardized Tests *Required:* Wonderlic aptitude test (for admission).

Costs (2003–04) *Tuition:* Total Program Cost varies depending on course of study. Consult school catalog.

Applying *Options:* deferred entrance. *Application fee:* $100. *Required:* high school transcript, interview. *Recommended:* letters of recommendation.

Admissions Contact Ms. Patricia Hyman, ITT Technical Institute, 1522 East Big Beaver Road, Troy, MI 48083. *Phone:* 248-524-1800. *Toll-free phone:* 800-832-6817. *Fax:* 248-524-1965.

JACKSON COMMUNITY COLLEGE
Jackson, Michigan

- **County-supported** 2-year, founded 1928, part of Michigan Department of Education
- **Calendar** semesters
- **Degree** certificates and associate
- **Suburban** 580-acre campus with easy access to Detroit
- **Endowment** $8.1 million
- **Coed,** 5,899 undergraduate students, 35% full-time, 64% women, 36% men

Undergraduates 2,062 full-time, 3,837 part-time. 1% are from out of state, 6% African American, 1% Asian American or Pacific Islander, 3% Hispanic American, 0.8% Native American, 34% transferred in.

Freshmen *Admission:* 672 enrolled.

Faculty *Total:* 374, 25% full-time, 4% with terminal degrees. *Student/faculty ratio:* 15:1.

Majors Accounting and finance; administrative assistant and secretarial science; airline pilot and flight crew; automobile/automotive mechanics technology; business administration and management; computer and information sciences and support services related; construction trades related; corrections; criminal justice/law enforcement administration; data processing and data processing technology; diagnostic medical sonography and ultrasound technology; early childhood education; electrical, electronic and communications engineering technology; emergency medical technology (EMT paramedic); executive assistant/executive secretary; general studies; graphic design; heating, air conditioning and refrigeration technology; liberal arts and sciences/liberal studies; marketing/marketing management; medical/clinical assistant; medical insurance/medical billing; medical radiologic technology; medical transcription; nursing (licensed practical/vocational nurse training); nursing (registered nurse training).

Academic Programs *Special study options:* academic remediation for entering students, adult/continuing education programs, advanced placement credit, cooperative education, distance learning, external degree program, honors programs, internships, part-time degree program, services for LD students, summer session for credit.

Library Atkinson Learning Resources Center plus 1 other with 66,000 titles, 300 serial subscriptions, 4,600 audiovisual materials, an OPAC, a Web page.

Computers on Campus 338 computers available on campus for general student use. A campuswide network can be accessed from off campus. Internet access, online (class) registration, at least one staffed computer lab available.

Student Life *Housing:* college housing not available. *Activities and Organizations:* drama/theater group, student-run newspaper, choral group. *Campus security:* 24-hour patrols.

Standardized Tests *Recommended:* ACT (for placement).

Costs (2003–04) *Tuition:* area resident $2070 full-time, $69 per credit hour part-time; state resident $2655 full-time, $89 per credit hour part-time; nonresident $3270 full-time, $109 per credit hour part-time. Full-time tuition and fees vary according to location. Part-time tuition and fees vary according to location. *Required fees:* $5 per credit part-time, $15 per term part-time. *Payment plan:* deferred payment. *Waivers:* employees or children of employees.

Financial Aid Of all full-time matriculated undergraduates who enrolled, 60 Federal Work-Study jobs (averaging $1304). 19 state and other part-time jobs (averaging $1192).

Applying *Options:* electronic application, early admission. *Application deadline:* rolling (freshmen), rolling (transfers). *Notification:* continuous (freshmen), continuous (transfers).

Admissions Contact Mr. Steven Bloomfield, Director of enrollment Management and Student Life, Jackson Community College, 2111 Emmons Road, Jackson, MI 49201. *Phone:* 517-796-8628. *Toll-free phone:* 888-522-7344. *Fax:* 517-796-8631.

KALAMAZOO VALLEY COMMUNITY COLLEGE
Kalamazoo, Michigan

- **State and locally supported** 2-year, founded 1966
- **Calendar** semesters
- **Degree** certificates and associate
- **Suburban** 187-acre campus
- **Coed,** 10,438 undergraduate students, 36% full-time, 53% women, 47% men

Undergraduates 3,753 full-time, 6,685 part-time. Students come from 3 states and territories, 46 other countries, 1% are from out of state, 9% African American, 1% Asian American or Pacific Islander, 3% Hispanic American, 1% Native American, 1% international.

Freshmen *Admission:* 1,853 enrolled.

Faculty *Total:* 134, 96% full-time. *Student/faculty ratio:* 45:1.

Majors Accounting technology and bookkeeping; automobile/automotive mechanics technology; business administration and management; chemical technology; commercial and advertising art; computer programming; criminal justice/police science; dental hygiene; drafting and design technology; electrical, electronic and communications engineering technology; elementary education; emergency medical technology (EMT paramedic); executive assistant/executive secretary; fire science; health science; heating, air conditioning and refrigeration technology; legal administrative assistant/secretary; liberal arts and sciences/liberal studies; machine tool technology; management information systems; marketing/marketing management; mechanical engineering/mechanical technology; medical administrative assistant and medical secretary; medical/clinical assistant; nursing (registered nurse training); plastics engineering technology; pre-engineering; respiratory care therapy; welding technology.

Academic Programs *Special study options:* academic remediation for entering students, advanced placement credit, cooperative education, distance learning, English as a second language, honors programs, independent study, internships, off-campus study, part-time degree program, services for LD students, student-designed majors, summer session for credit. *ROTC:* Army (c).

Library Kalamazoo Valley Community College Library with 88,791 titles, 420 serial subscriptions, an OPAC, a Web page.

Computers on Campus 1000 computers available on campus for general student use. A campuswide network can be accessed from off campus. Internet access, at least one staffed computer lab available.

Student Life *Housing:* college housing not available. *Activities and Organizations:* student-run newspaper, choral group. *Campus security:* 24-hour emergency response devices and patrols, late-night transport/escort service. *Student services:* personal/psychological counseling, women's center.

Athletics Member NJCAA. *Intercollegiate sports:* baseball M(s), basketball M(s)/W(s), golf M, softball W(s), tennis M(s)/W(s), volleyball W(s). *Intramural sports:* basketball M/W.

Standardized Tests *Recommended:* ACT (for placement).

Costs (2003–04) *Tuition:* area resident $1224 full-time, $51 per credit part-time; state resident $2088 full-time, $87 per credit part-time; nonresident $2904 full-time, $121 per credit part-time. *Payment plan:* installment. *Waivers:* senior citizens and employees or children of employees.

Financial Aid Of all full-time matriculated undergraduates who enrolled, 77 Federal Work-Study jobs (averaging $1400). 11 state and other part-time jobs (averaging $1528).

Applying *Options:* early admission, deferred entrance. *Application deadline:* rolling (freshmen), rolling (transfers). *Notification:* continuous (freshmen), continuous (transfers).

Admissions Contact Mr. Michael McCall, Director of Admissions, Registration and Records, Kalamazoo Valley Community College, PO Box 4070, Kalamazoo, MI 49003-4070. *Phone:* 269-488-4207. *Fax:* 616-372-5161. *E-mail:* admissions@kvcc.edu.

KELLOGG COMMUNITY COLLEGE
Battle Creek, Michigan

- **State and locally supported** 2-year, founded 1956, part of Michigan Department of Education
- **Calendar** semesters
- **Degree** certificates and associate
- **Urban** 120-acre campus
- **Endowment** $91,005
- **Coed,** 5,523 undergraduate students, 33% full-time, 71% women, 29% men

Undergraduates 1,824 full-time, 3,699 part-time. Students come from 3 states and territories, 11 other countries, 1% are from out of state, 7% African American, 1% Asian American or Pacific Islander, 2% Hispanic American, 0.5% Native American, 0.8% international, 3% transferred in.

Freshmen *Admission:* 1,512 applied, 1,512 admitted, 824 enrolled.

Faculty *Total:* 382, 24% full-time, 7% with terminal degrees. *Student/faculty ratio:* 15:1.

Majors Accounting; accounting technology and bookkeeping; administrative assistant and secretarial science; anthropology; art; art teacher education; biology/biological sciences; business administration and management; chemical technology; chemistry; clinical/medical laboratory technology; commercial and advertising art; communication/speech communication and rhetoric; computer engineering technology; computer graphics; computer programming; computer programming (specific applications); computer software and media applications related; corrections; criminal justice/police science; criminal justice/safety; data entry/microcomputer applications related; dental hygiene; drafting and design technology; dramatic/theatre arts; elementary education; emergency medical technology (EMT paramedic); engineering; English; executive assistant/executive secretary; fire protection and safety technology; general studies; heating, air conditioning, ventilation and refrigeration maintenance technology; history; human services; industrial technology; international relations and affairs; journalism; kindergarten/preschool education; legal administrative assistant/secretary; legal assistant/paralegal; liberal arts and sciences/liberal studies; machine tool technology; mathematics; medical administrative assistant and medical secretary; medical radiologic technology; music; nursing (licensed practical/vocational nurse training); nursing (registered nurse training); philosophy; physical education teaching and coaching; physical therapist assistant; physics; pipefitting and sprinkler fitting; plastics engineering technology; political science and government; pre-law studies; pre-medical studies; pre-pharmacy studies; pre-theology/pre-ministerial studies; pre-veterinary studies; psychology; public relations/image management; radio and television broadcasting technology; robotics technology; secondary education; sheet metal technology; social work; sociology; special education; technology/industrial arts teacher education; welding technology; word processing.

Academic Programs *Special study options:* academic remediation for entering students, accelerated degree program, adult/continuing education programs, advanced placement credit, distance learning, double majors, freshman honors college, honors programs, independent study, internships, off-campus study, part-time degree program, services for LD students, summer session for credit.

Library Emory W. Morris Learning Resource Center with 42,131 titles, 172 serial subscriptions, 4,145 audiovisual materials, an OPAC, a Web page.

Computers on Campus 550 computers available on campus for general student use. A campuswide network can be accessed from off campus. At least one staffed computer lab available.

Student Life *Housing:* college housing not available. *Activities and Organizations:* drama/theater group, student-run newspaper, choral group, Tech Club, Phi Theta Kappa, Student Nurses Association, Crude Arts Club, Art League. *Campus security:* 24-hour emergency response devices and patrols, late-night transport/escort service. *Student services:* personal/psychological counseling.

Athletics Member NJCAA. *Intercollegiate sports:* baseball M(s), basketball M(s)/W(s), soccer M, softball W(s), volleyball W(s).

Standardized Tests *Required for some:* SAT I or ACT (for admission).

Costs (2004–05) *Tuition:* area resident $1984 full-time; state resident $3124 full-time; nonresident $4627 full-time. Full-time tuition and fees vary according to reciprocity agreements. Part-time tuition and fees vary according to reciprocity agreements. *Required fees:* $150 full-time. *Payment plan:* deferred payment. *Waivers:* senior citizens and employees or children of employees.

Kellogg Community College (continued)

Financial Aid Of all full-time matriculated undergraduates who enrolled, 41 Federal Work-Study jobs (averaging $2251). 43 state and other part-time jobs (averaging $2058).

Applying *Options:* common application, early admission, deferred entrance. *Required for some:* high school transcript, minimum 2.0 GPA. *Application deadline:* 8/30 (freshmen), rolling (transfers). *Notification:* continuous (freshmen), continuous (transfers).

Admissions Contact Mr. Sedgwick Harris, Director of Admissions, Kellogg Community College, 450 North Avenue, Battle Creek, MI 49017. *Phone:* 269-965-3931 Ext. 2641. *Fax:* 269-965-4133.

KIRTLAND COMMUNITY COLLEGE
Roscommon, Michigan

- **District-supported** 2-year, founded 1966, part of Michigan Department of Education
- **Calendar** semesters
- **Degree** certificates and associate
- **Rural** 180-acre campus
- **Coed,** 1,918 undergraduate students, 32% full-time, 58% women, 42% men

Undergraduates 609 full-time, 1,309 part-time. 0.8% African American, 0.1% Asian American or Pacific Islander, 0.6% Hispanic American, 1% Native American, 0.1% international.

Freshmen *Admission:* 355 applied, 355 admitted, 355 enrolled.

Faculty *Total:* 95, 41% full-time.

Majors Accounting; administrative assistant and secretarial science; art; automobile/automotive mechanics technology; biological and physical sciences; business administration and management; corrections; cosmetology; creative writing; criminal justice/law enforcement administration; drafting and design technology; industrial technology; information science/studies; legal administrative assistant/secretary; liberal arts and sciences/liberal studies; marketing/marketing management; medical administrative assistant and medical secretary; nursing (licensed practical/vocational nurse training); nursing (registered nurse training); welding technology.

Academic Programs *Special study options:* academic remediation for entering students, adult/continuing education programs, advanced placement credit, cooperative education, internships, part-time degree program, services for LD students, summer session for credit.

Library Kirtland Community College Library with 35,000 titles, 317 serial subscriptions.

Computers on Campus 125 computers available on campus for general student use.

Student Life *Activities and Organizations:* drama/theater group, student-run newspaper, choral group. *Campus security:* student patrols, late-night transport/escort service. *Student services:* personal/psychological counseling.

Standardized Tests *Required:* ACT ASSET (for placement). *Recommended:* SAT I or ACT (for placement).

Costs (2004–05) *Tuition:* area resident $2008 full-time, $63 per credit part-time; state resident $3685 full-time, $115 per credit part-time; nonresident $4552 full-time, $142 per credit part-time. *Required fees:* $631 full-time. *Room and board:* $4350.

Financial Aid Of all full-time matriculated undergraduates who enrolled, 46 Federal Work-Study jobs (averaging $1282). 82 state and other part-time jobs (averaging $1578).

Applying *Options:* early admission, deferred entrance. *Application deadline:* rolling (freshmen), rolling (transfers). *Notification:* continuous until 8/22 (freshmen), continuous until 8/22 (transfers).

Admissions Contact Ms. Stacey Thompson, Registrar, Kirtland Community College, 10775 North St Helen Road, Roscommon, MI 48653-9699. *Phone:* 517-275-5121 Ext. 248.

LAKE MICHIGAN COLLEGE
Benton Harbor, Michigan

- **District-supported** 2-year, founded 1946, part of Michigan Department of Education
- **Calendar** semesters
- **Degree** certificates and associate
- **Small-town** 260-acre campus
- **Coed**

Athletics Member NJCAA.

Standardized Tests *Required:* ACT ASSET (for placement). *Recommended:* ACT (for placement).

Applying *Options:* common application, early admission, deferred entrance. *Required:* high school transcript. *Required for some:* interview.

Admissions Contact Mrs. Linda Steinberger, Manager of Admissions, Lake Michigan College, 2755 East Napier, Benton Harbor, MI 49022-1899. *Phone:* 616-927-8100 Ext. 5205. *Toll-free phone:* 800-252-1LMC. *Fax:* 269-927-6874.

LANSING COMMUNITY COLLEGE
Lansing, Michigan

- **State and locally supported** 2-year, founded 1957, part of Michigan Department of Education
- **Calendar** semesters
- **Degree** certificates and associate
- **Urban** 28-acre campus
- **Endowment** $3.5 million
- **Coed,** 18,575 undergraduate students, 31% full-time, 56% women, 44% men

Undergraduates 5,836 full-time, 12,739 part-time. Students come from 14 states and territories, 69 other countries, 1% are from out of state, 9% African American, 3% Asian American or Pacific Islander, 4% Hispanic American, 1% Native American, 2% international.

Freshmen *Admission:* 10,810 applied, 10,810 admitted, 1,072 enrolled.

Faculty *Total:* 1,370, 17% full-time. *Student/faculty ratio:* 14:1.

Majors Accounting; administrative assistant and secretarial science; airline pilot and flight crew; architectural engineering technology; art; automobile/automotive mechanics technology; avionics maintenance technology; biological and physical sciences; biology/biological sciences; biology/biotechnology laboratory technician; broadcast journalism; business administration and management; carpentry; chemical engineering; chemistry; child development; cinematography and film/video production; civil engineering technology; clinical laboratory science/medical technology; commercial and advertising art; computer engineering technology; computer graphics; computer management; computer programming; computer typography and composition equipment operation; construction engineering technology; consumer merchandising/retailing management; corrections; court reporting; criminal justice/law enforcement administration; criminal justice/police science; dance; dental hygiene; developmental and child psychology; diagnostic medical sonography and ultrasound technology; drafting and design technology; dramatic/theatre arts; education; electrical, electronic and communications engineering technology; electromechanical technology; elementary education; emergency medical technology (EMT paramedic); engineering; engineering technology; English; film/cinema studies; finance; fine/studio arts; fire science; geography; geology/earth science; gerontology; heating, air conditioning, ventilation and refrigeration maintenance technology; heavy equipment maintenance technology; horticultural science; hospitality administration; hotel/motel administration; human resources management; human services; industrial technology; information science/studies; international business/trade/commerce; journalism; kindergarten/preschool education; labor and industrial relations; landscape architecture; legal administrative assistant/secretary; legal assistant/paralegal; liberal arts and sciences/liberal studies; machine tool technology; management information systems; marketing/marketing management; mass communication/media; mathematics; mechanical design technology; mechanical engineering/mechanical technology; medical/clinical assistant; medical radiologic technology; music; nursing (licensed practical/vocational nurse training); nursing (registered nurse training); philosophy; photography; physical education teaching and coaching; pre-engineering; public administration; public relations/image management; quality control technology; radio and television; real estate; religious studies; respiratory care therapy; sign language interpretation and translation; social work; special products marketing; speech and rhetoric; surgical technology; survey technology; teacher assistant/aide; telecommunications; tourism and travel services management; veterinary technology; voice and opera; welding technology.

Academic Programs *Special study options:* academic remediation for entering students, adult/continuing education programs, advanced placement credit, cooperative education, distance learning, double majors, English as a second language, external degree program, honors programs, independent study, internships, part-time degree program, services for LD students, study abroad, summer session for credit. *ROTC:* Army (c), Air Force (c).

Library Abel Sykes Technology and Learning Center plus 1 other with 98,125 titles, 600 serial subscriptions, 11,653 audiovisual materials, an OPAC, a Web page.

Computers on Campus 1146 computers available on campus for general student use. A campuswide network can be accessed from off campus. At least one staffed computer lab available.

Student Life *Housing:* college housing not available. *Activities and Organizations:* drama/theater group, student-run newspaper, radio station, choral group, Student Marketing, Legal Assistants Club, Student Nursing Club, Phi Theta Kappa, Student Advising Club, national fraternities, national sororities. *Campus security:* 24-hour emergency response devices and patrols, student patrols, late-night transport/escort service. *Student services:* personal/psychological counseling, women's center.

Athletics Member NJCAA. *Intercollegiate sports:* basketball M(s)/W(s), cross-country running M(s)/W(s), golf M(s), track and field M(s)/W(s), volleyball W(s). *Intramural sports:* baseball M, basketball M/W, cross-country running M/W, ice hockey M, soccer M/W, softball W, track and field M/W, volleyball W.

Standardized Tests *Required for some:* SAT I or ACT (for placement).

Costs (2004–05) *Tuition:* area resident $1705 full-time, $55 per contact hour part-time; state resident $2728 full-time, $88 per contact hour part-time; nonresident $3720 full-time, $120 per contact hour part-time. *Required fees:* $40 full-time.

Financial Aid Of all full-time matriculated undergraduates who enrolled, 125 Federal Work-Study jobs (averaging $2636). 122 state and other part-time jobs (averaging $2563).

Applying *Options:* common application, electronic application, early admission, deferred entrance. *Required for some:* essay or personal statement, high school transcript, 2 letters of recommendation, interview. *Application deadline:* rolling (freshmen), rolling (transfers).

Admissions Contact Mr. Lucian Leon, Director of Marketing and Admissions, Lansing Community College, PO Box 40010, Lansing, MI 48901-7210. *Phone:* 517-483-1058. *Toll-free phone:* 800-644-4LCC. *Fax:* 517-483-9668. *E-mail:* jhearns@lcc.edu.

LEWIS COLLEGE OF BUSINESS
Detroit, Michigan

- **Independent** 2-year, founded 1929
- **Calendar** semesters
- **Degree** associate
- **Urban** 11-acre campus
- **Coed**

Faculty *Student/faculty ratio:* 15:1.

Student Life *Campus security:* parking lot security.

Financial Aid Of all full-time matriculated undergraduates who enrolled, 80 Federal Work-Study jobs (averaging $2000). 40 state and other part-time jobs (averaging $1000).

Applying *Options:* common application, early admission, deferred entrance. *Application fee:* $15. *Required:* high school transcript.

Admissions Contact Ms. Frances Ambrose, Admissions Secretary, Lewis College of Business, 17370 Meyers Road, Detroit, MI 48235-1423. *Phone:* 313-862-6300.

MACOMB COMMUNITY COLLEGE
Warren, Michigan

- **District-supported** 2-year, founded 1954
- **Calendar** semesters
- **Degree** certificates and associate
- **Suburban** 384-acre campus with easy access to Detroit
- **Endowment** $8.0 million
- **Coed,** 22,245 undergraduate students, 28% full-time, 53% women, 47% men

Undergraduates 6,270 full-time, 15,975 part-time. Students come from 2 states and territories, 5% African American, 3% Asian American or Pacific Islander, 1% Hispanic American, 0.7% Native American, 1% international.

Freshmen *Admission:* 1,418 enrolled.

Faculty *Total:* 935, 24% full-time, 11% with terminal degrees. *Student/faculty ratio:* 28:1.

Majors Accounting; administrative assistant and secretarial science; agriculture; architectural drafting and CAD/CADD; automobile/automotive mechanics technology; automotive engineering technology; biology/biological sciences; business administration and management; business automation/technology/data entry; business/commerce; cabinetmaking and millwork; chemistry; child care and support services management; civil engineering technology; commercial and advertising art; communication/speech communication and rhetoric; computer programming; computer programming (specific applications); construction engineering technology; criminal justice/law enforcement administration; criminal justice/police science; culinary arts; drafting and design technology; electrical, electronic and communications engineering technology; electrical/electronics equipment installation and repair; electromechanical technology; emergency medical technology (EMT paramedic); energy management and systems technology; engineering related; finance; fire protection and safety technology; forensic science and technology; general studies; graphic and printing equipment operation/production; heating, air conditioning and refrigeration technology; heating, air conditioning, ventilation and refrigeration maintenance technology; industrial mechanics and maintenance technology; industrial technology; international/global studies; legal assistant/paralegal; legal studies; liberal arts and sciences/liberal studies; machine tool technology; manufacturing technology; marketing/marketing management; mathematics; mechanical design technology; mechanical drafting and CAD/CADD; mechanical engineering/mechanical technology; mechanic and repair technologies related; medical/clinical assistant; mental health/rehabilitation; metallurgical technology; music

performance; nursing (registered nurse training); occupational therapist assistant; operations management; physical therapist assistant; plastics engineering technology; plumbing technology; pre-engineering; quality control technology; respiratory care therapy; robotics technology; safety/security technology; sheet metal technology; social psychology; surgical technology; survey technology; tool and die technology; veterinary/animal health technology; veterinary sciences; welding technology.

Academic Programs *Special study options:* academic remediation for entering students, adult/continuing education programs, advanced placement credit, cooperative education, English as a second language, honors programs, internships, off-campus study, part-time degree program, services for LD students, student-designed majors, summer session for credit.

Library 159,226 titles, 4,240 serial subscriptions, an OPAC.

Computers on Campus 1800 computers available on campus for general student use. A campuswide network can be accessed from off campus. At least one staffed computer lab available.

Student Life *Housing:* college housing not available. *Activities and Organizations:* drama/theater group, Phi Beta Kappa, Adventure Unlimited, Alpha Rho Rho, SADD. *Campus security:* 24-hour emergency response devices and patrols, late-night transport/escort service, security phones in parking lots, surveillance cameras. *Student services:* health clinic, personal/psychological counseling.

Athletics Member NJCAA. *Intercollegiate sports:* baseball M(s), basketball M(s), cross-country running M(s)/W(s), soccer M(s), softball W(s), track and field M(s)/W(s), volleyball W(s). *Intramural sports:* baseball M, basketball M, bowling M/W, cross-country running M/W, football M/W, skiing (cross-country) M/W, skiing (downhill) M/W, volleyball M/W.

Standardized Tests *Required for some:* ACT ASSET, ACT COMPASS.

Costs (2003–04) *Tuition:* area resident $1860 full-time, $60 per semester hour part-time; state resident $2727 full-time, $88 per semester hour part-time; nonresident $3193 full-time, $103 per semester hour part-time. *Required fees:* $15 per term part-time.

Financial Aid Of all full-time matriculated undergraduates who enrolled, 954 Federal Work-Study jobs (averaging $2610).

Applying *Options:* common application, early admission, deferred entrance. *Application fee:* $15. *Application deadline:* rolling (freshmen), rolling (transfers).

Admissions Contact Mr. Richard P. Stevens, Coordinator of Admissions and Assessment, Macomb Community College, G312, 14500 East 12 Mile Road, Warren, MI 48088-3896. *Phone:* 586-445-7246. *Toll-free phone:* 866-622-6624. *Fax:* 586-445-7140.

MID MICHIGAN COMMUNITY COLLEGE
Harrison, Michigan

- **State and locally supported** 2-year, founded 1965, part of Michigan Department of Education
- **Calendar** semesters
- **Degree** certificates and associate
- **Rural** 560-acre campus
- **Coed,** 3,064 undergraduate students, 45% full-time, 61% women, 39% men

Undergraduates 1,368 full-time, 1,696 part-time. Students come from 6 states and territories, 0.5% are from out of state, 2% African American, 0.8% Asian American or Pacific Islander, 2% Hispanic American, 1% Native American, 6% transferred in. *Retention:* 8% of 2002 full-time freshmen returned.

Freshmen *Admission:* 1,066 applied, 1,066 admitted, 892 enrolled. *Test scores:* ACT scores over 18: 69%; ACT scores over 24: 9%; ACT scores over 30: 2%.

Faculty *Total:* 252, 24% full-time, 2% with terminal degrees. *Student/faculty ratio:* 15:1.

Majors Accounting; administrative assistant and secretarial science; art; automobile/automotive mechanics technology; biochemical technology; biological and physical sciences; biology/biological sciences; biology/biotechnology laboratory technician; business administration and management; chemistry; child care provision; child development; commercial and advertising art; computer graphics; computer science; corrections; criminal justice/law enforcement administration; drafting and design technology; dramatic/theatre arts; education (K-12); elementary education; emergency medical technology (EMT paramedic); engineering technologies related; engineering technology; environmental studies; fire science; fish/game management; general studies; heating, air conditioning, ventilation and refrigeration maintenance technology; hospitality administration; hospitality and recreation marketing; industrial radiologic technology; information science/studies; legal administrative assistant/secretary; liberal arts and sciences/liberal studies; machine tool technology; marketing/marketing management; mathematics; medical administrative assistant and medical secretary; medical/clinical assistant; medical transcription; nursing (licensed practical/vocational nurse training); nursing (registered nurse training); ophthalmic and optometric support services and allied professions related; pharmacy; physical therapy; pre-engineering; psychology; secondary education; sociology; speech and rhetoric; speech/theater education.

Mid Michigan Community College (continued)

Academic Programs *Special study options:* academic remediation for entering students, adult/continuing education programs, advanced placement credit, cooperative education, distance learning, honors programs, independent study, internships, part-time degree program, services for LD students, summer session for credit.

Library Charles A. Amble Library with 29,450 titles, 200 serial subscriptions.

Computers on Campus 175 computers available on campus for general student use. A campuswide network can be accessed. At least one staffed computer lab available.

Student Life *Housing:* college housing not available. *Activities and Organizations:* drama/theater group, student-run newspaper, choral group, Commission of Student Activities Services, Phi Theta Kappa. *Campus security:* 24-hour emergency response devices.

Standardized Tests *Recommended:* ACT (for placement).

Costs (2004–05) *Tuition:* area resident $1460 full-time, $61 per credit part-time; state resident $2507 full-time, $104 per credit part-time; nonresident $4200 full-time, $175 per credit part-time. Full-time tuition and fees vary according to program. Part-time tuition and fees vary according to program. *Payment plan:* installment. *Waivers:* senior citizens and employees or children of employees.

Financial Aid Of all full-time matriculated undergraduates who enrolled, 50 Federal Work-Study jobs (averaging $3600). 50 state and other part-time jobs (averaging $3600).

Applying *Options:* early admission. *Required for some:* interview. *Recommended:* high school transcript. *Application deadline:* rolling (freshmen), rolling (transfers). *Notification:* continuous (freshmen), continuous (transfers).

Admissions Contact Ms. Brenda Mather, Admissions Specialist, Mid Michigan Community College, 1375 South Clare Avenue, Harrison, MI 48625. *Phone:* 989-386-6661. *Fax:* 989-386-6613. *E-mail:* apply@midmich.edu.

MONROE COUNTY COMMUNITY COLLEGE
Monroe, Michigan

- **County-supported** 2-year, founded 1964, part of Michigan Department of Education
- **Calendar** semesters
- **Degree** certificates and associate
- **Small-town** 150-acre campus with easy access to Detroit and Toledo
- **Coed,** 3,943 undergraduate students, 38% full-time, 56% women, 44% men

Undergraduates 1,501 full-time, 2,442 part-time. Students come from 3 states and territories, 1 other country, 4% are from out of state, 5% transferred in.

Freshmen *Admission:* 1,700 applied, 1,698 admitted, 555 enrolled. *Average high school GPA:* 2.5.

Faculty *Total:* 201, 27% full-time.

Majors Accounting; administrative assistant and secretarial science; architectural engineering technology; art; biology/biological sciences; business administration and management; child development; clinical laboratory science/medical technology; computer and information sciences related; computer engineering technology; computer graphics; computer programming (specific applications); criminal justice/police science; criminal justice/safety; culinary arts; data processing and data processing technology; drafting and design technology; electrical, electronic and communications engineering technology; elementary education; English; finance; funeral service and mortuary science; industrial technology; information technology; journalism; legal administrative assistant/secretary; liberal arts and sciences/liberal studies; marketing/marketing management; mass communication/media; mathematics; medical administrative assistant and medical secretary; nursing (registered nurse training); physical therapy; pre-engineering; psychology; respiratory care therapy; social work; speech and rhetoric; veterinary sciences; web/multimedia management and webmaster; web page, digital/multimedia and information resources design; welding technology; word processing.

Academic Programs *Special study options:* academic remediation for entering students, advanced placement credit, independent study, part-time degree program, services for LD students, summer session for credit.

Library Campbell Learning Resource Center with 47,352 titles, 321 serial subscriptions, an OPAC.

Computers on Campus 140 computers available on campus for general student use. At least one staffed computer lab available.

Student Life *Housing:* college housing not available. *Activities and Organizations:* drama/theater group, student-run newspaper, choral group, student government, Society of Auto Engineers, Oasis, Nursing Students Organization. *Campus security:* police patrols during open hours.

Standardized Tests *Required:* ACT ASSET, ACT COMPASS (for admission). *Required for some:* ACT (for admission). *Recommended:* ACT (for admission).

Costs (2004–05) *Tuition:* area resident $1440 full-time, $60 per credit part-time; state resident $2256 full-time, $96 per credit part-time; nonresident $2448 full-time, $104 per credit part-time. *Required fees:* $146 full-time. *Waivers:* senior citizens and employees or children of employees.

Applying *Options:* early admission, deferred entrance. *Application fee:* $25. *Required:* high school transcript. *Application deadline:* rolling (transfers). *Notification:* continuous (freshmen), continuous (transfers).

Admissions Contact Mr. Randell W. Daniels, Director of Admissions and Guidance Services, Monroe County Community College, 155 South Raisinville Road, Monroe, MI 48161-9047. *Phone:* 734-384-4261. *Toll-free phone:* 877-YES MCCC. *Fax:* 734-242-9711. *E-mail:* rdaniels@monroeccc.edu.

MONTCALM COMMUNITY COLLEGE
Sidney, Michigan

- **State and locally supported** 2-year, founded 1965, part of Michigan Department of Education
- **Calendar** semesters
- **Degree** certificates and associate
- **Rural** 240-acre campus with easy access to Grand Rapids
- **Endowment** $3.3 million
- **Coed,** 1,802 undergraduate students, 30% full-time, 67% women, 33% men

Undergraduates 533 full-time, 1,269 part-time. Students come from 1 other state, 0.3% African American, 0.5% Asian American or Pacific Islander, 1% Hispanic American, 0.7% Native American, 16% transferred in.

Freshmen *Admission:* 429 applied, 429 admitted, 298 enrolled. *Average high school GPA:* 2.19. *Test scores:* ACT scores over 18: 74%; ACT scores over 24: 15%.

Faculty *Total:* 114, 22% full-time, 6% with terminal degrees. *Student/faculty ratio:* 13:1.

Majors Accounting; administrative assistant and secretarial science; business administration and management; child care and support services management; child care provision; computer installation and repair technology; corrections; cosmetology; criminal justice/law enforcement administration; data processing and data processing technology; drafting and design technology; electrical, electronic and communications engineering technology; emergency medical technology (EMT paramedic); entrepreneurship; executive assistant/executive secretary; industrial radiologic technology; industrial technology; liberal arts and sciences/liberal studies; management information systems; medical administrative assistant and medical secretary; medical radiologic technology; nursing (registered nurse training).

Academic Programs *Special study options:* academic remediation for entering students, adult/continuing education programs, advanced placement credit, cooperative education, distance learning, double majors, independent study, internships, off-campus study, part-time degree program, services for LD students, summer session for credit.

Library Montcalm Community College Library with 29,848 titles, 3,670 serial subscriptions, 580 audiovisual materials, an OPAC, a Web page.

Computers on Campus 450 computers available on campus for general student use. A campuswide network can be accessed from off campus. Internet access, online (class) registration, at least one staffed computer lab available.

Student Life *Housing:* college housing not available. *Activities and Organizations:* drama/theater group, choral group, Nursing Club, Native American Club, Phi Theta Kappa, Business Club, Judo Club. *Student services:* personal/psychological counseling.

Athletics *Intramural sports:* volleyball M/W.

Standardized Tests *Required:* ACT ASSET, ACT COMPASS (for placement). *Recommended:* ACT (for placement).

Costs (2003–04) *Tuition:* area resident $1680 full-time, $60 per credit hour part-time; state resident $2548 full-time, $91 per credit hour part-time; nonresident $3276 full-time, $117 per credit hour part-time. *Required fees:* $148 full-time, $6 per credit hour part-time. *Payment plan:* installment. *Waivers:* senior citizens and employees or children of employees.

Financial Aid Of all full-time matriculated undergraduates who enrolled, 57 Federal Work-Study jobs (averaging $2000).

Applying *Options:* early admission, deferred entrance. *Recommended:* high school transcript. *Application deadline:* rolling (freshmen), rolling (transfers). *Notification:* continuous (freshmen), continuous (transfers).

Admissions Contact Ms. Kathie Lofts, Director of Admissions, Montcalm Community College, 2800 College Drive, Sidney, MI 48885. *Phone:* 989-328-1250. *Toll-free phone:* 877-328-2111. *Fax:* 989-328-2950. *E-mail:* admissions@montcalm.edu.

MOTT COMMUNITY COLLEGE
Flint, Michigan

- **District-supported** 2-year, founded 1923, part of Michigan Labor and Economic Growth Department

- **Calendar** semesters
- **Degree** certificates and associate
- **Urban** 20-acre campus with easy access to Detroit
- **Endowment** $31.5 million
- **Coed,** 10,188 undergraduate students, 34% full-time, 62% women, 38% men

Undergraduates 3,445 full-time, 6,743 part-time. Students come from 8 states and territories, 24 other countries, 0.2% are from out of state, 18% African American, 0.7% Asian American or Pacific Islander, 3% Hispanic American, 1% Native American, 0.4% international, 4% transferred in.

Freshmen *Admission:* 4,630 applied, 1,640 admitted, 1,640 enrolled.

Faculty *Total:* 453, 33% full-time, 10% with terminal degrees. *Student/faculty ratio:* 23:1.

Majors Accounting technology and bookkeeping; administrative assistant and secretarial science; architectural engineering technology; autobody/collision and repair technology; automobile/automotive mechanics technology; business administration and management; business/commerce; child care provision; communications technology; community health services counseling; computer and information sciences and support services related; computer systems networking and telecommunications; criminal justice/police science; culinary arts; dental assisting; dental hygiene; drafting and design technology; early childhood education; electrical, electronic and communications engineering technology; elementary education; emergency medical technology (EMT paramedic); engineering technologies related; entrepreneurship; fire protection and safety technology; foodservice systems administration; general studies; graphic design; heating, air conditioning and refrigeration technology; histologic technician; information resources management; international business/trade/commerce; legal administrative assistant/secretary; legal assistant/paralegal; liberal arts and sciences/liberal studies; management information systems; manufacturing technology; marketing/marketing management; mechanical engineering/mechanical technology; medical administrative assistant and medical secretary; medical radiologic technology; nursing (licensed practical/vocational nurse training); nursing (registered nurse training); occupational therapist assistant; office management; photography; physical therapist assistant; precision production related; quality control technology; respiratory care therapy; sign language interpretation and translation; survey technology.

Academic Programs *Special study options:* academic remediation for entering students, accelerated degree program, adult/continuing education programs, advanced placement credit, cooperative education, distance learning, double majors, English as a second language, honors programs, independent study, internships, part-time degree program, services for LD students, summer session for credit.

Library Charles Stewart Mott Library with 118,861 titles, 325 serial subscriptions, an OPAC, a Web page.

Computers on Campus 1090 computers available on campus for general student use. A campuswide network can be accessed from off campus. Internet access, online (class) registration, at least one staffed computer lab available.

Student Life *Housing:* college housing not available. *Activities and Organizations:* choral group, Criminal Justice Association, Phi Theta Kappa, Dental Assisting Club, Connoisseur's Club, Social Work Club. *Campus security:* 24-hour emergency response devices and patrols, student patrols, late-night transport/escort service. *Student services:* health clinic, personal/psychological counseling.

Athletics Member NJCAA. *Intercollegiate sports:* baseball M(s), basketball M(s)/W(s), cross-country running M(s)/W(s), golf M(s), softball W(s), volleyball W(s).

Standardized Tests *Required:* Michigan Test of English Language Proficiency, CPT (for placement). *Recommended:* SAT I or ACT (for placement).

Costs (2004–05) *Tuition:* area resident $2070 full-time, $69 per contact hour part-time; state resident $3096 full-time, $104 per contact hour part-time; nonresident $4131 full-time, $138 per contact hour part-time. *Required fees:* $93 full-time, $47 per term part-time. *Payment plan:* installment. *Waivers:* senior citizens and employees or children of employees.

Financial Aid Of all full-time matriculated undergraduates who enrolled, 300 Federal Work-Study jobs (averaging $1000). 300 state and other part-time jobs (averaging $1000).

Applying *Options:* electronic application, early admission, deferred entrance. *Required:* high school transcript. *Application deadline:* 8/31 (freshmen). *Notification:* continuous (transfers).

Admissions Contact Mr. Marc Payne, Executive Director of Admissions, Mott Community College, 1401 East Court Street, Flint, MI 48503. *Phone:* 810-762-0316. *Toll-free phone:* 800-852-8614. *Fax:* 810-232-9442. *E-mail:* admissions@mcc.edu.

MUSKEGON COMMUNITY COLLEGE
Muskegon, Michigan

Admissions Contact Ms. Lynda Schwartz, Admissions Coordinator, Muskegon Community College, 221 South Quarterline Road, Muskegon, MI 49442-1493. *Phone:* 231-773-9131 Ext. 366.

NORTH CENTRAL MICHIGAN COLLEGE
Petoskey, Michigan

- **County-supported** 2-year, founded 1958, part of Michigan Department of Education
- **Calendar** semesters
- **Degree** certificates and associate
- **Small-town** 270-acre campus
- **Coed**

Faculty *Student/faculty ratio:* 17:1.

Student Life *Campus security:* 24-hour emergency response devices.

Standardized Tests *Required:* ACT (for placement).

Costs (2004–05) *Tuition:* area resident $1779 full-time, $59 per credit hour part-time; state resident $2763 full-time, $92 per credit hour part-time; nonresident $3438 full-time, $115 per credit hour part-time.

Financial Aid Of all full-time matriculated undergraduates who enrolled, 25 Federal Work-Study jobs (averaging $2400). 20 state and other part-time jobs (averaging $2400).

Applying *Required:* high school transcript.

Admissions Contact Ms. Julieanne Tobin, Director of Enrollment Management, North Central Michigan College, 1515 Howard Street, Petoskey, MI 49770-8717. *Phone:* 231-439-6511. *Toll-free phone:* 888-298-6605. *E-mail:* advisor@ncmc.cc.mi.us.

NORTHWESTERN MICHIGAN COLLEGE
Traverse City, Michigan

- **State and locally supported** 2-year, founded 1951
- **Calendar** semesters
- **Degree** certificates and associate
- **Small-town** 180-acre campus
- **Coed,** 4,471 undergraduate students, 40% full-time, 59% women, 41% men

Undergraduates 1,796 full-time, 2,675 part-time. Students come from 19 states and territories, 2% are from out of state, 0.6% African American, 0.8% Asian American or Pacific Islander, 1% Hispanic American, 3% Native American, 11% transferred in, 5% live on campus. *Retention:* 49% of 2002 full-time freshmen returned.

Freshmen *Admission:* 2,562 applied, 2,431 admitted, 950 enrolled.

Faculty *Total:* 349, 27% full-time. *Student/faculty ratio:* 23:1.

Majors Accounting technology and bookkeeping; agricultural production related; airline pilot and flight crew; art; automobile/automotive mechanics technology; biology/biological sciences; business administration and management; business and personal/financial services marketing; business automation/technology/data entry; business, management, and marketing related; child care and support services management; commercial and advertising art; communication/speech communication and rhetoric; corrections and criminal justice related; crop production; culinary arts; dental assisting; drafting and design technology; dramatic/theatre arts; education; electrical, electronic and communications engineering technology; electromechanical and instrumentation and maintenance technologies related; engineering; English; executive assistant/executive secretary; forest/forest resources management; health professions related; industrial technology; landscaping and groundskeeping; legal administrative assistant/secretary; liberal arts and sciences/liberal studies; machine shop technology; management information systems; marine science/merchant marine officer; marine transportation related; maritime science; marketing/marketing management; mathematics; medical/clinical assistant; music; nursing (registered nurse training); physical sciences; social sciences; turf and turfgrass management.

Academic Programs *Special study options:* academic remediation for entering students, adult/continuing education programs, advanced placement credit, cooperative education, distance learning, honors programs, independent study, internships, part-time degree program, services for LD students, summer session for credit.

Library Mark and Helen Osterlin Library plus 1 other with 97,458 titles, 9,820 serial subscriptions, 3,000 audiovisual materials, an OPAC, a Web page.

Computers on Campus 625 computers available on campus for general student use. A campuswide network can be accessed from student residence rooms and from off campus. Internet access, online (class) registration, at least one staffed computer lab available.

Student Life *Housing Options:* coed, men-only, women-only. Campus housing is university owned. *Activities and Organizations:* drama/theater group, student-run newspaper, radio station, choral group, Residence Hall Council, honors fraternity, student newspaper, student magazine, student radio station. *Campus security:* 24-hour emergency response devices and patrols, student patrols, late-night transport/escort service, controlled dormitory access, well-lit campus. *Student services:* health clinic, personal/psychological counseling.

Athletics *Intramural sports:* basketball M/W, cheerleading W, football M/W, golf M/W, sailing M(c)/W(c), skiing (downhill) M(c)/W(c), softball M/W, volleyball M/W.

Northwestern Michigan College (continued)

Standardized Tests *Required:* ACT COMPASS (for placement).

Costs (2004–05) *Tuition:* area resident $2196 full-time, $65 per contact hour part-time; state resident $3828 full-time, $113 per contact hour part-time; nonresident $4777 full-time, $141 per contact hour part-time. Full-time tuition and fees vary according to location. Part-time tuition and fees vary according to course load and location. *Required fees:* $362 full-time, $10 per contact hour part-time, $16 per term part-time. *Room and board:* $5700. Room and board charges vary according to board plan and housing facility. *Payment plans:* installment, deferred payment. *Waivers:* employees or children of employees.

Financial Aid Of all full-time matriculated undergraduates who enrolled, 77 Federal Work-Study jobs (averaging $1489). 9 state and other part-time jobs (averaging $556).

Applying *Options:* common application, early admission, deferred entrance. *Application fee:* $15. *Required for some:* high school transcript. *Recommended:* minimum 2.0 GPA. *Application deadline:* rolling (freshmen), rolling (transfers). *Notification:* continuous until 8/28 (freshmen), continuous until 8/28 (transfers).

Admissions Contact Northwestern Michigan College, 1701 East Front Street, Traverse City, MI 49686. *Phone:* 231-995-1034. *Toll-free phone:* 800-748-0566. *Fax:* 616-955-1339. *E-mail:* welcome@nmc.edu.

OAKLAND COMMUNITY COLLEGE
Bloomfield Hills, Michigan

- **State and locally supported** 2-year, founded 1964, part of Michigan Department of Education
- **Calendar** semesters
- **Degrees** certificates, associate, and postbachelor's certificates
- **Suburban** 540-acre campus with easy access to Detroit
- **Endowment** $18.6 million
- **Coed,** 24,145 undergraduate students, 30% full-time, 59% women, 41% men

Undergraduates 7,212 full-time, 16,933 part-time. Students come from 7 states and territories, 94 other countries, 16% African American, 3% Asian American or Pacific Islander, 2% Hispanic American, 0.6% Native American, 7% international, 11% transferred in.

Freshmen *Admission:* 3,264 applied, 3,264 admitted, 1,641 enrolled.

Faculty *Total:* 886, 32% full-time. *Student/faculty ratio:* 27:1.

Majors Accounting; allied health diagnostic, intervention, and treatment professions related; applied horticulture; architectural engineering technology; architecture; automobile/automotive mechanics technology; aviation/airway management; business administration and management; business automation/technology/data entry; cabinetmaking and millwork; carpentry; ceramic arts and ceramics; child care and support services management; clinical/medical laboratory science and allied professions related; computer and information sciences; computer programming; computer technology/computer systems technology; construction management; consumer merchandising/retailing management; corrections and criminal justice related; cosmetology; court reporting; criminal justice/law enforcement administration; criminal justice/police science; culinary arts; dental hygiene; diagnostic medical sonography and ultrasound technology; electrical, electronic and communications engineering technology; electromechanical technology; electroneurodiagnostic/electroencephalographic technology; emergency medical technology (EMT paramedic); engineering; entrepreneurship; environmental control technologies related; fashion merchandising; fine arts related; fire science; foodservice systems administration; forensic science and technology; general studies; gerontology; graphic design; health and physical education related; health/health care administration; health professions related; heating, air conditioning and refrigeration technology; histologic technician; hotel/motel administration; industrial electronics technology; industrial technology; interior design; international business/trade/commerce; kinesiology and exercise science; landscape architecture; landscaping and groundskeeping; legal assistant/paralegal; liberal arts and sciences and humanities related; liberal arts and sciences/liberal studies; library assistant; machine tool technology; management information systems and services related; management science; manufacturing technology; marketing related; massage therapy; mechanical drafting and CAD/CADD; medical/clinical assistant; medical radiologic technology; medical transcription; mental and social health services and allied professions related; nuclear medical technology; nursing (licensed practical/vocational nurse training); nursing (registered nurse training); office management; operations management; ornamental horticulture; pharmacy technician; photography; precision metal working related; pre-engineering; radio and television broadcasting technology; respiratory care therapy; restaurant/food services management; robotics technology; salon/beauty salon management; sport and fitness administration; surgical technology; tool and die technology; welding technology; woodworking related.

Academic Programs *Special study options:* academic remediation for entering students, adult/continuing education programs, advanced placement credit, cooperative education, distance learning, double majors, English as a second language, internships, off-campus study, part-time degree program, services for LD students, study abroad, summer session for credit.

Library Main Library plus 5 others with 248,494 titles, 3,880 serial subscriptions, 7,529 audiovisual materials, an OPAC, a Web page.

Computers on Campus 1500 computers available on campus for general student use. A campuswide network can be accessed from off campus. Internet access, at least one staffed computer lab available.

Student Life *Housing:* college housing not available. *Activities and Organizations:* drama/theater group, choral group, Phi Theta Kappa, International Student Organization, organizations related to student majors. *Campus security:* 24-hour emergency response devices, late-night transport/escort service. *Student services:* personal/psychological counseling, women's center.

Athletics Member NJCAA. *Intercollegiate sports:* basketball M(s)/W(s), cross-country running M(s)/W(s), golf M(s), soccer M, softball W(s), tennis W(s), volleyball W(s). *Intramural sports:* basketball M/W, cross-country running M/W, golf M, racquetball M/W, soccer M/W, softball W, tennis W, volleyball W.

Standardized Tests *Required:* ACT ASSET (for placement).

Costs (2003–04) *Tuition:* area resident $1628 full-time, $53 per credit hour part-time; state resident $2756 full-time, $89 per credit hour part-time; nonresident $3866 full-time, $125 per credit hour part-time. *Required fees:* $70 full-time, $35 per term part-time. *Waivers:* senior citizens and employees or children of employees.

Financial Aid Of all full-time matriculated undergraduates who enrolled, 135 Federal Work-Study jobs (averaging $2800). 70 state and other part-time jobs (averaging $2800).

Applying *Options:* early admission, deferred entrance. *Recommended:* high school transcript. *Application deadline:* rolling (freshmen), rolling (transfers). *Notification:* continuous (freshmen), continuous (transfers).

Admissions Contact Dr. Maurice H. McCall, Registrar and Director of Enrollment Services, Oakland Community College, 2480 Opdyke Road, Bloomfield Hills, MI 48304-2266. *Phone:* 248-341-2186.

SAGINAW CHIPPEWA TRIBAL COLLEGE
Mount Pleasant, Michigan

Admissions Contact Tracy Reed, Director of Admissions/Registrar, Saginaw Chippewa Tribal College, 2274 Enterprise Drive, Mount Pleasant, MI 48858. *Phone:* 989-775-4123.

ST. CLAIR COUNTY COMMUNITY COLLEGE
Port Huron, Michigan

- **State and locally supported** 2-year, founded 1923, part of Michigan Department of Education
- **Calendar** semesters
- **Degree** certificates and associate
- **Small-town** 25-acre campus with easy access to Detroit
- **Endowment** $2.5 million
- **Coed,** 4,523 undergraduate students

Undergraduates Students come from 6 other countries, 0.1% are from out of state.

Freshmen *Admission:* 2,696 applied, 2,696 admitted.

Faculty *Total:* 276, 29% full-time, 4% with terminal degrees.

Majors Accounting; administrative assistant and secretarial science; advertising; agricultural business and management; agricultural mechanization; agriculture; architectural engineering technology; art; artificial intelligence and robotics; biological and physical sciences; broadcast journalism; business administration and management; child development; commercial and advertising art; computer typography and composition equipment operation; corrections; criminal justice/law enforcement administration; drafting and design technology; electrical, electronic and communications engineering technology; fire science; horticultural science; industrial technology; information science/studies; journalism; legal administrative assistant/secretary; liberal arts and sciences/liberal studies; machine tool technology; marketing/marketing management; mass communication/media; medical administrative assistant and medical secretary; mental health/rehabilitation; nursing (registered nurse training); pharmacy; plastics engineering technology; quality control technology; welding technology.

Academic Programs *Special study options:* academic remediation for entering students, accelerated degree program, adult/continuing education programs, advanced placement credit, cooperative education, distance learning, double majors, honors programs, independent study, internships, part-time degree program, services for LD students, student-designed majors, summer session for credit.

Library Learning Resources Center with 59,134 titles, 610 serial subscriptions, 4,311 audiovisual materials, an OPAC.

Computers on Campus 450 computers available on campus for general student use. A campuswide network can be accessed. Internet access, at least one staffed computer lab available.

Student Life *Activities and Organizations:* drama/theater group, student-run newspaper, radio station, choral group, ADN Nursing Club, LPN Nursing Club, Phi Theta Kappa, DECA, student government. *Campus security:* patrols by security until 10 p.m. *Student services:* personal/psychological counseling.

Athletics Member NJCAA. *Intercollegiate sports:* baseball M(s), basketball M(s)/W(s), golf M, softball W(s), volleyball W(s). *Intramural sports:* rock climbing M/W.

Standardized Tests *Recommended:* ACT (for placement).

Costs (2004–05) *Tuition:* area resident $2106 full-time; state resident $3216 full-time; nonresident $4295 full-time. *Required fees:* $58 full-time. *Payment plan:* deferred payment. *Waivers:* senior citizens and employees or children of employees.

Financial Aid Of all full-time matriculated undergraduates who enrolled, 61 Federal Work-Study jobs (averaging $2543). 14 state and other part-time jobs (averaging $2113).

Applying *Options:* early admission. *Required:* high school transcript. *Application deadline:* rolling (freshmen), rolling (transfers).

Admissions Contact Mr. Pete Lacey, Registrar, St. Clair County Community College, 323 Erie Street, PO Box 5015, PO Box 5015, Port Huron, MI 48061-5015. *Phone:* 810-989-5500. *Toll-free phone:* 800-553-2427. *Fax:* 810-984-4730. *E-mail:* enrollment@stclair.cc.mi.us.

SCHOOLCRAFT COLLEGE
Livonia, Michigan

- **District-supported** 2-year, founded 1961, part of Michigan Department of Career Development
- **Calendar** semesters
- **Degree** certificates and associate
- **Suburban** 183-acre campus with easy access to Detroit
- **Endowment** $8.9 million
- **Coed,** 10,159 undergraduate students, 34% full-time, 57% women, 43% men

Undergraduates 3,434 full-time, 6,725 part-time. Students come from 4 states and territories, 8% African American, 3% Asian American or Pacific Islander, 2% Hispanic American, 0.6% Native American, 0.3% international, 8% transferred in.

Freshmen *Admission:* 2,921 applied, 2,921 admitted, 1,645 enrolled. *Average high school GPA:* 2.94.

Faculty *Total:* 465, 22% full-time, 4% with terminal degrees. *Student/faculty ratio:* 21:1.

Majors Accounting; administrative assistant and secretarial science; biomedical technology; business administration and management; child care and support services management; commercial and advertising art; computer programming; computer technology/computer systems technology; corrections; criminal justice/police science; culinary arts; data processing and data processing technology; drafting and design technology; education; electrical, electronic and communications engineering technology; electromechanical technology; emergency medical technology (EMT paramedic); engineering; entrepreneurship; environmental engineering technology; fire science; health information/medical records technology; industrial technology; laser and optical technology; liberal arts and sciences/liberal studies; marketing/marketing management; mechanical engineering/mechanical technology; medical laboratory technology; metallurgical technology; music teacher education; nursing (registered nurse training); occupational therapist assistant; physical sciences related; radio and television broadcasting technology; robotics technology; welding technology.

Academic Programs *Special study options:* academic remediation for entering students, accelerated degree program, adult/continuing education programs, advanced placement credit, cooperative education, distance learning, part-time degree program, services for LD students, summer session for credit.

Library Bradner Library plus 1 other with 96,216 titles, 634 serial subscriptions, an OPAC.

Computers on Campus 775 computers available on campus for general student use. A campuswide network can be accessed from off campus. At least one staffed computer lab available.

Student Life *Housing:* college housing not available. *Activities and Organizations:* drama/theater group, student-run newspaper, choral group, Student Activities Board, Ski Club, student newspaper, Music Club, Phi Theta Kappa, national fraternities. *Campus security:* 24-hour emergency response devices and patrols, late-night transport/escort service. *Student services:* health clinic, women's center, legal services.

Athletics Member NJCAA. *Intercollegiate sports:* basketball M(s)/W(s), cross-country running W(s), golf M(s)/W(s), soccer M(s)/W(s), volleyball W(s).

Standardized Tests *Required:* ACT, ACT ASSET, or CPT (for placement).

Costs (2004–05) *Tuition:* area resident $1890 full-time, $61 per credit hour part-time; state resident $2790 full-time, $91 per credit hour part-time; nonresident $4080 full-time, $134 per credit hour part-time. *Required fees:* $50 full-time. *Waivers:* senior citizens and employees or children of employees.

Financial Aid Of all full-time matriculated undergraduates who enrolled, 42 Federal Work-Study jobs (averaging $1722).

Applying *Options:* early admission, deferred entrance. *Required for some:* high school transcript. *Recommended:* high school transcript. *Application deadline:* rolling (freshmen), rolling (transfers).

Admissions Contact Ms. Cheryl Hagen, Associate Dean of Enrollment Management, Schoolcraft College, 18600 Hagerty Road, Livonia, MI 48152-2696. *Phone:* 734-462-4426. *Fax:* 734-462-4553. *E-mail:* admissions@schoolcraft.edu.

SOUTHWESTERN MICHIGAN COLLEGE
Dowagiac, Michigan

- **State and locally supported** 2-year, founded 1964, part of Michigan Department of Education
- **Calendar** semesters
- **Degree** certificates and associate
- **Rural** 240-acre campus
- **Endowment** $7.0 million
- **Coed,** 2,948 undergraduate students, 37% full-time, 66% women, 34% men

Undergraduates 1,077 full-time, 1,871 part-time. Students come from 3 states and territories, 19 other countries, 12% are from out of state, 7% African American, 0.8% Asian American or Pacific Islander, 5% Hispanic American, 1% Native American, 2% international, 43% transferred in.

Freshmen *Admission:* 500 applied, 500 admitted, 500 enrolled.

Faculty *Total:* 184, 27% full-time, 21% with terminal degrees. *Student/faculty ratio:* 19:1.

Majors Accounting technology and bookkeeping; administrative assistant and secretarial science; airframe mechanics and aircraft maintenance technology; automobile/automotive mechanics technology; business administration and management; business, management, and marketing related; child care and support services management; computer and information sciences related; computer programming; data entry/microcomputer applications related; drafting and design technology; electrical and electronic engineering technologies related; engineering technology; general studies; graphic and printing equipment operation/production; health professions related; heavy/industrial equipment maintenance technologies related; industrial mechanics and maintenance technology; legal assistant/paralegal; liberal arts and sciences and humanities related; liberal arts and sciences/liberal studies; machine shop technology; merchandising, sales, and marketing operations related (general); nursing (registered nurse training); precision production related; precision systems maintenance and repair technologies related; welding technology.

Academic Programs *Special study options:* academic remediation for entering students, accelerated degree program, adult/continuing education programs, advanced placement credit, cooperative education, distance learning, double majors, English as a second language, honors programs, independent study, internships, part-time degree program, services for LD students, student-designed majors, summer session for credit.

Library Fred L. Mathews Library with 38,000 titles, 1,100 serial subscriptions, 1,750 audiovisual materials, an OPAC, a Web page.

Computers on Campus 355 computers available on campus for general student use. A campuswide network can be accessed. Internet access available.

Student Life *Housing:* college housing not available. *Activities and Organizations:* drama/theater group, student-run newspaper, television station, choral group, Phi Theta Kappa. *Campus security:* 24-hour emergency response devices, evening police patrols.

Athletics *Intramural sports:* archery M/W, badminton M/W, basketball M/W, bowling M/W, cross-country running M/W, field hockey M/W, football M/W, golf M/W, racquetball M/W, skiing (cross-country) M/W, skiing (downhill) M/W, soccer M/W, softball M/W, tennis M/W, track and field M/W, volleyball M/W, weight lifting M/W.

Standardized Tests *Recommended:* SAT I or ACT (for placement).

Costs (2004–05) *Tuition:* area resident $1919 full-time; state resident $2210 full-time; nonresident $2387 full-time. *Required fees:* $403 full-time.

Financial Aid Of all full-time matriculated undergraduates who enrolled, 75 Federal Work-Study jobs (averaging $1250). 44 state and other part-time jobs (averaging $1300).

Applying *Options:* electronic application, deferred entrance. *Required:* high school transcript. *Required for some:* letters of recommendation, interview. *Application deadline:* rolling (freshmen), rolling (transfers). *Notification:* continuous until 9/10 (freshmen), continuous until 9/10 (transfers).

Admissions Contact Mrs. Margaret Hay, Dean of Academic Support, Southwestern Michigan College, 58900 Cherry Grove Road, Dowagiac, MI 49047. *Phone:* 269-782-1000 Ext. 1306. *Toll-free phone:* 800-456-8675. *Fax:* 616-782-1331. *E-mail:* cchurch@swmich.edu.

WASHTENAW COMMUNITY COLLEGE
Ann Arbor, Michigan

- **State and locally supported** 2-year, founded 1965
- **Calendar** semesters

Washtenaw Community College (continued)
- **Degree** certificates and associate
- **Suburban** 235-acre campus with easy access to Detroit
- **Endowment** $3.5 million
- **Coed,** 12,070 undergraduate students, 28% full-time, 56% women, 44% men

Undergraduates 3,432 full-time, 8,638 part-time. Students come from 12 states and territories, 37 other countries, 1% are from out of state, 15% African American, 3% Asian American or Pacific Islander, 2% Hispanic American, 1% Native American, 5% international.

Freshmen *Admission:* 1,788 enrolled.

Faculty *Total:* 772, 21% full-time, 2% with terminal degrees. *Student/faculty ratio:* 17:1.

Majors Accounting; administrative assistant and secretarial science; applied art; architectural engineering technology; artificial intelligence and robotics; automobile/automotive mechanics technology; biology/biological sciences; business administration and management; business machine repair; child development; commercial and advertising art; computer engineering technology; computer graphics; computer programming; computer programming (vendor/product certification); computer science; computer/technical support; computer typography and composition equipment operation; construction management; corrections; criminal justice/law enforcement administration; criminal justice/police science; culinary arts; data processing and data processing technology; dental assisting; drafting and design technology; electrical, electronic and communications engineering technology; electromechanical technology; engineering technology; food services technology; graphic and printing equipment operation/production; heating, air conditioning, ventilation and refrigeration maintenance technology; hotel/motel administration; industrial arts; industrial design; industrial technology; information science/studies; kindergarten/preschool education; liberal arts and sciences/liberal studies; machine tool technology; marketing/marketing management; mechanical engineering/mechanical technology; medical administrative assistant and medical secretary; nursing (registered nurse training); pharmacy technician; photography; pre-engineering; quality control technology; radiologic technology/science; respiratory care therapy; substance abuse/addiction counseling; surgical technology; system administration; technical and business writing; web/multimedia management and webmaster; web page, digital/multimedia and information resources design; welding technology; word processing.

Academic Programs *Special study options:* academic remediation for entering students, adult/continuing education programs, advanced placement credit, cooperative education, distance learning, English as a second language, external degree program, honors programs, independent study, internships, part-time degree program, services for LD students, student-designed majors, summer session for credit. *ROTC:* Army (c), Navy (c), Air Force (c).

Library Media Resource Center with 76,500 titles, 565 serial subscriptions, an OPAC, a Web page.

Computers on Campus 300 computers available on campus for general student use. A campuswide network can be accessed from off campus. Internet access, online (class) registration, at least one staffed computer lab available.

Student Life *Housing:* college housing not available. *Activities and Organizations:* drama/theater group, student-run newspaper, radio station, choral group, African-American Student Association, Delta Epsilon Chi, Muslim Student Association, Phi Theta Kappa, Anime Club. *Campus security:* 24-hour emergency response devices and patrols, late-night transport/escort service. *Student services:* personal/psychological counseling, women's center.

Athletics *Intramural sports:* basketball M/W, cross-country running M/W, ice hockey M/W, soccer M/W, softball M/W, track and field M/W, volleyball M/W.

Standardized Tests *Recommended:* SAT I or ACT (for admission), SAT I or ACT (for placement).

Costs (2004–05) *Tuition:* area resident $1800 full-time, $60 per credit hour part-time; state resident $3030 full-time, $101 per credit hour part-time; nonresident $4020 full-time, $134 per credit hour part-time. *Required fees:* $210 full-time, $7 per credit hour part-time.

Financial Aid Of all full-time matriculated undergraduates who enrolled, 120 Federal Work-Study jobs (averaging $4100).

Applying *Options:* common application, electronic application, early admission, deferred entrance. *Required for some:* high school transcript. *Application deadline:* rolling (freshmen), rolling (transfers). *Notification:* continuous (freshmen), continuous (transfers).

Admissions Contact Mr. Bradley D. Hoth, Admissions Representative, Washtenaw Community College, 4800 East Huron River Drive, PO Box D-1, Ann Arbor, MI 48106. *Phone:* 734-973-3676. *Fax:* 734-677-5408.

WAYNE COUNTY COMMUNITY COLLEGE DISTRICT
Detroit, Michigan

- **State and locally supported** 2-year, founded 1967
- **Calendar** semesters
- **Degree** certificates and associate
- **Urban** campus
- **Coed**

Student Life *Campus security:* 24-hour emergency response devices.

Athletics Member NJCAA.

Standardized Tests *Required:* ACT ASSET (for placement).

Costs (2004–05) *Tuition:* $54 per credit hour part-time.

Financial Aid Of all full-time matriculated undergraduates who enrolled, 239 Federal Work-Study jobs (averaging $2360). 147 state and other part-time jobs (averaging $1200).

Applying *Options:* common application, early admission, deferred entrance. *Application fee:* $10.

Admissions Contact Office of Enrollment Management and Student Services, Wayne County Community College District, 801 West Fort Street, Detroit, MI 48226-2539. *Phone:* 313-496-2600. *Fax:* 313-961-2791. *E-mail:* caafjh@wccc.edu.

▶ **See page 612 for a narrative description.**

WEST SHORE COMMUNITY COLLEGE
Scottville, Michigan

- **District-supported** 2-year, founded 1967, part of Michigan Department of Education
- **Calendar** semesters
- **Degree** certificates and associate
- **Rural** 375-acre campus
- **Endowment** $291,972
- **Coed**

Faculty *Student/faculty ratio:* 25:1.

Student Life *Campus security:* 24-hour emergency response devices and patrols.

Standardized Tests *Required for some:* ACT ASSET. *Recommended:* ACT (for placement).

Costs (2004–05) *Tuition:* $62 per credit hour part-time; state resident $2025 full-time, $102 per credit hour part-time; nonresident $3213 full-time, $135 per credit hour part-time. *Required fees:* $4 per credit hour part-time, $13 per term part-time.

Financial Aid Of all full-time matriculated undergraduates who enrolled, 80 Federal Work-Study jobs (averaging $3000). 40 state and other part-time jobs (averaging $3000).

Applying *Options:* common application, early admission, deferred entrance. *Application fee:* $10. *Required:* high school transcript.

Admissions Contact Mr. Tom Bell, Director of Admissions, West Shore Community College, PO Box 277, 3000 North Stiles Road, Scottville, MI 49454-0277. *Phone:* 231-845-6211 Ext. 3117. *Fax:* 231-845-3944. *E-mail:* admissions@westshore.cc.mi.us.

MINNESOTA

ACADEMY COLLEGE
Minneapolis, Minnesota

- **Proprietary** primarily 2-year
- **Calendar** quarters
- **Degrees** certificates, associate, and bachelor's
- **Urban** campus
- **Coed,** 320 undergraduate students, 71% full-time, 20% women, 80% men

Undergraduates 226 full-time, 94 part-time. 10% African American, 3% Asian American or Pacific Islander, 3% Hispanic American, 1% Native American.

Freshmen *Admission:* 35 enrolled.

Faculty *Total:* 55, 11% full-time. *Student/faculty ratio:* 8:1.

Majors Accounting; airline pilot and flight crew; aviation/airway management; business administration and management; business/commerce; commercial and advertising art; computer and information sciences; computer and information sciences and support services related; computer and information systems security; computer graphics; computer programming; computer science; computer systems networking and telecommunications; data processing and data processing technology; design and visual communications; finance; graphic design; intermedia/multimedia; management information systems; office management; sales, distribution and marketing; system administration; system, networking, and LAN/wan management; web/multimedia management and webmaster; web page, digital/multimedia and information resources design.

Academic Programs *Special study options:* academic remediation for entering students, accelerated degree program, adult/continuing education programs, cooperative education, double majors, English as a second language, honors programs, internships, part-time degree program, services for LD students, summer session for credit.

Library Learning Resource Center.

Computers on Campus A campuswide network can be accessed. Internet access, at least one staffed computer lab available.

Student Life *Housing:* college housing not available.

Costs (2003–04) *Tuition:* \$13,618 full-time, \$270 per credit part-time. Full-time tuition and fees vary according to course level. Part-time tuition and fees vary according to course level. *Required fees:* \$275 full-time. *Payment plan:* installment.

Applying *Options:* common application, electronic application, early admission, deferred entrance. *Required:* high school transcript, interview.

Admissions Contact Mary Erickson, Director of Administration, Academy College, 1101 East 78th Street, Suite e100, Minneapolis, MN 55420. *Phone:* 952-851-0066. *Toll-free phone:* 800-292-9149. *Fax:* 952-851-0094. *E-mail:* admissions@academycollege.edu.

ALEXANDRIA TECHNICAL COLLEGE
Alexandria, Minnesota

- **State-supported** 2-year, founded 1961, part of Minnesota State Colleges and Universities System
- **Calendar** semesters
- **Degree** certificates, diplomas, and associate
- **Small-town** 40-acre campus
- **Coed,** 2,164 undergraduate students, 75% full-time, 42% women, 58% men

Undergraduates 1,630 full-time, 534 part-time. Students come from 15 states and territories, 6% are from out of state, 0.2% African American, 0.5% Asian American or Pacific Islander, 0.5% Hispanic American, 0.6% Native American.

Freshmen *Admission:* 1,986 applied, 1,378 admitted.

Faculty *Total:* 95, 96% full-time, 4% with terminal degrees. *Student/faculty ratio:* 20:1.

Majors Accounting; administrative assistant and secretarial science; banking and financial support services; business administration and management; CAD/CADD drafting/design technology; carpentry; cartography; child care and support services management; child care provision; clinical/medical laboratory technology; commercial and advertising art; computer and information sciences; computer programming (specific applications); computer systems networking and telecommunications; computer technology/computer systems technology; criminal justice/police science; diesel mechanics technology; dietitian assistant; farm and ranch management; fashion merchandising; health and physical education; hospitality administration; hotel/motel administration; human services; hydraulics and fluid power technology; industrial technology; interior design; legal administrative assistant/secretary; legal assistant/paralegal; machine tool technology; marine maintenance and ship repair technology; marketing/marketing management; masonry; mechanical drafting and CAD/CADD; medical administrative assistant and medical secretary; medical insurance coding; medical reception; medical transcription; nursing assistant/aide and patient care assistant; nursing (licensed practical/vocational nurse training); office management; office occupations and clerical services; operations management; phlebotomy; receptionist; selling skills and sales; small business administration; small engine mechanics and repair technology; telecommunications technology; truck and bus driver/commercial vehicle operation; web page, digital/multimedia and information resources design; welding technology.

Academic Programs *Special study options:* academic remediation for entering students, advanced placement credit, distance learning, double majors, internships, part-time degree program, services for LD students.

Library Learning Resource Center with 12,430 titles, 173 serial subscriptions, 943 audiovisual materials, an OPAC.

Computers on Campus 600 computers available on campus for general student use. A campuswide network can be accessed from off campus. Internet access, online (class) registration, at least one staffed computer lab available. Computer purchase or lease plan available.

Student Life *Housing:* college housing not available. *Activities and Organizations:* VICA (Vocational Industrial Clubs of America) Skills USA, BPA (Business Professionals of America), DECA (Delta Epsilon Club), Student Senate, Phi Theta Kappa. *Campus security:* late-night transport/escort service, security cameras inside and outside. *Student services:* personal/psychological counseling.

Athletics *Intercollegiate sports:* basketball M, volleyball M/W. *Intramural sports:* basketball M/W, football M/W, golf M/W, softball M/W, volleyball M/W.

Standardized Tests *Required:* ACT COMPASS (for placement).

Costs (2004–05) *Tuition:* state resident \$3774 full-time, \$111 per credit part-time; nonresident \$7548 full-time, \$222 per credit part-time. Full-time tuition and fees vary according to reciprocity agreements. Part-time tuition and fees vary according to reciprocity agreements. *Required fees:* \$282 full-time, \$8 per credit part-time. *Payment plan:* deferred payment. *Waivers:* senior citizens and employees or children of employees.

Financial Aid Of all full-time matriculated undergraduates who enrolled, 94 Federal Work-Study jobs (averaging \$1871).

Applying *Options:* common application, electronic application, early admission. *Application fee:* \$20. *Required:* high school transcript, interview. *Application deadline:* rolling (freshmen).

Admissions Contact Mr. Bruce Smith, Associate Dean of Marketing and Enrollment, Alexandria Technical College, 1601 Jefferson Street, Alexandria, MN 56308. *Phone:* 320-762-0221 Ext. 4483. *Toll-free phone:* 888-234-1222. *Fax:* 320-762-4603. *E-mail:* michelleg@alx.tec.mn.us.

ANOKA-RAMSEY COMMUNITY COLLEGE
Coon Rapids, Minnesota

- **State-supported** 2-year, founded 1965, part of Minnesota State Colleges and Universities System
- **Calendar** semesters
- **Degree** certificates and associate
- **Suburban** 100-acre campus with easy access to Minneapolis-St. Paul
- **Coed**

Anoka-Ramsey Community College, with campuses in Coon Rapids and Cambridge, has been a leading provider of higher education and training in the northern suburban area of Minneapolis/St. Paul since 1965 and east-central Minnesota since 1977. The College serves more than 8,000 learners of all ages each year as they pursue associate degrees that transfer as the first two years of a bachelor's degree or certificate programs that lead immediately to rewarding careers.

Faculty *Student/faculty ratio:* 25:1.

Student Life *Campus security:* 24-hour emergency response devices and patrols, late-night transport/escort service.

Athletics Member NJCAA.

Costs (2003–04) *Tuition:* state resident \$3170 full-time; nonresident \$5963 full-time. Full-time tuition and fees vary according to program and reciprocity agreements. Part-time tuition and fees vary according to course load, program, and reciprocity agreements.

Financial Aid Of all full-time matriculated undergraduates who enrolled, 88 Federal Work-Study jobs (averaging \$4000). 106 state and other part-time jobs (averaging \$4000).

Applying *Options:* common application, early admission, deferred entrance. *Application fee:* \$20. *Required for some:* high school transcript.

Admissions Contact Mr. Tom Duval, Admissions Counselor, Anoka-Ramsey Community College, 11200 Mississippi Boulevard NW, Coon Rapids, MN 55433. *Phone:* 763-422-3458. *Fax:* 763-422-3636. *E-mail:* patrick.mcvary@anokaramsey.edu.

ANOKA-RAMSEY COMMUNITY COLLEGE, CAMBRIDGE CAMPUS
Cambridge, Minnesota

Admissions Contact Ms. Judy Gall, Admissions/Records, Anoka-Ramsey Community College, Cambridge Campus, 300 Polk Street South, Cambridge, MN 55008. *Phone:* 763-689-7027. *Fax:* 763-689-7050. *E-mail:* judy.gall@anokaramsey.edu.

ANOKA TECHNICAL COLLEGE
Anoka, Minnesota

- **State-supported** 2-year, founded 1967, part of Minnesota State Colleges and Universities System
- **Calendar** semesters
- **Degree** certificates, diplomas, and associate
- **Small-town** campus with easy access to Minneapolis-St. Paul
- **Coed,** 2,371 undergraduate students, 45% full-time, 49% women, 51% men

Undergraduates 1,058 full-time, 1,313 part-time. 8% African American, 2% Asian American or Pacific Islander, 0.8% Hispanic American, 0.3% Native American, 1% international. *Retention:* 59% of 2002 full-time freshmen returned.

Freshmen *Admission:* 1,165 applied, 951 admitted, 799 enrolled.

Faculty *Total:* 110, 62% full-time. *Student/faculty ratio:* 16:1.

Majors Accounting; administrative assistant and secretarial science; air traffic control; applied horticulture; architectural drafting and CAD/CADD; automobile/automotive mechanics technology; aviation/airway management; business administration and management; child care and support services management;

Anoka Technical College (continued)

communications systems installation and repair technology; computer technology/ computer systems technology; court reporting; electrical, electronic and communications engineering technology; electrical/electronics drafting and CAD/ CADD; health information/medical records technology; human services; landscaping and groundskeeping; legal administrative assistant/secretary; mechanical drafting and CAD/CADD; medical administrative assistant and medical secretary; medical/clinical assistant; occupational therapist assistant; turf and turfgrass management; welding technology.

Academic Programs *Special study options:* academic remediation for entering students, advanced placement credit, cooperative education, distance learning, double majors, English as a second language, internships, part-time degree program, services for LD students.

Computers on Campus 100 computers available on campus for general student use. A campuswide network can be accessed. Internet access, online (class) registration, at least one staffed computer lab available.

Student Life *Housing:* college housing not available. *Campus security:* late-night transport/escort service. *Student services:* personal/psychological counseling.

Costs (2003–04) *Tuition:* state resident $3159 full-time, $119 per credit part-time; nonresident $6317 full-time, $224 per credit part-time. Full-time tuition and fees vary according to program and reciprocity agreements. Part-time tuition and fees vary according to program and reciprocity agreements. *Required fees:* $406 full-time.

Applying *Options:* common application, electronic application, deferred entrance. *Application fee:* $20. *Required:* high school transcript. *Required for some:* interview. *Application deadline:* 8/1 (freshmen).

Admissions Contact Mr. Robert Hoenie, Director of Admissions, Anoka Technical College, 1355 West Highway 10, Anoka, MN 55303. *Phone:* 763-576-4746. *Fax:* 763-576-4756. *E-mail:* info@ank.tec.mn.us.

ARGOSY UNIVERSITY/TWIN CITIES
Eagan, Minnesota

- **Proprietary** university, founded 1961, part of Education Management Corporation, Pittsburgh, PA
- **Calendar** semesters
- **Degrees** associate, bachelor's, master's, doctoral, and post-master's certificates
- **Suburban** campus with easy access to Minneapolis-St. Paul, MN
- **Coed,** 919 undergraduate students, 40% full-time, 85% women, 15% men

Undergraduates 367 full-time, 552 part-time. Students come from 20 states and territories, 1 other country, 10% are from out of state, 4% African American, 2% Asian American or Pacific Islander, 0.9% Hispanic American, 0.8% Native American.

Freshmen *Admission:* 570 applied, 492 admitted. *Test scores:* ACT scores over 18: 98%; ACT scores over 24: 38%; ACT scores over 30: 1%.

Faculty *Total:* 140, 38% full-time, 38% with terminal degrees. *Student/faculty ratio:* 12:1.

Majors Cardiovascular technology; clinical/medical laboratory technology; dental hygiene; diagnostic medical sonography and ultrasound technology; histologic technology/histotechnologist; medical laboratory technology; medical radiologic technology; psychology; veterinary technology.

Academic Programs *Special study options:* academic remediation for entering students, double majors, internships, part-time degree program, services for LD students, summer session for credit.

Library MIM/MSPP Library with 2,000 titles, 15 serial subscriptions, an OPAC, a Web page.

Computers on Campus 50 computers available on campus for general student use. At least one staffed computer lab available.

Student Life *Housing:* college housing not available. *Campus security:* 24-hour emergency response devices, late-night transport/escort service.

Athletics *Intramural sports:* rock climbing M/W, ultimate Frisbee M/W.

Standardized Tests *Required:* SAT I or ACT (for admission), Wonderlic Scholastic Level Exam (for admission). *Recommended:* SAT I or ACT (for admission).

Costs (2003–04) *Tuition:* $10,867 full-time, $360 per semester hour part-time. Full-time tuition and fees vary according to course load and program. *Required fees:* $365 full-time. *Payment plans:* installment, deferred payment. *Waivers:* employees or children of employees.

Financial Aid Of all full-time matriculated undergraduates who enrolled, 20 Federal Work-Study jobs (averaging $3000). 20 state and other part-time jobs (averaging $1500).

Applying *Options:* common application, electronic application, deferred entrance. *Application fee:* $50. *Required:* high school transcript, interview. *Required for some:* essay or personal statement, letters of recommendation. *Application deadline:* rolling (freshmen), rolling (out-of-state freshmen), rolling (transfers). *Notification:* continuous (transfers).

Admissions Contact Ms. Jeanne Stoneking, Director of Admissions, Argosy University/Twin Cities, 1515 Central Parkway, Eagan, MN 55121. *Phone:* 651-846-3331. *Toll-free phone:* 651-846-3300 (in-state); 888-844-2004 (out-of-state). *Fax:* 651-994-7956. *E-mail:* tcadmissions@argosyu.edu.

▶ **See page 500 for a narrative description.**

THE ART INSTITUTES INTERNATIONAL MINNESOTA
Minneapolis, Minnesota

- **Proprietary** primarily 2-year, founded 1964, part of The Art Institute
- **Calendar** quarters
- **Degrees** certificates, associate, and bachelor's
- **Urban** campus
- **Coed,** 1,162 undergraduate students

Undergraduates Students come from 35 states and territories, 8 other countries, 6% are from out of state, 1% African American, 2% Asian American or Pacific Islander, 1% Hispanic American, 0.4% Native American, 1% international, 13% live on campus.

Freshmen *Admission:* 680 applied, 350 admitted. *Average high school GPA:* 2.6.

Faculty *Total:* 66, 38% full-time. *Student/faculty ratio:* 20:1.

Majors Animation, interactive technology, video graphics and special effects; commercial and advertising art; computer graphics; culinary arts; digital communication and media/multimedia; graphic communications related; graphic design; interior design; intermedia/multimedia; restaurant, culinary, and catering management; web page, digital/multimedia and information resources design.

Academic Programs *Special study options:* academic remediation for entering students, advanced placement credit, cooperative education, internships, part-time degree program, services for LD students, summer session for credit.

Library Learning Resource Center with 1,450 titles, 25 serial subscriptions, a Web page.

Computers on Campus 75 computers available on campus for general student use. A campuswide network can be accessed from off campus. Internet access, at least one staffed computer lab available.

Student Life *Housing Options:* coed. Campus housing is leased by the school. *Activities and Organizations:* Siggraph, AIGA, ASID, ACF Jr., GSA. *Campus security:* security personnel during hours of operation. *Student services:* personal/psychological counseling.

Standardized Tests *Required:* Thurston Mental Alertness Test (for admission). *Recommended:* ACT (for admission).

Costs (2003–04) *Tuition:* $16,128 full-time, $336 per credit part-time. Full-time tuition and fees vary according to course load, degree level, and program. Part-time tuition and fees vary according to course load, degree level, and program. No tuition increase for student's term of enrollment. *Room only:* $6550. *Payment plans:* tuition prepayment, installment, deferred payment. *Waivers:* employees or children of employees.

Financial Aid Of all full-time matriculated undergraduates who enrolled, 55 Federal Work-Study jobs (averaging $3200).

Applying *Options:* common application, electronic application, deferred entrance. *Application fee:* $50. *Required:* essay or personal statement, high school transcript, interview. *Application deadline:* rolling (freshmen), rolling (transfers).

Admissions Contact Mr. Russ Gill, Director of Admissions, The Art Institutes International Minnesota, 15 South 9th Street, Minneapolis, MN 55402. *Phone:* 612-332-3361 Ext. 6820. *Toll-free phone:* 800-777-3643. *Fax:* 612-332-3934. *E-mail:* kozela@aii.edu.

BROWN COLLEGE
Mendota Heights, Minnesota

- **Proprietary** primarily 2-year, founded 1946, part of Career Education Corporation
- **Calendar** quarters
- **Degrees** certificates, associate, and bachelor's
- **Suburban** 20-acre campus with easy access to Minneapolis-St. Paul
- **Coed**

Faculty *Student/faculty ratio:* 24:1.

Student Life *Campus security:* 24-hour emergency response devices, student patrols, late-night transport/escort service.

Standardized Tests *Required:* CPAt, SAT I, or ACT (for admission).

Costs (2003–04) *Tuition:* $16,800 full-time. *Required fees:* $50 full-time.

Financial Aid Of all full-time matriculated undergraduates who enrolled, 20 Federal Work-Study jobs (averaging $2000).

Applying *Options:* deferred entrance. *Application fee:* $50. *Required:* high school transcript, interview. *Required for some:* minimum 2.0 GPA. *Recommended:* letters of recommendation.

Admissions Contact Mr. Mike Price, Director of Admissions, Brown College, 1440 Northland Drive, Mendota Heights, MN 55120. *Phone:* 651-905-3400. *Toll-free phone:* 800-6BROWN6. *Fax:* 651-905-3510.

CENTRAL LAKES COLLEGE
Brainerd, Minnesota

- **State-supported** 2-year, founded 1938, part of Minnesota State Colleges and Universities System
- **Calendar** semesters
- **Degree** certificates, diplomas, and associate
- **Small-town** 1-acre campus
- **Coed,** 2,947 undergraduate students, 66% full-time, 56% women, 44% men

Undergraduates 1,957 full-time, 990 part-time. Students come from 10 states and territories, 1 other country, 0.3% are from out of state, 1% African American, 0.7% Asian American or Pacific Islander, 0.8% Hispanic American, 2% Native American.

Faculty *Total:* 140. *Student/faculty ratio:* 17:1.

Majors Accounting; administrative assistant and secretarial science; business administration and management; developmental and child psychology; horticultural science; legal administrative assistant/secretary; liberal arts and sciences/liberal studies; marketing/marketing management; medical administrative assistant and medical secretary; nursing (registered nurse training).

Academic Programs *Special study options:* academic remediation for entering students, advanced placement credit, external degree program, off-campus study, part-time degree program, summer session for credit.

Library Learning Resource Center with 16,052 titles, 286 serial subscriptions, an OPAC.

Computers on Campus 100 computers available on campus for general student use. A campuswide network can be accessed. Internet access, at least one staffed computer lab available.

Student Life *Housing:* college housing not available. *Activities and Organizations:* drama/theater group, student-run newspaper, choral group. *Campus security:* late-night transport/escort service.

Athletics Member NJCAA. *Intercollegiate sports:* baseball M, basketball M/W, football M, softball W, tennis M/W, volleyball W. *Intramural sports:* basketball M/W, bowling M/W, football M, golf M/W, softball M/W, tennis M/W, volleyball M/W.

Standardized Tests *Recommended:* ACT (for placement).

Costs (2003–04) *Tuition:* state resident $3017 full-time, $94 per credit part-time; nonresident $6035 full-time, $189 per credit part-time. *Required fees:* $440 full-time, $14 per credit part-time.

Applying *Options:* deferred entrance. *Application fee:* $20. *Application deadline:* rolling (freshmen), rolling (transfers).

Admissions Contact Charlotte Daniels, Director of Admissions, Central Lakes College, 501 West College Drive, Brainerd, MN 56401-3904. *Phone:* 218-828-2525. *Toll-free phone:* 800-933-0346 Ext. 2586. *E-mail:* rtretter@clcmn.edu.

CENTURY COLLEGE
White Bear Lake, Minnesota

- **State-supported** 2-year, founded 1970, part of Minnesota State Colleges and Universities System
- **Calendar** semesters
- **Degree** certificates, diplomas, and associate
- **Suburban** 150-acre campus with easy access to Minneapolis-St. Paul
- **Endowment** $500,000
- **Coed,** 8,490 undergraduate students, 48% full-time, 58% women, 42% men

Undergraduates 4,035 full-time, 4,455 part-time. 7% African American, 8% Asian American or Pacific Islander, 1% Hispanic American, 0.9% Native American, 2% international. *Retention:* 48% of 1999 full-time freshmen returned.

Freshmen *Admission:* 2,828 applied, 2,828 admitted, 1,897 enrolled.

Faculty *Total:* 292. *Student/faculty ratio:* 24:1.

Majors Accounting; administrative assistant and secretarial science; autobody/collision and repair technology; automobile/automotive mechanics technology; business administration and management; computer engineering technology; cosmetology; criminal justice/police science; dental assisting; dental hygiene; dental laboratory technology; diesel mechanics technology; educational/instructional media design; emergency medical technology (EMT paramedic); environmental studies; fashion merchandising; general retailing/wholesaling; heating, air conditioning, ventilation and refrigeration maintenance technology; industrial technology; interior design; legal administrative assistant/secretary; liberal arts and sciences/liberal studies; machine tool technology; management information systems; medical administrative assistant and medical secretary; medical/clinical assistant; medical radiologic technology; music management and merchandising; nursing (registered nurse training); orthotics/prosthetics;

pharmacy technician; quality control technology; selling skills and sales; small engine mechanics and repair technology; social work; substance abuse/addiction counseling.

Academic Programs *Special study options:* academic remediation for entering students, adult/continuing education programs, advanced placement credit, distance learning, double majors, English as a second language, honors programs, internships, part-time degree program, services for LD students, summer session for credit. *ROTC:* Air Force (c).

Library Century College Main Library plus 1 other with 56,867 titles, 486 serial subscriptions, 3,569 audiovisual materials, an OPAC, a Web page.

Computers on Campus 450 computers available on campus for general student use. A campuswide network can be accessed from off campus. Internet access, online (class) registration, at least one staffed computer lab available.

Student Life *Housing:* college housing not available. *Activities and Organizations:* drama/theater group, student-run newspaper, choral group, Student Senate, Phi Theta Kappa, Dental Assistants Club, Creative Arts Alliance, Christian Club. *Campus security:* late-night transport/escort service, day patrols. *Student services:* personal/psychological counseling, women's center.

Athletics *Intramural sports:* badminton M/W, basketball M/W, golf M/W, soccer M/W, softball M/W.

Costs (2003–04) *Tuition:* $96 per credit part-time. *Required fees:* $366 full-time, $12 per credit part-time.

Financial Aid Of all full-time matriculated undergraduates who enrolled, 134 Federal Work-Study jobs (averaging $1324). 48 state and other part-time jobs (averaging $1324).

Applying *Application fee:* $20. *Required:* high school transcript. *Application deadline:* rolling (freshmen), rolling (transfers).

Admissions Contact Ms. Christine Paulos, Admissions Director, Century College, 3300 Century Avenue North, White Bear Lake, MN 55110. *Phone:* 651-779-2619. *Toll-free phone:* 800-228-1978. *Fax:* 651-779-5810.

DAKOTA COUNTY TECHNICAL COLLEGE
Rosemount, Minnesota

- **State-supported** 2-year, founded 1970, part of Minnesota State Colleges and Universities System
- **Calendar** semesters
- **Degree** certificates, diplomas, and associate
- **Suburban** 100-acre campus with easy access to Minneapolis and St. Paul
- **Endowment** $1.3 million
- **Coed,** 6,069 undergraduate students, 49% full-time, 42% women, 58% men

Undergraduates 2,956 full-time, 3,113 part-time. Students come from 8 states and territories, 21 other countries, 3% are from out of state, 2% African American, 1% Asian American or Pacific Islander, 1% Hispanic American, 0.5% Native American, 0.7% international, 8% transferred in.

Freshmen *Admission:* 2,578 applied, 2,283 enrolled.

Faculty *Total:* 199, 43% full-time, 80% with terminal degrees. *Student/faculty ratio:* 20:1.

Majors Accounting; accounting technology and bookkeeping; administrative assistant and secretarial science; applied horticulture/horticultural business services related; architectural drafting and CAD/CADD; architectural technology; autobody/collision and repair technology; automobile/automotive mechanics technology; biomedical technology; child care and support services management; child care provision; commercial and advertising art; commercial photography; communications systems installation and repair technology; computer and information systems security; computer graphics; computer programming related; computer programming (specific applications); computer programming (vendor/product certification); computer software and media applications related; computer systems networking and telecommunications; concrete finishing; data entry/microcomputer applications; data entry/microcomputer applications related; data modeling/warehousing and database administration; desktop publishing and digital imaging design; diesel mechanics technology; drafting and design technology; electrical/electronics equipment installation and repair; electrician; engineering technology; entrepreneurial and small business related; entrepreneurship; executive assistant/executive secretary; furniture design and manufacturing; graphic design; housing and human environments; industrial mechanics and maintenance technology; interior design; landscaping and groundskeeping; lineworker; marketing/marketing management; masonry; medical insurance coding; medical transcription; medium/heavy vehicle and truck technology; nursing (licensed practical/vocational nurse training); photographic and film/video technology; photography; plant nursery management; sales, distribution and marketing; system administration; tourism and travel services management; tourism and travel services marketing; truck and bus driver/commercial vehicle operation; vehicle and vehicle parts and accessories marketing; web/multimedia management and webmaster; web page, digital/multimedia and information resources design; word processing.

Academic Programs *Special study options:* academic remediation for entering students, cooperative education, distance learning, double majors, English as a second language, independent study, internships, part-time degree program, services for LD students, summer session for credit.

Minnesota

Dakota County Technical College (continued)
Library DCTC Library with 15,693 titles, 258 serial subscriptions, 1,164 audiovisual materials, an OPAC, a Web page.
Computers on Campus 200 computers available on campus for general student use. A campuswide network can be accessed from off campus. Internet access, online (class) registration, at least one staffed computer lab available.
Student Life *Housing:* college housing not available. *Activities and Organizations:* student-run newspaper, Student Senate, Visual Communications Club, SKILLS/VICA, Landscape Horticulture Club, Multicultural Club. *Campus security:* 24-hour emergency response devices, late-night transport/escort service. *Student services:* health clinic, personal/psychological counseling.
Athletics Member NJCAA. *Intercollegiate sports:* baseball M, soccer M/W, wrestling M.
Standardized Tests *Required for some:* ACCUPLACER/CPT.
Costs (2004–05) *Tuition:* state resident $3702 full-time, $116 per semester hour part-time; nonresident $7405 full-time, $231 per semester hour part-time. Full-time tuition and fees vary according to reciprocity agreements. Part-time tuition and fees vary according to reciprocity agreements. *Required fees:* $538 full-time, $17 per semester hour part-time. *Payment plans:* installment, deferred payment. *Waivers:* senior citizens.
Financial Aid Of all full-time matriculated undergraduates who enrolled, 29 Federal Work-Study jobs (averaging $2589).
Applying *Options:* common application, electronic application. *Application fee:* $20. *Required for some:* high school transcript, letters of recommendation. *Recommended:* interview.
Admissions Contact Mr. Patrick Lair, Admissions Director, Dakota County Technical College, 1300 145th Street East, Rosemount, MN 55068. *Phone:* 651-423-8399. *Toll-free phone:* 877-YES-DCTC Ext. 302 (in-state); 877-YES-DCTC (out-of-state). *Fax:* 651-423-8775. *E-mail:* admissions@dctc.mnscu.edu.

DULUTH BUSINESS UNIVERSITY
Duluth, Minnesota
- **Proprietary** 2-year, founded 1891
- **Calendar** quarters
- **Degree** diplomas and associate
- **Urban** campus
- **Coed, primarily women,** 325 undergraduate students

Majors Accounting; administrative assistant and secretarial science; business administration and management; computer systems networking and telecommunications; dental assisting; design and visual communications; medical/clinical assistant; veterinary/animal health technology; web page, digital/multimedia and information resources design.
Costs (2003–04) *Tuition:* $244 per credit part-time.
Admissions Contact Mr. Mark Traux, Director of Admissions, Duluth Business University, 4724 Mike Colalillo Drive, Duluth, MN 55807. *Phone:* 800-777-8406. *Toll-free phone:* 800-777-8406.

DUNWOODY COLLEGE OF TECHNOLOGY
Minneapolis, Minnesota
- **Independent** 2-year, founded 1914
- **Calendar** quarters
- **Degree** diplomas and associate
- **Urban** 12-acre campus
- **Endowment** $31.2 million
- **Coed, primarily men,** 1,611 undergraduate students, 77% full-time, 10% women, 90% men

Undergraduates 1,236 full-time, 375 part-time. Students come from 12 states and territories, 3 other countries, 5% are from out of state, 7% African American, 5% Asian American or Pacific Islander, 1% Hispanic American, 2% Native American, 0.3% international, 8% transferred in. *Retention:* 67% of 2002 full-time freshmen returned.
Freshmen *Admission:* 798 applied, 492 admitted, 397 enrolled. *Average high school GPA:* 2.67.
Faculty *Total:* 105, 77% full-time, 4% with terminal degrees. *Student/faculty ratio:* 15:1.
Majors Appliance installation and repair technology; architectural drafting and CAD/CADD; autobody/collision and repair technology; automobile/automotive mechanics technology; computer and information sciences; computer programming (specific applications); electrical and power transmission installation; electrical, electronic and communications engineering technology; engineering related; graphic and printing equipment operation/production; heating, air conditioning and refrigeration technology; heating, air conditioning, ventilation and refrigeration maintenance technology; industrial technology; tool and die technology; welding technology.

Academic Programs *Special study options:* academic remediation for entering students, English as a second language, independent study, internships, summer session for credit.
Library Learning Resource Center with 8,000 titles, 115 serial subscriptions, 250 audiovisual materials, an OPAC.
Computers on Campus 300 computers available on campus for general student use. A campuswide network can be accessed from off campus. Internet access, at least one staffed computer lab available.
Student Life *Housing:* college housing not available. *Campus security:* 24-hour emergency response devices, late-night transport/escort service. *Student services:* personal/psychological counseling.
Costs (2004–05) *Tuition:* $20,742 full-time, $227 per credit part-time. *Required fees:* $1155 full-time, $1155 per year part-time.
Financial Aid Of all full-time matriculated undergraduates who enrolled, 20 Federal Work-Study jobs (averaging $3000). 20 state and other part-time jobs (averaging $3000).
Applying *Options:* electronic application, early admission, deferred entrance. *Application fee:* $50. *Required:* high school transcript, interview, institutional entrance test. *Application deadline:* rolling (freshmen). *Notification:* continuous (freshmen).
Admissions Contact Ms. Yun-bok Christenson, Records Coordinator, Dunwoody College of Technology, 818 Dunwoody Boulevard, Minneapolis, MN 55403. *Phone:* 612-374-5800 Ext. 2019. *Toll-free phone:* 800-292-4625. *Fax:* 612-374-4128. *E-mail:* aylreb@dunwoody.tec.mn.us.

FOND DU LAC TRIBAL AND COMMUNITY COLLEGE
Cloquet, Minnesota
- **State-supported** 2-year, founded 1987, part of Minnesota State Colleges and Universities System
- **Calendar** semesters
- **Degree** certificates and associate
- **Rural** 31-acre campus
- **Endowment** $270,000
- **Coed**

Faculty *Student/faculty ratio:* 21:1.
Student Life *Campus security:* 24-hour emergency response devices, late-night transport/escort service, controlled dormitory access, video surveillance system.
Standardized Tests *Required:* ASAP (for placement).
Costs (2003–04) *Tuition:* state resident $2475 full-time, $113 per credit part-time; nonresident $5051 full-time, $210 per credit part-time. *Payment plans:* installment, deferred payment.
Applying *Options:* common application, electronic application, early admission, deferred entrance. *Application fee:* $20. *Required for some:* high school transcript.
Admissions Contact Ms. Nancy Gordon, Admissions Representative, Fond du Lac Tribal and Community College, 2101 14th Street, Cloquet, MN 55720. *Phone:* 218-879-0808. *Toll-free phone:* 800-657-3712. *Fax:* 218-879-0814. *E-mail:* admissions@fdltcc.edu.

GLOBE COLLEGE
Oakdale, Minnesota
- **Private** primarily 2-year, founded 1885
- **Calendar** quarters
- **Degrees** certificates, diplomas, associate, bachelor's, and master's
- **Suburban** campus
- **Coed,** 997 undergraduate students

Undergraduates Students come from 1 other country, 8% are from out of state.
Faculty *Student/faculty ratio:* 15:1.
Majors Accounting; administrative assistant and secretarial science; business administration and management; business systems networking/ telecommunications; computer graphics; computer software engineering; computer systems networking and telecommunications; cosmetology; information technology; intermedia/multimedia; kinesiology and exercise science; legal administrative assistant/secretary; massage therapy; medical administrative assistant; music related; paralegal/legal assistant; physician assistant; taxation; veterinary technology; web page, digital/multimedia and information resources design.
Academic Programs *Special study options:* academic remediation for entering students, adult/continuing education programs, advanced placement credit, distance learning, external degree program, independent study, internships, part-time degree program.

Library Globe College Library with 1,700 titles, 85 serial subscriptions, 100 audiovisual materials, a Web page.
Computers on Campus 180 computers available on campus for general student use. Internet access, online (class) registration, at least one staffed computer lab available.
Standardized Tests *Recommended:* SAT I or ACT (for admission).
Costs (2003–04) *Tuition:* $11,340 full-time, $315 per credit part-time. Full-time tuition and fees vary according to course load. Part-time tuition and fees vary according to course load. *Payment plan:* installment. *Waivers:* employees or children of employees.
Applying *Options:* common application, electronic application. *Required:* interview.
Admissions Contact Mr. Rob Harker, Director of Admissions, Globe College, 7166 10th Street North, Oakdale, MN 55128. *Phone:* 651-714-7313. *Fax:* 651-730-5151. *E-mail:* admissions@globecollege.edu.

HENNEPIN TECHNICAL COLLEGE
Brooklyn Park, Minnesota

- **State-supported** 2-year, founded 1972, part of Minnesota State Colleges and Universities System
- **Calendar** semesters
- **Degree** certificates, diplomas, and associate
- **Urban** 100-acre campus with easy access to Minneapolis-St. Paul
- **Coed**

Faculty *Student/faculty ratio:* 25:1.
Student Life *Campus security:* late-night transport/escort service, security service.
Costs (2004–05) *Tuition:* state resident $111 per credit part-time; nonresident $222 per credit part-time. Full-time tuition and fees vary according to course load and reciprocity agreements. Part-time tuition and fees vary according to course load and reciprocity agreements. *Required fees:* $6 per credit part-time.
Financial Aid Of all full-time matriculated undergraduates who enrolled, 72 Federal Work-Study jobs (averaging $3000).
Applying *Application fee:* $20. *Recommended:* high school transcript, interview.
Admissions Contact Mrs. Joy Bodin, Director of Admissions, Hennepin Technical College, 9000 Brooklyn Boulevard, Brooklyn Park, MN 55445. *Phone:* 763-488-2415. *Fax:* 763-550-2119.

HERZING COLLEGE, LAKELAND MEDICAL-DENTAL DIVISION
Minneapolis, Minnesota

Admissions Contact Mr. Thomas Kosel, President, Herzing College, Lakeland Medical-Dental Division, 1402 West Lake Street, Minneapolis, MN 55408-2682. *Phone:* 763-535-3000.

HERZING COLLEGE, MINNEAPOLIS DRAFTING SCHOOL DIVISION
Minneapolis, Minnesota

- **Proprietary** primarily 2-year, part of Herzing College
- **Calendar** semesters
- **Degrees** certificates, diplomas, associate, and bachelor's
- **Suburban** 1-acre campus
- **Coed, primarily women,** 346 undergraduate students, 59% full-time, 79% women, 21% men

Undergraduates 205 full-time, 141 part-time. Students come from 3 states and territories, 1% are from out of state, 14% African American, 5% Asian American or Pacific Islander, 1% Hispanic American, 1% Native American.
Freshmen *Admission:* 128 applied, 96 admitted, 96 enrolled.
Faculty *Total:* 32, 66% full-time, 25% with terminal degrees. *Student/faculty ratio:* 14:1.
Majors Computer and information sciences; computer systems networking and telecommunications; dental assisting; dental hygiene; management information systems; massage therapy; medical/clinical assistant; medical insurance coding.
Academic Programs *Special study options:* adult/continuing education programs, part-time degree program.
Library Main Library plus 1 other.
Computers on Campus 50 computers available on campus for general student use. Internet access, at least one staffed computer lab available.
Student Life *Housing:* college housing not available. *Campus security:* 24-hour emergency response devices, late-night transport/escort service. *Student services:* personal/psychological counseling.

Standardized Tests *Required:* ACCUPLACER (for admission). *Recommended:* SAT I and SAT II or ACT (for admission), SAT II: Writing Test (for admission).
Costs (2004–05) *Tuition:* $9680 full-time, $303 per credit part-time. Full-time tuition and fees vary according to course load and program. Part-time tuition and fees vary according to course load and program. *Required fees:* $25 full-time. *Payment plan:* installment. *Waivers:* employees or children of employees.
Applying *Required:* high school transcript, interview.
Admissions Contact Mr. James Decker, Director of Admissions, Herzing College, Minneapolis Drafting School Division, 5700 West Broadway, Minneapolis, MN 55428. *Phone:* 763-231-3152. *Toll-free phone:* 800-878-DRAW. *Fax:* 763-535-9205. *E-mail:* info@mpls.herzing.edu.

HIBBING COMMUNITY COLLEGE
Hibbing, Minnesota

- **State-supported** 2-year, founded 1916, part of Minnesota State Colleges and Universities System
- **Calendar** semesters
- **Degree** certificates, diplomas, and associate
- **Small-town** 100-acre campus
- **Coed,** 1,832 undergraduate students

Undergraduates Students come from 20 states and territories, 11% are from out of state, 2% African American, 0.3% Asian American or Pacific Islander, 0.4% Hispanic American, 1% Native American, 10% live on campus.
Freshmen *Admission:* 1,029 applied, 1,029 admitted.
Faculty *Total:* 86, 73% full-time, 2% with terminal degrees. *Student/faculty ratio:* 17:1.
Majors Administrative assistant and secretarial science; business administration and management; clinical/medical laboratory technology; computer and information sciences; computer installation and repair technology; computer systems networking and telecommunications; criminal justice/police science; culinary arts; dental assisting; drafting and design technology; educational/instructional media design; foodservice systems administration; legal administrative assistant/secretary; liberal arts and sciences/liberal studies; medical administrative assistant and medical secretary; nursing (registered nurse training); pre-engineering; selling skills and sales; web page, digital/multimedia and information resources design.
Academic Programs *Special study options:* academic remediation for entering students, adult/continuing education programs, advanced placement credit, cooperative education, distance learning, internships, off-campus study, part-time degree program, services for LD students, study abroad, summer session for credit.
Library Hibbing Community College Library with 19,536 titles, 190 serial subscriptions, a Web page.
Computers on Campus 150 computers available on campus for general student use. A campuswide network can be accessed from off campus. At least one staffed computer lab available.
Student Life *Activities and Organizations:* drama/theater group, student-run newspaper, choral group, Phi Theta Kappa, Performing Music Ensembles Club, Student Senate, Engineering Club, VICA. *Campus security:* late-night transport/escort service. *Student services:* personal/psychological counseling.
Athletics Member NJCAA. *Intercollegiate sports:* baseball M, basketball M/W, football M, golf M/W, softball W, volleyball W. *Intramural sports:* basketball M/W, bowling M/W, field hockey M/W, football W, golf M/W, skiing (cross-country) M/W, skiing (downhill) M/W, tennis M/W, volleyball M/W.
Standardized Tests *Recommended:* SAT I or ACT (for placement).
Costs (2003–04) *Tuition:* state resident $2873 full-time; nonresident $2873 full-time. Full-time tuition and fees vary according to course load and reciprocity agreements. Part-time tuition and fees vary according to course load and reciprocity agreements. *Required fees:* $429 full-time. *Room and board:* $4275. *Payment plan:* installment. *Waivers:* senior citizens and employees or children of employees.
Applying *Options:* common application, early admission, deferred entrance. *Application fee:* $20. *Required:* high school transcript. *Application deadline:* rolling (freshmen), rolling (transfers). *Notification:* continuous (freshmen), continuous (transfers).
Admissions Contact Ms. Shelly Corradi, Admissions, Hibbing Community College, 1515 East 25th Street, Hibbing, MN 55746. *Phone:* 218-262-7207. *Toll-free phone:* 800-224-4HCC. *Fax:* 218-262-6717. *E-mail:* admissions@hcc.mnscu.edu.

HIGH-TECH INSTITUTE
St. Louis Park, Minnesota

Admissions Contact 5100 Gamble Drive, St. Louis Park, MN 55416. *Toll-free phone:* 800-987-0110.

INVER HILLS COMMUNITY COLLEGE
Inver Grove Heights, Minnesota

- **State-supported** 2-year, founded 1969, part of Minnesota State Colleges and Universities System
- **Calendar** semesters
- **Degree** certificates and associate
- **Suburban** 100-acre campus with easy access to Minneapolis-St. Paul
- **Coed**

Student Life *Campus security:* late-night transport/escort service, evening police patrol.

Costs (2003–04) *Tuition:* state resident $3525 full-time; nonresident $6593 full-time. Full-time tuition and fees vary according to course load and reciprocity agreements. Part-time tuition and fees vary according to course load and reciprocity agreements.

Financial Aid Of all full-time matriculated undergraduates who enrolled, 80 Federal Work-Study jobs (averaging $2000). 75 state and other part-time jobs (averaging $2000).

Applying *Application fee:* $20. *Required for some:* high school transcript. *Recommended:* high school transcript.

Admissions Contact Ms. Susan Merkling, Admissions, Inver Hills Community College, 2500 East 80th Street, Inver Grove Heights, MN 55076-3224. *Phone:* 651-450-8501. *Fax:* 651-450-8677. *E-mail:* shandwe@inverhills.mnscu.edu.

ITASCA COMMUNITY COLLEGE
Grand Rapids, Minnesota

- **State-supported** 2-year, founded 1922, part of Minnesota State Colleges and Universities System
- **Calendar** semesters
- **Degree** certificates, diplomas, and associate
- **Rural** 24-acre campus
- **Coed,** 1,131 undergraduate students, 74% full-time, 54% women, 46% men

Undergraduates 837 full-time, 294 part-time. Students come from 10 states and territories, 3 other countries, 3% are from out of state, 0.1% African American, 0.2% Asian American or Pacific Islander, 0.4% Hispanic American, 3% Native American, 0.3% international. *Retention:* 54% of 2002 full-time freshmen returned.

Freshmen *Admission:* 566 applied, 566 admitted. *Average high school GPA:* 2.78.

Faculty *Total:* 75, 57% full-time, 3% with terminal degrees. *Student/faculty ratio:* 16:1.

Majors Accounting; American Indian/Native American studies; business administration and management; chemical engineering; civil engineering; computer engineering; computer engineering related; education; education (K-12); engineering; engineering related; engineering science; engineering technology; environmental studies; fish/game management; forestry; forestry technology; general studies; geography; human services; liberal arts and sciences/liberal studies; mechanical engineering; natural resources/conservation; natural resources management and policy; nuclear engineering; nursing (licensed practical/vocational nurse training); pre-engineering; psychology; wildlife and wildlands science and management.

Academic Programs *Special study options:* academic remediation for entering students, adult/continuing education programs, advanced placement credit, cooperative education, double majors, independent study, internships, off-campus study, part-time degree program, services for LD students, study abroad, summer session for credit.

Library Itasca Community College Library with 28,790 titles, 280 serial subscriptions, 2,443 audiovisual materials, an OPAC, a Web page.

Computers on Campus 135 computers available on campus for general student use. A campuswide network can be accessed from student residence rooms and from off campus. Internet access, online (class) registration, at least one staffed computer lab available.

Student Life *Housing Options:* Campus housing is university owned. *Activities and Organizations:* student association, Circle K, Student Ambassadors, Minority Student Club, Psychology Club. *Campus security:* late-night transport/escort service, evening patrols by trained security personnel.

Athletics Member NJCAA. *Intercollegiate sports:* baseball M, basketball M/W, football M, softball W, volleyball W, wrestling M. *Intramural sports:* basketball M, bowling M/W, golf W, softball M/W, table tennis M/W, volleyball M/W.

Costs (2004–05) *Tuition:* state resident $3790 full-time; nonresident $7580 full-time. Full-time tuition and fees vary according to reciprocity agreements. Part-time tuition and fees vary according to reciprocity agreements. *Room and board:* room only: $2200. *Payment plans:* installment, deferred payment. *Waivers:* employees or children of employees.

Financial Aid Of all full-time matriculated undergraduates who enrolled, 83 Federal Work-Study jobs (averaging $1352). 180 state and other part-time jobs (averaging $705).

Applying *Options:* common application, electronic application. *Application fee:* $20. *Required:* high school transcript. *Required for some:* essay or personal statement, 3 letters of recommendation. *Application deadline:* rolling (freshmen). *Notification:* continuous (freshmen), continuous (transfers).

Admissions Contact Ms. Candace Perry, Director of Enrollment Services, Itasca Community College, 1851 East Highway 169, Grand Rapids, MN 55744. *Phone:* 218-327-4464 Ext. 4464. *Toll-free phone:* 800-996-6422 Ext. 4464. *Fax:* 218-327-4350. *E-mail:* iccinfo@it.cc.mn.us.

ITT TECHNICAL INSTITUTE
Eden Prairie, Minnesota

Admissions Contact 8911 Columbine Road, Eden Prairie, MN 55347.

LAKE SUPERIOR COLLEGE
Duluth, Minnesota

- **State-supported** 2-year, founded 1995, part of Minnesota State Colleges and Universities System
- **Calendar** semesters
- **Degree** certificates, diplomas, and associate
- **Urban** 105-acre campus
- **Endowment** $133,182
- **Coed,** 4,215 undergraduate students, 55% full-time, 58% women, 42% men

Undergraduates 2,324 full-time, 1,891 part-time. 13% are from out of state, 0.9% African American, 0.9% Asian American or Pacific Islander, 0.4% Hispanic American, 2% Native American.

Freshmen *Admission:* 921 admitted.

Faculty *Total:* 247, 38% full-time, 4% with terminal degrees. *Student/faculty ratio:* 22:1.

Majors Accounting; airline pilot and flight crew; architectural drafting and CAD/CADD; automobile/automotive mechanics technology; business administration and management; carpentry; civil engineering technology; clinical/medical laboratory technology; computer programming (specific applications); computer technology/computer systems technology; dental hygiene; electrical, electronic and communications engineering technology; electrician; emergency medical technology (EMT paramedic); executive assistant/executive secretary; fire science; fire services administration; human resources management and services related; legal administrative assistant/secretary; legal assistant/paralegal; liberal arts and sciences and humanities related; liberal arts and sciences/liberal studies; machine tool technology; management information systems; mechanical drafting and CAD/CADD; medical administrative assistant and medical secretary; medical radiologic technology; nursing (registered nurse training); occupational therapist assistant; physical therapist assistant; quality control and safety technologies related; respiratory care therapy; selling skills and sales; surgical technology.

Academic Programs *Special study options:* academic remediation for entering students, advanced placement credit, distance learning, double majors, English as a second language, independent study, internships, part-time degree program, services for LD students, summer session for credit.

Library Harold P. Erickson Library with 2,869 titles, 100 serial subscriptions, 280 audiovisual materials, an OPAC, a Web page.

Computers on Campus 230 computers available on campus for general student use. A campuswide network can be accessed from off campus. Internet access, at least one staffed computer lab available.

Student Life *Housing:* college housing not available. *Activities and Organizations:* Business Professionals of America, Gus Gus Players, Art Club, All Nations, PTK Phi Theta Kappa. *Campus security:* late-night transport/escort service, 15-hour patrols by trained security personnel. *Student services:* health clinic, personal/psychological counseling, women's center.

Athletics *Intramural sports:* basketball M/W, softball M/W, volleyball M/W.

Standardized Tests *Required:* ASAP, ACCUPLACER (for placement).

Costs (2004–05) *Tuition:* state resident $2738 full-time, $91 per credit part-time; nonresident $5475 full-time, $183 per credit part-time. *Required fees:* $463 full-time, $15 per credit part-time.

Financial Aid Of all full-time matriculated undergraduates who enrolled, 100 Federal Work-Study jobs (averaging $2380). 100 state and other part-time jobs (averaging $2380).

Applying *Options:* early admission, deferred entrance. *Application fee:* $20. *Required for some:* high school transcript. *Application deadline:* rolling (freshmen), rolling (transfers). *Notification:* continuous (freshmen), continuous (transfers).

Admissions Contact Ms. Melissa Leno, Director of Admissions, Lake Superior College, 2101 Trinity Road, Duluth, MN 55811. *Phone:* 218-723-4895. *Toll-free phone:* 800-432-2884. *Fax:* 218-733-5945. *E-mail:* enroll@lsc.admin.

LEECH LAKE TRIBAL COLLEGE
Cass Lake, Minnesota

Admissions Contact Admissions Director, Leech Lake Tribal College, PO Box 180, Cass Lake, MN 56633-0180. *Phone:* 218-335-4200. *Toll-free phone:* 888-829-4240.

MESABI RANGE COMMUNITY AND TECHNICAL COLLEGE
Virginia, Minnesota

■ **State-supported** 2-year, founded 1918, part of Minnesota State Colleges and Universities System
■ **Calendar** semesters
■ **Degree** certificates, diplomas, and associate
■ **Small-town** 30-acre campus
■ **Coed,** 1,509 undergraduate students, 65% full-time, 48% women, 52% men

Undergraduates 988 full-time, 521 part-time. Students come from 6 states and territories, 10% live on campus.
Faculty *Total:* 77, 64% full-time. *Student/faculty ratio:* 18:1.
Majors Administrative assistant and secretarial science; business/commerce; computer graphics; computer/information technology services administration related; computer programming related; computer programming (specific applications); computer software and media applications related; computer systems networking and telecommunications; electrical/electronics equipment installation and repair; human services; information technology; instrumentation technology; liberal arts and sciences/liberal studies; pre-engineering; substance abuse/addiction counseling; web page, digital/multimedia and information resources design.
Academic Programs *Special study options:* academic remediation for entering students, adult/continuing education programs, advanced placement credit, cooperative education, internships, off-campus study, part-time degree program, services for LD students, student-designed majors, summer session for credit.
Library Mesabi Library with 23,000 titles, 167 serial subscriptions.
Computers on Campus 120 computers available on campus for general student use. At least one staffed computer lab available.
Student Life *Housing Options:* coed. Campus housing is provided by a third party. *Activities and Organizations:* drama/theater group, choral group, Student Senate, Human Services Club, Native American Club, Student Life Club, Black Awareness Club. *Campus security:* late-night transport/escort service. *Student services:* personal/psychological counseling.
Athletics Member NJCAA. *Intercollegiate sports:* baseball M, basketball M/W, football M, softball W, volleyball W. *Intramural sports:* badminton M/W, basketball M/W, bowling M/W, field hockey M/W, football M/W, golf M/W, ice hockey M/W, skiing (cross-country) M/W, skiing (downhill) M/W, tennis M/W, volleyball M/W.
Standardized Tests *Recommended:* ACT (for placement).
Costs (2003–04) *Tuition:* state resident $3437 full-time, $100 per credit hour part-time; nonresident $100 per credit hour part-time. Full-time tuition and fees vary according to reciprocity agreements. Part-time tuition and fees vary according to reciprocity agreements. *Required fees:* $14 per credit part-time. *Room and board:* room only: $2530. *Waivers:* senior citizens and employees or children of employees.
Financial Aid Of all full-time matriculated undergraduates who enrolled, 209 Federal Work-Study jobs (averaging $1725). 100 state and other part-time jobs (averaging $2100).
Applying *Options:* common application, early admission, deferred entrance. *Application fee:* $20. *Application deadline:* rolling (freshmen), rolling (transfers). *Notification:* continuous (freshmen), continuous (transfers).
Admissions Contact Mesabi Range Community and Technical College, 1001 Chestnut Street West, Virginia, MN 55792. *Phone:* 218-749-0314. *Toll-free phone:* 800-657-3860. *Fax:* 218-749-0318.

MINNEAPOLIS BUSINESS COLLEGE
Roseville, Minnesota

■ **Proprietary** 2-year, founded 1874, part of The Bradford School
■ **Degree** diplomas and associate
■ **Coed, primarily women,** 300 undergraduate students

Undergraduates Students come from 2 states and territories, 4% are from out of state, 4% African American, 6% Asian American or Pacific Islander, 2% Hispanic American.
Faculty *Total:* 17, 53% full-time. *Student/faculty ratio:* 30:1.
Majors Accounting; business administration and management; computer programming; tourism and travel services management.

Student Life *Housing Options:* Campus housing is leased by the school. *Campus security:* 24-hour emergency response devices.
Costs (2003–04) *Tuition:* $10,360 full-time. *Room only:* $5040.
Applying *Application fee:* $50.
Admissions Contact Mr. David Whitman, President, Minneapolis Business College, 1711 West County Road B, Roseville, MN 55113. *Phone:* 651-604-4118. *Toll-free phone:* 800-279-5200. *Fax:* 651-636-8185. *E-mail:* info@mplsbusinesscollege.com.

MINNEAPOLIS COMMUNITY AND TECHNICAL COLLEGE
Minneapolis, Minnesota

■ **State-supported** 2-year, founded 1965, part of Minnesota State Colleges and Universities System
■ **Calendar** semesters
■ **Degree** certificates, diplomas, and associate
■ **Urban** 4-acre campus
■ **Endowment** $1.5 million
■ **Coed,** 7,446 undergraduate students

Undergraduates Students come from 45 states and territories, 81 other countries, 6% are from out of state, 23% African American, 5% Asian American or Pacific Islander, 2% Hispanic American, 2% Native American, 3% international. *Retention:* 51% of 2002 full-time freshmen returned.
Freshmen *Admission:* 3,882 applied, 3,870 admitted.
Faculty *Total:* 352, 38% full-time. *Student/faculty ratio:* 24:1.
Majors Accounting technology and bookkeeping; administrative assistant and secretarial science; aircraft powerplant technology; airframe mechanics and aircraft maintenance technology; automobile/automotive mechanics technology; avionics maintenance technology; business administration and management; business/commerce; child guidance; cinematography and film/video production; commercial and advertising art; computer and information sciences related; computer programming; criminal justice/police science; criminal justice/safety; culinary arts; human services; information science/studies; legal administrative assistant/secretary; liberal arts and sciences/liberal studies; nursing (registered nurse training); parks, recreation and leisure; substance abuse/addiction counseling; web/multimedia management and webmaster; web page, digital/multimedia and information resources design.
Academic Programs *Special study options:* academic remediation for entering students, adult/continuing education programs, advanced placement credit, distance learning, English as a second language, honors programs, independent study, internships, off-campus study, part-time degree program, services for LD students, student-designed majors, summer session for credit.
Library Minneapolis Community and Technical College Library with 42,000 titles, 400 serial subscriptions, an OPAC.
Computers on Campus 150 computers available on campus for general student use. A campuswide network can be accessed. Internet access, online (class) registration, at least one staffed computer lab available.
Student Life *Housing:* college housing not available. *Activities and Organizations:* drama/theater group, student-run newspaper, choral group, Student Senate, National Vocational-Technical Honor Society, Phi Theta Kappa, Association of Black Collegiates, Soccer Club. *Campus security:* 24-hour emergency response devices, late-night transport/escort service. *Student services:* personal/psychological counseling, women's center.
Athletics Member NJCAA. *Intercollegiate sports:* basketball M/W, golf M/W. *Intramural sports:* soccer M(c)/W(c).
Standardized Tests *Required:* (for placement).
Costs (2003–04) *Tuition:* state resident $3466 full-time, $104 per credit part-time; nonresident $6571 full-time, $207 per credit part-time. Full-time tuition and fees vary according to program. Part-time tuition and fees vary according to program. *Required fees:* $12 per credit part-time. *Payment plan:* installment. *Waivers:* senior citizens and employees or children of employees.
Financial Aid Of all full-time matriculated undergraduates who enrolled, 190 Federal Work-Study jobs (averaging $5000). 201 state and other part-time jobs (averaging $5000).
Applying *Options:* early admission, deferred entrance. *Application fee:* $20. *Required:* high school transcript. *Application deadline:* 8/31 (freshmen), rolling (transfers). *Notification:* continuous (freshmen), continuous (transfers).
Admissions Contact Treka McMillian, Admission Representative, Minneapolis Community and Technical College, 1501 Hennepin Avenue, Minneapolis, MN 55403. *Phone:* 612-659-1325. *Toll-free phone:* 800-247-0911. *Fax:* 612-659-1357.

MINNESOTA SCHOOL OF BUSINESS-BROOKLYN CENTER
Brooklyn Center, Minnesota

- **Proprietary** primarily 2-year, founded 1989
- **Calendar** quarters
- **Degrees** certificates, diplomas, associate, bachelor's, and master's
- **Suburban** campus
- **Coed,** 809 undergraduate students

Faculty *Student/faculty ratio:* 16:1.

Majors Accounting; administrative assistant and secretarial science; business administration and management; business systems networking/ telecommunications; computer graphics; computer software engineering; computer systems networking and telecommunications; cosmetology; information technology; intermedia/multimedia; legal administrative assistant/secretary; massage therapy; medical administrative assistant; music related; paralegal/legal assistant; physician assistant; taxation; veterinary technology; web page, digital/multimedia and information resources design.

Costs (2003–04) *Tuition:* $11,340 full-time, $315 per credit part-time.

Admissions Contact Mr. Jeffrey Georgeson, Director of Admissions, Minnesota School of Business-Brooklyn Center, 5910 Shingle Creek Parkway, Brooklyn Center, MN 55430. *Phone:* 763-585-7777.

MINNESOTA SCHOOL OF BUSINESS-PLYMOUTH
Minneapolis, Minnesota

- **Proprietary** primarily 2-year, founded 2002
- **Calendar** quarters
- **Degrees** certificates, diplomas, associate, bachelor's, and master's
- **Suburban** 3-acre campus
- **Coed,** 500 undergraduate students

Faculty *Student/faculty ratio:* 10:1.

Majors Accounting; administrative assistant and secretarial science; business administration and management; business systems networking/ telecommunications; computer graphics; computer software engineering; computer systems networking and telecommunications; cosmetology; information technology; intermedia/multimedia; kinesiology and exercise science; legal administrative assistant/secretary; massage therapy; medical administrative assistant; music related; paralegal/legal assistant; physician assistant; taxation; veterinary technology; web page, digital/multimedia and information resources design.

Costs (2003–04) *Tuition:* $11,340 full-time, $315 per credit part-time.

Admissions Contact Mr. Don Baker, Director of Admissions, Minnesota School of Business-Plymouth, 1455 Country Road 101 North, Minneapolis, MN 55447. *Phone:* 763-476-2000.

MINNESOTA SCHOOL OF BUSINESS-RICHFIELD
Richfield, Minnesota

- **Proprietary** primarily 2-year, founded 1877
- **Calendar** quarters
- **Degrees** certificates, diplomas, associate, bachelor's, and master's
- **Urban** 3-acre campus with easy access to Minneapolis-St. Paul
- **Coed,** 944 undergraduate students

Undergraduates Students come from 5 states and territories.

Faculty *Student/faculty ratio:* 15:1.

Majors Accounting; administrative assistant and secretarial science; business administration and management; business systems networking/ telecommunications; computer graphics; computer software engineering; computer systems networking and telecommunications; cosmetology; information science/studies; intermedia/multimedia; kinesiology and exercise science; legal administrative assistant/secretary; legal assistant/paralegal; massage therapy; medical/clinical assistant; medical office management; music related; taxation; veterinary/animal health technology; web page, digital/multimedia and information resources design.

Academic Programs *Special study options:* academic remediation for entering students, accelerated degree program, adult/continuing education programs, cooperative education, distance learning, internships.

Library Main Library plus 1 other with 3,000 titles, 5 serial subscriptions, an OPAC, a Web page.

Computers on Campus 150 computers available on campus for general student use. A campuswide network can be accessed from off campus. Internet access, online (class) registration, at least one staffed computer lab available.

Student Life *Housing:* college housing not available.

Standardized Tests *Required:* CPAt (for admission).

Costs (2003–04) *Tuition:* $11,340 full-time, $315 per credit part-time.

Applying *Options:* common application. *Application fee:* $50. *Required:* high school transcript, interview. *Required for some:* essay or personal statement. *Application deadline:* 10/6 (freshmen).

Admissions Contact Ms. Patricia Murray, Director of Admissions, Minnesota School of Business-Richfield, 1401 West 76th Street, Richfield, MN 55430. *Phone:* 612-861-2000 Ext. 720. *Toll-free phone:* 800-752-4223. *Fax:* 612-861-5548. *E-mail:* rkuhl@msbcollege.com.

MINNESOTA STATE COLLEGE-SOUTHEAST TECHNICAL
Winona, Minnesota

- **State-supported** 2-year, founded 1992, part of Minnesota State Colleges and Universities System
- **Calendar** semesters
- **Degree** certificates, diplomas, and associate
- **Small-town** campus with easy access to Minneapolis-St. Paul
- **Endowment** $110,000
- **Coed,** 1,875 undergraduate students, 53% full-time, 49% women, 51% men

Undergraduates 985 full-time, 890 part-time. Students come from 20 states and territories, 2% African American, 0.9% Asian American or Pacific Islander, 1% Hispanic American, 1% Native American, 0.1% international.

Freshmen *Admission:* 1,263 applied, 1,104 admitted, 757 enrolled. *Average high school GPA:* 2.56.

Faculty *Total:* 118, 47% full-time.

Majors Accounting; administrative assistant and secretarial science; automobile/automotive mechanics technology; avionics maintenance technology; business machine repair; carpentry; child development; computer engineering technology; computer programming; computer typography and composition equipment operation; consumer merchandising/retailing management; cosmetology; drafting and design technology; electrical, electronic and communications engineering technology; emergency medical technology (EMT paramedic); heating, air conditioning, ventilation and refrigeration maintenance technology; industrial technology; kindergarten/preschool education; legal administrative assistant/secretary; machine tool technology; marketing/marketing management; mechanical design technology; medical administrative assistant and medical secretary; musical instrument fabrication and repair; nursing (licensed practical/vocational nurse training); nursing (registered nurse training); violin, viola, guitar and other stringed instruments; welding technology.

Academic Programs *Special study options:* academic remediation for entering students, English as a second language, internships, part-time degree program, services for LD students.

Library Learning Resource Center plus 1 other with 8,000 titles, 150 serial subscriptions, an OPAC, a Web page.

Computers on Campus 50 computers available on campus for general student use. A campuswide network can be accessed from off campus. Internet access, at least one staffed computer lab available.

Student Life *Housing:* college housing not available. *Activities and Organizations:* Student Senate. *Campus security:* 24-hour emergency response devices, late-night transport/escort service.

Costs (2004–05) *Tuition:* state resident $115 per credit part-time; nonresident $230 per credit part-time. Full-time tuition and fees vary according to reciprocity agreements. Part-time tuition and fees vary according to reciprocity agreements. *Required fees:* $12 per credit part-time.

Financial Aid Of all full-time matriculated undergraduates who enrolled, 65 Federal Work-Study jobs (averaging $2500). 65 state and other part-time jobs (averaging $2500).

Applying *Application fee:* $20. *Required:* high school transcript. *Application deadline:* rolling (freshmen), rolling (transfers).

Admissions Contact Ms. Christine Humble, Student Services Specialist, Minnesota State College-Southeast Technical, PO Box 409, Winona, MN 55987. *Phone:* 507-453-2732. *Toll-free phone:* 800-372-8164. *Fax:* 507-453-2715. *E-mail:* EnrollmentServices@southeasttech.mnscu.edu.

MINNESOTA STATE COMMUNITY AND TECHNICAL COLLEGE-DETROIT LAKES
Detroit Lakes, Minnesota

Admissions Contact 900 Highway 34, E, Detroit Lakes, MN 56501. *Toll-free phone:* 888-MY-MSCTC.

MINNESOTA STATE COMMUNITY AND TECHNICAL COLLEGE-FERGUS FALLS
Fergus Falls, Minnesota

- **State-supported** 2-year, founded 1960, part of Minnesota State Colleges and Universities System
- **Calendar** semesters
- **Degree** certificates, diplomas, and associate
- **Rural** 146-acre campus
- **Endowment** $1.4 million
- **Coed,** 1,739 undergraduate students, 54% full-time, 61% women, 39% men

Undergraduates 937 full-time, 802 part-time. Students come from 12 states and territories, 2 other countries, 4% are from out of state, 2% African American, 0.5% Asian American or Pacific Islander, 0.6% Hispanic American, 0.6% Native American, 4% transferred in, 22% live on campus.

Freshmen *Admission:* 744 applied, 744 admitted, 428 enrolled.

Faculty *Total:* 92, 47% full-time, 5% with terminal degrees. *Student/faculty ratio:* 18:1.

Majors Administrative assistant and secretarial science; biological and physical sciences; business administration and management; clinical/medical laboratory technology; criminal justice/police science; legal administrative assistant/secretary; liberal arts and sciences/liberal studies; marketing/marketing management; medical administrative assistant and medical secretary; medical laboratory technology; nursing (licensed practical/vocational nurse training); nursing (registered nurse training); pre-engineering.

Academic Programs *Special study options:* academic remediation for entering students, advanced placement credit, English as a second language, independent study, off-campus study, part-time degree program, services for LD students, study abroad, summer session for credit.

Library Fergus Falls Community College Library with 30,000 titles, 173 serial subscriptions, an OPAC.

Computers on Campus 144 computers available on campus for general student use. A campuswide network can be accessed from off campus. Internet access, online (class) registration, at least one staffed computer lab available.

Student Life *Housing Options:* coed. Campus housing is university owned. *Activities and Organizations:* drama/theater group, student-run newspaper, choral group, Student Senate, Students In Free Enterprise, Phi Theta Kappa. *Campus security:* late-night transport/escort service, security for special events. *Student services:* personal/psychological counseling, women's center.

Athletics Member NJCAA. *Intercollegiate sports:* baseball M, basketball M/W, football M, golf M/W, softball W, volleyball W. *Intramural sports:* badminton M/W, basketball M, bowling M/W, football M/W, golf M/W, skiing (cross-country) M/W, skiing (downhill) M/W, softball M/W, table tennis M/W, tennis M/W, volleyball M/W, weight lifting M/W.

Standardized Tests *Recommended:* ACT (for placement).

Costs (2004–05) *Tuition:* state resident $3840 full-time, $120 per credit part-time; nonresident $7680 full-time, $240 per credit part-time. Full-time tuition and fees vary according to course load, location, and reciprocity agreements. Part-time tuition and fees vary according to course load, location, and reciprocity agreements. *Required fees:* $560 full-time, $18 per credit part-time. *Room and board:* Room and board charges vary according to housing facility. *Waivers:* employees or children of employees.

Financial Aid Of all full-time matriculated undergraduates who enrolled, 80 Federal Work-Study jobs (averaging $1900). 80 state and other part-time jobs (averaging $1900).

Applying *Options:* common application, electronic application, early admission, deferred entrance. *Application fee:* $20. *Required:* high school transcript. *Application deadline:* rolling (freshmen), rolling (transfers). *Notification:* continuous (freshmen), continuous (transfers).

Admissions Contact Ms. Carrie Brimhall, Director of Enrollment Management, Minnesota State Community and Technical College-Fergus Falls, 1414 College Way, Fergus Falls, MN 56537-1009. *Phone:* 218-739-7425. *Toll-free phone:* 888-MY-MSCTC. *Fax:* 218-739-7475.

MINNESOTA STATE COMMUNITY AND TECHNICAL COLLEGE-MOORHEAD
Moorhead, Minnesota

Admissions Contact 1900 28th Avenue, South, Moorhead, MN 56560. *Toll-free phone:* 888-MY-MSCTC.

MINNESOTA STATE COMMUNITY AND TECHNICAL COLLEGE-WADENA
Wadena, Minnesota

Admissions Contact 405 Colfax Avenue, SW, PO Box 566, Wadena, MN 56482. *Toll-free phone:* 888-MY-MSCTC.

MINNESOTA WEST COMMUNITY AND TECHNICAL COLLEGE
Pipestone, Minnesota

- **State-supported** 2-year, founded 1967, part of Minnesota State Colleges and Universities System
- **Calendar** semesters
- **Degrees** certificates, diplomas, and associate (profile contains information from Canby, Granite Falls, Jackson, and Worthington campuses)
- **Rural** 103-acre campus
- **Coed,** 3,175 undergraduate students, 46% full-time, 49% women, 51% men

Undergraduates 1,457 full-time, 1,718 part-time. Students come from 17 states and territories, 7 other countries, 11% are from out of state, 1% African American, 1% Asian American or Pacific Islander, 1% Hispanic American, 0.6% Native American, 0.7% international, 5% transferred in. *Retention:* 63% of 2002 full-time freshmen returned.

Freshmen *Admission:* 1,911 applied, 1,580 admitted, 714 enrolled. *Average high school GPA:* 2.56.

Faculty *Total:* 263, 36% full-time. *Student/faculty ratio:* 15:1.

Majors Accounting; administrative assistant and secretarial science; clinical/medical laboratory technology; medical administrative assistant and medical secretary; medical/clinical assistant.

Academic Programs *Special study options:* academic remediation for entering students, advanced placement credit, cooperative education, distance learning, double majors, English as a second language, external degree program, honors programs, independent study, internships, part-time degree program, services for LD students, summer session for credit.

Library Minnesota West Library with an OPAC.

Computers on Campus A campuswide network can be accessed. Internet access, online (class) registration, at least one staffed computer lab available. Computer purchase or lease plan available.

Student Life *Housing:* college housing not available. *Student services:* personal/psychological counseling.

Athletics Member NJCAA. *Intercollegiate sports:* baseball M, basketball M/W, football M, softball W, volleyball M/W, wrestling M. *Intramural sports:* softball M/W, volleyball M/W.

Costs (2004–05) *Tuition:* state resident $3814 full-time. *Required fees:* $305 full-time. *Payment plan:* deferred payment.

Applying *Options:* common application, electronic application. *Application fee:* $20. *Required:* high school transcript. *Application deadline:* rolling (freshmen), rolling (transfers).

Admissions Contact Mr. Gary Gillin, Dean of Communication and Enrollment, Minnesota West Community and Technical College, 1314 North Hiawatha Avenue, Pipestone, MN 56164. *Phone:* 507-825-6804. *Toll-free phone:* 800-658-2330. *Fax:* 507-825-4656. *E-mail:* garyg@ps.mnwest.mnscu.edu.

MUSICTECH COLLEGE
Saint Paul, Minnesota

- **Proprietary** 2-year, founded 1985
- **Calendar** semesters
- **Degree** certificates, diplomas, and associate
- **Urban** campus
- **Coed,** 405 undergraduate students, 84% full-time, 14% women, 86% men

Undergraduates 340 full-time, 65 part-time. Students come from 15 states and territories, 1 other country, 40% are from out of state, 3% African American, 2% Asian American or Pacific Islander, 2% Hispanic American, 1% Native American, 0.2% international, 9% transferred in.

Freshmen *Admission:* 133 enrolled.

Faculty *Total:* 86, 60% full-time. *Student/faculty ratio:* 6:1.

Majors Engineering technologies related; music management and merchandising.

Academic Programs *Special study options:* adult/continuing education programs, advanced placement credit, independent study, internships, summer session for credit.

Library Musictech College Learning Center plus 1 other.

Computers on Campus 20 computers available on campus for general student use. Internet access, at least one staffed computer lab available.

Musictech College (continued)

Student Life *Housing:* college housing not available. *Activities and Organizations:* student-run newspaper, Student Advisory Board, Audio Engineering Society, Minnesota Songwriters Association. *Campus security:* 24-hour emergency response devices. *Student services:* personal/psychological counseling.

Standardized Tests *Recommended:* ACT (for admission).

Costs (2004–05) *Tuition:* $15,725 full-time, $590 per credit part-time. Full-time tuition and fees vary according to course load and program. Part-time tuition and fees vary according to course load and program. No tuition increase for student's term of enrollment. *Required fees:* $75 full-time. *Payment plan:* installment. *Waivers:* employees or children of employees.

Applying *Application fee:* $25. *Required:* essay or personal statement, high school transcript, 2 letters of recommendation, interview. *Required for some:* audition. *Application deadline:* 8/1 (freshmen). *Notification:* 8/1 (freshmen).

Admissions Contact Ms. Debbie Sandridge, Director of Admissions, Musictech College, 19 Exchange Street East, St. Paul, MN 55101. *Phone:* 651-291-0177 Ext. 2382. *Toll-free phone:* 800-594-9500. *Fax:* 651-291-0366. *E-mail:* dsandridge@musictech.edu.

NORMANDALE COMMUNITY COLLEGE
Bloomington, Minnesota

- **State-supported** 2-year, founded 1968, part of Minnesota State Colleges and Universities System
- **Calendar** semesters
- **Degree** certificates and associate
- **Suburban** 90-acre campus with easy access to Minneapolis-St. Paul
- **Endowment** $1.4 million
- **Coed,** 7,811 undergraduate students

Undergraduates Students come from 22 states and territories, 2% are from out of state, 7% African American, 6% Asian American or Pacific Islander, 2% Hispanic American, 0.7% Native American, 1% international.

Freshmen *Admission:* 4,186 applied, 2,954 admitted.

Faculty *Total:* 230, 74% full-time, 18% with terminal degrees. *Student/faculty ratio:* 28:1.

Majors Accounting; architectural drafting and CAD/CADD; automobile/automotive mechanics technology; business administration and management; business automation/technology/data entry; child care and support services management; commercial photography; computer and information sciences; computer programming (specific applications); computer science; computer systems networking and telecommunications; criminal justice/police science; criminal justice/safety; dental assisting; dental hygiene; dietetics; electrical, electronic and communications engineering technology; general retailing/wholesaling; hospitality administration; hydraulics and fluid power technology; legal administrative assistant/secretary; liberal arts and sciences/liberal studies; management information systems; marketing/marketing management; mechanical drafting and CAD/CADD; mechanical engineering/mechanical technology; medical administrative assistant and medical secretary; medical radiologic technology; nursing (registered nurse training).

Academic Programs *Special study options:* academic remediation for entering students, accelerated degree program, adult/continuing education programs, advanced placement credit, cooperative education, distance learning, English as a second language, independent study, internships, off-campus study, part-time degree program, services for LD students, student-designed majors, study abroad, summer session for credit. *ROTC:* Army (c), Air Force (c).

Library Library plus 1 other with 98,141 titles, 623 serial subscriptions, 43,561 audiovisual materials, an OPAC.

Computers on Campus 450 computers available on campus for general student use. A campuswide network can be accessed from off campus. Internet access, online (class) registration, at least one staffed computer lab available.

Student Life *Housing:* college housing not available. *Activities and Organizations:* drama/theater group, student-run newspaper, choral group, Program Board (NPB), Student Senate, Phi Theta Kappa, Inter-Varsity Christian Fellowship Club, Spanish Club. *Campus security:* 24-hour emergency response devices, student patrols, late-night transport/escort service. *Student services:* personal/psychological counseling.

Athletics *Intramural sports:* archery M/W, badminton M/W, basketball M/W, bowling M/W, football M/W, ice hockey M/W, lacrosse M/W, racquetball M/W, soccer M/W, softball M/W, table tennis M/W, tennis M/W, volleyball M/W.

Standardized Tests *Recommended:* ACT (for placement).

Costs (2004–05) *Tuition:* state resident $3675 full-time; nonresident $7079 full-time. *Waivers:* senior citizens.

Financial Aid Of all full-time matriculated undergraduates who enrolled, 480 Federal Work-Study jobs (averaging $4000). 1,200 state and other part-time jobs (averaging $4000).

Applying *Options:* common application, early admission, deferred entrance. *Application fee:* $20. *Required for some:* high school transcript. *Application deadline:* rolling (freshmen), rolling (transfers). *Notification:* continuous (freshmen), continuous (transfers).

Admissions Contact Information Center, Normandale Community College, 9700 France Avenue South, Bloomington, MN 55431. *Phone:* 952-487-8201. *Toll-free phone:* 866-880-8740. *Fax:* 952-487-8230. *E-mail:* information@normandale.edu.

NORTH HENNEPIN COMMUNITY COLLEGE
Brooklyn Park, Minnesota

- **State-supported** 2-year, founded 1966, part of Minnesota State Colleges and Universities System
- **Calendar** semesters
- **Degree** certificates and associate
- **Suburban** 80-acre campus
- **Endowment** $230,000
- **Coed,** 7,787 undergraduate students, 37% full-time, 60% women, 40% men

Undergraduates 2,896 full-time, 4,891 part-time. Students come from 9 states and territories, 35 other countries, 3% are from out of state, 10% African American, 5% Asian American or Pacific Islander, 1% Hispanic American, 0.4% Native American, 0.8% international.

Freshmen *Admission:* 2,726 applied, 2,726 admitted, 1,763 enrolled.

Faculty *Total:* 198, 42% full-time. *Student/faculty ratio:* 28:1.

Majors Accounting; administrative assistant and secretarial science; architectural drafting and CAD/CADD; automobile/automotive mechanics technology; business administration and management; cardiovascular technology; clinical/medical laboratory technology; commercial and advertising art; construction management; consumer merchandising/retailing management; criminal justice/police science; electrical, electronic and communications engineering technology; fire science; health information/medical records technology; hydraulics and fluid power technology; industrial technology; legal assistant/paralegal; liberal arts and sciences/liberal studies; management information systems; marketing/marketing management; materials science; mechanical drafting and CAD/CADD; medical radiologic technology; nursing (registered nurse training); pre-engineering; transportation technology.

Academic Programs *Special study options:* academic remediation for entering students, accelerated degree program, adult/continuing education programs, advanced placement credit, distance learning, English as a second language, honors programs, off-campus study, part-time degree program, services for LD students, study abroad, summer session for credit. *ROTC:* Air Force (c).

Library Main Library plus 1 other with 35,000 titles, 250 serial subscriptions, an OPAC, a Web page.

Computers on Campus 200 computers available on campus for general student use. A campuswide network can be accessed. Internet access, at least one staffed computer lab available.

Student Life *Housing:* college housing not available. *Activities and Organizations:* drama/theater group, student-run newspaper, choral group. *Campus security:* 24-hour patrols, late-night transport/escort service. *Student services:* personal/psychological counseling.

Athletics Member NJCAA. *Intramural sports:* basketball M/W, bowling M/W, football M, golf M/W, soccer M, tennis M/W, volleyball M/W.

Costs (2004–05) *Tuition:* state resident $3616 full-time, $121 per credit part-time; nonresident $6694 full-time, $121 per credit part-time. *Required fees:* $223 per credit part-time.

Applying *Options:* early admission, deferred entrance. *Application fee:* $20. *Required for some:* high school transcript. *Application deadline:* rolling (freshmen), rolling (transfers). *Notification:* continuous (freshmen), continuous (transfers).

Admissions Contact Lori Kirkeby, Director of Admissions and Registration, North Hennepin Community College, 7411 85th Avenue North, Brooklyn Park, MN 55445-2231. *Phone:* 763-424-0713.

NORTHLAND COMMUNITY AND TECHNICAL COLLEGE-EAST GRAND FORKS
East Grand Forks, Minnesota

Admissions Contact 2022 Central Avenue, NW, East Grand Forks, MN 56721-2702. *Toll-free phone:* 800-451-3441.

NORTHLAND COMMUNITY AND TECHNICAL COLLEGE-THIEF RIVER FALLS
Thief River Falls, Minnesota

- **State-supported** 2-year, founded 1965, part of Minnesota State Colleges and Universities System

- **Calendar** semesters
- **Degree** diplomas and associate
- **Rural** campus
- **Coed**

Faculty *Student/faculty ratio:* 23:1.

Student Life *Campus security:* student patrols, late-night transport/escort service.

Athletics Member NJCAA.

Standardized Tests *Recommended:* SAT I or ACT (for placement).

Costs (2003–04) *Tuition:* state resident $3200 full-time, $100 per credit part-time. *Required fees:* $480 full-time, $15 per credit part-time.

Financial Aid Of all full-time matriculated undergraduates who enrolled, 75 Federal Work-Study jobs (averaging $2500). 40 state and other part-time jobs (averaging $2500).

Applying *Options:* common application, electronic application, early admission, deferred entrance. *Application fee:* $20. *Required:* high school transcript.

Admissions Contact Mr. Eugene Klinke, Director of Enrollment Management, Northland Community and Technical College-Thief River Falls, 1101 Highway #1 East, Thief River Falls, MN 56701. *Phone:* 218-681-0862. *Toll-free phone:* 800-959-6282. *Fax:* 218-681-0774. *E-mail:* eugene.klinke@northlandcollege.edu.

NORTHWEST TECHNICAL COLLEGE
Bemidji, Minnesota

Admissions Contact Northwest Technical College, 905 Grant Avenue, SE, Bemidji, MN 56601. *Phone:* 218-846-7444. *Toll-free phone:* 800-942-8324.

NORTHWEST TECHNICAL INSTITUTE
Eden Prairie, Minnesota

- **Proprietary** 2-year, founded 1957
- **Calendar** semesters
- **Degree** associate
- **Suburban** 2-acre campus with easy access to Minneapolis-St. Paul
- **Coed,** 108 undergraduate students, 100% full-time, 11% women, 89% men

Undergraduates 108 full-time. Students come from 2 states and territories, 25% are from out of state, 2% African American, 0.9% Hispanic American, 6% transferred in.

Freshmen *Admission:* 25 applied, 25 admitted, 25 enrolled. *Average high school GPA:* 3.0.

Faculty *Total:* 9, 89% full-time, 22% with terminal degrees. *Student/faculty ratio:* 12:1.

Majors Architectural drafting and CAD/CADD; mechanical drafting and CAD/CADD.

Academic Programs *Special study options:* honors programs, independent study.

Library 565 titles, 4 serial subscriptions.

Computers on Campus 120 computers available on campus for general student use. A campuswide network can be accessed. At least one staffed computer lab available.

Student Life *Housing:* college housing not available. *Campus security:* 24-hour emergency response devices and patrols, late-night transport/escort service.

Costs (2004–05) *Tuition:* $13,200 full-time. *Required fees:* $25 full-time.

Applying *Application fee:* $25. *Required:* high school transcript, interview. *Application deadline:* rolling (freshmen), rolling (transfers). *Notification:* continuous (freshmen), continuous (transfers).

Admissions Contact Mr. John Hartman, Director of Admissions, Northwest Technical Institute, 11995 Singletree Lane, Eden Prairie, MN 55344-5351. *Phone:* 952-944-0080 Ext. 103. *Toll-free phone:* 800-443-4223. *Fax:* 952-944-9274. *E-mail:* info@nti.edu.

PINE TECHNICAL COLLEGE
Pine City, Minnesota

- **State-supported** 2-year, founded 1965, part of Minnesota State Colleges and Universities System
- **Calendar** semesters
- **Degree** certificates, diplomas, and associate
- **Small-town** 6-acre campus with easy access to Minneapolis-St. Paul
- **Coed**

Faculty *Student/faculty ratio:* 16:1.

Student Life *Campus security:* late-night transport/escort service.

Standardized Tests *Required:* ASAP (for placement).

Costs (2003–04) *Tuition:* state resident $3328 full-time, $104 per semester hour part-time; nonresident $6656 full-time, $208 per semester hour part-time. Full-time tuition and fees vary according to program. Part-time tuition and fees vary according to program. *Required fees:* $448 full-time, $14 per semester hour part-time.

Financial Aid Of all full-time matriculated undergraduates who enrolled, 6 Federal Work-Study jobs (averaging $2000). 10 state and other part-time jobs.

Applying *Options:* early admission. *Application fee:* $20. *Required:* high school transcript. *Required for some:* letters of recommendation.

Admissions Contact Mr. Phil Schroeder, Dean, Student Affairs, Pine Technical College, 900 Fourth Street, SE, Pine City, MN 55063. *Phone:* 320-629-5100. *Toll-free phone:* 800-521-7463.

RAINY RIVER COMMUNITY COLLEGE
International Falls, Minnesota

- **State-supported** 2-year, founded 1967, part of Minnesota State Colleges and Universities System
- **Calendar** semesters
- **Degree** certificates, diplomas, and associate
- **Small-town** 80-acre campus
- **Coed,** 384 undergraduate students, 69% full-time, 56% women, 44% men

Undergraduates 265 full-time, 119 part-time. Students come from 8 states and territories, 18% African American, 0.5% Asian American or Pacific Islander, 1% Hispanic American, 3% Native American, 10% live on campus.

Freshmen *Admission:* 230 applied, 230 admitted.

Faculty *Total:* 32, 53% full-time.

Majors Administrative assistant and secretarial science; biological and physical sciences; business administration and management; liberal arts and sciences/liberal studies; pre-engineering; real estate.

Academic Programs *Special study options:* academic remediation for entering students, adult/continuing education programs, advanced placement credit, cooperative education, English as a second language, honors programs, independent study, internships, part-time degree program, services for LD students, summer session for credit.

Library Rainy River Community College Library with 20,000 titles, an OPAC.

Computers on Campus 70 computers available on campus for general student use. A campuswide network can be accessed from off campus. Internet access, at least one staffed computer lab available.

Student Life *Housing Options:* coed, disabled students. *Activities and Organizations:* drama/theater group, Anishinaabe Student Coalition, Student Senate, Black Student Association. *Campus security:* 24-hour emergency response devices, late-night transport/escort service, controlled dormitory access. *Student services:* personal/psychological counseling.

Athletics Member NJCAA. *Intercollegiate sports:* basketball M/W, softball W, volleyball W. *Intramural sports:* archery M/W, badminton M/W, bowling M/W, skiing (cross-country) M/W, skiing (downhill) M/W, swimming M/W, tennis M/W, volleyball M/W, weight lifting M/W.

Standardized Tests *Required:* CPT (for placement). *Recommended:* ACT (for placement).

Costs (2003–04) *Tuition:* $118 per credit part-time; state resident $3782 full-time. *Room and board:* room only: $2190.

Financial Aid Of all full-time matriculated undergraduates who enrolled, 110 Federal Work-Study jobs (averaging $2000). 55 state and other part-time jobs (averaging $2000).

Applying *Options:* common application, early admission, deferred entrance. *Application fee:* $20. *Required:* high school transcript. *Application deadline:* rolling (freshmen), rolling (transfers). *Notification:* continuous (freshmen), continuous (transfers).

Admissions Contact Ms. Berta Hagen, Registrar, Rainy River Community College, 1501 Highway 71, International Falls, MN 56649. *Phone:* 218-285-2207. *Toll-free phone:* 800-456-3996. *Fax:* 218-285-2239. *E-mail:* djohnson@rrcc.mnscu.edu.

RASMUSSEN COLLEGE EAGAN
Eagan, Minnesota

Admissions Contact Ms. Jacinda Miller, Admissions Coordinator, Rasmussen College Eagan, 3500 Federal Drive, Eagan, MN 55122-1346. *Phone:* 651-687-9000. *Toll-free phone:* 651-687-0507 (in-state); 800-852-6367 (out-of-state). *E-mail:* admission@rasmussen.edu.

RASMUSSEN COLLEGE MANKATO
Mankato, Minnesota

- **Proprietary** 2-year, founded 1904, part of Rasmussen College System
- **Calendar** quarters

Minnesota

Rasmussen College Mankato *(continued)*
- **Degree** certificates, diplomas, and associate
- **Suburban** campus with easy access to Minneapolis-St. Paul
- **Coed, primarily women,** 330 undergraduate students

Undergraduates 0.6% Asian American or Pacific Islander, 2% Hispanic American.
Faculty *Total:* 42, 31% full-time. *Student/faculty ratio:* 18:1.
Majors Accounting; administrative assistant and secretarial science; business administration and management; child care and support services management; child care provision; child development; computer graphics; computer software and media applications related; computer systems networking and telecommunications; computer/technical support; computer typography and composition equipment operation; data entry/microcomputer applications; data entry/microcomputer applications related; data processing and data processing technology; health information/medical records administration; health unit coordinator/ward clerk; hospitality administration; hospitality and recreation marketing; hotel/motel administration; legal administrative assistant/secretary; legal assistant/paralegal; legal studies; marketing/marketing management; medical administrative assistant and medical secretary; medical/clinical assistant; restaurant, culinary, and catering management; system administration; tourism and travel services management; tourism and travel services marketing; tourism promotion; web page, digital/multimedia and information resources design; word processing.
Academic Programs *Special study options:* academic remediation for entering students, advanced placement credit, cooperative education, internships, part-time degree program, services for LD students, summer session for credit.
Library Media Center with 1,000 titles, 3 serial subscriptions.
Computers on Campus 70 computers available on campus for general student use. Internet access, at least one staffed computer lab available.
Student Life *Housing:* college housing not available. *Activities and Organizations:* student-run newspaper, Student Senate, Student Ambassadors, Student Life Organization. *Campus security:* limited access to buildings after hours.
Standardized Tests *Required:* ACT COMPASS (for admission).
Costs (2004–05) *Tuition:* $13,200 full-time, $275 per credit part-time. *Required fees:* $60 full-time.
Financial Aid Of all full-time matriculated undergraduates who enrolled, 5 Federal Work-Study jobs (averaging $4000). 3 state and other part-time jobs (averaging $4000).
Applying *Options:* common application, deferred entrance. *Application fee:* $60. *Required:* high school transcript, minimum 2.0 GPA, interview.
Admissions Contact Ms. Kathy Clifford, Director of Admissions, Rasmussen College Mankato, 501 Holly Lane, Mankato, MN 56001-6803. *Phone:* 507-625-6556. *Toll-free phone:* 800-657-6767. *E-mail:* rascoll@ic.mankato.mn.us.

RASMUSSEN COLLEGE MINNETONKA
Minnetonka, Minnesota
- **Proprietary** 2-year, founded 1904, part of Rasmussen College System
- **Calendar** quarters
- **Degree** certificates, diplomas, and associate
- **Suburban** 2-acre campus with easy access to Minneapolis-St. Paul
- **Coed,** 325 undergraduate students, 58% full-time, 76% women, 24% men

Undergraduates 189 full-time, 136 part-time. Students come from 1 other state, 10% African American, 2% Asian American or Pacific Islander, 2% Hispanic American, 2% Native American.
Freshmen *Admission:* 75 enrolled. *Average high school GPA:* 3.10.
Faculty *Total:* 32, 47% full-time, 31% with terminal degrees. *Student/faculty ratio:* 11:1.
Majors Accounting; administrative assistant and secretarial science; business administration and management; child development; court reporting; legal administrative assistant/secretary; marketing/marketing management; medical administrative assistant and medical secretary.
Academic Programs *Special study options:* academic remediation for entering students, internships, part-time degree program, summer session for credit.
Library 3,400 titles, 10 serial subscriptions.
Computers on Campus 300 computers available on campus for general student use. Internet access, at least one staffed computer lab available.
Student Life *Housing:* college housing not available. *Campus security:* late-night transport/escort service.
Costs (2004–05) *Tuition:* $18,360 full-time.
Applying *Options:* early admission, deferred entrance. *Application fee:* $60. *Required:* high school transcript, interview. *Application deadline:* rolling (freshmen), rolling (transfers).
Admissions Contact Mr. Ethan Campbell, Director of Admissions, Rasmussen College Minnetonka, 12450 Wayzata Boulevard, Suite 315, Minnetonka, MN 55305-1928. *Phone:* 952-545-2000. *Toll-free phone:* 800-852-0929.

RASMUSSEN COLLEGE ST. CLOUD
St. Cloud, Minnesota
- **Proprietary** 2-year, founded 1904, part of Rasmussen College System
- **Calendar** quarters
- **Degree** certificates, diplomas, and associate
- **Urban** campus with easy access to Minneapolis-St. Paul
- **Coed, primarily women,** 454 undergraduate students, 67% full-time, 79% women, 21% men

Undergraduates 302 full-time, 152 part-time. Students come from 2 states and territories, 2% African American, 0.7% Asian American or Pacific Islander, 1% Hispanic American, 1% Native American.
Freshmen *Admission:* 136 enrolled.
Faculty *Total:* 28, 36% full-time, 50% with terminal degrees. *Student/faculty ratio:* 16:1.
Majors Accounting; administrative assistant and secretarial science; business administration and management; court reporting; health information/medical records administration; legal administrative assistant/secretary; marketing/marketing management; medical administrative assistant and medical secretary; tourism and travel services management.
Academic Programs *Special study options:* academic remediation for entering students, adult/continuing education programs, distance learning, double majors, internships, part-time degree program, summer session for credit.
Library St. Cloud Rasmussen College Library with 494 titles, 49 serial subscriptions, 125 audiovisual materials, an OPAC, a Web page.
Computers on Campus 75 computers available on campus for general student use. A campuswide network can be accessed from off campus that provide access to Web-based e-mail, remote file access. Internet access, at least one staffed computer lab available.
Student Life *Activities and Organizations:* student-run newspaper, Student Senate.
Standardized Tests *Required:* ACT COMPASS (for admission).
Costs (2004–05) *Comprehensive fee:* $16,875 includes full-time tuition ($12,375) and room and board ($4500). Full-time tuition and fees vary according to course load. Part-time tuition: $275 per credit. Part-time tuition and fees vary according to course load. *Payment plan:* installment. *Waivers:* employees or children of employees.
Financial Aid Of all full-time matriculated undergraduates who enrolled, 34 Federal Work-Study jobs (averaging $866). 51 state and other part-time jobs (averaging $700).
Applying *Options:* common application, electronic application, early admission, deferred entrance. *Application fee:* $60. *Required:* high school transcript, minimum 2.0 GPA, interview. *Application deadline:* rolling (freshmen), rolling (transfers).
Admissions Contact Rasmussen College St. Cloud, 226 Park Avenue South, St. Cloud, MN 56301. *Phone:* 320-251-5600. *Toll-free phone:* 800-852-0460. *Fax:* 320-251-3702. *E-mail:* admstc@rasmussen.edu.

RIDGEWATER COLLEGE
Willmar, Minnesota
- **State-supported** 2-year, founded 1961, part of Minnesota State Colleges and Universities System
- **Calendar** semesters
- **Degree** certificates, diplomas, and associate
- **Small-town** 83-acre campus
- **Coed**

Faculty *Student/faculty ratio:* 19:1.
Student Life *Campus security:* late-night transport/escort service.
Athletics Member NJCAA.
Costs (2003–04) *Tuition:* state resident $3113 full-time; nonresident $6226 full-time. Full-time tuition and fees vary according to program and reciprocity agreements. Part-time tuition and fees vary according to program and reciprocity agreements. *Required fees:* $46 full-time.
Financial Aid Of all full-time matriculated undergraduates who enrolled, 350 Federal Work-Study jobs (averaging $3000). 133 state and other part-time jobs (averaging $2400).
Applying *Options:* early admission, deferred entrance. *Application fee:* $20. *Required:* high school transcript. *Required for some:* letters of recommendation, interview.
Admissions Contact Ms. Linda Barron, Admissions Assistant, Ridgewater College, PO Box 1097, Willmar, MN 56201-1097. *Phone:* 320-231-2906 Ext. 2906. *Toll-free phone:* 800-722-1151 Ext. 2906. *Fax:* 320-231-7677. *E-mail:* skerfield@ridgewater.mnscu.edu.

RIVERLAND COMMUNITY COLLEGE
Austin, Minnesota

- **State-supported** 2-year, founded 1940, part of Minnesota State Colleges and Universities System
- **Calendar** semesters
- **Degree** certificates, diplomas, and associate
- **Small-town** 187-acre campus with easy access to Minneapolis-St. Paul
- **Coed,** 4,000 undergraduate students, 58% full-time, 52% women, 48% men

Undergraduates 2,320 full-time, 1,680 part-time. Students come from 5 states and territories, 10 other countries, 3% African American, 0.3% Asian American or Pacific Islander, 3% Hispanic American, 0.3% Native American.

Freshmen *Admission:* 2,400 admitted. *Average high school GPA:* 3.08.

Faculty *Total:* 158, 64% full-time. *Student/faculty ratio:* 18:1.

Majors Administrative assistant and secretarial science; autobody/collision and repair technology; business administration and management; computer and information systems security; computer installation and repair technology; computer programming (specific applications); computer programming (vendor/product certification); computer software and media applications related; computer systems networking and telecommunications; computer/technical support; corrections; criminal justice/police science; data entry/microcomputer applications; data entry/microcomputer applications related; diesel mechanics technology; electrical/electronics equipment installation and repair; health unit coordinator/ward clerk; human services; industrial mechanics and maintenance technology; legal administrative assistant/secretary; liberal arts and sciences/liberal studies; machine shop technology; medical administrative assistant and medical secretary; medical radiologic technology; nursing (registered nurse training); web/multimedia management and webmaster; web page, digital/multimedia and information resources design; word processing.

Academic Programs *Special study options:* academic remediation for entering students, adult/continuing education programs, advanced placement credit, English as a second language, internships, off-campus study, part-time degree program, services for LD students, study abroad, summer session for credit.

Library Riverland Community College Library plus 2 others with 33,500 titles, 278 serial subscriptions, an OPAC.

Computers on Campus 175 computers available on campus for general student use. A campuswide network can be accessed from student residence rooms. At least one staffed computer lab available.

Student Life *Housing Options:* Campus housing is provided by a third party. *Activities and Organizations:* drama/theater group, student-run newspaper, choral group, College Choir, student newspaper, Student Activities Board, Phi Theta Kappa, Theater Club. *Campus security:* late-night transport/escort service. *Student services:* personal/psychological counseling, women's center.

Athletics Member NJCAA. *Intercollegiate sports:* baseball M, basketball M/W, softball W, tennis M/W, volleyball W. *Intramural sports:* basketball M.

Standardized Tests *Required:* ASAP (for placement). *Recommended:* ACT (for placement).

Costs (2004–05) *Tuition:* state resident $3390 full-time, $113 per credit part-time; nonresident $6780 full-time, $226 per credit part-time. Full-time tuition and fees vary according to program and reciprocity agreements. Part-time tuition and fees vary according to program and reciprocity agreements. *Required fees:* $480 full-time, $16 per credit part-time. *Room and board:* room only: $2590. *Payment plans:* installment, deferred payment.

Applying *Options:* early admission. *Application fee:* $20. *Required:* high school transcript. *Application deadline:* rolling (freshmen), rolling (transfers).

Admissions Contact Ms. Sharon Jahnke, Admission Secretary, Riverland Community College, 1900 8th Avenue NW, Austin, MN 55912. *Phone:* 507-433-0820. *Toll-free phone:* 800-247-5039. *Fax:* 507-433-0515. *E-mail:* admissions@river.cc.mn.us.

ROCHESTER COMMUNITY AND TECHNICAL COLLEGE
Rochester, Minnesota

- **State-supported** primarily 2-year, founded 1915, part of Minnesota State Colleges and Universities System
- **Calendar** semesters
- **Degrees** certificates, diplomas, associate, and bachelor's (also offers 13 programs that lead to a bachelor's degree with Winona State University or University of Minnesota)
- **Small-town** 460-acre campus
- **Endowment** $437,000
- **Coed,** 5,862 undergraduate students

Undergraduates Students come from 39 states and territories, 36 other countries, 10% are from out of state.

Freshmen *Admission:* 2,428 applied, 2,400 admitted.

Faculty *Total:* 225, 41% full-time.

Majors Administrative assistant and secretarial science; business administration and management; child guidance; civil engineering technology; clinical/medical laboratory technology; computer science; criminal justice/police science; dental hygiene; developmental and child psychology; electrical, electronic and communications engineering technology; fashion merchandising; general studies; greenhouse management; human services; landscaping and groundskeeping; legal administrative assistant/secretary; liberal arts and sciences/liberal studies; mechanical engineering/mechanical technology; medical administrative assistant and medical secretary; natural resources/conservation; nursing (registered nurse training); pre-engineering; respiratory care therapy; surgical technology; turf and turfgrass management.

Academic Programs *Special study options:* academic remediation for entering students, advanced placement credit, distance learning, English as a second language, honors programs, independent study, internships, off-campus study, part-time degree program, services for LD students, summer session for credit.

Library Goddard Library plus 1 other with 62,000 titles, 600 serial subscriptions.

Computers on Campus 170 computers available on campus for general student use. A campuswide network can be accessed. At least one staffed computer lab available.

Student Life *Housing:* college housing not available. *Activities and Organizations:* drama/theater group, student-run newspaper, choral group, choir, band, football, theater, Program Council. *Campus security:* student patrols, late-night transport/escort service. *Student services:* health clinic, personal/psychological counseling.

Athletics Member NJCAA. *Intercollegiate sports:* baseball M, basketball M/W, football M, golf M/W, soccer W, softball W, volleyball W, wrestling M. *Intramural sports:* basketball M/W, football M, soccer M(c)/W(c), softball M/W, table tennis M/W, tennis M/W, volleyball M/W.

Costs (2003–04) *Tuition:* state resident $2823 full-time, $117 per credit part-time; nonresident $5257 full-time, $219 per credit part-time.

Financial Aid Of all full-time matriculated undergraduates who enrolled, 500 Federal Work-Study jobs (averaging $3000). 300 state and other part-time jobs (averaging $3000).

Applying *Options:* early admission. *Application fee:* $20. *Required:* high school transcript. *Application deadlines:* 8/24 (freshmen), 8/24 (transfers). *Notification:* continuous (freshmen), continuous (transfers).

Admissions Contact Mr. Troy Tynsky, Director of Admissions, Rochester Community and Technical College, 851 30th Avenue, SE, Rochester, MN 55904-4999. *Phone:* 507-280-3509. *Fax:* 507-285-7496.

ST. CLOUD TECHNICAL COLLEGE
St. Cloud, Minnesota

- **State-supported** 2-year, founded 1948, part of Minnesota State Colleges and Universities System
- **Calendar** semesters
- **Degree** certificates, diplomas, and associate
- **Urban** 35-acre campus with easy access to Minneapolis-St. Paul
- **Coed,** 3,205 undergraduate students, 68% full-time, 51% women, 49% men

Undergraduates 2,165 full-time, 1,040 part-time. Students come from 5 states and territories, 10 other countries, 3% are from out of state, 0.7% African American, 1% Asian American or Pacific Islander, 0.7% Hispanic American, 0.6% Native American, 0.5% international, 9% transferred in.

Freshmen *Admission:* 3,711 applied, 1,626 admitted, 889 enrolled. *Average high school GPA:* 2.70.

Faculty *Total:* 237, 47% full-time. *Student/faculty ratio:* 21:1.

Majors Accounting; accounting technology and bookkeeping; administrative assistant and secretarial science; advertising; architectural drafting and CAD/CADD; architectural engineering technology; autobody/collision and repair technology; automobile/automotive mechanics technology; banking and financial support services; business administration and management; carpentry; child care and support services management; child development; civil engineering technology; commercial and advertising art; computer/information technology services administration related; computer programming; computer programming related; computer programming (specific applications); computer systems networking and telecommunications; computer/technical support; computer typography and composition equipment operation; construction engineering technology; consumer merchandising/retailing management; culinary arts; dental assisting; dental hygiene; diagnostic medical sonography and ultrasound technology; diesel mechanics technology; electrical and power transmission installation; electrical, electronic and communications engineering technology; emergency medical technology (EMT paramedic); finance; general retailing/wholesaling; graphic and printing equipment operation/production; heating, air conditioning and refrigeration technology; heating, air conditioning, ventilation and refrigeration maintenance technology; information technology; instrumentation technology; kindergarten/preschool education; legal administrative assistant/secretary; machine tool technology; marketing/marketing management; mechanical design technology; mechanical drafting and CAD/CADD; medical administrative assis-

St. Cloud Technical College (continued)

tant and medical secretary; medical office management; nursing (licensed practical/vocational nurse training); office management; ophthalmic laboratory technology; pipefitting and sprinkler fitting; surgical technology; teacher assistant/ aide; water quality and wastewater treatment management and recycling technology; welding technology; word processing.

Academic Programs *Special study options:* academic remediation for entering students, adult/continuing education programs, cooperative education, internships, part-time degree program, services for LD students, summer session for credit.

Library Learning Resource Center with 10,000 titles, 600 serial subscriptions, an OPAC.

Computers on Campus 500 computers available on campus for general student use. A campuswide network can be accessed. Internet access, online (class) registration, at least one staffed computer lab available.

Student Life *Housing:* college housing not available. *Activities and Organizations:* student-run newspaper, Student Senate, Distributive Education Club of America, Business Professionals of America, Child and Adult Care Education, Central Minnesota Builders Association. *Campus security:* late-night transport/ escort service. *Student services:* personal/psychological counseling, women's center.

Athletics *Intercollegiate sports:* basketball M/W, golf M/W, softball M/W, volleyball M/W.

Standardized Tests *Required:* ACT ASSET (for placement).

Costs (2003–04) *Tuition:* state resident $3061 full-time, $102 per credit part-time; nonresident $6121 full-time, $204 per credit part-time. *Required fees:* $275 full-time, $9 per credit part-time.

Financial Aid Of all full-time matriculated undergraduates who enrolled, 38 Federal Work-Study jobs (averaging $4000). 38 state and other part-time jobs (averaging $4000).

Applying *Options:* early admission, deferred entrance. *Application fee:* $20. *Required:* high school transcript. *Recommended:* interview. *Application deadline:* rolling (freshmen), rolling (transfers). *Notification:* continuous until 8/24 (freshmen), 8/24 (transfers).

Admissions Contact Ms. Jodi Elness, Admissions Office, St. Cloud Technical College, 1540 Northway Drive, St. Cloud, MN 56303. *Phone:* 320-308-5089. *Toll-free phone:* 800-222-1009. *Fax:* 320-654-5981. *E-mail:* jme@cloud.tec.mn.us.

SAINT PAUL COLLEGE-A COMMUNITY & TECHNICAL COLLEGE
St. Paul, Minnesota

- **State-related** 2-year, founded 1919, part of Minnesota State Colleges and Universities System
- **Calendar** semesters
- **Degree** certificates, diplomas, and associate
- **Urban** campus
- **Coed,** 5,552 undergraduate students, 28% full-time, 46% women, 54% men

Undergraduates 1,541 full-time, 4,011 part-time. 18% African American, 9% Asian American or Pacific Islander, 3% Hispanic American, 1% Native American, 1% international, 4% transferred in.

Freshmen *Admission:* 3,601 applied, 2,397 admitted, 545 enrolled.

Faculty *Total:* 251, 36% full-time, 45% with terminal degrees. *Student/faculty ratio:* 20:1.

Majors Accounting; administrative assistant and secretarial science; child development; civil engineering technology; clinical/medical laboratory technology; computer programming; electrical, electronic and communications engineering technology; human resources management; industrial technology; international business/trade/commerce; medical administrative assistant and medical secretary; respiratory care therapy; sign language interpretation and translation.

Academic Programs *Special study options:* academic remediation for entering students, adult/continuing education programs, English as a second language, internships, services for LD students.

Library St. Paul Technical College Library with 12,000 titles, 110 serial subscriptions, 260 audiovisual materials, an OPAC.

Computers on Campus A campuswide network can be accessed. Internet access, at least one staffed computer lab available.

Student Life *Housing:* college housing not available. *Activities and Organizations:* Student Senate. *Campus security:* late-night transport/escort service. *Student services:* personal/psychological counseling, women's center.

Standardized Tests *Required:* CPT, ACCUPLACER (for placement).

Costs (2004–05) *Tuition:* state resident $3263 full-time; nonresident $6527 full-time. *Required fees:* $235 full-time.

Financial Aid Of all full-time matriculated undergraduates who enrolled, 48 Federal Work-Study jobs (averaging $2500). 94 state and other part-time jobs (averaging $2500).

Applying *Options:* early admission. *Application fee:* $20. *Required for some:* high school transcript, interview. *Application deadline:* rolling (freshmen).

Admissions Contact Ms. Lisa Netzley, Admissions Counselor, Saint Paul College-A Community & Technical College, 235 Marshall Avenue, St. Paul, MN 55102-1800. *Phone:* 651-221-1333. *Toll-free phone:* 800-227-6029. *Fax:* 651-221-1416. *E-mail:* admiss@stp.tec.mn.us.

SOUTH CENTRAL TECHNICAL COLLEGE
North Mankato, Minnesota

- **State-supported** 2-year, founded 1946, part of Minnesota State Colleges and Universities System
- **Calendar** semesters
- **Degree** certificates, diplomas, and associate
- **Urban** campus
- **Coed,** 2,350 undergraduate students, 100% full-time, 57% women, 43% men

Undergraduates 2,350 full-time. 1% African American, 1% Asian American or Pacific Islander, 1% Hispanic American, 0.2% Native American.

Freshmen *Admission:* 1,100 applied, 1,100 admitted, 900 enrolled.

Faculty *Total:* 250. *Student/faculty ratio:* 18:1.

Majors Accounting; administrative assistant and secretarial science; agribusiness; agricultural mechanization; agricultural production; architectural drafting and CAD/CADD; autobody/collision and repair technology; automobile/ automotive mechanics technology; business administration and management; computer programming; culinary arts; dental assisting; emergency medical technology (EMT paramedic); heating, air conditioning, ventilation and refrigeration maintenance technology; machine tool technology; mechanical drafting and CAD/CADD; nursing (registered nurse training).

Computers on Campus 300 computers available on campus for general student use. A campuswide network can be accessed. Internet access, at least one staffed computer lab available.

Costs (2003–04) *Tuition:* state resident $2826 full-time; nonresident $5653 full-time. *Required fees:* $338 full-time.

Admissions Contact Ms. Beverly Herda, Director of Admissions, South Central Technical College, 1920 Lee Boulevard, North Mankato, MN 56003. *Phone:* 507-389-7334.

VERMILION COMMUNITY COLLEGE
Ely, Minnesota

- **State-supported** 2-year, founded 1922, part of Minnesota State Colleges and Universities System
- **Calendar** semesters
- **Degree** certificates, diplomas, and associate
- **Rural** 5-acre campus
- **Coed,** 1,191 undergraduate students, 53% full-time, 33% women, 67% men

Undergraduates 635 full-time, 556 part-time. Students come from 42 states and territories, 3 other countries, 50% live on campus.

Freshmen *Admission:* 595 applied, 341 admitted. *Average high school GPA:* 2.8.

Faculty *Total:* 102, 31% full-time.

Majors Accounting; aeronautics/aviation/aerospace science and technology; agricultural business and management; agricultural economics; agricultural teacher education; agronomy and crop science; airline pilot and flight crew; architectural engineering technology; art; art history, criticism and conservation; art teacher education; aviation/airway management; biological and physical sciences; biology/biological sciences; business administration and management; business/managerial economics; chemistry; computer engineering technology; computer management; computer science; criminal justice/law enforcement administration; criminal justice/police science; criminal justice/safety; data processing and data processing technology; dramatic/theatre arts; drawing; ecology; economics; education; elementary education; engineering; environmental education; environmental engineering technology; environmental studies; family and consumer sciences/human sciences; finance; fish/game management; forest/forest resources management; forestry; forestry technology; forest sciences and biology; geography; geology/earth science; health information/medical records administration; health teacher education; history; human ecology; hydrology and water resources science; industrial arts; industrial technology; interdisciplinary studies; kindergarten/preschool education; land use planning and management; liberal arts and sciences/liberal studies; mass communication/media; mathematics; medical administrative assistant and medical secretary; music; natural resources/conservation; natural resources management and policy; parks, recreation and leisure; parks, recreation and leisure facilities management; physical education teaching and coaching; physical sciences; physics; political science and government; pre-engineering; psychology; range science and management; science teacher education; sociology; soil conservation; special products marketing; speech and rhetoric; water quality and wastewater treatment management and recycling technology; wildlife and wildlands science and management; wildlife biology.

Academic Programs *Special study options:* academic remediation for entering students, adult/continuing education programs, advanced placement credit, cooperative education, honors programs, internships, off-campus study, part-time degree program, services for LD students, summer session for credit.

Library Vermilion Community College Library with 19,500 titles, 100 serial subscriptions, an OPAC.

Computers on Campus 60 computers available on campus for general student use. A campuswide network can be accessed from student residence rooms and from off campus. At least one staffed computer lab available.

Student Life *Housing:* on-campus residence required for freshman year. *Options:* coed. Campus housing is university owned and leased by the school. *Activities and Organizations:* Student Life Committee, student government, Drama Club. *Campus security:* student patrols, late-night transport/escort service, controlled dormitory access. *Student services:* personal/psychological counseling, women's center.

Athletics Member NJCAA. *Intercollegiate sports:* baseball M, basketball M/W, football M, softball W, volleyball W. *Intramural sports:* basketball M/W, bowling M/W, cross-country running M/W, football M, golf M/W, ice hockey M, skiing (cross-country) M/W, skiing (downhill) M/W, softball M/W, tennis M/W, volleyball M/W, weight lifting M/W, wrestling M.

Standardized Tests *Recommended:* SAT I and SAT II or ACT (for placement).

Costs (2003–04) *Tuition:* state resident $3648 full-time, $121 per credit part-time; nonresident $6753 full-time, $225 per credit part-time. *Room and board:* $4370; room only: $2800.

Financial Aid Of all full-time matriculated undergraduates who enrolled, 150 Federal Work-Study jobs (averaging $1000). 30 state and other part-time jobs (averaging $1000).

Applying *Options:* common application, electronic application, early admission, deferred entrance. *Application fee:* $20. *Required:* high school transcript. *Application deadline:* rolling (freshmen), rolling (transfers). *Notification:* continuous (freshmen), continuous (transfers).

Admissions Contact Mr. Todd Heiman, Director of Enrollment Services, Vermilion Community College, 1900 East Camp Street, Ely, MN 55731-1996. *Phone:* 218-365-7224. *Toll-free phone:* 800-657-3608.

MISSISSIPPI

ANTONELLI COLLEGE
Hattiesburg, Mississippi

Admissions Contact Ms. Connie Sharp, Director of Admissions, Antonelli College, 1500 North 31st Avenue, Hattiesburg, MS 39401. *Phone:* 601-583-4100.

ANTONELLI COLLEGE
Jackson, Mississippi

- **Proprietary** 2-year
- **Calendar** quarters
- **Degree** diplomas and associate
- **Coed**

Admissions Contact Ms. Page McDaniel, Senior Admissions Officer, Antonelli College, 480 East Woodrow Wilson Drive, Jackson, MS 39216. *Phone:* 601-362-9991.

COAHOMA COMMUNITY COLLEGE
Clarksdale, Mississippi

- **State and locally supported** 2-year, founded 1949, part of Mississippi State Board for Community and Junior Colleges
- **Calendar** semesters
- **Degree** certificates and associate
- **Small-town** 29-acre campus with easy access to Memphis
- **Coed**

Student Life *Campus security:* 24-hour patrols.

Athletics Member NJCAA.

Standardized Tests *Required:* SAT I or ACT (for placement).

Financial Aid Of all full-time matriculated undergraduates who enrolled, 350 Federal Work-Study jobs (averaging $600). 45 state and other part-time jobs (averaging $1000).

Applying *Options:* common application. *Required:* high school transcript.

Admissions Contact Mrs. Wanda Holmes, Director of Admissions and Records, Coahoma Community College, Route 1, PO Box 616, Clarksdale, MS 38614-9799. *Phone:* 662-621-4205. *Toll-free phone:* 800-844-1222.

COPIAH-LINCOLN COMMUNITY COLLEGE
Wesson, Mississippi

- **State and locally supported** 2-year, founded 1928, part of Mississippi State Board for Community and Junior Colleges
- **Calendar** semesters
- **Degree** certificates and associate
- **Rural** 525-acre campus with easy access to Jackson
- **Coed**, 2,161 undergraduate students, 66% full-time, 60% women, 40% men

Undergraduates 1,430 full-time, 731 part-time. Students come from 7 states and territories, 2 other countries, 2% are from out of state, 35% African American, 0.4% Asian American or Pacific Islander, 0.4% Hispanic American, 0.2% Native American, 0.1% international, 30% live on campus.

Freshmen *Admission:* 1,108 enrolled.

Faculty *Total:* 127, 65% full-time.

Majors Accounting; agribusiness; agricultural business and management; agricultural business and management related; agricultural business technology; agricultural economics; agricultural/farm supplies retailing and wholesaling; agriculture; architecture; art teacher education; biological and physical sciences; biology/biological sciences; business administration and management; chemistry; child development; civil engineering technology; clinical/medical laboratory technology; computer programming; cosmetology; criminal justice/police science; data processing and data processing technology; drafting and design technology; economics; education; electrical, electronic and communications engineering technology; elementary education; engineering; English; family and consumer sciences/home economics teacher education; farm and ranch management; food technology and processing; forestry; French; health teacher education; history; industrial radiologic technology; journalism; liberal arts and sciences/liberal studies; library science; music teacher education; nursing (registered nurse training); physical education teaching and coaching; special products marketing; trade and industrial teacher education; wood science and wood products/pulp and paper technology.

Academic Programs *Special study options:* academic remediation for entering students, adult/continuing education programs, advanced placement credit, honors programs, part-time degree program, student-designed majors, summer session for credit.

Library Oswalt Memorial Library with 38,900 titles, 255 serial subscriptions.

Computers on Campus 300 computers available on campus for general student use. At least one staffed computer lab available.

Student Life *Housing Options:* Campus housing is university owned. *Activities and Organizations:* drama/theater group, student-run newspaper, radio station, choral group, marching band. *Campus security:* 24-hour patrols. *Student services:* health clinic, personal/psychological counseling.

Athletics Member NJCAA. *Intercollegiate sports:* baseball M(s), basketball M(s)/W(s), football M(s), golf M/W, softball W, tennis M/W, track and field M. *Intramural sports:* basketball M/W, football M, golf M/W, tennis M/W, volleyball M/W.

Standardized Tests *Required for some:* ACT (for placement).

Costs (2004–05) *Tuition:* state resident $3650 full-time. Part-time tuition and fees vary according to program. *Room and board:* $2150; room only: $1000.

Financial Aid Of all full-time matriculated undergraduates who enrolled, 125 Federal Work-Study jobs (averaging $1000).

Applying *Options:* early admission. *Required:* high school transcript. *Application deadline:* rolling (freshmen), rolling (transfers).

Admissions Contact Dr. Phillilp H. Broome, Director of Admissions and Records, Copiah-Lincoln Community College, PO Box 371, Wesson, MS 39191-0457. *Phone:* 601-643-8307.

COPIAH-LINCOLN COMMUNITY COLLEGE-NATCHEZ CAMPUS
Natchez, Mississippi

- **State and locally supported** 2-year, founded 1972, part of Mississippi State Board for Community and Junior Colleges
- **Calendar** semesters
- **Degree** certificates and associate
- **Small-town** 24-acre campus
- **Coed**, 900 undergraduate students, 62% full-time, 73% women, 27% men

Undergraduates 554 full-time, 346 part-time. Students come from 4 states and territories, 53% African American, 0.3% Asian American or Pacific Islander, 0.3% Hispanic American.

Copiah-Lincoln Community College-Natchez Campus (continued)

Freshmen *Admission:* 363 enrolled.

Faculty *Total:* 53, 45% full-time, 100% with terminal degrees. *Student/faculty ratio:* 20:1.

Majors Administrative assistant and secretarial science; elementary education; family and consumer sciences/human sciences; forestry; general studies; hotel/motel administration; instrumentation technology; liberal arts and sciences/liberal studies; marketing/marketing management; political science and government; respiratory care therapy.

Academic Programs *Special study options:* academic remediation for entering students, adult/continuing education programs, advanced placement credit, distance learning, internships, part-time degree program, student-designed majors, summer session for credit.

Library Willie Mae Dunn Library with 19,000 titles, 112 serial subscriptions, 700 audiovisual materials, an OPAC, a Web page.

Computers on Campus 175 computers available on campus for general student use. A campuswide network can be accessed from off campus. Internet access, at least one staffed computer lab available.

Student Life *Housing Options:* Campus housing is provided by a third party. *Activities and Organizations:* student-run newspaper, student newspaper. *Campus security:* 24-hour patrols.

Athletics Member NJCAA.

Standardized Tests *Required for some:* ACT (for admission), TABE.

Costs (2004–05) *Tuition:* state resident $1600 full-time, $100 per semester hour part-time; nonresident $3000 full-time, $145 per semester hour part-time. *Required fees:* $100 full-time, $5 per semester hour part-time, $10 per year part-time. *Room and board:* $3600. *Payment plan:* deferred payment. *Waivers:* senior citizens and employees or children of employees.

Financial Aid Of all full-time matriculated undergraduates who enrolled, 96 Federal Work-Study jobs, 14 state and other part-time jobs.

Applying *Options:* early admission. *Required:* high school transcript. *Application deadline:* rolling (freshmen), rolling (transfers). *Notification:* continuous (freshmen), continuous (transfers).

Admissions Contact Mrs. Gwen S. McCalip, Director of Admissions and Records, Copiah-Lincoln Community College-Natchez Campus, 11 Co-Lin Circle, Natchez, MS 39120. *Phone:* 601-442-9111 Ext. 224. *Fax:* 601-446-1222. *E-mail:* gwen.mccalip@colin.edu.

EAST CENTRAL COMMUNITY COLLEGE
Decatur, Mississippi

Admissions Contact Ms. Donna Luke, Director of Admissions, Records, and Research, East Central Community College, PO Box 129, Decatur, MS 39327-0129. *Phone:* 601-635-2111 Ext. 206. *Toll-free phone:* 877-462-3222. *Fax:* 601-635-2150.

EAST MISSISSIPPI COMMUNITY COLLEGE
Scooba, Mississippi

- **State and locally supported** 2-year, founded 1927, part of Mississippi State Board for Community and Junior Colleges
- **Calendar** semesters
- **Degree** certificates and associate
- **Rural** 25-acre campus
- **Endowment** $134,022
- **Coed,** 3,417 undergraduate students, 61% full-time, 60% women, 40% men

Undergraduates 2,068 full-time, 1,349 part-time. Students come from 4 states and territories, 1% are from out of state, 51% African American, 0.4% Asian American or Pacific Islander, 0.5% Hispanic American, 0.1% Native American, 25% live on campus.

Freshmen *Admission:* 2,245 applied, 1,402 admitted. *Test scores:* ACT scores over 18: 39%; ACT scores over 24: 5%.

Faculty *Total:* 191, 48% full-time. *Student/faculty ratio:* 22:1.

Majors Accounting; administrative assistant and secretarial science; art; automobile/automotive mechanics technology; banking and financial support services; biological and physical sciences; business administration and management; business teacher education; computer programming; computer science; cosmetology; criminal justice/law enforcement administration; drafting and design technology; economics; education; electrical, electronic and communications engineering technology; elementary education; English; fire science; forestry technology; funeral service and mortuary science; health teacher education; history; hotel/motel administration; instrumentation technology; liberal arts and sciences/liberal studies; mathematics; music; office occupations and clerical services; ophthalmic laboratory technology; pre-engineering; psychology; reading teacher education; real estate; social sciences; sociology.

Academic Programs *Special study options:* academic remediation for entering students, adult/continuing education programs, advanced placement credit, cooperative education, distance learning, double majors, honors programs, part-time degree program, services for LD students, summer session for credit.

Library Tubb-May Library with 27,840 titles, 116 serial subscriptions, 3,478 audiovisual materials, an OPAC, a Web page.

Computers on Campus 100 computers available on campus for general student use. A campuswide network can be accessed from student residence rooms and from off campus. Internet access available.

Student Life *Housing Options:* men-only, women-only. Campus housing is university owned. *Activities and Organizations:* drama/theater group, student-run newspaper, choral group, marching band. *Campus security:* 24-hour emergency response devices and patrols. *Student services:* personal/psychological counseling.

Athletics Member NJCAA. *Intercollegiate sports:* baseball M(s), basketball M(s)/W(s), cheerleading W(s), football M(s), golf M(s), soccer M(s)/W(s), softball W(s). *Intramural sports:* basketball M/W, football M, golf M, gymnastics M/W, tennis M/W.

Standardized Tests *Required for some:* ACT (for placement).

Costs (2003–04) *Tuition:* state resident $1100 full-time; nonresident $2850 full-time. *Required fees:* $160 full-time. *Room and board:* $2370. Room and board charges vary according to board plan. *Payment plan:* installment. *Waivers:* senior citizens and employees or children of employees.

Financial Aid Of all full-time matriculated undergraduates who enrolled, 200 Federal Work-Study jobs (averaging $1200).

Applying *Options:* common application, electronic application, deferred entrance. *Required:* high school transcript. *Application deadline:* rolling (freshmen), rolling (transfers).

Admissions Contact Ms. Melinda Sciple, Admissions Officer, East Mississippi Community College, PO Box 158, Scooba, MS 39358-0158. *Phone:* 662-476-5041.

HINDS COMMUNITY COLLEGE
Raymond, Mississippi

- **State and locally supported** 2-year, founded 1917, part of Mississippi State Board for Community and Junior Colleges
- **Calendar** semesters
- **Degree** certificates, diplomas, and associate
- **Small-town** 671-acre campus
- **Endowment** $948,556
- **Coed,** 9,961 undergraduate students, 72% full-time, 65% women, 35% men

Undergraduates 7,145 full-time, 2,816 part-time. Students come from 16 states and territories, 1 other country, 3% are from out of state, 52% African American, 0.5% Asian American or Pacific Islander, 0.6% Hispanic American, 0.2% Native American, 15% live on campus.

Freshmen *Admission:* 4,298 enrolled. *Average high school GPA:* 2.7. *Test scores:* ACT scores over 18: 16%; ACT scores over 24: 3%.

Faculty *Total:* 656, 54% full-time, 13% with terminal degrees. *Student/faculty ratio:* 17:1.

Majors Accounting; administrative assistant and secretarial science; agricultural business and management; agricultural economics; agricultural mechanization; agricultural teacher education; agronomy and crop science; art; avionics maintenance technology; biology/biological sciences; business administration and management; carpentry; child development; civil engineering technology; clinical/medical laboratory technology; clothing/textiles; commercial and advertising art; computer and information sciences related; computer graphics; computer programming; computer programming related; computer science; computer/technical support; criminal justice/law enforcement administration; criminal justice/police science; data entry/microcomputer applications; data entry/microcomputer applications related; data processing and data processing technology; dental hygiene; developmental and child psychology; dietetics; drafting and design technology; dramatic/theatre arts; economics; electrical, electronic and communications engineering technology; emergency medical technology (EMT paramedic); English; family and consumer sciences/human sciences; fashion/apparel design; finance; food services technology; graphic and printing equipment operation/production; health information/medical records administration; hotel/motel administration; humanities; industrial arts; industrial radiologic technology; information technology; journalism; landscaping and groundskeeping; legal assistant/paralegal; liberal arts and sciences/liberal studies; machine tool technology; marketing/marketing management; mass communication/media; mathematics; music; nursing (licensed practical/vocational nurse training); nursing (registered nurse training); political science and government; postal management; pre-engineering; psychology; public administration; real estate; respiratory care therapy; social sciences; sociology; special products marketing; surgical technology; system administration; telecommunications; veterinary sciences; veterinary technology; welding technology.

Academic Programs *Special study options:* academic remediation for entering students, accelerated degree program, adult/continuing education programs,

advanced placement credit, cooperative education, distance learning, double majors, freshman honors college, honors programs, independent study, part-time degree program, services for LD students, summer session for credit. *ROTC:* Army (c).

Library McLendon Library with 165,260 titles, 1,178 serial subscriptions, an OPAC.

Computers on Campus 55 computers available on campus for general student use. A campuswide network can be accessed. Internet access, online (class) registration, at least one staffed computer lab available.

Student Life *Housing Options:* men-only, women-only. *Activities and Organizations:* drama/theater group, student-run newspaper, choral group, marching band, Phi Theta Kappa, Baptist Student Union, Residence Hall Association, Hi-Steppers Dance Team, band. *Campus security:* 24-hour emergency response devices and patrols, controlled dormitory access. *Student services:* personal/psychological counseling, women's center.

Athletics Member NJCAA. *Intercollegiate sports:* baseball M(s), basketball M(s)/W(s), cross-country running M(s), football M(s), golf M(s), soccer M(s), softball W(s), tennis M(s)/W(s), track and field M(s). *Intramural sports:* basketball M/W, football M/W, softball M/W, volleyball M/W.

Standardized Tests *Required for some:* SAT I and SAT II or ACT (for admission).

Costs (2003–04) *Tuition:* state resident $1460 full-time, $75 per semester hour part-time; nonresident $3666 full-time, $160 per semester hour part-time. *Room and board:* $2142; room only: $912.

Financial Aid Of all full-time matriculated undergraduates who enrolled, 300 Federal Work-Study jobs (averaging $1250). 200 state and other part-time jobs (averaging $1000).

Applying *Options:* common application, early admission. *Required:* high school transcript. *Application deadline:* rolling (freshmen), rolling (transfers). *Notification:* continuous (freshmen), continuous (transfers).

Admissions Contact Mr. Jay Allen, Director of Admissions and Records, Hinds Community College, PO Box 1100, Raymond, MS 39154-1100. *Phone:* 601-857-3280. *Toll-free phone:* 800-HINDSCC. *Fax:* 601-857-3539.

HOLMES COMMUNITY COLLEGE
Goodman, Mississippi

- **State and locally supported** 2-year, founded 1928, part of Mississippi State Board for Community and Junior Colleges
- **Calendar** semesters
- **Degree** certificates and associate
- **Small-town** 196-acre campus
- **Endowment** $2.1 million
- **Coed,** 3,805 undergraduate students, 20% full-time, 16% women, 12% men

Undergraduates 773 full-time, 273 part-time. Students come from 13 states and territories, 42% African American, 0.4% Hispanic American, 0.1% Native American, 20% live on campus. *Retention:* 55% of 2002 full-time freshmen returned.

Freshmen *Admission:* 2,504 applied, 1,807 admitted, 1,046 enrolled.

Faculty *Total:* 156, 74% full-time, 6% with terminal degrees. *Student/faculty ratio:* 28:1.

Majors Administrative assistant and secretarial science; agriculture; biology/biological sciences; business administration and management; business teacher education; child development; clinical laboratory science/medical technology; computer and information sciences related; computer science; computer/technical support; data processing and data processing technology; drafting and design technology; elementary education; engineering; finance; forestry; health information/medical records administration; liberal arts and sciences/liberal studies; music teacher education; nursing (registered nurse training); pharmacy; physical therapy; radio and television; respiratory care therapy; science teacher education; social work; system administration; veterinary sciences; wildlife biology.

Academic Programs *Special study options:* academic remediation for entering students, adult/continuing education programs, advanced placement credit, cooperative education, distance learning, services for LD students, summer session for credit.

Library McMorrough Library plus 2 others with 53,000 titles, 550 serial subscriptions, an OPAC.

Computers on Campus 150 computers available on campus for general student use. A campuswide network can be accessed from off campus. Internet access, online (class) registration, at least one staffed computer lab available.

Student Life *Housing Options:* Campus housing is university owned. *Activities and Organizations:* drama/theater group, student-run newspaper, choral group, marching band, Student Government Association, Drama/Theater Club, Baptist Student Union, FCA, Vocational Industrial Clubs of America. *Campus security:* 24-hour emergency response devices and patrols. *Student services:* personal/psychological counseling.

Athletics Member NJCAA. *Intercollegiate sports:* baseball M(s), basketball M(s)/W, football M(s), golf M(s)/W(s), soccer M(s)/W(s), softball W(s), tennis M(s)/W(s). *Intramural sports:* basketball M/W, football M/W, softball M/W, volleyball M/W.

Standardized Tests *Required:* ACT (for placement).

Costs (2003–04) *Tuition:* state resident $1430 full-time, $65 per semester hour part-time. Part-time tuition and fees vary according to course load. *Required fees:* $270 full-time, $10 per term part-time. *Room and board:* $3800; room only: $800. *Waivers:* employees or children of employees.

Financial Aid Of all full-time matriculated undergraduates who enrolled, 160 Federal Work-Study jobs (averaging $700).

Applying *Options:* early admission. *Required:* high school transcript. *Application deadline:* rolling (freshmen), rolling (transfers). *Notification:* continuous (freshmen), continuous (transfers).

Admissions Contact Dr. Lynn Wright, Dean of Admissions and Records, Holmes Community College, PO Box 369, Goodman, MS 39079-0369. *Phone:* 601-472-2312 Ext. 1023.

ITAWAMBA COMMUNITY COLLEGE
Fulton, Mississippi

Admissions Contact Mr. Max Munn, Director of Recruiting, Itawamba Community College, 602 West Hill Street, Fulton, MS 38843. *Phone:* 601-862-8252.

JONES COUNTY JUNIOR COLLEGE
Ellisville, Mississippi

- **State and locally supported** 2-year, founded 1928, part of Mississippi State Board for Community and Junior Colleges
- **Calendar** semesters
- **Degree** certificates and associate
- **Small-town** 360-acre campus
- **Coed**

Faculty *Student/faculty ratio:* 25:1.

Student Life *Campus security:* 24-hour patrols.

Athletics Member NJCAA.

Standardized Tests *Required:* SAT I or ACT (for admission).

Costs (2004–05) *Tuition:* state resident $1288 full-time, $65 per semester hour part-time; nonresident $3188 full-time, $144 per semester hour part-time. *Required fees:* $132 full-time, $18 per term part-time. *Room and board:* $1332.

Financial Aid Of all full-time matriculated undergraduates who enrolled, 325 Federal Work-Study jobs (averaging $1850).

Applying *Options:* common application, early admission. *Required:* high school transcript.

Admissions Contact Mrs. Dianne Speed, Director of Admissions and Records, Jones County Junior College, 900 South Court Street, Ellisville, MS 39437. *Phone:* 601-477-4025. *Fax:* 601-477-4258.

MERIDIAN COMMUNITY COLLEGE
Meridian, Mississippi

- **State and locally supported** 2-year, founded 1937, part of Mississippi State Board for Community and Junior Colleges
- **Calendar** semesters
- **Degree** certificates and associate
- **Small-town** 62-acre campus
- **Endowment** $4.8 million
- **Coed,** 3,635 undergraduate students, 73% full-time, 69% women, 31% men

Undergraduates 2,636 full-time, 999 part-time. Students come from 16 states and territories, 3% are from out of state, 40% African American, 0.4% Asian American or Pacific Islander, 0.8% Hispanic American, 2% Native American, 0.2% international, 12% live on campus.

Freshmen *Admission:* 882 admitted.

Faculty *Total:* 256, 56% full-time, 3% with terminal degrees.

Majors Administrative assistant and secretarial science; athletic training; broadcast journalism; clinical/medical laboratory technology; computer engineering technology; computer graphics; dental hygiene; drafting and design technology; electrical, electronic and communications engineering technology; emergency medical technology (EMT paramedic); fire science; health information/medical records administration; horticultural science; hotel/motel administration; machine tool technology; marketing/marketing management; medical radiologic technology; nursing (registered nurse training); physical therapy; respiratory care therapy; telecommunications.

Meridian Community College (continued)

Academic Programs *Special study options:* academic remediation for entering students, adult/continuing education programs, advanced placement credit, cooperative education, part-time degree program, services for LD students, summer session for credit.

Library L.O. Todd Library with 50,000 titles, 600 serial subscriptions.

Computers on Campus 123 computers available on campus for general student use.

Student Life *Housing Options:* coed, men-only, women-only. Campus housing is university owned and leased by the school. *Activities and Organizations:* drama/theater group, student-run newspaper, radio station, choral group, Phi Theta Kappa, Vocational Industrial Clubs of America, Health Occupations Students of America, Organization of Student Nurses, Distributive Education Clubs of America. *Campus security:* 24-hour patrols, student patrols. *Student services:* health clinic, personal/psychological counseling.

Athletics Member NJCAA. *Intercollegiate sports:* baseball M(s), basketball M(s)/W(s), cross-country running M(s)/W(s), golf M(s), soccer M(s), softball W(s), tennis M(s)/W(s), track and field M(s)/W(s). *Intramural sports:* basketball M/W, bowling M/W, cross-country running M/W, swimming M/W, tennis M/W, volleyball M/W.

Standardized Tests *Required:* SAT I or ACT (for placement). *Recommended:* ACCUPLACER.

Costs (2003–04) *Tuition:* state resident $1200 full-time, $65 per credit hour part-time; nonresident $2640 full-time, $132 per credit hour part-time. *Required fees:* $146 full-time, $4 per credit hour part-time, $15 per term part-time. *Room and board:* $2550.

Financial Aid Of all full-time matriculated undergraduates who enrolled, 100 Federal Work-Study jobs (averaging $2100).

Applying *Options:* early admission. *Required:* high school transcript, minimum 2.0 GPA. *Required for some:* essay or personal statement. *Application deadline:* rolling (freshmen), rolling (transfers).

Admissions Contact Ms. Mary Faye Wilson, Director of Admissions, Meridian Community College, 910 Highway 19 North, Meridian, MS 39307. *Phone:* 601-484-8621. *Toll-free phone:* 800-622-8731. *E-mail:* dwalton@mcc.cc.ms.us.

MISSISSIPPI DELTA COMMUNITY COLLEGE
Moorhead, Mississippi

- **District-supported** 2-year, founded 1926, part of Mississippi State Board for Community and Junior Colleges
- **Calendar** semesters
- **Degree** certificates, diplomas, and associate
- **Small-town** 425-acre campus
- **Coed**

Student Life *Campus security:* 24-hour emergency response devices and patrols, late-night transport/escort service.

Athletics Member NJCAA.

Standardized Tests *Required for some:* ACT (for admission).

Financial Aid Of all full-time matriculated undergraduates who enrolled, 100 Federal Work-Study jobs (averaging $1400). 100 state and other part-time jobs (averaging $1400).

Applying *Options:* deferred entrance. *Required:* high school transcript.

Admissions Contact Mr. Joseph F. Ray Jr., Vice President of Admissions, Mississippi Delta Community College, PO Box 668, Moorhead, MS 38761-0668. *Phone:* 662-246-6308.

MISSISSIPPI GULF COAST COMMUNITY COLLEGE
Perkinston, Mississippi

- **District-supported** 2-year, founded 1911, part of Mississippi State Board for Community and Junior Colleges
- **Calendar** semesters
- **Degree** certificates, diplomas, and associate
- **Small-town** 600-acre campus with easy access to New Orleans
- **Endowment** $3.0 million
- **Coed**, 10,231 undergraduate students

Undergraduates Students come from 15 states and territories, 4% are from out of state, 20% African American, 2% Asian American or Pacific Islander, 2% Hispanic American, 0.4% Native American, 7% live on campus. *Retention:* 62% of 2002 full-time freshmen returned.

Faculty *Total:* 472, 57% full-time. *Student/faculty ratio:* 26:1.

Majors Accounting; administrative assistant and secretarial science; advertising; agricultural business and management; art; art teacher education; automobile/

automotive mechanics technology; biological and physical sciences; business administration and management; business teacher education; chemical engineering; clinical/medical laboratory technology; computer and information sciences related; computer engineering technology; computer graphics; computer programming related; computer science; computer systems networking and telecommunications; court reporting; criminal justice/law enforcement administration; criminal justice/police science; data entry/microcomputer applications; data entry/microcomputer applications related; drafting and design technology; education; electrical, electronic and communications engineering technology; elementary education; emergency medical technology (EMT paramedic); fashion merchandising; finance; horticultural science; hotel/motel administration; human services; industrial radiologic technology; information technology; kindergarten/preschool education; legal assistant/paralegal; liberal arts and sciences/liberal studies; marketing/marketing management; nursing (registered nurse training); ornamental horticulture; postal management; pre-engineering; respiratory care therapy; welding technology; word processing.

Academic Programs *Special study options:* academic remediation for entering students, adult/continuing education programs, advanced placement credit, cooperative education, distance learning, English as a second language, honors programs, internships, part-time degree program, services for LD students, summer session for credit.

Library Main Library plus 3 others with 100,472 titles, 933 serial subscriptions, an OPAC.

Computers on Campus 435 computers available on campus for general student use. A campuswide network can be accessed from student residence rooms. At least one staffed computer lab available.

Student Life *Housing Options:* men-only, women-only. Campus housing is university owned. *Activities and Organizations:* drama/theater group, student-run newspaper, choral group, marching band, VICA, SIFE, Student Government Association. *Campus security:* 24-hour emergency response devices and patrols. *Student services:* personal/psychological counseling, women's center.

Athletics Member NJCAA. *Intercollegiate sports:* baseball M(s), basketball M(s)/W(s), football M(s), golf M(s), soccer M(s)/W(s), softball W(s), tennis M(s)/W(s), track and field M(s). *Intramural sports:* basketball M/W, football M, soccer M/W, softball M/W, volleyball M/W.

Standardized Tests *Required for some:* ACT (for placement).

Costs (2003–04) *Tuition:* state resident $1290 full-time, $65 per semester hour part-time; nonresident $3136 full-time, $142 per semester hour part-time. *Required fees:* $142 full-time, $3 per semester hour part-time, $20 per term part-time. *Room and board:* $2050; room only: $770. Room and board charges vary according to board plan. *Payment plan:* installment. *Waivers:* senior citizens and employees or children of employees.

Applying *Options:* common application, electronic application, early admission. *Required:* high school transcript. *Application deadline:* rolling (freshmen), rolling (transfers). *Notification:* continuous (freshmen), continuous (transfers).

Admissions Contact Ms. Michelle Sekul, Director of Admissions, Mississippi Gulf Coast Community College, PO Box 548, Perkinston, MS 39573. *Phone:* 601-928-6264. *E-mail:* michelle.sekul@mgccc.edu.

NORTHEAST MISSISSIPPI COMMUNITY COLLEGE
Booneville, Mississippi

- **State-supported** 2-year, founded 1948, part of Mississippi State Board for Community and Junior Colleges
- **Calendar** semesters
- **Degree** certificates and associate
- **Small-town** 100-acre campus
- **Coed,** 3,224 undergraduate students, 86% full-time, 59% women, 41% men

Undergraduates 2,777 full-time, 447 part-time. Students come from 18 states and territories, 18% African American, 0.4% Asian American or Pacific Islander, 0.4% Hispanic American, 0.4% Native American, 25% live on campus.

Freshmen *Admission:* 1,101 enrolled.

Faculty *Total:* 142, 94% full-time.

Majors Accounting; administrative assistant and secretarial science; agricultural teacher education; agriculture; agronomy and crop science; art; artificial intelligence and robotics; art teacher education; biblical studies; biological and physical sciences; biology/biological sciences; broadcast journalism; business administration and management; business/managerial economics; business teacher education; carpentry; chemistry; child development; civil engineering technology; clinical laboratory science/medical technology; clinical/medical laboratory technology; commercial and advertising art; computer management; computer programming; computer science; criminal justice/law enforcement administration; criminal justice/police science; dairy science; data processing and data processing technology; dental hygiene; developmental and child psychology; drafting and design technology; dramatic/theatre arts; drawing; economics; education; electrical, electronic and communications engineering technology; elementary education; engineering; engineering technology; English; entomology; family and consumer sciences/home economics teacher education; family and consumer sciences/human sciences; fashion/apparel design; fashion merchandising; food science; forestry; forestry technology; health science; health teacher education; heating, air conditioning, ventilation and refrigeration maintenance technology; history; horticultural science; hospitality and recreation marketing; hotel/motel administration; industrial radiologic technology; industrial technology; information science/studies; insurance; interior design; journalism; kindergarten/preschool education; kinesiology and exercise science; landscape architecture; legal administrative assistant/secretary; legal assistant/paralegal; liberal arts and sciences/liberal studies; library science; mass communication/media; mathematics; medical administrative assistant and medical secretary; medical/clinical assistant; music; music teacher education; nursing (registered nurse training); occupational therapy; oceanography (chemical and physical); parks, recreation and leisure; pharmacy; photography; physical education teaching and coaching; physical therapy; political science and government; pre-engineering; psychology; public administration; public relations/image management; radio and television; religious education; respiratory care therapy; science teacher education; social sciences; social work; special products marketing; speech therapy; teacher assistant/aide; theology; trade and industrial teacher education; wildlife and wildlands science and management; wildlife biology; zoology/animal biology.

Academic Programs *Special study options:* academic remediation for entering students, adult/continuing education programs, advanced placement credit, cooperative education, part-time degree program, services for LD students, student-designed majors, summer session for credit.

Library Eula Dees Library with 29,879 titles, 378 serial subscriptions.

Computers on Campus 350 computers available on campus for general student use. At least one staffed computer lab available.

Student Life *Housing Options:* Campus housing is university owned. *Activities and Organizations:* drama/theater group, student-run newspaper, choral group, marching band. *Campus security:* 24-hour patrols, student patrols, controlled dormitory access. *Student services:* personal/psychological counseling.

Athletics Member NJCAA. *Intercollegiate sports:* baseball M(s), basketball M(s)/W(s), football M(s), golf M, softball W, tennis M/W. *Intramural sports:* archery M/W, badminton M/W, basketball M/W, soccer M/W, softball M/W, tennis M/W, volleyball M/W.

Standardized Tests *Required for some:* SAT I or ACT (for admission).

Costs (2004–05) *Tuition:* state resident $1500 full-time, $83 per hour part-time; nonresident $3220 full-time, $179 per hour part-time. *Required fees:* $104 full-time. *Room and board:* $2862; room only: $2862.

Applying *Options:* early admission. *Application deadline:* rolling (freshmen), rolling (transfers). *Notification:* continuous (freshmen), continuous (transfers).

Admissions Contact Ms. Lynn Gibson, Director of Enrollment Services, Northeast Mississippi Community College, 101 Cunningham Boulevard, Booneville, MS 38829. *Phone:* 662-728-7751 Ext. 7239. *Toll-free phone:* 800-555-2154.

NORTHWEST MISSISSIPPI COMMUNITY COLLEGE
Senatobia, Mississippi

- **State and locally supported** 2-year, founded 1927, part of Mississippi State Board for Community and Junior Colleges
- **Calendar** semesters
- **Degree** associate
- **Rural** 75-acre campus with easy access to Memphis
- **Coed**

Faculty *Student/faculty ratio:* 20:1.

Student Life *Campus security:* 24-hour emergency response devices, late-night transport/escort service, controlled dormitory access.

Athletics Member NJCAA.

Standardized Tests *Required:* ACT (for placement).

Applying *Options:* common application, early admission, deferred entrance. *Required:* high school transcript.

Admissions Contact Ms. Deanna Ferguson, Director of Admissions and Recruiting, Northwest Mississippi Community College, 4975 Highway 51 North, Senatobia, MS 38668-1701. *Phone:* 662-562-3222.

PEARL RIVER COMMUNITY COLLEGE
Poplarville, Mississippi

- **State and locally supported** 2-year, founded 1909, part of Mississippi State Board for Community and Junior Colleges
- **Calendar** semesters
- **Degree** certificates and associate
- **Rural** 240-acre campus with easy access to New Orleans
- **Coed**

Student Life *Campus security:* 24-hour patrols.

Athletics Member NJCAA.

Standardized Tests *Required:* ACT (for placement).

Costs (2003–04) *Tuition:* state resident $1410 full-time; nonresident $3810 full-time. *Room and board:* $2064.

Financial Aid Of all full-time matriculated undergraduates who enrolled, 200 Federal Work-Study jobs (averaging $2000).

Applying *Options:* early admission, deferred entrance. *Required:* high school transcript.

Admissions Contact Mr. J. Dow Ford, Director of Admissions, Pearl River Community College, 101 Highway 11 North, Poplarville, MS 39470. *Phone:* 601-795-6801 Ext. 216. *E-mail:* jdowford@teclink.net.

SOUTHWEST MISSISSIPPI COMMUNITY COLLEGE
Summit, Mississippi

- **State and locally supported** 2-year, founded 1918, part of Mississippi State Board for Community and Junior Colleges
- **Calendar** semesters
- **Degree** certificates and associate
- **Rural** 701-acre campus
- **Coed,** 2,268 undergraduate students, 61% full-time, 64% women, 36% men

Undergraduates 1,387 full-time, 881 part-time. Students come from 6 states and territories, 10% are from out of state, 43% African American, 0.1% Asian American or Pacific Islander, 0.2% Hispanic American, 0.2% Native American, 35% live on campus.

Faculty *Total:* 94, 87% full-time, 6% with terminal degrees. *Student/faculty ratio:* 25:1.

Majors Accounting; administrative assistant and secretarial science; advertising; automobile/automotive mechanics technology; biological and physical sciences; biology/biological sciences; business administration and management; business teacher education; carpentry; chemistry; computer programming related; computer science; construction engineering technology; cosmetology; education; electrical, electronic and communications engineering technology; elementary education; emergency medical technology (EMT paramedic); engineering; English; fashion merchandising; finance; health science; history; humanities; information technology; legal administrative assistant/secretary; liberal arts and sciences/liberal studies; machine tool technology; marketing/marketing management; music; music teacher education; nursing (registered nurse training); physical education teaching and coaching; physical sciences; social sciences; system administration; welding technology.

Academic Programs *Special study options:* academic remediation for entering students, adult/continuing education programs, distance learning, part-time degree program, summer session for credit.

Library Library Learning Resources Center (LLRC) with 34,000 titles, 150 serial subscriptions, an OPAC.

Computers on Campus 300 computers available on campus for general student use. A campuswide network can be accessed from off campus. Internet access, online (class) registration, at least one staffed computer lab available.

Student Life *Activities and Organizations:* student-run newspaper, choral group, marching band. *Campus security:* 24-hour patrols.

Athletics Member NJCAA. *Intercollegiate sports:* baseball M, basketball M(s)/W(s), football M(s), golf M, softball W, tennis M/W. *Intramural sports:* basketball M/W.

Standardized Tests *Required for some:* ACT (for placement).

Costs (2004–05) *Tuition:* state resident $750 full-time, $70 per hour part-time; nonresident $1850 full-time, $165 per hour part-time. *Required fees:* $50 full-time, $25 per term part-time. *Room and board:* $1050.

Financial Aid Of all full-time matriculated undergraduates who enrolled, 85 Federal Work-Study jobs (averaging $698). 6 state and other part-time jobs (averaging $550).

Applying *Required:* high school transcript. *Application deadlines:* 8/1 (freshmen), 8/1 (transfers).

Admissions Contact Alicia C. Shows, Director of Admissions, Southwest Mississippi Community College, College Drive, Summit, MS 39666. *Phone:* 601-276-2000. *Fax:* 601-276-3888.

VIRGINIA COLLEGE AT JACKSON
Jackson, Mississippi

- **Proprietary** 2-year, founded 2000
- **Calendar** quarters
- **Degree** diplomas and associate
- **Urban** 3-acre campus
- **Coed,** 1,108 undergraduate students

Faculty *Total:* 85. *Student/faculty ratio:* 11:1.

Virginia College at Jackson (continued)

Majors Accounting related; administrative assistant and secretarial science; business operations support and secretarial services related; computer systems networking and telecommunications; educational/instructional media design; health information/medical records administration; human resources management; medical/clinical assistant; medical office management.

Student Life *Housing:* college housing not available. *Campus security:* 24-hour emergency response devices and patrols.

Standardized Tests *Required:* CPAt (for admission).

Costs (2003–04) *Tuition:* $8820 full-time, $245 per quarter hour part-time.

Applying *Application fee:* $100. *Required:* high school transcript, interview, GED.

Admissions Contact Mr. Bill Milstead, Vice President of Admissions, Virginia College at Jackson, Interstate 55 North, Jackson, MS 39211. *Phone:* 601-977-0960 Ext. 2704. *E-mail:* bmilstead@vc.edu.

MISSOURI

ALLIED COLLEGE
Saint Ann, Missouri

Admissions Contact Mr. Larkin Hicks, President, Allied College, 500 Northwest Plaza Tower, Suite 400, Saint Ann, MO 63074. *Phone:* 314-739-4450.

BLUE RIVER COMMUNITY COLLEGE
Blue Springs, Missouri

- **State and locally supported** 2-year, part of Metropolitan Community Colleges System
- **Calendar** semesters
- **Degree** certificates and associate
- **Suburban** campus with easy access to Kansas City
- **Endowment** $1.4 million
- **Coed,** 2,323 undergraduate students, 44% full-time, 62% women, 38% men

Undergraduates 1,015 full-time, 1,308 part-time. Students come from 2 states and territories, 1 other country, 0.2% are from out of state, 2% African American, 0.9% Asian American or Pacific Islander, 2% Hispanic American, 0.3% Native American, 0.1% international, 0.5% transferred in. *Retention:* 48% of 2002 full-time freshmen returned.

Freshmen *Admission:* 409 applied, 409 admitted, 409 enrolled.

Faculty *Total:* 292, 10% full-time. *Student/faculty ratio:* 20:1.

Majors Accounting technology and bookkeeping; administrative assistant and secretarial science; business administration and management; computer and information sciences related; computer science; criminal justice/police science; fire science; information science/studies; liberal arts and sciences/liberal studies.

Academic Programs *Special study options:* academic remediation for entering students, accelerated degree program, adult/continuing education programs, advanced placement credit, cooperative education, distance learning, English as a second language, honors programs, internships, off-campus study, part-time degree program, services for LD students, summer session for credit.

Library Blue River Community College Library with 9,333 titles, 12,776 serial subscriptions, 512 audiovisual materials, an OPAC, a Web page.

Computers on Campus 543 computers available on campus for general student use. A campuswide network can be accessed from off campus. Internet access, at least one staffed computer lab available.

Student Life *Housing:* college housing not available. *Activities and Organizations:* choral group. *Campus security:* 24-hour emergency response devices and patrols.

Standardized Tests *Required:* ACT ASSET (for placement). *Recommended:* ACT (for placement).

Costs (2004–05) *Tuition:* area resident $2070 full-time, $69 per hour part-time; state resident $3750 full-time, $125 per hour part-time; nonresident $5100 full-time, $170 per hour part-time. Full-time tuition and fees vary according to course level and program. Part-time tuition and fees vary according to course level and program. *Required fees:* $150 full-time, $5 per hour part-time. *Payment plan:* installment. *Waivers:* senior citizens and employees or children of employees.

Applying *Options:* early admission, deferred entrance. *Application deadline:* rolling (freshmen), rolling (transfers).

Admissions Contact Mr. Jon Burke, Dean of Student Services, Blue River Community College, 1501 West Jefferson Street, Blue Spring, MO 64015. *Phone:* 816-655-6118. *Fax:* 816-655-6014.

CONCORDE CAREER INSTITUTE
Kansas City, Missouri

Admissions Contact 3239 Broadway, Kansas City, MO 64111-2407.

COTTEY COLLEGE
Nevada, Missouri

- **Independent** 2-year, founded 1884
- **Calendar** semesters
- **Degree** associate
- **Small-town** 51-acre campus
- **Endowment** $67.4 million
- **Women only**

Faculty *Student/faculty ratio:* 10:1.

Student Life *Campus security:* 24-hour emergency response devices and patrols, late-night transport/escort service, controlled dormitory access.

Athletics Member NAIA.

Standardized Tests *Required:* SAT I or ACT (for admission).

Costs (2004–05) *Comprehensive fee:* $16,380 includes full-time tuition ($10,800), mandatory fees ($580), and room and board ($5000).

Financial Aid Of all full-time matriculated undergraduates who enrolled, 26 Federal Work-Study jobs (averaging $1500). 131 state and other part-time jobs (averaging $1500).

Applying *Options:* electronic application, early admission, deferred entrance. *Application fee:* $20. *Required:* essay or personal statement, high school transcript, 1 letter of recommendation. *Recommended:* minimum 2.6 GPA, interview.

Admissions Contact Ms. Marjorie J. Cooke, Dean of Enrollment Management, Cottey College, 1000 West Austin, Nevada, MO 64772. *Phone:* 417-667-8181. *Toll-free phone:* 888-526-8839. *Fax:* 417-667-8103. *E-mail:* enrollmgt@cottey.edu.

CROWDER COLLEGE
Neosho, Missouri

- **State and locally supported** 2-year, founded 1963, part of Missouri Coordinating Board for Higher Education
- **Calendar** semesters
- **Degree** certificates and associate
- **Rural** 608-acre campus
- **Coed,** 2,616 undergraduate students, 53% full-time, 63% women, 37% men

Undergraduates 1,378 full-time, 1,238 part-time. Students come from 14 states and territories, 14 other countries, 2% are from out of state, 1% African American, 0.7% Asian American or Pacific Islander, 4% Hispanic American, 2% Native American, 0.7% international, 5% transferred in, 10% live on campus.

Freshmen *Admission:* 1,356 applied, 1,356 admitted, 607 enrolled.

Faculty *Total:* 199, 31% full-time.

Majors Administrative assistant and secretarial science; agribusiness; agriculture; art; biology/biological sciences; business administration and management; business automation/technology/data entry; computer systems networking and telecommunications; construction engineering technology; drafting and design technology; dramatic/theatre arts; education; electrical, electronic and communications engineering technology; elementary education; environmental engineering technology; environmental health; executive assistant/executive secretary; farm and ranch management; fire science; general studies; industrial technology; legal administrative assistant/secretary; liberal arts and sciences/liberal studies; mass communication/media; mathematics; mathematics and computer science; medical administrative assistant and medical secretary; music; nursing (registered nurse training); physical education teaching and coaching; physical sciences; poultry science; pre-engineering; psychology; public relations/image management.

Academic Programs *Special study options:* academic remediation for entering students, adult/continuing education programs, advanced placement credit, cooperative education, English as a second language, freshman honors college, honors programs, internships, part-time degree program, study abroad, summer session for credit.

Library Crowder College Learning Resources Center with 32,093 titles, 307 serial subscriptions, 4,789 audiovisual materials, an OPAC, a Web page.

Computers on Campus 261 computers available on campus for general student use. A campuswide network can be accessed. At least one staffed computer lab available.

Student Life *Housing Options:* men-only, women-only. Campus housing is university owned. *Activities and Organizations:* drama/theater group, student-run newspaper, choral group, Phi Beta Lambda, Students in Free Enterprise, Baptist Student Union, Student Senate, Student Ambassadors. *Campus security:* 24-hour patrols. *Student services:* personal/psychological counseling.

Athletics Member NJCAA. *Intercollegiate sports:* baseball M(s), basketball W(s). *Intramural sports:* soccer M.

Standardized Tests *Required:* ACT COMPASS (for placement).

Costs (2003–04) *Tuition:* area resident $1710 full-time, $51 per semester hour part-time; state resident $2430 full-time, $73 per semester hour part-time; nonresident $3180 full-time, $96 per semester hour part-time. *Required fees:* $180 full-time, $6 per semester hour part-time. *Room and board:* $3750.

Financial Aid Of all full-time matriculated undergraduates who enrolled, 150 Federal Work-Study jobs (averaging $1000).

Applying *Application fee:* $25. *Required:* high school transcript. *Application deadline:* rolling (freshmen), rolling (transfers). *Notification:* continuous (freshmen).

Admissions Contact Mr. Jim Riggs, Admissions Coordinator, Crowder College, 601 Laclede, Neosho, MO 64850. *Phone:* 417-451-3223 Ext. 5466. *Toll-free phone:* 866-238-7788. *Fax:* 417-455-5731.

EAST CENTRAL COLLEGE
Union, Missouri

- **District-supported** 2-year, founded 1959, part of Missouri Coordinating Board for Higher Education
- **Calendar** semesters
- **Degree** certificates and associate
- **Rural** 207-acre campus with easy access to St. Louis
- **Endowment** $1.8 million
- **Coed**

Faculty *Student/faculty ratio:* 18:1.

Student Life *Campus security:* 24-hour emergency response devices, late-night transport/escort service.

Athletics Member NJCAA.

Standardized Tests *Required:* ACT ASSET, ACT COMPASS (for placement). *Recommended:* ACT (for placement).

Costs (2003–04) *Tuition:* area resident $1416 full-time, $59 per credit hour part-time; state resident $2040 full-time, $85 per credit hour part-time; nonresident $3096 full-time, $129 per credit hour part-time. Full-time tuition and fees vary according to course load. Part-time tuition and fees vary according to course load. *Required fees:* $240 full-time, $10 per credit hour part-time.

Financial Aid Of all full-time matriculated undergraduates who enrolled, 35 Federal Work-Study jobs (averaging $1500). 35 state and other part-time jobs (averaging $1500).

Applying *Options:* common application, early admission, deferred entrance. *Required:* high school transcript.

Admissions Contact Mrs. Karen Wieda, Registrar, East Central College, 1964 Prairie Dell Road, Union, MO 63084. *Phone:* 636-583-5195 Ext. 2220. *Fax:* 636-583-1897. *E-mail:* wiedaks@eastcentral.edu.

HERITAGE COLLEGE
Kansas City, Missouri

Admissions Contact 534 East 99th Street, Kansas City, MO 64131-4203.

HICKEY COLLEGE
St. Louis, Missouri

- **Proprietary** primarily 2-year, founded 1933
- **Calendar** semesters
- **Degrees** diplomas, associate, and bachelor's
- **Suburban** campus
- **Coed,** 500 undergraduate students

Diploma and associate degree programs. Founded 1933. Eight- to sixteen-month programs include accounting, administrative assistant studies, computer applications specialist studies, computer applications and programming, graphic design, legal administrative assistant studies, and paralegal studies. Tuition and fees vary by program. Financial assistance for those who qualify. Housing available. Accredited member, ACICS. Call 314-434-2212 or 800-777-1544 (toll-free) for more information.

Faculty *Total:* 18, 67% full-time. *Student/faculty ratio:* 30:1.

Majors Accounting; business administration and management; computer programming; executive assistant/executive secretary; graphic design; legal administrative assistant/secretary; legal assistant/paralegal.

Academic Programs *Special study options:* accelerated degree program.

Computers on Campus 109 computers available on campus for general student use.

Costs (2004–05) *Tuition:* $10,480 full-time, $300 per credit hour part-time. *Room only:* $4800.

Applying *Application fee:* $50. *Required:* high school transcript, interview. *Application deadline:* rolling (freshmen), rolling (transfers).

Admissions Contact Ms. Michelle Hayes, Director of Admissions, Hickey College, 940 West Port Plaza Drive, St. Louis, MO 63146. *Phone:* 314-434-2212 Ext. 136. *Toll-free phone:* 800-777-1544. *Fax:* 314-434-1974. *E-mail:* admin@hickeycollege.com.

HIGH-TECH INSTITUTE
Kansas City, Missouri

Admissions Contact 9001 State Line Road, Kansas City, MO 64114.

IHM HEALTH STUDIES CENTER
St. Louis, Missouri

- **Independent** 2-year, founded 1977
- **Calendar** trimesters
- **Degree** certificates and associate
- **Suburban** campus
- **Coed,** 136 undergraduate students, 53% full-time, 40% women, 60% men

Undergraduates 72 full-time, 64 part-time. 18% African American, 1% Asian American or Pacific Islander, 0.7% Hispanic American, 0.7% Native American.

Faculty *Total:* 7, 57% full-time.

Majors Emergency medical technology (EMT paramedic).

Costs (2004–05) *Required fees:* $210 full-time. *Room and board:* $8622.

Admissions Contact Mr. Taz A. Meyer, Director of Education, IHM Health Studies Center, 2500 Abbott Place, St. Louis, MO 63143-2636. *Phone:* 314-768-1234 Ext. 1128.

ITT TECHNICAL INSTITUTE
Arnold, Missouri

- **Proprietary** primarily 2-year, part of ITT Educational Services, Inc.
- **Calendar** quarters
- **Degrees** associate and bachelor's
- **Coed**

Standardized Tests *Required:* Wonderlic aptitude test (for admission).

Costs (2003–04) *Tuition:* Total Program Cost varies depending on course of study. Consult school catalog.

Applying *Options:* deferred entrance. *Application fee:* $100. *Required:* high school transcript, interview. *Recommended:* letters of recommendation.

Admissions Contact Mr. James R. Rowe, Director of Recruitment, ITT Technical Institute, 1930 Meyer Drury Drive, Arnold, MO 63010. *Phone:* 636-464-6600. *Toll-free phone:* 888-488-1082. *Fax:* 636-464-6611.

ITT TECHNICAL INSTITUTE
Earth City, Missouri

- **Proprietary** primarily 2-year, founded 1936, part of ITT Educational Services, Inc.
- **Calendar** quarters
- **Degrees** associate and bachelor's
- **Suburban** 2-acre campus with easy access to St. Louis
- **Coed**

Standardized Tests *Required:* Wonderlic aptitude test (for admission).

Costs (2003–04) *Tuition:* Total Program Cost varies depending on course of study. Consult school catalog.

Applying *Options:* deferred entrance. *Application fee:* $100. *Required:* high school transcript, interview. *Recommended:* letters of recommendation.

Admissions Contact Mr. Randal Hayes, ITT Technical Institute, 13505 Lakefront Drive, Earth City, MO 63045. *Phone:* 314-298-7800. *Toll-free phone:* 800-235-5488. *Fax:* 314-298-0559.

JEFFERSON COLLEGE
Hillsboro, Missouri

- **State-supported** 2-year, founded 1963, part of Missouri Coordinating Board for Higher Education
- **Calendar** semesters
- **Degree** certificates and associate
- **Rural** 480-acre campus with easy access to St. Louis
- **Endowment** $769,631
- **Coed,** 4,065 undergraduate students, 54% full-time, 61% women, 39% men

Missouri

Jefferson College (continued)

Undergraduates 2,176 full-time, 1,889 part-time. Students come from 6 states and territories, 1% are from out of state, 1% African American, 0.3% Asian American or Pacific Islander, 0.8% Hispanic American, 0.6% Native American, 0.6% international, 5% transferred in, 15% live on campus.

Freshmen *Admission:* 2,927 applied, 2,927 admitted, 1,005 enrolled. *Average high school GPA:* 2.34. *Test scores:* ACT scores over 18: 73%; ACT scores over 24: 20%; ACT scores over 30: 1%.

Faculty *Total:* 218, 39% full-time, 5% with terminal degrees. *Student/faculty ratio:* 18:1.

Majors Administrative assistant and secretarial science; art; automobile/automotive mechanics technology; biological and physical sciences; business administration and management; business/commerce; business teacher education; CAD/CADD drafting/design technology; child care and support services management; civil engineering technology; computer systems networking and telecommunications; consumer merchandising/retailing management; criminal justice/law enforcement administration; criminal justice/police science; culinary arts; dramatic/theatre arts; education; electrical, electronic and communications engineering technology; elementary education; emergency medical technology (EMT paramedic); engineering; English; fire protection and safety technology; forestry; geography; health aide; health unit coordinator/ward clerk; heating, air conditioning, ventilation and refrigeration maintenance technology; history; hospitality administration; industrial mechanics and maintenance technology; institutional food workers; interdisciplinary studies; journalism; kindergarten/preschool education; laser and optical technology; legal administrative assistant/secretary; liberal arts and sciences/liberal studies; machine tool technology; mathematics; mechanical design technology; medical administrative assistant and medical secretary; music; nursing assistant/aide and patient care assistant; nursing (licensed practical/vocational nurse training); nursing (registered nurse training); physical education teaching and coaching; physical sciences; political science and government; precision metal working related; precision production related; pre-engineering; psychology; public administration; robotics technology; social work; sociology; Spanish; speech and rhetoric; telecommunications; veterinary/animal health technology; veterinary technology; welding technology.

Academic Programs *Special study options:* academic remediation for entering students, adult/continuing education programs, advanced placement credit, distance learning, double majors, English as a second language, freshman honors college, honors programs, independent study, internships, off-campus study, part-time degree program, services for LD students, study abroad, summer session for credit.

Library Jefferson College Library plus 1 other with 70,402 titles, 242 serial subscriptions, 5,085 audiovisual materials, an OPAC, a Web page.

Computers on Campus 350 computers available on campus for general student use. A campuswide network can be accessed. Internet access, at least one staffed computer lab available.

Student Life *Housing Options:* Campus housing is university owned. *Activities and Organizations:* drama/theater group, student-run newspaper, television station, choral group, Student Senate, nursing associations, Baptist Student Unit, Phi Beta Lambda, Phi Theta Kappa. *Campus security:* 24-hour patrols. *Student services:* personal/psychological counseling.

Athletics Member NJCAA. *Intercollegiate sports:* baseball M(s), basketball W(s), volleyball W(s).

Standardized Tests *Required:* ACT COMPASS (for placement). *Recommended:* ACT (for placement).

Costs (2004–05) *Tuition:* area resident $1530 full-time, $51 per credit part-time; state resident $2230 full-time, $76 per credit part-time; nonresident $3060 full-time, $102 per credit part-time. Full-time tuition and fees vary according to program. Part-time tuition and fees vary according to program. *Required fees:* $300 full-time, $10 per credit part-time. *Room and board:* $6111. Room and board charges vary according to housing facility. *Payment plan:* installment. *Waivers:* employees or children of employees.

Financial Aid Of all full-time matriculated undergraduates who enrolled, 89 Federal Work-Study jobs (averaging $1095).

Applying *Options:* electronic application, early admission. *Application fee:* $20. *Required:* high school transcript. *Application deadline:* rolling (freshmen), rolling (transfers).

Admissions Contact Ms. Amy Martin-Small, Director of Admissions and Financial Aid, Jefferson College, 1000 Viking Drive, Hillsboro, MO 63050. *Phone:* 636-797-3000 Ext. 218. *Toll-free phone:* 636-797-3000 Ext. 217. *Fax:* 636-789-5103. *E-mail:* admissions@jeffco.edu.

LINN STATE TECHNICAL COLLEGE
Linn, Missouri

- **State-supported** 2-year, founded 1961
- **Calendar** semesters
- **Degree** certificates and associate
- **Rural** 249-acre campus
- **Endowment** $43,580

- **Coed, primarily men,** 872 undergraduate students, 90% full-time, 9% women, 91% men

Undergraduates 783 full-time, 89 part-time. Students come from 5 states and territories, 1% are from out of state, 1% African American, 0.7% Asian American or Pacific Islander, 0.5% Hispanic American, 0.6% Native American, 8% transferred in, 26% live on campus. *Retention:* 58% of 2002 full-time freshmen returned.

Freshmen *Admission:* 597 applied, 420 admitted, 392 enrolled. *Average high school GPA:* 2.77. *Test scores:* ACT scores over 18: 58%; ACT scores over 24: 9%.

Faculty *Total:* 77, 94% full-time. *Student/faculty ratio:* 12:1.

Majors Aircraft powerplant technology; autobody/collision and repair technology; automobile/automotive mechanics technology; civil engineering technology; computer programming; computer systems analysis; drafting and design technology; electrical, electronic and communications engineering technology; electrical/electronics equipment installation and repair; electrician; heating, air conditioning, ventilation and refrigeration maintenance technology; heavy equipment maintenance technology; industrial production technologies related; information science/studies; laser and optical technology; lineworker; machine tool technology; nuclear and industrial radiologic technologies related; physical therapist assistant; turf and turfgrass management.

Student Life *Housing Options:* coed, men-only, women-only, disabled students. Campus housing is university owned. *Activities and Organizations:* Skills USA-VICA, Phi Theta Kappa, Student Government Association, Aviation Club, Electricity Club. *Campus security:* 24-hour emergency response devices, student patrols, controlled dormitory access, indoor and outdoor surveillance cameras. *Student services:* personal/psychological counseling.

Athletics *Intramural sports:* archery M/W, basketball M/W, golf M/W, riflery M/W, softball M/W, table tennis M/W.

Standardized Tests *Required:* ACT ASSET, ACT COMPASS (for admission). *Required for some:* ACT (for admission).

Costs (2003–04) *Tuition:* state resident $3300 full-time; nonresident $6600 full-time. *Required fees:* $590 full-time. *Room and board:* $1925; room only: $1325. Room and board charges vary according to board plan. *Payment plan:* installment. *Waivers:* employees or children of employees.

Financial Aid Of all full-time matriculated undergraduates who enrolled, 70 Federal Work-Study jobs (averaging $769).

Applying *Required:* high school transcript. *Required for some:* essay or personal statement, 3 letters of recommendation, interview, driving record, physical examination. *Notification:* continuous (freshmen), continuous (transfers).

Admissions Contact Ms. Becky Dunn, Assistant Director of Admissions and Student Services, Linn State Technical College, One Technology Drive, Linn, MO 65051. *Phone:* 573-897-5196. *Toll-free phone:* 800-743-TECH. *Fax:* 573-897-5026. *E-mail:* admissions@linnstate.edu.

LONGVIEW COMMUNITY COLLEGE
Lee's Summit, Missouri

- **State and locally supported** 2-year, founded 1969, part of Metropolitan Community Colleges System
- **Calendar** semesters
- **Degree** certificates and associate
- **Suburban** 147-acre campus with easy access to Kansas City
- **Endowment** $1.4 million
- **Coed,** 5,713 undergraduate students, 41% full-time, 58% women, 42% men

Undergraduates 2,346 full-time, 3,367 part-time. Students come from 1 other state, 1 other country, 1% are from out of state, 11% African American, 0.8% Asian American or Pacific Islander, 2% Hispanic American, 0.5% Native American. *Retention:* 42% of 2002 full-time freshmen returned.

Freshmen *Admission:* 686 applied, 686 admitted, 686 enrolled.

Faculty *Total:* 328, 23% full-time. *Student/faculty ratio:* 35:1.

Majors Accounting; administrative assistant and secretarial science; agricultural mechanization; automobile/automotive mechanics technology; biological and physical sciences; biology/biological sciences; business administration and management; chemistry; computer and information sciences related; computer programming; computer science; computer typography and composition equipment operation; corrections; criminal justice/law enforcement administration; criminal justice/police science; data processing and data processing technology; drafting and design technology; electrical, electronic and communications engineering technology; engineering; heavy equipment maintenance technology; human services; legal administrative assistant/secretary; liberal arts and sciences/liberal studies; marketing/marketing management; medical administrative assistant and medical secretary; postal management; pre-engineering; quality control technology.

Academic Programs *Special study options:* academic remediation for entering students, accelerated degree program, adult/continuing education programs, advanced placement credit, cooperative education, distance learning, English as a second language, honors programs, internships, off-campus study, part-time degree program, services for LD students, summer session for credit.

Library Longview Community College Library with 6,567 serial subscriptions, 451 audiovisual materials, an OPAC.

Computers on Campus 543 computers available on campus for general student use. A campuswide network can be accessed from off campus. Internet access, at least one staffed computer lab available.

Student Life *Housing:* college housing not available. *Activities and Organizations:* drama/theater group, student-run newspaper, choral group, student newspaper, student government, Phi Theta Kappa, Longview Mighty Voices Choir, Longview Broadcasting Network, national fraternities. *Campus security:* 24-hour patrols. *Student services:* personal/psychological counseling.

Athletics Member NJCAA. *Intercollegiate sports:* baseball M(s), volleyball W(s). *Intramural sports:* basketball M/W, swimming M/W, volleyball M/W.

Standardized Tests *Required:* ACT ASSET (for placement). *Recommended:* ACT (for placement).

Costs (2004–05) *Tuition:* area resident $2070 full-time, $69 per hour part-time; state resident $3750 full-time, $125 per hour part-time; nonresident $5100 full-time, $170 per hour part-time. Full-time tuition and fees vary according to degree level and program. Part-time tuition and fees vary according to degree level and program. *Required fees:* $150 full-time, $5 per hour part-time.

Applying *Options:* early admission, deferred entrance. *Application deadline:* rolling (freshmen), rolling (transfers).

Admissions Contact Ms. Kathy Hale, Registrar, Longview Community College, 500 Southwest Longview Road, Lee's Summit, MO 64081-2105. *Phone:* 816-672-2249. *Fax:* 816-672-2040.

MAPLE WOODS COMMUNITY COLLEGE
Kansas City, Missouri

- **State and locally supported** 2-year, founded 1969, part of Metropolitan Community Colleges System
- **Calendar** semesters
- **Degree** certificates and associate
- **Suburban** 205-acre campus
- **Endowment** $1.4 million
- **Coed,** 4,747 undergraduate students, 43% full-time, 59% women, 41% men

Undergraduates 2,019 full-time, 2,728 part-time. Students come from 4 states and territories, 1% are from out of state, 4% African American, 2% Asian American or Pacific Islander, 2% Hispanic American, 0.5% Native American, 0.1% international, 0.6% transferred in. *Retention:* 40% of 2002 full-time freshmen returned.

Freshmen *Admission:* 500 applied, 500 admitted, 500 enrolled.

Faculty *Total:* 288, 17% full-time. *Student/faculty ratio:* 36:1.

Majors Accounting; administrative assistant and secretarial science; avionics maintenance technology; biological and physical sciences; biology/biological sciences; business administration and management; chemistry; computer and information sciences related; computer programming; computer science; criminal justice/law enforcement administration; criminal justice/police science; data processing and data processing technology; electrical, electronic and communications engineering technology; heating, air conditioning, ventilation and refrigeration maintenance technology; legal administrative assistant/secretary; liberal arts and sciences/liberal studies; machine shop technology; machine tool technology; marketing/marketing management; medical administrative assistant and medical secretary; pre-engineering; tourism and travel services management; veterinary technology.

Academic Programs *Special study options:* academic remediation for entering students, accelerated degree program, adult/continuing education programs, advanced placement credit, cooperative education, distance learning, English as a second language, honors programs, internships, off-campus study, part-time degree program, services for LD students, summer session for credit.

Library Maple Woods Community College Library with 29,000 titles, 265 serial subscriptions, 3,170 audiovisual materials, an OPAC.

Computers on Campus 398 computers available on campus for general student use. A campuswide network can be accessed from off campus. Internet access, at least one staffed computer lab available.

Student Life *Housing:* college housing not available. *Activities and Organizations:* drama/theater group, student-run newspaper, choral group, Student Activities Council, Art Club, Friends of All Cultures, Phi Theta Kappa, Engineering Club, national fraternities. *Campus security:* 24-hour patrols, late-night transport/escort service. *Student services:* personal/psychological counseling.

Athletics Member NJCAA. *Intercollegiate sports:* baseball M(s). *Intramural sports:* softball M/W, volleyball M/W.

Standardized Tests *Required:* ACT ASSET (for placement).

Costs (2004–05) *Tuition:* area resident $2070 full-time, $69 per hour part-time; state resident $3750 full-time, $125 per hour part-time; nonresident $5100 full-time, $170 per hour part-time. Full-time tuition and fees vary according to course level and program. Part-time tuition and fees vary according to course

level and program. *Required fees:* $150 full-time, $5 per hour part-time. *Payment plan:* installment. *Waivers:* senior citizens and employees or children of employees.

Applying *Options:* early admission, deferred entrance. *Application deadline:* rolling (freshmen), rolling (transfers). *Notification:* continuous (freshmen), continuous (transfers).

Admissions Contact Ms. Dawn Hatterman, Registrar, Maple Woods Community College, 2601 Northeast Barry Road, Kansas City, MO 64156-1299. *Phone:* 816-437-3108. *Fax:* 816-437-3351.

METRO BUSINESS COLLEGE
Cape Girardeau, Missouri

- **Proprietary** primarily 2-year
- **Calendar** quarters
- **Degrees** certificates, diplomas, associate, and bachelor's
- **Coed**

Admissions Contact Ms. Kyla Evans, Admissions Director, Metro Business College, 1732 North Kings Highway, Cape Girardeau, MO 63701. *Phone:* 573-334-9181.

METRO BUSINESS COLLEGE
Jefferson City, Missouri

Admissions Contact Ms. Cherie Chockley, Campus Director, Metro Business College, 1407 Southwest Boulevard, Jefferson City, MO 65109. *Phone:* 573-635-6600. *Toll-free phone:* 800-467-0786.

METRO BUSINESS COLLEGE
Rolla, Missouri

Admissions Contact Ms. Cristie Barker, Director, Metro Business College, 1202 East State Route 72, Rolla, MO 65401. *Phone:* 314-364-8464. *Toll-free phone:* 800-467-0785.

METROPOLITAN COMMUNITY COLLEGE-BUSINESS & TECHNOLOGY COLLEGE
Kansas City, Missouri

- **State and locally supported** 2-year, founded 1995, part of Metropolitan Community Colleges
- **Calendar** semesters
- **Degree** certificates and associate
- **Urban** 23-acre campus
- **Endowment** $1.4 million
- **Coed, primarily men,** 401 undergraduate students, 27% full-time, 15% women, 85% men

Undergraduates 108 full-time, 293 part-time. Students come from 1 other state, 2% are from out of state, 8% African American, 0.4% Asian American or Pacific Islander, 4% Hispanic American, 0.4% Native American.

Freshmen *Admission:* 47 applied, 47 admitted, 47 enrolled.

Faculty *Total:* 33, 30% full-time. *Student/faculty ratio:* 24:1.

Majors Accounting; accounting technology and bookkeeping; artificial intelligence and robotics; building/construction site management; business administration and management; business/commerce; carpentry; computer and information sciences; computer and information sciences and support services related; computer and information sciences related; computer and information systems security; computer graphics; computer/information technology services administration related; computer programming; computer programming related; computer programming (specific applications); computer programming (vendor/product certification); computer science; computer software and media applications related; computer systems analysis; computer systems networking and telecommunications; data entry/microcomputer applications; data entry/microcomputer applications related; data modeling/warehousing and database administration; data processing and data processing technology; drafting and design technology; electrical, electronic and communications engineering technology; engineering; engineering-related technologies; environmental engineering technology; glazier; information science/studies; information technology; liberal arts and sciences/liberal studies; machine shop technology; management information systems and services related; masonry; quality control technology; system administration; system, networking, and LAN/wan management; web/multimedia management and webmaster; web page, digital/multimedia and information resources design; word processing.

Student Life *Housing:* college housing not available. *Campus security:* 24-hour patrols, late-night transport/escort service.

Metropolitan Community College-Business & Technology College (continued)

Standardized Tests *Required:* ACT ASSET and ACT COMPASS (for placement). *Recommended:* ACT (for placement).

Costs (2004–05) *Tuition:* area resident $2070 full-time, $69 per hour part-time; state resident $3750 full-time, $125 per hour part-time; nonresident $5100 full-time, $170 per hour part-time. Full-time tuition and fees vary according to course level and program. Part-time tuition and fees vary according to course level and program. *Required fees:* $150 full-time, $5 per hour part-time. *Payment plan:* installment. *Waivers:* senior citizens and employees or children of employees.

Admissions Contact Mr. Jim Everett, Technical Education and Enrollment Management, Metropolitan Community College-Business & Technology College, 1775 Universal Avenue, Kansas City, MO 64120. *Toll-free phone:* 800-841-7158.

MIDWEST INSTITUTE
Earth City, Missouri

Admissions Contact 4260 Shoreline Drive, Earth City, MO 63045.

MIDWEST INSTITUTE
Kirkwood, Missouri

Admissions Contact Midwest Institute, 10910 Manchester Road, Kirkwood, MO 63122.

MINERAL AREA COLLEGE
Park Hills, Missouri

- **District-supported** 2-year, founded 1922, part of Missouri Coordinating Board for Higher Education
- **Calendar** semesters
- **Degree** certificates and associate
- **Rural** 240-acre campus with easy access to St. Louis
- **Endowment** $2.1 million
- **Coed,** 2,946 undergraduate students, 56% full-time, 67% women, 33% men

Undergraduates 1,645 full-time, 1,301 part-time. Students come from 6 states and territories, 11 other countries, 1% are from out of state, 2% African American, 0.3% Asian American or Pacific Islander, 0.5% Hispanic American, 0.5% Native American, 0.4% international, 3% transferred in.

Freshmen *Admission:* 663 applied, 663 admitted, 663 enrolled. *Average high school GPA:* 2.90. *Test scores:* ACT scores over 18: 67%; ACT scores over 24: 14%; ACT scores over 30: 1%.

Faculty *Total:* 178, 29% full-time. *Student/faculty ratio:* 22:1.

Majors Accounting; administrative assistant and secretarial science; agribusiness; applied horticulture; banking and financial support services; business administration and management; child care provision; clinical laboratory science/medical technology; clinical/medical laboratory technology; commercial and advertising art; computer management; computer programming; construction engineering technology; corrections; criminal justice/police science; drafting and design technology; electrical, electronic and communications engineering technology; fire science; health/health care administration; hospitality administration related; industrial technology; liberal arts and sciences/liberal studies; marketing/marketing management; mass communication/media; medical radiologic technology; nursing assistant/aide and patient care assistant; nursing (licensed practical/vocational nurse training); nursing (registered nurse training); occupational safety and health technology; operations management; parks, recreation and leisure; radio and television broadcasting technology; system administration; tourism and travel services management.

Academic Programs *Special study options:* academic remediation for entering students, advanced placement credit, distance learning, honors programs, internships, off-campus study, part-time degree program, services for LD students, summer session for credit.

Library C. H. Cozen Learning Resource Center with 32,228 titles, 214 serial subscriptions, 4,859 audiovisual materials, an OPAC, a Web page.

Computers on Campus 226 computers available on campus for general student use. A campuswide network can be accessed from student residence rooms and from off campus. Internet access, at least one staffed computer lab available.

Student Life *Housing Options:* coed. *Activities and Organizations:* drama/theater group, choral group, Student Senate, Phi Theta Kappa, Psi Beta, MAC Ambassadors, Phi Beta Lambda. *Campus security:* 24-hour patrols. *Student services:* personal/psychological counseling.

Athletics Member NJCAA. *Intercollegiate sports:* baseball M(s), basketball M(s)/W(s), volleyball W(s).

Standardized Tests *Required for some:* ACT (for placement), ACT COMPASS.

Costs (2003–04) *Tuition:* area resident $1980 full-time; state resident $2700 full-time; nonresident $3420 full-time. *Room and board:* room only: $3474. *Payment plans:* installment, deferred payment. *Waivers:* senior citizens and employees or children of employees.

Financial Aid Of all full-time matriculated undergraduates who enrolled, 65 Federal Work-Study jobs (averaging $3708).

Applying *Options:* electronic application, early admission. *Application fee:* $15. *Required:* high school transcript. *Application deadline:* rolling (freshmen), rolling (transfers). *Notification:* continuous (freshmen).

Admissions Contact Mrs. Linda Huffman, Registrar, Mineral Area College, PO Box 1000, Park Hills, MO 63601-1000. *Phone:* 573-518-2130. *Toll-free phone:* 573-518-2206. *Fax:* 573-518-2166. *E-mail:* jsheets@mail.mac.cc.mo.us.

MISSOURI COLLEGE
St. Louis, Missouri

- **Proprietary** 2-year, founded 1963
- **Degree** diplomas and associate
- **Coed, primarily women**

Faculty *Student/faculty ratio:* 20:1.

Costs (2003–04) *Tuition:* $8675 full-time.

Financial Aid Of all full-time matriculated undergraduates who enrolled, 12 Federal Work-Study jobs (averaging $1000).

Applying *Application fee:* $35. *Required:* essay or personal statement, interview.

Admissions Contact Mr. Doug Brinker, Admissions Director, Missouri College, 10121 Manchester Road, St. Louis, MO 63122-1583. *Phone:* 314-821-7700.

MOBERLY AREA COMMUNITY COLLEGE
Moberly, Missouri

- **State and locally supported** 2-year, founded 1927
- **Calendar** semesters
- **Degree** certificates and associate
- **Small-town** 32-acre campus
- **Endowment** $648,360
- **Coed,** 3,588 undergraduate students, 49% full-time, 63% women, 37% men

Undergraduates 1,749 full-time, 1,839 part-time. Students come from 20 states and territories, 13 other countries, 1% are from out of state, 6% African American, 1% Asian American or Pacific Islander, 0.9% Hispanic American, 0.3% Native American, 0.2% international, 5% transferred in, 1% live on campus. *Retention:* 57% of 2002 full-time freshmen returned.

Freshmen *Admission:* 951 admitted, 951 enrolled. *Average high school GPA:* 3.00. *Test scores:* ACT scores over 18: 64%; ACT scores over 24: 12%; ACT scores over 30: 1%.

Faculty *Total:* 251, 21% full-time, 9% with terminal degrees. *Student/faculty ratio:* 20:1.

Majors Accounting technology and bookkeeping; administrative assistant and secretarial science; child guidance; computer and information sciences; criminal justice/police science; drafting and design technology; electrical, electronic and communications engineering technology; graphic and printing equipment operation/production; industrial technology; liberal arts and sciences/liberal studies; marketing/marketing management; nursing (registered nurse training); pre-engineering; welding technology.

Academic Programs *Special study options:* academic remediation for entering students, adult/continuing education programs, advanced placement credit, cooperative education, distance learning, internships, part-time degree program, services for LD students, study abroad, summer session for credit.

Library Kate Stamper Wilhite Library with 29,307 titles, 239 serial subscriptions, 1,161 audiovisual materials, an OPAC, a Web page.

Computers on Campus 550 computers available on campus for general student use. A campuswide network can be accessed from off campus. Internet access, at least one staffed computer lab available.

Student Life *Housing Options:* men-only, women-only. Campus housing is university owned. *Activities and Organizations:* drama/theater group, student-run newspaper, choral group, Phi Theta Kappa, Student Nurses Association, Child Care Club, Delta Epsilon Chi, Brother Ox. *Campus security:* student patrols, extensive surveillance.

Athletics Member NJCAA. *Intercollegiate sports:* basketball M(s)/W(s), cheerleading M(s)/W(s). *Intramural sports:* basketball M/W, volleyball M/W.

Standardized Tests *Required for some:* ACT (for placement), ACT ASSET. *Recommended:* ACT (for placement), ACT ASSET.

Costs (2004–05) *Tuition:* area resident $1590 full-time, $53 per credit hour part-time; state resident $2370 full-time, $79 per credit hour part-time; nonresident $3780 full-time, $126 per credit hour part-time. *Required fees:* $240 full-time, $8 per credit hour part-time. *Room and board:* room only: $1800. *Payment plan:* installment. *Waivers:* senior citizens and employees or children of employees.

Financial Aid Of all full-time matriculated undergraduates who enrolled, 89 Federal Work-Study jobs (averaging $4193).

Applying *Options:* electronic application. *Required:* high school transcript. *Application deadline:* rolling (freshmen), rolling (transfers). *Notification:* continuous until 9/1 (freshmen), continuous until 9/1 (transfers).

Admissions Contact Dr. James Grant, Dean of Student Services, Moberly Area Community College, 101 College Avenue, Moberly, MO 65270-1304. *Phone:* 660-263-4110 Ext. 235. *Toll-free phone:* 800-622-2070 Ext. 270. *Fax:* 660-263-2406. *E-mail:* info@macc.edu.

NORTH CENTRAL MISSOURI COLLEGE
Trenton, Missouri

- **District-supported** 2-year, founded 1925, part of Missouri Coordinating Board for Higher Education
- **Calendar** semesters
- **Degree** certificates and associate
- **Small-town** 2-acre campus
- **Endowment** $437,671
- **Coed,** 1,319 undergraduate students, 47% full-time, 68% women, 32% men

Undergraduates 617 full-time, 702 part-time. Students come from 11 states and territories, 3 other countries, 1% are from out of state, 1% African American, 0.2% Asian American or Pacific Islander, 0.4% Hispanic American, 0.4% Native American, 1% international, 4% transferred in, 11% live on campus.

Freshmen *Admission:* 516 applied, 505 admitted, 320 enrolled.

Faculty *Student/faculty ratio:* 20:1.

Majors Accounting; administrative assistant and secretarial science; agricultural business and management; automobile/automotive mechanics technology; business administration and management; carpentry; computer engineering technology; construction engineering technology; criminal justice/law enforcement administration; data processing and data processing technology; drafting and design technology; electrical, electronic and communications engineering technology; emergency medical technology (EMT paramedic); farm and ranch management; liberal arts and sciences/liberal studies; marketing/marketing management; nursing (registered nurse training).

Academic Programs *Special study options:* academic remediation for entering students, accelerated degree program, adult/continuing education programs, advanced placement credit, cooperative education, distance learning, internships, off-campus study, part-time degree program, services for LD students, summer session for credit.

Library North Central Missouri College Library with 20,627 titles, 104 serial subscriptions.

Computers on Campus 101 computers available on campus for general student use. A campuswide network can be accessed. Internet access, at least one staffed computer lab available.

Student Life *Housing Options:* men-only, women-only. *Activities and Organizations:* drama/theater group, student-run newspaper. *Campus security:* controlled dormitory access. *Student services:* personal/psychological counseling.

Athletics Member NJCAA. *Intercollegiate sports:* baseball M(s), basketball M(s)/W(s), softball W(s).

Standardized Tests *Required for some:* ACT (for placement), nursing exam, ACT ASSET. *Recommended:* ACT (for placement).

Costs (2003–04) *Tuition:* $64 per credit part-time; state resident $91 per credit part-time; nonresident $123 per credit part-time. *Room and board:* $3844; room only: $1830.

Financial Aid Of all full-time matriculated undergraduates who enrolled, 40 Federal Work-Study jobs (averaging $1500). 25 state and other part-time jobs (averaging $1200).

Applying *Options:* early admission. *Required:* high school transcript. *Application deadline:* rolling (freshmen), rolling (transfers).

Admissions Contact Tim Asher, Director of Admissions, North Central Missouri College, 1301 Main Street, Trenton, MO 64683. *Phone:* 660-359-3948 Ext. 401. *Toll-free phone:* 800-880-6180 Ext. 401. *E-mail:* kkrohn@mail.ncmc.cc.mo.us.

OZARKS TECHNICAL COMMUNITY COLLEGE
Springfield, Missouri

- **District-supported** 2-year, founded 1990, part of Missouri Coordinating Board for Higher Education
- **Calendar** semesters
- **Degree** certificates, diplomas, and associate
- **Urban** 20-acre campus
- **Endowment** $3867
- **Coed**

Student Life *Campus security:* 24-hour emergency response devices.

Standardized Tests *Required:* ACT ASSET, ACT COMPASS (for placement).

Costs (2003–04) *Tuition:* area resident $1065 full-time; state resident $1365 full-time; nonresident $1815 full-time. *Required fees:* $150 full-time.

Financial Aid Of all full-time matriculated undergraduates who enrolled, 168 Federal Work-Study jobs.

Applying *Options:* common application, early admission. *Required:* high school transcript.

Admissions Contact Mr. Jeff Jochems, Dean of Student Development, Ozarks Technical Community College, PO Box 5958, Springfield, MO 65801. *Phone:* 417-895-7136. *Fax:* 417-895-7161.

PATRICIA STEVENS COLLEGE
St. Louis, Missouri

- **Proprietary** 2-year, founded 1947
- **Calendar** quarters
- **Degree** diplomas and associate
- **Urban** campus
- **Coed, primarily women,** 212 undergraduate students, 54% full-time, 97% women, 3% men

Undergraduates 114 full-time, 98 part-time. Students come from 4 states and territories, 42% are from out of state, 47% African American, 0.5% Asian American or Pacific Islander, 0.5% Hispanic American.

Freshmen *Average high school GPA:* 2.50.

Faculty *Total:* 32, 16% full-time, 16% with terminal degrees. *Student/faculty ratio:* 9:1.

Majors Business/commerce; fashion merchandising; interior design; legal assistant/paralegal; medical office management; retailing; tourism and travel services management.

Academic Programs *Special study options:* academic remediation for entering students, adult/continuing education programs, advanced placement credit, cooperative education, honors programs, independent study, internships, part-time degree program, summer session for credit.

Computers on Campus 35 computers available on campus for general student use. Internet access, at least one staffed computer lab available.

Student Life *Campus security:* 24-hour emergency response devices and patrols. *Student services:* personal/psychological counseling.

Costs (2004–05) *Tuition:* $8993 full-time, $180 per credit hour part-time.

Applying *Options:* deferred entrance. *Application fee:* $15. *Required:* high school transcript, interview. *Recommended:* essay or personal statement, letters of recommendation. *Application deadline:* rolling (freshmen).

Admissions Contact Mr. John Willmon, Director of Admissions, Patricia Stevens College, 330 North Fourth Street, Suite 306, St. Louis, MO 63102. *Phone:* 314-421-0949 Ext. 12. *Toll-free phone:* 800-871-0949. *Fax:* 314-421-0304. *E-mail:* info@patriciastevenscollege.com.

PENN VALLEY COMMUNITY COLLEGE
Kansas City, Missouri

- **State and locally supported** 2-year, founded 1969, part of Metropolitan Community Colleges System
- **Calendar** semesters
- **Degree** certificates and associate
- **Urban** 25-acre campus
- **Endowment** $1.4 million
- **Coed,** 4,559 undergraduate students, 34% full-time, 72% women, 28% men

Undergraduates 1,529 full-time, 3,030 part-time. Students come from 1 other state, 46 other countries, 3% are from out of state, 36% African American, 4% Asian American or Pacific Islander, 4% Hispanic American, 0.5% Native American, 2% international, 1% transferred in. *Retention:* 39% of 2002 full-time freshmen returned.

Freshmen *Admission:* 532 applied, 532 admitted, 532 enrolled.

Faculty *Total:* 381, 25% full-time. *Student/faculty ratio:* 24:1.

Majors Accounting; administrative assistant and secretarial science; biological and physical sciences; biology/biological sciences; business administration and management; chemistry; child care provision; commercial and advertising art; computer and information sciences related; computer science; corrections; criminal justice/law enforcement administration; criminal justice/police science; culinary arts; data processing and data processing technology; electrical, electronic and communications engineering technology; emergency medical technology (EMT paramedic); engineering; family and consumer sciences/human sciences; fashion/apparel design; fashion merchandising; fire science; health

Penn Valley Community College (continued)
information/medical records administration; heating, air conditioning, ventilation and refrigeration maintenance technology; hotel/motel administration; industrial radiologic technology; kindergarten/preschool education; legal administrative assistant/secretary; legal assistant/paralegal; liberal arts and sciences/liberal studies; marketing/marketing management; medical administrative assistant and medical secretary; nursing (registered nurse training); occupational therapy; ophthalmic technology; physical therapy; respiratory care therapy; special products marketing.

Academic Programs *Special study options:* academic remediation for entering students, accelerated degree program, adult/continuing education programs, advanced placement credit, cooperative education, distance learning, English as a second language, honors programs, internships, off-campus study, part-time degree program, services for LD students, summer session for credit.

Library Penn Valley Community College Library with 5,606 serial subscriptions, 24 audiovisual materials, an OPAC.

Computers on Campus 749 computers available on campus for general student use. A campuswide network can be accessed from off campus. Internet access, at least one staffed computer lab available.

Student Life *Housing:* college housing not available. *Activities and Organizations:* drama/theater group, student-run newspaper, choral group, Black Student Association, Los Americanos, Phi Theta Kappa, Fashion Club, national fraternities. *Campus security:* 24-hour patrols. *Student services:* personal/psychological counseling.

Athletics Member NJCAA. *Intercollegiate sports:* basketball M(s).

Standardized Tests *Required:* ACT ASSET (for placement).

Costs (2004–05) *Tuition:* area resident $2070 full-time, $69 per hour part-time; state resident $3750 full-time, $125 per hour part-time; nonresident $5100 full-time, $170 per hour part-time. Full-time tuition and fees vary according to course level and program. Part-time tuition and fees vary according to course level and program. *Required fees:* $150 full-time, $5 per hour part-time. *Payment plan:* installment. *Waivers:* senior citizens and employees or children of employees.

Applying *Options:* common application, early admission. *Required:* high school transcript. *Application deadline:* rolling (freshmen), rolling (transfers).

Admissions Contact Mrs. Carroll O'Neal, Registrar, Penn Valley Community College, 3201 Southwest Trafficway, Kansas City, MO 64111. *Phone:* 816-759-4101. *Fax:* 816-759-4478.

PINNACLE CAREER INSTITUTE
Kansas City, Missouri

- **Proprietary** 2-year
- **Degree** certificates and associate
- **Coed**

Costs (2004–05) *Tuition:* $9000 full-time.

Admissions Contact Ms. Ruth Matous, Director of Admissions, Pinnacle Career Institute, 15329 Kensington Avenue, Kansas City, MO 64147-1212. *Phone:* 816-331-5700 Ext. 212.

RANKEN TECHNICAL COLLEGE
St. Louis, Missouri

- **Independent** primarily 2-year, founded 1907
- **Calendar** semesters
- **Degrees** certificates, associate, and bachelor's
- **Urban** 10-acre campus
- **Endowment** $39.0 million
- **Coed, primarily men,** 1,423 undergraduate students, 52% full-time, 4% women, 96% men

Undergraduates 743 full-time, 680 part-time. Students come from 3 states and territories, 40% are from out of state, 1% live on campus.

Freshmen *Admission:* 920 applied, 850 admitted, 321 enrolled.

Faculty *Total:* 67, 88% full-time. *Student/faculty ratio:* 15:1.

Majors Architectural engineering technology; autobody/collision and repair technology; automobile/automotive mechanics technology; carpentry; computer and information sciences; computer and information sciences and support services related; computer engineering technology; electrical, electronic and communications engineering technology; heating, air conditioning, ventilation and refrigeration maintenance technology; machine tool technology; pipefitting and sprinkler fitting.

Academic Programs *Special study options:* academic remediation for entering students, adult/continuing education programs, advanced placement credit, cooperative education, distance learning, independent study, internships, part-time degree program, services for LD students, summer session for credit.

Library Ashley Gray Jr. Learning Center with 11,000 titles, 182 serial subscriptions, an OPAC, a Web page.

Computers on Campus 85 computers available on campus for general student use. A campuswide network can be accessed. Internet access, at least one staffed computer lab available.

Student Life *Housing Options:* men-only, women-only. Campus housing is provided by a third party. *Activities and Organizations:* student-run newspaper, Phi Theta Kappa, student government, Women's Support Group, Instrumentation Society of America, Vocational Industrial Clubs of America. *Campus security:* 24-hour emergency response devices and patrols. *Student services:* personal/psychological counseling, women's center.

Standardized Tests *Required:* SAT I or ACT (for placement).

Costs (2004–05) *Tuition:* $9500 full-time, $695 per term part-time. *Required fees:* $140 full-time, $95 per term part-time. *Payment plan:* installment.

Financial Aid Of all full-time matriculated undergraduates who enrolled, 30 Federal Work-Study jobs (averaging $2000).

Applying *Options:* common application, electronic application. *Application fee:* $95. *Required:* essay or personal statement, high school transcript, interview. *Application deadline:* rolling (freshmen). *Notification:* continuous (transfers).

Admissions Contact Ms. Elizabeth Keserauskis, Director of Admissions, Ranken Technical College, 4431 Finney Avenue, St. Louis, MO 63113. *Phone:* 314-371-0233 Ext. 4811. *Toll-free phone:* 866-4RANKEN. *Fax:* 314-371-0241. *E-mail:* admissions@ranken.edu.

SAINT CHARLES COMMUNITY COLLEGE
St. Peters, Missouri

- **State-supported** 2-year, founded 1986, part of Missouri Coordinating Board for Higher Education
- **Calendar** semesters
- **Degree** certificates and associate
- **Small-town** 234-acre campus with easy access to St. Louis
- **Endowment** $6.6 million
- **Coed,** 6,696 undergraduate students, 47% full-time, 61% women, 39% men

Undergraduates 3,146 full-time, 3,550 part-time. Students come from 4 states and territories, 6 other countries, 3% African American, 1% Asian American or Pacific Islander, 2% Hispanic American, 0.5% Native American, 0.3% international, 6% transferred in.

Freshmen *Admission:* 1,465 applied, 1,465 admitted, 1,465 enrolled.

Faculty *Total:* 364, 21% full-time. *Student/faculty ratio:* 22:1.

Majors Accounting; administrative assistant and secretarial science; business administration and management; child development; commercial and advertising art; computer programming related; computer programming (specific applications); computer science; computer systems networking and telecommunications; criminal justice/law enforcement administration; criminal justice/police science; drafting and design technology; health information/medical records administration; human services; liberal arts and sciences/liberal studies; marketing/marketing management; medical transcription; nursing (registered nurse training); occupational therapy; office management; pre-engineering; web/multimedia management and webmaster.

Academic Programs *Special study options:* academic remediation for entering students, adult/continuing education programs, advanced placement credit, distance learning, double majors, English as a second language, independent study, internships, part-time degree program, services for LD students, summer session for credit.

Library Learning Resource Center with 54,110 titles, 8,282 serial subscriptions, 7,624 audiovisual materials, an OPAC, a Web page.

Computers on Campus 117 computers available on campus for general student use. A campuswide network can be accessed from off campus. Internet access, online (class) registration, at least one staffed computer lab available.

Student Life *Housing:* college housing not available. *Activities and Organizations:* drama/theater group, student-run newspaper, choral group, Phi Theta Kappa, SCCCC Roller Hockey Club, Student Senate, Criminal Justice Student Organization, Human Services Student Organization. *Campus security:* 24-hour emergency response devices and patrols, late-night transport/escort service. *Student services:* personal/psychological counseling.

Athletics Member NJCAA. *Intercollegiate sports:* baseball M(s), softball W(s). *Intramural sports:* basketball M/W, football M, soccer M/W, softball M/W, volleyball M/W.

Standardized Tests *Required:* ACT COMPASS (for placement). *Recommended:* ACT (for placement).

Costs (2004–05) *Tuition:* area resident $1950 full-time, $65 per credit hour part-time; state resident $2850 full-time, $95 per credit hour part-time; nonresident $4200 full-time, $140 per credit hour part-time. *Waivers:* employees or children of employees.

Financial Aid Of all full-time matriculated undergraduates who enrolled, 21 Federal Work-Study jobs (averaging $1848).

Applying *Options:* common application, early admission, deferred entrance. *Required for some:* high school transcript. *Recommended:* high school transcript. *Application deadline:* rolling (freshmen), rolling (transfers). *Notification:* continuous (freshmen), continuous (transfers).

Admissions Contact Ms. Kathy Brockgreitens, Director of Admissions/Registrar/Financial Assistance, Saint Charles Community College, 4601 Mid Rivers Mall Drive, St. Peters, MO 63376-0975. *Phone:* 636-922-8229. *Fax:* 636-922-8236. *E-mail:* regist@stchas.edu.

St. Louis Community College at Florissant Valley

St. Louis, Missouri

- **District-supported** 2-year, founded 1963, part of St. Louis Community College System
- **Calendar** semesters
- **Degree** certificates and associate
- **Suburban** 108-acre campus
- **Coed**

Undergraduates Students come from 31 other countries.

Majors Accounting; administrative assistant and secretarial science; art; broadcast journalism; business administration and management; chemical engineering; child development; cinematography and film/video production; civil engineering technology; commercial and advertising art; computer engineering technology; computer programming; computer science; construction engineering technology; corrections; criminal justice/law enforcement administration; criminal justice/police science; data processing and data processing technology; dietetics; dramatic/theatre arts; electrical, electronic and communications engineering technology; elementary education; emergency medical technology (EMT paramedic); engineering; engineering science; engineering technology; fashion merchandising; finance; fire science; food science; food services technology; human services; information science/studies; journalism; legal studies; liberal arts and sciences/liberal studies; mass communication/media; mathematics; mechanical engineering/mechanical technology; music; nursing (registered nurse training); photography; pre-engineering; radio and television; real estate; sign language interpretation and translation; special products marketing; telecommunications.

Academic Programs *Special study options:* academic remediation for entering students, adult/continuing education programs, advanced placement credit, cooperative education, English as a second language, honors programs, part-time degree program, services for LD students, study abroad, summer session for credit. *ROTC:* Army (c).

Library 90,021 titles, 655 serial subscriptions.

Computers on Campus 470 computers available on campus for general student use. A campuswide network can be accessed. At least one staffed computer lab available.

Student Life *Housing:* college housing not available. *Activities and Organizations:* drama/theater group, student-run newspaper, radio station, Phi Theta Kappa, Student Nurses Association, Women in New Goals, Florissant Valley Association of the Deaf, Student Government Association, national fraternities, national sororities. *Campus security:* 24-hour emergency response devices and patrols, late-night transport/escort service. *Student services:* health clinic, personal/psychological counseling.

Athletics Member NAIA, NJCAA. *Intercollegiate sports:* baseball M, basketball M(s)/W(s), cross-country running M(s)/W(s), soccer M(s)/W(s), softball W(s), track and field M(s)/W(s), volleyball W(s). *Intramural sports:* volleyball W.

Standardized Tests *Recommended:* SAT I or ACT (for placement).

Costs (2004–05) *Tuition:* $72 per credit hour part-time; state resident $93 per credit hour part-time; nonresident $128 per credit hour part-time. *Waivers:* senior citizens and employees or children of employees.

Applying *Options:* electronic application, early admission. *Required:* high school transcript. *Application deadlines:* 8/19 (freshmen), 8/19 (transfers). *Notification:* continuous (freshmen), continuous (transfers).

Admissions Contact Mr. Mitchell Egeston, Manager of Admissions and Registration, St. Louis Community College at Florissant Valley, 3400 Pershall Road, St. Louis, MO 63135-1499. *Phone:* 314-595-4245. *Fax:* 314-595-2224.

St. Louis Community College at Forest Park

St. Louis, Missouri

- **District-supported** 2-year, founded 1962, part of St. Louis Community College System
- **Calendar** semesters
- **Degree** associate
- **Suburban** 34-acre campus
- **Coed**

Faculty *Student/faculty ratio:* 19:1.

Student Life *Campus security:* 24-hour patrols.

Athletics Member NJCAA.

Financial Aid Of all full-time matriculated undergraduates who enrolled, 165 Federal Work-Study jobs (averaging $3000).

Applying *Options:* electronic application, early admission. *Required:* high school transcript.

Admissions Contact Mr. Glenn Marshall, Coordinator of Enrollment Services, St. Louis Community College at Forest Park, 5600 Oakland Avenue, St. Louis, MO 63110. *Phone:* 314-644-9125. *Fax:* 314-644-9375.

St. Louis Community College at Meramec

Kirkwood, Missouri

- **District-supported** 2-year, founded 1963, part of St. Louis Community College System
- **Calendar** semesters
- **Degree** certificates and associate
- **Suburban** 80-acre campus with easy access to St. Louis
- **Coed**

Student Life *Campus security:* 24-hour emergency response devices and patrols.

Athletics Member NJCAA.

Standardized Tests *Required for some:* Michigan Test of English Language Proficiency.

Applying *Options:* early admission, deferred entrance. *Required for some:* high school transcript, interview.

Admissions Contact Mr. Mike Cundiff, Coordinator of Admissions, St. Louis Community College at Meramec, 11333 Big Bend Boulevard, Kirkwood, MO 63122-5720. *Phone:* 314-984-7608. *Fax:* 314-984-7051.

Sanford-Brown College

Fenton, Missouri

- **Proprietary** primarily 2-year, founded 1868
- **Calendar** quarters
- **Degrees** certificates, diplomas, associate, and bachelor's
- **Suburban** 6-acre campus with easy access to St. Louis
- **Coed**

Faculty *Student/faculty ratio:* 9:1.

Student Life *Campus security:* late-night transport/escort service, trained security personnel from 7:30 p.m. to 10:30 p.m.

Standardized Tests *Required:* CPAt (for admission).

Applying *Options:* common application, deferred entrance. *Application fee:* $25. *Required:* high school transcript, interview.

Admissions Contact Ms. Judy Wilga, Director of Admissions, Sanford-Brown College, 1203 Smizer Mill Road, Fenton, MO 63026. *Phone:* 636-349-4900 Ext. 102. *Toll-free phone:* 800-456-7222. *Fax:* 636-349-9170.

Sanford-Brown College

Hazelwood, Missouri

- **Proprietary** 2-year, founded 1868
- **Calendar** quarters
- **Degree** diplomas and associate
- 1-acre campus with easy access to St. Louis
- **Coed,** 600 undergraduate students

Undergraduates Students come from 3 other countries.

Majors Accounting; administrative assistant and secretarial science; business administration and management; computer programming; health teacher education; legal assistant/paralegal; physical therapy.

Academic Programs *Special study options:* academic remediation for entering students, adult/continuing education programs, internships, part-time degree program, services for LD students.

Library Learning Resource Center.

Computers on Campus 32 computers available on campus for general student use. At least one staffed computer lab available.

Student Life *Activities and Organizations:* Paralegal Club, peer advisors, student council, Accounting Club. *Campus security:* 24-hour emergency response devices and patrols. *Student services:* personal/psychological counseling.

Athletics *Intercollegiate sports:* basketball M.

Sanford-Brown College (continued)

Costs (2003–04) *Tuition:* $300 per credit hour part-time. Full-time tuition and fees vary according to program. Part-time tuition and fees vary according to program. *Payment plans:* installment, deferred payment. *Waivers:* employees or children of employees.

Applying *Options:* common application, deferred entrance. *Required:* high school transcript, interview. *Application deadline:* rolling (freshmen).

Admissions Contact Mr. Sherri Bremer, Director of Admissions, Sanford-Brown College, 75 Village Square, Hazelwood, MO 63042. *Phone:* 314-731-5200 Ext. 201.

SANFORD-BROWN COLLEGE
North Kansas City, Missouri

Admissions Contact Mr. Edward A. Beauchamp, Director of Admissions, Sanford-Brown College, 520 East 19th Avenue, North Kansas City, MO 64116. *Phone:* 816-472-0275. *Toll-free phone:* 800-456-7222.

SANFORD-BROWN COLLEGE
St. Charles, Missouri

Admissions Contact Karl J. Petersen, Executive Director, Sanford-Brown College, 3555 Franks Drive, St. Charles, MO 63301. *Phone:* 636-949-2620. *Toll-free phone:* 800-456-7222.

SOUTHEAST MISSOURI HOSPITAL COLLEGE OF NURSING AND HEALTH SCIENCES
Cape Girardeau, Missouri

Admissions Contact Tonya L. Buttry, President, Southeast Missouri Hospital College of Nursing and Health Sciences, 1819 Broadway, Cape Girardeau, MO 63701. *Phone:* 534-334-6825.

SOUTHWEST MISSOURI STATE UNIVERSITY-WEST PLAINS
West Plains, Missouri

- **State-supported** 2-year, founded 1963, part of Southwest Missouri State University
- **Calendar** semesters
- **Degree** certificates and associate
- **Small-town** 11-acre campus
- **Endowment** $448,596
- **Coed**, 1,701 undergraduate students

Undergraduates Students come from 15 states and territories, 6 other countries, 4% are from out of state, 1% African American, 1% Asian American or Pacific Islander, 0.8% Hispanic American, 1% Native American, 0.4% international, 6% live on campus.

Freshmen *Admission:* 500 applied, 500 admitted. *Test scores:* ACT scores over 18: 72%; ACT scores over 24: 19%.

Faculty *Total:* 114, 23% full-time. *Student/faculty ratio:* 17:1.

Majors Agriculture; business/commerce; computer programming (specific applications); criminal justice/police science; engineering; general studies; industrial technology; legal assistant/paralegal; nursing (registered nurse training).

Academic Programs *Special study options:* academic remediation for entering students, advanced placement credit, cooperative education, distance learning, honors programs, internships, part-time degree program, services for LD students, study abroad, summer session for credit.

Library Garnett Library with 21,210 titles, 189 serial subscriptions, 714 audiovisual materials, an OPAC, a Web page.

Computers on Campus 58 computers available on campus for general student use. A campuswide network can be accessed from student residence rooms and from off campus. At least one staffed computer lab available.

Student Life *Housing Options:* coed. Campus housing is university owned. *Activities and Organizations:* drama/theater group, choral group, Student Government Association, Chi Alpha, Adult Students in Higher Education, Lambda Lambda Lambda, Programming Board. *Campus security:* late-night transport/escort service, controlled dormitory access.

Athletics Member NJCAA. *Intercollegiate sports:* basketball M(s), volleyball W(s).

Standardized Tests *Required for some:* ACT (for placement).

Costs (2004–05) *Tuition:* state resident $2910 full-time, $97 per credit hour part-time; nonresident $5820 full-time, $194 per credit hour part-time. Full-time tuition and fees vary according to course load. Part-time tuition and fees vary according to course load. *Required fees:* $210 full-time. *Room and board:* $4512. *Payment plan:* deferred payment. *Waivers:* senior citizens and employees or children of employees.

Financial Aid Of all full-time matriculated undergraduates who enrolled, 63 Federal Work-Study jobs (averaging $2000).

Applying *Application fee:* $15. *Required for some:* high school transcript. *Application deadline:* rolling (freshmen), rolling (transfers).

Admissions Contact Ms. Melissa Jett, Admissions Assistant, Southwest Missouri State University-West Plains, 128 Garfield, West Plains, MO 65775. *Phone:* 417-255-7955. *Fax:* 417-255-7959. *E-mail:* admissions@wp.smsu.edu.

SPRINGFIELD COLLEGE
Springfield, Missouri

Admissions Contact Gerald F. Terrebrood, President, Springfield College, 1010 West Sunshine Street, Springfield, MO 65807. *Phone:* 417-864-7220. *Toll-free phone:* 800-864-5697 (in-state); 800-475-2669 (out-of-state). *Fax:* 417-864-5697.

STATE FAIR COMMUNITY COLLEGE
Sedalia, Missouri

- **District-supported** 2-year, founded 1966, part of Missouri Coordinating Board for Higher Education
- **Calendar** semesters
- **Degree** certificates and associate
- **Small-town** 128-acre campus
- **Coed**

Faculty *Student/faculty ratio:* 17:1.

Student Life *Campus security:* security during evening class hours.

Athletics Member NJCAA.

Standardized Tests *Required for some:* ACT (for placement), ACT ASSET, ACT COMPASS.

Costs (2004–05) *Tuition:* area resident $2240 full-time, $70 per semester hour part-time; state resident $3104 full-time, $97 per credit hour part-time; nonresident $4800 full-time, $150 per credit hour part-time. *Room and board:* $4300; room only: $2500.

Financial Aid Of all full-time matriculated undergraduates who enrolled, 50 Federal Work-Study jobs (averaging $1000).

Applying *Options:* early admission. *Required:* high school transcript.

Admissions Contact Mrs. Sharon Peacock, Registrar, State Fair Community College, 3201 West 16th, Sedalia, MO 65301. *Phone:* 660-530-5800 Ext. 293. *Toll-free phone:* 877-311-SFCC Ext. 217 (in-state); 877-311-SFCC (out-of-state). *Fax:* 660-530-5546.

THREE RIVERS COMMUNITY COLLEGE
Poplar Bluff, Missouri

- **State and locally supported** 2-year, founded 1966, part of Missouri Coordinating Board for Higher Education
- **Calendar** semesters
- **Degree** certificates and associate
- **Rural** 70-acre campus
- **Coed**, 3,235 undergraduate students, 51% full-time, 69% women, 31% men

Undergraduates 1,657 full-time, 1,578 part-time. Students come from 41 states and territories, 8 other countries.

Freshmen *Admission:* 1,892 enrolled.

Faculty *Total:* 67, 78% full-time. *Student/faculty ratio:* 18:1.

Majors Accounting; administrative assistant and secretarial science; agricultural business and management; agricultural mechanization; business administration and management; clinical/medical laboratory technology; computer and information sciences related; computer engineering technology; computer/technical support; construction engineering technology; criminal justice/law enforcement administration; criminal justice/police science; data entry/microcomputer applications; data entry/microcomputer applications related; education; elementary education; engineering technology; industrial technology; information technology; liberal arts and sciences/liberal studies; marketing/marketing management; music; nursing (registered nurse training); word processing.

Academic Programs *Special study options:* academic remediation for entering students, accelerated degree program, adult/continuing education programs, advanced placement credit, distance learning, English as a second language, external degree program, honors programs, independent study, internships, off-campus study, part-time degree program, services for LD students, summer session for credit.

Library Rutland Library with 27,000 titles, 385 serial subscriptions, a Web page.
Computers on Campus 21 computers available on campus for general student use. A campuswide network can be accessed from student residence rooms and from off campus. Internet access, online (class) registration, at least one staffed computer lab available.
Student Life *Housing Options:* Campus housing is provided by a third party. *Activities and Organizations:* student government, PTK, PBL, Alpha Beta Gamma, Lambda Alpha Epsilon. *Campus security:* 24-hour patrols.
Athletics Member NJCAA. *Intercollegiate sports:* baseball M(s), basketball M(s)/W(s), cheerleading M(s)/W(s), softball W(s), volleyball W(s). *Intramural sports:* baseball M, basketball M/W.
Standardized Tests *Recommended:* ACT (for placement), ACT ASSET, ACT COMPASS.
Costs (2004–05) *Tuition:* area resident $1740 full-time; state resident $2790 full-time; nonresident $3480 full-time. *Required fees:* $356 full-time. *Room and board:* room only: $3948. Room and board charges vary according to board plan. *Waivers:* employees or children of employees.
Applying *Options:* early admission. *Application fee:* $20. *Required:* high school transcript. *Application deadlines:* 8/15 (freshmen), 8/15 (transfers). *Notification:* continuous (freshmen), continuous (transfers).
Admissions Contact Ms. Marcia Fields, Director of Admissions and Recruiting, Three Rivers Community College, 2080 Three Rivers Boulevard, Poplar Bluff, MO 63901. *Phone:* 573-840-9675. *Toll-free phone:* 877-TRY-TRCC Ext. 605 (in-state); 573-840-9604 (out-of-state). *E-mail:* sinman@trcc.edu.

VATTEROTT COLLEGE
Kansas City, Missouri

Admissions Contact 8955 East 38th Terrace, Kansas City, MO 64129. *Toll-free phone:* 800-466-3997.

VATTEROTT COLLEGE
St. Ann, Missouri

- **Proprietary** primarily 2-year, founded 1969
- **Calendar** continuous
- **Degrees** diplomas, associate, and bachelor's
- **Suburban** 5-acre campus with easy access to St. Louis
- **Coed,** 580 undergraduate students, 100% full-time, 19% women, 81% men

Undergraduates 580 full-time. 56% African American, 0.2% Asian American or Pacific Islander, 0.3% Hispanic American.
Freshmen *Admission:* 126 enrolled.
Faculty *Total:* 24. *Student/faculty ratio:* 25:1.
Majors CAD/CADD drafting/design technology; computer engineering; computer programming; electrical and power transmission installation related; electrical, electronic and communications engineering technology; heating, air conditioning and refrigeration technology; medical office assistant; plumbing technology; welding technology.
Library Main Library plus 7 others with a Web page.
Computers on Campus 240 computers available on campus for general student use. A campuswide network can be accessed. Internet access, at least one staffed computer lab available.
Student Life *Housing:* college housing not available.
Applying *Options:* common application.
Admissions Contact Mrs. Shari H. Cobb, Director of Admissions, Vatterott College, 3925 Industrial Drive, St. Ann, MO 63074-1807. *Phone:* 314-428-5900 Ext. 215. *Toll-free phone:* 800-345-6018. *Fax:* 314-428-5956.

VATTEROTT COLLEGE
St. Joseph, Missouri

- **Proprietary** 2-year
- **Calendar** semesters
- **Degree** diplomas and associate
- **Urban** campus
- **Coed**

Faculty *Total:* 19.
Majors Administrative assistant and secretarial science; computer systems networking and telecommunications; computer technology/computer systems technology; medical/clinical assistant.
Admissions Contact Ms. Sandra Wisdom, Director of Admissions, Vatterott College, 3131 Frederick Avenue, St. Joseph, MO 64506. *Phone:* 816-364-5399 Ext. 110. *Toll-free phone:* 800-282-5327.

VATTEROTT COLLEGE
Sunset Hills, Missouri

- **Proprietary** primarily 2-year
- **Calendar** semesters
- **Degrees** diplomas, associate, and bachelor's
- **Coed**

Admissions Contact Ms. Michelle Tinsley, Director of Admission, Vatterott College, 12970 Maurer Industrial Drive, St. Louis, MO 63127. *Phone:* 314-843-4200. *Fax:* 843-1709. *E-mail:* sunsethills@vatterott-college.edu.

VATTEROTT COLLEGE
Springfield, Missouri

- **Proprietary** 2-year, part of Vatterott College
- **Calendar** quarters
- **Degree** diplomas and associate
- **Urban** 2-acre campus
- **Coed**

Freshmen *Admission:* 48 applied, 47 admitted.
Faculty *Total:* 23, 61% full-time, 4% with terminal degrees.
Majors CAD/CADD drafting/design technology; computer programming; medical/clinical assistant; pharmacy technician; system, networking, and LAN/wan management.
Student Life *Housing:* college housing not available. *Activities and Organizations:* Computer Club. *Campus security:* alarm devices and personnel during open hours; security alarms during closed hours.
Costs (2004–05) *Tuition:* $8397 full-time. Full-time tuition and fees vary according to degree level and program. *Required fees:* $525 full-time. *Payment plan:* installment.
Applying *Required:* high school transcript, interview. *Notification:* continuous (transfers).
Admissions Contact Mr. Kevin Asberry, Director of Admissions, Vatterott College, 3850 South Campbell, Springfield, MO 65807. *Phone:* 417-831-8116 Ext. 235. *Toll-free phone:* 800-766-5829. *E-mail:* adm@vatterott-college.edu.

WENTWORTH MILITARY ACADEMY AND JUNIOR COLLEGE
Lexington, Missouri

- **Independent** 2-year, founded 1880
- **Calendar** semesters
- **Degree** associate
- **Small-town** 130-acre campus with easy access to Kansas City
- **Coed**

Faculty *Student/faculty ratio:* 9:1.
Student Life *Campus security:* 24-hour emergency response devices and patrols.
Athletics Member NJCAA.
Standardized Tests *Recommended:* SAT I or ACT (for admission).
Applying *Options:* common application. *Application fee:* $100. *Required:* high school transcript.
Admissions Contact Maj. Todd Kitchen, Dean of Admissions, Wentworth Military Academy and Junior College, 1880 Washington Avenue, Lexington, MO 64067. *Phone:* 660-259-2221. *Fax:* 660-259-2677. *E-mail:* admissions@wma1880.org.

MONTANA

BLACKFEET COMMUNITY COLLEGE
Browning, Montana

- **Independent** 2-year, founded 1974
- **Calendar** semesters
- **Degree** certificates, diplomas, and associate
- **Small-town** 5-acre campus
- **Endowment** $300,688
- **Coed,** 503 undergraduate students, 84% full-time, 64% women, 36% men

Undergraduates 424 full-time, 79 part-time. Students come from 2 states and territories, 0.4% Hispanic American, 92% Native American, 6% transferred in.

Montana

Blackfeet Community College (continued)
Freshmen *Admission:* 137 enrolled.
Faculty *Total:* 63, 43% full-time, 2% with terminal degrees. *Student/faculty ratio:* 12:1.
Majors Administrative assistant and secretarial science; American Indian/ Native American studies; bilingual and multilingual education; business administration and management; computer and information sciences and support services related; construction engineering technology; elementary education; entrepreneurship; general studies; health/medical preparatory programs related; hospitality administration; human services; kindergarten/preschool education; liberal arts and sciences/liberal studies; natural resources management and policy; teacher assistant/aide.
Academic Programs *Special study options:* academic remediation for entering students, adult/continuing education programs, off-campus study, part-time degree program.
Library 10,000 titles, 175 serial subscriptions.
Computers on Campus 55 computers available on campus for general student use. A campuswide network can be accessed. At least one staffed computer lab available.
Student Life *Housing:* college housing not available. *Campus security:* 16 hour patrols by security personnel.
Athletics *Intramural sports:* basketball M/W.
Costs (2004–05) *Tuition:* $1650 full-time. Full-time tuition and fees vary according to course load. Part-time tuition and fees vary according to course load. *Required fees:* $350 full-time, $80 per term part-time, $175 per term part-time. *Payment plan:* installment. *Waivers:* senior citizens and employees or children of employees.
Financial Aid Of all full-time matriculated undergraduates who enrolled, 10 Federal Work-Study jobs (averaging $2316). *Financial aid deadline:* 6/30.
Applying *Options:* early admission. *Application fee:* $20. *Required:* high school transcript, application, immunization with 2nd MMR, certificate of Indian blood. *Application deadline:* 8/29 (freshmen), rolling (transfers). *Notification:* continuous (freshmen), continuous (transfers).
Admissions Contact Ms. Deana M. McNabb, Registrar and Admissions Officer, Blackfeet Community College, PO Box 819, Browning, MT 59417. *Phone:* 406-338-5421 Ext. 243. *Toll-free phone:* 800-549-7457. *Fax:* 406-338-3272. *E-mail:* helen_morris@bfcc.org.

CHIEF DULL KNIFE COLLEGE
Lame Deer, Montana

Admissions Contact Mr. William L. Wertman, Registrar and Director of Admissions, Chief Dull Knife College, PO Box 98, Lame Deer, MT 59043-0098. *Phone:* 406-477-6215.

DAWSON COMMUNITY COLLEGE
Glendive, Montana

- **State and locally supported** 2-year, founded 1940, part of Montana University System
- **Calendar** semesters
- **Degree** certificates and associate
- **Rural** 300-acre campus
- **Endowment** $344,944
- **Coed**, 475 undergraduate students, 69% full-time, 51% women, 49% men

Undergraduates 326 full-time, 149 part-time. Students come from 10 states and territories, 2 other countries, 1% African American, 0.5% Asian American or Pacific Islander, 1% Hispanic American, 3% Native American, 7% transferred in, 19% live on campus.
Freshmen *Admission:* 208 applied, 208 admitted, 158 enrolled. *Test scores:* ACT scores over 18: 67%; ACT scores over 24: 17%.
Faculty *Total:* 49, 43% full-time. *Student/faculty ratio:* 16:1.
Majors Administrative assistant and secretarial science; agricultural business and management; automobile/automotive mechanics technology; business/ commerce; child care and support services management; clinical/medical social work; computer and information sciences; criminal justice/police science; liberal arts and sciences/liberal studies; substance abuse/addiction counseling.
Academic Programs *Special study options:* academic remediation for entering students, adult/continuing education programs, independent study, internships, part-time degree program, services for LD students, summer session for credit.
Library Jane Carey Memorial Library with 18,870 titles, 1,112 audiovisual materials, an OPAC, a Web page.
Computers on Campus 70 computers available on campus for general student use. A campuswide network can be accessed from student residence rooms and from off campus. Internet access, at least one staffed computer lab available.

Student Life *Housing Options:* coed. Campus housing is university owned. *Activities and Organizations:* drama/theater group, choral group, Human Services Club, Law Enforcement Club, Associated Student Body, VICA, United Badlands Indian Club. *Campus security:* 24-hour emergency response devices.
Athletics Member NJCAA. *Intercollegiate sports:* baseball M, basketball M(s)/W(s), equestrian sports M(s)/W(s), softball W. *Intramural sports:* basketball M/W, bowling M/W, golf M/W, racquetball M/W, softball M/W, table tennis M/W, tennis M/W, volleyball M/W.
Standardized Tests *Required for some:* ACT (for placement). *Recommended:* ACT (for placement).
Costs (2004–05) *Room and board:* room only: $1650.
Financial Aid Of all full-time matriculated undergraduates who enrolled, 45 Federal Work-Study jobs (averaging $1200). 17 state and other part-time jobs (averaging $1200).
Applying *Options:* deferred entrance. *Application fee:* $30. *Required:* high school transcript. *Application deadline:* rolling (freshmen), rolling (transfers). *Notification:* continuous (freshmen), continuous (transfers).
Admissions Contact Ms. Jolene Myers, Director of Admissions and Financial Aid, Dawson Community College, Box 421, Glendive, MT 59330-0421. *Phone:* 406-377-3396 Ext. 410. *Toll-free phone:* 800-821-8320. *Fax:* 406-377-8132.

FLATHEAD VALLEY COMMUNITY COLLEGE
Kalispell, Montana

- **State and locally supported** 2-year, founded 1967
- **Calendar** semesters
- **Degree** certificates and associate
- **Small-town** 40-acre campus
- **Endowment** $865,025
- **Coed**

Established in 1967, FVCC is an accredited, comprehensive community college located at the foot of the Rockies and just minutes from Glacier National Park, 2 major ski resorts, and the Bob Marshall Wilderness. The architectural award-winning, handicapped-accessible campus serves more than 2,000 students in many different academic transfer and occupational programs.

Faculty *Student/faculty ratio:* 16:1.
Athletics Member NJCAA.
Standardized Tests *Required:* ACT ASSET, ACT COMPASS (for placement).
Costs (2004–05) *Tuition:* area resident $1589 full-time, $57 per credit part-time; state resident $2605 full-time, $93 per credit part-time; nonresident $6525 full-time, $233 per credit part-time. Part-time tuition and fees vary according to course load. *Required fees:* $603 full-time, $26 per credit part-time.
Financial Aid Of all full-time matriculated undergraduates who enrolled, 63 Federal Work-Study jobs (averaging $1200). 50 state and other part-time jobs (averaging $1200).
Applying *Options:* early admission, deferred entrance. *Application fee:* $15. *Required:* high school transcript.
Admissions Contact Ms. Marlene C. Stoltz, Admissions/Graduation Coordinator, Flathead Valley Community College, 777 Grandview Avenue, Kalispell, MT 59901-2622. *Phone:* 406-756-3846. *Toll-free phone:* 800-313-3822. *Fax:* 406-756-3965. *E-mail:* rharper@fvcc.edu.

FORT BELKNAP COLLEGE
Harlem, Montana

- **Federally supported** 2-year, founded 1984
- **Calendar** quarters
- **Degree** certificates and associate
- **Rural** 3-acre campus
- **Endowment** $291,263
- **Coed**

Student Life *Campus security:* 24-hour patrols.
Standardized Tests *Required:* TABE (for placement).
Applying *Options:* early admission, deferred entrance. *Application fee:* $10. *Required:* high school transcript.
Admissions Contact Ms. Dixie Brockie, Registrar and Admissions Officer, Fort Belknap College, PO Box 159, Harlem, MT 59526-0159. *Phone:* 406-353-2607 Ext. 219.

FORT PECK COMMUNITY COLLEGE
Poplar, Montana

Admissions Contact Mr. Robert McAnally, Dean of Students, Fort Peck Community College, PO Box 398, Poplar, MT 59255-0398. *Phone:* 406-768-5553.

LITTLE BIG HORN COLLEGE
Crow Agency, Montana

- **Independent** 2-year, founded 1980
- **Calendar** quarters
- **Degree** certificates and associate
- **Rural** 5-acre campus
- **Coed**

Faculty *Student/faculty ratio:* 25:1.
Standardized Tests *Required:* ACT ASSET (for placement).
Applying *Required:* high school transcript.
Admissions Contact Ms. Ann Bullis, Dean of Student Services, Little Big Horn College, Box 370, Crow Agency, MT 59022-0370. *Phone:* 406-638-2228 Ext. 50.

MILES COMMUNITY COLLEGE
Miles City, Montana

- **State and locally supported** 2-year, founded 1939, part of Montana University System
- **Calendar** semesters
- **Degree** certificates and associate
- **Small-town** 8-acre campus
- **Endowment** $2.7 million
- **Coed,** 474 undergraduate students, 76% full-time, 60% women, 40% men

Undergraduates 360 full-time, 114 part-time. Students come from 6 states and territories, 5% are from out of state, 0.7% African American, 0.5% Asian American or Pacific Islander, 0.7% Hispanic American, 1% Native American, 2% international, 11% transferred in, 20% live on campus.
Freshmen *Admission:* 205 applied, 205 admitted, 118 enrolled. *Average high school GPA:* 2.73.
Faculty *Total:* 40, 68% full-time. *Student/faculty ratio:* 14:1.
Majors Administrative assistant and secretarial science; agricultural mechanization; automobile/automotive mechanics technology; building/property maintenance and management; business administration and management; carpentry; commercial and advertising art; computer engineering technology; computer graphics; computer management; construction engineering technology; consumer merchandising/retailing management; electrical, electronic and communications engineering technology; electrical/electronics equipment installation and repair; energy management and systems technology; fire science; human services; information technology; liberal arts and sciences/liberal studies; marketing/marketing management; medical administrative assistant and medical secretary; nursing (registered nurse training); telecommunications.
Academic Programs *Special study options:* academic remediation for entering students, accelerated degree program, adult/continuing education programs, advanced placement credit, cooperative education, distance learning, double majors, English as a second language, independent study, internships, off-campus study, part-time degree program, services for LD students, summer session for credit.
Library Library Resource Center with 17,563 titles, 310 serial subscriptions, 174 audiovisual materials, an OPAC, a Web page.
Computers on Campus 165 computers available on campus for general student use. A campuswide network can be accessed from off campus. Internet access, at least one staffed computer lab available.
Student Life *Housing Options:* coed. *Activities and Organizations:* drama/theater group, student-run newspaper, choral group, Campus Ministry, Multicultural Club, Student Nurses Association, Vocational Industrial Club, Western Club. *Campus security:* 24-hour emergency response devices. *Student services:* personal/psychological counseling.
Athletics Member NJCAA. *Intercollegiate sports:* basketball M(s)/W(s), golf M/W. *Intramural sports:* basketball M/W, bowling M/W, golf M/W, ice hockey M/W, racquetball M/W, soccer M/W, tennis M/W, track and field M/W, volleyball M/W, weight lifting M/W.
Standardized Tests *Required for some:* SAT I or ACT (for placement). *Recommended:* SAT I or ACT (for placement).
Costs (2004–05) *Tuition:* area resident $2550 full-time, $85 per credit part-time; state resident $3300 full-time, $110 per credit part-time; nonresident $5250 full-time, $175 per credit part-time. *Room and board:* Room and board charges vary according to board plan, housing facility, and location. *Payment plans:* installment, deferred payment. *Waivers:* senior citizens and employees or children of employees.

Financial Aid Of all full-time matriculated undergraduates who enrolled, 25 Federal Work-Study jobs (averaging $1400). 22 state and other part-time jobs (averaging $1300).
Applying *Options:* common application, early admission, deferred entrance. *Application fee:* $40. *Required:* high school transcript. *Application deadline:* rolling (freshmen), rolling (transfers).
Admissions Contact Miles Community College, 2715 Dickinson, Miles City, MT 59301-4799. *Phone:* 406-874-6159. *Toll-free phone:* 800-541-9281. *Fax:* 406-234-3599.

MONTANA STATE UNIVERSITY-GREAT FALLS COLLEGE OF TECHNOLOGY
Great Falls, Montana

- **State-supported** 2-year, founded 1969, part of Montana University System
- **Calendar** semesters
- **Degree** certificates and associate
- **Urban** 35-acre campus
- **Coed,** 1,463 undergraduate students, 49% full-time, 69% women, 31% men

Undergraduates 716 full-time, 747 part-time. Students come from 10 states and territories, 1% are from out of state, 2% African American, 1% Asian American or Pacific Islander, 2% Hispanic American, 3% Native American, 8% transferred in. *Retention:* 47% of 2002 full-time freshmen returned.
Freshmen *Admission:* 422 applied, 421 admitted, 220 enrolled.
Faculty *Total:* 83, 48% full-time. *Student/faculty ratio:* 15:1.
Majors Accounting; administrative assistant and secretarial science; autobody/collision and repair technology; biology/biotechnology laboratory technician; business/commerce; computer and information sciences; computer management; computer systems networking and telecommunications; data entry/microcomputer applications related; dental assisting; dental hygiene; drafting and design technology; elementary education; emergency medical technology (EMT paramedic); fire science; general studies; health information/medical records administration; health information/medical records technology; interior design; legal administrative assistant/secretary; medical administrative assistant and medical secretary; medical/clinical assistant; medical transcription; nursing (licensed practical/vocational nurse training); physical therapist assistant; respiratory care therapy; web page, digital/multimedia and information resources design.
Academic Programs *Special study options:* academic remediation for entering students, adult/continuing education programs, advanced placement credit, distance learning, double majors, independent study, internships, off-campus study, part-time degree program, services for LD students, summer session for credit.
Library Montana State University College of Technology—Great Falls Library with 4,000 titles, 200 serial subscriptions, an OPAC, a Web page.
Computers on Campus 150 computers available on campus for general student use. A campuswide network can be accessed from off campus. Internet access, online (class) registration, at least one staffed computer lab available.
Student Life *Housing:* college housing not available. *Activities and Organizations:* student-run newspaper. *Campus security:* 24-hour emergency response devices.
Standardized Tests *Required:* SAT I, ACT, or ACT ASSET (for placement).
Costs (2004–05) *Tuition:* state resident $2370 full-time, $99 per credit part-time; nonresident $7556 full-time, $315 per credit part-time. Full-time tuition and fees vary according to program. Part-time tuition and fees vary according to program. *Required fees:* $438 full-time, $20 per credit part-time, $38 per term part-time.
Financial Aid Of all full-time matriculated undergraduates who enrolled, 48 Federal Work-Study jobs (averaging $2000). 13 state and other part-time jobs (averaging $2000).
Applying *Options:* deferred entrance. *Application fee:* $30. *Required:* high school transcript, proof of immunization. *Required for some:* essay or personal statement, 3 letters of recommendation. *Application deadline:* rolling (freshmen).
Admissions Contact Montana State University-Great Falls College of Technology, 2100 16th Avenue South, Great Falls, MT 59405. *Phone:* 406-771-4300. *Toll-free phone:* 800-446-2698. *Fax:* 406-771-4317. *E-mail:* information@msugf.edu.

SALISH KOOTENAI COLLEGE
Pablo, Montana

- **Independent** primarily 2-year, founded 1977
- **Calendar** quarters
- **Degrees** certificates, associate, and bachelor's
- **Rural** 4-acre campus
- **Coed**

Salish Kootenai College (continued)

Standardized Tests *Required:* TABE (for placement).

Financial Aid Of all full-time matriculated undergraduates who enrolled, 64 Federal Work-Study jobs (averaging $1387).

Applying *Options:* deferred entrance. *Required:* high school transcript, proof of immunization, tribal enrollment.

Admissions Contact Ms. Jackie Moran, Admissions Officer, Salish Kootenai College, PO 117, Highway 93, Pablo, MT 59855. *Phone:* 406-275-4866. *Fax:* 406-275-4810. *E-mail:* jackie_moran@skc.edu.

STONE CHILD COLLEGE
Box Elder, Montana

Admissions Contact Mr. Ted Whitford, Director of Admissions/Registrar, Stone Child College, RR1, Box 1082, Box Elder, MT 59521. *Phone:* 406-395-4313 Ext. 110. *Fax:* 406-395-4836. *E-mail:* uanet337@quest.ocsc.montana.edu.

THE UNIVERSITY OF MONTANA-HELENA COLLEGE OF TECHNOLOGY
Helena, Montana

- **State-supported** 2-year, founded 1939, part of Montana University System
- **Calendar** semesters
- **Degree** certificates and associate
- **Small-town** campus
- **Coed**

Faculty *Student/faculty ratio:* 18:1.

Standardized Tests *Required:* ACT ASSET (for placement).

Costs (2003–04) *Tuition:* state resident $2800 full-time; nonresident $6900 full-time. *Required fees:* $60 full-time.

Financial Aid Of all full-time matriculated undergraduates who enrolled, 60 Federal Work-Study jobs (averaging $1500). 15 state and other part-time jobs (averaging $1500).

Applying *Options:* early admission, deferred entrance. *Application fee:* $30.

Admissions Contact Ms. Vicki Cavanaugh, Director of Admissions, The University of Montana-Helena College of Technology, 1115 North Roberts Street, Helena, MT 59601. *Phone:* 406-444-6800. *Toll-free phone:* 800-241-4882. *Fax:* 406-444-6892.

NEBRASKA

CENTRAL COMMUNITY COLLEGE-COLUMBUS CAMPUS
Columbus, Nebraska

- **State and locally supported** 2-year, founded 1968, part of Central Community College
- **Calendar** semesters plus six-week summer session
- **Degree** certificates, diplomas, and associate
- **Small-town** 90-acre campus
- **Coed,** 1,937 undergraduate students, 25% full-time, 62% women, 38% men

Undergraduates 488 full-time, 1,449 part-time. Students come from 42 states and territories, 4% are from out of state, 0.8% African American, 0.8% Asian American or Pacific Islander, 5% Hispanic American, 0.4% Native American, 17% live on campus.

Freshmen *Admission:* 84 enrolled.

Faculty *Total:* 92, 41% full-time, 5% with terminal degrees. *Student/faculty ratio:* 15:1.

Majors Accounting; administrative assistant and secretarial science; agricultural business and management; automobile/automotive mechanics technology; business administration and management; commercial and advertising art; computer and information sciences; computer programming (specific applications); drafting and design technology; electrical, electronic and communications engineering technology; electromechanical technology; family and consumer sciences/human sciences; industrial technology; information technology; liberal arts and sciences/liberal studies; machine tool technology; marketing/marketing management; nursing (licensed practical/vocational nurse training); quality control technology; system administration; web/multimedia management and webmaster; welding technology.

Academic Programs *Special study options:* academic remediation for entering students, accelerated degree program, adult/continuing education programs,

advanced placement credit, cooperative education, distance learning, English as a second language, external degree program, independent study, internships, off-campus study, part-time degree program, services for LD students, student-designed majors, summer session for credit.

Library Learning Resources Center with 23,219 titles, 142 serial subscriptions, 1,365 audiovisual materials, an OPAC.

Computers on Campus 100 computers available on campus for general student use. A campuswide network can be accessed from student residence rooms and from off campus. Internet access, at least one staffed computer lab available.

Student Life *Housing Options:* coed. Campus housing is university owned. *Activities and Organizations:* choral group, Phi Theta Kappa, Drama Club, Art Club, Cantari, Chorale. *Campus security:* late-night transport/escort service, controlled dormitory access, night security. *Student services:* personal/psychological counseling, women's center.

Athletics Member NJCAA. *Intercollegiate sports:* basketball M(s), volleyball W(s). *Intramural sports:* basketball M/W, football M, softball M/W, table tennis M/W, volleyball M/W.

Standardized Tests *Required for some:* ACT (for placement). *Recommended:* ACT ASSET or ACT COMPASS.

Costs (2004–05) *Tuition:* state resident $1296 full-time, $54 per credit part-time; nonresident $1944 full-time, $81 per credit part-time. *Required fees:* $96 full-time, $4 per credit part-time. *Room and board:* $3744. Room and board charges vary according to board plan. *Payment plan:* deferred payment. *Waivers:* employees or children of employees.

Applying *Options:* common application, electronic application, early admission. *Required:* high school transcript. *Required for some:* 3 letters of recommendation, interview. *Application deadline:* rolling (freshmen), rolling (transfers). *Notification:* continuous (freshmen), continuous (transfers).

Admissions Contact Ms. Mary Young, Records Coordinator, Central Community College-Columbus Campus, PO Box 1027, Columbus, NE 68602-1027. *Phone:* 402-562-1296. *Toll-free phone:* 800-642-1083. *E-mail:* myoung@cccneb.edu.

CENTRAL COMMUNITY COLLEGE-GRAND ISLAND CAMPUS
Grand Island, Nebraska

- **State and locally supported** 2-year, founded 1976, part of Central Community College
- **Calendar** semesters plus six-week summer session
- **Degree** certificates, diplomas, and associate
- **Small-town** 64-acre campus
- **Coed,** 2,771 undergraduate students, 18% full-time, 68% women, 32% men

Undergraduates 487 full-time, 2,284 part-time. Students come from 42 states and territories, 4% are from out of state, 0.9% African American, 0.8% Asian American or Pacific Islander, 7% Hispanic American, 0.4% Native American.

Freshmen *Admission:* 136 enrolled.

Faculty *Total:* 115, 37% full-time, 4% with terminal degrees. *Student/faculty ratio:* 15:1.

Majors Accounting; administrative assistant and secretarial science; automobile/automotive mechanics technology; business administration and management; child development; clinical/medical social work; computer and information sciences; computer programming (specific applications); criminal justice/safety; data processing and data processing technology; drafting and design technology; electrical, electronic and communications engineering technology; heating, air conditioning, ventilation and refrigeration maintenance technology; industrial technology; information technology; legal assistant/paralegal; liberal arts and sciences/liberal studies; nursing (licensed practical/vocational nurse training); nursing (registered nurse training); system administration; web/multimedia management and webmaster; welding technology.

Academic Programs *Special study options:* academic remediation for entering students, accelerated degree program, adult/continuing education programs, advanced placement credit, cooperative education, distance learning, English as a second language, external degree program, independent study, internships, off-campus study, part-time degree program, services for LD students, student-designed majors, summer session for credit.

Library Central Community College-Grand Island Campus Library with 5,373 titles, 98 serial subscriptions, 807 audiovisual materials, an OPAC, a Web page.

Computers on Campus 156 computers available on campus for general student use. A campuswide network can be accessed from off campus. Internet access, at least one staffed computer lab available.

Student Life *Housing:* college housing not available. *Activities and Organizations:* Mid-Nebraska Users of Computers, Student Activities Organization, intramurals. *Student services:* personal/psychological counseling.

Athletics *Intramural sports:* bowling M/W, table tennis M/W, volleyball M/W.

Standardized Tests *Required for some:* ACT (for placement). *Recommended:* ACT ASSET or ACT COMPASS.

Costs (2004–05) *Tuition:* state resident $1296 full-time, $54 per credit part-time; nonresident $1944 full-time, $81 per credit part-time. *Required fees:* $96 full-time, $4 per credit part-time. *Payment plan:* deferred payment. *Waivers:* employees or children of employees.

Financial Aid Of all full-time matriculated undergraduates who enrolled, 155 Federal Work-Study jobs (averaging $1200). 40 state and other part-time jobs (averaging $1000).

Applying *Options:* common application, electronic application, early admission. *Required:* high school transcript. *Required for some:* 3 letters of recommendation, interview. *Application deadline:* rolling (freshmen), rolling (transfers). *Notification:* continuous (freshmen), continuous (transfers).

Admissions Contact Ms. Angie Pacheco, Admissions Director, Central Community College-Grand Island Campus, PO Box 4903, Grand Island, NE 68802-4903. *Phone:* 308-398-7406 Ext. 406. *Toll-free phone:* 800-652-9177. *Fax:* 308-398-7398. *E-mail:* apacheco@cccneb.edu.

CENTRAL COMMUNITY COLLEGE-HASTINGS CAMPUS
Hastings, Nebraska

- **State and locally supported** 2-year, founded 1966, part of Central Community College
- **Calendar** semesters plus six-week summer session
- **Degree** certificates, diplomas, and associate
- **Small-town** 600-acre campus
- **Coed,** 2,400 undergraduate students, 39% full-time, 56% women, 44% men

Undergraduates 942 full-time, 1,458 part-time. Students come from 42 states and territories, 4% are from out of state, 0.3% African American, 1% Asian American or Pacific Islander, 4% Hispanic American, 0.3% Native American, 26% live on campus.

Freshmen *Admission:* 233 enrolled.

Faculty *Total:* 92, 67% full-time, 4% with terminal degrees. *Student/faculty ratio:* 15:1.

Majors Accounting; administrative assistant and secretarial science; agricultural business and management; applied horticulture; autobody/collision and repair technology; automobile/automotive mechanics technology; business administration and management; child development; clinical/medical social work; commercial and advertising art; computer and information sciences; computer programming (specific applications); construction engineering technology; dental assisting; dental hygiene; diesel mechanics technology; drafting and design technology; electrical, electronic and communications engineering technology; graphic and printing equipment operation/production; health information/medical records technology; heating, air conditioning, ventilation and refrigeration maintenance technology; hospital and health care facilities administration; hospitality administration; hotel/motel administration; industrial technology; information technology; liberal arts and sciences/liberal studies; machine tool technology; mass communication/media; medical administrative assistant and medical secretary; medical/clinical assistant; radio and television broadcasting technology; system administration; vehicle/petroleum products marketing; web/multimedia management and webmaster; welding technology.

Academic Programs *Special study options:* academic remediation for entering students, accelerated degree program, adult/continuing education programs, advanced placement credit, cooperative education, distance learning, English as a second language, external degree program, independent study, internships, off-campus study, part-time degree program, services for LD students, student-designed majors, summer session for credit.

Library Nuckolls Library with 4,724 titles, 48 serial subscriptions, an OPAC.

Computers on Campus 190 computers available on campus for general student use. A campuswide network can be accessed from student residence rooms and from off campus. Internet access, at least one staffed computer lab available.

Student Life *Housing Options:* coed. Campus housing is university owned. *Activities and Organizations:* student-run radio station, Student Senate, Central Dormitory Council, Judicial Board, Seeds and Soils, Young Farmers and Ranchers. *Campus security:* 24-hour patrols, controlled dormitory access. *Student services:* personal/psychological counseling, women's center.

Athletics *Intramural sports:* basketball M/W, bowling M/W, golf M/W, softball M/W, volleyball M/W, weight lifting M/W.

Standardized Tests *Required for some:* ACT (for placement). *Recommended:* ACT ASSET or ACT COMPASS.

Costs (2004–05) *Tuition:* state resident $1296 full-time, $54 per credit part-time; nonresident $1944 full-time, $81 per credit part-time. *Required fees:* $96 full-time, $4 per credit part-time. *Room and board:* $3744. Room and board charges vary according to board plan. *Payment plan:* deferred payment. *Waivers:* employees or children of employees.

Financial Aid Of all full-time matriculated undergraduates who enrolled, 70 Federal Work-Study jobs (averaging $1200). 12 state and other part-time jobs (averaging $1250).

Applying *Options:* common application, electronic application, early admission. *Required:* high school transcript. *Required for some:* 3 letters of recommendation, interview. *Application deadline:* rolling (freshmen), rolling (transfers). *Notification:* continuous (freshmen), continuous (transfers).

Admissions Contact Mr. Robert Glenn, Admissions and Recruiting Director, Central Community College-Hastings Campus, PO Box 1024, East Highway 6, Hastings, NE 68902-1024. *Phone:* 402-461-2428. *Toll-free phone:* 800-742-7872. *E-mail:* bglenn@cccneb.edu.

THE CREATIVE CENTER
Omaha, Nebraska

- **Proprietary** 2-year
- **Calendar** semesters
- **Degree** associate
- **Urban** campus
- **Coed,** 131 undergraduate students, 99% full-time, 47% women, 53% men

Undergraduates 130 full-time, 1 part-time. 5% African American, 2% Asian American or Pacific Islander, 2% Hispanic American.

Freshmen *Admission:* 57 enrolled.

Faculty *Total:* 18, 28% full-time. *Student/faculty ratio:* 25:1.

Majors Computer graphics; design and visual communications; illustration.

Costs (2004–05) *Tuition:* $14,800 full-time, $1480 per course part-time. *Required fees:* $1100 full-time, $100 per course part-time.

Admissions Contact Ms. Debbie Carlson, Admissions, The Creative Center, 10850 Emmet Street, Omaha, NE 68164. *Phone:* 402-898-1000 Ext. 216. *Toll-free phone:* 888-898-1789.

HAMILTON COLLEGE
Omaha, Nebraska

- **Proprietary** primarily 2-year, founded 1891, part of Educational Medical, Inc
- **Calendar** quarters
- **Degrees** diplomas, associate, and bachelor's
- **Urban** 3-acre campus
- **Coed,** 700 undergraduate students, 100% full-time, 64% women, 36% men

Undergraduates 700 full-time. Students come from 5 states and territories.

Freshmen *Admission:* 850 applied, 700 enrolled.

Faculty *Total:* 35, 49% full-time. *Student/faculty ratio:* 20:1.

Majors Accounting; administrative assistant and secretarial science; business administration and management; computer programming; computer programming (specific applications); legal administrative assistant/secretary; legal assistant/paralegal; medical administrative assistant and medical secretary; medical/clinical assistant.

Academic Programs *Special study options:* academic remediation for entering students, adult/continuing education programs, advanced placement credit, cooperative education, internships, part-time degree program, summer session for credit.

Library Nebraska College of Business Library with 4,800 titles, 50 serial subscriptions, a Web page.

Computers on Campus 110 computers available on campus for general student use. Internet access, at least one staffed computer lab available.

Student Life *Housing:* college housing not available. *Activities and Organizations:* student-run newspaper. *Campus security:* 24-hour emergency response devices. *Student services:* personal/psychological counseling.

Standardized Tests *Required:* CPAt (for admission).

Applying *Options:* early admission, deferred entrance. *Application fee:* $50. *Required:* high school transcript, interview. *Application deadline:* rolling (freshmen), rolling (transfers).

Admissions Contact Mr. Mark Stoltenberger, Director of Admissions, Hamilton College, 3350 North 90 Street, Omaha, NE 68134. *Phone:* 402-572-8500. *Toll-free phone:* 800-642-1456. *Fax:* 402-573-1341.

HAMILTON COLLEGE-LINCOLN
Lincoln, Nebraska

- **Proprietary** 2-year, founded 1884, part of Quest Education Corporation
- **Calendar** quarters
- **Degree** certificates, diplomas, and associate
- **Urban** 5-acre campus with easy access to Omaha
- **Coed**

Faculty *Student/faculty ratio:* 19:1.

Student Life *Campus security:* late-night transport/escort service.

Standardized Tests *Required:* CPAt (for admission).

Hamilton College-Lincoln (continued)

Costs (2003–04) *Tuition:* $12,300 full-time. No tuition increase for student's term of enrollment. *Required fees:* $25 full-time. *Room only:* $1875.

Applying *Options:* early admission. *Application fee:* $25. *Required:* essay or personal statement, high school transcript, letters of recommendation, interview.

Admissions Contact Mr. Andy Bossler, Director of Admissions, Hamilton College-Lincoln, 1821 K Street, Lincoln, NE 68508. *Phone:* 402-474-5315. *Toll-free phone:* 800-742-7738. *Fax:* 402-474-5302. *E-mail:* lsc@ix.netcom.com.

ITT TECHNICAL INSTITUTE
Omaha, Nebraska

- **Proprietary** primarily 2-year, founded 1991, part of ITT Educational Services, Inc
- **Calendar** quarters
- **Degrees** associate and bachelor's
- **Urban** 1-acre campus
- **Coed**

Standardized Tests *Required:* Wonderlic aptitude test (for admission).

Costs (2003–04) *Tuition:* Total Program Cost varies depending on course of study. Consult school catalog.

Applying *Options:* deferred entrance. *Application fee:* $100. *Required:* high school transcript, interview. *Recommended:* letters of recommendation.

Admissions Contact Ms. Jacqueline M. Hawthorne, Director of Recruitment, ITT Technical Institute, 9814 M Street, Omaha, NE 68127. *Phone:* 402-331-2900. *Toll-free phone:* 800-677-9260. *Fax:* 402-331-9495.

LITTLE PRIEST TRIBAL COLLEGE
Winnebago, Nebraska

- **Independent** 2-year
- **Degree** certificates, diplomas, and associate
- **Rural** campus
- 130 undergraduate students, 52% full-time

Undergraduates 67 full-time, 63 part-time. 0.8% African American, 0.8% Asian American or Pacific Islander, 2% Hispanic American, 83% Native American.

Freshmen *Admission:* 24 applied, 24 admitted, 21 enrolled. *Average high school GPA:* 2.64.

Faculty *Total:* 16, 25% full-time. *Student/faculty ratio:* 11:1.

Costs (2003–04) *Tuition:* $2220 full-time, $74 per credit part-time. *Required fees:* $575 full-time, $18 per credit part-time.

Financial Aid Of all full-time matriculated undergraduates who enrolled, 8 Federal Work-Study jobs (averaging $750).

Admissions Contact Ms. Karen Kemling, Director of Admissions and Records, Little Priest Tribal College, PO Box 270, Winnebago, NE 68071. *Phone:* 402-878-2380.

METROPOLITAN COMMUNITY COLLEGE
Omaha, Nebraska

- **State and locally supported** 2-year, founded 1974, part of Nebraska Coordinating Commission for Postsecondary Education
- **Calendar** quarters
- **Degree** certificates, diplomas, and associate
- **Urban** 172-acre campus
- **Endowment** $1.2 million
- **Coed,** 12,838 undergraduate students, 36% full-time, 57% women, 43% men

Metropolitan Community College offers the advantages of a comprehensive, multicampus institution with small-college friendliness. Located in Omaha, Nebraska, Metro provides personalized services and high-quality programs in business administration, computer and office technologies, food arts, industrial and construction technologies, nursing and allied health, social sciences and services, and visual and electronic technologies as well as academic transfer programs. Many courses are offered through distance learning. Students can visit the College's Web site at http://www.mccneb.edu.

Undergraduates 4,661 full-time, 8,177 part-time. Students come from 27 states and territories, 4% are from out of state, 20% transferred in. *Retention:* 34% of 2002 full-time freshmen returned.

Freshmen *Admission:* 1,552 applied, 1,552 admitted, 1,552 enrolled.

Faculty *Total:* 697, 26% full-time. *Student/faculty ratio:* 16:1.

Majors Accounting; administrative assistant and secretarial science; architectural engineering technology; automobile/automotive mechanics technology; business administration and management; child development; civil engineering technology; commercial and advertising art; computer programming; construc-

tion engineering technology; criminal justice/police science; culinary arts; drafting and design technology; electrical, electronic and communications engineering technology; graphic and printing equipment operation/production; heating, air conditioning, ventilation and refrigeration maintenance technology; heavy equipment maintenance technology; human services; interior design; kindergarten/preschool education; legal administrative assistant/secretary; legal assistant/paralegal; legal studies; liberal arts and sciences/liberal studies; mental health/rehabilitation; nursing (licensed practical/vocational nurse training); nursing (registered nurse training); ornamental horticulture; photography; pre-engineering; respiratory care therapy; surgical technology; welding technology.

Academic Programs *Special study options:* academic remediation for entering students, adult/continuing education programs, advanced placement credit, cooperative education, distance learning, English as a second language, independent study, internships, part-time degree program, services for LD students, summer session for credit. *ROTC:* Army (c).

Library Metropolitan Community College plus 2 others with 47,652 titles, 733 serial subscriptions, 10,458 audiovisual materials, an OPAC, a Web page.

Computers on Campus 1500 computers available on campus for general student use. A campuswide network can be accessed from off campus that provide access to on-line classes, e-mail. Internet access, online (class) registration, at least one staffed computer lab available.

Student Life *Housing:* college housing not available. *Campus security:* 24-hour emergency response devices and patrols, late-night transport/escort service, security on duty 9 pm to 6 am. *Student services:* personal/psychological counseling.

Standardized Tests *Recommended:* ACT (for placement), ACT ASSET or ACT COMPASS.

Costs (2004–05) *Tuition:* state resident $1508 full-time, $37 per credit hour part-time; nonresident $2160 full-time, $51 per credit hour part-time. *Required fees:* $135 full-time, $3 per credit hour part-time. *Payment plan:* deferred payment. *Waivers:* senior citizens and employees or children of employees.

Financial Aid Of all full-time matriculated undergraduates who enrolled, 180 Federal Work-Study jobs (averaging $1339).

Applying *Options:* early admission. *Recommended:* high school transcript. *Application deadline:* rolling (freshmen), rolling (transfers). *Notification:* continuous (freshmen), continuous (transfers).

Admissions Contact Ms. Arlene Jordan, Director of Enrollment Management, Metropolitan Community College, PO Box 3777, Omaha, NE 69103-0777. *Phone:* 402-457-2563. *Toll-free phone:* 800-228-9553. *Fax:* 402-457-2564.

MID-PLAINS COMMUNITY COLLEGE
North Platte, Nebraska

- **District-supported** 2-year
- **Calendar** semesters
- **Degree** certificates, diplomas, and associate
- **Small-town** campus
- **Coed,** 3,084 undergraduate students, 35% full-time, 58% women, 42% men

Undergraduates 1,083 full-time, 2,001 part-time. Students come from 11 states and territories, 0.1% are from out of state, 1% African American, 0.4% Asian American or Pacific Islander, 2% Hispanic American, 0.5% Native American, 0.4% international, 8% live on campus.

Freshmen *Admission:* 816 applied, 630 admitted, 555 enrolled.

Faculty *Total:* 193, 32% full-time, 6% with terminal degrees. *Student/faculty ratio:* 14:1.

Majors Administrative assistant and secretarial science; autobody/collision and repair technology; automobile/automotive mechanics technology; building/construction finishing, management, and inspection related; business administration and management; clinical/medical laboratory technology; computer and information sciences; construction engineering technology; dental assisting; diesel mechanics technology; electrical, electronic and communications engineering technology; fire science; heating, air conditioning, ventilation and refrigeration maintenance technology; liberal arts and sciences/liberal studies; nursing (licensed practical/vocational nurse training); nursing (registered nurse training); transportation and materials moving related; welding technology.

Academic Programs *Special study options:* academic remediation for entering students, adult/continuing education programs, advanced placement credit, cooperative education, distance learning, independent study, internships, part-time degree program, summer session for credit.

Library McDonald-Belton L R C plus 1 other with 64,284 titles, 277 serial subscriptions, 6,318 audiovisual materials.

Computers on Campus 300 computers available on campus for general student use. A campuswide network can be accessed from off campus. Internet access, at least one staffed computer lab available.

Student Life *Housing Options:* coed. *Activities and Organizations:* drama/theater group, student-run newspaper, choral group, Student Senate, Phi Theta

Kappa, Phi Beta Lamda, SEAN. *Campus security:* controlled dormitory access, patrols by trained security personnel.
Athletics Member NJCAA. *Intercollegiate sports:* baseball M(s), basketball M(s)/W(s), golf M(s), softball W(s), volleyball W(s). *Intramural sports:* baseball M, basketball M/W, softball W, volleyball W.
Standardized Tests *Required:* ACT COMPASS (for placement). *Recommended:* ACT (for placement).
Costs (2004–05) *Tuition:* state resident $1620 full-time, $54 per semester hour part-time; nonresident $2025 full-time, $68 per semester hour part-time. *Required fees:* $6 per semester hour part-time. *Room and board:* $3200. Room and board charges vary according to housing facility and location. *Waivers:* senior citizens and employees or children of employees.
Applying *Required:* high school transcript. *Application deadline:* rolling (freshmen), rolling (transfers). *Notification:* continuous (freshmen), continuous (transfers).
Admissions Contact Ms. Mary Schriefer, Advisor, Mid-Plains Community College, 1101 Halligan Drive, North Platte, NE 69101. *Phone:* 308-535-3710. *Toll-free phone:* 800-658-4308 (in-state); 800-658-4348 (out-of-state). *Fax:* 308-634-2522.

MYOTHERAPY INSTITUTE
Lincoln, Nebraska

Admissions Contact Ms. Gerri Allen, Director of Admissions, Myotherapy Institute, 6020 South 58th Street, Lincoln, NE 68516. *Phone:* 801-485-6600. *Toll-free phone:* 800-896-3363.

NEBRASKA COLLEGE OF TECHNICAL AGRICULTURE
Curtis, Nebraska

Admissions Contact Mr. Gerald Sundquist, Director of Instruction, Nebraska College of Technical Agriculture, RR3, Box 23A, Curtis, NE 69025-9205. *Phone:* 308-367-4124 Ext. 205. *Toll-free phone:* 800-3CURTIS. *Fax:* 308-367-5203. *E-mail:* ncta@unlvm.unl.edu.

NEBRASKA INDIAN COMMUNITY COLLEGE
Macy, Nebraska

- **Federally supported** 2-year, founded 1979
- **Calendar** semesters
- **Degree** certificates and associate
- **Rural** 2-acre campus with easy access to Omaha, NE
- **Endowment** $68,020
- **Coed,** 190 undergraduate students, 51% full-time, 68% women, 32% men

Undergraduates 97 full-time, 93 part-time. Students come from 2 states and territories, 13% are from out of state, 4% African American, 0.5% Hispanic American, 82% Native American.
Freshmen *Admission:* 68 enrolled.
Faculty *Total:* 38, 16% full-time, 3% with terminal degrees. *Student/faculty ratio:* 8:1.
Majors American Indian/Native American studies; business administration and management; carpentry; corrections and criminal justice related; data entry/microcomputer applications; early childhood education; human services; information technology; liberal arts and sciences/liberal studies; natural resources/conservation; social work.
Academic Programs *Special study options:* academic remediation for entering students, adult/continuing education programs, double majors, part-time degree program, summer session for credit.
Computers on Campus 10 computers available on campus for general student use. Internet access, at least one staffed computer lab available.
Student Life *Housing:* college housing not available.
Costs (2003–04) *Tuition:* $1920 full-time, $80 per credit hour part-time. Full-time tuition and fees vary according to course load. Part-time tuition and fees vary according to course load. *Required fees:* $458 full-time, $17 per credit hour part-time, $25 per term part-time. *Payment plan:* installment. *Waivers:* senior citizens and employees or children of employees.
Applying *Options:* early admission, deferred entrance. *Application fee:* $10. *Required:* high school transcript, certificate of tribal enrollment if applicable. *Application deadline:* rolling (freshmen), rolling (transfers). *Notification:* continuous (freshmen), continuous (transfers).
Admissions Contact Mr. Ed Stevens, Admission Counselor, Nebraska Indian Community College, 2451 Saint Mary's Avenue, Omaha, NE 68105. *Phone:* 402-344-8428. *Toll-free phone:* 888-843-6432 Ext. 14. *Fax:* 402-344-8358.

NORTHEAST COMMUNITY COLLEGE
Norfolk, Nebraska

- **State and locally supported** 2-year, founded 1973, part of Nebraska Coordinating Commission for Postsecondary Education
- **Calendar** semesters
- **Degree** certificates, diplomas, and associate
- **Small-town** 205-acre campus
- **Endowment** $1.5 million
- **Coed,** 4,858 undergraduate students, 39% full-time, 45% women, 55% men

Undergraduates 1,886 full-time, 2,972 part-time. Students come from 15 states and territories, 15 other countries, 4% are from out of state, 1% African American, 0.4% Asian American or Pacific Islander, 3% Hispanic American, 1% Native American, 1% international, 11% live on campus.
Freshmen *Admission:* 788 enrolled.
Faculty *Total:* 337, 30% full-time. *Student/faculty ratio:* 20:1.
Majors Accounting; administrative assistant and secretarial science; agricultural business and management; agricultural mechanization; agricultural production; agriculture; agronomy and crop science; animal sciences; applied horticulture; art; art teacher education; audio engineering; autobody/collision and repair technology; automobile/automotive mechanics technology; biological and physical sciences; biology/biological sciences; broadcast journalism; business administration and management; business teacher education; carpentry; chemistry; computer and information sciences; computer programming; computer programming (specific applications); computer science; corrections; criminal justice/law enforcement administration; criminal justice/police science; crop production; diesel mechanics technology; drafting and design technology; dramatic/theatre arts; education; electrical, electronic and communications engineering technology; electrician; electromechanical technology; elementary education; emergency medical technology (EMT paramedic); engineering; English; entrepreneurship; farm and ranch management; general studies; health and physical education; heating, air conditioning, ventilation and refrigeration maintenance technology; horticultural science; journalism; legal administrative assistant/secretary; legal assistant/paralegal; liberal arts and sciences/liberal studies; lineworker; livestock management; marketing/marketing management; marketing related; mass communication/media; mathematics; medical administrative assistant and medical secretary; music; music management and merchandising; music performance; music teacher education; nursing (licensed practical/vocational nurse training); nursing (registered nurse training); physical education teaching and coaching; physical therapy; physics; pre-law studies; radio and television; real estate; retailing; social sciences; social work related; speech and rhetoric; surgical technology; veterinary technology; welding technology.
Academic Programs *Special study options:* academic remediation for entering students, accelerated degree program, adult/continuing education programs, advanced placement credit, cooperative education, distance learning, English as a second language, independent study, internships, off-campus study, part-time degree program, services for LD students, summer session for credit.
Library Resource Center plus 1 other with 28,000 titles, 3,025 serial subscriptions, 1,298 audiovisual materials, an OPAC, a Web page.
Computers on Campus 300 computers available on campus for general student use. A campuswide network can be accessed. Internet access, online (class) registration, at least one staffed computer lab available.
Student Life *Housing Options:* coed, disabled students. Campus housing is university owned. *Activities and Organizations:* drama/theater group, student-run newspaper, radio and television station, choral group, Phi Theta Kappa, Campus Crusade for Christ, Diversified Ag Club, Electricians Club, Utility Line Club. *Campus security:* 24-hour patrols, controlled dormitory access. *Student services:* personal/psychological counseling.
Athletics Member NJCAA. *Intercollegiate sports:* basketball M(s)/W(s), cheerleading W(s). *Intramural sports:* basketball M/W, bowling M/W, football M/W, soccer M/W, softball M/W, table tennis M/W, volleyball M/W.
Standardized Tests *Required:* ACT ASSET (for placement). *Recommended:* ACT (for placement).
Costs (2003–04) *Tuition:* state resident $1560 full-time, $52 per hour part-time; nonresident $1950 full-time, $65 per hour part-time. *Required fees:* $225 full-time, $8 per hour part-time. *Room and board:* $3500; room only: $1900. Room and board charges vary according to board plan and housing facility. *Waivers:* employees or children of employees.
Financial Aid Of all full-time matriculated undergraduates who enrolled, 90 Federal Work-Study jobs (averaging $1700).
Applying *Options:* electronic application, early admission. *Recommended:* high school transcript. *Application deadline:* rolling (freshmen), rolling (transfers). *Notification:* continuous (freshmen), continuous (transfers).
Admissions Contact Ms. Maureen Baker, Dean of Enrollment Management, Northeast Community College, PO Box 469, Norfolk, NE 68702-0469. *Phone:* 402-844-7258. *Toll-free phone:* 800-348-9033 Ext. 7260. *Fax:* 402-844-7400. *E-mail:* admission@northeastcollege.com.

Nebraska

SOUTHEAST COMMUNITY COLLEGE, BEATRICE CAMPUS

Beatrice, Nebraska

- **District-supported** 2-year, founded 1976, part of Southeast Community College System
- **Calendar** semesters
- **Degree** certificates, diplomas, and associate
- **Small-town** 640-acre campus
- **Coed,** 1,220 undergraduate students

Undergraduates Students come from 9 states and territories, 7 other countries, 3% are from out of state, 22% live on campus.

Faculty *Total:* 85, 76% full-time. *Student/faculty ratio:* 12:1.

Majors Accounting; administrative assistant and secretarial science; agricultural business and management; agricultural mechanization; agriculture; agronomy and crop science; animal sciences; art; biological and physical sciences; biology/biological sciences; biology/biotechnology laboratory technician; broadcast journalism; business administration and management; computer science; education; elementary education; finance; journalism; legal administrative assistant/secretary; liberal arts and sciences/liberal studies; medical administrative assistant and medical secretary; nursing (licensed practical/vocational nurse training); physical sciences; soil conservation.

Academic Programs *Special study options:* academic remediation for entering students, adult/continuing education programs, advanced placement credit, cooperative education, distance learning, internships, off-campus study, part-time degree program, services for LD students, summer session for credit.

Library Learning Resource Center with 13,287 titles, 225 serial subscriptions, 1,681 audiovisual materials, an OPAC.

Computers on Campus 75 computers available on campus for general student use. At least one staffed computer lab available.

Student Life *Housing Options:* coed. *Activities and Organizations:* drama/theater group, student-run newspaper, radio station, choral group, Student Senate, Agricultural Club, Residence Hall Association, Licensed Practical Association of Nebraska, International Student Association. *Campus security:* controlled dormitory access, evening security. *Student services:* personal/psychological counseling.

Athletics Member NJCAA. *Intercollegiate sports:* basketball M(s)/W(s), golf M(s), volleyball W(s). *Intramural sports:* archery M, softball M/W, table tennis M/W.

Standardized Tests *Required for some:* ACT ASSET, ACT COMPASS. *Recommended:* SAT I or ACT (for admission), ACT ASSET, ACT COMPASS.

Costs (2003–04) *Tuition:* state resident $1508 full-time, $50 per credit hour part-time; nonresident $1823 full-time, $61 per credit hour part-time. *Required fees:* $75 full-time, $3 per credit hour part-time. *Room and board:* room only: $2472.

Applying *Options:* common application, electronic application, early admission, deferred entrance. *Required:* high school transcript. *Recommended:* minimum 2.0 GPA. *Application deadline:* rolling (freshmen), rolling (transfers).

Admissions Contact Ms. Mary Ann Harms, Admissions Technician, Southeast Community College, Beatrice Campus, 4771 W. Scott Road, Beatrice, NE 68310-7042. *Phone:* 800-233-5027 Ext. 214. *Toll-free phone:* 800-233-5027 Ext. 214.

SOUTHEAST COMMUNITY COLLEGE, LINCOLN CAMPUS

Lincoln, Nebraska

- **District-supported** 2-year, founded 1973, part of Southeast Community College System
- **Calendar** quarters
- **Degree** certificates, diplomas, and associate
- **Suburban** 115-acre campus with easy access to Omaha
- **Coed,** 7,547 undergraduate students, 50% full-time, 58% women, 42% men

Undergraduates 3,806 full-time, 3,741 part-time. Students come from 23 states and territories, 4% are from out of state.

Freshmen *Admission:* 3,805 applied, 3,217 enrolled.

Faculty *Total:* 548, 25% full-time, 2% with terminal degrees. *Student/faculty ratio:* 15:1.

Majors Administrative assistant and secretarial science; automobile/automotive mechanics technology; business administration and management; child development; clinical/medical laboratory technology; computer and information sciences; culinary arts; dietetics; drafting and design technology; electrical, electronic and communications engineering technology; environmental studies; fire science; food services technology; human services; liberal arts and sciences/liberal studies; machine tool technology; medical radiologic technology; nursing (registered nurse training); respiratory care therapy; welding technology.

Academic Programs *Special study options:* academic remediation for entering students, adult/continuing education programs, advanced placement credit, cooperative education, distance learning, English as a second language, independent study, internships, off-campus study, part-time degree program, services for LD students, summer session for credit.

Library Lincoln Campus Learning Resource Center with 14,081 titles, 375 serial subscriptions, an OPAC.

Computers on Campus 380 computers available on campus for general student use. A campuswide network can be accessed. Internet access, online (class) registration, at least one staffed computer lab available.

Student Life *Housing:* college housing not available. *Activities and Organizations:* Student Senate, Phi Theta Kappa, Multicultural Student Organization, Single Parents Club, Vocational Industrial Clubs of America. *Campus security:* late-night transport/escort service. *Student services:* personal/psychological counseling.

Athletics *Intramural sports:* basketball M/W, softball M/W, table tennis M/W, tennis M/W, volleyball M/W.

Standardized Tests *Recommended:* SAT I or ACT (for placement).

Costs (2004–05) *Tuition:* state resident $1620 full-time, $36 per credit part-time; nonresident $1958 full-time, $44 per credit part-time. *Required fees:* $45 full-time, $1 per credit part-time. *Payment plan:* installment. *Waivers:* employees or children of employees.

Applying *Options:* electronic application, early admission, deferred entrance. *Required:* high school transcript. *Application deadline:* rolling (freshmen), rolling (transfers).

Admissions Contact Ms. Pat Frakes, Admissions Representative, Southeast Community College, Lincoln Campus, 8800 "O" Street, Lincoln, NE 68520. *Phone:* 402-437-2600 Ext. 2600. *Toll-free phone:* 800-642-4075 Ext. 2600.

SOUTHEAST COMMUNITY COLLEGE, MILFORD CAMPUS

Milford, Nebraska

- **District-supported** 2-year, founded 1941, part of Southeast Community College System
- **Calendar** quarters
- **Degree** diplomas and associate
- **Small-town** 50-acre campus with easy access to Omaha
- **Coed, primarily men**

Faculty *Student/faculty ratio:* 20:1.

Student Life *Campus security:* 24-hour patrols, late-night transport/escort service.

Standardized Tests *Recommended:* SAT I (for admission), ACT (for admission).

Costs (2003–04) *Tuition:* state resident $2010 full-time, $34 per quarter hour part-time; nonresident $2430 full-time. *Required fees:* $60 full-time, $1 per quarter hour part-time. *Room and board:* $2733.

Applying *Options:* common application. *Required:* high school transcript.

Admissions Contact Mr. Larry E. Meyer, Dean of Students, Southeast Community College, Milford Campus, 600 State Street, Milford, NE 68405. *Phone:* 402-761-2131 Ext. 8270. *Toll-free phone:* 800-933-7223 Ext. 8243. *Fax:* 402-761-2324. *E-mail:* lmeyer@southeast.edu.

VATTEROTT COLLEGE

Omaha, Nebraska

- **Proprietary** 2-year, founded 1967
- **Calendar** semesters
- **Degree** diplomas and associate
- **Urban** 1-acre campus
- **Coed,** 414 undergraduate students

Undergraduates Students come from 5 states and territories, 12% are from out of state, 29% African American, 0.2% Asian American or Pacific Islander, 4% Hispanic American, 1% Native American.

Freshmen *Admission:* 230 applied, 186 admitted.

Faculty *Total:* 21, 95% full-time. *Student/faculty ratio:* 14:1.

Majors Commercial and advertising art; heating, air conditioning, ventilation and refrigeration maintenance technology; medical administrative assistant and medical secretary; medical/clinical assistant; veterinary technology.

Academic Programs *Special study options:* internships, summer session for credit.

Library Main Library plus 1 other with 1,900 titles, 22 serial subscriptions, an OPAC.

Computers on Campus 50 computers available on campus for general student use. Internet access, at least one staffed computer lab available.

Student Life *Campus security:* 24-hour emergency response devices.

Standardized Tests *Required:* Wonderlic aptitude test (for admission). *Recommended:* SAT I or ACT (for admission).

Costs (2004–05) *Tuition:* $17,918 full-time. *Required fees:* $900 full-time.

Applying *Options:* early admission, deferred entrance. *Required:* high school transcript. *Application deadline:* rolling (freshmen), rolling (transfers). *Notification:* continuous (freshmen), continuous (transfers).

Admissions Contact Dr. James G. Hadley, Campus Director, Vatterott College, 225 North 80th Street, Omaha, NE 68114. *Phone:* 402-392-1300 Ext. 207. *Toll-free phone:* 800-865-8628.

VATTEROTT COLLEGE
Omaha, Nebraska

- **Proprietary** 2-year
- **Calendar** semesters
- **Coed**

Admissions Contact 5318 South 136th Street, Omaha, NE 68137.

WESTERN NEBRASKA COMMUNITY COLLEGE
Sidney, Nebraska

- **State and locally supported** 2-year, founded 1926, part of Western Community College Area System
- **Calendar** semesters
- **Degree** certificates, diplomas, and associate
- **Rural** 20-acre campus
- **Coed**

Faculty *Student/faculty ratio:* 15:1.

Student Life *Campus security:* 24-hour emergency response devices and patrols, late-night transport/escort service, controlled dormitory access, patrols by trained security personnel from 12:30 a.m. to 6 a.m.

Athletics Member NJCAA.

Standardized Tests *Required:* ACT ASSET (for placement). *Recommended:* SAT I and SAT II or ACT (for placement).

Costs (2004–05) *Tuition:* state resident $1530 full-time, $51 per credit hour part-time; nonresident $1800 full-time, $60 per credit hour part-time. Full-time tuition and fees vary according to course load. Part-time tuition and fees vary according to course load. *Required fees:* $240 full-time, $8 per credit hour part-time. *Room and board:* $3620; room only: $1170.

Financial Aid Of all full-time matriculated undergraduates who enrolled, 55 Federal Work-Study jobs (averaging $1800).

Applying *Options:* common application, electronic application. *Recommended:* high school transcript.

Admissions Contact Mr. Troy Archuleta, Admissions and Recruitment Director, Western Nebraska Community College, 371 College Drive, Sidney, NE 69162. *Phone:* 308-635-6015. *Toll-free phone:* 800-222-9682 (in-state); 800-348-4435 (out-of-state). *Fax:* 308-635-6100. *E-mail:* rhovey@wncc.net.

NEVADA

THE ART INSTITUTE OF LAS VEGAS
Henderson, Nevada

- **Proprietary** primarily 2-year, founded 2002
- **Calendar** quarters
- **Degrees** certificates, diplomas, associate, and bachelor's
- **Coed,** 678 undergraduate students, 95% full-time, 50% women, 50% men

Undergraduates 646 full-time, 32 part-time. 0.6% African American, 0.7% Asian American or Pacific Islander, 2% Hispanic American.

Freshmen *Admission:* 678 admitted, 172 enrolled.

Faculty *Total:* 45, 24% full-time. *Student/faculty ratio:* 21:1.

Costs (2004–05) *Tuition:* $16,464 full-time, $343 per credit part-time.

Admissions Contact Suzanne Noel, Director of Admissions, The Art Institute of Las Vegas, 2350 Corporate Circle Drive, Henderson, NV 89074. *Phone:* 702-369-9944 Ext. 8459.

CAREER COLLEGE OF NORTHERN NEVADA
Reno, Nevada

- **Proprietary** 2-year, founded 1984
- **Calendar** quarters six-week terms
- **Degree** diplomas and associate
- **Urban** 1-acre campus
- **Coed,** 389 undergraduate students, 100% full-time, 69% women, 31% men

Undergraduates 389 full-time. Students come from 2 states and territories, 5% are from out of state, 8% African American, 1% Asian American or Pacific Islander, 10% Hispanic American, 2% Native American, 3% international.

Freshmen *Admission:* 499 applied, 499 admitted.

Faculty *Total:* 19, 74% full-time, 11% with terminal degrees. *Student/faculty ratio:* 20:1.

Majors Business administration and management; computer and information sciences; data processing and data processing technology; electrical, electronic and communications engineering technology; management information systems; medical/clinical assistant.

Academic Programs *Special study options:* academic remediation for entering students, accelerated degree program, cooperative education, double majors, internships, summer session for credit.

Library 380 titles, 7 serial subscriptions.

Computers on Campus 120 computers available on campus for general student use. A campuswide network can be accessed. Internet access, at least one staffed computer lab available.

Student Life *Housing:* college housing not available. *Activities and Organizations:* student-run newspaper. *Campus security:* 24-hour emergency response devices.

Costs (2004–05) *Tuition:* $5580 full-time, $155 per credit hour part-time. *Required fees:* $150 full-time.

Financial Aid Of all full-time matriculated undergraduates who enrolled, 6 Federal Work-Study jobs (averaging $3000).

Applying *Application fee:* $25. *Required:* essay or personal statement, high school transcript, interview. *Application deadline:* rolling (freshmen), rolling (transfers). *Notification:* continuous (freshmen), continuous (transfers).

Admissions Contact Ms. Laura Goldhammer, Director of Admissions, Career College of Northern Nevada, 1195-A Corporate Boulevard, Reno, NV 89502. *Phone:* 775-856-2266 Ext. 11. *Fax:* 775-856-0935. *E-mail:* lgoldhammer@ccnn4u.com.

COMMUNITY COLLEGE OF SOUTHERN NEVADA
North Las Vegas, Nevada

Admissions Contact Mr. Arlie J. Stops, Associate Vice President for Admissions and Records, Community College of Southern Nevada, 3200 East Cheyenne Avenue, North Las Vegas, NV 89030-4296. *Phone:* 702-651-4060. *Toll-free phone:* 800-492-5728. *Fax:* 702-643-1474. *E-mail:* stops@ccsn.nevada.edu.

GREAT BASIN COLLEGE
Elko, Nevada

- **State-supported** primarily 2-year, founded 1967, part of University and Community College System of Nevada
- **Calendar** semesters
- **Degrees** certificates, associate, bachelor's, and first professional certificates
- **Small-town** 45-acre campus
- **Endowment** $150,000
- **Coed,** 2,731 undergraduate students, 100% full-time, 69% women, 31% men

Undergraduates 2,731 full-time. 0.7% African American, 1% Asian American or Pacific Islander, 9% Hispanic American, 4% Native American.

Faculty *Total:* 225, 24% full-time. *Student/faculty ratio:* 12:1.

Majors Anthropology; art; business administration and management; business/commerce; chemistry; criminal justice/safety; data processing and data processing technology; diesel mechanics technology; electrical, electronic and communications engineering technology; elementary education; English; environmental studies; geology/earth science; history; industrial technology; interdisciplinary studies; kindergarten/preschool education; mathematics; nursing (registered nurse training); office management; operations management; physics; psychology; sociology; welding technology.

Academic Programs *Special study options:* academic remediation for entering students, adult/continuing education programs, cooperative education, distance learning, English as a second language, external degree program, independent study, part-time degree program, services for LD students, summer session for credit.

Great Basin College (continued)

Library Learning Resources Center with 27,521 titles, 250 serial subscriptions, an OPAC.

Computers on Campus 95 computers available on campus for general student use. A campuswide network can be accessed from off campus. Internet access, online (class) registration, at least one staffed computer lab available.

Student Life *Housing Options:* Campus housing is university owned. *Activities and Organizations:* drama/theater group, choral group. *Campus security:* evening patrols by trained security personnel. *Student services:* personal/psychological counseling.

Athletics *Intramural sports:* badminton M/W, basketball M/W, volleyball M/W, weight lifting M/W.

Standardized Tests *Recommended:* SAT I or ACT (for placement).

Costs (2004–05) *Tuition:* $49 per credit part-time. Part-time tuition and fees vary according to course load. *Payment plans:* tuition prepayment, deferred payment. *Waivers:* senior citizens and employees or children of employees.

Financial Aid Of all full-time matriculated undergraduates who enrolled, 35 Federal Work-Study jobs (averaging $1000).

Applying *Options:* common application, electronic application, early admission, deferred entrance. *Application fee:* $5. *Required:* high school transcript. *Application deadline:* rolling (freshmen), rolling (transfers). *Notification:* continuous (freshmen), continuous (transfers).

Admissions Contact Ms. Julie Byrnes, Director of Enrollment Management, Great Basin College, 1500 College Parkway, Elko, NV 89801-3348. *Phone:* 775-753-2271. *Fax:* 775-753-2311. *E-mail:* stdsvc@gbcnv.edu.

HERITAGE COLLEGE
Las Vegas, Nevada

Admissions Contact 3305 Spring Mountain Road, Suite 7, Las Vegas, NV 89102.

HIGH-TECH INSTITUTE
Las Vegas, Nevada

Admissions Contact Mr. Alvin J. Hollander, Director, High-Tech Institute, 2320 South Ranch Drive, Las Vegas, NV 89102. *Phone:* 702-385-6700. *Toll-free phone:* 800-987-0110.

ITT TECHNICAL INSTITUTE
Henderson, Nevada

- **Proprietary** primarily 2-year, part of ITT Educational Services, Inc.
- **Degrees** associate and bachelor's
- **Coed**

Standardized Tests *Required:* Wonderlic aptitude test (for admission).

Costs (2003–04) *Tuition:* Total Program Cost varies depending on course of study. Consult school catalog.

Financial Aid Of all full-time matriculated undergraduates who enrolled, 6 Federal Work-Study jobs (averaging $5000).

Applying *Options:* deferred entrance. *Application fee:* $100. *Required:* high school transcript, interview. *Recommended:* letters of recommendation.

Admissions Contact Ms. Sandra Turkington, Director of Recruitment, ITT Technical Institute, 168 North Gibson Road, Henderson, NV 89014. *Phone:* 702-558-5404. *Toll-free phone:* 800-488-8459. *Fax:* 702-558-5412.

LAS VEGAS COLLEGE
Las Vegas, Nevada

- **Proprietary** 2-year, founded 1979, part of Corinthian Colleges, Inc
- **Calendar** quarters
- **Degree** diplomas and associate
- **Urban** campus
- **Coed**

Standardized Tests *Required:* CPAt (for placement).

Costs (2003–04) *Tuition:* $11,472 full-time, $239 per credit part-time. *Required fees:* $150 full-time.

Applying *Options:* common application. *Required:* high school transcript, interview.

Admissions Contact Mr. Bill Hall, Director of Admissions, Las Vegas College, 4100 West Flamingo Road, Suite 2100, Las Vegas, NV 89103-3926. *Phone:* 702-368-6200. *Toll-free phone:* 800-903-3101. *Fax:* 702-368-6464. *E-mail:* mmiloro@cci.edu.

LE CORDON BLEU COLLEGE OF CULINARY ARTS, LAS VEGAS
Las Vegas, Nevada

Admissions Contact 1451 Center Crossing Road, Las Vegas, NV 89144.

TRUCKEE MEADOWS COMMUNITY COLLEGE
Reno, Nevada

Admissions Contact Mr. Dave Harbeck, Director of Admissions and Records, Truckee Meadows Community College, Mail Station #15, 7000 Dandini Boulevard, MS RDMT 319, Reno, NV 89512-3901. *Phone:* 775-674-7623.

WESTERN NEVADA COMMUNITY COLLEGE
Carson City, Nevada

- **State-supported** 2-year, founded 1971, part of University and Community College System of Nevada
- **Calendar** semesters
- **Degree** certificates, diplomas, and associate
- **Small-town** 200-acre campus
- **Endowment** $101,000
- **Coed,** 4,714 undergraduate students, 19% full-time, 59% women, 41% men

Undergraduates 888 full-time, 3,826 part-time. 3% are from out of state.

Freshmen *Admission:* 635 applied, 635 admitted.

Faculty *Total:* 325, 23% full-time.

Majors Accounting; accounting technology and bookkeeping; administrative assistant and secretarial science; automobile/automotive mechanics technology; biology/biological sciences; business administration and management; business automation/technology/data entry; business/commerce; carpentry; child care and support services management; clinical/medical laboratory technology; computer and information sciences; computer programming; construction management; corrections; criminal justice/law enforcement administration; criminal justice/police science; drafting and design technology; electrical and power transmission installation; electrical, electronic and communications engineering technology; engineering; environmental studies; fire protection and safety technology; general studies; heating, air conditioning, ventilation and refrigeration maintenance technology; industrial technology; legal assistant/paralegal; liberal arts and sciences/liberal studies; machine tool technology; management information systems; management science; marketing/marketing management; masonry; mathematics; nursing (registered nurse training); parks, recreation and leisure facilities management; physical sciences; pipefitting and sprinkler fitting; real estate; sheet metal technology; vehicle/equipment operation; welding technology.

Academic Programs *Special study options:* academic remediation for entering students, adult/continuing education programs, advanced placement credit, cooperative education, distance learning, English as a second language, honors programs, independent study, internships, part-time degree program, services for LD students, summer session for credit.

Library Western Nevada Community College Library and Media Services plus 2 others with 35,712 titles, 199 serial subscriptions, 22,723 audiovisual materials, an OPAC, a Web page.

Computers on Campus 266 computers available on campus for general student use. A campuswide network can be accessed. Internet access, at least one staffed computer lab available.

Student Life *Housing:* college housing not available. *Activities and Organizations:* drama/theater group, choral group, Phi Theta Kappa, writers group, Infinity Society, Golf Club, Physics and Engineering Club. *Campus security:* late-night transport/escort service. *Student services:* personal/psychological counseling.

Standardized Tests *Recommended:* SAT I or ACT (for placement).

Costs (2004–05) *Tuition:* state resident $1470 full-time, $49 per credit part-time; nonresident $4692 full-time, $103 per credit part-time. *Required fees:* $120 full-time, $4 per credit part-time.

Financial Aid Of all full-time matriculated undergraduates who enrolled, 24 Federal Work-Study jobs (averaging $4500). 48 state and other part-time jobs (averaging $4500).

Applying *Options:* early admission. *Application fee:* $15. *Required for some:* high school transcript. *Application deadline:* rolling (freshmen), rolling (transfers).

Admissions Contact Mr. Dennis Hull, Interim Dean of Student Services/Registrar, Western Nevada Community College, 2201 West College Parkway, Carson City, NV 89703-7399. *Phone:* 775-445-3277. *Toll-free phone:* 800-748-5690. *Fax:* 775-887-3141. *E-mail:* wncc_aro@wncc.edu.

NEW HAMPSHIRE

Hesser College
Manchester, New Hampshire

- **Proprietary** primarily 2-year, founded 1900, part of Quest Education Corporation
- **Calendar** semesters
- **Degrees** certificates, diplomas, associate, and bachelor's (also offers a graduate law program with Massachusetts School of Law at Andover)
- **Urban** 1-acre campus with easy access to Boston
- **Coed,** 2,860 undergraduate students, 66% full-time, 67% women, 33% men

Undergraduates 1,880 full-time, 980 part-time. Students come from 12 states and territories, 3% African American, 1% Asian American or Pacific Islander, 7% Hispanic American, 0.2% Native American, 0.2% international, 50% live on campus.

Freshmen *Admission:* 1,725 applied, 1,562 admitted, 911 enrolled. *Average high school GPA:* 2.3.

Faculty *Total:* 215, 18% full-time. *Student/faculty ratio:* 18:1.

Majors Accounting; business administration and management; business and personal/financial services marketing; child care and support services management; commercial and advertising art; computer and information sciences; computer engineering technology; computer management; computer programming; computer science; computer systems analysis; corrections; criminal justice/law enforcement administration; criminal justice/police science; criminal justice/safety; human services; information science/studies; interior design; kindergarten/preschool education; legal assistant/paralegal; liberal arts and sciences/liberal studies; management information systems; marketing/marketing management; mass communication/media; medical administrative assistant and medical secretary; medical/clinical assistant; physical therapist assistant; psychology; radio and television; sales, distribution and marketing; security and loss prevention; social work; sport and fitness administration.

Academic Programs *Special study options:* accelerated degree program, adult/continuing education programs, advanced placement credit, cooperative education, double majors, internships, part-time degree program, student-designed majors, summer session for credit.

Library Kenneth W. Galeucia Memorial Library with 38,000 titles, 200 serial subscriptions, 60 audiovisual materials, an OPAC, a Web page.

Computers on Campus 60 computers available on campus for general student use. A campuswide network can be accessed from student residence rooms. Internet access, at least one staffed computer lab available.

Student Life *Housing Options:* coed. Campus housing is university owned. Freshman campus housing is guaranteed. *Activities and Organizations:* student-run radio and television station, student government, Ski Club, Amnesty International, yearbook, student ambassadors. *Campus security:* 24-hour emergency response devices and patrols, student patrols, late-night transport/escort service, controlled dormitory access. *Student services:* health clinic, personal/psychological counseling.

Athletics *Intercollegiate sports:* basketball M(s)/W(s), soccer M(s)/W(s), volleyball M(s)/W(s). *Intramural sports:* baseball M, basketball M/W, bowling M/W, skiing (downhill) M/W, softball M/W, table tennis M/W, volleyball M/W.

Standardized Tests *Recommended:* SAT I (for admission).

Costs (2003–04) *Comprehensive fee:* $17,490 includes full-time tuition ($10,290), mandatory fees ($1000), and room and board ($6200). Full-time tuition and fees vary according to program. Part-time tuition: $373 per credit. Part-time tuition and fees vary according to program. *Required fees:* $250 per term part-time. *Room and board:* college room only: $3400. *Payment plans:* tuition prepayment, installment, deferred payment. *Waivers:* children of alumni and employees or children of employees.

Financial Aid Of all full-time matriculated undergraduates who enrolled, 700 Federal Work-Study jobs (averaging $1000).

Applying *Options:* common application, electronic application, deferred entrance. *Application fee:* $10. *Required:* high school transcript, interview. *Required for some:* essay or personal statement, letters of recommendation. *Recommended:* minimum 2.0 GPA. *Application deadline:* rolling (freshmen), rolling (transfers). *Notification:* continuous (freshmen), continuous (transfers).

Admissions Contact Mr. Kevin Wilkenson, Director of Admissions, Hesser College, 3 Sundial Avenue, Manchester, NH 03103. *Phone:* 603-668-6660 Ext. 2101. *Toll-free phone:* 800-526-9231 Ext. 2110. *E-mail:* admissions@hesser.edu.

▶ See page 550 for a narrative description.

McIntosh College
Dover, New Hampshire

- **Proprietary** 2-year, founded 1896
- **Calendar** trimesters
- **Degree** certificates and associate
- **Small-town** 11-acre campus with easy access to Boston
- **Coed,** 1,386 undergraduate students, 87% full-time, 57% women, 43% men

Undergraduates 1,200 full-time, 186 part-time. Students come from 20 states and territories, 10% are from out of state, 5% African American, 0.9% Asian American or Pacific Islander, 3% Hispanic American, 0.9% Native American, 0.6% international, 4% transferred in. *Retention:* 96% of 2002 full-time freshmen returned.

Freshmen *Admission:* 1,612 applied, 1,612 admitted, 604 enrolled. *Average high school GPA:* 2.78.

Faculty *Total:* 100, 42% full-time, 3% with terminal degrees. *Student/faculty ratio:* 25:1.

Majors Accounting; administrative assistant and secretarial science; business administration and management; computer and information sciences; computer management; computer science; computer systems analysis; criminal justice/law enforcement administration; culinary arts; information science/studies; kindergarten/preschool education; legal administrative assistant/secretary; legal assistant/paralegal; medical administrative assistant and medical secretary; medical/clinical assistant; office management; sales, distribution and marketing; telecommunications; tourism and travel services management.

Academic Programs *Special study options:* accelerated degree program, adult/continuing education programs, advanced placement credit, cooperative education, double majors, internships, part-time degree program, services for LD students, summer session for credit.

Library McIntosh College Library with 11,000 titles, 130 serial subscriptions.

Computers on Campus 150 computers available on campus for general student use. Internet access, online (class) registration, at least one staffed computer lab available.

Student Life *Housing Options:* coed. Campus housing is university owned and leased by the school. *Activities and Organizations:* drama/theater group, Student Activities Committee, Drama Club, Business Club, Culture Club, Collegiate Secretaries International. *Campus security:* 24-hour emergency response devices and patrols, student patrols, controlled dormitory access. *Student services:* personal/psychological counseling.

Standardized Tests *Recommended:* SAT II: Writing Test (for placement).

Costs (2004–05) *Comprehensive fee:* $27,604 includes full-time tuition ($20,004), mandatory fees ($100), and room and board ($7500). Part-time tuition: $500 per credit.

Applying *Options:* common application, electronic application, early admission, deferred entrance. *Application fee:* $15. *Required:* high school transcript. *Recommended:* interview. *Application deadline:* rolling (freshmen). *Notification:* continuous (freshmen), continuous (transfers).

Admissions Contact Karen Arnold, Vice President of Admissions and Marketing, McIntosh College, 23 Cataract Avenue, Dover, NH 03820-3990. *Phone:* 603-742-1234. *Toll-free phone:* 800-McINTOSH. *Fax:* 603-743-0060. *E-mail:* admissions@mcintosh.dover.nh.us.

▶ See page 574 for a narrative description.

New Hampshire Community Technical College, Berlin/Laconia
Berlin, New Hampshire

- **State-supported** 2-year, founded 1966, part of New Hampshire Community Technical College System
- **Calendar** semesters
- **Degree** certificates, diplomas, and associate
- **Rural** 325-acre campus
- **Coed,** 2,080 undergraduate students, 34% full-time, 60% women, 40% men

Undergraduates 708 full-time, 1,372 part-time. Students come from 6 states and territories, 9% are from out of state, 0.1% African American, 0.2% Asian American or Pacific Islander, 0.1% Hispanic American, 0.1% Native American, 3% transferred in.

Freshmen *Admission:* 396 enrolled.

Faculty *Total:* 105, 31% full-time, 2% with terminal degrees.

Majors Accounting; administrative assistant and secretarial science; automobile/automotive mechanics technology; business administration and management; cartography; computer and information sciences; computer engineering technology; culinary arts; diesel mechanics technology; environmental studies; forestry; general studies; human services; industrial technology; kindergarten/preschool education; liberal arts and sciences/liberal studies; nursing (registered nurse training); survey technology; water quality and wastewater treatment management and recycling technology.

Academic Programs *Special study options:* academic remediation for entering students, adult/continuing education programs, advanced placement credit, distance learning, double majors, external degree program, independent study, internships, part-time degree program, services for LD students, summer session for credit.

New Hampshire Community Technical College, Berlin/Laconia (continued)

Library   Fortier Library with 10,000 titles, 160 serial subscriptions, 50 audiovisual materials, an OPAC.

Computers on Campus   65 computers available on campus for general student use. A campuswide network can be accessed from off campus. Internet access, at least one staffed computer lab available.

Student Life   *Housing:* college housing not available. *Activities and Organizations:* student-run newspaper, Student Senate. *Student services:* personal/psychological counseling, women's center.

Athletics   Member NSCAA. *Intercollegiate sports:* basketball M/W, ice hockey M/W, soccer M/W. *Intramural sports:* basketball M/W, bowling M/W, ice hockey M/W, skiing (cross-country) M/W, volleyball M/W.

Standardized Tests   *Required:* ACT ASSET (for admission).

Costs (2003–04)   *Tuition:* state resident $133 per credit part-time; nonresident $306 per credit part-time. *Required fees:* $2 per credit part-time. *Payment plans:* installment, deferred payment. *Waivers:* senior citizens and employees or children of employees.

Applying   *Application fee:* $10. *Required:* high school transcript, placement test. *Required for some:* essay or personal statement. *Application deadline:* rolling (freshmen), rolling (transfers). *Notification:* continuous (freshmen), continuous (transfers).

Admissions Contact   Ms. Martha P. Laflamme, Vice President of Student Affairs, New Hampshire Community Technical College, Berlin/Laconia, 2020 Riverside Drive, Berlin, NH 03570-3717. *Phone:* 603-752-1113 Ext. 1004. *Toll-free phone:* 800-445-4525. *Fax:* 603-752-6335. *E-mail:* berlin4u@nhctc.edu.

NEW HAMPSHIRE COMMUNITY TECHNICAL COLLEGE, MANCHESTER/STRATHAM
Manchester, New Hampshire

- **State-supported** 2-year, founded 1945, part of New Hampshire Community Technical College System
- **Calendar** semesters
- **Degree** certificates, diplomas, and associate
- **Urban** 60-acre campus with easy access to Boston
- **Coed,** 2,309 undergraduate students

Undergraduates   Students come from 5 states and territories.

Freshmen   *Admission:* 1,199 applied, 862 admitted.

Faculty   *Total:* 190, 25% full-time, 3% with terminal degrees. *Student/faculty ratio:* 14:1.

Majors   Accounting; administrative assistant and secretarial science; athletic training; automobile/automotive mechanics technology; business administration and management; child development; commercial and advertising art; community organization and advocacy; construction engineering technology; drafting and design technology; heating, air conditioning, ventilation and refrigeration maintenance technology; human services; information science/studies; kindergarten/preschool education; kinesiology and exercise science; liberal arts and sciences/liberal studies; management information systems; marketing/marketing management; mechanical design technology; medical administrative assistant and medical secretary; nursing (registered nurse training); physical therapy; welding technology.

Academic Programs   *Special study options:* academic remediation for entering students, adult/continuing education programs, advanced placement credit, cooperative education, external degree program, internships, part-time degree program, services for LD students, summer session for credit.

Library   New Hampshire Community Technical College Library plus 1 other with 15,000 titles, 200 serial subscriptions, an OPAC.

Computers on Campus   75 computers available on campus for general student use. A campuswide network can be accessed. Internet access, at least one staffed computer lab available.

Student Life   *Housing:* college housing not available. *Activities and Organizations:* Student Senate, Phi Theta Kappa, American Society of Welders, Student Nurses Association. *Campus security:* trained security personnel. *Student services:* personal/psychological counseling.

Athletics   *Intercollegiate sports:* baseball W, basketball M, skiing (downhill) M/W, soccer M/W, volleyball M/W. *Intramural sports:* basketball M/W, bowling M/W, ice hockey M, skiing (cross-country) M/W, skiing (downhill) M/W, volleyball M/W.

Standardized Tests   *Required for some:* SAT I or ACT (for placement).

Costs (2003–04)   *Tuition:* state resident $3192 full-time, $133 per credit part-time; nonresident $7344 full-time, $306 per credit part-time. *Required fees:* $72 full-time, $3 per credit part-time.

Applying   *Options:* early admission, deferred entrance. *Application fee:* $10. *Required:* high school transcript, interview. *Recommended:* letters of recom-

mendation. *Application deadline:* rolling (freshmen), rolling (transfers). *Notification:* continuous (freshmen), continuous (transfers).

Admissions Contact   Dr. Anita Kaplan, Vice President of Student and Community Services, New Hampshire Community Technical College, Manchester/Stratham, 1066 Front Street, Manchester, NH 03102-8518. *Phone:* 603-668-6706 Ext. 208.

NEW HAMPSHIRE COMMUNITY TECHNICAL COLLEGE, NASHUA/CLAREMONT
Nashua, New Hampshire

- **State-supported** 2-year, founded 1967, part of New Hampshire Community Technical College System
- **Calendar** semesters
- **Degree** certificates, diplomas, and associate
- **Urban** 66-acre campus with easy access to Boston
- **Coed**

Faculty   *Student/faculty ratio:* 9:1.

Student Life   *Campus security:* 24-hour emergency response devices.

Standardized Tests   *Required:* ACCUPLACER (for placement).

Costs (2003–04)   *Tuition:* state resident $4256 full-time; nonresident $9792 full-time. Full-time tuition and fees vary according to course load and reciprocity agreements. Part-time tuition and fees vary according to course load and reciprocity agreements. *Required fees:* $102 full-time.

Financial Aid   Of all full-time matriculated undergraduates who enrolled, 35 Federal Work-Study jobs (averaging $1000).

Applying   *Options:* deferred entrance. *Application fee:* $10. *Required:* high school transcript, interview. *Required for some:* letters of recommendation, nursing exam. *Recommended:* letters of recommendation.

Admissions Contact   Ms. Patricia Goodman, Director of Student Services, New Hampshire Community Technical College, Nashua/Claremont, 505 Amherst Street, Nashua, NH 03063. *Phone:* 603-882-6923 Ext. 1529. *Fax:* 603-882-8690. *E-mail:* nashua@nhctc.edu.

NEW HAMPSHIRE TECHNICAL INSTITUTE
Concord, New Hampshire

- **State-supported** 2-year, founded 1964, part of New Hampshire Community Technical College System
- **Calendar** semesters
- **Degree** certificates, diplomas, and associate
- **Small-town** 225-acre campus with easy access to Boston
- **Coed,** 3,650 undergraduate students, 42% full-time, 61% women, 39% men

Undergraduates   1,523 full-time, 2,127 part-time. Students come from 12 states and territories, 24 other countries, 2% are from out of state, 1% African American, 1% Asian American or Pacific Islander, 2% Hispanic American, 0.3% Native American, 23% live on campus.

Freshmen   *Admission:* 1,919 applied, 1,408 admitted. *Average high school GPA:* 2.50.

Faculty   *Total:* 146, 66% full-time, 8% with terminal degrees. *Student/faculty ratio:* 12:1.

Majors   Accounting; architectural engineering technology; business administration and management; computer and information sciences; computer engineering technology; computer programming (specific applications); computer systems networking and telecommunications; criminal justice/law enforcement administration; dental assisting; dental hygiene; diagnostic medical sonography and ultrasound technology; electrical, electronic and communications engineering technology; emergency medical technology (EMT paramedic); engineering technology; general studies; hotel/motel administration; human resources management; human services; kindergarten/preschool education; legal assistant/paralegal; liberal arts and sciences/liberal studies; marketing/marketing management; mechanical engineering/mechanical technology; mental health/rehabilitation; nursing (registered nurse training); real estate; sport and fitness administration; substance abuse/addiction counseling; teacher assistant/aide; tourism and travel services management.

Academic Programs   *Special study options:* academic remediation for entering students, adult/continuing education programs, advanced placement credit, distance learning, double majors, English as a second language, external degree program, part-time degree program, services for LD students, summer session for credit.

Library   Farnum Library plus 1 other with 32,000 titles, 500 serial subscriptions, 1,000 audiovisual materials, an OPAC, a Web page.

Computers on Campus   160 computers available on campus for general student use. Internet access, at least one staffed computer lab available.

Student Life *Housing Options:* coed. *Activities and Organizations:* drama/ theater group, Phi Theta Kappa, Student Senate, Student Nurses Association, Criminal Justice Club, Outing Club. *Campus security:* 24-hour patrols, late-night transport/escort service, controlled dormitory access. *Student services:* health clinic, personal/psychological counseling.

Athletics Member NSCAA. *Intercollegiate sports:* baseball M, basketball M/W, soccer M/W, softball W, volleyball M/W. *Intramural sports:* softball W, volleyball M/W.

Standardized Tests *Required for some:* National League of Nursing Exam. *Recommended:* SAT I or ACT (for admission).

Costs (2003–04) *Tuition:* state resident $3990 full-time, $133 per credit part-time; nonresident $9180 full-time, $306 per credit hour part-time. Full-time tuition and fees vary according to class time and program. Part-time tuition and fees vary according to class time and program. *Required fees:* $510 full-time, $15 per credit part-time. *Room and board:* $5420; room only: $3570. *Payment plan:* installment. *Waivers:* senior citizens and employees or children of employees.

Financial Aid Of all full-time matriculated undergraduates who enrolled, 150 Federal Work-Study jobs (averaging $1000).

Applying *Options:* electronic application. *Application fee:* $10. *Required:* high school transcript. *Required for some:* essay or personal statement, letters of recommendation, interview. *Recommended:* minimum 2.0 GPA. *Application deadline:* rolling (freshmen), rolling (transfers). *Notification:* continuous (freshmen), continuous (transfers).

Admissions Contact Mr. Francis P. Meyer, Director of Admissions, New Hampshire Technical Institute, 11 Institute Drive, Concord, NH 03301-7412. *Phone:* 603-271-7131. *Toll-free phone:* 800-247-0179. *Fax:* 603-271-7139. *E-mail:* nhtiadm@tec.nh.us.

NEW JERSEY

ASSUMPTION COLLEGE FOR SISTERS
Mendham, New Jersey

- **Independent Roman Catholic** 2-year, founded 1953
- **Calendar** semesters
- **Degree** certificates, diplomas, and associate
- **Rural** 112-acre campus with easy access to New York City
- **Women only,** 30 undergraduate students, 53% full-time

Undergraduates 16 full-time, 14 part-time. Students come from 6 states and territories, 2 other countries, 5% are from out of state, 17% Asian American or Pacific Islander, 6% Hispanic American, 61% international.

Freshmen *Admission:* 7 enrolled.

Faculty *Total:* 9, 22% with terminal degrees. *Student/faculty ratio:* 3:1.

Majors Liberal arts and sciences/liberal studies; theology.

Academic Programs *Special study options:* academic remediation for entering students, advanced placement credit, English as a second language, part-time degree program, services for LD students, summer session for credit.

Library Assumption College for Sisters Library with 28,400 titles, 91 serial subscriptions, 3,834 audiovisual materials.

Computers on Campus 14 computers available on campus for general student use. Internet access, at least one staffed computer lab available.

Student Life *Housing Options:* Campus housing is provided by a third party. *Activities and Organizations:* choral group. *Campus security:* 24-hour emergency response devices.

Costs (2003–04) *Tuition:* $3300 full-time, $100 per credit part-time. *Required fees:* $50 full-time.

Applying *Options:* deferred entrance. *Required:* high school transcript, 1 letter of recommendation, interview, intention of studying for Roman Catholic sisterhood. *Application deadline:* 10/15 (freshmen), rolling (transfers).

Admissions Contact Sr. Mary Theresa Wojcicki, Registrar and Academic Dean, Assumption College for Sisters, 350 Bernardsville Road, Mendham, NJ 07945-0800. *Phone:* 973-543-6528 Ext. 228. *Fax:* 973-543-1738.

ATLANTIC CAPE COMMUNITY COLLEGE
Mays Landing, New Jersey

- **County-supported** 2-year, founded 1964
- **Calendar** semesters
- **Degree** certificates, diplomas, and associate
- **Small-town** 537-acre campus with easy access to Philadelphia
- **Endowment** $576,000
- **Coed,** 6,177 undergraduate students

Undergraduates Students come from 3 states and territories, 1% are from out of state.

Freshmen *Admission:* 2,072 admitted.

Faculty *Total:* 308. *Student/faculty ratio:* 24:1.

Majors Accounting; biology/biological sciences; business administration and management; chemistry; child development; computer and information sciences and support services related; computer and information systems security; computer programming; corrections; criminal justice/police science; culinary arts; data entry/microcomputer applications; demography and population; education; fine/studio arts; foodservice systems administration; general studies; health services/allied health/health sciences; history; hospitality administration; humanities; legal assistant/paralegal; liberal arts and sciences/liberal studies; literature; mathematics; nursing (registered nurse training); physical therapist assistant; psychology; respiratory care therapy; social sciences; social work; sociology; visual and performing arts; web/multimedia management and webmaster.

Academic Programs *Special study options:* academic remediation for entering students, adult/continuing education programs, advanced placement credit, cooperative education, distance learning, double majors, English as a second language, independent study, internships, part-time degree program, services for LD students, summer session for credit.

Library William Spangler Library with 78,000 titles, 300 serial subscriptions, 1,000 audiovisual materials, an OPAC, a Web page.

Computers on Campus 350 computers available on campus for general student use. A campuswide network can be accessed from off campus. At least one staffed computer lab available.

Student Life *Housing:* college housing not available. *Activities and Organizations:* drama/theater group, student-run newspaper, radio station, Culinary Student Association, Phi Theta Kappa, History/Government Club, Student Nurses Club, Occupational Therapy Club. *Campus security:* 24-hour emergency response devices and patrols. *Student services:* personal/psychological counseling.

Athletics Member NJCAA. *Intercollegiate sports:* archery M/W, basketball M. *Intramural sports:* baseball M/W, cheerleading M/W, cross-country running M/W, football M/W, soccer M/W, softball M/W, table tennis M/W, volleyball M/W.

Standardized Tests *Recommended:* SAT I (for placement), ACCUPLACER.

Costs (2004–05) *Tuition:* area resident $2195 full-time, $73 per credit part-time; state resident $4390 full-time, $146 per credit part-time; nonresident $7680 full-time, $256 per credit part-time. Full-time tuition and fees vary according to program. Part-time tuition and fees vary according to program. *Required fees:* $420 full-time, $14 per credit part-time. *Payment plans:* installment, deferred payment. *Waivers:* senior citizens and employees or children of employees.

Financial Aid Of all full-time matriculated undergraduates who enrolled, 90 Federal Work-Study jobs (averaging $2000). 1,800 state and other part-time jobs (averaging $1500).

Applying *Options:* common application, electronic application, early admission, deferred entrance. *Application fee:* $35. *Recommended:* high school transcript. *Application deadlines:* 7/1 (freshmen), 7/1 (transfers).

Admissions Contact Mrs. Linda McLeod, Assistant Director of Admissions and College Recruiter, Atlantic Cape Community College, Mays Landing, NJ 08330-2699. *Phone:* 609-343-5000 Ext. 5009. *Fax:* 609-343-4921. *E-mail:* accadmit@atlantic.edu.

▶ See page 508 for a narrative description.

BERGEN COMMUNITY COLLEGE
Paramus, New Jersey

- **County-supported** 2-year, founded 1965
- **Calendar** semesters
- **Degree** certificates and associate
- **Suburban** 167-acre campus with easy access to New York City
- **Coed,** 13,991 undergraduate students, 49% full-time, 56% women, 44% men

Bergen Community College offers 3 types of degree programs in more than 70 fields of study and 1-year certificate programs. Students can earn an AA, AS, or AAS degree. Programs for international students and services for students with learning disabilities are available.

Undergraduates 6,907 full-time, 7,084 part-time. Students come from 120 other countries, 6% African American, 10% Asian American or Pacific Islander, 23% Hispanic American, 0.2% Native American, 8% international.

Freshmen *Admission:* 5,198 applied, 4,406 admitted, 2,554 enrolled.

Faculty *Total:* 705, 40% full-time, 20% with terminal degrees. *Student/faculty ratio:* 22:1.

Majors Accounting; administrative assistant and secretarial science; art; automobile/automotive mechanics technology; biology/biological sciences; broadcast journalism; business administration and management; chemistry; clinical/medical laboratory technology; commercial and advertising art; computer engineering technology; computer programming; computer science; computer typography and composition equipment operation; consumer merchandising/retailing management; criminal justice/law enforcement administration; dance;

New Jersey

Bergen Community College (continued)

dental hygiene; drafting and design technology; dramatic/theatre arts; economics; education; electrical, electronic and communications engineering technology; engineering science; finance; health science; history; hotel/motel administration; industrial radiologic technology; industrial technology; kindergarten/ preschool education; kinesiology and exercise science; legal administrative assistant/secretary; legal assistant/paralegal; liberal arts and sciences/liberal studies; literature; mass communication/media; mathematics; medical administrative assistant and medical secretary; medical/clinical assistant; music; nursing (registered nurse training); ornamental horticulture; parks, recreation and leisure; philosophy; photography; physics; political science and government; psychology; real estate; respiratory care therapy; sociology; special products marketing; tourism and travel services management; veterinary technology; women's studies.

Academic Programs *Special study options:* academic remediation for entering students, adult/continuing education programs, cooperative education, distance learning, English as a second language, honors programs, internships, part-time degree program, services for LD students, study abroad, summer session for credit.

Library Sidney Silverman Library and Learning Resources Center plus 1 other with 142,746 titles, 846 serial subscriptions, an OPAC.

Computers on Campus 225 computers available on campus for general student use. At least one staffed computer lab available.

Student Life *Housing:* college housing not available. *Activities and Organizations:* drama/theater group, student-run newspaper, choral group. *Campus security:* 24-hour patrols. *Student services:* health clinic, personal/psychological counseling.

Athletics Member NJCAA. *Intercollegiate sports:* baseball M, basketball M, cross-country running M/W, soccer M, softball W, track and field M/W, volleyball W, wrestling M. *Intramural sports:* basketball M, tennis M, volleyball M/W.

Costs (2004–05) *Tuition:* area resident $1982 full-time, $83 per credit part-time; state resident $4104 full-time, $171 per credit part-time; nonresident $4344 full-time, $181 per credit part-time. *Required fees:* $403 full-time, $17 per credit part-time.

Financial Aid Of all full-time matriculated undergraduates who enrolled, 159 Federal Work-Study jobs (averaging $1575).

Applying *Application fee:* $25. *Application deadlines:* 7/31 (freshmen), 7/31 (transfers). *Notification:* continuous (freshmen), continuous (transfers).

Admissions Contact Ms. Maxine Lisboa, Director of Admissions and Recruitment, Bergen Community College, 400 Paramus Road, Paramus, NJ 07652-1595. *Phone:* 201-612-5482. *Fax:* 201-444-7036.

BERKELEY COLLEGE
West Paterson, New Jersey

- **Proprietary** primarily 2-year, founded 1931
- **Calendar** quarters
- **Degrees** certificates, associate, and bachelor's
- **Suburban** 25-acre campus with easy access to New York City
- **Coed**, 2,198 undergraduate students, 85% full-time, 77% women, 23% men

Undergraduates 1,871 full-time, 327 part-time. Students come from 8 states and territories, 25 other countries, 16% African American, 5% Asian American or Pacific Islander, 34% Hispanic American, 0.3% Native American, 2% international, 1% live on campus.

Faculty *Total:* 158, 39% full-time. *Student/faculty ratio:* 24:1.

Majors Accounting; business administration and management; business/ commerce; computer management; fashion merchandising; interior design; international business/trade/commerce; legal assistant/paralegal; marketing/ marketing management; system administration; web page, digital/multimedia and information resources design.

Academic Programs *Special study options:* academic remediation for entering students, adult/continuing education programs, advanced placement credit, cooperative education, distance learning, English as a second language, internships, off-campus study, part-time degree program, study abroad, summer session for credit.

Library Walter A. Brower Library with 49,584 titles, 224 serial subscriptions, 2,659 audiovisual materials, an OPAC, a Web page.

Computers on Campus 300 computers available on campus for general student use. A campuswide network can be accessed from student residence rooms and from off campus. At least one staffed computer lab available.

Student Life *Housing Options:* coed. Campus housing is university owned. *Activities and Organizations:* student-run newspaper, Student Government Association, Athletics Club, Paralegal Student Association, International Club, Fashion and Marketing Club. *Campus security:* 24-hour emergency response devices, controlled dormitory access, security patrols. *Student services:* personal/ psychological counseling.

Athletics *Intramural sports:* basketball M/W, football M/W, soccer M/W, softball M/W, volleyball M/W.

Standardized Tests *Required:* SAT I or ACT (for admission).

Costs (2004–05) *One-time required fee:* $50. *Comprehensive fee:* $25,200 includes full-time tuition ($15,900) and room and board ($9300). Part-time tuition and fees vary according to class time. *Room and board:* Room and board charges vary according to housing facility. *Payment plan:* installment. *Waivers:* employees or children of employees.

Financial Aid Of all full-time matriculated undergraduates who enrolled, 150 Federal Work-Study jobs (averaging $1200).

Applying *Options:* electronic application, deferred entrance. *Application fee:* $40. *Required:* high school transcript. *Recommended:* interview. *Application deadline:* rolling (freshmen), rolling (transfers).

Admissions Contact Mrs. Carol Covino, Director of High School Admissions, Berkeley College, 44 Rifle Camp Road, West Paterson, NJ 07424. *Phone:* 973-278-5400 Ext. 1210. *Toll-free phone:* 800-446-5400. *E-mail:* info@ berkeleycollege.edu.

▶ **See page 516 for a narrative description.**

BROOKDALE COMMUNITY COLLEGE
Lincroft, New Jersey

- **County-supported** 2-year, founded 1967, part of New Jersey Commission on Higher Education
- **Calendar** semesters plus 1 ten-week and 2 six-week summer terms
- **Degree** certificates and associate
- **Small-town** 221-acre campus with easy access to New York City
- **Coed**, 12,724 undergraduate students, 52% full-time, 57% women, 43% men

Undergraduates 6,588 full-time, 6,136 part-time. Students come from 6 states and territories, 50 other countries, 0.1% are from out of state, 12% African American, 4% Asian American or Pacific Islander, 7% Hispanic American, 0.2% Native American, 1% international, 5% transferred in. *Retention:* 66% of 2002 full-time freshmen returned.

Freshmen *Admission:* 4,081 applied, 4,081 admitted, 2,806 enrolled.

Faculty *Total:* 713, 31% full-time. *Student/faculty ratio:* 22:1.

Majors Accounting; administrative assistant and secretarial science; architecture; art; audio engineering; automobile/automotive mechanics technology; biological and physical sciences; business administration and management; chemistry; clinical/medical laboratory technology; commercial and advertising art; computer engineering technology; computer programming; criminal justice/ law enforcement administration; culinary arts; design and visual communications; desktop publishing and digital imaging design; drafting and design technology; dramatic/theatre arts; education; educational/instructional media design; electrical, electronic and communications engineering technology; engineering; English; fashion merchandising; humanities; human services; interior design; international relations and affairs; journalism; kindergarten/preschool education; legal assistant/paralegal; liberal arts and sciences/liberal studies; library science; marketing/marketing management; mass communication/media; mathematics; mechanical drafting and CAD/CADD; modern languages; multi-/ interdisciplinary studies related; music; nursing (registered nurse training); photography; physics; political science and government; psychology; public relations/image management; radio and television broadcasting technology; radiologic technology/science; respiratory care therapy; social sciences; social work; sociology; special products marketing; speech and rhetoric; telecommunications; visual and performing arts.

Academic Programs *Special study options:* academic remediation for entering students, adult/continuing education programs, advanced placement credit, cooperative education, distance learning, English as a second language, honors programs, independent study, internships, part-time degree program, services for LD students, study abroad, summer session for credit. *ROTC:* Army (c), Air Force (c).

Library Brookdale Community College Library with 150,000 titles, 709 serial subscriptions, 33,000 audiovisual materials, an OPAC.

Computers on Campus 1100 computers available on campus for general student use. A campuswide network can be accessed from off campus. Internet access, online (class) registration, at least one staffed computer lab available.

Student Life *Housing:* college housing not available. *Activities and Organizations:* drama/theater group, student-run newspaper, radio station, Circle K, SAGE, Outdoor Club. *Campus security:* 24-hour emergency response devices and patrols. *Student services:* personal/psychological counseling, women's center.

Athletics Member NJCAA. *Intercollegiate sports:* baseball M, basketball M/W, cross-country running M/W, golf M, soccer M/W, softball W, tennis M/W. *Intramural sports:* basketball M/W, volleyball M/W.

Standardized Tests *Required for some:* ACCUPLACER.

Costs (2003–04) *Tuition:* area resident $2010 full-time, $84 per credit part-time; state resident $4020 full-time, $168 per credit part-time; nonresident $5400 full-time, $225 per credit part-time. Full-time tuition and fees vary according to course load. *Required fees:* $422 full-time, $18 per credit part-time. *Payment plans:* installment, deferred payment. *Waivers:* senior citizens and employees or children of employees.

Applying *Options:* early admission, deferred entrance. *Application fee:* $25. *Required:* high school transcript. *Application deadline:* rolling (freshmen), rolling (transfers). *Notification:* continuous (freshmen), continuous (transfers).

Admissions Contact Ms. Kim Heuser-Schuck, Registrar, Brookdale Community College, 765 Newman Springs Road, Lincroft, NJ 07738. *Phone:* 732-224-2268. *Fax:* 732-576-1643.

BURLINGTON COUNTY COLLEGE
Pemberton, New Jersey

- **County-supported** 2-year, founded 1966, part of New Jersey Commission on Higher Education
- **Calendar** semesters plus 2 summer terms
- **Degree** certificates and associate
- **Suburban** 225-acre campus with easy access to Philadelphia
- **Coed,** 7,519 undergraduate students, 45% full-time, 58% women, 42% men

Undergraduates 3,411 full-time, 4,108 part-time. Students come from 7 states and territories, 1% are from out of state, 22% African American, 4% Asian American or Pacific Islander, 5% Hispanic American, 0.4% Native American.

Freshmen *Admission:* 2,442 applied, 2,442 admitted, 1,498 enrolled.

Faculty *Total:* 423, 16% full-time. *Student/faculty ratio:* 27:1.

Majors Accounting; American Sign Language (ASL); art; automobile/automotive mechanics technology; biological and physical sciences; biology/biological sciences; biotechnology; business administration and management; chemical engineering; chemical technology; chemistry; civil engineering technology; commercial and advertising art; communications technology; computer graphics; computer science; drafting and design technology; dramatic/theatre arts; education; electrical, electronic and communications engineering technology; engineering; English; environmental studies; fashion/apparel design; fire science; foodservice systems administration; graphic and printing equipment operation/production; health information/medical records technology; history; hotel/motel administration; human services; information technology; journalism; legal assistant/paralegal; liberal arts and sciences/liberal studies; management information systems; mathematics; medical radiologic technology; music; nursing (registered nurse training); philosophy; physics; political science and government; psychology; sales, distribution and marketing; sign language interpretation and translation; sociology; special products marketing; survey technology.

Academic Programs *Special study options:* academic remediation for entering students, adult/continuing education programs, advanced placement credit, cooperative education, distance learning, double majors, English as a second language, honors programs, independent study, internships, part-time degree program, services for LD students, summer session for credit.

Library Burlington County College Library plus 1 other with 92,400 titles, 1,750 serial subscriptions, 11,600 audiovisual materials, an OPAC, a Web page.

Computers on Campus 500 computers available on campus for general student use. A campuswide network can be accessed from off campus. Internet access, at least one staffed computer lab available.

Student Life *Housing:* college housing not available. *Activities and Organizations:* drama/theater group, student-run radio station, Student Government Association, Phi Theta Kappa, Creative Writing Guild. *Campus security:* 24-hour emergency response devices and patrols, late-night transport/escort service, electronic entrances to buildings and rooms, surveillance cameras. *Student services:* health clinic, personal/psychological counseling.

Athletics Member NJCAA. *Intercollegiate sports:* baseball M, basketball M/W, golf M, soccer M/W, softball W.

Standardized Tests *Required:* New Jersey Basic Skills Exam (for placement).

Costs (2003–04) *Tuition:* area resident $1692 full-time, $65 per credit part-time; state resident $2400 full-time, $80 per credit part-time; nonresident $4350 full-time, $145 per credit part-time. Part-time tuition and fees vary according to course load. *Required fees:* $375 full-time, $13 per credit part-time. *Payment plans:* installment, deferred payment. *Waivers:* senior citizens and employees or children of employees.

Financial Aid Of all full-time matriculated undergraduates who enrolled, 100 Federal Work-Study jobs (averaging $1200). 100 state and other part-time jobs (averaging $2000).

Applying *Options:* common application, electronic application, early admission, deferred entrance. *Application fee:* $20. *Required:* high school transcript. *Application deadline:* rolling (freshmen), rolling (transfers). *Notification:* continuous (freshmen), continuous (transfers).

Admissions Contact Ms. Elva DeJesus-Lopez, Admissions Coordinator, Burlington County College, 601 Pemberton-Browns Mills Road, Pemberton, NJ 08068-1599. *Phone:* 609-894-9311 Ext. 7282.

CAMDEN COUNTY COLLEGE
Blackwood, New Jersey

- **State and locally supported** 2-year, founded 1967, part of New Jersey Commission on Higher Education

- **Calendar** semesters
- **Degree** certificates and associate
- **Suburban** 320-acre campus with easy access to Philadelphia
- **Coed,** 14,829 undergraduate students

New Jersey's largest community college enrolls nearly 15,000 students in more than 130 degree and certificate programs at locations in Blackwood, Camden, and Cherry Hill. In addition to credit programs in allied health, business, education, liberal arts and sciences, and technology, the College offers cultural programming, customized training, and professional and personal development courses.

Undergraduates Students come from 2 states and territories, 21 other countries, 4% are from out of state, 21% African American, 5% Asian American or Pacific Islander, 7% Hispanic American, 0.3% Native American.

Freshmen *Admission:* 9,472 applied, 9,472 admitted.

Faculty *Total:* 738, 18% full-time.

Majors Accounting; administrative assistant and secretarial science; animal sciences; applied art; art; artificial intelligence and robotics; automobile/automotive mechanics technology; business administration and management; clinical/medical laboratory technology; computer and information sciences related; computer engineering technology; computer graphics; computer/information technology services administration related; computer programming; computer programming related; computer programming (specific applications); computer typography and composition equipment operation; criminal justice/law enforcement administration; data entry/microcomputer applications; data entry/microcomputer applications related; data processing and data processing technology; dental hygiene; dietetics; dramatic/theatre arts; electrical, electronic and communications engineering technology; engineering science; environmental studies; finance; fire science; foods, nutrition, and wellness; forestry; gerontology; human services; information technology; kindergarten/preschool education; kinesiology and exercise science; laser and optical technology; liberal arts and sciences/liberal studies; marketing/marketing management; mass communication/media; mechanical engineering/mechanical technology; medical laboratory technology; medical radiologic technology; nursing (registered nurse training); occupational safety and health technology; parks, recreation and leisure; real estate; respiratory care therapy; special products marketing; system administration; web/multimedia management and webmaster; web page, digital/multimedia and information resources design; word processing.

Academic Programs *Special study options:* academic remediation for entering students, adult/continuing education programs, cooperative education, distance learning, double majors, English as a second language, external degree program, freshman honors college, honors programs, independent study, internships, off-campus study, part-time degree program, services for LD students, study abroad, summer session for credit.

Library Learning Resource Center with 91,366 titles, 449 serial subscriptions, 2,038 audiovisual materials, an OPAC.

Computers on Campus 700 computers available on campus for general student use. A campuswide network can be accessed. Internet access, at least one staffed computer lab available.

Student Life *Housing:* college housing not available. *Activities and Organizations:* drama/theater group, student-run radio station, choral group, Phi Theta Kappa, Circle K, Laser Club, Math Club, Chess Club. *Campus security:* 24-hour emergency response devices.

Athletics Member NJCAA. *Intercollegiate sports:* baseball M, basketball M/W, soccer M/W, softball W. *Intramural sports:* baseball M, basketball M/W, soccer M/W, softball W.

Costs (2003–04) *Tuition:* area resident $1980 full-time, $66 per credit part-time; state resident $2100 full-time, $70 per credit part-time; nonresident $2100 full-time, $70 per credit part-time. *Required fees:* $330 full-time, $11 per credit part-time.

Financial Aid Of all full-time matriculated undergraduates who enrolled, 117 Federal Work-Study jobs (averaging $1126).

Applying *Options:* common application, early admission. *Required for some:* high school transcript. *Application deadline:* rolling (freshmen), rolling (transfers).

Admissions Contact Jacqueline Baldwin, Enrollment Services, Camden County College, P.O. Box 200, College Drive, Blackwood, NJ 08012-0200. *Phone:* 856-227-7200 Ext. 4200. *Toll-free phone:* 888-228-2466. *Fax:* 856-374-4917.

COUNTY COLLEGE OF MORRIS
Randolph, New Jersey

- **County-supported** 2-year, founded 1966, part of New Jersey Commission on Higher Education
- **Calendar** semesters
- **Degree** certificates and associate
- **Suburban** 218-acre campus with easy access to New York City
- **Endowment** $1.3 million
- **Coed,** 8,496 undergraduate students

County College of Morris (continued)

Undergraduates Students come from 4 states and territories, 0.3% are from out of state, 4% African American, 7% Asian American or Pacific Islander, 11% Hispanic American, 0.4% Native American.

Freshmen *Test scores:* SAT verbal scores over 500: 34%; SAT math scores over 500: 39%; SAT verbal scores over 600: 6%; SAT math scores over 600: 6%; SAT verbal scores over 700: 1%; SAT math scores over 700: 1%.

Faculty *Total:* 497, 35% full-time. *Student/faculty ratio:* 17:1.

Majors Administrative assistant and secretarial science; agricultural business and management; airline pilot and flight crew; applied art; biology/biotechnology laboratory technician; business administration and management; chemical technology; clinical/medical laboratory technology; commercial and advertising art; criminal justice/police science; educational/instructional media design; electrical, electronic and communications engineering technology; engineering science; engineering technology; hotel/motel administration; interdisciplinary studies; kindergarten/preschool education; kinesiology and exercise science; liberal arts and sciences/liberal studies; management information systems; mechanical engineering/mechanical technology; nursing (registered nurse training); parks, recreation and leisure facilities management; photographic and film/video technology; public administration; radio and television broadcasting technology; respiratory care therapy; veterinary/animal health technology.

Academic Programs *Special study options:* academic remediation for entering students, adult/continuing education programs, advanced placement credit, cooperative education, distance learning, English as a second language, honors programs, internships, part-time degree program, services for LD students, summer session for credit.

Library Matsen Learning Resource Center with 102,550 titles, 819 serial subscriptions, an OPAC, a Web page.

Computers on Campus 51 computers available on campus for general student use. A campuswide network can be accessed from off campus. Internet access, online (class) registration, at least one staffed computer lab available.

Student Life *Housing:* college housing not available. *Activities and Organizations:* drama/theater group, student-run newspaper, radio station, choral group, Student Government Association, Student Activities Programming Board, Black Student Union, United Latino Organization, student newspaper. *Campus security:* 24-hour emergency response devices and patrols, late-night transport/escort service. *Student services:* health clinic, personal/psychological counseling, women's center.

Athletics Member NJCAA. *Intercollegiate sports:* baseball M(s), basketball M(s)/W(s), golf M/W, ice hockey M(s), soccer M, softball W(s), tennis M/W. *Intramural sports:* badminton M/W, basketball M/W, football M, soccer W, softball W, tennis M/W, volleyball M/W, weight lifting M/W, wrestling M/W.

Standardized Tests *Required:* New Jersey Basic Skills Exam (for placement). *Required for some:* SAT I or ACT (for placement).

Costs (2004–05) *Tuition:* $82 per credit hour part-time; state resident $164 per credit hour part-time; nonresident $229 per credit hour part-time. *Required fees:* $13 per credit hour part-time. *Waivers:* senior citizens and employees or children of employees.

Financial Aid Of all full-time matriculated undergraduates who enrolled, 848 Federal Work-Study jobs (averaging $1947).

Applying *Options:* common application, early admission. *Application fee:* $25. *Required:* high school transcript. *Required for some:* letters of recommendation. *Notification:* continuous (freshmen), continuous (transfers).

Admissions Contact Ms. Jessica Chambers, Director of Admissions, County College of Morris, 214 Center Grove Road, Randolph, NJ 07869-2086. *Phone:* 973-328-5100. *Toll-free phone:* 888-226-8001. *Fax:* 973-328-1282. *E-mail:* admiss@ccm.edu.

CUMBERLAND COUNTY COLLEGE
Vineland, New Jersey

- **State and locally supported** 2-year, founded 1963, part of New Jersey Commission on Higher Education
- **Calendar** semesters
- **Degree** certificates and associate
- **Small-town** 100-acre campus with easy access to Philadelphia
- **Coed,** 3,112 undergraduate students

Undergraduates Students come from 1 other state, 18% African American, 2% Asian American or Pacific Islander, 16% Hispanic American, 1% Native American. *Retention:* 64% of 2002 full-time freshmen returned.

Freshmen *Admission:* 1,111 applied, 1,111 admitted.

Faculty *Total:* 202, 21% full-time, 7% with terminal degrees. *Student/faculty ratio:* 19:1.

Majors Accounting; administrative assistant and secretarial science; agricultural business and management; agriculture; artificial intelligence and robotics; avionics maintenance technology; biological and physical sciences; broadcast journalism; business administration and management; cinematography and film/video production; community organization and advocacy; computer science;

computer systems networking and telecommunications; computer typography and composition equipment operation; corrections; criminal justice/police science; drafting and design technology; dramatic/theatre arts; education; elementary and middle school administration/principalship; engineering; fine/studio arts; horticultural science; hospitality and recreation marketing; human resources management; industrial radiologic technology; industrial technology; information science/studies; kindergarten/preschool education; legal administrative assistant/secretary; liberal arts and sciences/liberal studies; marketing/marketing management; mathematics; nursing (registered nurse training); ornamental horticulture; plastics engineering technology; pre-engineering; social work; system administration.

Academic Programs *Special study options:* academic remediation for entering students, adult/continuing education programs, advanced placement credit, cooperative education, distance learning, double majors, English as a second language, honors programs, part-time degree program, services for LD students, summer session for credit.

Library Cumberland County College Library with 51,000 titles, 213 serial subscriptions, 480 audiovisual materials, an OPAC, a Web page.

Computers on Campus 275 computers available on campus for general student use. A campuswide network can be accessed from off campus. Internet access, at least one staffed computer lab available.

Student Life *Housing:* college housing not available. *Activities and Organizations:* drama/theater group, student-run newspaper, choral group, Student Activities Board, Student Senate. *Campus security:* 24-hour emergency response devices, late-night transport/escort service. *Student services:* personal/psychological counseling.

Athletics Member NJCAA. *Intercollegiate sports:* baseball M, basketball M/W, softball W, track and field M. *Intramural sports:* fencing M/W, soccer M.

Costs (2004–05) *Tuition:* area resident $1776 full-time, $74 per credit part-time; state resident $3552 full-time, $148 per credit part-time; nonresident $7104 full-time, $296 per credit part-time. *Required fees:* $456 full-time, $19 per credit part-time. *Waivers:* employees or children of employees.

Financial Aid Of all full-time matriculated undergraduates who enrolled, 100 Federal Work-Study jobs (averaging $500). 100 state and other part-time jobs (averaging $600).

Applying *Options:* electronic application, early admission, deferred entrance. *Application fee:* $25. *Required:* high school transcript. *Application deadline:* rolling (freshmen), rolling (transfers). *Notification:* continuous (freshmen), continuous (transfers).

Admissions Contact Ms. Maud Fried-Goodnight, Executive Director of Enrollment Services, Cumberland County College, College Drive, Vineland, NJ 08362-1500. *Phone:* 856-691-8600 Ext. 228.

ESSEX COUNTY COLLEGE
Newark, New Jersey

- **County-supported** 2-year, founded 1966, part of New Jersey Commission on Higher Education
- **Calendar** semesters
- **Degree** certificates and associate
- **Urban** 22-acre campus with easy access to New York City
- **Coed,** 9,274 undergraduate students, 52% full-time, 65% women, 35% men

Undergraduates 4,840 full-time, 4,434 part-time. Students come from 10 states and territories, 88 other countries, 49% African American, 4% Asian American or Pacific Islander, 17% Hispanic American, 0.2% Native American, 8% international, 3% transferred in. *Retention:* 57% of 2002 full-time freshmen returned.

Freshmen *Admission:* 4,477 applied, 2,537 admitted, 1,810 enrolled.

Faculty *Total:* 473, 33% full-time. *Student/faculty ratio:* 28:1.

Majors Accounting; accounting technology and bookkeeping; administrative assistant and secretarial science; architectural engineering technology; art; biology/biological sciences; business administration and management; business teacher education; chemical technology; chemistry; civil engineering technology; communications technology; computer programming; computer programming (specific applications); computer science; criminal justice/law enforcement administration; criminal justice/police science; data processing and data processing technology; dental assisting; dental hygiene; education; electrical, electronic and communications engineering technology; elementary education; emergency medical technology (EMT paramedic); engineering; engineering technology; fire science; health/health care administration; health professions related; hotel/motel administration; human services; industrial production technologies related; information science/studies; kindergarten/preschool education; legal assistant/paralegal; legal professions and studies related; liberal arts and sciences/liberal studies; mathematics; medical administrative assistant and medical secretary; medical radiologic technology; music; nursing (registered nurse training); opticianry; physical education teaching and coaching; physical therapist assistant; physical therapy; pre-engineering; respiratory care therapy; secondary education; social sciences; social work.

Academic Programs *Special study options:* academic remediation for entering students, accelerated degree program, adult/continuing education programs,

advanced placement credit, cooperative education, distance learning, double majors, English as a second language, independent study, internships, off-campus study, part-time degree program, services for LD students, summer session for credit. *ROTC:* Army (c).

Library Martin Luther King, Jr. Library with 91,000 titles, 639 serial subscriptions, 3,618 audiovisual materials, an OPAC, a Web page.

Computers on Campus 450 computers available on campus for general student use. A campuswide network can be accessed from off campus. Internet access, at least one staffed computer lab available.

Student Life *Housing:* college housing not available. *Activities and Organizations:* drama/theater group, student-run newspaper, choral group, Fashion Entertainment Board, Phi Theta Kappa, Latin Student Union, DECA, Black Student Association. *Campus security:* 24-hour emergency response devices and patrols. *Student services:* health clinic, personal/psychological counseling, women's center.

Athletics Member NJCAA. *Intercollegiate sports:* basketball M(s)/W(s), cross-country running M(s)/W(s), soccer M, track and field M/W. *Intramural sports:* table tennis M, weight lifting M.

Standardized Tests *Required:* ACCUPLACER (for placement).

Costs (2003–04) *Tuition:* area resident $2318 full-time, $77 per credit hour part-time; state resident $4635 full-time, $155 per credit hour part-time. *Required fees:* $600 full-time, $20 per credit hour part-time.

Financial Aid Of all full-time matriculated undergraduates who enrolled, 250 Federal Work-Study jobs (averaging $2880).

Applying *Options:* deferred entrance. *Application fee:* $25. *Required:* high school transcript. *Application deadline:* 8/15 (freshmen), rolling (transfers). *Notification:* continuous (freshmen), continuous (transfers).

Admissions Contact Ms. Marva Mack, Director of Admissions, Essex County College, 303 University Avenue, Newark, NJ 07102. *Phone:* 973-877-3119. *Fax:* 973-623-6449.

GIBBS COLLEGE
Montclair, New Jersey

Admissions Contact Mrs. Mary-Jo Greco, President, Gibbs College, 33 Plymouth Street, Montclair, NJ 07042-2699. *Phone:* 201-744-2010.

GLOUCESTER COUNTY COLLEGE
Sewell, New Jersey

- **County-supported** 2-year, founded 1967, part of New Jersey Commission on Higher Education
- **Calendar** semesters
- **Degree** certificates and associate
- **Rural** 270-acre campus with easy access to Philadelphia
- **Coed,** 5,610 undergraduate students, 53% full-time, 60% women, 40% men

Undergraduates 2,950 full-time, 2,660 part-time. 9% African American, 2% Asian American or Pacific Islander, 2% Hispanic American, 0.4% Native American, 0.6% international.

Freshmen *Admission:* 2,219 applied, 2,219 admitted, 1,702 enrolled.

Faculty *Total:* 226, 26% full-time. *Student/faculty ratio:* 33:1.

Majors Accounting; accounting technology and bookkeeping; automobile/automotive mechanics technology; biology/biological sciences; business administration and management; chemical engineering; chemistry; civil engineering technology; communication/speech communication and rhetoric; computer graphics; computer science; consumer merchandising/retailing management; criminal justice/police science; data processing and data processing technology; diagnostic medical sonography and ultrasound technology; drafting and design technology; dramatic/theatre arts; education; engineering science; English; environmental engineering technology; finance; fine/studio arts; health and physical education; history; hospitality and recreation marketing; human development and family studies; information science/studies; kinesiology and exercise science; legal administrative assistant/secretary; legal assistant/paralegal; legal studies; liberal arts and sciences/liberal studies; marketing/marketing management; mathematics; medical administrative assistant and medical secretary; nuclear medical technology; nursing (registered nurse training); political science and government; psychology; respiratory care therapy; social sciences; sociology.

Academic Programs *Special study options:* academic remediation for entering students, advanced placement credit, cooperative education, distance learning, part-time degree program, services for LD students, summer session for credit.

Library Gloucester County College Library with 55,710 titles, 875 serial subscriptions, 13,407 audiovisual materials, an OPAC.

Computers on Campus 120 computers available on campus for general student use. A campuswide network can be accessed. Internet access, online (class) registration, at least one staffed computer lab available.

Student Life *Housing:* college housing not available. *Activities and Organizations:* drama/theater group, student-run newspaper, radio station, choral group,

Student Activities Board, student government, Accounting Club, Student Nurses Club, student newspaper. *Campus security:* 24-hour emergency response devices and patrols, late-night transport/escort service. *Student services:* health clinic, personal/psychological counseling, women's center.

Athletics Member NJCAA. *Intercollegiate sports:* baseball M, basketball M/W, cross-country running M/W, soccer M/W, softball W, tennis M/W, track and field M/W, wrestling M. *Intramural sports:* volleyball M/W.

Standardized Tests *Required for some:* SAT I or ACT (for admission).

Costs (2003–04) *Tuition:* $68 per credit part-time; state resident $69 per credit part-time; nonresident $260 per credit part-time. *Required fees:* $18 per credit part-time. *Waivers:* senior citizens and employees or children of employees.

Financial Aid Of all full-time matriculated undergraduates who enrolled, 25 Federal Work-Study jobs (averaging $1000). *Financial aid deadline:* 6/1.

Applying *Options:* electronic application, deferred entrance. *Application fee:* $10. *Required:* high school transcript. *Application deadline:* rolling (freshmen), rolling (transfers).

Admissions Contact Ms. Carol L. Lange, Admissions and Recruitment Coordinator, Gloucester County College, 1400 Tanyard Road, Sewell, NJ 08080. *Phone:* 856-468-5000. *Fax:* 856-468-8498. *E-mail:* hsimmons@gccnj.edu.

HUDSON COUNTY COMMUNITY COLLEGE
Jersey City, New Jersey

- **State and locally supported** 2-year, founded 1974, part of New Jersey Commission on Higher Education
- **Calendar** semesters
- **Degree** certificates, diplomas, and associate
- **Urban** campus with easy access to New York City
- **Endowment** $10,000
- **Coed,** 6,087 undergraduate students, 66% full-time, 66% women, 34% men

Undergraduates 4,028 full-time, 2,059 part-time. 19% African American, 15% Asian American or Pacific Islander, 41% Hispanic American, 0.1% Native American, 1% international.

Freshmen *Admission:* 1,705 applied, 1,705 admitted, 1,705 enrolled.

Faculty *Total:* 374, 23% full-time.

Majors Accounting; business administration and management; child development; computer engineering technology; computer science; criminal justice/safety; culinary arts; data processing and data processing technology; electrical, electronic and communications engineering technology; engineering science; health information/medical records technology; human services; legal assistant/paralegal; liberal arts and sciences/liberal studies; medical/clinical assistant; nursing (registered nurse training).

Academic Programs *Special study options:* academic remediation for entering students, adult/continuing education programs, advanced placement credit, distance learning, double majors, English as a second language, independent study, internships, part-time degree program, services for LD students, summer session for credit.

Library Hudson County Community College Library/Learning Resources Center with 17,000 titles, 251 serial subscriptions, 500 audiovisual materials.

Computers on Campus 367 computers available on campus for general student use. At least one staffed computer lab available.

Student Life *Housing:* college housing not available. *Activities and Organizations:* drama/theater group, student-run newspaper, choral group, Psychology Club, Hispanos Unidos Pura El Progreso, International Student Organization, Drama Society. *Campus security:* 24-hour emergency response devices. *Student services:* personal/psychological counseling.

Standardized Tests *Required:* ACCUPLACER (for placement).

Costs (2003–04) *Tuition:* area resident $2070 full-time; state resident $4140 full-time; nonresident $6210 full-time. *Required fees:* $888 full-time. *Payment plans:* installment, deferred payment.

Financial Aid Of all full-time matriculated undergraduates who enrolled, 102 Federal Work-Study jobs (averaging $3000).

Applying *Application fee:* $15. *Required:* high school transcript. *Application deadlines:* 9/1 (freshmen), 9/1 (transfers). *Notification:* continuous until 9/1 (freshmen), continuous until 9/1 (transfers).

Admissions Contact Mr. Robert Martin, Director of Admissions, Hudson County Community College, 162 Sip Avenue, Jersey City, NJ 07306. *Phone:* 201-714-2115. *Fax:* 201-714-2136. *E-mail:* rmartin@mail.hccc.edu.

MERCER COUNTY COMMUNITY COLLEGE
Trenton, New Jersey

Admissions Contact Mercer County Community College, 1200 Old Trenton Road, PO Box B, Trenton, NJ 08690-1004. *Phone:* 609-586-4800 Ext. 3209. *Toll-free phone:* 800-392-MCCC. *Fax:* 609-586-6944. *E-mail:* admiss@mccc.edu.

MIDDLESEX COUNTY COLLEGE
Edison, New Jersey

- **County-supported** 2-year, founded 1964
- **Calendar** semesters
- **Degree** certificates and associate
- **Suburban** 200-acre campus with easy access to New York City
- **Coed,** 11,276 undergraduate students

Undergraduates Students come from 4 states and territories.
Freshmen *Admission:* 9,394 applied, 6,481 admitted.
Faculty *Total:* 552, 37% full-time. *Student/faculty ratio:* 21:1.
Majors Accounting; administrative assistant and secretarial science; advertising; applied art; art; automobile/automotive mechanics technology; biological and physical sciences; biology/biological sciences; biology/biotechnology laboratory technician; business administration and management; chemistry; child development; civil engineering technology; clinical/medical laboratory technology; commercial and advertising art; computer engineering technology; computer graphics; computer programming; computer science; computer systems networking and telecommunications; construction engineering technology; consumer merchandising/retailing management; corrections; criminal justice/law enforcement administration; criminal justice/police science; culinary arts; dance; dental hygiene; dietetics; drafting and design technology; dramatic/theatre arts; education; electrical, electronic and communications engineering technology; engineering; engineering science; engineering technology; English; fashion/apparel design; fashion merchandising; fine/studio arts; fire science; general studies; history; hospitality administration; hotel/motel administration; information science/studies; journalism; kindergarten/preschool education; legal administrative assistant/secretary; legal assistant/paralegal; marketing/marketing management; mathematics; mechanical engineering/mechanical technology; modern languages; music; nursing (registered nurse training); photography; physical education teaching and coaching; physical sciences; physics; political science and government; psychology; radiologic technology/science; respiratory care therapy; social sciences; sociology; survey technology; teacher assistant/aide.
Academic Programs *Special study options:* academic remediation for entering students, adult/continuing education programs, advanced placement credit, cooperative education, distance learning, English as a second language, independent study, internships, off-campus study, part-time degree program, services for LD students, study abroad, summer session for credit. *ROTC:* Army (c).
Library Middlesex County College Library plus 1 other with 85,160 titles, 599 serial subscriptions, 5,642 audiovisual materials, an OPAC, a Web page.
Computers on Campus 1290 computers available on campus for general student use. A campuswide network can be accessed from off campus. Internet access, at least one staffed computer lab available.
Student Life *Housing:* college housing not available. *Activities and Organizations:* drama/theater group, student-run newspaper, radio station, choral group. *Campus security:* 24-hour emergency response devices and patrols. *Student services:* health clinic, personal/psychological counseling.
Athletics Member NJCAA. *Intercollegiate sports:* baseball M, basketball M(s)/W(s), cross-country running M/W(s), field hockey W, golf M/W, soccer M/W, softball W, tennis M/W, track and field M/W, wrestling M. *Intramural sports:* cheerleading M/W.
Standardized Tests *Required for some:* National League of Nursing Exam for most health-related programs.
Costs (2004–05) *Tuition:* area resident $1764 full-time, $74 per credit part-time; state resident $3528 full-time, $147 per credit part-time. Full-time tuition and fees vary according to course load. Part-time tuition and fees vary according to course load. *Required fees:* $420 full-time, $18 per credit part-time. *Payment plan:* installment. *Waivers:* senior citizens and employees or children of employees.
Financial Aid Of all full-time matriculated undergraduates who enrolled, 69 Federal Work-Study jobs (averaging $3350).
Applying *Options:* early admission, deferred entrance. *Application fee:* $25. *Required:* high school transcript. *Application deadline:* rolling (freshmen), rolling (transfers). *Notification:* continuous (freshmen), continuous (transfers).
Admissions Contact Mr. Peter W. Rice, Director of Admissions and Recruitment, Middlesex County College, 2600 Woodbridge Avenue, PO Box 3050, Edison, NJ 08818-3050. *Phone:* 732-906-4243. *Fax:* 732-906-7728. *E-mail:* admissions@middlesexcc.edu.

▶ See page 578 for a narrative description.

OCEAN COUNTY COLLEGE
Toms River, New Jersey

- **County-supported** 2-year, founded 1964, part of New Jersey Commission on Higher Education
- **Calendar** semesters
- **Degree** certificates, diplomas, and associate
- **Small-town** 275-acre campus with easy access to Philadelphia
- **Coed,** 8,436 undergraduate students, 49% full-time, 61% women, 39% men

Undergraduates 4,098 full-time, 4,338 part-time. Students come from 6 other countries, 4% African American, 3% Asian American or Pacific Islander, 6% Hispanic American, 0.3% Native American.
Faculty *Total:* 371, 32% full-time.
Majors Accounting; administrative assistant and secretarial science; business administration and management; business/commerce; child care and support services management; civil engineering technology; clinical/medical laboratory technology; commercial and advertising art; communications technology; computer and information sciences; computer programming; construction engineering technology; criminal justice/police science; electrical, electronic and communications engineering technology; engineering; fire protection and safety technology; general studies; health science; information science/studies; journalism; legal assistant/paralegal; liberal arts and sciences/liberal studies; medical/clinical assistant; nursing (registered nurse training); real estate; social work; teacher assistant/aide.
Academic Programs *Special study options:* academic remediation for entering students, accelerated degree program, adult/continuing education programs, advanced placement credit, cooperative education, distance learning, English as a second language, freshman honors college, honors programs, part-time degree program, services for LD students, study abroad, summer session for credit.
Library Ocean County College Library with 74,215 titles, 428 serial subscriptions.
Computers on Campus 100 computers available on campus for general student use. Internet access, at least one staffed computer lab available.
Student Life *Housing:* college housing not available. *Activities and Organizations:* drama/theater group, student-run newspaper, radio station, choral group. *Campus security:* 24-hour emergency response devices and patrols, late-night transport/escort service. *Student services:* health clinic, personal/psychological counseling.
Athletics Member NJCAA. *Intercollegiate sports:* baseball M, basketball M/W, golf M/W, soccer M/W, softball W, swimming M/W, tennis M/W. *Intramural sports:* basketball M/W, cross-country running M, tennis M/W, volleyball M/W.
Costs (2004–05) *Tuition:* area resident $2310 full-time, $77 per credit part-time; state resident $3159 full-time, $105 per credit part-time; nonresident $5190 full-time, $173 per credit part-time. *Required fees:* $40 full-time, $20 per term part-time.
Financial Aid Of all full-time matriculated undergraduates who enrolled, 76 Federal Work-Study jobs (averaging $1300). 45 state and other part-time jobs (averaging $850).
Applying *Options:* early admission, deferred entrance. *Application fee:* $15. *Required for some:* high school transcript, minimum 3.0 GPA. *Application deadline:* rolling (freshmen), rolling (transfers). *Notification:* continuous (freshmen), continuous (transfers).
Admissions Contact Mr. Carey Trevisan, Director of Admissions and Records, Ocean County College, College Drive, PO Box 2001, Toms River, NJ 08754-2001. *Phone:* 732-255-0304 Ext. 2016.

PASSAIC COUNTY COMMUNITY COLLEGE
Paterson, New Jersey

- **County-supported** 2-year, founded 1968
- **Calendar** semesters
- **Degree** certificates and associate
- **Urban** 6-acre campus with easy access to New York City
- **Endowment** $78,695
- **Coed**

Student Life *Campus security:* late-night transport/escort service.
Athletics Member NJCAA.
Standardized Tests *Required:* New Jersey Basic Skills Exam (for placement).
Costs (2003–04) *Tuition:* state resident $2025 full-time; nonresident $4050 full-time. *Required fees:* $420 full-time.
Financial Aid Of all full-time matriculated undergraduates who enrolled, 100 Federal Work-Study jobs (averaging $3000).
Applying *Options:* early admission, deferred entrance.

Admissions Contact Mr. Patrick Noonan, Director of Admissions, Passaic County Community College, One College Boulevard, Patterson, NJ 07505. *Phone:* 973-684-6304.

RARITAN VALLEY COMMUNITY COLLEGE
Somerville, New Jersey

- **County-supported** 2-year, founded 1965
- **Calendar** semesters
- **Degree** certificates and associate
- **Small-town** 225-acre campus with easy access to New York City and Philadelphia
- **Coed,** 6,470 undergraduate students, 39% full-time, 59% women, 41% men

Undergraduates 2,521 full-time, 3,949 part-time. 0.5% are from out of state, 9% African American, 6% Asian American or Pacific Islander, 7% Hispanic American, 0.2% Native American, 7% international. *Retention:* 66% of 2002 full-time freshmen returned.

Freshmen *Admission:* 2,300 applied, 2,300 admitted, 1,049 enrolled.

Faculty *Total:* 394, 30% full-time, 21% with terminal degrees. *Student/faculty ratio:* 18:1.

Majors Accounting; administrative assistant and secretarial science; aeronautics/ aviation/aerospace science and technology; artificial intelligence and robotics; automobile/automotive mechanics technology; biology/biological sciences; business administration and management; chemistry; commercial and advertising art; computer programming; computer science; construction engineering technology; consumer merchandising/retailing management; criminal justice/law enforcement administration; data processing and data processing technology; diesel mechanics technology; dramatic/theatre arts; education; electrical, electronic and communications engineering technology; electromechanical technology; elementary education; engineering; environmental studies; heating, air conditioning, ventilation and refrigeration maintenance technology; hospitality and recreation marketing; hotel/motel administration; human services; industrial technology; information science/studies; intermedia/multimedia; international business/trade/commerce; kindergarten/preschool education; legal assistant/ paralegal; liberal arts and sciences/liberal studies; management information systems; marketing/marketing management; mathematics; mechanical design technology; music; nursing (registered nurse training); ophthalmic laboratory technology; real estate; respiratory care therapy; social sciences; tourism and travel services management; visual and performing arts.

Academic Programs *Special study options:* academic remediation for entering students, adult/continuing education programs, advanced placement credit, cooperative education, distance learning, English as a second language, honors programs, independent study, internships, off-campus study, part-time degree program, services for LD students, summer session for credit. *ROTC:* Army (c), Air Force (c).

Library Evelyn S. Field Learning Resources Center with 84,150 titles, 325 serial subscriptions.

Computers on Campus 715 computers available on campus for general student use. A campuswide network can be accessed from off campus that provide access to library services, degree audits, grades, class schedules. Internet access, online (class) registration, at least one staffed computer lab available.

Student Life *Housing:* college housing not available. *Activities and Organizations:* drama/theater group, student-run newspaper, radio station, choral group, International Club, The Latin Pride Club, Student Nurses Association, The Record (student newspaper), Christian Fellowship Club. *Campus security:* 24-hour emergency response devices and patrols, 24-hour outdoor surveillance cameras. *Student services:* health clinic, personal/psychological counseling.

Athletics Member NJCAA. *Intercollegiate sports:* baseball M, basketball M, softball W. *Intramural sports:* golf M/W.

Costs (2003–04) *Tuition:* state resident $1980 full-time, $68 per credit part-time; nonresident $68 per credit part-time. *Required fees:* $530 full-time. *Waivers:* senior citizens and employees or children of employees.

Financial Aid Of all full-time matriculated undergraduates who enrolled, 12 Federal Work-Study jobs (averaging $1000).

Applying *Options:* electronic application, early admission. *Application fee:* $25. *Required:* high school transcript. *Application deadline:* rolling (freshmen), rolling (transfers).

Admissions Contact Mr. Steven Smith, Executive Director, Enrollment Services, Raritan Valley Community College, PO Box 3300, Somerville, NJ 08876-1265. *Phone:* 908-526-1200 Ext. 8217. *Fax:* 908-704-3442.

SALEM COMMUNITY COLLEGE
Carneys Point, New Jersey

- **County-supported** 2-year, founded 1972, part of New Jersey Commission on Higher Education

- **Calendar** semesters
- **Degree** certificates and associate
- **Small-town** campus with easy access to Philadelphia
- **Coed,** 1,150 undergraduate students, 18% full-time, 15% women, 11% men

Undergraduates 207 full-time, 94 part-time. Students come from 6 states and territories, 7% are from out of state, 19% African American, 1% Asian American or Pacific Islander, 4% Hispanic American, 1% Native American, 11% transferred in.

Freshmen *Admission:* 301 enrolled.

Faculty *Total:* 78, 33% full-time, 4% with terminal degrees.

Majors Accounting; biological and physical sciences; biology/biological sciences; business administration and management; chemistry; computer and information sciences; computer systems networking and telecommunications; criminal justice/law enforcement administration; early childhood education; education; English; family and community services; health and physical education; history; humanities; human resources management; journalism; kinesiology and exercise science; liberal arts and sciences/liberal studies; management information systems; marketing/marketing management; mathematics; physics; political science and government; pre-engineering; psychology; public administration; social sciences; sociology; web/multimedia management and webmaster.

Academic Programs *Special study options:* academic remediation for entering students, adult/continuing education programs, advanced placement credit, cooperative education, distance learning, double majors, English as a second language, independent study, off-campus study, part-time degree program, services for LD students, summer session for credit.

Library Michael S. Cettei Memorial Library with 28,951 titles, 240 serial subscriptions, an OPAC.

Computers on Campus 200 computers available on campus for general student use. A campuswide network can be accessed from off campus. Internet access, online (class) registration, at least one staffed computer lab available.

Student Life *Housing:* college housing not available. *Activities and Organizations:* drama/theater group, choral group, Drama Club, Science Club, Multicultural Exchange Club. *Campus security:* 24-hour emergency response devices and patrols, late-night transport/escort service. *Student services:* personal/ psychological counseling, women's center.

Athletics Member NJCAA. *Intercollegiate sports:* baseball M(s), basketball M(s)/W(s), softball W(s), tennis M(s)/W(s).

Standardized Tests *Required:* New Jersey Basic Skills Exam (for placement).

Costs (2003–04) *Tuition:* area resident $2175 full-time, $73 per credit part-time; state resident $2460 full-time, $82 per credit part-time; nonresident $2460 full-time, $82 per credit part-time. Full-time tuition and fees vary according to course load. Part-time tuition and fees vary according to course load. *Required fees:* $800 full-time, $25 per credit part-time, $25 per term part-time. *Payment plans:* installment, deferred payment. *Waivers:* senior citizens and employees or children of employees.

Financial Aid Of all full-time matriculated undergraduates who enrolled, 63 Federal Work-Study jobs (averaging $1000).

Applying *Options:* early admission, deferred entrance. *Application fee:* $25. *Required:* essay or personal statement, high school transcript. *Application deadline:* rolling (freshmen), rolling (transfers). *Notification:* continuous (freshmen), continuous (transfers).

Admissions Contact Salem Community College, 460 Hollywood Avenue, Carney's Point, NJ 08069. *Phone:* 856-351-2698. *Fax:* 856-299-9193. *E-mail:* info@salemcc.edu.

SOMERSET CHRISTIAN COLLEGE
Zarephath, New Jersey

- **Independent religious** 2-year, founded 1908
- **Calendar** semesters plus "FastTrack" semesters
- **Degree** associate
- **Coed**

Faculty *Student/faculty ratio:* 10:1.

Standardized Tests *Required for some:* SAT I or ACT (for admission).

Costs (2003–04) *Tuition:* $3840 full-time, $160 per credit part-time. *Required fees:* $120 full-time, $160 per credit part-time, $60 per semester part-time.

Financial Aid *Financial aid deadline:* 8/1.

Applying *Options:* electronic application, deferred entrance. *Application fee:* $20. *Required:* essay or personal statement, letters of recommendation. *Required for some:* high school transcript, minimum 2.5 GPA, interview.

Admissions Contact Ms. Cheryl L. Burdick, Dean of Enrollment Management, Somerset Christian College, 10 Liberty Square, Zarephath, NJ 08890. *Phone:* 732-356-1595 Ext. 106. *Toll-free phone:* 800-234-9305. *Fax:* 732-356-4846. *E-mail:* info@somerset.edu.

New Jersey

SUSSEX COUNTY COMMUNITY COLLEGE
Newton, New Jersey

- **State and locally supported** 2-year, founded 1981, part of New Jersey Commission on Higher Education
- **Calendar** semesters
- **Degree** certificates and associate
- **Small-town** 160-acre campus with easy access to New York City
- **Endowment** $349,969
- **Coed,** 2,924 undergraduate students, 46% full-time, 61% women, 39% men

Undergraduates 1,331 full-time, 1,593 part-time. Students come from 3 states and territories, 11% are from out of state, 2% African American, 0.9% Asian American or Pacific Islander, 4% Hispanic American, 0.6% international, 6% transferred in. *Retention:* 62% of 2002 full-time freshmen returned.
Freshmen *Admission:* 467 applied, 467 admitted, 467 enrolled.
Faculty *Total:* 188, 20% full-time, 19% with terminal degrees. *Student/faculty ratio:* 21:1.
Majors Accounting; administrative assistant and secretarial science; automotive engineering technology; biological and physical sciences; broadcast journalism; business administration and management; commercial and advertising art; computer and information sciences; consumer merchandising/retailing management; corrections and criminal justice related; English; environmental studies; fine/studio arts; fire protection related; health science; human services; journalism; legal assistant/paralegal; liberal arts and sciences/liberal studies; respiratory care therapy; veterinary/animal health technology.
Academic Programs *Special study options:* academic remediation for entering students, advanced placement credit, distance learning, double majors, English as a second language, internships, part-time degree program, services for LD students, summer session for credit.
Library Sussex County Community College Library with 34,346 titles, 266 serial subscriptions, 602 audiovisual materials, an OPAC, a Web page.
Computers on Campus 302 computers available on campus for general student use. A campuswide network can be accessed. Internet access, online (class) registration, at least one staffed computer lab available.
Student Life *Housing:* college housing not available. *Activities and Organizations:* drama/theater group, student-run newspaper, choral group, Student Government Association, "The College Hill" (newspaper), Human Services Club, Arts Club, Returning Adult Support Group. *Campus security:* late-night transport/escort service, trained security personnel. *Student services:* personal/psychological counseling, women's center.
Athletics Member NJCAA. *Intercollegiate sports:* baseball M, basketball M, soccer M/W, softball W. *Intramural sports:* football M/W, volleyball M/W.
Costs (2004–05) *Tuition:* area resident $2100 full-time, $70 per credit part-time; state resident $4200 full-time, $140 per credit part-time; nonresident $140 per credit part-time. Full-time tuition and fees vary according to course load and degree level. *Required fees:* $474 full-time, $9 per credit part-time, $15 per term part-time. *Payment plan:* installment. *Waivers:* senior citizens and employees or children of employees.
Financial Aid Of all full-time matriculated undergraduates who enrolled, 29 Federal Work-Study jobs (averaging $1500).
Applying *Application fee:* $15. *Required:* high school transcript. *Application deadline:* rolling (freshmen), rolling (transfers). *Notification:* continuous (freshmen), continuous (transfers).
Admissions Contact Mr. James J. Donohue, Director of Admissions and Registrar, Sussex County Community College, 1 College Hill, Newton, NJ 07860. *Phone:* 973-300-2219. *E-mail:* hdamato@sussex.cc.nj.us.

UNION COUNTY COLLEGE
Cranford, New Jersey

- **State and locally supported** 2-year, founded 1933, part of New Jersey Commission on Higher Education
- **Calendar** semesters
- **Degree** certificates, diplomas, and associate
- **Suburban** 48-acre campus with easy access to New York City
- **Coed,** 10,399 undergraduate students, 52% full-time, 66% women, 34% men

Undergraduates 5,430 full-time, 4,969 part-time. Students come from 8 states and territories, 82 other countries, 2% are from out of state, 24% African American, 5% Asian American or Pacific Islander, 24% Hispanic American, 0.2% Native American, 3% international, 7% transferred in. *Retention:* 77% of 2002 full-time freshmen returned.
Freshmen *Admission:* 5,999 applied, 5,952 admitted, 2,155 enrolled.
Faculty *Total:* 438, 42% full-time. *Student/faculty ratio:* 26:1.
Majors Accounting technology and bookkeeping; administrative assistant and secretarial science; allied health diagnostic, intervention, and treatment professions related; biology/biological sciences; business administration and management; business and personal/financial services marketing; business/commerce; chemistry; civil engineering technology; clinical/medical laboratory technology;

communication/speech communication and rhetoric; criminal justice/police science; dental hygiene; electromechanical technology; engineering; fire protection and safety technology; gerontology; hotel/motel administration; industrial technology; information science/studies; language interpretation and translation; liberal arts and sciences/liberal studies; management information systems; mechanical engineering/mechanical technology; medical/clinical assistant; medical radiologic technology; nuclear medical technology; nursing (licensed practical/vocational nurse training); nursing (registered nurse training); occupational therapist assistant; physical sciences; physical therapist assistant; rehabilitation and therapeutic professions related; respiratory care therapy; sign language interpretation and translation.
Academic Programs *Special study options:* academic remediation for entering students, accelerated degree program, adult/continuing education programs, advanced placement credit, distance learning, English as a second language, honors programs, internships, off-campus study, part-time degree program, services for LD students, student-designed majors, summer session for credit. *ROTC:* Air Force (c).
Library MacKay Library plus 2 others with 132,050 titles, 2,259 serial subscriptions, 2,259 audiovisual materials, an OPAC, a Web page.
Computers on Campus 750 computers available on campus for general student use. A campuswide network can be accessed from off campus. Internet access, at least one staffed computer lab available.
Student Life *Housing:* college housing not available. *Activities and Organizations:* drama/theater group, student-run newspaper, radio and television station, SIGN, Spanish Club, Black Students Heritage Organization, Student Government Organization, International Cultural Exchange Students. *Campus security:* 24-hour emergency response devices and patrols, late-night transport/escort service. *Student services:* personal/psychological counseling.
Athletics Member NJCAA. *Intercollegiate sports:* baseball M, basketball M/W(s), golf M/W, soccer M. *Intramural sports:* cheerleading W, rock climbing W, tennis M/W, volleyball W.
Standardized Tests *Required for some:* SAT I (for placement). *Recommended:* SAT I (for placement).
Costs (2003–04) *Tuition:* area resident $1752 full-time, $73 per credit part-time; state resident $3504 full-time, $146 per credit part-time; nonresident $146 per credit part-time. Full-time tuition and fees vary according to course load and program. Part-time tuition and fees vary according to course load and program. *Required fees:* $491 full-time, $20 per credit part-time. *Payment plan:* deferred payment. *Waivers:* senior citizens and employees or children of employees.
Financial Aid Of all full-time matriculated undergraduates who enrolled, 150 Federal Work-Study jobs (averaging $1700).
Applying *Options:* early admission, deferred entrance. *Application fee:* $25. *Required:* high school transcript. *Required for some:* interview. *Application deadline:* rolling (freshmen), rolling (transfers). *Notification:* continuous (freshmen), continuous (transfers).
Admissions Contact Ms. Jo Ann Davis, Director of Admissions, Records, and Registration, Union County College, 1033 Springfield Avenue, Cranford, NJ 07016. *Phone:* 908-709-7127. *Toll-free phone:* 908-309-7596. *Fax:* 908-709-7125.

WARREN COUNTY COMMUNITY COLLEGE
Washington, New Jersey

- **State and locally supported** 2-year, founded 1981, part of New Jersey Commission on Higher Education
- **Calendar** semesters
- **Degree** certificates and associate
- **Rural** 77-acre campus
- **Coed**

Faculty *Student/faculty ratio:* 13:1.
Student Life *Campus security:* evening and weekend security.
Standardized Tests *Required:* New Jersey Basic Skills Exam (for placement).
Financial Aid Of all full-time matriculated undergraduates who enrolled, 20 Federal Work-Study jobs (averaging $2000).
Applying *Options:* early admission, deferred entrance. *Application fee:* $15.
Admissions Contact Admissions Advisor, Warren County Community College, 475 Route 57 West, Washington, NJ 07882-9605. *Phone:* 908-835-2300. *Fax:* 908-689-5824.

NEW MEXICO

ALBUQUERQUE TECHNICAL VOCATIONAL INSTITUTE
Albuquerque, New Mexico

- **State-supported** 2-year, founded 1965
- **Calendar** trimesters
- **Degree** certificates and associate
- **Urban** 60-acre campus
- **Coed,** 22,077 undergraduate students, 30% full-time, 59% women, 41% men

Undergraduates 6,591 full-time, 15,486 part-time. 1% are from out of state, 3% African American, 2% Asian American or Pacific Islander, 41% Hispanic American, 8% Native American, 5% transferred in. *Retention:* 51% of 2002 full-time freshmen returned.
Freshmen *Admission:* 4,989 applied, 4,989 admitted, 2,632 enrolled.
Faculty *Total:* 1,018, 32% full-time. *Student/faculty ratio:* 21:1.
Majors Accounting; administrative assistant and secretarial science; architectural drafting and CAD/CADD; banking and financial support services; biotechnology; building/construction finishing, management, and inspection related; business administration and management; child care and support services management; clinical/medical laboratory technology; computer systems analysis; construction trades related; cosmetology; court reporting; criminal justice/safety; culinary arts; data processing and data processing technology; diagnostic medical sonography and ultrasound technology; electrical, electronic and communications engineering technology; electrical/electronics drafting and CAD/CADD; elementary education; engineering; engineering technologies related; environmental/environmental health engineering; fire protection and safety technology; health information/medical records administration; hospitality administration; industrial technology; information science/studies; laser and optical technology; legal assistant/paralegal; liberal arts and sciences/liberal studies; nursing (registered nurse training); parks, recreation, and leisure related; respiratory care therapy; vehicle maintenance and repair technologies related.
Academic Programs *Special study options:* academic remediation for entering students, adult/continuing education programs, advanced placement credit, cooperative education, distance learning, double majors, English as a second language, internships, part-time degree program, services for LD students, summer session for credit. *ROTC:* Air Force (c).
Library Main Campus Library plus 2 others with an OPAC, a Web page.
Computers on Campus A campuswide network can be accessed. Internet access, at least one staffed computer lab available.
Student Life *Housing:* college housing not available. *Activities and Organizations:* student-run newspaper, Phi Theta Kappa, student government, Hispanic Club, TVI Times (student newspaper). *Campus security:* 24-hour emergency response devices and patrols, late-night transport/escort service. *Student services:* health clinic, personal/psychological counseling.
Standardized Tests *Recommended:* SAT I or ACT (for placement).
Costs (2003–04) *Tuition:* state resident $1320 full-time, $37 per credit hour part-time; nonresident $5702 full-time, $158 per credit hour part-time. *Required fees:* $90 full-time, $30 per term part-time. *Payment plan:* deferred payment. *Waivers:* senior citizens and employees or children of employees.
Financial Aid Of all full-time matriculated undergraduates who enrolled, 145 Federal Work-Study jobs (averaging $6000). 210 state and other part-time jobs (averaging $6000).
Applying *Options:* early admission. *Recommended:* high school transcript. *Application deadline:* rolling (freshmen), rolling (transfers). *Notification:* continuous (freshmen).
Admissions Contact Ms. Jane Campbell, Director of Enrollment Services, Albuquerque Technical Vocational Institute, 900 University, SE, Albuquerque, NM 87106-4096. *Phone:* 505-224-3160. *Fax:* 505-224-4740.

THE ART CENTER DESIGN COLLEGE
Albuquerque, New Mexico

Admissions Contact Ms. Colleen Gimbel-Froebe, Associate Director of Admissions and Placement, The Art Center Design College, 5000 Marble NE, Albuquerque, NM 87110. *Phone:* 520-325-0123. *Toll-free phone:* 800-825-8753. *Fax:* 520-325-5535.

CLOVIS COMMUNITY COLLEGE
Clovis, New Mexico

- **State-supported** 2-year, founded 1990
- **Calendar** semesters
- **Degree** certificates and associate
- **Small-town** 25-acre campus
- **Endowment** $507,909
- **Coed,** 3,093 undergraduate students, 36% full-time, 67% women, 33% men

Undergraduates 1,128 full-time, 1,965 part-time. Students come from 47 states and territories, 32% are from out of state, 6% African American, 2% Asian American or Pacific Islander, 34% Hispanic American, 0.5% Native American, 6% transferred in. *Retention:* 45% of 2002 full-time freshmen returned.
Freshmen *Admission:* 252 applied, 252 admitted, 252 enrolled.
Faculty *Total:* 259, 21% full-time, 8% with terminal degrees. *Student/faculty ratio:* 15:1.
Majors Accounting; administrative assistant and secretarial science; automobile/automotive mechanics technology; bilingual and multilingual education; business administration and management; business automation/technology/data entry; carpentry; commercial and advertising art; computer and information sciences; computer typography and composition equipment operation; construction trades; corrections; cosmetology; criminal justice/police science; electrical, electronic and communications engineering technology; electromechanical technology; executive assistant/executive secretary; finance; fine/studio arts; health and physical education; heating, air conditioning, ventilation and refrigeration maintenance technology; legal administrative assistant/secretary; legal assistant/paralegal; liberal arts and sciences/liberal studies; library assistant; management information systems; mathematics; medical administrative assistant and medical secretary; medical office assistant; medical radiologic technology; nail technician and manicurist; nursing (registered nurse training); physical sciences; psychology; sign language interpretation and translation; teacher assistant/aide; technical and business writing; web/multimedia management and webmaster; web page, digital/multimedia and information resources design.
Academic Programs *Special study options:* academic remediation for entering students, advanced placement credit, cooperative education, distance learning, double majors, English as a second language, independent study, internships, part-time degree program, services for LD students, summer session for credit.
Library Clovis Community College Library and Learning Resources Center with 52,000 titles, 370 serial subscriptions, 2,900 audiovisual materials, an OPAC.
Computers on Campus 280 computers available on campus for general student use. A campuswide network can be accessed. Internet access, at least one staffed computer lab available.
Student Life *Housing:* college housing not available. *Activities and Organizations:* Student Senate, Student Nursing Association, Black Advisory Council, Hispanic Advisory Council, student ambassadors. *Campus security:* student patrols, late-night transport/escort service. *Student services:* personal/psychological counseling.
Athletics *Intramural sports:* basketball M/W, cross-country running M/W, racquetball M/W, tennis M/W, volleyball M/W.
Standardized Tests *Required for some:* TABE, ACCUPLACER. *Recommended:* TABE, ACCUPLACER.
Costs (2004–05) *Tuition:* area resident $616 full-time, $44 per credit hour part-time; state resident $664 full-time, $46 per credit hour part-time; nonresident $1120 full-time, $46 per credit hour part-time. *Required fees:* $20 full-time, $10 per term part-time. *Payment plans:* installment, deferred payment. *Waivers:* senior citizens and employees or children of employees.
Applying *Options:* common application. *Required:* high school transcript. *Notification:* continuous (transfers).
Admissions Contact Ms. Rosie Corrie, Director of Admissions, Registrar, Clovis Community College, 417 Schepps Boulevard, Clovis, NM 88101-8381. *Phone:* 505-769-4021. *Fax:* 505-769-4190. *E-mail:* admissions@clovis.edu.

CROWNPOINT INSTITUTE OF TECHNOLOGY
Crownpoint, New Mexico

Admissions Contact PO Box 849, Crownpoint, NM 87313.

DONA ANA BRANCH COMMUNITY COLLEGE
Las Cruces, New Mexico

- **State and locally supported** 2-year, founded 1973, part of New Mexico State University System
- **Calendar** semesters
- **Degree** certificates and associate
- **Urban** 15-acre campus with easy access to Ciudad Juarez and El Paso
- **Coed,** 5,872 undergraduate students, 56% full-time, 57% women, 43% men

Undergraduates 3,290 full-time, 2,582 part-time. 2% African American, 0.9% Asian American or Pacific Islander, 61% Hispanic American, 2% Native American, 1% international, 4% transferred in. *Retention:* 90% of 2002 full-time freshmen returned.

Dona Ana Branch Community College (continued)

Freshmen *Admission:* 1,496 enrolled. *Average high school GPA:* 2.75. *Test scores:* ACT scores over 18: 36%; ACT scores over 24: 2%.

Faculty *Total:* 380, 23% full-time. *Student/faculty ratio:* 67:1.

Majors Administrative assistant and secretarial science; architectural engineering technology; automobile/automotive mechanics technology; business administration and management; computer engineering technology; computer typography and composition equipment operation; consumer merchandising/retailing management; drafting and design technology; electrical, electronic and communications engineering technology; emergency medical technology (EMT paramedic); fashion merchandising; finance; fire science; heating, air conditioning, ventilation and refrigeration maintenance technology; hospitality administration; hydrology and water resources science; industrial radiologic technology; legal assistant/paralegal; library science; nursing (registered nurse training); respiratory care therapy; welding technology.

Academic Programs *Special study options:* academic remediation for entering students, adult/continuing education programs, advanced placement credit, cooperative education, English as a second language, freshman honors college, honors programs, internships, part-time degree program, services for LD students, summer session for credit. *ROTC:* Army (c), Air Force (c).

Library Library/Media Center with 17,140 titles, 213 serial subscriptions, an OPAC.

Computers on Campus 433 computers available on campus for general student use. A campuswide network can be accessed from off campus. Internet access, online (class) registration, at least one staffed computer lab available.

Student Life *Housing Options:* coed. *Activities and Organizations:* drama/theater group, student-run newspaper, radio station, choral group, marching band. *Campus security:* 24-hour emergency response devices and patrols, late-night transport/escort service. *Student services:* health clinic, personal/psychological counseling, women's center, legal services.

Standardized Tests *Recommended:* ACT, ACT ASSET, or ACT COMPASS.

Costs (2004–05) *Tuition:* area resident $480 full-time, $42 per credit part-time; state resident $540 full-time, $55 per credit part-time; nonresident $1260 full-time, $115 per credit part-time. *Required fees:* $18 per semester part-time.

Financial Aid Of all full-time matriculated undergraduates who enrolled, 15 Federal Work-Study jobs (averaging $2800). 106 state and other part-time jobs (averaging $2800). *Financial aid deadline:* 6/30.

Applying *Options:* deferred entrance. *Application fee:* $15. *Required:* high school transcript. *Required for some:* letters of recommendation. *Application deadline:* rolling (freshmen).

Admissions Contact Admissions Counselor, Dona Ana Branch Community College, MSC-3DA, Box 30001, Las Cruces, NM 88003-8001. *Phone:* 505-527-7532. *Toll-free phone:* 800-903-7503. *Fax:* 505-527-7515.

EASTERN NEW MEXICO UNIVERSITY-ROSWELL
Roswell, New Mexico

- **State-supported** 2-year, founded 1958, part of Eastern New Mexico University System
- **Calendar** semesters
- **Degree** certificates and associate
- **Small-town** 241-acre campus
- **Endowment** $494,460
- **Coed**

Faculty *Student/faculty ratio:* 16:1.

Student Life *Campus security:* 24-hour emergency response devices, student patrols, late-night transport/escort service.

Standardized Tests *Recommended:* ACT (for admission).

Costs (2003–04) *Tuition:* area resident $794 full-time, $33 per hour part-time; state resident $826 full-time, $34 per hour part-time; nonresident $3050 full-time, $127 per hour part-time. *Required fees:* $3 full-time, $3 per hour part-time. *Room and board:* $3200.

Financial Aid Of all full-time matriculated undergraduates who enrolled, 150 Federal Work-Study jobs (averaging $4000). 60 state and other part-time jobs (averaging $4000).

Applying *Options:* common application, early admission. *Required:* high school transcript.

Admissions Contact Mr. James Mares, Assistant Director, Eastern New Mexico University-Roswell, PO Box 6000, Roswell, NM 88202-6000. *Phone:* 505-624-7149. *Toll-free phone:* 800-243-6687. *Fax:* 505-624-7144.

INSTITUTE OF AMERICAN INDIAN ARTS
Santa Fe, New Mexico

Admissions Contact Mr. Ramus Suina, Director of Admissions, Institute of American Indian Arts, 83 Avan Nu Po Road, Santa Fe, NM 87508. *Phone:* 505-424-2335. *Fax:* 505-424-3535.

INTERNATIONAL INSTITUTE OF THE AMERICAS
Albuquerque, New Mexico

- **Independent** primarily 2-year
- **Calendar** continuous
- **Degrees** certificates, diplomas, associate, and bachelor's
- **Urban** 1-acre campus
- **Coed,** 163 undergraduate students, 100% full-time, 85% women, 15% men

Undergraduates 163 full-time. 4% African American, 2% Asian American or Pacific Islander, 55% Hispanic American, 17% Native American. *Retention:* 100% of 2002 full-time freshmen returned.

Freshmen *Admission:* 270 applied, 163 admitted, 19 enrolled.

Faculty *Total:* 9, 56% full-time, 22% with terminal degrees. *Student/faculty ratio:* 10:1.

Costs (2004–05) *Tuition:* $9000 full-time. *Required fees:* $350 full-time.

Admissions Contact Mr. Scott Yelton, Campus Director, International Institute of the Americas, 4201 Central Avenue NW, Suite J, Albuquerque, NM 87105-1649. *Phone:* 505-880-2877. *Toll-free phone:* 888-660-2428.

ITT TECHNICAL INSTITUTE
Albuquerque, New Mexico

- **Proprietary** primarily 2-year, founded 1989, part of ITT Educational Services, Inc.
- **Calendar** quarters
- **Degrees** associate and bachelor's
- **Coed**

Standardized Tests *Required:* Wonderlic aptitude test (for admission).

Costs (2003–04) *Tuition:* Total Program Cost varies depending on course of study. Consult school catalog.

Applying *Options:* deferred entrance. *Application fee:* $100. *Required:* high school transcript, interview. *Recommended:* letters of recommendation.

Admissions Contact Mr. John Crooks, Director of Recruitment, ITT Technical Institute, 5100 Masthead Street NE, Albuquerque, NM 87109. *Phone:* 505-828-1114. *Toll-free phone:* 800-636-1114. *Fax:* 505-828-1849.

LUNA COMMUNITY COLLEGE
Las Vegas, New Mexico

- **State-supported** 2-year, part of New Mexico Commission on Higher Education
- **Calendar** semesters
- **Degree** certificates, diplomas, and associate
- **Rural** 25-acre campus
- **Coed,** 1,815 undergraduate students, 21% full-time, 61% women, 39% men

Undergraduates 382 full-time, 1,433 part-time.

Freshmen *Admission:* 154 applied, 154 admitted, 88 enrolled.

Faculty *Total:* 121, 27% full-time. *Student/faculty ratio:* 13:1.

Majors Accounting; administrative assistant and secretarial science; architectural drafting; business administration and management; civil/structural drafting; computer and information sciences; criminal justice/police science; early childhood education; electrical, electronic and communications engineering technology; industrial arts; manufacturing technology; nursing (licensed practical/vocational nurse training); physical therapy.

Costs (2004–05) *Tuition:* area resident $300 full-time, $25 per hour part-time; state resident $444 full-time, $37 per hour part-time; nonresident $912 full-time, $76 per term part-time. *Required fees:* $44 full-time, $22 per term part-time.

Admissions Contact Ms. Henrietta Griego, Director of Admissions, Recruitment, and Retention, Luna Community College, PO Box 1510, Las Vegas, NM 87701. *Phone:* 505-454-2020 Ext. 1202.

MESALANDS COMMUNITY COLLEGE
Tucumcari, New Mexico

- **State-supported** 2-year, founded 1979
- **Calendar** semesters
- **Degree** certificates and associate
- **Small-town** campus
- **Endowment** $16,000
- **Coed,** 563 undergraduate students

Undergraduates Students come from 10 states and territories, 5% are from out of state, 2% African American, 1% Asian American or Pacific Islander, 35% Hispanic American, 3% Native American, 2% international.
Faculty *Total:* 27, 44% full-time. *Student/faculty ratio:* 10:1.
Majors Animal sciences; automobile/automotive mechanics technology; business administration and management; communication/speech communication and rhetoric; diesel mechanics technology; elementary education; geology/earth science; history; human resources management; information science/studies; metal and jewelry arts; paleontology; public administration; social work.
Student Life *Housing:* college housing not available. *Activities and Organizations:* Student Senate, Chi Alpha, Phi Theta Kappa, SHOE, Natural Sciences Club. *Campus security:* 24-hour emergency response devices.
Standardized Tests *Required:* ACT COMPASS (for placement).
Costs (2003–04) *Tuition:* state resident $1050 full-time, $35 per credit hour part-time; nonresident $1890 full-time, $63 per credit hour part-time. *Required fees:* $284 full-time, $6 per credit hour part-time, $25 per term part-time.
Applying *Required:* high school transcript. *Application deadline:* rolling (freshmen), rolling (transfers).
Admissions Contact Mr. Ken Brashear, Director of Enrollment Management, Mesalands Community College, 911 South Tenth Street, Tucumcari, NM 88401. *Phone:* 505-461-4413.

NEW MEXICO JUNIOR COLLEGE
Hobbs, New Mexico

- **State and locally supported** 2-year, founded 1965, part of New Mexico Commission on Higher Education
- **Calendar** semesters
- **Degree** certificates and associate
- **Small-town** 185-acre campus
- **Coed**

Faculty *Student/faculty ratio:* 19:1.
Student Life *Campus security:* 24-hour emergency response devices and patrols, late-night transport/escort service, controlled dormitory access.
Athletics Member NJCAA.
Standardized Tests *Recommended:* ACT (for placement).
Applying *Options:* early admission, deferred entrance.
Admissions Contact Mr. Robert Bensing, Dean of Enrollment Management, New Mexico Junior College, 5317 Lovington Highway, Hobbs, NM 88240-9123. *Phone:* 505-392-5092. *Fax:* 505-392-0322. *E-mail:* rbensing@nmjc.cc.nm.us.

NEW MEXICO MILITARY INSTITUTE
Roswell, New Mexico

- **State-supported** 2-year, founded 1891, part of New Mexico Commission on Higher Education
- **Calendar** semesters
- **Degree** associate
- **Small-town** 42-acre campus
- **Endowment** $243.6 million
- **Coed, primarily men**

Excellence is a process achieved in stages, sustained through effort, accentuated by detail, and celebrated by all. At NMMI, excellence is a universal goal. For more than 100 years, NMMI has built a community and a world-class institute of higher learning based on shared values and disciplined behavior, which foster the highest standards of achievement in its cadets.

Faculty *Student/faculty ratio:* 18:1.
Student Life *Campus security:* 24-hour emergency response devices and patrols, controlled dormitory access.
Athletics Member NJCAA.
Standardized Tests *Required:* SAT I or ACT (for admission).
Costs (2003–04) *Tuition:* state resident $1080 full-time; nonresident $3450 full-time. *Required fees:* $1220 full-time. *Room and board:* $3345.
Financial Aid Of all full-time matriculated undergraduates who enrolled, 16 Federal Work-Study jobs (averaging $440). 2 state and other part-time jobs (averaging $250).
Applying *Options:* early admission, deferred entrance. *Application fee:* $60. *Required:* high school transcript, minimum 2.0 GPA.
Admissions Contact Lt. Col. Craig C. Collins, Director of Admissions, New Mexico Military Institute, 101 West College Boulevard, Roswell, NM 88201-5173. *Phone:* 505-624-8050. *Toll-free phone:* 800-421-5376. *Fax:* 505-624-8058. *E-mail:* admissions@nmmi.edu.

▶ See page 584 for a narrative description.

NEW MEXICO STATE UNIVERSITY-ALAMOGORDO
Alamogordo, New Mexico

Admissions Contact Ms. Maureen Scott, Coordinator of Admissions and Records, New Mexico State University-Alamogordo, 2400 North Scenic Drive, Alamogordo, NM 88311-0477. *Phone:* 505-439-3700. *E-mail:* advisor@nmsua.nmsu.edu.

NEW MEXICO STATE UNIVERSITY-CARLSBAD
Carlsbad, New Mexico

- **State-supported** 2-year, founded 1950, part of New Mexico State University System
- **Calendar** semesters
- **Degree** certificates and associate
- **Small-town** 40-acre campus
- **Coed,** 1,228 undergraduate students

Undergraduates Students come from 6 states and territories, 2 other countries, 1% African American, 0.8% Asian American or Pacific Islander, 39% Hispanic American, 1% Native American, 0.2% international.
Freshmen *Admission:* 752 admitted.
Faculty *Total:* 73, 33% full-time, 92% with terminal degrees. *Student/faculty ratio:* 23:1.
Majors Administrative assistant and secretarial science; agriculture; business administration and management; computer science; criminal justice/law enforcement administration; education; electrical, electronic and communications engineering technology; engineering technology; environmental engineering technology; fire science; industrial technology; information science/studies; legal assistant/paralegal; liberal arts and sciences/liberal studies; nursing (registered nurse training); social work; welding technology.
Academic Programs *Special study options:* academic remediation for entering students, adult/continuing education programs, advanced placement credit, cooperative education, distance learning, double majors, English as a second language, honors programs, independent study, internships, part-time degree program, services for LD students, student-designed majors, summer session for credit.
Library Library/Media Center.
Computers on Campus 300 computers available on campus for general student use. A campuswide network can be accessed. Internet access, online (class) registration, at least one staffed computer lab available.
Student Life *Housing:* college housing not available. *Activities and Organizations:* drama/theater group, Student Nurses Association, Alpha Sigma Phi (criminal justice), Phi Theta Kappa, Associated Students. *Campus security:* 24-hour emergency response devices.
Standardized Tests *Required for some:* ACT (for placement). *Recommended:* ACT (for placement).
Costs (2003–04) *Tuition:* area resident $984 full-time, $41 per credit part-time; state resident $1104 full-time, $46 per credit part-time; nonresident $2352 full-time, $98 per credit part-time. *Required fees:* $48 full-time, $1 per credit part-time. *Payment plan:* deferred payment. *Waivers:* senior citizens and employees or children of employees.
Financial Aid Of all full-time matriculated undergraduates who enrolled, 4 Federal Work-Study jobs (averaging $2800). 36 state and other part-time jobs (averaging $2300).
Applying *Options:* electronic application, early admission, deferred entrance. *Application fee:* $15. *Required:* high school transcript. *Application deadline:* rolling (freshmen), rolling (transfers). *Notification:* continuous (freshmen), continuous (transfers).
Admissions Contact Ms. Everal Shannon, Records Specialist, New Mexico State University-Carlsbad, 1500 University Drive, Carlsbad, NM 88220-3509. *Phone:* 505-234-9222. *Fax:* 505-885-4951. *E-mail:* mcleary@nmsu.edu.

NEW MEXICO STATE UNIVERSITY-GRANTS
Grants, New Mexico

- **State-supported** 2-year, founded 1968, part of New Mexico State University System
- **Calendar** semesters
- **Degree** certificates and associate
- **Small-town** campus
- **Coed,** 636 undergraduate students, 37% full-time, 71% women, 29% men

New Mexico State University-Grants (continued)

Undergraduates 233 full-time, 403 part-time. Students come from 1 other state, 0.8% African American, 0.3% Asian American or Pacific Islander, 29% Hispanic American, 41% Native American.

Freshmen *Admission:* 93 enrolled.

Faculty *Total:* 57, 21% full-time.

Majors Administrative assistant and secretarial science; business administration and management; criminal justice/law enforcement administration; data processing and data processing technology; education; electrical, electronic and communications engineering technology; legal assistant/paralegal; liberal arts and sciences/liberal studies.

Academic Programs *Special study options:* part-time degree program, summer session for credit.

Library 30,000 titles, 20 serial subscriptions.

Computers on Campus 150 computers available on campus for general student use. A campuswide network can be accessed. Internet access, at least one staffed computer lab available.

Student Life *Housing:* college housing not available.

Standardized Tests *Required:* CPT (for admission).

Financial Aid Of all full-time matriculated undergraduates who enrolled, 3 Federal Work-Study jobs (averaging $1800). 6 state and other part-time jobs (averaging $1500).

Applying *Options:* common application, early admission. *Application fee:* $15. *Required:* high school transcript. *Application deadline:* 7/30 (freshmen).

Admissions Contact Ms. Irene Charles-Lutz, Campus Student Services Officer, New Mexico State University-Grants, 1500 3rd Street, Grants, NM 87020-2025. *Phone:* 505-287-7981. *E-mail:* bmontoya@grants.nmsu.edu.

NORTHERN NEW MEXICO COMMUNITY COLLEGE

Espanola, New Mexico

- **State-supported** 2-year, founded 1909, part of New Mexico Commission on Higher Education
- **Calendar** semesters
- **Degree** certificates and associate
- **Rural** 35-acre campus
- **Endowment** $829,791
- **Coed**

Student Life *Campus security:* 24-hour emergency response devices and patrols.

Costs (2003–04) *Tuition:* state resident $672 full-time, $28 per credit part-time; nonresident $1416 full-time, $59 per credit part-time. *Required fees:* $48 full-time. *Room and board:* $2928; room only: $1200.

Financial Aid Of all full-time matriculated undergraduates who enrolled, 150 Federal Work-Study jobs (averaging $3000). 140 state and other part-time jobs (averaging $3000).

Applying *Options:* early admission, deferred entrance. *Required:* high school transcript.

Admissions Contact Mr. Mike L. Costello, Registrar, Northern New Mexico Community College, 921 Paseo de Onate, Espanola, NM 87532. *Phone:* 505-747-2193. *Fax:* 505-747-2180. *E-mail:* tina@nnm.cc.nm.us.

PIMA MEDICAL INSTITUTE

Albuquerque, New Mexico

- **Proprietary** 2-year, founded 1985, part of Vocational Training Institutes, Inc
- **Calendar** modular
- **Degree** certificates and associate
- **Urban** campus
- **Coed**

Standardized Tests *Required:* (for admission).

Financial Aid Of all full-time matriculated undergraduates who enrolled, 6 Federal Work-Study jobs.

Applying *Required:* interview. *Required for some:* high school transcript.

Admissions Contact Ms. Martha Garcia, Admissions Office, Pima Medical Institute, 2201 San Pedro NE, Building 3, Suite 100, Albuquerque, NM 87110. *Phone:* 505-881-1234 Ext. 105.

SAN JUAN COLLEGE

Farmington, New Mexico

- **State-supported** 2-year, founded 1958, part of New Mexico Commission on Higher Education
- **Calendar** semesters
- **Degree** certificates and associate
- **Small-town** 698-acre campus
- **Endowment** $8.1 million
- **Coed**, 5,114 undergraduate students, 49% full-time, 60% women, 40% men

Undergraduates 2,511 full-time, 2,603 part-time. Students come from 17 states and territories, 6% are from out of state, 0.6% African American, 0.6% Asian American or Pacific Islander, 11% Hispanic American, 31% Native American, 0.3% international.

Freshmen *Admission:* 1,395 applied, 1,395 admitted, 846 enrolled.

Faculty *Total:* 317, 29% full-time. *Student/faculty ratio:* 17:1.

Majors Accounting technology and bookkeeping; administrative assistant and secretarial science; airline pilot and flight crew; anthropology; art; autobody/collision and repair technology; automobile/automotive mechanics technology; banking and financial support services; biology/biological sciences; business administration and management; carpentry; chemistry; commercial and advertising art; communication/speech communication and rhetoric; computer science; criminal justice/police science; criminal justice/safety; diesel mechanics technology; drafting and design technology; dramatic/theatre arts; economics; education; engineering; English; fire protection and safety technology; foreign languages and literatures; general studies; geology/earth science; health information/medical records technology; history; human services; information science/studies; instrumentation technology; kindergarten/preschool education; legal assistant/paralegal; mathematics; music; nursing (registered nurse training); parks, recreation and leisure; philosophy; physical sciences; physical therapist assistant; physics; political science and government; pre-medical studies; psychology; public administration; real estate; social work; sociology; water quality and wastewater treatment management and recycling technology; welding technology.

Academic Programs *Special study options:* academic remediation for entering students, adult/continuing education programs, advanced placement credit, cooperative education, distance learning, English as a second language, honors programs, independent study, internships, part-time degree program, services for LD students, summer session for credit.

Library San Juan College Library with 81,116 titles, 6,677 serial subscriptions, 1,779 audiovisual materials, an OPAC, a Web page.

Computers on Campus A campuswide network can be accessed from off campus. Internet access, at least one staffed computer lab available.

Student Life *Housing:* college housing not available. *Activities and Organizations:* drama/theater group, student-run newspaper, radio station, choral group, national fraternities, national sororities. *Campus security:* 24-hour patrols, late-night transport/escort service. *Student services:* personal/psychological counseling.

Athletics *Intramural sports:* archery M/W, badminton M/W, basketball M/W, bowling M/W, cross-country running M/W, football M/W, golf M/W, racquetball M/W, skiing (cross-country) M/W, skiing (downhill) M/W, soccer M/W, table tennis M/W, tennis M/W, volleyball M/W.

Standardized Tests *Required:* CPT (for placement).

Costs (2003–04) *Tuition:* state resident $600 full-time, $25 per credit hour part-time; nonresident $840 full-time, $35 per credit hour part-time. Full-time tuition and fees vary according to program and reciprocity agreements. Part-time tuition and fees vary according to program. *Payment plan:* tuition prepayment. *Waivers:* senior citizens.

Financial Aid Of all full-time matriculated undergraduates who enrolled, 150 Federal Work-Study jobs (averaging $2000). 100 state and other part-time jobs (averaging $2000).

Applying *Options:* early admission, deferred entrance. *Application fee:* $10. *Required:* high school transcript. *Application deadline:* rolling (freshmen), rolling (transfers). *Notification:* continuous (freshmen), continuous (transfers).

Admissions Contact Mr. Gary Golden, Vice President for Student Services, San Juan College, 4601 College Boulevard, Farmington, NM 87402. *Phone:* 505-566-3318. *Fax:* 505-566-3500. *E-mail:* drangc@sanjuancollege.edu.

SANTA FE COMMUNITY COLLEGE

Santa Fe, New Mexico

- **State and locally supported** 2-year, founded 1983
- **Calendar** semesters
- **Degree** certificates and associate
- **Suburban** 366-acre campus
- **Coed**, 5,452 undergraduate students, 17% full-time, 63% women, 37% men

Undergraduates 915 full-time, 4,537 part-time. Students come from 50 states and territories, 6 other countries, 10% are from out of state, 1% African American, 1% Asian American or Pacific Islander, 51% Hispanic American, 5% Native American, 0.5% international, 1% transferred in. *Retention:* 47% of 2002 full-time freshmen returned.

Freshmen *Admission:* 192 enrolled.

Faculty *Total:* 303, 18% full-time, 9% with terminal degrees. *Student/faculty ratio:* 18:1.

Majors Accounting; administrative assistant and secretarial science; area studies; art; biology/biological sciences; business administration and management; computer and information sciences; computer and information sciences related; construction engineering technology; criminal justice/safety; culinary arts; dance; design and visual communications; drafting and design technology; electrical, electronic and communications engineering technology; engineering; entrepreneurship; general studies; health and physical education; hotel/motel administration; interior design; kindergarten/preschool education; legal assistant/paralegal; natural resources management; nursing (registered nurse training); parks, recreation and leisure; physical sciences; radio and television broadcasting technology; sign language interpretation and translation; social work; Spanish; survey technology; visual and performing arts related.

Academic Programs *Special study options:* academic remediation for entering students, adult/continuing education programs, advanced placement credit, cooperative education, distance learning, double majors, English as a second language, external degree program, honors programs, independent study, internships, part-time degree program, services for LD students, summer session for credit.

Library Learning Resource Center with 38,226 titles, 206 serial subscriptions, 2,010 audiovisual materials, an OPAC, a Web page.

Computers on Campus 340 computers available on campus for general student use. A campuswide network can be accessed from off campus. Internet access, online (class) registration, at least one staffed computer lab available. Computer purchase or lease plan available.

Student Life *Housing:* college housing not available. *Activities and Organizations:* student-run radio station, choral group, Student Nurses Association, Native American Student Association, Service-Learning Club, MECHA (Movimiento Estudiantil Chicano de Aztlan), Phi Theta Kappa. *Campus security:* 24-hour emergency response devices and patrols, late-night transport/escort service. *Student services:* personal/psychological counseling, women's center.

Athletics *Intramural sports:* weight lifting M.

Costs (2004–05) *Tuition:* area resident $720 full-time, $27 per credit hour part-time; state resident $960 full-time, $40 per credit hour part-time; nonresident $1728 full-time, $65 per credit hour part-time. *Required fees:* $84 full-time, $4 per credit hour part-time, $5 per term part-time. *Payment plan:* deferred payment. *Waivers:* senior citizens and employees or children of employees.

Financial Aid Of all full-time matriculated undergraduates who enrolled, 20 Federal Work-Study jobs (averaging $3900). 50 state and other part-time jobs (averaging $3900).

Applying *Options:* early admission, deferred entrance. *Required:* high school transcript. *Application deadline:* rolling (freshmen), rolling (transfers). *Notification:* continuous (freshmen).

Admissions Contact Ms. Jennifer Nollette, Admissions Counselor, Santa Fe Community College, 6401 Richards Avenue, Santa Fe, NM 87505. *Phone:* 505-428-1410. *Fax:* 505-428-1237.

SOUTHWESTERN INDIAN POLYTECHNIC INSTITUTE
Albuquerque, New Mexico

Admissions Contact Southwestern Indian Polytechnic Institute, PO Box 10146, Albuquerque, NM 87120-3103. *Phone:* 505-346-2362. *Toll-free phone:* 800-586-7474. *Fax:* 505-346-2320.

UNIVERSITY OF NEW MEXICO-GALLUP
Gallup, New Mexico

- **State-supported** primarily 2-year, founded 1968, part of New Mexico Commission on Higher Education
- **Calendar** semesters
- **Degrees** certificates, diplomas, associate, and bachelor's
- **Small-town** 80-acre campus
- **Coed**

Faculty *Student/faculty ratio:* 25:1.

Student Life *Campus security:* late-night transport/escort service.

Standardized Tests *Required for some:* SAT I (for admission), ACT (for admission).

Costs (2003–04) *Tuition:* state resident $1032 full-time, $43 per credit hour part-time; nonresident $2436 full-time, $87 per credit hour part-time.

Applying *Options:* early admission. *Application fee:* $15. *Required for some:* high school transcript.

Admissions Contact Ms. Pearl A. Morris, Admissions Representative, University of New Mexico-Gallup, 200 College Road, Gallup, NM 87301-5603. *Phone:* 505-863-7576. *Fax:* 505-863-7610. *E-mail:* pmorris@gallup.unm.edu.

UNIVERSITY OF NEW MEXICO-LOS ALAMOS BRANCH
Los Alamos, New Mexico

- **State-supported** 2-year, founded 1980, part of New Mexico Commission on Higher Education
- **Calendar** semesters
- **Degree** certificates and associate
- **Small-town** 5-acre campus
- **Coed**

Standardized Tests *Required for some:* SAT I or ACT (for placement).

Financial Aid Of all full-time matriculated undergraduates who enrolled, 15 Federal Work-Study jobs (averaging $5000). 10 state and other part-time jobs (averaging $7000).

Applying *Options:* early admission, deferred entrance. *Application fee:* $15.

Admissions Contact Ms. Anna Mae Apodaca, Associate Campus Director for Student Services, University of New Mexico-Los Alamos Branch, 4000 University Drive, Los Alamos, NM 87544-2233. *Phone:* 505-661-4692.

UNIVERSITY OF NEW MEXICO-TAOS
Taos, New Mexico

Admissions Contact 115 Civic Plaza Drive, Taos, NM 87571.

UNIVERSITY OF NEW MEXICO-VALENCIA CAMPUS
Los Lunas, New Mexico

Admissions Contact Ms. Lucy Sanchez, Registrar, University of New Mexico-Valencia Campus, 280 La Entrada, Los Lunas, NM 87031-7633. *Phone:* 505-925-8580. *Fax:* 505-925-8563.

NEW YORK

ADIRONDACK COMMUNITY COLLEGE
Queensbury, New York

- **State and locally supported** 2-year, founded 1960, part of State University of New York System
- **Calendar** semesters
- **Degree** certificates and associate
- **Small-town** 141-acre campus
- **Endowment** $1.0 million
- **Coed**

Faculty *Student/faculty ratio:* 20:1.

Student Life *Campus security:* late-night transport/escort service, patrols by trained security personnel 8 a.m. to 10 p.m.

Athletics Member NJCAA.

Standardized Tests *Recommended:* SAT I or ACT (for placement).

Financial Aid Of all full-time matriculated undergraduates who enrolled, 98 Federal Work-Study jobs (averaging $462).

Applying *Options:* early admission, deferred entrance. *Application fee:* $30. *Required:* high school transcript. *Required for some:* minimum 2.0 GPA.

Admissions Contact Office of Admissions, Adirondack Community College, 640 Bay Road, Queensbury, NY 12804. *Phone:* 518-743-2264. *Fax:* 518-745-1433. *E-mail:* info@acc.sunyacc.edu.

AMERICAN ACADEMY MCALLISTER INSTITUTE OF FUNERAL SERVICE
New York, New York

- **Independent** 2-year, founded 1926
- **Calendar** semesters
- **Degree** diplomas and associate
- **Urban** campus
- **Coed**

Faculty *Student/faculty ratio:* 25:1.

American Academy McAllister Institute of Funeral Service (continued)

Applying *Options:* early admission, deferred entrance. *Application fee:* $35. *Required:* high school transcript, 2 letters of recommendation. *Recommended:* interview.

Admissions Contact Mr. Norman Provost, Registrar, American Academy McAllister Institute of Funeral Service, 450 West 56th Street, New York, NY 10019-3602. *Phone:* 212-757-1190. *Fax:* 212-765-5923.

AMERICAN ACADEMY OF DRAMATIC ARTS
New York, New York

- **Independent** 2-year, founded 1884
- **Calendar** continuous
- **Degree** certificates and associate
- **Urban** campus
- **Endowment** $4.3 million
- **Coed,** 224 undergraduate students, 100% full-time, 62% women, 38% men

Undergraduates 224 full-time. Students come from 2 states and territories, 14 other countries, 82% are from out of state, 4% African American, 3% Asian American or Pacific Islander, 6% Hispanic American, 18% international.
Freshmen *Admission:* 236 applied, 129 admitted, 60 enrolled. *Average high school GPA:* 2.80.
Faculty *Total:* 24, 25% full-time, 13% with terminal degrees. *Student/faculty ratio:* 16:1.
Majors Dramatic/theatre arts.
Library Academy/CBS Library with 7,467 titles, 24 serial subscriptions, 570 audiovisual materials.
Computers on Campus 2 computers available on campus for general student use. A campuswide network can be accessed. Internet access available.
Student Life *Housing:* college housing not available. *Campus security:* 24-hour emergency response devices, trained security guard during hours of operation.
Costs (2004–05) *Tuition:* $15,350 full-time. *Payment plan:* installment.
Financial Aid Of all full-time matriculated undergraduates who enrolled, 40 Federal Work-Study jobs (averaging $2000). 10 state and other part-time jobs (averaging $2000). *Financial aid deadline:* 5/15.
Applying *Options:* deferred entrance. *Application fee:* $50. *Required:* essay or personal statement, 2 letters of recommendation, interview, audition. *Required for some:* high school transcript. *Recommended:* high school transcript, minimum 2.0 GPA. *Application deadline:* rolling (freshmen), rolling (transfers). *Notification:* continuous (freshmen), continuous (transfers).
Admissions Contact Ms. Karen Higginbotham, Director of Admissions, American Academy of Dramatic Arts, 120 Madison Avenue, New York, NY 10016. *Phone:* 800-463-8990. *Toll-free phone:* 800-463-8990. *Fax:* 212-696-1284. *E-mail:* admissions-ny@aada.org.

▶ **See page 496 for a narrative description.**

THE ART INSTITUTE OF NEW YORK CITY
New York, New York

- **Proprietary** 2-year, founded 1980, part of Educational Management Corporation
- **Calendar** quarters
- **Degree** certificates, diplomas, and associate
- **Urban** campus
- **Coed,** 1,484 undergraduate students

Undergraduates Students come from 3 states and territories, 25% are from out of state.
Freshmen *Average high school GPA:* 2.5.
Faculty *Total:* 92, 83% full-time. *Student/faculty ratio:* 22:1.
Majors Animation, interactive technology, video graphics and special effects; cinematography and film/video production; fashion/apparel design; graphic design; restaurant, culinary, and catering management.
Academic Programs *Special study options:* advanced placement credit, cooperative education, internships.
Computers on Campus 20 computers available on campus for general student use. At least one staffed computer lab available.
Student Life *Housing:* college housing not available.
Costs (2004–05) *Tuition:* $393 per credit hour part-time.
Applying *Options:* common application. *Application fee:* $50. *Required:* high school transcript, interview. *Required for some:* essay or personal statement.

Admissions Contact Mr. Rich Clark, Director of Admissions, The Art Institute of New York City, 75 Varick Street, 16th Floor, New York, NY 10013. *Phone:* 212-226-5500 Ext. 6005. *Toll-free phone:* 800-654-2433. *Fax:* 212-966-0706.

ASA INSTITUTE, THE COLLEGE OF ADVANCED TECHNOLOGY
Brooklyn, New York

Admissions Contact Ms. Alice Perez, Director of Admissions, ASA Institute, The College of Advanced Technology, 151 Lawrence Street, 2nd Floor, Brooklyn, NY 11201. *Phone:* 718-534-0773.

BERKELEY COLLEGE-NEW YORK CITY CAMPUS
New York, New York

- **Proprietary** primarily 2-year, founded 1936
- **Calendar** quarters
- **Degrees** certificates, associate, and bachelor's
- **Urban** campus
- **Coed,** 1,807 undergraduate students, 88% full-time, 72% women, 28% men

Undergraduates 1,598 full-time, 209 part-time. Students come from 14 states and territories, 66 other countries, 9% are from out of state, 29% African American, 5% Asian American or Pacific Islander, 32% Hispanic American, 0.4% Native American, 13% international, 7% transferred in.
Freshmen *Admission:* 1,295 applied, 1,123 admitted, 411 enrolled.
Faculty *Total:* 140, 29% full-time. *Student/faculty ratio:* 24:1.
Majors Accounting; business administration and management; business/commerce; fashion merchandising; international business/trade/commerce; legal assistant/paralegal; marketing/marketing management; office management.
Academic Programs *Special study options:* academic remediation for entering students, adult/continuing education programs, advanced placement credit, cooperative education, distance learning, English as a second language, internships, off-campus study, part-time degree program, study abroad, summer session for credit.
Library 13,164 titles, 138 serial subscriptions, 949 audiovisual materials, an OPAC, a Web page.
Computers on Campus 200 computers available on campus for general student use. A campuswide network can be accessed from off campus. Internet access, at least one staffed computer lab available.
Student Life *Housing:* college housing not available. *Activities and Organizations:* student-run newspaper, student government, International Club, Paralegal Club, Accounting Club. *Campus security:* 24-hour emergency response devices. *Student services:* personal/psychological counseling.
Standardized Tests *Required:* SAT I or ACT (for admission).
Costs (2003–04) *Tuition:* $14,685 full-time, $380 per credit part-time. *Required fees:* $450 full-time, $75 per term part-time. *Payment plan:* installment. *Waivers:* employees or children of employees.
Financial Aid Of all full-time matriculated undergraduates who enrolled, 120 Federal Work-Study jobs (averaging $1500).
Applying *Options:* electronic application, deferred entrance. *Application fee:* $40. *Required:* high school transcript. *Recommended:* interview. *Application deadline:* rolling (freshmen), rolling (transfers).
Admissions Contact Mr. Stuart Siegman, Director, High School Admissions, Berkeley College-New York City Campus, 3 East 43rd Street, New York, NY 10017. *Phone:* 212-986-4343 Ext. 123. *Toll-free phone:* 800-446-5400. *Fax:* 212-818-1079. *E-mail:* info@berkeleycollege.edu.

▶ **See page 518 for a narrative description.**

BERKELEY COLLEGE-WESTCHESTER CAMPUS
White Plains, New York

- **Proprietary** primarily 2-year, founded 1945
- **Calendar** quarters
- **Degrees** certificates, associate, and bachelor's
- **Suburban** 10-acre campus with easy access to New York City
- **Coed,** 629 undergraduate students, 87% full-time, 70% women, 30% men

Undergraduates 547 full-time, 82 part-time. Students come from 9 states and territories, 28 other countries, 14% are from out of state, 28% African American, 3% Asian American or Pacific Islander, 23% Hispanic American, 0.2% Native American, 6% international, 14% transferred in, 10% live on campus.

Freshmen *Admission:* 517 applied, 455 admitted, 198 enrolled.

Faculty *Total:* 53, 32% full-time. *Student/faculty ratio:* 24:1.

Majors Accounting; business administration and management; business/commerce; fashion merchandising; international business/trade/commerce; legal assistant/paralegal; marketing/marketing management; office management.

Academic Programs *Special study options:* academic remediation for entering students, adult/continuing education programs, advanced placement credit, cooperative education, distance learning, English as a second language, internships, off-campus study, part-time degree program, services for LD students, study abroad, summer session for credit.

Library 9,526 titles, 66 serial subscriptions, 777 audiovisual materials, an OPAC, a Web page.

Computers on Campus 175 computers available on campus for general student use. A campuswide network can be accessed from off campus. Internet access, at least one staffed computer lab available.

Student Life *Housing Options:* coed. Campus housing is university owned. *Activities and Organizations:* student-run newspaper, student government, Paralegal Club, Fashion Club, Phi Theta Kappa. *Campus security:* monitored entrance with front desk security guard. *Student services:* personal/psychological counseling.

Standardized Tests *Required:* SAT I or ACT (for admission).

Costs (2003–04) *One-time required fee:* $50. *Comprehensive fee:* $24,435 includes full-time tuition ($14,685), mandatory fees ($450), and room and board ($9300). Part-time tuition: $380 per credit. *Required fees:* $75 per term part-time. *Room and board:* college room only: $6000. Room and board charges vary according to board plan. *Payment plan:* installment. *Waivers:* employees or children of employees.

Financial Aid Of all full-time matriculated undergraduates who enrolled, 40 Federal Work-Study jobs (averaging $1100).

Applying *Options:* electronic application, deferred entrance. *Application fee:* $40. *Required:* high school transcript. *Recommended:* interview. *Application deadline:* rolling (freshmen), rolling (transfers).

Admissions Contact Mr. David Bertrone, Director of High School Admissions, Berkeley College-Westchester Campus, 99 Church Street, White Plains, NY 10601. *Phone:* 914-694-1122 Ext. 3110. *Toll-free phone:* 800-446-5400. *Fax:* 914-328-9469. *E-mail:* info@berkeleycollege.edu.

▶ **See page 518 for a narrative description.**

BOROUGH OF MANHATTAN COMMUNITY COLLEGE OF THE CITY UNIVERSITY OF NEW YORK
New York, New York

- **State and locally supported** 2-year, founded 1963, part of City University of New York System
- **Calendar** semesters
- **Degree** certificates and associate
- **Urban** 5-acre campus
- **Endowment** $2.2 million
- **Coed,** 17,629 undergraduate students, 63% full-time, 64% women, 36% men

Undergraduates 11,140 full-time, 6,489 part-time. Students come from 3 states and territories, 100 other countries, 12% are from out of state, 37% African American, 10% Asian American or Pacific Islander, 29% Hispanic American, 0.1% Native American, 12% international, 11% transferred in.

Freshmen *Admission:* 6,446 applied, 5,718 admitted, 3,325 enrolled. *Average high school GPA:* 2.01. *Test scores:* SAT verbal scores over 500: 12%; SAT math scores over 500: 10%; SAT verbal scores over 600: 2%; SAT math scores over 600: 2%; SAT verbal scores over 700: 1%; SAT math scores over 700: 1%.

Faculty *Total:* 1,006, 33% full-time. *Student/faculty ratio:* 24:1.

Majors Accounting; administrative assistant and secretarial science; biological and physical sciences; business administration and management; child development; computer programming; data processing and data processing technology; emergency medical technology (EMT paramedic); engineering science; health science; human services; kindergarten/preschool education; liberal arts and sciences/liberal studies; marketing/marketing management; mathematics; nursing (registered nurse training); respiratory care therapy.

Academic Programs *Special study options:* academic remediation for entering students, adult/continuing education programs, advanced placement credit, cooperative education, distance learning, English as a second language, honors programs, independent study, internships, off-campus study, part-time degree program, services for LD students, study abroad, summer session for credit.

Library A. Philip Randolph Library with 101,869 titles, 8,594 serial subscriptions, 1,343 audiovisual materials, an OPAC, a Web page.

Computers on Campus Internet access, online (class) registration, at least one staffed computer lab available. Computer purchase or lease plan available.

Student Life *Housing:* college housing not available. *Activities and Organizations:* drama/theater group, student-run newspaper, choral group, Caribbean Students Association, Dominican Students Association, When One Voice is Not Enough (WOVINE), Students of Indian Descent Association, Asian Society. *Campus security:* 24-hour patrols. *Student services:* health clinic, personal/psychological counseling, women's center.

Athletics Member NJCAA. *Intercollegiate sports:* baseball M, basketball M/W, soccer M. *Intramural sports:* basketball M/W, soccer M, volleyball M/W.

Costs (2003–04) *Tuition:* state resident $2800 full-time, $120 per credit part-time; nonresident $4560 full-time, $190 per credit part-time. *Payment plan:* deferred payment.

Applying *Options:* electronic application, deferred entrance. *Application fee:* $40. *Required:* high school transcript. *Application deadline:* rolling (freshmen), rolling (transfers). *Notification:* continuous (freshmen), continuous (transfers).

Admissions Contact Mr. Eugenio Barrios, Director of Admissions, Borough of Manhattan Community College of the City University of New York, 199 Chambers Street, Room S-300, New York, NY 10007. *Phone:* 212-220-1265. *Fax:* 212-220-2366. *E-mail:* bmadmrpre@cunyum.cuny.edu.

BRAMSON ORT COLLEGE
Forest Hills, New York

- **Independent** 2-year, founded 1977
- **Calendar** semesters
- **Degree** certificates and associate
- **Coed**

Costs (2003–04) *Tuition:* $8160 full-time. *Required fees:* $330 full-time.

Applying *Options:* early admission, deferred entrance. *Application fee:* $50. *Required:* high school transcript.

Admissions Contact Admissions Office, Bramson ORT College, 69-30 Austin Street, Forest Hills, NY 11375-4239. *Phone:* 718-261-5800.

BRONX COMMUNITY COLLEGE OF THE CITY UNIVERSITY OF NEW YORK
Bronx, New York

- **State and locally supported** 2-year, founded 1959, part of City University of New York System
- **Calendar** semesters
- **Degree** certificates and associate
- **Urban** 50-acre campus
- **Coed,** 7,952 undergraduate students, 59% full-time, 65% women, 35% men

Undergraduates 4,725 full-time, 3,227 part-time. Students come from 16 states and territories, 100 other countries, 5% are from out of state, 38% African American, 3% Asian American or Pacific Islander, 49% Hispanic American, 0.1% Native American, 6% international, 6% transferred in. *Retention:* 65% of 2002 full-time freshmen returned.

Freshmen *Admission:* 1,409 enrolled.

Faculty *Total:* 548, 41% full-time.

Majors Accounting; administrative assistant and secretarial science; African-American/Black studies; art; biology/biological sciences; business administration and management; business teacher education; chemistry; child development; clinical/medical laboratory technology; computer science; data processing and data processing technology; electrical, electronic and communications engineering technology; history; human services; international relations and affairs; legal assistant/paralegal; liberal arts and sciences/liberal studies; marketing/marketing management; mathematics; medical administrative assistant and medical secretary; music; nuclear medical technology; nursing (registered nurse training); ornamental horticulture; pre-engineering; psychology.

Academic Programs *Special study options:* academic remediation for entering students, adult/continuing education programs, advanced placement credit, cooperative education, distance learning, English as a second language, honors programs, independent study, internships, part-time degree program, services for LD students, study abroad, summer session for credit.

Library 75,000 titles, 800 serial subscriptions.

Computers on Campus 300 computers available on campus for general student use.

Student Life *Housing:* college housing not available. *Activities and Organizations:* drama/theater group, student-run newspaper, radio station, choral group. *Campus security:* 24-hour patrols. *Student services:* personal/psychological counseling.

Athletics Member NJCAA. *Intercollegiate sports:* basketball M/W, soccer M, tennis M/W, track and field M/W, volleyball W, wrestling M. *Intramural sports:* basketball M/W, soccer M, tennis M/W, track and field M/W, volleyball W, wrestling M.

Costs (2003–04) *Tuition:* state resident $2800 full-time, $120 per credit part-time; nonresident $4560 full-time, $190 per credit part-time. *Required fees:* $284 full-time, $80 per term part-time.

Bronx Community College of the City University of New York (continued)

Applying *Application fee:* $40. *Required:* high school transcript. *Application deadline:* rolling (freshmen), rolling (transfers). *Notification:* continuous (freshmen), continuous (transfers).

Admissions Contact Ms. Alba N. Cancetty, Admissions Officer, Bronx Community College of the City University of New York, University Avenue and West 181st Street, Bronx, NY 10453. *Phone:* 718-289-5888. *E-mail:* admission@bcc.cuny.edu.

BROOME COMMUNITY COLLEGE
Binghamton, New York

- **State and locally supported** 2-year, founded 1946, part of State University of New York System
- **Calendar** semesters
- **Degree** certificates and associate
- **Suburban** 223-acre campus
- **Coed,** 6,542 undergraduate students, 63% full-time, 58% women, 42% men

Undergraduates 4,131 full-time, 2,411 part-time. Students come from 24 states and territories, 28 other countries, 4% are from out of state, 2% African American, 0.8% Asian American or Pacific Islander, 0.7% Hispanic American, 0.2% Native American, 2% international. *Retention:* 62% of 2002 full-time freshmen returned.

Freshmen *Admission:* 2,431 applied, 2,016 admitted, 1,336 enrolled.

Faculty *Total:* 398, 36% full-time. *Student/faculty ratio:* 21:1.

Majors Accounting technology and bookkeeping; business administration and management; child care and support services management; civil engineering technology; clinical/medical laboratory technology; communication/speech communication and rhetoric; communications systems installation and repair technology; computer and information sciences; computer engineering technology; corrections; criminal justice/police science; data processing and data processing technology; dental hygiene; electrical, electronic and communications engineering technology; emergency medical technology (EMT paramedic); engineering science; executive assistant/executive secretary; financial planning and services; fire science; health information/medical records technology; hotel/motel administration; industrial production technologies related; information science/studies; international finance; legal assistant/paralegal; liberal arts and sciences/liberal studies; mechanical engineering/mechanical technology; medical/clinical assistant; medical radiologic technology; mental and social health services and allied professions related; merchandising, sales, and marketing operations related (general); nursing (registered nurse training); physical therapist assistant; quality control technology; substance abuse/addiction counseling.

Academic Programs *Special study options:* academic remediation for entering students, adult/continuing education programs, advanced placement credit, distance learning, English as a second language, external degree program, honors programs, independent study, internships, off-campus study, part-time degree program, services for LD students, student-designed majors, study abroad, summer session for credit.

Library Cecil C. Tyrrell Learning Resources Center plus 1 other with 60,518 titles, 378 serial subscriptions, 239 audiovisual materials, an OPAC, a Web page.

Computers on Campus 550 computers available on campus for general student use. A campuswide network can be accessed from off campus. Internet access, at least one staffed computer lab available.

Student Life *Housing:* college housing not available. *Activities and Organizations:* student-run newspaper, choral group, Broome Early Childhood Organization, Differentially Disabled Student Association, Ecology Club, Phi Theta Kappa, Criminal Justice Club. *Campus security:* 24-hour emergency response devices and patrols. *Student services:* health clinic, personal/psychological counseling.

Athletics Member NJCAA. *Intercollegiate sports:* baseball M, basketball M/W, cheerleading W, cross-country running M/W, golf M, ice hockey M, lacrosse M, soccer M/W, softball W, tennis M/W, volleyball W. *Intramural sports:* basketball M/W, volleyball M/W.

Standardized Tests *Required for some:* ACCUPLACER.

Costs (2003–04) *One-time required fee:* $45. *Tuition:* state resident $2530 full-time, $106 per credit hour part-time; nonresident $5060 full-time, $212 per credit hour part-time. Full-time tuition and fees vary according to course load and location. Part-time tuition and fees vary according to course load and location. *Required fees:* $267 full-time, $5 per credit hour part-time, $29 per term part-time. *Waivers:* senior citizens and employees or children of employees.

Financial Aid Of all full-time matriculated undergraduates who enrolled, 164 Federal Work-Study jobs (averaging $796).

Applying *Options:* electronic application, early admission. *Required:* high school transcript. *Required for some:* interview. *Application deadline:* rolling (freshmen), rolling (transfers). *Notification:* continuous (freshmen), continuous (transfers).

Admissions Contact Mr. Anthony Fiorelli, Director of Admissions, Broome Community College, PO Box 1017, Upper Front Street, Binghamton, NY 13902. *Phone:* 607-778-5001. *E-mail:* admissions@sunybroome.edu.

BRYANT AND STRATTON COLLEGE
Albany, New York

- **Proprietary** 2-year, founded 1857, part of Bryant and Stratton College, Inc
- **Calendar** semesters
- **Degree** diplomas and associate
- **Suburban** campus
- **Coed**

Faculty *Student/faculty ratio:* 8:1.

Student Life *Campus security:* 24-hour emergency response devices.

Standardized Tests *Required:* TABE, CPAt (for admission). *Recommended:* SAT I or ACT (for admission).

Costs (2004–05) *Tuition:* $10,920 full-time, $364 per credit hour part-time. Full-time tuition and fees vary according to course load. Part-time tuition and fees vary according to course load. *Required fees:* $200 full-time, $100 per term part-time.

Financial Aid Of all full-time matriculated undergraduates who enrolled, 10 Federal Work-Study jobs (averaging $800).

Applying *Options:* deferred entrance. *Application fee:* $25. *Required:* high school transcript, interview. *Required for some:* letters of recommendation.

Admissions Contact Mr. Michael Gutierrez, Director of Admissions, Bryant and Stratton College, 1259 Central Avenue, Albany, NY 12205. *Phone:* 518-437-1802 Ext. 205. *Fax:* 518-437-1048.

BRYANT AND STRATTON COLLEGE
Buffalo, New York

- **Proprietary** 2-year, founded 1854, part of Bryant and Stratton Business Institute, Inc
- **Calendar** semesters
- **Degree** certificates, diplomas, and associate
- **Urban** 2-acre campus
- **Coed,** 567 undergraduate students, 91% full-time, 74% women, 26% men

Undergraduates 515 full-time, 52 part-time. 71% African American, 5% Hispanic American, 0.7% Native American, 2% transferred in.

Freshmen *Admission:* 228 enrolled.

Faculty *Total:* 45, 22% full-time. *Student/faculty ratio:* 10:1.

Majors Accounting; administrative assistant and secretarial science; business administration, management and operations related; computer and information sciences; medical/clinical assistant.

Academic Programs *Special study options:* academic remediation for entering students, adult/continuing education programs, distance learning, double majors, independent study, internships, part-time degree program, summer session for credit.

Library Learning Center/Library with 2,903 titles, 155 serial subscriptions, 252 audiovisual materials.

Computers on Campus 145 computers available on campus for general student use. A campuswide network can be accessed. Internet access, at least one staffed computer lab available.

Student Life *Housing:* college housing not available. *Activities and Organizations:* Med-Assisting Club, Secretarial Club, Accounting/Business Club.

Standardized Tests *Required:* TABE, CPAt (for admission). *Recommended:* SAT I or ACT (for admission).

Costs (2004–05) *Tuition:* $10,920 full-time, $364 per credit part-time. Full-time tuition and fees vary according to course load. Part-time tuition and fees vary according to course load. *Required fees:* $225 full-time. *Payment plan:* installment. *Waivers:* employees or children of employees.

Applying *Options:* common application, electronic application, deferred entrance. *Application fee:* $25. *Required:* high school transcript, interview. *Required for some:* letters of recommendation. *Recommended:* minimum 2.0 GPA. *Application deadline:* rolling (freshmen), rolling (transfers).

Admissions Contact Mr. Phil Strubel, Associate Director of Admissions, Bryant and Stratton College, 465 Main Street, Suite 400, Buffalo, NY 14203-1713. *Phone:* 716-884-9120 Ext. 225. *Fax:* 716-884-0091.

BRYANT AND STRATTON COLLEGE
Lackawanna, New York

- **Proprietary** 2-year, founded 1989, part of Bryant and Stratton Business Institute, Inc
- **Calendar** semesters
- **Degree** diplomas and associate
- **Suburban** campus with easy access to Buffalo
- **Coed,** 285 undergraduate students, 82% full-time, 47% women, 53% men

Undergraduates 234 full-time, 51 part-time. 6% African American, 7% Hispanic American, 2% Native American, 2% transferred in.

Freshmen *Admission:* 113 enrolled. *Average high school GPA:* 2.70.
Faculty *Total:* 40, 18% full-time.
Majors Accounting; administrative assistant and secretarial science; business administration, management and operations related; computer and information sciences; hotel/motel administration.
Academic Programs *Special study options:* academic remediation for entering students, cooperative education, distance learning, independent study, internships, part-time degree program, summer session for credit.
Library Southtowns Library with 1,402 titles, 42 serial subscriptions, 128 audiovisual materials, a Web page.
Computers on Campus 94 computers available on campus for general student use. A campuswide network can be accessed. Internet access, at least one staffed computer lab available.
Student Life *Housing:* college housing not available. *Activities and Organizations:* Accounting/Business Club, Administrative Professionals Club, Micro Club, Honor Society, student newsletter. *Campus security:* 24-hour emergency response devices, late-night transport/escort service.
Standardized Tests *Required:* TABE, CPAt (for admission). *Recommended:* SAT I or ACT (for admission).
Costs (2004–05) *Tuition:* $10,920 full-time, $364 per credit part-time. Full-time tuition and fees vary according to course load. Part-time tuition and fees vary according to course load. *Required fees:* $225 full-time. *Payment plan:* installment. *Waivers:* employees or children of employees.
Applying *Options:* common application, electronic application, deferred entrance. *Application fee:* $25. *Required:* essay or personal statement, high school transcript, interview. *Required for some:* letters of recommendation. *Recommended:* minimum 2.0 GPA. *Application deadline:* rolling (freshmen), rolling (transfers).
Admissions Contact Ms. Dee Edwards, Associate Director of Admissions, Bryant and Stratton College, 1214 Abbott Road, Lackawanna, NY 14218-1989. *Phone:* 716-884-9331 Ext. 217. *Fax:* 716-821-9343.

BRYANT AND STRATTON COLLEGE
Rochester, New York

- **Proprietary** 2-year, founded 1985, part of Bryant and Stratton College
- **Calendar** semesters
- **Degree** diplomas and associate
- **Suburban** 1-acre campus
- **Coed**

Faculty *Student/faculty ratio:* 11:1.
Student Life *Campus security:* late-night transport/escort service.
Standardized Tests *Required:* CPAt (for admission). *Recommended:* SAT I or ACT (for admission).
Costs (2003–04) *Tuition:* $10,410 full-time. *Required fees:* $200 full-time.
Financial Aid Of all full-time matriculated undergraduates who enrolled, 44 Federal Work-Study jobs (averaging $630).
Applying *Options:* electronic application, deferred entrance. *Application fee:* $25. *Required:* essay or personal statement, high school transcript, interview. *Required for some:* letters of recommendation. *Recommended:* minimum 2.0 GPA.
Admissions Contact Ms. Maria Scalise, Director of Admissions, Bryant and Stratton College, 150 Bellwood Drive, Greece Campus, Rochester, NY 14606. *Phone:* 585-720-0660 Ext. 220. *Fax:* 716-292-6015.

BRYANT AND STRATTON COLLEGE
Rochester, New York

- **Proprietary** 2-year, founded 1973, part of Bryant and Stratton College
- **Calendar** semesters
- **Degree** diplomas and associate
- **Urban** campus
- **Coed**

Faculty *Student/faculty ratio:* 12:1.
Student Life *Campus security:* 24-hour emergency response devices, late-night transport/escort service.
Standardized Tests *Required:* CPAt (for admission). *Recommended:* SAT I or ACT (for admission).
Costs (2003–04) *Tuition:* $10,410 full-time. *Required fees:* $200 full-time.
Financial Aid Of all full-time matriculated undergraduates who enrolled, 40 Federal Work-Study jobs (averaging $600).
Applying *Options:* electronic application, deferred entrance. *Application fee:* $25. *Required:* essay or personal statement, high school transcript, interview. *Required for some:* letters of recommendation. *Recommended:* minimum 2.0 GPA.

Admissions Contact Ms. Maria Scalise, Director of Admissions, Bryant and Stratton College, 1225 Jefferson Road, Henrietta Campus, Rochester, NY 14623. *Phone:* 585-292-5627 Ext. 103.

BRYANT AND STRATTON COLLEGE
Syracuse, New York

- **Proprietary** 2-year, founded 1854, part of Bryant and Stratton Business Institute, Inc
- **Calendar** semesters
- **Degree** diplomas and associate
- **Urban** campus
- **Coed,** 570 undergraduate students, 83% full-time, 73% women, 27% men

Undergraduates 475 full-time, 95 part-time. Students come from 1 other state, 2 other countries, 29% African American, 1% Asian American or Pacific Islander, 3% Hispanic American, 0.7% Native American, 0.7% international, 4% transferred in, 26% live on campus. *Retention:* 61% of 2002 full-time freshmen returned.
Freshmen *Admission:* 257 enrolled. *Average high school GPA:* 2.50.
Faculty *Total:* 20, 40% full-time. *Student/faculty ratio:* 15:1.
Majors Accounting; administrative assistant and secretarial science; business administration and management; computer programming; health information/medical records technology; hotel/motel administration; information science/studies; information technology; legal administrative assistant/secretary; medical administrative assistant and medical secretary; medical/clinical assistant; tourism and travel services management.
Academic Programs *Special study options:* academic remediation for entering students, distance learning, double majors, internships, part-time degree program, services for LD students, summer session for credit.
Library Bryant and Stratton, Syracuse Campus with 1,325 titles, 40 serial subscriptions, 40 audiovisual materials.
Computers on Campus 114 computers available on campus for general student use. At least one staffed computer lab available.
Student Life *Housing Options:* coed, disabled students. *Activities and Organizations:* Management Club, Travel Club, Medical Club, Computer Club. *Campus security:* 24-hour emergency response devices, controlled dormitory access.
Athletics Member NJCAA. *Intercollegiate sports:* soccer M(s)/W(s).
Standardized Tests *Required:* CPAt (for admission). *Recommended:* SAT I or ACT (for admission).
Costs (2004–05) *Comprehensive fee:* $17,870 includes full-time tuition ($12,120) and room and board ($5750). Part-time tuition: $364 per credit. *Room and board:* college room only: $3000.
Applying *Application fee:* $25. *Required:* essay or personal statement, high school transcript, interview, entrance, placement evaluations. *Required for some:* letters of recommendation. *Recommended:* minimum 2.0 GPA. *Application deadline:* rolling (freshmen), rolling (transfers). *Notification:* continuous (freshmen), continuous (transfers).
Admissions Contact Mrs. Amy Graham, Associate Director of Admissions, Bryant and Stratton College, 953 James Street, Syracuse, NY 13203-2502. *Phone:* 315-472-6603 Ext. 247.

BRYANT AND STRATTON COLLEGE, AMHERST CAMPUS
Clarence, New York

- **Proprietary** 2-year, founded 1977, part of Bryant and Stratton College
- **Calendar** semesters
- **Degree** diplomas and associate
- **Suburban** 12-acre campus with easy access to Buffalo
- **Coed,** 317 undergraduate students, 62% full-time, 66% women, 34% men

Undergraduates 196 full-time, 121 part-time. 10% African American, 0.9% Asian American or Pacific Islander, 3% Hispanic American, 0.6% Native American, 7% transferred in.
Freshmen *Admission:* 106 enrolled.
Faculty *Total:* 36, 17% full-time.
Majors Accounting; administrative assistant and secretarial science; business administration, management and operations related; commercial and advertising art; computer and information sciences; electrical, electronic and communications engineering technology; legal assistant/paralegal.
Academic Programs *Special study options:* academic remediation for entering students, adult/continuing education programs, cooperative education, independent study, internships, part-time degree program, summer session for credit.
Library Library Resource Center with 4,500 titles, 15 serial subscriptions, 150 audiovisual materials, an OPAC.

Bryant and Stratton College, Amherst Campus (continued)

Computers on Campus 125 computers available on campus for general student use. Internet access, at least one staffed computer lab available.

Student Life *Housing:* college housing not available. *Activities and Organizations:* Phi Beta Lambda, Student Government Association, Information Technology Club, Ambassadors.

Standardized Tests *Required:* TABE, CPAt (for admission). *Recommended:* SAT I or ACT (for admission).

Costs (2004–05) *Tuition:* $10,920 full-time, $364 per credit part-time. Full-time tuition and fees vary according to course load. Part-time tuition and fees vary according to course load. *Required fees:* $225 full-time. *Payment plan:* installment. *Waivers:* employees or children of employees.

Applying *Options:* common application, deferred entrance. *Application fee:* $25. *Required:* high school transcript. *Required for some:* essay or personal statement, interview. *Application deadline:* rolling (freshmen), rolling (transfers).

Admissions Contact Ms. Kathy Odo, Associate Director of Admissions, Bryant and Stratton College, Amherst Campus, 40 Hazelwood Drive, Amherst, NY 14228. *Phone:* 716-691-0012. *Fax:* 716-691-6716. *E-mail:* pvrichardson@bryantstratton.edu.

BRYANT AND STRATTON COLLEGE, NORTH CAMPUS
Liverpool, New York

- **Proprietary** 2-year, founded 1983, part of Bryant and Stratton Business Institute, Inc
- **Calendar** semesters
- **Degree** diplomas and associate
- **Rural** 1-acre campus with easy access to Syracuse
- **Coed**

Faculty *Student/faculty ratio:* 14:1.

Student Life *Campus security:* 24-hour emergency response devices.

Athletics Member NJCAA.

Standardized Tests *Required:* TABE, CPAt (for admission).

Costs (2003–04) *Tuition:* $10,410 full-time, $347 per semester hour part-time. Full-time tuition and fees vary according to course load. Part-time tuition and fees vary according to course load. *Required fees:* $200 full-time.

Applying *Options:* deferred entrance. *Application fee:* $25. *Required:* high school transcript, interview, entrance evaluation and placement evaluation. *Required for some:* letters of recommendation. *Recommended:* minimum 2.0 GPA.

Admissions Contact Ms. Heather Macnik, Director of Admissions, Bryant and Stratton College, North Campus, 8687 Carling Road, Liverpool, NY 13090-1315. *Phone:* 315-652-6500. *Fax:* 315-652-5500.

BUSINESS INFORMATICS CENTER, INC.
Valley Stream, New York

Admissions Contact Business Informatics Center, Inc., 134 South Central Avenue, Valley Stream, NY 11580-5431.

CAYUGA COUNTY COMMUNITY COLLEGE
Auburn, New York

- **State and locally supported** 2-year, founded 1953, part of State University of New York System
- **Calendar** semesters
- **Degree** certificates and associate
- **Small-town** 50-acre campus with easy access to Rochester and Syracuse
- **Endowment** $6.5 million
- **Coed**

Student Life *Campus security:* security from 8 a.m. to 9 p.m.

Athletics Member NJCAA.

Standardized Tests *Required for some:* ACT ASSET. *Recommended:* SAT I or ACT (for placement).

Costs (2004–05) *Tuition:* state resident $2900 full-time; nonresident $5800 full-time. *Required fees:* $520 full-time.

Financial Aid Of all full-time matriculated undergraduates who enrolled, 150 Federal Work-Study jobs (averaging $1800). 200 state and other part-time jobs (averaging $1000).

Applying *Options:* deferred entrance. *Required:* high school transcript. *Required for some:* interview.

Admissions Contact Mr. Dick Landers, Director of Admissions, Cayuga County Community College, 197 Franklin Street, Auburn, NY 13021-3099. *Phone:* 315-255-1743. *E-mail:* admissions@cayuga-cc.edu.

CLINTON COMMUNITY COLLEGE
Plattsburgh, New York

- **State and locally supported** 2-year, founded 1969, part of State University of New York System
- **Calendar** semesters
- **Degree** certificates and associate
- **Small-town** 100-acre campus
- **Endowment** $1.0 million
- **Coed,** 2,192 undergraduate students, 57% full-time, 57% women, 43% men

Undergraduates 1,259 full-time, 933 part-time. Students come from 5 states and territories, 9 other countries, 1% are from out of state, 3% African American, 0.6% Asian American or Pacific Islander, 2% Hispanic American, 0.9% Native American, 2% international, 6% transferred in, 6% live on campus.

Freshmen *Admission:* 1,714 applied, 1,406 admitted, 383 enrolled. *Average high school GPA:* 2.50.

Faculty *Total:* 142, 35% full-time, 8% with terminal degrees. *Student/faculty ratio:* 18:1.

Majors Accounting; administrative assistant and secretarial science; biological and physical sciences; business administration and management; clinical/medical laboratory technology; community organization and advocacy; computer/information technology services administration related; consumer merchandising/retailing management; criminal justice/law enforcement administration; criminal justice/police science; electrical, electronic and communications engineering technology; humanities; industrial technology; liberal arts and sciences/liberal studies; nursing (registered nurse training); physical education teaching and coaching; social sciences.

Academic Programs *Special study options:* academic remediation for entering students, adult/continuing education programs, advanced placement credit, cooperative education, distance learning, English as a second language, external degree program, independent study, internships, off-campus study, part-time degree program, services for LD students, student-designed majors, summer session for credit.

Library Clinton Community College Learning Resource Center plus 1 other with 33,862 titles, 288 serial subscriptions, 257 audiovisual materials, an OPAC, a Web page.

Computers on Campus 250 computers available on campus for general student use. A campuswide network can be accessed from off campus. Internet access, at least one staffed computer lab available.

Student Life *Housing Options:* coed, disabled students. Campus housing is provided by a third party. Freshman campus housing is guaranteed. *Activities and Organizations:* drama/theater group, student-run newspaper, choral group, Criminal Justice Club, Business Club, Tomorrow's New Teachers, Ski Club, Nursing Club. *Campus security:* 24-hour emergency response devices, late-night transport/escort service, controlled dormitory access, security during class hours. *Student services:* health clinic, personal/psychological counseling.

Athletics Member NJCAA. *Intercollegiate sports:* baseball M, basketball M/W, soccer M/W, softball W. *Intramural sports:* fencing M/W, volleyball M/W.

Standardized Tests *Recommended:* SAT I or ACT (for placement).

Costs (2004–05) *Tuition:* state resident $2920 full-time; nonresident $7400 full-time. *Required fees:* $155 full-time. *Room and board:* $6200; room only: $3700. Room and board charges vary according to board plan.

Financial Aid Of all full-time matriculated undergraduates who enrolled, 45 Federal Work-Study jobs (averaging $1260).

Applying *Options:* common application, electronic application, deferred entrance. *Required:* high school transcript. *Required for some:* essay or personal statement, minimum 2.5 GPA, 3 letters of recommendation, interview. *Application deadlines:* 8/26 (freshmen), 9/3 (transfers). *Notification:* continuous (freshmen), continuous (transfers).

Admissions Contact Ms. Maria M. Visco, Interim Associate Dean for Enrollment Management, Clinton Community College, 136 Clinton Point Drive, Plattsburgh, NY 12901. *Phone:* 518-562-4170. *Toll-free phone:* 800-552-1160. *Fax:* 518-562-4158. *E-mail:* cccadm@clintoncc.suny.edu.

COCHRAN SCHOOL OF NURSING
Yonkers, New York

- **Independent** 2-year, founded 1894
- **Calendar** semesters
- **Degree** associate
- **Urban** campus with easy access to New York City
- **Coed, primarily women,** 157 undergraduate students, 64% full-time, 87% women, 13% men

Undergraduates 101 full-time, 56 part-time. Students come from 2 states and territories, 25% African American, 12% Asian American or Pacific Islander, 14% Hispanic American, 50% transferred in. *Retention:* 75% of 2002 full-time freshmen returned.

Freshmen *Admission:* 16 applied, 2 admitted, 1 enrolled. *Average high school GPA:* 3.00.

Faculty *Total:* 34, 47% full-time. *Student/faculty ratio:* 5:1.

Majors Nursing (registered nurse training).

Academic Programs *Special study options:* advanced placement credit, part-time degree program.

Library Cochran School of Nursing Library with 4,314 titles, 115 serial subscriptions, 500 audiovisual materials, an OPAC.

Computers on Campus 6 computers available on campus for general student use. Internet access, at least one staffed computer lab available.

Student Life *Housing:* college housing not available. *Campus security:* 24-hour emergency response devices and patrols, late-night transport/escort service. *Student services:* health clinic, personal/psychological counseling.

Standardized Tests *Required:* nursing exam (for admission). *Required for some:* SAT I (for admission).

Costs (2003–04) *Tuition:* $10,440 full-time, $290 per credit part-time. Full-time tuition and fees vary according to course load. Part-time tuition and fees vary according to course load. *Required fees:* $620 full-time, $310 per term part-time. *Payment plan:* installment. *Waivers:* employees or children of employees.

Applying *Options:* deferred entrance. *Application fee:* $25. *Required:* essay or personal statement, high school transcript, interview. *Application deadline:* rolling (freshmen). *Notification:* continuous (freshmen), continuous (transfers).

Admissions Contact Ms. Sandra Sclafani, Registrar, Cochran School of Nursing, 967 North Broadway, Yonkers, NY 10701. *Phone:* 914-964-4296. *Fax:* 914-964-4796. *E-mail:* ssclafani@riversidehealth.org.

THE COLLEGE OF WESTCHESTER
White Plains, New York

- **Proprietary** 2-year, founded 1915
- **Calendar** quarters for day division, semesters for evening and weekend divisions
- **Degree** certificates and associate
- **Suburban** campus with easy access to New York City
- **Coed,** 973 undergraduate students, 94% full-time, 48% women, 52% men

Undergraduates 918 full-time, 55 part-time. Students come from 3 states and territories, 4 other countries, 8% are from out of state, 27% African American, 3% Asian American or Pacific Islander, 29% Hispanic American, 0.8% Native American, 7% transferred in.

Freshmen *Admission:* 209 enrolled.

Faculty *Total:* 89, 29% full-time, 8% with terminal degrees. *Student/faculty ratio:* 15:1.

Majors Accounting; administrative assistant and secretarial science; business administration and management; computer and information sciences related; computer graphics; computer/information technology services administration related; computer programming; computer programming related; computer programming (specific applications); computer programming (vendor/product certification); computer software and media applications related; computer systems networking and telecommunications; computer/technical support; computer typography and composition equipment operation; data entry/microcomputer applications; data entry/microcomputer applications related; data processing and data processing technology; information science/studies; information technology; management information systems; marketing/marketing management; medical administrative assistant and medical secretary; system administration; web/multimedia management and webmaster; web page, digital/multimedia and information resources design; word processing.

Academic Programs *Special study options:* academic remediation for entering students, accelerated degree program, adult/continuing education programs, cooperative education, double majors, honors programs, internships, part-time degree program, summer session for credit.

Library Westchester Business Institute Resource Center.

Computers on Campus 214 computers available on campus for general student use. A campuswide network can be accessed. Internet access, at least one staffed computer lab available.

Student Life *Housing:* college housing not available.

Standardized Tests *Recommended:* SAT I (for admission).

Costs (2004–05) *Tuition:* $16,203 full-time, $491 per credit part-time. Full-time tuition and fees vary according to course load and program. Part-time tuition and fees vary according to course load and program. *Required fees:* $780 full-time. *Payment plan:* installment. *Waivers:* employees or children of employees.

Applying *Options:* common application, electronic application, deferred entrance. *Application fee:* $30. *Required:* high school transcript, interview.

Required for some: essay or personal statement. *Application deadline:* rolling (freshmen), rolling (transfers).

Admissions Contact Mr. Dale T. Smith, Vice President, The College of Westchester, 325 Central Avenue, P.O. Box 710, White Plains, NY 10602. *Phone:* 914-948-4442 Ext. 311. *Toll-free phone:* 800-333-4924 Ext. 318. *Fax:* 914-948-5441. *E-mail:* admissions@wbi.org.

▶ **See page 528 for a narrative description.**

COLUMBIA-GREENE COMMUNITY COLLEGE
Hudson, New York

- **State and locally supported** 2-year, founded 1969, part of State University of New York System
- **Calendar** semesters
- **Degree** certificates and associate
- **Rural** 143-acre campus
- **Endowment** $450,000
- **Coed,** 1,715 undergraduate students, 55% full-time, 64% women, 36% men

Undergraduates 938 full-time, 777 part-time. Students come from 5 states and territories, 5 other countries, 1% are from out of state, 5% transferred in.

Freshmen *Admission:* 631 applied, 499 admitted, 366 enrolled.

Faculty *Total:* 107, 45% full-time. *Student/faculty ratio:* 18:1.

Majors Accounting; administrative assistant and secretarial science; art; automobile/automotive mechanics technology; biological and physical sciences; business administration and management; computer and information sciences related; computer graphics; computer science; computer systems networking and telecommunications; criminal justice/law enforcement administration; data processing and data processing technology; humanities; human services; information science/studies; interdisciplinary studies; kinesiology and exercise science; liberal arts and sciences/liberal studies; mathematics; nursing (registered nurse training); real estate; social sciences; web/multimedia management and webmaster.

Academic Programs *Special study options:* academic remediation for entering students, adult/continuing education programs, advanced placement credit, distance learning, honors programs, internships, part-time degree program, services for LD students, student-designed majors, summer session for credit.

Library 52,484 titles, 627 serial subscriptions, an OPAC, a Web page.

Computers on Campus 150 computers available on campus for general student use. A campuswide network can be accessed from off campus. Internet access, at least one staffed computer lab available.

Student Life *Housing:* college housing not available. *Activities and Organizations:* drama/theater group, student-run radio station, choral group, student council/government, Student Ambassadors, Nursing Club. *Campus security:* 24-hour patrols, late-night transport/escort service.

Athletics Member NJCAA. *Intercollegiate sports:* baseball M, basketball M, soccer M/W, softball W. *Intramural sports:* archery M/W, badminton M/W, baseball M, basketball M/W, fencing M/W, soccer M/W, table tennis M/W, tennis M/W, volleyball M/W, weight lifting M/W.

Standardized Tests *Required:* College Qualifying Test (for placement). *Recommended:* SAT I or ACT (for placement).

Costs (2004–05) *Tuition:* state resident $2472 full-time, $103 per credit hour part-time; nonresident $4944 full-time, $206 per credit hour part-time. *Required fees:* $140 full-time, $9 per semester part-time. *Payment plans:* installment, deferred payment. *Waivers:* senior citizens and employees or children of employees.

Applying *Options:* early admission, deferred entrance. *Application fee:* $30. *Required:* high school transcript. *Required for some:* interview. *Application deadline:* rolling (freshmen), rolling (transfers). *Notification:* continuous (freshmen), continuous (transfers).

Admissions Contact Mrs. Patricia Hallenbeck, Assistant Dean of Student Affairs, Columbia-Greene Community College, 4400 Route 23, Hudson, NY 12534-0327. *Phone:* 518-828-4181 Ext. 5513. *Fax:* 518-828-8543. *E-mail:* hallenbeck@vaxa.cis.sunycgcc.edu.

CORNING COMMUNITY COLLEGE
Corning, New York

- **State and locally supported** 2-year, founded 1956, part of State University of New York System
- **Calendar** semesters
- **Degree** certificates and associate
- **Rural** 275-acre campus
- **Endowment** $1.2 million
- **Coed,** 4,443 undergraduate students, 53% full-time, 59% women, 41% men

Corning Community College (continued)

Undergraduates 2,356 full-time, 2,087 part-time. Students come from 13 states and territories, 4% are from out of state, 3% African American, 0.7% Asian American or Pacific Islander, 0.7% Hispanic American, 0.2% Native American, 0.1% international, 4% transferred in. *Retention:* 67% of 2002 full-time freshmen returned.

Freshmen *Admission:* 1,622 applied, 1,464 admitted, 988 enrolled.

Faculty *Total:* 243, 39% full-time, 8% with terminal degrees. *Student/faculty ratio:* 19:1.

Majors Accounting; administrative assistant and secretarial science; automobile/automotive mechanics technology; automotive engineering technology; biological and physical sciences; business administration and management; chemical technology; child care provision; computer and information sciences; computer and information sciences related; computer graphics; computer/information technology services administration related; computer programming; computer programming related; computer science; computer systems networking and telecommunications; computer technology/computer systems technology; corrections and criminal justice related; criminal justice/law enforcement administration; drafting and design technology; education related; electrical, electronic and communications engineering technology; elementary education; emergency medical technology (EMT paramedic); fire science; general studies; health and physical education; humanities; human services; industrial technology; information technology; legal assistant/paralegal; liberal arts and sciences/liberal studies; machine shop technology; machine tool technology; mathematics; mechanical engineering/mechanical technology; nursing (registered nurse training); optical sciences; pre-engineering; social sciences; substance abuse/addiction counseling; tourism and travel services management; word processing.

Academic Programs *Special study options:* academic remediation for entering students, accelerated degree program, advanced placement credit, distance learning, double majors, honors programs, independent study, internships, part-time degree program, services for LD students, student-designed majors, summer session for credit. *ROTC:* Army (c), Navy (c), Air Force (c).

Library Arthur A. Houghton, Jr. Library with 71,233 titles, 2,500 serial subscriptions, 4,290 audiovisual materials, an OPAC, a Web page.

Computers on Campus 350 computers available on campus for general student use. A campuswide network can be accessed from off campus that provide access to e-mail, Internet courses. Internet access, at least one staffed computer lab available.

Student Life *Housing:* college housing not available. *Activities and Organizations:* drama/theater group, student-run newspaper, radio station, choral group, student association, WCEB, Two-Bit Players, Activities Programming Committee, Nursing Society. *Campus security:* 24-hour emergency response devices and patrols, late-night transport/escort service. *Student services:* health clinic, personal/psychological counseling.

Athletics Member NJCAA. *Intercollegiate sports:* basketball M/W, cheerleading W, soccer M/W, softball W, volleyball W. *Intramural sports:* archery M/W, badminton M/W, basketball M/W, bowling M/W, golf M/W, rock climbing M/W, soccer M/W, softball M/W, table tennis M/W, volleyball M/W, weight lifting M/W.

Costs (2003–04) *Tuition:* state resident $2864 full-time, $119 per credit hour part-time; nonresident $5728 full-time, $238 per credit hour part-time. Part-time tuition and fees vary according to course load. *Required fees:* $400 full-time, $75 per term part-time. *Payment plan:* installment. *Waivers:* employees or children of employees.

Financial Aid Of all full-time matriculated undergraduates who enrolled, 264 Federal Work-Study jobs (averaging $1128).

Applying *Options:* electronic application, early admission. *Application fee:* $25. *Required:* high school transcript. *Required for some:* interview. *Application deadline:* rolling (freshmen), rolling (transfers). *Notification:* continuous (freshmen), continuous (transfers).

Admissions Contact Ms. Donna A. Hastings, Interim Director of Admissions, Corning Community College, 1 Academic Drive, Corning, NY 14830. *Phone:* 607-962-9220. *Toll-free phone:* 800-358-7171 Ext. 220. *Fax:* 607-962-9520. *E-mail:* admissions@corning-cc.edu.

CROUSE HOSPITAL SCHOOL OF NURSING
Syracuse, New York

- **Independent** 2-year, founded 1913
- **Calendar** semesters
- **Degree** associate
- **Urban** campus
- **Coed, primarily women,** 222 undergraduate students, 57% full-time, 87% women, 13% men

Undergraduates 127 full-time, 95 part-time. Students come from 4 states and territories, 2% are from out of state, 9% African American, 2% Asian American or Pacific Islander, 2% Hispanic American, 0.9% Native American, 14% live on campus.

Freshmen *Admission:* 11 admitted, 11 enrolled.

Faculty *Total:* 23, 57% full-time. *Student/faculty ratio:* 9:1.

Majors Nursing (registered nurse training).

Academic Programs *Special study options:* part-time degree program.

Student Life *Campus security:* 24-hour emergency response devices and patrols, late-night transport/escort service, controlled dormitory access. *Student services:* health clinic, personal/psychological counseling.

Standardized Tests *Recommended:* SAT I or ACT (for admission).

Costs (2004–05) *Tuition:* $7352 full-time, $225 per credit hour part-time. *Required fees:* $300 full-time, $130 per term part-time. *Room only:* $1500.

Financial Aid Of all full-time matriculated undergraduates who enrolled, 18 Federal Work-Study jobs (averaging $880).

Applying *Options:* deferred entrance. *Application fee:* $20. *Required:* essay or personal statement, high school transcript, minimum 2.5 GPA, 3 letters of recommendation, interview. *Application deadlines:* 7/1 (freshmen), 7/1 (transfers).

Admissions Contact Ms. Karen Van Sise, Enrollment Management Coordinator, Crouse Hospital School of Nursing, 736 Irving Avenue, Syracuse, NY 13210. *Phone:* 315-470-7481. *Fax:* 315-470-7925.

DOROTHEA HOPFER SCHOOL OF NURSING AT THE MOUNT VERNON HOSPITAL
Mount Vernon, New York

- **Independent** 2-year
- 120 undergraduate students

Costs (2003–04) *Tuition:* $18,450 full-time.

Admissions Contact Office of Admissions, Dorothea Hopfer School of Nursing at The Mount Vernon Hospital, 53 Valentine Street, Mount Vernon, NY 10550. *Phone:* 914-664-8000 Ext. 3221. *Fax:* 914-665-7047.

DUTCHESS COMMUNITY COLLEGE
Poughkeepsie, New York

- **State and locally supported** 2-year, founded 1957, part of State University of New York System
- **Calendar** semesters
- **Degree** certificates and associate
- **Suburban** 130-acre campus with easy access to New York City
- **Coed,** 7,810 undergraduate students

Freshmen *Admission:* 1,030 applied, 1,012 admitted. *Average high school GPA:* 2.5.

Faculty *Total:* 396.

Majors Accounting; administrative assistant and secretarial science; architectural engineering technology; artificial intelligence and robotics; biological and physical sciences; business administration and management; business machine repair; child development; child guidance; clinical/medical laboratory technology; commercial and advertising art; communication/speech communication and rhetoric; computer and information sciences; computer science; construction engineering technology; consumer merchandising/retailing management; criminal justice/law enforcement administration; criminal justice/safety; dietetics; electrical, electronic and communications engineering technology; electrical, electronics and communications engineering; electromechanical technology; elementary education; emergency medical technology (EMT paramedic); engineering science; foods, nutrition, and wellness; humanities; information science/studies; kindergarten/preschool education; legal assistant/paralegal; liberal arts and sciences/liberal studies; mass communication/media; mathematics; medical/clinical assistant; mental health/rehabilitation; nursing (registered nurse training); parks, recreation and leisure; physical therapist assistant; psychiatric/mental health services technology; science teacher education; social sciences; special products marketing; telecommunications; tourism and travel services management.

Academic Programs *Special study options:* academic remediation for entering students, adult/continuing education programs, advanced placement credit, English as a second language, freshman honors college, honors programs, internships, off-campus study, part-time degree program, summer session for credit.

Library Dutchess Library with 103,272 titles, 540 serial subscriptions, an OPAC, a Web page.

Computers on Campus 50 computers available on campus for general student use. A campuswide network can be accessed from off campus. Internet access, at least one staffed computer lab available.

Student Life *Housing:* college housing not available. *Activities and Organizations:* drama/theater group, student-run newspaper, radio station, choral group.

Campus security: 24-hour emergency response devices and patrols, late-night transport/escort service. *Student services:* health clinic, personal/psychological counseling.

Athletics Member NJCAA. *Intercollegiate sports:* baseball M, basketball M/W, bowling M/W, golf M, soccer M/W, softball W, tennis M/W, volleyball W. *Intramural sports:* badminton M/W, basketball M/W, football M, soccer M/W, tennis M/W, volleyball M/W.

Costs (2003–04) *Tuition:* state resident $2450 full-time, $95 per credit hour part-time; nonresident $4900 full-time, $190 per credit hour part-time. *Required fees:* $115 full-time.

Financial Aid Of all full-time matriculated undergraduates who enrolled, 500 Federal Work-Study jobs (averaging $1500).

Applying *Options:* early admission, deferred entrance. *Required:* high school transcript. *Application deadline:* rolling (freshmen), rolling (transfers). *Notification:* continuous (freshmen), continuous (transfers).

Admissions Contact Ms. Rita Banner, Director of Admissions, Dutchess Community College, 53 Pendell Road, Poughkeepsie, NY 12601. *Phone:* 845-431-8010. *Toll-free phone:* 800-763-3933. *E-mail:* banner@sunydutchess.edu.

ELLIS HOSPITAL SCHOOL OF NURSING
Schenectady, New York

Admissions Contact Mary Lee Pollard, Director of School, Ellis Hospital School of Nursing, 1101 Nott Street, Schenectady, NY 12308. *Phone:* 518-243-4471.

ELMIRA BUSINESS INSTITUTE
Elmira, New York

- **Private** 2-year, founded 1858
- **Degree** certificates and associate
- **Coed, primarily women,** 340 undergraduate students, 100% full-time, 88% women, 12% men

Undergraduates 340 full-time. Students come from 2 states and territories, 40% are from out of state, 1% African American.

Freshmen *Admission:* 86 applied, 61 admitted. *Average high school GPA:* 2.50.

Faculty *Total:* 40, 18% full-time. *Student/faculty ratio:* 12:1.

Majors Accounting; administrative assistant and secretarial science; legal administrative assistant/secretary; medical administrative assistant and medical secretary; tourism and travel services management.

Academic Programs *Special study options:* academic remediation for entering students, advanced placement credit, internships, part-time degree program.

Library Elmira Business Institute Library with 800 titles, 14 serial subscriptions, 15 audiovisual materials.

Computers on Campus 50 computers available on campus for general student use. Internet access available.

Student Life *Housing:* college housing not available.

Costs (2003–04) *Tuition:* $8085 full-time, $245 per credit part-time. No tuition increase for student's term of enrollment. *Required fees:* $200 full-time. *Payment plan:* tuition prepayment.

Applying *Options:* common application, electronic application. *Required:* high school transcript, interview. *Application deadline:* rolling (freshmen).

Admissions Contact Ms. Lisa Roan, Admissions Director, Elmira Business Institute, 303 North Main Street, Langdon Plaza, Elmira, NY 14901. *Phone:* 800-843-1812 Ext. 210. *Toll-free phone:* 800-843-1812. *Fax:* 607-733-7178. *E-mail:* lroan@ebi-college.com.

ERIE COMMUNITY COLLEGE
Buffalo, New York

- **State and locally supported** 2-year, founded 1971, part of State University of New York System
- **Calendar** semesters
- **Degrees** certificates, diplomas, and associate (profile also includes information from North and South campuses)
- **Urban** 1-acre campus
- **Coed,** 12,284 undergraduate students, 66% full-time, 51% women, 49% men

Undergraduates 8,085 full-time, 4,199 part-time. Students come from 10 states and territories, 3 other countries, 1% are from out of state, 16% African American, 2% Asian American or Pacific Islander, 3% Hispanic American, 0.8% Native American, 0.7% international, 4% transferred in.

Freshmen *Admission:* 4,731 applied, 4,069 admitted, 2,867 enrolled.

Faculty *Total:* 1,104, 32% full-time. *Student/faculty ratio:* 17:1.

Majors Administrative assistant and secretarial science; building/property maintenance and management; business administration and management; child

care and support services management; community health services counseling; criminal justice/law enforcement administration; culinary arts; hotel/motel administration; humanities; industrial production technologies related; information science/studies; legal assistant/paralegal; liberal arts and sciences/liberal studies; medical radiologic technology; nursing (registered nurse training); office management; substance abuse/addiction counseling.

Academic Programs *Special study options:* academic remediation for entering students, adult/continuing education programs, advanced placement credit, cooperative education, distance learning, double majors, English as a second language, honors programs, independent study, internships, part-time degree program, services for LD students, student-designed majors, study abroad, summer session for credit. *ROTC:* Army (c).

Library Leon E. Butler Library with 24,927 titles, 208 serial subscriptions, 2,492 audiovisual materials, an OPAC, a Web page.

Computers on Campus 341 computers available on campus for general student use. A campuswide network can be accessed from off campus. Internet access, online (class) registration, at least one staffed computer lab available.

Student Life *Housing:* college housing not available. *Activities and Organizations:* student-run newspaper, Alpha Beta Gamma, Anthropology Club, Black Student Union, Business Club, Campus Ministry Club. *Campus security:* 24-hour emergency response devices and patrols, late-night transport/escort service. *Student services:* health clinic, personal/psychological counseling, women's center.

Athletics Member NJCAA. *Intercollegiate sports:* baseball M, basketball M/W, bowling M/W, cheerleading W, cross-country running M/W, football M, golf M/W, ice hockey M, soccer M/W, softball W, swimming M/W, track and field M/W, volleyball W.

Standardized Tests *Required:* ACT ASSET (for placement). *Recommended:* SAT I (for placement), SAT II: Subject Tests (for placement).

Costs (2003–04) *Tuition:* area resident $2700 full-time, $113 per credit hour part-time; state resident $5400 full-time, $226 per credit hour part-time; nonresident $5400 full-time, $226 per credit hour part-time. *Required fees:* $240 full-time, $5 per credit hour part-time, $20 per term part-time. *Payment plans:* installment, deferred payment. *Waivers:* senior citizens.

Financial Aid Of all full-time matriculated undergraduates who enrolled, 300 Federal Work-Study jobs (averaging $2000).

Applying *Options:* common application, electronic application. *Application fee:* $25. *Required:* high school transcript. *Required for some:* interview. *Application deadline:* rolling (freshmen). *Notification:* continuous (freshmen), continuous (transfers).

Admissions Contact Ms. Petrina Hill-Cheatom, Director of Admissions, Erie Community College, 121 Ellicott Street, Buffalo, NY 14203-2698. *Phone:* 716-851-1588. *Fax:* 716-851-1129.

EUGENIO MARIA DE HOSTOS COMMUNITY COLLEGE OF THE CITY UNIVERSITY OF NEW YORK
Bronx, New York

- **State and locally supported** 2-year, founded 1968, part of City University of New York System
- **Calendar** semesters
- **Degree** certificates and associate
- **Urban** 8-acre campus
- **Endowment** $172,149
- **Coed,** 3,705 undergraduate students, 72% full-time, 75% women, 25% men

Undergraduates 2,659 full-time, 1,046 part-time. Students come from 3 states and territories, 85 other countries, 1% are from out of state, 26% African American, 3% Asian American or Pacific Islander, 59% Hispanic American, 0.1% Native American, 9% international, 10% transferred in.

Freshmen *Admission:* 1,410 applied, 1,235 admitted, 629 enrolled.

Faculty *Total:* 310, 50% full-time, 36% with terminal degrees. *Student/faculty ratio:* 14:1.

Majors Accounting; administrative assistant and secretarial science; business administration and management; clinical/medical laboratory technology; data entry/microcomputer applications related; data processing and data processing technology; dental hygiene; electrical and electronic engineering technologies related; gerontology; kindergarten/preschool education; legal assistant/paralegal; liberal arts and sciences/liberal studies; medical administrative assistant and medical secretary; medical radiologic technology; nursing (licensed practical/vocational nurse training); nursing (registered nurse training); public administration.

Academic Programs *Special study options:* academic remediation for entering students, adult/continuing education programs, distance learning, double majors, English as a second language, internships, part-time degree program, services for LD students, study abroad, summer session for credit.

Eugenio Maria de Hostos Community College of the City University of New York (continued)

Library Hostos Community College Library with 54,202 titles, 321 serial subscriptions, 525 audiovisual materials, an OPAC, a Web page.

Computers on Campus 750 computers available on campus for general student use. A campuswide network can be accessed from off campus. Internet access, online (class) registration, at least one staffed computer lab available.

Student Life *Housing:* college housing not available. *Activities and Organizations:* student-run newspaper, Dominican Association, Puerto Rican Student Organization, Student Government Association, Black Student Union, Veterans Club. *Campus security:* 24-hour emergency response devices and patrols, late-night transport/escort service. *Student services:* health clinic, personal/psychological counseling, women's center, legal services.

Athletics Member NJCAA. *Intercollegiate sports:* baseball M, basketball M, volleyball W. *Intramural sports:* basketball M/W, cheerleading W, soccer M/W, volleyball W.

Costs (2003–04) *Tuition:* state resident $2500 full-time, $105 per credit part-time; nonresident $3076 full-time, $130 per credit part-time. *Required fees:* $172 full-time, $86 per term part-time. *Payment plans:* installment, deferred payment. *Waivers:* senior citizens and employees or children of employees.

Financial Aid Of all full-time matriculated undergraduates who enrolled, 1,600 Federal Work-Study jobs (averaging $1000).

Applying *Options:* common application. *Application fee:* $40. *Required:* high school transcript. *Application deadline:* rolling (freshmen), rolling (transfers). *Notification:* continuous until 2/15 (freshmen), continuous until 2/15 (transfers).

Admissions Contact Mr. Roland Velez, Director of Admissions, Eugenio Maria de Hostos Community College of the City University of New York, 120 149th Street, Room D-210, Bronx, NY 10451. *Phone:* 718-518-4406. *Fax:* 718-518-4256. *E-mail:* admissions2@hostos.cuny.edu.

FINGER LAKES COMMUNITY COLLEGE
Canandaigua, New York

- **State and locally supported** 2-year, founded 1965, part of State University of New York System
- **Calendar** semesters
- **Degree** certificates and associate
- **Small-town** 300-acre campus with easy access to Rochester
- **Coed,** 4,955 undergraduate students, 48% full-time, 59% women, 41% men

Undergraduates 2,356 full-time, 2,599 part-time. Students come from 6 states and territories, 3 other countries, 1% are from out of state.

Freshmen *Admission:* 3,109 applied, 3,000 admitted.

Faculty *Total:* 258, 41% full-time. *Student/faculty ratio:* 19:1.

Majors Accounting; administrative assistant and secretarial science; architectural engineering technology; banking and financial support services; biological and physical sciences; biology/biological sciences; biology/biotechnology laboratory technician; broadcast journalism; business administration and management; chemistry; commercial and advertising art; computer and information sciences; computer science; consumer merchandising/retailing management; criminal justice/law enforcement administration; criminal justice/police science; data processing and data processing technology; drafting and design technology; dramatic/theatre arts; engineering science; environmental studies; fine/studio arts; fish/game management; hotel/motel administration; humanities; human services; kindergarten/preschool education; legal assistant/paralegal; liberal arts and sciences/liberal studies; marketing/marketing management; mass communication/media; mathematics; mechanical engineering/mechanical technology; music; natural resources/conservation; natural resources management; natural resources management and policy; nursing (registered nurse training); ornamental horticulture; parks, recreation and leisure facilities management; physical education teaching and coaching; physics; political science and government; pre-engineering; psychology; social sciences; sociology; substance abuse/addiction counseling; tourism and travel services management.

Academic Programs *Special study options:* academic remediation for entering students, advanced placement credit, distance learning, English as a second language, honors programs, internships, off-campus study, part-time degree program, services for LD students, summer session for credit. *ROTC:* Army (c).

Library Charles Meder Library with 73,305 titles, 464 serial subscriptions, an OPAC.

Computers on Campus 425 computers available on campus for general student use. A campuswide network can be accessed from off campus. Internet access, at least one staffed computer lab available.

Student Life *Housing Options:* Campus housing is provided by a third party. *Activities and Organizations:* drama/theater group, student-run newspaper, radio station, choral group, national fraternities, national sororities. *Campus security:* 24-hour emergency response devices and patrols, late-night transport/escort service. *Student services:* health clinic, personal/psychological counseling, legal services.

Athletics Member NJCAA. *Intercollegiate sports:* baseball M, basketball M/W, cross-country running M/W, lacrosse M/W, soccer M/W, softball W. *Intramural sports:* basketball M/W, tennis M/W, volleyball M/W.

Standardized Tests *Recommended:* SAT I or ACT (for placement).

Costs (2003–04) *Tuition:* state resident $2700 full-time; nonresident $5400 full-time. *Required fees:* $230 full-time. *Waivers:* employees or children of employees.

Financial Aid Of all full-time matriculated undergraduates who enrolled, 150 Federal Work-Study jobs (averaging $1800). 150 state and other part-time jobs (averaging $1800).

Applying *Options:* electronic application, early admission, deferred entrance. *Required:* high school transcript. *Recommended:* interview. *Application deadline:* rolling (freshmen), rolling (transfers). *Notification:* continuous until 8/31 (freshmen), continuous until 8/31 (transfers).

Admissions Contact Ms. Bonnie B. Ritts, Director of Admissions, Finger Lakes Community College, 4355 Lake Shore Drive, Canandaigua, NY 14424-8395. *Phone:* 585-394-3500 Ext. 7278. *Fax:* 585-394-5005. *E-mail:* admissions@flcc.edu.

FIORELLO H. LAGUARDIA COMMUNITY COLLEGE OF THE CITY UNIVERSITY OF NEW YORK
Long Island City, New York

- **State and locally supported** 2-year, founded 1970, part of City University of New York System
- **Calendar** modified semester
- **Degree** certificates and associate
- **Urban** 6-acre campus
- **Coed,** 12,875 undergraduate students, 48% full-time, 63% women, 37% men

LaGuardia offers 30 degree programs; day, evening, and weekend classes; a world-renowned internship program; an Honors Program; a Career and Transfer Center; and strong support services to ensure student success. Recently recognized as 1 of 13 national Institutions of Excellence by the Policy Center for the First Year of College, LaGuardia, as part of CUNY, also has the lowest college tuition in New York City. Based in Queens, the College is less than 10 minutes from Manhattan and Brooklyn by subway or bus.

Undergraduates 6,190 full-time, 6,685 part-time. Students come from 9 states and territories, 135 other countries, 0.3% are from out of state, 15% African American, 11% Asian American or Pacific Islander, 33% Hispanic American, 0.1% Native American, 13% international, 7% transferred in. *Retention:* 62% of 2002 full-time freshmen returned.

Freshmen *Admission:* 6,281 applied, 6,281 admitted, 2,155 enrolled. *Average high school GPA:* 2.95.

Faculty *Total:* 758, 32% full-time, 23% with terminal degrees. *Student/faculty ratio:* 24:1.

Majors Accounting; administrative assistant and secretarial science; business administration and management; computer and information sciences related; computer engineering technology; computer programming; computer programming related; computer programming (specific applications); computer programming (vendor/product certification); computer science; computer systems networking and telecommunications; data entry/microcomputer applications; dietetics; education; emergency medical technology (EMT paramedic); fine/studio arts; funeral service and mortuary science; gerontology; human services; information science/studies; kindergarten/preschool education; legal administrative assistant/secretary; legal assistant/paralegal; liberal arts and sciences/liberal studies; mental health/rehabilitation; nursing (registered nurse training); occupational therapy; photography; physical therapy; special products marketing; system administration; tourism and travel services management; veterinary technology.

Academic Programs *Special study options:* academic remediation for entering students, adult/continuing education programs, advanced placement credit, cooperative education, double majors, English as a second language, honors programs, independent study, internships, off-campus study, part-time degree program, services for LD students, student-designed majors, study abroad.

Library Fiorello H. LaGuardia Community College Library Media Resources Center plus 1 other with 121,631 titles, 760 serial subscriptions, 5,529 audiovisual materials, an OPAC.

Computers on Campus 997 computers available on campus for general student use. A campuswide network can be accessed from off campus. At least one staffed computer lab available.

Student Life *Housing:* college housing not available. *Activities and Organizations:* drama/theater group, student-run newspaper, radio station, Latinos Unidos Club, Bangladesh Club, Dominican Club, Law Club. *Campus security:* 24-hour patrols. *Student services:* health clinic, personal/psychological counseling, women's center.

Athletics *Intramural sports:* basketball M/W, football M/W, golf M/W, soccer M/W, volleyball M/W, weight lifting M/W.

Standardized Tests *Recommended:* SAT I or ACT (for placement).
Costs (2003–04) *Tuition:* state resident $2500 full-time; nonresident $3076 full-time. *Required fees:* $272 full-time.
Financial Aid Of all full-time matriculated undergraduates who enrolled, 1,425 Federal Work-Study jobs (averaging $1194).
Applying *Options:* electronic application, early admission, deferred entrance. *Application fee:* $50. *Required:* high school transcript. *Application deadline:* rolling (freshmen), rolling (transfers). *Notification:* continuous (freshmen), continuous (transfers).
Admissions Contact Ms. LaVora Desvigne, Director of Admissions, Fiorello H. LaGuardia Community College of the City University of New York, RM-147, 31-10 Thomson Avenue, Long Island City, NY 11101. *Phone:* 718-482-7206. *Fax:* 718-482-5112. *E-mail:* admissions@lagcc.cuny.edu.

FULTON-MONTGOMERY COMMUNITY COLLEGE
Johnstown, New York

- **State and locally supported** 2-year, founded 1964, part of State University of New York System
- **Calendar** semesters plus winter session
- **Degree** certificates and associate
- **Rural** 195-acre campus
- **Endowment** $328,000
- **Coed,** 1,956 undergraduate students, 70% full-time, 57% women, 43% men

Undergraduates 1,361 full-time, 595 part-time. Students come from 3 states and territories, 20 other countries, 4% African American, 1% Asian American or Pacific Islander, 5% Hispanic American, 0.2% Native American, 8% international, 3% transferred in.
Freshmen *Admission:* 1,025 applied, 1,025 admitted, 512 enrolled.
Faculty *Total:* 110, 45% full-time, 12% with terminal degrees. *Student/faculty ratio:* 22:1.
Majors Accounting; administrative assistant and secretarial science; art; automobile/automotive mechanics technology; behavioral sciences; biological and physical sciences; biology/biological sciences; business administration and management; carpentry; commercial and advertising art; computer engineering technology; computer science; computer typography and composition equipment operation; construction engineering technology; criminal justice/law enforcement administration; data processing and data processing technology; developmental and child psychology; dramatic/theatre arts; electrical, electronic and communications engineering technology; elementary education; engineering science; English; environmental studies; finance; fine/studio arts; graphic and printing equipment operation/production; health teacher education; history; humanities; human services; information science/studies; kindergarten/preschool education; legal administrative assistant/secretary; liberal arts and sciences/liberal studies; mass communication/media; mathematics; medical administrative assistant and medical secretary; natural resources/conservation; nursing (registered nurse training); physical education teaching and coaching; physical sciences; psychology; social sciences; teacher assistant/aide.
Academic Programs *Special study options:* academic remediation for entering students, accelerated degree program, adult/continuing education programs, advanced placement credit, cooperative education, distance learning, double majors, English as a second language, external degree program, honors programs, independent study, internships, off-campus study, part-time degree program, services for LD students, student-designed majors, study abroad, summer session for credit. *ROTC:* Army (c), Air Force (c).
Library Evans Library with 53,485 titles, 167 serial subscriptions, 1,114 audiovisual materials, an OPAC, a Web page.
Computers on Campus 250 computers available on campus for general student use. A campuswide network can be accessed from off campus. Internet access, at least one staffed computer lab available.
Student Life *Housing:* college housing not available. *Activities and Organizations:* drama/theater group, student-run newspaper, choral group, Business Students' Association, Criminal Justice Club, WAU (We Are United), Ski Club. *Campus security:* weekend and night security. *Student services:* personal/psychological counseling.
Athletics Member NJCAA. *Intercollegiate sports:* baseball M, basketball M/W, soccer M/W, softball W, volleyball W. *Intramural sports:* baseball M, basketball M/W, fencing M(c)/W(c), golf M(c)/W(c), skiing (cross-country) M(c)/W(c), skiing (downhill) M(c)/W(c), volleyball M/W.
Costs (2003–04) *Tuition:* state resident $2800 full-time, $116 per credit hour part-time; nonresident $5600 full-time, $232 per credit hour part-time. Part-time tuition and fees vary according to course load. *Required fees:* $280 full-time, $2 per credit hour part-time, $38 per credit hour part-time. *Payment plans:* installment, deferred payment. *Waivers:* senior citizens and employees or children of employees.
Financial Aid Of all full-time matriculated undergraduates who enrolled, 87 Federal Work-Study jobs (averaging $1000).

Applying *Options:* common application, electronic application, early admission, deferred entrance. *Required:* high school transcript. *Application deadlines:* 9/10 (freshmen), 9/10 (transfers). *Notification:* continuous (freshmen), continuous (transfers).
Admissions Contact Ms. Jane Kelley, Associate Dean for Enrollment Management, Fulton-Montgomery Community College, 2805 State Highway 67, Johnstown, NY 12095-3790. *Phone:* 518-762-4651 Ext. 8301. *Fax:* 518-762-4334. *E-mail:* geninfo@fmcc.suny.edu.

GAMLA COLLEGE
Brooklyn, New York

Admissions Contact Gamla College, 1213 Elm Avenue, Brooklyn, NY 11230.

GENESEE COMMUNITY COLLEGE
Batavia, New York

- **State and locally supported** 2-year, founded 1966, part of State University of New York System
- **Calendar** semesters
- **Degree** certificates and associate
- **Small-town** 256-acre campus with easy access to Buffalo
- **Endowment** $890,901
- **Coed**

Faculty *Student/faculty ratio:* 19:1.
Student Life *Campus security:* 24-hour emergency response devices and patrols, late-night transport/escort service.
Athletics Member NJCAA.
Standardized Tests *Required:* ACT ASSET, ACT COMPASS (for placement).
Financial Aid Of all full-time matriculated undergraduates who enrolled, 140 Federal Work-Study jobs (averaging $1300).
Applying *Options:* common application, electronic application. *Required:* high school transcript. *Required for some:* 1 letter of recommendation.
Admissions Contact Mrs. Tanya Lane-Martin, Director of Admissions, Genesee Community College, 1 College Road, Batavia, NY 14020. *Phone:* 585-343-0055 Ext. 6413. *Toll-free phone:* 800-CALL GCC. *Fax:* 585-345-6892.

HELENE FULD COLLEGE OF NURSING OF NORTH GENERAL HOSPITAL
New York, New York

Admissions Contact Mrs. Gladys Pineda, Student Services, Helene Fuld College of Nursing of North General Hospital, 1879 Madison Avenue, New York, NY 10035. *Phone:* 212-423-2768.

HERKIMER COUNTY COMMUNITY COLLEGE
Herkimer, New York

- **State and locally supported** 2-year, founded 1966, part of State University of New York System
- **Calendar** semesters
- **Degree** certificates and associate
- **Small-town** 500-acre campus with easy access to Syracuse
- **Endowment** $1.7 million
- **Coed**

Faculty *Student/faculty ratio:* 24:1.
Student Life *Campus security:* 24-hour emergency response devices and patrols.
Athletics Member NJCAA.
Standardized Tests *Recommended:* SAT I or ACT (for placement).
Financial Aid Of all full-time matriculated undergraduates who enrolled, 150 Federal Work-Study jobs (averaging $700).
Applying *Options:* common application, early admission. *Required:* high school transcript.
Admissions Contact Mr. Philip G. Hubbard, Associate Dean for Enrollment Management and Marketing, Herkimer County Community College, Herkimer, NY 13350. *Phone:* 315-866-0300 Ext. 278. *Toll-free phone:* 888-464-4222 Ext. 278. *Fax:* 315-866-7253. *E-mail:* admission@hccc.suny.edu.

Hudson Valley Community College
Troy, New York

- **State and locally supported** 2-year, founded 1953, part of State University of New York System
- **Calendar** semesters
- **Degree** certificates and associate
- **Suburban** 135-acre campus
- **Coed**

Student Life *Campus security:* 24-hour emergency response devices and patrols, late-night transport/escort service.

Athletics Member NJCAA.

Standardized Tests *Required for some:* SAT I or ACT (for placement). *Recommended:* SAT I or ACT (for placement).

Costs (2003–04) *Tuition:* state resident $2500 full-time; nonresident $7500 full-time. *Required fees:* $106 full-time.

Financial Aid Of all full-time matriculated undergraduates who enrolled, 100 Federal Work-Study jobs (averaging $2000).

Applying *Options:* early admission, deferred entrance. *Application fee:* $30. *Required:* high school transcript.

Admissions Contact Ms. MaryClaire Bauer, Director of Admissions, Hudson Valley Community College, 80 Vandenburgh Avenue, Troy, NY 12180-6096. *Phone:* 518-629-4603. *E-mail:* panzajul@hvcc.edu.

Institute of Design and Construction
Brooklyn, New York

- **Independent** 2-year, founded 1947
- **Calendar** semesters
- **Degree** associate
- **Urban** campus
- **Coed, primarily men**

Applying *Options:* common application. *Application fee:* $30. *Required:* high school transcript. *Recommended:* interview.

Admissions Contact Mr. Kevin Giannetti, Director of Admissions, Institute of Design and Construction, 141 Willoughby Street, Brooklyn, NY 11201-5317. *Phone:* 718-855-3661. *Fax:* 718-852-5889.

Interboro Institute
New York, New York

- **Proprietary** 2-year, founded 1888
- **Calendar** semesters
- **Degree** associate
- **Urban** campus
- **Coed**

Faculty *Student/faculty ratio:* 36:1.

Student Life *Campus security:* student patrols.

Standardized Tests *Required for some:* CPAt.

Costs (2003–04) *Tuition:* $7800 full-time. *Required fees:* $35 full-time. *Payment plans:* installment, deferred payment.

Financial Aid Of all full-time matriculated undergraduates who enrolled, 156 Federal Work-Study jobs (averaging $2042).

Applying *Options:* deferred entrance. *Application fee:* $35. *Required:* essay or personal statement, interview. *Recommended:* high school transcript.

Admissions Contact Ms. Cheryl Ryan, Director of Admissions, Interboro Institute, 450 West 56th Street, New York, NY 10019. *Phone:* 212-399-0091 Ext. 6406. *Fax:* 212-399-9746. *E-mail:* ryan@interboro.com.

Island Drafting and Technical Institute
Amityville, New York

- **Proprietary** 2-year, founded 1957
- **Calendar** semesters
- **Degree** certificates, diplomas, and associate
- **Suburban** campus
- **Coed, primarily men,** 222 undergraduate students, 100% full-time, 14% women, 86% men

Undergraduates 222 full-time. Students come from 1 other state, 16% African American, 2% Asian American or Pacific Islander, 20% Hispanic American.

Freshmen *Admission:* 100 applied, 76 admitted, 76 enrolled. *Average high school GPA:* 3.50.

Faculty *Total:* 25, 20% full-time, 4% with terminal degrees. *Student/faculty ratio:* 15:1.

Majors Architectural drafting and CAD/CADD; computer and information systems security; computer systems networking and telecommunications; computer/technical support; computer technology/computer systems technology; electrical, electronic and communications engineering technology; mechanical drafting and CAD/CADD; system administration.

Academic Programs *Special study options:* accelerated degree program, adult/continuing education programs, summer session for credit.

Student Life *Housing:* college housing not available.

Costs (2004–05) *Tuition:* $10,800 full-time, $360 per credit part-time. No tuition increase for student's term of enrollment. *Required fees:* $350 full-time, $18 per credit part-time. *Payment plan:* installment.

Applying *Options:* early admission. *Required:* interview. *Recommended:* high school transcript. *Notification:* continuous (freshmen).

Admissions Contact Mr. Gary Weiller, Island Drafting and Technical Institute, 128 Broadway, Amityville, NY 11701. *Phone:* 631-691-8733. *Fax:* 631-691-8738. *E-mail:* info@islanddrafting.com.

ITT Technical Institute
Albany, New York

- **Proprietary** 2-year, part of ITT Educational Services, Inc
- **Calendar** quarters
- **Degree** associate
- **Coed**

Standardized Tests *Required:* Wonderlic aptitude test (for admission).

Costs (2003–04) *Tuition:* Total Program Cost varies depending on course of study. Consult school catalog.

Applying *Options:* deferred entrance. *Application fee:* $100. *Required:* high school transcript, interview. *Recommended:* letters of recommendation.

Admissions Contact Mr. John Henebry, Director of Recruitment, ITT Technical Institute, 13 Airline Drive, Albany, NY 12205. *Phone:* 518-452-9300. *Toll-free phone:* 800-489-1191. *Fax:* 518-452-9300.

ITT Technical Institute
Liverpool, New York

- **Proprietary** 2-year, part of ITT Educational Services, Inc
- **Calendar** semesters
- **Degree** associate
- **Coed**

Standardized Tests *Required:* Wonderlic aptitude test (for admission).

Costs (2003–04) *Tuition:* Total Program Cost varies depending on course of study. Consult school catalog.

Applying *Options:* deferred entrance. *Application fee:* $100. *Required:* high school transcript, interview. *Recommended:* letters of recommendation.

Admissions Contact Terry Riesel, Director of Recruitment, ITT Technical Institute, 235 Greenfield Parkway, Liverpool, NY 13088. *Phone:* 315-461-8000. *Toll-free phone:* 877-488-0011. *Fax:* 315-461-8008.

ITT Technical Institute
Getzville, New York

- **Proprietary** 2-year, part of ITT Educational Services, Inc
- **Degree** associate
- **Coed**

Standardized Tests *Required:* Wonderlic aptitude test (for admission).

Costs (2003–04) *Tuition:* Total Program Cost varies depending on course of study. Consult school catalog.

Applying *Options:* deferred entrance. *Application fee:* $100. *Required:* high school transcript, interview. *Recommended:* letters of recommendation.

Admissions Contact Ms. Suzanne Noel, Director of Recruitment, ITT Technical Institute, 2295 Millersport Highway, PO Box 327, Getzville, NY 14068. *Phone:* 716-689-2200. *Toll-free phone:* 800-469-7593. *Fax:* 716-689-2828.

Jamestown Business College
Jamestown, New York

- **Proprietary** 2-year, founded 1886
- **Calendar** quarters
- **Degree** certificates and associate

■ **Small-town** 1-acre campus
■ **Coed,** 327 undergraduate students, 100% full-time, 81% women, 19% men

Undergraduates 327 full-time. Students come from 2 states and territories, 17% are from out of state, 2% African American, 0.3% Asian American or Pacific Islander, 4% Hispanic American, 0.9% Native American, 14% transferred in.
Freshmen *Admission:* 112 applied, 81 admitted, 81 enrolled.
Faculty *Total:* 20, 35% full-time. *Student/faculty ratio:* 24:1.
Majors Accounting; administrative assistant and secretarial science; business administration and management; computer and information sciences; legal administrative assistant/secretary; marketing/marketing management; medical administrative assistant and medical secretary.
Academic Programs *Special study options:* academic remediation for entering students, advanced placement credit, double majors, internships, part-time degree program, summer session for credit.
Library James Prendergast Library with 279,270 titles, 372 serial subscriptions, an OPAC, a Web page.
Computers on Campus 106 computers available on campus for general student use. A campuswide network can be accessed from off campus. Internet access, at least one staffed computer lab available.
Student Life *Housing:* college housing not available. *Campus security:* 24-hour emergency response devices.
Athletics *Intramural sports:* basketball M(c)/W(c), bowling M(c)/W(c), racquetball M(c)/W(c), skiing (cross-country) M(c)/W(c), skiing (downhill) M(c)/W(c), softball M(c)/W(c), swimming M(c)/W(c), table tennis M(c)/W(c), volleyball M(c)/W(c), weight lifting M(c)/W(c).
Costs (2003–04) *Tuition:* $7500 full-time, $1300 per course part-time. *Required fees:* $360 full-time, $75 per term part-time.
Applying *Application fee:* $25. *Required:* essay or personal statement, high school transcript, interview. *Application deadline:* rolling (freshmen), rolling (transfers).
Admissions Contact Ms. Brenda Salemme, Director of Admissions and Placement, Jamestown Business College, 7 Fairmount Avenue, Jamestown, NY 14701. *Phone:* 716-664-5100. *Fax:* 716-664-3144. *E-mail:* admissions@jbcny.org.

JAMESTOWN COMMUNITY COLLEGE
Jamestown, New York

■ **State and locally supported** 2-year, founded 1950, part of State University of New York System
■ **Calendar** semesters
■ **Degree** certificates and associate
■ **Small-town** 107-acre campus
■ **Coed,** 3,598 undergraduate students, 69% full-time, 57% women, 43% men

Undergraduates 2,486 full-time, 1,112 part-time. 9% are from out of state, 2% African American, 0.7% Asian American or Pacific Islander, 2% Hispanic American, 0.9% Native American.
Freshmen *Admission:* 1,172 enrolled.
Faculty *Total:* 343, 22% full-time. *Student/faculty ratio:* 18:1.
Majors Accounting; airline pilot and flight crew; business administration and management; clinical/medical laboratory technology; communication/speech communication and rhetoric; computer and information sciences; computer and information sciences related; computer and information systems security; computer engineering technology; computer science; criminal justice/police science; criminal justice/safety; electrical, electronic and communications engineering technology; electrical, electronics and communications engineering; engineering; fine/studio arts; forestry; heating, air conditioning, ventilation and refrigeration maintenance technology; liberal arts and sciences/liberal studies; mechanical engineering/mechanical technology; music performance; nursing (registered nurse training); occupational therapist assistant; social sciences.
Academic Programs *Special study options:* academic remediation for entering students, adult/continuing education programs, advanced placement credit, cooperative education, distance learning, double majors, English as a second language, honors programs, independent study, internships, off-campus study, part-time degree program, services for LD students, student-designed majors, study abroad, summer session for credit.
Library Hultquist Library plus 1 other with 79,510 titles, 585 serial subscriptions, 7,126 audiovisual materials, an OPAC, a Web page.
Computers on Campus 400 computers available on campus for general student use. A campuswide network can be accessed from off campus. At least one staffed computer lab available.
Student Life *Housing:* college housing not available. *Activities and Organizations:* drama/theater group, student-run newspaper, radio station, choral group, Nursing Club, Inter-Varsity Christian Fellowship, Earth Awareness, Adult Student Network, Student Senate. *Student services:* health clinic, personal/psychological counseling.
Athletics Member NJCAA. *Intercollegiate sports:* baseball M, basketball M/W, cross-country running M/W, golf M/W, soccer M(s)/W, softball W,

swimming M/W, volleyball W. *Intramural sports:* basketball M/W, bowling M/W, softball M/W, table tennis M/W, tennis M/W, track and field M/W, volleyball M/W, water polo M/W, wrestling M.
Standardized Tests *Required:* ACT ASSET (for placement).
Costs (2003–04) *Tuition:* state resident $2850 full-time, $119 per credit hour part-time; nonresident $5700 full-time, $216 per credit hour part-time. Full-time tuition and fees vary according to program. *Required fees:* $450 full-time. *Payment plans:* installment, deferred payment. *Waivers:* employees or children of employees.
Financial Aid Of all full-time matriculated undergraduates who enrolled, 120 Federal Work-Study jobs (averaging $1000). 110 state and other part-time jobs (averaging $1000).
Applying *Options:* early admission, deferred entrance. *Application fee:* $40. *Required:* high school transcript. *Required for some:* standardized test scores. *Application deadline:* rolling (freshmen), rolling (transfers). *Notification:* continuous (freshmen), continuous (transfers).
Admissions Contact Ms. Wendy Martenson, Director of Admissions and Recruitment, Jamestown Community College, 525 Falconer Street, PO Box 20, Jamestown, NY 14702-0020. *Phone:* 716-665-5220 Ext. 2240. *Toll-free phone:* 800-388-8557. *E-mail:* admissions@mail.sunyjcc.edu.

JEFFERSON COMMUNITY COLLEGE
Watertown, New York

■ **State and locally supported** 2-year, founded 1961, part of State University of New York System
■ **Calendar** semesters
■ **Degree** certificates and associate
■ **Small-town** 90-acre campus with easy access to Syracuse
■ **Endowment** $2.3 million
■ **Coed,** 3,481 undergraduate students, 54% full-time, 62% women, 38% men

Undergraduates 1,868 full-time, 1,613 part-time. Students come from 26 states and territories, 3 other countries, 1% are from out of state, 5% African American, 1% Asian American or Pacific Islander, 4% Hispanic American, 0.5% Native American, 0.2% international, 4% transferred in.
Freshmen *Admission:* 692 enrolled.
Faculty *Total:* 180, 42% full-time, 9% with terminal degrees. *Student/faculty ratio:* 18:1.
Majors Accounting; administrative assistant and secretarial science; biology/biotechnology laboratory technician; business administration and management; chemical technology; computer science; computer systems networking and telecommunications; computer typography and composition equipment operation; consumer merchandising/retailing management; criminal justice/law enforcement administration; engineering science; forestry technology; hospitality administration; hotel/motel administration; humanities; human services; information science/studies; interdisciplinary studies; kindergarten/preschool education; legal assistant/paralegal; liberal arts and sciences/liberal studies; marketing/marketing management; mathematics; medical administrative assistant and medical secretary; medical laboratory technology; natural sciences; nursing (registered nurse training); pre-engineering; tourism and travel services management.
Academic Programs *Special study options:* academic remediation for entering students, advanced placement credit, cooperative education, distance learning, double majors, honors programs, independent study, internships, part-time degree program, services for LD students, student-designed majors, summer session for credit.
Library Melvil Dewey Library with 62,503 titles, 247 serial subscriptions, 4,097 audiovisual materials, an OPAC, a Web page.
Computers on Campus 354 computers available on campus for general student use. A campuswide network can be accessed. Internet access, at least one staffed computer lab available.
Student Life *Housing:* college housing not available. *Activities and Organizations:* drama/theater group, student-run newspaper, choral group, Student Nursing Association, newspaper, The Melting Pot, Paralegal Club, Criminal Justice Club. *Campus security:* 24-hour emergency response devices and patrols. *Student services:* health clinic, personal/psychological counseling.
Athletics Member NJCAA. *Intercollegiate sports:* baseball M, basketball M/W, golf M/W, lacrosse M/W, soccer M/W, softball W, tennis W, volleyball W. *Intramural sports:* badminton M/W, basketball M/W, soccer M/W, softball M/W, volleyball M/W.
Standardized Tests *Recommended:* SAT I or ACT (for admission).
Costs (2003–04) *Tuition:* state resident $2572 full-time, $107 per credit hour part-time; nonresident $3792 full-time, $158 per credit hour part-time. *Required fees:* $234 full-time, $8 per credit hour part-time. *Payment plan:* installment. *Waivers:* senior citizens.
Financial Aid Of all full-time matriculated undergraduates who enrolled, 125 Federal Work-Study jobs (averaging $1200). 50 state and other part-time jobs (averaging $1000).

Jefferson Community College (continued)

Applying *Options:* early admission, deferred entrance. *Required:* high school transcript. *Required for some:* letters of recommendation, interview. *Application deadline:* 9/6 (freshmen), rolling (transfers). *Notification:* continuous (freshmen), continuous (transfers).

Admissions Contact Ms. Rosanne N. Weir, Director of Admissions, Jefferson Community College, 1220 Coffeen Street, Watertown, NY 13601. *Phone:* 315-786-2277. *Fax:* 315-786-2459. *E-mail:* admissions@sunyjefferson.edu.

KATHARINE GIBBS SCHOOL
Melville, New York

■ **Proprietary** 2-year, founded 1971, part of Career Education Corporation
■ **Calendar** quarters
■ **Degree** certificates and associate
■ **Suburban** campus with easy access to New York City
■ **Coed, primarily women**

Faculty *Student/faculty ratio:* 24:1.
Student Life *Campus security:* security guard.
Standardized Tests *Required for some:* CPAt. *Recommended:* SAT I (for admission).
Applying *Options:* deferred entrance. *Application fee:* $50. *Required:* high school transcript, interview. *Recommended:* letters of recommendation.
Admissions Contact Ms. Cynthia Gamache, Director of Admissions, Katharine Gibbs School, 320 South Service Road, Melville, NY 11747-3785. *Phone:* 631-370-3307. *Fax:* 516-293-2709.

KATHARINE GIBBS SCHOOL
New York, New York

Admissions Contact Ms. Pat Martin, Admissions Director, Katharine Gibbs School, 50 West 40th Street, New York, NY 10018. *Phone:* 212-867-9300.

KINGSBOROUGH COMMUNITY COLLEGE OF THE CITY UNIVERSITY OF NEW YORK
Brooklyn, New York

■ **State and locally supported** 2-year, founded 1963, part of City University of New York System
■ **Calendar** semesters
■ **Degree** associate
■ **Urban** 72-acre campus with easy access to New York City
■ **Coed,** 14,944 undergraduate students, 50% full-time, 60% women, 40% men

Undergraduates 7,481 full-time, 7,463 part-time. 2% are from out of state, 34% African American, 9% Asian American or Pacific Islander, 14% Hispanic American, 0.1% Native American, 6% international, 8% transferred in.
Freshmen *Admission:* 2,978 applied, 1,810 enrolled. *Average high school GPA:* 2.70. *Test scores:* SAT verbal scores over 500: 8%; SAT math scores over 500: 12%; SAT verbal scores over 600: 1%; SAT math scores over 600: 2%.
Faculty *Total:* 805, 29% full-time, 38% with terminal degrees. *Student/faculty ratio:* 24:1.
Majors Accounting; administrative assistant and secretarial science; applied art; art; biology/biological sciences; broadcast journalism; business administration and management; chemistry; commercial and advertising art; community health services counseling; computer and information sciences; computer science; data processing and data processing technology; dramatic/theatre arts; early childhood education; education; elementary education; engineering science; fashion merchandising; health and physical education related; human services; journalism; labor and industrial relations; liberal arts and sciences/liberal studies; marine technology; marketing/marketing management; mathematics; mental health/rehabilitation; music; nursing (registered nurse training); parks, recreation and leisure; physical therapist assistant; physical therapy; physics; psychiatric/mental health services technology; sport and fitness administration; teacher assistant/aide; tourism and travel services management.
Academic Programs *Special study options:* academic remediation for entering students, adult/continuing education programs, advanced placement credit, English as a second language, honors programs, internships, off-campus study, part-time degree program, services for LD students, student-designed majors, summer session for credit.
Library Robert J. Kibbee Library with 158,463 titles, 441 serial subscriptions, 2,388 audiovisual materials, an OPAC.
Computers on Campus 730 computers available on campus for general student use. A campuswide network can be accessed. Internet access, at least one staffed computer lab available.

Student Life *Housing:* college housing not available. *Activities and Organizations:* drama/theater group, student-run newspaper, radio station, choral group, Peer Advisors, Caribbean Club, DECA. *Campus security:* 24-hour emergency response devices and patrols. *Student services:* health clinic, personal/psychological counseling, women's center.
Athletics Member NJCAA. *Intercollegiate sports:* baseball M, basketball M/W, soccer M, softball W, tennis M/W, track and field M/W, volleyball W. *Intramural sports:* baseball M, basketball M/W, cheerleading W, soccer M, softball W, tennis M/W, track and field M/W, volleyball W.
Costs (2003–04) *Tuition:* state resident $2800 full-time, $120 per credit part-time; nonresident $4560 full-time, $190 per credit part-time. *Required fees:* $280 full-time, $70 per term part-time. *Payment plan:* installment. *Waivers:* senior citizens.
Applying *Options:* common application. *Application fee:* $50. *Required:* high school transcript. *Application deadline:* 8/23 (freshmen), rolling (transfers).
Admissions Contact Mr. Robert Ingenito, Director of Admissions Information Center, Kingsborough Community College of the City University of New York, 2001 Oriental Boulevard, Brooklyn, NY 11235. *Phone:* 718-368-4600. *E-mail:* info@kbcc.cuny.edu.

LONG ISLAND BUSINESS INSTITUTE
Commack, New York

■ **Proprietary** 2-year, founded 1968
■ **Calendar** trimesters
■ **Degree** certificates, diplomas, and associate
■ **Suburban** campus with easy access to New York City
■ **Coed, primarily women,** 169 undergraduate students, 47% full-time, 96% women, 4% men

Undergraduates 80 full-time, 89 part-time. Students come from 1 other state, 15% African American, 1% Asian American or Pacific Islander, 9% Hispanic American, 0.6% international.
Freshmen *Admission:* 55 applied, 43 admitted.
Faculty *Total:* 21, 29% full-time. *Student/faculty ratio:* 15:1.
Majors Accounting; administrative assistant and secretarial science; business administration and management; court reporting.
Academic Programs *Special study options:* academic remediation for entering students, adult/continuing education programs, advanced placement credit, independent study, internships, part-time degree program, summer session for credit.
Library Mendon W. Smith Memorial Library with 1,484 titles, 15 serial subscriptions, 184 audiovisual materials, an OPAC.
Computers on Campus 77 computers available on campus for general student use. Internet access, at least one staffed computer lab available.
Student Life *Housing:* college housing not available. *Campus security:* 24-hour emergency response devices. *Student services:* personal/psychological counseling.
Standardized Tests *Required:* CPAt (for placement).
Costs (2004–05) *Tuition:* $8500 full-time, $275 per credit part-time. Full-time tuition and fees vary according to course load and program. Part-time tuition and fees vary according to course load and program. *Required fees:* $50 full-time, $50 per year part-time. *Payment plans:* installment, deferred payment.
Applying *Application fee:* $50. *Required:* essay or personal statement, high school transcript, interview. *Application deadline:* rolling (freshmen), rolling (transfers).
Admissions Contact Mr. Barry Packer, Admissions Representative, Long Island Business Institute, 6500 Jericho Turnpike, Commack, NY 11725. *Phone:* 631-499-7100. *Fax:* 631-499-7114.

LONG ISLAND COLLEGE HOSPITAL SCHOOL OF NURSING
Brooklyn, New York

Admissions Contact Ms. Barbara J. Evans, Admissions Assistant, Long Island College Hospital School of Nursing, 397 Hicks Street, Brooklyn, NY 11201-5940. *Phone:* 718-780-1898. *Fax:* 718-780-1936.

MARIA COLLEGE
Albany, New York

■ **Independent** 2-year, founded 1958
■ **Calendar** semesters
■ **Degree** certificates and associate
■ **Urban** 9-acre campus

■ Coed

Clinical facilities for nursing, physical therapist studies, and occupational therapy assistant studies majors are among the institutional leaders. Laboratory school for education majors is among the finest in the Capital District. Liberal arts, early childhood education, and business majors are highly transferable. Also offered are associate degrees in computer information systems and legal assistant studies. One-year certificate programs include legal assistant studies, bereavement studies, complementary therapy, and gerontology.

Faculty *Student/faculty ratio:* 9:1.

Student Life *Campus security:* late-night transport/escort service.

Standardized Tests *Required:* SAT I or ACT (for admission), SAT I or ACT (for placement).

Costs (2003–04) *Tuition:* $6900 full-time, $250 per credit part-time. Full-time tuition and fees vary according to program. Part-time tuition and fees vary according to program. *Required fees:* $150 full-time, $40 per term part-time.

Financial Aid Of all full-time matriculated undergraduates who enrolled, 32 Federal Work-Study jobs (averaging $1000).

Applying *Options:* early admission. *Application fee:* $25. *Required:* essay or personal statement, high school transcript, minimum 2.0 GPA, 1 letter of recommendation, interview.

Admissions Contact Ms. Laurie A. Gilmore, Director of Admissions, Maria College, 700 New Scotland Avenue, Albany, NY 12208. *Phone:* 518-438-3111 Ext. 17. *Fax:* 518-453-1366. *E-mail:* admissions@mariacollege.org.

▶ See page 570 for a narrative description.

MEMORIAL HOSPITAL SCHOOL OF NURSING
Albany, New York

Admissions Contact Memorial Hospital School of Nursing, 600 Northern Boulevard, Albany, NY 12204.

MILDRED ELLEY
Latham, New York

- **Private** 2-year
- **Degree** certificates, diplomas, and associate
- **Suburban** campus with easy access to Albany
- 394 undergraduate students, 100% full-time

Undergraduates 394 full-time. Students come from 3 states and territories, 3% are from out of state, 21% African American, 6% Hispanic American, 2% transferred in.

Freshmen *Admission:* 121 applied, 119 admitted, 110 enrolled.

Faculty *Total:* 31, 45% full-time, 16% with terminal degrees. *Student/faculty ratio:* 20:1.

Majors Administrative assistant and secretarial science; business administration and management; information technology; legal assistant/paralegal; medical/clinical assistant.

Student Life *Housing:* college housing not available. *Student services:* legal services.

Standardized Tests *Required:* CPAt (for admission).

Costs (2004–05) *Tuition:* $7800 full-time, $325 per credit part-time. Full-time tuition and fees vary according to program. *Required fees:* $300 full-time. *Payment plan:* installment.

Applying *Notification:* continuous (transfers).

Admissions Contact Mr. Michael Cahalan, Enrollment Manager, Mildred Elley, 800 New Loudon Road, Suite 5120, Latham, NY 12110. *Phone:* 518-786-3171 Ext. 227. *Toll-free phone:* 800-622-6327. *Fax:* 518-786-0011. *E-mail:* michael.cahalan@mildred-elley.edu.

MOHAWK VALLEY COMMUNITY COLLEGE
Utica, New York

- **State and locally supported** 2-year, founded 1946, part of State University of New York System
- **Calendar** semesters
- **Degree** certificates and associate
- **Suburban** 80-acre campus
- **Endowment** $2.3 million
- **Coed**, 5,842 undergraduate students, 66% full-time, 54% women, 46% men

Undergraduates 3,857 full-time, 1,985 part-time. Students come from 10 states and territories, 16 other countries, 1% are from out of state, 7% African American, 2% Asian American or Pacific Islander, 2% Hispanic American, 0.8% Native American, 2% international, 4% transferred in, 8% live on campus. *Retention:* 58% of 2002 full-time freshmen returned.

Freshmen *Admission:* 3,138 applied, 2,851 admitted, 1,484 enrolled.

Faculty *Total:* 266, 55% full-time. *Student/faculty ratio:* 24:1.

Majors Accounting technology and bookkeeping; administrative assistant and secretarial science; advertising; airframe mechanics and aircraft maintenance technology; art; banking and financial support services; building/property maintenance and management; business administration and management; chemical technology; civil engineering technology; commercial and advertising art; commercial photography; communications systems installation and repair technology; community organization and advocacy; computer and information sciences; computer and information sciences and support services related; computer programming; criminal justice/law enforcement administration; design and applied arts related; drafting and design technology; dramatic/theatre arts; electrical and electronic engineering technologies related; electrical, electronic and communications engineering technology; electrical/electronics maintenance and repair technology related; emergency medical technology (EMT paramedic); engineering; entrepreneurship; food services technology; foodservice systems administration; health information/medical records technology; heating, air conditioning and refrigeration technology; hotel/motel administration; humanities; human services; industrial production technologies related; liberal arts and sciences/liberal studies; management information systems and services related; mechanical design technology; mechanical engineering/mechanical technology; medical/clinical assistant; medical laboratory technology; medical radiologic technology; mental health/rehabilitation; nursing (registered nurse training); nutrition sciences; parks, recreation and leisure facilities management; pre-engineering; public administration; respiratory care therapy; restaurant, culinary, and catering management; substance abuse/addiction counseling; survey technology; telecommunications.

Academic Programs *Special study options:* academic remediation for entering students, adult/continuing education programs, advanced placement credit, English as a second language, internships, off-campus study, part-time degree program, services for LD students, summer session for credit. *ROTC:* Army (c).

Library Mohawk Valley Community College Library plus 2 others with 91,000 titles, 925 serial subscriptions, an OPAC, a Web page.

Computers on Campus 380 computers available on campus for general student use. A campuswide network can be accessed from off campus. Internet access, online (class) registration, at least one staffed computer lab available.

Student Life *Housing Options:* coed. *Activities and Organizations:* drama/theater group, student-run newspaper, radio station, choral group, Student Congress, Returning Adult Student Association, Black Student Union, Program Board. *Campus security:* 24-hour emergency response devices and patrols, late-night transport/escort service, controlled dormitory access. *Student services:* health clinic, personal/psychological counseling.

Athletics Member NJCAA. *Intercollegiate sports:* baseball M, basketball M/W, bowling M/W, cross-country running M/W, golf M/W, ice hockey M, lacrosse M, soccer M/W, softball W, tennis M/W, track and field M/W, volleyball W. *Intramural sports:* basketball M/W, cheerleading W, football M, racquetball M/W, softball M/W, table tennis M/W, tennis M/W, volleyball M/W, weight lifting M.

Costs (2003–04) *Tuition:* state resident $2800 full-time, $115 per credit hour part-time; nonresident $5600 full-time, $230 per credit hour part-time. Part-time tuition and fees vary according to course load. *Required fees:* $334 full-time, $1 per credit hour part-time, $35 per term part-time. *Room and board:* $6150; room only: $3550. Room and board charges vary according to board plan. *Payment plans:* installment, deferred payment. *Waivers:* employees or children of employees.

Applying *Options:* electronic application, early admission, deferred entrance. *Required:* high school transcript. *Application deadline:* rolling (freshmen), rolling (transfers).

Admissions Contact Mrs. Sandra Fiebiger, Electronic Data Processing Clerk, Admissions, Mohawk Valley Community College, 1101 Sherman Drive, Utica, NY 13501. *Phone:* 315-792-5640. *Toll-free phone:* 800-SEE-MVCC. *E-mail:* admissions@mvcc.edu.

▶ See page 580 for a narrative description.

MONROE COLLEGE
Bronx, New York

- **Proprietary** primarily 2-year, founded 1933
- **Calendar** trimesters
- **Degrees** associate and bachelor's
- **Urban** campus
- **Coed**, 4,028 undergraduate students, 87% full-time, 71% women, 29% men

Monroe is a private, coeducational institution that offers associate and bachelor's (2+2) degrees, with New York City and Westchester County campuses. Programs encompass

Monroe College (continued)

a variety of majors that develop the student's career. Monroe's dynamic faculty members and strong support services foster professional development opportunities for students. At Monroe, the focus is on each student's future.

Undergraduates 3,490 full-time, 538 part-time. Students come from 4 states and territories, 8 other countries, 1% are from out of state, 42% African American, 2% Asian American or Pacific Islander, 49% Hispanic American, 0.1% Native American, 1% international. *Retention:* 43% of 2002 full-time freshmen returned.

Faculty *Total:* 201, 33% full-time, 18% with terminal degrees. *Student/faculty ratio:* 21:1.

Majors Accounting; business administration and management; computer science; criminal justice/law enforcement administration; criminal justice/police science; hospitality administration; information science/studies; medical administrative assistant and medical secretary.

Academic Programs *Special study options:* academic remediation for entering students, adult/continuing education programs, cooperative education, English as a second language, internships, part-time degree program, summer session for credit.

Library Main Library plus 1 other with 28,000 titles, 301 serial subscriptions, an OPAC, a Web page.

Computers on Campus 541 computers available on campus for general student use. A campuswide network can be accessed. Internet access, at least one staffed computer lab available.

Student Life *Activities and Organizations:* drama/theater group, student-run newspaper. *Campus security:* late-night transport/escort service. *Student services:* personal/psychological counseling.

Athletics Member NJCAA. *Intercollegiate sports:* basketball M/W, soccer M/W. *Intramural sports:* basketball M/W, bowling M/W, soccer M/W, volleyball M/W.

Standardized Tests *Required:* ACT ASSET (for placement).

Costs (2003–04) *Comprehensive fee:* $18,480 includes full-time tuition ($7960), mandatory fees ($500), and room and board ($10,020). Part-time tuition: $332 per credit. *Required fees:* $125 per term part-time.

Financial Aid Of all full-time matriculated undergraduates who enrolled, 132 Federal Work-Study jobs (averaging $3100).

Applying *Options:* early admission, deferred entrance. *Application fee:* $25. *Required:* high school transcript, interview. *Application deadlines:* 8/26 (freshmen), 8/26 (transfers). *Notification:* continuous until 9/3 (freshmen), continuous until 9/3 (transfers).

Admissions Contact Ms. Lauren Rosenthal, Director of Admissions, Monroe College, Monroe College Way, 2501 Jerome Avenue, Bronx, NY 10468. *Phone:* 718-933-6700 Ext. 536. *Toll-free phone:* 800-55MONROE.

MONROE COLLEGE
New Rochelle, New York

- **Proprietary** primarily 2-year, founded 1983
- **Calendar** trimesters
- **Degrees** associate and bachelor's
- **Suburban** campus with easy access to New York City
- **Coed**, 1,433 undergraduate students, 83% full-time, 66% women, 34% men

Undergraduates 1,189 full-time, 244 part-time. Students come from 4 states and territories, 8 other countries, 1% are from out of state, 58% African American, 0.4% Asian American or Pacific Islander, 18% Hispanic American, 0.1% Native American, 12% international, 6% transferred in, 5% live on campus. *Retention:* 46% of 2002 full-time freshmen returned.

Freshmen *Admission:* 406 enrolled.

Faculty *Total:* 201, 33% full-time, 18% with terminal degrees. *Student/faculty ratio:* 20:1.

Majors Accounting; business administration and management; computer science; corrections and criminal justice related; hospitality administration; information science/studies; medical administrative assistant and medical secretary.

Academic Programs *Special study options:* academic remediation for entering students, adult/continuing education programs, cooperative education, English as a second language, internships, part-time degree program, summer session for credit.

Library Main Library plus 1 other with 8,400 titles, 211 serial subscriptions.

Computers on Campus 214 computers available on campus for general student use. A campuswide network can be accessed. At least one staffed computer lab available.

Student Life *Housing Options:* coed. *Activities and Organizations:* drama/theater group, student-run newspaper. *Campus security:* late-night transport/escort service. *Student services:* personal/psychological counseling.

Athletics Member NJCAA. *Intercollegiate sports:* basketball M/W, soccer M/W. *Intramural sports:* basketball M/W, bowling M/W, soccer M/W, volleyball M/W.

Standardized Tests *Required:* ACT ASSET (for placement).

Costs (2003–04) *Comprehensive fee:* $19,420 includes full-time tuition ($8900), mandatory fees ($500), and room and board ($10,020). Part-time tuition: $1050 per course. *Required fees:* $125 per term part-time.

Financial Aid Of all full-time matriculated undergraduates who enrolled, 50 Federal Work-Study jobs (averaging $4000).

Applying *Options:* common application, electronic application, early admission, deferred entrance. *Application fee:* $25. *Required:* high school transcript, interview. *Application deadlines:* 8/26 (freshmen), 8/26 (transfers). *Notification:* continuous until 9/3 (freshmen), continuous until 9/3 (transfers).

Admissions Contact Ms. Lisa Scorca, High School Admissions, Monroe College, 2468 Jerome Avenue, Bronx, NY 10468. *Phone:* 914-632-5400 Ext. 407. *Toll-free phone:* 800-55MONROE. *E-mail:* ejerome@monroecollege.edu.

MONROE COMMUNITY COLLEGE
Rochester, New York

- **State and locally supported** 2-year, founded 1961, part of State University of New York System
- **Calendar** semesters
- **Degree** certificates and associate
- **Suburban** 314-acre campus with easy access to Buffalo
- **Endowment** $3.6 million
- **Coed**

Faculty *Student/faculty ratio:* 20:1.

Student Life *Campus security:* 24-hour emergency response devices, late-night transport/escort service.

Athletics Member NJCAA.

Costs (2003–04) *Tuition:* state resident $2500 full-time, $105 per credit hour part-time; nonresident $5000 full-time, $210 per credit hour part-time. Part-time tuition and fees vary according to course load. *Required fees:* $96 full-time. *Room and board:* $6100; room only: $4000.

Financial Aid Of all full-time matriculated undergraduates who enrolled, 1,182 Federal Work-Study jobs (averaging $1450).

Applying *Options:* electronic application, early admission. *Application fee:* $20. *Required:* high school transcript.

Admissions Contact Mr. Anthony Felicetti, Associate Vice President, Enrollment Management, Monroe Community College, 1000 East Henrietta Road, Rochester, NY 14623-5780. *Phone:* 585-292-2000 Ext. 2221. *Fax:* 585-292-3860. *E-mail:* admissions@monroecc.edu.

NASSAU COMMUNITY COLLEGE
Garden City, New York

- **State and locally supported** 2-year, founded 1959, part of State University of New York System
- **Calendar** semesters
- **Degree** certificates and associate
- **Suburban** 225-acre campus with easy access to New York City
- **Coed**, 20,984 undergraduate students, 62% full-time, 54% women, 46% men

Undergraduates 13,055 full-time, 7,929 part-time. Students come from 99 other countries, 18% African American, 5% Asian American or Pacific Islander, 12% Hispanic American, 0.2% Native American, 5% international, 9% transferred in.

Freshmen *Admission:* 9,154 admitted, 4,860 enrolled.

Faculty *Total:* 1,242, 84% with terminal degrees. *Student/faculty ratio:* 20:1.

Majors Accounting; accounting technology and bookkeeping; administrative assistant and secretarial science; African-American/Black studies; art; business administration and management; civil engineering technology; clinical/medical laboratory technology; commercial and advertising art; communication/speech communication and rhetoric; computer and information sciences; computer and information sciences related; computer graphics; computer science; computer systems networking and telecommunications; criminal justice/law enforcement administration; criminal justice/safety; dance; data processing and data processing technology; design and visual communications; dramatic/theatre arts; engineering; entrepreneurship; fashion/apparel design; fashion merchandising; funeral service and mortuary science; general retailing/wholesaling; general studies; health science; hotel/motel administration; instrumentation technology; insurance; interior design; kindergarten/preschool education; legal administrative assistant/secretary; legal assistant/paralegal; liberal arts and sciences/liberal studies; management information systems; marketing/marketing management; mass communication/media; mathematics; medical administrative assistant and medical secretary; medical radiologic technology; music performance; nursing (registered nurse training); photography; physical therapist assistant; real estate; rehabilitation therapy; respiratory care therapy; security and loss prevention; surgical technology; theatre design and technology; transportation technology; visual and performing arts.

Academic Programs *Special study options:* academic remediation for entering students, adult/continuing education programs, advanced placement credit, cooperative education, distance learning, English as a second language, honors programs, internships, off-campus study, part-time degree program, services for LD students, summer session for credit. *ROTC:* Army (c).

Library A. Holly Patterson Library with 171,938 titles, 753 serial subscriptions, 55,514 audiovisual materials, an OPAC, a Web page.

Computers on Campus 700 computers available on campus for general student use. A campuswide network can be accessed from off campus. At least one staffed computer lab available.

Student Life *Housing:* college housing not available. *Activities and Organizations:* drama/theater group, student-run newspaper, radio station, choral group, Student Organization of Latinos, Student Government Association, Programming Board, Caribbean Student Organization, NYPIRG. *Campus security:* 24-hour emergency response devices and patrols, late-night transport/escort service. *Student services:* health clinic, personal/psychological counseling, women's center.

Athletics Member NJCAA. *Intercollegiate sports:* baseball M, basketball M/W, bowling M/W, cheerleading W, cross-country running M/W, equestrian sports M/W, football M, golf M/W, lacrosse M, soccer M/W, softball W, tennis M/W, track and field M/W, volleyball M/W, wrestling M. *Intramural sports:* badminton M/W, basketball M/W, cross-country running M/W, football M, ice hockey M, lacrosse M/W, racquetball M/W, soccer M/W, softball M/W, table tennis M/W, tennis M/W, volleyball M/W.

Standardized Tests *Recommended:* SAT I or ACT (for admission).

Costs (2003–04) *Tuition:* state resident $2650 full-time, $111 per credit part-time; nonresident $5300 full-time, $222 per credit part-time. *Required fees:* $230 full-time.

Financial Aid Of all full-time matriculated undergraduates who enrolled, 400 Federal Work-Study jobs (averaging $3300).

Applying *Options:* deferred entrance. *Application fee:* $20. *Required:* high school transcript. *Required for some:* minimum 3.0 GPA, interview. *Recommended:* minimum 2.0 GPA. *Application deadlines:* 8/1 (freshmen), 8/1 (transfers). *Notification:* continuous (freshmen), continuous (transfers).

Admissions Contact Mr. Craig Wright, Vice President of Student Academic Affairs, Nassau Community College, One Education Drive, Garden City, NY 11530. *Phone:* 516-572-7345. *E-mail:* admissions@sunynassau.edu.

NEW YORK CAREER INSTITUTE
New York, New York

Admissions Contact Ms. Cindy McMahon, Enrollment Coordinator, New York Career Institute, 15 Park Row, 4th Floor, New York, NY 10038-2301. *Phone:* 212-962-0002 Ext. 101.

NEW YORK CITY COLLEGE OF TECHNOLOGY OF THE CITY UNIVERSITY OF NEW YORK
Brooklyn, New York

- **State and locally supported** primarily 2-year, founded 1946, part of City University of New York System
- **Calendar** semesters
- **Degrees** certificates, associate, and bachelor's
- **Urban** campus
- **Endowment** $11.6 million
- **Coed**

Faculty *Student/faculty ratio:* 25:1.

Student Life *Campus security:* 24-hour emergency response devices and patrols.

Athletics Member NCAA. All Division III.

Costs (2003–04) *Tuition:* state resident $3400 full-time, $150 per credit hour part-time; nonresident $7000 full-time, $375 per credit hour part-time. *Required fees:* $150 full-time.

Applying *Application fee:* $40. *Required:* high school transcript.

Admissions Contact Mr. Joseph Lento, Director of Admissions, New York City College of Technology of the City University of New York, 300 Jay Street, Brooklyn, NY 11201-2983. *Phone:* 718-260-5500. *E-mail:* jlento@nyctc.cuny.edu.

NEW YORK COLLEGE OF HEALTH PROFESSIONS
Syosset, New York

- **Independent** founded 1981
- **Calendar** trimesters
- **Degrees** associate, incidental bachelor's, and master's
- **Suburban** campus with easy access to New York City
- **Coed**

Faculty *Total:* 95, 16% full-time.

Majors Health services/allied health/health sciences; massage therapy.

Academic Programs *Special study options:* academic remediation for entering students, accelerated degree program, adult/continuing education programs, advanced placement credit, distance learning, double majors, internships, part-time degree program, study abroad, summer session for credit.

Library James and Lenore Jacobson Library at the New Center with 4,600 titles, 100 serial subscriptions, an OPAC.

Computers on Campus 3 computers available on campus for general student use. Internet access, at least one staffed computer lab available.

Student Life *Housing:* college housing not available. *Campus security:* 24-hour patrols, security guard evening and weekend hours. *Student services:* health clinic.

Costs (2003–04) *Tuition:* $9900 full-time, $275 per credit part-time. *Required fees:* $400 full-time. *Payment plan:* installment. *Waivers:* employees or children of employees.

Financial Aid Of all full-time matriculated undergraduates who enrolled, 15 Federal Work-Study jobs.

Applying *Options:* common application, electronic application, deferred entrance. *Application fee:* $85. *Required:* high school transcript, minimum 2.5 GPA, interview. *Application deadline:* rolling (freshmen), rolling (transfers). *Notification:* continuous (freshmen), continuous (transfers).

Admissions Contact Dr. Mary Rodas, Director of Admissions, New York College of Health Professions, 6801 Jericho Turnpike, Syosset, NY 11791. *Phone:* 800-922-7337 Ext. 354. *Toll-free phone:* 800-922-7337 Ext. 351. *E-mail:* admission@nycollege.edu.

▶ **See page 586 for a narrative description.**

NIAGARA COUNTY COMMUNITY COLLEGE
Sanborn, New York

- **State and locally supported** 2-year, founded 1962, part of State University of New York System
- **Calendar** semesters
- **Degree** certificates and associate
- **Rural** 287-acre campus with easy access to Buffalo
- **Endowment** $2.0 million
- **Coed**, 5,252 undergraduate students, 64% full-time, 58% women, 42% men

Undergraduates 3,354 full-time, 1,898 part-time. Students come from 15 states and territories, 1% are from out of state, 6% African American, 0.8% Asian American or Pacific Islander, 0.9% Hispanic American, 1% Native American, 5% transferred in.

Freshmen *Admission:* 2,134 applied, 2,134 admitted, 1,079 enrolled. *Average high school GPA:* 2.48.

Faculty *Total:* 313, 42% full-time, 13% with terminal degrees. *Student/faculty ratio:* 18:1.

Majors Accounting; administrative assistant and secretarial science; animal sciences; biochemical technology; biological and physical sciences; business administration and management; computer science; consumer merchandising/retailing management; criminal justice/law enforcement administration; culinary arts; design and applied arts related; drafting and design technology; dramatic/theatre arts; electrical, electronic and communications engineering technology; electroneurodiagnostic/electroencephalographic technology; fine/studio arts; general studies; humanities; human services; information science/studies; liberal arts and sciences/liberal studies; mass communication/media; mathematics; mechanical design technology; medical/clinical assistant; music; natural resources/conservation; nursing (registered nurse training); occupational health and industrial hygiene; physical education teaching and coaching; physical therapist assistant; radiologic technology/science; social sciences; surgical technology; telecommunications.

Academic Programs *Special study options:* academic remediation for entering students, adult/continuing education programs, advanced placement credit, cooperative education, double majors, honors programs, independent study, internships, off-campus study, part-time degree program, services for LD students, student-designed majors, study abroad, summer session for credit. *ROTC:* Army (c).

Library Library Learning Center with 93,721 titles, 570 serial subscriptions, 24,571 audiovisual materials, an OPAC, a Web page.

Computers on Campus 414 computers available on campus for general student use. A campuswide network can be accessed. Internet access, at least one staffed computer lab available.

Student Life *Housing:* college housing not available. *Activities and Organizations:* drama/theater group, student-run newspaper, radio station, choral group,

Niagara County Community College (continued)
student radio station, Student Nurses Association, Phi Theta Kappa, Alpha Beta Gamma, Physical Education Club. *Campus security:* student patrols, late-night transport/escort service, emergency telephones. *Student services:* health clinic, personal/psychological counseling.

Athletics Member NJCAA. *Intercollegiate sports:* baseball M, basketball M(s)/W, golf M/W, soccer M/W, softball W, volleyball W, wrestling M(s). *Intramural sports:* basketball M/W, bowling M/W, cheerleading W, skiing (cross-country) M(c)/W(c), volleyball M/W.

Costs (2004–05) *Tuition:* state resident $2870 full-time, $116 per credit hour part-time; nonresident $4305 full-time, $174 per credit hour part-time. Full-time tuition and fees vary according to program. Part-time tuition and fees vary according to program. *Required fees:* $274 full-time, $55 per term part-time.

Financial Aid Of all full-time matriculated undergraduates who enrolled, 169 Federal Work-Study jobs (averaging $1000).

Applying *Options:* electronic application, early admission. *Required:* high school transcript. *Required for some:* minimum 2.0 GPA. *Notification:* continuous until 8/31 (freshmen), continuous until 8/31 (transfers).

Admissions Contact Ms. Kathy Saunders, Director of Enrollment Services, Niagara County Community College, 3111 Saunders Settlement Road, Sanborn, NY 14132. *Phone:* 716-614-6201. *Fax:* 716-614-6820. *E-mail:* admissions@niagaracc.suny.edu.

NORTH COUNTRY COMMUNITY COLLEGE
Saranac Lake, New York

- **State and locally supported** 2-year, founded 1967, part of State University of New York System
- **Calendar** semesters
- **Degree** certificates and associate
- **Rural** 100-acre campus
- **Coed**, 1,357 undergraduate students, 71% full-time, 64% women, 36% men

Undergraduates 962 full-time, 395 part-time. Students come from 20 states and territories, 2 other countries, 3% are from out of state, 1% African American, 0.7% Asian American or Pacific Islander, 1% Hispanic American, 2% Native American, 0.3% international, 9% transferred in, 7% live on campus.

Freshmen *Admission:* 709 applied, 567 admitted, 303 enrolled. *Test scores:* SAT verbal scores over 500: 27%; SAT math scores over 500: 33%; ACT scores over 18: 70%; SAT verbal scores over 600: 6%; SAT math scores over 600: 8%; ACT scores over 24: 12%; SAT verbal scores over 700: 2%; ACT scores over 30: 3%.

Faculty *Total:* 111, 35% full-time, 13% with terminal degrees. *Student/faculty ratio:* 17:1.

Majors Biological and physical sciences; business administration and management; computer graphics; consumer merchandising/retailing management; criminal justice/safety; interdisciplinary studies; kinesiology and exercise science; liberal arts and sciences/liberal studies; mathematics; medical radiologic technology; mental health/rehabilitation; nursing (registered nurse training); office occupations and clerical services; parks, recreation and leisure facilities management.

Academic Programs *Special study options:* academic remediation for entering students, advanced placement credit, distance learning, double majors, internships, part-time degree program, services for LD students, student-designed majors, summer session for credit.

Library North Country Community College Library with 58,556 titles, 177 serial subscriptions, 1,217 audiovisual materials.

Computers on Campus 125 computers available on campus for general student use. Internet access, at least one staffed computer lab available.

Student Life *Housing Options:* coed. Campus housing is university owned. *Activities and Organizations:* drama/theater group, student-run newspaper, Student Government Association, Wilderness Recreation Club, Nursing Club, Radiology Club, Criminal Justice Club. *Student services:* personal/psychological counseling.

Athletics Member NJCAA. *Intercollegiate sports:* basketball M/W, ice hockey M, soccer M/W, softball W, volleyball W. *Intramural sports:* archery M/W, badminton M/W, basketball M/W, bowling M/W, football M/W, soccer M/W, softball M/W, swimming M/W, tennis M/W, volleyball M/W, weight lifting M/W.

Standardized Tests *Recommended:* SAT I or ACT (for admission).

Costs (2004–05) *One-time required fee:* $35. *Tuition:* state resident $2850 full-time, $125 per credit hour part-time; nonresident $5700 full-time, $250 per credit hour part-time. *Required fees:* $535 full-time, $22 per credit hour part-time. *Room and board:* $3250. *Payment plan:* installment. *Waivers:* senior citizens and employees or children of employees.

Financial Aid Of all full-time matriculated undergraduates who enrolled, 104 Federal Work-Study jobs (averaging $1164). 27 state and other part-time jobs (averaging $1600).

Applying *Options:* electronic application, early admission, early decision, deferred entrance. *Required:* high school transcript. *Recommended:* essay or personal statement, 1 letter of recommendation, interview. *Application deadline:* rolling (freshmen), rolling (transfers). *Early decision:* 11/15. *Notification:* continuous (freshmen), 12/15 (early decision), continuous (transfers).

Admissions Contact Enrollment Management Assistant, North Country Community College, 23 Santanoni Avenue, PO Box 89, Saranac Lake, NY 12983-0089. *Phone:* 518-891-2915 Ext. 686. *Toll-free phone:* 888-TRY-NCCC Ext. 233. *Fax:* 518-891-0898. *E-mail:* info@nccc.edu.

OLEAN BUSINESS INSTITUTE
Olean, New York

- **Proprietary** 2-year, founded 1961
- **Calendar** semesters
- **Degree** diplomas and associate
- **Small-town** campus
- **Coed**

Student Life *Campus security:* 24-hour emergency response devices, late-night transport/escort service.

Costs (2003–04) *Tuition:* $8000 full-time, $300 per credit hour part-time. *Required fees:* $80 full-time.

Applying *Application fee:* $25. *Required:* high school transcript. *Required for some:* essay or personal statement, interview.

Admissions Contact Ms. Lori Kincaid, Director of Admissions, Olean Business Institute, 301 North Union Street, Olean, NY 14760-2691. *Phone:* 716-372-7978. *Fax:* 716-372-2120.

ONONDAGA COMMUNITY COLLEGE
Syracuse, New York

Admissions Contact Mr. Monty R. Flynn, Director of Admissions, Onondaga Community College, 4941 Onondaga Road, Syracuse, NY 13215. *Phone:* 315-498-2201. *Fax:* 315-498-2107. *E-mail:* admissions@sunyocc.edu.

ORANGE COUNTY COMMUNITY COLLEGE
Middletown, New York

- **State and locally supported** 2-year, founded 1950, part of State University of New York System
- **Calendar** semesters
- **Degree** certificates and associate
- **Suburban** 37-acre campus with easy access to New York City
- **Coed**, 6,109 undergraduate students, 50% full-time, 62% women, 38% men

Undergraduates 3,033 full-time, 3,076 part-time. Students come from 19 states and territories, 1% are from out of state, 9% African American, 3% Asian American or Pacific Islander, 12% Hispanic American, 0.4% Native American, 3% transferred in.

Freshmen *Admission:* 1,976 applied, 1,976 admitted, 1,501 enrolled. *Average high school GPA:* 2.25.

Faculty *Total:* 338, 40% full-time. *Student/faculty ratio:* 15:1.

Majors Accounting; administrative assistant and secretarial science; architectural engineering technology; biological and physical sciences; biology/biological sciences; business administration and management; child development; clinical/medical laboratory technology; computer and information sciences; computer and information sciences related; computer engineering related; computer engineering technology; computer programming; computer science; construction engineering technology; consumer merchandising/retailing management; criminal justice/law enforcement administration; criminal justice/police science; data entry/microcomputer applications; data processing and data processing technology; dental hygiene; drafting and design technology; electrical, electronic and communications engineering technology; elementary education; engineering science; finance; humanities; industrial radiologic technology; information science/studies; information technology; kinesiology and exercise science; liberal arts and sciences/liberal studies; marketing/marketing management; mental health/rehabilitation; nursing (registered nurse training); occupational therapy; parks, recreation and leisure; physical sciences; physical therapy; real estate; word processing.

Academic Programs *Special study options:* academic remediation for entering students, accelerated degree program, adult/continuing education programs, English as a second language, external degree program, honors programs, internships, part-time degree program, services for LD students, summer session for credit.

Library Learning Resource Center with 98,628 titles, 370 serial subscriptions, 225 audiovisual materials, an OPAC, a Web page.

Computers on Campus 200 computers available on campus for general student use. A campuswide network can be accessed. Internet access, at least one staffed computer lab available.

Student Life *Housing:* college housing not available. *Activities and Organizations:* drama/theater group, student-run newspaper, radio station, choral group, Phi Theta Kappa, Masters of the Elements, Computer Club, Agassiz Society, Apprentice Players. *Campus security:* 24-hour emergency response devices, late-night transport/escort service. *Student services:* health clinic, personal/psychological counseling.

Athletics Member NJCAA. *Intercollegiate sports:* baseball M(s), basketball M(s)/W(s), golf M/W, soccer M(s)/W(s), softball W(s), tennis M(s)/W(s), volleyball W. *Intramural sports:* basketball M/W, field hockey M, football M, racquetball M/W, soccer M/W, tennis M/W, volleyball M/W.

Costs (2003–04) *Tuition:* state resident $2700 full-time; nonresident $5400 full-time. *Required fees:* $175 full-time.

Financial Aid Of all full-time matriculated undergraduates who enrolled, 70 Federal Work-Study jobs (averaging $2000). 25 state and other part-time jobs (averaging $2000).

Applying *Options:* common application, early admission, deferred entrance. *Application fee:* $30. *Required:* high school transcript. *Application deadlines:* 8/1 (freshmen), 8/1 (transfers). *Notification:* continuous (freshmen), continuous (transfers).

Admissions Contact Ms. Margot St. Lawrence, Director of Admissions, Orange County Community College, 115 South Street, Middletown, NY 10940. *Phone:* 914-341-4030. *E-mail:* admssns@sunyorange.edu.

PHILLIPS BETH ISRAEL SCHOOL OF NURSING
New York, New York

- **Independent** 2-year, founded 1904
- **Calendar** semesters
- **Degree** associate
- **Urban** campus
- **Endowment** $1.2 million
- **Coed, primarily women,** 133 undergraduate students, 20% full-time, 83% women, 17% men

Undergraduates 27 full-time, 106 part-time. Students come from 8 states and territories, 5 other countries, 10% are from out of state, 17% African American, 23% Asian American or Pacific Islander, 9% Hispanic American, 6% international, 47% transferred in.

Freshmen *Admission:* 45 applied, 1 admitted, 1 enrolled. *Average high school GPA:* 2.90. *Test scores:* SAT verbal scores over 500: 100%; SAT math scores over 500: 100%.

Faculty *Total:* 14, 71% full-time, 14% with terminal degrees. *Student/faculty ratio:* 6:1.

Majors Nursing (registered nurse training).

Academic Programs *Special study options:* advanced placement credit, off-campus study, part-time degree program.

Library Phillips Health Science Library with 600 serial subscriptions, an OPAC.

Computers on Campus 15 computers available on campus for general student use. Internet access, at least one staffed computer lab available.

Student Life *Housing:* college housing not available. *Activities and Organizations:* student-run newspaper, choral group, Student Government Organization, National Student Nurses Association. *Campus security:* 24-hour emergency response devices. *Student services:* health clinic, personal/psychological counseling.

Standardized Tests *Required:* nursing exam (for admission). *Recommended:* SAT I (for admission).

Costs (2004–05) *Tuition:* $10,865 full-time, $265 per credit part-time. Full-time tuition and fees vary according to course level and student level. Part-time tuition and fees vary according to student level. *Required fees:* $1945 full-time. *Payment plan:* installment. *Waivers:* employees or children of employees.

Financial Aid *Financial aid deadline:* 6/1.

Applying *Options:* deferred entrance. *Application fee:* $35. *Required:* essay or personal statement, high school transcript, minimum 2.5 GPA, 2 letters of recommendation, interview. *Application deadlines:* 4/1 (freshmen), 4/1 (transfers). *Notification:* continuous (freshmen), continuous (transfers).

Admissions Contact Mrs. Bernice Pass-Stern, Director of Student Services, Phillips Beth Israel School of Nursing, 310 East 22nd Street, 9th Floor, New York, NY 10010-5702. *Phone:* 212-614-6108. *Fax:* 212-614-6109. *E-mail:* bstern@bethisraelny.org.

PLAZA BUSINESS INSTITUTE
Jackson Heights, New York

Admissions Contact Mr. Michael Talarico, Director of Admissions, Plaza Business Institute, 74-09 37th Avenue, Jackson Heights, NY 11372-6300. *Phone:* 718-779-1430.

QUEENSBOROUGH COMMUNITY COLLEGE OF THE CITY UNIVERSITY OF NEW YORK
Bayside, New York

- **State and locally supported** 2-year, founded 1958, part of City University of New York System
- **Calendar** semesters
- **Degree** certificates and associate
- **Urban** 34-acre campus with easy access to New York City
- **Endowment** $1.0 million
- **Coed,** 11,704 undergraduate students, 52% full-time, 58% women, 42% men

Undergraduates 6,074 full-time, 5,630 part-time. Students come from 2 states and territories, 132 other countries, 1% are from out of state, 5% transferred in. *Retention:* 70% of 2002 full-time freshmen returned.

Freshmen *Admission:* 4,263 applied, 3,725 admitted, 2,251 enrolled. *Average high school GPA:* 1.96. *Test scores:* SAT verbal scores over 500: 12%; SAT math scores over 500: 17%; SAT verbal scores over 600: 1%; SAT math scores over 600: 2%.

Faculty *Total:* 769, 33% full-time. *Student/faculty ratio:* 18:1.

Majors Accounting; business administration and management; business, management, and marketing related; clinical/medical laboratory technology; communication and journalism related; computer engineering technology; electrical, electronic and communications engineering technology; engineering science; environmental design/architecture; environmental health; fine/studio arts; health science; information science/studies; information technology; laser and optical technology; liberal arts and sciences/liberal studies; mechanical engineering/mechanical technology; musical instrument fabrication and repair; nursing (registered nurse training); telecommunications; visual and performing arts.

Academic Programs *Special study options:* academic remediation for entering students, adult/continuing education programs, advanced placement credit, cooperative education, English as a second language, honors programs, internships, part-time degree program, services for LD students, student-designed majors, summer session for credit. *ROTC:* Army (c).

Library The Kurt R. Schmeller with 140,000 titles, 600 serial subscriptions.

Computers on Campus 1001 computers available on campus for general student use. Internet access, online (class) registration, at least one staffed computer lab available.

Student Life *Housing:* college housing not available. *Activities and Organizations:* drama/theater group, student-run newspaper, radio station, choral group, Student Orientation Leaders, Student Nurses Association, Newman Club, Accounting Club, Flip Culture Society. *Campus security:* 24-hour patrols, late-night transport/escort service. *Student services:* health clinic, personal/psychological counseling.

Athletics Member NJCAA. *Intercollegiate sports:* baseball M, basketball M/W, cross-country running M/W, soccer M, softball W, tennis M/W, track and field M/W, volleyball M/W. *Intramural sports:* archery M/W, badminton M/W, basketball M/W, fencing M/W, soccer M/W, softball M/W, swimming M/W, table tennis M/W, tennis M/W, track and field M/W, volleyball M/W, weight lifting M/W.

Costs (2003–04) *Tuition:* state resident $2800 full-time. *Required fees:* $106 full-time.

Applying *Options:* electronic application, deferred entrance. *Application fee:* $40. *Required:* high school transcript. *Application deadline:* rolling (freshmen), rolling (transfers). *Notification:* continuous (freshmen), continuous (transfers).

Admissions Contact Ms. Ann Tullio, Director of Registration, Queensborough Community College of the City University of New York, 222-05 56th Avenue, Bayside, NY 11364. *Phone:* 718-631-6307. *Fax:* 718-281-5189.

ROCHESTER BUSINESS INSTITUTE
Rochester, New York

- **Proprietary** 2-year, founded 1863, part of Corinthian Colleges, Inc
- **Calendar** quarters
- **Degree** certificates, diplomas, and associate
- **Suburban** 2-acre campus
- **Coed,** 1,223 undergraduate students, 84% full-time, 70% women, 30% men

Undergraduates 1,032 full-time, 191 part-time. Students come from 2 states and territories, 38% African American, 1% Asian American or Pacific Islander, 10% Hispanic American, 0.3% Native American.

Rochester Business Institute (continued)

Freshmen *Admission:* 72 enrolled.

Faculty *Total:* 63, 19% full-time, 13% with terminal degrees. *Student/faculty ratio:* 18:1.

Majors Accounting; business administration and management; computer programming; data processing and data processing technology; management information systems.

Academic Programs *Special study options:* academic remediation for entering students, adult/continuing education programs, advanced placement credit, cooperative education, distance learning, double majors, independent study, internships, part-time degree program, summer session for credit.

Library Rochester Business Institute Library plus 2 others with 7,500 titles, 26 serial subscriptions, an OPAC.

Computers on Campus 125 computers available on campus for general student use. A campuswide network can be accessed. Internet access, at least one staffed computer lab available.

Student Life *Housing:* college housing not available.

Athletics *Intramural sports:* basketball M, softball M/W.

Standardized Tests *Required:* CPAt (for admission).

Costs (2003–04) *Tuition:* $10,464 full-time, $230 per credit hour part-time. Part-time tuition and fees vary according to course load. *Required fees:* $375 full-time, $25 per credit hour part-time, $100 per term part-time. *Payment plan:* installment. *Waivers:* employees or children of employees.

Applying *Options:* early admission, deferred entrance. *Required:* high school transcript, interview. *Application deadline:* rolling (freshmen), rolling (transfers). *Notification:* continuous (freshmen), continuous (transfers).

Admissions Contact Ms. Deanna Pfluke, Director of Admissions, Rochester Business Institute, 1630 Portland Avenue, Rochester, NY 14621. *Phone:* 585-266-0430. *Fax:* 585-266-8243. *E-mail:* csilvio@cci.edu.

ROCKLAND COMMUNITY COLLEGE
Suffern, New York

- **State and locally supported** 2-year, founded 1959, part of State University of New York System
- **Calendar** semesters
- **Degree** certificates and associate
- **Suburban** 150-acre campus with easy access to New York City
- **Coed**

Faculty *Student/faculty ratio:* 17:1.

Student Life *Campus security:* 24-hour emergency response devices and patrols, student patrols, late-night transport/escort service.

Athletics Member NJCAA.

Standardized Tests *Recommended:* SAT I or ACT (for placement).

Applying *Options:* early admission, deferred entrance. *Application fee:* $25. *Required:* high school transcript.

Admissions Contact Ms. Lucy Hirsch, Admissions Office Secretary, Rockland Community College, 145 College Road, Suffern, NY 10901-3699. *Phone:* 845-574-4237. *Toll-free phone:* 800-722-7666. *Fax:* 845-574-4433. *E-mail:* info@sunyrockland.edu.

ST. ELIZABETH COLLEGE OF NURSING
Utica, New York

Admissions Contact Ms. Marianne Monahan, Dean, St. Elizabeth College of Nursing, 2215 Genesee Street, Utica, NY 13501. *Phone:* 315-798-8253.

SAINT JOSEPH'S HOSPITAL HEALTH CENTER SCHOOL OF NURSING
Syracuse, New York

- **Independent** 2-year
- **Calendar** semesters
- **Degree** associate
- **Urban** campus
- **Coed, primarily women,** 293 undergraduate students, 61% full-time, 86% women, 14% men

Undergraduates 179 full-time, 114 part-time. Students come from 2 states and territories, 3% African American, 1% Asian American or Pacific Islander, 2% Hispanic American, 2% Native American, 37% transferred in, 25% live on campus.

Freshmen *Admission:* 38 applied, 26 admitted, 19 enrolled. *Test scores:* SAT verbal scores over 500: 56%; SAT math scores over 500: 50%; ACT scores over 18: 100%; ACT scores over 24: 1%.

Faculty *Total:* 29, 55% full-time. *Student/faculty ratio:* 9:1.

Majors Nursing (registered nurse training).

Academic Programs *Special study options:* academic remediation for entering students, adult/continuing education programs, advanced placement credit, cooperative education, internships, part-time degree program, services for LD students.

Library St. Joseph's Hospital Health Center School of Nursing Library with 4,500 titles, 230 serial subscriptions, 500 audiovisual materials, an OPAC.

Computers on Campus 30 computers available on campus for general student use. Internet access, at least one staffed computer lab available.

Student Life *Housing Options:* coed. *Activities and Organizations:* New York State Student Nurse's Association, Syracuse Area Black Nurses Association, Student Body Organization. *Campus security:* 24-hour patrols. *Student services:* health clinic, personal/psychological counseling, legal services.

Standardized Tests *Required:* SAT I or ACT (for admission).

Costs (2003–04) *Tuition:* state resident $6141 full-time, $240 per credit hour part-time. *Required fees:* $1050 full-time, $525 per term part-time. *Room and board:* room only: $3100.

Applying *Options:* deferred entrance. *Application fee:* $30. *Required:* essay or personal statement, high school transcript, minimum 3.0 GPA, 4 letters of recommendation, interview.

Admissions Contact Ms. JoAnne Kiggins, Admission and Recruitment Coordinator, Saint Joseph's Hospital Health Center School of Nursing, 206 Prospect Avenue, Syracuse, NY 13203. *Phone:* 315-448-5040.

SAINT VINCENT CATHOLIC MEDICAL CENTERS SCHOOL OF NURSING
Fresh Meadows, New York

- **Independent** 2-year, founded 1969
- **Calendar** semesters
- **Degree** associate
- **Suburban** 2-acre campus
- **Coed,** 93 undergraduate students, 32% full-time, 88% women, 12% men

Undergraduates 30 full-time, 63 part-time. Students come from 1 other state, 22% African American, 23% Asian American or Pacific Islander, 18% Hispanic American.

Freshmen *Admission:* 37 applied, 6 admitted.

Faculty *Total:* 13, 77% full-time. *Student/faculty ratio:* 10:1.

Majors Nursing (registered nurse training).

Academic Programs *Special study options:* part-time degree program.

Library Crouse Library with 2,326 titles, 42 serial subscriptions.

Computers on Campus 6 computers available on campus for general student use.

Student Life *Housing:* college housing not available. *Campus security:* 24-hour patrols.

Standardized Tests *Required:* nursing exam (for admission).

Costs (2003–04) *Tuition:* $11,000 full-time, $185 per credit part-time.

Financial Aid Of all full-time matriculated undergraduates who enrolled, 11 Federal Work-Study jobs (averaging $900).

Applying *Options:* deferred entrance. *Application fee:* $20. *Required:* essay or personal statement, high school transcript. *Application deadlines:* 4/30 (freshmen), 4/30 (transfers). *Notification:* continuous (freshmen), continuous (transfers).

Admissions Contact Nancy Wolinski, Chairperson of Admissions, Saint Vincent Catholic Medical Centers School of Nursing, 175-05 Horace Harding Expressway, Fresh Meadows, NY 11365. *Phone:* 718-357-0500 Ext. 131. *Fax:* 718-357-4683.

SAMARITAN HOSPITAL SCHOOL OF NURSING
Troy, New York

Admissions Contact Ms. Jennifer DeBlois, Student Services Coordinator, Samaritan Hospital School of Nursing, 2215 Burdett Avenue, Troy, NY 12180. *Phone:* 518-271-3734. *E-mail:* gallagherl@nehealth.com.

SCHENECTADY COUNTY COMMUNITY COLLEGE
Schenectady, New York

- **State and locally supported** 2-year, founded 1969, part of State University of New York System

■ **Calendar** semesters
■ **Degree** certificates and associate
■ **Urban** 50-acre campus
■ **Coed,** 4,140 undergraduate students, 50% full-time, 57% women, 43% men

Undergraduates 2,052 full-time, 2,088 part-time. 8% African American, 2% Asian American or Pacific Islander, 3% Hispanic American, 0.8% Native American, 9% transferred in. *Retention:* 43% of 2002 full-time freshmen returned.
Freshmen *Admission:* 2,190 applied, 2,144 admitted, 494 enrolled.
Faculty *Total:* 205, 32% full-time, 100% with terminal degrees. *Student/faculty ratio:* 22:1.
Majors Accounting; administrative assistant and secretarial science; aviation/airway management; biological and physical sciences; business administration and management; computer and information sciences; computer and information sciences related; computer/information technology services administration related; computer programming related; computer science; counseling psychology; criminal justice/law enforcement administration; culinary arts; dramatic/theatre arts; education; electrical, electronic and communications engineering technology; fire science; foods and nutrition related; hotel/motel administration; humanities; human services; information technology; legal assistant/paralegal; liberal arts and sciences/liberal studies; mathematics; music; music management and merchandising; music performance; securities services administration; telecommunications; tourism and travel services management; word processing.
Academic Programs *Special study options:* academic remediation for entering students, adult/continuing education programs, advanced placement credit, distance learning, double majors, English as a second language, honors programs, internships, off-campus study, part-time degree program, services for LD students, summer session for credit.
Library Begley Library with 85,000 titles, 640 serial subscriptions, 2,600 audiovisual materials, an OPAC, a Web page.
Computers on Campus 400 computers available on campus for general student use. A campuswide network can be accessed from off campus. Internet access, at least one staffed computer lab available.
Student Life *Housing:* college housing not available. *Activities and Organizations:* drama/theater group, choral group, Black and Latino Student Alliance, Culinary Arts Club, Student Government Association, Spanish Club, Rhythms Literary Magazine. *Campus security:* 24-hour emergency response devices and patrols, late-night transport/escort service. *Student services:* personal/psychological counseling.
Athletics Member NJCAA. *Intercollegiate sports:* baseball M, basketball M/W, bowling M/W, softball W. *Intramural sports:* soccer M/W, volleyball M/W.
Standardized Tests *Recommended:* SAT I or ACT (for placement).
Costs (2003–04) *Tuition:* state resident $2540 full-time, $100 per credit part-time; nonresident $5080 full-time. Part-time tuition and fees vary according to course load. *Required fees:* $100 full-time.
Financial Aid Of all full-time matriculated undergraduates who enrolled, 50 Federal Work-Study jobs.
Applying *Options:* electronic application, early admission, deferred entrance. *Required:* high school transcript. *Application deadline:* rolling (freshmen), rolling (transfers). *Notification:* continuous (freshmen), continuous (transfers).
Admissions Contact Mr. David Sampson, Director of Admissions, Schenectady County Community College, 78 Washington Avenue, Schenectady, NY 12305. *Phone:* 518-381-1370. *E-mail:* sampsodg@gw.sunysccc.edu.

SIMMONS INSTITUTE OF FUNERAL SERVICE
Syracuse, New York

■ **Proprietary** 2-year, founded 1900
■ **Calendar** semesters
■ **Degree** associate
■ **Urban** 1-acre campus
■ **Coed**

Student Life *Campus security:* 24-hour emergency response devices.
Costs (2003–04) *One-time required fee:* $100. *Tuition:* $9400 full-time, $397 per credit hour part-time.
Applying *Application fee:* $50. *Required:* essay or personal statement, high school transcript, interview.
Admissions Contact Ms. Vera Wightman, Director of Admissions, Simmons Institute of Funeral Service, 1828 South Avenue, Syracuse, NY 13207. *Phone:* 315-475-5142. *Toll-free phone:* 800-727-3536. *Fax:* 315-477-3817. *E-mail:* vwightman6@aol.com.

STATE UNIVERSITY OF NEW YORK COLLEGE OF AGRICULTURE AND TECHNOLOGY AT MORRISVILLE
Morrisville, New York

■ **State-supported** primarily 2-year, founded 1908, part of State University of New York System
■ **Calendar** semesters
■ **Degrees** certificates, associate, and bachelor's
■ **Rural** 185-acre campus with easy access to Syracuse
■ **Endowment** $681,026
■ **Coed,** 3,269 undergraduate students, 86% full-time, 46% women, 54% men

Undergraduates 2,820 full-time, 449 part-time. Students come from 14 states and territories, 11 other countries, 1% are from out of state, 12% African American, 0.9% Asian American or Pacific Islander, 4% Hispanic American, 0.8% Native American, 1% international, 9% transferred in, 60% live on campus.
Freshmen *Admission:* 3,028 applied, 1,278 admitted, 1,216 enrolled. *Average high school GPA:* 2.70. *Test scores:* SAT verbal scores over 500: 31%; SAT math scores over 500: 38%; SAT verbal scores over 600: 5%; SAT math scores over 600: 7%.
Faculty *Total:* 246, 52% full-time. *Student/faculty ratio:* 19:1.
Majors Accounting; administrative assistant and secretarial science; agricultural business and management; agricultural mechanization; agriculture; agronomy and crop science; animal sciences; architectural engineering technology; automobile/automotive mechanics technology; biology/biological sciences; biology/biotechnology laboratory technician; business administration and management; chemistry; clinical/medical laboratory technology; computer engineering technology; computer programming; computer science; computer typography and composition equipment operation; construction engineering technology; dairy science; data processing and data processing technology; dietetics; drafting and design technology; electrical, electronic and communications engineering technology; engineering; engineering science; engineering technology; environmental studies; equestrian studies; fish/game management; food services technology; foods, nutrition, and wellness; forestry; forestry technology; horticultural science; hospitality administration; hotel/motel administration; humanities; information science/studies; journalism; landscape architecture; landscaping and groundskeeping; legal administrative assistant/secretary; liberal arts and sciences/liberal studies; marketing/marketing management; mathematics; mechanical engineering/mechanical technology; medical administrative assistant and medical secretary; natural resources/conservation; natural resources management and policy; nursing (registered nurse training); parks, recreation and leisure facilities management; physics; plastics engineering technology; pre-engineering; social sciences; special products marketing; technical and business writing; tourism and travel services management; wildlife and wildlands science and management; wood science and wood products/pulp and paper technology.
Academic Programs *Special study options:* academic remediation for entering students, advanced placement credit, cooperative education, distance learning, double majors, honors programs, internships, off-campus study, part-time degree program, services for LD students, student-designed majors, summer session for credit. *ROTC:* Army (c).
Library SUNY Morrisville Library plus 1 other with 99,258 titles, 568 serial subscriptions, 2,100 audiovisual materials, an OPAC, a Web page.
Computers on Campus 90 computers available on campus for general student use. A campuswide network can be accessed from student residence rooms and from off campus that provide access to various software applications. Internet access, online (class) registration, at least one staffed computer lab available. Computer purchase or lease plan available.
Student Life *Housing:* on-campus residence required for freshman year. *Options:* coed. Campus housing is university owned. Freshman campus housing is guaranteed. *Activities and Organizations:* drama/theater group, student-run newspaper, radio station, choral group, African Student Union Black Alliance, Student Government Organization, Agriculture Club, Latino-American Student Association, WCVM (student radio station). *Campus security:* 24-hour emergency response devices and patrols, late-night transport/escort service, controlled dormitory access. *Student services:* health clinic, personal/psychological counseling.
Athletics Member NJCAA. *Intercollegiate sports:* baseball M, basketball M/W, cross-country running M/W, equestrian sports M/W, field hockey W, football M, ice hockey M, lacrosse M/W, skiing (downhill) M/W, soccer M/W, softball W, swimming M/W, tennis W, track and field M/W, volleyball W, wrestling M. *Intramural sports:* basketball M/W, riflery M/W, skiing (cross-country) M/W, skiing (downhill) M/W, soccer M/W, softball M/W, swimming M/W, tennis M/W, volleyball M/W, weight lifting M/W.
Standardized Tests *Required for some:* SAT I (for admission). *Recommended:* SAT I and SAT II or ACT (for admission).
Costs (2003–04) *Tuition:* state resident $4350 full-time, $140 per credit part-time; nonresident $7000 full-time, $292 per credit part-time. Full-time tuition and fees vary according to degree level and student level. Part-time tuition and fees vary according to course load. *Required fees:* $15 per term part-time.

State University of New York College of Agriculture and Technology at Morrisville (continued)

Room and board: $3150; room only: $3550. Room and board charges vary according to board plan and housing facility. *Payment plan:* deferred payment. *Waivers:* children of alumni and employees or children of employees.

Financial Aid Of all full-time matriculated undergraduates who enrolled, 300 Federal Work-Study jobs (averaging $1500).

Applying *Options:* electronic application, early admission, deferred entrance. *Application fee:* $40. *Required:* high school transcript. *Required for some:* essay or personal statement, letters of recommendation. *Recommended:* minimum 2.0 GPA, letters of recommendation, interview. *Application deadline:* rolling (freshmen), rolling (transfers). *Notification:* continuous (freshmen), continuous (transfers).

Admissions Contact Mr. Timothy Williams, Dean of Enrollment Management, State University of New York College of Agriculture and Technology at Morrisville, Box 901, Morrisville, NY 13408. *Phone:* 315-684-6046. *Toll-free phone:* 800-258-0111. *Fax:* 315-684-6427. *E-mail:* admissions@morrisville.edu.

STATE UNIVERSITY OF NEW YORK COLLEGE OF ENVIRONMENTAL SCIENCE & FORESTRY, RANGER SCHOOL
Wanakena, New York

- **State-supported** 2-year, founded 1912, part of State University of New York System
- **Calendar** semesters
- **Degree** associate
- **Rural** 2800-acre campus
- **Endowment** $524,891
- **Coed, primarily men,** 43 undergraduate students, 100% full-time, 14% women, 86% men

Undergraduates 43 full-time. Students come from 4 states and territories, 6% are from out of state, 126% transferred in, 100% live on campus.

Freshmen *Admission:* 87 applied, 62 admitted.

Faculty *Total:* 6, 83% full-time, 33% with terminal degrees. *Student/faculty ratio:* 7:1.

Majors Forestry technology; survey technology.

Academic Programs *Special study options:* advanced placement credit, distance learning.

Library Ranger School Library with 5,000 titles, 60 serial subscriptions, an OPAC.

Computers on Campus 20 computers available on campus for general student use. A campuswide network can be accessed from student residence rooms and from off campus. Internet access available.

Student Life *Housing Options:* coed. *Student services:* health clinic, personal/psychological counseling, legal services.

Athletics *Intramural sports:* basketball M/W, ice hockey M/W, skiing (cross-country) M/W, skiing (downhill) M/W, softball M/W, volleyball M/W, weight lifting M/W.

Standardized Tests *Required:* SAT I or ACT (for admission).

Costs (2004–05) *Tuition:* state resident $4350 full-time, $181 per credit hour part-time; nonresident $10,300 full-time, $429 per credit hour part-time. *Required fees:* $869 full-time. *Room and board:* $7650.

Financial Aid Of all full-time matriculated undergraduates who enrolled, 30 Federal Work-Study jobs (averaging $1500). 15 state and other part-time jobs (averaging $1200).

Applying *Options:* electronic application, deferred entrance. *Application fee:* $30. *Application deadline:* rolling (freshmen), rolling (transfers).

Admissions Contact State University of New York College of Environmental Science & Forestry, Ranger School, Bray 106, Syracuse, NY 13210-2779. *Phone:* 315-470-6600. *Toll-free phone:* 800-777-7373. *Fax:* 315-470-6933. *E-mail:* esfinfo@mailbox.syr.edu.

▶ See page 604 for a narrative description.

STATE UNIVERSITY OF NEW YORK COLLEGE OF TECHNOLOGY AT ALFRED
Alfred, New York

- **State-supported** primarily 2-year, founded 1908, part of State University of New York System
- **Calendar** semesters
- **Degrees** certificates, associate, and bachelor's
- **Rural** 175-acre campus
- **Endowment** $2.6 million
- **Coed,** 3,471 undergraduate students, 89% full-time, 35% women, 65% men

Undergraduates 3,074 full-time, 397 part-time. Students come from 29 states and territories, 1% are from out of state, 5% African American, 1% Asian American or Pacific Islander, 3% Hispanic American, 0.3% Native American, 70% live on campus. *Retention:* 96% of 2002 full-time freshmen returned.

Freshmen *Admission:* 4,300 applied, 2,867 admitted.

Faculty *Total:* 191, 77% full-time, 14% with terminal degrees. *Student/faculty ratio:* 19:1.

Majors Accounting; agricultural business and management; agriculture; animal sciences; architectural engineering technology; autobody/collision and repair technology; automobile/automotive mechanics technology; biological and physical sciences; biology/biotechnology laboratory technician; business administration and management; carpentry; civil engineering technology; computer and information sciences; computer engineering technology; computer graphics; computer hardware engineering; computer/information technology services administration related; computer installation and repair technology; computer science; computer/technical support; computer typography and composition equipment operation; construction engineering; construction engineering technology; court reporting; culinary arts; dairy science; data processing and data processing technology; drafting and design technology; electrical, electronic and communications engineering technology; electrical/electronics equipment installation and repair; electromechanical technology; engineering science; environmental studies; finance; health information/medical records administration; heating, air conditioning, ventilation and refrigeration maintenance technology; heavy equipment maintenance technology; humanities; human services; industrial electronics technology; landscaping and groundskeeping; liberal arts and sciences/liberal studies; machine tool technology; marketing/marketing management; masonry; mathematics; mechanical design technology; mechanical engineering/mechanical technology; medical/clinical assistant; nursing (registered nurse training); pipefitting and sprinkler fitting; restaurant, culinary, and catering management; sales, distribution and marketing; social sciences; sport and fitness administration; survey technology; system administration; veterinary sciences; welding technology.

Academic Programs *Special study options:* academic remediation for entering students, adult/continuing education programs, advanced placement credit, distance learning, external degree program, honors programs, independent study, off-campus study, part-time degree program, services for LD students, student-designed majors, summer session for credit. *ROTC:* Army (c).

Library Walter C. Hinkle Memorial Library plus 1 other with 71,243 titles, 594 serial subscriptions, 8,148 audiovisual materials, an OPAC, a Web page.

Computers on Campus 1600 computers available on campus for general student use. A campuswide network can be accessed from student residence rooms and from off campus. Internet access, online (class) registration, at least one staffed computer lab available.

Student Life *Housing Options:* coed, disabled students. Campus housing is university owned. Freshman campus housing is guaranteed. *Activities and Organizations:* drama/theater group, student-run newspaper, radio station, choral group, Outdoor Activity Club, BACCHUS, Sondai Society, Drama Club, choir. *Campus security:* 24-hour emergency response devices and patrols, late-night transport/escort service, residence hall entrance guards. *Student services:* health clinic, personal/psychological counseling.

Athletics Member NJCAA. *Intercollegiate sports:* baseball M, basketball M(s)/W(s), cheerleading M/W, cross-country running M(s)/W(s), football M(s), lacrosse M(s), soccer M(s)/W(s), softball W(s), swimming M/W, track and field M(s)/W(s), volleyball W, wrestling M. *Intramural sports:* basketball M/W, bowling M/W, cross-country running M/W, football M, golf M/W, lacrosse M/W, racquetball M/W, rugby M/W, skiing (cross-country) M/W, soccer M/W, softball M/W, table tennis M/W, tennis M/W, volleyball M/W, water polo M/W.

Standardized Tests *Recommended:* SAT I or ACT (for admission).

Costs (2003–04) *Tuition:* state resident $4350 full-time; nonresident $7000 full-time. Full-time tuition and fees vary according to degree level. *Required fees:* $930 full-time. *Room and board:* $6376. Room and board charges vary according to board plan and housing facility. *Payment plan:* installment.

Financial Aid Of all full-time matriculated undergraduates who enrolled, 350 Federal Work-Study jobs (averaging $1000).

Applying *Options:* common application, electronic application, deferred entrance. *Application fee:* $40. *Required:* high school transcript. *Required for some:* minimum 2.0 GPA. *Recommended:* essay or personal statement, letters of recommendation, interview. *Application deadline:* rolling (freshmen), rolling (transfers). *Notification:* continuous (freshmen), continuous (transfers).

Admissions Contact Ms. Deborah J. Goodrich, Director of Admissions, State University of New York College of Technology at Alfred, Huntington Administration Building, 10 Upper College Drive, Alfred, NY 14802. *Phone:* 607-587-4215. *Toll-free phone:* 800-4-ALFRED. *Fax:* 607-587-4299. *E-mail:* admissions@alfredstate.edu.

STATE UNIVERSITY OF NEW YORK COLLEGE OF TECHNOLOGY AT CANTON
Canton, New York

- **State-supported** primarily 2-year, founded 1906, part of State University of New York System
- **Calendar** semesters
- **Degrees** certificates, associate, and bachelor's
- **Small-town** 555-acre campus
- **Endowment** $5.0 million
- **Coed,** 2,538 undergraduate students, 84% full-time, 48% women, 52% men

Undergraduates 2,139 full-time, 399 part-time. Students come from 20 states and territories, 2 other countries, 3% are from out of state, 8% African American, 0.6% Asian American or Pacific Islander, 3% Hispanic American, 2% Native American, 0.7% international, 8% transferred in, 48% live on campus. *Retention:* 82% of 2002 full-time freshmen returned.

Freshmen *Admission:* 1,936 applied, 1,902 admitted, 873 enrolled.

Faculty *Total:* 136, 57% full-time. *Student/faculty ratio:* 23:1.

Majors Accounting; automobile/automotive mechanics technology; banking and financial support services; biological and physical sciences; business administration and management; business/managerial economics; carpentry; civil engineering technology; clinical/medical laboratory technology; computer/information technology services administration related; construction engineering technology; corrections; criminal justice/law enforcement administration; criminal justice/police science; electrical, electronic and communications engineering technology; engineering science; engineering technology; environmental studies; forestry technology; funeral service and mortuary science; health/health care administration; heating, air conditioning, ventilation and refrigeration maintenance technology; humanities; industrial technology; information science/studies; interdisciplinary studies; kindergarten/preschool education; liberal arts and sciences/liberal studies; mechanical engineering/mechanical technology; nursing (registered nurse training); occupational therapist assistant; office management; physical therapist assistant; pipefitting and sprinkler fitting; social sciences; veterinary technology.

Academic Programs *Special study options:* academic remediation for entering students, adult/continuing education programs, advanced placement credit, distance learning, internships, off-campus study, part-time degree program, services for LD students, student-designed majors, summer session for credit. *ROTC:* Army (c), Air Force (c).

Library Southworth Library with 71,200 titles, 397 serial subscriptions, 2,042 audiovisual materials, an OPAC, a Web page.

Computers on Campus 300 computers available on campus for general student use. A campuswide network can be accessed. Internet access, at least one staffed computer lab available.

Student Life *Housing:* on-campus residence required through sophomore year. *Options:* coed, men-only, women-only. Campus housing is university owned. *Activities and Organizations:* drama/theater group, student-run newspaper, radio station, choral group, Karate Club, Automotive Club, Outing Club, WATC Radio, Afro-Latin Society, national fraternities, national sororities. *Campus security:* 24-hour emergency response devices and patrols, late-night transport/escort service, controlled dormitory access. *Student services:* health clinic, personal/psychological counseling.

Athletics Member NJCAA. *Intercollegiate sports:* baseball M, basketball M/W, bowling M/W, golf M/W, ice hockey M, lacrosse M/W, soccer M/W, softball W, volleyball W. *Intramural sports:* badminton M/W, basketball M/W, golf M/W, skiing (cross-country) M/W, soccer M/W, softball M/W, tennis M/W, volleyball M/W.

Costs (2003–04) *Tuition:* state resident $4350 full-time; nonresident $10,300 full-time. Full-time tuition and fees vary according to degree level, location, and program. Part-time tuition and fees vary according to degree level, location, and program. *Required fees:* $925 full-time. *Room and board:* $6910; room only: $3980. Room and board charges vary according to housing facility. *Payment plans:* installment, deferred payment. *Waivers:* employees or children of employees.

Financial Aid Of all full-time matriculated undergraduates who enrolled, 250 Federal Work-Study jobs (averaging $1200). 10 state and other part-time jobs (averaging $1200).

Applying *Options:* electronic application, early admission, deferred entrance. *Application fee:* $40. *Required:* high school transcript. *Required for some:* interview. *Recommended:* minimum 2.0 GPA. *Application deadline:* rolling (freshmen), rolling (transfers). *Notification:* continuous (freshmen), continuous (transfers).

Admissions Contact Mr. David M. Gerlach, Dean of Enrollment Management, State University of New York College of Technology at Canton, Canton, NY 13617. *Phone:* 315-386-7123. *Toll-free phone:* 800-388-7123. *Fax:* 315-386-7929. *E-mail:* williama@scanva.canton.edu.

STATE UNIVERSITY OF NEW YORK COLLEGE OF TECHNOLOGY AT DELHI
Delhi, New York

- **State-supported** primarily 2-year, founded 1913, part of State University of New York System
- **Calendar** semesters
- **Degrees** certificates, associate, and bachelor's
- **Rural** 405-acre campus
- **Endowment** $1.2 million
- **Coed,** 2,281 undergraduate students, 90% full-time, 42% women, 58% men

Undergraduates 2,046 full-time, 235 part-time. Students come from 7 states and territories, 3 other countries, 2% are from out of state, 11% African American, 2% Asian American or Pacific Islander, 6% Hispanic American, 0.3% Native American, 2% international, 7% transferred in, 61% live on campus.

Freshmen *Admission:* 3,462 applied, 2,091 admitted, 945 enrolled.

Faculty *Total:* 130, 75% full-time. *Student/faculty ratio:* 17:1.

Majors Accounting; architectural engineering technology; business administration and management; carpentry; computer/information technology services administration related; construction engineering technology; construction management; culinary arts; drafting and design technology; electrical and power transmission installation; engineering science; engineering technology; forestry; general studies; health and physical education; heating, air conditioning and refrigeration technology; heating, air conditioning, ventilation and refrigeration maintenance technology; horticultural science; hospitality and recreation marketing; hotel/motel administration; humanities; information science/studies; landscape architecture; landscaping and groundskeeping; marketing/marketing management; masonry; mathematics; nursing (registered nurse training); parks, recreation and leisure; parks, recreation and leisure facilities management; physical education teaching and coaching; pipefitting and sprinkler fitting; restaurant, culinary, and catering management; social sciences; tourism and travel services management; turf and turfgrass management; veterinary technology; web page, digital/multimedia and information resources design; welding technology; woodworking.

Academic Programs *Special study options:* academic remediation for entering students, adult/continuing education programs, advanced placement credit, distance learning, English as a second language, honors programs, internships, part-time degree program, services for LD students, student-designed majors, summer session for credit.

Library Louis and Mildred Resnick Library with 47,909 titles, 384 serial subscriptions, an OPAC.

Computers on Campus 350 computers available on campus for general student use. A campuswide network can be accessed from off campus. Internet access, online (class) registration, at least one staffed computer lab available.

Student Life *Housing:* on-campus residence required through sophomore year. *Options:* coed. *Activities and Organizations:* drama/theater group, student-run newspaper, radio station, Latin American Student Organization, Hotel Sales Management Association, student radio station, Phi Theta Kappa, Student Programming Board, national fraternities. *Campus security:* 24-hour emergency response devices and patrols. *Student services:* health clinic, personal/psychological counseling, legal services.

Athletics Member NAIA, NJCAA. *Intercollegiate sports:* basketball M/W, cross-country running M/W, golf M/W, lacrosse M, soccer M/W, softball W, swimming M/W, tennis M/W, track and field M/W, volleyball W, wrestling M. *Intramural sports:* basketball M/W, bowling M/W, cheerleading M/W, cross-country running M/W, football M/W, golf M/W, racquetball M/W, skiing (cross-country) M/W, skiing (downhill) M/W, swimming M/W, tennis M/W, volleyball M/W, weight lifting M/W.

Costs (2004–05) *Tuition:* state resident $4350 full-time; nonresident $10,300 full-time. *Required fees:* $975 full-time. *Room and board:* $6390.

Financial Aid Of all full-time matriculated undergraduates who enrolled, 150 Federal Work-Study jobs (averaging $1050).

Applying *Options:* electronic application, early admission, deferred entrance. *Application fee:* $30. *Required:* high school transcript. *Required for some:* minimum 2.0 GPA. *Application deadline:* rolling (freshmen), rolling (transfers). *Notification:* continuous (freshmen), continuous (transfers).

Admissions Contact Mr. Larry Barrett, Dean of Enrollment, State University of New York College of Technology at Delhi, 2 Main Street, Delhi, NY 13753. *Phone:* 607-746-4000 Ext. 4856. *Toll-free phone:* 800-96-DELHI. *Fax:* 607-746-4104. *E-mail:* enroll@delhi.edu.

SUFFOLK COUNTY COMMUNITY COLLEGE
Selden, New York

- **State and locally supported** 2-year, founded 1959, part of State University of New York System
- **Calendar** semesters

Suffolk County Community College (continued)
- **Degree** certificates, diplomas, and associate
- **Small-town** 500-acre campus with easy access to New York City
- **Coed**

Faculty *Student/faculty ratio:* 18:1.

Student Life *Campus security:* 24-hour emergency response devices and patrols.

Athletics Member NJCAA.

Standardized Tests *Required for some:* SAT I or ACT (for placement). *Recommended:* SAT I or ACT (for placement).

Costs (2003–04) *Tuition:* area resident $2600 full-time; state resident $5200 full-time. *Required fees:* $450 full-time.

Financial Aid Of all full-time matriculated undergraduates who enrolled, 109 Federal Work-Study jobs (averaging $1377).

Applying *Options:* deferred entrance. *Application fee:* $30. *Required:* high school transcript.

Admissions Contact Executive Director of Admissions and Enrollment Management, Suffolk County Community College, 533 College Road, Selden, NY 11784-2899. *Phone:* 631-451-4000. *Fax:* 631-451-4415.

SULLIVAN COUNTY COMMUNITY COLLEGE
Loch Sheldrake, New York

- **State and locally supported** 2-year, founded 1962, part of State University of New York System
- **Calendar** 4-1-4
- **Degree** certificates and associate
- **Rural** 405-acre campus
- **Endowment** $657,688
- **Coed,** 1,902 undergraduate students, 62% full-time, 64% women, 36% men

Undergraduates 1,178 full-time, 724 part-time. Students come from 6 states and territories, 9 other countries, 1% are from out of state, 21% African American, 0.9% Asian American or Pacific Islander, 9% Hispanic American, 0.3% Native American, 0.9% international, 5% transferred in.

Freshmen *Admission:* 2,093 applied, 1,393 admitted, 832 enrolled.

Faculty *Total:* 134, 37% full-time. *Student/faculty ratio:* 16:1.

Majors Accounting; administrative assistant and secretarial science; baking and pastry arts; business administration and management; commercial and advertising art; computer graphics; computer programming (specific applications); consumer merchandising/retailing management; corrections; culinary arts; data entry/microcomputer applications; electrical, electronic and communications engineering technology; elementary education; engineering science; environmental studies; hospitality administration; human services; information science/studies; kindergarten/preschool education; legal assistant/paralegal; liberal arts and sciences/liberal studies; marketing/marketing management; mathematics; nursing (registered nurse training); photography; radio and television; sport and fitness administration; substance abuse/addiction counseling; survey technology; tourism and travel services management; web/multimedia management and webmaster.

Academic Programs *Special study options:* academic remediation for entering students, adult/continuing education programs, advanced placement credit, distance learning, double majors, honors programs, internships, part-time degree program, services for LD students, summer session for credit.

Library Hermann Memorial Library with 65,699 titles, 400 serial subscriptions, an OPAC, a Web page.

Computers on Campus 205 computers available on campus for general student use. A campuswide network can be accessed. Internet access, online (class) registration, at least one staffed computer lab available.

Student Life *Housing:* college housing not available. *Activities and Organizations:* student-run radio station, Science Alliance, Black Student Union, Drama Club, Baking Club, Honor Society. *Campus security:* 24-hour emergency response devices and patrols. *Student services:* health clinic, personal/psychological counseling, legal services.

Athletics Member NJCAA. *Intercollegiate sports:* basketball M/W, cheerleading W, cross-country running M/W, golf M, softball W, volleyball W. *Intramural sports:* basketball M/W, bowling M/W, cross-country running M/W, football M, golf M/W, racquetball M/W, skiing (downhill) M/W, soccer M/W, softball M/W, table tennis M/W, tennis M/W, volleyball M/W, weight lifting M/W.

Standardized Tests *Recommended:* SAT I or ACT (for placement).

Costs (2003–04) *Tuition:* state resident $2900 full-time; nonresident $5800 full-time. *Required fees:* $276 full-time. *Payment plans:* installment, deferred payment. *Waivers:* senior citizens and employees or children of employees.

Financial Aid Of all full-time matriculated undergraduates who enrolled, 105 Federal Work-Study jobs (averaging $800). 57 state and other part-time jobs (averaging $841).

Applying *Options:* common application, electronic application, early admission, deferred entrance. *Required:* high school transcript. *Application deadline:* rolling (freshmen), rolling (transfers). *Notification:* continuous (freshmen), continuous (transfers).

Admissions Contact Mr. Ray Sheenan, Director of Admissions and Registration Services, Sullivan County Community College, 112 College Road, Loch Sheldrake, NY 12759. *Phone:* 914-434-5750 Ext. 4480. *Toll-free phone:* 800-577-5243. *Fax:* 914-434-4806. *E-mail:* dbrown@sullivan.suny.edu.

TAYLOR BUSINESS INSTITUTE
New York, New York

Admissions Contact Mr. Orlando Mangual, Director of Admissions, Taylor Business Institute, 269 West 40th Street, New York, NY 10018. *Phone:* 212-302-4000.

TCI–THE COLLEGE OF TECHNOLOGY
New York, New York

- **Proprietary** 2-year, founded 1909
- **Calendar** semesters
- **Degree** certificates, diplomas, and associate
- **Urban** campus
- **Coed**

Faculty *Student/faculty ratio:* 30:1.

Student Life *Campus security:* 24-hour patrols.

Athletics Member NJCAA.

Financial Aid Of all full-time matriculated undergraduates who enrolled, 380 Federal Work-Study jobs (averaging $1697).

Applying *Options:* common application, deferred entrance. *Required:* essay or personal statement, high school transcript, interview.

Admissions Contact Ms. Sandra Germer, Director of Admission, TCI-The College of Technology, 320 West 31st Street, New York, NY 10001-2705. *Phone:* 212-594-4000 Ext. 437. *Fax:* 212-629-3937. *E-mail:* admissions@ tciedu.com.

TOMPKINS CORTLAND COMMUNITY COLLEGE
Dryden, New York

- **State and locally supported** 2-year, founded 1968, part of State University of New York System
- **Calendar** semesters
- **Degree** certificates and associate
- **Rural** 250-acre campus with easy access to Syracuse
- **Endowment** $2.0 million
- **Coed,** 3,227 undergraduate students, 66% full-time, 61% women, 39% men

Undergraduates 2,137 full-time, 1,090 part-time. Students come from 22 states and territories, 43 other countries, 1% are from out of state, 6% African American, 2% Asian American or Pacific Islander, 3% Hispanic American, 0.3% Native American, 3% international, 10% transferred in, 4% live on campus.

Freshmen *Admission:* 816 enrolled. *Average high school GPA:* 2.48. *Test scores:* SAT verbal scores over 500: 38%; SAT math scores over 500: 32%; ACT scores over 18: 65%; SAT verbal scores over 600: 7%; SAT math scores over 600: 4%; ACT scores over 24: 7%; SAT verbal scores over 700: 1%.

Faculty *Total:* 256, 27% full-time, 19% with terminal degrees. *Student/faculty ratio:* 21:1.

Majors Accounting; administrative assistant and secretarial science; aeronautics/aviation/aerospace science and technology; biological and physical sciences; business administration and management; child care provision; child development; commercial and advertising art; computer and information sciences related; computer and information systems security; computer graphics; computer hardware engineering; computer/information technology services administration related; computer programming related; computer science; computer software engineering; computer/technical support; construction engineering technology; criminal justice/law enforcement administration; data entry/microcomputer applications; electrical, electronic and communications engineering technology; engineering science; environmental studies; hotel/motel administration; humanities; human services; information science/studies; international business/trade/commerce; kindergarten/preschool education; legal assistant/paralegal; liberal arts and sciences/liberal studies; marketing/marketing management; mass communication/media; mathematics; nursing (registered nurse training); parks, recreation and leisure; radio and television; social sciences; sport and fitness administration; substance abuse/addiction counseling; system administration; tourism and travel services management; tourism and travel services marketing; web page, digital/multimedia and information resources design; women's studies.

Academic Programs *Special study options:* academic remediation for entering students, adult/continuing education programs, advanced placement credit, cooperative education, English as a second language, honors programs, internships, off-campus study, part-time degree program, services for LD students, summer session for credit. *ROTC:* Army (c).

Library Gerald A. Barry Memorial Library with 50,630 titles, 489 serial subscriptions, an OPAC, a Web page.

Computers on Campus 350 computers available on campus for general student use. A campuswide network can be accessed from student residence rooms. Internet access, online (class) registration, at least one staffed computer lab available.

Student Life *Housing Options:* coed. Campus housing is provided by a third party. *Activities and Organizations:* drama/theater group, Art Works, Accounting Club, Nurse's Association. *Campus security:* 24-hour emergency response devices and patrols. *Student services:* personal/psychological counseling.

Athletics Member NJCAA. *Intercollegiate sports:* basketball M/W, golf M/W, soccer M/W, softball W, tennis W, volleyball W, wrestling M. *Intramural sports:* badminton M/W, basketball M/W, bowling M/W, football M/W, golf M/W, lacrosse M/W, racquetball M/W, rock climbing M/W, skiing (cross-country) M/W, soccer M/W, softball M/W, swimming M/W, table tennis M/W, tennis M/W, volleyball M/W, water polo M/W.

Standardized Tests *Required for some:* SAT I or ACT (for placement). *Recommended:* ACT (for placement).

Costs (2004–05) *Tuition:* state resident $2950 full-time, $110 per credit part-time; nonresident $6200 full-time, $230 per credit part-time. Part-time tuition and fees vary according to course load. *Required fees:* $396 full-time, $10 per credit part-time. *Room and board:* room only: $4200. Room and board charges vary according to housing facility. *Payment plans:* installment, deferred payment. *Waivers:* employees or children of employees.

Financial Aid Of all full-time matriculated undergraduates who enrolled, 150 Federal Work-Study jobs (averaging $1000). 150 state and other part-time jobs (averaging $1000).

Applying *Options:* early admission, deferred entrance. *Application fee:* $15. *Required:* high school transcript. *Application deadline:* rolling (freshmen), rolling (transfers). *Notification:* continuous (freshmen), continuous (transfers).

Admissions Contact Mr. Sandy Drumluk, Director of Admissions, Tompkins Cortland Community College, 170 North Street, PO Box 139, Dryden, NY 13053-0139. *Phone:* 607-844-8222. *Toll-free phone:* 888-567-8211. *Fax:* 607-844-6538. *E-mail:* admissions@sunytcccc.edu.

TROCAIRE COLLEGE
Buffalo, New York

- **Independent** 2-year, founded 1958
- **Calendar** semesters
- **Degree** certificates and associate
- **Urban** 1-acre campus
- **Endowment** $4.2 million
- **Coed, primarily women**

Faculty *Student/faculty ratio:* 15:1.

Student Life *Campus security:* 24-hour emergency response devices and patrols, late-night transport/escort service.

Standardized Tests *Required for some:* SAT I or ACT (for admission).

Costs (2003–04) *Tuition:* $9290 full-time, $350 per credit hour part-time. Full-time tuition and fees vary according to program. Part-time tuition and fees vary according to program. *Required fees:* $160 full-time, $50 per term part-time.

Financial Aid Of all full-time matriculated undergraduates who enrolled, 33 Federal Work-Study jobs (averaging $1500).

Applying *Options:* deferred entrance. *Application fee:* $25. *Required:* high school transcript. *Recommended:* interview.

Admissions Contact Mrs. Theresa Horner, Director of Records, Trocaire College, 360 Choate Avenue, Buffalo, NY 14220. *Phone:* 716-826-1200 Ext. 1259. *Fax:* 716-828-6107. *E-mail:* info@trocaire.edu.

ULSTER COUNTY COMMUNITY COLLEGE
Stone Ridge, New York

- **State and locally supported** 2-year, founded 1961, part of State University of New York System
- **Calendar** semesters
- **Degree** certificates, diplomas, and associate
- **Rural** 165-acre campus
- **Endowment** $2.4 million
- **Coed**

Faculty *Student/faculty ratio:* 15:1.

Student Life *Campus security:* 24-hour emergency response devices and patrols.

Athletics Member NJCAA.

Standardized Tests *Required for some:* ACT ASSET, ACT COMPASS.

Costs (2004–05) *Tuition:* state resident $2900 full-time, $100 per credit hour part-time; nonresident $5800 full-time, $200 per credit hour part-time.

Financial Aid Of all full-time matriculated undergraduates who enrolled, 125 Federal Work-Study jobs (averaging $1000).

Applying *Options:* early admission, deferred entrance.

Admissions Contact Admissions Office, Ulster County Community College, Stone Ridge, NY 12484. *Phone:* 914-687-5022. *Toll-free phone:* 800-724-0833. *Fax:* 914-687-5083. *E-mail:* reqinfo@sunyulster.edu.

UTICA SCHOOL OF COMMERCE
Utica, New York

- **Proprietary** 2-year, founded 1896
- **Calendar** quarters
- **Degree** certificates, diplomas, and associate
- **Urban** 2-acre campus
- **Endowment** $21,000
- **Coed, primarily women**

Faculty *Student/faculty ratio:* 15:1.

Student Life *Campus security:* security during class hours.

Costs (2003–04) *Tuition:* $9400 full-time, $180 per semester hour part-time. *Required fees:* $360 full-time, $15 per credit hour part-time.

Financial Aid Of all full-time matriculated undergraduates who enrolled, 40 Federal Work-Study jobs (averaging $2000).

Applying *Options:* electronic application, early admission, deferred entrance. *Application fee:* $20. *Required:* high school transcript, interview. *Recommended:* essay or personal statement, letters of recommendation.

Admissions Contact Chris Tacea, Dean of Enrollment Management, Utica School of Commerce, 201 Bleecker Street, Utica, NY 13501. *Phone:* 315-733-2300. *Toll-free phone:* 800-321-4USC. *Fax:* 315-733-9281. *E-mail:* swilliams@uscny.edu.

VILLA MARIA COLLEGE OF BUFFALO
Buffalo, New York

- **Independent** 2-year, founded 1960, affiliated with Roman Catholic Church
- **Calendar** semesters
- **Degree** certificates and associate
- **Suburban** 9-acre campus
- **Endowment** $625,361
- **Coed,** 459 undergraduate students, 73% full-time, 75% women, 25% men

Undergraduates 335 full-time, 124 part-time. Students come from 1 other state, 25% African American, 2% Asian American or Pacific Islander, 2% Hispanic American, 0.2% Native American, 11% transferred in.

Freshmen *Admission:* 240 applied, 213 admitted, 124 enrolled. *Average high school GPA:* 2.46. *Test scores:* SAT verbal scores over 500: 15%; SAT math scores over 500: 10%; ACT scores over 18: 50%; SAT verbal scores over 600: 5%.

Faculty *Total:* 66, 41% full-time, 29% with terminal degrees. *Student/faculty ratio:* 9:1.

Majors Administrative assistant and secretarial science; business administration and management; commercial and advertising art; computer management; education; health science; interior design; kindergarten/preschool education; liberal arts and sciences/liberal studies; music; music management and merchandising; photography; physical therapist assistant.

Academic Programs *Special study options:* academic remediation for entering students, advanced placement credit, cooperative education, double majors, independent study, internships, off-campus study, part-time degree program, services for LD students, study abroad, summer session for credit.

Library Villa Maria College Library with 40,000 titles, 200 serial subscriptions, 5,000 audiovisual materials, an OPAC, a Web page.

Computers on Campus 80 computers available on campus for general student use. A campuswide network can be accessed from off campus. Internet access, at least one staffed computer lab available.

Student Life *Housing:* college housing not available. *Activities and Organizations:* drama/theater group, student-run newspaper, radio station, choral group, Design and Beyond, Teachers Love Children, Multicultural Club, Phi Theta Kappa, Helping Adults New Dreams Succeed. *Campus security:* late-night transport/escort service. *Student services:* health clinic, personal/psychological counseling.

Standardized Tests *Required:* (for placement). *Recommended:* SAT I or ACT (for admission).

Costs (2004–05) *Tuition:* $10,150 full-time, $340 per credit hour part-time. *Required fees:* $400 full-time. *Payment plan:* installment. *Waivers:* employees or children of employees.

Villa Maria College of Buffalo (continued)

Financial Aid Of all full-time matriculated undergraduates who enrolled, 71 Federal Work-Study jobs (averaging $1278).

Applying *Options:* deferred entrance. *Application fee:* $35. *Required:* high school transcript, interview, writing sample. *Application deadline:* rolling (freshmen), rolling (transfers). *Notification:* continuous (freshmen), continuous (transfers).

Admissions Contact Mr. Kevin Donovan, Director of Admissions, Villa Maria College of Buffalo, Villa Maria College, 240 Pine Ridge Road, Buffalo, NY 14225-3999. *Phone:* 716-896-0700 Ext. 1802. *Fax:* 716-896-0705. *E-mail:* admissions@villa.edu.

WESTCHESTER COMMUNITY COLLEGE
Valhalla, New York

- **State and locally supported** 2-year, founded 1946, part of State University of New York System
- **Calendar** semesters
- **Degree** certificates and associate
- **Suburban** 218-acre campus with easy access to New York City
- **Endowment** $8.5 million
- **Coed**

Faculty *Student/faculty ratio:* 16:1.

Student Life *Campus security:* 24-hour emergency response devices and patrols, late-night transport/escort service.

Athletics Member NJCAA.

Costs (2004–05) *Tuition:* state resident $2950 full-time, $123 per credit part-time; nonresident $7376 full-time, $308 per credit part-time. *Required fees:* $343 full-time, $76 per term part-time.

Financial Aid Of all full-time matriculated undergraduates who enrolled, 200 Federal Work-Study jobs (averaging $1000).

Applying *Options:* electronic application, early admission. *Application fee:* $25. *Required:* high school transcript. *Recommended:* interview.

Admissions Contact Ms. Terre Wisell, Director of Admissions, Westchester Community College, 75 Grasslands Road, Administration Building, Valhalla, NY 10595-1698. *Phone:* 914-785-6735. *E-mail:* admissions@sunywcc.edu.

WOOD TOBE-COBURN SCHOOL
New York, New York

- **Proprietary** 2-year, founded 1879, part of Bradford Schools, Inc
- **Calendar** semesters
- **Degree** diplomas and associate
- **Urban** campus
- **Coed, primarily women**

Student Life *Campus security:* 24-hour emergency response devices and patrols.

Costs (2003–04) *Tuition:* $12,360 full-time. *Required fees:* $150 full-time.

Applying *Required:* high school transcript, interview.

Admissions Contact Ms. Sandra L. Wendland, Director of Admissions, Wood Tobe-Coburn School, 8 East 40th Street, New York, NY 10016. *Phone:* 212-686-9040 Ext. 103.

NORTH CAROLINA

ALAMANCE COMMUNITY COLLEGE
Graham, North Carolina

- **State-supported** 2-year, founded 1959, part of North Carolina Community College System
- **Calendar** semesters
- **Degree** certificates, diplomas, and associate
- **Small-town** 48-acre campus
- **Endowment** $2.0 million
- **Coed**, 4,627 undergraduate students, 34% full-time, 65% women, 35% men

Undergraduates 1,570 full-time, 3,057 part-time. Students come from 23 states and territories, 3 other countries, 1% are from out of state, 23% African American, 1% Asian American or Pacific Islander, 2% Hispanic American, 0.4% Native American, 0.5% international.

Freshmen *Admission:* 1,733 applied, 1,733 admitted, 774 enrolled.

Faculty *Total:* 238, 39% full-time, 6% with terminal degrees. *Student/faculty ratio:* 16:1.

Majors Accounting technology and bookkeeping; animal sciences; applied horticulture; automobile/automotive mechanics technology; banking and financial support services; biotechnology; business administration and management; carpentry; clinical/medical laboratory technology; commercial and advertising art; computer programming; criminal justice/safety; culinary arts; electrical, electronic and communications engineering technology; electromechanical technology; executive assistant/executive secretary; general retailing/wholesaling; heating, air conditioning and refrigeration technology; information science/studies; kindergarten/preschool education; legal administrative assistant/secretary; liberal arts and sciences/liberal studies; machine tool technology; mechanical engineering/mechanical technology; medical administrative assistant and medical secretary; medical/clinical assistant; nursing (registered nurse training); office occupations and clerical services; operations management; real estate; social work; teacher assistant/aide; welding technology.

Academic Programs *Special study options:* academic remediation for entering students, adult/continuing education programs, cooperative education, distance learning, double majors, English as a second language, independent study, off-campus study, part-time degree program, services for LD students, summer session for credit.

Library Learning Resources Center with 22,114 titles, 185 serial subscriptions, 3,033 audiovisual materials, an OPAC, a Web page.

Computers on Campus A campuswide network can be accessed. At least one staffed computer lab available.

Student Life *Housing:* college housing not available. *Campus security:* 24-hour emergency response devices and patrols, student patrols, late-night transport/escort service. *Student services:* personal/psychological counseling.

Athletics *Intramural sports:* basketball M/W, bowling M/W, tennis M/W, volleyball M/W.

Standardized Tests *Recommended:* SAT I or ACT (for placement).

Costs (2004–05) *Tuition:* state resident $1136 full-time, $36 per credit hour part-time; nonresident $6304 full-time, $197 per credit hour part-time. Part-time tuition and fees vary according to course load. *Required fees:* $30 full-time, $1 per credit part-time. *Waivers:* senior citizens.

Financial Aid Of all full-time matriculated undergraduates who enrolled, 150 Federal Work-Study jobs (averaging $3000).

Applying *Options:* common application, deferred entrance. *Required:* high school transcript. *Application deadline:* rolling (freshmen), rolling (transfers). *Notification:* continuous (freshmen), continuous (transfers).

Admissions Contact Ms. Suzanne Lucier, Director for Enrollment Management, Alamance Community College, Jimmy Kerr Road, Graham, NC 27253-8000. *Phone:* 336-578-2002 Ext. 4138. *Fax:* 336-578-1987. *E-mail:* admissions@alamance.cc.nc.us.

THE ART INSTITUTE OF CHARLOTTE
Charlotte, North Carolina

- **Proprietary** 2-year, founded 1973
- **Calendar** quarters
- **Degree** associate
- **Suburban** campus
- **Coed**, 697 undergraduate students, 67% full-time, 64% women, 36% men

Undergraduates 466 full-time, 231 part-time. 28% African American, 2% Asian American or Pacific Islander, 2% Hispanic American, 0.4% Native American, 0.1% international.

Freshmen *Admission:* 196 enrolled.

Faculty *Total:* 48, 48% full-time, 13% with terminal degrees. *Student/faculty ratio:* 18:1.

Costs (2004–05) *Tuition:* $21,376 full-time, $334 per credit part-time. *Required fees:* $200 full-time, $50 per term part-time. *Room only:* $5336.

Admissions Contact Mrs. Elizabeth Guinan, College President, The Art Institute of Charlotte, 2110 Water Ridge Parkway, Charlotte, NC 28217. *Phone:* 704-357-8020 Ext. 2541.

ASHEVILLE-BUNCOMBE TECHNICAL COMMUNITY COLLEGE
Asheville, North Carolina

- **State-supported** 2-year, founded 1959, part of North Carolina Community College System
- **Calendar** semesters
- **Degree** certificates, diplomas, and associate
- **Urban** 126-acre campus
- **Endowment** $98,442
- **Coed**, 5,627 undergraduate students, 36% full-time, 55% women, 45% men

Undergraduates 2,042 full-time, 3,585 part-time. 2% are from out of state, 6% African American, 0.5% Asian American or Pacific Islander, 1% Hispanic American, 0.5% Native American, 0.6% international.

Freshmen *Admission:* 2,792 applied, 2,792 admitted, 522 enrolled.
Faculty *Total:* 584, 21% full-time, 5% with terminal degrees. *Student/faculty ratio:* 17:1.
Majors Accounting technology and bookkeeping; automobile/automotive mechanics technology; business administration and management; child care and support services management; civil engineering technology; clinical/medical laboratory technology; computer programming; computer systems networking and telecommunications; criminal justice/police science; culinary arts; dental hygiene; emergency medical technology (EMT paramedic); executive assistant/executive secretary; general retailing/wholesaling; heating, air conditioning, ventilation and refrigeration maintenance technology; hotel/motel administration; institutional food workers; liberal arts and sciences/liberal studies; machine tool technology; mechanical design technology; mechanical engineering/mechanical technology; medical radiologic technology; nursing (registered nurse training); operations management; social work; survey technology; tool and die technology.
Academic Programs *Special study options:* academic remediation for entering students, adult/continuing education programs, advanced placement credit, cooperative education, distance learning, double majors, independent study, internships, part-time degree program, services for LD students, summer session for credit.
Library Holly Learning Resources Center with 37,439 titles, 195 serial subscriptions, an OPAC.
Computers on Campus 414 computers available on campus for general student use. A campuswide network can be accessed from off campus. Internet access, at least one staffed computer lab available.
Student Life *Housing:* college housing not available. *Activities and Organizations:* drama/theater group, student-run newspaper, Student Government Association, Phi Beta Lambda. *Campus security:* 24-hour emergency response devices and patrols. *Student services:* personal/psychological counseling.
Athletics *Intramural sports:* basketball M/W, softball M/W, volleyball M/W.
Standardized Tests *Required:* CPT, SAT I, or ACT (for placement).
Costs (2003–04) *Tuition:* state resident $1316 full-time, $36 per credit hour part-time; nonresident $7130 full-time, $197 per credit hour part-time. *Required fees:* $27 full-time.
Applying *Options:* deferred entrance. *Required:* high school transcript. *Required for some:* letters of recommendation, interview. *Application deadline:* rolling (freshmen), rolling (transfers). *Notification:* continuous (freshmen), continuous (transfers).
Admissions Contact Ms. Martha B. McLean, Director of Enrollment Management, Asheville-Buncombe Technical Community College, 340 Victoria Road, Asheville, NC 28801. *Phone:* 828-254-1921 Ext. 147. *Fax:* 828-251-6718. *E-mail:* admissions@abtech.edu.

BEAUFORT COUNTY COMMUNITY COLLEGE
Washington, North Carolina

- **State-supported** 2-year, founded 1967, part of North Carolina Community College System
- **Calendar** semesters
- **Degree** certificates, diplomas, and associate
- **Rural** 67-acre campus
- **Coed,** 1,756 undergraduate students

Undergraduates 1% are from out of state, 35% African American, 0.1% Asian American or Pacific Islander, 1% Hispanic American, 0.2% international.
Faculty *Total:* 136, 43% full-time, 3% with terminal degrees.
Majors Accounting; administrative assistant and secretarial science; agricultural mechanization; automobile/automotive mechanics technology; business administration and management; clinical/medical laboratory technology; computer programming; computer systems networking and telecommunications; criminal justice/police science; drafting and design technology; electrical, electronic and communications engineering technology; heavy equipment maintenance technology; human resources management; information science/studies; kindergarten/preschool education; liberal arts and sciences/liberal studies; medical administrative assistant and medical secretary; medical office management; nursing (registered nurse training); social work; welding technology.
Academic Programs *Special study options:* academic remediation for entering students, advanced placement credit, cooperative education, distance learning, part-time degree program, services for LD students, summer session for credit.
Library Beaufort Community College Library with 25,734 titles, 214 serial subscriptions, an OPAC, a Web page.
Computers on Campus 60 computers available on campus for general student use. A campuswide network can be accessed from off campus. Internet access, at least one staffed computer lab available.
Student Life *Housing:* college housing not available. *Activities and Organizations:* Student Government Association, Gama Beta Phi, Phi Beta Lambda,

Hope Club. *Campus security:* 24-hour emergency response devices and patrols, late-night transport/escort service. *Student services:* personal/psychological counseling.
Standardized Tests *Required:* CPT (for admission).
Costs (2003–04) *Tuition:* state resident $1136 full-time, $35 per credit hour part-time; nonresident $6608 full-time, $207 per credit hour part-time. Part-time tuition and fees vary according to course load. *Required fees:* $28 full-time, $14 per credit hour part-time. *Waivers:* employees or children of employees.
Financial Aid Of all full-time matriculated undergraduates who enrolled, 21 Federal Work-Study jobs (averaging $1600). *Financial aid deadline:* 7/15.
Applying *Options:* early admission, deferred entrance. *Required:* high school transcript. *Required for some:* essay or personal statement, letters of recommendation, interview. *Application deadline:* 8/18 (freshmen), rolling (transfers). *Notification:* continuous (freshmen), continuous (transfers).
Admissions Contact Mr. Gary Burbage, Director of Admissions, Beaufort County Community College, PO Box 1069, 5337 US Highway 264 East, Washington, NC 27889-1069. *Phone:* 252-940-6233. *Fax:* 252-940-6393. *E-mail:* garyb@email.beaufort.cc.nc.us.

BLADEN COMMUNITY COLLEGE
Dublin, North Carolina

- **State and locally supported** 2-year, founded 1967, part of North Carolina Community College System
- **Calendar** semesters
- **Degree** certificates, diplomas, and associate
- **Rural** 45-acre campus
- **Endowment** $72,151
- **Coed,** 1,407 undergraduate students, 60% full-time, 77% women, 23% men

Undergraduates 838 full-time, 569 part-time. Students come from 3 states and territories, 48% African American, 0.2% Asian American or Pacific Islander, 0.6% Hispanic American, 10% Native American. *Retention:* 35% of 2002 full-time freshmen returned.
Freshmen *Admission:* 267 enrolled. *Average high school GPA:* 2.6.
Faculty *Total:* 85, 38% full-time, 5% with terminal degrees. *Student/faculty ratio:* 15:1.
Majors Administrative assistant and secretarial science; biotechnology; business administration and management; child care provision; computer programming; computer programming (specific applications); cosmetology; criminal justice/police science; electrical, electronic and communications engineering technology; general studies; industrial technology; information technology; liberal arts and sciences/liberal studies; nursing (registered nurse training); welding technology.
Academic Programs *Special study options:* academic remediation for entering students, adult/continuing education programs, advanced placement credit, distance learning, double majors, independent study, part-time degree program, services for LD students, summer session for credit.
Library Learning Resource Center with 19,881 titles, 52 serial subscriptions, 2,364 audiovisual materials, an OPAC, a Web page.
Computers on Campus 150 computers available on campus for general student use. A campuswide network can be accessed from off campus. Internet access, at least one staffed computer lab available.
Student Life *Housing:* college housing not available. *Campus security:* 14-hour patrols. *Student services:* personal/psychological counseling.
Standardized Tests *Required:* ACT COMPASS (for placement).
Costs (2004–05) *Tuition:* area resident $1136 full-time; state resident $36 per semester hour part-time; nonresident $6304 full-time, $197 per semester hour part-time. *Required fees:* $58 full-time, $22 per term part-time. *Waivers:* senior citizens and employees or children of employees.
Financial Aid Of all full-time matriculated undergraduates who enrolled, 30 Federal Work-Study jobs (averaging $1200).
Applying *Options:* common application, electronic application, deferred entrance. *Required:* high school transcript. *Recommended:* minimum 2.0 GPA. *Application deadlines:* 8/1 (freshmen), 8/1 (transfers). *Notification:* continuous until 8/15 (freshmen), continuous until 8/15 (transfers).
Admissions Contact Ms. Yvonne Willoughby, Admissions Secretary, Bladen Community College, PO Box 266, Dublin, NC 28332. *Phone:* 910-879-5593. *Fax:* 910-879-5564. *E-mail:* ywilloughby@bladen.cc.nc.us.

BLUE RIDGE COMMUNITY COLLEGE
Flat Rock, North Carolina

- **State and locally supported** 2-year, founded 1969, part of North Carolina Community College System
- **Calendar** semesters
- **Degree** certificates, diplomas, and associate
- **Small-town** 109-acre campus

Blue Ridge Community College (continued)
- **Endowment** $51,500
- **Coed,** 2,083 undergraduate students, 47% full-time, 59% women, 41% men

Undergraduates 971 full-time, 1,112 part-time. Students come from 18 states and territories, 14 other countries, 4% African American, 0.6% Asian American or Pacific Islander, 2% Hispanic American, 0.3% Native American, 2% international, 5% transferred in.

Freshmen *Admission:* 904 applied, 787 admitted, 434 enrolled.

Faculty *Total:* 255, 25% full-time, 9% with terminal degrees. *Student/faculty ratio:* 12:1.

Majors Administrative assistant and secretarial science; art; business administration and management; computer programming; computer programming related; cosmetology; drafting and design technology; electrical, electronic and communications engineering technology; environmental engineering technology; horticultural science; industrial technology; information science/studies; kindergarten/preschool education; liberal arts and sciences/liberal studies; machine tool technology; marketing/marketing management; mechanical engineering/mechanical technology; nursing (registered nurse training); sign language interpretation and translation; surgical technology; system administration; tourism and travel services management.

Academic Programs *Special study options:* academic remediation for entering students, adult/continuing education programs, advanced placement credit, cooperative education, distance learning, double majors, English as a second language, internships, part-time degree program, services for LD students, summer session for credit.

Library Blue Ridge Community College Library plus 1 other with 47,655 titles, 3,875 serial subscriptions, 1,692 audiovisual materials, an OPAC.

Computers on Campus 225 computers available on campus for general student use. A campuswide network can be accessed. Internet access available.

Student Life *Housing:* college housing not available. *Activities and Organizations:* drama/theater group, student-run newspaper, Student Government Association, Phi Theta Kappa, Spanish Club, Rotaract. *Campus security:* sheriff's deputy during class hours. *Student services:* personal/psychological counseling.

Athletics Member NJCAA. *Intercollegiate sports:* baseball M.

Costs (2003–04) *Tuition:* state resident $1136 full-time, $36 per credit hour part-time; nonresident $3152 full-time, $197 per credit hour part-time. *Required fees:* $104 full-time.

Financial Aid Of all full-time matriculated undergraduates who enrolled, 35 Federal Work-Study jobs (averaging $1920). 34 state and other part-time jobs (averaging $1920).

Applying *Options:* common application, early admission. *Required:* high school transcript. *Application deadline:* rolling (freshmen), rolling (transfers). *Notification:* continuous (freshmen), continuous (transfers).

Admissions Contact Ms. Sarah Jones, Registrar, Blue Ridge Community College, 180 West Campus Drive, Flat Rock, NC 28731. *Phone:* 828-694-1810. *E-mail:* sarahj@blueridge.edu.

BRUNSWICK COMMUNITY COLLEGE
Supply, North Carolina

- **State-supported** 2-year, founded 1979, part of North Carolina Community College System
- **Calendar** semesters
- **Degree** certificates, diplomas, and associate
- **Rural** 266-acre campus
- **Endowment** $944,888
- **Coed,** 1,109 undergraduate students, 49% full-time, 72% women, 28% men

Undergraduates 545 full-time, 564 part-time. Students come from 4 states and territories, 1% are from out of state, 23% African American, 0.2% Asian American or Pacific Islander, 0.8% Hispanic American, 0.5% Native American, 0.1% international, 4% transferred in.

Freshmen *Admission:* 259 enrolled.

Faculty *Total:* 108, 27% full-time, 9% with terminal degrees. *Student/faculty ratio:* 13:1.

Majors Administrative assistant and secretarial science; applied horticulture; aquaculture; business administration and management; child care provision; computer/information technology services administration related; computer programming; computer programming related; electrical, electronic and communications engineering technology; engineering technology; fishing and fisheries sciences and management; health information/medical records administration; industrial technology; liberal arts and sciences/liberal studies; nursing (registered nurse training); teacher assistant/aide; turf and turfgrass management.

Academic Programs *Special study options:* academic remediation for entering students, advanced placement credit, cooperative education, distance learning, English as a second language, independent study, internships, part-time degree program, services for LD students, summer session for credit.

Library Brunswick Community College Library plus 1 other with 18,679 titles, 71 serial subscriptions, 986 audiovisual materials, an OPAC.

Computers on Campus 128 computers available on campus for general student use. A campuswide network can be accessed. Internet access, at least one staffed computer lab available.

Student Life *Housing:* college housing not available. *Activities and Organizations:* Student Government Association, Phi Theta Kappa Honor Society, National Vocational-Technical Honor Society. *Campus security:* late-night transport/escort service, campus police. *Student services:* personal/psychological counseling.

Athletics Member NJCAA. *Intercollegiate sports:* basketball M(s), golf M(s), softball W. *Intramural sports:* volleyball M/W.

Standardized Tests *Required:* ACT ASSET (for placement).

Costs (2004–05) *Tuition:* state resident $36 per semester hour part-time; nonresident $197 per semester hour part-time. *Required fees:* $73 full-time, $23 per term part-time. *Payment plan:* deferred payment. *Waivers:* senior citizens and employees or children of employees.

Applying *Options:* electronic application. *Required:* high school transcript. *Required for some:* letters of recommendation, interview. *Application deadline:* rolling (freshmen), rolling (transfers). *Notification:* continuous (freshmen), continuous (transfers).

Admissions Contact Ms. Julie Olsen, Admissions Counselor, Brunswick Community College, PO Box 30, Supply, NC 28462. *Phone:* 910-755-7324. *Toll-free phone:* 800-754-1050 Ext. 324. *Fax:* 910-754-9609. *E-mail:* olsenj@brunswick.cc.nc.us.

CABARRUS COLLEGE OF HEALTH SCIENCES
Concord, North Carolina

- **Independent** primarily 2-year, founded 1942
- **Calendar** semesters
- **Degrees** certificates, diplomas, associate, and bachelor's
- **Suburban** 5-acre campus with easy access to Charlotte
- **Coed, primarily women,** 242 undergraduate students, 76% full-time, 95% women, 5% men

Undergraduates 183 full-time, 59 part-time. Students come from 2 states and territories, 2% are from out of state, 7% African American, 0.4% Hispanic American, 19% transferred in.

Freshmen *Admission:* 242 enrolled. *Average high school GPA:* 3.37. *Test scores:* SAT verbal scores over 500: 51%; SAT math scores over 500: 49%; SAT verbal scores over 600: 9%; SAT math scores over 600: 10%; SAT verbal scores over 700: 2%; SAT math scores over 700: 5%.

Faculty *Total:* 43, 37% full-time, 9% with terminal degrees. *Student/faculty ratio:* 9:1.

Majors Health/health care administration; medical/clinical assistant; nursing assistant/aide and patient care assistant; nursing (registered nurse training); occupational therapist assistant; surgical technology.

Academic Programs *Special study options:* advanced placement credit, distance learning, double majors, independent study, part-time degree program.

Library Northeast Medical Center Library with 7,676 titles, 2,127 serial subscriptions, 923 audiovisual materials.

Computers on Campus 30 computers available on campus for general student use. A campuswide network can be accessed from off campus. Internet access, at least one staffed computer lab available.

Student Life *Housing:* college housing not available. *Activities and Organizations:* student-run newspaper, Student Nurse Association, Christian Student Union, student government, Honor Society, Allied Health Student Association. *Campus security:* 24-hour emergency response devices and patrols. *Student services:* health clinic, personal/psychological counseling.

Standardized Tests *Required:* SAT I or ACT (for admission). *Required for some:* ACT ASSET.

Costs (2004–05) *Tuition:* $6200 full-time, $190 per credit hour part-time.

Financial Aid Of all full-time matriculated undergraduates who enrolled, 20 Federal Work-Study jobs.

Applying *Application fee:* $35. *Required:* essay or personal statement, high school transcript, minimum 2.0 GPA, 2 letters of recommendation. *Required for some:* interview. *Recommended:* minimum 3.0 GPA. *Application deadlines:* 3/1 (freshmen), 3/1 (transfers). *Notification:* 4/15 (freshmen), 4/15 (transfers).

Admissions Contact Mr. Mark Ellison, Director of Admissions, Cabarrus College of Health Sciences, 431 Copperfield Boulevard, NE, Concord, NC 28025-2405. *Phone:* 704-783-1616. *Fax:* 704-783-1764. *E-mail:* dbowman@northeastmedical.org.

CALDWELL COMMUNITY COLLEGE AND TECHNICAL INSTITUTE
Hudson, North Carolina

- **State-supported** 2-year, founded 1964, part of North Carolina Community College System
- **Calendar** semesters
- **Degree** certificates, diplomas, and associate
- **Small-town** 50-acre campus
- **Coed,** 3,636 undergraduate students, 44% full-time, 56% women, 44% men

Undergraduates 1,617 full-time, 2,019 part-time. Students come from 24 states and territories, 2 other countries, 5% African American, 0.7% Asian American or Pacific Islander, 0.9% Hispanic American, 0.3% Native American, 0.2% international, 9% transferred in.

Freshmen *Admission:* 846 applied, 846 admitted, 610 enrolled.

Faculty *Total:* 329, 33% full-time, 6% with terminal degrees. *Student/faculty ratio:* 8:1.

Majors Accounting; aeronautics/aviation/aerospace science and technology; art; biological and physical sciences; biomedical technology; business administration and management; business systems networking/ telecommunications; cardiovascular technology; child care/guidance; computer programming (specific applications); cosmetology; diagnostic medical sonography and ultrasound technology; drafting and design technology; electrical, electronic and communications engineering technology; health/health care administration; information technology; landscaping and groundskeeping; legal assistant/paralegal; liberal arts and sciences/liberal studies; medical radiologic technology; music; nuclear medical technology; nursing (registered nurse training); physical therapy; pre-engineering.

Academic Programs *Special study options:* academic remediation for entering students, adult/continuing education programs, advanced placement credit, cooperative education, distance learning, double majors, independent study, part-time degree program, services for LD students, summer session for credit.

Library Broyhill Center for Learning Resources with 50,770 titles, 251 serial subscriptions, 5,352 audiovisual materials, an OPAC, a Web page.

Computers on Campus 750 computers available on campus for general student use. A campuswide network can be accessed from off campus. Internet access, online (class) registration, at least one staffed computer lab available.

Student Life *Housing:* college housing not available. *Activities and Organizations:* drama/theater group, choral group. *Campus security:* trained security personnel during open hours.

Athletics Member NJCAA. *Intercollegiate sports:* basketball M, volleyball W. *Intramural sports:* basketball M/W, tennis M/W.

Standardized Tests *Required:* CPT (for placement).

Costs (2004–05) *Tuition:* state resident $1278 full-time, $36 per credit hour part-time; nonresident $7092 full-time, $197 per credit hour part-time.

Financial Aid Of all full-time matriculated undergraduates who enrolled, 40 Federal Work-Study jobs (averaging $960).

Applying *Options:* early admission. *Required:* high school transcript. *Application deadline:* rolling (freshmen), rolling (transfers). *Notification:* continuous (freshmen), continuous (transfers).

Admissions Contact Mrs. Johnna Coffey, Director of Enrollment Management Services, Caldwell Community College and Technical Institute, 2855 Hickory Boulevard, Hudson, NC 28638. *Phone:* 828-726-2702. *Fax:* 828-726-2709.

CAPE FEAR COMMUNITY COLLEGE
Wilmington, North Carolina

- **State-supported** 2-year, founded 1959, part of North Carolina Community College System
- **Calendar** semesters
- **Degree** certificates, diplomas, and associate
- **Urban** 150-acre campus
- **Endowment** $1.1 million
- **Coed,** 7,010 undergraduate students, 52% full-time, 56% women, 44% men

Undergraduates 3,657 full-time, 3,353 part-time. Students come from 26 states and territories, 2 other countries, 5% are from out of state.

Freshmen *Admission:* 1,103 admitted, 1,103 enrolled.

Faculty *Total:* 578, 37% full-time. *Student/faculty ratio:* 15:1.

Majors Accounting technology and bookkeeping; architectural engineering technology; automobile/automotive mechanics technology; business administration and management; chemical technology; child care and support services management; computer systems analysis; computer systems networking and telecommunications; computer technology/computer systems technology; criminal justice/police science; dental hygiene; diagnostic medical sonography and ultrasound technology; electrical, electronic and communications engineering technology; electrical/electronics equipment installation and repair; engineering/

industrial management; environmental studies; executive assistant/executive secretary; hotel/motel administration; industrial production technologies related; institutional food workers; instrumentation technology; interior design; landscaping and groundskeeping; liberal arts and sciences/liberal studies; machine shop technology; marine maintenance and ship repair technology; marine technology; mechanical engineering/mechanical technology; medical radiologic technology; nursing (registered nurse training); occupational therapist assistant.

Academic Programs *Special study options:* academic remediation for entering students, adult/continuing education programs, cooperative education, distance learning, part-time degree program, services for LD students.

Library Cape Fear Community College Library with 707 serial subscriptions, 5,126 audiovisual materials, an OPAC, a Web page.

Computers on Campus 80 computers available on campus for general student use. A campuswide network can be accessed from off campus. At least one staffed computer lab available.

Student Life *Housing:* college housing not available. *Activities and Organizations:* student-run newspaper, choral group, Nursing Club, Dental Hygiene Club, Pineapple Guild. *Campus security:* 24-hour emergency response devices and patrols, late-night transport/escort service. *Student services:* personal/psychological counseling.

Athletics Member NJCAA. *Intercollegiate sports:* basketball M, cheerleading M/W, golf M, softball M/W, tennis M/W, volleyball M/W. *Intramural sports:* soccer M.

Standardized Tests *Required:* ACT ASSET (for placement).

Costs (2003–04) *Tuition:* state resident $1065 full-time, $36 per credit hour part-time; nonresident $5910 full-time, $197 per credit hour part-time. *Required fees:* $34 full-time, $7 per credit part-time. *Waivers:* senior citizens and employees or children of employees.

Financial Aid Of all full-time matriculated undergraduates who enrolled, 50 Federal Work-Study jobs.

Applying *Options:* electronic application, early admission, deferred entrance. *Required:* high school transcript, placement testing. *Application deadline:* 8/21 (freshmen), rolling (transfers). *Notification:* continuous (freshmen), continuous (transfers).

Admissions Contact Ms. Linda Kasyan, Director of Enrollment Management, Cape Fear Community College, 411 North Front Street, Wilmington, NC 28401-3993. *Phone:* 910-362-7054. *Toll-free phone:* 910-362-7557. *Fax:* 910-362-7080. *E-mail:* admissions@cfcc.edu.

CAROLINAS COLLEGE OF HEALTH SCIENCES
Charlotte, North Carolina

- **Independent** 2-year, founded 1990, part of Carolinas Healthcare System
- **Calendar** semesters
- **Degree** certificates, diplomas, and associate
- **Urban** 3-acre campus
- **Endowment** $1.5 million
- **Coed, primarily women,** 405 undergraduate students, 31% full-time, 88% women, 12% men

Undergraduates 127 full-time, 278 part-time. Students come from 2 states and territories, 6% are from out of state, 14% African American, 0.7% Asian American or Pacific Islander, 3% Hispanic American, 0.5% Native American.

Freshmen *Admission:* 62 applied, 24 admitted, 24 enrolled. *Average high school GPA:* 2.96. *Test scores:* SAT verbal scores over 500: 63%; SAT math scores over 500: 53%; ACT scores over 18: 63%; SAT verbal scores over 600: 3%; SAT math scores over 600: 3%; ACT scores over 24: 13%.

Faculty *Total:* 51, 59% full-time, 6% with terminal degrees. *Student/faculty ratio:* 8:1.

Majors Medical radiologic technology; nursing (registered nurse training); radiologic technology/science.

Academic Programs *Special study options:* advanced placement credit, distance learning, independent study, internships.

Library AHEC Library with 9,810 titles, 503 serial subscriptions, an OPAC.

Computers on Campus 36 computers available on campus for general student use. A campuswide network can be accessed. Internet access, at least one staffed computer lab available.

Student Life *Housing:* college housing not available. *Options:* Campus housing is provided by a third party. *Activities and Organizations:* Student Government Association. *Campus security:* 24-hour emergency response devices and patrols, student patrols, late-night transport/escort service. *Student services:* health clinic, personal/psychological counseling, legal services.

Standardized Tests *Required:* SAT I or ACT (for admission).

Costs (2003–04) *Tuition:* $5400 full-time. Full-time tuition and fees vary according to course load and program. Part-time tuition and fees vary according to course load and program. *Required fees:* $250 full-time. *Payment plan:* installment. *Waivers:* employees or children of employees.

Carolinas College of Health Sciences (continued)

Financial Aid Of all full-time matriculated undergraduates who enrolled, 12 Federal Work-Study jobs (averaging $1500).

Applying *Options:* early admission, early decision. *Application fee:* $35. *Required:* high school transcript. *Required for some:* letters of recommendation, interview. *Recommended:* minimum 2.5 GPA. *Application deadline:* 2/6 (freshmen). *Early decision:* 12/5. *Notification:* 3/15 (freshmen), 1/15 (early decision).

Admissions Contact Ms. Vicki Striffler, Admissions Officer, Carolinas College of Health Sciences, PO Box 32861, Charlotte, NC 28232-2861. *Phone:* 704-355-5043. *Fax:* 704-355-9336. *E-mail:* cchsinformation@carolinashealthcare.org.

CARTERET COMMUNITY COLLEGE
Morehead City, North Carolina

- **State-supported** 2-year, founded 1963, part of North Carolina Community College System
- **Calendar** semesters
- **Degree** certificates, diplomas, and associate
- **Small-town** 25-acre campus
- **Coed,** 1,732 undergraduate students, 39% full-time, 69% women, 31% men

Undergraduates 679 full-time, 1,053 part-time. Students come from 24 states and territories, 12% African American, 1% Asian American or Pacific Islander, 2% Hispanic American, 0.3% Native American.

Faculty *Total:* 94, 41% full-time.

Majors Administrative assistant and secretarial science; business administration and management; computer engineering technology; computer software and media applications related; computer systems networking and telecommunications; criminal justice/law enforcement administration; industrial radiologic technology; information technology; interior design; legal administrative assistant/ secretary; legal assistant/paralegal; liberal arts and sciences/liberal studies; medical/clinical assistant; nursing (licensed practical/vocational nurse training); photography; respiratory care therapy; teacher assistant/aide; therapeutic recreation.

Academic Programs *Special study options:* academic remediation for entering students, adult/continuing education programs, cooperative education, distance learning, double majors, internships, part-time degree program, services for LD students, summer session for credit.

Library Michael J. Smith Learning Resource Center with 22,000 titles, 168 serial subscriptions.

Computers on Campus 150 computers available on campus for general student use. A campuswide network can be accessed. Internet access, at least one staffed computer lab available.

Student Life *Housing:* college housing not available. *Activities and Organizations:* student-run newspaper.

Athletics *Intercollegiate sports:* softball M/W, volleyball M/W.

Standardized Tests *Recommended:* SAT I (for placement).

Costs (2003–04) *Tuition:* state resident $1183 full-time, $50 per semester hour part-time; nonresident $6351 full-time, $211 per semester hour part-time.

Financial Aid Of all full-time matriculated undergraduates who enrolled, 40 Federal Work-Study jobs (averaging $750).

Applying *Options:* common application, electronic application, early admission. *Required:* high school transcript. *Application deadline:* rolling (freshmen), rolling (transfers). *Notification:* continuous (freshmen), continuous (transfers).

Admissions Contact Mr. Rick Hill, Director of Student Enrollment Resources, Carteret Community College, 3505 Arendell Street, Morehead City, NC 28557-2989. *Phone:* 252-222-6153 Ext. 6153. *Fax:* 252-222-6265. *E-mail:* mhw@carteret.edu.

CATAWBA VALLEY COMMUNITY COLLEGE
Hickory, North Carolina

Admissions Contact Mrs. Caroline Farmer, Director of Admissions and Records, Catawba Valley Community College, 2550 Highway 70 SE, Hickory, NC 28602-9699. *Phone:* 828-327-7000 Ext. 4218. *Fax:* 828-327-7000 Ext. 4224. *E-mail:* cfarmer@cvcc.cc.nc.us.

CENTRAL CAROLINA COMMUNITY COLLEGE
Sanford, North Carolina

- **State and locally supported** 2-year, founded 1962, part of North Carolina Community College System
- **Calendar** semesters
- **Degree** certificates, diplomas, and associate

- **Small-town** 41-acre campus
- **Endowment** $1.0 million
- **Coed**

Faculty *Student/faculty ratio:* 8:1.

Student Life *Campus security:* patrols by trained security personnel during operating hours.

Athletics Member NJCAA.

Standardized Tests *Required:* CPT, ACCUPLACER, ACT COMPASS, ACT ASSET (for placement). *Recommended:* SAT I or ACT (for placement).

Costs (2004–05) *Tuition:* state resident $1140 full-time, $36 per credit hour part-time; nonresident $6308 full-time, $197 per credit hour part-time. *Required fees:* $36 full-time.

Financial Aid Of all full-time matriculated undergraduates who enrolled, 47 Federal Work-Study jobs (averaging $1574). *Financial aid deadline:* 5/4.

Applying *Options:* electronic application, early admission, deferred entrance. *Required:* high school transcript.

Admissions Contact Mr. Ken R. Hoyle Jr., Dean of Student Services, Central Carolina Community College, 1105 Kelly Drive, Sanford, NC 27330. *Phone:* 919-775-5401. *Toll-free phone:* 800-682-8353 Ext. 7300. *Fax:* 919-718-7380. *E-mail:* tgraves@cccc.edu.

CENTRAL PIEDMONT COMMUNITY COLLEGE
Charlotte, North Carolina

- **State and locally supported** 2-year, founded 1963, part of North Carolina Community College System
- **Calendar** semesters
- **Degree** certificates, diplomas, and associate
- **Urban** 37-acre campus
- **Endowment** $12.2 million
- **Coed,** 16,245 undergraduate students, 35% full-time, 58% women, 42% men

Undergraduates 5,721 full-time, 10,524 part-time. Students come from 15 states and territories, 125 other countries, 2% are from out of state, 31% African American, 3% Asian American or Pacific Islander, 2% Hispanic American, 0.4% Native American, 8% international, 23% transferred in.

Freshmen *Admission:* 1,210 enrolled.

Faculty *Total:* 1,067, 28% full-time. *Student/faculty ratio:* 21:1.

Majors Accounting; administrative assistant and secretarial science; advertising; applied art; architectural engineering technology; art; automobile/automotive mechanics technology; biology/biological sciences; business administration and management; business machine repair; child development; civil engineering technology; clinical laboratory science/medical technology; clinical/medical laboratory technology; commercial and advertising art; computer engineering technology; computer programming; computer programming (specific applications); computer science; consumer merchandising/retailing management; criminal justice/law enforcement administration; criminal justice/police science; culinary arts; dance; data processing and data processing technology; dental hygiene; drafting and design technology; electrical, electronic and communications engineering technology; electromechanical technology; engineering technology; environmental engineering technology; fashion merchandising; finance; fire science; food science; food services technology; graphic and printing equipment operation/production; health/health care administration; health information/medical records administration; horticultural science; hospitality administration; hotel/motel administration; human services; industrial technology; insurance; interior design; kindergarten/preschool education; legal administrative assistant/secretary; legal assistant/paralegal; liberal arts and sciences/ liberal studies; machine tool technology; marketing/marketing management; mechanical engineering/mechanical technology; medical administrative assistant and medical secretary; medical/clinical assistant; music; nursing (licensed practical/vocational nurse training); nursing (registered nurse training); physical therapy; postal management; real estate; respiratory care therapy; sign language interpretation and translation; social work; special products marketing; survey technology; tourism and travel services management; transportation technology; welding technology.

Academic Programs *Special study options:* academic remediation for entering students, adult/continuing education programs, advanced placement credit, cooperative education, distance learning, English as a second language, honors programs, off-campus study, part-time degree program, services for LD students, student-designed majors, summer session for credit.

Library Hageneyer Learning Center plus 5 others with 102,649 titles, 750 serial subscriptions, 17,802 audiovisual materials, an OPAC, a Web page.

Computers on Campus A campuswide network can be accessed from off campus. At least one staffed computer lab available.

Student Life *Housing:* college housing not available. *Activities and Organizations:* drama/theater group, student-run newspaper, choral group, Phi Theta Kappa, Black Students Organization, Students for Environmental Sanity, Sierra

Club, Nursing Club. *Campus security:* 24-hour emergency response devices and patrols. *Student services:* personal/psychological counseling, women's center.

Athletics Member NJCAA. *Intramural sports:* soccer M/W.

Standardized Tests *Required for some:* Nelson Denny Reading Test or CPT.

Costs (2004–05) *Tuition:* state resident $1136 full-time, $36 per semester hour part-time; nonresident $6304 full-time, $197 per semester hour part-time. *Required fees:* $138 full-time, $40 per semester part-time. *Waivers:* senior citizens and employees or children of employees.

Financial Aid Of all full-time matriculated undergraduates who enrolled, 97 Federal Work-Study jobs (averaging $2737).

Applying *Options:* common application. *Required for some:* high school transcript. *Application deadline:* rolling (freshmen), rolling (transfers). *Notification:* continuous (freshmen), continuous (transfers).

Admissions Contact Ms. Linda McComb, Director of Admission, Registration, and Records, Central Piedmont Community College, PO Box 35009, Charlotte, NC 28235-5009. *Phone:* 704-330-6784.

CLEVELAND COMMUNITY COLLEGE
Shelby, North Carolina

- **State-supported** 2-year, founded 1965, part of North Carolina Community College System
- **Calendar** semesters
- **Degree** certificates, diplomas, and associate
- **Small-town** 43-acre campus with easy access to Charlotte
- **Endowment** $450,000
- **Coed,** 2,793 undergraduate students, 39% full-time, 63% women, 37% men

Undergraduates 1,095 full-time, 1,698 part-time. Students come from 2 states and territories, 1% are from out of state, 26% African American, 0.3% Asian American or Pacific Islander, 0.9% Hispanic American, 0.3% Native American, 0.8% transferred in.

Freshmen *Admission:* 278 applied, 278 admitted, 278 enrolled. *Average high school GPA:* 2.71.

Faculty *Total:* 64, 6% with terminal degrees.

Majors Accounting; administrative assistant and secretarial science; biological and physical sciences; business administration and management; communications technology; computer engineering technology; computer programming (specific applications); criminal justice/law enforcement administration; criminal justice/safety; data entry/microcomputer applications; electrical, electronic and communications engineering technology; electrician; engineering technologies related; executive assistant/executive secretary; fashion merchandising; fire protection and safety technology; industrial radiologic technology; information science/studies; information technology; liberal arts and sciences and humanities related; liberal arts and sciences/liberal studies; management information systems and services related; mechanical engineering/mechanical technology; medical administrative assistant and medical secretary; medical radiologic technology; nursing (registered nurse training); operations management; Spanish; special education; system administration; teacher assistant/aide.

Academic Programs *Special study options:* academic remediation for entering students, adult/continuing education programs, advanced placement credit, distance learning, double majors, English as a second language, independent study, off-campus study, part-time degree program, summer session for credit.

Library Cleveland Community College Library with 29,438 titles, 276 serial subscriptions, 3,619 audiovisual materials, an OPAC, a Web page.

Computers on Campus 300 computers available on campus for general student use. A campuswide network can be accessed. Internet access, at least one staffed computer lab available.

Student Life *Housing:* college housing not available. *Activities and Organizations:* drama/theater group, student-run television station, choral group, Gamma Beta Phi Honor Society, Student Government Association, Lamplighters, Mu Epsilon Delta, Black Awareness Club. *Campus security:* security personnel during open hours. *Student services:* personal/psychological counseling.

Standardized Tests *Required for some:* SAT I and SAT II or ACT (for placement).

Costs (2004–05) *Tuition:* state resident $1233 full-time, $34 per credit hour part-time; nonresident $6867 full-time, $191 per credit hour part-time. Full-time tuition and fees vary according to course load. Part-time tuition and fees vary according to course load. *Required fees:* $38 full-time, $10 per term part-time. *Waivers:* senior citizens.

Financial Aid Of all full-time matriculated undergraduates who enrolled, 18 Federal Work-Study jobs.

Applying *Options:* common application, electronic application, deferred entrance. *Required:* high school transcript. *Application deadline:* rolling (freshmen), rolling (transfers). *Notification:* continuous (freshmen), continuous (transfers).

Admissions Contact Mr. Alan Price, Dean of Enrollment Management, Cleveland Community College, 137 South Post Road, Shelby, NC 28152. *Phone:* 704-484-4073. *Fax:* 704-484-5305. *E-mail:* price@cleveland.cc.nc.us.

COASTAL CAROLINA COMMUNITY COLLEGE
Jacksonville, North Carolina

- **State and locally supported** 2-year, founded 1964, part of North Carolina Community College System
- **Calendar** semesters
- **Degree** certificates, diplomas, and associate
- **Small-town** 98-acre campus
- **Endowment** $1.6 million
- **Coed,** 4,231 undergraduate students, 49% full-time, 66% women, 34% men

Undergraduates 2,091 full-time, 2,140 part-time. Students come from 50 states and territories, 2 other countries, 32% are from out of state, 22% African American, 3% Asian American or Pacific Islander, 8% Hispanic American, 0.9% Native American, 0.6% international, 16% transferred in.

Freshmen *Admission:* 3,951 applied, 2,968 admitted, 1,040 enrolled.

Faculty *Total:* 285, 39% full-time, 8% with terminal degrees. *Student/faculty ratio:* 16:1.

Majors Accounting; architectural engineering technology; business administration and management; child care provision; clinical/medical laboratory technology; computer/information technology services administration related; computer programming (specific applications); computer systems analysis; computer systems networking and telecommunications; criminal justice/law enforcement administration; dental hygiene; emergency medical technology (EMT paramedic); executive assistant/executive secretary; fire science; legal assistant/paralegal; liberal arts and sciences/liberal studies; medical administrative assistant and medical secretary; nursing (registered nurse training); surgical technology.

Academic Programs *Special study options:* academic remediation for entering students, adult/continuing education programs, advanced placement credit, distance learning, double majors, English as a second language, independent study, internships, part-time degree program, services for LD students, summer session for credit.

Library C. Louis Shields Learning Resources Center with 43,420 titles, 265 serial subscriptions, 8,437 audiovisual materials, an OPAC.

Computers on Campus 646 computers available on campus for general student use. A campuswide network can be accessed from off campus. Internet access, at least one staffed computer lab available.

Student Life *Housing:* college housing not available. *Activities and Organizations:* drama/theater group, SHELL (environmental group), SPYS (social sciences group), student government, Star of Life, Association of Nursing Students. *Campus security:* 24-hour emergency response devices and patrols, late-night transport/escort service. *Student services:* personal/psychological counseling.

Standardized Tests *Required:* ACT ASSET (for placement).

Costs (2003–04) *Tuition:* state resident $1136 full-time, $36 per semester hour part-time; nonresident $6304 full-time, $197 per semester hour part-time. *Required fees:* $30 full-time, $5 per term part-time. *Waivers:* senior citizens.

Applying *Options:* deferred entrance. *Required:* high school transcript. *Required for some:* 2 letters of recommendation, interview. *Application deadline:* rolling (freshmen), rolling (transfers). *Notification:* continuous (freshmen), continuous (transfers).

Admissions Contact Mr. Jerry W. Snead, Director of Admissions, Coastal Carolina Community College, 444 Western Boulevard, Jacksonville, NC 28546. *Phone:* 910-938-6246. *Fax:* 910-455-2767.

COLLEGE OF THE ALBEMARLE
Elizabeth City, North Carolina

- **State-supported** 2-year, founded 1960, part of North Carolina Community College System
- **Calendar** semesters
- **Degree** certificates, diplomas, and associate
- **Small-town** 40-acre campus
- **Coed**

Student Life *Campus security:* 24-hour patrols.

Standardized Tests *Recommended:* SAT I or ACT (for placement).

Costs (2003–04) *Tuition:* state resident $822 full-time, $34 per credit part-time; nonresident $4578 full-time, $190 per credit part-time.

Financial Aid Of all full-time matriculated undergraduates who enrolled, 68 Federal Work-Study jobs (averaging $553).

Applying *Options:* early admission, deferred entrance. *Required:* high school transcript.

Admissions Contact Mr. Kenny Krentz, Director of Admissions and International Students, College of The Albemarle, PO Box 2327, 1208 N. Road Street, Elizabeth City, NC 27909-2327. *Phone:* 252-335-0821 Ext. 2220. *Fax:* 252-335-2011. *E-mail:* kkrentz@albemarle.edu.

CRAVEN COMMUNITY COLLEGE
New Bern, North Carolina

Admissions Contact Ms. Millicent Fulford, Recruiter, Craven Community College, 800 College Court, New Bern, NC 28562-4984. *Phone:* 252-638-7232. *Fax:* 252-638-4649.

DAVIDSON COUNTY COMMUNITY COLLEGE
Lexington, North Carolina

Admissions Contact Mr. Rick Travis, Director, Career Services, Davidson County Community College, PO Box 1287, Lexington, NC 27293-1287. *Phone:* 336-249-8186 Ext. 224. *Fax:* 336-249-0379.

DURHAM TECHNICAL COMMUNITY COLLEGE
Durham, North Carolina

- **State-supported** 2-year, founded 1961, part of North Carolina Community College System
- **Calendar** semesters
- **Degree** certificates, diplomas, and associate
- **Urban** campus
- **Coed,** 5,642 undergraduate students, 26% full-time, 63% women, 37% men

Undergraduates 1,464 full-time, 4,178 part-time. Students come from 50 states and territories, 1% are from out of state, 41% African American, 3% Asian American or Pacific Islander, 2% Hispanic American, 0.2% Native American, 8% international, 59% transferred in.
Freshmen *Admission:* 732 enrolled.
Faculty *Total:* 477, 25% full-time. *Student/faculty ratio:* 16:1.
Majors Accounting; administrative assistant and secretarial science; architectural engineering technology; automobile/automotive mechanics technology; business administration and management; child development; computer programming; computer programming related; computer typography and composition equipment operation; criminal justice/law enforcement administration; criminal justice/police science; data processing and data processing technology; dental hygiene; electrical, electronic and communications engineering technology; fire science; general studies; health information/medical records administration; information science/studies; information technology; kindergarten/preschool education; laser and optical technology; legal assistant/paralegal; liberal arts and sciences/liberal studies; machine tool technology; medical administrative assistant and medical secretary; nursing (licensed practical/vocational nurse training); nursing (registered nurse training); occupational safety and health technology; occupational therapy; operations management; ophthalmic laboratory technology; pharmacy; real estate; respiratory care therapy; surgical technology; system administration; teacher assistant/aide.
Academic Programs *Special study options:* academic remediation for entering students, accelerated degree program, adult/continuing education programs, advanced placement credit, cooperative education, distance learning, English as a second language, internships, off-campus study, part-time degree program, services for LD students, student-designed majors, summer session for credit.
Library Educational Resource Center with 36,388 titles, 1,348 audiovisual materials, an OPAC.
Computers on Campus 664 computers available on campus for general student use. A campuswide network can be accessed from off campus. Internet access, at least one staffed computer lab available.
Student Life *Housing:* college housing not available. *Activities and Organizations:* drama/theater group, Amigos Unidos, Gamma Beta Phi, Student Senate, Student Nurses Association, Practical Nurses Students Club. *Campus security:* 24-hour patrols, late-night transport/escort service. *Student services:* personal/psychological counseling.
Standardized Tests *Required:* ACT ASSET or ACT COMPASS (for placement).
Costs (2003–04) *Tuition:* state resident $1136 full-time, $36 per credit hour part-time; nonresident $6304 full-time, $197 per credit hour part-time. Full-time tuition and fees vary according to course load. *Required fees:* $42 full-time, $21 per term part-time. *Waivers:* senior citizens and employees or children of employees.
Financial Aid Of all full-time matriculated undergraduates who enrolled, 35 Federal Work-Study jobs (averaging $2000).
Applying *Options:* deferred entrance. *Required:* high school transcript. *Recommended:* interview. *Application deadline:* rolling (freshmen), rolling (transfers). *Notification:* continuous (freshmen), continuous (transfers).
Admissions Contact Ms. Penny Augustine, Director of Admissions, Durham Technical Community College, 1637 Lawson Street, Durham, NC 27703. *Phone:* 919-686-3619. *Toll-free phone:* 919-686-3333.

ECPI TECHNICAL COLLEGE
Raleigh, North Carolina

- **Proprietary** 2-year, founded 1990
- **Calendar** trimesters
- **Degree** diplomas and associate
- **Coed**

Applying *Options:* common application, electronic application. *Required:* high school transcript, interview.
Admissions Contact Mr. Rich Wechner, Campus Director, ECPI Technical College, 4101 Doie Cope Road, Raleigh, NC 27613-7387. *Phone:* 919-571-0057. *Toll-free phone:* 800-986-1200.

EDGECOMBE COMMUNITY COLLEGE
Tarboro, North Carolina

- **State and locally supported** 2-year, founded 1968, part of North Carolina Community College System
- **Calendar** semesters
- **Degree** certificates, diplomas, and associate
- **Small-town** 90-acre campus
- **Endowment** $1.0 million
- **Coed,** 2,498 undergraduate students, 41% full-time, 74% women, 26% men

Undergraduates 1,025 full-time, 1,473 part-time. Students come from 1 other state, 1% are from out of state, 62% African American, 0.2% Asian American or Pacific Islander, 1% Hispanic American, 1% Native American, 0.1% international, 3% transferred in.
Freshmen *Admission:* 453 applied, 413 admitted, 288 enrolled.
Faculty *Total:* 271, 31% full-time. *Student/faculty ratio:* 16:1.
Majors Accounting; administrative assistant and secretarial science; business administration and management; criminal justice/law enforcement administration; data entry/microcomputer applications; electrical, electronic and communications engineering technology; health information/medical records administration; human services; information technology; kindergarten/preschool education; liberal arts and sciences/liberal studies; mechanical drafting and CAD/CADD; mechanical engineering/mechanical technology; mechanical engineering technologies related; medical/clinical assistant; nursing (licensed practical/vocational nurse training); nursing (registered nurse training); plastics engineering technology; radiologic technology/science; respiratory care therapy; respiratory therapy technician; social work; surgical technology; system administration; word processing.
Academic Programs *Special study options:* academic remediation for entering students, adult/continuing education programs, advanced placement credit, cooperative education, distance learning, double majors, English as a second language, independent study, off-campus study, part-time degree program, services for LD students, summer session for credit.
Library 40,421 titles, 245 serial subscriptions, 2,527 audiovisual materials, an OPAC, a Web page.
Computers on Campus 160 computers available on campus for general student use. A campuswide network can be accessed from off campus. Internet access, at least one staffed computer lab available.
Student Life *Housing:* college housing not available. *Activities and Organizations:* Student Government Association.
Athletics *Intramural sports:* basketball M.
Standardized Tests *Recommended:* SAT I or ACT (for placement), MAPS.
Costs (2003–04) *Tuition:* state resident $1136 full-time, $36 per credit part-time; nonresident $6304 full-time, $197 per credit part-time. *Required fees:* $24 full-time. *Payment plan:* installment. *Waivers:* senior citizens and employees or children of employees.
Financial Aid Of all full-time matriculated undergraduates who enrolled, 45 Federal Work-Study jobs (averaging $800).
Applying *Options:* common application, electronic application. *Required:* high school transcript, minimum 2.0 GPA. *Required for some:* letters of recommendation. *Application deadline:* rolling (freshmen), rolling (transfers). *Notification:* continuous (freshmen), continuous (transfers).
Admissions Contact Ms. Jackie Heath, Admissions Officer, Edgecombe Community College, 2009 West Wilson Street, Tarboro, NC 27886. *Phone:* 252-823-5166 Ext. 254. *Fax:* 252-823-6817. *E-mail:* heathj@edgecombe.edu.

FAYETTEVILLE TECHNICAL COMMUNITY COLLEGE
Fayetteville, North Carolina

- **State-supported** 2-year, founded 1961, part of North Carolina Community College System
- **Calendar** semesters

■ **Degree** certificates, diplomas, and associate
■ **Suburban** 135-acre campus with easy access to Raleigh
■ **Endowment** $39,050
■ **Coed,** 10,141 undergraduate students, 44% full-time, 67% women, 33% men

Undergraduates 4,491 full-time, 5,650 part-time. Students come from 50 states and territories, 9 other countries, 21% are from out of state, 39% African American, 2% Asian American or Pacific Islander, 7% Hispanic American, 3% Native American, 1% international, 21% transferred in.

Freshmen *Admission:* 6,707 applied, 6,707 admitted, 2,290 enrolled. *Average high school GPA:* 2.43.

Faculty *Total:* 776, 36% full-time. *Student/faculty ratio:* 20:1.

Majors Accounting; advertising; anatomy; applied horticulture; architectural engineering technology; autobody/collision and repair technology; automobile/automotive mechanics technology; business administration and management; business automation/technology/data entry; cabinetmaking and millwork; carpentry; child care and support services management; child care provision; civil engineering technology; commercial and advertising art; communications systems installation and repair technology; computer and information sciences; computer and information sciences related; computer engineering related; computer graphics; computer programming; computer programming related; computer programming (specific applications); computer software and media applications related; computer systems networking and telecommunications; computer/technical support; cosmetology; criminal justice/safety; culinary arts related; data entry/microcomputer applications; dental assisting; dental hygiene; electrical, electronic and communications engineering technology; electrical, electronics and communications engineering; emergency medical technology (EMT paramedic); engineering technology; finance; food services technology; funeral service and mortuary science; general studies; health information/medical records technology; heating, air conditioning, ventilation and refrigeration maintenance technology; horticultural science; hospitality administration related; human resources management and services related; industrial mechanics and maintenance technology; industrial technology; information science/studies; information technology; kindergarten/preschool education; legal assistant/paralegal; liberal arts and sciences/liberal studies; machine tool technology; management information systems; management science; marketing/marketing management; masonry; medical laboratory technology; medical office management; nursing (licensed practical/vocational nurse training); nursing (registered nurse training); parks, recreation and leisure; pharmacy technician; physical therapist assistant; pipefitting and sprinkler fitting; postal management; public administration; radiologic technology/science; respiratory care therapy; sales, distribution and marketing; speech-language pathology; surgical technology; survey technology; system administration; tool and die technology; web/multimedia management and webmaster; web page, digital/multimedia and information resources design; welding technology; word processing.

Academic Programs *Special study options:* academic remediation for entering students, adult/continuing education programs, advanced placement credit, cooperative education, distance learning, double majors, English as a second language, independent study, internships, off-campus study, part-time degree program, services for LD students, student-designed majors, summer session for credit.

Library Paul H. Thompson Library with 61,580 titles, 398 serial subscriptions, 6,657 audiovisual materials, an OPAC, a Web page.

Computers on Campus 400 computers available on campus for general student use. A campuswide network can be accessed from off campus. Internet access, at least one staffed computer lab available.

Student Life *Housing:* college housing not available. *Activities and Organizations:* Criminal Justice Association, Early Childhood Club, Phi Beta Lambda, Student Nurses Club, Data Processing Management Association. *Campus security:* 24-hour emergency response devices and patrols, late-night transport/escort service. *Student services:* health clinic, personal/psychological counseling.

Athletics *Intramural sports:* basketball M/W, table tennis M/W, volleyball M/W.

Standardized Tests *Required:* ACCUPLACER (for placement).

Costs (2003–04) *Tuition:* state resident $1136 full-time, $35 per credit hour part-time; nonresident $6304 full-time, $197 per credit hour part-time. *Required fees:* $18 full-time, $18 per term part-time. *Waivers:* senior citizens and employees or children of employees.

Financial Aid Of all full-time matriculated undergraduates who enrolled, 75 Federal Work-Study jobs (averaging $2000). *Financial aid deadline:* 6/1.

Applying *Options:* electronic application, deferred entrance. *Required for some:* high school transcript. *Application deadline:* rolling (freshmen), rolling (transfers). *Notification:* continuous (freshmen), continuous (transfers).

Admissions Contact Mr. James Kelley, Director of Admissions, Fayetteville Technical Community College, PO Box 35236, Fayetteville, NC 28303. *Phone:* 910-678-8274. *Fax:* 910-678-8407. *E-mail:* collinsv@faytechcc.edu.

FORSYTH TECHNICAL COMMUNITY COLLEGE
Winston-Salem, North Carolina

■ **State-supported** 2-year, founded 1964, part of North Carolina Community College System
■ **Calendar** semesters
■ **Degree** certificates, diplomas, and associate
■ **Suburban** 38-acre campus
■ **Coed,** 7,157 undergraduate students, 39% full-time, 64% women, 36% men

Undergraduates 2,784 full-time, 4,373 part-time. 25% African American, 1% Asian American or Pacific Islander, 3% Hispanic American, 0.6% Native American.

Freshmen *Admission:* 9,275 applied, 5,268 admitted.

Faculty *Total:* 360, 48% full-time. *Student/faculty ratio:* 19:1.

Majors Accounting; administrative assistant and secretarial science; architectural engineering technology; automobile/automotive mechanics technology; business administration and management; carpentry; child development; commercial and advertising art; computer engineering technology; computer science; construction engineering technology; criminal justice/law enforcement administration; criminal justice/police science; data processing and data processing technology; drafting and design technology; electrical, electronic and communications engineering technology; electromechanical technology; engineering technology; finance; funeral service and mortuary science; graphic and printing equipment operation/production; heating, air conditioning, ventilation and refrigeration maintenance technology; horticultural science; industrial radiologic technology; industrial technology; kindergarten/preschool education; legal assistant/paralegal; machine tool technology; marketing/marketing management; mechanical design technology; medical/clinical assistant; nuclear medical technology; nursing (registered nurse training); ornamental horticulture; pipefitting and sprinkler fitting; real estate; respiratory care therapy; welding technology.

Academic Programs *Special study options:* academic remediation for entering students, adult/continuing education programs, English as a second language, part-time degree program, services for LD students, summer session for credit.

Library Forsyth Technical Community College Library plus 1 other with 41,606 titles, 358 serial subscriptions.

Computers on Campus 450 computers available on campus for general student use. At least one staffed computer lab available.

Student Life *Housing:* college housing not available. *Activities and Organizations:* student-run newspaper. *Campus security:* 24-hour patrols. *Student services:* personal/psychological counseling.

Athletics *Intramural sports:* basketball M/W, bowling M/W, softball W, volleyball M/W.

Standardized Tests *Required:* Assessment and Placement Services for Community Colleges (for placement). *Recommended:* SAT I or ACT (for placement).

Costs (2003–04) *Tuition:* state resident $822 full-time, $34 per credit hour part-time; nonresident $4578 full-time, $191 per credit hour part-time. *Required fees:* $60 full-time, $60 per term part-time.

Financial Aid Of all full-time matriculated undergraduates who enrolled, 42 Federal Work-Study jobs (averaging $2083).

Applying *Required:* high school transcript. *Application deadlines:* 8/25 (freshmen), 9/1 (transfers). *Notification:* continuous until 8/25 (freshmen), continuous until 9/8 (transfers).

Admissions Contact Ms. Patrice Mitchell, Director of Admissions, Forsyth Technical Community College, 2100 Silas Creek Parkway, Winston-Salem, NC 27103-5197. *Phone:* 336-734-7331. *Fax:* 336-761-2098. *E-mail:* admissions@forsythtech.edu.

GASTON COLLEGE
Dallas, North Carolina

■ **State and locally supported** 2-year, founded 1963, part of North Carolina Community College System
■ **Calendar** semesters
■ **Degree** certificates, diplomas, and associate
■ **Small-town** 166-acre campus with easy access to Charlotte
■ **Endowment** $716,546
■ **Coed,** 5,025 undergraduate students, 33% full-time, 69% women, 31% men

Undergraduates 1,640 full-time, 3,385 part-time. Students come from 10 states and territories, 17% African American, 1% Asian American or Pacific Islander, 2% Hispanic American, 0.4% Native American. *Retention:* 80% of 2002 full-time freshmen returned.

Freshmen *Admission:* 990 enrolled. *Average high school GPA:* 2.60.

Faculty *Total:* 357, 33% full-time. *Student/faculty ratio:* 18:1.

Majors Accounting; architectural engineering technology; art; automobile/automotive mechanics technology; business administration and management; civil engineering technology; computer programming; criminal justice/law

Gaston College (continued)

enforcement administration; data processing and data processing technology; dietetics; electrical, electronic and communications engineering technology; fire science; information science/studies; kindergarten/preschool education; legal assistant/paralegal; mechanical drafting and CAD/CADD; mechanical engineering/ mechanical technology; medical/clinical assistant; medical office management; nursing (registered nurse training); operations management; veterinary technology.

Academic Programs *Special study options:* academic remediation for entering students, adult/continuing education programs, advanced placement credit, cooperative education, English as a second language, off-campus study, part-time degree program, services for LD students, summer session for credit.

Library Gaston College Library with 49,434 titles, 561 serial subscriptions, 3,343 audiovisual materials, an OPAC.

Computers on Campus A campuswide network can be accessed. Internet access, online (class) registration, at least one staffed computer lab available.

Student Life *Housing:* college housing not available. *Activities and Organizations:* student-run radio station, Student Government Association. *Campus security:* 24-hour patrols.

Standardized Tests *Required:* ACT COMPASS (for placement). *Required for some:* ACT (for placement).

Costs (2003–04) *Tuition:* state resident $1136 full-time, $36 per credit hour part-time; nonresident $6304 full-time, $197 per credit hour part-time. Full-time tuition and fees vary according to course load. Part-time tuition and fees vary according to course load. *Required fees:* $26 full-time, $13 per term part-time. *Payment plan:* deferred payment. *Waivers:* senior citizens and employees or children of employees.

Applying *Required for some:* high school transcript. *Application deadline:* rolling (freshmen), rolling (transfers). *Notification:* continuous (freshmen), continuous (transfers).

Admissions Contact Ms. Alice D. Hopper, Admissions Specialist, Gaston College, 201 Highway 321 South, Dallas, NC 28034. *Phone:* 704-922-6214.

GUILFORD TECHNICAL COMMUNITY COLLEGE
Jamestown, North Carolina

- **State and locally supported** 2-year, founded 1958, part of North Carolina Community College System
- **Calendar** semesters
- **Degree** certificates, diplomas, and associate
- **Suburban** 158-acre campus
- **Coed,** 9,380 undergraduate students, 48% full-time, 57% women, 43% men

Undergraduates 4,469 full-time, 4,911 part-time. Students come from 21 states and territories, 32% African American, 3% Asian American or Pacific Islander, 2% Hispanic American, 0.6% Native American, 0.7% international.

Freshmen *Admission:* 1,346 enrolled.

Faculty *Total:* 478, 50% full-time, 6% with terminal degrees. *Student/faculty ratio:* 19:1.

Majors Accounting; airline pilot and flight crew; architectural engineering technology; automobile/automotive mechanics technology; aviation/airway management; avionics maintenance technology; biological and physical sciences; biology/biotechnology laboratory technician; building/construction finishing, management, and inspection related; business administration and management; business operations support and secretarial services related; chemistry related; cinematography and film/video production; civil engineering technology; clinical/ medical laboratory technology; commercial and advertising art; computer/ information technology services administration related; computer programming; computer systems networking and telecommunications; cosmetology; criminal justice/law enforcement administration; criminal justice/police science; culinary arts; dental hygiene; drafting and design technology; dramatic/theatre arts; education related; electrical, electronic and communications engineering technology; electrical/electronics equipment installation and repair; emergency medical technology (EMT paramedic); fire science; heating, air conditioning, ventilation and refrigeration maintenance technology; heavy equipment maintenance technology; human services; industrial arts; industrial mechanics and maintenance technology; industrial technology; information science/studies; kindergarten/ preschool education; legal assistant/paralegal; liberal arts and sciences/liberal studies; machine tool technology; medical/clinical assistant; nursing (registered nurse training); occupational therapist assistant; physical therapist assistant; respiratory care therapy; speech-language pathology; surgical technology; survey technology; turf and turfgrass management; web page, digital/multimedia and information resources design.

Academic Programs *Special study options:* academic remediation for entering students, adult/continuing education programs, advanced placement credit, cooperative education, distance learning, English as a second language, external degree program, independent study, internships, off-campus study, part-time degree program, services for LD students, student-designed majors, summer session for credit. *ROTC:* Army (c), Air Force (c).

Library M. W. Bell Library plus 2 others with 74,958 titles, 381 serial subscriptions, 7,286 audiovisual materials, an OPAC, a Web page.

Computers on Campus 90 computers available on campus for general student use. A campuswide network can be accessed from off campus. Internet access, at least one staffed computer lab available.

Student Life *Housing:* college housing not available. *Activities and Organizations:* drama/theater group.

Standardized Tests *Required:* ACT COMPASS (for placement).

Costs (2003–04) *Tuition:* state resident $1212 full-time, $36 per credit hour part-time; nonresident $6380 full-time, $197 per credit hour part-time. *Required fees:* $15 per term part-time. *Payment plan:* installment. *Waivers:* senior citizens and employees or children of employees.

Financial Aid Of all full-time matriculated undergraduates who enrolled, 94 Federal Work-Study jobs (averaging $2640).

Applying *Options:* early admission, deferred entrance. *Required:* high school transcript. *Required for some:* interview. *Application deadline:* rolling (freshmen), rolling (transfers). *Notification:* continuous (freshmen), continuous (transfers).

Admissions Contact Ms. Jean Groome, Director of Admissions, Guilford Technical Community College, PO Box 309, Jamestown, NC 27282. *Phone:* 336-334-4822 Ext. 2396. *E-mail:* knighte@gtcc.cc.nc.us.

HALIFAX COMMUNITY COLLEGE
Weldon, North Carolina

- **State and locally supported** 2-year, founded 1967, part of North Carolina Community College System
- **Calendar** semesters
- **Degree** certificates, diplomas, and associate
- **Rural** 109-acre campus
- **Coed**

Student Life *Campus security:* 12-hour patrols by trained security personnel.

Applying *Options:* deferred entrance. *Required:* high school transcript.

Admissions Contact Mrs. Scottie Dickens, Director of Admissions, Halifax Community College, PO Drawer 809, Weldon, NC 27890-0809. *Phone:* 252-536-2551 Ext. 220.

HAYWOOD COMMUNITY COLLEGE
Clyde, North Carolina

- **State and locally supported** 2-year, founded 1964, part of North Carolina Community College System
- **Calendar** semesters
- **Degree** certificates, diplomas, and associate
- **Rural** 85-acre campus
- **Coed**

Faculty *Student/faculty ratio:* 12:1.

Student Life *Campus security:* 24-hour patrols.

Costs (2004–05) *Tuition:* state resident $1136 full-time, $36 per credit hour part-time; nonresident $6304 full-time, $197 per credit hour part-time. Part-time tuition and fees vary according to course load. *Required fees:* $28 full-time, $7 per term part-time.

Financial Aid Of all full-time matriculated undergraduates who enrolled, 25 Federal Work-Study jobs (averaging $1200).

Applying *Required:* high school transcript. *Required for some:* interview.

Admissions Contact Ms. Debbie Rowland, Coordinator of Admissions, Haywood Community College, 185 Freedlander Drive, Clyde, NC 28721-9453. *Phone:* 828-627-4505. *Fax:* 828-627-4513. *E-mail:* drowland@haywood.cc.nc.us.

ISOTHERMAL COMMUNITY COLLEGE
Spindale, North Carolina

- **State-supported** 2-year, founded 1965, part of North Carolina Community College System
- **Calendar** semesters
- **Degree** certificates, diplomas, and associate
- **Rural** 120-acre campus
- **Coed,** 2,005 undergraduate students, 49% full-time, 65% women, 35% men

Undergraduates 988 full-time, 1,017 part-time. Students come from 40 states and territories, 3 other countries, 16% African American, 0.3% Asian American or Pacific Islander, 0.9% Hispanic American, 0.3% Native American, 0.3% international. *Retention:* 33% of 2002 full-time freshmen returned.

Freshmen *Admission:* 274 enrolled.

Faculty *Total:* 114, 53% full-time, 7% with terminal degrees. *Student/faculty ratio:* 17:1.

Majors Administrative assistant and secretarial science; automobile/automotive mechanics technology; biological and physical sciences; broadcast journalism; business administration and management; business teacher education; commercial and advertising art; computer programming; computer science; cosmetology; criminal justice/law enforcement administration; criminal justice/police science; drafting and design technology; education; electrical, electronic and communications engineering technology; elementary education; insurance; kindergarten/preschool education; liberal arts and sciences/liberal studies; machine tool technology; marketing/marketing management; mechanical design technology; mechanical engineering/mechanical technology; music; nursing (licensed practical/vocational nurse training); pharmacy; plastics engineering technology; pre-engineering; radio and television; real estate; teacher assistant/aide; trade and industrial teacher education; veterinary sciences; welding technology.

Academic Programs *Special study options:* academic remediation for entering students, adult/continuing education programs, advanced placement credit, cooperative education, English as a second language, external degree program, honors programs, part-time degree program, services for LD students, student-designed majors, summer session for credit.

Library 35,200 titles, 289 serial subscriptions, an OPAC, a Web page.

Computers on Campus Internet access, at least one staffed computer lab available.

Student Life *Housing:* college housing not available. *Activities and Organizations:* student-run newspaper, radio station, choral group. *Student services:* personal/psychological counseling.

Athletics *Intramural sports:* basketball M/W, football M/W, volleyball M/W.

Standardized Tests *Required:* ACT ASSET (for placement).

Costs (2004–05) *Tuition:* state resident $1136 full-time, $36 per hour part-time; nonresident $6304 full-time, $197 per hour part-time. *Required fees:* $28 full-time.

Financial Aid Of all full-time matriculated undergraduates who enrolled, 21 Federal Work-Study jobs.

Applying *Options:* early admission, deferred entrance. *Required:* high school transcript. *Application deadline:* rolling (freshmen), rolling (transfers). *Notification:* continuous (freshmen), continuous (transfers).

Admissions Contact Ms. Betty Gabriel, Director of Counseling, Isothermal Community College, PO Box 804, Spindale, NC 28160-0804. *Phone:* 828-286-3636 Ext. 243. *Fax:* 828-286-8109. *E-mail:* smonday@isothermal.cc.nc.us.

JAMES SPRUNT COMMUNITY COLLEGE
Kenansville, North Carolina

- **State-supported** 2-year, founded 1964, part of North Carolina Community College System
- **Calendar** semesters
- **Degree** certificates, diplomas, and associate
- **Rural** 51-acre campus
- **Endowment** $16,587
- **Coed,** 1,405 undergraduate students, 54% full-time, 71% women, 29% men

Undergraduates 754 full-time, 651 part-time. Students come from 3 states and territories, 1% are from out of state, 44% African American, 0.1% Asian American or Pacific Islander, 2% Hispanic American, 0.3% Native American, 0.3% international, 6% transferred in.

Freshmen *Admission:* 325 applied, 284 admitted, 202 enrolled.

Faculty *Total:* 144, 37% full-time, 1% with terminal degrees. *Student/faculty ratio:* 21:1.

Majors Accounting; administrative assistant and secretarial science; agribusiness; animal sciences; business administration and management; commercial and advertising art; computer systems analysis; cosmetology; criminal justice/police science; kindergarten/preschool education; liberal arts and sciences/liberal studies; medical/clinical assistant; nursing (registered nurse training).

Academic Programs *Special study options:* academic remediation for entering students, accelerated degree program, adult/continuing education programs, advanced placement credit, cooperative education, distance learning, double majors, English as a second language, external degree program, independent study, internships, part-time degree program, summer session for credit.

Library James Sprunt Community College Library with 23,433 titles, 230 serial subscriptions, 1,392 audiovisual materials, an OPAC.

Computers on Campus 100 computers available on campus for general student use. A campuswide network can be accessed from off campus. Internet access, at least one staffed computer lab available.

Student Life *Housing:* college housing not available. *Activities and Organizations:* student-run newspaper, Student Nurses Association, Art Club, Alumni Association, National Technical-Vocational Honor Society, Phi Theta Kappa. *Campus security:* trained security personnel. *Student services:* personal/psychological counseling.

Athletics *Intercollegiate sports:* softball W, volleyball M/W.

Standardized Tests *Required:* ACT ASSET (for placement).

Costs (2004–05) *Tuition:* state resident $1206 full-time; nonresident $6374 full-time. *Required fees:* $70 full-time. *Waivers:* employees or children of employees.

Financial Aid Of all full-time matriculated undergraduates who enrolled, 55 Federal Work-Study jobs (averaging $1650).

Applying *Options:* common application, early admission, deferred entrance. *Required:* high school transcript. *Application deadline:* rolling (freshmen), rolling (transfers). *Notification:* continuous (freshmen), continuous (transfers).

Admissions Contact Ms. Rita B. Brown, Director of Admissions and Records, James Sprunt Community College, Highway 11 South, 133 James Sprunt Drive. *Phone:* 910-296-2500. *Fax:* 910-296-1222. *E-mail:* rbrown@jscc.cc.nc.us.

JOHNSTON COMMUNITY COLLEGE
Smithfield, North Carolina

- **State-supported** 2-year, founded 1969, part of North Carolina Community College System
- **Calendar** semesters
- **Degree** certificates, diplomas, and associate
- **Rural** 100-acre campus
- **Endowment** $1.7 million
- **Coed,** 3,806 undergraduate students, 44% full-time, 62% women, 38% men

Undergraduates 1,657 full-time, 2,149 part-time. Students come from 10 states and territories, 1 other country, 1% are from out of state, 21% African American, 0.6% Asian American or Pacific Islander, 3% Hispanic American, 0.7% Native American, 0.4% international.

Freshmen *Admission:* 1,610 enrolled.

Faculty *Total:* 319, 39% full-time, 96% with terminal degrees. *Student/faculty ratio:* 18:1.

Majors Accounting technology and bookkeeping; administrative assistant and secretarial science; business administration and management; commercial and advertising art; computer programming; criminal justice/police science; diesel mechanics technology; electrical, electronic and communications engineering technology; heating, air conditioning, ventilation and refrigeration maintenance technology; kindergarten/preschool education; landscaping and groundskeeping; legal assistant/paralegal; liberal arts and sciences/liberal studies; machine tool technology; medical administrative assistant and medical secretary; medical/clinical assistant; medical radiologic technology; nursing (registered nurse training); operations management.

Academic Programs *Special study options:* academic remediation for entering students, adult/continuing education programs, advanced placement credit, cooperative education, distance learning, honors programs, independent study, part-time degree program, services for LD students, summer session for credit.

Library Johnston Community College Library plus 1 other with 31,333 titles, 366 serial subscriptions, 4,315 audiovisual materials, an OPAC, a Web page.

Computers on Campus 186 computers available on campus for general student use. Internet access, at least one staffed computer lab available.

Student Life *Housing:* college housing not available. *Campus security:* 24-hour patrols. *Student services:* personal/psychological counseling.

Athletics *Intercollegiate sports:* golf M/W, softball M/W, volleyball M/W. *Intramural sports:* basketball M/W.

Standardized Tests *Required for some:* ACCUPLACER.

Costs (2003–04) *Tuition:* state resident $1136 full-time, $36 per semester hour part-time; nonresident $6304 full-time. Full-time tuition and fees vary according to course load. Part-time tuition and fees vary according to course load. *Required fees:* $70 full-time, $1 per semester hour part-time, $19 per term part-time. *Waivers:* senior citizens and employees or children of employees.

Financial Aid Of all full-time matriculated undergraduates who enrolled, 27 Federal Work-Study jobs (averaging $5000).

Applying *Options:* electronic application, early admission. *Required:* high school transcript. *Application deadline:* rolling (freshmen), rolling (transfers). *Notification:* continuous (freshmen), continuous (transfers).

Admissions Contact Dr. Lawrence Rouse, Dean of Students Services, Johnston Community College, PO Box 2350, Smithfield, NC 27577-2350. *Phone:* 919-209-2048. *Fax:* 919-989-7862.

KING'S COLLEGE
Charlotte, North Carolina

Admissions Contact Ms. Barbara Rockecharlie, School Director, King's College, 322 Lamar Avenue, Charlotte, NC 28204-2436. *Phone:* 704-688-3613. *Toll-free phone:* 800-768-2255.

LENOIR COMMUNITY COLLEGE
Kinston, North Carolina

- **State-supported** 2-year, founded 1960, part of North Carolina Community College System

North Carolina

Lenoir Community College (continued)
- **Calendar** semesters
- **Degree** certificates, diplomas, and associate
- **Small-town** 86-acre campus
- **Coed,** 2,607 undergraduate students, 51% full-time, 69% women, 31% men

Undergraduates 1,337 full-time, 1,270 part-time.
Faculty *Total:* 85.
Majors Accounting; administrative assistant and secretarial science; agricultural business and management; agriculture; airline pilot and flight crew; art; aviation/airway management; avionics maintenance technology; business administration and management; commercial and advertising art; computer programming; consumer merchandising/retailing management; cosmetology; court reporting; criminal justice/law enforcement administration; criminal justice/police science; drafting and design technology; electrical, electronic and communications engineering technology; elementary education; finance; fire science; food services technology; graphic and printing equipment operation/production; heavy equipment maintenance technology; horticultural science; hydrology and water resources science; industrial technology; instrumentation technology; insurance; landscape architecture; legal administrative assistant/secretary; liberal arts and sciences/liberal studies; library science; marketing/marketing management; mechanical design technology; medical administrative assistant and medical secretary; medical/clinical assistant; mental health/rehabilitation; nursing (registered nurse training); ornamental horticulture; postal management; pre-engineering; trade and industrial teacher education; welding technology.
Academic Programs *Special study options:* academic remediation for entering students, adult/continuing education programs, advanced placement credit, cooperative education, English as a second language, part-time degree program, summer session for credit.
Library Learning Resources Center plus 1 other with 55,053 titles, 381 serial subscriptions.
Computers on Campus 116 computers available on campus for general student use. At least one staffed computer lab available.
Student Life *Housing:* college housing not available. *Activities and Organizations:* student-run newspaper, choral group, Student Government Association, Automotive Club, Electronics Club, Drafting Club, Cosmetology Club. *Campus security:* 24-hour emergency response devices and patrols, student patrols. *Student services:* personal/psychological counseling.
Athletics Member NJCAA. *Intercollegiate sports:* baseball M, basketball M(s), volleyball M/W. *Intramural sports:* basketball M, softball W, volleyball M/W.
Standardized Tests *Required:* Assessment and Placement Services for Community Colleges (for placement). *Recommended:* SAT I or ACT (for placement).
Costs (2003–04) *Tuition:* state resident $36 per credit hour part-time; nonresident $197 per credit hour part-time. *Required fees:* $3 per credit hour part-time.
Applying *Options:* early admission. *Required:* high school transcript. *Application deadline:* rolling (freshmen), rolling (transfers). *Notification:* continuous (freshmen), continuous (transfers).
Admissions Contact Ms. Tammy Buck, Director of Enrollment Management, Lenoir Community College, PO Box 188, Kinston, NC 28502-0188. *Phone:* 252-527-6223 Ext. 309.

LOUISBURG COLLEGE
Louisburg, North Carolina

- **Independent United Methodist** 2-year, founded 1787
- **Calendar** semesters
- **Degree** associate
- **Small-town** 75-acre campus with easy access to Raleigh
- **Endowment** $6.8 million
- **Coed**

Faculty *Student/faculty ratio:* 15:1.
Student Life *Campus security:* 24-hour emergency response devices and patrols, controlled dormitory access.
Athletics Member NJCAA.
Standardized Tests *Required:* SAT I or ACT (for admission).
Costs (2004–05) *Comprehensive fee:* $16,530 includes full-time tuition ($10,230) and room and board ($6300). Part-time tuition: $426 per semester hour. *Required fees:* $448 per term part-time. *Room and board:* college room only: $3815. Room and board charges vary according to housing facility.
Financial Aid Of all full-time matriculated undergraduates who enrolled, 100 Federal Work-Study jobs (averaging $1200). 50 state and other part-time jobs (averaging $1500).
Applying *Options:* common application, deferred entrance. *Application fee:* $25. *Required:* high school transcript. *Required for some:* letters of recommendation, interview.

Admissions Contact Ms. Stephanie Buchanan, Director of Admissions, Louisburg College, 501 North Main Street, Louisburg, NC 27549-2399. *Phone:* 919-497-3228. *Toll-free phone:* 800-775-0208. *Fax:* 919-496-1788. *E-mail:* admissions@earthlink.net.

MARTIN COMMUNITY COLLEGE
Williamston, North Carolina

- **State-supported** 2-year, founded 1968, part of North Carolina Community College System
- **Calendar** semesters
- **Degree** certificates, diplomas, and associate
- **Rural** 65-acre campus
- **Endowment** $32,015
- **Coed**

Faculty *Student/faculty ratio:* 14:1.
Student Life *Campus security:* 24-hour emergency response devices, part-time patrols by trained security personnel.
Standardized Tests *Required for some:* ACT COMPASS.
Costs (2003–04) *Tuition:* state resident $1136 full-time, $36 per credit hour part-time; nonresident $6192 full-time, $194 per credit hour part-time. *Required fees:* $38 full-time, $6 per credit hour part-time.
Financial Aid Of all full-time matriculated undergraduates who enrolled, 30 Federal Work-Study jobs (averaging $1200).
Applying *Required:* high school transcript. *Required for some:* interview.
Admissions Contact Ms. Sonya C. Atkinson, Registrar and Admissions Officer, Martin Community College, 1161 Kehukee Park Road, Williamston, NC 27892. *Phone:* 252-792-1521 Ext. 243. *Fax:* 252-792-0826.

MAYLAND COMMUNITY COLLEGE
Spruce Pine, North Carolina

- **State and locally supported** 2-year, founded 1971, part of North Carolina Community College System
- **Calendar** semesters
- **Degree** certificates, diplomas, and associate
- **Rural** 38-acre campus
- **Coed,** 1,494 undergraduate students

Undergraduates Students come from 3 states and territories, 4% African American, 0.4% Asian American or Pacific Islander, 0.8% Hispanic American, 0.8% Native American.
Freshmen *Admission:* 355 applied, 310 admitted.
Faculty *Total:* 132, 36% full-time. *Student/faculty ratio:* 10:1.
Majors Accounting; administrative assistant and secretarial science; business administration and management; carpentry; computer programming; criminal justice/law enforcement administration; criminal justice/police science; electrical, electronic and communications engineering technology; electrical, electronics and communications engineering; finance; horticultural science; information technology; kindergarten/preschool education; liberal arts and sciences/liberal studies; medical administrative assistant and medical secretary; medical/clinical assistant; nursing (registered nurse training); plumbing technology.
Academic Programs *Special study options:* academic remediation for entering students, adult/continuing education programs, advanced placement credit, part-time degree program, services for LD students, summer session for credit.
Library Learning Resources Center plus 1 other with 19,238 titles, 290 serial subscriptions, 1,820 audiovisual materials, an OPAC, a Web page.
Computers on Campus 200 computers available on campus for general student use. A campuswide network can be accessed. Internet access, at least one staffed computer lab available.
Student Life *Housing:* college housing not available. *Student services:* personal/psychological counseling.
Standardized Tests *Required for some:* CPT required for all for placement, required for admission to nursing program.
Costs (2004–05) *Tuition:* state resident $548 full-time, $35 per hour part-time; nonresident $3052 full-time, $191 per hour part-time. Full-time tuition and fees vary according to course load. Part-time tuition and fees vary according to course load. *Required fees:* $28 full-time, $10 per term part-time.
Financial Aid Of all full-time matriculated undergraduates who enrolled, 20 Federal Work-Study jobs (averaging $1350).
Applying *Options:* common application, deferred entrance. *Required:* high school transcript. *Application deadline:* rolling (freshmen), rolling (transfers). *Notification:* continuous (freshmen), continuous (transfers).
Admissions Contact Ms. Paula Crowder, Admissions Retention, Mayland Community College, PO Box 547, Spruce Pine, NC 28777. *Phone:* 828-765-7351. *E-mail:* mayland@cc.nc.us.

MCDOWELL TECHNICAL COMMUNITY COLLEGE
Marion, North Carolina

Admissions Contact Ms. Lisa D. Byrd, Admissions Officer, McDowell Technical Community College, Route 1, Box 170, Marion, NC 28752-9724. *Phone:* 828-652-6024. *Fax:* 828-652-1014.

MITCHELL COMMUNITY COLLEGE
Statesville, North Carolina

- **State-supported** 2-year, founded 1852, part of North Carolina Community College System
- **Calendar** semesters
- **Degree** certificates, diplomas, and associate
- **Small-town** 8-acre campus with easy access to Charlotte
- **Coed,** 2,243 undergraduate students, 44% full-time, 68% women, 32% men

Undergraduates 993 full-time, 1,250 part-time. Students come from 5 states and territories, 1 other country, 0.1% are from out of state, 20% African American, 2% Asian American or Pacific Islander, 2% Hispanic American, 0.2% Native American, 0.1% international, 4% transferred in. *Retention:* 61% of 2002 full-time freshmen returned.
Freshmen *Admission:* 610 enrolled.
Faculty *Total:* 140, 45% full-time, 2% with terminal degrees. *Student/faculty ratio:* 17:1.
Majors Accounting; administrative assistant and secretarial science; art; biological and physical sciences; business administration and management; child development; computer science; criminal justice/law enforcement administration; data processing and data processing technology; drafting and design technology; electrical, electronic and communications engineering technology; elementary education; engineering; human services; industrial technology; kindergarten/preschool education; liberal arts and sciences/liberal studies; machine tool technology; mathematics; medical/clinical assistant; nursing (registered nurse training); physical education teaching and coaching; psychology; social work.
Academic Programs *Special study options:* academic remediation for entering students, adult/continuing education programs, advanced placement credit, distance learning, English as a second language, part-time degree program, services for LD students, summer session for credit. *ROTC:* Army (c).
Library Main Library plus 1 other with 37,760 titles, 218 serial subscriptions, 2,225 audiovisual materials, an OPAC.
Computers on Campus 40 computers available on campus for general student use. A campuswide network can be accessed. At least one staffed computer lab available.
Student Life *Housing:* college housing not available. *Activities and Organizations:* choral group, Circle K, Phi Beta Lambda, Medical Assisting Club, Ebony Kinship. *Campus security:* day and evening security guards. *Student services:* personal/psychological counseling.
Costs (2004–05) *Tuition:* state resident $1136 full-time, $36 per credit hour part-time; nonresident $6304 full-time, $197 per credit hour part-time. *Required fees:* $62 full-time, $2 per credit hour part-time.
Financial Aid Of all full-time matriculated undergraduates who enrolled, 30 Federal Work-Study jobs.
Applying *Required:* high school transcript. *Application deadline:* rolling (freshmen), rolling (transfers). *Notification:* continuous (freshmen), continuous (transfers).
Admissions Contact Mr. Doug Rhoney, Counselor, Mitchell Community College, 500 West Broad, Statesville, NC 28677-5293. *Phone:* 704-878-3280. *Fax:* 704-878-0872.

MONTGOMERY COMMUNITY COLLEGE
Troy, North Carolina

- **State-supported** 2-year, founded 1967, part of North Carolina Community College System
- **Calendar** semesters
- **Degree** certificates, diplomas, and associate
- **Rural** 159-acre campus
- **Endowment** $13,000
- **Coed**

Standardized Tests *Required:* ACT ASSET or ACT COMPASS (for placement).
Costs (2003–04) *Tuition:* state resident $1136 full-time; nonresident $6304 full-time. Full-time tuition and fees vary according to course load. Part-time tuition and fees vary according to course load. *Required fees:* $57 full-time.
Financial Aid Of all full-time matriculated undergraduates who enrolled, 24 Federal Work-Study jobs (averaging $500).

Applying *Options:* early admission, deferred entrance. *Required:* high school transcript.
Admissions Contact Ms. Karen Frye, Admissions Officer, Montgomery Community College, 1011 Page Street, Troy, NC 27371. *Phone:* 910-576-6222 Ext. 240. *Toll-free phone:* 800-839-6222. *E-mail:* fryek@mcc.montgomery.cc.nc.us.

NASH COMMUNITY COLLEGE
Rocky Mount, North Carolina

- **State-supported** 2-year, founded 1967, part of North Carolina Community College System
- **Calendar** semesters
- **Degree** certificates, diplomas, and associate
- **Rural** 69-acre campus
- **Endowment** $147,220
- **Coed,** 2,567 undergraduate students, 35% full-time, 65% women, 35% men

Undergraduates 904 full-time, 1,663 part-time. Students come from 3 states and territories, 36% African American, 0.3% Asian American or Pacific Islander, 1% Hispanic American, 2% Native American, 1% transferred in.
Freshmen *Admission:* 360 applied, 360 admitted, 360 enrolled.
Faculty *Total:* 120, 58% full-time, 96% with terminal degrees. *Student/faculty ratio:* 22:1.
Majors Accounting; administrative assistant and secretarial science; architectural engineering technology; business administration and management; cosmetology; criminal justice/police science; electrical, electronic and communications engineering technology; information technology; kindergarten/preschool education; legal administrative assistant/secretary; liberal arts and sciences/liberal studies; marketing/marketing management; medical administrative assistant and medical secretary; nursing (registered nurse training); physical therapy; teacher assistant/aide.
Academic Programs *Special study options:* academic remediation for entering students, adult/continuing education programs, advanced placement credit, distance learning, double majors, English as a second language, independent study, part-time degree program, services for LD students, summer session for credit.
Library Nash Community College Library plus 1 other with 34,000 titles, 110 serial subscriptions, an OPAC.
Computers on Campus 110 computers available on campus for general student use. A campuswide network can be accessed. Internet access, at least one staffed computer lab available.
Student Life *Housing:* college housing not available. *Activities and Organizations:* student-run newspaper, Student Government Association, Gamma, Phi Beta Lambda, Student Nurses Organization/Physical Therapist Assistant Club, Criminal Justice Club. *Campus security:* 24-hour emergency response devices, late-night transport/escort service.
Standardized Tests *Required for some:* SAT I or ACT (for admission), SAT I and SAT II or ACT (for admission), ACT ASSET or ACT COMPASS.
Costs (2003–04) *Tuition:* state resident $1136 full-time, $36 per credit hour part-time; nonresident $6304 full-time, $197 per credit hour part-time. *Required fees:* $32 full-time, $1 per credit hour part-time.
Applying *Options:* common application, deferred entrance. *Required:* high school transcript. *Recommended:* interview. *Application deadline:* rolling (freshmen), rolling (transfers). *Notification:* continuous (freshmen), continuous (transfers).
Admissions Contact Ms. Mary Blount, Admissions Officer, Nash Community College, PO Box 7488, Rocky Mount, NC 27804-0488. *Phone:* 252-443-4011 Ext. 300. *Fax:* 252-443-0828.

PAMLICO COMMUNITY COLLEGE
Grantsboro, North Carolina

- **State-supported** 2-year, founded 1963, part of North Carolina Community College System
- **Calendar** semesters
- **Degree** certificates, diplomas, and associate
- **Rural** 44-acre campus
- **Coed**

Student Life *Campus security:* evening security guard.
Standardized Tests *Required:* ACT ASSET (for placement).
Financial Aid Of all full-time matriculated undergraduates who enrolled, 15 Federal Work-Study jobs (averaging $4353).
Applying *Options:* early admission, deferred entrance. *Required:* high school transcript.
Admissions Contact Mr. Floyd H. Hardison, Admissions Counselor, Pamlico Community College, PO Box 185, Grantsboro, NC 28529-0185. *Phone:* 252-249-1851 Ext. 28. *Fax:* 252-249-2377. *E-mail:* jjones@pamilcocommunitycollege.cc.nc.us.

PIEDMONT COMMUNITY COLLEGE
Roxboro, North Carolina

- **State-supported** 2-year, founded 1970, part of North Carolina Community College System
- **Calendar** semesters
- **Degree** certificates, diplomas, and associate
- **Small-town** 178-acre campus
- **Endowment** $1.8 million
- **Coed**

Faculty *Student/faculty ratio:* 28:1.

Student Life *Campus security:* security guard during certain evening and weekend hours.

Standardized Tests *Required:* ACT ASSET (for placement).

Financial Aid Of all full-time matriculated undergraduates who enrolled, 30 Federal Work-Study jobs (averaging $1500).

Applying *Options:* early admission, deferred entrance. *Required for some:* high school transcript.

Admissions Contact Ms. Sheila Williamson, Director of Admissions, Piedmont Community College, PO Box 1197, 1715 College Drive, Roxboro, NC 27573. *Phone:* 336-599-1181 Ext. 219. *Fax:* 336-598-9283.

PITT COMMUNITY COLLEGE
Greenville, North Carolina

- **State and locally supported** 2-year, founded 1961, part of North Carolina Community College System
- **Calendar** semesters
- **Degree** certificates, diplomas, and associate
- **Small-town** 172-acre campus
- **Endowment** $199,213
- **Coed,** 5,980 undergraduate students, 54% full-time, 60% women, 40% men

Undergraduates 3,200 full-time, 2,780 part-time. Students come from 13 states and territories, 2% are from out of state, 32% African American, 0.8% Asian American or Pacific Islander, 1% Hispanic American, 0.6% Native American, 0.4% international, 27% transferred in. *Retention:* 57% of 2002 full-time freshmen returned.

Freshmen *Admission:* 1,415 applied, 1,415 admitted, 163 enrolled.

Faculty *Total:* 328, 52% full-time, 5% with terminal degrees. *Student/faculty ratio:* 18:1.

Majors Accounting; administrative assistant and secretarial science; architectural engineering technology; business administration and management; child care and support services management; commercial and advertising art; computer programming (specific applications); computer systems analysis; computer systems networking and telecommunications; construction trades related; criminal justice/police science; diagnostic medical sonography and ultrasound technology; electrical, electronic and communications engineering technology; electromechanical technology; engineering/industrial management; environmental control technologies related; general retailing/wholesaling; health information/medical records technology; health professions related; industrial technology; legal assistant/paralegal; liberal arts and sciences/liberal studies; machine shop technology; machine tool technology; medical administrative assistant and medical secretary; medical/clinical assistant; medical radiologic technology; mental and social health services and allied professions related; nuclear medical technology; nursing (registered nurse training); occupational therapist assistant; operations management; psychiatric/mental health services technology; respiratory care therapy; retailing.

Academic Programs *Special study options:* academic remediation for entering students, adult/continuing education programs, advanced placement credit, cooperative education, distance learning, double majors, English as a second language, external degree program, independent study, internships, part-time degree program, services for LD students, summer session for credit. *ROTC:* Army (b).

Library Learning Resources Center with 43,558 titles, 275 serial subscriptions, 5,225 audiovisual materials, an OPAC, a Web page.

Computers on Campus 60 computers available on campus for general student use. A campuswide network can be accessed from off campus. Internet access, online (class) registration available.

Student Life *Housing:* college housing not available. *Campus security:* 24-hour patrols, student patrols, late-night transport/escort service. *Student services:* personal/psychological counseling.

Athletics Member NJCAA. *Intercollegiate sports:* baseball M(s), golf M(s)/W(s), volleyball W(s). *Intramural sports:* basketball M/W, softball W, volleyball M/W.

Standardized Tests *Required:* ACT ASSET or ACT COMPASS (for placement).

Costs (2003–04) *Tuition:* state resident $1136 full-time, $36 per semester hour part-time; nonresident $6304 full-time, $197 per semester hour part-time. *Required fees:* $40 full-time, $16 per term part-time.

Financial Aid Of all full-time matriculated undergraduates who enrolled, 117 Federal Work-Study jobs (averaging $1593).

Applying *Options:* electronic application, deferred entrance. *Required:* high school transcript. *Application deadline:* rolling (freshmen), rolling (transfers).

Admissions Contact Ms. Mary Tate, Director of Counseling, Pitt Community College, PO Drawer 7007, 1986 Pitt Tech Road, Greenville, NC 27835-7007. *Phone:* 252-321-4217. *Fax:* 252-321-4612. *E-mail:* pittadm@pcc.pitt.cc.nc.us.

RANDOLPH COMMUNITY COLLEGE
Asheboro, North Carolina

- **State-supported** 2-year, founded 1962, part of North Carolina Community College System
- **Calendar** semesters
- **Degree** certificates, diplomas, and associate
- **Small-town** 27-acre campus
- **Endowment** $6.4 million
- **Coed**

Faculty *Student/faculty ratio:* 23:1.

Student Life *Campus security:* security officer during open hours.

Standardized Tests *Required for some:* ACT ASSET or ACT COMPASS.

Costs (2003–04) *Tuition:* state resident $1704 full-time, $36 per semester hour part-time; nonresident $9456 full-time, $197 per semester hour part-time. *Required fees:* $80 full-time.

Applying *Options:* common application, deferred entrance. *Required:* high school transcript.

Admissions Contact Mrs. Carol M. Elmore, Director of Admissions and Registrar, Randolph Community College, PO Box 1009, Asheboro, NC 27204-1009. *Phone:* 336-633-0213. *Fax:* 336-629-4695. *E-mail:* info@randolph.edu.

RICHMOND COMMUNITY COLLEGE
Hamlet, North Carolina

- **State-supported** 2-year, founded 1964, part of North Carolina Community College System
- **Calendar** semesters
- **Degree** diplomas and associate
- **Rural** 163-acre campus
- **Coed,** 1,690 undergraduate students, 53% full-time, 72% women, 28% men

Undergraduates 891 full-time, 799 part-time. Students come from 3 states and territories, 31% African American, 1% Asian American or Pacific Islander, 0.5% Hispanic American, 9% Native American, 6% transferred in.

Freshmen *Admission:* 154 enrolled.

Faculty *Total:* 47, 85% full-time, 6% with terminal degrees. *Student/faculty ratio:* 30:1.

Majors Accounting; administrative assistant and secretarial science; business administration and management; child care and support services management; computer engineering technology; computer systems analysis; criminal justice/law enforcement administration; electrical, electronic and communications engineering technology; human services; industrial production technologies related; liberal arts and sciences/liberal studies; machine tool technology; mechanical engineering/mechanical technology; medical/clinical assistant; nursing (registered nurse training); web page, digital/multimedia and information resources design.

Academic Programs *Special study options:* academic remediation for entering students, adult/continuing education programs, advanced placement credit, cooperative education, distance learning, double majors, English as a second language, independent study, internships, part-time degree program, student-designed majors, summer session for credit.

Library Richmond Community College Library with 26,381 titles, 192 serial subscriptions, 1,676 audiovisual materials, an OPAC.

Computers on Campus 600 computers available on campus for general student use. A campuswide network can be accessed from off campus. Internet access, at least one staffed computer lab available.

Student Life *Housing:* college housing not available. *Activities and Organizations:* Criminal Justice Club, Human Services Club, Native American Club. *Campus security:* 24-hour emergency response devices, security guard during evening hours. *Student services:* personal/psychological counseling.

Costs (2004–05) *Tuition:* $38 per credit hour part-time; state resident $1125 full-time; nonresident $5910 full-time, $197 per credit hour part-time. *Required fees:* $38 full-time.

Financial Aid Of all full-time matriculated undergraduates who enrolled, 35 Federal Work-Study jobs (averaging $2000).

Applying *Options:* deferred entrance. *Required:* high school transcript. *Application deadline:* rolling (freshmen), rolling (transfers). *Notification:* continuous until 8/1 (freshmen), continuous until 8/1 (transfers).

Admissions Contact Ms. Wanda B. Watts, Director of Admissions/Registrar, Richmond Community College, PO Box 1189, Hamlet, NC 28345. *Phone:* 910-582-7113. *Fax:* 910-582-7102.

ROANOKE-CHOWAN COMMUNITY COLLEGE
Ahoskie, North Carolina

- **State-supported** 2-year, founded 1967, part of North Carolina Community College System
- **Calendar** semesters
- **Degree** certificates, diplomas, and associate
- **Rural** 39-acre campus
- **Endowment** $125,000
- **Coed,** 989 undergraduate students, 51% full-time, 74% women, 26% men

Undergraduates 502 full-time, 487 part-time. 67% African American, 0.5% Asian American or Pacific Islander, 0.4% Hispanic American, 0.6% Native American. *Retention:* 59% of 2002 full-time freshmen returned.

Freshmen *Admission:* 174 enrolled.

Faculty *Total:* 83, 48% full-time. *Student/faculty ratio:* 12:1.

Majors Administrative assistant and secretarial science; architectural engineering technology; automobile/automotive mechanics technology; business administration and management; computer programming; construction engineering technology; cosmetology; criminal justice/law enforcement administration; education; electrical, electronic and communications engineering technology; environmental engineering technology; heating, air conditioning, ventilation and refrigeration maintenance technology; kindergarten/preschool education; liberal arts and sciences/liberal studies; nursing (registered nurse training); welding technology.

Academic Programs *Special study options:* academic remediation for entering students, adult/continuing education programs, cooperative education, distance learning, part-time degree program, summer session for credit.

Library 29,268 titles, 207 serial subscriptions, an OPAC, a Web page.

Computers on Campus 90 computers available on campus for general student use. A campuswide network can be accessed. Internet access available.

Student Life *Housing:* college housing not available.

Athletics *Intramural sports:* basketball M/W, volleyball M/W.

Standardized Tests *Required:* ACT ASSET (for placement).

Costs (2003–04) *Tuition:* state resident $1136 full-time, $36 per credit part-time; nonresident $6304 full-time, $197 per credit part-time. Part-time tuition and fees vary according to course load. *Required fees:* $69 full-time, $3 per credit part-time.

Financial Aid Of all full-time matriculated undergraduates who enrolled, 50 Federal Work-Study jobs (averaging $1120).

Applying *Options:* early admission. *Required for some:* interview. *Application deadline:* rolling (freshmen), rolling (transfers). *Notification:* continuous (freshmen), continuous (transfers).

Admissions Contact Miss Sandra Copeland, Director, Counseling Services, Roanoke-Chowan Community College, 109 Community College Road, Ahoskie, NC 27910. *Phone:* 252-862-1225.

ROBESON COMMUNITY COLLEGE
Lumberton, North Carolina

- **State-supported** 2-year, founded 1965, part of North Carolina Community College System
- **Calendar** semesters
- **Degree** associate
- **Small-town** 78-acre campus
- **Coed**

Standardized Tests *Required:* ACT ASSET, ACT COMPASS (for placement).

Costs (2003–04) *Tuition:* state resident $852 full-time, $36 per credit hour part-time; nonresident $4728 full-time, $197 per credit hour part-time. *Required fees:* $60 full-time, $25 per term part-time.

Applying *Options:* early admission.

Admissions Contact Ms. Judy Revels, Director of Admissions, Robeson Community College, PO Box 1420, 5160 Fayetteville Road, Lumberton, NC 28359. *Phone:* 910-618-5680 Ext. 251. *Fax:* 910-618-5686.

ROCKINGHAM COMMUNITY COLLEGE
Wentworth, North Carolina

- **State-supported** 2-year, founded 1964, part of North Carolina Community College System
- **Calendar** semesters
- **Degree** certificates, diplomas, and associate
- **Rural** 257-acre campus
- **Coed,** 2,060 undergraduate students, 51% full-time, 65% women, 35% men

Undergraduates 1,050 full-time, 1,010 part-time. Students come from 9 states and territories, 1 other country, 20% African American, 0.2% Asian American or Pacific Islander, 0.7% Hispanic American, 0.3% Native American, 1% international.

Freshmen *Admission:* 505 enrolled.

Faculty *Total:* 106, 59% full-time, 6% with terminal degrees. *Student/faculty ratio:* 18:1.

Majors Accounting; administrative assistant and secretarial science; art; biological and physical sciences; business administration and management; business machine repair; carpentry; child development; construction engineering technology; consumer services and advocacy; cosmetology; criminal justice/law enforcement administration; criminal justice/police science; electromechanical technology; heating, air conditioning, ventilation and refrigeration maintenance technology; horticultural science; human resources management; industrial arts; information science/studies; labor and industrial relations; legal administrative assistant/secretary; legal assistant/paralegal; liberal arts and sciences/liberal studies; medical administrative assistant and medical secretary; medical/clinical assistant; nursing (licensed practical/vocational nurse training); nursing (registered nurse training); occupational therapist assistant; physical therapist assistant; respiratory care therapy; teacher assistant/aide; tourism and travel services management.

Academic Programs *Special study options:* academic remediation for entering students, adult/continuing education programs, advanced placement credit, cooperative education, part-time degree program, student-designed majors, summer session for credit.

Library Gerald B. James Library with 43,044 titles, 374 serial subscriptions, 3,990 audiovisual materials, an OPAC, a Web page.

Computers on Campus 150 computers available on campus for general student use. A campuswide network can be accessed. Internet access, at least one staffed computer lab available.

Student Life *Housing:* college housing not available. *Activities and Organizations:* student-run newspaper, Phi Theta Kappa, Cultural Diversity Club, Paralegal Club. *Campus security:* late-night transport/escort service. *Student services:* personal/psychological counseling.

Athletics Member NJCAA. *Intercollegiate sports:* baseball M, basketball M/W, volleyball W. *Intramural sports:* archery M/W, badminton M/W, basketball M/W, cheerleading W, table tennis M/W, tennis M/W, volleyball M/W.

Standardized Tests *Required for some:* CGP.

Costs (2003–04) *Tuition:* state resident $1136 full-time; nonresident $6305 full-time. *Required fees:* $37 full-time.

Financial Aid Of all full-time matriculated undergraduates who enrolled, 37 Federal Work-Study jobs (averaging $2300).

Applying *Options:* early admission, deferred entrance. *Application deadline:* rolling (freshmen), rolling (transfers). *Notification:* continuous (freshmen), continuous (transfers).

Admissions Contact Mrs. Leigh Hawkins, Director of Enrollment Services, Rockingham Community College, PO Box 38, Wentworth, NC 27375-0038. *Phone:* 336-342-4261 Ext. 2333.

ROWAN-CABARRUS COMMUNITY COLLEGE
Salisbury, North Carolina

- **State-supported** 2-year, founded 1963, part of North Carolina Community College System
- **Calendar** semesters
- **Degree** diplomas and associate
- **Small-town** 100-acre campus
- **Coed,** 5,200 undergraduate students, 43% full-time, 67% women, 33% men

Undergraduates 2,255 full-time, 2,945 part-time. Students come from 2 other countries, 20% African American, 1% Asian American or Pacific Islander, 2% Hispanic American, 0.4% Native American.

Freshmen *Admission:* 1,909 applied, 1,909 admitted, 1,561 enrolled.

Faculty *Total:* 251, 48% full-time.

Majors Accounting; automobile/automotive mechanics technology; biomedical technology; business administration and management; criminal justice/law enforcement administration; electrical, electronic and communications engineering technology; health information/medical records technology; industrial tech-

Rowan-Cabarrus Community College (continued)
nology; information science/studies; kindergarten/preschool education; legal assistant/paralegal; liberal arts and sciences/liberal studies; mechanical drafting and CAD/CADD; medical laboratory technology; nursing (registered nurse training); radiologic technology/science.

Academic Programs *Special study options:* academic remediation for entering students, adult/continuing education programs, advanced placement credit, cooperative education, distance learning, English as a second language, internships, part-time degree program, services for LD students, summer session for credit.

Library Learning Resource Center with 23,005 titles, 313 serial subscriptions.

Computers on Campus 200 computers available on campus for general student use. Internet access, at least one staffed computer lab available.

Student Life *Housing:* college housing not available. *Campus security:* on-campus security during operating hours. *Student services:* personal/psychological counseling.

Athletics *Intramural sports:* basketball M/W.

Standardized Tests *Required:* ACT ASSET (for placement).

Costs (2004–05) *Tuition:* state resident $1136 full-time; nonresident $6304 full-time. No tuition increase for student's term of enrollment. *Required fees:* $64 full-time. *Payment plan:* deferred payment. *Waivers:* senior citizens.

Applying *Required:* high school transcript. *Application deadline:* rolling (freshmen), rolling (transfers).

Admissions Contact Mr. Kenneth C. Hayes, Director of Admissions and Recruitment, Rowan-Cabarrus Community College, P.O. Box 1595, Salisbury, NC 28145. *Phone:* 704-637-0760 Ext. 212. *Fax:* 704-633-6804.

SAMPSON COMMUNITY COLLEGE
Clinton, North Carolina

- **State and locally supported** 2-year, founded 1965, part of North Carolina Community College System
- **Calendar** semesters
- **Degree** certificates, diplomas, and associate
- **Rural** 55-acre campus
- **Coed**

Faculty *Student/faculty ratio:* 20:1.

Student Life *Campus security:* local police patrol.

Standardized Tests *Required:* ACT ASSET (for placement).

Costs (2003–04) *Tuition:* state resident $1205 full-time, $36 per credit part-time; nonresident $6373 full-time, $197 per credit part-time. *Required fees:* $36 full-time.

Financial Aid Of all full-time matriculated undergraduates who enrolled, 37 Federal Work-Study jobs (averaging $1201). 8 state and other part-time jobs (averaging $463).

Applying *Options:* common application, deferred entrance. *Required:* high school transcript, interview. *Recommended:* minimum 2.0 GPA.

Admissions Contact Mr. William R. Jordan, Director of Admissions, Sampson Community College, PO Box 318, Clinton, NC 28329. *Phone:* 910-592-8084 Ext. 2022. *Fax:* 910-592-8048. *E-mail:* bjordan@sampson.cc.nc.us.

SANDHILLS COMMUNITY COLLEGE
Pinehurst, North Carolina

- **State and locally supported** 2-year, founded 1963, part of North Carolina Community College System
- **Calendar** semesters
- **Degree** certificates, diplomas, and associate
- **Small-town** campus
- **Endowment** $4.1 million
- **Coed**

Faculty *Student/faculty ratio:* 18:1.

Student Life *Campus security:* 24-hour emergency response devices, security on duty until 12 a.m.

Standardized Tests *Required:* ACT ASSET or ACT COMPASS (for placement).

Costs (2003–04) *Tuition:* state resident $36 per credit hour part-time; nonresident $197 per credit hour part-time. *Required fees:* $30 per term part-time.

Financial Aid Of all full-time matriculated undergraduates who enrolled, 59 Federal Work-Study jobs (averaging $1750).

Applying *Options:* common application, deferred entrance. *Required:* high school transcript.

Admissions Contact Ms. Rosa McAllister-McRae, Admissions Coordinator, Sandhills Community College, 3395 Airport Road, Pinehurst, NC 28374. *Phone:* 910-692-6185 Ext. 729. *Toll-free phone:* 800-338-3944. *Fax:* 910-692-5076. *E-mail:* mcallisterr@sandhills.edu.

SCHOOL OF COMMUNICATION ARTS
Raleigh, North Carolina

Admissions Contact 3000 Wakefield Crossing Drive, Raleigh, NC 27614. *Toll-free phone:* 800-288-7442.

SOUTH COLLEGE-ASHEVILLE
Asheville, North Carolina

- **Proprietary** 2-year, founded 1905
- **Calendar** quarters
- **Degree** certificates and associate
- **Urban** 8-acre campus
- **Coed,** 112 undergraduate students, 79% full-time, 87% women, 13% men

Undergraduates 88 full-time, 24 part-time. Students come from 2 states and territories, 15% African American, 0.9% Hispanic American.

Freshmen *Admission:* 19 applied, 19 admitted, 19 enrolled.

Faculty *Total:* 28, 29% full-time, 14% with terminal degrees. *Student/faculty ratio:* 9:1.

Majors Accounting; business administration and management; computer and information sciences; legal assistant/paralegal; medical/clinical assistant; office management.

Academic Programs *Special study options:* adult/continuing education programs, cooperative education, double majors, independent study, internships, part-time degree program, summer session for credit.

Library Hilde V. Kopf with 4,550 titles, 37 serial subscriptions.

Computers on Campus 28 computers available on campus for general student use. A campuswide network can be accessed. Internet access, at least one staffed computer lab available.

Student Life *Housing:* college housing not available. *Activities and Organizations:* C-Med, C-Cap, C-Com. *Campus security:* night security.

Standardized Tests *Required:* CPAt (for admission).

Costs (2003–04) *Tuition:* $9900 full-time, $260 per credit hour part-time. Part-time tuition and fees vary according to course load. *Payment plan:* installment. *Waivers:* employees or children of employees.

Applying *Options:* deferred entrance. *Application fee:* $40. *Required:* high school transcript. *Application deadline:* rolling (freshmen), rolling (transfers).

Admissions Contact Mr. Michael Darnell, Director of Admissions, South College-Asheville, 1567 Patton Avenue, Asheville, NC 28806. *Phone:* 828-252-2486. *Fax:* 828-252-8558. *E-mail:* ccdean@ioa.com.

SOUTHEASTERN COMMUNITY COLLEGE
Whiteville, North Carolina

- **State-supported** 2-year, founded 1964, part of North Carolina Community College System
- **Calendar** semesters
- **Degree** certificates, diplomas, and associate
- **Rural** 106-acre campus
- **Coed,** 2,460 undergraduate students, 88% full-time, 61% women, 39% men

Undergraduates 2,170 full-time, 290 part-time. Students come from 2 states and territories, 1% are from out of state, 30% African American, 0.2% Hispanic American, 4% Native American, 0.1% international.

Freshmen *Admission:* 985 applied, 985 admitted.

Faculty *Total:* 88, 82% full-time, 2% with terminal degrees.

Majors Administrative assistant and secretarial science; art; biological and physical sciences; business administration and management; clinical/medical laboratory technology; computer engineering technology; cosmetology; criminal justice/law enforcement administration; electrical, electronic and communications engineering technology; environmental studies; forestry technology; industrial technology; kindergarten/preschool education; liberal arts and sciences/liberal studies; music; nursing (registered nurse training); parks, recreation and leisure; parks, recreation and leisure facilities management; teacher assistant/aide; welding technology.

Academic Programs *Special study options:* academic remediation for entering students, adult/continuing education programs, advanced placement credit, cooperative education, distance learning, double majors, English as a second language, honors programs, independent study, internships, part-time degree program, services for LD students, summer session for credit.

Library Southeastern Community College Library with 50,297 titles, 192 serial subscriptions, an OPAC.

Computers on Campus 80 computers available on campus for general student use. A campuswide network can be accessed. Internet access, at least one staffed computer lab available.

Student Life *Housing:* college housing not available. *Activities and Organizations:* drama/theater group, choral group, Student Government Association,

Forestry Club, Nursing Club, Environmental Club. *Campus security:* 24-hour emergency response devices. *Student services:* personal/psychological counseling.
Athletics Member NJCAA. *Intercollegiate sports:* baseball M(s), softball W, squash W, volleyball W(s).
Standardized Tests *Required:* ACT ASSET, ACT COMPASS (for placement).
Costs (2003–04) *Tuition:* state resident $1198 full-time, $36 per semester hour part-time; nonresident $6366 full-time, $197 per semester hour part-time. *Required fees:* $62 full-time, $35 per term part-time.
Financial Aid Of all full-time matriculated undergraduates who enrolled, 80 Federal Work-Study jobs (averaging $1580).
Applying *Options:* common application, electronic application, early admission, deferred entrance. *Required:* high school transcript. *Application deadline:* rolling (freshmen), rolling (transfers).
Admissions Contact Ms. Linda Nelms, Coordinator of Student Records, Southeastern Community College, PO Box 151, Whiteville, NC 28472. *Phone:* 910-642-7141 Ext. 264. *Fax:* 910-642-5658. *E-mail:* jfowler@mail.southeast.cc.nc.us.

SOUTH PIEDMONT COMMUNITY COLLEGE
Polkton, North Carolina

Admissions Contact Ms. Jeania Martin, Admissions Coordinator, South Piedmont Community College, PO Box 126, Polkton, NC 28135. *Phone:* 704-272-7635. *Toll-free phone:* 800-766-0319. *Fax:* 704-272-8904. *E-mail:* j-martin@spcc.cc.nc.us.

SOUTHWESTERN COMMUNITY COLLEGE
Sylva, North Carolina

- **State-supported** 2-year, founded 1964, part of North Carolina Community College System
- **Calendar** semesters
- **Degree** certificates, diplomas, and associate
- **Small-town** 55-acre campus
- **Coed,** 1,939 undergraduate students, 46% full-time, 65% women, 35% men

Undergraduates 886 full-time, 1,053 part-time. Students come from 6 states and territories, 1 other country, 1% are from out of state, 1% African American, 0.4% Asian American or Pacific Islander, 0.8% Hispanic American, 12% Native American, 0.1% international, 8% transferred in.
Freshmen *Admission:* 342 enrolled. *Average high school GPA:* 2.90. *Test scores:* SAT verbal scores over 500: 5%; SAT math scores over 500: 5%; ACT scores over 18: 20%.
Faculty *Total:* 263, 25% full-time, 5% with terminal degrees. *Student/faculty ratio:* 12:1.
Majors Accounting; administrative assistant and secretarial science; automobile/automotive mechanics technology; business administration and management; child development; clinical/medical laboratory technology; commercial and advertising art; computer engineering technology; cosmetology; criminal justice/police science; culinary arts; electrical, electronic and communications engineering technology; emergency medical technology (EMT paramedic); environmental studies; health information/medical records administration; health information/medical records technology; information science/studies; legal assistant/paralegal; liberal arts and sciences/liberal studies; marketing/marketing management; massage therapy; medical radiologic technology; mental health/rehabilitation; nursing (licensed practical/vocational nurse training); nursing (registered nurse training); parks, recreation, and leisure related; physical therapist assistant; physical therapy; respiratory care therapy; substance abuse/addiction counseling; system, networking, and LAN/wan management; trade and industrial teacher education.
Academic Programs *Special study options:* academic remediation for entering students, adult/continuing education programs, cooperative education, distance learning, double majors, English as a second language, independent study, off-campus study, part-time degree program, services for LD students, summer session for credit.
Library Learning Resources Center with 27,428 titles, 257 serial subscriptions, 18,410 audiovisual materials, an OPAC.
Computers on Campus 400 computers available on campus for general student use. A campuswide network can be accessed from off campus. Internet access, at least one staffed computer lab available.
Student Life *Housing:* college housing not available. *Activities and Organizations:* Electronics Club, EMT Club, HIT Club, Cyber Crime Club, National Vocational-Technical Honor Society. *Campus security:* security during hours college is open. *Student services:* personal/psychological counseling.
Standardized Tests *Recommended:* SAT I or ACT (for admission).

Costs (2003–04) *Tuition:* state resident $1136 full-time, $34 per credit hour part-time; nonresident $6304 full-time, $191 per credit hour part-time. Full-time tuition and fees vary according to course load. Part-time tuition and fees vary according to course load. *Required fees:* $32 full-time, $1 per credit hour part-time.
Financial Aid Of all full-time matriculated undergraduates who enrolled, 55 Federal Work-Study jobs (averaging $900).
Applying *Options:* common application, early admission, deferred entrance. *Required:* high school transcript. *Required for some:* minimum 2.0 GPA, letters of recommendation, interview. *Application deadline:* rolling (freshmen), rolling (transfers). *Notification:* continuous (freshmen), continuous (transfers).
Admissions Contact Dr. Phil Weast, Director of Enrollment Management, Southwestern Community College, 447 College Drive, Sylva, NC 28779. *Phone:* 828-586-4091 Ext. 431. *Fax:* 828-586-3129. *E-mail:* pweast@southwest.cc.nc.us.

STANLY COMMUNITY COLLEGE
Albemarle, North Carolina

- **State-supported** 2-year, founded 1971, part of North Carolina Community College System
- **Calendar** semesters
- **Degree** certificates, diplomas, and associate
- **Small-town** 150-acre campus with easy access to Charlotte
- **Coed,** 2,000 undergraduate students

Undergraduates Students come from 13 states and territories, 3 other countries, 3% are from out of state.
Freshmen *Admission:* 642 applied, 642 admitted.
Faculty *Total:* 106, 50% full-time. *Student/faculty ratio:* 9:1.
Majors Accounting technology and bookkeeping; autobody/collision and repair technology; biomedical technology; business administration and management; child care and support services management; computer hardware engineering; computer/information technology services administration related; computer programming related; computer programming (specific applications); computer systems networking and telecommunications; computer/technical support; computer technology/computer systems technology; cosmetology; criminal justice/police science; electrical, electronic and communications engineering technology; executive assistant/executive secretary; human services; industrial technology; information science/studies; legal administrative assistant/secretary; mechanical drafting and CAD/CADD; medical administrative assistant and medical secretary; medical/clinical assistant; nursing (registered nurse training); occupational therapist assistant; physical therapist assistant; respiratory care therapy; system administration; web/multimedia management and webmaster; web page, digital/multimedia and information resources design; word processing.
Academic Programs *Special study options:* academic remediation for entering students, adult/continuing education programs, advanced placement credit, cooperative education, distance learning, double majors, English as a second language, independent study, internships, part-time degree program, services for LD students, summer session for credit.
Library 23,966 titles, 200 serial subscriptions, 2,500 audiovisual materials, an OPAC, a Web page.
Computers on Campus 100 computers available on campus for general student use. A campuswide network can be accessed. Internet access, at least one staffed computer lab available.
Student Life *Housing:* college housing not available. *Activities and Organizations:* student-run newspaper, television station. *Student services:* personal/psychological counseling.
Standardized Tests *Required:* ACT ASSET (for placement). *Recommended:* SAT I (for placement).
Costs (2003–04) *Tuition:* state resident $36 per credit hour part-time; nonresident $197 per credit hour part-time.
Financial Aid Of all full-time matriculated undergraduates who enrolled, 20 Federal Work-Study jobs (averaging $1800).
Applying *Options:* early admission, deferred entrance. *Required:* high school transcript. *Application deadline:* rolling (freshmen), rolling (transfers). *Notification:* continuous (freshmen), continuous (transfers).
Admissions Contact Mr. Ronnie Hinson, Director of Admissions, Stanly Community College, 141 College Drive, Albemarle, NC 28001. *Phone:* 704-982-0121 Ext. 233. *Fax:* 704-982-0819. *E-mail:* parksdf@stanly.cc.nc.us.

SURRY COMMUNITY COLLEGE
Dobson, North Carolina

- **State-supported** 2-year, founded 1965, part of North Carolina Community College System
- **Calendar** semesters

North Carolina

Surry Community College (continued)
- **Degree** certificates, diplomas, and associate
- **Rural** 100-acre campus
- **Coed**

Faculty *Student/faculty ratio:* 27:1.
Student Life *Campus security:* security guard during day and evening hours.
Athletics Member NJCAA.
Standardized Tests *Required:* CPT (for placement).
Financial Aid Of all full-time matriculated undergraduates who enrolled, 35 Federal Work-Study jobs (averaging $2800).
Applying *Options:* electronic application, early admission, deferred entrance. *Required:* high school transcript.
Admissions Contact Mr. Michael McHone, Vice President of Student Services, Surry Community College, PO Box 304, Dobson, NC 27017-0304. *Phone:* 336-386-3238. *Fax:* 336-386-8951. *E-mail:* mchonem@surry.cc.nc.us.

TRI-COUNTY COMMUNITY COLLEGE
Murphy, North Carolina

- **State-supported** 2-year, founded 1964, part of 278sck
- **Calendar** semesters
- **Degree** certificates, diplomas, and associate
- **Rural** 40-acre campus
- **Coed,** 1,234 undergraduate students, 45% full-time, 66% women, 34% men

Undergraduates 550 full-time, 684 part-time. Students come from 8 states and territories, 3% are from out of state, 0.9% African American, 1% Hispanic American, 2% Native American.
Freshmen *Admission:* 546 applied, 546 admitted. *Average high school GPA:* 2.9.
Faculty *Total:* 80, 58% full-time, 5% with terminal degrees. *Student/faculty ratio:* 21:1.
Majors Accounting; automobile/automotive mechanics technology; business administration and management; computer management; early childhood education; electrical, electronic and communications engineering technology; information technology; liberal arts and sciences/liberal studies; medical/clinical assistant; nursing (registered nurse training); welding technology.
Academic Programs *Special study options:* academic remediation for entering students, adult/continuing education programs, distance learning, double majors, part-time degree program, services for LD students, summer session for credit.
Library 16,224 titles, 306 serial subscriptions.
Computers on Campus 33 computers available on campus for general student use. A campuswide network can be accessed. Internet access available.
Student Life *Housing:* college housing not available. *Activities and Organizations:* student-run newspaper. *Student services:* personal/psychological counseling.
Standardized Tests *Required for some:* Assessment and Placement Services for Community Colleges. *Recommended:* SAT I (for placement).
Costs (2004–05) *Tuition:* state resident $852 full-time, $36 per credit hour part-time; nonresident $4728 full-time, $197 per credit hour part-time. *Required fees:* $60 full-time, $29 per term part-time.
Financial Aid Of all full-time matriculated undergraduates who enrolled, 11 Federal Work-Study jobs.
Applying *Required:* high school transcript. *Application deadline:* rolling (freshmen), rolling (transfers). *Notification:* continuous (freshmen), continuous (transfers).
Admissions Contact Mr. Jason Chambers, Director of Admissions, Tri-County Community College, 4600 East US 64, Murphy, NC 28906-7919. *Phone:* 828-837-6810 Ext. 4225.

VANCE-GRANVILLE COMMUNITY COLLEGE
Henderson, North Carolina

- **State-supported** 2-year, founded 1969, part of North Carolina Community College System
- **Calendar** semesters
- **Degree** certificates, diplomas, and associate
- **Rural** 83-acre campus with easy access to Raleigh
- **Endowment** $3.0 million
- **Coed,** 4,315 undergraduate students, 45% full-time, 66% women, 34% men

Undergraduates 1,921 full-time, 2,394 part-time. Students come from 10 states and territories, 15 other countries, 2% are from out of state, 48% African American, 0.4% Asian American or Pacific Islander, 1% Hispanic American, 1% Native American, 1% international, 2% transferred in.

Freshmen *Admission:* 1,765 applied, 1,765 admitted, 521 enrolled. *Average high school GPA:* 2.50.
Faculty *Total:* 353, 40% full-time, 5% with terminal degrees. *Student/faculty ratio:* 9:1.
Majors Accounting; administrative assistant and secretarial science; automobile/automotive mechanics technology; business administration and management; carpentry; child development; computer engineering technology; construction engineering technology; corrections; cosmetology; criminal justice/law enforcement administration; criminal justice/police science; data processing and data processing technology; education; electrical, electronic and communications engineering technology; elementary education; heating, air conditioning, ventilation and refrigeration maintenance technology; human services; industrial radiologic technology; industrial technology; kindergarten/preschool education; legal administrative assistant/secretary; liberal arts and sciences/liberal studies; medical administrative assistant and medical secretary; medical/clinical assistant; nursing (licensed practical/vocational nurse training); nursing (registered nurse training); parks, recreation and leisure; teacher assistant/aide; welding technology.
Academic Programs *Special study options:* academic remediation for entering students, accelerated degree program, adult/continuing education programs, advanced placement credit, cooperative education, distance learning, double majors, English as a second language, internships, part-time degree program, services for LD students, summer session for credit.
Library Vance-Granville Community College Learning Resource Center plus 1 other with 38,720 titles, 317 serial subscriptions, an OPAC, a Web page.
Computers on Campus 184 computers available on campus for general student use. A campuswide network can be accessed from off campus. Internet access, at least one staffed computer lab available.
Student Life *Housing:* college housing not available. *Activities and Organizations:* drama/theater group, Vocational Club, Phi Theta Kappa, Computer Club, Criminal Justice Club, Business Club. *Campus security:* 24-hour emergency response devices and patrols. *Student services:* personal/psychological counseling.
Athletics *Intramural sports:* basketball M/W, volleyball M/W.
Standardized Tests *Required for some:* ACT (for placement), nursing exam, Health Occupations Exam.
Costs (2004–05) *Tuition:* state resident $852 full-time, $36 per credit hour part-time; nonresident $4728 full-time, $197 per credit hour part-time. *Required fees:* $38 full-time, $14 per term part-time.
Financial Aid Of all full-time matriculated undergraduates who enrolled, 38 Federal Work-Study jobs (averaging $1750).
Applying *Options:* common application, early admission, deferred entrance. *Required:* high school transcript. *Application deadline:* rolling (freshmen), rolling (transfers). *Notification:* continuous (freshmen), continuous (transfers).
Admissions Contact Ms. Brenda W. Beck, Admissions Officer, Vance-Granville Community College, PO Box 917, State Road 1126, Henderson, NC 27536. *Phone:* 252-492-2061 Ext. 267. *Fax:* 252-430-0460.

WAKE TECHNICAL COMMUNITY COLLEGE
Raleigh, North Carolina

- **State and locally supported** 2-year, founded 1958, part of North Carolina Community College System
- **Calendar** semesters
- **Degree** certificates, diplomas, and associate
- **Suburban** 79-acre campus
- **Coed**

Faculty *Student/faculty ratio:* 11:1.
Student Life *Campus security:* 24-hour patrols.
Standardized Tests *Required:* ACT ASSET or ACT COMPASS (for placement). *Recommended:* SAT I or ACT (for placement).
Financial Aid Of all full-time matriculated undergraduates who enrolled, 35 Federal Work-Study jobs (averaging $2000). 15 state and other part-time jobs (averaging $2000).
Applying *Options:* common application, electronic application, early admission. *Required:* high school transcript.
Admissions Contact Ms. Susan Bloomfield, Director of Admissions, Wake Technical Community College, 9101 Fayetteville Road, Raleigh, NC 27603-5696. *Phone:* 919-662-3357. *Fax:* 919-662-3529. *E-mail:* reirelan@gwmail.wake.tec.nc.us.

WAYNE COMMUNITY COLLEGE
Goldsboro, North Carolina

- **State and locally supported** 2-year, founded 1957, part of North Carolina Community College System

- **Calendar** semesters
- **Degree** certificates, diplomas, and associate
- **Small-town** 125-acre campus
- **Endowment** $45,924
- **Coed**

Faculty *Student/faculty ratio:* 18:1.

Student Life *Campus security:* 24-hour emergency response devices and patrols, student patrols.

Standardized Tests *Required:* ACT ASSET (for placement).

Costs (2003–04) *Tuition:* state resident $1136 full-time, $34 per semester hour part-time; nonresident $6304 full-time, $191 per semester hour part-time. *Required fees:* $32 full-time, $8 per term part-time.

Financial Aid Of all full-time matriculated undergraduates who enrolled, 100 Federal Work-Study jobs (averaging $2000).

Applying *Options:* deferred entrance. *Required:* high school transcript, interview.

Admissions Contact Ms. Susan Mooring Sasser, Director of Admissions and Records, Wayne Community College, PO Box 8002, Goldsboro, NC 27533-8002. *Phone:* 919-735-5151 Ext. 216. *Fax:* 919-736-3204. *E-mail:* msm@wcc.wayne.cc.nc.us.

WESTERN PIEDMONT COMMUNITY COLLEGE
Morganton, North Carolina

- **State-supported** 2-year, founded 1964, part of North Carolina Community College System
- **Calendar** semesters
- **Degree** certificates, diplomas, and associate
- **Small-town** 130-acre campus
- **Coed**

Standardized Tests *Required:* ACT ASSET (for placement).

Costs (2004–05) *Tuition:* state resident $36 per credit hour part-time; nonresident $197 per credit hour part-time.

Financial Aid Of all full-time matriculated undergraduates who enrolled, 35 Federal Work-Study jobs (averaging $2150).

Applying *Required:* high school transcript.

Admissions Contact Mrs. Susan Williams, Director of Admissions, Western Piedmont Community College, 1001 Burkemont Avenue, Morganton, NC 28655-4511. *Phone:* 828-438-6051.

WILKES COMMUNITY COLLEGE
Wilkesboro, North Carolina

- **State-supported** 2-year, founded 1965, part of North Carolina Community College System
- **Calendar** semesters
- **Degree** certificates, diplomas, and associate
- **Small-town** 140-acre campus
- **Endowment** $2.5 million
- **Coed**

Faculty *Student/faculty ratio:* 8:1.

Student Life *Campus security:* 24-hour emergency response devices, student patrols, late-night transport/escort service.

Athletics Member NJCAA.

Standardized Tests *Required:* ACT COMPASS (for placement).

Costs (2003–04) *Tuition:* state resident $1136 full-time, $36 per credit hour part-time; nonresident $6304 full-time, $197 per credit hour part-time. Full-time tuition and fees vary according to course load. Part-time tuition and fees vary according to course load. *Required fees:* $45 full-time, $2 per credit hour part-time, $5 per term part-time. *Payment plans:* installment, deferred payment.

Financial Aid Of all full-time matriculated undergraduates who enrolled, 50 Federal Work-Study jobs (averaging $1800).

Applying *Options:* electronic application, deferred entrance. *Required:* high school transcript.

Admissions Contact Mr. Mac Warren, Director of Admissions, Wilkes Community College, PO Box 120, Wilkesboro, NC 28697. *Phone:* 336-838-6141. *Fax:* 336-838-6547. *E-mail:* mac.warren@wilkescc.edu.

WILSON TECHNICAL COMMUNITY COLLEGE
Wilson, North Carolina

- **State-supported** 2-year, founded 1958, part of North Carolina Community College System

- **Calendar** semesters
- **Degree** certificates, diplomas, and associate
- **Small-town** 35-acre campus
- **Endowment** $755,387
- **Coed,** 2,103 undergraduate students

Undergraduates Students come from 4 states and territories.

Freshmen *Admission:* 494 applied, 331 admitted.

Faculty *Total:* 90, 56% full-time, 4% with terminal degrees. *Student/faculty ratio:* 19:1.

Majors Accounting; administrative assistant and secretarial science; business administration and management; computer programming; criminal justice/law enforcement administration; electrical, electronic and communications engineering technology; emergency medical technology (EMT paramedic); fire science; general studies; industrial technology; information science/studies; kindergarten/preschool education; language interpretation and translation; legal assistant/paralegal; liberal arts and sciences/liberal studies; mechanical engineering/mechanical technology; nursing (registered nurse training); sign language interpretation and translation; tool and die technology.

Academic Programs *Special study options:* academic remediation for entering students, advanced placement credit, cooperative education, distance learning, double majors, English as a second language, independent study, internships, part-time degree program, services for LD students, summer session for credit.

Library 33,907 titles, 33,084 serial subscriptions, 7,117 audiovisual materials, an OPAC.

Computers on Campus 350 computers available on campus for general student use. A campuswide network can be accessed. Internet access, at least one staffed computer lab available.

Student Life *Housing:* college housing not available. *Campus security:* 11-hour patrols by trained security personnel. *Student services:* personal/psychological counseling.

Standardized Tests *Required:* ACT COMPASS (for placement).

Costs (2003–04) *Tuition:* state resident $1065 full-time; nonresident $5910 full-time. *Required fees:* $24 full-time.

Financial Aid Of all full-time matriculated undergraduates who enrolled, 65 Federal Work-Study jobs (averaging $1500).

Applying *Options:* common application, electronic application, deferred entrance. *Required:* high school transcript, interview. *Application deadline:* rolling (freshmen), rolling (transfers). *Notification:* continuous (freshmen), continuous (transfers).

Admissions Contact Ms. Denise Askew, Dean of Student Services, Wilson Technical Community College, PO Box 4305, Wilson, NC 27893-0305. *Phone:* 252-246-1275. *Fax:* 252-246-1285. *E-mail:* bpage@wilsontech.edu.

NORTH DAKOTA

AAKERS BUSINESS COLLEGE
Fargo, North Dakota

Admissions Contact Ms. Elizabeth Largent, Director, Aakers Business College, 4012 19th Avenue, SW, Fargo, ND 58103. *Phone:* 701-277-3889. *Toll-free phone:* 800-817-0009.

BISMARCK STATE COLLEGE
Bismarck, North Dakota

- **State-supported** 2-year, founded 1939, part of North Dakota University System
- **Calendar** semesters
- **Degree** certificates, diplomas, and associate
- **Suburban** 100-acre campus
- **Coed,** 3,430 undergraduate students, 67% full-time, 49% women, 51% men

Undergraduates 2,287 full-time, 1,143 part-time. Students come from 18 states and territories, 11 other countries, 8% are from out of state, 1% African American, 0.6% Asian American or Pacific Islander, 0.8% Hispanic American, 3% Native American, 0.2% international, 11% transferred in, 8% live on campus.

Freshmen *Admission:* 1,050 applied, 1,050 admitted, 1,050 enrolled.

Faculty *Total:* 198, 52% full-time, 9% with terminal degrees. *Student/faculty ratio:* 18:1.

Majors Administrative assistant and secretarial science; agricultural business and management; autobody/collision and repair technology; automobile/automotive mechanics technology; business automation/technology/data entry; business/commerce; carpentry; clinical/medical laboratory technology; commercial and advertising art; computer systems networking and telecommunications;

construction engineering technology; emergency medical technology (EMT paramedic); energy management and systems technology; heating, air conditioning, ventilation and refrigeration maintenance technology; hotel/motel administration; industrial technology; legal administrative assistant/secretary; liberal arts and sciences/liberal studies; lineworker; medical administrative assistant and medical secretary; nursing (licensed practical/vocational nurse training); surgical technology; welding technology.

Academic Programs *Special study options:* academic remediation for entering students, adult/continuing education programs, advanced placement credit, cooperative education, distance learning, part-time degree program, services for LD students, summer session for credit. *ROTC:* Army (c), Air Force (c).

Library Bismarck State College Library with 69,142 titles, 374 serial subscriptions, 6,518 audiovisual materials, an OPAC, a Web page.

Computers on Campus 420 computers available on campus for general student use. A campuswide network can be accessed from student residence rooms and from off campus. Internet access, online (class) registration, at least one staffed computer lab available.

Student Life *Housing Options:* men-only, women-only. Campus housing is university owned. *Activities and Organizations:* drama/theater group, student-run newspaper, choral group, Phi Theta Kappa, Drama Club, Art Club, Anime Club. *Campus security:* 24-hour emergency response devices and patrols, controlled dormitory access.

Athletics Member NJCAA. *Intercollegiate sports:* baseball M, basketball M(s)/W(s), golf M/W, tennis M/W, volleyball W(s). *Intramural sports:* basketball M, softball M, volleyball M/W.

Standardized Tests *Required:* SAT I or ACT (for admission).

Costs (2003–04) *Tuition:* state resident $2278 full-time; nonresident $5382 full-time. *Required fees:* $417 full-time. *Room and board:* $3300. *Waivers:* employees or children of employees.

Financial Aid Of all full-time matriculated undergraduates who enrolled, 84 Federal Work-Study jobs (averaging $1096).

Applying *Options:* common application, electronic application. *Application fee:* $35. *Required:* high school transcript. *Application deadlines:* rolling (freshmen), 8/1 (transfers). *Notification:* continuous (freshmen), continuous (transfers).

Admissions Contact Ms. Karla Gabriel, Dean of Admissions and Enrollment Services, Bismarck State College, PO Box 5587, Bismarck, ND 58506-5587. *Phone:* 701-224-5426. *Toll-free phone:* 800-445-5073 Ext. 45429 (in-state); 800-445-5073 (out-of-state). *Fax:* 701-224-5643. *E-mail:* karla.gabriel@bsc.nodak.edu.

CANKDESKA CIKANA COMMUNITY COLLEGE
Fort Totten, North Dakota

Admissions Contact Mr. Ermen Brown Jr., Registrar, Cankdeska Cikana Community College, PO Box 269, Fort Totten, ND 58335-0269. *Phone:* 701-766-1342.

FORT BERTHOLD COMMUNITY COLLEGE
New Town, North Dakota

Admissions Contact Mr. Russell Mason Jr., Registrar and Admissions Director, Fort Berthold Community College, PO Box 490, New Town, ND 58763-0490. *Phone:* 701-627-3665. *Fax:* 701-627-3609. *E-mail:* rmason@nt1.fort.berthold.cc.nd.us.

LAKE REGION STATE COLLEGE
Devils Lake, North Dakota

- **State-supported** 2-year, founded 1941, part of North Dakota University System
- **Calendar** semesters
- **Degree** certificates, diplomas, and associate
- **Small-town** 120-acre campus
- **Endowment** $2.2 million
- **Coed,** 1,473 undergraduate students, 27% full-time, 55% women, 45% men

Undergraduates 404 full-time, 1,069 part-time. Students come from 19 states and territories, 13 other countries, 15% are from out of state, 2% African American, 0.9% Asian American or Pacific Islander, 1% Hispanic American, 6% Native American, 4% international, 8% transferred in, 30% live on campus. *Retention:* 47% of 2002 full-time freshmen returned.

Freshmen *Admission:* 176 enrolled.

Faculty *Total:* 112, 27% full-time, 5% with terminal degrees. *Student/faculty ratio:* 15:1.

Majors Accounting; accounting technology and bookkeeping; administrative assistant and secretarial science; agricultural business and management; automobile/automotive mechanics technology; avionics maintenance technology; business administration and management; child care and support services management; child care provision; computer and information sciences; computer programming (specific applications); computer programming (vendor/product certification); computer science; computer systems networking and telecommunications; criminal justice/police science; diesel mechanics technology; electrical, electronics and communications engineering; electrical/electronics equipment installation and repair; executive assistant/executive secretary; fashion merchandising; information technology; legal administrative assistant/secretary; legal assistant/paralegal; liberal arts and sciences/liberal studies; management information systems; marketing research; medical administrative assistant and medical secretary; nursing assistant/aide and patient care assistant; nursing (licensed practical/vocational nurse training); office management; office occupations and clerical services; sales, distribution and marketing; sign language interpretation and translation; small business administration; technical teacher education.

Academic Programs *Special study options:* academic remediation for entering students, adult/continuing education programs, cooperative education, distance learning, double majors, English as a second language, freshman honors college, honors programs, internships, part-time degree program, summer session for credit.

Library Paul Hoghaug Library plus 1 other with 40,000 titles, 500 serial subscriptions, 8,000 audiovisual materials, an OPAC.

Computers on Campus 154 computers available on campus for general student use. A campuswide network can be accessed from student residence rooms. Internet access, online (class) registration, at least one staffed computer lab available. Computer purchase or lease plan available.

Student Life *Housing Options:* men-only, women-only. Campus housing is university owned. *Activities and Organizations:* drama/theater group, DECA, drama, SOTA (Students Other than Average), Student Senate, Computer Club. *Campus security:* 24-hour emergency response devices, controlled dormitory access. *Student services:* personal/psychological counseling.

Athletics Member NJCAA. *Intercollegiate sports:* basketball M(s)/W(s), volleyball W(s). *Intramural sports:* basketball M/W, bowling M, football M/W, golf M/W, ice hockey M/W, softball M/W, table tennis M/W, volleyball M/W.

Standardized Tests *Required:* SAT I or ACT (for admission).

Costs (2003–04) *Tuition:* state resident $2040 full-time, $85 per credit part-time; nonresident $2040 full-time, $85 per credit part-time. Full-time tuition and fees vary according to location and reciprocity agreements. Part-time tuition and fees vary according to location and reciprocity agreements. *Required fees:* $683 full-time, $22 per credit part-time, $341 per term part-time. *Room and board:* $3470. Room and board charges vary according to board plan and housing facility. *Waivers:* minority students, senior citizens, and employees or children of employees.

Financial Aid Of all full-time matriculated undergraduates who enrolled, 40 Federal Work-Study jobs (averaging $1600).

Applying *Options:* common application, electronic application. *Application fee:* $35. *Required:* high school transcript, immunizations. *Application deadline:* rolling (freshmen), rolling (transfers). *Notification:* continuous (freshmen), continuous (transfers).

Admissions Contact Ms. Denise Anderson, Administrative Assistant, Lake Region State College, 1801 College Drive North, Devils Lake, ND 58301. *Phone:* 701-662-1514. *Toll-free phone:* 800-443-1313 Ext. 514. *Fax:* 701-662-1570. *E-mail:* denise.d.anderson@lrsc.nodak.edu.

MINOT STATE UNIVERSITY-BOTTINEAU CAMPUS
Bottineau, North Dakota

- **State-supported** 2-year, founded 1906, part of North Dakota University System
- **Calendar** semesters
- **Degree** certificates, diplomas, and associate
- **Rural** 35-acre campus
- **Endowment** $1.0 million
- **Coed,** 620 undergraduate students, 62% full-time, 48% women, 52% men

Undergraduates 387 full-time, 233 part-time. Students come from 26 states and territories, 1 other country, 13% are from out of state, 2% African American, 1% Asian American or Pacific Islander, 0.6% Hispanic American, 5% Native American, 6% international, 7% transferred in, 45% live on campus.

Freshmen *Admission:* 298 applied, 298 admitted, 184 enrolled.

Faculty *Total:* 44, 59% full-time, 7% with terminal degrees. *Student/faculty ratio:* 11:1.

Majors Accounting technology and bookkeeping; administrative assistant and secretarial science; applied horticulture; applied horticulture/horticultural business services related; business administration and management; computer engineering related; computer engineering technology; computer systems networking and telecommunications; environmental engineering technology; executive assistant/executive secretary; fish/game management; forestry; greenhouse management; horticultural science; information science/studies; information technology; liberal arts and sciences/liberal studies; marketing/marketing management; medical administrative assistant and medical secretary; medical/clinical assistant; medical office management; natural resources/conservation; office occupations and clerical services; ornamental horticulture; receptionist; surveying engineering; system administration; turf and turfgrass management; water quality and wastewater treatment management and recycling technology; web/multimedia management and webmaster; web page, digital/multimedia and information resources design; wildlife and wildlands science and management.

Academic Programs *Special study options:* academic remediation for entering students, cooperative education, distance learning, double majors, internships, off-campus study, part-time degree program, services for LD students, summer session for credit.

Library Minot State University-Bottineau Library plus 1 other with 45,000 titles, 250 serial subscriptions, 800 audiovisual materials, an OPAC, a Web page.

Computers on Campus 60 computers available on campus for general student use. A campuswide network can be accessed from student residence rooms and from off campus. Internet access, at least one staffed computer lab available.

Student Life *Housing:* on-campus residence required through sophomore year. *Options:* coed, men-only, women-only. Campus housing is university owned. Freshman campus housing is guaranteed. *Activities and Organizations:* drama/theater group, choral group, Student Senate, Wildlife Club, Paul Bunyan Club, Horticulture Club, DECA. *Campus security:* controlled dormitory access. *Student services:* personal/psychological counseling.

Athletics Member NJCAA. *Intercollegiate sports:* baseball M, basketball M(s)/W(s), cheerleading M(s)/W(s), ice hockey M(s), volleyball W(s). *Intramural sports:* archery M/W, badminton M/W, basketball M/W, skiing (downhill) M/W, softball M/W, volleyball M/W.

Standardized Tests *Recommended:* SAT I or ACT (for placement).

Costs (2003–04) *Tuition:* state resident $2042 full-time, $85 per credit part-time; nonresident $5452 full-time, $227 per credit part-time. *Required fees:* $512 full-time, $21 per credit part-time. *Room and board:* $3166.

Financial Aid Of all full-time matriculated undergraduates who enrolled, 50 Federal Work-Study jobs (averaging $1100).

Applying *Options:* common application, electronic application, early admission, deferred entrance. *Application fee:* $35. *Required:* high school transcript. *Application deadline:* rolling (freshmen), rolling (transfers).

Admissions Contact Ms. Jody Klier, Admissions Counselor, Minot State University-Bottineau Campus, 105 Simrall Boulevard, Bottineau, ND 58318. *Phone:* 701-228-5426. *Toll-free phone:* 800-542-6866. *Fax:* 701-228-5499. *E-mail:* bergpla@misu.nodak.edu.

NORTH DAKOTA STATE COLLEGE OF SCIENCE
Wahpeton, North Dakota

- **State-supported** primarily 2-year, founded 1903, part of North Dakota University System
- **Calendar** semesters
- **Degrees** bachelor's, master's, doctoral, and first professional
- **Rural** 125-acre campus
- **Endowment** $4000
- **Coed**, 2,398 undergraduate students

Undergraduates Students come from 21 states and territories, 8 other countries, 27% are from out of state, 2% African American, 0.3% Asian American or Pacific Islander, 0.6% Hispanic American, 2% Native American, 1% international, 56% live on campus.

Freshmen *Average high school GPA:* 2.73. *Test scores:* ACT scores over 18: 58%; ACT scores over 24: 10%.

Faculty *Total:* 140, 91% full-time, 1% with terminal degrees. *Student/faculty ratio:* 15:1.

Majors Administrative assistant and secretarial science; agricultural business and management related; agricultural/farm supplies retailing and wholesaling; agricultural mechanization; agricultural production; architectural engineering technology; autobody/collision and repair technology; automobile/automotive mechanics technology; business/commerce; civil engineering technology; computer programming (specific applications); construction engineering technology; dental hygiene; diesel mechanics technology; electrical, electronic and communications engineering technology; foodservice systems administration; health information/medical records technology; heating, air conditioning and refrigeration technology; heating, air conditioning, ventilation and refrigeration maintenance technology; industrial electronics technology; industrial technology; liberal arts and sciences/liberal studies; machine shop technology; nursing (licensed practical/vocational nurse training); occupational therapist assistant; pharmacy technician; psychiatric/mental health services technology; small engine mechanics and repair technology; technical teacher education; vehicle maintenance and repair technologies related; welding technology.

Academic Programs *Special study options:* academic remediation for entering students, accelerated degree program, adult/continuing education programs, advanced placement credit, cooperative education, distance learning, English as a second language, internships, part-time degree program, services for LD students, student-designed majors, summer session for credit.

Library Mildred Johnson Library with 124,508 titles, 852 serial subscriptions, 4,178 audiovisual materials, an OPAC, a Web page.

Computers on Campus 450 computers available on campus for general student use. A campuswide network can be accessed from student residence rooms and from off campus. Internet access, at least one staffed computer lab available.

Student Life *Housing:* on-campus residence required for freshman year. *Options:* coed, men-only, women-only. Campus housing is university owned. *Activities and Organizations:* drama/theater group, choral group, marching band, Student Health Advisory Club, Drama Club, Inter-Varsity Christian Fellowship, Cultural Diversity, Habitat for Humanity. *Campus security:* 24-hour emergency response devices and patrols, student patrols, late-night transport/escort service, controlled dormitory access. *Student services:* health clinic, personal/psychological counseling, legal services.

Athletics Member NJCAA. *Intercollegiate sports:* basketball M(s)/W(s), football M(s), volleyball W(s). *Intramural sports:* basketball M/W, football M, racquetball M/W, softball M/W, volleyball M/W.

Standardized Tests *Required:* ACT (for placement).

Costs (2003–04) *Tuition:* state resident $2052 full-time; nonresident $5478 full-time. Full-time tuition and fees vary according to reciprocity agreements. Part-time tuition and fees vary according to reciprocity agreements. *Required fees:* $450 full-time. *Room and board:* $4066; room only: $1269. *Payment plans:* installment, deferred payment. *Waivers:* employees or children of employees.

Financial Aid Of all full-time matriculated undergraduates who enrolled, 90 Federal Work-Study jobs (averaging $1500).

Applying *Options:* common application, electronic application, early admission. *Application fee:* $35. *Required:* high school transcript. *Application deadline:* rolling (freshmen), rolling (transfers). *Notification:* continuous (freshmen), continuous (transfers).

Admissions Contact Mr. Keath Borchert, Director of Enrollment Services, North Dakota State College of Science, 800 North 6th Street, Wahpeton, ND 58076. *Phone:* 701-671-2189 Ext. 2189. *Toll-free phone:* 800-342-4325 Ext. 2202. *Fax:* 701-671-2332.

SITTING BULL COLLEGE
Fort Yates, North Dakota

- **Independent** 2-year, founded 1973
- **Calendar** semesters
- **Degree** certificates and associate
- **Rural** campus
- **Endowment** $541,000
- **Coed**

Faculty *Student/faculty ratio:* 6:1.

Standardized Tests *Required:* TABE (for placement).

Financial Aid Of all full-time matriculated undergraduates who enrolled, 20 Federal Work-Study jobs (averaging $2000).

Applying *Options:* early admission. *Required:* high school transcript, medical questionnaire.

Admissions Contact Ms. Melody Silk, Director of Registration and Admissions, Sitting Bull College, 1341 92nd Street, Fort Yates, ND 58538-9701. *Phone:* 701-854-3864.

TURTLE MOUNTAIN COMMUNITY COLLEGE
Belcourt, North Dakota

Admissions Contact Ms. Joni LaFontaine, Admissions/Records Officer, Turtle Mountain Community College, Box 340, Belcourt, ND 58316-0340. *Phone:* 701-477-5605 Ext. 217. *Fax:* 701-477-8967.

UNITED TRIBES TECHNICAL COLLEGE
Bismarck, North Dakota

- **Federally supported** 2-year, founded 1969
- **Calendar** semesters
- **Degree** certificates and associate
- **Small-town** 105-acre campus
- **Coed**, 678 undergraduate students

United Tribes Technical College (continued)

Freshmen *Admission:* 149 applied, 117 admitted.

Faculty *Total:* 37, 100% full-time. *Student/faculty ratio:* 8:1.

Majors Automobile/automotive mechanics technology; business administration and management; carpentry; child care provision; computer systems analysis; computer systems networking and telecommunications; criminal justice/law enforcement administration; criminal justice/police science; developmental and child psychology; dietetics; entrepreneurship; fine arts related; health information/medical records administration; health information/medical records technology; hospitality administration; hotel/motel administration; human services; kindergarten/preschool education; legal professions and studies related; nursing (licensed practical/vocational nurse training); nursing (registered nurse training); office occupations and clerical services; welding technology.

Academic Programs *Special study options:* academic remediation for entering students, cooperative education, honors programs, internships, part-time degree program, summer session for credit.

Library United Tribes Technical College Library plus 1 other with 6,000 titles, 86 serial subscriptions, an OPAC, a Web page.

Computers on Campus 210 computers available on campus for general student use. At least one staffed computer lab available.

Student Life *Housing Options:* men-only, women-only. *Activities and Organizations:* student-run newspaper. *Campus security:* 24-hour emergency response devices and patrols. *Student services:* personal/psychological counseling.

Athletics Member NJCAA. *Intercollegiate sports:* basketball M, cross-country running M/W. *Intramural sports:* basketball M, volleyball M/W.

Standardized Tests *Recommended:* TABE.

Costs (2003–04) *One-time required fee:* $100. *Tuition:* $88 per credit part-time; state resident $2100 full-time, $88 per credit part-time; nonresident $2100 full-time. No tuition increase for student's term of enrollment. *Required fees:* $530 full-time. *Room and board:* $3000. Room and board charges vary according to housing facility. *Payment plan:* installment.

Applying *Required:* high school transcript. *Application deadline:* rolling (freshmen), rolling (transfers).

Admissions Contact Ms. Vivian Gillett, Director of Admissions, United Tribes Technical College, 3315 University Drive, Bismarck, ND 58504. *Phone:* 701-255-3285 Ext. 1334. *Fax:* 701-530-0640. *E-mail:* ndvivian@hotmail.com.

WILLISTON STATE COLLEGE
Williston, North Dakota

- **State-supported** 2-year, founded 1957, part of North Dakota University System
- **Calendar** semesters
- **Degree** certificates, diplomas, and associate
- **Small-town** 80-acre campus
- **Endowment** $52,200
- **Coed,** 871 undergraduate students, 69% full-time, 65% women, 35% men

Undergraduates 603 full-time, 268 part-time. Students come from 9 states and territories, 3 other countries, 14% are from out of state, 0.7% African American, 0.7% Asian American or Pacific Islander, 0.9% Hispanic American, 5% Native American, 2% international, 64% transferred in, 13% live on campus.

Freshmen *Admission:* 295 applied, 285 admitted, 249 enrolled.

Faculty *Total:* 93, 32% full-time. *Student/faculty ratio:* 14:1.

Majors Accounting technology and bookkeeping; administrative assistant and secretarial science; agriculture; automobile/automotive mechanics technology; computer and information sciences and support services related; data processing and data processing technology; diesel mechanics technology; entrepreneurial and small business related; health information/medical records technology; liberal arts and sciences/liberal studies; marketing/marketing management; medical transcription; multi-/interdisciplinary studies related; nursing (licensed practical/vocational nurse training); physical therapist assistant.

Academic Programs *Special study options:* academic remediation for entering students, advanced placement credit, cooperative education, distance learning, honors programs, independent study, off-campus study, part-time degree program, services for LD students, student-designed majors, summer session for credit.

Library Williston State College Library with 16,218 titles, 214 serial subscriptions, 475 audiovisual materials, an OPAC, a Web page.

Computers on Campus 150 computers available on campus for general student use. A campuswide network can be accessed from student residence rooms and from off campus. Internet access, at least one staffed computer lab available. Computer purchase or lease plan available.

Student Life *Housing Options:* coed, men-only, women-only, cooperative. Campus housing is university owned. *Activities and Organizations:* drama/theater group, student-run newspaper, choral group, PTK, PBL, Student Senate, VICA, Student Nurses Association, national sororities. *Campus security:* controlled dormitory access. *Student services:* personal/psychological counseling.

Athletics Member NJCAA. *Intercollegiate sports:* baseball M(s), basketball M(s)/W(s), golf M/W, volleyball W(s). *Intramural sports:* basketball M/W, volleyball M/W.

Standardized Tests *Required for some:* ACT (for placement).

Costs (2004–05) *Tuition:* state resident $2074 full-time, $80 per credit part-time; nonresident $3111 full-time, $120 per credit part-time. *Required fees:* $530 full-time, $22 per credit part-time. *Room and board:* $2500; room only: $1000.

Financial Aid Of all full-time matriculated undergraduates who enrolled, 30 Federal Work-Study jobs (averaging $1500). 15 state and other part-time jobs (averaging $1000).

Applying *Options:* common application, electronic application. *Application fee:* $35. *Required:* high school transcript. *Application deadline:* rolling (freshmen), rolling (transfers). *Notification:* continuous (freshmen), continuous (transfers).

Admissions Contact Ms. Jan Solem, Director for Admission and Records, Williston State College, PO Box 1326, Williston, ND 58802-1326. *Phone:* 701-774-4554. *Toll-free phone:* 888-863-9455. *Fax:* 701-774-4211. *E-mail:* wsc.admission@wsc.nodak.edu.

OHIO

ACADEMY OF COURT REPORTING
Cleveland, Ohio

Admissions Contact Ms. Sheila Woods, Director of Admissions, Academy of Court Reporting, 2044 Euclid Avenue, Cleveland, OH 44115. *Phone:* 216-861-3222.

AEC SOUTHERN OHIO COLLEGE
North Canton, Ohio

- **Proprietary** 2-year, founded 1929, part of Educational Management Corporation
- **Calendar** quarters
- **Degree** diplomas and associate
- **Suburban** campus
- **Coed,** 700 undergraduate students

Undergraduates Students come from 1 other state.

Faculty *Total:* 35, 34% full-time.

Majors Business administration and management; computer programming related; computer programming (specific applications); computer systems networking and telecommunications; criminal justice/safety; drafting and design technology; electrical, electronic and communications engineering technology; graphic design; legal assistant/paralegal; medical administrative assistant and medical secretary; medical/clinical assistant.

Academic Programs *Special study options:* adult/continuing education programs, advanced placement credit, independent study.

Computers on Campus 65 computers available on campus for general student use. Internet access available.

Student Life *Housing:* college housing not available. *Activities and Organizations:* student-run newspaper.

Standardized Tests *Required:* ACT ASSET (for admission).

Costs (2004–05) *Tuition:* $14,976 full-time, $156 per credit hour part-time.

Applying *Options:* common application. *Application deadline:* rolling (freshmen).

Admissions Contact Mr. Greg Laudermilt, Admissions Director, AEC Southern Ohio College, 1320 West Maple Street, NW, North Canton, OH 44720-2854. *Phone:* 330-494-1214.

AEC SOUTHERN OHIO COLLEGE, AKRON CAMPUS
Akron, Ohio

- **Proprietary** 2-year, founded 1968
- **Calendar** quarters
- **Degree** certificates, diplomas, and associate
- **Suburban** 3-acre campus with easy access to Cleveland
- **Coed**

Faculty *Student/faculty ratio:* 12:1.

Student Life *Campus security:* late-night transport/escort service.

Standardized Tests *Required:* CCAP (for placement). *Recommended:* SAT I or ACT (for placement).
Applying *Options:* early admission, deferred entrance. *Application fee:* $20. *Recommended:* minimum 2.0 GPA.
Admissions Contact Ms. Sheila Freeman, Director of Admissions, AEC Southern Ohio College, Akron Campus, 2791 Mogadore Road, Akron, OH 44312-1596. *Phone:* 330-733-8766.

AEC SOUTHERN OHIO COLLEGE, CINCINNATI CAMPUS
Cincinnati, Ohio

- **Proprietary** 2-year, founded 1927, part of American Education Centers, Inc
- **Calendar** quarters
- **Degree** certificates, diplomas, and associate
- **Suburban** 3-acre campus
- **Coed**

Faculty *Student/faculty ratio:* 16:1.
Student Life *Campus security:* 24-hour emergency response devices, night security guard on-campus.
Financial Aid Of all full-time matriculated undergraduates who enrolled, 4 Federal Work-Study jobs.
Applying *Options:* common application, early admission, deferred entrance. *Application fee:* $20. *Required:* high school transcript, interview.
Admissions Contact Ms. Cherie McNeel, Director of Admissions, AEC Southern Ohio College, Cincinnati Campus, 1011 Glendale-Milford Road, Cincinnati, OH 45215. *Phone:* 513-771-2424. *Fax:* 513-771-3413.

AEC SOUTHERN OHIO COLLEGE, FINDLAY CAMPUS
Findlay, Ohio

- **Proprietary** 2-year, founded 1929
- **Calendar** continuous
- **Degree** diplomas and associate
- **Rural** 1-acre campus
- **Coed**

Faculty *Student/faculty ratio:* 15:1.
Student Life *Campus security:* 24-hour emergency response devices.
Standardized Tests *Required:* CPAt (for placement).
Costs (2003–04) *Tuition:* $7700 full-time. *Required fees:* $480 full-time.
Applying *Options:* common application. *Application fee:* $25. *Required:* high school transcript, interview.
Admissions Contact Ms. Kathy Pichacz, Senior Admissions, AEC Southern Ohio College, Findlay Campus, 1637 Tiffin Avenue, Findlay, OH 45840. *Phone:* 419-423-2211. *Toll-free phone:* 800-842-3687. *Fax:* 419-423-0725. *E-mail:* stautfin@ohio.tds.net.

ANTONELLI COLLEGE
Cincinnati, Ohio

- **Proprietary** 2-year, founded 1947
- **Calendar** quarters
- **Degree** diplomas and associate
- **Urban** campus
- **Coed,** 387 undergraduate students, 56% full-time, 76% women, 24% men

Undergraduates 216 full-time, 171 part-time. Students come from 6 states and territories, 20% are from out of state, 12% African American, 3% Asian American or Pacific Islander, 1% Hispanic American, 1% Native American.
Freshmen *Admission:* 130 applied, 118 admitted.
Faculty *Total:* 58, 24% full-time, 2% with terminal degrees. *Student/faculty ratio:* 10:1.
Majors Accounting and business/management; commercial and advertising art; computer and information sciences; computer systems networking and telecommunications; graphic design; interior design; photography; web/multimedia management and webmaster.
Academic Programs *Special study options:* honors programs, internships, part-time degree program, summer session for credit.
Library Main Library plus 1 other with 2,000 titles, 30 serial subscriptions.
Computers on Campus 46 computers available on campus for general student use. Internet access, at least one staffed computer lab available.
Student Life *Housing:* college housing not available. *Campus security:* 24-hour emergency response devices, security personnel while classes are in session. *Student services:* personal/psychological counseling.

Costs (2003–04) *Tuition:* $15,400 full-time, $325 per credit hour part-time. Full-time tuition and fees vary according to course load and program. Part-time tuition and fees vary according to course load and program. *Required fees:* $1440 full-time, $350 per term part-time. *Payment plan:* installment.
Applying *Options:* early admission, deferred entrance. *Application fee:* $100. *Required:* high school transcript, interview. *Required for some:* art portfolio. *Application deadline:* rolling (freshmen), rolling (transfers). *Notification:* continuous (transfers).
Admissions Contact Ms. Connie D. Sharp, Director, Antonelli College, 124 East Seventh Street, Cincinnati, OH 45202. *Phone:* 513-241-4338. *Toll-free phone:* 800-505-4338. *Fax:* 513-241-9396. *E-mail:* tess@antonellic.com.

THE ART INSTITUTE OF CINCINNATI
Cincinnati, Ohio

- **Proprietary** 2-year
- **Degree** associate
- **Coed**

Faculty *Student/faculty ratio:* 20:1.
Student Life *Campus security:* 24-hour emergency response devices.
Costs (2003–04) *Tuition:* $13,596 full-time. *Required fees:* $2530 full-time.
Applying *Required:* high school transcript, letters of recommendation, interview, portfolio.
Admissions Contact Ms. Cyndi Mendell, Admissions, The Art Institute of Cincinnati, 1171 East Kemper Road, Cincinnati, OH 45246. *Phone:* 513-751-1206. *E-mail:* acacollege@fuse.net.

ATS INSTITUTE OF TECHNOLOGY
Highland Heights, Ohio

Admissions Contact 230 Alpha Park, Highland Heights, OH 44143.

BELMONT TECHNICAL COLLEGE
St. Clairsville, Ohio

- **State-supported** 2-year, founded 1971, part of Ohio Board of Regents
- **Calendar** quarters
- **Degree** diplomas and associate
- **Rural** 55-acre campus
- **Coed**

Standardized Tests *Required:* ACT COMPASS (for placement).
Costs (2003–04) *Tuition:* state resident $2496 full-time, $52 per credit hour part-time; nonresident $4770 full-time, $106 per credit hour part-time. *Required fees:* $480 full-time, $10 per credit hour part-time, $5 per term part-time.
Financial Aid Of all full-time matriculated undergraduates who enrolled, 15 Federal Work-Study jobs (averaging $4500).
Applying *Options:* early admission.
Admissions Contact Mr. Thomas J. Tarowsky, Dean of Student Success, Belmont Technical College, 120 Fox Shannon Place, St. Clairsville, OH 43950-9735. *Phone:* 740-695-9500 Ext. 1064. *Toll-free phone:* 800-423-1188. *E-mail:* ttarowsk@belmont.tech.oh.us.

BOHECKER'S BUSINESS COLLEGE
Ravenna, Ohio

Admissions Contact 326 East Main Street, Ravenna, OH 44266.

BOWLING GREEN STATE UNIVERSITY-FIRELANDS COLLEGE
Huron, Ohio

- **State-supported** 2-year, founded 1968, part of Bowling Green State University System
- **Calendar** semesters
- **Degrees** certificates and associate (also offers some upper-level and graduate courses)
- **Rural** 216-acre campus with easy access to Cleveland and Toledo
- **Endowment** $1.2 million
- **Coed,** 1,738 undergraduate students, 52% full-time, 68% women, 32% men

Bowling Green State University-Firelands College (continued)

Undergraduates 912 full-time, 826 part-time. Students come from 2 states and territories, 7% African American, 0.4% Asian American or Pacific Islander, 3% Hispanic American, 0.4% Native American, 21% transferred in. *Retention:* 42% of 2002 full-time freshmen returned.

Freshmen *Admission:* 447 applied, 432 admitted, 352 enrolled. *Average high school GPA:* 2.73. *Test scores:* SAT verbal scores over 500: 47%; SAT math scores over 500: 47%; ACT scores over 18: 79%; SAT math scores over 600: 7%; ACT scores over 24: 18%.

Faculty *Total:* 106, 36% full-time, 29% with terminal degrees. *Student/faculty ratio:* 20:1.

Majors Accounting technology and bookkeeping; biological and physical sciences; business operations support and secretarial services related; communications technologies and support services related; computer engineering technology; computer programming; computer systems networking and telecommunications; computer/technical support; criminal justice/safety; design and visual communications; education; electrical, electronic and communications engineering technology; engineering technologies related; family and community services; health information/medical records administration; health professions related; humanities; human services; industrial technology; interdisciplinary studies; kindergarten/preschool education; liberal arts and sciences/liberal studies; mechanical design technology; nursing (registered nurse training); operations management; pre-engineering; respiratory care therapy; social sciences.

Academic Programs *Special study options:* academic remediation for entering students, adult/continuing education programs, advanced placement credit, distance learning, double majors, independent study, internships, part-time degree program, services for LD students, student-designed majors, summer session for credit. *ROTC:* Army (c), Air Force (c).

Library Firelands College Library with 38,658 titles, 230 serial subscriptions, 2,752 audiovisual materials, an OPAC, a Web page.

Computers on Campus 300 computers available on campus for general student use. A campuswide network can be accessed from off campus. Internet access, at least one staffed computer lab available.

Student Life *Housing:* college housing not available. *Activities and Organizations:* drama/theater group, Speech Activities Organization, Allied Health Club, student government, Intramural Club, Campus Fellowship. *Campus security:* 24-hour emergency response devices, late-night transport/escort service, patrols by trained security personnel.

Athletics *Intramural sports:* basketball M/W, football M/W, skiing (downhill) M(c)/W(c), softball M/W, volleyball M/W, weight lifting M(c)/W(c).

Standardized Tests *Required for some:* SAT I or ACT (for placement).

Costs (2003–04) *Tuition:* state resident $3790 full-time, $177 per credit hour part-time; nonresident $10,750 full-time, $509 per credit hour part-time. Full-time tuition and fees vary according to course load. Part-time tuition and fees vary according to course load. *Required fees:* $170 full-time, $10 per credit hour part-time, $85 per term part-time. *Payment plans:* installment, deferred payment. *Waivers:* children of alumni and employees or children of employees.

Applying *Options:* electronic application, early admission, deferred entrance. *Application fee:* $35. *Required:* high school transcript. *Application deadlines:* 8/15 (freshmen), 8/15 (transfers). *Notification:* continuous until 8/15 (freshmen), continuous until 8/15 (transfers).

Admissions Contact Ms. Debralee Divers, Director of Admissions and Financial Aid, Bowling Green State University-Firelands College, One University Drive, Huron, OH 44839. *Phone:* 419-433-5560. *Toll-free phone:* 800-322-4787. *Fax:* 419-372-0604. *E-mail:* divers@bgnet.bgsu.edu.

BRADFORD SCHOOL
Columbus, Ohio

- **Proprietary** 2-year, founded 1911
- **Calendar** semesters
- **Degree** diplomas and associate
- **Suburban** campus
- **Coed,** 312 undergraduate students, 100% full-time, 76% women, 24% men

Undergraduates 312 full-time. Students come from 2 states and territories, 5 other countries, 32% African American, 2% Asian American or Pacific Islander, 3% Hispanic American, 1% transferred in, 41% live on campus.

Freshmen *Admission:* 613 applied, 548 admitted, 223 enrolled. *Average high school GPA:* 2.60.

Faculty *Total:* 11, 55% full-time, 64% with terminal degrees. *Student/faculty ratio:* 25:1.

Majors Accounting; administrative assistant and secretarial science; computer programming; computer programming (specific applications); graphic design; legal administrative assistant/secretary; legal assistant/paralegal; medical/clinical assistant; tourism and travel services management.

Academic Programs *Special study options:* adult/continuing education programs, cooperative education, internships.

Library Resource Center with 2,000 titles, 15 serial subscriptions, 100 audiovisual materials, an OPAC.

Computers on Campus 102 computers available on campus for general student use. Internet access available.

Student Life *Housing Options:* coed, women-only, disabled students. Campus housing is leased by the school. Freshman applicants given priority for college housing. *Activities and Organizations:* International Association of Administrative Professionals. *Campus security:* 24-hour patrols.

Costs (2004–05) *Tuition:* $11,000 full-time. No tuition increase for student's term of enrollment. *Room only:* $5000. *Payment plan:* installment. *Waivers:* employees or children of employees.

Applying *Options:* common application, electronic application. *Application fee:* $50. *Required:* high school transcript, interview. *Application deadline:* rolling (freshmen), rolling (transfers).

Admissions Contact Ms. Raeann Lee, Director of Admissions, Bradford School, 2469 Stelzer Road, Columbus, OH 43219. *Phone:* 614-416-6200. *Toll-free phone:* 800-678-7981. *Fax:* 614-416-6210. *E-mail:* info@bradfordschoolcolumbus.edu.

BRYANT AND STRATTON COLLEGE
Parma, Ohio

- **Proprietary** 2-year, founded 1981, part of Bryant and Stratton Business Institute, Inc
- **Calendar** semesters
- **Degree** associate
- **Suburban** 4-acre campus with easy access to Cleveland
- **Coed,** 225 undergraduate students, 55% full-time, 79% women, 21% men

Undergraduates 123 full-time, 102 part-time. Students come from 1 other state, 22% African American, 0.4% Asian American or Pacific Islander, 8% Hispanic American, 3% transferred in. *Retention:* 47% of 2002 full-time freshmen returned.

Freshmen *Admission:* 83 applied, 78 enrolled. *Average high school GPA:* 2.39.

Faculty *Total:* 27, 22% full-time. *Student/faculty ratio:* 11:1.

Majors Accounting; administrative assistant and secretarial science; business administration and management; computer and information sciences; medical administrative assistant and medical secretary; medical/clinical assistant.

Academic Programs *Special study options:* academic remediation for entering students, cooperative education, distance learning, double majors, independent study, internships, part-time degree program, summer session for credit.

Library Main Library plus 1 other with 1,500 titles, 20 serial subscriptions, an OPAC.

Computers on Campus 96 computers available on campus for general student use. Internet access available.

Student Life *Housing:* college housing not available. *Activities and Organizations:* student-run newspaper, Business Professionals of America, Association for Computing Machinery, Baccus Gamma. *Campus security:* 24-hour emergency response devices. *Student services:* personal/psychological counseling.

Standardized Tests *Required:* CPAt (for admission). *Recommended:* SAT I or ACT (for admission).

Costs (2004–05) *Tuition:* $10,920 full-time, $364 per credit part-time. Full-time tuition and fees vary according to course load. Part-time tuition and fees vary according to course load. *Required fees:* $225 full-time. *Payment plan:* installment. *Waivers:* employees or children of employees.

Applying *Options:* deferred entrance. *Application fee:* $25. *Required:* essay or personal statement, high school transcript, interview. *Required for some:* 2 letters of recommendation. *Recommended:* minimum 2.0 GPA. *Application deadline:* 6/30 (freshmen), rolling (transfers).

Admissions Contact Ms. Shari Grasso, Director of Admissions, Bryant and Stratton College, 12955 Snow Road, Parma, OH 44130. *Phone:* 216-265-3151 Ext. 229. *Toll-free phone:* 800-327-3151. *Fax:* 216-265-0325. *E-mail:* slgrasso@bryantstratton.edu.

BRYANT AND STRATTON COLLEGE
Willoughby Hills, Ohio

Admissions Contact Mr. James Pettit, Director of Admissions, Bryant and Stratton College, 27557 Chardon Road, Willoughby Hills, OH 44092. *Phone:* 440-944-6800. *Fax:* 440-944-9260. *E-mail:* jwpettit@bryantstratton.edu.

CENTRAL OHIO TECHNICAL COLLEGE
Newark, Ohio

- **State-supported** 2-year, founded 1971, part of Ohio Board of Regents
- **Calendar** quarters
- **Degree** certificates and associate
- **Small-town** 155-acre campus with easy access to Columbus

■ **Coed**

Faculty *Student/faculty ratio:* 45:1.
Student Life *Campus security:* 24-hour emergency response devices, student patrols, late-night transport/escort service.
Standardized Tests *Required:* ACT ASSET or ACT COMPASS (for placement).
Costs (2003–04) *Tuition:* state resident $2862 full-time, $73 per credit part-time; nonresident $5022 full-time, $133 per credit part-time. *Required fees:* $216 full-time, $6 per credit part-time.
Applying *Options:* common application, electronic application, early admission, deferred entrance. *Application fee:* $15. *Required:* high school transcript.
Admissions Contact Admissions Representative, Central Ohio Technical College, 1179 University Drive, Newark, OH 43055-1767. *Phone:* 740-366-9222. *Toll-free phone:* 800-9NEWARK. *Fax:* 740-366-5047. *E-mail:* lnelson@ bigvax.newark.ohio-state.edu.

CHATFIELD COLLEGE
St. Martin, Ohio

■ **Independent** 2-year, founded 1970, affiliated with Roman Catholic Church
■ **Calendar** semesters
■ **Degree** associate
■ **Rural** 200-acre campus with easy access to Cincinnati and Dayton
■ **Endowment** $700,000
■ **Coed, primarily women,** 230 undergraduate students

Undergraduates Students come from 1 other state, 30% African American.
Freshmen *Admission:* 129 applied, 129 admitted.
Faculty *Total:* 43, 7% full-time. *Student/faculty ratio:* 12:1.
Majors Business administration and management; human services; kindergarten/ preschool education; liberal arts and sciences/liberal studies.
Academic Programs *Special study options:* academic remediation for entering students, adult/continuing education programs, advanced placement credit, internships, off-campus study, part-time degree program, summer session for credit.
Library Chatfield College Library with 15,000 titles, 30 serial subscriptions, an OPAC.
Computers on Campus 16 computers available on campus for general student use. A campuswide network can be accessed from off campus. Internet access, at least one staffed computer lab available.
Student Life *Housing:* college housing not available. *Activities and Organizations:* drama/theater group, student-run newspaper. *Campus security:* 12-hour night patrols by security. *Student services:* personal/psychological counseling.
Costs (2004–05) *Tuition:* $235 per credit hour part-time. *Required fees:* $130 per term part-time.
Financial Aid Of all full-time matriculated undergraduates who enrolled, 10 Federal Work-Study jobs (averaging $800). 4 state and other part-time jobs (averaging $600). *Financial aid deadline:* 8/1.
Applying *Options:* common application, early admission, deferred entrance. *Application fee:* $10. *Required:* high school transcript. *Application deadline:* rolling (freshmen), rolling (transfers). *Notification:* continuous (freshmen), continuous (transfers).
Admissions Contact Mr. Bill F. Balzano PhD, Director of Admissions, Chatfield College, St. Martin, OH 45118. *Phone:* 513-875-3344. *Fax:* 513-875-3912. *E-mail:* chatfield@chatfield.edu.

CINCINNATI COLLEGE OF MORTUARY SCIENCE
Cincinnati, Ohio

■ **Independent** primarily 2-year, founded 1882
■ **Calendar** quarters
■ **Degrees** associate and bachelor's
■ **Urban** 10-acre campus
■ **Coed,** 121 undergraduate students, 100% full-time, 37% women, 63% men

Undergraduates 121 full-time. Students come from 17 states and territories, 8% African American, 75% transferred in.
Freshmen *Admission:* 30 applied, 14 admitted, 14 enrolled.
Faculty *Total:* 12, 58% full-time. *Student/faculty ratio:* 5:1.
Majors Funeral service and mortuary science.
Academic Programs *Special study options:* academic remediation for entering students, adult/continuing education programs, advanced placement credit, summer session for credit.
Library 5,000 titles, 30 serial subscriptions, a Web page.
Computers on Campus 16 computers available on campus for general student use. At least one staffed computer lab available.

Student Life *Housing:* college housing not available.
Athletics *Intramural sports:* basketball M/W, bowling M/W, football M/W, softball M/W.
Costs (2004–05) *Tuition:* $12,900 full-time, $172 per credit hour part-time. *Required fees:* $120 full-time, $60 per term part-time.
Applying *Options:* deferred entrance. *Application fee:* $25. *Required:* high school transcript. *Recommended:* letters of recommendation. *Application deadline:* rolling (freshmen), rolling (transfers).
Admissions Contact Ms. Pat Leon, Director of Financial Aid, Cincinnati College of Mortuary Science, 645 West North Bend Road, Cincinnati, OH 45224-1462. *Phone:* 513-761-2020. *Fax:* 513-761-3333.

CINCINNATI STATE TECHNICAL AND COMMUNITY COLLEGE
Cincinnati, Ohio

■ **State-supported** 2-year, founded 1966, part of Ohio Board of Regents
■ **Calendar** 5 ten-week terms
■ **Degree** certificates and associate
■ **Urban** 46-acre campus
■ **Endowment** $947,117
■ **Coed,** 7,722 undergraduate students, 38% full-time, 56% women, 44% men

Undergraduates 2,964 full-time, 4,758 part-time. Students come from 7 states and territories, 71 other countries, 12% are from out of state, 28% African American, 0.9% Asian American or Pacific Islander, 0.7% Hispanic American, 0.2% Native American, 2% international. *Retention:* 48% of 2002 full-time freshmen returned.
Freshmen *Admission:* 1,569 enrolled.
Faculty *Total:* 599, 34% full-time. *Student/faculty ratio:* 14:1.
Majors Accounting; administrative assistant and secretarial science; aeronautical/ aerospace engineering technology; allied health and medical assisting services related; applied horticulture/horticultural business services related; architectural engineering technology; automotive engineering technology; biomedical technology; business administration and management; business, management, and marketing related; chemical technology; child care provision; cinematography and film/video production; civil engineering technology; clinical/medical laboratory technology; commercial and advertising art; computer and information sciences; computer engineering technology; computer programming; computer programming (specific applications); criminal justice/police science; culinary arts; diagnostic medical sonography and ultrasound technology; dietetics; electrical and electronic engineering technologies related; electrical, electronic and communications engineering technology; electromechanical technology; emergency medical technology (EMT paramedic); entrepreneurship; environmental engineering technology; executive assistant/executive secretary; fire science; general studies; health information/medical records technology; health professions related; heating, air conditioning and refrigeration technology; hotel/motel administration; information science/studies; international business/trade/ commerce; landscaping and groundskeeping; laser and optical technology; liberal arts and sciences/liberal studies; management information systems; marketing/marketing management; mechanical engineering/mechanical technology; mechanic and repair technologies related; medical/clinical assistant; nursing (registered nurse training); nursing (registered nurse training); occupational therapist assistant; office management; parks, recreation, and leisure related; plastics engineering technology; purchasing, procurement/acquisitions and contracts management; real estate; respiratory care therapy; restaurant, culinary, and catering management; science technologies related; security and loss prevention; sign language interpretation and translation; surgical technology; survey technology; technical and business writing; telecommunications; turf and turfgrass management.
Academic Programs *Special study options:* academic remediation for entering students, advanced placement credit, cooperative education, distance learning, double majors, English as a second language, internships, off-campus study, part-time degree program, services for LD students, student-designed majors, summer session for credit. *ROTC:* Army (c), Air Force (c).
Library Johnnie Mae Berry Library with 26,431 titles, 400 serial subscriptions, an OPAC, a Web page.
Computers on Campus 750 computers available on campus for general student use. A campuswide network can be accessed from off campus. Internet access, at least one staffed computer lab available.
Student Life *Housing:* college housing not available. *Activities and Organizations:* drama/theater group, student government, Nursing Student Association, Phi Theta Kappa, American Society of Civil Engineers, Students in Free Enterprise. *Campus security:* 24-hour emergency response devices and patrols, late-night transport/escort service. *Student services:* personal/psychological counseling.
Athletics Member NJCAA. *Intercollegiate sports:* basketball M/W, golf M/W, soccer M. *Intramural sports:* cheerleading W, soccer M.
Standardized Tests *Required:* ACT COMPASS (for placement).
Costs (2004–05) *Tuition:* state resident $3995 full-time; nonresident $7865 full-time. Full-time tuition and fees vary according to reciprocity agreements.

Ohio

Cincinnati State Technical and Community College (continued)

Part-time tuition and fees vary according to reciprocity agreements. *Required fees:* $155 full-time. *Waivers:* senior citizens and employees or children of employees.

Financial Aid Of all full-time matriculated undergraduates who enrolled, 71 Federal Work-Study jobs (averaging $3500).

Applying *Required:* high school transcript. *Application deadline:* rolling (freshmen), rolling (transfers). *Notification:* continuous (freshmen).

Admissions Contact Ms. Gabriele Boeckermann, Director of Admission, Cincinnati State Technical and Community College, 3520 Central Parkway, Cincinnati, OH 45223-2690. *Phone:* 513-569-1550. *Fax:* 513-569-1562. *E-mail:* adm@cincinnatistate.edu.

CLARK STATE COMMUNITY COLLEGE
Springfield, Ohio

- **State-supported** 2-year, founded 1962, part of Ohio Board of Regents
- **Calendar** quarters
- **Degree** certificates and associate
- **Suburban** 60-acre campus with easy access to Columbus and Dayton
- **Coed,** 3,309 undergraduate students, 41% full-time, 69% women, 31% men

Undergraduates 1,343 full-time, 1,966 part-time. 13% African American, 0.3% Asian American or Pacific Islander, 2% Hispanic American, 0.5% Native American, 0.3% international, 4% transferred in.

Freshmen *Admission:* 1,461 applied, 1,461 admitted, 707 enrolled.

Faculty *Total:* 321, 17% full-time. *Student/faculty ratio:* 23:1.

Majors Accounting; administrative assistant and secretarial science; agricultural business and management; agricultural mechanization; agriculture; business administration and management; civil engineering technology; clinical/medical laboratory technology; commercial and advertising art; computer programming; computer programming related; computer systems networking and telecommunications; computer/technical support; corrections; court reporting; criminal justice/law enforcement administration; criminal justice/police science; drafting and design technology; dramatic/theatre arts; electrical, electronic and communications engineering technology; emergency medical technology (EMT paramedic); horticultural science; human services; industrial technology; information science/studies; information technology; kindergarten/preschool education; kinesiology and exercise science; landscaping and groundskeeping; legal assistant/paralegal; liberal arts and sciences/liberal studies; mechanical engineering/mechanical technology; medical administrative assistant and medical secretary; nursing (licensed practical/vocational nurse training); nursing (registered nurse training); physical therapy; social work.

Academic Programs *Special study options:* academic remediation for entering students, adult/continuing education programs, advanced placement credit, cooperative education, distance learning, off-campus study, part-time degree program, services for LD students, summer session for credit. *ROTC:* Army (c).

Library Clark State Community College Library with 31,988 titles, 378 serial subscriptions, an OPAC, a Web page.

Computers on Campus 350 computers available on campus for general student use. A campuswide network can be accessed from off campus. Internet access, at least one staffed computer lab available.

Student Life *Housing:* college housing not available. *Activities and Organizations:* drama/theater group, student-run newspaper, choral group, Student Government Association, Minority Student Forum. *Campus security:* late-night transport/escort service. *Student services:* health clinic, personal/psychological counseling.

Athletics Member NJCAA. *Intercollegiate sports:* basketball M/W, softball W, volleyball W. *Intramural sports:* basketball M/W, tennis M/W, volleyball M/W.

Standardized Tests *Required for some:* SAT I or ACT (for placement). *Recommended:* SAT I or ACT (for placement).

Costs (2004–05) *Tuition:* state resident $3324 full-time, $70 per credit hour part-time; nonresident $6156 full-time, $129 per credit hour part-time. *Required fees:* $1100 full-time.

Applying *Options:* common application, electronic application, early admission, deferred entrance. *Application fee:* $15. *Required:* high school transcript. *Application deadline:* rolling (freshmen), rolling (transfers). *Notification:* continuous (freshmen), continuous (transfers).

Admissions Contact Mr. Todd Jones, Director of Admissions, Clark State Community College, PO Box 570, Springfield, OH 45501-0570. *Phone:* 937-328-6027. *Fax:* 937-328-3853. *E-mail:* admissions@clarkstate.edu.

CLEVELAND INSTITUTE OF ELECTRONICS
Cleveland, Ohio

- **Proprietary** 2-year, founded 1934
- **Calendar** continuous

- **Degrees** associate (offers only external degree programs conducted through home study)
- **Coed, primarily men,** 2,612 undergraduate students

Undergraduates Students come from 52 states and territories, 70 other countries, 97% are from out of state.

Faculty *Total:* 4, 75% full-time.

Majors Electrical, electronic and communications engineering technology.

Academic Programs *Special study options:* adult/continuing education programs, external degree program, part-time degree program.

Library 5,000 titles, 38 serial subscriptions.

Student Life *Housing:* college housing not available.

Costs (2003–04) *Tuition:* $1645 per term part-time.

Applying *Options:* common application, electronic application, early admission. *Required:* high school transcript. *Application deadline:* rolling (freshmen), rolling (transfers). *Notification:* continuous (freshmen), continuous (transfers).

Admissions Contact Mr. Scott Katzenmeyer, Registrar, Cleveland Institute of Electronics, 1776 East 17th Street, Cleveland, OH 44114. *Phone:* 216-781-9400. *Toll-free phone:* 800-243-6446. *Fax:* 216-781-0331. *E-mail:* instruct@cie-wc.edu.

COLLEGE OF ART ADVERTISING
Cincinnati, Ohio

Admissions Contact Ms. Janet Bussberg, Director of Admissions, College of Art Advertising, 4343 Bridgetown Road, Cincinnati, OH 45211-4427. *Phone:* 937-294-0592.

COLUMBUS STATE COMMUNITY COLLEGE
Columbus, Ohio

- **State-supported** 2-year, founded 1963, part of Ohio Board of Regents
- **Calendar** quarters
- **Degree** certificates and associate
- **Urban** 75-acre campus
- **Coed,** 23,297 undergraduate students, 39% full-time, 58% women, 42% men

Undergraduates 9,103 full-time, 14,194 part-time. 2% are from out of state, 23% African American, 3% Asian American or Pacific Islander, 2% Hispanic American, 0.6% Native American, 0.9% international, 4% transferred in. *Retention:* 48% of 2002 full-time freshmen returned.

Freshmen *Admission:* 4,877 applied, 4,877 admitted, 3,215 enrolled. *Average high school GPA:* 2.58. *Test scores:* ACT scores over 18: 55%; ACT scores over 24: 6%.

Faculty *Total:* 1,667, 16% full-time. *Student/faculty ratio:* 19:1.

Majors Accounting; accounting and computer science; accounting technology and bookkeeping; administrative assistant and secretarial science; aircraft powerplant technology; airframe mechanics and aircraft maintenance technology; architectural engineering technology; architectural technology; automobile/automotive mechanics technology; avionics maintenance technology; business administration and management; child development; civil engineering technology; clinical laboratory science/medical technology; clinical/medical laboratory assistant; clinical/medical laboratory technology; commercial and advertising art; computer engineering technology; computer programming; construction management; consumer merchandising/retailing management; corrections; criminal justice/police science; culinary arts; dental hygiene; dental laboratory technology; dietetics; dietetic technician; electrical and electronic engineering technologies related; electrical, electronic and communications engineering technology; electromechanical technology; emergency care attendant (EMT ambulance); emergency medical technology (EMT paramedic); environmental engineering technology; finance; food services technology; gerontology; health information/medical records administration; health information/medical records technology; heating, air conditioning, ventilation and refrigeration maintenance technology; histologic technician; hotel/motel administration; human resources management; industrial radiologic technology; kindergarten/preschool education; landscape architecture; legal administrative assistant/secretary; legal assistant/paralegal; liberal arts and sciences/liberal studies; logistics and materials management; marketing/marketing management; massage therapy; mechanical engineering/mechanical technology; medical administrative assistant and medical secretary; medical insurance coding; mental health/rehabilitation; nursing (licensed practical/vocational nurse training); nursing (registered nurse training); phlebotomy; purchasing, procurement/acquisitions and contracts management; quality control technology; radiologic technology/science; real estate; respiratory care therapy; respiratory therapy technician; restaurant/food services management; sign language interpretation and translation; sport and fitness administration; substance abuse/addiction counseling; surgical technology; technical and business writing; tourism and travel services management; veterinary/animal health technology; veterinary technology.

Academic Programs *Special study options:* academic remediation for entering students, adult/continuing education programs, advanced placement credit, cooperative education, distance learning, English as a second language, honors programs, internships, off-campus study, part-time degree program, services for LD students, student-designed majors, summer session for credit. *ROTC:* Army (b), Air Force (c).

Library Educational Resource Center plus 1 other with 27,102 titles, 489 serial subscriptions, 30,538 audiovisual materials, an OPAC, a Web page.

Computers on Campus 960 computers available on campus for general student use. A campuswide network can be accessed from off campus. At least one staffed computer lab available.

Student Life *Housing:* college housing not available. *Activities and Organizations:* choral group, Phi Theta Kappa, Alpha Xi Tau, African-American Women's Support Group, Society of Manufacturing Engineers, Student Organization for Legal Assistants. *Campus security:* 24-hour emergency response devices and patrols, late-night transport/escort service. *Student services:* health clinic, personal/psychological counseling.

Athletics Member NJCAA. *Intercollegiate sports:* baseball M, basketball M(s)/W(s), cross-country running M/W, equestrian sports M/W, golf M, soccer M, softball W, volleyball W. *Intramural sports:* basketball M/W, volleyball M/W, weight lifting M/W.

Standardized Tests *Required:* ACT COMPASS (for placement).

Costs (2003–04) *One-time required fee:* $35. *Tuition:* state resident $2484 full-time, $69 per credit part-time; nonresident $5472 full-time, $152 per credit part-time. *Waivers:* employees or children of employees.

Financial Aid Of all full-time matriculated undergraduates who enrolled, 133 Federal Work-Study jobs (averaging $1500).

Applying *Options:* common application, early admission, deferred entrance. *Application fee:* $10. *Recommended:* high school transcript. *Application deadline:* rolling (freshmen), rolling (transfers). *Notification:* continuous (freshmen), continuous (transfers).

Admissions Contact Mr. Kenneth Conner, Dean of Enrollment Services, Columbus State Community College, 550 East Spring Street, Madison Hall, Columbus, OH 43215. *Phone:* 614-287-2669 Ext. 3669. *Toll-free phone:* 800-621-6407 Ext. 2669. *Fax:* 614-287-6019.

CUYAHOGA COMMUNITY COLLEGE
Cleveland, Ohio

- **State and locally supported** 2-year, founded 1963
- **Calendar** semesters
- **Degree** certificates and associate
- **Urban** campus
- **Coed,** 23,808 undergraduate students, 39% full-time, 66% women, 34% men

Undergraduates 9,314 full-time, 14,494 part-time. Students come from 12 states and territories, 2% are from out of state, 30% African American, 2% Asian American or Pacific Islander, 4% Hispanic American, 0.6% Native American, 3% international, 3% transferred in.

Freshmen *Admission:* 9,474 applied, 9,474 admitted, 2,212 enrolled.

Faculty *Total:* 1,537, 22% full-time, 5% with terminal degrees. *Student/faculty ratio:* 19:1.

Majors Accounting; administrative assistant and secretarial science; automobile/automotive mechanics technology; avionics maintenance technology; business administration and management; clinical laboratory science/medical technology; commercial and advertising art; computer engineering technology; computer typography and composition equipment operation; court reporting; criminal justice/police science; engineering technology; finance; fire science; industrial radiologic technology; kindergarten/preschool education; legal assistant/paralegal; liberal arts and sciences/liberal studies; marketing/marketing management; merchandising; nursing (registered nurse training); opticianry; photography; physician assistant; real estate; respiratory care therapy; restaurant, culinary, and catering management; safety/security technology; sales, distribution and marketing; selling skills and sales; surgical technology; veterinary technology.

Academic Programs *Special study options:* adult/continuing education programs, advanced placement credit, cooperative education, distance learning, English as a second language, external degree program, independent study, part-time degree program, services for LD students, summer session for credit.

Library 177,767 titles, 1,135 serial subscriptions, an OPAC, a Web page.

Computers on Campus 1275 computers available on campus for general student use. A campuswide network can be accessed from off campus. Internet access, at least one staffed computer lab available.

Student Life *Housing:* college housing not available. *Activities and Organizations:* drama/theater group, student-run newspaper, choral group, Student Senate, Student Nursing Organization, Business Focus, Phi Theta Kappa. *Campus security:* 24-hour emergency response devices and patrols, late-night transport/escort service. *Student services:* health clinic, personal/psychological counseling.

Athletics Member NJCAA. *Intercollegiate sports:* baseball M(s), basketball M(s), cross-country running M(s)/W(s), soccer M(s), softball W(s). *Intramural sports:* basketball M, tennis M/W, track and field M/W, volleyball M/W.

Costs (2004–05) *Tuition:* area resident $2192 full-time, $73 per credit hour part-time; state resident $2897 full-time, $97 per credit hour part-time; nonresident $5933 full-time, $198 per credit hour part-time.

Financial Aid Of all full-time matriculated undergraduates who enrolled, 250 Federal Work-Study jobs.

Applying *Options:* early admission, deferred entrance. *Required for some:* high school transcript. *Application deadline:* rolling (freshmen), rolling (transfers). *Notification:* continuous (freshmen), continuous (transfers).

Admissions Contact Mrs. Rena Waghani-Mason, Acting Director of Admissions and Records, Cuyahoga Community College, 2900 Community College Avenue, Cleveland, OH 44115. *Phone:* 216-987-4030. *Toll-free phone:* 800-954-8742. *Fax:* 216-696-2567.

DAVIS COLLEGE
Toledo, Ohio

- **Proprietary** 2-year, founded 1858
- **Calendar** quarters
- **Degree** diplomas and associate
- **Urban** 1-acre campus with easy access to Detroit
- **Coed,** 417 undergraduate students, 45% full-time, 79% women, 21% men

Undergraduates 187 full-time, 230 part-time. Students come from 2 states and territories, 8% are from out of state, 23% African American, 0.5% Asian American or Pacific Islander, 2% Hispanic American, 0.2% Native American, 28% transferred in.

Freshmen *Admission:* 110 applied, 110 admitted, 106 enrolled.

Faculty *Total:* 25, 52% full-time, 4% with terminal degrees. *Student/faculty ratio:* 14:1.

Majors Accounting; administrative assistant and secretarial science; business administration and management; commercial and advertising art; computer systems networking and telecommunications; data processing and data processing technology; fashion merchandising; information technology; interior design; legal administrative assistant/secretary; medical administrative assistant and medical secretary; medical/clinical assistant; system administration; web page, digital/multimedia and information resources design.

Academic Programs *Special study options:* academic remediation for entering students, adult/continuing education programs, advanced placement credit, distance learning, internships, part-time degree program, summer session for credit.

Library Davis College Resource Center with 3,207 titles, 164 serial subscriptions, 341 audiovisual materials, an OPAC.

Computers on Campus 78 computers available on campus for general student use. Internet access, at least one staffed computer lab available.

Student Life *Housing:* college housing not available. *Activities and Organizations:* Student Advisory Board. *Campus security:* 24-hour emergency response devices, security cameras for parking lot. *Student services:* personal/psychological counseling.

Standardized Tests *Required:* CPAt (for admission).

Costs (2003–04) *Tuition:* $7452 full-time, $207 per credit hour part-time. *Required fees:* $480 full-time.

Financial Aid Of all full-time matriculated undergraduates who enrolled, 10 Federal Work-Study jobs (averaging $3500).

Applying *Options:* common application, electronic application, early admission, deferred entrance. *Application fee:* $30. *Required:* high school transcript, interview. *Application deadline:* rolling (freshmen), rolling (transfers). *Notification:* continuous (freshmen), continuous (transfers).

Admissions Contact Ms. Dana Stern, Senior Career Coordinator, Davis College, 4747 Monroe Street, Toledo, OH 43623-4307. *Phone:* 419-473-2700. *Toll-free phone:* 800-477-7021. *Fax:* 419-473-2472. *E-mail:* dstern@daviscollege.edu.

EDISON STATE COMMUNITY COLLEGE
Piqua, Ohio

- **State-supported** 2-year, founded 1973, part of Ohio Board of Regents
- **Calendar** semesters
- **Degree** certificates and associate
- **Small-town** 130-acre campus with easy access to Cincinnati and Dayton
- **Coed,** 3,000 undergraduate students, 34% full-time, 64% women, 36% men

Undergraduates 1,028 full-time, 1,972 part-time. Students come from 5 states and territories, 2% African American, 0.7% Asian American or Pacific Islander, 0.5% Hispanic American, 0.3% Native American, 4% transferred in.

Freshmen *Admission:* 611 enrolled.

Faculty *Total:* 298, 14% full-time. *Student/faculty ratio:* 19:1.

Majors Accounting; administrative assistant and secretarial science; advertising; art; business administration and management; commercial and advertising

Edison State Community College (continued)

art; computer engineering technology; computer graphics; computer programming; computer science; consumer merchandising/retailing management; criminal justice/law enforcement administration; criminal justice/police science; data processing and data processing technology; drafting and design technology; electrical, electronic and communications engineering technology; elementary education; engineering; engineering related; engineering technology; English; finance; health information/medical records administration; human resources management; human services; industrial technology; kindergarten/preschool education; legal assistant/paralegal; legal studies; liberal arts and sciences/liberal studies; marketing/marketing management; mathematics; mechanical design technology; medical administrative assistant and medical secretary; nursing (registered nurse training); pre-engineering; quality control technology; real estate.

Academic Programs *Special study options:* academic remediation for entering students, accelerated degree program, adult/continuing education programs, advanced placement credit, distance learning, double majors, independent study, internships, off-campus study, part-time degree program, services for LD students, student-designed majors, summer session for credit. *ROTC:* Army (c), Air Force (c).

Library Edison Community College Library with 29,851 titles, 542 serial subscriptions, 2,424 audiovisual materials, an OPAC, a Web page.

Computers on Campus 251 computers available on campus for general student use. A campuswide network can be accessed from off campus. Internet access, online (class) registration, at least one staffed computer lab available. Computer purchase or lease plan available.

Student Life *Housing:* college housing not available. *Activities and Organizations:* drama/theater group. *Campus security:* late-night transport/escort service, 18-hour patrols by trained security personnel. *Student services:* personal/psychological counseling.

Athletics Member NJCAA. *Intercollegiate sports:* basketball M/W, volleyball W.

Standardized Tests *Required for some:* SAT I or ACT (for placement), ACT ASSET, ACT COMPASS. *Recommended:* ACT ASSET, ACT COMPASS.

Costs (2003–04) *Tuition:* state resident $1956 full-time, $81 per credit hour part-time; nonresident $3912 full-time, $163 per credit hour part-time. Full-time tuition and fees vary according to course load. Part-time tuition and fees vary according to course load. *Required fees:* $384 full-time, $16 per credit hour part-time. *Payment plan:* deferred payment. *Waivers:* senior citizens and employees or children of employees.

Financial Aid Of all full-time matriculated undergraduates who enrolled, 42 Federal Work-Study jobs (averaging $3000).

Applying *Options:* electronic application, early admission, deferred entrance. *Application fee:* $15. *Required:* high school transcript. *Application deadline:* rolling (freshmen), rolling (transfers).

Admissions Contact Ms. Beth Iams Culbertson, Director of Admissions, Edison State Community College, 1973 Edison Drive, Piqua, OH 45356. *Phone:* 937-778-8600 Ext. 317. *Toll-free phone:* 800-922-3722. *Fax:* 937-778-4692. *E-mail:* info@edisonohio.edu.

ETI TECHNICAL COLLEGE OF NILES
Niles, Ohio

Admissions Contact Ms. Diane Marstellar, Director of Admissions, ETI Technical College of Niles, 2076 Youngstown-Warren Road, Niles, OH 44446-4398. *Phone:* 330-652-9919. *Fax:* 330-652-4399.

GALLIPOLIS CAREER COLLEGE
Gallipolis, Ohio

- **Independent** 2-year, founded 1962
- **Calendar** quarters
- **Degree** certificates, diplomas, and associate
- **Small-town** campus
- **Coed, primarily women,** 161 undergraduate students, 96% full-time, 86% women, 14% men

Undergraduates 154 full-time, 7 part-time. Students come from 2 states and territories, 5% African American.

Freshmen *Admission:* 34 enrolled.

Faculty *Total:* 16, 13% full-time. *Student/faculty ratio:* 8:1.

Majors Accounting; administrative assistant and secretarial science; business administration and management; business/commerce; computer science; computer software and media applications related; computer/technical support; data entry/microcomputer applications; medical administrative assistant and medical secretary.

Academic Programs *Special study options:* academic remediation for entering students, adult/continuing education programs, double majors, independent study, internships, part-time degree program, summer session for credit.

Library Gallipolis Career College Library with 94 audiovisual materials.

Computers on Campus 28 computers available on campus for general student use. A campuswide network can be accessed. Internet access, at least one staffed computer lab available.

Student Life *Housing:* college housing not available.

Standardized Tests *Required:* Wonderlic aptitude test (for admission).

Costs (2004–05) *Tuition:* $8160 full-time, $170 per credit hour part-time. *Required fees:* $100 full-time.

Applying *Application fee:* $50. *Required:* high school transcript, interview. *Application deadline:* rolling (freshmen), rolling (transfers).

Admissions Contact Mr. Jack Henson, Director of Admissions, Gallipolis Career College, 1176 Jackson Pike, Suite 312, Gallipolis, OH 45631. *Phone:* 740-446-4124 Ext. 12. *Toll-free phone:* 800-214-0452. *E-mail:* admissions@gallipoliscareercollege.com.

HOCKING COLLEGE
Nelsonville, Ohio

- **State-supported** 2-year, founded 1968, part of Ohio Board of Regents
- **Calendar** quarters
- **Degree** certificates, diplomas, and associate
- **Rural** 1600-acre campus with easy access to Columbus
- **Endowment** $2.3 million
- **Coed**

Student Life *Campus security:* 24-hour emergency response devices and patrols, student patrols, late-night transport/escort service.

Standardized Tests *Required for some:* nursing exam. *Recommended:* SAT I or ACT (for placement).

Costs (2003–04) *Tuition:* state resident $3024 full-time; nonresident $6048 full-time. *Required fees:* $3000 full-time.

Financial Aid Of all full-time matriculated undergraduates who enrolled, 125 Federal Work-Study jobs (averaging $1700). 225 state and other part-time jobs (averaging $1700).

Applying *Options:* electronic application. *Application fee:* $15. *Required:* high school transcript.

Admissions Contact Ms. Lyn Hull, Director of Admissions, Hocking College, 3301 Hocking Parkway, Nelsonville, OH 45764-9588. *Phone:* 740-753-3591 Ext. 2803. *Toll-free phone:* 800-282-4163. *Fax:* 740-753-1452. *E-mail:* admissions@hocking.edu.

HONDROS COLLEGE
Westerville, Ohio

- **Proprietary** 2-year
- **Calendar** quarters
- **Degree** certificates and associate
- **Coed**

Student Life *Campus security:* 24-hour emergency response devices.

Admissions Contact Ms. Carol Thomas, Operations Manager, Hondros College, 4140 Executive Parkway, Westerville, OH 43081. *Phone:* 614-508-7244. *Toll-free phone:* 800-783-0095. *Fax:* 614-508-7279. *E-mail:* hondras@hondras.com.

INTERNATIONAL COLLEGE OF BROADCASTING
Dayton, Ohio

- **Private** 2-year
- **Calendar** semesters
- **Degree** diplomas and associate
- **Urban** 1-acre campus
- **Coed,** 87 undergraduate students, 100% full-time, 26% women, 74% men

Undergraduates 87 full-time. 31% African American, 1% Hispanic American.

Freshmen *Admission:* 21 applied, 14 admitted, 11 enrolled. *Average high school GPA:* 2.30.

Faculty *Total:* 12, 50% full-time. *Student/faculty ratio:* 9:1.

Majors Audio engineering; radio and television.

Costs (2003–04) *Tuition:* $7800 full-time.

Admissions Contact Mr. Aan McIntosh, Director of Admissions, International College of Broadcasting, 6 South Smithville Road, Dayton, OH 45431. *Phone:* 937-258-8251. *Fax:* 937-258-8714. *E-mail:* micicb@aol.com.

ITT Technical Institute
Norwood, Ohio

- **Proprietary** 2-year, part of ITT Educational Services, Inc
- **Calendar** quarters
- **Degree** associate
- **Coed**

Standardized Tests *Required:* Wonderlic aptitude test (for admission).
Costs (2003–04) *Tuition:* Total Program Cost varies depending on course of study. Consult school catalog.
Applying *Options:* deferred entrance. *Application fee:* $100. *Required:* high school transcript, interview. *Recommended:* letters of recommendation.
Admissions Contact Mr. Bill Bradford, Director of Recruitment, ITT Technical Institute, 4750 Wesley Avenue, Norwood, OH 45212. *Phone:* 513-531-8300. *Toll-free phone:* 800-314-8324. *Fax:* 513-531-8368.

ITT Technical Institute
Strongsville, Ohio

- **Proprietary** 2-year, part of ITT Educational Services, Inc
- **Calendar** quarters
- **Degree** associate
- **Coed**

Standardized Tests *Required:* Wonderlic aptitude test (for admission).
Costs (2003–04) *Tuition:* Total Program Cost varies depending on course of study. Consult school catalog.
Applying *Options:* deferred entrance. *Application fee:* $100. *Required:* high school transcript, interview. *Recommended:* letters of recommendation.
Admissions Contact Mr. James Tussing, Director of Recruitment, ITT Technical Institute, 14955 Sprague Road, Strongsville, OH 44136. *Phone:* 440-234-9091. *Toll-free phone:* 800-331-1488. *Fax:* 440-234-7568.

ITT Technical Institute
Hillard, Ohio

Admissions Contact Jim Tussing, Director of Recruitment, ITT Technical Institute, 3781 Park Mill Run Drive, Hillard, OH 43026. *Phone:* 614-771-4888. *Toll-free phone:* 888-483-4888.

ITT Technical Institute
Dayton, Ohio

- **Proprietary** 2-year, founded 1935, part of ITT Educational Services, Inc
- **Calendar** quarters
- **Degree** associate
- **Suburban** 7-acre campus
- **Coed**

Standardized Tests *Required:* Wonderlic aptitude test (for admission).
Costs (2003–04) *Tuition:* Total Program Cost varies depending on course of study. Consult school catalog.
Applying *Options:* deferred entrance. *Application fee:* $100. *Required:* high school transcript, interview. *Recommended:* letters of recommendation.
Admissions Contact Mr. Sean G. Kuhn, Director of Recruitment, ITT Technical Institute, 3325 Stop 8 Road, Dayton, OH 45414. *Phone:* 937-454-2267. *Toll-free phone:* 800-568-3241. *Fax:* 937-454-2278.

ITT Technical Institute
Youngstown, Ohio

- **Proprietary** 2-year, founded 1967, part of ITT Educational Services, Inc
- **Calendar** quarters
- **Degree** associate
- **Suburban** campus with easy access to Cleveland and Pittsburgh
- **Coed**

Standardized Tests *Required:* Wonderlic aptitude test (for admission).
Costs (2003–04) *Tuition:* Total Program Cost varies depending on course of study. Consult school catalog.
Financial Aid Of all full-time matriculated undergraduates who enrolled, 5 Federal Work-Study jobs (averaging $3979).
Applying *Options:* deferred entrance. *Application fee:* $100. *Required:* high school transcript, interview. *Recommended:* letters of recommendation.
Admissions Contact Mr. Tom Flynn, Director of Recruitment, ITT Technical Institute, 1030 North Meridian Road, Youngstown, OH 44509. *Phone:* 330-270-1600. *Toll-free phone:* 800-832-5001. *Fax:* 330-270-8333.

James A. Rhodes State College
Lima, Ohio

- **State-supported** 2-year, founded 1971
- **Calendar** quarters
- **Degree** certificates and associate
- **Rural** 565-acre campus
- **Endowment** $849,362
- **Coed,** 2,842 undergraduate students, 50% full-time, 69% women, 31% men

Undergraduates 1,417 full-time, 1,425 part-time. Students come from 8 states and territories, 0.3% are from out of state, 7% African American, 0.7% Asian American or Pacific Islander, 1% Hispanic American, 0.2% Native American, 6% transferred in.
Freshmen *Admission:* 1,092 applied, 1,092 admitted, 469 enrolled. *Average high school GPA:* 2.82.
Faculty *Total:* 226, 25% full-time, 7% with terminal degrees. *Student/faculty ratio:* 25:1.
Majors Accounting; administrative assistant and secretarial science; artificial intelligence and robotics; business administration and management; child development; civil engineering technology; computer graphics; computer programming; consumer merchandising/retailing management; corrections; criminal justice/police science; dental hygiene; drafting and design technology; electrical, electronic and communications engineering technology; emergency medical technology (EMT paramedic); engineering technology; fashion merchandising; finance; human services; industrial radiologic technology; industrial technology; information science/studies; information technology; legal administrative assistant/secretary; legal assistant/paralegal; marketing/marketing management; mechanical design technology; mechanical engineering/mechanical technology; medical administrative assistant and medical secretary; nursing (registered nurse training); physical therapy; quality control technology; respiratory care therapy.
Academic Programs *Special study options:* academic remediation for entering students, adult/continuing education programs, advanced placement credit, cooperative education, distance learning, independent study, internships, off-campus study, part-time degree program, services for LD students, student-designed majors, summer session for credit.
Library Rhodes State/Ohio State Library/ with 80,000 titles, an OPAC.
Computers on Campus 150 computers available on campus for general student use. A campuswide network can be accessed from off campus. Internet access, online (class) registration, at least one staffed computer lab available.
Student Life *Housing:* college housing not available. *Activities and Organizations:* drama/theater group, student-run newspaper, choral group, Student Senate, Social Activities Board, Ski Club, Society of Manufacturing Engineers, Psychology Club. *Campus security:* student patrols, late-night transport/escort service.
Athletics *Intercollegiate sports:* baseball M(c), basketball M(c)/W(c), golf M(c). *Intramural sports:* baseball M, basketball M/W, bowling M/W, football M/W, golf M/W, softball M/W, volleyball M/W.
Standardized Tests *Required for some:* ACT (for placement), ACT ASSET and ACT COMPASS.
Costs (2004–05) *Tuition:* area resident $3461 full-time; nonresident $6800 full-time. Full-time tuition and fees vary according to course load. *Required fees:* $318 full-time. *Payment plan:* deferred payment. *Waivers:* senior citizens and employees or children of employees.
Financial Aid Of all full-time matriculated undergraduates who enrolled, 110 Federal Work-Study jobs (averaging $1000).
Applying *Options:* common application, early admission, deferred entrance. *Application fee:* $25. *Required:* high school transcript. *Application deadline:* rolling (freshmen), rolling (transfers). *Notification:* continuous until 9/22 (freshmen), continuous until 9/22 (transfers).
Admissions Contact Mr. Scot Lingrell, Director, Student Advising and Development, James A. Rhodes State College, 4240 Campus Drive, Lima, OH 45804-3597. *Phone:* 419-995-8050. *Fax:* 419-995-8098. *E-mail:* lingrel.s@rhodesstate.edu.

Jefferson Community College
Steubenville, Ohio

- **State and locally supported** 2-year, founded 1966, part of Ohio Board of Regents
- **Calendar** semesters
- **Degree** certificates and associate
- **Small-town** 83-acre campus with easy access to Pittsburgh
- **Endowment** $197,077
- **Coed,** 1,604 undergraduate students, 53% full-time, 63% women, 37% men

Undergraduates 851 full-time, 753 part-time. Students come from 3 states and territories, 16% are from out of state, 5% African American, 0.4% Asian American or Pacific Islander, 0.4% Hispanic American, 0.1% Native American, 30% transferred in.

Jefferson Community College (continued)

Freshmen *Admission:* 774 applied, 774 admitted, 445 enrolled. *Average high school GPA:* 2.53.

Faculty *Total:* 124, 28% full-time, 6% with terminal degrees. *Student/faculty ratio:* 16:1.

Majors Accounting; administrative assistant and secretarial science; business administration and management; child care and support services management; computer engineering related; consumer merchandising/retailing management; corrections; criminal justice/police science; data processing and data processing technology; dental assisting; developmental and child psychology; drafting and design technology; electrical, electronic and communications engineering technology; emergency medical technology (EMT paramedic); finance; industrial radiologic technology; industrial technology; legal administrative assistant/secretary; mechanical engineering/mechanical technology; medical administrative assistant and medical secretary; medical/clinical assistant; nursing (licensed practical/vocational nurse training); real estate; respiratory care therapy; special products marketing.

Academic Programs *Special study options:* academic remediation for entering students, adult/continuing education programs, internships, off-campus study, part-time degree program, services for LD students, summer session for credit.

Library Jefferson Community College Library with 12,000 titles, 180 serial subscriptions, 246 audiovisual materials, an OPAC.

Computers on Campus 250 computers available on campus for general student use. At least one staffed computer lab available.

Student Life *Housing:* college housing not available. *Activities and Organizations:* Student Senate, SADD, AITP (Association for Information Technology Professionals), American Drafting and Design Association, Writers Club. *Campus security:* student patrols.

Athletics *Intercollegiate sports:* basketball M/W. *Intramural sports:* basketball M/W, rock climbing M/W, softball M/W, tennis M/W, volleyball M/W.

Standardized Tests *Required for some:* SAT I or ACT (for admission), SAT I and SAT II or ACT (for admission).

Costs (2004–05) *Tuition:* area resident $2430 full-time, $81 per credit part-time; state resident $2580 full-time, $86 per credit part-time; nonresident $3240 full-time, $108 per credit part-time.

Financial Aid Of all full-time matriculated undergraduates who enrolled, 30 Federal Work-Study jobs (averaging $1500).

Applying *Options:* early admission, deferred entrance. *Application fee:* $20. *Required for some:* high school transcript. *Application deadlines:* 8/20 (freshmen), 8/20 (transfers). *Notification:* continuous until 8/20 (freshmen), continuous until 8/20 (transfers).

Admissions Contact Mr. Chuck Mascellino, Director of Admissions, Jefferson Community College, 4000 Sunset Boulevard, Steubenville, OH 43952. *Phone:* 740-264-5591 Ext. 142. *Toll-free phone:* 800-68-COLLEGE Ext. 142. *Fax:* 740-266-2944.

KENT STATE UNIVERSITY, ASHTABULA CAMPUS
Ashtabula, Ohio

- **State-supported** primarily 2-year, founded 1958, part of Kent State University System
- **Calendar** semesters
- **Degrees** certificates, associate, and bachelor's (also offers some upper-level and graduate courses)
- **Small-town** 120-acre campus with easy access to Cleveland
- **Coed**

Student Life *Campus security:* 24-hour emergency response devices.

Standardized Tests *Recommended:* SAT I or ACT (for placement).

Costs (2004–05) *Tuition:* state resident $4326 full-time; nonresident $11,338 full-time.

Financial Aid Of all full-time matriculated undergraduates who enrolled, 1,042 Federal Work-Study jobs (averaging $2316).

Applying *Options:* early admission, deferred entrance.

Admissions Contact Ms. Kelly Sanford, Director, Enrollment Management and Student Services, Kent State University, Ashtabula Campus, 3325 West 13th Street, Ashtabula, OH 44004-2299. *Phone:* 440-964-4217. *E-mail:* robinson@ashtabula.kent.edu.

KENT STATE UNIVERSITY, EAST LIVERPOOL CAMPUS
East Liverpool, Ohio

- **State-supported** 2-year, founded 1967, part of Kent State University System
- **Calendar** semesters

- **Degrees** certificates and associate (also offers some upper-level and graduate courses)
- **Small-town** 4-acre campus with easy access to Pittsburgh
- **Coed**

Faculty *Student/faculty ratio:* 15:1.

Student Life *Campus security:* student patrols, late-night transport/escort service.

Standardized Tests *Recommended:* ACT (for placement).

Financial Aid Of all full-time matriculated undergraduates who enrolled, 16 Federal Work-Study jobs (averaging $2727).

Applying *Options:* early admission, deferred entrance. *Application fee:* $30. *Required:* high school transcript.

Admissions Contact Mrs. Jamie Kenneally, Director of Enrollment Management and Student Services, Kent State University, East Liverpool Campus, 400 East Fourth Street, East Liverpool, OH 43920. *Phone:* 330-382-7414. *Fax:* 330-385-6348. *E-mail:* admissions@eliv.kent.edu.

KENT STATE UNIVERSITY, GEAUGA CAMPUS
Burton, Ohio

- **State-supported** founded 1964, part of Kent State University System
- **Calendar** semesters
- **Degrees** associate, bachelor's, and master's
- **Rural** 87-acre campus with easy access to Cleveland
- **Coed**

Faculty *Student/faculty ratio:* 14:1.

Student Life *Campus security:* 24-hour emergency response devices.

Standardized Tests *Recommended:* ACT (for placement).

Costs (2003–04) *Tuition:* state resident $3968 full-time; nonresident $10,400 full-time.

Financial Aid Of all full-time matriculated undergraduates who enrolled, 189 applied for aid, 157 were judged to have need, 17 had their need fully met. 11 Federal Work-Study jobs (averaging $1554). In 2001, 3. *Average percent of need met:* 56. *Average financial aid package:* $5391. *Average need-based loan:* $3147. *Average need-based gift aid:* $3785. *Average non-need-based aid:* $2415. *Average indebtedness upon graduation:* $19,489.

Applying *Options:* early admission, deferred entrance. *Application fee:* $30. *Required:* high school transcript, interview. *Recommended:* minimum 2.0 GPA.

Admissions Contact Ms. Betty Landrus, Admissions and Records Secretary, Kent State University, Geauga Campus, 14111 Claridon-Troy Road, Burton, OH 44021. *Phone:* 440-834-4187. *Fax:* 440-834-8846. *E-mail:* cbaker@geauga.kent.edu.

KENT STATE UNIVERSITY, SALEM CAMPUS
Salem, Ohio

- **State-supported** primarily 2-year, founded 1966, part of Kent State University System
- **Calendar** semesters
- **Degrees** associate and bachelor's (also offers some upper-level and graduate courses)
- **Rural** 98-acre campus
- **Coed**, 1,320 undergraduate students

Undergraduates Students come from 2 states and territories, 2 other countries, 3% African American, 0.4% Asian American or Pacific Islander, 0.4% Hispanic American, 0.1% Native American.

Freshmen *Admission:* 507 applied, 490 admitted. *Average high school GPA:* 2.73.

Faculty *Total:* 106, 47% full-time. *Student/faculty ratio:* 13:1.

Majors Accounting; administrative assistant and secretarial science; applied horticulture; applied horticulture/horticultural business services related; business administration and management; computer and information sciences; education; environmental studies; family and consumer sciences/human sciences; greenhouse management; horticultural science; human services; industrial technology; kindergarten/preschool education; liberal arts and sciences/liberal studies; manufacturing engineering; medical insurance coding; medical insurance/medical billing; medical radiologic technology; nursing (registered nurse training); ornamental horticulture; turf and turfgrass management.

Academic Programs *Special study options:* academic remediation for entering students, adult/continuing education programs, advanced placement credit, distance learning, freshman honors college, honors programs, internships, part-time degree program, services for LD students, summer session for credit. *ROTC:* Army (c), Air Force (c).

Library 19,000 titles, 163 serial subscriptions, 158 audiovisual materials, an OPAC, a Web page.

Computers on Campus 100 computers available on campus for general student use. A campuswide network can be accessed. Internet access, online (class) registration, at least one staffed computer lab available.

Student Life *Housing:* college housing not available. *Activities and Organizations:* drama/theater group, student government, NEXUS, Ski Club, Art Club, Drama Club. *Campus security:* 24-hour emergency response devices, late-night transport/escort service. *Student services:* personal/psychological counseling, women's center.

Athletics *Intramural sports:* basketball M/W, skiing (downhill) M/W, table tennis M/W, tennis M/W, volleyball M/W.

Standardized Tests *Required for some:* ACT (for admission), SAT I or ACT (for placement). *Recommended:* SAT I or ACT (for placement).

Costs (2003–04) *Tuition:* state resident $3968 full-time, $181 per credit part-time; nonresident $10,400 full-time, $474 per credit part-time. Full-time tuition and fees vary according to course level. Part-time tuition and fees vary according to course level. *Payment plans:* installment, deferred payment. *Waivers:* employees or children of employees.

Financial Aid Of all full-time matriculated undergraduates who enrolled, 16 Federal Work-Study jobs (averaging $3021).

Applying *Options:* early admission, deferred entrance. *Application fee:* $30. *Required:* high school transcript. *Required for some:* essay or personal statement, minimum X GPA, letters of recommendation. *Application deadline:* rolling (freshmen), rolling (transfers).

Admissions Contact Mrs. Judy Heisler, Admissions Secretary, Kent State University, Salem Campus, 2491 State Route 45 South, Salem, OH 44460-9412. *Phone:* 330-332-0361 Ext. 74201.

KENT STATE UNIVERSITY, STARK CAMPUS
Canton, Ohio

- **State-supported** primarily 2-year, founded 1967, part of Kent State University System
- **Calendar** semesters
- **Degrees** associate and bachelor's (also offers some graduate courses)
- **Suburban** 200-acre campus with easy access to Cleveland
- **Coed,** 3,736 undergraduate students

Undergraduates Students come from 2 states and territories.

Freshmen *Admission:* 1,510 applied, 1,510 admitted. *Average high school GPA:* 2.90. *Test scores:* SAT verbal scores over 500: 3%; SAT math scores over 500: 2%; ACT scores over 18: 60%; SAT verbal scores over 600: 1%; ACT scores over 24: 13%.

Faculty *Total:* 200, 43% full-time. *Student/faculty ratio:* 19:1.

Majors Art; biological and physical sciences; business administration and management; education; interdisciplinary studies; liberal arts and sciences/liberal studies.

Academic Programs *Special study options:* academic remediation for entering students, adult/continuing education programs, advanced placement credit, English as a second language, freshman honors college, honors programs, independent study, internships, off-campus study, part-time degree program, services for LD students, student-designed majors, study abroad, summer session for credit. *ROTC:* Army (c), Air Force (c).

Library Kent State University Library with 72,807 titles, 313 serial subscriptions, an OPAC, a Web page.

Computers on Campus 100 computers available on campus for general student use. A campuswide network can be accessed from off campus. Internet access, online (class) registration, at least one staffed computer lab available.

Student Life *Housing:* college housing not available. *Activities and Organizations:* drama/theater group, choral group, Psychology Club, Pan African Student Alliance, Criminal Justice Society, Women's Studies Club, History Club. *Campus security:* 24-hour emergency response devices, late-night transport/escort service.

Standardized Tests *Required for some:* SAT I or ACT (for admission).

Costs (2003–04) *Tuition:* state resident $3968 full-time, $181 per hour part-time; nonresident $10,400 full-time, $474 per hour part-time. No tuition increase for student's term of enrollment. *Payment plan:* installment. *Waivers:* employees or children of employees.

Financial Aid Of all full-time matriculated undergraduates who enrolled, 54 Federal Work-Study jobs (averaging $2389).

Applying *Options:* early admission, deferred entrance. *Application fee:* $30. *Required:* high school transcript. *Required for some:* interview. *Application deadline:* rolling (freshmen), rolling (transfers).

Admissions Contact Ms. Deborah Ann Speck, Director of Admissions, Kent State University, Stark Campus, 6000 Frank Avenue NW, Canton, OH 44720-7599. *Phone:* 330-499-9600 Ext. 53259. *Fax:* 330-499-0301. *E-mail:* aspeck@stark.kent.edu.

KENT STATE UNIVERSITY, TRUMBULL CAMPUS
Warren, Ohio

- **State-supported** 2-year, founded 1954, part of Kent State University System
- **Calendar** semesters
- **Degrees** certificates and associate (also offers some upper-level and graduate courses)
- **Suburban** 200-acre campus with easy access to Cleveland
- **Endowment** $1.1 million
- **Coed,** 2,270 undergraduate students, 50% full-time, 60% women, 40% men

Undergraduates 1,145 full-time, 1,125 part-time. Students come from 4 states and territories, 10% African American, 0.7% Asian American or Pacific Islander, 0.9% Hispanic American, 0.1% Native American.

Faculty *Total:* 155, 52% full-time.

Majors Accounting; administrative assistant and secretarial science; automobile/automotive mechanics technology; business administration and management; computer engineering technology; criminal justice/law enforcement administration; electrical, electronic and communications engineering technology; engineering; environmental engineering technology; finance; industrial technology; liberal arts and sciences/liberal studies; marketing/marketing management; mechanical engineering/mechanical technology; real estate; tourism and travel services management.

Academic Programs *Special study options:* academic remediation for entering students, adult/continuing education programs, advanced placement credit, cooperative education, distance learning, freshman honors college, honors programs, independent study, internships, part-time degree program, services for LD students, student-designed majors, summer session for credit. *ROTC:* Army (c), Air Force (c).

Library Trumbull Campus Library with 65,951 titles, 759 serial subscriptions, an OPAC, a Web page.

Computers on Campus 300 computers available on campus for general student use. Internet access, at least one staffed computer lab available.

Student Life *Housing:* college housing not available. *Activities and Organizations:* drama/theater group, student-run newspaper, Student Senate, Trumbull Environmental Club, Union Activities Board, Gamemasters, Kent Christian Fellowship. *Campus security:* 24-hour emergency response devices, late-night transport/escort service, patrols by trained security personnel during open hours.

Athletics *Intramural sports:* basketball M/W, bowling M/W, skiing (downhill) M/W, volleyball M/W.

Standardized Tests *Required:* ACT COMPASS (for placement). *Required for some:* SAT I or ACT (for placement).

Costs (2003–04) *Tuition:* state resident $3968 full-time; nonresident $5200 full-time.

Financial Aid Of all full-time matriculated undergraduates who enrolled, 31 Federal Work-Study jobs (averaging $2708).

Applying *Options:* early admission, deferred entrance. *Application fee:* $30. *Required:* high school transcript. *Application deadline:* 7/30 (freshmen), rolling (transfers). *Notification:* continuous until 8/30 (freshmen), continuous until 8/30 (transfers).

Admissions Contact Ms. Kerrianne Aulet, Admissions Specialist, Kent State University, Trumbull Campus, 4314 Mahoning Avenue, NW, Warren, OH 44483-1998. *Phone:* 330-847-0571 Ext. 2367. *E-mail:* info@lyceum.trumbull.kent.edu.

KENT STATE UNIVERSITY, TUSCARAWAS CAMPUS
New Philadelphia, Ohio

- **State-supported** primarily 2-year, founded 1962, part of Kent State University System
- **Calendar** semesters
- **Degrees** certificates, diplomas, associate, bachelor's, and master's (also offers some upper-level and graduate courses)
- **Small-town** 172-acre campus with easy access to Cleveland
- **Coed,** 2,008 undergraduate students

Undergraduates 1% African American, 0.3% Asian American or Pacific Islander, 0.4% Hispanic American, 0.4% Native American.

Freshmen *Admission:* 499 applied, 474 admitted.

Faculty *Total:* 144, 31% full-time, 24% with terminal degrees. *Student/faculty ratio:* 16:1.

Kent State University, Tuscarawas Campus (continued)

Majors Accounting; administrative assistant and secretarial science; animation, interactive technology, video graphics and special effects; business administration and management; communications technology; computer engineering technology; criminal justice/police science; early childhood education; electrical, electronic and communications engineering technology; engineering technology; environmental studies; industrial technology; liberal arts and sciences/liberal studies; mechanical engineering/mechanical technology; nursing (registered nurse training); plastics engineering technology.

Academic Programs *Special study options:* academic remediation for entering students, accelerated degree program, adult/continuing education programs, advanced placement credit, distance learning, double majors, freshman honors college, honors programs, internships, part-time degree program, services for LD students, student-designed majors, summer session for credit. *ROTC:* Army (c), Air Force (c).

Library Tuscarawas Campus Library with 58,946 titles, 400 serial subscriptions, 520 audiovisual materials, an OPAC, a Web page.

Computers on Campus 161 computers available on campus for general student use. A campuswide network can be accessed from off campus. Internet access, online (class) registration, at least one staffed computer lab available.

Student Life *Housing:* college housing not available. *Activities and Organizations:* choral group, Society of Mechanical Engineers, IEEE, Imagineers, Criminal Justice Club, Salt and Light.

Athletics *Intercollegiate sports:* basketball M/W, golf M/W. *Intramural sports:* basketball M/W, volleyball M/W.

Standardized Tests *Required for some:* SAT I or ACT (for placement).

Costs (2003–04) *Tuition:* state resident $3968 full-time, $181 per credit part-time; nonresident $10,400 full-time, $474 per credit part-time. Full-time tuition and fees vary according to course level, course load, and location. Part-time tuition and fees vary according to course level, course load, and location. *Payment plan:* installment. *Waivers:* senior citizens and employees or children of employees.

Financial Aid Of all full-time matriculated undergraduates who enrolled, 26 Federal Work-Study jobs (averaging $2699).

Applying *Options:* common application, early admission, deferred entrance. *Application fee:* $30. *Required:* high school transcript. *Application deadlines:* 9/1 (freshmen), 9/1 (transfers). *Notification:* continuous (freshmen), continuous (transfers).

Admissions Contact Ms. Denise L. Testa, Director of Admissions, Kent State University, Tuscarawas Campus, 330 University Drive NE, New Philadelphia, OH 44663-9403. *Phone:* 330-339-3391 Ext. 47425. *Fax:* 330-339-3321.

KETTERING COLLEGE OF MEDICAL ARTS
Kettering, Ohio

- **Independent Seventh-day Adventist** primarily 2-year, founded 1967
- **Calendar** semesters
- **Degrees** certificates, associate, bachelor's, and postbachelor's certificates
- **Suburban** 35-acre campus
- **Coed, primarily women,** 653 undergraduate students

Undergraduates Students come from 29 states and territories, 3 other countries, 7% African American, 3% Asian American or Pacific Islander, 2% Hispanic American, 0.3% Native American, 0.5% international, 20% live on campus.

Freshmen *Average high school GPA:* 3.27.

Faculty *Total:* 51, 49% full-time, 22% with terminal degrees.

Majors General studies; health science; nuclear medical technology; nursing (registered nurse training); physician assistant; radiologic technology/science; respiratory care therapy.

Academic Programs *Special study options:* advanced placement credit, internships, off-campus study, part-time degree program, summer session for credit.

Library Learning Resources Center plus 1 other with 29,390 titles, 266 serial subscriptions, an OPAC, a Web page.

Computers on Campus 30 computers available on campus for general student use. Internet access, at least one staffed computer lab available.

Student Life *Housing Options:* coed. *Activities and Organizations:* drama/theater group, choral group, student association/student life, campus ministries. *Campus security:* 24-hour emergency response devices and patrols, late-night transport/escort service. *Student services:* health clinic, personal/psychological counseling.

Athletics *Intramural sports:* basketball M/W, tennis M/W, volleyball M/W.

Standardized Tests *Required:* ACT (for admission). *Recommended:* SAT I (for admission).

Costs (2004–05) *Comprehensive fee:* $18,138 includes full-time tuition ($10,824), mandatory fees ($960), and room and board ($6354). Part-time

tuition: $260 per credit hour. *Required fees:* $110 per semester part-time. *Room and board:* college room only: $2994.

Applying *Options:* early admission. *Application fee:* $25. *Required:* high school transcript, minimum 2.0 GPA, 3 letters of recommendation. *Recommended:* minimum 3.0 GPA, interview. *Application deadline:* rolling (freshmen), rolling (transfers). *Notification:* continuous (freshmen), continuous (transfers).

Admissions Contact Mr. David Lofthouse, Director of Enrollment Services, Kettering College of Medical Arts, 3737 Southern Boulevard, Kettering, OH 45429-1299. *Phone:* 937-296-7228. *Toll-free phone:* 800-433-5262. *Fax:* 937-296-4238.

LAKELAND COMMUNITY COLLEGE
Kirtland, Ohio

- **State and locally supported** 2-year, founded 1967, part of Ohio Board of Regents
- **Calendar** semesters
- **Degree** certificates and associate
- **Suburban** 380-acre campus with easy access to Cleveland
- **Endowment** $1.4 million
- **Coed,** 8,635 undergraduate students, 36% full-time, 60% women, 40% men

Undergraduates 3,098 full-time, 5,537 part-time. Students come from 5 states and territories, 31 other countries, 1% are from out of state, 8% African American, 0.9% Asian American or Pacific Islander, 0.9% Hispanic American, 0.2% Native American, 3% international.

Freshmen *Admission:* 1,434 enrolled.

Faculty *Total:* 624, 19% full-time. *Student/faculty ratio:* 17:1.

Majors Accounting; administrative assistant and secretarial science; biological and physical sciences; biotechnology; business administration and management; civil engineering technology; clinical/medical laboratory technology; commercial and advertising art; computer graphics; computer programming related; computer programming (specific applications); computer systems networking and telecommunications; corrections; criminal justice/law enforcement administration; criminal justice/police science; dental hygiene; electrical, electronic and communications engineering technology; engineering technology; fire science; hospitality administration; human services; industrial technology; information science/studies; kindergarten/preschool education; legal assistant/paralegal; liberal arts and sciences/liberal studies; machine tool technology; mechanical engineering/mechanical technology; nursing (registered nurse training); ophthalmic laboratory technology; radiologic technology/science; respiratory care therapy; safety/security technology; system administration; tourism and travel services management; web/multimedia management and webmaster; web page, digital/multimedia and information resources design.

Academic Programs *Special study options:* academic remediation for entering students, adult/continuing education programs, advanced placement credit, cooperative education, distance learning, external degree program, internships, part-time degree program, services for LD students, summer session for credit.

Library Lakeland Community College Library with 70,874 titles, 2,205 serial subscriptions, 3,453 audiovisual materials, an OPAC, a Web page.

Computers on Campus 500 computers available on campus for general student use. A campuswide network can be accessed from off campus. Online (class) registration, at least one staffed computer lab available.

Student Life *Housing:* college housing not available. *Activities and Organizations:* drama/theater group, student-run newspaper, radio station, choral group, Campus Activities Board, Gamers Guild, Computers Users Group, Veterans Group, Aikido Club. *Campus security:* 24-hour emergency response devices and patrols, student patrols, late-night transport/escort service. *Student services:* health clinic, personal/psychological counseling, women's center.

Athletics Member NJCAA. *Intercollegiate sports:* baseball M(s), basketball M(s)/W(s), golf M(s)/W(s), soccer M(s), softball W(s), volleyball W(s). *Intramural sports:* basketball M/W, racquetball M/W, rock climbing W, volleyball M/W, wrestling M.

Standardized Tests *Required for some:* SAT I or ACT (for placement), ACT ASSET or ACT COMPASS. *Recommended:* SAT I or ACT (for placement).

Costs (2004–05) *Tuition:* area resident $2243 full-time, $70 per semester hour part-time; state resident $2748 full-time, $87 per semester hour part-time; nonresident $5873 full-time, $200 per semester hour part-time. Full-time tuition and fees vary according to course load. Part-time tuition and fees vary according to course load. *Required fees:* $10 per semester hour part-time, $14 per term part-time. *Payment plan:* installment. *Waivers:* senior citizens and employees or children of employees.

Financial Aid Of all full-time matriculated undergraduates who enrolled, 71 Federal Work-Study jobs (averaging $2500). 166 state and other part-time jobs (averaging $1700).

Applying *Options:* common application, electronic application, early admission, deferred entrance. *Application fee:* $15. *Required:* high school transcript. *Application deadlines:* 9/1 (freshmen), 9/1 (transfers). *Notification:* continuous until 9/1 (freshmen), continuous until 9/1 (transfers).

Admissions Contact Ms. Tracey Cooper, Director for Admissions/Registrar, Lakeland Community College, 7700 Clocktower Drive, Kirtland, OH 44094. *Phone:* 440-525-7230. *Toll-free phone:* 800-589-8520. *Fax:* 440-975-4330. *E-mail:* tcooper@lakelandcc.edu.

LORAIN COUNTY COMMUNITY COLLEGE
Elyria, Ohio

- **State and locally supported** 2-year, founded 1963, part of Ohio Board of Regents
- **Calendar** semesters
- **Degree** certificates and associate
- **Suburban** 480-acre campus with easy access to Cleveland
- **Coed,** 9,409 undergraduate students, 36% full-time, 67% women, 33% men

Undergraduates 3,432 full-time, 5,977 part-time. Students come from 20 states and territories, 7 other countries, 7% African American, 0.9% Asian American or Pacific Islander, 6% Hispanic American, 0.8% Native American, 0.7% international.
Freshmen *Admission:* 2,734 enrolled.
Faculty *Total:* 571, 21% full-time. *Student/faculty ratio:* 19:1.
Majors Accounting; administrative assistant and secretarial science; art; artificial intelligence and robotics; athletic training; biological and physical sciences; biology/biological sciences; business administration and management; chemistry; civil engineering technology; clinical/medical laboratory technology; computer and information sciences related; computer engineering technology; computer programming; computer programming related; computer programming (specific applications); computer programming (vendor/product certification); computer science; computer systems networking and telecommunications; computer technology/computer systems technology; consumer merchandising/retailing management; corrections; cosmetology; cosmetology and personal grooming arts related; criminal justice/police science; data entry/microcomputer applications; data entry/microcomputer applications related; diagnostic medical sonography and ultrasound technology; drafting and design technology; dramatic/theatre arts; education; electrical, electronic and communications engineering technology; elementary education; engineering; engineering technology; finance; fire science; history; human services; industrial radiologic technology; industrial technology; information science/studies; information technology; journalism; kindergarten/preschool education; liberal arts and sciences/liberal studies; machine tool technology; marketing/marketing management; mass communication/media; mathematics; mechanical design technology; music; nuclear medical technology; nursing (registered nurse training); personal/miscellaneous services; pharmacy; physical education teaching and coaching; physical therapist assistant; physics; plastics engineering technology; political science and government; pre-engineering; psychology; quality control technology; real estate; social sciences; social work; sociology; sport and fitness administration; surgical technology; tourism and travel services management; urban studies/affairs; veterinary sciences; word processing.
Academic Programs *Special study options:* academic remediation for entering students, adult/continuing education programs, advanced placement credit, cooperative education, distance learning, English as a second language, honors programs, independent study, part-time degree program, services for LD students, student-designed majors, summer session for credit.
Library Learning Resource Center with 198,984 titles, 3,289 audiovisual materials, an OPAC.
Computers on Campus 400 computers available on campus for general student use. A campuswide network can be accessed from off campus. Internet access, online (class) registration, at least one staffed computer lab available.
Student Life *Housing:* college housing not available. *Activities and Organizations:* drama/theater group, student-run newspaper, radio station, choral group, Phi Beta Kappa, Black Progressives, Hispanic Club, national fraternities, national sororities. *Campus security:* 24-hour emergency response devices and patrols, late-night transport/escort service. *Student services:* health clinic, personal/psychological counseling, women's center, legal services.
Athletics *Intramural sports:* archery M/W, basketball M/W, softball M/W, volleyball M/W, weight lifting M/W, wrestling M.
Standardized Tests *Required for some:* ACT ASSET, ACT COMPASS. *Recommended:* SAT I or ACT (for placement).
Costs (2004–05) *Tuition:* area resident $2106 full-time, $81 per credit hour part-time; state resident $2560 full-time, $99 per credit hour part-time; nonresident $5288 full-time, $203 per credit hour part-time. *Required fees:* $111 full-time, $4 per credit hour part-time. *Payment plans:* installment, deferred payment. *Waivers:* senior citizens and employees or children of employees.
Financial Aid Of all full-time matriculated undergraduates who enrolled, 100 Federal Work-Study jobs.
Applying *Options:* early admission, deferred entrance. *Required for some:* high school transcript. *Application deadline:* rolling (freshmen), rolling (transfers). *Notification:* continuous (freshmen), continuous (transfers).

Admissions Contact Ms. Dione Somervile, Director of Enrollment Services, Lorain County Community College, 1005 Abbe Road, North, Elyria, OH 44035. *Phone:* 440-366-7566. *Toll-free phone:* 800-995-5222 Ext. 4032. *Fax:* 440-365-6519.

MARION TECHNICAL COLLEGE
Marion, Ohio

- **State-supported** 2-year, founded 1971, part of Ohio Board of Regents
- **Calendar** quarters
- **Degree** certificates and associate
- **Small-town** 180-acre campus with easy access to Columbus
- **Coed,** 2,121 undergraduate students, 46% full-time, 61% women, 39% men

Undergraduates 981 full-time, 1,140 part-time. Students come from 4 states and territories, 7% African American, 0.3% Asian American or Pacific Islander, 1% Hispanic American, 0.4% Native American, 2% transferred in. *Retention:* 56% of 2002 full-time freshmen returned.
Freshmen *Admission:* 850 applied, 835 admitted, 387 enrolled.
Faculty *Total:* 190, 21% full-time. *Student/faculty ratio:* 18:1.
Majors Accounting; administrative assistant and secretarial science; business administration and management; clinical/medical laboratory technology; computer programming (vendor/product certification); computer software and media applications related; computer systems networking and telecommunications; data entry/microcomputer applications; data entry/microcomputer applications related; data processing and data processing technology; drafting and design technology; electrical, electronic and communications engineering technology; engineering technology; finance; human services; industrial radiologic technology; industrial technology; information technology; legal assistant/paralegal; marketing/marketing management; mechanical engineering/mechanical technology; medical administrative assistant and medical secretary; nursing (registered nurse training); physical therapist assistant; radiologic technology/science; social work; telecommunications technology.
Academic Programs *Special study options:* academic remediation for entering students, adult/continuing education programs, cooperative education, distance learning, internships, part-time degree program, services for LD students, student-designed majors, summer session for credit.
Library Marion Campus Library with 38,000 titles, 200 serial subscriptions, an OPAC.
Computers on Campus 270 computers available on campus for general student use. A campuswide network can be accessed. At least one staffed computer lab available.
Student Life *Housing:* college housing not available. *Activities and Organizations:* Student Ambassadors. *Campus security:* 24-hour emergency response devices.
Athletics *Intercollegiate sports:* basketball M/W, golf M/W, volleyball W. *Intramural sports:* badminton M/W, basketball M/W, bowling M/W, cheerleading W, football M, golf M, racquetball M/W, rugby M/W, skiing (cross-country) M/W, skiing (downhill) M/W, table tennis M/W, tennis M/W, track and field M/W, volleyball M/W.
Standardized Tests *Required for some:* ACT (for placement).
Costs (2003–04) *Tuition:* state resident $3096 full-time, $86 per credit hour part-time; nonresident $4788 full-time, $133 per credit hour part-time. *Required fees:* $425 full-time. *Payment plan:* deferred payment. *Waivers:* senior citizens.
Financial Aid Of all full-time matriculated undergraduates who enrolled, 28 Federal Work-Study jobs (averaging $1200). 45 state and other part-time jobs (averaging $1000).
Applying *Options:* early admission, deferred entrance. *Application fee:* $20. *Required:* high school transcript. *Application deadline:* rolling (freshmen), rolling (transfers). *Notification:* continuous (freshmen), continuous (transfers).

Admissions Contact Mr. Joel O. Liles, Director of Admissions and Career Services, Marion Technical College, 1467 Mt. Vernon Avenue, Marion, OH 43302. *Phone:* 740-389-4636 Ext. 249. *E-mail:* enroll@mtc.tec.oh.us.

MERCY COLLEGE OF NORTHWEST OHIO
Toledo, Ohio

- **Independent** primarily 2-year, founded 1993, affiliated with Roman Catholic Church
- **Calendar** semesters
- **Degrees** certificates, associate, and bachelor's
- **Urban** campus with easy access to Detroit
- **Endowment** $2.2 million
- **Coed, primarily women,** 565 undergraduate students, 50% full-time, 91% women, 9% men

Undergraduates 283 full-time, 282 part-time. Students come from 5 states and territories, 12% are from out of state, 7% African American, 0.7% Asian

Mercy College of Northwest Ohio (continued)
American or Pacific Islander, 4% Hispanic American, 0.5% Native American, 23% transferred in, 10% live on campus. *Retention:* 100% of 2002 full-time freshmen returned.

Freshmen *Admission:* 84 applied, 66 admitted, 66 enrolled. *Average high school GPA:* 3.32. *Test scores:* ACT scores over 18: 87%; ACT scores over 24: 18%; ACT scores over 30: 1%.

Faculty *Total:* 43, 100% full-time, 21% with terminal degrees. *Student/faculty ratio:* 13:1.

Majors General studies; health/health care administration; health information/medical records technology; massage therapy; medical radiologic technology; nursing (registered nurse training).

Academic Programs *Special study options:* academic remediation for entering students, advanced placement credit, independent study, internships, part-time degree program, services for LD students, summer session for credit.

Library Mercy College of Northwest Ohio Library with 5,900 titles, 171 serial subscriptions, 331 audiovisual materials, an OPAC.

Computers on Campus 22 computers available on campus for general student use. A campuswide network can be accessed from student residence rooms and from off campus. Internet access, at least one staffed computer lab available.

Student Life *Housing Options:* coed. Campus housing is provided by a third party. *Activities and Organizations:* student-run newspaper, Campus Ministry, Student Senate, Mercy College Musical Ensemble, Student Nurses Association, Stress Busters. *Campus security:* 24-hour patrols, late-night transport/escort service, controlled dormitory access. *Student services:* personal/psychological counseling.

Standardized Tests *Required for some:* SAT I or ACT (for admission). *Recommended:* SAT I or ACT (for admission).

Costs (2003–04) *One-time required fee:* $60. *Tuition:* $6234 full-time, $242 per credit hour part-time. Full-time tuition and fees vary according to course load. Part-time tuition and fees vary according to course load. *Required fees:* $160 full-time, $5 per credit hour part-time. *Room only:* $2800. Room and board charges vary according to housing facility. *Payment plan:* installment. *Waivers:* employees or children of employees.

Financial Aid Of all full-time matriculated undergraduates who enrolled, 18 Federal Work-Study jobs.

Applying *Application fee:* $25. *Required:* high school transcript. *Required for some:* minimum 2.3 GPA. *Application deadline:* rolling (freshmen), rolling (transfers). *Notification:* continuous (freshmen), continuous (transfers).

Admissions Contact Ms. Janice Bernard, Secretary, Mercy College of Northwest Ohio, 2221 Madison Avenue, Toledo, OH 43624-1197. *Phone:* 419-251-1313 Ext. 11723. *Toll-free phone:* 888-80-Mercy. *Fax:* 419-251-1462. *E-mail:* admissions@mercycollege.edu.

MIAMI-JACOBS COLLEGE
Dayton, Ohio

- **Proprietary** 2-year, founded 1860
- **Calendar** quarters
- **Degree** certificates, diplomas, and associate
- **Small-town** campus
- **Coed**

Faculty *Student/faculty ratio:* 13:1.

Student Life *Campus security:* late-night transport/escort service.

Standardized Tests *Required:* Wonderlic aptitude test (for admission). *Required for some:* ACT (for admission). *Recommended:* SAT I or ACT (for admission).

Costs (2004–05) *Tuition:* $9000 full-time, $250 per credit part-time. *Required fees:* $2000 full-time.

Applying *Options:* early admission, deferred entrance. *Application fee:* $50. *Required:* essay or personal statement, high school transcript, interview. *Recommended:* letters of recommendation.

Admissions Contact Mary Percell, Vice President of Information Services, Miami-Jacobs College, 110 North Patterson Street, PO Box 1433, Dayton, OH 45402. *Phone:* 937-461-5174 Ext. 118.

MIAMI UNIVERSITY HAMILTON
Hamilton, Ohio

- **State-supported** founded 1968, part of Miami University System
- **Calendar** semesters plus summer sessions
- **Degrees** certificates, associate, bachelor's, and master's (degrees awarded by Miami University main campus)
- **Suburban** 78-acre campus with easy access to Cincinnati
- **Coed**, 3,322 undergraduate students, 43% full-time, 57% women, 43% men

Undergraduates 1,427 full-time, 1,895 part-time. 6% African American, 2% Asian American or Pacific Islander, 1% Hispanic American, 0.3% Native American, 4% transferred in.

Freshmen *Admission:* 968 applied, 962 admitted, 649 enrolled.

Faculty *Total:* 222, 41% full-time. *Student/faculty ratio:* 15:1.

Majors Accounting; American studies; anthropology; architectural history and criticism; architecture; art; art teacher education; athletic training; audiology and speech-language pathology; biochemistry; botany/plant biology related; business administration and management; business administration, management and operations related; business/commerce; business/managerial economics; chemistry; chemistry teacher education; city/urban, community and regional planning; classics and languages, literatures and linguistics; clinical laboratory science/medical technology; communication/speech communication and rhetoric; computer and information sciences related; computer engineering; computer science; computer systems analysis; computer technology/computer systems technology; creative writing; dietetics; early childhood education; econometrics and quantitative economics; economics; education (multiple levels); electrical and electronic engineering technologies related; electromechanical technology; engineering/industrial management; engineering physics; engineering technology; English; English composition; English/language arts teacher education; environmental science; environmental studies; ethnic, cultural minority, and gender studies related; exercise physiology; finance; French; French language teacher education; general studies; geography; geology/earth science; German; German language teacher education; gerontology; graphic design; health teacher education; history; human resources management and services related; interior design; international/global studies; journalism; Latin; Latin teacher education; linguistics; management information systems; marketing/marketing management; marketing related; mass communication/media; mathematics; mathematics and statistics related; mathematics teacher education; mechanical engineering/mechanical technology; microbiology; multi-/interdisciplinary studies related; music; music teacher education; office management; philosophy; physical education teaching and coaching; physics; physics teacher education; political science and government; psychology; public administration; purchasing, procurement/acquisitions and contracts management; real estate; Russian; science teacher education; economics; education (multiple levels); social work related; sociology; Spanish; Spanish language teacher education; special education; speech-language pathology; statistics; technical and business writing; theatre/theatre arts management; work and family studies; zoology/animal biology.

Academic Programs *Special study options:* academic remediation for entering students, adult/continuing education programs, advanced placement credit, cooperative education, double majors, English as a second language, honors programs, internships, part-time degree program, services for LD students, student-designed majors, study abroad, summer session for credit. *ROTC:* Navy (c), Air Force (c).

Library Rentschler Library with 68,000 titles, 400 serial subscriptions, an OPAC, a Web page.

Computers on Campus 250 computers available on campus for general student use. A campuswide network can be accessed from off campus. Internet access, online (class) registration, at least one staffed computer lab available.

Student Life *Housing:* college housing not available. *Activities and Organizations:* drama/theater group, choral group, student government, Campus Activities Committee, Ski Club, Student Nursing Association, Minority Action Committee. *Campus security:* 24-hour emergency response devices and patrols, late-night transport/escort service. *Student services:* personal/psychological counseling.

Athletics *Intercollegiate sports:* baseball M, basketball M/W, cheerleading W, golf M, tennis M/W, volleyball W. *Intramural sports:* basketball M/W, bowling M/W, skiing (cross-country) M/W, soccer M/W, softball M/W, tennis M/W, volleyball M/W, weight lifting M/W.

Standardized Tests *Required for some:* SAT I or ACT (for placement).

Costs (2003–04) *Tuition:* state resident $3150 full-time, $131 per credit part-time; nonresident $12,901 full-time, $538 per credit part-time. *Required fees:* $382 full-time, $15 per credit part-time, $17 per term part-time. *Payment plan:* installment. *Waivers:* employees or children of employees.

Applying *Options:* electronic application. *Application fee:* $25. *Required:* high school transcript. *Application deadline:* rolling (freshmen). *Notification:* continuous (freshmen), continuous (transfers).

Admissions Contact Ms. Triana Adlon, Director of Admission and Financial Aid, Miami University Hamilton, 1601 Peck Boulevard, Hamilton, OH 45011-3399. *Phone:* 513-785-3111. *Fax:* 513-785-3148. *E-mail:* adlontm@muohio.edu.

MIAMI UNIVERSITY-MIDDLETOWN CAMPUS
Middletown, Ohio

- **State-supported** primarily 2-year, founded 1966, part of Miami University System
- **Calendar** semesters
- **Degrees** certificates, diplomas, associate, and bachelor's (also offers up to 2 years of most bachelor's degree programs offered at Miami University main campus)
- **Small-town** 141-acre campus with easy access to Cincinnati and Dayton

■ **Endowment** $779,742
■ **Coed**

Faculty *Student/faculty ratio:* 13:1.
Student Life *Campus security:* 24-hour patrols, late-night transport/escort service.
Standardized Tests *Recommended:* SAT I or ACT (for placement).
Costs (2003–04) *Tuition:* state resident $3498 full-time, $146 per credit hour part-time; nonresident $13,248 full-time, $552 per credit hour part-time. Full-time tuition and fees vary according to student level. Part-time tuition and fees vary according to student level. *Required fees:* $201 full-time.
Applying *Options:* electronic application, early admission, deferred entrance. *Application fee:* $25. *Required:* high school transcript.
Admissions Contact Mrs. Mary Lou Flynn, Director of Enrollment Services, Miami University-Middletown Campus, 4200 East University Boulevard, Middletown, OH 45042. *Phone:* 513-727-3346. *Toll-free phone:* 800-622-2262. *Fax:* 513-727-3223. *E-mail:* flynnml@muohio.edu.

NATIONAL INSTITUTE OF TECHNOLOGY
Cuyahoga Falls, Ohio

Admissions Contact 2545 Bailey Road, Cuyahoga Falls, OH 44221.

NORTH CENTRAL STATE COLLEGE
Mansfield, Ohio

■ **State-supported** 2-year, founded 1961, part of Ohio Board of Regents
■ **Calendar** quarters
■ **Degree** certificates and associate
■ **Suburban** 600-acre campus with easy access to Cleveland and Columbus
■ **Endowment** $624,998
■ **Coed,** 3,249 undergraduate students, 29% full-time, 68% women, 32% men

Undergraduates 953 full-time, 2,296 part-time. Students come from 1 other state, 5% African American, 0.7% Asian American or Pacific Islander, 1% Hispanic American, 0.6% Native American.
Freshmen *Admission:* 2,099 applied, 2,097 admitted.
Faculty *Total:* 221, 31% full-time.
Majors Accounting; administrative assistant and secretarial science; business administration and management; computer systems networking and telecommunications; criminal justice/law enforcement administration; criminal justice/safety; drafting and design technology; electrical, electronic and communications engineering technology; finance; heating, air conditioning, ventilation and refrigeration maintenance technology; human services; industrial technology; information science/studies; kindergarten/preschool education; legal assistant/paralegal; machine tool technology; mechanical engineering/mechanical technology; nursing (registered nurse training); operations management; pharmacy technician; physical therapist assistant; quality control technology; radiologic technology/science; respiratory care therapy; therapeutic recreation; welding technology.
Academic Programs *Special study options:* academic remediation for entering students, adult/continuing education programs, advanced placement credit, distance learning, independent study, internships, part-time degree program, services for LD students, student-designed majors, summer session for credit.
Library Bromfield Library plus 1 other with 52,700 titles, 410 serial subscriptions, an OPAC.
Computers on Campus 144 computers available on campus for general student use. A campuswide network can be accessed. Internet access, at least one staffed computer lab available.
Student Life *Housing:* college housing not available. *Activities and Organizations:* student-run radio station, choral group, Student Programming Board, choral group. *Campus security:* 24-hour emergency response devices and patrols, late-night transport/escort service. *Student services:* personal/psychological counseling.
Athletics *Intramural sports:* basketball M/W, football M/W, golf M/W, softball M/W, table tennis M/W, tennis M/W, volleyball M/W.
Standardized Tests *Required:* ACT COMPASS (for placement). *Required for some:* ACT (for placement).
Costs (2003–04) *Tuition:* state resident $1356 full-time, $57 per credit hour part-time; nonresident $2712 full-time, $113 per credit hour part-time. Full-time tuition and fees vary according to course load. Part-time tuition and fees vary according to course load. *Required fees:* $245 full-time, $10 per credit hour part-time. *Payment plan:* deferred payment. *Waivers:* employees or children of employees.
Applying *Options:* early admission, deferred entrance. *Required for some:* high school transcript. *Application deadline:* rolling (freshmen), rolling (transfers). *Notification:* continuous (freshmen), continuous (transfers).
Admissions Contact North Central State College, PO Box 698, Mansfield, OH 44901-0698. *Phone:* 419-755-4896. *Toll-free phone:* 888-755-4899.

NORTHWEST STATE COMMUNITY COLLEGE
Archbold, Ohio

■ **State-supported** 2-year, founded 1968, part of Ohio Board of Regents
■ **Calendar** semesters
■ **Degree** certificates and associate
■ **Rural** 80-acre campus with easy access to Toledo
■ **Endowment** $496,733
■ **Coed,** 3,347 undergraduate students, 33% full-time, 52% women, 48% men

Undergraduates 1,100 full-time, 2,247 part-time. Students come from 6 states and territories, 2% are from out of state, 1% African American, 0.5% Asian American or Pacific Islander, 6% Hispanic American, 0.3% Native American, 2% transferred in. *Retention:* 55% of 2002 full-time freshmen returned.
Freshmen *Admission:* 722 applied, 722 admitted, 554 enrolled. *Average high school GPA:* 2.81. *Test scores:* ACT scores over 18: 74%; ACT scores over 24: 21%.
Faculty *Total:* 185, 23% full-time, 14% with terminal degrees. *Student/faculty ratio:* 18:1.
Majors Accounting; business administration and management; business/commerce; business, management, and marketing related; child development; computer programming; corrections; criminal justice/law enforcement administration; criminal justice/police science; criminal justice/safety; design and visual communications; education; electrical, electronic and communications engineering technology; engineering related; executive assistant/executive secretary; health professions related; human development and family studies related; legal administrative assistant/secretary; legal assistant/paralegal; machine tool technology; marketing/marketing management; mechanical engineering; mechanical engineering/mechanical technology; medical administrative assistant and medical secretary; nursing (registered nurse training); plastics engineering technology; precision metal working related; quality control technology; sheet metal technology; social work; tool and die technology; transportation management.
Academic Programs *Special study options:* academic remediation for entering students, adult/continuing education programs, advanced placement credit, cooperative education, distance learning, external degree program, independent study, internships, off-campus study, part-time degree program, services for LD students, student-designed majors, summer session for credit.
Library Northwest State Community College Library with 15,321 titles, 1,680 serial subscriptions, 1,913 audiovisual materials, an OPAC, a Web page.
Computers on Campus 425 computers available on campus for general student use. A campuswide network can be accessed. Internet access, online (class) registration, at least one staffed computer lab available.
Student Life *Housing:* college housing not available. *Activities and Organizations:* Student Body Organization, Phi Theta Kappa, Campus Crusade for Christ. *Campus security:* security patrols. *Student services:* personal/psychological counseling.
Athletics *Intramural sports:* basketball M/W, bowling M/W, table tennis M/W, volleyball M/W.
Costs (2004–05) *Tuition:* state resident $3360 full-time, $112 per credit part-time; nonresident $6540 full-time, $224 per credit part-time. Full-time tuition and fees vary according to course load. Part-time tuition and fees vary according to course load. *Required fees:* $180 full-time, $6 per credit part-time, $10 per term part-time. *Payment plan:* deferred payment. *Waivers:* senior citizens and employees or children of employees.
Financial Aid Of all full-time matriculated undergraduates who enrolled, 54 Federal Work-Study jobs (averaging $685).
Applying *Options:* common application, early admission, deferred entrance. *Application fee:* $20. *Required:* high school transcript. *Application deadline:* rolling (freshmen), rolling (transfers). *Notification:* continuous (transfers).
Admissions Contact Mr. Dennis Gable, Director of Admissions, Northwest State Community College, 22600 State Route 34, Archbold, OH 43502-9542. *Phone:* 419-267-5511 Ext. 318. *Fax:* 419-267-5604. *E-mail:* admissions@nscc.cc.oh.us.

OHIO BUSINESS COLLEGE
Lorain, Ohio

■ **Proprietary** 2-year, founded 1903, part of Tri State Educational Systems
■ **Calendar** quarters
■ **Degree** diplomas and associate
■ **Coed, primarily women**

Faculty *Student/faculty ratio:* 18:1.
Standardized Tests *Required:* CPAt (for placement).
Costs (2003–04) *Tuition:* $7827 full-time, $145 per credit hour part-time. *Required fees:* $300 full-time.
Applying *Options:* common application, electronic application. *Application fee:* $25. *Required:* high school transcript, interview.

Ohio Business College (continued)

Admissions Contact Mr. Jim Unger, Admissions Director, Ohio Business College, 1907 North Ridge Road, Lorain, OH 44055. *Toll-free phone:* 888-514-3126.

OHIO BUSINESS COLLEGE
Sandusky, Ohio

- **Proprietary** 2-year, founded 1982
- **Calendar** quarters
- **Degree** diplomas and associate
- **Suburban** 1-acre campus
- **Coed,** 198 undergraduate students

Majors Accounting; administrative assistant and secretarial science; business administration and management; computer programming; data entry/microcomputer applications; health/medical claims examination; legal administrative assistant; medical administrative assistant and medical secretary.

Costs (2003–04) *Tuition:* $5580 full-time.

Applying *Application fee:* $25.

Admissions Contact Ms. Cecilia Blevins, Director of Admissions, Ohio Business College, 4020 Milan Road, Sandusky, OH 44870-5894. *Toll-free phone:* 888-627-8345.

OHIO COLLEGE OF MASSOTHERAPY
Akron, Ohio

Admissions Contact Ms. Sherri Becker, Vice President, Ohio College of Massotherapy, 225 Heritage Woods Drive, Akron, OH 44321. *Phone:* 330-665-1084.

OHIO INSTITUTE OF PHOTOGRAPHY AND TECHNOLOGY
Dayton, Ohio

- **Proprietary** 2-year, founded 1971, part of Kaplan Higher Education
- **Calendar** quarters
- **Degree** diplomas and associate
- **Urban** 2-acre campus with easy access to Cincinnati and Columbus
- **Coed,** 581 undergraduate students, 100% full-time, 74% women, 26% men

Undergraduates 581 full-time. Students come from 20 states and territories, 19% are from out of state, 14% African American, 1% Hispanic American, 0.7% Native American.

Freshmen *Admission:* 270 applied, 153 admitted, 111 enrolled.

Faculty *Total:* 53, 38% full-time.

Majors Criminal justice/law enforcement administration; graphic design; medical/clinical assistant; photography.

Academic Programs *Special study options:* cooperative education, internships, part-time degree program, student-designed majors, summer session for credit.

Library Main Library with 640 titles, 35 serial subscriptions.

Computers on Campus 90 computers available on campus for general student use. Internet access, at least one staffed computer lab available.

Student Life *Housing:* college housing not available. *Campus security:* 24-hour emergency response devices.

Costs (2003–04) *Tuition:* $29,890 per degree program part-time. Full-time tuition and fees vary according to program.

Applying *Options:* common application, early admission, deferred entrance. *Required:* high school transcript, interview, entrance exam. *Application deadline:* rolling (freshmen), rolling (transfers). *Notification:* continuous (freshmen), continuous (transfers).

Admissions Contact Mr. Norman Dorn, Director of Admissions, Ohio Institute of Photography and Technology, 2029 Edgefield Road, Dayton, OH 45439-1917. *Phone:* 937-294-6155. *Toll-free phone:* 800-932-9698. *Fax:* 937-294-2259. *E-mail:* info@oipt.com.

THE OHIO STATE UNIVERSITY AGRICULTURAL TECHNICAL INSTITUTE
Wooster, Ohio

- **State-supported** 2-year, founded 1971, part of Ohio State University
- **Calendar** quarters
- **Degree** certificates and associate
- **Small-town** campus with easy access to Cleveland and Columbus

- **Endowment** $2.1 million
- **Coed,** 830 undergraduate students, 88% full-time, 34% women, 66% men

Undergraduates 730 full-time, 100 part-time. Students come from 13 states and territories, 2 other countries, 2% are from out of state, 0.6% African American, 0.2% Asian American or Pacific Islander, 0.4% Hispanic American, 0.2% Native American, 0.5% international, 7% transferred in, 22% live on campus. *Retention:* 65% of 2002 full-time freshmen returned.

Freshmen *Admission:* 492 applied, 471 admitted, 295 enrolled. *Test scores:* SAT verbal scores over 500: 22%; SAT math scores over 500: 22%; SAT verbal scores over 600: 11%.

Faculty *Total:* 68, 49% full-time, 32% with terminal degrees. *Student/faculty ratio:* 17:1.

Majors Agribusiness; agricultural business and management; agricultural business technology; agricultural communication/journalism; agricultural economics; agricultural mechanization; agricultural power machinery operation; agricultural teacher education; agronomy and crop science; animal/livestock husbandry and production; animal sciences; biology/biotechnology laboratory technician; building/construction site management; clinical/medical laboratory technology; construction engineering technology; construction management; crop production; dairy husbandry and production; dairy science; environmental science; equestrian studies; floriculture/floristry management; greenhouse management; heavy equipment maintenance technology; horse husbandry/equine science and management; horticultural science; hydraulics and fluid power technology; industrial technology; landscaping and groundskeeping; livestock management; medical laboratory technology; natural resources management; natural resources management and policy; plant nursery management; pre-veterinary studies; soil conservation; turf and turfgrass management.

Academic Programs *Special study options:* academic remediation for entering students, accelerated degree program, adult/continuing education programs, advanced placement credit, cooperative education, honors programs, internships, part-time degree program, services for LD students, student-designed majors, summer session for credit. *ROTC:* Army (c), Navy (c), Air Force (c).

Library Agricultural Technical Institute Library with 19,009 titles, 595 serial subscriptions, an OPAC.

Computers on Campus 85 computers available on campus for general student use.

Student Life *Housing:* on-campus residence required for freshman year. *Options:* coed. Campus housing is university owned. *Activities and Organizations:* Hoof-n-Hide Club, Horticulture Club, Campus Crusade for Christ, Phi Theta Kappa, Artist de Fleur Club. *Campus security:* 24-hour emergency response devices and patrols, controlled dormitory access. *Student services:* health clinic, personal/psychological counseling.

Athletics *Intramural sports:* basketball M/W, football M/W, racquetball M/W, softball M/W, volleyball M/W.

Standardized Tests *Required for some:* SAT I or ACT (for admission).

Costs (2003–04) *Tuition:* state resident $4452 full-time; nonresident $14,529 full-time. Full-time tuition and fees vary according to course load. Part-time tuition and fees vary according to course load. *Required fees:* $27 full-time. *Room and board:* $5070; room only: $4170. Room and board charges vary according to board plan. *Payment plan:* installment. *Waivers:* employees or children of employees.

Applying *Options:* early admission. *Application fee:* $40. *Required:* high school transcript. *Application deadlines:* 7/1 (freshmen), 7/1 (transfers). *Notification:* continuous until 9/15 (freshmen).

Admissions Contact The Ohio State University Agricultural Technical Institute, 1328 Dover Road, Wooster, OH 44691. *Phone:* 330-264-3911 Ext. 1236. *Toll-free phone:* 800-647-8283 Ext. 1327. *Fax:* 330-262-7634. *E-mail:* ati@ohio-state.edu.

OHIO TECHNICAL COLLEGE
Cleveland, Ohio

Admissions Contact Mr. Marc Brenner, President, Ohio Technical College, 1374 East 51st Street, Cleveland, OH 44103. *Phone:* 216-881-1700. *Toll-free phone:* 800-322-7000.

OHIO VALLEY COLLEGE OF TECHNOLOGY
East Liverpool, Ohio

- **Proprietary** 2-year, founded 1886
- **Calendar** semesters
- **Degree** diplomas and associate
- **Small-town** campus with easy access to Pittsburgh
- **Coed, primarily women,** 126 undergraduate students, 96% full-time, 91% women, 9% men

Undergraduates 121 full-time, 5 part-time. Students come from 3 states and territories, 10% are from out of state, 3% African American, 0.8% Native American, 26% transferred in.

Freshmen *Admission:* 34 enrolled. *Average high school GPA:* 2.5.

Faculty *Total:* 11, 36% full-time. *Student/faculty ratio:* 18:1.

Majors Accounting; data processing and data processing technology; dental assisting; executive assistant/executive secretary; information technology; medical administrative assistant and medical secretary; medical/clinical assistant.

Academic Programs *Special study options:* internships, part-time degree program, summer session for credit.

Computers on Campus Internet access, at least one staffed computer lab available.

Student Life *Housing:* college housing not available. *Student services:* personal/psychological counseling.

Standardized Tests *Required:* CPAt (for admission).

Costs (2003–04) *Tuition:* $6500 full-time. Full-time tuition and fees vary according to course load. Part-time tuition and fees vary according to course load. No tuition increase for student's term of enrollment. *Required fees:* $390 full-time. *Payment plan:* installment. *Waivers:* employees or children of employees.

Applying *Required:* high school transcript, interview. *Application deadline:* rolling (freshmen). *Notification:* continuous (transfers).

Admissions Contact Ms. Jessica M. Ewing, Program Information Coordinator, Ohio Valley College of Technology, PO Box 7000, East Liverpool, OH 43920. *Phone:* 330-385-1070. *Toll-free phone:* 877-777-8451. *E-mail:* info@ohiovalleytech.com.

OWENS COMMUNITY COLLEGE
Findlay, Ohio

- **State-supported** 2-year, founded 1983, part of Owens Community College System
- **Calendar** semesters
- **Degree** certificates and associate
- **Small-town** 9-acre campus
- **Coed,** 2,623 undergraduate students, 43% full-time, 62% women, 38% men

Undergraduates 1,117 full-time, 1,506 part-time. Students come from 4 states and territories, 11 other countries, 5% African American, 0.9% Asian American or Pacific Islander, 5% Hispanic American, 0.6% Native American, 0.6% international.

Freshmen *Admission:* 1,105 enrolled. *Average high school GPA:* 2.6.

Faculty *Total:* 112, 24% full-time. *Student/faculty ratio:* 29:1.

Majors Accounting; accounting technology and bookkeeping; administrative assistant and secretarial science; business administration and management; business/commerce; commercial and advertising art; corrections; criminal justice/law enforcement administration; criminal justice/police science; early childhood education; electrical, electronic and communications engineering technology; electromechanical technology; fashion merchandising; general studies; marketing/marketing management; mechanical engineering/mechanical technology; medical administrative assistant and medical secretary; nursing (registered nurse training); operations management.

Academic Programs *Special study options:* academic remediation for entering students, adult/continuing education programs, advanced placement credit, cooperative education, distance learning, double majors, external degree program, honors programs, independent study, internships, part-time degree program, services for LD students, summer session for credit. *ROTC:* Army (c), Air Force (b).

Library an OPAC, a Web page.

Computers on Campus 100 computers available on campus for general student use. A campuswide network can be accessed from off campus. Internet access, at least one staffed computer lab available.

Student Life *Housing:* college housing not available. *Campus security:* 24-hour emergency response devices and patrols, student patrols. *Student services:* health clinic, personal/psychological counseling.

Athletics Member NJCAA. *Intercollegiate sports:* baseball M, basketball M(s)/W(s), soccer M, softball W, volleyball W. *Intramural sports:* basketball M/W, bowling M/W, football M/W, golf M/W, softball M/W, table tennis M/W, tennis M/W, volleyball M/W, weight lifting M/W.

Standardized Tests *Required for some:* ACT (for placement). *Recommended:* ACT (for placement), ACT ASSET.

Costs (2004–05) *Tuition:* state resident $2280 full-time, $110 per credit hour part-time; nonresident $4560 full-time, $205 per credit hour part-time. *Required fees:* $380 full-time, $15 per credit hour part-time.

Financial Aid Of all full-time matriculated undergraduates who enrolled, 75 Federal Work-Study jobs (averaging $4500).

Applying *Options:* common application, early admission, deferred entrance. *Required:* high school transcript. *Required for some:* minimum 2.0 GPA.

Recommended: essay or personal statement, letters of recommendation, interview. *Application deadline:* rolling (freshmen), rolling (transfers). *Notification:* continuous (freshmen), continuous (transfers).

Admissions Contact Owens Community College, 300 Davis Street, Findlay, OH 45840. *Phone:* 419-429-3509. *Toll-free phone:* 800-FINDLAY. *Fax:* 419-423-0246.

OWENS COMMUNITY COLLEGE
Toledo, Ohio

- **State-supported** 2-year, founded 1966, part of Owens Community College System
- **Calendar** semesters
- **Degree** certificates and associate
- **Small-town** 100-acre campus
- **Coed,** 16,992 undergraduate students, 34% full-time, 47% women, 53% men

Undergraduates 5,751 full-time, 11,241 part-time. Students come from 11 states and territories, 13% African American, 0.7% Asian American or Pacific Islander, 4% Hispanic American, 0.7% Native American, 0.5% international.

Freshmen *Admission:* 6,692 enrolled. *Average high school GPA:* 2.62.

Faculty *Total:* 933, 17% full-time. *Student/faculty ratio:* 23:1.

Majors Accounting technology and bookkeeping; agricultural business and management; automotive engineering technology; business/commerce; CAD/CADD drafting/design technology; commercial and advertising art; criminal justice/law enforcement administration; early childhood education; electrical, electronic and communications engineering technology; fashion merchandising; fire protection and safety technology; food services technology; general studies; health information/medical records technology; management information systems; manufacturing technology; marketing/marketing management; mechanical design technology; mechanical engineering/mechanical technology; nursing (registered nurse training); occupational therapist assistant; physical therapist assistant; survey technology; telecommunications.

Academic Programs *Special study options:* academic remediation for entering students, adult/continuing education programs, advanced placement credit, cooperative education, distance learning, double majors, English as a second language, external degree program, freshman honors college, honors programs, independent study, internships, part-time degree program, services for LD students, summer session for credit. *ROTC:* Army (c), Air Force (b).

Library 42,500 titles, 450 serial subscriptions, 2,986 audiovisual materials, an OPAC, a Web page.

Computers on Campus 308 computers available on campus for general student use. A campuswide network can be accessed from off campus. Internet access, at least one staffed computer lab available.

Student Life *Housing:* college housing not available. *Activities and Organizations:* drama/theater group, student-run newspaper, choral group, intramurals, Alpha Beta Gamma, Drama Club, Student Association for Young Children, Phi Theta Kappa. *Campus security:* 24-hour emergency response devices and patrols, student patrols. *Student services:* health clinic, personal/psychological counseling.

Athletics Member NJCAA. *Intercollegiate sports:* baseball M, basketball M(s)/W(s), soccer M, softball W, volleyball W. *Intramural sports:* basketball M/W, bowling M/W, football M/W, golf M/W, softball M/W, table tennis M/W, tennis M/W, volleyball M/W, weight lifting M/W.

Standardized Tests *Required for some:* SAT I or ACT (for placement). *Recommended:* SAT I or ACT (for placement), ACT ASSET.

Costs (2004–05) *Tuition:* state resident $2280 full-time, $110 per credit hour part-time; nonresident $4560 full-time, $205 per credit hour part-time. *Required fees:* $380 full-time, $15 per credit hour part-time.

Financial Aid Of all full-time matriculated undergraduates who enrolled, 200 Federal Work-Study jobs (averaging $4500).

Applying *Options:* common application, early admission. *Required:* high school transcript. *Required for some:* minimum 2.0 GPA. *Recommended:* essay or personal statement, letters of recommendation, interview. *Application deadline:* rolling (freshmen), rolling (transfers). *Notification:* continuous (freshmen), continuous (transfers).

Admissions Contact Mr. Jim Welling, Admissions Coordinator, Owens Community College, PO Box 10000, Toledo, OH 43699-1947. *Phone:* 419-429-3509. *Toll-free phone:* 800-GO-OWENS. *Fax:* 419-661-7607.

PROFESSIONAL SKILLS INSTITUTE
Toledo, Ohio

Admissions Contact Ms. Hope Finch, Director of Marketing, Professional Skills Institute, 20 Arco Drive, Toledo, OH 43607. *Phone:* 419-531-9610. *Fax:* 419-531-4732.

REMINGTON COLLEGE-CLEVELAND CAMPUS
Cleveland, Ohio

- **Proprietary** 2-year
- **Calendar** continuous
- **Degree** diplomas and associate
- **Urban** 2-acre campus
- **Coed,** 750 undergraduate students

Undergraduates 57% African American, 1% Hispanic American.
Faculty *Total:* 65, 62% full-time, 2% with terminal degrees. *Student/faculty ratio:* 15:1.
Costs (2003–04) *Tuition:* $14,945 full-time.
Admissions Contact Mr. Dave McDaniel, Director of Recruitment, Remington College-Cleveland Campus, 14445 Broadway Avenue, Cleveland, OH 44125. *Phone:* 216-475-7520.

REMINGTON COLLEGE-CLEVELAND WEST CAMPUS
North Olmstead, Ohio

Admissions Contact Mr. Gary Azotea, Vice President, Remington College-Cleveland West Campus, 26350 Brookpark Road, North Olmstead, OH 44070. *Phone:* 440-777-2560.

RETS TECH CENTER
Centerville, Ohio

- **Proprietary** 2-year, founded 1953
- **Calendar** semesters
- **Degree** diplomas and associate
- **Suburban** 4-acre campus with easy access to Dayton
- **Coed,** 464 undergraduate students, 100% full-time, 53% women, 47% men

Undergraduates 464 full-time. Students come from 2 states and territories, 1% are from out of state, 20% African American, 2% Hispanic American, 1% transferred in.
Freshmen *Admission:* 327 enrolled.
Faculty *Total:* 82, 15% full-time, 6% with terminal degrees. *Student/faculty ratio:* 19:1.
Majors Computer engineering technology; computer programming; computer science; electrical, electronic and communications engineering technology; legal assistant/paralegal; medical/clinical assistant.
Academic Programs *Special study options:* advanced placement credit, internships, summer session for credit.
Library RETS Library with 2,200 titles, 27 serial subscriptions, 66 audiovisual materials.
Computers on Campus 220 computers available on campus for general student use. A campuswide network can be accessed. Internet access, at least one staffed computer lab available.
Student Life *Housing:* college housing not available. *Campus security:* 24-hour emergency response devices. *Student services:* personal/psychological counseling.
Standardized Tests *Required:* (for placement).
Costs (2003–04) *Tuition:* $6995 full-time. *Required fees:* $300 full-time. *Payment plan:* installment.
Applying *Options:* early admission, deferred entrance. *Required:* high school transcript, interview. *Application deadline:* rolling (freshmen), rolling (transfers).
Admissions Contact Mr. Rich Elkin, Director of Admissions, RETS Tech Center, 555 East Alex Bell Road, Centerville, OH 45459-2712. *Phone:* 937-433-3410. *Toll-free phone:* 800-837-7387. *Fax:* 937-435-6516. *E-mail:* rets@erinet.com.

ROSEDALE BIBLE COLLEGE
Irwin, Ohio

Admissions Contact Mr. John Showalter, Director of Enrollment Services, Rosedale Bible College, 2270 Rosedale Road, Irwin, OH 43029-9501. *Phone:* 740-857-1311.

SCHOOL OF ADVERTISING ART
Kettering, Ohio

- **Proprietary** 2-year, founded 1983
- **Calendar** trimesters
- **Degree** diplomas and associate
- **Suburban** 5-acre campus with easy access to Dayton, Ohio; Cincinnati, Ohio
- **Coed,** 125 undergraduate students, 100% full-time, 48% women, 52% men

Undergraduates 125 full-time. Students come from 4 states and territories, 2% are from out of state, 2% African American, 0.8% Asian American or Pacific Islander, 2% Hispanic American. *Retention:* 75% of 2002 full-time freshmen returned.
Freshmen *Admission:* 190 applied, 152 admitted, 65 enrolled. *Average high school GPA:* 2.75.
Faculty *Total:* 16, 50% full-time. *Student/faculty ratio:* 12:1.
Majors Commercial and advertising art.
Student Life *Housing:* college housing not available. *Student services:* personal/psychological counseling.
Costs (2004–05) *Tuition:* $16,155 full-time. *Required fees:* $400 full-time. *Payment plan:* installment.
Applying *Application fee:* $90. *Required:* interview, portfolio. *Required for some:* essay or personal statement, high school transcript, minimum 2.0 GPA, 1 letter of recommendation. *Application deadlines:* 8/15 (freshmen), 8/15 (transfers). *Notification:* continuous until 8/15 (freshmen), continuous until 8/15 (transfers).
Admissions Contact Mrs. Jayne Fahncke, Admissions, School of Advertising Art, 1725 East David Road, Kettering, OH 45440. *Phone:* 937-294-0592 Ext. 102. *Toll-free phone:* 877-300-9326 Ext. 102. *Fax:* 937-294-5869. *E-mail:* nathan@saacollege.com.

SINCLAIR COMMUNITY COLLEGE
Dayton, Ohio

- **State and locally supported** 2-year, founded 1887, part of Ohio Board of Regents
- **Calendar** quarters
- **Degree** certificates and associate
- **Urban** 50-acre campus with easy access to Cincinnati
- **Endowment** $18.8 million
- **Coed,** 19,860 undergraduate students, 38% full-time, 57% women, 43% men

Undergraduates 7,452 full-time, 12,408 part-time. Students come from 25 states and territories, 4% are from out of state, 16% African American, 1% Asian American or Pacific Islander, 1% Hispanic American, 0.5% Native American, 0.6% international, 7% transferred in. *Retention:* 56% of 2002 full-time freshmen returned.
Freshmen *Admission:* 6,271 applied, 6,271 admitted, 2,495 enrolled.
Faculty *Total:* 1,061, 42% full-time, 85% with terminal degrees. *Student/faculty ratio:* 23:1.
Majors Accounting; administrative assistant and secretarial science; African studies; applied art; architectural engineering technology; art; artificial intelligence and robotics; automobile/automotive mechanics technology; aviation/airway management; biotechnology; business administration and management; child development; civil engineering technology; commercial and advertising art; computer and information sciences; computer and information sciences related; computer engineering related; computer graphics; computer hardware engineering; computer/information technology services administration related; computer programming related; computer programming (specific applications); computer programming (vendor/product certification); computer software engineering; computer systems networking and telecommunications; consumer merchandising/retailing management; corrections; criminal justice/law enforcement administration; criminal justice/police science; culinary arts; dance; data entry/microcomputer applications; data entry/microcomputer applications related; dental hygiene; dietetics; drafting and design technology; dramatic/theatre arts; education; electrical, electronic and communications engineering technology; electromechanical technology; emergency medical technology (EMT paramedic); engineering; finance; fine/studio arts; fire science; foods, nutrition, and wellness; gerontology; graphic and printing equipment operation/production; health information/medical records administration; hotel/motel administration; human services; industrial radiologic technology; industrial technology; information science/studies; information technology; interior design; kindergarten/preschool education; labor and industrial relations; legal administrative assistant/secretary; legal assistant/paralegal; liberal arts and sciences/liberal studies; logistics and materials management; machine tool technology; marketing/marketing management; mass communication/media; mechanical engineering/mechanical technology; medical administrative assistant and medical secretary; medical/clinical assistant; mental health/rehabilitation; music; nursing (registered nurse training); occupational therapy; physical education teaching and coaching; physical therapy; plastics engineering technology; public administration; quality control technology; radiologic technology/science; real estate; respiratory care therapy; sign language interpretation and translation; special products marketing; surgical technology; survey technology; system administration; tourism and travel services management; transportation technology; web/multimedia management and webmaster; word processing.

Academic Programs *Special study options:* academic remediation for entering students, adult/continuing education programs, cooperative education, distance learning, English as a second language, external degree program, honors programs, independent study, internships, off-campus study, part-time degree program, services for LD students, student-designed majors, summer session for credit. *ROTC:* Army (c), Air Force (c).

Library Learning Resources Center with 146,606 titles, 576 serial subscriptions, 8,745 audiovisual materials, an OPAC, a Web page.

Computers on Campus 1800 computers available on campus for general student use. A campuswide network can be accessed from off campus that provide access to Portal. Internet access, at least one staffed computer lab available.

Student Life *Housing:* college housing not available. *Activities and Organizations:* drama/theater group, student-run newspaper, choral group, African-American Men of the Future, Ohio Fellows, Phi Theta Kappa, student government, student newspaper. *Campus security:* 24-hour emergency response devices and patrols, student patrols, late-night transport/escort service. *Student services:* personal/psychological counseling.

Athletics Member NJCAA. *Intercollegiate sports:* baseball M(s), basketball M(s)/W(s), golf M(s), tennis M(s)/W(s), volleyball W(s).

Standardized Tests *Required for some:* ACT COMPASS.

Costs (2004–05) *Tuition:* area resident $1803 full-time, $40 per credit part-time; state resident $2943 full-time, $65 per credit part-time; nonresident $5310 full-time, $118 per credit part-time. Full-time tuition and fees vary according to course load. Part-time tuition and fees vary according to course load.

Financial Aid Of all full-time matriculated undergraduates who enrolled, 50 Federal Work-Study jobs (averaging $800). *Financial aid deadline:* 8/15.

Applying *Options:* electronic application, early admission, deferred entrance. *Application fee:* $10. *Required for some:* high school transcript, interview. *Application deadline:* rolling (freshmen), rolling (transfers). *Notification:* continuous (freshmen), continuous (transfers).

Admissions Contact Ms. Sara P. Smith, Director and Systems Manager, Outreach Services, Sinclair Community College, 444 West Third Street, Dayton, OH 45402-1460. *Phone:* 937-512-3060. *Toll-free phone:* 800-315-3000. *Fax:* 937-512-2393.

SOUTHEASTERN BUSINESS COLLEGE
Chillicothe, Ohio

- **Proprietary** 2-year, founded 1976
- **Calendar** quarters
- **Degree** associate
- **Coed**

Faculty *Student/faculty ratio:* 10:1.

Costs (2003–04) *Tuition:* $8000 full-time, $660 per course part-time. *Required fees:* $1200 full-time, $150 per course part-time.

Admissions Contact Ms. Elizabeth Scott, Admissions Representative, Southeastern Business College, 1855 Western Avenue, Chillicothe, OH 45601-1038. *Phone:* 740-774-6300.

SOUTHEASTERN BUSINESS COLLEGE
Jackson, Ohio

Admissions Contact Mr. Todd A. Riegel, Director of Education, Southeastern Business College, 504 McCarty Lane, Jackson, OH 45640. *Phone:* 740-286-1554.

SOUTHEASTERN BUSINESS COLLEGE
Lancaster, Ohio

Admissions Contact Mr. Ray Predmore, Director, Southeastern Business College, 1522 Sheridan Drive, Lancaster, OH 43130-1303. *Phone:* 740-687-6126.

SOUTHERN STATE COMMUNITY COLLEGE
Hillsboro, Ohio

- **State-supported** 2-year, founded 1975
- **Calendar** quarters
- **Degree** certificates and associate
- **Rural** 60-acre campus
- **Endowment** $61,195
- **Coed,** 2,234 undergraduate students, 51% full-time, 73% women, 27% men

Undergraduates 1,150 full-time, 1,084 part-time. 1% African American, 0.4% Asian American or Pacific Islander, 0.4% Hispanic American, 0.3% Native American.

Freshmen *Admission:* 912 applied.

Faculty *Total:* 132, 36% full-time, 5% with terminal degrees. *Student/faculty ratio:* 20:1.

Majors Accounting technology and bookkeeping; agricultural production; business/commerce; computer programming (specific applications); corrections; drafting and design technology; emergency medical technology (EMT paramedic); executive assistant/executive secretary; human services; kindergarten/preschool education; liberal arts and sciences/liberal studies; medical/clinical assistant; nursing (registered nurse training); real estate.

Academic Programs *Special study options:* academic remediation for entering students, advanced placement credit, cooperative education, distance learning, double majors, independent study, internships, off-campus study, part-time degree program, services for LD students, student-designed majors, summer session for credit.

Library Learning Resources Center plus 2 others with 62,300 titles, 1,075 serial subscriptions, 2,577 audiovisual materials, an OPAC, a Web page.

Computers on Campus 200 computers available on campus for general student use. A campuswide network can be accessed from off campus. Internet access, at least one staffed computer lab available.

Student Life *Housing:* college housing not available. *Activities and Organizations:* drama/theater group, choral group, Student Leadership, Student Nurses Association, Drama Club, Association of Medical Assistants, Phi Theta Kappa, national fraternities. *Student services:* personal/psychological counseling.

Athletics Member NJCAA. *Intercollegiate sports:* basketball M(s)/W(s), soccer M(s), softball W(s), volleyball W(s). *Intramural sports:* table tennis M/W.

Standardized Tests *Required for some:* ACT (for placement). *Recommended:* ACT (for placement).

Costs (2004–05) *Tuition:* state resident $3120 full-time, $80 per credit hour part-time; nonresident $6009 full-time, $154 per credit hour part-time. Full-time tuition and fees vary according to course load. Part-time tuition and fees vary according to course load. *Payment plan:* deferred payment. *Waivers:* senior citizens and employees or children of employees.

Applying *Options:* common application, early admission, deferred entrance. *Application fee:* $15. *Recommended:* high school transcript. *Application deadline:* rolling (freshmen), rolling (transfers). *Notification:* continuous (freshmen), continuous (transfers).

Admissions Contact Ms. Wendy Johnson, Director of Admissions, Southern State Community College, 100 Hobart Drive, Hillsboro, OH 45133. *Phone:* 937-393-3431 Ext. 2720. *Toll-free phone:* 800-628-7722. *Fax:* 937-393-6682. *E-mail:* info@sscc.edu.

SOUTHWESTERN COLLEGE OF BUSINESS
Cincinnati, Ohio

Admissions Contact Mr. Greg Petree, Director of Admissions, Southwestern College of Business, 149 Northland Boulevard, Cincinnati, OH 45246-1122. *Phone:* 513-874-0432.

SOUTHWESTERN COLLEGE OF BUSINESS
Cincinnati, Ohio

Admissions Contact Ms. Betty Streber, Director of Admissions, Southwestern College of Business, 632 Vine Street, Suite 200, Cincinnati, OH 45202-4304. *Phone:* 513-421-3212.

SOUTHWESTERN COLLEGE OF BUSINESS
Dayton, Ohio

- **Proprietary** 2-year, founded 1972
- **Calendar** quarters
- **Degree** certificates, diplomas, and associate
- **Urban** campus
- **Coed**

Faculty *Student/faculty ratio:* 15:1.

Costs (2003–04) *Tuition:* $5775 full-time. *Required fees:* $1149 full-time.

Applying *Options:* deferred entrance.

Southwestern College of Business (continued)
Admissions Contact Ms. Kathie Day, Director of Admissions, Southwestern College of Business, 111 West First Street, Dayton, OH 45402-3003. *Phone:* 937-224-0061 Ext. 17.

SOUTHWESTERN COLLEGE OF BUSINESS
Middletown, Ohio

Admissions Contact Ms. Susan Knodel, Director of Admissions, Southwestern College of Business, 201 East Second Street, Franklin, OH 45005. *Phone:* 937-746-6633. *Fax:* 937-746-6757.

STARK STATE COLLEGE OF TECHNOLOGY
Canton, Ohio

- **State and locally supported** 2-year, founded 1970, part of Ohio Board of Regents
- **Calendar** semesters
- **Degree** certificates and associate
- **Suburban** 34-acre campus with easy access to Cleveland
- **Coed,** 5,667 undergraduate students, 33% full-time, 58% women, 42% men

Undergraduates 1,890 full-time, 3,777 part-time. Students come from 4 states and territories, 14% transferred in.
Freshmen *Admission:* 1,232 enrolled.
Faculty *Total:* 353, 33% full-time. *Student/faculty ratio:* 19:1.
Majors Accounting; administrative assistant and secretarial science; architectural engineering technology; automobile/automotive mechanics technology; biomedical technology; business administration and management; child development; civil engineering technology; clinical/medical laboratory technology; computer and information sciences related; computer engineering related; computer hardware engineering; computer/information technology services administration related; computer programming; computer programming related; computer programming (specific applications); computer programming (vendor/product certification); computer software and media applications related; computer software engineering; computer systems networking and telecommunications; computer/technical support; consumer merchandising/retailing management; court reporting; data entry/microcomputer applications; data entry/microcomputer applications related; dental hygiene; drafting and design technology; environmental studies; finance; fire science; food services technology; health information/medical records administration; human services; industrial technology; information technology; international business/trade/commerce; legal administrative assistant/secretary; marketing/marketing management; mechanical engineering/mechanical technology; medical/clinical assistant; nursing (registered nurse training); occupational therapy; operations management; physical therapy; respiratory care therapy; survey technology; web/multimedia management and webmaster; web page, digital/multimedia and information resources design; word processing.
Academic Programs *Special study options:* academic remediation for entering students, adult/continuing education programs, distance learning, external degree program, independent study, off-campus study, part-time degree program, services for LD students, student-designed majors, summer session for credit.
Library Learning Resource Center with 70,000 titles, 425 serial subscriptions, an OPAC.
Computers on Campus 500 computers available on campus for general student use. A campuswide network can be accessed from off campus. Internet access, online (class) registration, at least one staffed computer lab available.
Student Life *Housing:* college housing not available. *Activities and Organizations:* student-run newspaper. *Campus security:* 24-hour emergency response devices, late-night transport/escort service. *Student services:* personal/psychological counseling.
Standardized Tests *Recommended:* SAT I or ACT (for placement).
Costs (2004–05) *Tuition:* state resident $3528 full-time, $114 per credit hour part-time; nonresident $4608 full-time, $144 per credit hour part-time. *Required fees:* $288 full-time, $16 per credit hour part-time. *Payment plan:* installment. *Waivers:* senior citizens and employees or children of employees.
Applying *Options:* electronic application, early admission, deferred entrance. *Application fee:* $35. *Required:* high school transcript. *Application deadline:* rolling (freshmen), rolling (transfers).
Admissions Contact Mr. Wallace Hoffer, Dean of Student Services, Stark State College of Technology, 6200 Frank Road, N.W., Canton, OH 44720. *Phone:* 330-966-5450. *Toll-free phone:* 800-797-8275. *Fax:* 330-497-6313.

STAUTZENBERGER COLLEGE
Toledo, Ohio

- **Proprietary** 2-year
- **Calendar** quarters
- **Degree** certificates, diplomas, and associate
- **Urban** campus
- **Coed,** 792 undergraduate students, 56% full-time, 76% women, 24% men

Undergraduates 444 full-time, 348 part-time. 14% African American, 0.6% Asian American or Pacific Islander, 3% Hispanic American, 0.4% Native American.
Freshmen *Admission:* 150 applied, 143 admitted.
Faculty *Total:* 47, 13% full-time, 83% with terminal degrees. *Student/faculty ratio:* 28:1.
Majors Business, management, and marketing related; computer systems networking and telecommunications; legal assistant/paralegal; massage therapy; medical/clinical assistant; medical office assistant; veterinary technology; web page, digital/multimedia and information resources design.
Costs (2004–05) *Tuition:* $7200 full-time. *Required fees:* $100 full-time.
Financial Aid Of all full-time matriculated undergraduates who enrolled, 2 Federal Work-Study jobs (averaging $5000).
Admissions Contact Ms. Karen Fitzgerald, Director of Admissions and Marketing, Stautzenberger College, 5355 Southwyck Boulevard, Toledo, OH 43614. *Phone:* 419-866-0261. *Toll-free phone:* 800-552-5099.

TECHNOLOGY EDUCATION COLLEGE
Columbus, Ohio

Admissions Contact Michael Mongomery, Executive Director, Technology Education College, 288 South Hamilton Road, Columbus, OH 43213-2087. *Phone:* 614-456-4600. *Toll-free phone:* 800-838-3233.

TERRA STATE COMMUNITY COLLEGE
Fremont, Ohio

- **State-supported** 2-year, founded 1968, part of Ohio Board of Regents
- **Calendar** quarters
- **Degree** certificates, diplomas, and associate
- **Small-town** 100-acre campus with easy access to Toledo
- **Endowment** $907,000
- **Coed,** 2,549 undergraduate students, 42% full-time, 51% women, 49% men

Undergraduates 1,075 full-time, 1,474 part-time. Students come from 5 states and territories, 0.1% are from out of state, 2% African American, 0.2% Asian American or Pacific Islander, 5% Hispanic American, 0.3% Native American, 13% transferred in. *Retention:* 41% of 2002 full-time freshmen returned.
Freshmen *Admission:* 648 enrolled.
Faculty *Total:* 142, 29% full-time. *Student/faculty ratio:* 21:1.
Majors Accounting; administrative assistant and secretarial science; architectural engineering technology; automobile/automotive mechanics technology; automotive engineering technology; banking and financial support services; business administration and management; chemistry; commercial and advertising art; computer and information sciences; criminal justice/police science; electromechanical technology; engineering; engineering technology; English; entrepreneurship; finance; general studies; heating, air conditioning and refrigeration technology; heating, air conditioning, ventilation and refrigeration maintenance technology; industrial technology; information science/studies; kindergarten/preschool education; marketing/marketing management; mathematics; mechanical engineering/mechanical technology; medical administrative assistant and medical secretary; office occupations and clerical services; plastics engineering technology; psychology; quality control technology; robotics technology; sign language interpretation and translation; social work; technical and business writing; tool and die technology; welding technology.
Academic Programs *Special study options:* academic remediation for entering students, accelerated degree program, adult/continuing education programs, advanced placement credit, cooperative education, distance learning, double majors, honors programs, independent study, internships, part-time degree program, services for LD students, student-designed majors, summer session for credit.
Library Learning Resource Center with 22,675 titles, 383 serial subscriptions, 1,957 audiovisual materials, an OPAC, a Web page.
Computers on Campus 250 computers available on campus for general student use. A campuswide network can be accessed from off campus. Internet access, online (class) registration, at least one staffed computer lab available.
Student Life *Housing:* college housing not available. *Activities and Organizations:* choral group, Phi Theta Kappa, Student Activities Club, Society of Plastic Engineers, Koinonia, Student Senate, national fraternities. *Campus security:* 24-hour emergency response devices, late-night transport/escort service. *Student services:* personal/psychological counseling.
Athletics Member NJCAA. *Intercollegiate sports:* golf M, volleyball W(s). *Intramural sports:* basketball M/W, bowling M/W, football M, golf M/W, softball M/W, table tennis M/W, volleyball M/W.

Standardized Tests *Required:* ACT COMPASS (for placement). *Recommended:* SAT I or ACT (for placement).

Costs (2004–05) *Tuition:* state resident $3025 full-time, $63 per credit hour part-time; nonresident $7095 full-time, $148 per credit hour part-time. Full-time tuition and fees vary according to course load. Part-time tuition and fees vary according to course load. *Required fees:* $305 full-time, $6 per credit hour part-time. *Payment plans:* installment, deferred payment. *Waivers:* senior citizens and employees or children of employees.

Financial Aid Of all full-time matriculated undergraduates who enrolled, 45 Federal Work-Study jobs (averaging $2000).

Applying *Options:* electronic application, early admission, deferred entrance. *Application fee:* $15. *Required:* high school transcript. *Application deadline:* rolling (freshmen), rolling (transfers).

Admissions Contact Mr. Dale Stearns, Associate Dean of Student Services, Terra State Community College, 2830 Napoleon Road, Fremont, OH 43420. *Phone:* 419-334-8400 Ext. 347. *Toll-free phone:* 800-334-3886. *Fax:* 419-334-9035. *E-mail:* cstine@terra.edu.

TRUMBULL BUSINESS COLLEGE
Warren, Ohio

- **Proprietary** 2-year, founded 1972
- **Calendar** quarters
- **Degree** diplomas and associate
- **Small-town** 6-acre campus
- **Coed, primarily women,** 411 undergraduate students, 84% full-time, 84% women, 16% men

Undergraduates 347 full-time, 64 part-time. Students come from 2 states and territories, 1% are from out of state, 19% African American, 0.5% Asian American or Pacific Islander, 1% Hispanic American.

Freshmen *Admission:* 97 applied, 97 admitted, 97 enrolled.

Faculty *Total:* 13, 69% full-time. *Student/faculty ratio:* 28:1.

Majors Accounting; administrative assistant and secretarial science; computer/information technology services administration related; legal administrative assistant/secretary; management information systems; medical administrative assistant and medical secretary; word processing.

Student Life *Housing:* college housing not available. *Activities and Organizations:* student-run newspaper, Student Senate, MADD/SADD.

Costs (2004–05) *Tuition:* $6480 full-time, $180 per credit hour part-time. Full-time tuition and fees vary according to program. Part-time tuition and fees vary according to program. No tuition increase for student's term of enrollment. *Payment plan:* installment.

Financial Aid Of all full-time matriculated undergraduates who enrolled, 2 Federal Work-Study jobs. *Financial aid deadline:* 9/30.

Applying *Application fee:* $70. *Required:* high school transcript, interview. *Application deadline:* rolling (freshmen). *Notification:* continuous until 10/1 (freshmen).

Admissions Contact Admissions Office, Trumbull Business College, 3200 Ridge Road, Warren, OH 44484. *Phone:* 330-369-3200 Ext. 0. *E-mail:* admissions@tbc-trumbullbusiness.com.

THE UNIVERSITY OF AKRON-WAYNE COLLEGE
Orrville, Ohio

- **State-supported** 2-year, founded 1972, part of The University of Akron
- **Calendar** semesters
- **Degree** certificates and associate
- **Rural** 157-acre campus
- **Coed,** 1,884 undergraduate students, 56% full-time, 62% women, 38% men

Undergraduates 1,061 full-time, 823 part-time. Students come from 1 other state, 3% African American, 0.7% Asian American or Pacific Islander, 0.4% Hispanic American, 0.5% Native American, 5% transferred in.

Freshmen *Admission:* 415 applied, 415 admitted, 258 enrolled. *Average high school GPA:* 2.90. *Test scores:* ACT scores over 18: 72%; ACT scores over 24: 16%; ACT scores over 30: 1%.

Faculty *Total:* 145, 21% full-time, 21% with terminal degrees. *Student/faculty ratio:* 28:1.

Majors Accounting; accounting technology and bookkeeping; administrative assistant and secretarial science; business administration and management; business automation/technology/data entry; computer science; computer systems networking and telecommunications; data processing and data processing technology; engineering; environmental health; executive assistant/executive secretary; general studies; interdisciplinary studies; legal administrative assistant/secretary; liberal arts and sciences/liberal studies; management information

systems; medical administrative assistant and medical secretary; medical office management; occupational safety and health technology; office management; social work.

Academic Programs *Special study options:* academic remediation for entering students, adult/continuing education programs, advanced placement credit, cooperative education, distance learning, double majors, English as a second language, honors programs, independent study, internships, off-campus study, part-time degree program, services for LD students, summer session for credit. *ROTC:* Army (c), Air Force (c).

Library Wayne College Library with 23,450 titles, 472 serial subscriptions, an OPAC.

Computers on Campus 240 computers available on campus for general student use. A campuswide network can be accessed from off campus. Internet access, online (class) registration, at least one staffed computer lab available.

Student Life *Housing:* college housing not available. *Campus security:* late-night transport/escort service. *Student services:* personal/psychological counseling.

Athletics *Intercollegiate sports:* basketball M/W, cheerleading W, golf M, volleyball W. *Intramural sports:* basketball M/W, golf M, volleyball M/W.

Standardized Tests *Required for some:* SAT I or ACT (for admission). *Recommended:* SAT I or ACT (for admission).

Costs (2004–05) *Tuition:* state resident $2372 full-time; nonresident $5051 full-time. Full-time tuition and fees vary according to course load. Part-time tuition and fees vary according to course load. *Payment plan:* installment. *Waivers:* minority students, adult students, senior citizens, and employees or children of employees.

Financial Aid Of all full-time matriculated undergraduates who enrolled, 8 Federal Work-Study jobs (averaging $2200).

Applying *Options:* common application, electronic application, early admission, deferred entrance. *Application fee:* $30. *Required for some:* high school transcript. *Application deadlines:* 8/30 (freshmen), 8/30 (transfers). *Notification:* continuous until 8/30 (freshmen), continuous until 8/30 (transfers).

Admissions Contact Ms. Alicia Broadus, Admissions Student Services Office, The University of Akron-Wayne College, 1901 Smucker Road, Orrville, OH 44667. *Phone:* 800-221-8308 Ext. 8901. *Toll-free phone:* 800-221-8308 Ext. 8900.

UNIVERSITY OF CINCINNATI CLERMONT COLLEGE
Batavia, Ohio

- **State-supported** 2-year, founded 1972, part of University of Cincinnati System
- **Calendar** quarters
- **Degree** certificates and associate
- **Rural** 65-acre campus with easy access to Cincinnati
- **Endowment** $338,141
- **Coed**

Student Life *Campus security:* 12-hour patrols by trained security personnel.

Standardized Tests *Required for some:* SAT I or ACT (for placement). *Recommended:* SAT I or ACT (for placement).

Applying *Options:* deferred entrance. *Required:* high school transcript.

Admissions Contact Ms. Tanya Bohart, Admissions Assistant, University of Cincinnati Clermont College, 4200 Clermont College Drive, Batavia, OH 45103-1785. *Phone:* 513-732-5202. *E-mail:* tanya.bohart@uc.edu.

UNIVERSITY OF CINCINNATI RAYMOND WALTERS COLLEGE
Cincinnati, Ohio

Admissions Contact Ms. Julie Martin, Enrollment Services Counselor, University of Cincinnati Raymond Walters College, 9555 Plainfield Road, Cincinnati, OH 45236-1007. *Phone:* 513-745-5700.

UNIVERSITY OF NORTHWESTERN OHIO
Lima, Ohio

- **Independent** primarily 2-year, founded 1920
- **Calendar** quarters
- **Degrees** diplomas, associate, and bachelor's
- **Small-town** 35-acre campus with easy access to Dayton and Toledo
- **Coed,** 2,665 undergraduate students, 89% full-time, 22% women, 78% men

The University of Northwestern Ohio (UNOH) is a private, nonprofit university established in 1920. Located in Lima, Ohio, UNOH has a population of 3,000 students and offers associate degrees and diplomas in automotive, high performance, diesel, agricul-

University of Northwestern Ohio (continued)

ture, alternative fuels, and HVAC/R. Associate degrees and diplomas are awarded in the College of Business for accounting, business, computers, and medical, as well as various other majors.

Undergraduates 2,370 full-time, 295 part-time. Students come from 37 states and territories, 15% are from out of state, 0.6% African American, 0.2% Hispanic American, 3% transferred in, 45% live on campus.
Freshmen *Admission:* 3,000 applied, 2,800 admitted, 1,875 enrolled. *Average high school GPA:* 2.5.
Faculty *Total:* 95, 72% full-time, 9% with terminal degrees. *Student/faculty ratio:* 24:1.
Majors Accounting; administrative assistant and secretarial science; agricultural business and management; automobile/automotive mechanics technology; business administration and management; computer programming; diesel mechanics technology; health/health care administration; heating, air conditioning, ventilation and refrigeration maintenance technology; legal administrative assistant/secretary; legal assistant/paralegal; marketing/marketing management; medical administrative assistant and medical secretary; medical/clinical assistant; pharmacy technician; tourism and travel services management.
Academic Programs *Special study options:* academic remediation for entering students, accelerated degree program, adult/continuing education programs, advanced placement credit, cooperative education, distance learning, double majors, part-time degree program, summer session for credit.
Library University of Northwestern Ohio Library with 8,857 titles, 117 serial subscriptions, 10 audiovisual materials.
Computers on Campus 149 computers available on campus for general student use. A campuswide network can be accessed from off campus. Internet access, at least one staffed computer lab available.
Student Life *Housing Options:* men-only, women-only, disabled students. Campus housing is university owned and leased by the school. Freshman campus housing is guaranteed. *Activities and Organizations:* student-run newspaper, Students in Free Enterprise. *Campus security:* 24-hour emergency response devices and patrols, late-night transport/escort service. *Student services:* personal/psychological counseling.
Athletics *Intramural sports:* basketball M, bowling M/W, volleyball M/W.
Costs (2003–04) *Tuition:* $10,200 full-time, $175 per credit part-time. No tuition increase for student's term of enrollment. *Room only:* $2520. *Payment plan:* installment. *Waivers:* employees or children of employees.
Financial Aid Of all full-time matriculated undergraduates who enrolled, 40 Federal Work-Study jobs (averaging $2000).
Applying *Options:* electronic application, early admission, deferred entrance. *Application fee:* $50. *Required:* high school transcript. *Application deadline:* rolling (freshmen), rolling (transfers).
Admissions Contact Mr. Dan Klopp, Vice President for Enrollment Management, University of Northwestern Ohio, 1441 North Cable Road, Lima, OH 45805-1498. *Phone:* 419-227-3141. *Fax:* 419-229-6926. *E-mail:* info@nc.edu.

VATTEROTT COLLEGE
Broadview Heights, Ohio

Admissions Contact Mr. Jack Chalk, Director of Admissions, Vatterott College, 5025 East Royalton Road, Broadview Heights, OH 44147. *Phone:* 440-526-1660. *Toll-free phone:* 800-864-5644.

VIRGINIA MARTI COLLEGE OF ART AND DESIGN
Lakewood, Ohio

Admissions Contact Quinn Marti, Head of Admissions, Virginia Marti College of Art and Design, 11724 Detroit Avenue, PO Box 580, Lakewood, OH 44107-3002. *Phone:* 216-221-8584. *E-mail:* dmarti@vmcad.edu.

WASHINGTON STATE COMMUNITY COLLEGE
Marietta, Ohio

- **State-supported** 2-year, founded 1971, part of Ohio Board of Regents
- **Calendar** quarters
- **Degree** certificates and associate
- **Small-town** campus
- **Coed**

Faculty *Student/faculty ratio:* 14:1.
Standardized Tests *Required:* ACT ASSET (for placement).
Financial Aid Of all full-time matriculated undergraduates who enrolled, 50 Federal Work-Study jobs (averaging $2040).

Applying *Options:* early admission, deferred entrance. *Required for some:* high school transcript. *Recommended:* high school transcript.
Admissions Contact Ms. Rebecca Peroni, Director of Admissions, Washington State Community College, 710 Colegate Drive, Marietta, OH 45750-9225. *Phone:* 740-374-8716. *Fax:* 740-376-0257.

WRIGHT STATE UNIVERSITY, LAKE CAMPUS
Celina, Ohio

Admissions Contact Mrs. B.J. Hobler, Student Services Officer, Wright State University, Lake Campus, 7600 State Route 703, Celina, OH 45822-2921. *Phone:* 419-586-0324. *Toll-free phone:* 800-237-1477.

ZANE STATE COLLEGE
Zanesville, Ohio

- **State and locally supported** 2-year, founded 1969
- **Calendar** quarters
- **Degree** certificates and associate
- **Small-town** 170-acre campus with easy access to Columbus
- **Coed**

Faculty *Student/faculty ratio:* 18:1.
Standardized Tests *Recommended:* SAT I or ACT (for admission).
Costs (2003–04) *Tuition:* state resident $3240 full-time, $72 per credit hour part-time; nonresident $6480 full-time, $144 per credit hour part-time.
Financial Aid Of all full-time matriculated undergraduates who enrolled, 65 Federal Work-Study jobs (averaging $2010).
Applying *Options:* early admission. *Required:* high school transcript. *Required for some:* letters of recommendation, interview.
Admissions Contact Mr. Paul Young, Director of Admissions, Zane State College, 1555 Newark Road, Zanesville, OH 43701-2626. *Phone:* 740-454-2501 Ext. 1225. *Toll-free phone:* 800-686-TECH Ext. 1225.

OKLAHOMA

CARL ALBERT STATE COLLEGE
Poteau, Oklahoma

Admissions Contact Ms. Dee Ann Dickerson, Director of Admissions, Carl Albert State College, 1507 South McKenna, Poteau, OK 74953-5208. *Phone:* 918-647-1301. *Fax:* 918-647-1306. *E-mail:* ddickerson@carlalbert.edu.

CONNORS STATE COLLEGE
Warner, Oklahoma

- **State-supported** 2-year, founded 1908, part of Oklahoma State Regents for Higher Education
- **Calendar** semesters
- **Degree** certificates, diplomas, and associate
- **Rural** 1658-acre campus
- **Endowment** $19,200
- **Coed,** 2,335 undergraduate students

Undergraduates Students come from 36 states and territories, 4 other countries, 3% are from out of state, 11% African American, 0.6% Asian American or Pacific Islander, 2% Hispanic American, 25% Native American, 0.5% international, 12% live on campus.
Freshmen *Admission:* 727 applied, 727 admitted. *Average high school GPA:* 3.05.
Faculty *Total:* 116, 47% full-time, 5% with terminal degrees. *Student/faculty ratio:* 21:1.
Majors Animal sciences; biology/biological sciences; business administration and management; chemistry; child development; computer science; criminal justice/police science; education; engineering; family and consumer sciences/human sciences; general studies; health services/allied health/health sciences; history; horticultural science; journalism; mathematics; nursing (registered nurse training); pre-nursing studies; psychology; social work; sociology.
Academic Programs *Special study options:* academic remediation for entering students, accelerated degree program, adult/continuing education programs, advanced placement credit, internships, part-time degree program, summer session for credit.

Library Carl Westbrook Library with 63,728 titles, 319 serial subscriptions, an OPAC.

Computers on Campus 206 computers available on campus for general student use. At least one staffed computer lab available.

Student Life *Housing Options:* coed, men-only, women-only, disabled students. Campus housing is university owned. Freshman campus housing is guaranteed. *Activities and Organizations:* drama/theater group, student-run newspaper, Aggie Club, CD Club, Twilight Angels, McClarren Club, Library Club. *Campus security:* late-night transport/escort service, trained security personnel. *Student services:* health clinic.

Athletics Member NJCAA. *Intercollegiate sports:* baseball M(s), basketball M(s)/W(s), softball W(s). *Intramural sports:* basketball M/W, football M/W, golf M/W, softball W, tennis M/W, volleyball M/W.

Standardized Tests *Required for some:* SAT I or ACT (for placement), ACT COMPASS.

Costs (2004–05) *Tuition:* state resident $1169 full-time, $39 per credit hour part-time; nonresident $3814 full-time, $127 per credit hour part-time. Full-time tuition and fees vary according to course level. Part-time tuition and fees vary according to course level. *Required fees:* $600 full-time, $20 per credit hour part-time. *Room and board:* $5636; room only: $3436. Room and board charges vary according to board plan. *Payment plan:* installment. *Waivers:* employees or children of employees.

Financial Aid Of all full-time matriculated undergraduates who enrolled, 100 Federal Work-Study jobs (averaging $800).

Applying *Options:* early admission, deferred entrance. *Required for some:* high school transcript. *Application deadline:* rolling (freshmen), rolling (transfers).

Admissions Contact Mr. John A. Turnbull, Director of Admissions/Registrar, Connors State College, Route 1 Box 1000 College Road, Warner, OK 74469. *Phone:* 918-463-6233 Ext. 6233. *Toll-free phone:* 918-463-2931 Ext. 6241.

EASTERN OKLAHOMA STATE COLLEGE
Wilburton, Oklahoma

- **State-supported** 2-year, founded 1908, part of Oklahoma State Regents for Higher Education
- **Calendar** semesters
- **Degree** certificates and associate
- **Rural** 4000-acre campus
- **Coed,** 2,639 undergraduate students

Undergraduates Students come from 8 states and territories, 2 other countries, 20% live on campus.

Faculty *Total:* 51, 100% full-time.

Majors Accounting; administrative assistant and secretarial science; agricultural business and management; agricultural economics; agricultural teacher education; agronomy and crop science; animal sciences; art; art teacher education; biology/biological sciences; business administration and management; business teacher education; chemistry; clinical laboratory science/medical technology; clinical/medical laboratory technology; computer engineering technology; computer science; corrections; criminal justice/law enforcement administration; dramatic/theatre arts; economics; education; electrical, electronic and communications engineering technology; elementary education; English; environmental studies; farm and ranch management; fashion merchandising; forestry; forestry technology; history; horticultural science; industrial arts; journalism; legal administrative assistant/secretary; marketing/marketing management; mathematics; medical/clinical assistant; music; nursing (registered nurse training); physical education teaching and coaching; physical sciences; political science and government; pre-engineering; psychology; range science and management; science teacher education; sociology; speech and rhetoric; survey technology; veterinary sciences; wildlife and wildlands science and management.

Academic Programs *Special study options:* academic remediation for entering students, adult/continuing education programs, advanced placement credit, cooperative education, double majors, honors programs, internships, off-campus study, part-time degree program, summer session for credit.

Library Bill H. Hill Library with 41,639 titles, 220 serial subscriptions, an OPAC.

Computers on Campus 250 computers available on campus for general student use. A campuswide network can be accessed from off campus. Internet access, at least one staffed computer lab available.

Student Life *Housing:* on-campus residence required through sophomore year. *Options:* men-only, women-only. *Activities and Organizations:* drama/theater group, student-run newspaper, choral group, Student Senate, Aggie Club, Phi Beta Lambda. *Student services:* personal/psychological counseling.

Athletics Member NJCAA. *Intercollegiate sports:* baseball M(s), basketball M(s)/W(s), cheerleading M/W, equestrian sports M/W, softball W(s). *Intramural sports:* baseball M/W, basketball M/W, football M/W, golf M/W, soccer M/W, softball M/W, swimming M/W, tennis M/W, track and field M/W, volleyball M/W.

Standardized Tests *Required:* ACT (for placement).

Applying *Options:* common application, early admission, deferred entrance. *Application fee:* $25. *Required:* high school transcript. *Application deadline:* rolling (freshmen), rolling (transfers).

Admissions Contact Ms. Leah Miller, Director of Admissions, Eastern Oklahoma State College, 1301 West Main, Wilburton, OK 74578-4999. *Phone:* 918-465-2361 Ext. 240. *Fax:* 918-465-2431. *E-mail:* edavis@eosc.cc.ok.us.

HERITAGE COLLEGE OF HAIR DESIGN
Oklahoma City, Oklahoma

Admissions Contact 7100 I-35 Services Road, Suite 7118, Oklahoma City, OK 73149.

MURRAY STATE COLLEGE
Tishomingo, Oklahoma

- **State-supported** 2-year, founded 1908, part of Oklahoma State Regents for Higher Education
- **Calendar** semesters
- **Degree** associate
- **Rural** 120-acre campus
- **Coed**

Faculty *Student/faculty ratio:* 27:1.

Student Life *Campus security:* 24-hour patrols.

Athletics Member NJCAA.

Standardized Tests *Required:* ACT (for placement).

Financial Aid Of all full-time matriculated undergraduates who enrolled, 81 Federal Work-Study jobs (averaging $2880). 15 state and other part-time jobs (averaging $2880).

Applying *Options:* common application, early admission, deferred entrance. *Required:* high school transcript.

Admissions Contact Mrs. Ann Beck, Registrar and Director of Admissions, Murray State College, 1Murray Campus, Tishomingo, OK 73460. *Phone:* 580-371-2371 Ext. 171. *Fax:* 580-371-9844.

NORTHEASTERN OKLAHOMA AGRICULTURAL AND MECHANICAL COLLEGE
Miami, Oklahoma

- **State-supported** 2-year, founded 1919, part of Oklahoma State Regents for Higher Education
- **Calendar** semesters
- **Degree** certificates and associate
- **Small-town** 340-acre campus
- **Coed,** 2,102 undergraduate students, 70% full-time, 57% women, 43% men

Undergraduates 1,473 full-time, 629 part-time. Students come from 25 states and territories, 19 other countries, 15% are from out of state.

Freshmen *Admission:* 670 enrolled.

Faculty *Total:* 115, 70% full-time, 8% with terminal degrees. *Student/faculty ratio:* 23:1.

Majors Accounting; administrative assistant and secretarial science; agricultural business and management; agricultural economics; agronomy and crop science; American Indian/Native American studies; animal sciences; art; art teacher education; biology/biological sciences; botany/plant biology; broadcast journalism; business administration and management; chemistry; child development; clothing/textiles; computer programming; computer science; computer typography and composition equipment operation; construction engineering technology; criminal justice/law enforcement administration; dairy science; drafting and design technology; dramatic/theatre arts; economics; electrical, electronic and communications engineering technology; elementary education; forestry; graphic and printing equipment operation/production; horticultural science; hotel/motel administration; industrial arts; journalism; legal administrative assistant/secretary; marketing/marketing management; mathematics; mechanical engineering/mechanical technology; medical administrative assistant and medical secretary; music; nursing (registered nurse training); philosophy; photography; physical education teaching and coaching; physical sciences; physical therapy; piano and organ; plastics engineering technology; political science and government; pre-engineering; psychology; social sciences; social work; sociology; trade and industrial teacher education; veterinary sciences; welding technology; wildlife and wildlands science and management; wildlife biology.

Academic Programs *Special study options:* academic remediation for entering students, adult/continuing education programs, advanced placement credit, distance learning, double majors, external degree program, internships, part-time degree program, services for LD students, summer session for credit.

Northeastern Oklahoma Agricultural and Mechanical College (continued)

Library Learning Resource Center with 74,000 titles, 450 serial subscriptions, an OPAC, a Web page.

Computers on Campus 65 computers available on campus for general student use. Internet access, at least one staffed computer lab available.

Student Life *Housing:* on-campus residence required through sophomore year. *Options:* Campus housing is university owned. Freshman campus housing is guaranteed. *Activities and Organizations:* drama/theater group, student-run newspaper, choral group, marching band. *Campus security:* 24-hour patrols. *Student services:* health clinic, personal/psychological counseling, women's center, legal services.

Athletics Member NJCAA. *Intercollegiate sports:* baseball M(s), basketball M(s)/W(s), cheerleading M(s)/W(s), football M(s), golf M(s), softball W(s), volleyball W(s). *Intramural sports:* basketball M/W, football M, golf M, softball W.

Standardized Tests *Required:* SAT I or ACT (for placement).

Costs (2004–05) *Tuition:* state resident $1838 full-time, $61 per credit part-time; nonresident $4478 full-time, $149 per credit part-time. Full-time tuition and fees vary according to location. Part-time tuition and fees vary according to location. *Room and board:* Room and board charges vary according to board plan. *Payment plan:* installment. *Waivers:* senior citizens and employees or children of employees.

Financial Aid Of all full-time matriculated undergraduates who enrolled, 100 Federal Work-Study jobs (averaging $2500). 100 state and other part-time jobs (averaging $1000).

Applying *Options:* electronic application. *Required:* high school transcript. *Application deadline:* rolling (freshmen), rolling (transfers).

Admissions Contact Amy Ishmael, Dean of Enrollment Management, Northeastern Oklahoma Agricultural and Mechanical College, PO Box 3842, 200 I Street NE, Miami, OK 74354. *Phone:* 918-540-6212. *Toll-free phone:* 800-464-6636. *Fax:* 918-540-6946. *E-mail:* neoadmission@neoam.edu.

NORTHERN OKLAHOMA COLLEGE
Tonkawa, Oklahoma

Admissions Contact Ms. Sheri Snyder, Director of College Relations, Northern Oklahoma College, PO Box 310, Tonkawa, OK 74653. *Phone:* 580-628-6290. *Toll-free phone:* 800-429-5715. *Fax:* 580-628-6371.

OKLAHOMA CITY COMMUNITY COLLEGE
Oklahoma City, Oklahoma

- **State-supported** 2-year, founded 1969, part of Oklahoma State Regents for Higher Education
- **Calendar** semesters
- **Degree** certificates and associate
- **Urban** 143-acre campus
- **Endowment** $91,544
- **Coed,** 12,048 undergraduate students, 40% full-time, 57% women, 43% men

Undergraduates 4,863 full-time, 7,185 part-time. Students come from 8 states and territories, 16 other countries, 8% African American, 6% Asian American or Pacific Islander, 4% Hispanic American, 5% Native American, 4% international, 6% transferred in.

Freshmen *Admission:* 2,882 enrolled. *Test scores:* ACT scores over 18: 70%; ACT scores over 24: 16%.

Faculty *Total:* 518, 22% full-time, 10% with terminal degrees. *Student/faculty ratio:* 23:1.

Majors Accounting; airframe mechanics and aircraft maintenance technology; applied art; area studies related; art; automobile/automotive mechanics technology; avionics maintenance technology; biology/biological sciences; biomedical technology; broadcast journalism; business administration and management; chemistry; child development; commercial and advertising art; computer engineering technology; computer science; drafting and design technology; dramatic/theatre arts; electrical, electronic and communications engineering technology; emergency medical technology (EMT paramedic); finance; fine/studio arts; gerontology; health information/medical records administration; history; humanities; insurance; liberal arts and sciences/liberal studies; literature; mass communication/media; mathematics; modern languages; music; nursing (registered nurse training); occupational therapy; orthoptics; physical therapy; physics; political science and government; pre-engineering; psychology; respiratory care therapy; sociology; surgical technology.

Academic Programs *Special study options:* academic remediation for entering students, accelerated degree program, advanced placement credit, cooperative education, distance learning, double majors, English as a second language, external degree program, honors programs, independent study, part-time degree program, student-designed majors, summer session for credit.

Library an OPAC.

Computers on Campus A campuswide network can be accessed from off campus. Internet access, online (class) registration, at least one staffed computer lab available.

Student Life *Housing:* college housing not available. *Activities and Organizations:* drama/theater group, student-run newspaper, choral group, Phi Theta Kappa, College Republicans, Future Teachers, Hispanic Organization to Promote Education, Student Activities Board. *Campus security:* 24-hour emergency response devices and patrols, late-night transport/escort service. *Student services:* personal/psychological counseling.

Athletics *Intramural sports:* basketball M/W, football M, soccer M/W, softball M/W, swimming M/W, volleyball M/W.

Standardized Tests *Required for some:* ACT (for placement), ACT COMPASS.

Costs (2003–04) *Tuition:* state resident $1082 full-time, $36 per credit hour part-time; nonresident $3486 full-time, $116 per credit hour part-time. *Required fees:* $423 full-time, $14 per credit hour part-time. *Payment plan:* installment. *Waivers:* employees or children of employees.

Financial Aid Of all full-time matriculated undergraduates who enrolled, 268 Federal Work-Study jobs (averaging $2167).

Applying *Options:* early admission, deferred entrance. *Application fee:* $25. *Required:* high school transcript. *Application deadline:* rolling (freshmen), rolling (transfers).

Admissions Contact Ms. Gloria Cardenas-Barton, Dean of Admissions/Registrar, Oklahoma City Community College, 7777 South May Avenue, Oklahoma City, OK 73159. *Phone:* 405-682-7515. *E-mail:* sedwards@okccc.edu.

OKLAHOMA STATE UNIVERSITY, OKLAHOMA CITY
Oklahoma City, Oklahoma

- **State-supported** 2-year, founded 1961, part of Oklahoma State University
- **Calendar** semesters
- **Degree** certificates and associate
- **Urban** 80-acre campus
- **Coed,** 5,654 undergraduate students

Undergraduates Students come from 18 states and territories, 15 other countries, 1% are from out of state, 13% African American, 3% Asian American or Pacific Islander, 3% Hispanic American, 6% Native American, 0.8% international.

Freshmen *Average high school GPA:* 2.44.

Faculty *Total:* 250, 26% full-time. *Student/faculty ratio:* 20:1.

Majors Accounting; architectural engineering technology; business administration and management; business automation/technology/data entry; civil engineering technology; computer and information sciences; computer/technical support; construction engineering technology; criminal justice/police science; data entry/microcomputer applications; early childhood education; education; electrical and power transmission installation; electrical, electronic and communications engineering technology; engineering; fire science; floristry marketing; horticultural science; industrial design; landscape architecture; medical/health management and clinical assistant; nursing (registered nurse training); occupational safety and health technology; quality control technology; sign language interpretation and translation; substance abuse/addiction counseling; survey technology; turf and turfgrass management; veterinary technology.

Academic Programs *Special study options:* academic remediation for entering students, advanced placement credit, distance learning, double majors, honors programs, independent study, part-time degree program, services for LD students, summer session for credit.

Library Oklahoma State University-Oklahoma City Campus with 11,973 titles, 244 serial subscriptions, an OPAC, a Web page.

Computers on Campus 75 computers available on campus for general student use. A campuswide network can be accessed from off campus. Internet access, at least one staffed computer lab available.

Student Life *Housing:* college housing not available. *Activities and Organizations:* Phi Theta Kappa, Deaf/Hearing Social Club, American Criminal Justice Association, Horticulture Club, Vet-Tech Club. *Campus security:* 24-hour patrols, late-night transport/escort service.

Athletics *Intramural sports:* basketball M/W, volleyball M/W.

Standardized Tests *Required for some:* SAT I or ACT (for placement), ACT COMPASS.

Costs (2004–05) *Tuition:* state resident $2304 full-time, $77 per credit hour part-time; nonresident $5754 full-time, $192 per credit hour part-time. *Required fees:* $35 full-time.

Financial Aid Of all full-time matriculated undergraduates who enrolled, 75 Federal Work-Study jobs (averaging $2500).

Applying *Options:* early admission. *Application deadline:* rolling (freshmen), rolling (transfers). *Notification:* continuous (freshmen), continuous (transfers).

Admissions Contact Ms. Jeanne Kubier, Director of Admissions and Registrar, Oklahoma State University, Oklahoma City, 900 North Portland Avenue, Oklahoma City, OK 73107. *Phone:* 405-945-3287. *Fax:* 405-945-3277.

OKLAHOMA STATE UNIVERSITY, OKMULGEE
Okmulgee, Oklahoma

Admissions Contact Kelly Hildebrant, Director of Admissions, Oklahoma State University, Okmulgee, 1801 East Fourth Street, Okmulgee, OK 74447-3901. *Phone:* 918-293-5298. *Toll-free phone:* 800-722-4471. *Fax:* 918-293-4650. *E-mail:* francie@okway.okstate.edu.

PLATT COLLEGE
Oklahoma City, Oklahoma

Admissions Contact Ms. Jane Nowlin, Director, Platt College, 309 South Ann Arbor Avenue, Oklahoma City, OK 73128. *Phone:* 405-946-7799.

PLATT COLLEGE
Tulsa, Oklahoma

Admissions Contact Mrs. Susan Rone, Director, Platt College, 3801 South Sheridan Road, Tulsa, OK 74145-111. *Phone:* 918-663-9000.

REDLANDS COMMUNITY COLLEGE
El Reno, Oklahoma

- **State-supported** 2-year, founded 1938, part of Oklahoma State Regents for Higher Education
- **Calendar** semesters
- **Degree** certificates and associate
- **Suburban** 55-acre campus with easy access to Oklahoma City
- **Coed**

Faculty *Student/faculty ratio:* 18:1.
Student Life *Campus security:* 24-hour patrols.
Athletics Member NJCAA.
Standardized Tests *Required:* ACT (for placement).
Costs (2003–04) *Tuition:* state resident $1200 full-time, $40 per credit hour part-time; nonresident $3450 full-time, $115 per credit hour part-time. *Required fees:* $870 full-time, $24 per credit hour part-time, $5 per credit hour part-time.
Financial Aid Of all full-time matriculated undergraduates who enrolled, 25 Federal Work-Study jobs (averaging $2000). 70 state and other part-time jobs (averaging $2000).
Applying *Options:* common application, electronic application, early admission, deferred entrance. *Required:* high school transcript.
Admissions Contact Vice President for Student Services, Redlands Community College, El Reno, OK 73036. *Phone:* 405-262-2552 Ext. 1282. *E-mail:* frenchr@redlands.cc.net.

ROSE STATE COLLEGE
Midwest City, Oklahoma

- **State and locally supported** 2-year, founded 1968, part of Oklahoma State Regents for Higher Education
- **Calendar** semesters
- **Degree** certificates and associate
- **Suburban** 110-acre campus with easy access to Oklahoma City
- **Coed**

Student Life *Campus security:* 24-hour patrols.
Athletics Member NJCAA.
Standardized Tests *Required:* SAT I, ACT, or ACT COMPASS (for placement).
Financial Aid Of all full-time matriculated undergraduates who enrolled, 150 Federal Work-Study jobs (averaging $4000).
Applying *Options:* common application, electronic application, early admission, deferred entrance. *Application fee:* $15. *Required:* high school transcript.
Admissions Contact Ms. Evelyn K. Hutchings, Registrar and Director of Admissions, Rose State College, 6420 Southeast 15th Street, Midwest City, OK 73110-2799. *Phone:* 405-733-7673. *Fax:* 405-736-0309. *E-mail:* ekhutchings@ms.rose.cc.ok.us.

SEMINOLE STATE COLLEGE
Seminole, Oklahoma

- **State-supported** 2-year, founded 1931, part of Oklahoma State Regents for Higher Education
- **Calendar** semesters
- **Degree** diplomas and associate
- **Small-town** 40-acre campus with easy access to Oklahoma City
- **Coed**

Faculty *Student/faculty ratio:* 22:1.
Student Life *Campus security:* 24-hour patrols.
Athletics Member NJCAA.
Standardized Tests *Required:* SAT I, ACT, or ACT COMPASS (for placement).
Costs (2003–04) *Tuition:* state resident $1230 full-time, $64 per credit hour part-time; nonresident $2733 full-time. *Required fees:* $719 full-time. *Room and board:* $4110.
Applying *Options:* common application, early admission, deferred entrance. *Application fee:* $15. *Required:* high school transcript.
Admissions Contact Mr. Chris Lindley, Director of Enrollment Management, Seminole State College, PO Box 351, 2701 Boren Boulevard, Seminole, OK 74818-0351. *Phone:* 405-382-9272. *Fax:* 405-382-9524. *E-mail:* lindley_c@ssc.cc.ok.us.

SOUTHWESTERN OKLAHOMA STATE UNIVERSITY AT SAYRE
Sayre, Oklahoma

- **State and locally supported** 2-year, founded 1938, part of Southwestern Oklahoma State University
- **Calendar** semesters
- **Degree** diplomas and associate
- **Rural** 6-acre campus
- **Coed**

Faculty *Student/faculty ratio:* 18:1.
Standardized Tests *Required for some:* ACT (for admission).
Costs (2003–04) *Tuition:* state resident $91 per credit hour part-time.
Applying *Options:* common application, early admission, deferred entrance. *Application fee:* $15. *Required:* high school transcript.
Admissions Contact Ms. Kim Seymour, Registrar, Southwestern Oklahoma State University at Sayre, 409 East Mississippi Street, Sayre, OK 73662-1236. *Phone:* 580-928-5533 Ext. 101. *Fax:* 580-928-1140.

SPARTAN SCHOOL OF AERONAUTICS
Tulsa, Oklahoma

- **Proprietary** primarily 2-year, founded 1928
- **Calendar** calendar terms
- **Degrees** certificates, associate, and bachelor's
- **Urban** 26-acre campus
- **Coed, primarily men**

Standardized Tests *Required:* ACT ASSET (for placement).
Costs (2003–04) *Tuition:* Full-time tuition varies with program. Single student housing available from $290 to $350 per month.
Financial Aid Of all full-time matriculated undergraduates who enrolled, 15 Federal Work-Study jobs (averaging $5739).
Applying *Options:* deferred entrance. *Application fee:* $100. *Required:* high school transcript. *Recommended:* interview.
Admissions Contact Mr. Mark Fowler, Vice President of Student Records and Finance, Spartan School of Aeronautics, 8820 East Pine Street, PO Box 582833, Tulsa, OK 74158-2833. *Phone:* 918-836-6886.

TULSA COMMUNITY COLLEGE
Tulsa, Oklahoma

- **State-supported** 2-year, founded 1968, part of Oklahoma State Regents for Higher Education
- **Calendar** semesters
- **Degree** certificates and associate
- **Urban** 160-acre campus
- **Coed**

Faculty *Student/faculty ratio:* 20:1.
Student Life *Campus security:* 24-hour emergency response devices and patrols, student patrols, late-night transport/escort service.

Tulsa Community College (continued)

Standardized Tests *Required:* SAT I or ACT (for placement), CPT (for placement).
Costs (2003–04) *Tuition:* state resident $1208 full-time; nonresident $4208 full-time. *Required fees:* $711 full-time.
Financial Aid Of all full-time matriculated undergraduates who enrolled, 200 Federal Work-Study jobs (averaging $1500).
Applying *Options:* common application, early admission. *Application fee:* $20. *Required:* high school transcript.
Admissions Contact Ms. Leanne Brewer, Director of Admissions and Records, Tulsa Community College, 6111 East Skelly Drive, Tulsa, OK 74135. *Phone:* 918-595-7811. *E-mail:* lbrewer@tulsacc.edu.

TULSA WELDING SCHOOL
Tulsa, Oklahoma

- **Proprietary** 2-year, founded 1949
- **Calendar** continuous (phased start every 3 weeks)
- **Degree** diplomas and associate
- **Urban** 5-acre campus
- **Coed, primarily men,** 362 undergraduate students, 100% full-time, 4% women, 96% men

Undergraduates 362 full-time. Students come from 21 states and territories, 41% are from out of state, 13% African American, 0.6% Asian American or Pacific Islander, 3% Hispanic American, 9% Native American.
Faculty *Total:* 17, 94% full-time.
Majors Welding technology.
Student Life *Housing:* college housing not available. *Campus security:* 24-hour emergency response devices.
Costs (2003–04) *Tuition:* $21,200 per degree program part-time.
Admissions Contact Mr. Mike Thurber, Director of Admissions, Tulsa Welding School, 2545 East 11th Street, Tulsa, OK 74104. *Phone:* 800-331-2934 Ext. 240. *Toll-free phone:* 800-WELD-PRO. *E-mail:* tws@ionet.net.

VATTEROTT COLLEGE
Oklahoma City, Oklahoma

- **Proprietary** 2-year
- **Calendar** semesters
- **Degrees** diplomas, associate, and first professional
- **Urban** campus
- **Coed,** 191 undergraduate students, 100% full-time, 38% women, 62% men

Undergraduates 191 full-time. 31% African American, 2% Asian American or Pacific Islander, 4% Hispanic American, 6% Native American.
Freshmen *Admission:* 191 enrolled.
Faculty *Total:* 21, 71% full-time, 14% with terminal degrees. *Student/faculty ratio:* 12:1.
Majors Computer programming; electrical and electronic engineering technologies related; heating, air conditioning and refrigeration technology; information technology; medical office assistant.
Costs (2004–05) *Tuition:* $20,000 full-time. *Required fees:* $900 full-time.
Admissions Contact Mark Hybers, Director of Admissions, Vatterott College, 4629 Northwest 23rd Street, Oklahoma City, OK 73127. *Phone:* 405-945-0088. *Toll-free phone:* 888-948-0088.

VATTEROTT COLLEGE
Tulsa, Oklahoma

- **Proprietary** 2-year
- **Calendar** semesters
- **Degree** diplomas and associate
- **Urban** 3-acre campus
- **Coed, primarily women,** 267 undergraduate students, 100% full-time, 15% women, 85% men

Undergraduates 267 full-time. 23% African American, 4% Hispanic American, 9% Native American. *Retention:* 71% of 2002 full-time freshmen returned.
Freshmen *Admission:* 117 applied, 80 admitted, 80 enrolled.
Faculty *Total:* 18, 100% full-time. *Student/faculty ratio:* 15:1.
Majors Computer engineering technology; computer programming; electrical, electronic and communications engineering technology; heating, air conditioning and refrigeration technology; medical administrative assistant and medical secretary.
Costs (2004–05) *Tuition:* $7729 full-time. *Required fees:* $450 full-time.

Admissions Contact Mr. Tim Maloukis, Director of Admissions, Vatterott College, 555 South Memorial Drive, Tulsa, OK 74112. *Phone:* 918-836-6656. *Toll-free phone:* 888-857-4016.

WESTERN OKLAHOMA STATE COLLEGE
Altus, Oklahoma

- **State-supported** 2-year, founded 1926, part of Oklahoma State Regents for Higher Education
- **Calendar** semesters
- **Degree** certificates and associate
- **Rural** 142-acre campus
- **Endowment** $2.5 million
- **Coed**

Faculty *Student/faculty ratio:* 20:1.
Student Life *Campus security:* 24-hour emergency response devices.
Athletics Member NJCAA.
Standardized Tests *Required for some:* ACT (for admission).
Costs (2003–04) *Tuition:* state resident $1629 full-time, $54 per credit hour part-time; nonresident $4034 full-time, $134 per credit hour part-time. *Room and board:* $4120.
Financial Aid Of all full-time matriculated undergraduates who enrolled, 85 Federal Work-Study jobs (averaging $1978).
Applying *Options:* electronic application, early admission. *Application fee:* $15. *Required:* high school transcript.
Admissions Contact Mr. Larry W. Paxton, Director of Admissions/Registrar, Western Oklahoma State College, 2801 North Main Street, Altus, OK 73521-1397. *Phone:* 580-477-7720. *Fax:* 580-477-7723. *E-mail:* larry.paxton@wosc.edu.

OREGON

BLUE MOUNTAIN COMMUNITY COLLEGE
Pendleton, Oregon

- **State and locally supported** 2-year, founded 1962
- **Calendar** quarters
- **Degree** certificates and associate
- **Rural** 170-acre campus
- **Endowment** $1.7 million
- **Coed**

Faculty *Student/faculty ratio:* 25:1.
Athletics Member NJCAA.
Standardized Tests *Required:* ACT ASSET and ACT COMPASS (for placement).
Costs (2003–04) *Tuition:* state resident $2588 full-time, $58 per credit hour part-time; nonresident $5175 full-time, $115 per credit hour part-time. *Required fees:* $165 full-time, $2 per credit hour part-time.
Financial Aid Of all full-time matriculated undergraduates who enrolled, 60 Federal Work-Study jobs (averaging $1800). 30 state and other part-time jobs (averaging $1200).
Applying *Options:* electronic application. *Required:* high school transcript.
Admissions Contact Ms. Valerie Fouquette, Director, Admissions and Records, Blue Mountain Community College, PO Box 100, Pendleton, OR 97801. *Phone:* 541-278-5774. *Fax:* 541-278-5871. *E-mail:* onlineinquiry@bluecc.edu.

CENTRAL OREGON COMMUNITY COLLEGE
Bend, Oregon

- **District-supported** 2-year, founded 1949, part of Oregon Community College Association
- **Calendar** quarters
- **Degree** certificates and associate
- **Small-town** 193-acre campus
- **Endowment** $4.6 million
- **Coed,** 4,076 undergraduate students, 35% full-time, 60% women, 40% men

Located in Bend, Oregon, Central Oregon Community College (COCC) offers more than 50 certificate and degree options, affordable tuition, outstanding faculty members, small classes, and access to more than 20 bachelor's degree programs through Oregon

State University's Cascades campus. COCC also features on-campus housing, intramural sports, and exceptional outdoor recreation opportunities.

Undergraduates 1,438 full-time, 2,638 part-time. Students come from 15 states and territories, 3% are from out of state, 0.3% African American, 2% Asian American or Pacific Islander, 3% Hispanic American, 2% Native American, 7% transferred in, 3% live on campus.
Freshmen *Admission:* 1,428 applied, 1,428 admitted, 767 enrolled.
Faculty *Total:* 317, 26% full-time. *Student/faculty ratio:* 18:1.
Majors Accounting; administrative assistant and secretarial science; art; automobile/automotive mechanics technology; biological and physical sciences; business administration and management; cartography; computer and information sciences related; computer science; criminal justice/law enforcement administration; culinary arts; dental assisting; early childhood education; education; emergency medical technology (EMT paramedic); fire science; fish/game management; forestry; forestry technology; health information/medical records technology; hospitality administration; hospitality and recreation marketing; hotel/motel administration; humanities; industrial technology; kinesiology and exercise science; liberal arts and sciences/liberal studies; marketing/marketing management; mathematics; medical/clinical assistant; nursing (licensed practical/vocational nurse training); nursing (registered nurse training); physical sciences; pre-engineering; social sciences; sport and fitness administration; tourism promotion; welding technology.
Academic Programs *Special study options:* academic remediation for entering students, advanced placement credit, cooperative education, distance learning, double majors, English as a second language, independent study, internships, part-time degree program, services for LD students, student-designed majors, study abroad, summer session for credit.
Library COCC Library plus 1 other with 73,606 titles, 346 serial subscriptions, 3,339 audiovisual materials, an OPAC, a Web page.
Computers on Campus 335 computers available on campus for general student use. A campuswide network can be accessed from student residence rooms and from off campus that provide access to e-mail. Internet access, online (class) registration, at least one staffed computer lab available.
Student Life *Housing Options:* coed. Campus housing is university owned. *Activities and Organizations:* student-run newspaper, choral group, student government, club sports, Phi Theta Kappa, DEC, Science Learning Center. *Campus security:* 24-hour emergency response devices and patrols, late-night transport/escort service. *Student services:* health clinic, personal/psychological counseling.
Athletics *Intercollegiate sports:* baseball M(c)/W(c), basketball M(c)/W(c), cross-country running M(c)/W(c), golf M(c)/W(c), soccer M(c)/W(c), tennis M(c)/W(c), volleyball M(c)/W(c). *Intramural sports:* badminton M/W, basketball M/W, cross-country running M/W, football M, golf M/W, soccer M/W, softball M/W, table tennis M/W, tennis M/W, ultimate Frisbee M/W, volleyball M/W, water polo M/W, weight lifting M/W.
Standardized Tests *Required:* ACT ASSET (for placement).
Costs (2004–05) *Tuition:* area resident $2430 full-time, $54 per credit part-time; state resident $3330 full-time, $74 per credit part-time; nonresident $6930 full-time, $154 per credit part-time. *Required fees:* $114 full-time, $4 per credit part-time. *Room and board:* $5883. Room and board charges vary according to housing facility. *Payment plan:* deferred payment. *Waivers:* employees or children of employees.
Financial Aid Of all full-time matriculated undergraduates who enrolled, 400 Federal Work-Study jobs (averaging $1900).
Applying *Application fee:* $25. *Required for some:* high school transcript, minimum 2.0 GPA. *Recommended:* high school transcript. *Application deadline:* rolling (freshmen), rolling (transfers). *Notification:* continuous (freshmen), continuous (transfers).
Admissions Contact Ms. Alicia Moore, Director of Admissions and Records, Central Oregon Community College, 2600 Northwest College Way, Bend, OR 97701-5998. *Phone:* 541-383-7500. *Fax:* 541-383-7506. *E-mail:* welcome@cocc.edu.

CHEMEKETA COMMUNITY COLLEGE
Salem, Oregon

- **State and locally supported** 2-year, founded 1955
- **Calendar** quarters
- **Degree** certificates, diplomas, and associate
- **Urban** 72-acre campus with easy access to Portland
- **Coed,** 14,454 undergraduate students, 25% full-time, 54% women, 46% men

Undergraduates 3,647 full-time, 10,807 part-time. Students come from 5 states and territories, 1% are from out of state, 1% African American, 3% Asian American or Pacific Islander, 8% Hispanic American, 2% Native American, 0.1% international.
Freshmen *Admission:* 781 enrolled.
Faculty *Total:* 632, 36% full-time. *Student/faculty ratio:* 25:1.

Majors Accounting; administrative assistant and secretarial science; agricultural teacher education; art teacher education; automobile/automotive mechanics technology; business administration and management; civil engineering technology; computer engineering technology; computer programming; computer science; construction engineering technology; criminal justice/law enforcement administration; dental hygiene; drafting and design technology; economics; education; electrical, electronic and communications engineering technology; emergency medical technology (EMT paramedic); engineering; English; finance; fire science; forestry; forestry technology; graphic and printing equipment operation/production; health/health care administration; health information/medical records administration; health teacher education; hospitality administration; hotel/motel administration; humanities; human services; industrial technology; kindergarten/preschool education; liberal arts and sciences/liberal studies; mathematics; mechanical design technology; medical administrative assistant and medical secretary; medical/clinical assistant; nursing (licensed practical/vocational nurse training); nursing (registered nurse training); physical education teaching and coaching; political science and government; real estate; science teacher education; social sciences; teacher assistant/aide; welding technology.
Academic Programs *Special study options:* academic remediation for entering students, adult/continuing education programs, advanced placement credit, cooperative education, distance learning, double majors, English as a second language, independent study, internships, part-time degree program, services for LD students, summer session for credit.
Library Chemeketa Community College Library plus 1 other with 801 audiovisual materials, an OPAC, a Web page.
Computers on Campus A campuswide network can be accessed from off campus. Internet access, at least one staffed computer lab available.
Student Life *Housing:* college housing not available. *Activities and Organizations:* drama/theater group, student-run newspaper, choral group, Health Occupations Students of America, International Conference of Building Officials, Ski Club, Christian Fellowship. *Campus security:* 24-hour emergency response devices and patrols, late-night transport/escort service. *Student services:* personal/psychological counseling, women's center.
Athletics *Intercollegiate sports:* baseball M(s), basketball M(s)/W(s), cross-country running M(s)/W(s), track and field M(s)/W(s), volleyball W(s).
Standardized Tests *Required for some:* ACT ASSET.
Costs (2003–04) *Tuition:* state resident $2430 full-time, $50 per credit hour part-time; nonresident $7920 full-time, $172 per credit hour part-time. *Required fees:* $180 full-time, $4 per credit hour part-time.
Financial Aid Of all full-time matriculated undergraduates who enrolled, 316 Federal Work-Study jobs (averaging $1290).
Applying *Options:* deferred entrance. *Required for some:* high school transcript. *Application deadline:* rolling (freshmen), rolling (transfers). *Notification:* continuous (freshmen), continuous (transfers).
Admissions Contact Ms. Carolyn Brownell, Admissions Specialist, Chemeketa Community College, 4000 Lancaster Drive, NE, Salem, OR 97305-7070. *Phone:* 503-399-5006. *Fax:* 503-399-3918. *E-mail:* broc@chemeketa.edu.

CLACKAMAS COMMUNITY COLLEGE
Oregon City, Oregon

- **District-supported** 2-year, founded 1966
- **Calendar** quarters
- **Degree** certificates, diplomas, and associate
- **Suburban** 175-acre campus with easy access to Portland
- **Endowment** $5.6 million
- **Coed**

Faculty *Student/faculty ratio:* 19:1.
Student Life *Campus security:* 24-hour emergency response devices and patrols, student patrols, late-night transport/escort service.
Athletics Member NJCAA.
Standardized Tests *Required:* Assessment and Placement Services for Community Colleges (for placement). *Recommended:* SAT I or ACT (for placement).
Financial Aid Of all full-time matriculated undergraduates who enrolled, 115 Federal Work-Study jobs (averaging $1330).
Applying *Options:* early admission. *Recommended:* high school transcript.
Admissions Contact Ms. Diane Drebin, Registrar, Clackamas Community College, 19600 South Molalla Avenue, Oregon City, OR 97045. *Phone:* 503-657-6958 Ext. 2742. *Fax:* 503-650-6654. *E-mail:* pattyw@clackamas.edu.

CLATSOP COMMUNITY COLLEGE
Astoria, Oregon

- **County-supported** 2-year, founded 1958
- **Calendar** quarters
- **Degree** certificates and associate
- **Small-town** 20-acre campus

Clatsop Community College (continued)
- **Endowment** $2.0 million
- **Coed**

Student Life *Campus security:* 24-hour emergency response devices, late-night transport/escort service.

Standardized Tests *Required:* ACT ASSET (for admission).

Costs (2003–04) *Tuition:* state resident $2340 full-time, $52 per credit part-time; nonresident $4500 full-time, $100 per credit part-time. *Required fees:* $90 full-time, $2 per credit part-time.

Financial Aid Of all full-time matriculated undergraduates who enrolled, 220 Federal Work-Study jobs (averaging $2175).

Applying *Options:* early admission. *Recommended:* high school transcript.

Admissions Contact Ms. Joanne Swenson, Admissions Coordinator/Registrar, Clatsop Community College, 1653 Jerome, Astoria, OR 97103-3698. *Phone:* 503-338-2325. *Toll-free phone:* 866-252-8767. *Fax:* 503-325-5738. *E-mail:* admissions@clatsop.cc.or.us.

COLUMBIA GORGE COMMUNITY COLLEGE
The Dalles, Oregon

Admissions Contact 400 East Scenic Drive, The Dalles, OR 97058.

HEALD COLLEGE-PORTLAND
Portland, Oregon

- **Independent** 2-year, founded 1863
- **Degree** certificates, diplomas, and associate
- **Coed**

Standardized Tests *Required:* (for admission).

Financial Aid Of all full-time matriculated undergraduates who enrolled, 15 Federal Work-Study jobs.

Applying *Options:* electronic application, early admission, deferred entrance. *Application fee:* $100. *Required:* high school transcript, interview.

Admissions Contact Director of Admissions, Heald College-Portland, 625 Southwest Broadway, Suite 200, Portland, OR 97205. *Phone:* 503-229-0492. *Toll-free phone:* 800-755-3550. *E-mail:* info@heald.edu.

ITT TECHNICAL INSTITUTE
Portland, Oregon

- **Proprietary** primarily 2-year, founded 1971, part of ITT Educational Services, Inc.
- **Calendar** quarters
- **Degrees** associate and bachelor's
- **Urban** 4-acre campus
- **Coed**

Standardized Tests *Required:* Wonderlic aptitude test (for admission).

Costs (2003–04) *Tuition:* Total Program Cost varies depending on course of study. Consult school catalog.

Financial Aid Of all full-time matriculated undergraduates who enrolled, 15 Federal Work-Study jobs (averaging $4000).

Applying *Options:* deferred entrance. *Application fee:* $100. *Required:* high school transcript, interview. *Recommended:* letters of recommendation.

Admissions Contact Mr. Ed Yakimchick, Director of Recruitment, ITT Technical Institute, 6035 Northeast 78th Court, Portland, OR 97218. *Phone:* 503-255-6500. *Toll-free phone:* 800-234-5488. *Fax:* 503-255-8381.

KLAMATH COMMUNITY COLLEGE
Klamath Falls, Oregon

Admissions Contact Mr. Greg Brown, Dean for Student Services, Klamath Community College, 7390 South 6th Street, Klamath Falls, OR 97603. *Phone:* 541-882-3521.

LANE COMMUNITY COLLEGE
Eugene, Oregon

Admissions Contact Ms. Helen Garrett, Director of Admissions/Registrar, Lane Community College, 4000 East 30th Avenue, Eugene, OR 97405-0640. *Phone:* 541-747-4501 Ext. 2686. *E-mail:* williamss@lanecc.edu.

LINN-BENTON COMMUNITY COLLEGE
Albany, Oregon

- **State and locally supported** 2-year, founded 1966
- **Calendar** quarters
- **Degree** certificates and associate
- **Small-town** 104-acre campus
- **Endowment** $1.9 million
- **Coed**, 5,453 undergraduate students, 55% full-time, 54% women, 46% men

Undergraduates 2,989 full-time, 2,464 part-time. Students come from 5 states and territories, 1% are from out of state, 1% African American, 3% Asian American or Pacific Islander, 4% Hispanic American, 2% Native American, 0.3% international, 5% transferred in.

Freshmen *Admission:* 3,014 applied, 2,740 admitted, 845 enrolled.

Faculty *Total:* 506, 36% full-time.

Majors Accounting; administrative assistant and secretarial science; agricultural business and management; agricultural teacher education; agriculture; animal sciences; art; automobile/automotive mechanics technology; biological and physical sciences; biology/biological sciences; business administration and management; chemistry; child care and support services management; civil engineering technology; commercial and advertising art; computer and information sciences; computer programming (specific applications); computer/technical support; criminal justice/police science; criminal justice/safety; culinary arts; culinary arts related; dairy husbandry and production; desktop publishing and digital imaging design; diesel mechanics technology; drafting and design technology; dramatic/theatre arts; economics; education; elementary education; engineering; English; family and consumer sciences/human sciences; foreign languages and literatures; graphic communications related; horse husbandry/equine science and management; horticultural science; industrial technology; journalism; juvenile corrections; legal administrative assistant/secretary; liberal arts and sciences/liberal studies; machine tool technology; mathematics; medical administrative assistant and medical secretary; medical/clinical assistant; metallurgical technology; multi-/interdisciplinary studies related; nursing (registered nurse training); photography; physical education teaching and coaching; physical sciences; physics; pre-engineering; restaurant, culinary, and catering management; speech and rhetoric; system administration; teacher assistant/aide; technical and business writing; water quality and wastewater treatment management and recycling technology; welding technology.

Academic Programs *Special study options:* academic remediation for entering students, adult/continuing education programs, advanced placement credit, cooperative education, distance learning, English as a second language, independent study, internships, part-time degree program, services for LD students, student-designed majors, summer session for credit. *ROTC:* Army (c), Air Force (c).

Library Linn-Benton Community College Library with 40,560 titles, 179 serial subscriptions, 6,756 audiovisual materials, an OPAC, a Web page.

Computers on Campus 500 computers available on campus for general student use. A campuswide network can be accessed from off campus. Internet access, online (class) registration, at least one staffed computer lab available.

Student Life *Housing:* college housing not available. *Activities and Organizations:* drama/theater group, student-run newspaper, choral group, EBOP Club, Multicultural Club, Campus Family Co-op, Horticulture Club, Collegiate Secretary Club. *Campus security:* 24-hour emergency response devices and patrols, student patrols, late-night transport/escort service. *Student services:* personal/psychological counseling.

Athletics *Intercollegiate sports:* baseball M(s), basketball M(s)/W(s), volleyball W(s). *Intramural sports:* basketball M/W, table tennis M/W, tennis M/W, ultimate Frisbee M/W.

Standardized Tests *Required:* CPT (for placement).

Costs (2003–04) *Tuition:* state resident $2250 full-time, $47 per credit hour part-time; nonresident $6795 full-time, $148 per credit hour part-time. Full-time tuition and fees vary according to course load. *Required fees:* $3 per credit part-time. *Payment plan:* installment. *Waivers:* senior citizens and employees or children of employees.

Financial Aid Of all full-time matriculated undergraduates who enrolled, 290 Federal Work-Study jobs (averaging $1800).

Applying *Options:* deferred entrance. *Application fee:* $25. *Required for some:* high school transcript. *Application deadline:* rolling (freshmen), rolling (transfers).

Admissions Contact Ms. Christine Baker, Outreach Coordinator, Linn-Benton Community College, 6500 Pacific Boulevard, SW, Albany, OR 97321. *Phone:* 541-917-4813. *E-mail:* admissions@linnbenton.edu.

MT. HOOD COMMUNITY COLLEGE
Gresham, Oregon

Admissions Contact Dr. Craig Kolins, Associate Vice President of Enrollment Services, Mt. Hood Community College, 26000 Southeast Stark Street, Gresham, OR 97030-3300. *Phone:* 503-491-7265.

PIONEER PACIFIC COLLEGE
Wilsonville, Oregon

- **Proprietary** primarily 2-year, founded 1981
- **Calendar** continuous
- **Degrees** diplomas, associate, and bachelor's
- **Suburban** campus with easy access to Portland
- **Coed,** 760 undergraduate students, 100% full-time, 73% women, 28% men

Undergraduates 759 full-time, 1 part-time. Students come from 2 states and territories, 1 other country, 6% are from out of state, 26% transferred in.
Freshmen *Admission:* 963 applied, 746 admitted, 316 enrolled.
Faculty *Total:* 74, 50% full-time, 11% with terminal degrees. *Student/faculty ratio:* 15:1.
Majors Accounting; business administration and management; criminal justice/police science; health/health care administration; information science/studies; information technology; legal assistant/paralegal; medical/clinical assistant; sales, distribution and marketing; web/multimedia management and webmaster.
Academic Programs *Special study options:* accelerated degree program.
Library 2,500 titles.
Computers on Campus 200 computers available on campus for general student use. A campuswide network can be accessed. Internet access available. Computer purchase or lease plan available.
Student Life *Housing:* college housing not available. *Activities and Organizations:* Phi Beta Lambda.
Standardized Tests *Required:* CPAt (for admission).
Costs (2004–05) *One-time required fee:* $150. *Tuition:* $7200 full-time, $160 per credit hour part-time. *Required fees:* $150 full-time.
Applying *Application fee:* $50. *Required:* high school transcript, interview. *Application deadline:* rolling (freshmen). *Notification:* continuous (transfers).
Admissions Contact Pioneer Pacific College, 27501 Southwest Parkway Avenue, Wilsonville, OR 97070. *Phone:* 503-682-3903. *Toll-free phone:* 866-772-4636. *Fax:* 503-682-1514. *E-mail:* inquiries@pioneerpacific.edu.

PORTLAND COMMUNITY COLLEGE
Portland, Oregon

- **State and locally supported** 2-year, founded 1961
- **Calendar** quarters
- **Degree** certificates, diplomas, and associate
- **Urban** 400-acre campus
- **Coed,** 96,764 undergraduate students

Portland Community College provides lower-division college transfer courses, 2-year associate degree programs, career training, and adult education courses. Low tuition, an extensive class schedule, and convenient locations combined with high-quality instruction are among its trademarks. For admissions information, contact 503-977-4519 or visit the Web site (http://www.pcc.edu).

Undergraduates Students come from 54 states and territories, 34 other countries, 12% are from out of state, 4% African American, 7% Asian American or Pacific Islander, 9% Hispanic American, 0.9% Native American, 0.4% international.
Freshmen *Admission:* 15,762 applied, 15,762 admitted.
Faculty *Total:* 1,745, 24% full-time. *Student/faculty ratio:* 25:1.
Majors Accounting; administrative assistant and secretarial science; aeronautics/aviation/aerospace science and technology; automobile/automotive mechanics technology; avionics maintenance technology; biological and physical sciences; biology/biotechnology laboratory technician; business administration and management; carpentry; child development; civil engineering technology; clinical/medical laboratory technology; commercial and advertising art; computer engineering technology; computer programming; construction engineering technology; criminal justice/law enforcement administration; dental hygiene; dietetics; drafting and design technology; educational/instructional media design; electrical, electronic and communications engineering technology; elementary education; engineering; engineering technology; family and consumer economics related; family and consumer sciences/human sciences; fire science; gerontology; health information/medical records administration; industrial design; industrial radiologic technology; information science/studies; landscape architecture; laser and optical technology; legal administrative assistant/secretary; legal assistant/paralegal; liberal arts and sciences/liberal studies; library science; machine tool technology; marketing/marketing management; mechanical engineering/mechanical technology; medical administrative assistant and medical secretary; medical/clinical assistant; medical laboratory technology; nursing (registered nurse training); ophthalmic laboratory technology; physical sciences; pre-engineering; real estate; sign language interpretation and translation; trade and industrial teacher education; welding technology.
Academic Programs *Special study options:* academic remediation for entering students, adult/continuing education programs, advanced placement credit, cooperative education, distance learning, double majors, English as a second

language, external degree program, independent study, internships, off-campus study, part-time degree program, services for LD students, study abroad, summer session for credit.
Library Main Library plus 4 others with 91,472 titles, 820 serial subscriptions, 247 audiovisual materials, an OPAC, a Web page.
Computers on Campus 1572 computers available on campus for general student use. A campuswide network can be accessed from off campus. Internet access, online (class) registration, at least one staffed computer lab available. Computer purchase or lease plan available.
Student Life *Housing:* college housing not available. *Activities and Organizations:* drama/theater group, student-run newspaper, television station, choral group. *Campus security:* 24-hour emergency response devices and patrols, late-night transport/escort service. *Student services:* personal/psychological counseling, women's center.
Athletics Member NJCAA. *Intercollegiate sports:* basketball M(s)/W(s). *Intramural sports:* archery M/W, badminton M/W, baseball M, basketball M/W, bowling M/W, cross-country running M/W, racquetball M/W, rock climbing M/W, skiing (cross-country) M/W, skiing (downhill) M/W, soccer M/W, softball W, swimming M/W, table tennis M/W, track and field M/W, ultimate Frisbee M/W, volleyball M/W, weight lifting M/W, wrestling M.
Costs (2004–05) *Tuition:* $62 per credit part-time; state resident $2790 full-time, $62 per credit part-time; nonresident $8550 full-time, $190 per credit part-time. *Required fees:* $240 full-time, $4 per credit part-time. *Payment plan:* installment. *Waivers:* senior citizens and employees or children of employees.
Applying *Options:* electronic application. *Application deadline:* rolling (freshmen).
Admissions Contact Mr. Dennis Bailey-Fournier, Director of Admissions, Portland Community College, PO Box 19000, Portland, OR 97280. *Phone:* 503-977-4519. *Fax:* 503-977-4740. *E-mail:* admissions@pcc.edu.

ROGUE COMMUNITY COLLEGE
Grants Pass, Oregon

- **State and locally supported** 2-year, founded 1970
- **Calendar** quarters
- **Degree** certificates, diplomas, and associate
- **Rural** 90-acre campus
- **Coed,** 4,383 undergraduate students, 41% full-time, 59% women, 41% men

Undergraduates 1,818 full-time, 2,565 part-time. Students come from 3 states and territories, 0.8% African American, 2% Asian American or Pacific Islander, 6% Hispanic American, 3% Native American, 0.2% international.
Freshmen *Admission:* 477 applied, 477 admitted, 477 enrolled.
Faculty *Total:* 457, 21% full-time. *Student/faculty ratio:* 12:1.
Majors Accounting; administrative assistant and secretarial science; art history, criticism and conservation; automobile/automotive mechanics technology; biological and physical sciences; business administration and management; child development; computer science; criminal justice/law enforcement administration; education related; electrical, electronic and communications engineering technology; fire science; heavy equipment maintenance technology; humanities; human services; industrial technology; journalism related; liberal arts and sciences/liberal studies; massage therapy; mathematics; nursing (registered nurse training); respiratory care therapy; social sciences; substance abuse/addiction counseling; welding technology.
Academic Programs *Special study options:* academic remediation for entering students, adult/continuing education programs, advanced placement credit, cooperative education, English as a second language, internships, part-time degree program, services for LD students, summer session for credit.
Library Rogue Community College Library with 33,000 titles, 275 serial subscriptions, an OPAC.
Computers on Campus 96 computers available on campus for general student use. A campuswide network can be accessed. Internet access, at least one staffed computer lab available.
Student Life *Housing:* college housing not available. *Activities and Organizations:* drama/theater group, student-run newspaper, choral group. *Campus security:* 24-hour patrols, late-night transport/escort service. *Student services:* personal/psychological counseling, women's center.
Athletics *Intramural sports:* badminton M/W, basketball M/W, skiing (cross-country) M/W, tennis M/W, volleyball M/W.
Standardized Tests *Required:* ACT ASSET (for placement).
Costs (2004–05) *Tuition:* state resident $2124 full-time, $59 per credit hour part-time; nonresident $2556 full-time, $71 per credit hour part-time. *Required fees:* $294 full-time, $4 per credit hour part-time.
Financial Aid Of all full-time matriculated undergraduates who enrolled, 210 Federal Work-Study jobs (averaging $3200). 300 state and other part-time jobs (averaging $3000).
Applying *Options:* early admission. *Application deadline:* rolling (freshmen), rolling (transfers).

Rogue Community College (continued)

Admissions Contact Claudia Sullivan, Director of Admissions, Rogue Community College, 3345 Redwood Highway, Grants Pass, OR 97527-9298. *Phone:* 541-956-7176. *E-mail:* ebunton@rogue.cc.or.us.

SOUTHWESTERN OREGON COMMUNITY COLLEGE
Coos Bay, Oregon

- **State and locally supported** 2-year, founded 1961
- **Calendar** quarters
- **Degree** certificates, diplomas, and associate
- **Small-town** 125-acre campus
- **Endowment** $637,301
- **Coed,** 2,068 undergraduate students, 42% full-time, 59% women, 41% men

Undergraduates 862 full-time, 1,206 part-time. Students come from 4 other countries, 1% African American, 1% Asian American or Pacific Islander, 3% Hispanic American, 4% Native American, 1% international.

Freshmen *Admission:* 636 applied, 636 admitted, 422 enrolled. *Average high school GPA:* 2.40.

Faculty *Total:* 216, 31% full-time. *Student/faculty ratio:* 23:1.

Majors Accounting; adult development and aging; athletic training; banking and financial support services; biological and physical sciences; business administration and management; criminal justice/police science; engineering; environmental studies; fire science; forestry; industrial technology; kindergarten/preschool education; liberal arts and sciences/liberal studies; machine tool technology; management information systems; marketing/marketing management; mathematics; medical/clinical assistant; music; nursing (registered nurse training); office management; social work; substance abuse/addiction counseling; turf and turfgrass management; welding technology.

Academic Programs *Special study options:* academic remediation for entering students, adult/continuing education programs, advanced placement credit, cooperative education, distance learning, English as a second language, internships, part-time degree program, services for LD students, summer session for credit.

Library Southwestern Oregon Community College Library with 40,505 titles, 218 serial subscriptions, 3,673 audiovisual materials, an OPAC, a Web page.

Computers on Campus 65 computers available on campus for general student use. A campuswide network can be accessed. Internet access, online (class) registration, at least one staffed computer lab available.

Student Life *Housing:* on-campus residence required for freshman year. *Options:* coed. Campus housing is university owned. *Activities and Organizations:* drama/theater group, student-run newspaper, choral group. *Campus security:* controlled dormitory access. *Student services:* personal/psychological counseling.

Athletics Member NJCAA. *Intercollegiate sports:* baseball M(s), basketball M(s)/W(s), soccer M(s)/W(s), softball W(s), track and field M(s)/W(s), volleyball W(s), wrestling M(s). *Intramural sports:* basketball M, volleyball M/W.

Standardized Tests *Recommended:* SAT I or ACT (for placement).

Costs (2004–05) *Tuition:* area resident $2520 full-time, $56 per credit part-time. *Required fees:* $315 full-time, $7 per credit part-time. *Room and board:* $5750. Room and board charges vary according to board plan and housing facility. *Payment plans:* installment, deferred payment. *Waivers:* employees or children of employees.

Financial Aid Of all full-time matriculated undergraduates who enrolled, 140 Federal Work-Study jobs (averaging $874). 42 state and other part-time jobs (averaging $545).

Applying *Options:* early admission. *Application fee:* $27. *Required for some:* high school transcript. *Application deadline:* rolling (freshmen), rolling (transfers). *Notification:* continuous (freshmen), continuous (transfers).

Admissions Contact Mr. Tom Nicholls, Recruitment, Southwestern Oregon Community College, Student 1st Stop, 1988 Newmark Avenue, Coos Bay, OR 97420. *Phone:* 541-888-7611. *Toll-free phone:* 800-962-2838. *E-mail:* jayjohnson@socc.edu.

TILLAMOOK BAY COMMUNITY COLLEGE
Tillamook, Oregon

- **District-supported** 2-year, founded 1984
- **Calendar** quarters
- **Degree** certificates, diplomas, and associate
- **Coed,** 250 undergraduate students, 12% full-time, 67% women, 33% men

Undergraduates 31 full-time, 219 part-time. Students come from 2 states and territories, 1 other country, 2% are from out of state, 2% African American, 0.8% Asian American or Pacific Islander, 3% Hispanic American, 0.8% Native American, 4% transferred in.

Freshmen *Admission:* 52 applied, 52 admitted, 52 enrolled.

Faculty *Total:* 27, 19% full-time, 19% with terminal degrees. *Student/faculty ratio:* 8:1.

Majors Accounting; accounting technology and bookkeeping; administrative assistant and secretarial science; business automation/technology/data entry; criminal justice/law enforcement administration; early childhood education; emergency medical technology (EMT paramedic); general studies; liberal arts and sciences/liberal studies; management science; marketing related; nursing related; office management; substance abuse/addiction counseling.

Student Life *Housing:* college housing not available. *Activities and Organizations:* student-run newspaper. *Campus security:* Evening security guard.

Costs (2003–04) *Tuition:* $54 per credit part-time; state resident $2592 full-time; nonresident $6192 full-time, $129 per credit part-time. Full-time tuition and fees vary according to program. Part-time tuition and fees vary according to program. *Required fees:* $618 full-time, $13 per credit part-time. *Payment plan:* deferred payment.

Admissions Contact Shiela Fitch, Enrollment Services Supervisor, Tillamook Bay Community College, 2510 First Street, Tillamook, OR 97141. *Phone:* -842-8222. *Fax:* 503-842-2214. *E-mail:* sfitch@tbcc.cc.or.us.

TREASURE VALLEY COMMUNITY COLLEGE
Ontario, Oregon

- **State and locally supported** 2-year, founded 1962
- **Calendar** quarters
- **Degree** certificates and associate
- **Small-town** 95-acre campus
- **Coed**

Student Life *Campus security:* student patrols, controlled dormitory access.

Athletics Member NJCAA.

Standardized Tests *Required for some:* SAT I, SAT II, ACT or ACT ASSET.

Costs (2003–04) *Tuition:* state resident $2700 full-time, $60 per quarter hour part-time; nonresident $3150 full-time, $70 per quarter hour part-time. *Required fees:* $360 full-time, $8 per quarter hour part-time. *Room and board:* $4203; room only: $2451.

Financial Aid Of all full-time matriculated undergraduates who enrolled, 90 Federal Work-Study jobs (averaging $1500).

Applying *Options:* common application, early admission, deferred entrance. *Application fee:* $10.

Admissions Contact Ms. Suzanne Bergam, Office of Admissions and Student Services, Treasure Valley Community College, 650 College Boulevard, Ontario, OR 97914. *Phone:* 541-881-8822 Ext. 239. *Fax:* 541-881-2721.

UMPQUA COMMUNITY COLLEGE
Roseburg, Oregon

- **State and locally supported** 2-year, founded 1964
- **Calendar** quarters
- **Degree** certificates and associate
- **Rural** 100-acre campus
- **Endowment** $2.9 million
- **Coed,** 2,141 undergraduate students, 46% full-time, 58% women, 42% men

Undergraduates 987 full-time, 1,154 part-time. Students come from 5 states and territories, 1% are from out of state, 1% African American, 1% Asian American or Pacific Islander, 2% Hispanic American, 2% Native American.

Faculty *Student/faculty ratio:* 18:1.

Majors Accounting; administrative assistant and secretarial science; agriculture; anthropology; art; art history, criticism and conservation; art teacher education; automobile/automotive mechanics technology; behavioral sciences; biological and physical sciences; biology/biological sciences; business administration and management; chemistry; child development; civil engineering technology; computer engineering technology; computer science; cosmetology; criminal justice/law enforcement administration; desktop publishing and digital imaging design; dramatic/theatre arts; economics; education; electrical, electronic and communications engineering technology; elementary education; emergency medical technology (EMT paramedic); engineering; English; fire science; forestry; health teacher education; history; humanities; human resources management; journalism; kindergarten/preschool education; legal administrative assistant/secretary; liberal arts and sciences/liberal studies; marketing/marketing management; mathematics; medical administrative assistant and medical secretary; music; music teacher education; natural sciences; nursing (registered nurse training); physical education teaching and coaching; physical sciences; political science and government; pre-engineering; psychology; social sciences; social work; sociology.

Academic Programs *Special study options:* academic remediation for entering students, accelerated degree program, adult/continuing education programs,

advanced placement credit, cooperative education, distance learning, English as a second language, honors programs, part-time degree program, services for LD students, student-designed majors, summer session for credit.
Library Umpqua Community College Library with 41,000 titles, 350 serial subscriptions, an OPAC, a Web page.
Computers on Campus 300 computers available on campus for general student use. A campuswide network can be accessed. Internet access, at least one staffed computer lab available.
Student Life *Housing:* college housing not available. *Activities and Organizations:* drama/theater group, student-run newspaper, choral group, Phi Theta Kappa, Computer Club, Phi Beta Lambda, Nursing Club, Umpqua Accounting Associates. *Student services:* personal/psychological counseling.
Athletics *Intercollegiate sports:* basketball M(s)/W(s). *Intramural sports:* basketball M/W, soccer M.
Costs (2004–05) *Tuition:* state resident $2655 full-time, $59 per credit part-time; nonresident $159 per credit part-time. *Required fees:* $45 full-time, $15 per term part-time. *Payment plan:* deferred payment. *Waivers:* senior citizens and employees or children of employees.
Financial Aid Of all full-time matriculated undergraduates who enrolled, 120 Federal Work-Study jobs (averaging $2700).
Applying *Options:* early admission, deferred entrance. *Application fee:* $25. *Recommended:* high school transcript. *Application deadline:* rolling (freshmen), rolling (transfers).
Admissions Contact Mr. David Farrington, Director of Admissions and Records, Umpqua Community College, PO Box 967, Roseburg, OR 97470-0226. *Phone:* 541-440-4616. *Fax:* 541-440-4612. *E-mail:* shiplel@umpqua.cc.or.us.

WESTERN BUSINESS COLLEGE
Portland, Oregon

Admissions Contact 425 Southwest Washington, Portland, OR 97204.

WESTERN CULINARY INSTITUTE
Portland, Oregon

Admissions Contact 1235 Southwest 12th Avenue, Suite 100, Portland, OR 97201. *Toll-free phone:* 800-666-0312.

PENNSYLVANIA

WINNER INSTITUTE OF ARTS & SCIENCES
Transfer, Pennsylvania

Admissions Contact One Winner Place, Transfer, PA 16154. *Toll-free phone:* 888-414-2433.

ACADEMY OF MEDICAL ARTS AND BUSINESS
Harrisburg, Pennsylvania

- **Proprietary** 2-year, founded 1980
- **Calendar** continuous
- **Degree** diplomas and associate
- **Suburban** 8-acre campus
- **Coed, primarily women,** 491 undergraduate students, 100% full-time, 86% women, 14% men

Undergraduates 491 full-time. Students come from 1 other state, 19% African American, 2% Asian American or Pacific Islander, 6% Hispanic American. *Retention:* 74% of 2002 full-time freshmen returned.
Faculty *Total:* 27, 52% full-time, 63% with terminal degrees. *Student/faculty ratio:* 20:1.
Majors Child care and support services management; child care provision; computer programming related; computer programming (specific applications); computer programming (vendor/product certification); data entry/microcomputer applications; data entry/microcomputer applications related; data processing and data processing technology; dental assisting; legal assistant/paralegal; medical administrative assistant and medical secretary; medical/clinical assistant; medical office management; word processing.

Academic Programs *Special study options:* advanced placement credit, internships.
Library Resource Center with 1,620 titles, 30 serial subscriptions, 30 audiovisual materials, an OPAC.
Computers on Campus 75 computers available on campus for general student use. Internet access, at least one staffed computer lab available.
Student Life *Housing:* college housing not available. *Activities and Organizations:* student-run newspaper.
Costs (2004–05) *Tuition:* $8650 full-time. *Required fees:* $1790 full-time.
Financial Aid Of all full-time matriculated undergraduates who enrolled, 25 Federal Work-Study jobs (averaging $6000).
Applying *Options:* common application. *Application fee:* $150. *Required:* high school transcript, interview. *Application deadline:* rolling (freshmen), rolling (transfers).
Admissions Contact Mr. Gary Kay, Director of Admissions, Academy of Medical Arts and Business, 2301 Academy Drive, Harrisburg, PA 17112. *Phone:* 717-545-4747. *Toll-free phone:* 800-400-3322. *Fax:* 717-901-9090. *E-mail:* info@acadcampus.com.

ALLENTOWN BUSINESS SCHOOL
Center Valley, Pennsylvania

- **Proprietary** 2-year, founded 1869, part of Career Education Corporation
- **Calendar** quarters
- **Degree** diplomas and associate
- **Urban** 30-acre campus with easy access to Philadelphia
- **Coed,** 1,511 undergraduate students, 89% full-time, 57% women, 43% men

Undergraduates 1,340 full-time, 171 part-time. Students come from 3 states and territories, 1% are from out of state, 3% African American, 0.3% Asian American or Pacific Islander, 6% Hispanic American, 0.1% Native American.
Freshmen *Admission:* 324 enrolled. *Average high school GPA:* 2.00.
Faculty *Total:* 92, 42% full-time, 2% with terminal degrees. *Student/faculty ratio:* 26:1.
Majors Accounting; administrative assistant and secretarial science; business administration and management; computer and information sciences; computer and information sciences and support services related; computer programming; criminal justice/law enforcement administration; design and visual communications; hospitality administration related; information science/studies; legal assistant/paralegal; marketing/marketing management; medical administrative assistant and medical secretary; tourism and travel services management.
Academic Programs *Special study options:* academic remediation for entering students, adult/continuing education programs, advanced placement credit, cooperative education, independent study, internships, services for LD students.
Library Main Library plus 1 other.
Computers on Campus 100 computers available on campus for general student use. A campuswide network can be accessed. Internet access, at least one staffed computer lab available. Computer purchase or lease plan available.
Student Life *Housing:* college housing not available. *Options:* Campus housing is provided by a third party. *Activities and Organizations:* Student Government, Travel Club. *Campus security:* evening security guard.
Standardized Tests *Required:* ACCUPLACER (for admission).
Costs (2004–05) *Tuition:* $25,200 full-time. Full-time tuition and fees vary according to course load. Part-time tuition and fees vary according to course load. No tuition increase for student's term of enrollment. *Room only:* Room and board charges vary according to housing facility. *Waivers:* employees or children of employees.
Financial Aid Of all full-time matriculated undergraduates who enrolled, 30 Federal Work-Study jobs (averaging $2500).
Applying *Options:* common application, electronic application, deferred entrance. *Required:* high school transcript. *Recommended:* interview. *Application deadline:* rolling (freshmen), rolling (transfers). *Notification:* continuous (freshmen), continuous (transfers).
Admissions Contact Mr. Michael Venier, Vice President Admissions, Allentown Business School, 2809 East Saucon Valley Road, Center Valley, PA 18034. *Phone:* 610-791-5100. *Toll-free phone:* 800-227-9109. *Fax:* 610-791-7810.

▶ **See page 494 for a narrative description.**

ALLIED MEDICAL AND TECHNICAL CAREERS
Forty Fort, Pennsylvania

Admissions Contact 166 Slocum Street, Forty Fort, PA 18704-2936.

ANTONELLI INSTITUTE
Erdenheim, Pennsylvania

- **Proprietary** 2-year, founded 1938
- **Calendar** semesters
- **Degree** associate
- **Suburban** 15-acre campus with easy access to Philadelphia
- **Coed**, 191 undergraduate students, 100% full-time, 63% women, 37% men

Undergraduates 191 full-time. Students come from 9 states and territories, 23% are from out of state, 5% African American, 2% Asian American or Pacific Islander, 2% Hispanic American, 40% live on campus. *Retention:* 100% of 1999 full-time freshmen returned.

Freshmen *Admission:* 160 applied, 122 admitted, 93 enrolled. *Average high school GPA:* 2.71.

Faculty *Total:* 17, 65% full-time. *Student/faculty ratio:* 11:1.

Majors Commercial and advertising art; photography.

Academic Programs *Special study options:* adult/continuing education programs, part-time degree program.

Library Antonelli Institute Library with 4,000 titles, 70 serial subscriptions, 50 audiovisual materials.

Computers on Campus 21 computers available on campus for general student use. A campuswide network can be accessed. Internet access, at least one staffed computer lab available. Computer purchase or lease plan available.

Student Life *Housing Options:* coed. Campus housing is leased by the school. Freshman applicants given priority for college housing. *Campus security:* 24-hour emergency response devices. *Student services:* personal/psychological counseling.

Costs (2004–05) *Tuition:* $15,600 full-time. Full-time tuition and fees vary according to program. *Room only:* $5300. *Payment plan:* installment.

Financial Aid Of all full-time matriculated undergraduates who enrolled, 5 Federal Work-Study jobs (averaging $2000).

Applying *Options:* common application, deferred entrance. *Application fee:* $25. *Required:* high school transcript, interview. *Recommended:* 1 letter of recommendation. *Application deadlines:* 9/1 (freshmen), 9/1 (transfers).

Admissions Contact Mr. Anthony Detore, Director of Admissions, Antonelli Institute, 300 Montgomery Avenue, Erdenheim, PA 19038. *Phone:* 215-836-2222. *Toll-free phone:* 800-722-7871. *Fax:* 215-836-2794.

THE ART INSTITUTE OF PHILADELPHIA
Philadelphia, Pennsylvania

- **Proprietary** primarily 2-year, founded 1966, part of The Art Institutes
- **Calendar** quarters
- **Degrees** associate and bachelor's
- **Urban** campus
- **Coed**, 3,007 undergraduate students, 68% full-time, 42% women, 58% men

The Art Institute of Philadelphia is one of the Art Institutes, a system of 30 schools nationwide that provide an important source of design, media arts, fashion, and culinary professionals. The parent company of the Art Institutes, Education Management Corp. (EDMC), is among the largest providers of proprietary postsecondary education in the US, offering bachelor's, associate, and nondegree programs. The company has provided career-oriented education programs for more than 35 years. Its schools have graduated more than 100,000 students.

Undergraduates 2,054 full-time, 953 part-time. Students come from 30 states and territories, 17% African American, 5% Asian American or Pacific Islander, 5% Hispanic American, 0.8% Native American, 0.3% international, 0.4% transferred in, 26% live on campus.

Freshmen *Admission:* 2,100 applied, 1,760 admitted, 775 enrolled. *Average high school GPA:* 2.7. *Test scores:* SAT verbal scores over 500: 54%; SAT math scores over 500: 54%; SAT verbal scores over 600: 24%; SAT math scores over 600: 24%; SAT verbal scores over 700: 1%; SAT math scores over 700: 1%.

Faculty *Total:* 171, 50% full-time. *Student/faculty ratio:* 20:1.

Majors Applied art; art; cinematography and film/video production; commercial and advertising art; commercial photography; culinary arts; fashion/apparel design; fashion merchandising; film/video and photographic arts related; graphic design; industrial design; interior design; intermedia/multimedia; photography; visual and performing arts related.

Academic Programs *Special study options:* academic remediation for entering students, adult/continuing education programs, advanced placement credit, cooperative education, external degree program, independent study, internships, off-campus study, part-time degree program, services for LD students, summer session for credit.

Library The Art Institute of Philadelphia Library with 19,200 titles, 150 serial subscriptions, 2,000 audiovisual materials, an OPAC, a Web page.

Computers on Campus 368 computers available on campus for general student use. Internet access, at least one staffed computer lab available. Computer purchase or lease plan available.

Student Life *Housing Options:* coed, disabled students. Campus housing is university owned. Freshman campus housing is guaranteed. *Activities and Organizations:* drama/theater group, student-run newspaper. *Campus security:* 24-hour patrols, controlled dormitory access. *Student services:* personal/psychological counseling.

Athletics *Intramural sports:* basketball M/W, softball M/W.

Standardized Tests *Recommended:* SAT I or ACT (for placement).

Costs (2004–05) *One-time required fee:* $100. *Tuition:* $22,280 full-time, $371 per credit part-time. Full-time tuition and fees vary according to course load and program. No tuition increase for student's term of enrollment. *Room only:* $8400. Room and board charges vary according to housing facility. *Payment plans:* tuition prepayment, installment.

Financial Aid Of all full-time matriculated undergraduates who enrolled, 230 Federal Work-Study jobs (averaging $3500).

Applying *Options:* common application, electronic application, early decision, deferred entrance. *Application fee:* $50. *Required:* essay or personal statement, high school transcript, interview. *Recommended:* minimum 2.5 GPA, letters of recommendation. *Application deadline:* rolling (freshmen), rolling (transfers). *Notification:* continuous (freshmen), continuous (transfers).

Admissions Contact Mr. Tim Howard, Director of Admissions, The Art Institute of Philadelphia, 1622 Chestnut Street, Philadelphia, PA 19103. *Phone:* 215-567-7080 Ext. 6337. *Toll-free phone:* 800-275-2474. *Fax:* 215-405-6399.

▶ See page 502 for a narrative description.

THE ART INSTITUTE OF PITTSBURGH
Pittsburgh, Pennsylvania

- **Proprietary** primarily 2-year, founded 1921, part of The Art Institutes International Education Management Corporation
- **Calendar** quarters
- **Degrees** diplomas, associate, and bachelor's
- **Urban** campus
- **Coed**, 3,405 undergraduate students, 62% full-time, 49% women, 51% men

Undergraduates 2,098 full-time, 1,307 part-time. Students come from 36 states and territories, 9 other countries, 42% are from out of state, 6% African American, 0.5% Asian American or Pacific Islander, 0.8% Hispanic American, 0.1% Native American, 0.4% international, 5% transferred in, 29% live on campus.

Freshmen *Admission:* 1,010 enrolled. *Average high school GPA:* 2.57. *Test scores:* SAT verbal scores over 500: 49%; SAT math scores over 500: 39%; ACT scores over 18: 50%; SAT verbal scores over 600: 13%; SAT math scores over 600: 8%; SAT verbal scores over 700: 1%.

Faculty *Total:* 136, 66% full-time, 7% with terminal degrees. *Student/faculty ratio:* 20:1.

Majors Advertising; applied art; architectural drafting and CAD/CADD; baking and pastry arts; CAD/CADD drafting/design technology; cinematography and film/video production; commercial and advertising art; commercial photography; computer graphics; cooking and related culinary arts; culinary arts; culinary arts related; design and visual communications; digital communication and media/multimedia; film/video and photographic arts related; food preparation; food service and dining room management; graphic design; hospitality administration; hospitality administration related; hotel/motel administration; illustration; industrial design; institutional food workers; interior design; intermedia/multimedia; painting; personal and culinary services related; photography; public relations/image management; radio and television; resort management; restaurant, culinary, and catering management; restaurant/food services management; web/multimedia management and webmaster; web page, digital/multimedia and information resources design.

Academic Programs *Special study options:* academic remediation for entering students, adult/continuing education programs, advanced placement credit, English as a second language, internships, part-time degree program, services for LD students, student-designed majors, summer session for credit.

Library Student Resource Center with 6,997 titles, 199 serial subscriptions.

Computers on Campus 240 computers available on campus for general student use. Internet access, at least one staffed computer lab available.

Student Life *Housing:* on-campus residence required for freshman year. *Options:* coed. Campus housing is leased by the school. *Activities and Organizations:* drama/theater group, student-run newspaper, radio station, American Society of Interior Designers, The Cel Group, AIPIK, Production Monsters, Video Visions. *Campus security:* 24-hour emergency response devices and patrols, student patrols, late-night transport/escort service, controlled dormitory access. *Student services:* personal/psychological counseling.

Standardized Tests *Required:* ACCUPLACER (for placement). *Recommended:* SAT I or ACT (for placement).

Costs (2004–05) *Tuition:* $16,335 full-time, $363 per credit part-time. Full-time tuition and fees vary according to course load. Part-time tuition and fees vary according to course load. *Required fees:* $185 full-time. *Room only:*

$5175. Room and board charges vary according to board plan and housing facility. *Payment plans:* installment, deferred payment. *Waivers:* employees or children of employees.
Applying *Options:* common application, deferred entrance. *Application fee:* $50. *Required:* essay or personal statement, high school transcript; minimum 2.0 GPA. *Required for some:* art portfolio. *Recommended:* interview. *Application deadline:* rolling (freshmen), rolling (transfers). *Notification:* continuous (freshmen), continuous (transfers).
Admissions Contact Mr. Newton I. Myvett, Director of Admissions, The Art Institute of Pittsburgh, 420 Boulevard of The Allies, Pittsburgh, PA 15219. *Phone:* 800-275-2470 Ext. 6220. *Toll-free phone:* 800-275-2470. *Fax:* 412-263-6667. *E-mail:* admissions@aii.edu.

> ▶ **See page 504 for a narrative description.**

BEREAN INSTITUTE
Philadelphia, Pennsylvania

- **Independent** 2-year, founded 1899
- **Calendar** quarters
- **Degree** certificates, diplomas, and associate
- **Urban** 3-acre campus
- **Endowment** $135,000
- **Coed,** 208 undergraduate students, 82% full-time, 73% women, 27% men

Undergraduates 171 full-time, 37 part-time. Students come from 3 states and territories.
Freshmen *Admission:* 69 enrolled.
Faculty *Total:* 26, 69% full-time. *Student/faculty ratio:* 15:1.
Majors Accounting; administrative assistant and secretarial science; computer science; court reporting; electrical, electronic and communications engineering technology; legal administrative assistant/secretary; medical administrative assistant and medical secretary.
Academic Programs *Special study options:* academic remediation for entering students, adult/continuing education programs, advanced placement credit, honors programs, internships, part-time degree program.
Library 3,500 titles, 48 serial subscriptions, an OPAC, a Web page.
Computers on Campus 30 computers available on campus for general student use. At least one staffed computer lab available.
Student Life *Housing:* college housing not available. *Activities and Organizations:* drama/theater group, student-run newspaper, television station, choral group, Berean Student Government, Berean Choir. *Campus security:* 24-hour emergency response devices and patrols. *Student services:* personal/psychological counseling.
Athletics *Intramural sports:* basketball M/W.
Costs (2003–04) *Tuition:* $4000 full-time, $1000 per term part-time. Full-time tuition and fees vary according to program. No tuition increase for student's term of enrollment. *Required fees:* $225 full-time. *Payment plans:* tuition prepayment, installment.
Applying *Options:* common application, deferred entrance. *Application fee:* $20. *Required:* high school transcript, interview. *Application deadline:* rolling (freshmen), rolling (transfers). *Notification:* continuous (freshmen), continuous (transfers).
Admissions Contact Berean Institute, 1901 West Girard Avenue, Philadelphia, PA 19130. *Phone:* 215-763-4833 Ext. 135. *Fax:* 215-236-6011 Ext. 104.

BERKS TECHNICAL INSTITUTE
Wyomissing, Pennsylvania

Admissions Contact Mr. Freddy Gonzales, Director of Admissions, Berks Technical Institute, 2205 Ridgewood Road, Wyomissing, PA 19610-1168. *Phone:* 610-372-1722. *Toll-free phone:* 800-284-4672 (in-state); 800-821-4662 (out-of-state).

BIDWELL TRAINING CENTER
Pittsburgh, Pennsylvania

Admissions Contact Bidwell Training Center, 1815 Metropolitan Street, Pittsburgh, PA 15233-2234.

BRADFORD SCHOOL
Pittsburgh, Pennsylvania

Admissions Contact Mr. Vincent S. Graziano, President, Bradford School, 707 Grant Street, Gulf Tower, Pittsburgh, PA 15219. *Phone:* 412-391-6710. *E-mail:* info@bradfordschoolpgh.com.

BRADLEY ACADEMY FOR THE VISUAL ARTS
York, Pennsylvania

- **Proprietary** 2-year, founded 1952
- **Calendar** quarters
- **Degree** associate
- **Suburban** 7-acre campus with easy access to Baltimore
- **Coed**

Faculty *Student/faculty ratio:* 15:1.
Standardized Tests *Required for some:* Wonderlic aptitude test. *Recommended:* SAT I or ACT (for admission).
Costs (2003–04) *Tuition:* $13,320 full-time, $370 per credit part-time. No tuition increase for student's term of enrollment. *Payment plans:* tuition prepayment, installment.
Financial Aid Of all full-time matriculated undergraduates who enrolled, 21 Federal Work-Study jobs (averaging $600).
Applying *Options:* deferred entrance. *Application fee:* $25. *Required:* essay or personal statement, high school transcript, 2 letters of recommendation, interview. *Required for some:* minimum 2.5 GPA, portfolio. *Recommended:* minimum 2.5 GPA.
Admissions Contact Ms. Alicia Laughman, Senior Admissions Representative, Bradley Academy for the Visual Arts, 1409 Williams Road, York, PA 17402. *Phone:* 717-755-2711. *Toll-free phone:* 800-864-7725. *Fax:* 717-840-1951. *E-mail:* info@bradleyacademy.net.

> ▶ **See page 520 for a narrative description.**

BUCKS COUNTY COMMUNITY COLLEGE
Newtown, Pennsylvania

- **County-supported** 2-year, founded 1964
- **Calendar** semesters
- **Degree** certificates and associate
- **Suburban** 200-acre campus with easy access to Philadelphia
- **Endowment** $2.3 million
- **Coed,** 10,096 undergraduate students, 40% full-time, 58% women, 42% men

Undergraduates 4,059 full-time, 6,037 part-time. Students come from 2 states and territories, 38 other countries, 1% are from out of state, 3% African American, 2% Asian American or Pacific Islander, 2% Hispanic American, 0.3% Native American, 5% international, 3% transferred in.
Freshmen *Admission:* 5,273 applied, 5,204 admitted, 2,646 enrolled.
Faculty *Total:* 572, 24% full-time. *Student/faculty ratio:* 19:1.
Majors Accounting; administrative assistant and secretarial science; American studies; art; banking and financial support services; biology/biological sciences; business administration and management; chemistry; cinematography and film/video production; commercial and advertising art; computer and information sciences; computer and information sciences related; computer engineering technology; computer/information technology services administration related; computer programming; computer programming related; computer programming (specific applications); computer science; consumer merchandising/retailing management; corrections; criminal justice/law enforcement administration; criminal justice/police science; culinary arts; data processing and data processing technology; dramatic/theatre arts; education; electrical, electronic and communications engineering technology; engineering; entrepreneurship; environmental studies; health science; health teacher education; historic preservation and conservation; hospitality administration; hotel/motel administration; humanities; information science/studies; information technology; journalism; kindergarten/preschool education; legal assistant/paralegal; liberal arts and sciences/liberal studies; marketing/marketing management; mass communication/media; mathematics; medical/clinical assistant; music; nursing (registered nurse training); physical education teaching and coaching; psychology; radio and television; social sciences; social work; sport and fitness administration; teacher assistant/aide; visual and performing arts; woodworking.
Academic Programs *Special study options:* academic remediation for entering students, adult/continuing education programs, advanced placement credit, cooperative education, distance learning, English as a second language, external degree program, independent study, internships, part-time degree program, services for LD students, student-designed majors, summer session for credit.
Library Bucks County Community College Library with 185,377 titles, 491 serial subscriptions, 5,546 audiovisual materials, an OPAC, a Web page.
Computers on Campus 450 computers available on campus for general student use. A campuswide network can be accessed from off campus that provide access to e-mail. Internet access, online (class) registration, at least one staffed computer lab available.
Student Life *Housing:* college housing not available. *Activities and Organizations:* drama/theater group, student-run newspaper, radio station, choral group, Phi Theta Kappa, Students in Free Enterprise, student council, The Centurion

Bucks County Community College (continued)
(student newspaper). *Campus security:* 24-hour emergency response devices and patrols, late-night transport/escort service. *Student services:* personal/psychological counseling.

Athletics Member NJCAA. *Intercollegiate sports:* baseball M, basketball M, equestrian sports M/W, golf M/W, soccer M/W, tennis M/W, volleyball W. *Intramural sports:* basketball M/W, bowling M/W, skiing (cross-country) M/W, skiing (downhill) M/W, soccer M/W, softball M/W, swimming M/W, tennis M/W, volleyball M/W.

Costs (2004–05) *Tuition:* area resident $2550 full-time, $85 per credit part-time; state resident $5100 full-time, $170 per credit part-time; nonresident $7650 full-time, $255 per credit part-time. *Required fees:* $434 full-time. *Payment plan:* installment. *Waivers:* senior citizens and employees or children of employees.

Financial Aid Of all full-time matriculated undergraduates who enrolled, 200 Federal Work-Study jobs.

Applying *Options:* electronic application, early admission. *Application fee:* $30. *Required:* high school transcript. *Required for some:* essay or personal statement, interview. *Application deadlines:* 5/1 (freshmen), 5/1 (transfers).

Admissions Contact Ms. Amy Wilson, Assistant Director of Admissions, Bucks County Community College, 275 Swamp Road, Newtown, PA 18940. *Phone:* 215-968-8119 Ext. 8119. *Fax:* 215-968-8110. *E-mail:* gleasonj@bucks.edu.

BUSINESS INSTITUTE OF PENNSYLVANIA
Meadville, Pennsylvania

Admissions Contact 628 Arch Street, Suite B105, Meadville, PA 16335.

BUSINESS INSTITUTE OF PENNSYLVANIA
Sharon, Pennsylvania

- **Proprietary** 2-year, founded 1926
- **Calendar** quarters
- **Degree** certificates, diplomas, and associate
- **Small-town** 2-acre campus
- **Coed**

Faculty *Student/faculty ratio:* 13:1.
Standardized Tests *Required:* ACT (for admission).
Costs (2003–04) *Tuition:* $6300 full-time, $175 per credit part-time. *Required fees:* $475 full-time.
Applying *Required:* high school transcript, interview.
Admissions Contact Ms. Shannon P. McNamara, President, Business Institute of Pennsylvania, 335 Boyd Drive, Sharon, PA 16146. *Phone:* 724-983-0700. *Toll-free phone:* 800-289-2069. *Fax:* 724-983-8355.

BUTLER COUNTY COMMUNITY COLLEGE
Butler, Pennsylvania

Admissions Contact Mr. William L. Miller, Director of Admissions, Butler County Community College, College Drive, PO Box 1203, Butler, PA 16003-1203. *Phone:* 724-287-8711 Ext. 344. *Toll-free phone:* 888-826-2829. *Fax:* 724-287-4961.

CAMBRIA COUNTY AREA COMMUNITY COLLEGE
Johnstown, Pennsylvania

- **State and locally supported** 2-year
- **Calendar** semesters
- **Degree** certificates, diplomas, and associate
- **Small-town** campus
- **Coed,** 1,327 undergraduate students, 45% full-time, 62% women, 38% men

Undergraduates 594 full-time, 733 part-time.
Freshmen *Admission:* 459 applied, 459 admitted, 386 enrolled.
Faculty *Total:* 145, 17% full-time. *Student/faculty ratio:* 14:1.
Majors Accounting; banking and financial support services; computer and information sciences; computer/information technology services administration related; computer programming; computer programming related; computer programming (specific applications); computer/technical support; construction engineering technology; consumer merchandising/retailing management; court

reporting; electrical, electronic and communications engineering technology; environmental engineering technology; geography; health/health care administration; heating, air conditioning and refrigeration technology; hospitality administration; human services; industrial technology; liberal arts and sciences/liberal studies; system administration; web/multimedia management and webmaster.
Academic Programs *Special study options:* academic remediation for entering students, adult/continuing education programs, advanced placement credit, cooperative education, distance learning, honors programs, independent study, internships, part-time degree program, services for LD students.
Library Cambria County Area Community College Main Library plus 3 others with an OPAC.
Computers on Campus 100 computers available on campus for general student use. A campuswide network can be accessed. Internet access, at least one staffed computer lab available.
Costs (2004–05) *Tuition:* area resident $1512 full-time, $63 per credit part-time; state resident $3024 full-time, $126 per credit part-time; nonresident $4536 full-time, $189 per credit part-time. *Required fees:* $390 full-time, $15 per credit part-time, $15 per term part-time. *Payment plan:* installment.
Financial Aid Of all full-time matriculated undergraduates who enrolled, 25 Federal Work-Study jobs (averaging $2500).
Applying *Options:* common application. *Application fee:* $20. *Recommended:* high school transcript, interview. *Application deadline:* 8/20 (freshmen).
Admissions Contact Mr. Jeff Maul, Admissions Officer, Cambria County Area Community College, PO Box 68, Johnstown, PA 15907. *Phone:* 814-532-5327. *Fax:* 814-262-3220. *E-mail:* jmaul@mail.ccacc.cc.pa.us.

CAMBRIA-ROWE BUSINESS COLLEGE
Indiana, Pennsylvania

- **Proprietary** 2-year, founded 1959
- **Calendar** quarters
- **Degree** diplomas and associate
- **Small-town** 1-acre campus
- **Coed, primarily women,** 118 undergraduate students, 94% full-time, 88% women, 12% men

Undergraduates 111 full-time, 7 part-time. 0.8% African American.
Freshmen *Admission:* 58 applied, 42 admitted, 42 enrolled.
Faculty *Total:* 8, 100% full-time, 38% with terminal degrees. *Student/faculty ratio:* 14:1.
Costs (2004–05) *Tuition:* $6900 full-time, $195 per credit part-time. *Required fees:* $990 full-time, $840 per term part-time.
Admissions Contact Laurie Price, Representative at Indiana Campus, Cambria-Rowe Business College, 422 South 13th Street, Indiana, PA 15701. *Phone:* 724-483-0222.

CAMBRIA-ROWE BUSINESS COLLEGE
Johnstown, Pennsylvania

- **Proprietary** 2-year, founded 1891
- **Calendar** quarters
- **Degree** diplomas and associate
- **Small-town** campus with easy access to Pittsburgh
- **Coed, primarily women,** 230 undergraduate students, 100% full-time, 89% women, 11% men

Undergraduates 230 full-time. Students come from 1 other state, 3% African American, 4% transferred in.
Freshmen *Admission:* 125 enrolled.
Faculty *Total:* 11, 100% full-time. *Student/faculty ratio:* 20:1.
Majors Accounting; administrative assistant and secretarial science; business administration and management; legal administrative assistant/secretary; medical administrative assistant and medical secretary.
Academic Programs *Special study options:* accelerated degree program, adult/continuing education programs, advanced placement credit, part-time degree program, summer session for credit.
Computers on Campus 105 computers available on campus for general student use. Computer purchase or lease plan available.
Student Life *Housing:* college housing not available.
Costs (2004–05) *One-time required fee:* $25. *Tuition:* $9200 full-time, $195 per credit part-time. *Required fees:* $1200 full-time. *Payment plan:* installment.
Financial Aid *Financial aid deadline:* 8/1.
Applying *Options:* common application, electronic application, early admission. *Application fee:* $15. *Required:* high school transcript, entrance exam. *Recommended:* minimum 2.0 GPA, interview. *Application deadline:* rolling (freshmen). *Notification:* continuous (freshmen).

Admissions Contact Mrs. Amanda C. Artim, Director of Admissions, Cambria-Rowe Business College, 221 Central Avenue, Johnstown, PA 15902-2494. *Phone:* 814-536-5168. *Fax:* 814-536-5160. *E-mail:* admissions@crbc.net.

CAREER TRAINING ACADEMY
Monroeville, Pennsylvania

Admissions Contact 105 Mall Boulevard, Suite 300 West, Expo Mart, Monroeville, PA 15146.

CAREER TRAINING ACADEMY
New Kensington, Pennsylvania

Admissions Contact 950 Fifth Avenue, New Kensington, PA 15068-6301.

CAREER TRAINING ACADEMY
Pittsburgh, Pennsylvania

Admissions Contact 1500 Northway Mall, Suite 200, Pittsburgh, PA 15237.

CENTER FOR ADVANCED MANUFACTURING & TECHNOLOGY
Erie, Pennsylvania

Admissions Contact Ms. Lisa Peszel, Director of Admissions, Center for Advanced Manufacturing & Technology, 5451 Merwin Lane, Erie, PA 16510. *Phone:* 814-897-0391 Ext. 226. *Toll-free phone:* 888-834-4226.

CENTRAL PENNSYLVANIA COLLEGE
Summerdale, Pennsylvania

- **Proprietary** primarily 2-year, founded 1881
- **Calendar** quarters
- **Degrees** certificates, associate, and bachelor's
- **Small-town** 35-acre campus
- **Coed,** 822 undergraduate students, 83% full-time, 66% women, 34% men

Central Pennsylvania College is a private, coeducational institution offering students bachelor's and associate degree programs in the business administration, communications, legal, medical, and information technology fields. Central Penn focuses on a fast-track career education that provides students with the experience employers seek through hands-on learning and internships.

Undergraduates 686 full-time, 136 part-time. Students come from 5 states and territories, 4% are from out of state, 11% African American, 1% Asian American or Pacific Islander, 2% Hispanic American, 2% Native American, 5% transferred in, 51% live on campus.

Freshmen *Admission:* 1,797 applied, 960 admitted, 208 enrolled.

Faculty *Total:* 97, 30% full-time. *Student/faculty ratio:* 17:1.

Majors Accounting; accounting related; business administration and management; child development; computer programming related; consumer merchandising/retailing management; criminal justice/law enforcement administration; executive assistant/executive secretary; finance; hotel/motel administration; information science/studies; legal administrative assistant/secretary; legal assistant/paralegal; management science; marketing/marketing management; mass communication/media; medical administrative assistant and medical secretary; medical/clinical assistant; ophthalmic laboratory technology; physical therapist assistant; sales, distribution and marketing; tourism and travel services management; web/multimedia management and webmaster.

Academic Programs *Special study options:* academic remediation for entering students, advanced placement credit, double majors, independent study, internships, part-time degree program, summer session for credit.

Library Charles T Jones Leadership Library plus 1 other with 6,122 titles, 94 serial subscriptions, 1,404 audiovisual materials, an OPAC.

Computers on Campus 150 computers available on campus for general student use. A campuswide network can be accessed. Internet access, at least one staffed computer lab available.

Student Life *Housing Options:* coed. Campus housing is university owned. *Activities and Organizations:* student-run newspaper, choral group, Campus Christian Fellowship, College Council, Student Ambassadors, Phi Beta Lambda, Travel Club. *Campus security:* 24-hour emergency response devices and patrols. *Student services:* personal/psychological counseling.

Athletics Member NJCAA. *Intercollegiate sports:* basketball M, volleyball W. *Intramural sports:* cheerleading M/W, golf M/W, volleyball M/W.

Costs (2004–05) *Comprehensive fee:* $17,160 includes full-time tuition ($10,440), mandatory fees ($570), and room and board ($6150). Full-time tuition

and fees vary according to program. Part-time tuition: $290 per credit hour. Part-time tuition and fees vary according to course load and program. *Required fees:* $190 per term part-time. *Room and board:* college room only: $4500. Room and board charges vary according to board plan and housing facility. *Payment plan:* deferred payment. *Waivers:* employees or children of employees.

Financial Aid Of all full-time matriculated undergraduates who enrolled, 50 Federal Work-Study jobs (averaging $1500). *Financial aid deadline:* 5/15.

Applying *Options:* electronic application. *Required:* high school transcript, interview. *Required for some:* minimum 2.0 GPA. *Application deadlines:* 9/20 (freshmen), 9/20 (transfers). *Notification:* continuous (freshmen), continuous (transfers).

Admissions Contact Ms. Jennifer Verhagen, Director of Admissions, Central Pennsylvania College, Campus on College Hill and Valley Roads, Summerdale, PA 17093. *Phone:* 717-728-2213. *Toll-free phone:* 800-759-2727. *Fax:* 717-732-5254.

CHI INSTITUTE
Southampton, Pennsylvania

- **Proprietary** 2-year, founded 1981, part of Quest Education
- **Calendar** quarters
- **Degree** certificates, diplomas, and associate
- **Suburban** 6-acre campus with easy access to Philadelphia
- **Coed,** 700 undergraduate students, 57% full-time, 36% women, 64% men

Undergraduates 400 full-time, 300 part-time. Students come from 3 states and territories, 2 other countries, 22% are from out of state, 25% African American, 3% Asian American or Pacific Islander, 7% Hispanic American, 1% international.

Freshmen *Admission:* 650 applied, 560 admitted. *Average high school GPA:* 2.5.

Faculty *Total:* 65, 69% full-time. *Student/faculty ratio:* 20:1.

Majors Clinical laboratory science/medical technology; commercial and advertising art; computer engineering technology; computer graphics; computer/information technology services administration related; computer programming; computer programming (specific applications); computer systems networking and telecommunications; computer typography and composition equipment operation; electrical, electronic and communications engineering technology; health information/medical records administration; heating, air conditioning, ventilation and refrigeration maintenance technology; medical administrative assistant and medical secretary; medical/clinical assistant; system administration; telecommunications.

Academic Programs *Special study options:* academic remediation for entering students, adult/continuing education programs.

Library 2,500 titles, 25 serial subscriptions.

Computers on Campus 70 computers available on campus for general student use.

Student Life *Housing:* college housing not available. *Activities and Organizations:* student-run newspaper. *Student services:* personal/psychological counseling.

Costs (2003–04) *Tuition:* $21,550 per degree program part-time. Full-time tuition and fees vary according to program.

Financial Aid Of all full-time matriculated undergraduates who enrolled, 30 Federal Work-Study jobs (averaging $2050).

Applying *Options:* common application, deferred entrance. *Required:* high school transcript, interview. *Application deadline:* rolling (freshmen), rolling (transfers).

Admissions Contact Mr. Michael Herbert, Director of Admissions, CHI Institute, 520 Street Road, Southampton, PA 18966. *Phone:* 215-357-5100 Ext. 114. *Toll-free phone:* 800-336-7696.

CHI INSTITUTE, RETS CAMPUS
Broomall, Pennsylvania

Admissions Contact Mr. Stuart Kahn, Director of Admissions, CHI Institute, RETS Campus, 1991 Lawrence Road, Suite 42, Broomall, PA 19008. *Phone:* 610-353-7630.

CHURCHMAN BUSINESS SCHOOL
Easton, Pennsylvania

- **Proprietary** 2-year, founded 1911
- **Calendar** trimesters
- **Degree** diplomas and associate
- **Small-town** campus with easy access to Allentown and Bethlehem
- **Coed**

Student Life *Campus security:* 24-hour emergency response devices.

Churchman Business School (continued)

Costs (2003–04) *Tuition:* $6885 full-time. Full-time tuition and fees vary according to class time. Part-time tuition and fees vary according to class time. *Required fees:* $690 full-time.

Applying *Options:* common application. *Application fee:* $25. *Required:* high school transcript. *Recommended:* interview.

Admissions Contact Ellis Plowman, President, Churchman Business School, 355 Spring Garden Street, Easton, PA 18042. *Phone:* 610-258-5345. *Fax:* 610-258-8086. *E-mail:* cbs4u@enter.net.

COMMONWEALTH TECHNICAL INSTITUTE
Johnstown, Pennsylvania

- **State-supported** 2-year
- **Calendar** trimesters
- **Degree** certificates, diplomas, and associate
- **Coed,** 231 undergraduate students, 100% full-time, 39% women, 61% men

Undergraduates 231 full-time. 14% African American, 1% Asian American or Pacific Islander. *Retention:* 64% of 2002 full-time freshmen returned.

Freshmen *Admission:* 102 enrolled.

Faculty *Total:* 30, 100% full-time.

Majors Accounting; architectural drafting and CAD/CADD; computer science; culinary arts; dental laboratory technology; mechanical drafting and CAD/CADD; medical/clinical assistant.

Library Hiram G. Andrews Center/Cambria County-Area Community College Library.

Student Life *Campus security:* 24-hour patrols.

Costs (2003–04) *Comprehensive fee:* $31,110 includes full-time tuition ($16,836) and room and board ($14,274).

Financial Aid Of all full-time matriculated undergraduates who enrolled, 20 Federal Work-Study jobs.

Admissions Contact Ms. Barbara Peterson, Director of Admissions, Commonwealth Technical Institute, 727 Goucher Street, Johnstown, PA 15905-3092. *Phone:* 814-255-8200 Ext. 8372. *Toll-free phone:* 800-762-4211 Ext. 8237.

COMMUNITY COLLEGE OF ALLEGHENY COUNTY
Pittsburgh, Pennsylvania

- **County-supported** 2-year, founded 1966
- **Calendar** semesters
- **Degree** certificates, diplomas, and associate
- **Urban** 242-acre campus
- **Coed,** 18,964 undergraduate students, 41% full-time, 56% women, 44% men

Undergraduates 7,818 full-time, 11,146 part-time. Students come from 17 states and territories, 79 other countries, 2% are from out of state, 15% African American, 1% Asian American or Pacific Islander, 0.6% Hispanic American, 0.7% Native American, 0.9% international, 11% transferred in.

Freshmen *Admission:* 6,273 applied, 5,392 admitted, 2,383 enrolled.

Faculty *Total:* 2,180, 13% full-time. *Student/faculty ratio:* 4:1.

Majors Accounting technology and bookkeeping; administrative assistant and secretarial science; airline pilot and flight crew; applied horticulture; architectural drafting and CAD/CADD; art; athletic training; automotive engineering technology; aviation/airway management; banking and financial support services; biology/biological sciences; building/property maintenance and management; business administration and management; business automation/technology/data entry; business machine repair; carpentry; chemical technology; chemistry; child care provision; child development; civil drafting and CAD/CADD; civil engineering technology; clinical/medical laboratory technology; commercial and advertising art; communications technologies and support services related; community health services counseling; computer engineering technology; computer systems networking and telecommunications; computer technology/computer systems technology; construction engineering technology; construction trades related; corrections; cosmetology and personal grooming arts related; court reporting; criminal justice/police science; culinary arts; diagnostic medical sonography and ultrasound technology; dietitian assistant; drafting and design technology; drafting/design engineering technologies related; dramatic/theatre arts; education (specific levels and methods) related; education (specific subject areas) related; electrical, electronic and communications engineering technology; electroneurodiagnostic/electroencephalographic technology; energy management and systems technology; engineering technologies related; English; entrepreneurship; environmental engineering technology; fire protection and safety technology; foodservice systems administration; foreign languages and literatures; general studies; greenhouse management; health and physical education; health information/medical records technology; health professions related;

health unit coordinator/ward clerk; heating, air conditioning, ventilation and refrigeration maintenance technology; hotel/motel administration; housing and human environments related; human development and family studies related; humanities; human resources management; industrial technology; insurance; journalism; landscaping and groundskeeping; legal administrative assistant/secretary; legal assistant/paralegal; liberal arts and sciences/liberal studies; machine shop technology; management information systems; marketing/marketing management; mathematics; mechanical design technology; mechanical drafting and CAD/CADD; medical administrative assistant and medical secretary; medical/clinical assistant; medical radiologic technology; music; nuclear medical technology; nursing assistant/aide and patient care assistant; nursing (licensed practical/vocational nurse training); nursing (registered nurse training); occupational therapist assistant; office management; ornamental horticulture; perioperative/operating room and surgical nursing; pharmacy technician; physical therapist assistant; physics; plant nursery management; psychiatric/mental health services technology; psychology; quality control technology; real estate; respiratory care therapy; restaurant, culinary, and catering management; retailing; robotics technology; science technologies related; sheet metal technology; sign language interpretation and translation; social sciences; social work; sociology; solar energy technology; substance abuse/addiction counseling; surgical technology; therapeutic recreation; tourism promotion; turf and turfgrass management; visual and performing arts related; welding technology.

Academic Programs *Special study options:* academic remediation for entering students, advanced placement credit, distance learning, English as a second language, external degree program, honors programs, independent study, off-campus study, part-time degree program, services for LD students, study abroad, summer session for credit.

Library Community College of Allegheny County Library plus 4 others with 272,697 titles, 933 serial subscriptions, 13,165 audiovisual materials, an OPAC, a Web page.

Computers on Campus 3100 computers available on campus for general student use. A campuswide network can be accessed from off campus. Internet access, online (class) registration, at least one staffed computer lab available.

Student Life *Housing:* college housing not available. *Activities and Organizations:* drama/theater group, student-run newspaper, choral group, Phi Theta Kappa. *Campus security:* 24-hour emergency response devices and patrols, late-night transport/escort service. *Student services:* health clinic, personal/psychological counseling, women's center.

Athletics Member NJCAA. *Intercollegiate sports:* baseball M, basketball M/W, bowling M/W, golf M/W, ice hockey M, softball W, table tennis M/W, tennis M/W, volleyball W. *Intramural sports:* badminton M/W, basketball M/W, bowling M/W, cross-country running M/W, football M, golf M/W, lacrosse M, racquetball M/W, softball M/W, table tennis M/W, tennis M/W, volleyball M/W, weight lifting M/W.

Costs (2004–05) *Tuition:* area resident $2325 full-time, $78 per credit part-time; state resident $4650 full-time, $155 per credit part-time; nonresident $6975 full-time, $233 per credit part-time. Full-time tuition and fees vary according to course load. Part-time tuition and fees vary according to course load. *Required fees:* $296 full-time. *Waivers:* employees or children of employees.

Applying *Options:* deferred entrance. *Recommended:* high school transcript. *Application deadline:* rolling (freshmen), rolling (transfers). *Notification:* continuous (freshmen), continuous (transfers).

Admissions Contact Community College of Allegheny County, 800 Allegheny Avenue, Pittsburgh, PA 15233.

▶ **See page 532 for a narrative description.**

COMMUNITY COLLEGE OF BEAVER COUNTY
Monaca, Pennsylvania

Admissions Contact Mr. Scott F. Ensworth, Dean of Enrollment, Community College of Beaver County, One Campus Drive, Monaca, PA 15061-2588. *Phone:* 724-775-8561 Ext. 330. *Toll-free phone:* 800-335-0222. *Fax:* 724-775-4055.

COMMUNITY COLLEGE OF PHILADELPHIA
Philadelphia, Pennsylvania

Admissions Contact Ms. Victoria King-Garwood, Director of Recruitment and Admissions, Community College of Philadelphia, 1700 Spring Garden Street, Philadelphia, PA 19130-3991. *Phone:* 215-751-8199.

CONSOLIDATED SCHOOL OF BUSINESS
Lancaster, Pennsylvania

- **Proprietary** 2-year, founded 1986
- **Calendar** continuous

■ **Degree** diplomas and associate
■ **Suburban** campus with easy access to Philadelphia
■ **Coed, primarily women**

Faculty *Student/faculty ratio:* 15:1.
Standardized Tests *Required:* TABE (for placement).
Costs (2003–04) *Tuition:* $10,200 full-time. No tuition increase for student's term of enrollment.
Applying *Options:* common application. *Application fee:* $25. *Required:* high school transcript, interview.
Admissions Contact Ms. Millie Liberatore, Director of Admission, Consolidated School of Business, 2124 Ambassador Circle, Lancaster, PA 17603. *Phone:* 717-764-9550. *Toll-free phone:* 800-541-8298. *Fax:* 717-394-6213. *E-mail:* admissions@csb.edu.

CONSOLIDATED SCHOOL OF BUSINESS
York, Pennsylvania

■ **Proprietary** 2-year, founded 1981
■ **Calendar** continuous
■ **Degree** diplomas and associate
■ **Suburban** 6-acre campus with easy access to Baltimore
■ **Coed, primarily women,** 202 undergraduate students, 100% full-time, 87% women, 13% men

Undergraduates 202 full-time. 5% African American, 0.5% Asian American or Pacific Islander, 7% Hispanic American.
Freshmen *Average high school GPA:* 2.8.
Faculty *Total:* 21, 86% full-time. *Student/faculty ratio:* 15:1.
Majors Accounting; business administration and management; health/health care administration; legal administrative assistant/secretary; medical administrative assistant and medical secretary; office management; tourism and travel services management.
Academic Programs *Special study options:* accelerated degree program, honors programs, independent study, internships, part-time degree program, services for LD students, student-designed majors.
Computers on Campus 120 computers available on campus for general student use. Internet access, at least one staffed computer lab available.
Student Life *Housing:* college housing not available. *Activities and Organizations:* Community Service Club.
Standardized Tests *Required:* TABE (for placement).
Costs (2004–05) *Tuition:* $15,500 full-time. No tuition increase for student's term of enrollment.
Applying *Options:* common application. *Application fee:* $25. *Required:* high school transcript, interview. *Application deadline:* rolling (freshmen), rolling (transfers).
Admissions Contact Ms. Millie Liberatore, Director of Admissions, Consolidated School of Business, 1605 Clugston Road, York, PA 17404. *Phone:* 717-764-9550. *Toll-free phone:* 800-520-0691. *Fax:* 717-764-9469. *E-mail:* admissions@csb.edu.

DEAN INSTITUTE OF TECHNOLOGY
Pittsburgh, Pennsylvania

■ **Proprietary** 2-year, founded 1947
■ **Calendar** quarters
■ **Degree** diplomas and associate
■ **Urban** 2-acre campus
■ **Coed,** 228 undergraduate students

Undergraduates Students come from 3 states and territories, 1 other country.
Faculty *Total:* 22, 73% full-time. *Student/faculty ratio:* 10:1.
Majors Electromechanical technology; heating, air conditioning and refrigeration technology.
Academic Programs *Special study options:* part-time degree program.
Library 2,500 titles, 25 serial subscriptions.
Computers on Campus 18 computers available on campus for general student use.
Student Life *Housing:* college housing not available. *Campus security:* 24-hour emergency response devices.
Applying *Options:* early admission, deferred entrance. *Application fee:* $50. *Application deadline:* rolling (freshmen), rolling (transfers).
Admissions Contact Mr. Richard D. Ali, Admissions Director, Dean Institute of Technology, 1501 West Liberty Avenue, Pittsburgh, PA 15226-1103. *Phone:* 412-531-4433. *Fax:* 412-531-4435.

DELAWARE COUNTY COMMUNITY COLLEGE
Media, Pennsylvania

■ **State and locally supported** 2-year, founded 1967
■ **Calendar** semesters
■ **Degree** certificates and associate
■ **Suburban** 123-acre campus with easy access to Philadelphia
■ **Endowment** $676,410
■ **Coed,** 10,608 undergraduate students, 40% full-time, 56% women, 44% men

Undergraduates 4,263 full-time, 6,345 part-time. Students come from 13 states and territories, 46 other countries, 1% are from out of state, 15% African American, 4% Asian American or Pacific Islander, 2% Hispanic American, 0.2% Native American, 1% international.
Freshmen *Admission:* 3,840 applied, 3,840 admitted, 2,616 enrolled.
Faculty *Total:* 665, 22% full-time. *Student/faculty ratio:* 20:1.
Majors Accounting technology and bookkeeping; anthropology; architectural engineering technology; automobile/automotive mechanics technology; biological and physical sciences; biomedical technology; building/property maintenance and management; business administration and management; business administration, management and operations related; commercial and advertising art; communication and journalism related; communication/speech communication and rhetoric; computer and information sciences; computer programming (specific applications); computer systems networking and telecommunications; computer technology/computer systems technology; construction engineering technology; criminal justice/police science; drafting and design technology; education (multiple levels); electrical, electronic and communications engineering technology; energy management and systems technology; engineering; entrepreneurship; fire protection and safety technology; general studies; health unit management/ward supervision; heating, air conditioning and refrigeration technology; heating, air conditioning, ventilation and refrigeration maintenance technology; hotel/motel administration; information science/studies; journalism; legal assistant/paralegal; liberal arts and sciences/liberal studies; machine tool technology; management information systems; mechanical engineering/mechanical technology; mechanical engineering technologies related; medical/clinical assistant; nursing (registered nurse training); office management; psychology; respiratory care therapy; robotics technology; science technologies related; sociology; surgical technology; teacher assistant/aide; web page, digital/multimedia and information resources design.
Academic Programs *Special study options:* academic remediation for entering students, adult/continuing education programs, advanced placement credit, cooperative education, distance learning, double majors, English as a second language, independent study, internships, part-time degree program, services for LD students, student-designed majors, summer session for credit.
Library Delaware County Community College Library with 58,692 titles, 421 serial subscriptions, 3,251 audiovisual materials, an OPAC, a Web page.
Computers on Campus 1200 computers available on campus for general student use. A campuswide network can be accessed from off campus. Internet access, online (class) registration, at least one staffed computer lab available.
Student Life *Housing:* college housing not available. *Activities and Organizations:* drama/theater group, student-run newspaper, radio station, choral group, student government, student radio station, Phi Theta Kappa, Business Society, Student Pennsylvania State Education Association. *Campus security:* 24-hour emergency response devices and patrols, late-night transport/escort service. *Student services:* health clinic, personal/psychological counseling.
Athletics Member NJCAA. *Intercollegiate sports:* baseball M, basketball M/W, golf M/W, soccer M, softball W, tennis M/W, volleyball W. *Intramural sports:* basketball M/W, lacrosse M(c), volleyball W.
Costs (2004–05) *Tuition:* area resident $1887 full-time, $75 per credit part-time; state resident $3800 full-time, $150 per credit part-time; nonresident $5715 full-time, $225 per credit part-time. Full-time tuition and fees vary according to course load. Part-time tuition and fees vary according to course load. *Required fees:* $365 full-time, $18 per credit part-time, $20 per term part-time. *Payment plan:* installment. *Waivers:* senior citizens and employees or children of employees.
Financial Aid Of all full-time matriculated undergraduates who enrolled, 95 Federal Work-Study jobs (averaging $900).
Applying *Options:* early admission, deferred entrance. *Application fee:* $20. *Required:* high school transcript. *Application deadline:* rolling (freshmen), rolling (transfers). *Notification:* continuous (freshmen), continuous (transfers).
Admissions Contact Ms. Hope Lentine, Director of Admissions, Delaware County Community College, Admissions Office, 901 South Media Line Road, Media, PA 19063-1094. *Phone:* 610-359-5333. *Toll-free phone:* 800-872-1102 (in-state); 800-543-0146 (out-of-state). *Fax:* 610-359-5343. *E-mail:* admiss@dccc.edu.

DOUGLAS EDUCATION CENTER
Monessen, Pennsylvania

- **Proprietary** 2-year
- **Degree** certificates, diplomas, and associate
- **Coed**

Faculty *Student/faculty ratio:* 10:1.
Standardized Tests *Required:* Wonderlic aptitude test (for admission).
Financial Aid Of all full-time matriculated undergraduates who enrolled, 5 Federal Work-Study jobs (averaging $2500).
Applying *Required:* high school transcript, interview.
Admissions Contact Ms. Linda Gambattista, Director of Admissions, Douglas Education Center, 130 Seventh Street, Monessen, PA 15062. *Phone:* 724-684-3684. *Fax:* 724-684-7463. *E-mail:* dec@douglas-school.com.

DUBOIS BUSINESS COLLEGE
DuBois, Pennsylvania

- **Proprietary** 2-year, founded 1885
- **Calendar** quarters
- **Degree** diplomas and associate
- **Rural** 4-acre campus
- **Coed, primarily women**

Faculty *Student/faculty ratio:* 15:1.
Student Life *Campus security:* late-night transport/escort service, controlled dormitory access.
Costs (2004–05) *Tuition:* $6900 full-time, $160 per credit part-time. *Required fees:* $475 full-time, $150 per term part-time. *Room only:* $2340.
Applying *Options:* common application, electronic application, deferred entrance. *Application fee:* $25. *Required:* high school transcript, interview. *Recommended:* letters of recommendation.
Admissions Contact Ms. Lisa Stanford, Director of Admissions, DuBois Business College, 1 Beaver Drive, DuBois, PA 15801-2401. *Phone:* 814-371-6920. *Toll-free phone:* 800-692-6213.

DUFF'S BUSINESS INSTITUTE
Pittsburgh, Pennsylvania

- **Proprietary** 2-year, founded 1840, part of Phillips Colleges, Inc
- **Calendar** quarters
- **Degree** diplomas and associate
- **Urban** campus
- **Coed, primarily women**

Faculty *Student/faculty ratio:* 14:1.
Student Life *Campus security:* 24-hour emergency response devices.
Standardized Tests *Required:* CPAt (for admission).
Costs (2003–04) *Tuition:* $223 per credit part-time. *Required fees:* $90 per term part-time.
Financial Aid Of all full-time matriculated undergraduates who enrolled, 40 Federal Work-Study jobs (averaging $5760). 15 state and other part-time jobs (averaging $5760).
Applying *Options:* deferred entrance. *Application fee:* $25.
Admissions Contact Ms. Lynn Fischer, Director of Admissions, Duff's Business Institute, 100 Forbes Avenue, Suite 1200, Pittsburgh, PA 15222. *Phone:* 412-261-4520 Ext. 212. *Toll-free phone:* 888-279-3314.

EDUCATION DIRECT CENTER FOR DEGREE STUDIES
Scranton, Pennsylvania

- **Proprietary** 2-year, founded 1975
- **Calendar** semesters
- **Degrees** associate (offers only external degree programs conducted through home study)
- **Coed,** 18,058 undergraduate students, 65% women, 35% men

Undergraduates 18,058 part-time. Students come from 52 states and territories, 15 other countries.
Freshmen *Admission:* 18,058 applied, 18,058 admitted.
Faculty *Total:* 29, 59% full-time.
Majors Accounting technology and bookkeeping; business/commerce; child care and support services management; civil engineering technology; computer and information sciences and support services related; computer science; crimi-

nal justice/police science; electrical, electronic and communications engineering technology; hotel/motel administration; industrial engineering; legal assistant/paralegal; mechanical engineering/mechanical technology; veterinary/animal health technology.
Academic Programs *Special study options:* academic remediation for entering students, adult/continuing education programs, distance learning, external degree program, independent study, part-time degree program, summer session for credit.
Student Life *Housing:* college housing not available.
Costs (2003–04) *Tuition:* $3425 per degree program part-time. Part-time tuition and fees vary according to program. *Payment plan:* installment.
Applying *Required:* high school transcript. *Application deadline:* rolling (freshmen), rolling (transfers).
Admissions Contact Ms. Connie Dempsey, Director of Compliance and Academic Affairs, Education Direct Center for Degree Studies, 925 Oak Street, Scranton, PA 18515. *Phone:* 570-342-7701 Ext. 4692. *Toll-free phone:* 800-233-4191.

▶ **See page 538 for a narrative description.**

ELECTRONIC INSTITUTE
Middletown, Pennsylvania

- **Independent** 2-year, founded 1959
- **Calendar** trimesters
- **Degree** diplomas and associate
- **Small-town** campus with easy access to Baltimore and Philadelphia
- **Coed, primarily men**

Faculty *Student/faculty ratio:* 10:1.
Costs (2003–04) *Tuition:* $8800 full-time, $1748 per term part-time. *Required fees:* $150 full-time.
Applying *Options:* deferred entrance. *Application fee:* $10. *Required:* high school transcript, interview.
Admissions Contact Mr. Tom Bogush, Chief Admissions Officer and School President, Electronic Institute, 1519 West Harrisburg Pike, Middletown, PA 17057. *Phone:* 717-944-2731. *Toll-free phone:* 800-884-2731. *Fax:* 717-944-2542. *E-mail:* tom.bogush@verizon.net.

ERIE BUSINESS CENTER, MAIN
Erie, Pennsylvania

- **Proprietary** 2-year, founded 1884
- **Calendar** trimesters
- **Degree** diplomas and associate
- **Urban** 1-acre campus with easy access to Cleveland and Buffalo
- **Coed**

Faculty *Student/faculty ratio:* 15:1.
Student Life *Campus security:* 24-hour emergency response devices, security guard.
Standardized Tests *Required:* Wonderlic aptitude test (for admission).
Costs (2003–04) *Tuition:* $6540 full-time. *Required fees:* $560 full-time. *Room only:* $2480.
Financial Aid Of all full-time matriculated undergraduates who enrolled, 15 Federal Work-Study jobs (averaging $600).
Applying *Options:* common application, deferred entrance. *Application fee:* $25. *Required:* essay or personal statement, high school transcript, interview.
Admissions Contact Ms. Amy Tevis, Director of Admissions, Erie Business Center, Main, 246 West Ninth Street, Erie, PA 16501-1392. *Phone:* 814-456-7504 Ext. 12. *Toll-free phone:* 800-352-ERIE Ext. 12 (in-state); 800-352-ERIE (out-of-state). *Fax:* 814-456-4882. *E-mail:* tevisa@eriebc.com.

ERIE BUSINESS CENTER SOUTH
New Castle, Pennsylvania

- **Proprietary** 2-year, founded 1894
- **Calendar** quarters
- **Degree** diplomas and associate
- **Small-town** 1-acre campus with easy access to Pittsburgh
- **Coed, primarily women,** 64 undergraduate students, 100% full-time, 75% women, 25% men

Undergraduates 64 full-time. 19% African American. *Retention:* 80% of 2002 full-time freshmen returned.
Freshmen *Admission:* 45 applied, 34 admitted.
Faculty *Total:* 6, 50% full-time. *Student/faculty ratio:* 13:1.
Majors Accounting; administrative assistant and secretarial science; advertising; business administration and management; computer science; health

information/medical records administration; legal administrative assistant/secretary; marketing/marketing management; medical administrative assistant and medical secretary; tourism and travel services management.

Academic Programs *Special study options:* academic remediation for entering students, adult/continuing education programs, internships, part-time degree program.

Library 1,725 titles, 20 serial subscriptions.

Computers on Campus 26 computers available on campus for general student use. Internet access, at least one staffed computer lab available.

Student Life *Housing:* college housing not available. *Activities and Organizations:* student government, Business Club, Medical Club, Travel Club, Ambassadors Club. *Campus security:* 24-hour patrols. *Student services:* personal/psychological counseling.

Athletics *Intramural sports:* basketball M/W, bowling M/W, softball M/W, volleyball M/W.

Standardized Tests *Recommended:* SAT I and SAT II or ACT (for admission).

Costs (2004–05) *Tuition:* $4560 full-time, $456 per course part-time. Full-time tuition and fees vary according to course load. Part-time tuition and fees vary according to course load. *Required fees:* $300 full-time, $152 per credit part-time. *Payment plan:* installment. *Waivers:* employees or children of employees.

Applying *Options:* common application, deferred entrance. *Application fee:* $25. *Required:* high school transcript. *Recommended:* interview. *Application deadline:* rolling (freshmen), rolling (transfers).

Admissions Contact Ms. Rose Hall, Admissions Representative, Erie Business Center South, 170 Cascade Galleria, New Castle, PA 16101-3950. *Phone:* 724-658-3595. *Toll-free phone:* 800-722-6227. *E-mail:* hallr@eriebcs.com.

ERIE INSTITUTE OF TECHNOLOGY
Erie, Pennsylvania

- **Proprietary** 2-year
- **Calendar** 4 3-month terms
- **Degree** diplomas and associate
- **Suburban** campus
- **Coed,** 173 undergraduate students

Undergraduates 2% African American, 3% Asian American or Pacific Islander, 2% Hispanic American, 92% international.

Faculty *Total:* 16. *Student/faculty ratio:* 15:1.

Majors Electrical, electronic and communications engineering technology.

Applying *Application fee:* $25. *Application deadline:* rolling (freshmen). *Notification:* continuous (freshmen).

Admissions Contact Mr. Ken Haas, Admissions Representative, Erie Institute of Technology, 5539 Peach Street, Erie, PA 16509. *Phone:* 814-868-9900. *Toll-free phone:* 866-868-3743.

HARCUM COLLEGE
Bryn Mawr, Pennsylvania

- **Independent** 2-year, founded 1915
- **Calendar** semesters
- **Degree** certificates and associate
- **Suburban** 12-acre campus with easy access to Philadelphia
- **Endowment** $9.0 million
- **Coed, primarily women,** 542 undergraduate students, 68% full-time, 90% women, 10% men

Undergraduates 366 full-time, 176 part-time. Students come from 8 states and territories, 6 other countries, 10% are from out of state, 16% African American, 3% Asian American or Pacific Islander, 3% Hispanic American, 0.4% Native American, 0.4% international, 22% transferred in, 23% live on campus. *Retention:* 90% of 2002 full-time freshmen returned.

Freshmen *Admission:* 361 applied, 207 admitted, 109 enrolled. *Average high school GPA:* 2.38. *Test scores:* SAT verbal scores over 500: 27%; SAT math scores over 500: 16%; SAT verbal scores over 600: 5%; SAT math scores over 600: 1%.

Faculty *Total:* 100, 27% full-time, 12% with terminal degrees. *Student/faculty ratio:* 9:1.

Majors Allied health diagnostic, intervention, and treatment professions related; animal sciences; business administration and management; child development; clinical/medical laboratory technology; consumer merchandising/retailing management; dental assisting; dental hygiene; fashion/apparel design; fashion merchandising; health science; information science/studies; interdisciplinary studies; interior design; kindergarten/preschool education; liberal arts and sciences/liberal studies; nursing (registered nurse training); occupational therapist assistant; physical therapist assistant; psychology; veterinary technology.

Academic Programs *Special study options:* academic remediation for entering students, adult/continuing education programs, advanced placement credit,

distance learning, double majors, English as a second language, honors programs, independent study, internships, off-campus study, part-time degree program, services for LD students, summer session for credit.

Library Main Library plus 1 other with 39,000 titles, 300 serial subscriptions, 1,000 audiovisual materials.

Computers on Campus 65 computers available on campus for general student use. Internet access, at least one staffed computer lab available.

Student Life *Housing Options:* coed, women-only. Campus housing is university owned. Freshman campus housing is guaranteed. *Activities and Organizations:* student-run newspaper, choral group, OATS (Organization for Animal Tech Students), Student Association of Dental Hygienist of America, Ebony Club, Dental Assisting Club, FLA International Club. *Campus security:* 24-hour emergency response devices and patrols, controlled dormitory access. *Student services:* health clinic, personal/psychological counseling, women's center.

Athletics *Intramural sports:* badminton W, basketball W, soccer W, softball W, tennis W, volleyball W.

Standardized Tests *Required:* SAT I or ACT (for admission).

Costs (2004–05) *Comprehensive fee:* $23,060.

Financial Aid Of all full-time matriculated undergraduates who enrolled, 161 Federal Work-Study jobs (averaging $1100).

Applying *Options:* common application, electronic application, early admission, deferred entrance. *Application fee:* $25. *Required:* essay or personal statement, high school transcript, letters of recommendation. *Recommended:* interview. *Application deadline:* rolling (freshmen), rolling (transfers). *Notification:* continuous (freshmen), continuous (transfers).

Admissions Contact Office of Enrollment Management, Harcum College, 750 Montgomery Avenue, Melville Hall, Bryn Mawr, PA 19010-3476. *Phone:* 610-526-6050. *Toll-free phone:* 800-345-2600. *Fax:* 610-526-6147. *E-mail:* enroll@harcum.edu.

▶ See page 548 for a narrative description.

HARRISBURG AREA COMMUNITY COLLEGE
Harrisburg, Pennsylvania

- **State and locally supported** 2-year, founded 1964
- **Calendar** semesters
- **Degree** certificates, diplomas, and associate
- **Urban** 212-acre campus
- **Endowment** $25.0 million
- **Coed,** 14,918 undergraduate students, 39% full-time, 64% women, 36% men

Undergraduates 5,768 full-time, 9,150 part-time. Students come from 6 states and territories, 15 other countries, 1% are from out of state, 10% African American, 2% Asian American or Pacific Islander, 5% Hispanic American, 0.3% Native American, 0.9% international, 29% transferred in.

Freshmen *Admission:* 6,989 applied, 6,526 admitted, 1,442 enrolled.

Faculty *Total:* 893, 26% full-time, 3% with terminal degrees. *Student/faculty ratio:* 20:1.

Majors Accounting; actuarial science; administrative assistant and secretarial science; agricultural business and management; architectural engineering technology; architecture; art; automobile/automotive mechanics technology; automotive engineering technology; banking and financial support services; biology/biological sciences; business administration and management; business/commerce; business, management, and marketing related; business teacher education; cardiovascular technology; chemistry; civil engineering technology; clinical/medical laboratory assistant; clinical/medical laboratory technology; commercial and advertising art; computer and information sciences; computer and information sciences and support services related; computer installation and repair technology; computer systems networking and telecommunications; construction engineering technology; consumer merchandising/retailing management; criminal justice/law enforcement administration; criminal justice/police science; culinary arts; dental hygiene; design and visual communications; dietetics; dramatic/theatre arts; education; electrical, electronic and communications engineering technology; elementary education; emergency medical technology (EMT paramedic); engineering; engineering technologies related; engineering technology; environmental studies; fire science; foods, nutrition, and wellness; general retailing/wholesaling; health information/medical records administration; heating, air conditioning and refrigeration technology; hospital and health care facilities administration; hotel/motel administration; human services; industrial mechanics and maintenance technology; information technology; institutional food workers; international relations and affairs; journalism; kindergarten/preschool education; legal administrative assistant/secretary; legal assistant/paralegal; liberal arts and sciences/liberal studies; management information systems; management science; marketing/marketing management; mass communication/media; mathematics; mechanical engineering/mechanical technology; medical office assistant; medical radiologic technology; music; nuclear medical technology; nursing (registered nurse training); opticianry; pharmacy technician; photography; physical education teaching and coaching;

Harrisburg Area Community College (continued)

physical sciences; psychology; real estate; respiratory care therapy; respiratory therapy technician; science teacher education; social sciences; social work; tourism and travel services management; tourism and travel services marketing; tourism/travel marketing; web/multimedia management and webmaster.

Academic Programs *Special study options:* academic remediation for entering students, adult/continuing education programs, advanced placement credit, cooperative education, English as a second language, honors programs, internships, part-time degree program, services for LD students, student-designed majors, study abroad, summer session for credit. *ROTC:* Army (b).

Library McCormick Library with 110,000 titles, 700 serial subscriptions, 16,335 audiovisual materials.

Computers on Campus 350 computers available on campus for general student use. A campuswide network can be accessed from off campus. Internet access, online (class) registration, at least one staffed computer lab available.

Student Life *Housing:* college housing not available. *Activities and Organizations:* drama/theater group, student-run newspaper, radio station, Student Government Association, Phi Theta Kappa, African American Student Association, Mosiaco Club, Fourth Estate. *Campus security:* 24-hour emergency response devices and patrols, late-night transport/escort service. *Student services:* personal/psychological counseling.

Athletics *Intercollegiate sports:* basketball M/W, soccer M, tennis M/W, volleyball W. *Intramural sports:* basketball M/W, football M/W, golf M/W, racquetball M/W, skiing (downhill) M/W, soccer M, softball M/W, squash M/W, swimming M/W, tennis M/W, volleyball M/W.

Standardized Tests *Required for some:* ACT (for placement).

Costs (2004–05) *Tuition:* area resident $2265 full-time, $76 per credit hour part-time; state resident $4530 full-time, $151 per credit hour part-time; nonresident $6795 full-time, $227 per credit hour part-time. *Required fees:* $360 full-time, $12 per credit hour part-time. *Waivers:* employees or children of employees.

Applying *Options:* early admission. *Application fee:* $30. *Required:* high school transcript. *Application deadline:* rolling (freshmen), rolling (transfers).

Admissions Contact Mrs. Vanita Cowan, Administrative Clerk, Admissions, Harrisburg Area Community College, 1 HACC Drive, Harrisburg, PA 17110. *Phone:* 717-780-2406. *Toll-free phone:* 800-ABC-HACC.

HUSSIAN SCHOOL OF ART
Philadelphia, Pennsylvania

- **Proprietary** 2-year, founded 1946
- **Calendar** semesters
- **Degree** associate
- **Urban** 1-acre campus
- **Coed,** 138 undergraduate students, 100% full-time, 33% women, 67% men

Undergraduates 138 full-time. Students come from 4 states and territories, 40% are from out of state, 9% African American, 3% Asian American or Pacific Islander, 4% Hispanic American. *Retention:* 90% of 2002 full-time freshmen returned.

Freshmen *Admission:* 81 applied, 43 admitted, 39 enrolled. *Average high school GPA:* 2.7.

Faculty *Total:* 29, 10% full-time, 17% with terminal degrees. *Student/faculty ratio:* 18:1.

Majors Advertising; commercial and advertising art.

Academic Programs *Special study options:* independent study, internships.

Library Main Library plus 1 other with 194,587 titles, 1,612 serial subscriptions, 4,588 audiovisual materials.

Computers on Campus 55 computers available on campus for general student use. A campuswide network can be accessed. Internet access, at least one staffed computer lab available.

Student Life *Housing:* college housing not available. *Campus security:* security guard during open hours.

Costs (2004–05) *Tuition:* $9200 full-time, $297 per credit part-time. *Required fees:* $355 full-time, $12 per contact hour part-time. *Payment plan:* installment.

Applying *Options:* common application, deferred entrance. *Application fee:* $25. *Required:* high school transcript, interview, art portfolio. *Application deadline:* rolling (freshmen), rolling (transfers). *Notification:* continuous (freshmen), continuous (transfers).

Admissions Contact Ms. Lynne D. Wartman, Director of Admissions, Hussian School of Art, 1118 Market Street, Philadelphia, PA 19107. *Phone:* 215-981-0900. *Fax:* 215-864-9115. *E-mail:* hussian@pond.com.

ICM SCHOOL OF BUSINESS & MEDICAL CAREERS
Pittsburgh, Pennsylvania

Admissions Contact Mrs. Marcia Rosenberg, Director of Admissions, ICM School of Business & Medical Careers, 10 Wood Street, Pittsburgh, PA 15222. *Phone:* 412-261-2647 Ext. 229. *Toll-free phone:* 800-441-5222. *E-mail:* icm@citynet.com.

INFORMATION COMPUTER SYSTEMS INSTITUTE
Allentown, Pennsylvania

Admissions Contact Bill Barber, Director, Information Computer Systems Institute, 2201 Hangar Place, Allentown, PA 18103-9504. *Phone:* 610-264-8029.

INTERNATIONAL ACADEMY OF DESIGN & TECHNOLOGY
Pittsburgh, Pennsylvania

Admissions Contact Ms. Debbie Love, Chief Admissions Officer, International Academy of Design & Technology, 555 Grant Street, Pittsburgh, PA 15219. *Phone:* 412-391-4197. *Toll-free phone:* 800-447-8324.

JNA INSTITUTE OF CULINARY ARTS
Philadelphia, Pennsylvania

Admissions Contact JNA Institute of Culinary Arts, 1212 South Broad Street, Philadelphia, PA 19146.

JOHNSON COLLEGE
Scranton, Pennsylvania

- **Independent** 2-year, founded 1912
- **Calendar** semesters
- **Degree** associate
- **Urban** 65-acre campus
- **Coed**

Faculty *Student/faculty ratio:* 17:1.

Student Life *Campus security:* 24-hour emergency response devices.

Standardized Tests *Required for some:* SAT I (for admission), College Qualifying Test. *Recommended:* SAT I (for admission).

Costs (2004–05) *Tuition:* $10,900 full-time, $300 per credit part-time. Full-time tuition and fees vary according to program. Part-time tuition and fees vary according to program. No tuition increase for student's term of enrollment. *Required fees:* $670 full-time. *Room only:* $3600.

Financial Aid Of all full-time matriculated undergraduates who enrolled, 40 Federal Work-Study jobs (averaging $800).

Applying *Options:* common application, electronic application, deferred entrance. *Application fee:* $30. *Required:* essay or personal statement, high school transcript, letters of recommendation, interview.

Admissions Contact Johnson College, 3427 North Main Avenue, Scranton, PA 18508. *Phone:* 570-342-6404 Ext. 122. *Toll-free phone:* 800-2-WE-WORK Ext. 125. *Fax:* 570-348-2181. *E-mail:* admit@johnson.edu.

▶ **See page 558 for a narrative description.**

KATHARINE GIBBS SCHOOL
Norristown, Pennsylvania

Admissions Contact Mr. Joseph Carretta, President, Katharine Gibbs School, 2501 Monroe Boulevard, Norristown, PA 19403. *Phone:* 610-676-0500. *Toll-free phone:* 866-PAGIBBS.

KEYSTONE COLLEGE
La Plume, Pennsylvania

- **Independent** primarily 2-year, founded 1868
- **Calendar** semesters
- **Degrees** certificates, associate, bachelor's, and postbachelor's certificates
- **Rural** 270-acre campus
- **Endowment** $8.9 million

■ **Coed,** 1,445 undergraduate students, 69% full-time, 63% women, 37% men

Undergraduates 998 full-time, 447 part-time. Students come from 12 states and territories, 7 other countries, 10% are from out of state, 5% African American, 0.3% Asian American or Pacific Islander, 1% Hispanic American, 0.1% Native American, 1% international, 8% transferred in, 34% live on campus. *Retention:* 58% of 2002 full-time freshmen returned.
Freshmen *Admission:* 788 applied, 746 admitted, 468 enrolled. *Test scores:* SAT verbal scores over 500: 21%; SAT math scores over 500: 16%; ACT scores over 18: 45%; SAT verbal scores over 600: 3%; SAT math scores over 600: 2%.
Faculty *Total:* 186, 31% full-time, 21% with terminal degrees. *Student/faculty ratio:* 12:1.
Majors Accounting; accounting and business/management; accounting related; art; art teacher education; biological and physical sciences; biology/biological sciences; business administration and management; business administration, management and operations related; business/commerce; communication and journalism related; communication and media related; communication/speech communication and rhetoric; computer/information technology services administration related; computer programming; computer programming (specific applications); computer systems networking and telecommunications; criminal justice/law enforcement administration; criminal justice/safety; culinary arts; culinary arts related; data processing and data processing technology; diagnostic medical sonography and ultrasound technology; drawing; early childhood education; education; education (K-12); elementary education; environmental studies; family and community services; fine/studio arts; food preparation; forensic science and technology; forestry; forestry technology; graphic design; hotel/motel administration; human resources management; illustration; information technology; journalism; kindergarten/preschool education; landscape architecture; liberal arts and sciences and humanities related; liberal arts and sciences/liberal studies; medical radiologic technology; natural resources management; occupational therapy; painting; parks, recreation and leisure facilities management; photography; physical therapy; physician assistant; pre-medical studies; pre-nursing studies; pre-pharmacy studies; pre-veterinary studies; printmaking; public relations, advertising, and applied communication related; radio and television; radiologic technology/science; radio, television, and digital communication related; restaurant, culinary, and catering management; restaurant/food services management; sculpture; sport and fitness administration; system administration; therapeutic recreation; water, wetlands, and marine resources management; wildlife and wildlands science and management; wildlife biology.
Academic Programs *Special study options:* academic remediation for entering students, adult/continuing education programs, advanced placement credit, cooperative education, distance learning, English as a second language, external degree program, independent study, internships, part-time degree program, services for LD students, student-designed majors, summer session for credit. *ROTC:* Army (c), Air Force (c).
Library Miller Library with 65,000 titles, 309 serial subscriptions, 10,000 audiovisual materials, an OPAC, a Web page.
Computers on Campus 120 computers available on campus for general student use. A campuswide network can be accessed from student residence rooms and from off campus that provide access to wireless campus. Internet access, online (class) registration, at least one staffed computer lab available. Computer purchase or lease plan available.
Student Life *Housing Options:* coed, women-only, disabled students. Campus housing is university owned. Freshman campus housing is guaranteed. *Activities and Organizations:* drama/theater group, student-run newspaper, radio station, choral group, Campus Activity Board, Student Senate, Art Society, Inter-Hall Council, Commuter Council. *Campus security:* 24-hour emergency response devices and patrols, student patrols, late-night transport/escort service, controlled dormitory access. *Student services:* health clinic, personal/psychological counseling, women's center.
Athletics Member NCAA. *Intercollegiate sports:* baseball M, basketball M/W, cross-country running M/W, golf M, soccer M/W, softball W, tennis M/W, track and field M/W, volleyball W. *Intramural sports:* basketball M/W, cheerleading M(c)/W(c), equestrian sports M(c)/W(c), football M/W, lacrosse M/W, skiing (downhill) M(c)/W(c), soccer M/W, softball M/W, table tennis M/W, tennis M/W, volleyball M/W, weight lifting M/W.
Standardized Tests *Required for some:* SAT I or ACT (for admission). *Recommended:* SAT I or ACT (for admission).
Costs (2004–05) *Comprehensive fee:* $21,980 includes full-time tuition ($13,450), mandatory fees ($970), and room and board ($7560). Part-time tuition: $315 per credit. *Required fees:* $110 per term part-time. *Room and board:* college room only: $3880. Room and board charges vary according to board plan and housing facility. *Payment plan:* installment. *Waivers:* senior citizens and employees or children of employees.
Financial Aid Of all full-time matriculated undergraduates who enrolled, 125 Federal Work-Study jobs (averaging $1000). 100 state and other part-time jobs (averaging $1000).
Applying *Options:* common application, electronic application, early admission, deferred entrance. *Application fee:* $25. *Required:* high school transcript. *Required for some:* interview, art portfolio. *Recommended:* essay or personal

statement, minimum 2.0 GPA, 1 letter of recommendation, interview. *Application deadline:* rolling (freshmen), rolling (transfers).
Admissions Contact Ms. Sarah Keating, Director of Admissions, Keystone College, One College Green, La Plume, PA 18440-1099. *Phone:* 570-945-5141 Ext. 2403. *Toll-free phone:* 877-4COLLEGE Ext. 1. *Fax:* 570-945-7916. *E-mail:* admissions@keystone.edu.

▶ **See page 560 for a narrative description.**

LACKAWANNA COLLEGE
Scranton, Pennsylvania

- **Independent** 2-year, founded 1894
- **Calendar** semesters
- **Degree** certificates, diplomas, and associate
- **Urban** 4-acre campus
- **Endowment** $594,255
- **Coed,** 1,108 undergraduate students, 58% full-time, 52% women, 48% men

Undergraduates 646 full-time, 462 part-time. Students come from 12 states and territories, 3% are from out of state, 10% African American, 0.8% Asian American or Pacific Islander, 2% Hispanic American, 0.2% Native American, 0.1% international, 7% transferred in.
Freshmen *Admission:* 767 admitted, 389 enrolled.
Faculty *Total:* 47, 38% full-time, 13% with terminal degrees. *Student/faculty ratio:* 16:1.
Majors Accounting technology and bookkeeping; administrative assistant and secretarial science; banking and financial support services; biotechnology; business administration and management; business/commerce; communication/speech communication and rhetoric; communications technology; computer and information sciences; criminal justice/safety; diagnostic medical sonography and ultrasound technology; early childhood education; education; emergency medical technology (EMT paramedic); general studies; humanities; industrial technology; legal assistant/paralegal; liberal arts and sciences/liberal studies; management information systems; mass communication/media; medical administrative assistant and medical secretary; mental health/rehabilitation.
Academic Programs *Special study options:* academic remediation for entering students, adult/continuing education programs, advanced placement credit, cooperative education, double majors, English as a second language, internships, part-time degree program, services for LD students, summer session for credit. *ROTC:* Army (c), Air Force (c).
Library Seeley Memorial Library with 15,276 titles, 58 serial subscriptions, 491 audiovisual materials, an OPAC, a Web page.
Computers on Campus 120 computers available on campus for general student use. A campuswide network can be accessed from student residence rooms and from off campus. Internet access, at least one staffed computer lab available.
Student Life *Housing Options:* Campus housing is university owned. *Activities and Organizations:* drama/theater group, student-run newspaper, student government, Student/Alumni Association, Diversity Club, student newspaper, Phi Beta Lambda. *Campus security:* 24-hour emergency response devices, late-night transport/escort service, patrols by college liaison staff. *Student services:* personal/psychological counseling.
Athletics Member NJCAA. *Intercollegiate sports:* baseball M(s), basketball M(s)/W(s), football M(s), golf M(s)/W(s), softball W(s), volleyball W(s). *Intramural sports:* weight lifting M/W.
Standardized Tests *Recommended:* SAT I or ACT (for placement).
Costs (2003–04) *Tuition:* $8900 full-time, $290 per credit part-time. *Required fees:* $100 full-time, $60 per term part-time. *Room only:* $6995. Room and board charges vary according to board plan. *Payment plan:* installment. *Waivers:* employees or children of employees.
Financial Aid Of all full-time matriculated undergraduates who enrolled, 96 Federal Work-Study jobs (averaging $995).
Applying *Options:* early admission, deferred entrance. *Application fee:* $30. *Required:* high school transcript, interview. *Application deadline:* rolling (freshmen), rolling (transfers).
Admissions Contact Lackawanna College, 501 Vine Street, Scranton, PA 18509. *Phone:* 570-961-7852. *Toll-free phone:* 877-346-3552. *Fax:* 570-961-7853. *E-mail:* dudam@lackawanna.edu.

LANSDALE SCHOOL OF BUSINESS
North Wales, Pennsylvania

Admissions Contact Ms. Marianne H. Johnson, Director of Admissions, Lansdale School of Business, 201 Church Road, North Wales, PA 19454-4148. *Phone:* 215-699-5700 Ext. 112. *Fax:* 215-699-8770.

LAUREL BUSINESS INSTITUTE
Uniontown, Pennsylvania

- **Proprietary** 2-year, founded 1985
- **Calendar** trimesters
- **Degree** certificates, diplomas, and associate
- **Small-town** campus with easy access to Pittsburgh
- **Coed**

Faculty *Student/faculty ratio:* 12:1.

Standardized Tests *Required:* Wonderlic aptitude test (for placement).

Costs (2003–04) *Tuition:* $13,375 full-time. *Required fees:* $285 full-time.

Financial Aid Of all full-time matriculated undergraduates who enrolled, 60 Federal Work-Study jobs (averaging $710).

Applying *Options:* common application, electronic application, deferred entrance. *Application fee:* $25. *Required:* high school transcript, interview.

Admissions Contact Mr. Christopher Decker, President and Acting Director of Admission, Laurel Business Institute, 11-15 Penn Street, PO Box 877, Uniontown, PA 15401. *Phone:* 724-439-4900. *Fax:* 724-439-3607. *E-mail:* lbi@laurelbusiness.net.

LEHIGH CARBON COMMUNITY COLLEGE
Schnecksville, Pennsylvania

- **State and locally supported** 2-year, founded 1967
- **Calendar** semesters
- **Degree** certificates, diplomas, and associate
- **Suburban** 153-acre campus with easy access to Philadelphia
- **Endowment** $20,000
- **Coed,** 6,353 undergraduate students, 37% full-time, 61% women, 39% men

Undergraduates 2,358 full-time, 3,995 part-time. Students come from 6 states and territories, 5 other countries, 1% are from out of state, 4% African American, 2% Asian American or Pacific Islander, 7% Hispanic American, 0.1% Native American, 0.1% international, 33% transferred in.

Freshmen *Admission:* 4,398 applied, 3,463 admitted, 2,231 enrolled.

Faculty *Total:* 454, 23% full-time, 2% with terminal degrees. *Student/faculty ratio:* 18:1.

Majors Accounting; accounting technology and bookkeeping; administrative assistant and secretarial science; adult development and aging; airline pilot and flight crew; art; aviation/airway management; avionics maintenance technology; biology/biological sciences; biomedical technology; biotechnology; business administration and management; chemical technology; child care provision; clinical/medical laboratory technology; commercial and advertising art; communication/speech communication and rhetoric; computer engineering technology; computer technology/computer systems technology; construction engineering technology; corrections; criminal justice/law enforcement administration; criminal justice/police science; culinary arts; digital communication and media/multimedia; drafting and design technology; education; electrical, electronic and communications engineering technology; electrical, electronics and communications engineering; engineering; executive assistant/executive secretary; forensic science and technology; general studies; health information/medical records technology; heating, air conditioning, ventilation and refrigeration maintenance technology; horticultural science; hotel/motel administration; humanities; human resources management; industrial technology; information science/studies; interior architecture; kindergarten/preschool education; legal administrative assistant/secretary; legal assistant/paralegal; liberal arts and sciences/liberal studies; lineworker; logistics and materials management; manufacturing technology; mathematics; mechanical engineering; mechanical engineering/mechanical technology; medical/clinical assistant; medical transcription; nursing (licensed practical/vocational nurse training); nursing (registered nurse training); occupational therapist assistant; office occupations and clerical services; operations management; physical sciences; physical therapist assistant; real estate; respiratory care therapy; restaurant/food services management; social sciences; social work; special education; sport and fitness administration; tourism promotion; tourism/travel marketing; veterinary/animal health technology.

Academic Programs *Special study options:* academic remediation for entering students, adult/continuing education programs, advanced placement credit, cooperative education, distance learning, English as a second language, independent study, internships, part-time degree program, services for LD students, summer session for credit. *ROTC:* Army (c).

Library Learning Resource Center with 99,615 titles, 515 serial subscriptions, 6,613 audiovisual materials, an OPAC, a Web page.

Computers on Campus 500 computers available on campus for general student use. At least one staffed computer lab available.

Student Life *Housing:* college housing not available. *Activities and Organizations:* student-run newspaper, radio station, Phi Theta Kappa, STEP Student Association, student radio station, student government, College Activity Board. *Campus security:* 24-hour emergency response devices and patrols, student patrols, late-night transport/escort service. *Student services:* personal/psychological counseling.

Athletics Member NJCAA. *Intercollegiate sports:* baseball M/W, basketball M/W, golf M/W, soccer M, softball W, volleyball W. *Intramural sports:* archery M/W, badminton M/W, baseball M, basketball M/W, bowling M/W, field hockey W, football M/W, golf M/W, racquetball M/W, skiing (downhill) M/W, soccer M/W, softball M/W, swimming M/W, table tennis M/W, tennis M/W, track and field M, volleyball M/W, weight lifting M/W.

Standardized Tests *Required for some:* ACT or ACT COMPASS.

Costs (2004–05) *Tuition:* area resident $2160 full-time, $72 per credit part-time; state resident $4320 full-time, $144 per credit part-time; nonresident $6480 full-time, $216 per credit part-time. Full-time tuition and fees vary according to course load and reciprocity agreements. Part-time tuition and fees vary according to course load and reciprocity agreements. *Required fees:* $315 full-time, $11 per credit hour part-time. *Payment plan:* installment. *Waivers:* employees or children of employees.

Applying *Application fee:* $25. *Required for some:* essay or personal statement, high school transcript, interview. *Application deadline:* rolling (freshmen), rolling (transfers). *Notification:* continuous (freshmen), continuous (transfers).

Admissions Contact Mr. David Solove, Director of Recruitment and Admissions, Lehigh Carbon Community College, 4525 Education Park Drive, Schnecksville, PA 18078-2598. *Phone:* 610-799-1575. *Fax:* 610-799-1527. *E-mail:* admis@lex.lccc.edu.

LINCOLN TECHNICAL INSTITUTE
Allentown, Pennsylvania

- **Proprietary** 2-year, founded 1949, part of Lincoln Technical Institute, Inc
- **Calendar** semesters
- **Degree** diplomas and associate
- **Suburban** 10-acre campus with easy access to Philadelphia
- **Coed**

Faculty *Student/faculty ratio:* 20:1.

Financial Aid Of all full-time matriculated undergraduates who enrolled, 5 Federal Work-Study jobs.

Applying *Options:* common application, early admission. *Application fee:* $100. *Required:* high school transcript, interview. *Recommended:* letters of recommendation.

Admissions Contact Admissions Office, Lincoln Technical Institute, 5151 Tilghman Street, Allentown, PA 18104-3298. *Phone:* 610-398-5301.

LINCOLN TECHNICAL INSTITUTE
Philadelphia, Pennsylvania

Admissions Contact Mr. James Kuntz, Executive Director, Lincoln Technical Institute, 9191 Torresdale Avenue, Philadelphia, PA 19136-1595. *Phone:* 215-335-0800. *Toll-free phone:* 800-238-8381.

LUZERNE COUNTY COMMUNITY COLLEGE
Nanticoke, Pennsylvania

- **County-supported** 2-year, founded 1966
- **Calendar** semesters
- **Degree** certificates, diplomas, and associate
- **Suburban** 122-acre campus with easy access to Philadelphia
- **Coed,** 6,170 undergraduate students, 48% full-time, 58% women, 42% men

Undergraduates 2,940 full-time, 3,230 part-time. Students come from 2 states and territories, 1 other country, 2% African American, 1% Asian American or Pacific Islander, 1% Hispanic American, 0.1% Native American, 0.1% international, 6% transferred in.

Freshmen *Admission:* 2,337 applied, 1,574 admitted, 1,447 enrolled.

Faculty *Total:* 475, 22% full-time. *Student/faculty ratio:* 19:1.

Majors Accounting; administrative assistant and secretarial science; airline pilot and flight crew; architectural engineering; architectural engineering technology; automobile/automotive mechanics technology; aviation/airway management; baking and pastry arts; banking and financial support services; biological and physical sciences; building/property maintenance and management; business administration and management; child care provision; commercial and advertising art; commercial photography; computer and information sciences; computer and information sciences related; computer graphics; computer programming related; computer science; computer systems networking and telecommunications; computer technology/computer systems technology; court reporting; criminal justice/law enforcement administration; culinary arts; data entry/microcomputer applications; data processing and data processing technology;

dental assisting; dental hygiene; drafting and design technology; drawing; early childhood education; education; electrical, electronic and communications engineering technology; electrician; emergency medical technology (EMT paramedic); engineering technology; executive assistant/executive secretary; fire science; food services technology; funeral service and mortuary science; general studies; graphic and printing equipment operation/production; graphic design; health and physical education; health/health care administration; heating, air conditioning, ventilation and refrigeration maintenance technology; horticultural science; hospitality and recreation marketing; hotel/motel administration; humanities; human services; industrial design; international business/trade/commerce; journalism; legal assistant/paralegal; liberal arts and sciences and humanities related; liberal arts and sciences/liberal studies; mathematics; mechanical design technology; medical administrative assistant and medical secretary; nursing (registered nurse training); ophthalmic/optometric services; painting; photography; physical education teaching and coaching; plumbing technology; prepharmacy studies; radio and television broadcasting technology; real estate; respiratory care therapy; social sciences; surgical technology; tourism and travel services management; tourism and travel services marketing.

Academic Programs *Special study options:* academic remediation for entering students, accelerated degree program, advanced placement credit, distance learning, external degree program, internships, part-time degree program, services for LD students, summer session for credit. *ROTC:* Air Force (c).

Library Learning Resources Center plus 1 other with 60,000 titles, 744 serial subscriptions, 3,000 audiovisual materials, an OPAC, a Web page.

Computers on Campus 150 computers available on campus for general student use. A campuswide network can be accessed. Internet access, at least one staffed computer lab available.

Student Life *Housing:* college housing not available. *Activities and Organizations:* student-run newspaper, radio and television station, student government, Circle K, Nursing Forum, Science Club, SADAH. *Campus security:* 24-hour patrols.

Athletics Member NJCAA. *Intercollegiate sports:* baseball M, basketball M/W, cross-country running M/W, golf M/W, soccer M/W, softball W, volleyball W. *Intramural sports:* badminton M/W, basketball M/W, bowling M/W, cheerleading M/W, softball M/W, tennis M/W, volleyball M/W.

Standardized Tests *Recommended:* ACCUPLACER.

Costs (2004–05) *Tuition:* area resident $2100 full-time, $70 per credit part-time; state resident $4200 full-time, $140 per credit part-time; nonresident $6300 full-time, $210 per credit part-time. *Required fees:* $270 full-time, $9 per credit part-time. *Waivers:* senior citizens and employees or children of employees.

Applying *Options:* early admission, deferred entrance. *Application fee:* $40. *Recommended:* high school transcript. *Application deadline:* rolling (freshmen), rolling (transfers).

Admissions Contact Mr. Francis Curry, Director of Admissions, Luzerne County Community College, 1333 South Prospect Street, Nanticoke, PA 18634. *Phone:* 570-740-0200 Ext. 343. *Toll-free phone:* 800-377-5222 Ext. 337. *Fax:* 570-740-0238. *E-mail:* admissions@luzerne.edu.

MANOR COLLEGE
Jenkintown, Pennsylvania

- **Independent Byzantine Catholic** 2-year, founded 1947
- **Calendar** semesters
- **Degrees** certificates, diplomas, associate, and postbachelor's certificates
- **Small-town** 35-acre campus with easy access to Philadelphia
- **Coed**

Manor College, located in Jenkintown, a suburb of Philadelphia, offers associate degree and transfer programs in the allied health, business, and liberal arts fields. Areas of study include accounting, allied health, business administration, computer science, dental hygiene, early child care/human services, expanded functions dental assisting, healthcare management, human resource management, marketing management, paralegal studies, psychology, and veterinary technology.

Faculty *Student/faculty ratio:* 14:1.

Student Life *Campus security:* 24-hour emergency response devices and patrols.

Standardized Tests *Required:* SAT I or ACT (for admission).

Costs (2004–05) *Comprehensive fee:* $15,296 includes full-time tuition ($10,046), mandatory fees ($350), and room and board ($4900). Part-time tuition: $220 per credit hour. *Required fees:* $35 per term part-time.

Financial Aid Of all full-time matriculated undergraduates who enrolled, 45 Federal Work-Study jobs (averaging $1000). 11 state and other part-time jobs (averaging $2260). *Financial aid deadline:* 9/30.

Applying *Options:* electronic application, deferred entrance. *Application fee:* $20. *Required:* high school transcript, interview.

Admissions Contact Ms. I. Jerry Czenstuch, Vice President of Enrollment Management, Manor College, 700 Fox Chase Road, Jenkintown, PA 19046. *Phone:* 215-884-2216. *Fax:* 215-576-6564. *E-mail:* ftadmiss@manor.edu.

▶ **See page 568 for a narrative description.**

MCCANN SCHOOL OF BUSINESS & TECHNOLOGY
Pottsville, Pennsylvania

- **Proprietary** 2-year, founded 1897
- **Calendar** quarters
- **Degree** certificates, diplomas, and associate
- **Small-town** campus
- **Coed**

Faculty *Student/faculty ratio:* 12:1.

Standardized Tests *Required:* Wonderlic aptitude test (for admission).

Costs (2003–04) *One-time required fee:* $175. *Tuition:* $7425 full-time, $165 per credit part-time. Full-time tuition and fees vary according to course load. Part-time tuition and fees vary according to course load. No tuition increase for student's term of enrollment. *Required fees:* $450 full-time.

Applying *Options:* common application, electronic application. *Application fee:* $40. *Required:* high school transcript, minimum 2.0 GPA, interview.

Admissions Contact Ms. Rachel M. Schoffstall, Director, Pottsville Campus, McCann School of Business & Technology, 2650 Woodglen Road, Pottsville, PA 17901. *Phone:* 570-622-7622. *Toll-free phone:* 888-622-2664. *Fax:* 570-622-7770.

MEDIAN SCHOOL OF ALLIED HEALTH CAREERS
Pittsburgh, Pennsylvania

- **Proprietary** 2-year, founded 1958
- **Calendar** quarters
- **Degree** diplomas and associate
- **Urban** campus
- **Coed**

Faculty *Student/faculty ratio:* 12:1.

Student Life *Campus security:* security during class hours.

Standardized Tests *Required:* Wonderlic aptitude test (for admission).

Financial Aid Of all full-time matriculated undergraduates who enrolled, 15 Federal Work-Study jobs.

Applying *Options:* deferred entrance. *Application fee:* $75. *Required:* essay or personal statement, high school transcript, interview. *Recommended:* minimum 2.0 GPA.

Admissions Contact Ms. Kris Jackson, Admission Coordinator, Median School of Allied Health Careers, 125 7th Street, Pittsburgh, PA 15222-3400. *Phone:* 800-570-0693. *Toll-free phone:* 800-570-0693. *Fax:* 412-232-4348. *E-mail:* median@sgi.net.

METROPOLITAN CAREER CENTER
Philadelphia, Pennsylvania

Admissions Contact Mr. Ken Huselton, Director of Student Services, Metropolitan Career Center, 100 South Broad Street, Philadelphia, PA 19110. *Phone:* 215-843-6615.

MONTGOMERY COUNTY COMMUNITY COLLEGE
Blue Bell, Pennsylvania

- **County-supported** 2-year, founded 1964
- **Calendar** semesters
- **Degree** certificates and associate
- **Suburban** 186-acre campus with easy access to Philadelphia
- **Coed,** 10,622 undergraduate students, 42% full-time, 59% women, 41% men

Undergraduates 4,428 full-time, 6,194 part-time. Students come from 14 states and territories, 33 other countries, 0.2% are from out of state, 8% African American, 6% Asian American or Pacific Islander, 2% Hispanic American, 0.3% Native American, 1% international.

Freshmen *Admission:* 4,967 applied, 4,967 admitted, 3,747 enrolled.

Faculty *Total:* 662, 22% full-time. *Student/faculty ratio:* 23:1.

Montgomery County Community College (continued)

Majors Accounting; accounting technology and bookkeeping; administrative assistant and secretarial science; architectural drafting and CAD/CADD; art; automotive engineering technology; baking and pastry arts; biology/biological sciences; biotechnology; business administration and management; business/commerce; business/corporate communications; child care and support services management; clinical/medical laboratory technology; commercial and advertising art; communication/speech communication and rhetoric; communications technologies and support services related; computer and information sciences; computer engineering technology; computer programming; computer systems networking and telecommunications; criminal justice/police science; culinary arts; dental hygiene; electrical, electronic and communications engineering technology; electromechanical technology; elementary education; engineering science; engineering technologies related; fire protection and safety technology; food sales operations; hospitality and recreation marketing; hotel/motel services marketing operations; humanities; information science/studies; liberal arts and sciences/liberal studies; management information systems and services related; mathematics; mechanical drafting and CAD/CADD; mechanical engineering/mechanical technology; medical radiologic technology; nursing (registered nurse training); physical education teaching and coaching; physical sciences; psychiatric/mental health services technology; radiologic technology/science; real estate; respiratory care therapy; sales, distribution and marketing; secondary education; social sciences; surgical technology; teacher assistant/aide.

Academic Programs *Special study options:* academic remediation for entering students, adult/continuing education programs, advanced placement credit, distance learning, English as a second language, honors programs, independent study, internships, part-time degree program, services for LD students, student-designed majors, study abroad, summer session for credit.

Library Learning Resources Center with 173,770 titles, 453 serial subscriptions, 23,219 audiovisual materials, an OPAC, a Web page.

Computers on Campus 800 computers available on campus for general student use. A campuswide network can be accessed from off campus. Internet access, online (class) registration, at least one staffed computer lab available.

Student Life *Housing:* college housing not available. *Activities and Organizations:* drama/theater group, student-run newspaper, radio and television station, choral group, student government, Meridians Non-traditional Age Club, student radio station. *Campus security:* 24-hour emergency response devices and patrols, late-night transport/escort service. *Student services:* health clinic, personal/psychological counseling.

Athletics *Intercollegiate sports:* cheerleading W(s). *Intramural sports:* badminton M/W, basketball M/W, bowling M/W, cross-country running M/W, football M, racquetball M/W, soccer M/W, softball M/W, table tennis M/W, tennis M/W, volleyball M/W, weight lifting M/W.

Standardized Tests *Recommended:* SAT I or ACT (for placement).

Costs (2003–04) *Tuition:* area resident $2370 full-time, $79 per credit part-time; state resident $4740 full-time, $158 per credit part-time; nonresident $7110 full-time, $237 per credit part-time. Full-time tuition and fees vary according to course load. Part-time tuition and fees vary according to course load. *Required fees:* $330 full-time, $11 per credit part-time. *Payment plan:* deferred payment. *Waivers:* employees or children of employees.

Financial Aid Of all full-time matriculated undergraduates who enrolled, 58 Federal Work-Study jobs (averaging $2121).

Applying *Options:* electronic application, early admission, deferred entrance. *Application fee:* $20. *Required for some:* high school transcript, interview. *Application deadline:* 5/1 (freshmen), rolling (transfers). *Notification:* continuous (freshmen), continuous (transfers).

Admissions Contact Mr. Joe Rodriguez, Director of Admissions and Records, Montgomery County Community College, Office of Admissions and Records, Blue Bell, PA 19422. *Phone:* 215-641-6550. *Fax:* 215-619-7188. *E-mail:* admrec@admin.mc3.edu.

NEW CASTLE SCHOOL OF TRADES
Pulaski, Pennsylvania

- **Independent** 2-year, founded 1945, part of Educational Enterprises Incorporated
- **Calendar** quarters
- **Degree** diplomas and associate
- **Rural** 20-acre campus with easy access to Youngstown
- **Coed, primarily men,** 451 undergraduate students, 100% full-time, 7% women, 93% men

Undergraduates 451 full-time. Students come from 3 states and territories, 40% are from out of state, 14% African American, 1% Asian American or Pacific Islander, 4% Hispanic American, 0.4% Native American.

Freshmen *Admission:* 87 applied, 84 admitted. *Average high school GPA:* 2.90.

Faculty *Total:* 36, 69% full-time. *Student/faculty ratio:* 18:1.

Majors Automotive engineering technology; construction engineering technology; electrical, electronic and communications engineering technology; heating, air conditioning and refrigeration technology; machine tool technology.

Student Life *Housing:* college housing not available. *Campus security:* 24-hour emergency response devices. *Student services:* personal/psychological counseling.

Standardized Tests *Required:* Wonderlic aptitude test (for admission).

Costs (2004–05) *Tuition:* $12,999 full-time, $2200 per term part-time. No tuition increase for student's term of enrollment. *Required fees:* $9 per hour part-time. *Payment plans:* tuition prepayment, installment, deferred payment. *Waivers:* employees or children of employees.

Applying *Application fee:* $25. *Required:* high school transcript, interview. *Required for some:* essay or personal statement, letters of recommendation. *Notification:* continuous (transfers).

Admissions Contact Mr. James Catheline, Admissions Director, New Castle School of Trades, RD 1, Route 422, Pulaski, PA 16143. *Phone:* 800-837-8299 Ext. 12. *Toll-free phone:* 800-837-8299 Ext. 12. *Fax:* 724-964-8777.

NEWPORT BUSINESS INSTITUTE
Lower Burrell, Pennsylvania

- **Proprietary** 2-year, founded 1895
- **Calendar** quarters
- **Degree** certificates, diplomas, and associate
- **Small-town** 4-acre campus with easy access to Pittsburgh
- **Coed,** 89 undergraduate students, 100% full-time, 85% women, 15% men

Undergraduates 89 full-time. Students come from 1 other state, 7% African American, 3% transferred in.

Freshmen *Admission:* 29 applied, 19 admitted, 19 enrolled. *Average high school GPA:* 2.8.

Faculty *Total:* 7. *Student/faculty ratio:* 14:1.

Majors Accounting; business administration and management; computer programming; consumer merchandising/retailing management; data entry/microcomputer applications; data entry/microcomputer applications related; executive assistant/executive secretary; legal administrative assistant/secretary; medical administrative assistant and medical secretary; medical/clinical assistant; medical office management; tourism and travel services management; word processing.

Academic Programs *Special study options:* advanced placement credit, double majors, internships, student-designed majors.

Library Jean H. Mullen Memorial Library with 962 titles, 18 serial subscriptions.

Computers on Campus 85 computers available on campus for general student use. Internet access, at least one staffed computer lab available.

Student Life *Housing:* college housing not available. *Activities and Organizations:* student-run newspaper, student services, Returning Adults Club, new student mentoring, peer liaison. *Campus security:* security system. *Student services:* personal/psychological counseling.

Costs (2004–05) *Tuition:* $6900 full-time, $580 per course part-time. Full-time tuition and fees vary according to program. *Required fees:* $1400 full-time. *Waivers:* employees or children of employees.

Applying *Options:* common application, early admission. *Application fee:* $25. *Required:* high school transcript. *Recommended:* interview. *Application deadline:* rolling (freshmen), rolling (transfers). *Notification:* continuous (freshmen), continuous (transfers).

Admissions Contact Mr. William Bates, Admissions Coordinator, Newport Business Institute, Lower Burrell, PA 15068. *Phone:* 724-339-7542. *Toll-free phone:* 800-752-7695. *Fax:* 724-339-2950.

NEWPORT BUSINESS INSTITUTE
Williamsport, Pennsylvania

- **Proprietary** 2-year, founded 1955
- **Calendar** quarters
- **Degree** associate
- **Small-town** campus
- **Coed, primarily women,** 112 undergraduate students, 98% full-time, 90% women, 10% men

Undergraduates 110 full-time, 2 part-time. Students come from 1 other state, 7% African American, 0.9% Asian American or Pacific Islander, 10% transferred in. *Retention:* 88% of 2002 full-time freshmen returned.

Freshmen *Admission:* 33 applied, 33 admitted, 33 enrolled.

Faculty *Total:* 6, 100% full-time. *Student/faculty ratio:* 20:1.

Majors Administrative assistant and secretarial science; business administration and management; legal administrative assistant/secretary; medical administrative assistant and medical secretary.

Academic Programs *Special study options:* internships, part-time degree program, summer session for credit.
Computers on Campus 60 computers available on campus for general student use. Internet access, at least one staffed computer lab available.
Student Life *Housing:* college housing not available. *Activities and Organizations:* Student Council.
Costs (2004–05) *Tuition:* $7950 full-time, $663 per course part-time. *Required fees:* $400 full-time.
Financial Aid *Financial aid deadline:* 8/1.
Applying *Options:* deferred entrance. *Application fee:* $25. *Required:* high school transcript. *Application deadline:* rolling (freshmen), rolling (transfers).
Admissions Contact Mrs. Connie Yorke, Admissions Representative, Newport Business Institute, 941 West Third Street, Williamsport, PA 17701-5855. *Phone:* 570-326-2869. *Toll-free phone:* 800-962-6971. *Fax:* 570-326-2136.

NORTHAMPTON COUNTY AREA COMMUNITY COLLEGE
Bethlehem, Pennsylvania

- **State and locally supported** 2-year, founded 1967
- **Calendar** semesters
- **Degree** certificates, diplomas, and associate
- **Suburban** 165-acre campus with easy access to Philadelphia
- **Endowment** $10.6 million
- **Coed,** 7,621 undergraduate students, 43% full-time, 63% women, 37% men

Undergraduates 3,268 full-time, 4,353 part-time. Students come from 21 states and territories, 36 other countries, 2% are from out of state, 6% African American, 2% Asian American or Pacific Islander, 7% Hispanic American, 0.2% Native American, 1% international, 34% transferred in, 3% live on campus.
Freshmen *Admission:* 2,774 applied, 2,741 admitted, 2,506 enrolled.
Faculty *Total:* 436, 23% full-time, 16% with terminal degrees. *Student/faculty ratio:* 22:1.
Majors Accounting technology and bookkeeping; acting; architectural engineering technology; automotive engineering technology; banking and financial support services; biological and biomedical sciences related; biology/biological sciences; business administration and management; business/commerce; chemical technology; chemistry; child care and support services management; commercial and advertising art; communication disorders; computer and information sciences; computer installation and repair technology; criminal justice/law enforcement administration; culinary arts; data processing and data processing technology; dental hygiene; drafting and design technology; education (specific levels and methods) related; electrical and electronic engineering technologies related; electrical, electronic and communications engineering technology; electromechanical technology; engineering; executive assistant/executive secretary; fine/studio arts; fire services administration; funeral service and mortuary science; general studies; hotel/motel administration; interior architecture; journalism; legal administrative assistant/secretary; legal assistant/paralegal; liberal arts and sciences and humanities related; liberal arts and sciences/liberal studies; mathematics; medical administrative assistant and medical secretary; medical radiologic technology; nursing (registered nurse training); occupational health and industrial hygiene; physics; quality control technology; radio and television broadcasting technology; social work; special education; sport and fitness administration; veterinary/animal health technology.
Academic Programs *Special study options:* academic remediation for entering students, accelerated degree program, adult/continuing education programs, advanced placement credit, cooperative education, distance learning, English as a second language, internships, part-time degree program, services for LD students, student-designed majors, study abroad, summer session for credit.
Library Learning Resources Center with 51,103 titles, 376 serial subscriptions, 7,866 audiovisual materials, an OPAC, a Web page.
Computers on Campus 1100 computers available on campus for general student use. A campuswide network can be accessed. Internet access, online (class) registration, at least one staffed computer lab available.
Student Life *Housing Options:* coed. Campus housing is university owned. *Activities and Organizations:* drama/theater group, student-run newspaper, radio station, choral group, Phi Theta Kappa, Nursing Student Organization, NAVTA (Veterinary Technology Club), Student American Dental Hygiene Association, Video Waves. *Campus security:* 24-hour emergency response devices and patrols, controlled dormitory access. *Student services:* health clinic, personal/psychological counseling.
Athletics *Intercollegiate sports:* baseball M, basketball M/W, bowling M/W, golf M/W, ice hockey M/W, soccer M, softball W, tennis M/W, volleyball M/W, wrestling M. *Intramural sports:* basketball M/W, bowling M/W, cheerleading W, golf M/W, racquetball M/W, soccer M/W.
Standardized Tests *Required for some:* ACT (for placement).
Costs (2003–04) *Tuition:* area resident $2040 full-time, $68 per credit hour part-time; state resident $4080 full-time, $136 per credit hour part-time; nonresident $6120 full-time, $204 per credit hour part-time. *Required fees:* $600

full-time, $20 per credit hour part-time. *Room and board:* $5376; room only: $3168. Room and board charges vary according to board plan and housing facility. *Payment plans:* installment, deferred payment. *Waivers:* senior citizens and employees or children of employees.
Financial Aid Of all full-time matriculated undergraduates who enrolled, 300 Federal Work-Study jobs (averaging $3000). 90 state and other part-time jobs (averaging $2100).
Applying *Options:* common application, electronic application, deferred entrance. *Application fee:* $25. *Required:* high school transcript. *Required for some:* interview, art evaluation for communication design and fine arts programs; audition for theatre program. *Application deadline:* rolling (freshmen), rolling (transfers). *Notification:* continuous (freshmen), continuous (transfers).
Admissions Contact Mr. James McCarthy, Director of Admissions, Northampton County Area Community College, 3835 Green Pond Road, Bethlehem, PA 18020-7599. *Phone:* 610-861-5506. *Fax:* 610-861-5551. *E-mail:* adminfo@northampton.edu.

NORTH CENTRAL INDUSTRIAL TECHNICAL EDUCATION CENTER
Ridgway, Pennsylvania

Admissions Contact Lugene Inzana, Director, North Central Industrial Technical Education Center, 651 Montmorenci Avenue, Ridgway, PA 15853. *Phone:* 814-772-1012. *Toll-free phone:* 800-242-5872.

OAKBRIDGE ACADEMY OF ARTS
Lower Burrell, Pennsylvania

- **Proprietary** 2-year, founded 1972
- **Calendar** quarters
- **Degree** associate
- **Small-town** 2-acre campus with easy access to Pittsburgh
- **Coed,** 103 undergraduate students, 99% full-time, 59% women, 41% men

Undergraduates 102 full-time, 1 part-time. Students come from 4 states and territories, 1% African American, 6% transferred in.
Freshmen *Admission:* 111 applied, 103 admitted, 32 enrolled. *Average high school GPA:* 2.30.
Faculty *Total:* 9, 67% full-time. *Student/faculty ratio:* 9:1.
Majors Commercial and advertising art; commercial photography; computer graphics.
Academic Programs *Special study options:* academic remediation for entering students, advanced placement credit, internships.
Library Robert J. Mullen Memorial Library plus 1 other with 3,000 titles, 15 serial subscriptions, 80 audiovisual materials, a Web page.
Computers on Campus 40 computers available on campus for general student use. Internet access, at least one staffed computer lab available.
Student Life *Housing:* college housing not available. *Campus security:* 24-hour emergency response devices.
Costs (2003–04) *Tuition:* $7800 full-time, $700 per course part-time. Full-time tuition and fees vary according to course load and program. Part-time tuition and fees vary according to course load and program. *Required fees:* $600 full-time. *Payment plan:* installment. *Waivers:* employees or children of employees.
Financial Aid *Financial aid deadline:* 8/1.
Applying *Options:* common application, electronic application. *Required:* high school transcript, portfolio. *Application deadline:* 8/31 (freshmen).
Admissions Contact Jan Schoeneberger, Admissions Representative, Oakbridge Academy of Arts, 1250 Greensburg Road, Lower Burrell, PA 15068. *Phone:* 724-335-5336. *Toll-free phone:* 800-734-5601. *Fax:* 724-335-3367.

ORLEANS TECHNICAL INSTITUTE-CENTER CITY CAMPUS
Philadelphia, Pennsylvania

- **Proprietary** 2-year
- **Calendar** trimesters
- **Degree** associate
- **Urban** campus
- **Coed, primarily women,** 207 undergraduate students, 58% full-time, 96% women, 4% men

Undergraduates 121 full-time, 86 part-time. Students come from 3 states and territories, 60% are from out of state, 25% African American, 1% Asian American or Pacific Islander, 6% Hispanic American, 0.5% Native American, 4% transferred in.

Orleans Technical Institute-Center City Campus (continued)

Freshmen *Admission:* 48 applied, 25 admitted, 18 enrolled.

Faculty *Total:* 25, 20% full-time.

Academic Programs *Special study options:* academic remediation for entering students, internships, part-time degree program, summer session for credit.

Library Library plus 1 other with 625 titles, 14 serial subscriptions.

Computers on Campus 46 computers available on campus for general student use. Internet access, at least one staffed computer lab available.

Student Life *Housing:* college housing not available.

Standardized Tests *Required:* CPAt (for admission).

Costs (2003–04) *One-time required fee:* $100. *Tuition:* $5800 full-time, $4060 per year part-time. Full-time tuition and fees vary according to program. Part-time tuition and fees vary according to program. *Required fees:* $200 full-time. *Payment plan:* installment. *Waivers:* employees or children of employees.

Financial Aid Of all full-time matriculated undergraduates who enrolled, 5 Federal Work-Study jobs (averaging $4800). *Financial aid deadline:* 8/1.

Applying *Application fee:* $150. *Required:* high school transcript, interview. *Application deadline:* rolling (freshmen), rolling (transfers).

Admissions Contact Mr. Gary Bello, Admissions Representative, Orleans Technical Institute-Center City Campus, 1845 Walnut Street, 7th Floor, Philadephia, PA 19103. *Phone:* 215-854-1853. *Fax:* 215-854-1880. *E-mail:* gary.bello@jevs.org.

PACE INSTITUTE
Reading, Pennsylvania

- **Private** 2-year
- **Degree** diplomas and associate
- **Coed**

Faculty *Student/faculty ratio:* 18:1.

Costs (2003–04) *Tuition:* $5880 full-time, $245 per credit part-time. *Required fees:* $1080 full-time, $45 per credit part-time.

Admissions Contact Mr. Ed Levandowski, Director of Enrollment Management, Pace Institute, 606 Court Street, Reading, PA 19601. *Phone:* 610-375-1212.

PENN COMMERCIAL BUSINESS AND TECHNICAL SCHOOL
Washington, Pennsylvania

- **Proprietary** 2-year, founded 1929
- **Calendar** quarters
- **Degree** certificates, diplomas, and associate
- **Small-town** 1-acre campus with easy access to Pittsburgh
- **Coed**

Faculty *Student/faculty ratio:* 16:1.

Financial Aid *Financial aid deadline:* 8/1.

Applying *Options:* early admission, deferred entrance. *Application fee:* $25. *Required:* high school transcript.

Admissions Contact Mr. Michael John Joyce, Director of Admissions, Penn Commercial Business and Technical School, 242 Oak Spring Road, Washington, PA 15301. *Phone:* 724-222-5330 Ext. 1. *Fax:* 724-225-3561. *E-mail:* pcadmissions@penncommercial.net.

PENNCO TECH
Bristol, Pennsylvania

Admissions Contact Mr. Nate R. Aldsworth, Corporate Director of Admissions and Marketing, Pennco Tech, 3815 Otter Street, Bristol, PA 19007-3696. *Phone:* 215-824-3200. *E-mail:* admissions@penncotech.com.

PENNSYLVANIA COLLEGE OF TECHNOLOGY
Williamsport, Pennsylvania

- **State-related** primarily 2-year, founded 1965
- **Calendar** semesters
- **Degrees** associate and bachelor's
- **Small-town** 958-acre campus
- **Endowment** $650,434
- **Coed**, 6,255 undergraduate students, 83% full-time, 35% women, 65% men

Undergraduates 5,198 full-time, 1,057 part-time. Students come from 32 states and territories, 16 other countries, 7% are from out of state, 3% African American, 1% Asian American or Pacific Islander, 0.9% Hispanic American, 0.5% Native American, 0.5% international, 8% transferred in, 19% live on campus.

Freshmen *Admission:* 5,483 applied, 2,777 admitted, 1,651 enrolled.

Faculty *Total:* 468, 60% full-time. *Student/faculty ratio:* 18:1.

Majors Accounting; accounting technology and bookkeeping; administrative assistant and secretarial science; adult health nursing; aeronautical/aerospace engineering technology; aircraft powerplant technology; allied health diagnostic, intervention, and treatment professions related; applied horticulture/horticultural business services related; architectural engineering technology; autobody/collision and repair technology; automotive engineering technology; avionics maintenance technology; baking and pastry arts; banking and financial support services; biology/biological sciences; biomedical technology; broadcast journalism; business administration and management; business administration, management and operations related; business automation/technology/data entry; cabinetmaking and millwork; cardiovascular technology; carpentry; child care and support services management; child care provision; civil engineering technology; commercial and advertising art; computer and information sciences; computer and information sciences and support services related; computer/information technology services administration related; computer programming (specific applications); computer systems analysis; computer systems networking and telecommunications; computer technology/computer systems technology; construction engineering technology; culinary arts; dental hygiene; diesel mechanics technology; dietitian assistant; drafting and design technology; drafting/design engineering technologies related; education (specific subject areas) related; electrical and electronic engineering technologies related; electrical, electronic and communications engineering technology; electrician; emergency medical technology (EMT paramedic); engineering science; engineering technologies related; environmental control technologies related; environmental engineering technology; forestry technology; general studies; graphic and printing equipment operation/production; health and medical administrative services related; health and physical education related; health information/medical records administration; health professions related; heating, air conditioning and refrigeration technology; heavy equipment maintenance technology; heavy/industrial equipment maintenance technologies related; industrial electronics technology; industrial mechanics and maintenance technology; industrial production technologies related; industrial technology; information technology; institutional food workers; instrumentation technology; laser and optical technology; legal assistant/paralegal; legal professions and studies related; legal studies; liberal arts and sciences and humanities related; liberal arts and sciences/liberal studies; machine shop technology; management information systems; manufacturing technology; masonry; mass communication/media; mechanical drafting and CAD/CADD; mechanical engineering/mechanical technology; mechanic and repair technologies related; medical administrative assistant and medical secretary; medical radiologic technology; mental and social health services and allied professions related; multi-/interdisciplinary studies related; nursing (licensed practical/vocational nurse training); nursing (registered nurse training); occupational therapist assistant; office occupations and clerical services; ornamental horticulture; physical sciences; plant nursery management; plastics engineering technology; platemaking/imaging; plumbing technology; psychiatric/mental health services technology; quality control technology; solar energy technology; survey technology; technical and business writing; tool and die technology; tourism and travel services management; turf and turfgrass management; vehicle and vehicle parts and accessories marketing; vehicle maintenance and repair technologies related; web page, digital/multimedia and information resources design; welding technology; woodworking related.

Academic Programs *Special study options:* academic remediation for entering students, advanced placement credit, cooperative education, distance learning, double majors, English as a second language, independent study, internships, off-campus study, part-time degree program, services for LD students, student-designed majors, summer session for credit. *ROTC:* Army (c).

Library Penn College Library plus 1 other with 64,462 titles, 6,985 audiovisual materials, an OPAC, a Web page.

Computers on Campus A campuswide network can be accessed from student residence rooms and from off campus. At least one staffed computer lab available.

Student Life *Housing Options:* coed. Campus housing is university owned. *Activities and Organizations:* student-run newspaper, radio station, Student Government Association, Resident Hall Association (RHA), Wildcats Event Board (WEB), Phi Beta Lambda, Early Educators. *Campus security:* 24-hour emergency response devices and patrols, late-night transport/escort service. *Student services:* personal/psychological counseling, women's center.

Athletics *Intercollegiate sports:* archery M/W, baseball M, basketball M/W, bowling M/W, cross-country running M/W, golf M/W, soccer M/W, softball W, tennis M/W, volleyball M/W. *Intramural sports:* archery M/W, badminton M/W, basketball M/W, bowling M/W, football M/W, golf M/W, lacrosse M/W, racquetball M/W, soccer M/W, softball M/W, table tennis M/W, tennis M/W, volleyball M/W, weight lifting M/W, wrestling M.

Standardized Tests *Required for some:* SAT I (for admission).

Costs (2003–04) *Tuition:* state resident $7860 full-time, $298 per credit part-time; nonresident $9990 full-time, $375 per credit part-time. Full-time tuition and fees vary according to course load and program. Part-time tuition and fees vary according to course load and program. *Required fees:* $1260 full-time. *Room and board:* $6186; room only: $3686. Room and board charges vary according to board plan, housing facility, and location. *Payment plan:* deferred payment. *Waivers:* employees or children of employees.

Financial Aid Of all full-time matriculated undergraduates who enrolled in 2002, 326 Federal Work-Study jobs (averaging $1339).

Applying *Options:* electronic application, early admission, deferred entrance. *Application fee:* $50. *Required:* high school transcript. *Application deadlines:* rolling (freshmen), 7/1 (out-of-state freshmen), rolling (transfers). *Early decision:* 7/1.

Admissions Contact Mr. Chester D. Schuman, Director of Admissions, Pennsylvania College of Technology, One College Avenue, DIF #119, Williamsport, PA 17701. *Phone:* 570-327-4761. *Toll-free phone:* 800-367-9222. *Fax:* 570-321-5551. *E-mail:* cschuman@pct.edu.

▶ **See page 590 for a narrative description.**

PENNSYLVANIA CULINARY INSTITUTE
Pittsburgh, Pennsylvania

- **Proprietary** 2-year, founded 1986
- **Calendar** semesters
- **Degree** associate
- **Urban** campus
- **Coed,** 991 undergraduate students, 100% full-time, 33% women, 67% men

Undergraduates 991 full-time. Students come from 23 states and territories, 2 other countries, 62% are from out of state, 15% African American, 0.8% Asian American or Pacific Islander, 3% Hispanic American, 0.4% Native American.

Freshmen *Admission:* 991 admitted.

Faculty *Total:* 46, 100% full-time. *Student/faculty ratio:* 18:1.

Majors Culinary arts; hotel/motel administration.

Academic Programs *Special study options:* academic remediation for entering students, double majors, internships.

Library Learning Resource Center with 6,000 titles, 73 serial subscriptions, 3 audiovisual materials, a Web page.

Computers on Campus 90 computers available on campus for general student use. A campuswide network can be accessed from off campus. Internet access, at least one staffed computer lab available.

Costs (2003–04) *Comprehensive fee:* $27,449 includes full-time tuition ($17,500), mandatory fees ($100), and room and board ($9849). No tuition increase for student's term of enrollment. *Room and board:* college room only: $6177. *Waivers:* employees or children of employees.

Applying *Options:* electronic application. *Application fee:* $100. *Required:* essay or personal statement, high school transcript, interview.

Admissions Contact Ms. Sharon Vito, Enrollment Manager, Pennsylvania Culinary Institute, 717 Liberty Avenue, Pittsburgh, PA 15222-3500. *Phone:* 412-566-2433 Ext. 4727. *Toll-free phone:* 800-432-2433. *Fax:* 412-566-2434. *E-mail:* info@paculinary.com.

PENNSYLVANIA INSTITUTE OF TECHNOLOGY
Media, Pennsylvania

- **Independent** 2-year, founded 1953
- **Calendar** semesters
- **Degree** certificates and associate
- **Small-town** 12-acre campus with easy access to Philadelphia
- **Coed,** 282 undergraduate students, 60% full-time, 38% women, 62% men

Undergraduates 168 full-time, 114 part-time. Students come from 3 states and territories, 36% African American, 2% Asian American or Pacific Islander, 2% Hispanic American, 1% international. *Retention:* 56% of 2002 full-time freshmen returned.

Freshmen *Admission:* 323 applied, 172 admitted, 111 enrolled.

Faculty *Total:* 30, 37% full-time, 3% with terminal degrees. *Student/faculty ratio:* 14:1.

Majors Architectural engineering technology; business administration and management; electrical, electronic and communications engineering technology; engineering technology; mechanical engineering/mechanical technology; mechanical engineering technologies related; medical office management; office occupations and clerical services; web page, digital/multimedia and information resources design.

Academic Programs *Special study options:* academic remediation for entering students, adult/continuing education programs, advanced placement credit, cooperative education, part-time degree program, summer session for credit.

Library Pennsylvania Institute of Technology Library/Learning Resource Center with 16,500 titles, 217 serial subscriptions, an OPAC, a Web page.

Computers on Campus 85 computers available on campus for general student use. At least one staffed computer lab available.

Student Life *Housing:* college housing not available. *Campus security:* 24-hour emergency response devices. *Student services:* personal/psychological counseling.

Athletics *Intramural sports:* basketball M/W, volleyball M/W.

Standardized Tests *Recommended:* SAT I or ACT (for placement).

Costs (2004–05) *Tuition:* $9000 full-time, $300 per credit part-time. Part-time tuition and fees vary according to course load. *Required fees:* $330 full-time, $11 per credit part-time. *Payment plan:* installment. *Waivers:* employees or children of employees.

Financial Aid Of all full-time matriculated undergraduates who enrolled, 15 Federal Work-Study jobs (averaging $1025). *Financial aid deadline:* 8/1.

Applying *Options:* common application, electronic application, deferred entrance. *Application fee:* $25. *Required:* high school transcript, interview. *Required for some:* 2 letters of recommendation. *Recommended:* essay or personal statement. *Application deadline:* 8/1 (freshmen), rolling (transfers). *Notification:* continuous until 9/1 (freshmen).

Admissions Contact Mr. Matthew Kadlubowski, Director of Admissions, Pennsylvania Institute of Technology, 800 Manchester Avenue, Media, PA 19063-4036. *Phone:* 610-892-1550 Ext. 1553. *Toll-free phone:* 800-422-0025. *Fax:* 610-892-1510. *E-mail:* info@pit.edu.

THE PENNSYLVANIA STATE UNIVERSITY BEAVER CAMPUS OF THE COMMONWEALTH COLLEGE
Monaca, Pennsylvania

- **State-related** primarily 2-year, founded 1964, part of Pennsylvania State University
- **Calendar** semesters
- **Degrees** associate and bachelor's (also offers up to 2 years of most bachelor's degree programs offered at University Park campus)
- **Small-town** 91-acre campus with easy access to Pittsburgh
- **Coed,** 735 undergraduate students, 88% full-time, 35% women, 65% men

Undergraduates 646 full-time, 89 part-time. 4% are from out of state, 4% African American, 2% Asian American or Pacific Islander, 2% Hispanic American, 0.5% Native American, 0.3% international, 4% transferred in, 26% live on campus. *Retention:* 71% of 2001 full-time freshmen returned.

Freshmen *Admission:* 572 applied, 523 admitted, 216 enrolled. *Average high school GPA:* 2.94. *Test scores:* SAT verbal scores over 500: 56%; SAT math scores over 500: 57%; SAT verbal scores over 600: 13%; SAT math scores over 600: 18%; SAT verbal scores over 700: 1%; SAT math scores over 700: 1%.

Faculty *Total:* 59, 61% full-time, 42% with terminal degrees. *Student/faculty ratio:* 16:1.

Majors Accounting; acting; actuarial science; adult and continuing education administration; advertising; aerospace, aeronautical and astronautical engineering; African-American/Black studies; agribusiness; agricultural and extension education; agricultural/biological engineering and bioengineering; agricultural business and management related; agricultural mechanization; agriculture; American studies; animal sciences; animal sciences related; anthropology; applied economics; archeology; architectural engineering; art; art history, criticism and conservation; art teacher education; Asian studies (East); astronomy; atmospheric sciences and meteorology; biochemistry; biological and biomedical sciences related; biological and physical sciences; biology/biological sciences; biology/biotechnology laboratory technician; biomedical/medical engineering; biomedical technology; business administration and management; business/commerce; business/managerial economics; chemical engineering; chemistry; civil engineering; classics and languages, literatures and linguistics; communication and journalism related; communication/speech communication and rhetoric; comparative literature; computer and information sciences; computer engineering; criminal justice/law enforcement administration; economics; electrical, electronic and communications engineering technology; electrical, electronics and communications engineering; elementary education; engineering science; English; environmental/environmental health engineering; film/cinema studies; finance; food science; forestry technology; forest sciences and biology; French; geography; geological and earth sciences/geosciences related; geology/earth science; German; graphic design; health/health care administration; history; horticultural science; hospitality administration related; human development and family studies; human nutrition; industrial engineering; information science/studies; international business/trade/commerce; international relations and affairs; Italian; Japanese; Jewish/Judaic studies; journalism; kinesiology and exercise science; labor and industrial relations; landscape architecture; landscaping and groundskeeping; Latin American studies; liberal arts and sciences/liberal studies; logistics and materials management; management information systems; management sciences and quantitative methods related; marketing/marketing manage-

The Pennsylvania State University Beaver Campus of the Commonwealth College (continued)

ment; materials science; mathematics; mechanical engineering; medical microbiology and bacteriology; medieval and Renaissance studies; mining and mineral engineering; natural resources and conservation related; natural resources/conservation; nuclear engineering; nursing (registered nurse training); organizational behavior; parks, recreation and leisure facilities management; petroleum engineering; philosophy; physics; political science and government; pre-medical studies; psychology; rehabilitation and therapeutic professions related; religious studies; Russian; secondary education; sociology; soil science and agronomy; Spanish; special education; statistics; telecommunications technology; theatre design and technology; turf and turfgrass management; visual and performing arts; women's studies.

Academic Programs *Special study options:* academic remediation for entering students, accelerated degree program, adult/continuing education programs, advanced placement credit, distance learning, double majors, English as a second language, honors programs, independent study, internships, services for LD students, summer session for credit.

Library 39,861 titles, 222 serial subscriptions, 6,683 audiovisual materials.

Computers on Campus 106 computers available on campus for general student use. A campuswide network can be accessed from student residence rooms and from off campus. Internet access, online (class) registration, at least one staffed computer lab available. Computer purchase or lease plan available.

Student Life *Housing Options:* coed. Campus housing is university owned. Freshman campus housing is guaranteed. *Activities and Organizations:* drama/theater group, student-run newspaper, radio station. *Campus security:* 24-hour patrols, controlled dormitory access.

Athletics Member NJCAA. *Intercollegiate sports:* baseball M, basketball M, golf M, softball W, volleyball W. *Intramural sports:* basketball M/W, cheerleading M(c)/W(c), cross-country running M/W, football M, golf M/W, soccer M/W, softball M/W, table tennis M/W.

Standardized Tests *Required:* SAT I or ACT (for admission).

Costs (2003–04) *Tuition:* state resident $8620 full-time, $348 per credit part-time; nonresident $13,250 full-time, $552 per credit part-time. *Required fees:* $408 full-time. *Room and board:* $5940; room only: $3080. *Waivers:* senior citizens.

Financial Aid Of all full-time matriculated undergraduates who enrolled, 38 Federal Work-Study jobs (averaging $1098).

Applying *Options:* electronic application, early admission, deferred entrance. *Application fee:* $50. *Required:* high school transcript. *Application deadline:* rolling (freshmen), rolling (transfers). *Notification:* continuous (freshmen), continuous (transfers).

Admissions Contact The Pennsylvania State University Beaver Campus of the Commonwealth College, 100 University Drive, Suite 113, Monaca, PA 15061-2799. *Phone:* 814-865-5471. *Toll-free phone:* 877-564-6778. *Fax:* 724-773-3658. *E-mail:* br-admissions@psu.edu.

THE PENNSYLVANIA STATE UNIVERSITY DELAWARE COUNTY CAMPUS OF THE COMMONWEALTH COLLEGE
Media, Pennsylvania

- **State-related** primarily 2-year, founded 1966, part of Pennsylvania State University
- **Calendar** semesters
- **Degrees** associate and bachelor's (also offers up to 2 years of most bachelor's degree programs offered at University Park campus)
- **Small-town** 87-acre campus with easy access to Philadelphia
- **Coed**, 1,733 undergraduate students, 83% full-time, 44% women, 56% men

Undergraduates 1,439 full-time, 294 part-time. 4% are from out of state, 13% African American, 9% Asian American or Pacific Islander, 2% Hispanic American, 0.1% Native American, 0.7% international, 3% transferred in. *Retention:* 72% of 2001 full-time freshmen returned.

Freshmen *Admission:* 1,573 applied, 1,221 admitted, 465 enrolled. *Average high school GPA:* 2.87. *Test scores:* SAT verbal scores over 500: 31%; SAT math scores over 500: 37%; SAT verbal scores over 600: 7%; SAT math scores over 600: 10%; SAT verbal scores over 700: 1%; SAT math scores over 700: 2%.

Faculty *Total:* 132, 52% full-time, 42% with terminal degrees. *Student/faculty ratio:* 17:1.

Majors Accounting; acting; actuarial science; adult and continuing education administration; advertising; aerospace, aeronautical and astronautical engineering; African-American/Black studies; agribusiness; agricultural and extension education; agricultural/biological engineering and bioengineering; agricultural business and management related; agricultural mechanization; agriculture; American studies; animal sciences; animal sciences related; anthropology; applied economics; archeology; architectural engineering; art; art history, criticism and

conservation; art teacher education; Asian studies (East); astronomy; atmospheric sciences and meteorology; biochemistry; biological and biomedical sciences related; biological and physical sciences; biology/biological sciences; biology/biotechnology laboratory technician; biomedical/medical engineering; business administration and management; business/commerce; business/managerial economics; chemical engineering; chemistry; civil engineering; classics and languages, literatures and linguistics; communication and journalism related; communication disorders; communication/speech communication and rhetoric; comparative literature; computer and information sciences; computer engineering; criminal justice/law enforcement administration; economics; electrical, electronics and communications engineering; elementary education; engineering science; English; environmental/environmental health engineering; film/cinema studies; finance; food science; forestry technology; forest sciences and biology; French; geography; geological and earth sciences/geosciences related; geology/earth science; German; graphic design; health/health care administration; history; horticultural science; hospitality administration related; human development and family studies; human nutrition; industrial engineering; information science/studies; international business/trade/commerce; international relations and affairs; Italian; Japanese; Jewish/Judaic studies; journalism; kinesiology and exercise science; labor and industrial relations; landscape architecture; landscaping and groundskeeping; Latin American studies; liberal arts and sciences/liberal studies; logistics and materials management; management information systems; management sciences and quantitative methods related; marketing/marketing management; materials science; mathematics; mechanical engineering; medical microbiology and bacteriology; medieval and Renaissance studies; mining and mineral engineering; natural resources and conservation related; natural resources/conservation; nuclear engineering; nursing (registered nurse training); organizational behavior; parks, recreation and leisure facilities management; petroleum engineering; philosophy; physics; political science and government; pre-medical studies; psychology; rehabilitation and therapeutic professions related; religious studies; Russian; secondary education; sociology; soil science and agronomy; Spanish; special education; statistics; theatre design and technology; turf and turfgrass management; visual and performing arts; women's studies.

Academic Programs *Special study options:* academic remediation for entering students, accelerated degree program, adult/continuing education programs, advanced placement credit, distance learning, double majors, English as a second language, honors programs, independent study, internships, services for LD students, student-designed majors, study abroad, summer session for credit. *ROTC:* Army (c).

Library 59,930 titles, 457 serial subscriptions, 3,987 audiovisual materials.

Computers on Campus 180 computers available on campus for general student use. A campuswide network can be accessed from off campus. Internet access, online (class) registration, at least one staffed computer lab available. Computer purchase or lease plan available.

Student Life *Housing:* college housing not available. *Activities and Organizations:* drama/theater group, student-run newspaper. *Campus security:* late-night transport/escort service, part-time trained security personnel.

Athletics Member NJCAA. *Intercollegiate sports:* baseball M, basketball M/W, lacrosse M(c)/W(c), soccer M/W, tennis M/W, volleyball W. *Intramural sports:* basketball M/W, cheerleading M(c)/W(c), golf M/W, ice hockey M(c)/W(c), lacrosse M/W, soccer M/W, softball W(c), tennis M/W, volleyball M(c)/W.

Standardized Tests *Required:* SAT I or ACT (for admission).

Costs (2003–04) *Tuition:* state resident $8620 full-time, $348 per credit part-time; nonresident $13,250 full-time, $552 per credit part-time. *Required fees:* $398 full-time.

Financial Aid Of all full-time matriculated undergraduates who enrolled, 28 Federal Work-Study jobs (averaging $615).

Applying *Options:* electronic application, early admission, deferred entrance. *Application fee:* $50. *Application deadline:* rolling (freshmen), rolling (transfers). *Notification:* continuous (freshmen), continuous (transfers).

Admissions Contact The Pennsylvania State University Delaware County Campus of the Commonwealth College, 25 Yearsley Mill Road, Media, PA 19063-5596. *Phone:* 814-865-5471. *Fax:* 610-892-1357. *E-mail:* admissions-delco@psu.edu.

THE PENNSYLVANIA STATE UNIVERSITY DUBOIS CAMPUS OF THE COMMONWEALTH COLLEGE
DuBois, Pennsylvania

- **State-related** primarily 2-year, founded 1935, part of Pennsylvania State University
- **Calendar** semesters
- **Degrees** associate and bachelor's (also offers up to 2 years of most bachelor's degree programs offered at University Park campus)
- **Small-town** 20-acre campus
- **Coed**, 919 undergraduate students, 75% full-time, 51% women, 49% men

Undergraduates 688 full-time, 231 part-time. 1% are from out of state, 0.8% African American, 0.9% Asian American or Pacific Islander, 0.4% Hispanic American, 0.3% Native American, 3% transferred in. *Retention:* 75% of 2001 full-time freshmen returned.

Freshmen *Admission:* 417 applied, 385 admitted, 216 enrolled. *Average high school GPA:* 2.87. *Test scores:* SAT verbal scores over 500: 48%; SAT math scores over 500: 50%; SAT verbal scores over 600: 9%; SAT math scores over 600: 12%.

Faculty *Total:* 90, 52% full-time, 39% with terminal degrees. *Student/faculty ratio:* 13:1.

Majors Accounting; acting; actuarial science; adult and continuing education administration; advertising; aerospace, aeronautical and astronautical engineering; African-American/Black studies; agribusiness; agricultural and extension education; agricultural/biological engineering and bioengineering; agricultural business and management related; agricultural mechanization; agriculture; American studies; animal sciences; animal sciences related; anthropology; applied economics; archeology; architectural engineering; art; art history, criticism and conservation; art teacher education; Asian studies (East); astronomy; atmospheric sciences and meteorology; biochemistry; biological and biomedical sciences related; biological and physical sciences; biology/biological sciences; biology/biotechnology laboratory technician; biomedical/medical engineering; biomedical technology; business administration and management; business/commerce; business/managerial economics; chemical engineering; chemistry; civil engineering; classics and languages, literatures and linguistics; clinical/medical laboratory technology; communication and journalism related; communication disorders; communication/speech communication and rhetoric; comparative literature; computer and information sciences; computer engineering; criminal justice/law enforcement administration; economics; electrical, electronic and communications engineering technology; electrical, electronics and communications engineering; elementary education; engineering science; English; environmental/environmental health engineering; film/cinema studies; finance; food science; forestry technology; forest sciences and biology; French; geography; geological and earth sciences/geosciences related; geology/earth science; German; graphic design; health/health care administration; history; horticultural science; hospitality administration related; human development and family studies; human nutrition; industrial engineering; information science/studies; international business/trade/commerce; international relations and affairs; Italian; Japanese; Jewish/Judaic studies; journalism; kinesiology and exercise science; labor and industrial relations; landscape architecture; landscaping and groundskeeping; Latin American studies; liberal arts and sciences/liberal studies; logistics and materials management; management information systems; management sciences and quantitative methods related; marketing/marketing management; materials science; mathematics; mechanical engineering; mechanical engineering/mechanical technology; medical microbiology and bacteriology; medieval and Renaissance studies; metallurgical technology; mining and mineral engineering; natural resources and conservation related; natural resources/conservation; nuclear engineering; nursing (registered nurse training); occupational therapist assistant; organizational behavior; parks, recreation and leisure facilities management; petroleum engineering; philosophy; physical therapist assistant; physics; political science and government; pre-medical studies; psychology; rehabilitation and therapeutic professions related; religious studies; Russian; secondary education; sociology; soil science and agronomy; Spanish; special education; statistics; telecommunications technology; theatre design and technology; turf and turfgrass management; visual and performing arts; wildlife and wildlands science and management; women's studies.

Academic Programs *Special study options:* academic remediation for entering students, accelerated degree program, adult/continuing education programs, advanced placement credit, distance learning, double majors, honors programs, independent study, internships, services for LD students, student-designed majors, summer session for credit.

Library 43,710 titles, 224 serial subscriptions, 1,091 audiovisual materials.

Computers on Campus 126 computers available on campus for general student use. A campuswide network can be accessed from off campus. Internet access, online (class) registration, at least one staffed computer lab available. Computer purchase or lease plan available.

Student Life *Housing:* college housing not available. *Activities and Organizations:* student-run newspaper, choral group.

Athletics Member NJCAA. *Intercollegiate sports:* basketball M, cross-country running M/W, golf M/W, volleyball W. *Intramural sports:* basketball M/W, football M, soccer M/W, table tennis M/W, volleyball M/W.

Standardized Tests *Required:* SAT I or ACT (for admission).

Costs (2003–04) *Tuition:* state resident $8620 full-time, $348 per credit part-time; nonresident $13,250 full-time, $552 per credit part-time. *Required fees:* $388 full-time.

Financial Aid Of all full-time matriculated undergraduates who enrolled, 79 Federal Work-Study jobs (averaging $1252).

Applying *Options:* electronic application, early admission, deferred entrance. *Application fee:* $50. *Required:* high school transcript. *Application deadline:* rolling (freshmen), rolling (transfers). *Notification:* continuous (freshmen), continuous (transfers).

Admissions Contact The Pennsylvania State University DuBois Campus of the Commonwealth College, 101 Hiller Building, College Place, DuBois, PA 15801-3199. *Phone:* 814-865-5471. *Toll-free phone:* 800-346-7627. *Fax:* 814-375-4784. *E-mail:* ds-admissions@psu.edu.

THE PENNSYLVANIA STATE UNIVERSITY FAYETTE CAMPUS OF THE COMMONWEALTH COLLEGE
Uniontown, Pennsylvania

- **State-related** primarily 2-year, founded 1934, part of Pennsylvania State University
- **Calendar** semesters
- **Degrees** associate and bachelor's (also offers up to 2 years of most bachelor's degree programs offered at University Park campus)
- **Small-town** 92-acre campus
- **Coed,** 1,156 undergraduate students, 75% full-time, 62% women, 38% men

Undergraduates 869 full-time, 287 part-time. 1% are from out of state, 5% African American, 0.8% Asian American or Pacific Islander, 0.5% Hispanic American, 4% transferred in. *Retention:* 67% of 2001 full-time freshmen returned.

Freshmen *Admission:* 398 applied, 347 admitted, 212 enrolled. *Average high school GPA:* 2.87. *Test scores:* SAT verbal scores over 500: 33%; SAT math scores over 500: 39%; SAT verbal scores over 600: 2%; SAT math scores over 600: 5%; SAT verbal scores over 700: 2%; SAT math scores over 700: 1%.

Faculty *Total:* 88, 60% full-time, 39% with terminal degrees. *Student/faculty ratio:* 15:1.

Majors Accounting; acting; actuarial science; adult and continuing education administration; advertising; aerospace, aeronautical and astronautical engineering; African-American/Black studies; agribusiness; agricultural and extension education; agricultural/biological engineering and bioengineering; agricultural business and management related; agricultural mechanization; agriculture; American studies; animal sciences; animal sciences related; anthropology; applied economics; archeology; architectural engineering; architectural engineering technology; art; art history, criticism and conservation; art teacher education; Asian studies (East); astronomy; atmospheric sciences and meteorology; biochemistry; biological and biomedical sciences related; biological and physical sciences; biology/biological sciences; biology/biotechnology laboratory technician; biomedical/medical engineering; biomedical technology; business administration and management; business/commerce; business/managerial economics; chemical engineering; chemistry; civil engineering; classics and languages, literatures and linguistics; communication and journalism related; communication disorders; communication/speech communication and rhetoric; comparative literature; computer and information sciences; computer engineering; criminal justice/law enforcement administration; criminal justice/safety; economics; electrical, electronic and communications engineering technology; electrical, electronics and communications engineering; elementary education; engineering science; English; environmental/environmental health engineering; film/cinema studies; finance; food science; forestry technology; forest sciences and biology; French; geography; geological and earth sciences/geosciences related; geology/earth science; German; graphic design; health/health care administration; history; horticultural science; hospitality administration related; human development and family studies; human nutrition; industrial engineering; information science/studies; international business/trade/commerce; international relations and affairs; Italian; Japanese; Jewish/Judaic studies; journalism; kinesiology and exercise science; labor and industrial relations; landscape architecture; landscaping and groundskeeping; Latin American studies; liberal arts and sciences/liberal studies; logistics and materials management; management information systems; management sciences and quantitative methods related; manufacturing engineering; marketing/marketing management; materials science; mathematics; mechanical engineering; medical microbiology and bacteriology; medieval and Renaissance studies; metallurgical technology; mining and mineral engineering; natural resources and conservation related; natural resources/conservation; nuclear engineering; nursing (registered nurse training); organizational behavior; parks, recreation and leisure facilities management; petroleum engineering; philosophy; physics; political science and government; pre-medical studies; psychology; rehabilitation and therapeutic professions related; religious studies; Russian; secondary education; sociology; soil science and agronomy; Spanish; special education; statistics; telecommunications technology; theatre design and technology; turf and turfgrass management; visual and performing arts; women's studies.

Academic Programs *Special study options:* academic remediation for entering students, accelerated degree program, adult/continuing education programs, advanced placement credit, distance learning, double majors, honors programs, independent study, internships, services for LD students, student-designed majors, summer session for credit.

Library 54,610 titles, 187 serial subscriptions, 6,721 audiovisual materials.

Computers on Campus 103 computers available on campus for general student use. A campuswide network can be accessed from off campus. Internet

The Pennsylvania State University Fayette Campus of the Commonwealth College (continued)

access, online (class) registration, at least one staffed computer lab available. Computer purchase or lease plan available.

Student Life *Housing:* college housing not available. *Activities and Organizations:* drama/theater group, student-run newspaper. *Campus security:* student patrols, 8-hour patrols by trained security personnel.

Athletics Member NJCAA. *Intercollegiate sports:* baseball M, basketball M, softball W, volleyball W. *Intramural sports:* badminton M/W, basketball M/W, cheerleading M(c)/W(c), equestrian sports M(c)/W(c), football M/W, golf M(c)/W(c), softball M/W, tennis M/W, volleyball M/W, weight lifting M/W.

Standardized Tests *Required:* SAT I or ACT (for admission).

Costs (2003–04) *Tuition:* state resident $8620 full-time, $348 per credit part-time; nonresident $13,250 full-time, $552 per credit part-time. *Required fees:* $388 full-time.

Financial Aid Of all full-time matriculated undergraduates who enrolled, 63 Federal Work-Study jobs (averaging $1017).

Applying *Options:* electronic application, early admission, deferred entrance. *Application fee:* $50. *Required:* high school transcript. *Application deadline:* rolling (freshmen), rolling (transfers). *Notification:* continuous (freshmen), continuous (transfers).

Admissions Contact The Pennsylvania State University Fayette Campus of the Commonwealth College, PO Box 519, Route 119 North, 108 Williams Building, Uniontown, PA 15401-0519. *Phone:* 814-865-5471. *Toll-free phone:* 877-568-4130. *Fax:* 724-430-4175. *E-mail:* feadm@psu.edu.

THE PENNSYLVANIA STATE UNIVERSITY HAZLETON CAMPUS OF THE COMMONWEALTH COLLEGE
Hazleton, Pennsylvania

- **State-related** primarily 2-year, founded 1934, part of Pennsylvania State University
- **Calendar** semesters
- **Degrees** associate and bachelor's (also offers up to 2 years of most bachelor's degree programs offered at University Park campus)
- **Small-town** 98-acre campus
- **Coed,** 1,214 undergraduate students, 94% full-time, 40% women, 60% men

Undergraduates 1,141 full-time, 73 part-time. 21% are from out of state, 6% African American, 4% Asian American or Pacific Islander, 4% Hispanic American, 0.2% Native American, 0.3% international, 2% transferred in, 37% live on campus. *Retention:* 80% of 2001 full-time freshmen returned.

Freshmen *Admission:* 1,243 applied, 1,125 admitted, 506 enrolled. *Average high school GPA:* 2.87. *Test scores:* SAT verbal scores over 500: 47%; SAT math scores over 500: 49%; SAT verbal scores over 600: 9%; SAT math scores over 600: 15%; SAT math scores over 700: 1%.

Faculty *Total:* 96, 60% full-time, 42% with terminal degrees. *Student/faculty ratio:* 17:1.

Majors Accounting; acting; actuarial science; adult and continuing education administration; advertising; aerospace, aeronautical and astronautical engineering; African-American/Black studies; agribusiness; agricultural and extension education; agricultural/biological engineering and bioengineering; agricultural business and management related; agricultural mechanization; agriculture; American studies; animal sciences; animal sciences related; anthropology; applied economics; archeology; architectural engineering; art; art history, criticism and conservation; art teacher education; Asian studies (East); astronomy; atmospheric sciences and meteorology; biochemistry; biological and biomedical sciences related; biological and physical sciences; biology/biological sciences; biology/biotechnology laboratory technician; biomedical/medical engineering; biomedical technology; business administration and management; business/commerce; business/managerial economics; chemical engineering; chemistry; civil engineering; classics and languages, literatures and linguistics; clinical/medical laboratory technology; communication and journalism related; communication disorders; communication/speech communication and rhetoric; comparative literature; computer and information sciences; computer engineering; criminal justice/law enforcement administration; economics; electrical, electronic and communications engineering technology; electrical, electronics and communications engineering; elementary education; engineering science; English; environmental/environmental health engineering; film/cinema studies; finance; food science; forestry technology; forest sciences and biology; French; geography; geological and earth sciences/geosciences related; geology/earth science; German; graphic design; health/health care administration; history; horticultural science; hospitality administration related; human development and family studies; human nutrition; industrial engineering; information science/studies; international business/trade/commerce; international relations and affairs; Italian; Japanese; Jewish/Judaic studies; journalism; kinesiology and exercise science; labor and industrial relations; landscape architecture; landscaping and groundskeeping; Latin American studies; liberal arts and sciences/liberal studies;

logistics and materials management; management information systems; management sciences and quantitative methods related; manufacturing engineering; marketing/marketing management; materials science; mathematics; mechanical engineering; mechanical engineering/mechanical technology; medical microbiology and bacteriology; medieval and Renaissance studies; metallurgical technology; mining and mineral engineering; natural resources and conservation related; natural resources/conservation; nuclear engineering; nursing (registered nurse training); organizational behavior; parks, recreation and leisure facilities management; petroleum engineering; philosophy; physical therapist assistant; physics; political science and government; pre-medical studies; psychology; rehabilitation and therapeutic professions related; religious studies; Russian; secondary education; sociology; soil science and agronomy; Spanish; special education; statistics; telecommunications technology; theatre design and technology; turf and turfgrass management; visual and performing arts; women's studies.

Academic Programs *Special study options:* academic remediation for entering students, accelerated degree program, adult/continuing education programs, advanced placement credit, distance learning, double majors, honors programs, independent study, internships, services for LD students, summer session for credit. *ROTC:* Army (b).

Library 83,266 titles, 996 serial subscriptions, 6,771 audiovisual materials.

Computers on Campus 131 computers available on campus for general student use. A campuswide network can be accessed from student residence rooms and from off campus. Internet access, online (class) registration, at least one staffed computer lab available. Computer purchase or lease plan available.

Student Life *Housing Options:* coed. Campus housing is university owned. Freshman campus housing is guaranteed. *Activities and Organizations:* drama/theater group, student-run newspaper, radio station, choral group. *Campus security:* 24-hour patrols, late-night transport/escort service, controlled dormitory access.

Athletics Member NJCAA. *Intercollegiate sports:* baseball M, basketball M/W, cheerleading M/W, soccer M, softball W, tennis M/W, volleyball M(c)/W. *Intramural sports:* basketball M/W, skiing (downhill) M(c)/W(c), soccer M/W, volleyball M/W.

Standardized Tests *Required:* SAT I or ACT (for admission).

Costs (2003–04) *Tuition:* state resident $8620 full-time, $348 per credit part-time; nonresident $13,250 full-time, $552 per credit part-time. *Required fees:* $398 full-time. *Room and board:* $5940; room only: $3080.

Financial Aid Of all full-time matriculated undergraduates who enrolled, 111 Federal Work-Study jobs (averaging $1151).

Applying *Options:* electronic application, early admission, deferred entrance. *Application fee:* $50. *Required:* high school transcript. *Application deadline:* rolling (freshmen), rolling (transfers). *Notification:* continuous (freshmen), continuous (transfers).

Admissions Contact The Pennsylvania State University Hazleton Campus of the Commonwealth College, 110 Administration Building, 76 University Drive, Hazleton, PA 18202. *Phone:* 814-865-5471. *Toll-free phone:* 800-279-8495. *Fax:* 570-450-3182. *E-mail:* admissions-hn@psu.edu.

THE PENNSYLVANIA STATE UNIVERSITY MCKEESPORT CAMPUS OF THE COMMONWEALTH COLLEGE
McKeesport, Pennsylvania

- **State-related** primarily 2-year, founded 1947, part of Pennsylvania State University
- **Calendar** semesters
- **Degrees** associate and bachelor's (also offers up to 2 years of most bachelor's degree programs offered at University Park campus)
- **Small-town** 40-acre campus with easy access to Pittsburgh
- **Coed,** 826 undergraduate students, 91% full-time, 38% women, 62% men

Undergraduates 749 full-time, 77 part-time. 8% are from out of state, 14% African American, 3% Asian American or Pacific Islander, 0.9% Hispanic American, 0.3% international, 3% transferred in, 16% live on campus. *Retention:* 79% of 2001 full-time freshmen returned.

Freshmen *Admission:* 578 applied, 510 admitted, 245 enrolled. *Average high school GPA:* 2.92. *Test scores:* SAT verbal scores over 500: 45%; SAT math scores over 500: 47%; SAT verbal scores over 600: 9%; SAT math scores over 600: 15%; SAT verbal scores over 700: 1%; SAT math scores over 700: 3%.

Faculty *Total:* 75, 52% full-time, 40% with terminal degrees. *Student/faculty ratio:* 15:1.

Majors Accounting; acting; actuarial science; adult and continuing education administration; advertising; aerospace, aeronautical and astronautical engineering; African-American/Black studies; agribusiness; agricultural and extension education; agricultural/biological engineering and bioengineering; agricultural business and management related; agricultural mechanization; agriculture; American studies; animal sciences; animal sciences related; anthropology; applied economics; archeology; architectural engineering; art; art history, criticism and conservation; art teacher education; Asian studies (East); astronomy; atmospheric sciences and meteorology; biochemistry; biological and biomedical sciences related; biological and physical sciences; biology/biological sciences; biology/biotechnology laboratory technician; biomedical/medical engineering; business administration and management; business/commerce; business/managerial economics; chemical engineering; chemistry; civil engineering; classics and languages, literatures and linguistics; communication and journalism related; communication disorders; communication/speech communication and rhetoric; comparative literature; computer and information sciences; computer engineering; criminal justice/law enforcement administration; economics; electrical, electronics and communications engineering; elementary education; engineering science; English; environmental/environmental health engineering; film/cinema studies; finance; food science; forestry technology; forest sciences and biology; French; geography; geological and earth sciences/geosciences related; geology/earth science; German; graphic design; health/health care administration; history; horticultural science; hospitality administration related; human development and family studies; human nutrition; industrial engineering; information science/studies; international business/trade/commerce; international relations and affairs; Italian; Japanese; Jewish/Judaic studies; journalism; kinesiology and exercise science; labor and industrial relations; landscape architecture; landscaping and groundskeeping; Latin American studies; liberal arts and sciences/liberal studies; logistics and materials management; management information systems; management sciences and quantitative methods related; marketing/marketing management; materials science; mathematics; mechanical engineering; medical microbiology and bacteriology; medieval and Renaissance studies; mining and mineral engineering; natural resources and conservation related; natural resources/conservation; nuclear engineering; nursing (registered nurse training); organizational behavior; parks, recreation and leisure facilities management; petroleum engineering; philosophy; physics; political science and government; pre-medical studies; psychology; rehabilitation and therapeutic professions related; religious studies; Russian; secondary education; sociology; soil science and agronomy; Spanish; special education; statistics; theatre design and technology; turf and turfgrass management; visual and performing arts; women's studies.

Academic Programs *Special study options:* academic remediation for entering students, accelerated degree program, adult/continuing education programs, advanced placement credit, distance learning, double majors, honors programs, independent study, services for LD students, summer session for credit. *ROTC:* Army (c), Air Force (c).

Library 40,851 titles, 300 serial subscriptions, 2,783 audiovisual materials.

Computers on Campus 167 computers available on campus for general student use. A campuswide network can be accessed from student residence rooms and from off campus. Internet access, online (class) registration, at least one staffed computer lab available. Computer purchase or lease plan available.

Student Life *Housing Options:* coed. Campus housing is university owned. Freshman campus housing is guaranteed. *Activities and Organizations:* drama/theater group, student-run newspaper, radio station. *Campus security:* 24-hour patrols, controlled dormitory access.

Athletics Member NJCAA. *Intercollegiate sports:* baseball M, basketball M, softball W, volleyball W. *Intramural sports:* basketball M/W, cheerleading M(c)/W(c), football M/W, ice hockey M(c), racquetball M/W, skiing (cross-country) M(c)/W(c), skiing (downhill) M(c)/W(c), soccer M(c)/W(c), softball M/W, tennis M/W, volleyball M/W.

Standardized Tests *Required:* SAT I or ACT (for admission).

Costs (2003–04) *Tuition:* state resident $8620 full-time, $348 per credit part-time; nonresident $13,250 full-time, $552 per credit part-time. *Required fees:* $388 full-time. *Room and board:* $5940; room only: $3080.

Financial Aid Of all full-time matriculated undergraduates who enrolled, 63 Federal Work-Study jobs (averaging $1017).

Applying *Options:* electronic application, early admission, deferred entrance. *Application fee:* $50. *Required:* high school transcript. *Application deadline:* rolling (freshmen), rolling (transfers). *Notification:* continuous (freshmen), continuous (transfers).

Admissions Contact The Pennsylvania State University McKeesport Campus of the Commonwealth College, 101 Frable Building, 4000 University Drive, McKeesport, PA 15132-7698. *Phone:* 814-865-5471. *Fax:* 412-9056. *E-mail:* psumk@psu.edu.

THE PENNSYLVANIA STATE UNIVERSITY MONT ALTO CAMPUS OF THE COMMONWEALTH COLLEGE
Mont Alto, Pennsylvania

- **State-related** primarily 2-year, founded 1929, part of Pennsylvania State University
- **Calendar** semesters
- **Degrees** associate and bachelor's (also offers up to 2 years of most bachelor's degree programs offered at University Park campus)
- **Small-town** 64-acre campus

- **Coed,** 1,098 undergraduate students, 69% full-time, 56% women, 44% men

Undergraduates 757 full-time, 341 part-time. 14% are from out of state, 8% African American, 3% Asian American or Pacific Islander, 2% Hispanic American, 0.2% Native American, 0.3% international, 5% transferred in, 34% live on campus. *Retention:* 78% of 2001 full-time freshmen returned.

Freshmen *Admission:* 700 applied, 606 admitted, 339 enrolled. *Average high school GPA:* 2.84. *Test scores:* SAT verbal scores over 500: 46%; SAT math scores over 500: 48%; SAT verbal scores over 600: 11%; SAT math scores over 600: 15%; SAT verbal scores over 700: 1%; SAT math scores over 700: 1%.

Faculty *Total:* 96, 57% full-time, 31% with terminal degrees. *Student/faculty ratio:* 13:1.

Majors Accounting; acting; actuarial science; adult and continuing education administration; advertising; aerospace, aeronautical and astronautical engineering; African-American/Black studies; agribusiness; agricultural and extension education; agricultural/biological engineering and bioengineering; agricultural business and management related; agricultural mechanization; agriculture; American studies; animal sciences; animal sciences related; anthropology; applied economics; archeology; architectural engineering; art; art history, criticism and conservation; art teacher education; Asian studies (East); astronomy; atmospheric sciences and meteorology; biochemistry; biological and biomedical sciences related; biological and physical sciences; biology/biological sciences; biology/biotechnology laboratory technician; biomedical/medical engineering; business administration and management; business/commerce; business/managerial economics; chemical engineering; chemistry; civil engineering; classics and languages, literatures and linguistics; communication and journalism related; communication disorders; communication/speech communication and rhetoric; comparative literature; computer and information sciences; computer engineering; criminal justice/law enforcement administration; economics; electrical, electronics and communications engineering; elementary education; engineering science; English; environmental/environmental health engineering; film/cinema studies; finance; food science; forestry technology; forest sciences and biology; French; geography; geological and earth sciences/geosciences related; geology/earth science; German; graphic design; health/health care administration; history; horticultural science; hospitality administration related; human development and family studies; human nutrition; industrial engineering; information science/studies; international business/trade/commerce; international relations and affairs; Italian; Japanese; Jewish/Judaic studies; journalism; kinesiology and exercise science; labor and industrial relations; landscape architecture; landscaping and groundskeeping; Latin American studies; liberal arts and sciences/liberal studies; logistics and materials management; management information systems; management sciences and quantitative methods related; marketing/marketing management; materials science; mathematics; mechanical engineering; medical microbiology and bacteriology; medieval and Renaissance studies; mining and mineral engineering; natural resources and conservation related; natural resources/conservation; nuclear engineering; nursing (registered nurse training); occupational therapist assistant; occupational therapy; organizational behavior; parks, recreation and leisure facilities management; petroleum engineering; philosophy; physical therapist assistant; physics; political science and government; pre-medical studies; psychology; rehabilitation and therapeutic professions related; religious studies; Russian; secondary education; sociology; soil science and agronomy; Spanish; special education; statistics; theatre design and technology; turf and turfgrass management; visual and performing arts; women's studies.

Academic Programs *Special study options:* academic remediation for entering students, accelerated degree program, adult/continuing education programs, advanced placement credit, distance learning, double majors, honors programs, independent study, internships, services for LD students, summer session for credit. *ROTC:* Army (c).

Library 38,962 titles, 273 serial subscriptions, 1,418 audiovisual materials.

Computers on Campus 182 computers available on campus for general student use. A campuswide network can be accessed from student residence rooms and from off campus. Internet access, online (class) registration, at least one staffed computer lab available. Computer purchase or lease plan available.

Student Life *Housing Options:* coed. Campus housing is university owned. Freshman campus housing is guaranteed. *Activities and Organizations:* student-run radio station. *Campus security:* 24-hour patrols, controlled dormitory access.

Athletics Member NJCAA. *Intercollegiate sports:* basketball M/W, cheerleading M/W, cross-country running M/W, golf M/W, soccer M/W, softball W, tennis M/W, volleyball W. *Intramural sports:* badminton M/W, basketball M/W, cheerleading M(c)/W(c), racquetball M/W, soccer M/W, softball W, volleyball M/W.

Standardized Tests *Required:* SAT I or ACT (for admission).

Costs (2003–04) *Tuition:* state resident $8620 full-time, $348 per credit part-time; nonresident $13,250 full-time, $552 per credit part-time. *Required fees:* $398 full-time. *Room and board:* $5940; room only: $3080.

Financial Aid Of all full-time matriculated undergraduates who enrolled, 89 Federal Work-Study jobs (averaging $844).

The Pennsylvania State University Mont Alto Campus of the Commonwealth College (continued)

Applying *Options:* electronic application, early admission, deferred entrance. *Application fee:* $50. *Required:* high school transcript. *Application deadline:* rolling (freshmen), rolling (transfers). *Notification:* continuous (freshmen), continuous (transfers).

Admissions Contact The Pennsylvania State University Mont Alto Campus of the Commonwealth College, 1 Campus Drive, Mont Alto, PA 17237-9703. *Phone:* 814-865-5471. *Toll-free phone:* 800-392-6173. *Fax:* 717-749-6132. *E-mail:* psuma@psu.edu.

THE PENNSYLVANIA STATE UNIVERSITY NEW KENSINGTON CAMPUS OF THE COMMONWEALTH COLLEGE
New Kensington, Pennsylvania

- **State-related** primarily 2-year, founded 1958, part of Pennsylvania State University
- **Calendar** semesters
- **Degrees** associate and bachelor's (also offers up to 2 years of most bachelor's degree programs offered at University Park campus)
- **Small-town** 71-acre campus with easy access to Pittsburgh
- **Coed,** 1,082 undergraduate students, 73% full-time, 43% women, 57% men

Undergraduates 788 full-time, 294 part-time. 1% are from out of state, 2% African American, 0.6% Asian American or Pacific Islander, 0.7% Hispanic American, 4% transferred in. *Retention:* 77% of 2001 full-time freshmen returned.

Freshmen *Admission:* 463 applied, 409 admitted, 224 enrolled. *Average high school GPA:* 2.98. *Test scores:* SAT verbal scores over 500: 51%; SAT math scores over 500: 54%; SAT verbal scores over 600: 9%; SAT math scores over 600: 14%; SAT verbal scores over 700: 1%.

Faculty *Total:* 103, 42% full-time, 38% with terminal degrees. *Student/faculty ratio:* 14:1.

Majors Accounting; acting; actuarial science; adult and continuing education administration; advertising; aerospace, aeronautical and astronautical engineering; African-American/Black studies; agribusiness; agricultural and extension education; agricultural/biological engineering and bioengineering; agricultural business and management related; agricultural mechanization; agriculture; American studies; animal sciences; animal sciences related; anthropology; applied economics; archeology; architectural engineering; art; art history, criticism and conservation; art teacher education; Asian studies (East); astronomy; atmospheric sciences and meteorology; biochemistry; biological and biomedical sciences related; biological and physical sciences; biology/biological sciences; biology/biotechnology laboratory technician; biomedical/medical engineering; biomedical technology; business administration and management; business/commerce; business/managerial economics; chemical engineering; chemistry; civil engineering; classics and languages, literatures and linguistics; communication and journalism related; communication disorders; communication/speech communication and rhetoric; comparative literature; computer and information sciences; computer engineering; computer engineering technology; criminal justice/law enforcement administration; economics; electrical, electronic and communications engineering technology; electrical, electronics and communications engineering; elementary education; engineering science; English; environmental/environmental health engineering; film/cinema studies; finance; food science; forestry technology; forest sciences and biology; French; geography; geological and earth sciences/geosciences related; geology/earth science; German; graphic design; health/health care administration; history; horticultural science; hospitality administration related; human development and family studies; human nutrition; industrial engineering; information science/studies; international business/trade/commerce; international relations and affairs; Italian; Japanese; Jewish/Judaic studies; journalism; kinesiology and exercise science; labor and industrial relations; landscape architecture; landscaping and groundskeeping; Latin American studies; liberal arts and sciences/liberal studies; logistics and materials management; management information systems; management sciences and quantitative methods related; marketing/marketing management; materials science; mathematics; mechanical engineering; mechanical engineering/mechanical technology; medical microbiology and bacteriology; medical radiologic technology; medieval and Renaissance studies; metallurgical technology; mining and mineral engineering; natural resources and conservation related; natural resources/conservation; nuclear engineering; nursing (registered nurse training); organizational behavior; parks, recreation and leisure facilities management; petroleum engineering; philosophy; physics; political science and government; pre-medical studies; psychology; rehabilitation and therapeutic professions related; religious studies; Russian; secondary education; sociology; soil science and agronomy; Spanish; special education; statistics; telecommunications technology; theatre design and technology; turf and turfgrass management; visual and performing arts; women's studies.

Academic Programs *Special study options:* academic remediation for entering students, accelerated degree program, adult/continuing education programs,

advanced placement credit, distance learning, double majors, honors programs, independent study, internships, services for LD students, summer session for credit.

Library 28,897 titles, 404 serial subscriptions, 4,294 audiovisual materials.

Computers on Campus 264 computers available on campus for general student use. A campuswide network can be accessed from off campus. Internet access, online (class) registration, at least one staffed computer lab available. Computer purchase or lease plan available.

Student Life *Housing:* college housing not available. *Activities and Organizations:* drama/theater group, student-run newspaper, choral group. *Campus security:* part-time trained security personnel.

Athletics Member NJCAA. *Intercollegiate sports:* baseball M, basketball M/W, cheerleading M/W, golf M/W, softball W, volleyball W. *Intramural sports:* badminton M/W, basketball M/W, bowling M/W, cheerleading M(c)/W(c), football M/W, ice hockey M(c)/W(c), racquetball M/W, skiing (downhill) M(c)/W(c), soccer M/W, softball W, volleyball M/W.

Standardized Tests *Required:* SAT I or ACT (for admission).

Costs (2003–04) *Tuition:* state resident $8620 full-time, $348 per credit part-time; nonresident $13,250 full-time, $552 per credit part-time. *Required fees:* $408 full-time.

Financial Aid Of all full-time matriculated undergraduates who enrolled, 44 Federal Work-Study jobs (averaging $1297).

Applying *Options:* electronic application, early admission, deferred entrance. *Application fee:* $50. *Required:* high school transcript. *Application deadline:* rolling (freshmen), rolling (transfers). *Notification:* continuous (freshmen), continuous (transfers).

Admissions Contact The Pennsylvania State University New Kensington Campus of the Commonwealth College, 3550 7th Street Road, Route 780, New Kensington, PA 15068. *Phone:* 814-865-5471. *Toll-free phone:* 888-968-7297. *Fax:* 724-334-6111. *E-mail:* nkadmissions@psu.edu.

THE PENNSYLVANIA STATE UNIVERSITY SHENANGO CAMPUS OF THE COMMONWEALTH COLLEGE
Sharon, Pennsylvania

- **State-related** primarily 2-year, founded 1965, part of Pennsylvania State University
- **Calendar** semesters
- **Degrees** associate and bachelor's (also offers up to 2 years of most bachelor's degree programs offered at University Park campus)
- **Small-town** 14-acre campus
- **Coed,** 904 undergraduate students, 58% full-time, 62% women, 38% men

Undergraduates 520 full-time, 384 part-time. 11% are from out of state, 4% African American, 0.7% Asian American or Pacific Islander, 1% Hispanic American, 0.1% Native American, 4% transferred in. *Retention:* 74% of 2001 full-time freshmen returned.

Freshmen *Admission:* 256 applied, 220 admitted, 141 enrolled. *Average high school GPA:* 2.87. *Test scores:* SAT verbal scores over 500: 36%; SAT math scores over 500: 44%; SAT verbal scores over 600: 5%; SAT math scores over 600: 5%.

Faculty *Total:* 82, 35% full-time, 30% with terminal degrees. *Student/faculty ratio:* 14:1.

Majors Accounting; acting; actuarial science; adult and continuing education administration; advertising; aerospace, aeronautical and astronautical engineering; African-American/Black studies; agribusiness; agricultural and extension education; agricultural/biological engineering and bioengineering; agricultural business and management related; agricultural mechanization; agriculture; American studies; animal sciences; animal sciences related; anthropology; applied economics; archeology; architectural engineering; art; art history, criticism and conservation; art teacher education; Asian studies (East); astronomy; atmospheric sciences and meteorology; biochemistry; biological and biomedical sciences related; biological and physical sciences; biology/biological sciences; biology/biotechnology laboratory technician; biomedical/medical engineering; biomedical technology; business administration and management; business/commerce; business/managerial economics; chemical engineering; chemistry; civil engineering; classics and languages, literatures and linguistics; communication and journalism related; communication disorders; communication/speech communication and rhetoric; comparative literature; computer and information sciences; computer engineering; criminal justice/law enforcement administration; economics; electrical, electronics and communications engineering; elementary education; engineering science; English; environmental/environmental health engineering; film/cinema studies; finance; food science; forestry technology; forest sciences and biology; French; geography; geological and earth sciences/geosciences related; geology/earth science; German; graphic design; health/health care administration; history; horticultural science; hospitality administration related; human development and family studies; human nutrition; industrial engineering; information science/studies; international business/trade/commerce;

international relations and affairs; Italian; Japanese; Jewish/Judaic studies; journalism; kinesiology and exercise science; labor and industrial relations; landscape architecture; landscaping and groundskeeping; Latin American studies; liberal arts and sciences/liberal studies; logistics and materials management; management information systems; management sciences and quantitative methods related; marketing/marketing management; materials science; mathematics; mechanical engineering; mechanical engineering/mechanical technology; medical microbiology and bacteriology; medieval and Renaissance studies; metallurgical technology; mining and mineral engineering; natural resources and conservation related; natural resources/conservation; nuclear engineering; nursing (registered nurse training); organizational behavior; parks, recreation and leisure facilities management; petroleum engineering; philosophy; physical therapist assistant; physics; political science and government; pre-medical studies; psychology; rehabilitation and therapeutic professions related; religious studies; Russian; secondary education; sociology; soil science and agronomy; Spanish; special education; statistics; telecommunications technology; theatre design and technology; turf and turfgrass management; visual and performing arts; women's studies.

Academic Programs *Special study options:* academic remediation for entering students, accelerated degree program, adult/continuing education programs, advanced placement credit, distance learning, double majors, honors programs, independent study, internships, services for LD students, study abroad, summer session for credit.

Library 25,273 titles, 346 serial subscriptions, 2,064 audiovisual materials.

Computers on Campus 102 computers available on campus for general student use. A campuswide network can be accessed from off campus. Internet access, online (class) registration, at least one staffed computer lab available. Computer purchase or lease plan available.

Student Life *Housing:* college housing not available. *Campus security:* part-time trained security personnel.

Athletics *Intramural sports:* basketball M(c)/W, bowling M/W, football M(c), golf M/W, softball M/W, tennis M/W, volleyball M/W.

Standardized Tests *Required:* SAT I or ACT (for admission).

Costs (2003–04) *Tuition:* state resident $8620 full-time, $348 per credit part-time; nonresident $13,250 full-time, $552 per credit part-time. *Required fees:* $398 full-time.

Financial Aid Of all full-time matriculated undergraduates who enrolled, 24 Federal Work-Study jobs (averaging $1166).

Applying *Options:* electronic application, early admission, deferred entrance. *Application fee:* $50. *Required:* high school transcript. *Application deadline:* rolling (freshmen), rolling (transfers). *Notification:* continuous (freshmen), continuous (transfers).

Admissions Contact The Pennsylvania State University Shenango Campus of the Commonwealth College, 147 Shenango Avenue, Sharon, PA 16146-1597. *Phone:* 814-865-5471. *Fax:* 724-983-2820. *E-mail:* psushenango@psu.edu.

THE PENNSYLVANIA STATE UNIVERSITY WILKES-BARRE CAMPUS OF THE COMMONWEALTH COLLEGE
Lehman, Pennsylvania

- **State-related** primarily 2-year, founded 1916, part of Pennsylvania State University
- **Calendar** semesters
- **Degrees** associate and bachelor's (also offers up to 2 years of most bachelor's degree programs offered at University Park campus)
- **Rural** 156-acre campus
- **Coed,** 782 undergraduate students, 75% full-time, 31% women, 69% men

Undergraduates 586 full-time, 196 part-time. 3% are from out of state, 0.5% African American, 2% Asian American or Pacific Islander, 0.5% Hispanic American, 0.2% Native American, 3% transferred in. *Retention:* 79% of 2001 full-time freshmen returned.

Freshmen *Admission:* 524 applied, 434 admitted, 190 enrolled. *Average high school GPA:* 2.98. *Test scores:* SAT verbal scores over 500: 53%; SAT math scores over 500: 54%; SAT verbal scores over 600: 11%; SAT math scores over 600: 17%; SAT verbal scores over 700: 1%; SAT math scores over 700: 2%.

Faculty *Total:* 78, 53% full-time, 33% with terminal degrees. *Student/faculty ratio:* 13:1.

Majors Accounting; acting; actuarial science; adult and continuing education administration; advertising; aerospace, aeronautical and astronautical engineering; African-American/Black studies; agribusiness; agricultural and extension education; agricultural/biological engineering and bioengineering; agricultural business and management related; agricultural mechanization; agriculture; American studies; animal sciences; animal sciences related; anthropology; applied economics; archeology; architectural engineering; art; art history, criticism and conservation; art teacher education; Asian studies (East); astronomy; atmospheric sciences and meteorology; biochemistry; biological and biomedical sciences related; biological and physical sciences; biology/biological sciences;

biology/biotechnology laboratory technician; biomedical/medical engineering; business administration and management; business/commerce; business/managerial economics; chemical engineering; chemistry; civil engineering; classics and languages, literatures and linguistics; communication and journalism related; communication disorders; communication/speech communication and rhetoric; comparative literature; computer and information sciences; computer engineering; criminal justice/law enforcement administration; economics; electrical, electronic and communications engineering technology; electrical, electronics and communications engineering; elementary education; engineering science; English; environmental/environmental health engineering; film/cinema studies; finance; food science; forestry technology; forest sciences and biology; French; geography; geological and earth sciences/geosciences related; geology/earth science; German; graphic design; health/health care administration; history; horticultural science; hospitality administration related; human development and family studies; human nutrition; industrial engineering; information science/studies; international business/trade/commerce; international relations and affairs; Italian; Japanese; Jewish/Judaic studies; journalism; kinesiology and exercise science; labor and industrial relations; landscape architecture; landscaping and groundskeeping; Latin American studies; liberal arts and sciences/liberal studies; logistics and materials management; management information systems; management sciences and quantitative methods related; manufacturing engineering; marketing/marketing management; materials science; mathematics; mechanical engineering; medical microbiology and bacteriology; medieval and Renaissance studies; metallurgical technology; mining and mineral engineering; natural resources and conservation related; natural resources/conservation; nuclear engineering; nursing (registered nurse training); organizational behavior; parks, recreation and leisure facilities management; petroleum engineering; philosophy; physics; political science and government; pre-medical studies; psychology; rehabilitation and therapeutic professions related; religious studies; Russian; secondary education; sociology; soil science and agronomy; Spanish; special education; statistics; survey technology; telecommunications technology; theatre design and technology; turf and turfgrass management; visual and performing arts; women's studies.

Academic Programs *Special study options:* academic remediation for entering students, accelerated degree program, adult/continuing education programs, advanced placement credit, distance learning, double majors, honors programs, independent study, internships, services for LD students, summer session for credit. *ROTC:* Air Force (c).

Library 35,697 titles, 199 serial subscriptions, 394 audiovisual materials.

Computers on Campus 137 computers available on campus for general student use. A campuswide network can be accessed from off campus. Internet access, online (class) registration, at least one staffed computer lab available. Computer purchase or lease plan available.

Student Life *Housing:* college housing not available. *Activities and Organizations:* student-run newspaper, radio station. *Campus security:* part-time trained security personnel.

Athletics Member NJCAA. *Intercollegiate sports:* baseball M, basketball M, cross-country running M/W, golf M/W, soccer M/W, volleyball W. *Intramural sports:* basketball M/W, bowling M(c)/W(c), cheerleading M(c)/W(c), football M, racquetball M/W, softball W, volleyball M(c)/W.

Standardized Tests *Required:* SAT I or ACT (for admission).

Costs (2003–04) *Tuition:* state resident $8620 full-time, $348 per credit part-time; nonresident $13,250 full-time, $552 per credit part-time. *Required fees:* $408 full-time.

Financial Aid Of all full-time matriculated undergraduates who enrolled, 22 Federal Work-Study jobs (averaging $971).

Applying *Options:* electronic application, early admission, deferred entrance. *Application fee:* $50. *Required:* high school transcript. *Application deadline:* rolling (freshmen), rolling (transfers). *Notification:* continuous (freshmen), continuous (transfers).

Admissions Contact The Pennsylvania State University Wilkes-Barre Campus of the Commonwealth College, PO Box PSU, Lehman, PA 18627-0217. *Phone:* 814-865-5471. *Toll-free phone:* 800-966-6613. *Fax:* 570-675-9113. *E-mail:* wbadmissions@psu.edu.

THE PENNSYLVANIA STATE UNIVERSITY WORTHINGTON SCRANTON CAMPUS OF THE COMMONWEALTH COLLEGE
Dunmore, Pennsylvania

- **State-related** primarily 2-year, founded 1923, part of Pennsylvania State University
- **Calendar** semesters
- **Degrees** associate and bachelor's (also offers up to 2 years of most bachelor's degree programs offered at University Park campus)
- **Small-town** 43-acre campus
- **Coed,** 1,338 undergraduate students, 76% full-time, 50% women, 50% men

Pennsylvania

The Pennsylvania State University Worthington Scranton Campus of the Commonwealth College (continued)

Undergraduates 1,018 full-time, 320 part-time. 1% are from out of state, 1% African American, 1% Asian American or Pacific Islander, 1% Hispanic American, 0.1% Native American, 0.1% international, 5% transferred in. *Retention:* 77% of 2001 full-time freshmen returned.

Freshmen *Admission:* 681 applied, 543 admitted, 254 enrolled. *Average high school GPA:* 2.83. *Test scores:* SAT verbal scores over 500: 43%; SAT math scores over 500: 41%; SAT verbal scores over 600: 8%; SAT math scores over 600: 10%.

Faculty *Total:* 116, 59% full-time, 36% with terminal degrees. *Student/faculty ratio:* 14:1.

Majors Accounting; acting; actuarial science; adult and continuing education administration; advertising; aerospace, aeronautical and astronautical engineering; African-American/Black studies; agribusiness; agricultural and extension education; agricultural/biological engineering and bioengineering; agricultural business and management related; agricultural mechanization; agriculture; American studies; animal sciences; animal sciences related; anthropology; applied economics; archeology; architectural engineering; architectural engineering technology; art; art history, criticism and conservation; art teacher education; Asian studies (East); astronomy; atmospheric sciences and meteorology; biochemistry; biological and biomedical sciences related; biological and physical sciences; biology/biological sciences; biology/biotechnology laboratory technician; biomedical/medical engineering; business administration and management; business/commerce; business/managerial economics; chemical engineering; chemistry; civil engineering; classics and languages, literatures and linguistics; communication and journalism related; communication disorders; communication/speech communication and rhetoric; comparative literature; computer and information sciences; computer engineering; criminal justice/law enforcement administration; economics; electrical, electronics and communications engineering; elementary education; engineering science; English; environmental/environmental health engineering; film/cinema studies; finance; food science; forestry technology; forest sciences and biology; French; geography; geological and earth sciences/geosciences related; geology/earth science; German; graphic design; health/health care administration; history; horticultural science; hospitality administration related; human development and family studies; human nutrition; industrial engineering; information science/studies; international business/trade/commerce; international relations and affairs; Italian; Japanese; Jewish/Judaic studies; journalism; kinesiology and exercise science; labor and industrial relations; landscape architecture; landscaping and groundskeeping; Latin American studies; liberal arts and sciences/liberal studies; logistics and materials management; management information systems; management sciences and quantitative methods related; marketing/marketing management; materials science; mathematics; mechanical engineering; medical microbiology and bacteriology; medieval and Renaissance studies; mining and mineral engineering; natural resources and conservation related; natural resources/conservation; nuclear engineering; nursing (registered nurse training); occupational therapist assistant; organizational behavior; parks, recreation and leisure facilities management; petroleum engineering; philosophy; physics; political science and government; pre-medical studies; psychology; rehabilitation and therapeutic professions related; religious studies; Russian; secondary education; sociology; soil science and agronomy; Spanish; special education; statistics; theatre design and technology; turf and turfgrass management; visual and performing arts; women's studies.

Academic Programs *Special study options:* academic remediation for entering students, accelerated degree program, adult/continuing education programs, advanced placement credit, distance learning, double majors, honors programs, independent study, internships, services for LD students, summer session for credit. *ROTC:* Army (c), Air Force (c).

Library 53,572 titles, 102 serial subscriptions, 3,048 audiovisual materials.

Computers on Campus 104 computers available on campus for general student use. A campuswide network can be accessed from off campus. Internet access, online (class) registration, at least one staffed computer lab available. Computer purchase or lease plan available.

Student Life *Housing:* college housing not available. *Activities and Organizations:* drama/theater group, student-run newspaper. *Campus security:* part-time trained security personnel.

Athletics Member NJCAA. *Intercollegiate sports:* baseball M, basketball M/W, cheerleading M/W, cross-country running M/W, soccer M, softball W, volleyball W. *Intramural sports:* basketball M/W, bowling M(c)/W(c), skiing (downhill) M(c)/W(c), soccer M/W, softball M/W, volleyball M/W(c), weight lifting M(c)/W(c).

Standardized Tests *Required:* SAT I or ACT (for admission).

Costs (2003–04) *Tuition:* state resident $8620 full-time, $348 per credit part-time; nonresident $13,250 full-time, $552 per credit part-time. *Required fees:* $388 full-time.

Financial Aid Of all full-time matriculated undergraduates who enrolled, 24 Federal Work-Study jobs (averaging $957).

Applying *Options:* electronic application, early admission, deferred entrance. *Application fee:* $50. *Required:* high school transcript. *Application deadline:* rolling (freshmen), rolling (transfers). *Notification:* continuous (freshmen), continuous (transfers).

Admissions Contact The Pennsylvania State University Worthington Scranton Campus of the Commonwealth College, 120 Ridge View Drive, Dunmore, PA 18512-1699. *Phone:* 814-865-5471. *Fax:* 570-963-2524. *E-mail:* wsadmissions@psu.edu.

THE PENNSYLVANIA STATE UNIVERSITY YORK CAMPUS OF THE COMMONWEALTH COLLEGE
York, Pennsylvania

- **State-related** primarily 2-year, founded 1926, part of Pennsylvania State University
- **Calendar** semesters
- **Degrees** associate and bachelor's (also offers up to 2 years of most bachelor's degree programs offered at University Park campus)
- **Suburban** 53-acre campus
- **Coed,** 1,730 undergraduate students, 58% full-time, 44% women, 56% men

Undergraduates 1,000 full-time, 730 part-time. 2% are from out of state, 4% African American, 6% Asian American or Pacific Islander, 2% Hispanic American, 0.4% Native American, 0.1% international, 2% transferred in. *Retention:* 74% of 2001 full-time freshmen returned.

Freshmen *Admission:* 979 applied, 835 admitted, 347 enrolled. *Average high school GPA:* 2.81. *Test scores:* SAT verbal scores over 500: 52%; SAT math scores over 500: 56%; SAT verbal scores over 600: 16%; SAT math scores over 600: 19%; SAT verbal scores over 700: 1%.

Faculty *Total:* 127, 49% full-time, 39% with terminal degrees. *Student/faculty ratio:* 16:1.

Majors Accounting; acting; actuarial science; adult and continuing education administration; advertising; aerospace, aeronautical and astronautical engineering; African-American/Black studies; agribusiness; agricultural and extension education; agricultural/biological engineering and bioengineering; agricultural business and management related; agricultural mechanization; agriculture; American studies; animal sciences; animal sciences related; anthropology; applied economics; archeology; architectural engineering; art; art history, criticism and conservation; art teacher education; Asian studies (East); astronomy; atmospheric sciences and meteorology; biochemistry; biological and biomedical sciences related; biological and physical sciences; biology/biological sciences; biology/biotechnology laboratory technician; biomedical/medical engineering; biomedical technology; business/commerce; business/managerial economics; chemical engineering; chemistry; civil engineering; classics and languages, literatures and linguistics; communication and journalism related; communication disorders; communication/speech communication and rhetoric; comparative literature; computer and information sciences; computer engineering; criminal justice/law enforcement administration; economics; electrical, electronic and communications engineering technology; electrical, electronics and communications engineering; elementary education; engineering science; English; environmental/environmental health engineering; film/cinema studies; finance; food science; forestry technology; forest sciences and biology; French; geography; geological and earth sciences/geosciences related; geology/earth science; German; graphic design; health/health care administration; history; horticultural science; hospitality administration related; human development and family studies; human nutrition; industrial engineering; industrial technology; information science/studies; international business/trade/commerce; international relations and affairs; Italian; Japanese; Jewish/Judaic studies; journalism; kinesiology and exercise science; labor and industrial relations; landscape architecture; landscaping and groundskeeping; Latin American studies; liberal arts and sciences/liberal studies; logistics and materials management; management information systems; management sciences and quantitative methods related; manufacturing engineering; marketing/marketing management; materials science; mathematics; mechanical engineering; mechanical engineering/mechanical technology; medical microbiology and bacteriology; medieval and Renaissance studies; metallurgical technology; mining and mineral engineering; natural resources and conservation related; natural resources/conservation; nuclear engineering; nursing (registered nurse training); organizational behavior; parks, recreation and leisure facilities management; petroleum engineering; philosophy; physics; political science and government; pre-medical studies; psychology; rehabilitation and therapeutic professions related; religious studies; Russian; secondary education; sociology; soil science and agronomy; Spanish; special education; statistics; telecommunications technology; theatre design and technology; turf and turfgrass management; visual and performing arts; women's studies.

Academic Programs *Special study options:* academic remediation for entering students, accelerated degree program, adult/continuing education programs, advanced placement credit, distance learning, double majors, English as a second language, honors programs, independent study, internships, services for LD students, student-designed majors, study abroad, summer session for credit.

Library 49,996 titles, 243 serial subscriptions, 3,567 audiovisual materials.

Computers on Campus 155 computers available on campus for general student use. A campuswide network can be accessed from off campus. Internet access, online (class) registration, at least one staffed computer lab available. Computer purchase or lease plan available.

Student Life *Housing:* college housing not available. *Activities and Organizations:* student-run newspaper. *Campus security:* part-time trained security personnel.

Athletics Member NJCAA. *Intercollegiate sports:* basketball M/W, cross-country running M/W, soccer M, tennis M/W, volleyball W. *Intramural sports:* badminton M/W, basketball M/W, cheerleading M(c)/W(c), football M, soccer M/W, softball M/W, tennis M/W, ultimate Frisbee M/W, volleyball M/W.

Standardized Tests *Required:* SAT I or ACT (for admission).

Costs (2003–04) *Tuition:* state resident $8620 full-time, $348 per credit part-time; nonresident $13,250 full-time, $552 per credit part-time. *Required fees:* $388 full-time.

Financial Aid Of all full-time matriculated undergraduates who enrolled, 37 Federal Work-Study jobs (averaging $772).

Applying *Options:* electronic application, early admission, deferred entrance. *Application fee:* $50. *Required:* high school transcript. *Application deadline:* rolling (freshmen), rolling (transfers). *Notification:* continuous (freshmen), continuous (transfers).

Admissions Contact The Pennsylvania State University York Campus of the Commonwealth College, 1031 Edgecomb Avenue, York, PA 17403-3398. *Phone:* 814-865-5471. *Toll-free phone:* 800-778-6227. *Fax:* 717-771-4005. *E-mail:* ykadmission@psu.edu.

PITTSBURGH INSTITUTE OF AERONAUTICS
Pittsburgh, Pennsylvania

- **Independent** 2-year, founded 1929
- **Calendar** quarters
- **Degree** associate
- **Suburban** campus
- **Coed, primarily men**

Faculty *Student/faculty ratio:* 17:1.

Costs (2003–04) *Tuition:* $9234 full-time, $1837 per term part-time. *Payment plans:* tuition prepayment, installment.

Applying *Options:* deferred entrance. *Application fee:* $150. *Recommended:* high school transcript, interview.

Admissions Contact Ms. Michaelene F. Kalinowski, Director of Admissions, Pittsburgh Institute of Aeronautics, PO Box 10897, Pittsburgh, PA 15236. *Phone:* 412-346-2100 Ext. 2123. *Toll-free phone:* 800-444-1440. *Fax:* 412-466-0513. *E-mail:* admissions@piainfo.org.

PITTSBURGH INSTITUTE OF MORTUARY SCIENCE, INCORPORATED
Pittsburgh, Pennsylvania

- **Independent** 2-year, founded 1939
- **Calendar** trimesters
- **Degree** diplomas and associate
- **Urban** campus
- **Coed**

Faculty *Student/faculty ratio:* 13:1.

Student Life *Campus security:* 24-hour emergency response devices.

Costs (2003–04) *Tuition:* $10,380 full-time, $230 per credit part-time. Full-time tuition and fees vary according to course load and program. Part-time tuition and fees vary according to course load and program.

Applying *Application fee:* $40. *Required:* high school transcript, 2 letters of recommendation, interview, immunizations.

Admissions Contact Pittsburgh Institute of Mortuary Science, Incorporated, 5808 Baum Boulevard, Pittsburgh, PA 15206-3706. *Phone:* 412-362-8500 Ext. 101. *Toll-free phone:* 800-933-5808. *Fax:* 412-362-1684. *E-mail:* pims5808@aol.com.

PITTSBURGH TECHNICAL INSTITUTE
Oakdale, Pennsylvania

- **Proprietary** 2-year, founded 1946
- **Calendar** quarters
- **Coed,** 1,975 undergraduate students

Faculty *Total:* 92.

Admissions Contact Mary Lou Zook, Vice President of Admissions, Pittsburgh Technical Institute, 1111 McKee Road, Oakdale, PA 15071. *Phone:* 412-809-5100. *Toll-free phone:* 800-784-9675.

THE PJA SCHOOL
Upper Darby, Pennsylvania

Admissions Contact Mr. David Hudiak, Director, The PJA School, 7900 West Chester Pike, Upper Darby, PA 19082-1926. *Phone:* 610-789-6700. *Toll-free phone:* 800-RING-PJA.

READING AREA COMMUNITY COLLEGE
Reading, Pennsylvania

- **County-supported** 2-year, founded 1971
- **Calendar** quarters
- **Degree** certificates, diplomas, and associate
- **Urban** 14-acre campus with easy access to Philadelphia
- **Endowment** $745,770
- **Coed,** 4,158 undergraduate students, 38% full-time, 67% women, 33% men

Undergraduates 1,578 full-time, 2,580 part-time. Students come from 10 other countries, 9% African American, 2% Asian American or Pacific Islander, 13% Hispanic American, 1% Native American, 0.8% international.

Freshmen *Admission:* 2,318 applied, 2,318 admitted, 1,345 enrolled.

Faculty *Total:* 223, 27% full-time.

Majors Accounting; administrative assistant and secretarial science; airline pilot and flight crew; behavioral sciences; biology/biological sciences; business administration and management; business teacher education; chemistry; child development; clinical laboratory science/medical technology; clinical/medical laboratory technology; communications technology; computer programming; computer science; consumer merchandising/retailing management; culinary arts; data processing and data processing technology; education; electrical, electronic and communications engineering technology; elementary education; engineering; engineering science; engineering technology; finance; health information/medical records administration; humanities; human resources management; human services; industrial radiologic technology; industrial technology; information science/studies; kindergarten/preschool education; legal administrative assistant/secretary; legal studies; liberal arts and sciences/liberal studies; machine tool technology; marketing/marketing management; mechanical engineering/mechanical technology; medical administrative assistant and medical secretary; medical laboratory technology; mental health/rehabilitation; nursing (licensed practical/vocational nurse training); nursing (registered nurse training); political science and government; pre-engineering; pre-pharmacy studies; psychology; public administration; respiratory care therapy; social sciences; social work; telecommunications; tourism and travel services management; veterinary sciences.

Academic Programs *Special study options:* academic remediation for entering students, adult/continuing education programs, cooperative education, English as a second language, external degree program, part-time degree program, services for LD students, student-designed majors, summer session for credit.

Library Yocum Library with 25,541 titles, 284 serial subscriptions, an OPAC, a Web page.

Computers on Campus 80 computers available on campus for general student use. At least one staffed computer lab available.

Student Life *Housing:* college housing not available. *Activities and Organizations:* student-run newspaper. *Campus security:* 24-hour patrols. *Student services:* personal/psychological counseling, women's center.

Athletics *Intercollegiate sports:* basketball M, soccer M, volleyball W. *Intramural sports:* cross-country running M/W.

Costs (2004–05) *Tuition:* area resident $1704 full-time, $72 per credit part-time; state resident $3192 full-time, $133 per credit part-time; nonresident $4680 full-time, $195 per credit part-time. *Required fees:* $504 full-time, $21 per credit part-time.

Financial Aid Of all full-time matriculated undergraduates who enrolled, 100 Federal Work-Study jobs (averaging $3300). 5 state and other part-time jobs (averaging $3300).

Applying *Options:* electronic application, early admission, deferred entrance. *Application fee:* $20. *Application deadline:* rolling (freshmen), rolling (transfers).

Admissions Contact Mr. David J. Adams, Director of Admissions, Reading Area Community College, PO Box 1706, Reading, PA 19603-1706. *Phone:* 610-607-6224. *Toll-free phone:* 800-626-1665. *Fax:* 610-375-8255.

THE RESTAURANT SCHOOL AT WALNUT HILL COLLEGE
Philadelphia, Pennsylvania

- **Proprietary** primarily 2-year, founded 1974
- **Calendar** semesters
- **Degrees** associate and bachelor's
- **Urban** 2-acre campus

The Restaurant School at Walnut Hill College (continued)
- **Coed,** 585 undergraduate students

Undergraduates Students come from 10 states and territories, 5 other countries, 57% are from out of state, 20% live on campus.
Freshmen *Average high school GPA:* 2.65.
Faculty *Total:* 27, 78% full-time, 37% with terminal degrees. *Student/faculty ratio:* 25:1.
Majors Baking and pastry arts; culinary arts; hotel/motel administration.
Academic Programs *Special study options:* academic remediation for entering students, internships, part-time degree program.
Library Alumni Resource Center with 5,000 titles, 200 serial subscriptions.
Computers on Campus 24 computers available on campus for general student use. Internet access, at least one staffed computer lab available.
Student Life *Housing Options:* coed. *Activities and Organizations:* student-run newspaper, Community Action Society, Les Gastronome, Culinary Salon, Tastevin, Pastry Club.
Standardized Tests *Recommended:* SAT I or ACT (for admission).
Costs (2004–05) *Tuition:* $12,100 full-time.
Applying *Options:* common application, early admission, early decision, deferred entrance. *Application fee:* $50. *Required:* essay or personal statement, high school transcript, 2 letters of recommendation, interview. *Required for some:* entrance exam. *Recommended:* minimum 2.0 GPA. *Application deadline:* rolling (freshmen).
Admissions Contact Mr. Karl D. Becker, Director of Admissions, The Restaurant School at Walnut Hill College, 4207 Walnut Street, Philadelphia, PA 19104. *Phone:* 215-222-4200 Ext. 3011. *Toll-free phone:* 877-925-6884 Ext. 3011. *Fax:* 215-222-4219. *E-mail:* info@walnuthillcollege.edu.

▶ **See page 598 for a narrative description.**

RETS INSTITUTE OF TECHNOLOGY
Pittsburgh, Pennsylvania

Admissions Contact 777 Penn Center Boulevard, Pittsburgh, PA 15235. *Toll-free phone:* 888-300-4255.

ROSEDALE TECHNICAL INSTITUTE
Pittsburgh, Pennsylvania

- **Independent** 2-year
- **Calendar** semesters
- **Degree** associate
- **Suburban** 6-acre campus
- **Coed, primarily women,** 205 undergraduate students, 100% full-time, 7% women, 93% men

Undergraduates 205 full-time.
Freshmen *Admission:* 145 applied, 95 admitted.
Faculty *Total:* 18, 78% full-time, 33% with terminal degrees. *Student/faculty ratio:* 20:1.
Majors Automobile/automotive mechanics technology; diesel mechanics technology.
Costs (2004–05) *Tuition:* $20,140 per degree program part-time.
Admissions Contact Mr. Kevin Auld, Director, Rosedale Technical Institute, 4634 Browns Hill Road, Pittsburgh, PA 15217-2919. *Phone:* 412-521-6200. *Toll-free phone:* 800-521-6262.

SCHUYLKILL INSTITUTE OF BUSINESS AND TECHNOLOGY
Pottsville, Pennsylvania

- **Proprietary** 2-year, part of Fore Front Education, Inc.
- **Calendar** quarters
- **Degree** diplomas and associate
- **Rural** campus
- **Coed,** 135 undergraduate students, 100% full-time, 56% women, 44% men

Undergraduates 135 full-time. Students come from 1 other state.
Freshmen *Admission:* 105 enrolled. *Average high school GPA:* 3.0.
Faculty *Total:* 19, 84% full-time. *Student/faculty ratio:* 8:1.
Majors Administrative assistant and secretarial science; business administration and management; commercial and advertising art; computer and information sciences and support services related; drafting and design technology; electrical, electronic and communications engineering technology; legal assistant/paralegal; medical office management.

Academic Programs *Special study options:* academic remediation for entering students, advanced placement credit, cooperative education, independent study, internships, services for LD students.
Library Schuylkill Institute of Business and Technology Learning Resource Cent with 920 titles, 20 serial subscriptions, 300 audiovisual materials, an OPAC.
Computers on Campus 41 computers available on campus for general student use. A campuswide network can be accessed from off campus. Internet access, at least one staffed computer lab available.
Student Life *Housing:* college housing not available.
Costs (2003–04) *One-time required fee:* $200. *Tuition:* $7000 full-time. Full-time tuition and fees vary according to degree level and program. No tuition increase for student's term of enrollment. *Required fees:* $250 full-time. *Payment plans:* installment, deferred payment. *Waivers:* employees or children of employees.
Applying *Options:* common application. *Application fee:* $50. *Required:* high school transcript, interview. *Application deadlines:* 10/25 (freshmen), 10/25 (transfers).
Admissions Contact Regina Gargano, Director of Admissions, Schuylkill Institute of Business and Technology, 171 Red Horse Road, Pottsville, PA 17901. *Phone:* 570-622-4835. *Fax:* 570-622-6563.

SOUTH HILLS SCHOOL OF BUSINESS & TECHNOLOGY
Atloona, Pennsylvania

- **Proprietary** 2-year, founded 2001
- **Calendar** trimesters
- **Degree** diplomas and associate
- **Coed**

Faculty *Student/faculty ratio:* 13:1.
Standardized Tests *Required for some:* CPAt.
Costs (2003–04) *Tuition:* $10,050 full-time, $203 per credit part-time. Full-time tuition and fees vary according to program. Part-time tuition and fees vary according to program. *Required fees:* $75 full-time.
Applying *Options:* common application, electronic application. *Application fee:* $25. *Required:* high school transcript, minimum 1.5 GPA, interview. *Required for some:* essay or personal statement. *Recommended:* minimum 3.0 GPA.
Admissions Contact Ms. Marianne M. Beyer, Director, South Hills School of Business & Technology, 508 58th Street, Altoona, PA 16602. *Phone:* 814-944-6134. *Fax:* 814-944-4684. *E-mail:* admissions@southhills.edu.

SOUTH HILLS SCHOOL OF BUSINESS & TECHNOLOGY
State College, Pennsylvania

- **Proprietary** 2-year, founded 1970
- **Calendar** quarters
- **Degrees** certificates, diplomas, and associate (also includes Altoona campus)
- **Small-town** 6-acre campus
- **Coed,** 754 undergraduate students, 93% full-time, 69% women, 31% men

Undergraduates 701 full-time, 53 part-time. Students come from 1 other state, 0.8% African American, 0.7% Asian American or Pacific Islander, 0.1% Hispanic American, 0.1% Native American, 15% transferred in. *Retention:* 83% of 2002 full-time freshmen returned.
Freshmen *Admission:* 586 applied, 477 admitted, 378 enrolled. *Average high school GPA:* 2.75.
Faculty *Total:* 64, 64% full-time. *Student/faculty ratio:* 17:1.
Majors Accounting; administrative assistant and secretarial science; business administration and management; computer and information sciences; computer programming (specific applications); diagnostic medical sonography and ultrasound technology; engineering technology; health information/medical records technology; legal administrative assistant/secretary; marketing/marketing management; medical administrative assistant and medical secretary; office management.
Academic Programs *Special study options:* advanced placement credit, double majors, independent study, internships, part-time degree program.
Computers on Campus 360 computers available on campus for general student use. Internet access available.
Student Life *Housing:* college housing not available. *Activities and Organizations:* student-run newspaper, Phi Beta Lambda, South Hills Executives, Student Forum, newspaper. *Campus security:* 24-hour emergency response devices.
Standardized Tests *Required for some:* CPAt.

Costs (2004–05) *Tuition:* $10,554 full-time, $213 per credit part-time. Full-time tuition and fees vary according to course load and program. Part-time tuition and fees vary according to course load and program. *Required fees:* $75 full-time, $25 per term part-time. *Waivers:* employees or children of employees.
Applying *Options:* electronic application. *Application fee:* $25. *Required:* high school transcript, minimum 1.5 GPA, interview. *Required for some:* essay or personal statement, 2 letters of recommendation. *Recommended:* minimum 3.0 GPA. *Application deadline:* 9/2 (freshmen).
Admissions Contact Ms. Diane M. Brown, Director of Admissions, South Hills School of Business & Technology, 480 Waupelani Drive, State College, PA 16801-4516. *Phone:* 814-234-7755 Ext. 2020. *Toll-free phone:* 888-282-7427 Ext. 2020. *Fax:* 814-234-0926. *E-mail:* admissions@southhills.edu.

THADDEUS STEVENS COLLEGE OF TECHNOLOGY
Lancaster, Pennsylvania

- **State-supported** 2-year, founded 1905
- **Calendar** semesters
- **Degree** associate
- **Urban** 33-acre campus with easy access to Philadelphia
- **Coed, primarily men**

Faculty *Student/faculty ratio:* 12:1.
Student Life *Campus security:* 24-hour emergency response devices.
Athletics Member NJCAA.
Standardized Tests *Required:* ACT ASSET (for admission).
Applying *Options:* common application, electronic application, deferred entrance. *Application fee:* $25. *Required:* essay or personal statement, high school transcript, minimum 2.0 GPA, letters of recommendation. *Required for some:* interview.
Admissions Contact Ms. Erin Kate Nelsen, Director of Enrollment, Thaddeus Stevens College of Technology, Enrollment Services, 750 East King Street, Lancaster, PA 17602-3198. *Phone:* 717-299-7772. *Toll-free phone:* 800-842-3832. *Fax:* 717-391-6929. *E-mail:* nelsen@stevenscollege.edu.

THOMPSON INSTITUTE
Harrisburg, Pennsylvania

- **Proprietary** primarily 2-year, founded 1918, part of Kaplan Higher Education Corporation
- **Calendar** quarters
- **Degrees** certificates, diplomas, associate, and bachelor's
- **Suburban** 5-acre campus
- **Coed,** 485 undergraduate students

Undergraduates Students come from 2 states and territories, 2% are from out of state.
Freshmen *Admission:* 165 applied, 145 admitted.
Faculty *Total:* 27, 89% full-time. *Student/faculty ratio:* 25:1.
Majors Accounting; business administration and management; computer management; computer programming; computer systems networking and telecommunications; drafting and design technology; electrical, electronic and communications engineering technology; health information/medical records administration; medical/clinical assistant.
Academic Programs *Special study options:* academic remediation for entering students, adult/continuing education programs, advanced placement credit, internships, services for LD students, summer session for credit.
Library 950 titles, 20 serial subscriptions, an OPAC.
Computers on Campus 113 computers available on campus for general student use. A campuswide network can be accessed from off campus. Internet access, at least one staffed computer lab available. Computer purchase or lease plan available.
Student Life *Housing Options:* coed. Campus housing is leased by the school. *Activities and Organizations:* Electronics Club, CAD Club, DPMA, Math Club, national sororities. *Campus security:* campus facilities manager. *Student services:* personal/psychological counseling.
Costs (2004–05) *Tuition:* $8200 full-time. *Required fees:* $800 full-time. *Room only:* $1600. *Payment plans:* installment, deferred payment.
Applying *Options:* common application, electronic application, deferred entrance. *Application fee:* $50. *Required:* high school transcript. *Recommended:* minimum 2.0 GPA. *Application deadline:* rolling (freshmen), rolling (transfers).
Admissions Contact Mr. Charles Zimmerman, Admissions Director, Thompson Institute, 5650 Derry Street, Harrisburg, PA 17111. *Phone:* 717-564-4112. *Toll-free phone:* 800-272-4632. *Fax:* 717-564-3779. *E-mail:* czimmerman@thompsoninstitute.org.

TRIANGLE TECH, INC.
Pittsburgh, Pennsylvania

- **Proprietary** 2-year, founded 1944, part of Triangle Tech, Inc
- **Calendar** semesters
- **Degree** diplomas and associate
- **Urban** 5-acre campus
- **Coed, primarily men,** 394 undergraduate students, 100% full-time, 2% women, 98% men

Undergraduates 394 full-time. Students come from 3 states and territories, 6% are from out of state, 12% African American, 0.3% Asian American or Pacific Islander.
Freshmen *Admission:* 136 applied, 123 admitted, 123 enrolled. *Average high school GPA:* 2.00.
Faculty *Total:* 32, 88% full-time, 3% with terminal degrees. *Student/faculty ratio:* 11:1.
Majors Architectural engineering technology; carpentry; drafting and design technology; electrical, electronic and communications engineering technology; heating, air conditioning, ventilation and refrigeration maintenance technology; mechanical design technology.
Academic Programs *Special study options:* academic remediation for entering students, advanced placement credit.
Library 2,000 titles, 30 serial subscriptions.
Computers on Campus 50 computers available on campus for general student use. A campuswide network can be accessed from off campus. Internet access, at least one staffed computer lab available.
Student Life *Housing:* college housing not available. *Activities and Organizations:* student council. *Campus security:* 16-hour patrols by trained security personnel.
Costs (2003–04) *Tuition:* $10,346 full-time. *Required fees:* $290 full-time.
Financial Aid Of all full-time matriculated undergraduates who enrolled, 16 Federal Work-Study jobs (averaging $1500). *Financial aid deadline:* 7/1.
Applying *Options:* early admission, deferred entrance. *Required:* high school transcript, minimum 2.0 GPA, interview. *Application deadline:* rolling (freshmen), rolling (transfers).
Admissions Contact Mr. John A. Mazzarese, Vice President of Admissions, Triangle Tech, Inc., 1940 Perrysville Avenue, Pittsburgh, PA 15214. *Phone:* 412-359-1000 Ext. 7174. *Toll-free phone:* 800-874-8324. *Fax:* 412-359-1012. *E-mail:* info@triangle-tech.com.

TRIANGLE TECH, INC.-DUBOIS SCHOOL
DuBois, Pennsylvania

- **Proprietary** 2-year, founded 1944, part of Triangle Tech, Inc
- **Calendar** semesters
- **Degree** associate
- **Small-town** 5-acre campus
- **Coed, primarily men,** 291 undergraduate students, 100% full-time, 4% women, 96% men

Undergraduates 291 full-time. Students come from 3 states and territories, 1% are from out of state, 0.3% African American, 0.3% Asian American or Pacific Islander.
Freshmen *Admission:* 156 applied, 152 admitted, 152 enrolled. *Average high school GPA:* 2.00.
Faculty *Total:* 25, 100% full-time. *Student/faculty ratio:* 15:1.
Majors Carpentry; drafting and design technology; electrical, electronic and communications engineering technology; welding technology.
Academic Programs *Special study options:* academic remediation for entering students, advanced placement credit, off-campus study.
Library 1,200 titles, 15 serial subscriptions.
Computers on Campus 40 computers available on campus for general student use. A campuswide network can be accessed from off campus. At least one staffed computer lab available.
Costs (2003–04) *Comprehensive fee:* $15,919 includes full-time tuition ($10,346), mandatory fees ($285), and room and board ($5288). Full-time tuition and fees vary according to program. *Payment plan:* installment. *Waivers:* employees or children of employees.
Applying *Options:* deferred entrance. *Required:* high school transcript, minimum 2.0 GPA, interview. *Application deadline:* rolling (freshmen), rolling (transfers).
Admissions Contact Mr. John Conway, Director of Admissions, Triangle Tech, Inc.-DuBois School, PO Box 551, DuBois, PA 15801. *Phone:* 412-359-1000. *Toll-free phone:* 800-874-8324. *Fax:* 814-371-9227. *E-mail:* info@triangle-tech.com.

TRIANGLE TECH, INC.-ERIE SCHOOL
Erie, Pennsylvania

- **Proprietary** 2-year, founded 1976, part of Triangle Tech, Inc
- **Calendar** semesters
- **Degree** associate
- **Urban** 1-acre campus
- **Coed, primarily men**

Faculty *Student/faculty ratio:* 12:1.

Student Life *Campus security:* 24-hour emergency response devices.

Costs (2003–04) *Tuition:* $10,346 full-time.

Financial Aid Of all full-time matriculated undergraduates who enrolled, 5 Federal Work-Study jobs (averaging $2000).

Applying *Options:* deferred entrance. *Required:* high school transcript, minimum 2.0 GPA, interview.

Admissions Contact Jennifer Provost, Admissions Representative, Triangle Tech, Inc.-Erie School, 2000 Liberty St., Erie, PA 16502. *Phone:* 814-453-6016. *Toll-free phone:* 800-874-8324 (in-state); 800-TRI-TECH (out-of-state). *Fax:* 814-454-2818. *E-mail:* pfitzgerald@triangle-tech.com.

TRIANGLE TECH, INC.-GREENSBURG CENTER
Greensburg, Pennsylvania

- **Proprietary** 2-year, founded 1944, part of Triangle Tech, Inc
- **Calendar** semesters
- **Degree** diplomas and associate
- **Small-town** 1-acre campus with easy access to Pittsburgh
- **Coed, primarily men,** 283 undergraduate students, 100% full-time, 6% women, 94% men

Undergraduates 283 full-time. 0.7% African American.

Freshmen *Admission:* 89 applied, 89 enrolled.

Faculty *Total:* 29, 97% full-time. *Student/faculty ratio:* 10:1.

Majors Carpentry; construction trades; drafting and design technology; electrical/electronics equipment installation and repair; electrical/electronics maintenance and repair technology related; heating, air conditioning and refrigeration technology; heating, air conditioning, ventilation and refrigeration maintenance technology; mechanical drafting and CAD/CADD.

Academic Programs *Special study options:* academic remediation for entering students, adult/continuing education programs, advanced placement credit, summer session for credit.

Library Triangle Tech Library plus 2 others with 550 titles, 15 serial subscriptions.

Computers on Campus 40 computers available on campus for general student use. A campuswide network can be accessed from off campus. Internet access, at least one staffed computer lab available.

Student Life *Student services:* personal/psychological counseling.

Costs (2003–04) *Tuition:* $10,346 full-time. *Required fees:* $1167 full-time.

Financial Aid Of all full-time matriculated undergraduates who enrolled, 5 Federal Work-Study jobs (averaging $2000).

Applying *Options:* deferred entrance. *Application fee:* $75. *Required:* high school transcript. *Application deadline:* rolling (freshmen), rolling (transfers).

Admissions Contact Mr. John A. Mazzarese, Vice President of Admissions, Triangle Tech, Inc.-Greensburg Center, 222 East Pittsburgh Street, Greensburg, PA 15601. *Phone:* 412-359-1000. *Toll-free phone:* 800-874-8324.

TRIANGLE TECH, INC.-SUNBURY
Sunbury, Pennsylvania

Admissions Contact RR #1, Box 51, Sunbury, PA 17801.

TRI-STATE BUSINESS INSTITUTE
Erie, Pennsylvania

Admissions Contact Guy M. Euliano, President, Tri-State Business Institute, 5757 West 26th Street, Erie, PA 16506. *Phone:* 814-838-7673.

UNIVERSITY OF PITTSBURGH AT TITUSVILLE
Titusville, Pennsylvania

- **State-related** 2-year, founded 1963, part of University of Pittsburgh System
- **Calendar** semesters

- **Degree** certificates and associate
- **Small-town** 10-acre campus
- **Endowment** $45,326
- **Coed,** 516 undergraduate students, 76% full-time, 57% women, 43% men

Undergraduates 392 full-time, 124 part-time. Students come from 8 states and territories, 7% are from out of state, 12% African American, 2% Asian American or Pacific Islander, 1% Hispanic American, 0.2% Native American, 6% transferred in, 47% live on campus.

Freshmen *Admission:* 3,431 applied, 3,391 admitted, 233 enrolled. *Average high school GPA:* 2.74. *Test scores:* SAT verbal scores over 500: 35%; SAT math scores over 500: 32%; ACT scores over 18: 67%; SAT verbal scores over 600: 5%; SAT math scores over 600: 5%; ACT scores over 24: 17%.

Faculty *Total:* 61, 34% full-time, 31% with terminal degrees. *Student/faculty ratio:* 12:1.

Majors Accounting; business administration and management; liberal arts and sciences/liberal studies; natural sciences; physical therapist assistant.

Academic Programs *Special study options:* academic remediation for entering students, advanced placement credit, independent study, internships, part-time degree program, study abroad, summer session for credit.

Library Haskell Memorial Library with 49,256 titles, 126 serial subscriptions, 505 audiovisual materials, an OPAC.

Computers on Campus 62 computers available on campus for general student use. A campuswide network can be accessed from student residence rooms and from off campus. Internet access, at least one staffed computer lab available.

Student Life *Housing:* on-campus residence required through sophomore year. *Options:* coed. Campus housing is university owned. Freshman campus housing is guaranteed. *Activities and Organizations:* drama/theater group, choral group, Phi Theta Kappa, Weight Club, SAB, SIFE, Diversity Club. *Campus security:* 24-hour emergency response devices and patrols, controlled dormitory access. *Student services:* health clinic, personal/psychological counseling.

Athletics Member NJCAA. *Intercollegiate sports:* basketball M(s)/W(s), golf M(s), volleyball W(s). *Intramural sports:* badminton M/W, basketball M/W, bowling M/W, football M/W, golf M/W, racquetball M/W, softball M/W, table tennis M/W, tennis M/W, volleyball M/W, weight lifting M/W.

Standardized Tests *Required:* SAT I or ACT (for admission). *Recommended:* SAT I (for admission).

Costs (2003–04) *Tuition:* state resident $7754 full-time; nonresident $16,132 full-time. *Required fees:* $670 full-time. *Room and board:* $6560. *Payment plan:* installment.

Applying *Options:* deferred entrance. *Application fee:* $35. *Required:* high school transcript, minimum 2.0 GPA. *Required for some:* essay or personal statement, 1 letter of recommendation. *Recommended:* interview. *Application deadline:* rolling (freshmen), rolling (transfers). *Notification:* continuous (freshmen).

Admissions Contact Mr. John R. Mumford, Executive Director of Enrollment Management, University of Pittsburgh at Titusville, PO Box 287, Titusville, PA 16354. *Phone:* 814-827-4409. *Toll-free phone:* 888-878-0462. *Fax:* 814-827-4519. *E-mail:* uptadm@pitt.edu.

VALLEY FORGE MILITARY COLLEGE
Wayne, Pennsylvania

- **Independent** 2-year, founded 1928
- **Calendar** 4-1-4
- **Degree** associate
- **Suburban** 119-acre campus with easy access to Philadelphia
- **Endowment** $7.2 million
- **Men only,** 240 undergraduate students

The College's primary goal is to prepare young men to transfer to and succeed at the 4-year college or university of their choice. For more than 95% of the graduates, that goal is achieved through challenging academic programs, a structured environment that builds confidence and character and fosters academic success, and personal transfer counseling and transfer agreements with major universities. The only 2-year Army ROTC commissioning program in the Northeast US, with full tuition scholarships for qualified applicants.

Undergraduates Students come from 6 other countries, 85% are from out of state, 100% live on campus.

Freshmen *Average high school GPA:* 2.00. *Test scores:* SAT verbal scores over 500: 49%; SAT math scores over 500: 51%; ACT scores over 18: 71%; SAT verbal scores over 600: 23%; SAT math scores over 600: 30%; ACT scores over 24: 48%; SAT verbal scores over 700: 4%; SAT math scores over 700: 4%; ACT scores over 30: 7%.

Faculty *Total:* 25, 56% full-time. *Student/faculty ratio:* 10:1.

Majors Biological and physical sciences; business administration and management; criminal justice/law enforcement administration; engineering; liberal arts and sciences/liberal studies.

Academic Programs *Special study options:* academic remediation for entering students, advanced placement credit, English as a second language. *ROTC:* Army (b), Air Force (c).

Library Baker Library with 75,830 titles, 189 serial subscriptions, 326 audiovisual materials, an OPAC.

Computers on Campus 44 computers available on campus for general student use. A campuswide network can be accessed from student residence rooms and from off campus. Internet access, at least one staffed computer lab available.

Student Life *Housing:* on-campus residence required through sophomore year. *Options:* men-only. *Activities and Organizations:* drama/theater group, student-run newspaper, choral group, marching band, Rotoract, Young Republicans, Phi Theta Kappa, Business Club, Criminal Justice Club, national fraternities. *Campus security:* 24-hour patrols, student patrols. *Student services:* health clinic, personal/psychological counseling.

Athletics *Intercollegiate sports:* basketball M(s), cross-country running M, equestrian sports M, football M(s), golf M, lacrosse M, riflery M, soccer M(s), tennis M, wrestling M. *Intramural sports:* basketball M, football M, rugby M, soccer M, volleyball M, water polo M, weight lifting M.

Standardized Tests *Required:* SAT I or ACT (for admission).

Costs (2003–04) *Comprehensive fee:* $26,790 includes full-time tuition ($16,830), mandatory fees ($1110), and room and board ($8850). *Payment plans:* installment, deferred payment. *Waivers:* employees or children of employees.

Financial Aid Of all full-time matriculated undergraduates who enrolled, 20 Federal Work-Study jobs (averaging $1500).

Applying *Options:* common application, early admission, deferred entrance. *Application fee:* $25. *Required:* high school transcript, guidance counselor/teacher evaluation form. *Recommended:* minimum 2.0 GPA, interview. *Application deadline:* 8/2 (freshmen), rolling (transfers). *Notification:* continuous (freshmen), continuous (transfers).

Admissions Contact Maj. Kelly M. DeShane, Associate Director for College Enrollment, Valley Forge Military College, 1001 Eagle Road, Wayne, PA 19087-3695. *Phone:* 610-989-1300. *Toll-free phone:* 800-234-8362. *Fax:* 610-688-1545. *E-mail:* admissions@vfmac.edu.

▶ **See page 606 for a narrative description.**

WESTERN SCHOOL OF HEALTH AND BUSINESS CAREERS
Monroeville, Pennsylvania

Admissions Contact 1 Monroeville Center, Suite 250, Route 22, 3824 Northern Pike, Monroeville, PA 15146-2142.

WESTERN SCHOOL OF HEALTH AND BUSINESS CAREERS
Pittsburgh, Pennsylvania

- **Proprietary** 2-year, founded 1980
- **Calendar** continuous
- **Degree** associate
- **Urban** campus
- **Coed**

Faculty *Student/faculty ratio:* 20:1.

Student Life *Campus security:* 24-hour emergency response devices, 14-hour security patrols Monday through Friday.

Standardized Tests *Recommended:* SAT I or ACT (for admission), SAT II: Subject Tests (for admission).

Financial Aid Of all full-time matriculated undergraduates who enrolled, 25 Federal Work-Study jobs (averaging $1200).

Applying *Options:* common application, electronic application, early admission, deferred entrance. *Required:* high school transcript, interview. *Required for some:* letters of recommendation. *Recommended:* letters of recommendation.

Admissions Contact Mr. Bruce E. Jones, Director of Admission, Western School of Health and Business Careers, 421 Seventh Avenue, Pittsburgh, PA 15219. *Phone:* 412-281-7083 Ext. 114. *Toll-free phone:* 800-333-6607. *Fax:* 412-281-0319. *E-mail:* adm@westernschool.com.

WESTMORELAND COUNTY COMMUNITY COLLEGE
Youngwood, Pennsylvania

- **County-supported** 2-year, founded 1970
- **Calendar** semesters
- **Degree** certificates, diplomas, and associate

- **Rural** 85-acre campus with easy access to Pittsburgh
- **Coed,** 6,257 undergraduate students, 41% full-time, 64% women, 36% men

Undergraduates 2,580 full-time, 3,677 part-time. Students come from 5 states and territories, 2% African American, 0.4% Asian American or Pacific Islander, 0.3% Hispanic American, 0.1% Native American. *Retention:* 58% of 2002 full-time freshmen returned.

Freshmen *Admission:* 1,931 applied, 1,931 admitted, 1,743 enrolled.

Faculty *Total:* 410, 20% full-time. *Student/faculty ratio:* 17:1.

Majors Accounting; administrative assistant and secretarial science; architectural engineering technology; artificial intelligence and robotics; business administration and management; child development; commercial and advertising art; computer and information sciences; computer engineering technology; computer graphics; computer science; consumer merchandising/retailing management; criminal justice/law enforcement administration; criminal justice/police science; culinary arts; data processing and data processing technology; dental hygiene; dietetics; drafting and design technology; electrical, electronic and communications engineering technology; engineering; environmental engineering technology; fashion/apparel design; fashion merchandising; finance; fire science; graphic and printing equipment operation/production; health information/medical records administration; health teacher education; heating, air conditioning, ventilation and refrigeration maintenance technology; horticultural science; hospitality administration; hotel/motel administration; human services; information science/studies; legal administrative assistant/secretary; legal assistant/paralegal; liberal arts and sciences/liberal studies; marketing/marketing management; mechanical design technology; mechanical engineering/mechanical technology; medical administrative assistant and medical secretary; nuclear/nuclear power technology; nursing (licensed practical/vocational nurse training); nursing (registered nurse training); ophthalmic laboratory technology; photography; public administration; publishing; real estate; special products marketing; tourism and travel services management; welding technology.

Academic Programs *Special study options:* academic remediation for entering students, adult/continuing education programs, advanced placement credit, cooperative education, distance learning, double majors, English as a second language, honors programs, internships, off-campus study, part-time degree program, services for LD students, summer session for credit.

Library 34,522 titles, 643 serial subscriptions.

Computers on Campus 600 computers available on campus for general student use. A campuswide network can be accessed. Internet access, at least one staffed computer lab available.

Student Life *Housing:* college housing not available. *Activities and Organizations:* student-run newspaper, radio station, choral group. *Campus security:* 24-hour emergency response devices and patrols. *Student services:* personal/psychological counseling.

Athletics Member NJCAA. *Intercollegiate sports:* baseball M, golf M/W, softball W, tennis M/W, volleyball W. *Intramural sports:* basketball M/W, bowling M/W, football M/W, racquetball M/W, skiing (downhill) M/W, softball M/W, table tennis M/W, volleyball M/W, weight lifting M/W.

Standardized Tests *Required:* ACT ASSET (for placement).

Costs (2004–05) *Tuition:* area resident $1830 full-time, $61 per credit part-time; state resident $3810 full-time, $129 per credit part-time; nonresident $5640 full-time, $191 per credit part-time. Full-time tuition and fees vary according to course load. Part-time tuition and fees vary according to course load. *Required fees:* $120 full-time, $4 per credit part-time. *Waivers:* employees or children of employees.

Applying *Options:* early admission. *Application deadline:* rolling (freshmen), rolling (transfers). *Notification:* continuous (freshmen), continuous (transfers).

Admissions Contact Ms. Susan Kuhn, Admissions Coordinator, Westmoreland County Community College, 400 Armbrust Road, Youngwood, PA 15697. *Phone:* 724-925-4064. *Toll-free phone:* 800-262-2103. *Fax:* 724-925-1150. *E-mail:* admission@wccc-pa.edu.

THE WILLIAMSON FREE SCHOOL OF MECHANICAL TRADES
Media, Pennsylvania

- **Independent** 2-year, founded 1888
- **Calendar** semesters
- **Degree** diplomas and associate
- **Small-town** 240-acre campus with easy access to Philadelphia
- **Men only,** 253 undergraduate students, 100% full-time

Undergraduates 253 full-time. Students come from 5 states and territories, 11% African American, 3% Hispanic American, 100% live on campus.

Freshmen *Admission:* 106 enrolled. *Average high school GPA:* 2.3.

Faculty *Total:* 29. *Student/faculty ratio:* 14:1.

Majors Carpentry; construction engineering technology; electrical, electronic and communications engineering technology; energy management and systems technology; horticultural science; landscaping and groundskeeping; machine tool technology; turf and turfgrass management.

The Williamson Free School of Mechanical Trades (continued)

Academic Programs *Special study options:* academic remediation for entering students, internships, off-campus study.

Library Shrigley Library plus 3 others with 1,600 titles, 70 serial subscriptions.

Computers on Campus 20 computers available on campus for general student use. At least one staffed computer lab available.

Student Life *Activities and Organizations:* student-run newspaper, choral group, Campus Crusade for Christ, Vocational Industrial Clubs of America. *Campus security:* evening patrols, gate security. *Student services:* health clinic, personal/psychological counseling.

Athletics Member NJCAA. *Intercollegiate sports:* baseball M, basketball M, cross-country running M, football M, golf M, lacrosse M, soccer M, wrestling M. *Intramural sports:* archery M, badminton M, baseball M, basketball M, cross-country running M, football M, golf M, lacrosse M, racquetball M, soccer M, table tennis M, volleyball M, weight lifting M, wrestling M.

Standardized Tests *Required:* Armed Services Vocational Aptitude Battery (for admission).

Costs (2003–04) *Tuition:* All students attend on full scholarship which covers tuition, room and board, and textbooks.

Applying *Required:* essay or personal statement, high school transcript, minimum 2.0 GPA, 3 letters of recommendation, interview. *Application deadline:* 3/15 (freshmen). *Notification:* 4/15 (freshmen).

Admissions Contact Mr. Edward D. Bailey, Director of Enrollments, The Williamson Free School of Mechanical Trades, 106 South New Middletown Road, Media, PA 19063. *Phone:* 610-566-1776 Ext. 235. *E-mail:* wiltech@libertynet.org.

WYOTECH
Blairsville, Pennsylvania

Admissions Contact 500 Innovation Drive, Blairsville, PA 15717. *Toll-free phone:* 800-822-8253.

YORK TECHNICAL INSTITUTE
York, Pennsylvania

- **Private** 2-year
- **Calendar** continuous
- **Degree** diplomas and associate
- **Suburban** campus
- **Coed**, 1,296 undergraduate students, 100% full-time, 30% women, 70% men

Undergraduates 1,296 full-time. Students come from 5 states and territories, 10% are from out of state.

Freshmen *Admission:* 904 enrolled.

Faculty *Total:* 87, 100% full-time. *Student/faculty ratio:* 25:1.

Majors Artificial intelligence and robotics; computer and information sciences related; computer and information systems security; computer/information technology services administration related; computer systems networking and telecommunications; computer/technical support; information technology; system administration; web page, digital/multimedia and information resources design.

Academic Programs *Special study options:* academic remediation for entering students, advanced placement credit, cooperative education, internships.

Computers on Campus 250 computers available on campus for general student use. A campuswide network can be accessed. Internet access, at least one staffed computer lab available.

Costs (2004–05) *Tuition:* $22,000 full-time. *Required fees:* $1200 full-time. *Payment plan:* installment. *Waivers:* employees or children of employees.

Financial Aid Of all full-time matriculated undergraduates who enrolled, 68 Federal Work-Study jobs (averaging $1938).

Applying *Required:* high school transcript, minimum 2.0 GPA, interview. *Required for some:* essay or personal statement.

Admissions Contact Ms. Sharon Mulligan, Associate Director of Admissions, York Technical Institute, 1405 Williams Road, York, PA 17402. *Phone:* 717-757-1100 Ext. 318. *Toll-free phone:* 800-229-9675 (in-state); 800-227-9675 (out-of-state). *E-mail:* crb@yhi.edu.

YORKTOWNE BUSINESS INSTITUTE
York, Pennsylvania

- **Proprietary** 2-year, founded 1976
- **Calendar** semesters
- **Degree** diplomas and associate
- **Small-town** 1-acre campus with easy access to Baltimore
- **Coed**

Faculty *Student/faculty ratio:* 11:1.

Costs (2003–04) *Tuition:* $13,050 full-time. *Required fees:* $150 full-time.

Applying *Required:* high school transcript, interview. *Required for some:* admissions test.

Admissions Contact Ms. Bonnie Gillespie, Director of Admissions, Yorktowne Business Institute, West Seventh Avenue, York, PA 17404. *Phone:* 717-846-5000 Ext. 124. *Toll-free phone:* 800-840-1004. *Fax:* 717-848-4584. *E-mail:* info@ybi.edu.

RHODE ISLAND

COMMUNITY COLLEGE OF RHODE ISLAND
Warwick, Rhode Island

- **State-supported** 2-year, founded 1964
- **Calendar** semesters
- **Degree** certificates and associate
- **Suburban** 205-acre campus with easy access to Boston
- **Endowment** $886,069
- **Coed**, 16,223 undergraduate students, 35% full-time, 63% women, 37% men

Undergraduates 5,681 full-time, 10,542 part-time. Students come from 15 states and territories, 34 other countries, 7% are from out of state, 7% African American, 2% Asian American or Pacific Islander, 10% Hispanic American, 0.5% Native American, 0.2% international, 3% transferred in.

Freshmen *Admission:* 7,037 applied, 4,863 admitted, 3,239 enrolled.

Faculty *Total:* 697, 46% full-time.

Majors Accounting; administrative assistant and secretarial science; adult development and aging; art; banking and financial support services; biological and physical sciences; business administration and management; business/commerce; chemical technology; clinical/medical laboratory technology; computer engineering technology; computer programming; criminal justice/police science; dental hygiene; dramatic/theatre arts; electrical, electronic and communications engineering technology; engineering; fashion merchandising; fire science; general retailing/wholesaling; general studies; instrumentation technology; kindergarten/preschool education; labor and industrial relations; legal administrative assistant/secretary; legal assistant/paralegal; liberal arts and sciences/liberal studies; marketing/marketing management; medical administrative assistant and medical secretary; medical radiologic technology; music; nursing (registered nurse training); occupational therapist assistant; physical therapist assistant; psychiatric/mental health services technology; rehabilitation and therapeutic professions related; respiratory care therapy; retailing; social work; special education; substance abuse/addiction counseling; theatre design and technology; urban studies/affairs.

Academic Programs *Special study options:* academic remediation for entering students, adult/continuing education programs, advanced placement credit, cooperative education, distance learning, double majors, English as a second language, external degree program, honors programs, independent study, internships, off-campus study, part-time degree program, services for LD students, study abroad, summer session for credit. *ROTC:* Army (c).

Library Community College of Rhode Island Learning Resources Center plus 2 others with 120,803 titles, 904 serial subscriptions, 12,502 audiovisual materials, an OPAC, a Web page.

Computers on Campus 1050 computers available on campus for general student use. A campuswide network can be accessed from off campus that provide access to e-mail. Internet access, online (class) registration, at least one staffed computer lab available.

Student Life *Housing:* college housing not available. *Activities and Organizations:* drama/theater group, choral group, Distributive Education Clubs of America, theater group, ABLE, Phi Theta Kappa. *Campus security:* 24-hour emergency response devices and patrols. *Student services:* health clinic, personal/psychological counseling.

Athletics Member NJCAA. *Intercollegiate sports:* baseball M, basketball M(s)/W(s), cross-country running M/W, golf M/W, soccer M(s)/W(s), softball W(s), swimming M/W, tennis M/W, track and field M/W, volleyball W(s).

Costs (2003–04) *Tuition:* state resident $1870 full-time; nonresident $5490 full-time. Part-time tuition and fees vary according to course load. *Required fees:* $250 full-time. *Payment plan:* deferred payment. *Waivers:* senior citizens and employees or children of employees.

Financial Aid Of all full-time matriculated undergraduates who enrolled, 500 Federal Work-Study jobs (averaging $2500). 70 state and other part-time jobs (averaging $2000).

Applying *Options:* deferred entrance. *Application fee:* $20. *Application deadline:* rolling (freshmen), rolling (transfers). *Notification:* continuous (freshmen).

Admissions Contact Ms. Donnamarie Allen, Senior Admission Officer/Financial Aid Officer, Community College of Rhode Island, 400 East Avenue, Warwick, RI 02886. *Phone:* 401-333-7121. *Fax:* 401-825-2394. *E-mail:* webadmission@ccri.cc.ri.us.

NEW ENGLAND INSTITUTE OF TECHNOLOGY
Warwick, Rhode Island

- **Independent** primarily 2-year, founded 1940
- **Calendar** quarters
- **Degrees** associate and bachelor's
- **Suburban** 10-acre campus with easy access to Boston
- **Coed**

Student Life *Campus security:* security personnel during open hours.
Costs (2004–05) *Tuition:* $13,200 full-time. *Required fees:* $1435 full-time.
Financial Aid Of all full-time matriculated undergraduates who enrolled, 250 Federal Work-Study jobs (averaging $2290).
Applying *Options:* early admission, deferred entrance. *Application fee:* $25. *Required:* high school transcript, interview.
Admissions Contact Mr. Michael Kwiatkowski, Director of Admissions, New England Institute of Technology, 2500 Post Road, Warwick, RI 02886-2266. *Phone:* 401-739-5000. *E-mail:* neit@ids.net.

SOUTH CAROLINA

AIKEN TECHNICAL COLLEGE
Aiken, South Carolina

Admissions Contact Mr. Dennis Harville, Director of Admissions and Records, Aiken Technical College, PO Drawer 696, Aiken, SC 29802-0696. *Phone:* 803-593-9231. *E-mail:* harden@aik.tec.sc.us.

CENTRAL CAROLINA TECHNICAL COLLEGE
Sumter, South Carolina

- **State-supported** 2-year, founded 1963, part of South Carolina State Board for Technical and Comprehensive Education
- **Calendar** semesters
- **Degree** certificates, diplomas, and associate
- **Small-town** 70-acre campus
- **Coed**, 3,191 undergraduate students, 32% full-time, 68% women, 32% men

Undergraduates 1,022 full-time, 2,169 part-time. Students come from 1 other state, 1% are from out of state, 48% African American, 1% Asian American or Pacific Islander, 2% Hispanic American, 0.3% Native American, 0.3% international, 4% transferred in.
Freshmen *Admission:* 653 enrolled. *Test scores:* SAT verbal scores over 500: 24%; SAT math scores over 500: 22%; ACT scores over 18: 40%; SAT verbal scores over 600: 10%; SAT math scores over 600: 3%; ACT scores over 24: 3%.
Faculty Total: 167, 47% full-time. *Student/faculty ratio:* 21:1.
Majors Accounting; administrative assistant and secretarial science; business administration and management; child care and support services management; civil engineering technology; criminal justice/safety; data processing and data processing technology; environmental control technologies related; industrial electronics technology; legal assistant/paralegal; liberal arts and sciences/liberal studies; mechanical drafting and CAD/CADD; multi-/interdisciplinary studies related; natural resources management and policy; nursing (registered nurse training); sales, distribution and marketing; surgical technology.
Academic Programs *Special study options:* academic remediation for entering students, adult/continuing education programs, advanced placement credit, cooperative education, distance learning, external degree program, independent study, internships, off-campus study, part-time degree program, summer session for credit.
Library Central Carolina Technical College Library with 20,356 titles, 245 serial subscriptions, 1,317 audiovisual materials, an OPAC, a Web page.
Computers on Campus 350 computers available on campus for general student use. A campuswide network can be accessed from off campus that provide access to course registration, student account and grade information. Internet access, online (class) registration, at least one staffed computer lab available.

Student Life *Housing:* college housing not available. *Activities and Organizations:* Creative Arts Society, Phi Theta Kappa, Computer Club, National Student Nurses Association (local chapter), Natural Resources Management Club. *Campus security:* 24-hour emergency response devices. *Student services:* personal/psychological counseling.
Standardized Tests *Required:* ACT COMPASS (for placement). *Required for some:* SAT I or ACT (for placement).
Costs (2004–05) *Tuition:* area resident $2500 full-time; state resident $2980 full-time; nonresident $5188 full-time. *Required fees:* $100 full-time. *Payment plan:* installment. *Waivers:* senior citizens.
Applying *Options:* electronic application. *Application fee:* $25. *Required:* high school transcript. *Application deadline:* rolling (freshmen), rolling (transfers).
Admissions Contact Admissions and Counseling Office, Central Carolina Technical College, 506 North Guignard Drive, Sumter, SC 29150. *Phone:* 803-778-1961 Ext. 455. *Toll-free phone:* 800-221-8711 Ext. 455 (in-state); 803-778-1961 Ext. 455 (out-of-state). *Fax:* 803-778-6696. *E-mail:* colmanjh@cctech.edu.

CLINTON JUNIOR COLLEGE
Rock Hill, South Carolina

Admissions Contact Dr. Janis Pen, President, Clinton Junior College, PO Box 968, 1029 Crawford Road, Rock Hill, SC 29730. *Phone:* 803-327-7402.

DENMARK TECHNICAL COLLEGE
Denmark, South Carolina

- **State-supported** 2-year, founded 1948, part of South Carolina State Board for Technical and Comprehensive Education
- **Calendar** semesters
- **Degree** certificates, diplomas, and associate
- **Rural** 53-acre campus
- **Coed**

Faculty *Student/faculty ratio:* 19:1.
Student Life *Campus security:* 24-hour patrols.
Standardized Tests *Required:* ACT ASSET (for placement).
Financial Aid Of all full-time matriculated undergraduates who enrolled, 250 Federal Work-Study jobs (averaging $2000).
Applying *Options:* early admission, deferred entrance. *Application fee:* $10. *Required:* high school transcript.
Admissions Contact Mrs. Michelle McDowell, Director of Admission and Records, Denmark Technical College, Solomon Blatt Boulevard, Box 327, Denmark, SC 29042-0327. *Phone:* 803-793-5176. *Fax:* 803-793-5942.

FLORENCE-DARLINGTON TECHNICAL COLLEGE
Florence, South Carolina

- **State-supported** 2-year, founded 1963, part of South Carolina State Board for Technical and Comprehensive Education
- **Calendar** semesters
- **Degree** certificates, diplomas, and associate
- **Small-town** 100-acre campus with easy access to Columbia
- **Endowment** $1000
- **Coed**

Faculty *Student/faculty ratio:* 17:1.
Student Life *Campus security:* 24-hour emergency response devices and patrols, late-night transport/escort service.
Standardized Tests *Required for some:* SAT I or ACT (for admission), CPT.
Costs (2003–04) *Tuition:* area resident $2370 full-time, $83 per credit hour part-time; state resident $2632 full-time, $94 per credit hour part-time; nonresident $4466 full-time, $170 per credit hour part-time. *Required fees:* $100 full-time, $50 per term part-time.
Financial Aid Of all full-time matriculated undergraduates who enrolled, 95 Federal Work-Study jobs (averaging $2500).
Applying *Options:* common application, deferred entrance. *Application fee:* $15. *Required for some:* high school transcript.
Admissions Contact Mr. Kevin Qualls, Director of Enrollment Services, Florence-Darlington Technical College, 2715 West Lucas Street, PO Box 100548, Florence, SC 29501-0548. *Phone:* 843-661-8153. *Toll-free phone:* 800-228-5745. *Fax:* 843-661-8041. *E-mail:* kirvenp@flo.tec.sc.us.

FORREST JUNIOR COLLEGE
Anderson, South Carolina

- **Proprietary** 2-year, founded 1946
- **Calendar** quarters

Forrest Junior College (continued)
- **Degree** certificates, diplomas, and associate
- **Small-town** 3-acre campus
- **Coed, primarily women,** 207 undergraduate students, 50% full-time, 92% women, 8% men

Undergraduates 103 full-time, 104 part-time. Students come from 2 states and territories, 26% are from out of state, 40% African American, 0.5% Hispanic American, 0.5% Native American.

Freshmen *Admission:* 26 applied, 23 admitted.

Faculty *Total:* 18, 22% full-time. *Student/faculty ratio:* 16:1.

Majors Business administration and management.

Academic Programs *Special study options:* accelerated degree program, advanced placement credit, cooperative education, distance learning, double majors, English as a second language, freshman honors college, internships, part-time degree program, summer session for credit.

Library Forrest Junior College Library plus 1 other with an OPAC.

Computers on Campus 37 computers available on campus for general student use. A campuswide network can be accessed from off campus. Internet access, online (class) registration, at least one staffed computer lab available.

Student Life *Housing:* college housing not available. *Campus security:* late-night transport/escort service. *Student services:* health clinic, legal services.

Costs (2003–04) *Tuition:* $8500 full-time, $110 per credit hour part-time.

Financial Aid Of all full-time matriculated undergraduates who enrolled, 13 Federal Work-Study jobs.

Applying *Options:* deferred entrance. *Application fee:* $25. *Required:* essay or personal statement, high school transcript, letters of recommendation, interview. *Application deadline:* 9/30 (freshmen).

Admissions Contact Ms. Janie Turmon, Admissions Representative, Forrest Junior College, 601 East River Street, Anderson, SC 29624. *Phone:* 864-225-7653 Ext. 206. *Fax:* 864-261-7471. *E-mail:* janieturmon@forrestcollege.com.

GREENVILLE TECHNICAL COLLEGE
Greenville, South Carolina

- **State-supported** 2-year, founded 1962, part of South Carolina State Board for Technical and Comprehensive Education
- **Calendar** semesters
- **Degree** certificates, diplomas, and associate
- **Urban** 407-acre campus
- **Coed**

Student Life *Campus security:* 24-hour emergency response devices and patrols, student patrols, late-night transport/escort service.

Standardized Tests *Recommended:* SAT I, ACT ASSET, or ACT COMPASS.

Financial Aid Of all full-time matriculated undergraduates who enrolled, 120 Federal Work-Study jobs (averaging $3270). *Financial aid deadline:* 5/1.

Applying *Options:* early admission, deferred entrance. *Application fee:* $25. *Required:* high school transcript.

Admissions Contact Ms. Martha S. White, Director of Admissions, Greenville Technical College, PO Box 5616, Greenville, SC 29606-5616. *Phone:* 864-250-8109. *Toll-free phone:* 800-922-1183 (in-state); 800-723-0673 (out-of-state). *Fax:* 864-250-8534.

HORRY-GEORGETOWN TECHNICAL COLLEGE
Conway, South Carolina

- **State and locally supported** 2-year, founded 1966, part of South Carolina State Board for Technical and Comprehensive Education
- **Calendar** semesters
- **Degree** certificates, diplomas, and associate
- **Small-town** campus
- **Endowment** $2.4 million
- **Coed**

Faculty *Student/faculty ratio:* 18:1.

Standardized Tests *Required:* CPT (for placement).

Costs (2004–05) *Tuition:* area resident $2496 full-time, $104 per credit hour part-time; state resident $3144 full-time, $131 per credit hour part-time; nonresident $4104 full-time, $171 per credit hour part-time. *Required fees:* $144 full-time, $3 per credit hour part-time, $35 per term part-time.

Applying *Options:* early admission. *Application fee:* $25. *Required for some:* high school transcript.

Admissions Contact Ms. Teresa Hilburn, Associate Vice President for Enrollment Development, Horry-Georgetown Technical College, 2050 Highway 501 East, PO Box 261966, Conway, SC 29528-6066. *Phone:* 843-349-5277. *Fax:* 843-234-2213. *E-mail:* jackson@hor.tec.sc.us.

ITT TECHNICAL INSTITUTE
Greenville, South Carolina

- **Proprietary** primarily 2-year, founded 1992, part of ITT Educational Services, Inc.
- **Calendar** quarters
- **Degrees** associate and bachelor's
- **Coed**

Standardized Tests *Required:* Wonderlic aptitude test (for admission).

Costs (2003–04) *Tuition:* Total Program Cost varies depending on course of study. Consult school catalog.

Financial Aid Of all full-time matriculated undergraduates who enrolled, 3 Federal Work-Study jobs.

Applying *Options:* deferred entrance. *Application fee:* $100. *Required:* high school transcript, interview. *Recommended:* letters of recommendation.

Admissions Contact Ms. Pamela Carpenter, Director of Recruitment, ITT Technical Institute, One Marcus Drive, Building 4, Suite 402, Greenville, SC 29615. *Phone:* 864-288-0777. *Toll-free phone:* 800-932-4488. *Fax:* 864-297-0930.

MIDLANDS TECHNICAL COLLEGE
Columbia, South Carolina

- **State and locally supported** 2-year, founded 1974, part of South Carolina State Board for Technical and Comprehensive Education
- **Calendar** semesters
- **Degree** certificates, diplomas, and associate
- **Suburban** 113-acre campus
- **Endowment** $2.1 million
- **Coed,** 10,925 undergraduate students, 44% full-time, 62% women, 38% men

Undergraduates 4,859 full-time, 6,066 part-time. Students come from 26 states and territories, 1% are from out of state, 36% African American, 1% Asian American or Pacific Islander, 2% Hispanic American, 1% Native American, 0.6% international.

Freshmen *Admission:* 2,070 admitted, 2,070 enrolled.

Faculty *Total:* 662, 32% full-time, 100% with terminal degrees. *Student/faculty ratio:* 20:1.

Majors Accounting; architectural engineering technology; automobile/automotive mechanics technology; business administration and management; business/commerce; child care provision; civil engineering technology; clinical/medical laboratory technology; commercial and advertising art; computer and information sciences and support services related; computer systems networking and telecommunications; construction engineering technology; data processing and data processing technology; dental assisting; dental hygiene; electrical, electronic and communications engineering technology; electrician; engineering technology; graphic and printing equipment operation/production; health information/medical records technology; heating, air conditioning, ventilation and refrigeration maintenance technology; industrial electronics technology; legal assistant/paralegal; liberal arts and sciences/liberal studies; mechanical drafting and CAD/CADD; mechanical engineering/mechanical technology; medical radiologic technology; multi-/interdisciplinary studies related; nuclear medical technology; nursing assistant/aide and patient care assistant; nursing (licensed practical/vocational nurse training); nursing (registered nurse training); occupational therapist assistant; pharmacy technician; physical therapist assistant; precision production related; respiratory care therapy; surgical technology.

Academic Programs *Special study options:* academic remediation for entering students, adult/continuing education programs, advanced placement credit, cooperative education, distance learning, double majors, English as a second language, internships, part-time degree program, services for LD students, student-designed majors, summer session for credit.

Library 77,000 titles, 509 serial subscriptions, 1,067 audiovisual materials, an OPAC.

Computers on Campus 125 computers available on campus for general student use. A campuswide network can be accessed from off campus. Internet access, online (class) registration, at least one staffed computer lab available.

Student Life *Housing:* college housing not available. *Activities and Organizations:* student-run newspaper. *Campus security:* 24-hour emergency response devices and patrols. *Student services:* personal/psychological counseling, women's center.

Athletics *Intramural sports:* basketball M, football M, softball M/W, volleyball M/W.

Standardized Tests *Required:* ACT ASSET (for admission). *Recommended:* SAT I or ACT (for admission).

Costs (2003–04) *Tuition:* area resident $2736 full-time, $114 per credit part-time; state resident $3420 full-time, $143 per credit part-time; nonresident $8208 full-time, $342 per credit part-time. *Required fees:* $100 full-time.

Financial Aid Of all full-time matriculated undergraduates who enrolled, 171 Federal Work-Study jobs (averaging $2079).

Applying *Options:* common application, early admission, deferred entrance. *Application fee:* $25. *Recommended:* high school transcript. *Application deadline:* rolling (freshmen), rolling (transfers). *Notification:* continuous (freshmen), continuous (transfers).

Admissions Contact Ms. Sylvia Littlejohn, Director of Admissions, Midlands Technical College, PO Box 2408, Columbia, SC 29202. *Phone:* 803-738-8324. *Fax:* 803-738-7840.

MILLER-MOTTE TECHNICAL COLLEGE
Charleston, South Carolina

- **Proprietary** 2-year, founded 2000
- **Calendar** quarters
- **Degree** diplomas
- **Urban** campus
- **Coed**

Costs (2003–04) *Tuition:* $2520 full-time.

Admissions Contact Ms. Julie Corner, Campus President, Miller-Motte Technical College, 8085 Rivers Avenue, Suite E, Charleston, SC 29418. *Phone:* 843-574-0101. *Toll-free phone:* 877-617-4740.

NORTHEASTERN TECHNICAL COLLEGE
Cheraw, South Carolina

- **State and locally supported** 2-year, founded 1967, part of South Carolina State Board for Technical and Comprehensive Education
- **Calendar** semesters
- **Degree** certificates, diplomas, and associate
- **Rural** 59-acre campus
- **Coed,** 1,098 undergraduate students, 52% full-time, 68% women, 32% men

Undergraduates 574 full-time, 524 part-time. Students come from 2 states and territories, 1% are from out of state, 42% African American, 0.4% Asian American or Pacific Islander, 0.4% Hispanic American, 2% Native American, 4% transferred in.

Freshmen *Admission:* 291 enrolled.

Faculty *Total:* 103, 27% full-time, 3% with terminal degrees. *Student/faculty ratio:* 25:1.

Majors Accounting; administrative assistant and secretarial science; business administration and management; computer programming; computer science; data processing and data processing technology; electrical, electronic and communications engineering technology; liberal arts and sciences/liberal studies; machine tool technology; marketing/marketing management; mechanical design technology.

Academic Programs *Special study options:* academic remediation for entering students, adult/continuing education programs, advanced placement credit, part-time degree program, summer session for credit.

Library Northeastern Technical College Library with 20,502 titles, 261 serial subscriptions, 690 audiovisual materials, an OPAC, a Web page.

Computers on Campus 125 computers available on campus for general student use. A campuswide network can be accessed from off campus. Internet access, at least one staffed computer lab available.

Student Life *Housing:* college housing not available. *Campus security:* 24-hour emergency response devices. *Student services:* personal/psychological counseling.

Standardized Tests *Required for some:* SAT I (for admission).

Costs (2004–05) *Tuition:* area resident $2346 full-time, $98 per hour part-time; state resident $2448 full-time, $102 per hour part-time; nonresident $3936 full-time, $164 per hour part-time. *Required fees:* $100 full-time, $4 per hour part-time.

Financial Aid Of all full-time matriculated undergraduates who enrolled, 25 Federal Work-Study jobs (averaging $2700).

Applying *Options:* early admission. *Required:* high school transcript, interview. *Application deadline:* rolling (transfers).

Admissions Contact Mrs. Mary K. Newton, Dean of Students, Northeastern Technical College, PO Drawer 1007, Cheraw, SC 29520-1007. *Phone:* 843-921-6935. *Fax:* 843-537-6148. *E-mail:* mpace@netc.edu.

ORANGEBURG-CALHOUN TECHNICAL COLLEGE
Orangeburg, South Carolina

- **State and locally supported** 2-year, founded 1968, part of State Board for Technical and Comprehensive Education, South Carolina
- **Calendar** semesters
- **Degree** certificates, diplomas, and associate

- **Small-town** 100-acre campus with easy access to Columbia
- **Endowment** $2.5 million
- **Coed,** 2,491 undergraduate students, 55% full-time, 72% women, 28% men

Undergraduates 1,380 full-time, 1,111 part-time. Students come from 5 states and territories, 1% are from out of state, 58% African American, 0.5% Asian American or Pacific Islander, 0.3% Hispanic American, 0.6% Native American, 4% transferred in.

Freshmen *Admission:* 640 enrolled.

Faculty *Total:* 129, 60% full-time, 2% with terminal degrees.

Majors Accounting; administrative assistant and secretarial science; automobile/automotive mechanics technology; business/commerce; clinical/medical laboratory technology; computer programming related; criminal justice/safety; electrical, electronic and communications engineering technology; instrumentation technology; kindergarten/preschool education; legal assistant/paralegal; liberal arts and sciences/liberal studies; machine tool technology; medical radiologic technology; nursing (registered nurse training); respiratory care therapy.

Academic Programs *Special study options:* academic remediation for entering students, adult/continuing education programs, advanced placement credit, cooperative education, distance learning, independent study, internships, part-time degree program, services for LD students, student-designed majors, summer session for credit.

Library Gressette Learning Center with 43,500 titles, 143 serial subscriptions, 2,253 audiovisual materials, an OPAC.

Computers on Campus 361 computers available on campus for general student use. A campuswide network can be accessed from off campus. Internet access available.

Student Life *Housing:* college housing not available. *Activities and Organizations:* Student Advisory Council. *Campus security:* 24-hour emergency response devices and patrols. *Student services:* personal/psychological counseling.

Standardized Tests *Required for some:* ACT ASSET. *Recommended:* SAT I and SAT II or ACT (for placement).

Costs (2003–04) *Tuition:* area resident $2496 full-time; state resident $3096 full-time; nonresident $4464 full-time. *Required fees:* $96 full-time.

Applying *Options:* common application, early admission. *Application fee:* $15. *Required:* high school transcript. *Required for some:* interview. *Application deadline:* rolling (freshmen), rolling (transfers). *Notification:* continuous (freshmen), continuous (transfers).

Admissions Contact Dana Rickards, Director of Recruitment, Orangeburg-Calhoun Technical College, 3250 St. Matthews Road, Highway 601, Orangeburg, SC 29118. *Phone:* 803-535-1219. *Toll-free phone:* 800-813-6519. *Fax:* 803-535-1388. *E-mail:* rickardsd@octech.edu.

PIEDMONT TECHNICAL COLLEGE
Greenwood, South Carolina

Admissions Contact Mr. Steve Coleman, Director of Admissions, Piedmont Technical College, PO Box 1467, Emerald Road, Greenwood, SC 29648. *Phone:* 864-941-8603. *Toll-free phone:* 800-868-5528. *E-mail:* coleman_s@piedmont.tec.sc.us.

SOUTH UNIVERSITY
Columbia, South Carolina

- **Proprietary** primarily 2-year, founded 1935
- **Calendar** quarters
- **Degrees** certificates, associate, and bachelor's
- **Urban** 2-acre campus
- **Coed,** 318 undergraduate students, 80% full-time, 84% women, 16% men

Undergraduates 254 full-time, 64 part-time. Students come from 1 other state, 71% African American, 0.9% Asian American or Pacific Islander, 0.9% Hispanic American, 2% transferred in.

Freshmen *Admission:* 58 applied, 41 admitted, 28 enrolled. *Average high school GPA:* 2.8.

Faculty *Total:* 32, 34% full-time, 34% with terminal degrees. *Student/faculty ratio:* 15:1.

Majors Accounting; business administration and management; information technology; legal assistant/paralegal; legal studies; medical/clinical assistant.

Academic Programs *Special study options:* academic remediation for entering students, accelerated degree program, adult/continuing education programs, advanced placement credit, cooperative education, double majors, internships, part-time degree program, services for LD students, summer session for credit.

Library 10,500 titles, 100 serial subscriptions, 200 audiovisual materials.

Computers on Campus 40 computers available on campus for general student use. A campuswide network can be accessed. Internet access available.

Student Life *Housing:* college housing not available. *Campus security:* 24-hour emergency response devices. *Student services:* personal/psychological counseling.

South University (continued)

Standardized Tests *Required:* SAT I or ACT (for admission).

Costs (2003–04) *Tuition:* $10,185 full-time. *Waivers:* employees or children of employees.

Applying *Options:* deferred entrance. *Application fee:* $25. *Required:* high school transcript, interview, admissions test. *Application deadline:* rolling (freshmen), rolling (transfers). *Notification:* continuous (transfers).

Admissions Contact South University, 3810 Main Street, Columbia, SC 29203-6443. *Phone:* 803-799-9082. *Toll-free phone:* 866-629-3031. *Fax:* 803-799-9038.

SPARTANBURG METHODIST COLLEGE
Spartanburg, South Carolina

- **Independent Methodist** 2-year, founded 1911
- **Calendar** semesters
- **Degree** diplomas and associate
- **Urban** 111-acre campus with easy access to Charlotte, NC
- **Endowment** $13.0 million
- **Coed,** 732 undergraduate students, 95% full-time, 46% women, 54% men

Spartanburg Methodist College (SMC) is the only private, 2-year, residential, liberal arts, coeducational college in South Carolina. Located in the college town of Spartanburg, South Carolina, and affiliated with the United Methodist Church, the College offers the Associate in Arts, the Associate in Science, and the Associate in Criminal Justice degrees. SMC offers a caring, nurturing environment that promotes success, with more than 90 percent of its graduates continuing their education at some of the finest colleges and universities in the nation.

Undergraduates 694 full-time, 38 part-time. Students come from 11 states and territories, 7 other countries, 8% are from out of state, 32% African American, 0.8% Asian American or Pacific Islander, 2% Hispanic American, 0.4% Native American, 3% international, 6% transferred in, 75% live on campus. *Retention:* 74% of 2002 full-time freshmen returned.

Freshmen *Admission:* 1,111 applied, 858 admitted, 414 enrolled. *Average high school GPA:* 3.02. *Test scores:* SAT verbal scores over 500: 17%; SAT math scores over 500: 18%; ACT scores over 18: 35%; SAT verbal scores over 600: 3%; SAT math scores over 600: 3%; ACT scores over 24: 2%; SAT verbal scores over 700: 1%; ACT scores over 30: 1%.

Faculty *Total:* 47, 45% full-time, 21% with terminal degrees. *Student/faculty ratio:* 18:1.

Majors Administrative assistant and secretarial science; criminal justice/law enforcement administration; information technology; liberal arts and sciences/liberal studies.

Academic Programs *Special study options:* academic remediation for entering students, advanced placement credit, English as a second language, honors programs, independent study, part-time degree program, services for LD students, summer session for credit. *ROTC:* Army (c).

Library Marie Blair Burgess Learning Resource Center with 75,000 titles, 5,000 serial subscriptions, 3,150 audiovisual materials, an OPAC, a Web page.

Computers on Campus 72 computers available on campus for general student use. A campuswide network can be accessed from student residence rooms and from off campus. Internet access, at least one staffed computer lab available.

Student Life *Housing:* on-campus residence required through sophomore year. *Options:* coed, men-only, women-only. Campus housing is university owned. *Activities and Organizations:* drama/theater group, student-run newspaper, choral group, College Christian Movement, Alpha Phi Omega, Campus Union, Fellowship of Christian Athletes, Kappa Sigma Alpha. *Campus security:* 24-hour emergency response devices and patrols, student patrols, late-night transport/escort service, controlled dormitory access. *Student services:* health clinic, personal/psychological counseling.

Athletics Member NJCAA. *Intercollegiate sports:* baseball M(s), basketball M(s)/W(s), cheerleading M(s)/W(s), cross-country running M(s)/W(s), golf M(s)/W(s), soccer M(s)/W(s), softball W(s), tennis M(s)/W(s), volleyball W(s), wrestling M(s). *Intramural sports:* basketball M/W, football M/W, golf M/W, racquetball M/W, soccer M/W, softball M/W, table tennis M/W, tennis M/W, volleyball M/W.

Standardized Tests *Required:* SAT I or ACT (for admission).

Costs (2004–05) *Comprehensive fee:* $14,464 includes full-time tuition ($9322), mandatory fees ($150), and room and board ($4992). Part-time tuition: $247 per credit. *Room and board:* college room only: $2566. Room and board charges vary according to housing facility. *Payment plan:* installment. *Waivers:* employees or children of employees.

Financial Aid Of all full-time matriculated undergraduates who enrolled, 80 Federal Work-Study jobs (averaging $1600). 90 state and other part-time jobs (averaging $1600). *Financial aid deadline:* 8/25.

Applying *Options:* common application, electronic application, deferred entrance. *Application fee:* $20. *Required:* high school transcript, minimum 2.0 GPA, rank in top 75% of high school class. *Required for some:* essay or personal statement, letters of recommendation, interview. *Recommended:* interview. *Application deadline:* rolling (freshmen), rolling (transfers). *Notification:* continuous (freshmen), continuous (transfers).

Admissions Contact Mr. Daniel L. Philbeck, Dean of Admissions and Financial Aid, Spartanburg Methodist College, 1200 Textile Road, Spartanburg, SC 29301-0009. *Phone:* 864-587-4223. *Toll-free phone:* 800-772-7286. *Fax:* 864-587-4355. *E-mail:* admiss@smcsc.edu.

▶ See page 602 for a narrative description.

SPARTANBURG TECHNICAL COLLEGE
Spartanburg, South Carolina

- **State-supported** 2-year, founded 1961, part of South Carolina State Board for Technical and Comprehensive Education
- **Calendar** semesters plus summer sessions
- **Degree** certificates, diplomas, and associate
- **Suburban** 104-acre campus
- **Coed,** 4,123 undergraduate students, 53% full-time, 63% women, 37% men

Undergraduates 2,166 full-time, 1,957 part-time. 2% are from out of state, 29% African American, 2% Asian American or Pacific Islander, 1% Hispanic American, 0.4% Native American.

Faculty *Total:* 100.

Majors Accounting; administrative assistant and secretarial science; architectural engineering technology; automobile/automotive mechanics technology; biological and physical sciences; business administration and management; civil engineering technology; clinical/medical laboratory technology; computer and information sciences; drafting and design technology; electrical, electronic and communications engineering technology; engineering technology; heating, air conditioning, ventilation and refrigeration maintenance technology; horticultural science; liberal arts and sciences/liberal studies; machine tool technology; marketing/marketing management; mechanical engineering/mechanical technology; medical administrative assistant and medical secretary; medical radiologic technology; respiratory care therapy; robotics technology; sign language interpretation and translation; trade and industrial teacher education.

Academic Programs *Special study options:* academic remediation for entering students, adult/continuing education programs, advanced placement credit, cooperative education, part-time degree program, services for LD students, summer session for credit.

Library Spartanburg Technical College Library with 36,000 titles, 400 serial subscriptions, an OPAC, a Web page.

Computers on Campus 360 computers available on campus for general student use. A campuswide network can be accessed from off campus. At least one staffed computer lab available.

Student Life *Housing:* college housing not available. *Activities and Organizations:* drama/theater group, student-run newspaper. *Campus security:* 24-hour patrols. *Student services:* personal/psychological counseling, women's center.

Standardized Tests *Required:* ACT ASSET, ACT COMPASS (for placement).

Costs (2004–05) *Tuition:* area resident $2616 full-time, $109 per hour part-time; state resident $3270 full-time, $137 per hour part-time; nonresident $5180 full-time, $216 per hour part-time. *Required fees:* $140 full-time, $5 per hour part-time, $20 per term part-time.

Financial Aid Of all full-time matriculated undergraduates who enrolled, 70 Federal Work-Study jobs (averaging $2600).

Applying *Options:* early admission. *Required:* high school transcript. *Application deadline:* rolling (freshmen), rolling (transfers). *Notification:* continuous (freshmen), continuous (transfers).

Admissions Contact Ms. Celia Bauss, Dean of Enrollment Management, Spartanburg Technical College, PO Box 4386, Spartanburg, SC 29305. *Phone:* 864-591-3800. *Toll-free phone:* 800-922-3679. *Fax:* 864-591-3916.

TECHNICAL COLLEGE OF THE LOWCOUNTRY
Beaufort, South Carolina

Admissions Contact Mr. Les Brediger, Director of Admissions, Technical College of the Lowcountry, 921 Ribaut Road, PO Box 1288, Beaufort, SC 29901-1288. *Phone:* 843-525-8307.

TRI-COUNTY TECHNICAL COLLEGE
Pendleton, South Carolina

- **State-supported** 2-year, founded 1962, part of South Carolina State Board for Technical and Comprehensive Education
- **Calendar** semesters
- **Degree** certificates, diplomas, and associate

- **Rural** 100-acre campus
- **Coed**

Faculty *Student/faculty ratio:* 25:1.
Student Life *Campus security:* 24-hour emergency response devices and patrols.
Standardized Tests *Required for some:* SAT I (for placement), National League of Nursing Exam.
Applying *Options:* early admission.
Admissions Contact Ms. Rachel Campbell, Director, Admission and Counseling, Tri-County Technical College, PO Box 587, Highway 76, Pendleton, SC 29670-0587. *Phone:* 864-646-1500. *Fax:* 864-646-8256. *E-mail:* admstaff@ tricty.tricounty.tec.sc.us.

TRIDENT TECHNICAL COLLEGE
Charleston, South Carolina

- **State and locally supported** 2-year, founded 1964, part of South Carolina State Board for Technical and Comprehensive Education
- **Calendar** semesters
- **Degree** certificates, diplomas, and associate
- **Urban** campus
- **Coed,** 11,791 undergraduate students, 44% full-time, 63% women, 37% men

Undergraduates 5,167 full-time, 6,624 part-time. 1% are from out of state, 29% African American, 2% Asian American or Pacific Islander, 2% Hispanic American, 0.6% Native American.
Freshmen *Admission:* 2,099 enrolled.
Faculty *Total:* 607, 42% full-time.
Majors Accounting; administrative assistant and secretarial science; airframe mechanics and aircraft maintenance technology; automobile/automotive mechanics technology; biological and physical sciences; broadcast journalism; business administration and management; child care provision; civil engineering technology; clinical/medical laboratory technology; commercial and advertising art; computer engineering technology; computer graphics; computer/information technology services administration related; computer programming (specific applications); computer systems networking and telecommunications; criminal justice/law enforcement administration; culinary arts; dental hygiene; electrical, electronic and communications engineering technology; engineering technology; horticultural science; hotel/motel administration; human services; industrial technology; legal assistant/paralegal; legal studies; liberal arts and sciences/ liberal studies; machine tool technology; marketing/marketing management; mechanical engineering/mechanical technology; medical administrative assistant and medical secretary; nursing (registered nurse training); occupational therapy; physical therapy; respiratory care therapy; telecommunications; veterinary technology; web/multimedia management and webmaster; web page, digital/multimedia and information resources design.
Academic Programs *Special study options:* academic remediation for entering students, advanced placement credit, cooperative education, English as a second language, part-time degree program, services for LD students, summer session for credit.
Library Learning Resources Center plus 3 others with 68,462 titles, 868 serial subscriptions.
Computers on Campus 500 computers available on campus for general student use. A campuswide network can be accessed. At least one staffed computer lab available. Computer purchase or lease plan available.
Student Life *Housing:* college housing not available. *Activities and Organizations:* student-run newspaper. *Campus security:* 24-hour emergency response devices and patrols, late-night transport/escort service. *Student services:* personal/ psychological counseling.
Standardized Tests *Required:* SAT I, ACT, or in-house test (for placement).
Costs (2004–05) *Tuition:* area resident $2688 full-time, $109 per credit hour part-time; state resident $2984 full-time, $121 per credit hour part-time; nonresident $5274 full-time, $216 per credit hour part-time. Full-time tuition and fees vary according to course load. Part-time tuition and fees vary according to course load. *Required fees:* $50 full-time, $5 per credit hour part-time. *Waivers:* senior citizens.
Financial Aid Of all full-time matriculated undergraduates who enrolled, 117 Federal Work-Study jobs (averaging $3000).
Applying *Options:* common application, early admission. *Application fee:* $25. *Required for some:* high school transcript. *Application deadlines:* 8/4 (freshmen), 8/4 (transfers). *Notification:* continuous (freshmen), continuous (transfers).
Admissions Contact Ms. Mary Stewart, Admissions Director, Trident Technical College, 7000 Rivers Avenue, Charleston, SC 29423-8067. *Phone:* 843-574-6383.

UNIVERSITY OF SOUTH CAROLINA LANCASTER
Lancaster, South Carolina

Admissions Contact Ms. Rebecca D. Parker, Director of Admissions, University of South Carolina Lancaster, PO Box 889, Lancaster, SC 29721-0889. *Phone:* 803-313-7000. *E-mail:* bparker@gwm.sc.edu.

UNIVERSITY OF SOUTH CAROLINA SALKEHATCHIE
Allendale, South Carolina

- **State-supported** 2-year, founded 1965, part of University of South Carolina System
- **Calendar** semesters
- **Degree** associate
- **Rural** 95-acre campus
- **Coed,** 777 undergraduate students, 36% full-time, 75% women, 25% men

Undergraduates 283 full-time, 494 part-time. Students come from 3 states and territories, 1% are from out of state, 41% African American.
Freshmen *Average high school GPA:* 2.50. *Test scores:* SAT verbal scores over 500: 1%; SAT math scores over 500: 1%.
Faculty *Total:* 38, 47% full-time, 45% with terminal degrees.
Majors Biological and physical sciences; liberal arts and sciences/liberal studies; mathematics.
Academic Programs *Special study options:* academic remediation for entering students, accelerated degree program, adult/continuing education programs, advanced placement credit, internships, part-time degree program, services for LD students, student-designed majors, summer session for credit. *ROTC:* Army (c), Navy (c), Air Force (c).
Library Salkehatchie Learning Resource Center with 47,877 titles, 832 audiovisual materials, an OPAC, a Web page.
Computers on Campus 70 computers available on campus for general student use. Internet access, at least one staffed computer lab available.
Student Life *Housing:* college housing not available. *Activities and Organizations:* student-run newspaper. *Campus security:* 24-hour emergency response devices.
Athletics Member NJCAA. *Intercollegiate sports:* baseball M, golf M. *Intramural sports:* basketball M/W, football M/W, tennis M/W, volleyball M/W.
Standardized Tests *Required:* SAT I or ACT (for admission).
Costs (2003–04) *Tuition:* state resident $3456 full-time, $144 per semester hour part-time; nonresident $8554 full-time, $356 per semester hour part-time. *Required fees:* $200 full-time, $8 per semester hour part-time.
Financial Aid Of all full-time matriculated undergraduates who enrolled, 53 Federal Work-Study jobs (averaging $2500). 68 state and other part-time jobs.
Applying *Required:* high school transcript, minimum 2.0 GPA. *Application deadline:* rolling (freshmen), rolling (transfers).
Admissions Contact Ms. Jane T. Brewer, Associate Dean for Student Services, University of South Carolina Salkehatchie, PO Box 617, Allendale, SC 29810-0617. *Phone:* 803-584-3446. *Toll-free phone:* 800-922-5500.

UNIVERSITY OF SOUTH CAROLINA SUMTER
Sumter, South Carolina

- **State-supported** 2-year, founded 1966, part of University of South Carolina System
- **Calendar** semesters
- **Degree** associate
- **Urban** 50-acre campus
- **Endowment** $1.7 million
- **Coed,** 1,184 undergraduate students, 48% full-time, 63% women, 37% men

Undergraduates 571 full-time, 613 part-time. Students come from 2 states and territories, 9 other countries, 1% are from out of state, 24% African American, 2% Asian American or Pacific Islander, 4% Hispanic American, 0.4% Native American, 0.7% international, 8% transferred in. *Retention:* 58% of 2002 full-time freshmen returned.
Freshmen *Admission:* 381 applied, 199 enrolled. *Average high school GPA:* 3.07. *Test scores:* SAT verbal scores over 500: 43%; SAT math scores over 500: 43%; ACT scores over 18: 61%; SAT verbal scores over 600: 1%; SAT math scores over 600: 1%; ACT scores over 24: 8%.
Faculty *Total:* 68, 59% full-time, 59% with terminal degrees. *Student/faculty ratio:* 18:1.
Majors Interdisciplinary studies; liberal arts and sciences/liberal studies.

University of South Carolina Sumter (continued)

Academic Programs *Special study options:* adult/continuing education programs, advanced placement credit, distance learning, English as a second language, freshman honors college, honors programs, independent study, off-campus study, part-time degree program, services for LD students, summer session for credit. *ROTC:* Army (c), Air Force (c).

Library University of South Carolina at Sumter Library with 51,666 titles, 2,130 serial subscriptions, 649 audiovisual materials, an OPAC, a Web page.

Computers on Campus 305 computers available on campus for general student use. A campuswide network can be accessed from off campus. Internet access, online (class) registration, at least one staffed computer lab available.

Student Life *Housing:* college housing not available. *Activities and Organizations:* drama/theater group, choral group, Association of African-American Students, Baptist Student Union, Student Education Association, Gamecock Ambassadors, Environmental Club. *Campus security:* late-night transport/escort service. *Student services:* personal/psychological counseling.

Athletics Member NSCAA. *Intramural sports:* badminton M/W, basketball M/W, bowling M/W, football M, gymnastics M/W, racquetball M/W, rock climbing M/W, soccer M, softball M/W, table tennis M/W, volleyball M/W.

Standardized Tests *Required:* SAT I or ACT (for admission).

Costs (2003–04) *Tuition:* state resident $3456 full-time; nonresident $8554 full-time. *Required fees:* $200 full-time. *Waivers:* senior citizens.

Financial Aid Of all full-time matriculated undergraduates who enrolled, 47 Federal Work-Study jobs (averaging $1337).

Applying *Options:* electronic application. *Application fee:* $40. *Required:* high school transcript, minimum 2.0 GPA. *Application deadline:* 8/8 (freshmen), rolling (transfers).

Admissions Contact Dr. Robert Ferrell, Director of Admissions, University of South Carolina Sumter, 200 Miller Road, Sumter, SC 29150-2498. *Phone:* 803-938-3762. *Fax:* 803-938-3901. *E-mail:* bobf@usc.sumter.edu.

UNIVERSITY OF SOUTH CAROLINA UNION
Union, South Carolina

- **State-supported** 2-year, founded 1965, part of University of South Carolina System
- **Calendar** semesters
- **Degree** associate
- **Small-town** campus with easy access to Charlotte
- **Coed,** 313 undergraduate students, 21% full-time, 66% women, 34% men

Undergraduates 67 full-time, 246 part-time. Students come from 2 states and territories, 16% African American, 0.3% Asian American or Pacific Islander, 0.6% Native American.

Freshmen *Admission:* 235 applied, 225 admitted. *Test scores:* SAT verbal scores over 500: 15%; SAT math scores over 500: 18%.

Faculty *Total:* 25, 52% full-time. *Student/faculty ratio:* 14:1.

Majors Biological and physical sciences; liberal arts and sciences/liberal studies.

Academic Programs *Special study options:* part-time degree program.

Computers on Campus 30 computers available on campus for general student use. A campuswide network can be accessed from off campus.

Student Life *Housing:* college housing not available. *Activities and Organizations:* drama/theater group, student-run newspaper, choral group.

Standardized Tests *Required:* SAT I or ACT (for admission).

Costs (2003–04) *Tuition:* state resident $3456 full-time; nonresident $8554 full-time. *Required fees:* $200 full-time.

Financial Aid Of all full-time matriculated undergraduates who enrolled, 16 Federal Work-Study jobs (averaging $3400).

Applying *Application fee:* $40. *Required:* high school transcript. *Application deadline:* rolling (freshmen).

Admissions Contact Mr. Terry E. Young, Director of Enrollment Services, University of South Carolina Union, PO Drawer 729, Union, SC 29379-0729. *Phone:* 864-429-8728.

WILLIAMSBURG TECHNICAL COLLEGE
Kingstree, South Carolina

- **State-supported** 2-year, founded 1969, part of South Carolina State Board for Technical and Comprehensive Education
- **Calendar** semesters
- **Degree** certificates, diplomas, and associate
- **Rural** 41-acre campus
- **Endowment** $52,987
- **Coed, primarily women,** 595 undergraduate students, 45% full-time, 73% women, 27% men

Undergraduates 269 full-time, 326 part-time. Students come from 1 other state, 71% African American, 0.3% Asian American or Pacific Islander, 0.2% Hispanic American.

Freshmen *Admission:* 140 admitted.

Faculty *Total:* 48, 29% full-time, 13% with terminal degrees. *Student/faculty ratio:* 13:1.

Majors Administrative assistant and secretarial science; business/commerce; computer management; computer programming (specific applications); data entry/microcomputer applications; drafting and design technology; heating, air conditioning, ventilation and refrigeration maintenance technology; information technology; liberal arts and sciences/liberal studies.

Academic Programs *Special study options:* academic remediation for entering students, adult/continuing education programs, advanced placement credit, cooperative education, distance learning, independent study, internships, part-time degree program, services for LD students, summer session for credit.

Library Learning Resource Center with 25,456 titles, 109 serial subscriptions, 3,601 audiovisual materials, an OPAC.

Computers on Campus 100 computers available on campus for general student use. A campuswide network can be accessed. Internet access, at least one staffed computer lab available.

Student Life *Housing:* college housing not available. *Activities and Organizations:* Student Government Association, National Vocational-Technical Honor Society, Phi Theta Kappa International Honor Society, Computer Club, national fraternities. *Campus security:* late-night transport/escort service. *Student services:* personal/psychological counseling.

Standardized Tests *Required:* ACT ASSET, ACT COMPASS (for placement). *Recommended:* SAT I or ACT (for placement).

Costs (2004–05) *Tuition:* state resident $2550 full-time, $106 per credit hour part-time; nonresident $4848 full-time, $202 per credit hour part-time. *Required fees:* $4 per credit hour part-time, $10 per term part-time.

Financial Aid Of all full-time matriculated undergraduates who enrolled, 22 Federal Work-Study jobs (averaging $2800).

Applying *Options:* common application, early admission, deferred entrance. *Application fee:* $10. *Required:* high school transcript. *Application deadline:* rolling (freshmen), rolling (transfers). *Notification:* continuous (freshmen), continuous (transfers).

Admissions Contact Ms. Elaine M. Hanna, Director of Admissions, Williamsburg Technical College, 601 Martin Luther King, Jr. Avenue, Kingstree, SC 29556-4197. *Phone:* 843-355-4110 Ext. 4162. *Toll-free phone:* 800-768-2021 Ext. 4162. *Fax:* 843-355-4269. *E-mail:* admissions@wil.tec.sc.us.

YORK TECHNICAL COLLEGE
Rock Hill, South Carolina

- **State-supported** 2-year, founded 1961, part of South Carolina State Board for Technical and Comprehensive Education
- **Calendar** semesters
- **Degree** certificates, diplomas, and associate
- **Small-town** 110-acre campus with easy access to Charlotte
- **Coed,** 4,171 undergraduate students, 49% full-time, 65% women, 35% men

Undergraduates 2,027 full-time, 2,144 part-time. 26% African American, 0.9% Asian American or Pacific Islander, 1% Hispanic American, 2% Native American, 0.1% international.

Freshmen *Admission:* 827 enrolled.

Faculty *Total:* 218, 44% full-time.

Majors Accounting; automobile/automotive mechanics technology; business administration and management; child care and support services management; child care provision; clinical/medical laboratory technology; computer engineering related; computer engineering technology; computer/information technology services administration related; data processing and data processing technology; dental hygiene; drafting and design technology; electrical, electronic and communications engineering technology; electrical/electronics equipment installation and repair; engineering technology; forestry technology; industrial electronics technology; industrial mechanics and maintenance technology; liberal arts and sciences/liberal studies; machine tool technology; mechanical drafting and CAD/CADD; mechanical engineering/mechanical technology; medical radiologic technology; nursing (registered nurse training).

Academic Programs *Special study options:* academic remediation for entering students, adult/continuing education programs, advanced placement credit, cooperative education, distance learning, English as a second language, honors programs, internships, off-campus study, part-time degree program, services for LD students, summer session for credit.

Library Anne Springs Close Library with 26,947 titles, 475 serial subscriptions, 1,813 audiovisual materials, an OPAC, a Web page.

Computers on Campus 250 computers available on campus for general student use. A campuswide network can be accessed from off campus that provide access to grades, course search, account detail, placement test scores. Internet access, online (class) registration, at least one staffed computer lab available.

Student Life *Housing:* college housing not available. *Activities and Organizations:* Jacobin Society, Phi Theta Kappa, Student Government Association, Phi Beta Lambda, Student Activities Board. *Campus security:* 24-hour patrols. *Student services:* personal/psychological counseling.

Standardized Tests *Required:* SAT I, ACT, or ACT ASSET, ACT COMPASS (for admission).

Costs (2004–05) *Tuition:* area resident $2600 full-time, $109 per credit part-time; state resident $2928 full-time, $122 per credit part-time; nonresident $5880 full-time, $245 per credit part-time. *Required fees:* $136 full-time, $4 per credit part-time, $20 per term part-time. *Payment plan:* installment. *Waivers:* senior citizens.

Financial Aid Of all full-time matriculated undergraduates who enrolled, 56 Federal Work-Study jobs (averaging $3500).

Applying *Options:* electronic application. *Required for some:* high school transcript. *Application deadline:* rolling (freshmen), rolling (transfers). *Notification:* continuous (freshmen), continuous (transfers).

Admissions Contact Mr. Kenny Aldridge, Admissions Department Manager, York Technical College, 452 South Anderson Road, Rock Hill, SC 29730. *Phone:* 803-327-8008. *Toll-free phone:* 800-922-8324. *Fax:* 803-981-7237. *E-mail:* kaldridge@yorktech.com.

SOUTH DAKOTA

KILIAN COMMUNITY COLLEGE
Sioux Falls, South Dakota

- **Independent** 2-year, founded 1977
- **Calendar** trimesters
- **Degree** certificates and associate
- **Urban** 2-acre campus
- **Endowment** $1587
- **Coed,** 444 undergraduate students

Undergraduates Students come from 3 states and territories, 6% are from out of state.

Freshmen *Admission:* 245 applied, 188 admitted.

Faculty *Total:* 71, 8% full-time. *Student/faculty ratio:* 8:1.

Majors Accounting; administrative assistant and secretarial science; business administration and management; computer science; computer software and media applications related; counseling psychology; criminal justice/law enforcement administration; information technology; liberal arts and sciences/liberal studies; medical insurance coding; medical office management; medical transcription; social work.

Academic Programs *Special study options:* academic remediation for entering students, cooperative education, double majors, independent study, internships, part-time degree program, services for LD students, summer session for credit.

Library University of Sioux Falls Mears Library with 78,000 titles, 395 serial subscriptions, an OPAC, a Web page.

Computers on Campus 37 computers available on campus for general student use. A campuswide network can be accessed. Internet access, at least one staffed computer lab available.

Student Life *Housing:* college housing not available. *Campus security:* late-night transport/escort service.

Standardized Tests *Required for some:* ACT ASSET.

Costs (2004–05) *Tuition:* $6660 full-time, $185 per credit part-time. *Required fees:* $150 full-time.

Financial Aid Of all full-time matriculated undergraduates who enrolled, 31 Federal Work-Study jobs (averaging $1200).

Applying *Options:* early admission, deferred entrance. *Application fee:* $25. *Required:* high school transcript. *Application deadline:* rolling (freshmen), rolling (transfers).

Admissions Contact Ms. Jacque Danielson, Director of Admissions, Kilian Community College, 224 North Phillips Avenue, Sioux Falls, SD 57104-6014. *Phone:* 605-221-3100. *Toll-free phone:* 800-888-1147. *Fax:* 605-336-2606. *E-mail:* info@kilian.edu.

LAKE AREA TECHNICAL INSTITUTE
Watertown, South Dakota

- **State-supported** 2-year, founded 1964
- **Calendar** semesters
- **Degree** diplomas and associate
- **Small-town** 16-acre campus
- **Coed,** 1,057 undergraduate students

Freshmen *Admission:* 549 admitted.

Faculty *Total:* 65. *Student/faculty ratio:* 15:1.

Majors Accounting; agricultural business and management; automobile/automotive mechanics technology; avionics maintenance technology; biology/biotechnology laboratory technician; carpentry; clinical/medical laboratory technology; computer programming; computer programming related; computer programming (specific applications); computer systems networking and telecommunications; cosmetology; data entry/microcomputer applications related; dental assisting; drafting and design technology; electrical, electronic and communications engineering technology; finance; information technology; machine tool technology; marketing/marketing management; medical/clinical assistant; nursing (licensed practical/vocational nurse training); occupational therapist assistant; physical therapist assistant; system administration; web/multimedia management and webmaster; welding technology.

Academic Programs *Special study options:* academic remediation for entering students, internships, services for LD students.

Library Leonard H. Timmerman Library plus 1 other with 5,000 titles, 128 serial subscriptions.

Computers on Campus 650 computers available on campus for general student use. A campuswide network can be accessed from off campus. Internet access, online (class) registration, at least one staffed computer lab available.

Student Life *Housing:* college housing not available. *Activities and Organizations:* PBL, VICA, Rodeo Club.

Athletics *Intramural sports:* basketball M/W, softball M/W, volleyball M/W.

Standardized Tests *Required:* ACT (for admission).

Costs (2004–05) *Tuition:* Full-time tuition and fees vary according to program. tuition varies by program. *Payment plan:* installment.

Financial Aid Of all full-time matriculated undergraduates who enrolled, 100 Federal Work-Study jobs (averaging $1200).

Applying *Options:* electronic application. *Application fee:* $15. *Required:* high school transcript. *Required for some:* essay or personal statement, 3 letters of recommendation, interview.

Admissions Contact Ms. Debra Shephard, Assistant Director, Lake Area Technical Institute, 230 11th Street Northeast, Watertown, SD 57201. *Phone:* 605-882-5284. *Toll-free phone:* 800-657-4344. *E-mail:* latiinfo@lati.tec.sd.us.

MITCHELL TECHNICAL INSTITUTE
Mitchell, South Dakota

- **District-supported** 2-year, founded 1968
- **Calendar** semesters
- **Degree** diplomas and associate
- **Rural** 90-acre campus
- **Coed,** 832 undergraduate students, 86% full-time, 31% women, 69% men

Undergraduates 712 full-time, 120 part-time. Students come from 18 states and territories, 2 other countries, 0.7% Asian American or Pacific Islander, 0.2% Hispanic American, 2% Native American.

Faculty *Total:* 57, 95% full-time. *Student/faculty ratio:* 16:1.

Majors Accounting; administrative assistant and secretarial science; agricultural business and management; agricultural production; appliance installation and repair technology; architectural drafting and CAD/CADD; carpentry; clinical/medical laboratory technology; communications technologies and support services related; computer and information sciences; computer and information sciences and support services related; computer/information technology services administration related; computer software and media applications related; computer systems networking and telecommunications; computer/technical support; computer technology/computer systems technology; construction trades related; culinary arts; data entry/microcomputer applications; drafting and design technology; electrical and electronic engineering technologies; electrical and power transmission installation; electrical, electronic and communications engineering technology; electrician; electromechanical technology; engineering technologies related; farm and ranch management; heating, air conditioning and refrigeration technology; heating, air conditioning, ventilation and refrigeration maintenance technology; industrial electronics technology; information science/studies; lineworker; medical administrative assistant and medical secretary; medical/clinical assistant; radiologic technology/science; system, networking, and LAN/wan management; telecommunications; telecommunications technology.

Academic Programs *Special study options:* academic remediation for entering students, advanced placement credit, cooperative education, distance learning, internships, services for LD students, summer session for credit.

Library Instructional Services Center with 100 serial subscriptions, an OPAC.

Computers on Campus 110 computers available on campus for general student use. A campuswide network can be accessed. Internet access, at least one staffed computer lab available. Computer purchase or lease plan available.

Student Life *Housing:* college housing not available. *Activities and Organizations:* Student Representative Board, Vocational Industrial Clubs of America,

Mitchell Technical Institute (continued)

Phi Beta Lambda, Post-Secondary Agricultural Students, Rodeo Club. *Student services:* personal/psychological counseling.

Athletics *Intercollegiate sports:* equestrian sports M/W. *Intramural sports:* basketball M/W, riflery M/W, softball M/W, volleyball M/W.

Standardized Tests *Required for some:* TABE. *Recommended:* ACT (for admission).

Costs (2003–04) *Tuition:* state resident $2500 full-time; nonresident $2500 full-time. *Required fees:* $400 full-time. *Payment plan:* installment. *Waivers:* employees or children of employees.

Financial Aid Of all full-time matriculated undergraduates who enrolled, 56 Federal Work-Study jobs (averaging $1600).

Applying *Options:* electronic application. *Application fee:* $25. *Required:* high school transcript. *Required for some:* essay or personal statement, interview. *Recommended:* minimum 2.0 GPA. *Application deadline:* rolling (freshmen), rolling (transfers). *Notification:* continuous (freshmen), continuous (transfers).

Admissions Contact Mr. Clayton Deuter, Admissions Representative, Mitchell Technical Institute, 821 North Capital, Mitchell, SD 57301. *Phone:* 605-995-3025. *Toll-free phone:* 800-952-0042. *Fax:* 605-996-3299. *E-mail:* questions@mti.tec.sd.us.

SISSETON-WAHPETON COMMUNITY COLLEGE
Sisseton, South Dakota

- **Federally supported** 2-year, founded 1979
- **Calendar** semesters
- **Degree** certificates and associate
- **Rural** 2-acre campus
- **Endowment** $253,820
- **Coed,** 287 undergraduate students, 57% full-time, 69% women, 31% men

Undergraduates 163 full-time, 124 part-time. Students come from 2 states and territories, 84% Native American, 7% transferred in.

Freshmen *Admission:* 61 applied, 61 admitted, 61 enrolled.

Faculty *Total:* 30, 40% full-time. *Student/faculty ratio:* 10:1.

Majors Accounting; American Indian/Native American studies; business administration and management; electrical, electronic and communications engineering technology; hospitality administration; information science/studies; kindergarten/preschool education; liberal arts and sciences/liberal studies; natural sciences; nursing (registered nurse training); nutrition sciences; substance abuse/addiction counseling.

Academic Programs *Special study options:* academic remediation for entering students, adult/continuing education programs, cooperative education, double majors, internships, off-campus study, part-time degree program, summer session for credit.

Library Sisseton-Wahpeton Community College Library with 14,255 titles, 165 serial subscriptions, 885 audiovisual materials.

Computers on Campus 28 computers available on campus for general student use. A campuswide network can be accessed from off campus. Internet access, at least one staffed computer lab available.

Student Life *Housing:* college housing not available. *Activities and Organizations:* Student Senate. *Campus security:* 24-hour emergency response devices. *Student services:* personal/psychological counseling.

Standardized Tests *Required:* Assessment and Placement Services for Community Colleges (for placement).

Costs (2004–05) *Tuition:* $2880 full-time, $96 per credit hour part-time. *Required fees:* $210 full-time.

Financial Aid Of all full-time matriculated undergraduates who enrolled, 5 Federal Work-Study jobs (averaging $1200).

Applying *Options:* common application, deferred entrance. *Required:* high school transcript. *Recommended:* minimum 2.0 GPA, letters of recommendation, interview. *Application deadline:* rolling (freshmen), rolling (transfers).

Admissions Contact Ms. Darlene Redday, Director of Admissions, Sisseton-Wahpeton Community College, Old Agency Box 689, Sisseton, SD 57262. *Phone:* 605-698-3966 Ext. 1110.

SOUTHEAST TECHNICAL INSTITUTE
Sioux Falls, South Dakota

- **State-supported** 2-year, founded 1968
- **Calendar** semesters
- **Degree** certificates, diplomas, and associate
- **Urban** 169-acre campus
- **Endowment** $145,000
- **Coed**

Faculty *Student/faculty ratio:* 17:1.

Student Life *Campus security:* 24-hour emergency response devices and patrols.

Standardized Tests *Recommended:* ACT (for admission).

Costs (2003–04) *Tuition:* state resident $1920 full-time. Full-time tuition and fees vary according to course load and program. Part-time tuition and fees vary according to course load and program. *Required fees:* $1195 full-time.

Financial Aid Of all full-time matriculated undergraduates who enrolled, 35 Federal Work-Study jobs (averaging $750).

Applying *Required:* high school transcript, minimum 2.0 GPA. *Required for some:* interview.

Admissions Contact Mr. Darrell Borgen, Career Counselor, Southeast Technical Institute, 2320 North Career Avenue, Sioux Falls, SD 57107. *Phone:* 605-367-6115. *Toll-free phone:* 800-247-0789. *Fax:* 605-367-8305. *E-mail:* darrell.borgen@southeasttech.com.

WESTERN DAKOTA TECHNICAL INSTITUTE
Rapid City, South Dakota

- **State-supported** 2-year, founded 1968
- **Calendar** semesters
- **Degree** certificates, diplomas, and associate
- **Small-town** 5-acre campus
- **Coed,** 1,057 undergraduate students, 71% full-time, 50% women, 50% men

Undergraduates 752 full-time, 305 part-time. Students come from 20 states and territories, 13% are from out of state, 12% transferred in. *Retention:* 62% of 2002 full-time freshmen returned.

Freshmen *Admission:* 901 applied, 669 admitted, 412 enrolled.

Faculty *Total:* 85, 68% full-time, 5% with terminal degrees. *Student/faculty ratio:* 15:1.

Majors Agricultural business and management; animal/livestock husbandry and production; automobile/automotive mechanics technology; business administration and management; computer installation and repair technology; computer/technical support; criminal justice/police science; drafting and design technology; electrical, electronic and communications engineering technology; electrical/electronics equipment installation and repair; farm and ranch management; industrial electronics technology; legal assistant/paralegal; machine shop technology; medical transcription; sales, distribution and marketing.

Academic Programs *Special study options:* academic remediation for entering students, advanced placement credit, independent study, internships, part-time degree program, services for LD students, summer session for credit.

Library Western Dakota Technical Institute Library with 10,000 titles, 40 serial subscriptions, 170 audiovisual materials, an OPAC.

Computers on Campus 140 computers available on campus for general student use. A campuswide network can be accessed. Internet access, at least one staffed computer lab available.

Student Life *Housing:* college housing not available. *Activities and Organizations:* student council, intercollegiate rodeo. *Student services:* personal/psychological counseling, women's center.

Athletics *Intercollegiate sports:* equestrian sports M/W.

Standardized Tests *Required:* TABE/NET for nursing applicants, HOBET for other medical programs (for placement). *Recommended:* ACT (for placement).

Costs (2003–04) *Tuition:* state resident $2052 full-time, $57 per credit hour part-time; nonresident $2052 full-time, $57 per credit hour part-time. Full-time tuition and fees vary according to program. Part-time tuition and fees vary according to program. *Payment plan:* deferred payment. *Waivers:* employees or children of employees.

Financial Aid Of all full-time matriculated undergraduates who enrolled, 85 Federal Work-Study jobs (averaging $1400).

Applying *Options:* common application, electronic application. *Application fee:* $10. *Required:* essay or personal statement, high school transcript. *Required for some:* letters of recommendation, interview. *Recommended:* minimum 2.0 GPA. *Application deadlines:* 8/1 (freshmen), 8/1 (transfers). *Notification:* continuous until 8/15 (freshmen), continuous until 8/15 (transfers).

Admissions Contact Janell Oberlander, Director of Admissions, Western Dakota Technical Institute, 800 Mickelson Drive, Rapid City, SD 57703. *Phone:* 605-394-4034 Ext. 111. *Toll-free phone:* 800-544-8765. *E-mail:* joberlander@wdti.tec.sd.us.

TENNESSEE

AMERICAN ACADEMY OF NUTRITION, COLLEGE OF NUTRITION
Knoxville, Tennessee

- **Proprietary** 2-year, founded 1984
- **Calendar** continuous
- **Degrees** certificates, diplomas, and associate (offers only external degree programs conducted through home study)
- **Suburban** campus
- **Coed,** 241 undergraduate students

Undergraduates Students come from 49 states and territories, 15 other countries.
Freshmen *Admission:* 33 applied, 33 admitted.
Faculty *Total:* 6, 33% full-time. *Student/faculty ratio:* 29:1.
Majors Foods, nutrition, and wellness.
Academic Programs *Special study options:* academic remediation for entering students, adult/continuing education programs, distance learning, external degree program, independent study, part-time degree program, student-designed majors, summer session for credit.
Costs (2003–04) *Tuition:* $2990 full-time, $115 per credit hour part-time. *Required fees:* $200 full-time. *Payment plan:* installment.
Applying *Options:* common application, electronic application, deferred entrance. *Required for some:* high school transcript, interview. *Recommended:* minimum 2.0 GPA. *Application deadline:* rolling (freshmen). *Notification:* continuous (freshmen).
Admissions Contact Ms. Jennifer Green, Faculty, American Academy of Nutrition, College of Nutrition, 1204-D Kenesaw Avenue, Knoxville, TN 37919. *Phone:* 865-524-8079. *Toll-free phone:* 800-290-4226. *Fax:* 865-524-8339. *E-mail:* info@nutritioneducation.com.

CHATTANOOGA STATE TECHNICAL COMMUNITY COLLEGE
Chattanooga, Tennessee

- **State-supported** 2-year, founded 1965, part of Tennessee Board of Regents
- **Calendar** semesters
- **Degree** certificates, diplomas, and associate
- **Urban** 100-acre campus
- **Coed**

Faculty *Student/faculty ratio:* 22:1.
Student Life *Campus security:* 24-hour emergency response devices and patrols, late-night transport/escort service.
Athletics Member NJCAA.
Standardized Tests *Required for some:* SAT I or ACT (for placement).
Costs (2003–04) *Tuition:* state resident $1824 full-time; nonresident $5464 full-time. *Required fees:* $225 full-time.
Financial Aid Of all full-time matriculated undergraduates who enrolled, 377 Federal Work-Study jobs (averaging $652).
Applying *Options:* early admission, deferred entrance. *Application fee:* $10. *Required:* high school transcript.
Admissions Contact Ms. Diane Norris, Director of Admissions, Chattanooga State Technical Community College, 4501 Amnicola Highway, Chattanooga, TN 37406-1097. *Phone:* 423-697-4422 Ext. 3107. *Fax:* 423-697-4709. *E-mail:* admsis@cstcc.cc.tn.us.

CLEVELAND STATE COMMUNITY COLLEGE
Cleveland, Tennessee

- **State-supported** 2-year, founded 1967, part of Tennessee Board of Regents
- **Calendar** semesters
- **Degree** certificates and associate
- **Small-town** 105-acre campus
- **Endowment** $4.4 million
- **Coed,** 3,161 undergraduate students, 55% full-time, 60% women, 40% men

Undergraduates 1,723 full-time, 1,438 part-time. Students come from 9 states and territories, 1% are from out of state, 5% African American, 0.8% Asian American or Pacific Islander, 1% Hispanic American, 0.5% Native American, 5% transferred in.
Freshmen *Admission:* 587 admitted, 587 enrolled. *Average high school GPA:* 2.8.

Faculty *Total:* 168, 38% full-time, 14% with terminal degrees. *Student/faculty ratio:* 19:1.
Majors Administrative assistant and secretarial science; business administration and management; child development; community organization and advocacy; general studies; industrial arts; industrial technology; kindergarten/preschool education; liberal arts and sciences/liberal studies; nursing (registered nurse training); public administration and social service professions related.
Academic Programs *Special study options:* academic remediation for entering students, adult/continuing education programs, advanced placement credit, cooperative education, distance learning, double majors, English as a second language, external degree program, honors programs, independent study, internships, off-campus study, part-time degree program, services for LD students, summer session for credit.
Library Cleveland State Community College Library with 65,347 titles, 368 serial subscriptions, 10,116 audiovisual materials, an OPAC, a Web page.
Computers on Campus 450 computers available on campus for general student use. A campuswide network can be accessed from off campus. Internet access, online (class) registration, at least one staffed computer lab available.
Student Life *Housing:* college housing not available. *Activities and Organizations:* student-run newspaper, television station, choral group, Student Senate, International Association of Administration Professionals, Phi Theta Kappa, Student Nursing Association. *Campus security:* 24-hour emergency response devices and patrols, late-night transport/escort service. *Student services:* personal/psychological counseling.
Athletics Member NJCAA. *Intercollegiate sports:* baseball M(s), basketball M(s)/W(s), softball W(s). *Intramural sports:* archery M/W, badminton M/W, basketball M/W, bowling M/W, golf M/W, softball M/W, table tennis M/W, tennis M/W, volleyball M/W.
Standardized Tests *Required for some:* ACT (for placement).
Costs (2003–04) *Tuition:* state resident $1824 full-time, $78 per semester hour part-time; nonresident $7288 full-time, $314 per semester hour part-time. *Required fees:* $263 full-time, $19 per semester hour part-time. *Payment plan:* deferred payment. *Waivers:* children of alumni and employees or children of employees.
Financial Aid Of all full-time matriculated undergraduates who enrolled, 52 Federal Work-Study jobs (averaging $1025).
Applying *Options:* early admission, deferred entrance. *Application fee:* $10. *Required:* high school transcript. *Application deadline:* rolling (freshmen), rolling (transfers). *Notification:* continuous (freshmen), continuous (transfers).
Admissions Contact Ms. Midge Burnette, Director of Admissions and Recruitment, Cleveland State Community College, 3535 Adkisson Drive, Cleveland, TN 37320-3570. *Phone:* 423-478-6212. *Toll-free phone:* 800-604-2722. *Fax:* 423-478-6255. *E-mail:* mburnette@clevelandstatecc.edu.

COLUMBIA STATE COMMUNITY COLLEGE
Columbia, Tennessee

- **State-supported** 2-year, founded 1966
- **Calendar** semesters
- **Degree** certificates and associate
- **Small-town** 179-acre campus with easy access to Nashville
- **Endowment** $707,627
- **Coed,** 4,613 undergraduate students, 53% full-time, 66% women, 34% men

Undergraduates 2,423 full-time, 2,190 part-time. Students come from 6 states and territories, 2 other countries, 8% African American, 0.7% Asian American or Pacific Islander, 2% Hispanic American, 0.4% Native American, 0.1% international, 10% transferred in. *Retention:* 61% of 2002 full-time freshmen returned.
Freshmen *Admission:* 837 enrolled. *Average high school GPA:* 2.84. *Test scores:* SAT verbal scores over 500: 33%; SAT math scores over 500: 33%; ACT scores over 18: 67%; SAT verbal scores over 600: 17%; ACT scores over 24: 12%; SAT verbal scores over 700: 17%; ACT scores over 30: 1%.
Faculty *Total:* 257, 38% full-time.
Majors Accounting; administrative assistant and secretarial science; agricultural business and management; art; biology/biological sciences; business/commerce; chemistry; clinical/medical laboratory technology; dental hygiene; economics; electrical, electronic and communications engineering technology; elementary education; geography; history; industrial radiologic technology; information science/studies; kindergarten/preschool education; liberal arts and sciences/liberal studies; mass communication/media; mathematics; music; nursing (registered nurse training); pharmacy; physical education teaching and coaching; physical therapy; physics; political science and government; pre-engineering; psychology; respiratory care therapy; sociology; speech and rhetoric; veterinary technology.
Academic Programs *Special study options:* academic remediation for entering students, adult/continuing education programs, advanced placement credit, double majors, honors programs, part-time degree program, services for LD students, summer session for credit.

Columbia State Community College (continued)

Library John W. Finney Memorial Learning Resources Center with 61,200 titles, 460 serial subscriptions, an OPAC.

Computers on Campus 260 computers available on campus for general student use. A campuswide network can be accessed from off campus. Internet access, at least one staffed computer lab available.

Student Life *Housing:* college housing not available. *Activities and Organizations:* drama/theater group, Student Government Association, Student Tennessee Education Association, Circle K, Gamma Beta Phi, Students in Free Enterprise. *Campus security:* 24-hour patrols. *Student services:* health clinic, personal/psychological counseling.

Athletics Member NJCAA. *Intercollegiate sports:* baseball M(s), basketball M(s)/W(s), softball W(s). *Intramural sports:* basketball M/W, softball M/W, table tennis M/W, volleyball M/W.

Standardized Tests *Required for some:* SAT I or ACT (for placement).

Costs (2003–04) *Tuition:* state resident $912 full-time, $78 per semester hour part-time; nonresident $3644 full-time, $314 per semester hour part-time. *Required fees:* $6 full-time, $3 per term part-time.

Financial Aid Of all full-time matriculated undergraduates who enrolled, 50 Federal Work-Study jobs (averaging $1250).

Applying *Options:* early admission. *Application fee:* $10. *Required:* high school transcript. *Application deadline:* rolling (freshmen), rolling (transfers).

Admissions Contact Mr. Joey Scruggs, Coordinator of Recruitment, Columbia State Community College, P.O. Box 1315, Columbia, TN 38402-1315. *Phone:* 931-540-2540. *Fax:* 931-540-2830. *E-mail:* scruggs@columbiastate.edu.

CONCORDE CAREER COLLEGE

Memphis, Tennessee

Admissions Contact 5100 Poplar Avenue, Suite 132, Memphis, TN 38137.

DRAUGHONS JUNIOR COLLEGE

Clarksville, Tennessee

- **Proprietary** 2-year, founded 1987
- **Calendar** semesters
- **Degree** associate
- **Coed**

Costs (2003–04) *Tuition:* Contact school as tuition and fees vary according to program.

Financial Aid Of all full-time matriculated undergraduates who enrolled, 20 Federal Work-Study jobs (averaging $1000).

Applying *Required:* high school transcript, interview.

Admissions Contact Admissions Office, Draughons Junior College, 1860 Wilma Rudolph Boulevard, Clarksville, TN 37040. *Fax:* 931-552-3624.

DRAUGHONS JUNIOR COLLEGE

Nashville, Tennessee

- **Proprietary** 2-year, founded 1884
- **Calendar** semesters
- **Degree** associate
- **Suburban** 5-acre campus
- **Coed**

Student Life *Campus security:* 24-hour emergency response devices.

Costs (2003–04) *Tuition:* Contact College as tuition and fees vary according to program.

Financial Aid Of all full-time matriculated undergraduates who enrolled, 28 Federal Work-Study jobs (averaging $2950).

Applying *Options:* deferred entrance. *Application fee:* $20. *Required:* high school transcript.

Admissions Contact Admissions Office, Draughons Junior College, 340 Plus Park, Nashville, TN 37217. *Phone:* 615-361-7555. *Fax:* 615-367-2736.

DYERSBURG STATE COMMUNITY COLLEGE

Dyersburg, Tennessee

- **State-supported** 2-year, founded 1969, part of Tennessee Board of Regents
- **Calendar** semesters
- **Degree** certificates and associate
- **Small-town** 100-acre campus with easy access to Memphis
- **Endowment** $3.2 million

- **Coed**

Faculty *Student/faculty ratio:* 24:1.

Student Life *Campus security:* 24-hour patrols.

Athletics Member NJCAA.

Standardized Tests *Required for some:* ACT (for placement).

Costs (2003–04) *Tuition:* state resident $1824 full-time; nonresident $7288 full-time. Part-time tuition and fees vary according to course load. *Required fees:* $241 full-time.

Financial Aid Of all full-time matriculated undergraduates who enrolled, 84 Federal Work-Study jobs (averaging $997). 115 state and other part-time jobs (averaging $837).

Applying *Options:* common application, early admission. *Application fee:* $10. *Required:* high school transcript.

Admissions Contact Mr. Dan J. Gullett, Director of Admissions and Records, Dyersburg State Community College, 1510 Lake Road, Dyersburg, TN 38024. *Phone:* 731-286-3327. *Fax:* 731-286-3325. *E-mail:* gulett@dscc.edu.

ELECTRONIC COMPUTER PROGRAMMING COLLEGE

Chattanooga, Tennessee

- **Proprietary** 2-year
- **Degree** associate
- 178 undergraduate students, 100% full-time

Faculty *Student/faculty ratio:* 20:1.

Costs (2004–05) *Tuition:* $5400 full-time.

Admissions Contact Toney McFadden, Admission Director, Electronic Computer Programming College, 3805 Brainerd Road, Chattanooga, TN 37411-3798. *Phone:* 423-624-0077.

FOUNTAINHEAD COLLEGE OF TECHNOLOGY

Knoxville, Tennessee

- **Proprietary** primarily 2-year, founded 1947
- **Calendar** semesters
- **Degrees** associate and bachelor's
- **Suburban** 1-acre campus
- **Coed**, 120 undergraduate students

Undergraduates Students come from 1 other state.

Faculty *Total:* 10, 90% full-time, 100% with terminal degrees.

Majors Communications technology; computer engineering technology; electrical, electronic and communications engineering technology; industrial technology; information science/studies.

Academic Programs *Special study options:* summer session for credit.

Library 1,200 titles, 1,000 serial subscriptions, a Web page.

Computers on Campus 15 computers available on campus for general student use. A campuswide network can be accessed from off campus. Internet access, at least one staffed computer lab available.

Student Life *Housing:* college housing not available. *Campus security:* 24-hour emergency response devices.

Applying *Application fee:* $100. *Recommended:* high school transcript. *Application deadline:* rolling (freshmen), rolling (transfers). *Notification:* continuous (freshmen), continuous (transfers).

Admissions Contact Ms. Casey Rackley, Director of Administration, Fountainhead College of Technology, 3203 Tazewell Pike, Knoxville, TN 37918-2530. *Phone:* 865-688-9422. *Toll-free phone:* 888-218-7335.

HIGH-TECH INSTITUTE

Memphis, Tennessee

Admissions Contact 5865 Shelby Oaks Circle, Memphis, TN 38134.

HIGH-TECH INSTITUTE

Nashville, Tennessee

Admissions Contact Mr. David Martinez, College Director, High-Tech Institute, 2710 Old Lebanon Road, Suite 12, Nashville, TN 37214. *Phone:* 615-902-9705. *Toll-free phone:* 800-987-0110.

HIWASSEE COLLEGE
Madisonville, Tennessee

- **Independent Methodist** 2-year, founded 1849
- **Calendar** semesters
- **Degree** associate
- **Rural** 410-acre campus
- **Endowment** $5.1 million
- **Coed,** 398 undergraduate students, 88% full-time, 57% women, 43% men

Undergraduates 350 full-time, 48 part-time. Students come from 11 states and territories, 8 other countries, 8% are from out of state, 13% African American, 0.5% Asian American or Pacific Islander, 3% Hispanic American, 0.3% Native American, 6% international, 6% transferred in, 40% live on campus.
Freshmen *Admission:* 562 applied, 392 admitted, 190 enrolled. *Average high school GPA:* 3.02. *Test scores:* SAT verbal scores over 500: 18%; SAT math scores over 500: 55%; ACT scores over 18: 63%; ACT scores over 24: 15%; ACT scores over 30: 1%.
Faculty *Total:* 28, 75% full-time, 43% with terminal degrees. *Student/faculty ratio:* 15:1.
Majors Accounting; agriculture; animal sciences; apparel and textiles; biology/biological sciences; business administration and management; chemistry; clinical laboratory science/medical technology; communication/speech communication and rhetoric; computer and information sciences; criminal justice/law enforcement administration; dental hygiene; dramatic/theatre arts; economics; elementary education; English; family and consumer sciences/human sciences; finance; fishing and fisheries sciences and management; food/nutrition; forestry; health and physical education; health information/medical records technology; history; hospitality administration; human services; kinesiology and exercise science; liberal arts and sciences/liberal studies; marketing/marketing management; music; nursing (registered nurse training); optometric technician; physical therapy; pre-dentistry studies; pre-engineering; pre-law; pre-medical studies; pre-nursing studies; pre-pharmacy studies; pre-theology/pre-ministerial studies; pre-veterinary studies; psychology; secondary education; sociology; wildlife and wildlands science and management.
Academic Programs *Special study options:* academic remediation for entering students, adult/continuing education programs, advanced placement credit, double majors, English as a second language, honors programs, part-time degree program, summer session for credit.
Library Hardwick-Johnston Memorial Library with 40,000 titles, 250 serial subscriptions, a Web page.
Computers on Campus 61 computers available on campus for general student use. A campuswide network can be accessed from student residence rooms and from off campus. Internet access, at least one staffed computer lab available.
Student Life *Housing:* on-campus residence required through sophomore year. *Options:* men-only, women-only. Campus housing is university owned. *Activities and Organizations:* drama/theater group, student-run newspaper, choral group, Baptist Student Union, Christian Student Movement, Future Farmers of America, Theatre Hiwassee, Student Government Association. *Campus security:* 24-hour emergency response devices, controlled dormitory access, late night security. *Student services:* health clinic, personal/psychological counseling.
Athletics Member NJCAA. *Intercollegiate sports:* baseball M(s), basketball M(s)/W(s), cross-country running M/W, golf M/W, soccer M(s)/W(s), softball W(s). *Intramural sports:* basketball M/W, football M/W, table tennis M/W, tennis M/W, volleyball M/W.
Standardized Tests *Required:* SAT I or ACT (for admission).
Costs (2003–04) *Comprehensive fee:* $12,600 includes full-time tuition ($7800) and room and board ($4800). Part-time tuition: $325 per credit. Part-time tuition and fees vary according to class time. *Payment plan:* installment. *Waivers:* adult students, senior citizens, and employees or children of employees.
Financial Aid Of all full-time matriculated undergraduates who enrolled, 150 Federal Work-Study jobs (averaging $750).
Applying *Options:* common application, electronic application, early admission, deferred entrance. *Required:* high school transcript, minimum 2.25 GPA. *Required for some:* 2 letters of recommendation, interview. *Application deadline:* rolling (freshmen), rolling (transfers).
Admissions Contact Jamie Williamson, Director of Admission, Hiwassee College, 225 Hiwassee College Drive, Madisonville, TN 37354. *Phone:* 423-420-1891. *Toll-free phone:* 800-356-2187. *Fax:* 423-442-8521. *E-mail:* enroll@hiwassee.edu.

ITT TECHNICAL INSTITUTE
Memphis, Tennessee

- **Proprietary** primarily 2-year, founded 1994, part of ITT Educational Services, Inc.
- **Calendar** quarters
- **Degrees** associate and bachelor's
- **Suburban** 1-acre campus
- **Coed**

Standardized Tests *Required:* Wonderlic aptitude test (for admission).
Costs (2003–04) *Tuition:* Total Program Cost varies depending on course of study. Consult school catalog.
Applying *Options:* deferred entrance. *Application fee:* $100. *Required:* high school transcript, interview. *Recommended:* letters of recommendation.
Admissions Contact Mr. James R. Mills, Director of Recruitment, ITT Technical Institute, 1255 Lynnfield Road, Suite 192, Memphis, TN 38119. *Phone:* 901-762-0556. *Fax:* 901-762-0566.

ITT TECHNICAL INSTITUTE
Nashville, Tennessee

- **Proprietary** primarily 2-year, founded 1984, part of ITT Educational Services, Inc.
- **Calendar** quarters
- **Degrees** associate and bachelor's
- **Urban** 21-acre campus
- **Coed**

Standardized Tests *Required:* Wonderlic aptitude test (for admission).
Costs (2003–04) *Tuition:* Total Program Cost varies depending on course of study. Consult school catalog.
Applying *Options:* deferred entrance. *Application fee:* $100. *Required:* high school transcript, interview. *Recommended:* letters of recommendation.
Admissions Contact Mr. Ronald Binkley, Director of Recruitment, ITT Technical Institute, 441 Donnelson Pike, Nashville, TN 37214. *Phone:* 615-889-8700. *Toll-free phone:* 800-331-8386. *Fax:* 615-872-7209.

ITT TECHNICAL INSTITUTE
Knoxville, Tennessee

- **Proprietary** primarily 2-year, founded 1988, part of ITT Educational Services, Inc.
- **Calendar** quarters
- **Degrees** associate and bachelor's
- **Suburban** 5-acre campus
- **Coed**

Standardized Tests *Required:* Wonderlic aptitude test (for admission).
Costs (2003–04) *Tuition:* Total Program Cost varies depending on course of study. Consult school catalog.
Applying *Options:* deferred entrance. *Application fee:* $100. *Required:* high school transcript, interview. *Recommended:* letters of recommendation.
Admissions Contact Mr. Mike Burke, Director of Recruitment, ITT Technical Institute, 10208 Technology Drive, Knoxville, TN 37932. *Phone:* 865-671-2800. *Toll-free phone:* 800-671-2801. *Fax:* 865-671-2811.

JACKSON STATE COMMUNITY COLLEGE
Jackson, Tennessee

- **State-supported** 2-year, founded 1967, part of Tennessee Board of Regents
- **Calendar** semesters
- **Degree** certificates and associate
- **Small-town** 104-acre campus
- **Endowment** $515,641
- **Coed,** 4,004 undergraduate students, 55% full-time, 65% women, 35% men

Undergraduates 2,201 full-time, 1,803 part-time. Students come from 9 states and territories, 0.4% are from out of state, 19% African American, 0.3% Asian American or Pacific Islander, 1% Hispanic American, 0.3% Native American, 9% transferred in. *Retention:* 57% of 2002 full-time freshmen returned.
Freshmen *Admission:* 1,252 applied, 1,252 admitted, 788 enrolled. *Average high school GPA:* 2.64. *Test scores:* ACT scores over 18: 57%; ACT scores over 24: 8%.
Faculty *Total:* 222, 51% full-time, 6% with terminal degrees. *Student/faculty ratio:* 19:1.
Majors Agricultural business and management; business administration and management; child development; clinical/medical laboratory technology; commercial and advertising art; computer science; electromechanical technology; industrial technology; liberal arts and sciences/liberal studies; management information systems; medical radiologic technology; nursing (registered nurse training); physical therapist assistant; respiratory care therapy; tool and die technology.
Academic Programs *Special study options:* academic remediation for entering students, adult/continuing education programs, advanced placement credit,

Jackson State Community College (continued)

cooperative education, distance learning, honors programs, internships, part-time degree program, summer session for credit.

Library Jackson State Community College Library with 63,583 titles, 250 serial subscriptions, 1,829 audiovisual materials, an OPAC, a Web page.

Computers on Campus 60 computers available on campus for general student use. A campuswide network can be accessed from off campus. Internet access, online (class) registration, at least one staffed computer lab available. Computer purchase or lease plan available.

Student Life *Housing:* college housing not available. *Activities and Organizations:* drama/theater group, student-run newspaper, choral group, Student Government Organization, Spanish Club, Biology Club, Art Club, Black Student Association. *Campus security:* 24-hour patrols. *Student services:* health clinic, personal/psychological counseling.

Athletics Member NJCAA. *Intercollegiate sports:* baseball M(s), basketball M(s)/W(s), cheerleading W(s), softball W(s). *Intramural sports:* basketball M/W, football M, golf M, tennis M/W, volleyball W.

Standardized Tests *Required for some:* SAT I or ACT (for placement).

Costs (2003–04) *Tuition:* state resident $1824 full-time, $78 per semester hour part-time; nonresident $5464 full-time, $236 per semester hour part-time. *Required fees:* $253 full-time, $23 per semester hour part-time, $127 per term part-time. *Payment plan:* deferred payment. *Waivers:* senior citizens and employees or children of employees.

Financial Aid Of all full-time matriculated undergraduates who enrolled, 60 Federal Work-Study jobs (averaging $3000). 10 state and other part-time jobs (averaging $3000).

Applying *Options:* electronic application, early admission, deferred entrance. *Application fee:* $10. *Required for some:* high school transcript. *Application deadline:* 8/22 (freshmen), rolling (transfers). *Notification:* continuous (freshmen), continuous (transfers).

Admissions Contact Ms. Monica Ray, Director of Admissions and Records, Jackson State Community College, 2046 North Parkway, Jackson, TN 38301. *Phone:* 731-425-2644. *Toll-free phone:* 800-355-5722. *Fax:* 731-425-9559. *E-mail:* mray@jscc.edu.

John A. Gupton College
Nashville, Tennessee

- **Independent** 2-year, founded 1946
- **Calendar** semesters
- **Degree** diplomas and associate
- **Urban** 1-acre campus
- **Endowment** $60,000
- **Coed**

Faculty *Student/faculty ratio:* 13:1.

Student Life *Campus security:* controlled dormitory access, day patrols.

Standardized Tests *Required:* ACT (for admission).

Financial Aid *Financial aid deadline:* 6/1.

Applying *Options:* common application, deferred entrance. *Application fee:* $20. *Required:* essay or personal statement, high school transcript, 2 letters of recommendation, health forms.

Admissions Contact Ms. Lisa Bolin, Registrar, John A. Gupton College, 1616 Church Street, Nashville, TN 37203. *Phone:* 615-327-3927. *Toll-free phone:* 615-327-3927. *E-mail:* spann@guptoncollege.com.

MedVance Institute
Cookeville, Tennessee

Admissions Contact Ms. Sharon Mellott, Director of Admissions, MedVance Institute, 1065 East 10th Street, Cookeville, TN 38501-1907. *Phone:* 931-526-3660. *Toll-free phone:* 800-259-3659 (in-state); 800-256-9085 (out-of-state). *Fax:* 931-372-2603. *E-mail:* briddell@medvance.org.

Mid-America Baptist Theological Seminary
Germantown, Tennessee

- **Independent Southern Baptist** founded 1972
- **Calendar** semesters
- **Degrees** associate, master's, doctoral, and first professional
- **Suburban** campus with easy access to Memphis
- **Endowment** $3.6 million
- **Coed, primarily men,** 43 undergraduate students, 67% full-time, 100% men

Undergraduates 29 full-time, 14 part-time. Students come from 26 states and territories, 1 other country, 9% African American.

Faculty *Total:* 27, 100% full-time. *Student/faculty ratio:* 14:1.

Majors Theology.

Academic Programs *Special study options:* summer session for credit.

Library Ora Byram Allison Memorial Library with 119,000 titles, 931 serial subscriptions, an OPAC, a Web page.

Computers on Campus 10 computers available on campus for general student use. At least one staffed computer lab available.

Student Life *Housing Options:* Campus housing is university owned. *Campus security:* 24-hour emergency response devices.

Costs (2003–04) *Tuition:* $2800 full-time. Full-time tuition and fees vary according to course load. Part-time tuition and fees vary according to course load.

Applying *Options:* common application. *Application fee:* $25. *Required:* high school transcript, 2 letters of recommendation. *Application deadline:* 8/7 (freshmen).

Admissions Contact Miss Kim Powers, Admissions Counselor, Mid-America Baptist Theological Seminary, 2216 Germantown Road South, Germantown, TN 38138. *Phone:* 901-751-8453 Ext. 3066. *Fax:* 901-751-8454. *E-mail:* info@mabts.edu.

Miller-Motte Technical College
Clarksville, Tennessee

Admissions Contact Ms. Lisa Teague, Director of Admissions, Miller-Motte Technical College, 1820 Business Park Drive, Clarksville, TN 37040. *Phone:* 800-558-0071.

Motlow State Community College
Tullahoma, Tennessee

- **State-supported** 2-year, founded 1969, part of Tennessee Board of Regents
- **Calendar** semesters
- **Degree** certificates and associate
- **Small-town** 187-acre campus with easy access to Nashville
- **Endowment** $2.7 million
- **Coed,** 3,478 undergraduate students, 57% full-time, 63% women, 37% men

Undergraduates 1,970 full-time, 1,508 part-time. Students come from 5 states and territories, 3 other countries, 0.5% are from out of state, 8% African American, 0.9% Asian American or Pacific Islander, 1% Hispanic American, 0.4% Native American, 0.4% international, 7% transferred in. *Retention:* 62% of 2002 full-time freshmen returned.

Freshmen *Admission:* 1,315 applied, 877 admitted, 867 enrolled. *Average high school GPA:* 2.81. *Test scores:* SAT verbal scores over 500: 20%; SAT math scores over 500: 26%; ACT scores over 18: 61%; SAT verbal scores over 600: 13%; SAT math scores over 600: 7%; ACT scores over 24: 11%; ACT scores over 30: 1%.

Faculty *Total:* 181, 45% full-time. *Student/faculty ratio:* 14:1.

Majors Business administration and management; engineering technology; liberal arts and sciences/liberal studies; nursing (registered nurse training); special education (early childhood).

Academic Programs *Special study options:* academic remediation for entering students, adult/continuing education programs, advanced placement credit, cooperative education, distance learning, double majors, honors programs, independent study, off-campus study, part-time degree program, services for LD students, summer session for credit.

Library Crouch Library with 54,471 titles, 126 serial subscriptions, 4,305 audiovisual materials, an OPAC, a Web page.

Computers on Campus 550 computers available on campus for general student use. A campuswide network can be accessed from off campus. Internet access, online (class) registration, at least one staffed computer lab available.

Student Life *Housing:* college housing not available. *Activities and Organizations:* drama/theater group, student-run newspaper, choral group, Photography Club, Psychology Club, Student Government Association, Outing Club, Baptist Student Union. *Campus security:* 24-hour patrols, late-night transport/escort service. *Student services:* health clinic, personal/psychological counseling.

Athletics Member NJCAA. *Intercollegiate sports:* baseball M(s), basketball M(s)/W(s), softball W(s). *Intramural sports:* archery M/W, badminton M/W, basketball M/W, bowling M/W, golf M/W, tennis M/W, volleyball M/W.

Standardized Tests *Required for some:* SAT I or ACT (for placement).

Costs (2003–04) *Tuition:* state resident $1824 full-time, $78 per credit part-time; nonresident $7310 full-time, $314 per credit part-time. Full-time tuition and fees vary according to program. Part-time tuition and fees vary according to course load and program. *Required fees:* $147 full-time, $9 per credit part-time, $11 per term part-time. *Payment plans:* installment, deferred payment. *Waivers:* senior citizens and employees or children of employees.

Financial Aid Of all full-time matriculated undergraduates who enrolled, 62 Federal Work-Study jobs (averaging $1331).

Applying *Options:* electronic application, early admission, deferred entrance. *Application fee:* $10. *Required:* high school transcript. *Application deadline:* 8/13 (freshmen), rolling (transfers). *Notification:* continuous (freshmen), continuous (transfers).

Admissions Contact Wendi Patton, Director of New Student Admissions, Motlow State Community College, PO Box 8500, Lynchburg, TN 37352. *Phone:* 931-393-1764. *Toll-free phone:* 800-654-4877. *Fax:* 931-393-1681. *E-mail:* galsup@mscc.edu.

NASHVILLE AUTO DIESEL COLLEGE
Nashville, Tennessee

- **Proprietary** 2-year, founded 1919
- **Calendar** continuous
- **Degree** diplomas and associate
- **Urban** 13-acre campus
- **Coed, primarily men,** 1,306 undergraduate students, 100% full-time, 0% women, 100% men

Undergraduates 1,306 full-time. Students come from 50 states and territories, 83% are from out of state, 30% African American, 0.8% Asian American or Pacific Islander, 0.8% Hispanic American, 1% Native American, 21% live on campus.

Freshmen *Admission:* 2,924 applied, 2,602 admitted, 95 enrolled. *Average high school GPA:* 2.3.

Faculty *Total:* 77, 95% full-time. *Student/faculty ratio:* 30:1.

Majors Autobody/collision and repair technology; automobile/automotive mechanics technology; diesel mechanics technology.

Academic Programs *Special study options:* advanced placement credit, cooperative education, honors programs.

Library NADC Library with 1,309 titles, 69 serial subscriptions.

Computers on Campus 40 computers available on campus for general student use. A campuswide network can be accessed. Internet access, at least one staffed computer lab available.

Student Life *Housing Options:* men-only. Campus housing is university owned. *Campus security:* 24-hour emergency response devices and patrols.

Costs (2004–05) *Tuition:* $17,750 full-time. Full-time tuition and fees vary according to degree level and program. No tuition increase for student's term of enrollment. *Required fees:* $100 full-time. *Room only:* $4372. Room and board charges vary according to housing facility. *Payment plan:* installment. *Waivers:* employees or children of employees.

Applying *Options:* deferred entrance. *Application fee:* $100. *Required:* high school transcript, interview. *Required for some:* 2.3 letters of recommendation. *Application deadline:* rolling (freshmen).

Admissions Contact Ms. Peggie Werrbach, Director of Admissions, Nashville Auto Diesel College, 1524 Gallatin Road, Nashville, TN 37206. *Phone:* 615-226-3990 Ext. 8465. *Toll-free phone:* 800-228-NADC. *Fax:* 615-262-8466. *E-mail:* wpruitt@nadcedu.com.

NASHVILLE STATE TECHNICAL COMMUNITY COLLEGE
Nashville, Tennessee

- **State-supported** 2-year, founded 1970, part of Tennessee Board of Regents
- **Calendar** semesters
- **Degree** certificates and associate
- **Urban** 85-acre campus
- **Coed,** 6,766 undergraduate students, 32% full-time, 57% women, 43% men

Undergraduates 2,195 full-time, 4,571 part-time. Students come from 29 states and territories, 56 other countries, 5% are from out of state, 25% African American, 3% Asian American or Pacific Islander, 2% Hispanic American, 0.3% Native American, 3% international, 3% transferred in.

Freshmen *Admission:* 758 enrolled.

Faculty *Total:* 412, 33% full-time.

Majors Accounting; administrative assistant and secretarial science; architectural engineering technology; automobile/automotive mechanics technology; business administration and management; civil engineering technology; commercial and advertising art; computer engineering technology; computer systems networking and telecommunications; criminal justice/police science; culinary arts; electrical, electronic and communications engineering technology; industrial engineering; industrial technology; information science/studies; kindergarten/preschool education; occupational therapy; photography; sign language interpretation and translation.

Academic Programs *Special study options:* academic remediation for entering students, adult/continuing education programs, advanced placement credit, cooperative education, distance learning, off-campus study, part-time degree program, services for LD students, summer session for credit.

Library 38,502 titles, 275 serial subscriptions, an OPAC, a Web page.

Computers on Campus 518 computers available on campus for general student use. A campuswide network can be accessed from off campus.

Student Life *Housing:* college housing not available. *Activities and Organizations:* student-run newspaper, Data Processing Management Association, Occupational Therapy Club, Phi Theta Kappa, Student Government Association, Black Student Association. *Campus security:* 24-hour emergency response devices and patrols, late-night transport/escort service. *Student services:* personal/psychological counseling.

Athletics *Intramural sports:* table tennis M/W, volleyball M/W.

Standardized Tests *Required for some:* SAT I or ACT (for placement).

Costs (2003–04) *Tuition:* state resident $88 per semester hour part-time; nonresident $324 per semester hour part-time.

Financial Aid Of all full-time matriculated undergraduates who enrolled, 66 Federal Work-Study jobs (averaging $806). 97 state and other part-time jobs (averaging $917).

Applying *Options:* electronic application, deferred entrance. *Application fee:* $5. *Required:* high school transcript. *Application deadline:* rolling (freshmen), rolling (transfers). *Notification:* continuous (freshmen), continuous (transfers).

Admissions Contact Mrs. Nancy Jewell, Assistant Director of Admissions, Nashville State Technical Community College, 120 White Bridge Road, Nashville, TN 37209. *Phone:* 615-353-3214. *Toll-free phone:* 800-272-7363. *Fax:* 615-353-3243. *E-mail:* jewell_n@nsti.tec.tn.us.

NATIONAL COLLEGE OF BUSINESS & TECHNOLOGY
Knoxville, Tennessee

- **Proprietary** 2-year, founded 2003, part of National College of Business and Technology
- **Calendar** quarters
- **Degree** diplomas and associate
- **Suburban** 2-acre campus
- **Coed,** 209 undergraduate students

Faculty *Student/faculty ratio:* 12:1.

Computers on Campus 55 computers available on campus for general student use. Internet access, at least one staffed computer lab available.

Costs (2004–05) *Tuition:* $170 per quarter hour part-time. Part-time tuition and fees vary according to course load. *Required fees:* $15 per term part-time.

Admissions Contact Mr. Andy W. Wills, Director, National College of Business & Technology, 8415 Kingston Pike, Knoxville, TN 37919. *Phone:* 865-539-2011. *Toll-free phone:* 800-664-1886.

NATIONAL COLLEGE OF BUSINESS & TECHNOLOGY
Nashville, Tennessee

- **Proprietary** 2-year, founded 1915, part of National College of Business and Technology
- **Calendar** quarters
- **Degree** diplomas and associate
- **Urban** 1-acre campus
- **Coed,** 434 undergraduate students

Faculty *Total:* 25, 12% full-time. *Student/faculty ratio:* 10:1.

Majors Administrative assistant and secretarial science; business administration and management; computer and information sciences related; medical/clinical assistant.

Academic Programs *Special study options:* double majors, honors programs, part-time degree program, services for LD students, summer session for credit.

Computers on Campus 35 computers available on campus for general student use. Internet access, at least one staffed computer lab available.

Student Life *Housing:* college housing not available.

Costs (2004–05) *Tuition:* $6120 full-time, $170 per credit hour part-time. Full-time tuition and fees vary according to course load. Part-time tuition and fees vary according to course load. *Required fees:* $75 full-time. *Payment plans:* installment, deferred payment. *Waivers:* employees or children of employees.

Financial Aid Of all full-time matriculated undergraduates who enrolled, 3 Federal Work-Study jobs.

Applying *Options:* electronic application. *Application fee:* $30. *Recommended:* interview. *Application deadline:* rolling (freshmen), rolling (transfers). *Notification:* continuous (freshmen), continuous (transfers).

Admissions Contact Mr. Robert Leonard, Campus Director, National College of Business & Technology, 3748 Nolensville Pike, Nashville, TN 37211. *Phone:* 615-333-3344. *Toll-free phone:* 800-664-1886. *Fax:* 615-333-3429. *E-mail:* adm@educorp.edu.

NORTH CENTRAL INSTITUTE
Clarksville, Tennessee

- **Proprietary** 2-year, founded 1988
- **Calendar** continuous
- **Degree** associate
- **Suburban** 14-acre campus
- **Coed, primarily men,** 107 undergraduate students, 49% full-time, 13% women, 87% men

Undergraduates 52 full-time, 55 part-time. Students come from 50 states and territories, 95% are from out of state, 17% African American, 0.9% Asian American or Pacific Islander, 12% Hispanic American, 8% Native American.

Freshmen *Admission:* 14 enrolled.

Faculty *Total:* 18, 39% full-time. *Student/faculty ratio:* 10:1.

Majors Aircraft powerplant technology; airframe mechanics and aircraft maintenance technology.

Academic Programs *Special study options:* advanced placement credit, external degree program, independent study, part-time degree program, summer session for credit.

Library Media Resource Center plus 1 other with 200 titles, 12 serial subscriptions, 20 audiovisual materials.

Student Life *Housing:* college housing not available. *Activities and Organizations:* Alpha Eta Rho (aviation fraternity). *Campus security:* 24-hour emergency response devices. *Student services:* personal/psychological counseling.

Costs (2003–04) *Tuition:* $6000 full-time.

Applying *Options:* common application, electronic application, early admission. *Application fee:* $35.

Admissions Contact Mrs. Sheri Nash-Kutch, Faculty Advisor/Dean, North Central Institute, 168 Jack Miller Boulevard, Clarksville, TN 37042. *Phone:* 931-431-9700 Ext. 235. *Fax:* 931-431-9771. *E-mail:* admissions@nci.edu.

NORTHEAST STATE TECHNICAL COMMUNITY COLLEGE
Blountville, Tennessee

- **State-supported** 2-year, founded 1966, part of Tennessee Board of Regents
- **Calendar** semesters
- **Degree** certificates and associate
- **Small-town** 100-acre campus
- **Endowment** $2.1 million
- **Coed,** 4,836 undergraduate students, 52% full-time, 54% women, 46% men

Undergraduates 2,537 full-time, 2,299 part-time. Students come from 3 states and territories, 3% are from out of state, 3% African American, 0.5% Asian American or Pacific Islander, 0.6% Hispanic American, 0.2% Native American, 5% transferred in. *Retention:* 58% of 2002 full-time freshmen returned.

Freshmen *Admission:* 2,544 applied, 2,544 admitted, 886 enrolled. *Average high school GPA:* 2.51. *Test scores:* ACT scores over 18: 57%; ACT scores over 24: 8%; ACT scores over 30: 1%.

Faculty *Total:* 221, 42% full-time, 12% with terminal degrees. *Student/faculty ratio:* 22:1.

Majors Accounting; administrative assistant and secretarial science; automobile/automotive mechanics technology; business administration and management; cardiovascular technology; chemistry; computer programming; computer programming related; computer systems networking and telecommunications; data processing and data processing technology; drafting and design technology; electrical, electronic and communications engineering technology; emergency medical technology (EMT paramedic); engineering technology; industrial technology; instrumentation technology; kindergarten/preschool education; liberal arts and sciences/liberal studies; machine tool technology; medical/clinical assistant; surgical technology; welding technology.

Academic Programs *Special study options:* academic remediation for entering students, advanced placement credit, cooperative education, distance learning, honors programs, part-time degree program, services for LD students, summer session for credit.

Library Main Library plus 1 other with 40,018 titles, 427 serial subscriptions, 7,904 audiovisual materials, an OPAC, a Web page.

Computers on Campus 830 computers available on campus for general student use. A campuswide network can be accessed from off campus. At least one staffed computer lab available.

Student Life *Housing:* college housing not available. *Activities and Organizations:* drama/theater group, Phi Theta Kappa, Student Government Association, Student Tennessee Education Association, Students in Free Enterprise, Student Ambassadors. *Campus security:* 24-hour patrols, late-night transport/escort service. *Student services:* health clinic, personal/psychological counseling.

Athletics *Intramural sports:* basketball M/W, golf M/W, volleyball M/W.

Standardized Tests *Required:* SAT I or ACT (for placement).

Costs (2003–04) *Tuition:* state resident $1824 full-time, $78 per credit hour part-time; nonresident $7288 full-time, $314 per credit hour part-time. Full-time tuition and fees vary according to course load. Part-time tuition and fees vary according to course load. *Required fees:* $262 full-time, $12 per credit hour part-time, $18 per term part-time.

Financial Aid Of all full-time matriculated undergraduates who enrolled, 109 Federal Work-Study jobs (averaging $1318). 35 state and other part-time jobs.

Applying *Application fee:* $10. *Required:* high school transcript, minimum 2.0 GPA. *Application deadline:* rolling (freshmen), rolling (transfers). *Notification:* continuous (freshmen), continuous (transfers).

Admissions Contact Dr. Jon P. Harr, Dean of Admissions and Records, Northeast State Technical Community College, PO Box 246, Blountville, TN 37617. *Phone:* 423-323-0231. *Toll-free phone:* 800-836-7822. *Fax:* 423-323-0215. *E-mail:* jpharr@nstcc.edu.

NOSSI COLLEGE OF ART
Goodlettsville, Tennessee

Admissions Contact Ms. Mary Alexander, Admissions Director, Nossi College of Art, 907 Rivergate Parkway, Goodlettsville, TN 37072. *Phone:* 615-851-1088. *E-mail:* admissions@nossi.com.

PELLISSIPPI STATE TECHNICAL COMMUNITY COLLEGE
Knoxville, Tennessee

- **State-supported** 2-year, founded 1974, part of Tennessee Board of Regents
- **Calendar** semesters
- **Degree** certificates and associate
- **Suburban** 144-acre campus
- **Endowment** $2.8 million
- **Coed,** 7,563 undergraduate students, 100% full-time, 53% women, 47% men

Undergraduates 7,563 full-time. Students come from 23 states and territories, 7% African American, 2% Asian American or Pacific Islander, 1% Hispanic American, 0.6% Native American.

Freshmen *Admission:* 1,152 applied, 1,150 admitted. *Average high school GPA:* 2.50.

Faculty *Total:* 412, 41% full-time. *Student/faculty ratio:* 21:1.

Majors Accounting; accounting technology and bookkeeping; administrative assistant and secretarial science; automobile/automotive mechanics technology; business administration and management; business machine repair; chemical engineering; chemical technology; cinematography and film/video production; civil engineering technology; commercial and advertising art; computer and information sciences; computer and information sciences related; computer engineering technology; computer graphics; computer programming; computer science; computer software and media applications related; computer systems networking and telecommunications; construction engineering technology; data entry/microcomputer applications; data entry/microcomputer applications related; data processing and data processing technology; drafting and design technology; electrical, electronic and communications engineering technology; environmental engineering technology; finance; geography; hospitality administration; hotel/motel administration; industrial arts; industrial technology; interior design; legal administrative assistant/secretary; legal assistant/paralegal; liberal arts and sciences/liberal studies; machine tool technology; marketing/marketing management; mechanical engineering/mechanical technology.

Academic Programs *Special study options:* academic remediation for entering students, adult/continuing education programs, advanced placement credit, cooperative education, distance learning, double majors, English as a second language, freshman honors college, honors programs, internships, part-time degree program, services for LD students, student-designed majors, summer session for credit.

Library Educational Resources Center plus 1 other with 43,000 titles, 527 serial subscriptions, an OPAC, a Web page.

Computers on Campus 1200 computers available on campus for general student use. A campuswide network can be accessed from off campus. Internet access, online (class) registration, at least one staffed computer lab available.

Student Life *Housing:* college housing not available. *Activities and Organizations:* drama/theater group, student-run newspaper, choral group, Student Government Association, Active Black Students Association, Phi Theta Kappa, Baptist Student Union, Vision. *Campus security:* 24-hour patrols. *Student services:* personal/psychological counseling.

Athletics *Intramural sports:* basketball M/W, golf M/W, soccer M/W, softball M/W, tennis M/W, volleyball M/W.

Standardized Tests *Required for some:* ACT (for placement).

Costs (2003–04) *Tuition:* state resident $1048 full-time; nonresident $3384 full-time.

Applying *Options:* common application, electronic application, early admission, deferred entrance. *Application fee:* $5. *Required:* high school transcript. *Application deadline:* rolling (freshmen), rolling (transfers). *Notification:* continuous (freshmen), continuous (transfers).

Admissions Contact Admissions Coordinator, Pellissippi State Technical Community College, PO Box 22990, Knoxville, TN 37933. *Phone:* 865-694-6681. *E-mail:* latouzeau@pstcc.cc.tn.us.

REMINGTON COLLEGE-MEMPHIS CAMPUS
Memphis, Tennessee

Admissions Contact Dr. Lori May, Campus President, Remington College-Memphis Campus, 2731 Nonconnah Boulevard, Memphis, TN 38132-2131. *Phone:* 901-291-4225.

REMINGTON COLLEGE-NASHVILLE CAMPUS
Nashville, Tennessee

Admissions Contact Mr. Frank Vivelo, Campus President, Remington College-Nashville Campus, 441 Donnelson Pike, Suite 150, Nashville, TN 37214. *Phone:* 615-889-5520.

ROANE STATE COMMUNITY COLLEGE
Harriman, Tennessee

- **State-supported** 2-year, founded 1971, part of Tennessee Board of Regents
- **Calendar** semesters
- **Degree** certificates and associate
- **Rural** 104-acre campus with easy access to Knoxville
- **Endowment** $18,123
- **Coed,** 5,385 undergraduate students, 55% full-time, 69% women, 31% men

Undergraduates 2,971 full-time, 2,414 part-time. Students come from 6 states and territories, 5 other countries, 1% are from out of state, 3% African American, 0.8% Asian American or Pacific Islander, 0.6% Hispanic American, 0.3% Native American, 0.4% international, 5% transferred in.

Freshmen *Admission:* 2,953 applied, 2,950 admitted, 1,039 enrolled. *Average high school GPA:* 2.97. *Test scores:* ACT scores over 18: 67%; ACT scores over 24: 11%.

Faculty *Total:* 333, 38% full-time. *Student/faculty ratio:* 19:1.

Majors Accounting; administrative assistant and secretarial science; art; art teacher education; biology/biological sciences; business administration and management; business teacher education; chemistry; clinical/medical laboratory technology; computer engineering technology; computer science; corrections; criminal justice/law enforcement administration; criminal justice/police science; dental hygiene; education; elementary education; emergency medical technology (EMT paramedic); engineering; environmental health; health information/medical records administration; industrial radiologic technology; kindergarten/preschool education; laser and optical technology; legal administrative assistant/secretary; liberal arts and sciences/liberal studies; mathematics; medical administrative assistant and medical secretary; music teacher education; nursing (registered nurse training); occupational therapy; pharmacy technician; physical education teaching and coaching; physical sciences; physical therapy; pre-engineering; respiratory care therapy; social sciences; technology/industrial arts teacher education.

Academic Programs *Special study options:* academic remediation for entering students, accelerated degree program, adult/continuing education programs, advanced placement credit, cooperative education, distance learning, double majors, external degree program, freshman honors college, honors programs, independent study, internships, off-campus study, part-time degree program, services for LD students, summer session for credit. *ROTC:* Army (c), Air Force (c).

Library Roane State Community College Library plus 1 other with 66,024 titles, 595 serial subscriptions, 8,808 audiovisual materials, an OPAC, a Web page.

Computers on Campus 750 computers available on campus for general student use. A campuswide network can be accessed. Internet access, online (class) registration, at least one staffed computer lab available.

Student Life *Housing:* college housing not available. *Activities and Organizations:* drama/theater group, student-run newspaper, choral group, Baptist Student Union, American Chemical Society, Physical Therapy Student Association, Student Artists At Roane State (S.T.A.R.S.), Phi Theta Kappa. *Campus security:* 24-hour patrols. *Student services:* health clinic, personal/psychological counseling.

Athletics Member NJCAA. *Intercollegiate sports:* baseball M(s), basketball M(s)/W(s), cheerleading W(s), softball W(s). *Intramural sports:* basketball M/W, football M, golf M, soccer M, softball M/W, volleyball M/W, weight lifting M.

Standardized Tests *Required for some:* SAT I or ACT (for placement).

Costs (2004–05) *Tuition:* state resident $1824 full-time, $78 per semester hour part-time; nonresident $7288 full-time, $314 per semester hour part-time. Full-time tuition and fees vary according to course load. *Required fees:* $265 full-time, $15 per semester hour part-time, $10 per term part-time. *Payment plan:* deferred payment. *Waivers:* senior citizens and employees or children of employees.

Financial Aid Of all full-time matriculated undergraduates who enrolled, 150 Federal Work-Study jobs (averaging $3000).

Applying *Options:* common application, electronic application, early admission, deferred entrance. *Application fee:* $10. *Required:* high school transcript. *Application deadline:* rolling (freshmen), rolling (transfers). *Notification:* continuous (freshmen), continuous (transfers).

Admissions Contact Ms. Brenda Rector, Director of Records and Registration, Roane State Community College, 276 Patton Lane, Harriman, TN 37748. *Phone:* 865-882-4526. *Toll-free phone:* 800-343-9104. *Fax:* 865-882-4562. *E-mail:* marine_gl@a1.rscc.cc.tn.us.

SOUTH COLLEGE
Knoxville, Tennessee

- **Proprietary** primarily 2-year, founded 1882
- **Calendar** quarters
- **Degrees** certificates, associate, and bachelor's
- **Urban** 2-acre campus
- **Coed, primarily women,** 443 undergraduate students, 100% full-time, 79% women, 21% men

Undergraduates 443 full-time. Students come from 2 states and territories, 14% African American, 0.5% Asian American or Pacific Islander, 0.7% Hispanic American, 0.2% Native American, 0.5% international.

Freshmen *Admission:* 32 admitted.

Faculty *Total:* 68, 26% full-time. *Student/faculty ratio:* 11:1.

Majors Accounting; administrative assistant and secretarial science; business administration and management; computer management; computer science; elementary education; hotel/motel administration; information science/studies; legal administrative assistant/secretary; legal assistant/paralegal; medical administrative assistant and medical secretary; medical/clinical assistant; nursing (registered nurse training); physical therapist assistant; radiologic technology/science.

Academic Programs *Special study options:* adult/continuing education programs, advanced placement credit, double majors, internships, part-time degree program, summer session for credit.

Library Knoxville Business College Library with 6,500 titles, 127 serial subscriptions, 16 audiovisual materials, a Web page.

Computers on Campus 50 computers available on campus for general student use. Internet access, at least one staffed computer lab available.

Student Life *Housing:* college housing not available. *Activities and Organizations:* Collegiate Secretaries International, Paralegal Club, Students of Medical Assisting, Empowerment. *Campus security:* evening and morning security patrols. *Student services:* personal/psychological counseling.

Standardized Tests *Recommended:* SAT I, ACT, or CPT.

Applying *Options:* common application, early admission, deferred entrance. *Application fee:* $40. *Required:* high school transcript, interview. *Application deadline:* 10/1 (freshmen), rolling (transfers). *Notification:* continuous (transfers).

Admissions Contact Mr. Walter Hosea, Director of Admissions, South College, 720 North Fifth Avenue, Knoxville, TN 37917. *Phone:* 865-524-3043 Ext. 1825. *Fax:* 865-637-0127.

SOUTHEASTERN CAREER COLLEGE
Nashville, Tennessee

Admissions Contact 2416 South 21st Avenue, Suite 300, Nashville, TN 37212. *Toll-free phone:* 800-336-4457.

SOUTHWEST TENNESSEE COMMUNITY COLLEGE
Memphis, Tennessee

- **State-supported** 2-year, part of Tennessee Board of Regents
- **Calendar** semesters
- **Degree** certificates and associate
- **Urban** 100-acre campus
- **Endowment** $61,798
- **Coed**

Southwest Tennessee Community College (continued)

Faculty *Student/faculty ratio:* 19:1.

Student Life *Campus security:* 24-hour emergency response devices and patrols, late-night transport/escort service.

Athletics Member NJCAA.

Standardized Tests *Required:* ACT (for placement).

Costs (2003–04) *Tuition:* state resident $1824 full-time; nonresident $7288 full-time. *Required fees:* $251 full-time.

Financial Aid Of all full-time matriculated undergraduates who enrolled, 201 Federal Work-Study jobs (averaging $2600).

Applying *Options:* common application, early admission, deferred entrance. *Application fee:* $5. *Required:* high school transcript.

Admissions Contact Ms. Cindy Meziere, Assistant Director of Recruiting, Southwest Tennessee Community College, PO Box 780, Memphis, TN 38103-0780. *Phone:* 901-333-4195. *Toll-free phone:* 877-717-STCC. *Fax:* 901-333-4473.

VATTEROTT COLLEGE
Memphis, Tennessee

Admissions Contact 6152 Macon Road, Memphis, TN 38134.

VOLUNTEER STATE COMMUNITY COLLEGE
Gallatin, Tennessee

- **State-supported** 2-year, founded 1970, part of Tennessee Board of Regents
- **Calendar** semesters
- **Degree** certificates and associate
- **Small-town** 100-acre campus with easy access to Nashville
- **Endowment** $97,286
- **Coed,** 6,991 undergraduate students, 48% full-time, 64% women, 36% men

Undergraduates 3,343 full-time, 3,648 part-time. Students come from 8 states and territories, 6 other countries, 1% are from out of state, 10% African American, 1% Asian American or Pacific Islander, 1% Hispanic American, 0.4% Native American, 0.6% international, 10% transferred in. *Retention:* 54% of 2002 full-time freshmen returned.

Freshmen *Admission:* 1,754 applied, 1,754 admitted, 1,308 enrolled. *Average high school GPA:* 2.76. *Test scores:* ACT scores over 18: 63%; ACT scores over 24: 9%; ACT scores over 30: 1%.

Faculty *Total:* 405, 36% full-time. *Student/faculty ratio:* 20:1.

Majors Business administration and management; fire science; health information/medical records technology; health professions related; industrial arts; legal assistant/paralegal; liberal arts and sciences/liberal studies; medical radiologic technology; ophthalmic technology; physical therapist assistant; respiratory care therapy.

Academic Programs *Special study options:* academic remediation for entering students, accelerated degree program, adult/continuing education programs, advanced placement credit, distance learning, double majors, English as a second language, honors programs, independent study, part-time degree program, services for LD students, summer session for credit.

Library Thigpen Learning Resource Center with 50,849 titles, 308 serial subscriptions, 3,147 audiovisual materials, an OPAC, a Web page.

Computers on Campus 400 computers available on campus for general student use. A campuswide network can be accessed from off campus. Internet access, online (class) registration, at least one staffed computer lab available.

Student Life *Housing:* college housing not available. *Activities and Organizations:* drama/theater group, student-run newspaper, radio station, choral group, Gamma Beta Phi, Returning Women's Organization, Phi Theta Kappa, Student Government Association, The Settler. *Campus security:* 24-hour emergency response devices and patrols, late-night transport/escort service. *Student services:* health clinic, personal/psychological counseling.

Athletics Member NJCAA. *Intercollegiate sports:* baseball M(s), basketball M(s)/W(s), softball W(s). *Intramural sports:* basketball M/W.

Standardized Tests *Required for some:* ACT (for placement).

Costs (2003–04) *Tuition:* state resident $1824 full-time, $78 per hour part-time; nonresident $7288 full-time, $314 per hour part-time. *Required fees:* $241 full-time, $9 per hour part-time, $8 per term part-time. *Payment plan:* deferred payment. *Waivers:* employees or children of employees.

Financial Aid Of all full-time matriculated undergraduates who enrolled, 45 Federal Work-Study jobs (averaging $1900). 15 state and other part-time jobs (averaging $2000).

Applying *Options:* electronic application, early admission, deferred entrance. *Application fee:* $10. *Required:* high school transcript. *Required for some:* essay or personal statement, minimum 2.0 GPA. *Application deadlines:* 7/31 (freshmen), 7/31 (transfers). *Notification:* continuous (freshmen), continuous (transfers).

Admissions Contact Mr. Tim Amyx, Director of Admission and Records, Volunteer State Community College, 1480 Nashville Pike, Gallatin, TN 37066-3188. *Phone:* 615-452-8600 Ext. 3614. *Toll-free phone:* 888-335-8722. *Fax:* 615-230-3577.

WALTERS STATE COMMUNITY COLLEGE
Morristown, Tennessee

- **State-supported** 2-year, founded 1970, part of Tennessee Board of Regents
- **Calendar** semesters
- **Degree** certificates and associate
- **Small-town** 100-acre campus
- **Endowment** $6.2 million
- **Coed,** 6,214 undergraduate students, 52% full-time, 63% women, 37% men

Undergraduates 3,242 full-time, 2,972 part-time. Students come from 7 states and territories, 8 other countries, 1% are from out of state, 4% African American, 0.7% Asian American or Pacific Islander, 1% Hispanic American, 0.3% Native American, 0.2% international, 4% transferred in.

Freshmen *Admission:* 1,818 applied, 1,818 admitted, 1,233 enrolled. *Average high school GPA:* 2.80. *Test scores:* SAT verbal scores over 500: 50%; SAT math scores over 500: 50%; ACT scores over 18: 55%; SAT verbal scores over 600: 20%; SAT math scores over 600: 20%; ACT scores over 24: 21%; SAT verbal scores over 700: 10%; SAT math scores over 700: 10%; ACT scores over 30: 1%.

Faculty *Total:* 288, 44% full-time, 15% with terminal degrees. *Student/faculty ratio:* 22:1.

Majors Administrative assistant and secretarial science; agricultural mechanization; art; art teacher education; business administration and management; child development; clinical/medical laboratory technology; computer and information sciences related; computer science; criminal justice/law enforcement administration; education; industrial radiologic technology; information technology; interdisciplinary studies; liberal arts and sciences/liberal studies; medical administrative assistant and medical secretary; music teacher education; nursing (registered nurse training); physical education teaching and coaching; pre-engineering.

Academic Programs *Special study options:* academic remediation for entering students, accelerated degree program, adult/continuing education programs, advanced placement credit, distance learning, freshman honors college, honors programs, part-time degree program, summer session for credit. *ROTC:* Army (c).

Library Walters State Library with 47,559 titles, 189 serial subscriptions, 22,677 audiovisual materials, an OPAC, a Web page.

Computers on Campus 686 computers available on campus for general student use. A campuswide network can be accessed from off campus. Internet access, online (class) registration, at least one staffed computer lab available.

Student Life *Housing:* college housing not available. *Activities and Organizations:* student-run newspaper, choral group. *Campus security:* 24-hour emergency response devices. *Student services:* health clinic.

Athletics Member NJCAA. *Intercollegiate sports:* baseball M(s), basketball M(s)/W(s), golf M(s), softball W(s). *Intramural sports:* baseball M, basketball M/W.

Standardized Tests *Required:* SAT I or ACT (for admission).

Costs (2003–04) *Tuition:* state resident $1824 full-time; nonresident $7288 full-time. *Required fees:* $238 full-time. *Waivers:* senior citizens.

Financial Aid Of all full-time matriculated undergraduates who enrolled, 60 Federal Work-Study jobs (averaging $2400).

Applying *Options:* early admission. *Application fee:* $10. *Required:* high school transcript. *Application deadline:* rolling (freshmen), rolling (transfers). *Notification:* continuous (freshmen), continuous (transfers).

Admissions Contact Mr. Michael Campbell, Director of Admissions and Registration Services, Walters State Community College, 500 South Davy Crockett Parkway, Morristown, TN 37813-6899. *Phone:* 423-585-2682. *Toll-free phone:* 800-225-4770. *Fax:* 423-585-6876. *E-mail:* mary.hopper@ws.edu.

TEXAS

THE ACADEMY OF HEALTH CARE PROFESSIONS
Houston, Texas

Admissions Contact Ms. Wanda Federick, Director of Admissions, The Academy of Health Care Professions, 1900 North Loop West, Suite 100, Houston, TX 77018. *Phone:* 713-425-3111.

ALVIN COMMUNITY COLLEGE
Alvin, Texas

- **State and locally supported** 2-year, founded 1949
- **Calendar** semesters
- **Degree** certificates, diplomas, and associate
- **Small-town** 114-acre campus with easy access to Houston
- **Coed,** 3,902 undergraduate students, 40% full-time, 59% women, 41% men

Undergraduates 1,578 full-time, 2,324 part-time. Students come from 15 states and territories, 0.5% are from out of state, 6% African American, 2% Asian American or Pacific Islander, 19% Hispanic American, 0.3% Native American, 0.4% international, 28% transferred in.

Freshmen *Admission:* 660 admitted, 660 enrolled.

Faculty *Total:* 251, 36% full-time. *Student/faculty ratio:* 16:1.

Majors Accounting; administrative assistant and secretarial science; aeronautics/aviation/aerospace science and technology; art; biology/biological sciences; business administration and management; chemical technology; child development; computer engineering technology; computer programming; corrections; court reporting; criminal justice/police science; drafting and design technology; dramatic/theatre arts; electrical, electronic and communications engineering technology; emergency medical technology (EMT paramedic); legal administrative assistant/secretary; legal assistant/paralegal; legal studies; liberal arts and sciences/liberal studies; marketing/marketing management; mathematics; medical administrative assistant and medical secretary; mental health/rehabilitation; music; nursing (registered nurse training); physical education teaching and coaching; physical sciences; radio and television; respiratory care therapy; substance abuse/addiction counseling; voice and opera.

Academic Programs *Special study options:* academic remediation for entering students, accelerated degree program, adult/continuing education programs, advanced placement credit, distance learning, double majors, English as a second language, honors programs, independent study, internships, part-time degree program, services for LD students, student-designed majors, study abroad, summer session for credit.

Library Alvin Community College Library with 29,440 titles, 226 serial subscriptions, an OPAC, a Web page.

Computers on Campus 622 computers available on campus for general student use. A campuswide network can be accessed from off campus. Internet access, at least one staffed computer lab available.

Student Life *Housing:* college housing not available. *Activities and Organizations:* drama/theater group, student-run radio and television station, choral group, Student Government Association, Baptist Student Union, Pan American College Forum, Catholic Newman Association, Phi Theta Kappa. *Campus security:* 24-hour patrols, late-night transport/escort service. *Student services:* personal/psychological counseling.

Athletics Member NJCAA. *Intercollegiate sports:* baseball M(s), softball W(s), volleyball W(s). *Intramural sports:* soccer M(c)/W(c).

Standardized Tests *Required:* THEA, ACCUPLACER (for placement).

Costs (2003–04) *Tuition:* area resident $624 full-time, $26 per credit part-time; state resident $1248 full-time, $52 per credit part-time; nonresident $2304 full-time, $96 per credit part-time. *Required fees:* $276 full-time, $98 per credit hour part-time. *Payment plan:* installment.

Financial Aid Of all full-time matriculated undergraduates who enrolled, 50 Federal Work-Study jobs (averaging $2200). 1 state and other part-time job (averaging $2500).

Applying *Required for some:* high school transcript. *Application deadline:* rolling (freshmen), rolling (transfers).

Admissions Contact Ms. Stephanie Stockstill, Director of Admissions and Advising, Alvin Community College, 3110 Mustang Road, Alvin, TX 77511. *Phone:* 281-756-3531. *Fax:* 281-756-3531. *E-mail:* admiss@alvincollege.edu.

AMARILLO COLLEGE
Amarillo, Texas

- **State and locally supported** 2-year, founded 1929
- **Calendar** semesters
- **Degree** certificates and associate
- **Suburban** 58-acre campus
- **Endowment** $13.6 million
- **Coed,** 9,348 undergraduate students

Undergraduates Students come from 9 states and territories, 1% are from out of state, 4% African American, 3% Asian American or Pacific Islander, 20% Hispanic American, 1% Native American.

Faculty *Total:* 237. *Student/faculty ratio:* 17:1.

Majors Accounting; administrative assistant and secretarial science; airframe mechanics and aircraft maintenance technology; architectural engineering technology; art; automobile/automotive mechanics technology; behavioral sciences; biblical studies; biology/biological sciences; broadcast journalism; business administration and management; business teacher education; chemical technol-

ogy; chemistry; child development; clinical laboratory science/medical technology; commercial and advertising art; computer engineering technology; computer programming; computer science; computer systems analysis; corrections; criminal justice/law enforcement administration; criminal justice/police science; dental hygiene; drafting and design technology; dramatic/theatre arts; electrical, electronic and communications engineering technology; elementary education; emergency medical technology (EMT paramedic); engineering; English; environmental health; fine/studio arts; fire science; funeral service and mortuary science; general studies; geology/earth science; health information/medical records administration; heating, air conditioning, ventilation and refrigeration maintenance technology; heavy equipment maintenance technology; history; industrial radiologic technology; information science/studies; instrumentation technology; interior design; journalism; laser and optical technology; legal administrative assistant/secretary; liberal arts and sciences/liberal studies; machine tool technology; mass communication/media; mathematics; medical administrative assistant and medical secretary; modern languages; music; music teacher education; natural sciences; nuclear medical technology; nursing (licensed practical/vocational nurse training); nursing (registered nurse training); occupational therapy; photography; physical education teaching and coaching; physical sciences; physical therapy; physics; pre-engineering; pre-pharmacy studies; psychology; public relations/image management; radio and television; radiologic technology/science; real estate; religious studies; respiratory care therapy; social sciences; social work; speech and rhetoric; substance abuse/addiction counseling; telecommunications; tourism and travel services management; visual and performing arts.

Academic Programs *Special study options:* academic remediation for entering students, adult/continuing education programs, advanced placement credit, distance learning, English as a second language, honors programs, part-time degree program, services for LD students, summer session for credit.

Library Lynn Library Learning Center plus 1 other with 75,200 titles, 325 serial subscriptions, an OPAC.

Computers on Campus 450 computers available on campus for general student use. A campuswide network can be accessed. Internet access, at least one staffed computer lab available.

Student Life *Housing:* college housing not available. *Options:* coed. *Activities and Organizations:* drama/theater group, student-run newspaper, radio station, choral group, Student Government Association, College Republicans. *Campus security:* 24-hour patrols, late-night transport/escort service. *Student services:* personal/psychological counseling.

Athletics *Intramural sports:* basketball M/W, tennis M/W, volleyball M/W.

Standardized Tests *Required:* THEA, MAPS (for placement).

Costs (2003–04) *Tuition:* area resident $792 full-time, $51 per credit part-time; state resident $1080 full-time, $63 per credit part-time; nonresident $1800 full-time, $223 per credit part-time.

Financial Aid Of all full-time matriculated undergraduates who enrolled, 100 Federal Work-Study jobs (averaging $3000).

Applying *Options:* early admission, deferred entrance. *Required:* high school transcript. *Notification:* continuous (freshmen), continuous (transfers).

Admissions Contact Mr. Robert Austin, Registrar and Director of Admissions, Amarillo College, PO Box 447, Amarillo, TX 79178-0001. *Phone:* 806-371-5024. *Fax:* 806-371-5066. *E-mail:* austin-rc@actx.edu.

ANGELINA COLLEGE
Lufkin, Texas

- **State and locally supported** 2-year, founded 1968
- **Calendar** semesters
- **Degree** certificates, diplomas, and associate
- **Small-town** 140-acre campus
- **Endowment** $2.6 million
- **Coed**

Student Life *Campus security:* 24-hour patrols.

Athletics Member NJCAA.

Standardized Tests *Required:* ACT COMPASS, THEA (for placement).

Applying *Options:* common application, electronic application, early admission, deferred entrance. *Required:* high school transcript.

Admissions Contact Ms. Judith Cutting, Registrar/Enrollment Director, Angelina College, PO Box 1768, Lufkin, TX 75902-1768. *Phone:* 936-639-1301 Ext. 213. *Fax:* 936-639-4299.

THE ART INSTITUTE OF DALLAS
Dallas, Texas

- **Proprietary** 2-year, founded 1978, part of Education Management Corporation
- **Calendar** quarters
- **Degree** associate

Texas

The Art Institute of Dallas (continued)
- **Urban** 2-acre campus
- **Coed**

Faculty *Student/faculty ratio:* 18:1.

Student Life *Campus security:* 24-hour emergency response devices and patrols, late-night transport/escort service.

Standardized Tests *Required:* ACT ASSET (for placement). *Recommended:* SAT I or ACT (for placement).

Costs (2003–04) *Tuition:* $4569 full-time.

Financial Aid Of all full-time matriculated undergraduates who enrolled, 33 Federal Work-Study jobs (averaging $2000).

Applying *Options:* deferred entrance. *Application fee:* $50. *Required:* essay or personal statement, high school transcript, interview.

Admissions Contact Mr. Keith Petovello, Director of Admissions, The Art Institute of Dallas, Two NorthPark, 8080 Park Lane, Suite 100, Dallas, TX 75231-9959. *Phone:* 214-692-8080 Ext. 1184. *Toll-free phone:* 800-275-4243. *Fax:* 214-750-9460.

THE ART INSTITUTE OF HOUSTON
Houston, Texas

- **Proprietary** primarily 2-year, founded 1978, part of The Art Institutes International
- **Calendar** quarters
- **Degrees** diplomas, associate, and bachelor's
- **Urban** campus
- **Coed,** 1,651 undergraduate students, 64% full-time, 43% women, 57% men

Undergraduates 1,053 full-time, 598 part-time. Students come from 12 states and territories, 25 other countries, 10% are from out of state, 15% live on campus.

Freshmen *Admission:* 849 applied, 816 admitted, 424 enrolled.

Faculty *Total:* 95, 47% full-time. *Student/faculty ratio:* 20:1.

Majors Applied art; commercial and advertising art; computer graphics; culinary arts; interior design; intermedia/multimedia; special products marketing; web page, digital/multimedia and information resources design.

Academic Programs *Special study options:* academic remediation for entering students, adult/continuing education programs, advanced placement credit, cooperative education, distance learning, internships, off-campus study.

Library Resource Center with 10,000 titles, 188 serial subscriptions, an OPAC.

Computers on Campus 194 computers available on campus for general student use. A campuswide network can be accessed from student residence rooms and from off campus. Internet access, at least one staffed computer lab available.

Student Life *Housing Options:* coed, men-only, women-only. Campus housing is leased by the school. *Activities and Organizations:* Texas Chef's Association, Association of Interior Designers, Computer Animation Society, Houston Ad Federation, International Television Association. *Campus security:* 24-hour emergency response devices. *Student services:* personal/psychological counseling.

Athletics *Intramural sports:* basketball M, football M/W, softball M/W, volleyball M/W.

Standardized Tests *Recommended:* SAT I or ACT (for admission).

Costs (2004–05) *Tuition:* $17,424 full-time, $363 per credit part-time. Full-time tuition and fees vary according to course load. No tuition increase for student's term of enrollment. *Room only:* $4545. Room and board charges vary according to housing facility. *Payment plans:* tuition prepayment, installment. *Waivers:* employees or children of employees.

Applying *Options:* common application, electronic application. *Application fee:* $50. *Required:* essay or personal statement, high school transcript, letters of recommendation, interview. *Required for some:* minimum 2.5 GPA, portfolio. *Recommended:* minimum 2.0 GPA. *Application deadline:* rolling (freshmen), rolling (transfers).

Admissions Contact Mr. Aaron McCardell, Director of Admissions, The Art Institute of Houston, 1900 Yorktown Street, Houston, TX 77056-4115. *Phone:* 713-623-2040 Ext. 3612. *Toll-free phone:* 800-275-4244. *Fax:* 713-966-2797. *E-mail:* aihadm@aih.aii.edu.

ATI TECHNICAL TRAINING CENTER
Dallas, Texas

Admissions Contact Mr. Brian DeLozier, Director, ATI Technical Training Center, 6627 Maple Avenue, Dallas, TX 75235. *Phone:* 214-352-2222.

AUSTIN BUSINESS COLLEGE
Austin, Texas

Admissions Contact Ms. Pam Binns, Director of Admissions, Austin Business College, 2101 Interstate Highway 35, Suite 300, Austin, TX 78741. *Phone:* 512-447-9415. *Toll-free phone:* 512-447-9415. *Fax:* 512-447-0194. *E-mail:* abc@austinbusinesscollege.org.

AUSTIN COMMUNITY COLLEGE
Austin, Texas

- **District-supported** 2-year, founded 1972
- **Calendar** semesters
- **Degree** certificates and associate
- **Urban** campus
- **Coed,** 35,576 undergraduate students

Undergraduates Students come from 93 other countries, 0.2% are from out of state, 7% African American, 6% Asian American or Pacific Islander, 22% Hispanic American, 0.9% Native American, 2% international.

Freshmen *Admission:* 4,701 applied, 4,701 admitted.

Faculty *Total:* 1,479, 28% full-time. *Student/faculty ratio:* 20:1.

Majors Accounting; administrative assistant and secretarial science; art; astronomy; automobile/automotive mechanics technology; biology/biological sciences; business administration and management; chemistry; clinical/medical laboratory technology; commercial and advertising art; computer and information sciences related; computer programming; computer programming related; computer science; computer systems networking and telecommunications; construction engineering technology; consumer merchandising/retailing management; criminal justice/law enforcement administration; criminal justice/police science; data entry/microcomputer applications; developmental and child psychology; drafting and design technology; economics; electrical, electronic and communications engineering technology; emergency medical technology (EMT paramedic); English; fashion merchandising; finance; fire science; French; geology/earth science; German; graphic and printing equipment operation/production; heating, air conditioning, ventilation and refrigeration maintenance technology; history; hospitality and recreation marketing; hotel/motel administration; human services; industrial radiologic technology; industrial technology; information science/studies; information technology; insurance; Japanese; journalism; legal administrative assistant/secretary; legal assistant/paralegal; liberal arts and sciences/liberal studies; marketing/marketing management; mass communication/media; mathematics; medical/clinical assistant; music; nursing (registered nurse training); occupational therapy; photography; physical sciences; physics; political science and government; pre-engineering; psychology; quality control technology; radio and television; real estate; Russian; sign language interpretation and translation; social work; sociology; Spanish; speech and rhetoric; surgical technology; survey technology; system administration; technical and business writing; welding technology.

Academic Programs *Special study options:* academic remediation for entering students, accelerated degree program, adult/continuing education programs, advanced placement credit, cooperative education, distance learning, English as a second language, external degree program, honors programs, independent study, internships, part-time degree program, services for LD students, summer session for credit. *ROTC:* Army (c), Air Force (c).

Library Main Library plus 6 others with 115,567 titles, 1,974 serial subscriptions, 14,044 audiovisual materials, an OPAC, a Web page.

Computers on Campus 225 computers available on campus for general student use. A campuswide network can be accessed from off campus. Internet access, at least one staffed computer lab available.

Student Life *Housing:* college housing not available. *Activities and Organizations:* drama/theater group, student-run newspaper. *Student services:* personal/psychological counseling.

Athletics *Intramural sports:* basketball M/W, football M, golf M, racquetball M/W, volleyball M/W, weight lifting M/W.

Costs (2003–04) *Tuition:* area resident $768 full-time, $32 per credit hour part-time; state resident $2016 full-time, $84 per credit hour part-time; nonresident $4104 full-time, $171 per credit hour part-time. Full-time tuition and fees vary according to course load. Part-time tuition and fees vary according to course load. *Required fees:* $294 full-time, $12 per credit hour part-time. *Payment plan:* installment. *Waivers:* senior citizens and employees or children of employees.

Financial Aid Of all full-time matriculated undergraduates who enrolled, 296 Federal Work-Study jobs (averaging $2000). 12 state and other part-time jobs (averaging $2000).

Applying *Options:* electronic application. *Application deadline:* rolling (freshmen), rolling (transfers).

Admissions Contact Ms. Linda Kluck, Director, Admissions and Records, Austin Community College, 5930 Middle Fiskville Road, Austin, TX 78752-4390. *Phone:* 512-223-7765. *Fax:* 512-223-7665.

BLINN COLLEGE
Brenham, Texas

- **State and locally supported** 2-year, founded 1883
- **Calendar** semesters

- **Degree** certificates, diplomas, and associate
- **Small-town** 100-acre campus with easy access to Houston
- **Endowment** $29.8 million
- **Coed**

Faculty *Student/faculty ratio:* 27:1.
Student Life *Campus security:* 24-hour emergency response devices and patrols, controlled dormitory access.
Athletics Member NJCAA.
Standardized Tests *Required:* THEA (for placement).
Costs (2004–05) *Tuition:* state resident $1728 full-time, $67 per hour part-time; nonresident $4000 full-time, $135 per hour part-time. *Room and board:* $3700. Room and board charges vary according to board plan, gender, and housing facility.
Applying *Options:* common application, electronic application, early admission, deferred entrance. *Required:* high school transcript.
Admissions Contact Ms. Brandi Bothe, Coordinator, Recruitment and Admissions, Blinn College, 902 College Avenue, Brenham, TX 77833-4049. *Phone:* 979-830-4152. *Fax:* 979-830-4110. *E-mail:* recruit@blinn.edu.

BORDER INSTITUTE OF TECHNOLOGY
El Paso, Texas

- **Proprietary** 2-year
- **Calendar** quarters
- **Degree** certificates, diplomas, and associate
- **Suburban** campus
- **Coed, primarily men,** 250 undergraduate students

Faculty *Total:* 20, 100% full-time. *Student/faculty ratio:* 7:1.
Majors Business administration and management; data entry/microcomputer applications; interior design; retailing.
Costs (2003–04) *Tuition:* $160 per credit hour part-time. *Required fees:* $10 per term part-time.
Financial Aid Of all full-time matriculated undergraduates who enrolled, 83 Federal Work-Study jobs (averaging $410).
Admissions Contact Mr. Miguel Gamino, Admissions Director, Border Institute of Technology, 9611 Acer Avenue, El Paso, TX 79925-6744. *Phone:* 915-593-7328 Ext. 24.

BRAZOSPORT COLLEGE
Lake Jackson, Texas

- **State and locally supported** 2-year, founded 1968
- **Calendar** semesters
- **Degree** certificates and associate
- **Small-town** 160-acre campus with easy access to Houston
- **Endowment** $3.1 million
- **Coed**

Faculty *Student/faculty ratio:* 18:1.
Student Life *Campus security:* 24-hour patrols.
Standardized Tests *Required for some:* THEA.
Costs (2003–04) *Tuition:* area resident $1020 full-time, $24 per hour part-time; state resident $1530 full-time, $41 per hour part-time; nonresident $2940 full-time, $88 per hour part-time. Full-time tuition and fees vary according to course load. Part-time tuition and fees vary according to course load. *Required fees:* $9 per hour part-time, $15 per term part-time.
Applying *Options:* early admission, deferred entrance. *Required for some:* high school transcript.
Admissions Contact Ms. Patricia S. Leyendecker, Director of Admissions/Registrar, Brazosport College, 500 College Drive, Lake Jackson, TX 77566. *Phone:* 979-230-3217. *Fax:* 979-230-3376. *E-mail:* regist@brazosport.edu.

BROOKHAVEN COLLEGE
Farmers Branch, Texas

Admissions Contact Thoa Vo, Registrar, Brookhaven College, 3939 Valley View Lane, Farmers Branch, TX 75244-4997. *Phone:* 972-860-4604. *Fax:* 972-860-4897. *E-mail:* bhc2310@dcccd.edu.

CEDAR VALLEY COLLEGE
Lancaster, Texas

- **State-supported** 2-year, founded 1977, part of Dallas County Community College District System
- **Calendar** semesters

- **Degree** certificates and associate
- **Suburban** 353-acre campus with easy access to Dallas-Fort Worth
- **Coed,** 4,405 undergraduate students, 33% full-time, 42% women, 58% men

Undergraduates 1,462 full-time, 2,943 part-time. Students come from 5 other countries, 2% are from out of state, 50% African American, 2% Asian American or Pacific Islander, 11% Hispanic American, 0.4% Native American, 0.6% international.
Freshmen *Admission:* 1,565 applied, 1,565 admitted.
Faculty *Total:* 153, 41% full-time. *Student/faculty ratio:* 26:1.
Majors Accounting; administrative assistant and secretarial science; automobile/automotive mechanics technology; business administration and management; computer programming; computer programming (specific applications); criminal justice/law enforcement administration; data processing and data processing technology; heating, air conditioning, ventilation and refrigeration maintenance technology; liberal arts and sciences/liberal studies; management information systems and services related; marketing/marketing management; music; radio and television broadcasting technology; real estate; veterinary/animal health technology.
Academic Programs *Special study options:* academic remediation for entering students, advanced placement credit, cooperative education, distance learning, English as a second language, part-time degree program, services for LD students, summer session for credit. *ROTC:* Army (c).
Library Cedar Valley College Library with 43,788 titles, 217 serial subscriptions, 16,460 audiovisual materials, an OPAC, a Web page.
Computers on Campus 600 computers available on campus for general student use. A campuswide network can be accessed from off campus. Internet access, online (class) registration, at least one staffed computer lab available.
Student Life *Housing:* college housing not available. *Activities and Organizations:* drama/theater group, choral group, African-American Student Organization, Latin-American Student Organization, Veterinary Technology Club, Phi Theta Kappa, Police Academy Club. *Campus security:* 24-hour emergency response devices and patrols. *Student services:* health clinic, personal/psychological counseling.
Athletics Member NJCAA. *Intercollegiate sports:* baseball M, basketball M, soccer W, volleyball W. *Intramural sports:* cheerleading W.
Standardized Tests *Required:* THEA (for admission). *Recommended:* SAT I or ACT (for admission).
Costs (2003–04) *Tuition:* area resident $900 full-time, $30 per credit part-time; state resident $1500 full-time, $50 per credit part-time; nonresident $2400 full-time, $200 per credit part-time. *Payment plan:* installment.
Applying *Options:* electronic application, early admission. *Required for some:* letters of recommendation, interview. *Recommended:* high school transcript. *Application deadline:* rolling (freshmen), rolling (transfers). *Notification:* continuous (freshmen), continuous (transfers).
Admissions Contact Ms. Carolyn Ward, Director of Admissions/Registrar, Cedar Valley College, 3030 North Dallas Avenue, Lancaster, TX 75134-3799. *Phone:* 972-860-8201. *E-mail:* jww3310@dcccd.edu.

CENTER FOR ADVANCED LEGAL STUDIES
Houston, Texas

Admissions Contact 3910 Kirby Drive, Suite 200, Houston, TX 77098-4151.

CENTRAL TEXAS COLLEGE
Killeen, Texas

- **State and locally supported** 2-year, founded 1967
- **Calendar** semesters
- **Degree** certificates and associate
- **Suburban** 500-acre campus with easy access to Austin
- **Endowment** $1.5 million
- **Coed**

Faculty *Student/faculty ratio:* 40:1.
Student Life *Campus security:* 24-hour emergency response devices and patrols.
Standardized Tests *Required:* THEA (for placement). *Recommended:* SAT I or ACT (for placement), SAT II: Subject Tests (for placement), SAT II: Writing Test (for placement).
Costs (2004–05) *Tuition:* area resident $900 full-time, $22 per hour part-time; state resident $1050 full-time, $27 per hour part-time; nonresident $3300 full-time, $75 per hour part-time. *Required fees:* $390 full-time, $8 per hour part-time. *Room and board:* $3548.
Financial Aid Of all full-time matriculated undergraduates who enrolled, 68 Federal Work-Study jobs.

Central Texas College (continued)

Applying *Options:* electronic application, early admission, deferred entrance. *Required:* high school transcript, minimum 2.0 GPA.

Admissions Contact Mr. David McClure, Associate Dean of Guidance and Counseling, Central Texas College, PO Box 1800, Killeen, TX 76540-1800. *Phone:* 254-526-1452. *Toll-free phone:* 800-792-3348 Ext. 1696 (in-state); 800-792-3348 Ext. 1132 (out-of-state). *Fax:* 254-526-1481. *E-mail:* guid_cou@ctcd.cc.tx.us.

▶ **See page 526 for a narrative description.**

CISCO JUNIOR COLLEGE
Cisco, Texas

- **State and locally supported** 2-year, founded 1940
- **Calendar** semesters
- **Degree** certificates and associate
- **Rural** 40-acre campus
- **Coed**

Faculty *Student/faculty ratio:* 18:1.

Student Life *Campus security:* late-night transport/escort service.

Athletics Member NJCAA.

Standardized Tests *Required:* THEA (for placement). *Recommended:* SAT I and SAT II or ACT (for placement).

Costs (2003–04) *Tuition:* area resident $2304 full-time, $96 per hour part-time; state resident $2448 full-time, $102 per hour part-time; nonresident $6120 full-time, $255 per hour part-time. Full-time tuition and fees vary according to course load. Part-time tuition and fees vary according to course load. *Room and board:* Room and board charges vary according to gender.

Applying *Options:* early admission.

Admissions Contact Mr. Olin O. Odom III, Dean of Admission/Registrar, Cisco Junior College, Box 3, Route 3, Cisco, TX 76437-9321. *Phone:* 254-442-2567 Ext. 130.

CLARENDON COLLEGE
Clarendon, Texas

- **State and locally supported** 2-year, founded 1898
- **Calendar** semesters
- **Degree** certificates and associate
- **Rural** 88-acre campus
- **Coed,** 963 undergraduate students, 40% full-time, 46% women, 54% men

Undergraduates 388 full-time, 575 part-time. Students come from 19 states and territories, 16% African American, 1% Asian American or Pacific Islander, 16% Hispanic American, 1% Native American, 1% international.

Freshmen *Admission:* 370 applied, 359 admitted, 130 enrolled.

Faculty *Total:* 71, 46% full-time, 3% with terminal degrees. *Student/faculty ratio:* 15:1.

Majors Accounting; agribusiness; agricultural economics; agriculture; behavioral sciences; biology/biological sciences; business administration and management; chemistry; computer and information sciences; dramatic/theatre arts; education; electrical, electronic and communications engineering technology; elementary education; English; farm and ranch management; finance; health services/allied health/health sciences; history; horse husbandry/equine science and management; kinesiology and exercise science; liberal arts and sciences/liberal studies; marketing/marketing management; mathematics; music; nursing (registered nurse training); physical education teaching and coaching; physical therapy; political science and government related; pre-dentistry studies; pre-medical studies; psychology; secondary education; social sciences; social work related; sociology; speech and rhetoric.

Academic Programs *Special study options:* academic remediation for entering students, adult/continuing education programs, part-time degree program, summer session for credit.

Library Clarendon College Library/Learning Resource Center with 20,000 titles.

Computers on Campus 30 computers available on campus for general student use. At least one staffed computer lab available.

Student Life *Housing:* on-campus residence required through sophomore year. *Options:* Campus housing is university owned. *Activities and Organizations:* drama/theater group, choral group. *Campus security:* 8-hour patrols by trained security personnel.

Athletics Member NJCAA. *Intercollegiate sports:* baseball M, basketball M(s)/W(s), softball W, volleyball M/W. *Intramural sports:* basketball M/W, cheerleading W, football M/W, volleyball M/W.

Standardized Tests *Required:* ACT (for placement), THEA (for placement).

Costs (2003–04) *Tuition:* area resident $1050 full-time, $35 per credit hour part-time; state resident $1500 full-time, $50 per credit hour part-time; nonresident $1950 full-time, $65 per credit hour part-time. Full-time tuition and fees

vary according to program. Part-time tuition and fees vary according to course load and program. *Required fees:* $480 full-time, $15 per credit hour part-time, $45 per term part-time. *Room and board:* $2900; room only: $1000. *Payment plan:* installment. *Waivers:* senior citizens.

Financial Aid Of all full-time matriculated undergraduates who enrolled, 41 Federal Work-Study jobs (averaging $985). 9 state and other part-time jobs (averaging $860).

Applying *Options:* early admission, deferred entrance. *Required:* high school transcript. *Required for some:* letters of recommendation, interview. *Application deadline:* rolling (freshmen), rolling (transfers). *Notification:* continuous (freshmen), continuous (transfers).

Admissions Contact Ms. Sharon Hannon, Admissions Director/Registrar, Clarendon College, PO Box 968, Clarendon, TX 79226-0968. *Phone:* 806-874-3571 Ext. 232. *Toll-free phone:* 800-687-9737. *Fax:* 806-874-3201.

COASTAL BEND COLLEGE
Beeville, Texas

- **County-supported** 2-year, founded 1965
- **Calendar** semesters
- **Degree** certificates and associate
- **Rural** 100-acre campus
- **Endowment** $825,011
- **Coed,** 3,660 undergraduate students, 47% full-time, 58% women, 42% men

Undergraduates 1,719 full-time, 1,941 part-time. Students come from 15 states and territories, 3 other countries, 1% are from out of state, 5% African American, 0.4% Asian American or Pacific Islander, 60% Hispanic American, 0.5% Native American, 0.1% international, 60% transferred in, 5% live on campus. *Retention:* 62% of 2002 full-time freshmen returned.

Freshmen *Admission:* 1,002 enrolled.

Faculty *Total:* 187, 53% full-time, 5% with terminal degrees. *Student/faculty ratio:* 18:1.

Majors Accounting; administrative assistant and secretarial science; agriculture; applied art; art; art teacher education; automobile/automotive mechanics technology; biological and physical sciences; biology/biological sciences; business administration and management; chemistry; child development; commercial and advertising art; computer and information sciences related; computer engineering technology; computer programming related; computer programming (specific applications); computer programming (vendor/product certification); computer science; computer systems networking and telecommunications; cosmetology; criminal justice/law enforcement administration; criminal justice/police science; data entry/microcomputer applications; data entry/microcomputer applications related; data processing and data processing technology; dental hygiene; developmental and child psychology; drafting and design technology; dramatic/theatre arts; economics; education; elementary education; engineering; English; environmental engineering technology; finance; fine/studio arts; French; geology/earth science; German; health teacher education; history; information technology; journalism; legal administrative assistant/secretary; liberal arts and sciences/liberal studies; mathematics; music; music teacher education; nursing (licensed practical/vocational nurse training); nursing (registered nurse training); parks, recreation and leisure; petroleum technology; pharmacy; physical education teaching and coaching; physical sciences; physics; political science and government; psychology; public relations/image management; sociology; speech and rhetoric; system administration; voice and opera; welding technology; word processing.

Academic Programs *Special study options:* academic remediation for entering students, adult/continuing education programs, advanced placement credit, cooperative education, distance learning, internships, part-time degree program, services for LD students, summer session for credit. *ROTC:* Army (c), Air Force (c).

Library Grady C. Hogue Learning Resource Center with 37,971 titles, 268 serial subscriptions, 2,974 audiovisual materials, an OPAC.

Computers on Campus 970 computers available on campus for general student use. A campuswide network can be accessed from off campus. Internet access, online (class) registration, at least one staffed computer lab available.

Student Life *Housing Options:* coed, men-only, women-only, disabled students. Campus housing is university owned. *Activities and Organizations:* drama/theater group, choral group, student government, Computer Science Club, Creative Writing Club, Drama Club, Art Club. *Campus security:* 24-hour emergency response devices. *Student services:* personal/psychological counseling.

Athletics *Intramural sports:* archery M/W, badminton M/W, basketball M/W, bowling M/W, cross-country running M/W, golf M/W, soccer M/W, softball M/W, table tennis M/W, tennis M/W, track and field M/W, volleyball M/W, weight lifting M/W.

Standardized Tests *Required:* THEA or ACT COMPASS (for placement).

Costs (2003–04) *Tuition:* area resident $1044 full-time, $44 per hour part-time; state resident $1684 full-time, $69 per hour part-time; nonresident $1948 full-time, $110 per hour part-time. *Required fees:* $40 full-time. *Room and board:* room only: $1300.

Financial Aid Of all full-time matriculated undergraduates who enrolled, 80 Federal Work-Study jobs (averaging $1484). 11 state and other part-time jobs (averaging $1159).

Applying *Options:* deferred entrance. *Required:* high school transcript. *Application deadline:* rolling (freshmen), rolling (transfers). *Notification:* continuous (freshmen), continuous (transfers).

Admissions Contact Ms. Alicia Ulloa, Director of Admissions/Registrar, Coastal Bend College, 3800 Charco Road, Beeville, TX 78102-2197. *Phone:* 361-354-2251. *Fax:* 361-354-2254. *E-mail:* register@cbc.cc.tx.us.

COLLEGE OF THE MAINLAND
Texas City, Texas

- **State and locally supported** 2-year, founded 1967
- **Calendar** semesters
- **Degree** certificates, diplomas, and associate
- **Small-town** 120-acre campus with easy access to Houston
- **Coed**

Faculty *Student/faculty ratio:* 12:1.

Student Life *Campus security:* 24-hour emergency response devices and patrols, student patrols.

Standardized Tests *Required for some:* SAT I and SAT II or ACT (for placement), THEA.

Costs (2003–04) *Tuition:* area resident $528 full-time, $22 per credit part-time; state resident $1224 full-time, $51 per credit part-time; nonresident $1842 full-time, $76 per credit part-time. Full-time tuition and fees vary according to course load. Part-time tuition and fees vary according to course load. *Required fees:* $143 full-time, $10 per credit part-time, $58 per term part-time.

Financial Aid Of all full-time matriculated undergraduates who enrolled, 137 Federal Work-Study jobs (averaging $1127). 145 state and other part-time jobs (averaging $936).

Applying *Options:* electronic application, early admission, deferred entrance. *Required for some:* high school transcript.

Admissions Contact College of the Mainland, 1200 Amburn Road, Texas City, TX 77591. *Phone:* 409-938-1211 Ext. 469. *Toll-free phone:* 888-258-8859 Ext. 264. *Fax:* 409-938-3126. *E-mail:* sem@com.edu.

COLLIN COUNTY COMMUNITY COLLEGE DISTRICT
Plano, Texas

- **State and locally supported** 2-year, founded 1985
- **Calendar** semesters
- **Degree** certificates and associate
- **Suburban** 333-acre campus with easy access to Dallas-Fort Worth
- **Endowment** $925,270
- **Coed,** 16,574 undergraduate students, 40% full-time, 57% women, 43% men

Undergraduates 6,621 full-time, 9,953 part-time. Students come from 44 states and territories, 86 other countries, 3% are from out of state, 7% African American, 6% Asian American or Pacific Islander, 8% Hispanic American, 0.6% Native American, 8% international, 11% transferred in.

Freshmen *Admission:* 2,966 admitted, 2,966 enrolled.

Faculty *Total:* 799, 25% full-time, 22% with terminal degrees. *Student/faculty ratio:* 25:1.

Majors Biology/biotechnology laboratory technician; business administration and management; business automation/technology/data entry; commercial and advertising art; computer and information sciences; computer engineering technology; computer programming; computer systems networking and telecommunications; dental hygiene; drafting and design technology; educational/instructional media design; electrical, electronic and communications engineering technology; electrical/electronics drafting and CAD/CADD; electrical/electronics equipment installation and repair; emergency medical technology (EMT paramedic); environmental engineering technology; family and community services; fire protection and safety technology; hospitality administration; interior design; legal assistant/paralegal; liberal arts and sciences/liberal studies; music management and merchandising; nursing (registered nurse training); real estate; respiratory care therapy; sales, distribution and marketing; sign language interpretation and translation; telecommunications technology; water quality and wastewater treatment management and recycling technology; web page, digital/multimedia and information resources design.

Academic Programs *Special study options:* academic remediation for entering students, adult/continuing education programs, advanced placement credit, cooperative education, distance learning, English as a second language, honors programs, internships, part-time degree program, services for LD students, study abroad, summer session for credit.

Library Main Library plus 3 others with 129,032 titles, 940 serial subscriptions, 17,342 audiovisual materials, an OPAC, a Web page.

Computers on Campus 1858 computers available on campus for general student use. A campuswide network can be accessed from student residence rooms. Internet access, online (class) registration, at least one staffed computer lab available. Computer purchase or lease plan available.

Student Life *Housing:* college housing not available. *Activities and Organizations:* drama/theater group, choral group, Phi Theta Kappa, LULAC/BSN, Baptist Student Ministry, Psi Beta, Collin Nursing Student Association. *Campus security:* 24-hour emergency response devices and patrols, late-night transport/escort service, controlled dormitory access. *Student services:* personal/psychological counseling.

Athletics Member NJCAA. *Intercollegiate sports:* basketball M(s)/W(s), tennis M(s)/W(s), volleyball W(s).

Standardized Tests *Required:* THEA (for admission).

Costs (2003–04) *Tuition:* area resident $750 full-time, $25 per credit hour part-time; state resident $930 full-time, $31 per credit hour part-time; nonresident $2340 full-time, $78 per credit hour part-time. *Required fees:* $304 full-time, $10 per credit hour part-time, $2 per term part-time. *Payment plan:* installment. *Waivers:* senior citizens.

Financial Aid Of all full-time matriculated undergraduates who enrolled, 80 Federal Work-Study jobs (averaging $3490).

Applying *Options:* electronic application. *Application deadline:* rolling (freshmen). *Notification:* continuous (freshmen), continuous (transfers).

Admissions Contact Ms. Stephanie Meinhardt, Registrar, Collin County Community College District, 2200 West University Drive, McKinney, TX 75070-8001. *Phone:* 972-881-5174. *Fax:* 972-881-5175. *E-mail:* smeinhardt@ccccd.edu.

COMMONWEALTH INSTITUTE OF FUNERAL SERVICE
Houston, Texas

- **Independent** 2-year, founded 1988
- **Calendar** quarters
- **Degree** certificates and associate
- **Urban** campus
- **Coed,** 152 undergraduate students, 95% full-time, 51% women, 49% men

Undergraduates 144 full-time, 8 part-time. Students come from 11 states and territories, 20% are from out of state, 39% African American, 20% Hispanic American, 0.7% Native American, 7% transferred in.

Freshmen *Admission:* 58 enrolled.

Faculty *Total:* 9, 44% full-time. *Student/faculty ratio:* 34:1.

Majors Funeral service and mortuary science.

Academic Programs *Special study options:* adult/continuing education programs, external degree program.

Library Commonwealth Institute Library and York Learning Resource Center with 1,500 titles, 12 serial subscriptions.

Computers on Campus 15 computers available on campus for general student use. At least one staffed computer lab available.

Student Life *Housing:* college housing not available. *Activities and Organizations:* student council. *Campus security:* 24-hour emergency response devices.

Standardized Tests *Required for some:* Wonderlic aptitude test or THEA. *Recommended:* SAT I or ACT (for admission).

Costs (2004–05) *Tuition:* $9400 full-time, $13 per contact hour part-time. *Required fees:* $100 full-time.

Applying *Options:* common application. *Application fee:* $50. *Required:* high school transcript. *Application deadline:* rolling (freshmen). *Notification:* continuous (freshmen).

Admissions Contact Mrs. Patricia Moreno, Registrar, Commonwealth Institute of Funeral Service, 415 Barren Springs Drive, Houston, TX 77090. *Phone:* 281-873-0262. *Toll-free phone:* 800-628-1580. *Fax:* 281-873-5232.

COMPUTER CAREER CENTER
El Paso, Texas

- **Proprietary** 2-year
- **Calendar** 8 six-week terms
- **Degree** certificates, diplomas, and associate
- **Urban** campus
- **Coed**

Admissions Contact Ms. Sarah Hernandez, Registrar, Computer Career Center, 6101 Montana Avenue, El Paso, TX 79925. *Phone:* 915-779-8031.

COURT REPORTING INSTITUTE OF DALLAS
Dallas, Texas

- **Proprietary** 2-year, founded 1978
- **Calendar** quarters
- **Degree** associate
- **Urban** campus
- **Coed, primarily women,** 526 undergraduate students, 100% full-time, 97% women, 3% men

Undergraduates 526 full-time. Students come from 15 states and territories, 10% are from out of state, 28% African American, 1% Asian American or Pacific Islander, 22% Hispanic American, 0.4% Native American, 0.2% international, 19% transferred in.
Freshmen *Admission:* 116 enrolled.
Faculty *Total:* 30, 50% full-time, 13% with terminal degrees. *Student/faculty ratio:* 35:1.
Majors Court reporting.
Student Life *Housing:* college housing not available. *Activities and Organizations:* student-run newspaper. *Campus security:* 24-hour patrols, late-night transport/escort service.
Costs (2003–04) *Tuition:* $2222 full-time, $1500 per term part-time. Part-time tuition and fees vary according to program. *Required fees:* $100 full-time, $25 per term part-time. *Payment plan:* installment.
Applying *Options:* early decision. *Application fee:* $100. *Required:* high school transcript, interview.
Admissions Contact Ms. Debra Smith-Armstrong, Director of Admissions, Court Reporting Institute of Dallas, 8585 North Stemmons, #200 North, Dallas, TX 75247. *Phone:* 214-350-9722 Ext. 227. *Toll-free phone:* 800-880-9722.

COURT REPORTING INSTITUTE OF HOUSTON
Houston, Texas

Admissions Contact 13101 Northwest Freeway, Suite 100, Houston, TX 77040. *Toll-free phone:* 866-996-8300.

CY-FAIR COLLEGE
Houston, Texas

- **State and locally supported** 2-year, founded 2002, part of North Harris Montgomery Community Course District
- **Calendar** semesters
- **Degree** certificates, diplomas, and associate
- **Suburban** 200-acre campus
- **Coed,** 6,900 undergraduate students

Undergraduates Students come from 36 other countries, 9% African American, 10% Asian American or Pacific Islander, 22% Hispanic American, 3% Native American, 3% international.
Faculty *Total:* 368, 30% full-time.
Academic Programs *Special study options:* academic remediation for entering students, adult/continuing education programs, advanced placement credit, cooperative education, distance learning, English as a second language, external degree program, honors programs, independent study, internships, part-time degree program, services for LD students.
Standardized Tests *Required for some:* SAT I or ACT (for placement).
Costs (2004–05) *Tuition:* area resident $768 full-time, $32 per credit hour part-time; state resident $1728 full-time, $72 per credit hour part-time; nonresident $2088 full-time, $87 per credit hour part-time. *Required fees:* $216 full-time, $8 per credit hour part-time, $12 per term part-time.
Applying *Options:* electronic application.
Admissions Contact Dr. Earl Campa, Vice President of Student Success, Cy-Fair College, 9191 Barker Cypress Road, Cypress, TX 77433-1383. *Phone:* 281-290-3950.

DALLAS INSTITUTE OF FUNERAL SERVICE
Dallas, Texas

- **Independent** 2-year, founded 1945
- **Calendar** quarters
- **Degree** associate
- **Urban** 8-acre campus with easy access to Dallas/Ft. Worth

- **Coed,** 221 undergraduate students, 100% full-time, 45% women, 55% men

Undergraduates 220 full-time, 1 part-time. Students come from 12 states and territories, 10% are from out of state, 29% African American, 0.5% Asian American or Pacific Islander, 11% Hispanic American, 11% transferred in.
Freshmen *Admission:* 63 applied, 50 admitted, 50 enrolled.
Faculty *Total:* 10, 50% full-time, 20% with terminal degrees. *Student/faculty ratio:* 16:1.
Majors Funeral service and mortuary science.
Student Life *Housing:* college housing not available. *Campus security:* 24-hour emergency response devices.
Costs (2004–05) *Tuition:* $9400 full-time, $175 per hour part-time. Part-time tuition and fees vary according to course load. No tuition increase for student's term of enrollment. *Payment plan:* installment.
Applying *Application fee:* $50. *Required:* high school transcript.
Admissions Contact Terry Parrish, Director of Admissions, Dallas Institute of Funeral Service, 3909 S. Buckner Blvd., Dallas, TX 75227. *Phone:* 214-388-5466. *Toll-free phone:* 800-235-5444. *E-mail:* difs@dallasinstitute.edu.

DEL MAR COLLEGE
Corpus Christi, Texas

- **State and locally supported** 2-year, founded 1935
- **Calendar** semesters
- **Degree** certificates and associate
- **Urban** 159-acre campus
- **Endowment** $29.1 million
- **Coed,** 11,338 undergraduate students, 34% full-time, 60% women, 40% men

Undergraduates 3,819 full-time, 7,519 part-time. Students come from 46 states and territories, 57 other countries, 1% are from out of state, 2% African American, 1% Asian American or Pacific Islander, 57% Hispanic American, 0.1% Native American, 0.9% international.
Freshmen *Admission:* 1,770 applied, 1,770 admitted.
Faculty *Total:* 697, 45% full-time. *Student/faculty ratio:* 18:1.
Majors Accounting; accounting technology and bookkeeping; administrative assistant and secretarial science; applied art; architectural engineering technology; art; art teacher education; automobile/automotive mechanics technology; biology/biological sciences; building/property maintenance and management; business administration and management; business/commerce; business machine repair; chemical technology; chemistry; child development; clinical laboratory science/medical technology; clinical/medical laboratory technology; community organization and advocacy; computer and information sciences related; computer programming; computer programming related; computer programming (specific applications); computer programming (vendor/product certification); computer science; computer systems networking and telecommunications; computer/technical support; computer typography and composition equipment operation; consumer merchandising/retailing management; cosmetology; court reporting; criminal justice/law enforcement administration; criminal justice/police science; culinary arts; data entry/microcomputer applications; dental hygiene; diagnostic medical sonography and ultrasound technology; drafting and design technology; dramatic/theatre arts; e-commerce; education; electrical, electronic and communications engineering technology; elementary education; emergency medical technology (EMT paramedic); English; finance; fine/studio arts; fire protection and safety technology; fire science; geography; geology/earth science; health information/medical records technology; health teacher education; heavy equipment maintenance technology; history; hotel/motel administration; industrial radiologic technology; information science/studies; information technology; interdisciplinary studies; journalism; kindergarten/preschool education; legal administrative assistant/secretary; legal studies; liberal arts and sciences/liberal studies; machine tool technology; management information systems; mathematics; medical administrative assistant and medical secretary; medical radiologic technology; mental health/rehabilitation; music; music teacher education; nursing (registered nurse training); occupational safety and health technology; occupational therapist assistant; office occupations and clerical services; parks, recreation and leisure; physical education teaching and coaching; physics; political science and government; pre-engineering; psychology; public administration; public policy analysis; radio and television; real estate; respiratory care therapy; sign language interpretation and translation; social work; sociology; special products marketing; speech and rhetoric; system administration; trade and industrial teacher education; transportation management; veterinary sciences; voice and opera; web/multimedia management and webmaster; web page, digital/multimedia and information resources design; welding technology; word processing.
Academic Programs *Special study options:* academic remediation for entering students, accelerated degree program, adult/continuing education programs, advanced placement credit, cooperative education, distance learning, English as a second language, freshman honors college, honors programs, internships, part-time degree program, services for LD students, summer session for credit. *ROTC:* Army (b).

Library White Library plus 1 other with 127,717 titles, 739 serial subscriptions, an OPAC.

Computers on Campus 450 computers available on campus for general student use. Internet access, online (class) registration, at least one staffed computer lab available.

Student Life *Housing:* college housing not available. *Activities and Organizations:* drama/theater group, student-run newspaper, radio station. *Campus security:* 24-hour emergency response devices and patrols.

Athletics *Intramural sports:* archery M/W, badminton M/W, basketball M/W, bowling M/W, fencing M/W, football M/W, golf M/W, gymnastics M/W, sailing M/W, swimming M/W, tennis M/W, track and field M/W, volleyball M/W, weight lifting M/W.

Standardized Tests *Required:* THEA or ACT ASSET (for placement).

Costs (2003–04) *Tuition:* area resident $1290 full-time; state resident $2490 full-time; nonresident $3480 full-time. Full-time tuition and fees vary according to program. *Required fees:* $540 full-time. *Payment plan:* installment. *Waivers:* senior citizens and employees or children of employees.

Financial Aid Of all full-time matriculated undergraduates who enrolled, 259 Federal Work-Study jobs (averaging $960). 449 state and other part-time jobs (averaging $1082).

Applying *Options:* early admission, deferred entrance. *Required:* high school transcript. *Application deadline:* rolling (freshmen), rolling (transfers).

Admissions Contact Ms. Frances P. Jordan, Assistant Dean of Enrollment Services and Registrar, Del Mar College, 101 Baldwin Boulevard, Corpus Christi, TX 78404-3897. *Phone:* 361-698-1248. *Toll-free phone:* 800-652-3357.

EASTFIELD COLLEGE
Mesquite, Texas

- **State and locally supported** 2-year, founded 1970, part of Dallas County Community College District System
- **Calendar** semesters
- **Degree** certificates and associate
- **Suburban** 244-acre campus with easy access to Dallas-Fort Worth
- **Coed,** 11,708 undergraduate students, 28% full-time, 61% women, 39% men

Undergraduates 3,270 full-time, 8,438 part-time. Students come from 18 states and territories, 1% are from out of state, 20% African American, 5% Asian American or Pacific Islander, 18% Hispanic American, 0.7% Native American, 1% international, 3% transferred in.

Freshmen *Admission:* 1,697 enrolled.

Faculty *Total:* 486, 20% full-time. *Student/faculty ratio:* 19:1.

Majors Accounting; autobody/collision and repair technology; automobile/automotive mechanics technology; business administration and management; child care and support services management; computer and information sciences related; computer engineering technology; computer hardware engineering; computer/information technology services administration related; computer programming; computer programming related; computer systems networking and telecommunications; criminal justice/safety; data entry/microcomputer applications; data processing and data processing technology; drafting and design technology; electrical, electronic and communications engineering technology; electrical/electronics drafting and CAD/CADD; executive assistant/executive secretary; graphic and printing equipment operation/production; heating, air conditioning, ventilation and refrigeration maintenance technology; legal administrative assistant/secretary; liberal arts and sciences/liberal studies; psychiatric/mental health services technology; sign language interpretation and translation; social work; substance abuse/addiction counseling; system administration; word processing.

Academic Programs *Special study options:* academic remediation for entering students, adult/continuing education programs, advanced placement credit, cooperative education, distance learning, English as a second language, honors programs, part-time degree program, services for LD students, summer session for credit.

Library Eastfield College Learning Resource Center with 66,988 titles, 415 serial subscriptions, 2,620 audiovisual materials, an OPAC, a Web page.

Computers on Campus 50 computers available on campus for general student use. A campuswide network can be accessed from off campus. Internet access, at least one staffed computer lab available.

Student Life *Housing:* college housing not available. *Activities and Organizations:* drama/theater group, student-run newspaper, choral group, LULAC, Rodeo Club, PTK, Rising Star, Communications Club. *Campus security:* 24-hour emergency response devices and patrols. *Student services:* health clinic, personal/psychological counseling, women's center.

Athletics Member NJCAA. *Intercollegiate sports:* baseball M, basketball M, golf M, tennis M/W, volleyball M/W. *Intramural sports:* basketball M, football M, softball M/W, volleyball M.

Costs (2003–04) *Tuition:* area resident $900 full-time, $30 per credit part-time; state resident $1500 full-time, $50 per credit part-time; nonresident $2400 full-time, $80 per credit part-time.

Applying *Options:* early admission, deferred entrance. *Recommended:* high school transcript. *Application deadline:* rolling (freshmen), rolling (transfers). *Notification:* continuous (freshmen), continuous (transfers).

Admissions Contact Ms. Linda Richardson, Director of Admissions/Registrar, Eastfield College, 3737 Motley Drive, Mesquite, TX 75150-2099. *Phone:* 972-860-7105. *Fax:* 912-860-8306. *E-mail:* efc@dcccd.edu.

EL CENTRO COLLEGE
Dallas, Texas

- **County-supported** 2-year, founded 1966, part of Dallas County Community College District System
- **Calendar** semesters
- **Degree** certificates and associate
- **Urban** 2-acre campus
- **Coed,** 5,884 undergraduate students, 27% full-time, 70% women, 30% men

Undergraduates 1,567 full-time, 4,317 part-time. Students come from 20 states and territories, 40 other countries, 3% are from out of state, 35% African American, 4% Asian American or Pacific Islander, 24% Hispanic American, 0.4% Native American, 3% international, 16% transferred in.

Freshmen *Admission:* 668 applied, 668 admitted, 668 enrolled.

Faculty *Total:* 390, 29% full-time, 7% with terminal degrees. *Student/faculty ratio:* 16:1.

Majors Accounting; administrative assistant and secretarial science; architectural engineering technology; baking and pastry arts; business administration and management; business automation/technology/data entry; cardiovascular technology; clinical laboratory science/medical technology; clinical/medical laboratory technology; clothing/textiles; computer/information technology services administration related; computer programming; computer science; criminal justice/police science; criminal justice/safety; culinary arts; data processing and data processing technology; diagnostic medical sonography and ultrasound technology; drafting and design technology; emergency medical technology (EMT paramedic); fashion/apparel design; food science; food services technology; health information/medical records administration; hospitality administration; hotel/motel administration; information science/studies; information technology; interior design; legal administrative assistant/secretary; legal assistant/paralegal; legal studies; liberal arts and sciences/liberal studies; medical administrative assistant and medical secretary; medical/clinical assistant; medical radiologic technology; medical transcription; nursing (licensed practical/vocational nurse training); nursing (registered nurse training); office occupations and clerical services; radiologic technology/science; respiratory care therapy; special products marketing; surgical technology; teacher assistant/aide; web page, digital/multimedia and information resources design.

Academic Programs *Special study options:* academic remediation for entering students, adult/continuing education programs, advanced placement credit, cooperative education, distance learning, double majors, English as a second language, freshman honors college, honors programs, internships, part-time degree program, services for LD students, summer session for credit. *ROTC:* Army (c).

Library El Centro College Library with 72,176 titles, 371 serial subscriptions, 5,463 audiovisual materials, an OPAC, a Web page.

Computers on Campus 832 computers available on campus for general student use. A campuswide network can be accessed from off campus. Internet access, online (class) registration, at least one staffed computer lab available.

Student Life *Housing:* college housing not available. *Activities and Organizations:* choral group, Phi Theta Kappa, Radiology Club, SPAR (Student Programs and Resources Office), Organization of Latin American Students. *Campus security:* 24-hour emergency response devices and patrols, late-night transport/escort service. *Student services:* health clinic, personal/psychological counseling.

Athletics *Intramural sports:* basketball M/W, table tennis M/W, volleyball M/W, weight lifting M/W.

Standardized Tests *Required:* THEA, ACCUPLACER (for placement). *Recommended:* SAT I or ACT (for placement).

Costs (2003–04) *Tuition:* area resident $720 full-time, $30 per credit part-time; state resident $1200 full-time, $50 per credit part-time; nonresident $1920 full-time, $80 per credit part-time. *Required fees:* $10 full-time, $5 per term part-time. *Payment plan:* installment. *Waivers:* employees or children of employees.

Applying *Options:* electronic application, early admission. *Required for some:* high school transcript, 1 letter of recommendation. *Application deadline:* rolling (freshmen), rolling (transfers).

Admissions Contact Ms. Stevie Stewart, Director of Admissions and Registrar, El Centro College, 801 Main Street, Dallas, TX 75202. *Phone:* 214-860-2618. *Fax:* 214-860-2233. *E-mail:* sgs5310@dcccd.edu.

EL PASO COMMUNITY COLLEGE
El Paso, Texas

Admissions Contact Daryle Hendry, Director of Admissions, El Paso Community College, PO Box 20500, El Paso, TX 79998-0500. *Phone:* 915-831-2580.

EVEREST COLLEGE
Arlington, Texas

Admissions Contact 2801 East Division Street, Suite 250, Arlington, TX 76011.

EVEREST COLLEGE
Dallas, Texas

Admissions Contact 6060 North Central Expressway, Suite 101, Dallas, TX 75206-5209.

FRANK PHILLIPS COLLEGE
Borger, Texas

Admissions Contact Mrs. Daytha Trimble, Director of Admissions, Frank Phillips College, Borger, TX 79008-5118. *Phone:* 806-274-5311. *Toll-free phone:* 800-687-2056. *Fax:* 806-274-6835. *E-mail:* dtrimble@fpc.cc.tx.us.

GALVESTON COLLEGE
Galveston, Texas

- **State and locally supported** 2-year, founded 1967
- **Calendar** semesters
- **Degree** certificates and associate
- **Urban** 11-acre campus with easy access to Houston
- **Coed,** 2,214 undergraduate students, 37% full-time, 65% women, 35% men

Undergraduates 814 full-time, 1,400 part-time. Students come from 29 states and territories, 19 other countries, 3% are from out of state, 19% African American, 3% Asian American or Pacific Islander, 24% Hispanic American, 0.4% Native American, 2% international, 14% transferred in.
Freshmen *Admission:* 477 applied, 477 admitted, 477 enrolled.
Faculty *Total:* 148, 38% full-time.
Majors Administrative assistant and secretarial science; behavioral sciences; biological and physical sciences; business administration and management; computer and information sciences related; computer science; computer/technical support; criminal justice/police science; culinary arts; data entry/microcomputer applications; dramatic/theatre arts; education; emergency medical technology (EMT paramedic); English; history; hotel/motel administration; humanities; information technology; liberal arts and sciences/liberal studies; mathematics; medical radiologic technology; modern languages; music; natural sciences; nuclear medical technology; nursing (licensed practical/vocational nurse training); nursing (registered nurse training); physical education teaching and coaching; physical sciences; social sciences; social work; web page, digital/multimedia and information resources design; word processing.
Academic Programs *Special study options:* academic remediation for entering students, adult/continuing education programs, advanced placement credit, cooperative education, distance learning, English as a second language, internships, off-campus study, part-time degree program, services for LD students, summer session for credit.
Library David Glenn Hunt Memorial Library with 45,193 titles, 4,000 serial subscriptions, 1,500 audiovisual materials, an OPAC, a Web page.
Computers on Campus 173 computers available on campus for general student use. A campuswide network can be accessed. Internet access, at least one staffed computer lab available.
Student Life *Housing:* college housing not available. *Activities and Organizations:* drama/theater group, choral group, student government, Phi Theta Kappa, Student Nurses Association, ATTC, Hispanic Student Organization. *Campus security:* 24-hour emergency response devices, late-night transport/escort service. *Student services:* personal/psychological counseling.
Athletics Member NJCAA. *Intercollegiate sports:* baseball M(s), softball W(s), volleyball W(s). *Intramural sports:* basketball M/W, bowling M/W, volleyball M/W.
Costs (2004–05) *Tuition:* state resident $900 full-time, $180 per term part-time; nonresident $1800 full-time, $360 per term part-time. *Required fees:* $478 full-time, $102 per term part-time.
Financial Aid Of all full-time matriculated undergraduates who enrolled, 36 Federal Work-Study jobs (averaging $2000).

Applying *Options:* common application. *Required for some:* high school transcript. *Application deadline:* rolling (freshmen), rolling (transfers). *Notification:* continuous (freshmen), continuous (transfers).
Admissions Contact MaEsther Francis, Dean of Enrollment Management and Student Success, Galveston College, 4015 Avenue Q, Galveston, TX 77550. *Phone:* 409-944-1238. *Fax:* 409-944-1501. *E-mail:* lhumphries@gc.edu.

GRAYSON COUNTY COLLEGE
Denison, Texas

- **State and locally supported** 2-year, founded 1964
- **Calendar** semesters
- **Degree** certificates, diplomas, and associate
- **Rural** 500-acre campus
- **Coed**

Faculty *Student/faculty ratio:* 16:1.
Athletics Member NJCAA.
Standardized Tests *Required:* THEA (for placement). *Recommended:* SAT I or ACT (for placement).
Costs (2003–04) *Tuition:* area resident $672 full-time, $37 per semester hour part-time; state resident $816 full-time, $43 per semester hour part-time; nonresident $1584 full-time, $81 per semester hour part-time. *Required fees:* $216 full-time. *Room and board:* $2520.
Applying *Options:* early admission, deferred entrance.
Admissions Contact Dr. David Petrash, Associate Vice President for Admissions, Records and Institutional Research, Grayson County College, 6101 Grayson Drive, Denison, TX 75020. *Phone:* 903-465-6030. *Fax:* 903-463-5284.

HALLMARK INSTITUTE OF AERONAUTICS
San Antonio, Texas

Admissions Contact Mr. David McSorley, Director, Hallmark Institute of Aeronautics, 8901 Wetmore Road, San Antonio, TX 78216. *Phone:* 210-690-9000. *Toll-free phone:* 800-683-3600.

HALLMARK INSTITUTE OF TECHNOLOGY
San Antonio, Texas

- **Proprietary** 2-year, founded 1969
- **Calendar** continuous
- **Degree** diplomas and associate
- **Suburban** campus
- **Coed**

Standardized Tests *Required:* Wonderlic aptitude test (for admission).
Applying *Required:* high school transcript, interview.
Admissions Contact Ms. Sonya Ross, Director of Admissions, Hallmark Institute of Technology, 10401 IH 10 West, San Antonio, TX 78230-1737. *Phone:* 210-690-9000 Ext. 212. *Toll-free phone:* 800-880-6600. *Fax:* 210-697-8225.

HIGH-TECH INSTITUTE
Irving, Texas

Admissions Contact Ms. Cindy M. Lewellen, Director, High-Tech Institute, 4250 North Belt Line Road, Irving, TX 75038. *Phone:* 972-871-2824. *Toll-free phone:* 800-987-0110.

HILL COLLEGE OF THE HILL JUNIOR COLLEGE DISTRICT
Hillsboro, Texas

- **District-supported** 2-year, founded 1923
- **Calendar** semesters
- **Degree** certificates and associate
- **Small-town** 80-acre campus with easy access to Dallas-Fort Worth
- **Endowment** $416,886
- **Coed,** 3,236 undergraduate students, 48% full-time, 60% women, 40% men

Undergraduates 1,569 full-time, 1,667 part-time. Students come from 8 states and territories, 28 other countries, 6% are from out of state, 6% African American, 1% Asian American or Pacific Islander, 11% Hispanic American,

0.7% Native American, 2% international, 6% transferred in, 14% live on campus. *Retention:* 90% of 2002 full-time freshmen returned.

Freshmen *Admission:* 1,237 enrolled.

Faculty *Total:* 243, 65% full-time, 3% with terminal degrees. *Student/faculty ratio:* 25:1.

Majors Accounting; administrative assistant and secretarial science; agricultural business and management; agricultural economics; agriculture; animal sciences; applied art; art; art history, criticism and conservation; artificial intelligence and robotics; art teacher education; autobody/collision and repair technology; automobile/automotive mechanics technology; behavioral sciences; biological and physical sciences; biology/biological sciences; botany/plant biology; business administration and management; business/managerial economics; ceramic arts and ceramics; chemistry; child care provision; child development; civil engineering technology; commercial and advertising art; computer programming; computer programming related; computer science; computer typography and composition equipment operation; cosmetology; criminal justice/law enforcement administration; criminal justice/police science; dairy science; data processing and data processing technology; developmental and child psychology; drafting and design technology; dramatic/theatre arts; economics; education; electrical, electronic and communications engineering technology; elementary education; engineering; engineering science; English; family and consumer sciences/human sciences; farm and ranch management; finance; fire science; geography; geology/earth science; health science; health teacher education; heating, air conditioning, ventilation and refrigeration maintenance technology; history; horticultural science; humanities; information science/studies; journalism; liberal arts and sciences/liberal studies; machine tool technology; mass communication/media; mathematics; music; music history, literature, and theory; music teacher education; music theory and composition; nursing (licensed practical/vocational nurse training); photography; physical education teaching and coaching; physical sciences; physics; piano and organ; political science and government; pre-engineering; psychology; public health; public policy analysis; real estate; social sciences; social work; sociology; Spanish; speech and rhetoric; voice and opera; welding technology; zoology/animal biology.

Academic Programs *Special study options:* academic remediation for entering students, adult/continuing education programs, advanced placement credit, cooperative education, distance learning, double majors, English as a second language, honors programs, internships, part-time degree program, services for LD students, summer session for credit.

Library Hill College Library plus 1 other with 40,000 titles, 300 serial subscriptions, 500 audiovisual materials, an OPAC, a Web page.

Computers on Campus 250 computers available on campus for general student use. A campuswide network can be accessed from off campus. Internet access, at least one staffed computer lab available.

Student Life *Housing:* on-campus residence required through sophomore year. *Options:* men-only, women-only. *Activities and Organizations:* drama/theater group, choral group, International Club, Sigma Phi Omega, Phi Theta Kappa, Fellowship of Christian Athletes, Psi Beta. *Campus security:* late-night transport/escort service, controlled dormitory access, security officers.

Athletics Member NJCAA. *Intercollegiate sports:* baseball M(s), basketball M(s)/W(s), soccer W(s), softball W(s), volleyball W(s). *Intramural sports:* basketball M/W, volleyball W.

Standardized Tests *Required:* THEA (for placement). *Recommended:* SAT I or ACT (for placement).

Costs (2003–04) *Tuition:* area resident $1032 full-time, $43 per credit hour part-time; state resident $1224 full-time, $51 per credit hour part-time; nonresident $1224 full-time, $51 per credit hour part-time. Full-time tuition and fees vary according to course load. Part-time tuition and fees vary according to course load. *Room and board:* $1980; room only: $700. Room and board charges vary according to board plan. *Payment plan:* installment. *Waivers:* senior citizens and employees or children of employees.

Financial Aid Of all full-time matriculated undergraduates who enrolled, 51 Federal Work-Study jobs (averaging $858). 20 state and other part-time jobs (averaging $230).

Applying *Options:* early admission, deferred entrance. *Required:* high school transcript. *Application deadline:* rolling (freshmen), rolling (transfers).

Admissions Contact Ms. Diane Harvey, Director of Admissions/Registrar, Hill College of the Hill Junior College District, PO Box 619, Hillsboro, TX 76645-0619. *Phone:* 254-582-2555 Ext. 315. *Fax:* 254-582-7591. *E-mail:* diharvey@hill-college.cc.tx.us.

HOUSTON COMMUNITY COLLEGE SYSTEM
Houston, Texas

- **State and locally supported** 2-year, founded 1971
- **Calendar** semesters
- **Degree** certificates and associate
- **Urban** campus
- **Coed,** 37,846 undergraduate students, 32% full-time, 59% women, 41% men

Undergraduates 12,153 full-time, 25,693 part-time. Students come from 134 other countries, 22% African American, 12% Asian American or Pacific Islander, 24% Hispanic American, 0.3% Native American, 11% international.

Freshmen *Admission:* 5,095 applied, 5,095 admitted, 5,095 enrolled.

Faculty *Total:* 2,511, 28% full-time, 14% with terminal degrees. *Student/faculty ratio:* 20:1.

Majors Accounting; administrative assistant and secretarial science; agriculture; automobile/automotive mechanics technology; business administration and management; business/corporate communications; cartography; child care and support services management; child development; civil engineering technology; clinical/medical laboratory technology; commercial and advertising art; commercial photography; computer and information sciences; computer engineering technology; computer science; construction engineering technology; court reporting; criminal justice/police science; drafting and design technology; dramatic/theatre arts; electrical, electronic and communications engineering technology; emergency medical technology (EMT paramedic); engineering technology; family and consumer sciences/human sciences; fashion/apparel design; fashion merchandising; finance; fire science; graphic and printing equipment operation/production; health/health care administration; health information/medical records administration; health information/medical records technology; horticultural science; hotel/motel administration; human resources management; industrial radiologic technology; industrial technology; insurance; interior design; kinesiology and exercise science; legal assistant/paralegal; liberal arts and sciences/liberal studies; logistics and materials management; marketing/marketing management; mass communication/media; medical administrative assistant and medical secretary; medical radiologic technology; mental health/rehabilitation; music management and merchandising; music theory and composition; nuclear medical technology; nursing (registered nurse training); occupational safety and health technology; occupational therapist assistant; physical therapist assistant; psychiatric/mental health services technology; radio and television broadcasting technology; real estate; respiratory care therapy; sign language interpretation and translation; social sciences; technical and business writing; tourism and travel services management; transportation technology.

Academic Programs *Special study options:* academic remediation for entering students, adult/continuing education programs, advanced placement credit, cooperative education, distance learning, English as a second language, honors programs, independent study, internships, part-time degree program, services for LD students, study abroad, summer session for credit. *ROTC:* Army (c).

Library Main Library plus 19 others with 140,674 titles, 2,012 serial subscriptions, 16,334 audiovisual materials, an OPAC, a Web page.

Computers on Campus 3200 computers available on campus for general student use. A campuswide network can be accessed from off campus. At least one staffed computer lab available.

Student Life *Housing:* college housing not available. *Activities and Organizations:* drama/theater group, student-run newspaper, television station, Phi Theta Kappa, Eastwood Student Association, Eagle's Club, Society of Hispanic Professional Engineers, International Student Association. *Campus security:* 24-hour emergency response devices and patrols, late-night transport/escort service. *Student services:* personal/psychological counseling.

Standardized Tests *Required:* TSI, ACT ASSET (for placement). *Required for some:* ACT (for placement). *Recommended:* SAT I (for placement).

Costs (2003–04) *Tuition:* area resident $1410 full-time, $47 per semester hour part-time; state resident $3030 full-time, $101 per semester hour part-time; nonresident $3630 full-time, $121 per semester hour part-time.

Financial Aid *Financial aid deadline:* 8/15.

Applying *Required for some:* high school transcript, interview. *Application deadline:* rolling (freshmen). *Notification:* continuous (transfers).

Admissions Contact Ms. Mary Lemburg, Registrar, Houston Community College System, 3100 Main Street, PO Box 667517, Houston, TX 77266-7517. *Phone:* 713-718-8500. *Fax:* 713-718-2111.

HOWARD COLLEGE
Big Spring, Texas

- **State and locally supported** 2-year, founded 1945, part of Howard County Junior College District System
- **Calendar** semesters
- **Degree** certificates and associate
- **Small-town** 120-acre campus
- **Endowment** $928,972
- **Coed,** 2,659 undergraduate students, 42% full-time, 64% women, 36% men

Undergraduates 1,113 full-time, 1,546 part-time. Students come from 21 states and territories, 6 other countries, 9% are from out of state, 4% African American, 1% Asian American or Pacific Islander, 28% Hispanic American, 0.3% Native American, 0.2% international, 30% transferred in, 15% live on campus.

Freshmen *Admission:* 515 applied, 515 admitted, 515 enrolled.

Faculty *Total:* 146, 66% full-time. *Student/faculty ratio:* 14:1.

Howard College (continued)

Majors Accounting; agriculture; art; automobile/automotive mechanics technology; behavioral sciences; biology/biological sciences; business administration and management; chemistry; child development; computer and information sciences related; computer programming; computer science; cosmetology; criminal justice/police science; dental hygiene; drafting and design technology; dramatic/theatre arts; English; finance; health information/medical records administration; industrial arts; mathematics; music teacher education; nursing (licensed practical/vocational nurse training); nursing (registered nurse training); ornamental horticulture; physical education teaching and coaching; respiratory care therapy; social sciences; speech and rhetoric; substance abuse/addiction counseling.

Academic Programs *Special study options:* academic remediation for entering students, adult/continuing education programs, advanced placement credit, cooperative education, distance learning, English as a second language, independent study, internships, part-time degree program, services for LD students, summer session for credit.

Library Howard College Library with 27,481 titles, 232 serial subscriptions.

Computers on Campus 40 computers available on campus for general student use. A campuswide network can be accessed from student residence rooms. Internet access, at least one staffed computer lab available.

Student Life *Housing:* on-campus residence required for freshman year. *Options:* men-only, women-only. Campus housing is university owned. Freshman applicants given priority for college housing. *Activities and Organizations:* drama/theater group, choral group, Phi Theta Kappa, Student Government Association, Mexican-American Student Association, Baptist Student Ministries. *Campus security:* 24-hour patrols. *Student services:* personal/psychological counseling.

Athletics Member NJCAA. *Intercollegiate sports:* baseball M(s), basketball M(s)/W(s), softball W(s). *Intramural sports:* basketball M/W, bowling M/W, football M/W, racquetball M/W, softball W, volleyball M/W.

Standardized Tests *Required:* THEA (for placement). *Required for some:* SAT I or ACT (for placement).

Costs (2003–04) *Tuition:* area resident $600 full-time; state resident $780 full-time, $23 per credit hour part-time; nonresident $1100 full-time, $32 per credit hour part-time. Full-time tuition and fees vary according to course load, location, and program. Part-time tuition and fees vary according to course load, location, and program. *Required fees:* $372 full-time. *Room and board:* $3070. *Payment plan:* installment. *Waivers:* senior citizens.

Applying *Options:* early admission. *Required:* high school transcript. *Application deadline:* rolling (freshmen), rolling (transfers). *Notification:* continuous until 8/31 (freshmen), continuous until 8/31 (transfers).

Admissions Contact Ms. Lisa Currie, Registrar, Howard College, 1001 Birdwell Lane, Big Spring, TX 79720-3702. *Phone:* 432-264-5109.

ITT TECHNICAL INSTITUTE
Austin, Texas

- **Proprietary** 2-year, founded 1985, part of ITT Educational Services, Inc
- **Calendar** quarters
- **Degree** associate
- **Urban** campus
- **Coed**

Standardized Tests *Required:* Wonderlic aptitude test (for admission).

Costs (2003–04) *Tuition:* Total Program Cost varies depending on course of study. Consult school catalog.

Financial Aid Of all full-time matriculated undergraduates who enrolled, 1 Federal Work-Study job.

Applying *Options:* deferred entrance. *Application fee:* $100. *Required:* high school transcript, interview. *Recommended:* letters of recommendation.

Admissions Contact Mr. Steve Shanabarger, Director of Recruitment, ITT Technical Institute, 6330 Highway 290 East, Suite 150, Austin, TX 78723. *Phone:* 512-467-6800. *Toll-free phone:* 800-431-0677. *Fax:* 512-467-6677.

ITT TECHNICAL INSTITUTE
Houston, Texas

- **Proprietary** 2-year, founded 1985, part of ITT Educational Services, Inc
- **Calendar** quarters
- **Degree** associate
- **Suburban** 1-acre campus
- **Coed**

Standardized Tests *Required:* Wonderlic aptitude test (for admission).

Costs (2003–04) *Tuition:* Total Program Cost varies depending on course of study. Consult school catalog.

Applying *Options:* deferred entrance. *Application fee:* $100. *Required:* high school transcript, interview. *Recommended:* letters of recommendation.

Admissions Contact Mr. Robert Roloff, Director of Recruitment, ITT Technical Institute, 15621 Blue Ash Drive, Suite 160, Houston, TX 77090. *Phone:* 281-873-0512. *Toll-free phone:* 800-879-6486. *Fax:* 281-873-0518.

ITT TECHNICAL INSTITUTE
Arlington, Texas

- **Proprietary** 2-year, founded 1982, part of ITT Educational Services, Inc
- **Calendar** quarters
- **Degree** associate
- **Suburban** campus with easy access to Dallas-Fort Worth
- **Coed**

Standardized Tests *Required:* Wonderlic aptitude test (for admission).

Costs (2003–04) *Tuition:* Total Program Cost varies depending on course of study. Consult school catalog.

Applying *Options:* deferred entrance. *Application fee:* $100. *Required:* high school transcript, interview. *Recommended:* letters of recommendation.

Admissions Contact Mr. Ed Leal, Director of Recruitment, ITT Technical Institute, 551 Ryan Plaza Drive, Arlington, TX 76011. *Phone:* 817-794-5100. *Toll-free phone:* 888-288-4950. *Fax:* 817-275-8446.

ITT TECHNICAL INSTITUTE
Houston, Texas

- **Proprietary** 2-year, founded 1983, part of ITT Educational Services, Inc
- **Calendar** quarters
- **Degree** associate
- **Urban** 4-acre campus
- **Coed**

Standardized Tests *Required:* Wonderlic aptitude test (for admission).

Costs (2003–04) *Tuition:* Total Program Cost varies depending on course of study. Consult school catalog.

Applying *Options:* deferred entrance. *Application fee:* $100. *Required:* high school transcript, interview. *Recommended:* letters of recommendation.

Admissions Contact Gaynelle Sanders, Director of Recruitment, ITT Technical Institute, 2950 South Gessner, Houston, TX 77063. *Phone:* 713-952-2294. *Toll-free phone:* 800-235-4787. *Fax:* 713-952-2393.

ITT TECHNICAL INSTITUTE
San Antonio, Texas

- **Proprietary** 2-year, founded 1988, part of ITT Educational Services, Inc
- **Calendar** quarters
- **Degree** associate
- **Urban** campus
- **Coed**

Standardized Tests *Required:* Wonderlic aptitude test (for admission).

Costs (2003–04) *Tuition:* Total Program Cost varies depending on course of study. Consult school catalog.

Applying *Options:* deferred entrance. *Application fee:* $100. *Required:* high school transcript, interview. *Recommended:* letters of recommendation.

Admissions Contact Mr. Doug Howard, Director of Recruitment, ITT Technical Institute, 5700 Northwest Parkway, San Antonio, TX 78249. *Phone:* 210-694-4612. *Toll-free phone:* 800-880-0570. *Fax:* 210-694-4651.

ITT TECHNICAL INSTITUTE
Richardson, Texas

- **Proprietary** 2-year, founded 1989, part of ITT Educational Services, Inc
- **Calendar** quarters
- **Degree** associate
- **Suburban** campus with easy access to Dallas-Fort Worth
- **Coed**

Standardized Tests *Required:* Wonderlic aptitude test (for admission).

Costs (2003–04) *Tuition:* Total Program Cost varies depending on course of study. Consult school catalog.

Financial Aid Of all full-time matriculated undergraduates who enrolled, 5 Federal Work-Study jobs (averaging $5000).

Applying *Options:* deferred entrance. *Application fee:* $100. *Required:* high school transcript, interview. *Recommended:* letters of recommendation.

Admissions Contact Mr. Fred Garcia, Director of Recruitment, ITT Technical Institute, 2101 Waterview Parkway, Richardson, TX 75080. *Phone:* 972-690-9100. *Toll-free phone:* 888-488-5761. *Fax:* 972-690-0853.

ITT Technical Institute
Houston, Texas

- **Proprietary** 2-year, founded 1995, part of ITT Educational Services, Inc
- **Calendar** quarters
- **Degree** associate
- **Coed**

Standardized Tests *Required:* Wonderlic aptitude test (for admission).

Costs (2003–04) *Tuition:* Total Program Cost varies depending on course of study. Consult school catalog.

Applying *Options:* deferred entrance. *Application fee:* $100. *Required:* high school transcript, interview. *Recommended:* letters of recommendation.

Admissions Contact Mr. Ricky J. Kana, Director of Recruitment, ITT Technical Institute, 2222 Bay Area Boulevard, Houston, TX 77058. *Phone:* 281-486-2630. *Toll-free phone:* 888-488-9347. *Fax:* 281-486-6099.

Jacksonville College
Jacksonville, Texas

- **Independent Baptist** 2-year, founded 1899
- **Calendar** semesters
- **Degree** diplomas and associate
- **Small-town** 20-acre campus
- **Coed,** 323 undergraduate students, 74% full-time, 67% women, 33% men

Undergraduates 240 full-time, 83 part-time. Students come from 16 states and territories, 15 other countries, 6% are from out of state, 16% African American, 0.3% Asian American or Pacific Islander, 11% Hispanic American, 0.3% Native American, 5% international, 39% live on campus.

Freshmen *Admission:* 281 applied, 106 admitted, 106 enrolled.

Faculty *Total:* 25, 44% full-time, 8% with terminal degrees. *Student/faculty ratio:* 14:1.

Majors Biological and physical sciences; liberal arts and sciences/liberal studies.

Academic Programs *Special study options:* academic remediation for entering students, adult/continuing education programs, advanced placement credit, part-time degree program, summer session for credit.

Library Weatherby Memorial Building plus 1 other with 22,000 titles, 170 serial subscriptions.

Computers on Campus 20 computers available on campus for general student use. A campuswide network can be accessed. Internet access, at least one staffed computer lab available.

Student Life *Housing:* on-campus residence required through sophomore year. *Activities and Organizations:* drama/theater group, choral group, Drama Club, Ministerial Alliance, Mission Band. *Campus security:* 24-hour emergency response devices, evening security personnel. *Student services:* health clinic, personal/psychological counseling.

Athletics Member NJCAA. *Intercollegiate sports:* basketball M(s)/W, volleyball W(s). *Intramural sports:* basketball M/W, table tennis M/W, tennis M/W, volleyball M/W.

Standardized Tests *Required:* THEA (for placement).

Costs (2004–05) *Comprehensive fee:* $6778 includes full-time tuition ($3750), mandatory fees ($400), and room and board ($2628). Part-time tuition: $165 per hour. Part-time tuition and fees vary according to course load. *Payment plan:* installment. *Waivers:* employees or children of employees.

Applying *Options:* electronic application, early admission. *Application fee:* $15. *Application deadlines:* 8/15 (freshmen), 7/1 (transfers). *Notification:* continuous until 7/1 (freshmen), continuous until 7/1 (transfers).

Admissions Contact Mrs. Johnnie Ross, Director of Admissions, Jacksonville College, 105 B.J. Albritton Drive, Jacksonville, TX 75766. *Phone:* 903-586-2518 Ext. 7134. *Toll-free phone:* 800-256-8522. *Fax:* 903-586-0743. *E-mail:* admissions@jacksonville-college.org.

KD Studio
Dallas, Texas

- **Proprietary** 2-year, founded 1979
- **Calendar** semesters
- **Degree** associate
- **Urban** campus
- **Coed,** 129 undergraduate students

Undergraduates Students come from 10 states and territories, 4% are from out of state, 54% African American, 2% Asian American or Pacific Islander, 16% Hispanic American.

Freshmen *Admission:* 65 applied, 65 admitted.

Faculty *Total:* 23, 100% full-time, 96% with terminal degrees. *Student/faculty ratio:* 15:1.

Majors Acting.

Academic Programs *Special study options:* cooperative education.

Library KD Studio Library with 800 titles, 15 serial subscriptions.

Computers on Campus 1 computer available on campus for general student use. . Internet access, at least one staffed computer lab available.

Student Life *Housing:* college housing not available. *Activities and Organizations:* drama/theater group, Student Council. *Campus security:* 24-hour emergency response devices and patrols.

Costs (2004–05) *Tuition:* $19,400 full-time. No tuition increase for student's term of enrollment. *Required fees:* $250 full-time. *Payment plan:* installment. *Waivers:* employees or children of employees.

Applying *Options:* common application, deferred entrance. *Application fee:* $100. *Required:* essay or personal statement, high school transcript, interview, audition. *Required for some:* letters of recommendation. *Application deadline:* rolling (freshmen), rolling (transfers).

Admissions Contact Mr. T. A. Taylor, Director of Education, KD Studio, 2600 Stemmons Freeway, #117, Dallas, TX 75207. *Phone:* 214-638-0484. *Fax:* 214-630-5140. *E-mail:* information@kdstudio.com.

Kilgore College
Kilgore, Texas

- **State and locally supported** 2-year, founded 1935
- **Calendar** semesters
- **Degree** certificates and associate
- **Small-town** 35-acre campus with easy access to Dallas-Fort Worth
- **Endowment** $5.2 million
- **Coed**

Faculty *Student/faculty ratio:* 19:1.

Student Life *Campus security:* 24-hour emergency response devices and patrols.

Athletics Member NJCAA.

Standardized Tests *Required:* THEA (for placement). *Recommended:* SAT I or ACT (for placement).

Costs (2003–04) *Tuition:* area resident $480 full-time; state resident $1290 full-time; nonresident $1770 full-time. *Required fees:* $510 full-time. *Room and board:* $2950.

Financial Aid Of all full-time matriculated undergraduates who enrolled, 80 Federal Work-Study jobs (averaging $2500). *Financial aid deadline:* 6/1.

Applying *Options:* early admission. *Required:* high school transcript. *Required for some:* interview.

Admissions Contact Ms. Jeanna Centers, Admissions Specialist, Kilgore College, 1100 Broadway, Kilgore, TX 75662. *Phone:* 903-983-8202. *Fax:* 903-983-8607. *E-mail:* register@kilgore.cc.tx.us.

Kingwood College
Kingwood, Texas

- **State and locally supported** 2-year, founded 1984, part of North Harris Montgomery Community College District
- **Calendar** semesters
- **Degree** certificates and associate
- **Suburban** 264-acre campus with easy access to Houston
- **Coed,** 6,056 undergraduate students, 24% full-time, 64% women, 36% men

Undergraduates 1,476 full-time, 4,580 part-time. Students come from 32 other countries, 0.4% are from out of state, 7% African American, 3% Asian American or Pacific Islander, 13% Hispanic American, 0.6% Native American, 2% international, 5% transferred in.

Freshmen *Admission:* 6,056 applied, 6,056 admitted, 977 enrolled.

Faculty *Total:* 269, 31% full-time. *Student/faculty ratio:* 16:1.

Majors Accounting; biology/biological sciences; business administration and management; computer and information sciences; computer engineering technology; computer graphics; computer typography and composition equipment operation; education; English; foreign languages and literatures; information science/studies; mathematics; nursing (licensed practical/vocational nurse training); occupational therapy; psychology; social sciences; visual and performing arts.

Academic Programs *Special study options:* academic remediation for entering students, accelerated degree program, advanced placement credit, cooperative education, distance learning, double majors, English as a second language, external degree program, honors programs, independent study, internships, part-time degree program, services for LD students, summer session for credit.

Library Kingwood College Library with 35,000 titles, 500 serial subscriptions, an OPAC, a Web page.

Computers on Campus 540 computers available on campus for general student use. A campuswide network can be accessed from off campus. At least one staffed computer lab available.

Kingwood College (continued)

Student Life *Housing:* college housing not available. *Activities and Organizations:* drama/theater group, student-run television station, choral group, Phi Theta Kappa, Office Administration Club, African American Student Association, Student Government Association, Delta Epsilon Chi. *Campus security:* 24-hour emergency response devices and patrols, late-night transport/escort service. *Student services:* personal/psychological counseling.

Athletics *Intramural sports:* baseball M.

Standardized Tests *Required for some:* SAT I or ACT (for placement), ACT ASSET.

Costs (2004–05) *Tuition:* area resident $984 full-time, $52 per credit part-time; state resident $1944 full-time, $92 per credit part-time; nonresident $2304 full-time, $220 per credit part-time. Full-time tuition and fees vary according to course load and program. Part-time tuition and fees vary according to course load. *Payment plans:* installment, deferred payment. *Waivers:* employees or children of employees.

Financial Aid Of all full-time matriculated undergraduates who enrolled, 13 Federal Work-Study jobs, 4 state and other part-time jobs. *Financial aid deadline:* 5/15.

Applying *Options:* common application, early admission. *Required:* high school transcript. *Required for some:* essay or personal statement. *Application deadline:* rolling (freshmen), rolling (transfers).

Admissions Contact Dr. Ron Shade, Dean of Student Development, Kingwood College, 20000 Kingwood Drive, Kingwood, TX 77339. *Phone:* 281-312-1444. *Fax:* 281-312-1477. *E-mail:* ronald.shade@nhmccd.edu.

LAMAR INSTITUTE OF TECHNOLOGY
Beaumont, Texas

Admissions Contact Mr. James Rush, Director of Admissions, Lamar Institute of Technology, PO Box 10043, Beaumont, TX 77710. *Phone:* 409-880-8354. *Toll-free phone:* 800-950-8321.

LAMAR STATE COLLEGE-ORANGE
Orange, Texas

- **State-supported** 2-year, founded 1969, part of The Texas State University System
- **Calendar** semesters
- **Degree** certificates and associate
- **Small-town** 21-acre campus
- **Endowment** $5524
- **Coed**, 1,853 undergraduate students, 50% full-time, 70% women, 30% men

Undergraduates 919 full-time, 934 part-time. Students come from 1 other state, 9% are from out of state, 16% African American, 1% Asian American or Pacific Islander, 3% Hispanic American, 0.2% Native American, 0.1% international, 8% transferred in.

Freshmen *Admission:* 411 applied, 362 admitted, 362 enrolled.

Faculty *Total:* 98, 48% full-time, 13% with terminal degrees. *Student/faculty ratio:* 18:1.

Majors Accounting; administrative assistant and secretarial science; architectural engineering technology; business administration and management; clinical/medical laboratory technology; computer science; data processing and data processing technology; environmental studies; information science/studies; liberal arts and sciences/liberal studies; literature; mass communication/media; mathematics; nursing (registered nurse training); real estate; social sciences.

Academic Programs *Special study options:* academic remediation for entering students, distance learning, double majors, internships, part-time degree program, summer session for credit.

Library Lamar State College-Orange Library plus 1 other with 71,092 titles, 1,306 serial subscriptions, 288 audiovisual materials, an OPAC.

Computers on Campus 70 computers available on campus for general student use. A campuswide network can be accessed from off campus. Internet access, at least one staffed computer lab available.

Student Life *Housing:* college housing not available. *Activities and Organizations:* student-run newspaper. *Campus security:* 24-hour emergency response devices, late-night transport/escort service.

Athletics *Intramural sports:* archery M, basketball M/W, volleyball M/W, weight lifting M/W.

Standardized Tests *Required for some:* THEA.

Costs (2004–05) *Tuition:* state resident $1152 full-time; nonresident $8400 full-time. Full-time tuition and fees vary according to course load. Part-time tuition and fees vary according to course load. *Required fees:* $1292 full-time. *Payment plan:* installment.

Financial Aid Of all full-time matriculated undergraduates who enrolled, 20 Federal Work-Study jobs (averaging $3000). 2 state and other part-time jobs (averaging $2000).

Applying *Options:* common application, early admission, deferred entrance. *Required:* high school transcript. *Recommended:* minimum 2.0 GPA. *Application deadline:* rolling (freshmen), rolling (transfers). *Notification:* continuous (freshmen), continuous (transfers).

Admissions Contact Kerry Olson, Director of Admissions and Financial Aid, Lamar State College-Orange, 410 Front Street, Orange, TX 77632. *Phone:* 409-882-3362.

LAMAR STATE COLLEGE-PORT ARTHUR
Port Arthur, Texas

- **State-supported** 2-year, founded 1909, part of The Texas State University System
- **Calendar** semesters
- **Degree** certificates and associate
- **Suburban** 34-acre campus with easy access to Houston
- **Coed**, 2,429 undergraduate students, 41% full-time, 65% women, 35% men

Undergraduates 990 full-time, 1,439 part-time. 1% are from out of state, 33% African American, 6% Asian American or Pacific Islander, 10% Hispanic American, 0.3% Native American, 0.4% international.

Freshmen *Admission:* 484 admitted.

Faculty *Total:* 118, 16% with terminal degrees. *Student/faculty ratio:* 30:1.

Majors Accounting; administrative assistant and secretarial science; automobile/automotive mechanics technology; business administration and management; business administration, management and operations related; child development; child guidance; computer and information sciences; computer technology/computer systems technology; cosmetology; criminal justice/law enforcement administration; electrical and electronic engineering technologies related; electrical, electronic and communications engineering technology; environmental engineering technology; family and consumer sciences/human sciences; general studies; health information/medical records administration; heating, air conditioning and refrigeration technology; heating, air conditioning, ventilation and refrigeration maintenance technology; hospitality administration; instrumentation technology; legal administrative assistant/secretary; legal assistant/paralegal; management science; medical administrative assistant and medical secretary; nursing (licensed practical/vocational nurse training); nursing (registered nurse training); nursing related; substance abuse/addiction counseling; surgical technology; welding technology.

Academic Programs *Special study options:* academic remediation for entering students, accelerated degree program, adult/continuing education programs, advanced placement credit, cooperative education, distance learning, double majors, English as a second language, honors programs, independent study, internships, off-campus study, part-time degree program, services for LD students, summer session for credit. *ROTC:* Army (c).

Library Gates Memorial Library with 43,726 titles, 3,400 serial subscriptions, 1,493 audiovisual materials, an OPAC, a Web page.

Computers on Campus A campuswide network can be accessed from off campus. Internet access, online (class) registration, at least one staffed computer lab available.

Student Life *Housing:* college housing not available. *Activities and Organizations:* drama/theater group, student-run newspaper, Historical Society, Chi Alpha, tennis, Student Government Association, Baptist Student Ministry. *Campus security:* 24-hour emergency response devices, student patrols, late-night transport/escort service. *Student services:* personal/psychological counseling.

Standardized Tests *Required for some:* SAT I (for placement), THEA.

Costs (2004–05) *Tuition:* state resident $2160 full-time, $72 per credit part-time; nonresident $9900 full-time, $330 per credit part-time. *Required fees:* $820 full-time, $48 per term part-time. *Waivers:* senior citizens and employees or children of employees.

Applying *Options:* common application, early admission, deferred entrance. *Required:* high school transcript. *Required for some:* interview. *Application deadline:* rolling (freshmen), rolling (transfers). *Notification:* continuous (freshmen), continuous (transfers).

Admissions Contact Ms. Connie Nicholas, Registrar, Lamar State College-Port Arthur, PO Box 310, Port Arthur, TX 77641-0310. *Phone:* 409-984-6165. *Toll-free phone:* 800-477-5872. *Fax:* 409-984-6025. *E-mail:* connie.nicholas@lamarpa.edu.

LAREDO COMMUNITY COLLEGE
Laredo, Texas

- **State and locally supported** 2-year, founded 1946
- **Calendar** semesters
- **Degree** certificates and associate
- **Urban** 186-acre campus
- **Endowment** $389,879
- **Coed**, 8,297 undergraduate students, 37% full-time, 59% women, 41% men

Undergraduates 3,029 full-time, 5,268 part-time. Students come from 4 states and territories, 5 other countries, 0.2% African American, 0.3% Asian American or Pacific Islander, 95% Hispanic American, 3% international. *Retention:* 82% of 2002 full-time freshmen returned.

Freshmen *Admission:* 1,017 applied, 1,017 admitted, 1,017 enrolled.

Faculty *Total:* 322, 58% full-time, 11% with terminal degrees. *Student/faculty ratio:* 22:1.

Majors Administrative assistant and secretarial science; child development; clinical/medical laboratory technology; computer programming; computer programming related; computer software and media applications related; computer systems networking and telecommunications; construction engineering technology; criminal justice/police science; data entry/microcomputer applications; data entry/microcomputer applications related; data processing and data processing technology; electrical, electronic and communications engineering technology; emergency medical technology (EMT paramedic); fashion merchandising; fire science; hotel/motel administration; industrial radiologic technology; information science/studies; information technology; international business/trade/commerce; liberal arts and sciences/liberal studies; marketing/marketing management; medical/clinical assistant; nursing (registered nurse training); physical therapy; radiologic technology/science; real estate; social sciences.

Academic Programs *Special study options:* academic remediation for entering students, adult/continuing education programs, advanced placement credit, distance learning, double majors, English as a second language, freshman honors college, honors programs, independent study, internships, part-time degree program, services for LD students, summer session for credit.

Library Yeary Library with 88,006 titles, 555 serial subscriptions, an OPAC.

Student Life *Housing Options:* coed. *Activities and Organizations:* drama/theater group, student-run newspaper, choral group. *Campus security:* 24-hour emergency response devices and patrols, student patrols. *Student services:* personal/psychological counseling, women's center.

Athletics Member NJCAA. *Intercollegiate sports:* baseball M(s), tennis M(s)/W(s), volleyball W(s). *Intramural sports:* cross-country running M/W, gymnastics M/W, swimming M/W, tennis M/W, track and field M/W, volleyball M/W.

Standardized Tests *Recommended:* ACT (for placement).

Costs (2004–05) *Tuition:* area resident $1140 full-time, $30 per credit hour part-time; state resident $1860 full-time, $60 per credit hour part-time; nonresident $2340 full-time, $80 per credit hour part-time. *Required fees:* $20 per credit hour part-time, $24 per term part-time. *Room and board:* $3922. *Payment plans:* installment, deferred payment. *Waivers:* senior citizens and employees or children of employees.

Financial Aid Of all full-time matriculated undergraduates who enrolled, 282 Federal Work-Study jobs (averaging $1854). 127 state and other part-time jobs (averaging $1884).

Applying *Options:* common application, early admission, deferred entrance. *Required:* high school transcript. *Application deadline:* rolling (freshmen), rolling (transfers).

Admissions Contact Ms. Josie Soliz, Admissions Records Supervisor, Laredo Community College, West End Washington Street, Laredo, TX 78040-4395. *Phone:* 956-721-5177. *Fax:* 956-721-5493.

LEE COLLEGE
Baytown, Texas

Admissions Contact Ms. Becki Griffith, Registrar, Lee College, PO Box 818, Baytown, TX 77522-0818. *Phone:* 281-425-6399. *Toll-free phone:* 800-621-8724. *Fax:* 281-425-6831.

LON MORRIS COLLEGE
Jacksonville, Texas

- **Independent United Methodist** 2-year, founded 1854
- **Calendar** semesters
- **Degree** associate
- **Small-town** 76-acre campus
- **Endowment** $20.1 million
- **Coed,** 432 undergraduate students, 91% full-time, 50% women, 50% men

Undergraduates 394 full-time, 38 part-time. Students come from 5 states and territories, 5% are from out of state, 21% African American, 0.5% Asian American or Pacific Islander, 11% Hispanic American, 0.9% Native American, 5% international, 90% live on campus. *Retention:* 53% of 2002 full-time freshmen returned.

Freshmen *Admission:* 261 applied, 225 admitted, 216 enrolled. *Average high school GPA:* 3.20. *Test scores:* SAT verbal scores over 500: 25%; SAT math scores over 500: 23%; ACT scores over 18: 38%; SAT verbal scores over 600: 5%; SAT math scores over 600: 5%; ACT scores over 24: 4%.

Faculty *Total:* 57, 60% full-time, 25% with terminal degrees. *Student/faculty ratio:* 10:1.

Majors Accounting; applied art; art; art history, criticism and conservation; art teacher education; biblical studies; biology/biological sciences; botany/plant biology; business administration and management; chemistry; commercial and advertising art; computer science; creative writing; dance; divinity/ministry; dramatic/theatre arts; drawing; economics; education; elementary education; engineering; English; fine/studio arts; history; humanities; liberal arts and sciences/liberal studies; literature; mass communication/media; mathematics; modern languages; music; music teacher education; philosophy; physical education teaching and coaching; physics; piano and organ; political science and government; pre-engineering; psychology; religious education; religious studies; Romance languages; social sciences; sociology; Spanish; speech and rhetoric; theology; voice and opera; western civilization.

Academic Programs *Special study options:* academic remediation for entering students, advanced placement credit, English as a second language, independent study, part-time degree program, services for LD students, study abroad, summer session for credit.

Library Henderson Library with 26,000 titles, 265 serial subscriptions, an OPAC, a Web page.

Computers on Campus 28 computers available on campus for general student use. Internet access, at least one staffed computer lab available.

Student Life *Housing:* on-campus residence required through sophomore year. *Options:* men-only, women-only. Campus housing is university owned. Freshman applicants given priority for college housing. *Activities and Organizations:* drama/theater group, student-run newspaper, choral group. *Campus security:* late-night transport/escort service, controlled dormitory access. *Student services:* personal/psychological counseling.

Athletics Member NJCAA. *Intercollegiate sports:* baseball M(s), basketball M(s), cheerleading M(s)/W(s), golf M(s)/W(s), soccer M(s)/W(s), softball W(s), volleyball W(s). *Intramural sports:* basketball M/W, cross-country running M/W, football M/W, softball W, tennis M/W, volleyball M/W, weight lifting M/W.

Standardized Tests *Required:* SAT I or ACT (for admission).

Costs (2003–04) *Comprehensive fee:* $13,400 includes full-time tuition ($6800), mandatory fees ($1800), and room and board ($4800). Full-time tuition and fees vary according to course load. Part-time tuition: $275 per credit hour. Part-time tuition and fees vary according to course load. *Required fees:* $150 per credit hour part-time. *Room and board:* college room only: $2300. Room and board charges vary according to board plan. *Payment plans:* installment, deferred payment. *Waivers:* employees or children of employees.

Financial Aid Of all full-time matriculated undergraduates who enrolled, 63 Federal Work-Study jobs (averaging $1300). 9 state and other part-time jobs (averaging $700).

Applying *Options:* common application, electronic application, deferred entrance. *Application fee:* $35. *Required:* high school transcript. *Application deadline:* rolling (freshmen), rolling (transfers).

Admissions Contact Mr. Craig Lee, Director of Admissions, Lon Morris College, 800 College Avenue, Jacksonville, TX 75766-2923. *Phone:* 903-589-4000 Ext. 4063. *Toll-free phone:* 800-259-5753. *Fax:* 903-589-4006.

MCLENNAN COMMUNITY COLLEGE
Waco, Texas

- **County-supported** 2-year, founded 1965
- **Calendar** semesters
- **Degree** certificates and associate
- **Urban** 200-acre campus
- **Coed,** 7,052 undergraduate students, 44% full-time, 68% women, 32% men

Undergraduates 3,073 full-time, 3,979 part-time. Students come from 10 other countries, 16% African American, 1% Asian American or Pacific Islander, 14% Hispanic American, 0.3% Native American, 0.6% international.

Freshmen *Admission:* 2,163 applied, 2,163 admitted, 1,229 enrolled.

Faculty *Total:* 340, 16% with terminal degrees.

Majors Accounting; administrative assistant and secretarial science; art teacher education; business administration and management; clinical/medical laboratory technology; computer engineering technology; criminal justice/law enforcement administration; criminal justice/police science; developmental and child psychology; finance; health information/medical records administration; industrial radiologic technology; information science/studies; kindergarten/preschool education; legal administrative assistant/secretary; legal assistant/paralegal; liberal arts and sciences/liberal studies; medical administrative assistant and medical secretary; mental health/rehabilitation; music; nursing (registered nurse training); physical education teaching and coaching; physical therapy; real estate; respiratory care therapy; sign language interpretation and translation.

Academic Programs *Special study options:* academic remediation for entering students, adult/continuing education programs, advanced placement credit, cooperative education, distance learning, honors programs, internships, off-campus study, part-time degree program, services for LD students, student-designed majors, study abroad, summer session for credit. *ROTC:* Air Force (c).

McLennan Community College (continued)

Library McLennan Community College Library with 93,000 titles, 400 serial subscriptions, an OPAC, a Web page.

Computers on Campus 425 computers available on campus for general student use. A campuswide network can be accessed from off campus. Internet access, at least one staffed computer lab available.

Student Life *Housing:* college housing not available. *Activities and Organizations:* drama/theater group, student-run newspaper, choral group. *Campus security:* 24-hour emergency response devices and patrols. *Student services:* personal/psychological counseling.

Athletics Member NJCAA. *Intercollegiate sports:* baseball M(s), basketball M(s)/W(s), golf M(s)/W(s), softball W(s). *Intramural sports:* basketball M/W, football M, gymnastics M, volleyball M/W.

Standardized Tests *Required:* THEA (for placement).

Costs (2004–05) *Tuition:* area resident $1272 full-time, $53 per semester hour part-time; state resident $1560 full-time, $65 per semester hour part-time; nonresident $2712 full-time, $113 per semester hour part-time. *Required fees:* $216 full-time, $9 per semester hour part-time.

Financial Aid Of all full-time matriculated undergraduates who enrolled, 265 Federal Work-Study jobs (averaging $850). 25 state and other part-time jobs (averaging $500).

Applying *Options:* early admission. *Required:* high school transcript. *Application deadline:* rolling (freshmen), rolling (transfers). *Notification:* continuous until 9/2 (freshmen), continuous until 9/2 (transfers).

Admissions Contact Ms. Vivian G. Jefferson, Director, Admissions and Recruitment, McLennan Community College, 1400 College Drive, Waco, TX 76708-1499. *Phone:* 254-299-8689. *Fax:* 254-299-8694. *E-mail:* ad1@mclennan.edu.

MIDLAND COLLEGE
Midland, Texas

- **State and locally supported** 2-year, founded 1969
- **Calendar** semesters
- **Degree** certificates and associate
- **Suburban** 163-acre campus
- **Endowment** $3.2 million
- **Coed,** 5,405 undergraduate students, 38% full-time, 58% women, 42% men

Undergraduates 2,068 full-time, 3,337 part-time. Students come from 23 states and territories, 30 other countries, 1% are from out of state, 4% African American, 1% Asian American or Pacific Islander, 30% Hispanic American, 0.4% Native American, 1% international, 6% transferred in.

Freshmen *Admission:* 2,612 applied, 2,612 admitted, 1,025 enrolled.

Faculty *Total:* 334, 33% full-time, 11% with terminal degrees. *Student/faculty ratio:* 18:1.

Majors Airline pilot and flight crew; anthropology; art; automobile/automotive mechanics technology; behavioral sciences; biology/biological sciences; business automation/technology/data entry; business/commerce; chemistry; child care provision; commercial and advertising art; computer programming (specific applications); criminal justice/police science; data modeling/warehousing and database administration; developmental and child psychology; drafting and design technology; drawing; economics; electrical, electronic and communications engineering technology; emergency medical technology (EMT paramedic); English; fine/studio arts; fire science; fire services administration; foreign languages and literatures; French; geology/earth science; German; health information/medical records technology; heating, air conditioning, ventilation and refrigeration maintenance technology; history; journalism; legal assistant/paralegal; liberal arts and sciences/liberal studies; literature; mass communication/media; mathematics; medical radiologic technology; modern languages; music; music teacher education; nursing (registered nurse training); physical education teaching and coaching; physics; political science and government; pre-engineering; psychology; radiologic technology/science; respiratory care therapy; sociology; Spanish; speech and rhetoric; substance abuse/addiction counseling; system administration; system, networking, and LAN/wan management; veterinary/animal health technology; veterinary technology; welding technology.

Academic Programs *Special study options:* academic remediation for entering students, adult/continuing education programs, advanced placement credit, cooperative education, distance learning, double majors, English as a second language, honors programs, internships, part-time degree program, services for LD students, student-designed majors, summer session for credit.

Library Murray Fasken Learning Resource Center plus 1 other with 53,800 titles, 331 serial subscriptions, an OPAC.

Computers on Campus 250 computers available on campus for general student use. A campuswide network can be accessed from student residence rooms and from off campus. Internet access, online (class) registration, at least one staffed computer lab available. Computer purchase or lease plan available.

Student Life *Housing Options:* Campus housing is university owned. *Activities and Organizations:* drama/theater group, student-run newspaper, choral group, OIKOS, Midland College Latin American Student Society, Student Government Association, Student Nurses Association, Baptist Student Ministries. *Campus security:* 24-hour patrols. *Student services:* personal/psychological counseling.

Athletics Member NJCAA. *Intercollegiate sports:* baseball M(s), basketball M(s)/W(s), cheerleading M(s)/W(s), golf M(s), softball W(s), volleyball W(s). *Intramural sports:* basketball M/W, football M/W, soccer M/W, table tennis M/W, tennis M/W, ultimate Frisbee M, volleyball M/W.

Standardized Tests *Required:* THEA or ACT COMPASS (for placement). *Recommended:* ACT (for placement).

Costs (2003–04) *Tuition:* area resident $1320 full-time, $43 per credit hour part-time; state resident $1470 full-time, $48 per credit hour part-time; nonresident $2070 full-time, $68 per credit hour part-time. Full-time tuition and fees vary according to course load. Part-time tuition and fees vary according to course load. *Room and board:* $3200. *Payment plan:* installment. *Waivers:* senior citizens and employees or children of employees.

Financial Aid Of all full-time matriculated undergraduates who enrolled, 75 Federal Work-Study jobs (averaging $2000). 5 state and other part-time jobs (averaging $2000).

Applying *Options:* common application. *Required:* high school transcript. *Application deadline:* rolling (freshmen), rolling (transfers). *Notification:* continuous (freshmen), continuous (transfers).

Admissions Contact Freshmen Admissions, Midland College, 3600 North Garfield, Midland, TX 79705-6399. *Phone:* 432-685-5502. *Fax:* 432-685-6401. *E-mail:* twetendorf@midland.edu.

MONTGOMERY COLLEGE
Conroe, Texas

Admissions Contact Ms. Suzy Englert, Admissions/Advising Coordinator, Montgomery College, 3200 College Park Drive, Conroe, TX 77384. *Phone:* 936-273-7236. *E-mail:* suzye@nhmccd.edu.

MOUNTAIN VIEW COLLEGE
Dallas, Texas

- **State and locally supported** 2-year, founded 1970, part of Dallas County Community College District System
- **Calendar** semesters
- **Degree** certificates and associate
- **Urban** 200-acre campus
- **Coed,** 6,410 undergraduate students, 100% full-time, 61% women, 39% men

Undergraduates 6,410 full-time. Students come from 9 states and territories, 36 other countries, 0.8% are from out of state, 30% African American, 3% Asian American or Pacific Islander, 41% Hispanic American, 0.6% Native American, 2% international.

Faculty *Total:* 304, 25% full-time.

Majors Accounting; artificial intelligence and robotics; aviation/airway management; avionics maintenance technology; computer programming; criminal justice/law enforcement administration; drafting and design technology; electrical, electronic and communications engineering technology; electromechanical technology; engineering technology; health information/medical records technology; information science/studies; legal administrative assistant/secretary; liberal arts and sciences/liberal studies; quality control technology; welding technology.

Academic Programs *Special study options:* academic remediation for entering students, adult/continuing education programs, advanced placement credit, cooperative education, distance learning, double majors, English as a second language, external degree program, freshman honors college, honors programs, independent study, internships, part-time degree program, services for LD students, summer session for credit. *ROTC:* Army (c).

Computers on Campus 200 computers available on campus for general student use. Internet access, at least one staffed computer lab available.

Student Life *Housing:* college housing not available. *Activities and Organizations:* drama/theater group, choral group. *Campus security:* 24-hour patrols, late-night transport/escort service. *Student services:* personal/psychological counseling, women's center.

Athletics Member NJCAA. *Intramural sports:* basketball M, football M, golf M, tennis M/W.

Standardized Tests *Required:* SAT I, ACT, THEA, or MAPS (for placement).

Costs (2004–05) *Tuition:* area resident $360 full-time, $30 per credit hour part-time; state resident $600 full-time, $50 per credit hour part-time; nonresident $960 full-time, $200 per credit hour part-time.

Financial Aid Of all full-time matriculated undergraduates who enrolled, 145 Federal Work-Study jobs (averaging $2700).

Applying *Options:* common application, electronic application, early admission, deferred entrance. *Required:* high school transcript. *Application deadline:* rolling (freshmen), rolling (transfers). *Notification:* continuous (freshmen), continuous (transfers).

Admissions Contact Ms. Glenda Hall, Associate Dean Student Services, Mountain View College, 4849 West Illinois Avenue, Dallas, TX 75211-6599. *Phone:* 214-860-8666. *Fax:* 214-860-8570. *E-mail:* jctorres@dcccd.edu.

MTI COLLEGE OF BUSINESS AND TECHNOLOGY
Houston, Texas

- **Proprietary** 2-year, founded 1984, part of MTI College of Business and Technology-Houston Campus
- **Calendar** semesters
- **Degree** certificates, diplomas, and associate
- **Suburban** 3-acre campus
- **Coed,** 287 undergraduate students, 100% full-time, 53% women, 47% men

Undergraduates 287 full-time. 15% African American, 8% Asian American or Pacific Islander, 45% Hispanic American.

Freshmen *Admission:* 619 applied, 453 admitted.

Faculty *Total:* 16, 63% full-time. *Student/faculty ratio:* 24:1.

Majors Administrative assistant and secretarial science; business operations support and secretarial services related; computer technology/computer systems technology; medical office assistant.

Academic Programs *Special study options:* advanced placement credit, cooperative education.

Computers on Campus 120 computers available on campus for general student use. Internet access, at least one staffed computer lab available.

Student Life *Housing:* college housing not available.

Applying *Options:* electronic application. *Required:* high school transcript, interview. *Application deadline:* rolling (freshmen).

Admissions Contact Mr. Derrell Beck, Admissions Manager, MTI College of Business and Technology, 1275 Space Park Drive, Houston, TX 77058. *Phone:* 281-333-3363. *Toll-free phone:* 888-532-7675. *Fax:* 281-333-4118. *E-mail:* info@mti.edu.

MTI COLLEGE OF BUSINESS AND TECHNOLOGY
Houston, Texas

- **Proprietary** 2-year
- **Calendar** semesters
- **Urban** 6-acre campus with easy access to Houston
- 718 undergraduate students, 100% full-time

Undergraduates 718 full-time. Students come from 1 other state.

Freshmen *Admission:* 521 enrolled.

Faculty *Total:* 31. *Student/faculty ratio:* 23:1.

Majors Administrative assistant and secretarial science; business automation/technology/data entry; computer and information systems security; medical office assistant; system administration; system, networking, and LAN/wan management.

Student Life *Housing:* college housing not available. *Campus security:* late-night transport/escort service.

Costs (2004–05) *Tuition:* $22,500 full-time. *Payment plan:* installment. *Waivers:* employees or children of employees.

Admissions Contact Mr. David Wood, Director of Admissions, MTI College of Business and Technology, 7277 Regency Square Boulevard, Houston, TX 77036-3163. *Phone:* 713-974-7181. *Toll-free phone:* 800-344-1990.

NAVARRO COLLEGE
Corsicana, Texas

Admissions Contact Mr. Dewayne Gragg, Registrar, Navarro College, 3200 West 7th Avenue, Corsicana, TX 75110-4899. *Phone:* 903-874-6501 Ext. 221. *Toll-free phone:* 800-NAVARRO (in-state); 800-628-2776 (out-of-state).

NORTH CENTRAL TEXAS COLLEGE
Gainesville, Texas

- **County-supported** 2-year, founded 1924
- **Calendar** semesters
- **Degree** certificates, diplomas, and associate
- **Rural** 132-acre campus with easy access to Dallas-Fort Worth
- **Endowment** $2.4 million
- **Coed**

Student Life *Campus security:* late-night transport/escort service, late night security.

Athletics Member NJCAA.

Standardized Tests *Required:* THEA (for placement). *Recommended:* SAT I or ACT (for placement).

Financial Aid Of all full-time matriculated undergraduates who enrolled, 108 Federal Work-Study jobs (averaging $1253). 29 state and other part-time jobs (averaging $392).

Applying *Options:* early admission. *Required:* high school transcript.

Admissions Contact Condoa Parrent, Director of Admissions/Registrar, North Central Texas College, 1525 West California Street, Gainesville, TX 76240-4699. *Phone:* 940-668-4222. *Fax:* 940-668-6049. *E-mail:* cparrent@nctc.cc.tx.us.

NORTHEAST TEXAS COMMUNITY COLLEGE
Mount Pleasant, Texas

- **State and locally supported** 2-year, founded 1985
- **Calendar** semesters
- **Degree** certificates and associate
- **Rural** 175-acre campus
- **Coed,** 2,512 undergraduate students, 54% full-time, 65% women, 35% men

Undergraduates 1,351 full-time, 1,161 part-time. Students come from 21 states and territories, 6 other countries, 2% are from out of state, 11% African American, 0.4% Asian American or Pacific Islander, 10% Hispanic American, 0.6% Native American, 1% international, 7% transferred in, 3% live on campus. *Retention:* 54% of 2002 full-time freshmen returned.

Freshmen *Admission:* 872 applied, 872 admitted, 844 enrolled.

Faculty *Total:* 134, 38% full-time.

Majors Accounting; administrative assistant and secretarial science; agriculture; automobile/automotive mechanics technology; computer science; cosmetology; criminal justice/law enforcement administration; dairy science; dental hygiene; education; elementary education; finance; information science/studies; legal administrative assistant/secretary; mathematics teacher education; medical administrative assistant and medical secretary; middle school education; nursing (registered nurse training); poultry science; range science and management; secondary education; special education (early childhood).

Academic Programs *Special study options:* academic remediation for entering students, adult/continuing education programs, advanced placement credit, cooperative education, distance learning, English as a second language, independent study, part-time degree program, services for LD students, summer session for credit.

Library Learning Resource Center with 24,501 titles, 325 serial subscriptions.

Computers on Campus 126 computers available on campus for general student use. Internet access, online (class) registration, at least one staffed computer lab available.

Student Life *Housing Options:* Campus housing is university owned. *Activities and Organizations:* drama/theater group, student-run newspaper, choral group, Phi Theta Kappa, Student Government, Psi Beta, Chemistry Club, Hispanic Culture Organization. *Campus security:* 24-hour patrols. *Student services:* personal/psychological counseling, women's center.

Athletics Member NJCAA. *Intercollegiate sports:* baseball M(s), cheerleading M(s)/W(s), softball W(s). *Intramural sports:* table tennis M/W, tennis M/W, volleyball M/W.

Standardized Tests *Required for some:* SAT I or ACT (for placement).

Costs (2004–05) *Tuition:* area resident $555 full-time, $45 per hour part-time; state resident $783 full-time, $64 per hour part-time; nonresident $903 full-time, $74 per hour part-time. *Room and board:* $1630. *Payment plan:* installment. *Waivers:* senior citizens.

Financial Aid Of all full-time matriculated undergraduates who enrolled, 79 Federal Work-Study jobs (averaging $1600). 8 state and other part-time jobs (averaging $1600).

Applying *Options:* early admission. *Required:* high school transcript. *Application deadline:* rolling (freshmen), rolling (transfers).

Admissions Contact Ms. Sherry Keys, Director of Admissions, Northeast Texas Community College, PO Box 1307, 1735 Farm to Market Road, Mount Pleasant, TX 75456-1307. *Phone:* 903-572-1911 Ext. 263. *Fax:* 903-572-6712. *E-mail:* skeys@ntcc.edu.

NORTH HARRIS COLLEGE
Houston, Texas

- **State and locally supported** 2-year, founded 1972, part of North Harris Montgomery Community College District
- **Calendar** semesters

North Harris College (continued)
- **Degree** certificates and associate
- **Suburban** 185-acre campus
- **Coed,** 10,591 undergraduate students

Undergraduates 0.5% are from out of state, 21% African American, 7% Asian American or Pacific Islander, 23% Hispanic American, 0.3% Native American, 4% international.

Freshmen *Admission:* 1,641 applied, 1,641 admitted.

Faculty *Total:* 534, 36% full-time.

Majors Accounting; administrative assistant and secretarial science; art; art teacher education; automobile/automotive mechanics technology; biological and physical sciences; child development; computer and information sciences; computer science; cosmetology; criminal justice/law enforcement administration; criminal justice/police science; drafting and design technology; dramatic/theatre arts; education; electrical, electronic and communications engineering technology; emergency medical technology (EMT paramedic); finance; heating, air conditioning, ventilation and refrigeration maintenance technology; human services; information science/studies; interior design; journalism; legal administrative assistant/secretary; legal studies; liberal arts and sciences/liberal studies; management information systems; marketing/marketing management; mathematics; music; nursing (registered nurse training); photography; physical education teaching and coaching; political science and government; pre-engineering; respiratory care therapy; sociology; speech and rhetoric; tourism and travel services management; veterinary sciences; welding technology.

Academic Programs *Special study options:* academic remediation for entering students, adult/continuing education programs, advanced placement credit, cooperative education, distance learning, double majors, English as a second language, external degree program, honors programs, independent study, internships, off-campus study, part-time degree program, services for LD students, summer session for credit. *ROTC:* Army (c).

Library Marion M. Donaldson Memorial Library with 131,851 titles, 1,203 serial subscriptions, 11,869 audiovisual materials, an OPAC, a Web page.

Computers on Campus 300 computers available on campus for general student use. A campuswide network can be accessed from student residence rooms and from off campus. Internet access, online (class) registration, at least one staffed computer lab available.

Student Life *Activities and Organizations:* drama/theater group, student-run newspaper, choral group, Phi Theta Kappa, Student Ambassadors, Hispanic Student Forum, Vietnamese Student Association, Earth Alliance. *Campus security:* 24-hour emergency response devices and patrols, late-night transport/escort service. *Student services:* personal/psychological counseling, women's center.

Athletics *Intramural sports:* badminton M/W, baseball M/W, basketball M/W, bowling M/W, football M/W, golf M/W, gymnastics M/W, racquetball M/W, soccer M/W, softball M/W, table tennis M/W, tennis M/W, track and field M/W, volleyball M/W, weight lifting M/W.

Standardized Tests *Required for some:* SAT I or ACT (for placement), ACT ASSET/THEA/ACCUPLACER/MAPS/ACT COMPASS.

Costs (2003–04) *Tuition:* area resident $1236 full-time; state resident $2436 full-time; nonresident $2886 full-time. *Required fees:* $276 full-time. *Payment plan:* installment. *Waivers:* employees or children of employees.

Financial Aid Of all full-time matriculated undergraduates who enrolled, 61 Federal Work-Study jobs (averaging $1390). 9 state and other part-time jobs (averaging $1153).

Applying *Options:* electronic application, early admission. *Required for some:* high school transcript, interview. *Application deadline:* rolling (freshmen), rolling (transfers).

Admissions Contact Mr. Michael Code, Assistant Dean, North Harris College, 2700 W.W. Thorne Drive, Houston, TX 77073. *Phone:* 281-618-5794. *Fax:* 281-618-7141. *E-mail:* nhc.startcollege@nhmccd.edu.

NORTH LAKE COLLEGE
Irving, Texas

Admissions Contact Mr. Steve Twenge, Director of Admissions and Registration, North Lake College, 5001 North MacArthur Boulevard, Irving, TX 75038-3899. *Phone:* 972-273-3109.

NORTHWEST VISTA COLLEGE
San Antonio, Texas

Admissions Contact Ms. Jill Weston, Director of Enrollment Management, Northwest Vista College, 3535 North Ellison Drive, San Antonio, TX 78251. *Phone:* 210-348-2016.

ODESSA COLLEGE
Odessa, Texas

- **State and locally supported** 2-year, founded 1946
- **Calendar** semesters

- **Degree** certificates and associate
- **Urban** 87-acre campus
- **Endowment** $2.5 million
- **Coed,** 4,858 undergraduate students, 46% full-time, 60% women, 40% men

Undergraduates 2,251 full-time, 2,607 part-time. Students come from 32 states and territories, 1% are from out of state, 5% African American, 0.7% Asian American or Pacific Islander, 44% Hispanic American, 0.6% Native American, 0.2% international, 3% live on campus.

Freshmen *Admission:* 1,186 applied, 1,186 admitted.

Faculty *Total:* 287, 8% with terminal degrees. *Student/faculty ratio:* 14:1.

Majors Accounting; administrative assistant and secretarial science; agriculture; applied art; art; athletic training; automobile/automotive mechanics technology; biology/biological sciences; business administration and management; chemistry; child development; clinical/medical laboratory technology; computer and information sciences; computer science; computer systems networking and telecommunications; construction engineering technology; cosmetology; criminal justice/law enforcement administration; criminal justice/police science; culinary arts; data processing and data processing technology; drafting and design technology; education; electrical, electronic and communications engineering technology; emergency medical technology (EMT paramedic); English; fashion merchandising; fire science; geology/earth science; hazardous materials management and waste technology; heating, air conditioning, ventilation and refrigeration maintenance technology; history; human services; industrial radiologic technology; information science/studies; kindergarten/preschool education; legal administrative assistant/secretary; liberal arts and sciences/liberal studies; machine tool technology; mathematics; modern languages; music; nursing (registered nurse training); petroleum technology; photography; physical education teaching and coaching; physical therapy; physics; political science and government; pre-engineering; psychology; radio and television; respiratory care therapy; social sciences; sociology; speech and rhetoric; substance abuse/addiction counseling; surgical technology; teacher assistant/aide; welding technology.

Academic Programs *Special study options:* academic remediation for entering students, adult/continuing education programs, advanced placement credit, cooperative education, internships, part-time degree program, services for LD students, student-designed majors, summer session for credit.

Library Murray H. Fly Learning Resource Center with 79,882 titles, 496 serial subscriptions.

Computers on Campus 300 computers available on campus for general student use. A campuswide network can be accessed from off campus. Internet access, at least one staffed computer lab available.

Student Life *Housing Options:* coed. Campus housing is university owned and is provided by a third party. *Activities and Organizations:* choral group, Baptist Student Union, Student Government Association, Rodeo Club, Physical Therapy Assistant Club, American Chemical Society. *Campus security:* 24-hour emergency response devices and patrols, late-night transport/escort service. *Student services:* personal/psychological counseling.

Athletics Member NJCAA. *Intercollegiate sports:* baseball M(s), basketball M(s)/W(s), golf M(s), softball W(s). *Intramural sports:* basketball M/W, bowling M/W, football M, racquetball M/W, softball M/W, table tennis M/W, volleyball M/W, weight lifting M/W.

Costs (2004–05) *Comprehensive fee:* $4530 includes full-time tuition ($1230) and room and board ($3300). Full-time tuition and fees vary according to course load. Part-time tuition and fees vary according to course load. *Room and board:* college room only: $1500. Room and board charges vary according to board plan, housing facility, and location. *Payment plan:* deferred payment.

Financial Aid Of all full-time matriculated undergraduates who enrolled, 105 Federal Work-Study jobs (averaging $1667). 11 state and other part-time jobs (averaging $2046).

Applying *Options:* common application, electronic application, early admission, deferred entrance. *Application deadline:* rolling (freshmen), rolling (transfers). *Notification:* continuous (freshmen), continuous (transfers).

Admissions Contact Ms. Tanya Hughes, Director of Admissions, Odessa College, 201 West University Avenue, Odessa, TX 79764-7127. *Phone:* 915-335-6815. *Fax:* 432-335-6824. *E-mail:* thughes@odessa.edu.

PALO ALTO COLLEGE
San Antonio, Texas

- **State and locally supported** 2-year, founded 1987, part of Alamo Community College District System
- **Calendar** semesters
- **Degree** associate
- **Urban** campus
- **Coed,** 7,727 undergraduate students

Undergraduates Students come from 50 states and territories, 2% are from out of state, 2% African American, 1% Asian American or Pacific Islander, 66% Hispanic American, 0.3% Native American, 0.2% international.

Freshmen *Admission:* 1,194 applied, 1,194 admitted.

Faculty *Total:* 474, 39% full-time. *Student/faculty ratio:* 18:1.
Majors Agriculture; architectural engineering technology; art; aviation/airway management; avionics maintenance technology; biology/biological sciences; business administration and management; chemistry; computer and information sciences related; computer engineering technology; computer management; computer science; economics; education; engineering; English; finance; geology/earth science; health science; history; horticultural science; information science/studies; information technology; journalism; legal studies; liberal arts and sciences/liberal studies; library science; mathematics; modern languages; music; philosophy; physical education teaching and coaching; physics; psychology; sociology; speech and rhetoric; trade and industrial teacher education; veterinary sciences.
Academic Programs *Special study options:* academic remediation for entering students, adult/continuing education programs, cooperative education, English as a second language, part-time degree program, summer session for credit.
Library Ozuna Learning and Resource Center.
Computers on Campus 300 computers available on campus for general student use. A campuswide network can be accessed from off campus. Internet access, online (class) registration, at least one staffed computer lab available.
Student Life *Housing:* college housing not available. *Activities and Organizations:* drama/theater group, student-run newspaper, Catholic Campus Ministries, International Club, Veterinary Technician Association, Movimiento Estudiantil Chicano De Aztlan, Phi Theta Kappa. *Campus security:* 24-hour emergency response devices and patrols. *Student services:* health clinic, personal/psychological counseling.
Athletics Member NJCAA. *Intercollegiate sports:* cross-country running M/W, swimming M/W, track and field M/W. *Intramural sports:* fencing M(c)/W(c).
Standardized Tests *Required:* ACT ASSET (for placement). *Required for some:* SAT I or ACT (for placement).
Costs (2004–05) *Tuition:* area resident $1140 full-time; state resident $2280 full-time; nonresident $4560 full-time. *Required fees:* $210 full-time. *Payment plan:* installment.
Financial Aid Of all full-time matriculated undergraduates who enrolled, 272 Federal Work-Study jobs (averaging $2000).
Applying *Options:* early admission. *Required:* high school transcript. *Application deadline:* rolling (freshmen).
Admissions Contact Ms. Rachel Montejano, Associate Director of Admissions and Records, Palo Alto College, 1400 West Villaret Boulevard, San Antonio, TX 78224. *Phone:* 210-921-5279. *Fax:* 210-921-5310. *E-mail:* pacar@accd.edu.

PANOLA COLLEGE
Carthage, Texas

- **State and locally supported** 2-year, founded 1947
- **Calendar** semesters
- **Degree** certificates and associate
- **Small-town** 35-acre campus
- **Endowment** $1.3 million
- **Coed,** 1,682 undergraduate students, 52% full-time, 67% women, 33% men

Undergraduates 877 full-time, 805 part-time. Students come from 22 states and territories, 1% are from out of state, 19% African American, 0.5% Asian American or Pacific Islander, 3% Hispanic American, 0.5% Native American, 0.4% international, 12% live on campus.
Freshmen *Admission:* 463 applied, 463 admitted, 463 enrolled.
Faculty *Total:* 61, 100% full-time, 5% with terminal degrees. *Student/faculty ratio:* 19:1.
Majors Administrative assistant and secretarial science; cosmetology; forestry technology; information science/studies; nursing (registered nurse training).
Academic Programs *Special study options:* academic remediation for entering students, adult/continuing education programs, advanced placement credit, distance learning, part-time degree program, services for LD students, summer session for credit.
Library M. P. Baker Library with 88,897 titles, 347 serial subscriptions, 4,133 audiovisual materials, an OPAC, a Web page.
Computers on Campus 500 computers available on campus for general student use. A campuswide network can be accessed from off campus. Internet access, online (class) registration, at least one staffed computer lab available.
Student Life *Housing:* on-campus residence required through sophomore year. *Options:* men-only, women-only. Campus housing is university owned. *Activities and Organizations:* drama/theater group, student-run newspaper, choral group, Student Senate, Excel Club, Baptist Student Union, Panola Pipers, Phi Theta Kappa. *Campus security:* controlled dormitory access.
Athletics Member NJCAA. *Intercollegiate sports:* basketball M(s)/W(s), volleyball W(s). *Intramural sports:* baseball M, basketball M/W, football M/W, racquetball M/W, volleyball M/W, weight lifting M/W.

Standardized Tests *Required:* THEA, ACT ASSET, or ACT COMPASS (for placement). *Required for some:* SAT I or ACT (for placement). *Recommended:* SAT I or ACT (for placement).
Costs (2003–04) *Tuition:* area resident $936 full-time, $78 per semester hour part-time; state resident $744 full-time, $101 per semester hour part-time; nonresident $900 full-time, $254 per semester hour part-time. Full-time tuition and fees vary according to course load. Part-time tuition and fees vary according to course load. *Room and board:* $3090; room only: $1100.
Financial Aid Of all full-time matriculated undergraduates who enrolled, 71 Federal Work-Study jobs (averaging $829).
Applying *Options:* common application, early admission. *Required for some:* high school transcript. *Recommended:* high school transcript. *Application deadline:* rolling (freshmen), rolling (transfers). *Notification:* continuous (freshmen), continuous (transfers).
Admissions Contact Ms. Barbara Simpson, Registrar/Director of Admissions, Panola College, 1109 West Panola Street, Carthage, TX 75633-2397. *Phone:* 903-693-2009. *Fax:* 903-693-2031.

PARIS JUNIOR COLLEGE
Paris, Texas

- **State and locally supported** 2-year, founded 1924
- **Calendar** semesters
- **Degree** certificates, diplomas, and associate
- **Rural** 54-acre campus
- **Coed,** 3,862 undergraduate students, 37% full-time, 63% women, 37% men

Undergraduates 1,430 full-time, 2,432 part-time. Students come from 16 states and territories, 13% African American, 0.6% Asian American or Pacific Islander, 4% Hispanic American, 1% Native American, 0.1% international.
Freshmen *Admission:* 1,591 applied, 1,591 admitted, 1,591 enrolled.
Faculty *Total:* 147, 48% full-time. *Student/faculty ratio:* 24:1.
Majors Agricultural mechanization; art; biological and physical sciences; business administration and management; business teacher education; computer engineering technology; computer typography and composition equipment operation; construction management; cosmetology; drafting and design technology; education; electrical, electronic and communications engineering technology; elementary education; engineering; heating, air conditioning, ventilation and refrigeration maintenance technology; information science/studies; liberal arts and sciences/liberal studies; mathematics; medical insurance coding; metal and jewelry arts; nursing (registered nurse training); real estate; surgical technology; welding technology.
Academic Programs *Special study options:* academic remediation for entering students, adult/continuing education programs, English as a second language, external degree program, part-time degree program, summer session for credit.
Library 38,150 titles, 404 serial subscriptions.
Computers on Campus 82 computers available on campus for general student use. At least one staffed computer lab available.
Student Life *Housing:* on-campus residence required for freshman year. *Activities and Organizations:* drama/theater group, choral group. *Campus security:* 24-hour emergency response devices and patrols, late-night transport/escort service. *Student services:* personal/psychological counseling, women's center.
Athletics Member NJCAA. *Intercollegiate sports:* basketball M(s)/W(s), golf M(s), softball W(s). *Intramural sports:* badminton M/W, basketball M, football M, table tennis M/W, tennis M/W, volleyball M/W.
Standardized Tests *Required:* THEA (for placement).
Costs (2004–05) *Tuition:* area resident $1068 full-time; state resident $1596 full-time; nonresident $2436 full-time. *Required fees:* $260 full-time. *Room and board:* $2000; room only: $500.
Applying *Options:* early admission. *Required:* high school transcript. *Application deadline:* rolling (freshmen), rolling (transfers).
Admissions Contact Ms. Sheila Reece, Director of Admissions, Paris Junior College, 2400 Clarksville Street, Paris, TX 75460-6298. *Phone:* 903-782-0425. *Toll-free phone:* 800-232-5804.

RANGER COLLEGE
Ranger, Texas

Admissions Contact Dr. Jim Davis, Dean of Students, Ranger College, College Circle, Ranger, TX 76470. *Phone:* 254-647-3234 Ext. 110.

REMINGTON COLLEGE-DALLAS CAMPUS
Garland, Texas

Admissions Contact Mr. Skip Walls, Campus President, Remington College-Dallas Campus, 1800 East Gate Drive, Garland, TX 75041-5513. *Phone:* 972-686-7878.

REMINGTON COLLEGE-FORT WORTH CAMPUS
Fort Worth, Texas

Admissions Contact Ms. Lynn Wey, Campus President, Remington College-Fort Worth Campus, 300 East Loop 820, Fort Worth, TX 76112. *Phone:* 817-451-0017.

REMINGTON COLLEGE-HOUSTON CAMPUS
Houston, Texas

- **Proprietary** 2-year
- **Degree** certificates and associate
- **Coed**

Admissions Contact Mr. Lance Stribling, Director of Recruitment, Remington College-Houston Campus, 9421 West Sam Houston Parkway, Houston, TX 77099. *Phone:* 281-89-1240.

RICHLAND COLLEGE
Dallas, Texas

- **State and locally supported** 2-year, founded 1972, part of Dallas County Community College District System
- **Calendar** semesters
- **Degree** associate
- **Suburban** 250-acre campus
- **Coed**

Student Life *Campus security:* 24-hour emergency response devices and patrols, late-night transport/escort service, emergency call boxes.

Athletics Member NJCAA.

Standardized Tests *Recommended:* SAT I or ACT (for placement).

Costs (2003–04) *Tuition:* area resident $720 full-time, $30 per credit hour part-time; state resident $1200 full-time, $50 per credit hour part-time; nonresident $1920 full-time, $80 per credit hour part-time.

Financial Aid Of all full-time matriculated undergraduates who enrolled, 123 Federal Work-Study jobs (averaging $2000).

Applying *Options:* early admission. *Required for some:* high school transcript.

Admissions Contact Ms. Carol McKinney, Department Assistant, Richland College, 12800 Abrams Road, Dallas, TX 75243-2199. *Phone:* 972-238-6100.

ST. PHILIP'S COLLEGE
San Antonio, Texas

- **District-supported** 2-year, founded 1898, part of Alamo Community College District System
- **Calendar** semesters
- **Degree** certificates, diplomas, and associate
- **Urban** 16-acre campus
- **Coed**, 9,490 undergraduate students, 44% full-time, 56% women, 44% men

Undergraduates 4,176 full-time, 5,314 part-time. Students come from 50 states and territories, 9 other countries, 17% African American, 2% Asian American or Pacific Islander, 50% Hispanic American, 0.5% Native American, 0.1% international, 10% transferred in.

Freshmen *Admission:* 1,935 admitted, 1,935 enrolled.

Faculty *Total:* 572, 36% full-time, 8% with terminal degrees. *Student/faculty ratio:* 18:1.

Majors Accounting; administrative assistant and secretarial science; aircraft powerplant technology; airframe mechanics and aircraft maintenance technology; art; autobody/collision and repair technology; automobile/automotive mechanics technology; biology/biological sciences; biomedical technology; business administration and management; CAD/CADD drafting/design technology; chemistry; clinical/medical laboratory technology; communications technology; computer and information systems security; computer maintenance technology; computer systems networking and telecommunications; construction engineering technology; construction management; criminal justice/law enforcement administration; culinary arts; data entry/microcomputer applications; diesel mechanics technology; dramatic/theatre arts; dramatic/theatre arts and stagecraft related; early childhood education; e-commerce; economics; education; electrical/electronics equipment installation and repair; electromechanical technology; English; environmental science; health information/medical records technology; heating, air conditioning, ventilation and refrigeration maintenance technology; history; home furnishings and equipment installation; hotel/motel administration; interior architecture; interior design; kinesiology and exercise science; leatherworking/upholstery; legal administrative assistant/secretary; liberal arts and sciences/liberal studies; mathematics; medical administrative assistant and medical secretary; medical radiologic technology; music; nursing (licensed practical/vocational nurse training); occupational therapist assistant; philosophy; physical therapist assistant; political science and government; pre-dentistry studies; pre-engineering; pre-law; pre-medical studies; pre-nursing studies; pre-pharmacy studies; psychology; respiratory care therapy; restaurant/food services management; social work; sociology; Spanish; speech and rhetoric; system, networking, and LAN/wan management; teacher assistant/aide; tourism and travel services management; urban studies/affairs; web/multimedia management and webmaster; welding technology.

Academic Programs *Special study options:* academic remediation for entering students, adult/continuing education programs, advanced placement credit, cooperative education, distance learning, double majors, freshman honors college, honors programs, internships, part-time degree program, services for LD students, summer session for credit. *ROTC:* Army (c).

Library St. Philip's College Learning Resource Center plus 1 other with 104,526 titles, 1,122 serial subscriptions, 11,674 audiovisual materials, an OPAC, a Web page.

Computers on Campus 885 computers available on campus for general student use. A campuswide network can be accessed from off campus that provide access to e-mail. Internet access, online (class) registration, at least one staffed computer lab available.

Student Life *Housing:* college housing not available. *Activities and Organizations:* drama/theater group, student-run newspaper, choral group, student government, Delta Epsilon Chi, Radiography Club, Respiratory Therapy Club, Diagnostic Imaging Club. *Campus security:* 24-hour emergency response devices and patrols, late-night transport/escort service. *Student services:* health clinic, women's center.

Athletics *Intramural sports:* basketball M/W, cheerleading M/W, table tennis M/W, tennis M/W, volleyball M/W, weight lifting M/W.

Costs (2004–05) *Tuition:* area resident $1140 full-time, $38 per hour part-time; state resident $2280 full-time, $76 per hour part-time; nonresident $4560 full-time, $152 per hour part-time. *Required fees:* $258 full-time. *Waivers:* employees or children of employees.

Applying *Options:* common application, early admission. *Required:* high school transcript. *Application deadline:* rolling (freshmen), rolling (transfers). *Notification:* continuous (freshmen), continuous (transfers).

Admissions Contact Mr. Xuri M. Allen, Director of Admissions and Enrollment Services, St. Philip's College, 1801 Martin Luther King Drive, San Antonio, TX 78203-2098. *Phone:* 210-531-4834. *Fax:* 210-531-4836. *E-mail:* xallen@accd.edu.

SAN ANTONIO COLLEGE
San Antonio, Texas

- **State and locally supported** 2-year, founded 1925, part of Alamo Community College District System
- **Calendar** semesters
- **Degree** certificates and associate
- **Urban** 45-acre campus
- **Coed**

Student Life *Campus security:* 24-hour patrols, late-night transport/escort service.

Standardized Tests *Required for some:* ACT ASSET, THEA, ACCUPLACER. *Recommended:* SAT I or ACT (for placement), ACT ASSET, THEA, ACCUPLACER.

Costs (2004–05) *Tuition:* area resident $912 full-time, $38 per semester hour part-time; state resident $1824 full-time, $76 per credit hour part-time; nonresident $3648 full-time, $152 per credit hour part-time.

Financial Aid Of all full-time matriculated undergraduates who enrolled, 500 Federal Work-Study jobs (averaging $3000).

Applying *Options:* early admission. *Required:* minimum 2.0 GPA.

Admissions Contact Ms. Rosemarie Hoopes, Director of Admissions and Records, San Antonio College, 1300 San Pedro Avenue, San Antonio, TX 78212-4299. *Phone:* 210-733-2582.

SOUTHEASTERN CAREER INSTITUTE
Dallas, Texas

Admissions Contact 5440 Harvest Hill, Suite 200, Dallas, TX 75230-1600. *Toll-free phone:* 800-525-1446.

SOUTH PLAINS COLLEGE
Levelland, Texas

- **State and locally supported** 2-year, founded 1958
- **Calendar** semesters

- **Degree** certificates and associate
- **Small-town** 177-acre campus
- **Endowment** $3.0 million
- **Coed,** 9,636 undergraduate students, 47% full-time, 53% women, 47% men

Undergraduates 4,512 full-time, 5,124 part-time. Students come from 21 states and territories, 8 other countries, 3% are from out of state, 4% African American, 0.9% Asian American or Pacific Islander, 23% Hispanic American, 0.4% Native American, 0.8% international, 10% live on campus.
Freshmen *Admission:* 3,937 enrolled.
Faculty *Total:* 423. *Student/faculty ratio:* 23:1.
Majors Accounting; administrative assistant and secretarial science; advertising; agricultural economics; agriculture; agronomy and crop science; art; audio engineering; automobile/automotive mechanics technology; biological and physical sciences; biology/biological sciences; business administration and management; carpentry; chemistry; child development; commercial and advertising art; computer engineering technology; computer programming; computer science; consumer merchandising/retailing management; cosmetology; criminal justice/law enforcement administration; criminal justice/police science; data processing and data processing technology; developmental and child psychology; dietetics; drafting and design technology; education; electrical, electronic and communications engineering technology; engineering; fashion merchandising; fire science; health/health care administration; health information/medical records administration; heating, air conditioning, ventilation and refrigeration maintenance technology; industrial radiologic technology; journalism; legal administrative assistant/secretary; liberal arts and sciences/liberal studies; machine tool technology; marketing/marketing management; mass communication/media; medical administrative assistant and medical secretary; mental health/rehabilitation; music; nursing (licensed practical/vocational nurse training); nursing (registered nurse training); petroleum technology; physical education teaching and coaching; physical therapy; postal management; pre-engineering; real estate; respiratory care therapy; social work; special products marketing; surgical technology; telecommunications; welding technology.
Academic Programs *Special study options:* academic remediation for entering students, accelerated degree program, adult/continuing education programs, advanced placement credit, distance learning, part-time degree program, services for LD students, student-designed majors, summer session for credit. *ROTC:* Army (c), Air Force (c).
Library 70,000 titles, 310 serial subscriptions, an OPAC.
Computers on Campus 130 computers available on campus for general student use. A campuswide network can be accessed. Internet access, at least one staffed computer lab available.
Student Life *Housing:* on-campus residence required through sophomore year. *Options:* men-only, women-only. Campus housing is university owned. *Activities and Organizations:* drama/theater group, student-run newspaper, television station, choral group, student government, Phi Beta Kappa, Bleacher Bums, Law Enforcement Association. *Campus security:* 24-hour emergency response devices and patrols. *Student services:* health clinic.
Athletics Member NJCAA. *Intercollegiate sports:* basketball M(s)/W(s), cross-country running M(s)/W(s), track and field M(s)/W(s). *Intramural sports:* basketball M/W, cross-country running M/W, football M/W, golf M/W, racquetball M/W, softball M/W, table tennis M/W, tennis M/W, volleyball M/W.
Standardized Tests *Required:* THEA (for placement). *Recommended:* SAT I and SAT II or ACT (for placement).
Costs (2004–05) *Tuition:* area resident $4600 full-time; state resident $5000 full-time; nonresident $5400 full-time. *Room and board:* $2900.
Financial Aid Of all full-time matriculated undergraduates who enrolled, 80 Federal Work-Study jobs (averaging $2000). 22 state and other part-time jobs (averaging $2000).
Applying *Options:* early admission. *Required:* high school transcript. *Application deadline:* rolling (freshmen), rolling (transfers).
Admissions Contact Mrs. Andrea Rangel, Dean of Admissions and Records, South Plains College, 1401 College Avenue, Levelland, TX 78336. *Phone:* 806-894-9611 Ext. 2370. *Fax:* 806-897-3167. *E-mail:* arangel@southplainscollege.edu.

SOUTH TEXAS COMMUNITY COLLEGE
McAllen, Texas

- **District-supported** 2-year, founded 1993
- **Calendar** semesters
- **Degree** certificates and associate
- **Suburban** 20-acre campus
- **Endowment** $17,971
- **Coed,** 15,334 undergraduate students, 46% full-time, 62% women, 38% men

Undergraduates 6,991 full-time, 8,343 part-time. 0.1% African American, 0.8% Asian American or Pacific Islander, 94% Hispanic American, 0.4% international. *Retention:* 56% of 2002 full-time freshmen returned.
Freshmen *Admission:* 1,844 enrolled. *Test scores:* SAT verbal scores over 500: 8%; SAT math scores over 500: 9%; SAT verbal scores over 600: 1%; SAT math scores over 600: 1%.

Faculty *Total:* 542, 61% full-time. *Student/faculty ratio:* 11:1.
Majors Accounting; automobile/automotive mechanics technology; behavioral sciences; business administration and management; clinical laboratory science/medical technology; computer science; computer typography and composition equipment operation; developmental and child psychology; education; emergency medical technology (EMT paramedic); heating, air conditioning, ventilation and refrigeration maintenance technology; heavy equipment maintenance technology; hospitality administration; hotel/motel administration; human services; industrial radiologic technology; industrial technology; information science/studies; interdisciplinary studies; legal administrative assistant/secretary; legal assistant/paralegal; liberal arts and sciences/liberal studies; machine tool technology; nursing (registered nurse training); occupational therapy; plastics engineering technology.
Academic Programs *Special study options:* academic remediation for entering students, accelerated degree program, adult/continuing education programs, cooperative education, off-campus study, part-time degree program, services for LD students, summer session for credit. *ROTC:* Army (c).
Library Learning Resources Center with 12,611 titles, 177 serial subscriptions, an OPAC, a Web page.
Computers on Campus 240 computers available on campus for general student use. A campuswide network can be accessed from off campus. At least one staffed computer lab available.
Student Life *Housing:* college housing not available. *Activities and Organizations:* Beta Epsilon Mu Honor Society, Automotive Technology Club, Child Care and Development Association Club, Heating, Air Conditioning, and Ventilation Club, Writing in Literary Discussion Club. *Campus security:* 24-hour emergency response devices and patrols, late-night transport/escort service. *Student services:* personal/psychological counseling.
Athletics *Intramural sports:* badminton M/W, basketball M/W, bowling M/W, football M/W, golf M/W, racquetball M/W, soccer M/W, softball M/W, table tennis M/W, volleyball M/W.
Standardized Tests *Required for some:* THEA.
Costs (2003–04) *One-time required fee:* $75. *Tuition:* area resident $1069 full-time; state resident $1241 full-time; nonresident $2436 full-time. Part-time tuition and fees vary according to course load.
Applying *Options:* common application, early admission, deferred entrance. *Required:* high school transcript. *Application deadline:* rolling (freshmen), rolling (transfers).
Admissions Contact Ms. Sarah Gomez, Director of Enrollment Services and Registrar, South Texas Community College, 3201 West Pecan, McAllen, TX 78501. *Phone:* 956-688-2011. *Toll-free phone:* 800-742-7822.

SOUTHWEST INSTITUTE OF TECHNOLOGY
Austin, Texas

- **Proprietary** 2-year
- **Calendar** continuous
- **Degree** diplomas and associate
- **Urban** 1-acre campus
- **Coed, primarily men,** 63 undergraduate students, 100% full-time, 14% women, 86% men

Undergraduates 63 full-time. 24% African American, 14% Asian American or Pacific Islander, 27% Hispanic American.
Freshmen *Admission:* 77 applied, 63 admitted, 63 enrolled.
Faculty *Total:* 10, 100% full-time. *Student/faculty ratio:* 6:1.
Costs (2004–05) *Tuition:* $28,500 per degree program part-time.
Admissions Contact Fredrico Garcia, Director of Admissions, Southwest Institute of Technology, 5424 Highway 290 West, Suite 200, Austin, TX 78735-8800. *Phone:* 512-892-2640.

SOUTHWEST TEXAS JUNIOR COLLEGE
Uvalde, Texas

- **State and locally supported** 2-year, founded 1946
- **Calendar** semesters
- **Degree** certificates and associate
- **Small-town** 97-acre campus with easy access to San Antonio
- **Coed**

Student Life *Campus security:* 24-hour patrols, controlled dormitory access.
Standardized Tests *Required:* THEA (for placement). *Recommended:* SAT I or ACT (for placement).
Costs (2003–04) *Tuition:* state resident $1184 full-time; nonresident $1560 full-time.

Southwest Texas Junior College (continued)

Financial Aid Of all full-time matriculated undergraduates who enrolled, 150 Federal Work-Study jobs (averaging $1250). 75 state and other part-time jobs (averaging $1250).

Applying *Options:* electronic application, early admission, deferred entrance. *Required:* high school transcript.

Admissions Contact Mr. Joe C. Barker, Dean of Admissions and Student Services, Southwest Texas Junior College, 2401 Garner Field Road, Uvalde, TX 78801. *Phone:* 830-278-4401 Ext. 7284.

TARRANT COUNTY COLLEGE DISTRICT
Fort Worth, Texas

- **County-supported** 2-year, founded 1967
- **Calendar** semesters
- **Degree** certificates and associate
- **Urban** 667-acre campus
- **Coed**

Faculty *Student/faculty ratio:* 22:1.

Student Life *Campus security:* 24-hour emergency response devices and patrols.

Standardized Tests *Required:* THEA (for placement).

Costs (2003–04) *Tuition:* area resident $744 full-time, $31 per semester hour part-time; state resident $1032 full-time, $43 per semester hour part-time; nonresident $3360 full-time, $140 per semester hour part-time. *Required fees:* $180 full-time, $8 per semester hour part-time, $15 per term part-time.

Financial Aid Of all full-time matriculated undergraduates who enrolled, 372 Federal Work-Study jobs (averaging $1325). 39 state and other part-time jobs (averaging $927).

Applying *Options:* early admission. *Application fee:* $10.

Admissions Contact Dr. Cathie Jackson, Director of Admissions and Records, Tarrant County College District, 1500 Houston Street, Fort Worth, TX 76102-6599. *Phone:* 817-515-5291.

TEMPLE COLLEGE
Temple, Texas

- **District-supported** 2-year, founded 1926
- **Calendar** semesters
- **Degree** certificates and associate
- **Suburban** 114-acre campus
- **Coed**, 3,934 undergraduate students, 38% full-time, 63% women, 37% men

Undergraduates 1,492 full-time, 2,442 part-time. Students come from 32 states and territories, 7 other countries, 1% are from out of state, 14% African American, 1% Asian American or Pacific Islander, 14% Hispanic American, 0.4% Native American, 0.2% international, 8% transferred in, 1% live on campus. *Retention:* 51% of 2002 full-time freshmen returned.

Freshmen *Admission:* 680 applied, 680 admitted, 680 enrolled.

Faculty *Total:* 215, 37% full-time, 15% with terminal degrees. *Student/faculty ratio:* 18:1.

Majors Administrative assistant and secretarial science; art; automobile/automotive mechanics technology; business administration and management; clinical laboratory science/medical technology; clinical/medical laboratory technology; computer programming; computer science; criminal justice/law enforcement administration; criminal justice/police science; data processing and data processing technology; dental hygiene; drafting and design technology; electrical, electronic and communications engineering technology; industrial technology; liberal arts and sciences/liberal studies; medical administrative assistant and medical secretary; nursing (licensed practical/vocational nurse training); nursing (registered nurse training); respiratory care therapy.

Academic Programs *Special study options:* academic remediation for entering students, adult/continuing education programs, internships, off-campus study, part-time degree program, summer session for credit.

Library Hubert Dawson Library with 55,536 titles, 391 serial subscriptions, 2,170 audiovisual materials, an OPAC, a Web page.

Computers on Campus 100 computers available on campus for general student use. Internet access, at least one staffed computer lab available.

Student Life *Housing Options:* Campus housing is provided by a third party. *Activities and Organizations:* drama/theater group. *Campus security:* 24-hour emergency response devices and patrols. *Student services:* personal/psychological counseling.

Athletics Member NJCAA. *Intercollegiate sports:* baseball M(s), basketball M(s)/W(s), golf M(s), softball W(s), tennis M(s)/W(s). *Intramural sports:* basketball M/W, golf M/W, racquetball M/W, soccer M/W, tennis M/W, volleyball M/W.

Standardized Tests *Required:* THEA (for placement). *Recommended:* ACT (for placement).

Costs (2003–04) *Tuition:* area resident $1650 full-time, $55 per hour part-time; state resident $2490 full-time, $73 per hour part-time; nonresident $4410 full-time, $147 per hour part-time. *Required fees:* $50 full-time.

Financial Aid Of all full-time matriculated undergraduates who enrolled, 86 Federal Work-Study jobs (averaging $826). 7 state and other part-time jobs (averaging $951).

Applying *Options:* early admission. *Required for some:* high school transcript. *Application deadlines:* 8/19 (freshmen), 8/23 (transfers).

Admissions Contact Ms. Angela Balch, Director of Admissions and Records, Temple College, 2600 South First Street, Temple, TX 76504-7435. *Phone:* 254-298-8308. *Toll-free phone:* 800-460-4636. *Fax:* 254-298-8288. *E-mail:* angela.balch@templejc.edu.

TEXARKANA COLLEGE
Texarkana, Texas

- **State and locally supported** 2-year, founded 1927
- **Calendar** semesters
- **Degree** certificates and associate
- **Urban** 88-acre campus
- **Coed**

Faculty *Student/faculty ratio:* 15:1.

Student Life *Campus security:* 24-hour patrols.

Athletics Member NJCAA.

Standardized Tests *Required:* THEA (for placement).

Costs (2003–04) *Tuition:* area resident $800 full-time, $27 per credit hour part-time; state resident $1000 full-time, $42 per credit hour part-time; nonresident $1750 full-time, $62 per credit hour part-time. Full-time tuition and fees vary according to course load. Part-time tuition and fees vary according to course load. *Required fees:* $50 full-time, $3 per credit hour part-time. *Room and board:* room only: $1300.

Financial Aid Of all full-time matriculated undergraduates who enrolled, 30 Federal Work-Study jobs (averaging $3090).

Applying *Options:* early admission. *Required:* high school transcript.

Admissions Contact Mr. Van Miller, Director of Admissions, Texarkana College, 2500 North Robison Road, Texarkana, TX 75599. *Phone:* 903-838-4541 Ext. 3358. *Fax:* 903-832-5030. *E-mail:* vmiller@texarkanacollege.edu.

TEXAS CULINARY ACADEMY
Austin, Texas

- **Independent** 2-year
- **Calendar** continuous
- **Degree** certificates, diplomas, and associate
- **Urban** campus
- **Coed**, 200 undergraduate students, 100% full-time, 45% women, 55% men

Undergraduates 200 full-time.

Faculty *Total:* 41, 85% full-time. *Student/faculty ratio:* 16:1.

Majors Culinary arts.

Student Life *Campus security:* 24-hour emergency response devices.

Costs (2004–05) *Tuition:* $37,500 full-time, $9375 per term part-time. *Required fees:* $2500 full-time.

Applying *Application fee:* $100. *Required:* essay or personal statement, high school transcript. *Application deadline:* rolling (freshmen).

Admissions Contact Paula Paulette, Vice President of Marketing and Admissions, Texas Culinary Academy, 11400 Burnet Road, Austin, TX 78758. *Phone:* 512-837-2665. *Toll-free phone:* 888-553-2433.

TEXAS SOUTHMOST COLLEGE
Brownsville, Texas

Admissions Contact Mr. Rene Villarreal, Director of Admissions, Texas Southmost College, 80 Fort Brown, Brownsville, TX 78520-4991. *Phone:* 956-544-8992. *E-mail:* admissions@utb.edu.

TEXAS STATE TECHNICAL COLLEGE-HARLINGEN
Harlingen, Texas

- **State-supported** 2-year, founded 1967, part of Texas State Technical College System
- **Calendar** semesters
- **Degree** certificates and associate

■ **Small-town** 125-acre campus
■ **Coed,** 4,028 undergraduate students, 43% full-time, 51% women, 49% men

Undergraduates 1,729 full-time, 2,299 part-time. Students come from 10 states and territories, 0.5% African American, 0.3% Asian American or Pacific Islander, 85% Hispanic American, 0.1% Native American, 4% international, 12% transferred in, 8% live on campus.

Freshmen *Admission:* 1,492 applied, 1,492 admitted, 749 enrolled.

Faculty *Total:* 179, 88% full-time, 6% with terminal degrees. *Student/faculty ratio:* 17:1.

Majors Administrative assistant and secretarial science; airframe mechanics and aircraft maintenance technology; autobody/collision and repair technology; biomedical technology; chemical engineering; commercial and advertising art; computer and information sciences; computer and information sciences related; computer graphics; computer/information technology services administration related; computer programming; computer programming related; computer programming (specific applications); computer programming (vendor/product certification); computer science; computer software and media applications related; computer systems networking and telecommunications; computer/technical support; computer technology/computer systems technology; construction engineering technology; data processing and data processing technology; dental assisting; dental hygiene; dental laboratory technology; drafting and design technology; electrical, electronic and communications engineering technology; electromechanical technology; environmental engineering technology; farm and ranch management; food services technology; health information/medical records administration; heating, air conditioning, ventilation and refrigeration maintenance technology; industrial technology; information technology; institutional food workers; instrumentation technology; legal administrative assistant/secretary; machine tool technology; surgical technology; system administration; web/multimedia management and webmaster; web page, digital/multimedia and information resources design; welding technology; word processing.

Academic Programs *Special study options:* academic remediation for entering students, adult/continuing education programs, cooperative education, distance learning, double majors, English as a second language, internships, part-time degree program, services for LD students, summer session for credit.

Library Texas State Technical College Learning Resource Center with 25,000 titles, 413 serial subscriptions, an OPAC, a Web page.

Computers on Campus 250 computers available on campus for general student use. A campuswide network can be accessed. Internet access, at least one staffed computer lab available.

Student Life *Housing Options:* men-only, women-only, disabled students. *Activities and Organizations:* student-run newspaper, Student Congress, Vocational Industrial Clubs of America, Business Professionals of America. *Campus security:* 24-hour emergency response devices and patrols, late-night transport/escort service, night watchman for housing area. *Student services:* health clinic, personal/psychological counseling, women's center.

Athletics *Intramural sports:* badminton M/W, basketball M/W, bowling M/W, cross-country running M/W, football M/W, golf M/W, racquetball M/W, soccer M/W, softball M/W, table tennis M/W, tennis M/W, track and field M/W, volleyball M/W, weight lifting M/W.

Standardized Tests *Required:* THEA (for placement). *Recommended:* SAT I or ACT (for placement).

Costs (2004–05) *Tuition:* state resident $2088 full-time, $58 per credit hour part-time; nonresident $5832 full-time, $162 per credit hour part-time. *Required fees:* $270 full-time, $8 per credit hour part-time, $1 per credit hour part-time. *Room and board:* $3795; room only: $2085.

Financial Aid Of all full-time matriculated undergraduates who enrolled, 150 Federal Work-Study jobs (averaging $2800). 5 state and other part-time jobs (averaging $2800).

Applying *Options:* common application, early admission, deferred entrance. *Required:* high school transcript. *Application deadline:* rolling (freshmen), rolling (transfers). *Notification:* continuous (freshmen), continuous (transfers).

Admissions Contact Mrs. Elva Short, Director of Admissions, Texas State Technical College-Harlingen, 1902 North Loop 499, Harlingen, TX 78550-3697. *Phone:* 956-364-4100. *Toll-free phone:* 800-852-8784. *Fax:* 956-364-5117. *E-mail:* arangel@harlingen.tstc.edu.

TEXAS STATE TECHNICAL COLLEGE-WACO
Waco, Texas

■ **State-supported** 2-year, founded 1965, part of Texas State Technical College System
■ **Calendar** trimesters
■ **Degree** certificates and associate
■ **Suburban** 200-acre campus
■ **Coed,** 4,129 undergraduate students, 73% full-time, 23% women, 77% men

Undergraduates 3,003 full-time, 1,126 part-time. Students come from 28 states and territories, 4 other countries, 13% African American, 1% Asian American or Pacific Islander, 14% Hispanic American, 0.6% Native American, 0.9% international.

Freshmen *Admission:* 2,623 applied, 2,623 admitted.

Faculty *Total:* 290, 86% full-time. *Student/faculty ratio:* 30:1.

Majors Aeronautics/aviation/aerospace science and technology; agricultural and food products processing; aircraft powerplant technology; airframe mechanics and aircraft maintenance technology; airline pilot and flight crew; audio engineering; autobody/collision and repair technology; automobile/automotive mechanics technology; avionics maintenance technology; biomedical technology; chemical engineering; chemical technology; commercial and advertising art; computer and information sciences; computer engineering technology; computer programming; computer science; computer technology/computer systems technology; culinary arts; dental assisting; diesel mechanics technology; drafting and design technology; educational/instructional media design; electrical, electronic and communications engineering technology; electrical/electronics drafting and CAD/CADD; food services technology; graphic and printing equipment operation/production; heating, air conditioning and refrigeration technology; heating, air conditioning, ventilation and refrigeration maintenance technology; heavy equipment maintenance technology; industrial technology; information science/studies; institutional food workers; instrumentation technology; laser and optical technology; machine tool technology; mechanical engineering/mechanical technology; nuclear/nuclear power technology; occupational safety and health technology; ornamental horticulture; photographic and film/video technology; quality control technology; turf and turfgrass management; welding technology.

Academic Programs *Special study options:* academic remediation for entering students, adult/continuing education programs, cooperative education, distance learning, internships, part-time degree program, services for LD students, summer session for credit.

Library Texas State Technical College-Waco Campus Library with 53,654 titles, 384 serial subscriptions, 2,324 audiovisual materials, an OPAC, a Web page.

Computers on Campus 900 computers available on campus for general student use. A campuswide network can be accessed from student residence rooms that provide access to various software packages. At least one staffed computer lab available.

Student Life *Housing:* on-campus residence required for freshman year. *Options:* coed, men-only, women-only, disabled students. *Activities and Organizations:* student-run newspaper, Automotive VICA, Society of Mexican-American Engineers and Scientists, Texas Association of Black Persons In Higher Education, Phi Theta Kappa. *Campus security:* 24-hour emergency response devices and patrols, late-night transport/escort service, controlled dormitory access. *Student services:* health clinic, personal/psychological counseling, women's center.

Athletics *Intramural sports:* basketball M/W, football M, golf M/W, racquetball M/W, softball M/W, volleyball M/W, weight lifting M.

Standardized Tests *Required:* CPT, THEA, ACCUPLACER (for placement).

Costs (2004–05) *Tuition:* state resident $53 per credit hour part-time; nonresident $148 per credit hour part-time. *Room and board:* $1800; room only: $1500.

Financial Aid Of all full-time matriculated undergraduates who enrolled, 125 Federal Work-Study jobs (averaging $2500). 150 state and other part-time jobs.

Applying *Options:* common application, electronic application, early admission. *Required:* high school transcript. *Required for some:* interview. *Application deadline:* rolling (freshmen), rolling (transfers). *Notification:* continuous (freshmen), continuous (transfers).

Admissions Contact Mr. Rick Gauer, Director, Recruiting Services, Texas State Technical College-Waco, 3801 Campus Drive, Waco, TX 76705. *Phone:* 254-867-2026. *Toll-free phone:* 800-792-8784 Ext. 2362.

TEXAS STATE TECHNICAL COLLEGE-WEST TEXAS
Sweetwater, Texas

■ **State-supported** 2-year, founded 1970, part of Texas State Technical College System
■ **Calendar** semesters
■ **Degree** certificates and associate
■ **Small-town** 115-acre campus
■ **Endowment** $50,000
■ **Coed**

Faculty *Student/faculty ratio:* 10:1.

Student Life *Campus security:* 24-hour patrols.

Standardized Tests *Required:* THEA (for admission).

Costs (2003–04) *Tuition:* state resident $1576 full-time, $53 per semester hour part-time; nonresident $4072 full-time, $157 per semester hour part-time. Full-time tuition and fees vary according to course load. Part-time tuition and

Texas State Technical College-West Texas (continued)
fees vary according to course load. *Required fees:* $270 full-time, $9 per semester hour part-time. *Room and board:* Room and board charges vary according to board plan and housing facility.
Financial Aid Of all full-time matriculated undergraduates who enrolled, 127 Federal Work-Study jobs (averaging $1350).
Applying *Options:* early admission, deferred entrance. *Required:* high school transcript.
Admissions Contact Ms. Maria Aguirre-Acuna, Coordinator of New Students, Texas State Technical College-West Texas, 300 College Drive, Sweetwater, TX 79556-4108. *Phone:* 915-235-7349. *Toll-free phone:* 800-592-8784. *Fax:* 915-235-7416. *E-mail:* juanita.garcia@sweetwater.tstc.edu.

TOMBALL COLLEGE
Tomball, Texas

- **State and locally supported** 2-year, founded 1988, part of North Harris Montgomery Community College District
- **Calendar** semesters
- **Degree** certificates and associate
- **Suburban** 210-acre campus with easy access to Houston
- **Coed**

Student Life *Campus security:* 24-hour emergency response devices, late-night transport/escort service, trained security personnel during open hours.
Standardized Tests *Recommended:* SAT I or ACT (for admission), THEA, ACT COMPASS.
Costs (2004–05) *Tuition:* area resident $984 full-time, $32 per credit hour part-time; state resident $1944 full-time, $72 per credit hour part-time; nonresident $2304 full-time, $87 per credit hour part-time. Full-time tuition and fees vary according to course load. Part-time tuition and fees vary according to course load. *Required fees:* $8 per credit hour part-time, $12 per term part-time.
Financial Aid Of all full-time matriculated undergraduates who enrolled, 34 Federal Work-Study jobs (averaging $3000).
Applying *Options:* common application, early admission.
Admissions Contact Mr. Larry Rideaux, Dean of Enrollment Services, Tomball College, 30555 Tomball Parkway, Tomball, TX 77375-4036. *Phone:* 281-351-3334. *Fax:* 281-357-3773. *E-mail:* tc.advisors@nhmccd.edu.

TRINITY VALLEY COMMUNITY COLLEGE
Athens, Texas

- **State and locally supported** 2-year, founded 1946
- **Calendar** semesters
- **Degree** certificates, diplomas, and associate
- **Small-town** 65-acre campus with easy access to Dallas-Fort Worth
- **Coed**

Faculty *Student/faculty ratio:* 21:1.
Student Life *Campus security:* 24-hour emergency response devices and patrols, controlled dormitory access.
Athletics Member NJCAA.
Standardized Tests *Required:* THEA (for placement). *Recommended:* ACT (for placement).
Costs (2003–04) *Tuition:* area resident $900 full-time; state resident $1500 full-time; nonresident $2250 full-time. *Room and board:* $3330.
Financial Aid Of all full-time matriculated undergraduates who enrolled, 80 Federal Work-Study jobs (averaging $1544). 40 state and other part-time jobs (averaging $1544).
Applying *Options:* common application, early admission. *Application fee:* $80.
Admissions Contact Dr. Collette Hilliard, Dean of Enrollment Management and Registrar, Trinity Valley Community College, 100 Cardinal Drive, Athens, TX 75751-2765. *Phone:* 903-675-6209.

TYLER JUNIOR COLLEGE
Tyler, Texas

- **State and locally supported** 2-year, founded 1926
- **Calendar** semesters
- **Degree** certificates and associate
- **Suburban** 85-acre campus
- **Coed**

Faculty *Student/faculty ratio:* 21:1.
Student Life *Campus security:* 24-hour patrols, controlled dormitory access.
Athletics Member NJCAA.
Standardized Tests *Required:* THEA (for placement). *Recommended:* SAT I and SAT II or ACT (for placement).

Costs (2004–05) *Tuition:* area resident $1460 full-time, $44 per semester hour part-time; state resident $2330 full-time, $73 per semester hour part-time; nonresident $2630 full-time, $83 per semester hour part-time. *Required fees:* $70 per term part-time. *Room and board:* $3700.
Financial Aid Of all full-time matriculated undergraduates who enrolled, 39 Federal Work-Study jobs (averaging $1117). 23 state and other part-time jobs (averaging $992).
Applying *Options:* common application, early admission. *Required:* high school transcript.
Admissions Contact Ms. Janna Chancey, Director of Enrollment Management, Tyler Junior College, PO Box 9020, Tyler, TX 75711. *Phone:* 903-510-2396. *Toll-free phone:* 800-687-5680. *Fax:* 903-510-2634. *E-mail:* klew@tjc.edu.

UNIVERSAL TECHNICAL INSTITUTE
Houston, Texas

Admissions Contact Randy Whitman, Director of Admissions, Universal Technical Institute, 721 Lockhaven Drive, Houston, TX 77073-5598. *Phone:* 281-443-6262 Ext. 261.

VERNON COLLEGE
Vernon, Texas

Admissions Contact Mr. Joe Hite, Dean of Admissions/Registrar, Vernon College, 4400 College Drive, Vernon, TX 76384-4092. *Phone:* 940-552-6291 Ext. 2204. *Fax:* 940-553-1753. *E-mail:* sdavenport@vrjc.cc.tx.us.

VICTORIA COLLEGE
Victoria, Texas

- **County-supported** 2-year, founded 1925
- **Calendar** semesters
- **Degree** certificates and associate
- **Urban** 80-acre campus
- **Coed**

Student Life *Campus security:* 24-hour emergency response devices.
Standardized Tests *Required:* THEA (for placement). *Required for some:* SAT I or ACT (for placement).
Costs (2004–05) *Tuition:* area resident $810 full-time, $81 per credit hour part-time; state resident $1230 full-time, $123 per credit hour part-time; nonresident $1650 full-time, $220 per credit hour part-time. *Required fees:* $360 full-time, $12 per credit hour part-time.
Applying *Required:* high school transcript.
Admissions Contact Laverne Dentler, Registrar, Victoria College, 2200 East Red River, Victoria, TX 77901-4494. *Phone:* 361-573-3291 Ext. 6407. *Fax:* 361-582-2525.

VIRGINIA COLLEGE AT AUSTIN
Austin, Texas

Admissions Contact 6301 East Highway 290, Austin, TX 78723.

WADE COLLEGE
Dallas, Texas

- **Proprietary** 2-year, founded 1965
- **Calendar** trimesters
- **Degree** associate
- **Urban** 175-acre campus
- **Coed, primarily women**

Faculty *Student/faculty ratio:* 16:1.
Student Life *Campus security:* 24-hour emergency response devices and patrols, late-night transport/escort service, controlled dormitory access.
Costs (2003–04) *Tuition:* $7950 full-time. No tuition increase for student's term of enrollment. *Required fees:* $125 full-time. *Room only:* $3360.
Applying *Options:* common application, electronic application. *Required:* high school transcript, interview.
Admissions Contact Ms. Suzan Wade, Admissions Director, Wade College, International Apparel Mart at Dallas Market Center, 2350 Stemmons Expressway, Suite M5120, PO Box 586343, Dallas, TX 75258. *Phone:* 214-637-3530. *Toll-free phone:* 800-624-4850. *Fax:* 214-637-0827. *E-mail:* lfreeman@wadecollege.edu.

▶ **See page 610 for a narrative description.**

WEATHERFORD COLLEGE
Weatherford, Texas

- **State and locally supported** 2-year, founded 1869
- **Calendar** semesters
- **Degree** certificates, diplomas, and associate
- **Small-town** 94-acre campus with easy access to Dallas-Fort Worth
- **Endowment** $42.5 million
- **Coed**, 3,999 undergraduate students, 51% full-time, 61% women, 39% men

Undergraduates 2,047 full-time, 1,952 part-time. 2% African American, 0.6% Asian American or Pacific Islander, 6% Hispanic American, 0.8% Native American, 1% international, 7% live on campus.
Freshmen *Admission:* 2,962 admitted.
Faculty *Total:* 201, 48% full-time. *Student/faculty ratio:* 42:1.
Majors Administrative assistant and secretarial science; biological and physical sciences; business administration and management; computer graphics; computer programming; corrections; cosmetology; criminal justice/law enforcement administration; emergency medical technology (EMT paramedic); fire science; information science/studies; liberal arts and sciences/liberal studies; nursing (registered nurse training); pharmacy technician; respiratory care therapy.
Academic Programs *Special study options:* academic remediation for entering students, adult/continuing education programs, cooperative education, distance learning, freshman honors college, honors programs, internships, part-time degree program, services for LD students, student-designed majors, summer session for credit. *ROTC:* Air Force (c).
Library Weatherford College Library with 59,499 titles, 362 serial subscriptions, an OPAC, a Web page.
Computers on Campus 85 computers available on campus for general student use. A campuswide network can be accessed from off campus. Internet access, at least one staffed computer lab available.
Student Life *Housing Options:* coed. *Activities and Organizations:* drama/theater group, choral group, Black Awareness Student Organization, Criminal Justice Club, Phi Theta Kappa. *Campus security:* 24-hour emergency response devices and patrols, late-night transport/escort service. *Student services:* personal/psychological counseling.
Athletics Member NJCAA. *Intercollegiate sports:* baseball M(s), basketball M(s)/W(s), cheerleading W(s), tennis W(s).
Standardized Tests *Required:* THEA (for placement). *Recommended:* SAT I or ACT (for placement).
Costs (2004–05) *Tuition:* area resident $1232 full-time, $44 per hour part-time; state resident $1624 full-time, $58 per hour part-time; nonresident $2660 full-time, $95 per hour part-time. *Required fees:* $50 full-time. *Room and board:* $5700. *Waivers:* senior citizens.
Applying *Options:* early admission. *Application deadline:* rolling (freshmen), rolling (transfers). *Notification:* continuous (freshmen), continuous (transfers).
Admissions Contact Mr. Ralph Willingham, Dean of Admissions, Weatherford College, 225 College Park Drive, Weatherford, TX 76086-5699. *Phone:* 817-598-6248. *Toll-free phone:* 800-287-5471 Ext. 248. *Fax:* 817-598-6205.

WESTERN TECHNICAL INSTITUTE
El Paso, Texas

Admissions Contact Bill Terrell, Senior Vice President, Western Technical Institute, 1000 Texas Avenue, El Paso, TX 79901-1536. *Phone:* 915-532-3737.

WESTERN TECHNICAL INSTITUTE
El Paso, Texas

Admissions Contact Mr. Bill Terrell, Chief Admissions Officer, Western Technical Institute, 9451 Diana, El Paso, TX 79930-2610. *Phone:* 800-225-5984.

WESTERN TEXAS COLLEGE
Snyder, Texas

- **State and locally supported** 2-year, founded 1969
- **Calendar** semesters
- **Degree** certificates and associate
- **Small-town** 165-acre campus
- **Endowment** $653,379
- **Coed**

Faculty *Student/faculty ratio:* 17:1.
Student Life *Campus security:* 24-hour emergency response devices and patrols.
Athletics Member NJCAA.

Standardized Tests *Required:* THEA (for placement). *Required for some:* ACT (for placement).
Financial Aid Of all full-time matriculated undergraduates who enrolled, 30 Federal Work-Study jobs (averaging $1600).
Applying *Options:* early admission, deferred entrance. *Required:* high school transcript.
Admissions Contact Dr. Jim Clifton, Dean of Student Services, Western Texas College, 6200 College Avenue, Snyder, TX 79549-6105. *Phone:* 915-573-8511 Ext. 204. *Toll-free phone:* 888-GO-TO-WTC.

WESTWOOD COLLEGE-DALLAS
Dallas, Texas

- **Proprietary** 2-year, founded 2002
- **Calendar** continuous
- **Degree** associate
- **Urban** campus with easy access to Dallas
- **Coed**, 404 undergraduate students, 98% full-time, 34% women, 66% men

Undergraduates 397 full-time, 7 part-time. 30% African American, 4% Asian American or Pacific Islander, 31% Hispanic American, 0.5% Native American, 0.2% international.
Freshmen *Admission:* 468 applied, 397 enrolled.
Faculty *Total:* 31.
Majors Architectural drafting and CAD/CADD; computer programming; computer systems networking and telecommunications; graphic design.
Applying *Required:* interview, HS diploma or GED, AND passing score on ACT/SAT or Accuplacer test.
Admissions Contact Eric Southwell, Director of Admissions, Westwood College-Dallas, Executive Plaza I, Suite 100, Dallas, TX 75243. *Phone:* 800-803.3140.

▶ **See page 624 for a narrative description.**

WESTWOOD COLLEGE-FORT WORTH
Euless, Texas

- **Proprietary** 2-year
- **Calendar** continuous
- **Degree** associate
- **Urban** campus with easy access to Dallas, TX
- **Coed**, 472 undergraduate students, 79% full-time, 33% women, 67% men

Undergraduates 375 full-time, 97 part-time. 13% African American, 2% Asian American or Pacific Islander, 26% Hispanic American, 1% Native American.
Freshmen *Admission:* 478 applied, 259 enrolled.
Faculty *Total:* 35.
Majors Architectural drafting and CAD/CADD; commercial and advertising art; computer programming; computer systems networking and telecommunications; graphic design; intermedia/multimedia.
Applying *Required:* interview, H.S. diploma/GED and passing scores on ACT/SAT or Accuplacer exam.
Admissions Contact Ms. Lisa Hecht, Director of Admissions, Westwood College-Fort Worth, 1331 Airport Freeway, Suite 402, Euless, TX 76040. *Phone:* 817-685-9994. *Toll-free phone:* 866-533-9997. *Fax:* 817-685-8929. *E-mail:* info@westwood.edu.

▶ **See page 630 for a narrative description.**

WESTWOOD COLLEGE-HOUSTON SOUTH CAMPUS
Houston, Texas

- **Proprietary** 2-year, founded 2003
- **Calendar** continuous
- **Degree** associate
- **Urban** campus with easy access to Houston, TX
- **Coed**, 16 undergraduate students, 100% full-time, 31% women, 69% men

Undergraduates 16 full-time. 56% African American, 13% Hispanic American.
Freshmen *Admission:* 29 applied, 19 admitted, 16 enrolled.
Faculty *Total:* 18.
Majors Architectural drafting and CAD/CADD; computer programming; computer systems networking and telecommunications; graphic design.
Applying *Required:* interview, HS diploma/GED and passing ACT/SAT or Accuplacer scores.

Westwood College-Houston South Campus (continued)

Admissions Contact Westwood College-Houston South Campus, 7322 Southwest Freeway #1900, Houston, TX 77074. *Phone:* 713-777-4433. *E-mail:* info@westwood.edu.

▶ See page 632 for a narrative description.

WHARTON COUNTY JUNIOR COLLEGE
Wharton, Texas

- **State and locally supported** 2-year, founded 1946
- **Calendar** semesters
- **Degree** certificates and associate
- **Rural** 90-acre campus with easy access to Houston
- **Coed**

Faculty *Student/faculty ratio:* 21:1.

Student Life *Campus security:* 24-hour patrols.

Athletics Member NJCAA.

Standardized Tests *Required:* THEA (for placement). *Recommended:* SAT I or ACT (for placement).

Costs (2004–05) *Tuition:* area resident $1296 full-time; state resident $2160 full-time, $32 per credit hour part-time; nonresident $2928 full-time, $64 per credit hour part-time. *Required fees:* $22 per credit hour part-time. *Room and board:* $2500; room only: $600.

Applying *Application fee:* $10. *Required:* high school transcript, minimum 2.0 GPA.

Admissions Contact Mr. Albert Barnes, Dean of Admissions and Registration, Wharton County Junior College, 911 Boling Highway, Wharton, TX 77488-3298. *Phone:* 979-532-6381.

UTAH

COLLEGE OF EASTERN UTAH
Price, Utah

- **State-supported** 2-year, founded 1937, part of Utah System of Higher Education
- **Calendar** semesters
- **Degree** certificates and associate
- **Small-town** 15-acre campus
- **Coed,** 2,692 undergraduate students, 54% full-time, 55% women, 45% men

Undergraduates 1,463 full-time, 1,229 part-time. Students come from 21 states and territories, 6% are from out of state, 1% African American, 1% Asian American or Pacific Islander, 4% Hispanic American, 15% Native American, 8% transferred in, 15% live on campus.

Freshmen *Admission:* 488 enrolled. *Average high school GPA:* 3.15. *Test scores:* ACT scores over 18: 61%; ACT scores over 24: 14%.

Faculty *Total:* 171, 46% full-time, 15% with terminal degrees. *Student/faculty ratio:* 17:1.

Majors Administrative assistant and secretarial science; automobile/automotive mechanics technology; business administration and management; carpentry; child development; computer graphics; construction engineering technology; cosmetology; kindergarten/preschool education; liberal arts and sciences/liberal studies; machine tool technology; mining technology; nursing (registered nurse training); pre-engineering; welding technology.

Academic Programs *Special study options:* academic remediation for entering students, adult/continuing education programs, advanced placement credit, cooperative education, distance learning, English as a second language, independent study, part-time degree program, services for LD students, summer session for credit.

Library College of Eastern Utah Library with 44,490 titles, 1,464 audiovisual materials, an OPAC, a Web page.

Computers on Campus 200 computers available on campus for general student use. A campuswide network can be accessed from student residence rooms and from off campus. Internet access, online (class) registration, at least one staffed computer lab available.

Student Life *Housing Options:* coed. Campus housing is university owned. *Activities and Organizations:* drama/theater group, student-run newspaper, choral group. *Campus security:* 24-hour emergency response devices and patrols, late-night transport/escort service. *Student services:* health clinic, personal/psychological counseling, women's center.

Athletics Member NJCAA. *Intercollegiate sports:* baseball M(s), basketball M(s)/W(s), golf M/W, volleyball W(s). *Intramural sports:* basketball M/W, racquetball M/W, soccer M, tennis M/W.

Standardized Tests *Required:* ACT ASSET or ABLE (for placement). *Recommended:* SAT I or ACT (for placement).

Costs (2003–04) *Tuition:* state resident $1406 full-time, $76 per credit hour part-time; nonresident $5894 full-time, $296 per credit hour part-time. Part-time tuition and fees vary according to course load. *Required fees:* $334 full-time, $17 per credit hour part-time. *Room and board:* $3268; room only: $1568. Room and board charges vary according to board plan, housing facility, and location. *Waivers:* senior citizens and employees or children of employees.

Financial Aid Of all full-time matriculated undergraduates who enrolled, 66 Federal Work-Study jobs (averaging $1369). 27 state and other part-time jobs (averaging $773).

Applying *Options:* electronic application, early admission. *Application fee:* $25. *Recommended:* high school transcript. *Application deadline:* rolling (freshmen).

Admissions Contact Mr. Todd Olsen, Director of Admissions, High School Relations, College of Eastern Utah, 451 East 400 North, Price, UT 84501. *Phone:* 435-613-5217. *Fax:* 435-613-5814. *E-mail:* janyoung@ceu.edu.

DIXIE STATE COLLEGE OF UTAH
St. George, Utah

- **State-supported** primarily 2-year, founded 1911, part of Utah System of Higher Education
- **Calendar** semesters
- **Degrees** certificates, associate, and bachelor's
- **Small-town** 60-acre campus
- **Endowment** $9.9 million
- **Coed**

Faculty *Student/faculty ratio:* 24:1.

Student Life *Campus security:* 24-hour emergency response devices and patrols.

Athletics Member NJCAA.

Standardized Tests *Required:* SAT I, ACT, CPT or ACT COMPASS (for placement). *Recommended:* SAT I or ACT (for placement).

Costs (2004–05) *Tuition:* state resident $1524 full-time, $64 per credit part-time; nonresident $6672 full-time, $278 per credit part-time. Full-time tuition and fees vary according to course level. Part-time tuition and fees vary according to course level and course load. *Required fees:* $362 full-time. *Room and board:* $2380.

Financial Aid Of all full-time matriculated undergraduates who enrolled, 100 Federal Work-Study jobs (averaging $2700). 20 state and other part-time jobs (averaging $2700).

Applying *Options:* electronic application, early admission, deferred entrance. *Application fee:* $25. *Required:* high school transcript.

Admissions Contact Ms. Darla Rollins, Admissions Coordinator, Dixie State College of Utah, 225 South 700 East Street, St. George, UT 84770-3876. *Phone:* 435-652-7702. *Toll-free phone:* 888-GO2DIXIE. *Fax:* 435-656-4005. *E-mail:* admissions@dixie.edu.

ITT TECHNICAL INSTITUTE
Murray, Utah

- **Proprietary** primarily 2-year, founded 1984, part of ITT Educational Services, Inc.
- **Calendar** quarters
- **Degrees** associate and bachelor's
- **Suburban** 3-acre campus with easy access to Salt Lake City
- **Coed**

Standardized Tests *Required:* Wonderlic aptitude test (for admission).

Costs (2003–04) *Tuition:* Total Program Cost varies depending on course of study. Consult school catalog.

Applying *Options:* deferred entrance. *Application fee:* $100. *Required:* high school transcript, interview. *Recommended:* letters of recommendation.

Admissions Contact Ms. JoAnn Meron, Director of Recruitment, ITT Technical Institute, 920 West LeVoy Drive, Murray, UT 84123. *Phone:* 801-263-3313. *Toll-free phone:* 800-365-2136. *Fax:* 801-263-3497.

LDS BUSINESS COLLEGE
Salt Lake City, Utah

- **Independent** 2-year, founded 1886, affiliated with The Church of Jesus Christ of Latter-day Saints, part of Latter-day Saints Church Educational System
- **Calendar** semesters
- **Degree** certificates and associate
- **Urban** campus
- **Coed,** 1,282 undergraduate students, 75% full-time, 61% women, 39% men

Undergraduates 960 full-time, 322 part-time. Students come from 40 states and territories, 45 other countries, 53% are from out of state, 0.9% African American, 2% Asian American or Pacific Islander, 4% Hispanic American, 0.2% Native American, 22% international, 11% transferred in, 13% live on campus.
Freshmen *Admission:* 630 applied, 515 admitted, 467 enrolled.
Faculty *Total:* 95, 15% full-time, 3% with terminal degrees. *Student/faculty ratio:* 20:1.
Majors Accounting; accounting and business/management; accounting technology and bookkeeping; administrative assistant and secretarial science; computer and information sciences and support services related; entrepreneurship; executive assistant/executive secretary; health information/medical records administration; information technology; interior design; legal administrative assistant/secretary; liberal arts and sciences/liberal studies; medical administrative assistant and medical secretary; medical/clinical assistant; medical insurance coding; medical office assistant; medical transcription; sales, distribution and marketing; system, networking, and LAN/wan management; web page, digital/multimedia and information resources design.
Academic Programs *Special study options:* academic remediation for entering students, adult/continuing education programs, advanced placement credit, cooperative education, internships, part-time degree program, summer session for credit.
Library LDS Business College Library with 24,000 titles, 130 serial subscriptions, 300 audiovisual materials, an OPAC, a Web page.
Computers on Campus 350 computers available on campus for general student use. A campuswide network can be accessed from student residence rooms. Internet access, at least one staffed computer lab available.
Student Life *Housing Options:* women-only. Campus housing is university owned. *Activities and Organizations:* student-run newspaper, choral group, Institute Women's Association, Institute Men's Association. *Campus security:* 24-hour emergency response devices, controlled dormitory access.
Standardized Tests *Recommended:* ACT (for placement).
Costs (2004–05) *Tuition:* $2400 full-time, $100 per credit hour part-time. Full-time tuition and fees vary according to course load. Part-time tuition and fees vary according to course load. *Room only:* $2236. *Payment plan:* installment. *Waivers:* employees or children of employees.
Applying *Options:* electronic application, early admission, deferred entrance. *Application fee:* $25. *Required:* high school transcript, interview. *Application deadline:* rolling (freshmen), rolling (transfers).
Admissions Contact Mr. Matt D. Tittle, Assistant Dean of Students, LDS Business College, 411 East South Temple, Salt Lake City, UT 84111-1392. *Phone:* 801-524-8146. *Toll-free phone:* 800-999-5767. *Fax:* 801-524-1900. *E-mail:* admissions@ldsbc.edu.

MOUNTAIN WEST COLLEGE
West Valley City, Utah

- **Proprietary** 2-year, founded 1982, part of Corinthian Colleges, Inc
- **Calendar** quarters
- **Degree** diplomas and associate
- **Suburban** campus
- **Coed,** 773 undergraduate students

Freshmen *Admission:* 169 applied, 149 admitted. *Average high school GPA:* 3.00.
Faculty *Total:* 77, 16% full-time. *Student/faculty ratio:* 15:1.
Majors Accounting; administrative assistant and secretarial science; business administration and management; computer systems networking and telecommunications; information science/studies; legal assistant/paralegal; medical/clinical assistant; tourism and travel services management.
Academic Programs *Special study options:* academic remediation for entering students, accelerated degree program, English as a second language, independent study, internships, part-time degree program, summer session for credit.
Library Learning Resource Center with 5,250 titles, 41 serial subscriptions.
Computers on Campus 76 computers available on campus for general student use. A campuswide network can be accessed. Internet access, at least one staffed computer lab available.
Student Life *Housing:* college housing not available. *Activities and Organizations:* Student Activity Committee.
Standardized Tests *Required:* CPAt (for admission). *Recommended:* SAT I or ACT (for admission).
Costs (2004–05) *Tuition:* $9144 full-time, $254 per quarter hour part-time. *Required fees:* $100 full-time, $25 per term part-time.
Applying *Options:* deferred entrance. *Required:* high school transcript, interview. *Application deadline:* rolling (freshmen), rolling (transfers).
Admissions Contact Mr. Jason Peterson, Director of Admissions, Mountain West College, 3280 West 3500 South, West Valley City, UT 84119. *Phone:* 801-840-4800. *Toll-free phone:* 888-741-4271. *Fax:* 801-840-4800. *E-mail:* jrios@cci.edu.

PROVO COLLEGE
Provo, Utah

Admissions Contact Mr. Gordon Peters, College Director, Provo College, 1450 West 820 North, Provo, UT 84601. *Phone:* 801-375-1861. *Toll-free phone:* 800-748-4834.

SALT LAKE COMMUNITY COLLEGE
Salt Lake City, Utah

- **State-supported** 2-year, founded 1948, part of Utah System of Higher Education
- **Calendar** semesters
- **Degree** certificates, diplomas, and associate
- **Urban** 114-acre campus
- **Endowment** $5.1 million
- **Coed**

Faculty *Student/faculty ratio:* 19:1.
Student Life *Campus security:* 24-hour emergency response devices and patrols, late-night transport/escort service.
Athletics Member NJCAA.
Standardized Tests *Recommended:* ACT (for placement), CPT.
Applying *Options:* electronic application, early admission, deferred entrance. *Application fee:* $20.
Admissions Contact Ms. Terri Blau, Assistant Director of Admissions for School Relations, Salt Lake Community College, Salt Lake City, UT 84130. *Phone:* 801-957-4299. *Fax:* 801-957-4958.

SNOW COLLEGE
Ephraim, Utah

- **State-supported** 2-year, founded 1888, part of Utah System of Higher Education
- **Calendar** semesters
- **Degree** certificates, diplomas, and associate
- **Rural** 50-acre campus
- **Endowment** $3.8 million
- **Coed,** 2,990 undergraduate students, 82% full-time, 58% women, 42% men

Undergraduates 2,448 full-time, 542 part-time. Students come from 55 states and territories, 10 other countries, 11% are from out of state, 0.5% African American, 2% Asian American or Pacific Islander, 2% Hispanic American, 0.6% Native American, 2% international, 1% transferred in, 22% live on campus.
Freshmen *Admission:* 2,038 applied, 2,038 admitted, 1,333 enrolled. *Average high school GPA:* 2.99. *Test scores:* ACT scores over 18: 71%; ACT scores over 24: 21%; ACT scores over 30: 1%.
Faculty *Total:* 148, 74% full-time, 13% with terminal degrees. *Student/faculty ratio:* 21:1.
Majors Accounting; administrative assistant and secretarial science; agricultural business and management; agricultural economics; agriculture; agronomy and crop science; animal physiology; animal sciences; art; automobile/automotive mechanics technology; biology/biological sciences; botany/plant biology; business administration and management; business teacher education; carpentry; chemistry; child development; computer science; construction engineering technology; construction management; criminal justice/law enforcement administration; dance; dramatic/theatre arts; economics; education; electrical, electronic and communications engineering technology; elementary education; engineering; entomology; family and community services; family and consumer sciences/human sciences; farm and ranch management; foods, nutrition, and wellness; forestry; French; geography; geology/earth science; history; humanities; information science/studies; Japanese; kindergarten/preschool education; liberal arts and sciences/liberal studies; mass communication/media; mathematics; music; music history, literature, and theory; music teacher education; natural resources management and policy; natural sciences; philosophy; physical education teaching and coaching; physical sciences; physics; political science and government; pre-engineering; range science and management; science teacher education; sociology; soil conservation; Spanish; trade and industrial teacher education; veterinary sciences; voice and opera; wildlife and wildlands science and management; zoology/animal biology.
Academic Programs *Special study options:* academic remediation for entering students, adult/continuing education programs, advanced placement credit, cooperative education, English as a second language, external degree program, honors programs, independent study, part-time degree program, services for LD students, summer session for credit.
Library Lucy Phillips Library with 31,911 titles, 1,870 audiovisual materials, an OPAC, a Web page.
Computers on Campus 220 computers available on campus for general student use. A campuswide network can be accessed from off campus. At least one staffed computer lab available.

Snow College (continued)

Student Life *Housing Options:* coed. Campus housing is university owned. *Activities and Organizations:* drama/theater group, student-run newspaper, radio station, choral group, marching band, Drama Club, Latter-Day Saints Singers, Dead Cats Society, Associated Women Students, Associated Men Students. *Campus security:* student patrols. *Student services:* health clinic, personal/psychological counseling.

Athletics Member NJCAA. *Intercollegiate sports:* baseball M, basketball M(s)/W(s), football M(s), golf M(s), softball W, volleyball W(s). *Intramural sports:* badminton M/W, basketball M/W, bowling M/W, football M/W, golf M/W, racquetball M/W, soccer M, softball M/W, tennis M/W, volleyball M/W, wrestling M.

Standardized Tests *Required:* ACT (for placement).

Costs (2003–04) *Tuition:* state resident $1370 full-time, $136 per credit hour part-time; nonresident $6072 full-time, $552 per credit hour part-time. Part-time tuition and fees vary according to class time, location, and program. *Required fees:* $300 full-time, $15 per credit hour part-time. *Room and board:* $3800. Room and board charges vary according to board plan. *Payment plan:* installment. *Waivers:* employees or children of employees.

Financial Aid Of all full-time matriculated undergraduates who enrolled, 92 Federal Work-Study jobs (averaging $1200).

Applying *Options:* early admission. *Application fee:* $20. *Required:* high school transcript. *Application deadlines:* 6/15 (freshmen), 6/1 (transfers). *Notification:* continuous (freshmen), continuous (transfers).

Admissions Contact Mr. Brach Schleuter, Coordinator of High School Relations, Snow College, 150 East College Avenue, Ephraim, UT 84627. *Phone:* 435-283-7151. *Fax:* 435-283-6879.

STEVENS-HENAGER COLLEGE
Ogden, Utah

- **Proprietary** primarily 2-year, founded 1891, part of CollegeAmerica, Inc.
- **Calendar** quarters
- **Degrees** associate and bachelor's
- **Urban** 1-acre campus with easy access to Salt Lake City
- **Coed**

Faculty *Student/faculty ratio:* 17:1.

Standardized Tests *Required:* Wonderlic aptitude test (for admission). *Recommended:* SAT I or ACT (for admission).

Applying *Options:* common application, early admission, deferred entrance. *Application fee:* $25. *Required:* high school transcript.

Admissions Contact Admissions Office, Stevens-Henager College, PO Box 9428, Ogden, UT 84409. *Phone:* 801-394-7791. *Toll-free phone:* 800-371-7791.

UTAH CAREER COLLEGE
West Jordan, Utah

- **Proprietary** 2-year
- **Calendar** quarters
- **Degree** certificates, diplomas, and associate
- **Suburban** 1-acre campus with easy access to Salt Lake City
- **Coed,** 482 undergraduate students, 40% full-time, 76% women, 24% men

Undergraduates 195 full-time, 287 part-time. Students come from 2 states and territories, 1% are from out of state, 2% African American, 3% Asian American or Pacific Islander, 9% Hispanic American, 1% Native American.

Freshmen *Admission:* 302 applied, 302 admitted.

Faculty *Total:* 51, 16% full-time, 12% with terminal degrees. *Student/faculty ratio:* 9:1.

Majors Agriculture; athletic training; business administration and management; computer graphics; massage therapy; medical/clinical assistant; veterinary/animal health technology.

Student Life *Housing:* college housing not available.

Costs (2003–04) *Tuition:* $9360 full-time, $260 per credit part-time. Full-time tuition and fees vary according to course load. Part-time tuition and fees vary according to course load. *Payment plans:* tuition prepayment, installment. *Waivers:* employees or children of employees.

Applying *Required:* high school transcript, interview. *Application deadline:* 10/1 (freshmen). *Notification:* 10/15 (freshmen), continuous (transfers).

Admissions Contact Mr. Richard Flanders, Director of Admissions, Utah Career College, 1902 West 7800 South, West Jordan, UT 84088. *Phone:* 801-304-4224 Ext. 103. *Toll-free phone:* 866-304-4224. *E-mail:* rflanders@utahcollege.com.

UTAH VALLEY STATE COLLEGE
Orem, Utah

- **State-supported** primarily 2-year, founded 1941, part of Utah System of Higher Education
- **Calendar** semesters
- **Degrees** certificates, diplomas, associate, and bachelor's
- **Suburban** 200-acre campus with easy access to Salt Lake City
- **Endowment** $5.1 million
- **Coed,** 23,803 undergraduate students, 52% full-time, 42% women, 58% men

Undergraduates 12,477 full-time, 11,326 part-time. Students come from 50 states and territories, 99 other countries, 11% are from out of state, 0.4% African American, 2% Asian American or Pacific Islander, 3% Hispanic American, 0.9% Native American, 2% international, 11% transferred in. *Retention:* 44% of 2002 full-time freshmen returned.

Freshmen *Admission:* 5,638 applied, 5,638 admitted, 2,629 enrolled. *Average high school GPA:* 2.76. *Test scores:* ACT scores over 18: 74%; ACT scores over 24: 16%; ACT scores over 30: 1%.

Faculty *Total:* 972, 38% full-time, 17% with terminal degrees. *Student/faculty ratio:* 19:1.

Majors Accounting; accounting technology and bookkeeping; airline pilot and flight crew; autobody/collision and repair technology; automobile/automotive mechanics technology; banking and financial support services; biology/biological sciences; biology teacher education; building/home/construction inspection; building/property maintenance and management; business administration and management; business automation/technology/data entry; business/commerce; business/managerial economics; business teacher education; cabinetmaking and millwork; chemistry; chemistry teacher education; commercial and advertising art; communication/speech communication and rhetoric; community health and preventive medicine; computer and information sciences; computer programming; computer science; computer systems analysis; computer systems networking and telecommunications; construction trades; criminal justice/law enforcement administration; culinary arts; dance; data processing and data processing technology; dental hygiene; diesel mechanics technology; digital communication and media/multimedia; drafting and design technology; dramatic/theatre arts; early childhood education; electrical, electronic and communications engineering technology; electromechanical technology; elementary education; engineering; English; English/language arts teacher education; entrepreneurship; environmental engineering technology; executive assistant/executive secretary; finance; fire science; fire services administration; general studies; graphic design; health and physical education; heating, air conditioning, ventilation and refrigeration maintenance technology; history; history teacher education; hospitality administration; hotel/motel administration; humanities; international business/trade/commerce; legal assistant/paralegal; lineworker; machine tool technology; management information systems; manufacturing technology; marketing/marketing management; mathematics; mathematics teacher education; medical administrative assistant and medical secretary; music; nursing (registered nurse training); office management; operations management; philosophy; physical sciences; physics; psychology; restaurant, culinary, and catering management; science teacher education; secondary education; social sciences; web page, digital/multimedia and information resources design; welding technology.

Academic Programs *Special study options:* academic remediation for entering students, accelerated degree program, advanced placement credit, cooperative education, distance learning, English as a second language, honors programs, independent study, internships, off-campus study, part-time degree program, services for LD students, student-designed majors, study abroad, summer session for credit. *ROTC:* Army (b), Air Force (c).

Library Utah Valley State College Library with 173,000 titles, 6,000 serial subscriptions, 9,000 audiovisual materials, an OPAC, a Web page.

Computers on Campus 173 computers available on campus for general student use. A campuswide network can be accessed from off campus. Internet access, online (class) registration, at least one staffed computer lab available.

Student Life *Housing:* college housing not available. *Activities and Organizations:* drama/theater group, student-run newspaper, television station, choral group. *Campus security:* 24-hour patrols. *Student services:* health clinic, personal/psychological counseling, women's center.

Athletics Member NCAA. All Division I. *Intercollegiate sports:* baseball M(s), basketball M(s)/W(s), cross-country running M(s)/W(s), golf M(s), soccer W(s), softball W(s), track and field M(s)/W(s), volleyball W(s), wrestling M(s). *Intramural sports:* badminton M/W, basketball M/W, bowling M/W, cheerleading M/W, football M/W, golf M/W, lacrosse M/W, racquetball M/W, soccer M/W, softball M/W, table tennis M/W, tennis M/W, volleyball M/W.

Standardized Tests *Required:* SAT I, ACT, or in-house tests (for placement).

Costs (2004–05) *Tuition:* state resident $2788 full-time; nonresident $8718 full-time. Full-time tuition and fees vary according to course level. Part-time tuition and fees vary according to course level. *Payment plans:* installment, deferred payment. *Waivers:* employees or children of employees.

Applying *Options:* electronic application, deferred entrance. *Application fee:* $30. *Recommended:* high school transcript. *Application deadline:* rolling (freshmen), rolling (transfers). *Notification:* continuous (freshmen), continuous (transfers).

Admissions Contact Mrs. Liz Childs, Director of Admissions, Utah Valley State College, 800 West University Parkway, Orem, UT 84058-5999. *Phone:* 801-863-8460. *Fax:* 801-225-4677. *E-mail:* info@uvsc.edu.

VERMONT

COMMUNITY COLLEGE OF VERMONT
Waterbury, Vermont

- **State-supported** 2-year, founded 1970, part of Vermont State Colleges System
- **Calendar** semesters
- **Degree** certificates, diplomas, and associate
- **Rural** campus
- **Coed**

Standardized Tests *Required:* (for placement).

Costs (2004–05) *Tuition:* state resident $3696 full-time, $154 per credit part-time; nonresident $7392 full-time, $308 per credit part-time. *Required fees:* $100 full-time, $50 per term part-time.

Financial Aid Of all full-time matriculated undergraduates who enrolled, 35 Federal Work-Study jobs (averaging $2000).

Admissions Contact Ms. Susan Henry, Dean of Administration, Community College of Vermont, PO Box 120, Waterbury, VT 05676-0120. *Phone:* 802-865-4422.

LANDMARK COLLEGE
Putney, Vermont

- **Independent** 2-year, founded 1983
- **Calendar** semesters
- **Degrees** associate (offers degree program for high-potential students with dyslexia, ADHD, or specific learning disabilities)
- **Rural** 125-acre campus
- **Endowment** $662,051
- **Coed**, 336 undergraduate students, 67% full-time, 27% women, 73% men

Undergraduates 226 full-time, 110 part-time. Students come from 42 states and territories, 8 other countries, 95% are from out of state, 4% African American, 1% Asian American or Pacific Islander, 2% Hispanic American, 0.3% Native American, 5% international, 9% transferred in, 94% live on campus. *Retention:* 40% of 2002 full-time freshmen returned.

Freshmen *Admission:* 255 applied, 169 admitted, 92 enrolled.

Faculty *Total:* 107, 94% full-time, 10% with terminal degrees. *Student/faculty ratio:* 5:1.

Majors Liberal arts and sciences/liberal studies.

Academic Programs *Special study options:* academic remediation for entering students, adult/continuing education programs, advanced placement credit, English as a second language, honors programs, internships, services for LD students, study abroad, summer session for credit.

Library Landmark College Academic Resource Center with 32,000 titles, 202 serial subscriptions, 400 audiovisual materials.

Computers on Campus 56 computers available on campus for general student use. A campuswide network can be accessed from student residence rooms and from off campus. Internet access, at least one staffed computer lab available.

Student Life *Housing:* on-campus residence required for freshman year. *Options:* coed. Campus housing is university owned. *Activities and Organizations:* drama/theater group, Student Government Association, Campus Activities Board, Phi Theta Kappa Honor Society, Jazz Band Club, Cultural Diversity Club. *Campus security:* 24-hour emergency response devices and patrols, controlled dormitory access. *Student services:* health clinic, personal/psychological counseling, women's center.

Athletics *Intercollegiate sports:* baseball M, basketball M/W, cross-country running M/W, equestrian sports M/W, soccer M/W. *Intramural sports:* basketball M/W, cross-country running M/W, fencing M/W, golf M/W, skiing (cross-country) M/W, soccer M/W, softball M/W, tennis M/W, volleyball M/W, weight lifting M/W.

Standardized Tests *Required:* Wechsler Adult Intelligence Scale III and Nelson Denny Reading Test (for admission).

Costs (2004–05) *Comprehensive fee:* $43,250 includes full-time tuition ($36,000), mandatory fees ($750), and room and board ($6500). *Room and board:* college room only: $3250.

Financial Aid Of all full-time matriculated undergraduates who enrolled, 60 Federal Work-Study jobs (averaging $1600). *Financial aid deadline:* 3/1.

Applying *Options:* deferred entrance. *Application fee:* $75. *Required:* essay or personal statement, high school transcript, 3 letters of recommendation, interview. *Application deadline:* rolling (transfers). *Notification:* continuous (freshmen), continuous (transfers).

Admissions Contact Mrs. Dale Herold, Vice President for Enrollment Management, Landmark College, 1 River Road South, Putney, VT 05346. *Phone:* 802-387-6716. *Fax:* 802-387-6868. *E-mail:* admissions@landmark.edu.

▶ See page 562 for a narrative description.

NEW ENGLAND CULINARY INSTITUTE
Montpelier, Vermont

- **Proprietary** primarily 2-year, founded 1980
- **Calendar** quarters
- **Degrees** certificates, associate, and bachelor's
- **Small-town** campus
- **Endowment** $291,550
- **Coed**, 606 undergraduate students, 100% full-time, 26% women, 74% men

Undergraduates 606 full-time. Students come from 49 states and territories, 93% are from out of state, 2% African American, 2% Asian American or Pacific Islander, 3% Hispanic American, 0.2% Native American, 0.5% international, 80% live on campus.

Freshmen *Admission:* 426 applied, 101 admitted, 101 enrolled.

Faculty *Total:* 84, 81% full-time, 4% with terminal degrees. *Student/faculty ratio:* 6:1.

Majors Baking and pastry arts; culinary arts; hotel/motel administration; restaurant, culinary, and catering management.

Academic Programs *Special study options:* accelerated degree program, advanced placement credit, cooperative education, honors programs, internships, services for LD students.

Library New England Culinary Institute Library with 2,400 titles, 30 serial subscriptions, 35 audiovisual materials, an OPAC.

Computers on Campus 14 computers available on campus for general student use. A campuswide network can be accessed from student residence rooms. Internet access, at least one staffed computer lab available. Computer purchase or lease plan available.

Student Life *Housing Options:* coed, men-only, women-only. Campus housing is university owned and leased by the school. *Activities and Organizations:* student-run newspaper, American Culinary Federation, Toastmasters, Ice Carving Club. *Campus security:* 24-hour emergency response devices, student patrols, Mod patrols in the evening. *Student services:* personal/psychological counseling.

Standardized Tests *Recommended:* SAT I (for placement).

Costs (2003–04) *Comprehensive fee:* $26,365 includes full-time tuition ($20,450), mandatory fees ($390), and room and board ($5525). Full-time tuition and fees vary according to program. *Room and board:* college room only: $3500. *Payment plan:* installment. *Waivers:* children of alumni and employees or children of employees.

Financial Aid Of all full-time matriculated undergraduates who enrolled, 320 Federal Work-Study jobs (averaging $1000).

Applying *Options:* common application, electronic application, early admission, deferred entrance. *Required:* essay or personal statement, high school transcript, 1 letter of recommendation, interview. *Required for some:* minimum TOEFL scores for foreign students. *Application deadline:* rolling (freshmen).

Admissions Contact Ms. Dawn Hayward, Director of Admissions, New England Culinary Institute, 250 Main Street, Montpelier, VT 05602. *Phone:* 877-223-6324 Ext. 3211. *Toll-free phone:* 877-223-6324. *Fax:* 802-225-3280. *E-mail:* info@neci.edu.

NEW ENGLAND CULINARY INSTITUTE AT ESSEX
Essex Junction, Vermont

Admissions Contact 48½ Park Street, Essex Junction, VT 05452.

VIRGINIA

BLUE RIDGE COMMUNITY COLLEGE
Weyers Cave, Virginia

- **State-supported** 2-year, founded 1967, part of Virginia Community College System

Blue Ridge Community College (continued)
- **Calendar** semesters
- **Degree** certificates, diplomas, and associate
- **Rural** 65-acre campus
- **Endowment** $1.4 million
- **Coed**

Faculty *Student/faculty ratio:* 21:1.

Student Life *Campus security:* 24-hour emergency response devices and patrols, late-night transport/escort service.

Standardized Tests *Recommended:* SAT I (for placement).

Costs (2003–04) *Tuition:* state resident $1788 full-time; nonresident $6167 full-time. *Required fees:* $146 full-time.

Financial Aid Of all full-time matriculated undergraduates who enrolled, 25 Federal Work-Study jobs (averaging $1582).

Applying *Options:* electronic application, early admission. *Required for some:* high school transcript, interview.

Admissions Contact Mr. Robert Clemmer, Coordinator of Admissions and Records, Blue Ridge Community College, PO Box 80, Weyers Cave, VA 24486-0080. *Phone:* 540-453-2251.

BRYANT AND STRATTON COLLEGE, RICHMOND
Richmond, Virginia

Admissions Contact Mr. Mark Sarver, Director of Admissions, Bryant and Stratton College, Richmond, 8141 Hull Street Road, Richmond, VA 23235-6411. *Phone:* 804-745-2444. *Fax:* 804-745-6884.

BRYANT AND STRATTON COLLEGE, VIRGINIA BEACH
Virginia Beach, Virginia

- **Proprietary** primarily 2-year, founded 1952, part of Bryant and Stratton Business Institute, Inc.
- **Calendar** semesters
- **Degrees** associate and bachelor's
- **Suburban** campus
- **Coed, primarily women**

Faculty *Student/faculty ratio:* 10:1.

Student Life *Campus security:* late-night transport/escort service.

Standardized Tests *Required:* CPAt (for admission).

Costs (2003–04) *One-time required fee:* $100. *Tuition:* $9900 full-time, $330 per credit hour part-time. Full-time tuition and fees vary according to class time and course load. *Required fees:* $200 full-time, $100 per term part-time.

Financial Aid Of all full-time matriculated undergraduates who enrolled, 30 Federal Work-Study jobs (averaging $5000).

Applying *Options:* common application, electronic application. *Application fee:* $25. *Required:* interview. *Required for some:* high school transcript.

Admissions Contact Mr. Greg Smith, Director of Admissions, Bryant and Stratton College, Virginia Beach, 301 Centre Pointe Drive, Virginia Beach, VA 23462-4417. *Phone:* 757-499-7900.

CENTRAL VIRGINIA COMMUNITY COLLEGE
Lynchburg, Virginia

Admissions Contact Ms. Judy Wilhelm, Enrollment Services Coordinator, Central Virginia Community College, 3506 Wards Road, Lynchburg, VA 24502-2498. *Phone:* 434-832-7630. *Toll-free phone:* 800-562-3060. *Fax:* 804-386-4681.

DABNEY S. LANCASTER COMMUNITY COLLEGE
Clifton Forge, Virginia

- **State-supported** 2-year, founded 1964, part of Virginia Community College System
- **Calendar** semesters
- **Degree** certificates, diplomas, and associate
- **Rural** 117-acre campus
- **Coed**

Standardized Tests *Required:* CGP (for placement).

Costs (2003–04) *Tuition:* state resident $1535 full-time; nonresident $5002 full-time.

Applying *Options:* early admission, deferred entrance.

Admissions Contact Dr. Robert Goralewicz, Director of Student Services, Dabney S. Lancaster Community College, 100 Dabney Drive, PO Box 1000, Clifton Forge, VA 24422. *Phone:* 540-863-2815.

DANVILLE COMMUNITY COLLEGE
Danville, Virginia

- **State-supported** 2-year, founded 1967, part of Virginia Community College System
- **Calendar** semesters
- **Degree** certificates, diplomas, and associate
- **Urban** 76-acre campus
- **Coed,** 4,089 undergraduate students, 33% full-time, 61% women, 39% men

Undergraduates 1,366 full-time, 2,723 part-time. Students come from 9 states and territories, 3 other countries, 2% are from out of state, 34% African American, 0.3% Asian American or Pacific Islander, 0.5% Hispanic American, 0.1% Native American. *Retention:* 100% of 2002 full-time freshmen returned.

Freshmen *Admission:* 404 enrolled.

Faculty *Total:* 201, 26% full-time. *Student/faculty ratio:* 19:1.

Majors Accounting; administrative assistant and secretarial science; biological and physical sciences; business administration and management; computer programming; education; engineering technology; liberal arts and sciences/liberal studies; marketing/marketing management.

Academic Programs *Special study options:* academic remediation for entering students, adult/continuing education programs, advanced placement credit, cooperative education, distance learning, honors programs, part-time degree program, summer session for credit.

Library Learning Resource Center with 41,600 titles, 345 serial subscriptions, an OPAC, a Web page.

Computers on Campus 265 computers available on campus for general student use. Internet access, at least one staffed computer lab available.

Student Life *Housing:* college housing not available. *Campus security:* 24-hour patrols.

Athletics *Intramural sports:* basketball M/W, bowling M/W, football M, golf M, rock climbing M/W, softball M/W, volleyball M/W.

Standardized Tests *Required for some:* ACT ASSET.

Costs (2003–04) *Tuition:* $63 per credit hour part-time; state resident $1898 full-time, $211 per credit hour part-time; nonresident $6321 full-time. *Required fees:* $7 full-time, $0 per credit hour part-time.

Applying *Options:* early admission, deferred entrance. *Required:* high school transcript. *Application deadline:* rolling (freshmen), rolling (transfers). *Notification:* continuous (freshmen), continuous (transfers).

Admissions Contact Mr. Peter Castiglione, Director of Student Development and Enrollment Management, Danville Community College, 1008 South Main Street, Danville, VA 24541-4088. *Phone:* 434-797-8490. *Toll-free phone:* 800-560-4291.

EASTERN SHORE COMMUNITY COLLEGE
Melfa, Virginia

- **State-supported** 2-year, founded 1971, part of Virginia Community College System
- **Calendar** semesters
- **Degree** certificates and associate
- **Rural** 117-acre campus
- **Coed,** 807 undergraduate students, 32% full-time, 72% women, 28% men

Undergraduates 260 full-time, 547 part-time. 44% African American, 0.7% Asian American or Pacific Islander, 1% Hispanic American. *Retention:* 36% of 2002 full-time freshmen returned.

Freshmen *Admission:* 390 applied, 322 admitted. *Average high school GPA:* 2.60.

Faculty *Total:* 57, 32% full-time, 7% with terminal degrees. *Student/faculty ratio:* 13:1.

Majors Administrative assistant and secretarial science; biological and physical sciences; business administration and management; computer/information technology services administration related; computer/technical support; education; electrical, electronic and communications engineering technology; liberal arts and sciences/liberal studies; nursing (registered nurse training).

Academic Programs *Special study options:* academic remediation for entering students, adult/continuing education programs, advanced placement credit, cooperative education, distance learning, English as a second language, off-campus study, part-time degree program, services for LD students, summer session for credit.

Library Learning Resources Center with 20,479 titles, 95 serial subscriptions, an OPAC, a Web page.
Computers on Campus 53 computers available on campus for general student use. A campuswide network can be accessed. At least one staffed computer lab available.
Student Life *Housing:* college housing not available. *Campus security:* night security guard. *Student services:* personal/psychological counseling.
Costs (2003–04) *Tuition:* state resident $1788 full-time, $60 per semester hour part-time; nonresident $6167 full-time, $206 per semester hour part-time. *Required fees:* $140 full-time, $5 per semester hour part-time.
Financial Aid Of all full-time matriculated undergraduates who enrolled, 11 Federal Work-Study jobs.
Applying *Required:* high school transcript. *Application deadline:* rolling (freshmen), rolling (transfers). *Notification:* continuous (freshmen), continuous (transfers).
Admissions Contact Ms. Faye Wilson, Enrollment Services Assistant for Admissions, Eastern Shore Community College, 29300 Lankford Highway, Melfa, VA 23410. *Phone:* 757-789-1731. *Toll-free phone:* 877-871-8455. *Fax:* 757-787-5984. *E-mail:* eswilsf@es.cc.va.us.

ECPI COLLEGE OF TECHNOLOGY
Newport News, Virginia

- **Proprietary** 2-year, founded 1966
- **Calendar** trimesters
- **Degree** certificates, diplomas, and associate
- **Suburban** campus
- **Coed,** 493 undergraduate students, 100% full-time, 33% women, 67% men

Undergraduates 493 full-time. Students come from 34 states and territories, 2% are from out of state, 46% African American, 2% Asian American or Pacific Islander, 6% Hispanic American, 0.2% Native American, 87% transferred in.
Freshmen *Admission:* 701 applied, 527 admitted, 79 enrolled. *Average high school GPA:* 2.5.
Faculty *Total:* 130, 51% full-time, 2% with terminal degrees. *Student/faculty ratio:* 16:1.
Majors Accounting; communications technology; computer and information sciences; computer engineering technology; computer management; computer science; computer typography and composition equipment operation; electrical, electronic and communications engineering technology; electromechanical technology; engineering technology; health/health care administration; health information/medical records administration; information science/studies; mechanical engineering/mechanical technology; medical administrative assistant and medical secretary; telecommunications; trade and industrial teacher education.
Academic Programs *Special study options:* adult/continuing education programs, advanced placement credit, freshman honors college, honors programs, internships, part-time degree program, summer session for credit.
Library ECPI-Virginia Beach Library with 13,014 titles, 168 serial subscriptions, an OPAC, a Web page.
Computers on Campus 100 computers available on campus for general student use. A campuswide network can be accessed from off campus. Internet access, at least one staffed computer lab available.
Student Life *Housing:* college housing not available. *Activities and Organizations:* SETA, IEEE, NVTHS, Accounting Society, CSI. *Campus security:* building and parking lot security. *Student services:* personal/psychological counseling.
Financial Aid Of all full-time matriculated undergraduates who enrolled, 30 Federal Work-Study jobs (averaging $2000).
Applying *Options:* common application, deferred entrance. *Application fee:* $100. *Required:* high school transcript, minimum 2.0 GPA, interview. *Notification:* continuous (freshmen), continuous (transfers).
Admissions Contact Ms. Teresa Cohn, Director of Admissions, ECPI College of Technology, 1001 Omni Boulevard, #100, Newport News, VA 23606. *Phone:* 757-838-9191.

ECPI COLLEGE OF TECHNOLOGY
Virginia Beach, Virginia

- **Proprietary** 2-year, founded 1966
- **Calendar** trimesters
- **Degree** certificates, diplomas, and associate
- **Suburban** 8-acre campus
- **Coed,** 3,223 undergraduate students, 93% full-time, 34% women, 66% men

Undergraduates 2,996 full-time, 227 part-time. Students come from 6 states and territories, 10% are from out of state, 34% African American, 3% Asian American or Pacific Islander, 4% Hispanic American, 0.4% Native American.
Freshmen *Admission:* 566 applied, 425 admitted, 425 enrolled.

Faculty *Total:* 130, 51% full-time, 2% with terminal degrees. *Student/faculty ratio:* 16:1.
Majors Accounting; biomedical technology; business machine repair; communications technology; computer and information sciences; computer engineering technology; computer management; computer programming; computer science; computer typography and composition equipment operation; data processing and data processing technology; electrical, electronic and communications engineering technology; electromechanical technology; engineering technology; health/health care administration; health information/medical records administration; information science/studies; mechanical engineering/mechanical technology; medical administrative assistant and medical secretary; telecommunications.
Academic Programs *Special study options:* adult/continuing education programs, advanced placement credit, distance learning, freshman honors college, internships, part-time degree program, summer session for credit.
Library ECPI-Virginia Beach Library with an OPAC, a Web page.
Computers on Campus 600 computers available on campus for general student use. A campuswide network can be accessed from off campus. Internet access, at least one staffed computer lab available.
Student Life *Housing Options:* Campus housing is provided by a third party. *Activities and Organizations:* SETA, IEEE, NVTHS, ITE, Accounting Society. *Campus security:* building and parking lot security. *Student services:* personal/psychological counseling.
Standardized Tests *Recommended:* SAT I or ACT (for admission).
Financial Aid Of all full-time matriculated undergraduates who enrolled, 80 Federal Work-Study jobs (averaging $2000).
Applying *Options:* common application, electronic application, deferred entrance. *Application fee:* $100. *Required:* high school transcript, interview. *Notification:* continuous (freshmen), continuous (transfers).
Admissions Contact Mr. Ronald Ballance, Vice President, ECPI College of Technology, 5555 Greenwich Road, Suite 100, Virginia Beach, VA 23462. *Phone:* 804-330-5533. *Toll-free phone:* 800-986-1200.

ECPI TECHNICAL COLLEGE
Glen Allen, Virginia

- **Proprietary** 2-year
- **Calendar** semesters
- **Degree** certificates, diplomas, and associate
- **Urban** campus with easy access to Richmond
- **Coed,** 360 undergraduate students, 100% full-time, 30% women, 70% men

Undergraduates 360 full-time. Students come from 2 states and territories, 1% are from out of state, 36% African American, 4% Asian American or Pacific Islander, 3% Hispanic American, 0.6% Native American.
Freshmen *Admission:* 105 applied, 57 admitted, 57 enrolled.
Faculty *Student/faculty ratio:* 15:1.
Majors Computer and information systems security; computer programming; computer technology/computer systems technology; data entry/microcomputer applications; telecommunications technology; web page, digital/multimedia and information resources design.
Student Life *Housing:* college housing not available. *Activities and Organizations:* CSI, OPMA, SETA, NVTHS, ITE. *Campus security:* building and parking lot security.
Standardized Tests *Recommended:* SAT I and SAT II or ACT (for admission).
Applying *Required:* high school transcript, interview. *Application deadline:* rolling (freshmen), rolling (transfers). *Notification:* continuous (freshmen), continuous (transfers).
Admissions Contact Mr. Jacob Pope, Director, ECPI Technical College, 4305 Cox Road, Glen Allen, VA 23060. *Phone:* 804-934-0100. *Toll-free phone:* 800-986-1200.

ECPI TECHNICAL COLLEGE
Richmond, Virginia

- **Proprietary** 2-year, founded 1966
- **Calendar** semesters
- **Degree** certificates, diplomas, and associate
- **Urban** campus
- **Coed,** 448 undergraduate students, 100% full-time, 33% women, 67% men

Undergraduates 448 full-time. Students come from 2 states and territories, 1% are from out of state, 43% African American, 1% Asian American or Pacific Islander, 2% Hispanic American, 0.2% Native American.
Freshmen *Admission:* 185 applied, 85 admitted, 85 enrolled.
Faculty *Student/faculty ratio:* 15:1.
Majors Accounting; business machine repair; communications technology; computer and information sciences; computer and information sciences related;

ECPI Technical College (continued)

computer and information systems security; computer management; computer programming; computer science; computer technology/computer systems technology; computer typography and composition equipment operation; data entry/microcomputer applications; data processing and data processing technology; electrical, electronic and communications engineering technology; electromechanical technology; engineering technology; health/health care administration; health information/medical records administration; information science/studies; mechanical engineering/mechanical technology; medical administrative assistant and medical secretary; telecommunications; telecommunications technology; trade and industrial teacher education; web page, digital/multimedia and information resources design.

Academic Programs *Special study options:* adult/continuing education programs, advanced placement credit, freshman honors college, honors programs, internships, part-time degree program, summer session for credit.

Library ECPI-Richmond Library with 3,165 titles, 81 serial subscriptions, an OPAC, a Web page.

Computers on Campus 190 computers available on campus for general student use. A campuswide network can be accessed from off campus. Internet access, at least one staffed computer lab available.

Student Life *Housing:* college housing not available. *Activities and Organizations:* Collegiate Secretaries International, Data Processing Management Association, Student Electronics Technicians Association, Future Office Assistants, National Vocational-Technical Honor Society. *Campus security:* building and parking lot security.

Standardized Tests *Recommended:* SAT I and SAT II or ACT (for admission).

Costs (2004–05) *Tuition:* Tuition varies by program. *Payment plan:* installment. *Waivers:* employees or children of employees.

Financial Aid Of all full-time matriculated undergraduates who enrolled, 40 Federal Work-Study jobs (averaging $2000).

Applying *Options:* common application, deferred entrance. *Application fee:* $100. *Required:* high school transcript, interview. *Application deadline:* rolling (freshmen), rolling (transfers). *Notification:* continuous (freshmen), continuous (transfers).

Admissions Contact Ms. Ada Gerard, Director, ECPI Technical College, 800 Moorefield Park Drive, Richmond, VA 23236. *Phone:* 804-330-5533. *Toll-free phone:* 800-986-1200.

ECPI TECHNICAL COLLEGE
Roanoke, Virginia

- **Proprietary** 2-year, founded 1966
- **Calendar** semesters
- **Degree** certificates, diplomas, and associate
- **Suburban** 3-acre campus
- **Coed,** 356 undergraduate students, 100% full-time, 25% women, 75% men

Undergraduates 356 full-time. Students come from 4 states and territories, 1% are from out of state, 23% African American, 0.6% Asian American or Pacific Islander, 1% Hispanic American, 0.3% Native American.

Freshmen *Admission:* 108 applied, 51 admitted, 51 enrolled.

Faculty *Student/faculty ratio:* 15:1.

Majors Accounting; communications technology; computer and information sciences; computer and information sciences related; computer and information systems security; computer engineering technology; computer science; computer technology/computer systems technology; computer typography and composition equipment operation; data entry/microcomputer applications; electrical, electronic and communications engineering technology; electromechanical technology; engineering technology; health/health care administration; health information/medical records administration; information science/studies; mechanical engineering/mechanical technology; medical administrative assistant and medical secretary; medical/clinical assistant; telecommunications; telecommunications technology.

Academic Programs *Special study options:* accelerated degree program, adult/continuing education programs, advanced placement credit, distance learning, internships, part-time degree program, summer session for credit.

Library ECPI-Roanoke Library plus 1 other with 1,703 titles, 43 serial subscriptions, a Web page.

Computers on Campus 80 computers available on campus for general student use. A campuswide network can be accessed from off campus. Internet access, at least one staffed computer lab available.

Student Life *Housing:* college housing not available. *Activities and Organizations:* SETA, NVTHS, SAFA, FOAMA, ITE. *Campus security:* building and parking lot security.

Standardized Tests *Recommended:* SAT I and SAT II or ACT (for admission).

Costs (2003–04) *Tuition:* Tuition varies by program. *Payment plan:* installment.

Financial Aid Of all full-time matriculated undergraduates who enrolled, 20 Federal Work-Study jobs (averaging $2000).

Applying *Options:* common application, electronic application, deferred entrance. *Application fee:* $100. *Required:* high school transcript, interview. *Application deadline:* rolling (freshmen), rolling (transfers). *Notification:* continuous (freshmen), continuous (transfers).

Admissions Contact ECPI Technical College, 5234 Airport Road, Roanoke, VA 24012. *Phone:* 540-362-5400. *Toll-free phone:* 800-986-1200.

GERMANNA COMMUNITY COLLEGE
Locust Grove, Virginia

- **State-supported** 2-year, founded 1970, part of Virginia Community College System
- **Calendar** semesters
- **Degree** certificates and associate
- **Rural** 100-acre campus with easy access to Washington, DC
- **Coed,** 4,520 undergraduate students, 29% full-time, 66% women, 34% men

Undergraduates 1,313 full-time, 3,207 part-time. Students come from 5 states and territories, 13% African American, 2% Asian American or Pacific Islander, 3% Hispanic American.

Freshmen *Admission:* 2,969 applied, 2,969 admitted, 767 enrolled.

Faculty *Total:* 282, 16% full-time.

Majors Accounting; administrative assistant and secretarial science; biological and physical sciences; business administration and management; criminal justice/police science; data processing and data processing technology; education; electrical, electronic and communications engineering technology; general studies; liberal arts and sciences/liberal studies; nursing (registered nurse training).

Academic Programs *Special study options:* academic remediation for entering students, adult/continuing education programs, off-campus study, part-time degree program, summer session for credit.

Library 22,412 titles, 160 serial subscriptions.

Computers on Campus 55 computers available on campus for general student use. At least one staffed computer lab available.

Student Life *Housing:* college housing not available. *Activities and Organizations:* student-run newspaper, Student Nurses Association, Student Government Association, Phi Theta Kappa, Students Against Substance Abuse. *Campus security:* 24-hour patrols. *Student services:* personal/psychological counseling.

Athletics *Intramural sports:* archery M/W, basketball M/W, bowling M/W, football M/W, golf M/W, tennis M/W, volleyball M/W.

Costs (2003–04) *Tuition:* state resident $1788 full-time, $60 per credit part-time; nonresident $6167 full-time, $206 per credit part-time. *Required fees:* $6 per credit part-time.

Financial Aid Of all full-time matriculated undergraduates who enrolled, 35 Federal Work-Study jobs (averaging $1212). 15 state and other part-time jobs (averaging $1667).

Applying *Options:* early admission. *Required for some:* high school transcript. *Application deadline:* rolling (freshmen), rolling (transfers). *Notification:* continuous (freshmen), continuous (transfers).

Admissions Contact Ms. Rita Dunston, Registrar, Germanna Community College, 2130 Germanna Highway, Locust Grove, VA 22508-2102. *Phone:* 540-727-3034.

ITT TECHNICAL INSTITUTE
Richmond, Virginia

- **Proprietary** primarily 2-year, part of ITT Educational Services, Inc.
- **Calendar** quarters
- **Degrees** associate and bachelor's
- **Coed**

Standardized Tests *Required:* Wonderlic aptitude test (for admission).

Costs (2003–04) *Tuition:* Total Program Cost varies depending on course of study. Consult school catalog.

Applying *Options:* deferred entrance. *Application fee:* $100. *Required:* high school transcript, interview. *Recommended:* letters of recommendation.

Admissions Contact Mr. Marc Wright, Director of Recruitment, ITT Technical Institute, 300 Gateway Centre Parkway, Richmond, VA 23235. *Phone:* 804-330-4992. *Toll-free phone:* 888-330-4888. *Fax:* 804-330-4993.

ITT TECHNICAL INSTITUTE
Chantilly, Virginia

- **Proprietary** 2-year, founded 2002, part of ITT Educational Services, Inc
- **Calendar** quarters
- **Degree** associate
- **Coed**

Standardized Tests *Required:* (for admission).

Costs (2003–04) *Tuition:* Total Program Cost varies depending on course of study. Consult school catalog.

Applying *Options:* deferred entrance. *Application fee:* $100. *Required:* high school transcript, interview. *Recommended:* letters of recommendation.

Admissions Contact Foy Ann Roach, Director of Recruitment, ITT Technical Institute, 14420 Albemarle Point Place, Chantilly, VA 20151. *Phone:* 703-263-2541. *Toll-free phone:* 888-895-8324. *Fax:* 703-263-0846.

ITT TECHNICAL INSTITUTE
Springfield, Virginia

- **Proprietary** primarily 2-year, founded 2002, part of ITT Educational Services, Inc.
- **Calendar** quarters
- **Degrees** associate and bachelor's
- **Coed**

Standardized Tests *Required:* Wonderlic aptitude test (for admission).

Costs (2003–04) *Tuition:* Total Program Cost varies depending on course of study. Consult school catalog.

Applying *Options:* deferred entrance. *Application fee:* $100. *Required:* high school transcript, interview. *Recommended:* letters of recommendation.

Admissions Contact Mr. Paul M. Ochoa, Director of Recruitment, ITT Technical Institute, 7300 Boston Boulevard, Springfield, VA 22153. *Phone:* 703-440-9535. *Toll-free phone:* 866-817-8324. *Fax:* 703-440-9561.

ITT TECHNICAL INSTITUTE
Norfolk, Virginia

- **Proprietary** primarily 2-year, founded 1988, part of ITT Educational Services, Inc.
- **Calendar** quarters
- **Degrees** associate and bachelor's
- **Suburban** 2-acre campus
- **Coed**

Standardized Tests *Required:* Wonderlic aptitude test (for admission).

Costs (2003–04) *Tuition:* Total Program Cost varies depending on course of study. Consult school catalog.

Financial Aid Of all full-time matriculated undergraduates who enrolled, 3 Federal Work-Study jobs (averaging $5000).

Applying *Options:* deferred entrance. *Application fee:* $100. *Required:* high school transcript, interview. *Recommended:* letters of recommendation.

Admissions Contact Mr. Jack Keesee, Director of Recruitment, ITT Technical Institute, 863 Glenrock Road, Norfolk, VA 23502. *Phone:* 757-466-1260. *Toll-free phone:* 888-253-8324. *Fax:* 757-466-7630.

JOHN TYLER COMMUNITY COLLEGE
Chester, Virginia

- **State-supported** 2-year, founded 1967, part of Virginia Community College System
- **Calendar** semesters
- **Degree** certificates and associate
- **Suburban** 160-acre campus with easy access to Richmond
- **Endowment** $2.0 million
- **Coed,** 6,054 undergraduate students, 24% full-time, 63% women, 37% men

Undergraduates 1,428 full-time, 4,626 part-time. Students come from 38 states and territories, 2% are from out of state, 25% African American, 3% Asian American or Pacific Islander, 2% Hispanic American, 0.5% Native American, 0.3% international, 15% transferred in.

Freshmen *Admission:* 378 enrolled.

Faculty *Total:* 402, 14% full-time. *Student/faculty ratio:* 27:1.

Majors Administrative assistant and secretarial science; architectural engineering technology; biology/biotechnology laboratory technician; business/commerce; electrical, electronics and communications engineering; environmental engineering technology; funeral service and mortuary science; human services; liberal arts and sciences/liberal studies; management information systems; mechanical engineering/mechanical technology; nursing (registered nurse training); physical therapy; safety/security technology.

Academic Programs *Special study options:* academic remediation for entering students, adult/continuing education programs, advanced placement credit, distance learning, external degree program, honors programs, off-campus study, part-time degree program, services for LD students, study abroad, summer session for credit. *ROTC:* Army (c).

Library John Tyler Community College Learning Resource and Technology Center with 49,393 titles, 179 serial subscriptions, 1,544 audiovisual materials, an OPAC, a Web page.

Computers on Campus 465 computers available on campus for general student use. A campuswide network can be accessed from off campus. Internet access, at least one staffed computer lab available.

Student Life *Housing:* college housing not available. *Campus security:* 24-hour patrols. *Student services:* personal/psychological counseling.

Athletics *Intramural sports:* golf M/W, softball M/W, tennis M/W, volleyball M/W.

Costs (2003–04) *Tuition:* area resident $1506 full-time; nonresident $5045 full-time. *Required fees:* $25 full-time.

Applying *Options:* common application, early admission, deferred entrance. *Recommended:* high school transcript. *Application deadline:* rolling (freshmen). *Notification:* continuous (freshmen).

Admissions Contact Ms. Joy James, Registrar and Enrollment Services Coordinator, John Tyler Community College, 13101 Jefferson Davis Highway, Chester, VA 23831. *Phone:* 804-796-4150. *Toll-free phone:* 800-552-3490. *Fax:* 804-796-4163.

J. SARGEANT REYNOLDS COMMUNITY COLLEGE
Richmond, Virginia

- **State-supported** 2-year, founded 1972, part of Virginia Community College System
- **Calendar** semesters
- **Degree** certificates and associate
- **Suburban** 207-acre campus
- **Endowment** $1.7 million
- **Coed,** 11,132 undergraduate students, 25% full-time, 59% women, 41% men

Undergraduates 2,786 full-time, 8,346 part-time. Students come from 34 states and territories, 49 other countries, 3% are from out of state, 36% African American, 3% Asian American or Pacific Islander, 2% Hispanic American, 0.6% Native American, 1% international.

Freshmen *Admission:* 2,452 applied, 1,073 admitted.

Faculty *Total:* 514, 21% full-time. *Student/faculty ratio:* 19:1.

Majors Accounting technology and bookkeeping; administrative assistant and secretarial science; architectural engineering technology; biological and physical sciences; business administration and management; child care and support services management; civil engineering technology; clinical/medical laboratory technology; community organization and advocacy; computer and information sciences; computer and information sciences related; computer engineering technology; computer programming; computer programming related; construction engineering technology; criminal justice/safety; culinary arts; data processing and data processing technology; dental laboratory technology; dietetics; electrical, electronic and communications engineering technology; engineering; executive assistant/executive secretary; fashion merchandising; fire science; hospitality administration; hotel/motel administration; information technology; landscaping and groundskeeping; legal assistant/paralegal; liberal arts and sciences/liberal studies; marketing/marketing management; music; nursing (registered nurse training); occupational therapist assistant; opticianry; ornamental horticulture; respiratory care therapy; social sciences.

Academic Programs *Special study options:* academic remediation for entering students, adult/continuing education programs, advanced placement credit, distance learning, English as a second language, independent study, internships, off-campus study, part-time degree program, services for LD students, summer session for credit. *ROTC:* Army (c).

Library Learning Resource Center plus 2 others with 80,736 titles, 465 serial subscriptions, 1,575 audiovisual materials, an OPAC, a Web page.

Computers on Campus 1100 computers available on campus for general student use. A campuswide network can be accessed from off campus that provide access to telephone registration for returning students. At least one staffed computer lab available.

Student Life *Housing:* college housing not available. *Activities and Organizations:* drama/theater group, choral group, Phi Theta Kappa, Student Nurses Association, SGA, Phi Beta Lambda. *Campus security:* security during open hours. *Student services:* personal/psychological counseling.

Athletics *Intramural sports:* basketball M/W, bowling M/W, soccer M/W, softball M/W, table tennis M/W, tennis M/W, volleyball M/W.

Costs (2003–04) *Tuition:* state resident $2000 full-time, $67 per hour part-time; nonresident $6423 full-time, $214 per hour part-time. *Required fees:* $9 per hour part-time. *Waivers:* senior citizens.

Financial Aid Of all full-time matriculated undergraduates who enrolled, 527 Federal Work-Study jobs (averaging $1711).

Applying *Required:* high school transcript. *Required for some:* interview. *Application deadline:* rolling (freshmen), rolling (transfers). *Notification:* continuous (freshmen), continuous (transfers).

J. Sargeant Reynolds Community College (continued)

Admissions Contact Ms. Suzan Marshall, Director of Admissions and Records, J. Sargeant Reynolds Community College, PO Box 85622, Richmond, VA 23285-5622. *Phone:* 804-371-3029. *Fax:* 804-371-3650. *E-mail:* smarshall@jsr.vccs.edu.

LORD FAIRFAX COMMUNITY COLLEGE
Middletown, Virginia

- **State-supported** 2-year, founded 1969, part of Virginia Community College System
- **Calendar** semesters
- **Degree** certificates and associate
- **Rural** 100-acre campus with easy access to Washington, DC
- **Coed,** 5,500 undergraduate students

Undergraduates 6% are from out of state. *Retention:* 52% of 2002 full-time freshmen returned.

Faculty *Total:* 198, 27% full-time.

Majors Accounting; administrative assistant and secretarial science; agricultural business and management; applied horticulture; biological and physical sciences; business administration and management; civil engineering technology; commercial and advertising art; communication/speech communication and rhetoric; computer and information sciences; computer programming; dental hygiene; education; environmental engineering technology; information science/studies; liberal arts and sciences/liberal studies; mechanical engineering/mechanical technology; natural resources management and policy; nursing (registered nurse training); office management; philosophy.

Academic Programs *Special study options:* academic remediation for entering students, adult/continuing education programs, advanced placement credit, cooperative education, distance learning, honors programs, part-time degree program, services for LD students, summer session for credit.

Library Learning Resources Center with 41,000 titles, 300 serial subscriptions, an OPAC.

Computers on Campus 450 computers available on campus for general student use. A campuswide network can be accessed from off campus. Internet access, at least one staffed computer lab available.

Student Life *Housing:* college housing not available. *Activities and Organizations:* drama/theater group, Phi Theta Kappa, Phi Beta Lambda, Performing Arts Club, Scientific Society, Ambassadors Club. *Campus security:* late-night transport/escort service. *Student services:* personal/psychological counseling, women's center.

Costs (2003–04) *Tuition:* state resident $1430 full-time, $60 per credit part-time; nonresident $4933 full-time, $206 per credit part-time. Full-time tuition and fees vary according to course load and location. Part-time tuition and fees vary according to course load and location. *Required fees:* $91 full-time, $4 per credit part-time. *Payment plan:* deferred payment. *Waivers:* senior citizens.

Financial Aid Of all full-time matriculated undergraduates who enrolled, 28 Federal Work-Study jobs (averaging $1600).

Applying *Options:* early admission. *Recommended:* high school transcript. *Application deadline:* rolling (freshmen), rolling (transfers). *Notification:* continuous (freshmen), continuous (transfers).

Admissions Contact Ms. Cynthia Bambara, Vice President of Student Success, Lord Fairfax Community College, 173 Skirmisher Lane, Middletown, VA 22645. *Phone:* 540-868-7105. *Toll-free phone:* 800-906-5322 Ext. 7107. *Fax:* 540-868-7005. *E-mail:* lfsmitt@lfcc.edu.

MEDICAL CAREERS INSTITUTE
Newport News, Virginia

Admissions Contact 1001 Omni Boulevard, Suite 200, Newport News, VA 23606.

MEDICAL CAREERS INSTITUTE
Richmond, Virginia

Admissions Contact David K. Mayle, Director of Admissions, Medical Careers Institute, 800 Moorefield Park Drive, Suite 302, Richmond, VA 23236-3659. *Phone:* 804-521-0400.

MEDICAL CAREERS INSTITUTE
Virginia Beach, Virginia

Admissions Contact 5501 Greenwich Road, Virginia Beach, VA 23462.

MOUNTAIN EMPIRE COMMUNITY COLLEGE
Big Stone Gap, Virginia

- **State-supported** 2-year, founded 1972, part of Virginia Community College System
- **Calendar** semesters
- **Degree** certificates, diplomas, and associate
- **Small-town** campus with easy access to Kingsport
- **Coed,** 2,885 undergraduate students, 41% full-time, 68% women, 32% men

Undergraduates 1,195 full-time, 1,690 part-time. Students come from 3 states and territories, 1 other country, 1% are from out of state.

Faculty *Total:* 150, 47% full-time, 15% with terminal degrees. *Student/faculty ratio:* 18:1.

Majors Accounting; administrative assistant and secretarial science; biological and physical sciences; biology/biological sciences; business administration and management; business teacher education; chemistry; computer systems networking and telecommunications; computer/technical support; corrections; criminal justice/law enforcement administration; criminal justice/police science; data entry/microcomputer applications; drafting and design technology; education; electrical, electronic and communications engineering technology; elementary education; engineering technology; English; environmental studies; forestry; hydrology and water resources science; industrial technology; information science/studies; information technology; land use planning and management; legal administrative assistant/secretary; liberal arts and sciences/liberal studies; marketing/marketing management; mathematics; mining technology; nursing (registered nurse training); pre-engineering; public administration.

Academic Programs *Special study options:* academic remediation for entering students, adult/continuing education programs, advanced placement credit, cooperative education, distance learning, internships, part-time degree program, student-designed majors, summer session for credit.

Library Robb Hall with 21,600 titles, 105 serial subscriptions, 200 audiovisual materials, an OPAC.

Computers on Campus 400 computers available on campus for general student use. A campuswide network can be accessed from off campus. Internet access, at least one staffed computer lab available.

Student Life *Housing:* college housing not available. *Activities and Organizations:* drama/theater group, student-run television station, Phi Theta Kappa, Lambda Alpha Epsilon, MECC Group Artists, Phi Beta Lambda, Players on the Mountain. *Campus security:* 24-hour emergency response devices and patrols. *Student services:* personal/psychological counseling.

Athletics *Intramural sports:* basketball M/W, football M/W, golf M/W, tennis M/W, volleyball M/W.

Standardized Tests *Required:* ACT ASSET, ACT COMPASS (for placement).

Costs (2004–05) *Tuition:* state resident $2367 full-time, $66 per credit hour part-time; nonresident $7675 full-time, $213 per credit hour part-time.

Financial Aid Of all full-time matriculated undergraduates who enrolled, 150 Federal Work-Study jobs (averaging $1200). 30 state and other part-time jobs (averaging $650).

Applying *Options:* early admission, deferred entrance. *Required:* high school transcript. *Required for some:* minimum 2.0 GPA. *Application deadline:* rolling (freshmen), rolling (transfers). *Notification:* continuous (freshmen), continuous (transfers).

Admissions Contact Mr. Perry Carroll, Director of Enrollment Services, Mountain Empire Community College, 3441 Mountain Empire Road, Big Stone Gap, VA 24219. *Phone:* 276-523-2400 Ext. 219. *E-mail:* pcarroll@me.vccs.edu.

NATIONAL COLLEGE OF BUSINESS & TECHNOLOGY
Bluefield, Virginia

- **Proprietary** 2-year, founded 1886, part of National College of Business and Technology
- **Calendar** quarters
- **Degree** diplomas and associate
- **Small-town** campus
- **Coed,** 216 undergraduate students

Faculty *Total:* 20. *Student/faculty ratio:* 10:1.

Majors Accounting; administrative assistant and secretarial science; business administration and management; computer and information sciences related; medical/clinical assistant.

Academic Programs *Special study options:* advanced placement credit, double majors, honors programs, internships, part-time degree program, services for LD students, summer session for credit.

Computers on Campus 35 computers available on campus for general student use. A campuswide network can be accessed. Internet access, at least one staffed computer lab available.

Student Life *Housing:* college housing not available.

Costs (2004–05) *Tuition:* $6120 full-time, $170 per credit hour part-time. Full-time tuition and fees vary according to course load. Part-time tuition and fees vary according to course load. *Required fees:* $75 full-time. *Payment plans:* installment, deferred payment. *Waivers:* employees or children of employees.

Financial Aid Of all full-time matriculated undergraduates who enrolled, 5 Federal Work-Study jobs.

Applying *Options:* electronic application. *Application fee:* $30. *Recommended:* interview. *Application deadline:* rolling (freshmen), rolling (transfers).

Admissions Contact Ms. Jennifer Hooper, Admissions Representative, National College of Business & Technology, 100 Logan Street, Bluefield, VA 24605. *Phone:* 540-326-6321. *Toll-free phone:* 800-664-1886. *Fax:* 540-322-5731. *E-mail:* adm@educorp.edu.

NATIONAL COLLEGE OF BUSINESS & TECHNOLOGY
Bristol, Virginia

- **Proprietary** 2-year, founded 1992, part of National College of Business and Technology
- **Calendar** quarters
- **Degree** diplomas and associate
- **Small-town** campus
- **Coed**, 267 undergraduate students

Faculty *Total:* 10. *Student/faculty ratio:* 10:1.

Majors Accounting; administrative assistant and secretarial science; business administration and management; computer and information sciences related; medical/clinical assistant.

Academic Programs *Special study options:* advanced placement credit, double majors, honors programs, internships, part-time degree program, services for LD students, summer session for credit.

Library National Business College-Bristol Campus Library.

Computers on Campus 35 computers available on campus for general student use. A campuswide network can be accessed. Internet access, at least one staffed computer lab available.

Student Life *Housing:* college housing not available.

Costs (2004–05) *Tuition:* $6120 full-time, $170 per credit hour part-time. Full-time tuition and fees vary according to course load. Part-time tuition and fees vary according to course load. *Required fees:* $75 full-time. *Payment plans:* installment, deferred payment. *Waivers:* employees or children of employees.

Financial Aid Of all full-time matriculated undergraduates who enrolled, 3 Federal Work-Study jobs.

Applying *Options:* electronic application. *Application fee:* $30. *Required:* high school transcript. *Recommended:* interview. *Application deadline:* rolling (freshmen), rolling (transfers).

Admissions Contact Mr. Steven Griffin, Campus Director, National College of Business & Technology, 300 A Piedmont Avenue, Bristol, VA 24201. *Phone:* 540-669-5333. *Toll-free phone:* 800-664-1886. *Fax:* 540-669-4793. *E-mail:* adm@educorp.edu.

NATIONAL COLLEGE OF BUSINESS & TECHNOLOGY
Charlottesville, Virginia

- **Proprietary** 2-year, founded 1975, part of National College of Business and Technology
- **Calendar** quarters
- **Degree** certificates, diplomas, and associate
- **Small-town** campus with easy access to Richmond
- **Coed**, 144 undergraduate students

Faculty *Total:* 14, 14% full-time. *Student/faculty ratio:* 10:1.

Majors Accounting; administrative assistant and secretarial science; business/commerce; computer and information sciences related; medical/clinical assistant.

Academic Programs *Special study options:* advanced placement credit, double majors, honors programs, internships, part-time degree program, services for LD students, summer session for credit.

Computers on Campus 35 computers available on campus for general student use. A campuswide network can be accessed. Internet access, at least one staffed computer lab available.

Costs (2004–05) *Tuition:* $6120 full-time, $170 per credit hour part-time. Full-time tuition and fees vary according to course load. Part-time tuition and

fees vary according to course load. *Required fees:* $75 full-time. *Payment plans:* installment, deferred payment. *Waivers:* employees or children of employees.

Financial Aid Of all full-time matriculated undergraduates who enrolled, 4 Federal Work-Study jobs.

Applying *Options:* electronic application. *Application fee:* $30. *Required for some:* high school transcript. *Recommended:* interview. *Application deadline:* rolling (freshmen), rolling (transfers).

Admissions Contact Ms. Paula Soukup, Campus Director, National College of Business & Technology, 1819 Emmet Street, Charlottesville, VA 22903. *Phone:* 434-295-0136. *Toll-free phone:* 800-664-1886. *Fax:* 434-979-8061. *E-mail:* mthomas@educorp.edu.

NATIONAL COLLEGE OF BUSINESS & TECHNOLOGY
Danville, Virginia

Admissions Contact Ms. Amy Bracey, Campus Director, National College of Business & Technology, 734 Main Street, Danville, VA 24541. *Phone:* 434-793-6822. *Toll-free phone:* 800-664-1886. *Fax:* 434-793-3634. *E-mail:* adm@educorp.edu.

NATIONAL COLLEGE OF BUSINESS & TECHNOLOGY
Harrisonburg, Virginia

- **Proprietary** 2-year, founded 1988, part of National College of Business and Technology
- **Calendar** quarters
- **Degree** diplomas and associate
- **Small-town** campus
- **Coed**, 193 undergraduate students

Faculty *Total:* 20, 10% full-time. *Student/faculty ratio:* 10:1.

Majors Accounting; administrative assistant and secretarial science; business administration and management; computer and information sciences related; medical/clinical assistant.

Academic Programs *Special study options:* advanced placement credit, double majors, honors programs, internships, part-time degree program, services for LD students, summer session for credit.

Computers on Campus 35 computers available on campus for general student use. A campuswide network can be accessed. Internet access, at least one staffed computer lab available.

Student Life *Housing:* college housing not available.

Costs (2004–05) *Tuition:* $6120 full-time, $170 per credit hour part-time. Full-time tuition and fees vary according to course load. Part-time tuition and fees vary according to course load. *Required fees:* $75 full-time. *Payment plans:* installment, deferred payment. *Waivers:* employees or children of employees.

Financial Aid Of all full-time matriculated undergraduates who enrolled, 2 Federal Work-Study jobs.

Applying *Options:* electronic application. *Application fee:* $30. *Required for some:* high school transcript. *Recommended:* interview. *Application deadline:* rolling (freshmen), rolling (transfers). *Notification:* continuous (freshmen), continuous (transfers).

Admissions Contact Jack Evey, Campus Director, National College of Business & Technology, 51 B Burgess Road, Harrisonburg, VA 22801. *Phone:* 540-432-0943. *Toll-free phone:* 800-664-1886. *Fax:* 540-432-1133. *E-mail:* adm@educorp.edu.

NATIONAL COLLEGE OF BUSINESS & TECHNOLOGY
Lynchburg, Virginia

- **Proprietary** 2-year, founded 1979, part of National College of Business and Technology
- **Calendar** quarters
- **Degree** diplomas and associate
- **Small-town** 2-acre campus
- **Coed**, 312 undergraduate students

Undergraduates Students come from 15 other countries.

Faculty *Total:* 20, 10% full-time. *Student/faculty ratio:* 10:1.

Majors Accounting; administrative assistant and secretarial science; business administration and management; computer and information sciences related; medical/clinical assistant.

Academic Programs *Special study options:* advanced placement credit, double majors, honors programs, internships, part-time degree program, services for LD students, summer session for credit.

National College of Business & Technology (continued)
Library 10 serial subscriptions.
Computers on Campus 35 computers available on campus for general student use. A campuswide network can be accessed. Internet access, at least one staffed computer lab available.
Student Life *Housing:* college housing not available.
Costs (2004–05) *Tuition:* $6120 full-time, $170 per credit hour part-time. Full-time tuition and fees vary according to course load. Part-time tuition and fees vary according to course load. *Required fees:* $75 full-time. *Payment plans:* installment, deferred payment. *Waivers:* employees or children of employees.
Financial Aid Of all full-time matriculated undergraduates who enrolled, 3 Federal Work-Study jobs.
Applying *Options:* electronic application. *Application fee:* $30. *Required for some:* high school transcript. *Recommended:* interview. *Application deadline:* rolling (freshmen), rolling (transfers).
Admissions Contact Mr. George Wheelous, Admissions Representative, National College of Business & Technology, 104 Candlewood Court, Lynchburg, VA 24502. *Phone:* 804-239-3500. *Toll-free phone:* 800-664-1886. *Fax:* 434-239-3948. *E-mail:* adm@educorp.edu.

NATIONAL COLLEGE OF BUSINESS & TECHNOLOGY
Martinsville, Virginia

- **Proprietary** 2-year, founded 1975, part of National College of Business and Technology
- **Calendar** quarters
- **Degree** diplomas and associate
- **Small-town** campus
- **Coed,** 302 undergraduate students

Faculty *Total:* 15, 13% full-time. *Student/faculty ratio:* 10:1.
Majors Accounting; administrative assistant and secretarial science; business administration and management; computer and information sciences related.
Academic Programs *Special study options:* advanced placement credit, double majors, honors programs, internships, part-time degree program, services for LD students, summer session for credit.
Computers on Campus 35 computers available on campus for general student use. A campuswide network can be accessed. Internet access, at least one staffed computer lab available.
Student Life *Housing:* college housing not available.
Costs (2004–05) *Tuition:* $6120 full-time, $170 per credit hour part-time. Full-time tuition and fees vary according to course load. Part-time tuition and fees vary according to course load. *Required fees:* $75 full-time. *Payment plans:* installment, deferred payment. *Waivers:* employees or children of employees.
Financial Aid Of all full-time matriculated undergraduates who enrolled, 2 Federal Work-Study jobs.
Applying *Options:* electronic application. *Application fee:* $30. *Required for some:* high school transcript. *Recommended:* interview. *Application deadline:* rolling (freshmen), rolling (transfers).
Admissions Contact Mr. John Scott, Campus Director, National College of Business & Technology, 10 Church Street, Martinsville, VA 24114. *Phone:* 276-632-5621. *Toll-free phone:* 800-664-1886 (in-state); 800-664-1866 (out-of-state). *Fax:* 276-632-7915. *E-mail:* adm@educorp.edu.

NATIONAL COLLEGE OF BUSINESS & TECHNOLOGY
Salem, Virginia

- **Proprietary** primarily 2-year, founded 1886, part of National College of Business and Technology
- **Calendar** quarters
- **Degrees** certificates, diplomas, associate, and bachelor's
- **Urban** 3-acre campus
- **Coed,** 756 undergraduate students

Undergraduates Students come from 15 other countries, 24% are from out of state. *Retention:* 70% of 2002 full-time freshmen returned.
Freshmen *Admission:* 346 applied, 346 admitted.
Faculty *Student/faculty ratio:* 12:1.
Majors Accounting; accounting technology and bookkeeping; administrative assistant and secretarial science; business/commerce; computer and information sciences; executive assistant/executive secretary; hospitality administration; hotel/motel administration; marketing/marketing management; medical/clinical assistant; office management; tourism/travel marketing.
Academic Programs *Special study options:* academic remediation for entering students, advanced placement credit, double majors, internships, part-time degree program, summer session for credit.

Library Main Library plus 1 other with 25,867 titles, 40 serial subscriptions.
Computers on Campus 35 computers available on campus for general student use. A campuswide network can be accessed. Internet access, at least one staffed computer lab available.
Student Life *Housing Options:* coed.
Costs (2004–05) *Tuition:* $6120 full-time, $170 per credit hour part-time. *Required fees:* $75 full-time.
Financial Aid Of all full-time matriculated undergraduates who enrolled, 6 Federal Work-Study jobs.
Applying *Application fee:* $30. *Required:* high school transcript. *Recommended:* interview. *Application deadline:* rolling (freshmen), rolling (transfers). *Notification:* continuous (freshmen).
Admissions Contact Ms. Bunnie Hancock, Admissions Representative, National College of Business & Technology, PO Box 6400, Roanoke, VA 24017. *Phone:* 540-986-1800. *Toll-free phone:* 800-664-1886. *Fax:* 540-986-1344. *E-mail:* market@educorp.edu.

NEW RIVER COMMUNITY COLLEGE
Dublin, Virginia

- **State-supported** 2-year, founded 1969, part of Virginia Community College System
- **Calendar** semesters
- **Degree** certificates, diplomas, and associate
- **Rural** 100-acre campus
- **Endowment** $1.9 million
- **Coed,** 4,345 undergraduate students, 46% full-time, 53% women, 47% men

Undergraduates 2,008 full-time, 2,337 part-time. Students come from 22 states and territories, 21 other countries, 3% are from out of state, 5% African American, 1% Asian American or Pacific Islander, 0.8% Hispanic American, 0.2% Native American, 5% transferred in.
Freshmen *Admission:* 617 applied, 850 enrolled.
Faculty *Total:* 206, 25% full-time. *Student/faculty ratio:* 22:1.
Majors Accounting; administrative assistant and secretarial science; architectural engineering technology; automobile/automotive mechanics technology; biological and physical sciences; business administration and management; child development; community organization and advocacy; computer engineering technology; computer graphics; computer typography and composition equipment operation; criminal justice/law enforcement administration; criminal justice/police science; drafting and design technology; education; electrical, electronic and communications engineering technology; engineering; forensic science and technology; general studies; gerontology; information science/studies; instrumentation technology; legal assistant/paralegal; liberal arts and sciences/liberal studies; machine tool technology; marketing/marketing management; medical administrative assistant and medical secretary; nursing (licensed practical/vocational nurse training); sign language interpretation and translation; welding technology.
Academic Programs *Special study options:* academic remediation for entering students, adult/continuing education programs, advanced placement credit, cooperative education, distance learning, double majors, external degree program, internships, part-time degree program, services for LD students, summer session for credit.
Library New River Community College Library with 33,993 titles, 258 serial subscriptions, an OPAC.
Computers on Campus 120 computers available on campus for general student use. A campuswide network can be accessed. At least one staffed computer lab available.
Student Life *Housing:* college housing not available. *Activities and Organizations:* Student Government Association, Phi Beta Lambda, Instrument Society of America, Human Service Organization, Sign Language Club. *Campus security:* 24-hour patrols. *Student services:* personal/psychological counseling.
Athletics *Intramural sports:* archery M/W, basketball M/W, bowling M/W, football M, golf M, soccer M/W, table tennis M/W, tennis M/W, volleyball M/W, weight lifting M/W.
Costs (2003–04) *Tuition:* state resident $1788 full-time, $60 per semester hour part-time; nonresident $6167 full-time, $206 per semester hour part-time. Part-time tuition and fees vary according to course load. *Required fees:* $144 full-time, $5 per semester hour part-time. *Waivers:* senior citizens.
Financial Aid Of all full-time matriculated undergraduates who enrolled, 150 Federal Work-Study jobs (averaging $2000).
Applying *Options:* early admission, deferred entrance. *Required for some:* high school transcript. *Application deadline:* rolling (freshmen), rolling (transfers). *Notification:* continuous (freshmen), continuous (transfers).
Admissions Contact Ms. Margaret G. Taylor, Coordinator of Admissions and Records and Student Services, New River Community College, PO Box 1127, 5251 College Drive, Dublin, VA 24084. *Phone:* 540-674-3600 Ext. 4205. *Fax:* 540-674-3644. *E-mail:* nrtaylm@nr.cc.va.us.

NORTHERN VIRGINIA COMMUNITY COLLEGE
Annandale, Virginia

- **State-supported** 2-year, founded 1965, part of Virginia Community College System
- **Calendar** semesters
- **Degree** certificates and associate
- **Suburban** 435-acre campus with easy access to Washington, DC
- **Endowment** $1.1 million
- **Coed**

Student Life *Campus security:* 24-hour emergency response devices, campus police.

Costs (2003–04) *Tuition:* state resident $1430 full-time, $60 per credit part-time; nonresident $4933 full-time, $206 per credit part-time. *Required fees:* $108 full-time, $4 per credit part-time.

Applying *Options:* common application, early admission, deferred entrance. *Required for some:* high school transcript.

Admissions Contact Dr. Max L. Bassett, Dean of Academic and Student Services, Northern Virginia Community College, 4001 Wakefield Chapel Road, Annandale, VA 22003-3796. *Phone:* 703-323-3195.

PARKS COLLEGE
Arlington, Virginia

- **Proprietary** 2-year, founded 2001
- **Calendar** quarters
- **Degree** certificates and associate
- **Urban** campus
- **Coed**

Undergraduates 75% African American, 2% Asian American or Pacific Islander, 7% Hispanic American.

Faculty *Total:* 34, 18% full-time.

Costs (2003–04) *Tuition:* $11,280 full-time, $235 per credit hour part-time. *Required fees:* $25 per term part-time.

Admissions Contact Lachelle Green, Director of Admissions, Parks College, 801 North Quincy Street, Arlington, VA 22203. *Phone:* 703-248-8887.

PATRICK HENRY COMMUNITY COLLEGE
Martinsville, Virginia

- **State-supported** 2-year, founded 1962, part of Virginia Community College System
- **Calendar** semesters
- **Degree** associate
- **Rural** 137-acre campus
- **Coed**

Student Life *Campus security:* 24-hour emergency response devices and patrols, late-night transport/escort service.

Standardized Tests *Required:* ACT ASSET (for placement).

Costs (2003–04) *Tuition:* state resident $1430 full-time, $60 per credit hour part-time; nonresident $4933 full-time, $206 per credit hour part-time. Full-time tuition and fees vary according to course load. Part-time tuition and fees vary according to course load. *Required fees:* $86 full-time, $3 per credit hour part-time, $5 per term part-time.

Financial Aid Of all full-time matriculated undergraduates who enrolled, 41 Federal Work-Study jobs (averaging $2000).

Applying *Options:* early admission, deferred entrance. *Required:* high school transcript.

Admissions Contact Dr. Joanne B. Whitley, Vice President of Academic and Student Development, Patrick Henry Community College, PO Box 5311, 645 Patriot Avenue, Martinsville, VA 24115. *Phone:* 276-656-0315. *Toll-free phone:* 800-232-7997. *Fax:* 276-656-0247. *E-mail:* qvalentine@ph.vccs.edu.

PAUL D. CAMP COMMUNITY COLLEGE
Franklin, Virginia

- **State-supported** 2-year, founded 1971, part of Virginia Community College System
- **Calendar** semesters
- **Degree** certificates and associate
- **Small-town** 99-acre campus
- **Endowment** $16,121
- **Coed,** 1,636 undergraduate students, 24% full-time, 66% women, 34% men

Undergraduates 391 full-time, 1,245 part-time. Students come from 2 states and territories, 2 other countries, 0.5% are from out of state, 41% African American, 0.7% Asian American or Pacific Islander, 0.6% Hispanic American, 0.7% Native American, 0.1% international, 3% transferred in.

Freshmen *Admission:* 410 applied, 410 admitted, 287 enrolled. *Average high school GPA:* 2.20. *Test scores:* SAT verbal scores over 500: 27%; SAT math scores over 500: 19%; SAT verbal scores over 600: 2%.

Faculty *Total:* 74, 32% full-time. *Student/faculty ratio:* 17:1.

Majors Administrative assistant and secretarial science; business administration and management; criminal justice/law enforcement administration; data processing and data processing technology; education; liberal arts and sciences/liberal studies.

Academic Programs *Special study options:* academic remediation for entering students, adult/continuing education programs, advanced placement credit, cooperative education, distance learning, honors programs, independent study, internships, off-campus study, part-time degree program, summer session for credit.

Library Paul D. Camp Community College Library with 22,000 titles, 200 serial subscriptions, an OPAC.

Computers on Campus 90 computers available on campus for general student use. A campuswide network can be accessed. At least one staffed computer lab available.

Student Life *Housing:* college housing not available. *Activities and Organizations:* student-run newspaper, African-American History Club, Phi Beta Lambda, Phi Theta Kappa, Student Government Association. *Campus security:* security staff until 7 p.m.

Standardized Tests *Required:* ACT COMPASS (for placement).

Costs (2004–05) *Tuition:* state resident $1883 full-time, $63 per credit hour part-time; nonresident $6306 full-time, $210 per credit hour part-time. *Required fees:* $95 full-time, $3 per credit hour part-time.

Financial Aid Of all full-time matriculated undergraduates who enrolled, 20 Federal Work-Study jobs (averaging $1000).

Applying *Options:* deferred entrance. *Required:* high school transcript. *Application deadline:* rolling (freshmen), rolling (transfers). *Notification:* continuous (freshmen), continuous (transfers).

Admissions Contact Ms. Monette Williams, Acting Director of Admissions and Records, Paul D. Camp Community College, PO Box 737, 100 North College Drive, Franklin, VA 23851-0737. *Phone:* 757-569-6725. *Fax:* 757-569-6795. *E-mail:* jstandahl@pc.cc.va.us.

PIEDMONT VIRGINIA COMMUNITY COLLEGE
Charlottesville, Virginia

- **State-supported** 2-year, founded 1972, part of Virginia Community College System
- **Calendar** semesters
- **Degree** certificates and associate
- **Suburban** 114-acre campus with easy access to Richmond
- **Coed,** 4,343 undergraduate students, 26% full-time, 63% women, 37% men

Undergraduates 1,122 full-time, 3,221 part-time. 2% are from out of state, 15% African American, 2% Asian American or Pacific Islander, 2% Hispanic American, 0.4% Native American, 0.8% international, 37% transferred in.

Freshmen *Admission:* 357 admitted, 357 enrolled.

Faculty *Total:* 222, 23% full-time, 10% with terminal degrees. *Student/faculty ratio:* 20:1.

Majors Accounting; administrative assistant and secretarial science; art; automobile/automotive mechanics technology; biological and physical sciences; business administration and management; computer programming; construction management; criminal justice/law enforcement administration; criminal justice/police science; data processing and data processing technology; dramatic/theatre arts; education; electrical, electronic and communications engineering technology; liberal arts and sciences/liberal studies; marketing/marketing management; nursing (registered nurse training); pre-engineering.

Academic Programs *Special study options:* academic remediation for entering students, adult/continuing education programs, advanced placement credit, cooperative education, distance learning, English as a second language, honors programs, independent study, part-time degree program, services for LD students, summer session for credit. *ROTC:* Army (c).

Library Jessup Library with 58,263 titles, 294 serial subscriptions, 19,457 audiovisual materials, an OPAC, a Web page.

Computers on Campus 110 computers available on campus for general student use. A campuswide network can be accessed from off campus that provide access to e-mail. Internet access, at least one staffed computer lab available.

Student Life *Housing:* college housing not available. *Activities and Organizations:* drama/theater group, student-run newspaper, choral group, Phi Theta

Piedmont Virginia Community College (continued)
Kappa, Black Student Alliance, Science Club, Masquers, Christian Fellowship Club. *Campus security:* 24-hour patrols.

Athletics *Intramural sports:* basketball M/W, bowling M/W, football M/W, golf M/W, lacrosse M/W, skiing (cross-country) M/W, soccer M/W, softball M/W, tennis M/W, volleyball M/W, weight lifting M/W.

Costs (2004–05) *Tuition:* state resident $1911 full-time; nonresident $6335 full-time. Full-time tuition and fees vary according to location. Part-time tuition and fees vary according to course load and location. *Required fees:* $134 full-time. *Waivers:* senior citizens.

Financial Aid Of all full-time matriculated undergraduates who enrolled, 50 Federal Work-Study jobs.

Applying *Options:* common application, electronic application, early admission. *Required for some:* high school transcript. *Application deadline:* 8/23 (transfers). *Notification:* continuous (freshmen), continuous (transfers).

Admissions Contact Ms. Mary Lee Walsh, Director of Student Services, Piedmont Virginia Community College, 501 College Drive, Charlottesville, VA 22902-7589. *Phone:* 434-961-5400. *Fax:* 434-961-5425.

RAPPAHANNOCK COMMUNITY COLLEGE
Glenns, Virginia

- **State-related** 2-year, founded 1970, part of Virginia Community College System
- **Calendar** semesters
- **Degree** certificates, diplomas, and associate
- **Rural** 217-acre campus
- **Coed**

Student Life *Campus security:* 24-hour emergency response devices.

Standardized Tests *Required:* CPT (for placement).

Costs (2004–05) *Tuition:* state resident $1529 full-time, $64 per credit part-time; nonresident $5032 full-time, $210 per credit part-time. *Required fees:* $98 full-time, $4 per credit part-time, $4 per term part-time.

Financial Aid Of all full-time matriculated undergraduates who enrolled, 40 Federal Work-Study jobs (averaging $1015).

Applying *Options:* early admission.

Admissions Contact Ms. Wilnet Willis, Admissions and Records Officer, Rappahannock Community College, Glenns Campus, 12745 College Drive, Glenns, VA 23149-2616. *Phone:* 804-758-6742. *Fax:* 804-758-3852.

RICHARD BLAND COLLEGE OF THE COLLEGE OF WILLIAM AND MARY
Petersburg, Virginia

- **State-supported** 2-year, founded 1961, part of College of William and Mary
- **Calendar** semesters
- **Degree** associate
- **Rural** 712-acre campus with easy access to Richmond
- **Endowment** $377,780
- **Coed,** 1,342 undergraduate students, 58% full-time, 66% women, 34% men

Undergraduates 781 full-time, 561 part-time. Students come from 8 states and territories, 4 other countries, 1% are from out of state, 20% African American, 2% Asian American or Pacific Islander, 2% Hispanic American, 0.2% Native American, 0.2% international, 7% transferred in. *Retention:* 64% of 2002 full-time freshmen returned.

Freshmen *Admission:* 1,125 applied, 439 enrolled. *Average high school GPA:* 2.71. *Test scores:* SAT verbal scores over 500: 40%; SAT math scores over 500: 32%; SAT verbal scores over 600: 9%; SAT math scores over 600: 5%; SAT verbal scores over 700: 1%; SAT math scores over 700: 1%.

Faculty *Total:* 61, 54% full-time, 31% with terminal degrees. *Student/faculty ratio:* 21:1.

Majors Liberal arts and sciences/liberal studies.

Academic Programs *Special study options:* academic remediation for entering students, accelerated degree program, advanced placement credit, part-time degree program, services for LD students, summer session for credit. *ROTC:* Army (c).

Library Richard Bland College Library with 91,000 titles, 9,000 serial subscriptions, 2,400 audiovisual materials, an OPAC, a Web page.

Computers on Campus 128 computers available on campus for general student use. A campuswide network can be accessed from off campus that provide access to e-mail, Blackboard. Internet access, at least one staffed computer lab available.

Student Life *Housing:* college housing not available. *Activities and Organizations:* drama/theater group, student-run newspaper, choral group, RBC Newspaper, Multicultural Alliance, student government, Spanish Club, Biology Club. *Campus security:* 24-hour patrols.

Athletics *Intramural sports:* basketball M/W, golf M/W, rock climbing M/W, tennis M/W, volleyball M/W.

Standardized Tests *Required:* ACT COMPASS (for admission). *Recommended:* SAT I or ACT (for admission).

Costs (2004–05) *Tuition:* state resident $2036 full-time, $82 per credit hour part-time; nonresident $8779 full-time, $372 per credit hour part-time. *Required fees:* $164 full-time, $4 per credit hour part-time. *Waivers:* senior citizens.

Financial Aid Of all full-time matriculated undergraduates who enrolled, 10 Federal Work-Study jobs (averaging $2000).

Applying *Application fee:* $20. *Required:* essay or personal statement, high school transcript, minimum 2.0 GPA. *Required for some:* letters of recommendation, interview. *Application deadline:* 8/15 (freshmen), rolling (transfers). *Notification:* continuous (freshmen), continuous (transfers).

Admissions Contact Mr. Randy Dean, Director of Admissions and Student Services, Richard Bland College of The College of William and Mary, 11301 Johnson Road, Petersburg, VA 23805-7100. *Phone:* 804-862-6225. *Fax:* 804-862-6490. *E-mail:* admit@rbc.edu.

SOUTHSIDE VIRGINIA COMMUNITY COLLEGE
Alberta, Virginia

- **State-supported** 2-year, founded 1970, part of Virginia Community College System
- **Calendar** semesters
- **Degree** certificates, diplomas, and associate
- **Rural** 207-acre campus
- **Endowment** $412,823
- **Coed,** 4,894 undergraduate students, 30% full-time, 64% women, 36% men

Undergraduates 1,447 full-time, 3,447 part-time. Students come from 3 states and territories, 2 other countries, 1% are from out of state, 49% African American, 0.6% Asian American or Pacific Islander, 0.5% Hispanic American, 0.2% Native American, 0.1% international.

Freshmen *Admission:* 393 enrolled.

Faculty *Total:* 283, 23% full-time, 6% with terminal degrees. *Student/faculty ratio:* 14:1.

Majors Administrative assistant and secretarial science; biological and physical sciences; business administration and management; criminal justice/law enforcement administration; drafting and design technology; education; electrical, electronic and communications engineering technology; general studies; human services; information science/studies; information technology; liberal arts and sciences/liberal studies; nursing (registered nurse training); respiratory care therapy.

Academic Programs *Special study options:* academic remediation for entering students, adult/continuing education programs, advanced placement credit, distance learning, double majors, honors programs, off-campus study, part-time degree program, services for LD students, study abroad, summer session for credit. *ROTC:* Army (c).

Library Julian M. Howell Library plus 1 other with 25,500 titles, 195 serial subscriptions, 850 audiovisual materials, an OPAC, a Web page.

Computers on Campus 200 computers available on campus for general student use. A campuswide network can be accessed. Internet access, at least one staffed computer lab available.

Student Life *Housing:* college housing not available. *Activities and Organizations:* choral group, Student Forum, Phi Theta Kappa, Phi Beta Lambda, Alpha Delta Omega.

Athletics *Intramural sports:* basketball M, softball M/W, table tennis M/W, tennis M/W, volleyball M/W.

Standardized Tests *Required:* ACT ASSET, ACT COMPASS (for placement).

Costs (2004–05) *Tuition:* state resident $1943 full-time, $65 per credit part-time; nonresident $6167 full-time, $206 per credit part-time. Full-time tuition and fees vary according to course load. Part-time tuition and fees vary according to course load. *Required fees:* $155 full-time, $5 per credit part-time. *Waivers:* senior citizens.

Applying *Options:* common application, electronic application, early admission, deferred entrance. *Required:* high school transcript, interview. *Application deadline:* rolling (freshmen), rolling (transfers). *Notification:* continuous (freshmen), continuous (transfers).

Admissions Contact Dr. Ronald E. Mattox, Dean of Admissions, Records, and Institutional Research, Southside Virginia Community College, Southside Virginia Community College, 109 Campus Drive, Alberta, VA 23821. *Phone:* 434-949-1012. *Fax:* 434-949-7863. *E-mail:* pat.watson@sv.vccs.edu.

SOUTHWEST VIRGINIA COMMUNITY COLLEGE
Richlands, Virginia

- **State-supported** 2-year, founded 1968, part of Virginia Community College System
- **Calendar** semesters
- **Degree** certificates, diplomas, and associate
- **Rural** 100-acre campus
- **Coed**

Student Life *Campus security:* 24-hour emergency response devices and patrols, student patrols.

Standardized Tests *Required:* SAT I or ACT (for placement), ACT ASSET (for placement).

Costs (2004–05) *Tuition:* $64 per credit hour part-time; state resident $1913 full-time, $64 per credit hour part-time; nonresident $6045 full-time, $210 per credit hour part-time. Full-time tuition and fees vary according to course load. Part-time tuition and fees vary according to course load. *Required fees:* $5 per credit hour part-time.

Financial Aid Of all full-time matriculated undergraduates who enrolled, 250 Federal Work-Study jobs (averaging $1236).

Applying *Options:* early admission, deferred entrance. *Required:* high school transcript, interview.

Admissions Contact Mr. Roderick B. Moore, Director of Admissions, Records, and Financial Aid, Southwest Virginia Community College, Box SVCC, Richlands, VA 24641. *Phone:* 276-964-7294. *Toll-free phone:* 800-822-7822. *Fax:* 540-964-7716.

TESST COLLEGE OF TECHNOLOGY
Alexandria, Virginia

Admissions Contact Mr. Bob Somers, Director, TESST College of Technology, 6315 Bren Mar Drive, Alexandria, VA 22312-6342. *Phone:* 703-548-4800. *Toll-free phone:* 800-48-TESST.

THOMAS NELSON COMMUNITY COLLEGE
Hampton, Virginia

- **State-supported** 2-year, founded 1968, part of Virginia Community College System
- **Calendar** semesters
- **Degree** certificates, diplomas, and associate
- **Suburban** 85-acre campus with easy access to Virginia Beach
- **Coed,** 7,889 undergraduate students, 36% full-time, 61% women, 39% men

Undergraduates 2,856 full-time, 5,033 part-time. 38% African American, 3% Asian American or Pacific Islander, 4% Hispanic American, 0.6% Native American, 0.2% international.

Freshmen *Admission:* 1,315 enrolled.

Faculty *Total:* 433, 21% full-time.

Majors Accounting; administrative assistant and secretarial science; art; automobile/automotive mechanics technology; biological and physical sciences; business administration and management; clinical/medical laboratory technology; commercial and advertising art; computer science; criminal justice/police science; drafting and design technology; electrical, electronic and communications engineering technology; engineering; fire science; information science/studies; kindergarten/preschool education; liberal arts and sciences/liberal studies; mechanical engineering/mechanical technology; nursing (registered nurse training); ophthalmic laboratory technology; photography; public administration; social sciences.

Academic Programs *Special study options:* academic remediation for entering students, adult/continuing education programs, advanced placement credit, cooperative education, English as a second language, external degree program, honors programs, internships, off-campus study, part-time degree program, services for LD students, summer session for credit.

Library Learning Resource Center with 66,281 titles, 467 serial subscriptions.

Computers on Campus 80 computers available on campus for general student use. A campuswide network can be accessed. At least one staffed computer lab available.

Student Life *Housing:* college housing not available. *Activities and Organizations:* student-run newspaper, choral group, Phi Theta Kappa, Future Nurses Association, Human Services Education Club, Student Government Association, Health Care Advocates. *Campus security:* 24-hour patrols. *Student services:* personal/psychological counseling.

Athletics *Intramural sports:* basketball M/W, sailing M/W, soccer M/W, tennis M/W, volleyball M/W.

Standardized Tests *Recommended:* SAT I (for placement).

Costs (2004–05) *Tuition:* $60 per credit hour part-time; state resident $1788 full-time, $60 per credit hour part-time; nonresident $6212 full-time, $207 per credit hour part-time. *Required fees:* $116 full-time, $3 per credit hour part-time, $11 per term part-time.

Financial Aid Of all full-time matriculated undergraduates who enrolled, 110 Federal Work-Study jobs (averaging $3000).

Applying *Options:* early admission, deferred entrance. *Required:* high school transcript. *Application deadline:* rolling (freshmen), rolling (transfers). *Notification:* continuous (freshmen), continuous (transfers).

Admissions Contact Ms. Aileen Girard, Admissions Office Manager, Thomas Nelson Community College, PO Box 9407, 99 Thomas Nelson Drive, Hampton, VA 23670. *Phone:* 757-825-2800.

TIDEWATER COMMUNITY COLLEGE
Norfolk, Virginia

- **State-supported** 2-year, founded 1968, part of Virginia Community College System
- **Calendar** semesters
- **Degree** certificates, diplomas, and associate
- **Suburban** 520-acre campus
- **Coed,** 23,029 undergraduate students, 34% full-time, 60% women, 40% men

Undergraduates 7,795 full-time, 15,234 part-time. Students come from 53 states and territories, 30% African American, 6% Asian American or Pacific Islander, 4% Hispanic American, 0.6% Native American.

Faculty *Total:* 1,233, 22% full-time.

Majors Accounting; administrative assistant and secretarial science; advertising; art; automobile/automotive mechanics technology; biological and physical sciences; business administration and management; commercial and advertising art; computer programming; data processing and data processing technology; drafting and design technology; education; electrical, electronic and communications engineering technology; engineering; finance; kindergarten/preschool education; liberal arts and sciences/liberal studies; marketing/marketing management; music; nursing (registered nurse training); real estate.

Academic Programs *Special study options:* academic remediation for entering students, accelerated degree program, adult/continuing education programs, advanced placement credit, cooperative education, distance learning, English as a second language, honors programs, independent study, internships, off-campus study, part-time degree program, services for LD students, summer session for credit.

Library 147,126 titles, 913 serial subscriptions.

Computers on Campus A campuswide network can be accessed from off campus. Internet access, online (class) registration, at least one staffed computer lab available.

Student Life *Housing:* college housing not available. *Activities and Organizations:* drama/theater group, student-run newspaper. *Campus security:* 24-hour patrols. *Student services:* personal/psychological counseling, women's center.

Athletics *Intramural sports:* basketball M/W, cheerleading W, rock climbing W, soccer M, softball W, tennis M/W, volleyball W.

Standardized Tests *Required for some:* ACT COMPASS. *Recommended:* ACT COMPASS.

Costs (2003–04) *Tuition:* state resident $1430 full-time, $60 per credit part-time; nonresident $4933 full-time, $206 per credit part-time. *Required fees:* $240 full-time, $9 per credit part-time.

Financial Aid Of all full-time matriculated undergraduates who enrolled, 64 Federal Work-Study jobs (averaging $2000).

Applying *Options:* early admission, deferred entrance. *Application deadline:* rolling (freshmen), rolling (transfers). *Notification:* continuous (freshmen), continuous (transfers).

Admissions Contact Mr. Randy Shannon, Associate Dean, Student Services, Tidewater Community College, 7000 College Drive, Portsmouth, VA 23703. *Phone:* 757-822-1068.

TIDEWATER TECH
Virginia Beach, Virginia

Admissions Contact Tidewater Tech, 2697 Dean Drive, Suite 100, Virginia Beach, VA 23452.

VIRGINIA HIGHLANDS COMMUNITY COLLEGE
Abingdon, Virginia

- **State-supported** 2-year, founded 1967, part of Virginia Community College System

Virginia Highlands Community College (continued)
- **Calendar** semesters
- **Degree** certificates, diplomas, and associate
- **Small-town** 100-acre campus
- **Coed**

Standardized Tests *Required for some:* SCAT, ACT ASSET. *Recommended:* SCAT, ACT ASSET.

Applying *Options:* early admission, deferred entrance. *Required:* high school transcript.

Admissions Contact Mr. David N. Matlock, Director of Admissions, Records, and Financial Aid, Virginia Highlands Community College, PO Box 828, Abingdon, VA 24212-0828. *Phone:* 276-739-2414 Ext. 290. *Toll-free phone:* 877-207-6115. *Fax:* 540-676-5591.

VIRGINIA WESTERN COMMUNITY COLLEGE
Roanoke, Virginia

- **State-supported** 2-year, founded 1966, part of Virginia Community College System
- **Calendar** semesters
- **Degree** certificates and associate
- **Suburban** 70-acre campus
- **Coed,** 8,124 undergraduate students, 26% full-time, 58% women, 42% men

Undergraduates 2,128 full-time, 5,996 part-time. 1% are from out of state, 10% African American, 2% Asian American or Pacific Islander, 0.7% Hispanic American, 0.3% Native American, 16% transferred in.

Freshmen *Admission:* 729 enrolled. *Average high school GPA:* 2.50.

Faculty *Total:* 406, 21% full-time. *Student/faculty ratio:* 25:1.

Majors Accounting; administrative assistant and secretarial science; art; automobile/automotive mechanics technology; biological and physical sciences; business administration and management; child development; civil engineering technology; commercial and advertising art; computer science; criminal justice/law enforcement administration; data processing and data processing technology; dental hygiene; education; electrical, electronic and communications engineering technology; engineering; industrial radiologic technology; kindergarten/preschool education; liberal arts and sciences/liberal studies; mechanical engineering/mechanical technology; mental health/rehabilitation; nursing (registered nurse training); pre-engineering; radio and television; radiologic technology/science.

Academic Programs *Special study options:* academic remediation for entering students, adult/continuing education programs, advanced placement credit, cooperative education, distance learning, double majors, English as a second language, independent study, internships, part-time degree program, services for LD students, summer session for credit.

Library Brown Library with 67,129 titles, 402 serial subscriptions, an OPAC, a Web page.

Computers on Campus 200 computers available on campus for general student use. A campuswide network can be accessed from off campus. Internet access, at least one staffed computer lab available.

Student Life *Housing:* college housing not available. *Activities and Organizations:* drama/theater group, student-run newspaper. *Student services:* personal/psychological counseling.

Athletics *Intramural sports:* baseball M, basketball M/W.

Standardized Tests *Recommended:* SAT I or ACT (for placement).

Costs (2003–04) *Tuition:* state resident $1930 full-time, $64 per credit part-time; nonresident $6353 full-time, $212 per credit part-time. *Waivers:* senior citizens.

Applying *Options:* common application, early admission, deferred entrance. *Required:* high school transcript. *Application deadline:* rolling (freshmen), rolling (transfers). *Notification:* continuous (freshmen), continuous (transfers).

Admissions Contact Admissions Office, Virginia Western Community College, 3095 Colonial Avenue, Roanoke, VA 24038. *Phone:* 540-857-7231. *Fax:* 540-857-6102. *E-mail:* infocenter@vw.vccs.edu.

WYTHEVILLE COMMUNITY COLLEGE
Wytheville, Virginia

- **State-supported** 2-year, founded 1967, part of Virginia Community College System
- **Calendar** semesters
- **Degree** certificates and associate
- **Rural** 141-acre campus
- **Coed**

Faculty *Student/faculty ratio:* 16:1.

Student Life *Campus security:* 24-hour emergency response devices and patrols.

Financial Aid Of all full-time matriculated undergraduates who enrolled, 125 Federal Work-Study jobs (averaging $2592).

Applying *Options:* early admission. *Required:* high school transcript. *Required for some:* interview.

Admissions Contact Ms. Sherry K. Dix, Registrar, Wytheville Community College, 1000 East Main Street, Wytheville, VA 24382-3308. *Phone:* 276-223-4755. *Toll-free phone:* 800-468-1195. *Fax:* 276-223-4860. *E-mail:* wcdixxs@wcc.vccs.edu.

WASHINGTON

APOLLO COLLEGE
Spokane, Washington

Admissions Contact Deanna Baker, Campus Director, Apollo College, 1101 North Francher Road, Spokane, WA 99212. *Phone:* 509-532-8888.

THE ART INSTITUTE OF SEATTLE
Seattle, Washington

- **Proprietary** primarily 2-year, founded 1982, part of Art Institutes International
- **Calendar** quarters
- **Degrees** diplomas, associate, and bachelor's
- **Urban** campus
- **Endowment** $1950
- **Coed,** 2,520 undergraduate students, 54% full-time, 48% women, 52% men

Undergraduates 1,359 full-time, 1,161 part-time. Students come from 49 states and territories, 21 other countries, 19% are from out of state, 3% African American, 8% Asian American or Pacific Islander, 3% Hispanic American, 2% Native American, 6% international, 2% transferred in. *Retention:* 66% of 2002 full-time freshmen returned.

Freshmen *Admission:* 701 applied, 541 admitted, 446 enrolled. *Average high school GPA:* 2.40.

Faculty *Total:* 172, 48% full-time, 12% with terminal degrees. *Student/faculty ratio:* 19:1.

Majors Audio engineering; culinary arts; design and applied arts related; fashion/apparel design; fashion merchandising; film/video and photographic arts related; graphic design; industrial design; interior design; intermedia/multimedia; photography.

Academic Programs *Special study options:* academic remediation for entering students, adult/continuing education programs, honors programs, internships, off-campus study, part-time degree program, services for LD students, summer session for credit.

Library AIS Library plus 1 other with 17,164 titles, 303 serial subscriptions, 5,416 audiovisual materials, an OPAC, a Web page.

Computers on Campus 475 computers available on campus for general student use. A campuswide network can be accessed. Internet access, online (class) registration, at least one staffed computer lab available.

Student Life *Housing Options:* coed. Campus housing is leased by the school. Freshman campus housing is guaranteed. *Activities and Organizations:* Multicultural Affairs Organization, American Society of Interior Designers, DECA, Student Advisory Board. *Campus security:* 24-hour emergency response devices and patrols, controlled dormitory access, patrols by trained security personnel for 17 hours. *Student services:* personal/psychological counseling.

Athletics *Intramural sports:* soccer M/W.

Standardized Tests *Recommended:* SAT I or ACT (for admission).

Costs (2004–05) *Tuition:* $15,750 full-time, $350 per credit part-time. *Room only:* $8355. *Payment plans:* installment, deferred payment. *Waivers:* employees or children of employees.

Financial Aid Of all full-time matriculated undergraduates who enrolled, 18 Federal Work-Study jobs (averaging $1795).

Applying *Options:* electronic application, deferred entrance. *Application fee:* $50. *Required:* essay or personal statement, high school transcript, interview. *Recommended:* 3 letters of recommendation. *Application deadline:* rolling (freshmen). *Notification:* continuous (freshmen), continuous (transfers).

Admissions Contact Ms. Laine Morgan, Director of Admissions, The Art Institute of Seattle, 2323 Elliott Avenue, Seattle, WA 98121-1622. *Phone:* 800-275-2471. *Toll-free phone:* 800-275-2471. *Fax:* 206-269-0275. *E-mail:* adm@ais.edu.

▶ See page 506 for a narrative description.

BATES TECHNICAL COLLEGE
Tacoma, Washington

- **State-supported** 2-year, part of Washington State Board for Community and Technical Colleges
- **Calendar** quarters
- **Degree** certificates, diplomas, and associate
- **Urban** campus with easy access to Seattle
- **Coed**, 16,162 undergraduate students

Faculty *Total:* 389, 41% full-time, 17% with terminal degrees. *Student/faculty ratio:* 18:1.

Majors Accounting technology and bookkeeping; administrative assistant and secretarial science; architectural engineering technology; autobody/collision and repair technology; automobile/automotive mechanics technology; biology/biotechnology laboratory technician; biomedical technology; building/property maintenance and management; carpentry; child care provision; civil engineering technology; computer programming; computer systems networking and telecommunications; computer technology/computer systems technology; court reporting; culinary arts; data modeling/warehousing and database administration; data processing and data processing technology; dental laboratory technology; diesel mechanics technology; electrical and power transmission installation; electrical, electronic and communications engineering technology; electrical/electronics equipment installation and repair; electrician; fire science; heating, air conditioning, ventilation and refrigeration maintenance technology; industrial electronics technology; information science/studies; legal administrative assistant/secretary; manufacturing technology; mechanical engineering/mechanical technology; nursing (licensed practical/vocational nurse training); occupational safety and health technology; radio and television broadcasting technology; retailing; small engine mechanics and repair technology; survey technology; web/multimedia management and webmaster.

Student Life *Housing:* college housing not available. *Activities and Organizations:* student-run newspaper, radio and television station, Associated Student Government. *Campus security:* 24-hour emergency response devices, on-campus weekday security to 10 p.m.

Standardized Tests *Required:* ACT ASSET (for placement).

Costs (2003–04) *Tuition:* state resident $3000 full-time. Full-time tuition and fees vary according to program.

Financial Aid Of all full-time matriculated undergraduates who enrolled, 15 Federal Work-Study jobs (averaging $3500). 35 state and other part-time jobs (averaging $3500).

Applying *Application fee:* $49. *Application deadline:* rolling (freshmen). *Notification:* continuous (freshmen), continuous (transfers).

Admissions Contact Ms. Gwen Sailer, Vice President for Student Services, Bates Technical College, 1101 South Yakima Avenue, Tacoma, WA 98405. *Phone:* 253-680-7000. *Toll-free phone:* 800-562-7099. *Fax:* 253-680-7101. *E-mail:* sashpole@bates.ctc.edu.

BELLEVUE COMMUNITY COLLEGE
Bellevue, Washington

- **State-supported** 2-year, founded 1966, part of Washington State Board for Community and Technical Colleges
- **Calendar** quarters
- **Degree** certificates and associate
- **Suburban** 96-acre campus with easy access to Seattle
- **Coed**, 13,716 undergraduate students

Undergraduates Students come from 32 states and territories, 64 other countries, 0.7% are from out of state, 4% African American, 14% Asian American or Pacific Islander, 0.7% Hispanic American, 0.9% Native American, 2% international.

Faculty *Total:* 516, 30% full-time, 2% with terminal degrees. *Student/faculty ratio:* 36:1.

Majors Accounting; administrative assistant and secretarial science; business administration and management; computer programming; criminal justice/law enforcement administration; criminal justice/police science; data processing and data processing technology; educational/instructional media design; fashion merchandising; fire science; industrial radiologic technology; information science/studies; interior design; kindergarten/preschool education; liberal arts and sciences/liberal studies; marketing/marketing management; nursing (registered nurse training); parks, recreation and leisure; real estate.

Academic Programs *Special study options:* academic remediation for entering students, advanced placement credit, cooperative education, distance learning, English as a second language, honors programs, independent study, internships, part-time degree program, services for LD students, summer session for credit.

Library Bellevue Community College Library with 42,000 titles, 485 serial subscriptions, an OPAC, a Web page.

Computers on Campus 600 computers available on campus for general student use. A campuswide network can be accessed from off campus. Internet access, online (class) registration, at least one staffed computer lab available.

Student Life *Housing:* college housing not available. *Activities and Organizations:* drama/theater group, student-run newspaper, radio station. *Student services:* health clinic, personal/psychological counseling, women's center.

Athletics Member NJCAA. *Intercollegiate sports:* baseball M(s), basketball M(s)/W(s), cross-country running M(s)/W(s), golf M(s), soccer M(s), softball W(s), tennis M(s)/W(s), track and field M(s)/W(s), volleyball W(s). *Intramural sports:* basketball M/W, cross-country running M/W, skiing (cross-country) M/W, skiing (downhill) M/W, soccer W, tennis M/W, track and field M/W, volleyball M/W.

Costs (2004–05) *Tuition:* state resident $2523 full-time, $76 per credit part-time; nonresident $7731 full-time, $248 per credit part-time. *Payment plan:* installment. *Waivers:* senior citizens and employees or children of employees.

Financial Aid Of all full-time matriculated undergraduates who enrolled, 75 Federal Work-Study jobs (averaging $3400). 23 state and other part-time jobs (averaging $3000).

Applying *Options:* electronic application. *Application deadline:* rolling (freshmen), rolling (transfers).

Admissions Contact Ms. Tika Esler, Associate Dean of Enrollment Services, Bellevue Community College, 3000 Landerholm Circle SE, Bellerne, WA 98007. *Phone:* 425-564-2222. *Fax:* 425-564-4065.

BELLINGHAM TECHNICAL COLLEGE
Bellingham, Washington

- **State-supported** 2-year
- **Degree** certificates and associate
- 4,159 undergraduate students, 23% full-time

Faculty *Student/faculty ratio:* 20:1.

Standardized Tests *Required:* (for placement).

Costs (2003–04) *Tuition:* state resident $2398 full-time. *Required fees:* $600 full-time.

Financial Aid Of all full-time matriculated undergraduates who enrolled, 40 state and other part-time jobs (averaging $2300).

Applying *Options:* early admission, deferred entrance. *Application fee:* $33.

Admissions Contact Bellingham Technical College, 3028 Lindbergh Avenue, Bellingham, WA 98225-1599. *Phone:* 360-738-3105 Ext. 440. *E-mail:* beltcadm@belltc.ctc.edu.

BIG BEND COMMUNITY COLLEGE
Moses Lake, Washington

- **State-supported** 2-year, founded 1962
- **Calendar** quarters
- **Degree** certificates and associate
- **Small-town** 159-acre campus
- **Endowment** $951,594
- **Coed**, 2,090 undergraduate students, 62% full-time, 57% women, 43% men

Undergraduates 1,302 full-time, 788 part-time. Students come from 4 states and territories, 3 other countries, 3% are from out of state, 0.4% African American, 1% Asian American or Pacific Islander, 19% Hispanic American, 1% Native American, 0.6% international, 6% transferred in, 5% live on campus.

Freshmen *Admission:* 393 applied, 393 admitted, 312 enrolled.

Faculty *Total:* 131, 37% full-time, 2% with terminal degrees. *Student/faculty ratio:* 20:1.

Majors Accounting technology and bookkeeping; airline pilot and flight crew; automobile/automotive mechanics technology; avionics maintenance technology; civil engineering technology; heavy/industrial equipment maintenance technologies related; industrial electronics technology; information science/studies; liberal arts and sciences/liberal studies; nursing (licensed practical/vocational nurse training); nursing (registered nurse training); office management; teacher assistant/aide; welding technology.

Academic Programs *Special study options:* academic remediation for entering students, advanced placement credit, cooperative education, distance learning, double majors, English as a second language, part-time degree program, services for LD students, summer session for credit.

Library Big Bend Community College Library with 41,900 titles, 3,700 serial subscriptions, 3,150 audiovisual materials, an OPAC, a Web page.

Computers on Campus 430 computers available on campus for general student use. A campuswide network can be accessed from off campus. Internet access, online (class) registration, at least one staffed computer lab available.

Student Life *Housing Options:* coed. Campus housing is university owned. *Activities and Organizations:* student-run newspaper, choral group. *Campus security:* 24-hour emergency response devices, student patrols. *Student services:* personal/psychological counseling.

Big Bend Community College (continued)

Athletics *Intercollegiate sports:* baseball M(s), basketball M(s)/W(s), softball W(s), volleyball W(s).

Costs (2004–05) *Tuition:* state resident $2330 full-time, $72 per credit part-time; nonresident $2820 full-time, $86 per credit part-time. *Room and board:* $4760. *Waivers:* senior citizens.

Financial Aid Of all full-time matriculated undergraduates who enrolled, 50 Federal Work-Study jobs (averaging $2700). 100 state and other part-time jobs (averaging $3240).

Applying *Options:* early admission, deferred entrance. *Application fee:* $10. *Required for some:* high school transcript. *Application deadline:* rolling (freshmen), rolling (transfers). *Notification:* continuous (freshmen), continuous (transfers).

Admissions Contact Ms. Candis Lacher, Dean of Enrollment Services, Big Bend Community College, 7662 Chanute Street, Moses Lake, WA 98837. *Phone:* 509-762-5351 Ext. 226. *Fax:* 509-762-6243. *E-mail:* admissions@bigbend.edu.

CASCADIA COMMUNITY COLLEGE
Bothell, Washington

- **State-supported** 2-year, founded 1999
- **Calendar** quarters
- **Degree** certificates and associate
- **Suburban** 128-acre campus
- **Coed,** 1,964 undergraduate students, 55% full-time, 47% women, 53% men

Undergraduates 1,080 full-time, 884 part-time. 2% African American, 7% Asian American or Pacific Islander, 4% Hispanic American, 0.7% Native American, 0.1% international. *Retention:* 60% of 2002 full-time freshmen returned.

Freshmen *Admission:* 374 enrolled.

Faculty *Total:* 98, 22% full-time, 27% with terminal degrees. *Student/faculty ratio:* 29:1.

Majors Liberal arts and sciences and humanities related; liberal arts and sciences/liberal studies; science technologies related.

Student Life *Housing:* college housing not available. *Campus security:* 24-hour emergency response devices, late-night transport/escort service.

Costs (2003–04) *Tuition:* state resident $2023 full-time, $67 per credit part-time; nonresident $7535 full-time, $251 per credit part-time. *Required fees:* $75 full-time.

Admissions Contact Ms. Marla Coan, Dean for Student Success, Cascadia Community College, 18345 Campus Way, NE, Bothell, WA 98011. *Phone:* 425-352-8000. *Fax:* 425-352-8137. *E-mail:* admissions@cascadia.ctc.edu.

CENTRALIA COLLEGE
Centralia, Washington

- **State-supported** 2-year, founded 1925, part of Washington State Board for Community and Technical Colleges
- **Calendar** quarters
- **Degree** certificates and associate
- **Small-town** 31-acre campus
- **Endowment** $3.0 million
- **Coed,** 4,097 undergraduate students

Undergraduates Students come from 4 states and territories, 1% are from out of state, 0.7% African American, 1% Asian American or Pacific Islander, 9% Hispanic American, 2% Native American. *Retention:* 57% of 2002 full-time freshmen returned.

Freshmen *Admission:* 2,257 applied, 2,257 admitted.

Faculty *Total:* 190, 29% full-time, 7% with terminal degrees. *Student/faculty ratio:* 24:1.

Majors Administrative assistant and secretarial science; applied art; art; biological and physical sciences; biology/biological sciences; botany/plant biology; broadcast journalism; business administration and management; business and personal/financial services marketing; business/commerce; chemistry; child care and support services management; child development; civil engineering technology; commercial and advertising art; computer and information sciences related; computer programming related; computer systems networking and telecommunications; consumer merchandising/retailing management; corrections; criminal justice/law enforcement administration; diesel mechanics technology; dramatic/theatre arts; electrical, electronic and communications engineering technology; engineering; English; family living/parenthood; French; geology/earth science; German; heavy equipment maintenance technology; history; humanities; kindergarten/preschool education; legal administrative assistant/secretary; liberal arts and sciences/liberal studies; marketing/marketing management; mass communication/media; mathematics; medical administrative assistant and medical secretary; music; natural sciences; nursing (licensed practical/vocational nurse training); nursing (registered nurse training); parks,

recreation and leisure; physical sciences; political science and government; pre-dentistry studies; pre-engineering; pre-law studies; pre-medical studies; pre-pharmacy studies; pre-veterinary studies; psychology; radio and television; receptionist; retailing; sales, distribution and marketing; social sciences; sociology; Spanish; survey technology; system administration; teacher assistant/aide; welding technology; zoology/animal biology.

Academic Programs *Special study options:* academic remediation for entering students, adult/continuing education programs, advanced placement credit, cooperative education, distance learning, English as a second language, external degree program, freshman honors college, honors programs, independent study, part-time degree program, services for LD students, study abroad, summer session for credit.

Library Kirk Library with 38,000 titles, 225 serial subscriptions, an OPAC, a Web page.

Computers on Campus 125 computers available on campus for general student use. A campuswide network can be accessed from off campus that provide access to online degree audits, transcripts. Internet access, online (class) registration, at least one staffed computer lab available. Computer purchase or lease plan available.

Student Life *Housing:* college housing not available. *Activities and Organizations:* drama/theater group, student-run newspaper, radio and television station, choral group, marching band, Phi Theta Kappa, Diesel Tech Club, Business Management Association, Student Activities/Admissions Team, International Club. *Campus security:* 24-hour patrols, late-night transport/escort service. *Student services:* personal/psychological counseling, women's center.

Athletics Member NJCAA. *Intercollegiate sports:* baseball M(s), basketball M(s)/W(s), golf W(s), softball W(s), volleyball W(s).

Standardized Tests *Required:* ACT ASSET or ACT COMPASS (for placement).

Costs (2004–05) *Tuition:* state resident $2313 full-time, $69 per credit part-time; nonresident $2702 full-time, $82 per credit part-time. *Required fees:* $135 full-time. *Waivers:* senior citizens.

Applying *Options:* electronic application. *Required:* high school transcript. *Application deadline:* rolling (freshmen), rolling (transfers). *Notification:* continuous until 9/15 (freshmen), continuous until 9/15 (transfers).

Admissions Contact Mr. Scott A. Copeland, Director of Enrollment Services, Centralia College, 600 West Locust, Centralia, WA 98531. *Phone:* 360-736-9391 Ext. 682. *Fax:* 360-330-7503. *E-mail:* admissions@centralia.ctc.edu.

CLARK COLLEGE
Vancouver, Washington

- **State-supported** 2-year, founded 1933, part of Washington State Board for Community and Technical Colleges
- **Calendar** quarters
- **Degree** certificates, diplomas, and associate
- **Urban** 80-acre campus with easy access to Portland
- **Endowment** $35.8 million
- **Coed,** 10,043 undergraduate students, 44% full-time, 60% women, 40% men

Undergraduates 4,405 full-time, 5,638 part-time. Students come from 9 states and territories, 15 other countries, 0.6% are from out of state, 2% African American, 6% Asian American or Pacific Islander, 0.5% Hispanic American, 1% Native American, 0.3% international, 7% transferred in. *Retention:* 64% of 2002 full-time freshmen returned.

Freshmen *Admission:* 2,825 applied, 2,825 admitted, 1,077 enrolled.

Faculty *Total:* 544, 32% full-time, 9% with terminal degrees. *Student/faculty ratio:* 23:1.

Majors Accounting technology and bookkeeping; applied horticulture; automobile/automotive mechanics technology; baking and pastry arts; business administration and management; business automation/technology/data entry; computer systems networking and telecommunications; construction engineering technology; culinary arts; data entry/microcomputer applications; dental hygiene; diesel mechanics technology; early childhood education; electrical, electronic and communications engineering technology; emergency medical technology (EMT paramedic); executive assistant/executive secretary; human resources management; landscaping and groundskeeping; legal assistant/paralegal; liberal arts and sciences/liberal studies; machine tool technology; manufacturing technology; medical administrative assistant and medical secretary; medical/clinical assistant; nursing (registered nurse training); substance abuse/addiction counseling; telecommunications technology; welding technology.

Academic Programs *Special study options:* academic remediation for entering students, adult/continuing education programs, advanced placement credit, cooperative education, distance learning, English as a second language, independent study, internships, part-time degree program, services for LD students, study abroad, summer session for credit. *ROTC:* Army (b), Air Force (c).

Library Lewis D. Cannell Library with 61,465 titles, 512 serial subscriptions, 2,048 audiovisual materials, an OPAC, a Web page.

Computers on Campus 730 computers available on campus for general student use. A campuswide network can be accessed from off campus. Internet access, online (class) registration, at least one staffed computer lab available.

Student Life *Housing:* college housing not available. *Activities and Organizations:* drama/theater group, student-run newspaper, choral group, Phi Theta Kappa, Baptist Student Ministries, Multicultural Students United, Peace Project, Students for Political Activism Now (SPAN). *Campus security:* 24-hour patrols, late-night transport/escort service, security staff during hours of operation. *Student services:* health clinic, personal/psychological counseling, legal services.

Athletics *Intercollegiate sports:* basketball M(s)/W(s), cross-country running M(s)/W(s), fencing M(c)/W(c), soccer M(s)/W(s), track and field M(s)/W(s), volleyball W(s). *Intramural sports:* basketball M/W, fencing M/W, football M/W, soccer M/W, softball M/W, table tennis M/W, volleyball M/W.

Standardized Tests *Required:* ACT ASSET (for placement).

Costs (2004–05) *Tuition:* state resident $2572 full-time, $75 per quarter hour part-time; nonresident $2572 full-time, $75 per quarter hour part-time. Full-time tuition and fees vary according to course load and reciprocity agreements. Part-time tuition and fees vary according to course load and reciprocity agreements. *Waivers:* senior citizens and employees or children of employees.

Financial Aid Of all full-time matriculated undergraduates who enrolled, 170 Federal Work-Study jobs (averaging $1900). 164 state and other part-time jobs (averaging $2150).

Applying *Options:* early admission, deferred entrance. *Required for some:* high school transcript, interview. *Application deadlines:* 8/8 (freshmen), 8/8 (transfers). *Notification:* continuous (freshmen), continuous (transfers).

Admissions Contact Ms. Sheryl Anderson, Director of Admissions, Clark College, 1800 East McLoughlin Boulevard, Vancouver, WA 98663. *Phone:* 360-992-2308. *Toll-free phone:* 360-992-2107. *Fax:* 360-992-2867. *E-mail:* sanderson@clark.edu.

CLOVER PARK TECHNICAL COLLEGE
Lakewood, Washington

- **State-supported** 2-year, founded 1942, part of Washington State Community and Technical College System
- **Degree** certificates and associate
- **Coed,** 7,342 undergraduate students, 26% full-time, 62% women, 38% men

Undergraduates 1,939 full-time, 5,403 part-time. Students come from 3 states and territories, 10% African American, 8% Asian American or Pacific Islander, 5% Hispanic American, 1% Native American, 0.4% international.

Freshmen *Admission:* 537 enrolled.

Faculty *Total:* 311, 37% full-time. *Student/faculty ratio:* 22:1.

Majors Accounting technology and bookkeeping; agriculture; airline pilot and flight crew; architectural engineering technology; automobile/automotive mechanics technology; avionics maintenance technology; business machine repair; clinical/medical laboratory assistant; computer and information sciences and support services related; computer and information systems security; computer programming; computer systems networking and telecommunications; early childhood education; environmental engineering technology; graphic and printing equipment operation/production; heating, air conditioning, ventilation and refrigeration maintenance technology; heavy equipment maintenance technology; interior design; landscaping and groundskeeping; legal administrative assistant/secretary; machine tool technology; marketing/marketing management; massage therapy; mechanical engineering/mechanical technology; office management; radio and television broadcasting technology; rehabilitation and therapeutic professions related; security and protective services related; teacher assistant/aide; web page, digital/multimedia and information resources design.

Academic Programs *Special study options:* academic remediation for entering students, accelerated degree program, cooperative education, distance learning, English as a second language, internships, part-time degree program, services for LD students.

Library CPTC Library with 11,219 titles, 97 serial subscriptions, 2,322 audiovisual materials, an OPAC, a Web page.

Computers on Campus 1510 computers available on campus for general student use. A campuswide network can be accessed from off campus. Internet access, at least one staffed computer lab available.

Student Life *Housing:* college housing not available. *Activities and Organizations:* student-run newspaper, Accounting Numbers Club, Auto Tech Club, Computer Users Club, Social Services Club. *Campus security:* 24-hour patrols, late-night transport/escort service. *Student services:* personal/psychological counseling.

Standardized Tests *Required:* ACT COMPASS (for placement).

Costs (2003–04) *Tuition:* state resident $2214 full-time. *Required fees:* $501 full-time.

Applying *Options:* common application, electronic application. *Application fee:* $36. *Required for some:* high school transcript, interview. *Application deadline:* 9/27 (freshmen). *Notification:* continuous until 9/27 (freshmen).

Admissions Contact Ms. Judy Richardson, Registrar, Clover Park Technical College, 4500 Steilacoom Boulevard Southwest, Lakewood, WA 98499. *Phone:* 253-589-5570. *Fax:* 253-589-5852. *E-mail:* admissions@cptc.edu.

COLUMBIA BASIN COLLEGE
Pasco, Washington

Admissions Contact Ms. Donna Korstad, Program Support Supervisor, Enrollment Management, Columbia Basin College, 2600 North 20th Avenue, Pasco, WA 99301. *Phone:* 509-547-0511 Ext. 2250. *Toll-free phone:* 509-547-0511 Ext. 2250. *Fax:* 509-546-0401.

CROWN COLLEGE
Tacoma, Washington

- **Proprietary** primarily 2-year, founded 1969
- **Calendar** continuous
- **Degrees** associate and bachelor's (bachelor's degree in public administration only)
- **Urban** campus with easy access to Seattle
- **Coed,** 316 undergraduate students

Undergraduates Students come from 39 states and territories, 1 other country.

Freshmen *Admission:* 21 applied, 20 admitted.

Faculty *Total:* 23, 30% full-time. *Student/faculty ratio:* 20:1.

Majors Criminal justice/safety; legal administrative assistant/secretary; legal assistant/paralegal; public administration.

Academic Programs *Special study options:* academic remediation for entering students, cooperative education, distance learning, double majors, honors programs, internships, off-campus study, study abroad.

Library Crown College Library plus 1 other with 9,500 titles, 37 serial subscriptions, 70 audiovisual materials, an OPAC, a Web page.

Computers on Campus 12 computers available on campus for general student use. A campuswide network can be accessed from student residence rooms and from off campus. Internet access, online (class) registration, at least one staffed computer lab available.

Student Life *Housing:* college housing not available. *Campus security:* 24-hour emergency response devices.

Applying *Options:* common application, electronic application. *Application fee:* $135. *Required:* high school transcript, interview. *Required for some:* essay or personal statement. *Notification:* continuous (freshmen).

Admissions Contact Ms. Sheila Millineaux, Admissions Director, Crown College, 8739 South Hosmer, Tacoma, WA 98444. *Phone:* 253-531-3123. *Toll-free phone:* 800-755-9525 (in-state); 888-689-3688 (out-of-state). *Fax:* 253-531-3521. *E-mail:* admissions@crowncollege.edu.

DIGIPEN INSTITUTE OF TECHNOLOGY
Redmond, Washington

Admissions Contact Ms. Gina Corpening, Admissions and Outreach Coordinator, DigiPen Institute of Technology, 5001-150th Avenue, NE, Redmond, WA 98052. *Phone:* 425-558-0299.

EDMONDS COMMUNITY COLLEGE
Lynnwood, Washington

- **State and locally supported** 2-year, founded 1967, part of Washington State Board for Community and Technical Colleges
- **Calendar** quarters
- **Degree** certificates and associate
- **Suburban** 115-acre campus with easy access to Seattle
- **Coed,** 8,385 undergraduate students, 45% full-time, 56% women, 44% men

Undergraduates 3,787 full-time, 4,598 part-time. Students come from 55 other countries, 4% African American, 11% Asian American or Pacific Islander, 5% Hispanic American, 1% Native American, 5% international.

Faculty *Total:* 419, 34% full-time. *Student/faculty ratio:* 24:1.

Majors Accounting technology and bookkeeping; business administration and management; chemical technology; child care and support services management; community health services counseling; computer and information sciences and support services related; computer technology/computer systems technology; construction engineering technology; culinary arts; data processing and data processing technology; electrical, electronic and communications engineering technology; entrepreneurship; fire services administration; gerontology; health aide; hospitality and recreation marketing; human resources management; international business/trade/commerce; landscaping and groundskeeping; legal admin-

Edmonds Community College (continued)

istrative assistant/secretary; legal assistant/paralegal; liberal arts and sciences/liberal studies; marketing/marketing management; office management; plant nursery management; retailing; social work; substance abuse/addiction counseling; therapeutic recreation; tourism and travel services marketing; tourism/travel marketing; vocational rehabilitation counseling.

Academic Programs *Special study options:* academic remediation for entering students, adult/continuing education programs, advanced placement credit, cooperative education, distance learning, English as a second language, honors programs, internships, off-campus study, part-time degree program, services for LD students, student-designed majors, study abroad, summer session for credit.

Library Edmonds Community College Library with 47,947 titles, 312 serial subscriptions, 7,735 audiovisual materials, an OPAC, a Web page.

Computers on Campus 1129 computers available on campus for general student use. A campuswide network can be accessed from off campus. Internet access, online (class) registration, at least one staffed computer lab available.

Student Life *Housing:* college housing not available. *Activities and Organizations:* student-run newspaper, choral group, Phi Theta Kappa, AITP, AAWCC, International Club, Pottery/Art Club. *Campus security:* 24-hour emergency response devices and patrols, student patrols, late-night transport/escort service. *Student services:* personal/psychological counseling, women's center.

Athletics *Intercollegiate sports:* baseball M(s), basketball M(s)/W(s), golf M(s)/W(s), soccer M(s)/W(s), softball W(s), volleyball W(s). *Intramural sports:* badminton M/W, baseball M, basketball M/W, bowling M/W, football M/W, golf M/W, soccer M, softball W, table tennis M/W, volleyball M/W.

Costs (2004–05) *Tuition:* state resident $2081 full-time; nonresident $7232 full-time.

Financial Aid Of all full-time matriculated undergraduates who enrolled, 125 Federal Work-Study jobs (averaging $7200). 100 state and other part-time jobs (averaging $7200).

Applying *Options:* common application, electronic application, early admission, deferred entrance. *Application fee:* $15. *Application deadline:* rolling (freshmen), rolling (transfers). *Notification:* continuous (freshmen).

Admissions Contact Ms. Sharon Bench, Admissions Director, Edmonds Community College, 20000 68th Avenue West, Lynnwood, WA 98036-5999. *Phone:* 425-640-1416. *Fax:* 425-640-1159. *E-mail:* info@edcc.edu.

EVERETT COMMUNITY COLLEGE
Everett, Washington

- **State-supported** 2-year, founded 1941, part of Washington State Board for Community and Technical Colleges
- **Calendar** quarters
- **Degree** certificates, diplomas, and associate
- **Suburban** 25-acre campus with easy access to Seattle
- **Endowment** $1.5 million
- **Coed**, 7,188 undergraduate students, 45% full-time, 62% women, 38% men

Undergraduates 3,262 full-time, 3,926 part-time. Students come from 17 states and territories, 13 other countries, 3% are from out of state, 2% African American, 5% Asian American or Pacific Islander, 4% Hispanic American, 2% Native American, 0.4% international, 3% transferred in. *Retention:* 59% of 2002 full-time freshmen returned.

Freshmen *Admission:* 612 admitted, 612 enrolled.

Faculty *Total:* 363, 36% full-time. *Student/faculty ratio:* 20:1.

Majors Accounting; animal sciences; anthropology; art; atmospheric sciences and meteorology; avionics maintenance technology; biology/biological sciences; botany/plant biology; business administration and management; chemistry; cinematography and film/video production; civil engineering technology; commercial and advertising art; computer science; consumer merchandising/retailing management; cosmetology; criminal justice/law enforcement administration; criminal justice/police science; data processing and data processing technology; dental hygiene; drafting and design technology; dramatic/theatre arts; drawing; ecology; economics; education; elementary education; engineering; engineering science; engineering technology; English; environmental studies; fire science; funeral service and mortuary science; geology/earth science; German; history; human services; industrial arts; industrial technology; Japanese; journalism; kindergarten/preschool education; liberal arts and sciences/liberal studies; marketing/marketing management; mathematics; medical administrative assistant and medical secretary; medical/clinical assistant; modern languages; music; nursing (licensed practical/vocational nurse training); nursing (registered nurse training); occupational therapy; oceanography (chemical and physical); ophthalmic laboratory technology; pharmacy technician; philosophy; photography; physical education teaching and coaching; physical therapist assistant; physics; political science and government; pre-engineering; psychology; Russian; sociology; Spanish; speech and rhetoric; veterinary/animal health technology; welding technology; wildlife biology; zoology/animal biology.

Academic Programs *Special study options:* academic remediation for entering students, adult/continuing education programs, advanced placement credit, cooperative education, distance learning, English as a second language, indepen-

dent study, internships, part-time degree program, services for LD students, study abroad, summer session for credit.

Library John Terrey Library/Media Center with 49,600 titles, 279 serial subscriptions, 5,997 audiovisual materials, an OPAC, a Web page.

Computers on Campus 600 computers available on campus for general student use. A campuswide network can be accessed from off campus. Internet access, online (class) registration, at least one staffed computer lab available.

Student Life *Housing:* college housing not available. *Activities and Organizations:* drama/theater group, student-run newspaper, choral group, United Native American Council, Nippon Friendship Club, Student Nurses Association, International Students Club, Math, Engineering and Science Student Organization. *Campus security:* 24-hour emergency response devices and patrols, late-night transport/escort service. *Student services:* personal/psychological counseling, women's center.

Athletics Member NJCAA. *Intercollegiate sports:* baseball M(s), basketball M(s)/W(s), cross-country running M(s)/W(s), soccer M(s)/W(s), softball W(s), volleyball W(s). *Intramural sports:* basketball M/W, bowling M/W, crew M(c)/W(c), football M/W, golf M/W, soccer M/W, softball M/W, tennis M/W, volleyball M/W, weight lifting M/W.

Standardized Tests *Recommended:* ACT ASSET, ACT COMPASS.

Costs (2003–04) *Tuition:* state resident $2048 full-time, $66 per credit part-time; nonresident $7221 full-time, $238 per credit part-time. Full-time tuition and fees vary according to course load. Part-time tuition and fees vary according to course load. *Waivers:* senior citizens.

Financial Aid Of all full-time matriculated undergraduates who enrolled, 152 Federal Work-Study jobs (averaging $3000). 48 state and other part-time jobs (averaging $3000).

Applying *Options:* common application, electronic application, early admission, deferred entrance. *Recommended:* high school transcript. *Application deadline:* rolling (freshmen), rolling (transfers). *Notification:* continuous (freshmen), continuous (transfers).

Admissions Contact Ms. Linda Baca, Admissions Manager, Everett Community College, 2000 Tower Street, Everett, WA 98201-1352. *Phone:* 425-388-9219. *Fax:* 425-388-9173. *E-mail:* admissions@everettcc.edu.

GRAYS HARBOR COLLEGE
Aberdeen, Washington

- **State-supported** 2-year, founded 1930, part of Washington State Board for Community and Technical Colleges
- **Calendar** quarters
- **Degree** certificates, diplomas, and associate
- **Small-town** 125-acre campus
- **Endowment** $927,238
- **Coed**

Faculty *Student/faculty ratio:* 16:1.

Student Life *Campus security:* 24-hour emergency response devices, late-night transport/escort service.

Standardized Tests *Required:* ACT ASSET, CPT (for placement).

Financial Aid Of all full-time matriculated undergraduates who enrolled, 67 Federal Work-Study jobs (averaging $1064). 135 state and other part-time jobs (averaging $1693).

Applying *Options:* common application, electronic application, early admission. *Recommended:* high school transcript.

Admissions Contact Ms. Brenda Dell, Admissions Officer, Grays Harbor College, 1620 Edward P. Smith Drive, Aberdeen, WA 98520-7599. *Phone:* 360-532-9020 Ext. 4026. *Toll-free phone:* 800-562-4830. *Fax:* 360-538-4293. *E-mail:* bdell@ghc.ctc.edu.

GREEN RIVER COMMUNITY COLLEGE
Auburn, Washington

- **State-supported** 2-year, founded 1965, part of Washington State Board for Community and Technical Colleges
- **Calendar** quarters
- **Degree** certificates, diplomas, and associate
- **Rural** 168-acre campus with easy access to Seattle
- **Coed**, 6,621 undergraduate students, 59% full-time, 56% women, 44% men

Undergraduates 3,883 full-time, 2,738 part-time. Students come from 30 other countries, 1% are from out of state, 3% African American, 7% Asian American or Pacific Islander, 5% Hispanic American, 1% Native American, 4% international.

Freshmen *Admission:* 1,098 enrolled.

Faculty *Total:* 368, 35% full-time. *Student/faculty ratio:* 22:1.

Majors Accounting technology and bookkeeping; airline pilot and flight crew; air traffic control; autobody/collision and repair technology; automobile/automotive mechanics technology; carpentry; child care and support services management; court reporting; criminal justice/police science; drafting and design technology; forestry technology; information science/studies; legal administrative assistant/secretary; liberal arts and sciences/liberal studies; machine tool technology; marketing/marketing management; mechanical engineering/mechanical technology; medical administrative assistant and medical secretary; nursing (licensed practical/vocational nurse training); occupational therapist assistant; office management; physical therapist assistant; water quality and wastewater treatment management and recycling technology; welding technology.

Academic Programs *Special study options:* academic remediation for entering students, adult/continuing education programs, advanced placement credit, cooperative education, distance learning, English as a second language, internships, off-campus study, part-time degree program, services for LD students, summer session for credit.

Library Holman Library with 32,500 titles, 2,100 serial subscriptions, 4,471 audiovisual materials, an OPAC, a Web page.

Computers on Campus 104 computers available on campus for general student use. A campuswide network can be accessed. Internet access, at least one staffed computer lab available.

Student Life *Housing:* college housing not available. *Activities and Organizations:* drama/theater group, student-run newspaper, radio station, choral group, Phi Theta Kappa, Green River Active Christian Encounter, Vocational and Industrial Clubs of America (VICA), Multicultural Student Alliance. *Campus security:* 24-hour emergency response devices and patrols, student patrols, late-night transport/escort service. *Student services:* health clinic, personal/psychological counseling, women's center.

Athletics Member NJCAA. *Intercollegiate sports:* baseball M(s), basketball M(s)/W(s), golf M(s)/W(s), soccer M(s)/W(s), softball W(s), tennis M(s)/W(s), volleyball W(s). *Intramural sports:* badminton M/W, basketball M/W, football M/W, tennis M/W, volleyball M/W, weight lifting M/W.

Standardized Tests *Required:* ACT ASSET or ACT COMPASS (for placement).

Costs (2003–04) *Tuition:* state resident $2142 full-time, $66 per credit part-time; nonresident $2571 full-time, $79 per credit part-time. Part-time tuition and fees vary according to course load. *Required fees:* $198 full-time. *Payment plan:* installment.

Financial Aid Of all full-time matriculated undergraduates who enrolled, 113 Federal Work-Study jobs (averaging $2356). 174 state and other part-time jobs.

Applying *Options:* electronic application, early admission, deferred entrance. *Required for some:* high school transcript. *Application deadline:* rolling (freshmen), rolling (transfers). *Notification:* continuous (freshmen), continuous (transfers).

Admissions Contact Ms. Peggy Morgan, Program Support Supervisor, Green River Community College, 12401 Southeast 320th Street, Auburn, WA 98092-3699. *Phone:* 253-833-9111 Ext. 2513. *Fax:* 253-288-3454.

HIGHLINE COMMUNITY COLLEGE
Des Moines, Washington

- **State-supported** 2-year, founded 1961, part of Washington State Board for Community and Technical Colleges
- **Calendar** quarters
- **Degree** certificates, diplomas, and associate
- **Suburban** 81-acre campus with easy access to Seattle
- **Coed**

Highline Community College, founded in 1961 as the first community college in King County, is one of the premier 2-year schools in Washington State, with an 80-acre wooded campus overlooking the waters of the Puget Sound. High-quality transfer, professional/technical, and international programs and facilities; exceptional faculty and student services staff members who serve a diverse student body; affordable cost; and convenient location combine to make Highline a great choice for a promising future.

Student Life *Campus security:* 24-hour patrols.
Athletics Member NJCAA.
Standardized Tests *Recommended:* ACT COMPASS.
Costs (2003–04) *Tuition:* state resident $2235 full-time; nonresident $7914 full-time.
Applying *Application fee:* $20.
Admissions Contact Highline Community College, PO Box 98000, 2400 South 240th Street, Des Moines, WA 98198-9800. *Phone:* 206-878-3710 Ext. 3363. *Fax:* 206-870-4855. *E-mail:* dfaison@hcc.ctc.edu.

ITT TECHNICAL INSTITUTE
Seattle, Washington

- **Proprietary** primarily 2-year, founded 1932, part of ITT Educational Services, Inc.
- **Calendar** quarters
- **Degrees** associate and bachelor's
- **Urban** campus
- **Coed**

Standardized Tests *Required:* Wonderlic aptitude test (for admission).
Costs (2003–04) *Tuition:* Total Program Cost varies depending on course of study. Consult school catalog.
Applying *Options:* deferred entrance. *Application fee:* $100. *Required:* high school transcript, interview. *Recommended:* letters of recommendation.
Admissions Contact Mr. Rocco Liace, Director of Recruitment, ITT Technical Institute, 12720 Gateway Drive, Suite 100, Seattle, WA 98168. *Phone:* 206-244-3300. *Toll-free phone:* 800-422-2029. *Fax:* 206-246-7635.

ITT TECHNICAL INSTITUTE
Spokane, Washington

- **Proprietary** primarily 2-year, founded 1985, part of ITT Educational Services, Inc.
- **Calendar** quarters
- **Degrees** associate and bachelor's
- **Suburban** 3-acre campus
- **Coed**

Standardized Tests *Required:* Wonderlic aptitude test (for admission).
Costs (2003–04) *Tuition:* Total Program Cost varies depending on course of study. Consult school catalog.
Financial Aid Of all full-time matriculated undergraduates who enrolled, 9 Federal Work-Study jobs (averaging $4000).
Applying *Options:* deferred entrance. *Application fee:* $100. *Required:* high school transcript, interview. *Recommended:* letters of recommendation.
Admissions Contact Mr. Gregory L. Alexander, Director of Recruitment, ITT Technical Institute, North 1050 Argonne Road, Spokane, WA 99212. *Phone:* 509-926-2900. *Toll-free phone:* 800-777-8324. *Fax:* 509-926-2908.

ITT TECHNICAL INSTITUTE
Bothell, Washington

- **Proprietary** primarily 2-year, founded 1993, part of ITT Educational Services, Inc.
- **Calendar** quarters
- **Degrees** associate and bachelor's
- **Coed**

Standardized Tests *Required:* Wonderlic aptitude test (for admission).
Costs (2003–04) *Tuition:* Total Program Cost varies depending on course of study. Consult school catalog.
Applying *Options:* deferred entrance. *Application fee:* $100. *Required:* high school transcript, interview. *Recommended:* letters of recommendation.
Admissions Contact Mr. Jon L. Scherrer, Director of Recruitment, ITT Technical Institute, 2525 223rd Street SE, Bothell, WA 98021. *Phone:* 425-485-0303. *Toll-free phone:* 800-272-3791. *Fax:* 425-485-3438.

LAKE WASHINGTON TECHNICAL COLLEGE
Kirkland, Washington

- **District-supported** 2-year, founded 1949, part of Washington State Board for Community and Technical Colleges
- **Calendar** quarters
- **Degree** certificates and associate
- **Suburban** 57-acre campus with easy access to Seattle
- **Endowment** $198,295
- **Coed,** 4,860 undergraduate students, 42% full-time, 56% women, 44% men

Undergraduates 2,020 full-time, 2,840 part-time. Students come from 4 states and territories, 12 other countries, 3% African American, 13% Asian American or Pacific Islander, 9% Hispanic American, 0.7% Native American, 1% international.
Freshmen *Admission:* 3,256 applied, 2,648 enrolled.
Faculty *Total:* 221, 27% full-time. *Student/faculty ratio:* 8:1.
Majors Accounting; administrative assistant and secretarial science; autobody/collision and repair technology; automobile/automotive mechanics technology; child development; computer engineering technology; computer science; culinary arts; dental assisting; dental hygiene; diesel mechanics technology; drafting and design technology; electrical, electronic and communications engineering technology; environmental studies; horticultural science; hotel/motel administration; legal administrative assistant/secretary; machine tool technology; medical/clinical assistant.

Lake Washington Technical College (continued)

Academic Programs *Special study options:* academic remediation for entering students, advanced placement credit, cooperative education, English as a second language, internships, services for LD students, summer session for credit.

Library Lake Washington Technical College Library/Media Center with 18,300 titles, 770 serial subscriptions, an OPAC, a Web page.

Computers on Campus 400 computers available on campus for general student use. A campuswide network can be accessed from off campus. Internet access, at least one staffed computer lab available.

Student Life *Housing:* college housing not available. *Campus security:* 24-hour emergency response devices, late-night transport/escort service, parking lot security, security cameras. *Student services:* personal/psychological counseling, women's center.

Standardized Tests *Required:* ACT ASSET (for placement).

Costs (2004–05) *Tuition:* state resident $3193 full-time, $64 per credit part-time. Full-time tuition and fees vary according to course load and program. Part-time tuition and fees vary according to course load and program. *Waivers:* senior citizens and employees or children of employees.

Financial Aid Of all full-time matriculated undergraduates who enrolled, 38 Federal Work-Study jobs (averaging $1800). 69 state and other part-time jobs (averaging $2259).

Applying *Options:* common application, early admission. *Required for some:* high school transcript. *Application deadline:* rolling (freshmen), rolling (transfers). *Notification:* continuous (freshmen), continuous (transfers).

Admissions Contact Mr. Jim West, Director of Admissions and Registration, Lake Washington Technical College, 11605 132nd Avenue NE, Kirkland, WA 98034-8506. *Phone:* 425-739-8233.

LOWER COLUMBIA COLLEGE
Longview, Washington

- **State-supported** 2-year, founded 1934, part of Washington State Board for Community and Technical Colleges
- **Calendar** quarters
- **Degree** certificates, diplomas, and associate
- **Small-town** 30-acre campus with easy access to Portland
- **Endowment** $2.4 million
- **Coed,** 3,320 undergraduate students, 54% full-time, 59% women, 41% men

Undergraduates 1,809 full-time, 1,511 part-time. Students come from 5 states and territories, 15% are from out of state, 1% African American, 2% Asian American or Pacific Islander, 2% Hispanic American, 1% Native American, 11% transferred in. *Retention:* 48% of 2002 full-time freshmen returned.

Freshmen *Admission:* 349 applied, 349 admitted, 294 enrolled.

Faculty *Total:* 163, 48% full-time. *Student/faculty ratio:* 22:1.

Majors Accounting; accounting technology and bookkeeping; administrative assistant and secretarial science; anthropology; art; automobile/automotive mechanics technology; biology/biological sciences; business administration and management; business/commerce; CAD/CADD drafting/design technology; computer and information sciences; computer engineering technology; computer programming; computer science; computer systems analysis; computer systems networking and telecommunications; computer technology/computer systems technology; corrections; criminal justice/law enforcement administration; criminal justice/police science; criminal justice/safety; data entry/microcomputer applications; data processing and data processing technology; diesel mechanics technology; dramatic/theatre arts; early childhood education; economics; electrical, electronic and communications engineering technology; electrician; engineering; engineering technology; English; environmental studies; fire science; fire services administration; foreign languages and literatures; geography; geology/earth science; heavy equipment maintenance technology; history; industrial mechanics and maintenance technology; industrial technology; information science/studies; information technology; instrumentation technology; kindergarten/preschool education; legal administrative assistant/secretary; liberal arts and sciences/liberal studies; lineworker; machine tool technology; management information systems; mathematics; mechanical engineering/mechanical technology; medical administrative assistant and medical secretary; medical/clinical assistant; medical reception; medical transcription; music; nursing (licensed practical/vocational nurse training); nursing (registered nurse training); office management; philosophy; photography; physical education teaching and coaching; physics; political science and government; pre-engineering; pre-law studies; psychology; receptionist; social sciences; sociology; speech and rhetoric; substance abuse/addiction counseling; teacher assistant/aide; welding technology; wood science and wood products/pulp and paper technology; word processing.

Academic Programs *Special study options:* academic remediation for entering students, adult/continuing education programs, cooperative education, English as a second language, honors programs, part-time degree program, services for LD students, study abroad, summer session for credit.

Library Allan Thompson Library plus 1 other with 41,991 titles, 217 serial subscriptions, 3,376 audiovisual materials, an OPAC.

Computers on Campus 250 computers available on campus for general student use. A campuswide network can be accessed. At least one staffed computer lab available.

Student Life *Housing:* college housing not available. *Activities and Organizations:* drama/theater group, student-run newspaper, choral group, Campus Entertainment, Phi Theta Kappa, Services and Relations Club, Multicultural Students Club, Theater Club. *Campus security:* 24-hour emergency response devices and patrols. *Student services:* health clinic, personal/psychological counseling.

Athletics *Intercollegiate sports:* baseball M(s), basketball M(s)/W(s), soccer M(s)/W(s), softball W(s), volleyball W(s).

Standardized Tests *Required:* ACT COMPASS (for placement).

Costs (2003–04) *Tuition:* state resident $2268 full-time, $70 per credit hour part-time; nonresident $2606 full-time, $83 per credit hour part-time. *Required fees:* $56 full-time. *Payment plan:* deferred payment. *Waivers:* senior citizens and employees or children of employees.

Financial Aid Of all full-time matriculated undergraduates who enrolled, 440 Federal Work-Study jobs (averaging $708). 447 state and other part-time jobs (averaging $2415).

Applying *Options:* early admission, deferred entrance. *Recommended:* high school transcript. *Application deadline:* rolling (freshmen), rolling (transfers). *Notification:* continuous (freshmen).

Admissions Contact Ms. Mary Harding, Vice President for Student Success, Lower Columbia College, 1600 Maple Street, Longview, WA 98632. *Phone:* 360-442-2301. *Fax:* 360-442-2379. *E-mail:* jmccall@lcc.ctc.edu.

NORTH SEATTLE COMMUNITY COLLEGE
Seattle, Washington

- **State-supported** 2-year, founded 1970, part of Seattle Community College District System
- **Calendar** quarters
- **Degree** certificates, diplomas, and associate
- **Urban** 65-acre campus
- **Coed,** 6,465 undergraduate students, 50% full-time, 59% women, 41% men

Undergraduates 3,239 full-time, 3,226 part-time. Students come from 50 states and territories, 1% are from out of state, 7% African American, 18% Asian American or Pacific Islander, 5% Hispanic American, 2% Native American, 0.3% international, 36% transferred in.

Freshmen *Admission:* 1,269 admitted, 1,269 enrolled.

Faculty *Total:* 278, 36% full-time, 3% with terminal degrees. *Student/faculty ratio:* 22:1.

Majors Accounting technology and bookkeeping; art; biomedical technology; business administration and management; civil drafting and CAD/CADD; communications systems installation and repair technology; computer systems networking and telecommunications; culinary arts; data processing and data processing technology; early childhood education; electrical, electronic and communications engineering technology; electrical/electronics drafting and CAD/CADD; heating, air conditioning, ventilation and refrigeration maintenance technology; industrial electronics technology; information science/studies; liberal arts and sciences/liberal studies; mechanical drafting and CAD/CADD; medical/clinical assistant; music; nursing (licensed practical/vocational nurse training); nursing (registered nurse training); office management; pharmacy technician; watchmaking and jewelrymaking; web/multimedia management and webmaster; web page, digital/multimedia and information resources design.

Academic Programs *Special study options:* academic remediation for entering students, adult/continuing education programs, advanced placement credit, cooperative education, distance learning, English as a second language, external degree program, independent study, internships, part-time degree program, services for LD students, summer session for credit. *ROTC:* Army (c).

Library North Seattle Community College Library with 52,496 titles, 594 serial subscriptions, 2,957 audiovisual materials, an OPAC, a Web page.

Computers on Campus 1600 computers available on campus for general student use. A campuswide network can be accessed from off campus. Internet access, online (class) registration, at least one staffed computer lab available.

Student Life *Housing:* college housing not available. *Activities and Organizations:* drama/theater group, student-run newspaper, television station, choral group, Muslim Students Association, Indonesian Community Club, Literary Guild, Phi Theta Kappa, Vietnamese Student Association, national sororities. *Campus security:* 24-hour emergency response devices and patrols, student patrols, late-night transport/escort service, patrols by security. *Student services:* personal/psychological counseling, women's center, legal services.

Athletics *Intercollegiate sports:* basketball M/W. *Intramural sports:* basketball M/W.

Costs (2003–04) *Tuition:* state resident $2131 full-time, $69 per credit part-time; nonresident $7339 full-time, $238 per credit part-time. Part-time tuition and fees vary according to course load. *Required fees:* $35 full-time. *Waivers:* employees or children of employees.

Applying *Options:* common application, electronic application, early admission, deferred entrance. *Required:* high school transcript. *Required for some:* essay or personal statement. *Application deadline:* rolling (freshmen), rolling (transfers). *Notification:* continuous until 9/24 (freshmen), continuous until 9/24 (transfers).

Admissions Contact Ms. Betsy Abts, Assistant Registrar, Admissions/ Registration, North Seattle Community College, 9600 College Way North, Seattle, WA 98103-3599. *Phone:* 206-527-3796. *Fax:* 206-527-3671. *E-mail:* babts@sccd.ctc.edu.

NORTHWEST AVIATION COLLEGE
Auburn, Washington

Admissions Contact Mr. Shawn Pratt, Assistant Director of Education, Northwest Aviation College, 506 23rd, NE, Auburn, WA 98002. *Phone:* 253-854-4960. *Toll-free phone:* 800-246-4960. *Fax:* 253-931-0768. *E-mail:* afsnac@ nventure.com.

NORTHWEST INDIAN COLLEGE
Bellingham, Washington

- **Federally supported** 2-year, founded 1978
- **Calendar** quarters
- **Degrees** certificates and associate (also offers bachelor's degree in elementary education in conjunction with Washington State University)
- **Rural** 5-acre campus
- **Endowment** $3.0 million
- **Coed**

Standardized Tests *Required:* TABE (for placement).

Applying *Application fee:* $25. *Required:* high school transcript.

Admissions Contact Ms. Lisa Santana, Director of Admissions, Northwest Indian College, 2522 Kwina Road, Bellingham, WA 98226. *Phone:* 360-676-2772 Ext. 4270. *Toll-free phone:* 866-676-2772 Ext. 4264. *E-mail:* admissions@ orca.nwic.edu.

NORTHWEST SCHOOL OF WOODEN BOATBUILDING
Port Townsend, Washington

Admissions Contact Ms. Gretchen Siegfried, Student Services Coordinator, Northwest School of Wooden Boatbuilding, 251 Otto Street, Port Townsend, WA 98368. *Phone:* 360-385-4948.

OLYMPIC COLLEGE
Bremerton, Washington

- **State-supported** 2-year, founded 1946, part of Washington State Board for Community and Technical Colleges
- **Calendar** quarters
- **Degree** certificates, diplomas, and associate
- **Suburban** 32-acre campus with easy access to Seattle
- **Endowment** $3.3 million
- **Coed,** 7,102 undergraduate students

Undergraduates Students come from 50 states and territories, 4 other countries, 3% African American, 10% Asian American or Pacific Islander, 5% Hispanic American, 2% Native American, 0.3% international.

Faculty *Total:* 307, 32% full-time. *Student/faculty ratio:* 25:1.

Majors Accounting technology and bookkeeping; administrative assistant and secretarial science; aesthetician/esthetician and skin care; animation, interactive technology, video graphics and special effects; audiovisual communications technologies related; automobile/automotive mechanics technology; barbering; business administration and management; child care and support services management; computer and information sciences related; computer graphics; computer programming; computer programming related; computer software and media applications related; computer systems networking and telecommunications; cosmetology; cosmetology, barber/styling, and nail instruction; criminal justice/law enforcement administration; criminal justice/police science; culinary arts; culinary arts related; digital communication and media/multimedia; drafting and design technology; early childhood education; electrical, electronic and communications engineering technology; engineering; fire science; fire services administration; industrial technology; information science/studies; information technology; legal administrative assistant/secretary; liberal arts and sciences/ liberal studies; marine maintenance and ship repair technology; medical/clinical

assistant; nail technician and manicurist; nursing (licensed practical/vocational nurse training); nursing (registered nurse training); office management; photographic and film/video technology; recording arts technology; special education (early childhood); system administration; system, networking, and LAN/wan management; web/multimedia management and webmaster; welding technology.

Academic Programs *Special study options:* academic remediation for entering students, adult/continuing education programs, advanced placement credit, cooperative education, distance learning, English as a second language, honors programs, independent study, off-campus study, part-time degree program, services for LD students, summer session for credit.

Library Haselwood Library with 51,443 titles, 541 serial subscriptions, 3,007 audiovisual materials, an OPAC, a Web page.

Computers on Campus 634 computers available on campus for general student use. A campuswide network can be accessed from off campus. Internet access, online (class) registration, at least one staffed computer lab available.

Student Life *Housing:* college housing not available. *Activities and Organizations:* drama/theater group, student-run newspaper, choral group, Phi Theta Kappa, Aware, Oceans (Nursing), ASOC, ASAD. *Campus security:* 24-hour emergency response devices and patrols, student patrols, late-night transport/ escort service. *Student services:* personal/psychological counseling, women's center.

Athletics *Intercollegiate sports:* baseball M(s), basketball M(s)/W(s), cheerleading W, softball W(s), volleyball W(s). *Intramural sports:* basketball M/W, rock climbing M/W, volleyball M/W.

Standardized Tests *Required for some:* ACT ASSET.

Costs (2003–04) *Tuition:* state resident $2142 full-time, $63 per credit part-time; nonresident $7350 full-time, $234 per credit part-time. Full-time tuition and fees vary according to course load. Part-time tuition and fees vary according to course load. *Required fees:* $180 full-time, $60 per term part-time. *Waivers:* senior citizens and employees or children of employees.

Financial Aid Of all full-time matriculated undergraduates who enrolled, 105 Federal Work-Study jobs (averaging $2380). 31 state and other part-time jobs (averaging $2880).

Applying *Options:* early admission. *Required for some:* high school transcript. *Application deadline:* rolling (freshmen), rolling (transfers). *Notification:* continuous (freshmen), continuous (transfers).

Admissions Contact Ms. Gerry Stamm, Director of Admissions and Outreach, Olympic College, Bremerton, WA 98337-1699. *Phone:* 360-475-7126. *Toll-free phone:* 800-259-6718. *Fax:* 360-475-7020. *E-mail:* gstamm@ oc.ctc.edu.

PENINSULA COLLEGE
Port Angeles, Washington

- **State-supported** 2-year, founded 1961
- **Calendar** quarters
- **Degree** certificates and associate
- **Small-town** 75-acre campus
- **Coed,** 4,591 undergraduate students, 35% full-time, 55% women, 45% men

Undergraduates 1,609 full-time, 2,982 part-time. Students come from 5 other countries, 4% African American, 3% Asian American or Pacific Islander, 4% Hispanic American, 4% Native American, 1% international.

Freshmen *Admission:* 1,214 applied, 1,214 admitted, 1,164 enrolled.

Faculty *Total:* 212, 31% full-time, 7% with terminal degrees. *Student/faculty ratio:* 13:1.

Majors Accounting; automobile/automotive mechanics technology; biological and physical sciences; business administration and management; child care and support services management; child development; civil engineering technology; commercial fishing; computer programming (vendor/product certification); criminal justice/law enforcement administration; data entry/microcomputer applications related; diesel mechanics technology; electrical, electronic and communications engineering technology; engineering technology; fishing and fisheries sciences and management; nursing (registered nurse training); office management; substance abuse/addiction counseling; web page, digital/multimedia and information resources design.

Academic Programs *Special study options:* academic remediation for entering students, adult/continuing education programs, advanced placement credit, distance learning, English as a second language, honors programs, internships, part-time degree program, services for LD students, summer session for credit.

Library 33,736 titles, 383 serial subscriptions.

Computers on Campus 38 computers available on campus for general student use. A campuswide network can be accessed from student residence rooms and from off campus. At least one staffed computer lab available.

Student Life *Housing Options:* coed. Campus housing is university owned. *Activities and Organizations:* drama/theater group, student-run newspaper, choral group, Phi Theta Kappa, SAGE (Students Advocating Global Environmentalism). *Campus security:* 8-hour patrols by trained security personnel. *Student services:* women's center.

Peninsula College (continued)

Athletics *Intercollegiate sports:* baseball W, basketball M/W. *Intramural sports:* badminton M/W, basketball M/W, bowling M/W, football M, golf M, skiing (cross-country) M/W, soccer M/W, softball M/W, table tennis M/W, tennis M/W, volleyball M/W.

Standardized Tests *Required:* ACT ASSET or ACT COMPASS (for placement). *Recommended:* SAT I (for placement).

Costs (2004–05) *Tuition:* state resident $2313 full-time, $69 per credit part-time; nonresident $2702 full-time, $83 per credit part-time. *Required fees:* $127 full-time, $3 per credit part-time, $13 per term part-time.

Financial Aid Of all full-time matriculated undergraduates who enrolled, 30 Federal Work-Study jobs (averaging $3600). 25 state and other part-time jobs (averaging $3600).

Applying *Options:* common application, electronic application, deferred entrance. *Required for some:* high school transcript. *Application deadline:* rolling (freshmen), rolling (transfers). *Notification:* continuous (freshmen), continuous (transfers).

Admissions Contact Mr. Jack Huls, Vice President of Student Services, Peninsula College, 1502 East Lauridsen Boulevard, Port Angeles, WA 98362-2779. *Phone:* 360-417-6225. *Fax:* 360-457-8100. *E-mail:* admissions@pcadmin.ctc.edu.

PIERCE COLLEGE
Puyallup, Washington

- **State-supported** 2-year, founded 1967, part of Washington State Board for Community and Technical Colleges
- **Calendar** quarters
- **Degree** certificates, diplomas, and associate
- **Suburban** 140-acre campus with easy access to Seattle
- **Endowment** $4540
- **Coed**

Student Life *Campus security:* 24-hour emergency response devices and patrols, late-night transport/escort service.

Standardized Tests *Required for some:* ACT ASSET. *Recommended:* ACT ASSET.

Costs (2003–04) *Tuition:* area resident $2142 full-time; state resident $2595 full-time; nonresident $7350 full-time. *Required fees:* $255 full-time.

Financial Aid Of all full-time matriculated undergraduates who enrolled, 242 Federal Work-Study jobs (averaging $810). 48 state and other part-time jobs (averaging $3055).

Applying *Options:* early admission.

Admissions Contact Ms. Cindy Burbank, Director of Admissions, Pierce College, 1601 39th Avenue SE, Puyallup, WA 98374-2222. *Phone:* 253-964-6686. *Fax:* 253-964-6427.

PIMA MEDICAL INSTITUTE
Seattle, Washington

- **Proprietary** 2-year, founded 1989, part of Vocational Training Institutes, Inc
- **Calendar** modular
- **Degree** certificates and associate
- **Urban** campus
- **Coed, primarily women,** 292 undergraduate students, 100% full-time, 82% women, 18% men

Undergraduates 292 full-time.

Freshmen *Admission:* 24 admitted.

Faculty *Total:* 19, 16% full-time. *Student/faculty ratio:* 15:1.

Majors Radiologic technology/science.

Student Life *Housing:* college housing not available.

Admissions Contact Ms. Donna Murray, Admissions Office Director, Pima Medical Institute, 1627 Eastlake Avenue, East, Seattle, WA 98102. *Phone:* 206-322-6100.

RENTON TECHNICAL COLLEGE
Renton, Washington

Admissions Contact Mr. Jon Pozega, Vice President for Student Services, Renton Technical College, 3000 Fourth Street, NE, Renton, WA 98056. *Phone:* 425-235-2463. *Fax:* 425-235-7832. *E-mail:* cdaniels@rtc.ctc.edu.

SEATTLE CENTRAL COMMUNITY COLLEGE
Seattle, Washington

- **State-supported** 2-year, founded 1966, part of Seattle Community College District System
- **Calendar** quarters
- **Degree** certificates and associate
- **Urban** 15-acre campus
- **Coed**

Student Life *Campus security:* 24-hour emergency response devices.

Standardized Tests *Required:* ACT ASSET (for placement).

Admissions Contact Admissions Office, Seattle Central Community College, 1701 Broadway, Seattle, WA 98122-2400. *Phone:* 206-587-5450.

SHORELINE COMMUNITY COLLEGE
Shoreline, Washington

- **State-supported** 2-year, founded 1964, part of Washington State Board for Community and Technical Colleges
- **Calendar** quarters
- **Degree** certificates, diplomas, and associate
- **Suburban** 80-acre campus
- **Coed**

Faculty *Student/faculty ratio:* 21:1.

Student Life *Campus security:* 24-hour emergency response devices and patrols.

Standardized Tests *Required for some:* SAT I or ACT (for placement), ACT ASSET or ACT COMPASS.

Applying *Options:* early admission. *Required:* high school transcript.

Admissions Contact Ms. Robin Young, Registrar, Shoreline Community College, 16101 Greenwood Avenue North, Seattle, WA 98133. *Phone:* 206-546-4581. *Fax:* 206-546-5835. *E-mail:* sccadmis@ctc.edu.

SKAGIT VALLEY COLLEGE
Mount Vernon, Washington

- **State-supported** 2-year, founded 1926, part of Washington State Board for Community and Technical Colleges
- **Calendar** quarters
- **Degree** certificates, diplomas, and associate
- **Small-town** 85-acre campus with easy access to Seattle
- **Endowment** $3.2 million
- **Coed**

Faculty *Student/faculty ratio:* 22:1.

Student Life *Campus security:* 24-hour patrols, late-night transport/escort service, telephone/pager system.

Standardized Tests *Required:* ACT ASSET (for placement).

Costs (2003–04) *Tuition:* state resident $2310 full-time; nonresident $2610 full-time. *Required fees:* $155 full-time. *Room and board:* $5700.

Financial Aid Of all full-time matriculated undergraduates who enrolled, 100 Federal Work-Study jobs (averaging $2800).

Applying *Options:* common application, electronic application, deferred entrance. *Required for some:* high school transcript, interview.

Admissions Contact Ms. Karen Ackelson, Admissions and Recruitment Coordinator, Skagit Valley College, 2405 College Way, Mount Vernon, WA 98273-5899. *Phone:* 360-416-7620. *Fax:* 360-416-7890. *E-mail:* ackelson@skagit.ctc.edu.

SOUTH PUGET SOUND COMMUNITY COLLEGE
Olympia, Washington

- **State-supported** 2-year, founded 1970, part of Washington State Board for Community and Technical Colleges
- **Calendar** quarters
- **Degree** certificates, diplomas, and associate
- **Suburban** 86-acre campus with easy access to Seattle
- **Coed,** 6,351 undergraduate students, 39% full-time, 62% women, 38% men

Undergraduates 2,495 full-time, 3,856 part-time. Students come from 19 other countries.

Freshmen *Admission:* 3,732 applied, 3,732 admitted.

Faculty *Total:* 201, 45% full-time, 10% with terminal degrees. *Student/faculty ratio:* 20:1.

Majors Accounting; administrative assistant and secretarial science; automobile/automotive mechanics technology; business administration and management; communications technology; computer and information sciences; computer programming; culinary arts; data processing and data processing technology; dental hygiene; drafting and design technology; electrical, electronic and communications engineering technology; fire science; food services technology; horticultural science; information science/studies; kindergarten/preschool education; landscaping and groundskeeping; legal administrative assistant/secretary; legal assistant/paralegal; liberal arts and sciences/liberal studies; medical administrative assistant and medical secretary; medical/clinical assistant; nursing (licensed practical/vocational nurse training); nursing (registered nurse training); purchasing, procurement/acquisitions and contracts management; sign language interpretation and translation; special products marketing; telecommunications; welding technology.

Academic Programs *Special study options:* academic remediation for entering students, adult/continuing education programs, advanced placement credit, cooperative education, English as a second language, internships, part-time degree program, services for LD students, study abroad, summer session for credit. *ROTC:* Army (c).

Library Media Center plus 1 other with 30,000 titles, 340 serial subscriptions, an OPAC.

Computers on Campus 450 computers available on campus for general student use. A campuswide network can be accessed from off campus. Internet access, at least one staffed computer lab available.

Student Life *Housing:* college housing not available. *Activities and Organizations:* drama/theater group, student-run newspaper. *Campus security:* 24-hour emergency response devices and patrols, late-night transport/escort service. *Student services:* personal/psychological counseling.

Athletics *Intercollegiate sports:* basketball M(s)/W(s), soccer M(s), softball W(s). *Intramural sports:* basketball M/W, softball W.

Standardized Tests *Required:* CPT, ACCUPLACER (for placement). *Recommended:* SAT I or ACT (for placement).

Costs (2003–04) *Tuition:* state resident $2134 full-time, $66 per credit part-time; nonresident $2530 full-time, $79 per credit part-time. *Required fees:* $35 full-time, $3 per credit part-time.

Financial Aid Of all full-time matriculated undergraduates who enrolled, 42 Federal Work-Study jobs (averaging $3150). 14 state and other part-time jobs (averaging $4400). *Financial aid deadline:* 6/29.

Applying *Options:* electronic application, early admission, deferred entrance. *Application fee:* $15. *Application deadline:* rolling (freshmen), rolling (transfers). *Notification:* continuous (freshmen), continuous (transfers).

Admissions Contact Mr. Jerry Haynes, Dean of Enrollment Services, South Puget Sound Community College, 2011 Mottman Road, SW. *Phone:* 360-754-7711 Ext. 5240. *Fax:* 360-596-5709. *E-mail:* lsmith@spscc.ctc.edu.

SOUTH SEATTLE COMMUNITY COLLEGE
Seattle, Washington

Admissions Contact Ms. Kim Manderbach, Dean of Student Services/Registration, South Seattle Community College, 6000 16th Avenue, SW, Seattle, WA 98106-1499. *Phone:* 206-764-5378.

SPOKANE COMMUNITY COLLEGE
Spokane, Washington

- **State-supported** 2-year, founded 1963, part of Washington State Board for Community and Technical Colleges
- **Calendar** quarters
- **Degree** certificates, diplomas, and associate
- **Urban** 108-acre campus
- **Endowment** $33,508
- **Coed,** 7,258 undergraduate students

Undergraduates Students come from 5 states and territories, 20 other countries, 17% are from out of state, 2% African American, 3% Asian American or Pacific Islander, 3% Hispanic American, 3% Native American, 0.5% international. *Retention:* 35% of 2002 full-time freshmen returned.

Faculty *Total:* 361, 53% full-time. *Student/faculty ratio:* 21:1.

Majors Accounting technology and bookkeeping; administrative assistant and secretarial science; agricultural business and management; agronomy and crop science; applied horticulture; architectural engineering technology; artificial intelligence and robotics; automobile/automotive mechanics technology; avionics maintenance technology; biomedical technology; business administration and management; carpentry; civil engineering technology; computer programming; computer typography and composition equipment operation; construction engineering technology; corrections; cosmetology; criminal justice/police science; culinary arts; data processing and data processing technology; dental hygiene; dietetics; drafting and design technology; electrical, electronic and communications engineering technology; fire science; food services technology; forestry; health information/medical records administration; heating, air conditioning, ventilation and refrigeration maintenance technology; heavy equipment maintenance technology; hotel/motel administration; hydrology and water resources science; industrial technology; landscaping and groundskeeping; legal administrative assistant/secretary; legal assistant/paralegal; liberal arts and

sciences/liberal studies; machine tool technology; marketing/marketing management; mechanical design technology; mechanical engineering/mechanical technology; medical administrative assistant and medical secretary; natural resources management and policy; nursing (licensed practical/vocational nurse training); nursing (registered nurse training); ophthalmic laboratory technology; ornamental horticulture; parks, recreation and leisure facilities management; respiratory care therapy; surgical technology; welding technology; wildlife and wildlands science and management.

Academic Programs *Special study options:* academic remediation for entering students, adult/continuing education programs, advanced placement credit, cooperative education, distance learning, English as a second language, independent study, internships, part-time degree program, services for LD students, student-designed majors, summer session for credit. *ROTC:* Army (c).

Library Learning Resources Center plus 1 other with 38,967 titles, 466 serial subscriptions, an OPAC.

Computers on Campus 700 computers available on campus for general student use. A campuswide network can be accessed. Internet access, online (class) registration, at least one staffed computer lab available.

Student Life *Housing:* college housing not available. *Activities and Organizations:* drama/theater group, student-run newspaper, VICA, Delta Epsilon Chi, Intercultural Student Organization, Rho Beta Psi, Student Awareness League. *Campus security:* 24-hour emergency response devices and patrols, student patrols, late-night transport/escort service.

Athletics Member NJCAA. *Intercollegiate sports:* baseball M(s), basketball M(s)/W(s), cross-country running M(s)/W(s), soccer M(s)/W(s), softball W(s), tennis M(s)/W(s), track and field M(s)/W(s), volleyball W(s). *Intramural sports:* badminton M/W, basketball M/W, bowling M/W, softball M/W, table tennis M/W, tennis M/W, volleyball M/W, water polo M/W.

Costs (2003–04) *Tuition:* state resident $2134 full-time, $66 per credit part-time; nonresident $3193 full-time. *Required fees:* $367 full-time.

Financial Aid Of all full-time matriculated undergraduates who enrolled, 291 Federal Work-Study jobs (averaging $3600). 250 state and other part-time jobs (averaging $3600).

Applying *Options:* early admission, deferred entrance. *Application fee:* $15. *Recommended:* high school transcript. *Application deadline:* rolling (freshmen), rolling (transfers). *Notification:* continuous (freshmen).

Admissions Contact Ms. Colleen Straight, Manager, District Institutional Research, Spokane Community College, North 1810 Greene Street, Spokane, WA 99217-5399. *Phone:* 509-434-5240. *Toll-free phone:* 800-248-5644.

SPOKANE FALLS COMMUNITY COLLEGE
Spokane, Washington

- **State-supported** 2-year, founded 1967, part of State Board for Washington Community and Technical Colleges
- **Calendar** quarters
- **Degree** certificates, diplomas, and associate
- **Urban** 125-acre campus
- **Endowment** $33,407
- **Coed,** 5,734 undergraduate students, 72% full-time, 57% women, 43% men

Undergraduates 4,142 full-time, 1,592 part-time. Students come from 6 states and territories, 14 other countries, 5% are from out of state, 2% African American, 3% Asian American or Pacific Islander, 4% Hispanic American, 2% Native American, 1% international. *Retention:* 29% of 2002 full-time freshmen returned.

Faculty *Total:* 431, 34% full-time. *Student/faculty ratio:* 22:1.

Majors Accounting technology and bookkeeping; administrative assistant and secretarial science; art; business administration and management; business and personal/financial services marketing; child care and support services management; commercial and advertising art; commercial photography; consumer merchandising/retailing management; fashion merchandising; gerontology; heavy equipment maintenance technology; information science/studies; interior design; international business/trade/commerce; leatherworking/upholstery; liberal arts and sciences/liberal studies; library assistant; marketing/marketing management; mass communication/media; music; office occupations and clerical services; orthotics/prosthetics; physical therapist assistant; real estate; sign language interpretation and translation; social work; sport and fitness administration; substance abuse/addiction counseling; vocational rehabilitation counseling; welding technology.

Academic Programs *Special study options:* academic remediation for entering students, adult/continuing education programs, advanced placement credit, cooperative education, English as a second language, internships, part-time degree program, services for LD students, student-designed majors, summer session for credit. *ROTC:* Army (c).

Library Learning Resources Center plus 1 other with 58,000 titles, 705 serial subscriptions, an OPAC.

Computers on Campus 400 computers available on campus for general student use. A campuswide network can be accessed. Internet access, online (class) registration, at least one staffed computer lab available.

Spokane Falls Community College (continued)

Student Life *Housing:* college housing not available. *Activities and Organizations:* drama/theater group, student-run newspaper, radio station, choral group, DECA, Associated Men Students, Associated Women Students, chorale, Forensics Club. *Campus security:* late-night transport/escort service, 24-hour emergency dispatch. *Student services:* personal/psychological counseling, women's center.

Athletics Member NJCAA. *Intercollegiate sports:* baseball M(s), basketball M(s)/W(s), cross-country running M(s)/W(s), soccer M(s)/W(s), softball W(s), tennis M(s)/W(s), track and field M(s)/W(s), volleyball W(s). *Intramural sports:* badminton M/W, basketball M/W, bowling M/W, soccer M/W, softball M/W, table tennis M/W, tennis M/W, volleyball M/W.

Standardized Tests *Required:* ACT ASSET (for placement).

Costs (2003–04) *Tuition:* state resident $2134 full-time; nonresident $3193 full-time. *Required fees:* $367 full-time.

Financial Aid Of all full-time matriculated undergraduates who enrolled, 250 Federal Work-Study jobs (averaging $3600). 260 state and other part-time jobs (averaging $4500).

Applying *Options:* early admission, deferred entrance. *Application fee:* $15. *Recommended:* high school transcript. *Application deadline:* rolling (freshmen), rolling (transfers). *Notification:* continuous (freshmen), continuous (transfers).

Admissions Contact Ms. Carol Green, Vice President of Student Services, Spokane Falls Community College, 3410 West Fort George Wright Drive, Spokane, WA 99224-5288. *Phone:* 509-533-3682. *Toll-free phone:* 888-509-7944.

TACOMA COMMUNITY COLLEGE
Tacoma, Washington

- **State-supported** 2-year, founded 1965, part of Washington State Board for Community and Technical Colleges
- **Calendar** quarters
- **Degree** certificates, diplomas, and associate
- **Urban** 150-acre campus with easy access to Seattle
- **Coed**

Faculty *Student/faculty ratio:* 27:1.

Student Life *Campus security:* Sonitrol electronic system.

Standardized Tests *Required:* ACCUPLACER (for placement).

Costs (2003–04) *Tuition:* state resident $2201 full-time; nonresident $2597 full-time. *Required fees:* $68 full-time.

Financial Aid Of all full-time matriculated undergraduates who enrolled, 81 Federal Work-Study jobs (averaging $2916). 146 state and other part-time jobs (averaging $2830). *Financial aid deadline:* 5/14.

Applying *Options:* early admission.

Admissions Contact Ms. Annette Hayward, Admissions Officer, Tacoma Community College, 6501 South 19th Street, Tacoma, WA 98466. *Phone:* 253-566-5108. *Fax:* 253-566-6011. *E-mail:* admissions@tcc.ctc.edu.

WALLA WALLA COMMUNITY COLLEGE
Walla Walla, Washington

- **State-supported** 2-year, founded 1967, part of Washington State Board for Community and Technical Colleges
- **Calendar** quarters
- **Degree** certificates, diplomas, and associate
- **Small-town** 125-acre campus
- **Endowment** $4.0 million
- **Coed**

Faculty *Student/faculty ratio:* 21:1.

Student Life *Campus security:* student patrols, late-night transport/escort service.

Athletics Member NJCAA.

Standardized Tests *Required:* ACT ASSET and ACT COMPASS (for placement).

Financial Aid Of all full-time matriculated undergraduates who enrolled, 95 Federal Work-Study jobs (averaging $1600). 20 state and other part-time jobs (averaging $2000).

Applying *Options:* common application, electronic application. *Application fee:* $40. *Required for some:* interview. *Recommended:* high school transcript.

Admissions Contact Ms. Sally Wagoner, Director of Admissions and Records, Walla Walla Community College, 500 Tausick Way, Walla Walla, WA 99362-9267. *Phone:* 509-527-4283. *Toll-free phone:* 877-992-9282 (in-state); 877-992-9292 (out-of-state). *Fax:* 509-527-3361. *E-mail:* admissions@wwcc.ctc.edu.

WENATCHEE VALLEY COLLEGE
Wenatchee, Washington

- **State and locally supported** 2-year, founded 1939, part of Washington State Board for Community and Technical Colleges
- **Calendar** quarters
- **Degree** certificates, diplomas, and associate
- **Rural** 56-acre campus
- **Endowment** $358,000
- **Coed**

Student Life *Campus security:* evening and late night security patrols.

Standardized Tests *Required:* ACT ASSET (for placement).

Applying *Options:* common application, electronic application, early admission, deferred entrance. *Required for some:* high school transcript.

Admissions Contact Ms. Marlene Sinko, Registrar/Admissions Coordinator, Wenatchee Valley College, 1300 Fifth Street, Wenatchee, WA 98801-1799. *Phone:* 509-664-2564. *Fax:* 509-664-2511. *E-mail:* atyrrell@wvcmail.ctc.edu.

WESTERN BUSINESS COLLEGE
Vancouver, Washington

- **Proprietary** 2-year, founded 1979
- **Calendar** quarters
- **Degree** diplomas and associate
- **Coed**

Faculty *Student/faculty ratio:* 19:1.

Costs (2003–04) *Tuition:* $10,560 full-time, $220 per credit part-time. $25 application fee per term.

Applying *Recommended:* interview.

Admissions Contact Ms. Maryann Green, Director of Admission, Western Business College, 120 Northeast 136th Avenue, Suite300, Vancouver, WA 98684. *Phone:* 360-254-3282. *Fax:* 360-254-3035.

WHATCOM COMMUNITY COLLEGE
Bellingham, Washington

- **State-supported** 2-year, founded 1970, part of Washington State Board for Community and Technical Colleges
- **Calendar** quarters
- **Degree** certificates and associate
- **Small-town** 52-acre campus with easy access to Vancouver
- **Coed**

Student Life *Campus security:* 24-hour emergency response devices.

Costs (2003–04) *Tuition:* state resident $2181 full-time; nonresident $7389 full-time.

Financial Aid Of all full-time matriculated undergraduates who enrolled, 50 Federal Work-Study jobs (averaging $3300). 80 state and other part-time jobs (averaging $3500).

Applying *Options:* common application, electronic application.

Admissions Contact Entry and Advising Center, Whatcom Community College, 237 West Kellogg Road, Bellingham, WA 98226. *Phone:* 360-650-5358. *Fax:* 360-676-2171. *E-mail:* admit@whatcom.ctc.edu.

YAKIMA VALLEY COMMUNITY COLLEGE
Yakima, Washington

- **State-supported** 2-year, founded 1928, part of Washington State Board for Community and Technical Colleges
- **Calendar** quarters
- **Degree** certificates and associate
- **Small-town** 20-acre campus
- **Endowment** $1.7 million
- **Coed**, 7,133 undergraduate students, 54% full-time, 64% women, 36% men

Undergraduates 3,882 full-time, 3,251 part-time. Students come from 10 other countries, 2% are from out of state, 2% African American, 2% Asian American or Pacific Islander, 39% Hispanic American, 3% Native American, 1% live on campus.

Freshmen *Admission:* 1,834 applied, 1,834 admitted.

Faculty *Total:* 120. *Student/faculty ratio:* 20:1.

Majors Accounting; administrative assistant and secretarial science; agricultural business and management; agricultural mechanization; agriculture; agronomy and crop science; animal sciences; automobile/automotive mechanics technology; broadcast journalism; business administration and management; child development; civil engineering technology; computer engineering technology;

computer graphics; computer science; criminal justice/law enforcement administration; criminal justice/police science; dental hygiene; electrical, electronic and communications engineering technology; family and consumer economics related; fire science; hotel/motel administration; industrial radiologic technology; industrial technology; instrumentation technology; kindergarten/preschool education; legal administrative assistant/secretary; liberal arts and sciences/liberal studies; management information systems; marketing/marketing management; medical administrative assistant and medical secretary; nursing (registered nurse training); occupational therapy; pre-engineering; special products marketing; substance abuse/addiction counseling; tourism and travel services management; veterinary technology.

Academic Programs *Special study options:* academic remediation for entering students, adult/continuing education programs, advanced placement credit, cooperative education, distance learning, English as a second language, internships, part-time degree program, services for LD students, summer session for credit. *ROTC:* Air Force (c).

Library Raymond Library with 31,716 titles, 860 serial subscriptions, an OPAC.

Computers on Campus 369 computers available on campus for general student use. A campuswide network can be accessed. Internet access, online (class) registration, at least one staffed computer lab available.

Student Life *Housing:* on-campus residence required for freshman year. *Options:* coed. *Activities and Organizations:* drama/theater group, student-run newspaper, choral group, Veterans with Supporters, Business Management/Marketing Club, Image Makers, Agri-Business Club. *Campus security:* 24-hour emergency response devices, student patrols, late-night transport/escort service, controlled dormitory access. *Student services:* health clinic, personal/psychological counseling, women's center.

Athletics Member NJCAA. *Intercollegiate sports:* baseball M(s), basketball M(s)/W(s), softball W(s), tennis M(s)/W(s), volleyball W(s), wrestling M. *Intramural sports:* badminton M/W, basketball M/W, table tennis M/W, tennis M/W, volleyball M/W, wrestling M.

Standardized Tests *Required:* ACT ASSET (for placement).

Costs (2003–04) *Tuition:* state resident $2247 full-time, $70 per credit part-time; nonresident $2643 full-time, $241 per credit part-time. *Room and board:* $4425.

Financial Aid Of all full-time matriculated undergraduates who enrolled, 133 Federal Work-Study jobs (averaging $1164). 156 state and other part-time jobs (averaging $2083).

Applying *Options:* common application, deferred entrance. *Required for some:* high school transcript, minimum 2.0 GPA, letters of recommendation, interview. *Recommended:* high school transcript. *Application deadlines:* 9/15 (freshmen), 9/15 (transfers). *Notification:* continuous until 9/15 (freshmen), continuous until 9/15 (transfers).

Admissions Contact Ms. Judy Morehead, Admissions Assistant, Yakima Valley Community College, PO Box 22520, Yakima, WA 98907-2520. *Phone:* 509-574-4713. *Fax:* 509-574-6860.

WEST VIRGINIA

EASTERN WEST VIRGINIA COMMUNITY AND TECHNICAL COLLEGE
Moorefield, West Virginia

- **State-supported** 2-year, founded 1999
- **Calendar** semesters
- **Degree** certificates and associate
- **Rural** campus
- **Coed,** 405 undergraduate students, 12% full-time, 73% women, 27% men

Undergraduates 48 full-time, 357 part-time. 2% African American, 0.5% Hispanic American.

Freshmen *Admission:* 51 applied, 51 admitted, 49 enrolled.

Faculty *Total:* 33, 6% with terminal degrees.

Costs (2004–05) *Tuition:* state resident $1560 full-time, $65 per credit part-time; nonresident $5496 full-time, $229 per credit part-time.

Admissions Contact Ms. Sharon Bungard, Admissions, Eastern West Virginia Community and Technical College, HC 65 Box 402, Moorefield, WV 26836. *Phone:* 304-434-8000. *Toll-free phone:* 877-982-2322.

FAIRMONT STATE COMMUNITY & TECHNICAL COLLEGE
Fairmont, West Virginia

- **State-supported** 2-year
- **Calendar** semesters
- **Degree** certificates and associate
- **Small-town** 90-acre campus
- **Endowment** $91,000
- **Coed,** 3,355 undergraduate students, 56% full-time, 57% women, 43% men

Undergraduates 1,878 full-time, 1,477 part-time. Students come from 11 states and territories, 5% African American, 1% Asian American or Pacific Islander, 0.6% Hispanic American, 0.5% Native American.

Freshmen *Admission:* 1,267 applied, 1,120 admitted, 513 enrolled.

Faculty *Total:* 242, 17% full-time.

Majors Aeronautical/aerospace engineering technology; American Sign Language (ASL); architectural engineering technology; business/commerce; child development; civil engineering technology; communications technology; drafting/design engineering technologies related; electrical and electronic engineering technologies related; electrical, electronic and communications engineering technology; emergency medical technology (EMT paramedic); finance; food service and dining room management; general studies; graphic communications; mechanical engineering/mechanical technology; nursing (registered nurse training); physician assistant.

Academic Programs *Special study options:* adult/continuing education programs, external degree program, part-time degree program, summer session for credit.

Student Life *Housing Options:* Campus housing is university owned. *Activities and Organizations:* drama/theater group, student-run newspaper, choral group, marching band, national fraternities, national sororities. *Student services:* health clinic, personal/psychological counseling.

Athletics Member NCAA.

Standardized Tests *Required:* SAT I or ACT (for admission). *Required for some:* ACT COMPASS.

Costs (2003–04) *Tuition:* state resident $3130 full-time; nonresident $7038 full-time. *Room and board:* $4846; room only: $2420. Room and board charges vary according to board plan and housing facility. *Payment plan:* installment.

Applying *Options:* common application, electronic application, deferred entrance. *Recommended:* high school transcript, 2.25 letters of recommendation. *Application deadline:* rolling (freshmen), rolling (transfers). *Notification:* continuous (freshmen), continuous (transfers).

Admissions Contact Mr. Douglas Dobbins, Executive Director of Enrollment Services, Fairmont State Community & Technical College, 1201 Locust Avenue, Fairmont, WV 26554. *Phone:* 304-367-4062. *Toll-free phone:* 800-641-5678. *Fax:* 304-367-4584. *E-mail:* fscinfo@mail.fscwv.edu.

▶ **See page 540 for a narrative description.**

HUNTINGTON JUNIOR COLLEGE
Huntington, West Virginia

- **Proprietary** 2-year, founded 1936
- **Calendar** quarters
- **Degree** associate
- **Urban** campus
- **Coed**

Faculty *Student/faculty ratio:* 18:1.

Applying *Required:* high school transcript.

Admissions Contact Mr. James Garrett, Educational Services Director, Huntington Junior College, 900 Fifth Avenue, Huntington, WV 25701-2004. *Phone:* 304-697-7550.

INTERNATIONAL ACADEMY OF DESIGN & TECHNOLOGY
Fairmont, West Virginia

Admissions Contact Mr. Dennis A. Hirsh, President, International Academy of Design & Technology, 2000 Green River Drive, Fairmont, WV 26554-9790. *Phone:* 888-406-8324. *Toll-free phone:* 888-406-8324.

MOUNTAIN STATE COLLEGE
Parkersburg, West Virginia

- **Proprietary** 2-year, founded 1888
- **Calendar** quarters
- **Degree** diplomas and associate
- **Small-town** campus
- **Coed, primarily women,** 150 undergraduate students, 100% full-time, 91% women, 9% men

Undergraduates 150 full-time. 5% African American. *Retention:* 70% of 2002 full-time freshmen returned.

Mountain State College (continued)

Freshmen *Admission:* 29 enrolled.
Faculty *Total:* 11, 64% full-time, 27% with terminal degrees. *Student/faculty ratio:* 17:1.
Majors Accounting and business/management; administrative assistant and secretarial science; computer and information sciences; legal assistant/paralegal; medical/clinical assistant; medical transcription.
Computers on Campus Internet access available.
Student Life *Housing:* college housing not available.
Standardized Tests *Required:* CPAt (for admission).
Costs (2003–04) *Tuition:* $7050 full-time.
Applying *Required:* interview.
Admissions Contact Ms. Linda Craig, Director, Student Services, Mountain State College, 1508 Spring Street, Parkersburg, WV 26101-3993. *Phone:* 304-485-5487. *Toll-free phone:* 800-841-0201. *Fax:* 304-485-3524. *E-mail:* adm@mountainstate.org.

NATIONAL INSTITUTE OF TECHNOLOGY
Cross Lanes, West Virginia

- **Proprietary** 2-year, founded 1938, part of Corinthian Schools, Inc.
- **Calendar** quarters
- **Degree** certificates, diplomas, and associate
- **Small-town** campus
- **Coed,** 520 undergraduate students, 100% full-time, 62% women, 38% men

Undergraduates 520 full-time. Students come from 4 states and territories, 2% are from out of state, 2% African American, 1% Asian American or Pacific Islander, 2% Hispanic American.
Faculty *Total:* 27, 56% full-time.
Majors Electrical, electronic and communications engineering technology; medical/clinical assistant.
Academic Programs *Special study options:* advanced placement credit, internships.
Computers on Campus 140 computers available on campus for general student use. Internet access, at least one staffed computer lab available. Computer purchase or lease plan available.
Student Life *Housing:* college housing not available. *Activities and Organizations:* student-run newspaper.
Costs (2003–04) *Tuition:* $18,470 full-time.
Financial Aid Of all full-time matriculated undergraduates who enrolled, 4 Federal Work-Study jobs (averaging $4000).
Applying *Options:* deferred entrance. *Required:* high school transcript, interview. *Application deadline:* rolling (freshmen), rolling (transfers). *Notification:* continuous (freshmen), continuous (transfers).
Admissions Contact Mrs. Karen Wilkinson, Director of Admissions, National Institute of Technology, 5514 Big Tyler Road, Cross Lanes, WV 25313. *Phone:* 304-776-6290. *Toll-free phone:* 888-741-4271. *Fax:* 304-776-6262.

POTOMAC STATE COLLEGE OF WEST VIRGINIA UNIVERSITY
Keyser, West Virginia

Admissions Contact Ms. Beth Little, Director of Enrollment Services, Potomac State College of West Virginia University, One Grand Central Business Center, Suite 2090, Keyser, WV 26726. *Phone:* 304-788-6820. *Toll-free phone:* 800-262-7332 Ext. 6820. *Fax:* 304-788-6939. *E-mail:* go2psc@mail.wvu.edu.

SOUTHERN WEST VIRGINIA COMMUNITY AND TECHNICAL COLLEGE
Mount Gay, West Virginia

- **State-supported** 2-year, founded 1971, part of State College System of West Virginia
- **Calendar** semesters
- **Degree** certificates and associate
- **Rural** 23-acre campus
- **Coed,** 2,042 undergraduate students, 66% full-time, 67% women, 33% men

Undergraduates 1,340 full-time, 702 part-time. Students come from 2 states and territories, 10% are from out of state, 2% African American, 0.1% Asian American or Pacific Islander, 0.3% Hispanic American, 0.2% Native American, 7% transferred in.
Freshmen *Admission:* 1,465 applied, 1,465 admitted, 437 enrolled. *Average high school GPA:* 2.90.

Faculty *Total:* 163, 39% full-time. *Student/faculty ratio:* 25:1.
Majors Accounting; administrative assistant and secretarial science; automobile/automotive mechanics technology; business administration and management; clinical/medical laboratory technology; communications technology; computer programming (specific applications); criminal justice/law enforcement administration; drafting and design technology; engineering technology; finance; industrial radiologic technology; information science/studies; liberal arts and sciences/liberal studies; nursing (registered nurse training); welding technology.
Academic Programs *Special study options:* academic remediation for entering students, adult/continuing education programs, advanced placement credit, cooperative education, external degree program, part-time degree program, services for LD students, summer session for credit.
Library 70,576 titles, 233 serial subscriptions.
Computers on Campus 92 computers available on campus for general student use. A campuswide network can be accessed from off campus. Internet access, at least one staffed computer lab available.
Student Life *Housing:* college housing not available. *Activities and Organizations:* drama/theater group, student-run television station. *Student services:* personal/psychological counseling.
Standardized Tests *Required for some:* ACT (for placement).
Costs (2004–05) *Tuition:* $68 per credit hour part-time; state resident $1634 full-time; nonresident $6486 full-time, $270 per credit hour part-time.
Financial Aid *Financial aid deadline:* 3/1.
Applying *Options:* early admission, deferred entrance. *Required:* high school transcript. *Application deadline:* rolling (freshmen), rolling (transfers). *Notification:* continuous (freshmen), continuous (transfers).
Admissions Contact Mr. Roy Simmons, Registrar, Southern West Virginia Community and Technical College, PO Box 2900, Mt. Gay, WV 25637. *Phone:* 304-792-7160 Ext. 120. *E-mail:* admissions@southern.wvnet.edu.

VALLEY COLLEGE OF TECHNOLOGY
Martinsburg, West Virginia

- **Proprietary** 2-year, founded 1983
- **Calendar** continuous
- **Degree** certificates and associate
- **Suburban** campus
- **Coed, primarily women,** 47 undergraduate students, 100% full-time, 94% women, 6% men

Undergraduates 47 full-time. 13% African American, 2% Hispanic American, 4% Native American.
Freshmen *Admission:* 40 enrolled.
Faculty *Total:* 6, 67% full-time. *Student/faculty ratio:* 14:1.
Majors Business administration and management.
Costs (2003–04) *Tuition:* $7488 full-time, $208 per credit part-time. *Required fees:* $100 full-time.
Admissions Contact Ms. Leslie C. See, Admissions Director, Valley College of Technology, 2600 Aikens Center, Edwin Miller Boulevard, Martinsburg, WV 25401. *Phone:* 304-263-0979.

WEST VIRGINIA BUSINESS COLLEGE
Nutter Fort, West Virginia

Admissions Contact 116 Pennsylvania Avenue, Nutter Fort, WV 26301.

WEST VIRGINIA BUSINESS COLLEGE
Wheeling, West Virginia

- **Proprietary** 2-year, founded 1881
- **Calendar** quarters
- **Degree** diplomas and associate
- **Urban** 5-acre campus
- **Coed, primarily women,** 56 undergraduate students, 93% full-time, 96% women, 4% men

Undergraduates 52 full-time, 4 part-time. 2% African American.
Freshmen *Admission:* 12 applied, 12 admitted, 10 enrolled.
Faculty *Total:* 10, 100% with terminal degrees. *Student/faculty ratio:* 6:1.
Majors Accounting; administrative assistant and secretarial science; business administration and management; legal assistant/paralegal.
Costs (2004–05) *Tuition:* $15,000 full-time. *Required fees:* $175 full-time.
Admissions Contact Ms. Karen D. Shaw, Director, West Virginia Business College, 1052 Main Street, Wheeling, WV 26003. *Phone:* 304-232-0361. *E-mail:* wbbcwheeling@juno.com.

WEST VIRGINIA JUNIOR COLLEGE
Bridgeport, West Virginia

Admissions Contact Ms. Cheryl Stickley, Executive Assistant, West Virginia Junior College, 176 Thompson Drive, Bridgeport, WV 26330. *Phone:* 304-363-8824.

WEST VIRGINIA JUNIOR COLLEGE
Charleston, West Virginia

Admissions Contact Admission Department, West Virginia Junior College, 1000 Virginia Street East, Charleston, WV 25301-2817. *Phone:* 304-345-2820.

WEST VIRGINIA JUNIOR COLLEGE
Morgantown, West Virginia

- **Proprietary** 2-year, founded 1922
- **Calendar** quarters
- **Degrees** associate (also offers non-degree programs with significant enrollment not reflected in profile)
- **Small-town** campus with easy access to Pittsburgh
- **Coed**

Faculty *Student/faculty ratio:* 14:1.
Applying *Required:* high school transcript, interview. *Recommended:* letters of recommendation.
Admissions Contact Admissions Office, West Virginia Junior College, 148 Willey Street, Morgantown, WV 26505-5521. *Phone:* 304-296-8282.

WEST VIRGINIA NORTHERN COMMUNITY COLLEGE
Wheeling, West Virginia

- **State-supported** 2-year, founded 1972
- **Calendar** semesters
- **Degree** certificates and associate
- **Small-town** campus with easy access to Pittsburgh
- **Endowment** $700,706
- **Coed,** 2,879 undergraduate students, 43% full-time, 65% women, 35% men

Undergraduates 1,239 full-time, 1,640 part-time. Students come from 5 states and territories, 17% are from out of state, 4% African American, 0.5% Asian American or Pacific Islander, 0.4% Hispanic American, 0.3% Native American, 8% transferred in. *Retention:* 51% of 2002 full-time freshmen returned.
Freshmen *Admission:* 606 applied, 391 admitted, 381 enrolled. *Average high school GPA:* 2.80. *Test scores:* SAT verbal scores over 500: 28%; SAT math scores over 500: 11%; ACT scores over 18: 60%; SAT verbal scores over 600: 6%; SAT math scores over 600: 6%; ACT scores over 24: 7%.
Faculty *Total:* 149, 36% full-time, 11% with terminal degrees. *Student/faculty ratio:* 21:1.
Majors Accounting technology and bookkeeping; administrative assistant and secretarial science; applied horticulture; banking and financial support services; business administration and management; computer programming; criminal justice/police science; electrical, electronic and communications engineering technology; health information/medical records technology; heating, air conditioning, ventilation and refrigeration maintenance technology; hospitality administration; industrial technology; information technology; institutional food workers; liberal arts and sciences/liberal studies; nursing (registered nurse training); social work; word processing.
Academic Programs *Special study options:* academic remediation for entering students, accelerated degree program, adult/continuing education programs, advanced placement credit, distance learning, double majors, honors programs, internships, part-time degree program, student-designed majors, summer session for credit.
Library Wheeling B and O Campus Library plus 2 others with 36,650 titles, 188 serial subscriptions, 3,495 audiovisual materials, an OPAC, a Web page.
Computers on Campus 250 computers available on campus for general student use. A campuswide network can be accessed from off campus. Internet access, at least one staffed computer lab available.
Student Life *Housing:* college housing not available. *Campus security:* security personnel during evening and night classes. *Student services:* personal/psychological counseling, women's center.
Athletics *Intramural sports:* basketball M/W, bowling M/W, softball M/W, volleyball M/W.
Standardized Tests *Required:* ACT ASSET (for placement). *Required for some:* SAT I or ACT (for placement).
Costs (2004–05) *Tuition:* state resident $1752 full-time, $73 per credit part-time; nonresident $5592 full-time, $233 per credit part-time. Full-time

tuition and fees vary according to course load and reciprocity agreements. Part-time tuition and fees vary according to course load and reciprocity agreements. *Required fees:* $6 full-time, $3 per term part-time. *Payment plan:* installment. *Waivers:* employees or children of employees.
Financial Aid Of all full-time matriculated undergraduates who enrolled, 35 Federal Work-Study jobs (averaging $1650).
Applying *Options:* common application, electronic application, early admission, deferred entrance. *Required for some:* high school transcript. *Application deadline:* rolling (freshmen), rolling (transfers).
Admissions Contact Ms. Janet M. Fike, Associate Dean of Enrollment Management, West Virginia Northern Community College, 1704 Market Street, Wheeling, WV 26003-3699. *Phone:* 304-233-5900 Ext. 4363. *Fax:* 304-233-5900.

WEST VIRGINIA UNIVERSITY AT PARKERSBURG
Parkersburg, West Virginia

- **State-supported** primarily 2-year, founded 1961
- **Calendar** semesters
- **Degrees** certificates, associate, and bachelor's
- **Small-town** 140-acre campus
- **Coed**

Faculty *Student/faculty ratio:* 17:1.
Standardized Tests *Required:* ACT (for placement).
Costs (2003–04) *Tuition:* state resident $1620 full-time; nonresident $5604 full-time. Full-time tuition and fees vary according to degree level. Part-time tuition and fees vary according to degree level.
Applying *Options:* common application, electronic application, early admission, deferred entrance. *Required for some:* high school transcript.
Admissions Contact Ms. Violet Mosser, Senior Admissions Counselor, West Virginia University at Parkersburg, 300 Campus Drive, Parkersburg, WV 26101. *Phone:* 304-424-8223 Ext. 223. *Toll-free phone:* 800-WVA-WVUP. *Fax:* 304-424-8332.

WISCONSIN

BLACKHAWK TECHNICAL COLLEGE
Janesville, Wisconsin

- **District-supported** 2-year, founded 1968, part of Wisconsin Technical College System
- **Calendar** semesters
- **Degree** associate
- **Rural** 84-acre campus
- **Coed,** 2,627 undergraduate students, 39% full-time, 59% women, 41% men

Undergraduates 1,015 full-time, 1,612 part-time. Students come from 4 states and territories, 6% African American, 0.7% Asian American or Pacific Islander, 3% Hispanic American, 0.4% Native American.
Freshmen *Admission:* 860 enrolled.
Faculty *Total:* 341, 27% full-time.
Majors Accounting; administrative assistant and secretarial science; avionics maintenance technology; computer and information sciences; criminal justice/police science; culinary arts; dental hygiene; electrical, electronic and communications engineering technology; electromechanical technology; fire science; industrial technology; legal administrative assistant/secretary; marketing/marketing management; mechanical design technology; nursing (registered nurse training); physical therapy; radiologic technology/science.
Academic Programs *Special study options:* academic remediation for entering students, accelerated degree program, adult/continuing education programs, advanced placement credit, cooperative education, distance learning, English as a second language, external degree program, independent study, internships, part-time degree program, services for LD students, student-designed majors, summer session for credit.
Library Blackhawk Technical College Library with 25,000 titles, 435 serial subscriptions, an OPAC.
Computers on Campus 180 computers available on campus for general student use. A campuswide network can be accessed. Internet access, online (class) registration, at least one staffed computer lab available.
Student Life *Housing:* college housing not available. *Activities and Organizations:* student-run newspaper. *Student services:* personal/psychological counseling, women's center.

Blackhawk Technical College (continued)

Costs (2004–05) *Tuition:* state resident $76 per credit part-time; nonresident $488 per credit part-time.

Financial Aid Of all full-time matriculated undergraduates who enrolled, 40 Federal Work-Study jobs (averaging $1900).

Applying *Options:* common application, electronic application. *Application fee:* $30. *Required:* high school transcript. *Application deadline:* rolling (freshmen), rolling (transfers). *Notification:* continuous (freshmen), continuous (transfers).

Admissions Contact Ms. Barbara Erlandson, Student Services Manager, Blackhawk Technical College, PO Box 5009, Janesville, WI 53547-5009. *Phone:* 608-757-7713. *Toll-free phone:* 800-472-0024. *Fax:* 608-743-4407.

BRYANT AND STRATTON COLLEGE
Milwaukee, Wisconsin

- **Proprietary** primarily 2-year, founded 1863, part of Bryant and Stratton Business Institute, Inc.
- **Calendar** semesters
- **Degrees** associate and bachelor's
- **Urban** 2-acre campus
- **Coed,** 656 undergraduate students, 61% full-time, 76% women, 24% men

Undergraduates 400 full-time, 256 part-time. Students come from 1 other state, 85% African American, 2% Asian American or Pacific Islander, 1% Hispanic American, 0.3% Native American. *Retention:* 70% of 2002 full-time freshmen returned.

Freshmen *Admission:* 402 applied, 331 admitted. *Average high school GPA:* 2.0.

Faculty *Total:* 69, 12% full-time. *Student/faculty ratio:* 14:1.

Majors Accounting; administrative assistant and secretarial science; business administration, management and operations related; computer and information sciences; legal administrative assistant/secretary; medical administrative assistant and medical secretary; medical/clinical assistant.

Academic Programs *Special study options:* academic remediation for entering students, adult/continuing education programs, advanced placement credit, cooperative education, distance learning, double majors, independent study, internships, part-time degree program, summer session for credit.

Library Bryant and Stratton College Library with 120 serial subscriptions, 100 audiovisual materials.

Computers on Campus 130 computers available on campus for general student use. A campuswide network can be accessed. Internet access, at least one staffed computer lab available.

Student Life *Housing:* college housing not available. *Activities and Organizations:* Phi Beta Lambda, Association of Information Technology Professionals, Allied Health Association, Institute of Management Accountants, Student Advisory Board. *Campus security:* 24-hour emergency response devices and patrols. *Student services:* personal/psychological counseling.

Standardized Tests *Required:* TABE (for admission). *Recommended:* SAT I or ACT (for admission).

Costs (2003–04) *One-time required fee:* $25. *Tuition:* $10,440 full-time, $350 per credit hour part-time. Full-time tuition and fees vary according to class time and course load. Part-time tuition and fees vary according to class time and course load. *Required fees:* $200 full-time, $100 per term part-time. *Payment plan:* installment. *Waivers:* employees or children of employees.

Applying *Application fee:* $25. *Required:* high school transcript. *Required for some:* letters of recommendation, interview. *Recommended:* minimum 2.0 GPA. *Application deadline:* rolling (freshmen), rolling (transfers).

Admissions Contact Ms. Kathryn Cotey, Director of Admissions, Bryant and Stratton College, 310 West Wisconsin Avenue, Milwaukee, WI 53203-2214. *Phone:* 414-276-5200.

CHIPPEWA VALLEY TECHNICAL COLLEGE
Eau Claire, Wisconsin

- **District-supported** 2-year, founded 1912, part of Wisconsin Technical College System
- **Calendar** semesters
- **Degree** certificates, diplomas, and associate
- **Urban** 160-acre campus
- **Coed**

Faculty *Student/faculty ratio:* 12:1.

Student Life *Campus security:* 24-hour emergency response devices, late-night transport/escort service.

Standardized Tests *Required:* ACT COMPASS (for placement). *Required for some:* ACT (for placement).

Costs (2003–04) *Tuition:* Contact college as tuition and fees vary by program.

Financial Aid Of all full-time matriculated undergraduates who enrolled, 218 Federal Work-Study jobs (averaging $943).

Applying *Options:* common application, early admission, deferred entrance. *Application fee:* $30. *Required:* high school transcript. *Required for some:* interview.

Admissions Contact Mr. Timothy Shepardson, Director of Admissions, Chippewa Valley Technical College, 620 West Clairemont Avenue, Eau Claire, WI 54701-6162. *Phone:* 715-833-6245. *Toll-free phone:* 800-547-2882. *Fax:* 715-833-6470.

COLLEGE OF MENOMINEE NATION
Keshena, Wisconsin

- **Independent** 2-year
- **Calendar** semesters
- **Degree** certificates and associate
- **Coed**

Standardized Tests *Required:* TABE (for placement).

Costs (2003–04) *Tuition:* state resident $3584 full-time, $149 per credit part-time.

Financial Aid Of all full-time matriculated undergraduates who enrolled, 10 Federal Work-Study jobs.

Applying *Application fee:* $10.

Admissions Contact Ms. Cynthia Norton, Admissions Representative, College of Menominee Nation, PO Box 1179, Keshena, WI 54135. *Phone:* 715-799-5600 Ext. 3053. *Fax:* 715-799-1326.

FOX VALLEY TECHNICAL COLLEGE
Appleton, Wisconsin

- **State and locally supported** 2-year, founded 1967, part of Wisconsin Technical College System
- **Calendar** semesters
- **Degree** certificates, diplomas, and associate
- **Suburban** 100-acre campus
- **Endowment** $1.3 million
- **Coed**

Faculty *Student/faculty ratio:* 10:1.

Student Life *Campus security:* late-night transport/escort service, 16-hour patrols by trained security personnel.

Standardized Tests *Required:* ACT or ACT ASSET (for placement).

Costs (2003–04) *Tuition:* state resident $2380 full-time, $70 per credit part-time; nonresident $16,652 full-time, $490 per credit part-time. *Required fees:* $306 full-time, $9 per credit part-time.

Financial Aid Of all full-time matriculated undergraduates who enrolled, 165 Federal Work-Study jobs (averaging $2300).

Applying *Options:* common application, electronic application, early admission, deferred entrance. *Application fee:* $30. *Required:* high school transcript.

Admissions Contact Mr. Robert Burdick, Dean of Student Services, Fox Valley Technical College, 1825 North Bluemound Drive, PO Box 2277, Appleton, WI 54912-2277. *Phone:* 920-735-5643. *Fax:* 920-735-2582.

GATEWAY TECHNICAL COLLEGE
Kenosha, Wisconsin

- **State and locally supported** 2-year, founded 1911, part of Wisconsin Technical College System
- **Calendar** semesters
- **Degree** certificates, diplomas, and associate
- **Urban** 10-acre campus with easy access to Chicago and Milwaukee
- **Coed**

Student Life *Campus security:* 24-hour emergency response devices and patrols, late-night transport/escort service.

Standardized Tests *Required:* ACT ASSET or ACT COMPASS (for placement). *Recommended:* ACT (for placement).

Costs (2003–04) *Tuition:* state resident $2100 full-time, $70 per credit part-time; nonresident $14,693 full-time, $490 per credit part-time. Full-time tuition and fees vary according to course load. Part-time tuition and fees vary according to course load. *Required fees:* $239 full-time, $4 per credit part-time. *Payment plans:* installment, deferred payment.

Financial Aid Of all full-time matriculated undergraduates who enrolled, 75 Federal Work-Study jobs (averaging $1500).

Applying *Options:* electronic application, early admission, deferred entrance. *Application fee:* $30. *Required for some:* high school transcript, minimum 2.0 GPA, interview.
Admissions Contact Ms. Susan Roberts, Manager Admissions and Testing, Gateway Technical College, 3520 30th Avenue, Kenosha, WI 53144-1690. *Phone:* 262-564-3224. *Fax:* 262-564-2301. *E-mail:* admissions@gateway.tec.wi.us.

HERZING COLLEGE
Madison, Wisconsin

- **Proprietary** primarily 2-year, founded 1948, part of Herzing Institutes, Inc.
- **Calendar** semesters
- **Degrees** diplomas, associate, and bachelor's
- **Suburban** campus with easy access to Milwaukee
- **Coed, primarily men**

Faculty *Student/faculty ratio:* 13:1.
Student Life *Campus security:* 24-hour emergency response devices.
Costs (2003–04) *Tuition:* $10,000 full-time. Full-time tuition and fees vary according to course level and program. Part-time tuition and fees vary according to course level and program. *Required fees:* $100 full-time.
Financial Aid *Financial aid deadline:* 6/30.
Applying *Options:* common application, electronic application, early admission. *Required:* high school transcript, interview.
Admissions Contact Ms. Renee Herzing, Admissions Director, Herzing College, 5218 East Terrace Drive, Madison, WI 53718. *Phone:* 608-249-6611. *Toll-free phone:* 800-582-1227. *E-mail:* mailbag@msn.herzing.edu.

ITT TECHNICAL INSTITUTE
Green Bay, Wisconsin

- **Proprietary** primarily 2-year, founded 2000, part of ITT Educational Services, Inc.
- **Calendar** quarters
- **Degrees** associate and bachelor's
- **Coed**

Standardized Tests *Required:* (for admission).
Costs (2003–04) *Tuition:* Total Program Cost varies depending on course of study. Consult school catalog.
Applying *Options:* deferred entrance. *Application fee:* $100. *Required:* high school transcript, interview. *Recommended:* letters of recommendation.
Admissions Contact Mr. Raymond Sweetman, ITT Technical Institute, 470 Security Boulevard, Green Bay, WI 54313. *Phone:* 920-662-9000. *Toll-free phone:* 888-884-3626. *Fax:* 920-662-9384.

ITT TECHNICAL INSTITUTE
Greenfield, Wisconsin

- **Proprietary** primarily 2-year, founded 1968, part of ITT Educational Services, Inc.
- **Calendar** quarters
- **Degrees** associate and bachelor's
- **Suburban** campus with easy access to Milwaukee
- **Coed**

Standardized Tests *Required:* Wonderlic aptitude test (for admission).
Costs (2003–04) *Tuition:* Total Program Cost varies depending on course of study. Consult school catalog.
Applying *Options:* deferred entrance. *Application fee:* $100. *Required:* high school transcript, interview. *Recommended:* letters of recommendation.
Admissions Contact Mr. Al Hedin, Director of Recruitment, ITT Technical Institute, 6300 West Layton Avenue, Greenfield, WI 53220. *Phone:* 414-282-9494. *Fax:* 414-282-9698.

LAC COURTE OREILLES OJIBWA COMMUNITY COLLEGE
Hayward, Wisconsin

- **Federally supported** 2-year, founded 1982
- **Calendar** semesters
- **Degree** certificates and associate
- **Rural** 2-acre campus
- **Endowment** $950,616
- **Coed,** 561 undergraduate students, 57% full-time, 71% women, 29% men

Undergraduates 321 full-time, 240 part-time. Students come from 1 other state, 0.7% African American, 0.4% Hispanic American, 75% Native American, 0.2% international.
Freshmen *Admission:* 158 admitted, 158 enrolled.
Faculty *Student/faculty ratio:* 20:1.
Majors Administrative assistant and secretarial science; American Indian/Native American studies; business administration and management; liberal arts and sciences/liberal studies; medical/clinical assistant; natural resources management and policy; nursing (registered nurse training); social work; substance abuse/addiction counseling.
Academic Programs *Special study options:* academic remediation for entering students, adult/continuing education programs, distance learning, double majors, external degree program, honors programs, independent study, part-time degree program.
Library Lac Courte Oreilles Ojibwa Community College Library with 13,800 titles, 100 serial subscriptions, an OPAC.
Computers on Campus 25 computers available on campus for general student use. A campuswide network can be accessed. Internet access, at least one staffed computer lab available.
Student Life *Housing:* college housing not available. *Activities and Organizations:* student association. *Campus security:* 24-hour emergency response devices.
Athletics *Intramural sports:* basketball M, softball W, volleyball M/W, weight lifting M/W.
Standardized Tests *Required:* TABE (for placement).
Financial Aid Of all full-time matriculated undergraduates who enrolled, 15 Federal Work-Study jobs (averaging $1400).
Applying *Options:* common application, early admission. *Application fee:* $10. *Required:* high school transcript. *Application deadline:* rolling (freshmen), rolling (transfers).
Admissions Contact Ms. Annette Wiggins, Registrar, Lac Courte Oreilles Ojibwa Community College, 13466 West Trepania Road, Hayward, WI 54843-2181. *Phone:* 715-634-4790 Ext. 104. *Toll-free phone:* 888-526-6221.

LAKESHORE TECHNICAL COLLEGE
Cleveland, Wisconsin

- **State and locally supported** 2-year, founded 1967, part of Wisconsin Technical College System
- **Calendar** semesters
- **Degree** certificates, diplomas, and associate
- **Rural** 160-acre campus with easy access to Milwaukee
- **Coed,** 3,069 undergraduate students, 26% full-time, 61% women, 39% men

Undergraduates 807 full-time, 2,262 part-time. Students come from 3 states and territories, 2% are from out of state, 0.4% African American, 2% Asian American or Pacific Islander, 2% Hispanic American, 0.5% Native American.
Freshmen *Admission:* 2,151 applied, 1,130 admitted, 839 enrolled.
Faculty *Total:* 318, 33% full-time. *Student/faculty ratio:* 14:1.
Majors Accounting; administrative assistant and secretarial science; computer and information sciences related; computer management; computer programming; computer programming related; computer systems analysis; court reporting; criminal justice/police science; dental hygiene; electrical, electronic and communications engineering technology; electromechanical technology; finance; legal assistant/paralegal; management science; marketing/marketing management; mechanical design technology; medical administrative assistant and medical secretary; nursing (registered nurse training); quality control technology; radiologic technology/science.
Academic Programs *Special study options:* academic remediation for entering students, accelerated degree program, adult/continuing education programs, advanced placement credit, cooperative education, distance learning, double majors, English as a second language, external degree program, independent study, internships, part-time degree program, services for LD students, student-designed majors, summer session for credit.
Library 15,749 titles, 220 serial subscriptions, 9,931 audiovisual materials, an OPAC.
Computers on Campus 720 computers available on campus for general student use. A campuswide network can be accessed. Internet access, at least one staffed computer lab available.
Student Life *Housing:* college housing not available. *Activities and Organizations:* student government, Business Professionals of America, Police Science Club, Lakeshore Student Nurse Association, Dairy Herd Club. *Campus security:* 24-hour patrols. *Student services:* health clinic, personal/psychological counseling.
Standardized Tests *Required:* SAT I or ACT (for admission), ACCUPLACER/ACT ASSET (for admission).
Costs (2003–04) *Tuition:* state resident $2110 full-time, $70 per credit part-time; nonresident $16,990 full-time, $540 per credit part-time. Full-time tuition and fees vary according to course load and program. Part-time tuition and

Lakeshore Technical College (continued)

fees vary according to course load and program. *Required fees:* $270 full-time, $7 per credit part-time. *Payment plan:* deferred payment.

Financial Aid Of all full-time matriculated undergraduates who enrolled, 37 Federal Work-Study jobs.

Applying *Options:* common application, electronic application, early admission, deferred entrance. *Application fee:* $30. *Required for some:* high school transcript, interview. *Application deadline:* rolling (freshmen), rolling (transfers). *Notification:* continuous (freshmen), continuous (transfers).

Admissions Contact Ms. Donna Gorzelitz, Enrollment Specialist, Lakeshore Technical College, 1290 North Avenue, Cleveland, WI 53015. *Phone:* 920-693-1339. *Toll-free phone:* 888-GO TO LTC. *Fax:* 920-693-3561. *E-mail:* enroll@ltc.tec.wi.us.

MADISON AREA TECHNICAL COLLEGE
Madison, Wisconsin

- **District-supported** 2-year, founded 1911, part of Wisconsin Technical College System
- **Calendar** semesters
- **Degree** certificates, diplomas, and associate
- **Urban** 150-acre campus
- **Coed**

Student Life *Campus security:* 24-hour emergency response devices and patrols, late-night transport/escort service.

Athletics Member NJCAA.

Standardized Tests *Required for some:* ACT (for admission).

Financial Aid Of all full-time matriculated undergraduates who enrolled, 60 Federal Work-Study jobs (averaging $2000). 240 state and other part-time jobs (averaging $2000).

Applying *Options:* early admission. *Application fee:* $25. *Required for some:* high school transcript.

Admissions Contact Ms. Maureen Menendez, Interim Admissions Administrator, Madison Area Technical College, 3550 Anderson Street, Madison, WI 53704-2599. *Phone:* 608-246-6212.

MADISON MEDIA INSTITUTE
Madison, Wisconsin

Admissions Contact Mr. Chris K Hutchings, President / Director, Madison Media Institute, 2702 Agriculture Drive, Suite 1, Madison, WI 53718. *Phone:* 608-663-2000. *Toll-free phone:* 800-236-4997.

MID-STATE TECHNICAL COLLEGE
Wisconsin Rapids, Wisconsin

- **State and locally supported** 2-year, founded 1917, part of Wisconsin Technical College System
- **Calendar** semesters
- **Degree** certificates, diplomas, and associate
- **Small-town** 155-acre campus
- **Endowment** $1.2 million
- **Coed**

Athletics Member NJCAA.

Standardized Tests *Required:* ACT ASSET (for placement). *Recommended:* SAT I or ACT (for placement).

Costs (2003–04) *Tuition:* state resident $1680 full-time, $70 per credit part-time; nonresident $12,480 full-time, $520 per credit part-time.

Financial Aid Of all full-time matriculated undergraduates who enrolled, 315 Federal Work-Study jobs (averaging $2000).

Applying *Options:* electronic application, early admission, deferred entrance. *Application fee:* $25. *Required:* high school transcript.

Admissions Contact Ms. Carole Prochnow, Admissions Assistant, Mid-State Technical College, 500 32nd Street North, Wisconsin Rapids, WI 54494-5599. *Phone:* 715-422-5444. *Toll-free phone:* 888-575-6782. *Fax:* 715-422-5440.

MILWAUKEE AREA TECHNICAL COLLEGE
Milwaukee, Wisconsin

- **District-supported** 2-year, founded 1912, part of Wisconsin Technical College System
- **Calendar** semesters
- **Degree** certificates, diplomas, and associate
- **Urban** campus
- **Coed,** 56,862 undergraduate students

Freshmen *Admission:* 11,000 applied, 11,000 admitted.

Faculty *Total:* 1,946, 32% full-time. *Student/faculty ratio:* 16:1.

Majors Accounting technology and bookkeeping; administrative assistant and secretarial science; agricultural business and management; automobile/automotive mechanics technology; baking and pastry arts; barbering; biomedical technology; business administration and management; business, management, and marketing related; cardiovascular technology; chemical engineering; child development; civil engineering technology; clinical/medical laboratory technology; commercial and advertising art; communications technology; computer and information sciences related; computer graphics; computer/information technology services administration related; computer programming related; computer programming (specific applications); computer programming (vendor/product certification); computer science; computer systems analysis; construction engineering technology; consumer merchandising/retailing management; cooking and related culinary arts; cosmetology; cosmetology and personal grooming arts related; criminal justice/law enforcement administration; criminal justice/police science; culinary arts; data entry/microcomputer applications; data processing and data processing technology; dental assisting; dental hygiene; dietetics; dietetic technician; drafting and design technology; e-commerce; educational/instructional media design; electrical, electronic and communications engineering technology; electrical/electronics equipment installation and repair; electrocardiograph technology; electromechanical technology; environmental engineering technology; environmental health; fashion merchandising; film/cinema studies; finance; fire science; food services technology; funeral service and mortuary science; funeral service and mortuary science related; furniture design and manufacturing; graphic and printing equipment operation/production; hair styling and hair design; health unit coordinator/ward clerk; heating, air conditioning and refrigeration technology; heating, air conditioning, ventilation and refrigeration maintenance technology; hospitality and recreation marketing; hotel/motel administration; human services; hydrology and water resources science; industrial design; industrial radiologic technology; industrial technology; information technology; landscaping and groundskeeping; legal administrative assistant/secretary; legal assistant/paralegal; liberal arts and sciences/liberal studies; machine tool technology; marketing/marketing management; mechanical engineering/mechanical technology; medical administrative assistant and medical secretary; music; nursing (licensed practical/vocational nurse training); nursing (registered nurse training); occupational therapy; opticianry; photography; physical therapy; pre-engineering; publishing; radio and television broadcasting technology; real estate; respiratory care therapy; substance abuse/addiction counseling; survey technology; system administration; tool and die technology; tourism and travel services marketing; transportation management; transportation technology; web/multimedia management and webmaster; welding technology; word processing.

Academic Programs *Special study options:* academic remediation for entering students, adult/continuing education programs, advanced placement credit, cooperative education, distance learning, double majors, English as a second language, external degree program, freshman honors college, honors programs, independent study, internships, off-campus study, part-time degree program, services for LD students, student-designed majors, summer session for credit.

Library William F. Rasche Library plus 4 others with 60,847 titles, 856 serial subscriptions, an OPAC.

Computers on Campus 1000 computers available on campus for general student use. A campuswide network can be accessed. Internet access, online (class) registration, at least one staffed computer lab available.

Student Life *Housing:* college housing not available. *Activities and Organizations:* student-run newspaper, television station, choral group. *Campus security:* 24-hour emergency response devices and patrols, student patrols, late-night transport/escort service. *Student services:* personal/psychological counseling, women's center, legal services.

Athletics Member NJCAA. *Intercollegiate sports:* baseball M/W, basketball M/W, bowling M/W, cross-country running M/W, golf M/W, soccer M, softball M/W, tennis M/W, track and field M/W, volleyball W. *Intramural sports:* badminton M/W, baseball M/W, basketball M, bowling M/W, soccer M/W, table tennis M/W, tennis M/W, volleyball M/W.

Standardized Tests *Required:* ACCUPLACER (for admission).

Costs (2004–05) *Tuition:* state resident $2240 full-time, $76 per credit hour part-time; nonresident $15,680 full-time, $495 per credit hour part-time. Full-time tuition and fees vary according to course level and program. Part-time tuition and fees vary according to course level and program. *Payment plan:* installment.

Financial Aid Of all full-time matriculated undergraduates who enrolled, 300 Federal Work-Study jobs (averaging $3900).

Applying *Options:* common application, electronic application. *Application fee:* $30. *Required:* high school transcript. *Application deadline:* rolling (freshmen), rolling (transfers). *Notification:* continuous until 8/20 (freshmen), continuous until 8/20 (transfers).

Admissions Contact Mr. Robert Bullock, Director of Admissions, Milwaukee Area Technical College, 700 West State Street, Milwaukee, WI 53233. *Phone:* 414-297-6274. *Fax:* 414-297-6371. *E-mail:* apply@matc.edu.

MORAINE PARK TECHNICAL COLLEGE
Fond du Lac, Wisconsin

- **State and locally supported** 2-year, founded 1967, part of Wisconsin Technical College System
- **Calendar** semesters
- **Degree** certificates, diplomas, and associate
- **Small-town** 40-acre campus with easy access to Milwaukee
- **Endowment** $21,500
- **Coed,** 7,277 undergraduate students, 19% full-time, 52% women, 48% men

Undergraduates 1,354 full-time, 5,923 part-time. Students come from 5 states and territories, 1% are from out of state, 5% African American, 0.6% Asian American or Pacific Islander, 2% Hispanic American, 0.7% Native American, 0.4% transferred in.

Freshmen *Admission:* 1,606 applied, 1,606 admitted, 570 enrolled.

Faculty *Total:* 555, 28% full-time.

Majors Accounting; administrative assistant and secretarial science; agriculture; automobile/automotive mechanics technology; child guidance; civil engineering technology; commercial and advertising art; computer engineering; computer engineering technology; computer programming; corrections; culinary arts; data processing and data processing technology; drafting and design technology; electromechanical technology; emergency medical technology (EMT paramedic); food science; health information/medical records administration; hotel/motel administration; hydrology and water resources science; industrial technology; machine tool technology; marketing/marketing management; mechanical design technology; medical administrative assistant and medical secretary; nursing (registered nurse training); substance abuse/addiction counseling.

Academic Programs *Special study options:* academic remediation for entering students, accelerated degree program, adult/continuing education programs, advanced placement credit, distance learning, English as a second language, external degree program, independent study, internships, part-time degree program, services for LD students, summer session for credit.

Library Moraine Park Technical College Library/Learning Resource Center with 32,166 titles, 630 serial subscriptions, 13,330 audiovisual materials, an OPAC, a Web page.

Computers on Campus A campuswide network can be accessed. Internet access, online (class) registration, at least one staffed computer lab available.

Student Life *Housing:* college housing not available. *Activities and Organizations:* Student Programming Board, student government, Corrections Club, HVAC Club, Food Service Executives. *Campus security:* 24-hour emergency response devices. *Student services:* personal/psychological counseling, women's center.

Athletics *Intramural sports:* bowling M/W, volleyball M/W.

Standardized Tests *Required:* ACT ASSET, ACCUPLACER (for admission). *Required for some:* ACT (for admission).

Costs (2004–05) *Tuition:* state resident $2280 full-time, $76 per credit part-time; nonresident $16,923 full-time, $564 per credit part-time. *Required fees:* $114 full-time, $4 per credit part-time.

Financial Aid Of all full-time matriculated undergraduates who enrolled, 47 Federal Work-Study jobs (averaging $989).

Applying *Options:* electronic application, deferred entrance. *Application fee:* $30. *Required:* interview. *Recommended:* high school transcript. *Application deadline:* rolling (freshmen), rolling (transfers). *Notification:* continuous (freshmen), continuous (transfers).

Admissions Contact Ms. Karen Jarvis, Student Services, Moraine Park Technical College, 235 North National Ave, PO Box 1940, Fond du Lac, WI 54936-1940. *Phone:* 920-924-3200. *Toll-free phone:* 800-472-4554. *Fax:* 920-924-3421.

NICOLET AREA TECHNICAL COLLEGE
Rhinelander, Wisconsin

- **State and locally supported** 2-year, founded 1968, part of Wisconsin Technical College System
- **Calendar** semesters
- **Degree** certificates, diplomas, and associate
- **Rural** 280-acre campus
- **Coed**

Student Life *Campus security:* 24-hour emergency response devices.

Athletics Member NJCAA.

Standardized Tests *Recommended:* ACT (for admission).

Costs (2003–04) *Tuition:* state resident $2328 full-time, $97 per credit part-time; nonresident $9600 full-time, $300 per credit part-time.

Applying *Options:* electronic application, early admission. *Application fee:* $25. *Required:* essay or personal statement, high school transcript, minimum 2.0 GPA.

Admissions Contact Ms. Susan Kordula, Director of Admissions and Marketing, Nicolet Area Technical College, Box 518, Rhinelander, WI 54501-0518. *Phone:* 715-365-4451. *Toll-free phone:* 800-544-3039 Ext. 4451. *Fax:* 715-365-4411. *E-mail:* inquire@nicolet.tec.wi.us.

NORTHCENTRAL TECHNICAL COLLEGE
Wausau, Wisconsin

- **District-supported** 2-year, founded 1912, part of Wisconsin Technical College System
- **Calendar** semesters
- **Degree** certificates, diplomas, and associate
- **Rural** 96-acre campus
- **Endowment** $1.4 million
- **Coed,** 3,734 undergraduate students, 34% full-time, 61% women, 39% men

Undergraduates 1,276 full-time, 2,458 part-time. Students come from 3 states and territories, 2 other countries, 1% are from out of state, 0.1% African American, 2% Asian American or Pacific Islander, 0.5% Hispanic American, 1% Native American, 0.6% international, 4% transferred in.

Freshmen *Admission:* 708 enrolled.

Faculty *Total:* 172, 88% full-time. *Student/faculty ratio:* 13:1.

Majors Accounting; administrative assistant and secretarial science; architectural engineering technology; automobile/automotive mechanics technology; business administration and management; criminal justice/police science; dental hygiene; drafting and design technology; electrical, electronic and communications engineering technology; electromechanical technology; graphic and printing equipment operation/production; human services; industrial radiologic technology; industrial technology; information science/studies; kindergarten/preschool education; laser and optical technology; legal administrative assistant/secretary; machine tool technology; marketing/marketing management; mechanical design technology; medical administrative assistant and medical secretary; nursing (licensed practical/vocational nurse training); nursing (registered nurse training); radiologic technology/science; sign language interpretation and translation.

Academic Programs *Special study options:* academic remediation for entering students, adult/continuing education programs, advanced placement credit, distance learning, double majors, English as a second language, independent study, internships, part-time degree program, services for LD students, student-designed majors, summer session for credit.

Library Northcentral Technical College, Wausau Campus plus 1 other with 30,000 titles, 400 serial subscriptions, an OPAC, a Web page.

Computers on Campus 1200 computers available on campus for general student use. A campuswide network can be accessed from off campus. Internet access, at least one staffed computer lab available.

Student Life *Housing:* college housing not available. *Activities and Organizations:* student-run newspaper, Student Governing Board, International Club, Habitat for Humanity, Nursing Club, Delta Epsilon Chi (marketing club). *Campus security:* 24-hour emergency response devices, late-night transport/escort service. *Student services:* health clinic, personal/psychological counseling, women's center.

Athletics *Intramural sports:* badminton M/W, basketball M/W, bowling M/W, racquetball M/W, softball M/W, table tennis M/W, tennis M/W, volleyball M/W.

Standardized Tests *Required for some:* ACCUPLACER.

Costs (2003–04) *Tuition:* state resident $2670 full-time, $70 per credit part-time; nonresident $16,765 full-time, $490 per credit part-time. *Required fees:* $115 full-time, $4 per credit part-time.

Financial Aid Of all full-time matriculated undergraduates who enrolled, 366 Federal Work-Study jobs (averaging $2000).

Applying *Options:* common application, electronic application, early admission, deferred entrance. *Application fee:* $25. *Required:* high school transcript. *Required for some:* interview. *Application deadline:* rolling (freshmen), rolling (transfers). *Notification:* continuous (freshmen), continuous (transfers).

Admissions Contact Ms. Carolyn Michalski, Team Leader, Student Services, Northcentral Technical College, 1000 West Campus Drive, Wausau, WI 54401-1899. *Phone:* 715-675-3331 Ext. 4285. *Fax:* 715-675-9776.

NORTHEAST WISCONSIN TECHNICAL COLLEGE
Green Bay, Wisconsin

- **State and locally supported** 2-year, founded 1913, part of Wisconsin Technical College System
- **Calendar** semesters
- **Degree** certificates, diplomas, and associate
- **Suburban** 192-acre campus
- **Coed,** 8,760 undergraduate students, 34% full-time, 60% women, 40% men

Northeast Wisconsin Technical College (continued)

Undergraduates 3,001 full-time, 5,759 part-time. Students come from 3 states and territories, 89% are from out of state, 0.8% African American, 1% Asian American or Pacific Islander, 0.9% Hispanic American, 3% Native American.

Freshmen *Admission:* 4,258 applied, 1,978 admitted, 1,075 enrolled.

Faculty *Total:* 2,340, 11% full-time. *Student/faculty ratio:* 39:1.

Majors Accounting; accounting related; accounting technology and bookkeeping; administrative assistant and secretarial science; agribusiness; agricultural business and management; agricultural mechanization; agriculture; apparel and accessories marketing; architectural engineering technology; autobody/collision and repair technology; automobile/automotive mechanics technology; automotive engineering technology; business administration and management; business administration, management and operations related; business, management, and marketing related; carpentry; child care and support services management; civil engineering technology; clinical/medical laboratory technology; communications technologies and support services related; computer and information sciences and support services related; computer programming; corrections; criminal justice/police science; data processing and data processing technology; dental assisting; dental hygiene; diesel mechanics technology; drafting and design technology; electrical, electronic and communications engineering technology; electromechanical technology; emergency medical technology (EMT paramedic); environmental studies; farm and ranch management; fashion merchandising; finance; finance and financial management services related; fire science; fire services administration; health information/medical records technology; heating, air conditioning and refrigeration technology; heating, air conditioning, ventilation and refrigeration maintenance technology; heavy/industrial equipment maintenance technologies related; industrial design; industrial technology; instrumentation technology; legal administrative assistant/secretary; legal assistant/paralegal; lineworker; logistics and materials management; machine shop technology; machine tool technology; marine maintenance and ship repair technology; marketing/marketing management; mass communication/media; mechanical design technology; mechanical drafting and CAD/CADD; mechanical engineering/mechanical technology; mechanic and repair technologies related; medical administrative assistant and medical secretary; medical/clinical assistant; medical office management; merchandising, sales, and marketing operations related (general); nursing assistant/aide and patient care assistant; nursing (licensed practical/vocational nurse training); nursing (registered nurse training); office occupations and clerical services; petroleum technology; physical therapist assistant; physical therapy; precision metal working related; precision production related; precision systems maintenance and repair technologies related; quality control technology; respiratory care therapy; surgical technology; systems science and theory; telecommunications; tourism and travel services management; transportation technology; vehicle and vehicle parts and accessories marketing; watchmaking and jewelrymaking; welding technology.

Academic Programs *Special study options:* academic remediation for entering students, accelerated degree program, adult/continuing education programs, advanced placement credit, distance learning, English as a second language, part-time degree program, services for LD students, student-designed majors, summer session for credit.

Library 22,250 titles, 450 serial subscriptions.

Computers on Campus 395 computers available on campus for general student use. Internet access, at least one staffed computer lab available.

Student Life *Housing:* college housing not available. *Activities and Organizations:* Skills USA, Wisconsin Marketing Management Association, Business Professionals of America, Auto Club, Architectural Club. *Campus security:* 24-hour emergency response devices, late-night transport/escort service. *Student services:* health clinic, personal/psychological counseling.

Athletics *Intramural sports:* basketball W, volleyball M/W.

Standardized Tests *Required for some:* SAT I or ACT (for placement).

Costs (2004–05) *Tuition:* state resident $2205 full-time, $74 per credit part-time; nonresident $13,222 full-time, $441 per credit part-time. *Required fees:* $375 full-time, $8 per credit part-time. *Payment plan:* installment.

Financial Aid Of all full-time matriculated undergraduates who enrolled, 44 Federal Work-Study jobs (averaging $1500).

Applying *Options:* early admission. *Application fee:* $30. *Required for some:* high school transcript. *Application deadline:* rolling (freshmen). *Notification:* continuous (transfers).

Admissions Contact Ms. Heather Hill, Program Enrollment Team Supervisor, Northeast Wisconsin Technical College, 2740 West Mason Street, PO Box 19042, Green Bay, WI 54307-9042. *Phone:* 920-498-5612. *Toll-free phone:* 800-498-5444 (in-state); 800-422-6982 (out-of-state). *Fax:* 920-498-6882. *E-mail:* heather.hill@nwtc.edu.

SOUTHWEST WISCONSIN TECHNICAL COLLEGE
Fennimore, Wisconsin

- **State and locally supported** 2-year, founded 1967, part of Wisconsin Technical College System
- **Calendar** semesters
- **Degree** certificates, diplomas, and associate
- **Rural** 53-acre campus
- **Endowment** $935,000
- **Coed**

Faculty *Student/faculty ratio:* 13:1.

Standardized Tests *Required:* TABE (for placement).

Costs (2003–04) *Tuition:* state resident $2520 full-time, $70 per credit part-time; nonresident $17,631 full-time, $490 per credit part-time. Full-time tuition and fees vary according to program. Part-time tuition and fees vary according to program. *Required fees:* $216 full-time, $6 per credit part-time. *Room and board:* room only: $2425. *Payment plans:* installment, deferred payment.

Applying *Options:* electronic application, early admission. *Application fee:* $30. *Required:* high school transcript, interview.

Admissions Contact Ms. Kathy Kreul, Admissions, Southwest Wisconsin Technical College, 1800 Bronson Boulevard, Fennimore, WI 53813. *Phone:* 608-822-3262 Ext. 2355. *Toll-free phone:* 800-362-3322 Ext. 2355. *Fax:* 608-822-6019. *E-mail:* kkreul@southwest.tec.wi.us.

UNIVERSITY OF WISCONSIN-BARABOO/ SAUK COUNTY
Baraboo, Wisconsin

- **State-supported** 2-year, founded 1968, part of University of Wisconsin System
- **Calendar** semesters
- **Degree** associate
- **Small-town** 68-acre campus
- **Coed,** 566 undergraduate students, 58% full-time, 57% women, 43% men

Undergraduates 331 full-time, 235 part-time. Students come from 2 states and territories, 3 other countries, 1% are from out of state, 0.9% African American, 1% Asian American or Pacific Islander, 2% Hispanic American, 2% Native American, 0.4% international.

Faculty *Total:* 42, 45% full-time, 50% with terminal degrees. *Student/faculty ratio:* 21:1.

Majors Liberal arts and sciences/liberal studies.

Academic Programs *Special study options:* academic remediation for entering students, advanced placement credit, distance learning, external degree program, honors programs, independent study, off-campus study, part-time degree program, services for LD students, student-designed majors, study abroad, summer session for credit.

Library T. N. Savides Library with 45,000 titles, 300 serial subscriptions, 940 audiovisual materials, an OPAC.

Computers on Campus 45 computers available on campus for general student use. A campuswide network can be accessed from off campus that provide access to financial aid application. Internet access, online (class) registration, at least one staffed computer lab available.

Student Life *Housing:* college housing not available. *Activities and Organizations:* drama/theater group, student-run newspaper, choral group, Student Government Association, chorus and band, dance team, Gaming Club, Business Club.

Athletics Member NJCAA. *Intercollegiate sports:* basketball M, cross-country running M/W, golf M/W, soccer M/W, tennis M/W, volleyball W. *Intramural sports:* basketball W, bowling M/W, racquetball M/W, softball M/W, table tennis M/W, volleyball M/W, weight lifting M/W.

Standardized Tests *Required:* SAT I or ACT (for admission).

Costs (2003–04) *Tuition:* state resident $3461 full-time, $144 per credit part-time; nonresident $12,162 full-time, $507 per credit part-time. Part-time tuition and fees vary according to course load. *Payment plans:* installment, deferred payment. *Waivers:* senior citizens.

Applying *Options:* electronic application, early admission, deferred entrance. *Application fee:* $35. *Required:* high school transcript. *Required for some:* interview. *Application deadline:* rolling (freshmen), rolling (transfers). *Notification:* continuous until 8/31 (freshmen), continuous until 8/31 (transfers).

Admissions Contact Ms. Jan Gerlach, Assistant Director of Student Services, University of Wisconsin-Baraboo/Sauk County, 1006 Connie Road, Baraboo, WI 53913-1015. *Phone:* 608-356-8724 Ext. 270. *Fax:* 608-356-4074. *E-mail:* boouinfo@uwc.edu.

UNIVERSITY OF WISCONSIN-BARRON COUNTY
Rice Lake, Wisconsin

- **State-supported** 2-year, founded 1966, part of University of Wisconsin System

- **Calendar** semesters
- **Degree** associate
- **Small-town** 142-acre campus
- **Coed,** 644 undergraduate students, 49% full-time, 59% women, 41% men

Undergraduates   318 full-time, 326 part-time. Students come from 5 states and territories, 1 other country, 0.5% African American, 0.9% Asian American or Pacific Islander, 0.8% Hispanic American, 0.8% Native American.

Freshmen   *Admission:* 299 applied, 293 admitted.

Faculty   *Total:* 25.

Majors   Liberal arts and sciences/liberal studies.

Academic Programs   *Special study options:* academic remediation for entering students, adult/continuing education programs, advanced placement credit, distance learning, English as a second language, independent study, internships, off-campus study, part-time degree program, services for LD students, summer session for credit.

Library   Main Library plus 1 other with 39,479 titles, 233 serial subscriptions, an OPAC.

Computers on Campus   50 computers available on campus for general student use. Internet access, at least one staffed computer lab available.

Student Life   *Housing:* college housing not available. *Activities and Organizations:* drama/theater group, student-run newspaper, choral group, Phi Theta Kappa, student government, Encore, Delta Psi Omega, Sociology Club. *Student services:* health clinic.

Athletics   Member NJCAA. *Intercollegiate sports:* baseball M, basketball M/W, golf M/W, volleyball W. *Intramural sports:* football M/W, softball M/W, table tennis M/W, volleyball M/W.

Standardized Tests   *Required:* SAT I or ACT (for placement).

Costs (2003–04)   *Tuition:* state resident $3200 full-time, $133 per credit part-time; nonresident $11,900 full-time, $495 per credit part-time. Full-time tuition and fees vary according to reciprocity agreements. Part-time tuition and fees vary according to reciprocity agreements. *Required fees:* $328 full-time, $14 per credit part-time. *Payment plan:* installment.

Applying   *Options:* electronic application, early admission, deferred entrance. *Application fee:* $35. *Required:* high school transcript. *Application deadlines:* 9/2 (freshmen), 9/2 (transfers). *Notification:* continuous (freshmen), continuous (transfers).

Admissions Contact   Ms. June Brunette, Program Assistant, University of Wisconsin-Barron County, 1800 College Drive, Rice Lake, WI 54868-2497. *Phone:* 715-234-8176 Ext. 430.

UNIVERSITY OF WISCONSIN-FOND DU LAC
Fond du Lac, Wisconsin

Admissions Contact   Ms. Linda A. Reiss, Director of Student Services, University of Wisconsin-Fond du Lac, 400 University Drive, Fond du Lac, WI 54935-2950. *Phone:* 920-929-3606. *E-mail:* lreiss@uwc.edu.

UNIVERSITY OF WISCONSIN-FOX VALLEY
Menasha, Wisconsin

- **State-supported** 2-year, founded 1933, part of University of Wisconsin System
- **Calendar** semesters
- **Degree** associate
- **Urban** 33-acre campus
- **Coed**

Athletics   Member NJCAA.

Standardized Tests   *Required:* ACT (for admission).

Applying   *Options:* common application, early admission. *Required:* high school transcript.

Admissions Contact   Ms. Rhonda Uschan, Director of Student Services, University of Wisconsin-Fox Valley, 1478 Midway Road, Menasha, WI 54952. *Phone:* 920-832-2620. *Toll-free phone:* 888-INFOUWC. *E-mail:* foxinfo@uwc.edu.

UNIVERSITY OF WISCONSIN-MANITOWOC
Manitowoc, Wisconsin

- **State-supported** 2-year, founded 1935, part of University of Wisconsin System

- **Calendar** semesters
- **Degree** associate
- **Small-town** 50-acre campus with easy access to Milwaukee
- **Coed,** 635 undergraduate students, 71% full-time, 55% women, 45% men

Undergraduates   451 full-time, 184 part-time. Students come from 3 states and territories, 0.2% African American, 4% Asian American or Pacific Islander, 0.9% Hispanic American, 0.3% Native American.

Freshmen   *Admission:* 320 applied, 290 admitted. *Test scores:* ACT scores over 18: 87%; ACT scores over 24: 27%; ACT scores over 30: 2%.

Faculty   *Total:* 26, 73% full-time. *Student/faculty ratio:* 21:1.

Majors   Liberal arts and sciences/liberal studies.

Academic Programs   *Special study options:* academic remediation for entering students, adult/continuing education programs, advanced placement credit, distance learning, off-campus study, part-time degree program, services for LD students, student-designed majors, summer session for credit.

Library   25,750 titles, 150 serial subscriptions, an OPAC.

Computers on Campus   50 computers available on campus for general student use. A campuswide network can be accessed from off campus. At least one staffed computer lab available.

Student Life   *Housing:* college housing not available. *Activities and Organizations:* drama/theater group, student-run newspaper, choral group, Business Club, Drama Club, Music Club, Phi Kappa Theta, Environmental Awareness. *Student services:* personal/psychological counseling.

Athletics   *Intercollegiate sports:* basketball M/W, golf M, tennis M/W, volleyball W.

Standardized Tests   *Required:* SAT I or ACT (for admission).

Costs (2004–05)   *Tuition:* state resident $3870 full-time, $161 per credit part-time; nonresident $12,300 full-time, $516 per credit part-time. *Payment plan:* installment.

Applying   *Options:* electronic application, early admission. *Application fee:* $35. *Required:* high school transcript. *Notification:* continuous until 7/1 (freshmen), continuous until 7/1 (transfers).

Admissions Contact   Dr. Michael A. Herrity, Director of Student Services, University of Wisconsin-Manitowoc, 705 Viebahn Street, Manitowoc, WI 54220-6699. *Phone:* 920-683-4708. *E-mail:* mherrity@uwc.edu.

UNIVERSITY OF WISCONSIN-MARATHON COUNTY
Wausau, Wisconsin

- **State-supported** 2-year, founded 1933, part of University of Wisconsin System
- **Calendar** semesters
- **Degree** associate
- **Small-town** 7-acre campus
- **Coed,** 1,295 undergraduate students

Undergraduates   0.7% African American, 8% Asian American or Pacific Islander, 0.5% Hispanic American, 0.3% Native American, 16% live on campus. *Retention:* 100% of 2002 full-time freshmen returned.

Freshmen   *Admission:* 1,187 applied, 790 admitted. *Average high school GPA:* 2.80.

Faculty   *Total:* 81, 72% full-time. *Student/faculty ratio:* 24:1.

Majors   Liberal arts and sciences/liberal studies.

Academic Programs   *Special study options:* academic remediation for entering students, adult/continuing education programs, advanced placement credit, honors programs, off-campus study, part-time degree program, student-designed majors, study abroad, summer session for credit. *ROTC:* Army (c).

Library   University of Wisconsin-Marathon Library with 37,000 titles, 150 serial subscriptions, an OPAC, a Web page.

Computers on Campus   50 computers available on campus for general student use. A campuswide network can be accessed. Internet access, at least one staffed computer lab available.

Student Life   *Housing Options:* coed. Campus housing is university owned. *Activities and Organizations:* drama/theater group, student-run newspaper, choral group, Fiercely Independent Theatre, Ski Club, Ten Percent Society, Unity, Tempo. *Campus security:* 24-hour emergency response devices, controlled dormitory access. *Student services:* personal/psychological counseling.

Athletics   Member NJCAA. *Intercollegiate sports:* basketball M/W, golf M/W, soccer M/W, tennis M/W, volleyball W. *Intramural sports:* archery M/W, badminton M/W, basketball M/W, bowling M/W, cross-country running M/W, fencing M/W, football M/W, golf M/W, racquetball M/W, skiing (cross-country) M/W, skiing (downhill) M/W, soccer M/W, squash M/W, swimming M/W, table tennis M/W, tennis M/W, volleyball M/W, water polo M/W, weight lifting M/W.

Standardized Tests   *Required:* ACT (for admission).

Costs (2003–04)   *Tuition:* state resident $3406 full-time; nonresident $12,106 full-time. *Required fees:* $25 full-time. *Room and board:* $3400.

University of Wisconsin-Marathon County (continued)

Applying *Options:* common application, electronic application, early admission, deferred entrance. *Application fee:* $35. *Required for some:* interview. *Recommended:* minimum 2.0 GPA. *Application deadline:* rolling (transfers).

Admissions Contact Dr. Nolan Beck, Director of Student Services, University of Wisconsin-Marathon County, 518 South Seventh Avenue, Wausau, WI 54401-5396. *Phone:* 715-261-6238. *Toll-free phone:* 888-367-8962. *Fax:* 715-848-3568.

UNIVERSITY OF WISCONSIN-MARINETTE

Marinette, Wisconsin

- **State-supported** 2-year, founded 1965, part of University of Wisconsin System
- **Calendar** semesters
- **Degree** associate
- **Small-town** 36-acre campus
- **Endowment** $200,000
- **Coed**

Faculty *Student/faculty ratio:* 24:1.

Standardized Tests *Recommended:* SAT I or ACT (for admission).

Applying *Options:* electronic application. *Application fee:* $35. *Required:* high school transcript.

Admissions Contact Ms. Cynthia M. Bailey, Director of Student Services, University of Wisconsin-Marinette, 750 West Bay Shore, Marinette, WI 54143-4299. *Phone:* 715-735-4301. *E-mail:* ssinfo@mai.uwc.edu.

UNIVERSITY OF WISCONSIN-MARSHFIELD/WOOD COUNTY

Marshfield, Wisconsin

- **State-supported** 2-year, founded 1964, part of University of Wisconsin System
- **Calendar** semesters
- **Degree** associate
- **Small-town** 71-acre campus
- **Endowment** $500,000
- **Coed**

Faculty *Student/faculty ratio:* 17:1.

Student Life *Campus security:* 24-hour patrols, patrols by city police.

Standardized Tests *Required:* SAT I or ACT (for admission).

Applying *Options:* common application, electronic application, early admission, deferred entrance. *Application fee:* $35. *Required:* high school transcript. *Required for some:* essay or personal statement, letters of recommendation, interview.

Admissions Contact Mr. Jeff Meece, Director of Student Services, University of Wisconsin-Marshfield/Wood County, 2000 West Fifth Street, Marshfield, WI 54449. *Phone:* 715-389-6500. *Fax:* 715-384-1718.

UNIVERSITY OF WISCONSIN-RICHLAND

Richland Center, Wisconsin

- **State-supported** 2-year, founded 1967, part of University of Wisconsin System
- **Calendar** semesters
- **Degree** associate
- **Rural** 135-acre campus
- **Coed**, 517 undergraduate students, 65% full-time, 54% women, 46% men

Undergraduates 338 full-time, 179 part-time. Students come from 4 states and territories, 15 other countries, 1% are from out of state, 0.2% African American, 0.8% Asian American or Pacific Islander, 0.4% Hispanic American, 0.4% Native American, 3% international, 6% transferred in, 35% live on campus. *Retention:* 55% of 2002 full-time freshmen returned.

Freshmen *Admission:* 280 enrolled. *Test scores:* ACT scores over 18: 91%; ACT scores over 24: 19%.

Faculty *Total:* 26, 50% full-time, 35% with terminal degrees. *Student/faculty ratio:* 18:1.

Majors Biological and physical sciences; liberal arts and sciences/liberal studies.

Academic Programs *Special study options:* academic remediation for entering students, adult/continuing education programs, advanced placement credit, distance learning, external degree program, independent study, off-campus study, part-time degree program, services for LD students, study abroad, summer session for credit.

Library Miller Memorial Library with 45,000 titles, 200 serial subscriptions, an OPAC, a Web page.

Computers on Campus 45 computers available on campus for general student use. A campuswide network can be accessed from off campus. Internet access, at least one staffed computer lab available.

Student Life *Housing Options:* coed. Campus housing is provided by a third party. *Activities and Organizations:* drama/theater group, student-run newspaper, choral group. *Student services:* personal/psychological counseling.

Athletics *Intercollegiate sports:* basketball M/W, soccer M/W, volleyball W. *Intramural sports:* badminton M/W, basketball M/W, football M/W, golf M/W, racquetball M/W, swimming M/W, table tennis M/W, tennis M/W, volleyball M/W.

Standardized Tests *Required:* SAT I or ACT (for admission). *Recommended:* ACT (for admission).

Costs (2003–04) *Tuition:* state resident $3560 full-time; nonresident $12,260 full-time. *Required fees:* $362 full-time. *Room and board:* $4100; room only: $2800. *Payment plan:* installment. *Waivers:* senior citizens.

Applying *Options:* electronic application, early admission. *Application fee:* $35. *Required:* high school transcript. *Required for some:* letters of recommendation, interview. *Application deadlines:* rolling (freshmen), 9/1 (transfers). *Notification:* continuous until 9/1 (freshmen), continuous until 9/1 (transfers).

Admissions Contact Mr. John D. Poole, Director of Student Services, University of Wisconsin-Richland, 1200 Highway 14 West, Richland Center, WI 53581. *Phone:* 608-647-8422 Ext. 223. *Fax:* 608-647-6225. *E-mail:* jpoole@uwc.edu.

UNIVERSITY OF WISCONSIN-ROCK COUNTY

Janesville, Wisconsin

- **State-supported** 2-year, founded 1966, part of University of Wisconsin System
- **Calendar** semesters
- **Degree** certificates and associate
- **Suburban** 50-acre campus with easy access to Milwaukee
- **Coed**

Faculty *Student/faculty ratio:* 16:1.

Standardized Tests *Required:* ACT (for admission).

Costs (2003–04) *Tuition:* state resident $3405 full-time; nonresident $7019 full-time. *Required fees:* $140 full-time.

Applying *Options:* electronic application, deferred entrance. *Application fee:* $35. *Required:* high school transcript.

Admissions Contact Ms. Donna Johnson, Program Manager, University of Wisconsin-Rock County, 2909 Kellogg Avenue, Janesville, WI 53456. *Phone:* 608-758-6523. *Toll-free phone:* 888-INFO-UWC. *Fax:* 608-755-2732. *E-mail:* tpickart@uwc.edu.

UNIVERSITY OF WISCONSIN-SHEBOYGAN

Sheboygan, Wisconsin

Admissions Contact Dr. Ronald P. Campopiano, Director of Student Services, University of Wisconsin-Sheboygan, One University Drive, Sheboygan, WI 53081-4789. *Phone:* 920-459-6633. *Fax:* 920-459-6602. *E-mail:* rcampopi@uwc.edu.

UNIVERSITY OF WISCONSIN-WASHINGTON COUNTY

West Bend, Wisconsin

- **State-supported** 2-year, founded 1968, part of University of Wisconsin System
- **Calendar** semesters
- **Degree** associate
- **Small-town** 87-acre campus with easy access to Milwaukee
- **Coed**, 968 undergraduate students

Undergraduates Students come from 2 states and territories, 2 other countries, 1% are from out of state, 0.6% African American, 1% Asian American or Pacific Islander, 1% Hispanic American, 0.4% Native American, 1% international.

Freshmen *Admission:* 431 applied, 410 admitted.

Faculty *Total:* 47, 51% full-time, 66% with terminal degrees. *Student/faculty ratio:* 25:1.

Majors Liberal arts and sciences/liberal studies.

Academic Programs *Special study options:* academic remediation for entering students, advanced placement credit, distance learning, double majors, honors programs, independent study, off-campus study, part-time degree program, services for LD students, summer session for credit.

Library University of Wisconsin-Washington County Library with 46,429 titles, 247 serial subscriptions, 4,998 audiovisual materials, an OPAC, a Web page.

Computers on Campus 78 computers available on campus for general student use. A campuswide network can be accessed from off campus. Internet access, at least one staffed computer lab available.

Student Life *Housing:* college housing not available. *Activities and Organizations:* drama/theater group, student-run newspaper, choral group, Student Government Association, Business Club, Phi Theta Kappa, Writers' Guild, Student Impact. *Student services:* personal/psychological counseling.

Athletics Member NAIA. *Intercollegiate sports:* basketball M/W, cheerleading W(s), golf M/W, soccer M/W, tennis M/W, volleyball W. *Intramural sports:* basketball M/W, football M/W, softball M/W, volleyball M/W.

Standardized Tests *Required:* ACT (for admission).

Costs (2003–04) *Tuition:* state resident $3442 full-time, $145 per credit hour part-time; nonresident $12,142 full-time, $507 per credit hour part-time. Part-time tuition and fees vary according to course load. *Payment plans:* installment, deferred payment.

Applying *Options:* electronic application, deferred entrance. *Application fee:* $35. *Required:* high school transcript. *Required for some:* essay or personal statement, interview. *Application deadline:* rolling (freshmen), rolling (transfers).

Admissions Contact Mr. Dan Cebrario, Associate Director of Student Services, University of Wisconsin-Washington County, Student Services Office, 400 University Drive, West Bend, WI 53095. *Phone:* 262-335-5201. *Fax:* 262-335-5220.

UNIVERSITY OF WISCONSIN-WAUKESHA
Waukesha, Wisconsin

- **State-supported** 2-year, founded 1966, part of University of Wisconsin System
- **Calendar** semesters
- **Degree** associate
- **Suburban** 86-acre campus with easy access to Milwaukee
- **Coed,** 2,214 undergraduate students, 58% full-time, 53% women, 47% men

Undergraduates 1,278 full-time, 936 part-time. Students come from 5 states and territories, 1% are from out of state, 2% African American, 2% Asian American or Pacific Islander, 3% Hispanic American, 0.4% Native American, 0.1% international.

Freshmen *Admission:* 1,886 applied, 1,254 admitted.

Faculty *Total:* 90, 43% full-time, 54% with terminal degrees. *Student/faculty ratio:* 14:1.

Majors Liberal arts and sciences/liberal studies.

Academic Programs *Special study options:* academic remediation for entering students, adult/continuing education programs, advanced placement credit, honors programs, off-campus study, part-time degree program, services for LD students, student-designed majors, summer session for credit.

Library University of Wisconsin-Waukesha Library plus 1 other with 41,000 titles, 300 serial subscriptions.

Computers on Campus 90 computers available on campus for general student use. A campuswide network can be accessed. Internet access, at least one staffed computer lab available.

Student Life *Housing:* college housing not available. *Activities and Organizations:* drama/theater group, student-run newspaper, radio station, choral group, student government, Student Activities Committee, Campus Crusade, Phi Theta Kappa, Circle K. *Campus security:* late-night transport/escort service, part-time patrols by trained security personnel.

Athletics Member NJCAA. *Intercollegiate sports:* basketball M/W, golf M/W, soccer M/W, tennis M/W, volleyball W. *Intramural sports:* basketball M, bowling M/W, football M/W, skiing (downhill) M/W, table tennis M/W, volleyball M(c).

Standardized Tests *Required:* ACT (for admission). *Required for some:* SAT I (for admission).

Costs (2003–04) *Tuition:* state resident $3395 full-time, $142 per credit part-time; nonresident $16,161 full-time, $504 per credit part-time. *Required fees:* $197 full-time.

Applying *Options:* early admission, deferred entrance. *Application fee:* $35. *Required:* high school transcript. *Required for some:* letters of recommendation, interview. *Application deadlines:* 8/15 (freshmen), 9/1 (transfers). *Notification:* continuous until 8/11 (freshmen), continuous until 9/1 (transfers).

Admissions Contact Ms. Susan Adams, Coordinator of Admissions, University of Wisconsin-Waukesha, 1500 North University Drive, Waukesha, WI 53188. *Phone:* 262-521-5200. *Fax:* 262-521-5491. *E-mail:* sadams@uwc.edu.

WAUKESHA COUNTY TECHNICAL COLLEGE
Pewaukee, Wisconsin

- **State and locally supported** 2-year, founded 1923, part of Wisconsin Technical College System
- **Calendar** semesters
- **Degree** certificates, diplomas, and associate
- **Small-town** 137-acre campus with easy access to Milwaukee
- **Coed**

Student Life *Campus security:* patrols by police officers 8 a.m. to 10 p.m.

Athletics Member NJCAA.

Standardized Tests *Required for some:* ACT ASSET.

Financial Aid Of all full-time matriculated undergraduates who enrolled, 50 Federal Work-Study jobs (averaging $3000).

Applying *Options:* early admission. *Application fee:* $25. *Required:* high school transcript. *Required for some:* interview.

Admissions Contact Ms. Dianna Skornicka, Interim Director of Admissions, Waukesha County Technical College, 800 Main Street, Pewaukee, WI 53072-4601. *Phone:* 262-691-5464. *Toll-free phone:* 888-892-WCTC.

WESTERN WISCONSIN TECHNICAL COLLEGE
La Crosse, Wisconsin

- **District-supported** 2-year, founded 1911, part of Wisconsin Technical College System
- **Calendar** semesters
- **Degree** certificates, diplomas, and associate
- **Urban** 10-acre campus
- **Coed,** 5,286 undergraduate students, 39% full-time, 55% women, 45% men

Undergraduates 2,066 full-time, 3,220 part-time. Students come from 4 states and territories, 7% are from out of state, 1% African American, 3% Asian American or Pacific Islander, 0.7% Hispanic American, 1% Native American, 9% transferred in, 2% live on campus.

Freshmen *Admission:* 3,443 applied, 1,816 admitted, 1,096 enrolled.

Faculty *Total:* 920, 22% full-time. *Student/faculty ratio:* 16:1.

Majors Accounting; administrative assistant and secretarial science; agricultural mechanization; automobile/automotive mechanics technology; business administration and management; business administration, management and operations related; child care provision; child development; clinical/medical laboratory technology; commercial and advertising art; communications technologies and support services related; computer programming; consumer merchandising/retailing management; criminal justice/police science; data processing and data processing technology; dental hygiene; electrical, electronic and communications engineering technology; electromechanical technology; electroneurodiagnostic/electroencephalographic technology; fashion merchandising; finance; fire protection and safety technology; food services technology; heating, air conditioning, ventilation and refrigeration maintenance technology; hospital and health care facilities administration; human resources management; interior design; legal assistant/paralegal; marketing/marketing management; mass communication/media; mechanical design technology; medical administrative assistant and medical secretary; nursing (registered nurse training); occupational therapy; office management; physical therapist assistant; precision production related; public health related; radiologic technology/science; respiratory care therapy; retailing; sales, distribution and marketing; surgical technology; system administration.

Academic Programs *Special study options:* academic remediation for entering students, accelerated degree program, adult/continuing education programs, advanced placement credit, cooperative education, distance learning, English as a second language, external degree program, internships, off-campus study, part-time degree program, services for LD students, student-designed majors, summer session for credit.

Library Western Wisconsin Technical College Library plus 1 other with 31,243 titles, 313 serial subscriptions, 3,750 audiovisual materials, an OPAC.

Computers on Campus 800 computers available on campus for general student use. A campuswide network can be accessed from student residence rooms and from off campus. Internet access, online (class) registration, at least one staffed computer lab available.

Student Life *Housing Options:* coed. *Activities and Organizations:* student-run newspaper, Wisconsin Marketing Management Association (WMMA), Air Conditioning, Refrigeration Organization (ACRO), Multicultural Club, Business

Western Wisconsin Technical College (continued)
Professionals of America (BPA), Advertising Club. *Campus security:* 24-hour emergency response devices and patrols, student patrols, late-night transport/escort service, controlled dormitory access. *Student services:* personal/psychological counseling.

Athletics Member NJCAA. *Intercollegiate sports:* baseball M, basketball M/W, volleyball W. *Intramural sports:* basketball M/W, rock climbing M/W, volleyball M/W.

Standardized Tests *Required for some:* ACT ASSET. *Recommended:* ACT (for admission).

Costs (2004–05) *Tuition:* state resident $2280 full-time, $76 per credit part-time; nonresident $14,894 full-time, $488 per credit part-time. *Required fees:* $251 full-time. *Room and board:* room only: $2200.

Financial Aid Of all full-time matriculated undergraduates who enrolled, 102 Federal Work-Study jobs (averaging $1444).

Applying *Options:* common application, electronic application, early admission. *Application fee:* $30. *Required:* high school transcript. *Recommended:* interview. *Application deadline:* rolling (freshmen), rolling (transfers).

Admissions Contact Ms. Jane Wells, Manager of Admissions, Registration and Records, Western Wisconsin Technical College, PO Box 908, La Crosse, WI 54602-0908. *Phone:* 608-785-9158. *Toll-free phone:* 800-322-9982 (in-state); 800-248-9982 (out-of-state). *Fax:* 608-785-9094. *E-mail:* mildes@wwtc.edu.

WISCONSIN INDIANHEAD TECHNICAL COLLEGE
Shell Lake, Wisconsin

- **District-supported** 2-year, founded 1912, part of Wisconsin Technical College System
- **Calendar** semesters
- **Degree** certificates, diplomas, and associate
- **Urban** 113-acre campus
- **Endowment** $1.7 million
- **Coed,** 3,606 undergraduate students, 46% full-time, 59% women, 41% men

Undergraduates 1,659 full-time, 1,947 part-time. 0.3% African American, 0.6% Asian American or Pacific Islander, 0.7% Hispanic American, 2% Native American.

Faculty *Total:* 974, 16% full-time. *Student/faculty ratio:* 6:1.

Majors Accounting; administrative assistant and secretarial science; agricultural/farm supplies retailing and wholesaling; architectural engineering technology; business and personal/financial services marketing; business operations support and secretarial services related; child care and support services management; communications systems installation and repair technology; computer programming (specific applications); computer systems networking and telecommunications; corrections and criminal justice related; court reporting; criminal justice/police science; electromechanical technology; emergency medical technology (EMT paramedic); engineering technologies related; finance; heating, air conditioning and refrigeration technology; management information systems and services related; mechanical engineering/mechanical technology; medical administrative assistant and medical secretary; merchandising, sales, and marketing operations related (general); occupational therapy; quality control technology; retailing.

Costs (2004–05) *Tuition:* state resident $2432 full-time; nonresident $15,619 full-time. *Required fees:* $200 full-time.

Applying *Application fee:* $35. *Application deadline:* rolling (freshmen).

Admissions Contact Ms. Mimi Crandall, Dean, Student Services, Wisconsin Indianhead Technical College, 505 Pine Ridge Drive, Shell Lake, WI 54871. *Phone:* 715-468-2815 Ext. 2280. *Toll-free phone:* 800-243-9482. *Fax:* 715-468-2819.

WYOMING

CASPER COLLEGE
Casper, Wyoming

- **District-supported** 2-year, founded 1945, part of Wyoming Community College Commission
- **Calendar** semesters
- **Degree** certificates and associate
- **Small-town** 125-acre campus
- **Endowment** $50,000
- **Coed,** 4,158 undergraduate students, 49% full-time, 61% women, 39% men

Undergraduates 2,041 full-time, 2,117 part-time. Students come from 41 states and territories, 10 other countries, 7% are from out of state, 0.8% African

American, 0.5% Asian American or Pacific Islander, 3% Hispanic American, 1% Native American, 0.6% international, 35% transferred in, 16% live on campus. *Retention:* 59% of 2002 full-time freshmen returned.

Freshmen *Admission:* 1,087 applied, 1,087 admitted, 772 enrolled. *Average high school GPA:* 3.00.

Faculty *Total:* 243, 60% full-time, 15% with terminal degrees. *Student/faculty ratio:* 15:1.

Majors Accounting; administrative assistant and secretarial science; agricultural business and management; agricultural mechanization; agriculture; airline pilot and flight crew; animal sciences; anthropology; applied art; art; automobile/automotive mechanics technology; behavioral sciences; biological and physical sciences; biology/biological sciences; botany/plant biology; business administration and management; business teacher education; carpentry; ceramic arts and ceramics; chemistry; clinical laboratory science/medical technology; commercial and advertising art; computer engineering technology; computer programming; computer science; construction engineering technology; consumer merchandising/retailing management; corrections; criminal justice/law enforcement administration; criminal justice/police science; data processing and data processing technology; drafting and design technology; dramatic/theatre arts; ecology; economics; education; electrical, electronic and communications engineering technology; elementary education; emergency medical technology (EMT paramedic); engineering; English; fire science; French; geology/earth science; German; history; humanities; industrial arts; industrial radiologic technology; Italian; journalism; kindergarten/preschool education; legal administrative assistant/secretary; legal assistant/paralegal; liberal arts and sciences/liberal studies; machine tool technology; marketing/marketing management; mass communication/media; mathematics; mining technology; music; music teacher education; natural sciences; nursing (licensed practical/vocational nurse training); nursing (registered nurse training); occupational therapy; pharmacy; pharmacy technician; photography; physical education teaching and coaching; physical sciences; physical therapy; physics; political science and government; pre-engineering; psychology; social sciences; social work; sociology; Spanish; speech and rhetoric; veterinary sciences; welding technology; wildlife and wildlands science and management; zoology/animal biology.

Academic Programs *Special study options:* academic remediation for entering students, accelerated degree program, adult/continuing education programs, advanced placement credit, cooperative education, distance learning, English as a second language, external degree program, honors programs, internships, off-campus study, part-time degree program, services for LD students, study abroad, summer session for credit. *ROTC:* Army (c).

Library Goodstein Library with 82,336 titles, 460 serial subscriptions, an OPAC, a Web page.

Computers on Campus 130 computers available on campus for general student use. A campuswide network can be accessed from student residence rooms. At least one staffed computer lab available.

Student Life *Housing Options:* coed. Campus housing is university owned. *Activities and Organizations:* drama/theater group, student-run newspaper, choral group, Student Senate, Student Activities Board, Agriculture Club, Theater Club, Phi Theta Kappa. *Campus security:* 24-hour patrols, late-night transport/escort service. *Student services:* health clinic, personal/psychological counseling, women's center.

Athletics Member NJCAA. *Intercollegiate sports:* basketball M(s)/W(s), volleyball W(s). *Intramural sports:* badminton M/W, basketball M/W, bowling M/W, field hockey M/W, football M/W, golf M/W, gymnastics M/W, racquetball M/W, skiing (cross-country) M/W, skiing (downhill) M/W, soccer M/W, softball M/W, swimming M/W, table tennis M/W, tennis M/W, volleyball M/W, water polo M/W, weight lifting M/W.

Standardized Tests *Required:* SAT I and SAT II or ACT (for placement).

Costs (2004–05) *Tuition:* state resident $1320 full-time, $55 per credit part-time; nonresident $3960 full-time, $165 per credit part-time. *Required fees:* $144 full-time, $6 per credit part-time. *Room and board:* $3210. Room and board charges vary according to board plan. *Payment plan:* installment. *Waivers:* children of alumni, senior citizens, and employees or children of employees.

Financial Aid Of all full-time matriculated undergraduates who enrolled, 112 Federal Work-Study jobs (averaging $2400).

Applying *Options:* electronic application, early admission. *Required:* high school transcript. *Required for some:* minimum 2.0 GPA. *Application deadlines:* 8/15 (freshmen), 8/15 (transfers). *Notification:* continuous until 8/15 (freshmen), continuous until 8/15 (transfers).

Admissions Contact Ms. Donna Hoffman, Admission Specialist, Casper College, 125 College Drive, Casper, WY 82601. *Phone:* 307-268-2458. *Toll-free phone:* 800-442-2963.

CENTRAL WYOMING COLLEGE
Riverton, Wyoming

- **State and locally supported** 2-year, founded 1966, part of Wyoming Community College Commission
- **Calendar** semesters
- **Degree** certificates and associate

- **Small-town** 200-acre campus
- **Endowment** $2.4 million
- **Coed,** 1,808 undergraduate students, 45% full-time, 65% women, 35% men

Undergraduates 807 full-time, 1,001 part-time. Students come from 20 states and territories, 3 other countries, 5% are from out of state, 0.2% African American, 0.5% Asian American or Pacific Islander, 4% Hispanic American, 19% Native American, 0.8% international, 7% transferred in, 9% live on campus. *Retention:* 57% of 2002 full-time freshmen returned.

Freshmen *Admission:* 394 applied, 394 admitted, 265 enrolled. *Average high school GPA:* 2.98. *Test scores:* SAT verbal scores over 500: 100%; ACT scores over 18: 70%; ACT scores over 24: 18%; ACT scores over 30: 1%.

Faculty *Total:* 127, 30% full-time, 54% with terminal degrees. *Student/faculty ratio:* 17:1.

Majors Accounting; accounting technology and bookkeeping; agricultural business and management; agriculture; American Indian/Native American studies; art; automobile/automotive mechanics technology; biology/biological sciences; business administration and management; business automation/technology/data entry; child care and support services management; computer science; computer systems networking and telecommunications; computer technology; computer systems technology; criminal justice/law enforcement administration; dramatic/theatre arts; elementary education; English; environmental science; equestrian studies; general studies; horse husbandry/equine science and management; human services; management information systems; music; nursing (registered nurse training); parts, warehousing, and inventory management; physical sciences; pre-law studies; psychology; radio and television broadcasting technology; range science and management; secondary education; social sciences; surgical technology; web page, digital/multimedia and information resources design; welding technology.

Academic Programs *Special study options:* academic remediation for entering students, adult/continuing education programs, advanced placement credit, cooperative education, distance learning, English as a second language, honors programs, independent study, off-campus study, part-time degree program, services for LD students, student-designed majors, summer session for credit.

Library Central Wyoming College Library with 53,909 titles, 233 serial subscriptions, 1,217 audiovisual materials, an OPAC, a Web page.

Computers on Campus 283 computers available on campus for general student use. A campuswide network can be accessed from off campus. Internet access, online (class) registration, at least one staffed computer lab available.

Student Life *Housing Options:* coed. Campus housing is university owned. *Activities and Organizations:* drama/theater group, student-run radio and television station, choral group, Multi-Cultural Club, La Vida Nueva Club, Fellowship of College Christians, Quality Leaders, Science Club. *Campus security:* 24-hour patrols. *Student services:* personal/psychological counseling.

Athletics *Intercollegiate sports:* equestrian sports M(s)/W(s). *Intramural sports:* badminton M/W, basketball M/W, football M/W, skiing (downhill) M/W, soccer M/W, softball M/W, swimming M/W, table tennis M/W, tennis M/W, volleyball M/W, weight lifting M/W.

Standardized Tests *Required for some:* ACT COMPASS. *Recommended:* SAT I or ACT (for placement).

Costs (2004–05) *Tuition:* state resident $1320 full-time, $55 per credit part-time; nonresident $3960 full-time, $165 per credit part-time. Full-time tuition and fees vary according to program and reciprocity agreements. Part-time tuition and fees vary according to course load, program, and reciprocity agreements. *Required fees:* $480 full-time, $20 per credit part-time. *Room and board:* $2690; room only: $1300. Room and board charges vary according to board plan and housing facility. *Payment plans:* installment, deferred payment. *Waivers:* senior citizens and employees or children of employees.

Financial Aid Of all full-time matriculated undergraduates who enrolled, 51 Federal Work-Study jobs (averaging $1074).

Applying *Options:* early admission, deferred entrance. *Recommended:* high school transcript. *Application deadline:* rolling (freshmen), rolling (transfers).

Admissions Contact Admissions Officer, Central Wyoming College, 2660 Peck Avenue, Riverton, WY 82501-2273. *Phone:* 307-855-2119. *Toll-free phone:* 800-735-8418 Ext. 2119. *Fax:* 307-855-2065. *E-mail:* admit@cwc.edu.

EASTERN WYOMING COLLEGE
Torrington, Wyoming

- **State and locally supported** 2-year, founded 1948, part of Wyoming Community College Commission
- **Calendar** semesters
- **Degree** certificates, diplomas, and associate
- **Rural** 40-acre campus
- **Coed,** 1,448 undergraduate students, 36% full-time, 66% women, 34% men

Undergraduates 519 full-time, 929 part-time. Students come from 23 states and territories, 3 other countries, 25% are from out of state, 1% African American, 0.4% Asian American or Pacific Islander, 5% Hispanic American, 0.6% Native American, 0.3% international, 4% transferred in, 26% live on campus.

Freshmen *Admission:* 181 enrolled. *Average high school GPA:* 2.83.

Faculty *Total:* 124, 30% full-time, 6% with terminal degrees. *Student/faculty ratio:* 13:1.

Majors Accounting; administrative assistant and secretarial science; agribusiness; agricultural economics; agricultural teacher education; agriculture; animal sciences; art; biology/biological sciences; business administration and management; business teacher education; child development; communication/speech communication and rhetoric; cosmetology; criminal justice/police science; criminal justice/safety; economics; elementary education; English; farm and ranch management; foreign languages and literatures; general studies; health/medical preparatory programs related; history; liberal arts and sciences/liberal studies; management information systems; management information systems and services related; mathematics; mathematics teacher education; middle school education; music; music teacher education; physical education teaching and coaching; political science and government; pre-dentistry studies; pre-medical studies; pre-pharmacy studies; pre-veterinary studies; psychology; secondary education; sociology; special education; statistics; veterinary/animal health technology; welding technology; wildlife and wildlands science and management.

Academic Programs *Special study options:* academic remediation for entering students, accelerated degree program, adult/continuing education programs, advanced placement credit, cooperative education, distance learning, English as a second language, independent study, internships, part-time degree program, services for LD students, student-designed majors, summer session for credit.

Library Eastern Wyoming College Library with an OPAC, a Web page.

Computers on Campus 124 computers available on campus for general student use. A campuswide network can be accessed. Internet access, at least one staffed computer lab available.

Student Life *Housing Options:* coed, men-only, women-only. Campus housing is university owned. *Activities and Organizations:* student-run newspaper, choral group, Criminal Justice Technology Club, Veterinary Technology Club, Student Senate, Music Club, Rodeo Club. *Campus security:* 24-hour emergency response devices, controlled dormitory access. *Student services:* personal/psychological counseling.

Athletics Member NJCAA. *Intercollegiate sports:* basketball M(s), cheerleading M(s)/W(s), equestrian sports M(s)/W(s), golf M(s), volleyball W(s). *Intramural sports:* badminton M/W, basketball M/W, bowling M/W, football M, racquetball M/W, softball M/W, table tennis M/W, tennis M/W, volleyball M/W.

Standardized Tests *Recommended:* ACT (for placement).

Costs (2004–05) *Tuition:* state resident $1320 full-time, $55 per credit hour part-time; nonresident $3960 full-time, $165 per credit hour part-time. Full-time tuition and fees vary according to reciprocity agreements. Part-time tuition and fees vary according to reciprocity agreements. *Required fees:* $512 full-time, $16 per credit hour part-time. *Room and board:* $3124; room only: $1364. *Payment plan:* installment. *Waivers:* children of alumni, senior citizens, and employees or children of employees.

Financial Aid Of all full-time matriculated undergraduates who enrolled, 100 Federal Work-Study jobs (averaging $700). 60 state and other part-time jobs (averaging $700).

Applying *Options:* electronic application, early admission. *Recommended:* high school transcript, minimum 2.0 GPA. *Application deadline:* rolling (freshmen), rolling (transfers).

Admissions Contact Mrs. Marilyn Cotant, Dean of Students, Eastern Wyoming College, 3200 West C Street, Torrington, WY 82240. *Phone:* 307-532-8257. *Toll-free phone:* 800-658-3195. *Fax:* 307-532-8222. *E-mail:* bbates@ewc.cc.wy.us.

LARAMIE COUNTY COMMUNITY COLLEGE
Cheyenne, Wyoming

- **State-supported** 2-year, founded 1968, part of Wyoming Community College Commission
- **Calendar** semesters
- **Degree** certificates and associate
- **Small-town** 270-acre campus
- **Endowment** $4.4 million
- **Coed,** 4,485 undergraduate students, 34% full-time, 58% women, 42% men

Undergraduates 1,527 full-time, 2,958 part-time. Students come from 37 states and territories, 7% are from out of state, 5% transferred in, 2% live on campus.

Freshmen *Admission:* 2,450 applied, 2,450 admitted, 378 enrolled.

Faculty *Total:* 255, 31% full-time. *Student/faculty ratio:* 18:1.

Majors Accounting; agribusiness; agricultural business technology; agricultural production; agriculture; anthropology; art; autobody/collision and repair technology; automobile/automotive mechanics technology; biological and physical sciences; biology/biological sciences; business administration and management; business/commerce; business operations support and secretarial services

Laramie County Community College (continued)

related; carpentry; chemistry; civil engineering technology; communication/speech communication and rhetoric; computer and information sciences; computer and information sciences and support services related; computer hardware technology; computer programming; computer science; computer systems analysis; construction engineering technology; construction trades; construction trades related; corrections; criminal justice/law enforcement administration; customer service support/call center/teleservice operation; data modeling/warehousing and database administration; dental assisting; dental hygiene; diagnostic medical sonography and ultrasound technology; diesel mechanics technology; digital communication and media/multimedia; dramatic/theatre arts; early childhood education; economics; education; education (specific levels and methods) related; electrician; engineering; engineering technology; English; entrepreneurship; equestrian studies; health/medical preparatory programs related; history; humanities; industrial radiologic technology; information technology; journalism; mass communication/media; mathematics; multi-/interdisciplinary studies related; music; nursing assistant/aide and patient care assistant; nursing (registered nurse training); philosophy; physical education teaching and coaching; political science and government; pre-dentistry studies; pre-engineering; pre-law studies; pre-medical studies; pre-pharmacy studies; pre-veterinary studies; psychology; public administration; radiologic technology/science; religious studies; social sciences; sociology; Spanish; visual and performing arts; web/multimedia management and webmaster; web page, digital/multimedia and information resources design; wildlife and wildlands science and management.

Academic Programs *Special study options:* academic remediation for entering students, adult/continuing education programs, advanced placement credit, cooperative education, distance learning, English as a second language, independent study, internships, off-campus study, part-time degree program, services for LD students, summer session for credit. *ROTC:* Air Force (c).

Library 49,000 titles, 397 serial subscriptions, 3,983 audiovisual materials, an OPAC, a Web page.

Computers on Campus 600 computers available on campus for general student use. A campuswide network can be accessed from off campus. Internet access, online (class) registration, at least one staffed computer lab available.

Student Life *Housing Options:* coed. Campus housing is university owned. *Activities and Organizations:* drama/theater group, student-run newspaper, choral group, Block and Bridle Club, Phi Theta Kappa, music, Student Nurses Association, STAR Club. *Campus security:* 24-hour patrols, controlled dormitory access. *Student services:* personal/psychological counseling.

Athletics Member NJCAA. *Intercollegiate sports:* basketball M(s), soccer M(s)/W(s), volleyball W(s). *Intramural sports:* basketball M/W, skiing (cross-country) M/W, soccer M/W, volleyball M/W.

Standardized Tests *Recommended:* ACT (for admission), ACT (for placement).

Costs (2004–05) *Tuition:* state resident $1320 full-time, $55 per credit hour part-time; nonresident $3960 full-time, $165 per credit hour part-time. Part-time tuition and fees vary according to course load. *Required fees:* $516 full-time, $22 per credit hour part-time. *Room and board:* $4512. *Payment plan:* installment. *Waivers:* senior citizens and employees or children of employees.

Applying *Options:* electronic application, early admission. *Application fee:* $20. *Required:* high school transcript. *Required for some:* interview. *Application deadline:* rolling (freshmen), rolling (transfers). *Notification:* continuous until 8/31 (freshmen), continuous until 8/31 (transfers).

Admissions Contact Ms. Jenny Hargett, Assistant Director of Enrollment Management, Laramie County Community College, 1400 East College Drive, Cheyenne, WY 82007. *Phone:* 307-778-5222 Ext. 1117. *Toll-free phone:* 800-522-2993 Ext. 1357. *Fax:* 307-778-1360. *E-mail:* learnmore@lccc.wy.edu.

NORTHWEST COLLEGE
Powell, Wyoming

- **State and locally supported** 2-year, founded 1946, part of Wyoming Community College Commission
- **Calendar** semesters
- **Degree** certificates and associate
- **Rural** 75-acre campus
- **Endowment** $6.1 million
- **Coed,** 1,711 undergraduate students, 66% full-time, 61% women, 39% men

Undergraduates 1,121 full-time, 590 part-time. Students come from 23 states and territories, 27% are from out of state, 0.6% African American, 1% Asian American or Pacific Islander, 4% Hispanic American, 0.8% Native American, 0.4% international, 6% transferred in, 46% live on campus.

Freshmen *Admission:* 1,160 applied, 963 admitted, 443 enrolled. *Average high school GPA:* 2.97. *Test scores:* ACT scores over 18: 66%; ACT scores over 24: 21%.

Faculty *Total:* 154, 50% full-time. *Student/faculty ratio:* 16:1.

Majors Accounting; administrative assistant and secretarial science; agricultural business and management; agricultural economics; agricultural mechanization; agricultural teacher education; agriculture; agronomy and crop science;

American studies; animal sciences; art; art teacher education; biological and physical sciences; biology/biological sciences; botany/plant biology; business administration and management; business teacher education; chemistry; commercial and advertising art; desktop publishing and digital imaging design; drafting and design technology; early childhood education; ecology; economics; education; elementary education; engineering; English; environmental studies; equestrian studies; farm and ranch management; forestry; graphic and printing equipment operation/production; health teacher education; history; humanities; information science/studies; journalism; kindergarten/preschool education; kinesiology and exercise science; liberal arts and sciences/liberal studies; marketing/marketing management; mass communication/media; mathematics; modern languages; music; music teacher education; natural resources management and policy; natural sciences; nursing (licensed practical/vocational nurse training); nursing (registered nurse training); parks, recreation and leisure; parks, recreation and leisure facilities management; photography; physical anthropology; physical education teaching and coaching; physical sciences; physics; political science and government; pre-engineering; psychology; range science and management; science teacher education; social sciences; sociology; speech and rhetoric; tourism and travel services management; trade and industrial teacher education; welding technology; wildlife and wildlands science and management.

Academic Programs *Special study options:* academic remediation for entering students, adult/continuing education programs, advanced placement credit, cooperative education, distance learning, double majors, English as a second language, external degree program, honors programs, internships, part-time degree program, services for LD students, study abroad, summer session for credit.

Library John Taggart Hinckley Library plus 1 other with 55,330 titles, 1,738 serial subscriptions, 741 audiovisual materials, an OPAC, a Web page.

Computers on Campus 300 computers available on campus for general student use. A campuswide network can be accessed from student residence rooms. Internet access, online (class) registration, at least one staffed computer lab available. Computer purchase or lease plan available.

Student Life *Housing:* on-campus residence required for freshman year. *Options:* coed, women-only. Campus housing is university owned. Freshman campus housing is guaranteed. *Activities and Organizations:* drama/theater group, student-run newspaper, choral group. *Campus security:* 24-hour emergency response devices and patrols, late-night transport/escort service, controlled dormitory access. *Student services:* health clinic, personal/psychological counseling.

Athletics Member NJCAA. *Intercollegiate sports:* basketball M(s)/W(s), equestrian sports M(s)/W(s), riflery M/W, volleyball W(s), wrestling M(s). *Intramural sports:* archery M/W, badminton M/W, baseball M/W, basketball M/W, bowling M/W, cheerleading M/W, football M/W, golf M/W, gymnastics M/W, racquetball M/W, riflery M/W, skiing (cross-country) M/W, skiing (downhill) M/W, soccer M/W, softball M/W, table tennis M/W, tennis M/W, volleyball M/W, weight lifting M/W.

Standardized Tests *Required for some:* SAT I or ACT (for admission), ACT COMPASS.

Costs (2003–04) *Tuition:* state resident $1272 full-time, $71 per credit part-time; nonresident $3816 full-time, $177 per credit part-time. *Required fees:* $488 full-time, $18 per credit part-time. *Room and board:* $3358. Room and board charges vary according to board plan and housing facility. *Waivers:* children of alumni, senior citizens, and employees or children of employees.

Financial Aid Of all full-time matriculated undergraduates who enrolled, 107 Federal Work-Study jobs (averaging $1200). 245 state and other part-time jobs (averaging $1200).

Applying *Options:* common application, electronic application, early admission, deferred entrance. *Required:* high school transcript. *Recommended:* minimum 2.0 GPA. *Application deadlines:* 8/15 (freshmen), 8/1 (transfers). *Notification:* continuous (freshmen), continuous (transfers).

Admissions Contact Assistant Director of Admissions, Northwest College, 231 West Sixth Street, Powell, WY 82435. *Phone:* 307-754-6043. *Toll-free phone:* 800-560-4692. *Fax:* 307-754-6249. *E-mail:* admissions@northwestcollege.edu.

SHERIDAN COLLEGE
Sheridan, Wyoming

- **State and locally supported** 2-year, founded 1948, part of Wyoming Community College Commission
- **Calendar** semesters
- **Degree** certificates and associate
- **Small-town** 124-acre campus
- **Coed,** 2,665 undergraduate students, 36% full-time, 62% women, 38% men

Undergraduates 967 full-time, 1,698 part-time. Students come from 30 states and territories, 6 other countries, 9% are from out of state, 3% transferred in, 20% live on campus.

Freshmen *Admission:* 375 enrolled.

Faculty *Total:* 173, 41% full-time, 6% with terminal degrees. *Student/faculty ratio:* 16:1.

Majors Administrative assistant and secretarial science; agricultural business and management; agriculture; art; biological and physical sciences; biology/biological sciences; business administration and management; business/commerce; computer programming (specific applications); computer software and media applications related; computer systems networking and telecommunications; criminal justice/law enforcement administration; criminal justice/police science; data entry/microcomputer applications; dental hygiene; diesel mechanics technology; drafting and design technology; education; elementary education; engineering; engineering technology; English; foreign languages and literatures; general studies; health and physical education; heavy equipment maintenance technology; history; hospitality administration; humanities; information science/studies; liberal arts and sciences/liberal studies; machine tool technology; mathematics; music; nursing (registered nurse training); respiratory care therapy; sign language interpretation and translation; social sciences; system administration; web/multimedia management and webmaster; web page, digital/multimedia and information resources design; welding technology.

Academic Programs *Special study options:* academic remediation for entering students, adult/continuing education programs, advanced placement credit, cooperative education, distance learning, double majors, English as a second language, independent study, internships, off-campus study, part-time degree program, services for LD students, student-designed majors, summer session for credit.

Library Griffith Memorial Library plus 1 other with 46,589 titles, 545 serial subscriptions, 17,122 audiovisual materials, an OPAC, a Web page.

Computers on Campus 200 computers available on campus for general student use. A campuswide network can be accessed from student residence rooms and from off campus. Internet access, at least one staffed computer lab available.

Student Life *Housing Options:* coed, women-only, disabled students. *Activities and Organizations:* drama/theater group, student-run newspaper, choral group, student government, Phi Theta Kappa, Art Club, Nursing Club, Police Science Club. *Campus security:* 24-hour emergency response devices, student patrols, controlled dormitory access, night patrols by certified officers. *Student services:* personal/psychological counseling.

Athletics Member NJCAA. *Intercollegiate sports:* basketball M(s)/W(s), volleyball W(s). *Intramural sports:* basketball M/W, bowling M/W, soccer M/W, softball M/W, table tennis M/W, tennis M/W, volleyball M/W.

Costs (2004–05) *Tuition:* state resident $1320 full-time, $55 per credit hour part-time; nonresident $3960 full-time, $165 per credit hour part-time. Full-time tuition and fees vary according to course load and reciprocity agreements. Part-time tuition and fees vary according to reciprocity agreements. *Required fees:* $360 full-time, $15 per credit hour part-time. *Room and board:* $3720. Room and board charges vary according to board plan and housing facility. *Payment plans:* installment, deferred payment. *Waivers:* senior citizens and employees or children of employees.

Financial Aid Of all full-time matriculated undergraduates who enrolled, 86 Federal Work-Study jobs (averaging $1044).

Applying *Options:* electronic application, early admission, deferred entrance. *Required for some:* high school transcript. *Recommended:* high school transcript. *Application deadline:* rolling (freshmen), rolling (transfers). *Notification:* continuous (freshmen), continuous (transfers).

Admissions Contact Mr. Zane Garstad, Director of Admissions, Sheridan College, PO Box 1500, Sheridan, WY 82801-1500. *Phone:* 307-674-6446 Ext. 6318. *Toll-free phone:* 800-913-9139 Ext. 6138. *Fax:* 307-674-7205. *E-mail:* admissions@sheridan.edu.

WESTERN WYOMING COMMUNITY COLLEGE
Rock Springs, Wyoming

- **State and locally supported** 2-year, founded 1959
- **Calendar** semesters
- **Degree** certificates, diplomas, and associate
- **Small-town** 10-acre campus
- **Endowment** $6.0 million
- **Coed**, 2,315 undergraduate students, 45% full-time, 65% women, 35% men

Western Wyoming Community College is a public, 2-year, comprehensive community college located in Rock Springs, Wyoming. This rural campus provides easy access to a variety of outdoor recreational opportunities, and its location makes travel to metropolitan areas such as Denver and Salt Lake City very easy. The modern, fully enclosed campus is designed to provide comfort and safety for college students as well as up-to-date equipment and facilities. The low student-teacher ratio of 15:1 ensures that students get individualized attention in their classes. Students major in transfer programs as well as occupational programs designed to lead directly to the workforce. Western is committed to both quality and success.

Undergraduates 1,046 full-time, 1,269 part-time. Students come from 12 states and territories, 10 other countries, 6% are from out of state, 0.4% African American, 0.7% Asian American or Pacific Islander, 5% Hispanic American, 2%

Native American, 3% international, 5% transferred in, 13% live on campus. *Retention:* 47% of 2002 full-time freshmen returned.

Freshmen *Admission:* 1,016 applied, 769 admitted, 409 enrolled. *Average high school GPA:* 2.95. *Test scores:* ACT scores over 18: 90%; ACT scores over 24: 10%.

Faculty *Total:* 167, 38% full-time. *Student/faculty ratio:* 15:1.

Majors Accounting; administrative assistant and secretarial science; anthropology; archeology; art; automobile/automotive mechanics technology; biological and physical sciences; biology/biological sciences; business administration and management; chemistry; communication/speech communication and rhetoric; computer and information sciences; computer programming (specific applications); computer science; criminal justice/law enforcement administration; criminology; dance; data entry/microcomputer applications; data processing and data processing technology; diesel mechanics technology; dramatic/theatre arts; early childhood education; economics; education; education (multiple levels); electrical, electronic and communications engineering technology; electrical/electronics equipment installation and repair; electrician; elementary education; engineering technology; English; environmental science; forestry; general studies; geography; geology/earth science; health/medical preparatory programs related; health services/allied health/health sciences; heavy equipment maintenance technology; history; humanities; human services; industrial electronics technology; industrial mechanics and maintenance technology; information science/studies; information technology; instrumentation technology; international relations and affairs; journalism; kinesiology and exercise science; legal administrative assistant/secretary; liberal arts and sciences/liberal studies; marketing/marketing management; mathematics; mechanics and repair; medical administrative assistant and medical secretary; medical/clinical assistant; medical office assistant; medical office computer specialist; mining technology; music; nursing assistant/aide and patient care assistant; nursing (licensed practical/vocational nurse training); photography; political science and government; pre-dentistry studies; pre-engineering; pre-law studies; pre-medical studies; pre-nursing studies; pre-pharmacy studies; pre-veterinary studies; psychology; secondary education; social sciences; social work; sociology; Spanish; special education; theatre design and technology; visual and performing arts; web/multimedia management and webmaster; web page, digital/multimedia and information resources design; welding technology; wildlife and wildlands science and management; word processing.

Academic Programs *Special study options:* academic remediation for entering students, adult/continuing education programs, advanced placement credit, cooperative education, distance learning, English as a second language, freshman honors college, honors programs, independent study, internships, part-time degree program, services for LD students, summer session for credit.

Library Hay Library with 114,000 titles, 210 serial subscriptions, 3,093 audiovisual materials, an OPAC, a Web page.

Computers on Campus 300 computers available on campus for general student use. A campuswide network can be accessed from off campus. Internet access, online (class) registration, at least one staffed computer lab available.

Student Life *Housing Options:* coed, disabled students. Campus housing is university owned. *Activities and Organizations:* drama/theater group, student-run newspaper, choral group, Phi Theta Kappa, Students Without Borders (international club), Residence Hall Association, Associated Student Government, LDSSA. *Campus security:* 24-hour emergency response devices, late-night transport/escort service, controlled dormitory access, patrols by trained security personnel from 4 p.m. to 8 a.m., 24-hour patrols on weekends and holidays. *Student services:* personal/psychological counseling.

Athletics Member NJCAA. *Intercollegiate sports:* basketball M(s)/W(s), soccer M(s)(c)/W(s), volleyball W(s), wrestling M(s). *Intramural sports:* badminton M/W, basketball M/W, bowling M/W, football M/W, rock climbing M/W, skiing (downhill) M/W, soccer M/W, softball M/W, table tennis M/W, tennis M/W, ultimate Frisbee M/W, volleyball M/W, water polo M/W.

Standardized Tests *Required:* ACT COMPASS (for placement). *Recommended:* SAT I or ACT (for placement).

Costs (2004–05) *Tuition:* state resident $1594 full-time, $67 per credit hour part-time; nonresident $4234 full-time, $177 per credit hour part-time. Full-time tuition and fees vary according to reciprocity agreements. Part-time tuition and fees vary according to course load and reciprocity agreements. *Room and board:* $2999; room only: $1440. Room and board charges vary according to board plan and housing facility. *Payment plan:* installment. *Waivers:* children of alumni, senior citizens, and employees or children of employees.

Financial Aid Of all full-time matriculated undergraduates who enrolled, 20 Federal Work-Study jobs (averaging $1500).

Applying *Options:* common application, electronic application, early admission, deferred entrance. *Required:* high school transcript. *Application deadline:* rolling (freshmen), rolling (transfers).

Admissions Contact Western Wyoming Community College, PO Box 428, 2500 College Drive, Rock Springs, WY 82902-0428. *Phone:* 307-382-1647. *Toll-free phone:* 800-226-1181. *Fax:* 307-382-1636. *E-mail:* admissions@wwcc.cc.wy.us.

WYOTECH
Laramie, Wyoming

- **Proprietary** 2-year, founded 1966
- **Calendar** 9-month program
- **Degree** diplomas and associate
- **Rural** campus
- **Coed, primarily men**

Faculty *Student/faculty ratio:* 14:1.
Costs (2003–04) *Tuition:* $19,000 full-time. *Required fees:* $100 full-time. *Room only:* $2475.
Financial Aid Of all full-time matriculated undergraduates who enrolled, 139 Federal Work-Study jobs (averaging $1001).
Applying *Options:* common application. *Application fee:* $100. *Required:* high school transcript.
Admissions Contact Mr. Troy Chaney, Director of Admissions, WyoTech, 4373 North Third Street, Laramie, WY 82072-9519. *Phone:* 307-742-3776. *Toll-free phone:* 800-521-7158.

AMERICAN SAMOA

AMERICAN SAMOA COMMUNITY COLLEGE
Pago Pago, American Samoa

Admissions Contact Mrs. Sina P. Ward, Registrar, American Samoa Community College, PO Box 2609, Pago Pago, AS 96799-2609. *Phone:* 684-699-1141.

FEDERATED STATES OF MICRONESIA

COLLEGE OF MICRONESIA-FSM
Kolonia Pohnpei, Federated States of Micronesia

Admissions Contact Mr. Wilson J. Kalio, Coordinator of Admissions and Records, College of Micronesia-FSM, PO Box 159, Kolonia Pohnpei, FM 96941-0159. *Phone:* 691-320-2480 Ext. 6200. *Fax:* 691-320-2479.

GUAM

GUAM COMMUNITY COLLEGE
Barrigada, Guam

Admissions Contact Ms. Deborah D. Leon Guerrero, Registrar, Guam Community College, PO Box 23069, Sesame Street, Barrigada 96921, Guam. *Phone:* 671-735-5531. *Fax:* 671-734-0540. *E-mail:* deborah@guamcc.net.

NORTHERN MARIANA ISLANDS

NORTHERN MARIANAS COLLEGE
Saipan, Northern Mariana Islands

- **Territory-supported** primarily 2-year, founded 1981
- **Calendar** semesters
- **Degrees** certificates, diplomas, associate, and bachelor's
- **Rural** 14-acre campus
- **Coed**

Student Life *Campus security:* patrols by trained security personnel.

Costs (2003–04) *Tuition:* territory resident $1560 full-time, $65 per credit part-time; nonresident $2340 full-time, $130 per credit part-time. Full-time tuition and fees vary according to course level. Part-time tuition and fees vary according to course level. *Required fees:* $210 full-time, $2 per credit part-time, $25 per term part-time.
Applying *Options:* early admission, deferred entrance. *Application fee:* $25. *Required:* high school transcript.
Admissions Contact Ms. Joyce Taro, Admission Specialist, Northern Marianas College, PO Box 501250, Saipan, MP 96950-1250. *Phone:* 670-234-3690 Ext. 1528. *Fax:* 670-235-4967. *E-mail:* joycet@nmcnet.edu.

PUERTO RICO

CENTRO DE ESTUDIOS MULTIDISCIPLINARIOS
San Juan, Puerto Rico

Admissions Contact URB San Agustin, 1206 13th Street, San Juan, PR 00926.

COLUMBIA COLLEGE
Yauco, Puerto Rico

Admissions Contact Box 3062, Yauco, PR 00698.

ELECTRONIC DATA PROCESSING COLLEGE OF PUERTO RICO-SAN SEBASTIAN
San Sebastian, Puerto Rico

Admissions Contact 48 Betances Street, PO Box 1674, San Sebastian, PR 00685.

HUERTAS JUNIOR COLLEGE
Caguas, Puerto Rico

Admissions Contact Mrs. Barbara Hassim, Director of Admissions, Huertas Junior College, PO Box 8429, Caguas, PR 00726. *Phone:* 787-743-1242.

HUMACAO COMMUNITY COLLEGE
Humacao, Puerto Rico

Admissions Contact Ms. Paula Serrano, Director of Admissions, Humacao Community College, PO Box 9139, Humacao, PR 00792. *Phone:* 787-852-2525.

INSTITUTO COMERCIAL DE PUERTO RICO JUNIOR COLLEGE
San Juan, Puerto Rico

Admissions Contact Admissions Office, Instituto Comercial de Puerto Rico Junior College, PO Box 190304, San Juan, PR 00919-0304. *Phone:* 787-753-6335. *Fax:* 787-763-7249. *E-mail:* 1a_f_mena@icprjc.edu.

INTERNATIONAL JUNIOR COLLEGE
San Juan, Puerto Rico

Admissions Contact PO Box 8245, San Juan, PR 00910.

NATIONAL COLLEGE OF BUSINESS & TECHNOLOGY
Bayamon, Puerto Rico

Admissions Contact Mr. Desi Lopez, Vice President of Financial Aid and Compliance, National College of Business & Technology, PO Box 2036, Bayamon, PR 00960. *Phone:* 787-780-5134. *Toll-free phone:* 800-780-5188.

PUERTO RICO TECHNICAL JUNIOR COLLEGE
Mayaguez, Puerto Rico

Admissions Contact Calle Santiago R. Palmer #15 Est, Mayaguez, PR 00680.

PUERTO RICO TECHNICAL JUNIOR COLLEGE
San Juan, Puerto Rico

Admissions Contact 703 Ponce De Leon Avenue, Hato Rey, San Juan, PR 00917.

RAMIREZ COLLEGE OF BUSINESS AND TECHNOLOGY
San Juan, Puerto Rico

Admissions Contact Mrs. Evelyn Mercado, Director of Admissions, Ramirez College of Business and Technology, PO Box 8340, San Juan, PR 00910-0340. *Phone:* 787-763-3120.

TECHNOLOGICAL COLLEGE OF SAN JUAN
San Juan, Puerto Rico

Admissions Contact Mrs. Nilsa E. Rivera-Almenas, Director of Enrollment Management, Technological College of San Juan, 180 Jose R. Oliver Street, Tres Monjitas Industrial Park, San Juan, PR 00918. *Phone:* 787-250-7111 Ext. 2271. *Fax:* 787-250-7395.

UNIVERSITY COLLEGE OF CRIMINAL JUSTICE OF PUERTO RICO
Gurabo, Puerto Rico

Admissions Contact University College of Criminal Justice of Puerto Rico, HC 02 Box 12000, Gurabo, PR 00778-9601.

UNIVERSITY OF PUERTO RICO AT CAROLINA
Carolina, Puerto Rico

Admissions Contact Mrs. Ivonne Calderon, Admissions Officer, University of Puerto Rico at Carolina, PO Box 4800, Carolina, PR 00984-4800. *Phone:* 787-257-0000 Ext. 3347.

INTERNATIONAL

MARSHALL ISLANDS

COLLEGE OF THE MARSHALL ISLANDS
Majuro, Marshall Islands

Admissions Contact PO Box 1258, Majuro 96960, Marshall Islands.

MEXICO

WESTHILL UNIVERSITY
Sante Fe, Mexico

Admissions Contact 56 Domingo Garcia Ramos, Zona Escolar, Prados de la Montana I, Sante Fe, Cuajimalpa CP 05610, Mexico.

PALAU

PALAU COMMUNITY COLLEGE
Koror, Palau

- **Territory-supported** 2-year, founded 1969
- **Calendar** semesters
- **Degree** certificates and associate
- **Small-town** 30-acre campus
- **Endowment** $297,156
- **Coed**

Faculty *Student/faculty ratio:* 12:1.
Student Life *Campus security:* late-night transport/escort service, evening patrols by trained security personnel.
Costs (2003–04) *Tuition:* area resident $1800 full-time, $60 per credit part-time. Full-time tuition and fees vary according to course load. Part-time tuition and fees vary according to course load. *Required fees:* $450 full-time, $225 per term part-time. *Room and board:* $2352; room only: $588. Room and board charges vary according to housing facility.
Financial Aid Of all full-time matriculated undergraduates who enrolled, 200 Federal Work-Study jobs (averaging $200).
Applying *Options:* early admission, deferred entrance. *Application fee:* $10. *Required:* high school transcript, minimum 2.00 GPA.
Admissions Contact Ms. Elsie Skang, Admissions Counselor, Palau Community College, PO Box 9, Koror, PW 96940-0009, Palau. *Phone:* 680-488-2470 Ext. 265. *Fax:* 680-488-4468.

SWITZERLAND

SCHILLER INTERNATIONAL UNIVERSITY
Engelberg, Switzerland

- **Independent** 2-year, founded 1988, part of Schiller International University
- **Calendar** semesters
- **Degree** certificates, diplomas, and associate
- **Urban** campus with easy access to Zurich
- **Coed,** 58 undergraduate students

Undergraduates Students come from 2 states and territories, 17 other countries, 100% are from out of state.
Freshmen *Admission:* 130 applied, 40 admitted.
Faculty *Total:* 14, 36% full-time. *Student/faculty ratio:* 7:1.
Majors Hotel/motel administration; international business/trade/commerce; tourism and travel services management.
Academic Programs *Special study options:* accelerated degree program, adult/continuing education programs, advanced placement credit, cooperative education, English as a second language, independent study, internships, study abroad, summer session for credit.
Library Bellevue Library with 3,000 titles, 17 serial subscriptions, 60 audiovisual materials, an OPAC.
Computers on Campus 11 computers available on campus for general student use. At least one staffed computer lab available.
Student Life *Housing Options:* coed. Campus housing is university owned. Freshman campus housing is guaranteed. *Activities and Organizations:* student-run newspaper, student government, student newspaper. *Campus security:* 24-hour emergency response devices. *Student services:* personal/psychological counseling.
Athletics *Intramural sports:* badminton M/W, basketball M/W, golf M/W, rock climbing M/W, skiing (cross-country) M/W, skiing (downhill) M/W, soccer M/W, swimming M/W, tennis M/W, volleyball M/W, weight lifting M/W.
Costs (2003–04) *Comprehensive fee:* $25,650 includes full-time tuition ($18,675), mandatory fees ($750), and room and board ($6225). Full-time tuition and fees vary according to program and student level. Part-time tuition: $820 per credit. No tuition increase for student's term of enrollment. *Required fees:* $150 per term part-time. *Room and board:* Room and board charges vary according to housing facility, location, and student level.
Financial Aid *Financial aid deadline:* 6/1.
Applying *Options:* common application, deferred entrance. *Application fee:* $55. *Required:* high school transcript, interview. *Application deadline:* rolling (freshmen), rolling (transfers).
Admissions Contact Ms. Annelies Muff, Administrative Assistant, Schiller International University, Hotel Europe, Dorfstrasse 40, Engelberg 6390, Switzerland. *Phone:* 41-41-639 74 74. *Fax:* 41-41-639 7475. *E-mail:* info@schiller-university.ch.

In-Depth Descriptions of Two-Year
COLLEGES

ALLENTOWN BUSINESS SCHOOL
CENTER VALLEY, PENNSYLVANIA

The College and Its Mission

Located in the Lehigh Valley for more than 134 years, Allentown Business School (ABS) is steeped in a tradition of education excellence. ABS is dedicated to developing people for career positions using hands-on teaching methods, industry-current technology, and externships. The vast majority of graduates are either employed or continuing their education within one year of graduation. Because ABS is a private school, it can put students first and promote an atmosphere in which students can learn, grow, and meet or even exceed their expectations of achievement. The Allentown Business School is accredited by the Accrediting Council for Independent Colleges and Schools.

Academic Programs

ABS provides career training leading to a diploma or an Associate in Specialized Business or Technology degree. All programs follow the quarterly schedule. These programs are nine to twenty-four months long. Associate degree programs are eighteen months long and consist of prescribed subjects that are divided into periods of instruction approximately eleven weeks in length and offered every eleven weeks.

Associate Degree Programs Accounting: eighteen months (day), 1,680 clock hours, 99 credits. Graduates are qualified for such positions as junior accountant, accounts receivable/payable clerk, bookkeeper, and payroll clerk upon completion of the course.

Computer Programming: eighteen months (day), 1,680 clock hours, 93 credits. The program prepares students for careers in the field of application development and system design. The program enhances the basic philosophies with a detailed study of modern programming languages. Programming skills are applicable to the PC market, the mainframe market, or the emerging Internet programming market. Graduates are awarded the Associate in Specialized Technology degree.

Criminal Justice: 18 months (day), 24 months (evening), 1750 clock hours, 94 credits. This program prepares students for positions as corrections officers; local, county, and state police officers; campus police; investigators; detectives; child case workers; juvenile service officers; drug task officers; customs inspectors; loss prevention managers; and U.S. marshals.

Hospitality and Tourism Management: eighteen months (day), 1,750 clock hours, 96 credits. After completing their internship, students are prepared for positions in the hospitality industry and tourism field.

Medical Assisting and Office Administration: eighteen months (day), 1,750 clock hours, 92 credits. After an internship is completed in the health-care field, graduates take positions in hospitals, doctors' offices, clinics, and insurance agencies.

Management/Marketing: eighteen months (day), 1,680 clock hours, 102 credits. Graduates of this program are qualified for entry-level positions in business, banking, insurance, finance, and government.

Personal Computers and Network Technology: eighteen months (day), 1,680 clock hours, 95 credits. Students are provided with the latest technology, software, and core business subjects to perform entry-level tasks in PC and LAN setups, diagnoses, upgrades, configurations, and repairs.

Visual Communications: eighteen months (day), 1,680 clock hours, 92 credits. Graduates of this program find employment as entry-level production artists, layout artists, illustrators, and freelance graphic designers. Employment opportunities are in advertising agencies, design studios, art departments, printing companies, and newspaper/magazine publishers.

Web Administration: eighteen months (day), 1,680 clock hours, 94 credits. The high level of instruction and variety of courses in this program help students gain successful employment by providing skills to design, launch, and manage Web sites for businesses.

Diploma Programs Computer Administration: nine months (day), 12 months (evening), 840 clock hours, 46.5 credits.

Computer Programming Specialist Studies: eighteen months (evening), 896 clock hours, 49 credits. Students prepare for entry-level positions in the fields of development and system design in the PC market, the mainframe market, or the emerging Internet programming market by being exposed to the modern programming languages that are widely used today.

Graphic Design : eighteen months (evening), 1,008 clock hours, 54 credits. Students prepare for entry-level positions as production artists, layout artists, illustrators, or electronic or freelance graphic designers by being exposed to the most current industry-standard software applications, the elements of graphic design, and conceptual skills.

Local Area Network (LAN) Technology: eighteen months (evening), 1,008 clock hours, 56 credits.

Paralegal Studies: eighteen months (day), 1,750 clock hours, 96 credits. This program prepares students for a career in the legal field, doing work with closings, hearings, trials, and corporate meetings; in the business field, helping with contracts; and in the government field, analyzing legal material, doing research, collecting evidence, and writing memoranda.

Web Design and Technology: twelve months (evening), 672 clock hours, 37 credits.

Costs

The following costs are estimates and subject to change. Costs for diploma programs include: computer administration studies, $10,530 (estimated cost of books/supplies, $750; laptop, $2325); computer programming, $20,130 (estimated cost of books/supplies, $1800; laptop, $2325); computer programming specialist studies, $18,720 (estimated cost of books/supplies, $1275; laptop, $2325); local area network technology, $18,630 (estimated cost of books/supplies, $2450; laptop, $2325); graphic design, $17,010 (estimated cost of books/supplies, $1900; laptop, $2800); management/marketing, $19,530 (estimated cost of books/supplies, $1800; laptop, $2325); Web administration, $24,120 (estimated cost of books/supplies, $1800; laptop, $2650); and Web design and technology, $15,000 (estimated cost of books/supplies, $900; laptop, $2650). Business associate degree programs are estimated at $18,900 (estimated cost of books/supplies, $1500; laptop, $2325); personal computer and network technology, $23,010 (estimated cost of books/supplies, $2900; laptop, $2325); and the visual communications program, $23,910 (estimated cost of books/supplies, $2925; laptop, $2800). All books and supplies and laptop costs are estimates. All costs are for the entire program. Additional fees include a registration fee of $50 and a graduation fee of $100.

The Education Department evaluates any previous education and training that may be applicable to an educational program. If the education and/or training meets the standards for transfer of credit, the program may be shortened and the tuition reduced accordingly. Students who request credit for previous education or training are required to provide the School with an official transcript from the educational institution.

Financial Aid

The Financial Aid Department devotes personal attention to every student by individually mapping out financial options. In addition to more than $100,000 in scholarships, grants and loans available to those who qualify include Federal Pell Grant, Federal Stafford Student Loan, Federal Supplemental Educational Opportunity Grant, Federal Parent Loan for Undergraduate Students, Federal Work-Study Program, and alternative funding. Scholarships from Allentown Business School and Future Business Leaders of America for graduating high school seniors are also available.

Faculty

Allentown Business School has more than 100 full- and part-time instructors with either bachelor's, master's, or doctoral degrees in addition to occupational qualifications.

Student Body Profile

There are currently more than 1,500 students enrolled at the School. The students who attend Allentown Business School come from a number of areas within a 50-mile radius. All students reside off campus; however, ABS assists with housing when necessary.

Student Activities

ABS has a number of activities and organizations for the students to participate in, such as SIFE, Student Government Association, and various organizations in the program specialties. The students are also encouraged to participate in community events and help raise money for worthy causes.

Throughout the school year, activities that encourage school spirit and develop student leadership may be offered. The School believes that participation in these activities is an important part of the educational process, and student involvement is encouraged.

Facilities and Resources

Students are provided with facilities that have the latest industry-standard equipment. ABS's new facility houses a variety of teaching and resource tools, including a library, a bookstore, and student lounges. The building also houses six PC labs, three Mac labs, two art studios, and a photography studio. The wireless environment allows students to work freely throughout the campus with access to the network at all times.

Career Planning ABS provides career planning services to all students and graduates. While in school, students may take advantage of job fairs and part-time job postings. As students prepare for graduation, career planning representatives assist them with resume writing, interviewing skills, and all other job search techniques to help maximize employment opportunities. Through relationships developed and maintained with employers, the career planning department stays informed about current hiring and industry trends to better serve students and graduates.

Allentown Business School assists students in finding part-time employment while they attend school. Assistance includes advice in preparing for an interview, aid with securing an interview, and offering a list of available jobs.

The school encourages students to maintain satisfactory attendance, conduct, and academic progress so they may be viewed favorably by prospective employers. While the school cannot guarantee employment, it has been successful in placing the majority of its graduates in their field of training. All graduating students participate in the following career planning activities: preparation of resumes and letters of introduction, an important step in a well-planned job search; interviewing techniques, where students acquire effective interviewing skills through practice exercises; job referral, as the Career Planning Services Department compiles job openings from employers in the area; and on-campus interviews, in which companies visit the school to interview graduates for employment opportunities.

All students are expected to participate in the career-planning program, and failure to do so may jeopardize these privileges.

Alumni may continue to utilize the school's career-planning program at no additional cost.

Location

Allentown Business School is located at 2809 East Saucon Valley Road, Center Valley, Pennsylvania. Its new 97,000-square foot building is easily accessible from I-78 and the Pennsylvania Turnpike. It is on a local bus route and within a short driving distance of the Poconos, Philadelphia, and New York. Nearby are Blue Mountain Ski Area, Doe Mountain Ski Area, Dorney Park and Wildwater Kingdom, and the Lehigh County Velodrome. Year-round activities include Musikfest, the Celtic Classic, the Great Allentown Fair, Mayfair, and the Pennsylvania Shakespeare Festival.

Admission Requirements

Students are required to have a personal interview to be accepted into the School. This can be done by meeting with an admissions representative in person. This is also a time to tour the facilities and ask any questions that the student, spouse, or parents may have. Personal interviews enable the School representative to determine whether an applicant is likely to benefit from enrollment into the program. The following items must be included at the time of application: a high school transcript or General Educational Development (GED) test scores, an enrollment agreement (if the applicant is under 18 years of age, it must be signed by the parent or guardian), financial aid forms (if the applicant wishes to apply for financial aid), and the registration fee of $60.

The School reserves the right to reject students if the requirements listed above are not successfully completed.

Prior to beginning school or upon receipt of the student's records, diagnostic testing may be used to assess basic learning skills and the student's ability to benefit from enrolling in the School. The diagnostic tests used are the Test of English as a Foreign Language (TOEFL) and the Career Programs Assessment Test (CPAt).

Students who graduate from a high school outside of the United States must have successfully completed the TOEFL with a minimum score of 450. Any student who is required to take but has not taken the TOEFL is required to take the CPAt.

Application and Information

Allentown Business School follows an open enrollment system; applications to the School are accepted at all times. Students should apply for admission as soon as possible in order to be officially accepted for a specific program and starting date. To apply, students should call to set up an interview with one of the admissions representatives. To meet with one of the representatives and tour the School or to get additional information, interested students should contact the address below.

Admissions Department
Allentown Business School
2809 East Saucon Valley Road
Center Valley, Pennsylvania 18034

Telephone: 610-791-5100
Fax: 610-791-7810
World Wide Web: http://www.chooseabs.com

AMERICAN ACADEMY OF DRAMATIC ARTS
NEW YORK, NEW YORK, AND HOLLYWOOD, CALIFORNIA

The American
Academy
of Dramatic
Arts

The College and Its Mission

Founded in New York in 1884, the American Academy of Dramatic Arts (AADA) was the first school in the United States to provide a professional education for actors. Since 1974, the Academy has operated an additional campus in the Los Angeles area, making AADA the only degree granting conservatory for actors offering programs in both of the major centers of theatrical activity in the country. Now in its second century, the Academy remains dedicated to a single purpose: training actors. The love of acting, as an art and as an occupation, is the spirit that impels the school. For the serious, well-motivated student ready to make a commitment to acting and to concentrated professional training, the Academy offers more than a century of success; a well-balanced, carefully structured curriculum; and a vital, dedicated, and caring faculty. Academy training involves the student intellectually, physically, and emotionally. Designed for the individual, it stresses self-discovery and self-discipline. Underlying the training are the beliefs that an actor prepared to work on the stage has the best foundation for acting in any medium and that classroom learning must be put to the test in the practical arena of a theater. The soundness of this approach is reflected in the achievements of the alumni, a diverse body of professionals unmatched by the alumni of any other institution. (Performances by Academy alumni have received nominations for 72 Oscars, 57 Tonys, and 195 Emmys.) The time spent at the Academy can be an important period of development for those who become professional actors as well as for those who eventually choose other paths. All students are expected to make a commitment to professionalism, excellence, and discipline while enrolled at the Academy. The American Academy of Dramatic Arts is a nonprofit educational institution, chartered in New York by the Board of Regents of the University of the State of New York. In New York the Academy is accredited by the Middle States Association of Colleges and Schools and in California by the Western Association of Schools and Colleges. Both schools are accredited by the National Association of Schools of Theatre.

Academic Programs

The Professional Training Program requires two years to complete. Students who meet the requirements of the program receive an associate degree. A third-year performance program is offered to selected graduates. Students who successfully complete this program earn the Certificate of Advanced Studies in Actor training.

The first year consists of two 12-week terms and one 6-week term, providing a total of 30 transferable college credits. Classes include acting, movement, voice and speech, vocal production, acting styles, and theater history. The primary goals of the first-year program are to achieve relaxed, free, and truthful use of oneself in imaginary circumstances; to gain awareness of the body in terms of alignment, flexibility, and strength; to develop an open, well-placed, and well-supported vocal tone; to acquire clearly articulated standard American speech; and to increase understanding of the historical and stylistic backgrounds of drama. Students may enter the first year in mid-September or late January for the course in Pasadena; late October or early February for New York. Admission to the second year is by invitation. Selection is made on the basis of progress, potential, and readiness to benefit from advanced training, as evidenced by the quality of first-year classwork and examination play performances. The second year begins with advanced classwork designed to reinforce and build upon the learning experiences of the first year. Emphasis is gradually shifted to performance opportunities. Additional courses are given in fencing and stage makeup. The second-year course provides 30 transferable undergraduate credits. Workshops to deal with specific acting problems are set up as needed, and, toward the end of the second year, seminars are scheduled to familiarize students with basic procedures for attaining professional employment. Upon completion of the second year, students graduate from the Professional Training Program with associate degrees. Admission to the third-year program, which emphasizes performance, is also by invitation. Students who undertake a third year of study become members of the Academy Company, the school's performance ensemble. Selection is based on the individual's potential and the overall concept of a balanced acting company. The practical development of the actor is continued through study, rehearsal, and performance of fully-produced plays in Academy theaters over a thirty-week period from late summer to late winter. Agents, casting directors, and other professional personnel are invited to see Academy Company productions, and counseling is offered to assist third-year students in launching professional careers. Students completing the third-year program earn an additional 30 college credits and are awarded a certificate. Guest speakers from the professional world are regularly invited to the Academy to share insights with the students at special assemblies.

The Academy also offers a six-week summer conservatory for those who would like to begin to study, to refresh basic skills, or to test interest and ability in an environment of professional training. Classes begin shortly after the Fourth of July and are open to anyone of high school age or older. Teaching standards are identical to those of the Academy's degree and certificate programs.

Costs

In 2004–05, the cost of the full-time program was $14,900 for tuition and $450 for the general fee. (The general fee covers the cost of accident insurance, costume and production costs, use of the library, and student identification.) Students need to budget an additional $600 for purchasing books and scripts, dance attire for movement class, a makeup kit, and other expenses related to the training. The cost of housing varies. On the average, housing, food, transportation, and personal expenses can amount to approximately $11,000 to $13,000.

Financial Aid

The Academy makes every effort to assist students in need of financial aid. The Academy participates in various financial aid programs, including government administered grants, loans, and college work-study. Grant awards are determined by financial need. (Only United States citizens and permanent residents are eligible for government-sponsored aid programs.) Payment plans (for those eligible) assist students by extending the payment of tuition over a period of time. Scholarships, awarded on the basis of both need and merit, are available to qualified students, including a limited number of Trustee Awards to first-year students. New York City and Los Angeles offer numerous job opportunities for students desiring part-time employment, including on-campus employment (work-study).

Faculty

To achieve its objectives, the Academy requires that its faculty members be well trained in the various performing arts disciplines; seasoned by professional experience; mature, objective, and sympathetic in their relations with students; and exemplars of the commitment to excellence that the Academy hopes to instill in its students. In their own training, the Academy's faculty members represent all of the master teachers and significant systems and philosophies of the performing arts of the past half-century. Their professional experience is diversified, encompassing a variety of positions in film, television, and theater. In selecting faculty members to support its specialized programs, the Academy places more importance on an instructor's professional training and experience and teaching ability than on traditional academic credentials. The student-faculty ratio ranges from 16:1 in classroom instruction, to 4:1 or 3:1 in some performance situations.

Student Body Profile

Academy students reflect a wide diversity of backgrounds and geographical origin; they come from every region of the United States, from Canada, and from many other countries. Enrollment in 2003 was 239 in California and 216 in New York, with a combined average of 20 percent members of minority groups and 20 percent international students. Forty percent of the students are men. The average age of an entering Academy student is 22. Less than half of all first-year students come directly after high school; others enroll after a range of experiences, including college, military service, or other careers.

Student Activities

Students at the American Academy of Dramatic Arts are bonded by their love of acting. A common interest and the collaborative nature of the training contribute to genial social relations among the student body, and, accordingly, school-arranged activities are usually related to the performing arts. Academy students are frequently invited to attend all types of theatrical events for free or given the opportunity to purchase reduced-priced tickets. Every effort is made by the school to facilitate the cultural enrichment of the students.

Facilities and Resources

The Academy in New York is housed in a six-story building that is a registered New York City landmark. It includes classrooms, rehearsal studios, dance studios, a video studio, a student lounge, locker areas, and dressing rooms. A library, made possible by a grant from CBS, is a handsome facility, organized to serve the special research and study needs of the actor. Three theaters—a 160-seat proscenium theater, an intimate 160-seat thrust-stage theater, and a semiarena theater that seats 103—are used for classes, rehearsals, and productions. Production facilities include a prop department, a costume department, a scene shop, and a sound room.

After housing its West Coast operation in leased space in Pasadena for more than twenty-five years, the Academy purchased a campus in the heart of Hollywood and took residence in 2000. Situated on 2.25 acres adjacent to the historic Charlie Chaplin Studios, the new campus includes a theater, ample parking, a library, and spacious classrooms and studios.

In place of on-campus housing, AADA offers a variety of attractive off-campus options through special arrangements with local housing resources.

Location

Located in midtown Manhattan, the New York home of the Academy is within walking distance of the Grand Central and Pennsylvania train stations, the Port Authority bus terminal, and Broadway and off-Broadway theaters.

AADA Hollywood is located in the center of the motion picture and television production capital of the world. The new campus is a short walk from Hollywood Boulevard and is surrounded by film and television production companies. The California Freeway system affords access to beaches, deserts, and mountains.

At each location, the training at the Academy is enhanced by the exciting variety of nearby cultural and recreational opportunities afforded by New York and Los Angeles.

Admission Requirements

AADA seeks talented and highly motivated applicants. An audition/interview is the cornerstone of the admission process. The overall policy is to admit individuals who seem both artistically and academically qualified to undertake a rigorous conservatory program of professional training. Readiness to benefit fully from such training is assessed in the audition/interview. Auditions, whether for entrance into the program in New York City or Hollywood, may be held at either school. In addition, regional auditions are held annually in major cities in the United States, Canada, and London. The audition requires the performance of two contrasting, memorized speeches (one comedic and one dramatic) from published plays (one period and one contemporary), the total performance time to be no more than 4 minutes. The audition appointment includes an interview. In the audition/interview, special attention is given to the quality of the applicant's instinctive emotional connection to the audition material. Since good listening is so fundamental to good acting, the auditioner notes how well the applicant listens in the "real world" context of the interview. Other criteria include sensitivity, sense of language, sense of humor, vitality, presence, vocal quality, cultural interests, a realistic sense of self, and the challenge involved in pursuing an acting career.

All entering students must hold a diploma from an accredited secondary school or its equivalent. Transcripts of all previous academic work must be submitted; previous college credits may not be transferred. High school seniors should submit SAT I or ACT scores. Two letters of recommendation are required before an audition is scheduled. International students who are fluent in English are welcome to apply. AADA is approved for the training of veterans.

Application and Information

The Academy operates on a rolling admission basis, but early application is encouraged. There is a nonrefundable application fee of $50. Admission decisions are made within four weeks of the audition. Further information may be obtained from:

For AADA New York:
Karen Higginbotham
Director of Admissions
American Academy of Dramatic Arts
120 Madison Avenue
New York, New York 10016
Telephone: 212-686-0620
            800-463-8990 (toll-free)
E-mail: admissions-ny@aada.org

For AADA Hollywood:
Dan Justin
Director of Admissions
American Academy of Dramatic Arts
1336 North La Brea Avenue
Hollywood, California 90028
Telephone: 800-222-2867 (toll-free)
E-mail: admissions-ca@aada.org
World Wide Web: http://www.aada.org (both campuses)

Robert Redford presents fellow AADA alumnus Jason Robards with the Alumni Achievement Award at the Centennial Gala.

ANDREW COLLEGE

CUTHBERT, GEORGIA

The College and Its Mission

Founded in 1854, Andrew College is a small, two-year, residential college related to the United Methodist Church. Its mission is to provide an academically challenging liberal arts curriculum within a nurturing community. As a two-year, senior college–parallel, church-related college, Andrew exists to provide students with a better beginning to their college careers. Andrew specializes in the education of freshmen and sophomores. Historically, 100 percent of Andrew College's graduates are accepted into four-year colleges and universities.

For a quarter of a century, the Andrew College chapter of Phi Theta Kappa, the international honor society for two-year colleges, has won national recognition and was the number one chapter during five of those years. There are more than 1,000 chapters of Phi Theta Kappa, and no other chapter, in public or private institutions, has established a more impressive record. Andrew College seeks to achieve its goals by providing several advantages, many of which are unique to a small campus with a church-related environment: the opportunity for intellectual, social, and spiritual development; a professionally competent faculty that is dedicated to teaching; individual attention to students at all levels of operation within the College; a two-year curriculum that parallels that of four-year colleges and universities; a cultural enrichment program that encourages students to appreciate the arts; the opportunity to learn leisure-time skills that lead to the development of a healthy body; remediation in the basic skills; orientation experiences for successful adjustment to college life; academic advising; a student community committed to the earning of a college education; and cultural and academic resources for the community and churches in the area.

Andrew College is accredited by the Commission on Colleges of the Southern Association of Colleges and Schools (1866 Southern Lane, Decatur, Georgia 30033-4097; telephone: 404-679-4501) to award associate degrees. Andrew College is listed by the University Senate of the United Methodist Church.

Academic Programs

The academic program at Andrew College is specifically designed for freshman and sophomore students. The faculty members serve at Andrew because they enjoy teaching freshmen and sophomores. This attitude and expertise contribute significantly to the quality of education that students receive.

Andrew College offers programs that lead to advanced degrees in the arts and sciences. The College offers the Associate of Arts degree, the Associate of Science degree, and the Associate of Music degree. To be eligible for graduation, a student must have earned at least a 2.0 cumulative grade point average on the work attempted at Andrew College. All associate degrees have a core curriculum of liberal studies, including a required curriculum of essential skills, humanities/fine arts, science/mathematics/technology, social science, and physical education. Each student must satisfactorily complete a course in religion or philosophy and satisfy Cultural Enrichment Program requirements. All students who graduate from Andrew College must demonstrate proficiency in computer and oral communication skills.

All students entering Andrew College are assigned a faculty adviser who assists students in all matters relating to their academic progress. Andrew College schedules free tutoring during each term for students who need extra help with their studies. Some students, including students on academic probation and those admitted on a conditional basis, are assigned to mandatory study and tutoring sessions. Enrichment seminars are offered in areas beyond those covered in regular class study. These courses provide students with a challenge to do in-depth study and carry institutional credit only. Andrew College offers a number of programs that assist students in reaching their educational potential. For a variety of reasons, some applicants to Andrew College may need to improve their academic skills in order to be successful in a full-time schedule of college-level courses. The Strategic Studies Program serves students who need to improve their academic skills before embarking on a full-time

schedule of college-level courses. The program contains a selected schedule of college-level course work as well as other specially designed courses that provide intensive study and individual guidance at a pace that is compatible with the students' abilities. Tutorial assistance is provided.

Andrew College has established an intensive level of academic support services designed for and limited to specifically identified and accepted students with documented learning disabilities and/or attention deficit disorders. While the Focus Program supplements and complements the tutorial and advising services available to all students, it provides an additional level of professional assistance and monitoring to enhance the students' probability for success.

Andrew College offers an English as a Second Language (ESL) Program for students whose native language is not English and gives them a choice in the selection of the instructional program.

Through the Cultural Enrichment Program (CEP), Andrew College recognizes the fact that exposure to the cultural arts is an essential part of a liberal arts education. As a graduation requirement, all degree-seeking students must attend designated programs relating to the cultural arts during their enrollment.

Costs

Although Andrew College is a private college, an Andrew education is affordable. Tuition and fees for the 2004–05 academic year are $8150. Room and board are $5130 for the academic year. Books and supplies average $600 to $700 per academic year. Approximately $2300 per year should be allowed for other costs, including transportation and personal expenses.

Financial Aid

Approximately 90 percent of Andrew College students receive some type of federal or institutional aid. Students from Georgia are eligible for the Georgia Tuition Equalization Grant and may be eligible for the HOPE Scholarship. Scholarships are given for academic excellence, community service, intercollegiate sports, spiritual life, and programs such as chorus, art, drama, piano, photography, yearbook, and journalism.

Every year, the Office of Admission holds a Scholarship Day program, where students who have a 3.0 GPA or above and at least a 1000 on the SAT I are invited to compete for academic scholarships. Four Andrew Scholar awards (full tuition, room, and board scholarships) are presented at the competition, along with other academic awards. Scholarships or loans may be awarded to students who are members of the United Methodist Church. Other churches, religious and community organizations, and fraternal or business groups may also sponsor financial awards. Government programs at the federal and state levels provide a variety of grants, low-interest educational loans, and work-study employment opportunities for students. Eligibility for many of these programs is based on need.

Faculty

The faculty at Andrew College is committed to the education of freshmen and sophomores. The success of the students at the next level and beyond is the focus of the faculty and the academic program at Andrew.

The College employs 29 full-time and 5 part-time faculty members. The student-faculty ratio varies each year but is maintained at or below 16:1, resulting in lively discussions, teacher-student interaction, and individual attention. The student-faculty ratio for 2002–03 was 13:1. Eight members of the full-time faculty hold doctoral degrees, two have terminal degrees in their field, and the remainder hold master's degrees in their area of specialty.

Student Body Profile

Andrew College has a diverse population of students from all over the world. Approximately 5 percent of the College population is international students from countries such as Japan, Nigeria, Trinidad, Mexico, Guatemala, and Korea. Based on figures from fall 2002, 84 percent of students were from Georgia, 6 percent were from Florida,

3 percent were from Alabama, and 2 percent were from other states. The total student population in fall 2002 was 395 students. The College plans to grow to 500 students by 2004. Ninety percent of Andrew College students live in a College residence hall.

While most students transfer to schools in Georgia, graduates have chosen to transfer to schools as far away as New England or California.

Student Activities

The student life program at Andrew College is designed to promote activities and programs that are supportive of the College's aims and purposes. The first two years of college are critical for academic success; therefore, programs that support and enhance students' lives are very important.

Andrew College is committed to the idea that total education involves more than academic pursuit. Activities, including intramural recreation, student activities, religious activities, career and transfer services, student government, and residential and commuter student programs, are among the many programs offered. All freshman students are required to complete a student orientation program.

Informal recreation opportunities available to students include basketball, indoor and outdoor volleyball, racquetball, walleyball, weight training, and tennis. Formalized recreational opportunities exist under the umbrella of intramurals and include team and individual sports and exercise programs. Off-campus recreational opportunities are promoted throughout the year. A wide variety of student activities take place at Andrew. Many organizations and various offices of the College provide a diversity of programs. The Student Events and Activities (SEA) Board is the chief programming committee in the student life area and sponsors events such as Homecoming, major dances, movies, coffeehouse performers, speakers, and comedy acts. Student organizations at Andrew College offer many leadership opportunities and operate under the jurisdiction of the Student Development Committee. Such organizations include the Student Government Association, International Student Association, Outdoor Adventure Club, Phi Theta Kappa Honor Society, AndrewServes, and the Residence Hall Association.

Sports Andrew College maintains membership in the National Junior College Athletic Association and the Georgia Junior College Athletic Association. Andrew offers scholarships in all intercollegiate sports in which the College participates. Andrew participates competitively in baseball, golf, and soccer for men and soccer and fast-pitch softball for women.

Facilities and Resources

Pitts Library subscribes to more than 100 periodicals, five daily newspapers, and three weekly newspapers. These publications supplement the library's holdings and provide reading and sources for the students and faculty members. Library computers provide students with access to holdings at other libraries and access to the World Wide Web through the Internet. A substantial collection of audiovisual and microfilm materials is maintained. An attractive main reading room provides areas for individual study, and a special reference section supplies ample space for research work.

The Andrew College Interactive Distance Learning Center is located adjacent to the main reading room and contains videoconferencing and Web-based instructional program development facilities.

In 1999, the College completed construction of an athletic complex, which contains baseball, soccer, and softball fields. The Fort Residence

Building was completed and ready for occupancy by 142 students in fall 2000. The Phyllis and Jack Jones Chapel was completed in September 2001.

Location

Andrew College is located in southwest Georgia in the town of Cuthbert. Cuthbert is the county seat of Randolph County, which has a total population of 8,000 people. The Cuthbert area is a safe, friendly community located 40 miles east of Albany, Georgia; 161 miles southwest of Atlanta; 60 miles south of Columbus, Georgia; and 30 miles east of Eufaula, Alabama. The weather year-round is ideally suited to the many recreational opportunities in the region. A championship state park golf course is located 20 minutes from the campus of Andrew College. Lake George is also 20 minutes away and provides an ideal place for fishing, boating, and waterskiing. Large cities and shopping malls are within 1 hour's drive. Providence Canyon, for hiking, picnicking, and nature watching, is only a 20-minute drive from the campus.

Admission Requirements

Andrew College admits applicants who demonstrate abilities that are necessary for successful completion of the program. Admission decisions are based on the applicant's previous academic record, test scores, recommendations, and, in some cases, a personal interview. Equal educational opportunities are offered to students regardless of race, color, religion, disability, gender, age, creed, or national origin.

Applicants may be admitted for any term. In order to ensure proper processing, all credentials should be on file in the Office of Admission approximately thirty days prior to semester registration. All applicants must submit the following materials: a completed application for admission, a $20 application fee, transcripts of high school (or GED) and/or college course work attempted, and scores from either the SAT I or ACT. Transfer students who have successfully completed college-level courses in English and math need not submit SAT I/ACT scores. In addition, applicants whose native language is not English must submit scores from the Test of English as a Foreign Language (TOEFL) or an acceptable score on an equivalent English language examination.

Admission to Andrew College is gained through an individual selection process. Minimum academic requirements for nonconditional acceptance include a high school diploma, graduation from an accredited high school, an evaluated high school GPA of 2.0 or better on a 4.0 scale, and SAT I scores of at least 460 on verbal and 430 on math or the ACT equivalent. Students not meeting the minimum academic requirements for nonconditional acceptance may be conditionally accepted but are required to take placement examinations prior to registering for their first semester.

Application and Information

A new student may enter Andrew College at the beginning of the fall, spring, and summer semesters. There is an application deadline set at two weeks prior to the registration date for each term.

For an application and further information about Andrew College, students should contact:

Office of Admission and Financial Aid
Andrew College
413 College Street
Cuthbert, Georgia 39840
Telephone: 800-664-9250 (toll-free)
Fax: 229-732-2176
E-mail: admissions@andrewcollege.edu
World Wide Web: http://www.andrewcollege.edu

ARGOSY UNIVERSITY/TWIN CITIES
School of Health Sciences
EAGAN, MINNESOTA

The University and Its Mission

Argosy University is a private institution of higher education dedicated to providing high-quality professional educational programs at doctoral, masters, baccalaureate, and associate degree levels, as well as continuing education to individuals who seek to advance their professional and personal lives. The University emphasizes programs in the behavioral sciences, business, education, and the health-are professions. A limited number of preprofessional programs and general education offerings are provided to permit students to prepare for entry into these professional fields. The programs of Argosy University are designed to instill the knowledge, skills, and ethical values of professional practice and to foster values of social responsibility in a supportive, learning-centered environment of mutual respect and professional excellence.

The University has a strong base of full-time practitioner-oriented faculty and staff members, an attractive learning environment, and a rich array of program offerings. At Argosy University/Twin Cities, students are able to choose from a variety of programs of study and have the opportunity to learn with a diverse group of students and faculty members. The School of Health Sciences at Argosy University /Twin Cities offers programs ranging from dental hygiene to veterinary technology to radiation therapy.

Argosy University is accredited by the Higher Learning Commission and is a member of the North Central Association (NCA) of Colleges and Schools (30 North LaSalle Street, Chicago, Illinois 60602; telephone: 312-263-0456; Web site: http://www.ncahlc.org).

Argosy University/Twin Cities is registered with the Minnesota Higher Education Services Office (1450 Energy Park Drive, Suite 350, St. Paul, Minnesota 55108; telephone: 651-642-0533). Registration is not an endorsement of the institution. Registration does not mean that credits earned at the institution can be transferred to other institutions or that the quality of the educational programs would meet the standards of every student, educational institution, or employer.

The Associate of Science in dental hygiene degree program is accredited by the Commission on Dental Accreditation (211 East Chicago Avenue, Chicago, Illinois, 60611; telephone: 312-440-4653). The Commission is a specialized accrediting body recognized by the United States Department of Education.

The Associate of Applied Science in diagnostic medical sonography degree program is accredited by the Commission on Accreditation of Allied Health Education Programs on recommendation of the Joint Review Committee on Education in Diagnostic Medical Sonography (35 East Wacker Drive, Suite 1970, Chicago, Illinois 60601-2208; telephone: 312-553-9355).

The Associate of Applied Science in histotechnology and medical laboratory degree programs are accredited by the National Accrediting Agency for Clinical Laboratory Sciences (8410 West Bryn Mawr, Suite 670, Chicago, Illinois, 60631; telephone: 773-714-8880).

The Associate of Applied Science in medical assisting degree program is accredited by the Commission on Accreditation of Allied Health Education Programs on recommendation of the

Committee on Accreditation for Medical Assistant Education (35 East Wacker Drive, Suite 1970, Chicago, Illinois, 60601-2208; telephone: 312-553-9355).

The Associate of Science in radiation therapy and the Associate of Applied Science radiologic technology degree programs are accredited by the Joint Review Committee on Education in Radiologic Technology (20 North Wacker Drive, Suite 900, Chicago, Illinois, 60606; telephone: 312-704-5300).

The Associate of Applied Science in veterinary technology degree program is accredited through the Council on Education of the American Veterinary Medical Association (1931 North Meachum Road, Suite 100, Schaumburg, Illinois, 60173; telephone: 847-925-8070).

Academic Programs

The programs at Argosy University/Twin Cities are designed to develop skills in high-demand fields and to provide students with industry-relevant instruction from experienced professors. Since 1961, nearly 6,000 students have successfully completed the health science programs and joined the health-care community as practicing health-care and veterinary professionals.

Associate Degree Programs The Argosy University/Twin Cities School of Health Sciences offers associate degree programs in dental hygiene, diagnostic medical sonography, histotechnology, medical assisting, medical laboratory technology, radiation therapy, radiologic technology, and veterinary technology. Typically, associate degree programs are completed in one to two years. These programs follow a semester calendar.

Costs

For the current academic year, tuition for full-time students is $360 per semester credit hour. Fees include, but are not limited to, laboratory fee ($40 per semester lab credit), clinic fee (dental hygiene program, $390 per term), graduation fee ($150), and application fee ($50). Books and related supplies are not included. Argosy University reserves the right to add or change any of the fees or charges at any time without prior written notice.

Financial Aid

Through Argosy University's Central Office of Student Finance, eligible students receive help in obtaining financial assistance through a variety of programs. The Central Office of Student Finance coordinates the administration of all federal, state, and institutional aid, including grants, scholarships, and loans. The first step in this process is to complete the Free Application for Federal Student Aid (FAFSA). Applications can be obtained electronically on the Web at http://fafsa.ed.gov or at the campus. It is best to submit the application as early as possible to receive consideration for the maximum amount of aid possible and to ensure timely receipt of funds. Argosy University/Twin Cities is dedicated to providing students with timely, efficient, and courteous assistance throughout the financial aid process.

Faculty

The most outstanding aspect of the institution is the dedication of the faculty members and their ability to cultivate a supportive learning environment. From them, students learn to integrate formal knowledge with professional practice. Argosy University/Twin Cities faculty members believe that their primary roles are those of mentor, teacher, and colearner. They are dedicated to training students to assume leadership roles within various health science fields. Students have access to faculty members and counseling with regard to course and program matters. In addition, the Student Services Office personnel advise students in a number of areas.

Student Body Profile

In 2002, Argosy University/Twin Cities' total undergraduate enrollment was 850. Its students come from many different states, territories, and countries. Approximately 5 percent of the total student body comes from outside the state of Minnesota. One hundred percent of the student body lives off campus.

Student Activities

There are a number of opportunities for students to serve as part of the campus governance process. A primary purpose of the student organizations is to represent student concerns, facilitate communication, and assist the faculty and administration in promoting the welfare of the campus.

Facilities and Resources

The new Argosy University/Twin Cities facility is a 90,000-square-foot building that houses 1,300 students. It features large classrooms and an expansive new laboratory and library as well as additional student and faculty service facilities. Features include forty-four labs and classrooms, large student lounge areas, an outdoor picnic/study area, an expanded student resource center, an on-site student bookstore store, a smart classroom and an expansive library.

Location

The new 90,000-square-foot campus facility at Argosy University/Twin Cities in suburban Eagan, Minnesota, is located on Central Parkway near the intersection of Yankee Doodle and Pilot Knob Roads, next to the new Eagan Community Center near Interstate 494.

Admission Requirements

Students who have successfully completed a program of secondary education or the equivalent (GED) are eligible for admission to the health sciences programs. Entrance requirements include either an ACT composite score of 18 or above, a combined math and verbal SAT score of 850 or above, or a passing score on the Argosy University entrance exam. In addition, a minimum TOEFL score of 173 (computer version) or 500 (paper version) is required for applicants whose native language is not English or who have not graduated from an institution in which English is the language of instruction. All applicants must include a completed application form, proof of high school graduation or GED, official postsecondary transcripts, and SAT, ACT, or Argosy University exam scores. Additional materials are required prior to matriculation. Some programs have additional application requirements. An admissions representative can provide further detailed information.

Application and Information

Prospective students may apply online at the Web site listed below or submit an application and $50 application fee by mail to the address listed below. For more information, applicants should contact:

Admissions Office
Argosy University/Twin Cities
1515 Central Parkway
Eagan, Minnesota 55121
Telephone: 651-846-2882
         888-844-2004 (toll-free)
E-mail: tcadmissions@argosyu.edu
World Wide Web: http://www.argosyu.edu/pg

THE ART INSTITUTE OF PHILADELPHIA

PHILADELPHIA, PENNSYLVANIA

The Institute and Its Mission

For more than twenty-nine years, the Art Institute has supplied the marketplace with graduates whose skills take creative technologies to the next level. The Art Institute has trained thousands of talented individuals, seamlessly integrating technology into their lives and teaching the skills employers look for in new hires. Employers consistently return for qualified graduates. This is a testament to the Institute's educational philosophies and how well it analyzes industry directions to prepare students for an increasingly competitive and high-tech career market.

Conveniently located in downtown Philadelphia, the Institute was founded by artist Philip Trachtman in 1971. In 1979, The Art Institutes International acquired the school, which had an enrollment of approximately 275. The Institute moved to its present location in 1982 and today serves approximately 2,500 students in eleven major academic programs.

In addition to the Art Institute of Philadelphia, the Art Institutes system includes thirty other Art Institutes. All member schools share a board of advisers that oversees curricula and assists in the placement of graduates.

The Art Institute is accredited by the Accrediting Council for Independent Colleges and Schools (ACICS) to award the Associate of Science and the Bachelor of Science degrees. The Art Institute is authorized by the Commonwealth of Pennsylvania Department of Education to confer the Associate of Science and Bachelor of Science degrees.

Academic Programs

Each school quarter is eleven weeks long, and programs are between six and twelve quarters in length. All programs are offered on a year-round basis, which provides students with strong continuity and the ability to work uninterrupted toward their degrees.

Associate Degree Programs The **Associate of Science** degree is offered in computer animation (eight quarters/120 credits), culinary arts (six quarters/90 credits), fashion design (seven quarters/99 credits), fashion marketing (seven quarters/99 credits), graphic design (eight quarters/120 credits), interior design (eight quarters/120 credits), multimedia and Web design (eight quarters/120 credits), photography (eight quarters/120 credits), video production (seven quarters/111 credits), and visual merchandising (six quarters/99 credits).

Bachelor's Degree Programs The **Bachelor of Science** degree is offered in computer animation, digital media production, graphic design, industrial design, interior design, multimedia and Web design, and visual effects and motion graphics. All degrees require twelve quarters of study and 180 credits.

Transfer Arrangements In the U.S. higher education system, transferability of credit is always determined by the receiving institution. The mission of the Art Institute of Philadelphia is to help students to prepare for entry-level employment in their chosen field of study. It is very unlikely that the academic credits earned at the Art Institute of Philadelphia can be transferred to another school. The Art Institute of Philadelphia does not imply, promise, or guarantee transferability of credits to any other institution.

Special Programs and Services The Institute offers a skills enhancement program designed to help students prepare for college-level English and math courses, and confidential counseling is available when academic or personal problems create roadblocks to success.

Academic counseling is provided by faculty members, the academic department director, and the dean of education. The student and instructor evaluate the student's projects for the purpose of preparing a professional portfolio. Each student develops techniques and strategies for self-marketing in his or her chosen field. Emphasis is placed on each student assessing his or her own marketable skills, developing a network of contacts, generating interviews, writing cover letters and resumes, preparing for interviews, developing a professional appearance, closing, and following up. Students receive instruction in self-confidence, flexibility, and the effort required to conduct a successful job search. Special workshops are offered each summer for art teachers and educators and for high school juniors and seniors.

Off-Campus Programs

The Institute arranges student trips to local cultural and commercial sites. These visits are an integral part of each student's learning experience. In addition to local student trips to support the curriculum, out-of-town seminars and visits are planned in individual programs.

Costs

The cost of tuition and fees varies depending on the student's program. Current costs are available from the Art Institute of Philadelphia Admissions Office. The quarterly tuition is subject to adjustment each academic year, and students are given ninety days' notice in the event of an adjustment.

Financial Aid

All students may apply for financial assistance under various federal and state programs, including Federal Stafford Student Loan (formerly Guaranteed Student Loan), Federal Pell Grant, Federal Supplemental Educational Opportunity Grant (FSEOG), Federal Perkins Loan (FNDSL), Federal Work-Study Program (FWS), Federal PLUS (Parent) Loan Program, state-funded assistance programs, vocational rehabilitation assistance, and Veterans Administration Benefits. Awards under these programs are based on individual need and the availability of funds. Students should contact the Institute's Student Financial Services Office for complete details about financial aid resources.

Full- and half-tuition High School Senior Scholarships may be offered annually in each of the following: graphic design, interior design, industrial design technology, fashion design, computer animation, photography, fashion marketing, digital media production, multimedia and Web design, and video production. Merit scholarships are available to incoming students based on previous academic performance and demonstrated financial need. Presidential scholarships are awarded to upper-quarter students based on criteria selected by the program director and the dean of education.

Faculty

The faculty includes full- and part-time members. Many are experienced in their industry, with outstanding credentials and reputations in their fields, and many of them have achieved regional and national recognition. Each student is assigned a faculty adviser. The year-round average class size is 20–25 students.

Student Body Profile

Students come to the Art Institute of Philadelphia from all over the U.S. and abroad and include men and women who have enrolled directly after completing high school, have transferred from colleges and universities, or have left employment situations to prepare for new careers.

Student Activities

The Art Institute of Philadelphia students have the opportunity to join professional organizations such as the American Society of Interior Designers (ASID), the American Society of Media Photographers (ASMP), and the Fashion Group of Philadelphia.

Facilities and Resources

Housing an impressive gallery, the Institute occupies nearly 86,000 square feet of space on Chestnut Street in a building originally designed in 1928 as the CBS flagship radio station affiliate. Designated as a historical site by the Philadelphia Historical Commission, the Art Deco building became home to the Art Institute in 1982. In addition to classrooms, studios, laboratories, offices, a learning resource center, and the exhibition gallery, the Institute maintains an art supply store for the convenience of the students. Administration and classroom facilities have been designed to accommodate the special needs of individuals with disabilities. A recently acquired space at 1610 Chestnut Street adds approximately 40,000 square feet for offices, classrooms, and computer labs for all bachelor's and associate programs. Whether in the student lounge, the gallery, the Art Institute Supply Store, or the extensive resource center, the daily gathering of students and faculty and staff members makes it easy to feel the energy, caring, and commitment that underlies education at the Art Institute of Philadelphia.

The culinary arts program is housed at 2300 Market Street and has three large kitchens that include a bake shop, a skills kitchen, and an a la carte kitchen. The building also houses the general education, fashion, and interior design classes.

Students enrolled at the Art Institute of Philadelphia are given assistance in locating housing by members of the Student Services Department. Options include Art Institute–sponsored apartment-style housing and independent apartment living.

Classes are structured to be more like life, and the environment is as close to professional as possible. What students learn in class, they put into practice in labs and studios using today's computer technologies. Computer lab facilities at the Art Institute include PAD System (computerized patternmaking) as well as Intergraph Visual Workstations, Pentium-based and Macintosh G4 PCs, Avid Video Labs, Adobe Premier, and a TV station equipped with the latest technology, including digital applications and equipment.

Career Planning/Employment Assistance The Art Institute maintains a Career Services Center for graduates and students. Although the school offers no guarantee of employment, considerable effort is put forth to bring together potential employers and graduates who have the skills employers are seeking. Employment assistance is a priority at the Art Institute. Of all 2000 Art Institute of Philadelphia graduates available for placement, 85.8 percent were working in their field within six months of graduation, earning an average salary of $26,262.

Location

The Art Institute is located in Philadelphia, the birthplace of American Democracy, which was founded in 1682. The City of Brotherly Love has grown up around the Liberty Bell and Independence Hall and surrounds the largest municipal landscaped park in the world. With tree-lined streets and an elegant blend of contemporary and historic architecture, this fifth-largest city in the U.S. offers the finest in symphony orchestras, theater, film, jazz, and opera. The movie *Sixth Sense* was filmed in Philadelphia, which also claims rights to the original Philly cheesesteak. This city of art, with thirty-two major museums, including the expansive collections at the Museum of Art, also provides some of the finest shopping in the nation, from the Market Street Gallery, one of the nation's largest urban shopping malls, to the European-style Bourse with its fifty international boutiques and restaurants. Sports enthusiasts can follow their favorite teams, often right through league playoffs. Baseball's Phillies, NFL's Eagles, NBA's 76ers, and NHL's Flyers play on Broad Street, at the new Citizen's Bank Park and Lincoln Financial Field and at the Wachovia Center.

Admission Requirements

High school graduation or a General Educational Development (GED) certificate is a prerequisite for admission. All applicants are evaluated on the basis of their previous education and their background or stated or demonstrated interest in animation, culinary studies, fashion design or marketing, graphic design, industrial design technology, interior design, multimedia and Web design, photography, video production, visual effects and motion graphics, or visual merchandising. Portfolios are welcome but not required. The Art Institute reserves the right to request any additional information necessary to evaluate an applicant's potential for academic success.

Application and Information

The Institute operates on a rolling admission basis. Applications for admission must be completed and signed by candidates and their parents or guardians (if applicable) and sent to the Institute with a $50 application fee. A tuition deposit of $100 is due within ten days after the enrollment agreement has been submitted. High school and/or college transcripts should be submitted to the Institute at least a month prior to starting classes. For more information, candidates should contact:

Office of Admissions
The Art Institute of Philadelphia
1622 Chestnut Street
Philadelphia, Pennsylvania 19103-5198
Telephone: 215-567-7080
              800-275-2474 (toll-free)
Fax: 215-405-6399
World Wide Web: http://www.aiph.aii.edu

The environment at the Art Institute of Philadelphia is conducive to innovation and growth and ensures that graduates have skills that fit the needs of today's competitive marketplace.

THE ART INSTITUTE OF PITTSBURGH

PITTSBURGH, PENNSYLVANIA

The Institute

At the Art Institute of Pittsburgh, there are 2,500 students, who are learning new ways to apply creative talent, energy, and skill to a new world of commercial and culinary arts, design, and technology. Today's Art Institute of Pittsburgh student draws upon the academic advantage of nine bachelor's degree programs. By becoming the first postsecondary career school in Pennsylvania to offer a baccalaureate degree, the Institute is creating a world with enhanced academic study and greater earning potential for its graduates. Students can take advantage of a world of convenience through online course work. Students anywhere can take a variety of general education courses as well as full degree programs in game art and design, graphic design, and multimedia and Web design courses in the virtual classroom through the Art Institute Online, a division of the Art Institute of Pittsburgh.

The campus resides in a newly renovated historic landmark building with ten floors of fully networked, industry-standard computer labs and specialty facilities, such as four new kitchens, editing suites, digital photography labs, a television production studio, an industrial design machine shop, and more. With graduates located worldwide, the Art Institute of Pittsburgh's alumni network spans more than three quarters of a century and includes more than 26,000 members. From the golden age of illustration to the technological revolution, the graduates have helped to create and shape the world of American popular culture. More than eighty years later, the Art Institute of Pittsburgh's mission to train students for career success remains exactly the same. The Institute is still graduating message makers and tailoring its programs to the needs of an ever-evolving job market. With a history rich in experience and alumni success, the school continues to provide outcome-oriented education leading to the creative careers of tomorrow.

The Art Institute of Pittsburgh is accredited by the Accrediting Council for Independent Colleges (ACICS). The Art Institute of Pittsburgh is a candidate of Middle States Accreditation by the Commissions on Higher Education of the Middle States Association of Colleges and Schools. A candidate for accreditation is a status of affiliation with a regional accrediting commission, which indicates that an institution has achieved recognition and is progressing toward, but is not assured of, accreditation. It has provided evidence of sound planning, seems to have the resources to implement the plan, and appears to have the potential for obtaining its goals within a reasonable time. Candidacy was granted in June 2003.

Academic Programs

The Institute offers Bachelor of Science degree programs (thirty-six months) in culinary management, digital media production, game art and design, graphics design, industrial design, interior design, media arts and animation, interactive media design, photography, and visual effects and motion graphics. Associate of Science degree programs (twenty-one months) are offered in culinary arts, graphic design, industrial design, interactive media design, photography, and video production. Diploma programs (twelve months) are offered in the art of cooking, digital design, residential planning, and Web design.

Off-Campus Programs

Students at the Art Institute of Pittsburgh can find reasonably priced housing through the services of the school's Housing Department. School-sponsored housing is available at Allegheny Center Apartments, complete with fully furnished rental units and free evening shuttle service. Downtown Pittsburgh is serviced by a well-networked Port Authority Transit and subway system, making all of Allegheny County's suburbs accessible to students of the Art Institute of Pittsburgh.

Cost of Study

Tuition for all degree programs is $354 per credit (with an average of 15 credits per quarter). There is a $50 application fee and a $100 enrollment fee. Upon enrollment, each student receives a program-specific supply kit, with prices ranging from $180 to $875, depending on the program of study.

Financial Aid

The Art Institute of Pittsburgh provides financial planning for its students and encourages them to become familiar with the financial aid programs that are available. The Student Financial Services Department helps the student and his or her family plan for the projected costs of education. The department uses a required formula specified by the U.S. Department of Education that compares the cost of education to family size, income, and assets to determine how much of the estimated cost of education should be financed by the student or family and how much should be paid for using aid programs. A financial planner then works with the student to devise a student financial plan to help cover education expenses, based on financial aid eligibility and family income circumstances. This plan carefully matches the student's personal financial contributions with probable outside forms of assistance. Financial aid programs are designed to supplement—rather than replace—the resources of the family. Various merit-based and need-based scholarships are available at the Art Institute of Pittsburgh. Information about the school's scholarships can be obtained in the Admissions Office.

Faculty

The faculty and staff of the Art Institute of Pittsburgh have grown proportionately, both having nearly doubled over the last twenty years alone, to approximately 250 people. Many of the Art Institute faculty members are drawn from the ranks of industry professionals, so they are able to teach students how to use current technology while cultivating their conceptual, creative, and problem-solving skills. To support its educational mission, the Art Institute staff comprises nearly 150 dedicated individuals, all working toward the success of students from admissions to career services. The year-round average class size is 25 students. The Art Institute has an active employer count of more than 9,700, indicating another area of enhancement—career services. The one-time advising approach to graduate placement has become an aggressive and far more sophisticated marketing effort. Approximately 88 percent of all graduates are working in field-related jobs within six months of graduation.

Student Body Profile

What started as a relatively local student body now draws a substantial portion of its enrollment from areas beyond 100 miles of the school and from all over the nation. International students also represent a growing percentage of the Art Institute's population. The average age of the Art Institute student fluctuates between 18 and 24. Approximately 600 of the Art Institute's 2,400 enrolled students reside in a school-sponsored apartment complex located on Pittsburgh's North Shore.

Student Activities

The Art Institute of Pittsburgh's Student Life Department offers collegiate activities and events. The department also employs a Student Activities Coordinator, who plans various events, theme parties, and clubs. Events are communicated via weekly and quarterly newsletters as well as a college television network. The school supports approximately twenty clubs and intramural sports teams as well as a housing department that oversees the activities and concerns of school-sponsored housing residents. A cross-program Student Council represents the needs and issues of the entire student body and meets biweekly. The Student Life Department also offers counseling services.

Academic Facilities

The Art Institute of Pittsburgh is currently located at 420 Boulevard of the Allies in a ten-story building. This fully networked building is a sprawling 170,000-square-foot, historic landmark. The facility has interchangeable classroom and computer and cell animation labs, with extended access to Macintosh and PC computer and design and animation software. Photography students have access to a digital darkroom as well as traditional wet labs and printing stations. Interior design students utilize a fabric and textile research facility and computer-aided drawing software. The building is equipped with a television studio, digital editing suites, and Foley audio studio to support the video production curriculum. A full industrial design shop is available as well. The Art Institute of Pittsburgh's library is program oriented and is undergoing an aggressive purchase of related volumes.

Location

The Art Institute of Pittsburgh is nestled in the heart of downtown Pittsburgh's Golden Triangle. A visitor to the greater Pittsburgh area finds a thriving metropolis that sprawls over 55 square miles. The thirteenth-largest city in the nation, Pittsburgh is situated halfway between New York City and Chicago and is within a 2-hour flight or a day's drive of more than 70 percent of the U.S. population.

By day, Pittsburgh follows the rush of the downtown business crowd and is the international headquarters of many new technology-driven businesses. There are free summer concerts in downtown's Market Square; an abundance of theaters; thriving nightlife districts, such as the South Side and the Strip District; and quaint coffee shops and retail merchants on every corner. A football stadium for the Pittsburgh Steelers and a waterfront baseball park for the Pirates adorn the city's North Shore. Pittsburgh is serviced by Greater Pittsburgh International Airport, one of the largest and most retail-developed airports in the U.S. Directions to the school are available at the Web site listed below.

Admission Requirements

A prospective student seeking admission to the Art Institute of Pittsburgh must be a high school graduate with a high school QPA of 2.0 or higher and a 2.5 or higher for admission into game art and design or hold a General Educational Development (GED), or have a bachelor's degree or higher as a prerequisite for admission. Students who have completed high school or its equivalent but cannot provide the necessary documentation may provide alternate documentation to satisfy this requirement. The President of the Art Institute of Pittsburgh must approve all exceptions. A student who holds a bachelor's degree or higher may submit proof of the bachelor's degree to satisfy the high school or GED requirement. In addition, there is a portfolio requirement for media arts and animation and game art and design.

The Art Institute of Pittsburgh seeks students who are serious about entering the commercial art, culinary, design, or media fields as a career. Prospective students should be serious about achieving career goals as efficiently and effectively as possible. They should also desire a practical and skills-oriented education,

while understanding the importance of a general education component in a well-rounded education. All Art Institute of Pittsburgh applicants are evaluated on the basis of their previous education, background, and stated or demonstrated interest in their program of choice. Portfolios are welcome but not required. Applicants who have taken the SAT I or ACT are encouraged to submit scores to the Admissions Office for evaluation.

Application and Information

Applications are accepted on a rolling basis. An application for admission must be completed, signed by the applicant, and sent to the Art Institute of Pittsburgh with a $50 application fee. As part of the application, the applicant is required to independently conceive and write an essay, stating how the applicant believes his or her education at the Art Institute will help to attain career goals. Applicants must submit a completed enrollment agreement and a high school transcript or GED scores and are assessed a $100 enrollment fee within ten days of application. Applicants who are not accepted for admission receive a full refund. Prospective students are encouraged to visit the Art Institute, although a visit is not required. The Art Institute conducts four open houses per year and has a solid commitment to visiting high schools to conduct presentations.

Arrangements for an interview or tour of the school may be made by contacting:

Director of Admissions
The Art Institute of Pittsburgh
420 Boulevard of the Allies
Pittsburgh, Pennsylvania 15219
Telephone: 412-263-6600
World Wide Web: http://www.aip.aii.edu.

AIP students enjoy a landmark building.

THE ART INSTITUTE OF SEATTLE
SEATTLE, WASHINGTON

The College and Its Mission

Originally founded in 1946 as the Burnley School of Professional Art, the Art Institute of Seattle has a proud history as part of the Seattle community and as a contributor to the creative industries in the Northwest. From the early days of 100 students to today's enrollment of nearly 3,000, the Art Institute has held the commitment of offering high-quality programs based on the real-world needs of business.

The Art Institute of Seattle is accredited by the Commission on Colleges of the Northwest Association of Schools and Colleges and is licensed by the Washington Workforce Training and Education Coordinating Board. The Art Institute of Seattle is approved for the training of veterans and eligible veterans' dependents and is authorized to enroll nonimmigrant international students.

Academic Programs

The Art Institute of Seattle operates on a year-round, quarter basis, with each quarter equaling eleven weeks. Bachelor of Fine Art degree programs are twelve quarters. Associate degree program lengths include six, seven, eight, and nine quarters. Diploma programs are four quarters.

Bachelor of Fine Arts Degree Programs The following programs are offered as a B.F.A. degree: graphic design (180 credits, twelve quarters), interior design (180 credits, twelve quarters), and media arts and animation (180 credits, twelve quarters).

Associate of Applied Arts Degree Programs The following programs are offered as an A.A.A. degree: animation art and design (120 credits, eight quarters), audio production (90 credits, six quarters), culinary arts (108 credits, seven quarters), fashion design (90 credits, six quarters), fashion marketing (90 credits, six quarters), graphic design (120 credits, eight quarters), industrial design technology (120 credits, eight quarters), interior design (135 credits, nine quarters), multimedia and Web design (120 credits, eight quarters), photography (120 credits, eight quarters), and video production (90 credits, six quarters). The animation art and design, culinary arts, graphic design, and multimedia and Web design programs are also offered as evening programs for those students who work full-time or have other obligations during the day.

Diploma Programs The following programs are offered as diploma programs and are offered solely at night: baking and pastry (36 credits, four quarters), computer design technology (36 credits, four quarters), desktop production (36 credits, four quarters), residential design (36 credits, four quarters), and the art of cooking (36 credits, four quarters).

Costs

The Art Institute of Seattle currently follows a "lock-in" tuition policy. As the cost of higher education continues to rise, many colleges, including the Art Institute, are adopting a tuition system that allows students to lock in their tuition. Stated simply, when students enroll, start, and stay in school, the Art Institute of Seattle locks in their tuition at a constant level throughout the duration of their studies. As long as students stay in school, they are unaffected by any future tuition increases.

Tuition is charged on a per-credit-hour basis. The costs for tuition and fees vary depending on the student's program. For current costs, students should contact the Art Institute of Seattle Admissions Office or visit the Art Institute of Seattle Web site at the address below.

Financial Aid

Students understand that a college education is an investment in themselves, one that will support them for the rest of their lives. The Student Financial Services Department works to make that investment not only possible, but accessible. The Student Financial Planners are somewhat unique in their approach. They take a holistic approach to developing a plan to meet the cost of a student's college education. They work with students and their families to develop a financial blueprint to take the student from admission through graduation and beyond, a plan that meets both the student's direct and indirect educational expenses. They begin by carefully reviewing the student's needs and personal resources. In addition, because many of the Art Institute's students also rely on other sources to help with their educational needs, the experienced staff presents the various options available for the student's evaluation.

Eligible students may apply for financial assistance under various federal and state programs, including the Federal Pell Grant, Federal Supplemental Educational Opportunity Grant (FSEOG), Federal Perkins Loan, Federal Subsidized Stafford Student Loan, Federal Unsubsidized Stafford Student Loan, Federal Work-Study Program (FWS), Alaska State Student Loan, Federal PLUS Program (parents), Washington State Need Grant, Vocational Rehabilitation Assistance, Veterans Administration Benefits, and Bureau of Indian Affairs. Awards under these programs are based on individual need and the availability of funds.

The Art Institute of Seattle offers scholarships based on merit, motivation, and financial need to new and continuing students. The selection committee reviews applications for these scholarships. The Art Institute offers the following scholarships: Advantage Grant Program, the Art Institute Excellence Award, the Art Institute's Scholarship Competition, the Art Institute's Culinary Scholarship Competition, the National Art Honor Society Scholarship, the Evelyn Keedy Memorial Scholarship, VICA Skills USA Championship, Scholastic Arts Competition, HERO, IACP Foundation, C-Cap, ProStart, Technology Student Association Competition, and the New York City Schools Scholarship Competition.

For more information about financial aid and scholarships, students should contact either the Student Financial Services Department or the Admissions Department.

Faculty

The faculty includes both full- and part-time instructors. This group of more than 140 professionals are experienced in what they teach, bringing their real-world knowledge into the classroom. The average class size is 19.

Student Body Profile

The student body at the Art Institute of Seattle includes people who are just out of high school, people who have some previous college experience and are looking to finish and focus their education, and people who have worked for twenty years and have returned to college to change their careers. The Art Institute of Seattle enrolls students from all across the United States and from countries around the world, all sharing a desire to start a creative career.

Student Activities

The Art Institute of Seattle places a high value on student life both in and out of the classroom setting by providing an environment that encourages involvement in a wide variety of activities of both an academic and nonacademic nature. These include clubs and organizations, community service opportunities, and various committees designed to enhance the quality of student life. Numerous all-school programs and events are planned throughout the year to meet the needs and desires of students.

Facilities and Resources

The Art Institute of Seattle is an urban campus that comprises three facilities. These facilities contain classrooms; audio and video studios; a student store; student lounges; copy centers; a gallery; a woodshop; a sculpture room; fashion display windows; a resource center; culinary facilities, including professionally equipped kitchens and a public restaurant; and a technology center equipped with PC and Macintosh computers.

The Student Services Department offers a variety of services to students to help them make the most of their educational experience. These services include student housing (school-sponsored housing and independent housing referrals), counseling, part-time job assistance (while enrolled), tutoring and learning services, and special needs services. The faculty members, Academic Directors, and the Dean of Education provide academic advising.

The Career Services Department works with students as they are completing their educational program to refine their presentations to potential employers as well as to give the advisers insight into each student's specialized skills and interests. Specific career advising occurs during the last two quarters of a student's education. Interviewing techniques and resume writing skills are developed, and students receive extensive portfolio advising from faculty members. Although the Art Institute offers no guarantee of employment, considerable effort is put forth to cultivate employment opportunities and to match job leads with qualified graduates.

Location

The Art Institute of Seattle is located on Seattle's waterfront in the Belltown district. Seattle is a great city in which to live and study. It is large enough to offer outstanding cultural opportunities, and it has an innovative business environment that is also outstanding. At the same time, Seattle is small enough to make strangers quickly feel at home. Founded by Native Americans and traders, it has retained respect for each new cultural group that has made Seattle home. People from all over the world come to study, work, and live here in a city known for the friendliness of its people and the beauty of its natural surroundings.

World-class companies, such as Microsoft, Boeing, Starbucks, Amazon.com, and Nordstrom, make their global headquarters in Seattle. As a gateway on the Pacific Rim, Seattle is a crossroads where creativity, technology, and business meet.

Admission Requirements

Each individual who seeks admission to the Art Institute of Seattle is required to have an admissions interview (in person or over the phone) to explore the prospective student's background and interests, to assist the student in identifying the appropriate area of study consistent with their stated or demonstrated interest, and to provide information concerning program offerings and support services available. Applicants are also required to have a high school diploma or a General Education Diploma (GED) and to submit an admissions application, a $50 application fee, and an essay (a written paragraph of approximately 150 words describing what the prospective student's career goals are and how the Art Institute of Seattle can help the student achieve those goals). Applicants must also complete an Enrollment Agreement and pay a $100 tuition deposit (due within ten days after the application is submitted, for all degree programs). For advanced placement, additional information, such as college transcripts, letters of recommendation, or portfolio work, may be required. Students may apply online at the Web site listed below.

Application and Information

The Art Institute of Seattle follows a rolling admissions schedule, allowing students to begin their education at a time best suited to their circumstances. Students are encouraged to apply for their chosen quarter early so that they can take advantage of orientation activities, but students can apply up to the actual start date for any given quarter, depending on space availability. For more information, students should contact:

Office of Admissions
The Art Institute of Seattle
2323 Elliott Avenue
Seattle, Washington 98121
Telephone: 206-448-6600
     800-275-2471 (toll-free)
Fax: 206-269-0275
World Wide Web: http://www.ais.edu

The Art Institute of Seattle's faculty members bring their professional experience into the classroom to create a collaborative, real-world learning environment.

ATLANTIC CAPE COMMUNITY COLLEGE

MAYS LANDING, ATLANTIC CITY, AND CAPE MAY COUNTY,
NEW JERSEY

The College and Its Mission

Founded in 1964, Atlantic Cape Community College (ACCC) held its first classes in fall 1966 in rented facilities in Atlantic City, New Jersey. In February 1968, the College moved to its present main campus location in Mays Landing, the Atlantic County seat. ACCC was the second community college organized in the state.

ACCC is a comprehensive, two-year public institution serving the residents of Atlantic and Cape May counties, enrolling more than 6,000 credit students. The College operates nationally recognized casino career and culinary arts programs and is a leader in online education. In addition to the College's main campus in Mays Landing, ACCC operates extension centers in Atlantic City and Cape May County.

The Casino Career Institute (CCI), located at the Charles D. Worthington Atlantic City Center, was the first casino gaming school in the nation affiliated with a community college and the only licensed slot training school in New Jersey. Opened in 1978, CCI has trained more than 46,000 people for careers in the casino industry. It has provided training for members of several federal governments and many state police forces as other jurisdictions prepare themselves for legalized gaming.

In 1981, as another extension of its role to train workers for the southern New Jersey hospitality industry, ACCC opened the Academy of Culinary Arts, a chefs' training program that has graduated more than 2,300 students. The Academy of Culinary Arts has a full-time enrollment of nearly 300 students.

Academic Programs

ACCC offers twenty-one transfer and career degree programs with twenty options and thirty-one professional series programs as well as noncredit professional development and customized training services. ACCC requires a minimum of 64 credits for its associate degrees.

Associate Degree Programs Associate in Arts degree programs are designed for students who wish to continue their education at a four-year college or university and pursue studies in the liberal arts, humanities, or social sciences. The A.A. degree requires a minimum of 45 credits in general education. One basic program of study in liberal arts is available, with options in business administration, child development/child care, education, history, humanities, literature, performing arts, psychology, social science, sociology, or studio art.

Associate in Science degrees are awarded to students who successfully complete programs that emphasize mathematics, the biological or physical sciences, and business programs intended as prebaccalaureate work. The A.S. degree requires a minimum of 30 credits in general education. Degree programs are available in business administration (with an option in economics), computer information systems, criminal justice (with an option in corrections in criminal justice), general studies, health sciences, paralegal studies, science and mathematics (with options in biology, chemistry, and mathematics), and social work.

Associate in Applied Science degree programs emphasize preparation for careers, typically at the technical or semiprofessional level. The A.A.S. degree requires a minimum of 20 credits in general education. Degree programs are available in accounting (with an option in accounting information systems), business administration, computer programming, computer systems support (with options in microcomputer technologies and Web technologies), culinary arts, food service management, hospitality management, nursing, office systems technology, paralegal studies, physical therapist assistant studies, and respiratory therapy.

In addition, ACCC offers a number of certificate programs to meet the short-term training needs of the local workforce.

The largest cooking school in New Jersey, the Academy of Culinary Arts, was founded in 1981 to meet the growing need for highly skilled chefs and food service professionals for the Atlantic City hospitality industry. Facilities include six teaching kitchens with overhead mirrors, a bake shop, and classrooms. A $4.6-million facility, constructed in 1991, features more than 28,250 square feet of space, including teaching kitchens, classrooms, a gourmet restaurant, a banquet room, administrative and faculty offices, a computer lab, and a retail store.

The culinary arts program features hands-on and academic training and an externship program. Classes meet 5 hours a day, Monday through Friday, in a morning or afternoon session from January through May and August/September through December. As part of their training, students operate a gourmet restaurant on the College's campus. Specialized certificate programs are available in catering, food service management, hot foods, and baking and pastry.

The food service management program combines liberal arts classes, hands-on culinary training, and management-related courses in the specifics of the hospitality industry. The combination of front-of-the-house and back-of-the-house courses provides students with the broad-based knowledge of the industry that is key to succeeding in the field.

Off-Campus Programs

Cooperative education is an academic program that allows students to receive college credits for working in jobs related to their major while pursuing their studies at ACCC. A cooperative education component is required for the culinary arts program but is optional for all other majors.

ACCC, a leader in educational technology, now offers eleven associate degrees and several professional series programs through distance education. Courses are offered online. The degree programs available through distance education are business administration (A.A.S. and A.S.), computer information systems (A.S.), general studies (A.S.), liberal arts (A.A., with options in business administration, history, humanities, literature, psychology, and social science), and office systems technology (A.A.S.). ACCC offers more than 100 online courses and has trained faculty members from colleges across New Jersey to use the technology for instruction. It hosts the New Jersey Virtual Community College Consortium (NJVCCC).

Costs

In 2004–05, full-time tuition for Atlantic and Cape May County residents or out-of-county New Jersey residents with a chargeback is $2200 per year. Part-time tuition is $73.15 per credit. Out-of-county New Jersey residents without chargebacks pay $146.30 per credit. Out-of-state and out-of-country residents pay $256 per credit.

The 2004–05 tuition and fees for the Academy of Culinary Arts are $219.45 per credit for Atlantic and Cape May County residents, $292.60 per credit for out-of-county residents without chargeback, and $402.35 per credit for out-of-state and out-of-country residents. Students also pay required fees of $14 per credit and a program fee of $133.50 per credit for culinary arts courses only.

There are also parking and mandatory accident and health insurance fees. Some classes require special lab or material costs or other fees.

Tuition for online courses is $90 per credit.

Financial Aid

About 65 percent of ACCC students who apply receive some form of financial aid, including scholarships, grants, loans, and work-study assistance. Funds are available from federal, state, and private sources for those with a demonstrated need or who meet eligibility requirements. All applicants for aid must complete the Free Application for Federal Student Aid (FAFSA), available online or from ACCC's financial aid office or most high school guidance offices.

Faculty

ACCC has 80 full-time and approximately 228 part-time faculty members. Full-time faculty members hold master's degrees, and many also have doctoral degrees in the field of study. Most faculty members also serve as academic advisers. ACCC's student-faculty ratio is 24:1.

Student Body Profile

In 2003, there were 6,177 students at Atlantic Cape Community College. Atlantic County residents accounted for 71 percent of the student body; Cape May County residents accounted for 21 percent. Members of minority groups were as follows: Hispanic, 10 percent; Asian, 8 percent; Native American, .3 percent; and African American, 15 percent. International students made up .8 percent of the total. The average age of students was 27.

Student Activities

Every ACCC student is a member of the Student Government Association (SGA). The main policy making body of the SGA is the Student Senate, which charters student clubs and organizations, approves budgets, determines student policy, and works with the faculty and administration to improve the College. There are numerous special interest clubs and organizations open to all students, an on-campus radio station, and a student newspaper.

Facilities and Resources

ACCC is built around a quadrangle of lawn. The buildings, designed of split-face brick, natural cedar shakes, and tinted glass, are joined by a system of walkways. A central loop connects buildings and parking areas with the Black Horse Pike (Route 322). ACCC's indoor athletic facilities include a gymnasium with a seating capacity of 800 and a weight room with lockers and showers. Outdoor facilities include baseball, softball, and soccer fields; two basketball courts; a nature trail; and an archery range. ACCC's housing program assists culinary and hospitality major students who are not Atlantic or Cape May County residents in obtaining high-quality living arrangements in an off-campus setting. There is no on-campus housing available.

The College's cultural events are staged in a 500-seat theater located in Walter E. Edge Hall. The resources and facilities of the William Spangler Library are available to the College community and to the residents of Atlantic and Cape May counties. The library currently houses more than 78,000 books, 1,000 CDs, audiocassettes and phonograph records, and subscriptions to more than 300 periodicals. Students have access to Science Direct, Dialog, EBSCO Host, Literature Resource Center, and LexisNexis (1,000 full-text journals); a variety of CD-ROM databases; and the World Wide Web.

Location

Located on 537 acres in the picturesque New Jersey Pinelands, Atlantic Cape Community College is in Atlantic County, New Jersey, 17 miles west of Atlantic City's boardwalk, 45 miles from Philadelphia, and 115 miles from New York City. It operates extension centers in Atlantic City and Cape May County and is building a full-service campus in Middle Township, Cape May County, which is scheduled to open in fall 2005.

Admission Requirements

Admission is available to all applicants who are 18 years of age and older whose high school class has graduated. Applicants who have graduated from an accredited secondary or preparatory school, or those with a state equivalency certificate, are accepted to ACCC. Applicants under 18 years of age, not currently enrolled in a high school or not having a high school diploma or GED certificate do not qualify for admission to a community college. Applicants who are 18 years of age and older and do not have a high school diploma or GED certificate may apply to the College for admission under special conditions.

Admission to specific programs, such as culinary arts or nursing, is dependent upon students meeting the necessary program requirements and completing course prerequisites.

Application and Information

Applications are reviewed on a continuous basis. The preferred deadline for fall admission is July 1; for spring admission, November 1. There is a $35 application fee, which includes the cost of administering the placement test. Culinary applicants must pay an additional, nonrefundable $300 deposit. The deposit reserves a seat for a maximum of two semesters and is applied toward the semester tuition bill when the student registers. Seats are assigned on a first-come, first-served basis according to the completion of the steps toward admission.

For an application or additional information, students should contact:

Admissions Office
Atlantic Cape Community College
5100 Black Horse Pike
Mays Landing, New Jersey 08330-2699
Telephone: 609-343-5000
 800-645-CHEF (toll-free)
E-mail: accadmit@atlantic.edu
World Wide Web: http://www.atlantic.edu

The Academy of Culinary Arts, housed at Atlantic Cape Community College, is New Jersey's largest cooking school, with nearly 300 students.

BALTIMORE INTERNATIONAL COLLEGE
BALTIMORE, MARYLAND; VIRGINIA, COUNTY CAVAN, IRELAND

The College and Its Mission

The Baltimore International College, a regionally accredited, independent college, was founded in 1972 to provide theoretical and technical skills education for individuals seeking careers as hospitality professionals. The College is committed to providing students with the knowledge and ability necessary for employment and success in the hospitality industry.

In 1985, the College was authorized by the state of Maryland to grant associate degrees. As part of the College's continued growth, restaurant and food service management and innkeeping management were added to its curriculum. In 1987, the Virginia Park Campus in Ireland was founded, enabling students to study under European chefs and hoteliers in a European environment. In 1996, the College was granted accreditation by the Commission on Higher Education of the Middle States Association of College and Schools. In 1998, the College was authorized by the state of Maryland to grant four-year baccalaureate degrees. In addition to classrooms, offices, and dorms, the College's campus in Baltimore includes a campus bookstore, a student union, a hotel, an inn, two restaurants, parking, student dining facilities, a Career Development Center, and a Learning Resource Center comprising a library, two academic computer labs, and an art gallery.

Freshman students who are single, under 21, and live farther than 50 miles from campus are required to live in student housing.

Academic Programs

The College provides a comprehensive curriculum, which includes an honors study abroad program at the Baltimore International College Virginia Park Campus near Dublin, Ireland.

The College's professional cooking program and the combined programs in professional cooking and baking and baking and pastry operate throughout the calendar year; new classes begin in the spring, summer, and fall. The College's business and management programs accept freshmen in the fall and spring semesters. The culinary arts certificate, which combines cooking and baking, and the certificate in professional marketing are available through evening classes and begin in the fall and spring semesters.

Associate Degree Programs Baltimore International College awards the associate degree in the following programs: food and beverage management, hotel/motel/innkeeping management, professional baking and pastry, professional cooking, and professional cooking and baking. The associate degree is offered separately and as part of the 2+2 program at Baltimore International College. In the 2+2 program, students receive their two-year associate degree and then continue two additional years to complete the four-year bachelor's degree. Bachelor's degree programs require 125 to 133 credits.

To earn an associate degree in professional cooking, professional baking and pastry, or professional cooking and baking, the student must complete 62–66 credits. To earn an associate degree in food and beverage management or hotel/motel/innkeeping management, the student must complete approximately 65 credits. Certificate candidates must complete 54 credits. The certificate program concentrates on technical courses and is intended for students who already have a strong academic background. The associate degree program combines technical hands-on courses with general education courses such as nutrition, sanitation, psychology, English, and mathematics, as well as an internship or externship.

Off-Campus Programs

The Honors Program has been developed for qualified culinary arts and business and management majors. The Honors Program is taught at the College's historic, 100-acre Virginia Park campus in County Cavan, Ireland. Culinary students who are selected for the Honors Program further enhance their skills in and knowledge of European cuisine, baking and pastry, and a la carte service. Business and management students selected for the honors program have the opportunity to learn the day-to-day operation of a hotel and restaurant, from reception to housekeeping and from restaurant management to accounting. Students fully enjoy the cross-cultural experience of living in an English-speaking foreign country.

Costs

Tuition for 2002–03 was $6371. Student housing costs ranged from $2812 to $4713 per semester for dormitory-style housing (includes meal plan).

Financial Aid

Students receive financial aid from federal, state, institutional, and private sources and may be employed during their attendance as full-time students. The forms of financial aid available at the College through federal sources include the Federal Pell Grant, the Federal Supplemental Educational Opportunity Grant, the Federal Work-Study Program, the Federal Subsidized and Unsubsidized Stafford Student Loans, FPLUS loans, and veterans' educational benefits. Students are encouraged to investigate the scholarship programs in their home state and apply for state scholarships if the grants can be used in Maryland. The College also offers its own series of scholarships and payment options. In 2002–03, College-funded scholarships averaged $2678 per academic year for in-state students and $4707 per academic year for out-of-state students. Students can request a financial aid application from the Student Financial Planning Office. The College employs the Federal Methodology of Need Analysis, approved by the U.S. Department of Education, as a fair and equitable means of determining the family's ability to contribute to the student's educational expenses, as well as eligibility for other financial aid programs.

Faculty

Baltimore International College faculty members include 29 chefs and academic instructors of high academic distinction. The student-faculty ratio averages 16:1 in culinary labs and 25:1 in academic classes. Each student is assigned a faculty adviser who oversees the student's progress and answers questions about academic and career concerns. Students are encouraged to discuss program-related issues with the Director of Student Counseling.

Student Body Profile

Current enrollment is 750 annually, with 52 percent men and 48 percent women. Approximately 17 percent of students are from out-of-state, representing twenty-four states and several other countries. Students can join the Greater Baltimore Chapter of the American Culinary Federation and can participate in a variety of other activities through Student Affairs.

Student Activities

The College offers general academic counseling for all students, peer tutoring on request, and a variety of referrals for support services. In addition, student services provide many recreation and leisure activities, including the student union, a series of activities sponsored by the College, and information about cultural programs around the city. Student services also provides ongoing support to the College's alumni through surveys, mailings about the College's growth, and involvement in College-sponsored events such as open houses, resume referrals, and career fairs.

Facilities and Resources

The Baltimore campus includes kitchens, storerooms, cooking demonstration theaters, academic classrooms, multipurpose rooms, a library, computer labs, a student union, and auxiliary services. Public operations that function as in-house training for students include the Mount Vernon Hotel, the Bay Atlantic Club Restaurant, and the Hopkins Inn.

The Virginia Park Campus is located on 100 acres, 50 miles from Dublin student housing, with laboratory kitchens and lecture facilities. The complex also includes the Park Hotel, with public operations that function as in-house training for students, including the Marquis Dining Room and the Marchioness Ballroom. The Park Hotel has thirty-six guest rooms. All students enjoy unlimited golf and fishing as well as hiking trails.

Career Planning/Placement Offices The College's Career Development Center offers students access to information about careers in food service and hospitality management. The College's career development services are located in the Career Information Center where coordinators organize on-campus recruiting and offer workshops and assistance in resume writing and interviewing skills.

Library and Audiovisual Services The College's Learning Resource Center is a member of an interlibrary loan network that enables users to borrow from public, academic, and private libraries throughout Maryland. The library's current core collection has approximately 13,000 volumes, 200 periodicals, and almost 800 audiovisual selections. The library offers students access to the Internet, a worldwide network of electronic information. In-house services include two academic computer labs, electronic databases for research, and a photocopier.

The College's art gallery is part of the Learning Resource Center and features a permanent display of edible art. Student participation in all exhibits is encouraged.

Location

The College's main campus, located in downtown Baltimore, is just two blocks from the city's famous Inner Harbor, a location that puts the College in the midst of numerous hotels and restaurants. The city offers year-round cultural and entertainment opportunities, such as theater, opera, the Baltimore Symphony Orchestra, museums, sporting events, and festivals. Other attractions in Baltimore, within walking distance of the College, are the National Aquarium, Harborplace, Oriole Park at Camden Yards, Ravens Stadium, Maryland Science Center, and many historic sites, including Fort McHenry, Mount Vernon, and the Walters Art Museum. Baltimore also has parks and miles of waterfront for those who enjoy outdoor recreation. Washington, D.C., the nation's capital, is just 30 miles from downtown Baltimore. The city of Baltimore is easily accessed by major highways and bus, rail, and air service. Baltimore/Washington International Airport is a short drive from the campus.

Admission Requirements

Creativity and skill of students must be matched by dedication. The College seeks candidates who desire a professional career in the hospitality industry.

Individuals seeking admission to the College must have earned a high school diploma or have passed the GED. Applicants must either pass the College's Admissions Test, take developmental courses during their first semester, or have one of the following: minimum SAT I scores of 430 verbal and 420 math, a minimum composite ACT score of 16, minimum CLEP scores in the 50th percentile in math and English composition with essay, a secondary degree, or 16 credit hours at the postsecondary level with a minimum average of C in math and English. Transfer students must submit an official college transcript as well as catalog course descriptions for credits they wish to transfer.

The College affords equally to all students the rights, privileges, programs, activities, scholarships and loan programs, and other programs administered by the College without regard to race, color, creed, sex, age, handicap, or national or ethnic origin.

Application and Information

Applicants are required to submit an application form along with a $35 nonrefundable fee. Requests by the College for additional information must be handled in a timely manner. An admission decision is made as soon as a file is complete. Upon acceptance, applicants are asked to submit a $100 tuition deposit.

For additional information, students should contact:

Office of Admissions
Commerce Exchange
Baltimore International College
17 Commerce Street
Baltimore, Maryland 21202-3230
Telephone: 410-752-4710 Ext. 120
           800-624-9926 Ext. 120 (toll-free)
E-mail: admissions@bic.edu
World Wide Web: http://www.bic.edu

Small classes at Baltimore International College enable students to receive individual instruction that helps them perfect their skills.

BAY STATE COLLEGE
BOSTON, MASSACHUSETTS

The College and Its Mission

Bay State College, a private, two-year, independent, coeducational institution, is located in Boston's historic Back Bay. Since 1946, Bay State College has been preparing young men and women with the skills necessary to attain outstanding careers in the business and allied health disciplines.

The College's goal is to prepare and educate students for successful and rewarding professional opportunities. Bay State College accomplishes this by providing the best possible education, which enables students to go out into the working world equipped with all the skills needed to succeed professionally or to transfer to a four-year college of choice. Bay State College assists, encourages, supports, and educates students in all their academic, professional, and personal goals and aspirations.

Bay State College is accredited by the New England Association of Schools and Colleges, is authorized to award the Associate in Science and Associate in Applied Science degrees by the Commonwealth of Massachusetts, and is a member of several professional educational associations.

Bay State College's allied health programs are accredited by the Accrediting Bureau of Health Education Schools (ABHES). The Physical Therapist Assistant Program is accredited by the Commission on Accreditation in Physical Therapy Education (CAPTE) of the American Physical Therapy Association (APTA).

Academic Programs

Bay State College offers unique courses preparing students for careers in accounting, business, criminal justice, early childhood education, fashion design, fashion merchandising, general studies, medical assisting studies, and physical therapist assistant studies. In addition, students are exceptionally prepared to transfer to four-year colleges and universities.

The College's current programs include accounting (A.A.S.), business administration (A.A.S.), computer and Internet management (A.A.S.), early childhood education (A.S.), entertainment management (A.A.S.), fashion design (A.S.), fashion merchandising (A.A.S.), general studies (A.S.), medical assisting studies (A.S.), physical therapist assistant studies (A.S.), retail business management (A.A.S.), and travel and hospitality management (A.A.S.).

Bay State College's Day and Continuing Education Divisions offer day and evening classes. Two satellite campuses for continuing education are located in Gloucester and Middleborough, Massachusetts.

Off-Campus Programs

The internship program, available in all major areas of study, provides practical field experience so that the students gain the skills and experience with the technologies used in the business and medical settings.

Students from Bay State College are among the 250 students participating in the Walt Disney World College Program. During their stay at Walt Disney World, students receive on-the-job training and classroom experience. This is just one of the many internship possibilities for students each year at Bay State College.

Costs

For the 2004–05 academic year, the College's Day Division charges a comprehensive fee of $24,400, which includes full-time tuition ($14,900) and room and board ($9500). There is an allied health lab fee of $475 per year (medical assisting studies and physical therapist assistant studies only). Textbooks are estimated at $600 per year. Bay State College's Continuing Education Division, the Boston, Middleborough, and Gloucester campuses, charges $220 per credit. Tuition, dormitory charges, and fees are subject to change.

Financial Aid

Personal financial planning and counseling is completed with all students and families. Approximately 85 percent of students receive some form of financial assistance. Bay State College requires a completed Free Application for Federal Student Aid (FAFSA) form and signed federal tax forms. The College's institutional financial aid priority deadline is March 1. Financial aid is granted on a rolling basis.

Faculty

There are 50 faculty members, with 53 percent holding advanced degrees and 6 percent holding doctoral degrees. The student-faculty ratio is 15:1.

Student Body Profile

There are 567 students in terminal programs. The average age is 18. The student body is ethnically and culturally diverse; 85 percent are state residents, 9 percent are transfer students, 4 percent are international students, 60 percent are women, 19 percent are African American, 11 percent are Hispanic, and 10 percent are Asian American. In the past year, 33 percent of Bay State College's graduating class continued on to a four-year college.

Bay State College's residence halls are located on Commonwealth Avenue. There are 174 college housing spaces available. Each residence hall is designed to accommodate from 1 to 5 students per room. Housing is guaranteed to freshmen who complete and submit a dorm contract by May 1.

Each hall is staffed by professional live-in directors and a paraprofessional staff of resident assistants. The staff members strive to foster a living and learning environment that complements the academic mission. All residents have the opportunity to experience a wide variety of programs such as in-house educational, cultural, and awareness seminars; study breaks; discounts to area movies and theater productions; and holiday celebrations. Twenty-four-hour quiet hours are in effect during midterm and final periods. A campus dining facility is available, as are microwaves, laundry facilities, cable-ready outlets, and computer labs.

Student Activities

Students participate in a multitude of activities offered by the College through student groups. These include the Travel Club, Fashion Club, Early Childhood Education Club, Accounting Club, Student Leader Organization, Medical Assisting Society, Physical Therapist Assistant Club, a talent show, a student-produced fashion show, a literary magazine, literary readings, and access to a gym.

Facilities and Resources

Advisement/Counseling Trained staff members assist students in selecting courses and programs of study to satisfy their educational objectives. A counseling center is available to provide mental and physical health referrals to all Bay State students in need of such services. Referral networks are extensive, within a wide range of geographic areas, and provide access to a variety of public and private health agencies.

Specialized Services The Learning Center has been renamed the Center for Learning and Academic Support (CLAS). A learning center serves as a supplementary learning tool for those individuals wishing to improve their skills through self-paced individualized instruction. The center offers assistance through the use of peer and faculty tutors, individualized learning packets, and audio, visual, and other self-study resources. Introductory studies courses are designed for a diverse population of students, including workers returning to school, recent high school graduates seeking academic reinforcement, and ESL students. Their individual needs are met so they can be successful in the traditional course of study leading to an associate degree.

Career Planning/Placement Of the number of students seeking assistance from the Career Services Office, there was a 95 percent job placement rate. The primary purpose of the Career Services Office at Bay State College is to see that every graduating senior secures the best possible position in his or her chosen career. The Career Services Office, offering lifelong service to all alumni, continually posts job openings for current students and graduates. An average of 10,000 job openings are posted every year. The Career Services Office,

under the guidance of Mr. Timothy Mosehauer, Assistant Director of Student Career Services (telephone: 617-236-8030), assists each student through one-on-one career counseling. Services include career fairs on campus, with more than seventy attending companies; resume preparation; career counseling; the career library; and a professional dynamics course.

Library and Audiovisual Services The library has a combined book collection of approximately 5,300 books. In addition, Bay State College has 100 periodicals and 200 audiovisual titles. The College's sixty computers have access to the Internet and several databases for magazine and journal articles, including ProQuest, LexisNexis Academic, and Westlaw legal database.

Location

The location of Bay State College makes it the perfect place to attend to get a complete education. While the academics are great, students are also within a mile of major-league sports, free concerts, museums, the Freedom Trail, Boston Symphony Hall, the Boston Public Library, the Boston Public Garden, and much more. The city is known for its college atmosphere. Tree-lined streets are mirrored in the skyscrapers of the Back Bay. Major shopping, cultural, and sporting events make College life an experience that students will always remember. The College's location is accessible by public transportation and in proximity to Boston Logan International Airport.

Admission Requirements

Students must be in pursuit of a high school diploma or GED certificate in order to apply and must receive it before the start of classes at Bay State College. A personal interview is strongly recommended for all students. Transcripts are requested once a student has applied. A decision is made by the Admissions Office upon completion and receipt of all documents. International students must complete an International Student Application and provide a transcript, a TOEFL score, and final documents in order to be considered for admission.

Application and Information

Bay State College accepts applications on a rolling basis, so students may apply at any time. A $25 fee is required at the time of application, but application fee waivers are available upon request.

Applications should be submitted to:

Admissions Office
Bay State College
122 Commonwealth Avenue
Boston, Massachusetts 02116
Telephone: 800-81-LEARN (toll-free)
Fax: 617-536-1735
World Wide Web: http://www.baystate.edu

BENJAMIN FRANKLIN INSTITUTE OF TECHNOLOGY

BOSTON, MASSACHUSETTS

The Institute and Its Mission

Benjamin Franklin Institute of Technology is a small, technical college offering a variety of instructional programs based on science, engineering, and technology. Programs of one-, two-, three-, and four-years' duration are provided for various levels of interest, abilities, and objectives. The aim of Franklin Institute is to prepare the students in each program for immediate employment upon graduation in a chosen career field and at the same time to give students a technical education upon which they can continue to build. Because of the Institute's student-teacher ratio of 11:1, students receive a great deal of individual attention with a hands-on approach to learning.

The objectives of the Franklin Institute are threefold: to provide educational opportunities in science and technology for men and women in order that they may better themselves both economically and socially; to provide a sound educational foundation upon which the graduates of the Institute's programs may continue to grow both in personal terms as well as professional and educational terms; and to assess the present and future needs of industry and technology in order to anticipate and respond to those needs through curriculum revisions and the addition of new programs.

Academic Programs

Bachelor's Degree Programs Franklin Institute is one of the few colleges in the nation to offer a **Bachelor of Science** degree in automotive technology. The program follows completion of all requirements at the Franklin associate level. Its primary objective is to prepare students for middle management positions in the automotive industry and raise the standards for education industry-wide in an increasingly complex and technical profession. The curriculum is a combination of technical and business management courses. A total of eight semesters and 134 credit hours must be successfully completed for graduation.

Associate Degree Programs Franklin Institute grants the **Associate in Science** degree in automotive technology. The **Associate in Engineering** degree is awarded in architectural technology, computer engineering technology, computer technology, electrical engineering technology, electronic engineering technology, mechanical engineering technology, and medical electronics engineering technology.

The engineering technology associate degree programs require four semesters for completion with a total of 74 semester hours of credit. Half of the total curriculum in each engineering technology program is devoted to the technical specialty. One fourth of the total curriculum is devoted to physical science and mathematics, courses in college algebra and trigonometry, analytic geometry, calculus, and college physics. The remaining fourth of the curriculum includes English, humanities, and social studies. Most of the graduates of the engineering technology associate degree programs are employed by industry in various capacities in engineering and scientific fields. A high percentage of graduates continue their education at other colleges and universities.

The computer engineering technology program includes both fundamental and advanced courses in digital computer circuits, systems and languages, and electronic devices and circuit theory.

The electrical engineering technology program includes basic and advanced courses in the design and construction of electrical distribution systems for modern commercial and industrial buildings, commercial lighting design, and electrical estimating.

The electronic engineering technology program includes basic and advanced courses in electric and electronic circuit theory, semiconductor devices, principles and design of electrical and electronic equipment, and measurement techniques up to and including microwave frequencies.

The mechanical engineering technology program includes fundamental and advanced courses in applied mechanics, mechanics of materials, thermodynamics, heat transfer, machine design, fluid power, and instrumentation.

The medical electronics engineering technology curriculum incorporates basic and advanced courses in minicomputers and microcomputers, electronic devices, electric and electronic circuit theory, medical instrumentation, human physiology, medical instrument safety and grounding techniques, semiconductor circuitry, and principles and design of medical electronic instruments.

The industrial technology associate degree programs require four semesters for completion with a total of 70 semester hours of credit. More than half of the total curriculum in each industrial technology program is devoted to the technical specialty. About one fourth of the total curriculum is devoted to basic science and mathematics, including algebra, trigonometry, and precalculus mathematics. The remainder of the curriculum includes English, humanities, and social studies.

More than half of the automotive technology two-year program is devoted to automotive technical specialties, including actual work on vehicles in the student instructional garage. About one third of the program is devoted to basic mathematics, physics, humanities, and social sciences, and the remaining time is devoted to basic mechanical technology studies.

The computer technology program prepares students to meet the rapidly growing demand for technicians who can install, maintain, and repair computer equipment and digital electronic systems.

The architectural technology program is designed to enable its graduates to become skilled and knowledgeable architectural draftspersons, capable of making important contributions to the architectural and/or engineering team that produces the complete working drawings from which buildings, residences, and other structures are erected.

Transfer Arrangements Transfer credit received for courses completed at Franklin Institute is dependent on the policies of the transferring institution. Many graduates receive a full two years' credit toward a baccalaureate degree.

Certificate Programs The Certificate of Proficiency programs require two to three semesters for completion with a total of 18 to 36 semester hours of credit. Instruction is concentrated in the student's main area of interest. Graduates of these programs are generally immediately employable in their field of training.

The objective of the practical electricity program is to produce qualified technicians capable of assisting licensed electricians or electrical engineers in the layout, installation, maintenance, or testing of electrical equipment or systems. Upon satisfactory completion of the one-year program, students are given 600 hours of credit for educational training toward application for the Journeyman Electrician License in Massachusetts.

Costs

For the 2003–04 academic year, tuition was $11,950 per year. Books and supplies average $600. While the Institute does not maintain its own residence halls, various housing options exist within walking distance of the Institute.

Financial Aid

Franklin Institute offers financial assistance to students on the basis of demonstrated financial need and satisfactory academic progress. All students are encouraged to file the Free Application for Federal Student Aid (FAFSA). The Institute participates in the Federal Pell Grant, Federal Supplemental Educational Opportunity Grant, Federal Direct Loan, and Federal Work-Study programs and offers Franklin Institute grants and academic scholarships. State scholarships, VA assistance, rehabilitation funding, and payment plans are available for eligible students.

Faculty

The faculty at Franklin Institute consists of instructors with practical experience in their field of expertise and many years of instruction. Instructors meet annually with the Industrial Advisory Board for each program to review and update the curricula. There are 32 full-time and 9 part-time faculty members.

Student Body Profile

Ninety-two percent of students are state residents, 8 percent are transfer students, and 3 percent are international students. Fourteen percent of the student body are 25 years of age or older, and 14 percent are women. The student body is ethnically and culturally diverse: 30 percent are African American, 15 percent are Hispanic, and 14 percent are Asian American. Thirty-five percent of students work full-time.

Student Activities

All students are encouraged to participate in the campus environment. Activities include student government, Women's Support Group, engineering week competitions, yearbook, professional honor societies, and athletics.

Sports Franklin Institute offers outdoor recreation programs, including basketball, soccer, and volleyball. Indoor activities include table tennis.

Facilities and Resources

The Union building houses the library, which holds 10,000 bound volumes, 160 periodical subscriptions, 85 computer terminals, and a word processing lab for student use. Other labs associated with individual programs include digital and analog electronics, electrical wiring, computer systems, materials testing, machine tool, CAD, automotive engines, transmissions, drivability, and electrical as well as a full-service garage.

Location

The land on which the Institute stands, at the corner of Berkeley and Appleton Streets in the South End of Boston, was provided by the city in 1906. The Institute complex consists of three buildings, a plaza, a landscaped mall connecting the buildings on Berkeley and Appleton Streets, and a modern underground automotive technology shop. The facilities of the Kendall Administration Building and the Dunham Building are handicapped accessible. The Institute is readily accessible by public transportation and is within close walking distance of many cultural, social, and recreational activities offered in the city of Boston. Franklin Institute students have the opportunity to meet other college students from around the world, as there are more than seventy postsecondary institutions in the greater Boston area.

Admission Requirements

All applicants must possess a high school diploma or its equivalent and must have completed four full-year courses in high school English. For associate degrees in engineering technology, satisfactory completion of the following courses in mathematics and science is also required: algebra I, algebra II, and a laboratory science, preferably physics, although courses in chemistry or biology are acceptable. Additional courses in mathematics, such as trigonometry, math analysis, or precalculus, are helpful but not required.

Admission requirements for associate degree in industrial technology programs include a minimum of two high school courses in mathematics, including the study of elementary algebra, and one course in science.

Admission requirements for the Certificate of Proficiency include a minimum of two high school courses in mathematics and one course in science. The study of elementary algebra is recommended and in some cases required.

Application and Information

All applicants should complete a Franklin Institute Application for Admission and submit it with the required $25 processing fee to the Office of Admission. Official transcripts of high school records, including first-term senior year grades, should be requested by the student and sent directly from the high school to the Office of Admission. Because applications are processed on a rolling basis, applicants are notified of their admission status shortly after all required documents have been received. International applicants are also required to demonstrate English language proficiency and provide a financial statement showing proof of ability to pay the first year's costs.

State and institutional financial aid resources can be exhausted early in the application process. For financial aid priority consideration, applicants should apply for admission and financial aid no later than April 15, 2003.

Requests for additional information and application forms should be addressed to:

Office of Admission
Benjamin Franklin Institute of Technology
41 Berkeley Street
Boston, Massachusetts 02116
Telephone: 617-423-4630
Fax: 617-482-3706
E-mail: admis@bfit.edu
World Wide Web: http://www.bfit.edu

BERKELEY COLLEGE

WEST PATERSON, PARAMUS, AND WOODBRIDGE, NEW JERSEY

The College and Its Mission

Since its inception in 1931, Berkeley College has been committed to providing an exceptional undergraduate business education. Today, Berkeley College is recognized across the nation as a premier school, preparing students for successful careers in business in the modern world. Berkeley College's strong academic program succeeds through a blend of traditional education, professional training, and real-world experience.

At Berkeley, students benefit from small class sizes, personalized academic and career counseling, and the chance to develop their analytical and creative skills. Berkeley believes that teaching should provide a practical perspective to traditional material, and Berkeley's distinguished faculty brings academic preparation and professional experience to the classroom. Faculty members are chosen not just for their academic achievements, but also for their applicable backgrounds in the business world.

All campuses are accredited by the Middle States Commission on Higher Education. The New Jersey campuses are licensed as a college and are authorized by the New Jersey Commission on Higher Education to confer the degrees of Associate in Science (A.S.), Associate in Applied Science (A.A.S.), and Bachelor of Business Administration (B.B.A.). The American Bar Association (ABA) approves the paralegal studies program at all campuses.

Berkeley programs provide the comprehensive foundation necessary to begin a successful business career or to advance in a current career. The Academic Resource Centers and Learning Labs provide students with a wide range of support services to help improve their study skills as well as their reading, writing, and mathematical abilities. Academic, career, individual advisement, and free tutorial services are also available. At Berkeley, the traditional undergraduate curriculum is enhanced with professional training and experience. Berkeley's internship requirement provides valuable work experience and often leads to a full-time position. Students work in their fields of study, earn academic credits toward their degrees, establish a network of business connections for the future, and offset college costs.

Academic Programs

Berkeley offers a wide range of career-focused associate and bachelor's degree programs that prepare students for immediate marketability and professional growth. The academic curriculum combines leading-edge theory, real-world practicality, and extensive training in the latest computer technologies. Berkeley's commitment to excellence constitutes the primary objective of the College. Small classes, individualized advisement and counseling, and the development of the students' creative and analytical skills support this commitment.

Berkeley College provides exceptional flexibility and convenience as students have the option of combining day, evening, weekend, and online classes—offering everything students need to pursue a wide range of associate or bachelor's degrees, backed by Berkeley's commitment to excellence in education and value. The Bachelor of Science (B.S.) degree in business administration is offered entirely online.

The College operates year-round on the quarter system, with classes starting in September, January, April, and July. The flexible quarter system provides students enrolled in the day division the options of completing their associate degree in only eighteen months or of earning their bachelor's degree in as little as three years or in the traditional four years. Associate degree credits are easily transferred to bachelor's degree programs. Evening/weekend students have the options of completing their associate degrees in only two years or of completing their bachelor's degrees in less than four years.

Associate Degree Programs Associate degrees are offered in business administration, with specializations in accounting, information systems management, management, and marketing. Additional associate degree programs include fashion marketing and management, interior design, international business, network management, paralegal studies, and Web design.

Bachelor's Degree Programs Bachelor of Science degrees are offered in accounting, business administration, fashion marketing and management, international business, management, and marketing. Not all programs are offered at all campuses. A highly student-supportive and flexible online program offering the bachelor's degree in business administration is also available for those whose busy lives and daily responsibilities do not allow for access to on-site classes.

Certificate Programs Berkeley College offers certificate programs in computer applications. These programs, which can be completed in a year or less, provide students with the opportunity to get a head start in a gratifying career. Credits earned in certificate programs are transferable to Berkeley's degree programs. Students enrolled in certificate programs receive all the benefits of a Berkeley education, including lifetime placement assistance and software refresher courses.

Costs

In 2004-05, full-time students pay $15,900 in tuition and fees for the academic year. Berkeley offers protection from any tuition increase to students who maintain continuous, full-time enrollment. A variety of housing options are available, depending on the campus attended. Students who choose to live in residence housing pay an additional $5400 to $7200 per academic year for a double- or single-room preference and an additional $3300 per academic year for fifteen meals weekly. Students are securely housed in Garret Hall and Knuppel Hall, which are three-story, brick, coed residence halls. Rooms are designed to house 1 or 2 students and are comfortably furnished. The buildings also include lounges, kitchens, and a laundry room in addition to overnight security.

Financial Aid

Berkeley is committed to helping students find the financing options that will make their education possible. Financial assistance programs are available from federal and state sources and through Berkeley in the form of scholarships, grants, loans, and other awards. Berkeley College allocates approximately $12 million annually for student aid, based on need and/or merit. Financial aid administrators are available to meet one-on-one with students and their families to develop a plan best suited to meet their individual educational expenses.

Faculty

Because Berkeley believes that teaching should encompass both a conceptual and practical perspective, faculty members are chosen for both their professional experience and their academic credentials. Their business experience brings an added intellectual reality to the classroom, resulting in a challenging and stimulating learning environment. Several of Berkeley's administrators are nationally recognized authors, lecturers, consultants, and leaders in business education.

Student Body Profile

Berkeley's total enrollment of nearly 4,700 students at five campuses in New Jersey and New York, includes day and evening and full- and part-time students who represent seventy-six countries.

Student Activities

All students are members of the Student Government Association (SGA). Elected SGA officers meet regularly and act as liaisons between students and the administration concerning social and academic matters. Berkeley offers a number of organizations, clubs, and activities designed to meet the educational, cultural, and social needs and interests of students. Activities include, but are not limited to, picnics, intramural sports, ski weekends, theater events, and charity drives.

Facilities and Resources

Libraries and Computer Labs Berkeley College maintains comprehensive libraries on each campus. Each library houses a collection of print and nonprint resources, periodicals, study areas, computers, and audiovisual equipment. The libraries provide a variety of services, including orientations, reference assistance, and course-related, course-integrated, and point-of-use instruction. A systemwide catalog, encompassing the holdings of all Berkeley libraries, consists of approximately 85,000 items. Library Web pages provide 24-hours-a-day, seven-days-a-week access to the online catalogs, electronic databases, reference tools, Internet search engines, and links to the institution-wide portals. Each academic facility is staffed with librarians committed to teaching independent research and literacy skills. Throughout Berkeley's campuses are state-of-the-art computer labs with more than 700 classroom computer stations.

Advisement/Counseling From academic, career, and individual counseling to free tutorial services, Berkeley is committed to providing a supportive, highly personalized environment.

Placement Berkeley's full-service Career Services Division has 20 placement advisers who specialize in each major field of study. Berkeley's Career Services professionals work with students to identify career options, develop and refine resume and interviewing skills, set up and place students in internship positions, and schedule interviews in the areas surrounding the five New York/New Jersey locations. Lifetime career assistance is available to all Berkeley graduates. Last year, more than 96 percent of all graduates available for placement were employed in positions related to their studies at Berkeley College.

Location

The West Paterson campus offers all the amenities of college life and is located on 25 acres of wooded countryside and situated atop Garret Mountain in the suburban West Paterson–Little Falls region. Students enjoy the complete college experience with diverse student activities, residence halls, student center, full-service cafeteria, and the friendliness and warmth of the Berkeley community. The Woodbridge and Paramus campuses are ideal for students who prefer a smaller setting and the intimacy and the extrapersonalized attention that comes with it. The central New Jersey campus of Berkeley is located in downtown Woodbridge. It is within easy reach of Woodbridge Center, which is the focus for fashion, the arts, shopping, recreation, and government in the region. The Paramus campus is in the heart of Bergen County's business district. The corporate atmosphere of the campus reflects the area. Internship and employment opportunities can be found nearby.

Admission Requirements

The basic requirements for admission to Berkeley College include graduation from an accredited high school or the equivalent and an entrance exam or SAT/ACT scores. A personal interview is strongly recommended. The following credentials must be submitted as part of the application process: a completed application form, a nonrefundable $40 application fee, and an unofficial transcript for currently enrolled high school students or an official high school transcript or its (GED) equivalent for high school graduates.

Students who graduated from an accredited high school or who have earned a GED and then attended another college or university, are considered transfer students. Transfer students must submit an application for admission and the nonrefundable $40 application fee, a final transcript from each college or university attended, and a final high school transcript or GED certificate.

Berkeley accepts transfer credits from regionally accredited postsecondary institutions for courses in which the student earned a minimum grade of C and that are applicable to a student's program at Berkeley. Academic advisers can also explore with transfer students the possibility of receiving credit for acceptable scores on national standardized exams and professional certification exams. Knowledge gained outside the classroom, either through work or life experience, can often translate into college credit at Berkeley. A prior-learning academic adviser counsels students, reviews the possibilities for credit recognition, and determines the best method for assessment.

Application and Information

Applications are accepted on an ongoing basis. Prospective students should contact the Director of Admissions at the campus that is most convenient to them or visit the College's Web site at the address below.

West Paterson Campus
Berkeley College
44 Rifle Camp Road
West Paterson, New Jersey

Woodbridge Campus
Berkeley College
430 Rahway Avenue
Woodbridge, New Jersey

Paramus Campus
Berkeley College
64 East Midland Avenue
Paramus, New Jersey

To reach all campuses:
Telephone: 800-446-5400 Ext. G28 (toll-free)
E-mail: info@berkeleycollege.edu
World Wide Web: http://www.berkeleycollege.edu

Berkeley College's programs balance traditional academic preparation with professional training and hands-on experience.

BERKELEY COLLEGE

NEW YORK CITY AND WHITE PLAINS, NEW YORK

The College and Its Mission

Since its inception in 1931, Berkeley College has been committed to providing an exceptional undergraduate business education. Today, Berkeley College is recognized across the nation as a premier school that prepares students for successful careers in business in the modern world. Berkeley College's strong academic program succeeds through a blend of traditional education, professional training, and real-world experience.

At Berkeley, students benefit from small class sizes, personal academic and career counseling, and the chance to develop their analytical and creative skills. Berkeley believes that teaching should provide a practical perspective to traditional material, and Berkeley's distinguished faculty members bring academic preparation and professional experience to the classroom. Faculty members are chosen not just for their academic achievements but also for their applicable background in the business world.

The Middle States Commission on Higher Education of the Middle States Association of Colleges and Schools accredits Berkeley College, and the New York State Board of Regents authorizes the New York City and Westchester campuses to confer the degrees of Associate in Science (A.S.), Associate in Applied Science (A.A.S.), and Bachelor of Business Administration (B.B.A.). Their programs are registered by the New York State Education Department. The paralegal studies program at all campuses is approved by the American Bar Association (ABA).

Berkeley programs provide the comprehensive foundation necessary to begin a successful business career or to advance in a current career. At Berkeley, the traditional undergraduate curriculum is enhanced with professional training and experience. Berkeley's internship requirement provides valuable work experience and often leads to a full-time position. Students work in their fields of study, earn academic credits toward their degrees, establish a network of business connections for the future, and offset college costs.

Academic Programs

Berkeley offers a wide range of career-focused associate and bachelor's degrees that prepare students for immediate marketability and professional growth. The academic curriculum combines leading-edge theory, real-world practicality, and extensive training in the latest computer technologies. Berkeley's commitment to excellence constitutes the primary objective of the College. Small classes, individualized advisement and counseling, and the development of the students' creative and analytical skills support this commitment.

Berkeley College provides exceptional flexibility and convenience, as students have the option of combining day, evening, weekend, and online classes that provide everything students need to pursue a wide range of associate or bachelor's degrees backed by Berkeley's commitment to excellence in education and value.

The College operates year-round on the quarter system, with classes starting in September, January, April, and July. The flexible quarter system provides students enrolled in the day division with the opportunity to complete their associate degree in only eighteen months or earn their bachelor's degree either in as little as three years or in the traditional four years. Associate degree credits are easily transferred to bachelor's degree programs. Evening/weekend students have the opportunity to complete their associate degree in only two years or earn their bachelor's degree in less than four years.

Majors and Degrees Associate degree programs are offered in business administration, with specializations in accounting, information systems management, management, and marketing. Additional associate degree programs include fashion marketing and management, international business, and paralegal studies. Bachelor of Business Administration degree programs are offered in accounting, fashion marketing and management, general business, information systems management, international business, management, and marketing. Not all programs are offered at all campuses.

Certificate Programs Berkeley College offers certificate programs in computer applications and software management. These programs, which can be completed in a year or less, provide students with the opportunity to get a head start in a gratifying career. Credits earned in certificate programs are transferable to Berkeley's degree programs, and students enrolled in certificate programs receive all the benefits of a Berkeley education, including lifetime placement assistance and software refresher courses.

Credit for Nontraditional Learning Experiences

Knowledge gained outside the classroom, through either work or life experience, can often translate into college credit at Berkeley. A Prior-Learning Academic Adviser counsels students, reviews the possibilities for credit recognition, and determines the best method for assessment.

Costs

In 2004–05, full-time students pay $15,900 in tuition and fees for the academic year. Berkeley offers protection from any tuition increase to students who maintain continuous full-time enrollment. A variety of housing options are available, depending on the campus attended. Westchester students are housed in Cottage Place Apartments, a new six-story residence adjacent to the White Plains campus. Cottage Place comprises studio apartments with kitchenettes and two- and three-bedroom apartments with full kitchens and living rooms. All studios and bedrooms are designed for double occupancy, and the three-bedroom apartments have two bathrooms. Bright, cheerful, and attractively furnished, each apartment is air conditioned and wired for voice, data, and cable TV. Amenities include overnight security, laundry facilities, and electronic key-card access. Cottage Place is within easy walking distance of commuter train and bus lines. Housing costs are $5850 per academic year. Living expenses can vary considerably.

Financial Aid

Berkeley is committed to helping students find the financing options that make their education possible. Financial assistance programs are available from federal and state sources and through Berkeley in the forms of scholarships, grants, loans, and other awards. Berkeley College allocates approximately $12 million annually for student aid, based on need and/or merit. Financial aid administrators are available to meet one-on-one with students and their families to develop a plan that is best suited to meet their individual educational expenses.

Faculty

Because Berkeley believes that teaching should encompass a conceptual and practical perspective, faculty members are chosen for both their professional experience and their academic credentials. Their business experience brings an added intellectual reality to the classroom, creating a challenging and stimulating learning environment. Several of Berkeley's administrators are nationally recognized authors, lecturers, consultants, and leaders in business education.

Student Body Profile

Berkeley's total enrollment of nearly 4,700 students at five campuses in New York and New Jersey includes day and evening and full- and part-time students, who represent seventy-six countries.

Student Activities

Berkeley offers a number of organizations, clubs, and activities designed to meet the educational, cultural, and social needs and interests of students. Activities include, but are not limited to, picnics, intramural sports, ski weekends, theater events, and charity drives. All students are members of the Student Government Association (SGA). Elected SGA officers meet regularly and act as liaisons between students and the administration concerning social and academic matters.

Facilities and Resources

Berkeley College maintains comprehensive libraries on each campus. Each library houses a collection of print and nonprint resources, periodicals, study areas, computers, and audiovisual equipment. The libraries provide a variety of services, including orientations, reference assistance, and course-related, course-integrated, and point-of-use instruction. A systemwide catalog encompassing the holdings of all Berkeley libraries consists of approximately 85,000 items. Library Web pages provide access 24 hours a day, seven days a week to online catalogs, electronic databases, reference tools, Internet search engines, and links to institution-wide portals. Each academic facility is staffed with librarians committed to teaching independent research and literacy skills.

The Academic Resource Centers and Learning Labs provide students with a wide range of support services to help improve their study skills as well as their reading, writing, and mathematical abilities. Academic, career, individual advisement, and free tutorial services are also available. Throughout Berkeley's campuses are state-of-the-art computer labs with more than 700 classroom computer stations.

Berkeley's full-service Career Services division has 20 placement advisers who specialize in each major field of study. Berkeley's Career Services professionals work with students to identify career options, develop and refine resume and interviewing skills, set up and place students in internship positions, and schedule interviews in the areas surrounding the five New York/New Jersey locations. Lifetime career assistance is available to all Berkeley graduates. Last year, more than 96 percent of all graduates available for placement were employed in positions related to their studies at Berkeley College.

Location

Berkeley College provides students with the choices and opportunities of both urban and suburban campuses. The New York City campus, found in the heart of Manhattan's east side next to Grand Central Station, is for students who want to take advantage of the total metropolitan experience. Berkeley's Westchester campus, which was recently relocated to the heart of the business district in downtown White Plains, is easily accessible from all directions and is centrally located near commuter train and bus lines.

Admission Requirements

The basic requirements for admission to Berkeley College include graduation from an accredited high school or the equivalent and entrance exam or SAT/ACT scores. A personal interview is strongly recommended. The following must be submitted as part of the application process: a completed application form, a nonrefundable $40 application fee, and an unofficial transcript for currently enrolled high school students or an official high school transcript or its equivalent for high school graduates.

Students who graduated from an accredited high school or the equivalent and then attended another college or university are considered transfer students. Transfer students must submit an application for admission and the nonrefundable $40 application fee, a final transcript from each college or university attended, and a final high school transcript or GED certificate.

Berkeley accepts transfer credits from regionally accredited postsecondary institutions for courses in which the student earned a minimum grade of C and that are applicable to a student's program at Berkeley. Academic advisers can also explore with transfer students the possibility of receiving credit for acceptable scores on national standardized exams and professional certification exams.

Application and Information

Applications are accepted on an ongoing basis. Prospective students should contact the Director of Admissions at the Berkeley College campus that is most convenient to them.

New York City Campus
Berkeley College
3 East 43rd Street
New York, New York 10017
Telephone: 800-446-5400 Ext. G28 (toll-free)
E-mail: info@berkeleycollege.edu
Internet: http://www.berkeleycollege.edu

White Plains Campus
Berkeley College
99 Church Street
White Plains, New York 10601
Telephone: 800-446-5400 Ext. G28 (toll-free)
E-mail: info@berkeleycollege.edu
World Wide Web: http://www.berkeleycollege.edu

Berkeley College's career-oriented curriculum includes training in the latest computer technologies.

BRADLEY ACADEMY FOR THE VISUAL ARTS

YORK, PENNSYLVANIA

The College and Its Mission

Bradley Academy maintains its tradition of excellence. In 1952, the York Academy of Arts was established by local artists to meet the community's needs for trained visual artists. Thirty years later, the school became part of the Antonelli Institute of Art and Photography group, with headquarters in Philadelphia. In 1988, Bradley Academy once again became an independent school continuing to provide area employers with well-trained graduates.

It is Bradley Academy's mission to be responsive to the needs of employers by teaching, within a supportive environment, the creative, technical, and workplace skills required for a successful career. Bradley's success is measured by the number of students who complete their programs and get jobs in their chosen fields—graphic design, interior design, multimedia design, fashion marketing, print technology, or Web technology. In recent years, 85 to 95 percent of each year's available graduating students are working in their chosen professional fields within six months after graduation.

Bradley Academy is people. A staff of dedicated professionals strives to help students realize their full potential and master the skills needed for their first job in their chosen fields. Faculty and staff members believe in their responsibility to provide practical, hands-on career training; develop social skills, good work habits, and technical skills; provide equal opportunity for success based on performance; provide a supportive environment; and prepare students in the classroom for the workplace.

Bradley Academy for the Visual Arts is a private, proprietary institution specializing in career-oriented programs in the visual arts. Most course work is directly related to the student's major field of study. Bradley Academy is accredited by the Accrediting Commission for Career Schools and Colleges of Technology (ACCSCT).

Academic Programs

All programs are geared toward career preparation, and general education requirements are held to five courses out of the total of twenty-four courses taken in the two-year specialized associate degree programs. Students select their major fields at the time of enrollment, and their courses are block scheduled.

Whenever possible and appropriate, courses are taught in a studio or lab setting providing hands-on instruction. Two years ago, Bradley Academy became the first school in its region to require students to have a laptop computer. While at school, students can access the wireless network to check e-mail, hand in assignments, and check grades or attendance or work on a project anywhere on campus. This technology creates an environment in which each classroom also functions as a computer lab.

Associate Degree Programs Programs offered for the **Associate in Specialized Technology** degree include digital arts and animation, graphic design, interior design, and Web design. The program for the **Associate in Specialized Business** degree is fashion marketing.

Specialized associate degree programs require successful completion of 72 credits, taken over six 11-week terms. The diploma program requires successful completion of 768 clock hours, taken over four 11-week terms.

Special Programs and Services A Summer Studio Program for students who are entering their senior year of high school is held each year. Students take classes in one of four areas: graphic design, interior design, fashion marketing, or interactive design.

Credit for Nontraditional Learning Experiences

Advanced standing or academic credit for work done elsewhere is considered on a case-by-case basis by the Dean of Education. A portfolio evaluation is usually part of the process; testing may also be required.

Costs

Tuition for the 2003–04 academic year was $370 per credit. Students in the degree programs usually take 12 credits per term, making total tuition for the academic year $13,320. Tuition is anticipated to increase to $390 per credit beginning with the October 2004 starting class. Starting students can purchase a supply kit that costs $550 to $900, depending on the program. The purchase of a laptop computer with appropriate software is also required.

Bradley Academy does not operate facilities for student housing, but does assist students in finding suitable accommodations and roommates upon request. The suburban area surrounding Bradley Academy has sufficient rental units available to students at reasonable costs, averaging $350 to $550 per month per student.

Financial Aid

Bradley Academy participates in the Federal Pell Grant, Federal Student Educational Opportunity Grant, Federal College Work-Study, Federal Stafford Student Loan, and PLUS Programs; the Pennsylvania PHEAA grant program; and other sources of aid that may be available to qualified students. Institutional aid is also available and is awarded based on need and merit. The financial planner can assist students in determining eligibility and completing applications and can help families create a personal plan that outlines expenses and identifies financial resources available to students.

Faculty

Total faculty members number 53. Of these, 11 are full-time and 42 are adjunct. The student-faculty ratio is approximately 15:1. Faculty members are required to have a minimum of three years' professional experience in the fields in which they teach, in addition to appropriate academic credentials. Many faculty members have earned bachelor's degrees in their respective fields; approximately one third have earned master's degrees.

Student Body Profile

The average age of students at Bradley Academy is 22. About 55 percent are women, and 45 percent are men. The total number of full-time students enrolled in fall 2003 was 477. Approximately 55 percent of students commute from their homes in south-central Pennsylvania and northern Maryland; the other 45 percent rent apartments within a short distance of the school.

Student Activities

Students may get involved with professional organizations such as the American Institute of Graphic Artists (AIGA), American Society of Interior Designers (ASID), National Kitchen and Bath Association (NKBA), Special Interest Group on Computer Graphics (SIGGRAPH), and the Student Government Association. The school also has a chapter of Alpha Beta Kappa (ABK), a national honor society that promotes and rewards personal integrity and academic excellence. Students maintaining a 3.5 cumulative GPA or higher at the end of the fifth term are considered for induction into ABK. School activities include a school picnic each term, a Halloween party, and a variety of field trips within each department. Life Skills seminars are also offered, including financial planning, planned parenthood, and safety, to name a few. Students are also encouraged to get involved with the community through freelance work and frequent community service opportunities.

Facilities and Resources

Bradley Academy is housed in a 38,000-square-foot facility that was built in 1997 on 7 acres in a suburban area of York, Pennsylvania. Twenty-one spacious classrooms and studios, accommodating an average class size of 25 or fewer, are well suited for studio work as well as lecture classes. Computer labs provide state-of-the-industry hardware and software, including printers, scanners, and CD-ROM players. Students routinely work with industry-standard software applications, which are regularly upgraded to reflect current industry practice. There is wireless connectivity throughout the building. All computers are networked and have Internet access. Other resources include a community gallery, a student gallery, and an art supply/bookstore. A graphics lab, display windows, and vignette spaces allow students to apply the skills learned in the classroom.

Library and Audiovisual Services The library occupies about 1,000 square feet near the front of the school. It contains more than 3,000 general reference books as well as titles specifically related to the programs offered at the Academy. The library also includes more than 70 periodicals routinely received by the school, plus a collection of popular DVDs/videos and bestselling books. The library has eight Windows NT workstations, which are connected by cable modem to the Internet. A CD-ROM server enables students to access many additional types of reference materials. Operated through a partnership agreement with the public library system and the township, the library is staffed by professionals and offers interlibrary loan.

In addition to the library, each program has additional resource areas that contain materials specific to that course of study. For example, the Interior Design Resource Room has catalogs of furniture manufacturers and a wide selection of fabric samples used for window treatments, wall covering or upholstery, tile samples, and paint swatches. The Fashion Marketing Resource Area includes commercial sewing machines, mannequins, and materials used for visual merchandising as well as industry-specific publications. Student artwork is proudly displayed throughout the school as well as in the student gallery. It is used to demonstrate the students' achievements and the nature of their work to prospective employers and students.

Location

The York area offers a unique blend of small-city convenience, safety, and lifestyle with easy access to the larger population centers of Baltimore, Maryland (45 minutes), and Lancaster and Harrisburg (each 30 minutes). York was founded in pre-Revolutionary times. It has a rich historic past and a strong commitment to preserving its traditions. York County also offers several major shopping malls and many outlet shopping opportunities. It has a strong manufacturing and industrial base as well, and consistently has one of the lowest unemployment rates in Pennsylvania. Book publishers, furniture manufacturers, and apparel manufacturers are among the many employers in the area.

Admission Requirements

Typically, the admissions procedure begins with a visit to Bradley Academy. At that time, prospective students and their families can tour the school and gather the information needed to make a decision. Likewise, the admissions staff can become acquainted with the student's qualifications. To be considered for admission, all applicants must have a high school diploma or hold a GED certificate approved by the state. All applicants are evaluated on their educational backgrounds and demonstrated interest in their chosen fields. A portfolio review is required as part of the admissions process for applicants to the animation program. In addition, students accepted to the graphic design program are asked to submit a portfolio prior to starting school for academic placement. High school transcripts are requested, and students are encouraged but not required to submit SAT scores. Bradley Academy reserves the right to request additional information or assessment as deemed necessary by the Admissions Committee. Qualified students are accepted at any time. However, early application is strongly encouraged. Bradley Academy is a small school, and some classes fill well in advance of the starting date. An early decision also has the advantage of allowing time for proper processing of financial aid.

Application and Information

Prospective students should contact:

Director of Admissions
Bradley Academy for the Visual Arts
1409 Williams Road
York, Pennsylvania 17402

Telephone: 800-864-7725 (toll-free)
Fax: 717-840-1951
E-mail: info@bradleyacademy.edu
World Wide Web: http://www.bradleyacademy.edu

BRIARWOOD COLLEGE
SOUTHINGTON, CONNECTICUT

The College and Its Mission

Briarwood College is a coed, two-year private college whose mission is to develop students' critical thinking, self-discipline, and communication skills within the context of career and technical programs. An emphasis on small classes, comprehensive academic support services, and programs closely connected to opportunities in the employment market account for more than 85 percent of Briarwood's graduates being placed in jobs in their field within six months of graduation.

The College offers full- and part-time opportunities, evening classes, an accelerated option on Saturdays that is designed for working adults, and a variety of continuing education offerings through the Division of Lifelong Learning. In addition, alumni of the College receive a unique benefit, *Education for Life*®, which allows them to return for further course work tuition-free for the rest of their lives.

Academic Programs

Briarwood College offers a variety of career-oriented programs, both full- and part-time, leading to a certificate, diploma, or associate degree. In general, an associate degree program requires two years of study and a certificate program one year. Diploma programs may take up to one year.

Associate Degree Programs Briarwood College offers associate degrees in twenty-seven majors. The **Associate in Arts** (A.A.) degree is offered in general studies with concentrations in ballet, biotechnology, computer information systems, English, environmental technology, fine arts, history, mathematics, psychology, and science. The **Associate in Applied Science** (A.A.S.) degree is offered in accounting, administrative technology (with concentrations in executive, legal, and management), child development, communication, criminal justice, dental administrative assistant studies, dietetic technician studies, executive medical assistant studies, fashion merchandising, fitness technician studies, health information technology, hospitality (with concentrations in hotel and restaurant management and travel and tourism management), marketing, medical office management, mortuary science, occupational therapy assistant studies, and paralegal studies.

Certificate Programs The following programs lead to a certificate after one year: administrative legal professional studies, administrative medical professional studies, child development assistant studies, dental chairside assistant studies, health information coding, health information processing, medical assistant studies, medical transcription, pharmacy technician studies, and word processing. Most of these programs may be applied toward an associate degree program.

Diploma Programs Briarwood also offers diploma courses in computer information systems leading to certification in Microsoft certified systems engineer, Microsoft certified system administrator, certified Novell administrator, and Computer Technology Industry Association: A+ certification for hardware repair.

Saturday College Saturday College is an accelerated degree program for mature adults who want to complete their studies while continuing to work full-time. Students complete two courses every eight weeks, enabling them to complete an associate degree in twenty months.

Education for Life® is a unique benefit offered to graduates of Briarwood College who complete associate degrees after at least three full-time semesters of study. Graduates are able to return to Briarwood for additional credit or noncredit courses tuition-free for the rest of their lives.

Costs

For the 2004–05 academic year, costs are as follows: tuition is $14,625 for resident and commuter students; part-time students pay $485 per credit. Resident students are also charged a $3200 residency fee. The nonrefundable registration fee for resident and commuter students is $95; part-time students pay $95 per semester.

Financial Aid

The following types of financial aid are available individually or in combination with other resources: presidential scholarships, state scholarships, and the Capitol Scholarship Program. Briarwood College, in conjunction with outside professional associations, also awards several scholarships in the business, health, and office administration fields. As other scholarships become available in specific program fields, they are announced in Briarwood College publications and posted outside the Financial Aid Office. A number of scholarships are awarded annually to students by local civic groups, churches, and fraternal and union organizations. Students are encouraged to explore all outside possibilities, utilizing the assistance of high school guidance officers or the Briarwood College Financial Aid Office. Recipients of the scholarships are chosen on the basis of high scholastic achievement, need, and potential for success.

Eligible students are encouraged to seek, and are assisted in obtaining, educational benefits from the Veterans Administration, G.I. Bill, and state agencies. There are also grants and loans available, including Connecticut Independent College Student Grants (CICS), Federal Pell Grants, Federal Stafford Student Loans, Federal PLUS loans, Federal Supplemental Educational Opportunity Grant, and Federal Perkins Loans. For more information, students should contact the Financial Aid Office at 860-628-4751 or 800-952-2444 (toll-free).

Faculty

The faculty includes 1 professor, 6 associate professors, 16 assistant professors, and 80 other instructors. The teaching experience among the faculty members at Briarwood College is distinct in its variety of professional, business, and years of teaching experience. There are several faculty members who remain active in their line of work. For example, the Allied Health Division has on its staff several faculty members who are currently active in their vocation who bring expertise to their students. The faculty in this category include the Program Director of the Pharmacy Technician Program, who is a practicing pharmacist; the Program Director of Travel and Tourism, who has more than twenty years of experience in the travel industry and is still active in the field; and adjunct faculty members in the Mortuary Science Program, who are presently working in the funeral service business.

Student Body Profile

There are 565 students currently enrolled. Nineteen percent are members of minority groups, 1 percent are international students, and 33 percent live on campus.

Student Activities

Students are encouraged to join and participate in clubs, student organizations, and other activities that interest them, including Student Government, Student Ambassador Program, Hall Council,

Allied Health Club, Fashion Club (F.A.M.E.), Phi Beta Lambda, Psi Beta (a national honor society for the field of psychology), and yearbook staff.

Sports Briarwood College is in the process of applying to the National Junior College Athletic Association to enable its men's basketball team to compete with other colleges in Region 21. Briarwood College is also in the process of starting a women's basketball team and men's and women's soccer teams. Students may become involved in a wide variety of outdoor/indoor recreational activities such as softball, volleyball, and golf. Skiing is available locally at Mount Southington, only 1 mile from the College. Weekend trips to ski resorts in Vermont are also scheduled. Indoor activities include weight lifting and exercise machines, aerobics, racquetball, and swimming, made available through a special affiliation with the Southington YMCA and Gold's Gym.

Facilities and Resources

The College is located at the base of Mount Southington, near Lake Compounce Theme Park in Southington, Connecticut. There are two residential facilities on campus: Eder Hall, with its townhouse–style apartments, and Dominic DiVerene Hall. All units have furnished bedrooms, kitchens, and living rooms as well as laundry facilities. The residence halls also have Internet and cable access. A student center provides recreation space, pool tables, lounge chairs, and a large-screen television. A softball field is located adjacent to the residence halls.

Career Services The Career Service Office at Briarwood College provides a comprehensive career development program designed to assist students in making appropriate career choices and in developing plans to achieve their goals. The goal of Career Services is to assist student with having a meaningful college experience that leads to successful employment and/or continued education. To enhance potential and marketability, students are encouraged—through numerous outreach methods—to take advantage of services early in their college careers.

Counseling Services Students who experience academic, personal, learning, or study problems are urged to seek help as soon as the problem is recognized. Counselors provide academic intervention activities designed to assist students who are experiencing academic difficulties. These activities include Early Alert notices, midterm intervention sessions, and individual assistance. A counselor is available to assist students who are having academic difficulties by working with them to develop a personal plan for success.

College counselors are available to aid students in resolving many types of problems. Such problems may involve social, emotional, vocational, and personal concerns. All information is handled in a confidential setting. Services of the Counseling Center include short term personal counseling, crisis intervention, career development, and administering and interpreting self-assessment inventories.

In some cases, a counselor determines that the needs of a student would be best met through a community agency off campus. Referrals are made when the student is in crisis; has a long-term, ongoing problem; or can otherwise benefit from the resources of an outside agency. Counselors assist students in obtaining such services when appropriate.

Disability Services The Disability Services Office is responsible for all disability-related concerns of Briarwood College students. Briarwood College encourages qualified students with disabilities to take advantage of its educational programs. The College is responsible for ensuring that courses, programs, services, activities, and facilities are available and usable in the most integrated and appropriate settings. Students with disabilities seeking accommodations must identify themselves as individuals with disabilities, request needed accommodations, and provide documentation from the appropriate professional as to how the disabilities limit their participation in courses, programs, activities, and use of facilities. Upon receipt of documentation of a disability, it is the responsibility of the Disability Services Office to explore and facilitate reasonable accommodations, academic adjustments, and/or auxiliary aids and services for individuals with disabilities in courses, programs, services, activities, and facilities. Students anticipating the need for accommodations, both before and after enrollment, are encouraged to contact the Dean of Student Services, whose office is located in the lower level of Eder Hall Center, ext. 219.

Health and Wellness Services The Health Office provides basic first aid and health education information to Briarwood College students. In some cases, a nurse determines that the needs of a student would be best met through an off-campus community facility. All students are required by federal law to provide their medical history and documentation of illnesses and immunizations prior to matriculation at Briarwood College. This information is used by the nurse in providing routine and emergency care.

Library and Audiovisual Services The Dr. Anthony A. Pupillo Library, staffed by a professional librarian and knowledgeable library assistants, plays an integral part in the education process of the students. The library is committed to providing support for the various courses and programs of study offered by Briarwood College. Although the library's resources are richest in the curricula taught at the College, a wide variety of works for individual interest and personal growth are also offered. The library offers a wide variety of electronic resources to facilitate student research. Novice users quickly learn to utilize the capabilities of the library's computer technology. The library offers research-only computers for student use and one-on-one sessions with students to familiarize them with its resources. Interlibrary loan is available to the students.

Location

Briarwood College is located in Southington, Connecticut, only 2 hours from Boston and New York. Students find skiing and Connecticut beaches readily accessible, and the school is minutes from the Hartford and New Haven metropolitan areas. The picturesque 35-acre campus is nestled at the base of Mount Southington and provides students the opportunity to take 2-hour daily or weekend excursions to the cultural and entertainment meccas of New York and Boston.

Admission Requirements

The College requires applicants for full-time study to submit a completed application form, a $25 application fee, official high school transcripts or GED scores, a personal statement, and one letter of recommendation. SAT I scores are not required, but are recommended for students interested in scholarship opportunities. International students for whom English is not the first language are required to show proof of English competency. Part-time and transfer applicants are ordinarily not required to submit a personal statement and recommendation letter. Transfer applicants are also required to submit transcripts from all colleges or universities previously attended. Interviews with the program directors are also required for applicants to the dental assisting and occupational therapy assisting programs. Applications are reviewed on a rolling basis and acceptances are mailed, usually within one week of receipt of all required documents. Applicants for fall semester are encouraged to apply by March 30 for priority scholarship consideration.

Application and Information

For more information, students should contact:

Admissions Department
Briarwood College
2279 Mt. Vernon Road
Southington, Connecticut 06489
Telephone: 860-628-4751
          800-952-2444 (toll-free)
E-mail: admis@briarwood.edu
World Wide Web: http://www.briarwood.edu

BUNKER HILL COMMUNITY COLLEGE

BOSTON, MASSACHUSETTS

The College and Its Mission

A public institution of higher education, Bunker Hill Community College (BHCC) offers wide-ranging workforce education curricula interwoven throughout comprehensive programs and courses of study, including nursing and allied health, an extensive information technology program, criminal justice, hospitality and culinary arts, business, and early childhood development. Accredited by the Commission on Institutions of Higher Education of the New England Association of Schools and Colleges, BHCC supports open access to postsecondary education by providing a strong liberal arts foundation and a range of educational opportunities that include distance learning, self-directed learning, an Honors Program, and, for nonnative English-speaking students, a variety of levels of English as a second language (ESL) instruction. BHCC graduates have gone on to continue their education at many four-year institutions, including the University of Massachusetts, Brandeis University, Northeastern University, Tufts University, Smith College, Suffolk University, and Wellesley College. BHCC seeks to enhance its position as a primary educational and economic asset for the commonwealth through cooperative planning and program implementation involving neighboring institutions of higher education, the public schools, community organizations, and area businesses and industries.

Academic Programs

BHCC offers numerous programs of study. They include Associate in Arts (A.A.) degrees, Associate in Science (A.S.) degrees, and certificate programs. Associate in Arts concentrations are designed to permit the student to transfer smoothly to four-year colleges and universities. Although extreme care has been taken in fashioning these transfer-focused degrees, students are advised to consult the institution to which they wish to transfer to ensure the wisest choice of courses at BHCC. These students should also work with the BHCC transfer counselor and academic advisers in planning both the curriculum at BHCC and the transfer process.

Associate in Science programs are designed to develop the knowledge and skills required for employment at the conclusion of the associate degree. In addition to employment preparation, many Associate in Science programs have transfer options. To ensure smooth transfer to four-year programs, students are advised to consult the institution to which they wish to transfer.

A wide variety of certificate programs provide skills training and job-upgrade opportunities for students who successfully complete these programs.

The Honors Program offers students the opportunity to study and learn in an academically challenging and enriching learning environment.

All programs of study include courses from three requirement areas: general education requirements, career or liberal arts electives, and program requirements, which are outlined in each program grid included on the College's Web site and in the College catalog. Each degree or certificate has requirements for courses and number of credits taken.

Associate Degree Programs **Associate in Arts** degrees are available in biological science, business, chemical science, communication, computer information systems, computer science, education, English, fine arts, foreign language, general concentration, history and government, human services,

mathematics, music, physics/engineering, psychology, sociology, and theater. Students enrolling in any A.A. degree program can earn world studies emphasis certification simultaneously.

Associate in Science degrees are offered in business administration (accounting, finance, international business, management), computer information technology (computer support specialist studies, database programming and administration, network technology and administration), criminal justice, culinary arts, early childhood development, fire protection and safety, graphic arts and visual communication, hotel/restaurant/travel (hotel/restaurant management, travel and tourism management), human services, media technology, medical imaging (medical imaging core curriculum, cardiac sonography, medical radiography, medical radiography–part-time evening), nursing (day, evening, or weekend), office management (administrative information management, medical information management), and pharmacy technology.

Certificate Programs Certificates are available in allied health (medical assistant studies, medical lab assistant studies, patient-care assistant studies, phlebotomy technician studies), business administration (accounting, computer-based accounting, e-commerce marketing management, international business, paralegal studies), computer information technology (computer support specialist studies, database programming and administration, network technology and administration, object-oriented computer programming and design certificate program), culinary arts, diagnostic medical sonography (ultrasound), early childhood development, office and information management (information management specialist studies, medical information management assistant studies), surgical technology (central processing (sterile processing and distribution management), surgical technology), and travel and tourism management.

Off-Campus Programs

Bunker Hill Community College offers eCollege and distance learning courses online as a convenient alternative to the traditional classroom. These courses are designed for self-directed, motivated learners. The courses are equivalent in content and academic rigor to traditional classroom courses but offer students the flexibility and convenience of learning virtually anytime and anywhere. The eCollege also offers hybrid courses. These courses incorporate both traditional classroom and online components. Hybrid courses generally meet on-site for 50 percent of the instructional time, with the remaining instruction conducted online.

BHCC offers a range of educational opportunities at its five satellite campuses, each intended to serve the distinct needs and interests of the host communities—Cambridge, Chinatown, Revere, Somerville, and Boston's South End. The curricula available at the satellites allow students to prepare for workforce advancement while earning credits toward an associate degree or certificate in several of the wide variety of fields offered by the College. Programs include foundation courses that fulfill general education requirements as well as courses in response to community interest, such as offerings in computer technology, business management, and hospitality.

Bunker Hill Community College has a comprehensive study-abroad program that allows students to experience different cultures. Each year, approximately twenty scholarships are awarded to further assist BHCC students in realizing their dream of studying abroad. Faculty, staff, and interested community members are also invited to take part in the programs, although scholarships are available only to qualified BHCC students.

Credit for Nontraditional Learning Experiences

The Prior Learning Assessment Program provides an opportunity to students to condense their time of study by granting credits for college-level knowledge and skills. This program assists students in examining their outside learning experiences and identifying those that might be considered for college credits. Common sources for this kind of learning are jobs, volunteer work, skills training, workshops or study groups, and community involvement.

Students can earn college credits in four ways: portfolio evaluation, the College-Level Examination Program (CLEP), military evaluation, and departmental challenge exams.

Costs

Tuition for Massachusetts residents is $100 per credit; for non-Massachusetts residents, it is $306 per credit. The New England Regional Student Program costs $112 per credit. The health course fee is $35 per credit (for health program courses only).

Financial Aid

The Financial Aid Office at Bunker Hill Community College assists students and their families in meeting the costs of a college education. Bunker Hill Community College participates in a wide variety of federal, state, and private financial aid programs. Students should be aware that all institutions, including Bunker Hill Community College, are subject to adjustments in funding allocations from both the commonwealth of Massachusetts and the United States Department of Education.

In order to be eligible for financial aid, an applicant must be a United States citizen or an eligible noncitizen enrolled or accepted for enrollment in an eligible program. In addition, the applicant must maintain satisfactory academic progress, comply with Federal Selective Service Law, and not be in default on any educational loans or owe a refund on any federal grants or loans to any institution. Students who have obtained a previous bachelor's degree at any U.S. or international institution are not eligible for financial aid.

Financial aid awards are subject to change if any of the factors used to calculate eligibility from the Free Application for Federal Student Aid (FAFSA) change after the date of original application. Other examples of factors that impact eligibility include increases in income and changes in family size and/or in the number of family members enrolled in college. Students are strongly advised to consult with the Financial Aid Office if they are contemplating a change in enrollment status.

Faculty

There are 120 full-time faculty members and more than 200 adjunct faculty members at BHCC. The student-faculty ratio is 30:1.

Student Body Profile

The student body reflects the diversity of the urban community, and an essential part of the College's mission is to encourage this diversity. The average student age is 28. Nearly 60 percent of the students are women, more than half are people of color, and most are employed while attending school.

Student Activities

Bunker Hill Community College has an active student life program. The activities coordinated through the Student Activities and Athletics Office provide students with the opportunity to have fun, meet people, and make a difference in campus life at the College. BHCC celebrates cultural diversity and encourages cultural interaction.

There are more than twenty-eight student organizations and athletic teams at Bunker Hill Community College, which provide the campus with social, cultural, and educational programs as well as competitive sports, intramural/recreational programs, and leisure-time activities. New members are always welcome.

Athletic programs provide opportunities for students to participate in competitive or recreational activities on the intercollegiate and intramural levels. The Intercollegiate Athletic Program consists of men's soccer, baseball, and basketball and women's soccer, softball, and basketball. The Intramural Athletic Program includes basketball, flag football, table tennis, tennis, and walk/jog.

Student clubs and organizations include ACT (Activism, Commitment, and Teamwork); African-American Cultural Society; Alpha Kappa Mu Honor Society; Arab Students Association; Asian-Pacific Students Association; Campus Activities Board; Campus Crusade for Christ/Real Life Club; Computer Science Club; Criminal Justice Club; Disabled Students Activities Club; Drama Club; Environmental Club; Epsilon Science Club; Gay, Lesbian and Bisexual Student Union; Haitian Club; Hospitality Club; International Students Club; Italian-American Society; Investment Club; Latinos Unidos Club; Music Club; Nursing Mentor; Student Government; Television Production Club; Upsidedown Club; and WBCC radio.

Facilities and Resources

Facilities available at BHCC include the library and information center, advising and counseling center, tutoring and academic support center, career center, international center, and academic computing center.

Location

All Bunker Hill Community College sites are located in urban communities within 5 miles of downtown Boston. The main campus is located in the historic Charlestown neighborhood of Boston. An annex campus is located in Bellingham Square in Chelsea. The satellites are in Cambridge, Chinatown, Revere, Somerville, and the South End. All locations are easily accessible via public transportation. A subway stop is located steps from the Charlestown Campus.

Admission Requirements

All students admitted to degree or certificate programs are required to take computerized placement tests (CPTs) in English, reading, and mathematics. The purpose of the tests is to determine the levels at which students will begin their study. Based upon test results, the College may prescribe development courses or limit a student's enrollment, in an effort to enhance that student's ability to succeed. Applicants to health careers and technical programs must comply with program entrance requirements and application deadlines.

Application and Information

Although the College has a rolling admissions process, students should contact the Admissions and Transfer Counseling Office for program-specific application deadlines.

Admissions and Transfer Counseling
Bunker Hill Community College
Charlestown Campus, Room B130
250 New Rutherford Avenue
Boston, Massachusetts 02129
Telephone: 617-228-2019
Fax: 617-228-3336
E-mail: admissions@bhcc.mass.edu
World Wide Web: http://www.bhcc.mass.edu

CENTRAL TEXAS COLLEGE

KILLEEN, TEXAS

The College and Its Mission

Founded in 1965, Central Texas College (CTC) is a public, open-admission community college, offering associate degrees and certificate programs in academic, professional, and vocational/technical fields. Central Texas College consists of six campuses: Central Campus in Killeen, Texas; the Continental Campus; the Europe Campus; the Fort Hood and Service Area Campus; the Navy Campus; and the Pacific Far East Campus. With more than 100 locations around the world, CTC serves more than 50,000 students on military installations, in correctional facilities, in embassies, and on ships at sea. Central Texas College is evolving and expanding to meet its role in the changing needs of the local, national, and military communities. Its mission is to provide students with high-quality education.

Academic Programs

Central Texas College confers the Associate in Arts degree, the Associate in Science degree, the Associate in Applied Science degree, and the Associate of General Studies degree upon students who have successfully completed the minimum requirements and all the specific requirements for graduation. In addition, a Certificate of Completion is awarded to students who fulfill the curricular requirements of special courses and programs.

Degree programs are offered in the major subjects of agriculture science, art, auto collision studies, automotive mechanic studies, aviation science, biology, business administration, business management, chemistry, computer science, criminal justice, diesel studies, drafting and design, drama, early childhood studies, electronics, emergency medical technician studies, engineering, environmental science, geology, graphics and printing, heating and air conditioning, hospitality management, interdisciplinary studies, journalism/communication, legal assistant studies, kinesiology, maintenance technology, mathematics, medical laboratory technician studies, mental health services, modern language, music, nursing, office technology, radio and television broadcasting, social science, and welding.

The English as a second language (ESL) program provides training for non-English speaking students. New students who have not taken the TOEFL, or those with TOEFL scores below 520 on the paper-based test, are required to take the Comprehensive English Language Test (CELT) upon arrival to determine the appropriate level of English instruction required. The ESL program is comprised of three levels of English, which include listening and speaking, reading and vocabulary, and grammar/writing. Classes operate under the traditional semester system. Fall and spring semesters are sixteen weeks, and summer semester is ten weeks. Students with a TOEFL score of 520 or higher are required to take a placement test. ESL classes are only offered on Central Campus in Killeen, Texas.

Costs

Tuition ranges from $30 per credit hour (minimum of $90) for a Texas resident to $1325 (full-time) for a non-Texas resident or international student per semester. Fees are not included in these amounts. The complete tuition and fee schedule may be found on the College Web site. Books are not included in the cost of tuition and fees.

Financial Aid

Central Texas College participates in numerous financial aid programs designed to assist students who demonstrate financial need. To be considered for financial aid, students must complete the Free Application for Federal Student Aid (FAFSA). International students (visa or nonimmigrant) are not eligible to receive federal financial aid.

The CTC Foundation offers scholarships to students currently enrolled in CTC and who are in good academic standing. Application guidelines and a current list of scholarships offered are listed in the Alumni/CTC Foundation section on the CTC Web site.

Faculty

Central Texas College's faculty members strive to provide high-quality instruction with individual attention while serving a culturally diverse and mobile population. The College faculty and staff members share a common commitment to the personal development of each student. Most of CTC's instructors hold advanced degrees in their areas of specialization and continually seek further education and professional development

Student Body Profile

At the CTC Central Campus, there are 9,500 students, of whom 62.9 percent are women and 37.1 percent are men. The ethnicity of the student body is made up of 5.5 percent Asian, 31.7 percent black, 17 percent Hispanic, 0.8 percent Native American, 43.6 percent white, and 1.4 percent international.

Student Activities

The Office of Student Life supports student development by providing opportunities through student organizations, tournaments, multicultural celebrations, and other social activities. The Roy J. Smith Student Center is the social center of the campus. The first floor contains the Student Life Office, the campus bookstore, the cafeteria, the snack bar, and offices for Student Support Services. The second floor contains the Student Government Association Office, a game room, a recreational center, and a television lounge and is the main site for student organization meetings and activities.

A host of intramural sports activities, which take place in and around the new Natatorium and Physical Education Complex, are available and include volleyball, three-on-three basketball, and softball.

Facilities and Resources

Central Texas College seeks constant improvement by building new facilities and upgrading existing structures. The attractively landscaped campus provides a modern classroom, a laboratory, a library, on-campus housing, and athletic and recreational facilities. The most recent addition to Central Campus was the $8.5-million Technology Complex and Planetarium. Other examples of CTC's commitment to growth include the recently opened Natatorium and Physical Education Center, and the expanded Oveta Culp Hobby Library. on the Central Campus, Central Texas College operates an air-conditioned, coeducational residence hall that accommodates approximately 120 students. A comprehensive campus tour is available on the College Web site, listed under the Alumni and Community section.

Project PASS (Partners in Academic Success Services) provides a wide range of tutoring, textbook lending and library services, and noncredit refresher courses in math and English. Disability Support Services assist students with physical and/or learning disabilities through the lending of equipment, such as Braille textbooks, tape recorders, tutoring, and providing note-taker services. Other services include Single Parent/Homemaker Support Services, the Gender Equity Program, the Learning Resource Center, and transportation assistance, which offers bus service to CTC from many pick-up points in the area. All of these services are free to CTC students.

Location

The CTC Central Campus is located in Killeen, Texas, approximately 60 miles north of the capital city of Austin and adjacent to Fort Hood, the largest Army installation in the U.S.

Admission Requirements

Application forms and procedures are available on the College Web site, listed under Admissions and Registration. International students must meet additional admission requirements and should contact the Office of International Student Services for assistance.

Application and Information

Admissions and Records
Central Texas College
P.O. Box 1800
Killeen, Texas 76540-1800
Telephone: 254-526-1696
        800-792-3348 Ext. 1696 (toll-free)
E-mail: admrec@ctcd.edu
World Wide Web: http://www.ctcd.edu

International Student Services
Central Texas College
P.O. Box 1800
Killeen, Texas 76540-1800
Telephone: 254-526-1107
        800-792-3348 Ext. 1107 (toll-free)
E-mail: ctcinternational@ctcd.edu

THE COLLEGE OF WESTCHESTER

WHITE PLAINS, NEW YORK

The College and Its Mission

Founded in 1915, the College of Westchester (CW), formerly the Westchester Business College, has a rich history of providing the community with affordable, private education at the collegiate level. The beautiful, state-of-the-art campus in White Plains offers an environment that is conducive to learning. Programs are designed for college-bound students with an interest in a career-focused education leading to long-term security and financial success.

The College's mission is to offer high-quality career-oriented business and computer-related programs that challenge both the traditional and returning student to advanced levels of intellectual and personal development. This commitment to educational excellence is reflected in a carefully constructed and distinctive curriculum that is designed to provide students with sophisticated, marketable skills and to promote in students those attributes that contribute to personal and career success and a desire for lifelong learning. In order to maximize student success, the college maintains a student-centered environment.

CW is a junior college accredited by the Accrediting Council for Independent Colleges and Schools (ACICS) to award associate degrees, certificates, and diplomas. It is also registered by the New York State Education Department Office of Higher Education and the Professions.

Academic Programs

The Associate in Applied Science (A.A.S.) degree or the Associate in Occupational Studies (A.O.S.) degree is awarded upon successful completion of a two-year program. The requirements include courses in basic college skills, courses pertaining to the student's major, and, for those students pursuing an A.A.S. degree, courses in general education.

The Business Administration–Management/Marketing program provides students with an opportunity to concentrate in either e-commerce marketing, entrepreneurial management, or information systems. Graduates pursue management training, Internet marketing, and sales positions. The program also affords self-employment opportunities through an appropriate educational background.

The Computer Network Administration program provides students with a leading-edge career education for today's technical world. Students study administration, design, support, and maintenance of local area networks through lectures and by using Microsoft Windows 2000 systems and software. The program includes additional nontechnical courses to enhance the student's career opportunities.

The Multimedia Development and Management program provides students with the tools to design and develop multimedia applications for the general media, business, education, the Internet, and entertainment markets. The program utilizes the most current multimedia technologies that enable students to create portfolios of their work.

The Computer Applications Management program prepares students for various professional-level employment opportunities in the rapidly expanding information processing and office technology fields. Graduates of this program are qualified to seek office technology and information processing positions that require expert computer applications skills and knowledge of technical office procedures.

The Computer Systems–Management Applications program prepares students to become competent business-applications programmers and systems specialists. Instruction in computer languages in microcomputer environments gives students the flexibility to become competent in diverse business usages.

The Business Administration–Accounting/Computer Applications program provides students with a business administration accounting curriculum, which places a strong focus on computer applications. Upon graduation, students are prepared for a variety of career possibilities in which a thorough understanding of the principles of accounting are essential.

The Office Administration program prepares students for various professional-level employment opportunities. Graduates of the program are qualified to seek office administration, executive administrative assistant, executive assistant, or office management positions.

Students in nondegree programs receive a certificate from CW if all courses are successfully completed. Credits may be transferred to the associate degree programs, providing a 2.0 or better cumulative grade point average has been achieved in addition to the successful completion of all required courses.

In a short certificate program, students can obtain specialized job skills to launch or upgrade their career. These programs are popular among students who already have some advanced skills or education as well as those who want to be employable and promotable in the shortest possible time.

Certificate programs include Computer Applications Specialist, Computer Networking Specialist, Computer Programming, E-Commerce, Intensive Accounting/Computer Applications, Multimedia Technology, and Word Processing Specialist.

Costs

The cost of tuition and fees varies, depending on the student's program. Current costs are available from the CW admissions office.

Financial Aid

All students at CW are encouraged to apply for financial assistance and meet with a financial assistance counselor who conducts a confidential analysis detailing the funds available to finance their education. In addition to federal- and state-funded programs, the college offers a variety of institutional scholarships, grants, and payment plans each year.

Faculty

CW instructors are highly qualified, dedicated, and respected educators who are committed to excellence in teaching and service to students. Most faculty members have advanced degrees and all have extensive business experience. A comprehensive faculty development program ensures that all instructors remain current in their field of expertise and utilizes state-of-the-art technology and teaching methodologies.

Student Body Profile

Students come to CW from throughout the New York metropolitan area. The present student body represents 117 high schools, five states, and six countries. The breadth of racial, ethnic, and socioeconomic backgrounds represented in the student body creates a genuinely diverse institution. There are nearly equal numbers of women and men enrolled and a sizable population of mature, nontraditional students who primarily attend convenient evening and weekend classes.

Student Activities

CW offers an array of student activities and support services designed to help students achieve their fullest potential for growth. Activities include Student Government Association, Alpha Beta Kappa honor society, business- and technology-related clubs, field trips to businesses and corporations, and social events.

Facilities and Resources

The College of Westchester is located in a newly renovated, five-story, 50,000-square-foot building. The college's academic facilities include nineteen classrooms; a library; a student life center that houses all student organizations and clubs; an academic advancement center, an open computer lab that also serves as a tutoring and study center; a student lounge; and faculty offices. The facility also includes the Admissions Office; the Academic Center, where the academic administrators, including academic advisers, are housed; the Financial Services Center; and Career Placement Services.

CW's Career Placement Services specializes in finding part-time work for currently enrolled students and full-time, career-related positions for graduates. The staff members work with students to secure paid internships, co-op opportunities, and work-study positions while they are attending the college and also carefully guide students through the many facets of planning and preparing for job searches. This may include guidance in areas such as properly completing resumes, writing letters of application, securing job interviews, researching companies, and conducting interviews. CW's record indicates that 95 percent of graduates who seek employment find positions related to their studies.

At CW, leading-edge technology defines the teaching and learning environment. The computer classrooms feature Pentium-based personal computers, outfitted with an extensive selection of current software applications. The College maintains state-of-the-art computer networking and multimedia classrooms, each of which is equipped with a Pentium Pro file server that uses the Microsoft Windows 2000 operating system. High-speed fiber-optic networks connect the College's students not only to the Internet, but directly to their instructors, online course work, and even their classmates.

Location

CW is located in White Plains, the county seat and hub of Westchester County. Many of the College's graduates work for area corporations, including IBM, Verizon, Kraft General Foods USA, the Bank of New York, PepsiCo, AT&T, the Reader's Digest Association, Philip Morris, MasterCard, Citibank, Con Ed, CIBA, Texaco, MCI, Bayer Corporation, MBIA, Lillian Vernon, Fuji Film USA, Sunburst Communications, Hitachi America, Ltd., MetLife Corporation, MTA, Nine West, Avon Products, Carolee Designs, Online Design, Pitney Bowes, American Express, Coca Cola Corporation, Dannon Corporation, Doral Arrowwood, FedEx, International Paper, *The Journal News*, KPMG Peat Marwick, Lincoln Center for the Performing Arts, MCS Cannon, Manulife Wood Logan, Marsh & McLennan, the United Way, Xerox, and Zurich Reinsurance.

The New York Metro North Railroad Station and the transportation center are both a short walk from CW.

Admission Requirements

To properly assist applicants in selecting the program that is best suited to their needs, a personal interview is conducted with an admissions associate. Prospective students should call the Admissions Office for an appointment. In addition to the interview, all applicants must be graduates of an accredited high school or its equivalent, or have received a high school equivalency diploma (GED). In some cases, mature, non–high school graduates who have demonstrated an ability to benefit based upon an interview, counseling, and testing may be admitted. These individuals may qualify for a high school equivalency diploma through CW from the New York State Education Department by successfully completing 36 quarter hours of academic work with a minimum of a 2.0 GPA in one of the college programs.

Application and Information

CW has a rolling admissions policy. Students may apply at any time up to the beginning of the quarter; although, students are strongly encouraged to apply as early as possible. To be considered for admission, the following must be submitted: an application for admission; a $30 nonrefundable application fee; and an official high school transcript, its equivalent, or GED equivalency diploma. If transferring credits from a prior college, students must submit an official college transcript. Students seeking to transfer credits from another institution of higher education should request that an official transcript be mailed to Transfer Credits, Office of Admissions, at the College of Westchester address listed below. Students who have attended another accredited college or university may obtain credit toward graduation for courses taken at that institution. Credit is transferable for comparable courses in the student's selected curriculum in which the applicant has obtained a grade of C (2.0) or higher. A maximum of 50 percent of the credits required for program completion may be transferred. Official documentation of successful completion of high school or the equivalent must be received prior to the completion of the first quarter at the college.

For application materials and additional information, prospective students should contact:

Office of Admissions
The College of Westchester
325 Central Park Avenue
White Plains, New York 10606
Telephone: 800-333-4924
E-mail: admissions@wbi.org
World Wide Web: http://www.wbi.org

COLORADO MOUNTAIN COLLEGE
GLENWOOD SPRINGS, COLORADO

The College and Its Mission

There is a different view of the Rocky Mountains at each Colorado Mountain College campus. Learning is personal; classes are small; faculty members are friendly. Colorado Mountain College is a multicampus community college with three residential campuses and twelve commuter locations. This coeducational public institution began operation in 1967. Colorado Mountain College is a district-supported college with its own governing board. Colorado Mountain College operates on a semester system with a limited summer session and is accredited by the North Central Association of Colleges and Secondary Schools.

The three residential campuses include Alpine Campus in Steamboat Springs, Spring Valley Campus outside of Glenwood Springs, and Timberline Campus in Leadville. At these locations, students still find a traditional college experience, including residence halls, cafeterias, extensive libraries, laboratories, and many opportunities to participate in campus life. The commuter campuses serve primarily local residents, and classes are scheduled for the convenience of working adults. Commuter sites are located in Aspen, Basalt, Breckenridge, Buena Vista, Carbondale, Dillon, Eagle, Glenwood Springs, Rifle, Salida, and Vail.

Colorado Mountain College offers academic programs for transfer, career training in several specialty areas, and courses to enrich the lives and livelihoods of local residents. Students can begin their four-year degree because the State Guaranteed Transfer courses are guaranteed to satisfy general education requirements at all Colorado public higher-education institutions.

Students may also choose to start a career with occupational training programs. In one or two years, students can learn the skills for employment in some unique and exciting programs. The mountain environment gives students many opportunities to learn outside the classroom.

Academic Programs

Colorado Mountain College offers both occupational and transfer programs. Degrees awarded include the **Associate in Arts** degree, **Associate in Science** degree, **Associate in General Studies** degree, **Associate in Applied Science** degree, and a one-year Occupational Proficiency certificate. The Associate in Arts degree is available at all Colorado Mountain College campuses.

Degrees and programs vary by campus, with the residential campuses offering the fullest range of degrees and certificates. Alpine Campus offerings include the Associate in Arts (areas of specialization are business, fine arts, liberal arts, and wilderness studies), the Associate in Science (areas of specialization are biology, chemistry, geology, and mathematics), and the Associate in Applied Science and Certificates of Occupational Proficiency (offerings include accounting, business, microcomputer support specialist, resort management, and ski and snowboard business). The Alpine Campus also offers an Honors Program. Spring Valley Campus offerings include the Associate in Arts (areas of specialization are business, liberal arts, outdoor education, and theater), Associate in Science (areas of specialization are biology, chemistry, geology, mathematics, and nursing), and Associate in Applied Science and Certificates of Occupational Proficiency (offerings include accounting, business, graphic design, law enforcement, microcomputer support specialist studies, photography, practical nursing, and veterinary technology). Timberline Campus offerings include the Associate in Arts (areas of specialization are business, liberal arts, and Outdoor Semester in the Rockies), the Associate in General Studies degree in

outdoor recreational leadership, the Associate in Science (areas of specialization are biology, chemistry, geology, and mathematics), and the Associate in Applied Science and Certificates of Occupational Proficiency (offerings include accounting, business, microcomputer support specialist studies, natural resources management, natural resources recreation management, and ski area operations).

Off-Campus Programs

One of the most popular off-campus programs is the Outdoor Semester in the Rockies. This program blends outdoor adventure with the disciplines of college classes such as science and philosophy. Colorado Mountain College encourages students to take advantage of several study-abroad class tours. The College also offers exciting distance education opportunities to district and residential campus students through telecourses, an interactive video system, and some Internet courses.

Credit for Nontraditional Learning Experiences

Colorado Mountain College awards credit through national standardized exams, challenge exams, and credit for life experience. To be awarded credit, testing options are used if possible, and students must be enrolled in a degree or certificate program. Credits posted to a student's academic record through one of these nontraditional methods are noted, indicating the method by which they were awarded.

Costs

Colorado Mountain College's tuition for the academic year 2003–04 was $41 per credit hour for in-district students, $69 per credit hour for in-state students, and $220 per credit hour for out-of-state students. Residential campuses had student activity fees of $180 per academic year. Room and board costs averaged $6000 per year, and the housing reservation deposit was $300. Books average $650 per academic year.

Financial Aid

Colorado Mountain College is approved for participation in all major federal and state financial aid programs, including Federal Pell Grant, loan programs, and work-study. Financial assistance is awarded through a central district office for all Colorado Mountain College campuses and education centers. The application for financial assistance is the Free Application for Federal Student Aid (FAFSA). First priority is given to those students applying on or before March 31. Applications received after this date are processed pending availability of funds. Questions may be addressed to Student Financial Assistance, District Office, P.O. 10001, Glenwood Springs, Colorado 81602.

Faculty

Colorado Mountain College faculty members are accessible to students. They are at Colorado Mountain College because they believe in teaching. There are 59 full-time faculty members and 144 part-time faculty members at the three residential campuses. The faculty members pride themselves on the high-quality education students receive in the classroom, with classes averaging 15 students. The student-faculty ratio is 12:1. Many faculty members have taught at colleges and universities and have chosen to teach at Colorado Mountain College because of their love for teaching and the blend of invigorating environments and stimulating learning.

Student Body Profile

Colorado Mountain College students are from the local area, forty-eight states, and six other countries. Undergraduate full-time and part-time students at the residential campuses number 1,500 at the Alpine Campus, 1,000 at the Spring Valley Campus, and 1,100 at the Timberline Campus. Alpine has approximately 500 full-time students, and Timberline has about 300 full-time students. Colorado Mountain College opened new residence halls in fall 1997 at all three residential locations. The Alpine Campus can house about 220 students on campus, the Spring Valley Campus about 240 students, and the Timberline Campus about 140 students.

Student Activities

Each residential campus has active student government organizations. Each student government determines the student activity fee and how the funds are utilized on each campus. Student government helps to sponsor student activities, clubs and organizations, and guest speakers. Colorado Mountain College's ski team holds six national titles. But there is more than snow available for outdoor activities. Students actively participate in hiking, biking, and water sports. Student Activities Offices organize basketball and volleyball intramurals. Men's and women's club soccer teams are offered, and the soccer clubs compete for the CMC title and with other colleges. Every season brings new activities and celebrations to the mountain resort towns.

Facilities and Resources

The residential campuses offer a full college experience with residence halls, cafeterias, libraries, academic classrooms, learning labs, laboratories, and student center facilities.

The Alpine Campus offers residence halls and classroom buildings. Fall 1992 marked the opening of an academic building that includes faculty offices, a library, classrooms, instructional and computer laboratories, and recreational space. Spring 1995 saw the opening of a remodeled cafeteria, bookstore, and student center. At the Spring Valley Campus, students can enjoy the hot springs pool in Glenwood Springs, the charm of Carbondale, and the culture of Aspen. Spring Valley offers residence halls, a cafeteria, a gymnasium and climbing wall, a student center, a bookstore, classrooms, a working farm, laboratories, and an extensive library. A new academic building opened in fall 1998. This building houses a theater, photography labs and studio, a graphic design computer lab, a student computer center, and classrooms. The faculty offices surround the classrooms so students can easily access their instructors and professors. At the Timberline Campus, many students combine their environmental interests and their college education. Colorado's highest mountain peak is in the backyard, cross-country skiing begins at the edge of campus, and many of Colorado's big name slopes are no more than an hour away. The campus offers classroom facilities, a library and learning lab, a computer lab, and a bookstore. In fall 1999, a new academic building opened at the Timberline Campus. It houses classrooms, a computer center, laboratories, student services, and faculty offices. Students enjoy a relaxing student center and cafeteria and have access to Leadville's modern recreation complex.

Location

Like the Rockies that surround it, Colorado Mountain College is wide open and full of possibilities. There are miles of spruce and aspen, wildflowers, backroads, whitewater and bareback ranchland, three national forests, six wilderness areas, and most of Colorado's major ski resorts. There is a spirit among the teachers and students, an atmosphere of encouragement, and an attitude of confidence. **Alpine Campus** is situated above the downtown area on the west end of Steamboat Springs. In Leadville, **Timberline Campus** is less than an hour's drive from Vail and is surrounded by Colorado's highest peaks and the legends of a town built by silver. High above the Roaring Fork River, **Spring Valley Campus** is located 10 miles south of Glenwood Springs and within 40 miles of Aspen. All Colorado Mountain College locations are resort or mountain communities accessible by air, rail, or bus, and provide excellent outdoor opportunities.

Admission Requirements

Colorado Mountain College seeks, encourages, and assists all interested students beyond high-school age who demonstrate a desire to learn. With a few exceptions, admission follows an open-door policy. Even though Colorado Mountain College has open admission, certain occupational programs have selective admission. Programs with selection or testing requirements and admission deadlines include culinary arts, nursing, outdoor recreation leadership, paramedicine, professional photography, and veterinary technology.

To apply for admission, students must complete and return the Colorado Mountain College admissions application and high school and/or college transcripts. There is no application fee. All entering students should submit ACT or SAT I scores for scholarship, advising, and placement purposes. Some programs require testing for admission.

Transfer students are welcome and should have attained a cumulative grade point average of at least 2.0 on any college work attempted. Nongraduates may take the General Educational Development test (GED) to meet graduation equivalence. International students may be considered for admission to the residential campuses. International admission packets are available and must be completed and returned to apply for admission, and a minimum TOEFL score of 500 on the paper exam or a minimum score of 173 on the computerized exam is required for admission.

Students are encouraged to apply as soon as possible to secure on-campus housing. After applying for admission to a residential campus, students receive housing reservation information.

Application and Information

For more information, students should contact:

Director of Pre-Enrollment Services
Colorado Mountain College
P.O. Box 10001 PG
Glenwood Springs, Colorado 81602
Telephone: 970-945-8691
             800-621-8559 (toll-free)
Fax: 970-947-8324
E-mail: joinus@coloradomtn.edu
World Wide Web: http://www.coloradomtn.edu

The Colorado Rockies are a classroom for Colorado Mountain College students.

COMMUNITY COLLEGE
OF ALLEGHENY COUNTY

PITTSBURGH, MONROEVILLE, NORTH HILLS, AND WEST MIFFLIN, PENNSYLVANIA

The College and Its Mission

The Community College of Allegheny County (CCAC) has been helping students plan their futures for thirty-five years. CCAC's educational influence extends far beyond the 350 acres that compose its four campuses. The College reaches deep into the communities. Classes are offered at **Allegheny Campus** in Pittsburgh's North Shore, **Boyce Campus** in Monroeville, **South Campus** in West Mifflin, and **North Campus** in the North Hills section of Pittsburgh. Classes are also offered at more than 400 other locations in Allegheny County. CCAC is the largest community college in Pennsylvania. Its size is a great advantage in terms of the depth and breadth of academic opportunities. However, it is the deep personal commitment that CCAC brings to each student's academic life that makes this college especially effective. High school graduates seeking to begin their college studies find themselves challenged by supporting faculty members who have made a commitment to teaching. Nontraditional students who are returning to school and have family responsibilities can find a wide range of course offerings scheduled at convenient times and locations. CCAC is fully accredited by the Middle States Association of Colleges and Schools.

Academic Programs

CCAC offers academic, career, and technical programs that prepare students for the work force or to transfer into baccalaureate degree programs at other colleges or universities. The College offers both full- and part-time programs leading to certificates or associate degrees. Program requirements vary, but in general, an associate degree program requires two years of study, and a certificate program requires one year or less.

Associate Degree Programs The associate degrees offered by CCAC can be grouped into seven different areas. University Parallel and transfer programs offer associate degrees in accounting, administration of justice, Africana and ethnic studies, art, biology, business, chemistry, computer information science, cosmetology management, criminal justice and corrections, engineering science, engineering technology, foreign language, humanities, journalism, liberal arts and sciences, mathematics, music, physics, pre–athletic training, pre–health professions, psychology, social sciences, sociology/anthropology, teacher education, and theater.

Career programs in business offer associate degrees in accounting specialist studies, administrative office professional studies, aviation management, banking management, business management, court reporter studies, culinary arts, flight technology, health services management, hotel management, hotel-restaurant management, marketing management, paralegal studies, personnel management, public administration, and travel and tourism.

Career programs in computer information technology offer associate degrees in application software development, e-commerce development, network administration, and user support.

Career programs in health offer associate degrees in biotechnology; diagnostic medical sonographer studies; dietary manager studies; fitness, sports, and lifetime recreation specialist studies; health information technology; massage therapy; medical assistant studies; medical laboratory technician studies; nuclear medicine technologist studies; nursing; occupational therapy assistant studies; pharmacy technician studies; physical therapy assistant studies; radiation therapy technologist studies; radiologic technologist studies; respiratory therapy technician studies; and surgical technologist studies.

Career programs in social service offer associate degrees in administration of criminal justice, child and family studies, corrections administration, fire science and administration, interpreter for the deaf training, mental health/mental retardation specialist studies, social work technician studies and teacher's assistant studies.

Career programs in applied arts technologies offer associate degrees in graphics communications, horticulture technology (floriculture), horticulture technology (landscape design), horticulture technology (landscape management), horticulture technology (landscape and turfgrass management), industrial design and art, and multimedia communications.

Career programs in applied service and trade technologies offer associate degrees in automotive service education, automotive technology, building construction estimating, building construction supervision, building construction technology, electrical distribution technology, heating and air-conditioning technology, mechanical electronics technology, mechanical maintenance technology, motor winding technology, and welding technology.

Career programs in engineering and science technologies offer associate degrees in architectural drafting and design technology, chemical technology, civil engineering technology, computer-aided drafting and design technology, electronic engineering technology, laboratory technology, mechanical drafting and design technology, microcomputer electronics technology, robotics and automated systems technology, and science and engineering technology.

Certificate Programs CCAC offers the following certificate programs: accounting, activities professional studies, Africana and ethnic studies, anesthesia professional studies, automotive technology, banking management, basic CAD, basic electronics, basic preparation cook studies, biotechnology, building construction, building maintenance technology, business management, carpentry, case management, CAT scanning, central services technology, child and family studies, child care, child development, CIT application software development, CIT computer programming, CIT e-commerce development, CIT network administration, CIT user support, CIT Web designer, commercial art and design, commercial cook studies, computer numerical control programming, construction estimating, court reporting, deaf studies, dental assistant studies, diagnostic medical sonography, dietary manager studies, digital electronics, digital graphic design, drafting and/or surveying, drug and alcohol, educational assistant studies, electroneurodiagnostic EEG studies, electronics (basic or digital), families of prisoners intervention, families with children with special needs, family intervention, floral art and design, foreman training, geriatric studies, health services management, health unit coordinator studies, heating and air conditioning, hotel management, ironworking, landscape maintenance, machine studies (basic), massage therapy, mechanical electronic technology, mechanical maintenance technology, medical assistant studies, medical insurance specialist studies, medical transcription, mental health specialist studies, mental retardation technician studies, motor winding technology, MRI scanning, nanofabrication, network cable, nuclear medicine, office technology professional studies, operating room nursing, paralegal studies, personnel administration, pharmacy technician studies, phlebotomist studies, plumbing, practical nursing, private pilot, public administration, radiation therapy, rehabilitation aide studies, restaurant management, sheet-metal studies, social work, surgical technology, technical theater, training for persons needing learning support (food service, greenhouse/nursery, human services aide, janitorial/housekeeping, or nursing assistant), travel specialist studies, turfgrass maintenance, and welding.

Costs

For residents of Allegheny County, CCAC's tuition is $71.50 per credit. Residents of other Pennsylvania counties that do not have a community college pay $85.50 per credit. Residents of Pennsylvania counties with community colleges pay $143 per credit. Students living out of state pay $214.50 per credit. A College fee of $50.40 per semester is charged to students taking classes at each campus location. Some courses offered by CCAC require special course or lab fees in addition to the tuition and College fee. All of these costs were estimated for the 2002–03 academic year. CCAC reserves the right to change the tuition and fees at any time and without prior notice.

Financial Aid

Financial aid programs at CCAC are designed to assist students whose family circumstances limit their ability to contribute toward educational costs. Under federal guidelines, students are expected to seek assistance first from funds that are available through their own personal resources and then from the government. Most awards are need-based, which means that a determination of the expected family contribution is made through a formula established by the U.S. Department of Education. Financial aid consists of scholarships, grants, loans, and employment. Aid may be offered in some combination of these sources, depending on the student's financial need and the requirements for each program. Awards are based on the enrollment of the student, the expected family contribution of the student, and the availability of funding at the time the application for aid is received. Students who have taken out student loans in the past and who are in default on those loans are not eligible for any type of federal, state, or institutional financial aid. Students must complete the Free Application for Federal Student Aid (FAFSA) to be considered for financial aid. Other supporting documents may be required by the Financial Aid Office. Students are notified as to which forms are required once the FAFSA results are received.

Faculty

CCAC has 287 full-time professors and a staff of part-time educators who are experienced, knowledgeable, and committed to teaching. While most faculty members continue their studies and research to remain current in their respective fields, their first commitment is to the students. The average class size is 17.

Student Body Profile

There are currently almost 17,600 students enrolled as full- and part-time credit students. The average age of this student population is 29. In a typical fall semester, the CCAC minority group enrollment is approximately 18 percent. Ninety-one percent of the students enrolled in credit courses live within Allegheny County. More than 26,710 students are currently enrolled in noncredit course work.

Student Activities

CCAC student activities include acquiring leadership potential as part of student government or participation in creative endeavors, including student publications, drama productions, and art programs. Many cultural clubs and organizations exist as well. Students may also enrich their chosen field of studies as a member of an academically related club or organization. For those who prefer the competitive edge, athletic programs for both men and women are available at designated CCAC campuses. Basketball, baseball, golf, tennis, bowling, softball, volleyball, cross-country, racquetball, and weightlifting are just some of the intramural and intercollegiate athletic programs available at designated campuses.

Facilities and Resources

The Community College of Allegheny County is committed to students' success. The modern facilities available provide the stimulus to enhance the educational experience. Each of the four CCAC campuses provides a developmental child-care center, staffed by professionals who not only care for each child's physical needs but also provide a stimulating learning environment. CCAC Adult Re-entry Services provide educational and emotional support for these students returning to an academic environment after a long absence. Services offered include career and educational planning, basic skills instruction, and confidence building. Facilities at CCAC are designed to accommodate students with physical disabilities. Paved walkways, accessible building entrances, and elevator systems provide easy access to classrooms and laboratories. In addition, interpreters for the deaf, Braille materials, note-taking, scanning, voice output, and use of technology are available for students with documented disabilities. The College maintains excellent computer facilities at each of its four campuses. Students receive hands-on experience on state-of-the-art computers and instructional equipment ranging from a powerful IBM mainframe computer that is used for both instructional and administrative purposes to microcomputers. Campus and center computer labs offer convenient day and evening hours.

CCAC's four campus libraries house more than 200,000 volumes and subscribe to 847 periodicals. Quiet private reading and study areas are available with knowledgeable librarians who provide the research assistance to help students succeed. Tutoring services and workshops in test taking, study techniques, and basic academic skills are provided at no cost to students through CCAC's Learning Assistance Centers. In support of classroom instruction, audiovisual instructional and technical support services are provided to faculty members.

CCAC provides valuable job search assistance for its students and graduates through its Career Services Departments. In 2003 through early 2004, local employers posted more than 2,000 jobs on the CCAC Job Bank Web site. Through the CCAC Career Services Departments, CCAC belongs as a community center to Pennsylvania CareerLink, which maintains a database containing more than 5,000 annual job listings.

Location

The College is composed of four main campuses and eight college centers located strategically throughout Allegheny County. The city of Pittsburgh, located in Allegheny County, is one of the largest sites of corporate headquarters in the United States and has an abundance of cultural activities.

Admission Requirements

The College has an open admissions policy. Entrance tests are not required, but applicants are encouraged to participate in these testing programs. To enroll as a full-time student, applicants must have a high school diploma or Pennsylvania GED certificate or must be at least 18 years of age with experience reasonably equivalent to a GED. Students should request an admission application form from the admission office on any CCAC campus and should return the completed application to the Admission Office. There is no application fee. An applicant is also required to take the College's placement test to determine the level of study suitable for his or her skills and to meet with a College adviser, as scheduled at registration time, to select classes for the coming term. Applicants with prior college experience or a minimum SAT score may be exempt from placement testing.

Application and Information

Application forms and additional information are available at the following CCAC campus locations:

Allegheny Campus (North Shore)
Community College of Allegheny County
808 Ridge Avenue
Pittsburgh, Pennsylvania 15212
Telephone: 412-237-2511

North Campus (North Hills)
Community College of Allegheny County
8701 Perry Highway
Pittsburgh, Pennsylvania 15237
Telephone: 412-369-3600

Boyce Campus (Monroeville)
Community College of Allegheny County
595 Beatty Road
Monroeville, Pennsylvania 15146
Telephone: 724-325-6614

South Campus (West Mifflin)
Community College of Allegheny County
1750 Clairton Road and Route 885
West Mifflin, Pennsylvania 15122
Telephone: 412-469-4301
World Wide Web: http://www.ccac.edu

COOKING AND HOSPITALITY INSTITUTE OF CHICAGO

CHICAGO, ILLINOIS

The Institute and Its Mission

The mission of the Cooking and Hospitality Institute of Chicago (CHIC) is to prepare students to fulfill their career ambitions and meet the needs of the food service industry. To this end, the Institute has set up a dynamic curriculum that continually adapts to the needs of employers while providing students with the flexibility to receive the education that best meets their career needs. Founded in 1983, the Institute was established to provide culinary education using the traditional European hands-on approach. In 1991, the Institute received degree-granting authority from the Illinois Board of Higher Education and began offering an Associate of Applied Science degree in culinary arts. In 2000, CHIC introduced the Le Cordon Bleu Culinary Program to its Associate of Applied Science degree program. With its reputation for excellence, the demand for CHIC graduates by employers far exceeds the number of graduates available.

CHIC is accredited by the Higher Learning Commission of the North Central Association. The Institute is also accredited by the Accrediting Commission of Career Schools and Colleges of Technology (ACCSCT) and the American Culinary Federation (ACF).

Academic Programs

CHIC offers accredited Associate of Applied Sciences (A.A.S.) degrees in Le Cordon Bleu culinary arts and Le Cordon Bleu patisserie and baking. CHIC is devoted to fostering a lifelong love of learning and holding students to high academic standards. CHIC's premier Le Cordon Bleu A.A.S. program combines course work in three areas: culinary, baking and pastry, and management. CHIC operates on a trisemester basis with rolling midsemester starts. Students may begin their studies every other month (January, March, May, July, September, or October). Classes are offered seven days a week and five evenings a week. Students enrolled in CHIC's programs show commitment to those programs, as well as to the culinary profession, by completing their education in a timely manner.

Associate Degree Programs CHIC offers an associate degree program in baking and pastry. This program teaches the principles and techniques of professional pastry and baking production and is intended for students who have an interest in large-quantity baking or who want to work for establishments that have in-house baking and pastry operations.

CHIC also offers an Associate of Applied Science degree in Le Cordon Bleu culinary arts. The program includes professional cooking skills, baking and pastry skills, restaurant management skills, nutrition sciences, and general education. This well-rounded program is designed to give students the technical skills and theoretical expertise that are necessary for a career in the food service industry. Graduates can expect immediate employment in entry-level to midlevel positions as well as rapid advancement into management and sous chef positions and further. Students with or without prior experience find that this program offers everything that they need to begin a fast-track career in the fastest-growing industry in the United States.

Transfer Arrangements CHIC accepts transfer credits from any accredited college provided that the credits are in courses comparable to the courses required under the student's program of study at the Institute.

Off-Campus Programs

CHIC has entered into cooperative agreements with three area colleges that allow students to transfer CHIC credits toward a bachelor's degree. At Dominican University in River Forest, Illinois, students can continue on for a Bachelor of General Studies (B.G.S.) in culinary arts and management or a Bachelor of Science (B.S.) in nutrition and dietetics, food science management, or food science and nutrition. Students may opt to include in these programs elective courses for nursing home administrator licensure in Illinois. Students may also continue their studies at Robert Morris College, which has campuses in Chicago, Orland Park, Naperville, and Springfield, Illinois, to pursue a Bachelor of Business Administration (B.B.A.). CHIC graduates who transfer to Robert Morris with a GPA of at least 3.0 may also receive a tuition scholarship of up to $4800. Students also have the opportunity to continue their studies at Roosevelt University, which accepts 39 CHIC credits toward their B.S. in hospitality and tourism.

Credit for Nontraditional Learning Experiences

The Institute awards credit to students who have demonstrated proficiency through the Advanced Placement (AP) program and the College-Level Examination Program (CLEP).

Costs

For the 2003–04 academic year, tuition was $12,250 per semester. (Typically, students graduate in three semesters.) In addition, students can expect a one-time purchase of a supply kit. Books and uniforms can cost up to approximately $3200 per year.

Financial Aid

Tuition planning is provided free of charge to all applicants. The Institute participates in Federal Title IV assistance programs such as Federal Stafford Student Loans, Federal PLUS loans, Federal Pell Grants, Federal Supplemental Educational Opportunity Grants, and the Federal Work-Study Program. Students may also receive funding from a variety of institutional and industry-related scholarships, which include the Nancy Abrams Academic Excellence Scholarship, Charlie Trotter's Culinary Education Foundation, the Educational Foundation's ProMgmt. Scholarship, and the Career College Association's Imagine America Scholarships for high school seniors as well as scholarships from the James Beard Foundation, the International Association of Culinary Professionals, the Illinois Restaurant Association, and the National Restaurant Association. Scholarships range from $500 to $10,000.

Nongovernmental loans are available through Sallie Mae. These loans may be used to supplement federal financial aid and in cases where students do not qualify for federal aid. The loan terms are similar to federal student loans, but the application procedure is greatly simplified.

Faculty

Faculty members are selected for their professional backgrounds, academic experience, and certification from the American

Culinary Federation as culinary educators. This allows faculty members to bring daily real-life experiences to their students.

Student Body Profile

CHIC is both ethnically and culturally diverse, with international students representing more than fifteen different countries. Students range in age from 17 to 70. Twenty percent of the students are recent high school graduates, while more than half are career changers whose average age is about 30. In addition, 20 percent of the students are from out of state and have relocated to Chicago in order to participate in the Institute's programs.

Student Activities

The Institute supports many student organizations that provide students with interesting networking and experiential opportunities. Under the advisement of the Dean of Education and faculty advisers, these organizations are the Student Recipe Development Association, the Alpha Beta Kappa Society, the Student Board, the Cellar Club, the Pastry Display Club, the Bread Guild, and the Culinary Competition Team. The Culinary Competition Team has won medals and certificates around the country.

Facilities and Resources

The Institute is housed on the ground, first, and second floors of a two-story building. The 60,000-square-foot facility features large air-conditioned classrooms, a student lounge, men's and women's locker rooms, a student communication center, the Learning Resource Center (LRC), and eight kitchens. In addition, the Institute's showcase is the 100-seat student-run restaurant, the CHIC Café, which is open for lunch seven days a week as well as for dinner on Friday and Saturday nights.

Student Housing A student housing program is available to CHIC students through a Real Estate Firm. Apartments (shared housing) are competitively priced and accessible to CHIC via public transportation.

Learning Resource Center Students and faculty members have full access to a collection of more than 5,000 volumes, forty related periodicals and newsletters, and reference materials in hospitality-related areas as well as CD-ROMs and numerous online resources. Online services include a reference catalog, Internet access, ProQuest, and Infotrac. In addition to the current holdings, the library has cooperative arrangements with various local libraries and professional associations. Interlibrary loan service is available through Illinet (Illinois Library and Information Network). The LRC also maintains a staffed computer laboratory for student use, with access to the Internet, various hospitality and purchasing software, word processing, and scanners.

Career Planning/Placement Offices The Career Services Department serves as the liaison between employers and graduates and students seeking career positions. The Institute has developed relationships with many industry leaders who support the educational endeavors of the students. Current students are encouraged to seek part-time positions through the department. Permanent placement upon graduation is readily available, and alumni who wish to advance their careers find a number of opportunities through the department. The Institute currently receives more employer inquiries than it has students and graduates to fill them. For this reason, the Institute screens employers so that they meet the desires of its students.

Location

The Institute is located in the River North area of Chicago, within walking distance of some of the finest restaurants and art galleries in the city. It is eight blocks west of Chicago's famed shopping district, the Magnificent Mile, and only a few blocks north of Chicago's business district, the Loop. It is easily accessible by public transportation and the major expressways.

Admission Requirements

All applicants must be beyond compulsory school age and must furnish documentation of at least a high school diploma or a GED diploma. In addition, applicants must demonstrate their math and English abilities by providing high school or college transcripts or ACT or SAT I scores, or they may take the Institute's math and/or English placement exams. International students may submit TOEFL scores for initial acceptance and issuance of an I-20 visa, but they must take the Institute's placement tests upon arrival for course determination.

Application and Information

Applications are accepted on an ongoing basis. Prospective students should contact:

Director of Admissions
Cooking and Hospitality Institute of Chicago
361 West Chestnut
Chicago, Illinois 60610
Telephone: 312-944-0882
       877-828-7772 (toll-free)
Fax: 312-944-8557
E-mail: chic@chicnet.org
World Wide Web: http://www.chic.edu

Students receive hands-on instruction in the kitchens of the Cooking and Hospitality Institute of Chicago.

DEAN COLLEGE
FRANKLIN, MASSACHUSETTS

The College and Its Mission

Dean College is committed to being the leader among private two-year residential colleges, promoting academic success, and building student confidence. The focus of the College is on educating students for transfer to baccalaureate institutions and entry into full-time employment in their major field of study. To support this mission, Dean offers a campus environment that is attractive, safe, and alive with activity. The suburban location near Boston and Providence allows students to take advantage of the cities for recreation, education, and work opportunities. Dean students are part of an academic community that has high expectations of them and a record of helping students achieve success. The academic preparation that students receive enables them to transfer to outstanding private colleges and major state universities across the country. The College is committed to providing personal and academic support, advice and counseling, and the opportunity to discover strengths that may not be evident in high school. Dean students study, work, and play hard. They are part of a vital, active community. This sense of community is evident from the first day on campus. With more than thirty clubs and organizations, it is difficult for anyone to feel left out. Dean provides an outstanding educational value to families. The College does whatever is in its power to help students meet the cost of attending Dean and provide them with a high-quality education in a student-oriented setting that emphasizes customer service.

Academic Programs

Associate Degree Programs Associate in Arts and Associate in Science degrees are offered in business, business technology, computer information systems, criminal justice, dance (A.A. and B.A.), early childhood education, liberal arts (with concentrations in education, English, history, math/science, psychology, and social science), liberal studies, sport/fitness studies (with concentrations in athletic training, fitness studies, personal trainer studies, physical education, and sports management), and theater arts (with concentrations in musical theater and theater).

The Dean Arch Program is a college-preparatory program that supports students with learning disabilities. It is specifically designed for students who need or desire one or two semesters of intensive academic skill development in preparation of an associate degree program. The program combines course work in the liberal arts with course work in reading, writing, mathematics, technology, study strategies, and personal development.

Bachelor's Degree Programs Dean College offers a Bachelor of Arts degree in dance. The program includes the disciplines of tap, ballet, modern, and modern jazz dance within a broad liberal arts environment. The B.A. program is appropriate for students interested in teaching, arts management, movement therapy, dance journalism, and performance.

The Suffolk/Dean Program was established by Dean College through a unique collaboration with Suffolk University. Students who have completed a Dean College associate degree program may continue on to earn a baccalaureate degree from Suffolk University, while remaining on the Dean College campus.

Options are offered in business, communications/public relations, computer information systems, criminology and law, and psychology.

Credit for Nontraditional Learning Experiences

Credit is available through the CLEP program, which is sponsored by the College Board.

Costs

In 2003–04, tuition was $18,150, a room costs $5500, board was $3200, the comprehensive fee was $1840, and student health insurance was $425. Approximately $1500 is needed to cover other expenses such as books, travel, and personal expenses. The comprehensive fee does not include the cost of optional programs and services, such as academic support services, instrumental music and voice instruction, laboratory fees, physical education uniforms, private lessons, field trips, and the cost of materials used in art courses.

Financial Aid

Academic scholarships, athletic scholarships, loans, and part-time jobs are available at Dean, and 80 percent of the student body receives some form of assistance. Students are required to submit the Free Application for Federal Student Aid (FAFSA). To qualify for aid, the form should be on file in the Financial Aid Office by March 1. Although every effort is made to meet the financial needs of students, campus-based funds are awarded on the basis of demonstrated need, academic promise, and the availability of funds. Students must be admitted before an offer of financial aid can be made. For more information, students should contact the Student Financial Services Office (telephone: 508-541-1518).

Faculty

The student-faculty ratio is 18:1. Faculty members are dedicated to teaching and supporting students throughout the academic year. They serve as academic counselors and are available outside of class to assist students. Many faculty members also act as coaches and advisers for student clubs and organizations. Most faculty members hold advanced degrees.

Student Body Profile

Students from more than twenty-five states represent approximately 92 percent of the student population. International students from more than twenty countries represent 8 percent of the student body. Approximately 71 percent of the student body is white (non-Hispanic), 10 percent is black, 1 percent is Asian, and 1 percent is Hispanic. More than 90 percent of students live on campus.

Student Activities

The Student Government Association, consisting of elected representatives from each residence hall and from the commuter student group, the Student Activities Committee, and the Leadership Council, composed of officers from student organizations, meet frequently to discuss matters of concern to the student body. Students in these groups provide leadership and direction in social activities and programs related to student interests. The President of the College holds informal group discussions with students, and members of the Student Affairs staff meet with residence hall groups and commuting student groups so that each student has an opportunity to be heard. Students are frequently asked to serve on all-College committees that make recommendations to the president.

Facilities and Resources

The E. Ross Anderson Library currently contains more than 54,000 volumes, 350 periodical subscriptions, microfilm, and electronic equipment that allows for a full range of teaching and learning aids on tape. Dean is the first two-year college in Massachusetts to offer a comprehensive wireless computing atmosphere to their students. Other facilities include the Campus Center, the Center for the Performing Arts, radio station WGAO, the Telecommunications Center, a language lab, and the Children's Center. The Academic Computer Center, open to all students, includes several computer classrooms equipped with IBM PCs and printers. Pieri Gymnasium includes facilities for basketball and volleyball, a pool, exercise equipment, and training facilities.

Location

The College is located on a 100-acre campus in Franklin, Massachusetts, a suburb of Boston. The College is easily reached from the interstate highway system, and Boston's Logan Airport is less than 30 miles away. Commuter rail service to and from Boston is within a block of the campus. Providence, Rhode Island, and Worcester, Massachusetts, are both within a 30-minute drive. Shopping, restaurants, movie theaters, golf, and many other recreational facilities are within walking distance of the College. The town of Franklin and the College enjoy a friendly relationship, with many local residents attending social and athletic events on campus and Dean students volunteering for various agencies and projects in and around the town.

Admission Requirements

The Office of Admissions accepts students who can reasonably be expected to satisfy the academic requirements established by the College. Students are selected based on their performance in secondary school, the quality of their curriculum, and a recommendation from their guidance counselor, principal, or headmaster. A student's overall grade point average and rank in class are considered in evaluating an application. SAT I or ACT scores are required. A personal interview is highly recommended. During the visit to campus, students gain a full understanding of the programs, academic expectations, and the support services offered by the College. While on campus for the interview, students have the opportunity to tour with a student guide and to meet with faculty and staff members. International students are encouraged to apply for all academic programs. Applicants for the B.A. in dance must also submit a video, photo, and resumé.

Application and Information

Dean College operates on a rolling admission plan. Applications may be submitted as early in the senior year as a student wishes, usually after first marking period grades are available. Applications are reviewed as soon as an application is complete, and the majority of students are notified in February and March. Applications are accepted as long as there is space available in the College.

Applications can be requested by contacting:

Office of Admissions
Dean College
99 Main Street
Franklin, Massachusetts 02038-1994

Telephone: 877-TRY-DEAN (toll-free)
Fax: 508-541-8726
E-mail: admission@dean.edu
World Wide Web: http://www.dean.edu

Students on the campus of Dean College.

EDUCATION DIRECT

SCRANTON, PENNSYLVANIA

The College and Its Mission

Education Direct, a division of Thomson Learning, is one of the oldest and largest distance learning institutions in the world. The School's programs and services are designed to meet the lifelong learning needs of the adult learner. Programs of study lead to specialized associate degrees and career-specific diplomas.

The mission of Education Direct is to empower adult learners to advance or change their careers, learn a new skill, or gain personal satisfaction. Thomson Education Direct strives to fulfill this mission by providing breadth and depth of courseware, applicable technology, and a wide array of flexible services aimed at the needs of the adult learner. Programs not only teach current marketplace skills, but also present liberal arts offerings that help develop critical thinking, writing, and mathematical abilities.

Education Direct was founded in 1890 by newspaperman Thomas J. Foster as a way of helping anthracite coal miners become mine superintendents and foremen. By 1894, the school was enrolling students in Mexico, British America, and Australia. By 1945, 5 million students had enrolled in Education Direct training programs, and as of today, that number has grown to more than 13 million.

Students in the Associate in Specialized Technology (A.S.T.) degree programs may be required to attend a two-week resident laboratory training at the Pennsylvania State University Harrisburg Campus in Middletown, Pennsylvania. However, training may be available at a college or university near the student, or previous experience in a student's field of study may result in exemption from lab work.

An overall QPA of 2.0 or above is required to earn an Associate in Specialized Business (A.S.B.) degree or an Associate in Specialized Technology (A.S.T.) degree.

Education Direct is accredited by the Accrediting Commission of the Distance Education and Training Council (DETC). Education Direct and the Center for Degree Studies are licensed by the Pennsylvania State Board of Private Licensed Schools.

Academic Programs

Associate Degree Programs   Associate degree programs consist of ten to fourteen instructional modules divided into four semesters of study. Upon completion of one semester, the materials for the next semester are sent to the student. Associate in Specialized Business (A.S.B.) degrees are available in accounting, applied computer science, business management, criminal justice, early childhood education, finance, hospitality management, marketing, and paralegal studies. Associate in Specialized Technology (A.S.T.) degrees are available in electrical engineering technology, civil engineering technology, electronics technology, industrial engineering technology, Internet technology/e-commerce administration, Internet technology/multimedia and design, Internet technology/Web programming, mechanical engineering technology, and veterinary technician studies.

Career Diploma Programs   Education Direct also offers an array of career-oriented distance learning programs in the trades, technology, and health-care fields. A Certificate of Completion is awarded at the successful end of the student's course of study.

Costs

Tuition varies from program to program; however, most programs range from $798 to $1098. This includes tuition of $455 to $890, a registration fee of $68 to $150, a credit application fee of $25, a technology fee of $25 to $35, and a shipping and handling charge of $25. Tuition includes all required materials.

Financial Aid

Education Direct does not participate in federal financial aid programs. It does, however, offer interest-free monthly payment plans and participates in the Veterans Administration (VA) and DANTES programs for qualified members of the U.S. military.

Faculty

Programs are written by experts in the field, and instructional support is available for students during the course of their program. Instructors evaluate and grade projects and papers, answer questions, and provide feedback.

Student Body Profile

Approximately 13 million students have enrolled in degree and certificate programs. The majority of degree students are working adults who want to establish or advance a lucrative career in business or technology. The distance learning format provides the means for flexible scheduling, enabling the student who would otherwise not be able to earn a degree to achieve that goal. A significant number of students are members of the armed forces; these individuals can complete their studies regardless of their location.

Facilities and Resources

Students have access to an online library for use during their studies with Education Direct. They can use this library to do the required research in the courses they need to complete, or they can use it for general reference and to link to valuable resources. The library contains helpful research assistance, articles, databases, books, Web links, and e-mail access to a librarian.

The Pennsylvania State University Harrisburg Campus in Middletown, Pennsylvania, hosts a two-week resident laboratory training program for students in the Associate in Specialized Technology (A.S.T.) program.

Location

Education Direct offers distance learning programs. The School is headquartered in Scranton, Pennsylvania. The instructional and student service staffs are housed there, and the texts and learning materials are shipped to students from a facility nearby.

Admission Requirements

Applicants to all associate degree programs, as well as certain career diploma programs, must submit proof of high school graduation or GED equivalency certificate. Degree students are accepted for the entire program but are financially obligated for one semester at a time. Familiarity with personal computers is recommended for some computer and information technology (IT) programs. Advanced standing may, on approval by faculty members, be granted to those applicants who have completed comparable work with a grade of C or higher from an accredited institution, as evidenced by the college transcript or evidence of the College-Level Examination Program (CLEP) certification.

Application and Information

Students may enter the program of their choice at any time by enrolling through the Web site at the address listed below. For more information, prospective students should contact:

Education Direct
P.O. Box 1900
Scranton, Pennsylvania 18501

Telephone: 570-961-4033
Fax: 570-343-8462
E-mail: infoims@educationdirect.com
World Wide Web: http://www.educationdirect.com

FAIRMONT STATE COMMUNITY & TECHNICAL COLLEGE

FAIRMONT, WEST VIRGINIA

The College and Its Mission

Fairmont State Community & Technical College (FSC&TC) is the largest state-supported two-year college in West Virginia, with an enrollment of approximately 3,130 students. Founded in 1974, the College is located in the north-central portion of the state in the city of Fairmont, West Virginia. The main campus includes thirteen major buildings.

Academic Programs

Fairmont State offers forty different programs leading to an associate degree or a certificate. These are offered in the areas of business, health careers, social science, and technology.

Associate Degree Programs Fairmont State offers three 2-year degree programs: Associate of Arts (A.A.), Associate of Science (A.S.), and Associate of Applied Science (A.A.S.). Students in the A.A. program may major in general studies or sign language interpreter studies. In the A.S. program, the majors are administrative support, architecture engineering technology, avionics maintenance technology, civil engineering technology, electronics engineering technology, graphics technology (emphases in commercial design, electronic publishing/imaging, and printing production), mechanical engineering technology, and nursing. Majors in the A.A.S. program consist of applied design (emphases in fashion design and interior design), aviation maintenance technology, business administration (emphases in accounting and general business), criminal justice, drafting/design engineering technology, early childhood, emergency medical services, food service management (emphases in culinary arts, dietary management, and institutional food management), health information technology, information systems (emphases in applications, networking, and system development), medical laboratory technology, occupational development (emphases in building and construction trades, childcare practitioner studies, correctional officer studies, emergency medical services, firefighter studies, and food service specialist studies), physical therapist assistant studies, technical studies (emphases in automotive technology, highway technician studies, information systems, water and wastewater, and wood production technology), and veterinary technology.

Certificate Programs Certificate programs generally take one year or two semesters of full-time course work to complete. They are designed for students seeking to learn basic skills or to increase their proficiency in a specific occupational area.

Baccalaureate Programs Many of Fairmont State Community & Technical College's two-year programs transfer to Fairmont State College's baccalaureate programs, providing a seamless educational transition for those students desiring to continue their education beyond an associate degree. The courses of study lead to bachelor's degrees in business, the fine arts, the humanities, industrial technology, the social and natural sciences, and teacher education.

Off-Campus Programs

In addition to the main campus, classes are offered at the Robert C. Byrd National Aerospace Education Center in Bridgeport as well as at the Gaston Caperton Center, a 36,000-square-foot state-of-the-art facility in Clarksburg. The College also has satellite facilities reaching across the north-central region of West Virginia and at the Center for Workforce Education at the I-79 Technology Park.

Costs

Fairmont State remains a very financially affordable institution. Tuition and fees for the 2003–04 academic year were $2712 for West Virginia residents and $6560 for out-of-state students. Average room and board costs were $4552 per year. Textbooks cost approximately $600 per year.

Financial Aid

Sixty-five percent of Fairmont State students receive some form of financial aid. Guidelines and forms for West Virginia and out-of-state residents are available from high school guidance counselors or Fairmont State's Financial Aid Office.

Faculty

Fairmont State Community & Technical College employs more than 40 full-time faculty members, ensuring a low student-teacher ratio. Each student is assigned a faculty adviser who helps schedule courses, oversees classroom performance, and offers academic counseling.

Student Body Profile

The total enrollment for Fairmont State Community & Technical College is 3,128 and breaks down to one half full-time students and one half part-time students. Students come to Fairmont State right out of high school, transfer from other colleges, or have been in the workforce and decide to pursue additional education. Women make up 56 percent of the enrollment, men are 44 percent. The College has students from all fifty states and from more than thirty-five countries. Approximately 25 percent of the students are nontraditional, and the average student's age is 24.

Student Activities

Fairmont State has a rich and proud athletic tradition. The College is a member of NCAA Division II and offers men's teams in baseball, basketball, cross-country, football, golf, tennis, and swimming. The College sponsors women's teams in basketball, cross-country, golf, softball, swimming, tennis, and volleyball. Fairmont State's cheerleaders are consistently among the top teams in the state and the nation. Fairmont State also has an extensive and well-organized intramural program and provides other recreational facilities across the campus.

The Newman Center and the Wesley Foundation are available to minister to the spiritual needs of students; both organizations are adjacent to the Fairmont State campus. There are also various student organizations, honor societies, and social fraternities and sororities to enhance extracurricular life at the College.

Facilities and Resources

The Ruth Ann Musick Library has a collection of more than 200,000 books and more than 15,000 bound periodicals, microfilms, and other materials, including a large collection of audiotapes and videotapes to supplement and enhance learning. The Computer Center allows students to use the latest in technology, including free access to the Internet. Music, theater, and other fine arts are showcased in Wallman Hall Theatre and the Gallery.

Students who live on campus are housed in one of three residence halls and take their meals at a centrally located dining hall or at the food court in the student center. For those students who prefer to live off campus, private accommodations close to the College are available. Parents who are taking classes at the College may find it convenient to enroll their young children in the day-care center located on the main campus.

Location

Fairmont is the county seat of Marion County and has a population of approximately 20,000. Located along Interstate 79, approximately 90 miles south of Pittsburgh, the city and College are easily accessible to all travelers.

Fairmont State and the city of Fairmont share a long history of mutual cooperation and respect. Shopping malls, restaurants, cultural entertainment, and nightlife are easily found throughout the city, while countless outdoor recreational pleasures are offered by such places as Pricketts Fort State Park, Valley Falls State Park, and a variety of city and county parks nearby.

Admission Requirements

Students must indicate on the admission application their degree or program objective—a two-year associate degree or one-year certificate program.

Admission to Fairmont State does not guarantee admission to specific programs, which may be restricted based on qualifications and available space.

Application and Information

Campus tours are available Monday through Friday at 10 a.m. and 2 p.m. by appointment. Fairmont State also sponsors a Saturday Campus Visitation Day during the fall semester. For more information or to schedule a tour, students should contact:

Office of Admissions
Fairmont State Community & Technical College
1201 Locust Avenue
Fairmont, West Virginia 26554

Telephone: 304-367-4892
　　　　　　800-641-5678 (toll-free)
　　　　　　304-367-4213 (financial aid)
　　　　　　304-367-4216 (housing)
　　　　　　304-367-4000 (campus operator)
　　　　　　304-623-5721 (Caperton Center)
　　　　　　304-842-8300 (Aerospace Education Center)

E-mail: fscinfo@mail.fscwv.edu
World Wide Web: http://www.fscwv.edu

Fairmont State students have an opportunity to relax and socialize in the inviting plaza in front of the Education Building.

FASHION INSTITUTE OF DESIGN AND MERCHANDISING

LOS ANGELES, CALIFORNIA

The Institute and Its Mission

The Fashion Institute of Design and Merchandising (FIDM) provides a dynamic and exciting community of learning in the fashion, graphics, interior design, and entertainment industries. The purpose of the Institute is to provide an educational environment designed to combine student goals with industry needs.

FIDM has a reputation for graduating professionally competent and confident men and women capable of creative thought. It has graduated more than 30,000 students in its thirty-five-year history.

FIDM is accredited by the Accrediting Commission for Community and Junior Colleges of the Western Association of Schools and Colleges (WASC) and the National Association of Schools of Art and Design (NASAD).

Academic Programs

FIDM operates on a four-quarter academic calendar. New students may begin their studies any quarter throughout the year. The requirement for a two-year Associate of Arts degree is the completion of 90 units.

Associate Degree Programs FIDM offers **Associate of Arts** degrees in apparel manufacturing management, beauty industry merchandising and marketing, fashion design, graphic design, interior design, international manufacturing and product development, merchandise marketing (fashion merchandising or product development), textile design, theater costume, TV and film costume design, footwear design, interactive multimedia, and visual communication. All of these programs offer the highly specialized curriculum of a specific major combined with a core general education/liberal arts foundation.

Transfer Arrangements FIDM accepts course work from other accredited colleges if there is an equivalent course at FIDM and the grade is a C or better. FIDM courses at the 100, 200, and 300 levels are certified by FIDM to be baccalaureate level. FIDM maintains articulation agreements with selected colleges with the intent of enhancing a student's transfer opportunities. Academic counselors will provide assistance to students interested in transferring to other institutions to attain a four-year degree.

Internship and Co-op Programs Internships are available within each of the various majors. Paid and volunteer positions provide work experience for students to gain practical application of classroom skills.

Special Programs and Services FIDM offers Associate of Arts professional designation degrees for individuals with substantial academic and professional experience who wish to add a new field of specialization. These are nine- or twelve-month programs of intensive study in one of the Institute's specialized majors. Students from other regionally accredited programs have the opportunity to complement their previous education by enrolling in a professional designation program. Requirements for completion range from 45 to 66 units, depending on the field of study. FIDM also offers Associate of Arts advanced study programs that develop specialized expertise in the student's unique area of study. These programs are open to students who possess extensive prior academic and professional experience within the discipline area. These areas include fashion design advanced study, interior design advanced study, theater costume advanced study, and international manufacturing and product development. Completion requirements for these programs are 45 units. Some classes are offered online.

In response to student needs, FIDM has established an evening program in addition to the regular daytime courses. The program has been designed to accommodate the time requirements of working students. The entire evening program for the Associate in Arts degree can be completed in 2½ years.

FIDM offers English as a second language (ESL) for students requiring English development to complete their major field of study. The program is concurrent and within FIDM's existing college-level course work. These classes focus on the special needs of students in the areas of oral communication, reading comprehension, and English composition.

Community Programs Community service programs are offered both independently and in cooperation with various community groups. General studies course credit may be awarded to participating students. Each FIDM campus identifies community projects that allow students to support local service agencies.

Off-Campus Programs

FIDM provides the opportunity for students to participate in academic study tours in Europe, Asia, and New York. These tours are specifically designed to broaden and enhance the specialized education offered at the Institute. Study tour participants may earn academic credit under faculty-supervised directed studies. Exchange programs are also available with Esmod, Paris; Instituto Artictico dell' Abbigliamento Marangoni, Milan; Accademia Internazionale d'Alta Mode e d'Arte del Costume Koefia, Rome; St. Martins School of Art, London; College of Distributive Trades, London; and Janette Klein Design School, Mexico City.

Credit for Nontraditional Learning Experiences

The Institute may give credit for demonstrated proficiency in areas related to college-level courses. Sources used to determine proficiency are the College-Level Examination Program (CLEP) and Credit for Academically Relevant Experience (CARE), an Institute-sponsored program.

Costs

For the 2004–05 academic year, tuition starts at $16,400, depending on the major selected by the student. Textbooks and supplies start at $1400 per year, depending on the major. Yearly fees are $500. First-year application fees start at $225 for California residents and range up to $525 for international students.

Financial Aid

There are several sources of financial funding available to the student, including federal financial aid and education loan programs, California state aid programs, institutional loan programs, and FIDM awards and scholarships.

Faculty

FIDM faculty members are selected as specialists in their fields. Many are actively employed in their respective fields of expertise. They bring daily exposure to their industry into the classroom for the benefit of the students. In pursuit of the best faculty members, consideration is given to both academic excellence as well as practical experience. FIDM has a 16:1 student-instructor ratio.

Student Body Profile

FIDM's ethnically and culturally diverse student body is one of the attractions to the Institute. Fifteen percent of the current student body are international students from more than thirty different countries. Twenty percent of the students are more than 25 years of age. Fifty percent of all students complete their associate degree. More than 90 percent find career positions within one year of graduation.

Student Activities

The Student Activities Committee plans and coordinates social activities, cultural events, and community projects, including the ASID Student Chapter, International Club, Delta Epsilon Chi (DEX), Association of Manufacturing Students, Honor Society, and the Alumni Association. The students also produce their own trend newsletter, *The Mode*.

Facilities and Resources

Advisement/Counseling Department Chairs and other trained staff members provide assistance to students in selecting the correct sequence of courses to allow each student to complete degree requirements. The counseling department provides personal guidance and referral to outside counseling services as well as matching peer tutors to specific students' needs. Individual Development and Education Assistance (IDEA) centers at each campus provide students with additional educational assistance to supplement classroom instruction. Services are available in the areas of writing, mathematics, computer competency, study skills, research skills, and reading comprehension.

Career Planning/Placement Offices Career planning and job placement are among the most important services offered by the Institute. Career assistance includes job search techniques, preparation for employment interviews, resume preparation, and job adjustment assistance. Services provided by the center include undergraduate placement, graduate placement, alumni placement, internships, and industry work/study programs.

Library and Audiovisual Services FIDM's library goes beyond the traditional sources of information. In addition to more than 12,000 books and reference materials, FIDM also features an international video library, subscriptions to major predictive services, international and domestic periodicals, interior design workrooms, textile samples, a trimmings/findings collection, and access to the Internet. FIDM's Costume Museum houses more than 4,500 garments from the seventeenth century to present day. The collection includes items from the California Historical Society (First Families), the Hollywood Collection, and the Rudi Gernreich Collection.

State-of-the-art computer labs support and enhance the educational programs of the Institute. Specialized labs offer computerized cutting and marking, graphic and textile design, word processing, and database management.

Location

Established in 1969, FIDM is a private college that now enrolls more than 5,000 students a year. The main campus is in the heart of downtown Los Angeles near the garment district. This campus is adjacent to the beautiful Grand Hope Park. There are additional branch campuses located in San Francisco, San Diego, and Irvine, California.

Admission Requirements

The Institute provides educational opportunities to high school graduates or applicants that meet the Institute's Ability to Benefit (ATB) criteria to pursue a two-year Associate of Arts degree. Qualifications for professional designation programs include students that meet the general education core requirements or who have a U.S. accredited degree. All applicants must have an initial interview with an admissions representative. In addition, students must submit references and specific portfolio projects if applicable to the chosen major. The Institute is on the approved list of the U.S. Department of Justice for nonimmigrant students and is authorized to issue Certificates of Eligibility (Form I-20).

Application and Information

Applications are accepted on an ongoing basis. All prospective students should contact:

Director of Admissions
Fashion Institute of Design and Merchandising
919 South Grand Avenue
Los Angeles, California 90015

Telephone: 800-624-1200 (toll-free)
Fax: 213-624-4799
World Wide Web: http://www.fidm.com/

Debut. Student designer: Kim Yen Cao.

FISHER COLLEGE
BOSTON, MASSACHUSETTS

The College and Its Mission

Fisher College, a small, private college for men and women, celebrated its centennial in 2003. Fisher has been a leader in preparing students for challenging careers and facilitating transfer options to four-year colleges. Transfer options also include the College's baccalaureate degree in management. Currently, more than 550 students comprise the College's student body. Students come from all parts of the United States and more than fifteen other countries.

The Academic Support Center is staffed by 20 learning skills specialists and provides a supportive environment in which students develop writing, mathematics, and test-taking skills. The majority of the tutors also serve as instructors, so the tutors have firsthand experience with the subject matter and the students themselves.

Fisher students who graduate with their associate degree have three options once they have completed their program. An increasing number of students are transferring into Fisher College's Management Program. Currently, there are three concentrations in the B.S. Management Program: management information systems, marketing, and travel hospitality. Other students join the workforce upon graduation. Still others transfer to a different four-year college or university. Fisher College is fully accredited by the New England Association of Schools and Colleges. Therefore, other institutions accept qualified courses with adequate grades for transfer credit. Academic advisers assist students with the transfer process. Fisher also has several articulation agreements with colleges and universities throughout New England and beyond.

Academic Programs

The programs at Fisher College are designed to help students develop academic and professional skills.

Associate Degree Programs Fisher offers associate degrees in accounting, business administration, computer technology, early childhood education, fashion design, fashion merchandising, health science, liberal arts (humanities, justice studies, and social science concentrations), psychology, and travel hospitality management.

Bachelor's Degree Programs Fisher College now offers a B.S. in management. There are three concentrations in the Management Program: management information systems, marketing, and travel hospitality.

Certificate programs are also available.

Internship Program Some of the majors offered at Fisher College require internships. Through the internship program, students gain professional experience that often becomes an employment opportunity upon graduation. Students learn valuable skills that help them build their resumes and they also have the opportunity to establish professional contacts.

Fisher's location in downtown Boston creates the opportunity for countless internship possibilities. Students who take internships gain professional skills, learn business practices, and benefit from hands-on experience. Students have secured internships at businesses such as American Express Financial, Louis of Boston, Bright Horizons, Hilton Hotels, Park Plaza Hotel, and Saks Fifth Avenue.

Special Programs and Services Fisher College offers a summer English as a second language program. The majority of the students attending the Summer Language Institute matriculate into the College full-time in the fall semester. Students entering this program are required to have taken the Test of English as Foreign Language (TOEFL) and attained a minimum score of 400 (paper-based test) or 97 (computer-based test). For further details, students should visit the College's Web site, which is listed at the end of this description.

Costs

For the 2004–05 academic year, tuition is $15,975, room and board are $9975, and the comprehensive fee is $1600.

Financial Aid

The vast majority of students at Fisher qualify for some form of financial aid. Fisher offers both need-based and merit-based scholarships. Need-based awards include the Fisher Trustee Scholarship, Federal Pell Grants, Federal Perkins Loans, Federal Stafford Student Loans, Massachusetts State (Gilbert) Grants, and Federal Work-Study Program positions. Merit-based funds include eight different types of scholarships for incoming freshmen and several different options for transfer students. Students who have graduated from a Massachusetts public high school after June 2003 must pass the MCAS in order to be eligible for state and federal financial aid.

Faculty

The instructors at Fisher College are aware of and are sensitive to students' needs and aspirations. Faculty members are chosen for their academic qualifications and experience. Students find that the instructors are involved in promoting the progress and success of each student. The student-faculty ratio is 20:1. Faculty members and course advisers counsel students during posted office hours and informally throughout the day. Many instructors also work as tutors in the Academic Support Center.

Student Body Profile

Ninety percent of all students enter Fisher immediately after high school. Students come from fifteen different states and twelve other countries. The mean GPA for students applying for the 2004–05 academic year is 2.51 on a 4.0 scale.

Fifty percent of all students complete a full-time two-year associate degree program. Sixty percent transfer to a four-year college or university. This includes the students who continue at Fisher and earn their bachelor's degree in the Management Program.

Student Activities

The Student Activities Office is the focal point of campus life and offers a full range of extracurricular activities. Clubs and activities offered vary from year to year, depending on the interest of the students. Recently, the active clubs have included intramural sports, the Multicultural Club, Outdoors Club, Management Club, Ski Club, the Honors Program, Phi Theta Kappa, and the Fashion Show.

Sports Fisher College offers intercollegiate men's and women's baseball, basketball, and softball. All teams are recognized by the NAIA and compete at the Division II level in the Sunrise Conference.

Facilities and Resources

Advisement/Counseling The Student Affairs Department consists of Residence Life, Student Activities, Athletics, Health and Counseling Service, and Career Placement. A faculty adviser is assigned to each student to assist with the selection of courses.

Career Planning/Placement Offices Fisher College's Placement Office offers students a full range of professional services designed to help guide students along the path to a successful career. Trained staff members assist students with developing resumes and interviewing techniques and identifying specific job opportunities. With a 98 percent placement success rate and lifetime assistance, the Placement Office is an invaluable resource.

Library and Audiovisual Services The Fisher College Library contains more than 35,000 volumes and 200 printed periodicals as well as a comprehensive supply of audiovisual materials. The library also provides students with Internet access in the computer labs and residence halls. Students have access to PCs in the computer labs when classes are not held and there are banks of computers in the library and the Academic Support Center. Students also use the Boston Public Library, which is located only a few blocks from the College.

Location

Located in the Back Bay section of Boston, Fisher is a small college in a world-class city. Within a 6-mile radius of Boston, there are more than thirty-six schools and colleges that draw more than 250,000 students to the city annually. This creates an environment that is truly unique—the individual attention and structure that only a small college can offer and the social, cultural, historical, and educational opportunities that make Boston famous.

The campus facilities, dorms, and classrooms overlook either Beacon Street or the Charles River and the Esplanade. The Back Bay is one of the most exclusive and safest neighborhoods of Boston. The city itself becomes a part of the student's college experience. Many of the city's world-famous attractions are within walking distance of the campus, and there is nothing in Boston that is not accessible via subway or bus.

Boston has an outstanding public transportation system; there is a subway stop within four blocks of the College. South Station and North Station offer both bus and rail service for local and interstate travel. Both are only a few stops away on the subway. Logan International Airport is approximately 20 minutes away via taxi. Airport shuttle service is available.

Admission Requirements

The College advocates an admission policy that focuses on the positive attributes in a student's record. Applicants are evaluated based on their academic performance in secondary school. Applicants must submit an official transcript for acceptance and a final, official copy upon graduation from high school.

Students must have a minimum grade point average (GPA) of 2.0 in college preparatory classes, 4 units of English, 3 units of math, 3 units of history/social science, and 2 units of science. Fisher College recalculates a student's GPA and does not factor electives into the new GPA. Improvements over the course of the applicant's high school career, recommendations, a personal statement, an interview, and other supporting credentials are also considered in the decision-making process but are not required.

International students are required to submit original copies of transcripts, state exam results, and results from the Test of English as a Foreign Language (TOEFL). Photocopies are not acceptable forms of documentation. International students should visit the College's Web site (listed at the end of this description) for examples of proper documentation.

Application and Information

Applications are received on a rolling basis. The Admissions Committee reviews an application when it is complete with proper documentation. Following a preliminary assessment, the Admissions Committee may request additional documents or require a personal interview. Students interested in Fisher College should contact:

Director of Admissions
Fisher College
118 Beacon Street
Boston, Massachusetts 02116

Telephone: 617-236-8818
Fax: 617-236-5473
E-mail: admissions@fisher.edu
World Wide Web: http://www.fisher.edu

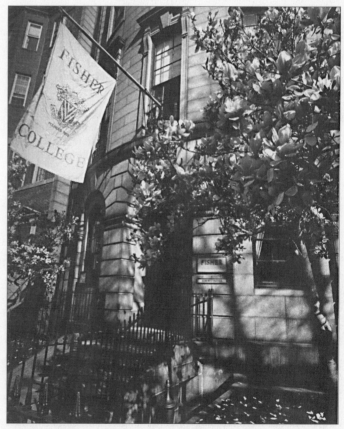

The Administration Building, located on Beacon Street in Boston's Back Bay.

FLORIDA NATIONAL COLLEGE

HIALEAH, FLORIDA

The College and Its Mission

Founded in 1982, Florida National College (FNC) has three campuses. The main campus is located in Hialeah; the second campus, known as the South Campus, is located in Miami; and the third campus, the Training Center, is also located in Hialeah. Florida National College is a two-year, proprietary, urban, commuter junior college offering Associate of Arts, Associate of Science, diploma, and certificate programs in the following fields: accounting, business, computer technology, criminal justice, dental technology, education, English as a second language, medical technology, paralegal, radiology, sonogram, and travel and tourism.

The purpose of Florida National College is to contribute to the education of a population of diverse, presently predominantly Hispanic, cultures. The college realizes this mission through the employment and development of a faculty of scholars who are proficient in the art of teaching. The College strives to prepare its students for entry-level positions in their chosen career or for upper-level studies through the acquisition of a system of technical and professional knowledge and skills, enriched with a liberal arts curriculum.

Florida National College strives to provide the educational facilities and resources that support intensive sessions of study in small classes, in order to foster in the student the attainment of a quality college education according to the student's personal goals and in congruence with the advancement of modern technology.

FNC offers several services, free of charge, to the communities surrounding its campuses, as a contribution to each community's development. Campus-based services may include, but are not limited to, literacy programs, GED classes, library services, health fairs, and citizenship and other seminars.

FNC is accredited by the Commission on Colleges of the Southern Association of Colleges and Schools to award the Associate of Arts and Associate of Science degrees, and it is licensed by the commission for Independent Education. In addition to holding memberships in a wide array of professional organizations, FNC maintains articulation agreements with various universities and its credits are transferable to any educational institution of higher learning.

Academic Programs

Florida National College offers associate degrees, diplomas, and certificates through five academic divisions: Allied Health, Business and Economics, Computer Science, Humanities and Fine Arts, and English as a Second Language.

The Allied Health Division offers Associate of Science degrees in dental technology, diagnostic medical sonographer studies, medical assisting technology, and radiologic technology. Diploma ares offered in basic X-ray technician studies; dental assistant studies; dental laboratory technician (DLT) studies; dental laboratory technician studies: full and partial dentures; dental laboratory technician studies: crown and bridge, and porcelain; medical assistant studies; medical secretary studies; medical sonographer technology; obstetric-gynecology medical sonographer studies; and patient care technician studies.

The Business and Economics Division is made up of the Department of Business Administration, the Department of Legal/Paralegal Studies (including criminal justice), and the Department of Travel and Tourism. Within these departments, FNC offers a variety of degrees that lead to interesting and profitable careers and/or higher education studies. These programs also provide students with the knowledge they need for starting their own businesses. FNC offers Associate of Science degrees in administrative assistant studies; business administration; accounting; legal assistant/paralegal studies; and travel and tourism. Associate of Arts degree programs are offered in business administration and in criminal justice. FNC offers diplomas within the division in executive secretary/information systems, legal secretary studies, office specialist studies, and travel and tourism-secretarial studies.

The Computer Science Division offers Associate of Science degree in computer programming, computer support specialist studies, networking system administrator studies, and Web page design. Diplomas are offered in computer office specialist studies, computer support specialist studies, networking systems administrator studies, and MCSA certification.

The Humanities and Fine Arts Division offers the Associate of Arts degree in education.

The English as a Second Language Division offers two certificate programs: English as a second language: basic level and English as a second language: intermediate level.

Costs

Registration fees range from $50 to $150, depending upon residency and ESL status. Tuition is $290 per credit, with tuition for certain majors in the Allied Health Division being slightly higher. Degree programs usually require 60–80 credits. Books (approximately $750–$900), supplies, lab fees, and other costs are additional. Students should contact the school for current costs, which are subject to change without notice.

Financial Aid

Florida National College is committed to assisting its students in meeting college expenses through federal aid, if the student qualifies, and/or other methods such as loans or deferred payment plans. Florida National College assists its qualified students in obtaining funds in the form of grants, loans, and work-study opportunities. FNC participates in six student financial aid programs supported by the United States Department of Education and the Florida Department of Education. Participation in most aid programs is dependent on the student filing the Free Application for Federal Financial Aid.

Faculty

Florida National College has more than 60 full- and part-time faculty members who come from the professions that they teach, including doctors, lawyers, physicians, and dentists. These faculty members work closely with the students in the academic programs as well as the English as a second language program to ensure each student's success.

Student Body Profile

The student body of Florida National College is primarily Hispanic. Most students come from the surrounding areas of Florida.

Student Activities

Florida National College's Student Government Association (SGA) is the self-governing student entity serving as a liaison between the student body, the faculty, and the administration. It seeks to foster professional development in an atmosphere of friendship and participation. The SGA is responsible for organizing such student activities as dances, sports, parties, picnics, and fund-raisers.

Facilities and Resources

Florida National College's library exists chiefly to support the curricula offered by the College. Its responsibilities include assisting faculty members and students in locating library materials as well as instructing them in the effective use of library resources, which include multimedia resources and Internet access. Library hours are scheduled to service day and evening students. During scheduled hours, a librarian or an assistant librarian is always available to assist students, faculty members, and staff members in the use of the library.

FNC offers employability training, job referrals, and participation in annual job fairs. Students are strongly urged to maintain contact with FNC when they obtain employment, change jobs, need further assistance, or relocate to another area so they can take advantage of this lifetime service. There is a placement office at each FNC campus.

Though students are not required to make their purchases on campus, textbooks, workbooks, supplies, and materials for all courses are available from the bookstore at each campus during the first ten days of each academic period.

Although FNC does not have residence halls, assistance with local housing information is provided to students on request. Each campus can be reached using city transportation services.

Location

Florida National College's Hialeah Campus is located in the northwest area of Miami-Dade County. The campus occupies approximately 56,000 square feet and includes a library; dental, medical, X-ray, and computer labs; a cafeteria; student lounge; reception area; conference room; bookstore; and administrative offices. There is ample lighted parking, and the building is equipped with elevators and wide aisles for accessibility by physically challenged persons.

The South Campus is located in the west area of Miami-Dade County. Occupying approximately 25,000 square feet, its space is used for a media center, medical lab, X-ray lab, computer and language labs, student lounge, reception area, and administrative offices.

The FNC Training Center is located at Hialeah and occupies approximately 6,000 square feet. The Training Center houses a Prometric Testing Center, two computer labs, a medical lab, student lounge, and administrative offices.

Admission Requirements

Florida National College has an open door admissions policy and welcomes all qualified applicants without regard to ethnic background, sex, religion, national origin, age, or physical handicap. Applications for admission are processed under a policy of continuous admissions.

For admission into an associate degree program, applicants must have a diploma from an accredited four-year high school, a GED certificate, or an equivalent. Prospective students must also complete an interview with an FNC admissions representative, submit a completed and signed Enrollment Agreement, and commit themselves to abide by the College's directives and regulations.

For diploma and certificate programs, applicants must be at least 16 years old, complete an interview with an FNC admissions representative, submit a completed and signed Enrollment Agreement, and commit themselves to abide by the College's directives and regulations.

Other requirements may apply, and interested students are urged to visit the College's Web site (listed below) for further information.

Application and Information

Office of Admissions
FNC Hialeah Campus (Main)
4425 West 20th Avenue
Hialeah, Florida 33012
Telephone: 305-821-3333 Ext. 3
Fax: 305-362-0595
World Wide Web: http://www.fnc.edu

Office of Admissions
FNC South Campus
11865 SW 26th Street, Unit H3
Miami, Florida 33173
Telephone: 305-226-9999 Ext. 3
Fax: 305-226-4439
World Wide Web: http://www.fnc.edu

Office of Admissions
FNC Training Center
4206 West 12th Avenue
Hialeah, Florida 33012
Telephone: 305-231-3326
Fax: 305-362-0595
World Wide Web: http://www.fnc.edu

HARCUM COLLEGE
BRYN MAWR, PENNSYLVANIA

The College and Its Mission

Harcum College provides an educational foundation and environment for learning that promotes academic, professional, and personal growth of its students. It is a two-year private, coeducational college that admits both residential and commuter students. Harcum College is fully accredited by the Middle States Association of Colleges and Schools.

Intent upon becoming the leading independent, two-year, career-preparation college in America, Harcum is especially focused in the health-care fields. Moreover, the College takes great pride in the close individual attention it gives to students who need it. All programs at Harcum, whether health-related or not, include practical, hands-on internships. Service learning is also emphasized. Styling itself as "the opportunity college," Harcum sends its graduates into careers that are socially useful, remunerative, and personally enriching.

Edith Hatcher Harcum and her husband, Marvin Harcum, founded Harcum in 1915. It was their vision to build a college of higher learning for women seeking financial and intellectual independence. Since then, Harcum College has been providing contemporary, career-oriented education supported by a strong liberal arts foundation. Harcum graduates find employment in their fields or transfer to four-year colleges and universities. Harcum was the first college in Pennsylvania to award the Associate in Arts and Associate in Science degrees. Today, Harcum is still the only two-year private women-centered college in Pennsylvania.

Academic Programs

Harcum's academic programs are diverse and fall under three schools: the School for Business and Professional Studies, the School for Allied Health Sciences, and the School for Liberal Studies and Education. Harcum graduates are prepared to immediately embark on careers or further their studies by transferring to a four-year institution. The **Associate in Arts** degree is offered in early childhood education, liberal studies, and psychology. The **Associate in Science** degree is offered in allied health science, animal center management, business administration, computer information systems, dental hygiene, expanded functions dental assisting, fashion design, fashion merchandising, health-care practice management, interior design, legal studies, medical laboratory technology, muscle therapy and integrated health care, nursing, physical therapist assistant, and veterinary technology. **Credit one-year certificates** are available in dental assisting studies and expanded functions dental assisting studies.

Transfer Arrangements The Career and Transfer Services staff assists students in preparing for transfer to a four-year institution. Harcum students have been accepted by more than 200 colleges and universities nationwide and abroad. Harcum has close relationships with many colleges and a growing number of articulation agreements with many that enable students to transfer without loss of academic credit.

Internship and Co-op Programs All of Harcum's programs require an internship as part of the curriculum. Students spend a period of time gaining valuable work experience in a workplace appropriate to their program, where they apply the knowledge they have acquired in the classroom. Many students subsequently receive job offers from their internship sponsors.

Special Programs and Services The College offers a number of special programs to assist students in succeeding at college. Summer Advance is a five-week summer program that gives students an opportunity to adjust to college life while strengthening their academic preparation in reading, writing, math, and other areas. Achieving Individual Motivation for Success (A.I.M.) develops academic and personal skills, cultural awareness, career plans, and lifelong learning tools for students who have disabilities, are economically disadvantaged, or are first-generation college attendees. The English Language Academy offers full- and part-time instruction in English as a second language. The Developmental Program provides courses to strengthen skills in English, math, and reading. Independent study is offered for students who want to study a topic that deeply interests them. A qualified, conscientious instructor guides students in their study, independent of regular classroom attendance. Periodic meetings and discussion seminars are held. The Center for Student Development and Counseling offers personal and individualized career and academic counseling.

Continuing Education Programs The College's Corporate and Community Services Division offers programs year-round. Courses are offered for professional development and personal enrichment. Continuing Education Units (CEUs) may be earned in the dental and veterinary fields, and in many other fields related to the College's degree programs. Other popular programs include the pharmacy technician training course, the phlebotomy technician training course, medical insurance claims processing, animal-assisted therapy, and holistic studies. Harcum College is an AutoDesk Authorized Training Center (ATC), and as such offers a well-established series of classes in AutoDesk's AutoCAD software, designed for professionals in the architecture, design, engineering, and construction fields. For adult students looking to further their education in the evenings and on weekends, Harcum College offers flexible scheduling, a large selection of Internet courses, and an accelerated core curriculum to make the associate's degree attainable.

Credit for Nontraditional Learning Experiences

The College awards credit for knowledge acquired outside the usual educational setting by accepting College-Level Examination Program (CLEP) scores for credit toward a degree. The College accepts general and subject examination CLEP scores based on the American Council on Education's recommended cut scores. Students working toward an associate degree may earn a total of 30 credits through CLEP, challenge exams, portfolio-assisted assessment, or traditional transfer.

Costs

The 2004–05 annual tuition for full-time students is $6945 per semester. Tuition for part-time students is $455 per credit. There are additional miscellaneous fees and deposits. Annual room and board charges are $3400 per semester in 2004–05. All fees and tuition are subject to change.

Financial Aid

More than 85 percent of students at Harcum receive some form of financial aid. Available aid includes Harcum grants-in-aid, scholarships, Federal Pell Grants, Federal Supplemental Educational Opportunity Grants, state grants, Federal Perkins Loans, and Federal Work-Study Program awards. The priority deadline for financial aid applications is May 1 for fall enrollment.

Faculty

All of Harcum's programs are led by full-time directors and have full-time professors. Their expertise is augmented by part-time adjunct instructors who usually are practicing professionals in their fields. There are 26 full-time faculty members. Eighty percent of full-time faculty members have advanced degrees, including 13 percent who hold doctorates. The student-faculty ratio is 9:1.

Student Body Profile

The student body is 90 percent women. The largest age group is between 18 and 26, but nearly as many are between 26 and 39 years of age. Seventy percent of the students are white; 16 percent are African American; 3 percent are Asian. Full-time students make up 68 percent of the total. Commuters account for 83 percent. Eighty-nine percent of the students are from Pennsylvania, primarily from the five-county Philadelphia region. The next largest group (4 percent) is from New Jersey. International students make up 2 percent. Sixty percent of those accepted to Harcum College enroll. Of those who enroll, 60 percent graduate.

Student Activities

It is easy to get involved on campus. Harcum has clubs and organizations for students with many different interests. Students make their mark on campus by joining one of more than twenty clubs, such as the student newspaper, the yearbook, the Organization for Animal Technician Students, or the Student American Dental Hygienists Association. The College has a chapter of Phi Theta Kappa, the national honor society for two-year colleges, and Chi Alpha Epsilon, a national honor society for A.I.M. students. The College also organizes many community service activities and events. Students participate in volunteer projects on and off campus, such as peer tutoring, clothing drives, and Earth Day.

Facilities and Resources

Harcum gives students full support throughout their time at the College and after graduation. At the Center for Student Development and Counseling, counselors give a hand with everything from advice on balancing a schedule to resolving a personal problem. The College also has academic tutors to help students with course work.

Students at Harcum have the option of living on campus in the residence halls, which is a great way to make friends and be in the middle of everything that is happening on campus. The residence hall staff plans programs and events, including seminars and discussion groups on topics ranging from study skills to current events, and stress-buster pizza parties.

Students feel at home at Harcum College. Even the students who commute say they do not feel like outsiders. Harcum is a small community, and students quickly find that they recognize friendly faces all over the campus.

Library and Audiovisual Services The library collection has 39,000 volumes, 300 periodicals, and more than 1,000 audiovisual items. It is a member of the Tri-State College Library Cooperative, a forty-two-college consortium, which provides access to more than 6 million volumes. Harcum's library also provides connections to the Internet and FirstSearch, an online database, and it is networked with 20 CD-ROM databases.

Location

Harcum is located in Bryn Mawr, Pennsylvania, 12 miles west of Philadelphia, in the heart of the Main Line, a string of attractive, safe, friendly suburban communities. The College is in the midst of one of the largest concentrations of educational institutions in the country. There are fifty-five colleges and universities in the Philadelphia area. The campus is on a parklike 12-acre site next to a commuter railroad station, which makes travel to Philadelphia and throughout the area easy. Available in Philadelphia are the world-renowned Philadelphia Orchestra, the Pennsylvania Ballet, the Opera Company of Philadelphia, and the world-famous Philadelphia Museum of Art. The city has major league teams in baseball, football, ice hockey, and basketball. There are numerous historic sites in and around Philadelphia to visit, including Independence Hall, the Liberty Bell, and Valley Forge National Park.

Admission Requirements

All applicants are required to submit official academic transcripts, results of any standardized tests taken, a written essay, and a letter of recommendation. An interview is recommended. The dental hygiene application deadline is February 15. All other programs follow a rolling admission policy. Prospective students should consult the enrollment office for additional requirements specific to each program.

Application and Information

For more information, students should contact:

Office of Enrollment Management
Harcum College
750 Montgomery Avenue
Bryn Mawr, Pennsylvania 19010-3476

Telephone: 610-526-6050
　　　　　　 800-345-2600 (toll-free)
Fax: 610-526-6147
E-mail: journey@harcum.edu
World Wide Web: http://www.harcum.edu

Library and Academic Center.

HESSER COLLEGE

MANCHESTER, NEW HAMPSHIRE

The College and Its Mission

The primary purpose of Hesser College is to provide a high-quality education that is personalized, cost effective, and employment oriented. Hesser College's innovative approach to higher education provides students increased flexibility compared to traditional colleges. After two years of college, students earn an associate degree and are prepared to enter the workplace, or, if they prefer, students can continue on in one of Hesser's 2+2 bachelor's degree programs.

Hesser College was established in 1900 as Hesser Business College, a private, nonsectarian college. Since 1972, Hesser College has expanded and enriched its curricula in keeping with its tradition of providing an affordable career education of high quality. The physical building encompasses more than fifteen different businesses that all create the Hesser Center of Commerce and Education. This is an unusual and beneficial partnership of business and education.

Hesser College is fully accredited by the New England Association of Schools and Colleges. The association is the official accrediting agency for schools and colleges in the six New England states and is widely considered to hold the strictest academic standards. Students who choose Hesser College are assured of a high-quality education.

Academic Programs

The primary goal of the curricula is to prepare students for success in specific career areas. The general education requirements are designed to provide the skills necessary for career growth and lifelong learning. Internships, practicums, and opportunities for part-time work experience are available in all majors. An education from Hesser College provides a solid career foundation. The College's goal is quite simple: to prepare people for careers and career advancement.

Many of the Hesser College programs are for the career-minded student who wants to concentrate on the skills required to be successful in the workplace. Seventy-five percent of the courses that students take are directly related to their career choices. Upon completion of the associate degree program, a student may pursue a four-year degree by enrolling in one of Hesser's 2+2 bachelor's degree programs.

Associate Degree Programs Hesser offers a wide range of programs that prepare students for high-demand careers. They include accounting; business administration; business computer applications; business science/individualized studies; communications and public relations; corrections, probation, and parole; early childhood education; graphic design; human services; interior design; law enforcement; liberal studies; marketing; medical assistant studies; medical office management; paralegal studies; physical therapist assistant studies; psychology; radio and video production and broadcasting; small-business management/entrepreneurship; and sports management. In addition, the College offers 2+2 bachelor's degree programs in accounting, business administration, and criminal justice.

Off-Campus Programs

The College offers opportunities for cooperative education and internships in most of its academic programs. The early childhood education program includes practicums and supervised fieldwork in the freshman and senior years, utilizing a variety of child-care facilities. The physical therapist assistant studies program requires students to participate in at least 265 hours of clinical experience in a health-care setting under the direct supervision of a certified instructor or therapist.

Credit for Nontraditional Learning Experiences

Hesser College offers a variety of options for students to earn college credit by means other than taking traditional college courses. These programs enable those students who have reached the college level of education in nontraditional ways (e.g., correspondence study, self-study, company, or military training) to assess the level of their achievement and to use the assessment and/or test results in seeking college credit. These programs allow the student to shorten the amount of time required to obtain a degree. These programs cannot be used to erase failing grades or upgrade other grades.

Costs

Part-time students are billed at the rate of $373 per credit for most majors. Information technology credit rates vary. Full-time expenses per semester in 2003–04 were as follows: tuition (12–16 credits), $5145, and room and board, $3400.

Financial Aid

Hesser College offers financial assistance to students based on demonstrated financial need. Seventy percent of students receive some form of aid. Scholarships are awarded each year to freshman and senior students based on academic and financial standing. The College offers low-interest loans from both internal and external sources. Federal Supplemental Educational Opportunity Grants, the Federal Work-Study Program, Federal Perkins Loans, Federal Stafford Student Loans, and state scholarship programs are available to those who qualify. Awards are made on a rolling basis and are subject to availability. In order to apply for financial aid and scholarships at Hesser College, students must complete a FAFSA and a Hesser College Institutional Financial Aid Application.

Faculty

The faculty members of Hesser College consistently receive high student evaluations for their interest in each student's success and for the high quality of their teaching. The majority of the faculty members have completed programs of advanced study, and all have practical experience in business or other career fields. Faculty members participate in national and regional conferences and associations and are continually involved with program review and curriculum development. The student-faculty ratio is 18:1.

Student Body Profile

Nearly 85 percent of the students work in the afternoons, evenings, or weekends while attending Hesser. The 890 men and women currently enrolled represent several states and more than fifteen countries. A large part of the student population is from the New England region.

Student Activities

Hesser College offers intercollegiate sports teams in men's and women's basketball, soccer, and volleyball; men's baseball; and women's softball. The basketball and volleyball teams have consistently been a major power in the Northern New England Small College Conference. Students also participate in a number of intramural sports programs. Extracurricular activities are varied and include social activities, clubs, trips, and programs in the residence halls. A freshman orientation program is conducted each fall before classes begin.

Facilities and Resources

The College includes dormitories for approximately 70 percent of the 890 students. A wide range of resources are located on campus. Academic advising is coordinated through department chairpersons and the Center for Teaching, Learning, and Assessment; the size of the College allows for individual attention to the financial and career counseling needs of each student.

The academic facilities located within the Hesser Commerce and Education Center include four computer labs, a Mac-based graphic design lab, a medical assistant lab, a physical therapist assistant lab, and a radio/video production lab. The College library contains more than 30,000 titles. The Center for Teaching, Learning, and Assessment provides special tutoring and programs in study skills, reading, writing, math, and computer skills.

The College has also developed a number of learning assistance programs to help students succeed in their studies. Tutoring and special classes are provided by the faculty throughout each semester. In addition, several departments offer honor programs and special opportunities for independent study. The College also sponsors an active chapter of the national honor society Phi Theta Kappa, which promotes scholarship and service to the College and the community.

Location

Hesser College is located in Manchester, New Hampshire. With a population of more than 100,000, Manchester is a medium-sized city that offers many cultural, historical, and social events. Hesser College's central location provides easy access to entertainment, shopping, and a variety of part-time jobs and academic work experiences.

Manchester was recently named by *Money* magazine as the number one small city in the northeast United States. In addition, Manchester was recently named as one of the best cities in the United States for business. According to *U.S. News & World Report*, Manchester is "at the hub of things" in the fast-growing, high-technology, financial, and information-oriented businesses of southern New Hampshire.

Manchester is within 1 hour of Boston, and the mountains and major ski resorts are within 1 or 2 hours of Hesser's campus. Manchester has been called the "Gateway to Northern New England," and several major carriers serve the Manchester Airport.

Admission Requirements

Hesser College's freshman class is selected by a committee made up of administrators and admission personnel. A high school transcript must be submitted. SAT scores are not required but may be considered in the admission decision if submitted. Transfer students are required to submit a high school and college transcript, with a minimum grade point average of 2.0 for college work.

All applicants are required to come to Hesser for an interview. Hesser recommends that all applicants submit one recommendation from a counselor, teacher, or employer. The College operates on a rolling admission basis, and notification is continuous.

Application and Information

Applicants must submit an application form with a $10 nonrefundable fee. Applications are reviewed on a first-come, first-served basis and normally take seven to fourteen days to be fully reviewed upon receipt of all required information.

Requests for additional information and application forms should be addressed to:

Director of Admissions
Hesser College
3 Sundial Avenue
Manchester, New Hampshire 03103
Telephone: 603-668-6660 Ext. 2110
             800-526-9231 Ext. 2110 (toll-free)
Fax: 603-666-4722
E-mail: admissions@hesser.edu
World Wide Web: http://www.hesser.edu

Students at Hesser College's main campus.

HOLY CROSS COLLEGE
NOTRE DAME, INDIANA

The College and Its Mission

Holy Cross College (HCC) is an independent, Catholic community of higher education founded by and operated in the tradition of the Brothers of Holy Cross. It accommodates a broad spectrum of needs, interests, and backgrounds by combining a demanding liberal arts program with cooperative and supportive instruction.

As a community, the College actively pursues the integrated spiritual, academic, and personal formation of students. The Associate of Arts degree program provides a liberal arts foundation that emphasizes core transferable skills and career exploration. The baccalaureate option offers a continued liberal arts experience that provides students with the competence and courage to face future challenges.

Holy Cross College encourages each member of its community to live the Gospel message by developing a personal understanding of his or her relationship to God, others, and self. Members of the community respect and honor one another through active spiritual and intellectual lives. Community members also engage one another in meaningful discourse and enlighten one another about their common responsibilities to further the Kingdom of God.

Academic Programs

The academic associate degree offered at Holy Cross College is the Associate of Arts. It is awarded to the student who has completed the required academic program. Since the liberal arts curriculum within the Associate of Arts is nonterminal, the student who has set the intermediate goal of an associate degree is able to transfer these credits and complete general education requirements in pursuit of a bachelor's degree at HCC or another institution.

Every student who enters Holy Cross begins on the Associate of Arts degree track and after two years decides to either apply to Holy Cross's baccalaureate in liberal studies program or apply for transfer into another four-year institution. The curriculum specified in the College Bulletin must be followed for a student to qualify for the Associate of Arts and bachelor's degrees.

An agreement existing between the U.S. Army and U.S. Air Force ROTC detachments at the University of Notre Dame and Holy Cross College permits students attending Holy Cross to affiliate with the ROTC program and to take courses in military science and aerospace studies. Credits earned in these courses are valid for ROTC programs at any college that offers the program.

Courses that the student has completed with a grade of C or above while attending another accredited collegiate institution are accepted in transfer if the courses are comparable to those of the HCC program. A transfer course that does not parallel a course offered at Holy Cross College may be accepted if it appears suitable for elective credit. No transfer credit is given for courses completed with a grade of less than C. Grades earned in transferred courses are not calculated into the Holy Cross College cumulative grade point average. For students transferring from institutions that employ the quarter system, the equivalent semester value is based on two thirds of the quarter hours of credits accepted.

Costs

Tuition and fee charges for the 2004–05 academic year are $5250 per semester for a full-time student and $345 per semester hour for a part-time student. A full-time student is enrolled for 12 or more semester hours. Room and board costs are approximately $3500 per semester.

Financial Aid

Federal, state, and Holy Cross financial aid, with the exception of the Unsubsidized Federal Stafford Student Loan Program, PLUS Loan Program, and Hoosier Scholarship Award, are need-based programs. Financial need is determined through approved need analysis as provided by Congress. The College utilizes the Free Application for Federal Student Aid (FAFSA). Federal regulations require all students applying for aid, including student loans, to have the results of the FAFSA on file to be eligible for any aid. Holy Cross College also offers merit-based scholarships to those students who academically excel as well as Leadership Scholarships to those students who demonstrate outstanding leadership qualities.

Faculty

The faculty of Holy Cross College is composed of religious, laymen, and laywomen, all of whom hold graduate degrees in their academic disciplines. The quality of teaching is the primary criterion for faculty selection. Also important in faculty selection is an ability to interact with students on a friendly and professional level. The reward in teaching is found in the student's ability to organize new knowledge, apply it to concrete situations, and enjoy the experience.

Student Body Profile

The majority of students entering Holy Cross College come directly from high school. Many students select Holy Cross because they have a desire to attend a small college. Some also select the College because they desire to attend a college close to home, cutting down on expenses while maintaining their ties with family and friends. Other students select Holy Cross College to have the opportunity to test their abilities while making progress toward a bachelor's degree. In addition, there are students at Holy Cross College who initially started their college work at other institutions but, for various reasons, did not achieve their potential at those institutions.

Each year, students from up to thirty-five states and twelve countries are represented at Holy Cross College.

Student Activities

Students at Holy Cross College have a variety of choices for social, athletic, and spiritual activities, including Student Government Association, Campus Ministry, and Phi Theta Kappa.

Intramural sports programs include basketball, flag football, lacrosse, soccer, and volleyball and are run by the students. Other activities are dependent on the wants and interests of the students. Due to the relatively small enrollment, Holy Cross College does not have an intercollegiate athletic program. Enrolled Holy Cross students are entitled to participate in the recognized athletic department club sports at the University of Notre Dame and intramural athletics at Saint Mary's College.

Holy Cross College students have the privilege of using certain athletic and recreational facilities on an individual basis at the University of Notre Dame, such as the Rolfs Aquatic Center, the Joyce Athletic and Convocation Center, swimming pools, and tennis courts. These facilities have racquetball and squash courts, weight-training and workout rooms, and basketball courts. Holy Cross students also have access to Notre Dame football season tickets.

Holy Cross College students are invited to participate in the University Bands Program at Notre Dame. A variety of ensembles are available, including the Notre Dame Marching Band, Concert Band, Varsity Band, Jazz Band, Woodwind Ensemble, and Brass Ensemble.

Facilities and Resources

In 1995, Holy Cross College completed construction of the Vincent Atrium and Classroom Building, which contains laboratories for science and art, a technology center, faculty offices, general classrooms, a learning center, a greenhouse, and student social space. It was part of an expansion project that also enlarged the library and renovated and expanded the Driscoll Auditorium and Classroom Building. The project more than doubled the academic facilities available on campus.

Construction of a second major academic building was completed in 2001. The addition includes six classrooms, a science lab and prep room, student lounge, faculty offices, and conference rooms.

In 1997, Holy Cross College opened its first residence hall for men and women. The facility includes a full-service dining room, lounge areas, and a chapel. A second residence hall was opened in 1998, and a third opened in 1999. Two 12-unit student apartment buildings, South Hall and Pulte Hall, opened in 2000 and 2003, respectively, and contain spacious 4-person suites with two bedrooms, two baths, a kitchen, and a living room.

In addition to the College's library facility, Holy Cross College students may use the Hesburgh Library at the University of Notre Dame and the Cushwa-Leighton Library at Saint Mary's College. Admittance to either of these library facilities may be gained by presenting a valid Holy Cross College ID card.

Location

Holy Cross College is located just north of the city limits of South Bend, Indiana. The College is adjacent to the campuses of the University of Notre Dame and Saint Mary's College. The proximity of Holy Cross College to the University of Notre Dame and Saint Mary's College has the advantage of providing Holy Cross students with an association with two major Catholic centers of learning. Holy Cross College is an autonomous institution and is not an adjunct to either institution. Holy Cross students who wish to transfer to these particular institutions must meet the same transfer academic requirements as any transfer student seeking admission. Many Holy Cross students have successfully transferred to the University of Notre Dame and Saint Mary's College.

Admission Requirements

The entering freshman is normally expected to have successfully completed a college-preparatory high school program of at least 16 academic units. One unit is equivalent to a full year of study in a college-preparatory subject. The following are recommended: 4 units of English (composition and literature), 3 units of college-preparatory mathematics, 2 units of history or social science, and 1 unit of laboratory science. The remaining 6 units should also be college-preparatory courses.

A student who has the General Educational Development (GED) certificate may be considered for admission to Holy Cross College. In addition to GED scores and certificate, an official transcript of completed high school course work is required.

Application and Information

Application forms and/or requests for additional information should be directed to the address below.

Office of Admissions
Holy Cross College
P.O. Box 308
Notre Dame, Indiana 46556

Telephone: 574-239-8400
Fax: 574-239-8323
E-mail: admissions@hcc-nd.edu
World Wide Web: http://www.hcc-nd.edu

The Vincent Atrium and Classroom Building.

INDIANA BUSINESS COLLEGE
INDIANAPOLIS, INDIANA

INDIANA BUSINESS COLLEGE

The College and Its Mission

Indiana Business College was founded in 1902 to serve the specific education and career needs and interests of students planning to enter the business community. Indiana Business College consists of ten campuses at convenient locations across the state. Full- and part-time programs as well as day and evening classes are available at all locations. The philosophy behind the curriculum at the College is one of individual attention, allowing for flexibility and higher achievement in the classroom. The career-oriented emphasis enables course work to be highly specialized. Indiana Business College has a commitment to providing career-related education; students are trained by practical application and hands-on experience. This commitment, coupled with a reputation for offering a high-quality education, contributes to the employment opportunities for graduates. The College offers a continuous placement assistance service to its graduates and is continually updating the curriculum to meet the demands of today's business world. Indiana Business College is accredited by the Accrediting Council for Independent Colleges and Schools and is regulated by the Indiana Commission on Proprietary Education. The medical assisting programs at the Evansville, Fort Wayne, Medical (Indianapolis), and Terre Haute campuses are accredited by the Commission on Accreditation of Allied Health Education Programs on the recommendation of the Committee on Accreditation for Medical Assistant Education.

Academic Programs

Indiana Business College offers Associate of Applied Science degrees in accounting, administrative assistant studies, business administration, business administration/network technology, business and information technology, medical assisting, health claims examiner studies, medical records technology, fashion merchandising, therapeutic massage and bodyworks, Cisco Network Associate studies, and organizational management.

Indiana Business College also offers diplomas in the areas of accounting assistant studies, medical coding specialist studies, medical office assistant studies, medical transcription, and office assistant studies.

Certificates are available in computer network technician studies and therapeutic massage practitioner studies.

Indiana Business College operates throughout the calendar year; classes begin quarterly in January, April, June, and September. To be awarded a degree, diploma, or certificate, students must maintain a minimum cumulative GPA of 2.0 (on a 4.0 scale).

The computer programs at Indiana Business College include courses in Cisco network administration, A+ computer technology, and Network+. The College has some of the state's top information technology programs available, including MCSE and MCSA. IBC is an associate member of CompTIA, offering A+ and Network+ certifications. The College is also a Microsoft IT Academy and one of the only Transcender Training partners in Indianapolis offering on-site testing for all IT certification programs.

The organizational management degree is designed to prepare individuals for careers in project management, where sound business principles and state-of-the-art computer skills are essential for success in today's high-speed, high-technology marketplace. Topics include project integration, human and material resource allocation, risk analysis, cost engineering, procurement management, information technology topics, and e-business. Project managers are employed in every aspect of the business community.

The accounting programs offered at Indiana Business College include courses in intermediate and cost accounting, income tax, and payroll. Both diploma and Associate of Applied Science degree accounting programs incorporate the courses necessary to prepare students for excellent positions in private business, public accounting, and departments within the government.

The Associate of Applied Science degree program in business administration includes courses in the areas of computers, accounting, marketing, management, and sales. This program helps students to develop the creativity and the supervisory skills needed for managerial positions.

Indiana Business College's administrative support programs include administrative assistant studies and office assistant studies. These programs provide students with the necessary foundation in keyboarding, information processing, and computer technology.

The Associate of Applied Science degree program in fashion merchandising prepares the graduate for a career in the fashion industry. Combining business classes with fashion studies prepares the student to succeed in this competitive field. Included in this curriculum are courses such as textiles, display and design, marketing, and apparel merchandising.

Indiana Business College's medical programs include health claims examiner studies, medical assistant studies, medical records technology, medical coding specialist studies, medical office assistant studies, medical transcription, and therapeutic massage studies. The medical assistant studies degree program provides the student with skills to be competent in both front and back office procedures. The medical assistant may assist the physician in minor surgery, perform laboratory tests, assess vital signs, administer medication, operate an EKG machine, or perform other therapeutic modalities prescribed by the physician. Programs in medical coding specialist studies and medical records technology provide training to analyze medical records, to assign codes to index diagnoses and procedures, and to provide information for reimbursement purposes. Courses in medical science, medical terminology, medical office administration, and medical insurance processing are offered to help students meet the needs of the industry. The therapeutic massage and bodyworks studies program at Indiana Business College allows graduates to possess the necessary skills for applications and treatment goals of muscular and general relaxation, stress reduction, pain management, recovery from injury, health promotion, education, and body awareness. The successful practitioner must therefore be proficient at more than a simple massage; he or she must understand the body and its functions, master a variety of techniques, and hone such skills as client assessment, communication, and self-evaluation.

Costs

For 2003–04 the cost per credit hour ranged from $146 to $210. Tuition varies according to the program chosen and does not include books or fees.

Financial Aid

Many Indiana Business College students qualify for some form of financial aid. The College participates in the Federal Pell Grant, Federal Supplemental Educational Opportunity Grant, Federal Stafford Student Loan, Federal PLUS programs, the Federal Work-Study Program, the Twenty-first Century Scholars Program, and state grants. Students' eligibility to participate in these programs is contingent upon demonstration of financial need. In addition, the College offers scholarships to both graduating high school seniors and nontraditional students.

Financial planning and financial aid personnel are available to assist the student in the application process.

Students are also encouraged to investigate possibilities for private scholarships.

Faculty

The faculty at Indiana Business College is composed of dedicated professionals who are committed to giving personal attention to every student. The selection of instructors is based not only on their academic credentials, professional training, and business experience, but also on their capacity to develop students' abilities in preparation for the world of work.

Student Body Profile

The student body consists of approximately 3,500 students. Fifty percent of the students are between 19 and 24 years old, and roughly 27 percent are between 25 and 34 years old.

Student Activities

Students may join independent student groups and student councils. Coordinating activities with an executive director or department head, student groups organize a variety of on-campus and off-campus events. Professional organizations are also available for student participation. Intramural sports and group functions vary by campus.

Facilities and Resources

Indiana Business College offers resource centers and computer labs for its students. These facilities provide access to up-to-date information and programs.

Career Planning/Placement Offices The Career Services Office at Indiana Business College assists graduates in securing employment. The Career Services Office is a lifetime service to all alumni and posts job openings for current students and graduates. Students are assisted in all aspects of the job search through career development classes focusing on goal setting, resumes, interviewing, and networking.

Location

Situated in the heart of Indianapolis, the main campus of Indiana Business College houses the Corporate Office for all branches of the College. The excitement of urban living, combined with the cultural and historical sites, makes Indiana Business College's location ideal. Indianapolis' Children's Museum, Indiana Repertory Theater, and White River Park Zoo provide a variety of educational and recreational activities. The College is within walking distance of downtown shopping centers and major sports centers, such as Circle Centre Mall, Conseco Field House, and the RCA Dome. It is also readily accessible from many different transportation systems.

In addition to the main campus and the medical campus, both located in Indianapolis, Indiana Business College has campuses in Anderson, Columbus, Evansville, Fort Wayne, Lafayette, Marion, Muncie, and Terre Haute.

Students may earn credits toward the completion of a program at more than one location. The convenience of having ten locations significantly lessens the cost of an education by eliminating additional housing and transportation expenses.

Admission Requirements

Applicants must be high school graduates or have obtained a General Educational Development (GED) certificate to be considered for admission to Indiana Business College. The College reviews each application for admission and bases the admission decision on a personal interview and scores from the Wonderlic Scholastic Level Exam.

The College is open to men and women of any race, faith, or national origin. All students are given equal opportunity to pursue their educational and career goals through the programs offered at Indiana Business College.

Application and Information

All applications must be accompanied by a $30 application fee. High school transcripts are requested directly from the student's school by Indiana Business College. Applicants are notified within two weeks of the completion of all application requirements.

All inquiries should be directed to:

Admissions Office
Indiana Business College
550 East Washington Street
Indianapolis, Indiana 46204

Telephone: 800-IBC-GRAD (toll-free)
Fax: 317-264-5650
World Wide Web: http://www.ibcschools.edu

INTERNATIONAL COLLEGE OF HOSPITALITY MANAGEMENT, CÉSAR RITZ

SUFFIELD, CONNECTICUT

The College and Its Mission

The International College of Hospitality Management *César Ritz* (ICHM), located in the town of Suffield in northwest Connecticut, is the only Swiss college of hospitality management in the U.S. It is one of four internationally acclaimed HOTELCONSULT *César Ritz* colleges, with affiliate campuses in Switzerland and Australia. The mission of ICHM is to prepare students for successful careers in the hospitality industry by combining the renowned Swiss art of hotel management with American business techniques.

With a maximum of 120 students on a 56-acre residential campus set among woods and rolling lawns, the College occupies a former seminary, St. Alphonsus College. Hospitality faculty members have extensive professional experience and instruct alongside liberal studies teachers of the highest caliber. Students receive intensive course training over four 11-week terms. This training is reinforced by a paid internship in prestigious hotels of the U.S.

The internship is an essential component in the program at ICHM. The resulting combination of professional, academic, and practical training provides graduates with a firm base for managing their careers. The internship also supplies ICHM students with a competitive edge in finding employment when they leave the College. The College's Director of Internships and Placements helps guide students in their career development, and HOTELCONSULT has a network of 10,000 alumni to give yet further guidance. In addition, the College organizes career fairs twice each year. The College has a 100 percent placement rate, a record of which it is very proud.

ICHM students are encouraged to actively participate in the social and recreational life of the College, in much the same way that they assume significant responsibilities in managing their academic progress and professional comportment. Because students are very involved in many aspects of College life, a great sense of community has developed at ICHM.

Academic Programs

Associate of Science Degree in Hospitality Management The first year of the program consists of two 11-week terms, followed by a six-month (800-hour) internship. The first two terms of study are very hands-on, with courses based in practical skills and hotel industry norms. The internship that follows is carefully structured and supervised and enhances the concepts previously introduced in the classroom.

In their second academic year, students develop skills in business planning and strategy, and learn about control procedures and staff management. The second academic year is followed by an optional 800-hour internship, with an option to prolong the internship contract by six or twelve months. Studying abroad is available to those qualifying students who want to take terms three and four in ICHM's affiliate campuses in Switzerland or Australia. (More information on study abroad is in the Off-Campus Programs section.)

Certificate in Hospitality Management Candidates holding a bachelor's degree in a different discipline or those with professional hospitality experience may choose to enroll in the certificate program in hospitality management. This one-year program consists of two 11-week terms followed by an internship of at least 800 hours. It is designed to provide graduates with the skills and experience necessary to enter the hospitality industry with confidence.

Special Program Services Career fairs are held twice each year, wherein students and alumni are selected for 800-hour paid internships and positions of longer duration. The fairs are attended by recruiters from approximately thirty leading hotel and resort properties, typically five-star hospitality establishments. Many students receive multiple internship offers. In addition, individual hotel and resort properties often recruit directly on campus.

Transfer Arrangements Course-credit transfers must be comparable to ICHM courses and must have been awarded by an accredited institution. The student must have earned a minimum C grade (2.0 GPA) for transfer credits to be considered. This information must be provided on official sealed transcripts mailed directly to ICHM's Office of Admissions.

Off-Campus Programs

Students with qualifying grades may wish to take their second year of studies at either the campus on Lake Geneva, Switzerland or at the campus in Sydney, Australia. The Switzerland option will enable students to gain a Swiss Diploma in Hospitality Management. Students electing to go to Sydney will receive an Australian Diploma in Hospitality Management. In addition, all students who successfully complete their program, having spent their first year of studies at ICHM, will receive an American Associate of Science degree. Students who wish to complete their studies in Switzerland or Australia must give written advice to the ICHM Dean of Academic Affairs before the end of the first term of their first year.

Credit for Nontraditional Learning Experiences

Credit may be awarded for prior professional experience in the hospitality industry. For details, applicants should consult the Registrar.

Costs

Expenses for the 2003–04 academic year included tuition of $14,900 and room and board of $4675. Each student is required to purchase books, uniforms, and supplies.

Financial Aid

To help eligible students meet their educational expense, the College offers financial assistance programs such as scholarships, grants, low-interest loans, and part-time employment opportunities. The College's Financial Aid Officer is happy to work with families on an individual basis to help them plan the cost of education.

Faculty

The student-faculty ratio at the College is 15:1. All full-time faculty members have student advising responsibilities and are involved in the administration of the College. The faculty members have a wide range of international hospitality experience, a diversity that supports the College's mission of offering students an intellectually challenging education in a multicultural environment.

Student Body Profile

The College attracts students from the United States and nearly thirty different countries each year, representing many different cultures. Most students are in their early twenties and, for many, English is a second language. Some are seeking a change of career, others have already obtained advanced qualifications in a different discipline, and all are drawn to the dynamics of international hospitality.

Student Activities

The Student Committee organizes sports, activities, theme nights, and excursions and serves as a representative of all students. Officers of the Student Committee are elected by a democratic vote and arrange meetings and activities with the Coordinator of Student Services. In addition, within the College is a voluntary organization called the Ritz Guild. Its members plan and coordinate events to benefit the local community, often with the help of civic organizations such as the Lions Club and the House of Bread. Each year, Ritz Guild members are given official recognition for their contributions. The College maintains several vans for student activities around the region.

Facilities and Resources

In 2003, the College moved from rural Washington, Connecticut, to a larger, more convenient campus in Suffield, Connecticut. The new location offers an array of activities and amenities to ICHM students.

The meal plan is provided by ICHM's sister school, the Connecticut Culinary Institute, with which it shares a campus. Students can enjoy an excellent regulation-size gymnasium, and a modern exercise facility. There are also sports fields and hiking trails on campus. The area has many fine theaters, music venues, restaurants, clubs, and dancing. There are also many well-regarded museums and historic sites within a short distance.

ICHM's spacious library offers more than 10,000 volumes plus numerous industry periodicals and videotapes. The College's computer labs are all connected to broadband Internet services, and the entire building is a wireless broadband environment as well.

Location

The College is situated on 56 wooded acres in Suffield, Connecticut, a charming New England town. Next door to the campus is Six Flags New England Amusement Park, with a new $140-million water park. The 135,000-square-foot building is located minutes from Springfield, Massachusetts, and Hartford, Connecticut. It is a short drive to Boston and New York City and only 10 minutes from Bradley International Airport.

Admission Requirements

The College requires U.S. applicants to submit a completed application form, $25 application fee, official high school transcripts or GED scores, and two letters of recommendation. SAT I scores are not required but are highly recommended. Students for whom English is not the first language are required to show proof of English competency. The College seeks applications from both U.S. and international citizens and welcomes motivated students who have a desire to succeed in international hospitality management. The cultural mix of ICHM benefits students as they move towards their chosen profession. Because of the unique nature of the College and its program, applicants are strongly encouraged to schedule an on-campus interview. Prospective students may take advantage of the Visitor Information Program (VIP), wherein they can stay on campus for up to two nights and participate in classes and campus activities. Applicants should contact the Office of Admissions for details.

Application and Information

The College accepts applications throughout the year for its August, November, February, and April starting dates. Applicants are notified of their admission status shortly after their forms are received, usually within two weeks. For application materials and additional information, students should contact:

Office of Admissions
International College of Hospitality Management
1760 Mapleton Avenue
Suffield, Connecticut 06078

Telephone: 860-668-3515
Fax: 860-668-7369
E-mail: admissions@ichm.edu
World Wide Web: http://www.ichm.edu

The elegant grounds of the International College of Hospitality Management, César Ritz.

JOHNSON COLLEGE
SCRANTON, PENNSYLVANIA

The College and Its Mission

Johnson College, a two-year technical college, was founded by Orlando S. Johnson, a wealthy coal baron in the Scranton area who died in 1912. Mr. Johnson left the bulk of his estate to establish and maintain a trade school, and his purpose became the mission of the College: to be an institution "where young men and women can be taught useful arts and trades that may enable them to make an honorable living and become contributing members of society."

A board of directors was created and a 65-acre tract in Scranton known as the William H. Richmond estate was selected as the site for the new enterprise. Opening in 1918, the school admitted young men and women who had completed a minimum of eight years of school and were at least 14 years old.

In 1964, the school became a postsecondary institution, requiring applicants to be high school graduates or to have equivalency certificates. The name of the institution changed from the Johnson Trade School to the Johnson School of Technology in 1966. The school was incorporated as a nonprofit corporation in 1967, and in 1968 it became licensed by the Commonwealth of Pennsylvania Bureau of Private Trade Schools. Approval to award an Associate in Specialized Technology degree came in 1974, with accreditation by the National Association of Trade and Technical Schools (NATTS) following in 1979. In 1985, the school changed its name to Johnson Technical Institute, and the three-year Associate in Specialized Technology degree programs were changed to two-year programs in 1987.

Responding to the continuing technological changes in society, the board, administration, faculty and staff members, and students conducted an intense two-year self-study, beginning in 1994, to assess the institution's strengths and weaknesses. The study led to a formal application to the Commission on Higher Education for two-year college status. The Pennsylvania Department of Education approved the application of Johnson Technical Institute as a two-year college in 1997. The graduating class of 1998 was the first class to receive either an Associate in Applied Science (A.A.S.) degree or an Associate in Science (A.S.) degree.

Continuing the expansion of technology programs, the College began offering veterinary science technology in 1994. Clinical classes were held off campus until the completion of a 6,500-square-foot Science Center on campus. The program received full accreditation from the American Veterinary Medical Association (AVMA) for the fall semester of 2000. In 1995, electromechanical technology was added to the curriculum, and the Bureau of Private Licensed Schools approved the diesel truck technology program in November 1996. A computer information technology program, specializing in enterprise computer networking, was approved in 2000, and a curriculum in radiographic technology received approval in 2002.

Today, approximately 400 students pursue careers in twelve different technical and clinical programs. The College has eight buildings on campus, including a library, a bookstore, a gymnasium, classrooms, shops, laboratories, administrative offices, and a student apartment complex for on-campus living.

Over the years, the College has served the region by providing a technical education program, and it continually evaluates its program to meet the technological needs of society. This evaluation process is assisted by the Program Advisory Committees of each program area, consisting of regional business and community leaders who meet several times during the year to advise the College on curriculum content, length of programs, and current materials and equipment. They also review placement and retention statistics. The College has maintained the initial intent of Mr. Johnson with a professional and dedicated staff to ensure up-to-date training that prepares graduates to readily step into responsible positions in business and industry.

The current student count is approximately 400, made up of about 60 percent men and 40 percent women. The students spend 70 percent of their time in technological programs and the remainder in general education classes. The College has extensive externships with a variety of businesses and professional organizations. One of the important success stories of Johnson College is its career placement rate. For the last reported year, 97 percent of the graduating class secured positions within twelve months of graduation (based on data gathered from the 125 graduates of the class of 2001).

Academic Programs

Johnson College offers twelve technical and clinical programs, awarding Associate in Applied Science and Associate in Science degrees.

The technology programs include architectural drafting and design, automotive technology, biomedical equipment technology, carpentry and cabinetmaking, diesel truck technology, electromechanical technology, electronic technology, machine tool technology, and tool and diemaking technology.

The science programs include computer information technology, radiographic technology, and veterinary science technology.

Johnson College is accredited by the Accrediting Commission of Career Schools and Colleges of Technology (ACCSCT), and the veterinary science technology program is accredited by the American Veterinary Medical Association (AVMA). The Pennsylvania Department of Education and the State Board of Education have approved Johnson College as a two-year college.

Transfer Arrangements The College maintains articulation agreements with the State University of New York Institute of Technology at Utica/Rome for the following programs: architectural drafting and design technology, biomedical equipment technology, and electronic technology.

Costs

The tuition for full-time attendance for 2004–05 (12 to 24 credit hours) is $5450 per semester for all programs. Books and supplies are approximately $1500 per school year; however, this amount varies by program. Program fees vary by department. On-campus housing is available in double-occupancy apartments at a rate of $300 per month per student. Students should consult the current College catalog for additional and recent financial information.

Financial Aid

Johnson College provides financial support through the Financial Aid Office, with several programs and opportunities available for students from all income categories. Scholarships are available and are awarded on the basis of merit, academic performance, and extracurricular involvement. The College also participates in the following federally sponsored programs: Federal Pell Grants, Federal Supplemental Educational Opportunity Grants (FSEOG), Federal PLUS loans, and Federal Stafford Student Loans. Other opportunities include employment programs and alternative loans at the College and state and College grants. For consideration for any financial assistance program, students must complete the Free Application for Federal Student Aid (FAFSA). In addition, the College offers $25,000 in merit scholarships for those who are eligible.

Faculty

There are 26 faculty members at the College, and the student-faculty ratio is 17:1. Counseling is available for academic, personal, and vocational issues. The College maintains strong interpersonal relationships among its students and faculty and staff members.

Student Activities

There are a variety of activities available for students on campus, including a Student Government Association, which consists of a student from each technical, trade, and clinical program. The Social Force Club, funded by Act 101, is a community service organization that involves students in on- and off-campus activities, including field trips. Students participate in an active intramural sports program, social functions, holiday parties, talent shows, clubs, and other events and functions.

Facilities and Resources

The Library Resource Center at the College is a technology-based library and is a participating member of the Northeastern Pennsylvania Library Network Consortium. Located in the Moffat Building, the collection consists of more than 4,000 volumes of books and more than 100 current periodical subscriptions. The library complements the curriculum of the academic and technical, trade, and clinical programs. This unique collection offers students the resources necessary to research issues that pertain to their fields of study and for which students should keep abreast of new technological developments. The library also offers online computer services and CD-ROM searching. A professionally staffed cafeteria is available for breakfast, lunch, and snacks. The Moffat Building contains two fitness centers that offer a variety of exercise equipment. A campus bookstore is available for student supplies, clothing items, and a variety of other items. Limited on-campus housing is available in fully furnished two-story apartment-style units.

Location

Johnson College is conveniently located in Scranton, Pennsylvania, at Exit 190 on Interstate 81. Highway exit ramps clearly indicate the location of the campus. The College is just under 2 hours from New York City and Philadelphia. The campus is minutes from great skiing and other recreational activities, along with a variety of sports, arts, music, cultural, and historical events at places like Lackawanna County Stadium (home of the Triple-A Red Barons baseball team), Montage Amphitheater, and the Steamtown National Park and Mall.

Admission Requirements

Johnson College accepts qualified students regardless of race, religion, handicap, or national origin, and admissions are on a rolling basis. The technical core of each program begins in the fall semester; however, students may enroll in general education courses at any time. Applicants should be secondary school seniors, secondary school graduates, or recipients of a secondary school equivalency certificate. Successful completion of one year of algebra is required for all programs. Veterinary science and radiographic technology applicants must have successfully completed one unit of biology and chemistry (a grade of C or better is considered successful completion). To complete the radiographic technology program in two years, including summers, entering students are required to have successfully completed one unit of chemistry or biology with a grade of C or better and a minimum of one year of algebra. Each applicant is encouraged to arrange for a campus visit and a personal interview with an admissions representative, and appointments may be made for meeting with appropriate faculty members and current students.

Application and Information

Applications may be submitted in person, by mail, or online at the Web site listed below. Accompanying information must include an official secondary school or equivalency transcript, satisfactory SAT or ACT test scores, one letter of recommendation, and a $30 nonrefundable processing fee. Applicants for veterinary science technology and radiographic technology are required to submit a questionnaire and observation hours as part of the application process. The College notifies prospective candidates of a decision within thirty days following the completion of the application procedures.

Additional information may be obtained by contacting:

Office of Admissions
Johnson College
3427 North Main Avenue
Scranton, Pennsylvania 18508
Telephone: 800-293-9675 (toll-free)
World Wide Web: http://www.johnson.edu

KEYSTONE COLLEGE
LA PLUME, PENNSYLVANIA

The College and Its Mission

Keystone College was founded in 1868 as Keystone Academy in Factoryville, Pennsylvania. Initially opened as the only high school between Binghamton, New York, and Scranton, Pennsylvania, Keystone flourished as a secondary school for more than sixty-five years. Rechartered as Scranton-Keystone Junior College in 1934 and then Keystone Junior College in 1944, the College served as one of the premier two-year institutions in the Northeast until 1995. In this year the school was again renamed, as Keystone College, and began its tenure as an "ideal" four-year degree-granting college. Keystone College has a current enrollment of 1,500, including students from fourteen states and seven other countries. Students can choose from twelve different four-year majors and more than twenty-five different two-year degree and certificate programs.

Academic Programs

Associate Degree Programs Associate of Applied Science degrees are offered in accounting, culinary arts, hotel and restaurant management, and information technology. The Associate in Fine Arts is offered in art. The Associate in Arts is offered in allied health with emphasis in nursing, occupational therapy, physical therapy, and radiological technology/diagnostic imaging; biological science with emphasis in biochemistry, biology, premedicine, and pre–pharmacy studies; business administration; communications; computer information systems; criminal justice; environmental studies; forestry/resource management; human resource management; human services; landscape architecture; liberal studies; liberal studies–education emphasis; sport and recreation management; and wildlife biology. The Associate in Science is offered in early childhood education. In addition, there are one-year programs in computer information systems, forestry technology, information technology, Microsoft Certified Systems Administrator, Microsoft Certified Systems Engineer, and pre–major studies (undeclared major).

Bachelor's Degree Programs The Bachelor of Arts degree is offered in humanities, professional studies–communication arts, and visual art. The Bachelor of Science degree is offered in accounting, business, business administration–human resource management, criminal justice administration, early childhood education, elementary education, professional studies–environmental resource management, professional studies–information technology, professional studies–natural sciences with emphasis in forensic biology and general biology, professional studies–sport and recreation management, and teaching–art education (K–12).

Postbaccalaureate certification is available in elementary education, early childhood education, and teaching–art education (K–12).

The College runs on a two-semester schedule (fall and spring) and has night and weekend classes available. The number of credit hours required to earn a degree is dependent on the field of study chosen, and students must have attained a minimum cumulative GPA of 2.0. Every student must complete a set of general core curriculum requirements as well as the courses specific to his or her major course of study. All students are required to complete one internship or co-op before graduation, depending on the course of study.

Students have the opportunity to participate in both the Army and Navy ROTC programs in conjunction with other local participating institutions. There are opportunities for double majors as well as minors in various fields of study.

Off-Campus Programs

The College maintains articulation agreements with Thomas Jefferson University and College Misericordia for students enrolling in the allied health curriculums. Students enrolled in the environmental programs may opt to pursue Keystone's articulation with State University of New York College of Environmental Science and Forestry (SUNY-ESF) in Syracuse. Other transfer opportunities exist with Marywood University, University of Scranton, Bloomsburg University, Wilkes University, Temple University, University of the Arts, Parson's School of Design, Penn State University, and many others.

Costs

Tuition and fees for Keystone College for the 2003–04 year were $6975 per semester, while room and board costs averaged $3700 per semester. Books and general supplies averaged $500 per semester and vary according to major.

Financial Aid

The Financial Aid Office provides adequate funds and resources to meet the financial needs of students from all income categories. Scholarships are awarded based on merit, academic performance, and extracurricular involvement. Keystone College also participates in the following federally sponsored programs: Federal Perkins Loan, Federal Pell Grant, Federal Supplemental Educational Opportunity Grant (FSEOG), Federal PLUS Loan, and Federal Stafford Student Loan. The College also offers college employment programs to students and alternative loans as well as state grants and Keystone grants. In order to be considered for financial aid, students must complete the Free Application for Federal Student Aid (FAFSA).

Faculty

There are 59 full-time professors and 151 part-time adjunct faculty members. The student-faculty ratio is 10:1, and the average class size is 15 students. Counseling is available for academic, personal, and vocational issues. Keystone College is supported by strong interpersonal relationships among its students and faculty and staff members. All faculty members post regular office hours and are generally available outside of these hours.

Student Activities

Student Senate is the central governing body of all student government organizations on the campus. It serves as the liaison between the student body and the College administration. Members of Student Senate are chosen by their peers and are responsible for improving and maintaining student life both on and off campus. Students may choose from more than twenty-five different clubs and organizations, including those with academic, service-oriented, and social interests.

Facilities and Resources

The Harry K. Miller Library is available on campus to all students. This facility offers standard print and online research opportunities. The Hibbard Campus Center is the setting for the student cafeteria, a full-service restaurant, and The Chef's Table (a student-run restaurant), as well as a U.S. post office, a print shop, a student-run radio station, and reception halls. The campus also includes an art gallery, a celestial observatory, and the Poinsard Greenhouse. Keystone College also serves as the home for the Urban Forestry Center, Willary Water Discovery Center, the Northeast Theatre (TNT), and the Countryside Conservancy.

There are more than 120 computers available on campus for general student use, and both the Internet and campus network can be accessed from all residence halls and most buildings on campus.

Location

Located at the foot of the Endless Mountains in northeastern Pennsylvania, the 270-acre campus is both scenic and historic, with buildings dating back to 1870. Located 13 miles from Scranton, Pennsylvania, the campus offers easy access to major East Coast cities, including New York, Philadelphia, and Baltimore.

Admission Requirements

Keystone accepts qualified students regardless of race, religion, handicap, or national origin, and admissions are on a rolling basis. Admission is based on prior academic performance and the ability of the applicant to profit from and contribute to the academic, interpersonal, and extracurricular life of the College. Keystone considers applicants who meet the following criteria: graduation from an approved secondary school or the equivalent (with official transcripts), satisfactory scores on the SAT or ACT (the SAT is preferred but is not required in all circumstances), one letter of recommendation, and evidence of potential for successful college achievement. All students are strongly encouraged to visit the campus for a personal interview with the admissions staff and a member of the faculty from the student's area of interest. Students applying to the art and teaching–art education programs are required to participate in a portfolio interview.

Transfer students in good academic and financial standing at their current institution are also encouraged to apply to Keystone. Transfer students should contact the Office of Admissions and may be required to submit either high school transcripts or transcripts from each college attended, or both.

Admissions decisions are made within two weeks from the day all required materials are received in the Office of Admissions.

Application and Information

Students wishing to be considered for admission must submit an application and a $25 processing fee, along with official high school transcripts, college transcripts (if applicable), a letter of recommendation from someone other than a friend or relative, and scores from either the SAT or ACT (submitted directly to the Office of Admissions; Keystone's CEEB code numbers are 2351 for the SAT, 2602 for the ACT).

Applications and any additional information about Keystone College may be obtained by contacting:

Office of Admissions
Keystone College
One College Green
La Plume, Pennsylvania 18440
Telephone: 570-945-5141
          800-824-2764 Option 1 (toll-free)
E-mail: admissions@keystone.edu
World Wide Web: http://www.keystone.edu

Students on the campus of Keystone College.

LANDMARK COLLEGE
PUTNEY, VERMONT

The College and Its Mission

Landmark College is the only accredited college in the country designed exclusively for students of average to superior intellectual potential with dyslexia, attention deficit hyperactivity disorder (AD/HD), or specific learning disabilities. Life-changing experiences are commonplace at Landmark College. Simply put, Landmark College, better than any other place on earth, knows how to serve students who learn differently.

Landmark's beautiful campus offers all the resources students might expect at a high-quality higher education institution, including a new athletics center, a student center, a dining facility, a café, residence halls, and an academic resource center (library). The College has also invested substantially in technology and offers a wireless network in all of its classrooms, along with LAN, telephone, and cable connections in all the residence rooms. Entering students are expected to bring a notebook computer, as these are used in nearly every class session. The College's programs extensively integrate assistive technologies, such as Dragon Naturally Speaking and Kurzweil text-to-speech software.

Landmark's faculty and staff members make it unique. The College's more than 100 full-time faculty members are all highly experienced in serving students with learning disabilities and attention deficit disorders. More than 100 staff members provide an array of support services that are unusually comprehensive for a student population of less than 400 students.

Academic Programs

Offering an associate degree in general studies, Landmark College builds strong literacy, organizational, study, and other skills—positioning students to successfully pursue a baccalaureate or advanced degree and to be successful in their professional careers. More than 90 percent of Landmark College graduates go on to a four-year college or university.

With more than 100 faculty members and less than 400 students, Landmark College's small classes and personalized instruction provide a uniquely challenging, yet supportive, academic program. At Landmark College, students learn how to learn.

The College's diverse curriculum includes English, communications, the humanities, math, science, foreign language, theater, video, music, art, physical education, and other classes taught in a multimodal, multimedia environment that is highly interactive. There is no "back of the room" in a Landmark College classroom, and all students participate in class discussions, while building strong academic skills.

Landmark College has articulation agreements with a number of other colleges. These colleges have agreed to admit Landmark College graduates as juniors and transfer all of their credits if they attain a specific grade point average on graduation from Landmark.

Through a carefully sequenced, integrated curriculum, students develop the confidence and independence needed to meet the demands of college work. When students graduate with an associate degree from Landmark College, they are ready to succeed in a four-year college, a technical or professional program, or the workforce.

Off-Campus Programs

The Landmark Study Abroad Program has developed programs with students' diverse learning styles in mind. Landmark College's faculty members design and teach experiential courses in their specific disciplines that fulfill Landmark core requirements, while helping students gain confidence and independence in new academic structures. College faculty members accompany students abroad, providing them with the Landmark College academic experience in an international setting. The College offers summer credit programs in England, Greece, India, Ireland, Italy, and Spain and a semester abroad program in London, England.

Costs

Landmark College's tuition for the 2002–03 academic year was $34,000. Room and board costs were $5500. Single rooms or suites were available at an added cost of between $1000 and $1500. A guarantee fee (contingency deposit) of $300 was required.

Since admission to Landmark College requires a medical diagnosis of a learning disability or attention deficit disorder, in most cases all of the costs of a Landmark College education are tax deductible as a medical expense. For more information, students should consult a tax attorney.

Financial Aid

Landmark College participates in all major federal and state financial aid programs, including the Federal Pell Grant, Federal Family Education Loans, and work-study. Institutional scholarships are available. To apply for financial assistance, students should submit the Free Application for Federal Student Aid (FAFSA), the Landmark College Financial Aid Application, and federal tax returns.

Faculty

With the College's low student-faculty ratio, Landmark College faculty members are unusually accessible to students. There are more than 100 full-time faculty members who provide classroom teaching, professional advising, and office hours to students. In addition, faculty members provide individualized instruction throughout the day and into the evening at one of three learning centers: the Coursework Support Center, the Reading and Study Skills Center, and the Writing Center. Landmark College does not typically employ adjunct faculty members or student teaching assistants. Regular faculty members deliver all instruction. Their depth of experience in serving students with learning differences ensures that students receive the individualized education that is most appropriate to their learning style.

Student Body Profile

Landmark College students come from around the country and from an average of twelve other countries annually. Approximately two thirds of the student body is men. Ninety percent of all students are residential students living on campus in one of seven residence halls. Representatives of multicultural groups make up approximately 10 percent of Landmark College students.

Student Activities

Landmark College closely integrates academics and student life. Academic deans, advisers, and faculty members work closely with student life deans and directors to provide a comprehensive program that serves the whole student. The goal is not simply to support academic success, but also to guide and challenge students in their personal and social development. Each student has access to a comprehensive support team, including an academic adviser, classroom instructors, a resident dean, an extensive program of athletics, adventure education, and activities; a highly trained, experienced counseling department; and an alcohol and other drug counselor.

For a college its size, Landmark College has an extraordinary range of student-development resources, providing general educational, social, and recreational opportunities. Clubs at Landmark are active. In the past, they have included the Running Club, Monday Night Art, the Multicultural Awareness Club, the Gay/Lesbian/Bisexual/Transgender Alliance, the Mountain Biking Club, the Jazz Ensemble, *Impressions Literary Magazine,* the Coffee House Writers Group, the International Club, the Small Business Management Club, Choral Singing, the Weight Lifting Group, and the Spirituality Group.

Landmark College outdoor programs provide students with a diverse range of outdoor and experiential learning opportunities, including wilderness first-aid training, a ropes course, rock-climbing instruction, an indoor climbing wall, and a full inventory of camping equipment, cross-country skis, snowshoes, and mountain bikes. The College has an active intercollegiate and intramural athletics program that is supported by a well-equipped athletics center that opened in 2001.

Facilities and Resources

Landmark College's residence halls, academic buildings, athletics center, and student center provide a rich array of resources and educational, recreational, and social opportunities. The traditional brick campus, designed by noted architect Edward Durell Stone in the 1960s and entirely renovated beginning in the mid-1980s, includes such amenities as a 400-seat theater, an NCAA regulation basketball court, an exercise pool, three fitness centers, a tennis court, science laboratories, an infirmary, an academic resource center, a bookstore, learning centers, a café, a game room, an indoor climbing wall, and a ropes course.

Location

Located in scenic southeastern Vermont, Landmark College overlooks the Connecticut River Valley, with sweeping views of the mountains and valleys of southern Vermont and northern Massachusetts. Wilderness areas, national forests, ski areas, lakes and streams, and other natural attractions abound. Nearby Brattleboro, Vermont, and the five-college region in the Amherst, Massachusetts, area offer opportunities for culture, the arts, fine dining, and more. Putney is a picturesque Vermont village with several shops, stores, restaurants, a bakery/coffeehouse, a bookstore, and other resources.

The College is located just off Exit 4 on Interstate 91. The most convenient airport is Bradley International Airport in Hartford, Connecticut, about 1½ hours away by car. Metropolitan areas within a 4-hour driving radius include Boston, New York, and Providence.

Admission Requirements

Applicants to Landmark College must have a diagnosis of dyslexia, attention deficit disorder, or other specific learning disability. Diagnostic testing within the last three years is required, along with a diagnosis of a learning disability or AD/HD. One of the Wechsler Scales (WAIS-III or WISC-III) administered within three years of application is required. Scores and subtest scores and their analysis are required to be submitted as well. Alternately, the Woodcock Johnson Cognitive Assessment may be substituted if administered within three years of application. Other criteria for admission include average to superior intellectual potential and high motivation to undertake the program.

The College offers rolling admission and enrolls academic semester students for fall and spring semesters. Students may begin in August (for the fall semester), January (for the spring semester), and June (for the summer session). A six-week skills-development program is offered in the summer. A high school program for students aged 16–18 is also offered in the summer.

Application and Information

For more information, students should contact:

Office of Admissions
Landmark College
P.O. Box 820
Putney, Vermont 05346-0820
Telephone: 802-387-6718
Fax: 802-387-6868
E-mail: admissions@landmark.edu
World Wide Web: http://www.landmark.edu

Learning *Your* Way.

LINCOLN COLLEGE
LINCOLN, ILLINOIS

The College and Its Mission

The mission of Lincoln College is to assist each student in the development and achievement of personal and educational goals and to ensure that its degree recipients are liberally educated and personally and academically prepared to succeed in four-year colleges. Lincoln College is an excellent beginning for those students with a 15–21 ACT score who desire a residential experience in a supportive atmosphere. Lincoln College has a solid reputation for a high percentage/retention of students who transfer to four-year institutions and is the only two-year residential institution in Illinois.

Academic Programs

Associate Degree Programs The majority of students graduate with an **Associate in Arts** degree. This is designed to provide the student with a liberal grounding in the fundamental areas of human knowledge and allow elective selection of courses of general interest or pre-major preparation. This degree is transfer-oriented and fulfills the general education requirements of most four-year colleges and universities nationwide.

A variety of courses and scholarships exist in the performing arts arena. Subjects include dance, music-vocal, music-instrumental, theater, technical theater, visual arts, creative writing, photography, and speech.

Costs

Costs for the 2004–05 academic year include tuition ($13,600), room and board ($5400), and fees ($570). Textbooks and supplies are estimated at $240.

Financial Aid

Financial assistance is generally determined by the need of the applicant, along with the availability of funds from federal, state, institutional, and private sources. Lincoln College considers the needs of each individual applicant in creating the financial package. Scholarships are awarded for academic, fine arts, and athletic excellence. Approximately 90 percent of Lincoln College students receive financial aid.

Faculty

The majority of Lincoln College faculty members are full-time. They are directly involved in instruction, advising, and counseling. Of full-time faculty members, 100 percent hold advanced degrees. The student-faculty ratio is 16:1, and the average class size is 16.

Student Body Profile

Fourteen different states and six other countries are represented through the Lincoln campus student body. Approximately 650 students attend Lincoln College, and 90 percent are classified as residential. The average age is 18.5. Approximately 89 percent of Lincoln College graduates enter immediately into four-year institutions.

Student Activities

Students may participate in a variety of fine arts activities, including music-vocal, music-instrumental, theater, technical theater, dance, photography, ceramics, visual art, and speech.

Sports Varsity sports for women include athletic training/management, basketball, cheerleading, cross-country, golf, soccer, softball, swimming/diving, tennis, and volleyball. Varsity sports for men include athletic training/management, baseball, basketball, cheerleading, cross-country, golf, soccer, swimming/diving, and wrestling.

Facilities and Resources

Lincoln College was established in 1865 and since that time has grown into a 60-acre campus with ten instructional buildings, a library, a swimming pool, a gymnasium, a performing arts center, a student center, two modern computer centers, an art gallery and studio, the Lincoln Museum and Museum of Presidents, administrative offices, a dance studio, a radio station, seven residential halls, a bookstore, a post office, softball and baseball diamonds, a soccer field, several intramural fields, a weight training center, tennis courts, and several supporting physical plant structures.

The original structure of Lincoln College, University Hall, has been in continuous use since 1866. For both its historic ties to Abraham Lincoln and its Italianate Victorian style of architecture, University Hall is listed on the National Registry of Historical Sites and Places.

Lincoln College is well established in its commitment to a supportive environment. Many programs are designed to assist the student both academically and socially. A very personal approach to education includes the residential component, outstanding faculty members and advising, tutorial services, enriched classes, detailed orientation, academic tracking, and a campus-wide commitment to student achievement.

Location

The city of Lincoln (population 16,000) is located in the geographic center of Illinois. The city is the hub of six major urban areas: Springfield, Decatur, Bloomington-Normal, Champaign-Urbana, Pekin, and Peoria. There are two airports within an hour's drive, and daily Amtrak service to Chicago and St. Louis is available. The College is located directly off of Interstate 55.

Admission Requirements

For freshman students, acceptance to Lincoln College is based on high school record, standardized test scores, a personal interview, and letters of recommendation. Students with an ACT composite score of 16 or better may be admitted without restriction. Those with an ACT composite score of 15 or lower may be admitted on provisional status. The admissions committee also considers high school transcript data, and high school counselor recommendations are given a high priority. Students entering Lincoln College provisionally are required to attend and successfully complete the Academic Development Seminar, which occurs one week prior to the fall semester. Students who are transferring to Lincoln College from another college or university may enter the College at the beginning of any semester. If they were on probation at the previous institution and/or maintained less than a 2.0 GPA (on a 4.0 scale), they may be admitted to Lincoln College on provisional status as well. Students for whom English is a second language must take the TOEFL examination and have their scores sent to Lincoln College. Any international student with a minimum score of 480 on the Test of English as a Foreign Language (TOEFL) will be granted admission to Lincoln College. Students whose scores are below 480 may be granted conditional acceptance if space is available.

Application and Information

Applications are accepted contingent on the availability of housing. Freshmen are encouraged to apply before July 1. Individuals interested in Lincoln College should contact:

Lincoln College Admissions
Lincoln College
300 Keokuk
Lincoln, Illinois 62656
Telephone: 217-732-3155
          800-569-0556 (toll-free)
Fax: 217-732-7715
E-mail: srachel@lincolncollege.com
World Wide Web: http://www.lincolncollege.edu

Lincoln College is well established in its commitment to a supportive environment.

LINCOLN COLLEGE AT NORMAL

NORMAL, ILLINOIS

The College and Its Mission

Lincoln College, a private two-year residential college, has been offering students the opportunity to study and succeed in a highly supportive environment since 1865. Accredited by the North Central Association of Colleges and Schools, Lincoln offers Associate in Arts, Associate in Science, Associate in Applied Science, Bachelor of Arts, and Bachelor of Science degrees.

The mission of Lincoln College is to assist each student in the development and achievement of personal and educational goals and to ensure that degree recipients are liberally educated and personally and academically prepared to succeed in four-year colleges and/or careers. The College is an excellent beginning for those students with a 15–21 ACT score who desire a residential experience in a supportive atmosphere.

Lincoln College has a national reputation for academic achievement, and the College's associate degree graduates have continued their studies at more than 200 different four-year colleges and universities in the last decade. Small class sizes, outstanding faculty advisement, free professional tutoring, and a residential experience result in approximately 89 percent of Lincoln College graduates entering immediately into four-year institutions. In addition, the College added new bachelor's degree programs for liberal arts and business management during the 2001–02 academic year.

Lincoln College at Normal opened in 1979 as an extension of Lincoln College in Lincoln, Illinois. Today, Lincoln College at Normal has two modern academic facilities on campus, which house classrooms, laboratories, and administrative offices. In addition, five student residential units are available on campus, offering apartment/suite-style living with private bedrooms and shared kitchens and living rooms. Students also enjoy a new Student Activity Center on campus. Coexisting in the Bloomington-Normal area with a major state university as well as a private four-year college, Lincoln College at Normal offers students the excitement and diversity of a large university community while still preserving the benefits of a small-college atmosphere.

Academic Programs

The College is on a two-semester schedule, with fall and spring components. A limited number of classes are also offered in the summer.

Bachelor's Degree Programs In the fall of 2001, Lincoln College at Normal established two new bachelor's degree programs: a Bachelor of Arts in liberal arts and a Bachelor of Science in business management. These programs are organized in a "2+2" structure, where students must first complete an Associate in Arts or an Associate in Science degree (or the equivalent) before being accepted to the bachelor's degree program.

Associate Degree Programs The Associate in Arts degree is designed to provide the student with a liberal grounding in the fundamental areas of human knowledge and allow a variety of elective selection of courses of general interest or premajor preparation. This degree is transfer-oriented and fulfills the general education requirements of most four-year colleges and universities nationwide. Typical premajor interests include American studies, art, biology, business administration, chemistry/physics, criminal justice, education, English/literature, environmental science, history/political science, law enforcement, mathematics, media/journalism, music, philosophy and religion, physical education, prenursing, psychology, sociology, speech, and theater. The College also offers an Associate in Science

degree, where more emphasis is placed upon math and science, as well as Associate in Applied Science degrees in cosmetology and travel/tourism.

Certificate and Diploma Programs These programs are typically completed in one year and include cosmetology, managerial training, and travel/tourism.

Costs

Costs for the 2003–04 academic year included tuition, $12,400; room and board, $5500; and fees, $570. Textbook rentals and supplies were estimated at $300.

Financial Aid

Approximately 91 percent of students at Lincoln College at Normal benefit from some type of financial aid each year. Financial assistance is generally determined by the need of the applicant (from the Free Application for Federal Student Aid) along with the availability of funds from federal, state, institutional, and private sources. Lincoln College considers the needs of each individual applicant in creating the financial aid package. Scholarships are also awarded for academic, fine arts, and athletic excellence.

Faculty

The majority of Lincoln College faculty members are full-time. Their direct involvement with students includes instruction, advisement, and counseling. Of the full-time faculty, 100 percent hold advanced degrees. The student-faculty ratio is 14:1, and the average class size is 16.

Student Body Profile

Six different states and three other countries are represented through the approximately 550 students enrolled at Lincoln College at Normal. Approximately 70 percent of students are full-time and 67 percent of the full-time students reside on campus. The average age of the student body is 19. Typically, 72 percent of students graduate on time with a two-year degree, with 89 percent of those students transferring successfully either to the bachelor's degree program on campus or to a four-year university the following semester.

Student Activities

Student Government The members of the Student Government Association are committed to proactively effecting change in the best interests of the student body, furthering the cultural and social growth of the student body, and generally advocating the interests of the student body to the College and community.

Student Activities The Student Activities Committee works to get the student body involved both in the College and in the various extracurricular activities. Student activities include intramural sports, outdoor activities (camping, canoeing, etc.), volunteering and community service events, music concerts, shopping trips, and athletic events.

Fine Arts Students may participate in a variety of fine arts activities, including the areas of visual arts, theater, and music.

Sports Opportunities in intramural athletics are available on campus as well as through the intramural programs offered at neighboring Illinois State University. Students also have access to the Student Recreation Complex at Illinois State University for exercise and workout needs. Opportunities in varsity athletics are available through the campus in Lincoln, Illinois.

Facilities and Resources

Lincoln College at Normal consists of two modern academic facilities with classrooms, laboratories, an art center, a state-of-the-art lecture hall, and administrative offices. In addition, five student residential buildings are located on campus, offering apartment/suite-style living with private bedrooms and shared kitchens and living rooms. This represents the primary housing option for students, with private off-campus apartment housing also available in the community. In addition, the Student Activity Center opened on campus in 2002. It houses the Student Activities office and also features workout facilities, a multimedia room, a game room, a snack bar, and meeting spaces.

Advisement/Counseling Trained full-time faculty members assist students in selecting courses and programs of study to satisfy their educational objectives. The Learning Center provides free professional tutoring to all students in any subject. This takes the form of one-on-one sessions as well as online tutorial programs. Students can also make up assignments and do extra credit projects under the direction of the Learning Center personnel.

Recreation/Career Counseling/Placement Services Students enjoy full access and privileges to each of these facilities and offices at Illinois State University as part of their enrollment at Lincoln College at Normal.

Dining/Health Services Lincoln College students at the campus in Normal may also elect to take certain other services from the programs at Illinois State University in Normal. These offerings are available on an à la carte basis and can be arranged with the assistance of the Lincoln College Housing personnel.

Library and Audiovisual Services Lincoln College students at the campus in Normal have library privileges for the Illinois State University library in Normal, with a combined book collection of 1,659,983 volumes. CD-ROM and online databases are also available for student use. The College offers two state-of-the-art computer labs for classroom, homework, and project use. These labs have more than forty computers for the students' use, all with Internet access. In addition, the student housing on campus features high-speed Internet access in every bedroom, and additional computers are also available in the Student Activity Center.

Location

Lincoln College at Normal is located in the city of Normal near the geographic center of Illinois, and with the adjoining city of Bloomington, has a population of more than 100,000. The College is situated on 10 acres of land approximately two blocks west of Route 51 (North Main Street) in north Normal, just off Interstate

55. The Bloomington/Normal area is served by three interstate highways, I-55, I-74, and I-39. It also features an airport, bus service, and Amtrak service. Driving time from Chicago and St. Louis is 2½ hours.

Admission Requirements

Associate Degree Program Acceptance to the associate degree program at Lincoln College at Normal is based on a student's high school record, standardized test scores, a personal interview, and letters of recommendation. Students with a minimum ACT composite score of 17 may be admitted without restriction. Those with an ACT composite score of 16 or less may be admitted on provisional status, based on the decision of the Admissions Committee. Students who are transferring to Lincoln College at Normal from another college or university may enter the College at the beginning of any semester. If they have been on academic probation at the previous institution and/or have maintained less than a 2.0 GPA (on a 4.0 scale), they may be admitted to the College on provisional status as well. Students for whom English is a second language must take the TOEFL examination and have their scores sent to the College. Any international student with a minimum score of 480 (paper-based) on the TOEFL may be granted admission to Lincoln College. Students whose scores are below 480 may be granted conditional acceptance if space is available.

Bachelor's Degree Program Students who are applying to the bachelor's degree program are required to have earned an Associate in Arts or Associate in Science degree or the equivalent at an accredited institution in order to be admitted without restriction. Students who have not yet met this requirement may be admitted on a conditional basis, based on the decision of the Admissions Committee.

Application and Information

Applications are accepted on a rolling basis and housing on campus is contingent on availability. All students are encouraged to apply before June 1 for the fall semester. Individuals interested in Lincoln College at Normal should contact:

Lincoln College Admissions
Lincoln College at Normal
715 West Raab Road
Normal, Illinois 61761
Telephone: 309-452-0500
           800-569-0558 (toll-free)
Fax: 309-454-5652
E-mail: admissions@lincoln.mclean.il.us
World Wide Web: http://www.lincoln.mclean.il.us

Students enjoy the residential life at Lincoln College at Normal.

MANOR COLLEGE
JENKINTOWN, PENNSYLVANIA

The College and Its Mission

Manor College is a private, coed Catholic college founded in 1947 by the Ukrainian Sisters of Saint Basil the Great. The College is characterized by its dedication to the education, growth, and self-actualization of the whole person through its personalized and nurturing atmosphere. Upon graduation, 40 percent of Manor's students are employed in their chosen fields; the remaining 60 percent of students transfer to four-year institutions to earn baccalaureate degrees. There are approximately 800 full- and part-time students enrolled at Manor. Extracurricular activities include honor societies, men's and women's intercollegiate soccer and basketball as well as intramural sports, the yearbook, and special interest and cultural clubs. Manor provides free counseling and tutoring services through an on-campus learning center. Trained counselors are available to assist students on an individual and confidential basis for academic, career, and personal concerns. Upon entering Manor, students are assigned an academic adviser, who provides guidance and support throughout their Manor experience. Transfer counseling is available for students interested in pursuing a four-year degree. The College's 35-acre campus includes a modern three-story dormitory, a library/administration building, and an academic building that also houses the bookstore, dining hall, an auditorium/gymnasium, and a student lounge. The Ukrainian Heritage Studies Center and the Manor Dental Health Center are also located on the campus grounds. Manor is accredited by the Middle States Association of Colleges and Schools.

Academic Programs

Manor offers career-oriented, two-year associate degrees, as well as transfer programs for the purpose of pursuing a bachelor's degree. Internships provide theory with practice, enhancing employment opportunities. The liberal arts core ensures a common breadth of knowledge along with mobility and future advancement. Manor offers ten programs with twenty-four majors/concentrations leading to associate degrees and transfer programs through its three divisions: Liberal Arts, Allied Health/Science/Mathematics, and Business.

The Liberal Arts Division offers **Associate in Arts** degrees in early childhood education, psychology, and liberal arts. In addition, the Liberal Arts Division provides a liberal arts and psychology transfer major, as well as an elementary education transfer major, an early child-care major, a three-year English as a second language (ESL) concentration, a concentration in catechetical education, and a concentration in communications. The Allied Health/Science/Mathematics Division offers **Associate in Science** degrees in dental hygiene, expanded functions dental assisting, and veterinary technology. This division also includes allied health and science transfer programs for students who seek preprofessional programs in biotechnology, cytotechnology, diagnostic imaging, funeral science, general sciences, medical technology, nursing, occupational therapy, physical therapy, prepharmacy, and pre–veterinary animal science. The Business Division offers **Associate in Science** degrees in accounting, business administration, business administration/computer science, business administration/health-care management, business administration/human resource management, business administration/international business, business administration/management, business administration/marketing management, and paralegal studies. There are four certificate programs. There is a PC technician/computer support specialist studies certificate and a certificate program in paralegal studies for students who have a bachelor's degree, as well as a legal nurse consultant certificate. A certificate program in catechist/educator development is offered for both Latin and Byzantine rites.

Manor also offers selected courses through three modes of distance learning: televideo, online Web-based learning, and teleconferencing.

The Office of Part-Time Admissions and Professional Development serves adult learners by providing educational options for those who want to attend college on a part-time basis. The office also supports the needs of the community and business and industry by offering noncredit classes and workshops, as well as on- and off-site corporate training programs, throughout the year. Approved as an authorized provider by the International Association for Continuing Education and Training, the office also grants continuing education units (CEUs) for selected professional development courses each semester.

Off-Campus Programs

Externships are incorporated into the academic studies programs. Students earn credits as they gain practical experience under the supervision of professionals in a specific field of study. Externships are offered in the career-oriented programs of study and in some transfer programs. Manor's affiliation with several area hospitals enables the allied health program student to fulfill clinical requirements at these sites. Students in other programs serve externships in law offices, courtrooms, day-care centers, businesses, health-care organizations, and veterinary facilities. Manor has dual admissions, 2+2, and 2+3 articulation agreements with major allied health universities, hospitals, and local universities.

Credit for Nontraditional Learning Experiences

Manor College awards credit by examination for college-level learning through the College-Level Examination Program (CLEP). Manor administers exemption tests for courses not available through CLEP. Adults may also receive college credit for military experience and education through the Army/American Council on Education Registry Transcript System (AARTS), by submitting a transcript to Manor for evaluation of credits, and by requesting assessment of previous life and job experiences through nontraditional means.

Costs

Tuition for the 2003–04 academic year was $9660 for full-time studies. Part-time study was $220 per credit hour. Students in certain allied health programs paid an additional $470 per year for full-time study or an additional $95 per credit hour for part-time study. On-campus room and board are available for men and women, and cost $4900 a year. There is an additional $800 fee for a private room. Other fees included a $350 general fee per year and a $100 graduation fee.

Financial Aid

Manor College offers need-based financial aid to eligible applicants in the form of grants, loans, and campus employment. Scholarships are awarded on the basis of academic promise. Approximately 85 percent of Manor's students receive some form of financial aid. Federally funded sources include the Federal Pell Grant, Federal Supplemental Educational Opportunity Grant, Federal Perkins Loan, Federal Stafford Student Loan, Federal PLUS loan, and Federal Work-Study. State-funded programs offered are the PHEAA State Grant and State Work-Study programs. The institutionally funded sources are the Manor Grant and the Resident Grant. Scholarships available for attendance at Manor include the following: Manor Presidential Scholarship; Joseph and Rose Wawriw Scholarships; Henry Lewandowski Memorial Scholarship; Elizabeth A. Stahlecker Memorial Scholarship; Mary Wolchonsky Scholarship; John Woloschuk Memorial Scholarship; George Harbison Memorial Scholarship; Alexander Wowk Memorial Scholarship; Eileen Freedman Memorial Scholarship; Manor Allied Health, Science, and Math Division Scholarship; Business Division Scholarship; Liberal Arts Division Scholarship; Basilian Scholarships; Scholar Athlete Award; St. Basil Academy Scholarship; Wasyl and Jozefa Soroka Scholarships; Wendy Holmes Oliva Memorial Scholarship; and International Scholarships. Scholarship eligibility requirements vary; details are available from the Admissions Office.

Faculty

There are 24 full-time and 87 part-time faculty members at Manor. Forty-nine percent of the faculty members have master's degrees and 30 percent possess doctorates in their field. Faculty members spend three fourths of their time teaching and the remainder counseling and advising students. The overall faculty-student ratio is 1:14. Small class size allows for personal attention in an environment conducive to learning.

Student Body Profile

Of the approximately 800 full- and part-time students enrolled at Manor, 207 entered the College as full-time freshman students in fall 2002. Twenty percent of that freshman class lived in the on-campus residence hall. Seventeen percent of the recent freshman class were members of minority groups, and 9 percent were international students from Albania, Brazil, India, Jamaica, Japan, Korea, Liberia, Nigeria, Poland, Sierra Leone, Ukraine, and Uzbekistan.

Student Activities

Manor encourages students to develop leadership skills through active participation in all aspects of college life. A variety of options for extracurricular participation fall under the umbrella of Manor's student services department, including the Student Senate, athletic teams, and clubs. The Student Senate forms an important part of the College community. The Senate, representing the student population, responds to student interests and concerns and acts as a liaison between the administration and the student body. Other extracurricular activities include intercollegiate men's and women's basketball and soccer. Manor's sports teams compete in the Eastern Pennsylvania Collegiate Conference. Additional extracurricular activities include the honor societies, intramural sports, the yearbook, and various special interest and cultural clubs. Student services is also responsible for the campus ministry, the counseling center, the residence hall, and the on-campus security force.

Facilities and Resources

The Academic Building (also called Mother of Perpetual Help Hall) includes classrooms, lecture rooms, laboratories, the chapel, and the Offices of Student Services, Campus Ministry, and Counseling. The Academic Building is equipped with up-to-date facilities, including biology, chemistry, and clinical laboratories, as well as modern IBM-compatible microsystems network labs. The Learning Center provides professional and student tutors in all College subjects and conducts workshops in study and research skills. Courses in English as a second language are also offered at the center.

The Basileiad Library has the capacity for 60,000 books, periodicals, and journals. The library includes a reserve room, reading areas, a micromedia room, and stack areas. The current library collection contains 50,000 volumes, including a special law collection, and subscriptions to 206 periodicals and newspapers. The library also houses the Small Business Resource Center, which helps local businesses with the solutions to everyday problems. An on-campus community Manor Dental Health Center was established in 1979 as an adjunct to the Expanded Functions Dental Assisting (EFDA) Program. Located on the lower level of St. Josaphat Hall, the center provides students enrolled in the EFDA Program or the Dental Hygiene Program at Manor with training under the direct supervision of faculty dentists. Currently, more than 2,000 patients receive care, including the following services: general dentistry, oral hygiene, orthodontics, prosthodontics, endodontics, and cosmetic dentistry. Because Manor Dental Health Center is a teaching facility, the fees charged for services are lower than those charged by private practitioners. Community residents are welcome as patients. The

Ukrainian Heritage Studies Center, located on the campus, preserves and promotes Ukrainian heritage, arts, and culture through four areas: academic programs, a museum collection, a library, and archives. Special events, exhibits, workshops, and seminars are offered throughout the year. The center is open to the public for tours and educational presentations by appointment.

Location

Manor is located in Jenkintown, Pennsylvania, 15 miles north of Center City, Philadelphia. Manor is accessible via public transportation and is located near the Pennsylvania Turnpike, Route 611, U.S. 1, and Route 232. Centers of cultural and historic interest are found in nearby Philadelphia, Valley Forge, and beautiful Bucks County. Manor's suburban campus is within walking distance of a large shopping mall, medical offices, and a township park.

Admission Requirements

Manor is open to qualified applicants of all races, creeds, and national origins. Candidates are required to have a high school diploma or its equivalent. Admission is based on the applicant's scholastic record, test scores, and interviews. The application procedure involves submission of a completed application form, a high school transcript, SAT I or ACT scores (required for students less than 21 years old), an interview, and Manor's entrance/placement test (waived for candidates who hold the baccalaureate degree). Transfer students must submit transcripts of all college work completed. International students must also submit results of the Test of English as a Foreign Language (TOEFL) or, for the Liberal Arts/ESL program, must have completed two years of English language study at the high school or college level in their native country.

Application and Information

Manor has a rolling admission policy. Students may apply for admission in either the fall or the spring semester. Interested students are invited to visit the campus and meet with admissions staff, faculty members, program directors, and students. Open houses, career days and nights, and classroom visits are scheduled throughout the year. The Admissions Office is open Monday through Friday, 8:30 a.m. to 6 p.m. (Saturday hours are by appointment). Admissions staff members can schedule visits and answer questions concerning admission, careers, programs, special features, and student life. For application forms, program-of-study bulletins, and catalogs, students should write to:

I. Jerry Czenstuch
Vice President of Enrollment Management
Manor College
700 Fox Chase Road
Jenkintown, Pennsylvania 19046
Telephone: 215-884-2216
E-mail: ftadmiss@manor.edu
World Wide Web: http://www.manor.edu

Manor College students relax between classes on the steps outside Mother of Perpetual Help Hall.

MARIA COLLEGE
ALBANY, NEW YORK

The College and Its Mission

Maria College was established in 1958 by the Religious Sisters of Mercy as an independent two-year, degree-granting institution. The College is career oriented and admits both men and women. The current enrollment is 688; about 90 percent are women. It is accredited by the Middle States Association of Colleges and Schools.

Located in a quiet corner of the New York State capital, Albany, Maria College concentrates on preparing its students for productive careers in health, education, and business. Nursing graduates are prepared for the state examination for licensure as registered nurses. The occupational therapy assistant and physical therapist assistant programs lead to certification by the state of New York upon graduation. In addition, following an examination, occupational therapy assistants are certified by the American Occupational Therapy Association.

The College's Career Planning and Placement Office is responsible for counseling students and alumni on career development, helping students obtain employment upon graduation, and assisting students in the process of transferring to other institutions. With the cooperation of program chairpersons, this office conducts seminars on resume preparation, interviewing techniques, and the job search. Individual counseling is available. Placement Office records show nearly 100 percent employment and/or transfer to four-year schools for Maria College graduates over the past fifteen years.

Academic Programs

Associate Degree Programs Maria College offers the **Associate in Applied Science (A.A.S.)** degree in allied health (nursing, occupational therapy assistant studies, and physical therapist assistant studies), business sciences (accounting, legal assistant studies, and management), computer information systems, and early childhood education. The **Associate in Arts (A.A.)** degree is offered in liberal arts. The **Associate in Science (A.S.)** degree is offered in general studies. Degrees are conferred on students who have completed at least 64 college credits through courses taken at Maria, transfer credit, credit earned through approved proficiency examinations, or life experience credit. Graduates also must complete the College's requirements of 6 credit hours in religious studies/philosophy and 6 credit hours in English. The required liberal arts core consists of 48 credit hours for an A.A., 32 credit hours for an A.S., and 22 credit hours for an A.A.S. An overall quality point average of at least 2.0 (on a 4.0 scale) is also required.

In addition to traditional day classes, Maria College's Evening Division offers degree programs in accounting, computer information systems, general studies, liberal arts, management, nursing, and physical therapist assistant studies. For those who are unable to attend during the day and seek programs for enrichment or a career change, credit-free evening courses, seminars, and workshops are also provided.

The first Weekend College to be established in northeastern New York is conducted at Maria. This innovative, degree-granting option allows students to complete degree programs in business, computer information systems, general studies, legal assistant studies, and liberal arts by attending classes every other weekend for two years. The occupational therapy assistant studies program takes three years to complete.

Students who wish to continue studies toward a baccalaureate degree may complete the first two years of study at Maria and then transfer to a senior institution for the next two years. To facilitate such a transfer, Maria College has articulation agreements with a wide range of senior colleges. For nursing students, for example, articulation agreements exist with the baccalaureate nursing program at Russell Sage College in Troy, New York, and with the College of Health Related Professions of the State University of New York Health Science Center at Syracuse.

Certificate Programs Certificate programs are available in bereavement studies, gerontology, complementary therapy, and legal assistant studies. The legal assistant studies certificate is available only for those with associate or bachelor's degrees.

Off-Campus Programs

Clinical laboratory experiences for nursing students are provided at Albany Medical Center, Our Lady of Mercy Life Center, and St. Peter's Hospital. Students in the occupational therapy assistant and physical therapist assistant programs receive clinical training in hospitals, developmental centers, nursing homes, and rehabilitation centers in New York State and at selected sites in other states. Senior students in the early childhood education program are trained in a variety of outside field agencies, which may include day-care centers, home-based centers, Head Start, and centers providing programs for infants and toddlers or for children with special needs.

Credit for Nontraditional Learning Experiences

Maria College recognizes college-level courses taken by students while they are still attending high school. Advanced Placement scores of 5, 4, and 3 normally earn college credit. Maria College grants credit for the Regents College Examinations and the College-Level Examination Programs (CLEP) when these examinations cover comparable material. Proficiency credits are treated as transfer credits.

Maria College recognizes that certain adult students may have gained valuable knowledge in their lives from diverse experiences. Some of this learning may qualify as college-level course work. Students requesting credit will be required to substantiate this learning experience. Total credit obtained through life experience is limited to a maximum of 16 nonduplicative transfer credits applied toward a degree, 25 percent of the required 64 credits.

The Nursing Program offers advanced placement for licensed practical nurses who may challenge seven credits in nursing. A series of classes is held twice a year to assist licensed practical nurses in meeting the requirements for challenge. Each candidate for advanced placement must be successful in both a written and a skill examination.

Costs

Tuition for the 2002–03 academic year was estimated at $6300 for full-time study and $230 per credit hour for part-time study. Fees were estimated at $100 per academic year (higher for those in the allied health programs). The College does not provide housing, but arrangements for off-campus housing may be made through the Admissions Office.

Financial Aid

Tuition Assistance Program (TAP) awards are available to New York State residents only. Financial aid is available to students through Federal Stafford Student Loans, Federal PLUS loans, Federal Perkins Loans, Federal Nursing Loans, Federal Pell Grants, Federal Supplemental Educational Opportunity Grants, and Federal Work-Study awards. Also available to those qualifying are the Regents Awards for Children of Deceased or Disabled Veterans and Disabled Policemen and Firefighters, State Aid to Native Americans, and Veterans Administration educational benefits. Approximately 50 percent of the College's students receive aid. To apply for aid, students must submit both the Free Application for Federal Student Aid (FAFSA) and the NYS TAP form.

Faculty

Maria College has full- and part-time faculty members. Every freshman is assigned to a faculty adviser, who encourages communication and a strong working relationship. The student-faculty ratio is 8:1.

Student Body Profile

For the entering fall 2001 class, 23 percent were first-time freshmen. Approximately 85 percent of all students were from a radius of 50 miles from the College. Nonresident aliens made up less than 1 percent of the student body, and approximately 22 percent of full-time enrollees belonged to a minority group. Seventy percent of students were older than 25. Maria College is a commuter-based institution; less than 10 percent of students seek housing through the Admissions Office.

Student Activities

Student government is handled on a departmental basis; each department operates independently of all other departments.

Facilities and Resources

Maria's facilities are located in three buildings. The Administration Building's modern facilities include offices, classrooms, computerized science laboratories, a computer center, a working library of 55,000 volumes, a multimedia center, and a multimedia large lecture hall. Marian Hall, Maria's allied health facility, has been renovated through grants from the Helene Fuld Foundation and gifts from the College's alumni and friends. It includes the Helene Fuld Audio-Visual Laboratory for nursing students, the Bearldean B. Burke Occupational Therapy Teaching Center, the Activities of Daily Living Suite, a multimedia auditorium, classrooms, offices, and nursing labs. Marian Hall also houses facilities for the physical therapist assistant program. The Campus School is a fully equipped teaching facility that provides preschool and full-day kindergarten classes and serves as a laboratory school for students majoring in early childhood education.

Location

Maria's urban location makes the many attractions of the capital district readily accessible. City buses provide convenient transportation to the area's sister cities of Schenectady and Troy, to many fine shopping centers, and to the impressive Nelson A. Rockefeller Empire State Plaza, which has the State Museum, indoor and outdoor entertainment areas, and performing arts facilities. Access to the Adirondack Northway—leading to the Saratoga Performing Arts Center and Canada—is minutes away. Amtrak trains are available from Schenectady and Rensselaer. Opportunities for outdoor activities in the area are numerous. The Catskills, the Helderbergs, the Adirondacks, and their many lakes provide four seasons of outdoor enjoyment.

Admission Requirements

Admission to full-time study at Maria College is based on a review of the applicant's high school and (when applicable) college performance, SAT I or ACT scores and other objective test data, letters of recommendation, and the applicant's interests, maturity, and objectives. Interviews are required. An early admission program is offered for qualified high school students. Part-time study is also available.

Application and Information

It is recommended that application be made early in the first semester of the last year of high school. Applicants must submit an application form and a nonrefundable $25 fee, offer evidence of completion or anticipated completion of a high school program or its equivalent, present at least 16 units of high school work (as specified by the program selected at the College), and arrange for transcripts and SAT I or ACT scores to be sent to Maria College. Students whose SAT or ACT scores fall below a particular level are required to take placement tests in the basic skills of reading, writing, and mathematics. Inquiries regarding academic programs or admission to Maria College may be directed to:

Director of Admissions
Maria College
700 New Scotland Avenue
Albany, New York 12208
Telephone: 518-438-3111
Fax: 518-453-1366
E-mail: admissions@mariacollege.edu
World Wide Web: http://www.mariacollege.edu

Students wait in college courtyard for exam doors to open.

MASSACHUSETTS BAY COMMUNITY COLLEGE

WELLESLEY HILLS, FRAMINGHAM, AND ASHLAND, MASSACHUSETTS

The College and Its Mission

Massachusetts Bay Community College (MassBay) provides a student-centered learning environment in which a diverse student body explores, develops, and achieves educational goals. MassBay is committed to academic excellence and student success. The College is a comprehensive, two-year public institution offering career programs for immediate employability and programs paralleling the first two years of a bachelor's degree. MassBay emphasizes technology and health-care programs and has strong transfer programs in the liberal arts and business. While the majority of the students hail from the Metro West and Boston areas, its reputation has attracted students from throughout the United States and worldwide. It has been serving the academic needs of the community since it was founded in 1961.

The student body at MassBay comprises a diverse group of individuals, all with various goals and educational needs. Some may be working towards an associate degree or certificate program by taking day or evening classes. Others may have plans to transfer to a four-year college or university to continue their education. Still others may have some college experience but want to broaden their professional skills. MassBay's programs are geared to meet the needs of this diverse population, ensuring access to education and flexibility to students by offering a variety of instructional delivery systems, including distance learning, day and night schedules, and online courses.

Each of MassBay's programs of study belongs to one of its specialized Centers of Excellence—the Science and Advanced Technology Institute (SATI), the Health and Human Services Institute (HHSI), the Academic Opportunity Institute (AOI), or the Language and Literacy Center (LLC). Whether a student's level of study is undergraduate, professional training, or continuing education, the goal of the Centers of Excellence is to provide students with a seamless learning and training experience. In addition, the Centers of Excellence enable students to easily plan their education to meet their career goals and at a pace that fits their lifestyle. For example, they can decide to complete a degree or certificate program to obtain an entry-level position, then return to the Center for more advanced training as they prepare for the next step of their career ladder. Because MassBay is committed to the success of its students, the Centers of Excellence are designed to provide open and enriching dialogue among faculty members and fellow students in similar programs of study. This allows for students to share experiences, compare similarities in career fields, or mentor each other in a particular project. Through the Centers of Excellence, students experience an innovative way of learning that provides a rewarding college experience and prepares them to excel in meeting the ever-changing demands of today's workforce.

MassBay students perform better than the state average on the registered nurse licensing exam (NCLEX-RN) and the practical nurse licensing exam (NCLEX-PN). All of MassBay's automotive technician training programs have received Automotive Service Excellence (ASE) MASTER certification, the highest level of achievement recognized by the National Institute for Automotive Service Excellence. MassBay students have received the prestigious and world-recognized Barry M. Goldwater Scholarship Award for mathematics, natural science, or engineering excellence. MassBay students regularly receive several Elizabeth Davis Scholarships from Wellesley College. There are only two other colleges in the world that offer an associate degree in forensic science. MassBay's athletics teams routinely contend for state, regional, and national honors and championships.

MassBay is accredited by the New England Association of Schools and Colleges (NEASC), the Council for Accreditation of Allied Health Education Programs (NEASC), the Council for Accreditation for Allied Health Education Programs (CAAHEP), the Joint Review Committee on Education in Radiologic Technology (JRCERT), the National League for Nursing (NLN), Commission on Accreditation in Physical Therapy Education (CAPTE), Accreditation Council for Occupational Therapy Education (ACOTE), and the National Automotive Technician Educational Foundation (NATEF).

Academic Programs

MassBay Community College offers two-year professional and liberal arts programs and certificate programs. From automotive technology, business, education, engineering, health, information systems and computer technology, liberal arts, and physical sciences, MassBay students have a wide range of choices. Many of the College's professional programs give students the opportunity to learn not only in the classroom but also in the field, with hands-on experience and state-of-the-art labs simulating the real experiences faced on the job. MassBay's liberal arts program provides the foundation for further learning and career advancement. Certificates can help students enter a new field or advance their current one. MassBay recommends that students work with an adviser in designing their specific course of study and planning for further college study or employment.

Students who complete a MassBay degree program may receive an Associate of Arts or an Associate of Science degree and are fully prepared for further study at four-year institutions for a baccalaureate degree. Students may be eligible for transfer status as a junior to many colleges and universities. Many of these programs also qualify students for immediate employment in their chosen field.

MassBay also participates in the Joint Admissions Program for students to transfer from MassBay to one of the four University of Massachusetts campuses or seven state colleges. The program is open to students who receive an associate degree in an approved major, with a 2.5 or higher grade point average. In addition, the Tuition Advantage Plan may help transferring graduates lower their tuition costs.

The associate degree programs offered are accounting, automotive technology, biotechnology, business administration, communications, computer information systems, computer science, criminal justice, early childhood education, electrical and computer engineering, electronics technology, electronics technology semiconductor, engineering, engineering design, environmental science and occupational safety, forensic science, general business, general studies, hospitality management, human services, information systems technology and management, liberal arts, life sciences, mechanical engineering, nursing, occupational therapy assistant, paralegal studies, physical therapist assistant, psychology/sociology/anthropology, radiologic technology, telecommunications, and technology.

The certificate programs offered are accounting, automotive technology, central processing technology, central service and material management, communications, computer-aided design, early childhood education, infant-toddler teacher, emergency medical technician, hospitality management, human services, information technology, interior design, liberal arts, medical coding, medical office administrative assistant, paralegal studies, paramedicine, phlebotomy, practical nursing, surgical technology, telecommuncations/photonics, and therapeutic massage.

Internships play a critical role in the MassBay learning experience. Counselors in the Office of Career Development can assist students in finding internship opportunities that fit into their career paths. Internships are valuable experiences that allow students to gain experience in the field of their interest and develop professional contacts.

Costs

The tuition per credit hour for Massachusetts residents is $104. For out-of-state/nonresidents, the tuition is $310 per credit hour. Fees for health insurance, student parking, lab, or material costs may be added. Continuing education tuition is $121 per credit hour for Massachusetts residents. For out-of-state/nonresidents, the cost of tuition per credit hour is $310. All evening tuition for AD nursing courses is $258 per credit hour plus additional fees. All evening tuition for practical nursing courses (CE, PN) is $210 per credit hour plus additional fees. Under the New England Regional Student Program, some New England students may attend MassBay for 150 percent of the in-state tuition rate, which is less than the out-of-state tuition rate.

Financial Aid

Financial assistance is available to all qualified students. Such aid is designed to help students meet basic college expenses. Financial assistance may be in the form of a grant, a scholarship, a loan, work-study employment, or any combination of these. MassBay's resources are obtained from federal, state, local, or private sources. Applicant eligibility and program guidelines are defined by the funding source. Grants and scholarships generally do not need to be paid back to MassBay or the sponsor. Loans can be made to the student or a student's parent and must be paid back. Loans can be need-based or non-need-based depending upon the individual circumstances of the student.

Faculty

The faculty members at MassBay total 228, with 78 full-time and 150 part-time. Many members of the faculty are affiliated with other colleges and universities in the state, providing MassBay students with a valuable resource.

Student Body Profile

The student body at MassBay comprises a diverse group of individuals, all with various goals and educational needs. There are more than 5,000 students enrolled at MassBay. While the majority of students hail from the Metro West and the Boston vicinity, there are many international students as well, representing countries such as Brazil, Haiti, Russia, Uganda, and India. Fifty percent of MassBay students are between 17 and 22 years of age.

Student Activities

The College supports intercollegiate athletic programs, including men's baseball; women's softball; and men's and women's soccer, basketball, volleyball, golf, tennis, and cross-country.

Some other student clubs and organizations offered by MassBay are the Student Senate and Student Government; honor societies, such as Alpha Beta Gamma, the National Business Honor Society, Alpha Kappa Lamda, Psi Beta, Sigma Delta Mus, and Silver Key; the student-run theater group, the MassBay Players; concert/lecture series; the International and Multicultural Student Development program; and the student newspaper, *The Beacon*.

Facilities and Resources

MassBay provides the College community with resources and facilities that support the academic programs and courses offered, including a Student Development Office; Student Advising, where students can speak with a personal adviser; an Academic Achievement Center that supplements classroom instruction with one-on-one support while accommodating MassBay students' diverse learning styles; the Reading and Writing Centers, which offer individual instruction on both campuses for students who like one-on-one help in completing a reading or writing assignment for any college course; smart classrooms, used by faculty members and students to enhance the classroom learning experience; a library with more than 49,000 volumes; and computer labs with over 400 computers for student use. A recreation and wellness center was built in 2003.

Location

MassBay serves students from three convenient locations. The Wellesley Hills Campus is located on Route 9 approximately 10 miles west of Boston. The Framingham Campus is near Routes 9 and 126. The Technology Center in Ashland is approximately 4 miles south of the Framingham Campus off Route 126.

Admission Requirements

MassBay maintains an open-door admissions policy, and there is no application deadline. If students have earned a GED, a high school diploma, or an associate degree or higher, they will be admitted to MassBay on a first-come, first-served basis, provided there is a vacancy in the program to which they have applied.

Application and Information

MassBay enrollment is open to Massachusetts residents at the in-state tuition rate. A Massachusetts resident is currently defined as a U.S. citizen or permanent resident having a minimum of six consecutive months of verifiable domicile in the Commonwealth. Others may attend MassBay at the out-of-state tuition rate.

Applicants must include a $20 fee with their application. For an application and information, students should contact the Office of Admissions at the address listed below.

Office of Admissions
Massachusetts Bay Community College
50 Oakland Street
Wellesley Hills, Massachusetts 02481
Telephone: 781-239-2500
World Wide Web: http://www.massbay.edu

The MassBay Wellesley campus.

McINTOSH COLLEGE
DOVER, NEW HAMPSHIRE

The College and Its Mission

For the residential or commuting student seeking the intimate personal experience of a small college and the technical training in practical skills needed to compete in today's computer-oriented job market, McIntosh College is the answer. For more than 100 years, McIntosh has provided an exciting variety of business and professional opportunities to recent high school graduates and adults seeking career changes or re-entry into the job market. McIntosh is a two-year degree-granting institution accredited by the New England Association of Schools and Colleges. The College currently enrolls more than 1,000 students at its campus in Dover, New Hampshire.

The mission of the College combines a clearly defined educational philosophy with a profound understanding of the College's role in providing effective business-oriented associate degree and certificate programs in a fully equipped learning facility. This integration allows the College to enhance the quality of personal and professional life of the business and academic communities that it serves.

McIntosh is a career-oriented institution dedicated to the personal, intellectual, and professional growth of its students. The College has a century-long tradition of providing academic programs that integrate the acquisition of job-related skills with the development of clear, critical thinking and effective reasoning. While McIntosh recognizes its obligation to provide the specific skills necessary for the student to function in a contemporary work environment, it operates under the philosophy that a college is more than a training facility. Students must leave the college experience with a sense of competence in their chosen fields, a belief in themselves as individuals, and an enhanced critical awareness of the world around them.

Academic Programs

McIntosh College offers a unique blend of courses and programs of study designed to prepare students for careers in business, hospitality and tourism management, the computer industry, public service, allied health, paralegal studies, and criminal justice. All programs of study provide students with academic credit, which allows them to continue their studies at four-year institutions.

Associate Degree Programs McIntosh College is authorized by the Postsecondary Education Commission of the State of New Hampshire to offer associate degree programs with major areas of concentration in accounting, business information management, business studies, criminal justice, culinary arts, desktop support specialist, general business, medical assisting, network administrator, paralegal studies, and visual communication.

Honors Programs The McIntosh College Beta Gamma Gamma Chapter of the Phi Theta Kappa Honor Society supports a number of scholarship opportunities and activities for honor students.

Transfer Arrangements McIntosh students can earn an associate degree and an articulated bachelor's degree in one continuous program of study at the Dover campus through the uniquely structured McIntosh/Southern New Hampshire University (formerly New Hampshire College) 2+2 Program. Academic counseling is available and full support is provided for students wishing to continue their education at other institutions of higher learning.

Internship and Co-op Programs All academic departments supporting degree programs support for-credit internship opportunities for qualified students. The Office of Career Development assists students in finding appropriate internships in accounting, business, computer studies, criminal justice, culinary arts, hospitality and tourism management, information systems, medical assisting, office technology, or paralegal studies.

Credit for Nontraditional Learning Experiences

The College grants credit to students who have passed authorized advanced placement courses in high school with grades of B or better or who present evidence of having received scores of 460 or better on CLEP examinations in subject areas that directly correspond to the content of individual McIntosh courses.

Costs

The 2002–03 annual tuition for a full-time degree candidate was $21,000–$24,000. Tuition and costs are subject to change.

Financial Aid

The Office of Financial Aid provides information and personal counseling with respect to the various federal grant and loan programs and institutional scholarships available to students attending McIntosh College. McIntosh College believes that every student should have access to the financial resources needed to pursue academic or career interests. Pell Grants, Supplemental Educational Opportunity Grants, Federal Work-Study, Stafford Student Loans, Plus Loans, State Incentive Programs, direct loans, scholarships, and family discounts are all available to students attending McIntosh College.

Faculty

There are 44 full-time faculty members at McIntosh College. Of these, 67 percent hold advanced degrees and specialized certifications.

Student Body Profile

McIntosh College attracts students from a wide age spectrum. Because the College offers parallel day and evening programs, there is a substantial mix of recent high school graduates and adult students returning to school. The average age of a McIntosh student is 26, slightly higher at night and slightly lower during the day program. Students are generally career oriented. More than 50 percent of graduates continue their studies at the bachelor's degree level.

Student Activities

The College supports a variety of social clubs, organizations, and other extracurricular activities designed to enhance and enrich the student's educational experience at McIntosh. The Student Activities Committee provides a forum for students interested in planning and implementing social and cultural events at the College. There is a chapter of Delta Epsilon Chi on campus. Departmental associations include the McIntosh Paralegal Association and the Criminal Justice Association.

Facilities and Resources

In recent years, McIntosh has anticipated changes in the business environment and the need for a newly oriented work force by establishing a superior computer facility consisting of seven computer labs housing more than 175 individual and networked stations. An integrated curriculum provides specific computer instruction related to each major field of study. In addition, McIntosh students can roam the Internet, explore online services such as WestLaw, or browse through an extensive CD-ROM collection in the McIntosh academic and paralegal library facilities. A fully equipped medical lab and a real-world operative teaching kitchen provide hands-on working environments for medical assisting and culinary arts majors. At McIntosh, emphasis is placed on the practical aspects of career development. Internships are available in all departments.

On-campus student housing facilities at McIntosh College have been carefully designed to provide a warm, supportive living and learning environment that serves to nurture students' personal development and to enhance their opportunities for academic and professional success. The residential facility includes spacious furnished living units that are cable-ready and have air-conditioning, a full bath, and access to a computer lab. Residential students may choose from a variety of meal plans. Initial inquiries about eligibility requirements and the availability of on-campus housing should be directed to the Office of Admissions. Room assignments are made on a first-come, first-served basis, depending on eligibility.

Advisement/Counseling The faculty and administration of the College are committed to the principle that students should be given every possible opportunity to achieve academic and professional success. For this reason, the College offers extensive academic and career counseling to its students. Free study skills workshops are regularly available. In addition, the College provides free tutorial assistance in accounting, computer applications, English, and math.

Career Planning/Placement Offices The College provides free career counseling and placement referral services to its students and graduates through the Office of Career Development. Workshops on resume writing are frequently offered to currently enrolled students.

Location

McIntosh College consists of two separate facilities situated next to the Spaulding Turnpike in Dover, New Hampshire. Dover is a city of about 26,000, located in the Seacoast area of New Hampshire about one hour north of Boston. The College is conveniently located just a short drive from coastal beaches and world-class skiing. The academic center is located on a 13-acre tract of land on Cataract Avenue.

Admission Requirements

A high school diploma or its equivalent (GED) is required of all students accepted for admission at McIntosh College with matriculated student status. Students can apply and can be admitted at any time during the year. A student attending a full-time degree program can expect to graduate in eighteen or twenty-four months.

Application and Information

Applications for admission are accepted on an ongoing basis. Most students may begin classes at the start of any term scheduled throughout the year. For application materials, students should contact:

Office of Admissions
McIntosh College
23 Cataract Avenue
Dover, New Hampshire 03820

Telephone: 800-MCINTOSH (toll-free)
Fax: 603-742-3755
E-mail: admissions@mcintoshcollege.com
World Wide Web: http://www.mcintoshcollege.com

McIntosh welcomes students from around the world.

MIAMI DADE COLLEGE
MIAMI, FLORIDA

The College and Its Mission

Miami Dade College, formerly known as Miami-Dade Community College, is nationally and internationally recognized as one of the largest and best community colleges in the country. At Miami Dade, student success is the priority. The mission of the College is to provide accessible, affordable, high-quality education by keeping the learner's needs at the center of the decision making and working in partnership with its dynamic, multicultural community. The College is accredited by the Southern Association of Colleges and Schools and offers undergraduate study in more than 200 areas and professions.

Academic Programs

The instructional program at the College is designed two-fold: one path is designed to prepare students to enter the professional field of teaching science and math in secondary schools and K–12 exceptional students; the other path is designed to prepare students to transfer to the upper division of senior colleges and universities or for immediate entry into career fields. The Associate in Arts (A.A.) degree, offered for students planning to transfer to a university, can be earned in 60 credits, including 36 credits of required general education and 24 credits of electives. The state of Florida has developed a set of common program prerequisites for each program to facilitate student transfer. A variety of Associate in Science (A.S.) and Associate in Applied Science (A.A.S.) degrees, college credit certificate programs, vocational credit certificate programs, and supplemental courses are offered to prepare students to enter the job market or upgrade skills. These programs vary in length. The A.S. degree includes 15 credits of general education requirements. Several A.S. and A.A.S. degree programs include courses that have articulation agreements for transfer to one or more universities; others offer advanced certificate training. The Medical Center Campus offers a wide range of allied health and nursing programs, with clinicals in major local hospitals and health-care centers. Courses are offered year-round in two major terms of sixteen weeks each and summer terms comprised of two 6-week terms or one 12-week term.

Miami Dade offers the A.A. degree, which prepares students for transfer to upper-division programs. The A.A.S. degree is designed to prepare individuals for employment in hospitality and business. The following A.S. degree programs, which prepare students for employment and may transfer to a four-year institution, are available at one or more campuses: accounting technology; air-conditioning, refrigeration, and heating; architectural design and construction technology; automotive service management technology; aviation administration; aviation maintenance management; biomedical engineering technology; building construction technology; business administration; civil engineering technology; computer engineering technology; computer information technology; computer programming and analysis; court reporting technology; criminal justice technology; dietetic technician studies; drafting and design technology; electronics engineering technology; environmental science technology; film production technology; financial services; fire science technology; funeral services; graphic arts technology; graphic design technology; graphic Internet technology; hospitality and tourism management; human services; industrial management technology; interior design technology; Internet services technology; landscape technology; legal assisting; marketing management; music business; networking services technology; office systems technology; photographic technology; professional pilot technology; radio and television broadcast programming; sign language interpretation; telecommunications engineering; theater and entertainment technology; translation/interpretation: English/Spanish track; and travel industry management.

Allied health A.S. degree programs offered at the Medical Center Campus include dental hygiene, diagnostic medical sonography technology, emergency medical services, health information management, histologic technology, medical laboratory technology, midwifery, nuclear medicine technology, nursing-RN, opticianry, physical therapist assistant studies, physician assistant studies, radiation therapy technology, respiratory care, and veterinary technology. In addition, an A.A.S. degree program is offered in radiography.

College credit certificates are offered in accounting applications, air cargo agent studies, airline reservation and ticketing agent studies, airline/aviation management, business management, Cisco network associate studies, computer specialist studies, computer programming, computer-aided design assistant studies, computer-aided design operator studies, embalming, emergency medical technician studies, information technology support, interpretation studies: English/Spanish, marketing operations, microcomputer repairer/installer studies, Microsoft database administrator studies, Microsoft solutions developer studies, mortgage finance, network systems developer studies, nuclear medicine technology specialist studies, office systems specialist studies, Oracle database administrator studies, Oracle database developer studies, passenger service agent studies, paramedic studies, translation studies: English/Spanish, and Web development specialist studies. An Applied Technology Diploma is offered in emergency medical technician studies.

Distance Education Through virtual college, high-quality online academic and vocational programs are offered to meet the needs of nontraditional and out-of-area students as well as students who find it difficult to attend classes during scheduled hours and at specific locations. The array of instructional activities in the Web courses is designed to engage students in interactive and collaborative learning. The courses cover the established competencies through the use of resource materials and Web activities.

Honors Programs Miami Dade's Honors College provides a rigorous and comprehensive curriculum, seminars, and enrichment activities in a scholarly and supportive environment where goal-oriented, academically gifted students explore new ideas and engage in inspired creativity and intellectual collaborations with experienced faculty members.

Transfer Arrangements A statewide articulation agreement among all Florida institutions of higher education facilitates transfers and ensures that a student who is awarded the Associate in Arts degree at Miami Dade has met general education requirements for admission to the upper division in public and private colleges and universities. In addition, Miami Dade has established articulation agreements with prestigious colleges and universities throughout the nation.

Certificate Programs Vocational credit certificate programs are offered at one or more campuses in academy of international marketing, accounting operations, administrative assistant studies, architectural drafting, bail bonding, business computer programming, business supervision and management, commercial art technology, community service officer/police service aide studies, correctional officer studies, correctional probation officer studies, crossover from correction officer to law enforcement officer studies, customer assistance, early childhood education, electronic technology, fire fighting, insurance marketing, law enforcement officer studies, legal secretary studies, massage therapy, mechanical drafting, medical assisting, medical coder/biller studies, medical record transcribing, medical secretary studies, network support services, PC support services, pharmacy technician studies, phlebotomy, practical nursing, private security officer studies, public safety telecommunications, real estate marketing, television production, teller operations, and travel and tourism industry operations. Applied Technology Diplomas are offered in medical coder/biller and medical record transcribing.

Internship and Co-op Programs Co-op programs provide an opportunity for students to obtain career-related work experience (paid or voluntary) while earning academic credit.

Special Programs and Services New World School of the Arts (NWSA) is a unique educational partnership of Miami-Dade County Public Schools, Miami Dade College, and the University of Florida. Through its sponsoring institutions, NWSA awards high school diplomas, Associate in Arts degrees, and Bachelor of Music and Bachelor of Fine Arts degrees. Students are admitted through audition or portfolio presentation. Other special programs and services include academic remediation for entering students, English as a second language, services for disabled students (including learning disabled), study abroad, and advanced placement.

Community Programs Community programs are offered both independently and in cooperation with community organizations. Workshops and seminars are held throughout the year in response to community needs.

Continuing Education Unit Certificate Programs Miami Dade provides students the opportunity to obtain Continuing Education Units (CEUs) for certain courses. Transcripts designating CEUs are provided.

Personal Enrichment/Noncredit Courses A wide array of noncredit courses and programs are offered both on and off campus.

Off-Campus Programs

Study-abroad programs, both short-term and full semester, are available in many countries. Internships and clinicals may be scheduled off campus.

Credit for Nontraditional Learning Experiences

The College may award credit for demonstrated proficiency in areas related to college-level courses. Sources used to determine such proficiency are the College-Level Examination Program, the Advanced Placement Program, the Proficiency Examination Program, the International Baccalaureate Program, Dual Enrollment, Tech Prep Articulation, the Defense Activity for Nontraditional Education Support, the United States Armed Forces Institute, the Institutional Credit by Exam, and the internal Miami Dade procedures for awarding credit related to specific programs for approval licensures.

Costs

For the 2003–04 academic year, tuition was $56.50 per college credit and $47.50 per vocational credit for Florida residents; it was $197.50 per college credit and $188.90 per vocational credit for nonresidents. Textbooks and supplies for full-time students were estimated at $1500. On-campus housing is not available; room and board costs vary, depending upon the type of off-campus housing desired.

Financial Aid

Financial aid that a student receives is determined through federal, state, and institutional guidelines and is offered to students in packages that may consist of grants, loans, employment, and scholarships. Financial aid is based upon financial need. In addition, the College offers merit-based aid to those who qualify, as funds are available. Available assistance includes Federal Pell Grants, Federal Supplemental Educational Opportunity Grants, the Florida Student Assistance Grant, the Florida Bright Futures Scholarship, the Federal Work-Study Program, the Florida Work Experience Program (FWEP), Federal Perkins Loans, Federal Family Education Loan Programs, and Federal PLUS Loans. In addition, the College offers Foundation and Institutional Grants, scholarships, short-term tuition loans, and employment to students as well as funding for the purchase of special equipment and services for disabled students.

Faculty

There are 707 full-time faculty members and 1,376 part-time faculty members. Of the full-time faculty members, 94 percent hold advanced degrees; 22 percent have earned doctorates.

Student Body Profile

More than 155,000 credit and noncredit students are enrolled at Miami Dade, including almost 2,300 international students from 100 countries. Seventy-three percent of students with an A.A. degree continue their education at a four-year college. Fifteen percent of the upper-division students in the Florida State University System started college at Miami Dade. The average age of students is 27, although about 30 percent of students are between 21 and 25 years old. Almost 65 percent attend on a part-time basis. Sixty-two percent are women. The student body is ethnically and culturally diverse. Miami Dade enrolls more Hispanic students than any other college or university, and is second in African-American enrollment, in the United States.

Student Activities

More than 100 organizations offer opportunities to participate in student government, student publications, music ensembles, drama productions (in English and Spanish), religious activities, service and political clubs, national and local fraternities and sororities, professional organizations, and honor societies.

Sports Intercollegiate and intramural athletics play an important role at Miami Dade College. Miami Dade is a member of NJCAA, competing at the Division I level. Intercollegiate teams include women's basketball, softball, and volleyball and men's baseball and basketball. In addition, sports facilities, such as wellness centers; racquetball, tennis, and handball courts; swimming pools; and a track field, are available.

Facilities and Resources

Career Planning/Placement Offices Trained staff members assist students in selecting courses and programs of study to satisfy their educational objectives. Each campus has a career center where students who are uncertain about their future careers may obtain career counseling and vocational interest testing and may review a variety of career materials. The campus Job Placement Centers provide part-time or full-time job referral services to actively enrolled students or graduates. The centers also provide training that prepares students for job search, resume writing, and effective job interviews. In addition, Career Fairs are scheduled on the campuses.

Library and Audiovisual Services The campus libraries have a combined book collection of more than 350,000 titles and more than 1,900 periodicals. Numerous CD-ROM, audiovisual materials, and online databases are available. Computers for student use are available in computer labs, learning resource centers, labs, classrooms, and the library.

Location

Blessed with a sunny, subtropical climate, beautiful beaches, and an international flavor, Miami has been a mecca for students and tourists for decades. A variety of exciting cultural, sporting, and intellectual activities take place each week. Opportunities to explore unique settings, such as the historic Art Deco District and Little Havana or the Everglades National Park, abound. Miami is a gateway city with easy access to most countries. Six campuses and numerous outreach centers are located throughout the greater Miami area. **North Campus** is located on a 245-acre, fully landscaped site with free, lighted parking areas and a lake around which the buildings are clustered. **Kendall Campus** is situated 23 miles southwest of the North Campus on a 185-acre site. Focal points of the campus' award-winning landscape designs are the lakes and lush tropical growth. **Wolfson Campus,** the only urban campus, is located in the heart of Miami's business community and has two award-winning buildings. **Medical Center Campus** is located in Miami's medical/civic center complex. **Homestead Campus** is located on an 8-acre site in the historic business district of Homestead. **InterAmerican Campus** is located in the heart of Little Havana, one of south Florida's most colorful and ethnically diverse communities. Off-campus commuter sites are located in the major suburbs.

Admission Requirements

Miami Dade has an open-door admission policy. The College provides educational opportunities to all high school graduates, including those who have a state high school equivalency diploma, and to transfer students from other colleges and universities. In addition to the application to the College, which carries a $20 application fee, students must have official transcripts from high school, college, university, or other postsecondary educational institutions sent directly to the Office of Admissions from the institutions. High school equivalency diploma or certificate holders must provide the original document and score report (which are returned) or an exact copy of the documents. Florida residents must complete a Florida residency statement. Test scores, such as SAT I, ACT, or TOEFL, should be sent directly to the Office of Admissions by the testing board. Students not presenting test scores are tested for placement purposes upon acceptance to the College.

Application and Information

Applications are accepted on an ongoing basis. All prospective students should contact:

District Office of Admissions and Registration Services
Miami Dade College
11101 S.W. 104th Street
Miami, Florida 33176-3393

Telephone: 305-237-8888
Fax: 305-237-2964
World Wide Web: http://www.mdc.edu

MIDDLESEX COUNTY COLLEGE
EDISON, NEW JERSEY

The College and Its Mission

Middlesex County College (MCC) is one of the largest and among the oldest county colleges in New Jersey. The College, a two-year publicly supported coeducational institution, is committed to serving all those who can benefit from postsecondary learning, and the student body reflects this belief. More than 550 courses are offered during the day, evening, and on weekends. Students have the opportunity to prepare academically and through cooperative work placements, clinical experience, and laboratory work for careers in business, health, social science, and science technologies.

Middlesex County College offers modern, well-equipped facilities located on a beautiful 200-acre campus, together with excellent learning resources and dedicated faculty members. Most students commute to the College from Middlesex County, although a growing number commute from out of county. Each year, more and more students from outside the United States enroll in the International Student Program. All students have the opportunity to add to their collegiate experience through participation in a variety of student activities and clubs. The College has a recreational facility with a 25-meter pool, dance studio, wrestling and weight rooms, and racquetball courts. The College philosophy is directed toward assisting each individual in reaching his or her maximum potential, and counselors work with students to ensure this goal.

Academic Programs

More than seventy different degree and certificate programs, either transfer or career oriented, may be taken full-time or part-time during the day, evening, and on weekends. Courses are offered during the fall and spring semesters, a January winter session, and summer sessions. The College offers **Associate in Arts (A.A.)** and **Associate in Science (A.S.)** degree programs designed specifically to transfer to four-year colleges and universities in the fields of arts, business education, engineering, and sciences. Students interested in preparing for careers in medicine and law begin study at MCC with courses in science and liberal arts. Graduates have an excellent success rate in transferring to colleges and universities nationwide. In selected programs there is a formal credit transfer agreement with four-year institutions such as Rutgers, The State University of New Jersey; New Jersey Institute of Technology; and New York University.

MCC has dual-degree programs with Rutgers University. MCC students who complete the designated transfer associate degree program and fulfill the necessary criteria are guaranteed admission with full junior status at Camden, Newark, and New Brunswick campuses of Rutgers University.

MCC also has a joint admission program with New Jersey Institute of Technology (NJIT). Under the terms of the agreement, MCC offers students who apply for admission to designated associate degree programs the opportunity to be admitted simultaneously to the related baccalaureate program at NJIT. Jointly admitted students who successfully complete the specified associate degree program at MCC and receive the recommendation of their program dean may then enroll in the third year of study in the designated program at NJIT without further admission review.

Adult students may earn up to 80 credits at Middlesex, which, with proper planning, may be applied toward a bachelor's degree at Thomas Edison College.

Many challenging programs and options designed to prepare students for entry into the job market are available in business education, engineering technologies, health technologies, and science. MCC has one of the few professional culinary arts programs in the state. MCC has the only Psychosocial Rehabilitation and Treatment Program in the state. Graduates of career programs receive an **Associate in Applied Science (A.A.S.)** degree. Many graduates holding the A.A.S. degree transfer to four-year colleges, which may accept all or part of the credits earned at MCC. Certificate programs are available.

In addition to associate degree and certificate curricula, the College offers students the opportunity to enroll in a plan of study through the Open College Program. Open College serves students who want to try out an individualized academic program prior to formally enrolling in a specific degree or certificate program. The College offers Project Connections, a nationally recognized program for students with learning disabilities. Students interested in military education may participate in the Army or Air Force ROTC program through cross-registration at Rutgers University.

Degree and certificate programs are offered in accounting; automotive technology; biological laboratory technology; biology; business administration; chemical technology; chemistry; civil/construction engineering technology; communication; computer programming; computer science; criminal justice (correction administration and police science); culinary arts; dance; dental hygiene; dietetic technology; education (practitioner in early childhood education, practitioner in special education, practitioner in general classroom education, teacher aide, and teacher assistant studies); electrical engineering technology (computer electronics technology); English; environmental technology; fashion merchandising; fine arts; fire science technology; graphic arts; health sciences; history; hotel, restaurant, and institution management (hotel/motel management and restaurant food service management); journalism; liberal arts; management; marketing; mathematics; mechanical engineering technology; mecomtronics engineering technology; media art and design (advertising graphics design and professional commercial photography); medical laboratory technology; modern languages; music; nursing; office administration; paralegal studies; pharmacy assistant studies; physical education/recreation; physics; political science; preprofessional biology; psychology; psychosocial rehabilitation and treatment; radiography education; respiratory care; retail management; small business administration; social and rehabilitation services; social services; sociology; surveying technology; telecommunication networking technology; theater; and visual arts.

Off-Campus Programs

In addition to the main campus in Edison, MCC offers classes at fourteen sites throughout the county in industry and schools. There are two outreach centers in New Brunswick and Perth Amboy. Both centers offer a comprehensive English as a Second Language Program. The College offers credit courses through a network of public adult schools, corporations, and hospitals.

MCC also offers study-abroad programs in England, France, Spain, and other countries.

Credit for Nontraditional Learning Experiences

There are several programs at the College through which applicants may earn credit for knowledge learned in nontraditional ways. Both Credit by Examination and the College-Level Examination Program (CLEP) are available.

Costs

The 2003–04 tuition was $73.50 per credit for in-county residents and $147 per credit for out-of-county residents. There are also mandatory accident and health insurance fees and parking and technology fees. Some classes require special lab or material costs or other fees. The per-credit cost is subject to change.

Financial Aid

Through its financial aid programs, MCC makes every effort to overcome economic barriers. Funds from federal, state, and private sources are available to those who have need and meet the eligibility requirements. To be considered for financial aid, a student must complete the Free Application for Federal Student Aid (FAFSA) and the MCC Financial Aid Form. The priority deadline for the fall semester is April 1 and November 1 for the spring semester. Before a financial aid application can be reviewed, the student must be accepted to a degree program and be matriculated for a minimum of 6 credits.

Faculty

There are 200 full-time and 500 part-time members of the faculty. The student-faculty ratio is 21:1. Of the full-time faculty members, nearly 90 percent are teaching faculty members and serve as academic advisers.

Student Body Profile

There are about 11,500 students on campus, including 5,000 full-time and 6,500 part-time. The campus population is diverse, with students from more than sixty countries in attendance. Approximately half of the students come directly from high school, with an average age of 25 for the entire student body.

Student Activities

There are more than sixty chartered clubs and organizations, a College Center Program Board, College Assembly, national honor societies, special minority student activities, and a College newspaper, radio station, and literary magazine. The College offers intercollegiate competition through membership in Region XIX of the National Junior College Athletic Association and Garden State Athletic Conference.

Facilities and Resources

The campus is composed of twenty-five buildings, including a state-of-the-art Technical Services Center, a fully equipped Recreation Center, and a 440-seat Performing Arts Center. The Career Counseling and Placement Center provides students with assistance in making decisions about career choices, education programs, college transfer, job placement, and other personal concerns. Bilingual counseling is available to Spanish-speaking students.

Location

The College is located just 15 minutes from New Brunswick, New Jersey. The College is conveniently located near numerous restaurants and shopping centers. The New Jersey shore is less than 30 minutes away. Mass transit to the College is available from many surrounding areas and easy transportation is available to New York City and Philadelphia.

Admission Requirements

The admission policy is based on the premise that the College should provide an opportunity for further education to all citizens of the community. Enrollment is open to anyone who holds a high school diploma or any non–high school graduates 18 years of age or older who can demonstrate an ability to benefit from a college education. SAT scores are optional. Applicants to most programs are not required to submit any standardized test scores.

Admission to programs that specify additional selective criteria may require a review of prior educational performance, standardized test scores, the completion of an appropriate developmental program, or, when suitable, an assessment of an applicant's aptitude and interest, as determined during an admission counseling interview.

Application and Information

Completed applications are reviewed on a continuous basis, with the exception of the limited-seat programs in dental hygiene, medical laboratory technology, nursing, psychosocial rehabilitation, radiography education, and respiratory care. A completed application form, a required $25 nonrefundable application fee, and all supporting materials should be sent to the officer of admissions.

For application forms or additional information, students should contact:

Admissions Office
Middlesex County College
2600 Woodbridge Avenue, P.O. Box 3050
Edison, New Jersey 08818-3050
Telephone: 732-906-4243

MOHAWK VALLEY COMMUNITY COLLEGE

UTICA AND ROME, NEW YORK

The College and Its Mission

Mohawk Valley Community College (MVCC) offers choice, opportunity, and hope by providing accessible and affordable higher education, training, and services that emphasize academic excellence, diversity, and a global view.

Mohawk Valley Community College strives to be a college of choice through innovative educational leadership, programs, and services that address the current and future needs of rapidly changing local, regional, and global communities.

The College was founded in 1946 as the New York State Institute of Applied Arts and Sciences at Utica. One of five postsecondary institutions established on an experimental basis after World War II, the public institute offered programs leading to technical and semiprofessional employment in business and industry. After name changes in the 1950s, redefining its mission, the College moved to its current 80-acre campus location in Utica in 1960. In 1961, the College was renamed Mohawk Valley Community College. Today, the College offers a full range of academic programs.

The College is accredited by the Middle States Association of Colleges and Schools. Individual program accreditations are as follows: civil, electrical, and mechanical engineering technology and surveying technology by the Commission for Technology Accreditation of the Accreditation Board for Engineering and Technology, Inc. (ABET); nursing by the National League for Nursing Accrediting Commission (NLNAC); and respiratory care and health information technology–medical records by the Commission on Accreditation of Allied Health Education Programs, in cooperation with the Committee on Accreditation for Respiratory Care and the American Health Information Association's Council on Accreditation, respectively.

Academic Programs

The College has been authorized to offer the following degrees and certificates: Associate in Arts (A.A.) degree, Associate in Science (A.S.) degree, Associate in Applied Science (A.A.S.) degree, Associate in Occupational Studies (A.O.S.) degree, and the MVCC Certificate.

The structure and goals of academic programming at MVCC have two main purposes. Certificate, A.O.S., and A.A.S. programs emphasize the development of employable skills through a combination of classroom and laboratory instruction. Some programs also include internship experiences. A.A. and A.S. programs provide students with the liberal arts, science, mathematics, business, engineering, or computer course work necessary for transfer into the junior year of a preprofessional program at a four-year public or private college or university upon the completion of their associate degree.

The minimum number of credits needed to earn an associate degree is 62. The maximum credits required for a degree differ by program and degree type.

Opportunities for specialization include the Honors Program, independent study, internships, study abroad, and ROTC (Army).

The College operates on a semester calendar. Fall classes begin before Labor Day and end before Christmas. Spring classes begin in mid-January and end in mid-May.

Career and transfer programs are available. Majors offered include accounting (A.A.S.); air conditioning technology (A.O.S.); banking and insurance (A.A.S.); building management (A.A.S.); business administration (A.S.); business management (A.A.S.); chemical dependency practitioner studies (A.A.S.); civil engineering technology (A.A.S.); computer-aided drafting (A.O.S.); computer information systems (A.A.S.); computer science (A.S.); criminal justice (A.A.S.); culinary arts management (A.O.S.); digital animation (A.A.S.); electrical service technician studies (A.O.S.), with options in electrical maintenance, fiber optics, and robotics; electrical engineering technology (A.A.S.); emergency medical services/paramedic studies (A.A.S.); engineering science (A.S.); environmental analysis–chemical technology (A.A.S.); fine art (A.S.); general studies (A.S.); general studies–childhood education (A.S., joint admission with the State University of New York (SUNY) College at Oneonta); graphic arts technology (A.A.S.); graphic design (A.A.S.); health information technology–medical records (A.A.S.); hotel technology–meeting services (A.A.S.); human services (A.A.S.); illustration (A.A.S.); individual studies (A.A., A.A.S., A.S., and A.O.S.); international studies (A.A.); liberal arts–humanities and social science (A.A.); manufacturing technology (A.O.S.); mathematics (A.S.); mechanical engineering technology (A.A.S.); mechanical technology–aircraft maintenance (A.A.S.); media marketing and management (A.A.S.); medical assisting studies (A.A.S.); nursing (A.A.S.); nutrition and dietetics (A.S.); office technologies (A.A.S.); photography (A.A.S.); pre–environmental science (A.S.); programming and systems (A.A.S.); radiologic technology (A.S.); recreation and leisure services (A.A.S.); respiratory care (A.A.S.); restaurant management (A.A.S.); science, with emphasis areas in biology, chemistry, physical education, physics, and sports medicine (A.S.); semiconductor manufacturing technology (A.A.S.); surveying technology (A.A.S.); telecommunications technology (A.A.S.); Web site design and management (A.A.S.); and welding technology (A.O.S.).

Certificate programs include appliance repair, refrigeration, and air conditioning; architectural drafting; carpentry and masonry; case management; chef training; clinical lab assistant; CNC machinist technology; coaching; computer electronic technician studies; electronic technician studies; engineering drawing; finance; graphic communication; heating and air conditioning; hotel technology–front office technology; individual studies: business and industry; industrial and commercial electricity; industrial engineering technician studies; insurance; machinist technology; managerial accounting; mechanical drafting; media marketing and management; medical assistant studies; metallurgy lab technician studies; office practice; phlebotomy; photography; production planning; refrigeration; small-business management; surveying; tool design; Web site design and management; welding; and word processing management.

The College offers an English as a Second Language (ESL) Summer Institute beginning in mid-July each year. A jointly registered degree program with SUNY College at Oneonta offers applicants the opportunity to complete a bachelor's degree in childhood education (grades 1–6) at MVCC.

Credit for Nontraditional Learning Experiences

MVCC offers adult students the opportunity to earn credits through the CLEP examination, MVCC-administered examinations, life experience, and course work completed in a noncollegiate setting. The accumulated credit earned cannot exceed 75 percent of the student's degree program.

Costs

Tuition for New York State residents is $1400 per semester for full-time students and $115 per credit hour for part-time students; for out-of-state and international students, it is $2800 per semester full-time and $230 per credit hour part-time. Student fees are $65 per semester for full-time students and $1 per credit hour for part-time students. Books and supplies range from $300 to $500 per semester, depending on the student's major. Residence hall occupants must purchase one of the available room and board packages each semester. Costs are approximately $3160 per semester, depending on type of accommodations and number of meals chosen. The residence hall technology fee is $100 per semester for Internet and phone access. The residence hall social fee is $10 per semester. The residence hall orientation fee is $40 and covers new-resident orientation programming and meals.

Financial Aid

One of MVCC's major objectives is to make college affordable for all. Approximately 90 percent of MVCC students receive some form of state or federal financial aid. The College offers a comprehensive financial assistance program of scholarships, loans, and grants. Most of the financial assistance received by MVCC students is need based. Non-need-based scholarships include the Presidential Scholarship Program for the top 10 percent of Oneida County (the College's sponsoring county) graduates, two similar Exceptional Student Scholarships for those not from Oneida County, and the Sodexho/MVCC Meal Plan Scholarships, which consider exceptional citizenship. Students eligible for non-need-based scholarships are expected to apply for state and federal financial assistance as applicable.

Faculty

The full-time faculty numbers 149, and the part-time faculty numbers 130. Approximately 8 percent of all faculty members have doctoral degrees. The student-faculty ratio is approximately 18:1.

Student Body Profile

MVCC enrolls approximately 5,500 students each year. Enrollment is divided between the main campus in Utica, New York, and the branch campus in Rome, New York, with approximately 80 percent of the student population enrolled on the main campus.

The College is designed to be predominantly commuter based; 85 percent of the students live within 60 miles of the campus in central New York State. For fall 2005, the College plans to add a fifth residence hall on the main campus in Utica, increasing housing capacity to 500 students. The residence life staff provides listings of off-campus apartment-style housing options.

The international student population has grown from 40 students to 122 since 1996. Twenty-one different countries are represented on campus.

The average age of students is about 22, with approximately 35 percent of the population being over the age of 25. Approximately 52 percent of the enrolled students are women. The racial/ethnic makeup of the campus is currently 80 percent white, non-Hispanic; 7 percent black, non-Hispanic; 1 percent American Indian/Alaskan native; 1 percent Asian/Pacific Islander; and 3 percent Hispanic. Of the total student body, 8 percent chose not to identify with any of the listed groups.

Enrolling students typically exhibit an 80 percent grade average in high school and a rank in the top 50 percent of their high school class.

Student Activities

The Student Activities program offers a wide variety of experiences for students through clubs, Student Congress, and other activities. On each campus, the staff assists students with the planning of events and programs. There are seventeen professional, curriculum-related clubs. In addition, there are thirty service/interest clubs that provide students with the opportunity to participate in a wide range of social, cultural, theatrical, athletic, and international activities to broaden their experiences.

MVCC participates in Division III of the National Junior College Athletic Association. Men's teams include baseball, basketball, bowling, cross-country, golf, ice hockey, indoor track, lacrosse, tennis, track and field, and soccer. Women's teams include basketball, bowling, cross-country, golf, indoor track, softball, soccer, tennis, track and field, and volleyball. The combined team win/loss record in 2003 was 461-138-2, for a .770 winning percentage.

Facilities and Resources

MVCC has undergone major renovations in the past three years as part of a $21-million campus master plan. As part of the plan, campus renovations have included new practice lab facilities for nursing and respiratory-care students, cadaver labs for anatomy and physiology, and a student service center in Payne Hall that includes admissions, financial aid, the registrar, counseling, the business office, an advisement center, and a help desk. Other renovations to the Alumni College Center provided an expanded bookstore and a new student health center.

A new 65,000-square-foot information technology and performing arts conference center, the main feature of the project, houses computer labs, conferencing facilities, a new state-of-the-art theater, and additional instructional computer support laboratories. It is a focal point of campus activities.

The campus collection includes 86,000 books and more than 700 periodical titles. CDs, audiotapes, and videotapes are available for loan. Each campus library has a bestseller collection for recreational reading. The main campus library in Utica maintains a Career Center for job-search assistance. Each library provides a number of electronic resources, including Internet access.

Academic tutoring is available at no cost to students in the Learning Centers on both campuses. The centers offer instructional support in mathematics, writing, reading, study skills, life sciences, and computer and social sciences.

Location

The main campus is in Utica, New York, a small city of 50,000 people. The branch campus in Rome, New York, is located in a community of 30,000 people. The small-city atmosphere, coupled with a wide range of cultural activities, museums, access to the Adirondack Mountains, good public transportation, and sports venues, provides an excellent location for student growth and development.

Admission Requirements

The College is an open-admission, full-opportunity college. The College does not require applicants to complete standardized admissions tests such as the ACT or SAT.

Application and Information

Students can apply in a variety of ways. MVCC provides its own admission application; no processing fee is required. It is available from the Admissions Office or high schools in New York State, or it can be printed out from the College's Web site. MVCC also participates in the SUNY application process. Students can use the SUNY application, which costs $40 per college choice, as well.

For further information, interested students should contact:

Admissions Office
Mohawk Valley Community College
1101 Sherman Drive
Utica, New York 13501

Telephone: 315-792-5354
Fax: 315-792-5527
E-mail: admissions@mvcc.edu (U.S.)
       international_admissions@mvcc.edu (international)
World Wide Web: http://www.mvcc.edu

MORRISON INSTITUTE OF TECHNOLOGY

MORRISON, ILLINOIS

The Institute and Its Mission

Morrison Institute of Technology is an independent, coeducational, not-for-profit, two-year college specializing in engineering technology. Founded in 1973, the college provides a cost-effective educational program that leads to a professional career in engineering technology. While many graduates go directly into industry, some transfer to four-year colleges offering a continuation of studies in the engineering technology fields.

All classes are day classes offered at the campus in Morrison, Illinois. Courses are offered on a semester basis, with semesters starting in January and August.

Morrison has an open admissions policy. Anyone with a valid high school diploma or equivalent may enroll. It has been found from experience that some students who have had an otherwise undistinguished high school career often thrive and blossom when challenged by a college program that specializes in the area in which they are interested. Many students who have found their niche at Morrison have gone on to earn advanced technical degrees and some have even founded thriving technical businesses.

The college is authorized to operate and grant degrees in the state of Illinois under the applicable state statutes administered by the Illinois Board of Higher Education. The Engineering Technology program is accredited by the Technology Accreditation Commission (TAC) of the Accreditation Board for Engineering and Technology (ABET), 111 Market Place, Suite 1050, Baltimore, Maryland 21201; telephone: 410-347-7700. In addition, the drafting design program at Morrison Institute of Technology is certified by the American Drafting Design Association, P.O. Box 11937, Columbia, South Carolina 29211 (telephone: 803-771-0008), at the design/drafter level. The college is also fully accredited by the Council on Occupational Education, 41 Perimeter Center, NE Suite 640, Atlanta, Georgia 30346; telephone: 800-917-2081 (toll-free). The state of Illinois, Department of Veterans Affairs, State Approving Agency, has approved Morrison Institute of Technology for veteran's training under Chapter 36 of Title #38, U.S. Code. The Division of Rehabilitation Services (DORS) and the Job Training Partnership Act (JTPA) both refer clients to the college for training. The college is listed in the Educational Directory, U.S. Department of Education, as a legally authorized institution of higher learning, allowing qualified students to participate in a number of federally funded student financial aid and grant programs. The college is also a member of the Service Members Opportunity Colleges (SOC), thus extending educational opportunities to service personnel while on active duty. The college is also a member of the Better Business Bureau.

Student housing facilities are available on campus in Odey Residence Hall. This facility has been designed to provide housing for students in an efficiency apartment arrangement. The residence hall is coeducational, but individual rooms are not coeducational and accommodations for married couples are not available.

Academic Programs

The engineering technology program has been developed and is kept current in accordance with suggested guidelines provided by nationally recognized technical education groups, accrediting organizations, and the college Industrial Advisory Board.

The curriculum for the engineering technology program has been designed with an appropriate balance of study in the areas of engineering and construction technology and manual drafting. In addition, to ensure that a student is prepared to assume a productive and contributing role as a citizen locally, nationally, and worldwide, a core of general education courses, including basic sciences, humanities, written and oral communications, mathematics, and computer literacy, are required to provide that academic foundation which the student must acquire to continue a lifelong learning process on a formal or informal basis. Extensive exposure to computer usage in computer-aided drafting (CAD) is also provided to all students.

The program has a very open architecture to permit students to concentrate their technical electives in the construction area or the design drafting area. A student may also elect to choose technical electives from both concentrations, if he or she desires a more general background. The minimum total number of technical elective credit hours required is 21 in order to meet the minimum total number of credit hours required to receive the Associate in Applied Science (A.A.S.) degree in engineering technology.

Costs

The tuition for 2003–04 was $4995 per semester, based upon taking a typical academic load of 12 to 19 semester credit hours. The computer usage fee was $100 per semester. Campus housing costs were $1000 per semester (not required if the student lives off campus). An additional $100 housing deposit is required for first-time residents. The housing cost figure does not include food, laundry, or general living expenses. Parking fees were $20 per semester (not required if the student does not park a car on campus). The recreation center/activity fee was $30 per semester, and the technology fee was $150.

Financial Aid

The curricula offered at Morrison Institute of Technology have been accredited by a nationally recognized accrediting agency. Qualified students, therefore, may take advantage of a number of federally funded student financial aid programs.

Grant programs at Morrison include the Federal Pell Grant, the Illinois Student Assistance Commission Monetary Award Program Grant, the Federal Supplemental Educational Opportunity Grant (FSEOG), the Federal Work-Study Program (FWS), tutorial and lab supervisors, the Department of Rehabilitation Services, the Job Training Partnership Act and the Veterans Educational Program.

Morrison Institute of Technology has available a limited number of scholarships for students now attending high school or the associated area vocational technical school, who wish to pursue engineering technology studies at Morrison Institute of Technology. These scholarships are independent of, and in addition to, any other financial aid a student may obtain. There are three areas in which a student can qualify for a Morrison Institute of Technology sponsored scholarship: the Morrison Institute of Technology Academic Scholarships, the Morrison

Institute of Technology Performance Scholarships, or the Morrison Institute of Technology Parent Scholarships.

Loan programs at Morrison include the Subsidized Federal Family Education Loan Program (student loan), the Unsubsidized Federal Family Education Loan Program (student loan), and the Federal PLUS loan.

All prospective students are encouraged to complete the Free Application for Federal Student Aid (FAFSA). Applications may be obtained from student's high school or the college Federal Aid Office or by downloading the FAFSA Express Software from the Web at http://www.ed.gov/offices/OPE/express.html.

Faculty

Morrison's faculty members are full-time employees. The student-faculty ratio is about 15:1, which means that students at Morrison receive a lot of personal attention. The faculty members are experienced in the areas they teach, and many are sought out by businesses to provide private consultative services; therefore, students learn what the profession is all about from persons who actually do the work. Approximately 30 percent of the faculty members are licensed professional engineers or surveyors. Approximately 23 percent have earned graduate-level degrees.

Student Body Profile

Morrison is a small college. The total full-time enrollment is about 200 students. The majority of the students attending are from the Midwest, mostly Illinois, Iowa, Wisconsin, and Indiana, with a few from the Eastern and Western states. Approximately 8–12 percent of the student enrollment is female, Hispanics make up 2–6 percent, African Americans number 6–10 percent, and Asians compose 1–2 percent. Approximately 75 percent of the students receive financial aid of some kind. About 60 percent are enrolled in the construction option while the remaining 40 percent are enrolled in the design drafting CAD option.

Student Activities

A student recreation center is provided for all students. The recreation center provides a place for students to relax; play pool, video games, Ping-Pong, card games, or chess; or watch TV. The facility also has a fitness room and laundromat. Vending machines are also available in the recreation center. Morrison Institute of Technology sponsors a student chapter of the Society of Manufacturing Engineers (SME). Activities associated with SME include attending regional meetings, field trips, and SME-sponsored exhibitions and seminars.

Facilities and Resources

The college has two main educational facilities, the A. E. Rambo Center, which also houses the administrative offices and student learning center, and the Technical Center, which houses mainly the computer laboratories, survey, soils laboratory, and multimedia lecture halls. The college also has the student recreation center complex and Odey Residence Hall.

Location

The campus is located on 17 acres on the south side of Morrison, Illinois. Morrison is about 45 minutes by car from the Quad-Cities area and about 2¼ hours by car from Chicago. Morrison is a picturesque small town with a population of 4,300. It is a neat, clean, and friendly town with tree-lined streets, neighborhood churches, and a small but busy business district. The college took its mascot emblem, "The Thoroughbreds," because there are many horse ranches in the area. The town is considered very safe: children play on the streets after dark here, and many people don't bother to lock their doors. Nearby is Rockwood State Park, several wildlife sanctuaries along the Mississippi River, and several park areas featuring Native American pre-Columbian settlements.

Admission Requirements

Admission to Morrison Institute of Technology is considered if the applicant has graduated from high school or has completed GED testing with scores that can be accepted as meeting high school requirements. It is recommended, but not required, that an applicant's educational background include at least one semester each of high school algebra and geometry. ACT or SAT test scores are required for academic counseling. Those students not having either test score are administered an institutional placement test.

All applicants are encouraged to schedule a tour of the campus. Tours are conducted during any of the formal open houses held by the college. If an applicant is unable to attend an open house, tours can be arranged on an individual basis by appointment. To complete the application process the following items are to be mailed to the college: a completed application for enrollment; the appropriate fees; an official high school transcript; if transfer analysis is requested, an official transcript from the institution granting the credit, mailed directly from the institution to Morrison Institute of Technology; a copy of the applicant's immunization record; and ACT, SAT, or placement test scores.

Application and Information

Students who wish to attend Morrison Institute of Technology may obtain the required admission application material and additional information by contacting:

Admissions Office
Morrison Institute of Technology
701 Portland Avenue
Morrison, Illinois 61270

Telephone: 815-772-7218
Fax: 815-772-7584
E-mail: admissions@morrison.tec.il.us
World Wide Web: http://www.morrison.tec.il.us

NEW MEXICO MILITARY INSTITUTE

ROSWELL, NEW MEXICO

The Institute and Its Mission

New Mexico Military Institute (NMMI) was established in 1891 and became a State (Territorial) School in 1893. Its purpose then and now was "for the education and training of the youth of this country with a mandate by law to be of as high a standard as like institutions in other states and territories of the United States." New Mexico Military Institute is primarily an academic institution operating within the framework of a military environment. NMMI is accredited by the North Central Association of Colleges and Schools, by the State of New Mexico Department of Education, and by the Department of the Army as a Military Junior college offering Junior and Senior ROTC. The Department of the Army has annually rated NMMI as an Honor School with Distinction or its equivalent since 1909.

Academic Programs

New Mexico Military Institute provides a comprehensive liberal arts curriculum including such disciplines as criminal justice, English, foreign language (Spanish, German, French), history, sociology, philosophy, political science, psychology, business administration, economics, computer science, chemistry, physics, biology, math through college calculus, geology, art, music, and physical education.

Associate Degree Programs The school awards an **Associate in Arts** degree, which requires 68 hours (6 in English, 6 to 8 in the humanities, 9 in social science/history, 8 in laboratory science, 6 to 12 in military science, 3 in mathematics, 2 in physical education, with the balance in electives). A normal load is 17 hours per semester. A cadet may choose to concentrate in a particular area while pursuing the Associate in Arts degree.

Many cadets are interested in pursuing a military career through the ROTC Basic Camp (Camp Challenge) approach. In order to qualify for the two-year commissioning program, a student must successfully complete a five-week training program conducted by the U.S. Army. This course occurs the summer before cadets enter their freshman (second class) year at New Mexico Military Institute. In special cases, students who have three or more years of high school ROTC or prior military service may apply for advanced placement credit. If accepted, they need not attend the Basic Camp. All eligible camp cadets can compete for a two-year scholarship that is awarded upon completion of the Basic Camp. The PMS has numerous Army ROTC two-year scholarships to award each year. Two years of advanced military science (MS III and MS IV), are required during the freshman and sophomore years, respectively. An advanced ROTC camp is required during the summer between MS III and MS IV. This camp is five weeks long. Upon successful completion of all phases, two years of college, Basic Camp, MS III, Advanced Camp, and MS IV, the cadet is commissioned as a second lieutenant in the United States Army Reserve.

Costs

For the academic year 2004–05, in-state tuition is $1130, out-of-state tuition is $3570, room was $1225, board is $2150, and the matriculation fee is $5. Accident insurance costs $200. Other fixed fees were $1131. Uniforms, books, and supplies cost $1700. This includes all uniform purchases. Additional funds are necessary for personal expenses. The amount needed varies depending on a cadet's spending habits. New Mexico Military Institute offers a deferred payment plan requiring an initial deposit of $2200. All costs are subject to change.

Financial Aid

Federal financial aid is available to all eligible college students. New Mexico Military Institute participates in the Federal Pell Grant, Federal Supplemental Educational Opportunity Grant, Federal Perkins Loan, Federal Work Study program, Stafford Loan, Parent Loan for Undergraduate Students program and specialized programs for New Mexico residents. New Mexico Military Institute offers a varied scholarship program for merit-based and need-based considerations. The New Mexico Legislator Scholarship Program is available only to New Mexico residents. Scholarships are renewable based on the continued eligibility of the recipient. In 2000–01, more than 76 percent of the college student body received either federal or scholarship assistance amounting to more than $1.3 million. Currently, 410 college students receive $1,368,295 in assistance, ranging from $500 scholarships to $7000 in federal financial aid. A full-time financial aid staff is available.

Faculty

NMMI has 63 full-time faculty members, many with terminal degrees, and all are required to have at least a master's degree. The student-faculty ratio is 18:1.

Student Body Profile

The junior college population of 450 to 500 at New Mexico Military Institute generally includes cadets from more than forty-four different states and twelve other countries. Typically, the ethnic breakdown includes 17 percent Hispanic, 8 percent African American, 6 percent Asian, and 2 percent Native American students. In 2003–04, there were 111 cadets representing thirteen different nations. Twenty-one percent of the Corps of Cadets were female. More than one third of college students are pursuing an Army commission. College cadets entering the Corps of Cadets for the first time are new cadets for one semester. New cadets receive yearling status at the completion of one semester and old cadet status with the completion of one year. The new cadet environment is stressful, formal, strict, and just. All cadets are held strictly accountable for their actions. NMMI operates with a Cadet Honor Code that states, "A cadet will not lie, cheat, or steal, or tolerate those who do. Every cadet is obligated to support and enforce the honor system." NMMI maintains a strict policy regarding the possession, use, or sale of alcoholic beverages and illegal drugs. All cadets live on campus.

Student Activities

Students enjoy video games, pool, bowling, and the snack bar during their free time. Movies on Saturday nights also contribute to weekend activities. Informal dances are held about twice a month. Recorded music is provided by students and professional disc jockeys. Two formal balls are held each year, the Homecoming Ball in the fall and the Final Ball in the spring. Escorts from all over the country attend. NMMI students can participate in outdoor activities at the nearby ski resort area of Ruidoso and the Mescalero Apache Indian Reservation. Other attractions include Carlsbad Caverns, Lincoln National Forest, Bottomless Lakes, Living Desert State Park, and the historical town of Lincoln, famous for the exploits of Billy the Kid, Pat Garrett, and John Chisum. Rounding out the Institute's extracurricular activities, students enjoy marching and concert bands, soccer, judo and karate clubs, color guards, and rifle and drill teams. Students may also participate in swimming, drama, and academic honorary societies. Student publications include *The Maverick* and the Bronco yearbook.

Facilities and Resources

NMMI's campus encompasses more than 40 acres and has some of the finest academic facilities in the country. The yellow brick buildings reflect a military style traditional to the campus since 1909. The Toles Learning Center houses the library and its 68,000-volume collection, TV/communication studio, academic computer center, 200-seat lecture hall, classrooms, and the Student Assistance Center. Available to cadets is an online catalog. Also located in the Toles Learning Center are the Computer Services Center and the Career Lab, housed in the Student Assistance Center. College faculty academic advisers are available to provide students with assistance in college exploration and selection. A computerized college scholarship search program is available in the center for cadet use. NMMI is a regional test center for the ACT, SAT, and GRE. College-Level Examination Program (CLEP) exams are available to those cadets wishing to challenge a course. A liaison officer is available whose duties include working with and assisting students interested in attending the national service academies. The Student Assistance Center provides professional advisers who offer academic and career counseling. Transfer guidance on colleges and service academy admission is also available. Approximately $15 million in cadet room renovations have allowed each cadet access to a state-of-the-art computer network, cable TV, and telephones. New Mexico Military Institute has excellent athletic facilities and athletic playing fields. They include a physical education building with four regulation basketball courts, four handball/racquetball courts, an Olympic-size swimming pool with sunning decks, Nautilus exercise equipment and Universal exercise machines. A separate building houses the varsity team locker and weight rooms and a gymnasium for varsity basketball games. The playing fields include twelve tennis courts, a baseball diamond, running tracks (quarter-mile and half-mile), football and soccer fields, and an eighteen-hole golf course.

Location

New Mexico Military Institute is located in the city of Roswell in the southeastern part of New Mexico. It is within 70 miles of skiing in the mountains of Ruidoso and within 200 miles of El Paso to the south and Albuquerque and Santa Fe to the north. The nearest regional airports are Albuquerque International Airport and Lubbock International Airport.

Admission Requirements

The minimum standards for normal admission to the college are graduation from high school with at least a 2.0 GPA (on a 4.0 scale) or equivalent and a composite score of 18 on the ACT, or a combined verbal/mathematics score of 870 on the recentered SAT I and a 2.0 GPA, or a minimum 2.5 GPA for all high school core courses and graduating in the top 50 percent of the high school class. Prospective students for the Army Commissioning program will need a composite score of 19 on the ACT, or a combined verbal/mathematics score of 920 on the recentered SAT I. Applicants and members of the Corps of Cadets must have never been married, have no dependent children, be in good physical condition, and be able to participate in athletic and leadership development activities. In addition, they cannot be more than the age of 22 at the time of admission. The admissions policy of New Mexico Military Institute is nondiscriminatory with respect to race, color, creed, or national or ethnic origin and is in compliance with federal laws with respect to sex and the handicapped. Priority of admission is given to New Mexico residents.

Application and Information

An initial inquiry is welcome at any time. Campus tours are conducted weekdays. Interested students should call to schedule an appointment at any time except for school holidays. Applications are accepted through July into all classes. Notification of acceptance is made on a rolling admissions basis.

For more information, students should contact:

Director of Admissions
New Mexico Military Institute
101 West College Boulevard
Roswell, New Mexico 88201-5173
Telephone: 505-624-8050
         800-421-5376 (toll-free)
Fax: 505-624-8058
E-mail: admissions@nmmi.edu
World Wide Web: http://www.nmmi.edu

Cadets find time to study in the New Mexico sunshine.

THE NEW YORK COLLEGE OF HEALTH PROFESSIONS
School of Massage Therapy
SYOSSET AND BROOKLYN, NEW YORK

New York
COLLEGE
of Health Professions

The College and Its Mission

New York College of Health Professions, a private nonprofit institution, is one of the nation's premier centers of holistic medicine. The College educates students, treats patients, and conducts innovative research. Founded in 1981, New York College is firmly rooted in the principles of holistic health care as well as the blending of Western and Eastern practices, or integrative medicine.

New York College offers accredited degree programs in the field of complementary medicine. Undergraduate programs include an associate degree in massage therapy and a bachelor's degree in advanced Asian bodywork. Graduate programs include combined bachelor's and master's degrees in acupuncture or oriental medicine (the combined study of acupuncture and herbs). All programs lead to New York State licensing and/or national certification.

The College also offers a 495-clock-hour continuing education program in holistic nursing for RNs and a selection of other continuing education courses and workshops for both health-care professionals and the general public. In 2003, New York College was awarded a grant from New York State to train all the RNs at Bellevue Hospital in New York City in an Introduction to Holistic Nursing course.

New York College is chartered by the Board of Regents of the University of the State of New York, and all programs are registered by the New York State Education Department. The acupuncture and Oriental medicine programs are accredited by the Accrediting Commission for Acupuncture and Oriental Medicine (ACAOM). The Oriental medicine program is also approved by the California Acupuncture Board. The College is approved as a provider of Continuing Education by the New York State Nurses Association Council on Continuing Education and the National Certification Board for Therapeutic Massage and Bodywork. The College is a member of numerous professional organizations related to the fields of Oriental medicine and massage therapy. There are an on-site café and a bookstore at the Syosset campus.

Academic Programs

The massage therapy program at New York College began in 1981 and was the School's first educational program. It has since become nationally recognized and was cited for academic excellence in 1997 by the National Certification Board for Therapeutic Massage and Bodywork. In 1996, New York College became the first college in the United States to award an associate degree in massage therapy. The program exceeds national certification and state licensing requirements. In August 2003, first-time candidates from New York College had an 88 percent pass rate on the New York State Massage Therapy Licensing Examination.

The benefits of massage therapy have become widely recognized. Documentation on the effects of massage shows that it improves circulation and lymph drainage and can help treat sports injuries and alleviate stress, headaches, and other aches and pains. When practiced in conjunction with Western medical treatment, massage can also be used to treat arthritis, hypertension, diabetes, asthma, bronchitis, and neuromuscular diseases, among others. Massage therapy most commonly falls into two categories: Western (Swedish), which focuses on the musculoskeletal system and is based on standard Western anatomy and physiology, and Eastern, or Oriental, which is based on the movement of energy through various channels in the body. At New York College, students learn both of these modalities as well as the specific techniques for sports massage, chair massage, shiatsu, reflexology, and more.

New York College's massage therapy program is a 72-credit program. Upon completion, graduates receive an Associate of Occupational Studies (A.O.S.) degree in massage therapy. They are eligible to sit for the New York State Licensing Exam in Massage Therapy, the National Certification Exam for Therapeutic Massage and Bodywork, and the NCCAOM National Certification Exam for Oriental Bodywork Therapy. Course work for the massage therapy program includes in-depth study of both Western and Eastern health sciences, Western and Oriental bodywork techniques, and tai chi chuan, qi gong, or yoga. Courses are also offered in ethics, professional development, and business practice. The culmination of the program is the intensive clinical internship that students undergo in the College's on-site teaching clinic.

New York College operates on a fifteen-week trimester system. New students are admitted to the College for the September, January, and May trimesters. Ten-week, second-cycle trimester admissions may be added when there is sufficient demand. The program can be completed in twenty months, twenty-four months, or thirty-six months on a part-time basis.

Off-Campus Programs

New York College offers study abroad at its Luo Yang Medical Center facility in the People's Republic of China. Programs range from three-week immersion programs to a full trimester in China. Students study in the hospitals of Luo Yang as well as attend lectures at the medical center. The clinic rotations give students the opportunity to observe and participate in patient treatments. The courses taken in China are those required by the student's curriculum, and the classes and clinic time count toward their required credits. Currently, only students in the School of Massage Therapy are eligible to study at the College's facility in China.

Costs

Tuition is based on a per-credit charge of $275 and is paid each semester. The application fee is $85, and required fees total approximately $110 per semester. Students should expect to incur an additional $1500 in expenses for texts and supplies.

Financial Aid

New York College is an eligible institution approved by the United States Department of Education and the New York State Education Department to participate in the following programs: Federal Pell Grant, Federal Supplemental Educational Opportunity Grant (FSEOG), Tuition Assistance Program (TAP), Aid for Part-Time Study, Federal Work-Study Program, Veterans Administration, Vocational Rehabilitation, Federal Stafford Student Loan, Federal PLUS loan, and alternative financing. For additional information, students should contact the College's Office of Financial Aid (800-922-7337 Ext. 244).

Faculty

New York College has a total of 90 faculty members, 15 of whom are full-time. The faculty-student ratio is 1:16 for technique classes, 1:45 for didactic classes, and up to 1:6 for clinical internships.

Student Body Profile

Total current enrollment at New York College is more than 800 students, most of whom are in the massage therapy program. New York College does not have student housing; therefore, most students are from the local area, with the majority coming from Long Island, Brooklyn, and Queens. However, the College attracts a percentage of both international and out-of-state students.

Facilities and Resources

The main campus of the College in Syosset occupies 70,000 square feet in a modern facility on three levels. Within the facility are the administrative offices, classrooms for all College educational programs, a physical arts deck, the Integrative Health Center, Academic Health Care Clinics, the Herbal Dispensary, the James and Lenore Jacobson Library, the café, the bookstore, and student and faculty lounges. Classrooms are designed and used specifically for lecture or technique work and contain the most recent instructional materials. The physical arts deck for the practice of tai chi, hatha yoga, and qi gong is specifically designed with space, light, and quiet.

The James and Lenore Jacobson Library contains the most extensive collection of materials about holistic medicine available on Long Island. The library houses a collection of books and journals specializing in Oriental medicine, complementary and alternative therapies, acupuncture, herbs, massage therapy, and holistic nursing. The library belongs to a consortium of special and medical libraries that provide interloans of additional books and journal articles. Several networked workstations provide access to the computerized book collection catalog and magazine subject index, various software and CD-ROM programs, the Internet, and various online professional databases.

The Academic Health Care Teaching Clinics are an integral part of a student's educational experience. The clinics provide affordable holistic health care to members of the community, treating more than 30,000 patients annually. Supervised student treatments include Swedish massage, Amma massage, acupuncture, herbal consultations, and holistic nursing.

In January 2004, New York College opened a center in Brooklyn, New York, and began conducting classes in all degree programs. Located in a private wing of the Brooklyn Hospital Center, Caledonian Campus, this additional location is convenient and easily reached by subway or bus for students from the outer boroughs of New York City as well as Manhattan. This facility has both didactic and technique classrooms, a solarium for physical arts, administration and faculty offices, a student lounge for studying, and a student locker room. It is located close to the Brooklyn Public Library and to stores and restaurants. The College offers day, evening, and weekend classes in Brooklyn.

The College has been a pioneer in the field of holistic health care since its inception. The Integrative Health Center is the professional family clinic of the College and offers the skills and services of licensed holistic practitioners to patients of all ages. For more than twenty-five years, this fully integrated clinic has provided patients with minimally invasive therapies, including acupuncture; herbal medicine; many modalities of massage therapy such as Swedish, sports, Amma, shiatsu, reflexology, and pregnancy massage; and chiropractic and holistic nursing. Special patient programs exist for smoking cessation, weight loss, and cancer support.

The Dean of Students is responsible for special-needs students, academic progress advisement, the organization of study groups, and tutoring services. New York College's Career Services Office offers graduates assistance with job placement. Currently, the College lists more than 300 employment and rental opportunities for its licensed graduates. Sponsorship opportunities for graduates waiting to sit for licensure are also available.

Location

Long Island The main campus of New York College is located in Syosset, on the North Shore of Long Island, approximately 30 miles from Manhattan. Its proximity to all major parkways and railroad service provides easy access to one of the world's most exciting cities, while capturing the serenity, beauty, and open space of the suburbs. Long Island stretches for 110 miles and is a wealth of natural, cultural, and historic treasures. Some of the world's most beautiful sandy beaches surround the island—from the popular Jones Beach to the chic Hamptons to the barrier isle of Fire Island with its pristine beaches and absence of automobiles. The island's fifteen state parks also offer an abundance of recreational opportunities and even include a polo field. There are nearly 100 museums on the island.

Brooklyn New York College operates a center in Brooklyn, located at the Brooklyn Hospital Center, Caledonian Campus, at 100 Parkside Avenue. This facility is located directly across the street from Prospect Park and is reached easily by bus or subway from all of the boroughs of New York City, including Manhattan.

China New York College owns the Luo Yang Medical Center in the People's Republic of China. Situated in the ancient capital of China,

the 35-acre site is surrounded by historic and important attractions. Modern buildings are fully equipped with Western fixtures.

Admission Requirements

New York College is deeply committed to recruiting the most highly qualified and motivated candidates for admission. The College is particularly proud of its diverse population that is made up of students from a variety of cultural backgrounds, who possess many unique gifts and strengths. New York College students contribute to the friendly and supportive atmosphere at the College.

Applicants who have graduated from high school must have achieved a minimum GPA of 2.0 or have equivalent qualifications. Students may earn their GED certificate while enrolled in a massage therapy degree program by successfully completing 24 credits of specified credit courses in six subject areas. Candidates must be at least 17 years of age and, in accordance with New York State guidelines, must hold U.S. citizenship, be an alien lawfully admitted for permanent residence in the U.S., or hold a valid visa. The College is authorized under federal law to enroll nonimmigrant alien students.

Candidates must complete and submit an application along with an $85 application fee and arrange for the submission of an official high school transcript (or proof of equivalency) and official transcripts from all previously attended higher educational institutions. Candidates are notified promptly of the receipt of their application and advised which, if any, of the required documents have not been received by the Admissions Department. An admissions interview is required. The College offers on-the-spot enrollment: a student can be interviewed and conditionally admitted and enrolled in one visit.

Application and Information

New students are admitted to New York College for the September, January, and May trimesters. Additional second-cycle trimesters may be added if there is sufficient demand. It is recommended that applications be submitted three to four months prior to the desired entrance date.

Admissions Department
The New York College of Health Professions
6801 Jericho Turnpike
Syosset, New York 11791

Telephone: 800-9-CAREER Ext. 351 (toll-free)
Fax: 516-364-0989
E-mail: admissions@nycollege.edu
World Wide Web: http://www.nycollege.edu

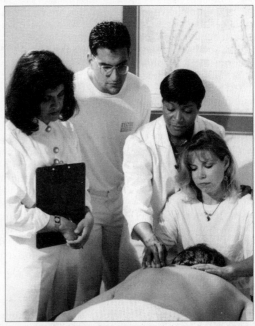

The Academic Health Care Clinics are an integral part of a student's education.

NORTHWESTERN BUSINESS COLLEGE

CHICAGO, ILLINOIS

The College and Its Mission

Northwestern Business College (NBC) was established in 1902 as Chicago's first private business college, and for nearly a century it has been helping ambitious students get started on the path to success. As business needs have changed over the years, so have the College's programs of study. Students will find today's NBC is much different from the traditional "business college" of years past. Just like its students, NBC is diversified, career-oriented, and right in step with the times. More than 2,200 students attend classes at the College's three easily accessible campuses–one in Jefferson Park, just northwest of the Chicago Loop; the other in suburban Bridgeview; and the third in Naperville on Mill Street and Diehl Road.

The College believes in its mission: "The professionals of Northwestern Business College, an institution of higher education, empower students to realize their career potential and individual goals. Our quality educational programs combined with our commitment, integrity, and personal attention provide a vital human resource to the community." These educational programs provide hands-on knowledge and training in many of today's most sought-after professions. A highly focused curriculum and career-relevant courses make it possible for students to earn an Associate in Applied Science degree in only eighteen months or complete a certificate in less than a year.

Northwestern Business College is accredited by the Higher Learning Commission and is a member of the North Central Association of Colleges and Schools (30 North LaSalle Street, Suite 2400, Chicago, Illinois 60602-2504; telephone: 312-263-0456). The medical assisting program is accredited by the Commission on Accreditation of Allied Health Education Programs (CAAHEP) on the recommendation of the Committee on Accreditation for Medical Assistant Education, also known as the Curriculum Review Board of the American Association of Assistants' Endowment (AAMAE) (35 East Wacker Drive, Suite1970, Chicago, Illinois 60601; telephone: 312-553-9355). Graduates of the medical assisting program are eligible to sit for the national certified medical assistant (CMA) exam. The health information technology program is accredited by the Commission on Accreditation of Allied Health Education Programs (CAAHEP), in cooperation with the Council on Accreditation of the American Health Information Management Association (AHIMA). Graduates of accredited programs are eligible to take the national qualifying examination for certification as an accredited record technician (ART). The business administration, executive accounting, computer, and administrative assisting programs are accredited by the Association of Collegiate Business Schools and Programs (ACBSP) (7007 College Boulevard, Suite 420, Overland Park, Kansas 66211; telephone: 913-339-9356). The paralegal and legal nurse consultant programs are approved by the American Bar Association (ABA). The College is also approved for veterans' training under the G.I. Bill for veterans' educational assistance, as well as by the United States Department of Justice Immigration and Naturalization Service as an institution of higher education for training international students. It is approved by the Board of Higher Education of the State of Illinois and authorized by the Board to award an Associate in Applied Science degree.

Academic Programs

The academic calendar year is divided into four quarters: fall, winter, spring, and summer. Each term is approximately twelve weeks in length. The fall, winter, and spring terms constitute a traditional academic year. The summer quarter is 10 weeks and students who wish to graduate early attend all four quarters.

Northwestern Business College is committed to providing students with both a foundation and the essential tools necessary for continued personal and intellectual growth. To that end, the College requires that a minimum of 34 percent of a student's course work be in general education. This general education core requirement includes courses in communications, humanities, social and behavioral sciences, mathematics, and life skills and is intended to help students build a foundation for learning through study and exploration.

Associate Degree Programs The College offers Associate in Applied Science degrees in administrative assisting, business administration, business computer programming, business information systems, computer technical support, criminal justice, cyber security, executive accounting, health information technology, hospitality tourism management, massage therapy, medical assisting, and paralegal studies. In order to graduate with an Associate in Applied Science degree, each student must successfully complete a minimum of 100 quarter-hours of credit, with a cumulative GPA of at least 2.0.

Certificate Programs Certificates are offered in accounting, business, coding specialist studies, gaming management, health care billing specialist studies, I.T. support specialist studies, legal nurse consultant studies, massage therapy, medical machine transcriptionist studies, and meeting planning and convention management.

Externship and Co-op Programs Many programs require students to complete an externship, which puts students on site with one of the area's major employers. Students work in their fields of study, earn college credit, and gain valuable business skills at the same time, while also opening doors to potential full-time employment. Externship participants are not paid and assume the costs of transportation, lunch, appropriate wardrobe, and other related expenses.

Credit for Nontraditional Learning Experiences

The College will evaluate life experience credits through written examination. Northwestern Business College offers two types of proficiency examinations to determine a student's prior knowledge of a subject. Advanced Status Examinations are given to determine advanced class placement, but do not provide college credit. Credit By Examination (CBE) is a comprehensive exam that relates specifically to the subject matter for which credit is sought, and students who pass the CBE will receive credit for that course. Students should contact the Student Services Department for the list of classes for which proficiency examinations may be taken.

Costs

For the 2004–05 academic year, tuition is $275 per credit hour for lecture classes and $375 per credit hour for laboratory and computer classes.

Financial Aid

Northwestern Business College recognizes that many students need financial assistance. The College's Financial Aid Office is available to assist those students and families requiring financial assistance in addition to their own contributions to cover the cost of their NBC education. Financial assistance is available to eligible students who are enrolled for 7 or more credit hours. Available assistance includes Federal Work-Study, Pell Grants, Supplemental Educational Opportunity Grants, PLUS Loans, TERI Loans, and Federal Stafford Student Loans, as well as Veteran's Benefits and State of Illinois MAP and IIA grants. In addition, the College offers institutional scholarships and a payment plan. All students applying for financial aid must complete and submit the FAFSA, as well as any other required forms, depending upon the type of aid sought.

Faculty

Because NBC's faculty comprises working professionals who have built successful careers in the same fields in which they teach, they are able to share insights and perspectives that give meaning to the "real world" outside of the classroom. The more than 130 faculty members at Northwestern include practicing lawyers, certified public accountants, travel agents, computer programmers, and medical personnel. Small class size (the College has an average student-faculty ratio of 18:1) and a comfortable atmosphere allow faculty members and students to work together on a more personal level.

Student Body Profile

The caliber of NBC's faculty members is matched by the quality of the students who enroll. The commitment, creativity, and seriousness of the student body is one of the school's greatest strengths. NBC's enrollment includes approximately 2,200 students. Seventy percent reside within Chicago city limits; others travel from neighboring suburbs, and some from as far away as Indiana. Several hundred of these students attend part-time.

Nearly twenty countries are represented in the student body. NBC's international students come from diverse ethnic heritages and pride themselves on their bilingual expertise. The College encourages and welcomes economic, racial, ethnic, and religious diversity in its student body.

Student Activities

NBC believes that college is about more than simply attending classes. It's also about participating in activities, sharing interests, helping others succeed, and building lasting friendships. The College's numerous organizations encourage students to explore their career interests outside of the classroom. NBC also sponsors a chapter of Alpha Beta Gamma, a national business society established in 1970 to recognize and encourage scholarship among college students in business curricula. In addition, the College sponsors Student Ambassadors, a service organization of students responsible for representing NBC at special community and college events, and Students Helping Students, a peer tutoring program.

Facilities and Resources

Advisement/Counseling All new students are assigned a faculty adviser who is available throughout the school year to provide advice and assistance with scheduling classes and other academic matters. The College provides personal counseling to help students with school-related problems and/or to provide referral assistance to appropriate outside agencies.

Career Development and Alumni Relations Offices Because the majority of NBC students are interested in gaining work experience while attending college, job placement is available after their first quarter. The NBC Office of Career Development and Alumni Relations also serves as an active liaison between employers and graduates. More than 95 percent of NBC's graduates have been successfully placed in the field of their choice. The College offers a lifetime placement assistance program that NBC graduates may use at any time in the future. In addition to on-campus recruitment and career fairs, NBC offers guidance in resume writing, interviewing, and job-search techniques, which build the confidence of students and enhance their professional images.

Library Services Each campus has a library equipped with current books, periodicals, reference material for students' use in classroom research, students also have access to the Internet as well as Westlaw, Lexis-Nexis, and ProQuest videotapes and audiotapes for student use.

Location

Chicago The Chicago campus, located on Milwaukee Avenue and Lawrence Avenue, is 7 miles northwest of Chicago's Loop, in a residential/commercial area. It is easily accessible by bus, rapid transit, commuter train, and car and is convenient to both the Kennedy and Edens Expressways.

Bridgeview Located at 79th and Harlem, the Bridgeview campus serves the southern suburbs. This totally renovated facility offers 88,000 square feet of educational opportunity, more than three times that of the former campus in Hickory Hills, which the Bridgeview campus replaced in fall 2003.

Naperville NBC's Naperville location was opened in 2002 on the corner of Mill Street and Diehl Road in an office complex near Interstate 88 and Naverville Road. This location serves DuPage, Kane, Will, and Cook Counties.

Admission Requirements

Northwestern Business College seeks students who have the desire for practical career preparation in their chosen fields and have the ability to achieve academic success. To be admitted to the College, a prospective student must be a high school graduate or hold a General Equivalency Development (GED) certificate and have the minimum required SAT I or ACT scores (minimum conditional scores are 550-700 on the SAT I and 15 on the ACT). If SAT I or ACT scores are not available, then the placement exam administered on campus may be used for admission.

Northwestern Business College may accept credit for classes taken at an accredited college or university if the grade earned is C or better; the class is college level and credit bearing; and is equivalent to a course taught at NBC in the student's major. Requirements are as follows: 50 percent of the entire program and 67 percent of the major must be completed at NBC. If the student changes majors, his/her transferred credit will then be reevaluated.

International applicants are expected to meet the same admissions requirements as all other students. In addition, applicants whose native language is not English are requested to take the Test of English as a Foreign Language (TOEFL) and must achieve a minimum score of 500 (or they may use the placement exam administered on campus in lieu of the TOEFL).

Application and Information

Applications are accepted on an ongoing basis. Interested students are invited to visit Northwestern Business College's Web site at http://www.northwesternbc.edu. All prospective students should contact the Admissions Department at:

Chicago Campus
Northwestern Business College
4839 North Milwaukee Avenue
Chicago, Illinois 60630
Telephone: 800-396-5613 (toll-free)

Bridgeview Campus
Northwestern Business College
7725 South Harlem Avenue
Bridgeview, Illinois 60455
Telephone: 800-682-9113 (toll-free)

Naperville Campus
Northwestern Business College
1805 F Mill Street
Naperville, Illinois 60563
Telephone: 866-622-6785 (toll-free)

PENNSYLVANIA COLLEGE OF TECHNOLOGY
An Affiliate of The Pennsylvania State University
WILLIAMSPORT, PENNSYLVANIA

Pennsylvania College of Technology
PENN**STATE**

The College and Its Mission

Pennsylvania College of Technology (Penn College) is an affiliate of the Pennsylvania State University (Penn State) and is Pennsylvania's premier technical college. Penn College is a special mission affiliate of Penn State, committed to applied technology education. Partnerships with industry leaders, including Toyota, Ford, Mack Trucks, and Caterpillar, provide students unique opportunities to advance their careers. Graduate surveys indicate a placement rate that exceeds 90 percent annually (100 percent in some majors). Among the keys to graduate success are Penn College's emphasis on small classes (18 students is the average size of freshman classes), personal attention, and hands-on experience using the latest technology. Student projects reflect real working situations. A number of campus buildings, including a conference center, a Victorian guest house, an athletic field house, and a rustic retreat used for professional gatherings, have been designed, constructed, and maintained by students. The facilities stand as testimony to the quality of a Penn College education. State-of-the-art classrooms and laboratories on the ultramodern campus located in Williamsport, Pennsylvania, reflect the expectations of the twenty-first-century workforce.

Academic Programs

Associate Degree Majors Associate degrees (A.A.S., A.A.A., A.A., or A.S.) are offered in accounting; advertising art; architectural technology; automated manufacturing technology; automotive service sales and marketing; automotive technology (including Ford and Toyota industry-sponsored majors); aviation technology; baking and pastry arts; building construction technology; building construction technology (masonry emphasis); business management; civil engineering technology; collision repair technology; computer-aided drafting; computer information systems (emphases in Cisco technology, information technology technician studies, network technology, technical support technology, and Web and applications technology); culinary arts technology; dental hygiene; diesel technology (including a Mack Trucks industry-sponsored major); early childhood education; electric power generation technology; electrical technology; electromechanical maintenance technology; electronics technology (emphases in Cisco systems, communications/fiber optics, computer-automation maintenance, electronics engineering technology, industrial process control, and semiconductor processing technology); environmental technology; floral design/interior plantscape; forest technology; general studies; graphic communications technology; health arts; health information technology; heating, ventilation, and air conditioning (HVAC) technology; heavy construction equipment technology (emphases in a Caterpillar industry-sponsored major, operator studies, and technician studies); hospitality management; human services; individual studies; landscape/nursery technology; landscape/nursery technology (turfgrass management emphasis); legal assistant (paralegal) studies; mass media communication; nursing; occupational therapy assistant studies; office information technology (emphases in medical office information, specialized office information, and Web design); paramedic technology; physical fitness specialist studies; plastics and polymer technology; radiography; surgical technology; surveying technology; toolmaking technology; and welding technology.

Bachelor's Degree Majors Many associate degree graduates choose to continue their education with exceptional **Bachelor of Science (B.S.) degrees** that focus on applied technology in traditional and emerging career fields. Majors include accounting; applied health studies; applied human services; automotive technology management; aviation maintenance technology; building automation technology; business administration (concentrations in banking and finance, human resource management, management, management information systems, marketing, and small business and entrepreneurship); civil engineering technology; computer-aided product design; computer information technology (concentrations in IT security specialist studies, network specialist studies, technical support specialist studies, and Web and applications development); construction management; culinary arts technology; dental hygiene

(concentrations in health policy and administration and special-population care); electronics engineering technology; environmental technology management; graphic communications management; graphic design; heating, ventilation, and air conditioning (HVAC) technology; legal assistant/paralegal studies; manufacturing engineering technology; nursing; physician assistant studies; plastics and polymer engineering technology; residential construction technology and management; technology management; and welding and fabrication engineering technology.

Certificate Majors Certificates are offered in automotive service technician studies, aviation maintenance technician studies, cabinetmaking and millwork, computer applications technology, collision repair technician studies, construction carpentry, diesel technician studies, electrical occupations, machinist general, nurse/health-care paralegal studies, plumbing, practical nursing, and welding.

Off-Campus Programs

Cooperative education and internships give students the opportunity to gain workforce experience. Penn College students have worked throughout Pennsylvania and in eighteen other states, the District of Columbia, Canada, and Puerto Rico.

Costs

Tuition and related fees are based on a per-credit-hour charge. Yearly tuition and fees, based upon 15 credits per semester for 2003–04 (not including housing, food, living expenses, lab fees, books, tools, uniforms, supplies, and major personal expenses), were $8940 for in-state students and $11,250 for out-of-state students. The exact costs depend upon the specific courses and number of credits taken. In 2003–04, costs ranged from $1563 to $2000 per semester for on-campus housing. All on-campus housing is apartment style (kitchen, living room, bedrooms, and bathroom). On-campus housing is alcohol-free, drug-free, noise controlled, and secure. Resident and nonresident students may purchase meal plans that are accepted in the College's dining facilities, which include the main dining hall, a bistro-style restaurant, a gourmet restaurant, two convenience stores, a coffeehouse, and on-campus pizza delivery. The College Store offers an Express Pay plan for student purchases. Students can add to their meal plan and Express Pay accounts during the semester and can place College Store orders via the Internet.

Financial Aid

Approximately 4 out of 5 Penn College students receive financial assistance. Types of aid available include Federal Pell Grants, Pennsylvania Higher Education Assistance Agency grants, Federal Supplemental Educational Opportunity Grants, Federal Work-Study Program awards, Federal Stafford Student Loans, Federal PLUS loans, veterans' benefits, and Bureau of Vocational Rehabilitation benefits. A deferred-payment plan allows students to spread their tuition cost over two payments each semester. Penn College offers academic, need-based, and technical scholarships to qualified students. For detailed information on scholarships, students should contact the Financial Aid Office or visit the Web at http://www.pct.edu/scholarships.

Faculty

Penn College's 455 faculty members (269 full-time and 186 part-time) provide individual attention that students need to be successful in the classroom and the workplace. Faculty members are experienced in their fields. Each year, Penn College recognizes excellence among the faculty members through distinguished faculty award programs. Small class sizes (with a current student-faculty ratio of 18:1) promote student success. Advisory committees of faculty members and business and industry leaders work together to ensure that programs meet current workplace needs.

Student Body Profile

In fall 2003, a total of 6,255 students attended Penn College. Another 4,659 students took part in the extensive noncredit and continuing education program, which includes customized business and industry courses offered through Penn College's Technology Transfer Center.

Student Activities

Penn College is a place where future technicians and designers mingle easily with chefs, health-care personnel, and business students. It is a place where students actually construct campus buildings, cater important campus functions, compute strategies for engineering technology problems, and care for children in an on-campus day-care center and kindergarten program. A magnificent Campus Center provides an opportunity to eat, shop, work out, and spend time with friends. A modern fitness center, College Store, convenience store, art gallery, TV lounge, Internet lounge, video rental and game room, coffeehouse, and bistro-style restaurant are among the features of the Campus Center. Impressive cultural activities are available both on the main campus and at Penn College's Community Arts Center, a restored 1920s-era theater in downtown Williamsport. Student ticket rates are available for performances that include Broadway shows, opera, ballet, symphony orchestras, and popular entertainers.

Student Government Association (SGA) and Wildcat Events Board (WEB) represent the student body in matters related to College policy and activities. Participation offers students the opportunity to develop leadership skills while contributing to the well-being of the College and the student body. In addition, more than forty student organizations offer opportunities for organized campus activity and leadership experiences.

The Penn College Wildcats compete in the Eastern Pennsylvania Collegiate Conference (EPCC) of the Pennsylvania Collegiate Athletic Association (PCAA). Varsity sports include archery, baseball, basketball, bowling, cross-country, golf, soccer, softball, team tennis, and volleyball. Penn College's men's compound-bow archery team is a former two-time national champion in the National Archery Association (NAA).

Facilities and Resources

The hands-on experience offered at Penn College creates a need for a variety of special academic facilities. Students enjoy access to an advanced computer network through both on-campus and dial-in services. On-campus computer labs offer an average of one computer for every 5 students. Besides extensive, accessible computer labs, the main campus has an automated manufacturing center, plastics manufacturing center, printing and publishing facility, dental hygiene clinic, automotive repair center, machine shop, welding shop, building trades center, architectural studio, computer-aided drafting labs, broadcast studio, modern science laboratories, fine-dining restaurant, campus guest house, aviation and avionics instructional facility located at the regional airport, greenhouses, working sawmill, diesel center, and heavy-equipment training site.

Library Services The library houses a collection of more than 110,000 items, including books, periodicals, and audiovisual and electronic materials. The collection grows at the rate of nearly 6,000 titles per year to keep pace with student needs. The fully automated catalog of library resources, including more than 7,000 online periodical subscriptions and other databases, is available through the library's Web site and is available on and off campus. Basic library instruction is offered to each first-year student. Library hours include late evenings and weekends.

Location

The main campus is in Williamsport, a city known internationally as the home of Little League Baseball. Williamsport (population 32,500) is the seat of Lycoming County (population 121,000); it offers the advantages of a city situated in a rural environment. The surrounding area is an outdoor-lovers' paradise, offering hunting, fishing, hiking, camping, backpacking, and more, just minutes from downtown. Besides the main campus in Williamsport, Penn College also offers classes at three other locations: the Advanced Automotive Technology Center at Wahoo Drive Industrial Park in Williamsport, the Aviation Center at the Williamsport Regional Airport in Montoursville, and the Earth Science Center, 10 miles south of Williamsport near Allenwood.

Admission Requirements

Penn College offers educational opportunities to anyone who has the interest, desire, and ability to pursue advanced study. Due to the wide variety of majors, admission criteria vary according to the major. At a minimum, applicants must have a high school diploma or its equivalent. Some majors are restricted to persons who meet certain academic skill levels and prerequisites, have attained certain levels of academic achievement, and have earned an acceptable score on the SAT I or ACT. Questions regarding the admission standards for specific majors should be directed to the Office of Admissions. To ensure that applicants have the entry-level skills needed for success in college majors, all students are required to take placement examinations, which are used to assess skills in math, English, and reading. The College provides opportunities for students to develop the basic skills necessary for enrollment in associate degree and certificate majors when the placement tests indicate that such help is needed. International students whose native language is not English are required to take the TOEFL, submit an affidavit of support, and comply with test regulations of the Immigration and Naturalization Service, along with meeting all other admission requirements. The College offers equal opportunity for admission without regard to age, race, color, creed, sex, national origin, disability, veteran status, or political affiliation.

Penn College offers opportunities for students to transfer the following course credits: credit earned at other institutions, college credit earned before high school graduation, service credit, DANTES credit, and credit earned through the College-Level Examination Program (CLEP).

Application and Information

College catalogs, viewbooks, financial aid information, and other informative brochures, along with applications for admission, are available from the Office of Admissions. Prospective students and their families should contact the Office of Admissions to arrange a personal interview or campus tour. Fall and spring visitation events are held annually.

All inquiries should be addressed to:

Office of Admissions
Pennsylvania College of Technology
One College Avenue
Williamsport, Pennsylvania 17701-5799
Telephone: 570-327-4761
           800-367-9222 (toll-free)
E-mail: admissions@pct.edu
World Wide Web: http://www.pct.edu

Banners representing each of the eight academic schools at Penn College adorn lampposts leading from the new main entrance to the heart of the campus.

PLATT COLLEGE
LOS ANGELES, CALIFORNIA

PLATT COLLEGE
NEWPORT BEACH . ONTARIO . LOS ANGELES

The College and its Mission

Platt College is a private school that was founded in Missouri in 1879. Today, Platt has three Southern California campuses, which are located in Los Angeles, Newport Beach, and Ontario (a branch of Platt College Los Angeles).

Platt College students participate in a career-focused and hands-on environment that prepares them to enter the workforce as quickly as possible.

Platt College is always looking to the future and revising its programs to meet the constant changes taking place in the related industries. Platt College is dedicated to the principle that education is the foundation for personal and professional growth and that students should have the opportunity to develop to their full potential. Platt College is accredited by the Accrediting Commission of Career Schools and Colleges of Technology and is state approved by the Bureau for Private Postsecondary and Vocational Education.

Academic Programs

Platt College offers the following programs: Bachelor of Arts (B.A.) in visual communication, Associate of Arts (A.A.) and a diploma in graphic design, Associate of Arts in paralegal studies, Associate of Science (A.S.) in information technology networking, a certificate in information technology networking, and a certificate in multimedia.

The programs vary in length from approximately five to thirty-one months, and total classroom hours vary from 350 to 2,400 hours. Classes start every five weeks, thus providing many opportunities for students to get started in fulfilling their educational and career goals.

Classes meet either two or four days each week, depending on the nature of the specific course. There are no classes on Friday, which is reserved as an open lab day so that students may work on class or individual projects.

Credit for Nontraditional Learning Experiences

Transfer and Experiential Learning Credit Many students enter Platt College having attended another college. In addition, many students with industry experience attend Platt College for the purpose of gaining a degree or enhancing their skills. Applicants with the appropriate amount of industry experience may be qualified for waiver of Platt College courses through experiential learning. Up to 50 percent of a student's program at Platt College may be waived through transfer credits from a previously attended school and/or through experiential learning.

Costs

Program costs (including tuition, books, supplies, and registration fee), as of the date of this publication, are B.A. in visual communication, $54,655; A.A. in graphic design, $25,085; A.A. in paralegal studies, $25,480; A.S. in information technology networking, $26,000; diploma in graphic design, $18,685; certificate in information technology networking, $7930; and certificate in multimedia, $10,350.

Financial Aid

Eligible applicants may benefit from the following federally sponsored programs, which provide grants, loans, and Federal Work-Study Program positions to cover portions of tuition and fees: Federal Pell Grant, Federal Supplemental Educational Opportunity Grant (FSEOG), Federal Stafford Student Loans (subsidized and unsubsidized), Federal PLUS loans for parents, and Consolidation Loans. Platt College can also provide private education loans through KeyBank and Sallie Mae. Applicants are required to complete a credit application to determine approval status.

Platt College also participates in the Cal Grant program which is offered by the State of California and administered through the California Student Aid Commission. Awards are based on need and academic achievement. Platt College also services students receiving Veterans Administration benefits.

Faculty

The faculty of the Los Angeles campus is composed of full- and part-time instructors who bring teaching and industry experience to the classrooms and computer labs. The faculty members are active in all campus activities, from new student orientation through to graduation. Platt College believes that the learning process is a partnership between the students and their instructors.

Student Body Profile

The Los Angeles campus has a student population that varies from 160 to 200 students. The average age of the student population is 23; 60 percent of the students are men and 40 percent are women; approximately 45 percent of the students have prior industry and/or college experience; and the ethnic breakdown is representative of Los Angeles County. All students are commuters.

Facilities and Resources

Facilities include general education rooms and computer labs, with each student having a dedicated workstation. The Library provides research materials, both in holdings and online as well as computers for Internet access and a service bureau.

Academic and financial aid advising is provided for the students. Campus activities focus on contacts with industries related to students' majors and opportunities for students to develop and present their portfolios.

Career Services strives to see that each graduate understands the job search process. Placement begins on orientation day, at which time the importance of attendance and productivity in class are stressed. During the course of training, the Career Services staff meets with each student, becoming familiar with his or her special skills, background, and goals. Students participate in resume preparation, letters of application, researching and contacting potential employers, interviewing skills, and portfolio preparation.

Location

Platt College Los Angeles is located in a gated campus setting that includes other learning institutions, businesses, restaurants, and other amenities. The area surrounding the campus is Greater Los Angeles, with easy access to the beautiful California beaches, parks, entertainment industry, and other attractions associated with a large metropolitan area.

Admission Requirements

All applicants to Platt College are required to visit the campus for a personal interview with the Admissions Department, complete an application form, and tour the facility to view the classrooms, equipment, and samples of student work.

Applicants are required to take a standardized entrance examination that measures language, reading comprehension, and numerical skills. In addition to the examination, all applicants are required to complete a written essay addressing their rationale for entering one of the offered programs of study. All applicants must provide proof of either a high school diploma or successful completion of the GED program.

An Acceptance Committee reviews the examination scores and essay and then informs the applicant regarding her or his acceptance or nonacceptance to Platt College.

Application and Information

Platt College programs are based on five-week modules with rolling start dates throughout the year. Interested students should contact:

Manfred Rodriguez, Campus Director
Platt College
1000 South Fremont Ave, A9 West
Alhambra, California 91803

Telephone: 626-300-5444
888-866-6697 (toll-free)

Fax: 626-300-3978

E-mail: mrodriguez@plattcollege.edu

World Wide Web: http://www.plattcollege.edu

PLATT COLLEGE
NEWPORT BEACH, CALIFORNIA

The College and its Mission

Platt College is a private school that was founded in Missouri in 1879. Today, Platt has three southern California campuses, which are located in Los Angeles, Newport Beach, and Ontario, a branch of Platt College Los Angeles.

Platt College students participate in a career-focused and hands-on environment that prepares them to enter the workforce as quickly as possible.

Platt College is always looking to the future and revising its programs to meet the constant changes taking place in the related industries. Platt College is dedicated to the principle that education is the foundation for personal and professional growth and that students should have the opportunity to develop to their full potential. Platt College is accredited by the Accrediting Commission of Career Schools and Colleges of Technology and is state approved by the Bureau for Private Postsecondary and Vocational Education.

Academic Programs

Platt College offers the following programs: the Bachelor of Arts (B.A.) degree in visual communication, the Associate of Arts (A.A.) degree and diploma in graphic design, the Associate of Arts (A.A.) degree in paralegal studies, the Associate of Science (A.S.) degree in information technology networking, a certificate in information technology networking, and a certificate in multimedia.

The programs vary in length from approximately five months to thirty-one months and total classroom hours vary from 350 to 2,400 hours. Classes start every five weeks, thus providing many opportunities for students to get started in fulfilling their educational and career goals.

Classes meet either two or four days each week, depending on the nature of the specific course. There are no classes on Friday, which is reserved as an open-lab day for students to work on class or individual projects.

While internships are not a requirement for graduation, students are encouraged to contact the Career Services Office to participate in an internship if their schedule allows.

Transfer Arrangements Many students enter Platt College having attended another college. Up to 50 percent of a student's program at Platt College may be waived through transfer credits from a previously attended school.

Credit for Nontraditional Learning Experiences

Many students with industry experience attend Platt College for the purpose of gaining a degree or enhancing their skills.

Experiential Learning Credit Applicants with the appropriate amount of industry experience may be qualified for waiver of Platt College courses through experiential learning. Up to 50 percent of a student's program at Platt College may be waived through experiential learning.

Costs

Program costs, including tuition, books, supplies, and registration fee, are as follows: B.A. in visual communication, $54,655; A.A. in graphic design, $25,085; diploma in graphic design, $18,685;

A.A. in paralegal studies, $25,480; A.S. in information technology networking, $26,000; certificate in information technology networking, $7930; and certificate in multimedia, $10,350.

Financial Aid

Eligible applicants may benefit from the following federally sponsored programs which provide grants, loans, and federal work-study opportunities to cover portions of a student's tuition and fees: Federal Pell Grant, Supplemental Educational Opportunity Grant (SEOG), subsidized and unsubsidized Stafford Student Loans, Parent Loan for Undergraduate Students (PLUS), and consolidation loans. Platt College can also provide private education loans through Key Bank and SallieMae. Applicants are required to complete a credit application to determine approval status.

Platt College also participates in the Cal Grant program, which is offered by the State of California and administered through the California Student Aid Commission. Awards are based on need and academic achievement. Platt College also services students who are receiving Veterans Administration benefits.

Faculty

The faculty of the Newport Beach campus is composed of full-time and part-time instructors who bring teaching and industry experience to the classrooms and computer labs. The faculty members are active in all campus activities, from the new student orientation program through graduation day. Platt College believes that the learning process is a partnership between the students and their instructors.

Student Body Profile

The Newport Beach campus has a student population that ranges from 180 to 200 students. The average age of the student population is 23; 60 percent of the students are men and 40 percent are women; approximately 45 percent of the students have prior industry and/or college experience; and the ethnic breakdown is representative of Orange County. All students are commuters.

Student Activities

Students participate in field trips related to art and science. Graphic design students display work in local art shows and often do work for charity groups that need design services. Students may also take advantage of on-campus guest speakers and Career Nights, which are arranged by the College.

Facilities and Resources

Facilities include general education classrooms and computer labs, with each student having a dedicated workstation. The library provides research materials, both in its holdings and online; it also provides computers for Internet access.

Academic and financial aid advising is made available to all students. Campus activities focus on contacts with the related industries and opportunities for students to develop and present their portfolios.

Career Services strives to see that each graduate understands the job search process. Placement begins on orientation day, at which time the importance of the student's attendance and productivity in class is stressed. During the course of training, members of the Career Services staff meet with each student and become familiar with his or her special skills, background, and goals. Students participate in writing resumes and letters of application, portfolio preparation, and researching and contacting potential employers. Students also gain valuable interviewing skills.

Location

The area surrounding the campus is the growing and vibrant area of Orange County. The campus is conveniently located within easy access to the beautiful California beaches, amusement parks, and other attractions. The campus is serviced by Los Angeles International Airport and nearby John Wayne Airport.

Admission Requirements

All applicants for admission to Platt College are required to visit the campus for a personal interview with the Admissions Department, complete an application form, and tour the facility to view the classrooms, equipment, and samples of student work.

Applicants are required to take a standardized entrance examination that measures language, reading comprehension, and numerical skills. In addition to the examination, all applicants are required to complete a written essay addressing their rationale for entering one of the offered programs of study. An Acceptance Committee reviews the examination scores and essay and then informs the applicants regarding their acceptance to Platt College.

All applicants must provide proof of either a high school diploma or GED.

Application and Information

Platt College programs are based on five-week modules with rolling start dates throughout the year.

Interested students should contact:

Lisa Rhodes, Campus Director
Platt College
3901 MacArthur Boulevard
Newport Beach, California 92660
Telephone: 949-851-4991
888-866-6697 (toll-free)
Fax: 949-833-0269
E-mail: lrhodes@plattcollege.edu
World Wide Web: http://www.plattcollege.edu

PLATT COLLEGE
ONTARIO, CALIFORNIA

The College and its Mission

Platt College is a private school that was founded in Missouri in 1879. Today, Platt has three southern California campuses, which are located in Los Angeles, Newport Beach, and Ontario, a branch of Platt College Los Angeles.

Platt College students participate in a career-focused and hands-on environment that prepares them to enter the workforce as quickly as possible.

Platt College is always looking to the future and revising its programs to meet the constant changes taking place in the related industries. Platt College is dedicated to the principle that education is the foundation for personal and professional growth and that students should have the opportunity to develop to their full potential. Platt College is accredited by the Accrediting Commission of Career Schools and Colleges of Technology and is state approved by the Bureau for Private Postsecondary and Vocational Education.

Academic Programs

Platt College offers the following programs: the Bachelor of Arts (B.A.) degree in visual communication, the Associate of Arts (A.A.) degree and diploma in graphic design, the Associate of Arts (A.A.) degree and diploma in paralegal studies, the Associate of Science (A.S.) degree in information technology networking, a certificate in information technology networking, and a certificate in multimedia.

The programs vary in length from approximately five months to thirty-one months and total classroom hours vary from 350 to 2,400 hours. Classes start every five weeks, thus providing many opportunities for students to get started in fulfilling their educational and career goals.

Classes meet either two or four days each week, depending on the nature of the specific course. There are no classes on Friday, which is reserved as an open-lab day for students to work on class or individual projects.

While internships are not a requirement for graduation, students are encouraged to contact the Career Services Office to participate in an internship if their schedule allows.

Transfer Arrangements Many students enter Platt College having attended another college. Up to 50 percent of a student's program at Platt College may be waived through transfer credits from a previously attended school.

Credit for Nontraditional Learning Experiences

Many students with industry experience attend Platt College for the purpose of gaining a degree or enhancing their skills.

Experiential Learning Credit Applicants with the appropriate amount of industry experience may be qualified for waiver of Platt College courses through experiential learning. Up to 50 percent of a student's program at Platt College may be waived through experiential learning.

Costs

Program costs, including tuition, books, supplies, and registration fee, are as follows: B.A. in visual communication, $54,655; A.A. in graphic design, $25,085; diploma in graphic design, $18,685; A.A. in paralegal studies, $25,480; diploma in paralegal studies, $19,080; A.S. in information technology networking, $26,000; certificate in information technology networking, $7930; and certificate in multimedia, $10,350.

Financial Aid

Eligible applicants may benefit from the following federally sponsored programs which provide grants, loans, and federal work-study opportunities to cover portions of a student's tuition and fees: Federal Pell Grant, Supplemental Educational Opportunity Grant (SEOG), subsidized and unsubsidized Stafford Student Loans, Parent Loan for Undergraduate Students (PLUS), and consolidation loans. Platt College can also provide private education loans through Key Bank and SallieMae. Applicants are required to complete a credit application to determine approval status.

Platt College also participates in the Cal Grant program, which is offered by the State of California and administered through the California Student Aid Commission. Awards are based on need and academic achievement. Platt College also services students who are receiving Veterans Administration benefits.

Faculty

The faculty of the Ontario campus is composed of full-time and part-time instructors who bring teaching and industry experience to the classrooms and computer labs. The faculty members are active in all campus activities, from the new student orientation program through graduation day. Platt College believes that the learning process is a partnership between the students and their instructors.

Student Body Profile

The Ontario campus has a student population that ranges from 380 to 425 students. The average age of the student population is 23; 55 percent of the students are men and 45 percent are women; approximately 45 percent of the students have prior industry and/or college experience; and the ethnic make-up is representative of the counties comprising southern California's Inland Empire. All students are commuters.

Student Activities

Students participate in field trips related to art and science. Graphic design students display work in local art shows and often do work for charity groups that need design services. Students may also take advantage of on-campus guest speakers and Career Nights, which are arranged by the College.

Facilities and Resources

Facilities include general education classrooms and computer labs, with each student having a dedicated workstation. The library provides research materials, both in its holdings and online; it also provides computers for Internet access.

Academic and financial aid advising is made available to all students. Campus activities focus on contacts with the related industries and opportunities for students to develop and present their portfolios.

Career Services strives to see that each graduate understands the job search process. Placement begins on orientation day, at which time the importance of the student's attendance and productivity in class is stressed. During the course of training, members of the Career Services staff meet with each student and become familiar with his or her special skills, background, and goals. Students participate in writing resumes and letters of application, portfolio preparation, and researching and contacting potential employers. Students also gain valuable interviewing skills.

Location

The area surrounding the campus is the growing city of Ontario and the greater Inland Empire. The campus is close, via the freeway, to Orange and Los Angeles counties and is serviced by Ontario International Airport and local bus lines.

Admission Requirements

All applicants for admission to Platt College are required to visit the campus for a personal interview with the Admissions Department, complete an application form, and tour the facility to view the classrooms, equipment, and samples of student work.

Applicants are required to take a standardized entrance examination that measures language, reading comprehension, and numerical skills. In addition to the examination, all applicants are required to complete a written essay addressing their rationale for entering one of the offered programs of study. An Acceptance Committee reviews the examination scores and essay and then informs the applicant regarding his or her acceptance to Platt College.

All applicants must provide proof of either a high school diploma or GED.

Application and Information

Platt College programs are based on five-week modules with rolling start dates throughout the year.

Interested students should contact:

Joe Blackman, Campus Director
Platt College
3700 Inland Empire Boulevard
Ontario, California 91764
Telephone: 909-941-9410
          888-866-6697 (toll-free)
Fax: 909-941-9660
E-mail: jblackman@plattcollege.edu
World Wide Web: http://www.plattcollege.edu

THE RESTAURANT SCHOOL AT WALNUT HILL COLLEGE

PHILADELPHIA, PENNSYLVANIA

The College and Its Mission

The Restaurant School at Walnut Hill College, *Philadelphia's Home of Hospitality Excellence*, was established in 1974 and is dedicated to inspiring the future of the restaurant and hotel industry through training that is dynamic, timely, and insightful, with a commitment of service to its students. The Restaurant School at Walnut Hill College combines both intensive classroom training and practical experience; students use their knowledge while they learn. Within eighteen months, graduates are working in the field, earning an income, building a resume, and gaining practical and professional experience.

A student's education is cultivated by the College's philosophy that hands-on training is an essential part of education. This approach has multiple benefits—it enhances learning abilities, creates marketable skills and experience for a resume, brings education to life, and, most importantly, puts the student at the center of it all.

The Restaurant School at Walnut Hill College is licensed by the Pennsylvania Department of Education State Board of Private License Schools, is a member of the Pennsylvania Association of Private School Administrators, is accredited by the Accrediting Commission of Career Schools and Colleges of Technology, is certified for veteran's training by the Veterans Administration, is approved by the United States Department of Justice to grant student visas, and is recognized as a Professional Management Development Partner of the Educational Foundation of the National Restaurant Association.

Academic Programs

Associate and Bachelor's Degree Programs There are four majors at the Restaurant School at Walnut Hill College: hotel management, restaurant management, culinary arts, and pastry arts. Each major provides the student with a broad-based knowledge of the overall workings of a fine restaurant or hotel. Beyond that, the programs prepare the student with the day-to-day skills and specific knowledge that are required as he or she develops a career as a restaurant manager, chef, pastry chef, hotel manager, or restaurateur. In partnership with the Educational Foundation of the National Restaurant Association, the College's curriculum includes up to twelve nationally recognized food service and hospitality management courses. Upon successful completion of the courses and the certification exam, students receive national certification.

All students must successfully complete four 15-week semesters to be awarded an Associate of Science degree or eight 15-week semesters to be awarded a Bachelor of Science degree.

Off-Campus Programs

The Restaurant School at Walnut Hill College was one of the first schools in the country to offer a travel experience as part of a curriculum. Culinary and pastry students participate in an eight-day tour of France, while hotel and restaurant management students participate in an eight-day Orlando resort and cruise tour. This travel experience enhances both training and resumes.

A study-abroad program to France and England is currently being formulated. Students may contact the College for detailed information.

Costs

Tuition for the two-year program for students who started September 8, 2003, was $23,200 ($11,600 per academic year). Equipment, books, activity fees, culinary whites, and management dining room attire cost approximately $960. Students may contact the College for information on on-campus housing.

Financial Aid

Financial aid programs are available to those who qualify. It is recommended that students apply early. The College participates in the Federal Pell Grant, the Pennsylvania PHEAA State Grant, the Subsidized Federal Stafford Student Loan, the Unsubsidized Federal Stafford Student Loan, and the parents' Federal PLUS loan programs. The financial aid officers assist students and their families with the creation of a personal plan that outlines expenses and identifies financial resources that are available to students. Scholarships and grants are available to incoming students; for more specific information, students may contact the College.

Faculty

Learning comes to life under the guiding hands and encouragement of the highly trained, technically skilled faculty; the Restaurant School at Walnut Hill College has on staff 1 of only 20 Certified Master Pastry Chefs in the country. The faculty members are seasoned professionals, having logged many years of experience in restaurants and food service. Through their instruction, students gain professional insight, which gives them a competitive edge upon entering the hospitality field. The chefs and instructors are committed to helping students achieve success. As professionals, they continuously keep pace with current trends in the hospitality industry and convey their professional dedication and work ethic to their students.

Student Body Profile

There is a diverse population at the Restaurant School at Walnut Hill College, with students coming from throughout the United States and abroad and ranging in age from the high school graduate to the adult who wants to change careers.

Student Activities

Whether it is a celebrity chef's cooking demonstration, dinner and a tour at a notable restaurant or hotel, or a winery tour and tasting, students at the Restaurant School at Walnut Hill College are exposed to the very best Philadelphia has to offer. There are activities and weekly special events that are sponsored by student clubs. The Culinary Salon Team holds the title of 2001–02 Pennsylvania State Champions, and the Wine Club is undefeated in their scholastic debates. Activities are both educational and fun, combining opportunities to learn and to establish camaraderie and professional development. Events are listed in the student newsletter and monthly calendar.

Facilities and Resources

Recently completing a yearlong renovation, the Restaurant School at Walnut Hill College is poised to offer one of the most dynamic hands-on learning opportunities in the country. The dining experience, situated in the breathtakingly restored 1853 Allison Mansion, turns into a dining event with the addition of three theme restaurants, including Terraza di Italia, a casual Italian trattoria that features classic pasta presentations set amidst an Italian terrace. Guests are invited to sit inside the restaurant, where they can enjoy homemade pasta or dine amongst the twinkling lights in the European Courtyard.

American cuisine is presented in an innovative new style in the American Heartland. Depicting a country farm with a painted blue sky and cornfields, this restaurant allows students to explore some of America's best cooking while guests enjoy the comfort of a country dining or veranda setting.

Most notable is the elegant Great Chefs of Philadelphia restaurant. Amidst glittering crystal chandeliers and a rich tapestry motif, guests enjoy wonderful cuisine and service designed by some of Philadelphia's and America's top chefs.

Also in the mansion is the student resource center, featuring state-of-the-art computer lab stations as well as the Alumni Library, which encompasses thousands of books, magazines, and videotapes on cooking, management, and wines. The building also houses a student conference room and a wines and bartending training salon.

The Pastry Shop and Café is filled each morning with buttery croissants, crisp French baguettes, and glistening pastries that are prepared by the pastry arts students. Also available is a selection of pastas, salads, soups, and entrées for an informal café lunch, prepared by the culinary arts students.

The education building is the focal point of a student's training. It houses four modern classroom kitchens, two lecture halls, and the College's purchasing center.

Hunter Hall is a turn-of-the-century masterpiece that features magnificent carved mahogany, marble, and fireplaces. The College's Office of Admissions, Financial Aid, and Independent Student Housing is located in this building.

Career Development and Job Placement Assistance at the Restaurant School at Walnut Hill College begins on the first day of school with training that is thorough and realistic. In the classroom, students learn how to develop effective resumes and portfolios as well as various interviewing techniques. Career development never ends—graduates can always contact the College for assistance with employment possibilities and resume updates. The College regularly invites personnel directors and proprietors of successful restaurants, hotels, and other food businesses to visit the College. Placement of Restaurant School at Walnut Hill College graduates averages 97 percent.

Location

Philadelphia is a great place to live and learn. As the fourth-largest city in the United States, Philadelphia has much to offer and is a city of firsts—the first public library, the first college, the first zoo—all in a first-class city.

The Restaurant School at Walnut Hill College is located in the University City section of Philadelphia, neighboring both the University of Pennsylvania and Drexel University. Located just across the Schuylkill River from Center City, University City has a wonderful college-town ambiance. Restaurants, museums, shops, and theaters abound, with local merchants offering discounts to students. The Amtrak train station is within walking distance of the campus, and the airport is 20 minutes away by car.

Center City is located just minutes from campus. Here, students find a bustling shopping and business district, complete with award-winning restaurant row, luxury hotels, and exclusive boutiques.

Ethnic diversity abounds in this city of neighborhoods, including Chinatown, complete with exotic restaurants and shops; South Philadelphia, with its famed Italian Market; and the ever-eclectic South Street, with blocks of restaurants, galleries, shops, and entertainment. There are also the historic district, which was the birthplace of the nation, and a waterfront that features exciting nightlife.

Philadelphia is rich in culture and heritage. Students find world-class art and science museums, theaters that feature major Broadway shows and renowned regional productions, and music, which includes everything from jazz to pop to the internationally acclaimed Philadelphia Orchestra.

Admission Requirements

Typically, the admissions procedure begins with a visit to the College. At that time, prospective students and their families tour the College, watch hands-on classes in action, and get a feel for campus life. Application for admission to the College is available to any individual with a high school diploma or its equivalent and an interest in developing a career or ownership options in fine restaurants, food service, or hospitality. Applicants are evaluated on their educational background and demonstrated or stated interest in their chosen field. Two references are required, as are high school transcripts.

Students may contact the College for information on the early decision program for high school juniors and seniors.

Application and Information

The Restaurant School at Walnut Hill College practices rolling admission; qualified applicants are accepted at any time. Applications for admission are submitted with a $50 application fee and a $150 registration fee. Prospective students should contact:

Office of Admissions
The Restaurant School at Walnut Hill College
4207 Walnut Street
Philadelphia, Pennsylvania 19104
Telephone: 215-222-4200 Ext. 3011
         877-925-6884 Ext. 3011 (toll-free)
Fax: 215-222-4219
E-mail: info@walnuthillcollege.com
World Wide Web: http://www.walnuthillcollege.com

The Restaurant School at Walnut Hill College.

SANTA MONICA COLLEGE
SANTA MONICA, CALIFORNIA

The College and Its Mission

Santa Monica College is a two-year community college, founded in 1929. The College is supported by the state of California and is accredited by the Western Association of Schools and Colleges. It has an enrollment of 25,550 students, including 2,921 students from 105 other countries.

Santa Monica College welcomes students from all countries in the world and provides special assistance to them through the International Student Center. New incoming students are given an orientation that includes an introduction to the College and its services. In addition, information on immigration issues, housing, and registration are also covered in these sessions.

Santa Monica College ranks first among the 109 community colleges in California in transferring students to the University of California. The College also has articulation agreements with the California State Universities as well as with outstanding private universities, including the University of Southern California and Pepperdine and Loyola Marymount Universities.

To a great extent, the reputation of Santa Monica as one of the leading community colleges in America is based on the quality of its teaching faculty. Unlike some universities that place more emphasis on research, Santa Monica College chooses its professors for their ability to teach as well as their expertise in their fields.

A high priority is placed on individual interaction between instructors and students. Smaller classes give students the opportunity to receive more personal attention than they would in introductory courses at large universities.

The College radio station, KCRW, is the leading public radio station in southern California, providing both local and national news and entertainment programs. The Santa Monica Associates, a community-based foundation, enables the College to bring some of the world's outstanding scientists, writers, and artists to the campus for lectures and interaction with students. Santa Monica College students also present symphony concerts, plays, and operas.

Academic Programs

Graduation from Santa Monica College with the **Associate in Arts** degree is granted upon successful completion of a program of studies that includes the mastery of minimum skill requirements in English and mathematics; a selection of courses from the natural sciences, social sciences, and humanities; and prescribed courses in the major field. Graduating students are required to complete a minimum of 60 units with at least a C (2.0) average. A unit is based on the number of hours of classroom instruction. Most courses offer 3 units of credit for classes that meet 3 hours a week for a semester. Full-time students take a minimum of 12 units per semester.

Santa Monica College offers programs of courses that parallel the lower division, or the first two years, of four-year universities and colleges. Students wishing to transfer must complete a minimum of 56 transfer-level units in fields including English, mathematics, humanities, the physical sciences, and the social sciences. Requirements vary among universities, and it is to the student's advantage to choose the university to which he or she plans to transfer as soon as possible.

All nine campuses of the University of California, including UCLA and Berkeley, give preference to California's community

college students over all other applicants for third-year transfer; however, students must complete the required courses with at least a 2.8 grade point average. In some majors, such as engineering and economics, a higher grade point average may be necessary for acceptance at high-demand campuses such as UCLA.

The twenty-three campuses of the California State University also give preference to community college students who have completed a prescribed program of lower-division courses with 56 transfer-level units and a minimum grade point average of 2.5. Campuses and majors in high demand by students may require higher grade point averages.

Associate Degree Programs Santa Monica College offers courses in seventy-six academic major fields of study, including accounting, anatomy, anthropology, art, astronomy, bilingual education, biological sciences, botany, broadcasting, business administration, chemistry, child development, Chinese, cinema, communication, computer information systems, economics, electronics, engineering, English, fashion merchandising, French, geography, geology, German, graphic design, history, interior design, Italian, Japanese, journalism, management, mathematics, merchandising, philosophy, photography, physical education, physics, physiology, political science, respiratory therapy, Russian, sociology, Spanish, speech, theater arts, and zoology. Courses for preprofessional study in such fields as chiropractic studies, medicine, optometry, pharmacy, physical therapy, and veterinary science are also offered.

Students who complete their first two years of undergraduate requirements may receive an Associate in Arts degree before transferring to a four-year university to complete their bachelor's degree. Occupational certificates are also granted in certain two-year programs including accounting, administration of justice, architecture, automotive technology, child development, computer information systems, cosmetology, electronics, fashion design, management, office information systems, photography, printing, real estate, recreational leadership, and supervision.

Credit for Nontraditional Learning Experiences

The cooperative work experience program at Santa Monica College makes it possible for students to earn College credit for work experience in technical, business, or professional settings. The program is a joint effort of the College and the community to combine on-the-job training with classroom instruction, enabling the student to acquire knowledge, skills, and attitudes necessary to enter into or progress in a chosen occupation.

Costs

For the 2004–05 academic year, California residents pay an enrollment fee of $18 per unit. Nonresidents paid an enrollment fee of $18 per unit plus $171 per unit in tuition. It is estimated that room and board in a homestay or apartment for this period cost $9244. Other costs include mandatory health insurance for F-1 international students ($660 per year) and textbooks and supplies ($1500). International students should have a minimum of $16,000 available to them to cover all of their costs for the year.

Financial Aid

U.S. students receive government support in the form of grants and loans based on their financial need. International students do not qualify for government support, but they are eligible to compete for 200 non-need scholarships (averaging $500) given by private donors.

Faculty

Santa Monica has 321 full-time faculty members and 581 part-time faculty members. All hold the equivalent of a master's degree or higher and are certified by the state of California. Although faculty members are chosen on the basis of their teaching ability, many of the professors hold doctoral degrees, particularly in the sciences. The student-faculty ratio is 40:1, although some classes are larger or smaller than 40, depending on the subject. Many faculty members maintain office hours to advise students on an individual basis. In addition, counselors on the faculty help students plan their schedules and provide special assistance for personal learning problems.

Student Body Profile

Santa Monica College has a total enrollment of 25,550 students, of whom 44 percent are men and 56 percent are women. The average age is 29. The racial breakdown of the student group includes Asian, 23 percent; African American, 9 percent; Hispanic, 24 percent; Native American, 1 percent; Pacific Islander, 1 percent; other (nonwhites), 2 percent; and white (non-Hispanic), 40 percent. Of the full-time students enrolled, 65 percent plan to transfer to a four-year college or university, 13 percent are undecided, 6 percent are taking classes for personal interest, 4 percent enroll for professional development, 3 percent enroll for a vocational certificate or an associate degree, and 9 percent enroll for other reasons. The international student population numbers 2,921.

Student Activities

All students are encouraged to join a variety of clubs supported by the Associated Students. The clubs are organized by students with special interests such as ecology, geology, biology, skiing, karate, dance, music, and drama. There is also an international club and clubs organized by students from Hong Kong, Indonesia, and India. The clubs normally meet once a week and conduct activities on and off campus throughout the year.

Sports   Sports facilities at the College include off-site tennis courts, a gymnasium, an Olympic-size swimming pool, and the track built for the 1984 Olympics in Los Angeles. The College competes on the varsity level in men's football and men's and women's basketball, tennis, track, and volleyball. All students have access to the sports facilities for classes and individual training.

Facilities and Resources

Santa Monica College has excellent teaching facilities, including laboratories for science, electronics, computers, and nursing. It also has a new state-of the-art library with 103,392 bound volumes, and a learning resources center provides media-assisted individual instruction and free tutoring. There are 160 terminals/PCs available for student use at various locations throughout the campus. Other facilities include an amphitheater, a music room and auditorium, a little theater, an art gallery, a planetarium, a media center, and a student activities building.

The Associated Student Center provides study areas and a computer laboratory with free use of Macintosh computers to all students. The Student Center also includes a cafeteria, conference center, and bookstore.

The Santa Monica College Transfer Center assists students who are seeking to continue their studies at a four-year college or university. Its services include workshops on the application process, opportunities to meet with representatives from the four-year institutions, and tours of the campuses throughout California.

A Mentor Program in the arts gives exceptionally talented students in the performing and applied arts an opportunity to further develop their abilities through individual instruction. Mentor programs exist in architecture, art, dance, fashion design, music, photography, and theater arts. Students wishing to be part of the Mentor Program must demonstrate exceptional abilities and commitment. The program of study is tailored to the goals of the individual and often results in a 1-person show of the student's work or a public performance.

Location

Santa Monica College is located on the beautiful coast of Southern California in the city of Santa Monica. Because of the nearness to the ocean, Santa Monica has clean air and a mild climate throughout the year. It is just to the west of Los Angeles, one of the most cosmopolitan cities in the world. The campus provides easy access to outstanding theater, music, and museum facilities in Los Angeles as well as to Universal Studios and other centers of the entertainment industry. Santa Monica College is less than 10 miles from UCLA, USC, Pepperdine University, Loyola Marymount University, and other fine institutions of higher education in the Los Angeles area.

Admission Requirements

Santa Monica College has an open admission policy. Math and English tests are given upon entry in order to counsel students and place them at the proper course levels. International students who are below the university level in English are able to take preuniversity courses in ESL while they are taking university transfer-level courses, such as mathematics, that are not as dependent on English skills. International students are required to have an English level equivalent to a TOEFL score of 450 in order to enroll in university transfer-level courses. Students who do not have the required English proficiency (TOEFL score) can enroll in the Intensive ESL Program at Santa Monica College.

Application and Information

Applications are accepted on an ongoing basis prior to the beginning of each semester. For the 2004–05 academic year, the fall semester begins August 30, the winter session begins January 3, the spring semester begins February 14, and the summer session begins June 20. All students should apply two months prior to the beginning of each semester or session in order to have the best selection of classes. International students must submit the documents required by the U.S. government for issuing I-20 student visas two months in advance. These documents include transcripts from high school and other colleges or universities attended, verification of financial support and a certification of the minimum English level. International student applications are processed within one week, and notification of acceptance can be made by fax or express mail when necessary.

For more information, students should contact:

Teresita Rodriguez
Dean of Admissions
Santa Monica College
1900 Pico Boulevard
Santa Monica, California 90405-1628
Telephone: 310-434-4380

International students should contact:

Dr. Elena M. Garate
Dean, International Education
International Student Center
Santa Monica College
1900 Pico Boulevard
Santa Monica, California 90405-1628
Telephone: 310-434-4217
Fax: 310-434-3651

SPARTANBURG METHODIST COLLEGE

SPARTANBURG, SOUTH CAROLINA

The College and Its Mission

Spartanburg Methodist College (SMC) is the only private, residential, two-year liberal arts college in South Carolina. SMC serves the educational needs of 750 students. Most students have as their primary goal to earn a baccalaureate degree. Students are generally traditional college-age students, 80 percent of whom live on campus.

Spartanburg Methodist College was founded in 1911 by Dr. David English Camak, a visionary Methodist minister, as a work-study cooperative to serve young adults. As the first cooperative education program in the country, students worked a week and then took classes for a week. In 1927, the curriculum provided graduates with an associate degree in liberal arts for transfer to senior-level colleges.

Today, SMC serves a highly diverse student body from many states and ten different nations. Spartanburg Methodist College seeks to enable students to meet the challenges of the future and to develop the worth and abilities of students through programs that are relevant to their academic and personal needs. The College provides a values-oriented atmosphere in the Christian tradition in which students develop sensitivity to the needs of others and from which they assume responsible positions in society. The academic program offers a university-parallel curriculum that is designed to transfer to a four-year college or university for continued study in the junior and senior year.

Since 1911, Spartanburg Methodist College has believed that the first two years of college are the most critical in determining college success. Therefore, the College places all of its effort into making this the best two years of a four-year degree for its students. More than 90 percent of graduates continue their education by enrolling in the junior class of some of the finest universities and colleges in the nation. The Spartanburg curriculum insures a smooth transfer of credits.

Academic Programs

SMC has a variety of academic and special education opportunities available to traditional age and adult students. The College helps students to discover and develop their personal skills and interests, to reflect on their personal values and goals, to make decisions about their educational and vocational goals, and to prepare for their futures. SMC has transfer articulation agreements and direct-transfer agreements with colleges across the state and region to facilitate the transfer process. SMC students are well prepared for the challenges of academic work at the senior college or university of their choice.

Spartanburg Methodist offers the Associate in Arts, Associate in Science, Associate in Criminal Justice, and Associate in Information Management degrees. The Associate in Arts degree prepares students for many majors, such as business administration, English, foreign language, history, political science or government, psychology, religious studies, and sociology. The Associate in Science degree leads to majors in allied health, business, computer science, mathematics, natural and physical sciences, and preprofessional degrees. The Associate in Criminal Justice degree prepares students to enter one of the many career fields in criminal justice or law enforcement or transfer to four-year degree programs in criminal justice. The Associate in Information Management degree meets the educational needs of students who are planning to work in the high-technology offices of the twenty-first century.

Candidates for the associate degrees must complete 64 hours of course work and maintain a 2.0 grade point average on work completed at Spartanburg Methodist College. Candidates must earn a minimum of 34 credit hours on the campus of SMC and demonstrate competency in reading, writing, basic mathematics, the basic use of computers, and oral communication.

Credit for Nontraditional Learning Experiences

Students may be granted academic credit by achieving successful scores on the CLEP and Advanced Placement tests of the College Board.

Costs

Tuition and fees for the 2003–04 year were $8870. For those students who reside on campus, there was an additional charge of $2466 for room and $2330 for board, making the total cost for a student living on campus $13,666.

Financial Aid

Financial aid assistance is determined by the financial need of the student. Determinations are made based on the filing of the Free Application for Federal Student Aid (FAFSA). Financial aid packages include funds from federal, state, institutional, and private sources. Sources include Federal Pell Grants, Federal Supplemental Educational Opportunity Grants, South Carolina State Tuition Grants, South Carolina LIFE Scholarships, Federal Subsidized and Unsubsidized Stafford Loans, Federal PLUS Loans, Perkins Loans, and the Federal College Work-Study program. In addition, the College offers academic, athletic, need-based, merit, and performance-related scholarship programs, the United Methodist Scholar Program, and College-funded work-study opportunities. Off-campus work positions also can be attained through the College Work/Campus Service Coordinator. South Carolina students who graduate with a rank in the top 75 percent of their high school class or with an SAT score of 900 or ACT score of 19 may qualify for a need-based state tuition grant of up to $2210. South Carolina LIFE Scholarships are awarded based on a student's graduation from high school with a GPA of at least 3.0 (on a 4.0 scale). South Carolina Education Lottery Scholarships are also available.

Faculty

Spartanburg Methodist College has 48 full-time faculty members and dedicated adjunct faculty members. All of the faculty members have earned graduate degrees and one fourth hold the doctorate in their subject area. The student-faculty ratio is 18:1.

Student Body Profile

Spartanburg Methodist has an enrollment of 750 students. The average age of the student body is 20. SMC has an ethnically and culturally diverse student body, with members of minority groups representing 20 percent of the student body, international students from ten countries represent 5 percent, and out-of-state students represent 30 percent. Full-time students make up

91 percent of the student body, and 48 percent are women. Seventy-six percent of the freshman class graduates with an associate degree, and 93 percent of these graduates transfer to senior colleges or universities.

Student Activities

Spartanburg Methodist College offers a variety of extracurricular activities that challenge students mentally, physically, socially, and spiritually. SMC offers students membership to academic honor societies, service fraternities, and numerous clubs associated with academic classes and activities on campus. As a member of the NJCAA, SMC fields five men's and six women's intercollegiate teams. Men's sports include baseball, basketball, cross-country, golf, and soccer. Women's sports include basketball, cross-country, soccer, softball, tennis, and volleyball. An active intramural program provides many opportunities for students who are not members of an intercollegiate team to participate in team events.

SMC enjoys a rich heritage that is closely connected to the United Methodist Church. Religious life activities include the Fellowship of Christian Athletes, the Gospel Choir, and the College Christian Movement. The Office of the Chaplain also sponsors a mission trip during spring break.

Because SMC believes that one learns how to be a leader through service, it has developed a leadership program that focuses heavily on community service. In addition to the Leadership Retreat, the Leadership Transcript, the Leadership Training Lab, and the Student Organization Fair, SMC's student leaders regularly volunteer their time to services such as the Downtown Rescue Mission, the Salvation Army, and the Red Cross.

SMC offers a fully staffed career/counseling center to assist students with selecting career paths and dealing with personal problems.

The Marie Blair Burgess Learning Resources Center includes books, periodicals, and study areas as well as a complete multimedia center, computer terminals, and the control center of the campus television cable system. The College also has state-of-the-art computer labs that are available to students throughout the day and evening with appropriate staff assistance. All dormitory rooms provide high-speed Internet access for each resident student.

Location

Spartanburg Methodist is located on a 110-acre campus in Spartanburg, South Carolina. Interstates I-26 and I-85 intersect near the campus and provide easy access to SMC. The Blue Ridge Mountains of North Carolina are within a 1-hour drive of the campus, while the beaches of South Carolina, such as Myrtle Beach and Hilton Head, are just four hours away. Two major airports serve the area, Charlotte International Airport in Charlotte, North Carolina, and Greenville-Spartanburg International Airport.

Admission Requirements

Spartanburg Methodist College is committed to providing opportunities to motivated, academically qualified students. The student's high school academic record, class rank, SAT or ACT scores, and extracurricular activities are all taken into consideration in admission decisions.

Application and Information

Consideration for admission to SMC requires a completed application, a $20 application fee, an official copy of the high school transcript, and scores from either the SAT or ACT. Transfer students with less than 16 transferable credit hours must submit official copies of both the college and high school transcripts. Transfer students with 16 or more transferable credit hours must submit official copies of all college transcripts. Qualified students are notified of their acceptance as soon as their files are completed and evaluated.

For more information, students should contact:

Dean of Admissions and Financial Aid
Spartanburg Methodist College
1200 Textile Road
Spartanburg, South Carolina 29301
Telephone: 864-587-4213
               800-772-7286 (toll-free)
Fax: 864-587-4355
E-mail: admiss@smcsc.edu
World Wide Web: http://www.smcsc.edu

The Walter S. Montgomery Science Building.

STATE UNIVERSITY OF NEW YORK COLLEGE OF ENVIRONMENTAL SCIENCE AND FORESTRY, RANGER SCHOOL

WANAKENA, NEW YORK

The College and Its Mission

The Forest Technology Program is offered through the State University of New York College of Environmental Science and Forestry (ESF) at the Ranger School campus. Throughout its history, the College has focused on the environmental issues of the time in each of its three mission areas: instruction, research, and public service. The College is dedicated to educating future scientists and managers who, through specialized skills, will be able to use a holistic approach to solving the environmental and resource problems facing society.

More than 3,200 students have graduated from the program over the past eighty-five years, including 180 women since 1974. Established in 1912 with the gift of 1,800 acres of land in the Adirondack Mountains, the ESF Forest Technology Program is the oldest in the nation. The Ranger School's managed forest includes both hardwood and coniferous trees and is bounded on two sides by the New York State Forest Preserve. It is also adjacent to several acres of virgin timber in the Adirondack Forest preserve.

The main campus building houses the central academic, dining, and recreational facilities. Dormitory wings are located on either side of the main campus building. Dorm rooms are designed to accommodate 1 or 2 people. All second-year students live on campus, with the exception of married students accompanied by their families. These students should arrange for rental accommodations well before the start of the academic year.

A $5-million renovation and expansion of the Ranger school was just completed. This project included renovations and an addition to the main campus building, a new dining hall, distance learning classrooms, additional residence hall facilities, and a new student recreational area.

Academic Programs

Associate Degree Programs Students who complete the program earn an **Associate in Applied Science (A.A.S.)** degree in forest technology.

The two-year curriculum offers concentrations in forest technology and surveying. Students may fulfill the program's freshman liberal arts and sciences requirements at any accredited college. The second year of study takes place on the Wanakena campus. Time is equally divided between classroom and laboratory work and experience in the field. Students must also devote several hours to evening and weekend study. Forestry agencies and the wood products industry employ graduates as forest technicians, and graduates of the surveying option join surveying firms and governmental agencies.

The ESF Ranger School's 1+1 plan requires 30 credit hours of course work in general studies at the College's Syracuse campus or any accredited college during the freshman year and an additional 48 credit hours at the Wanakena campus in the second year of the program. Field study is a large component of the curriculum. Several short field trips, made at no additional expense to the student, take place as part of the second year of study. The trips enhance courses in dendrology, silviculture, forest management and recreation, wildlife ecology, and

surveying. Students who are considering later transfer to a baccalaureate program should follow the suggestions for freshman course selection outlined in the ESF catalog.

Transfer Arrangements Counseling is available for students interested in pursuing a four-year degree on the main campus in Syracuse. Students should contact the ESF admissions office.

Costs

The cost of the first year varies according to the institution attended. Estimated tuition and fees for the 2004–05 academic year at the Wanakena campus total $5219 for residents of New York State and $11,169 for out-of-state residents. Room and board at the Wanakena campus are $7650 and the estimated cost of books, personal expenses, and travel is $2000. (Books and supplies are sold on campus.)

Financial Aid

More than 80 percent of Ranger School students receive some form of financial aid, including grants and scholarships, low-interest loans, and student employment. All students are encouraged to apply for financial aid by completing the Free Application for Federal Student Aid.

Faculty

Five full-time faculty members and 1 part-time instructor teach at the Wanakena campus. The student-faculty ratio is approximately 10:1. Students have ready access to faculty members for consultations. Faculty members are housed on campus, and faculty offices are located near student living quarters. There is close contact between students and faculty members in the classroom and at fieldwork sites.

Student Body Profile

Ninety percent of all students complete the forest technology program. About 50 percent go on to careers as forest technicians or aides with private companies or government agencies; some 30 percent become surveyors. Many graduates of the Forest Technology Program go on to receive Bachelor of Science and even graduate-level degrees at ESF's main campus in Syracuse or at other colleges and universities.

Student Activities

Students have a variety of activities available to them at the Wanakena campus. Many recreational activities are readily available, including hiking, camping, canoeing, cross-country skiing, and ice-skating. Students are assigned a canoe for their use during the year. Each class forms a student government, which plans a number of class activities. A small recreational facility is available for student use. Students in the second year of the Forest Technology Program follow the ESF code of student conduct and follow the house rules of the Wanakena campus.

Location

The 2,800-acre campus is situated on the banks of the Oswegatchie River near the Adirondack Mountain hamlet of Wanakena, approximately 65 miles east of Watertown, New York, and 35 miles west of Tupper Lake on New York State's Route 3. At the Wanakena campus, social and recreational activities utilize the area's year-round opportunities for outdoor enjoyment. An excellent hospital, located in Star Lake, New York, serves the community.

Admission Requirements

Students may apply to ESF for admission to the Ranger School's Forest Technology Program during their senior year in high school for guaranteed transfer admission or during their freshman year of college for transfer admission. Prospective students should consult the current catalog for specific information concerning the application process. ESF cooperates with more than fifty colleges in cooperative transfer programs. Acceptance to the Ranger School is contingent upon satisfactory completion of first-year courses. While in high school, applicants should successfully complete a college-preparatory program with an emphasis in mathematics and science. Electives in such areas as computer applications and mechanical drawing are recommended. Transfer students are considered on the basis of college course work and interest in the program. In addition to academic requirements, applicants must be able to meet the physical requirements of the Ranger School program and must submit a full medical report. Parents of applicants under 18 years old should be aware of the field nature of the program and its rigorous study-work regimen.

Application and Information

The Forest Technology Program accepts students for fall admission only. Fall admission decisions are made beginning around the middle of January and continue on a rolling basis until the class is filled. Application forms for New York State residents are available at all high schools in the state and at all colleges in the state university system. Out-of-state students should request application forms from the Office of Undergraduate Admissions at the address below. Prospective students who wish to visit the 2,800-acre campus can do so by contacting the Director, New York State Ranger School, Wanakena, New York 13695-0106 (telephone: 315-848-2566 or fax: 315-848-3249).

Office of Undergraduate Admissions
106 Bray Hall
State University of New York College of Environmental
    Science and Forestry
1 Forestry Drive
Syracuse, New York 13210-2779

Telephone: 315-470-6600
               800-777-7373 (toll-free)
Fax: 315-470-6933
E-mail: esfinfo@esf.edu
World Wide Web: http://rangerschool.esf.edu

VALLEY FORGE MILITARY COLLEGE
WAYNE, PENNSYLVANIA

The College and Its Mission

Valley Forge Military College (VFMC) is a private men's residential college that offers the freshman and sophomore years of college. The primary mission of the College is to prepare students for transfer to competitive senior colleges and universities. The College, established in 1935, has a long tradition of fostering personal growth through a comprehensive system built on the five cornerstones that make Valley Forge unique: academics, character development, self-discipline, physical development, and leadership to all students regardless of race, creed, or national origin. The diverse student body represents more than twenty-seven states and twenty-three countries. The College has an excellent transfer record, with 95 percent of cadets accepted to their first or second choice. More than 65 percent were admitted to the top- and second-tier schools in the country.

Valley Forge Military College is the only college in the northeastern United States that offers qualified freshmen the opportunity to participate in an Early Commissioning Program, leading to a commission as a second lieutenant in the U.S. Army Reserves at the end of their sophomore year. The U.S. Air Force Academy, the U.S. Military Academy, the U.S. Coast Guard Academy, and the U.S. Naval Academy have all sponsored young men through their Foundation Scholars Program to attend Valley Forge Military College.

The College is accredited by the Middle States Association of Colleges and Schools and is approved by the Pennsylvania State Council of Education and the Commission on Higher Education of the Pennsylvania State Department of Education. The College is a member of the National Association of Independent Colleges and Universities, the Commission on Independent Colleges and Universities, and the Association of Military Colleges and Schools in the United States.

Academic Programs

All students are required to complete a core program of approximately 45 credits that is designed to establish the essential competencies necessary for continued intellectual development and to facilitate the transfer process. Included in the core program are two semesters of English, one semester of literature, one semester of Western civilization, two semesters of mathematics, one semester of science, and one semester of computer science. Qualified cadets must also complete a minimum of two semesters of military science. All sophomores participate in the sophomore writing seminar, a guided research experience. To satisfy the requirement for an associate degree, cadets must complete at least 15 additional credits in courses related to their selected area of concentration. Associate degrees are awarded upon completion of the degree requirements with a quality point average of 2.0 or better.

Associate Degree Programs Valley Forge Military College offers programs of study in business, criminal justice, pre-engineering, liberal arts, and physical, environmental, and health sciences that lead to associate degrees in the arts and sciences.

Transfer Arrangements Transfer of academic credits and completion of the baccalaureate degree is facilitated by established relationships with a number of outstanding colleges and universities.

Credit for Nontraditional Learning Experiences

Valley Forge Military College may give credit for demonstrated proficiency in areas related to college-level courses. Sources used to determine such proficiency are College-Level Examination Program (CLEP), Advanced Placement Examination (AP), Defense Activity for Nontraditional Education Support (DANTES), and the Office of Education Credit and Credentials of the American Council on Education (ACE).

Costs

The annual charge for 2003–04 was $25,680. This charge included tuition, room and board, uniforms, maintenance, haircuts, and other fees. Optional expenses may include fee-based courses, such as scuba, aviation, and driver's education or membership in the cavalry troop or artillery battery. A fee is charged for Health Center confinement over 24 hours' duration. For information on the payment plan, students should contact the Finance Office.

Financial Aid

The College offers merit-based scholarships, merit- and need-based endowed scholarships, and need-based grants to help VFMC cadets finance their education. The Academic scholarship rewards incoming and returning cadets who have demonstrated academic excellence. Performance scholarships are awarded to eligible cadets who participate in the athletic teams, band, or choir. Many Friends of Valley Forge have established various special and endowed scholarships, with a range of merit- and/or need-based criteria, to help cadets finance their education. Need-based grants are offered to eligible cadets with demonstrated financial need based on the filing of the Free Application for Federal Student Aid (FAFSA). In addition, qualified cadets in the advanced ROTC commissioning program are eligible for two-year, full tuition scholarships. These scholarships are supplemented by assistance for room and board provided by the College.

Valley Forge Military College offers Federal student aid to eligible cadets in the form of Federal Pell Grants, Federal Supplemental Educational Opportunity Grants (FSEOG), Federal Work-Study (FWS), and federally guaranteed student and parent loans through the Federal Family Education Loan Program. Applicants must file the FAFSA and the VFMC financial aid application for consideration.

Faculty

There are 13 full-time and 17 part-time faculty members holding the academic rank of professor, associate professor, assistant professor, or instructor. These faculty members are selected for their professional ability and strong personal leadership qualities. Faculty members perform additional duties as athletic coaches and advisers of extracurricular activities. The Military Science Department has 5 active-duty Army officers and 4 noncommissioned officers assigned as full-time faculty members for the ROTC program. The faculty-student ratio is approximately 1:10. Classes are small, and the classroom atmosphere contributes to a harmonious relationship between faculty members and the students.

Student Body Profile

The military structure of Valley Forge provides extraordinary opportunities for the student to develop and exercise his leadership abilities. The Corps of Cadets is a self-administering body organized in nine company units along military lines, with a cadet officer and noncommissioned officer organization for cadet control and administration. The College's cadets are appointed to major command positions in the Corps. The first captain is generally a sophomore in the College. Cadet leadership and positive peer pressure within this structured setting results in a brotherhood and camaraderie among cadets. Cadets, through their student representatives, cooperate with the administration in enforcing regulations regarding student conduct. A Student Advisory Council represents the cadets in the school administration. The Dean's Council meets regularly to discuss aspects of academic life.

Student Activities

The proximity to many colleges and universities ensures a full schedule of local college-oriented events in addition to Valley Forge's own activities. Cadets are encouraged to become involved in community-service activities. The scholarship-supported Regimental Band has performed for U.S. presidents, royalty, and countless military and social events. The Regimental Chorus has performed at the Capitol Building in Washington, D.C.; the Philadelphia Academy of Music; and New York's Carnegie Hall. In addition, eligible students can participate in VFMC honor societies: Phi Theta Kappa, Lambda Alpha Epsilon, or Alpha Beta Gamma. Other available activities include business and political clubs, Rotoract, flight training, and the Mask and Spur Theater Society.

Sports Athletics and physical well-being are important elements in a Valley Forge education. The aim of the program is to develop all-around fitness, alertness, character, esprit de corps, leadership, courage, competitive spirit, and genuine desire for physical and mental achievement. For students aspiring to compete at the Division 1-A or Division 1-AA level, Valley Forge's residential college football and basketball programs offer a distinctive opportunity that combines such a strong academic transfer program with a highly successful athletic program that has habitually placed players at the national level. Continuing a legacy that began with its high school program, in only eight years, the College has placed 40 players on national level teams in basketball and football. In the last three years, the Valley Forge wrestling program has also produced two National Collegiate Wrestling Association Champions and one All American National Collegiate Wrestling Association Champion. Students may also compete at the collegiate level in cross country, lacrosse, soccer, tennis, and wrestling. Club and interscholastic teams are available in golf, polo, and riflery. The Valley Forge polo team is consistently among the top-ranked polo teams in the nation.

Facilities and Resources

Campus buildings are modern and well equipped to meet student needs. A fiber-optic, Internet capable computer network connects all classrooms, laboratories, library, and dormitory rooms on the campus. All rooms are computer accessible and provide access to CadetNET, the institutional local area network. This network provides access to the library and the Internet. College classrooms are located in two buildings and contain chemistry, biology, and physics laboratories. A recently renovated computer laboratory supports the computer science curriculum and student requirements through a local area network.

Library and Audiovisual Services The Mary H. Baker Memorial Library is a learning resource center for independent study and research. The library has more than 100,000 volumes and audiovisual materials, microfilm, and periodicals and houses the newly created Cadet Achievement Center. It provides online database access, membership in the Tri-State Library Consortium, and computer links to ACCESS Pennsylvania and other databases to support the College requirements.

Location

Valley Forge Military College is on a beautifully landscaped 120-acre campus in the Main Line community of Wayne, 15 miles west of Philadelphia and close to the Valley Forge National Historic Park. Ample opportunities exist for cadets to enjoy cultural and entertainment resources and activities in the Philadelphia area.

Admission Requirements

Admission to the College is based upon review of an applicant's SAT I or ACT scores, high school transcript, recommendations from a guidance counselor, and personal interview. Students may be accepted for midyear admission. Minimum requirements for admission on a nonprobational status are a high school diploma or equivalency diploma with a minimum 2.0 average, rank in the upper half of the class, and a minimum combined SAT I score of 850 or an ACT score of 17. An international student for whom English is a second language must have a minimum score of 500 on the Test of English as a Foreign Language (TOEFL). Up to 20 percent of an entering class may be admitted on a conditional or probationary status, and individual entrance requirements may be waived by the dean of the College for students who display a sincere commitment to pursuing a college degree.

Application and Information

Valley Forge Military College follows a program of rolling admissions. Applicants are notified of the admission decision as soon as their files are complete. A nonrefundable registration fee of $25 is required of all applicants.

For application forms and further information, students should contact:

William T. Gans
College Admissions Officer
Valley Forge Military College
1001 Eagle Road
Wayne, Pennsylvania 19087
Telephone: 800-234-VFMC (toll-free)
E-mail: bgans@vfmac.edu
World Wide Web: http://www.vfmac.edu

Valley Forge College cadet rappels down the Rappel Tower.

VINCENNES UNIVERSITY
VINCENNES, INDIANA

The University and Its Mission

By the time most of the nation's two-year colleges were founded, Vincennes University (VU) had already been around for 150 years. This unique institution is one of a select few whose roots can be traced to the turn of the nineteenth century and the open admission policy embraced by modern society.

In the early 1800s, higher education was a privilege afforded mostly to the clergy and men from influential families. It took a small group of visionaries from the Indiana Territory to establish a university that would serve everyone, including women and Native Americans as well as less affluent farmers and traders. Founded as Jefferson Academy in 1801, this extremely progressive pioneer college was incorporated by the Indiana territorial legislature five years later as Vincennes University.

Today VU is a modern 100-acre, state-supported college accredited by the North Central Association of Colleges and Schools. While it looks and feels more like a baccalaureate college than a two-year institution, its very roots—a mission of giving every capable person the opportunity to succeed—are what really separate it from other educational institutions.

Academic Programs

Associate Degree Programs Vincennes University awards the Associate in Arts, Associate in Science, and Associate in Applied Science degrees as well as the Certificate of Graduation and the Certificate of Program Completion. Students choose from more than 250 programs, each one designed specifically to prepare them to continue their education at a four-year college or to enter the job market immediately following graduation.

High school students who dream of a degree from one of the state's premier four-year universities can save thousands of dollars in tuition by completing their first two years at Vincennes University. For many families, especially those with more than one student in college at the same time, VU can mean the difference between a debt-free graduation and one buried under a pile of student loans. The quality of VU's transfer education programs is validated through articulation agreements with all of Indiana's four-year colleges. Many of these agreements include 2+2 arrangements that make it possible for students to transfer with automatic junior status, eliminating the need for individual course review. Research shows that students who transfer to a four-year college following graduation from VU are successful. Year after year, they do as well as or better than the students who are already there.

Vincennes University also specializes in many unique and high-demand career programs for students who are anxious to enter the job market. These programs combine liberal arts with applied learning to produce graduates who are extremely well prepared for the marketplace. Graduates with degrees in career areas such as surveying, computer networking, fire science, Webmaster, law enforcement, broadcasting, nursing, physical therapy assistant, machine trades, drafting, auto body, aviation maintenance, and accounting have been highly successful in obtaining employment with higher-than-average starting salaries. Job placement surveys are posted on the VU Web site each fall so prospective students and their families can review current information prior to making a college decision.

The Honors Program is available to a select group of students who want more of an academic challenge than the standard curriculum might provide, while the Freshman Year Experience (FYE) is designed to help incoming students feel more comfortable and make new friends. The FYE Living Community, for example, is made up of approximately 200 students who live in the same general area. As a group, they participate in special activities that help them connect with others who have similar interests and goals. All first-year students have the opportunity to sign up for the Freshman Seminar Class. One component of the class is that all students, regardless of major, share a common reading assignment. Approximately 500 students read the same book and then, ideally, have a common topic for discussion, whether it's in the classroom, dining center, coffee shop, or fitness center. Any student, regardless of major, is eligible to apply to any of these special programs.

Off-Campus Programs

In addition to the residential campus in Vincennes, VU operates a commuter campus in Jasper, an aviation maintenance center at the Indianapolis International Airport, and an American Sign Language program at the Indiana School for the Deaf in Indianapolis. VU offers evening classes in neighboring communities and partners with high schools throughout Indiana to offer college courses to high school students during regular school hours. The University provides distance education using the Internet, correspondence, and closed-circuit TV. For more information about any of these areas, students should visit the Web site listed at the end of this description.

Costs

In-state tuition for 2003–04 was $2875.50 plus a $2-per-credit-hour technology fee and any applicable course fees. Out-of-state students paid $7177.50 plus fees. Student activities fees were $75 per semester, and parking permits cost $20 per year. Room and board ranged from $5326 to $5810.

Financial Aid

Vincennes University is approved for participation in all major federal and state financial aid programs, including the Federal Pell Grant, loan programs, and work-study. In addition, VU annually awards more than $500,000 in academic, performance, and need-based scholarships and grants to students enrolled on the Vincennes campus.

Faculty

Unlike most two-year colleges, approximately 85 percent of the VU faculty members serve as full-time employees. Their primary responsibilities are teaching and advising, and they maintain regular office hours so students can schedule private meetings. Accessible faculty members, Internet chat rooms, group-study sessions, study labs, and free tutoring are integral parts of the institution's culture, which makes student learning a top priority.

Student Body Profile

In fall 2003, VU students came from all ninety-two Indiana counties, twenty-two states, and thirty-one other countries. Sixty-two percent of the 4,419 full-time students were men, 38 percent were women, and 95 percent were single. African-American students represented 8 percent of the population.

Student Activities

The Executive Council, Student Senate, Vice Presidents' Council, and Union Board form the nucleus of campus activities. Working closely with University staff and faculty members and other student organizations, these student leaders ensure that activity fees are spent on things that students want. They are responsible for sponsoring campus events, student activities, concerts, dances, clubs and organizations, and national celebrities.

Athletics and physical competition are also important at VU. From the newly remodeled Trailblazers Fitness Center to intramurals to eleven NJCAA intercollegiate sports teams, each season brings new thrills and challenges to students who thrive on an active lifestyle. For those with dramatic or musical talent, the University provides the opportunity to land the lead in the school play, go solo, or direct the dance and drill team—even as a first-year student.

Facilities and Resources

While Vincennes University is Indiana's first college, it is by no means its oldest. In fact, most of the buildings on this 100-acre campus were built in the last two decades, making it one of the most modern in the Midwest.

Rooms in each of the campus's six residence halls are individually climate controlled (air-conditioning and heat), have voice mail, and are Ethernet wired for high-speed Internet access. Other standard amenities include 24-hour front desk check-in, security cameras, kitchenettes, computer labs, and laundry facilities. Approximately 2,000 students reside on campus, taking advantage of the convenience, security, and cost savings offered.

Instructional buildings are also air-conditioned, with each building containing a smart classroom equipped with the latest technology to enhance teaching and learning. The University's recently completed Technology Center is part of a multistep remodeling campaign. In fall 2002, 25,000 additional square feet, along with new equipment and computer labs, greeted students studying computer-integrated manufacturing, electronics, and aviation flight. An additional 23,000 square feet were added with more computer labs, robotics, surveying, and drafting classes. Separate buildings were also completed for students in construction and automotive technology programs, with plans under way to provide new facilities for the aviation maintenance program as well. When finished, the extensive renovations will ensure that students continue to receive the high-quality education and practical experience employers have come to expect from VU graduates. For a virtual tour of the 2002 technology center, students may visit http://techserv.vinu.edu/.

The student union provides office space for both students and administrators involved in student life. The union also contains a room for formal receptions, a student lounge complete with a baby grand piano, a bookstore, a coffee shop, a food court, and a large activities room that can be sectioned for smaller events. Computers with Internet connections are stationed throughout the building. The two-story library contains a coffee shop, a computer lab, a computer commons, and the Center for Teaching and Learning, a twelve-month academy where instructors and professors learn how to incorporate technology into their teaching.

Location

Vincennes University borders the historic banks of the Wabash River in southwestern Indiana. It sits midway between Terre Haute and Evansville on Highway 41, less than an hour from the major interstates of I-70 and I-64. Located in historic Vincennes, this rural college offers a safe environment for students to concentrate on their studies while creating lifelong memories with classmates and friends.

Admission Requirements

With a few exceptions, Vincennes University maintains an open-door admissions policy. This means anyone who has a diploma from an accredited high school (Indiana graduates must pass the GQE) or a GED certificate or is transferring in good standing from another college is eligible for admission. All students are required to take a pre-enrollment test, and those enrolling in a health occupation program must have either SAT or ACT scores. International students must have a minimum TOEFL score of 528; however, the University does provide an ESL program for those who do not qualify for full admission. With proper documentation, VU also welcomes students who attended a nonaccredited high school or have been home-schooled. The application fee is $20.

Application and Information

Director of Admissions
Vincennes University
1002 North First Street, GOV 72
Vincennes, Indiana 47591

Telephone: 800-742-9198 (toll-free)
Fax: 812-888-5707
E-mail: vuadmit@vinu.edu
World Wide Web: http://www.vinu.edu
http://www.vinu.edu/apply.htm
(application)

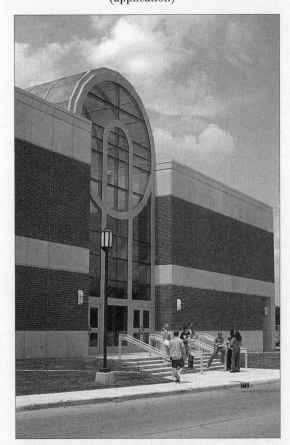

Vincennes University's Technology Center, which recently received a multimillion-dollar expansion.

WADE COLLEGE
DALLAS, TEXAS

The College and Its Mission

Wade College is a small private college offering an associate degree program in merchandising and design. The College is a teaching institution that emphasizes professional study and the liberal arts.

Wade College exists and operates to provide its students with the skills and knowledge that are needed to be productive members of society. It further seeks to provide them with an enriching cultural, moral, economic, and social experience. The College is committed to serving the changing requirements of the merchandising, fashion design, computer graphic design, and interior design fields.

The purpose of Wade College is to offer programs of instruction that are designed to allow students to develop the competencies necessary for immediate employment and career advancement in their chosen fields; continue and complete a formal education in upper-level and graduate colleges and universities, if so desired; develop intellectual, humanitarian, and leadership skills that will advance their potential for success; and engage in continual self-improvement.

Wade College emphasizes individual student attention. To facilitate this, class sizes are usually small.

Academic Programs

The educational program emphasizes the importance of both general education and specialized study. The values of the former are deemed important to the development of responsible citizens in a free society; the experience of the latter is regarded as indispensable to students preparing for active careers. General education is versatile and helps students to better adapt to change so that they may advance in their careers. Specialized study helps them develop the professional skills that are required in their career fields.

Through the integration of diverse disciplines in art, design, business, computers, and the liberal arts, the Associate of Arts degree program reaches beyond specialized professional skills to a broader spectrum of knowledge. The curriculum promotes a well-rounded perspective of the world in general and the field of merchandising and design in particular.

For more than forty years, Wade College has specialized in academic programs leading to careers in the fields of merchandising and design. The Associate of Arts degree is a balanced program with dual majors in merchandising and design. Concentrations are offered in fashion design, interior design, computer graphic design, merchandise marketing, fashion merchandising, and interior merchandising. A minimum of 63 semester credit hours is required for degree completion. The associate degree is normally completed in four consecutive trimesters of full-time study. Each trimester is fifteen weeks in length and is equivalent to a traditional semester. Full-time students are expected to graduate sixteen months after entering the program. Individual degree plans can be developed for students with special needs.

Costs

In 2004–05, tuition for the academic year is $8250. Optional student housing is $3360 per academic year. There are additional fees and deposits. Textbooks, supplies, and course fees are estimated at $1480 per academic year. All tuition and fee costs are subject to change. Wade College has a guaranteed tuition rate for the four trimesters of the student's program.

Financial Aid

Wade College offers financial aid counseling and assistance in applying for a variety of federal financial aid programs. The U.S. Department of Education offers several financial aid programs to help students meet educational expenses. Students at Wade College are eligible to apply for financial assistance under the following federal student aid programs: the Federal Pell Grant Program, Federal Supplemental Educational Opportunity Grants, Federal Work-Study Program, Federal Perkins Loan, William D. Ford Federal Direct Loan Program, and the Federal Parent Loan for Undergraduate Students (PLUS) program.

The College is committed to helping every student plan for educational expenses. An individual Student Financial Plan is prepared for each registered student prior to the start of classes. Various payment options are also available.

Faculty

Each educational area is headed by a full-time faculty member with an advanced degree in his or her field. There are seven full-time instructors. Numerous part-time adjunct instructors are also available. Usually, these are individuals who have advanced degrees and are also practicing professionals in their fields. Approximately 80 percent of the faculty members have advanced degrees.

Student Body Profile

The student body is 90 percent female and 10 percent male. The majority of students are from Texas, but students also come from Oklahoma, Louisiana, Arkansas, Colorado, New Mexico, and from almost every other part of the U.S. and several other countries. The average age is 20.5 years old. Most students are between the ages of 18 and 24, but there are many students over 30. The ethnic composition of the student body is similar to that of the North Texas area. Approximately 65 percent are white, 20 percent are African American, 10 percent are Hispanic, and 5 percent are Asian.

Student Activities

Numerous campus organizations and activities are available for student participation. The College has a chapter of Phi Theta Kappa, the national honor society for two-year colleges. Many students participate in the seasonal fashion apparel and furniture wholesale markets held on campus at the Dallas Market Center. They are assisted through the College's Career Planning and Placement Office.

Comprehensive student services are offered in the areas of housing, financial aid, part-time employment, counseling, and graduate placement. Student needs are given a high priority. Career planning and placement for students of Wade College is offered through the offices of the Executive Director and the Director of Student Services. Career development and professional job search assistance is provided to students and alumni though individual career counseling and exploration of various career opportunities. The office also provides instruction in writing resumes and cover letters, portfolio presentations and self-promotion, interviewing skills, and networking techniques to prepare students for the job market.

Facilities and Resources

Wade College is located at the Dallas Market Center, the world's largest merchandising and design wholesale complex. The Market Center features almost 5,000 showrooms for the wholesale display of merchandise. Students have the opportunity to learn right in the heart of the industry, where the education and business worlds come together. The Dallas area is one of the largest business markets for furnishings, apparel, merchandising, and computer technology in the United States.

The student residence apartments are located in the dynamic environment of North Dallas, 12 miles from downtown.

Wade College Library is located on the campus of Wade College. The library provides access to a specialty collection of materials reflecting the College's curriculum. The library's collection contains more than 7,000 bound volumes, 150 periodical subscriptions, and 400 audiovisual and computer items. The library is a member of AMIGOS, a regional network for resource sharing and technology. The library is also a member of OCLC, providing online search capabilities.

Location

Dallas, Texas is an international business, technology, and retail center. Dallas is known for its shopping, restaurants, and entertainment. Dallas is also home to the Cowboys, the Mavericks, the Rangers, and the Stars—major professional sports teams in the NFL, NBA, MLB, and NHL, respectively. The city and surrounding areas have a population of well over 2 million. The area is served by public transportation, including bus and light rail. Situated on a major interstate highway, the campus is easily accessible by car. Fort Worth, another major urban center, is within easy driving distance. The climate of Dallas is relatively mild in winter, warm in spring and fall, and hot in the summer.

Admission Requirements

Wade College adheres to a policy of open admissions for high school graduates or those students who have passed the GED test. This policy precludes admitting students on the basis of qualitative selection procedures. The philosophy of admission is that an educationally motivated individual is entitled to an opportunity for improved professional and personal success. The College provides a supportive educational environment so that individuals with a sincere interest have the opportunity to meet the educational rigors placed on them and successfully progress through course requirements.

Prospective students may apply for admission as early as one year in advance of the desired class starting date. Since annual enrollment is limited by facility space available in the International Apparel Mart, interested students are encouraged to submit their applications as early as possible. Wade College does not have an application fee. All applicants are required to interview with a representative from the Admissions Office prior to the start of classes. It is highly recommended that this interview take place at the College; however, in circumstances where the applicant's home is a great distance from the College, the interview may be conducted on the telephone or via the Internet.

Applicants are expected to register within 30 days of their acceptance by paying a nonrefundable $125 enrollment fee. Accepted applicants must submit verification of high school graduation or successful completion of the GED program prior to entry.

Application and Information

For more information, prospective students should contact:

Admissions Office
Wade College
Dallas Market Center
2350 Stemmons Expressway, Suite M5120
P.O. Box 421149
Dallas, Texas 75342
Telephone: 214-637-3530
        800-624-4850 (toll-free)
Fax: 214-637-0827
E-mail: admissions@wadecollege.edu
World Wide Web: http://www.wadecollege.edu

WAYNE COUNTY COMMUNITY COLLEGE DISTRICT

DETROIT, MICHIGAN

The College and Its Mission

Wayne County Community College District (WCCCD) has served as a leader in providing education services and training to residents of southeast Michigan. Distinctive in its purpose and history, WCCCD was established by a public mandate and chartered in 1967. In 1969, the first classes were offered by the institution known as the "college without walls" in that WCCCD had no buildings or facilities of its own. By 1982, the College had constructed five campuses within its 550-square-mile service district. As a two-year "open door" institution, WCCCD is committed to providing an affordable high-quality education in an atmosphere of friendly support and encouragement.

Academic Programs

The College operates on a two-semester system and also offers a summer term.

WCCCD offers **Associate of General Studies, Associate of Arts, Associate of Applied Science,** and **Associate of Science** degrees plus one-year and two-year certificates.

The certificate and degree programs offered at Wayne County Community College District include the following: accounting; agriscience; architectural construction technology; automotive service technology; aviation mechanics (options in airframe and power plant); business administration; business information systems (options in administrative assistant studies, general office clerical, legal secretarial, medical secretarial, and word/information processing); child-care training; computer graphic technology; computer information systems; criminal justice (options in law enforcement administration and corrections); dental assisting; dental hygiene; dental lab technology; electrical/electronics technology (options in computer technology, electronics engineering technology, industrial electronics and control technology, and telecommunications technology); emergency medical technology; environmental and natural resources; environmental, health, and safety technology; facility maintenance; fire protection; food service management; general studies; gerontology; heating, ventilating, and air-conditioning; heavy equipment maintenance technology; honors program; lawn and ornamental plant maintenance; machine tool technology/numerical control; manufacturing technology; mental health; Muslim world studies; nursing; nursing assistant studies; occupational therapy assistant studies; paralegal technology; pre-engineering (transfer); pharmacy assistant technology; pre–social work; substance abuse counseling; surgical technology; telecommunications technology; urban teacher studies (options in elementary education, secondary education, and special education); veterinary technology; and welding.

WCCCD offers a combination of programs oriented toward general education, transfer to baccalaureate institutions, and career preparation. All degree programs require the completion of at least 60 credit hours, including the last 15 at WCCCD, and specific program or academic group requirements; a varying number of credit hours in U.S. government; and a final grade point average of at least 2.0. Requirements for the Associate of Arts and Associate of Science degrees include a specified number of credit hours in English, humanities, mathematics/sciences, and natural and social sciences. Associate of Applied Science degree requirements include a specified number of credit hours in general education, specific courses, and occupational support courses.

Many students begin their education at Wayne County Community College District and later transfer to 4-year colleges or universities. Transfer is made possible in several ways. WCCCD participates in a number of articulation agreements with local colleges and universities (i.e. Wayne State, Michigan, Michigan State, etc.) These agreements provide ease of transfer to those students wishing to earn a baccalaureate degree. WCCCD is a member of the Michigan Association of Collegiate Registrars and Admissions Officers (MACRAO). Students wishing to transfer are advised of the requirements as stipulated in the MACRAO Agreement. Academic advising is made accessible to any student in any major who wishes to transfer so that the number of hours transferred into a 4-year degree program is maximized.

Certificate programs are designed for students seeking job-entry skills and those aiming to improve job performance or to qualify for advancement. Specific program requirements vary by program.

Costs

Tuition in 2004–05 is $54 per credit hour for Wayne County residents who live in WCCCD's service district. Average fees for the academic year are $90. The costs for two semesters for a full-time in-district student who is a dependent include $1506 for tuition and fees, $600 for books, $800 for transportation, and $675 for personal expenses.

Financial Aid

A student must apply to be considered for financial aid, which is granted based on need. Available assistance includes Federal Pell Grants, Federal Supplemental Educational Opportunity Grants, Federal Work-Study awards, Federal Stafford Student Loans, Michigan Part-time Student Grants, Michigan College Work-Study awards, and Michigan Educational Opportunity Grants. Michigan's Tuition Incentive Program (TIP) provides free community-college tuition for two years to eligible high school graduates. Though applications are accepted on an ongoing basis, students are encouraged to apply early and electronically. The priority date for fall semester enrollment is June 1.

Faculty

The WCCCD faculty includes 100 full-time and more than 300 part-time instructors.

Student Body Profile

WCCCD has a rich and diverse student population; approximately 70 percent are women and more than 50 percent are members of minority groups. While some 85 percent are Michigan residents, citizens from more than thirty countries are also enrolled in programs of study at the College. Seventy percent of all WCCCD students attend part-time. There are no on-campus housing facilities. Excellent child-care facilities in a safe and caring educational environment are available for a limited number of students at four of the campuses.

Student Activities

In addition to a variety of student clubs and organizations, there is a Student Government Association on each campus. Films, lectures, performing arts events, and other activities offer opportunities for students beyond the classroom.

Facilities and Resources

WCCCD offers a wide range of support services to help students have a meaningful and productive educational experience.

The Career Planning and Placement Office offers aid that includes computerized career information and exploration resources, such as the Michigan Occupational Information System, Sigi-Plus, and the Perfect Resume Service. A computer job-sharing network lists a variety of opportunities.

Multi-Learning Laboratories have filmstrips, slides, programmed texts, tapes, reading machines, and textbooks at varying levels of difficulty to help students improve academically. Tutoring is also available.

The Access College Careers and Educational Supportive Services (ACCESS) helps students who are displaced homemakers, people who speak English as a second language, and those who are physically handicapped. This department can provide tutors, note takers, braille and taped materials, and interpreters for the deaf.

The Learning Resource Center at each campus is a library and more. Features include the Detroit Area Library Network (DALNET), a computer link between all WCCCD libraries and the libraries of several local colleges, universities, and hospitals.

Location

Wayne County Community College District's five facilities are located in suburban, urban, and rural areas of Wayne County.

Metropolitan Detroit offers a broad choice of cultural institutions and recreational activities, including major sports teams. In addition to being the world's automotive capital, Detroit is host to leading medical institutions, high-technology manufacturers, and international-class financial institutions.

Wayne County Community College has five campuses located in the metropolitan Detroit area. The **Downtown Campus** is at the edge of Detroit's convention center. The **Eastern Campus** is part of a medical/retail/residential corridor on the east side of the city. The **Northwest Campus** is located in a business hub and near a diverse residential community in northwest Detroit. The **Downriver Campus** is located in suburban Taylor (an industrial and residential community), and the **Western Campus** sits on more than 100 acres in the growing industrial community of Belleville.

All College facilities are easily accessible via freeways.

Admission Requirements

WCCCD has an open admission policy—acceptance is automatic for those who are age 18 or older with a high school diploma or GED. Admission is granted on a nonselective basis. However, all students are assessed upon entry in English and math for placement into appropriate courses.

Students at other colleges or universities who wish to transfer credits to WCCCD should request that official copies of their transcripts be forwarded to WCCCD's Office of Admissions. Generally, credit earned from regionally accredited institutions and from all publicly supported junior and community colleges is readily accepted if it has been earned with a grade of C or better. Students should note that grades are not transferable; only credit hours can be transferred.

WCCCD welcomes applications from international students who have completed secondary education and are eligible for admission to college-level studies. International applicants should begin the admission process at the earliest possible date: from three to six months before a semester begins is recommended. In addition to meeting other admission criteria, international students must score 500 or above on the Test of English as a Foreign Language (TOEFL) or score at least 70 on the Michigan Test. The TOEFL is given in countries throughout the world. Testing information is available from TOEFL, Box 6151, Princeton, New Jersey 08541, and from the U.S. embassies or consulates. Michigan Test information is available from the English Language Institute, University of Michigan, Ann Arbor, Michigan 48109 (telephone: 313-764-2416).

Application and Information

Applications are accepted on an ongoing basis. For international students, correspondence concerning admission and all credentials in support of the application must be on file in the Office of Admissions prior to its issuance of an I-20 A-B.

For an application form and additional information, students should contact:

Division of Student Services
Wayne County Community College District
801 West Fort Street
Detroit, Michigan 48226-2539

Telephone: 313-496-2600
E-mail: info@wccc.edu
World Wide Web: http://www.wccc.edu

WESTWOOD COLLEGE–ANAHEIM

ANAHEIM, CALIFORNIA

The College and Its Mission

Today, the variables that define career success are ever changing. In order to get ahead and stay ahead, students need the right kind of preparation. To prepare them for the working world, students need a career-focused education program that teaches the skills employers demand and offers hands-on practical experience with real-world applications and the right kind of job-placement assistance to help them get started in their new careers.

Students also need a fast-track learning program that shortens the time from education to career, with an academic schedule that fits their lifestyle. They need a high level of student services to help them reach their goals and the right financial package to make it all possible.

All of these are the focus at Westwood College, which operates seventeen campuses, with locations in California, Colorado, Illinois, Georgia, and Texas. The fourteen campuses of Westwood College offer degree programs in high-technology fields, while the three aviation campuses (Westwood College of Aviation Technology–Denver, Westwood College of Aviation Technology–Los Angeles, and Westwood Aviation Institute–Houston) offer aviation maintenance training.

Such fields as computer networking, graphic design, computer-aided design, and e-business are featured at the Westwood College campuses located in Anaheim, Inland Empire (Upland), Long Beach, and Los Angeles, California; Atlanta, Georgia; DuPage, O'Hare Airport, River Oaks, and Chicago–Loop, Illinois; Denver–North and Denver–South, Colorado; and Dallas, Fort Worth, and Houston, Texas. The Westwood College of Aviation Technology offers the aviation curriculum at the Denver, Colorado and Los Angeles, California, campuses, while Westwood Aviation Institute offers the aviation curriculum in Houston.

The Anaheim campus is accredited by the Accrediting Commission of Career Schools and Colleges of Technology (ACCSCT).

Westwood College–Anaheim is a branch of Westwood College–Denver North.

Academic Programs

The Anaheim campus focuses on computer-based technology programs that prepare graduates to take advantage of southern California's unique, high-tech career opportunities. Bachelor's degree programs are offered in computer network management, criminal justice, e-business management, game art and design, game software development, information systems security, interior design, visual communications, and Web design and multimedia. Associate degree programs are offered in computer-aided design/architectural drafting, computer network engineering, graphic design and multimedia, and software engineering.

The programs, which feature hands-on learning experience, are designed to prepare students for entry-level positions in their chosen careers.

Costs

The standard fee for full-time students is $3729 per term. Books and lab and other fees are additional. The standard fee for part-time students is $2423 per term.

Financial Aid

Tuition assistance is available for those who qualify. Scholarships include the Westwood High School Scholarship Program, which offers two scholarships to every high school in the United States; the Colorado Undergraduate Merit State Scholarships for Colorado residents; and several loan programs.

Faculty

Westwood has 528 total faculty members. Half are full-time. Fifty-two teach at the Anaheim campus. Forty percent hold master's degrees and 5 percent doctorates.

Student Body Profile

Student enrollment at the Anaheim campus totals 782, of whom approximately 25 percent are women.

Student Activities

In addition to on-campus activities, the Anaheim area offers many cultural and recreational opportunities for students.

Facilities and Resources

The campus includes a primary building with approximately 25,000 square feet dedicated to classrooms, labs, and administrative offices. A nearby campus annex houses additional classroom space.

Location

The Anaheim campus is in Orange County, minutes from attractions such as Disneyland, Knott's Berry Farm, and Edison International Park. The area offers students an active lifestyle and is rich in career opportunities. The campus is easily accessible from Interstate 5 at La Palma Avenue.

Admission Requirements

Applicants must have either a diploma from an accredited high school or a GED certificate and passing scores on the College entrance exam (or qualifying ACT/SAT scores).

Application and Information

Paula Sallenbach, Director of Admissions
Westwood College–Anaheim
2461 West La Palma Avenue
Anaheim, California 92801-2610
Telephone: 714-226-9990
                877-650-6050 (toll-free)
Fax: 714-826-7398
E-mail: info@westwood.edu
World Wide Web: http://www.westwood.edu

WESTWOOD COLLEGE–CHICAGO DUPAGE

WOODRIDGE, ILLINOIS

The College and Its Mission

Today, the variables that define career success are ever changing. In order to get ahead and stay ahead, students need the right kind of preparation. To prepare for the working world, they need a career-focused education program that teaches the skills employers demand and offers hands-on, practical experience with real-world applications and the right kind of job-placement assistance to help students get started in their new careers.

Students also need a fast-track learning program that shortens the time from education to career, with an academic schedule that fits their lifestyle. They need a high level of student services to help them reach their goals and the right financial package to make it all possible.

All of these are the focus at Westwood College, which operates seventeen campuses, with locations in California, Colorado, Illinois, Georgia, and Texas. The fourteen campuses of Westwood College offer degree programs in high-technology fields, while the three aviation campuses (Westwood College of Aviation Technology–Denver, Westwood College of Aviation Technology–Los Angeles, and Westwood Aviation Institute–Houston) offer aviation maintenance training.

Such fields as computer networking, graphic design, computer-aided design, and e-business are featured at the Westwood College campuses located in Anaheim, Inland Empire (Upland), Long Beach, and Los Angeles, California; Atlanta, Georgia; DuPage, O'Hare Airport, River Oaks, and Chicago–Loop, Illinois; Denver–North and Denver–South, Colorado; and Dallas, Fort Worth, and Houston, Texas. The Westwood College of Aviation Technology offers the aviation curriculum at the Denver, Colorado, and Los Angeles, California, campuses, while Westwood Aviation Institute offers the aviation curriculum in Houston.

The DuPage Campus is accredited by the Accrediting Council for Independent Colleges and Schools (ACICS).

Academic Programs

The DuPage Campus focuses on computer-based technology programs that prepare graduates to take advantage of high-technology career opportunities. Both the faculty and campus have been designed specifically to meet the unique needs of Westwood's students. Associate degree programs in computer-assisted design/architectural drafting (CAD), computer network engineering, graphic design and multimedia, and software engineering are offered in addition to bachelor's degree programs in animation, computer network management, e-business management, visual communications, and Web design and multimedia.

Costs

The standard fee is $3729 per term, with lab fees, other fees, and books additional. The standard fee for half-time students is $2423 per term.

Financial Aid

Tuition assistance is available for those who qualify. Scholarships include the Westwood High School Scholarship Program, in which two scholarships are offered to every high school in the United States, and the Colorado Undergraduate Merit State Scholarships for Colorado residents. In addition, several loan programs are available.

Faculty

Westwood has a total of 528 faculty members (half are full-time and half are part-time); 60 percent teach at the DuPage campus. Of the total number of faculty members, 40 percent hold a master's degree and 5 percent hold the doctoral degree.

Student Body Profile

Student enrollment at the DuPage campus totals 422, of whom approximately 30 percent are women.

Student Activities

The greater Chicago area offers many cultural and recreational activities.

Facilities and Resources

The campus occupies 25,000 square feet of classroom, lab, and administrative space.

Location

One of three Westwood campuses in the greater Chicago area, the DuPage Campus is located an hour's drive southwest of Chicago in Woodridge, Illinois.

Admission Requirements

A diploma from an accredited four-year high school or a GED certificate and passing scores on the college entrance exam (or qualifying ACT/SAT scores) are required.

Application and Information

Scott Kawall, Director of Admissions
Westwood College–Chicago DuPage
7155 Janes Avenue
Woodridge, Illinois 60517-2321
Telephone: 630-434-8244
         888-721-7646 (toll-free)
Fax: 630-434-8255
E-mail: info@westwood.edu
World Wide Web: http://www.westwood.edu

WESTWOOD COLLEGE–
CHICAGO LOOP

CHICAGO, ILLINOIS

The College and Its Mission

Today, the variables that define career success are ever changing. In order to get ahead and stay ahead, students need the right kind of preparation. To prepare for the working world, they need a career-focused education program that teaches the skills employers demand. The curriculum should include hands-on, practical experience and real-world applications to help graduates get started in their new careers.

Students also need a fast-track learning program that shortens the time from education to career, with an academic schedule that fits their lifestyle. They need a high level of student services to help them reach their goals and the right financial package to make it all possible.

All of these are the focus at Westwood College, which operates seventeen campuses, with locations in California, Colorado, Illinois, Georgia, and Texas. The fourteen campuses of Westwood College offer degree programs in high-technology fields, while the three aviation campuses (Westwood College of Aviation Technology–Denver, Westwood College of Aviation Technology–Los Angeles, and Westwood Aviation Institute–Houston) offer aviation maintenance training.

Such fields as computer networking, graphic design, computer-aided design, and e-business are featured at the Westwood College campuses located in Anaheim, Inland Empire (Upland), Long Beach, and Los Angeles, California; Atlanta, Georgia; DuPage, O'Hare Airport, River Oaks, and Chicago-Loop, Illinois; Denver–North and Denver–South, Colorado; and Dallas, Fort Worth, and Houston, Texas. The Westwood College of Aviation Technology offers the aviation curriculum at the Denver, Colorado, and Los Angeles, California, campuses, while Westwood Aviation Institute offers the aviation curriculum in Houston.

Westwood College–Chicago Loop is a branch of Westwood College–Los Angeles and is accredited by the Accrediting Council for Independent Colleges and Schools (ACICS).

Academic Programs

At the Westwood College–Chicago Loop campus, students may obtain a bachelor's degree in less than three years and an associate degree in less than seventeen months through day and evening classes. The programs are designed to help adults move quickly into the high-tech world of work. Classes provide hands-on skills and career-focused training. Skilled technology workers with fine-tuned critical-thinking skills graduate from Westwood ready to succeed. Westwood College's career development services match students with employers to get graduates started on the right career path.

The Chicago Loop campus offers such programs as bachelor's degree programs in animation, computer network management, criminal justice, information systems security, interior design, visual communications, and Web design and multimedia. The College offers associate degree programs in computer-aided design/architectural drafting, computer network engineering, and graphic design and multimedia.

Costs

The standard fee is $3729 per term. Books, laboratory fees, and other fees are additional. The standard fee for half-time students is $2423 per term. Educators can attend Westwood classes tuition free.

Financial Aid

Westwood students who qualify take full advantage of loans, grants, and scholarships to pay their way. Two Westwood High School Scholarships are offered to every high school in the United States. Tuition reimbursement programs may be available through a student's employer. Students may also apply for federal aid through normal channels. The College is committed to extending higher education to all qualified candidates, regardless of their ability to pay. An online Financial Aid Contact Center helps students navigate their way through the loan/grant/scholarship process.

Faculty

Westwood campuses have a total of more than 500 faculty members, of whom 40 percent hold master's degrees and 5 percent hold doctorates.

Student Body Profile

Westwood College recruits recent high school graduates, young adults, and working adults who want to acquire new skills to take advantage of growing opportunities in the professional workplace. Students come to Westwood from all across the U.S. and many other countries.

Student Activities

In addition to the many on-campus activities available at Westwood College, the greater Chicago area abounds in cultural and recreational opportunities.

Facilities and Resources

Campus Resource Centers located on each Westwood campus contain a library of program-specific materials, books, and periodicals and Internet access. A virtual library provides remote access to several selected databases and links to Internet-based information that is specific to technology study. The Resource Center also contains the campus bookstore. Resource Center staff members can assist students in navigating all the research materials that are available.

Location

Westwood College's Chicago Loop campus is located on North State Street, in the heart of downtown Chicago, one of the nation's major urban hubs. Students find plenty of diversity and activity in Chicago's Loop area, the hub of central Chicago's shopping, dining, and commerce district. Arts and theater, nightlife, and city activities abound—all within easy access by foot, trolley, or public transit. Chicago is situated on Lake Michigan, providing plenty of outdoor recreational choices as well.

Admission Requirements

Admission requirements include a diploma from an accredited four-year high school or a GED certificate and passing scores on the College placement exam or qualifying SAT/ACT scores. Applicants fill out the Personal Career Assessment, which includes an application/evaluation form and the Entrance Assessment form, and complete the Financing Process form. Westwood admissions counselors help students choose the correct course of study, if needed. Admissions paperwork is available by contacting the College at the address below.

Application and Information

Director of Admissions
Westwood College–Chicago Loop
17 North State Street, 15th floor
Chicago, Illinois 60602
Telephone: 312-739-0850
          800-693-5415 (toll-free)
Fax: 312-739-1004
E-mail: info@westwood.edu
World Wide Web: http://www.westwood.edu

WESTWOOD COLLEGE– CHICAGO O'HARE AIRPORT

SCHILLER PARK, ILLINOIS

WESTWOOD COLLEGE

The College and Its Mission

Today, the variables that define career success are ever changing. In order to get ahead and stay ahead, students need the right kind of preparation. To prepare for the working world, students need a programmed, career-focused education that teaches the skills employers demand, that is, hands-on practical experience with real-world applications and the right kind of job-placement assistance to help them get started in their new career.

Students also need a fast-track learning program that shortens the time from education to career, with an academic schedule that fits their lifestyle. Students need a high level of student services to help them reach their goals, and the right financial package to make it all possible.

All of these are the focus at Westwood College, which operates seventeen campuses, with locations in California, Colorado, Illinois, Georgia, and Texas. The fourteen campuses of Westwood College offer degree programs in high-technology fields, while the three aviation campuses (Westwood College of Aviation Technology–Denver, Westwood College of Aviation Technology–Los Angeles, and Westwood Aviation Institute–Houston) offer aviation maintenance training.

Such fields as computer networking, graphic design, computer-aided design, and e-business are featured at the Westwood College campuses located in Anaheim, Inland Empire (Upland), Long Beach, and Los Angeles, California; Atlanta, Georgia; DuPage, O'Hare Airport, River Oaks, and Chicago–Loop, Illinois; Denver–North and Denver–South, Colorado; and Dallas, Fort Worth, and Houston, Texas. The Westwood College of Aviation Technology offers the aviation curriculum at the Denver, Colorado and Los Angeles, California, campuses, while Westwood Aviation Institute offers the aviation curriculum in Houston.

The Westwood–O'Hare Airport campus is accredited by the Accrediting Council for Independent Colleges and Schools (ACICS).

Academic Programs

The Westwood College–O'Hare Airport campus focuses on computer-based technology programs that prepare graduates to take advantage of their high-technology career opportunities. Associate degree programs are offered in computer-aided design/architectural drafting (CAD), computer network engineering, and graphic design and multimedia. Bachelor's degree programs are offered in animation, computer network management, e-business management, visual communications, and Web design and multimedia.

Costs

The standard fee is $3540 per term. Books, laboratory fees, and other fees are additional. The standard fee for half-time students is $2300 per term.

Financial Aid

Tuition assistance is available to those students who qualify. Scholarships include the Westwood High School Scholarship Program, in which two scholarships are offered to every high school in the United States, the Colorado Undergraduate Merit State Scholarships for Colorado residents, and several loan programs.

Faculty

Westwood has a total of 528 faculty members (half are full-time, half are part-time), of whom 32 teach at the O'Hare Airport campus. A total of 40 percent of the faculty members hold a master's degree, while 5 percent hold a doctorate.

Student Body Profile

A total of 573 students are enrolled at the O'Hare Airport campus, of whom approximately 75 percent are men and 25 percent are women.

Student Activities

In addition to on-campus activities, the greater Chicago area offers many cultural and recreational opportunities.

Facilities and Resources

The campus includes 27,000 square feet of classrooms, labs, and administrative offices. In addition to an on-campus Resource Center, students benefit through cooperation with the suburban Inter-Library Loan Consortium and Illinet.

Location

The campus is located in Schiller Park, close to major highways and O'Hare International Airport.

Admission Requirements

A diploma from an accredited four-year high school or GED certificate is required as are passing scores on the college entrance exam (or qualifying ACT/SAT scores).

Application and Information

David Traub, Director of Admissions
Westwood College–Chicago O'Hare Airport
4825 North Scott Street, Suite 100
Schiller Park, Illinois 60176-1209
Telephone: 847-928-0200
            877-877-8857 (toll-free)
Fax: 847-928-2120
E-mail: info@westwood.edu
World Wide Web: http://www.westwood.edu

WESTWOOD COLLEGE–CHICAGO RIVER OAKS

CALUMET CITY, ILLINOIS

The College and Its Mission

Today, the variables that define career success are ever changing. In order to get ahead and stay ahead, students need the right kind of preparation. To prepare for the working world, students need a career-focused education program that teaches the skills employers demand and offers hands-on, practical experience with real-world applications and the right kind of job-placement assistance to help them get started in their new careers.

Students also need a fast-track learning program that shortens the time from education to career, with an academic schedule that fits their lifestyle. They need a high level of student services to help them reach their goals and the right financial package to make it all possible.

All of these are the focus at Westwood College, which operates seventeen campuses, with locations in California, Colorado, Illinois, Georgia, and Texas. The fourteen campuses of Westwood College offer degree programs in high-technology fields, while the three aviation campuses (Westwood College of Aviation Technology–Denver, Westwood College of Aviation Technology–Los Angeles, and Westwood Aviation Institute–Houston) offer aviation maintenance training.

Such fields as computer networking, graphic design, computer-aided design, and e-business are featured at the Westwood College campuses located in Anaheim, Inland Empire (Upland), Long Beach, and Los Angeles, California; Atlanta, Georgia; DuPage, O'Hare Airport, River Oaks, and Chicago–Loop, Illinois; Denver–North and Denver–South, Colorado; and Dallas, Fort Worth, and Houston, Texas. The Westwood College of Aviation Technology offers the aviation curriculum at the Denver, Colorado and Los Angeles, California, campuses, while Westwood Aviation Institute offers the aviation curriculum in Houston.

The River Oaks campus is accredited by the Accrediting Council for Independent Colleges and Schools (ACICS).

Westwood College–River Oaks is a branch of Westwood College–Los Angeles.

Academic Programs

The River Oaks Campus focuses on computer-based technology programs that prepare students to take advantage of high-tech careers. Associate degree programs in computer-aided design/architectural drafting (CAD), computer network engineering, graphic design and multimedia, and software engineering are offered. Bachelor's degree programs are offered in animation, computer network management, e-business management, visual communications, and Web design and multimedia.

Costs

The standard fee is $3729 per term; lab fees and other fees and books are additional. The standard fee for half-time students is $2423 per term.

Financial Aid

Tuition assistance is available for those who qualify. Scholarships include the Westwood High School Scholarship Program, through which two scholarships are offered to every high school in the United States; the Colorado Undergraduate Merit State Scholarships for Colorado residents; and several loan programs.

Faculty

Westwood has 528 total faculty members (half full-time, half part-time), of whom 77 are at the River Oaks campus. Forty percent hold master's degrees and 5 percent doctorates.

Student Body Profile

There are 763 students enrolled at this campus, of whom 25 percent are women.

Student Activities

In addition to on-campus activities, many cultural and recreational opportunities are available in the Greater Chicago area.

Facilities and Resources

The campus includes 25,000 square feet of classrooms, labs, and administrative offices. In addition to an on-campus resource center, students benefit from cooperation with the suburban Inter-Library Loan Consortium and Illinet.

Location

The campus is located an hour south of Chicago at 80 River Oaks Center in Calumet City. It is easily reached by several major freeways.

Admission Requirements

A diploma from an accredited four-year high school or a GED certificate and passing scores on the college entrance exam (or qualifying ACT/SAT scores) are required.

Application and Information

Tash Uray, Director of Admissions
Westwood College–Chicago River Oaks
80 River Oaks Drive, Suite D-49
Calumet City, Illinois 60409-5802
Telephone: 708-832-1988
           888-549-6873 (toll-free)
Fax: 708-832-9617
E-mail: info@westwood.edu
World Wide Web: http://www.westwood.edu

WESTWOOD COLLEGE–DALLAS

DALLAS, TEXAS

The College and Its Mission

Today, the variables that define career success are ever changing. In order to get ahead and stay ahead, students need the right kind of preparation. To prepare for the working world, they need a career-focused education program that teaches the skills employers demand. The curriculum should include hands-on, practical experience and real-world applications to help graduates get started in their new career.

Students also need a fast-track learning program that shortens the time from education to career, with an academic schedule that fits their lifestyle. They need a high level of student services to help them reach their goals and the right financial package to make it all possible.

All of these are the focus at Westwood College, which operates seventeen campuses, with locations in California, Colorado, Illinois, Georgia, and Texas. The fourteen campuses of Westwood College offer degree programs in high-technology fields, while the three aviation campuses (Westwood College of Aviation Technology–Denver, Westwood College of Aviation Technology–Los Angeles, and Westwood Aviation Institute–Houston) offer aviation maintenance training.

Such fields as computer-aided design, computer networking, e-business, and graphic design are featured at the Westwood College campuses located in Anaheim, Inland Empire (Upland), Long Beach, and Los Angeles, California; Atlanta, Georgia; DuPage, O'Hare Airport, River Oaks, and Chicago–Loop, Illinois; Denver–North and Denver–South, Colorado; and Dallas, Fort Worth, and Houston, Texas. The Westwood College of Aviation Technology offers the aviation curriculum at the Denver, Colorado, and Los Angeles, California, campuses, while Westwood Aviation Institute offers the aviation curriculum in Houston.

Westwood College–Dallas is a branch of the Westwood College–O'Hare Airport and is accredited by the Accrediting Council for Independent Colleges and Schools (ACICS).

Academic Programs

At the Westwood College–Dallas campus, students may obtain an associate degree in less than seventeen months through day and evening classes. The programs are designed to help adults move into the high-tech world of work quickly. Classes provide hands-on skills and career-focused training. Skilled technology workers with fine-tuned critical-thinking skills graduate from Westwood ready to succeed. Westwood College's career development services work to match students with employers to get graduates started on the right career path.

The Dallas campus offers associate degree programs in computer-aided design/architectural drafting, computer network engineering, graphic design and multimedia, and software engineering.

Costs

The standard fee is $3729 per term. Books, laboratory fees, and other fees are additional. The standard fee for half-time students is $2423 per term. Educators can attend Westwood classes tuition free.

Financial Aid

Westwood students who qualify take full advantage of loans, grants, and scholarships to pay their way. Two Westwood High School Scholarships are offered to every high school in the United States. Tuition reimbursement programs may be available through a student's employer. Students may also apply for federal aid through normal channels. The College is committed to extending higher education to all qualified candidates, regardless of their ability to pay. An online Financial Aid Contact Center helps students navigate their way through the loan/grant/scholarship process.

Faculty

Westwood campuses have a total of more than 500 faculty members, of whom 40 percent hold master's degrees and 5 percent hold doctorates.

Student Body Profile

Westwood College recruits recent high school graduates, young adults, and working adults who want to acquire new skills to take advantage of growing opportunities in the professional workplace. Students come to Westwood from all across the U.S. and many other countries. Students enrolled at the Dallas campus total 370, of whom 30 percent are women.

Student Activities

In addition to the on-campus activities available at the College, the greater Dallas area offers unlimited recreational opportunities for students.

Facilities and Resources

Campus Resource Centers located on each Westwood campus contain a library of program-specific materials, books, and periodicals and Internet access. A virtual library provides remote access to several selected databases and links to Internet-based information that is specific to technology study. The Resource Center also contains the campus bookstore. Resource Center staff members can assist students in navigating all the research materials that are available.

Location

Westwood's Dallas campus is located on LBJ Freeway in the heart of Dallas, Texas. One of the largest cities in the southern United States, Dallas offers a wide range of cultural and recreational activities in an urban setting. A 60-acre arts district is home to theater, dance, music, sculpture, and museums. The city maintains more than 20,000 acres of lake and park space within its borders.

Admission Requirements

Admission requirements include a diploma from an accredited four-year high school or a GED certificate and passing scores on the College placement exam or qualifying SAT/ACT scores. Applicants fill out the Personal Career Assessment, which includes an application/evaluation form and the Entrance Assessment form, and complete the Financing Process form.

Westwood admissions counselors help students choose the correct course of study, if needed. Admissions paperwork is available by contacting the College at the address below.

Application and Information

Admissions Office
Westwood College–Dallas
Executive Center I, Suite 100
8390 LBJ Freeway
Dallas, Texas 75243
Telephone: 214-570-9100
          800-803-3140 (toll-free)
Fax: 214-570-8502
E-mail: info@westwood.edu
World Wide Web: http://www.westwood.edu

WESTWOOD COLLEGE–DENVER NORTH

DENVER, COLORADO

The College and Its Mission

Today, the variables that define career success are ever changing. In order to get ahead and stay ahead, students need the right kind of preparation. To prepare for the working world, they need a career-focused education program that teaches the skills employers demand and offers hands-on, practical experience with real-world applications and the right kind of job-placement assistance to help students get started in their new careers.

Students also need a fast-track learning program that shortens the time from education to career, with an academic schedule that fits their lifestyle. They need a high level of student services to help them reach their goals and the right financial package to make it all possible.

All of these are the focus at Westwood College, which operates seventeen campuses, with locations in California, Colorado, Illinois, Georgia, and Texas. The fourteen campuses of Westwood College offer degree programs in high-technology fields, while the three aviation campuses (Westwood College of Aviation Technology–Denver, Westwood College of Aviation Technology–Los Angeles, and Westwood Aviation Institute–Houston) offer aviation maintenance training.

Such fields as computer networking, graphic design, computer-aided design, and e-business are featured at the Westwood College campuses located in Anaheim, Inland Empire (Upland), Long Beach, and Los Angeles, California; Atlanta, Georgia; DuPage, O'Hare Airport, River Oaks, and Chicago–Loop, Illinois; Denver–North and Denver–South, Colorado; and Dallas, Fort Worth, and Houston, Texas. The Westwood College of Aviation Technology offers the aviation curriculum at the Denver, Colorado and Los Angeles, California, campuses, while Westwood Aviation Institute offers the aviation curriculum in Houston.

The Denver North campus is accredited by the Accrediting Commission of Career Schools and Colleges of Technology (ACCSCT).

Academic Programs

Denver North offers the largest variety of Westwood's bachelor's and associate degree programs. The campus, in addition to featuring high-technology opportunities, offers programs in high-demand industrial and medical fields. Bachelor's programs in animation, computer network management, criminal justice, e-business management, electronic engineering technology, game art and design, game software development, information systems security, interior design, visual communications, and Web design and multimedia are offered. Associate degree programs in technology are offered in computer-aided design/architectural drafting, computer-aided design/mechanical drafting, computer network engineering, electronic engineering technology, graphic design and

multimedia, and software engineering. Associate degree programs in service and industrial fields are offered in automotive technology; heating, ventilation, air conditioning, and refrigeration; hotel and restaurant management; medical assisting; medical transcription; and surveying.

Off-Campus Programs

Many of the College's degree programs are also available. This offers students the chance to obtain a degree at any time and location through a virtual campus. Students should call 800-992-5050 Ext. 244 for information.

Costs

The standard fee is $3729 per term, with lab; other fees and books are additional. The standard fee for half-time students is $2423 per term.

Financial Aid

Tuition assistance is available for those who qualify. Scholarships include the Westwood High School Scholarship Program, through which two scholarships are offered to every high school in the United States; the Colorado Undergraduate Merit State Scholarships for Colorado residents; and several loan programs.

Faculty

Westwood has 528 total faculty members (half are full-time), of whom 69 are at the Denver North campus. Forty percent hold master's degrees and 5 percent hold doctorates.

Student Body Profile

There are 1,369 students enrolled at the Denver North campus, of whom 25 percent are women.

Student Activities

With a diverse population of nearly 2 million and proximity to the Rocky Mountains, Denver offers students a unique opportunity to combine advanced learning with a healthy, active lifestyle. Skiing, snowboarding, mountain climbing, and other outdoor, recreational, and cultural activities abound.

Facilities and Resources

The Denver North campus is the largest of Westwood's campuses and recently underwent a $4-million renovation. The campus provides industry-standard classrooms and labs, which provides a completely functional learning environment that complements Westwood's mission.

Location

The campus is located at 7350 North Broadway in Denver, near the intersection of Interstate 25 and the Boulder Turnpike. Students have easy access to the downtown business districts, LoDo cultural activities, and the I-36 High-Tech Corridor.

Admission Requirements

A diploma from an accredited four-year high school or a GED certificate and passing scores on the college placement exam (or qualifying SAT/ACT scores) are required.

Application and Information

Ben Simms, Director of Admissions
Westwood College–Denver North
7350 North Broadway
Denver, Colorado 80221-3653
Telephone: 303-650-5050
             800-992-5050 (toll-free)
Fax: 303-487-0214
E-mail: info@westwood.edu
World Wide Web: http://www.westwood.edu

WESTWOOD COLLEGE–DENVER SOUTH

DENVER, COLORADO

The College and Its Mission

Today, the variables that define career success are ever changing. In order to get ahead and stay ahead, students need the right kind of preparation. To prepare for the working world, they need a program of career-focused education that teaches the skills employers demand and offers hands-on, practical experience with real-world applications and the right kind of job-placement assistance to help students get started in their new careers.

Students also need a fast-track learning program that shortens the time from education to career, with an academic schedule that fits their lifestyle. They need a high level of student services to help reach their goals and the right financial package to make it all possible.

All of these are the focus at Westwood College, which operates seventeen campuses, with locations in California, Colorado, Illinois, Georgia, and Texas. The fourteen campuses of Westwood College offer degree programs in high-technology fields, while the three aviation campuses (Westwood College of Aviation Technology–Denver, Westwood College of Aviation Technology–Los Angeles, and Westwood Aviation Institute–Houston) offer aviation maintenance training.

Such fields as computer networking, graphic design, computer-aided design, and e-business are featured at the Westwood College campuses located in Anaheim, Inland Empire (Upland), Long Beach, and Los Angeles, California; Atlanta, Georgia; DuPage, O'Hare Airport, River Oaks, and Chicago–Loop, Illinois; Denver–North and Denver–South, Colorado; and Dallas, Fort Worth, and Houston, Texas. The Westwood College of Aviation Technology offers the aviation curriculum at the Denver, Colorado and Los Angeles, California, campuses, while Westwood Aviation Institute offers the aviation curriculum in Houston.

The Denver–South Campus is accredited by the Accrediting Commission of Career Schools and Colleges of Technology (ACCSCT).

Academic Programs

Denver South concentrates on computer-based high-technology bachelor's and associate degree programs. It offers daytime, evening, and weekend class schedules in order to serve as many students as possible. Bachelor's programs in animation, computer network management, criminal justice, e-business management, game art and design, game software development, interior design, technical management, visual communications, and Web design and multimedia are offered. Associate degree programs in computer-aided design/architectural drafting (CAD), computer network engineering, graphic design and multimedia, and software engineering are available.

Costs

The standard fee is $3729 per term, with additional costs for lab and miscellaneous fees and books. The standard fee for half-time students is $2423 per term.

Financial Aid

Tuition assistance is available for those who qualify. Scholarships include the Westwood High School Scholarship Program, through which two scholarships are offered to every high school in the United States; the Colorado Undergraduate Merit State Scholarships for Colorado residents; and several loan programs.

Faculty

The Westwood College system has 528 total faculty members (half are full-time), of whom 38 are at Denver South. Forty percent hold a master's degree and 5 percent a doctorate.

Student Body Profile

Four hundred forty-seven students are enrolled at Denver South, of whom 75 percent are men and 25 percent women.

Student Activities

With a diverse population of nearly 2 million and proximity to the Rocky Mountains, students have a unique opportunity to combine advanced learning with a healthy, active lifestyle. Skiing, snowboarding, mountain climbing, and other outdoor, recreational, and cultural activities abound.

Facilities and Resources

The campus includes two dedicated buildings totaling more than 30,000 square feet of classrooms, labs, and administrative offices. There is also an annex containing classroom space.

Location

The campus is located at 3150 South Sheridan Boulevard in Denver, at the intersection of South Sheridan Boulevard and Hampden Avenue (Interstate Highway 85). It is easily accessible from Lakewood, Englewood, Littleton, and Denver's entire southwest metro area.

Admission Requirements

A diploma from an accredited four-year high school or a GED certificate and passing scores on the college entrance exam (or qualifying ACT/SAT scores) are required.

Application and Information

Ron DeJong, Director of Admissions
Westwood College–Denver South
3150 South Sheridan Boulevard
Denver, Colorado 80227-5548

Telephone: 303-934-2790
Fax: 303-934-2583
E-mail: info@westwood.edu
World Wide Web: http://www.westwood.edu

WESTWOOD COLLEGE–
FORT WORTH
EULESS, TEXAS

The College and Its Mission

Today, the variables that define career success are ever changing. In order to get ahead and stay ahead, students need the right kind of preparation. To prepare for the working world, students need a programmed, career-focused education that teaches the skills employers demand, that is, hands-on practical experience with real-world applications and the right kind of job-placement assistance to help them get started in their new career.

Students also need a fast-track leaning program that shortens the time from education to career, with an academic schedule that fits their lifestyle. Students need a high level of student services to help them reach their goals, and the right financial package to make it all possible.

All of these are the focus at Westwood College, which operates seventeen campuses, with locations in California, Colorado, Illinois, Georgia, and Texas. The fourteen campuses of Westwood College offer degree programs in high-technology fields, while the three aviation campuses (Westwood College of Aviation Technology–Denver, Westwood College of Aviation Technology–Los Angeles, and Westwood Aviation Institute–Houston) offer aviation maintenance training.

Such fields as computer networking, graphic design, computer-aided design, and e-business are featured at the Westwood College campuses located in Anaheim, Inland Empire (Upland), Long Beach, and Los Angeles, California; Atlanta, Georgia; DuPage, O'Hare Airport, River Oaks, and Chicago–Loop, Illinois; Denver–North and Denver–South, Colorado; and Dallas, Fort Worth, and Houston, Texas. The Westwood College of Aviation Technology offers the aviation curriculum at the Denver, Colorado and Los Angeles, California, campuses, while Westwood Aviation Institute offers the aviation curriculum in Houston.

The Fort Worth campus is accredited by the Accrediting Council for Independent Colleges and Schools (ACICS).

Westwood College–Fort Worth (Euless, Texas) is a branch of Westwood College–DuPage (Woodridge, Illinois).

Academic Programs

The Fort Worth campus focuses on computer-based technology programs that prepare graduates to take advantage of the high-technology career opportunities that exist in the Dallas–Fort Worth metroplex. Associate degree programs are offered in computer-assisted design/architectural drafting, computer network engineering, graphic design and multimedia, and software engineering.

Costs

The standard fee is $3729 per term. Books, laboratory fees, and other fees are additional. The standard fee for half-time students is $2423 per term.

Financial Aid

Tuition assistance is available for those who qualify. Scholarships include The Westwood High School Scholarship Program, in which two scholarships are offered to every high school in the United States, the Colorado Undergraduate Merit State Scholarships for Colorado residents, and several loan programs.

Faculty

Westwood has a total of 528 faculty members (half are full-time and half are part-time), of whom 35 teach in the Dallas and Fort Worth campuses. A total of 40 percent hold the master's degree, while 5 percent hold a doctoral degree.

Student Body Profile

Students enrolled at the Forth Worth campus total 395, of whom 30 percent are women.

Student Activities

In addition to on-campus activities, students can take advantage of a vast array of recreational and cultural activities in this dynamic area with a Southwestern flavor.

Facilities and Resources

Westwood College–Fort Worth currently occupies 12,000 square feet of administrative and instructional space. Also available is a Resource Center, with occupation-related reference materials and a number of resources that link students to library assets nationwide.

Location

The Fort Worth campus is located in Euless, Texas, between Dallas and Fort Worth.

Admission Requirements

A diploma from an accredited four-year high school or GED certificate and passing scores on the college entrance exam (or qualifying ACT/SAT scores) are required.

Application and Information

Lisa Hecht, Director of Admissions
Westwood College–Fort Worth
1331 Airport Freeway, Suite 402
Euless, Texas 76040
Telephone: 817-685-9994
              866-533-9997 (toll-free)
Fax: 817-685-8929
E-mail: info@westwood.edu
World Wide Web: http://www.westwood.edu

WESTWOOD COLLEGE–HOUSTON SOUTH

HOUSTON, TEXAS

The College and Its Mission

Today, the variables that define career success are ever changing. In order to get ahead and stay ahead, students need the right kind of preparation. To prepare for the working world, they need a career-focused education program that teaches the skills employers demand. The curriculum should include hands-on, practical experience and real-world applications to help graduates get started in their new careers.

Students also need a fast-track learning program that shortens the time from education to career, with an academic schedule that fits their lifestyle. They need a high level of student services to help them reach their goals and the right financial package to make it all possible.

All of these are the focus at Westwood College, which operates seventeen campuses, with locations in California, Colorado, Illinois, Georgia, and Texas. The fourteen campuses of Westwood College offer degree programs in high-technology fields, while the three aviation campuses (Westwood College of Aviation Technology–Denver, Westwood College of Aviation Technology–Los Angeles, and Westwood Aviation Institute–Houston) offer aviation maintenance training.

Such fields as computer networking, graphic design, computer-aided design, and e-business are featured at the Westwood College campuses located in Anaheim, Inland Empire (Upland), Long Beach, and Los Angeles, California; Atlanta, Georgia; DuPage, O'Hare Airport, River Oaks, and Chicago–Loop, Illinois; Denver–North and Denver–South, Colorado; and Dallas, Fort Worth, and Houston South, Texas. The Westwood College of Aviation Technology offers the aviation curriculum at the Denver, Colorado, and Los Angeles, California, campuses, while Westwood Aviation Institute offers the aviation curriculum in Houston.

Westwood College–Houston South is accredited by the Accrediting Commission of Career Schools and Colleges of Technology (ACCSCT) and is a branch of Westwood College–Denver North.

Academic Programs

At the Westwood College–Houston South campus, students may obtain an associate degree in less than seventeen months through day and evening classes. The programs are designed to help adults move into the high-technology world of work quickly. Classes provide hands-on skills and career-focused training. Skilled technology workers with fine-tuned critical-thinking skills graduate from Westwood ready to succeed. Westwood College's career development services work to match students with employers to get graduates started on the right career path.

The Houston South campus focuses on computer-based programs that prepare graduates to take advantage of the high-technology career opportunities available in Houston. Associate degree programs are offered in computer-aided design/architectural drafting (CAD), computer network engineering, and graphic design and multimedia.

Costs

The standard fee is $3894 for the August and October 2004 and January 2005 terms. Books, laboratory fees, and other fees are additional. The standard fee for half-time students is $2531 for the same terms.

Financial Aid

Westwood students who qualify take full advantage of loans, grants, and scholarships to pay their way. Two Westwood High School Scholarships are offered to every high school in the United States. Tuition reimbursement programs may be available through a student's employer. Students may also apply for federal aid through normal channels. The College is committed to extending higher education to all qualified candidates, regardless of their ability to pay. An online Financial Aid Contact Center helps students navigate their way through the loan/grant/scholarship process.

Faculty

Westwood has 18 faculty members; 50 percent hold master's degrees.

Student Body Profile

Student enrollment at the Houston South campus totals 70 students, 30 percent of whom are women.

Student Activities

In addition to on-campus activities, students can take advantage of the many cultural and recreational activities of the city and surrounding communities.

Facilities and Resources

The Campus Resource Center offers a library of program-specific materials that have been carefully selected to aid that school's career-focused educational mission. Typical learning aids include books, periodicals, and Internet access. A virtual library provides remote access to several selected databases, and staff members are available to assist with research and provide instruction on how to conduct research. Westwood offers tutoring at no charge, and specialized Student Success Workshops help students improve skills in areas such as test taking, time management, resume preparation, and general study skills.

Location

With the campus located in the nation's fourth-largest city, cultural and recreational opportunities abound for students. A cosmopolitan city of many cultures and world-class theater, music, museums, architecture, dance, art, sports, and shopping, Houston also offers nearby beaches, rivers, and outdoor activities.

Admission Requirements

Admission requirements include a diploma from an accredited four-year high school or a GED certificate and passing scores on the College placement exam or qualifying SAT/ACT scores. Applicants fill out the Personal Career Assessment, which includes an application/evaluation form and the Entrance Assessment form, and complete the Financing Process form. Westwood admissions counselors help students choose the correct course of study, if needed. Admissions paperwork is available by contacting the College.

Application and Information

Westwood College–Houston
One Arena Place
7322 Southwest Freeway #1900
Houston, Texas 77074

Telephone: 713-777-4433
E-mail: info@westwood.edu
World Wide Web: http://www.westwood.edu

WESTWOOD COLLEGE–
INLAND EMPIRE
UPLAND, CALIFORNIA

The College and Its Mission

Today, the variables that define career success are ever changing. In order to get ahead and stay ahead, students needs the right kind of preparation. To prepare for the working world, students need a career-focused education program that teaches the skills employers demand and offers hands-on, practical experience with real-world applications and the right kind of job-placement assistance to help them get started in their new careers.

Students also need a fast-track learning program that shortens the time from education to career, with an academic schedule that fits their lifestyle. They need a high level of student services to help them reach their goals and the right financial package to make it all possible.

All of these are the focus at Westwood College, which operates seventeen campuses, with locations in California, Colorado, Illinois, Georgia, and Texas. The fourteen campuses of Westwood College offer degree programs in high-technology fields, while the three aviation campuses (Westwood College of Aviation Technology–Denver, Westwood College of Aviation Technology–Los Angeles, and Westwood Aviation Institute–Houston) offer aviation maintenance training.

Such fields as computer networking, graphic design, computer-aided design, and e-business are featured at the Westwood College campuses located in Anaheim, Inland Empire (Upland), Long Beach, and Los Angeles, California; Atlanta, Georgia; DuPage, O'Hare Airport, River Oaks, and Chicago–Loop, Illinois; Denver–North and Denver–South, Colorado; and Dallas, Fort Worth, and Houston, Texas. The Westwood College of Aviation Technology offers the aviation curriculum at the Denver, Colorado, and Los Angeles, California, campuses, while Westwood Aviation Institute offers the aviation curriculum in Houston.

The Inland Empire campus is accredited by the Accrediting Commission of Career Schools and Colleges of Technology (ACCSCT).

Westwood College–Inland Empire is a branch of Westwood College–Denver North.

Academic Programs

The Inland Empire campus focuses on computer-based programs that prepare graduates to take advantage of Southern California's high-tech career opportunities. Bachelor's degree programs are offered in computer network management, criminal justice, e-business management, game art and design, game software development, information systems security, interior design, and visual communications. Associate degree programs are offered in computer-aided design/architectural drafting (CAD), computer network engineering, graphic design and multimedia, and software engineering.

Costs

The standard fee is $3729 per term; lab fees and other fees and books are additional. The standard fee for half-time students is $2423 per term.

Financial Aid

Tuition assistance is available to those students who qualify. Scholarships include the Westwood High School Scholarship Program, which offers two scholarships to every high school in the United States; the Colorado Undergraduate Merit State Scholarships for Colorado residents; and several loan programs.

Faculty

Westwood has 528 faculty members (half full-time, half part-time); 32 teach at the Inland Empire campus. Forty percent hold master's degrees, and 5 percent hold doctorates.

Student Body Profile

Student enrollment at the Inland Empire campus totals 633 students, 30 percent of whom are women.

Student Activities

In addition to on-campus activities, students can take advantage of many outdoor recreational activities. Several minor-league baseball teams play in the area. Many cultural opportunities are available as well.

Facilities and Resources

The campus features an all-new facility that was designed and built specifically for Westwood College. The design, layout, and features of the facility are the product of an extensive research project that evaluated the unique requirements of Westwood's students, faculty, and staff.

Location

The campus is located on the western edge of Southern California's Inland Empire, just minutes from the Ontario International Airport. It is easily reached by Interstate 10 and Interstate 15 from surrounding communities such as Ontario, Pomona, Rancho Cucamonga, Covina, Redlands, and San Bernardino.

Admission Requirements

A diploma from an accredited four-year high school or a GED certificate and passing scores on the college entrance exam (or qualifying ACT/SAT scores) are required.

Application and Information

Lyle Seavers, Director of Admissions
Westwood College–Inland Empire
20 West 7th Street
Upland, California 91786-7148
Telephone: 909-931-7550
          866-288-9488 (toll-free)
Fax: 909-931-9195
E-mail: info@westwood.edu
World Wide Web: http://www.westwood.edu

WESTWOOD COLLEGE–LONG BEACH

LONG BEACH, CALIFORNIA

The College and Its Mission

Today, the variables that define career success are ever changing. In order to get ahead and stay ahead, students need the right kind of preparation. To prepare for the working world, they need a career-focused education program that teaches the skills employers demand. The curriculum should include hands-on, practical experience and real-world applications to help graduates get started in their new careers.

Students also need a fast-track learning program that shortens the time from education to career, with an academic schedule that fits their lifestyle. They need a high level of student services to help them reach their goals and the right financial package to make it all possible.

All of these are the focus at Westwood College, which operates seventeen campuses, with locations in California, Colorado, Illinois, Georgia, and Texas. The fourteen campuses of Westwood College offer degree programs in high-technology fields, while the three aviation campuses (Westwood College of Aviation Technology–Denver, Westwood College of Aviation Technology–Los Angeles, and Westwood Aviation Institute–Houston) offer aviation maintenance training.

Such fields as computer networking, graphic design, computer-aided design, and e-business are featured at the Westwood College campuses located in Anaheim, Inland Empire (Upland), Long Beach, and Los Angeles, California; Atlanta, Georgia; DuPage, O'Hare Airport, River Oaks, and Chicago–Loop, Illinois; Denver–North and Denver–South, Colorado; and Dallas, Fort Worth, and Houston, Texas. The Westwood College of Aviation Technology offers the aviation curriculum at the Denver, Colorado, and Los Angeles, California, campuses, while Westwood Aviation Institute offers the aviation curriculum in Houston.

Westwood College–Long Beach is accredited by the Accrediting Commission of Career Schools and Colleges of Technology (ACCSCT) and has received temporary approval from the Bureau for Private Postsecondary and Vocational Education.

Academic Programs

At the Westwood College–Long Beach campus, students may obtain a bachelor's degree in less than three years and an associate degree in less than seventeen months through day and evening classes. The programs are designed to help adults move into the high-tech world of work quickly. Classes provide hands-on skills and career-focused training. Skilled technology workers with fine-tuned critical-thinking skills graduate from Westwood ready to succeed. Westwood College's career development services match students with employers to get graduates started on the right career path.

The Long Beach campus offers such bachelor's degree programs as animation, computer network management,

criminal justice, information systems security, and visual communications. The College offers associate degree programs in computer-aided design/architectural drafting, computer network engineering, and graphic design and multimedia.

Costs

The standard fee is $3729 per term. Books, laboratory fees, and other fees are additional. The standard fee for half-time students is $2423 per term. Educators can attend Westwood classes tuition free.

Financial Aid

Westwood students who qualify take full advantage of loans, grants, and scholarships to pay their way. Two Westwood High School Scholarships are offered to every high school in the United States. Tuition reimbursement programs may be available through a student's employer. Students may also apply for federal aid through normal channels. The College is committed to extending higher education to all qualified candidates, regardless of their ability to pay. An online Financial Aid Contact Center helps students navigate their way through the loan/grant/scholarship process.

Faculty

Westwood campuses have a total of more than 500 faculty members, of whom 40 percent hold master's degrees and 5 percent hold doctorates.

Student Body Profile

Westwood College recruits recent high school graduates, young adults, and working adults who want to acquire new skills to take advantage of growing opportunities in the professional workplace. Students come to Westwood from all across the U.S. and many other countries.

Student Activities

In addition to the many on-campus activities available at Westwood College, the greater Long Beach area abounds in cultural and recreational opportunities.

Facilities and Resources

Campus Resource Centers located on each Westwood campus contain a library of program-specific materials, books, and periodicals and Internet access. A virtual library provides remote access to several selected databases and links to Internet-based information that is specific to technology study. The Resource Center also contains the campus bookstore. Resource Center staff members can assist students in navigating all the research materials that are available.

Location

Long Beach is located in southern California, on the Pacific coast. Outstanding cultural arts and music festivals, plus a short boat ride to Catalina Island and gorgeous weather year-round, make Long Beach a paradise. Shopping, dining, sporting events, endless beaches, and an array of cultural diversity and nightlife make Long Beach a terrific place to begin a visitor's California adventure. Nearby Los Angeles as well as the many diverse towns and cities along the edge of the Pacific Ocean supply visitors with limitless opportunities for recreation, culture, and arts.

Admission Requirements

Admission requirements include a diploma from an accredited four-year high school or a GED certificate and passing scores on the College placement exam or qualifying SAT/ACT scores.

Applicants fill out the Personal Career Assessment, which includes an application/evaluation form and the Entrance Assessment form, and complete the Financing Process form. Westwood admissions counselors help students choose the correct course of study, if needed. Admissions paperwork is available by contacting the College at the address below.

Application and Information

Westwood College–Long Beach
3901 Via Oro Avenue, #103
Long Beach, California 90810
Telephone: 310-522-2088
         888-403-3339 (toll-free)
Fax: 310-522-2093
E-mail: info@westwood.edu
World Wide Web: http://www.westwood.edu

WESTWOOD COLLEGE–
LOS ANGELES

LOS ANGELES, CALIFORNIA

The College and Its Mission

Today, the variables that define career success are ever changing. In order to get ahead and stay ahead, students need the right kind of preparation. To prepare for the working world, they need a career-focused education program that teaches the skills employers demand and offers hands-on, practical experience with real-world applications and the right kind of job-placement assistance to help students get started in their new careers.

Students also need a fast-track learning program that shortens the time from education to career, with an academic schedule that fits their lifestyle. They need a high level of student services to help them reach their goals and the right financial package to make it all possible.

All of these are the focus at Westwood College, which operates seventeen campuses, with locations in California, Colorado, Illinois, Georgia, and Texas. The fourteen campuses of Westwood College offer degree programs in high-technology fields, while the three aviation campuses (Westwood College of Aviation Technology–Denver, Westwood College of Aviation Technology–Los Angeles, and Westwood Aviation Institute–Houston) offer aviation maintenance training.

Such fields as computer networking, graphic design, computer-aided design, and e-business are featured at the Westwood College campuses located in Anaheim, Inland Empire (Upland), Long Beach, and Los Angeles, California; Atlanta, Georgia; DuPage, O'Hare Airport, River Oaks, and Chicago–Loop, Illinois; Denver–North and Denver–South, Colorado; and Dallas, Fort Worth, and Houston, Texas. The Westwood College of Aviation Technology offers the aviation curriculum at the Denver, Colorado and Los Angeles, California, campuses, while Westwood Aviation Institute offers the aviation curriculum in Houston.

The Los Angeles campus is accredited by the Accrediting Council for Independent Colleges and Schools (ACICS).

Academic Programs

The Los Angeles campus focuses on computer-based technologies that prepare graduates to take advantage of southern California's unique career opportunities. Associate degree programs are offered in computer-aided designing/architectural drafting, computer network engineering, graphic design and multimedia, and software engineering. Bachelor's degree programs are offered in animation, computer network management, criminal justice, e-business management, game art and design, game software development, information systems security, visual communications, and Web design and multimedia.

Costs

The standard fee is $3729 per term, with lab; other fees and books are additional. The standard fee for half-time students is $2423 per term.

Financial Aid

Tuition assistance is available for those who qualify. Scholarships include the Westwood High School Scholarship Program, through which two scholarships are offered to every high school in the United States; the Colorado Undergraduate Merit State Scholarships for Colorado residents; and several loan programs.

Faculty

Westwood has 528 total faculty members (half are full-time), of whom 45 are at the Los Angeles campus. Forty percent hold master's degrees and 5 percent hold doctorates.

Student Body Profile

The campus has an enrollment of 694, of whom 75 percent are men and 25 percent are women.

Student Activities

The Los Angeles area, given its climate and recreational and cultural diversity, offers unlimited opportunities for students.

Facilities and Resources

The campus includes computer labs, featuring both PC and Macintosh machines running the most popular software applications used throughout industry to give students the hands-on experience that employers demand. The campus offers both day and evening classes.

Location

The campus is located at 3480 Wilshire Boulevard, Suite 700, in the Central Plaza Complex, just minutes from downtown Los Angeles in an urban environment.

Admission Requirements

A diploma from an accredited four-year high school or a GED certificate as well as passing scores on the college's entrance exam (or qualifying ACT/SAT scores) are required.

Application and Information

Ron Milman, Director of Admissions
Westwood College–Los Angeles
3460 Wilshire Boulevard, Suite 700
Los Angeles, California 90010-2210
Telephone: 213-739-9999
         877-377-4600 (toll-free)
Fax: 213-382-2468
E-mail: info@westwood.edu
World Wide Web: http://www.westwood.edu

WESTWOOD COLLEGE OF AVIATION TECHNOLOGY–DENVER

DENVER, COLORADO

WESTWOOD COLLEGE

The College and Its Mission

Today, the variables that define career success are ever changing. In order to get ahead and stay ahead, students need the right kind of preparation. To prepare for the working world, students need a career-focused education program that teaches the skills employers demand and offers hands-on practical experience with real-world applications and the right kind of job-placement assistance to help them get started in their new careers.

Students also need a fast-track learning program that shortens the time from education to career, with an academic schedule that fits their lifestyle. They need a high level of student services to help them reach their goals and the right financial package to make it all possible.

All of these are the focus at Westwood College, which operates seventeen campuses, with locations in California, Colorado, Illinois, Georgia, and Texas. The fourteen campuses of Westwood College offer degree programs in high-technology fields, while the three aviation campuses (Westwood College of Aviation Technology–Denver, Westwood College of Aviation Technology–Los Angeles, and Westwood Aviation Institute–Houston) offer aviation maintenance training.

Such fields as computer networking, graphic design, computer-aided design, and e-business are featured at the Westwood College campuses located in Anaheim, Inland Empire (Upland), Long Beach, and Los Angeles, California; Atlanta, Georgia; DuPage, O'Hare Airport, River Oaks, and Chicago–Loop, Illinois; Denver–North and Denver–South, Colorado; and Dallas, Fort Worth, and Houston, Texas. The Westwood College of Aviation Technology offers the aviation curriculum at the Denver, Colorado and Los Angeles, California, campuses, while Westwood Aviation Institute offers the aviation curriculum in Houston.

Westwood College of Aviation Technology–Denver is accredited by the Accrediting Commission of Career Schools and Colleges of Technology (ACCSCT).

Academic Programs

Students are drawn to this campus to train for a career in aviation maintenance or avionics. Graduates have gone on to careers with large commercial airlines, aerospace manufacturing companies, regional airlines, fixed-base carriers and a variety of other industry employers. Programs in airframe and power plant and advanced electronics technology (avionics) are offered.

Costs

For the combined airframe and powerplant program, costs total $27,568. This includes tuition, books, tools, registration fees, and student insurance.

Financial Aid

Tuition assistance is available for those who qualify. Scholarships include the Westwood High School Scholarship Program, which offers two scholarships to every high school in the United States; the Colorado Undergraduate Merit State Scholarships for Colorado residents; and several loan programs.

Faculty

Westwood has 528 total faculty members. Half are full-time. Thirty-two are based at the Denver Aviation campus. Forty percent hold master's degrees and 5 percent doctorates.

Student Body Profile

Student enrollment at the Denver Aviation campus totals 632, of whom approximately 10 percent are women.

Student Activities

Located near both the Rocky Mountain foothills and Denver, students attending this campus have a vast array of recreational and cultural opportunities at their disposal.

Facilities and Resources

The Denver Aviation campus gives students hands-on experience, with a variety of essential training aids, including reciprocating power plants and turbines from General Electric, Lycoming, Pratt & Whitney, and other manufacturers. The campus also features a complete Boeing 727 cockpit and operable subassemblies needed to learn Airframe and Power Plant and Avionics Maintenance.

Location

The campus is located a few minutes northwest of Denver in the suburb of Broomfield, Colorado, at 10851 West 120th Avenue, adjacent to the Jefferson County Airport. It is easily reached from Denver, Boulder, and surrounding communities via the Boulder Turnpike (Highway 36).

Admission Requirements

To enroll, students must be at least 17 years of age, have a high school diploma or GED certificate, and be able to speak, read, and write in English.

Application and Information

Susan Cottrell, Director of Admissions
Westwood College of Aviation Technology–Denver
10851 West 120th Avenue
Broomfield, Colorado 80021-3401

Telephone: 303-466-1714
Fax: 303-469-3797
E-mail: info@westwood.edu
World Wide Web: http://www.westwood.edu/aviation

Appendix

2003–04 Changes in Institutions

Following is an alphabetical listing of institutions that have recently closed, merged with other institutions, or changed their name or status. In the case of a name change, the former name appears first, followed by the new name.

Academy of Court Reporting (Cleveland, OH): no longer eligible for inclusion.

AEC Southern Ohio College, Northeast Campus (Akron, OH): name changed to AEC Southern Ohio College, Akron Campus.

Albany Technical Institute (Albany, GA): name changed to Albany Technical College.

Allied Medical College (Saint Ann, MO): name changed to Allied College.

Altamaha Technical Institute (Jesup, GA): name changed to Altamaha Technical College.

Anoka-Hennepin Technical College (Anoka, MN): name changed to Anoka Technical College.

Appalachian Technical Institute (Jasper, GA): name changed to Appalachian Technical College.

ATI Career Training Center (Dallas, TX): name changed to ATI Technical Training Center.

Bidwell Training Center, Inc. (Pittsburgh, PA): name changed to Bidwell Training Center.

Business Institute of Pennsylvania–Titusville (Meadville, PA): name changed to Business Institute of Pennsylvania.

California College Andon-Modesto (Modesto, CA): name changed to Maric College.

California College of Technology (Sacramento, CA): name changed to Maric College.

Career Training Academy–Monroeville Campus (Monroeville, PA): name changed to Career Training Academy.

Career Training Institute (Orlando, FL): name changed to Central Florida College.

CEI College (Anaheim, CA): name changed to Maric College.

Central Maine Technical College (Auburn, ME): name changed to Central Maine Community College.

Certified Careers Institute (Clearfield, UT): not eligible for inclusion.

Certified Careers Institute (Salt Lake City, UT): not eligible for inclusion.

Chipola Junior College (Marianna, FL): name changed to Chipola College.

CollegeAmerica-Colorado Springs (Colorado Spring, CO): name changed to CollegeAmerica–Colorado Springs.

Columbia Junior College (Columbia, SC): name changed to South University.

The Community College of Baltimore County–Catonsville Campus (Baltimore, MD): closed.

The Community College of Baltimore County–Dundalk Campus (Baltimore, MD): closed.

The Community College of Baltimore County–Essex Campus (Baltimore, MD): data reported under The Community College of Baltimore.

ConCorde Career Institute (Memphis, TN): name changed to ConCorde Career College.

Coosa Valley Technical Institute (Rome, GA): name changed to Coosa Valley Technical College.

Court Reporting Institute (Seattle, WA): name changed to Court Reporting Institute and Agency.

Court Reporting Institute (Seattle, WA): not eligible for inclusion.

Dull Knife Memorial College (Lame Deer, MT): name changed to Chief Dull Knife College.

Eastern Maine Technical College (Bangor, ME): name changed to Eastern Maine Community College.

Education Direct (Scranton, PA): name changed to Education Direct Center for Degree Studies.

Electronic Data Processing College of Puerto Rico, Inc.–San Sebastian (San Sebastian, PR): name changed to Electronic Data Processing College of Puerto Rico–San Sebastian.

Erie Community College, City Campus (Buffalo, NY): name changed to Erie Community College.

Erie Community College, North Campus (Williamsville, NY): data reported under Erie Community College.

Erie Community College, South Campus (Orchard Park, NY): data reported under Erie Community College.

ETI Technical College (North Canton, OH): name changed to AEC Southern Ohio College.

Fergus Falls Community College (Fergus Falls, MN): name changed to Minnesota State Community and Technical College–Fergus Falls.

Florida Computer & Business School (Miami, FL): name changed to Florida Career College.

The Florida School of Traditional Midwifery (Gainseville, FL): name changed to The Florida School of Midwifery.

Fountainhead College of Electronics (Knoxville, TN): name changed to Fountainhead College of Technology.

Hazard Community College (Hazard, KY): name changed to Hazard Community and Technical College.

Heald College-Milpitas (Milpitas, CA): name changed to Heald College-San Jose.

Heart of Georgia Technical Institute (Dublin, GA): name changed to Heart of Georgia Technical College.

Heritage College of Health Careers, Inc. (Denver, CO): name changed to Heritage College.

Herzing College, Minneapolis Drafting School Campus (Minneapolis, MN): name changed to Herzing College, Minneapolis Drafting School Division.

High-Tech Institute, Las Vegas (Las Vegas, NV): name changed to High-Tech Institute.

Huntington Junior College of Business (Huntington, WV): name changed to Huntington Junior College.

Institute of Career Education (West Palm Beach, FL): name changed to Summit Institute.

Instituto Fontecha (San Juan, PR): not eligible for inclusion.

Kennebec Valley Technical College (Fairfield, ME): name changed to Kennebec Valley Community College.

Kentucky Tech–Elizabethtown Campus (Elizabethtown, KY): name changed to Elizabethtown Technical College.

Lakeland Medical–Dental Academy (Minneapolis, MN): name changed to Herzing College, Lakeland Medical–Dental Division.

Lanier Technical Institute (Oakwood, GA): name changed to Lanier Technical College.

Lee College (West Hills, CA): name changed to Maric College.

Lincoln School of Commerce (Lincoln, NE): name changed to Hamilton College-Lincoln.

Louisiana Technical College–Sowela Campus (Lake Charles, LA): closed.

Maryland College of Art and Design (Silver Spring, MD): merged with Montgomery College.

McCann School of Business (Mahanoy City, PA): name changed to McCann School of Business & Technology.

Medical Careers Institute-Richmond (Richmond, VA): name changed to Medical Careers Institute.

Miami University–Hamilton Campus (Hamilton, OH): name changed to Miami University Hamilton.

Miami-Dade Community College (Miami, FL): name changed to Miami Dade College.

Mid-Plains Community College Area (North Platte, NE): name changed to Mid-Plains Community College.

Mid-State College (Auburn, ME): closed.

Mississippi County Community College (Blytheville, AR): name changed to Arkansas Northeastern College.

Modern Technology College (North Hollywood, CA): name changed to Maric College.

Moultrie Area Technical Institute (Moultrie, GA): name changed to Moultrie Technical College.

MTI College (Orange, CA): not eligible for inclusion.

Muskingum Area Technical College (Zanesville, OH): name changed to Zane State College.

Nebraska College of Business (Omaha, NE): name changed to Hamilton College.

NEI College of Technology (Columbia Heights, MN): closed.

New England Culinary Institute at Essex (Essex Junction, VT):

North Metro Technical Institute (Acworth, GA): name changed to North Metro Technical College.

Northeast Kansas Area Vocational Technical School (Atchison, KS): name changed to Northeast Kansas Technical College.

Northern Maine Technical College (Presque Isle, ME): name changed to Northern Maine Community College.

Northland Community and Technical College (Thief River Falls, MN): name changed to Northland Community and Technical College–Thief River Falls.

Northrop Rice Los Angeles (Inglewood, CA): name changed to Northrop Rice Aviation Institute of Technology.

Northwest Kansas Area Vocational Technical School (Goodland, KS): name changed to Northwest KansasTechnical College.

Northwest Technical College (East Grand Forks, MN): name changed to Northland Community and Technical College–East Grand Forks.

Northwest Technical College (Wadena, MN): name changed to Minnesota State Community and Technical College&-Wadena.

Northwest Technical College–Detroit Lakes (Detroit Lakes, MN): name changed to Minnesota State Community and Technical College–Detroit Lakes.

Ohio College of Massotherapy, Inc. (Akron, OH): name changed to Ohio College of Massotherapy.

Okefenokee Technical Institute (Waycross, GA): name changed to Okefenokee Technical College.

Owensboro Community College (Owensboro, KY): name changed to Owensboro Community and Technical College.

Pittsburgh Technical Institute (Pittsburgh, PA): closed.

Pittsburgh Technical Institute–Boyd School Division (Oakdale, PA): name changed to Pittsburgh Technical Institute.

Pratt Community College and Area Vocational School (Pratt, KS): name changed to Pratt Community College.

Prestonsburg Community College (Prestonsburg, KY): name changed to Big Sandy Community and Technical College.

Prospect Hall School of Business (Hollywood, FL): closed.

Puerto Rico Technical Junior College, Inc. (San Juan, PR): name changed to Puerto Rico Technical Junior College.

Remington College–Topeka Campus (Topeka, KS): closed.

RETS Electronic Institute (Louisville, KY): name changed to RETS Institute of Technology.

San Jacinto College Central Campus (Pasadena, TX): data reported under San Jacinto College District.

San Jacinto College North Campus (Houston, TX): data reported under San Jacinto College District.

San Jacinto College South Campus (Houston, TX): data reported under San Jacinto College District.

School of Advertising Art, Inc. (Kettering, OH): name changed to School of Advertising Art.

Silicon Valley College-Emeryville Campus (Emeryville, CA): name changed to Silicon Valley College.

Skadron College (San Bernardino, CA): name changed to Bryman College.

South Georgia Technical Institute (Americus, GA): name changed to South Georgia Technical College.

South University (Columbia, SC): closed.

Southeastern Technical Institute (Vidalia, GA): name changed to Southeastern Technical College.

Southern California College of Business and Law (Brea, CA): closed.

Southern California College of Court Reporting (Anaheim, CA): name changed to South Coast College.

Southern Maine Technical College (South Portland, ME): name changed to Southern Maine Community College.

St. Luke's College of Nursing and Health Sciences (Sioux City, IA): name changed to St. Luke's College.

Swainsboro Technical Institute (Swainsboro, GA): name changed to Swainsboro Technical College.

Trenholm State Technical College (Montgomery, AL): closed.

Trenholm State Technical College, Patterson Campus (Montgomery, AL): name changed to Trenholm State Technical College.

Valdosta Technical Institute (Valdosta, GA): name changed to Valdosta Technical College.

Vatterott College, Dodge Campus (Omaha, NE): name changed to Vatterott College.

Virginia Marti College of Fashion and Art (Lakewood, OH): name changed to Virginia Marti College of Art and Design.

Washington County Technical College (Calais, ME): name changed to Washington County Community College.

Webster Institute of Technology (Tampa, FL): name changed to Webster College.

West Side Institute of Technology (Cleveland, OH): closed.

The Westchester Business Institute (White Plains, NY): name changed to The College of Westchester.

Western Institute of Science & Health (Rohnert Park, CA): name changed to Sonoma College.

Westwood College of Aviation Technology–Denver (Broomfield, CO): name changed to Westwood College&-Denver.

Westwood College of Aviation Technology–Houston (Houston, TX): name changed to Westwood Aviation Institute.

Westwood College of Aviation Technology–Houston (Houston, TX): not eligible for inclusion.

Westwood College of Aviation Technology–Los Angeles (Inglewood, CA): name changed to Westwood College–Los Angeles.

Westwood College of Aviation Technology–Los Angeles (Inglewood, CA): not eligible for inclusion.

Westwood College of Technology–Anaheim (Anaheim, CA): name changed to Westwood College&-Anaheim.

Westwood College of Technology–Chicago O'Hare Airport (Schiller Park, IL): name changed to Westwood College–Chicago O'Hare Airport.

Westwood College of Technology–Chicago River Oaks (Calumet City, IL): name changed to Westwood College–Chicago River Oaks.

Westwood College of Technology–Dallas (Dallas, TX): name changed to Westwood College&-Dallas.

Westwood College of Technology–Denver North (Denver, CO): name changed to Westwood College–Denver North.

Westwood College of Technology–Denver South (Denver, CO): name changed to Westwood College–Denver South.

Westwood College of Technology–Fort Worth (Euless, TX): name changed to Westwood College–Fort Worth.

Westwood College of Technology–Inland Empire (Upland, CA): name changed to Westwood College–Inland Empire.

Westwood College of Technology–Long Beach (Long Beach, CA): name changed to Westwood College–Long Beach.

Westwood College of Technology–Los Angeles (Los Angeles, CA): name changed to Westwood College–Los Angeles.

Westwood College of Technology-Chicago Du Page (Woodridge, IL): name changed to Westwood College–Chicago Du Page.

Wyoming Technical Institute (Blairsville, PA): name changed to WyoTech.

Wyoming Technical Institute (Laramie, WY): name changed to WyoTech.

Indexes

Accounting

Abraham Baldwin Ag Coll (GA)
Academy Coll (MN)
AIB Coll of Business (IA)
Albuquerque Tech Vocational Inst (NM)
Alexandria Tech Coll (MN)
Allentown Business School (PA)
Alpena Comm Coll (MI)
Alvin Comm Coll (TX)
Amarillo Coll (TX)
American River Coll (CA)
Andover Coll (ME)
Anne Arundel Comm Coll (MD)
Anoka Tech Coll (MN)
Arapahoe Comm Coll (CO)
Asnuntuck Comm Coll (CT)
Atlantic Cape Comm Coll (NJ)
Augusta Tech Coll (GA)
Austin Comm Coll (TX)
Bainbridge Coll (GA)
Barton County Comm Coll (KS)
Bay State Coll (MA)
Beaufort County Comm Coll (NC)
Bellevue Comm Coll (WA)
Berean Inst (PA)
Bergen Comm Coll (NJ)
Berkeley Coll (NJ)
Berkeley Coll-New York City Campus (NY)
Berkeley Coll-Westchester Campus (NY)
Big Sandy Comm and Tech Coll (KY)
Blackhawk Tech Coll (WI)
Borough of Manhattan Comm Coll of City U of NY (NY)
Bradford School (OH)
Brevard Comm Coll (FL)
Briarwood Coll (CT)
Bristol Comm Coll (MA)
Bronx Comm Coll of City U of NY (NY)
Brookdale Comm Coll (NJ)
The Brown Mackie Coll-Lenexa Campus (KS)
Bryant & Stratton Business Inst, Buffalo (NY)
Bryant & Stratton Business Inst, Lackawanna (NY)
Bryant & Stratton Business Inst, Syracuse (NY)
Bryant and Stratton Coll, Parma (OH)
Bryant and Stratton Coll (WI)
Bryant & Stratton Business Inst, Amherst Cmps (NY)
Bucks County Comm Coll (PA)
Bunker Hill Comm Coll (MA)
Burlington County Coll (NJ)
Butler County Comm Coll (KS)
Butte Coll (CA)
Cabrillo Coll (CA)
Caldwell Comm Coll and Tech Inst (NC)
Calhoun Comm Coll (AL)

Cambria County Area Comm Coll (PA)
Cambria-Rowe Business Coll, Johnstown (PA)
Camden County Coll (NJ)
Cañada Coll (CA)
Cape Cod Comm Coll (MA)
Capital Comm Coll (CT)
Carl Sandburg Coll (IL)
Casper Coll (WY)
Cecil Comm Coll (MD)
Cedar Valley Coll (TX)
Central Arizona Coll (AZ)
Central Carolina Tech Coll (SC)
Central Comm Coll-Columbus Campus (NE)
Central Comm Coll-Grand Island Campus (NE)
Central Comm Coll-Hastings Campus (NE)
Central Georgia Tech Coll (GA)
Central Lakes Coll (MN)
Central Oregon Comm Coll (OR)
Central Pennsylvania Coll (PA)
Central Piedmont Comm Coll (NC)
Central Wyoming Coll (WY)
Century Coll (MN)
Chabot Coll (CA)
Chaparral Coll (AZ)
Chemeketa Comm Coll (OR)
Chesapeake Coll (MD)
Chipola Coll (FL)
Cincinnati State Tech and Comm Coll (OH)
City Colls of Chicago, Malcolm X Coll (IL)
City Colls of Chicago, Wilbur Wright Coll (IL)
Clarendon Coll (TX)
Clark State Comm Coll (OH)
Cleveland Comm Coll (NC)
Clinton Comm Coll (NY)
Clovis Comm Coll (NM)
Coastal Bend Coll (TX)
Coastal Carolina Comm Coll (NC)
Coffeyville Comm Coll (KS)
Colby Comm Coll (KS)
Coll of DuPage (IL)
Coll of Southern Idaho (ID)
Coll of Southern Maryland (MD)
Coll of the Canyons (CA)
Coll of the Sequoias (CA)
The Coll of Westchester (NY)
Colorado Mountn Coll, Alpine Cmps (CO)
Colorado Mountn Coll (CO)
Colorado Mountn Coll, Timberline Cmps (CO)
Colorado Northwestern Comm Coll (CO)
Columbia-Greene Comm Coll (NY)
Columbia State Comm Coll (TN)
Columbus State Comm Coll (OH)
Commonwealth Business Coll, Merrillville (IN)

Commonwealth Business Coll, Michigan City (IN)
Commonwealth Tech Inst (PA)
Comm Coll of Aurora (CO)
Comm Coll of Denver (CO)
Comm Coll of Rhode Island (RI)
Consolidated School of Business, York (PA)
Copiah-Lincoln Comm Coll (MS)
Corning Comm Coll (NY)
Cumberland County Coll (NJ)
Cuyahoga Comm Coll (OH)
Cuyamaca Coll (CA)
Dakota County Tech Coll (MN)
Danville Comm Coll (VA)
Darton Coll (GA)
Davis Coll (OH)
Daytona Beach Comm Coll (FL)
DeKalb Tech Coll (GA)
Delaware Tech & Comm Coll, Terry Cmps (DE)
Delgado Comm Coll (LA)
Del Mar Coll (TX)
Delta Coll (MI)
Des Moines Area Comm Coll (IA)
Donnelly Coll (KS)
Draughons Jr Coll (KY)
Duluth Business U (MN)
Durham Tech Comm Coll (NC)
Dutchess Comm Coll (NY)
Eastern Idaho Tech Coll (ID)
Eastern Oklahoma State Coll (OK)
Eastern Wyoming Coll (WY)
Eastfield Coll (TX)
East Los Angeles Coll (CA)
East Mississippi Comm Coll (MS)
ECPI Coll of Technology, Newport News (VA)
ECPI Coll of Technology, Virginia Beach (VA)
ECPI Tech Coll, Richmond (VA)
ECPI Tech Coll, Roanoke (VA)
Edgecombe Comm Coll (NC)
Edison Comm Coll (FL)
Edison State Comm Coll (OH)
Elaine P. Nunez Comm Coll (LA)
El Camino Coll (CA)
El Centro Coll (TX)
Elgin Comm Coll (IL)
Elmira Business Inst (NY)
Erie Business Center South (PA)
Essex County Coll (NJ)
Eugenio María de Hostos Comm Coll of City U of NY (NY)
Everest Coll (AZ)
Everett Comm Coll (WA)
Fayetteville Tech Comm Coll (NC)

Finger Lakes Comm Coll (NY)
Fiorello H LaGuardia Comm Coll of City U of NY (NY)
Fisher Coll (MA)
Florida National Coll (FL)
Foothill Coll (CA)
Forsyth Tech Comm Coll (NC)
Fort Scott Comm Coll (KS)
Frederick Comm Coll (MD)
Fulton-Montgomery Comm Coll (NY)
Gallipolis Career Coll (OH)
Garden City Comm Coll (KS)
Gaston Coll (NC)
Gavilan Coll (CA)
Gem City Coll (IL)
Germanna Comm Coll (VA)
Globe Coll (MN)
Gloucester County Coll (NJ)
Gogebic Comm Coll (MI)
Greenfield Comm Coll (MA)
Guilford Tech Comm Coll (NC)
Gulf Coast Comm Coll (FL)
Gwinnett Tech Coll (GA)
Hamilton Coll (NE)
Harrisburg Area Comm Coll (PA)
Hawaii Comm Coll (HI)
Hawkeye Comm Coll (IA)
Hesser Coll (NH)
Hickey Coll (MO)
Hill Coll of the Hill Jr College District (TX)
Hillsborough Comm Coll (FL)
Hinds Comm Coll (MS)
Hiwassee Coll (TN)
Holyoke Comm Coll (MA)
Houston Comm Coll System (TX)
Howard Coll (TX)
Howard Comm Coll (MD)
Hudson County Comm Coll (NJ)
Illinois Eastern Comm Colls, Olney Central Coll (IL)
Indiana Business Coll, Anderson (IN)
Indiana Business Coll, Columbus (IN)
Indiana Business Coll, Evansville (IN)
Indiana Business Coll, Fort Wayne (IN)
Indiana Business Coll, Indianapolis (IN)
Indiana Business Coll, Lafayette (IN)
Indiana Business Coll, Marion (IN)
Indiana Business Coll, Muncie (IN)
Indiana Business Coll, Terre Haute (IN)
Iowa Lakes Comm Coll (IA)
Itasca Comm Coll (MN)
Ivy Tech State Coll-Lafayette (IN)
James A. Rhodes State Coll (OH)
James Sprunt Comm Coll (NC)

Jamestown Business Coll (NY)
Jamestown Comm Coll (NY)
Jefferson Comm Coll (KY)
Jefferson Comm Coll (NY)
Jefferson Comm Coll (OH)
J. F. Drake State Tech Coll (AL)
John A. Logan Coll (IL)
John Wood Comm Coll (IL)
Kapiolani Comm Coll (HI)
Kaplan Coll (IA)
Kauai Comm Coll (HI)
Kellogg Comm Coll (MI)
Kent State U, Salem Campus (OH)
Kent State U, Trumbull Campus (OH)
Kent State U, Tuscarawas Campus (OH)
Keystone Coll (PA)
Kilian Comm Coll (SD)
Kingsborough Comm Coll of City U of NY (NY)
Kingwood Coll (TX)
Kirkwood Comm Coll (IA)
Kirtland Comm Coll (MI)
Lake Area Tech Inst (SD)
Lakeland Comm Coll (OH)
Lake Region State Coll (ND)
Lakeshore Tech Coll (WI)
Lake Superior Coll (MN)
Lake Washington Tech Coll (WA)
Lamar State Coll-Orange (TX)
Lamar State Coll-Port Arthur (TX)
Lanier Tech Coll (GA)
Lansing Comm Coll (MI)
Laramie County Comm Coll (WY)
Lawson State Comm Coll (AL)
LDS Business Coll (UT)
Lehigh Carbon Comm Coll (PA)
Lenoir Comm Coll (NC)
Lewis and Clark Comm Coll (IL)
Lincoln Coll, Lincoln (IL)
Linn-Benton Comm Coll (OR)
Long Island Business Inst (NY)
Longview Comm Coll (MO)
Lon Morris Coll (TX)
Lorain County Comm Coll (OH)
Lord Fairfax Comm Coll (VA)
Los Angeles Harbor Coll (CA)
Los Angeles Pierce Coll (CA)
Los Angeles Trade-Tech Coll (CA)
Los Angeles Valley Coll (CA)
Louisiana Tech Coll-Florida Parishes Campus (LA)
Lower Columbia Coll (WA)
Luna Comm Coll (NM)
Luzerne County Comm Coll (PA)
MacCormac Coll (IL)
Macomb Comm Coll (MI)
Manatee Comm Coll (FL)

Manchester Comm Coll (CT)
Maple Woods Comm Coll (MO)
Marion Tech Coll (OH)
Marshalltown Comm Coll (IA)
Massasoit Comm Coll (MA)
Mayland Comm Coll (NC)
Maysville Comm Coll (KY)
McIntosh Coll (NH)
McLennan Comm Coll (TX)
Merritt Coll (CA)
Metropolitan Comm Coll (NE)
Metropolitan Comm Coll-Business & Technology College (MO)
Michiana Coll, South Bend (IN)
Middlesex Comm Coll (CT)
Middlesex Comm Coll (MA)
Middlesex County Coll (NJ)
Midlands Tech Coll (SC)
Mid Michigan Comm Coll (MI)
Mineral Area Coll (MO)
Minneapolis Business Coll (MN)
Minnesota School of Business-Brooklyn Center (MN)
Minnesota School of Business-Plymouth (MN)
Minnesota School of Business-Richfield (MN)
Minnesota State Coll-Southeast Tech (MN)
Minnesota West Comm & Tech Coll-Pipestone Cmps (MN)
MiraCosta Coll (CA)
Mississippi Gulf Coast Comm Coll (MS)
Mitchell Comm Coll (NC)
Mitchell Tech Inst (SD)
Modesto Jr Coll (CA)
Mohave Comm Coll (AZ)
Monroe Coll, Bronx (NY)
Monroe Coll, New Rochelle (NY)
Monroe County Comm Coll (MI)
Montana State U Coll of Tech-Great Falls (MT)
Montcalm Comm Coll (MI)
Montgomery County Comm Coll (PA)
Moraine Park Tech Coll (WI)
Morgan Comm Coll (CO)
Morton Coll (IL)
Mountain Empire Comm Coll (VA)
Mountain View Coll (TX)
Mountain West Coll (UT)
Mt. San Antonio Coll (CA)
Mount Wachusett Comm Coll (MA)
Napa Valley Coll (CA)
Nash Comm Coll (NC)
Nashville State Tech Comm Coll (TN)
Nassau Comm Coll (NY)
National Coll of Business & Technology, Danville (KY)

National Coll of Business & Technology, Florence (KY)
National Coll of Business & Technology, Lexington (KY)
National Coll of Business & Technology, Louisville (KY)
National Coll of Business & Technology, Pikeville (KY)
National Coll of Business & Technology, Richmond (KY)
National Coll of Business & Technology, Bluefield (VA)
National Coll of Business & Technology, Bristol (VA)
National Coll of Business & Technology, Charlottesville (VA)
National Coll of Business & Technology, Harrisonburg (VA)
National Coll of Business & Technology, Lynchburg (VA)
National Coll of Business & Technology, Martinsville (VA)
National Coll of Business & Technology, Salem (VA)
Naugatuck Valley Comm Coll (CT)
New Hampshire Comm Tech Coll, Berlin/Laconia (NH)
New Hampshire Comm Tech Coll, Manchester/Stratham (NH)
New Hampshire Tech Inst (NH)
Newport Business Inst, Lower Burrell (PA)
New River Comm Coll (VA)
Niagara County Comm Coll (NY)
Normandale Comm Coll (MN)
North Central Missouri Coll (MO)
North Central State Coll (OH)
Northcentral Tech Coll (WI)
Northeast Comm Coll (NE)
Northeastern Oklahoma A&M Coll (OK)
Northeastern Tech Coll (SC)
Northeast Iowa Comm Coll (IA)
Northeast Mississippi Comm Coll (MS)
Northeast State Tech Comm Coll (TN)
Northeast Texas Comm Coll (TX)
Northeast Wisconsin Tech Coll (WI)
Northern Essex Comm Coll (MA)
Northern Maine Comm Coll (ME)
North Harris Coll (TX)
North Hennepin Comm Coll (MN)
North Iowa Area Comm Coll (IA)
North Shore Comm Coll (MA)
Northwest Coll (WY)
Northwestern Connecticut Comm-Tech Coll (CT)
Northwest Iowa Comm Coll (IA)
Northwest-Shoals Comm Coll (AL)
Northwest State Comm Coll (OH)
Oakland Comm Coll (MI)
Oakton Comm Coll (IL)
Ocean County Coll (NJ)
Odessa Coll (TX)
Ohio Business Coll, Sandusky (OH)
Ohio Valley Coll of Technology (OH)
Oklahoma City Comm Coll (OK)

Oklahoma State U, Oklahoma City (OK)
Orangeburg-Calhoun Tech Coll (SC)
Orange Coast Coll (CA)
Orange County Comm Coll (NY)
Ouachita Tech Coll (AR)
Owens Comm Coll, Findlay (OH)
Oxnard Coll (CA)
Palm Beach Comm Coll (FL)
Palomar Coll (CA)
Pasadena City Coll (CA)
Pellissippi State Tech Comm Coll (TN)
Peninsula Coll (WA)
Penn Valley Comm Coll (MO)
Pensacola Jr Coll (FL)
Phoenix Coll (AZ)
Piedmont Virginia Comm Coll (VA)
Pima Comm Coll (AZ)
Pioneer Pacific Coll (OR)
Pitt Comm Coll (NC)
Portland Comm Coll (OR)
Pratt Comm Coll and Area Vocational School (KS)
Prince George's Comm Coll (MD)
Queensborough Comm Coll of City U of NY (NY)
Quinebaug Valley Comm Coll (CT)
Quinsigamond Comm Coll (MA)
Raritan Valley Comm Coll (NJ)
Rasmussen Coll Mankato (MN)
Rasmussen Coll Minnetonka (MN)
Rasmussen Coll St. Cloud (MN)
Reading Area Comm Coll (PA)
Red Rocks Comm Coll (CO)
Richmond Comm Coll (NC)
Riverside Comm Coll (CA)
Roane State Comm Coll (TN)
Rochester Business Inst (NY)
Rockingham Comm Coll (NC)
Rogue Comm Coll (OR)
Rowan-Cabarrus Comm Coll (NC)
Saint Charles Comm Coll (MO)
St. Clair County Comm Coll (MI)
St. Cloud Tech Coll (MN)
St. Louis Comm Coll at Florissant Valley (MO)
Saint Paul Coll—A Comm & Tech College (MN)
St. Philip's Coll (TX)
Salem Comm Coll (NJ)
San Diego City Coll (CA)
Sanford-Brown Coll, Hazelwood (MO)
San Joaquin Delta Coll (CA)
San Jose City Coll (CA)
Santa Barbara City Coll (CA)
Santa Fe Comm Coll (NM)
Santa Monica Coll (CA)
Sauk Valley Comm Coll (IL)
Schenectady County Comm Coll (NY)
Schoolcraft Coll (MI)
Scottsdale Comm Coll (AZ)
Seminole Comm Coll (FL)
Seward County Comm Coll (KS)
Sierra Coll (CA)
Sinclair Comm Coll (OH)
Sisseton-Wahpeton Comm Coll (SD)
Snow Coll (UT)
South Central Tech Coll (MN)
South Coll (TN)
South Coll-Asheville (NC)

Southeast Comm Coll, Beatrice Campus (NE)
Southeastern Tech Coll (GA)
Southern West Virginia Comm and Tech Coll (WV)
South Hills School of Business & Technology, State College (PA)
South Plains Coll (TX)
South Puget Sound Comm Coll (WA)
South Suburban Coll (IL)
South Texas Comm Coll (TX)
South U (FL)
South U (SC)
Southwestern Coll (CA)
Southwestern Comm Coll (NC)
Southwestern Illinois Coll (IL)
Southwestern Oregon Comm Coll (OR)
Southwest Mississippi Comm Coll (MS)
Spartanburg Tech Coll (SC)
Spencerian Coll (KY)
Spoon River Coll (IL)
Springfield Tech Comm Coll (MA)
Stark State Coll of Technology (OH)
State U of NY Coll of A&T at Morrisville (NY)
State U of NY Coll of Technology at Alfred (NY)
State U of NY Coll of Technology at Canton (NY)
State U of NY Coll of Technology at Delhi (NY)
Sullivan County Comm Coll (NY)
Sussex County Comm Coll (NJ)
Terra State Comm Coll (OH)
Thomas Nelson Comm Coll (VA)
Thompson Inst (PA)
Three Rivers Comm Coll (MO)
Tidewater Comm Coll (VA)
Tillamook Bay Comm Coll (OR)
Tompkins Cortland Comm Coll (NY)
Tri-County Comm Coll (NC)
Trident Tech Coll (SC)
Trinidad State Jr Coll (CO)
Triton Coll (IL)
Trumbull Business Coll (OH)
Umpqua Comm Coll (OR)
The U of Akron—Wayne Coll (OH)
U of Alaska Anchorage, Matanuska-Susitna Coll (AK)
U of Kentucky, Lexington Comm Coll (KY)
U of Northwestern Ohio (OH)
U of Pittsburgh at Titusville (PA)
Utah Valley State Coll (UT)
Vance-Granville Comm Coll (NC)
Ventura Coll (CA)
Vermilion Comm Coll (MN)
Vincennes U (IN)
Virginia Western Comm Coll (VA)
Vista Comm Coll (CA)
Washtenaw Comm Coll (MI)
Waycross Coll (GA)
Western Nevada Comm Coll (NV)
Western Wisconsin Tech Coll (WI)
Western Wyoming Comm Coll (WY)
West Hills Comm Coll (CA)
West Kentucky Comm and Tech Coll (KY)
Westmoreland County Comm Coll (PA)
West Virginia Business Coll, Wheeling (WV)
Wilson Tech Comm Coll (NC)

Wisconsin Indianhead Tech Coll (WI)
Yakima Valley Comm Coll (WA)
Yavapai Coll (AZ)
York County Comm Coll (ME)
York Tech Coll (SC)
Yuba Coll (CA)

Accounting and Business/ Management
Antonelli Coll (OH)
LDS Business Coll (UT)
Mountain State Coll (WV)
Sawyer Coll, Hammond (IN)
Westwood Coll—Chicago Loop Campus (IL)

Accounting and Computer Science
Columbus State Comm Coll (OH)

Accounting and Finance
Jackson Comm Coll (MI)

Accounting Related
Central Pennsylvania Coll (PA)
International Inst of the Americas, Phoenix (AZ)
Northeast Wisconsin Tech Coll (WI)
Virginia Coll at Jackson (MS)

Accounting Technology and Bookkeeping
AEC Southern Ohio Coll, Northern Kentucky Campus (KY)
Alamance Comm Coll (NC)
Allegany Coll of Maryland (MD)
Asheville-Buncombe Tech Comm Coll (NC)
Bates Tech Coll (WA)
Big Bend Comm Coll (WA)
Blue River Comm Coll (MO)
Bowling Green State U-Firelands Coll (OH)
Broome Comm Coll (NY)
Cape Fear Comm Coll (NC)
Central Florida Comm Coll (FL)
Central Georgia Tech Coll (GA)
Central Wyoming Coll (WY)
Clark Coll (WA)
Clover Park Tech Coll (WA)
Coll of Lake County (IL)
Columbus State Comm Coll (OH)
Comm Coll of Allegheny County (PA)
Cuyamaca Coll (CA)
Dakota County Tech Coll (MN)
Delaware County Comm Coll (PA)
Del Mar Coll (TX)
Edmonds Comm Coll (WA)
Education Direct Center for Degree Studies (PA)
Elgin Comm Coll (IL)
Essex County Coll (NJ)
Front Range Comm Coll (CO)
Glendale Comm Coll (AZ)
Gloucester County Coll (NJ)
Goodwin Coll (CT)
Green River Comm Coll (WA)
Hagerstown Comm Coll (MD)
Harford Comm Coll (MD)
Inst of Business & Medical Careers (CO)
Iowa Lakes Comm Coll (IA)
Ivy Tech State Coll—Bloomington (IN)
Ivy Tech State Coll—Central Indiana (IN)
Ivy Tech State Coll—Columbus (IN)
Ivy Tech State Coll—Eastcentral (IN)

Ivy Tech State Coll—Kokomo (IN)
Ivy Tech State Coll—Lafayette (IN)
Ivy Tech State Coll—North Central (IN)
Ivy Tech State Coll—Northeast (IN)
Ivy Tech State Coll—Northwest (IN)
Ivy Tech State Coll—Southcentral (IN)
Ivy Tech State Coll—Southeast (IN)
Ivy Tech State Coll—Southwest (IN)
Ivy Tech State Coll—Wabash Valley (IN)
Ivy Tech State Coll—Whitewater (IN)
Jefferson State Comm Coll (AL)
Johnson County Comm Coll (KS)
Johnston Comm Coll (NC)
John Wood Comm Coll (IL)
J. Sargeant Reynolds Comm Coll (VA)
Kalamazoo Valley Comm Coll (MI)
Kellogg Comm Coll (MI)
Lackawanna Coll (PA)
Lake Land Coll (IL)
Lake Region State Coll (ND)
LDS Business Coll (UT)
Lehigh Carbon Comm Coll (PA)
Louisiana Tech Coll—Delta Ouachita Campus (LA)
Louisiana Tech Coll—Evangeline Campus (LA)
Louisiana Tech Coll—Lamar Salter Campus (LA)
Louisiana Tech Coll—Natchitoches Campus (LA)
Louisiana Tech Coll—North Central Campus (LA)
Louisiana Tech Coll—Northwest Louisiana Campus (LA)
Louisiana Tech Coll—Sabine Valley Campus (LA)
Louisiana Tech Coll—Sidney N. Collier Campus (LA)
Louisiana Tech Coll—Young Memorial Campus (LA)
Lower Columbia Coll (WA)
McHenry County Coll (IL)
Metropolitan Comm Coll-Business & Technology College (MO)
Miami Dade Coll (FL)
Milwaukee Area Tech Coll (WI)
Minneapolis Comm and Tech Coll (MN)
Minot State U-Bottineau Campus (ND)
Moberly Area Comm Coll (MO)
Mohawk Valley Comm Coll (NY)
Montgomery Coll (MD)
Montgomery County Comm Coll (PA)
Mott Comm Coll (MI)
Nassau Comm Coll (NY)
National Coll of Business & Technology, Salem (VA)
Northampton County Area Comm Coll (PA)
Northeast Wisconsin Tech Coll (WI)
North Florida Comm Coll (FL)
North Iowa Area Comm Coll (IA)
Northland Pioneer Coll (AZ)
North Seattle Comm Coll (WA)
Northwestern Michigan Coll (MI)
Olympic Coll (WA)

Owens Comm Coll, Findlay (OH)
Owens Comm Coll, Toledo (OH)
Parkland Coll (IL)
Pellissippi State Tech Comm Coll (TN)
Pennsylvania Coll of Technology (PA)
Pikes Peak Comm Coll (CO)
Polk Comm Coll (FL)
St. Cloud Tech Coll (MN)
St. Johns River Comm Coll (FL)
St. Petersburg Coll (FL)
San Juan Coll (NM)
Southern State Comm Coll (OH)
Southwestern Michigan Coll (MI)
Spokane Comm Coll (WA)
Spokane Falls Comm Coll (WA)
Stanly Comm Coll (NC)
Tillamook Bay Comm Coll (OR)
Trenholm State Tech Coll, Montgomery (AL)
Union County Coll (NJ)
The U of Akron–Wayne Coll (OH)
Utah Valley State Coll (UT)
Waubonsee Comm Coll (IL)
Western Nevada Comm Coll (NV)
West Virginia Northern Comm Coll (WV)
Williston State Coll (ND)
Wor-Wic Comm Coll (MD)

Acting
KD Studio (TX)
Northampton County Area Comm Coll (PA)
Santa Barbara City Coll (CA)

Actuarial Science
Harrisburg Area Comm Coll (PA)

Administrative Assistant and Secretarial Science
Abraham Baldwin Ag Coll (GA)
AIB Coll of Business (IA)
Albuquerque Tech Vocational Inst (NM)
Alexandria Tech Coll (MN)
Allegany Coll of Maryland (MD)
Allentown Business School (PA)
Alpena Comm Coll (MI)
Alvin Comm Coll (TX)
Amarillo Coll (TX)
American River Coll (CA)
Andover Coll (ME)
Anne Arundel Comm Coll (MD)
Anoka Tech Coll (MN)
Arapahoe Comm Coll (CO)
Arizona Western Coll (AZ)
Asnuntuck Comm Coll (CT)
Augusta Tech Coll (GA)
Austin Comm Coll (TX)
Bainbridge Coll (GA)
Barton County Comm Coll (KS)
Bates Tech Coll (WA)
Bay State Coll (MA)
Beaufort County Comm Coll (NC)
Bellevue Comm Coll (WA)
Berean Inst (PA)
Bergen Comm Coll (NJ)
Berkshire Comm Coll (MA)
Bismarck State Coll (ND)
Blackfeet Comm Coll (MT)
Blackhawk Tech Coll (WI)
Bladen Comm Coll (NC)
Blue Ridge Comm Coll (NC)
Blue River Comm Coll (MO)
Borough of Manhattan Comm Coll of City U of NY (NY)
Bradford School (OH)

Briarwood Coll (CT)
Bronx Comm Coll of City U of NY (NY)
Brookdale Comm Coll (NJ)
Brunswick Comm Coll (NC)
Bryant & Stratton Business Inst, Buffalo (NY)
Bryant & Stratton Business Inst, Lackawanna (NY)
Bryant & Stratton Business Inst, Syracuse (NY)
Bryant and Stratton Coll, Parma (OH)
Bryant and Stratton Coll (WI)
Bryant & Stratton Business Inst, Amherst Cmps (NY)
Bucks County Comm Coll (PA)
Butler County Comm Coll (KS)
Butte Coll (CA)
Cambria-Rowe Business Coll, Johnstown (PA)
Camden County Coll (NJ)
Cañada Coll (CA)
Cape Cod Comm Coll (MA)
Capital Comm Coll (CT)
Carl Sandburg Coll (IL)
Carteret Comm Coll (NC)
Casper Coll (WY)
Cecil Comm Coll (MD)
Cedar Valley Coll (TX)
Central Alabama Comm Coll (AL)
Central Arizona Coll (AZ)
Central Carolina Tech Coll (SC)
Central Comm Coll–Columbus Campus (NE)
Central Comm Coll–Grand Island Campus (NE)
Central Comm Coll–Hastings Campus (NE)
Centralia Coll (WA)
Central Lakes Coll (MN)
Central Oregon Comm Coll (OR)
Central Piedmont Comm Coll (NC)
Century Coll (MN)
Chabot Coll (CA)
Chaparral Coll (AZ)
Chemeketa Comm Coll (OR)
Chesapeake Coll (MD)
Cincinnati State Tech and Comm Coll (OH)
City Colls of Chicago, Malcolm X Coll (IL)
Clark State Comm Coll (OH)
Cleveland Comm Coll (NC)
Cleveland State Comm Coll (TN)
Clinton Comm Coll (NY)
Clovis Comm Coll (NM)
Coastal Bend Coll (TX)
Coffeyville Comm Coll (KS)
Coll of DuPage (IL)
Coll of Eastern Utah (UT)
Coll of Lake County (IL)
Coll of the Canyons (CA)
Coll of the Desert (CA)
Coll of the Sequoias (CA)
The Coll of Westchester (NY)
Columbia Coll (CA)
Columbia-Greene Comm Coll (NY)
Columbia State Comm Coll (TN)
Columbus State Comm Coll (OH)
Commonwealth Business Coll, Michigan City (IN)
Comm Coll of Allegheny County (PA)
Comm Coll of Aurora (CO)
Comm Coll of Denver (CO)
Comm Coll of Rhode Island (RI)
Contra Costa Coll (CA)
Copiah-Lincoln Comm Coll–Natchez Campus (MS)
Corning Comm Coll (NY)
County Coll of Morris (NJ)

Crowder Coll (MO)
Cuesta Coll (CA)
Cumberland County Coll (NJ)
Cuyahoga Comm Coll (OH)
Dakota County Tech Coll (MN)
Danville Comm Coll (VA)
Darton Coll (GA)
Davis Coll (OH)
Dawson Comm Coll (MT)
Daytona Beach Comm Coll (FL)
DeKalb Tech Coll (GA)
Delaware Tech & Comm Coll, Terry Cmps (DE)
Delgado Comm Coll (LA)
Del Mar Coll (TX)
Delta Coll (MI)
Des Moines Area Comm Coll (IA)
Doña Ana Branch Comm Coll (NM)
Draughons Jr Coll (KY)
Duluth Business U (MN)
Durham Tech Comm Coll (NC)
Dutchess Comm Coll (NY)
Eastern Idaho Tech Coll (ID)
Eastern Maine Comm Coll (ME)
Eastern Oklahoma State Coll (OK)
Eastern Shore Comm Coll (VA)
Eastern Wyoming Coll (WY)
East Los Angeles Coll (CA)
East Mississippi Comm Coll (MS)
Edgecombe Comm Coll (NC)
Edison State Comm Coll (OH)
Elaine P. Nunez Comm Coll (LA)
El Camino Coll (CA)
El Centro Coll (TX)
Elgin Comm Coll (IL)
Elizabethtown Comm Coll (KY)
Elmira Business Inst (NY)
Erie Business Center South (PA)
Erie Comm Coll (NY)
Essex County Coll (NJ)
Eugenio María de Hostos Comm Coll of City U of NY (NY)
Everest Coll (AZ)
Feather River Comm Coll District (CA)
Finger Lakes Comm Coll (NY)
Fiorello H LaGuardia Comm Coll of City U of NY (NY)
Florida National Coll (FL)
Forsyth Tech Comm Coll (NC)
Fort Scott Comm Coll (KS)
Frederick Comm Coll (MD)
Front Range Comm Coll (CO)
Fulton-Montgomery Comm Coll (NY)
Gadsden State Comm Coll (AL)
Gallipolis Career Coll (OH)
Galveston Coll (TX)
Garden City Comm Coll (KS)
Garrett Coll (MD)
Gavilan Coll (CA)
Gem City Coll (IL)
Germanna Comm Coll (VA)
Glendale Comm Coll (AZ)
Globe Coll (MN)
Gogebic Comm Coll (MI)
Goodwin Coll (CT)
Gordon Coll (GA)
Grand Rapids Comm Coll (MI)
Greenfield Comm Coll (MA)
Gulf Coast Comm Coll (FL)
Gwinnett Tech Coll (GA)
Hamilton Coll (NE)
Harford Comm Coll (MD)

Harrisburg Area Comm Coll (PA)
Hawaii Comm Coll (HI)
Hawkeye Comm Coll (IA)
Heartland Comm Coll (IL)
Henderson Comm Coll (KY)
Hibbing Comm Coll (MN)
Hill Coll of the Hill Jr College District (TX)
Hillsborough Comm Coll (FL)
Hinds Comm Coll (MS)
Holmes Comm Coll (MS)
Holyoke Comm Coll (MA)
Hopkinsville Comm Coll (KY)
Houston Comm Coll System (TX)
Howard Comm Coll (MD)
Hutchinson Comm Coll and Area Vocational School (KS)
Illinois Eastern Comm Colls, Frontier Comm Coll (IL)
Illinois Eastern Comm Colls, Olney Central Coll (IL)
Illinois Eastern Comm Colls, Wabash Valley Coll (IL)
Indiana Business Coll, Anderson (IN)
Indiana Business Coll, Columbus (IN)
Indiana Business Coll, Evansville (IN)
Indiana Business Coll, Fort Wayne (IN)
Indiana Business Coll, Indianapolis (IN)
Indiana Business Coll, Lafayette (IN)
Indiana Business Coll, Marion (IN)
Indiana Business Coll, Muncie (IN)
Indiana Business Coll, Terre Haute (IN)
Iowa Lakes Comm Coll (IA)
Isothermal Comm Coll (NC)
Jackson Comm Coll (MI)
James A. Rhodes State Coll (OH)
James H. Faulkner State Comm Coll (AL)
James Sprunt Comm Coll (NC)
Jamestown Business Coll (NY)
Jefferson Coll (MO)
Jefferson Comm Coll (NY)
Jefferson Comm Coll (OH)
Jefferson Davis Comm Coll (AL)
Jefferson State Comm Coll (AL)
J. F. Drake State Tech Coll (AL)
Johnson County Comm Coll (KS)
Johnston Comm Coll (NC)
John Tyler Comm Coll (VA)
John Wood Comm Coll (IL)
J. Sargeant Reynolds Comm Coll (VA)
Kansas City Kansas Comm Coll (KS)
Kauai Comm Coll (HI)
Kellogg Comm Coll (MI)
Kent State U, Salem Campus (OH)
Kent State U, Trumbull Campus (OH)
Kent State U, Tuscarawas Campus (OH)
Kilian Comm Coll (SD)
Kingsborough Comm Coll of City U of NY (NY)
Kirkwood Comm Coll (IA)
Kirtland Comm Coll (MI)
Kishwaukee Coll (IL)
Lac Courte Oreilles Ojibwa Comm Coll (WI)
Lackawanna Coll (PA)
Lake City Comm Coll (FL)
Lake Land Coll (IL)
Lakeland Comm Coll (OH)
Lake Region State Coll (ND)

Lakeshore Tech Coll (WI)
Lake Washington Tech Coll (WA)
Lamar State Coll–Orange (TX)
Lamar State Coll–Port Arthur (TX)
Lansing Comm Coll (MI)
Laredo Comm Coll (TX)
Lawson State Comm Coll (AL)
LDS Business Coll (UT)
Lehigh Carbon Comm Coll (PA)
Lenoir Comm Coll (NC)
Lewis and Clark Comm Coll (IL)
Lincoln Land Comm Coll (IL)
Linn-Benton Comm Coll (OR)
Long Island Business Inst (NY)
Longview Comm Coll (MO)
Lorain County Comm Coll (OH)
Lord Fairfax Comm Coll (VA)
Los Angeles Harbor Coll (CA)
Los Angeles Valley Coll (CA)
Louisiana Tech Coll–Bastrop Campus (LA)
Louisiana Tech Coll–North Central Campus (LA)
Lower Columbia Coll (WA)
Luna Comm Coll (NM)
Luzerne County Comm Coll (PA)
MacCormac Coll (IL)
Macomb Comm Coll (MI)
Manatee Comm Coll (FL)
Manchester Comm Coll (CT)
Maple Woods Comm Coll (MO)
Marion Tech Coll (OH)
Marshalltown Comm Coll (IA)
Massasoit Comm Coll (MA)
Mayland Comm Coll (NC)
Maysville Comm Coll (KY)
McHenry County Coll (IL)
McIntosh Coll (NH)
McLennan Comm Coll (TX)
Meridian Comm Coll (MS)
Merritt Coll (CA)
Mesabi Range Comm and Tech Coll (MN)
Metropolitan Comm Coll (NE)
Miami Dade Coll (FL)
Middlesex Comm Coll (CT)
Middlesex County Coll (NJ)
Mid Michigan Comm Coll (MI)
Mid-Plains Comm Coll, North Platte (NE)
Mildred Elley (NY)
Miles Comm Coll (MT)
Milwaukee Area Tech Coll (WI)
Mineral Area Coll (MO)
Minneapolis Comm and Tech Coll (MN)
Minnesota School of Business–Brooklyn Center (MN)
Minnesota School of Business-Plymouth (MN)
Minnesota School of Business-Richfield (MN)
Minnesota State Coll–Southeast Tech (MN)
Minnesota State Comm and Tech Coll–Fergus Falls (MN)
Minnesota West Comm & Tech Coll-Pipestone Cmps (MN)
Minot State U–Bottineau Campus (ND)
MiraCosta Coll (CA)
Mississippi Gulf Coast Comm Coll (MS)
Mitchell Comm Coll (NC)
Mitchell Tech Inst (SD)

Moberly Area Comm Coll (MO)
Modesto Jr Coll (CA)
Mohawk Valley Comm Coll (NY)
Monroe County Comm Coll (MI)
Montana State U Coll of Tech-Great Falls (MT)
Montcalm Comm Coll (MI)
Montgomery County Comm Coll (PA)
Moraine Park Tech Coll (WI)
Moraine Valley Comm Coll (IL)
Morgan Comm Coll (CO)
Morton Coll (IL)
Mott Comm Coll (MI)
Mountain Empire Comm Coll (VA)
Mountain State Coll (WV)
Mountain West Coll (UT)
Mt. San Antonio Coll (CA)
Mt. San Jacinto Coll (CA)
MTI Coll of Business and Technology, Houston (TX)
MTI Coll of Business and Technology, Houston (TX)
Napa Valley Coll (CA)
Nash Comm Coll (NC)
Nashville State Tech Comm Coll (TN)
Nassau Comm Coll (NY)
National Coll of Business & Technology, Danville (KY)
National Coll of Business & Technology, Florence (KY)
National Coll of Business & Technology, Lexington (KY)
National Coll of Business & Technology, Louisville (KY)
National Coll of Business & Technology, Pikeville (KY)
National Coll of Business & Technology, Richmond (KY)
National Coll of Business & Technology, Nashville (TN)
National Coll of Business & Technology, Bluefield (VA)
National Coll of Business & Technology, Bristol (VA)
National Coll of Business & Technology, Charlottesville (VA)
National Coll of Business & Technology, Harrisonburg (VA)
National Coll of Business & Technology, Lynchburg (VA)
National Coll of Business & Technology, Martinsville (VA)
National Coll of Business & Technology, Salem (VA)
Naugatuck Valley Comm Coll (CT)
New Hampshire Comm Tech Coll, Berlin/Laconia (NH)
New Hampshire Comm Tech Coll, Manchester/Stratham (NH)
New Mexico State U–Carlsbad (NM)
New Mexico State U–Grants (NM)
Newport Business Inst, Williamsport (PA)
New River Comm Coll (VA)
Niagara County Comm Coll (NY)
North Arkansas Coll (AR)
North Central Missouri Coll (MO)
North Central State Coll (OH)
Northcentral Tech Coll (WI)
North Dakota State Coll of Science (ND)
Northeast Alabama Comm Coll (AL)
Northeast Comm Coll (NE)
Northeastern Oklahoma A&M Coll (OK)

Northeastern Tech Coll (SC)
Northeast Mississippi Comm Coll (MS)
Northeast State Tech Comm Coll (TN)
Northeast Texas Comm Coll (TX)
Northeast Wisconsin Tech Coll (WI)
Northern Essex Comm Coll (MA)
Northern Maine Comm Coll (ME)
North Harris Coll (TX)
North Hennepin Comm Coll (MN)
North Idaho Coll (ID)
North Iowa Area Comm Coll (IA)
Northland Pioneer Coll (AZ)
North Shore Comm Coll (MA)
Northwest Coll (WY)
Northwestern Connecticut Comm-Tech Coll (CT)
Northwest Iowa Comm Coll (IA)
Northwest-Shoals Comm Coll (AL)
Oakton Comm Coll (IL)
Ocean County Coll (NJ)
Odessa Coll (TX)
Ohio Business Coll, Sandusky (OH)
Olympic Coll (WA)
Orangeburg-Calhoun Tech Coll (SC)
Orange Coast Coll (CA)
Orange County Comm Coll (NY)
Otero Jr Coll (CO)
Ouachita Tech Coll (AR)
Owens Comm Coll, Findlay (OH)
Oxnard Coll (CA)
Ozarka Coll (AR)
Palm Beach Comm Coll (FL)
Palomar Coll (CA)
Panola Coll (TX)
Parkland Coll (IL)
Pasadena City Coll (CA)
Paul D. Camp Comm Coll (VA)
Pellissippi State Tech Comm Coll (TN)
Pennsylvania Coll of Technology (PA)
Penn Valley Comm Coll (MO)
Pensacola Jr Coll (FL)
Phoenix Coll (AZ)
Piedmont Virginia Comm Coll (VA)
Pima Comm Coll (AZ)
Pitt Comm Coll (NC)
Portland Comm Coll (OR)
Pratt Comm Coll and Area Vocational School (KS)
Pulaski Tech Coll (AR)
Quinebaug Valley Comm Coll (CT)
Quinsigamond Comm Coll (MA)
Rainy River Comm Coll (MN)
Raritan Valley Comm Coll (NJ)
Rasmussen Coll Mankato (MN)
Rasmussen Coll Minnetonka (MN)
Rasmussen Coll St. Cloud (MN)
Reading Area Comm Coll (PA)
Red Rocks Comm Coll (CO)
Reid State Tech Coll (AL)
Rend Lake Coll (IL)
Richmond Comm Coll (NC)
Rich Mountain Comm Coll (AR)
Riverland Comm Coll (MN)
Roane State Comm Coll (TN)

Roanoke-Chowan Comm Coll (NC)
Rochester Comm and Tech Coll (MN)
Rockingham Comm Coll (NC)
Rogue Comm Coll (OR)
Saint Charles Comm Coll (MO)
St. Clair County Comm Coll (MI)
St. Cloud Tech Coll (MN)
St. Johns River Comm Coll (FL)
St. Louis Comm Coll at Florissant Valley (MO)
Saint Paul Coll–A Comm & Tech College (MN)
St. Philip's Coll (TX)
San Diego City Coll (CA)
Sanford-Brown Coll, Hazelwood (MO)
San Jose City Coll (CA)
San Juan Coll (NM)
Santa Barbara City Coll (CA)
Santa Fe Comm Coll (NM)
Santa Monica Coll (CA)
Sauk Valley Comm Coll (IL)
Schenectady County Comm Coll (NY)
Schoolcraft Coll (MI)
Schuylkill Inst of Business and Technology (PA)
Scottsdale Comm Coll (AZ)
Seminole Comm Coll (FL)
Seward County Comm Coll (KS)
Shelton State Comm Coll (AL)
Sheridan Coll (WY)
Sierra Coll (CA)
Sinclair Comm Coll (OH)
Snow Coll (UT)
South Arkansas Comm Coll (AR)
South Central Tech Coll (MN)
South Coll (TN)
Southeast Comm Coll (KY)
Southeast Comm Coll, Beatrice Campus (NE)
Southeast Comm Coll, Lincoln Campus (NE)
Southeastern Comm Coll (NC)
Southern West Virginia Comm and Tech Coll (WV)
South Hills School of Business & Technology, State College (PA)
South Plains Coll (TX)
South Puget Sound Comm Coll (WA)
Southside Virginia Comm Coll (VA)
South Suburban Coll (IL)
South U (FL)
Southwestern Coll (CA)
Southwestern Comm Coll (NC)
Southwestern Illinois Coll (IL)
Southwestern Michigan Coll (MI)
Southwest Mississippi Comm Coll (MS)
Spartanburg Methodist Coll (SC)
Spartanburg Tech Coll (SC)
Spokane Comm Coll (WA)
Spokane Falls Comm Coll (WA)
Spoon River Coll (IL)
Springfield Tech Comm Coll (MA)
Stark State Coll of Technology (OH)
State U of NY Coll of A&T at Morrisville (NY)
Sullivan County Comm Coll (NY)
Sussex County Comm Coll (NJ)
Temple Coll (TX)
Terra State Comm Coll (OH)

Texas State Tech Coll–Harlingen (TX)
Thomas Nelson Comm Coll (VA)
Three Rivers Comm Coll (MO)
Tidewater Comm Coll (VA)
Tillamook Bay Comm Coll (OR)
Tompkins Cortland Comm Coll (NY)
Trenholm State Tech Coll, Montgomery (AL)
Trident Tech Coll (SC)
Trinidad State Jr Coll (CO)
Triton Coll (IL)
Trumbull Business Coll (OH)
Umpqua Comm Coll (OR)
Union County Coll (NJ)
The U of Akron–Wayne Coll (OH)
U of Alaska Anchorage, Kenai Peninsula Coll (AK)
U of Alaska Anchorage, Matanuska-Susitna Coll (AK)
U of Alaska Southeast, Ketchikan Campus (AK)
U of Northwestern Ohio (OH)
Vance-Granville Comm Coll (NC)
Vatterott Coll, St. Joseph (MO)
Ventura Coll (CA)
Victor Valley Coll (CA)
Villa Maria Coll of Buffalo (NY)
Vincennes U (IN)
Virginia Coll at Jackson (MS)
Virginia Western Comm Coll (VA)
Walters State Comm Coll (TN)
Washtenaw Comm Coll (MI)
Waubonsee Comm Coll (IL)
Waycross Coll (GA)
Weatherford Coll (TX)
Western Nevada Comm Coll (NV)
Western Wisconsin Tech Coll (WI)
Western Wyoming Comm Coll (WY)
West Hills Comm Coll (CA)
West Kentucky Comm and Tech Coll (KY)
Westmoreland County Comm Coll (PA)
West Virginia Business Coll, Wheeling (WV)
West Virginia Northern Comm Coll (WV)
Williamsburg Tech Coll (SC)
Williston State Coll (ND)
Wilson Tech Comm Coll (NC)
Wisconsin Indianhead Tech Coll (WI)
Wor-Wic Comm Coll (MD)
Yakima Valley Comm Coll (WA)
Yavapai Coll (AZ)
Yuba Coll (CA)

Adult Development and Aging
Comm Coll of Rhode Island (RI)
Lehigh Carbon Comm Coll (PA)
Southwestern Oregon Comm Coll (OR)

Advertising
American River Coll (CA)
Central Piedmont Comm Coll (NC)
Chabot Coll (CA)
Daytona Beach Comm Coll (FL)
Edison State Comm Coll (OH)
El Camino Coll (CA)
Erie Business Center South (PA)

Fayetteville Tech Comm Coll (NC)
Hussian School of Art (PA)
Los Angeles Valley Coll (CA)
Manatee Comm Coll (FL)
Middlesex County Coll (NJ)
Mississippi Gulf Coast Comm Coll (MS)
Mohawk Valley Comm Coll (NY)
Mt. San Antonio Coll (CA)
Palomar Coll (CA)
Parkland Coll (IL)
Pasadena City Coll (CA)
St. Clair County Comm Coll (MI)
St. Cloud Tech Coll (MN)
South Plains Coll (TX)
South Suburban Coll (IL)
Southwest Mississippi Comm Coll (MS)
Tidewater Comm Coll (VA)
Vincennes U (IN)
Yuba Coll (CA)

Aeronautical/Aerospace Engineering Technology
Calhoun Comm Coll (AL)
Cincinnati State Tech and Comm Coll (OH)
Fairmont State Comm & Tech Coll (WV)
Pennsylvania Coll of Technology (PA)

Aeronautics/Aviation/Aerospace Science and Technology
Alvin Comm Coll (TX)
Caldwell Comm Coll and Tech Inst (NC)
Comm Coll of the Air Force (AL)
Delaware Tech & Comm Coll, Terry Cmps (DE)
Miami Dade Coll (FL)
Orange Coast Coll (CA)
Portland Comm Coll (OR)
Raritan Valley Comm Coll (NJ)
Texas State Tech Coll–Waco/Marshall Campus (TX)
Tompkins Cortland Comm Coll (NY)
Vermilion Comm Coll (MN)

Aerospace, Aeronautical and Astronautical Engineering
Prince George's Comm Coll (MD)

Aesthetician/Esthetician and Skin Care
Colorado Northwestern Comm Coll (CO)
Olympic Coll (WA)

African-American/Black Studies
Atlanta Metropolitan Coll (GA)
Bronx Comm Coll of City U of NY (NY)
Contra Costa Coll (CA)
El Camino Coll (CA)
Los Angeles Valley Coll (CA)
Manatee Comm Coll (FL)
Merritt Coll (CA)
Nassau Comm Coll (NY)
Pasadena City Coll (CA)
San Diego City Coll (CA)
Santa Barbara City Coll (CA)
Southwestern Coll (CA)
Yuba Coll (CA)

African Studies
MiraCosta Coll (CA)
Pasadena City Coll (CA)
Sinclair Comm Coll (OH)
Southwestern Coll (CA)

Agribusiness
Clarendon Coll (TX)
Copiah-Lincoln Comm Coll (MS)
Crowder Coll (MO)

Eastern Arizona Coll (AZ)
Eastern Wyoming Coll (WY)
Glendale Comm Coll (AZ)
Iowa Lakes Comm Coll (IA)
James Sprunt Comm Coll (NC)
Laramie County Comm Coll (WY)
Mineral Area Coll (MO)
Northeast Wisconsin Tech Coll (WI)
Ohio State U Ag Tech Inst (OH)
South Central Tech Coll (MN)
Yavapai Coll (AZ)

Agricultural and Extension Education
Vincennes U (IN)

Agricultural and Food Products Processing
Texas State Tech Coll–Waco/Marshall Campus (TX)

Agricultural Business and Management
Abraham Baldwin Ag Coll (GA)
Arizona Western Coll (AZ)
Barton County Comm Coll (KS)
Bismarck State Coll (ND)
Butler County Comm Coll (KS)
Butte Coll (CA)
Carl Sandburg Coll (IL)
Casper Coll (WY)
Central Comm Coll–Columbus Campus (NE)
Central Comm Coll–Hastings Campus (NE)
Central Wyoming Coll (WY)
Clark State Comm Coll (OH)
Coastal Georgia Comm Coll (GA)
Coffeyville Comm Coll (KS)
Colby Comm Coll (KS)
Coll of Southern Idaho (ID)
Coll of the Desert (CA)
Coll of the Sequoias (CA)
Columbia State Comm Coll (TN)
Copiah-Lincoln Comm Coll (MS)
County Coll of Morris (NJ)
Cumberland County Coll (NJ)
Dawson Comm Coll (MT)
Delta Coll (MI)
Des Moines Area Comm Coll (IA)
Eastern Oklahoma State Coll (OK)
Fort Scott Comm Coll (KS)
Frederick Comm Coll (MD)
Garden City Comm Coll (KS)
Harrisburg Area Comm Coll (PA)
Hawkeye Comm Coll (IA)
Hill Coll of the Hill Jr College District (TX)
Hinds Comm Coll (MS)
Illinois Eastern Comm Colls, Wabash Valley Coll (IL)
Iowa Lakes Comm Coll (IA)
Jackson State Comm Coll (TN)
Jefferson State Comm Coll (AL)
John Wood Comm Coll (IL)
Kaskaskia Coll (IL)
Kirkwood Comm Coll (IA)
Kishwaukee Coll (IL)
Lake Area Tech Inst (SD)
Lake Land Coll (IL)
Lake Region State Coll (ND)
Lenoir Comm Coll (NC)
Linn-Benton Comm Coll (OR)
Lord Fairfax Comm Coll (VA)
Milwaukee Area Tech Coll (WI)
Mississippi Gulf Coast Comm Coll (MS)

Mitchell Tech Inst (SD)
Modesto Jr Coll (CA)
Mt. San Antonio Coll (CA)
North Central Missouri Coll (MO)
Northeast Comm Coll (NE)
Northeastern Oklahoma A&M Coll (OK)
Northeast Iowa Comm Coll (IA)
Northeast Wisconsin Tech Coll (WI)
Northern Maine Comm Coll (ME)
Northwest Coll (WY)
Ohio State U Ag Tech Inst (OH)
Otero Jr Coll (CO)
Owens Comm Coll, Toledo (OH)
Oxnard Coll (CA)
Parkland Coll (IL)
Pratt Comm Coll and Area Vocational School (KS)
Rend Lake Coll (IL)
Riverside Comm Coll (CA)
St. Clair County Comm Coll (MI)
San Joaquin Delta Coll (CA)
Sheridan Coll (WY)
Snow Coll (UT)
Southeast Comm Coll, Beatrice Campus (NE)
Spokane Comm Coll (WA)
State U of NY Coll of A&T at Morrisville (NY)
State U of NY Coll of Technology at Alfred (NY)
Three Rivers Comm Coll (MO)
U of Northwestern Ohio (OH)
Ventura Coll (CA)
Vermilion Comm Coll (MN)
Vincennes U (IN)
Western Dakota Tech Inst (SD)
West Hills Comm Coll (CA)
Yakima Valley Comm Coll (WA)
Yavapai Coll (AZ)
Yuba Coll (CA)

Agricultural Business and Management Related
Copiah-Lincoln Comm Coll (MS)
Iowa Lakes Comm Coll (IA)
North Dakota State Coll of Science (ND)
Penn State U Beaver Campus of the Commonwealth Coll (PA)
Penn State U Delaware County Campus of the Commonwealth Coll (PA)
Penn State U DuBois Campus of the Commonwealth Coll (PA)
Penn State U Fayette Campus of the Commonwealth Coll (PA)
Penn State U Hazleton Campus of the Commonwealth Coll (PA)
Penn State U McKeesport Campus of the Commonwealth Coll (PA)
Penn State U Mont Alto Campus of the Commonwealth Coll (PA)
Penn State U New Kensington Campus of the Commonwealth Coll (PA)
Penn State U Shenango Campus of the Commonwealth Coll (PA)
Penn State U Wilkes-Barre Campus of the Commonwealth Coll (PA)
Penn State U Worthington Scranton Cmps Commonwealth Coll (PA)
Penn State U York Campus of the Commonwealth Coll (PA)

Agricultural Business Technology
Copiah-Lincoln Comm Coll (MS)
Iowa Lakes Comm Coll (IA)
Laramie County Comm Coll (WY)
North Iowa Area Comm Coll (IA)
Ohio State U Ag Tech Inst (OH)

Agricultural Communication/Journalism
Ohio State U Ag Tech Inst (OH)

Agricultural Economics
Abraham Baldwin Ag Coll (GA)
Butte Coll (CA)
Clarendon Coll (TX)
Coffeyville Comm Coll (KS)
Colby Comm Coll (KS)
Copiah-Lincoln Comm Coll (MS)
Eastern Oklahoma State Coll (OK)
Eastern Wyoming Coll (WY)
Fort Scott Comm Coll (KS)
Garden City Comm Coll (KS)
Hill Coll of the Hill Jr College District (TX)
Hinds Comm Coll (MS)
Iowa Lakes Comm Coll (IA)
Northeastern Oklahoma A&M Coll (OK)
North Iowa Area Comm Coll (IA)
Northwest Coll (WY)
Ohio State U Ag Tech Inst (OH)
Pratt Comm Coll and Area Vocational School (KS)
Snow Coll (UT)
South Plains Coll (TX)
Vermilion Comm Coll (MN)

Agricultural/Farm Supplies Retailing and Wholesaling
Copiah-Lincoln Comm Coll (MS)
Iowa Lakes Comm Coll (IA)
North Dakota State Coll of Science (ND)
Western Iowa Tech Comm Coll (IA)
Wisconsin Indianhead Tech Coll (WI)

Agricultural Mechanics and Equipment Technology
Iowa Lakes Comm Coll (IA)

Agricultural Mechanization
Abraham Baldwin Ag Coll (GA)
Beaufort County Comm Coll (NC)
Carl Sandburg Coll (IL)
Casper Coll (WY)
Clark State Comm Coll (OH)
Coffeyville Comm Coll (KS)
Coll of the Sequoias (CA)
Cuesta Coll (CA)
Delta Coll (MI)
Fort Scott Comm Coll (KS)
Garden City Comm Coll (KS)
Garrett Coll (MD)
Hawkeye Comm Coll (IA)
Hinds Comm Coll (MS)
Hutchinson Comm Coll and Area Vocational School (KS)
Indian Hills Comm Coll (IA)
Iowa Lakes Comm Coll (IA)
Kishwaukee Coll (IL)
Lake Land Coll (IL)
Longview Comm Coll (MO)
Miles Comm Coll (MT)
Modesto Jr Coll (CA)
Mt. San Antonio Coll (CA)
North Dakota State Coll of Science (ND)
Northeast Comm Coll (NE)
Northeast Wisconsin Tech Coll (WI)

Northwest Coll (WY)
Ohio State U Ag Tech Inst (OH)
Oxnard Coll (CA)
Paris Jr Coll (TX)
Parkland Coll (IL)
Pratt Comm Coll and Area Vocational School (KS)
Rend Lake Coll (IL)
St. Clair County Comm Coll (MI)
San Joaquin Delta Coll (CA)
Sierra Coll (CA)
South Central Tech Coll (MN)
Southeast Comm Coll, Beatrice Campus (NE)
Spoon River Coll (IL)
State U of NY Coll of A&T at Morrisville (NY)
Three Rivers Comm Coll (MO)
Vincennes U (IN)
Walters State Comm Coll (TN)
Western Wisconsin Tech Coll (WI)
West Hills Comm Coll (CA)
Yakima Valley Comm Coll (WA)
Yuba Coll (CA)

Agricultural Mechanization Related
Garden City Comm Coll (KS)

Agricultural Power Machinery Operation
Iowa Lakes Comm Coll (IA)
Ohio State U Ag Tech Inst (OH)

Agricultural Production
Hillsborough Comm Coll (FL)
Illinois Eastern Comm Colls, Wabash Valley Coll (IL)
Iowa Lakes Comm Coll (IA)
John Wood Comm Coll (IL)
Kishwaukee Coll (IL)
Lake Land Coll (IL)
Laramie County Comm Coll (WY)
Lincoln Land Comm Coll (IL)
Mitchell Tech Inst (SD)
Modesto Jr Coll (CA)
North Dakota State Coll of Science (ND)
Northeast Comm Coll (NE)
North Iowa Area Comm Coll (IA)
Rend Lake Coll (IL)
South Central Tech Coll (MN)
Southern State Comm Coll (OH)

Agricultural Production Related
Iowa Lakes Comm Coll (IA)
Northwestern Michigan Coll (MI)

Agricultural Teacher Education
Chemeketa Comm Coll (OR)
Coffeyville Comm Coll (KS)
Colby Comm Coll (KS)
Coll of the Sequoias (CA)
Eastern Oklahoma State Coll (OK)
Eastern Wyoming Coll (WY)
Fort Scott Comm Coll (KS)
Hinds Comm Coll (MS)
Iowa Lakes Comm Coll (IA)
Kirkwood Comm Coll (IA)
Linn-Benton Comm Coll (OR)
Northeast Mississippi Comm Coll (MS)
Northwest Coll (WY)
Northwest-Shoals Comm Coll (AL)
Ohio State U Ag Tech Inst (OH)
Pratt Comm Coll and Area Vocational School (KS)
Spoon River Coll (IL)
Vermilion Comm Coll (MN)
Victor Valley Coll (CA)

Agriculture
Abraham Baldwin Ag Coll (GA)
Andrew Coll (GA)
Arizona Western Coll (AZ)
Arkansas Northeastern Coll (AR)
Arkansas State U–Beebe
Bainbridge Coll (GA)
Barton County Comm Coll (KS)
Butte Coll (CA)
Calhoun Comm Coll (AL)
Casper Coll (WY)
Central Arizona Coll (AZ)
Central Wyoming Coll (WY)
Chipola Coll (FL)
Clarendon Coll (TX)
Clark State Comm Coll (OH)
Clover Park Tech Coll (WA)
Coastal Bend Coll (TX)
Coffeyville Comm Coll (KS)
Colby Comm Coll (KS)
Coll of Southern Idaho (ID)
Coll of the Sequoias (CA)
Copiah-Lincoln Comm Coll (MS)
Crowder Coll (MO)
Cumberland County Coll (NJ)
Darton Coll (GA)
Daytona Beach Comm Coll (FL)
Delta Coll (MI)
Eastern Arizona Coll (AZ)
Eastern Wyoming Coll (WY)
Fort Scott Comm Coll (KS)
Frederick Comm Coll (MD)
Garden City Comm Coll (KS)
Gordon Coll (GA)
Hawaii Comm Coll (HI)
Hill Coll of the Hill Jr College District (TX)
Hiwassee Coll (TN)
Holmes Comm Coll (MS)
Houston Comm Coll System (TX)
Howard Coll (TX)
Hutchinson Comm Coll and Area Vocational School (KS)
Iowa Lakes Comm Coll (IA)
John A. Logan Coll (IL)
Kirkwood Comm Coll (IA)
Laramie County Comm Coll (WY)
Lenoir Comm Coll (NC)
Linn-Benton Comm Coll (OR)
Los Angeles Pierce Coll (CA)
Macomb Comm Coll (MI)
Miami Dade Coll (FL)
Modesto Jr Coll (CA)
Moraine Park Tech Coll (WI)
Mt. San Antonio Coll (CA)
Napa Valley Coll (CA)
New Mexico State U–Carlsbad (NM)
North Arkansas Coll (AR)
Northeast Comm Coll (NE)
Northeast Mississippi Comm Coll (MS)
Northeast Texas Comm Coll (TX)
Northeast Wisconsin Tech Coll (WI)
North Idaho Coll (ID)
Northland Pioneer Coll (AZ)
Northwest Coll (WY)
Odessa Coll (TX)
Owensboro Comm and Tech Coll (KY)
Palo Alto Coll (TX)
Pensacola Jr Coll (FL)
Pratt Comm Coll and Area Vocational School (KS)
Rend Lake Coll (IL)
St. Clair County Comm Coll (MI)
San Joaquin Delta Coll (CA)
Seward County Comm Coll (KS)
Sheridan Coll (WY)

Snow Coll (UT)
Southeast Comm Coll, Beatrice Campus (NE)
South Plains Coll (TX)
Southwest Missouri State U–West Plains (MO)
State U of NY Coll of A&T at Morrisville (NY)
State U of NY Coll of Technology at Alfred (NY)
Umpqua Comm Coll (OR)
Utah Career Coll (UT)
Waycross Coll (GA)
Williston State Coll (ND)
Yakima Valley Comm Coll (WA)
Yavapai Coll (AZ)
Yuba Coll (CA)

Agronomy and Crop Science
Butte Coll (CA)
Chipola Coll (FL)
Colby Comm Coll (KS)
Eastern Oklahoma State Coll (OK)
Fort Scott Comm Coll (KS)
Hawkeye Comm Coll (IA)
Hinds Comm Coll (MS)
Iowa Lakes Comm Coll (IA)
Kirkwood Comm Coll (IA)
Modesto Jr Coll (CA)
Mt. San Antonio Coll (CA)
Northeast Comm Coll (NE)
Northeastern Oklahoma A&M Coll (OK)
Northeast Mississippi Comm Coll (MS)
Northwest Coll (WY)
Ohio State U Ag Tech Inst (OH)
Sierra Coll (CA)
Snow Coll (UT)
Southeast Comm Coll, Beatrice Campus (NE)
Southern Maine Comm Coll (ME)
South Plains Coll (TX)
Spokane Comm Coll (WA)
State U of NY Coll of A&T at Morrisville (NY)
Ventura Coll (CA)
Vermilion Comm Coll (MN)
West Hills Comm Coll (CA)
Yakima Valley Comm Coll (WA)
Yuba Coll (CA)

Aircraft Powerplant Technology
Colorado Northwestern Comm Coll (CO)
Columbus State Comm Coll (OH)
Linn State Tech Coll (MO)
Minneapolis Comm and Tech Coll (MN)
North Central Inst (TN)
Pennsylvania Coll of Technology (PA)
Pima Comm Coll (AZ)
St. Philip's Coll (TX)
Southern Arkansas U Tech (AR)
Texas State Tech Coll–Waco/Marshall Campus (TX)
Westwood Coll–Denver (CO)

Airframe Mechanics and Aircraft Maintenance Technology
Amarillo Coll (TX)
Colorado Northwestern Comm Coll (CO)
Columbus State Comm Coll (OH)
Comm Coll of the Air Force (AL)
Hawkeye Comm Coll (IA)
Ivy Tech State Coll–Wabash Valley (IN)
Johnson County Comm Coll (KS)
Minneapolis Comm and Tech Coll (MN)

Mohawk Valley Comm Coll (NY)
Mt. San Antonio Coll (CA)
North Central Inst (TN)
Oklahoma City Comm Coll (OK)
St. Philip's Coll (TX)
Southwestern Illinois Coll (IL)
Southwestern Michigan Coll (MI)
Texas State Tech Coll–Harlingen (TX)
Texas State Tech Coll–Waco/Marshall Campus (TX)
Trident Tech Coll (SC)
Vincennes U (IN)
Westwood Coll–Denver (CO)

Airline Pilot and Flight Crew
Academy Coll (MN)
Big Bend Comm Coll (WA)
Casper Coll (WY)
Central Florida Comm Coll (FL)
Clover Park Tech Coll (WA)
Colorado Northwestern Comm Coll (CO)
Comm Coll of Allegheny County (PA)
County Coll of Morris (NJ)
Green River Comm Coll (WA)
Guilford Tech Comm Coll (NC)
Indian Hills Comm Coll (IA)
Iowa Lakes Comm Coll (IA)
Jackson Comm Coll (MI)
Jamestown Comm Coll (NY)
Lake Superior Coll (MN)
Lansing Comm Coll (MI)
Lehigh Carbon Comm Coll (PA)
Lenoir Comm Coll (NC)
Luzerne County Comm Coll (PA)
Miami Dade Coll (FL)
Midland Coll (TX)
Mt. San Antonio Coll (CA)
North Shore Comm Coll (MA)
Northwestern Michigan Coll (MI)
Orange Coast Coll (CA)
Palm Beach Comm Coll (FL)
Pasadena City Coll (CA)
San Juan Coll (NM)
Texas State Tech Coll–Waco/Marshall Campus (TX)
Utah Valley State Coll (UT)
Vermilion Comm Coll (MN)
Vincennes U (IN)

Air Traffic Control
Anoka Tech Coll (MN)
Cecil Comm Coll (MD)
Comm Coll of the Air Force (AL)
Green River Comm Coll (WA)
Miami Dade Coll (FL)
Mt. San Antonio Coll (CA)

Allied Health and Medical Assisting Services Related
Cincinnati State Tech and Comm Coll (OH)
Florida National Coll (FL)
Wichita Area Tech Coll (KS)

Allied Health Diagnostic, Intervention, and Treatment Professions Related
Harcum Coll (PA)
Oakland Comm Coll (MI)
Pennsylvania Coll of Technology (PA)
Union County Coll (NJ)

American Government and Politics
Manatee Comm Coll (FL)

American Indian/Native American Studies
Blackfeet Comm Coll (MT)
Central Wyoming Coll (WY)
Itasca Comm Coll (MN)
Lac Courte Oreilles Ojibwa Comm Coll (WI)
Nebraska Indian Comm Coll (NE)
Northeastern Oklahoma A&M Coll (OK)
North Idaho Coll (ID)
Pima Comm Coll (AZ)
Santa Barbara City Coll (CA)
Sisseton-Wahpeton Comm Coll (SD)

American Sign Language (ASL)
Burlington County Coll (NJ)
Fairmont State Comm & Tech Coll (WV)

American Studies
Anne Arundel Comm Coll (MD)
Bucks County Comm Coll (PA)
El Camino Coll (CA)
Foothill Coll (CA)
Greenfield Comm Coll (MA)
Holyoke Comm Coll (MA)
Manatee Comm Coll (FL)
Miami Dade Coll (FL)
Naugatuck Valley Comm Coll (CT)
Northwest Coll (WY)

Anatomy
Cañada Coll (CA)
Fayetteville Tech Comm Coll (NC)
Riverside Comm Coll (CA)

Animal/Livestock Husbandry and Production
Feather River Comm Coll District (CA)
Hopkinsville Comm Coll (KY)
Iowa Lakes Comm Coll (IA)
John Wood Comm Coll (IL)
Ohio State U Ag Tech Inst (OH)
Pratt Comm Coll and Area Vocational School (KS)
Western Dakota Tech Inst (SD)

Animal Physiology
Chabot Coll (CA)
Snow Coll (UT)

Animal Sciences
Abraham Baldwin Ag Coll (GA)
Alamance Comm Coll (NC)
Arkansas State U–Beebe (AR)
Butte Coll (CA)
Camden County Coll (NJ)
Casper Coll (WY)
Coffeyville Comm Coll (KS)
Colby Comm Coll (KS)
Coll of the Sequoias (CA)
Connors State Coll (OK)
Eastern Oklahoma State Coll (OK)
Eastern Wyoming Coll (WY)
Everett Comm Coll (WA)
Fort Scott Comm Coll (KS)
Harcum Coll (PA)
Hawkeye Comm Coll (IA)
Hill Coll of the Hill Jr College District (TX)
Hiwassee Coll (TN)
Iowa Lakes Comm Coll (IA)
James Sprunt Comm Coll (NC)
Kirkwood Comm Coll (IA)
Linn-Benton Comm Coll (OR)
Los Angeles Pierce Coll (CA)
Mesalands Comm Coll (NM)
Modesto Jr Coll (CA)
Mt. San Antonio Coll (CA)
Niagara County Comm Coll (NY)

Northeast Comm Coll (NE)
Northeastern Oklahoma A&M Coll (OK)
Northwest Coll (WY)
Ohio State U Ag Tech Inst (OH)
Pratt Comm Coll and Area Vocational School (KS)
San Joaquin Delta Coll (CA)
Sierra Coll (CA)
Snow Coll (UT)
Southeast Comm Coll, Beatrice Campus (NE)
State U of NY Coll of A&T at Morrisville (NY)
State U of NY Coll of Technology at Alfred (NY)
Ventura Coll (CA)
West Hills Comm Coll (CA)
Yakima Valley Comm Coll (WA)
Yuba Coll (CA)

Animal Sciences Related
Front Range Comm Coll (CO)

Animation, Interactive Technology, Video Graphics and Special Effects
The Art Inst of New York City (NY)
Kent State U, Tuscarawas Campus (OH)
Louisville Tech Inst (KY)
Olympic Coll (WA)
Platt Coll San Diego (CA)
Silicon Valley Coll, Walnut Creek (CA)

Anthropology
Barton County Comm Coll (KS)
Cañada Coll (CA)
Casper Coll (WY)
Coll of Southern Idaho (ID)
Coll of the Desert (CA)
Columbia Coll (CA)
Contra Costa Coll (CA)
Darton Coll (GA)
Daytona Beach Comm Coll (FL)
Delaware County Comm Coll (PA)
Eastern Arizona Coll (AZ)
East Los Angeles Coll (CA)
El Camino Coll (CA)
Everett Comm Coll (WA)
Foothill Coll (CA)
Georgia Perimeter Coll (GA)
Great Basin Coll (NV)
Gulf Coast Comm Coll (FL)
Kellogg Comm Coll (MI)
Laramie County Comm Coll (WY)
Lower Columbia Coll (WA)
Miami Dade Coll (FL)
Midland Coll (TX)
North Idaho Coll (ID)
Orange Coast Coll (CA)
Oxnard Coll (CA)
Palomar Coll (CA)
Pasadena City Coll (CA)
Pima Comm Coll (AZ)
Riverside Comm Coll (CA)
San Diego City Coll (CA)
San Joaquin Delta Coll (CA)
San Juan Coll (NM)
Santa Barbara City Coll (CA)
Santa Monica Coll (CA)
Southwestern Coll (CA)
Triton Coll (IL)
Umpqua Comm Coll (OR)
Vincennes U (IN)
Western Wyoming Comm Coll (WY)

Apparel and Accessories Marketing
Fashion Inst of Design & Merchandising, LA Campus (CA)
Fashion Inst of Design & Merchandising, SD Campus (CA)

Fashion Inst of Design & Merchandising, SF Campus (CA)
Northeast Wisconsin Tech Coll (WI)

Apparel and Textile Marketing Management
Comm Coll of the Air Force (AL)
Delta Coll (MI)

Apparel and Textiles
Fashion Inst of Design & Merchandising, LA Campus (CA)
Fashion Inst of Design & Merchandising, SF Campus (CA)
Hiwassee Coll (TN)
Modesto Jr Coll (CA)
Mt. San Antonio Coll (CA)

Appliance Installation and Repair Technology
Dunwoody Coll of Technology (MN)
Mitchell Tech Inst (SD)

Applied Art
Anne Arundel Comm Coll (MD)
The Art Inst of Houston (TX)
The Art Inst of Philadelphia (PA)
The Art Inst of Pittsburgh (PA)
Bristol Comm Coll (MA)
Butte Coll (CA)
Camden County Coll (NJ)
Casper Coll (WY)
Centralia Coll (WA)
Central Piedmont Comm Coll (NC)
Coastal Bend Coll (TX)
Coffeyville Comm Coll (KS)
County Coll of Morris (NJ)
Cuesta Coll (CA)
Del Mar Coll (TX)
Delta Coll (MI)
Edison Comm Coll (FL)
Hill Coll of the Hill Jr College District (TX)
Howard Comm Coll (MD)
Iowa Lakes Comm Coll (IA)
Jefferson Davis Comm Coll (AL)
Kingsborough Comm Coll of City U of NY (NY)
Kirkwood Comm Coll (IA)
Lincoln Coll, Lincoln (IL)
Lon Morris Coll (TX)
Middlesex County Coll (NJ)
Odessa Coll (TX)
Oklahoma City Comm Coll (OK)
Palomar Coll (CA)
Pratt Comm Coll and Area Vocational School (KS)
St. Johns River Comm Coll (FL)
Sinclair Comm Coll (OH)
Washtenaw Comm Coll (MI)

Applied Horticulture
Alamance Comm Coll (NC)
Anoka Tech Coll (MN)
Arkansas Northeastern Coll (AR)
Brunswick Comm Coll (NC)
Central Comm Coll–Hastings Campus (NE)
Clark Coll (WA)
Comm Coll of Allegheny County (PA)
Delgado Comm Coll (LA)
Fayetteville Tech Comm Coll (NC)
Front Range Comm Coll (CO)
Glendale Comm Coll (AZ)
John Wood Comm Coll (IL)
Kaskaskia Coll (IL)
Kent State U, Salem Campus (OH)
Kishwaukee Coll (IL)

Lord Fairfax Comm Coll (VA)
McHenry County Coll (IL)
Mineral Area Coll (MO)
Minot State U–Bottineau Campus (ND)
Montgomery Coll (MD)
Northeast Comm Coll (NE)
North Shore Comm Coll (MA)
Oakland Comm Coll (MI)
Rend Lake Coll (IL)
Santa Barbara City Coll (CA)
Spokane Comm Coll (WA)
West Virginia Northern Comm Coll (WV)

Applied Horticulture/ Horticultural Business Services Related
Central Florida Comm Coll (FL)
Cincinnati State Tech and Comm Coll (OH)
Dakota County Tech Coll (MN)
Kent State U, Salem Campus (OH)
Minot State U–Bottineau Campus (ND)
Pennsylvania Coll of Technology (PA)

Applied Mathematics
Chabot Coll (CA)
Lincoln Coll, Lincoln (IL)

Aquaculture
Brunswick Comm Coll (NC)
Hillsborough Comm Coll (FL)
Yavapai Coll (AZ)

Archeology
Palomar Coll (CA)
Pima Comm Coll (AZ)
Western Wyoming Comm Coll (WY)

Architectural Drafting
Coll of Lake County (IL)
IntelliTec Coll, Grand Junction (CO)
Luna Comm Coll (NM)

Architectural Drafting and Cad/Cadd
Albuquerque Tech Vocational Inst (NM)
Anoka Tech Coll (MN)
Commonwealth Tech Inst (PA)
Comm Coll of Allegheny County (PA)
Dakota County Tech Coll (MN)
Dunwoody Coll of Technology (MN)
Glendale Comm Coll (AZ)
Island Drafting and Tech Inst (NY)
Kaskaskia Coll (IL)
Lake Superior Coll (MN)
Lincoln Land Comm Coll (IL)
Louisville Tech Inst (KY)
Macomb Comm Coll (MI)
Miami Dade Coll (FL)
Mitchell Tech Inst (SD)
Montgomery Coll (MD)
Montgomery County Comm Coll (PA)
New England Inst of Tech & Florida Culinary Inst (FL)
Normandale Comm Coll (MN)
North Florida Comm Coll (FL)
North Hennepin Comm Coll (MN)
Northwest Tech Inst (MN)
Pima Comm Coll (AZ)
St. Cloud Tech Coll (MN)
Silicon Valley Coll, Walnut Creek (CA)
South Central Tech Coll (MN)
U of Kentucky, Lexington Comm Coll (KY)
Westwood Coll–Anaheim (CA)

Westwood Coll–Atlanta Campus (GA)
Westwood Coll–Chicago Du Page (IL)
Westwood Coll–Chicago O'Hare Airport (IL)
Westwood Coll–Chicago River Oaks (IL)
Westwood Coll–Dallas (TX)
Westwood Coll–Fort Worth (TX)
Westwood Coll–Houston South Campus (TX)
Westwood Coll–Inland Empire (CA)
Westwood Coll–Los Angeles (CA)
Westwood Coll–Chicago Loop Campus (IL)
Westwood Coll–Denver North (CO)
Yavapai Coll (AZ)

Architectural Engineering
Luzerne County Comm Coll (PA)

Architectural Engineering Technology
Amarillo Coll (TX)
Anne Arundel Comm Coll (MD)
Arapahoe Comm Coll (CO)
Bates Tech Coll (WA)
Cape Fear Comm Coll (NC)
Central Piedmont Comm Coll (NC)
Chabot Coll (CA)
Chesapeake Coll (MD)
Cincinnati State Tech and Comm Coll (OH)
City Colls of Chicago, Wilbur Wright Coll (IL)
Clover Park Tech Coll (WA)
Coastal Carolina Comm Coll (NC)
Coll of the Desert (CA)
Coll of the Sequoias (CA)
Columbus State Comm Coll (OH)
Daytona Beach Comm Coll (FL)
Delaware County Comm Coll (PA)
Delaware Tech & Comm Coll, Terry Cmps (DE)
Delgado Comm Coll (LA)
Del Mar Coll (TX)
Delta Coll (MI)
Doña Ana Branch Comm Coll (NM)
Durham Tech Comm Coll (NC)
Dutchess Comm Coll (NY)
East Los Angeles Coll (CA)
El Camino Coll (CA)
El Centro Coll (TX)
Essex County Coll (NJ)
Fairmont State Comm & Tech Coll (WV)
Fayetteville Tech Comm Coll (NC)
Finger Lakes Comm Coll (NY)
Forsyth Tech Comm Coll (NC)
Fort Scott Comm Coll (KS)
Front Range Comm Coll (CO)
Gaston Coll (NC)
Grand Rapids Comm Coll (MI)
Guilford Tech Comm Coll (NC)
Harrisburg Area Comm Coll (PA)
Hawkeye Comm Coll (IA)
Hillsborough Comm Coll (FL)
Honolulu Comm Coll (HI)
John Tyler Comm Coll (VA)
J. Sargeant Reynolds Comm Coll (VA)
Lake Land Coll (IL)
Lamar State Coll–Orange (TX)

Lansing Comm Coll (MI)
Los Angeles Harbor Coll (CA)
Los Angeles Pierce Coll (CA)
Los Angeles Trade-Tech Coll (CA)
Louisville Tech Inst (KY)
Luzerne County Comm Coll (PA)
Massasoit Comm Coll (MA)
Metropolitan Comm Coll (NE)
Miami Dade Coll (FL)
Midlands Tech Coll (SC)
MiraCosta Coll (CA)
Modesto Jr Coll (CA)
Monroe County Comm Coll (MI)
Mott Comm Coll (MI)
Mt. San Antonio Coll (CA)
Nash Comm Coll (NC)
Nashville State Tech Comm Coll (TN)
New Hampshire Tech Inst (NH)
New River Comm Coll (VA)
Northampton County Area Comm Coll (PA)
Northcentral Tech Coll (WI)
North Dakota State Coll of Science (ND)
Northeast Wisconsin Tech Coll (WI)
Oakland Comm Coll (MI)
Oakton Comm Coll (IL)
Oklahoma State U, Oklahoma City (OK)
Orange Coast Coll (CA)
Orange County Comm Coll (NY)
Palo Alto Coll (TX)
Pasadena City Coll (CA)
Pennsylvania Coll of Technology (PA)
Pennsylvania Inst of Technology (PA)
Penn State U Fayette Campus of the Commonwealth Coll (PA)
Penn State U Worthington Scranton Cmps Commonwealth Coll (PA)
Phoenix Coll (AZ)
Pikes Peak Comm Coll (CO)
Pitt Comm Coll (NC)
Ranken Tech Coll (MO)
Roanoke-Chowan Comm Coll (NC)
St. Clair County Comm Coll (MI)
St. Cloud Tech Coll (MN)
St. Petersburg Coll (FL)
Santa Monica Coll (CA)
Seminole Comm Coll (FL)
Sinclair Comm Coll (OH)
Southern Maine Comm Coll (ME)
South Suburban Coll (IL)
Southwestern Coll (CA)
Spartanburg Tech Coll (SC)
Spokane Comm Coll (WA)
Springfield Tech Comm Coll (MA)
Stark State Coll of Technology (OH)
State U of NY Coll of A&T at Morrisville (NY)
State U of NY Coll of Technology at Alfred (NY)
State U of NY Coll of Technology at Delhi (NY)
Terra State Comm Coll (OH)
Triangle Tech, Inc. (PA)
Triton Coll (IL)
U of Kentucky, Lexington Comm Coll (KY)
Ventura Coll (CA)
Vermilion Comm Coll (MN)
Vincennes U (IN)
Washtenaw Comm Coll (MI)
Western Iowa Tech Comm Coll (IA)

Westmoreland County Comm Coll (PA)
Wisconsin Indianhead Tech Coll (WI)

Architectural Technology
City Colls of Chicago, Wilbur Wright Coll (IL)
Columbus State Comm Coll (OH)
Dakota County Tech Coll (MN)
Rend Lake Coll (IL)
Silicon Valley Coll, Walnut Creek (CA)

Architecture
Barton County Comm Coll (KS)
Brookdale Comm Coll (NJ)
Copiah-Lincoln Comm Coll (MS)
Harrisburg Area Comm Coll (PA)
Howard Comm Coll (MD)
Oakland Comm Coll (MI)
Riverside Comm Coll (CA)
Sauk Valley Comm Coll (IL)
Silicon Valley Coll, Walnut Creek (CA)

Architecture Related
Louisville Tech Inst (KY)
Silicon Valley Coll, Walnut Creek (CA)

Area Studies
Santa Fe Comm Coll (NM)

Area Studies Related
Oklahoma City Comm Coll (OK)

Art
Abraham Baldwin Ag Coll (GA)
Alvin Comm Coll (TX)
Amarillo Coll (TX)
American River Coll (CA)
Andrew Coll (GA)
Anne Arundel Comm Coll (MD)
Arizona Western Coll (AZ)
The Art Inst of Philadelphia (PA)
Asnuntuck Comm Coll (CT)
Atlanta Metropolitan Coll (GA)
Austin Comm Coll (TX)
Bainbridge Coll (GA)
Barton County Comm Coll (KS)
Bergen Comm Coll (NJ)
Blue Ridge Comm Coll (NC)
Bronx Comm Coll of City U of NY (NY)
Brookdale Comm Coll (NJ)
Bucks County Comm Coll (PA)
Bunker Hill Comm Coll (MA)
Burlington County Coll (NJ)
Butler County Comm Coll (KS)
Butte Coll (CA)
Caldwell Comm Coll and Tech Inst (NC)
Camden County Coll (NJ)
Cañada Coll (CA)
Cape Cod Comm Coll (MA)
Casper Coll (WY)
Cecil Comm Coll (MD)
Centralia Coll (WA)
Central Oregon Comm Coll (OR)
Central Piedmont Comm Coll (NC)
Central Wyoming Coll (WY)
Chabot Coll (CA)
Chesapeake Coll (MD)
Chipola Coll (FL)
City Colls of Chicago, Malcolm X Coll (IL)
City Colls of Chicago, Wilbur Wright Coll (IL)
Coastal Bend Coll (TX)
Coastal Georgia Comm Coll (GA)

Coffeyville Comm Coll (KS)
Coll of Lake County (IL)
Coll of Southern Idaho (ID)
Coll of the Canyons (CA)
Coll of the Desert (CA)
Coll of the Sequoias (CA)
Colorado Mountn Coll (CO)
Colorado Mountn Coll, Timberline Cmps (CO)
Colorado Northwestern Comm Coll (CO)
Columbia Coll (CA)
Columbia-Greene Comm Coll (NY)
Columbia State Comm Coll (TN)
Comm Coll of Allegheny County (PA)
Comm Coll of Rhode Island (RI)
Contra Costa Coll (CA)
Crowder Coll (MO)
Cuesta Coll (CA)
Darton Coll (GA)
Daytona Beach Comm Coll (FL)
Del Mar Coll (TX)
Eastern Arizona Coll (AZ)
Eastern Oklahoma State Coll (OK)
Eastern Wyoming Coll (WY)
East Los Angeles Coll (CA)
East Mississippi Comm Coll (MS)
Edison Comm Coll (FL)
Edison State Comm Coll (OH)
El Camino Coll (CA)
Elgin Comm Coll (IL)
Essex County Coll (NJ)
Everett Comm Coll (WA)
Foothill Coll (CA)
Frederick Comm Coll (MD)
Fulton-Montgomery Comm Coll (NY)
Garrett Coll (MD)
Gaston Coll (NC)
Gavilan Coll (CA)
Georgia Perimeter Coll (GA)
Gordon Coll (GA)
Grand Rapids Comm Coll (MI)
Great Basin Coll (NV)
Greenfield Comm Coll (MA)
Gulf Coast Comm Coll (FL)
Harrisburg Area Comm Coll (PA)
Hill Coll of the Hill Jr College District (TX)
Hillsborough Comm Coll (FL)
Hinds Comm Coll (MS)
Howard Coll (TX)
Howard Comm Coll (MD)
Iowa Lakes Comm Coll (IA)
Jefferson Coll (MO)
John A. Logan Coll (IL)
Kellogg Comm Coll (MI)
Kent State U, Stark Campus (OH)
Keystone Coll (PA)
Kingsborough Comm Coll of City U of NY (NY)
Kirkwood Comm Coll (IA)
Kirtland Comm Coll (MI)
Kishwaukee Coll (IL)
Lansing Comm Coll (MI)
Laramie County Comm Coll (WY)
Lawson State Comm Coll (AL)
Lehigh Carbon Comm Coll (PA)
Lenoir Comm Coll (NC)
Lewis and Clark Comm Coll (IL)
Lincoln Land Comm Coll (IL)
Linn-Benton Comm Coll (OR)
Lon Morris Coll (TX)
Lorain County Comm Coll (OH)
Los Angeles Pierce Coll (CA)
Los Angeles Valley Coll (CA)
Lower Columbia Coll (WA)

Manatee Comm Coll (FL)
McHenry County Coll (IL)
Miami Dade Coll (FL)
Middlesex Comm Coll (MA)
Middlesex County Coll (NJ)
Midland Coll (TX)
Mid Michigan Comm Coll (MI)
MiraCosta Coll (CA)
Mississippi Gulf Coast Comm Coll (MS)
Mitchell Comm Coll (NC)
Modesto Jr Coll (CA)
Mohave Comm Coll (AZ)
Mohawk Valley Comm Coll (NY)
Monroe County Comm Coll (MI)
Montgomery County Comm Coll (PA)
Morton Coll (IL)
Mt. San Jacinto Coll (CA)
Mount Wachusett Comm Coll (MA)
Napa Valley Coll (CA)
Nassau Comm Coll (NY)
Northeast Comm Coll (NE)
Northeastern Oklahoma A&M Coll (OK)
Northeast Mississippi Comm Coll (MS)
North Harris Coll (TX)
North Idaho Coll (ID)
North Seattle Comm Coll (WA)
Northwest Coll (WY)
Northwestern Connecticut Comm-Tech Coll (CT)
Northwestern Michigan Coll (MI)
Northwest-Shoals Comm Coll (AL)
Oakton Comm Coll (IL)
Odessa Coll (TX)
Oklahoma City Comm Coll (OK)
Orange Coast Coll (CA)
Palm Beach Comm Coll (FL)
Palo Alto Coll (TX)
Palomar Coll (CA)
Paris Jr Coll (TX)
Parkland Coll (IL)
Pasadena City Coll (CA)
Pensacola Jr Coll (FL)
Phoenix Coll (AZ)
Piedmont Virginia Comm Coll (VA)
Pima Comm Coll (AZ)
Platt Coll San Diego (CA)
Pratt Comm Coll and Area Vocational School (KS)
Quinebaug Valley Comm Coll (CT)
Quinsigamond Comm Coll (MA)
Red Rocks Comm Coll (CO)
Rend Lake Coll (IL)
Riverside Comm Coll (CA)
Roane State Comm Coll (TN)
Rockingham Comm Coll (NC)
St. Clair County Comm Coll (MI)
St. Johns River Comm Coll (FL)
St. Louis Comm Coll at Florissant Valley (MO)
St. Philip's Coll (TX)
San Diego City Coll (CA)
San Joaquin Delta Coll (CA)
San Juan Coll (NM)
Santa Fe Comm Coll (NM)
Santa Monica Coll (CA)
Sauk Valley Comm Coll (IL)
Seward County Comm Coll (KS)
Sheridan Coll (WY)
Sierra Coll (CA)
Sinclair Comm Coll (OH)
Snow Coll (UT)
Southeast Comm Coll, Beatrice Campus (NE)

Southeastern Comm Coll (NC)
South Plains Coll (TX)
Southwestern Coll (CA)
Spokane Falls Comm Coll (WA)
Spoon River Coll (IL)
Temple Coll (TX)
Thomas Nelson Comm Coll (VA)
Tidewater Comm Coll (VA)
Triton Coll (IL)
Umpqua Comm Coll (OR)
Ventura Coll (CA)
Vermilion Comm Coll (MN)
Victor Valley Coll (CA)
Vincennes U (IN)
Virginia Western Comm Coll (VA)
Vista Comm Coll (CA)
Walters State Comm Coll (TN)
Waubonsee Comm Coll (IL)
Western Wyoming Comm Coll (WY)
West Hills Comm Coll (CA)
Yuba Coll (CA)

Art History, Criticism and Conservation
Cañada Coll (CA)
El Camino Coll (CA)
Foothill Coll (CA)
Hill Coll of the Hill Jr College District (TX)
Iowa Lakes Comm Coll (IA)
Lincoln Coll, Lincoln (IL)
Lon Morris Coll (TX)
Manatee Comm Coll (FL)
Palm Beach Comm Coll (FL)
Pasadena City Coll (CA)
Rogue Comm Coll (OR)
Santa Barbara City Coll (CA)
Umpqua Comm Coll (OR)
Vermilion Comm Coll (MN)

Artificial Intelligence and Robotics
Arkansas State U–Beebe (AR)
Camden County Coll (NJ)
Cecil Comm Coll (MD)
Cuesta Coll (CA)
Cumberland County Coll (NJ)
Des Moines Area Comm Coll (IA)
Dutchess Comm Coll (NY)
Hill Coll of the Hill Jr College District (TX)
Indian Hills Comm Coll (IA)
James A. Rhodes State Coll (OH)
Kirkwood Comm Coll (IA)
Lorain County Comm Coll (OH)
Louisville Tech Inst (KY)
Metropolitan Comm Coll-Business & Technology College (MO)
Mountain View Coll (TX)
Northeast Mississippi Comm Coll (MS)
Raritan Valley Comm Coll (NJ)
St. Clair County Comm Coll (MI)
San Diego City Coll (CA)
Sinclair Comm Coll (OH)
Spokane Comm Coll (WA)
Vincennes U (IN)
Washtenaw Comm Coll (MI)
Westmoreland County Comm Coll (PA)
York Tech Inst (PA)

Arts Management
Cuesta Coll (CA)
Palomar Coll (CA)

Art Teacher Education
Chemeketa Comm Coll (OR)
Coastal Bend Coll (TX)
Copiah-Lincoln Comm Coll (MS)
Del Mar Coll (TX)

Delta Coll (MI)
Eastern Arizona Coll (AZ)
Eastern Oklahoma State Coll (OK)
Hill Coll of the Hill Jr College District (TX)
Iowa Lakes Comm Coll (IA)
John A. Logan Coll (IL)
Kellogg Comm Coll (MI)
Kirkwood Comm Coll (IA)
Kishwaukee Coll (IL)
Lincoln Coll, Lincoln (IL)
Lon Morris Coll (TX)
McLennan Comm Coll (TX)
Miami Dade Coll (FL)
Mississippi Gulf Coast Comm Coll (MS)
Northeast Comm Coll (NE)
Northeastern Oklahoma A&M Coll (OK)
Northeast Mississippi Comm Coll (MS)
North Harris Coll (TX)
Northwest Coll (WY)
Oxnard Coll (CA)
Palomar Coll (CA)
Parkland Coll (IL)
Pensacola Jr Coll (FL)
Pratt Comm Coll and Area Vocational School (KS)
Roane State Comm Coll (TN)
Shelton State Comm Coll (AL)
Trinidad State Jr Coll (CO)
Umpqua Comm Coll (OR)
Vermilion Comm Coll (MN)
Vincennes U (IN)
Walters State Comm Coll (TN)
Waubonsee Comm Coll (IL)

Asian-American Studies
Southwestern Coll (CA)

Asian Studies
East Los Angeles Coll (CA)
El Camino Coll (CA)
Manatee Comm Coll (FL)
Miami Dade Coll (FL)
Pima Comm Coll (AZ)

Astronomy
Anne Arundel Comm Coll (MD)
Austin Comm Coll (TX)
Daytona Beach Comm Coll (FL)
El Camino Coll (CA)
Iowa Lakes Comm Coll (IA)
Manatee Comm Coll (FL)
North Idaho Coll (ID)
Palomar Coll (CA)
Pasadena City Coll (CA)
Riverside Comm Coll (CA)
Santa Monica Coll (CA)
Southwestern Coll (CA)

Athletic Training
Andrew Coll (GA)
Barton County Comm Coll (KS)
Coffeyville Comm Coll (KS)
Coll of the Sequoias (CA)
Comm Coll of Allegheny County (PA)
Dean Coll (MA)
Foothill Coll (CA)
Fort Scott Comm Coll (KS)
Front Range Comm Coll (CO)
Garden City Comm Coll (KS)
Iowa Lakes Comm Coll (IA)
Lorain County Comm Coll (OH)
Meridian Comm Coll (MS)
New Hampshire Comm Tech Coll, Manchester/Stratham (NH)
North Idaho Coll (ID)
Odessa Coll (TX)
Orange Coast Coll (CA)
Pratt Comm Coll and Area Vocational School (KS)
Santa Barbara City Coll (CA)
Santa Monica Coll (CA)

Sauk Valley Comm Coll (IL)
Seward County Comm Coll (KS)
Southwestern Oregon Comm Coll (OR)
Utah Career Coll (UT)
Vincennes U (IN)

Atmospheric Sciences and Meteorology
Comm Coll of the Air Force (AL)
Daytona Beach Comm Coll (FL)
Everett Comm Coll (WA)

Audio Engineering
The Art Inst of Seattle (WA)
Brookdale Comm Coll (NJ)
Full Sail Real World Education (FL)
Harford Comm Coll (MD)
International Coll of Broadcasting (OH)
Mt. San Jacinto Coll (CA)
Northeast Comm Coll (NE)
South Plains Coll (TX)
Texas State Tech Coll–Waco/Marshall Campus (TX)

Audiology and Hearing Sciences
Arkansas State U–Mountain Home (AR)

Audiovisual Communications Technologies Related
Olympic Coll (WA)

Autobody/Collision and Repair Technology
Bates Tech Coll (WA)
Bismarck State Coll (ND)
Central Comm Coll–Hastings Campus (NE)
Century Coll (MN)
Coll of Southern Idaho (ID)
Dakota County Tech Coll (MN)
Dunwoody Coll of Technology (MN)
Eastfield Coll (TX)
Fayetteville Tech Comm Coll (NC)
Green River Comm Coll (WA)
Hawkeye Comm Coll (IA)
Hill Coll of the Hill Jr College District (TX)
Hutchinson Comm Coll and Area Vocational School (KS)
Illinois Eastern Comm Colls, Olney Central Coll (IL)
Iowa Lakes Comm Coll (IA)
Kaskaskia Coll (IL)
Kauai Comm Coll (HI)
Kishwaukee Coll (IL)
Lake Washington Tech Coll (WA)
Laramie County Comm Coll (WY)
Linn State Tech Coll (MO)
Louisiana Tech Coll–Delta Ouachita Campus (LA)
Manhattan Area Tech Coll (KS)
Mid-Plains Comm Coll, North Platte (NE)
Modesto Jr Coll (CA)
Montana State U Coll of Tech-Great Falls (MT)
Mott Comm Coll (MI)
Nashville Auto Diesel Coll (TN)
North Dakota State Coll of Science (ND)
Northeast Comm Coll (NE)
Northeast Wisconsin Tech Coll (WI)
Northwest Iowa Comm Coll (IA)
Parkland Coll (IL)
Pennsylvania Coll of Technology (PA)

Pikes Peak Comm Coll (CO)
Ranken Tech Coll (MO)
Riverland Comm Coll (MN)
St. Cloud Tech Coll (MN)
St. Philip's Coll (TX)
San Juan Coll (NM)
Somerset Comm Coll (KY)
South Central Tech Coll (MN)
Southwestern Illinois Coll (IL)
Stanly Comm Coll (NC)
State U of NY Coll of Technology at Alfred (NY)
Texas State Tech Coll–Harlingen (TX)
Texas State Tech Coll–Waco/Marshall Campus (TX)
Utah Valley State Coll (UT)
Waubonsee Comm Coll (IL)
Western Iowa Tech Comm Coll (IA)
Wichita Area Tech Coll (KS)

Automobile/Automotive Mechanics Technology
Alamance Comm Coll (NC)
Allegany Coll of Maryland (MD)
Alpena Comm Coll (MI)
Amarillo Coll (TX)
American River Coll (CA)
Anoka Tech Coll (MN)
Arapahoe Comm Coll (CO)
Arizona Western Coll (AZ)
Asheville-Buncombe Tech Comm Coll (NC)
Austin Comm Coll (TX)
Bainbridge Coll (GA)
Barton County Comm Coll (KS)
Bates Tech Coll (WA)
Beaufort County Comm Coll (NC)
Bergen Comm Coll (NJ)
Big Bend Comm Coll (WA)
Bismarck State Coll (ND)
Brookdale Comm Coll (NJ)
Burlington County Coll (NJ)
Butler County Comm Coll (KS)
Butte Coll (CA)
Camden County Coll (NJ)
Cape Fear Comm Coll (NC)
Carl Sandburg Coll (IL)
Casper Coll (WY)
Cedar Valley Coll (TX)
Central Arizona Coll (AZ)
Central Comm Coll–Columbus Campus (NE)
Central Comm Coll–Grand Island Campus (NE)
Central Comm Coll–Hastings Campus (NE)
Central Oregon Comm Coll (OR)
Central Piedmont Comm Coll (NC)
Central Wyoming Coll (WY)
Century Coll (MN)
Chabot Coll (CA)
Chemeketa Comm Coll (OR)
Clark Coll (WA)
Clover Park Tech Coll (WA)
Clovis Comm Coll (NM)
Coastal Bend Coll (TX)
Coffeyville Comm Coll (KS)
Coll of DuPage (IL)
Coll of Eastern Utah (UT)
Coll of Lake County (IL)
Coll of Southern Idaho (ID)
Coll of the Desert (CA)
Coll of the Sequoias (CA)
Columbia Coll (CA)
Columbia-Greene Comm Coll (NY)
Columbus State Comm Coll (OH)
Comm Coll of Aurora (CO)
Comm Coll of the Air Force (AL)
Contra Costa Coll (CA)
Corning Comm Coll (NY)
Cossatot Comm Coll of the U of Arkansas (AR)
Cuesta Coll (CA)

Cuyahoga Comm Coll (OH)
Cuyamaca Coll (CA)
Dakota County Tech Coll (MN)
Dawson Comm Coll (MT)
Daytona Beach Comm Coll (FL)
DeKalb Tech Coll (GA)
Delaware County Comm Coll (PA)
Delgado Comm Coll (LA)
Del Mar Coll (TX)
Delta Coll (MI)
Des Moines Area Comm Coll (IA)
Doña Ana Branch Comm Coll (NM)
Dunwoody Coll of Technology (MN)
Durham Tech Comm Coll (NC)
Eastern Arizona Coll (AZ)
Eastern Idaho Tech Coll (ID)
Eastern Maine Comm Coll (ME)
Eastfield Coll (TX)
East Los Angeles Coll (CA)
East Mississippi Comm Coll (MS)
El Camino Coll (CA)
Elgin Comm Coll (IL)
Fayetteville Tech Comm Coll (NC)
Forsyth Tech Comm Coll (NC)
Front Range Comm Coll (CO)
Fulton-Montgomery Comm Coll (NY)
Garden City Comm Coll (KS)
Gaston Coll (NC)
Gavilan Coll (CA)
Glendale Comm Coll (AZ)
Glen Oaks Comm Coll (MI)
Gloucester County Coll (NJ)
Gogebic Comm Coll (MI)
Grand Rapids Comm Coll (MI)
Green River Comm Coll (WA)
Guilford Tech Comm Coll (NC)
Gwinnett Tech Coll (GA)
Harrisburg Area Comm Coll (PA)
Hawaii Comm Coll (HI)
Hawkeye Comm Coll (IA)
Hill Coll of the Hill Jr College District (TX)
Honolulu Comm Coll (HI)
Houston Comm Coll System (TX)
Howard Coll (TX)
Hutchinson Comm Coll and Area Vocational School (KS)
Illinois Eastern Comm Colls, Olney Central Coll (IL)
Indian Hills Comm Coll (IA)
Iowa Lakes Comm Coll (IA)
Isothermal Comm Coll (NC)
Ivy Tech State Coll–Central Indiana (IN)
Ivy Tech State Coll–Columbus (IN)
Ivy Tech State Coll–Eastcentral (IN)
Ivy Tech State Coll–Kokomo (IN)
Ivy Tech State Coll–Lafayette (IN)
Ivy Tech State Coll–North Central (IN)
Ivy Tech State Coll–Northeast (IN)
Ivy Tech State Coll–Northwest (IN)
Ivy Tech State Coll–Southcentral (IN)
Ivy Tech State Coll–Southwest (IN)
Ivy Tech State Coll–Wabash Valley (IN)

Ivy Tech State Coll–Whitewater (IN)
Jackson Comm Coll (MI)
Jefferson Coll (MO)
John A. Logan Coll (IL)
Johnson County Comm Coll (KS)
Kalamazoo Valley Comm Coll (MI)
Kaskaskia Coll (IL)
Kauai Comm Coll (HI)
Kent State U, Trumbull Campus (OH)
Kirkwood Comm Coll (IA)
Kirtland Comm Coll (MI)
Kishwaukee Coll (IL)
Lake Area Tech Inst (SD)
Lake Land Coll (IL)
Lake Region State Coll (ND)
Lake Superior Coll (MN)
Lake Washington Tech Coll (WA)
Lamar State Coll–Port Arthur (TX)
Lansing Comm Coll (MI)
Laramie County Comm Coll (WY)
Lewis and Clark Comm Coll (IL)
Lincoln Land Comm Coll (IL)
Linn-Benton Comm Coll (OR)
Linn State Tech Coll (MO)
Longview Comm Coll (MO)
Los Angeles Harbor Coll (CA)
Los Angeles Pierce Coll (CA)
Los Angeles Trade-Tech Coll (CA)
Louisiana Tech Coll–Delta Ouachita Campus (LA)
Lower Columbia Coll (WA)
Luzerne County Comm Coll (PA)
Macomb Comm Coll (MI)
Manhattan Area Tech Coll (KS)
McHenry County Coll (IL)
Mesalands Comm Coll (NM)
Metropolitan Comm Coll (NE)
Middlesex Comm Coll (MA)
Middlesex County Coll (NJ)
Midland Coll (TX)
Midlands Tech Coll (SC)
Mid Michigan Comm Coll (MI)
Mid-Plains Comm Coll, North Platte (NE)
Miles Comm Coll (MT)
Milwaukee Area Tech Coll (WI)
Minneapolis Comm and Tech Coll (MN)
Minnesota State Coll–Southeast Tech (MN)
MiraCosta Coll (CA)
Mississippi Gulf Coast Comm Coll (MS)
Modesto Jr Coll (CA)
Mohave Comm Coll (AZ)
Montgomery Coll (MD)
Moraine Park Tech Coll (WI)
Moraine Valley Comm Coll (IL)
Morgan Comm Coll (CO)
Morton Coll (IL)
Mott Comm Coll (MI)
Mt. San Jacinto Coll (CA)
Mount Wachusett Comm Coll (MA)
Nashville Auto Diesel Coll (TN)
Nashville State Tech Comm Coll (TN)
Naugatuck Valley Comm Coll (CT)
New England Inst of Tech & Florida Culinary Inst (FL)
New Hampshire Comm Tech Coll, Berlin/Laconia (NH)
New Hampshire Comm Tech Coll, Manchester/Stratham (NH)

New River Comm Coll (VA)
Normandale Comm Coll (MN)
North Central Missouri Coll (MO)
Northcentral Tech Coll (WI)
North Dakota State Coll of Science (ND)
Northeast Comm Coll (NE)
Northeast State Tech Comm Coll (TN)
Northeast Texas Comm Coll (TX)
Northeast Wisconsin Tech Coll (WI)
Northern Maine Comm Coll (ME)
North Harris Coll (TX)
North Hennepin Comm Coll (MN)
North Idaho Coll (ID)
North Iowa Area Comm Coll (IA)
Northwestern Michigan Coll (MI)
Northwest Iowa Comm Coll (IA)
Oakland Comm Coll (MI)
Oakton Comm Coll (IL)
Odessa Coll (TX)
Oklahoma City Comm Coll (OK)
Olympic Coll (WA)
Orangeburg-Calhoun Tech Coll (SC)
Otero Jr Coll (CO)
Ouachita Tech Coll (AR)
Oxnard Coll (CA)
Ozarka Coll (AR)
Palomar Coll (CA)
Parkland Coll (IL)
Pasadena City Coll (CA)
Pellissippi State Tech Comm Coll (TN)
Peninsula Coll (WA)
Pensacola Jr Coll (FL)
Piedmont Virginia Comm Coll (VA)
Pikes Peak Comm Coll (CO)
Pima Comm Coll (AZ)
Portland Comm Coll (OR)
Pratt Comm Coll and Area Vocational School (KS)
Quinsigamond Comm Coll (MA)
Ranken Tech Coll (MO)
Raritan Valley Comm Coll (NJ)
Rend Lake Coll (IL)
Roanoke-Chowan Comm Coll (NC)
Rogue Comm Coll (OR)
Rosedale Tech Inst (PA)
Rowan-Cabarrus Comm Coll (NC)
St. Cloud Tech Coll (MN)
St. Philip's Coll (TX)
San Diego City Coll (CA)
San Joaquin Delta Coll (CA)
San Juan Coll (NM)
Santa Barbara City Coll (CA)
Santa Monica Coll (CA)
Seminole Comm Coll (FL)
Shelton State Comm Coll (AL)
Sierra Coll (CA)
Sinclair Comm Coll (OH)
Snow Coll (UT)
Somerset Comm Coll (KY)
South Central Tech Coll (MN)
Southeast Arkansas Coll (AR)
Southeast Comm Coll, Lincoln Campus (NE)
Southern Maine Comm Coll (ME)
Southern West Virginia Comm and Tech Coll (WV)
South Plains Coll (TX)
South Puget Sound Comm Coll (WA)
South Texas Comm Coll (TX)
Southwestern Coll (CA)

Southwestern Comm Coll (NC)
Southwestern Michigan Coll (MI)
Southwest Mississippi Comm Coll (MS)
Spartanburg Tech Coll (SC)
Spokane Comm Coll (WA)
Spoon River Coll (IL)
Stark State Coll of Technology (OH)
State U of NY Coll of A&T at Morrisville (NY)
State U of NY Coll of Technology at Alfred (NY)
State U of NY Coll of Technology at Canton (NY)
Temple Coll (TX)
Terra State Comm Coll (OH)
Texas State Tech Coll–Waco/Marshall Campus (TX)
Thomas Nelson Comm Coll (VA)
Tidewater Comm Coll (VA)
Trenholm State Tech Coll, Montgomery (AL)
Tri-County Comm Coll (NC)
Trident Tech Coll (SC)
Trinidad State Jr Coll (CO)
Triton Coll (IL)
Umpqua Comm Coll (OR)
United Tribes Tech Coll (ND)
U of Northwestern Ohio (OH)
Utah Valley State Coll (UT)
Vance-Granville Comm Coll (NC)
Ventura Coll (CA)
Victor Valley Coll (CA)
Vincennes U (IN)
Virginia Western Comm Coll (VA)
Washtenaw Comm Coll (MI)
Waubonsee Comm Coll (IL)
Waycross Coll (GA)
Western Dakota Tech Inst (SD)
Western Iowa Tech Comm Coll (IA)
Western Nevada Comm Coll (NV)
Western Wisconsin Tech Coll (WI)
Western Wyoming Comm Coll (WY)
West Hills Comm Coll (CA)
Westwood Coll–Denver North (CO)
Wichita Area Tech Coll (KS)
Williston State Coll (ND)
Yakima Valley Comm Coll (WA)
Yavapai Coll (AZ)
York Tech Coll (SC)
Yuba Coll (CA)

Automotive Engineering Technology
Central Florida Comm Coll (FL)
Cincinnati State Tech and Comm Coll (OH)
Comm Coll of Allegheny County (PA)
Corning Comm Coll (NY)
Harrisburg Area Comm Coll (PA)
Macomb Comm Coll (MI)
Montgomery County Comm Coll (PA)
New Castle School of Trades (PA)
Northampton County Area Comm Coll (PA)
Northeast Wisconsin Tech Coll (WI)
Owens Comm Coll, Toledo (OH)
Pennsylvania Coll of Technology (PA)
Rend Lake Coll (IL)
Springfield Tech Comm Coll (MA)
Sussex County Comm Coll (NJ)

Terra State Comm Coll (OH)
Trenholm State Tech Coll, Montgomery (AL)

Aviation/Airway Management
Academy Coll (MN)
Anoka Tech Coll (MN)
Comm Coll of Allegheny County (PA)
Delaware Tech & Comm Coll, Terry Cmps (DE)
Guilford Tech Comm Coll (NC)
Iowa Lakes Comm Coll (IA)
Lehigh Carbon Comm Coll (PA)
Lenoir Comm Coll (NC)
Luzerne County Comm Coll (PA)
Miami Dade Coll (FL)
Mountain View Coll (TX)
Oakland Comm Coll (MI)
Palo Alto Coll (TX)
Palomar Coll (CA)
Pasadena City Coll (CA)
Schenectady County Comm Coll (NY)
Sinclair Comm Coll (OH)
Vermilion Comm Coll (MN)

Avionics Maintenance Technology
Big Bend Comm Coll (WA)
Blackhawk Tech Coll (WI)
Clover Park Tech Coll (WA)
Columbus State Comm Coll (OH)
Comm Coll of the Air Force (AL)
Cumberland County Coll (NJ)
Cuyahoga Comm Coll (OH)
Delaware Tech & Comm Coll, Terry Cmps (DE)
Delta Coll (MI)
Everett Comm Coll (WA)
Foothill Coll (CA)
Frederick Comm Coll (MD)
Gavilan Coll (CA)
Guilford Tech Comm Coll (NC)
Hawkeye Comm Coll (IA)
Hinds Comm Coll (MS)
Honolulu Comm Coll (HI)
Indian Hills Comm Coll (IA)
Lake Area Tech Inst (SD)
Lake Region State Coll (ND)
Lansing Comm Coll (MI)
Lehigh Carbon Comm Coll (PA)
Lenoir Comm Coll (NC)
Maple Woods Comm Coll (MO)
Minneapolis Comm and Tech Coll (MN)
Minnesota State Coll–Southeast Tech (MN)
Mountain View Coll (TX)
Mt. San Antonio Coll (CA)
Oklahoma City Comm Coll (OK)
Orange Coast Coll (CA)
Palo Alto Coll (TX)
Palomar Coll (CA)
Pasadena City Coll (CA)
Pennsylvania Coll of Technology (PA)
Portland Comm Coll (OR)
Quinebaug Valley Comm Coll (CT)
Somerset Comm Coll (KY)
Southwestern Illinois Coll (IL)
Spokane Comm Coll (WA)
Texas State Tech Coll–Waco/Marshall Campus (TX)
Vincennes U (IN)
Westwood Coll–Denver (CO)

Baking and Pastry Arts
The Art Inst of Pittsburgh (PA)
Clark Coll (WA)
Coll of DuPage (IL)

The Cooking and Hospitality Inst of Chicago (IL)
El Centro Coll (TX)
Florida Culinary Inst (FL)
Luzerne County Comm Coll (PA)
Milwaukee Area Tech Coll (WI)
Montgomery County Comm Coll (PA)
New England Culinary Inst (VT)
Pennsylvania Coll of Technology (PA)
Sullivan County Comm Coll (NY)
Triton Coll (IL)
Vincennes U (IN)

Banking and Financial Support Services
Alamance Comm Coll (NC)
Albuquerque Tech Vocational Inst (NM)
Alexandria Tech Coll (MN)
Barton County Comm Coll (KS)
Bristol Comm Coll (MA)
Bucks County Comm Coll (PA)
Cambria County Area Comm Coll (PA)
Comm Coll of Allegheny County (PA)
Comm Coll of Rhode Island (RI)
Eastern Maine Comm Coll (ME)
East Mississippi Comm Coll (MS)
Finger Lakes Comm Coll (NY)
Harrisburg Area Comm Coll (PA)
Jefferson State Comm Coll (AL)
Lackawanna Coll (PA)
Lanier Tech Coll (GA)
Luzerne County Comm Coll (PA)
Mineral Area Coll (MO)
Modesto Jr Coll (CA)
Mohawk Valley Comm Coll (NY)
Northampton County Area Comm Coll (PA)
Ozarka Coll (AR)
Pennsylvania Coll of Technology (PA)
Pima Comm Coll (AZ)
St. Cloud Tech Coll (MN)
San Juan Coll (NM)
Seminole Comm Coll (FL)
Southwestern Illinois Coll (IL)
Southwestern Oregon Comm Coll (OR)
Terra State Comm Coll (OH)
Utah Valley State Coll (UT)
Waubonsee Comm Coll (IL)
West Virginia Northern Comm Coll (WV)

Barbering
Milwaukee Area Tech Coll (WI)
Olympic Coll (WA)

Behavioral Sciences
Amarillo Coll (TX)
Anne Arundel Comm Coll (MD)
Casper Coll (WY)
Chabot Coll (CA)
Clarendon Coll (TX)
Coffeyville Comm Coll (KS)
Colby Comm Coll (KS)
Colorado Mountn Coll, Alpine Cmps (CO)
Colorado Mountn Coll (CO)
Colorado Mountn Coll, Timberline Cmps (CO)
Daytona Beach Comm Coll (FL)
Fulton-Montgomery Comm Coll (NY)
Galveston Coll (TX)

Garrett Coll (MD)
Gordon Coll (GA)
Greenfield Comm Coll (MA)
Hill Coll of the Hill Jr College District (TX)
Howard Coll (TX)
Iowa Lakes Comm Coll (IA)
Lincoln Coll, Lincoln (IL)
Miami Dade Coll (FL)
Midland Coll (TX)
MiraCosta Coll (CA)
Modesto Jr Coll (CA)
Mt. San Jacinto Coll (CA)
Napa Valley Coll (CA)
Northwestern Connecticut Comm-Tech Coll (CT)
Orange Coast Coll (CA)
Oxnard Coll (CA)
Phoenix Coll (AZ)
Reading Area Comm Coll (PA)
San Diego City Coll (CA)
San Joaquin Delta Coll (CA)
South Texas Comm Coll (TX)
Umpqua Comm Coll (OR)
Vincennes U (IN)

Biblical Studies
Amarillo Coll (TX)
Crowley's Ridge Coll (AR)
Hesston Coll (KS)
Lon Morris Coll (TX)
Northeast Mississippi Comm Coll (MS)

Bilingual and Multilingual Education
Blackfeet Comm Coll (MT)
Clovis Comm Coll (NM)

Biochemical Technology
Mid Michigan Comm Coll (MI)
Niagara County Comm Coll (NY)

Biological and Biomedical Sciences Related
Northampton County Area Comm Coll (PA)

Biological and Physical Sciences
Abraham Baldwin Ag Coll (GA)
American River Coll (CA)
Andrew Coll (GA)
Anne Arundel Comm Coll (MD)
Arapahoe Comm Coll (CO)
Arizona Western Coll (AZ)
Borough of Manhattan Comm Coll of City U of NY (NY)
Bowling Green State U-Firelands Coll (OH)
Brookdale Comm Coll (NJ)
Burlington County Coll (NJ)
Cabrillo Coll (CA)
Caldwell Comm Coll and Tech Inst (NC)
Cañada Coll (CA)
Cape Cod Comm Coll (MA)
Casper Coll (WY)
Centralia Coll (WA)
Central Oregon Comm Coll (OR)
Chabot Coll (CA)
Chesapeake Coll (MD)
Chipola Coll (FL)
City Colls of Chicago, Wilbur Wright Coll (IL)
Cleveland Comm Coll (NC)
Clinton Comm Coll (NY)
Coastal Bend Coll (TX)
Coffeyville Comm Coll (KS)
Colby Comm Coll (KS)
Coll of DuPage (IL)
Coll of Lake County (IL)
Coll of the Canyons (CA)
Coll of the Sequoias (CA)
Colorado Mountn Coll, Alpine Cmps (CO)
Colorado Mountn Coll (CO)
Colorado Mountn Coll, Timberline Cmps (CO)

Columbia-Greene Comm Coll (NY)
Comm Coll of Aurora (CO)
Comm Coll of Rhode Island (RI)
Copiah-Lincoln Comm Coll (MS)
Corning Comm Coll (NY)
Cumberland County Coll (NJ)
Cuyamaca Coll (CA)
Danville Comm Coll (VA)
Daytona Beach Comm Coll (FL)
Delaware County Comm Coll (PA)
Delgado Comm Coll (LA)
Donnelly Coll (KS)
Dutchess Comm Coll (NY)
Eastern Shore Comm Coll (VA)
East Mississippi Comm Coll (MS)
Elgin Comm Coll (IL)
Elizabethtown Comm Coll (KY)
Finger Lakes Comm Coll (NY)
Fulton-Montgomery Comm Coll (NY)
Galveston Coll (TX)
Garden City Comm Coll (KS)
Gavilan Coll (CA)
Georgia Perimeter Coll (GA)
Germanna Comm Coll (VA)
Glen Oaks Comm Coll (MI)
Gordon Coll (GA)
Greenfield Comm Coll (MA)
Guilford Tech Comm Coll (NC)
Heartland Comm Coll (IL)
Hill Coll of the Hill Jr College District (TX)
Howard Comm Coll (MD)
Illinois Eastern Comm Colls, Frontier Comm Coll (IL)
Illinois Eastern Comm Colls, Lincoln Trail Coll (IL)
Illinois Eastern Comm Colls, Olney Central Coll (IL)
Illinois Eastern Comm Colls, Wabash Valley Coll (IL)
Iowa Lakes Comm Coll (IA)
Isothermal Comm Coll (NC)
Jacksonville Coll (TX)
Jefferson Coll (MO)
Jefferson Davis Comm Coll (AL)
John Wood Comm Coll (IL)
J. Sargeant Reynolds Comm Coll (VA)
Kaskaskia Coll (IL)
Kent State U, Stark Campus (OH)
Kirkwood Comm Coll (IA)
Kirtland Comm Coll (MI)
Lake Land Coll (IL)
Lakeland Comm Coll (OH)
Lansing Comm Coll (MI)
Laramie County Comm Coll (WY)
Lewis and Clark Comm Coll (IL)
Lincoln Coll, Lincoln (IL)
Lincoln Land Comm Coll (IL)
Linn-Benton Comm Coll (OR)
Longview Comm Coll (MO)
Lorain County Comm Coll (OH)
Lord Fairfax Comm Coll (VA)
Luzerne County Comm Coll (PA)
Maple Woods Comm Coll (MO)
Marshalltown Comm Coll (IA)
McHenry County Coll (IL)
Merritt Coll (CA)
Middlesex Comm Coll (CT)
Middlesex County Coll (NJ)
Mid Michigan Comm Coll (MI)

Minnesota State Comm and Tech Coll–Fergus Falls (MN)
Mississippi Gulf Coast Comm Coll (MS)
Mitchell Comm Coll (NC)
Moraine Valley Comm Coll (IL)
Morgan Comm Coll (CO)
Morton Coll (IL)
Mountain Empire Comm Coll (VA)
Mt. San Jacinto Coll (CA)
Napa Valley Coll (CA)
Naugatuck Valley Comm Coll (CT)
New River Comm Coll (VA)
Niagara County Comm Coll (NY)
North Country Comm Coll (NY)
Northeast Alabama Comm Coll (AL)
Northeast Comm Coll (NE)
Northeast Mississippi Comm Coll (MS)
Northern Essex Comm Coll (MA)
North Harris Coll (TX)
North Idaho Coll (ID)
Northland Pioneer Coll (AZ)
Northwest Coll (WY)
Oakton Comm Coll (IL)
Orange County Comm Coll (NY)
Otero Jr Coll (CO)
Paris Jr Coll (TX)
Parkland Coll (IL)
Pasadena City Coll (CA)
Peninsula Coll (WA)
Penn State U Beaver Campus of the Commonwealth Coll (PA)
Penn State U DuBois Campus of the Commonwealth Coll (PA)
Penn State U McKeesport Campus of the Commonwealth Coll (PA)
Penn State U New Kensington Campus of the Commonwealth Coll (PA)
Penn State U Shenango Campus of the Commonwealth Coll (PA)
Penn Valley Comm Coll (MO)
Piedmont Virginia Comm Coll (VA)
Portland Comm Coll (OR)
Pratt Comm Coll and Area Vocational School (KS)
Rainy River Comm Coll (MN)
Red Rocks Comm Coll (CO)
Rend Lake Coll (IL)
Riverside Comm Coll (CA)
Rockingham Comm Coll (NC)
Rogue Comm Coll (OR)
St. Clair County Comm Coll (MI)
Salem Comm Coll (NJ)
Schenectady County Comm Coll (NY)
Seward County Comm Coll (KS)
Sheridan Coll (WY)
Southeast Comm Coll, Beatrice Campus (NE)
Southeastern Comm Coll (NC)
South Plains Coll (TX)
Southside Virginia Comm Coll (VA)
Southwestern Coll (CA)
Southwestern Oregon Comm Coll (OR)
Southwest Mississippi Comm Coll (MS)
Spartanburg Tech Coll (SC)
Spoon River Coll (IL)
State U of NY Coll of Technology at Alfred (NY)

State U of NY Coll of Technology at Canton (NY)
Sussex County Comm Coll (NJ)
Thomas Nelson Comm Coll (VA)
Tidewater Comm Coll (VA)
Tompkins Cortland Comm Coll (NY)
Trident Tech Coll (SC)
Trinidad State Jr Coll (CO)
Triton Coll (IL)
Umpqua Comm Coll (OR)
U of South Carolina Salkehatchie (SC)
U of South Carolina at Union (SC)
U of Wisconsin Center–Richland (WI)
Valley Forge Military Coll (PA)
Vermilion Comm Coll (MN)
Victor Valley Coll (CA)
Virginia Western Comm Coll (VA)
Waubonsee Comm Coll (IL)
Weatherford Coll (TX)
Western Wyoming Comm Coll (WY)
Yuba Coll (CA)

Biology/Biological Sciences
Abraham Baldwin Ag Coll (GA)
Alpena Comm Coll (MI)
Alvin Comm Coll (TX)
Amarillo Coll (TX)
Ancilla Coll (IN)
Andrew Coll (GA)
Anne Arundel Comm Coll (MD)
Arizona Western Coll (AZ)
Arkansas State U–Beebe (AR)
Atlanta Metropolitan Coll (GA)
Atlantic Cape Comm Coll (NJ)
Austin Comm Coll (TX)
Bainbridge Coll (GA)
Barton County Comm Coll (KS)
Bergen Comm Coll (NJ)
Bronx Comm Coll of City U of NY (NY)
Bucks County Comm Coll (PA)
Burlington County Coll (NJ)
Butler County Comm Coll (KS)
Butte Coll (CA)
Calhoun Comm Coll (AL)
Cañada Coll (CA)
Casper Coll (WY)
Cecil Comm Coll (MD)
Centralia Coll (WA)
Central Piedmont Comm Coll (NC)
Central Wyoming Coll (WY)
Chabot Coll (CA)
Clarendon Coll (TX)
Coastal Bend Coll (TX)
Coastal Georgia Comm Coll (GA)
Coffeyville Comm Coll (KS)
Colby Comm Coll (KS)
Coll of Southern Idaho (ID)
Coll of the Canyons (CA)
Coll of the Desert (CA)
Coll of the Sequoias (CA)
Colorado Mountn Coll, Alpine Cmps (CO)
Colorado Mountn Coll (CO)
Colorado Mountn Coll, Timberline Cmps (CO)
Columbia Coll (CA)
Columbia State Comm Coll (TN)
Comm Coll of Allegheny County (PA)
Connors State Coll (OK)
Contra Costa Coll (CA)
Copiah-Lincoln Comm Coll (MS)
Crowder Coll (MO)

Cuesta Coll (CA)
Darton Coll (GA)
Daytona Beach Comm Coll (FL)
Del Mar Coll (TX)
Delta Coll (MI)
Eastern Arizona Coll (AZ)
Eastern Oklahoma State Coll (OK)
Eastern Wyoming Coll (WY)
East Los Angeles Coll (CA)
El Camino Coll (CA)
Essex County Coll (NJ)
Everett Comm Coll (WA)
Feather River Comm Coll District (CA)
Finger Lakes Comm Coll (NY)
Foothill Coll (CA)
Frederick Comm Coll (MD)
Fulton-Montgomery Comm Coll (NY)
Garrett Coll (MD)
Gavilan Coll (CA)
Georgia Perimeter Coll (GA)
Gloucester County Coll (NJ)
Gogebic Comm Coll (MI)
Gordon Coll (GA)
Gulf Coast Comm Coll (FL)
Harrisburg Area Comm Coll (PA)
Hawkeye Comm Coll (IA)
Hill Coll of the Hill Jr College District (TX)
Hinds Comm Coll (MS)
Hiwassee Coll (TN)
Holmes Comm Coll (MS)
Holyoke Comm Coll (MA)
Howard Coll (TX)
Hutchinson Comm Coll and Area Vocational School (KS)
Iowa Lakes Comm Coll (IA)
Jefferson Davis Comm Coll (AL)
John A. Logan Coll (IL)
Kellogg Comm Coll (MI)
Keystone Coll (PA)
Kingsborough Comm Coll of City U of NY (NY)
Kingwood Coll (TX)
Kirkwood Comm Coll (IA)
Lansing Comm Coll (MI)
Laramie County Comm Coll (WY)
Lawson State Comm Coll (AL)
Lehigh Carbon Comm Coll (PA)
Lewis and Clark Comm Coll (IL)
Lincoln Coll, Lincoln (IL)
Linn-Benton Comm Coll (OR)
Longview Comm Coll (MO)
Lon Morris Coll (TX)
Lorain County Comm Coll (OH)
Los Angeles Harbor Coll (CA)
Los Angeles Valley Coll (CA)
Lower Columbia Coll (WA)
Macomb Comm Coll (MI)
Manatee Comm Coll (FL)
Maple Woods Comm Coll (MO)
Miami Dade Coll (FL)
Middlesex County Coll (NJ)
Midland Coll (TX)
Mid Michigan Comm Coll (MI)
MiraCosta Coll (CA)
Modesto Jr Coll (CA)
Monroe County Comm Coll (MI)
Montgomery County Comm Coll (PA)
Mountain Empire Comm Coll (VA)
Northampton County Area Comm Coll (PA)
Northeast Comm Coll (NE)
Northeastern Oklahoma A&M Coll (OK)

Northeast Mississippi Comm Coll (MS)
North Idaho Coll (ID)
Northwest Coll (WY)
Northwestern Connecticut Comm-Tech Coll (CT)
Northwestern Michigan Coll (MI)
Odessa Coll (TX)
Oklahoma City Comm Coll (OK)
Orange Coast Coll (CA)
Orange County Comm Coll (NY)
Otero Jr Coll (CO)
Oxnard Coll (CA)
Palm Beach Comm Coll (FL)
Palo Alto Coll (TX)
Palomar Coll (CA)
Pasadena City Coll (CA)
Pennsylvania Coll of Technology (PA)
Penn Valley Comm Coll (MO)
Pensacola Jr Coll (FL)
Pratt Comm Coll and Area Vocational School (KS)
Raritan Valley Comm Coll (NJ)
Reading Area Comm Coll (PA)
Red Rocks Comm Coll (CO)
Roane State Comm Coll (TN)
St. Philip's Coll (TX)
Salem Comm Coll (NJ)
San Diego City Coll (CA)
San Joaquin Delta Coll (CA)
San Juan Coll (NM)
Santa Barbara City Coll (CA)
Santa Fe Comm Coll (NM)
Santa Monica Coll (CA)
Sauk Valley Comm Coll (IL)
Seward County Comm Coll (KS)
Shelton State Comm Coll (AL)
Sheridan Coll (WY)
Sierra Coll (CA)
Snow Coll (UT)
Southeast Comm Coll, Beatrice Campus (NE)
South Plains Coll (TX)
Southwestern Coll (CA)
Southwest Mississippi Comm Coll (MS)
Spoon River Coll (IL)
Springfield Tech Comm Coll (MA)
State U of NY Coll of A&T at Morrisville (NY)
Trinidad State Jr Coll (CO)
Triton Coll (IL)
Umpqua Comm Coll (OR)
Union County Coll (NJ)
Utah Valley State Coll (UT)
Ventura Coll (CA)
Vermilion Comm Coll (MN)
Victor Valley Coll (CA)
Vincennes U (IN)
Washtenaw Comm Coll (MI)
Waycross Coll (GA)
Western Nevada Comm Coll (NV)
Western Wyoming Comm Coll (WY)
West Hills Comm Coll (CA)
Yuba Coll (CA)

Biology/Biotechnology Laboratory Technician
Bates Tech Coll (WA)
Collin County Comm Coll District (TX)
Contra Costa Coll (CA)
County Coll of Morris (NJ)
Des Moines Area Comm Coll (IA)
Finger Lakes Comm Coll (NY)
Foothill Coll (CA)
Guilford Tech Comm Coll (NC)
Indian Hills Comm Coll (IA)
Jefferson Comm Coll (NY)

John Tyler Comm Coll (VA)
Kirkwood Comm Coll (IA)
Lake Area Tech Inst (SD)
Lansing Comm Coll (MI)
Middlesex Comm Coll (CT)
Middlesex County Coll (NJ)
Mid Michigan Comm Coll (MI)
Montana State U Coll of Tech-Great Falls (MT)
North Shore Comm Coll (MA)
Ohio State U Ag Tech Inst (OH)
Portland Comm Coll (OR)
Southeast Arkansas Coll (AR)
Southeast Comm Coll, Beatrice Campus (NE)
State U of NY Coll of A&T at Morrisville (NY)
State U of NY Coll of Technology at Alfred (NY)
Vista Comm Coll (CA)

Biology Teacher Education
Manatee Comm Coll (FL)

Biomedical Technology
Bates Tech Coll (WA)
Caldwell Comm Coll and Tech Inst (NC)
Cincinnati State Tech and Comm Coll (OH)
Comm Coll of the Air Force (AL)
Dakota County Tech Coll (MN)
Delaware County Comm Coll (PA)
Delgado Comm Coll (LA)
ECPI Coll of Technology, Virginia Beach (VA)
Hillsborough Comm Coll (FL)
Howard Comm Coll (MD)
Jefferson State Comm Coll (AL)
Lehigh Carbon Comm Coll (PA)
Miami Dade Coll (FL)
Middlesex Comm Coll (MA)
Milwaukee Area Tech Coll (WI)
Napa Valley Coll (CA)
North Seattle Comm Coll (WA)
Oklahoma City Comm Coll (OK)
Parkland Coll (IL)
Pennsylvania Coll of Technology (PA)
Penn State U Beaver Campus of the Commonwealth Coll (PA)
Penn State U DuBois Campus of the Commonwealth Coll (PA)
Penn State U Fayette Campus of the Commonwealth Coll (PA)
Penn State U Hazleton Campus of the Commonwealth Coll (PA)
Penn State U New Kensington Campus of the Commonwealth Coll (PA)
Penn State U Shenango Campus of the Commonwealth Coll (PA)
Penn State U York Campus of the Commonwealth Coll (PA)
Rowan-Cabarrus Comm Coll (NC)
St. Philip's Coll (TX)
Santa Barbara City Coll (CA)
Schoolcraft Coll (MI)
South Suburban Coll (IL)
Spokane Comm Coll (WA)
Stanly Comm Coll (NC)
Stark State Coll of Technology (OH)
Texas State Tech Coll–Harlingen (TX)

Texas State Tech Coll–
Waco/Marshall Campus
(TX)
Western Iowa Tech Comm
Coll (IA)

Biotechnology
Alamance Comm Coll (NC)
Albuquerque Tech Vocational
Inst (NM)
Bladen Comm Coll (NC)
Briarwood Coll (CT)
Burlington County Coll (NJ)
Howard Comm Coll (MD)
Lackawanna Coll (PA)
Lakeland Comm Coll (OH)
Lehigh Carbon Comm Coll
(PA)
Montgomery County Comm
Coll (PA)
Santa Barbara City Coll (CA)
Sinclair Comm Coll (OH)
Springfield Tech Comm Coll
(MA)

Boilermaking
Ivy Tech State Coll–
Southwest (IN)

Botany/Plant Biology
Anne Arundel Comm Coll
(MD)
Casper Coll (WY)
Centralia Coll (WA)
Coffeyville Comm Coll (KS)
Coll of Southern Idaho (ID)
El Camino Coll (CA)
Everett Comm Coll (WA)
Hill Coll of the Hill Jr College
District (TX)
Iowa Lakes Comm Coll (IA)
Lincoln Coll, Lincoln (IL)
Lon Morris Coll (TX)
Northeastern Oklahoma
A&M Coll (OK)
North Idaho Coll (ID)
Northwest Coll (WY)
Palm Beach Comm Coll (FL)
Riverside Comm Coll (CA)
San Joaquin Delta Coll (CA)
Snow Coll (UT)
Southern Maine Comm Coll
(ME)
Spoon River Coll (IL)

Broadcast Journalism
Amarillo Coll (TX)
Anne Arundel Comm Coll
(MD)
Arizona Western Coll (AZ)
Bergen Comm Coll (NJ)
Centralia Coll (WA)
Chabot Coll (CA)
Coffeyville Comm Coll (KS)
Colby Comm Coll (KS)
Cumberland County Coll
(NJ)
Delta Coll (MI)
Finger Lakes Comm Coll
(NY)
Iowa Lakes Comm Coll (IA)
Isothermal Comm Coll (NC)
Kingsborough Comm Coll of
City U of NY (NY)
Kirkwood Comm Coll (IA)
Lansing Comm Coll (MI)
Lincoln Coll, Lincoln (IL)
Los Angeles Valley Coll (CA)
Meridian Comm Coll (MS)
Middlesex Comm Coll (CT)
Mount Wachusett Comm Coll
(MA)
Northeast Comm Coll (NE)
Northeastern Oklahoma
A&M Coll (OK)
Northeast Mississippi Comm
Coll (MS)
Oklahoma City Comm Coll
(OK)
Pasadena City Coll (CA)
Pennsylvania Coll of
Technology (PA)
Pratt Comm Coll and Area
Vocational School (KS)
St. Clair County Comm Coll
(MI)

St. Louis Comm Coll at
Florissant Valley (MO)
San Joaquin Delta Coll (CA)
Santa Monica Coll (CA)
Southeast Comm Coll,
Beatrice Campus (NE)
Sussex County Comm Coll
(NJ)
Trident Tech Coll (SC)
Vincennes U (IN)
Yakima Valley Comm Coll
(WA)

**Building/Construction
Finishing, Management, and
Inspection Related**
Albuquerque Tech Vocational
Inst (NM)
Guilford Tech Comm Coll
(NC)
Manhattan Area Tech Coll
(KS)
Mid-Plains Comm Coll, North
Platte (NE)
Pima Comm Coll (AZ)

**Building/Construction Site
Management**
Metropolitan Comm
Coll-Business &
Technology College (MO)
Ohio State U Ag Tech Inst
(OH)

**Building/Home/Construction
Inspection**
Arapahoe Comm Coll (CO)
McHenry County Coll (IL)
Modesto Jr Coll (CA)
Orange Coast Coll (CA)
Utah Valley State Coll (UT)
Vincennes U (IN)

**Building/Property
Maintenance and
Management**
Bates Tech Coll (WA)
Coll of DuPage (IL)
Comm Coll of Allegheny
County (PA)
Delaware County Comm Coll
(PA)
Delgado Comm Coll (LA)
Del Mar Coll (TX)
Erie Comm Coll (NY)
Illinois Eastern Comm Colls,
Lincoln Trail Coll (IL)
Ivy Tech State Coll–
Bloomington (IN)
Ivy Tech State Coll–Central
Indiana (IN)
Ivy Tech State Coll–
Columbus (IN)
Ivy Tech State Coll–
Eastcentral (IN)
Ivy Tech State Coll–Kokomo
(IN)
Ivy Tech State Coll–Lafayette
(IN)
Ivy Tech State Coll–North
Central (IN)
Ivy Tech State Coll–
Northeast (IN)
Ivy Tech State Coll–
Northwest (IN)
Ivy Tech State Coll–
Southcentral (IN)
Ivy Tech State Coll–
Southwest (IN)
Ivy Tech State Coll–Wabash
Valley (IN)
Ivy Tech State Coll–
Whitewater (IN)
Luzerne County Comm Coll
(PA)
Miles Comm Coll (MT)
Mohawk Valley Comm Coll
(NY)
Northland Pioneer Coll (AZ)
Pikes Peak Comm Coll (CO)
Pima Comm Coll (AZ)
Utah Valley State Coll (UT)

**Business Administration
and Management**
Abraham Baldwin Ag Coll
(GA)

Academy Coll (MN)
AEC Southern Ohio Coll
(OH)
AEC Southern Ohio Coll,
Northern Kentucky
Campus (KY)
AIB Coll of Business (IA)
Alamance Comm Coll (NC)
Albuquerque Tech Vocational
Inst (NM)
Alexandria Tech Coll (MN)
Allegany Coll of Maryland
(MD)
Allentown Business School
(PA)
Alpena Comm Coll (MI)
Alvin Comm Coll (TX)
Amarillo Coll (TX)
American River Coll (CA)
Ancilla Coll (IN)
Andover Coll (ME)
Andrew Coll (GA)
Anne Arundel Comm Coll
(MD)
Anoka Tech Coll (MN)
Arapahoe Comm Coll (CO)
Arizona Western Coll (AZ)
Arkansas State U–Beebe
(AR)
Asheville-Buncombe Tech
Comm Coll (NC)
Asnuntuck Comm Coll (CT)
Atlanta Metropolitan Coll
(GA)
Atlantic Cape Comm Coll
(NJ)
Austin Comm Coll (TX)
Bainbridge Coll (GA)
Barton County Comm Coll
(KS)
Bay State Coll (MA)
Beaufort County Comm Coll
(NC)
Bellevue Comm Coll (WA)
Bergen Comm Coll (NJ)
Berkeley Coll (NJ)
Berkeley Coll-New York City
Campus (NY)
Berkeley Coll-Westchester
Campus (NY)
Berkshire Comm Coll (MA)
Big Sandy Comm and Tech
Coll (KY)
Blackfeet Comm Coll (MT)
Bladen Comm Coll (NC)
Blue Ridge Comm Coll (NC)
Blue River Comm Coll (MO)
Borough of Manhattan
Comm Coll of City U of NY
(NY)
Brevard Comm Coll (FL)
Briarwood Coll (CT)
Bristol Comm Coll (MA)
Bronx Comm Coll of City U of
NY (NY)
Brookdale Comm Coll (NJ)
Broome Comm Coll (NY)
The Brown Mackie Coll–
Lenexa Campus (KS)
Brunswick Comm Coll (NC)
Bryant & Stratton Business
Inst, Syracuse (NY)
Bryant and Stratton Coll,
Parma (OH)
Bucks County Comm Coll
(PA)
Bunker Hill Comm Coll (MA)
Burlington County Coll (NJ)
Butler County Comm Coll
(KS)
Cabrillo Coll (CA)
Caldwell Comm Coll and
Tech Inst (NC)
Calhoun Comm Coll (AL)
Cambria-Rowe Business
Coll, Johnstown (PA)
Camden County Coll (NJ)
Cañada Coll (CA)
Cape Cod Comm Coll (MA)
Cape Fear Comm Coll (NC)
Capital Comm Coll (CT)
Career Coll of Northern
Nevada (NV)
Carl Sandburg Coll (IL)

Carteret Comm Coll (NC)
Casper Coll (WY)
Cecil Comm Coll (MD)
Cedar Valley Coll (TX)
Central Alabama Comm Coll
(AL)
Central Arizona Coll (AZ)
Central Carolina Tech Coll
(SC)
Central Comm Coll–
Columbus Campus (NE)
Central Comm Coll–Grand
Island Campus (NE)
Central Comm Coll–Hastings
Campus (NE)
Central Florida Comm Coll
(FL)
Central Georgia Tech Coll
(GA)
Centralia Coll (WA)
Central Lakes Coll (MN)
Central Oregon Comm Coll
(OR)
Central Pennsylvania Coll
(PA)
Central Piedmont Comm Coll
(NC)
Central Wyoming Coll (WY)
Century Coll (MN)
Chabot Coll (CA)
Chaparral Coll (AZ)
Chatfield Coll (OH)
Chemeketa Comm Coll (OR)
Chesapeake Coll (MD)
Chipola Coll (FL)
Cincinnati State Tech and
Comm Coll (OH)
City Colls of Chicago, Wilbur
Wright Coll (IL)
Clarendon Coll (TX)
Clark Coll (WA)
Clark State Comm Coll (OH)
Cleveland Comm Coll (NC)
Cleveland State Comm Coll
(TN)
Clinton Comm Coll (NY)
Clovis Comm Coll (NM)
Coastal Bend Coll (TX)
Coastal Carolina Comm Coll
(NC)
Coastal Georgia Comm Coll
(GA)
Coffeyville Comm Coll (KS)
Colby Comm Coll (KS)
CollAmerica–Fort Collins
(CO)
Coll of DuPage (IL)
Coll of Eastern Utah (UT)
Coll of Lake County (IL)
Coll of Southern Idaho (ID)
Coll of Southern Maryland
(MD)
Coll of the Canyons (CA)
Coll of the Desert (CA)
Coll of the Sequoias (CA)
The Coll of Westchester (NY)
Collin County Comm Coll
District (TX)
Colorado Mountn Coll, Alpine
Cmps (CO)
Colorado Mountn Coll (CO)
Colorado Mountn Coll,
Timberline Cmps (CO)
Colorado Northwestern
Comm Coll (CO)
Columbia Coll (CA)
Columbia-Greene Comm
Coll (NY)
Columbus State Comm Coll
(OH)
Commonwealth Business
Coll, Merrillville (IN)
Commonwealth Business
Coll, Michigan City (IN)
Comm Coll of Allegheny
County (PA)
Comm Coll of Aurora (CO)
Comm Coll of Denver (CO)
Comm Coll of Rhode Island
(RI)
Connors State Coll (OK)
Consolidated School of
Business, York (PA)
Contra Costa Coll (CA)

Copiah-Lincoln Comm Coll
(MS)
Corning Comm Coll (NY)
Cossatot Comm Coll of the U
of Arkansas (AR)
County Coll of Morris (NJ)
Crowder Coll (MO)
Cuesta Coll (CA)
Cumberland County Coll
(NJ)
Cuyahoga Comm Coll (OH)
Cuyamaca Coll (CA)
Danville Comm Coll (VA)
Darton Coll (GA)
Davis Coll (OH)
Daytona Beach Comm Coll
(FL)
Dean Coll (MA)
Delaware County Comm Coll
(PA)
Delaware Tech & Comm
Coll, Terry Cmps (DE)
Delgado Comm Coll (LA)
Del Mar Coll (TX)
Delta Coll (MI)
Des Moines Area Comm Coll
(IA)
Doña Ana Branch Comm
Coll (NM)
Donnelly Coll (KS)
Draughons Jr Coll (KY)
Duluth Business U (MN)
Durham Tech Comm Coll
(NC)
Dutchess Comm Coll (NY)
East Arkansas Comm Coll
(AR)
Eastern Arizona Coll (AZ)
Eastern Maine Comm Coll
(ME)
Eastern Oklahoma State Coll
(OK)
Eastern Shore Comm Coll
(VA)
Eastern Wyoming Coll (WY)
Eastfield Coll (TX)
East Los Angeles Coll (CA)
East Mississippi Comm Coll
(MS)
Edgecombe Comm Coll (NC)
Edison Comm Coll (FL)
Edison State Comm Coll
(OH)
Edmonds Comm Coll (WA)
El Camino Coll (CA)
El Centro Coll (TX)
Elgin Comm Coll (IL)
Elizabethtown Comm Coll
(KY)
Erie Business Center South
(PA)
Erie Comm Coll (NY)
Essex County Coll (NJ)
Eugenio María de Hostos
Comm Coll of City U of NY
(NY)
Everett Comm Coll (WA)
Fayetteville Tech Comm Coll
(NC)
Finger Lakes Comm Coll
(NY)
Fiorello H LaGuardia Comm
Coll of City U of NY (NY)
Fisher Coll (MA)
Florida National Coll (FL)
Foothill Coll (CA)
Forrest Jr Coll (SC)
Forsyth Tech Comm Coll
(NC)
Fort Scott Comm Coll (KS)
Frederick Comm Coll (MD)
Front Range Comm Coll
(CO)
Fulton-Montgomery Comm
Coll (NY)
Gallipolis Career Coll (OH)
Galveston Coll (TX)
Garden City Comm Coll (KS)
Garrett Coll (MD)
Gaston Coll (NC)
Gavilan Coll (CA)
Gem City Coll (IL)
Georgia Perimeter Coll (GA)
Germanna Comm Coll (VA)

Glendale Comm Coll (AZ)
Glen Oaks Comm Coll (MI)
Globe Coll (MN)
Gloucester County Coll (NJ)
Gogebic Comm Coll (MI)
Gordon Coll (GA)
Grand Rapids Comm Coll
(MI)
Great Basin Coll (NV)
Greenfield Comm Coll (MA)
Guilford Tech Comm Coll
(NC)
Gulf Coast Comm Coll (FL)
Hagerstown Comm Coll
(MD)
Hamilton Coll (NE)
Harcum Coll (PA)
Harford Comm Coll (MD)
Harrisburg Area Comm Coll
(PA)
Hawkeye Comm Coll (IA)
Heartland Comm Coll (IL)
Henderson Comm Coll (KY)
Hesser Coll (NH)
Hesston Coll (KS)
Hibbing Comm Coll (MN)
Hill Coll of the Hill Jr College
District (TX)
Hillsborough Comm Coll (FL)
Hinds Comm Coll (MS)
Hiwassee Coll (TN)
Holmes Comm Coll (MS)
Holyoke Comm Coll (MA)
Hopkinsville Comm Coll (KY)
Houston Comm Coll System
(TX)
Howard Coll (TX)
Howard Comm Coll (MD)
Hudson County Comm Coll
(NJ)
Illinois Eastern Comm Colls,
Wabash Valley Coll (IL)
Indiana Business Coll,
Anderson (IN)
Indiana Business Coll,
Columbus (IN)
Indiana Business Coll,
Evansville (IN)
Indiana Business Coll, Fort
Wayne (IN)
Indiana Business Coll,
Indianapolis (IN)
Indiana Business Coll,
Lafayette (IN)
Indiana Business Coll,
Marion (IN)
Indiana Business Coll,
Muncie (IN)
Indiana Business Coll, Terre
Haute (IN)
Indian Hills Comm Coll (IA)
Inst of Business & Medical
Careers (CO)
Iowa Lakes Comm Coll (IA)
Isothermal Comm Coll (NC)
Itasca Comm Coll (MN)
Ivy Tech State Coll–
Bloomington (IN)
Ivy Tech State Coll–Central
Indiana (IN)
Ivy Tech State Coll–
Columbus (IN)
Ivy Tech State Coll–
Eastcentral (IN)
Ivy Tech State Coll–Kokomo
(IN)
Ivy Tech State Coll–Lafayette
(IN)
Ivy Tech State Coll–North
Central (IN)
Ivy Tech State Coll–
Northeast (IN)
Ivy Tech State Coll–
Northwest (IN)
Ivy Tech State Coll–
Southcentral (IN)
Ivy Tech State Coll–
Southeast (IN)
Ivy Tech State Coll–
Southwest (IN)
Ivy Tech State Coll–Wabash
Valley (IN)
Ivy Tech State Coll–
Whitewater (IN)

Associate Degree Programs at Two-Year Colleges
Business Administration and Management

Jackson Comm Coll (MI)
Jackson State Comm Coll (TN)
James A. Rhodes State Coll (OH)
James H. Faulkner State Comm Coll (AL)
James Sprunt Comm Coll (NC)
Jamestown Business Coll (NY)
Jamestown Comm Coll (NY)
Jefferson Coll (MO)
Jefferson Comm Coll (KY)
Jefferson Comm Coll (NY)
Jefferson Comm Coll (OH)
Jefferson Davis Comm Coll (AL)
John A. Logan Coll (IL)
Johnson County Comm Coll (KS)
Johnston Comm Coll (NC)
John Wood Comm Coll (IL)
J. Sargeant Reynolds Comm Coll (VA)
Kalamazoo Valley Comm Coll (MI)
Kansas City Kansas Comm Coll (KS)
Kaplan Coll (IA)
Kaskaskia Coll (IL)
Keiser Coll, Miami (FL)
Kellogg Comm Coll (MI)
Kent State U, Salem Campus (OH)
Kent State U, Stark Campus (OH)
Kent State U, Trumbull Campus (OH)
Kent State U, Tuscarawas Campus (OH)
Keystone Coll (PA)
Kilian Comm Coll (SD)
Kingsborough Comm Coll of City U of NY (NY)
Kingwood Coll (TX)
Kirkwood Comm Coll (IA)
Kirtland Comm Coll (MI)
Kishwaukee Coll (IL)
Lac Courte Oreilles Ojibwa Comm Coll (WI)
Lackawanna Coll (PA)
Lake City Comm Coll (FL)
Lake Land Coll (IL)
Lakeland Comm Coll (OH)
Lake Region State Coll (ND)
Lake-Sumter Comm Coll (FL)
Lake Superior Coll (MN)
Lamar State Coll–Orange (TX)
Lamar State Coll–Port Arthur (TX)
Lansing Comm Coll (MI)
Laramie County Comm Coll (WY)
Lawson State Comm Coll (AL)
Lehigh Carbon Comm Coll (PA)
Lenoir Comm Coll (NC)
Lewis and Clark Comm Coll (IL)
Lincoln Coll, Lincoln (IL)
Lincoln Land Comm Coll (IL)
Linn-Benton Comm Coll (OR)
Long Island Business Inst (NY)
Longview Comm Coll (MO)
Lon Morris Coll (TX)
Lorain County Comm Coll (OH)
Lord Fairfax Comm Coll (VA)
Los Angeles Harbor Coll (CA)
Los Angeles Trade-Tech Coll (CA)
Los Angeles Valley Coll (CA)
Lower Columbia Coll (WA)
Luna Comm Coll (NM)
Luzerne County Comm Coll (PA)
MacCormac Coll (IL)

Macomb Comm Coll (MI)
Manatee Comm Coll (FL)
Manchester Comm Coll (CT)
Maple Woods Comm Coll (MO)
Marion Tech Coll (OH)
Marshalltown Comm Coll (IA)
Massasoit Comm Coll (MA)
Mayland Comm Coll (NC)
Maysville Comm Coll (KY)
McHenry County Coll (IL)
McIntosh Coll (NH)
McLennan Comm Coll (TX)
Merritt Coll (CA)
Mesalands Comm Coll (NM)
Metropolitan Comm Coll (NE)
Metropolitan Comm Coll-Business & Technology College (MO)
Miami Dade Coll (FL)
Miami U Hamilton (OH)
Michiana Coll, South Bend (IN)
Middle Georgia Coll (GA)
Middlesex Comm Coll (CT)
Middlesex Comm Coll (MA)
Middlesex County Coll (NJ)
Midlands Tech Coll (SC)
Mid Michigan Comm Coll (MI)
Mid-Plains Comm Coll, North Platte (NE)
Mildred Elley (NY)
Miles Comm Coll (MT)
Milwaukee Area Tech Coll (WI)
Mineral Area Coll (MO)
Minneapolis Business Coll (MN)
Minneapolis Comm and Tech Coll (MN)
Minnesota School of Business–Brooklyn Center (MN)
Minnesota School of Business-Plymouth (MN)
Minnesota School of Business-Richfield (MN)
Minnesota State Comm and Tech Coll–Fergus Falls (MN)
Minot State U–Bottineau Campus (ND)
MiraCosta Coll (CA)
Mississippi Gulf Coast Comm Coll (MS)
Mitchell Comm Coll (NC)
Modesto Jr Coll (CA)
Mohave Comm Coll (AZ)
Mohawk Valley Comm Coll (NY)
Monroe Coll, Bronx (NY)
Monroe Coll, New Rochelle (NY)
Monroe County Comm Coll (MI)
Montcalm Comm Coll (MI)
Montgomery Coll (MD)
Montgomery County Comm Coll (PA)
Moraine Valley Comm Coll (IL)
Morgan Comm Coll (CO)
Morton Coll (IL)
Motlow State Comm Coll (TN)
Mott Comm Coll (MI)
Mountain Empire Comm Coll (VA)
Mountain West Coll (UT)
Mt. San Antonio Coll (CA)
Mt. San Jacinto Coll (CA)
Mount Wachusett Comm Coll (MA)
Napa Valley Coll (CA)
Nash Comm Coll (NC)
Nashville State Tech Comm Coll (TN)
Nassau Comm Coll (NY)
National Coll of Business & Technology, Danville (KY)

National Coll of Business & Technology, Florence (KY)
National Coll of Business & Technology, Lexington (KY)
National Coll of Business & Technology, Louisville (KY)
National Coll of Business & Technology, Pikeville (KY)
National Coll of Business & Technology, Richmond (KY)
National Coll of Business & Technology, Nashville (TN)
National Coll of Business & Technology, Bluefield (VA)
National Coll of Business & Technology, Bristol (VA)
National Coll of Business & Technology, Harrisonburg (VA)
National Coll of Business & Technology, Lynchburg (VA)
National Coll of Business & Technology, Martinsville (VA)
Naugatuck Valley Comm Coll (CT)
Nebraska Indian Comm Coll (NE)
New Hampshire Comm Tech Coll, Berlin/Laconia (NH)
New Hampshire Comm Tech Coll, Manchester/Stratham (NH)
New Hampshire Tech Inst (NH)
New Mexico State U–Carlsbad (NM)
New Mexico State U–Grants (NM)
Newport Business Inst, Lower Burrell (PA)
Newport Business Inst, Williamsport (PA)
New River Comm Coll (VA)
Niagara County Comm Coll (NY)
Normandale Comm Coll (MN)
Northampton County Area Comm Coll (PA)
North Arkansas Coll (AR)
North Central Missouri Coll (MO)
North Central State Coll (OH)
Northcentral Tech Coll (WI)
North Country Comm Coll (NY)
Northeast Alabama Comm Coll (AL)
Northeast Comm Coll (NE)
Northeastern Oklahoma A&M Coll (OK)
Northeastern Tech Coll (SC)
Northeast Mississippi Comm Coll (MS)
Northeast State Tech Comm Coll (TN)
Northeast Wisconsin Tech Coll (WI)
Northern Essex Comm Coll (MA)
Northern Maine Comm Coll (ME)
North Florida Comm Coll (FL)
North Hennepin Comm Coll (MN)
North Idaho Coll (ID)
North Iowa Area Comm Coll (IA)
Northland Pioneer Coll (AZ)
North Seattle Comm Coll (WA)
North Shore Comm Coll (MA)
Northwest Coll (WY)
Northwestern Connecticut Comm-Tech Coll (CT)
Northwestern Michigan Coll (MI)
Northwest Iowa Comm Coll (IA)

Northwest-Shoals Comm Coll (AL)
Northwest State Comm Coll (OH)
Oakland Comm Coll (MI)
Oakton Comm Coll (IL)
Ocean County Coll (NJ)
Odessa Coll (TX)
Ohio Business Coll, Sandusky (OH)
Oklahoma City Comm Coll (OK)
Oklahoma State U, Oklahoma City (OK)
Olympic Coll (WA)
Orange Coast Coll (CA)
Orange County Comm Coll (NY)
Otero Jr Coll (CO)
Ouachita Tech Coll (AR)
Owensboro Comm and Tech Coll (KY)
Owens Comm Coll, Findlay (OH)
Oxnard Coll (CA)
Ozarka Coll (AR)
Palm Beach Comm Coll (FL)
Palo Alto Coll (TX)
Palomar Coll (CA)
Paris Jr Coll (TX)
Parkland Coll (IL)
Pasadena City Coll (CA)
Pasco-Hernando Comm Coll (FL)
Paul D. Camp Comm Coll (VA)
Pellissippi State Tech Comm Coll (TN)
Peninsula Coll (WA)
Pennsylvania Coll of Technology (PA)
Pennsylvania Inst of Technology (PA)
Penn Valley Comm Coll (MO)
Pensacola Jr Coll (FL)
Phoenix Coll (AZ)
Piedmont Virginia Comm Coll (VA)
Pikes Peak Comm Coll (CO)
Pima Comm Coll (AZ)
Pioneer Pacific Coll (OR)
Pitt Comm Coll (NC)
Polk Comm Coll (FL)
Portland Comm Coll (OR)
Pratt Comm Coll and Area Vocational School (KS)
Prince George's Comm Coll (MD)
Queensborough Comm Coll of City U of NY (NY)
Quinebaug Valley Comm Coll (CT)
Quinsigamond Comm Coll (MA)
Rainy River Comm Coll (MN)
Raritan Valley Comm Coll (NJ)
Rasmussen Coll Mankato (MN)
Rasmussen Coll Minnetonka (MN)
Rasmussen Coll St. Cloud (MN)
Reading Area Comm Coll (PA)
Red Rocks Comm Coll (CO)
Remington Coll–Lafayette Campus (LA)
Rend Lake Coll (IL)
Richmond Comm Coll (NC)
Riverland Comm Coll (MN)
Riverside Comm Coll (CA)
Roane State Comm Coll (TN)
Roanoke-Chowan Comm Coll (NC)
Rochester Business Inst (NY)
Rochester Comm and Tech Coll (MN)
Rockingham Comm Coll (NC)
Rogue Comm Coll (OR)

Rowan-Cabarrus Comm Coll (NC)
Saint Charles Comm Coll (MO)
St. Clair County Comm Coll (MI)
St. Cloud Tech Coll (MN)
St. Johns River Comm Coll (FL)
St. Louis Comm Coll at Florissant Valley (MO)
St. Petersburg Coll (FL)
St. Philip's Coll (TX)
Salem Comm Coll (NJ)
San Diego City Coll (CA)
Sanford-Brown Coll, Hazelwood (MO)
San Joaquin Delta Coll (CA)
San Jose City Coll (CA)
San Juan Coll (NM)
Santa Barbara City Coll (CA)
Santa Fe Comm Coll (NM)
Santa Monica Coll (CA)
Sauk Valley Comm Coll (IL)
Schenectady County Comm Coll (NY)
Schoolcraft Coll (MI)
Schuylkill Inst of Business and Technology (PA)
Scottsdale Comm Coll (AZ)
Seminole Comm Coll (FL)
Seward County Comm Coll (KS)
Shelton State Comm Coll (AL)
Sheridan Coll (WY)
Sierra Coll (CA)
Sinclair Comm Coll (OH)
Sisseton-Wahpeton Comm Coll (SD)
Snead State Comm Coll (AL)
Snow Coll (UT)
South Central Tech Coll (MN)
South Coll (TN)
South Coll-Asheville (NC)
Southeast Arkansas Coll (AR)
Southeast Comm Coll (KY)
Southeast Comm Coll, Beatrice Campus (NE)
Southeast Comm Coll, Lincoln Campus (NE)
Southeastern Comm Coll (NC)
Southeastern Tech Coll (GA)
Southern Arkansas U Tech (AR)
Southern Maine Comm Coll (ME)
Southern West Virginia Comm and Tech Coll (WV)
South Hills School of Business & Technology, State College (PA)
South Plains Coll (TX)
South Puget Sound Comm Coll (WA)
Southside Virginia Comm Coll (VA)
South Texas Comm Coll (TX)
South U (FL)
South U (SC)
Southwestern Coll (CA)
Southwestern Comm Coll (NC)
Southwestern Illinois Coll (IL)
Southwestern Michigan Coll (MI)
Southwestern Oregon Comm Coll (OR)
Southwest Mississippi Comm Coll (MS)
Spartanburg Tech Coll (SC)
Spencerian Coll (KY)
Spokane Comm Coll (WA)
Spokane Falls Comm Coll (WA)
Spoon River Coll (IL)
Springfield Tech Comm Coll (MA)
Stanly Comm Coll (NC)
Stark State Coll of Technology (OH)

State U of NY Coll of A&T at Morrisville (NY)
State U of NY Coll of Technology at Alfred (NY)
State U of NY Coll of Technology at Canton (NY)
State U of NY Coll of Technology at Delhi (NY)
Sullivan County Comm Coll (NY)
Sussex County Comm Coll (NJ)
Temple Coll (TX)
Terra State Comm Coll (OH)
Thomas Nelson Comm Coll (VA)
Thompson Inst (PA)
Three Rivers Comm Coll (MO)
Tidewater Comm Coll (VA)
Tompkins Cortland Comm Coll (NY)
Tri-County Comm Coll (NC)
Trident Tech Coll (SC)
Trinidad State Jr Coll (CO)
Triton Coll (IL)
Umpqua Comm Coll (OR)
Union County Coll (NJ)
United Tribes Tech Coll (ND)
The U of Akron–Wayne Coll (OH)
U of Alaska Anchorage, Kenai Peninsula Coll (AK)
U of Alaska Anchorage, Matanuska-Susitna Coll (AK)
U of Alaska Southeast, Ketchikan Campus (AK)
U of Arkansas Comm Coll at Hope (AR)
U of Kentucky, Lexington Comm Coll (KY)
U of Northwestern Ohio (OH)
U of Pittsburgh at Titusville (PA)
Utah Career Coll (UT)
Utah Valley State Coll (UT)
Valley Coll of Technology (WV)
Valley Forge Military Coll (PA)
Vance-Granville Comm Coll (NC)
Ventura Coll (CA)
Vermilion Comm Coll (MN)
Victor Valley Coll (CA)
Villa Maria Coll of Buffalo (NY)
Vincennes U (IN)
Virginia Western Comm Coll (VA)
Vista Comm Coll (CA)
Volunteer State Comm Coll (TN)
Walters State Comm Coll (TN)
Washtenaw Comm Coll (MI)
Waubonsee Comm Coll (IL)
Waycross Coll (GA)
Weatherford Coll (TX)
Western Dakota Tech Inst (SD)
Western Iowa Tech Comm Coll (IA)
Western Nevada Comm Coll (NV)
Western Wisconsin Tech Coll (WI)
Western Wyoming Comm Coll (WY)
West Hills Comm Coll (CA)
West Kentucky Comm and Tech Coll (KY)
Westmoreland County Comm Coll (PA)
West Virginia Business Coll, Wheeling (WV)
West Virginia Northern Comm Coll (WV)
Wilson Tech Comm Coll (NC)
Wor-Wic Comm Coll (MD)
Yakima Valley Comm Coll (WA)
Yavapai Coll (AZ)

York County Comm Coll (ME)
York Tech Coll (SC)
Yuba Coll (CA)

Business Administration, Management and Operations Related
Bryant & Stratton Business Inst, Buffalo (NY)
Bryant & Stratton Business Inst, Lackawanna (NY)
Bryant and Stratton Coll (WI)
Bryant & Stratton Business Inst, Amherst Cmps (NY)
Delaware County Comm Coll (PA)
Indiana Business Coll, Anderson (IN)
Indiana Business Coll, Columbus (IN)
Indiana Business Coll, Indianapolis (IN)
Indiana Business Coll, Lafayette (IN)
Indiana Business Coll, Muncie (IN)
Indiana Business Coll, Terre Haute (IN)
Lamar State Coll–Port Arthur (TX)
Lanier Tech Coll (GA)
Massasoit Comm Coll (MA)
Northeast Wisconsin Tech Coll (WI)
Western Wisconsin Tech Coll (WI)

Business and Personal/ Financial Services Marketing
Centralia Coll (WA)
Heartland Comm Coll (IL)
Hesser Coll (NH)
Hutchinson Comm Coll and Area Vocational School (KS)
North Florida Comm Coll (FL)
Northland Pioneer Coll (AZ)
Northwestern Michigan Coll (MI)
Spokane Falls Comm Coll (WA)
Union County Coll (NJ)
Wisconsin Indianhead Tech Coll (WI)

Business Automation/ Technology/Data Entry
Alpena Comm Coll (MI)
Arkansas State U–Mountain Home (AR)
Berkshire Comm Coll (MA)
Bismarck State Coll (ND)
Bristol Comm Coll (MA)
Central Wyoming Coll (WY)
Clark Coll (WA)
Clovis Comm Coll (NM)
Coll of Lake County (IL)
Collin County Comm Coll District (TX)
Comm Coll of Allegheny County (PA)
Crowder Coll (MO)
Delta Coll (MI)
El Centro Coll (TX)
Fayetteville Tech Comm Coll (NC)
Front Range Comm Coll (CO)
Gogebic Comm Coll (MI)
Illinois Eastern Comm Colls, Frontier Comm Coll (IL)
Illinois Eastern Comm Colls, Lincoln Trail Coll (IL)
Illinois Eastern Comm Colls, Olney Central Coll (IL)
Illinois Eastern Comm Colls, Wabash Valley Coll (IL)
Iowa Lakes Comm Coll (IA)
Kaskaskia Coll (IL)
Lincoln Land Comm Coll (IL)
Macomb Comm Coll (MI)
Michiana Coll, South Bend (IN)

Midland Coll (TX)
MTI Coll of Business and Technology, Houston (TX)
Normandale Comm Coll (MN)
Northland Pioneer Coll (AZ)
Northwestern Michigan Coll (MI)
Oakland Comm Coll (MI)
Oklahoma State U, Oklahoma City (OK)
Parkland Coll (IL)
Pennsylvania Coll of Technology (PA)
Tillamook Bay Comm Coll (OR)
The U of Akron–Wayne Coll (OH)
Utah Valley State Coll (UT)
Waubonsee Comm Coll (IL)
Western Nevada Comm Coll (NV)

Business/Commerce
Academy Coll (MN)
Arkansas Northeastern Coll (AR)
Berkeley Coll (NJ)
Berkshire Comm Coll (MA)
Bismarck State Coll (ND)
Centralia Coll (WA)
Coll of Southern Idaho (ID)
Columbia State Comm Coll (TN)
Comm Coll of Rhode Island (RI)
Cuyamaca Coll (CA)
Dawson Comm Coll (MT)
DeKalb Tech Coll (GA)
Del Mar Coll (TX)
Education Direct Center for Degree Studies (PA)
Fairmont State Comm & Tech Coll (WV)
Feather River Comm Coll District (CA)
Gallipolis Career Coll (OH)
Glendale Comm Coll (AZ)
Goodwin Coll (CT)
Great Basin Coll (NV)
Hagerstown Comm Coll (MD)
Harford Comm Coll (MD)
Harrisburg Area Comm Coll (PA)
Hawkeye Comm Coll (IA)
Hutchinson Comm Coll and Area Vocational School (KS)
Jefferson Coll (MO)
Jefferson State Comm Coll (AL)
John Tyler Comm Coll (VA)
John Wood Comm Coll (IL)
Keystone Coll (PA)
Lackawanna Coll (PA)
Laramie County Comm Coll (WY)
Louisiana Tech Coll–Gulf Area Campus (LA)
Lower Columbia Coll (WA)
Macomb Comm Coll (MI)
Manatee Comm Coll (FL)
Mesabi Range Comm and Tech Coll (MN)
Metropolitan Comm Coll-Business & Technology College (MO)
Midland Coll (TX)
Midlands Tech Coll (SC)
Minneapolis Comm and Tech Coll (MN)
Montana State U Coll of Tech-Great Falls (MT)
Montgomery Coll (MD)
Montgomery County Comm Coll (PA)
Moraine Valley Comm Coll (IL)
Mott Comm Coll (MI)
National Coll of Business & Technology, Charlottesville (VA)
National Coll of Business & Technology, Salem (VA)

Northampton County Area Comm Coll (PA)
North Dakota State Coll of Science (ND)
Northland Pioneer Coll (AZ)
Northwest State Comm Coll (OH)
Ocean County Coll (NJ)
Orangeburg-Calhoun Tech Coll (SC)
Owens Comm Coll, Findlay (OH)
Owens Comm Coll, Toledo (OH)
Patricia Stevens Coll (MO)
Penn State U Beaver Campus of the Commonwealth Coll (PA)
Penn State U Delaware County Campus of the Commonwealth Coll (PA)
Penn State U DuBois Campus of the Commonwealth Coll (PA)
Penn State U Fayette Campus of the Commonwealth Coll (PA)
Penn State U Hazleton Campus of the Commonwealth Coll (PA)
Penn State U McKeesport Campus of the Commonwealth Coll (PA)
Penn State U Mont Alto Campus of the Commonwealth Coll (PA)
Penn State U New Kensington Campus of the Commonwealth Coll (PA)
Penn State U Shenango Campus of the Commonwealth Coll (PA)
Penn State U Wilkes-Barre Campus of the Commonwealth Coll (PA)
Penn State U Worthington Scranton Cmps Commonwealth Coll (PA)
Penn State U York Campus of the Commonwealth Coll (PA)
Pensacola Jr Coll (FL)
Sheridan Coll (WY)
Somerset Comm Coll (KY)
South Arkansas Comm Coll (AR)
Southeast Arkansas Coll (AR)
Southern State Comm Coll (OH)
Southwest Missouri State U–West Plains (MO)
Springfield Tech Comm Coll (MA)
Truett-McConnell Coll (GA)
Union County Coll (NJ)
U of Arkansas Comm Coll at Batesville (AR)
Utah Valley State Coll (UT)
Victor Valley Coll (CA)
Vista Comm Coll (CA)
Western Nevada Comm Coll (NV)
Williamsburg Tech Coll (SC)
Wor-Wic Comm Coll (MD)

Business Computer Programming
Barton County Comm Coll (KS)
Coll of Lake County (IL)

Business/Corporate Communications
Houston Comm Coll System (TX)
Middlesex Comm Coll (MA)
Montgomery County Comm Coll (PA)

Business Machine Repair
Cabrillo Coll (CA)
Cañada Coll (CA)
Central Piedmont Comm Coll (NC)
Chabot Coll (CA)

Clover Park Tech Coll (WA)
Coffeyville Comm Coll (KS)
Comm Coll of Allegheny County (PA)
Del Mar Coll (TX)
Dutchess Comm Coll (NY)
ECPI Coll of Technology, Virginia Beach (VA)
ECPI Tech Coll, Richmond (VA)
Iowa Lakes Comm Coll (IA)
Los Angeles Valley Coll (CA)
Minnesota State Coll–Southeast Tech (MN)
Palomar Coll (CA)
Pellissippi State Tech Comm Coll (TN)
Rockingham Comm Coll (NC)
Southern Maine Comm Coll (ME)
Washtenaw Comm Coll (MI)

Business, Management, and Marketing Related
Bristol Comm Coll (MA)
Cincinnati State Tech and Comm Coll (OH)
Eastern Arizona Coll (AZ)
Harrisburg Area Comm Coll (PA)
Heart of Georgia Tech Coll (GA)
Lanier Tech Coll (GA)
Milwaukee Area Tech Coll (WI)
Northeast Wisconsin Tech Coll (WI)
Northwestern Michigan Coll (MI)
Northwest State Comm Coll (OH)
Queensborough Comm Coll of City U of NY (NY)
Southwestern Michigan Coll (MI)
Stautzenberger Coll (OH)

Business/Managerial Economics
Anne Arundel Comm Coll (MD)
Chabot Coll (CA)
Colby Comm Coll (KS)
Coll of the Desert (CA)
Hill Coll of the Hill Jr College District (TX)
Lincoln Coll, Lincoln (IL)
Manatee Comm Coll (FL)
Morgan Comm Coll (CO)
Northeast Mississippi Comm Coll (MS)
San Joaquin Delta Coll (CA)
State U of NY Coll of Technology at Canton (NY)
Vermilion Comm Coll (MN)

Business Operations Support and Secretarial Services Related
Ancilla Coll (IN)
Bowling Green State U-Firelands Coll (OH)
Bristol Comm Coll (MA)
Eastern Arizona Coll (AZ)
Guilford Tech Comm Coll (NC)
Hillsborough Comm Coll (FL)
Laramie County Comm Coll (WY)
Louisiana Tech Coll–Florida Parishes Campus (LA)
MTI Coll of Business and Technology, Houston (TX)
Virginia Coll at Jackson (MS)
Wisconsin Indianhead Tech Coll (WI)

Business Systems Networking/ Telecommunications
Caldwell Comm Coll and Tech Inst (NC)
Coll of Lake County (IL)
Globe Coll (MN)

Minnesota School of Business–Brooklyn Center (MN)
Minnesota School of Business-Plymouth (MN)
Minnesota School of Business-Richfield (MN)

Business Teacher Education
Amarillo Coll (TX)
Bainbridge Coll (GA)
Bristol Comm Coll (MA)
Bronx Comm Coll of City U of NY (NY)
Butte Coll (CA)
Casper Coll (WY)
Chabot Coll (CA)
Coffeyville Comm Coll (KS)
Colby Comm Coll (KS)
Darton Coll (GA)
Delta Coll (MI)
Eastern Arizona Coll (AZ)
Eastern Oklahoma State Coll (OK)
Eastern Wyoming Coll (WY)
East Mississippi Comm Coll (MS)
Essex County Coll (NJ)
Harrisburg Area Comm Coll (PA)
Holmes Comm Coll (MS)
Holyoke Comm Coll (MA)
Iowa Lakes Comm Coll (IA)
Isothermal Comm Coll (NC)
Jefferson Coll (MO)
John A. Logan Coll (IL)
Kirkwood Comm Coll (IA)
Lawson State Comm Coll (AL)
Lincoln Coll, Lincoln (IL)
Merritt Coll (CA)
Mississippi Gulf Coast Comm Coll (MS)
Morgan Comm Coll (CO)
Mountain Empire Comm Coll (VA)
Mt. San Antonio Coll (CA)
Northeast Comm Coll (NE)
Northeast Mississippi Comm Coll (MS)
Northern Essex Comm Coll (MA)
North Idaho Coll (ID)
Northwest Coll (WY)
Palomar Coll (CA)
Paris Jr Coll (TX)
Pasadena City Coll (CA)
Pratt Comm Coll and Area Vocational School (KS)
Prince George's Comm Coll (MD)
Reading Area Comm Coll (PA)
Roane State Comm Coll (TN)
Shelton State Comm Coll (AL)
Snow Coll (UT)
Southwest Mississippi Comm Coll (MS)
Spoon River Coll (IL)
Vincennes U (IN)
Waycross Coll (GA)

Cabinetmaking and Millwork
Coll of Southern Idaho (ID)
Fayetteville Tech Comm Coll (NC)
Illinois Eastern Comm Colls, Olney Central Coll (IL)
Ivy Tech State Coll–Bloomington (IN)
Ivy Tech State Coll–Central Indiana (IN)
Ivy Tech State Coll–Columbus (IN)
Ivy Tech State Coll–Eastcentral (IN)
Ivy Tech State Coll–Kokomo (IN)
Ivy Tech State Coll–Lafayette (IN)
Ivy Tech State Coll–North Central (IN)

Ivy Tech State Coll–Northeast (IN)
Ivy Tech State Coll–0Northwest (IN)
Ivy Tech State Coll–Southcentral (IN)
Ivy Tech State Coll–Southwest (IN)
Ivy Tech State Coll–Wabash Valley (IN)
Ivy Tech State Coll–Whitewater (IN)
Macomb Comm Coll (MI)
Oakland Comm Coll (MI)
Pennsylvania Coll of Technology (PA)
Utah Valley State Coll (UT)

Cad/Cadd Drafting/Design Technology
Alexandria Tech Coll (MN)
Jefferson Coll (MO)
Louisville Tech Inst (KY)
Lower Columbia Coll (WA)
Morrison Inst of Technology (IL)
Oakton Comm Coll (IL)
Owens Comm Coll, Toledo (OH)
St. Philip's Coll (TX)
Silicon Valley Coll, Walnut Creek (CA)
Somerset Comm Coll (KY)
Springfield Tech Comm Coll (MA)
Vatterott Coll, St. Ann (MO)
Vatterott Coll, Springfield (MO)
Westwood Coll–Long Beach (CA)

Cardiovascular Technology
Bunker Hill Comm Coll (MA)
Caldwell Comm Coll and Tech Inst (NC)
Comm Coll of the Air Force (AL)
Darton Coll (GA)
El Centro Coll (TX)
Harrisburg Area Comm Coll (PA)
Howard Comm Coll (MD)
Milwaukee Area Tech Coll (WI)
Northeast State Tech Comm Coll (TN)
North Hennepin Comm Coll (MN)
Orange Coast Coll (CA)
Southern Maine Comm Coll (ME)

Carpentry
Alamance Comm Coll (NC)
Alexandria Tech Coll (MN)
American River Coll (CA)
Bates Tech Coll (WA)
Bismarck State Coll (ND)
Casper Coll (WY)
Cecil Comm Coll (MD)
Clovis Comm Coll (NM)
Coffeyville Comm Coll (KS)
Coll of Eastern Utah (UT)
Coll of the Sequoias (CA)
Comm Coll of Allegheny County (PA)
Comm Coll of Aurora (CO)
Cossatot Comm Coll of the U of Arkansas (AR)
Delta Coll (MI)
Des Moines Area Comm Coll (IA)
Eastern Maine Comm Coll (ME)
Fayetteville Tech Comm Coll (NC)
Forsyth Tech Comm Coll (NC)
Fulton-Montgomery Comm Coll (NY)
Gogebic Comm Coll (MI)
Green River Comm Coll (WA)
Hawaii Comm Coll (HI)
Hinds Comm Coll (MS)
Honolulu Comm Coll (HI)

Hutchinson Comm Coll and Area Vocational School (KS)
Iowa Lakes Comm Coll (IA)
Ivy Tech State Coll–Central Indiana (IN)
Ivy Tech State Coll–Eastcentral (IN)
Ivy Tech State Coll–Lafayette (IN)
Ivy Tech State Coll–North Central (IN)
Ivy Tech State Coll–Northwest (IN)
Ivy Tech State Coll–Southcentral (IN)
Ivy Tech State Coll–Southwest (IN)
Ivy Tech State Coll–Wabash Valley (IN)
Kaskaskia Coll (IL)
Kauai Comm Coll (HI)
Lake Area Tech Inst (SD)
Lake Superior Coll (MN)
Lansing Comm Coll (MI)
Laramie County Comm Coll (WY)
Lawson State Comm Coll (AL)
Los Angeles Trade-Tech Coll (CA)
Mayland Comm Coll (NC)
Metropolitan Comm Coll-Business & Technology College (MO)
Miles Comm Coll (MT)
Minnesota State Coll–Southeast Tech (MN)
Mitchell Tech Inst (SD)
Nebraska Indian Comm Coll (NE)
North Central Missouri Coll (MO)
Northeast Comm Coll (NE)
Northeast Mississippi Comm Coll (MS)
Northeast Wisconsin Tech Coll (WI)
Northern Maine Comm Coll (ME)
North Idaho Coll (ID)
North Iowa Area Comm Coll (IA)
Northland Pioneer Coll (AZ)
Oakland Comm Coll (MI)
Palomar Coll (CA)
Pasadena City Coll (CA)
Pennsylvania Coll of Technology (PA)
Portland Comm Coll (OR)
Ranken Tech Coll (MO)
Red Rocks Comm Coll (CO)
Rockingham Comm Coll (NC)
St. Cloud Tech Coll (MN)
San Diego City Coll (CA)
San Joaquin Delta Coll (CA)
San Juan Coll (NM)
Sierra Coll (CA)
Snow Coll (UT)
Somerset Comm Coll (KY)
Southern Maine Comm Coll (ME)
South Plains Coll (TX)
Southwestern Illinois Coll (IL)
Southwest Mississippi Comm Coll (MS)
Spokane Comm Coll (WA)
State U of NY Coll of Technology at Alfred (NY)
State U of NY Coll of Technology at Canton (NY)
State U of NY Coll of Technology at Delhi (NY)
Trenholm State Tech Coll, Montgomery (AL)
Triangle Tech, Inc. (PA)
Triangle Tech, Inc.–DuBois School (PA)
Triangle Tech, Inc.–Greensburg Center (PA)
Trinidad State Jr Coll (CO)
United Tribes Tech Coll (ND)

Vance-Granville Comm Coll (NC)
Western Nevada Comm Coll (NV)
Wichita Area Tech Coll (KS)
The Williamson Free School of Mecha Trades (PA)

Cartography
Alexandria Tech Coll (MN)
Cabrillo Coll (CA)
Central Oregon Comm Coll (OR)
Houston Comm Coll System (TX)
New Hampshire Comm Tech Coll, Berlin/Laconia (NH)

Ceramic Arts and Ceramics
Cabrillo Coll (CA)
Casper Coll (WY)
Garden City Comm Coll (KS)
Hill Coll of the Hill Jr College District (TX)
Iowa Lakes Comm Coll (IA)
Kirkwood Comm Coll (IA)
Lincoln Coll, Lincoln (IL)
Los Angeles Valley Coll (CA)
Mohave Comm Coll (AZ)
Oakland Comm Coll (MI)
Palm Beach Comm Coll (FL)
Palomar Coll (CA)
Pasadena City Coll (CA)
Ventura Coll (CA)

Ceramic Sciences and Engineering
Pasadena City Coll (CA)

Chemical Engineering
Alpena Comm Coll (MI)
Brevard Comm Coll (FL)
Burlington County Coll (NJ)
Delta Coll (MI)
Gloucester County Coll (NJ)
Itasca Comm Coll (MN)
Lansing Comm Coll (MI)
Los Angeles Trade-Tech Coll (CA)
Milwaukee Area Tech Coll (WI)
Mississippi Gulf Coast Comm Coll (MS)
Naugatuck Valley Comm Coll (CT)
Pellissippi State Tech Comm Coll (TN)
St. Louis Comm Coll at Florissant Valley (MO)
Texas State Tech Coll–Harlingen (TX)
Texas State Tech Coll–Waco/Marshall Campus (TX)

Chemical Technology
Alvin Comm Coll (TX)
Amarillo Coll (TX)
Burlington County Coll (NJ)
Cape Fear Comm Coll (NC)
Cincinnati State Tech and Comm Coll (OH)
Coll of Lake County (IL)
Comm Coll of Allegheny County (PA)
Comm Coll of Rhode Island (RI)
Corning Comm Coll (NY)
County Coll of Morris (NJ)
Del Mar Coll (TX)
Edmonds Comm Coll (WA)
Essex County Coll (NJ)
Jefferson Comm Coll (NY)
Johnson County Comm Coll (KS)
Kalamazoo Valley Comm Coll (MI)
Kellogg Comm Coll (MI)
Lehigh Carbon Comm Coll (PA)
Mohawk Valley Comm Coll (NY)
Northampton County Area Comm Coll (PA)
Pellissippi State Tech Comm Coll (TN)

Pensacola Jr Coll (FL)
St. Johns River Comm Coll (FL)
Texas State Tech Coll–Waco/Marshall Campus (TX)

Chemistry
Abraham Baldwin Ag Coll (GA)
Alpena Comm Coll (MI)
Amarillo Coll (TX)
Ancilla Coll (IN)
Andrew Coll (GA)
Anne Arundel Comm Coll (MD)
Arizona Western Coll (AZ)
Atlanta Metropolitan Coll (GA)
Atlantic Cape Comm Coll (NJ)
Austin Comm Coll (TX)
Bainbridge Coll (GA)
Barton County Comm Coll (KS)
Bergen Comm Coll (NJ)
Bronx Comm Coll of City U of NY (NY)
Brookdale Comm Coll (NJ)
Bucks County Comm Coll (PA)
Bunker Hill Comm Coll (MA)
Burlington County Coll (NJ)
Butler County Comm Coll (KS)
Cañada Coll (CA)
Casper Coll (WY)
Centralia Coll (WA)
Chabot Coll (CA)
Clarendon Coll (TX)
Coastal Bend Coll (TX)
Coastal Georgia Comm Coll (GA)
Coffeyville Comm Coll (KS)
Colby Comm Coll (KS)
Coll of Southern Idaho (ID)
Coll of the Canyons (CA)
Coll of the Desert (CA)
Coll of the Sequoias (CA)
Columbia Coll (CA)
Columbia State Comm Coll (TN)
Comm Coll of Allegheny County (PA)
Connors State Coll (OK)
Contra Costa Coll (CA)
Copiah-Lincoln Comm Coll (MS)
Cuesta Coll (CA)
Cuyamaca Coll (CA)
Darton Coll (GA)
Daytona Beach Comm Coll (FL)
Del Mar Coll (TX)
Delta Coll (MI)
Eastern Arizona Coll (AZ)
Eastern Oklahoma State Coll (OK)
East Los Angeles Coll (CA)
El Camino Coll (CA)
Essex County Coll (NJ)
Everett Comm Coll (WA)
Finger Lakes Comm Coll (NY)
Foothill Coll (CA)
Frederick Comm Coll (MD)
Gavilan Coll (CA)
Georgia Perimeter Coll (GA)
Gloucester County Coll (NJ)
Great Basin Coll (NV)
Harrisburg Area Comm Coll (PA)
Hill Coll of the Hill Jr College District (TX)
Hiwassee Coll (TN)
Holyoke Comm Coll (MA)
Howard Coll (TX)
Iowa Lakes Comm Coll (IA)
John A. Logan Coll (IL)
Kellogg Comm Coll (MI)
Kingsborough Comm Coll of City U of NY (NY)
Lansing Comm Coll (MI)
Laramie County Comm Coll (WY)

Lawson State Comm Coll (AL)
Lincoln Coll, Lincoln (IL)
Linn-Benton Comm Coll (OR)
Longview Comm Coll (MO)
Lon Morris Coll (TX)
Lorain County Comm Coll (OH)
Macomb Comm Coll (MI)
Manatee Comm Coll (FL)
Maple Woods Comm Coll (MO)
Miami Dade Coll (FL)
Middlesex County Coll (NJ)
Midland Coll (TX)
Mid Michigan Comm Coll (MI)
MiraCosta Coll (CA)
Mountain Empire Comm Coll (VA)
Northampton County Area Comm Coll (PA)
Northeast Comm Coll (NE)
Northeastern Oklahoma A&M Coll (OK)
Northeast Mississippi Comm Coll (MS)
Northeast State Tech Comm Coll (TN)
North Idaho Coll (ID)
Northwest Coll (WY)
Odessa Coll (TX)
Oklahoma City Comm Coll (OK)
Orange Coast Coll (CA)
Palm Beach Comm Coll (FL)
Palo Alto Coll (TX)
Palomar Coll (CA)
Pasadena City Coll (CA)
Penn Valley Comm Coll (MO)
Pensacola Jr Coll (FL)
Pratt Comm Coll and Area Vocational School (KS)
Raritan Valley Comm Coll (NJ)
Reading Area Comm Coll (PA)
Red Rocks Comm Coll (CO)
Rend Lake Coll (IL)
Riverside Comm Coll (CA)
Roane State Comm Coll (TN)
St. Philip's Coll (TX)
Salem Comm Coll (NJ)
San Joaquin Delta Coll (CA)
San Juan Coll (NM)
Santa Barbara City Coll (CA)
Santa Monica Coll (CA)
Sauk Valley Comm Coll (IL)
Seward County Comm Coll (KS)
Shelton State Comm Coll (AL)
Sierra Coll (CA)
Snow Coll (UT)
South Plains Coll (TX)
South Suburban Coll (IL)
Southwestern Coll (CA)
Southwest Mississippi Comm Coll (MS)
Spoon River Coll (IL)
Springfield Tech Comm Coll (MA)
State U of NY Coll of A&T at Morrisville (NY)
Terra State Comm Coll (OH)
Trinidad State Jr Coll (CO)
Triton Coll (IL)
Umpqua Comm Coll (OR)
Union County Coll (NJ)
Vermilion Comm Coll (MN)
Vincennes U (IN)
Waycross Coll (GA)
Western Wyoming Comm Coll (WY)
West Hills Coll (CA)
Yuba Coll (CA)

Chemistry Related
Guilford Tech Comm Coll (NC)

Chemistry Teacher Education
Manatee Comm Coll (FL)

Child Care and Guidance Related
Albany Tech Coll (GA)

Child Care and Support Services Management
Academy of Medical Arts and Business (PA)
Albuquerque Tech Vocational Inst (NM)
Alexandria Tech Coll (MN)
Anoka Tech Coll (MN)
Arapahoe Comm Coll (CO)
Arkansas Northeastern Coll (AR)
Asheville-Buncombe Tech Comm Coll (NC)
Barton County Comm Coll (KS)
Broome Comm Coll (NY)
Calhoun Comm Coll (AL)
Cape Fear Comm Coll (NC)
Central Carolina Tech Coll (SC)
Central Florida Comm Coll (FL)
Central Georgia Tech Coll (GA)
Centralia Coll (WA)
Central Wyoming Coll (WY)
Coll of DuPage (IL)
Colorado Northwestern Comm Coll (CO)
Dakota County Tech Coll (MN)
Dawson Comm Coll (MT)
Eastfield Coll (TX)
Edmonds Comm Coll (WA)
Education Direct Center for Degree Studies (PA)
Erie Comm Coll (NY)
Fayetteville Tech Comm Coll (NC)
Feather River Comm Coll District (CA)
Front Range Comm Coll (CO)
Gadsden State Comm Coll (AL)
Gogebic Comm Coll (MI)
Green River Comm Coll (WA)
Hagerstown Comm Coll (MD)
Harford Comm Coll (MD)
Hesser Coll (NH)
Hopkinsville Comm Coll (KY)
Houston Comm Coll System (TX)
Hutchinson Comm Coll and Area Vocational School (KS)
Ivy Tech State Coll–Bloomington (IN)
Ivy Tech State Coll–Central Indiana (IN)
Ivy Tech State Coll–Columbus (IN)
Ivy Tech State Coll–Eastcentral (IN)
Ivy Tech State Coll–Kokomo (IN)
Ivy Tech State Coll–Lafayette (IN)
Ivy Tech State Coll–North Central (IN)
Ivy Tech State Coll–Northeast (IN)
Ivy Tech State Coll–Northwest (IN)
Ivy Tech State Coll–Southcentral (IN)
Ivy Tech State Coll–Southeast (IN)
Ivy Tech State Coll–Southwest (IN)
Ivy Tech State Coll–Wabash Valley (IN)
Ivy Tech State Coll–Whitewater (IN)
Jefferson Coll (MO)

Jefferson Comm Coll (OH)
Jefferson State Comm Coll (AL)
J. Sargeant Reynolds Comm Coll (VA)
Kansas City Kansas Comm Coll (KS)
Kishwaukee Coll (IL)
Lake Land Coll (IL)
Lake Region State Coll (ND)
Linn-Benton Comm Coll (OR)
Macomb Comm Coll (MI)
Massasoit Comm Coll (MA)
McHenry County Coll (IL)
MiraCosta Coll (CA)
Modesto Jr Coll (CA)
Montcalm Comm Coll (MI)
Montgomery Coll (MD)
Montgomery County Comm Coll (PA)
Normandale Comm Coll (MN)
Northampton County Area Comm Coll (PA)
Northeast Wisconsin Tech Coll (WI)
Northland Pioneer Coll (AZ)
Northwestern Michigan Coll (MI)
Oakland Comm Coll (MI)
Ocean County Coll (NJ)
Olympic Coll (WA)
Orange Coast Coll (CA)
Ouachita Tech Coll (AR)
Peninsula Coll (WA)
Pennsylvania Coll of Technology (PA)
Pima Comm Coll (AZ)
Pitt Comm Coll (NC)
Rasmussen Coll Mankato (MN)
Richmond Comm Coll (NC)
St. Cloud Tech Coll (MN)
Santa Barbara City Coll (CA)
Schoolcraft Coll (MI)
Snead State Comm Coll (AL)
Southwestern Michigan Coll (MI)
Spokane Falls Comm Coll (WA)
Stanly Comm Coll (NC)
Trenholm State Tech Coll, Montgomery (AL)
Victor Valley Coll (CA)
Vincennes U (IN)
Western Iowa Tech Comm Coll (IA)
Western Nevada Comm Coll (NV)
Wisconsin Indianhead Tech Coll (WI)
Wor-Wic Comm Coll (MD)
York Tech Coll (SC)

Child Care/Guidance
Bristol Comm Coll (MA)
Caldwell Comm Coll and Tech Inst (NC)
Feather River Comm Coll District (CA)

Child Care Provider
Coll of Lake County (IL)

Child Care Provision
Academy of Medical Arts and Business (PA)
Alexandria Tech Coll (MN)
Arapahoe Comm Coll (CO)
Bates Tech Coll (WA)
Bladen Comm Coll (NC)
Brunswick Comm Coll (NC)
Central Florida Comm Coll (FL)
Cincinnati State Tech and Comm Coll (OH)
City Colls of Chicago, Malcolm X Coll (IL)
Coastal Carolina Comm Coll (NC)
Coll of DuPage (IL)
Comm Coll of Allegheny County (PA)
Corning Comm Coll (NY)

Dakota County Tech Coll (MN)
Eastern Arizona Coll (AZ)
Fayetteville Tech Comm Coll (NC)
Gulf Coast Comm Coll (FL)
Heartland Comm Coll (IL)
Hill Coll of the Hill Jr College District (TX)
Iowa Lakes Comm Coll (IA)
Lake Region State Coll (ND)
Lehigh Carbon Comm Coll (PA)
Lincoln Land Comm Coll (IL)
Luzerne County Comm Coll (PA)
Massasoit Comm Coll (MA)
McHenry County Coll (IL)
Midland Coll (TX)
Midlands Tech Coll (SC)
Mid Michigan Comm Coll (MI)
Mineral Area Coll (MO)
Modesto Jr Coll (CA)
Montcalm Comm Coll (MI)
Moraine Valley Comm Coll (IL)
Mott Comm Coll (MI)
Northland Pioneer Coll (AZ)
Orange Coast Coll (CA)
Parkland Coll (IL)
Pennsylvania Coll of Technology (PA)
Penn Valley Comm Coll (MO)
Pima Comm Coll (AZ)
Rasmussen Coll Mankato (MN)
Southern Arkansas U Tech (AR)
Tompkins Cortland Comm Coll (NY)
Trident Tech Coll (SC)
Triton Coll (IL)
United Tribes Tech Coll (ND)
U of Arkansas Comm Coll at Hope (AR)
Vincennes U (IN)
Waubonsee Comm Coll (IL)
Western Wisconsin Tech Coll (WI)
York Tech Coll (SC)

Child Development
Abraham Baldwin Ag Coll (GA)
Alvin Comm Coll (TX)
Amarillo Coll (TX)
American River Coll (CA)
Atlanta Metropolitan Coll (GA)
Atlantic Cape Comm Coll (NJ)
Augusta Tech Coll (GA)
Borough of Manhattan Comm Coll of City U of NY (NY)
Briarwood Coll (CT)
Bronx Comm Coll of City U of NY (NY)
Butler County Comm Coll (KS)
Cabrillo Coll (CA)
Central Arizona Coll (AZ)
Central Comm Coll–Grand Island Campus (NE)
Central Comm Coll–Hastings Campus (NE)
Centralia Coll (WA)
Central Pennsylvania Coll (PA)
Central Piedmont Comm Coll (NC)
Cleveland State Comm Coll (TN)
Coastal Bend Coll (TX)
Colby Comm Coll (KS)
Coll of DuPage (IL)
Coll of Eastern Utah (UT)
Coll of Southern Idaho (ID)
Coll of the Canyons (CA)
Colorado Mountn Coll, Timberline Cmps (CO)
Columbus State Comm Coll (OH)

Comm Coll of Allegheny County (PA)
Connors State Coll (OK)
Copiah-Lincoln Comm Coll (MS)
Cuesta Coll (CA)
Daytona Beach Comm Coll (FL)
Dean Coll (MA)
Del Mar Coll (TX)
Delta Coll (MI)
Des Moines Area Comm Coll (IA)
Durham Tech Comm Coll (NC)
Dutchess Comm Coll (NY)
Eastern Wyoming Coll (WY)
East Los Angeles Coll (CA)
Fairmont State Comm & Tech Coll (WV)
Foothill Coll (CA)
Forsyth Tech Comm Coll (NC)
Frederick Comm Coll (MD)
Garden City Comm Coll (KS)
Gavilan Coll (CA)
Gogebic Comm Coll (MI)
Harcum Coll (PA)
Hawkeye Comm Coll (IA)
Heartland Comm Coll (IL)
Hill Coll of the Hill Jr College District (TX)
Hillsborough Comm Coll (FL)
Hinds Comm Coll (MS)
Holmes Comm Coll (MS)
Houston Comm Coll System (TX)
Howard Coll (TX)
Howard Comm Coll (MD)
Hudson County Comm Coll (NJ)
Illinois Eastern Comm Colls, Wabash Valley Coll (IL)
Indian Hills Comm Coll (IA)
Iowa Lakes Comm Coll (IA)
Jackson State Comm Coll (TN)
James A. Rhodes State Coll (OH)
Jefferson Comm Coll (KY)
Kirkwood Comm Coll (IA)
Lake Washington Tech Coll (WA)
Lamar State Coll–Port Arthur (TX)
Lansing Comm Coll (MI)
Laredo Comm Coll (TX)
Lewis and Clark Comm Coll (IL)
Los Angeles Valley Coll (CA)
Marshalltown Comm Coll (IA)
Merritt Coll (CA)
Metropolitan Comm Coll (NE)
Miami Dade Coll (FL)
Middlesex County Coll (NJ)
Mid Michigan Comm Coll (MI)
Milwaukee Area Tech Coll (WI)
Minnesota State Coll–Southeast Tech (MN)
Mitchell Comm Coll (NC)
Modesto Jr Coll (CA)
Monroe County Comm Coll (MI)
Mt. San Antonio Coll (CA)
Napa Valley Coll (CA)
New Hampshire Comm Tech Coll, Manchester/Stratham (NH)
New River Comm Coll (VA)
Northeastern Oklahoma A&M Coll (OK)
Northeast Mississippi Comm Coll (MS)
North Harris Coll (TX)
Northland Pioneer Coll (AZ)
North Shore Comm Coll (MA)
Northwestern Connecticut Comm-Tech Coll (CT)

Northwest-Shoals Comm Coll (AL)
Northwest State Comm Coll (OH)
Odessa Coll (TX)
Oklahoma City Comm Coll (OK)
Orange County Comm Coll (NY)
Otero Jr Coll (CO)
Oxnard Coll (CA)
Peninsula Coll (WA)
Pensacola Jr Coll (FL)
Pikes Peak Comm Coll (CO)
Polk Comm Coll (FL)
Portland Comm Coll (OR)
Pratt Comm Coll and Area Vocational School (KS)
Rasmussen Coll Mankato (MN)
Rasmussen Coll Minnetonka (MN)
Reading Area Comm Coll (PA)
Rend Lake Coll (IL)
Riverside Comm Coll (CA)
Rockingham Comm Coll (NC)
Rogue Comm Coll (OR)
Saint Charles Comm Coll (MO)
St. Clair County Comm Coll (MI)
St. Cloud Tech Coll (MN)
St. Louis Comm Coll at Florissant Valley (MO)
Saint Paul Coll–A Comm & Tech College (MN)
San Joaquin Delta Coll (CA)
San Jose City Coll (CA)
Seminole Comm Coll (FL)
Seward County Comm Coll (KS)
Sinclair Comm Coll (OH)
Snow Coll (UT)
Southeast Comm Coll, Lincoln Campus (NE)
Southern Maine Comm Coll (ME)
South Plains Coll (TX)
South Suburban Coll (IL)
Southwestern Comm Coll (NC)
Southwestern Illinois Coll (IL)
Spoon River Coll (IL)
Stark State Coll of Technology (OH)
Tompkins Cortland Comm Coll (NY)
Umpqua Comm Coll (OR)
Vance-Granville Comm Coll (NC)
Victor Valley Coll (CA)
Vincennes U (IN)
Virginia Western Comm Coll (VA)
Walters State Comm Coll (TN)
Washtenaw Comm Coll (MI)
Western Wisconsin Tech Coll (WI)
West Hills Comm Coll (CA)
Westmoreland County Comm Coll (PA)
Yakima Valley Comm Coll (WA)
Yuba Coll (CA)

Child Guidance
Cuyamaca Coll (CA)
Dutchess Comm Coll (NY)
Elizabethtown Comm Coll (KY)
Gulf Coast Comm Coll (FL)
Ivy Tech State Coll–Central Indiana (IN)
John Wood Comm Coll (IL)
Lamar State Coll–Port Arthur (TX)
Lincoln Land Comm Coll (IL)
Manatee Comm Coll (FL)
Minneapolis Comm and Tech Coll (MN)
Moberly Area Comm Coll (MO)

Moraine Park Tech Coll (WI)
Northland Pioneer Coll (AZ)
Rochester Comm and Tech Coll (MN)

Chiropractic Assistant
Barton County Comm Coll (KS)
Iowa Lakes Comm Coll (IA)
Sauk Valley Comm Coll (IL)

Cinematography and Film/Video Production
Anne Arundel Comm Coll (MD)
The Art Inst of New York City (NY)
The Art Inst of Philadelphia (PA)
The Art Inst of Pittsburgh (PA)
Bucks County Comm Coll (PA)
Cincinnati State Tech and Comm Coll (OH)
Coll of DuPage (IL)
Coll of the Canyons (CA)
Cumberland County Coll (NJ)
Daytona Beach Comm Coll (FL)
Everett Comm Coll (WA)
Full Sail Real World Education (FL)
Glendale Comm Coll (AZ)
Guilford Tech Comm Coll (NC)
Holyoke Comm Coll (MA)
Lansing Comm Coll (MI)
Miami Dade Coll (FL)
Minneapolis Comm and Tech Coll (MN)
Orange Coast Coll (CA)
Pellissippi State Tech Comm Coll (TN)
Platt Coll San Diego (CA)
St. Louis Comm Coll at Florissant Valley (MO)
Southern Maine Comm Coll (ME)

Civil Drafting and Cad/Cadd
Comm Coll of Allegheny County (PA)
North Seattle Comm Coll (WA)

Civil Engineering
Itasca Comm Coll (MN)

Civil Engineering Related
Bristol Comm Coll (MA)

Civil Engineering Technology
Asheville-Buncombe Tech Comm Coll (NC)
Bates Tech Coll (WA)
Big Bend Comm Coll (WA)
Bristol Comm Coll (MA)
Broome Comm Coll (NY)
Burlington County Coll (NJ)
Butte Coll (CA)
Central Arizona Coll (AZ)
Central Carolina Tech Coll (SC)
Centralia Coll (WA)
Central Piedmont Comm Coll (NC)
Chabot Coll (CA)
Chemeketa Comm Coll (OR)
Cincinnati State Tech and Comm Coll (OH)
Clark State Comm Coll (OH)
Coll of Lake County (IL)
Columbus State Comm Coll (OH)
Comm Coll of Allegheny County (PA)
Copiah-Lincoln Comm Coll (MS)
Daytona Beach Comm Coll (FL)
Delaware Tech & Comm Coll, Terry Cmps (DE)
Delgado Comm Coll (LA)

Des Moines Area Comm Coll (IA)
Eastern Arizona Coll (AZ)
East Los Angeles Coll (CA)
Education Direct Center for Degree Studies (PA)
Essex County Coll (NJ)
Everett Comm Coll (WA)
Fairmont State Comm & Tech Coll (WV)
Fayetteville Tech Comm Coll (NC)
Gadsden State Comm Coll (AL)
Gaston Coll (NC)
Gloucester County Coll (NJ)
Guilford Tech Comm Coll (NC)
Gulf Coast Comm Coll (FL)
Harrisburg Area Comm Coll (PA)
Hawkeye Comm Coll (IA)
Hill Coll of the Hill Jr College District (TX)
Hinds Comm Coll (MS)
Houston Comm Coll System (TX)
James A. Rhodes State Coll (OH)
Jefferson Coll (MO)
Johnson County Comm Coll (KS)
J. Sargeant Reynolds Comm Coll (VA)
Lake Land Coll (IL)
Lakeland Comm Coll (OH)
Lake Superior Coll (MN)
Lansing Comm Coll (MI)
Laramie County Comm Coll (WY)
Linn-Benton Comm Coll (OR)
Linn State Tech Coll (MO)
Lorain County Comm Coll (OH)
Lord Fairfax Comm Coll (VA)
Los Angeles Valley Coll (CA)
Macomb Comm Coll (MI)
Manatee Comm Coll (FL)
Metropolitan Comm Coll (NE)
Miami Dade Coll (FL)
Middlesex County Coll (NJ)
Midlands Tech Coll (SC)
Milwaukee Area Tech Coll (WI)
Mohawk Valley Comm Coll (NY)
Montgomery Coll (MD)
Moraine Park Tech Coll (WI)
Mt. San Antonio Coll (CA)
Nashville State Tech Comm Coll (TN)
Nassau Comm Coll (NY)
North Dakota State Coll of Science (ND)
Northeast Mississippi Comm Coll (MS)
Northeast Wisconsin Tech Coll (WI)
Northern Essex Comm Coll (MA)
Ocean County Coll (NJ)
Oklahoma State U, Oklahoma City (OK)
Pasadena City Coll (CA)
Pellissippi State Tech Comm Coll (TN)
Peninsula Coll (WA)
Pennsylvania Coll of Technology (PA)
Pensacola Jr Coll (FL)
Phoenix Coll (AZ)
Portland Comm Coll (OR)
Rochester Comm and Tech Coll (MN)
St. Cloud Tech Coll (MN)
St. Louis Comm Coll at Florissant Valley (MO)
Saint Paul Coll–A Comm & Tech College (MN)
San Joaquin Delta Coll (CA)
Seminole Comm Coll (FL)
Sinclair Comm Coll (OH)

Spartanburg Tech Coll (SC)
Spokane Comm Coll (WA)
Springfield Tech Comm Coll (MA)
Stark State Coll of Technology (OH)
State U of NY Coll of Technology at Alfred (NY)
State U of NY Coll of Technology at Canton (NY)
Trident Tech Coll (SC)
Trinidad State Jr Coll (CO)
Umpqua Comm Coll (OR)
Union County Coll (NJ)
U of Kentucky, Lexington Comm Coll (KY)
Vincennes U (IN)
Virginia Western Comm Coll (VA)
Yakima Valley Comm Coll (WA)

Civil/Structural Drafting
Luna Comm Coll (NM)

Classics and Languages, Literatures And Linguistics
Foothill Coll (CA)

Clinical Laboratory Science/ Medical Technology
Amarillo Coll (TX)
Andrew Coll (GA)
Anne Arundel Comm Coll (MD)
Arapahoe Comm Coll (CO)
Butte Coll (CA)
Casper Coll (WY)
Central Piedmont Comm Coll (NC)
CHI Inst (PA)
Chipola Coll (FL)
Coll of Southern Idaho (ID)
Columbus State Comm Coll (OH)
Cuyahoga Comm Coll (OH)
Darton Coll (GA)
Del Mar Coll (TX)
Eastern Oklahoma State Coll (OK)
Edison Comm Coll (FL)
El Centro Coll (TX)
Fort Scott Comm Coll (KS)
Henderson Comm Coll (KY)
Hiwassee Coll (TN)
Holmes Comm Coll (MS)
Holyoke Comm Coll (MA)
Howard Comm Coll (MD)
Labouré Coll (MA)
Lansing Comm Coll (MI)
Lawson State Comm Coll (AL)
Mineral Area Coll (MO)
Monroe County Comm Coll (MI)
Northeast Mississippi Comm Coll (MS)
North Idaho Coll (ID)
Northwest-Shoals Comm Coll (AL)
Orange Coast Coll (CA)
Pensacola Jr Coll (FL)
Phoenix Coll (AZ)
Reading Area Comm Coll (PA)
South Texas Comm Coll (TX)
Temple Coll (TX)
Vincennes U (IN)
Waycross Coll (GA)

Clinical/Medical Laboratory Assistant
Allegany Coll of Maryland (MD)
Clover Park Tech Coll (WA)
Columbus State Comm Coll (OH)
Harrisburg Area Comm Coll (PA)
IntelliTec Coll, Grand Junction (CO)
Riverside Comm Coll (CA)
Somerset Comm Coll (KY)

Clinical/Medical Laboratory Science and Allied Professions Related
Oakland Comm Coll (MI)

Clinical/Medical Laboratory Technology
Alamance Comm Coll (NC)
Albuquerque Tech Vocational Inst (NM)
Alexandria Tech Coll (MN)
Allegany Coll of Maryland (MD)
Arapahoe Comm Coll (CO)
Arkansas State U–Beebe (AR)
Asheville-Buncombe Tech Comm Coll (NC)
Austin Comm Coll (TX)
Barton County Comm Coll (KS)
Beaufort County Comm Coll (NC)
Bergen Comm Coll (NJ)
Bismarck State Coll (ND)
Brevard Comm Coll (FL)
Bristol Comm Coll (MA)
Bronx Comm Coll of City U of NY (NY)
Brookdale Comm Coll (NJ)
Broome Comm Coll (NY)
Camden County Coll (NJ)
Central Georgia Tech Coll (GA)
Central Piedmont Comm Coll (NC)
Cincinnati State Tech and Comm Coll (OH)
City Colls of Chicago, Malcolm X Coll (IL)
Clark State Comm Coll (OH)
Clinton Comm Coll (NY)
Coastal Carolina Comm Coll (NC)
Coastal Georgia Comm Coll (GA)
Columbia State Comm Coll (TN)
Columbus State Comm Coll (OH)
Comm Coll of Allegheny County (PA)
Comm Coll of Rhode Island (RI)
Comm Coll of the Air Force (AL)
Copiah-Lincoln Comm Coll (MS)
County Coll of Morris (NJ)
DeKalb Tech Coll (GA)
Delgado Comm Coll (LA)
Del Mar Coll (TX)
Des Moines Area Comm Coll (IA)
Dutchess Comm Coll (NY)
Eastern Oklahoma State Coll (OK)
El Centro Coll (TX)
Elgin Comm Coll (IL)
Eugenio María de Hostos Comm Coll of City U of NY (NY)
Gadsden State Comm Coll (AL)
Guilford Tech Comm Coll (NC)
Harcum Coll (PA)
Harrisburg Area Comm Coll (PA)
Hawkeye Comm Coll (IA)
Hibbing Comm Coll (MN)
Hinds Comm Coll (MS)
Houston Comm Coll System (TX)
Ivy Tech State Coll–North Central (IN)
Ivy Tech State Coll–Wabash Valley (IN)
Jackson State Comm Coll (TN)
Jamestown Comm Coll (NY)
Jefferson State Comm Coll (AL)
John A. Logan Coll (IL)
John Wood Comm Coll (IL)

J. Sargeant Reynolds Comm Coll (VA)
Kapiolani Comm Coll (HI)
Kellogg Comm Coll (MI)
Lake Area Tech Inst (SD)
Lake City Comm Coll (FL)
Lakeland Comm Coll (OH)
Lake Superior Coll (MN)
Lamar State Coll–Orange (TX)
Laredo Comm Coll (TX)
Lehigh Carbon Comm Coll (PA)
Lorain County Comm Coll (OH)
Manchester Comm Coll (CT)
Marion Tech Coll (OH)
McLennan Comm Coll (TX)
Meridian Comm Coll (MS)
Miami Dade Coll (FL)
Middlesex County Coll (NJ)
Midlands Tech Coll (SC)
Mid-Plains Comm Coll, North Platte (NE)
Milwaukee Area Tech Coll (WI)
Mineral Area Coll (MO)
Minnesota State Comm and Tech Coll–Fergus Falls (MN)
Minnesota West Comm & Tech Coll-Pipestone Cmps (MN)
Mississippi Gulf Coast Comm Coll (MS)
Mitchell Tech Inst (SD)
Montgomery County Comm Coll (PA)
Nassau Comm Coll (NY)
North Arkansas Coll (AR)
Northeast Iowa Comm Coll (IA)
Northeast Mississippi Comm Coll (MS)
Northeast Wisconsin Tech Coll (WI)
North Hennepin Comm Coll (MN)
North Iowa Area Comm Coll (IA)
Oakton Comm Coll (IL)
Ocean County Coll (NJ)
Odessa Coll (TX)
Ohio State U Ag Tech Inst (OH)
Okefenokee Tech Coll (GA)
Orangeburg-Calhoun Tech Coll (SC)
Orange County Comm Coll (NY)
Penn State U Hazleton Campus of the Commonwealth Coll (PA)
Phoenix Coll (AZ)
Portland Comm Coll (OR)
Queensborough Comm Coll of City U of NY (NY)
Reading Area Comm Coll (PA)
Rend Lake Coll (IL)
Roane State Comm Coll (TN)
Rochester Comm and Tech Coll (MN)
Saint Paul Coll–A Comm & Tech College (MN)
St. Petersburg Coll (FL)
St. Philip's Coll (TX)
Seward County Comm Coll (KS)
Shelton State Comm Coll (AL)
South Arkansas Comm Coll (AR)
Southeast Comm Coll (KY)
Southeast Comm Coll, Lincoln Campus (NE)
Southeastern Comm Coll (NC)
Southern West Virginia Comm and Tech Coll (WV)
Southwestern Comm Coll (NC)
Southwestern Illinois Coll (IL)

Spartanburg Tech Coll (SC)
Springfield Tech Comm Coll (MA)
Stark State Coll of Technology (OH)
State U of NY Coll of A&T at Morrisville (NY)
State U of NY Coll of Technology at Canton (NY)
Temple Coll (TX)
Thomas Nelson Comm Coll (VA)
Three Rivers Comm Coll (MO)
Trident Tech Coll (SC)
Union County Coll (NJ)
Vincennes U (IN)
Walters State Comm Coll (TN)
Waycross Coll (GA)
Western Iowa Tech Comm Coll (IA)
Western Nevada Comm Coll (NV)
Western Wisconsin Tech Coll (WI)
Wichita Area Tech Coll (KS)
York Tech Coll (SC)

Clinical/Medical Social Work
Central Comm Coll–Grand Island Campus (NE)
Central Comm Coll–Hastings Campus (NE)
Dawson Comm Coll (MT)

Clothing/Textiles
Central Alabama Comm Coll (AL)
El Centro Coll (TX)
Hinds Comm Coll (MS)
Lawson State Comm Coll (AL)
Northeastern Oklahoma A&M Coll (OK)
Northland Pioneer Coll (AZ)
Palm Beach Comm Coll (FL)
Trenholm State Tech Coll, Montgomery (AL)

Commercial and Advertising Art
Academy Coll (MN)
Alamance Comm Coll (NC)
Alexandria Tech Coll (MN)
Amarillo Coll (TX)
Antonelli Coll (OH)
Antonelli Inst (PA)
Arapahoe Comm Coll (CO)
The Art Inst of Houston (TX)
The Art Inst of Philadelphia (PA)
The Art Inst of Pittsburgh (PA)
The Art Insts International Minnesota (MN)
Asnuntuck Comm Coll (CT)
Austin Comm Coll (TX)
Bergen Comm Coll (NJ)
Bismarck State Coll (ND)
Brookdale Comm Coll (NJ)
Bryant & Stratton Business Inst, Amherst Cmps (NY)
Bucks County Comm Coll (PA)
Burlington County Coll (NJ)
Butte Coll (CA)
Casper Coll (WY)
Central Comm Coll–Columbus Campus (NE)
Central Comm Coll–Hastings Campus (NE)
Centralia Coll (WA)
Central Piedmont Comm Coll (NC)
Chabot Coll (CA)
CHI Inst (PA)
Cincinnati State Tech and Comm Coll (OH)
Clark State Comm Coll (OH)
Clovis Comm Coll (NM)
Coastal Bend Coll (TX)
Colby Comm Coll (KS)
Coll of DuPage (IL)
Coll of Southern Idaho (ID)
Coll of the Sequoias (CA)

Collin County Comm Coll District (TX)
Colorado Mountn Coll (CO)
Columbus State Comm Coll (OH)
Comm Coll of Allegheny County (PA)
Comm Coll of Aurora (CO)
Comm Coll of Denver (CO)
Comm Coll of the Air Force (AL)
County Coll of Morris (NJ)
Cuyahoga Comm Coll (OH)
Cuyamaca Coll (CA)
Dakota County Tech Coll (MN)
Davis Coll (OH)
Daytona Beach Comm Coll (FL)
Delaware County Comm Coll (PA)
Delgado Comm Coll (LA)
Delta Coll of Arts and Technology (LA)
Des Moines Area Comm Coll (IA)
Dutchess Comm Coll (NY)
Eastern Arizona Coll (AZ)
Edison State Comm Coll (OH)
Elgin Comm Coll (IL)
Everett Comm Coll (WA)
Fashion Inst of Design & Merchandising, LA Campus (CA)
Fashion Inst of Design & Merchandising, SD Campus (CA)
Fashion Inst of Design & Merchandising, SF Campus (CA)
Fayetteville Tech Comm Coll (NC)
Finger Lakes Comm Coll (NY)
Foothill Coll (CA)
Forsyth Tech Comm Coll (NC)
Fort Scott Comm Coll (KS)
Full Sail Real World Education (FL)
Fulton-Montgomery Comm Coll (NY)
Garden City Comm Coll (KS)
Glendale Comm Coll (AZ)
Gogebic Comm Coll (MI)
Greenfield Comm Coll (MA)
Guilford Tech Comm Coll (NC)
Hagerstown Comm Coll (MD)
Harford Comm Coll (MD)
Harrisburg Area Comm Coll (PA)
Hawkeye Comm Coll (IA)
Hesser Coll (NH)
Hill Coll of the Hill Jr College District (TX)
Hillsborough Comm Coll (FL)
Hinds Comm Coll (MS)
Holyoke Comm Coll (MA)
Honolulu Comm Coll (HI)
Houston Comm Coll System (TX)
Hussian School of Art (PA)
Iowa Lakes Comm Coll (IA)
Isothermal Comm Coll (NC)
Jackson State Comm Coll (TN)
James H. Faulkner State Comm Coll (AL)
James Sprunt Comm Coll (NC)
Jefferson Comm Coll (KY)
J. F. Drake State Tech Coll (AL)
Johnson County Comm Coll (KS)
Johnston Comm Coll (NC)
Kalamazoo Valley Comm Coll (MI)
Kellogg Comm Coll (MI)
Kingsborough Comm Coll of City U of NY (NY)

Lakeland Comm Coll (OH)
Lake-Sumter Comm Coll (FL)
Lansing Comm Coll (MI)
Lehigh Carbon Comm Coll (PA)
Lenoir Comm Coll (NC)
Lincoln Coll, Lincoln (IL)
Linn-Benton Comm Coll (OR)
Lon Morris Coll (TX)
Lord Fairfax Comm Coll (VA)
Los Angeles Trade-Tech Coll (CA)
Los Angeles Valley Coll (CA)
Luzerne County Comm Coll (PA)
Macomb Comm Coll (MI)
Manatee Comm Coll (FL)
Manchester Comm Coll (CT)
Metropolitan Comm Coll (NE)
Miami Dade Coll (FL)
Middlesex Comm Coll (CT)
Middlesex Comm Coll (MA)
Middlesex County Coll (NJ)
Midland Coll (TX)
Midlands Tech Coll (SC)
Mid Michigan Comm Coll (MI)
Miles Comm Coll (MT)
Milwaukee Area Tech Coll (WI)
Mineral Area Coll (MO)
Minneapolis Comm and Tech Coll (MN)
Modesto Jr Coll (CA)
Mohawk Valley Comm Coll (NY)
Montgomery Coll (MD)
Montgomery County Comm Coll (PA)
Moraine Park Tech Coll (WI)
Mt. San Antonio Coll (CA)
Nashville State Tech Comm Coll (TN)
Nassau Comm Coll (NY)
New Hampshire Comm Tech Coll, Manchester/Stratham (NH)
Northampton County Area Comm Coll (PA)
Northeast Mississippi Comm Coll (MS)
Northern Essex Comm Coll (MA)
North Hennepin Comm Coll (MN)
North Idaho Coll (ID)
Northwest Coll (WY)
Northwestern Connecticut Comm-Tech Coll (CT)
Northwestern Michigan Coll (MI)
Oakbridge Academy of Arts (PA)
Ocean County Coll (NJ)
Oklahoma City Comm Coll (OK)
Orange Coast Coll (CA)
Owens Comm Coll, Findlay (OH)
Owens Comm Coll, Toledo (OH)
Palm Beach Comm Coll (FL)
Palomar Coll (CA)
Pellissippi State Tech Comm Coll (TN)
Pennsylvania Coll of Technology (PA)
Penn Valley Comm Coll (MO)
Pensacola Jr Coll (FL)
Pima Comm Coll (AZ)
Pitt Comm Coll (NC)
Platt Coll, Newport Beach (CA)
Platt Coll San Diego (CA)
Portland Comm Coll (OR)
Pratt Comm Coll and Area Vocational School (KS)
Quinsigamond Comm Coll (MA)

Raritan Valley Comm Coll (NJ)
Rend Lake Coll (IL)
Saint Charles Comm Coll (MO)
St. Clair County Comm Coll (MI)
St. Cloud Tech Coll (MN)
St. Johns River Comm Coll (FL)
St. Louis Comm Coll at Florissant Valley (MO)
St. Petersburg Coll (FL)
San Diego City Coll (CA)
San Joaquin Delta Coll (CA)
San Juan Coll (NM)
Santa Barbara City Coll (CA)
Santa Monica Coll (CA)
Schoolcraft Coll (MI)
School of Advertising Art (OH)
Schuylkill Inst of Business and Technology (PA)
Sinclair Comm Coll (OH)
Southern Arkansas U Tech (AR)
South Plains Coll (TX)
South Suburban Coll (IL)
Southwestern Coll (CA)
Southwestern Comm Coll (NC)
Spokane Falls Comm Coll (WA)
Springfield Tech Comm Coll (MA)
Sullivan County Comm Coll (NY)
Sussex County Comm Coll (NJ)
Terra State Comm Coll (OH)
Texas State Tech Coll–Harlingen (TX)
Texas State Tech Coll–Waco/Marshall Campus (TX)
Thomas Nelson Comm Coll (VA)
Tidewater Comm Coll (VA)
Tompkins Cortland Comm Coll (NY)
Trident Tech Coll (SC)
Trinidad State Jr Coll (CO)
Triton Coll (IL)
Utah Valley State Coll (UT)
Vatterott Coll, Omaha (NE)
Ventura Coll (CA)
Villa Maria Coll of Buffalo (NY)
Vincennes U (IN)
Virginia Western Comm Coll (VA)
Washtenaw Comm Coll (MI)
Western Wisconsin Tech Coll (WI)
Westmoreland County Comm Coll (PA)
Westwood Coll–Chicago Du Page (IL)
Westwood Coll–Chicago O'Hare Airport (IL)
Westwood Coll–Denver South (CO)
Westwood Coll–Fort Worth (TX)
Westwood Coll–Inland Empire (CA)
Yavapai Coll (AZ)

Commercial Fishing
Peninsula Coll (WA)

Commercial Photography
The Art Inst of Philadelphia (PA)
The Art Inst of Pittsburgh (PA)
Dakota County Tech Coll (MN)
Houston Comm Coll System (TX)
Luzerne County Comm Coll (PA)
Mohawk Valley Comm Coll (NY)
Montgomery Coll (MD)

Normandale Comm Coll (MN)

Oakbridge Academy of Arts (PA)

Spokane Falls Comm Coll (WA)

Communication and Journalism Related
Delaware County Comm Coll (PA)
Delgado Comm Coll (LA)
Iowa Lakes Comm Coll (IA)
Keystone Coll (PA)
Queensborough Comm Coll of City U of NY (NY)

Communication and Media Related
Keystone Coll (PA)
Platt Coll San Diego (CA)
Somerset Comm Coll (KY)

Communication Disorders
Northampton County Area Comm Coll (PA)

Communication Disorders Sciences and Services Related
Bristol Comm Coll (MA)

Communication/Speech Communication and Rhetoric
Atlanta Metropolitan Coll (GA)
Barton County Comm Coll (KS)
Briarwood Coll (CT)
Bristol Comm Coll (MA)
Broome Comm Coll (NY)
Bunker Hill Comm Coll (MA)
Coll of Southern Idaho (ID)
Dean Coll (MA)
Delaware County Comm Coll (PA)
Dutchess Comm Coll (NY)
Eastern Wyoming Coll (WY)
Foothill Coll (CA)
Gloucester County Coll (NJ)
Hiwassee Coll (TN)
Hutchinson Comm Coll and Area Vocational School (KS)
Jamestown Comm Coll (NY)
Kellogg Comm Coll (MI)
Keystone Coll (PA)
Lackawanna Coll (PA)
Laramie County Comm Coll (WY)
Lehigh Carbon Comm Coll (PA)
Lord Fairfax Comm Coll (VA)
Macomb Comm Coll (MI)
Manchester Comm Coll (CT)
Mesalands Comm Coll (NM)
Montgomery County Comm Coll (PA)
Nassau Comm Coll (NY)
Northwestern Michigan Coll (MI)
San Juan Coll (NM)
Santa Barbara City Coll (CA)
Sauk Valley Comm Coll (IL)
Union County Coll (NJ)
Utah Valley State Coll (UT)
Ventura Coll (CA)
Vincennes U (IN)
Waubonsee Comm Coll (IL)
Western Wyoming Comm Coll (WY)
Yuba Coll (CA)

Communications Systems Installation and Repair Technology
Anoka Tech Coll (MN)
Arapahoe Comm Coll (CO)
Bristol Comm Coll (MA)
Broome Comm Coll (NY)
Coll of DuPage (IL)
Dakota County Tech Coll (MN)
Fayetteville Tech Comm Coll (NC)
Modesto Jr Coll (CA)

Mohawk Valley Comm Coll (NY)
North Seattle Comm Coll (WA)
Wisconsin Indianhead Tech Coll (WI)

Communications Technologies and Support Services Related
Bowling Green State U-Firelands Coll (OH)
Comm Coll of Allegheny County (PA)
Harford Comm Coll (MD)
Mitchell Tech Inst (SD)
Montgomery County Comm Coll (PA)
Northeast Wisconsin Tech Coll (WI)
Springfield Tech Comm Coll (MA)
Western Wisconsin Tech Coll (WI)

Communications Technology
Allegany Coll of Maryland (MD)
Anne Arundel Comm Coll (MD)
Arapahoe Comm Coll (CO)
Burlington County Coll (NJ)
Cleveland Comm Coll (NC)
Coffeyville Comm Coll (KS)
Coll of DuPage (IL)
Comm Coll of the Air Force (AL)
ECPI Coll of Technology, Newport News (VA)
ECPI Coll of Technology, Virginia Beach (VA)
ECPI Tech Coll, Richmond (VA)
ECPI Tech Coll, Roanoke (VA)
Essex County Coll (NJ)
Fairmont State Comm & Tech Coll (WV)
Fountainhead Coll of Technology (TN)
Hutchinson Comm Coll and Area Vocational School (KS)
Kent State U, Tuscarawas Campus (OH)
Kirkwood Comm Coll (IA)
Lackawanna Coll (PA)
Milwaukee Area Tech Coll (WI)
Mott Comm Coll (MI)
Napa Valley Coll (CA)
Northwestern Connecticut Comm-Tech Coll (CT)
Ocean County Coll (NJ)
Orange Coast Coll (CA)
Pasadena City Coll (CA)
Reading Area Comm Coll (PA)
St. Philip's Coll (TX)
Southern Maine Comm Coll (ME)
Southern West Virginia Comm and Tech Coll (WV)
South Puget Sound Comm Coll (WA)
Vincennes U (IN)

Community Health and Preventive Medicine
Utah Valley State Coll (UT)

Community Health Services Counseling
Comm Coll of Allegheny County (PA)
Edmonds Comm Coll (WA)
Erie Comm Coll (NY)
Kingsborough Comm Coll of City U of NY (NY)
Manatee Comm Coll (FL)
Mott Comm Coll (MI)

Community Organization and Advocacy
Berkshire Comm Coll (MA)

Cleveland State Comm Coll (TN)
Clinton Comm Coll (NY)
Coll of the Sequoias (CA)
Cumberland County Coll (NJ)
Del Mar Coll (TX)
Honolulu Comm Coll (HI)
J. Sargeant Reynolds Comm Coll (VA)
Marshalltown Comm Coll (IA)
Merritt Coll (CA)
Mohawk Valley Comm Coll (NY)
New Hampshire Comm Tech Coll, Manchester/Stratham (NH)
New River Comm Coll (VA)

Computer and Information Sciences
Academy Coll (MN)
Albany Tech Coll (GA)
Alexandria Tech Coll (MN)
Allentown Business School (PA)
Alpena Comm Coll (MI)
Andrew Coll (GA)
Antonelli Coll (OH)
Atlanta Metropolitan Coll (GA)
Berkshire Comm Coll (MA)
Blackhawk Tech Coll (WI)
Bristol Comm Coll (MA)
Broome Comm Coll (NY)
Bryant & Stratton Business Inst, Buffalo (NY)
Bryant & Stratton Business Inst, Lackawanna (NY)
Bryant and Stratton Coll, Parma (OH)
Bryant and Stratton Coll (WI)
Bryant & Stratton Business Inst, Amherst Cmps (NY)
Bucks County Comm Coll (PA)
Butler County Comm Coll (KS)
Calhoun Comm Coll (AL)
Cambria County Area Comm Coll (PA)
Capital Comm Coll (CT)
Career Coll of Northern Nevada (NV)
Central Arizona Coll (AZ)
Central Comm Coll–Columbus Campus (NE)
Central Comm Coll–Grand Island Campus (NE)
Central Comm Coll–Hastings Campus (NE)
Cincinnati State Tech and Comm Coll (OH)
City Colls of Chicago, Wilbur Wright Coll (IL)
Clarendon Coll (TX)
Clovis Comm Coll (NM)
Coffeyville Comm Coll (KS)
Collin County Comm Coll District (TX)
Corning Comm Coll (NY)
Darton Coll (GA)
Dawson Comm Coll (MT)
Delaware County Comm Coll (PA)
Delta Coll (MI)
Dunwoody Coll of Technology (MN)
Dutchess Comm Coll (NY)
ECPI Coll of Technology, Newport News (VA)
ECPI Coll of Technology, Virginia Beach (VA)
ECPI Tech Coll, Richmond (VA)
ECPI Tech Coll, Roanoke (VA)
Fayetteville Tech Comm Coll (NC)
Finger Lakes Comm Coll (NY)
Gadsden State Comm Coll (AL)
Goodwin Coll (CT)

Hagerstown Comm Coll (MD)
Harford Comm Coll (MD)
Harrisburg Area Comm Coll (PA)
Heartland Comm Coll (IL)
Herzing Coll, Minneapolis Drafting School Division (MN)
Hesser Coll (NH)
Hibbing Comm Coll (MN)
Hiwassee Coll (TN)
Houston Comm Coll System (TX)
Hutchinson Comm Coll and Area Vocational School (KS)
Indiana Business Coll, Indianapolis (IN)
IntelliTec Coll, Grand Junction (CO)
Ivy Tech State Coll–Bloomington (IN)
Ivy Tech State Coll–Central Indiana (IN)
Ivy Tech State Coll–Columbus (IN)
Ivy Tech State Coll–Eastcentral (IN)
Ivy Tech State Coll–Kokomo (IN)
Ivy Tech State Coll–Lafayette (IN)
Ivy Tech State Coll–North Central (IN)
Ivy Tech State Coll–Northeast (IN)
Ivy Tech State Coll–Northwest (IN)
Ivy Tech State Coll–Southcentral (IN)
Ivy Tech State Coll–Southeast (IN)
Ivy Tech State Coll–Southwest (IN)
Ivy Tech State Coll–Wabash Valley (IN)
Ivy Tech State Coll–Whitewater (IN)
James H. Faulkner State Comm Coll (AL)
Jamestown Business Coll (NY)
Jamestown Comm Coll (NY)
Jefferson State Comm Coll (AL)
J. Sargeant Reynolds Comm Coll (VA)
Kaplan Coll (IA)
Kent State U, Salem Campus (OH)
Kingsborough Comm Coll of City U of NY (NY)
Kingwood Coll (TX)
Lackawanna Coll (PA)
Lake Region State Coll (ND)
Lamar State Coll–Port Arthur (TX)
Laramie County Comm Coll (WY)
Linn-Benton Comm Coll (OR)
Lord Fairfax Comm Coll (VA)
Louisville Tech Inst (KY)
Lower Columbia Coll (WA)
Luna Comm Coll (NM)
Luzerne County Comm Coll (PA)
MacCormac Coll (IL)
Manatee Comm Coll (FL)
Massasoit Comm Coll (MA)
McIntosh Coll (NH)
Metropolitan Comm Coll-Business & Technology College (MO)
Mid-Plains Comm Coll, North Platte (NE)
Mid-South Comm Coll (AR)
Mitchell Tech Inst (SD)
Moberly Area Comm Coll (MO)
Mohawk Valley Comm Coll (NY)

Montana State U Coll of Tech-Great Falls (MT)
Montgomery Coll (MD)
Montgomery County Comm Coll (PA)
Mountain State Coll (WV)
Nassau Comm Coll (NY)
National Coll of Business & Technology, Salem (VA)
New Hampshire Comm Tech Coll, Berlin/Laconia (NH)
New Hampshire Tech Inst (NH)
Normandale Comm Coll (MN)
Northampton County Area Comm Coll (PA)
Northeast Comm Coll (NE)
Northern Essex Comm Coll (MA)
North Harris Coll (TX)
North Iowa Area Comm Coll (IA)
Northland Pioneer Coll (AZ)
Northwest-Shoals Comm Coll (AL)
Oakland Comm Coll (MI)
Oakton Comm Coll (IL)
Ocean County Coll (NJ)
Odessa Coll (TX)
Oklahoma State U, Oklahoma City (OK)
Orange County Comm Coll (NY)
Ouachita Tech Coll (AR)
Owensboro Comm and Tech Coll (KY)
Parkland Coll (IL)
Pellissippi State Tech Comm Coll (TN)
Pennsylvania Coll of Technology (PA)
Phoenix Coll (AZ)
Pima Comm Coll (AZ)
Ranken Tech Coll (MO)
Remington Coll–Mobile Campus (AL)
Rend Lake Coll (IL)
Riverside Comm Coll (CA)
St. Johns River Comm Coll (FL)
Salem Comm Coll (NJ)
Santa Fe Comm Coll (NM)
Schenectady County Comm Coll (NY)
Sinclair Comm Coll (OH)
Snead State Comm Coll (AL)
South Coll-Asheville (NC)
Southeast Comm Coll, Lincoln Campus (NE)
South Hills School of Business & Technology, State College (PA)
South Puget Sound Comm Coll (WA)
Spartanburg Tech Coll (SC)
State U of NY Coll of Technology at Alfred (NY)
Sussex County Comm Coll (NJ)
Terra State Comm Coll (OH)
Texas State Tech Coll–Harlingen (TX)
Texas State Tech Coll–Waco/Marshall Campus (TX)
Trenholm State Tech Coll, Montgomery (AL)
Utah Valley State Coll (UT)
Ventura Coll (CA)
Victor Valley Coll (CA)
Vista Comm Coll (CA)
Waubonsee Comm Coll (IL)
Waycross Coll (GA)
Western Nevada Comm Coll (NV)
Western Wyoming Comm Coll (WY)
Westmoreland County Comm Coll (PA)
Wor-Wic Comm Coll (MD)

Computer and Information Sciences and Support Services Related
Academy Coll (MN)
Allentown Business School (PA)
Atlantic Cape Comm Coll (NJ)
Blackfeet Comm Coll (MT)
Bunker Hill Comm Coll (MA)
Clover Park Tech Coll (WA)
Edmonds Comm Coll (WA)
Education Direct Center for Degree Studies (PA)
Harrisburg Area Comm Coll (PA)
Indiana Business Coll, Columbus (IN)
Indiana Business Coll, Indianapolis (IN)
Indiana Business Coll, Lafayette (IN)
Indiana Business Coll, Muncie (IN)
Indiana Business Coll, Terre Haute (IN)
Jackson Comm Coll (MI)
Laramie County Comm Coll (WY)
LDS Business Coll (UT)
Louisville Tech Inst (KY)
Massasoit Comm Coll (MA)
Metropolitan Comm Coll-Business & Technology College (MO)
Midlands Tech Coll (SC)
Mitchell Tech Inst (SD)
Mohawk Valley Comm Coll (NY)
Mott Comm Coll (MI)
Northeast Wisconsin Tech Coll (WI)
Pennsylvania Coll of Technology (PA)
Ranken Tech Coll (MO)
Schuylkill Inst of Business and Technology (PA)
Southern Arkansas U Tech (AR)
Springfield Tech Comm Coll (MA)
Williston State Coll (ND)

Computer and Information Sciences Related
American River Coll (CA)
Anne Arundel Comm Coll (MD)
Austin Comm Coll (TX)
Blue River Comm Coll (MO)
Bristol Comm Coll (MA)
Bucks County Comm Coll (PA)
Camden County Coll (NJ)
Cape Cod Comm Coll (MA)
Capital Comm Coll (CT)
Centralia Coll (WA)
Central Oregon Comm Coll (OR)
Chabot Coll (CA)
Chipola Coll (FL)
Coastal Bend Coll (TX)
Colby Comm Coll (KS)
Coll of the Canyons (CA)
Coll of the Desert (CA)
The Coll of Westchester (NY)
Columbia-Greene Comm Coll (NY)
Corning Comm Coll (NY)
Daytona Beach Comm Coll (FL)
Del Mar Coll (TX)
Delta Coll (MI)
Donnelly Coll (KS)
Eastfield Coll (TX)
ECPI Tech Coll, Richmond (VA)
ECPI Tech Coll, Roanoke (VA)
Elaine P. Nunez Comm Coll (LA)
Fayetteville Tech Comm Coll (NC)
Fiorello H LaGuardia Comm Coll of City U of NY (NY)

Galveston Coll (TX)
Gavilan Coll (CA)
Gordon Coll (GA)
Heartland Comm Coll (IL)
Henderson Comm Coll (KY)
Hinds Comm Coll (MS)
Holmes Comm Coll (MS)
Howard Coll (TX)
Howard Comm Coll (MD)
Iowa Lakes Comm Coll (IA)
Jamestown Comm Coll (NY)
J. Sargeant Reynolds Comm Coll (VA)
Kishwaukee Coll (IL)
Lakeshore Tech Coll (WI)
Lake-Sumter Comm Coll (FL)
Lawson State Comm Coll (AL)
Longview Comm Coll (MO)
Lorain County Comm Coll (OH)
Los Angeles Valley Coll (CA)
Luzerne County Comm Coll (PA)
Manatee Comm Coll (FL)
Maple Woods Comm Coll (MO)
Massasoit Comm Coll (MA)
Metropolitan Comm Coll–Business & Technology College (MO)
Middle Georgia Coll (GA)
Milwaukee Area Tech Coll (WI)
Minneapolis Comm and Tech Coll (MN)
Mississippi Gulf Coast Comm Coll (MS)
Mohave Comm Coll (AZ)
Monroe County Comm Coll (MI)
Nassau Comm Coll (NY)
National Coll of Business & Technology, Danville (KY)
National Coll of Business & Technology, Florence (KY)
National Coll of Business & Technology, Lexington (KY)
National Coll of Business & Technology, Louisville (KY)
National Coll of Business & Technology, Pikeville (KY)
National Coll of Business & Technology, Richmond (KY)
National Coll of Business & Technology, Nashville (TN)
National Coll of Business & Technology, Bluefield (VA)
National Coll of Business & Technology, Bristol (VA)
National Coll of Business & Technology, Charlottesville (VA)
National Coll of Business & Technology, Harrisonburg (VA)
National Coll of Business & Technology, Lynchburg (VA)
National Coll of Business & Technology, Martinsville (VA)
North Idaho Coll (ID)
North Shore Comm Coll (MA)
Oakton Comm Coll (IL)
Olympic Coll (WA)
Orange County Comm Coll (NY)
Palo Alto Coll (TX)
Pellissippi State Tech Comm Coll (TN)
Penn Valley Comm Coll (MO)
Quinebaug Valley Comm Coll (CT)
Santa Fe Comm Coll (NM)
Santa Monica Coll (CA)
Sauk Valley Comm Coll (IL)
Schenectady County Comm Coll (NY)
Seminole Comm Coll (FL)

Sinclair Comm Coll (OH)
Southwestern Coll (CA)
Southwestern Michigan Coll (MI)
Stark State Coll of Technology (OH)
Three Rivers Comm Coll (MO)
Tompkins Cortland Comm Coll (NY)
Trinidad State Jr Coll (CO)
Vincennes U (IN)
Vista Comm Coll (CA)
Walters State Comm Coll (TN)
York Tech Inst (PA)
Yuba Coll (CA)

Computer and Information Systems Security
Academy Coll (MN)
American River Coll (CA)
Atlantic Cape Comm Coll (NJ)
City Colls of Chicago, Wilbur Wright Coll (IL)
Clover Park Tech Coll (WA)
Dakota County Tech Coll (MN)
ECPI Tech Coll, Glen Allen (VA)
ECPI Tech Coll, Richmond (VA)
ECPI Tech Coll, Roanoke (VA)
Florida National Coll (FL)
Island Drafting and Tech Inst (NY)
Jamestown Comm Coll (NY)
Louisville Tech Inst (KY)
Metropolitan Comm Coll–Business & Technology College (MO)
MTI Coll of Business and Technology, Houston (TX)
Riverland Comm Coll (MN)
St. Philip's Coll (TX)
Seminole Comm Coll (FL)
Southwestern Coll (CA)
Tompkins Cortland Comm Coll (NY)
Triton Coll (IL)
Vista Comm Coll (CA)
York Tech Inst (PA)

Computer Engineering
Itasca Comm Coll (MN)
Moraine Park Tech Coll (WI)
Santa Barbara City Coll (CA)
Vatterott Coll, St. Ann (MO)

Computer Engineering Related
Arkansas State U–Beebe (AR)
Coll of the Canyons (CA)
Daytona Beach Comm Coll (FL)
Fayetteville Tech Comm Coll (NC)
Florida Career Coll (FL)
Itasca Comm Coll (MN)
Jefferson Comm Coll (OH)
Middle Georgia Coll (GA)
Minot State U–Bottineau Campus (ND)
Orange County Comm Coll (NY)
Seminole Comm Coll (FL)
Sinclair Comm Coll (OH)
Stark State Coll of Technology (OH)
Vincennes U (IN)
York Tech Coll (SC)

Computer Engineering Technology
Abraham Baldwin Ag Coll (GA)
Allegany Coll of Maryland (MD)
Alvin Comm Coll (TX)
Amarillo Coll (TX)
American River Coll (CA)
Anne Arundel Comm Coll (MD)

Arkansas State U–Beebe (AR)
Bergen Comm Coll (NJ)
Bowling Green State U–Firelands Coll (OH)
Brevard Comm Coll (FL)
Brookdale Comm Coll (NJ)
Broome Comm Coll (NY)
Bucks County Comm Coll (PA)
Camden County Coll (NJ)
Cañada Coll (CA)
Capital Comm Coll (CT)
Carteret Comm Coll (NC)
Casper Coll (WY)
Cecil Comm Coll (MD)
Central Piedmont Comm Coll (NC)
Century Coll (MN)
Chabot Coll (CA)
Chemeketa Comm Coll (OR)
Chesapeake Coll (MD)
CHI Inst (PA)
Cincinnati State Tech and Comm Coll (OH)
Cleveland Comm Coll (NC)
Coastal Bend Coll (TX)
Coll of the Sequoias (CA)
Collin County Comm Coll District (TX)
Colorado Mountn Coll, Alpine Cmps (CO)
Colorado Mountn Coll (CO)
Colorado Mountn Coll, Timberline Cmps (CO)
Columbus State Comm Coll (OH)
Comm Coll of Allegheny County (PA)
Comm Coll of Rhode Island (RI)
Cuesta Coll (CA)
Cuyahoga Comm Coll (OH)
DeKalb Tech Coll (GA)
Delaware Tech & Comm Coll, Terry Cmps (DE)
Delgado Comm Coll (LA)
Des Moines Area Comm Coll (IA)
Doña Ana Branch Comm Coll (NM)
East Arkansas Comm Coll (AR)
Eastern Oklahoma State Coll (OK)
Eastfield Coll (TX)
East Los Angeles Coll (CA)
ECPI Coll of Technology, Newport News (VA)
ECPI Coll of Technology, Virginia Beach (VA)
ECPI Tech Coll, Roanoke (VA)
Edison State Comm Coll (OH)
Elaine P. Nunez Comm Coll (LA)
Everest Coll (AZ)
Fiorello H LaGuardia Comm Coll of City U of NY (NY)
Foothill Coll (CA)
Forsyth Tech Comm Coll (NC)
Foundation Coll, San Diego (CA)
Fountainhead Coll of Technology (TN)
Frederick Comm Coll (MD)
Fulton-Montgomery Comm Coll (NY)
Garden City Comm Coll (KS)
Gogebic Comm Coll (MI)
Grand Rapids Comm Coll (MI)
Gulf Coast Comm Coll (FL)
Hawkeye Comm Coll (IA)
Heartland Comm Coll (IL)
Hesser Coll (NH)
High-Tech Inst (AZ)
Hillsborough Comm Coll (FL)
Houston Comm Coll System (TX)
Hudson County Comm Coll (NJ)

Indian Hills Comm Coll (IA)
Jamestown Comm Coll (NY)
J. Sargeant Reynolds Comm Coll (VA)
Kansas City Kansas Comm Coll (KS)
Kellogg Comm Coll (MI)
Kent State U, Trumbull Campus (OH)
Kent State U, Tuscarawas Campus (OH)
Kingwood Coll (TX)
Lake Washington Tech Coll (WA)
Lansing Comm Coll (MI)
Lehigh Carbon Comm Coll (PA)
Lorain County Comm Coll (OH)
Los Angeles Harbor Coll (CA)
Los Angeles Pierce Coll (CA)
Los Angeles Trade-Tech Coll (CA)
Louisiana Tech Coll–Gulf Area Campus (LA)
Louisville Tech Inst (KY)
Lower Columbia Coll (WA)
Manatee Comm Coll (FL)
McLennan Comm Coll (TX)
Meridian Comm Coll (MS)
Merritt Coll (CA)
Miami Dade Coll (FL)
Middlesex Comm Coll (MA)
Middlesex County Coll (NJ)
Miles Comm Coll (MT)
Minnesota State Coll–Southeast Tech (MN)
Minot State U–Bottineau Campus (ND)
MiraCosta Coll (CA)
Mississippi Gulf Coast Comm Coll (MS)
Monroe County Comm Coll (MI)
Montgomery County Comm Coll (PA)
Moraine Park Tech Coll (WI)
Mt. San Antonio Coll (CA)
Nashville State Tech Comm Coll (TN)
New Hampshire Comm Tech Coll, Berlin/Laconia (NH)
New Hampshire Tech Inst (NH)
New River Comm Coll (VA)
North Central Missouri Coll (MO)
Northeast Iowa Comm Coll (IA)
Northern Essex Comm Coll (MA)
Northern Maine Comm Coll (ME)
North Shore Comm Coll (MA)
Northwestern Connecticut Comm-Tech Coll (CT)
Northwest-Shoals Comm Coll (AL)
Oklahoma City Comm Coll (OK)
Orange Coast Coll (CA)
Orange County Comm Coll (NY)
Palo Alto Coll (TX)
Paris Jr Coll (TX)
Pasadena City Coll (CA)
Pellissippi State Tech Comm Coll (TN)
Penn State U New Kensington Campus of the Commonwealth Coll (PA)
Portland Comm Coll (OR)
Prince George's Comm Coll (MD)
Pulaski Tech Coll (AR)
Queensborough Comm Coll of City U of NY (NY)
Ranken Tech Coll (MO)
Red Rocks Comm Coll (CO)
Remington Coll–Mobile Campus (AL)
Rend Lake Coll (IL)

RETS Tech Center (OH)
Richmond Comm Coll (NC)
Roane State Comm Coll (TN)
St. Johns River Comm Coll (FL)
St. Louis Comm Coll at Florissant Valley (MO)
St. Petersburg Coll (FL)
San Diego City Coll (CA)
San Joaquin Delta Coll (CA)
San Jose City Coll (CA)
Seminole Comm Coll (FL)
Sierra Coll (CA)
Southeast Comm Coll (KY)
Southeastern Comm Coll (NC)
Southern Maine Comm Coll (ME)
South Plains Coll (TX)
Southwestern Comm Coll (NC)
Springfield Tech Comm Coll (MA)
State U of NY Coll of A&T at Morrisville (NY)
State U of NY Coll of Technology at Alfred (NY)
Texas State Tech Coll–Waco/Marshall Campus (TX)
Three Rivers Comm Coll (MO)
Trident Tech Coll (SC)
Triton Coll (IL)
Umpqua Comm Coll (OR)
Vance-Granville Comm Coll (NC)
Vatterott Coll, Tulsa (OK)
Vermilion Comm Coll (MN)
Vincennes U (IN)
Washtenaw Comm Coll (MI)
Westmoreland County Comm Coll (PA)
Westwood Coll–Denver North (CO)
Yakima Valley Comm Coll (WA)
York County Comm Coll (ME)
York Tech Coll (SC)

Computer Graphics
Academy Coll (MN)
American River Coll (CA)
Arapahoe Comm Coll (CO)
Arkansas State U–Beebe (AR)
The Art Inst of Houston (TX)
The Art Inst of Pittsburgh (PA)
Burlington County Coll (NJ)
Calhoun Comm Coll (AL)
Camden County Coll (NJ)
Cape Cod Comm Coll (MA)
Cecil Comm Coll (MD)
CHI Inst (PA)
CollAmerica–Fort Collins (CO)
Coll of Eastern Utah (UT)
Coll of the Desert (CA)
Coll of the Sequoias (CA)
The Coll of Westchester (NY)
Columbia-Greene Comm Coll (NY)
Corning Comm Coll (NY)
The Creative Center (NE)
Dakota County Tech Coll (MN)
Daytona Beach Comm Coll (FL)
Delta Coll (MI)
Edison State Comm Coll (OH)
Elgin Comm Coll (IL)
Fayetteville Tech Comm Coll (NC)
Florida National Coll (FL)
Full Sail Real World Education (FL)
Garden City Comm Coll (KS)
Gavilan Coll (CA)
Globe Coll (MN)
Gloucester County Coll (NJ)
Gogebic Comm Coll (MI)

Hinds Comm Coll (MS)
Howard Comm Coll (MD)
Iowa Lakes Comm Coll (IA)
James A. Rhodes State Coll (OH)
Kellogg Comm Coll (MI)
Kingwood Coll (TX)
Lakeland Comm Coll (OH)
Lansing Comm Coll (MI)
Louisville Tech Inst (KY)
Luzerne County Comm Coll (PA)
Manatee Comm Coll (FL)
Meridian Comm Coll (MS)
Mesabi Range Comm and Tech Coll (MN)
Metropolitan Comm Coll–Business & Technology College (MO)
Miami Dade Coll (FL)
Middlesex County Coll (NJ)
Mid Michigan Comm Coll (MI)
Miles Comm Coll (MT)
Milwaukee Area Tech Coll (WI)
Minnesota School of Business–Brooklyn Center (MN)
Minnesota School of Business-Plymouth (MN)
Minnesota School of Business-Richfield (MN)
Mississippi Gulf Coast Comm Coll (MS)
Modesto Jr Coll (CA)
Monroe County Comm Coll (MI)
Mt. San Antonio Coll (CA)
Mount Wachusett Comm Coll (MA)
Nassau Comm Coll (NY)
New River Comm Coll (VA)
North Country Comm Coll (NY)
Northeast Alabama Comm Coll (AL)
Northern Essex Comm Coll (MA)
Northland Pioneer Coll (AZ)
North Shore Comm Coll (MA)
Northwestern Connecticut Comm-Tech Coll (CT)
Oakbridge Academy of Arts (PA)
Oakton Comm Coll (IL)
Olympic Coll (WA)
Orange Coast Coll (CA)
Parkland Coll (IL)
Pellissippi State Tech Comm Coll (TN)
Phoenix Coll (AZ)
Platt Coll, Newport Beach (CA)
Platt Coll San Diego (CA)
Quinebaug Valley Comm Coll (CT)
Rasmussen Coll Mankato (MN)
Riverside Comm Coll (CA)
Seminole Comm Coll (FL)
Sinclair Comm Coll (OH)
Southwestern Coll (CA)
State U of NY Coll of Technology at Alfred (NY)
Sullivan County Comm Coll (NY)
Texas State Tech Coll–Harlingen (TX)
Tompkins Cortland Comm Coll (NY)
Trident Tech Coll (SC)
Triton Coll (IL)
Utah Career Coll (UT)
Vincennes U (IN)
Vista Comm Coll (CA)
Washtenaw Comm Coll (MI)
Weatherford Coll (TX)
Westmoreland County Comm Coll (PA)
Yakima Valley Comm Coll (WA)

Computer Hardware Engineering

Cuesta Coll (CA)
Eastfield Coll (TX)
Lake City Comm Coll (FL)
Louisville Tech Inst (KY)
Seminole Comm Coll (FL)
Sinclair Comm Coll (OH)
Stanly Comm Coll (NC)
Stark State Coll of Technology (OH)
Tompkins Cortland Comm Coll (NY)
Vincennes U (IN)
Westwood Coll–Long Beach (CA)

Computer Hardware Technology

Central Florida Comm Coll (FL)
Laramie County Comm Coll (WY)
Louisville Tech Inst (KY)

Computer/Information Technology Services Administration Related

Alpena Comm Coll (MI)
Andover Coll (ME)
Arapahoe Comm Coll (CO)
Atlanta Metropolitan Coll (GA)
Barton County Comm Coll (KS)
Brevard Comm Coll (FL)
Brunswick Comm Coll (NC)
Bucks County Comm Coll (PA)
Cambria County Area Comm Coll (PA)
Camden County Coll (NJ)
CHI Inst (PA)
Clinton Comm Coll (NY)
Coastal Carolina Comm Coll (NC)
The Coll of Westchester (NY)
Corning Comm Coll (NY)
Daytona Beach Comm Coll (FL)
Eastern Shore Comm Coll (VA)
Eastfield Coll (TX)
Elaine P. Nunez Comm Coll (LA)
El Centro Coll (TX)
Georgia Perimeter Coll (GA)
Gogebic Comm Coll (MI)
Guilford Tech Comm Coll (NC)
Hawkeye Comm Coll (IA)
Henderson Comm Coll (KY)
Hesston Coll (KS)
Howard Comm Coll (MD)
International Inst of the Americas, Phoenix (AZ)
Iowa Lakes Comm Coll (IA)
Keystone Coll (PA)
Mesabi Range Comm and Tech Coll (MN)
Metropolitan Comm Coll-Business & Technology College (MO)
Middle Georgia Coll (GA)
Milwaukee Area Tech Coll (WI)
Mitchell Tech Inst (SD)
Modesto Jr Coll (CA)
Naugatuck Valley Comm Coll (CT)
Owensboro Comm and Tech Coll (KY)
Parkland Coll (IL)
Pennsylvania Coll of Technology (PA)
St. Cloud Tech Coll (MN)
Schenectady County Comm Coll (NY)
Seminole Comm Coll (FL)
Sinclair Comm Coll (OH)
Southeast Comm Coll (KY)
Stanly Comm Coll (NC)
Stark State Coll of Technology (OH)

State U of NY Coll of Technology at Canton (NY)
Texas State Tech Coll–Harlingen (TX)
Tompkins Cortland Comm Coll (NY)
Trident Tech Coll (SC)
Trumbull Business Coll (OH)
Vincennes U (IN)
York County Comm Coll (ME)
York Tech Coll (SC)
York Tech Inst (PA)

Computer Installation and Repair Technology

CollAmerica–Fort Collins (CO)
Coll of DuPage (IL)
Coll of Lake County (IL)
Daymar Coll, Louisville (KY)
Delgado Comm Coll (LA)
Harrisburg Area Comm Coll (PA)
Hibbing Comm Coll (MN)
Louisville Tech Inst (KY)
Modesto Jr Coll (CA)
Montcalm Comm Coll (MI)
Northampton County Area Comm Coll (PA)
Northland Pioneer Coll (AZ)
Riverland Comm Coll (MN)
State U of NY Coll of Technology at Alfred (NY)
Western Dakota Tech Inst (SD)

Computer Maintenance Technology

St. Philip's Coll (TX)

Computer Management

AIB Coll of Business (IA)
Andover Coll (ME)
Anne Arundel Comm Coll (MD)
Berkeley Coll (NJ)
Central Georgia Tech Coll (GA)
Cossatot Comm Coll of the U of Arkansas (AR)
Darton Coll (GA)
Delta Coll (MI)
ECPI Coll of Technology, Newport News (VA)
ECPI Coll of Technology, Virginia Beach (VA)
ECPI Tech Coll, Richmond (VA)
Hesser Coll (NH)
Lakeshore Tech Coll (WI)
Lansing Comm Coll (MI)
McIntosh Coll (NH)
Michiana Coll, South Bend (IN)
Miles Comm Coll (MT)
Mineral Area Coll (MO)
Montana State U Coll of Tech-Great Falls (MT)
Northeast Mississippi Comm Coll (MS)
Otero Jr Coll (CO)
Palo Alto Coll (TX)
Prince George's Comm Coll (MD)
South Coll (TN)
Southern Maine Comm Coll (ME)
Thompson Inst (PA)
Tri-County Comm Coll (NC)
Vermilion Comm Coll (MN)
Villa Maria Coll of Buffalo (NY)
Williamsburg Tech Coll (SC)

Computer Programming

Abraham Baldwin Ag Coll (GA)
Academy Coll (MN)
Alamance Comm Coll (NC)
Allentown Business School (PA)
Alvin Comm Coll (TX)
Amarillo Coll (TX)
American River Coll (CA)
Ancilla Coll (IN)

Andover Coll (ME)
Anne Arundel Comm Coll (MD)
Arapahoe Comm Coll (CO)
Asheville-Buncombe Tech Comm Coll (NC)
Atlantic Cape Comm Coll (NJ)
Augusta Tech Coll (GA)
Austin Comm Coll (TX)
Bates Tech Coll (WA)
Beaufort County Comm Coll (NC)
Bellevue Comm Coll (WA)
Bergen Comm Coll (NJ)
Bladen Comm Coll (NC)
Blue Ridge Comm Coll (NC)
Borough of Manhattan Comm Coll of City U of NY (NY)
Bowling Green State U-Firelands Coll (OH)
Bradford School (OH)
Brevard Comm Coll (FL)
Bristol Comm Coll (MA)
Brookdale Comm Coll (NJ)
Brunswick Comm Coll (NC)
Bryant & Stratton Business Inst, Syracuse (NY)
Bucks County Comm Coll (PA)
Bunker Hill Comm Coll (MA)
Cabrillo Coll (CA)
Cambria County Area Comm Coll (PA)
Camden County Coll (NJ)
Cañada Coll (CA)
Casper Coll (WY)
Cecil Comm Coll (MD)
Cedar Valley Coll (TX)
Central Alabama Comm Coll (AL)
Central Florida Comm Coll (FL)
Central Piedmont Comm Coll (NC)
Chemeketa Comm Coll (OR)
Chesapeake Coll (MD)
CHI Inst (PA)
Cincinnati State Tech and Comm Coll (OH)
Clark State Comm Coll (OH)
Clover Park Tech Coll (WA)
Coffeyville Comm Coll (KS)
CollAmerica–Fort Collins (CO)
Coll of Southern Maryland (MD)
Coll of the Sequoias (CA)
The Coll of Westchester (NY)
Collin County Comm Coll District (TX)
Columbus State Comm Coll (OH)
Comm Coll of Denver (CO)
Comm Coll of Rhode Island (RI)
Contra Costa Coll (CA)
Copiah-Lincoln Comm Coll (MS)
Corning Comm Coll (NY)
Danville Comm Coll (VA)
Darton Coll (GA)
Daymar Coll, Louisville (KY)
Daytona Beach Comm Coll (FL)
DeKalb Tech Coll (GA)
Delaware Tech & Comm Coll, Terry Cmps (DE)
Del Mar Coll (TX)
Delta Coll (MI)
Des Moines Area Comm Coll (IA)
Durham Tech Comm Coll (NC)
Eastfield Coll (TX)
East Los Angeles Coll (CA)
East Mississippi Comm Coll (MS)
ECPI Coll of Technology, Virginia Beach (VA)
ECPI Tech Coll, Glen Allen (VA)

ECPI Tech Coll, Richmond (VA)
Edison Comm Coll (FL)
Edison State Comm Coll (OH)
El Centro Coll (TX)
Essex County Coll (NJ)
Fayetteville Tech Comm Coll (NC)
Fiorello H LaGuardia Comm Coll of City U of NY (NY)
Florida Career Coll (FL)
Florida National Coll (FL)
Foundation Coll, San Diego (CA)
Garden City Comm Coll (KS)
Gaston Coll (NC)
Gavilan Coll (CA)
Grand Rapids Comm Coll (MI)
Greenfield Comm Coll (MA)
Guilford Tech Comm Coll (NC)
Gulf Coast Comm Coll (FL)
Gwinnett Tech Coll (GA)
Hamilton Coll (NE)
Heartland Comm Coll (IL)
Hesser Coll (NH)
Hickey Coll (MO)
Hill Coll of the Hill Jr College District (TX)
Hillsborough Comm Coll (FL)
Hinds Comm Coll (MS)
Howard Coll (TX)
Indiana Business Coll, Indianapolis (IN)
Indian Hills Comm Coll (IA)
Iowa Lakes Comm Coll (IA)
Isothermal Comm Coll (NC)
James A. Rhodes State Coll (OH)
Johnston Comm Coll (NC)
J. Sargeant Reynolds Comm Coll (VA)
Kalamazoo Valley Comm Coll (MI)
Kellogg Comm Coll (MI)
Keystone Coll (PA)
Kirkwood Comm Coll (IA)
Lake Area Tech Inst (SD)
Lake City Comm Coll (FL)
Lakeshore Tech Coll (WI)
Lansing Comm Coll (MI)
Laramie County Comm Coll (WY)
Laredo Comm Coll (TX)
Lenoir Comm Coll (NC)
Lewis and Clark Comm Coll (IL)
Lincoln Coll, Lincoln (IL)
Linn State Tech Coll (MO)
Longview Comm Coll (MO)
Lorain County Comm Coll (OH)
Lord Fairfax Comm Coll (VA)
Los Angeles Pierce Coll (CA)
Los Angeles Trade-Tech Coll (CA)
Los Angeles Valley Coll (CA)
Lower Columbia Coll (WA)
Macomb Comm Coll (MI)
Manatee Comm Coll (FL)
Maple Woods Comm Coll (MO)
Massasoit Comm Coll (MA)
Mayland Comm Coll (NC)
Merritt Coll (CA)
Metropolitan Comm Coll (NE)
Metropolitan Comm Coll-Business & Technology College (MO)
Miami Dade Coll (FL)
Michiana Coll, South Bend (IN)
Middlesex Comm Coll (CT)
Middlesex County Coll (NJ)
Mineral Area Coll (MO)
Minneapolis Business Coll (MN)
Minneapolis Comm and Tech Coll (MN)
Minnesota State Coll–Southeast Tech (MN)

Mohawk Valley Comm Coll (NY)
Montgomery County Comm Coll (PA)
Moraine Park Tech Coll (WI)
Mountain View Coll (TX)
Naugatuck Valley Comm Coll (CT)
Newport Business Inst, Lower Burrell (PA)
Northeast Comm Coll (NE)
Northeastern Oklahoma A&M Coll (OK)
Northeastern Tech Coll (SC)
Northeast Mississippi Comm Coll (MS)
Northeast State Tech Comm Coll (TN)
Northeast Wisconsin Tech Coll (WI)
Northern Essex Comm Coll (MA)
Northern Maine Comm Coll (ME)
North Idaho Coll (ID)
North Shore Comm Coll (MA)
Northwestern Connecticut Comm-Tech Coll (CT)
Northwest Iowa Comm Coll (IA)
Northwest-Shoals Comm Coll (AL)
Northwest State Comm Coll (OH)
Oakland Comm Coll (MI)
Oakton Comm Coll (IL)
Ocean County Coll (NJ)
Ohio Business Coll, Sandusky (OH)
Olympic Coll (WA)
Orange Coast Coll (CA)
Orange County Comm Coll (NY)
Palm Beach Comm Coll (FL)
Parkland Coll (IL)
Pasadena City Coll (CA)
Pellissippi State Tech Comm Coll (TN)
Piedmont Virginia Comm Coll (VA)
Portland Comm Coll (OR)
Prince George's Comm Coll (MD)
Quinsigamond Comm Coll (MA)
Raritan Valley Comm Coll (NJ)
Reading Area Comm Coll (PA)
Red Rocks Comm Coll (CO)
Remington Coll–Lafayette Campus (LA)
RETS Tech Center (OH)
Riverside Comm Coll (CA)
Roanoke-Chowan Comm Coll (NC)
Rochester Business Inst (NY)
St. Cloud Tech Coll (MN)
St. Johns River Comm Coll (FL)
St. Louis Comm Coll at Florissant Valley (MO)
Saint Paul Coll–A Comm & Tech College (MN)
St. Petersburg Coll (FL)
Sanford-Brown Coll, Hazelwood (MO)
San Joaquin Delta Coll (CA)
Santa Monica Coll (CA)
Sawyer Coll, Hammond (IN)
Schoolcraft Coll (MI)
Seminole Comm Coll (FL)
Seward County Comm Coll (KS)
South Central Tech Coll (MN)
Southern Arkansas U Tech (AR)
South Plains Coll (TX)
South Puget Sound Comm Coll (WA)
Southwestern Coll (CA)

Southwestern Michigan Coll (MI)
Spokane Comm Coll (WA)
Stark State Coll of Technology (OH)
State U of NY Coll of A&T at Morrisville (NY)
Temple Coll (TX)
Texas State Tech Coll–Harlingen (TX)
Texas State Tech Coll–Waco/Marshall Campus (TX)
Thompson Inst (PA)
Tidewater Comm Coll (VA)
U of Northwestern Ohio (OH)
Utah Valley State Coll (UT)
Vatterott Coll, St. Ann (MO)
Vatterott Coll, Springfield (MO)
Vatterott Coll, Oklahoma City (OK)
Vatterott Coll, Tulsa (OK)
Vincennes U (IN)
Washtenaw Comm Coll (MI)
Weatherford Coll (TX)
Western Nevada Comm Coll (NV)
Western Wisconsin Tech Coll (WI)
West Virginia Northern Comm Coll (WV)
Westwood Coll–Atlanta Campus (GA)
Westwood Coll–Chicago Du Page (IL)
Westwood Coll–Chicago O'Hare Airport (IL)
Westwood Coll–Chicago River Oaks (IL)
Westwood Coll–Dallas (TX)
Westwood Coll–Denver South (CO)
Westwood Coll–Fort Worth (TX)
Westwood Coll–Houston South Campus (TX)
Westwood Coll–Inland Empire (CA)
Westwood Coll–Los Angeles (CA)
Westwood Coll–Chicago Loop Campus (IL)
Westwood Coll–Denver North (CO)
Wilson Tech Comm Coll (NC)

Computer Programming Related

Academy of Medical Arts and Business (PA)
AEC Southern Ohio Coll (OH)
American River Coll (CA)
Arapahoe Comm Coll (CO)
Austin Comm Coll (TX)
Blue Ridge Comm Coll (NC)
The Brown Mackie Coll–Lenexa Campus (KS)
Brunswick Comm Coll (NC)
Bucks County Comm Coll (PA)
Cambria County Area Comm Coll (PA)
Camden County Coll (NJ)
Centralia Coll (WA)
Central Pennsylvania Coll (PA)
Clark State Comm Coll (OH)
Coastal Bend Coll (TX)
Coll of the Desert (CA)
The Coll of Westchester (NY)
Corning Comm Coll (NY)
Dakota County Tech Coll (MN)
Del Mar Coll (TX)
Delta Coll (MI)
Donnelly Coll (KS)
Durham Tech Comm Coll (NC)
Eastfield Coll (TX)
Fayetteville Tech Comm Coll (NC)
Fiorello H LaGuardia Comm Coll of City U of NY (NY)

Florida National Coll (FL)
Henderson Comm Coll (KY)
Hill Coll of the Hill Jr College District (TX)
Hinds Comm Coll (MS)
J. Sargeant Reynolds Comm Coll (VA)
Kishwaukee Coll (IL)
Lake Area Tech Inst (SD)
Lakeland Comm Coll (OH)
Lakeshore Tech Coll (WI)
Laredo Comm Coll (TX)
Lorain County Comm Coll (OH)
Luzerne County Comm Coll (PA)
Manatee Comm Coll (FL)
Mesabi Range Comm and Tech Coll (MN)
Metropolitan Comm Coll-Business & Technology College (MO)
Milwaukee Area Tech Coll (WI)
Mississippi Gulf Coast Comm Coll (MS)
Northeast State Tech Comm Coll (TN)
Northern Essex Comm Coll (MA)
Northwest Iowa Comm Coll (IA)
Olympic Coll (WA)
Orangeburg-Calhoun Tech Coll (SC)
Pasco-Hernando Comm Coll (FL)
Remington Coll–Lafayette Campus (LA)
Riverside Comm Coll (CA)
Saint Charles Comm Coll (MO)
St. Cloud Tech Coll (MN)
Schenectady County Comm Coll (NY)
Seminole Comm Coll (FL)
Sinclair Comm Coll (OH)
Southwest Mississippi Comm Coll (MS)
Stanly Comm Coll (NC)
Stark State Coll of Technology (OH)
Texas State Tech Coll–Harlingen (TX)
Tompkins Cortland Comm Coll (NY)
Triton Coll (IL)
Vincennes U (IN)

Computer Programming (Specific Applications)
Academy of Medical Arts and Business (PA)
AEC Southern Ohio Coll (OH)
AIB Coll of Business (IA)
Alexandria Tech Coll (MN)
American River Coll (CA)
Arapahoe Comm Coll (CO)
Bladen Comm Coll (NC)
Bradford School (OH)
Brevard Comm Coll (FL)
Bristol Comm Coll (MA)
Bucks County Comm Coll (PA)
Bunker Hill Comm Coll (MA)
Caldwell Comm Coll and Tech Inst (NC)
Cambria County Area Comm Coll (PA)
Camden County Coll (NJ)
Cedar Valley Coll (TX)
Central Comm Coll–Columbus Campus (NE)
Central Comm Coll–Grand Island Campus (NE)
Central Comm Coll–Hastings Campus (NE)
Central Piedmont Comm Coll (NC)
Chabot Coll (CA)
CHI Inst (PA)
Cincinnati State Tech and Comm Coll (OH)

City Colls of Chicago, Malcolm X Coll (IL)
Cleveland Comm Coll (NC)
Coastal Bend Coll (TX)
Coastal Carolina Comm Coll (NC)
CollAmerica–Fort Collins (CO)
Coll of DuPage (IL)
The Coll of Westchester (NY)
Dakota County Tech Coll (MN)
Daytona Beach Comm Coll (FL)
Delaware County Comm Coll (PA)
Del Mar Coll (TX)
Delta Coll (MI)
Des Moines Area Comm Coll (IA)
Dunwoody Coll of Technology (MN)
Edison Comm Coll (FL)
Elgin Comm Coll (IL)
Essex County Coll (NJ)
Fayetteville Tech Comm Coll (NC)
Fiorello H LaGuardia Comm Coll of City U of NY (NY)
Florida Career Coll (FL)
Florida National Coll (FL)
Gogebic Comm Coll (MI)
Gulf Coast Comm Coll (FL)
Hamilton Coll (NE)
Heartland Comm Coll (IL)
Henderson Comm Coll (KY)
Indiana Business Coll, Evansville (IN)
Indiana Business Coll, Indianapolis (IN)
Indiana Business Coll, Muncie (IN)
Indiana Business Coll, Terre Haute (IN)
Johnson County Comm Coll (KS)
John Wood Comm Coll (IL)
Kaskaskia Coll (IL)
Kellogg Comm Coll (MI)
Kishwaukee Coll (IL)
Lake Area Tech Inst (SD)
Lake City Comm Coll (FL)
Lake Land Coll (IL)
Lakeland Comm Coll (OH)
Lake Region State Coll (ND)
Lake Superior Coll (MN)
Lincoln Land Comm Coll (IL)
Linn-Benton Comm Coll (OR)
Lorain County Comm Coll (OH)
Macomb Comm Coll (MI)
McHenry County Coll (IL)
Mesabi Range Comm and Tech Coll (MN)
Metropolitan Comm Coll-Business & Technology College (MO)
Midland Coll (TX)
Milwaukee Area Tech Coll (WI)
Mohave Comm Coll (AZ)
Monroe County Comm Coll (MI)
Moraine Valley Comm Coll (IL)
Naugatuck Valley Comm Coll (CT)
New Hampshire Tech Inst (NH)
North Dakota State Coll of Science (ND)
Northeast Comm Coll (NE)
Northern Essex Comm Coll (MA)
North Shore Comm Coll (MA)
Oakton Comm Coll (IL)
Orange Coast Coll (CA)
Palm Beach Comm Coll (FL)
Parkland Coll (IL)
Pasco-Hernando Comm Coll (FL)

Pennsylvania Coll of Technology (PA)
Pitt Comm Coll (NC)
Rend Lake Coll (IL)
Riverland Comm Coll (MN)
Saint Charles Comm Coll (MO)
St. Cloud Tech Coll (MN)
Santa Monica Coll (CA)
Seminole Comm Coll (FL)
Sheridan Coll (WY)
Sinclair Comm Coll (OH)
Southern State Comm Coll (OH)
Southern West Virginia Comm and Tech Coll (WV)
South Hills School of Business & Technology, State College (PA)
Southwest Missouri State U–West Plains (MO)
Stanly Comm Coll (NC)
Stark State Coll of Technology (OH)
Sullivan County Comm Coll (NY)
Texas State Tech Coll–Harlingen (TX)
Trident Tech Coll (SC)
Victor Valley Coll (CA)
Vincennes U (IN)
Waubonsee Comm Coll (IL)
Western Iowa Tech Comm Coll (IA)
Western Wyoming Comm Coll (WY)
Williamsburg Tech Coll (SC)
Wisconsin Indianhead Tech Coll (WI)

Computer Programming (Vendor/Product Certification)
Academy of Medical Arts and Business (PA)
American River Coll (CA)
Arkansas State U–Beebe (AR)
Coastal Bend Coll (TX)
The Coll of Westchester (NY)
Dakota County Tech Coll (MN)
Del Mar Coll (TX)
Fiorello H LaGuardia Comm Coll of City U of NY (NY)
Heartland Comm Coll (IL)
Henderson Comm Coll (KY)
Lake City Comm Coll (FL)
Lake Region State Coll (ND)
Lorain County Comm Coll (OH)
Louisville Tech Inst (KY)
Marion Tech Coll (OH)
Metropolitan Comm Coll-Business & Technology College (MO)
Milwaukee Area Tech Coll (WI)
Parkland Coll (IL)
Peninsula Coll (WA)
Riverland Comm Coll (MN)
Seminole Comm Coll (FL)
Sinclair Comm Coll (OH)
Stark State Coll of Technology (OH)
Texas State Tech Coll–Harlingen (TX)
Vincennes U (IN)
Washtenaw Comm Coll (MI)

Computer Science
Abraham Baldwin Ag Coll (GA)
AEC Southern Ohio Coll, Northern Kentucky Campus (KY)
Amarillo Coll (TX)
Andover Coll (ME)
Anne Arundel Comm Coll (MD)
Arapahoe Comm Coll (CO)
Arizona Western Coll (AZ)
Asnuntuck Comm Coll (CT)
Atlanta Metropolitan Coll (GA)

Austin Comm Coll (TX)
Barton County Comm Coll (KS)
Berean Inst (PA)
Bergen Comm Coll (NJ)
Blue River Comm Coll (MO)
Bristol Comm Coll (MA)
Bronx Comm Coll of City U of NY (NY)
Bucks County Comm Coll (PA)
Bunker Hill Comm Coll (MA)
Burlington County Coll (NJ)
Butler County Comm Coll (KS)
Cabrillo Coll (CA)
Cañada Coll (CA)
Cape Cod Comm Coll (MA)
Casper Coll (WY)
Central Alabama Comm Coll (AL)
Central Arizona Coll (AZ)
Central Oregon Comm Coll (OR)
Central Piedmont Comm Coll (NC)
Central Wyoming Coll (WY)
Chabot Coll (CA)
Chemeketa Comm Coll (OR)
Chesapeake Coll (MD)
Chipola Coll (FL)
Coastal Bend Coll (TX)
Coastal Georgia Comm Coll (GA)
Coffeyville Comm Coll (KS)
Colby Comm Coll (KS)
Coll of Southern Idaho (ID)
Coll of the Canyons (CA)
Coll of the Desert (CA)
Coll of the Sequoias (CA)
Columbia Coll (CA)
Columbia-Greene Comm Coll (NY)
Commonwealth Tech Inst (PA)
Connors State Coll (OK)
Contra Costa Coll (CA)
Corning Comm Coll (NY)
Cuesta Coll (CA)
Cumberland County Coll (NJ)
Darton Coll (GA)
Daytona Beach Comm Coll (FL)
Del Mar Coll (TX)
Delta Coll (MI)
Donnelly Coll (KS)
Dutchess Comm Coll (NY)
Eastern Oklahoma State Coll (OK)
East Mississippi Comm Coll (MS)
ECPI Coll of Technology, Newport News (VA)
ECPI Coll of Technology, Virginia Beach (VA)
ECPI Tech Coll, Richmond (VA)
ECPI Tech Coll, Roanoke (VA)
Edison Comm Coll (FL)
Edison State Comm Coll (OH)
Education Direct Center for Degree Studies (PA)
Elaine P. Nunez Comm Coll (LA)
El Centro Coll (TX)
Erie Business Center South (PA)
Essex County Coll (NJ)
Everett Comm Coll (WA)
Finger Lakes Comm Coll (NY)
Fiorello H LaGuardia Comm Coll of City U of NY (NY)
Florida Career Coll (FL)
Florida National Coll (FL)
Foothill Coll (CA)
Forsyth Tech Comm Coll (NC)
Fort Scott Comm Coll (KS)
Foundation Coll, San Diego (CA)

Fulton-Montgomery Comm Coll (NY)
Gallipolis Career Coll (OH)
Galveston Coll (TX)
Garden City Comm Coll (KS)
Gavilan Coll (CA)
Gem City Coll (IL)
Georgia Perimeter Coll (GA)
Gloucester County Coll (NJ)
Gogebic Comm Coll (MI)
Gordon Coll (GA)
Grand Rapids Comm Coll (MI)
Gwinnett Tech Coll (GA)
Heartland Comm Coll (IL)
Hesser Coll (NH)
Hill Coll of the Hill Jr College District (TX)
Hinds Comm Coll (MS)
Holmes Comm Coll (MS)
Houston Comm Coll System (TX)
Howard Coll (TX)
Howard Comm Coll (MD)
Hudson County Comm Coll (NJ)
Iowa Lakes Comm Coll (IA)
Isothermal Comm Coll (NC)
Jackson State Comm Coll (TN)
Jamestown Comm Coll (NY)
Jefferson Comm Coll (NY)
John A. Logan Coll (IL)
Kilian Comm Coll (SD)
Kingsborough Comm Coll of City U of NY (NY)
Kirkwood Comm Coll (IA)
Lake Region State Coll (ND)
Lake-Sumter Comm Coll (FL)
Lake Washington Tech Coll (WA)
Lamar State Coll–Orange (TX)
Lanier Tech Coll (GA)
Laramie County Comm Coll (WY)
Lincoln Coll, Lincoln (IL)
Longview Comm Coll (MO)
Lon Morris Coll (TX)
Lorain County Comm Coll (OH)
Los Angeles Pierce Coll (CA)
Louisiana Tech Coll–Delta Ouachita Campus (LA)
Louisiana Tech Coll–Northwest Louisiana Campus (LA)
Louisiana Tech Coll–Sabine Valley Campus (LA)
Lower Columbia Coll (WA)
Luzerne County Comm Coll (PA)
Maple Woods Comm Coll (MO)
Marshalltown Comm Coll (IA)
McIntosh Coll (NH)
Metropolitan Comm Coll-Business & Technology College (MO)
Miami Dade Coll (FL)
Middle Georgia Coll (GA)
Middlesex Comm Coll (MA)
Middlesex County Coll (NJ)
Mid Michigan Comm Coll (MI)
Milwaukee Area Tech Coll (WI)
Mississippi Gulf Coast Comm Coll (MS)
Mitchell Comm Coll (NC)
Modesto Jr Coll (CA)
Mohave Comm Coll (AZ)
Monroe Coll, Bronx (NY)
Monroe Coll, New Rochelle (NY)
Mt. San Antonio Coll (CA)
Mt. San Jacinto Coll (CA)
Napa Valley Coll (CA)
Nassau Comm Coll (NY)
New Mexico State U–Carlsbad (NM)

Niagara County Comm Coll (NY)
Normandale Comm Coll (MN)
Northeast Alabama Comm Coll (AL)
Northeast Comm Coll (NE)
Northeastern Oklahoma A&M Coll (OK)
Northeastern Tech Coll (SC)
Northeast Mississippi Comm Coll (MS)
Northeast Texas Comm Coll (TX)
Northern Essex Comm Coll (MA)
North Harris Coll (TX)
North Idaho Coll (ID)
North Shore Comm Coll (MA)
Northwestern Connecticut Comm-Tech Coll (CT)
Northwest-Shoals Comm Coll (AL)
Oakton Comm Coll (IL)
Odessa Coll (TX)
Oklahoma City Comm Coll (OK)
Orange County Comm Coll (NY)
Palm Beach Comm Coll (FL)
Palo Alto Coll (TX)
Palomar Coll (CA)
Parkland Coll (IL)
Pasadena City Coll (CA)
Pellissippi State Tech Comm Coll (TN)
Penn Valley Comm Coll (MO)
Pensacola Jr Coll (FL)
Prince George's Comm Coll (MD)
Raritan Valley Comm Coll (NJ)
Reading Area Comm Coll (PA)
Red Rocks Comm Coll (CO)
Rend Lake Coll (IL)
RETS Tech Center (OH)
Roane State Comm Coll (TN)
Rochester Comm and Tech Coll (MN)
Rogue Comm Coll (OR)
Saint Charles Comm Coll (MO)
St. Louis Comm Coll at Florissant Valley (MO)
San Joaquin Delta Coll (CA)
San Jose City Coll (CA)
San Juan Coll (NM)
Santa Barbara City Coll (CA)
Schenectady County Comm Coll (NY)
Seward County Comm Coll (KS)
Shelton State Comm Coll (AL)
Sierra Coll (CA)
Snow Coll (UT)
South Coll (TN)
Southeast Comm Coll, Beatrice Campus (NE)
Southern Arkansas U Tech (AR)
South Plains Coll (TX)
South Texas Comm Coll (TX)
Southwestern Coll (CA)
Southwest Mississippi Comm Coll (MS)
Springfield Tech Comm Coll (MA)
State U of NY Coll of A&T at Morrisville (NY)
State U of NY Coll of Technology at Alfred (NY)
Temple Coll (TX)
Texas State Tech Coll–Harlingen (TX)
Texas State Tech Coll–Waco/Marshall Campus (TX)
Thomas Nelson Comm Coll (VA)

Tompkins Cortland Comm Coll (NY)
Trinidad State Jr Coll (CO)
Triton Coll (IL)
Umpqua Comm Coll (OR)
The U of Akron–Wayne Coll (OH)
Utah Valley State Coll (UT)
Vermilion Comm Coll (MN)
Victor Valley Coll (CA)
Vincennes U (IN)
Virginia Western Comm Coll (VA)
Walters State Comm Coll (TN)
Washtenaw Comm Coll (MI)
Waycross Coll (GA)
Western Wyoming Comm Coll (WY)
Westmoreland County Comm Coll (PA)
Yakima Valley Comm Coll (WA)
Yuba Coll (CA)

Computer Software and Media Applications Related
AIB Coll of Business (IA)
American River Coll (CA)
Ancilla Coll (IN)
Arapahoe Comm Coll (CO)
Brevard Comm Coll (FL)
Carteret Comm Coll (NC)
Coll of the Sequoias (CA)
The Coll of Westchester (NY)
Dakota County Tech Coll (MN)
Delta Coll (MI)
Fayetteville Tech Comm Coll (NC)
Gallipolis Career Coll (OH)
Kellogg Comm Coll (MI)
Kilian Comm Coll (SD)
Laredo Comm Coll (TX)
Louisiana Tech Coll–Florida Parishes Campus (LA)
Marion Tech Coll (OH)
Mesabi Range Comm and Tech Coll (MN)
Metropolitan Comm Coll-Business & Technology College (MO)
Mitchell Tech Inst (SD)
Olympic Coll (WA)
Parkland Coll (IL)
Pellissippi State Tech Comm Coll (TN)
Platt Coll San Diego (CA)
Rasmussen Coll Mankato (MN)
Riverland Comm Coll (MN)
Seminole Comm Coll (FL)
Sheridan Coll (WY)
Stark State Coll of Technology (OH)
Texas State Tech Coll–Harlingen (TX)
Triton Coll (IL)
Vincennes U (IN)
Vista Comm Coll (CA)

Computer Software Engineering
Globe Coll (MN)
Lake City Comm Coll (FL)
Minnesota School of Business–Brooklyn Center (MN)
Minnesota School of Business-Plymouth (MN)
Minnesota School of Business-Richfield (MN)
Mt. San Jacinto Coll (CA)
Seminole Comm Coll (FL)
Sinclair Comm Coll (OH)
Stark State Coll of Technology (OH)
Tompkins Cortland Comm Coll (NY)
Vincennes U (IN)
Westwood Coll–Chicago Du Page (IL)
Westwood Coll–Chicago O'Hare Airport (IL)

Computer Software Technology
Iowa Lakes Comm Coll (IA)
Miami Dade Coll (FL)
Middlesex Comm Coll (MA)
Westwood Coll–Denver North (CO)

Computer Systems Analysis
Albuquerque Tech Vocational Inst (NM)
Amarillo Coll (TX)
Brevard Comm Coll (FL)
Cape Fear Comm Coll (NC)
Central Florida Comm Coll (FL)
Coastal Carolina Comm Coll (NC)
Hesser Coll (NH)
James Sprunt Comm Coll (NC)
Lakeshore Tech Coll (WI)
Laramie County Comm Coll (WY)
Linn State Tech Coll (MO)
Lower Columbia Coll (WA)
McIntosh Coll (NH)
Metropolitan Comm Coll-Business & Technology College (MO)
Milwaukee Area Tech Coll (WI)
Pima Comm Coll (AZ)
Pitt Comm Coll (NC)
Remington Coll–Lafayette Campus (LA)
Richmond Comm Coll (NC)
United Tribes Tech Coll (ND)
Utah Valley State Coll (UT)
Wor-Wic Comm Coll (MD)

Computer Systems Networking and Telecommunications
Academy Coll (MN)
AEC Southern Ohio Coll (OH)
AIB Coll of Business (IA)
Alexandria Tech Coll (MN)
Alpena Comm Coll (MI)
American River Coll (CA)
Ancilla Coll (IN)
Antonelli Coll (OH)
Arapahoe Comm Coll (CO)
Arkansas State U–Beebe (AR)
Asheville-Buncombe Tech Comm Coll (NC)
Austin Comm Coll (TX)
Barton County Comm Coll (KS)
Bates Tech Coll (WA)
Beaufort County Comm Coll (NC)
Beckfield Coll (KY)
Bismarck State Coll (ND)
Bowling Green State U-Firelands Coll (OH)
Brevard Comm Coll (FL)
Bunker Hill Comm Coll (MA)
Cape Cod Comm Coll (MA)
Cape Fear Comm Coll (NC)
Carteret Comm Coll (NC)
Centralia Coll (WA)
Central Wyoming Coll (WY)
Chaparral Coll (AZ)
CHI Inst (PA)
Clark Coll (WA)
Clark State Comm Coll (OH)
Clover Park Tech Coll (WA)
Coastal Bend Coll (TX)
Coastal Carolina Comm Coll (NC)
CollAmerica–Fort Collins (CO)
The Coll of Westchester (NY)
Collin County Comm Coll District (TX)
Colorado Mountn Coll (CO)
Columbia-Greene Comm Coll (NY)
Comm Coll of Allegheny County (PA)
Corning Comm Coll (NY)
Crowder Coll (MO)

Cuesta Coll (CA)
Cumberland County Coll (NJ)
Dakota County Tech Coll (MN)
Davis Coll (OH)
Daymar Coll, Louisville (KY)
Daytona Beach Comm Coll (FL)
Delaware County Comm Coll (PA)
Del Mar Coll (TX)
Duluth Business U (MN)
Eastern Idaho Tech Coll (ID)
Eastfield Coll (TX)
Fayetteville Tech Comm Coll (NC)
Fiorello H LaGuardia Comm Coll of City U of NY (NY)
Florida National Coll (FL)
Foundation Coll, San Diego (CA)
Garden City Comm Coll (KS)
Glendale Comm Coll (AZ)
Globe Coll (MN)
Guilford Tech Comm Coll (NC)
Harrisburg Area Comm Coll (PA)
Hawkeye Comm Coll (IA)
Heartland Comm Coll (IL)
Henderson Comm Coll (KY)
Herzing Coll, Minneapolis Drafting School Division (MN)
Hibbing Comm Coll (MN)
High-Tech Inst (AZ)
Hillsborough Comm Coll (FL)
Howard Comm Coll (MD)
IntelliTec Coll, Grand Junction (CO)
Iowa Lakes Comm Coll (IA)
Island Drafting and Tech Inst (NY)
Jefferson Coll (MO)
Jefferson Comm Coll (NY)
Johnson County Comm Coll (KS)
Keiser Coll, Miami (FL)
Lake Area Tech Inst (SD)
Lake Land Coll (IL)
Lakeland Comm Coll (OH)
Lake Region State Coll (ND)
Lanier Tech Coll (GA)
Laredo Comm Coll (TX)
Lincoln Land Comm Coll (IL)
Lorain County Comm Coll (OH)
Louisville Tech Inst (KY)
Lower Columbia Coll (WA)
Luzerne County Comm Coll (PA)
Manhattan Area Tech Coll (KS)
Marion Tech Coll (OH)
Mesabi Range Comm and Tech Coll (MN)
Metropolitan Comm Coll-Business & Technology College (MO)
Michiana Coll, South Bend (IN)
Middlesex County Coll (NJ)
Midlands Tech Coll (SC)
Minnesota School of Business–Brooklyn Center (MN)
Minnesota School of Business-Plymouth (MN)
Minnesota School of Business-Richfield (MN)
Minot State U–Bottineau Campus (ND)
Mississippi Gulf Coast Comm Coll (MS)
Mitchell Tech Inst (SD)
Montana State U Coll of Tech-Great Falls (MT)
Montgomery County Comm Coll (PA)
Moraine Valley Comm Coll (IL)
Mott Comm Coll (MI)

Mountain Empire Comm Coll (VA)
Mountain West Coll (UT)
Nashville State Tech Comm Coll (TN)
Nassau Comm Coll (NY)
New England Inst of Tech & Florida Culinary Inst (FL)
New Hampshire Tech Inst (NH)
Normandale Comm Coll (MN)
North Central State Coll (OH)
Northeast State Tech Comm Coll (TN)
Northern Essex Comm Coll (MA)
Northland Pioneer Coll (AZ)
North Seattle Comm Coll (WA)
Northwest Iowa Comm Coll (IA)
Odessa Coll (TX)
Olympic Coll (WA)
Parkland Coll (IL)
Pasco-Hernando Comm Coll (FL)
Pellissippi State Tech Comm Coll (TN)
Pennsylvania Coll of Technology (PA)
Pima Comm Coll (AZ)
Pitt Comm Coll (NC)
Pratt Comm Coll and Area Vocational School (KS)
Quinebaug Valley Comm Coll (CT)
Rasmussen Coll Mankato (MN)
Remington Coll–Lafayette Campus (LA)
Remington Coll–Mobile Campus (AL)
Riverland Comm Coll (MN)
Riverside Comm Coll (CA)
Saint Charles Comm Coll (MO)
St. Cloud Tech Coll (MN)
St. Petersburg Coll (FL)
St. Philip's Coll (TX)
Salem Comm Coll (NJ)
Seminole Comm Coll (FL)
Sheridan Coll (WY)
Sinclair Comm Coll (OH)
Stanly Comm Coll (NC)
Stark State Coll of Technology (OH)
Stautzenberger Coll (OH)
Texas State Tech Coll–Harlingen (TX)
Thompson Inst (PA)
Trident Tech Coll (SC)
Trinidad State Jr Coll (CO)
Triton Coll (IL)
United Tribes Tech Coll (ND)
The U of Akron–Wayne Coll (OH)
U of Arkansas Comm Coll at Batesville (AR)
U of Kentucky, Lexington Comm Coll (KY)
Utah Valley State Coll (UT)
Vatterott Coll, St. Joseph (MO)
Vincennes U (IN)
Virginia Coll at Jackson (MS)
Westwood Coll–Anaheim (CA)
Westwood Coll–Atlanta Campus (GA)
Westwood Coll–Chicago Du Page (IL)
Westwood Coll–Chicago O'Hare Airport (IL)
Westwood Coll–Chicago River Oaks (IL)
Westwood Coll–Dallas (TX)
Westwood Coll–Denver South (CO)
Westwood Coll–Fort Worth (TX)
Westwood Coll–Houston South Campus (TX)

Westwood Coll–Inland Empire (CA)
Westwood Coll–Los Angeles (CA)
Westwood Coll–Chicago Loop Campus (IL)
Wisconsin Indianhead Tech Coll (WI)
York County Comm Coll (ME)
York Tech Inst (PA)

Computer/Technical Support
American River Coll (CA)
Anne Arundel Comm Coll (MD)
Arapahoe Comm Coll (CO)
Bowling Green State U-Firelands Coll (OH)
The Brown Mackie Coll–Lenexa Campus (KS)
Cambria County Area Comm Coll (PA)
Clark State Comm Coll (OH)
Coll of the Desert (CA)
The Coll of Westchester (NY)
Colorado Mountn Coll (CO)
Cuesta Coll (CA)
Del Mar Coll (TX)
Eastern Shore Comm Coll (VA)
Elaine P. Nunez Comm Coll (LA)
Fayetteville Tech Comm Coll (NC)
Florida National Coll (FL)
Gallipolis Career Coll (OH)
Galveston Coll (TX)
Goodwin Coll (CT)
Hawkeye Comm Coll (IA)
Heartland Comm Coll (IL)
Hinds Comm Coll (MS)
Holmes Comm Coll (MS)
Island Drafting and Tech Inst (NY)
Linn-Benton Comm Coll (OR)
Louisville Tech Inst (KY)
Massasoit Comm Coll (MA)
Mitchell Tech Inst (SD)
Mountain Empire Comm Coll (VA)
North Idaho Coll (ID)
Oakton Comm Coll (IL)
Oklahoma State U, Oklahoma City (OK)
Palm Beach Comm Coll (FL)
Parkland Coll (IL)
Pratt Comm Coll and Area Vocational School (KS)
Rasmussen Coll Mankato (MN)
Remington Coll–Lafayette Campus (LA)
Riverland Comm Coll (MN)
Riverside Comm Coll (CA)
St. Cloud Tech Coll (MN)
Seminole Comm Coll (FL)
Stanly Comm Coll (NC)
Stark State Coll of Technology (OH)
Texas State Tech Coll–Harlingen (TX)
Three Rivers Comm Coll (MO)
Tompkins Cortland Comm Coll (NY)
Triton Coll (IL)
Vincennes U (IN)
Washtenaw Comm Coll (MI)
Western Dakota Tech Inst (SD)
York Tech Inst (PA)

Computer Technology/ Computer Systems Technology
Alexandria Tech Coll (MN)
Anoka Tech Coll (MN)
Bates Tech Coll (WA)
Beckfield Coll (KY)
Cape Fear Comm Coll (NC)
Central Wyoming Coll (WY)

Comm Coll of Allegheny County (PA)
Corning Comm Coll (NY)
Delaware County Comm Coll (PA)
Eastern Maine Comm Coll (ME)
ECPI Tech Coll, Glen Allen (VA)
ECPI Tech Coll, Richmond (VA)
ECPI Tech Coll, Roanoke (VA)
Edmonds Comm Coll (WA)
Foundation Coll, San Diego (CA)
High-Tech Inst (AZ)
Island Drafting and Tech Inst (NY)
ITI Tech Coll (LA)
Lake Superior Coll (MN)
Lamar State Coll–Port Arthur (TX)
Lehigh Carbon Comm Coll (PA)
Lorain County Comm Coll (OH)
Louisville Tech Inst (KY)
Lower Columbia Coll (WA)
Luzerne County Comm Coll (PA)
Manhattan Area Tech Coll (KS)
Miami Dade Coll (FL)
Miami U Hamilton (OH)
Mitchell Tech Inst (SD)
Montgomery Coll (MD)
Mount Wachusett Comm Coll (MA)
MTI Coll of Business and Technology, Houston (TX)
Oakland Comm Coll (MI)
Okefenokee Tech Coll (GA)
Pennsylvania Coll of Technology (PA)
Pima Comm Coll (AZ)
Quinsigamond Comm Coll (MA)
Schoolcraft Coll (MI)
Southern Arkansas U Tech (AR)
Stanly Comm Coll (NC)
Texas State Tech Coll–Harlingen (TX)
Texas State Tech Coll–Waco/Marshall Campus (TX)
Vatterott Coll, St. Joseph (MO)

Computer Typography and Composition Equipment Operation
Abraham Baldwin Ag Coll (GA)
Bergen Comm Coll (NJ)
Bristol Comm Coll (MA)
The Brown Mackie Coll–Lenexa Campus (KS)
Camden County Coll (NJ)
Chabot Coll (CA)
CHI Inst (PA)
Clovis Comm Coll (NM)
Coll of DuPage (IL)
Coll of the Desert (CA)
Coll of the Sequoias (CA)
The Coll of Westchester (NY)
Commonwealth Business Coll, Michigan City (IN)
Comm Coll of Denver (CO)
Cumberland County Coll (NJ)
Cuyahoga Comm Coll (OH)
Daytona Beach Comm Coll (FL)
Del Mar Coll (TX)
Doña Ana Branch Comm Coll (NM)
Durham Tech Comm Coll (NC)
ECPI Coll of Technology, Newport News (VA)
ECPI Coll of Technology, Virginia Beach (VA)

Computer Typography and Composition Equipment Operation

ECPI Tech Coll, Richmond (VA)
ECPI Tech Coll, Roanoke (VA)
Elgin Comm Coll (IL)
Fulton-Montgomery Comm Coll (NY)
Gogebic Comm Coll (MI)
Hill Coll of the Hill Jr College District (TX)
Holyoke Comm Coll (MA)
Jefferson Comm Coll (NY)
Kingwood Coll (TX)
Lansing Comm Coll (MI)
Lincoln Coll, Lincoln (IL)
Longview Comm Coll (MO)
MacCormac Coll (IL)
Merritt Coll (CA)
Minnesota State Coll–Southeast Tech (MN)
New River Comm Coll (VA)
Northeast Alabama Comm Coll (AL)
Northeastern Oklahoma A&M Coll (OK)
Northern Essex Comm Coll (MA)
Northwest-Shoals Comm Coll (AL)
Orange Coast Coll (CA)
Paris Jr Coll (TX)
Pasadena City Coll (CA)
Platt Coll San Diego (CA)
Pratt Comm Coll and Area Vocational School (KS)
Prince George's Comm Coll (MD)
Rasmussen Coll Mankato (MN)
St. Clair County Comm Coll (MI)
St. Cloud Tech Coll (MN)
St. Johns River Comm Coll (FL)
South Texas Comm Coll (TX)
Spokane Comm Coll (WA)
State U of NY Coll of A&T at Morrisville (NY)
State U of NY Coll of Technology at Alfred (NY)
Triton Coll (IL)
Washtenaw Comm Coll (MI)
Western Iowa Tech Comm Coll (IA)

Concrete Finishing
Dakota County Tech Coll (MN)

Construction Engineering
State U of NY Coll of Technology at Alfred (NY)

Construction Engineering Technology
American River Coll (CA)
Austin Comm Coll (TX)
Bismarck State Coll (ND)
Blackfeet Comm Coll (MT)
Butte Coll (CA)
Cambria County Area Comm Coll (PA)
Casper Coll (WY)
Cecil Comm Coll (MD)
Central Comm Coll–Hastings Campus (NE)
Chemeketa Comm Coll (OR)
Clark Coll (WA)
Coffeyville Comm Coll (KS)
Coll of Eastern Utah (UT)
Coll of Lake County (IL)
Coll of the Sequoias (CA)
Comm Coll of Allegheny County (PA)
Comm Coll of the Air Force (AL)
Crowder Coll (MO)
Cuesta Coll (CA)
Daytona Beach Comm Coll (FL)
Delaware County Comm Coll (PA)
Delaware Tech & Comm Coll, Terry Cmps (DE)
Delta Coll (MI)
Dutchess Comm Coll (NY)

Eastern Maine Comm Coll (ME)
Edmonds Comm Coll (WA)
El Camino Coll (CA)
Feather River Comm Coll District (CA)
Forsyth Tech Comm Coll (NC)
Fulton-Montgomery Comm Coll (NY)
Gogebic Comm Coll (MI)
Gulf Coast Comm Coll (FL)
Harrisburg Area Comm Coll (PA)
Hillsborough Comm Coll (FL)
Houston Comm Coll System (TX)
Iowa Lakes Comm Coll (IA)
Jefferson State Comm Coll (AL)
J. Sargeant Reynolds Comm Coll (VA)
Kirkwood Comm Coll (IA)
Lansing Comm Coll (MI)
Laramie County Comm Coll (WY)
Laredo Comm Coll (TX)
Lehigh Carbon Comm Coll (PA)
Los Angeles Pierce Coll (CA)
Los Angeles Trade-Tech Coll (CA)
Macomb Comm Coll (MI)
Manatee Comm Coll (FL)
Metropolitan Comm Coll (NE)
Miami Dade Coll (FL)
Middlesex County Coll (NJ)
Midlands Tech Coll (SC)
Mid-Plains Comm Coll, North Platte (NE)
Miles Comm Coll (MT)
Milwaukee Area Tech Coll (WI)
Mineral Area Coll (MO)
Morrison Inst of Technology (IL)
New Castle School of Trades (PA)
New Hampshire Comm Tech Coll, Manchester/Stratham (NH)
North Central Missouri Coll (MO)
North Dakota State Coll of Science (ND)
Northeastern Oklahoma A&M Coll (OK)
Northeast Iowa Comm Coll (IA)
Ocean County Coll (NJ)
Odessa Coll (TX)
Ohio State U Ag Tech Inst (OH)
Oklahoma State U, Oklahoma City (OK)
Orange Coast Coll (CA)
Orange County Comm Coll (NY)
Palomar Coll (CA)
Pasadena City Coll (CA)
Pellissippi State Tech Comm Coll (TN)
Pennsylvania Coll of Technology (PA)
Pensacola Jr Coll (FL)
Phoenix Coll (AZ)
Pima Comm Coll (AZ)
Portland Comm Coll (OR)
Raritan Valley Comm Coll (NJ)
Roanoke-Chowan Comm Coll (NC)
Rockingham Comm Coll (NC)
St. Cloud Tech Coll (MN)
St. Louis Comm Coll at Florissant Valley (MO)
St. Petersburg Coll (FL)
St. Philip's Coll (TX)
San Joaquin Delta Coll (CA)
San Jose City Coll (CA)
Santa Fe Comm Coll (NM)
Santa Monica Coll (CA)

Seminole Comm Coll (FL)
Sierra Coll (CA)
Snow Coll (UT)
Southern Maine Comm Coll (ME)
South Suburban Coll (IL)
Southwestern Coll (CA)
Southwestern Illinois Coll (IL)
Southwest Mississippi Comm Coll (MS)
Spokane Comm Coll (WA)
State U of NY Coll of A&T at Morrisville (NY)
State U of NY Coll of Technology at Alfred (NY)
State U of NY Coll of Technology at Canton (NY)
State U of NY Coll of Technology at Delhi (NY)
Texas State Tech Coll–Harlingen (TX)
Three Rivers Comm Coll (MO)
Tompkins Cortland Comm Coll (NY)
Trenholm State Tech Coll, Montgomery (AL)
Trinidad State Jr Coll (CO)
Triton Coll (IL)
Vance-Granville Comm Coll (NC)
Ventura Coll (CA)
Victor Valley Coll (CA)
Vincennes U (IN)
The Williamson Free School of Mecha Trades (PA)
Yavapai Coll (AZ)

Construction/Heavy Equipment/Earthmoving Equipment Operation
Ivy Tech State Coll–Southwest (IN)
Ivy Tech State Coll–Wabash Valley (IN)
Northwest Iowa Comm Coll (IA)

Construction Management
Arapahoe Comm Coll (CO)
Cabrillo Coll (CA)
Coll of the Desert (CA)
Columbus State Comm Coll (OH)
Columbus State Comm Coll (OH)
Delaware Tech & Comm Coll, Terry Cmps (DE)
Delgado Comm Coll (LA)
Delta Coll (MI)
Frederick Comm Coll (MD)
Gogebic Comm Coll (MI)
Gwinnett Tech Coll (GA)
Iowa Lakes Comm Coll (IA)
Modesto Jr Coll (CA)
Montgomery Coll (MD)
Mt. San Antonio Coll (CA)
North Hennepin Comm Coll (MN)
Oakland Comm Coll (MI)
Oakton Comm Coll (IL)
Ohio State U Ag Tech Inst (OH)
Palm Beach Comm Coll (FL)
Paris Jr Coll (TX)
Parkland Coll (IL)
Piedmont Virginia Comm Coll (VA)
Pikes Peak Comm Coll (CO)
St. Philip's Coll (TX)
Seminole Comm Coll (FL)
Sierra Coll (CA)
Snow Coll (UT)
Southwestern Illinois Coll (IL)
State U of NY Coll of Technology at Delhi (NY)
Triton Coll (IL)
Victor Valley Coll (CA)
Washtenaw Comm Coll (MI)
Western Nevada Comm Coll (NV)

Construction Trades
Clovis Comm Coll (NM)
Delta Coll (MI)
Iowa Lakes Comm Coll (IA)

Ivy Tech State Coll–Eastcentral (IN)
Ivy Tech State Coll–Northeast (IN)
Ivy Tech State Coll–Northwest (IN)
Ivy Tech State Coll–Whitewater (IN)
Laramie County Comm Coll (WY)
Triangle Tech, Inc.–Greensburg Center (PA)
Utah Valley State Coll (UT)

Construction Trades Related
Albuquerque Tech Vocational Inst (NM)
Comm Coll of Allegheny County (PA)
Comm Coll of Denver (CO)
Jackson Comm Coll (MI)
Laramie County Comm Coll (WY)
Mitchell Tech Inst (SD)
Pitt Comm Coll (NC)

Consumer/Homemaking Education
MiraCosta Coll (CA)

Consumer Merchandising/Retailing Management
American River Coll (CA)
Anne Arundel Comm Coll (MD)
Arapahoe Comm Coll (CO)
Austin Comm Coll (TX)
Bay State Coll (MA)
Bergen Comm Coll (NJ)
Bucks County Comm Coll (PA)
Cabrillo Coll (CA)
Cambria County Area Comm Coll (PA)
Casper Coll (WY)
Centralia Coll (WA)
Central Pennsylvania Coll (PA)
Central Piedmont Comm Coll (NC)
Chabot Coll (CA)
Clinton Comm Coll (NY)
Coffeyville Comm Coll (KS)
Colorado Mountn Coll, Alpine Cmps (CO)
Columbus State Comm Coll (OH)
Del Mar Coll (TX)
Delta Coll (MI)
Des Moines Area Comm Coll (IA)
Doña Ana Branch Comm Coll (NM)
Dutchess Comm Coll (NY)
Edison State Comm Coll (OH)
Elgin Comm Coll (IL)
Everett Comm Coll (WA)
Fashion Inst of Design & Merchandising, LA Campus (CA)
Fashion Inst of Design & Merchandising, SD Campus (CA)
Fashion Inst of Design & Merchandising, SF Campus (CA)
Finger Lakes Comm Coll (NY)
Fort Scott Comm Coll (KS)
Garden City Comm Coll (KS)
Glendale Comm Coll (AZ)
Gloucester County Coll (NJ)
Harcum Coll (PA)
Harrisburg Area Comm Coll (PA)
Holyoke Comm Coll (MA)
Howard Comm Coll (MD)
Iowa Lakes Comm Coll (IA)
James A. Rhodes State Coll (OH)
Jefferson Comm Coll (MO)
Jefferson Comm Coll (NY)
Jefferson Comm Coll (OH)
John A. Logan Coll (IL)
Kirkwood Comm Coll (IA)

Lansing Comm Coll (MI)
Lenoir Comm Coll (NC)
Lorain County Comm Coll (OH)
Los Angeles Valley Coll (CA)
MacCormac Coll (IL)
Middlesex Comm Coll (MA)
Middlesex County Coll (NJ)
Miles Comm Coll (MT)
Milwaukee Area Tech Coll (WI)
Minnesota State Coll–Southeast Tech (MN)
Newport Business Inst, Lower Burrell (PA)
Niagara County Comm Coll (NY)
North Country Comm Coll (NY)
North Hennepin Comm Coll (MN)
Oakland Comm Coll (MI)
Orange County Comm Coll (NY)
Parkland Coll (IL)
Quinsigamond Comm Coll (MA)
Raritan Valley Comm Coll (NJ)
Reading Area Comm Coll (PA)
St. Cloud Tech Coll (MN)
Sinclair Comm Coll (OH)
South Plains Coll (TX)
South Suburban Coll (IL)
Spokane Falls Comm Coll (WA)
Stark State Coll of Technology (OH)
Sullivan County Comm Coll (NY)
Sussex County Comm Coll (NJ)
Triton Coll (IL)
Western Wisconsin Tech Coll (WI)
West Kentucky Comm and Tech Coll (KY)
Westmoreland County Comm Coll (PA)

Consumer Services and Advocacy
Rockingham Comm Coll (NC)
San Diego City Coll (CA)

Cooking and Related Culinary Arts
The Art Inst of Pittsburgh (PA)
Iowa Lakes Comm Coll (IA)
Milwaukee Area Tech Coll (WI)
Pikes Peak Comm Coll (CO)

Corrections
Alpena Comm Coll (MI)
Alvin Comm Coll (TX)
Amarillo Coll (TX)
Anne Arundel Comm Coll (MD)
Atlantic Cape Comm Coll (NJ)
Brevard Comm Coll (FL)
Broome Comm Coll (NY)
Bucks County Comm Coll (PA)
Casper Coll (WY)
Central Arizona Coll (AZ)
Centralia Coll (WA)
Chabot Coll (CA)
Chesapeake Coll (MD)
Clark State Comm Coll (OH)
Clovis Comm Coll (NM)
Coll of DuPage (IL)
Coll of the Sequoias (CA)
Columbus State Comm Coll (OH)
Comm Coll of Allegheny County (PA)
Cumberland County Coll (NJ)
Daytona Beach Comm Coll (FL)

Delaware Tech & Comm Coll, Terry Cmps (DE)
Delta Coll (MI)
Des Moines Area Comm Coll (IA)
Eastern Arizona Coll (AZ)
Eastern Oklahoma State Coll (OK)
Elgin Comm Coll (IL)
Gavilan Coll (CA)
Gogebic Comm Coll (MI)
Grand Rapids Comm Coll (MI)
Hawkeye Comm Coll (IA)
Heartland Comm Coll (IL)
Hesser Coll (NH)
Hillsborough Comm Coll (FL)
Illinois Eastern Comm Colls, Frontier Comm Coll (IL)
Illinois Eastern Comm Colls, Lincoln Trail Coll (IL)
Illinois Eastern Comm Colls, Olney Central Coll (IL)
Illinois Eastern Comm Colls, Wabash Valley Coll (IL)
Iowa Lakes Comm Coll (IA)
Jackson Comm Coll (MI)
James A. Rhodes State Coll (OH)
Jefferson Comm Coll (OH)
Kellogg Comm Coll (MI)
Kirkwood Comm Coll (IA)
Kirtland Comm Coll (MI)
Lake Land Coll (IL)
Lakeland Comm Coll (OH)
Lansing Comm Coll (MI)
Laramie County Comm Coll (WY)
Lehigh Carbon Comm Coll (PA)
Lincoln Coll, Lincoln (IL)
Longview Comm Coll (MO)
Lorain County Comm Coll (OH)
Lower Columbia Coll (WA)
Middlesex County Coll (NJ)
Mid Michigan Comm Coll (MI)
Mineral Area Coll (MO)
Modesto Jr Coll (CA)
Montcalm Comm Coll (MI)
Moraine Park Tech Coll (WI)
Moraine Valley Comm Coll (IL)
Mountain Empire Comm Coll (VA)
Mt. San Antonio Coll (CA)
Napa Valley Coll (CA)
Northeast Comm Coll (NE)
Northeast Wisconsin Tech Coll (WI)
Northland Pioneer Coll (AZ)
Northwest State Comm Coll (OH)
Owens Comm Coll, Findlay (OH)
Penn Valley Comm Coll (MO)
Phoenix Coll (AZ)
Polk Comm Coll (FL)
Rend Lake Coll (IL)
Riverland Comm Coll (MN)
Roane State Comm Coll (TN)
St. Clair County Comm Coll (MI)
St. Louis Comm Coll at Florissant Valley (MO)
St. Petersburg Coll (FL)
San Joaquin Delta Coll (CA)
Sauk Valley Comm Coll (IL)
Schoolcraft Coll (MI)
Sierra Coll (CA)
Sinclair Comm Coll (OH)
Southern State Comm Coll (OH)
Southwestern Coll (CA)
Spokane Comm Coll (WA)
State U of NY Coll of Technology at Canton (NY)
Sullivan County Comm Coll (NY)
Trinidad State Jr Coll (CO)

Vance-Granville Comm Coll (NC)
Vincennes U (IN)
Washtenaw Comm Coll (MI)
Weatherford Coll (TX)
Western Nevada Comm Coll (NV)
Yuba Coll (CA)

Corrections Administration
Michiana Coll, South Bend (IN)

Corrections and Criminal Justice Related
Albany Tech Coll (GA)
Corning Comm Coll (NY)
Delta Coll (MI)
Heart of Georgia Tech Coll (GA)
Lanier Tech Coll (GA)
Monroe Coll, New Rochelle (NY)
Nebraska Indian Comm Coll (NE)
Northwestern Michigan Coll (MI)
Oakland Comm Coll (MI)
Southeastern Tech Coll (GA)
Wisconsin Indianhead Tech Coll (WI)

Cosmetology
Albuquerque Tech Vocational Inst (NM)
Bladen Comm Coll (NC)
Blue Ridge Comm Coll (NC)
Butte Coll (CA)
Caldwell Comm Coll and Tech Inst (NC)
Carl Sandburg Coll (IL)
Century Coll (MN)
Clovis Comm Coll (NM)
Coastal Bend Coll (TX)
Coll of Eastern Utah (UT)
Coll of the Sequoias (CA)
Copiah-Lincoln Comm Coll (MS)
Daytona Beach Comm Coll (FL)
Del Mar Coll (TX)
Delta Coll (MI)
Eastern Wyoming Coll (WY)
East Mississippi Comm Coll (MS)
El Camino Coll (CA)
Everett Comm Coll (WA)
Fayetteville Tech Comm Coll (NC)
Fort Scott Comm Coll (KS)
Garden City Comm Coll (KS)
Gavilan Coll (CA)
Gem City Coll (IL)
Globe Coll (MN)
Guilford Tech Comm Coll (NC)
Hill Coll of the Hill Jr College District (TX)
Honolulu Comm Coll (HI)
Howard Coll (TX)
Isothermal Comm Coll (NC)
James Sprunt Comm Coll (NC)
John A. Logan Coll (IL)
Johnson County Comm Coll (KS)
Kirtland Comm Coll (MI)
Lake Area Tech Inst (SD)
Lamar State Coll–Port Arthur (TX)
Lawson State Comm Coll (AL)
Lenoir Comm Coll (NC)
Lincoln Coll, Lincoln (IL)
Lorain County Comm Coll (OH)
Los Angeles Trade-Tech Coll (CA)
Milwaukee Area Tech Coll (WI)
Minnesota School of Business–Brooklyn Center (MN)
Minnesota School of Business-Plymouth (MN)

Minnesota School of Business-Richfield (MN)
Minnesota State Coll–Southeast Tech (MN)
MiraCosta Coll (CA)
Montcalm Comm Coll (MI)
Napa Valley Coll (CA)
Nash Comm Coll (NC)
Northeast Texas Comm Coll (TX)
North Harris Coll (TX)
Northland Pioneer Coll (AZ)
Oakland Comm Coll (MI)
Odessa Coll (TX)
Olympic Coll (WA)
Panola Coll (TX)
Paris Jr Coll (TX)
Pasadena City Coll (CA)
Roanoke-Chowan Comm Coll (NC)
Rockingham Comm Coll (NC)
San Diego City Coll (CA)
San Jose City Coll (CA)
Santa Barbara City Coll (CA)
Santa Monica Coll (CA)
Shelton State Comm Coll (AL)
Somerset Comm Coll (KY)
Southeastern Comm Coll (NC)
South Plains Coll (TX)
Southwestern Comm Coll (NC)
Southwest Mississippi Comm Coll (MS)
Spokane Comm Coll (WA)
Springfield Tech Comm Coll (MA)
Stanly Comm Coll (NC)
Trenholm State Tech Coll, Montgomery (AL)
Trinidad State Jr Coll (CO)
Umpqua Comm Coll (OR)
Vance-Granville Comm Coll (NC)
Vincennes U (IN)
Waycross Coll (GA)
Weatherford Coll (TX)
Yuba Coll (CA)

Cosmetology and Personal Grooming Arts Related
Allegany Coll of Maryland (MD)
Bristol Comm Coll (MA)
Comm Coll of Allegheny County (PA)
Lorain County Comm Coll (OH)
Milwaukee Area Tech Coll (WI)

Cosmetology, Barber/Styling, and Nail Instruction
Olympic Coll (WA)

Counseling Psychology
Kilian Comm Coll (SD)
Schenectady County Comm Coll (NY)

Counselor Education/School Counseling and Guidance
East Los Angeles Coll (CA)
Pratt Comm Coll and Area Vocational School (KS)

Court Reporting
AIB Coll of Business (IA)
Albuquerque Tech Vocational Inst (NM)
Alvin Comm Coll (TX)
Anoka Tech Coll (MN)
Bates Tech Coll (WA)
Berean Inst (PA)
Butte Coll (CA)
Cambria County Area Comm Coll (PA)
Clark State Comm Coll (OH)
Comm Coll of Allegheny County (PA)
Court Reporting Inst of Dallas (TX)
Cuyahoga Comm Coll (OH)

Daytona Beach Comm Coll (FL)
Del Mar Coll (TX)
Gadsden State Comm Coll (AL)
Green River Comm Coll (WA)
Houston Comm Coll System (TX)
Illinois Eastern Comm Colls, Wabash Valley Coll (IL)
James H. Faulkner State Comm Coll (AL)
Kaplan Coll (IA)
Lakeshore Tech Coll (WI)
Lansing Comm Coll (MI)
Lenoir Comm Coll (NC)
Long Island Business Inst (NY)
Luzerne County Comm Coll (PA)
MacCormac Coll (IL)
Miami Dade Coll (FL)
Mississippi Gulf Coast Comm Coll (MS)
Northland Pioneer Coll (AZ)
Oakland Comm Coll (MI)
Pensacola Jr Coll (FL)
Prince Inst of Professional Studies (AL)
Rasmussen Coll Minnetonka (MN)
Rasmussen Coll St. Cloud (MN)
San Diego City Coll (CA)
South Suburban Coll (IL)
Stark State Coll of Technology (OH)
State U of NY Coll of Technology at Alfred (NY)
Triton Coll (IL)
Wisconsin Indianhead Tech Coll (WI)

Crafts, Folk Art and Artisanry
Lawson State Comm Coll (AL)

Creative Writing
Foothill Coll (CA)
Kirtland Comm Coll (MI)
Lincoln Coll, Lincoln (IL)
Lon Morris Coll (TX)
Vista Comm Coll (CA)

Criminal Justice/Law Enforcement Administration
Abraham Baldwin Ag Coll (GA)
Allentown Business School (PA)
Amarillo Coll (TX)
Ancilla Coll (IN)
Andover Coll (ME)
Anne Arundel Comm Coll (MD)
Arapahoe Comm Coll (CO)
Arizona Western Coll (AZ)
Arkansas State U–Mountain Home (AR)
Atlanta Metropolitan Coll (GA)
Austin Comm Coll (TX)
Bainbridge Coll (GA)
Bellevue Comm Coll (WA)
Bergen Comm Coll (NJ)
Big Sandy Comm and Tech Coll (KY)
Brevard Comm Coll (FL)
Briarwood Coll (CT)
Brookdale Comm Coll (NJ)
Bucks County Comm Coll (PA)
Bunker Hill Comm Coll (MA)
Butte Coll (CA)
Camden County Coll (NJ)
Cape Cod Comm Coll (MA)
Carl Sandburg Coll (IL)
Carteret Comm Coll (NC)
Casper Coll (WY)
Cecil Comm Coll (MD)
Cedar Valley Coll (TX)
Central Arizona Coll (AZ)
Central Florida Comm Coll (FL)

Centralia Coll (WA)
Central Oregon Comm Coll (OR)
Central Pennsylvania Coll (PA)
Central Piedmont Comm Coll (NC)
Central Wyoming Coll (WY)
Chabot Coll (CA)
Chemeketa Comm Coll (OR)
Chesapeake Coll (MD)
Clark State Comm Coll (OH)
Cleveland Comm Coll (NC)
Clinton Comm Coll (NY)
Coastal Bend Coll (TX)
Coastal Carolina Comm Coll (NC)
Coastal Georgia Comm Coll (GA)
Colby Comm Coll (KS)
Coll of DuPage (IL)
Coll of Southern Idaho (ID)
Coll of the Canyons (CA)
Coll of the Desert (CA)
Coll of the Sequoias (CA)
Colorado Mountn Coll (CO)
Colorado Northwestern Comm Coll (CO)
Columbia-Greene Comm Coll (NY)
Comm Coll of Aurora (CO)
Comm Coll of the Air Force (AL)
Contra Costa Coll (CA)
Corning Comm Coll (NY)
Darton Coll (GA)
Daytona Beach Comm Coll (FL)
Dean Coll (MA)
Delaware Tech & Comm Coll, Terry Cmps (DE)
Del Mar Coll (TX)
Delta Coll (MI)
Des Moines Area Comm Coll (IA)
Durham Tech Comm Coll (NC)
Dutchess Comm Coll (NY)
East Arkansas Comm Coll (AR)
Eastern Arizona Coll (AZ)
Eastern Oklahoma State Coll (OK)
East Los Angeles Coll (CA)
East Mississippi Comm Coll (MS)
Edgecombe Comm Coll (NC)
Edison Comm Coll (FL)
Edison State Comm Coll (OH)
Elgin Comm Coll (IL)
Erie Comm Coll (NY)
Essex County Coll (NJ)
Everett Comm Coll (WA)
Feather River Comm Coll District (CA)
Finger Lakes Comm Coll (NY)
Forsyth Tech Comm Coll (NC)
Fort Scott Comm Coll (KS)
Frederick Comm Coll (MD)
Fulton-Montgomery Comm Coll (NY)
Garden City Comm Coll (KS)
Gaston Coll (NC)
Gavilan Coll (CA)
Glendale Comm Coll (AZ)
Gogebic Comm Coll (MI)
Grand Rapids Comm Coll (MI)
Greenfield Comm Coll (MA)
Guilford Tech Comm Coll (NC)
Gulf Coast Comm Coll (FL)
Harrisburg Area Comm Coll (PA)
Hawaii Comm Coll (HI)
Hawkeye Comm Coll (IA)
Hesser Coll (NH)
Hill Coll of the Hill Jr College District (TX)
Hillsborough Comm Coll (FL)
Hinds Comm Coll (MS)

Hiwassee Coll (TN)
Howard Comm Coll (MD)
Indian Hills Comm Coll (IA)
International Inst of the Americas, Phoenix (AZ)
Iowa Lakes Comm Coll (IA)
Isothermal Comm Coll (NC)
Jackson Comm Coll (MI)
Jefferson Coll (MO)
Jefferson Comm Coll (NY)
John A. Logan Coll (IL)
Keiser Coll, Miami (FL)
Kent State U, Trumbull Campus (OH)
Kilian Comm Coll (SD)
Kirkwood Comm Coll (IA)
Kirtland Comm Coll (MI)
Lake City Comm Coll (FL)
Lakeland Comm Coll (OH)
Lake-Sumter Comm Coll (FL)
Lamar State Coll–Port Arthur (TX)
Lansing Comm Coll (MI)
Laramie County Comm Coll (WY)
Lawson State Comm Coll (AL)
Lehigh Carbon Comm Coll (PA)
Lenoir Comm Coll (NC)
Lewis and Clark Comm Coll (IL)
Lincoln Coll, Lincoln (IL)
Longview Comm Coll (MO)
Los Angeles Valley Coll (CA)
Lower Columbia Coll (WA)
Luzerne County Comm Coll (PA)
Macomb Comm Coll (MI)
Manchester Comm Coll (CT)
Maple Woods Comm Coll (MO)
Mayland Comm Coll (NC)
McIntosh Coll (NH)
McLennan Comm Coll (TX)
Miami Dade Coll (FL)
Middlesex Comm Coll (MA)
Middlesex County Coll (NJ)
Mid Michigan Comm Coll (MI)
Milwaukee Area Tech Coll (WI)
MiraCosta Coll (CA)
Mississippi Gulf Coast Comm Coll (MS)
Mitchell Comm Coll (NC)
Modesto Jr Coll (CA)
Mohawk Valley Comm Coll (NY)
Monroe Coll, Bronx (NY)
Montcalm Comm Coll (MI)
Mountain Empire Comm Coll (VA)
Mountain View Coll (TX)
Mount Wachusett Comm Coll (MA)
Napa Valley Coll (CA)
Nassau Comm Coll (NY)
Naugatuck Valley Comm Coll (CT)
New Hampshire Tech Inst (NH)
New Mexico State U–Carlsbad (NM)
New Mexico State U–Grants (NM)
New River Comm Coll (VA)
Niagara County Comm Coll (NY)
Northampton County Area Comm Coll (PA)
North Central Missouri Coll (MO)
North Central State Coll (OH)
Northeast Comm Coll (NE)
Northeastern Oklahoma A&M Coll (OK)
Northeast Mississippi Comm Coll (MS)
Northeast Texas Comm Coll (TX)
Northern Essex Comm Coll (MA)

North Harris Coll (TX)
North Idaho Coll (ID)
North Shore Comm Coll (MA)
Northwestern Connecticut Comm-Tech Coll (CT)
Northwest-Shoals Comm Coll (AL)
Northwest State Comm Coll (OH)
Oakland Comm Coll (MI)
Odessa Coll (TX)
Ohio Inst of Photography and Technology (OH)
Olympic Coll (WA)
Orange County Comm Coll (NY)
Owens Comm Coll, Findlay (OH)
Owens Comm Coll, Toledo (OH)
Ozarka Coll (AR)
Palm Beach Comm Coll (FL)
Palomar Coll (CA)
Pasadena City Coll (CA)
Pasco-Hernando Comm Coll (FL)
Paul D. Camp Comm Coll (VA)
Peninsula Coll (WA)
Penn Valley Comm Coll (MO)
Piedmont Virginia Comm Coll (VA)
Pikes Peak Comm Coll (CO)
Polk Comm Coll (FL)
Portland Comm Coll (OR)
Prince George's Comm Coll (MD)
Quinsigamond Comm Coll (MA)
Raritan Valley Comm Coll (NJ)
Red Rocks Comm Coll (CO)
Richmond Comm Coll (NC)
Riverside Comm Coll (CA)
Roane State Comm Coll (TN)
Roanoke-Chowan Comm Coll (NC)
Rockingham Comm Coll (NC)
Rogue Comm Coll (OR)
Rowan-Cabarrus Comm Coll (NC)
Saint Charles Comm Coll (MO)
St. Clair County Comm Coll (MI)
St. Johns River Comm Coll (FL)
St. Louis Comm Coll at Florissant Valley (MO)
St. Philip's Coll (TX)
Salem Comm Coll (NJ)
San Jose City Coll (CA)
Santa Barbara City Coll (CA)
Santa Monica Coll (CA)
Sauk Valley Comm Coll (IL)
Schenectady County Comm Coll (NY)
Scottsdale Comm Coll (AZ)
Seminole Comm Coll (FL)
Sheridan Coll (WY)
Sierra Coll (CA)
Sinclair Comm Coll (OH)
Snow Coll (UT)
Southeastern Comm Coll (NC)
Southern Maine Comm Coll (ME)
Southern West Virginia Comm and Tech Coll (WV)
South Plains Coll (TX)
Southside Virginia Comm Coll (VA)
South Suburban Coll (IL)
Southwestern Coll (CA)
Southwestern Illinois Coll (IL)
Spartanburg Methodist Coll (SC)
Spoon River Coll (IL)
State U of NY Coll of Technology at Canton (NY)

Temple Coll (TX)
Three Rivers Comm Coll (MO)
Tillamook Bay Comm Coll (OR)
Tompkins Cortland Comm Coll (NY)
Trident Tech Coll (SC)
Triton Coll (IL)
Umpqua Comm Coll (OR)
United Tribes Tech Coll (ND)
U of Arkansas Comm Coll at Hope (AR)
Utah Valley State Coll (UT)
Valley Forge Military Coll (PA)
Vance-Granville Comm Coll (NC)
Ventura Coll (CA)
Vermilion Comm Coll (MN)
Vincennes U (IN)
Virginia Western Comm Coll (VA)
Walters State Comm Coll (TN)
Washtenaw Comm Coll (MI)
Waycross Coll (GA)
Weatherford Coll (TX)
Western Iowa Tech Comm Coll (IA)
Western Nevada Comm Coll (NV)
Western Wyoming Comm Coll (WY)
West Hills Comm Coll (CA)
Westmoreland County Comm Coll (PA)
Wilson Tech Comm Coll (NC)
Yakima Valley Comm Coll (WA)
Yuba Coll (CA)

Criminal Justice/Police Science

Abraham Baldwin Ag Coll (GA)
Alexandria Tech Coll (MN)
Allegany Coll of Maryland (MD)
Alpena Comm Coll (MI)
Alvin Comm Coll (TX)
Amarillo Coll (TX)
Anne Arundel Comm Coll (MD)
Arapahoe Comm Coll (CO)
Arizona Western Coll (AZ)
Arkansas Northeastern Coll (AR)
Asheville-Buncombe Tech Comm Coll (NC)
Atlantic Cape Comm Coll (NJ)
Austin Comm Coll (TX)
Barton County Comm Coll (KS)
Beaufort County Comm Coll (NC)
Bellevue Comm Coll (WA)
Blackhawk Tech Coll (WI)
Bladen Comm Coll (NC)
Blue River Comm Coll (MO)
Brevard Comm Coll (FL)
Broome Comm Coll (NY)
Bucks County Comm Coll (PA)
Butler County Comm Coll (KS)
Butte Coll (CA)
Calhoun Comm Coll (AL)
Cape Fear Comm Coll (NC)
Carl Sandburg Coll (IL)
Casper Coll (WY)
Central Piedmont Comm Coll (NC)
Century Coll (MN)
Chabot Coll (CA)
Cincinnati State Tech and Comm Coll (OH)
City Colls of Chicago, Wilbur Wright Coll (IL)
Clark State Comm Coll (OH)
Clinton Comm Coll (NY)
Clovis Comm Coll (NM)
Coastal Bend Coll (TX)
Coll of DuPage (IL)

Coll of Lake County (IL)
Coll of Southern Idaho (ID)
Coll of the Canyons (CA)
Coll of the Desert (CA)
Coll of the Sequoias (CA)
Columbus State Comm Coll (OH)
Comm Coll of Allegheny County (PA)
Comm Coll of Rhode Island (RI)
Connors State Coll (OK)
Contra Costa Coll (CA)
Copiah-Lincoln Comm Coll (MS)
County Coll of Morris (NJ)
Cumberland County Coll (NJ)
Cuyahoga Comm Coll (OH)
Dawson Comm Coll (MT)
Daytona Beach Comm Coll (FL)
Dean Coll (MA)
Delaware County Comm Coll (PA)
Delgado Comm Coll (LA)
Del Mar Coll (TX)
Delta Coll (MI)
Des Moines Area Comm Coll (IA)
Durham Tech Comm Coll (NC)
East Arkansas Comm Coll (AR)
Eastern Arizona Coll (AZ)
Eastern Wyoming Coll (WY)
East Los Angeles Coll (CA)
Edison State Comm Coll (OH)
Education Direct Center for Degree Studies (PA)
El Camino Coll (CA)
El Centro Coll (TX)
Elgin Comm Coll (IL)
Elizabethtown Comm Coll (KY)
Essex County Coll (NJ)
Everett Comm Coll (WA)
Finger Lakes Comm Coll (NY)
Forsyth Tech Comm Coll (NC)
Gadsden State Comm Coll (AL)
Galveston Coll (TX)
Garden City Comm Coll (KS)
Gavilan Coll (CA)
Germanna Comm Coll (VA)
Glendale Comm Coll (AZ)
Gloucester County Coll (NJ)
Grand Rapids Comm Coll (MI)
Green River Comm Coll (WA)
Guilford Tech Comm Coll (NC)
Hagerstown Comm Coll (MD)
Harrisburg Area Comm Coll (PA)
Hawkeye Comm Coll (IA)
Hesser Coll (NH)
Hibbing Comm Coll (MN)
Hill Coll of the Hill Jr College District (TX)
Hillsborough Comm Coll (FL)
Hinds Comm Coll (MS)
Holyoke Comm Coll (MA)
Honolulu Comm Coll (HI)
Hopkinsville Comm Coll (KY)
Houston Comm Coll System (TX)
Howard Coll (TX)
Hutchinson Comm Coll and Area Vocational School (KS)
Illinois Eastern Comm Colls, Olney Central Coll (IL)
Iowa Lakes Comm Coll (IA)
Isothermal Comm Coll (NC)
James A. Rhodes State Coll (OH)
James Sprunt Comm Coll (NC)

Jamestown Comm Coll (NY)
Jefferson Coll (MO)
Jefferson Comm Coll (OH)
Jefferson Davis Comm Coll (AL)
Jefferson State Comm Coll (AL)
Johnson County Comm Coll (KS)
Johnston Comm Coll (NC)
John Wood Comm Coll (IL)
Kalamazoo Valley Comm Coll (MI)
Kansas City Kansas Comm Coll (KS)
Kaskaskia Coll (IL)
Kellogg Comm Coll (MI)
Kent State U, Tuscarawas Campus (OH)
Kirkwood Comm Coll (IA)
Kishwaukee Coll (IL)
Lake Land Coll (IL)
Lakeland Comm Coll (OH)
Lake Region State Coll (ND)
Lakeshore Tech Coll (WI)
Lansing Comm Coll (MI)
Laredo Comm Coll (TX)
Lawson State Comm Coll (AL)
Lehigh Carbon Comm Coll (PA)
Lenoir Comm Coll (NC)
Lincoln Coll, Lincoln (IL)
Lincoln Land Comm Coll (IL)
Linn-Benton Comm Coll (OR)
Longview Comm Coll (MO)
Lorain County Comm Coll (OH)
Los Angeles Harbor Coll (CA)
Los Angeles Valley Coll (CA)
Lower Columbia Coll (WA)
Luna Comm Coll (NM)
Macomb Comm Coll (MI)
Maple Woods Comm Coll (MO)
Massasoit Comm Coll (MA)
Mayland Comm Coll (NC)
McHenry County Coll (IL)
McLennan Comm Coll (TX)
Metropolitan Comm Coll (NE)
Miami Dade Coll (FL)
Middle Georgia Coll (GA)
Middlesex County Coll (NJ)
Midland Coll (TX)
Milwaukee Area Tech Coll (WI)
Mineral Area Coll (MO)
Minneapolis Comm and Tech Coll (MN)
Minnesota State Comm and Tech Coll—Fergus Falls (MN)
MiraCosta Coll (CA)
Mississippi Gulf Coast Comm Coll (MS)
Moberly Area Comm Coll (MO)
Modesto Jr Coll (CA)
Mohave Comm Coll (AZ)
Monroe Coll, Bronx (NY)
Monroe County Comm Coll (MI)
Montgomery Coll (MD)
Montgomery County Comm Coll (PA)
Moraine Valley Comm Coll (IL)
Morton Coll (IL)
Mott Comm Coll (MI)
Mountain Empire Comm Coll (VA)
Mt. San Antonio Coll (CA)
Mt. San Jacinto Coll (CA)
Napa Valley Coll (CA)
Nash Comm Coll (NC)
Nashville State Tech Comm Coll (TN)
New River Comm Coll (VA)
Normandale Comm Coll (MN)
Northcentral Tech Coll (WI)

Northeast Comm Coll (NE)
Northeast Mississippi Comm Coll (MS)
Northeast Wisconsin Tech Coll (WI)
North Harris Coll (TX)
North Hennepin Comm Coll (MN)
North Idaho Coll (ID)
North Iowa Area Comm Coll (IA)
Northwestern Connecticut Comm-Tech Coll (CT)
Northwest-Shoals Comm Coll (AL)
Northwest State Comm Coll (OH)
Oakland Comm Coll (MI)
Oakton Comm Coll (IL)
Ocean County Coll (NJ)
Odessa Coll (TX)
Okefenokee Tech Coll (GA)
Oklahoma State U, Oklahoma City (OK)
Olympic Coll (WA)
Orange County Comm Coll (NY)
Owensboro Comm and Tech Coll (KY)
Owens Comm Coll, Findlay (OH)
Palm Beach Comm Coll (FL)
Palomar Coll (CA)
Penn Valley Comm Coll (MO)
Phoenix Coll (AZ)
Piedmont Virginia Comm Coll (VA)
Pima Comm Coll (AZ)
Pioneer Pacific Coll (OR)
Pitt Comm Coll (NC)
Polk Comm Coll (FL)
Rend Lake Coll (IL)
Riverland Comm Coll (MN)
Roane State Comm Coll (TN)
Rochester Comm and Tech Coll (MN)
Rockingham Comm Coll (NC)
Saint Charles Comm Coll (MO)
St. Louis Comm Coll at Florissant Valley (MO)
St. Petersburg Coll (FL)
San Joaquin Delta Coll (CA)
San Juan Coll (NM)
Santa Monica Coll (CA)
Sauk Valley Comm Coll (IL)
Schoolcraft Coll (MI)
Seward County Comm Coll (KS)
Sheridan Coll (WY)
Sierra Coll (CA)
Sinclair Comm Coll (OH)
Somerset Comm Coll (KY)
South Arkansas Comm Coll (AR)
Southeast Comm Coll (KY)
Southern Maine Comm Coll (ME)
South Plains Coll (TX)
South Suburban Coll (IL)
Southwestern Comm Coll (NC)
Southwestern Oregon Comm Coll (OR)
Spokane Comm Coll (WA)
Spoon River Coll (IL)
Springfield Tech Comm Coll (MA)
Stanly Comm Coll (NC)
State U of NY Coll of Technology at Canton (NY)
Temple Coll (TX)
Terra State Comm Coll (OH)
Thomas Nelson Comm Coll (VA)
Three Rivers Comm Coll (MO)
Trinidad State Jr Coll (CO)
Triton Coll (IL)
Union County Coll (NJ)
United Tribes Tech Coll (ND)

Vance-Granville Comm Coll (NC)
Vermilion Comm Coll (MN)
Victor Valley Coll (CA)
Vincennes U (IN)
Washtenaw Comm Coll (MI)
Waubonsee Comm Coll (IL)
Western Dakota Tech Inst (SD)
Western Nevada Comm Coll (NV)
Western Wisconsin Tech Coll (WI)
Westmoreland County Comm Coll (PA)
West Virginia Northern Comm Coll (WV)
Wisconsin Indianhead Tech Coll (WI)
Wor-Wic Comm Coll (MD)
Yakima Valley Comm Coll (WA)
Yavapai Coll (AZ)
Yuba Coll (CA)

Criminal Justice/Safety

AEC Southern Ohio Coll (OH)
Alamance Comm Coll (NC)
Albuquerque Tech Vocational Inst (NM)
Arkansas State U–Mountain Home (AR)
Asnuntuck Comm Coll (CT)
Berkshire Comm Coll (MA)
Bowling Green State U-Firelands Coll (OH)
Bristol Comm Coll (MA)
Central Carolina Tech Coll (SC)
Central Comm Coll–Grand Island Campus (NE)
Chaparral Coll (AZ)
Cleveland Comm Coll (NC)
Crown Coll (WA)
Dutchess Comm Coll (NY)
Eastern Wyoming Coll (WY)
Eastfield Coll (TX)
El Centro Coll (TX)
Fayetteville Tech Comm Coll (NC)
Garrett Coll (MD)
Great Basin Coll (NV)
Hudson County Comm Coll (NJ)
Ivy Tech State Coll–Bloomington (IN)
Ivy Tech State Coll–Central Indiana (IN)
Ivy Tech State Coll–Eastcentral (IN)
Ivy Tech State Coll–Kokomo (IN)
Ivy Tech State Coll–North Central (IN)
Ivy Tech State Coll–Northwest (IN)
Ivy Tech State Coll–Southwest (IN)
Ivy Tech State Coll–Wabash Valley (IN)
Jamestown Comm Coll (NY)
J. Sargeant Reynolds Comm Coll (VA)
Kaplan Coll (IA)
Kellogg Comm Coll (MI)
Keystone Coll (PA)
Lackawanna Coll (PA)
Linn-Benton Comm Coll (OR)
Lower Columbia Coll (WA)
Manatee Comm Coll (FL)
Minneapolis Comm and Tech Coll (MN)
Monroe County Comm Coll (MI)
Nassau Comm Coll (NY)
Normandale Comm Coll (MN)
North Central State Coll (OH)
North Country Comm Coll (NY)
North Florida Comm Coll (FL)

Northwest State Comm Coll (OH)
Orangeburg-Calhoun Tech Coll (SC)
Parkland Coll (IL)
Pensacola Jr Coll (FL)
Phoenix Coll (AZ)
Pima Comm Coll (AZ)
San Juan Coll (NM)
Santa Fe Comm Coll (NM)
U of Arkansas Comm Coll at Batesville (AR)
Vermilion Comm Coll (MN)

Criminology

Daytona Beach Comm Coll (FL)
Lincoln Coll, Lincoln (IL)
Pensacola Jr Coll (FL)
Southeast Arkansas Coll (AR)
Western Wyoming Comm Coll (WY)

Crop Production

Barton County Comm Coll (KS)
Iowa Lakes Comm Coll (IA)
Northeast Comm Coll (NE)
Northwestern Michigan Coll (MI)
Ohio State U Ag Tech Inst (OH)

Culinary Arts

Alamance Comm Coll (NC)
Albany Tech Coll (GA)
Albuquerque Tech Vocational Inst (NM)
Allegany Coll of Maryland (MD)
American River Coll (CA)
The Art Inst of Houston (TX)
The Art Inst of Philadelphia (PA)
The Art Inst of Pittsburgh (PA)
The Art Inst of Seattle (WA)
The Art Insts International Minnesota (MN)
Asheville-Buncombe Tech Comm Coll (NC)
Atlantic Cape Comm Coll (NJ)
Baltimore International Coll (MD)
Bates Tech Coll (WA)
Blackhawk Tech Coll (WI)
Brevard Comm Coll (FL)
Brookdale Comm Coll (NJ)
Bucks County Comm Coll (PA)
Bunker Hill Comm Coll (MA)
California Culinary Academy (CA)
Central Oregon Comm Coll (OR)
Central Piedmont Comm Coll (NC)
Cincinnati State Tech and Comm Coll (OH)
Clark Coll (WA)
Coll of DuPage (IL)
Coll of Southern Idaho (ID)
Coll of the Desert (CA)
Coll of the Sequoias (CA)
Columbia Coll (CA)
Columbus State Comm Coll (OH)
Commonwealth Tech Inst (PA)
Comm Coll of Allegheny County (PA)
Contra Costa Coll (CA)
The Cooking and Hospitality Inst of Chicago (IL)
Daytona Beach Comm Coll (FL)
Del Mar Coll (TX)
Des Moines Area Comm Coll (IA)
Eastern Maine Comm Coll (ME)
Edmonds Comm Coll (WA)
El Camino Coll (CA)

El Centro Coll (TX)
Elgin Comm Coll (IL)
Erie Comm Coll (NY)
Florida Culinary Inst (FL)
Galveston Coll (TX)
Grand Rapids Comm Coll (MI)
Guilford Tech Comm Coll (NC)
Gulf Coast Comm Coll (FL)
Harrisburg Area Comm Coll (PA)
Hibbing Comm Coll (MN)
Hillsborough Comm Coll (FL)
Hudson County Comm Coll (NJ)
Illinois Eastern Comm Colls, Lincoln Trail Coll (IL)
Jefferson Coll (MO)
Jefferson Comm Coll (KY)
J. Sargeant Reynolds Comm Coll (VA)
Kapiolani Comm Coll (HI)
Kaskaskia Coll (IL)
Kauai Comm Coll (HI)
Keystone Coll (PA)
Kirkwood Comm Coll (IA)
Lake Washington Tech Coll (WA)
Lehigh Carbon Comm Coll (PA)
Linn-Benton Comm Coll (OR)
Los Angeles Trade-Tech Coll (CA)
Louisiana Tech Coll–Delta Ouachita Campus (LA)
Luzerne County Comm Coll (PA)
Macomb Comm Coll (MI)
Massasoit Comm Coll (MA)
McIntosh Coll (NH)
Metropolitan Comm Coll (NE)
Middlesex Comm Coll (MA)
Middlesex County Coll (NJ)
Milwaukee Area Tech Coll (WI)
Minneapolis Comm and Tech Coll (MN)
Mitchell Tech Inst (SD)
Monroe County Comm Coll (MI)
Montgomery County Comm Coll (PA)
Moraine Park Tech Coll (WI)
Mott Comm Coll (MI)
Nashville State Tech Comm Coll (TN)
New England Culinary Inst (VT)
New Hampshire Comm Tech Coll, Berlin/Laconia (NH)
Niagara County Comm Coll (NY)
Northampton County Area Comm Coll (PA)
North Idaho Coll (ID)
North Seattle Comm Coll (WA)
North Shore Comm Coll (MA)
Northwestern Michigan Coll (MI)
Oakland Comm Coll (MI)
Odessa Coll (TX)
Olympic Coll (WA)
Orange Coast Coll (CA)
Oxnard Coll (CA)
Ozarka Coll (AR)
Pennsylvania Coll of Technology (PA)
Pennsylvania Culinary Inst (PA)
Penn Valley Comm Coll (MO)
Pensacola Jr Coll (FL)
Reading Area Comm Coll (PA)
Rend Lake Coll (IL)
The Restaurant School at Walnut Hill Coll (PA)
Riverside Comm Coll (CA)
St. Cloud Tech Coll (MN)

St. Philip's Coll (TX)
San Joaquin Delta Coll (CA)
Santa Fe Comm Coll (NM)
Schenectady County Comm Coll (NY)
Schoolcraft Coll (MI)
Scottsdale Comm Coll (AZ)
Sinclair Comm Coll (OH)
South Central Tech Coll (MN)
Southeast Comm Coll, Lincoln Campus (NE)
Southern Maine Comm Coll (ME)
South Puget Sound Comm Coll (WA)
Southwestern Comm Coll (NC)
Spokane Comm Coll (WA)
State U of NY Coll of Technology at Alfred (NY)
State U of NY Coll of Technology at Delhi (NY)
Sullivan County Comm Coll (NY)
Texas Culinary Academy (TX)
Texas State Tech Coll–Waco/Marshall Campus (TX)
Trenholm State Tech Coll, Montgomery (AL)
Trident Tech Coll (SC)
Triton Coll (IL)
Utah Valley State Coll (UT)
Vincennes U (IN)
Washtenaw Comm Coll (MI)
Westmoreland County Comm Coll (PA)
York County Comm Coll (ME)

Culinary Arts Related
The Art Inst of Pittsburgh (PA)
Fayetteville Tech Comm Coll (NC)
Hillsborough Comm Coll (FL)
Iowa Lakes Comm Coll (IA)
Keystone Coll (PA)
Linn-Benton Comm Coll (OR)
Olympic Coll (WA)
Santa Barbara City Coll (CA)

Cultural Studies
Coll of the Sequoias (CA)
Foothill Coll (CA)
Orange Coast Coll (CA)
Pasadena City Coll (CA)
Riverside Comm Coll (CA)
Santa Barbara City Coll (CA)
Santa Monica Coll (CA)
Ventura Coll (CA)
Yuba Coll (CA)

Customer Service Support/Call Center/Teleservice Operation
Laramie County Comm Coll (WY)

Cytotechnology
Barton County Comm Coll (KS)

Dairy Husbandry and Production
Linn-Benton Comm Coll (OR)
Ohio State U Ag Tech Inst (OH)

Dairy Science
Coll of the Sequoias (CA)
Hill Coll of the Hill Jr College District (TX)
Modesto Jr Coll (CA)
Mt. San Antonio Coll (CA)
Northeastern Oklahoma A&M Coll (OK)
Northeast Iowa Comm Coll (IA)
Northeast Mississippi Comm Coll (MS)
Northeast Texas Comm Coll (TX)

Ohio State U Ag Tech Inst (OH)
State U of NY Coll of A&T at Morrisville (NY)
State U of NY Coll of Technology at Alfred (NY)

Dance
Barton County Comm Coll (KS)
Bergen Comm Coll (NJ)
Cañada Coll (CA)
Central Piedmont Comm Coll (NC)
Daytona Beach Comm Coll (FL)
Dean Coll (MA)
Hillsborough Comm Coll (FL)
Lansing Comm Coll (MI)
Lincoln Coll, Lincoln (IL)
Lon Morris Coll (TX)
Miami Dade Coll (FL)
Middlesex County Coll (NJ)
MiraCosta Coll (CA)
Mt. San Jacinto Coll (CA)
Nassau Comm Coll (NY)
Northern Essex Comm Coll (MA)
Orange Coast Coll (CA)
Palomar Coll (CA)
St. Johns River Comm Coll (FL)
San Joaquin Delta Coll (CA)
Santa Fe Comm Coll (NM)
Santa Monica Coll (CA)
Sinclair Comm Coll (OH)
Snow Coll (UT)
Southwestern Coll (CA)
Utah Valley State Coll (UT)
Western Wyoming Comm Coll (WY)

Data Entry/Microcomputer Applications
Academy of Medical Arts and Business (PA)
American River Coll (CA)
Anne Arundel Comm Coll (MD)
Atlantic Cape Comm Coll (NJ)
Austin Comm Coll (TX)
The Brown Mackie Coll–Lenexa Campus (KS)
Bunker Hill Comm Coll (MA)
Camden County Coll (NJ)
Clark Coll (WA)
Cleveland Comm Coll (NC)
Coastal Bend Coll (TX)
The Coll of Westchester (NY)
Colorado Mountn Coll, Timberline Cmps (CO)
Dakota County Tech Coll (MN)
Del Mar Coll (TX)
Delta Coll (MI)
Eastern Arizona Coll (AZ)
Eastfield Coll (TX)
ECPI Tech Coll, Glen Allen (VA)
ECPI Tech Coll, Richmond (VA)
ECPI Tech Coll, Roanoke (VA)
Edgecombe Comm Coll (NC)
Fayetteville Tech Comm Coll (NC)
Fiorello H LaGuardia Comm Coll of City U of NY (NY)
Florida National Coll (FL)
Gallipolis Career Coll (OH)
Galveston Coll (TX)
Heartland Comm Coll (IL)
Henderson Comm Coll (KY)
Hinds Comm Coll (MS)
Howard Comm Coll (MD)
IntelliTec Coll, Grand Junction (CO)
Iowa Lakes Comm Coll (IA)
Laredo Comm Coll (TX)
Lorain County Comm Coll (OH)
Lower Columbia Coll (WA)
Luzerne County Comm Coll (PA)

Marion Tech Coll (OH)
Metropolitan Comm Coll-Business & Technology College (MO)
Milwaukee Area Tech Coll (WI)
Mississippi Gulf Coast Comm Coll (MS)
Mitchell Tech Inst (SD)
Modesto Jr Coll (CA)
Mountain Empire Comm Coll (VA)
Nebraska Indian Comm Coll (NE)
Newport Business Inst, Lower Burrell (PA)
North Shore Comm Coll (MA)
Ohio Business Coll, Sandusky (OH)
Oklahoma State U, Oklahoma City (OK)
Orange County Comm Coll (NY)
Owensboro Comm and Tech Coll (KY)
Parkland Coll (IL)
Pellissippi State Tech Comm Coll (TN)
Pratt Comm Coll and Area Vocational School (KS)
Quinebaug Valley Comm Coll (CT)
Rasmussen Coll Mankato (MN)
Riverland Comm Coll (MN)
St. Philip's Coll (TX)
Seminole Comm Coll (FL)
Sheridan Coll (WY)
Sinclair Comm Coll (OH)
Southeastern Tech Coll (GA)
Stark State Coll of Technology (OH)
Sullivan County Comm Coll (NY)
Three Rivers Comm Coll (MO)
Tompkins Cortland Comm Coll (NY)
U of Arkansas Comm Coll at Batesville (AR)
Vincennes U (IN)
Western Wyoming Comm Coll (WY)
Williamsburg Tech Coll (SC)

Data Entry/Microcomputer Applications Related
Academy of Medical Arts and Business (PA)
AIB Coll of Business (IA)
The Brown Mackie Coll–Lenexa Campus (KS)
Camden County Coll (NJ)
Capital Comm Coll (CT)
Coastal Bend Coll (TX)
Coll of DuPage (IL)
The Coll of Westchester (NY)
Colorado Mountn Coll, Alpine Cmps (CO)
Colorado Mountn Coll (CO)
Colorado Mountn Coll, Timberline Cmps (CO)
Dakota County Tech Coll (MN)
Delta Coll (MI)
Donnelly Coll (KS)
Eugenio María de Hostos Comm Coll of City U of NY (NY)
Florida National Coll (FL)
Hawkeye Comm Coll (IA)
Heartland Comm Coll (IL)
Henderson Comm Coll (KY)
Hinds Comm Coll (MS)
Kellogg Comm Coll (MI)
Lake Area Tech Inst (SD)
Laredo Comm Coll (TX)
Lorain County Comm Coll (OH)
Marion Tech Coll (OH)
Metropolitan Comm Coll-Business & Technology College (MO)

Mississippi Gulf Coast Comm Coll (MS)
Montana State U Coll of Tech-Great Falls (MT)
Newport Business Inst, Lower Burrell (PA)
Orange Coast Coll (CA)
Pellissippi State Tech Comm Coll (TN)
Peninsula Coll (WA)
Pratt Comm Coll and Area Vocational School (KS)
Rasmussen Coll Mankato (MN)
Remington Coll–Lafayette Campus (LA)
Riverland Comm Coll (MN)
Seminole Comm Coll (FL)
Sinclair Comm Coll (OH)
Southwestern Michigan Coll (MI)
Stark State Coll of Technology (OH)
Three Rivers Comm Coll (MO)
Vincennes U (IN)
Vista Comm Coll (CA)

Data Modeling/Warehousing and Database Administration
Arapahoe Comm Coll (CO)
Bates Tech Coll (WA)
Coll of the Sequoias (CA)
Dakota County Tech Coll (MN)
Lanier Tech Coll (GA)
Laramie County Comm Coll (WY)
Metropolitan Comm Coll-Business & Technology College (MO)
Middlesex Comm Coll (MA)
Midland Coll (TX)
Northland Pioneer Coll (AZ)
Seminole Comm Coll (FL)

Data Processing and Data Processing Technology
Abraham Baldwin Ag Coll (GA)
Academy Coll (MN)
Academy of Medical Arts and Business (PA)
Albuquerque Tech Vocational Inst (NM)
Alpena Comm Coll (MI)
American River Coll (CA)
Anne Arundel Comm Coll (MD)
Bainbridge Coll (GA)
Bates Tech Coll (WA)
Bellevue Comm Coll (WA)
Borough of Manhattan Comm Coll of City U of NY (NY)
Bristol Comm Coll (MA)
Bronx Comm Coll of City U of NY (NY)
Broome Comm Coll (NY)
Bucks County Comm Coll (PA)
Butler County Comm Coll (KS)
Butte Coll (CA)
Cabrillo Coll (CA)
Camden County Coll (NJ)
Cañada Coll (CA)
Career Coll of Northern Nevada (NV)
Carl Sandburg Coll (IL)
Casper Coll (WY)
Cecil Comm Coll (MD)
Cedar Valley Coll (TX)
Central Carolina Tech Coll (SC)
Central Comm Coll–Grand Island Campus (NE)
Central Piedmont Comm Coll (NC)
Chabot Coll (CA)
Chesapeake Coll (MD)
City Colls of Chicago, Wilbur Wright Coll (IL)
Coastal Bend Coll (TX)

The Coll of Westchester (NY)
Columbia-Greene Comm Coll (NY)
Copiah-Lincoln Comm Coll (MS)
Cuesta Coll (CA)
Davis Coll (OH)
Delaware Tech & Comm Coll, Terry Cmps (DE)
Delgado Comm Coll (LA)
Delta Coll (MI)
Des Moines Area Comm Coll (IA)
Donnelly Coll (KS)
Durham Tech Comm Coll (NC)
Eastfield Coll (TX)
East Los Angeles Coll (CA)
ECPI Coll of Technology, Virginia Beach (VA)
ECPI Tech Coll, Richmond (VA)
Edison State Comm Coll (OH)
Edmonds Comm Coll (WA)
El Camino Coll (CA)
El Centro Coll (TX)
Essex County Coll (NJ)
Eugenio María de Hostos Comm Coll of City U of NY (NY)
Everett Comm Coll (WA)
Finger Lakes Comm Coll (NY)
Fisher Coll (MA)
Florida National Coll (FL)
Forsyth Tech Comm Coll (NC)
Foundation Coll, San Diego (CA)
Frederick Comm Coll (MD)
Fulton-Montgomery Comm Coll (NY)
Gaston Coll (NC)
Germanna Comm Coll (VA)
Gloucester County Coll (NJ)
Gogebic Comm Coll (MI)
Great Basin Coll (NV)
Henderson Comm Coll (KY)
Hill Coll of the Hill Jr College District (TX)
Hinds Comm Coll (MS)
Holmes Comm Coll (MS)
Hudson County Comm Coll (NJ)
Iowa Lakes Comm Coll (IA)
Jackson Comm Coll (MI)
Jefferson Comm Coll (KY)
Jefferson Comm Coll (OH)
John A. Logan Coll (IL)
J. Sargeant Reynolds Comm Coll (VA)
Kansas City Kansas Comm Coll (KS)
Kapiolani Comm Coll (HI)
Keystone Coll (PA)
Kingsborough Comm Coll of City U of NY (NY)
Kirkwood Comm Coll (IA)
Lamar State Coll–Orange (TX)
Laredo Comm Coll (TX)
Lewis and Clark Comm Coll (IL)
Lincoln Coll, Lincoln (IL)
Longview Comm Coll (MO)
Los Angeles Harbor Coll (CA)
Los Angeles Pierce Coll (CA)
Los Angeles Trade-Tech Coll (CA)
Los Angeles Valley Coll (CA)
Louisiana Tech Coll–Lamar Salter Campus (LA)
Louisiana Tech Coll–North Central Campus (LA)
Lower Columbia Coll (WA)
Luzerne County Comm Coll (PA)
Maple Woods Comm Coll (MO)
Marion Tech Coll (OH)

Metropolitan Comm Coll-Business & Technology College (MO)
Miami Dade Coll (FL)
Middle Georgia Coll (GA)
Midlands Tech Coll (SC)
Milwaukee Area Tech Coll (WI)
Mitchell Comm Coll (NC)
Monroe County Comm Coll (MI)
Montcalm Comm Coll (MI)
Moraine Park Tech Coll (WI)
Morton Coll (IL)
Mt. San Antonio Coll (CA)
Napa Valley Coll (CA)
Nassau Comm Coll (NY)
New Mexico State U–Grants (NM)
Northampton County Area Comm Coll (PA)
North Central Missouri Coll (MO)
Northeastern Tech Coll (SC)
Northeast Mississippi Comm Coll (MS)
Northeast State Tech Comm Coll (TN)
Northeast Wisconsin Tech Coll (WI)
Northern Essex Comm Coll (MA)
Northern Maine Comm Coll (ME)
North Seattle Comm Coll (WA)
Odessa Coll (TX)
Ohio Valley Coll of Technology (OH)
Orange Coast Coll (CA)
Orange County Comm Coll (NY)
Otero Jr Coll (CO)
Palm Beach Comm Coll (FL)
Pasadena City Coll (CA)
Paul D. Camp Comm Coll (VA)
Pellissippi State Tech Comm Coll (TN)
Penn Valley Comm Coll (MO)
Phoenix Coll (AZ)
Piedmont Virginia Comm Coll (VA)
Polk Comm Coll (FL)
Quinsigamond Comm Coll (MA)
Raritan Valley Comm Coll (NJ)
Rasmussen Coll Mankato (MN)
Reading Area Comm Coll (PA)
Rochester Business Inst (NY)
St. Louis Comm Coll at Florissant Valley (MO)
San Diego City Coll (CA)
San Jose City Coll (CA)
Santa Monica Coll (CA)
Schoolcraft Coll (MI)
Seminole Comm Coll (FL)
Seward County Comm Coll (KS)
Shelton State Comm Coll (AL)
Snead State Comm Coll (AL)
Southeast Comm Coll (KY)
South Plains Coll (TX)
South Puget Sound Comm Coll (WA)
South Suburban Coll (IL)
Southwestern Illinois Coll (IL)
Spokane Comm Coll (WA)
State U of NY Coll of A&T at Morrisville (NY)
State U of NY Coll of Technology at Alfred (NY)
Temple Coll (TX)
Texas State Tech Coll–Harlingen (TX)
Tidewater Comm Coll (VA)
Trinidad State Jr Coll (CO)
Triton Coll (IL)

The U of Akron–Wayne Coll (OH)
Utah Valley State Coll (UT)
Vance-Granville Comm Coll (NC)
Vermilion Comm Coll (MN)
Virginia Western Comm Coll (VA)
Washtenaw Comm Coll (MI)
Western Wisconsin Tech Coll (WI)
Western Wyoming Comm Coll (WY)
Westmoreland County Comm Coll (PA)
Williston State Coll (ND)
York Tech Coll (SC)

Demography and Population
Atlantic Cape Comm Coll (NJ)

Dental Assisting
Academy of Medical Arts and Business (PA)
Briarwood Coll (CT)
Calhoun Comm Coll (AL)
Central Comm Coll–Hastings Campus (NE)
Central Oregon Comm Coll (OR)
Century Coll (MN)
Coll of Southern Idaho (ID)
Comm Coll of the Air Force (AL)
Delta Coll (MI)
Duluth Business U (MN)
Essex County Coll (NJ)
Fayetteville Tech Comm Coll (NC)
Foothill Coll (CA)
Harcum Coll (PA)
Herzing Coll, Minneapolis Drafting School Division (MN)
Hibbing Comm Coll (MN)
James H. Faulkner State Comm Coll (AL)
Jefferson Comm Coll (OH)
Lake Area Tech Inst (SD)
Lake Washington Tech Coll (WA)
Laramie County Comm Coll (WY)
Luzerne County Comm Coll (PA)
Marshalltown Comm Coll (IA)
Massasoit Comm Coll (MA)
Middlesex Comm Coll (MA)
Midlands Tech Coll (SC)
Mid-Plains Comm Coll, North Platte (NE)
Milwaukee Area Tech Coll (WI)
Modesto Jr Coll (CA)
Montana State U Coll of Tech-Great Falls (MT)
Mott Comm Coll (MI)
New England Inst of Tech & Florida Culinary Inst (FL)
New Hampshire Tech Inst (NH)
Normandale Comm Coll (MN)
Northeast Wisconsin Tech Coll (WI)
Northern Essex Comm Coll (MA)
Northwestern Michigan Coll (MI)
Ohio Valley Coll of Technology (OH)
Oxnard Coll (CA)
Pikes Peak Comm Coll (CO)
St. Cloud Tech Coll (MN)
South Central Tech Coll (MN)
Texas State Tech Coll–Harlingen (TX)
Texas State Tech Coll–Waco/Marshall Campus (TX)
Trenholm State Tech Coll, Montgomery (AL)

Dental Hygiene
Allegany Coll of Maryland (MD)
Amarillo Coll (TX)
Andrew Coll (GA)
Asheville-Buncombe Tech Comm Coll (NC)
Barton County Comm Coll (KS)
Bergen Comm Coll (NJ)
Big Sandy Comm and Tech Coll (KY)
Blackhawk Tech Coll (WI)
Brevard Comm Coll (FL)
Bristol Comm Coll (MA)
Broome Comm Coll (NY)
The Brown Mackie Coll–Lenexa Campus (KS)
Cabrillo Coll (CA)
Camden County Coll (NJ)
Cape Cod Comm Coll (MA)
Cape Fear Comm Coll (NC)
Central Comm Coll–Hastings Campus (NE)
Central Piedmont Comm Coll (NC)
Century Coll (MN)
Chabot Coll (CA)
Chemeketa Comm Coll (OR)
Clark Coll (WA)
Coastal Bend Coll (TX)
Coastal Carolina Comm Coll (NC)
Coastal Georgia Comm Coll (GA)
Colby Comm Coll (KS)
Coll of DuPage (IL)
Coll of Lake County (IL)
Coll of Southern Idaho (ID)
Collin County Comm Coll District (TX)
Colorado Northwestern Comm Coll (CO)
Columbia State Comm Coll (TN)
Columbus State Comm Coll (OH)
Comm Coll of Denver (CO)
Comm Coll of Rhode Island (RI)
Contra Costa Coll (CA)
Delgado Comm Coll (LA)
Del Mar Coll (TX)
Delta Coll (MI)
Des Moines Area Comm Coll (IA)
Durham Tech Comm Coll (NC)
Edison Comm Coll (FL)
Elizabethtown Comm Coll (KY)
Essex County Coll (NJ)
Eugenio María de Hostos Comm Coll of City U of NY (NY)
Everett Comm Coll (WA)
Fayetteville Tech Comm Coll (NC)
Florida National Coll (FL)
Foothill Coll (CA)
Georgia Perimeter Coll (GA)
Grand Rapids Comm Coll (MI)
Guilford Tech Comm Coll (NC)
Gulf Coast Comm Coll (FL)
Gwinnett Tech Coll (GA)
Harcum Coll (PA)
Harrisburg Area Comm Coll (PA)
Hawkeye Comm Coll (IA)
Herzing Coll, Minneapolis Drafting School Division (MN)
Hillsborough Comm Coll (FL)
Hinds Comm Coll (MS)
Hiwassee Coll (TN)
Howard Coll (TX)
James A. Rhodes State Coll (OH)
John A. Logan Coll (IL)

Johnson County Comm Coll (KS)
Kalamazoo Valley Comm Coll (MI)
Kellogg Comm Coll (MI)
Lake Land Coll (IL)
Lakeland Comm Coll (OH)
Lakeshore Tech Coll (WI)
Lake Superior Coll (MN)
Lake Washington Tech Coll (WA)
Lansing Comm Coll (MI)
Laramie County Comm Coll (WY)
Lewis and Clark Comm Coll (IL)
Lord Fairfax Comm Coll (VA)
Luzerne County Comm Coll (PA)
Meridian Comm Coll (MS)
Miami Dade Coll (FL)
Middlesex Comm Coll (MA)
Middlesex Comm Coll (NJ)
Midlands Tech Coll (SC)
Milwaukee Area Tech Coll (WI)
Montana State U Coll of Tech-Great Falls (MT)
Montgomery County Comm Coll (PA)
Mott Comm Coll (MI)
New Hampshire Tech Inst (NH)
Normandale Comm Coll (MN)
Northampton County Area Comm Coll (PA)
Northcentral Tech Coll (WI)
North Dakota State Coll of Science (ND)
Northeast Mississippi Comm Coll (MS)
Northeast Texas Comm Coll (TX)
Northeast Wisconsin Tech Coll (WI)
Oakland Comm Coll (MI)
Orange Coast Coll (CA)
Orange County Comm Coll (NY)
Oxnard Coll (CA)
Palm Beach Comm Coll (FL)
Palomar Coll (CA)
Parkland Coll (IL)
Pasadena City Coll (CA)
Pasco-Hernando Comm Coll (FL)
Pennsylvania Coll of Technology (PA)
Pensacola Jr Coll (FL)
Phoenix Coll (AZ)
Pima Comm Coll (AZ)
Portland Comm Coll (OR)
Quinsigamond Comm Coll (MA)
Riverside Comm Coll (CA)
Roane State Comm Coll (TN)
Rochester Comm and Tech Coll (MN)
St. Cloud Tech Coll (MN)
St. Petersburg Coll (FL)
San Jose City Coll (CA)
Santa Monica Coll (CA)
Sheridan Coll (WY)
Sinclair Comm Coll (OH)
South Puget Sound Comm Coll (WA)
Southwestern Coll (CA)
Spokane Comm Coll (WA)
Springfield Tech Comm Coll (MA)
Stark State Coll of Technology (OH)
Temple Coll (TX)
Texas State Tech Coll–Harlingen (TX)
Trident Tech Coll (SC)
Union County Coll (NJ)
U of Kentucky, Lexington Comm Coll (KY)
Utah Valley State Coll (UT)
Vincennes U (IN)

Virginia Western Comm Coll (VA)
Western Wisconsin Tech Coll (WI)
Westmoreland County Comm Coll (PA)
Yakima Valley Comm Coll (WA)
York Tech Coll (SC)

Dental Laboratory Technology
Bates Tech Coll (WA)
Century Coll (MN)
Columbus State Comm Coll (OH)
Commonwealth Tech Inst (PA)
Comm Coll of the Air Force (AL)
Delgado Comm Coll (LA)
J. Sargeant Reynolds Comm Coll (VA)
Middlesex Comm Coll (MA)
Pima Comm Coll (AZ)
Texas State Tech Coll–Harlingen (TX)
Trenholm State Tech Coll, Montgomery (AL)
U of Kentucky, Lexington Comm Coll (KY)

Design and Applied Arts Related
The Art Inst of Seattle (WA)
Mohawk Valley Comm Coll (NY)
Niagara County Comm Coll (NY)
Platt Coll San Diego (CA)

Design and Visual Communications
Academy Coll (MN)
Allentown Business School (PA)
The Art Inst of Pittsburgh (PA)
Bristol Comm Coll (MA)
Brookdale Comm Coll (NJ)
Bunker Hill Comm Coll (MA)
Coll of DuPage (IL)
The Creative Center (NE)
Duluth Business U (MN)
Elgin Comm Coll (IL)
Fashion Inst of Design & Merchandising, LA Campus (CA)
Fashion Inst of Design & Merchandising, SD Campus (CA)
Fashion Inst of Design & Merchandising, SF Campus (CA)
Front Range Comm Coll (CO)
Harrisburg Area Comm Coll (PA)
Ivy Tech State Coll–Central Indiana (IN)
Ivy Tech State Coll–Columbus (IN)
Ivy Tech State Coll–North Central (IN)
Ivy Tech State Coll–Southcentral (IN)
Ivy Tech State Coll–Southwest (IN)
Ivy Tech State Coll–Wabash Valley (IN)
Moraine Valley Comm Coll (IL)
Nassau Comm Coll (NY)
Northwest State Comm Coll (OH)
Parkland Coll (IL)
Pensacola Jr Coll (FL)
Pima Comm Coll (AZ)
Platt Coll San Diego (CA)
Santa Fe Comm Coll (NM)
Trinidad State Jr Coll (CO)
Waubonsee Comm Coll (IL)
Westwood Coll–Chicago Du Page (IL)
Westwood Coll–Chicago O'Hare Airport (IL)

Desktop Publishing and Digital Imaging Design
Brookdale Comm Coll (NJ)
Coll of DuPage (IL)
Dakota County Tech Coll (MN)
Iowa Lakes Comm Coll (IA)
Lake Land Coll (IL)
Linn-Benton Comm Coll (OR)
Louisville Tech Inst (KY)
Northwest Coll (WY)
Parkland Coll (IL)
Platt Coll San Diego (CA)
Silicon Valley Coll, Walnut Creek (CA)
Southwestern Illinois Coll (IL)
Springfield Tech Comm Coll (MA)
Umpqua Comm Coll (OR)

Developmental and Child Psychology
Arizona Western Coll (AZ)
Austin Comm Coll (TX)
Carl Sandburg Coll (IL)
Central Georgia Tech Coll (GA)
Central Lakes Coll (MN)
Coastal Bend Coll (TX)
Coll of the Canyons (CA)
Coll of the Sequoias (CA)
Columbia Coll (CA)
East Los Angeles Coll (CA)
Fulton-Montgomery Comm Coll (NY)
Garden City Comm Coll (KS)
Gavilan Coll (CA)
Hill Coll of the Hill Jr College District (TX)
Hinds Comm Coll (MS)
Iowa Lakes Comm Coll (IA)
Jefferson Comm Coll (OH)
Kirkwood Comm Coll (IA)
Lansing Comm Coll (MI)
Lincoln Coll, Lincoln (IL)
Los Angeles Harbor Coll (CA)
Los Angeles Valley Coll (CA)
McLennan Comm Coll (TX)
Midland Coll (TX)
MiraCosta Coll (CA)
Northeast Mississippi Comm Coll (MS)
North Idaho Coll (ID)
Palomar Coll (CA)
Pasadena City Coll (CA)
Rochester Comm and Tech Coll (MN)
San Diego City Coll (CA)
San Joaquin Delta Coll (CA)
Santa Monica Coll (CA)
South Plains Coll (TX)
South Texas Comm Coll (TX)
United Tribes Tech Coll (ND)
Waycross Coll (GA)

Diagnostic Medical Sonography and Ultrasound Technology
Albuquerque Tech Vocational Inst (NM)
Caldwell Comm Coll and Tech Inst (NC)
Cape Fear Comm Coll (NC)
Cincinnati State Tech and Comm Coll (OH)
Comm Coll of Allegheny County (PA)
Darton Coll (GA)
Del Mar Coll (TX)
El Centro Coll (TX)
Florida Hospital Coll of Health Sciences (FL)
Florida National Coll (FL)
Foothill Coll (CA)
Gloucester County Coll (NJ)
Hillsborough Comm Coll (FL)
Jackson Comm Coll (MI)
Keystone Coll (PA)
Lackawanna Coll (PA)
Lansing Comm Coll (MI)
Laramie County Comm Coll (WY)

Lorain County Comm Coll (OH)
Miami Dade Coll (FL)
Middlesex Comm Coll (MA)
Montgomery Coll (MD)
New Hampshire Tech Inst (NH)
Oakland Comm Coll (MI)
Pitt Comm Coll (NC)
St. Cloud Tech Coll (MN)
South Hills School of Business & Technology, State College (PA)
Springfield Tech Comm Coll (MA)

Diesel Mechanics Technology
Alexandria Tech Coll (MN)
Bates Tech Coll (WA)
Central Comm Coll–Hastings Campus (NE)
Centralia Coll (WA)
Century Coll (MN)
Clark Coll (WA)
Coll of Southern Idaho (ID)
Dakota County Tech Coll (MN)
Eastern Idaho Tech Coll (ID)
Great Basin Coll (NV)
Illinois Eastern Comm Colls, Wabash Valley Coll (IL)
Johnston Comm Coll (NC)
Lake Region State Coll (ND)
Lake Washington Tech Coll (WA)
Laramie County Comm Coll (WY)
Linn-Benton Comm Coll (OR)
Louisiana Tech Coll–Delta Ouachita Campus (LA)
Lower Columbia Coll (WA)
Massasoit Comm Coll (MA)
Mesalands Comm Coll (NM)
Mid-Plains Comm Coll, North Platte (NE)
Nashville Auto Diesel Coll (TN)
New Hampshire Comm Tech Coll, Berlin/Laconia (NH)
North Dakota State Coll of Science (ND)
Northeast Comm Coll (NE)
Northeast Wisconsin Tech Coll (WI)
Northwest Iowa Comm Coll (IA)
Peninsula Coll (WA)
Pennsylvania Coll of Technology (PA)
Raritan Valley Comm Coll (NJ)
Rend Lake Coll (IL)
Riverland Comm Coll (MN)
Rosedale Tech Inst (PA)
St. Cloud Tech Coll (MN)
St. Philip's Coll (TX)
San Juan Coll (NM)
Sheridan Coll (WY)
Somerset Comm Coll (KY)
Texas State Tech Coll–Waco/Marshall Campus (TX)
U of Northwestern Ohio (OH)
Utah Valley State Coll (UT)
Western Iowa Tech Comm Coll (IA)
Western Wyoming Comm Coll (WY)
Wichita Area Tech Coll (KS)
Williston State Coll (ND)

Dietetics
Briarwood Coll (CT)
Camden County Coll (NJ)
Central Arizona Coll (AZ)
Cincinnati State Tech and Comm Coll (OH)
Coll of Southern Idaho (ID)
Columbus State Comm Coll (OH)
Comm Coll of the Air Force (AL)
Delgado Comm Coll (LA)

Delta Coll (MI)
Dutchess Comm Coll (NY)
Fiorello H LaGuardia Comm Coll of City U of NY (NY)
Gaston Coll (NC)
Harrisburg Area Comm Coll (PA)
Hinds Comm Coll (MS)
J. Sargeant Reynolds Comm Coll (VA)
Labouré Coll (MA)
Lawson State Comm Coll (AL)
Manatee Comm Coll (FL)
Miami Dade Coll (FL)
Middlesex County Coll (NJ)
Milwaukee Area Tech Coll (WI)
Normandale Comm Coll (MN)
Orange Coast Coll (CA)
Pensacola Jr Coll (FL)
Portland Comm Coll (OR)
Riverside Comm Coll (CA)
St. Louis Comm Coll at Florissant Valley (MO)
Sinclair Comm Coll (OH)
Southeast Comm Coll, Lincoln Campus (NE)
Southern Maine Comm Coll (ME)
South Plains Coll (TX)
Spokane Comm Coll (WA)
State U of NY Coll of A&T at Morrisville (NY)
United Tribes Tech Coll (ND)
Vincennes U (IN)
Westmoreland County Comm Coll (PA)
Wichita Area Tech Coll (KS)

Dietetic Technician
Columbus State Comm Coll (OH)
Miami Dade Coll (FL)
Milwaukee Area Tech Coll (WI)

Dietitian Assistant
Alexandria Tech Coll (MN)
Barton County Comm Coll (KS)
City Colls of Chicago, Malcolm X Coll (IL)
Comm Coll of Allegheny County (PA)
Front Range Comm Coll (CO)
Pennsylvania Coll of Technology (PA)

Digital Communication and Media/Multimedia
The Art Inst of Pittsburgh (PA)
The Art Insts International Minnesota (MN)
Brevard Comm Coll (FL)
Hillsborough Comm Coll (FL)
Laramie County Comm Coll (WY)
Lehigh Carbon Comm Coll (PA)
Louisville Tech Inst (KY)
Olympic Coll (WA)
Platt Coll San Diego (CA)
Utah Valley State Coll (UT)

Direct Entry Midwifery
The Florida School of Midwifery (FL)

Divinity/Ministry
Andrew Coll (GA)
Crestmont Coll (CA)
Lon Morris Coll (TX)

Drafting
Arkansas Northeastern Coll (AR)

Drafting and Design Technology
AEC Southern Ohio Coll (OH)
Albany Tech Coll (GA)
Alpena Comm Coll (MI)

Alvin Comm Coll (TX)
Amarillo Coll (TX)
American River Coll (CA)
Arapahoe Comm Coll (CO)
Arizona Western Coll (AZ)
Arkansas State U–Beebe (AR)
Austin Comm Coll (TX)
Bainbridge Coll (GA)
Beaufort County Comm Coll (NC)
Bergen Comm Coll (NJ)
Blue Ridge Comm Coll (NC)
Brevard Comm Coll (FL)
Brookdale Comm Coll (NJ)
Burlington County Coll (NJ)
Butler County Comm Coll (KS)
Butte Coll (CA)
Cabrillo Coll (CA)
Caldwell Comm Coll and Tech Inst (NC)
Calhoun Comm Coll (AL)
Carl Sandburg Coll (IL)
Casper Coll (WY)
Central Alabama Comm Coll (AL)
Central Comm Coll–Columbus Campus (NE)
Central Comm Coll–Grand Island Campus (NE)
Central Comm Coll–Hastings Campus (NE)
Central Piedmont Comm Coll (NC)
Chemeketa Comm Coll (OR)
Clark State Comm Coll (OH)
Coastal Bend Coll (TX)
Coffeyville Comm Coll (KS)
Coll of DuPage (IL)
Coll of Southern Idaho (ID)
Coll of the Canyons (CA)
Coll of the Desert (CA)
Coll of the Sequoias (CA)
Collin County Comm Coll District (TX)
Comm Coll of Allegheny County (PA)
Comm Coll of Denver (CO)
Contra Costa Coll (CA)
Copiah-Lincoln Comm Coll (MS)
Corning Comm Coll (NY)
Crowder Coll (MO)
Cumberland County Coll (NJ)
Cuyamaca Coll (CA)
Dakota County Tech Coll (MN)
Daytona Beach Comm Coll (FL)
Delaware County Comm Coll (PA)
Delaware Tech & Comm Coll, Terry Cmps (DE)
Delgado Comm Coll (LA)
Del Mar Coll (TX)
Delta Coll (MI)
Des Moines Area Comm Coll (IA)
Doña Ana Branch Comm Coll (NM)
Donnelly Coll (KS)
East Arkansas Comm Coll (AR)
Eastern Arizona Coll (AZ)
Eastern Maine Comm Coll (ME)
Eastfield Coll (TX)
East Los Angeles Coll (CA)
East Mississippi Comm Coll (MS)
Edison Comm Coll (FL)
Edison State Comm Coll (OH)
Elaine P. Nunez Comm Coll (LA)
El Camino Coll (CA)
El Centro Coll (TX)
Elgin Comm Coll (IL)
Everett Comm Coll (WA)
Finger Lakes Comm Coll (NY)

Forsyth Tech Comm Coll (NC)
Fort Scott Comm Coll (KS)
Frederick Comm Coll (MD)
Front Range Comm Coll (CO)
Garden City Comm Coll (KS)
Gavilan Coll (CA)
Gloucester County Coll (NJ)
Gogebic Comm Coll (MI)
Grand Rapids Comm Coll (MI)
Green River Comm Coll (WA)
Guilford Tech Comm Coll (NC)
Gulf Coast Comm Coll (FL)
Gwinnett Tech Coll (GA)
Hawaii Comm Coll (HI)
Hawkeye Comm Coll (IA)
Heartland Comm Coll (IL)
Hibbing Comm Coll (MN)
High-Tech Inst (AZ)
Hill Coll of the Hill Jr College District (TX)
Hinds Comm Coll (MS)
Holmes Comm Coll (MS)
Honolulu Comm Coll (HI)
Houston Comm Coll System (TX)
Howard Coll (TX)
Hutchinson Comm Coll and Area Vocational School (KS)
Indian Hills Comm Coll (IA)
IntelliTec Coll, Colorado Springs (CO)
Iowa Lakes Comm Coll (IA)
Isothermal Comm Coll (NC)
ITI Tech Coll (LA)
Ivy Tech State Coll–Central Indiana (IN)
Ivy Tech State Coll–Columbus (IN)
Ivy Tech State Coll–Eastcentral (IN)
Ivy Tech State Coll–Kokomo (IN)
Ivy Tech State Coll–Lafayette (IN)
Ivy Tech State Coll–North Central (IN)
Ivy Tech State Coll–Northeast (IN)
Ivy Tech State Coll–Northwest (IN)
Ivy Tech State Coll–Wabash Valley (IN)
James A. Rhodes State Coll (OH)
Jefferson Comm Coll (OH)
J. F. Drake State Tech Coll (AL)
John A. Logan Coll (IL)
Johnson County Comm Coll (KS)
Kalamazoo Valley Comm Coll (MI)
Kansas City Kansas Comm Coll (KS)
Kellogg Comm Coll (MI)
Kirkwood Comm Coll (IA)
Kirtland Comm Coll (MI)
Lake Area Tech Inst (SD)
Lake Land Coll (IL)
Lake Washington Tech Coll (WA)
Lansing Comm Coll (MI)
Lawson State Comm Coll (AL)
Lehigh Carbon Comm Coll (PA)
Lenoir Comm Coll (NC)
Lewis and Clark Comm Coll (IL)
Linn-Benton Comm Coll (OR)
Linn State Tech Coll (MO)
Longview Comm Coll (MO)
Lorain County Comm Coll (OH)
Los Angeles Harbor Coll (CA)
Los Angeles Pierce Coll (CA)

Los Angeles Trade-Tech Coll (CA)
Los Angeles Valley Coll (CA)
Louisiana Tech Coll–Delta Ouachita Campus (LA)
Louisville Tech Inst (KY)
Luzerne County Comm Coll (PA)
Macomb Comm Coll (MI)
Manatee Comm Coll (FL)
Manhattan Area Tech Coll (KS)
Marion Tech Coll (OH)
Marshalltown Comm Coll (IA)
Meridian Comm Coll (MS)
Metropolitan Comm Coll (NE)
Metropolitan Comm Coll-Business & Technology College (MO)
Miami Dade Coll (FL)
Michiana Coll, South Bend (IN)
Middlesex Comm Coll (MA)
Middlesex County Coll (NJ)
Midland Coll (TX)
Mid Michigan Comm Coll (MI)
Milwaukee Area Tech Coll (WI)
Mineral Area Coll (MO)
Minnesota State Coll–Southeast Tech (MN)
MiraCosta Coll (CA)
Mississippi Gulf Coast Comm Coll (MS)
Mitchell Comm Coll (NC)
Mitchell Tech Inst (SD)
Moberly Area Comm Coll (MO)
Modesto Jr Coll (CA)
Mohawk Valley Comm Coll (NY)
Monroe County Comm Coll (MI)
Montana State U Coll of Tech-Great Falls (MT)
Montcalm Comm Coll (MI)
Moraine Park Tech Coll (WI)
Morrison Inst of Technology (IL)
Morton Coll (IL)
Mott Comm Coll (MI)
Mountain Empire Comm Coll (VA)
Mountain View Coll (TX)
Mt. San Antonio Coll (CA)
Napa Valley Coll (CA)
Naugatuck Valley Comm Coll (CT)
New England Inst of Tech & Florida Culinary Inst (FL)
New Hampshire Comm Tech Coll, Manchester/Stratham (NH)
New River Comm Coll (VA)
Niagara County Comm Coll (NY)
Northampton County Area Comm Coll (PA)
North Central Missouri Coll (MO)
North Central State Coll (OH)
Northcentral Tech Coll (WI)
Northeast Comm Coll (NE)
Northeastern Oklahoma A&M Coll (OK)
Northeast Mississippi Comm Coll (MS)
Northeast State Tech Comm Coll (TN)
Northeast Wisconsin Tech Coll (WI)
Northern Maine Comm Coll (ME)
North Harris Coll (TX)
North Idaho Coll (ID)
Northland Pioneer Coll (AZ)
Northwest Coll (WY)
Northwestern Michigan Coll (MI)
Northwest-Shoals Comm Coll (AL)

Odessa Coll (TX)
Oklahoma City Comm Coll (OK)
Olympic Coll (WA)
Orange Coast Coll (CA)
Orange County Comm Coll (NY)
Palm Beach Comm Coll (FL)
Palomar Coll (CA)
Paris Jr Coll (TX)
Pasadena City Coll (CA)
Pasco-Hernando Comm Coll (FL)
Pellissippi State Tech Comm Coll (TN)
Pennsylvania Coll of Technology (PA)
Pensacola Jr Coll (FL)
Phoenix Coll (AZ)
Portland Comm Coll (OR)
Prince George's Comm Coll (MD)
Pulaski Tech Coll (AR)
Red Rocks Comm Coll (CO)
Remington Coll–Mobile Campus (AL)
Saint Charles Comm Coll (MO)
St. Clair County Comm Coll (MI)
St. Petersburg Coll (FL)
San Diego City Coll (CA)
San Joaquin Delta Coll (CA)
San Jose City Coll (CA)
San Juan Coll (NM)
Santa Barbara City Coll (CA)
Santa Fe Comm Coll (NM)
Santa Monica Coll (CA)
Schoolcraft Coll (MI)
Schuylkill Inst of Business and Technology (PA)
Seminole Comm Coll (FL)
Shelton State Comm Coll (AL)
Sheridan Coll (WY)
Sierra Coll (CA)
Silicon Valley Coll, Walnut Creek (CA)
Sinclair Comm Coll (OH)
Southeast Arkansas Coll (AR)
Southeast Comm Coll, Lincoln Campus (NE)
Southern Arkansas U Tech (AR)
Southern Maine Comm Coll (ME)
Southern State Comm Coll (OH)
Southern West Virginia Comm and Tech Coll (WV)
South Plains Coll (TX)
South Puget Sound Comm Coll (WA)
Southside Virginia Comm Coll (VA)
South Suburban Coll (IL)
Southwestern Illinois Coll (IL)
Southwestern Michigan Coll (MI)
Spartanburg Tech Coll (SC)
Spokane Comm Coll (WA)
Stark State Coll of Technology (OH)
State U of NY Coll of A&T at Morrisville (NY)
State U of NY Coll of Technology at Alfred (NY)
State U of NY Coll of Technology at Delhi (NY)
Temple Coll (TX)
Texas State Tech Coll–Harlingen (TX)
Texas State Tech Coll–Waco/Marshall Campus (TX)
Thomas Nelson Comm Coll (VA)
Thompson Inst (PA)
Tidewater Comm Coll (VA)
Trenholm State Tech Coll, Montgomery (AL)
Triangle Tech, Inc. (PA)

Triangle Tech, Inc.–DuBois School (PA)
Triangle Tech, Inc.– Greensburg Center (PA)
Trinidad State Jr Coll (CO)
Triton Coll (IL)
Utah Valley State Coll (UT)
Ventura Coll (CA)
Vincennes U (IN)
Washtenaw Comm Coll (MI)
Waycross Coll (GA)
Western Dakota Tech Inst (SD)
Western Nevada Comm Coll (NV)
Westmoreland County Comm Coll (PA)
Williamsburg Tech Coll (SC)
York County Comm Coll (ME)
York Tech Coll (SC)

Drafting/Design Engineering Technologies Related
Comm Coll of Allegheny County (PA)
Fairmont State Comm & Tech Coll (WV)
Louisville Tech Inst (KY)
Pennsylvania Coll of Technology (PA)

Dramatic/Theatre Arts
Alvin Comm Coll (TX)
Amarillo Coll (TX)
American Academy of Dramatic Arts (NY)
American Academy of Dramatic Arts/Hollywood (CA)
American River Coll (CA)
Andrew Coll (GA)
Arizona Western Coll (AZ)
Bainbridge Coll (GA)
Barton County Comm Coll (KS)
Bergen Comm Coll (NJ)
Brookdale Comm Coll (NJ)
Bucks County Comm Coll (PA)
Bunker Hill Comm Coll (MA)
Burlington County Coll (NJ)
Butler County Comm Coll (KS)
Calhoun Comm Coll (AL)
Camden County Coll (NJ)
Cañada Coll (CA)
Cape Cod Comm Coll (MA)
Casper Coll (WY)
Centralia Coll (WA)
Central Wyoming Coll (WY)
Clarendon Coll (TX)
Clark State Comm Coll (OH)
Coastal Bend Coll (TX)
Coffeyville Comm Coll (KS)
Colby Comm Coll (KS)
Coll of Southern Idaho (ID)
Coll of the Desert (CA)
Coll of the Sequoias (CA)
Colorado Mountn Coll (CO)
Columbia Coll (CA)
Comm Coll of Allegheny County (PA)
Comm Coll of Rhode Island (RI)
Crowder Coll (MO)
Cumberland County Coll (NJ)
Darton Coll (GA)
Daytona Beach Comm Coll (FL)
Dean Coll (MA)
Del Mar Coll (TX)
Delta Coll (MI)
Eastern Arizona Coll (AZ)
Eastern Oklahoma State Coll (OK)
East Los Angeles Coll (CA)
El Camino Coll (CA)
Everett Comm Coll (WA)
Finger Lakes Comm Coll (NY)
Foothill Coll (CA)
Fulton-Montgomery Comm Coll (NY)

Galveston Coll (TX)
Garden City Comm Coll (KS)
Georgia Perimeter Coll (GA)
Gloucester County Coll (NJ)
Gordon Coll (GA)
Guilford Tech Comm Coll (NC)
Harrisburg Area Comm Coll (PA)
Hill Coll of the Hill Jr Coll District (TX)
Hillsborough Comm Coll (FL)
Hinds Comm Coll (MS)
Hiwassee Coll (TN)
Holyoke Comm Coll (MA)
Houston Comm Coll System (TX)
Howard Coll (TX)
Howard Comm Coll (MD)
Jefferson Coll (MO)
Jefferson Davis Comm Coll (AL)
Kellogg Comm Coll (MI)
Kingsborough Comm Coll of City U of NY (NY)
Kirkwood Comm Coll (IA)
Lansing Comm Coll (MI)
Laramie County Comm Coll (WY)
Lincoln Coll, Lincoln (IL)
Linn-Benton Comm Coll (OR)
Lon Morris Coll (TX)
Lorain County Comm Coll (OH)
Los Angeles Pierce Coll (CA)
Los Angeles Valley Coll (CA)
Lower Columbia Coll (WA)
Manatee Comm Coll (FL)
Manchester Comm Coll (CT)
Massasoit Comm Coll (MA)
Miami Dade Coll (FL)
Middlesex Comm Coll (MA)
Middlesex County Coll (NJ)
Mid Michigan Comm Coll (MI)
MiraCosta Coll (CA)
Modesto Jr Coll (CA)
Mohawk Valley Comm Coll (NY)
Nassau Comm Coll (NY)
Niagara County Comm Coll (NY)
Northeast Comm Coll (NE)
Northeastern Oklahoma A&M Coll (OK)
Northeast Mississippi Comm Coll (MS)
Northern Essex Comm Coll (MA)
North Harris Coll (TX)
North Idaho Coll (ID)
Northwestern Michigan Coll (MI)
Oklahoma City Comm Coll (OK)
Orange Coast Coll (CA)
Otero Jr Coll (CO)
Oxnard Coll (CA)
Palm Beach Comm Coll (FL)
Palomar Coll (CA)
Pasadena City Coll (CA)
Pensacola Jr Coll (FL)
Piedmont Virginia Comm Coll (VA)
Pima Comm Coll (AZ)
Raritan Valley Comm Coll (NJ)
Riverside Comm Coll (CA)
St. Johns River Comm Coll (FL)
St. Louis Comm Coll at Florissant Valley (MO)
St. Philip's Coll (TX)
San Diego City Coll (CA)
San Joaquin Delta Coll (CA)
San Juan Coll (NM)
Santa Barbara City Coll (CA)
Santa Monica Coll (CA)
Sauk Valley Comm Coll (IL)
Schenectady County Comm Coll (NY)
Scottsdale Comm Coll (AZ)

Seward County Comm Coll (KS)
Sinclair Comm Coll (OH)
Snow Coll (UT)
Southwestern Coll (CA)
Spoon River Coll (IL)
Trinidad State Jr Coll (CO)
Triton Coll (IL)
Umpqua Comm Coll (OR)
Utah Valley State Coll (UT)
Ventura Coll (CA)
Vermilion Comm Coll (MN)
Victor Valley Coll (CA)
Vincennes U (IN)
Western Wyoming Comm Coll (WY)
Yuba Coll (CA)

Dramatic/Theatre Arts and Stagecraft Related
Bristol Comm Coll (MA)
St. Philip's Coll (TX)

Drawing
Cañada Coll (CA)
Chabot Coll (CA)
Coffeyville Comm Coll (KS)
Cuyamaca Coll (CA)
Everett Comm Coll (WA)
Iowa Lakes Comm Coll (IA)
Keystone Coll (PA)
Lincoln Coll, Lincoln (IL)
Lon Morris Coll (TX)
Luzerne County Comm Coll (PA)
Midland Coll (TX)
Northeast Mississippi Comm Coll (MS)
Palomar Coll (CA)
Pasadena City Coll (CA)
San Joaquin Delta Coll (CA)
Seward County Comm Coll (KS)
Vermilion Comm Coll (MN)

Early Childhood Education
Albany Tech Coll (GA)
Barton County Comm Coll (KS)
Brevard Comm Coll (FL)
Bristol Comm Coll (MA)
Bunker Hill Comm Coll (MA)
Central Oregon Comm Coll (OR)
Clark Coll (WA)
Clover Park Tech Coll (WA)
Colorado Northwestern Comm Coll (CO)
Heart of Georgia Tech Coll (GA)
Hopkinsville Comm Coll (KY)
Iowa Lakes Comm Coll (IA)
Jackson Comm Coll (MI)
John Wood Comm Coll (IL)
Kent State U, Tuscarawas Campus (OH)
Keystone Coll (PA)
Kingsborough Comm Coll of City U of NY (NY)
Lackawanna Coll (PA)
Lanier Tech Coll (GA)
Laramie County Comm Coll (WY)
Louisiana Tech Coll–Florida Parishes Campus (LA)
Lower Columbia Coll (WA)
Luna Comm Coll (NM)
Luzerne County Comm Coll (PA)
Mott Comm Coll (MI)
Nebraska Indian Comm Coll (NE)
Northland Pioneer Coll (AZ)
North Seattle Comm Coll (WA)
Northwest Coll (WY)
Oakton Comm Coll (IL)
Okefenokee Tech Coll (GA)
Oklahoma State U, Oklahoma City (OK)
Olympic Coll (WA)
Owens Comm Coll, Findlay (OH)
Owens Comm Coll, Toledo (OH)
Rend Lake Coll (IL)

St. Philip's Coll (TX)
Salem Comm Coll (NJ)
Sauk Valley Comm Coll (IL)
Somerset Comm Coll (KY)
Southeastern Tech Coll (GA)
Tillamook Bay Comm Coll (OR)
Tri-County Comm Coll (NC)
Utah Valley State Coll (UT)
Western Wyoming Comm Coll (WY)

Ecology
Abraham Baldwin Ag Coll (GA)
Casper Coll (WY)
Chabot Coll (CA)
Colorado Mountn Coll, Timberline Cmps (CO)
Everett Comm Coll (WA)
Iowa Lakes Comm Coll (IA)
Northwest Coll (WY)
Vermilion Comm Coll (MN)

E-Commerce
Colorado Northwestern Comm Coll (CO)
Del Mar Coll (TX)
Milwaukee Area Tech Coll (WI)
St. Philip's Coll (TX)

Economics
Anne Arundel Comm Coll (MD)
Austin Comm Coll (TX)
Barton County Comm Coll (KS)
Bergen Comm Coll (NJ)
Cañada Coll (CA)
Casper Coll (WY)
Chabot Coll (CA)
Chemeketa Comm Coll (OR)
Coastal Bend Coll (TX)
Coffeyville Comm Coll (KS)
Coll of the Desert (CA)
Columbia State Comm Coll (TN)
Copiah-Lincoln Comm Coll (MS)
Darton Coll (GA)
Daytona Beach Comm Coll (FL)
Eastern Oklahoma State Coll (OK)
Eastern Wyoming Coll (WY)
East Mississippi Comm Coll (MS)
El Camino Coll (CA)
Everett Comm Coll (WA)
Foothill Coll (CA)
Gulf Coast Comm Coll (FL)
Hill Coll of the Hill Jr Coll District (TX)
Hinds Comm Coll (MS)
Hiwassee Coll (TN)
Iowa Lakes Comm Coll (IA)
Laramie County Comm Coll (WY)
Lincoln Coll, Lincoln (IL)
Linn-Benton Comm Coll (OR)
Lon Morris Coll (TX)
Los Angeles Valley Coll (CA)
Lower Columbia Coll (WA)
Manatee Comm Coll (FL)
Marshalltown Comm Coll (IA)
Merritt Coll (CA)
Miami Dade Coll (FL)
Midland Coll (TX)
MiraCosta Coll (CA)
Northeastern Oklahoma A&M Coll (OK)
Northeast Mississippi Comm Coll (MS)
Northwest Coll (WY)
Orange Coast Coll (CA)
Oxnard Coll (CA)
Palm Beach Comm Coll (FL)
Palo Alto Coll (TX)
Palomar Coll (CA)
Pasadena City Coll (CA)
Red Rocks Comm Coll (CO)
Riverside Comm Coll (CA)

St. Philip's Coll (TX)
San Joaquin Delta Coll (CA)
San Juan Coll (NM)
Santa Barbara City Coll (CA)
Santa Monica Coll (CA)
Sauk Valley Comm Coll (IL)
Seward County Comm Coll (KS)
Snow Coll (UT)
Southwestern Coll (CA)
Triton Coll (IL)
Umpqua Comm Coll (OR)
Vermilion Comm Coll (MN)
Western Wyoming Comm Coll (WY)

Education
Abraham Baldwin Ag Coll (GA)
Andrew Coll (GA)
Anne Arundel Comm Coll (MD)
Arizona Western Coll (AZ)
Atlantic Cape Comm Coll (NJ)
Bainbridge Coll (GA)
Bergen Comm Coll (NJ)
Bowling Green State U–Firelands Coll (OH)
Brookdale Comm Coll (NJ)
Bucks County Comm Coll (PA)
Bunker Hill Comm Coll (MA)
Burlington County Coll (NJ)
Calhoun Comm Coll (AL)
Cape Cod Comm Coll (MA)
Casper Coll (WY)
Cecil Comm Coll (MD)
Central Oregon Comm Coll (OR)
Chabot Coll (CA)
Chemeketa Comm Coll (OR)
Chipola Coll (FL)
Clarendon Coll (TX)
Coastal Bend Coll (TX)
Coffeyville Comm Coll (KS)
Colby Comm Coll (KS)
Coll of Southern Idaho (ID)
Coll of Southern Maryland (MD)
Coll of the Desert (CA)
Colorado Northwestern Comm Coll (CO)
Connors State Coll (OK)
Copiah-Lincoln Comm Coll (MS)
Crowder Coll (MO)
Cumberland County Coll (NJ)
Danville Comm Coll (VA)
Darton Coll (GA)
Daytona Beach Comm Coll (FL)
Del Mar Coll (TX)
Delta Coll (MI)
Des Moines Area Comm Coll (IA)
Donnelly Coll (KS)
Eastern Oklahoma State Coll (OK)
Eastern Shore Comm Coll (VA)
East Mississippi Comm Coll (MS)
Essex County Coll (NJ)
Everett Comm Coll (WA)
Fiorello H LaGuardia Comm Coll of City U of NY (NY)
Florida National Coll (FL)
Fort Scott Comm Coll (KS)
Frederick Comm Coll (MD)
Galveston Coll (TX)
Garden City Comm Coll (KS)
Garrett Coll (MD)
Georgia Perimeter Coll (GA)
Germanna Comm Coll (VA)
Gloucester County Coll (NJ)
Gogebic Comm Coll (MI)
Gordon Coll (GA)
Greenfield Comm Coll (MA)
Hagerstown Comm Coll (MD)
Harford Comm Coll (MD)
Harrisburg Area Comm Coll (PA)

Hawkeye Comm Coll (IA)
Hill Coll of the Hill Jr College District (TX)
Hillsborough Comm Coll (FL)
Hutchinson Comm Coll and Area Vocational School (KS)
Iowa Lakes Comm Coll (IA)
Isothermal Comm Coll (NC)
Itasca Comm Coll (MN)
Jefferson Coll (MO)
Jefferson Davis Comm Coll (AL)
John A. Logan Coll (IL)
Johnson County Comm Coll (KS)
Kent State U, Salem Campus (OH)
Kent State U, Stark Campus (OH)
Kingsborough Comm Coll of City U of NY (NY)
Kingwood Coll (TX)
Kirkwood Comm Coll (IA)
Lackawanna Coll (PA)
Lansing Comm Coll (MI)
Laramie County Comm Coll (WY)
Lawson State Comm Coll (AL)
Lehigh Carbon Comm Coll (PA)
Lincoln Coll, Lincoln (IL)
Linn-Benton Comm Coll (OR)
Lon Morris Coll (TX)
Lorain County Comm Coll (OH)
Lord Fairfax Comm Coll (VA)
Luzerne County Comm Coll (PA)
Miami Dade Coll (FL)
Middlesex County Coll (NJ)
Mississippi Gulf Coast Comm Coll (MS)
Montgomery Coll (MD)
Mountain Empire Comm Coll (VA)
New Mexico State U– Carlsbad (NM)
New Mexico State U–Grants (NM)
New River Comm Coll (VA)
Northeast Comm Coll (NE)
Northeast Mississippi Comm Coll (MS)
Northeast Texas Comm Coll (TX)
Northern Essex Comm Coll (MA)
North Harris Coll (TX)
North Idaho Coll (ID)
Northwest Coll (WY)
Northwestern Michigan Coll (MI)
Northwest-Shoals Comm Coll (AL)
Northwest State Comm Coll (OH)
Odessa Coll (TX)
Oklahoma State U, Oklahoma City (OK)
Otero Jr Coll (CO)
Palm Beach Comm Coll (FL)
Palo Alto Coll (TX)
Paris Jr Coll (TX)
Paul D. Camp Comm Coll (VA)
Pensacola Jr Coll (FL)
Piedmont Virginia Comm Coll (VA)
Pratt Comm Coll and Area Vocational School (KS)
Prince George's Comm Coll (MD)
Raritan Valley Comm Coll (NJ)
Reading Area Comm Coll (PA)
Riverside Comm Coll (CA)
Roane State Comm Coll (TN)
Roanoke-Chowan Comm Coll (NC)

St. Philip's Coll (TX)
Salem Comm Coll (NJ)
San Juan Coll (NM)
Sauk Valley Comm Coll (IL)
Schenectady County Comm Coll (NY)
Schoolcraft Coll (MI)
Seward County Comm Coll (KS)
Shelton State Comm Coll (AL)
Sheridan Coll (WY)
Sinclair Comm Coll (OH)
Snow Coll (UT)
Southeast Comm Coll, Beatrice Campus (NE)
South Plains Coll (TX)
Southside Virginia Comm Coll (VA)
South Texas Comm Coll (TX)
Southwest Mississippi Comm Coll (MS)
Spoon River Comm Coll (IL)
Three Rivers Comm Coll (MO)
Tidewater Comm Coll (VA)
Trinidad State Jr Coll (CO)
Triton Coll (IL)
Truett-McConnell Coll (GA)
Umpqua Comm Coll (OR)
U of Arkansas Comm Coll at Batesville (AR)
Vance-Granville Comm Coll (NC)
Ventura Coll (CA)
Vermilion Comm Coll (MN)
Villa Maria Coll of Buffalo (NY)
Vincennes U (IN)
Virginia Western Comm Coll (VA)
Walters State Comm Coll (TN)
Waycross Coll (GA)
Western Wyoming Comm Coll (WY)
Wor-Wic Comm Coll (MD)
Yuba Coll (CA)

Educational/Instructional Media Design
Bellevue Comm Coll (WA)
Brookdale Comm Coll (NJ)
Century Coll (MN)
Collin County Comm Coll District (TX)
Comm Coll of the Air Force (AL)
County Coll of Morris (NJ)
Hibbing Comm Coll (MN)
Hutchinson Comm Coll and Area Vocational School (KS)
Ivy Tech State Coll–North Central (IN)
Milwaukee Area Tech Coll (WI)
Portland Comm Coll (OR)
Southern Arkansas U Tech (AR)
Texas State Tech Coll–Waco/Marshall Campus (TX)
Virginia Coll at Jackson (MS)

Educational Leadership and Administration
Comm Coll of the Air Force (AL)

Education (K–12)
Cecil Comm Coll (MD)
Itasca Comm Coll (MN)
Keystone Coll (PA)
Mid Michigan Comm Coll (MI)
Pratt Comm Coll and Area Vocational School (KS)
Vincennes U (IN)

Education (Multiple Levels)
Atlanta Metropolitan Coll (GA)
Coastal Georgia Comm Coll (GA)

Delaware County Comm Coll (PA)
Georgia Perimeter Coll (GA)
Western Wyoming Comm Coll (WY)

Education Related
Corning Comm Coll (NY)
Guilford Tech Comm Coll (NC)
Rogue Comm Coll (OR)
Yavapai Coll (AZ)

Education (Specific Levels and Methods) Related
Comm Coll of Allegheny County (PA)
Laramie County Comm Coll (WY)
Northampton County Area Comm Coll (PA)

Education (Specific Subject Areas) Related
Comm Coll of Allegheny County (PA)
Pennsylvania Coll of Technology (PA)

Electrical and Electronic Engineering Technologies Related
Albany Tech Coll (GA)
Cincinnati State Tech and Comm Coll (OH)
Columbus State Comm Coll (OH)
Eugenio María de Hostos Comm Coll of City U of NY (NY)
Fairmont State Comm & Tech Coll (WV)
Lamar State Coll–Port Arthur (TX)
Louisville Tech Inst (KY)
Massasoit Comm Coll (MA)
Miami Dade Coll (FL)
Miami U Hamilton (OH)
Mitchell Tech Inst (SD)
Mohawk Valley Comm Coll (NY)
Northampton County Area Comm Coll (PA)
Pennsylvania Coll of Technology (PA)
Southwestern Michigan Coll (MI)
Springfield Tech Comm Coll (MA)
Vatterott Coll, Oklahoma City (OK)

Electrical and Power Transmission Installation
Bates Tech Coll (WA)
Dunwoody Coll of Technology (MN)
Ivy Tech State Coll–Columbus (IN)
Johnson County Comm Coll (KS)
Mitchell Tech Inst (SD)
Oklahoma State U, Oklahoma City (OK)
Orange Coast Coll (CA)
St. Cloud Tech Coll (MN)
State U of NY Coll of Technology at Delhi (NY)
Western Nevada Comm Coll (NV)

Electrical and Power Transmission Installation Related
Calhoun Comm Coll (AL)
Manhattan Area Tech Coll (KS)
Vatterott Coll, St. Ann (MO)

Electrical, Electronic and Communications Engineering Technology
AEC Southern Ohio Coll (OH)
Alamance Comm Coll (NC)
Albuquerque Tech Vocational Inst (NM)
Alvin Comm Coll (TX)

Amarillo Coll (TX)
American River Coll (CA)
Anne Arundel Comm Coll (MD)
Anoka Tech Coll (MN)
Arapahoe Comm Coll (CO)
Arizona Western Coll (AZ)
Arkansas State U–Beebe (AR)
Augusta Tech Coll (GA)
Austin Comm Coll (TX)
Bainbridge Coll (GA)
Bates Tech Coll (WA)
Beaufort County Comm Coll (NC)
Berean Inst (PA)
Bergen Comm Coll (NJ)
Berkshire Comm Coll (MA)
Blackhawk Tech Coll (WI)
Bladen Comm Coll (NC)
Blue Ridge Comm Coll (NC)
Bowling Green State U–Firelands Coll (OH)
Brevard Comm Coll (FL)
Bristol Comm Coll (MA)
Bronx Comm Coll of City U of NY (NY)
Brookdale Comm Coll (NJ)
Broome Comm Coll (NY)
Brunswick Comm Coll (NC)
Bryant & Stratton Business Inst, Amherst Cmps (NY)
Bucks County Comm Coll (PA)
Burlington County Coll (NJ)
Butler County Comm Coll (KS)
Butte Coll (CA)
Cabrillo Coll (CA)
Caldwell Comm Coll and Tech Inst (NC)
Calhoun Comm Coll (AL)
Cambria County Area Comm Coll (PA)
Camden County Coll (NJ)
Cape Fear Comm Coll (NC)
Capital Comm Coll (CT)
Career Coll of Northern Nevada (NV)
Carl Sandburg Coll (IL)
Casper Coll (WY)
Cecil Comm Coll (MD)
Central Alabama Comm Coll (AL)
Central Comm Coll–Columbus Campus (NE)
Central Comm Coll–Grand Island Campus (NE)
Central Comm Coll–Hastings Campus (NE)
Central Florida Comm Coll (FL)
Centralia Coll (WA)
Central Piedmont Comm Coll (NC)
Chabot Coll (CA)
Chemeketa Comm Coll (OR)
Chesapeake Coll (MD)
CHI Inst (PA)
Cincinnati State Tech and Comm Coll (OH)
Clarendon Coll (TX)
Clark Coll (WA)
Clark State Comm Coll (OH)
Cleveland Comm Coll (NC)
Cleveland Inst of Electronics (OH)
Clinton Comm Coll (NY)
Clovis Comm Coll (NM)
Coll of DuPage (IL)
Coll of Lake County (IL)
Coll of Southern Idaho (ID)
Coll of Southern Maryland (MD)
Coll of the Canyons (CA)
Coll of the Sequoias (CA)
Collin County Comm Coll District (TX)
Columbia State Comm Coll (TN)
Columbus State Comm Coll (OH)
Comm Coll of Allegheny County (PA)

Comm Coll of Denver (CO)
Comm Coll of Rhode Island (RI)
Comm Coll of the Air Force (AL)
Contra Costa Coll (CA)
Copiah-Lincoln Comm Coll (MS)
Corning Comm Coll (NY)
County Coll of Morris (NJ)
Crowder Coll (MO)
Cuesta Coll (CA)
Daytona Beach Comm Coll (FL)
DeKalb Tech Coll (GA)
Delaware County Comm Coll (PA)
Delaware Tech & Comm Coll, Terry Cmps (DE)
Delgado Comm Coll (LA)
Del Mar Coll (TX)
Des Moines Area Comm Coll (IA)
Doña Ana Branch Comm Coll (NM)
Dunwoody Coll of Technology (MN)
Durham Tech Comm Coll (NC)
Dutchess Comm Coll (NY)
Eastern Idaho Tech Coll (ID)
Eastern Maine Comm Coll (ME)
Eastern Oklahoma State Coll (OK)
Eastern Shore Comm Coll (VA)
Eastfield Coll (TX)
East Los Angeles Coll (CA)
East Mississippi Comm Coll (MS)
ECPI Coll of Technology, Newport News (VA)
ECPI Coll of Technology, Virginia Beach (VA)
ECPI Tech Coll, Richmond (VA)
ECPI Tech Coll, Roanoke (VA)
Edgecombe Comm Coll (NC)
Edison Comm Coll (FL)
Edison State Comm Coll (OH)
Edmonds Comm Coll (WA)
Education Direct Center for Degree Studies (PA)
Elaine P. Nunez Comm Coll (LA)
El Camino Coll (CA)
Elgin Comm Coll (IL)
Erie Inst of Technology (PA)
Essex County Coll (NJ)
Fairmont State Comm & Tech Coll (WV)
Fayetteville Tech Comm Coll (NC)
Foothill Coll (CA)
Forsyth Tech Comm Coll (NC)
Fort Scott Comm Coll (KS)
Fountainhead Coll of Technology (TN)
Frederick Comm Coll (MD)
Front Range Comm Coll (CO)
Fulton-Montgomery Comm Coll (NY)
Garden City Comm Coll (KS)
Gaston Coll (NC)
Germanna Comm Coll (VA)
Glendale Comm Coll (AZ)
Grand Rapids Comm Coll (MI)
Great Basin Coll (NV)
Guilford Tech Comm Coll (NC)
Gulf Coast Comm Coll (FL)
Gwinnett Tech Coll (GA)
Harrisburg Area Comm Coll (PA)
Hawaii Comm Coll (HI)
Heartland Comm Coll (IL)
Henderson Comm Coll (KY)

Hill Coll of the Hill Jr College District (TX)
Hillsborough Comm Coll (FL)
Hinds Comm Coll (MS)
Honolulu Comm Coll (HI)
Hopkinsville Comm Coll (KY)
Houston Comm Coll System (TX)
Howard Comm Coll (MD)
Hudson County Comm Coll (NJ)
Illinois Eastern Comm Colls, Wabash Valley Coll (IL)
Indian Hills Comm Coll (IA)
IntelliTec Coll, Colorado Springs (CO)
IntelliTec Coll, Grand Junction (CO)
Island Drafting and Tech Inst (NY)
Isothermal Comm Coll (NC)
ITI Tech Coll (LA)
Ivy Tech State Coll–Bloomington (IN)
Ivy Tech State Coll–Central Indiana (IN)
Ivy Tech State Coll–Columbus (IN)
Ivy Tech State Coll–Eastcentral (IN)
Ivy Tech State Coll–Kokomo (IN)
Ivy Tech State Coll–Lafayette (IN)
Ivy Tech State Coll–North Central (IN)
Ivy Tech State Coll–Northeast (IN)
Ivy Tech State Coll–Northwest (IN)
Ivy Tech State Coll–Southcentral (IN)
Ivy Tech State Coll–Southeast (IN)
Ivy Tech State Coll–Southwest (IN)
Ivy Tech State Coll–Wabash Valley (IN)
Ivy Tech State Coll–Whitewater (IN)
Jackson Comm Coll (MI)
James A. Rhodes State Coll (OH)
Jamestown Comm Coll (NY)
Jefferson Coll (MO)
Jefferson Comm Coll (KY)
Jefferson Comm Coll (OH)
J. F. Drake State Tech Coll (AL)
John A. Logan Coll (IL)
Johnston Comm Coll (NC)
John Wood Comm Coll (IL)
J. Sargeant Reynolds Comm Coll (VA)
Kalamazoo Valley Comm Coll (MI)
Kaskaskia Coll (IL)
Kauai Comm Coll (HI)
Kent State U, Trumbull Campus (OH)
Kent State U, Tuscarawas Campus (OH)
Kirkwood Comm Coll (IA)
Lake Area Tech Inst (SD)
Lake City Comm Coll (FL)
Lake Land Coll (IL)
Lakeland Comm Coll (OH)
Lakeshore Tech Coll (WI)
Lake Superior Coll (MN)
Lake Washington Tech Coll (WA)
Lamar State Coll–Port Arthur (TX)
Lanier Tech Coll (GA)
Lansing Comm Coll (MI)
Laredo Comm Coll (TX)
Lawson State Comm Coll (AL)
Lehigh Carbon Comm Coll (PA)
Lenoir Comm Coll (NC)
Lincoln Land Comm Coll (IL)
Linn State Tech Coll (MO)
Longview Comm Coll (MO)

Lorain County Comm Coll (OH)
Los Angeles Harbor Coll (CA)
Los Angeles Pierce Coll (CA)
Los Angeles Trade-Tech Coll (CA)
Los Angeles Valley Coll (CA)
Louisiana Tech Coll–Gulf Area Campus (LA)
Louisville Tech Inst (KY)
Lower Columbia Coll (WA)
Luna Comm Coll (NM)
Luzerne County Comm Coll (PA)
Macomb Comm Coll (MI)
Manatee Comm Coll (FL)
Maple Woods Comm Coll (MO)
Marion Tech Coll (OH)
Marshalltown Comm Coll (IA)
Massasoit Comm Coll (MA)
Mayland Comm Coll (NC)
Maysville Comm Coll (KY)
McHenry County Coll (IL)
Meridian Comm Coll (MS)
Metropolitan Comm Coll (NE)
Metropolitan Comm Coll–Business & Technology College (MO)
Miami Dade Coll (FL)
Middlesex Comm Coll (MA)
Middlesex County Coll (NJ)
Midland Coll (TX)
Midlands Tech Coll (SC)
Mid-Plains Comm Coll, North Platte (NE)
Miles Comm Coll (MT)
Milwaukee Area Tech Coll (WI)
Mineral Area Coll (MO)
Minnesota State Coll–Southeast Tech (MN)
Mississippi Gulf Coast Comm Coll (MS)
Mitchell Comm Coll (NC)
Mitchell Tech Inst (SD)
Moberly Area Comm Coll (MO)
Modesto Jr Coll (CA)
Mohawk Valley Comm Coll (NY)
Monroe County Comm Coll (MI)
Montcalm Comm Coll (MI)
Montgomery Coll (MD)
Montgomery County Comm Coll (PA)
Mott Comm Coll (MI)
Mountain Empire Comm Coll (VA)
Mountain View Coll (TX)
Mt. San Antonio Coll (CA)
Mount Wachusett Comm Coll (MA)
Napa Valley Coll (CA)
Nash Comm Coll (NC)
Nashville State Tech Comm Coll (TN)
National Inst of Technology (WV)
Naugatuck Valley Comm Coll (CT)
New Castle School of Trades (PA)
New England Inst of Tech & Florida Culinary Inst (FL)
New Hampshire Tech Inst (NH)
New Mexico State U–Carlsbad (NM)
New Mexico State U–Grants (NM)
New River Comm Coll (VA)
Niagara County Comm Coll (NY)
Normandale Comm Coll (MN)
Northampton County Area Comm Coll (PA)
North Central Missouri Coll (MO)

Electrical, Electronic and Communications Engineering Technology

North Central State Coll (OH)
Northcentral Tech Coll (WI)
North Dakota State Coll of Science (ND)
Northeast Alabama Comm Coll (AL)
Northeast Comm Coll (NE)
Northeastern Oklahoma A&M Coll (OK)
Northeastern Tech Coll (SC)
Northeast Iowa Comm Coll (IA)
Northeast Mississippi Comm Coll (MS)
Northeast State Tech Comm Coll (TN)
Northeast Wisconsin Tech Coll (WI)
Northern Essex Comm Coll (MA)
Northern Maine Comm Coll (ME)
North Harris Coll (TX)
North Hennepin Comm Coll (MN)
North Idaho Coll (ID)
North Iowa Area Comm Coll (IA)
Northland Pioneer Coll (AZ)
North Seattle Comm Coll (WA)
Northwestern Connecticut Comm-Tech Coll (CT)
Northwestern Michigan Coll (MI)
Northwest Iowa Comm Coll (IA)
Northwest-Shoals Comm Coll (AL)
Northwest State Comm Coll (OH)
Oakland Comm Coll (MI)
Oakton Comm Coll (IL)
Ocean County Coll (NJ)
Odessa Coll (TX)
Oklahoma City Comm Coll (OK)
Oklahoma State U, Oklahoma City (OK)
Olympic Coll (WA)
Orangeburg-Calhoun Tech Coll (SC)
Orange Coast Coll (CA)
Orange County Comm Coll (NY)
Owensboro Comm and Tech Coll (KY)
Owens Comm Coll, Findlay (OH)
Owens Comm Coll, Toledo (OH)
Oxnard Coll (CA)
Palm Beach Comm Coll (FL)
Palomar Coll (CA)
Paris Jr Coll (TX)
Pasadena City Coll (CA)
Pellissippi State Tech Comm Coll (TN)
Peninsula Coll (WA)
Pennsylvania Coll of Technology (PA)
Pennsylvania Inst of Technology (PA)
Penn State U Beaver Campus of the Commonwealth Coll (PA)
Penn State U DuBois Campus of the Commonwealth Coll (PA)
Penn State U Fayette Campus of the Commonwealth Coll (PA)
Penn State U Hazleton Campus of the Commonwealth Coll (PA)
Penn State U New Kensington Campus of the Commonwealth Coll (PA)
Penn State U Wilkes-Barre Campus of the Commonwealth Coll (PA)
Penn State U York Campus of the Commonwealth Coll (PA)

Penn Valley Comm Coll (MO)
Pensacola Jr Coll (FL)
Piedmont Virginia Comm Coll (VA)
Pikes Peak Comm Coll (CO)
Pima Comm Coll (AZ)
Pitt Comm Coll (NC)
Portland Comm Coll (OR)
Prince George's Comm Coll (MD)
Queensborough Comm Coll of City U of NY (NY)
Quinsigamond Comm Coll (MA)
Ranken Tech Coll (MO)
Raritan Valley Comm Coll (NJ)
Reading Area Comm Coll (PA)
Red Rocks Comm Coll (CO)
Reid State Tech Coll (AL)
Remington Coll–Lafayette Campus (LA)
RETS Tech Center (OH)
Richmond Comm Coll (NC)
Roanoke-Chowan Comm Coll (NC)
Rochester Comm and Tech Coll (MN)
Rogue Comm Coll (OR)
Rowan-Cabarrus Comm Coll (NC)
St. Clair County Comm Coll (MI)
St. Cloud Tech Coll (MN)
St. Johns River Comm Coll (FL)
St. Louis Comm Coll at Florissant Valley (MO)
Saint Paul Coll–A Comm & Tech College (MN)
St. Petersburg Coll (FL)
San Diego City Coll (CA)
San Joaquin Delta Coll (CA)
San Jose City Coll (CA)
Santa Barbara City Coll (CA)
Santa Fe Comm Coll (NM)
Santa Monica Coll (CA)
Sauk Valley Comm Coll (IL)
Schenectady County Comm Coll (NY)
Schoolcraft Coll (MI)
Sisseton-Wahpeton Comm Coll (SD)
Snow Coll (UT)
Somerset Comm Coll (KY)
Southeast Arkansas Coll (AR)
Southeast Comm Coll, Lincoln Campus (NE)
Southeastern Comm Coll (NC)
Southeastern Tech Coll (GA)
Southern Maine Comm Coll (ME)
South Plains Coll (TX)
South Puget Sound Comm Coll (WA)
Southside Virginia Comm Coll (VA)
South Suburban Coll (IL)
Southwestern Coll (CA)
Southwestern Comm Coll (NC)
Southwestern Illinois Coll (IL)
Southwest Mississippi Comm Coll (MS)
Spartanburg Tech Coll (SC)
Spokane Comm Coll (WA)
Spoon River Coll (IL)
Springfield Tech Comm Coll (MA)
Stanly Comm Coll (NC)
State U of NY Coll of A&T at Morrisville (NY)

State U of NY Coll of Technology at Alfred (NY)
State U of NY Coll of Technology at Canton (NY)
Sullivan County Comm Coll (NY)
Temple Coll (TX)
Texas State Tech Coll–Harlingen (TX)
Texas State Tech Coll–Waco/Marshall Campus (TX)
Thomas Nelson Comm Coll (VA)
Thompson Inst (PA)
Tidewater Comm Coll (VA)
Tompkins Cortland Comm Coll (NY)
Trenholm State Tech Coll, Montgomery (AL)
Triangle Tech, Inc. (PA)
Triangle Tech, Inc.–DuBois School (PA)
Tri-County Comm Coll (NC)
Trident Tech Coll (SC)
Trinidad State Jr Coll (CO)
Triton Coll (IL)
Umpqua Comm Coll (OR)
U of Alaska Anchorage, Kenai Peninsula Coll (AK)
U of Alaska Anchorage, Matanuska-Susitna Coll (AK)
U of Kentucky, Lexington Comm Coll (KY)
Utah Valley State Coll (UT)
Vance-Granville Comm Coll (NC)
Vatterott Coll, St. Ann (MO)
Vatterott Coll, Tulsa (OK)
Victor Valley Coll (CA)
Vincennes U (IN)
Virginia Western Comm Coll (VA)
Washtenaw Comm Coll (MI)
Waubonsee Comm Coll (IL)
Waycross Coll (GA)
Western Dakota Tech Inst (SD)
Western Iowa Tech Comm Coll (IA)
Western Nevada Comm Coll (NV)
Western Wisconsin Tech Coll (WI)
Western Wyoming Comm Coll (WY)
West Kentucky Comm and Tech Coll (KY)
Westmoreland County Comm Coll (PA)
West Virginia Northern Comm Coll (WV)
Westwood Coll–Denver North (CO)
The Williamson Free School of Mecha Trades (PA)
Wilson Tech Comm Coll (NC)
Wor-Wic Comm Coll (MD)
Yakima Valley Comm Coll (WA)
York Tech Coll (SC)
Yuba Coll (CA)

Electrical, Electronics and Communications Engineering
Dutchess Comm Coll (NY)
Fayetteville Tech Comm Coll (NC)
Jamestown Comm Coll (NY)
John Tyler Comm Coll (VA)
Lake Region State Coll (ND)
Lehigh Carbon Comm Coll (PA)
Mayland Comm Coll (NC)
Michiana Coll, South Bend (IN)

Electrical/Electronics Drafting and Cad/Cadd
Albuquerque Tech Vocational Inst (NM)
Anoka Tech Coll (MN)
Brevard Comm Coll (FL)

Collin County Comm Coll District (TX)
Eastfield Coll (TX)
North Seattle Comm Coll (WA)
Texas State Tech Coll–Waco/Marshall Campus (TX)

Electrical/Electronics Equipment Installation and Repair
Bates Tech Coll (WA)
Bristol Comm Coll (MA)
Cape Fear Comm Coll (NC)
Coll of DuPage (IL)
Collin County Comm Coll District (TX)
Dakota County Tech Coll (MN)
Delgado Comm Coll (LA)
Guilford Tech Comm Coll (NC)
Hutchinson Comm Coll and Area Vocational School (KS)
Lake Region State Coll (ND)
Linn State Tech Coll (MO)
Louisville Tech Inst (KY)
Macomb Comm Coll (MI)
Mesabi Range Comm and Tech Coll (MN)
Miles Comm Coll (MT)
Milwaukee Area Tech Coll (WI)
Modesto Jr Coll (CA)
Orange Coast Coll (CA)
Riverland Comm Coll (MN)
St. Philip's Coll (TX)
Santa Barbara City Coll (CA)
State U of NY Coll of Technology at Alfred (NY)
Triangle Tech, Inc.–Greensburg Center (PA)
Western Dakota Tech Inst (SD)
Western Wyoming Comm Coll (WY)
York Tech Coll (SC)

Electrical/Electronics Maintenance and Repair Technology Related
Bunker Hill Comm Coll (MA)
Louisville Tech Inst (KY)
Mohawk Valley Comm Coll (NY)
Triangle Tech, Inc.–Greensburg Center (PA)

Electrician
Bates Tech Coll (WA)
Cleveland Comm Coll (NC)
Coll of Lake County (IL)
Dakota County Tech Coll (MN)
Delta Coll (MI)
Ivy Tech State Coll–Bloomington (IN)
Ivy Tech State Coll–Central Indiana (IN)
Ivy Tech State Coll–Eastcentral (IN)
Ivy Tech State Coll–Kokomo (IN)
Ivy Tech State Coll–Lafayette (IN)
Ivy Tech State Coll–North Central (IN)
Ivy Tech State Coll–Northeast (IN)
Ivy Tech State Coll–Northwest (IN)
Ivy Tech State Coll–Southcentral (IN)
Ivy Tech State Coll–Southwest (IN)
Ivy Tech State Coll–Wabash Valley (IN)
Ivy Tech State Coll–Whitewater (IN)
John Wood Comm Coll (IL)
Lake Superior Coll (MN)
Laramie County Comm Coll (WY)
Linn State Tech Coll (MO)

Lower Columbia Coll (WA)
Luzerne County Comm Coll (PA)
Midlands Tech Coll (SC)
Mitchell Tech Inst (SD)
Northeast Comm Coll (NE)
Northland Pioneer Coll (AZ)
Pennsylvania Coll of Technology (PA)
Rend Lake Coll (IL)
Trenholm State Tech Coll, Montgomery (AL)
Western Wyoming Comm Coll (WY)

Electrocardiograph Technology
Milwaukee Area Tech Coll (WI)

Electromechanical and Instrumentation And Maintenance Technologies Related
Calhoun Comm Coll (AL)
Gulf Coast Comm Coll (FL)
Louisville Tech Inst (KY)
Northwestern Michigan Coll (MI)

Electromechanical Technology
Alamance Comm Coll (NC)
Blackhawk Tech Coll (WI)
Central Comm Coll–Columbus Campus (NE)
Central Piedmont Comm Coll (NC)
Chabot Coll (CA)
Cincinnati State Tech and Comm Coll (OH)
Clovis Comm Coll (NM)
Coll of DuPage (IL)
Columbus State Comm Coll (OH)
Dean Inst of Technology (PA)
DeKalb Tech Coll (GA)
Delaware Tech & Comm Coll, Terry Cmps (DE)
Dutchess Comm Coll (NY)
ECPI Coll of Technology, Newport News (VA)
ECPI Coll of Technology, Virginia Beach (VA)
ECPI Tech Coll, Richmond (VA)
ECPI Tech Coll, Roanoke (VA)
Forsyth Tech Comm Coll (NC)
Hagerstown Comm Coll (MD)
Jackson State Comm Coll (TN)
Kirkwood Comm Coll (IA)
Lake Land Coll (IL)
Lakeshore Tech Coll (WI)
Lansing Comm Coll (MI)
Los Angeles Harbor Coll (CA)
Macomb Comm Coll (MI)
Maysville Comm Coll (KY)
Milwaukee Area Tech Coll (WI)
Mitchell Tech Inst (SD)
Montgomery Coll (MD)
Montgomery County Comm Coll (PA)
Moraine Park Tech Coll (WI)
Mountain View Coll (TX)
Northampton County Area Comm Coll (PA)
North Arkansas Coll (AR)
Northcentral Tech Coll (WI)
Northeast Comm Coll (NE)
Northeast Wisconsin Tech Coll (WI)
Oakland Comm Coll (MI)
Owens Comm Coll, Findlay (OH)
Pitt Comm Coll (NC)
Pulaski Tech Coll (AR)
Raritan Valley Comm Coll (NJ)
Rockingham Comm Coll (NC)

St. Philip's Coll (TX)
Schoolcraft Coll (MI)
Sinclair Comm Coll (OH)
Springfield Tech Comm Coll (MA)
State U of NY Coll of Technology at Alfred (NY)
Terra State Comm Coll (OH)
Texas State Tech Coll–Harlingen (TX)
Union County Coll (NJ)
Utah Valley State Coll (UT)
Washtenaw Comm Coll (MI)
Western Wisconsin Tech Coll (WI)
Wisconsin Indianhead Tech Coll (WI)

Electroneurodiagnostic/Electroencephalographic Technology
Comm Coll of Allegheny County (PA)
Harford Comm Coll (MD)
Niagara County Comm Coll (NY)
Oakland Comm Coll (MI)
Parkland Coll (IL)
Western Wisconsin Tech Coll (WI)

Elementary and Middle School Administration/Principalship
Cumberland County Coll (NJ)

Elementary Education
Abraham Baldwin Ag Coll (GA)
Albuquerque Tech Vocational Inst (NM)
Alpena Comm Coll (MI)
Amarillo Coll (TX)
Ancilla Coll (IN)
Anne Arundel Comm Coll (MD)
Bainbridge Coll (GA)
Barton County Comm Coll (KS)
Blackfeet Comm Coll (MT)
Bristol Comm Coll (MA)
Calhoun Comm Coll (AL)
Casper Coll (WY)
Cecil Comm Coll (MD)
Central Wyoming Coll (WY)
Chesapeake Coll (MD)
City Colls of Chicago, Malcolm X Coll (IL)
City Colls of Chicago, Wilbur Wright Coll (IL)
Clarendon Coll (TX)
Coastal Bend Coll (TX)
Coffeyville Comm Coll (KS)
Coll of Southern Idaho (ID)
Coll of Southern Maryland (MD)
Columbia State Comm Coll (TN)
Copiah-Lincoln Comm Coll (MS)
Copiah-Lincoln Comm Coll–Natchez Campus (MS)
Corning Comm Coll (NY)
Crowder Coll (MO)
Cuyamaca Coll (CA)
Del Mar Coll (TX)
Delta Coll (MI)
Dutchess Comm Coll (NY)
Eastern Arizona Coll (AZ)
Eastern Oklahoma State Coll (OK)
Eastern Wyoming Coll (WY)
East Mississippi Comm Coll (MS)
Edison State Comm Coll (OH)
Essex County Coll (NJ)
Everett Comm Coll (WA)
Frederick Comm Coll (MD)
Fulton-Montgomery Comm Coll (NY)
Garden City Comm Coll (KS)
Garrett Coll (MD)
Georgia Perimeter Coll (GA)

Great Basin Coll (NV)
Gulf Coast Comm Coll (FL)
Hagerstown Comm Coll (MD)
Harford Comm Coll (MD)
Harrisburg Area Comm Coll (PA)
Hill Coll of the Hill Jr College District (TX)
Hillsborough Comm Coll (FL)
Hiwassee Coll (TN)
Holmes Comm Coll (MS)
Holyoke Comm Coll (MA)
Howard Comm Coll (MD)
Iowa Lakes Comm Coll (IA)
Isothermal Comm Coll (NC)
Jefferson Coll (MO)
Jefferson Davis Comm Coll (AL)
John A. Logan Coll (IL)
Kalamazoo Valley Comm Coll (MI)
Kellogg Comm Coll (MI)
Kingsborough Comm Coll of City U of NY (NY)
Kirkwood Comm Coll (IA)
Lansing Comm Coll (MI)
Lenoir Comm Coll (NC)
Lincoln Coll, Lincoln (IL)
Linn-Benton Comm Coll (OR)
Lon Morris Coll (TX)
Lorain County Comm Coll (OH)
Mesalands Comm Coll (NM)
Miami Dade Coll (FL)
Middlesex Comm Coll (MA)
Mid Michigan Comm Coll (MI)
Mississippi Gulf Coast Comm Coll (MS)
Mitchell Comm Coll (NC)
Monroe County Comm Coll (MI)
Montana State U Coll of Tech-Great Falls (MT)
Montgomery County Comm Coll (PA)
Mott Comm Coll (MI)
Mountain Empire Comm Coll (VA)
Northeast Comm Coll (NE)
Northeastern Oklahoma A&M Coll (OK)
Northeast Mississippi Comm Coll (MS)
Northeast Texas Comm Coll (TX)
Northern Essex Comm Coll (MA)
North Idaho Coll (ID)
Northland Pioneer Coll (AZ)
Northwest Coll (WY)
Northwest-Shoals Comm Coll (AL)
Orange County Comm Coll (NY)
Otero Jr Coll (CO)
Palm Beach Comm Coll (FL)
Paris Jr Coll (TX)
Portland Comm Coll (OR)
Pratt Comm Coll and Area Vocational School (KS)
Prince George's Comm Coll (MD)
Raritan Valley Comm Coll (NJ)
Reading Area Comm Coll (PA)
Rend Lake Coll (IL)
Roane State Comm Coll (TN)
St. Louis Comm Coll at Florissant Valley (MO)
Sauk Valley Comm Coll (IL)
Seward County Comm Coll (KS)
Shelton State Comm Coll (AL)
Sheridan Coll (WY)
Snow Coll (UT)
South Coll (TN)
Southeast Comm Coll, Beatrice Campus (NE)

South Suburban Coll (IL)
Southwestern Coll (CA)
Southwestern Illinois Coll (IL)
Southwest Mississippi Comm Coll (MS)
Springfield Tech Comm Coll (MA)
Sullivan County Comm Coll (NY)
Three Rivers Comm Coll (MO)
Umpqua Comm Coll (OR)
Utah Valley State Coll (UT)
Vance-Granville Comm Coll (NC)
Vermilion Comm Coll (MN)
Vincennes U (IN)
Waycross Coll (GA)
Western Wyoming Comm Coll (WY)
Wor-Wic Comm Coll (MD)
Yuba Coll (CA)

Emergency Care Attendant (Emt Ambulance)
Columbus State Comm Coll (OH)
Iowa Lakes Comm Coll (IA)

Emergency Medical Technology (Emt Paramedic)
Alvin Comm Coll (TX)
Amarillo Coll (TX)
Anne Arundel Comm Coll (MD)
Arapahoe Comm Coll (CO)
Arkansas State U–Mountain Home (AR)
Asheville-Buncombe Tech Comm Coll (NC)
Augusta Tech Coll (GA)
Austin Comm Coll (TX)
Barton County Comm Coll (KS)
Bismarck State Coll (ND)
Borough of Manhattan Comm Coll of City U of NY (NY)
Brevard Comm Coll (FL)
Broome Comm Coll (NY)
Calhoun Comm Coll (AL)
Capital Comm Coll (CT)
Casper Coll (WY)
Central Arizona Coll (AZ)
Central Florida Comm Coll (FL)
Central Oregon Comm Coll (OR)
Century Coll (MN)
Chabot Coll (CA)
Chemeketa Comm Coll (OR)
Cincinnati State Tech and Comm Coll (OH)
City Colls of Chicago, Malcolm X Coll (IL)
Clark Coll (WA)
Clark State Comm Coll (OH)
Coastal Carolina Comm Coll (NC)
Coffeyville Comm Coll (KS)
Coll of DuPage (IL)
Coll of Oceaneering (CA)
Collin County Comm Coll District (TX)
Colorado Northwestern Comm Coll (CO)
Columbus State Comm Coll (OH)
Contra Costa Coll (CA)
Corning Comm Coll (NY)
Cossatot Comm Coll of the U of Arkansas (AR)
Daytona Beach Comm Coll (FL)
Delgado Comm Coll (LA)
Del Mar Coll (TX)
Delta Coll (MI)
Doña Ana Branch Comm Coll (NM)
Dutchess Comm Coll (NY)
Eastern Arizona Coll (AZ)
East Los Angeles Coll (CA)
Edison Comm Coll (FL)

Elaine P. Nunez Comm Coll (LA)
El Centro Coll (TX)
Elgin Comm Coll (IL)
Essex County Coll (NJ)
Fairmont State Comm & Tech Coll (WV)
Fayetteville Tech Comm Coll (NC)
Fiorello H LaGuardia Comm Coll of City U of NY (NY)
Foothill Coll (CA)
Fort Scott Comm Coll (KS)
Gadsden State Comm Coll (AL)
Galveston Coll (TX)
Garden City Comm Coll (KS)
Glendale Comm Coll (AZ)
Guilford Tech Comm Coll (NC)
Gulf Coast Comm Coll (FL)
Gwinnett Tech Coll (GA)
Hagerstown Comm Coll (MD)
Harrisburg Area Comm Coll (PA)
Hawkeye Comm Coll (IA)
Hillsborough Comm Coll (FL)
Hinds Comm Coll (MS)
Houston Comm Coll System (TX)
Howard Comm Coll (MD)
Hutchinson Comm Coll and Area Vocational School (KS)
IHM Health Studies Center (MO)
Iowa Lakes Comm Coll (IA)
Ivy Tech State Coll–Bloomington (IN)
Ivy Tech State Coll–Kokomo (IN)
Ivy Tech State Coll–North Central (IN)
Ivy Tech State Coll–Southwest (IN)
Ivy Tech State Coll–Wabash Valley (IN)
Jackson Comm Coll (MI)
James A. Rhodes State Coll (OH)
Jefferson Coll (MO)
Jefferson Comm Coll (OH)
John A. Logan Coll (IL)
Johnson County Comm Coll (KS)
John Wood Comm Coll (IL)
Kalamazoo Valley Comm Coll (MI)
Kansas City Kansas Comm Coll (KS)
Kellogg Comm Coll (MI)
Kishwaukee Coll (IL)
Lackawanna Coll (PA)
Lake City Comm Coll (FL)
Lake-Sumter Comm Coll (FL)
Lake Superior Coll (MN)
Lansing Comm Coll (MI)
Laredo Comm Coll (TX)
Lurleen B. Wallace Comm Coll (AL)
Luzerne County Comm Coll (PA)
Macomb Comm Coll (MI)
McHenry County Coll (IL)
Meridian Comm Coll (MS)
Miami Dade Coll (FL)
Midland Coll (TX)
Mid Michigan Comm Coll (MI)
Minnesota State Coll–Southeast Tech (MN)
Mississippi Gulf Coast Comm Coll (MS)
Modesto Jr Coll (CA)
Mohawk Valley Comm Coll (NY)
Montana State U Coll of Tech-Great Falls (MT)
Montcalm Comm Coll (MI)
Moraine Park Tech Coll (WI)
Mott Comm Coll (MI)
Mt. San Antonio Coll (CA)

Napa Valley Coll (CA)
New Hampshire Tech Inst (NH)
North Arkansas Coll (AR)
North Central Missouri Coll (MO)
Northeast Alabama Comm Coll (AL)
Northeast Comm Coll (NE)
Northeast State Tech Comm Coll (TN)
Northeast Wisconsin Tech Coll (WI)
Northern Maine Comm Coll (ME)
North Harris Coll (TX)
North Iowa Area Comm Coll (IA)
Northland Pioneer Coll (AZ)
Northwest Iowa Comm Coll (IA)
Oakland Comm Coll (MI)
Odessa Coll (TX)
Oklahoma City Comm Coll (OK)
Orange Coast Coll (CA)
Palomar Coll (CA)
Pasco-Hernando Comm Coll (FL)
Pennsylvania Coll of Technology (PA)
Penn Valley Comm Coll (MO)
Pensacola Jr Coll (FL)
Phoenix Coll (AZ)
Pikes Peak Comm Coll (CO)
Pima Comm Coll (AZ)
Polk Comm Coll (FL)
Prince George's Comm Coll (MD)
Quinsigamond Comm Coll (MA)
Rend Lake Coll (IL)
Roane State Comm Coll (TN)
St. Cloud Tech Coll (MN)
St. Johns River Comm Coll (FL)
St. Louis Comm Coll at Florissant Valley (MO)
St. Petersburg Coll (FL)
San Diego City Coll (CA)
San Joaquin Delta Coll (CA)
Schoolcraft Coll (MI)
Scottsdale Comm Coll (AZ)
Seminole Comm Coll (FL)
Shelton State Comm Coll (AL)
Sinclair Comm Coll (OH)
South Arkansas Comm Coll (AR)
South Central Tech Coll (MN)
Southeast Arkansas Coll (AR)
Southern Arkansas U Tech (AR)
Southern State Comm Coll (OH)
South Texas Comm Coll (TX)
Southwestern Coll (CA)
Southwestern Comm Coll (NC)
Southwest Mississippi Comm Coll (MS)
Tillamook Bay Comm Coll (OR)
Trenholm State Tech Coll, Montgomery (AL)
Umpqua Comm Coll (OR)
U of Arkansas Comm Coll at Batesville (AR)
Waycross Coll (GA)
Weatherford Coll (TX)
Western Iowa Tech Comm Coll (IA)
Wilson Tech Comm Coll (NC)
Wisconsin Indianhead Tech Coll (WI)
Wor-Wic Comm Coll (MD)

Energy Management and Systems Technology
Bismarck State Coll (ND)
Cabrillo Coll (CA)

Comm Coll of Allegheny County (PA)
Delaware County Comm Coll (PA)
Iowa Lakes Comm Coll (IA)
Macomb Comm Coll (MI)
Miles Comm Coll (MT)
Pratt Comm Coll and Area Vocational School (KS)
The Williamson Free School of Mecha Trades (PA)

Engineering
Albuquerque Tech Vocational Inst (NM)
Amarillo Coll (TX)
Arapahoe Comm Coll (CO)
Berkshire Comm Coll (MA)
Bristol Comm Coll (MA)
Brookdale Comm Coll (NJ)
Bucks County Comm Coll (PA)
Burlington County Coll (NJ)
Cañada Coll (CA)
Casper Coll (WY)
Central Arizona Coll (AZ)
Centralia Coll (WA)
Chabot Coll (CA)
Chemeketa Comm Coll (OR)
City Colls of Chicago, Wilbur Wright Coll (IL)
Coastal Bend Coll (TX)
Coffeyville Comm Coll (KS)
Coll of DuPage (IL)
Coll of Lake County (IL)
Coll of Southern Idaho (ID)
Coll of Southern Maryland (MD)
Coll of the Sequoias (CA)
Comm Coll of Rhode Island (RI)
Connors State Coll (OK)
Contra Costa Coll (CA)
Copiah-Lincoln Comm Coll (MS)
Cuesta Coll (CA)
Cumberland County Coll (NJ)
Daytona Beach Comm Coll (FL)
Delaware County Comm Coll (PA)
Delta Coll (MI)
Donnelly Coll (KS)
East Los Angeles Coll (CA)
Edison Comm Coll (FL)
Edison State Comm Coll (OH)
El Camino Coll (CA)
Essex County Coll (NJ)
Everett Comm Coll (WA)
Foothill Coll (CA)
Frederick Comm Coll (MD)
Garden City Comm Coll (KS)
Gogebic Comm Coll (MI)
Hagerstown Comm Coll (MD)
Harford Comm Coll (MD)
Harrisburg Area Comm Coll (PA)
Heartland Comm Coll (IL)
Hill Coll of the Hill Jr College District (TX)
Hillsborough Comm Coll (FL)
Holmes Comm Coll (MS)
Howard Comm Coll (MD)
Hutchinson Comm Coll and Area Vocational School (KS)
Iowa Lakes Comm Coll (IA)
Itasca Comm Coll (MN)
Jamestown Comm Coll (NY)
Jefferson Coll (MO)
J. Sargeant Reynolds Comm Coll (VA)
Kellogg Comm Coll (MI)
Kent State U, Trumbull Campus (OH)
Kirkwood Comm Coll (IA)
Kishwaukee Coll (IL)
Lansing Comm Coll (MI)
Laramie County Comm Coll (WY)
Lehigh Carbon Comm Coll (PA)

Linn-Benton Comm Coll (OR)
Longview Comm Coll (MO)
Lon Morris Coll (TX)
Lorain County Comm Coll (OH)
Los Angeles Trade-Tech Coll (CA)
Lower Columbia Coll (WA)
Manatee Comm Coll (FL)
McHenry County Coll (IL)
Metropolitan Comm Coll-Business & Technology College (MO)
Miami Dade Coll (FL)
Middlesex County Coll (NJ)
Mitchell Comm Coll (NC)
Modesto Jr Coll (CA)
Mohawk Valley Comm Coll (NY)
Montgomery Coll (MD)
Mt. San Jacinto Coll (CA)
Napa Valley Coll (CA)
Nassau Comm Coll (NY)
New River Comm Coll (VA)
Northampton County Area Comm Coll (PA)
Northeast Comm Coll (NE)
Northeast Mississippi Comm Coll (MS)
North Idaho Coll (ID)
Northwest Coll (WY)
Northwestern Connecticut Comm-Tech Coll (CT)
Northwestern Michigan Coll (MI)
Oakland Comm Coll (MI)
Oakton Comm Coll (IL)
Ocean County Coll (NJ)
Oklahoma State U, Oklahoma City (OK)
Olympic Coll (WA)
Orange Coast Coll (CA)
Palo Alto Coll (TX)
Palomar Coll (CA)
Paris Jr Coll (TX)
Pasadena City Coll (CA)
Penn Valley Comm Coll (MO)
Portland Comm Coll (OR)
Prince George's Comm Coll (MD)
Raritan Valley Comm Coll (NJ)
Reading Area Comm Coll (PA)
Rend Lake Coll (IL)
Riverside Comm Coll (CA)
Roane State Comm Coll (TN)
St. Louis Comm Coll at Florissant Valley (MO)
San Joaquin Delta Coll (CA)
San Jose City Coll (CA)
San Juan Coll (NM)
Santa Barbara City Coll (CA)
Santa Fe Comm Coll (NM)
Schoolcraft Coll (MI)
Sheridan Coll (WY)
Sierra Coll (CA)
Sinclair Comm Coll (OH)
Snow Coll (UT)
South Plains Coll (TX)
Southwestern Coll (CA)
Southwestern Oregon Comm Coll (OR)
Southwest Mississippi Comm Coll (MS)
Southwest Missouri State U–West Plains (MO)
Springfield Tech Comm Coll (MA)
State U of NY Coll of A&T at Morrisville (NY)
Terra State Comm Coll (OH)
Thomas Nelson Comm Coll (VA)
Tidewater Comm Coll (VA)
Trinidad State Jr Coll (CO)
Umpqua Comm Coll (OR)
Union County Coll (NJ)
The U of Akron–Wayne Coll (OH)
Utah Valley State Coll (UT)

Valley Forge Military Coll (PA)
Ventura Coll (CA)
Vermilion Comm Coll (MN)
Vincennes U (IN)
Virginia Western Comm Coll (VA)
Waubonsee Comm Coll (IL)
Western Nevada Comm Coll (NV)
Westmoreland County Comm Coll (PA)

Engineering/Industrial Management
Cape Fear Comm Coll (NC)
Pitt Comm Coll (NC)
St. Petersburg Coll (FL)

Engineering Physics
Rend Lake Coll (IL)

Engineering Related
Bristol Comm Coll (MA)
Dunwoody Coll of Technology (MN)
Edison State Comm Coll (OH)
Itasca Comm Coll (MN)
Los Angeles Valley Coll (CA)
Macomb Comm Coll (MI)
Miami Dade Coll (FL)
Northwest State Comm Coll (OH)
San Joaquin Delta Coll (CA)
Southern Maine Comm Coll (ME)
Triton Coll (IL)

Engineering-Related Technologies
Metropolitan Comm Coll-Business & Technology College (MO)

Engineering Science
Asnuntuck Comm Coll (CT)
Bergen Comm Coll (NJ)
Borough of Manhattan Comm Coll of City U of NY (NY)
Bristol Comm Coll (MA)
Broome Comm Coll (NY)
Camden County Coll (NJ)
County Coll of Morris (NJ)
Dutchess Comm Coll (NY)
Everett Comm Coll (WA)
Finger Lakes Comm Coll (NY)
Fulton-Montgomery Comm Coll (NY)
Gloucester County Coll (NJ)
Greenfield Comm Coll (MA)
Hill Coll of the Hill Jr College District (TX)
Holyoke Comm Coll (MA)
Hudson County Comm Coll (NJ)
Itasca Comm Coll (MN)
Jefferson Comm Coll (NY)
Kingsborough Comm Coll of City U of NY (NY)
Manchester Comm Coll (CT)
Middlesex Comm Coll (CT)
Middlesex County Coll (NJ)
Montgomery County Comm Coll (PA)
Northern Essex Comm Coll (MA)
North Shore Comm Coll (MA)
Orange County Comm Coll (NY)
Parkland Coll (IL)
Pennsylvania Coll of Technology (PA)
Queensborough Comm Coll of City U of NY (NY)
Reading Area Comm Coll (PA)
Rend Lake Coll (IL)
St. Louis Comm Coll at Florissant Valley (MO)
State U of NY Coll of A&T at Morrisville (NY)

State U of NY Coll of Technology at Alfred (NY)
State U of NY Coll of Technology at Canton (NY)
State U of NY Coll of Technology at Delhi (NY)
Sullivan County Comm Coll (NY)
Tompkins Cortland Comm Coll (NY)

Engineering Technologies Related
Albuquerque Tech Vocational Inst (NM)
Bowling Green State U-Firelands Coll (OH)
Bristol Comm Coll (MA)
Cleveland Comm Coll (NC)
Comm Coll of Allegheny County (PA)
Harford Comm Coll (MD)
Harrisburg Area Comm Coll (PA)
Louisville Tech Inst (KY)
Massasoit Comm Coll (MA)
Mid Michigan Comm Coll (MI)
Mitchell Tech Inst (SD)
Montgomery County Comm Coll (PA)
Mott Comm Coll (MI)
Musictech Coll (MN)
Southern Arkansas U Tech (AR)
Wisconsin Indianhead Tech Coll (WI)
Wor-Wic Comm Coll (MD)

Engineering Technology
American River Coll (CA)
Anne Arundel Comm Coll (MD)
Arizona Western Coll (AZ)
Atlanta Metropolitan Coll (GA)
Atlanta Metropolitan Coll (GA)
Barton County Comm Coll (KS)
Brunswick Comm Coll (NC)
Central Piedmont Comm Coll (NC)
Chabot Coll (CA)
Coll of the Desert (CA)
County Coll of Morris (NJ)
Cuyahoga Comm Coll (OH)
Dakota County Tech Coll (MN)
Danville Comm Coll (VA)
Darton Coll (GA)
DeKalb Tech Coll (GA)
Delaware Tech & Comm Coll, Terry Cmps (DE)
Delta Coll (MI)
ECPI Coll of Technology, Newport News (VA)
ECPI Coll of Technology, Virginia Beach (VA)
ECPI Tech Coll, Richmond (VA)
ECPI Tech Coll, Roanoke (VA)
Edison Comm Coll (FL)
Edison State Comm Coll (OH)
Essex County Coll (NJ)
Everett Comm Coll (WA)
Fayetteville Tech Comm Coll (NC)
Forsyth Tech Comm Coll (NC)
Garden City Comm Coll (KS)
Glendale Comm Coll (AZ)
Gulf Coast Comm Coll (FL)
Harrisburg Area Comm Coll (PA)
Hawkeye Comm Coll (IA)
Henderson Comm Coll (KY)
Honolulu Comm Coll (HI)
Houston Comm Coll System (TX)
Itasca Comm Coll (MN)
James A. Rhodes State Coll (OH)

Kent State U, Tuscarawas Campus (OH)
Lakeland Comm Coll (OH)
Lansing Comm Coll (MI)
Laramie County Comm Coll (WY)
Lorain County Comm Coll (OH)
Los Angeles Harbor Coll (CA)
Louisville Tech Inst (KY)
Louisville Tech Inst (KY)
Lower Columbia Coll (WA)
Luzerne County Comm Coll (PA)
Marion Tech Coll (OH)
Miami Dade Coll (FL)
Middlesex Comm Coll (CT)
Middlesex County Coll (NJ)
Midlands Tech Coll (SC)
Mid Michigan Comm Coll (MI)
Morrison Inst of Technology (IL)
Motlow State Comm Coll (TN)
Mountain Empire Comm Coll (VA)
Mountain View Coll (TX)
Mt. San Antonio Coll (CA)
Naugatuck Valley Comm Coll (CT)
New Hampshire Tech Inst (NH)
New Mexico State U-Carlsbad (NM)
Northeast Mississippi Comm Coll (MS)
Northeast State Tech Comm Coll (TN)
Pasadena City Coll (CA)
Peninsula Coll (WA)
Pennsylvania Inst of Technology (PA)
Portland Comm Coll (OR)
Quinebaug Valley Comm Coll (CT)
Reading Area Comm Coll (PA)
Rend Lake Coll (IL)
St. Louis Comm Coll at Florissant Valley (MO)
San Diego City Coll (CA)
San Joaquin Delta Coll (CA)
Santa Barbara City Coll (CA)
Sheridan Coll (WY)
Snead State Comm Coll (AL)
Snead State Comm Coll (AL)
Southern West Virginia Comm and Tech Coll (WV)
South Hills School of Business & Technology, State College (PA)
Southwestern Illinois Coll (IL)
Southwestern Michigan Coll (MI)
Spartanburg Tech Coll (SC)
State U of NY Coll of A&T at Morrisville (NY)
State U of NY Coll of Technology at Canton (NY)
State U of NY Coll of Technology at Delhi (NY)
Terra State Comm Coll (OH)
Three Rivers Comm Coll (MO)
Trident Tech Coll (SC)
Triton Coll (IL)
Triton Coll (IL)
Vincennes U (IN)
Vincennes U (IN)
Washtenaw Comm Coll (MI)
Waycross Coll (GA)
Western Wyoming Comm Coll (WY)
York Tech Coll (SC)

English
Abraham Baldwin Ag Coll (GA)
Alpena Comm Coll (MI)
Amarillo Coll (TX)
Andrew Coll (GA)
Anne Arundel Comm Coll (MD)

Arizona Western Coll (AZ)
Atlanta Metropolitan Coll (GA)
Austin Comm Coll (TX)
Bainbridge Coll (GA)
Barton County Comm Coll (KS)
Brookdale Comm Coll (NJ)
Bunker Hill Comm Coll (MA)
Burlington County Coll (NJ)
Butler County Comm Coll (KS)
Calhoun Comm Coll (AL)
Cañada Coll (CA)
Casper Coll (WY)
Centralia Coll (WA)
Central Wyoming Coll (WY)
Chabot Coll (CA)
Chemeketa Comm Coll (OR)
City Colls of Chicago, Wilbur Wright Coll (IL)
Clarendon Coll (TX)
Coastal Bend Coll (TX)
Coastal Georgia Comm Coll (GA)
Coffeyville Comm Coll (KS)
Colby Comm Coll (KS)
Coll of Southern Idaho (ID)
Coll of the Canyons (CA)
Coll of the Desert (CA)
Coll of the Sequoias (CA)
Colorado Mountn Coll, Alpine Cmps (CO)
Colorado Mountn Coll (CO)
Colorado Mountn Coll, Timberline Cmps (CO)
Colorado Northwestern Comm Coll (CO)
Columbia Coll (CA)
Comm Coll of Allegheny County (PA)
Contra Costa Coll (CA)
Copiah-Lincoln Comm Coll (MS)
Cuyamaca Coll (CA)
Darton Coll (GA)
Daytona Beach Comm Coll (FL)
Del Mar Coll (TX)
Delta Coll (MI)
Donnelly Coll (KS)
Eastern Arizona Coll (AZ)
Eastern Oklahoma State Coll (OK)
Eastern Wyoming Coll (WY)
East Los Angeles Coll (CA)
East Mississippi Comm Coll (MS)
Edison State Comm Coll (OH)
El Camino Coll (CA)
Everett Comm Coll (WA)
Feather River Comm Coll District (CA)
Foothill Coll (CA)
Frederick Comm Coll (MD)
Fulton-Montgomery Comm Coll (NY)
Galveston Coll (TX)
Garden City Comm Coll (KS)
Gavilan Coll (CA)
Georgia Perimeter Coll (GA)
Gloucester County Coll (NJ)
Gordon Coll (GA)
Great Basin Coll (NV)
Gulf Coast Comm Coll (FL)
Hill Coll of the Hill Jr College District (TX)
Hinds Comm Coll (MS)
Hiwassee Coll (TN)
Howard Coll (TX)
Hutchinson Comm Coll and Area Vocational School (KS)
Iowa Lakes Comm Coll (IA)
Jefferson Coll (MO)
John A. Logan Coll (IL)
Kellogg Comm Coll (MI)
Kingwood Coll (TX)
Kirkwood Comm Coll (IA)
Lansing Comm Coll (MI)
Laramie County Comm Coll (WY)

Lawson State Comm Coll (AL)
Lincoln Coll, Lincoln (IL)
Linn-Benton Comm Coll (OR)
Lon Morris Coll (TX)
Lower Columbia Coll (WA)
Manatee Comm Coll (FL)
Miami Dade Coll (FL)
Middlesex County Coll (NJ)
Midland Coll (TX)
MiraCosta Coll (CA)
Modesto Jr Coll (CA)
Mohave Comm Coll (AZ)
Monroe County Comm Coll (MI)
Mountain Empire Comm Coll (VA)
Northeast Comm Coll (NE)
Northeast Mississippi Comm Coll (MS)
North Idaho Coll (ID)
Northwest Coll (WY)
Northwestern Connecticut Comm-Tech Coll (CT)
Northwestern Michigan Coll (MI)
Odessa Coll (TX)
Orange Coast Coll (CA)
Oxnard Coll (CA)
Palm Beach Comm Coll (FL)
Palo Alto Coll (TX)
Pasadena City Coll (CA)
Pratt Comm Coll and Area Vocational School (KS)
Red Rocks Comm Coll (CO)
Rend Lake Coll (IL)
Riverside Comm Coll (CA)
St. Philip's Coll (TX)
Salem Comm Coll (NJ)
San Diego City Coll (CA)
San Joaquin Delta Coll (CA)
San Juan Coll (NM)
Santa Barbara City Coll (CA)
Santa Monica Coll (CA)
Sauk Valley Comm Coll (IL)
Seward County Comm Coll (KS)
Sheridan Coll (WY)
Southwestern Coll (CA)
Southwest Mississippi Comm Coll (MS)
Spoon River Coll (IL)
Sussex County Comm Coll (NJ)
Terra State Comm Coll (OH)
Trinidad State Jr Coll (CO)
Triton Coll (IL)
Umpqua Comm Coll (OR)
Utah Valley State Coll (UT)
Vincennes U (IN)
Vista Comm Coll (CA)
Waycross Coll (GA)
Western Wyoming Comm Coll (WY)
Yuba Coll (CA)

English Composition
Vista Comm Coll (CA)

English/Language Arts Teacher Education
Manatee Comm Coll (FL)

Entomology
Northeast Mississippi Comm Coll (MS)
Snow Coll (UT)

Entrepreneurial and Small Business Related
Dakota County Tech Coll (MN)
Northland Pioneer Coll (AZ)
Williston State Coll (ND)

Entrepreneurship
Blackfeet Comm Coll (MT)
Bristol Comm Coll (MA)
Bucks County Comm Coll (PA)
Calhoun Comm Coll (AL)
Cincinnati State Tech and Comm Coll (OH)
Colorado Northwestern Comm Coll (CO)

Comm Coll of Allegheny County (PA)
Cuyamaca Coll (CA)
Dakota County Tech Coll (MN)
Delaware County Comm Coll (PA)
Eastern Arizona Coll (AZ)
Edmonds Comm Coll (WA)
Front Range Comm Coll (CO)
Goodwin Coll (CT)
Laramie County Comm Coll (WY)
LDS Business Coll (UT)
Mohawk Valley Comm Coll (NY)
Montcalm Comm Coll (MI)
Moraine Valley Comm Coll (IL)
Mott Comm Coll (MI)
Nassau Comm Coll (NY)
Northeast Comm Coll (NE)
North Iowa Area Comm Coll (IA)
Oakland Comm Coll (MI)
Santa Fe Comm Coll (NM)
Schoolcraft Coll (MI)
Springfield Tech Comm Coll (MA)
Terra State Comm Coll (OH)
United Tribes Tech Coll (ND)
Waubonsee Comm Coll (IL)

Environmental Control Technologies Related
Central Carolina Tech Coll (SC)
Central Florida Comm Coll (FL)
Oakland Comm Coll (MI)
Pennsylvania Coll of Technology (PA)
Pitt Comm Coll (NC)

Environmental Design/Architecture
Abraham Baldwin Ag Coll (GA)
Iowa Lakes Comm Coll (IA)
Queensborough Comm Coll of City U of NY (NY)
Scottsdale Comm Coll (AZ)

Environmental Education
Colorado Mountn Coll, Timberline Cmps (CO)
Iowa Lakes Comm Coll (IA)
Vermilion Comm Coll (MN)

Environmental Engineering Technology
Arapahoe Comm Coll (CO)
Blue Ridge Comm Coll (NC)
Bristol Comm Coll (MA)
Cambria County Area Comm Coll (PA)
Cape Cod Comm Coll (MA)
Central Alabama Comm Coll (AL)
Central Piedmont Comm Coll (NC)
Cincinnati State Tech and Comm Coll (OH)
City Colls of Chicago, Wilbur Wright Coll (IL)
Clover Park Tech Coll (WA)
Coastal Bend Coll (TX)
Collin County Comm Coll District (TX)
Columbus State Comm Coll (OH)
Comm Coll of Allegheny County (PA)
Comm Coll of Denver (CO)
Crowder Coll (MO)
Cuyamaca Coll (CA)
Elaine P. Nunez Comm Coll (LA)
Front Range Comm Coll (CO)
Gloucester County Coll (NJ)
Harford Comm Coll (MD)
IntelliTec Coll, Colorado Springs (CO)
Iowa Lakes Comm Coll (IA)

James H. Faulkner State Comm Coll (AL)
John Tyler Comm Coll (VA)
Kent State U, Trumbull Campus (OH)
Lamar State Coll–Port Arthur (TX)
Lord Fairfax Comm Coll (VA)
Metropolitan Comm Coll–Business & Technology College (MO)
Miami Dade Coll (FL)
Milwaukee Area Tech Coll (WI)
Minot State U–Bottineau Campus (ND)
Napa Valley Coll (CA)
New Mexico State U–Carlsbad (NM)
Pellissippi State Tech Comm Coll (TN)
Pennsylvania Coll of Technology (PA)
Pima Comm Coll (AZ)
Roanoke-Chowan Comm Coll (NC)
San Diego City Coll (CA)
Schoolcraft Coll (MI)
Southern Arkansas U Tech (AR)
Southern Maine Comm Coll (ME)
Texas State Tech Coll–Harlingen (TX)
Utah Valley State Coll (UT)
Vermilion Comm Coll (MN)
Westmoreland County Comm Coll (PA)

Environmental/ Environmental Health Engineering
Albuquerque Tech Vocational Inst (NM)
Bristol Comm Coll (MA)
Santa Barbara City Coll (CA)

Environmental Health
Amarillo Coll (TX)
Comm Coll of the Air Force (AL)
Crowder Coll (MO)
Milwaukee Area Tech Coll (WI)
North Idaho Coll (ID)
Queensborough Comm Coll of City U of NY (NY)
Roane State Comm Coll (TN)
The U of Akron–Wayne Coll (OH)
Vincennes U (IN)

Environmental Science
Berkshire Comm Coll (MA)
Bristol Comm Coll (MA)
Central Wyoming Coll (WY)
City Colls of Chicago, Wilbur Wright Coll (IL)
Colorado Northwestern Comm Coll (CO)
Darton Coll (GA)
Delta Coll (MI)
Ohio State U Ag Tech Inst (OH)
St. Philip's Coll (TX)
Western Wyoming Comm Coll (WY)

Environmental Studies
Anne Arundel Comm Coll (MD)
Arizona Western Coll (AZ)
Bristol Comm Coll (MA)
Bucks County Comm Coll (PA)
Burlington County Coll (NJ)
Camden County Coll (NJ)
Cañada Coll (CA)
Cape Cod Comm Coll (MA)
Cape Fear Comm Coll (NC)
Century Coll (MN)
Coll of Southern Idaho (ID)
Coll of the Desert (CA)
Colorado Mountn Coll, Timberline Cmps (CO)

Columbia Coll (CA)
Comm Coll of the Air Force (AL)
Cossatot Comm Coll of the U of Arkansas (AR)
Delta Coll (MI)
Eastern Oklahoma State Coll (OK)
East Los Angeles Coll (CA)
Everett Comm Coll (WA)
Finger Lakes Comm Coll (NY)
Fulton-Montgomery Comm Coll (NY)
Great Basin Coll (NV)
Harrisburg Area Comm Coll (PA)
Hillsborough Comm Coll (FL)
Holyoke Comm Coll (MA)
Howard Comm Coll (MD)
Iowa Lakes Comm Coll (IA)
Itasca Comm Coll (MN)
Kent State U, Salem Campus (OH)
Kent State U, Tuscarawas Campus (OH)
Keystone Coll (PA)
Lake Washington Tech Coll (WA)
Lamar State Coll–Orange (TX)
Lower Columbia Coll (WA)
Middlesex Comm Coll (CT)
Mid Michigan Comm Coll (MI)
Mountain Empire Comm Coll (VA)
Mount Wachusett Comm Coll (MA)
Napa Valley Coll (CA)
Naugatuck Valley Comm Coll (CT)
New Hampshire Comm Tech Coll, Berlin/Laconia (NH)
Northeast Wisconsin Tech Coll (WI)
Northwest Coll (WY)
Pensacola Jr Coll (FL)
Raritan Valley Comm Coll (NJ)
Riverside Comm Coll (CA)
Santa Barbara City Coll (CA)
Santa Monica Coll (CA)
Southeast Comm Coll, Lincoln Campus (NE)
Southeastern Comm Coll (NC)
Southwestern Comm Coll (NC)
Southwestern Oregon Comm Coll (OR)
Stark State Coll of Technology (OH)
State U of NY Coll of A&T at Morrisville (NY)
State U of NY Coll of Technology at Alfred (NY)
State U of NY Coll of Technology at Canton (NY)
Sullivan County Comm Coll (NY)
Sussex County Comm Coll (NJ)
Tompkins Cortland Comm Coll (NY)
Vermilion Comm Coll (MN)
Vincennes U (IN)
Western Nevada Comm Coll (NV)

Equestrian Studies
Central Wyoming Coll (WY)
Coll of Southern Idaho (ID)
Kirkwood Comm Coll (IA)
Laramie County Comm Coll (WY)
Los Angeles Pierce Coll (CA)
Northwest Coll (WY)
Ohio State U Ag Tech Inst (OH)
Parkland Coll (IL)
Scottsdale Comm Coll (AZ)
Sierra Coll (CA)
State U of NY Coll of A&T at Morrisville (NY)

West Hills Comm Coll (CA)
Yavapai Coll (AZ)

European Studies
Anne Arundel Comm Coll (MD)

European Studies (Central and Eastern)
Manatee Comm Coll (FL)

Executive Assistant/ Executive Secretary
Alamance Comm Coll (NC)
Asheville-Buncombe Tech Comm Coll (NC)
Broome Comm Coll (NY)
Cape Cod Comm Coll (MA)
Cape Fear Comm Coll (NC)
Central Florida Comm Coll (FL)
Central Pennsylvania Coll (PA)
Cincinnati State Tech and Comm Coll (OH)
Clark Coll (WA)
Cleveland Comm Coll (NC)
Clovis Comm Coll (NM)
Coastal Carolina Comm Coll (NC)
Crowder Coll (MO)
Dakota County Tech Coll (MN)
Delta Coll (MI)
Eastfield Coll (TX)
Elgin Comm Coll (IL)
Hickey Coll (MO)
Ivy Tech State Coll–Bloomington (IN)
Ivy Tech State Coll–Central Indiana (IN)
Ivy Tech State Coll–Columbus (IN)
Ivy Tech State Coll–Eastcentral (IN)
Ivy Tech State Coll–Kokomo (IN)
Ivy Tech State Coll–Lafayette (IN)
Ivy Tech State Coll–North Central (IN)
Ivy Tech State Coll–Northeast (IN)
Ivy Tech State Coll–Northwest (IN)
Ivy Tech State Coll–Southcentral (IN)
Ivy Tech State Coll–Southeast (IN)
Ivy Tech State Coll–Southwest (IN)
Ivy Tech State Coll–Wabash Valley (IN)
Ivy Tech State Coll–Whitewater (IN)
Jackson Comm Coll (MI)
John Wood Comm Coll (IL)
J. Sargeant Reynolds Comm Coll (VA)
Kalamazoo Valley Comm Coll (MI)
Kaskaskia Coll (IL)
Kellogg Comm Coll (MI)
Lake Land Coll (IL)
Lake Region State Coll (ND)
Lake Superior Coll (MN)
LDS Business Coll (UT)
Lehigh Carbon Comm Coll (PA)
Luzerne County Comm Coll (PA)
Minot State U–Bottineau Campus (ND)
Montcalm Comm Coll (MI)
National Coll of Business & Technology, Salem (VA)
Newport Business Inst, Lower Burrell (PA)
Northampton County Area Comm Coll (PA)
Northwestern Michigan Coll (MI)
Northwest State Comm Coll (OH)
Ohio Valley Coll of Technology (OH)

Owensboro Comm and Tech Coll (KY)
Southern State Comm Coll (OH)
Stanly Comm Coll (NC)
The U of Akron–Wayne Coll (OH)
Utah Valley State Coll (UT)
Waubonsee Comm Coll (IL)
Western Iowa Tech Comm Coll (IA)

Family and Community Services
Bowling Green State U-Firelands Coll (OH)
Collin County Comm Coll District (TX)
Garden City Comm Coll (KS)
Oxnard Coll (CA)
Salem Comm Coll (NJ)
San Jose City Coll (CA)
Snow Coll (UT)

Family and Consumer Economics Related
Arizona Western Coll (AZ)
Butte Coll (CA)
Cuesta Coll (CA)
Los Angeles Valley Coll (CA)
Modesto Jr Coll (CA)
Orange Coast Coll (CA)
Palomar Coll (CA)
Portland Comm Coll (OR)
Vincennes U (IN)
Yakima Valley Comm Coll (WA)
Yuba Coll (CA)

Family and Consumer Sciences/Home Economics Teacher Education
American River Coll (CA)
Coll of the Sequoias (CA)
Copiah-Lincoln Comm Coll (MS)
Manatee Comm Coll (FL)
Northeast Mississippi Comm Coll (MS)

Family and Consumer Sciences/Human Sciences
Abraham Baldwin Ag Coll (GA)
Bainbridge Coll (GA)
Butte Coll (CA)
Central Comm Coll–Columbus Campus (NE)
Coffeyville Comm Coll (KS)
Colby Comm Coll (KS)
Coll of the Sequoias (CA)
Connors State Coll (OK)
Contra Costa Coll (CA)
Copiah-Lincoln Comm Coll–Natchez Campus (MS)
Delta Coll (MI)
East Los Angeles Coll (CA)
El Camino Coll (CA)
Garden City Comm Coll (KS)
Hill Coll of the Hill Jr College District (TX)
Hinds Comm Coll (MS)
Hiwassee Coll (TN)
Holyoke Comm Coll (MA)
Houston Comm Coll System (TX)
Hutchinson Comm Coll and Area Vocational School (KS)
Iowa Lakes Comm Coll (IA)
Kent State U, Salem Campus (OH)
Lamar State Coll–Port Arthur (TX)
Linn-Benton Comm Coll (OR)
Los Angeles Valley Coll (CA)
Mt. San Antonio Coll (CA)
Northeast Mississippi Comm Coll (MS)
Orange Coast Coll (CA)
Oxnard Coll (CA)
Palm Beach Comm Coll (FL)
Penn Valley Comm Coll (MO)

Phoenix Coll (AZ)
Portland Comm Coll (OR)
Pratt Comm Coll and Area Vocational School (KS)
Riverside Comm Coll (CA)
San Joaquin Delta Coll (CA)
Santa Monica Coll (CA)
Shelton State Comm Coll (AL)
Sierra Coll (CA)
Snow Coll (UT)
Ventura Coll (CA)
Vermilion Comm Coll (MN)
Vincennes U (IN)
Yuba Coll (CA)

Family and Consumer Sciences/Human Sciences Communication
Vincennes U (IN)

Family Living/Parenthood
Centralia Coll (WA)

Family Resource Management
Calhoun Comm Coll (AL)

Farm and Ranch Management
Abraham Baldwin Ag Coll (GA)
Alexandria Tech Coll (MN)
Butler County Comm Coll (KS)
Clarendon Coll (TX)
Colby Comm Coll (KS)
Copiah-Lincoln Comm Coll (MS)
Crowder Coll (MO)
Eastern Oklahoma State Coll (OK)
Eastern Wyoming Coll (WY)
Garden City Comm Coll (KS)
Hawkeye Comm Coll (IA)
Hill Coll of the Hill Jr College District (TX)
Hutchinson Comm Coll and Area Vocational School (KS)
Iowa Lakes Comm Coll (IA)
Kirkwood Comm Coll (IA)
Mitchell Tech Inst (SD)
North Central Missouri Coll (MO)
Northeast Comm Coll (NE)
Northeast Wisconsin Tech Coll (WI)
Northwest Coll (WY)
Pratt Comm Coll and Area Vocational School (KS)
Seward County Comm Coll (KS)
Snow Coll (UT)
Texas State Tech Coll–Harlingen (TX)
Trinidad State Jr Coll (CO)
Western Dakota Tech Inst (SD)

Fashion and Fabric Consulting
Coll of DuPage (IL)

Fashion/Apparel Design
American River Coll (CA)
The Art Inst of New York City (NY)
The Art Inst of Philadelphia (PA)
The Art Inst of Seattle (WA)
Bay State Coll (MA)
Burlington County Coll (NJ)
Butte Coll (CA)
Cañada Coll (CA)
Chabot Coll (CA)
Coll of DuPage (IL)
Coll of the Sequoias (CA)
Daytona Beach Comm Coll (FL)
East Los Angeles Coll (CA)
El Camino Coll (CA)
El Centro Coll (TX)
Fashion Careers of California Coll (CA)

Fashion Inst of Design & Merchandising, LA Campus (CA)
Fashion Inst of Design & Merchandising, SD Campus (CA)
Fashion Inst of Design & Merchandising, SF Campus (CA)
Fisher Coll (MA)
Garden City Comm Coll (KS)
Harcum Coll (PA)
Hinds Comm Coll (MS)
Honolulu Comm Coll (HI)
Houston Comm Coll System (TX)
Kirkwood Comm Coll (IA)
Los Angeles Trade-Tech Coll (CA)
Middlesex County Coll (NJ)
Nassau Comm Coll (NY)
Northeast Mississippi Comm Coll (MS)
Palm Beach Comm Coll (FL)
Palomar Coll (CA)
Penn Valley Comm Coll (MO)
Phoenix Coll (AZ)
Ventura Coll (CA)
Vincennes U (IN)
Westmoreland County Comm Coll (PA)

Fashion Merchandising
Abraham Baldwin Ag Coll (GA)
Alexandria Tech Coll (MN)
American River Coll (CA)
The Art Inst of Philadelphia (PA)
The Art Inst of Seattle (WA)
Austin Comm Coll (TX)
Bay State Coll (MA)
Bellevue Comm Coll (WA)
Berkeley Coll (NJ)
Berkeley Coll-New York City Campus (NY)
Berkeley Coll-Westchester Campus (NY)
Briarwood Coll (CT)
Brookdale Comm Coll (NJ)
Butte Coll (CA)
Carl Sandburg Coll (IL)
Central Piedmont Comm Coll (NC)
Century Coll (MN)
Chabot Coll (CA)
Cleveland Comm Coll (NC)
Coll of DuPage (IL)
Coll of the Sequoias (CA)
Comm Coll of Rhode Island (RI)
Cuesta Coll (CA)
Davis Coll (OH)
Delta Coll (MI)
Des Moines Area Comm Coll (IA)
Doña Ana Branch Comm Coll (NM)
Eastern Oklahoma State Coll (OK)
Fashion Careers of California Coll (CA)
Fashion Inst of Design & Merchandising, LA Campus (CA)
Fashion Inst of Design & Merchandising, SD Campus (CA)
Fashion Inst of Design & Merchandising, SF Campus (CA)
Fisher Coll (MA)
Garden City Comm Coll (KS)
Grand Rapids Comm Coll (MI)
Gwinnett Tech Coll (GA)
Harcum Coll (PA)
Houston Comm Coll System (TX)
Howard Comm Coll (MD)
Indiana Business Coll, Indianapolis (IN)
Iowa Lakes Comm Coll (IA)

James A. Rhodes State Coll (OH)
John A. Logan Coll (IL)
J. Sargeant Reynolds Comm Coll (VA)
Kingsborough Comm Coll of City U of NY (NY)
Kirkwood Comm Coll (IA)
Lake Region State Coll (ND)
Laredo Comm Coll (TX)
Los Angeles Trade-Tech Coll (CA)
Middle Georgia Coll (GA)
Middlesex Comm Coll (MA)
Middlesex County Coll (NJ)
Milwaukee Area Tech Coll (WI)
Mississippi Gulf Coast Comm Coll (MS)
Modesto Jr Coll (CA)
Mt. San Antonio Coll (CA)
Nassau Comm Coll (NY)
Northeast Mississippi Comm Coll (MS)
Northeast Wisconsin Tech Coll (WI)
Oakland Comm Coll (MI)
Odessa Coll (TX)
Orange Coast Coll (CA)
Owens Comm Coll, Findlay (OH)
Owens Comm Coll, Toledo (OH)
Oxnard Coll (CA)
Palm Beach Comm Coll (FL)
Palomar Coll (CA)
Pasadena City Coll (CA)
Patricia Stevens Coll (MO)
Penn Valley Comm Coll (MO)
Rochester Comm and Tech Coll (MN)
St. Louis Comm Coll at Florissant Valley (MO)
San Diego City Coll (CA)
San Joaquin Delta Coll (CA)
Santa Monica Coll (CA)
Scottsdale Comm Coll (AZ)
Sierra Coll (CA)
South Plains Coll (TX)
South Suburban Coll (IL)
Southwest Mississippi Comm Coll (MS)
Spokane Falls Comm Coll (WA)
Triton Coll (IL)
Vincennes U (IN)
Western Wisconsin Tech Coll (WI)
Westmoreland County Comm Coll (PA)

Fiber, Textile and Weaving Arts
Pasadena City Coll (CA)

Film/Cinema Studies
Lansing Comm Coll (MI)
Los Angeles Valley Coll (CA)
Milwaukee Area Tech Coll (WI)
Orange Coast Coll (CA)
Palomar Coll (CA)
Santa Barbara City Coll (CA)
Yavapai Coll (AZ)

Film/Video and Photographic Arts Related
The Art Inst of Pittsburgh (PA)
The Art Inst of Seattle (WA)

Finance
Academy Coll (MN)
AIB Coll of Business (IA)
American River Coll (CA)
Arapahoe Comm Coll (CO)
Arizona Western Coll (AZ)
Austin Comm Coll (TX)
Bergen Comm Coll (NJ)
Bunker Hill Comm Coll (MA)
Butte Coll (CA)
Camden County Coll (NJ)
Central Pennsylvania Coll (PA)

Central Piedmont Comm Coll (NC)
Chabot Coll (CA)
Chemeketa Comm Coll (OR)
Chipola Coll (FL)
Clarendon Coll (TX)
Clovis Comm Coll (NM)
Coastal Bend Coll (TX)
Coll of Southern Idaho (ID)
Columbus State Comm Coll (OH)
Comm Coll of Aurora (CO)
Comm Coll of the Air Force (AL)
Cuyahoga Comm Coll (OH)
Daytona Beach Comm Coll (FL)
Del Mar Coll (TX)
Delta Coll (MI)
Doña Ana Branch Comm Coll (NM)
East Los Angeles Coll (CA)
Edison Comm Coll (FL)
Edison State Comm Coll (OH)
El Camino Coll (CA)
Elizabethtown Comm Coll (KY)
Fairmont State Comm & Tech Coll (WV)
Fayetteville Tech Comm Coll (NC)
Forsyth Tech Comm Coll (NC)
Frederick Comm Coll (MD)
Fulton-Montgomery Comm Coll (NY)
Gloucester County Coll (NJ)
Hill Coll of the Hill Jr College District (TX)
Hillsborough Comm Coll (FL)
Hinds Comm Coll (MS)
Hiwassee Coll (TN)
Holmes Comm Coll (MS)
Hopkinsville Comm Coll (KY)
Houston Comm Coll System (TX)
Howard Coll (TX)
Iowa Lakes Comm Coll (IA)
James A. Rhodes State Coll (OH)
Jefferson Comm Coll (OH)
Jefferson Davis Comm Coll (AL)
John A. Logan Coll (IL)
Kent State U, Trumbull Campus (OH)
Kirkwood Comm Coll (IA)
Lake Area Tech Inst (SD)
Lakeshore Tech Coll (WI)
Lansing Comm Coll (MI)
Lenoir Comm Coll (NC)
Lorain County Comm Coll (OH)
Macomb Comm Coll (MI)
Manatee Comm Coll (FL)
Marion Tech Coll (OH)
Mayland Comm Coll (NC)
McLennan Comm Coll (TX)
Miami Dade Coll (FL)
Milwaukee Area Tech Coll (WI)
Mississippi Gulf Coast Comm Coll (MS)
Modesto Jr Coll (CA)
Monroe County Comm Coll (MI)
Morton Coll (IL)
Mt. San Antonio Coll (CA)
Naugatuck Valley Comm Coll (CT)
North Central State Coll (OH)
Northeast Alabama Comm Coll (AL)
Northeast Texas Comm Coll (TX)
Northeast Wisconsin Tech Coll (WI)
Northern Essex Comm Coll (MA)
North Harris Coll (TX)
Oakton Comm Coll (IL)
Oklahoma City Comm Coll (OK)

Orange County Comm Coll (NY)
Palm Beach Comm Coll (FL)
Palo Alto Coll (TX)
Pasadena City Coll (CA)
Pellissippi State Tech Comm Coll (TN)
Phoenix Coll (AZ)
Polk Comm Coll (FL)
Reading Area Comm Coll (PA)
St. Cloud Tech Coll (MN)
St. Louis Comm Coll at Florissant Valley (MO)
San Diego City Coll (CA)
Santa Barbara City Coll (CA)
Scottsdale Comm Coll (AZ)
Seminole Comm Coll (FL)
Seward County Comm Coll (KS)
Sinclair Comm Coll (OH)
Southeast Comm Coll, Beatrice Campus (NE)
Southern West Virginia Comm and Tech Coll (WV)
South Suburban Coll (IL)
Southwestern Coll (CA)
Southwest Mississippi Comm Coll (MS)
Spoon River Coll (IL)
Springfield Tech Comm Coll (MA)
Stark State Coll of Technology (OH)
State U of NY Coll of Technology at Alfred (NY)
Terra State Comm Coll (OH)
Tidewater Comm Coll (VA)
Vermilion Comm Coll (MN)
Western Wisconsin Tech Coll (WI)
Westmoreland County Comm Coll (PA)
Wisconsin Indianhead Tech Coll (WI)

Finance and Financial Management Services Related
Bristol Comm Coll (MA)
Northeast Wisconsin Tech Coll (WI)

Financial Planning and Services
Broome Comm Coll (NY)
Howard Comm Coll (MD)

Fine Arts Related
Ancilla Coll (IN)
Colorado Northwestern Comm Coll (CO)
Oakland Comm Coll (MI)
United Tribes Tech Coll (ND)
Yavapai Coll (AZ)

Fine/Studio Arts
Amarillo Coll (TX)
Atlantic Cape Comm Coll (NJ)
Bristol Comm Coll (MA)
Chabot Coll (CA)
Clovis Comm Coll (NM)
Coastal Bend Coll (TX)
Colorado Mountn Coll, Alpine Cmps (CO)
Cumberland County Coll (NJ)
Delgado Comm Coll (LA)
Del Mar Coll (TX)
Finger Lakes Comm Coll (NY)
Fiorello H LaGuardia Comm Coll of City U of NY (NY)
Foothill Coll (CA)
Fulton-Montgomery Comm Coll (NY)
Garden City Comm Coll (KS)
Gloucester County Coll (NJ)
Holyoke Comm Coll (MA)
Iowa Lakes Comm Coll (IA)
Jamestown Comm Coll (NY)
Lansing Comm Coll (MI)
Lincoln Coll, Lincoln (IL)
Lon Morris Coll (TX)
Manatee Comm Coll (FL)

Manchester Comm Coll (CT)
Massasoit Comm Coll (MA)
Middlesex Comm Coll (CT)
Middlesex County Coll (NJ)
Midland Coll (TX)
Morton Coll (IL)
Mount Wachusett Comm Coll (MA)
Niagara County Comm Coll (NY)
Northampton County Area Comm Coll (PA)
Oklahoma City Comm Coll (OK)
Pratt Comm Coll and Area Vocational School (KS)
Queensborough Comm Coll of City U of NY (NY)
Santa Barbara City Coll (CA)
Sinclair Comm Coll (OH)
South Suburban Coll (IL)
Southwestern Illinois Coll (IL)
Springfield Tech Comm Coll (MA)
Sussex County Comm Coll (NJ)
Vista Comm Coll (CA)

Fire Protection and Safety Technology
Albuquerque Tech Vocational Inst (NM)
Bunker Hill Comm Coll (MA)
Capital Comm Coll (CT)
Central Florida Comm Coll (FL)
Cleveland Comm Coll (NC)
Coll of Lake County (IL)
Collin County Comm Coll District (TX)
Comm Coll of Allegheny County (PA)
Delaware County Comm Coll (PA)
Delgado Comm Coll (LA)
Del Mar Coll (TX)
Elgin Comm Coll (IL)
Jefferson Coll (MO)
John Wood Comm Coll (IL)
Kellogg Comm Coll (MI)
Lincoln Land Comm Coll (IL)
Macomb Comm Coll (MI)
Montgomery Coll (MD)
Montgomery County Comm Coll (PA)
Moraine Valley Comm Coll (IL)
Mott Comm Coll (MI)
Ocean County Coll (NJ)
Owens Comm Coll, Toledo (OH)
Pikes Peak Comm Coll (CO)
San Juan Coll (NM)
Union County Coll (NJ)
Victor Valley Coll (CA)
Waubonsee Comm Coll (IL)
Western Nevada Comm Coll (NV)
Western Wisconsin Tech Coll (WI)

Fire Protection Related
Sussex County Comm Coll (NJ)

Fire Science
Amarillo Coll (TX)
American River Coll (CA)
Arizona Western Coll (AZ)
Austin Comm Coll (TX)
Barton County Comm Coll (KS)
Bates Tech Coll (WA)
Bellevue Comm Coll (WA)
Berkshire Comm Coll (MA)
Blackhawk Tech Coll (WI)
Blue River Comm Coll (MO)
Brevard Comm Coll (FL)
Bristol Comm Coll (MA)
Broome Comm Coll (NY)
Burlington County Coll (NJ)
Butler County Comm Coll (KS)
Butte Coll (CA)
Cabrillo Coll (CA)
Camden County Coll (NJ)

Cape Cod Comm Coll (MA)
Casper Coll (WY)
Central Oregon Comm Coll (OR)
Central Piedmont Comm Coll (NC)
Chabot Coll (CA)
Chemeketa Comm Coll (OR)
Cincinnati State Tech and Comm Coll (OH)
Coastal Carolina Comm Coll (NC)
Coll of DuPage (IL)
Coll of the Desert (CA)
Coll of the Sequoias (CA)
Colorado Northwestern Comm Coll (CO)
Columbia Coll (CA)
Comm Coll of Rhode Island (RI)
Comm Coll of the Air Force (AL)
Corning Comm Coll (NY)
Crowder Coll (MO)
Cuyahoga Comm Coll (OH)
Daytona Beach Comm Coll (FL)
Del Mar Coll (TX)
Delta Coll (MI)
Des Moines Area Comm Coll (IA)
Doña Ana Branch Comm Coll (NM)
Durham Tech Comm Coll (NC)
East Los Angeles Coll (CA)
East Mississippi Comm Coll (MS)
Edison Comm Coll (FL)
El Camino Coll (CA)
Elgin Comm Coll (IL)
Essex County Coll (NJ)
Everett Comm Coll (WA)
Gaston Coll (NC)
Georgia Perimeter Coll (GA)
Glendale Comm Coll (AZ)
Greenfield Comm Coll (MA)
Guilford Tech Comm Coll (NC)
Gulf Coast Comm Coll (FL)
Harrisburg Area Comm Coll (PA)
Hawaii Comm Coll (HI)
Hawkeye Comm Coll (IA)
Hill Coll of the Hill Jr College District (TX)
Hillsborough Comm Coll (FL)
Honolulu Comm Coll (HI)
Houston Comm Coll System (TX)
Hutchinson Comm Coll and Area Vocational School (KS)
J. Sargeant Reynolds Comm Coll (VA)
Kalamazoo Valley Comm Coll (MI)
Kansas City Kansas Comm Coll (KS)
Kirkwood Comm Coll (IA)
Lakeland Comm Coll (OH)
Lake-Sumter Comm Coll (FL)
Lake Superior Coll (MN)
Lanier Tech Coll (GA)
Lansing Comm Coll (MI)
Laredo Comm Coll (TX)
Lawson State Comm Coll (AL)
Lenoir Comm Coll (NC)
Lewis and Clark Comm Coll (IL)
Lorain County Comm Coll (OH)
Los Angeles Harbor Coll (CA)
Los Angeles Valley Coll (CA)
Lower Columbia Coll (WA)
Luzerne County Comm Coll (PA)
Manatee Comm Coll (FL)
Massasoit Comm Coll (MA)
McHenry County Coll (IL)
Meridian Comm Coll (MS)

Miami Dade Coll (FL)
Middlesex Comm Coll (MA)
Middlesex County Coll (NJ)
Midland Coll (TX)
Mid Michigan Comm Coll (MI)
Mid-Plains Comm Coll, North Platte (NE)
Miles Comm Coll (MT)
Milwaukee Area Tech Coll (WI)
Mineral Area Coll (MO)
Modesto Jr Coll (CA)
Mohave Comm Coll (AZ)
Montana State U Coll of Tech-Great Falls (MT)
Mt. San Antonio Coll (CA)
Mt. San Jacinto Coll (CA)
Mount Wachusett Comm Coll (MA)
Naugatuck Valley Comm Coll (CT)
New Mexico State U– Carlsbad (NM)
Northeast Wisconsin Tech Coll (WI)
North Hennepin Comm Coll (MN)
Northland Pioneer Coll (AZ)
North Shore Comm Coll (MA)
Northwest-Shoals Comm Coll (AL)
Oakland Comm Coll (MI)
Oakton Comm Coll (IL)
Odessa Coll (TX)
Oklahoma State U, Oklahoma City (OK)
Olympic Coll (WA)
Oxnard Coll (CA)
Palm Beach Comm Coll (FL)
Palomar Coll (CA)
Pasadena City Coll (CA)
Penn Valley Comm Coll (MO)
Pensacola Jr Coll (FL)
Phoenix Coll (AZ)
Pima Comm Coll (AZ)
Polk Comm Coll (FL)
Portland Comm Coll (OR)
Quinsigamond Comm Coll (MA)
Red Rocks Comm Coll (CO)
Rogue Comm Coll (OR)
St. Clair County Comm Coll (MI)
St. Johns River Comm Coll (FL)
St. Louis Comm Coll at Florissant Valley (MO)
St. Petersburg Coll (FL)
San Joaquin Delta Coll (CA)
Santa Monica Coll (CA)
Schenectady County Comm Coll (NY)
Schoolcraft Coll (MI)
Scottsdale Comm Coll (AZ)
Seminole Comm Coll (FL)
Sierra Coll (CA)
Sinclair Comm Coll (OH)
Southeast Comm Coll, Lincoln Campus (NE)
Southern Arkansas U Tech (AR)
Southern Maine Comm Coll (ME)
South Plains Coll (TX)
South Puget Sound Comm Coll (WA)
South Suburban Coll (IL)
Southwestern Coll (CA)
Southwestern Illinois Coll (IL)
Southwestern Oregon Comm Coll (OR)
Spokane Comm Coll (WA)
Springfield Tech Comm Coll (MA)
Stark State Coll of Technology (OH)
Thomas Nelson Comm Coll (VA)
Triton Coll (IL)
Umpqua Comm Coll (OR)

U of Alaska Anchorage, Matanuska-Susitna Coll (AK)
Utah Valley State Coll (UT)
Victor Valley Coll (CA)
Vincennes U (IN)
Volunteer State Comm Coll (TN)
Weatherford Coll (TX)
Westmoreland County Comm Coll (PA)
Wilson Tech Comm Coll (NC)
Yakima Valley Comm Coll (WA)
Yavapai Coll (AZ)
Yuba Coll (CA)

Fire Services Administration
Calhoun Comm Coll (AL)
Capital Comm Coll (CT)
Edmonds Comm Coll (WA)
Jefferson State Comm Coll (AL)
Johnson County Comm Coll (KS)
Lake Superior Coll (MN)
Lower Columbia Coll (WA)
Midland Coll (TX)
Northampton County Area Comm Coll (PA)
Northeast Wisconsin Tech Coll (WI)
North Iowa Area Comm Coll (IA)
Olympic Coll (WA)

Fish/Game Management
Abraham Baldwin Ag Coll (GA)
Central Oregon Comm Coll (OR)
Coll of Southern Idaho (ID)
Finger Lakes Comm Coll (NY)
Garrett Coll (MD)
Iowa Lakes Comm Coll (IA)
Itasca Comm Coll (MN)
Kirkwood Comm Coll (IA)
Mid Michigan Comm Coll (MI)
Minot State U–Bottineau Campus (ND)
North Idaho Coll (ID)
Pratt Comm Coll and Area Vocational School (KS)
Seward County Comm Coll (KS)
State U of NY Coll of A&T at Morrisville (NY)
Vermilion Comm Coll (MN)

Fishing and Fisheries Sciences And Management
Bristol Comm Coll (MA)
Brunswick Comm Coll (NC)
Hiwassee Coll (TN)
Iowa Lakes Comm Coll (IA)
Peninsula Coll (WA)

Flight Instruction
Iowa Lakes Comm Coll (IA)

Floriculture/Floristry Management
Ohio State U Ag Tech Inst (OH)

Floristry Marketing
Oklahoma State U, Oklahoma City (OK)

Food/Nutrition
Hiwassee Coll (TN)

Food Preparation
The Art Inst of Pittsburgh (PA)
Iowa Lakes Comm Coll (IA)
Keystone Coll (PA)

Food Sales Operations
Montgomery County Comm Coll (PA)

Foods and Nutrition Related
Front Range Comm Coll (CO)

Iowa Lakes Comm Coll (IA)
Schenectady County Comm Coll (NY)

Food Science
Cabrillo Coll (CA)
Central Piedmont Comm Coll (NC)
El Centro Coll (TX)
Greenfield Comm Coll (MA)
Hawkeye Comm Coll (IA)
Miami Dade Coll (FL)
Modesto Jr Coll (CA)
Moraine Park Tech Coll (WI)
Northeast Mississippi Comm Coll (MS)
Orange Coast Coll (CA)
St. Louis Comm Coll at Florissant Valley (MO)
Vincennes U (IN)

Food Service and Dining Room Management
Fairmont State Comm & Tech Coll (WV)
Iowa Lakes Comm Coll (IA)

Food Services Technology
Anne Arundel Comm Coll (MD)
Arapahoe Comm Coll (CO)
Cabrillo Coll (CA)
Central Piedmont Comm Coll (NC)
Columbia Coll (CA)
Columbus State Comm Coll (OH)
El Centro Coll (TX)
Fayetteville Tech Comm Coll (NC)
Hawaii Comm Coll (HI)
Hinds Comm Coll (MS)
Honolulu Comm Coll (HI)
Indian Hills Comm Coll (IA)
Kirkwood Comm Coll (IA)
Lenoir Comm Coll (NC)
Luzerne County Comm Coll (PA)
Milwaukee Area Tech Coll (WI)
Modesto Jr Coll (CA)
Mohawk Valley Comm Coll (NY)
Orange Coast Coll (CA)
Owens Comm Coll, Toledo (OH)
Palomar Coll (CA)
St. Louis Comm Coll at Florissant Valley (MO)
San Joaquin Delta Coll (CA)
Sierra Coll (CA)
Southeast Comm Coll, Lincoln Campus (NE)
Southern Maine Comm Coll (ME)
South Puget Sound Comm Coll (WA)
Spokane Comm Coll (WA)
Stark State Coll of Technology (OH)
State U of NY Coll of A&T at Morrisville (NY)
Texas State Tech Coll–Harlingen (TX)
Texas State Tech Coll–Waco/Marshall Campus (TX)
Ventura Coll (CA)
Victor Valley Coll (CA)
Washtenaw Comm Coll (MI)
Western Wisconsin Tech Coll (WI)

Foodservice Systems Administration
Atlantic Cape Comm Coll (NJ)
Burlington County Coll (NJ)
Comm Coll of Allegheny County (PA)
Hibbing Comm Coll (MN)
Mohawk Valley Comm Coll (NY)
Mott Comm Coll (MI)
North Dakota State Coll of Science (ND)

Oakland Comm Coll (MI)
Santa Barbara City Coll (CA)

Foods, Nutrition, and Wellness
American Academy of Nutrition, Coll of Nutrition (TN)
Camden County Coll (NJ)
Colby Comm Coll (KS)
Cuesta Coll (CA)
Daytona Beach Comm Coll (FL)
Dutchess Comm Coll (NY)
Harrisburg Area Comm Coll (PA)
Holyoke Comm Coll (MA)
Lincoln Coll, Lincoln (IL)
North Shore Comm Coll (MA)
Orange Coast Coll (CA)
Palm Beach Comm Coll (FL)
Sinclair Comm Coll (OH)
Snow Coll (UT)
State U of NY Coll of A&T at Morrisville (NY)

Food Technology and Processing
Copiah-Lincoln Comm Coll (MS)

Foreign Languages and Literatures
Atlanta Metropolitan Coll (GA)
Coastal Georgia Comm Coll (GA)
Coll of Southern Idaho (ID)
Comm Coll of Allegheny County (PA)
Darton Coll (GA)
Eastern Arizona Coll (AZ)
Eastern Wyoming Coll (WY)
Georgia Perimeter Coll (GA)
Gulf Coast Comm Coll (FL)
Hutchinson Comm Coll and Area Vocational School (KS)
Iowa Lakes Comm Coll (IA)
Kingwood Coll (TX)
Linn-Benton Comm Coll (OR)
Lower Columbia Coll (WA)
Midland Coll (TX)
Modesto Jr Coll (CA)
San Juan Coll (NM)
Sheridan Coll (WY)

Foreign Languages Related
Georgia Perimeter Coll (GA)

Foreign Language Teacher Education
Manatee Comm Coll (FL)

Forensic Science and Technology
Arkansas State U–Mountain Home (AR)
Darton Coll (GA)
Lehigh Carbon Comm Coll (PA)
Macomb Comm Coll (MI)
New River Comm Coll (VA)
Oakland Comm Coll (MI)
Prince George's Comm Coll (MD)

Forest/Forest Resources Management
Allegany Coll of Maryland (MD)
Lake City Comm Coll (FL)
Northwestern Michigan Coll (MI)
Vermilion Comm Coll (MN)

Forestry
Abraham Baldwin Ag Coll (GA)
Andrew Coll (GA)
Bainbridge Coll (GA)
Barton County Comm Coll (KS)
Camden County Coll (NJ)
Central Oregon Comm Coll (OR)

Chemeketa Comm Coll (OR)
Coastal Georgia Comm Coll (GA)
Colby Comm Coll (KS)
Coll of Southern Idaho (ID)
Copiah-Lincoln Comm Coll (MS)
Copiah-Lincoln Comm Coll–Natchez Campus (MS)
Darton Coll (GA)
Daytona Beach Comm Coll (FL)
Delta Coll (MI)
Eastern Arizona Coll (AZ)
Eastern Oklahoma State Coll (OK)
Feather River Comm Coll District (CA)
Grand Rapids Comm Coll (MI)
Hiwassee Coll (TN)
Holmes Comm Coll (MS)
Iowa Lakes Comm Coll (IA)
Itasca Comm Coll (MN)
Jamestown Comm Coll (NY)
Jefferson Coll (MO)
Keystone Coll (PA)
Kirkwood Comm Coll (IA)
Miami Dade Coll (FL)
Minot State U–Bottineau Campus (ND)
Modesto Jr Coll (CA)
Mountain Empire Comm Coll (VA)
New Hampshire Comm Tech Coll, Berlin/Laconia (NH)
Northeastern Oklahoma A&M Coll (OK)
Northeast Mississippi Comm Coll (MS)
North Idaho Coll (ID)
North Shore Comm Coll (MA)
Northwest Coll (WY)
Northwest-Shoals Comm Coll (AL)
Riverside Comm Coll (CA)
Sierra Coll (CA)
Snow Coll (UT)
Southwestern Oregon Comm Coll (OR)
Spokane Comm Coll (WA)
State U of NY Coll of A&T at Morrisville (NY)
State U of NY Coll of Technology at Delhi (NY)
Trinidad State Jr Coll (CO)
Umpqua Comm Coll (OR)
Vermilion Comm Coll (MN)
Vincennes U (IN)
Waycross Coll (GA)
Western Wyoming Comm Coll (WY)

Forestry Technology
Abraham Baldwin Ag Coll (GA)
Albany Tech Coll (GA)
American River Coll (CA)
Central Oregon Comm Coll (OR)
Chemeketa Comm Coll (OR)
Columbia Coll (CA)
Eastern Oklahoma State Coll (OK)
East Mississippi Comm Coll (MS)
El Camino Coll (CA)
Green River Comm Coll (WA)
Itasca Comm Coll (MN)
Jefferson Comm Coll (NY)
Keystone Coll (PA)
Lake City Comm Coll (FL)
Lurleen B. Wallace Comm Coll (AL)
Modesto Jr Coll (CA)
Mt. San Antonio Coll (CA)
Northeast Mississippi Comm Coll (MS)
Okefenokee Tech Coll (GA)
Panola Coll (TX)
Pasadena City Coll (CA)

Pennsylvania Coll of Technology (PA)
Penn State U Mont Alto Campus of the Commonwealth Coll (PA)
Pensacola Jr Coll (FL)
Sierra Coll (CA)
Southeastern Comm Coll (NC)
State U of NY Coll of A&T at Morrisville (NY)
State U of NY Coll of Environ Sci & For Ranger Sch (NY)
State U of NY Coll of Technology at Canton (NY)
Vermilion Comm Coll (MN)
Waycross Coll (GA)
York Tech Coll (SC)

Forest Sciences and Biology
Gogebic Comm Coll (MI)
Vermilion Comm Coll (MN)

French
Austin Comm Coll (TX)
Cañada Coll (CA)
Casper Coll (WY)
Centralia Coll (WA)
Coastal Bend Coll (TX)
Coll of the Canyons (CA)
Coll of the Desert (CA)
Coll of the Sequoias (CA)
Contra Costa Coll (CA)
Copiah-Lincoln Comm Coll (MS)
East Los Angeles Coll (CA)
Foothill Coll (CA)
Kirkwood Comm Coll (IA)
Los Angeles Valley Coll (CA)
Manatee Comm Coll (FL)
Merritt Coll (CA)
Miami Dade Coll (FL)
Midland Coll (TX)
MiraCosta Coll (CA)
North Idaho Coll (ID)
Orange Coast Coll (CA)
Pasadena City Coll (CA)
Red Rocks Comm Coll (CO)
Riverside Comm Coll (CA)
San Joaquin Delta Coll (CA)
Santa Barbara City Coll (CA)
Santa Monica Coll (CA)
Sauk Valley Comm Coll (IL)
Snow Coll (UT)
Southwestern Coll (CA)
Triton Coll (IL)
Vincennes U (IN)

Funeral Service and Mortuary Science
Amarillo Coll (TX)
Arapahoe Comm Coll (CO)
Arkansas State U–Mountain Home (AR)
Barton County Comm Coll (KS)
Briarwood Coll (CT)
Carl Sandburg Coll (IL)
Cincinnati Coll of Mortuary Science (OH)
City Colls of Chicago, Malcolm X Coll (IL)
Commonwealth Inst of Funeral Service (TX)
Dallas Inst of Funeral Service (TX)
Delgado Comm Coll (LA)
Delta Coll (MI)
East Mississippi Comm Coll (MS)
Everett Comm Coll (WA)
Fayetteville Tech Comm Coll (NC)
Fiorello H LaGuardia Comm Coll of City U of NY (NY)
Forsyth Tech Comm Coll (NC)
Gupton-Jones Coll of Funeral Service (GA)
Jefferson State Comm Coll (AL)
John Tyler Comm Coll (VA)
Kansas City Kansas Comm Coll (KS)

Luzerne County Comm Coll (PA)
Miami Dade Coll (FL)
Milwaukee Area Tech Coll (WI)
Monroe County Comm Coll (MI)
Nassau Comm Coll (NY)
Northampton County Area Comm Coll (PA)
St. Petersburg Coll (FL)
State U of NY Coll of Technology at Canton (NY)
U of Arkansas Comm Coll at Hope (AR)
Vincennes U (IN)
Worsham Coll of Mortuary Science (IL)

Funeral Service and Mortuary Science Related
Delta Coll (MI)
Milwaukee Area Tech Coll (WI)

Furniture Design and Manufacturing
Dakota County Tech Coll (MN)
Milwaukee Area Tech Coll (WI)

General Retailing/Wholesaling
Alamance Comm Coll (NC)
Asheville-Buncombe Tech Comm Coll (NC)
Century Coll (MN)
Comm Coll of Rhode Island (RI)
Elgin Comm Coll (IL)
Gadsden State Comm Coll (AL)
Harrisburg Area Comm Coll (PA)
Nassau Comm Coll (NY)
Normandale Comm Coll (MN)
Orange Coast Coll (CA)
Pitt Comm Coll (NC)
St. Cloud Tech Coll (MN)

General Studies
Alpena Comm Coll (MI)
Amarillo Coll (TX)
Arkansas Northeastern Coll (AR)
Asnuntuck Comm Coll (CT)
Atlanta Metropolitan Coll (GA)
Atlantic Cape Comm Coll (NJ)
Barton County Comm Coll (KS)
Blackfeet Comm Coll (MT)
Bladen Comm Coll (NC)
Briarwood Coll (CT)
Bristol Comm Coll (MA)
Bunker Hill Comm Coll (MA)
Calhoun Comm Coll (AL)
Cecil Comm Coll (MD)
Central Wyoming Coll (WY)
Cincinnati State Tech and Comm Coll (OH)
City Colls of Chicago, Malcolm X Coll (IL)
City Colls of Chicago, Wilbur Wright Coll (IL)
Cleveland State Comm Coll (TN)
Colorado Northwestern Comm Coll (CO)
Comm Coll of Allegheny County (PA)
Comm Coll of Rhode Island (RI)
Connors State Coll (OK)
Copiah-Lincoln Comm Coll–Natchez Campus (MS)
Corning Comm Coll (NY)
Crowder Coll (MO)
Crowley's Ridge Coll (AR)
Cuyamaca Coll (CA)
Darton Coll (GA)

Delaware County Comm Coll (PA)

Delgado Comm Coll (LA)

Durham Tech Comm Coll (NC)

Eastern Wyoming Coll (WY)

Estrella Mountain Comm Coll (AZ)

Fairmont State Comm & Tech Coll (WV)

Fayetteville Tech Comm Coll (NC)

Florida Hospital Coll of Health Sciences (FL)

Front Range Comm Coll (CO)

Gadsden State Comm Coll (AL)

Garrett Coll (MD)

Georgia Perimeter Coll (GA)

Germanna Comm Coll (VA)

Gordon Coll (GA)

Howard Comm Coll (MD)

Illinois Eastern Comm Colls, Frontier Comm Coll (IL)

Illinois Eastern Comm Colls, Lincoln Trail Coll (IL)

Illinois Eastern Comm Colls, Olney Central Coll (IL)

Illinois Eastern Comm Colls, Wabash Valley Coll (IL)

Iowa Lakes Comm Coll (IA)

Itasca Comm Coll (MN)

Jackson Comm Coll (MI)

James H. Faulkner State Comm Coll (AL)

Jefferson State Comm Coll (AL)

John Wood Comm Coll (IL)

Kaskaskia Coll (IL)

Kellogg Comm Coll (MI)

Kettering Coll of Medical Arts (OH)

Lackawanna Coll (PA)

Lake Land Coll (IL)

Lamar State Coll–Port Arthur (TX)

Lehigh Carbon Comm Coll (PA)

Lincoln Land Comm Coll (IL)

Luzerne County Comm Coll (PA)

Macomb Comm Coll (MI)

Manchester Comm Coll (CT)

McHenry County Coll (IL)

Mercy Coll of Northwest Ohio (OH)

Merritt Coll (CA)

Miami Dade Coll (FL)

Miami U Hamilton (OH)

Middlesex Comm Coll (MA)

Middlesex County Coll (NJ)

Mid Michigan Comm Coll (MI)

MiraCosta Coll (CA)

Modesto Jr Coll (CA)

Montana State U Coll of Tech-Great Falls (MT)

Montgomery Coll (MD)

Mott Comm Coll (MI)

Mount Wachusett Comm Coll (MA)

Nassau Comm Coll (NY)

New Hampshire Comm Tech Coll, Berlin/Laconia (NH)

New Hampshire Tech Inst (NH)

New River Comm Coll (VA)

Niagara County Comm Coll (NY)

Northampton County Area Comm Coll (PA)

North Arkansas Coll (AR)

Northeast Comm Coll (NE)

Northern Essex Comm Coll (MA)

Northland Pioneer Coll (AZ)

Northwest-Shoals Comm Coll (AL)

Oakland Comm Coll (MI)

Ocean County Coll (NJ)

Owens Comm Coll, Findlay (OH)

Owens Comm Coll, Toledo (OH)

Parkland Coll (IL)

Pennsylvania Coll of Technology (PA)

Pensacola Jr Coll (FL)

Pikes Peak Comm Coll (CO)

Pima Comm Coll (AZ)

Platt Coll San Diego (CA)

Quinsigamond Comm Coll (MA)

Rochester Comm and Tech Coll (MN)

San Juan Coll (NM)

Santa Fe Comm Coll (NM)

Sheridan Coll (WY)

Snead State Comm Coll (AL)

South Arkansas Comm Coll (AR)

Southeast Arkansas Coll (AR)

Southern Arkansas U Tech (AR)

Southern Maine Comm Coll (ME)

Southside Virginia Comm Coll (VA)

Southwestern Coll (CA)

Southwestern Michigan Coll (MI)

Southwest Missouri State U–West Plains (MO)

Springfield Tech Comm Coll (MA)

State U of NY Coll of Technology at Delhi (NY)

Terra State Comm Coll (OH)

Tillamook Bay Comm Coll (OR)

Truett-McConnell Coll (GA)

The U of Akron–Wayne Coll (OH)

Utah Valley State Coll (UT)

Vista Comm Coll (CA)

Waubonsee Comm Coll (IL)

Western Nevada Comm Coll (NV)

Western Wyoming Comm Coll (WY)

Wilson Tech Comm Coll (NC)

York County Comm Coll (ME)

Geography

Cambria County Area Comm Coll (PA)

Cañada Coll (CA)

Coll of Southern Idaho (ID)

Coll of the Canyons (CA)

Coll of the Desert (CA)

Columbia State Comm Coll (TN)

Contra Costa Coll (CA)

Darton Coll (GA)

Del Mar Coll (TX)

East Los Angeles Coll (CA)

El Camino Coll (CA)

Foothill Coll (CA)

Hill Coll of the Hill Jr College District (TX)

Itasca Comm Coll (MN)

Jefferson Coll (MO)

Lansing Comm Coll (MI)

Lincoln Coll, Lincoln (IL)

Los Angeles Valley Coll (CA)

Lower Columbia Coll (WA)

Orange Coast Coll (CA)

Pasadena City Coll (CA)

Pellissippi State Tech Comm Coll (TN)

Riverside Comm Coll (CA)

Santa Barbara City Coll (CA)

Santa Monica Coll (CA)

Snow Coll (UT)

Southwestern Coll (CA)

Triton Coll (IL)

Vermilion Comm Coll (MN)

Vincennes U (IN)

Western Wyoming Comm Coll (WY)

West Hills Comm Coll (CA)

Geology/Earth Science

Amarillo Coll (TX)

Arizona Western Coll (AZ)

Austin Comm Coll (TX)

Barton County Comm Coll (KS)

Cañada Coll (CA)

Casper Coll (WY)

Centralia Coll (WA)

Coastal Bend Coll (TX)

Coastal Georgia Comm Coll (GA)

Colby Comm Coll (KS)

Coll of Southern Idaho (ID)

Coll of the Canyons (CA)

Coll of the Desert (CA)

Colorado Mountn Coll, Alpine Cmps (CO)

Colorado Northwestern Comm Coll (CO)

Columbia Coll (CA)

Contra Costa Coll (CA)

Cuesta Coll (CA)

Daytona Beach Comm Coll (FL)

Del Mar Coll (TX)

Delta Coll (MI)

Eastern Arizona Coll (AZ)

East Los Angeles Coll (CA)

El Camino Coll (CA)

Everett Comm Coll (WA)

Foothill Coll (CA)

Georgia Perimeter Coll (GA)

Grand Rapids Comm Coll (MI)

Great Basin Coll (NV)

Hill Coll of the Hill Jr College District (TX)

Iowa Lakes Comm Coll (IA)

Lansing Comm Coll (MI)

Lincoln Coll, Lincoln (IL)

Los Angeles Valley Coll (CA)

Lower Columbia Coll (WA)

Mesalands Comm Coll (NM)

Miami Dade Coll (FL)

Midland Coll (TX)

North Idaho Coll (ID)

Odessa Coll (TX)

Orange Coast Coll (CA)

Palo Alto Coll (TX)

Palomar Coll (CA)

Pasadena City Coll (CA)

Pensacola Jr Coll (FL)

Red Rocks Comm Coll (CO)

Riverside Comm Coll (CA)

San Joaquin Delta Coll (CA)

San Juan Coll (NM)

Santa Barbara City Coll (CA)

Santa Monica Coll (CA)

Sierra Coll (CA)

Snow Coll (UT)

Southwestern Coll (CA)

Triton Coll (IL)

Vermilion Comm Coll (MN)

Vincennes U (IN)

Western Wyoming Comm Coll (WY)

West Hills Comm Coll (CA)

German

Austin Comm Coll (TX)

Cañada Coll (CA)

Casper Coll (WY)

Centralia Coll (WA)

Coastal Bend Coll (TX)

Coll of the Canyons (CA)

Contra Costa Coll (CA)

El Camino Coll (CA)

Everett Comm Coll (WA)

Foothill Coll (CA)

Manatee Comm Coll (FL)

Miami Dade Coll (FL)

Midland Coll (TX)

North Idaho Coll (ID)

Orange Coast Coll (CA)

Pasadena City Coll (CA)

Red Rocks Comm Coll (CO)

Riverside Comm Coll (CA)

San Joaquin Delta Coll (CA)

Santa Monica Coll (CA)

Vincennes U (IN)

Gerontological Services

Wichita Area Tech Coll (KS)

Gerontology

American River Coll (CA)

Camden County Coll (NJ)

City Colls of Chicago, Wilbur Wright Coll (IL)

Columbus State Comm Coll (OH)

Edmonds Comm Coll (WA)

El Camino Coll (CA)

Elgin Comm Coll (IL)

Eugenio María de Hostos Comm Coll of City U of NY (NY)

Fiorello H LaGuardia Comm Coll of City U of NY (NY)

Lansing Comm Coll (MI)

Mt. San Jacinto Coll (CA)

Naugatuck Valley Comm Coll (CT)

New River Comm Coll (VA)

North Shore Comm Coll (MA)

Oakland Comm Coll (MI)

Oklahoma City Comm Coll (OK)

Pima Comm Coll (AZ)

Portland Comm Coll (OR)

Sinclair Comm Coll (OH)

Spokane Falls Comm Coll (WA)

Union County Coll (NJ)

Glazier

Metropolitan Comm Coll-Business & Technology College (MO)

Graphic and Printing Equipment Operation/ Production

Austin Comm Coll (TX)

Burlington County Coll (NJ)

Central Comm Coll–Hastings Campus (NE)

Central Piedmont Comm Coll (NC)

Chemeketa Comm Coll (OR)

Clover Park Tech Coll (WA)

Coll of DuPage (IL)

Comm Coll of Denver (CO)

Delta Coll (MI)

Des Moines Area Comm Coll (IA)

Dunwoody Coll of Technology (MN)

Eastfield Coll (TX)

Forsyth Tech Comm Coll (NC)

Fulton-Montgomery Comm Coll (NY)

Gogebic Comm Coll (MI)

Hinds Comm Coll (MS)

Houston Comm Coll System (TX)

Iowa Lakes Comm Coll (IA)

Kirkwood Comm Coll (IA)

Lake Land Coll (IL)

Lenoir Comm Coll (NC)

Los Angeles Trade-Tech Coll (CA)

Louisville Tech Inst (KY)

Luzerne County Comm Coll (PA)

Macomb Comm Coll (MI)

Metropolitan Comm Coll (NE)

Midlands Tech Coll (SC)

Milwaukee Area Tech Coll (WI)

Moberly Area Comm Coll (MO)

Modesto Jr Coll (CA)

Montgomery Coll (MD)

Northcentral Tech Coll (WI)

Northeastern Oklahoma A&M Coll (OK)

Northwest Coll (WY)

Palomar Coll (CA)

Pennsylvania Coll of Technology (PA)

St. Cloud Tech Coll (MN)

San Diego City Coll (CA)

San Joaquin Delta Coll (CA)

Santa Monica Coll (CA)

Silicon Valley Coll, Walnut Creek (CA)

Sinclair Comm Coll (OH)

South Suburban Coll (IL)

Southwestern Michigan Coll (MI)

Texas State Tech Coll–Waco/Marshall Campus (TX)

Trenholm State Tech Coll, Montgomery (AL)

Triton Coll (IL)

Vincennes U (IN)

Washtenaw Comm Coll (MI)

Westmoreland County Comm Coll (PA)

Graphic Communications

Fairmont State Comm & Tech Coll (WV)

Iowa Lakes Comm Coll (IA)

Louisville Tech Inst (KY)

Pikes Peak Comm Coll (CO)

Platt Coll San Diego (CA)

Silicon Valley Coll, Walnut Creek (CA)

Graphic Communications Related

The Art Insts International Minnesota (MN)

Linn-Benton Comm Coll (OR)

Louisville Tech Inst (KY)

Platt Coll San Diego (CA)

Trenholm State Tech Coll, Montgomery (AL)

Graphic Design

Academy Coll (MN)

AEC Southern Ohio Coll (OH)

Antonelli Coll (OH)

The Art Inst of New York City (NY)

The Art Inst of Philadelphia (PA)

The Art Inst of Pittsburgh (PA)

The Art Inst of Seattle (WA)

The Art Insts International Minnesota (MN)

Barton County Comm Coll (KS)

Bradford School (OH)

Bristol Comm Coll (MA)

Calhoun Comm Coll (AL)

Dakota County Tech Coll (MN)

Hickey Coll (MO)

Iowa Lakes Comm Coll (IA)

Ivy Tech State Coll–Southwest (IN)

Jackson Comm Coll (MI)

Keystone Coll (PA)

Louisville Tech Inst (KY)

Luzerne County Comm Coll (PA)

Massasoit Comm Coll (MA)

Mott Comm Coll (MI)

Oakland Comm Coll (MI)

Ohio Inst of Photography and Technology (OH)

Platt Coll San Diego (CA)

Springfield Tech Comm Coll (MA)

Utah Valley State Coll (UT)

Westwood Coll–Anaheim (CA)

Westwood Coll–Atlanta Campus (GA)

Westwood Coll–Chicago Du Page (IL)

Westwood Coll–Chicago O'Hare Airport (IL)

Westwood Coll–Chicago River Oaks (IL)

Westwood Coll–Dallas (TX)

Westwood Coll–Denver South (CO)

Westwood Coll–Fort Worth (TX)

Westwood Coll–Houston South Campus (TX)

Westwood Coll–Inland Empire (CA)

Westwood Coll–Los Angeles (CA)

Westwood Coll–Chicago Loop Campus (IL)

Southwestern Michigan Coll (MI)

Texas State Tech Coll–Waco/Marshall Campus (TX)

Westwood Coll–Denver North (CO)

Westwood Coll–Long Beach (CA)

Yavapai Coll (AZ)

Greenhouse Management

Comm Coll of Allegheny County (PA)

Kent State U, Salem Campus (OH)

Kishwaukee Coll (IL)

Minot State U–Bottineau Campus (ND)

Ohio State U Ag Tech Inst (OH)

Rochester Comm and Tech Coll (MN)

Gunsmithing

Yavapai Coll (AZ)

Hair Styling and Hair Design

Colorado Northwestern Comm Coll (CO)

Milwaukee Area Tech Coll (WI)

Hazardous Materials Management and Waste Technology

Barton County Comm Coll (KS)

Kansas City Kansas Comm Coll (KS)

Odessa Coll (TX)

Health Aide

Central Arizona Coll (AZ)

Edmonds Comm Coll (WA)

Jefferson Coll (MO)

Springfield Tech Comm Coll (MA)

Health and Medical Administrative Services Related

Indiana Business Coll, Marion (IN)

Keiser Coll, Miami (FL)

Silicon Valley Coll, Walnut Creek (CA)

Health and Physical Education

Alexandria Tech Coll (MN)

Atlanta Metropolitan Coll (GA)

Clovis Comm Coll (NM)

Coastal Georgia Comm Coll (GA)

Comm Coll of Allegheny County (PA)

Corning Comm Coll (NY)

Darton Coll (GA)

Dean Coll (MA)

Eastern Arizona Coll (AZ)

Georgia Perimeter Coll (GA)

Gloucester County Coll (NJ)

Hiwassee Coll (TN)

Iowa Lakes Comm Coll (IA)

John Wood Comm Coll (IL)

Lawson State Comm Coll (AL)

Luzerne County Comm Coll (PA)

Northeast Comm Coll (NE)

Pensacola Jr Coll (FL)

Riverside Comm Coll (CA)

Salem Comm Coll (NJ)

Santa Fe Comm Coll (NM)

Sheridan Coll (WY)

State U of NY Coll of Technology at Delhi (NY)

Utah Valley State Coll (UT)

Health and Physical Education Related

Garden City Comm Coll (KS)

Indiana Business Coll-Medical (IN)

Kingsborough Comm Coll of City U of NY (NY)

Oakland Comm Coll (MI)

Pennsylvania Coll of Technology (PA)

Health/Health Care Administration

Cabarrus Coll of Health Sciences (NC)
Caldwell Comm Coll and Tech Inst (NC)
Cambria County Area Comm Coll (PA)
Central Piedmont Comm Coll (NC)
Chemeketa Comm Coll (OR)
Coll of DuPage (IL)
Coll of Southern Idaho (ID)
Comm Coll of the Air Force (AL)
Consolidated School of Business, York (PA)
Des Moines Area Comm Coll (IA)
ECPI Coll of Technology, Newport News (VA)
ECPI Coll of Technology, Virginia Beach (VA)
ECPI Tech Coll, Richmond (VA)
ECPI Tech Coll, Roanoke (VA)
Essex County Coll (NJ)
Houston Comm Coll System (TX)
Indian Hills Comm Coll (IA)
Iowa Lakes Comm Coll (IA)
Luzerne County Comm Coll (PA)
Manatee Comm Coll (FL)
Mineral Area Coll (MO)
National Coll of Business & Technology, Louisville (KY)
North Idaho Coll (ID)
Oakland Comm Coll (MI)
Pensacola Jr Coll (FL)
Pioneer Pacific Coll (OR)
St. Petersburg Coll (FL)
St. Vincent's Coll (CT)
South Plains Coll (TX)

Health Information/Medical Records Administration

Albuquerque Tech Vocational Inst (NM)
Amarillo Coll (TX)
Andover Coll (ME)
Arapahoe Comm Coll (CO)
Barton County Comm Coll (KS)
Bowling Green State U–Firelands Coll (OH)
Briarwood Coll (CT)
The Brown Mackie Coll–Lenexa Campus (KS)
Brunswick Comm Coll (NC)
Bunker Hill Comm Coll (MA)
Butler County Comm Coll (KS)
Cabrillo Coll (CA)
Central Florida Comm Coll (FL)
Central Piedmont Comm Coll (NC)
Chabot Coll (CA)
Chemeketa Comm Coll (OR)
CHI Inst (PA)
Coll of DuPage (IL)
Columbus State Comm Coll (OH)
Darton Coll (GA)
Daytona Beach Comm Coll (FL)
Draughons Jr Coll (KY)
Durham Tech Comm Coll (NC)
East Los Angeles Coll (CA)
ECPI Coll of Technology, Newport News (VA)
ECPI Coll of Technology, Virginia Beach (VA)
ECPI Tech Coll, Richmond (VA)
ECPI Tech Coll, Roanoke (VA)
Edgecombe Comm Coll (NC)
Edison State Comm Coll (OH)
Elaine P. Nunez Comm Coll (LA)

El Centro Coll (TX)
Elgin Comm Coll (IL)
Erie Business Center South (PA)
Gogebic Comm Coll (MI)
Harrisburg Area Comm Coll (PA)
Hinds Comm Coll (MS)
Holmes Comm Coll (MS)
Holyoke Comm Coll (MA)
Houston Comm Coll System (TX)
Howard Coll (TX)
Indiana Business Coll, Evansville (IN)
Indian Hills Comm Coll (IA)
John A. Logan Coll (IL)
Kirkwood Comm Coll (IA)
Labouré Coll (MA)
Lake-Sumter Comm Coll (FL)
Lamar State Coll–Port Arthur (TX)
LDS Business Coll (UT)
McLennan Comm Coll (TX)
Meridian Comm Coll (MS)
Miami Dade Coll (FL)
Montana State U Coll of Tech-Great Falls (MT)
Moraine Park Tech Coll (WI)
Northeast Iowa Comm Coll (IA)
Northern Essex Comm Coll (MA)
Northland Pioneer Coll (AZ)
Oakton Comm Coll (IL)
Oklahoma City Comm Coll (OK)
Pennsylvania Coll of Technology (PA)
Penn Valley Comm Coll (MO)
Pensacola Jr Coll (FL)
Phoenix Coll (AZ)
Polk Comm Coll (FL)
Portland Comm Coll (OR)
Prince George's Comm Coll (MD)
Rasmussen Coll Mankato (MN)
Rasmussen Coll St. Cloud (MN)
Reading Area Comm Coll (PA)
Roane State Comm Coll (TN)
Saint Charles Comm Coll (MO)
St. Johns River Comm Coll (FL)
St. Petersburg Coll (FL)
Shelton State Comm Coll (AL)
Sinclair Comm Coll (OH)
South Plains Coll (TX)
Southwestern Comm Coll (NC)
Southwestern Illinois Coll (IL)
Spokane Comm Coll (WA)
Stark State Coll of Technology (OH)
State U of NY Coll of Technology at Alfred (NY)
Texas State Tech Coll–Harlingen (TX)
Thompson Inst (PA)
United Tribes Tech Coll (ND)
Vermilion Comm Coll (MN)
Vincennes U (IN)
Virginia Coll at Jackson (MS)
Westmoreland County Comm Coll (PA)

Health Information/Medical Records Technology

Anoka Tech Coll (MN)
Bristol Comm Coll (MA)
Broome Comm Coll (NY)
Bryant & Stratton Business Inst, Syracuse (NY)
Burlington County Coll (NJ)
Central Comm Coll–Hastings Campus (NE)
Central Oregon Comm Coll (OR)

Cincinnati State Tech and Comm Coll (OH)
Coll of DuPage (IL)
Columbus State Comm Coll (OH)
Comm Coll of Allegheny County (PA)
Darton Coll (GA)
Delgado Comm Coll (LA)
Del Mar Coll (TX)
Fayetteville Tech Comm Coll (NC)
Hiwassee Coll (TN)
Houston Comm Coll System (TX)
Hudson County Comm Coll (NJ)
Hutchinson Comm Coll and Area Vocational School (KS)
Indiana Business Coll, Anderson (IN)
Indiana Business Coll, Muncie (IN)
Jefferson Comm Coll (KY)
Johnson County Comm Coll (KS)
Lehigh Carbon Comm Coll (PA)
Mercy Coll of Northwest Ohio (OH)
Midland Coll (TX)
Midlands Tech Coll (SC)
Mohawk Valley Comm Coll (NY)
Montana State U Coll of Tech-Great Falls (MT)
Montgomery Coll (MD)
Moraine Valley Comm Coll (IL)
Mountain View Coll (TX)
North Dakota State Coll of Science (ND)
Northeast Wisconsin Tech Coll (WI)
North Hennepin Comm Coll (MN)
Northwest Iowa Comm Coll (IA)
Owens Comm Coll, Toledo (OH)
Ozarka Coll (AR)
Pitt Comm Coll (NC)
Rend Lake Coll (IL)
Rowan-Cabarrus Comm Coll (NC)
St. Philip's Coll (TX)
San Juan Coll (NM)
Santa Barbara City Coll (CA)
Schoolcraft Coll (MI)
South Hills School of Business & Technology, State College (PA)
Southwestern Comm Coll (NC)
United Tribes Tech Coll (ND)
Volunteer State Comm Coll (TN)
West Virginia Northern Comm Coll (WV)
Williston State Coll (ND)

Health/Medical Claims Examination

Ohio Business Coll, Sandusky (OH)

Health/Medical Preparatory Programs Related

Ancilla Coll (IN)
Blackfeet Comm Coll (MT)
Eastern Arizona Coll (AZ)
Eastern Wyoming Coll (WY)
Laramie County Comm Coll (WY)
Western Wyoming Comm Coll (WY)

Health Professions Related

Allegany Coll of Maryland (MD)
Berkshire Comm Coll (MA)
Bowling Green State U–Firelands Coll (OH)
Cincinnati State Tech and Comm Coll (OH)

Comm Coll of Allegheny County (PA)
Essex County Coll (NJ)
Indiana Business Coll, Columbus (IN)
Indiana Business Coll, Fort Wayne (IN)
Indiana Business Coll, Terre Haute (IN)
Indiana Business Coll-Medical (IN)
International Inst of the Americas, Phoenix (AZ)
Lanier Tech Coll (GA)
Northwestern Michigan Coll (MI)
Northwest State Comm Coll (OH)
Oakland Comm Coll (MI)
Pitt Comm Coll (NC)
Southwestern Michigan Coll (MI)
Volunteer State Comm Coll (TN)

Health Science

Arizona Western Coll (AZ)
Bergen Comm Coll (NJ)
Borough of Manhattan Comm Coll of City U of NY (NY)
Bucks County Comm Coll (PA)
Butte Coll (CA)
Cabrillo Coll (CA)
Cañada Coll (CA)
Coll of the Canyons (CA)
Daytona Beach Comm Coll (FL)
Harcum Coll (PA)
Hill Coll of the Hill Jr College District (TX)
Kalamazoo Valley Comm Coll (MI)
Merritt Coll (CA)
Mohave Comm Coll (AZ)
Nassau Comm Coll (NY)
Northeast Mississippi Comm Coll (MS)
North Shore Comm Coll (MA)
Northwestern Connecticut Comm-Tech Coll (CT)
Ocean County Coll (NJ)
Orange Coast Coll (CA)
Palo Alto Coll (TX)
Queensborough Comm Coll of City U of NY (NY)
Riverside Comm Coll (CA)
San Joaquin Delta Coll (CA)
Southwest Mississippi Comm Coll (MS)
Spoon River Coll (IL)
Sussex County Comm Coll (NJ)
Villa Maria Coll of Buffalo (NY)
West Hills Comm Coll (CA)

Health Services/Allied Health/Health Sciences

Atlanta Metropolitan Coll (GA)
Atlantic Cape Comm Coll (NJ)
Clarendon Coll (TX)
Colorado Northwestern Comm Coll (CO)
Connors State Coll (OK)
Florida National Coll (FL)
Keiser Coll, Miami (FL)
New York Col Health Professions (NY)
Rend Lake Coll (IL)
South U (FL)
Western Wyoming Comm Coll (WY)

Health Teacher Education

Anne Arundel Comm Coll (MD)
Bainbridge Coll (GA)
Bucks County Comm Coll (PA)
Cañada Coll (CA)
Chabot Coll (CA)

Chemeketa Comm Coll (OR)
Chesapeake Coll (MD)
Coastal Bend Coll (TX)
Coll of the Sequoias (CA)
Columbia Coll (CA)
Copiah-Lincoln Comm Coll (MS)
Daytona Beach Comm Coll (FL)
Del Mar Coll (TX)
Donnelly Coll (KS)
East Mississippi Comm Coll (MS)
Fulton-Montgomery Comm Coll (NY)
Hill Coll of the Hill Jr College District (TX)
Howard Comm Coll (MD)
Manatee Comm Coll (FL)
Northeast Mississippi Comm Coll (MS)
Northwest Coll (WY)
Palm Beach Comm Coll (FL)
Pratt Comm Coll and Area Vocational School (KS)
Prince George's Comm Coll (MD)
Sanford-Brown Coll, Hazelwood (MO)
Umpqua Comm Coll (OR)
Vermilion Comm Coll (MN)
Waycross Coll (GA)
Westmoreland County Comm Coll (PA)
Yuba Coll (CA)

Health Unit Coordinator/Ward Clerk

The Brown Mackie Coll–Lenexa Campus (KS)
Comm Coll of Allegheny County (PA)
Jefferson Coll (MO)
Milwaukee Area Tech Coll (WI)
Rasmussen Coll Mankato (MN)
Riverland Comm Coll (MN)

Health Unit Management/Ward Supervision

The Brown Mackie Coll–Lenexa Campus (KS)
Delaware County Comm Coll (PA)

Heating, Air Conditioning and Refrigeration Technology

Alamance Comm Coll (NC)
Calhoun Comm Coll (AL)
Cambria County Area Comm Coll (PA)
Cincinnati State Tech and Comm Coll (OH)
Dean Inst of Technology (PA)
DeKalb Tech Coll (GA)
Delaware County Comm Coll (PA)
Delta Coll (MI)
Dunwoody Coll of Technology (MN)
Front Range Comm Coll (CO)
Gadsden State Comm Coll (AL)
Harrisburg Area Comm Coll (PA)
Jackson Comm Coll (MI)
Johnson County Comm Coll (KS)
Kalamazoo Valley Comm Coll (MI)
Lamar State Coll–Port Arthur (TX)
Macomb Comm Coll (MI)
Manhattan Area Tech Coll (KS)
Massasoit Comm Coll (MA)
Miami Dade Coll (FL)
Milwaukee Area Tech Coll (WI)
Mitchell Tech Inst (SD)
Mohawk Valley Comm Coll (NY)
Mott Comm Coll (MI)

New Castle School of Trades (PA)
North Dakota State Coll of Science (ND)
Northeast Wisconsin Tech Coll (WI)
Oakland Comm Coll (MI)
Oakton Comm Coll (IL)
Pennsylvania Coll of Technology (PA)
St. Cloud Tech Coll (MN)
Springfield Tech Comm Coll (MA)
State U of NY Coll of Technology at Delhi (NY)
Terra State Comm Coll (OH)
Texas State Tech Coll–Waco/Marshall Campus (TX)
Triangle Tech, Inc.–Greensburg Center (PA)
Vatterott Coll, St. Ann (MO)
Vatterott Coll, Oklahoma City (OK)
Vatterott Coll, Tulsa (OK)
Wisconsin Indianhead Tech Coll (WI)

Heating, Air Conditioning, Ventilation and Refrigeration Maintenance Technology

Amarillo Coll (TX)
Arizona Western Coll (AZ)
Asheville-Buncombe Tech Comm Coll (NC)
Austin Comm Coll (TX)
Bates Tech Coll (WA)
Bismarck State Coll (ND)
Calhoun Comm Coll (AL)
Cedar Valley Coll (TX)
Central Comm Coll–Grand Island Campus (NE)
Central Comm Coll–Hastings Campus (NE)
Century Coll (MN)
CHI Inst (PA)
Clover Park Tech Coll (WA)
Clovis Comm Coll (NM)
Coll of DuPage (IL)
Coll of Lake County (IL)
Coll of Southern Idaho (ID)
Coll of the Desert (CA)
Coll of the Sequoias (CA)
Columbus State Comm Coll (OH)
Comm Coll of Allegheny County (PA)
Comm Coll of Denver (CO)
Daytona Beach Comm Coll (FL)
Delaware County Comm Coll (PA)
Delta Coll (MI)
Des Moines Area Comm Coll (IA)
Doña Ana Branch Comm Coll (NM)
Dunwoody Coll of Technology (MN)
Eastern Maine Comm Coll (ME)
Eastfield Coll (TX)
Elaine P. Nunez Comm Coll (LA)
El Camino Coll (CA)
Elgin Comm Coll (IL)
Fayetteville Tech Comm Coll (NC)
Forsyth Tech Comm Coll (NC)
Grand Rapids Comm Coll (MI)
Guilford Tech Comm Coll (NC)
Hawkeye Comm Coll (IA)
Heartland Comm Coll (IL)
Hill Coll of the Hill Jr College District (TX)
Honolulu Comm Coll (HI)
Illinois Eastern Comm Colls, Lincoln Trail Coll (IL)
IntelliTec Coll, Grand Junction (CO)
Ivy Tech State Coll–Bloomington (IN)

Ivy Tech State Coll–Central Indiana (IN)
Ivy Tech State Coll–Columbus (IN)
Ivy Tech State Coll–Eastcentral (IN)
Ivy Tech State Coll–Kokomo (IN)
Ivy Tech State Coll–Lafayette (IN)
Ivy Tech State Coll–North Central (IN)
Ivy Tech State Coll–Northeast (IN)
Ivy Tech State Coll–Northwest (IN)
Ivy Tech State Coll–Southcentral (IN)
Ivy Tech State Coll–Southwest (IN)
Ivy Tech State Coll–Wabash Valley (IN)
Ivy Tech State Coll–Whitewater (IN)
Jamestown Comm Coll (NY)
Jefferson Coll (MO)
John A. Logan Coll (IL)
Johnston Comm Coll (NC)
Kellogg Comm Coll (MI)
Kirkwood Comm Coll (IA)
Lamar State Coll–Port Arthur (TX)
Lansing Comm Coll (MI)
Lehigh Carbon Comm Coll (PA)
Linn State Tech Coll (MO)
Los Angeles Trade-Tech Coll (CA)
Louisiana Tech Coll–Delta Ouachita Campus (LA)
Louisiana Tech Coll–Mansfield Campus (LA)
Luzerne County Comm Coll (PA)
Macomb Comm Coll (MI)
Maple Woods Comm Coll (MO)
Metropolitan Comm Coll (NE)
Miami Dade Coll (FL)
Midland Coll (TX)
Midlands Tech Coll (SC)
Mid Michigan Comm Coll (MI)
Mid-Plains Comm Coll, North Platte (NE)
Milwaukee Area Tech Coll (WI)
Minnesota State Coll–Southeast Tech (MN)
Mitchell Tech Inst (SD)
Modesto Jr Coll (CA)
Morton Coll (IL)
Mt. San Antonio Coll (CA)
New England Inst of Tech & Florida Culinary Inst (FL)
New Hampshire Comm Tech Coll, Manchester/Stratham (NH)
North Central State Coll (OH)
North Dakota State Coll of Science (ND)
Northeast Comm Coll (NE)
Northeast Mississippi Comm Coll (MS)
Northeast Wisconsin Tech Coll (WI)
Northern Maine Comm Coll (ME)
North Harris Coll (TX)
North Idaho Coll (ID)
North Iowa Area Comm Coll (IA)
North Seattle Comm Coll (WA)
Odessa Coll (TX)
Orange Coast Coll (CA)
Oxnard Coll (CA)
Paris Jr Coll (TX)
Penn Valley Comm Coll (MO)
Ranken Tech Coll (MO)
Raritan Valley Comm Coll (NJ)

Roanoke-Chowan Comm Coll (NC)
Rockingham Comm Coll (NC)
St. Cloud Tech Coll (MN)
St. Philip's Coll (TX)
San Joaquin Delta Coll (CA)
San Jose City Coll (CA)
Sauk Valley Comm Coll (IL)
Shelton State Comm Coll (AL)
Somerset Comm Coll (KY)
South Central Tech Coll (MN)
Southern Maine Comm Coll (ME)
South Plains Coll (TX)
South Texas Comm Coll (TX)
Southwestern Illinois Coll (IL)
Spartanburg Tech Coll (SC)
Spokane Comm Coll (WA)
State U of NY Coll of Technology at Alfred (NY)
State U of NY Coll of Technology at Canton (NY)
State U of NY Coll of Technology at Delhi (NY)
Terra State Comm Coll (OH)
Texas State Tech Coll–Harlingen (TX)
Texas State Tech Coll–Waco/Marshall Campus (TX)
Trenholm State Tech Coll, Montgomery (AL)
Triangle Tech, Inc. (PA)
Triangle Tech, Inc.–Greensburg Center (PA)
Triton Coll (IL)
U of Alaska Anchorage, Matanuska-Susitna Coll (AK)
U of Northwestern Ohio (OH)
Utah Valley State Coll (UT)
Vance-Granville Comm Coll (NC)
Vatterott Coll, Omaha (NE)
Washtenaw Comm Coll (MI)
Waubonsee Comm Coll (IL)
Western Iowa Tech Comm Coll (IA)
Western Nevada Comm Coll (NV)
Western Wisconsin Tech Coll (WI)
Westmoreland County Comm Coll (PA)
West Virginia Northern Comm Coll (WV)
Westwood Coll–Denver North (CO)
Williamsburg Tech Coll (SC)

Heavy Equipment Maintenance Technology
Amarillo Coll (TX)
Beaufort County Comm Coll (NC)
Centralia Coll (WA)
Clover Park Tech Coll (WA)
Del Mar Coll (TX)
Des Moines Area Comm Coll (IA)
Eastern Maine Comm Coll (ME)
Guilford Tech Comm Coll (NC)
Hawkeye Comm Coll (IA)
Illinois Eastern Comm Colls, Olney Central Coll (IL)
Indian Hills Comm Coll (IA)
Lansing Comm Coll (MI)
Lawson State Comm Coll (AL)
Lenoir Comm Coll (NC)
Linn State Tech Coll (MO)
Longview Comm Coll (MO)
Los Angeles Trade-Tech Coll (CA)
Lower Columbia Coll (WA)
Marshalltown Comm Coll (IA)
Metropolitan Comm Coll (NE)
Northern Maine Comm Coll (ME)

North Idaho Coll (ID)
Ohio State U Ag Tech Inst (OH)
Pennsylvania Coll of Technology (PA)
Red Rocks Comm Coll (CO)
Rend Lake Coll (IL)
Rogue Comm Coll (OR)
Sheridan Coll (WY)
South Texas Comm Coll (TX)
Spokane Comm Coll (WA)
Spokane Falls Comm Coll (WA)
State U of NY Coll of Technology at Alfred (NY)
Texas State Tech Coll–Waco/Marshall Campus (TX)
Trenholm State Tech Coll, Montgomery (AL)
Trinidad State Jr Coll (CO)
Vincennes U (IN)
Waycross Coll (GA)
Western Wyoming Comm Coll (WY)

Heavy/Industrial Equipment Maintenance Technologies Related
Big Bend Comm Coll (WA)
Northeast Wisconsin Tech Coll (WI)
Pennsylvania Coll of Technology (PA)
Southwestern Michigan Coll (MI)

Hebrew
Los Angeles Valley Coll (CA)

Hematology Technology
Comm Coll of the Air Force (AL)

Hispanic-American, Puerto Rican, and Mexican-American/Chicano Studies
City Colls of Chicago, Wilbur Wright Coll (IL)
Contra Costa Coll (CA)
East Los Angeles Coll (CA)
Pasadena City Coll (CA)
San Diego City Coll (CA)
Santa Barbara City Coll (CA)
Southwestern Coll (CA)
Yuba Coll (CA)

Histologic Technician
Columbus State Comm Coll (OH)
Darton Coll (GA)
Miami Dade Coll (FL)
Mott Comm Coll (MI)
Oakland Comm Coll (MI)

Historic Preservation and Conservation
Bucks County Comm Coll (PA)

History
Abraham Baldwin Ag Coll (GA)
Amarillo Coll (TX)
Andrew Coll (GA)
Atlanta Metropolitan Coll (GA)
Atlantic Cape Comm Coll (NJ)
Austin Comm Coll (TX)
Bainbridge Coll (GA)
Barton County Comm Coll (KS)
Bergen Comm Coll (NJ)
Bronx Comm Coll of City U of NY (NY)
Bunker Hill Comm Coll (MA)
Burlington County Coll (NJ)
Butler County Comm Coll (KS)
Cañada Coll (CA)
Cape Cod Comm Coll (MA)
Casper Coll (WY)
Centralia Coll (WA)
Chabot Coll (CA)
Clarendon Coll (TX)
Coastal Bend Coll (TX)

Coastal Georgia Comm Coll (GA)
Coffeyville Comm Coll (KS)
Colby Comm Coll (KS)
Coll of Southern Idaho (ID)
Coll of the Canyons (CA)
Coll of the Desert (CA)
Coll of the Sequoias (CA)
Colorado Northwestern Comm Coll (CO)
Columbia Coll (CA)
Columbia State Comm Coll (TN)
Connors State Coll (OK)
Contra Costa Coll (CA)
Copiah-Lincoln Comm Coll (MS)
Cuyamaca Coll (CA)
Darton Coll (GA)
Daytona Beach Comm Coll (FL)
Del Mar Coll (TX)
Donnelly Coll (KS)
Eastern Arizona Coll (AZ)
Eastern Oklahoma State Coll (OK)
Eastern Wyoming Coll (WY)
East Los Angeles Coll (CA)
East Mississippi Comm Coll (MS)
El Camino Coll (CA)
Everett Comm Coll (WA)
Feather River Comm Coll District (CA)
Foothill Coll (CA)
Fulton-Montgomery Comm Coll (NY)
Galveston Coll (TX)
Gavilan Coll (CA)
Georgia Perimeter Coll (GA)
Gloucester County Coll (NJ)
Gordon Coll (GA)
Great Basin Coll (NV)
Gulf Coast Comm Coll (FL)
Hill Coll of the Hill Jr College District (TX)
Hiwassee Coll (TN)
Iowa Lakes Comm Coll (IA)
Jefferson Coll (MO)
Jefferson Davis Comm Coll (AL)
John A. Logan Coll (IL)
Kellogg Comm Coll (MI)
Kirkwood Comm Coll (IA)
Laramie County Comm Coll (WY)
Lawson State Comm Coll (AL)
Lincoln Coll, Lincoln (IL)
Lon Morris Coll (TX)
Lorain County Comm Coll (OH)
Los Angeles Valley Coll (CA)
Lower Columbia Coll (WA)
Manatee Comm Coll (FL)
Mesalands Comm Coll (NM)
Miami Dade Coll (FL)
Middlesex County Coll (NJ)
Midland Coll (TX)
MiraCosta Coll (CA)
Mohave Comm Coll (AZ)
Naugatuck Valley Comm Coll (CT)
Northeast Mississippi Comm Coll (MS)
Northern Essex Comm Coll (MA)
North Idaho Coll (ID)
Northwest Coll (WY)
Odessa Coll (TX)
Oklahoma City Comm Coll (OK)
Orange Coast Coll (CA)
Otero Jr Coll (CO)
Oxnard Coll (CA)
Palm Beach Comm Coll (FL)
Palo Alto Coll (TX)
Pasadena City Coll (CA)
Pensacola Jr Coll (FL)
Pratt Comm Coll and Area Vocational School (KS)
Red Rocks Comm Coll (CO)
Rend Lake Coll (IL)
Riverside Comm Coll (CA)

St. Philip's Coll (TX)
Salem Comm Coll (NJ)
San Joaquin Delta Coll (CA)
San Jose City Coll (CA)
San Juan Coll (NM)
Santa Barbara City Coll (CA)
Santa Monica Coll (CA)
Sauk Valley Comm Coll (IL)
Seward County Comm Coll (KS)
Sheridan Coll (WY)
Snow Coll (UT)
Southwestern Coll (CA)
Southwest Mississippi Comm Coll (MS)
Spoon River Coll (IL)
Triton Coll (IL)
Umpqua Comm Coll (OR)
Vermilion Comm Coll (MN)
Vincennes U (IN)
Waycross Coll (GA)
Western Wyoming Comm Coll (WY)
Yuba Coll (CA)

Home Furnishings and Equipment Installation
Jefferson State Comm Coll (AL)
St. Philip's Coll (TX)

Home Health Aide
Barton County Comm Coll (KS)

Home Health Aide/Home Attendant
Mt. San Jacinto Coll (CA)

Horse Husbandry/Equine Science and Management
Central Wyoming Coll (WY)
Clarendon Coll (TX)
Linn-Benton Comm Coll (OR)
Ohio State U Ag Tech Inst (OH)
Yavapai Coll (AZ)

Horticultural Science
Abraham Baldwin Ag Coll (GA)
American River Coll (CA)
Anne Arundel Comm Coll (MD)
Blue Ridge Comm Coll (NC)
Butte Coll (CA)
Cabrillo Coll (CA)
Central Lakes Coll (MN)
Central Piedmont Comm Coll (NC)
Chabot Coll (CA)
Clark State Comm Coll (OH)
Coffeyville Comm Coll (KS)
Coll of the Desert (CA)
Coll of the Sequoias (CA)
Connors State Coll (OK)
Cumberland County Coll (NJ)
Des Moines Area Comm Coll (IA)
Eastern Oklahoma State Coll (OK)
Edison Comm Coll (FL)
El Camino Coll (CA)
Fayetteville Tech Comm Coll (NC)
Forsyth Tech Comm Coll (NC)
Gwinnett Tech Coll (GA)
Hawkeye Comm Coll (IA)
Hill Coll of the Hill Jr College District (TX)
Houston Comm Coll System (TX)
Indian Hills Comm Coll (IA)
Kent State U, Salem Campus (OH)
Kirkwood Comm Coll (IA)
Lake Washington Tech Coll (WA)
Lansing Comm Coll (MI)
Lehigh Carbon Comm Coll (PA)
Lenoir Comm Coll (NC)
Linn-Benton Comm Coll (OR)

Los Angeles Pierce Coll (CA)
Luzerne County Comm Coll (PA)
Mayland Comm Coll (NC)
Meridian Comm Coll (MS)
Merritt Coll (CA)
Miami Dade Coll (FL)
Minot State U–Bottineau Campus (ND)
MiraCosta Coll (CA)
Mississippi Gulf Coast Comm Coll (MS)
Mt. San Antonio Coll (CA)
Naugatuck Valley Comm Coll (CT)
Northeast Comm Coll (NE)
Northeastern Oklahoma A&M Coll (OK)
Northeast Mississippi Comm Coll (MS)
Ohio State U Ag Tech Inst (OH)
Oklahoma State U, Oklahoma City (OK)
Orange Coast Coll (CA)
Palo Alto Coll (TX)
Pensacola Jr Coll (FL)
Rockingham Comm Coll (NC)
St. Clair County Comm Coll (MI)
Sierra Coll (CA)
Southern Maine Comm Coll (ME)
South Puget Sound Comm Coll (WA)
Southwestern Illinois Coll (IL)
Spartanburg Tech Coll (SC)
State U of NY Coll of A&T at Morrisville (NY)
State U of NY Coll of Technology at Delhi (NY)
Trident Tech Coll (SC)
Ventura Coll (CA)
Victor Valley Coll (CA)
Vincennes U (IN)
Westmoreland County Comm Coll (PA)
The Williamson Free School of Mecha Trades (PA)

Hospital and Health Care Facilities Administration
Central Comm Coll–Hastings Campus (NE)
City Colls of Chicago, Malcolm X Coll (IL)
Coll of DuPage (IL)
Harrisburg Area Comm Coll (PA)
Manatee Comm Coll (FL)
Western Wisconsin Tech Coll (WI)

Hospitality Administration
Abraham Baldwin Ag Coll (GA)
Albuquerque Tech Vocational Inst (NM)
Alexandria Tech Coll (MN)
Allegany Coll of Maryland (MD)
Arizona Western Coll (AZ)
The Art Inst of Pittsburgh (PA)
Atlantic Cape Comm Coll (NJ)
Baltimore International Coll (MD)
Bay State Coll (MA)
Berkshire Comm Coll (MA)
Blackfeet Comm Coll (MT)
Bucks County Comm Coll (PA)
Bunker Hill Comm Coll (MA)
Cambria County Area Comm Coll (PA)
Central Comm Coll–Hastings Campus (NE)
Central Florida Comm Coll (FL)
Central Oregon Comm Coll (OR)
Central Piedmont Comm Coll (NC)

Chemeketa Comm Coll (OR)
Coll of DuPage (IL)
Collin County Comm Coll District (TX)
Colorado Mountn Coll, Alpine Cmps (CO)
Daytona Beach Comm Coll (FL)
Delgado Comm Coll (LA)
Des Moines Area Comm Coll (IA)
Doña Ana Branch Comm Coll (NM)
Edison Comm Coll (FL)
El Centro Coll (TX)
Fisher Coll (MA)
Florida National Coll (FL)
Gulf Coast Comm Coll (FL)
Hillsborough Comm Coll (FL)
Hiwassee Coll (TN)
Holyoke Comm Coll (MA)
Iowa Lakes Comm Coll (IA)
Ivy Tech State Coll–Eastcentral (IN)
Ivy Tech State Coll–North Central (IN)
Ivy Tech State Coll–Northeast (IN)
James H. Faulkner State Comm Coll (AL)
Jefferson Coll (MO)
Jefferson Comm Coll (NY)
Jefferson State Comm Coll (AL)
Johnson County Comm Coll (KS)
J. Sargeant Reynolds Comm Coll (VA)
Kauai Comm Coll (HI)
Lakeland Comm Coll (OH)
Lamar State Coll–Port Arthur (TX)
Lansing Comm Coll (MI)
Miami Dade Coll (FL)
Middlesex County Coll (NJ)
Mid Michigan Comm Coll (MI)
Monroe Coll, Bronx (NY)
Monroe Coll, New Rochelle (NY)
National Coll of Business & Technology, Salem (VA)
Naugatuck Valley Comm Coll (CT)
Normandale Comm Coll (MN)
North Idaho Coll (ID)
North Shore Comm Coll (MA)
Pellissippi State Tech Comm Coll (TN)
Pima Comm Coll (AZ)
Rasmussen Coll Mankato (MN)
Rend Lake Coll (IL)
St. Petersburg Coll (FL)
San Diego City Coll (CA)
Scottsdale Comm Coll (AZ)
Sheridan Coll (WY)
Sisseton-Wahpeton Comm Coll (SD)
Southern Maine Comm Coll (ME)
South Texas Comm Coll (TX)
Southwestern Illinois Coll (IL)
State U of NY Coll of A&T at Morrisville (NY)
Sullivan County Comm Coll (NY)
Triton Coll (IL)
United Tribes Tech Coll (ND)
Utah Valley State Coll (UT)
Westmoreland County Comm Coll (PA)
West Virginia Northern Comm Coll (WV)
Wor-Wic Comm Coll (MD)

Hospitality Administration Related
Allentown Business School (PA)
The Art Inst of Pittsburgh (PA)

Fayetteville Tech Comm Coll (NC)
Mineral Area Coll (MO)
Penn State U Beaver Campus of the Commonwealth Coll (PA)

Hospitality and Recreation Marketing
AIB Coll of Business (IA)
American River Coll (CA)
Austin Comm Coll (TX)
Central Oregon Comm Coll (OR)
Cumberland County Coll (NJ)
Edmonds Comm Coll (WA)
Gloucester County Coll (NJ)
Kirkwood Comm Coll (IA)
Luzerne County Comm Coll (PA)
Mid Michigan Comm Coll (MI)
Milwaukee Area Tech Coll (WI)
Montgomery County Comm Coll (PA)
Northeast Mississippi Comm Coll (MS)
Raritan Valley Comm Coll (NJ)
Rasmussen Coll Mankato (MN)
State U of NY Coll of Technology at Delhi (NY)
Vincennes U (IN)

Hospitality/Recreation Marketing
Middlesex Comm Coll (MA)

Hotel/Motel Administration
Alexandria Tech Coll (MN)
American River Coll (CA)
Anne Arundel Comm Coll (MD)
The Art Inst of Pittsburgh (PA)
Asheville-Buncombe Tech Comm Coll (NC)
Austin Comm Coll (TX)
Baltimore International Coll (MD)
Bay State Coll (MA)
Bergen Comm Coll (NJ)
Bismarck State Coll (ND)
Briarwood Coll (CT)
Broome Comm Coll (NY)
Bryant & Stratton Business Inst, Lackawanna (NY)
Bryant & Stratton Business Inst, Syracuse (NY)
Bucks County Comm Coll (PA)
Bunker Hill Comm Coll (MA)
Burlington County Coll (NJ)
Butler County Comm Coll (KS)
Cape Cod Comm Coll (MA)
Cape Fear Comm Coll (NC)
Central Arizona Coll (AZ)
Central Comm Coll–Hastings Campus (NE)
Central Oregon Comm Coll (OR)
Central Pennsylvania Coll (PA)
Central Piedmont Comm Coll (NC)
Chemeketa Comm Coll (OR)
Cincinnati State Tech and Comm Coll (OH)
Coll of DuPage (IL)
Coll of Southern Idaho (ID)
Coll of the Canyons (CA)
Colorado Mountn Coll, Alpine Cmps (CO)
Columbia Coll (CA)
Columbus State Comm Coll (OH)
Comm Coll of Allegheny County (PA)
Comm Coll of the Air Force (AL)

Copiah-Lincoln Comm Coll–Natchez Campus (MS)
County Coll of Morris (NJ)
Daytona Beach Comm Coll (FL)
Delaware County Comm Coll (PA)
Del Mar Coll (TX)
Des Moines Area Comm Coll (IA)
East Mississippi Comm Coll (MS)
Education Direct Center for Degree Studies (PA)
El Centro Coll (TX)
Elgin Comm Coll (IL)
Erie Comm Coll (NY)
Essex County Coll (NJ)
Finger Lakes Comm Coll (NY)
Galveston Coll (TX)
Garrett Coll (MD)
Gwinnett Tech Coll (GA)
Harrisburg Area Comm Coll (PA)
Hawaii Comm Coll (HI)
Hillsborough Comm Coll (FL)
Hinds Comm Coll (MS)
Holyoke Comm Coll (MA)
Houston Comm Coll System (TX)
Iowa Lakes Comm Coll (IA)
Jefferson Comm Coll (NY)
Johnson County Comm Coll (KS)
John Wood Comm Coll (IL)
J. Sargeant Reynolds Comm Coll (VA)
Kapiolani Comm Coll (HI)
Keystone Coll (PA)
Kirkwood Comm Coll (IA)
Lake Washington Tech Coll (WA)
Lansing Comm Coll (MI)
Laredo Comm Coll (TX)
Lehigh Carbon Comm Coll (PA)
Lincoln Land Comm Coll (IL)
Los Angeles Valley Coll (CA)
Louisiana Tech Coll–Northwest Louisiana Campus (LA)
Luzerne County Comm Coll (PA)
MacCormac Coll (IL)
Manchester Comm Coll (CT)
Massasoit Comm Coll (MA)
Meridian Comm Coll (MS)
Middlesex Comm Coll (MA)
Middlesex County Coll (NJ)
Milwaukee Area Tech Coll (WI)
MiraCosta Coll (CA)
Mississippi Gulf Coast Comm Coll (MS)
Mohawk Valley Comm Coll (NY)
Montgomery Coll (MD)
Moraine Park Tech Coll (WI)
Mt. San Antonio Coll (CA)
Nassau Comm Coll (NY)
National Coll of Business & Technology, Salem (VA)
Naugatuck Valley Comm Coll (CT)
New Hampshire Tech Inst (NH)
Northampton County Area Comm Coll (PA)
Northeastern Oklahoma A&M Coll (OK)
Northeast Mississippi Comm Coll (MS)
Northern Essex Comm Coll (MA)
Oakland Comm Coll (MI)
Orange Coast Coll (CA)
Oxnard Coll (CA)
Palm Beach Comm Coll (FL)
Pellissippi State Tech Comm Coll (TN)
Pennsylvania Culinary Inst (PA)

Penn Valley Comm Coll (MO)
Pensacola Jr Coll (FL)
Pima Comm Coll (AZ)
Quinsigamond Comm Coll (MA)
Raritan Valley Comm Coll (NJ)
Rasmussen Coll Mankato (MN)
The Restaurant School at Walnut Hill Coll (PA)
St. Philip's Coll (TX)
Santa Barbara City Coll (CA)
Santa Fe Comm Coll (NM)
Schenectady County Comm Coll (NY)
Schiller International USwitzerland)
Scottsdale Comm Coll (AZ)
Sinclair Comm Coll (OH)
South Coll (TN)
Southern Maine Comm Coll (ME)
South Texas Comm Coll (TX)
Spokane Comm Coll (WA)
State U of NY Coll of A&T at Morrisville (NY)
State U of NY Coll of Technology at Delhi (NY)
Tompkins Cortland Comm Coll (NY)
Trident Tech Coll (SC)
Triton Coll (IL)
Union County Coll (NJ)
United Tribes Tech Coll (ND)
Vincennes U (IN)
Washtenaw Comm Coll (MI)
Westmoreland County Comm Coll (PA)
Yakima Valley Comm Coll (WA)
York County Comm Coll (ME)

Hotel/Motel Services Marketing Operations
Montgomery County Comm Coll (PA)

Housing and Human Environments
Dakota County Tech Coll (MN)
Louisville Tech Inst (KY)
Modesto Jr Coll (CA)
Orange Coast Coll (CA)
Vincennes U (IN)

Housing and Human Environments Related
Comm Coll of Allegheny County (PA)

Human Development and Family Studies
Cuesta Coll (CA)
Gloucester County Coll (NJ)
Lincoln Coll, Lincoln (IL)
Orange Coast Coll (CA)
Penn State U Delaware County Campus of the Commonwealth Coll (PA)
Penn State U DuBois Campus of the Commonwealth Coll (PA)
Penn State U Fayette Campus of the Commonwealth Coll (PA)
Penn State U Mont Alto Campus of the Commonwealth Coll (PA)
Penn State U New Kensington Campus of the Commonwealth Coll (PA)
Penn State U Shenango Campus of the Commonwealth Coll (PA)
Penn State U Worthington Scranton Cmps Commonwealth Coll (PA)
Penn State U York Campus of the Commonwealth Coll (PA)

Human Development and Family Studies Related
Comm Coll of Allegheny County (PA)
Northwest State Comm Coll (OH)

Human Ecology
Greenfield Comm Coll (MA)
Vermilion Comm Coll (MN)

Humanities
Abraham Baldwin Ag Coll (GA)
Ancilla Coll (IN)
Andrew Coll (GA)
Anne Arundel Comm Coll (MD)
Atlantic Cape Comm Coll (NJ)
Bowling Green State U-Firelands Coll (OH)
Bristol Comm Coll (MA)
Brookdale Comm Coll (NJ)
Bucks County Comm Coll (PA)
Cañada Coll (CA)
Casper Coll (WY)
Centralia Coll (WA)
Central Oregon Comm Coll (OR)
Chabot Coll (CA)
Chemeketa Comm Coll (OR)
Chesapeake Coll (MD)
Clinton Comm Coll (NY)
Coffeyville Comm Coll (KS)
Colby Comm Coll (KS)
Coll of the Canyons (CA)
Coll of the Sequoias (CA)
Colorado Mountn Coll, Alpine Cmps (CO)
Colorado Mountn Coll (CO)
Colorado Mountn Coll, Timberline Cmps (CO)
Columbia Coll (CA)
Columbia-Greene Comm Coll (NY)
Comm Coll of Allegheny County (PA)
Contra Costa Coll (CA)
Corning Comm Coll (NY)
Daytona Beach Comm Coll (FL)
Dean Coll (MA)
Dutchess Comm Coll (NY)
Erie Comm Coll (NY)
Finger Lakes Comm Coll (NY)
Fisher Coll (MA)
Foothill Coll (CA)
Fulton-Montgomery Comm Coll (NY)
Galveston Coll (TX)
Garden City Comm Coll (KS)
Gogebic Comm Coll (MI)
Greenfield Comm Coll (MA)
Hill Coll of the Hill Jr College District (TX)
Hinds Comm Coll (MS)
Iowa Lakes Comm Coll (IA)
Jefferson Comm Coll (NY)
John A. Logan Coll (IL)
Kirkwood Comm Coll (IA)
Lackawanna Coll (PA)
Laramie County Comm Coll (WY)
Lehigh Carbon Comm Coll (PA)
Lincoln Coll, Lincoln (IL)
Lon Morris Coll (TX)
Luzerne County Comm Coll (PA)
Manatee Comm Coll (FL)
Merritt Coll (CA)
Miami Dade Coll (FL)
MiraCosta Coll (CA)
Modesto Jr Coll (CA)
Mohawk Valley Comm Coll (NY)
Montgomery County Comm Coll (PA)
Mt. San Jacinto Coll (CA)
Napa Valley Coll (CA)
Niagara County Comm Coll (NY)

Northwest Coll (WY)
Oklahoma City Comm Coll (OK)
Orange Coast Coll (CA)
Orange County Comm Coll (NY)
Otero Jr Coll (CO)
Pratt Comm Coll and Area Vocational School (KS)
Reading Area Comm Coll (PA)
Red Rocks Comm Coll (CO)
Riverside Comm Coll (CA)
Rogue Comm Coll (OR)
Salem Comm Coll (NJ)
San Joaquin Delta Coll (CA)
Schenectady County Comm Coll (NY)
Sheridan Coll (WY)
Snow Coll (UT)
Southwest Mississippi Comm Coll (MS)
State U of NY Coll of A&T at Morrisville (NY)
State U of NY Coll of Technology at Alfred (NY)
State U of NY Coll of Technology at Canton (NY)
State U of NY Coll of Technology at Delhi (NY)
Tompkins Cortland Comm Coll (NY)
Umpqua Comm Coll (OR)
Utah Valley State Coll (UT)
Victor Valley Coll (CA)
Western Wyoming Comm Coll (WY)
West Hills Comm Coll (CA)

Human Resources Management
Beaufort County Comm Coll (NC)
Central Georgia Tech Coll (GA)
Clark Coll (WA)
Columbus State Comm Coll (OH)
Comm Coll of Allegheny County (PA)
Comm Coll of the Air Force (AL)
Cumberland County Coll (NJ)
Edison State Comm Coll (OH)
Edmonds Comm Coll (WA)
Houston Comm Coll System (TX)
Keystone Coll (PA)
Lansing Comm Coll (MI)
Lehigh Carbon Comm Coll (PA)
Mesalands Comm Coll (NM)
Moraine Valley Comm Coll (IL)
New Hampshire Tech Inst (NH)
Reading Area Comm Coll (PA)
Rockingham Comm Coll (NC)
Saint Paul Coll–A Comm & Tech College (MN)
Salem Comm Coll (NJ)
Umpqua Comm Coll (OR)
Virginia Coll at Jackson (MS)
Western Wisconsin Tech Coll (WI)

Human Resources Management and Services Related
Barton County Comm Coll (KS)
Fayetteville Tech Comm Coll (NC)
Iowa Lakes Comm Coll (IA)
Lake Superior Coll (MN)

Human Services
Alexandria Tech Coll (MN)
American River Coll (CA)
Anne Arundel Comm Coll (MD)
Anoka Tech Coll (MN)

Arizona Western Coll (AZ)
Asnuntuck Comm Coll (CT)
Atlanta Metropolitan Coll (GA)
Austin Comm Coll (TX)
Big Sandy Comm and Tech Coll (KY)
Blackfeet Comm Coll (MT)
Borough of Manhattan Comm Coll of City U of NY (NY)
Bowling Green State U-Firelands Coll (OH)
Bristol Comm Coll (MA)
Bronx Comm Coll of City U of NY (NY)
Brookdale Comm Coll (NJ)
Bunker Hill Comm Coll (MA)
Bunker Hill Comm Coll (MA)
Burlington County Coll (NJ)
Cambria County Area Comm Coll (PA)
Camden County Coll (NJ)
Central Piedmont Comm Coll (NC)
Central Wyoming Coll (WY)
Chabot Coll (CA)
Chatfield Coll (OH)
Chemeketa Comm Coll (OR)
Chesapeake Coll (MD)
Clark State Comm Coll (OH)
Coll of DuPage (IL)
Coll of DuPage (IL)
Coll of Southern Idaho (ID)
Coll of Southern Maryland (MD)
Colorado Northwestern Comm Coll (CO)
Columbia-Greene Comm Coll (NY)
Comm Coll of Denver (CO)
Corning Comm Coll (NY)
Cuesta Coll (CA)
Daytona Beach Comm Coll (FL)
Delaware Tech & Comm Coll, Terry Cmps (DE)
Des Moines Area Comm Coll (IA)
Edgecombe Comm Coll (NC)
Edison Comm Coll (FL)
Edison State Comm Coll (OH)
Elgin Comm Coll (IL)
Essex County Coll (NJ)
Everett Comm Coll (WA)
Finger Lakes Comm Coll (NY)
Fiorello H LaGuardia Comm Coll of City U of NY (NY)
Frederick Comm Coll (MD)
Fulton-Montgomery Comm Coll (NY)
Glendale Comm Coll (AZ)
Greenfield Comm Coll (MA)
Guilford Tech Comm Coll (NC)
Gulf Coast Comm Coll (FL)
Gulf Coast Comm Coll (FL)
Harrisburg Area Comm Coll (PA)
Harrisburg Area Comm Coll (PA)
Henderson Comm Coll (KY)
Hesser Coll (NH)
Hillsborough Comm Coll (FL)
Hiwassee Coll (TN)
Holyoke Comm Coll (MA)
Honolulu Comm Coll (HI)
Hopkinsville Comm Coll (KY)
Hopkinsville Comm Coll (KY)
Hudson County Comm Coll (NJ)
Itasca Comm Coll (MN)
James A. Rhodes State Coll (OH)
Jefferson Comm Coll (NY)
John Tyler Comm Coll (VA)
Kellogg Comm Coll (MI)
Kent State U, Salem Campus (OH)
Kingsborough Comm Coll of City U of NY (NY)
Kirkwood Comm Coll (IA)

Lake Land Coll (IL)
Lakeland Comm Coll (OH)
Lansing Comm Coll (MI)
Longview Comm Coll (MO)
Lorain County Comm Coll (OH)
Luzerne County Comm Coll (PA)
Manchester Comm Coll (CT)
Marion Tech Coll (OH)
Massasoit Comm Coll (MA)
Massasoit Comm Coll (MA)
Mesabi Range Comm and Tech Coll (MN)
Metropolitan Comm Coll (NE)
Miami Dade Coll (FL)
Middlesex Comm Coll (CT)
Middlesex Comm Coll (MA)
Miles Comm Coll (MT)
Milwaukee Area Tech Coll (WI)
Minneapolis Comm and Tech Coll (MN)
Mississippi Gulf Coast Comm Coll (MS)
Mitchell Comm Coll (NC)
Modesto Jr Coll (CA)
Mohawk Valley Comm Coll (NY)
Mount Wachusett Comm Coll (MA)
Naugatuck Valley Comm Coll (CT)
Nebraska Indian Comm Coll (NE)
Nebraska Indian Comm Coll (NE)
New Hampshire Comm Tech Coll, Berlin/Laconia (NH)
New Hampshire Comm Tech Coll, Manchester/Stratham (NH)
New Hampshire Tech Inst (NH)
Niagara County Comm Coll (NY)
North Central State Coll (OH)
Northcentral Tech Coll (WI)
Northern Essex Comm Coll (MA)
North Harris Coll (TX)
North Idaho Coll (ID)
Northwestern Connecticut Comm-Tech Coll (CT)
Odessa Coll (TX)
Owensboro Comm and Tech Coll (KY)
Parkland Coll (IL)
Pasadena City Coll (CA)
Pasco-Hernando Comm Coll (FL)
Pratt Comm Coll and Area Vocational School (KS)
Quinebaug Valley Comm Coll (CT)
Quinsigamond Comm Coll (MA)
Raritan Valley Comm Coll (NJ)
Reading Area Comm Coll (PA)
Richmond Comm Coll (NC)
Riverland Comm Coll (MN)
Rochester Comm and Tech Coll (MN)
Rogue Comm Coll (OR)
Saint Charles Comm Coll (MO)
St. Louis Comm Coll at Florissant Valley (MO)
St. Petersburg Coll (FL)
San Jose City Coll (CA)
San Juan Coll (NM)
Sauk Valley Comm Coll (IL)
Schenectady County Comm Coll (NY)
Schenectady County Comm Coll (NY)
Sinclair Comm Coll (OH)
Southeast Comm Coll, Lincoln Campus (NE)
Southern State Comm Coll (OH)

Southside Virginia Comm Coll (VA)
South Suburban Coll (IL)
South Texas Comm Coll (TX)
Stanly Comm Coll (NC)
Stark State Coll of Technology (OH)
State U of NY Coll of Technology at Alfred (NY)
Sullivan County Comm Coll (NY)
Sussex County Comm Coll (NJ)
Tompkins Cortland Comm Coll (NY)
Trident Tech Coll (SC)
United Tribes Tech Coll (ND)
U of Alaska Anchorage, Matanuska-Susitna Coll (AK)
U of Arkansas Comm Coll at Hope (AR)
Urban Coll of Boston (MA)
Vance-Granville Comm Coll (NC)
Western Wyoming Comm Coll (WY)
Westmoreland County Comm Coll (PA)
Yuba Coll (CA)

Hydraulics and Fluid Power Technology
Alexandria Tech Coll (MN)
Normandale Comm Coll (MN)
North Hennepin Comm Coll (MN)
Ohio State U Ag Tech Inst (OH)

Hydrology and Water Resources Science
Cecil Comm Coll (MD)
Coll of Southern Idaho (ID)
Coll of the Canyons (CA)
Colorado Mountn Coll, Timberline Cmps (CO)
Delta Coll (MI)
Doña Ana Branch Comm Coll (NM)
Fort Scott Comm Coll (KS)
Iowa Lakes Comm Coll (IA)
Kirkwood Comm Coll (IA)
Lawson State Comm Coll (AL)
Lenoir Comm Coll (NC)
Los Angeles Trade-Tech Coll (CA)
Milwaukee Area Tech Coll (WI)
Moraine Park Tech Coll (WI)
Mountain Empire Comm Coll (VA)
Northeast Alabama Comm Coll (AL)
Palomar Coll (CA)
Red Rocks Comm Coll (CO)
St. Petersburg Coll (FL)
Spokane Comm Coll (WA)
Ventura Coll (CA)
Vermilion Comm Coll (MN)

Illustration
The Art Inst of Pittsburgh (PA)
The Creative Center (NE)
Keystone Coll (PA)

Industrial Arts
American River Coll (CA)
Casper Coll (WY)
Chabot Coll (CA)
Cleveland State Comm Coll (TN)
Coll of the Sequoias (CA)
Contra Costa Coll (CA)
Delta Coll (MI)
Eastern Oklahoma State Coll (OK)
El Camino Coll (CA)
Everett Comm Coll (WA)
Fort Scott Comm Coll (KS)
Garden City Comm Coll (KS)
Guilford Tech Comm Coll (NC)

Hinds Comm Coll (MS)
Honolulu Comm Coll (HI)
Howard Coll (TX)
Los Angeles Pierce Coll (CA)
Luna Comm Coll (NM)
Modesto Jr Coll (CA)
Mt. San Antonio Coll (CA)
Northeastern Oklahoma A&M Coll (OK)
Northern Maine Comm Coll (ME)
Ouachita Tech Coll (AR)
Pellissippi State Tech Comm Coll (TN)
Pratt Comm Coll and Area Vocational School (KS)
Rockingham Comm Coll (NC)
San Diego City Coll (CA)
Santa Monica Coll (CA)
Sierra Coll (CA)
Vermilion Comm Coll (MN)
Volunteer State Comm Coll (TN)
Washtenaw Comm Coll (MI)

Industrial Design
The Art Inst of Pittsburgh (PA)
The Art Inst of Seattle (WA)
Cabrillo Coll (CA)
Kishwaukee Coll (IL)
Luzerne County Comm Coll (PA)
Milwaukee Area Tech Coll (WI)
Mt. San Antonio Coll (CA)
Northeast Wisconsin Tech Coll (WI)
Oklahoma State U, Oklahoma City (OK)
Orange Coast Coll (CA)
Portland Comm Coll (OR)
Vincennes U (IN)
Washtenaw Comm Coll (MI)

Industrial Electronics Technology
Bates Tech Coll (WA)
Big Bend Comm Coll (WA)
Central Carolina Tech Coll (SC)
Coll of DuPage (IL)
John Wood Comm Coll (IL)
Louisville Tech Inst (KY)
Midlands Tech Coll (SC)
Mitchell Tech Inst (SD)
Modesto Jr Coll (CA)
North Dakota State Coll of Science (ND)
North Iowa Area Comm Coll (IA)
North Seattle Comm Coll (WA)
Northwest Iowa Comm Coll (IA)
Northwest-Shoals Comm Coll (AL)
Oakland Comm Coll (MI)
Pennsylvania Coll of Technology (PA)
Rend Lake Coll (IL)
State U of NY Coll of Technology at Alfred (NY)
Trenholm State Tech Coll, Montgomery (AL)
Vincennes U (IN)
Western Dakota Tech Inst (SD)
Western Wyoming Comm Coll (WY)
York Tech Coll (SC)

Industrial Engineering
Education Direct Center for Degree Studies (PA)
Manchester Comm Coll (CT)
Mount Wachusett Comm Coll (MA)
Nashville State Tech Comm Coll (TN)
Pima Comm Coll (AZ)
Santa Barbara City Coll (CA)

Industrial Mechanics and Maintenance Technology
Arkansas Northeastern Coll (AR)
Calhoun Comm Coll (AL)
Coll of Lake County (IL)
Dakota County Tech Coll (MN)
Fayetteville Tech Comm Coll (NC)
Guilford Tech Comm Coll (NC)
Harrisburg Area Comm Coll (PA)
Heartland Comm Coll (IL)
Illinois Eastern Comm Colls, Olney Central Coll (IL)
Ivy Tech State Coll–Eastcentral (IN)
Jefferson Coll (MO)
John Wood Comm Coll (IL)
Kaskaskia Coll (IL)
Louisville Tech Inst (KY)
Lower Columbia Coll (WA)
Macomb Comm Coll (MI)
Northland Pioneer Coll (AZ)
Northwest-Shoals Comm Coll (AL)
Pennsylvania Coll of Technology (PA)
Rend Lake Coll (IL)
Riverland Comm Coll (MN)
Southern Arkansas U Tech (AR)
Southwestern Michigan Coll (MI)
Trenholm State Tech Coll, Montgomery (AL)
U of Arkansas Comm Coll at Hope (AR)
Vincennes U (IN)
Waubonsee Comm Coll (IL)
Western Wyoming Comm Coll (WY)
York Tech Coll (SC)

Industrial Production Technologies Related
Arkansas Northeastern Coll (AR)
Broome Comm Coll (NY)
Cape Fear Comm Coll (NC)
Erie Comm Coll (NY)
Essex County Coll (NJ)
Linn State Tech Coll (MO)
Mohawk Valley Comm Coll (NY)
Pennsylvania Coll of Technology (PA)
Richmond Comm Coll (NC)

Industrial Radiologic Technology
Amarillo Coll (TX)
Anne Arundel Comm Coll (MD)
Austin Comm Coll (TX)
Bellevue Comm Coll (WA)
Bergen Comm Coll (NJ)
Cañada Coll (CA)
Carl Sandburg Coll (IL)
Carteret Comm Coll (NC)
Casper Coll (WY)
Central Florida Comm Coll (FL)
Cleveland Comm Coll (NC)
Columbia State Comm Coll (TN)
Columbus State Comm Coll (OH)
Comm Coll of Denver (CO)
Copiah-Lincoln Comm Coll (MS)
Cumberland County Coll (NJ)
Cuyahoga Comm Coll (OH)
Daytona Beach Comm Coll (FL)
Del Mar Coll (TX)
Delta Coll (MI)
Doña Ana Branch Comm Coll (NM)
Forsyth Tech Comm Coll (NC)
Gulf Coast Comm Coll (FL)

Gwinnett Tech Coll (GA)
Hillsborough Comm Coll (FL)
Hinds Comm Coll (MS)
Houston Comm Coll System (TX)
Indian Hills Comm Coll (IA)
James A. Rhodes State Coll (OH)
Jefferson Comm Coll (OH)
Kapiolani Comm Coll (HI)
Labouré Coll (MA)
Laramie County Comm Coll (WY)
Laredo Comm Coll (TX)
Lorain County Comm Coll (OH)
Marion Tech Coll (OH)
Marshalltown Comm Coll (IA)
McLennan Comm Coll (TX)
Merritt Coll (CA)
Middlesex Comm Coll (CT)
Mid Michigan Comm Coll (MI)
Milwaukee Area Tech Coll (WI)
Mississippi Gulf Coast Comm Coll (MS)
Montcalm Comm Coll (MI)
Mt. San Antonio Coll (CA)
Naugatuck Valley Comm Coll (CT)
Northcentral Tech Coll (WI)
Northeast Mississippi Comm Coll (MS)
Northern Essex Comm Coll (MA)
Odessa Coll (TX)
Orange Coast Coll (CA)
Orange County Comm Coll (NY)
Palm Beach Comm Coll (FL)
Pasadena City Coll (CA)
Penn Valley Comm Coll (MO)
Portland Comm Coll (OR)
Reading Area Comm Coll (PA)
Roane State Comm Coll (TN)
St. Petersburg Coll (FL)
San Joaquin Delta Coll (CA)
Sauk Valley Comm Coll (IL)
Sinclair Comm Coll (OH)
Southern Maine Comm Coll (ME)
Southern West Virginia Comm and Tech Coll (WV)
South Plains Coll (TX)
South Suburban Coll (IL)
South Texas Comm Coll (TX)
Southwestern Illinois Coll (IL)
Vance-Granville Comm Coll (NC)
Virginia Western Comm Coll (VA)
Walters State Comm Coll (TN)
West Kentucky Comm and Tech Coll (KY)
Yakima Valley Comm Coll (WA)
Yuba Coll (CA)

Industrial Technology
Albany Tech Coll (GA)
Albuquerque Tech Vocational Inst (NM)
Alexandria Tech Coll (MN)
Anne Arundel Comm Coll (MD)
Arkansas Northeastern Coll (AR)
Austin Comm Coll (TX)
Bergen Comm Coll (NJ)
Bismarck State Coll (ND)
Blackhawk Tech Coll (WI)
Bladen Comm Coll (NC)
Blue Ridge Comm Coll (NC)
Bowling Green State U-Firelands Coll (OH)
Brunswick Comm Coll (NC)
Cambria County Area Comm Coll (PA)
Central Arizona Coll (AZ)

Central Comm Coll–
Columbus Campus (NE)
Central Comm Coll–Grand
Island Campus (NE)
Central Comm Coll–Hastings
Campus (NE)
Central Georgia Tech Coll
(GA)
Central Oregon Comm Coll
(OR)
Central Piedmont Comm Coll
(NC)
Century Coll (MN)
Chabot Coll (CA)
Chemeketa Comm Coll (OR)
Clark State Comm Coll (OH)
Cleveland State Comm Coll
(TN)
Clinton Comm Coll (NY)
Coffeyville Comm Coll (KS)
Coll of DuPage (IL)
Comm Coll of Allegheny
County (PA)
Comm Coll of the Air Force
(AL)
Corning Comm Coll (NY)
Cossatot Comm Coll of the U
of Arkansas (AR)
Crowder Coll (MO)
Cuesta Coll (CA)
Cumberland County Coll
(NJ)
Delaware Tech & Comm
Coll, Terry Cmps (DE)
Dunwoody Coll of
Technology (MN)
Edison State Comm Coll
(OH)
Elgin Comm Coll (IL)
Everett Comm Coll (WA)
Fayetteville Tech Comm Coll
(NC)
Forsyth Tech Comm Coll
(NC)
Fountainhead Coll of
Technology (TN)
Front Range Comm Coll
(CO)
Garden City Comm Coll (KS)
Glendale Comm Coll (AZ)
Grand Rapids Comm Coll
(MI)
Great Basin Coll (NV)
Greenfield Comm Coll (MA)
Guilford Tech Comm Coll
(NC)
Heartland Comm Coll (IL)
Hopkinsville Comm Coll (KY)
Houston Comm Coll System
(TX)
Illinois Eastern Comm Colls,
Wabash Valley Coll (IL)
Ivy Tech State Coll–
Bloomington (IN)
Ivy Tech State Coll–Central
Indiana (IN)
Ivy Tech State Coll–
Columbus (IN)
Ivy Tech State Coll–
Eastcentral (IN)
Ivy Tech State Coll–Kokomo
(IN)
Ivy Tech State Coll–Lafayette
(IN)
Ivy Tech State Coll–North
Central (IN)
Ivy Tech State Coll–
Northeast (IN)
Ivy Tech State Coll–
Southcentral (IN)
Ivy Tech State Coll–
Southeast (IN)
Ivy Tech State Coll–
Southwest (IN)
Ivy Tech State Coll–Wabash
Valley (IN)
Ivy Tech State Coll–
Whitewater (IN)
Jackson State Comm Coll
(TN)
James A. Rhodes State Coll
(OH)
Jefferson Comm Coll (OH)
Kellogg Comm Coll (MI)

Kent State U, Salem
Campus (OH)
Kent State U, Trumbull
Campus (OH)
Kent State U, Tuscarawas
Campus (OH)
Kirkwood Comm Coll (IA)
Kirtland Comm Coll (MI)
Lackawanna Coll (PA)
Lake Land Coll (IL)
Lakeland Comm Coll (OH)
Lanier Tech Coll (GA)
Lansing Comm Coll (MI)
Lehigh Carbon Comm Coll
(PA)
Lenoir Comm Coll (NC)
Linn-Benton Comm Coll
(OR)
Lorain County Comm Coll
(OH)
Los Angeles Pierce Coll (CA)
Los Angeles Trade-Tech Coll
(CA)
Lower Columbia Coll (WA)
Macomb Comm Coll (MI)
Manchester Comm Coll (CT)
Marion Tech Coll (OH)
Miami Dade Coll (FL)
Milwaukee Area Tech Coll
(WI)
Mineral Area Coll (MO)
Minnesota State Coll–
Southeast Tech (MN)
MiraCosta Coll (CA)
Mitchell Comm Coll (NC)
Moberly Area Comm Coll
(MO)
Monroe County Comm Coll
(MI)
Montcalm Comm Coll (MI)
Moraine Park Tech Coll (WI)
Mountain Empire Comm Coll
(VA)
Mount Wachusett Comm Coll
(MA)
Nashville State Tech Comm
Coll (TN)
Naugatuck Valley Comm Coll
(CT)
New Hampshire Comm Tech
Coll, Berlin/Laconia (NH)
New Mexico State U–
Carlsbad (NM)
North Central State Coll (OH)
Northcentral Tech Coll (WI)
North Dakota State Coll of
Science (ND)
Northeast Mississippi Comm
Coll (MS)
Northeast State Tech Comm
Coll (TN)
Northeast Wisconsin Tech
Coll (WI)
North Florida Comm Coll
(FL)
North Hennepin Comm Coll
(MN)
Northland Pioneer Coll (AZ)
Northwestern Michigan Coll
(MI)
Oakland Comm Coll (MI)
Ohio State U Ag Tech Inst
(OH)
Olympic Coll (WA)
Ouachita Tech Coll (AR)
Parkland Coll (IL)
Pellissippi State Tech Comm
Coll (TN)
Pennsylvania Coll of
Technology (PA)
Penn State U York Campus
of the Commonwealth Coll
(PA)
Pensacola Jr Coll (FL)
Pitt Comm Coll (NC)
Pulaski Tech Coll (AR)
Raritan Valley Comm Coll
(NJ)
Reading Area Comm Coll
(PA)
Rend Lake Coll (IL)
Rogue Comm Coll (OR)
Rowan-Cabarrus Comm Coll
(NC)

St. Clair County Comm Coll
(MI)
Saint Paul Coll–A Comm &
Tech College (MN)
St. Petersburg Coll (FL)
San Diego City Coll (CA)
Santa Barbara City Coll (CA)
Schoolcraft Coll (MI)
Seminole Comm Coll (FL)
Sierra Coll (CA)
Sinclair Comm Coll (OH)
Somerset Comm Coll (KY)
South Arkansas Comm Coll
(AR)
Southeast Arkansas Coll
(AR)
Southeastern Comm Coll
(NC)
Southern Arkansas U Tech
(AR)
South Suburban Coll (IL)
South Texas Comm Coll (TX)
Southwestern Oregon Comm
Coll (OR)
Southwest Missouri State
U–West Plains (MO)
Spokane Comm Coll (WA)
Spoon River Coll (IL)
Stanly Comm Coll (NC)
Stark State Coll of
Technology (OH)
State U of NY Coll of
Technology at Canton (NY)
Temple Coll (TX)
Terra State Comm Coll (OH)
Texas State Tech Coll–
Harlingen (TX)
Texas State Tech Coll–
Waco/Marshall Campus
(TX)
Three Rivers Comm Coll
(MO)
Trident Tech Coll (SC)
Trinidad State Jr Coll (CO)
Triton Coll (IL)
Union County Coll (NJ)
U of Arkansas Comm Coll at
Batesville (AR)
Vance-Granville Comm Coll
(NC)
Vermilion Comm Coll (MN)
Washtenaw Comm Coll (MI)
Waubonsee Comm Coll (IL)
Western Nevada Comm Coll
(NV)
West Virginia Northern
Comm Coll (WV)
Wilson Tech Comm Coll (NC)
Yakima Valley Comm Coll
(WA)
Yuba Coll (CA)

**Information Resources
Management**
Mott Comm Coll (MI)

Information Science/Studies
AEC Southern Ohio Coll,
Northern Kentucky
Campus (KY)
Alamance Comm Coll (NC)
Albuquerque Tech Vocational
Inst (NM)
Allentown Business School
(PA)
Alpena Comm Coll (MI)
Amarillo Coll (TX)
Anne Arundel Comm Coll
(MD)
Arapahoe Comm Coll (CO)
Arizona Western Coll (AZ)
Arkansas State U–Beebe
(AR)
Arkansas State U–Mountain
Home (AR)
Atlanta Metropolitan Coll
(GA)
Augusta Tech Coll (GA)
Austin Comm Coll (TX)
Bainbridge Coll (GA)
Barton County Comm Coll
(KS)
Bates Tech Coll (WA)
Beaufort County Comm Coll
(NC)

Bellevue Comm Coll (WA)
Big Bend Comm Coll (WA)
Blue Ridge Comm Coll (NC)
Blue River Comm Coll (MO)
Bristol Comm Coll (MA)
Broome Comm Coll (NY)
Bryant & Stratton Business
Inst, Syracuse (NY)
Bucks County Comm Coll
(PA)
Cañada Coll (CA)
Cape Cod Comm Coll (MA)
Cecil Comm Coll (MD)
Central Alabama Comm Coll
(AL)
Central Georgia Tech Coll
(GA)
Central Pennsylvania Coll
(PA)
Chabot Coll (CA)
Cincinnati State Tech and
Comm Coll (OH)
Clark State Comm Coll (OH)
Cleveland Comm Coll (NC)
Coffeyville Comm Coll (KS)
Coll of Southern Maryland
(MD)
Coll of the Canyons (CA)
Coll of the Sequoias (CA)
The Coll of Westchester (NY)
Columbia-Greene Comm
Coll (NY)
Columbia State Comm Coll
(TN)
Commonwealth Business
Coll, Merrillville (IN)
Comm Coll of Aurora (CO)
Comm Coll of Denver (CO)
Cumberland County Coll
(NJ)
Cuyamaca Coll (CA)
Daytona Beach Comm Coll
(FL)
Delaware County Comm Coll
(PA)
Del Mar Coll (TX)
Delta Coll (MI)
Draughons Jr Coll (KY)
Durham Tech Comm Coll
(NC)
Dutchess Comm Coll (NY)
Eastern Arizona Coll (AZ)
ECPI Coll of Technology,
Newport News (VA)
ECPI Coll of Technology,
Virginia Beach (VA)
ECPI Tech Coll, Richmond
(VA)
ECPI Tech Coll, Roanoke
(VA)
Elaine P. Nunez Comm Coll
(LA)
El Centro Coll (TX)
Elgin Comm Coll (IL)
Elizabethtown Comm Coll
(KY)
Erie Comm Coll (NY)
Essex County Coll (NJ)
Fayetteville Tech Comm Coll
(NC)
Fiorello H LaGuardia Comm
Coll of City U of NY (NY)
Fulton-Montgomery Comm
Coll (NY)
Garden City Comm Coll (KS)
Gaston Coll (NC)
Gavilan Coll (CA)
Gem City Coll (IL)
Gloucester County Coll (NJ)
Greenfield Comm Coll (MA)
Green River Comm Coll
(WA)
Guilford Tech Comm Coll
(NC)
Harcum Coll (PA)
Heartland Comm Coll (IL)
Hesser Coll (NH)
Hill Coll of the Hill Jr College
District (TX)
Hillsborough Comm Coll (FL)
Holyoke Comm Coll (MA)
Howard Comm Coll (MD)
James A. Rhodes State Coll
(OH)

Jefferson Comm Coll (NY)
J. F. Drake State Tech Coll
(AL)
John A. Logan Coll (IL)
Kingwood Coll (TX)
Kirtland Comm Coll (MI)
Lakeland Comm Coll (OH)
Lamar State Coll–Orange
(TX)
Lansing Comm Coll (MI)
Laredo Comm Coll (TX)
Lawson State Comm Coll
(AL)
Lehigh Carbon Comm Coll
(PA)
Linn State Tech Coll (MO)
Lorain County Comm Coll
(OH)
Lord Fairfax Comm Coll (VA)
Los Angeles Harbor Coll
(CA)
Los Angeles Trade-Tech Coll
(CA)
Los Angeles Valley Coll (CA)
Louisiana Tech Coll–Florida
Parishes Campus (LA)
Lower Columbia Coll (WA)
Manatee Comm Coll (FL)
Manchester Comm Coll (CT)
McIntosh Coll (NH)
McLennan Comm Coll (TX)
Merritt Coll (CA)
Mesalands Comm Coll (NM)
Metropolitan Comm
Coll-Business &
Technology College (MO)
Miami Dade Coll (FL)
Middle Georgia Coll (GA)
Middlesex County Coll (NJ)
Mid Michigan Comm Coll
(MI)
Minneapolis Comm and Tech
Coll (MN)
Minnesota School of
Business-Richfield (MN)
Minot State U–Bottineau
Campus (ND)
MiraCosta Coll (CA)
Mitchell Tech Inst (SD)
Monroe Coll, Bronx (NY)
Monroe Coll, New Rochelle
(NY)
Montgomery County Comm
Coll (PA)
Mountain Empire Comm Coll
(VA)
Mountain View Coll (TX)
Mountain West Coll (UT)
Mount Wachusett Comm Coll
(MA)
Nashville State Tech Comm
Coll (TN)
Naugatuck Valley Comm Coll
(CT)
New Hampshire Comm Tech
Coll, Manchester/Stratham
(NH)
New Mexico State U–
Carlsbad (NM)
New River Comm Coll (VA)
Niagara County Comm Coll
(NY)
North Central State Coll (OH)
Northcentral Tech Coll (WI)
Northeast Alabama Comm
Coll (AL)
Northeast Mississippi Comm
Coll (MS)
Northeast Texas Comm Coll
(TX)
North Harris Coll (TX)
Northland Pioneer Coll (AZ)
North Seattle Comm Coll
(WA)
North Shore Comm Coll
(MA)
Northwest Coll (WY)
Northwestern Connecticut
Comm-Tech Coll (CT)
Northwest-Shoals Comm
Coll (AL)
Oakton Comm Coll (IL)
Ocean County Coll (NJ)
Odessa Coll (TX)

Olympic Coll (WA)
Orange Coast Coll (CA)
Orange County Comm Coll
(NY)
Oxnard Coll (CA)
Ozarka Coll (AR)
Palo Alto Coll (TX)
Palomar Coll (CA)
Panola Coll (TX)
Paris Jr Coll (TX)
Parkland Coll (IL)
Pasadena City Coll (CA)
Penn State U Beaver
Campus of the
Commonwealth Coll (PA)
Penn State U DuBois
Campus of the
Commonwealth Coll (PA)
Penn State U Fayette
Campus of the
Commonwealth Coll (PA)
Penn State U Hazleton
Campus of the
Commonwealth Coll (PA)
Penn State U Mont Alto
Campus of the
Commonwealth Coll (PA)
Penn State U New
Kensington Campus of the
Commonwealth Coll (PA)
Penn State U Shenango
Campus of the
Commonwealth Coll (PA)
Penn State U Wilkes-Barre
Campus of the
Commonwealth Coll (PA)
Penn State U Worthington
Scranton Cmps
Commonwealth Coll (PA)
Penn State U York Campus
of the Commonwealth Coll
(PA)
Pensacola Jr Coll (FL)
Phoenix Coll (AZ)
Pioneer Pacific Coll (OR)
Platt Coll, Newport Beach
(CA)
Polk Comm Coll (FL)
Portland Comm Coll (OR)
Prince George's Comm Coll
(MD)
Pulaski Tech Coll (AR)
Queensborough Comm Coll
of City U of NY (NY)
Quinsigamond Comm Coll
(MA)
Raritan Valley Comm Coll
(NJ)
Reading Area Comm Coll
(PA)
Remington Coll–Mobile
Campus (AL)
Rockingham Comm Coll
(NC)
Rowan-Cabarrus Comm Coll
(NC)
St. Clair County Comm Coll
(MI)
St. Louis Comm Coll at
Florissant Valley (MO)
St. Petersburg Coll (FL)
San Juan Coll (NM)
Santa Barbara City Coll (CA)
Santa Monica Coll (CA)
Scottsdale Comm Coll (AZ)
Seminole Comm Coll (FL)
Sheridan Coll (WY)
Sierra Coll (CA)
Sinclair Comm Coll (OH)
Sisseton-Wahpeton Comm
Coll (SD)
Snow Coll (UT)
South Coll (TN)
Southern Maine Comm Coll
(ME)
Southern West Virginia
Comm and Tech Coll (WV)
South Puget Sound Comm
Coll (WA)
Southside Virginia Comm
Coll (VA)
South Suburban Coll (IL)
South Texas Comm Coll (TX)
South U (FL)

Southwestern Coll (CA)
Southwestern Comm Coll (NC)
Southwestern Illinois Coll (IL)
Spokane Falls Comm Coll (WA)
Spoon River Coll (IL)
Stanly Comm Coll (NC)
State U of NY Coll of A&T at Morrisville (NY)
State U of NY Coll of Technology at Canton (NY)
State U of NY Coll of Technology at Delhi (NY)
Sullivan County Comm Coll (NY)
Terra State Comm Coll (OH)
Texas State Tech Coll–Waco/Marshall Campus (TX)
Thomas Nelson Comm Coll (VA)
Tompkins Cortland Comm Coll (NY)
Trenholm State Tech Coll, Montgomery (AL)
Trinidad State Jr Coll (CO)
Triton Coll (IL)
Union County Coll (NJ)
U of Kentucky, Lexington Comm Coll (KY)
Ventura Coll (CA)
Victor Valley Coll (CA)
Vincennes U (IN)
Washtenaw Comm Coll (MI)
Weatherford Coll (TX)
Western Wyoming Comm Coll (WY)
West Hills Comm Coll (CA)
West Kentucky Comm and Tech Coll (KY)
Westmoreland County Comm Coll (PA)
Wilson Tech Comm Coll (NC)
Yavapai Coll (AZ)

Information Technology
Arkansas State U–Beebe (AR)
Atlanta Metropolitan Coll (GA)
Austin Comm Coll (TX)
Big Sandy Comm and Tech Coll (KY)
Bladen Comm Coll (NC)
Bristol Comm Coll (MA)
The Brown Mackie Coll–Lenexa Campus (KS)
Bryant & Stratton Business Inst, Syracuse (NY)
Bucks County Comm Coll (PA)
Burlington County Coll (NJ)
Caldwell Comm Coll and Tech Inst (NC)
Camden County Coll (NJ)
Cape Cod Comm Coll (MA)
Capital Comm Coll (CT)
Carteret Comm Coll (NC)
Cecil Comm Coll (MD)
Central Comm Coll–Columbus Campus (NE)
Central Comm Coll–Grand Island Campus (NE)
Central Comm Coll–Hastings Campus (NE)
Clark State Comm Coll (OH)
Cleveland Comm Coll (NC)
Coastal Bend Coll (TX)
The Coll of Westchester (NY)
Corning Comm Coll (NY)
Cuesta Coll (CA)
Davis Coll (OH)
Daytona Beach Comm Coll (FL)
Del Mar Coll (TX)
Delta Coll (MI)
Draughons Jr Coll (KY)
Durham Tech Comm Coll (NC)
Edgecombe Comm Coll (NC)
Edison Comm Coll (FL)
El Centro Coll (TX)
Fayetteville Tech Comm Coll (NC)

Galveston Coll (TX)
Gavilan Coll (CA)
Globe Coll (MN)
Gogebic Comm Coll (MI)
Gordon Coll (GA)
Harrisburg Area Comm Coll (PA)
Hawkeye Comm Coll (IA)
Heartland Comm Coll (IL)
Henderson Comm Coll (KY)
Hinds Comm Coll (MS)
Howard Comm Coll (MD)
Indiana Business Coll, Columbus (IN)
Indiana Business Coll, Evansville (IN)
Indiana Business Coll, Indianapolis (IN)
Indiana Business Coll, Lafayette (IN)
Indiana Business Coll, Muncie (IN)
Indiana Business Coll, Terre Haute (IN)
International Inst of the Americas, Phoenix (AZ)
Iowa Lakes Comm Coll (IA)
ITI Tech Coll (LA)
James A. Rhodes State Coll (OH)
J. Sargeant Reynolds Comm Coll (VA)
Kaplan Coll (IA)
Keystone Coll (PA)
Kilian Comm Coll (SD)
Lake Area Tech Inst (SD)
Lake Land Coll (IL)
Lake Region State Coll (ND)
Laramie County Comm Coll (WY)
Laredo Comm Coll (TX)
LDS Business Coll (UT)
Lorain County Comm Coll (OH)
Louisville Tech Inst (KY)
Lower Columbia Coll (WA)
Marion Tech Coll (OH)
Mayland Comm Coll (NC)
Mesabi Range Comm and Tech Coll (MN)
Metropolitan Comm Coll-Business & Technology College (MO)
Mildred Elley (NY)
Miles Comm Coll (MT)
Milwaukee Area Tech Coll (WI)
Minnesota School of Business–Brooklyn Center (MN)
Minnesota School of Business-Plymouth (MN)
Minot State U–Bottineau Campus (ND)
Mississippi Gulf Coast Comm Coll (MS)
Mohave Comm Coll (AZ)
Monroe County Comm Coll (MI)
Mountain Empire Comm Coll (VA)
Nash Comm Coll (NC)
Naugatuck Valley Comm Coll (CT)
Nebraska Indian Comm Coll (NE)
Ohio Valley Coll of Technology (OH)
Olympic Coll (WA)
Orange County Comm Coll (NY)
Owensboro Comm and Tech Coll (KY)
Palo Alto Coll (TX)
Pasco-Hernando Comm Coll (FL)
Pennsylvania Coll of Technology (PA)
Platt Coll, Newport Beach (CA)
Queensborough Comm Coll of City U of NY (NY)
St. Cloud Tech Coll (MN)
Santa Barbara City Coll (CA)

Schenectady County Comm Coll (NY)
Seminole Comm Coll (FL)
Silicon Valley Coll, Walnut Creek (CA)
Sinclair Comm Coll (OH)
Somerset Comm Coll (KY)
Southeast Comm Coll (KY)
Southside Virginia Comm Coll (VA)
South U (FL)
South U (SC)
Southwestern Coll (CA)
Southwest Mississippi Comm Coll (MS)
Spartanburg Methodist Coll (SC)
Stark State Coll of Technology (OH)
Texas State Tech Coll–Harlingen (TX)
Three Rivers Comm Coll (MO)
Tri-County Comm Coll (NC)
Trinidad State Jr Coll (CO)
U of Arkansas Comm Coll at Batesville (AR)
Vatterott Coll, Oklahoma City (OK)
Vincennes U (IN)
Walters State Comm Coll (TN)
Western Wyoming Comm Coll (WY)
West Virginia Northern Comm Coll (WV)
Williamsburg Tech Coll (SC)
York Tech Inst (PA)

Institutional Food Workers
The Art Inst of Pittsburgh (PA)
Asheville-Buncombe Tech Comm Coll (NC)
Cape Fear Comm Coll (NC)
Delgado Comm Coll (LA)
Elaine P. Nunez Comm Coll (LA)
Harrisburg Area Comm Coll (PA)
Iowa Lakes Comm Coll (IA)
Jefferson Coll (MO)
MiraCosta Coll (CA)
Pennsylvania Coll of Technology (PA)
Santa Barbara City Coll (CA)
Texas State Tech Coll–Harlingen (TX)
Texas State Tech Coll–Waco/Marshall Campus (TX)
West Virginia Northern Comm Coll (WV)

Instrumentation Technology
Amarillo Coll (TX)
Cape Fear Comm Coll (NC)
Chabot Coll (CA)
Colorado Northwestern Comm Coll (CO)
Comm Coll of Rhode Island (RI)
Copiah-Lincoln Comm Coll–Natchez Campus (MS)
DeKalb Tech Coll (GA)
East Mississippi Comm Coll (MS)
ITI Tech Coll (LA)
Lamar State Coll–Port Arthur (TX)
Lenoir Comm Coll (NC)
Louisiana Tech Coll–Northwest Louisiana Campus (LA)
Lower Columbia Coll (WA)
Mesabi Range Comm and Tech Coll (MN)
Moraine Valley Comm Coll (IL)
Nassau Comm Coll (NY)
New River Comm Coll (VA)
Northeast State Tech Comm Coll (TN)

Northeast Wisconsin Tech Coll (WI)
Northern Maine Comm Coll (ME)
Orangeburg-Calhoun Tech Coll (SC)
Pennsylvania Coll of Technology (PA)
St. Cloud Tech Coll (MN)
San Juan Coll (NM)
Southwestern Illinois Coll (IL)
Texas State Tech Coll–Harlingen (TX)
Texas State Tech Coll–Waco/Marshall Campus (TX)
Trenholm State Tech Coll, Montgomery (AL)
U of Alaska Anchorage, Kenai Peninsula Coll (AK)
Western Wyoming Comm Coll (WY)
Yakima Valley Comm Coll (WA)

Insurance
Austin Comm Coll (TX)
Central Piedmont Comm Coll (NC)
Comm Coll of Allegheny County (PA)
Daytona Beach Comm Coll (FL)
Houston Comm Coll System (TX)
Isothermal Comm Coll (NC)
Lenoir Comm Coll (NC)
Nassau Comm Coll (NY)
Northeast Mississippi Comm Coll (MS)
Oklahoma City Comm Coll (OK)
San Diego City Coll (CA)

Interdisciplinary Studies
Bowling Green State U-Firelands Coll (OH)
Chabot Coll (CA)
Columbia-Greene Comm Coll (NY)
County Coll of Morris (NJ)
Del Mar Coll (TX)
Great Basin Coll (NV)
Harcum Coll (PA)
Hawkeye Comm Coll (IA)
Jefferson Coll (MO)
Jefferson Comm Coll (NY)
Mt. San Jacinto Coll (CA)
North Country Comm Coll (NY)
North Shore Comm Coll (MA)
Pasadena City Coll (CA)
South Texas Comm Coll (TX)
State U of NY Coll of Technology at Canton (NY)
Triton Coll (IL)
The U of Akron–Wayne Coll (OH)
U of South Carolina at Sumter (SC)
Vermilion Comm Coll (MN)
Walters State Comm Coll (TN)

Interior Architecture
Delgado Comm Coll (LA)
Lehigh Carbon Comm Coll (PA)
Northampton County Area Comm Coll (PA)
St. Philip's Coll (TX)

Interior Design
Alexandria Tech Coll (MN)
Amarillo Coll (TX)
American River Coll (CA)
Antonelli Coll (OH)
The Art Inst of Houston (TX)
The Art Inst of Philadelphia (PA)
The Art Inst of Pittsburgh (PA)
The Art Inst of Seattle (WA)
The Art Insts International Minnesota (MN)

Bellevue Comm Coll (WA)
Berkeley Coll (NJ)
Brookdale Comm Coll (NJ)
Cañada Coll (CA)
Cape Fear Comm Coll (NC)
Carteret Comm Coll (NC)
Central Piedmont Comm Coll (NC)
Century Coll (MN)
Clover Park Tech Coll (WA)
Coll of DuPage (IL)
Coll of the Canyons (CA)
Coll of the Desert (CA)
Coll of the Sequoias (CA)
Collin County Comm Coll District (TX)
Cuesta Coll (CA)
Dakota County Tech Coll (MN)
Davis Coll (OH)
Daytona Beach Comm Coll (FL)
Delta Coll (MI)
El Camino Coll (CA)
El Centro Coll (TX)
Fashion Inst of Design & Merchandising, LA Campus (CA)
Fashion Inst of Design & Merchandising, SD Campus (CA)
Fashion Inst of Design & Merchandising, SF Campus (CA)
Garden City Comm Coll (KS)
Gwinnett Tech Coll (GA)
Harcum Coll (PA)
Harford Comm Coll (MD)
Hawkeye Comm Coll (IA)
Hesser Coll (NH)
Hillsborough Comm Coll (FL)
Houston Comm Coll System (TX)
IntelliTec Coll, Colorado Springs (CO)
Ivy Tech State Coll–North Central (IN)
Ivy Tech State Coll–Southwest (IN)
Kirkwood Comm Coll (IA)
LDS Business Coll (UT)
Los Angeles Valley Coll (CA)
Louisville Tech Inst (KY)
Metropolitan Comm Coll (NE)
Miami Dade Coll (FL)
Modesto Jr Coll (CA)
Montana State U Coll of Tech-Great Falls (MT)
Mt. San Antonio Coll (CA)
Nassau Comm Coll (NY)
Northeast Mississippi Comm Coll (MS)
North Harris Coll (TX)
Oakland Comm Coll (MI)
Orange Coast Coll (CA)
Palm Beach Comm Coll (FL)
Palomar Coll (CA)
Pasadena City Coll (CA)
Patricia Stevens Coll (MO)
Pellissippi State Tech Comm Coll (TN)
Phoenix Coll (AZ)
Pikes Peak Comm Coll (CO)
St. Philip's Coll (TX)
San Diego City Coll (CA)
San Joaquin Delta Coll (CA)
Santa Barbara City Coll (CA)
Santa Fe Comm Coll (NM)
Santa Monica Coll (CA)
Scottsdale Comm Coll (AZ)
Seminole Comm Coll (FL)
Sierra Coll (CA)
Sinclair Comm Coll (OH)
Spokane Falls Comm Coll (WA)
Triton Coll (IL)
Villa Maria Coll of Buffalo (NY)
Vincennes U (IN)
Western Wisconsin Tech Coll (WI)

Intermedia/Multimedia
Academy Coll (MN)
The Art Inst of Houston (TX)
The Art Inst of Philadelphia (PA)
The Art Inst of Pittsburgh (PA)
The Art Inst of Seattle (WA)
The Art Insts International Minnesota (MN)
Bristol Comm Coll (MA)
Comm Coll of Denver (CO)
Full Sail Real World Education (FL)
Globe Coll (MN)
Hillsborough Comm Coll (FL)
Middlesex Comm Coll (CT)
Minnesota School of Business–Brooklyn Center (MN)
Minnesota School of Business-Plymouth (MN)
Minnesota School of Business-Richfield (MN)
Platt Coll San Diego (CA)
Raritan Valley Comm Coll (NJ)
Westwood Coll–Anaheim (CA)
Westwood Coll–Atlanta Campus (GA)
Westwood Coll–Chicago Du Page (IL)
Westwood Coll–Chicago O'Hare Airport (IL)
Westwood Coll–Chicago River Oaks (IL)
Westwood Coll–Denver South (CO)
Westwood Coll–Fort Worth (TX)
Westwood Coll–Inland Empire (CA)
Westwood Coll–Los Angeles (CA)
Westwood Coll–Chicago Loop Campus (IL)

International Business/Trade/Commerce
Berkeley Coll (NJ)
Berkeley Coll-New York City Campus (NY)
Berkeley Coll-Westchester Campus (NY)
Brevard Comm Coll (FL)
Bunker Hill Comm Coll (MA)
Cincinnati State Tech and Comm Coll (OH)
Edmonds Comm Coll (WA)
Foothill Coll (CA)
Frederick Comm Coll (MD)
Kansas City Kansas Comm Coll (KS)
Kirkwood Comm Coll (IA)
Lansing Comm Coll (MI)
Laredo Comm Coll (TX)
Luzerne County Comm Coll (PA)
MacCormac Coll (IL)
Mott Comm Coll (MI)
Oakland Comm Coll (MI)
Oakton Comm Coll (IL)
Palomar Coll (CA)
Pima Comm Coll (AZ)
Raritan Valley Comm Coll (NJ)
Saint Paul Coll–A Comm & Tech College (MN)
Schiller International USwitzerland)
Spokane Falls Comm Coll (WA)
Stark State Coll of Technology (OH)
Tompkins Cortland Comm Coll (NY)
Triton Coll (IL)
Vincennes U (IN)

International Finance
Broome Comm Coll (NY)

International/Global Studies
Macomb Comm Coll (MI)

International Relations and Affairs
Bronx Comm Coll of City U of NY (NY)
Brookdale Comm Coll (NJ)
Harrisburg Area Comm Coll (PA)
Kellogg Comm Coll (MI)
Miami Dade Coll (FL)
Naugatuck Valley Comm Coll (CT)
Northern Essex Comm Coll (MA)
Santa Barbara City Coll (CA)
Western Wyoming Comm Coll (WY)

Ironworking
Ivy Tech State Coll–Lafayette (IN)
Ivy Tech State Coll–North Central (IN)
Ivy Tech State Coll–Northeast (IN)
Ivy Tech State Coll–Northwest (IN)
Ivy Tech State Coll–Southwest (IN)
Ivy Tech State Coll–Wabash Valley (IN)

Italian
Casper Coll (WY)
Chabot Coll (CA)
Coll of the Desert (CA)
Contra Costa Coll (CA)
El Camino Coll (CA)
Los Angeles Valley Coll (CA)
Miami Dade Coll (FL)
San Joaquin Delta Coll (CA)
Triton Coll (IL)

Japanese
Austin Comm Coll (TX)
East Los Angeles Coll (CA)
El Camino Coll (CA)
Everett Comm Coll (WA)
Foothill Coll (CA)
MiraCosta Coll (CA)
San Joaquin Delta Coll (CA)
Snow Coll (UT)

Jazz/Jazz Studies
Iowa Lakes Comm Coll (IA)
Kirkwood Comm Coll (IA)
Lincoln Coll, Lincoln (IL)
Manatee Comm Coll (FL)

Jewish/Judaic Studies
Manatee Comm Coll (FL)

Journalism
Abraham Baldwin Ag Coll (GA)
Amarillo Coll (TX)
American River Coll (CA)
Andrew Coll (GA)
Austin Comm Coll (TX)
Bainbridge Coll (GA)
Barton County Comm Coll (KS)
Brookdale Comm Coll (NJ)
Bucks County Comm Coll (PA)
Burlington County Coll (NJ)
Butler County Comm Coll (KS)
Cañada Coll (CA)
Casper Coll (WY)
Chabot Coll (CA)
City Colls of Chicago, Wilbur Wright Coll (IL)
Coastal Bend Coll (TX)
Coffeyville Comm Coll (KS)
Colby Comm Coll (KS)
Coll of the Canyons (CA)
Coll of the Desert (CA)
Coll of the Sequoias (CA)
Comm Coll of Allegheny County (PA)
Connors State Coll (OK)
Contra Costa Coll (CA)
Copiah-Lincoln Comm Coll (MS)
Cuesta Coll (CA)
Darton Coll (GA)

Daytona Beach Comm Coll (FL)
Delaware County Comm Coll (PA)
Del Mar Coll (TX)
Delta Coll (MI)
Eastern Oklahoma State Coll (OK)
East Los Angeles Coll (CA)
El Camino Coll (CA)
Everett Comm Coll (WA)
Garden City Comm Coll (KS)
Gavilan Coll (CA)
Georgia Perimeter Coll (GA)
Gordon Coll (GA)
Harrisburg Area Comm Coll (PA)
Hill Coll of the Hill Jr College District (TX)
Hinds Comm Coll (MS)
Iowa Lakes Comm Coll (IA)
Jefferson Coll (MO)
John A. Logan Coll (IL)
Kellogg Comm Coll (MI)
Keystone Coll (PA)
Kingsborough Comm Coll of City U of NY (NY)
Kirkwood Comm Coll (IA)
Lansing Comm Coll (MI)
Laramie County Comm Coll (WY)
Lincoln Coll, Lincoln (IL)
Linn-Benton Comm Coll (OR)
Lorain County Comm Coll (OH)
Los Angeles Pierce Coll (CA)
Los Angeles Trade-Tech Coll (CA)
Los Angeles Valley Coll (CA)
Luzerne County Comm Coll (PA)
Manatee Comm Coll (FL)
Manchester Comm Coll (CT)
Miami Dade Coll (FL)
Middlesex County Coll (NJ)
Midland Coll (TX)
MiraCosta Coll (CA)
Monroe County Comm Coll (MI)
Mt. San Antonio Coll (CA)
Northampton County Area Comm Coll (PA)
Northeast Comm Coll (NE)
Northeastern Oklahoma A&M Coll (OK)
Northeast Mississippi Comm Coll (MS)
Northern Essex Comm Coll (MA)
North Harris Coll (TX)
North Idaho Coll (ID)
Northwest Coll (WY)
Ocean County Coll (NJ)
Orange Coast Coll (CA)
Oxnard Coll (CA)
Palm Beach Comm Coll (FL)
Palo Alto Coll (TX)
Palomar Coll (CA)
Pasadena City Coll (CA)
Pensacola Jr Coll (FL)
Pima Comm Coll (AZ)
Riverside Comm Coll (CA)
St. Clair County Comm Coll (MI)
St. Louis Comm Coll at Florissant Valley (MO)
Salem Comm Coll (NJ)
San Diego City Coll (CA)
San Joaquin Delta Coll (CA)
Santa Monica Coll (CA)
Seward County Comm Coll (KS)
Sierra Coll (CA)
Southeast Comm Coll, Beatrice Campus (NE)
South Plains Coll (TX)
Southwestern Coll (CA)
State U of NY Coll of A&T at Morrisville (NY)
Sussex County Comm Coll (NJ)
Trinidad State Jr Coll (CO)
Triton Coll (IL)

Umpqua Comm Coll (OR)
Ventura Coll (CA)
Vincennes U (IN)
Western Wyoming Comm Coll (WY)

Journalism Related
Rogue Comm Coll (OR)

Juvenile Corrections
Linn-Benton Comm Coll (OR)

Kindergarten/Preschool Education
Abraham Baldwin Ag Coll (GA)
Alamance Comm Coll (NC)
American River Coll (CA)
Andover Coll (ME)
Anne Arundel Comm Coll (MD)
Asnuntuck Comm Coll (CT)
Bainbridge Coll (GA)
Bay State Coll (MA)
Beaufort County Comm Coll (NC)
Bellevue Comm Coll (WA)
Bergen Comm Coll (NJ)
Blackfeet Comm Coll (MT)
Blue Ridge Comm Coll (NC)
Borough of Manhattan Comm Coll of City U of NY (NY)
Brookdale Comm Coll (NJ)
Bucks County Comm Coll (PA)
Butler County Comm Coll (KS)
Butte Coll (CA)
Cabrillo Coll (CA)
Camden County Coll (NJ)
Cañada Coll (CA)
Cape Cod Comm Coll (MA)
Capital Comm Coll (CT)
Casper Coll (WY)
Cecil Comm Coll (MD)
Central Arizona Coll (AZ)
Centralia Coll (WA)
Central Piedmont Comm Coll (NC)
Chabot Coll (CA)
Chatfield Coll (OH)
Chemeketa Comm Coll (OR)
Chesapeake Coll (MD)
Clark State Comm Coll (OH)
Cleveland State Comm Coll (TN)
Colby Comm Coll (KS)
Coll of Eastern Utah (UT)
Coll of Southern Maryland (MD)
Coll of the Canyons (CA)
Coll of the Desert (CA)
Coll of the Sequoias (CA)
Colorado Mountn Coll, Timberline Cmps (CO)
Columbia State Comm Coll (TN)
Columbus State Comm Coll (OH)
Comm Coll of Aurora (CO)
Comm Coll of Denver (CO)
Comm Coll of Rhode Island (RI)
Contra Costa Coll (CA)
County Coll of Morris (NJ)
Cuesta Coll (CA)
Cumberland County Coll (NJ)
Cuyahoga Comm Coll (OH)
Daytona Beach Comm Coll (FL)
Delaware Tech & Comm Coll, Terry Cmps (DE)
Delgado Comm Coll (LA)
Del Mar Coll (TX)
Donnelly Coll (KS)
Durham Tech Comm Coll (NC)
Dutchess Comm Coll (NY)
Eastern Maine Comm Coll (ME)
Edgecombe Comm Coll (NC)
Edison State Comm Coll (OH)

Elaine P. Nunez Comm Coll (LA)
El Camino Coll (CA)
Elgin Comm Coll (IL)
Essex County Coll (NJ)
Eugenio María de Hostos Comm Coll of City U of NY (NY)
Everett Comm Coll (WA)
Fayetteville Tech Comm Coll (NC)
Finger Lakes Comm Coll (NY)
Fiorello H LaGuardia Comm Coll of City U of NY (NY)
Fisher Coll (MA)
Forsyth Tech Comm Coll (NC)
Frederick Comm Coll (MD)
Fulton-Montgomery Comm Coll (NY)
Gaston Coll (NC)
Gavilan Coll (CA)
Glendale Comm Coll (AZ)
Gogebic Comm Coll (MI)
Great Basin Coll (NV)
Greenfield Comm Coll (MA)
Guilford Tech Comm Coll (NC)
Harcum Coll (PA)
Harrisburg Area Comm Coll (PA)
Hawaii Comm Coll (HI)
Heartland Comm Coll (IL)
Hesser Coll (NH)
Hesston Coll (KS)
Holyoke Comm Coll (MA)
Honolulu Comm Coll (HI)
Hopkinsville Comm Coll (KY)
Howard Comm Coll (MD)
Iowa Lakes Comm Coll (IA)
Isothermal Comm Coll (NC)
James Sprunt Comm Coll (NC)
Jefferson Coll (MO)
Jefferson Comm Coll (NY)
John A. Logan Coll (IL)
Johnston Comm Coll (NC)
Kauai Comm Coll (HI)
Kellogg Comm Coll (MI)
Kent State U, Salem Campus (OH)
Keystone Coll (PA)
Kirkwood Comm Coll (IA)
Lakeland Comm Coll (OH)
Lansing Comm Coll (MI)
Lehigh Carbon Comm Coll (PA)
Lewis and Clark Comm Coll (IL)
Lincoln Coll, Lincoln (IL)
Lorain County Comm Coll (OH)
Los Angeles Valley Coll (CA)
Louisiana Tech Coll–Natchitoches Campus (LA)
Lower Columbia Coll (WA)
Manatee Comm Coll (FL)
Manchester Comm Coll (CT)
Mayland Comm Coll (NC)
McIntosh Coll (NH)
McLennan Comm Coll (TX)
Merritt Coll (CA)
Metropolitan Comm Coll (NE)
Miami Dade Coll (FL)
Middlesex Comm Coll (MA)
Middlesex County Coll (NJ)
Minnesota State Coll–Southeast Tech (MN)
MiraCosta Coll (CA)
Mississippi Gulf Coast Comm Coll (MS)
Mitchell Comm Coll (NC)
Modesto Jr Coll (CA)
Mt. San Antonio Coll (CA)
Mt. San Jacinto Coll (CA)
Napa Valley Coll (CA)
Nash Comm Coll (NC)
Nashville State Tech Comm Coll (TN)
Nassau Comm Coll (NY)
Naugatuck Valley Comm Coll (CT)

New Hampshire Comm Tech Coll, Berlin/Laconia (NH)
New Hampshire Comm Tech Coll, Manchester/Stratham (NH)
New Hampshire Tech Inst (NH)
North Central State Coll (OH)
Northcentral Tech Coll (WI)
Northeast Mississippi Comm Coll (MS)
Northeast State Tech Comm Coll (TN)
Northern Essex Comm Coll (MA)
Northern Maine Comm Coll (ME)
Northland Pioneer Coll (AZ)
North Shore Comm Coll (MA)
Northwest Coll (WY)
Northwestern Connecticut Comm-Tech Coll (CT)
Oakton Comm Coll (IL)
Odessa Coll (TX)
Orangeburg-Calhoun Tech Coll (SC)
Orange Coast Coll (CA)
Otero Jr Coll (CO)
Owensboro Comm and Tech Coll (KY)
Oxnard Coll (CA)
Palm Beach Comm Coll (FL)
Palomar Coll (CA)
Pasadena City Coll (CA)
Penn Valley Comm Coll (MO)
Pensacola Jr Coll (FL)
Pratt Comm Coll and Area Vocational School (KS)
Prince George's Comm Coll (MD)
Quinsigamond Comm Coll (MA)
Raritan Valley Comm Coll (NJ)
Reading Area Comm Coll (PA)
Riverside Comm Coll (CA)
Roane State Comm Coll (TN)
Roanoke-Chowan Comm Coll (NC)
Rowan-Cabarrus Comm Coll (NC)
St. Cloud Tech Coll (MN)
St. Petersburg Coll (FL)
San Joaquin Delta Coll (CA)
San Jose City Coll (CA)
San Juan Coll (NM)
Santa Barbara City Coll (CA)
Santa Fe Comm Coll (NM)
Santa Monica Coll (CA)
Scottsdale Comm Coll (AZ)
Shelton State Comm Coll (AL)
Sierra Coll (CA)
Sinclair Comm Coll (OH)
Sisseton-Wahpeton Comm Coll (SD)
Snow Coll (UT)
Southeastern Comm Coll (NC)
Southern Maine Comm Coll (ME)
Southern State Comm Coll (OH)
South Puget Sound Comm Coll (WA)
South Suburban Coll (IL)
Southwestern Coll (CA)
Southwestern Oregon Comm Coll (OR)
Spoon River Coll (IL)
Springfield Tech Comm Coll (MA)
State U of NY Coll of Technology at Canton (NY)
Sullivan County Comm Coll (NY)
Terra State Comm Coll (OH)
Thomas Nelson Comm Coll (VA)
Tidewater Comm Coll (VA)

Tompkins Cortland Comm Coll (NY)
Trinidad State Jr Coll (CO)
Triton Coll (IL)
Umpqua Comm Coll (OR)
United Tribes Tech Coll (ND)
U of Arkansas Comm Coll at Batesville (AR)
Urban Coll of Boston (MA)
Vance-Granville Comm Coll (NC)
Ventura Coll (CA)
Vermilion Comm Coll (MN)
Victor Valley Coll (CA)
Villa Maria Coll of Buffalo (NY)
Vincennes U (IN)
Virginia Western Comm Coll (VA)
Washtenaw Comm Coll (MI)
Waubonsee Comm Coll (IL)
West Hills Comm Coll (CA)
Wilson Tech Comm Coll (NC)
Yakima Valley Comm Coll (WA)
York County Comm Coll (ME)
Yuba Coll (CA)

Kinesiology and Exercise Science
Barton County Comm Coll (KS)
Bergen Comm Coll (NJ)
Camden County Coll (NJ)
Cañada Coll (CA)
Central Oregon Comm Coll (OR)
Clarendon Coll (TX)
Clark State Comm Coll (OH)
Columbia-Greene Comm Coll (NY)
County Coll of Morris (NJ)
Globe Coll (MN)
Gloucester County Coll (NJ)
Hiwassee Coll (TN)
Houston Comm Coll System (TX)
Minnesota School of Business-Plymouth (MN)
Minnesota School of Business-Richfield (MN)
Mount Wachusett Comm Coll (MA)
Naugatuck Valley Comm Coll (CT)
New Hampshire Comm Tech Coll, Manchester/Stratham (NH)
North Country Comm Coll (NY)
Northeast Mississippi Comm Coll (MS)
Northwest Coll (WY)
Oakland Comm Coll (MI)
Orange Coast Coll (CA)
Orange County Comm Coll (NY)
St. Philip's Coll (TX)
Salem Comm Coll (NJ)
Santa Barbara City Coll (CA)
Vincennes U (IN)
Western Wyoming Comm Coll (WY)

Labor and Industrial Relations
Comm Coll of Rhode Island (RI)
El Camino Coll (CA)
Kingsborough Comm Coll of City U of NY (NY)
Lansing Comm Coll (MI)
Los Angeles Trade-Tech Coll (CA)
Rockingham Comm Coll (NC)
San Diego City Coll (CA)
San Jose City Coll (CA)
Sinclair Comm Coll (OH)

Landscape Architecture
American River Coll (CA)
Anne Arundel Comm Coll (MD)
Butte Coll (CA)

Columbus State Comm Coll (OH)
Foothill Coll (CA)
Keystone Coll (PA)
Kirkwood Comm Coll (IA)
Lansing Comm Coll (MI)
Lenoir Comm Coll (NC)
Los Angeles Pierce Coll (CA)
Merritt Coll (CA)
Modesto Jr Coll (CA)
Mt. San Antonio Coll (CA)
Northeast Mississippi Comm Coll (MS)
Oakland Comm Coll (MI)
Oklahoma State U, Oklahoma City (OK)
Pasadena City Coll (CA)
Portland Comm Coll (OR)
Riverside Comm Coll (CA)
Southwestern Coll (CA)
State U of NY Coll of A&T at Morrisville (NY)
State U of NY Coll of Technology at Delhi (NY)
Trinidad State Jr Coll (CO)
Triton Coll (IL)
Ventura Coll (CA)
Vincennes U (IN)

Landscaping and Groundskeeping
Abraham Baldwin Ag Coll (GA)
Anoka Tech Coll (MN)
Caldwell Comm Coll and Tech Inst (NC)
Cape Fear Comm Coll (NC)
Chabot Coll (CA)
Cincinnati State Tech and Comm Coll (OH)
Clark Coll (WA)
Clark State Comm Coll (OH)
Clover Park Tech Coll (WA)
Coll of DuPage (IL)
Coll of Lake County (IL)
Comm Coll of Allegheny County (PA)
Cuyamaca Coll (CA)
Dakota County Tech Coll (MN)
Edmonds Comm Coll (WA)
Glendale Comm Coll (AZ)
Hinds Comm Coll (MS)
Iowa Lakes Comm Coll (IA)
James H. Faulkner State Comm Coll (AL)
Johnston Comm Coll (NC)
J. Sargeant Reynolds Comm Coll (VA)
Kishwaukee Coll (IL)
Lake City Comm Coll (FL)
Lincoln Land Comm Coll (IL)
Los Angeles Pierce Coll (CA)
Merritt Coll (CA)
Miami Dade Coll (FL)
Milwaukee Area Tech Coll (WI)
MiraCosta Coll (CA)
North Shore Comm Coll (MA)
Northwestern Michigan Coll (MI)
Oakland Comm Coll (MI)
Ohio State U Ag Tech Inst (OH)
Parkland Coll (IL)
Pensacola Jr Coll (FL)
Pikes Peak Comm Coll (CO)
Rochester Comm and Tech Coll (MN)
St. Petersburg Coll (FL)
Santa Barbara City Coll (CA)
Southern Maine Comm Coll (ME)
South Puget Sound Comm Coll (WA)
Southwestern Coll (CA)
Spokane Comm Coll (WA)
Springfield Tech Comm Coll (MA)
State U of NY Coll of A&T at Morrisville (NY)
State U of NY Coll of Technology at Alfred (NY)

State U of NY Coll of Technology at Delhi (NY)
Triton Coll (IL)
The Williamson Free School of Mecha Trades (PA)

Land Use Planning and Management
Colorado Mountn Coll, Timberline Cmps (CO)
Merritt Coll (CA)
Mountain Empire Comm Coll (VA)
Vermilion Comm Coll (MN)

Language Interpretation and Translation
Union County Coll (NJ)
Wilson Tech Comm Coll (NC)

Laser and Optical Technology
Albuquerque Tech Vocational Inst (NM)
Amarillo Coll (TX)
Camden County Coll (NJ)
Cincinnati State Tech and Comm Coll (OH)
Durham Tech Comm Coll (NC)
Elaine P. Nunez Comm Coll (LA)
Front Range Comm Coll (CO)
Indian Hills Comm Coll (IA)
Jefferson Coll (MO)
Linn State Tech Coll (MO)
Northcentral Tech Coll (WI)
Pennsylvania Coll of Technology (PA)
Portland Comm Coll (OR)
Queensborough Comm Coll of City U of NY (NY)
Roane State Comm Coll (TN)
Schoolcraft Coll (MI)
Springfield Tech Comm Coll (MA)
Texas State Tech Coll–Waco/Marshall Campus (TX)
Vincennes U (IN)

Latin American Studies
Manatee Comm Coll (FL)
Miami Dade Coll (FL)
Pasadena City Coll (CA)
San Diego City Coll (CA)

Leatherworking/Upholstery
St. Philip's Coll (TX)
Spokane Falls Comm Coll (WA)

Legal Administrative Assistant
Ohio Business Coll, Sandusky (OH)
Sauk Valley Comm Coll (IL)

Legal Administrative Assistant/Secretary
AIB Coll of Business (IA)
Alamance Comm Coll (NC)
Alexandria Tech Coll (MN)
Alvin Comm Coll (TX)
Amarillo Coll (TX)
American River Coll (CA)
Andover Coll (ME)
Anoka Tech Coll (MN)
Arapahoe Comm Coll (CO)
Austin Comm Coll (TX)
Bates Tech Coll (WA)
Bay State Coll (MA)
Berean Inst (PA)
Bergen Comm Coll (NJ)
Bismarck State Coll (ND)
Blackhawk Tech Coll (WI)
Bradford School (OH)
Briarwood Coll (CT)
Bristol Comm Coll (MA)
Bryant & Stratton Business Inst, Syracuse (NY)
Bryant and Stratton Coll (WI)
Butte Coll (CA)
Cambria-Rowe Business Coll, Johnstown (PA)
Cape Cod Comm Coll (MA)

Carteret Comm Coll (NC)
Casper Coll (WY)
Central Arizona Coll (AZ)
Central Florida Comm Coll (FL)
Centralia Coll (WA)
Central Lakes Coll (MN)
Central Pennsylvania Coll (PA)
Central Piedmont Comm Coll (NC)
Century Coll (MN)
Chabot Coll (CA)
Chesapeake Coll (MD)
Clover Park Tech Coll (WA)
Clovis Comm Coll (NM)
Coastal Bend Coll (TX)
Coffeyville Comm Coll (KS)
Coll of DuPage (IL)
Columbus State Comm Coll (OH)
Commonwealth Business Coll, Michigan City (IN)
Comm Coll of Allegheny County (PA)
Comm Coll of Denver (CO)
Comm Coll of Rhode Island (RI)
Consolidated School of Business, York (PA)
Crowder Coll (MO)
Crown Coll (WA)
Cumberland County Coll (NJ)
Davis Coll (OH)
Daytona Beach Comm Coll (FL)
DeKalb Tech Coll (GA)
Del Mar Coll (TX)
Delta Coll (MI)
Des Moines Area Comm Coll (IA)
Draughons Jr Coll (KY)
Eastern Oklahoma State Coll (OK)
Eastfield Coll (TX)
East Los Angeles Coll (CA)
Edmonds Comm Coll (WA)
El Centro Coll (TX)
Elgin Comm Coll (IL)
Elmira Business Inst (NY)
Erie Business Center South (PA)
Fiorello H LaGuardia Comm Coll of City U of NY (NY)
Florida National Coll (FL)
Fort Scott Comm Coll (KS)
Frederick Comm Coll (MD)
Fulton-Montgomery Comm Coll (NY)
Garden City Comm Coll (KS)
Gavilan Coll (CA)
Gem City Coll (IL)
Globe Coll (MN)
Gloucester County Coll (NJ)
Gogebic Comm Coll (MI)
Grand Rapids Comm Coll (MI)
Green River Comm Coll (WA)
Hamilton Coll (NE)
Harrisburg Area Comm Coll (PA)
Hibbing Comm Coll (MN)
Hickey Coll (MO)
Hillsborough Comm Coll (FL)
Holyoke Comm Coll (MA)
Howard Comm Coll (MD)
Indiana Business Coll, Indianapolis (IN)
Inst of Business & Medical Careers (CO)
Iowa Lakes Comm Coll (IA)
James A. Rhodes State Coll (OH)
Jamestown Business Coll (NY)
Jefferson Coll (MO)
Jefferson Comm Coll (OH)
John A. Logan Coll (IL)
John Wood Comm Coll (IL)
Kalamazoo Valley Comm Coll (MI)
Kapiolani Comm Coll (HI)

Kellogg Comm Coll (MI)
Kirkwood Comm Coll (IA)
Kirtland Comm Coll (MI)
Lake Land Coll (IL)
Lake Region State Coll (ND)
Lake Superior Coll (MN)
Lake Washington Tech Coll (WA)
Lamar State Coll–Port Arthur (TX)
Lansing Comm Coll (MI)
Lawson State Comm Coll (AL)
LDS Business Coll (UT)
Lehigh Carbon Comm Coll (PA)
Lenoir Comm Coll (NC)
Lewis and Clark Comm Coll (IL)
Lincoln Land Comm Coll (IL)
Linn-Benton Comm Coll (OR)
Longview Comm Coll (MO)
Los Angeles Harbor Coll (CA)
Lower Columbia Coll (WA)
MacCormac Coll (IL)
Manchester Comm Coll (CT)
Maple Woods Comm Coll (MO)
McIntosh Coll (NH)
McLennan Comm Coll (TX)
Metropolitan Comm Coll (NE)
Miami Dade Coll (FL)
Middlesex Comm Coll (CT)
Middlesex County Coll (NJ)
Mid Michigan Comm Coll (MI)
Milwaukee Area Tech Coll (WI)
Minneapolis Comm and Tech Coll (MN)
Minnesota School of Business–Brooklyn Center (MN)
Minnesota School of Business-Plymouth (MN)
Minnesota School of Business-Richfield (MN)
Minnesota State Coll–Southeast Tech (MN)
Minnesota State Comm and Tech Coll–Fergus Falls (MN)
Monroe County Comm Coll (MI)
Montana State U Coll of Tech-Great Falls (MT)
Morton Coll (IL)
Mott Comm Coll (MI)
Mountain Empire Comm Coll (VA)
Mountain View Coll (TX)
Mt. San Antonio Coll (CA)
Napa Valley Coll (CA)
Nash Comm Coll (NC)
Nassau Comm Coll (NY)
Naugatuck Valley Comm Coll (CT)
Newport Business Inst, Lower Burrell (PA)
Newport Business Inst, Williamsport (PA)
Normandale Comm Coll (MN)
Northampton County Area Comm Coll (PA)
Northcentral Tech Coll (WI)
Northeast Alabama Comm Coll (AL)
Northeast Comm Coll (NE)
Northeastern Oklahoma A&M Coll (OK)
Northeast Mississippi Comm Coll (MS)
Northeast Texas Comm Coll (TX)
Northeast Wisconsin Tech Coll (WI)
Northern Maine Comm Coll (ME)
North Harris Coll (TX)
North Idaho Coll (ID)

Northland Pioneer Coll (AZ)
North Shore Comm Coll (MA)
Northwestern Michigan Coll (MI)
Northwest State Comm Coll (OH)
Odessa Coll (TX)
Olympic Coll (WA)
Orange Coast Coll (CA)
Otero Jr Coll (CO)
Ouachita Tech Coll (AR)
Palm Beach Comm Coll (FL)
Palomar Coll (CA)
Pasadena City Coll (CA)
Pellissippi State Tech Comm Coll (TN)
Penn Valley Comm Coll (MO)
Phoenix Coll (AZ)
Polk Comm Coll (FL)
Portland Comm Coll (OR)
Rasmussen Coll Mankato (MN)
Rasmussen Coll Minnetonka (MN)
Rasmussen Coll St. Cloud (MN)
Reading Area Comm Coll (PA)
Riverland Comm Coll (MN)
Roane State Comm Coll (TN)
Rochester Comm and Tech Coll (MN)
Rockingham Comm Coll (NC)
St. Clair County Comm Coll (MI)
St. Cloud Tech Coll (MN)
St. Petersburg Coll (FL)
St. Philip's Coll (TX)
San Diego City Coll (CA)
Sierra Coll (CA)
Sinclair Comm Coll (OH)
South Coll (TN)
Southeast Comm Coll, Beatrice Campus (NE)
South Hills School of Business & Technology, State College (PA)
South Plains Coll (TX)
South Puget Sound Comm Coll (WA)
South Texas Comm Coll (TX)
Southwestern Coll (CA)
Southwestern Illinois Coll (IL)
Southwest Mississippi Comm Coll (MS)
Spokane Comm Coll (WA)
Spoon River Coll (IL)
Stanly Comm Coll (NC)
Stark State Coll of Technology (OH)
State U of NY Coll of A&T at Morrisville (NY)
Texas State Tech Coll–Harlingen (TX)
Triton Coll (IL)
Trumbull Business Coll (OH)
Umpqua Comm Coll (OR)
The U of Akron–Wayne Coll (OH)
U of Northwestern Ohio (OH)
Vance-Granville Comm Coll (NC)
Vincennes U (IN)
Western Iowa Tech Comm Coll (IA)
Western Wyoming Comm Coll (WY)
Westmoreland County Comm Coll (PA)
Yakima Valley Comm Coll (WA)
Yavapai Coll (AZ)

Legal Assistant/Paralegal
Academy of Medical Arts and Business (PA)
AEC Southern Ohio Coll (OH)
Albuquerque Tech Vocational Inst (NM)
Alexandria Tech Coll (MN)

Allegany Coll of Maryland (MD)
Allentown Business School (PA)
Alvin Comm Coll (TX)
American River Coll (CA)
Andover Coll (ME)
Anne Arundel Comm Coll (MD)
Arapahoe Comm Coll (CO)
Atlantic Cape Comm Coll (NJ)
Austin Comm Coll (TX)
Beckfield Coll (KY)
Bergen Comm Coll (NJ)
Berkeley Coll (NJ)
Berkeley Coll-New York City Campus (NY)
Berkeley Coll-Westchester Campus (NY)
Bradford School (OH)
Brevard Comm Coll (FL)
Briarwood Coll (CT)
Bronx Comm Coll of City U of NY (NY)
Brookdale Comm Coll (NJ)
Broome Comm Coll (NY)
The Brown Mackie Coll–Lenexa Campus (KS)
Bryant & Stratton Business Inst, Amherst Cmps (NY)
Bucks County Comm Coll (PA)
Burlington County Coll (NJ)
Caldwell Comm Coll and Tech Inst (NC)
Calhoun Comm Coll (AL)
Cañada Coll (CA)
Cape Cod Comm Coll (MA)
Carteret Comm Coll (NC)
Casper Coll (WY)
Central Carolina Tech Coll (SC)
Central Comm Coll–Grand Island Campus (NE)
Central Florida Comm Coll (FL)
Central Pennsylvania Coll (PA)
Central Piedmont Comm Coll (NC)
Clark Coll (WA)
Clark State Comm Coll (OH)
Clovis Comm Coll (NM)
Coastal Carolina Comm Coll (NC)
Coll of Southern Maryland (MD)
Coll of the Sequoias (CA)
Collin County Comm Coll District (TX)
Colorado Northwestern Comm Coll (CO)
Columbus State Comm Coll (OH)
Commonwealth Business Coll, Merrillville (IN)
Comm Coll of Allegheny County (PA)
Comm Coll of Aurora (CO)
Comm Coll of Denver (CO)
Comm Coll of Rhode Island (RI)
Comm Coll of the Air Force (AL)
Corning Comm Coll (NY)
Crown Coll (WA)
Cuyahoga Comm Coll (OH)
Cuyamaca Coll (CA)
Daymar Coll, Louisville (KY)
Daytona Beach Comm Coll (FL)
Delaware County Comm Coll (PA)
Delta Coll (MI)
Des Moines Area Comm Coll (IA)
Doña Ana Branch Comm Coll (NM)
Durham Tech Comm Coll (NC)
Dutchess Comm Coll (NY)
Eastern Idaho Tech Coll (ID)

Edison State Comm Coll (OH)

Edmonds Comm Coll (WA)

Education Direct Center for Degree Studies (PA)

Elaine P. Nunez Comm Coll (LA)

El Camino Coll (CA)

El Centro Coll (TX)

Elgin Comm Coll (IL)

Erie Comm Coll (NY)

Essex County Coll (NJ)

Eugenio María de Hostos Comm Coll of City U of NY (NY)

Everest Coll (AZ)

Fayetteville Tech Comm Coll (NC)

Finger Lakes Comm Coll (NY)

Fiorello H LaGuardia Comm Coll of City U of NY (NY)

Fisher Coll (MA)

Florida National Coll (FL)

Forsyth Tech Comm Coll (NC)

Frederick Comm Coll (MD)

Gadsden State Comm Coll (AL)

Gaston Coll (NC)

Gem City Coll (IL)

Gloucester County Coll (NJ)

Guilford Tech Comm Coll (NC)

Gulf Coast Comm Coll (FL)

Hamilton Coll (NE)

Harford Comm Coll (MD)

Harrisburg Area Comm Coll (PA)

Hesser Coll (NH)

Hickey Coll (MO)

Hinds Comm Coll (MS)

Houston Comm Coll System (TX)

Hudson County Comm Coll (NJ)

Hutchinson Comm Coll and Area Vocational School (KS)

Inst of Business & Medical Careers (CO)

Iowa Lakes Comm Coll (IA)

Ivy Tech State Coll–Bloomington (IN)

Ivy Tech State Coll–Central Indiana (IN)

Ivy Tech State Coll–Columbus (IN)

Ivy Tech State Coll–Eastcentral (IN)

Ivy Tech State Coll–Kokomo (IN)

Ivy Tech State Coll–Lafayette (IN)

Ivy Tech State Coll–North Central (IN)

Ivy Tech State Coll–Northeast (IN)

Ivy Tech State Coll–Northwest (IN)

Ivy Tech State Coll–Southcentral (IN)

Ivy Tech State Coll–Southeast (IN)

Ivy Tech State Coll–Southwest (IN)

Ivy Tech State Coll–Wabash Valley (IN)

Ivy Tech State Coll–Whitewater (IN)

James A. Rhodes State Coll (OH)

James H. Faulkner State Comm Coll (AL)

Jefferson Comm Coll (NY)

Johnson County Comm Coll (KS)

Johnston Comm Coll (NC)

J. Sargeant Reynolds Comm Coll (VA)

Kansas City Kansas Comm Coll (KS)

Kapiolani Comm Coll (HI)

Kaplan Coll (IA)

Keiser Coll, Miami (FL)

Kellogg Comm Coll (MI)

Kirkwood Comm Coll (IA)

Lackawanna Coll (PA)

Lakeland Comm Coll (OH)

Lake Region State Coll (ND)

Lakeshore Tech Coll (WI)

Lake-Sumter Comm Coll (FL)

Lake Superior Coll (MN)

Lamar State Coll–Port Arthur (TX)

Lansing Comm Coll (MI)

Lehigh Carbon Comm Coll (PA)

Luzerne County Comm Coll (PA)

MacCormac Coll (IL)

Macomb Comm Coll (MI)

Manatee Comm Coll (FL)

Manchester Comm Coll (CT)

Marion Tech Coll (OH)

McIntosh Coll (NH)

McLennan Comm Coll (TX)

Merritt Coll (CA)

Metropolitan Comm Coll (NE)

Miami Dade Coll (FL)

Michiana Coll, South Bend (IN)

Middlesex Comm Coll (MA)

Middlesex County Coll (NJ)

Midland Coll (TX)

Midlands Tech Coll (SC)

Mildred Elley (NY)

Milwaukee Area Tech Coll (WI)

Minnesota School of Business-Richfield (MN)

Mississippi Gulf Coast Comm Coll (MS)

Montgomery Coll (MD)

Mott Comm Coll (MI)

Mountain State Coll (WV)

Mountain West Coll (UT)

Mt. San Antonio Coll (CA)

Mt. San Jacinto Coll (CA)

Mount Wachusett Comm Coll (MA)

Napa Valley Coll (CA)

Nassau Comm Coll (NY)

Naugatuck Valley Comm Coll (CT)

New Hampshire Tech Inst (NH)

New Mexico State U–Carlsbad (NM)

New Mexico State U–Grants (NM)

New River Comm Coll (VA)

Northampton County Area Comm Coll (PA)

North Central State Coll (OH)

Northeast Alabama Comm Coll (AL)

Northeast Comm Coll (NE)

Northeast Mississippi Comm Coll (MS)

Northeast Wisconsin Tech Coll (WI)

Northern Essex Comm Coll (MA)

North Hennepin Comm Coll (MN)

North Idaho Coll (ID)

Northland Pioneer Coll (AZ)

North Shore Comm Coll (MA)

Northwestern Connecticut Comm-Tech Coll (CT)

Northwest State Comm Coll (OH)

Oakland Comm Coll (MI)

Ocean County Coll (NJ)

Orangeburg-Calhoun Tech Coll (SC)

Ouachita Tech Coll (AR)

Palomar Coll (CA)

Pasco-Hernando Comm Coll (FL)

Patricia Stevens Coll (MO)

Pellissippi State Tech Comm Coll (TN)

Pennsylvania Coll of Technology (PA)

Penn Valley Comm Coll (MO)

Pensacola Jr Coll (FL)

Phoenix Coll (AZ)

Pikes Peak Comm Coll (CO)

Pima Comm Coll (AZ)

Pioneer Pacific Coll (OR)

Pitt Comm Coll (NC)

Platt Coll, Newport Beach (CA)

Portland Comm Coll (OR)

Prince George's Comm Coll (MD)

Raritan Valley Comm Coll (NJ)

Rasmussen Coll Mankato (MN)

Remington Coll–Lafayette Campus (LA)

RETS Tech Center (OH)

Rockingham Comm Coll (NC)

Rowan-Cabarrus Comm Coll (NC)

St. Petersburg Coll (FL)

San Diego City Coll (CA)

Sanford-Brown Coll, Hazelwood (MO)

San Juan Coll (NM)

Santa Fe Comm Coll (NM)

Sawyer Coll, Hammond (IN)

Schenectady County Comm Coll (NY)

Schuylkill Inst of Business and Technology (PA)

Seminole Comm Coll (FL)

Sinclair Comm Coll (OH)

South Coll (TN)

South Coll-Asheville (NC)

Southeast Arkansas Coll (AR)

South Puget Sound Comm Coll (WA)

South Suburban Coll (IL)

South Texas Comm Coll (TX)

South U (FL)

South U (SC)

Southwestern Comm Coll (NC)

Southwestern Illinois Coll (IL)

Southwestern Michigan Coll (MI)

Southwest Missouri State U–West Plains (MO)

Spokane Comm Coll (WA)

Stautzenberger Coll (OH)

Sullivan County Comm Coll (NY)

Sussex County Comm Coll (NJ)

Tompkins Cortland Comm Coll (NY)

Trident Tech Coll (SC)

U of Northwestern Ohio (OH)

Utah Valley State Coll (UT)

Vincennes U (IN)

Volunteer State Comm Coll (TN)

Western Dakota Tech Inst (SD)

Western Nevada Comm Coll (NV)

Western Wisconsin Tech Coll (WI)

Westmoreland County Comm Coll (PA)

West Virginia Business Coll, Wheeling (WV)

Wilson Tech Comm Coll (NC)

Yavapai Coll (AZ)

Legal Professions and Studies Related

Essex County Coll (NJ)

Florida National Coll (FL)

Northland Pioneer Coll (AZ)

United Tribes Tech Coll (ND)

Legal Studies

Alvin Comm Coll (TX)

Bay State Coll (MA)

Del Mar Coll (TX)

Delta Coll (MI)

Edison Comm Coll (FL)

Edison State Comm Coll (OH)

El Centro Coll (TX)

Florida National Coll (FL)

Foothill Coll (CA)

Gloucester County Coll (NJ)

Hillsborough Comm Coll (FL)

Iowa Lakes Comm Coll (IA)

Kirkwood Comm Coll (IA)

MacCormac Coll (IL)

Macomb Comm Coll (MI)

Metropolitan Comm Coll (NE)

North Harris Coll (TX)

Oxnard Coll (CA)

Palo Alto Coll (TX)

Pasadena City Coll (CA)

Rasmussen Coll Mankato (MN)

Reading Area Comm Coll (PA)

St. Louis Comm Coll at Florissant Valley (MO)

Santa Barbara City Coll (CA)

Trident Tech Coll (SC)

Liberal Arts and Sciences And Humanities Related

Cascade Comm Coll (WA)

Cleveland Comm Coll (NC)

Hagerstown Comm Coll (MD)

Harford Comm Coll (MD)

Iowa Lakes Comm Coll (IA)

Kansas City Kansas Comm Coll (KS)

Lake Superior Coll (MN)

Luzerne County Comm Coll (PA)

Massasoit Comm Coll (MA)

Northampton County Area Comm Coll (PA)

Oakland Comm Coll (MI)

Oakton Comm Coll (IL)

Pennsylvania Coll of Technology (PA)

Pikes Peak Comm Coll (CO)

Platt Coll San Diego (CA)

Southwestern Michigan Coll (MI)

Wor-Wic Comm Coll (MD)

Liberal Arts and Sciences/ Liberal Studies

Abraham Baldwin Ag Coll (GA)

Alamance Comm Coll (NC)

Albuquerque Tech Vocational Inst (NM)

Allegany Coll of Maryland (MD)

Alpena Comm Coll (MI)

Alvin Comm Coll (TX)

Amarillo Coll (TX)

American River Coll (CA)

Ancilla Coll (IN)

Anne Arundel Comm Coll (MD)

Arapahoe Comm Coll (CO)

Arizona Western Coll (AZ)

Arkansas State U–Beebe (AR)

Arkansas State U–Mountain Home (AR)

Asheville-Buncombe Tech Comm Coll (NC)

Asnuntuck Comm Coll (CT)

Assumption Coll for Sisters (NJ)

Atlantic Cape Comm Coll (NJ)

Austin Comm Coll (TX)

Bainbridge Coll (GA)

Barton County Comm Coll (KS)

Bay State Coll (MA)

Beaufort County Comm Coll (NC)

Bellevue Comm Coll (WA)

Bergen Comm Coll (NJ)

Berkshire Comm Coll (MA)

Big Bend Comm Coll (WA)

Big Sandy Comm and Tech Coll (KY)

Bismarck State Coll (ND)

Blackfeet Comm Coll (MT)

Bladen Comm Coll (NC)

Blue Ridge Comm Coll (NC)

Blue River Comm Coll (MO)

Borough of Manhattan Comm Coll of City U of NY (NY)

Bowling Green State U-Firelands Coll (OH)

Brevard Comm Coll (FL)

Bristol Comm Coll (MA)

Bronx Comm Coll of City U of NY (NY)

Brookdale Comm Coll (NJ)

Broome Comm Coll (NY)

Brunswick Comm Coll (NC)

Bucks County Comm Coll (PA)

Burlington County Coll (NJ)

Butler County Comm Coll (KS)

Butte Coll (CA)

Cabrillo Coll (CA)

Caldwell Comm Coll and Tech Inst (NC)

Calhoun Comm Coll (AL)

Cambria County Area Comm Coll (PA)

Camden County Coll (NJ)

Cañada Coll (CA)

Cape Cod Comm Coll (MA)

Cape Fear Comm Coll (NC)

Capital Comm Coll (CT)

Carl Sandburg Coll (IL)

Carteret Comm Coll (NC)

Cascadia Comm Coll (WA)

Casper Coll (WY)

Cecil Comm Coll (MD)

Cedar Valley Coll (TX)

Central Alabama Comm Coll (AL)

Central Arizona Coll (AZ)

Central Carolina Tech Coll (SC)

Central Comm Coll–Columbus Campus (NE)

Central Comm Coll–Grand Island Campus (NE)

Central Comm Coll–Hastings Campus (NE)

Central Florida Comm Coll (FL)

Centralia Coll (WA)

Central Lakes Coll (MN)

Central Oregon Comm Coll (OR)

Central Piedmont Comm Coll (NC)

Century Coll (MN)

Chabot Coll (CA)

Chatfield Coll (OH)

Chemeketa Comm Coll (OR)

Chesapeake Coll (MD)

Chipola Coll (FL)

Cincinnati State Tech and Comm Coll (OH)

City Colls of Chicago, Malcolm X Coll (IL)

City Colls of Chicago, Wilbur Wright Coll (IL)

Clarendon Coll (TX)

Clark Coll (WA)

Clark State Comm Coll (OH)

Cleveland Comm Coll (NC)

Cleveland State Comm Coll (TN)

Clinton Comm Coll (NY)

Clovis Comm Coll (NM)

Coastal Bend Coll (TX)

Coastal Carolina Comm Coll (NC)

Coastal Georgia Comm Coll (GA)

Coastline Comm Coll (CA)

Coffeyville Comm Coll (KS)

Colby Comm Coll (KS)

Coll of DuPage (IL)

Coll of Eastern Utah (UT)

Coll of Lake County (IL)

Coll of Southern Idaho (ID)

Coll of Southern Maryland (MD)

Coll of the Canyons (CA)

Coll of the Desert (CA)

Coll of the Sequoias (CA)

Collin County Comm Coll District (TX)

Colorado Mountn Coll, Alpine Cmps (CO)

Colorado Mountn Coll (CO)

Colorado Mountn Coll, Timberline Cmps (CO)

Colorado Northwestern Comm Coll (CO)

Columbia Coll (CA)

Columbia-Greene Comm Coll (NY)

Columbia State Comm Coll (TN)

Columbus State Comm Coll (OH)

Comm Coll of Allegheny County (PA)

Comm Coll of Aurora (CO)

Comm Coll of Denver (CO)

Comm Coll of Rhode Island (RI)

Contra Costa Coll (CA)

Copiah-Lincoln Comm Coll (MS)

Copiah-Lincoln Comm Coll–Natchez Campus (MS)

Corning Comm Coll (NY)

Cossatot Comm Coll of the U of Arkansas (AR)

County Coll of Morris (NJ)

Crowder Coll (MO)

Cuesta Coll (CA)

Cumberland County Coll (NJ)

Cuyahoga Comm Coll (OH)

Cuyamaca Coll (CA)

Danville Comm Coll (VA)

Dawson Comm Coll (MT)

Daytona Beach Comm Coll (FL)

Dean Coll (MA)

Delaware County Comm Coll (PA)

Del Mar Coll (TX)

Delta Coll (MI)

Des Moines Area Comm Coll (IA)

Diablo Valley Coll (CA)

Donnelly Coll (KS)

Durham Tech Comm Coll (NC)

Dutchess Comm Coll (NY)

East Arkansas Comm Coll (AR)

Eastern Arizona Coll (AZ)

Eastern Maine Comm Coll (ME)

Eastern Shore Comm Coll (VA)

Eastern Wyoming Coll (WY)

Eastfield Coll (TX)

East Los Angeles Coll (CA)

East Mississippi Comm Coll (MS)

Edgecombe Comm Coll (NC)

Edison Comm Coll (FL)

Edison State Comm Coll (OH)

Edmonds Comm Coll (WA)

Elaine P. Nunez Comm Coll (LA)

El Camino Coll (CA)

El Centro Coll (TX)

Elgin Comm Coll (IL)

Elizabethtown Comm Coll (KY)

Erie Comm Coll (NY)

Essex County Coll (NJ)

Estrella Mountain Comm Coll (AZ)

Eugenio María de Hostos Comm Coll of City U of NY (NY)

Everett Comm Coll (WA)

Fayetteville Tech Comm Coll (NC)

Feather River Comm Coll District (CA)

Finger Lakes Comm Coll (NY)

Fiorello H LaGuardia Comm Coll of City U of NY (NY)
Fisher Coll (MA)
Florida National Coll (FL)
Foothill Coll (CA)
Fort Scott Comm Coll (KS)
Frederick Comm Coll (MD)
Front Range Comm Coll (CO)
Fulton-Montgomery Comm Coll (NY)
Gadsden State Comm Coll (AL)
Galveston Coll (TX)
Garden City Comm Coll (KS)
Garrett Coll (MD)
Gavilan Coll (CA)
Germanna Comm Coll (VA)
Glendale Comm Coll (AZ)
Glen Oaks Comm Coll (MI)
Gloucester County Coll (NJ)
Gogebic Comm Coll (MI)
Grand Rapids Comm Coll (MI)
Greenfield Comm Coll (MA)
Green River Comm Coll (WA)
Guilford Tech Comm Coll (NC)
Gulf Coast Comm Coll (FL)
Hagerstown Comm Coll (MD)
Harcum Coll (PA)
Harford Comm Coll (MD)
Harrisburg Area Comm Coll (PA)
Hawaii Comm Coll (HI)
Hawaii Tokai International Coll (HI)
Hawkeye Comm Coll (IA)
Heartland Comm Coll (IL)
Hesser Coll (NH)
Hesston Coll (KS)
Hibbing Comm Coll (MN)
Hill Coll of the Hill Jr College District (TX)
Hillsborough Comm Coll (FL)
Hinds Comm Coll (MS)
Hiwassee Coll (TN)
Holmes Comm Coll (MS)
Holy Cross Coll (IN)
Holyoke Comm Coll (MA)
Honolulu Comm Coll (HI)
Hopkinsville Comm Coll (KY)
Houston Comm Coll System (TX)
Howard Comm Coll (MD)
Hudson County Comm Coll (NJ)
Hutchinson Comm Coll and Area Vocational School (KS)
Illinois Eastern Comm Colls, Frontier Comm Coll (IL)
Illinois Eastern Comm Colls, Lincoln Trail Coll (IL)
Illinois Eastern Comm Colls, Olney Central Coll (IL)
Illinois Eastern Comm Colls, Wabash Valley Coll (IL)
Indian Hills Comm Coll (IA)
Iowa Lakes Comm Coll (IA)
Isothermal Comm Coll (NC)
Itasca Comm Coll (MN)
Ivy Tech State Coll–Bloomington (IN)
Ivy Tech State Coll–Central Indiana (IN)
Ivy Tech State Coll–Columbus (IN)
Ivy Tech State Coll–Eastcentral (IN)
Ivy Tech State Coll–Kokomo (IN)
Ivy Tech State Coll–Lafayette (IN)
Ivy Tech State Coll–North Central (IN)
Ivy Tech State Coll–Northeast (IN)
Ivy Tech State Coll–Southcentral (IN)
Ivy Tech State Coll–Southeast (IN)

Ivy Tech State Coll–Southwest (IN)
Ivy Tech State Coll–Wabash Valley (IN)
Ivy Tech State Coll–Whitewater (IN)
Jackson Comm Coll (MI)
Jackson State Comm Coll (TN)
Jacksonville Coll (TX)
James H. Faulkner State Comm Coll (AL)
James Sprunt Comm Coll (NC)
Jamestown Comm Coll (NY)
Jefferson Coll (MO)
Jefferson Comm Coll (KY)
Jefferson Comm Coll (NY)
Jefferson Davis Comm Coll (AL)
Jefferson State Comm Coll (AL)
John A. Logan Coll (IL)
Johnson County Comm Coll (KS)
Johnston Comm Coll (NC)
John Tyler Comm Coll (VA)
John Wood Comm Coll (IL)
J. Sargeant Reynolds Comm Coll (VA)
Kalamazoo Valley Comm Coll (MI)
Kansas City Kansas Comm Coll (KS)
Kapiolani Comm Coll (HI)
Kaskaskia Coll (IL)
Kauai Comm Coll (HI)
Kellogg Comm Coll (MI)
Kent State U, Salem Campus (OH)
Kent State U, Stark Campus (OH)
Kent State U, Trumbull Campus (OH)
Kent State U, Tuscarawas Campus (OH)
Keystone Coll (PA)
Kilian Comm Coll (SD)
Kingsborough Comm Coll of City U of NY (NY)
Kirkwood Comm Coll (IA)
Kirtland Comm Coll (MI)
Kishwaukee Coll (IL)
Lac Courte Oreilles Ojibwa Comm Coll (WI)
Lackawanna Coll (PA)
Lake City Comm Coll (FL)
Lake Land Coll (IL)
Lakeland Comm Coll (OH)
Lake Region State Coll (ND)
Lake-Sumter Comm Coll (FL)
Lake Superior Coll (MN)
Lamar State Coll–Orange (TX)
Landmark Coll (VT)
Lansing Comm Coll (MI)
Laredo Comm Coll (TX)
Lawson State Comm Coll (AL)
LDS Business Coll (UT)
Lehigh Carbon Comm Coll (PA)
Lenoir Comm Coll (NC)
Lewis and Clark Comm Coll (IL)
Lincoln Coll, Lincoln (IL)
Lincoln Land Comm Coll (IL)
Linn-Benton Comm Coll (OR)
Longview Comm Coll (MO)
Lon Morris Coll (TX)
Lorain County Comm Coll (OH)
Lord Fairfax Comm Coll (VA)
Los Angeles Harbor Coll (CA)
Los Angeles Pierce Coll (CA)
Los Angeles Trade-Tech Coll (CA)
Los Angeles Valley Coll (CA)
Lower Columbia Coll (WA)
Lurleen B. Wallace Comm Coll (AL)

Luzerne County Comm Coll (PA)
Macomb Comm Coll (MI)
Manatee Comm Coll (FL)
Manchester Comm Coll (CT)
Maple Woods Comm Coll (MO)
Marshalltown Comm Coll (IA)
Massasoit Comm Coll (MA)
Mayland Comm Coll (NC)
Maysville Comm Coll (KY)
McHenry County Coll (IL)
McLennan Comm Coll (TX)
Merritt Coll (CA)
Mesabi Range Comm and Tech Coll (MN)
Metropolitan Comm Coll (NE)
Metropolitan Comm Coll-Business & Technology College (MO)
Middle Georgia Coll (GA)
Middlesex Comm Coll (CT)
Middlesex Comm Coll (MA)
Midland Coll (TX)
Midlands Tech Coll (SC)
Mid Michigan Comm Coll (MI)
Mid-Plains Comm Coll, North Platte (NE)
Mid-South Comm Coll (AR)
Miles Comm Coll (MT)
Milwaukee Area Tech Coll (WI)
Mineral Area Coll (MO)
Minneapolis Comm and Tech Coll (MN)
Minnesota State Comm and Tech Coll–Fergus Falls (MN)
Minot State U–Bottineau Campus (ND)
MiraCosta Coll (CA)
Mississippi Gulf Coast Comm Coll (MS)
Mitchell Comm Coll (NC)
Moberly Area Comm Coll (MO)
Mohave Comm Coll (AZ)
Mohawk Valley Comm Coll (NY)
Monroe County Comm Coll (MI)
Montcalm Comm Coll (MI)
Montgomery Coll (MD)
Montgomery County Comm Coll (PA)
Moraine Valley Comm Coll (IL)
Morgan Comm Coll (CO)
Morton Coll (IL)
Motlow State Comm Coll (TN)
Mott Comm Coll (MI)
Mountain Empire Comm Coll (VA)
Mountain View Coll (TX)
Mt. San Antonio Coll (CA)
Mount Wachusett Comm Coll (MA)
Nash Comm Coll (NC)
Nassau Comm Coll (NY)
Naugatuck Valley Comm Coll (CT)
Nebraska Indian Comm Coll (NE)
New Hampshire Comm Tech Coll, Berlin/Laconia (NH)
New Hampshire Comm Tech Coll, Manchester/Stratham (NH)
New Hampshire Tech Inst (NH)
New Mexico State U–Carlsbad (NM)
New Mexico State U–Grants (NM)
New River Comm Coll (VA)
Niagara County Comm Coll (NY)
Normandale Comm Coll (MN)

Northampton County Area Comm Coll (PA)
North Arkansas Coll (AR)
North Central Missouri Coll (MO)
North Country Comm Coll (NY)
North Dakota State Coll of Science (ND)
Northeast Alabama Comm Coll (AL)
Northeast Comm Coll (NE)
Northeastern Tech Coll (SC)
Northeast Iowa Comm Coll (IA)
Northeast Mississippi Comm Coll (MS)
Northeast State Tech Comm Coll (TN)
Northern Essex Comm Coll (MA)
North Florida Comm Coll (FL)
North Harris Coll (TX)
North Hennepin Comm Coll (MN)
North Idaho Coll (ID)
North Iowa Area Comm Coll (IA)
Northland Pioneer Coll (AZ)
North Seattle Comm Coll (WA)
North Shore Comm Coll (MA)
Northwest Coll (WY)
Northwestern Connecticut Comm-Tech Coll (CT)
Northwestern Michigan Coll (MI)
Northwest Iowa Comm Coll (IA)
Northwest-Shoals Comm Coll (AL)
Oakland Comm Coll (MI)
Oakton Comm Coll (IL)
Ocean County Coll (NJ)
Odessa Coll (TX)
Oklahoma City Comm Coll (OK)
Olympic Coll (WA)
Orangeburg-Calhoun Tech Coll (SC)
Orange Coast Coll (CA)
Orange County Comm Coll (NY)
Otero Jr Coll (CO)
Ouachita Tech Coll (AR)
Owensboro Comm and Tech Coll (KY)
Oxnard Coll (CA)
Ozarka Coll (AR)
Palm Beach Comm Coll (FL)
Palo Alto Coll (TX)
Palomar Coll (CA)
Paris Jr Coll (TX)
Parkland Coll (IL)
Pasadena City Coll (CA)
Pasco-Hernando Comm Coll (FL)
Paul D. Camp Comm Coll (VA)
Pellissippi State Tech Comm Coll (TN)
Pennsylvania Coll of Technology (PA)
Penn State U Beaver Campus of the Commonwealth Coll (PA)
Penn State U Delaware County Campus of the Commonwealth Coll (PA)
Penn State U DuBois Campus of the Commonwealth Coll (PA)
Penn State U Fayette Campus of the Commonwealth Coll (PA)
Penn State U Hazleton Campus of the Commonwealth Coll (PA)
Penn State U McKeesport Campus of the Commonwealth Coll (PA)

Penn State U Mont Alto Campus of the Commonwealth Coll (PA)
Penn State U New Kensington Campus of the Commonwealth Coll (PA)
Penn State U Shenango Campus of the Commonwealth Coll (PA)
Penn State U Wilkes-Barre Campus of the Commonwealth Coll (PA)
Penn State U Worthington Scranton Cmps Commonwealth Coll (PA)
Penn State U York Campus of the Commonwealth Coll (PA)
Penn Valley Comm Coll (MO)
Pensacola Jr Coll (FL)
Phoenix Coll (AZ)
Piedmont Virginia Comm Coll (VA)
Pikes Peak Comm Coll (CO)
Pima Comm Coll (AZ)
Pitt Comm Coll (NC)
Polk Comm Coll (FL)
Portland Comm Coll (OR)
Pratt Comm Coll and Area Vocational School (KS)
Prince George's Comm Coll (MD)
Queensborough Comm Coll of City U of NY (NY)
Quinebaug Valley Comm Coll (CT)
Quinsigamond Comm Coll (MA)
Rainy River Comm Coll (MN)
Raritan Valley Comm Coll (NJ)
Reading Area Comm Coll (PA)
Red Rocks Comm Coll (CO)
Richard Bland Coll of the Coll of William and Mary (VA)
Richmond Comm Coll (NC)
Rich Mountain Comm Coll (AR)
Riverland Comm Coll (MN)
Riverside Comm Coll (CA)
Roane State Comm Coll (TN)
Roanoke-Chowan Comm Coll (NC)
Rochester Comm and Tech Coll (MN)
Rockingham Comm Coll (NC)
Rogue Comm Coll (OR)
Rowan-Cabarrus Comm Coll (NC)
Saint Charles Comm Coll (MO)
St. Clair County Comm Coll (MI)
St. Johns River Comm Coll (FL)
St. Louis Comm Coll at Florissant Valley (MO)
St. Petersburg Coll (FL)
St. Philip's Coll (TX)
Salem Comm Coll (NJ)
San Diego City Coll (CA)
San Joaquin Delta Coll (CA)
San Jose City Coll (CA)
Santa Barbara City Coll (CA)
Santa Monica Coll (CA)
Sauk Valley Comm Coll (IL)
Schenectady County Comm Coll (NY)
Schoolcraft Coll (MI)
Seminole Comm Coll (FL)
Seward County Comm Coll (KS)
Shelton State Comm Coll (AL)
Sheridan Coll (WY)
Sierra Coll (CA)
Sinclair Comm Coll (OH)
Sisseton-Wahpeton Comm Coll (SD)

Snead State Comm Coll (AL)
Snow Coll (UT)
Southeast Comm Coll (KY)
Southeast Comm Coll, Beatrice Campus (NE)
Southeast Comm Coll, Lincoln Campus (NE)
Southeastern Comm Coll (NC)
Southern Maine Comm Coll (ME)
Southern State Comm Coll (OH)
Southern West Virginia Comm and Tech Coll (WV)
South Plains Coll (TX)
South Puget Sound Comm Coll (WA)
Southside Virginia Comm Coll (VA)
South Suburban Coll (IL)
South Texas Comm Coll (TX)
Southwestern Coll (CA)
Southwestern Comm Coll (NC)
Southwestern Illinois Coll (IL)
Southwestern Michigan Coll (MI)
Southwestern Oregon Comm Coll (OR)
Southwest Mississippi Comm Coll (MS)
Spartanburg Methodist Coll (SC)
Spartanburg Tech Coll (SC)
Spokane Comm Coll (WA)
Spokane Falls Comm Coll (WA)
Spoon River Coll (IL)
Springfield Tech Comm Coll (MA)
State U of NY Coll of A&T at Morrisville (NY)
State U of NY Coll of Technology at Alfred (NY)
State U of NY Coll of Technology at Canton (NY)
Sullivan County Comm Coll (NY)
Sussex County Comm Coll (NJ)
Temple Coll (TX)
Thomas Nelson Comm Coll (VA)
Three Rivers Comm Coll (MO)
Tidewater Comm Coll (VA)
Tillamook Bay Comm Coll (OR)
Tompkins Cortland Comm Coll (NY)
Tri-County Comm Coll (NC)
Trident Tech Coll (SC)
Trinidad State Jr Coll (CO)
Triton Coll (IL)
Truett-McConnell Coll (GA)
Umpqua Comm Coll (OR)
Union County Coll (NJ)
The U of Akron–Wayne Coll (OH)
U of Alaska Anchorage, Kenai Peninsula Coll (AK)
U of Alaska Anchorage, Matanuska-Susitna Coll (AK)
U of Alaska Southeast, Ketchikan Campus (AK)
U of Arkansas Comm Coll at Hope (AR)
U of Kentucky, Lexington Comm Coll (KY)
U of Pittsburgh at Titusville (PA)
U of South Carolina Salkehatchie (SC)
U of South Carolina at Sumter (SC)
U of South Carolina at Union (SC)
U of Wisconsin Center–Baraboo/ Sauk County (WI)
U of Wisconsin Center–Barron County (WI)

U of Wisconsin Center–Manitowoc (WI)
U of Wisconsin Center–Marathon County (WI)
U of Wisconsin Center–Richland (WI)
U of Wisconsin Center–Washington County (WI)
U of Wisconsin Center–Waukesha County (WI)
Urban Coll of Boston (MA)
Valley Forge Military Coll (PA)
Vance-Granville Comm Coll (NC)
Ventura Coll (CA)
Vermilion Comm Coll (MN)
Victor Valley Coll (CA)
Villa Maria Coll of Buffalo (NY)
Vincennes U (IN)
Virginia Western Comm Coll (VA)
Vista Comm Coll (CA)
Volunteer State Comm Coll (TN)
Walters State Comm Coll (TN)
Washtenaw Comm Coll (MI)
Waubonsee Comm Coll (IL)
Waycross Coll (GA)
Weatherford Coll (TX)
Western Iowa Tech Comm Coll (IA)
Western Nevada Comm Coll (NV)
Western Wyoming Comm Coll (WY)
West Hills Comm Coll (CA)
Westmoreland County Comm Coll (PA)
West Virginia Northern Comm Coll (WV)
Williamsburg Tech Coll (SC)
Williston State Coll (ND)
Wilson Tech Comm Coll (NC)
Yakima Valley Comm Coll (WA)
Yavapai Coll (AZ)
York Tech Coll (SC)

Library Assistant
Clovis Comm Coll (NM)
Coll of DuPage (IL)
Northland Pioneer Coll (AZ)
Oakland Comm Coll (MI)
Spokane Falls Comm Coll (WA)

Library Science
Brookdale Comm Coll (NJ)
City Colls of Chicago, Wilbur Wright Coll (IL)
Colby Comm Coll (KS)
Coll of DuPage (IL)
Coll of Southern Idaho (ID)
Copiah-Lincoln Comm Coll (MS)
Cuesta Coll (CA)
Doña Ana Branch Comm Coll (NM)
Foothill Coll (CA)
Lawson State Comm Coll (AL)
Lenoir Comm Coll (NC)
Los Angeles Valley Coll (CA)
Northeast Mississippi Comm Coll (MS)
Oxnard Coll (CA)
Palo Alto Coll (TX)
Palomar Coll (CA)
Pasadena City Coll (CA)
Portland Comm Coll (OR)
Riverside Comm Coll (CA)

Lineworker
Bismarck State Coll (ND)
Dakota County Tech Coll (MN)
Ivy Tech State Coll–Lafayette (IN)
Lehigh Carbon Comm Coll (PA)
Linn State Tech Coll (MO)
Lower Columbia Coll (WA)

Mitchell Tech Inst (SD)
Northeast Comm Coll (NE)
Northeast Wisconsin Tech Coll (WI)
Northwest Iowa Comm Coll (IA)
Utah Valley State Coll (UT)

Linguistics
Foothill Coll (CA)

Literature
Andrew Coll (GA)
Atlantic Cape Comm Coll (NJ)
Bergen Comm Coll (NJ)
Chabot Coll (CA)
Foothill Coll (CA)
Iowa Lakes Comm Coll (IA)
Lamar State Coll–Orange (TX)
Lincoln Land Comm Coll (IL)
Lon Morris Coll (TX)
Miami Dade Coll (FL)
Midland Coll (TX)
Oklahoma City Comm Coll (OK)
Otero Jr Coll (CO)
Palm Beach Comm Coll (FL)
Pratt Comm Coll and Area Vocational School (KS)
San Joaquin Delta Coll (CA)
Seward County Comm Coll (KS)
Southwestern Coll (CA)

Livestock Management
Barton County Comm Coll (KS)
Northeast Comm Coll (NE)
Ohio State U Ag Tech Inst (OH)

Logistics and Materials Management
Columbus State Comm Coll (OH)
Comm Coll of the Air Force (AL)
Houston Comm Coll System (TX)
Lehigh Carbon Comm Coll (PA)
Northeast Wisconsin Tech Coll (WI)
Sinclair Comm Coll (OH)
Springfield Tech Comm Coll (MA)
Waubonsee Comm Coll (IL)

Machine Shop Technology
Cape Fear Comm Coll (NC)
Coll of Lake County (IL)
Comm Coll of Allegheny County (PA)
Corning Comm Coll (NY)
Delgado Comm Coll (LA)
Eastern Arizona Coll (AZ)
Front Range Comm Coll (CO)
Illinois Eastern Comm Colls, Wabash Valley Coll (IL)
Ivy Tech State Coll–Central Indiana (IN)
Maple Woods Comm Coll (MO)
Metropolitan Comm Coll–Business & Technology College (MO)
Modesto Jr Coll (CA)
North Dakota State Coll of Science (ND)
Northeast Wisconsin Tech Coll (WI)
North Iowa Area Comm Coll (IA)
Northwestern Michigan Coll (MI)
Northwest Iowa Comm Coll (IA)
Orange Coast Coll (CA)
Pennsylvania Coll of Technology (PA)
Pikes Peak Comm Coll (CO)
Pima Comm Coll (AZ)
Pitt Comm Coll (NC)

Riverland Comm Coll (MN)
Southwestern Michigan Coll (MI)
U of Arkansas Comm Coll at Hope (AR)
Vincennes U (IN)
Western Dakota Tech Inst (SD)
Wichita Area Tech Coll (KS)

Machine Tool Technology
Alamance Comm Coll (NC)
Alexandria Tech Coll (MN)
Amarillo Coll (TX)
Asheville-Buncombe Tech Comm Coll (NC)
Blue Ridge Comm Coll (NC)
Calhoun Comm Coll (AL)
Casper Coll (WY)
Central Comm Coll–Columbus Campus (NE)
Central Comm Coll–Hastings Campus (NE)
Central Piedmont Comm Coll (NC)
Century Coll (MN)
City Colls of Chicago, Wilbur Wright Coll (IL)
Clark Coll (WA)
Clover Park Tech Coll (WA)
Coffeyville Comm Coll (KS)
Coll of DuPage (IL)
Coll of Eastern Utah (UT)
Corning Comm Coll (NY)
Delaware County Comm Coll (PA)
Delgado Comm Coll (LA)
Del Mar Coll (TX)
Delta Coll (MI)
Des Moines Area Comm Coll (IA)
Durham Tech Comm Coll (NC)
Eastern Maine Comm Coll (ME)
Elgin Comm Coll (IL)
Fayetteville Tech Comm Coll (NC)
Forsyth Tech Comm Coll (NC)
Green River Comm Coll (WA)
Guilford Tech Comm Coll (NC)
Gwinnett Tech Coll (GA)
Hawkeye Comm Coll (IA)
Heartland Comm Coll (IL)
Hill Coll of the Hill Jr College District (TX)
Hinds Comm Coll (MS)
Hutchinson Comm Coll and Area Vocational School (KS)
Indian Hills Comm Coll (IA)
Isothermal Comm Coll (NC)
Ivy Tech State Coll–Bloomington (IN)
Ivy Tech State Coll–Central Indiana (IN)
Ivy Tech State Coll–Columbus (IN)
Ivy Tech State Coll–Eastcentral (IN)
Ivy Tech State Coll–Kokomo (IN)
Ivy Tech State Coll–Lafayette (IN)
Ivy Tech State Coll–North Central (IN)
Ivy Tech State Coll–Northeast (IN)
Ivy Tech State Coll–Northwest (IN)
Ivy Tech State Coll–Southcentral (IN)
Ivy Tech State Coll–Southwest (IN)
Ivy Tech State Coll–Wabash Valley (IN)
Ivy Tech State Coll–Whitewater (IN)
Jefferson Coll (MO)
J. F. Drake State Tech Coll (AL)
John A. Logan Coll (IL)

Johnson County Comm Coll (KS)
Johnston Comm Coll (NC)
Kalamazoo Valley Comm Coll (MI)
Kellogg Comm Coll (MI)
Lake Area Tech Inst (SD)
Lakeland Comm Coll (OH)
Lake Superior Coll (MN)
Lake Washington Tech Coll (WA)
Lansing Comm Coll (MI)
Lewis and Clark Comm Coll (IL)
Linn-Benton Comm Coll (OR)
Linn State Tech Coll (MO)
Lorain County Comm Coll (OH)
Los Angeles Pierce Coll (CA)
Los Angeles Valley Coll (CA)
Louisiana Tech Coll–Delta Ouachita Campus (LA)
Lower Columbia Coll (WA)
Macomb Comm Coll (MI)
Maple Woods Comm Coll (MO)
Marshalltown Comm Coll (IA)
Meridian Comm Coll (MS)
Mid Michigan Comm Coll (MI)
Milwaukee Area Tech Coll (WI)
Minnesota State Coll–Southeast Tech (MN)
MiraCosta Coll (CA)
Mitchell Comm Coll (NC)
Modesto Jr Coll (CA)
Moraine Park Tech Coll (WI)
Mt. San Antonio Coll (CA)
Napa Valley Coll (CA)
New Castle School of Trades (PA)
New River Comm Coll (VA)
North Central State Coll (OH)
Northcentral Tech Coll (WI)
Northeastern Tech Coll (SC)
Northeast State Tech Comm Coll (TN)
Northeast Wisconsin Tech Coll (WI)
Northern Essex Comm Coll (MA)
North Idaho Coll (ID)
North Iowa Area Comm Coll (IA)
Northwest State Comm Coll (OH)
Oakland Comm Coll (MI)
Oakton Comm Coll (IL)
Odessa Coll (TX)
Orangeburg-Calhoun Tech Coll (SC)
Orange Coast Coll (CA)
Ouachita Tech Coll (AR)
Oxnard Coll (CA)
Pasadena City Coll (CA)
Pellissippi State Tech Comm Coll (TN)
Pitt Comm Coll (NC)
Portland Comm Coll (OR)
Ranken Tech Coll (MO)
Reading Area Comm Coll (PA)
Richmond Comm Coll (NC)
St. Clair County Comm Coll (MI)
St. Cloud Tech Coll (MN)
San Diego City Coll (CA)
San Joaquin Delta Coll (CA)
San Jose City Coll (CA)
Sheridan Coll (WY)
Sinclair Comm Coll (OH)
Somerset Comm Coll (KY)
South Central Tech Coll (MN)
Southeast Comm Coll, Lincoln Campus (NE)
Southern Maine Comm Coll (ME)
South Plains Coll (TX)
South Suburban Coll (IL)
South Texas Comm Coll (TX)
Southwestern Illinois Coll (IL)

Southwestern Oregon Comm Coll (OR)
Southwest Mississippi Comm Coll (MS)
Spartanburg Tech Coll (SC)
Spokane Comm Coll (WA)
State U of NY Coll of Technology at Alfred (NY)
Texas State Tech Coll–Harlingen (TX)
Texas State Tech Coll–Waco/Marshall Campus (TX)
Trenholm State Tech Coll, Montgomery (AL)
Trident Tech Coll (SC)
Triton Coll (IL)
U of Alaska Anchorage, Kenai Peninsula Coll (AK)
Utah Valley State Coll (UT)
Ventura Coll (CA)
Vincennes U (IN)
Washtenaw Comm Coll (MI)
Waycross Coll (GA)
Western Iowa Tech Comm Coll (IA)
Western Nevada Comm Coll (NV)
The Williamson Free School of Mecha Trades (PA)
York Tech Coll (SC)
Yuba Coll (CA)

Management Information Systems
Academy Coll (MN)
Allegany Coll of Maryland (MD)
Arapahoe Comm Coll (CO)
Big Sandy Comm and Tech Coll (KY)
Bristol Comm Coll (MA)
Burlington County Coll (NJ)
Career Coll of Northern Nevada (NV)
Central Wyoming Coll (WY)
Century Coll (MN)
Cincinnati State Tech and Comm Coll (OH)
Clovis Comm Coll (NM)
The Coll of Westchester (NY)
Commonwealth Business Coll, Merrillville (IN)
Comm Coll of Allegheny County (PA)
Comm Coll of the Air Force (AL)
County Coll of Morris (NJ)
Delaware County Comm Coll (PA)
Del Mar Coll (TX)
Eastern Wyoming Coll (WY)
Fayetteville Tech Comm Coll (NC)
Front Range Comm Coll (CO)
Glendale Comm Coll (AZ)
Gwinnett Tech Coll (GA)
Hagerstown Comm Coll (MD)
Harford Comm Coll (MD)
Harrisburg Area Comm Coll (PA)
Heartland Comm Coll (IL)
Hesser Coll (NH)
Hopkinsville Comm Coll (KY)
Hutchinson Comm Coll and Area Vocational School (KS)
Jackson State Comm Coll (TN)
John Tyler Comm Coll (VA)
Kalamazoo Valley Comm Coll (MI)
Kirkwood Comm Coll (IA)
Lackawanna Coll (PA)
Lake Region State Coll (ND)
Lake Superior Coll (MN)
Lansing Comm Coll (MI)
Louisiana Tech Coll–Evangeline Campus (LA)
Louisiana Tech Coll–Natchitoches Campus (LA)

Louisiana Tech Coll–Northwest Louisiana Campus (LA)
Louisiana Tech Coll–Sidney N. Collier Campus (LA)
Louisiana Tech Coll–Young Memorial Campus (LA)
Lower Columbia Coll (WA)
Manchester Comm Coll (CT)
Manhattan Area Tech Coll (KS)
Miami Dade Coll (FL)
Miami U Hamilton (OH)
Modesto Jr Coll (CA)
Montcalm Comm Coll (MI)
Montgomery Coll (MD)
Mott Comm Coll (MI)
Mount Wachusett Comm Coll (MA)
Napa Valley Coll (CA)
Nassau Comm Coll (NY)
New Hampshire Comm Tech Coll, Manchester/Stratham (NH)
Normandale Comm Coll (MN)
North Harris Coll (TX)
North Hennepin Comm Coll (MN)
Northland Pioneer Coll (AZ)
Northwestern Michigan Coll (MI)
Ouachita Tech Coll (AR)
Owens Comm Coll, Toledo (OH)
Pikes Peak Comm Coll (CO)
Raritan Valley Comm Coll (NJ)
Rochester Business Inst (NY)
Salem Comm Coll (NJ)
South Arkansas Comm Coll (AR)
Southeast Comm Coll (KY)
Southern Maine Comm Coll (ME)
South Suburban Coll (IL)
Southwestern Oregon Comm Coll (OR)
Trinidad State Jr Coll (CO)
Triton Coll (IL)
Trumbull Business Coll (OH)
Union County Coll (NJ)
The U of Akron–Wayne Coll (OH)
Victor Valley Coll (CA)
Vincennes U (IN)
Western Nevada Comm Coll (NV)
Yakima Valley Comm Coll (WA)

Management Information Systems and Services Related
Cedar Valley Coll (TX)
Central Florida Comm Coll (FL)
Cleveland Comm Coll (NC)
Eastern Wyoming Coll (WY)
Indiana Business Coll, Columbus (IN)
Indiana Business Coll, Indianapolis (IN)
Indiana Business Coll, Lafayette (IN)
Indiana Business Coll, Muncie (IN)
Indiana Business Coll, Terre Haute (IN)
International Inst of the Americas, Phoenix (AZ)
Metropolitan Comm Coll–Business & Technology College (MO)
Mid-South Comm Coll (AR)
Mohawk Valley Comm Coll (NY)
Montgomery County Comm Coll (PA)
Northland Pioneer Coll (AZ)
Oakland Comm Coll (MI)
Wisconsin Indianhead Tech Coll (WI)

Management Science

Cape Cod Comm Coll (MA)
Fayetteville Tech Comm Coll (NC)
Harrisburg Area Comm Coll (PA)
Lakeshore Tech Coll (WI)
Lamar State Coll–Port Arthur (TX)
Oakland Comm Coll (MI)
Oakton Comm Coll (IL)
Phoenix Coll (AZ)
Tillamook Bay Comm Coll (OR)
Western Nevada Comm Coll (NV)

Manufacturing Engineering

Bristol Comm Coll (MA)
Kent State U, Salem Campus (OH)
Penn State U Fayette Campus of the Commonwealth Coll (PA)
Penn State U Hazleton Campus of the Commonwealth Coll (PA)
Penn State U Wilkes-Barre Campus of the Commonwealth Coll (PA)
Penn State U York Campus of the Commonwealth Coll (PA)

Manufacturing Technology

Albany Tech Coll (GA)
Alpena Comm Coll (MI)
Bates Tech Coll (WA)
Brevard Comm Coll (FL)
Clark Coll (WA)
Coll of DuPage (IL)
Hopkinsville Comm Coll (KY)
Hutchinson Comm Coll and Area Vocational School (KS)
Lehigh Carbon Comm Coll (PA)
Luna Comm Coll (NM)
Macomb Comm Coll (MI)
Mott Comm Coll (MI)
Oakland Comm Coll (MI)
Owens Comm Coll, Toledo (OH)
Pennsylvania Coll of Technology (PA)
Rend Lake Coll (IL)
Utah Valley State Coll (UT)

Marine Biology and Biological Oceanography

Colorado Northwestern Comm Coll (CO)
Daytona Beach Comm Coll (FL)
Lincoln Coll, Lincoln (IL)
Southern Maine Comm Coll (ME)

Marine Maintenance and Ship Repair Technology

Alexandria Tech Coll (MN)
Cape Fear Comm Coll (NC)
Iowa Lakes Comm Coll (IA)
Northeast Wisconsin Tech Coll (WI)
Olympic Coll (WA)

Marine Science/Merchant Marine Officer

Anne Arundel Comm Coll (MD)
Northwestern Michigan Coll (MI)

Marine Technology

Cape Fear Comm Coll (NC)
Coll of Oceaneering (CA)
Honolulu Comm Coll (HI)
Kingsborough Comm Coll of City U of NY (NY)
Louisville Tech Inst (KY)
North Idaho Coll (ID)
Orange Coast Coll (CA)
Santa Barbara City Coll (CA)

Marine Transportation Related

Northwestern Michigan Coll (MI)

Maritime Science

Northwestern Michigan Coll (MI)

Marketing/Marketing Management

Abraham Baldwin Ag Coll (GA)
AIB Coll of Business (IA)
Alexandria Tech Coll (MN)
Allegany Coll of Maryland (MD)
Allentown Business School (PA)
Alvin Comm Coll (TX)
American River Coll (CA)
Anne Arundel Comm Coll (MD)
Arapahoe Comm Coll (CO)
Augusta Tech Coll (GA)
Austin Comm Coll (TX)
Bainbridge Coll (GA)
Barton County Comm Coll (KS)
Bellevue Comm Coll (WA)
Berkeley Coll (NJ)
Berkeley Coll-New York City Campus (NY)
Berkeley Coll-Westchester Campus (NY)
Blackhawk Tech Coll (WI)
Blue Ridge Comm Coll (NC)
Borough of Manhattan Comm Coll of City U of NY (NY)
Bristol Comm Coll (MA)
Bronx Comm Coll of City U of NY (NY)
Brookdale Comm Coll (NJ)
Bucks County Comm Coll (PA)
Butler County Comm Coll (KS)
Butte Coll (CA)
Camden County Coll (NJ)
Carl Sandburg Coll (IL)
Casper Coll (WY)
Cecil Comm Coll (MD)
Cedar Valley Coll (TX)
Central Arizona Coll (AZ)
Central Comm Coll–Columbus Campus (NE)
Central Florida Comm Coll (FL)
Centralia Coll (WA)
Central Lakes Coll (MN)
Central Oregon Comm Coll (OR)
Central Pennsylvania Coll (PA)
Central Piedmont Comm Coll (NC)
Cincinnati State Tech and Comm Coll (OH)
City Colls of Chicago, Wilbur Wright Coll (IL)
Clarendon Coll (TX)
Clover Park Tech Coll (WA)
Coffeyville Comm Coll (KS)
Colby Comm Coll (KS)
Coll of DuPage (IL)
Coll of Southern Idaho (ID)
Coll of the Desert (CA)
Coll of the Sequoias (CA)
The Coll of Westchester (NY)
Colorado Mountn Coll, Alpine Cmps (CO)
Columbus State Comm Coll (OH)
Comm Coll of Allegheny County (PA)
Comm Coll of Aurora (CO)
Comm Coll of Rhode Island (RI)
Copiah-Lincoln Comm Coll–Natchez Campus (MS)
Cuesta Coll (CA)
Cumberland County Coll (NJ)

Cuyahoga Comm Coll (OH)
Dakota County Tech Coll (MN)
Danville Comm Coll (VA)
Daytona Beach Comm Coll (FL)
DeKalb Tech Coll (GA)
Delta Coll (MI)
Des Moines Area Comm Coll (IA)
Eastern Idaho Tech Coll (ID)
Eastern Oklahoma State Coll (OK)
East Los Angeles Coll (CA)
Edison State Comm Coll (OH)
Edmonds Comm Coll (WA)
El Camino Coll (CA)
Elgin Comm Coll (IL)
Erie Business Center South (PA)
Everett Comm Coll (WA)
Fayetteville Tech Comm Coll (NC)
Finger Lakes Comm Coll (NY)
Forsyth Tech Comm Coll (NC)
Frederick Comm Coll (MD)
Garden City Comm Coll (KS)
Georgia Perimeter Coll (GA)
Gloucester County Coll (NJ)
Greenfield Comm Coll (MA)
Green River Comm Coll (WA)
Gwinnett Tech Coll (GA)
Harrisburg Area Comm Coll (PA)
Hawkeye Comm Coll (IA)
Hesser Coll (NH)
Hillsborough Comm Coll (FL)
Hinds Comm Coll (MS)
Hiwassee Coll (TN)
Houston Comm Coll System (TX)
Iowa Lakes Comm Coll (IA)
Isothermal Comm Coll (NC)
Jackson Comm Coll (MI)
James A. Rhodes State Coll (OH)
Jamestown Business Coll (NY)
Jefferson Comm Coll (NY)
Jefferson Davis Comm Coll (AL)
John A. Logan Coll (IL)
J. Sargeant Reynolds Comm Coll (VA)
Kalamazoo Valley Comm Coll (MI)
Kapiolani Comm Coll (HI)
Kent State U, Trumbull Campus (OH)
Kingsborough Comm Coll of City U of NY (NY)
Kirkwood Comm Coll (IA)
Kirtland Comm Coll (MI)
Lake Area Tech Inst (SD)
Lake Land Coll (IL)
Lakeshore Tech Coll (WI)
Lansing Comm Coll (MI)
Laredo Comm Coll (TX)
Lenoir Comm Coll (NC)
Lincoln Coll, Lincoln (IL)
Longview Comm Coll (MO)
Lorain County Comm Coll (OH)
Los Angeles Valley Coll (CA)
MacCormac Coll (IL)
Macomb Comm Coll (MI)
Manchester Comm Coll (CT)
Maple Woods Comm Coll (MO)
Marion Tech Coll (OH)
Marshalltown Comm Coll (IA)
Massasoit Comm Coll (MA)
Maysville Comm Coll (KY)
Meridian Comm Coll (MS)
Miami Dade Coll (FL)
Miami U Hamilton (OH)
Middlesex Comm Coll (CT)
Middlesex Comm Coll (MA)
Middlesex County Coll (NJ)

Mid Michigan Comm Coll (MI)
Miles Comm Coll (MT)
Milwaukee Area Tech Coll (WI)
Mineral Area Coll (MO)
Minnesota State Coll–Southeast Tech (MN)
Minnesota State Comm and Tech Coll–Fergus Falls (MN)
Minot State U–Bottineau Campus (ND)
MiraCosta Coll (CA)
Mississippi Gulf Coast Comm Coll (MS)
Moberly Area Comm Coll (MO)
Modesto Jr Coll (CA)
Mohave Comm Coll (AZ)
Monroe County Comm Coll (MI)
Moraine Park Tech Coll (WI)
Morton Coll (IL)
Mott Comm Coll (MI)
Mountain Empire Comm Coll (VA)
Mt. San Antonio Coll (CA)
Napa Valley Coll (CA)
Nash Comm Coll (NC)
Nassau Comm Coll (NY)
National Coll of Business & Technology, Salem (VA)
Naugatuck Valley Comm Coll (CT)
New Hampshire Comm Tech Coll, Manchester/Stratham (NH)
New Hampshire Tech Inst (NH)
New River Comm Coll (VA)
Normandale Comm Coll (MN)
North Central Missouri Coll (MO)
Northcentral Tech Coll (WI)
Northeast Comm Coll (NE)
Northeastern Oklahoma A&M Coll (OK)
Northeastern Tech Coll (SC)
Northeast Iowa Comm Coll (IA)
Northeast Wisconsin Tech Coll (WI)
Northern Essex Comm Coll (MA)
North Harris Coll (TX)
North Hennepin Comm Coll (MN)
North Shore Comm Coll (MA)
Northwest Coll (WY)
Northwestern Michigan Coll (MI)
Northwest State Comm Coll (OH)
Oakton Comm Coll (IL)
Orange Coast Coll (CA)
Orange County Comm Coll (NY)
Ouachita Tech Coll (AR)
Owens Comm Coll, Findlay (OH)
Owens Comm Coll, Toledo (OH)
Oxnard Coll (CA)
Palm Beach Comm Coll (FL)
Palomar Coll (CA)
Pasadena City Coll (CA)
Pasco-Hernando Comm Coll (FL)
Pellissippi State Tech Comm Coll (TN)
Penn Valley Comm Coll (MO)
Phoenix Coll (AZ)
Piedmont Virginia Comm Coll (VA)
Polk Comm Coll (FL)
Portland Comm Coll (OR)
Pratt Comm Coll and Area Vocational School (KS)
Prince George's Comm Coll (MD)

Raritan Valley Comm Coll (NJ)
Rasmussen Coll Mankato (MN)
Rasmussen Coll Minnetonka (MN)
Rasmussen Coll St. Cloud (MN)
Reading Area Comm Coll (PA)
Red Rocks Comm Coll (CO)
Saint Charles Comm Coll (MO)
St. Clair County Comm Coll (MI)
St. Cloud Tech Coll (MN)
St. Johns River Comm Coll (FL)
St. Petersburg Coll (FL)
Salem Comm Coll (NJ)
San Diego City Coll (CA)
San Joaquin Delta Coll (CA)
San Jose City Coll (CA)
Santa Barbara City Coll (CA)
Sauk Valley Comm Coll (IL)
Schoolcraft Coll (MI)
Seminole Comm Coll (FL)
Seward County Comm Coll (KS)
Sierra Coll (CA)
Sinclair Comm Coll (OH)
Southeastern Tech Coll (GA)
South Hills School of Business & Technology, State College (PA)
South Plains Coll (TX)
South Suburban Coll (IL)
Southwestern Coll (CA)
Southwestern Comm Coll (NC)
Southwestern Illinois Coll (IL)
Southwestern Oregon Comm Coll (OR)
Southwest Mississippi Comm Coll (MS)
Spartanburg Tech Coll (SC)
Spokane Comm Coll (WA)
Spokane Falls Comm Coll (WA)
Springfield Tech Comm Coll (MA)
Stark State Coll of Technology (OH)
State U of NY Coll of A&T at Morrisville (NY)
State U of NY Coll of Technology at Alfred (NY)
State U of NY Coll of Technology at Delhi (NY)
Sullivan County Comm Coll (NY)
Terra State Comm Coll (OH)
Three Rivers Comm Coll (MO)
Tidewater Comm Coll (VA)
Tompkins Cortland Comm Coll (NY)
Trident Tech Coll (SC)
Trinidad State Jr Coll (CO)
Triton Coll (IL)
Umpqua Comm Coll (OR)
U of Northwestern Ohio (OH)
Vincennes U (IN)
Washtenaw Comm Coll (MI)
Western Nevada Comm Coll (NV)
Western Wisconsin Tech Coll (WI)
Western Wyoming Comm Coll (WY)
Westmoreland County Comm Coll (PA)
Williston State Coll (ND)
Yakima Valley Comm Coll (WA)

Marketing Related

Northeast Comm Coll (NE)
Oakland Comm Coll (MI)
Tillamook Bay Comm Coll (OR)

Marketing Research

Lake Region State Coll (ND)
Riverside Comm Coll (CA)

Masonry

Alexandria Tech Coll (MN)
Dakota County Tech Coll (MN)
Fayetteville Tech Comm Coll (NC)
Ivy Tech State Coll–Central Indiana (IN)
Ivy Tech State Coll–Columbus (IN)
Ivy Tech State Coll–Eastcentral (IN)
Ivy Tech State Coll–Lafayette (IN)
Ivy Tech State Coll–North Central (IN)
Ivy Tech State Coll–Northeast (IN)
Ivy Tech State Coll–Northwest (IN)
Ivy Tech State Coll–Southcentral (IN)
Ivy Tech State Coll–Southwest (IN)
Ivy Tech State Coll–Wabash Valley (IN)
Metropolitan Comm Coll-Business & Technology College (MO)
Pennsylvania Coll of Technology (PA)
Somerset Comm Coll (KY)
State U of NY Coll of Technology at Alfred (NY)
State U of NY Coll of Technology at Delhi (NY)
Western Nevada Comm Coll (NV)

Massage Therapy

Clover Park Tech Coll (WA)
Coll of DuPage (IL)
Columbus State Comm Coll (OH)
Globe Coll (MN)
Herzing Coll, Minneapolis Drafting School Division (MN)
Indiana Business Coll-Medical (IN)
Inst of Business & Medical Careers (CO)
IntelliTec Coll, Grand Junction (CO)
Iowa Lakes Comm Coll (IA)
Mercy Coll of Northwest Ohio (OH)
Minnesota School of Business–Brooklyn Center (MN)
Minnesota School of Business-Plymouth (MN)
Minnesota School of Business-Richfield (MN)
National School of Technology, Inc., North Miami Beach (FL)
New York Col Health Professions (NY)
Northland Pioneer Coll (AZ)
Oakland Comm Coll (MI)
Rogue Comm Coll (OR)
Sawyer Coll, Hammond (IN)
Southwestern Comm Coll (NC)
Springfield Tech Comm Coll (MA)
Stautzenberger Coll (OH)
Utah Career Coll (UT)
Waubonsee Comm Coll (IL)

Mass Communication/Media

Amarillo Coll (TX)
Andrew Coll (GA)
Anne Arundel Comm Coll (MD)
Asnuntuck Comm Coll (CT)
Austin Comm Coll (TX)
Bergen Comm Coll (NJ)
Brookdale Comm Coll (NJ)
Bucks County Comm Coll (PA)
Bunker Hill Comm Coll (MA)
Butler County Comm Coll (KS)

Camden County Coll (NJ)
Cape Cod Comm Coll (MA)
Casper Coll (WY)
Central Comm Coll–Hastings Campus (NE)
Centralia Coll (WA)
Central Pennsylvania Coll (PA)
Chabot Coll (CA)
Chipola Coll (FL)
Coffeyville Comm Coll (KS)
Colby Comm Coll (KS)
Coll of the Desert (CA)
Coll of the Sequoias (CA)
Columbia State Comm Coll (TN)
Crowder Coll (MO)
Cuesta Coll (CA)
Daytona Beach Comm Coll (FL)
Dutchess Comm Coll (NY)
Finger Lakes Comm Coll (NY)
Frederick Comm Coll (MD)
Fulton-Montgomery Comm Coll (NY)
Grand Rapids Comm Coll (MI)
Greenfield Comm Coll (MA)
Harrisburg Area Comm Coll (PA)
Henderson Comm Coll (KY)
Hesser Coll (NH)
Hill Coll of the Hill Jr College District (TX)
Hillsborough Comm Coll (FL)
Hinds Comm Coll (MS)
Holyoke Comm Coll (MA)
Houston Comm Coll System (TX)
Iowa Lakes Comm Coll (IA)
Kirkwood Comm Coll (IA)
Lackawanna Coll (PA)
Lamar State Coll–Orange (TX)
Lansing Comm Coll (MI)
Laramie County Comm Coll (WY)
Lincoln Coll, Lincoln (IL)
Lon Morris Coll (TX)
Lorain County Comm Coll (OH)
Los Angeles Valley Coll (CA)
Manatee Comm Coll (FL)
Miami Dade Coll (FL)
Middlesex Comm Coll (CT)
Middlesex Comm Coll (MA)
Midland Coll (TX)
Mineral Area Coll (MO)
Modesto Jr Coll (CA)
Monroe County Comm Coll (MI)
Nassau Comm Coll (NY)
Niagara County Comm Coll (NY)
Northeast Comm Coll (NE)
Northeast Mississippi Comm Coll (MS)
Northeast Wisconsin Tech Coll (WI)
North Idaho Coll (ID)
Northwest Coll (WY)
Oklahoma City Comm Coll (OK)
Orange Coast Coll (CA)
Palm Beach Comm Coll (FL)
Pasadena City Coll (CA)
Pennsylvania Coll of Technology (PA)
Phoenix Coll (AZ)
Pratt Comm Coll and Area Vocational School (KS)
Red Rocks Comm Coll (CO)
St. Clair County Comm Coll (MI)
St. Louis Comm Coll at Florissant Valley (MO)
Santa Monica Coll (CA)
Seward County Comm Coll (KS)
Sierra Coll (CA)
Sinclair Comm Coll (OH)
Snow Coll (UT)
South Plains Coll (TX)

Spokane Falls Comm Coll (WA)
Spoon River Coll (IL)
Tompkins Cortland Comm Coll (NY)
Triton Coll (IL)
Vermilion Comm Coll (MN)
Vincennes U (IN)
Waubonsee Comm Coll (IL)
Western Wisconsin Tech Coll (WI)
West Kentucky Comm and Tech Coll (KY)
Yuba Coll (CA)

Materials Science
Central Arizona Coll (AZ)
Contra Costa Coll (CA)
Mt. San Antonio Coll (CA)
Northern Essex Comm Coll (MA)
North Hennepin Comm Coll (MN)

Mathematics
Abraham Baldwin Ag Coll (GA)
Alpena Comm Coll (MI)
Alvin Comm Coll (TX)
Amarillo Coll (TX)
American River Coll (CA)
Ancilla Coll (IN)
Andrew Coll (GA)
Anne Arundel Comm Coll (MD)
Arizona Western Coll (AZ)
Arkansas State U–Beebe (AR)
Atlanta Metropolitan Coll (GA)
Atlantic Cape Comm Coll (NJ)
Austin Comm Coll (TX)
Bainbridge Coll (GA)
Barton County Comm Coll (KS)
Bergen Comm Coll (NJ)
Borough of Manhattan Comm Coll of City U of NY (NY)
Bronx Comm Coll of City U of NY (NY)
Brookdale Comm Coll (NJ)
Bucks County Comm Coll (PA)
Bunker Hill Comm Coll (MA)
Burlington County Coll (NJ)
Butler County Comm Coll (KS)
Butte Coll (CA)
Calhoun Comm Coll (AL)
Cañada Coll (CA)
Cape Cod Comm Coll (MA)
Casper Coll (WY)
Cecil Comm Coll (MD)
Centralia Coll (WA)
Central Oregon Comm Coll (OR)
Chabot Coll (CA)
Chemeketa Comm Coll (OR)
Chesapeake Coll (MD)
Clarendon Coll (TX)
Clovis Comm Coll (NM)
Coastal Bend Coll (TX)
Coastal Georgia Comm Coll (GA)
Coffeyville Comm Coll (KS)
Colby Comm Coll (KS)
Coll of Southern Idaho (ID)
Coll of the Canyons (CA)
Coll of the Desert (CA)
Coll of the Sequoias (CA)
Colorado Mountn Coll, Alpine Cmps (CO)
Colorado Mountn Coll (CO)
Colorado Mountn Coll, Timberline Cmps (CO)
Columbia Coll (CA)
Columbia-Greene Comm Coll (NY)
Columbia State Comm Coll (TN)
Comm Coll of Allegheny County (PA)
Connors State Coll (OK)

Contra Costa Coll (CA)
Corning Comm Coll (NY)
Crowder Coll (MO)
Cuesta Coll (CA)
Cumberland County Coll (NJ)
Darton Coll (GA)
Daytona Beach Comm Coll (FL)
Del Mar Coll (TX)
Delta Coll (MI)
Donnelly Coll (KS)
Dutchess Comm Coll (NY)
Eastern Arizona Coll (AZ)
Eastern Oklahoma State Coll (OK)
Eastern Wyoming Coll (WY)
East Los Angeles Coll (CA)
East Mississippi Comm Coll (MS)
Edison State Comm Coll (OH)
El Camino Coll (CA)
Essex County Coll (NJ)
Everett Comm Coll (WA)
Feather River Comm Coll District (CA)
Finger Lakes Comm Coll (NY)
Foothill Coll (CA)
Frederick Comm Coll (MD)
Fulton-Montgomery Comm Coll (NY)
Galveston Coll (TX)
Garden City Comm Coll (KS)
Garrett Coll (MD)
Gavilan Coll (CA)
Georgia Perimeter Coll (GA)
Gloucester County Coll (NJ)
Gogebic Comm Coll (MI)
Gordon Coll (GA)
Great Basin Coll (NV)
Greenfield Comm Coll (MA)
Gulf Coast Comm Coll (FL)
Harrisburg Area Comm Coll (PA)
Hill Coll of the Hill Jr College District (TX)
Hinds Comm Coll (MS)
Howard Coll (TX)
Hutchinson Comm Coll and Area Vocational School (KS)
Iowa Lakes Comm Coll (IA)
Jefferson Coll (MO)
Jefferson Comm Coll (NY)
John A. Logan Coll (IL)
Kellogg Comm Coll (MI)
Kingsborough Comm Coll of City U of NY (NY)
Kingwood Coll (TX)
Kirkwood Comm Coll (IA)
Lamar State Coll–Orange (TX)
Lansing Comm Coll (MI)
Laramie County Comm Coll (WY)
Lawson State Comm Coll (AL)
Lehigh Carbon Comm Coll (PA)
Lincoln Coll, Lincoln (IL)
Linn-Benton Comm Coll (OR)
Lon Morris Coll (TX)
Lorain County Comm Coll (OH)
Los Angeles Valley Coll (CA)
Lower Columbia Coll (WA)
Luzerne County Comm Coll (PA)
Macomb Comm Coll (MI)
Merritt Coll (CA)
Miami Dade Coll (FL)
Middlesex County Coll (NJ)
Midland Coll (TX)
Mid Michigan Comm Coll (MI)
MiraCosta Coll (CA)
Mitchell Comm Coll (NC)
Modesto Jr Coll (CA)
Mohave Comm Coll (AZ)
Monroe County Comm Coll (MI)

Montgomery County Comm Coll (PA)
Mountain Empire Comm Coll (VA)
Mt. San Jacinto Coll (CA)
Nassau Comm Coll (NY)
Naugatuck Valley Comm Coll (CT)
Niagara County Comm Coll (NY)
Northampton County Area Comm Coll (PA)
North Country Comm Coll (NY)
Northeast Comm Coll (NE)
Northeastern Oklahoma A&M Coll (OK)
Northeast Mississippi Comm Coll (MS)
North Harris Coll (TX)
North Idaho Coll (ID)
Northwest Coll (WY)
Northwestern Connecticut Comm-Tech Coll (CT)
Northwestern Michigan Coll (MI)
Oakton Comm Coll (IL)
Odessa Coll (TX)
Oklahoma City Comm Coll (OK)
Orange Coast Coll (CA)
Otero Jr Coll (CO)
Oxnard Coll (CA)
Palm Beach Comm Coll (FL)
Palo Alto Coll (TX)
Palomar Coll (CA)
Paris Jr Coll (TX)
Pasadena City Coll (CA)
Pensacola Jr Coll (FL)
Pratt Comm Coll and Area Vocational School (KS)
Raritan Valley Comm Coll (NJ)
Red Rocks Comm Coll (CO)
Rend Lake Coll (IL)
Riverside Comm Coll (CA)
Roane State Comm Coll (TN)
Rogue Comm Coll (OR)
St. Louis Comm Coll at Florissant Valley (MO)
St. Philip's Coll (TX)
Salem Comm Coll (NJ)
San Diego City Coll (CA)
San Joaquin Delta Coll (CA)
San Juan Coll (NM)
Santa Barbara City Coll (CA)
Santa Monica Coll (CA)
Sauk Valley Comm Coll (IL)
Schenectady County Comm Coll (NY)
Scottsdale Comm Coll (AZ)
Seward County Comm Coll (KS)
Sheridan Coll (WY)
Snow Coll (UT)
South Suburban Coll (IL)
Southwestern Coll (CA)
Southwestern Oregon Comm Coll (OR)
Spoon River Coll (IL)
Springfield Tech Comm Coll (MA)
State U of NY Coll of A&T at Morrisville (NY)
State U of NY Coll of Technology at Alfred (NY)
State U of NY Coll of Technology at Delhi (NY)
Sullivan County Comm Coll (NY)
Terra State Comm Coll (OH)
Tompkins Cortland Comm Coll (NY)
Triton Coll (IL)
Umpqua Comm Coll (OR)
U of South Carolina Salkehatchie (SC)
Utah Valley State Coll (UT)
Vermilion Comm Coll (MN)
Victor Valley Coll (CA)
Vincennes U (IN)
Waycross Coll (GA)

Western Nevada Comm Coll (NV)
Western Wyoming Comm Coll (WY)
West Hills Comm Coll (CA)
Yuba Coll (CA)

Mathematics and Computer Science
Crowder Coll (MO)
Dean Coll (MA)

Mathematics and Statistics Related
Bristol Comm Coll (MA)

Mathematics Teacher Education
Eastern Wyoming Coll (WY)
Manatee Comm Coll (FL)
Northeast Texas Comm Coll (TX)

Mechanical Design Technology
Arapahoe Comm Coll (CO)
Asheville-Buncombe Tech Comm Coll (NC)
Blackhawk Tech Coll (WI)
Bowling Green State U-Firelands Coll (OH)
Chemeketa Comm Coll (OR)
Coll of DuPage (IL)
Comm Coll of Allegheny County (PA)
Cuyamaca Coll (CA)
Delta Coll (MI)
Edison State Comm Coll (OH)
Forsyth Tech Comm Coll (NC)
Garden City Comm Coll (KS)
Hawkeye Comm Coll (IA)
Heartland Comm Coll (IL)
Isothermal Comm Coll (NC)
James A. Rhodes State Coll (OH)
Jefferson Coll (MO)
Kirkwood Comm Coll (IA)
Lakeshore Tech Coll (WI)
Lansing Comm Coll (MI)
Lenoir Comm Coll (NC)
Lorain County Comm Coll (OH)
Los Angeles Valley Coll (CA)
Louisville Tech Inst (KY)
Luzerne County Comm Coll (PA)
Macomb Comm Coll (MI)
Minnesota State Coll–Southeast Tech (MN)
Mohawk Valley Comm Coll (NY)
Moraine Park Tech Coll (WI)
Mt. San Antonio Coll (CA)
New Hampshire Comm Tech Coll, Manchester/Stratham (NH)
Niagara County Comm Coll (NY)
Northcentral Tech Coll (WI)
Northeastern Tech Coll (SC)
Northeast Iowa Comm Coll (IA)
Northeast Wisconsin Tech Coll (WI)
Northwest Iowa Comm Coll (IA)
Oakton Comm Coll (IL)
Owens Comm Coll, Toledo (OH)
Phoenix Coll (AZ)
Raritan Valley Comm Coll (NJ)
St. Cloud Tech Coll (MN)
South Suburban Coll (IL)
Spokane Comm Coll (WA)
State U of NY Coll of Technology at Alfred (NY)
Triangle Tech, Inc. (PA)
Western Wisconsin Tech Coll (WI)
Westmoreland County Comm Coll (PA)

Mechanical Drafting
IntelliTec Coll, Grand Junction (CO)

Mechanical Drafting and Cad/Cadd
Alexandria Tech Coll (MN)
Anoka Tech Coll (MN)
Brookdale Comm Coll (NJ)
Central Carolina Tech Coll (SC)
Commonwealth Tech Inst (PA)
Comm Coll of Allegheny County (PA)
Edgecombe Comm Coll (NC)
Gaston Coll (NC)
Island Drafting and Tech Inst (NY)
John Wood Comm Coll (IL)
Lake Superior Coll (MN)
Louisville Tech Inst (KY)
Macomb Comm Coll (MI)
Midlands Tech Coll (SC)
Montgomery County Comm Coll (PA)
Morrison Inst of Technology (IL)
Normandale Comm Coll (MN)
Northeast Wisconsin Tech Coll (WI)
North Florida Comm Coll (FL)
North Hennepin Comm Coll (MN)
North Seattle Comm Coll (WA)
Northwest Tech Inst (MN)
Oakland Comm Coll (MI)
Oakton Comm Coll (IL)
Rowan-Cabarrus Comm Coll (NC)
St. Cloud Tech Coll (MN)
Silicon Valley Coll, Walnut Creek (CA)
South Central Tech Coll (MN)
Stanly Comm Coll (NC)
Triangle Tech, Inc.–Greensburg Center (PA)
Westwood Coll–Denver North (CO)
York Tech Coll (SC)

Mechanical Engineering
Bristol Comm Coll (MA)
Delta Coll (MI)
Itasca Comm Coll (MN)
Lehigh Carbon Comm Coll (PA)
Northwest State Comm Coll (OH)

Mechanical Engineering/Mechanical Technology
Alamance Comm Coll (NC)
Anne Arundel Comm Coll (MD)
Asheville-Buncombe Tech Comm Coll (NC)
Augusta Tech Coll (GA)
Bates Tech Coll (WA)
Blue Ridge Comm Coll (NC)
Broome Comm Coll (NY)
Camden County Coll (NJ)
Cape Fear Comm Coll (NC)
Central Piedmont Comm Coll (NC)
Cincinnati State Tech and Comm Coll (OH)
Clark State Comm Coll (OH)
Cleveland Comm Coll (NC)
Clover Park Tech Coll (WA)
Coffeyville Comm Coll (KS)
Coll of Lake County (IL)
Columbus State Comm Coll (OH)
Corning Comm Coll (NY)
County Coll of Morris (NJ)
Delaware County Comm Coll (PA)
Delta Coll (MI)
ECPI Coll of Technology, Newport News (VA)
ECPI Coll of Technology, Virginia Beach (VA)

ECPI Tech Coll, Richmond (VA)
ECPI Tech Coll, Roanoke (VA)
Edgecombe Comm Coll (NC)
Education Direct Center for Degree Studies (PA)
Fairmont State Comm & Tech Coll (WV)
Finger Lakes Comm Coll (NY)
Gadsden State Comm Coll (AL)
Garden City Comm Coll (KS)
Gaston Coll (NC)
Green River Comm Coll (WA)
Hagerstown Comm Coll (MD)
Harford Comm Coll (MD)
Harrisburg Area Comm Coll (PA)
Hawaii Comm Coll (HI)
Hawkeye Comm Coll (IA)
Illinois Eastern Comm Colls, Lincoln Trail Coll (IL)
Isothermal Comm Coll (NC)
James A. Rhodes State Coll (OH)
Jamestown Comm Coll (NY)
Jefferson Comm Coll (KY)
Jefferson Comm Coll (NY)
John Tyler Comm Coll (VA)
Kalamazoo Valley Comm Coll (MI)
Kent State U, Trumbull Campus (OH)
Kent State U, Tuscarawas Campus (OH)
Kirkwood Comm Coll (IA)
Lakeland Comm Coll (OH)
Lansing Comm Coll (MI)
Lehigh Carbon Comm Coll (PA)
Lord Fairfax Comm Coll (VA)
Los Angeles Trade-Tech Coll (CA)
Los Angeles Valley Coll (CA)
Louisville Tech Inst (KY)
Lower Columbia Coll (WA)
Macomb Comm Coll (MI)
Marion Tech Coll (OH)
McHenry County Coll (IL)
Miami U Hamilton (OH)
Middlesex County Coll (NJ)
Midlands Tech Coll (SC)
Milwaukee Area Tech Coll (WI)
Mohawk Valley Comm Coll (NY)
Montgomery County Comm Coll (PA)
Moraine Valley Comm Coll (IL)
Mott Comm Coll (MI)
Naugatuck Valley Comm Coll (CT)
New Hampshire Tech Inst (NH)
Normandale Comm Coll (MN)
North Central State Coll (OH)
Northeastern Oklahoma A&M Coll (OK)
Northeast Wisconsin Tech Coll (WI)
Northwest State Comm Coll (OH)
Owens Comm Coll, Findlay (OH)
Owens Comm Coll, Toledo (OH)
Pasadena City Coll (CA)
Pellissippi State Tech Comm Coll (TN)
Pennsylvania Inst of Technology (PA)
Penn State U DuBois Campus of the Commonwealth Coll (PA)
Penn State U Hazleton Campus of the Commonwealth Coll (PA)

Penn State U New Kensington Campus of the Commonwealth Coll (PA)
Penn State U Shenango Campus of the Commonwealth Coll (PA)
Penn State U York Campus of the Commonwealth Coll (PA)
Portland Comm Coll (OR)
Queensborough Comm Coll of City U of NY (NY)
Reading Area Comm Coll (PA)
Red Rocks Comm Coll (CO)
The Refrigeration School (AZ)
Richmond Comm Coll (NC)
Rochester Comm and Tech Coll (MN)
St. Louis Comm Coll at Florissant Valley (MO)
San Joaquin Delta Coll (CA)
Sauk Valley Comm Coll (IL)
Schoolcraft Coll (MI)
Sinclair Comm Coll (OH)
Spartanburg Tech Coll (SC)
Spokane Comm Coll (WA)
Springfield Tech Comm Coll (MA)
Stark State Coll of Technology (OH)
State U of NY Coll of A&T at Morrisville (NY)
State U of NY Coll of Technology at Alfred (NY)
State U of NY Coll of Technology at Canton (NY)
Terra State Comm Coll (OH)
Texas State Tech Coll–Waco/Marshall Campus (TX)
Thomas Nelson Comm Coll (VA)
Trident Tech Coll (SC)
Union County Coll (NJ)
Vincennes U (IN)
Virginia Western Comm Coll (VA)
Washtenaw Comm Coll (MI)
Westmoreland County Comm Coll (PA)
Wichita Area Tech Coll (KS)
Wilson Tech Comm Coll (NC)
Wisconsin Indianhead Tech Coll (WI)
York Tech Coll (SC)

Mechanical Engineering Technologies Related
Delaware County Comm Coll (PA)
Edgecombe Comm Coll (NC)
Pennsylvania Inst of Technology (PA)

Mechanic and Repair Technologies Related
Cincinnati State Tech and Comm Coll (OH)
Macomb Comm Coll (MI)
Northeast Wisconsin Tech Coll (WI)
Pennsylvania Coll of Technology (PA)

Mechanics and Repair
Ivy Tech State Coll–Bloomington (IN)
Ivy Tech State Coll–Central Indiana (IN)
Ivy Tech State Coll–Columbus (IN)
Ivy Tech State Coll–Kokomo (IN)
Ivy Tech State Coll–Lafayette (IN)
Ivy Tech State Coll–North Central (IN)
Ivy Tech State Coll–Northeast (IN)
Ivy Tech State Coll–Northwest (IN)
Ivy Tech State Coll–Southcentral (IN)

Ivy Tech State Coll–Southwest (IN)
Ivy Tech State Coll–Wabash Valley (IN)
Ivy Tech State Coll–Whitewater (IN)
Western Wyoming Comm Coll (WY)

Medical Administrative Assistant
Globe Coll (MN)
Minnesota School of Business–Brooklyn Center (MN)
Minnesota School of Business-Plymouth (MN)

Medical Administrative Assistant and Medical Secretary
Academy of Medical Arts and Business (PA)
AEC Southern Ohio Coll (OH)
AIB Coll of Business (IA)
Alamance Comm Coll (NC)
Alexandria Tech Coll (MN)
Allentown Business School (PA)
Alvin Comm Coll (TX)
Amarillo Coll (TX)
American River Coll (CA)
Andover Coll (ME)
Anoka Tech Coll (MN)
Barton County Comm Coll (KS)
Bay State Coll (MA)
Beaufort County Comm Coll (NC)
Berean Inst (PA)
Bergen Comm Coll (NJ)
Bismarck State Coll (ND)
Brevard Comm Coll (FL)
Briarwood Coll (CT)
Bristol Comm Coll (MA)
Bronx Comm Coll of City U of NY (NY)
The Brown Mackie Coll–Lenexa Campus (KS)
Bryant & Stratton Business Inst, Syracuse (NY)
Bryant and Stratton Coll, Parma (OH)
Bryant and Stratton Coll (WI)
Butler County Comm Coll (KS)
Butte Coll (CA)
Cabrillo Coll (CA)
Cambria-Rowe Business Coll, Johnstown (PA)
Cape Cod Comm Coll (MA)
Central Arizona Coll (AZ)
Central Comm Coll–Hastings Campus (NE)
Centralia Coll (WA)
Central Lakes Coll (MN)
Central Pennsylvania Coll (PA)
Central Piedmont Comm Coll (NC)
Century Coll (MN)
Chemeketa Comm Coll (OR)
Chesapeake Coll (MD)
CHI Inst (PA)
Clark Coll (WA)
Clark State Comm Coll (OH)
Cleveland Comm Coll (NC)
Clovis Comm Coll (NM)
Coastal Carolina Comm Coll (NC)
Coffeyville Comm Coll (KS)
The Coll of Westchester (NY)
Columbus State Comm Coll (OH)
Commonwealth Business Coll, Michigan City (IN)
Comm Coll of Allegheny County (PA)
Comm Coll of Aurora (CO)
Comm Coll of Denver (CO)
Comm Coll of Rhode Island (RI)
Consolidated School of Business, York (PA)

Crowder Coll (MO)
Davis Coll (OH)
Daytona Beach Comm Coll (FL)
Del Mar Coll (TX)
Delta Coll (MI)
Des Moines Area Comm Coll (IA)
Durham Tech Comm Coll (NC)
East Los Angeles Coll (CA)
ECPI Coll of Technology, Newport News (VA)
ECPI Coll of Technology, Virginia Beach (VA)
ECPI Tech Coll, Richmond (VA)
ECPI Tech Coll, Roanoke (VA)
Edison State Comm Coll (OH)
El Centro Coll (TX)
Elgin Comm Coll (IL)
Elmira Business Inst (NY)
Erie Business Center South (PA)
Essex County Coll (NJ)
Eugenio María de Hostos Comm Coll of City U of NY (NY)
Everett Comm Coll (WA)
Florida National Coll (FL)
Fort Scott Comm Coll (KS)
Frederick Comm Coll (MD)
Fulton-Montgomery Comm Coll (NY)
Gallipolis Career Coll (OH)
Gem City Coll (IL)
Gloucester County Coll (NJ)
Gogebic Comm Coll (MI)
Goodwin Coll (CT)
Grand Rapids Comm Coll (MI)
Green River Comm Coll (WA)
Hamilton Coll (NE)
Hawkeye Comm Coll (IA)
Hesser Coll (NH)
Hibbing Comm Coll (MN)
Hillsborough Comm Coll (FL)
Houston Comm Coll System (TX)
Howard Comm Coll (MD)
Illinois Eastern Comm Colls, Olney Central Coll (IL)
Inst of Business & Medical Careers (CO)
IntelliTec Coll, Grand Junction (CO)
Iowa Lakes Comm Coll (IA)
James A. Rhodes State Coll (OH)
Jamestown Business Coll (NY)
Jefferson Coll (MO)
Jefferson Comm Coll (NY)
Jefferson Comm Coll (OH)
Johnston Comm Coll (NC)
John Wood Comm Coll (IL)
Kalamazoo Valley Comm Coll (MI)
Kellogg Comm Coll (MI)
Kirkwood Comm Coll (IA)
Kirtland Comm Coll (MI)
Lackawanna Coll (PA)
Lake Land Coll (IL)
Lake Region State Coll (ND)
Lakeshore Tech Coll (WI)
Lake Superior Coll (MN)
Lamar State Coll–Port Arthur (TX)
LDS Business Coll (UT)
Lenoir Comm Coll (NC)
Lewis and Clark Comm Coll (IL)
Linn-Benton Comm Coll (OR)
Longview Comm Coll (MO)
Los Angeles Harbor Coll (CA)
Lower Columbia Coll (WA)
Luzerne County Comm Coll (PA)
MacCormac Coll (IL)

Manchester Comm Coll (CT)
Maple Woods Comm Coll (MO)
Marion Tech Coll (OH)
Mayland Comm Coll (NC)
McIntosh Coll (NH)
McLennan Comm Coll (TX)
Middlesex Comm Coll (CT)
Mid Michigan Comm Coll (MI)
Miles Comm Coll (MT)
Milwaukee Area Tech Coll (WI)
Minnesota State Coll–Southeast Tech (MN)
Minnesota State Comm and Tech Coll–Fergus Falls (MN)
Minnesota West Comm & Tech Coll-Pipestone Cmps (MN)
Minot State U–Bottineau Campus (ND)
Mitchell Tech Inst (SD)
Monroe Coll, Bronx (NY)
Monroe Coll, New Rochelle (NY)
Monroe County Comm Coll (MI)
Montana State U Coll of Tech-Great Falls (MT)
Montcalm Comm Coll (MI)
Moraine Park Tech Coll (WI)
Morton Coll (IL)
Mott Comm Coll (MI)
Mt. San Antonio Coll (CA)
Nash Comm Coll (NC)
Nassau Comm Coll (NY)
Naugatuck Valley Comm Coll (CT)
New Hampshire Comm Tech Coll, Manchester/Stratham (NH)
Newport Business Inst, Lower Burrell (PA)
Newport Business Inst, Williamsport (PA)
New River Comm Coll (VA)
Normandale Comm Coll (MN)
Northampton County Area Comm Coll (PA)
Northcentral Tech Coll (WI)
Northeast Alabama Comm Coll (AL)
Northeast Comm Coll (NE)
Northeastern Oklahoma A&M Coll (OK)
Northeast Mississippi Comm Coll (MS)
Northeast Texas Comm Coll (TX)
Northeast Wisconsin Tech Coll (WI)
Northern Essex Comm Coll (MA)
Northern Maine Comm Coll (ME)
North Idaho Coll (ID)
North Shore Comm Coll (MA)
Northwest State Comm Coll (OH)
Ohio Business Coll, Sandusky (OH)
Ohio Valley Coll of Technology (OH)
Orange Coast Coll (CA)
Otero Jr Coll (CO)
Ouachita Tech Coll (AR)
Owens Comm Coll, Findlay (OH)
Palomar Coll (CA)
Pennsylvania Coll of Technology (PA)
Penn Valley Comm Coll (MO)
Pensacola Jr Coll (FL)
Phoenix Coll (AZ)
Pima Comm Coll (AZ)
Pitt Comm Coll (NC)
Polk Comm Coll (FL)
Portland Comm Coll (OR)

Rasmussen Coll Mankato (MN)
Rasmussen Coll Minnetonka (MN)
Rasmussen Coll St. Cloud (MN)
Reading Area Comm Coll (PA)
Rend Lake Coll (IL)
Riverland Comm Coll (MN)
Roane State Comm Coll (TN)
Rochester Comm and Tech Coll (MN)
Rockingham Comm Coll (NC)
St. Clair County Comm Coll (MI)
St. Cloud Tech Coll (MN)
Saint Paul Coll–A Comm & Tech College (MN)
St. Philip's Coll (TX)
Scottsdale Comm Coll (AZ)
Shelton State Comm Coll (AL)
Sierra Coll (CA)
Silicon Valley Coll, Walnut Creek (CA)
Sinclair Comm Coll (OH)
South Coll (TN)
Southeast Comm Coll, Beatrice Campus (NE)
South Hills School of Business & Technology, State College (PA)
South Plains Coll (TX)
South Puget Sound Comm Coll (WA)
Southwestern Illinois Coll (IL)
Spartanburg Tech Coll (SC)
Spokane Comm Coll (WA)
Spoon River Coll (IL)
Springfield Tech Comm Coll (MA)
Stanly Comm Coll (NC)
State U of NY Coll of A&T at Morrisville (NY)
Temple Coll (TX)
Terra State Comm Coll (OH)
Trident Tech Coll (SC)
Trumbull Business Coll (OH)
Umpqua Comm Coll (OR)
The U of Akron–Wayne Coll (OH)
U of Northwestern Ohio (OH)
Utah Valley State Coll (UT)
Vance-Granville Comm Coll (NC)
Vatterott Coll, Omaha (NE)
Vatterott Coll, Tulsa (OK)
Vermilion Comm Coll (MN)
Vincennes U (IN)
Vista Comm Coll (CA)
Walters State Comm Coll (TN)
Washtenaw Comm Coll (MI)
Western Iowa Tech Comm Coll (IA)
Western Wisconsin Tech Coll (WI)
Western Wyoming Comm Coll (WY)
Westmoreland County Comm Coll (PA)
Wisconsin Indianhead Tech Coll (WI)
Yakima Valley Comm Coll (WA)

Medical/Clinical Assistant
Academy of Medical Arts and Business (PA)
AEC Southern Ohio Coll (OH)
AEC Southern Ohio Coll, Northern Kentucky Campus (KY)
Alamance Comm Coll (NC)
Andover Coll (ME)
Anne Arundel Comm Coll (MD)
Anoka Tech Coll (MN)
Arapahoe Comm Coll (CO)
Austin Comm Coll (TX)
Bay State Coll (MA)

Bergen Comm Coll (NJ)
Bradford School (OH)
Brevard Comm Coll (FL)
Briarwood Coll (CT)
Broome Comm Coll (NY)
The Brown Mackie Coll–
Lenexa Campus (KS)
Bryant & Stratton Business
Inst, Buffalo (NY)
Bryant & Stratton Business
Inst, Syracuse (NY)
Bryant and Stratton Coll,
Parma (OH)
Bryant and Stratton Coll (WI)
Bucks County Comm Coll
(PA)
Cabarrus Coll of Health
Sciences (NC)
Capital Comm Coll (CT)
Career Coll of Northern
Nevada (NV)
Carteret Comm Coll (NC)
Central Comm Coll–Hastings
Campus (NE)
Central Oregon Comm Coll
(OR)
Central Pennsylvania Coll
(PA)
Central Piedmont Comm Coll
(NC)
Century Coll (MN)
Chabot Coll (CA)
Chemeketa Comm Coll (OR)
CHI Inst (PA)
Cincinnati State Tech and
Comm Coll (OH)
City Colls of Chicago,
Malcolm X Coll (IL)
Clark Coll (WA)
CollAmerica–Fort Collins
(CO)
Coll of the Desert (CA)
Commonwealth Business
Coll, Merrillville (IN)
Commonwealth Business
Coll, Michigan City (IN)
Commonwealth Tech Inst
(PA)
Comm Coll of Allegheny
County (PA)
Comm Coll of Aurora (CO)
Cossatot Comm Coll of the U
of Arkansas (AR)
Cuesta Coll (CA)
Davis Coll (OH)
DeKalb Tech Coll (GA)
Delaware County Comm Coll
(PA)
Delta Coll (MI)
Des Moines Area Comm Coll
(IA)
Draughons Jr Coll (KY)
Duluth Business U (MN)
Dutchess Comm Coll (NY)
Eastern Idaho Tech Coll (ID)
Eastern Oklahoma State Coll
(OK)
East Los Angeles Coll (CA)
ECPI Tech Coll, Roanoke
(VA)
Edgecombe Comm Coll (NC)
El Camino Coll (CA)
El Centro Coll (TX)
Everett Comm Coll (WA)
Florida National Coll (FL)
Forsyth Tech Comm Coll
(NC)
Gaston Coll (NC)
Gem City Coll (IL)
Goodwin Coll (CT)
Guilford Tech Comm Coll
(NC)
Gwinnett Tech Coll (GA)
Hamilton Coll (NE)
Herzing Coll, Minneapolis
Drafting School Division
(MN)
Hesser Coll (NH)
Hudson County Comm Coll
(NJ)
Indiana Business Coll,
Anderson (IN)
Indiana Business Coll,
Columbus (IN)

Indiana Business Coll,
Evansville (IN)
Indiana Business Coll, Fort
Wayne (IN)
Indiana Business Coll, Terre
Haute (IN)
Indiana Business
Coll-Medical (IN)
Inst of Business & Medical
Careers (CO)
International Inst of the
Americas, Phoenix (AZ)
Iowa Lakes Comm Coll (IA)
Ivy Tech State Coll–Central
Indiana (IN)
Ivy Tech State Coll–
Columbus (IN)
Ivy Tech State Coll–
Eastcentral (IN)
Ivy Tech State Coll–Kokomo
(IN)
Ivy Tech State Coll–Lafayette
(IN)
Ivy Tech State Coll–North
Central (IN)
Ivy Tech State Coll–
Northeast (IN)
Ivy Tech State Coll–
Northwest (IN)
Ivy Tech State Coll–
Southcentral (IN)
Ivy Tech State Coll–
Southeast (IN)
Ivy Tech State Coll–
Southwest (IN)
Ivy Tech State Coll–Wabash
Valley (IN)
Ivy Tech State Coll–
Whitewater (IN)
Jackson Comm Coll (MI)
James Sprunt Comm Coll
(NC)
Jefferson Comm Coll (OH)
Jefferson Davis Comm Coll
(AL)
Johnston Comm Coll (NC)
Kalamazoo Valley Comm
Coll (MI)
Kapiolani Comm Coll (HI)
Kaplan Coll (IA)
Kirkwood Comm Coll (IA)
Lac Courte Oreilles Ojibwa
Comm Coll (WI)
Lake Area Tech Inst (SD)
Lake Washington Tech Coll
(WA)
Lansing Comm Coll (MI)
Laredo Comm Coll (TX)
LDS Business Coll (UT)
Lehigh Carbon Comm Coll
(PA)
Lenoir Comm Coll (NC)
Linn-Benton Comm Coll
(OR)
Lower Columbia Coll (WA)
Macomb Comm Coll (MI)
Massasoit Comm Coll (MA)
Mayland Comm Coll (NC)
McIntosh Coll (NH)
Miami Dade Coll (FL)
Michiana Coll, South Bend
(IN)
Middlesex Comm Coll (MA)
Mid Michigan Comm Coll
(MI)
Mildred Elley (NY)
Minnesota School of
Business-Richfield (MN)
Minnesota West Comm &
Tech Coll-Pipestone Cmps
(MN)
Minot State U–Bottineau
Campus (ND)
Mitchell Comm Coll (NC)
Mitchell Tech Inst (SD)
Modesto Jr Coll (CA)
Mohawk Valley Comm Coll
(NY)
Montana State U Coll of
Tech-Great Falls (MT)
Mountain State Coll (WV)
Mountain West Coll (UT)
Mount Wachusett Comm Coll
(MA)

National Coll of Business &
Technology, Danville (KY)
National Coll of Business &
Technology, Florence (KY)
National Coll of Business &
Technology, Louisville (KY)
National Coll of Business &
Technology, Pikeville (KY)
National Coll of Business &
Technology, Richmond
(KY)
National Coll of Business &
Technology, Nashville (TN)
National Coll of Business &
Technology, Bluefield (VA)
National Coll of Business &
Technology, Bristol (VA)
National Coll of Business &
Technology, Charlottesville
(VA)
National Coll of Business &
Technology, Harrisonburg
(VA)
National Coll of Business &
Technology, Lynchburg
(VA)
National Coll of Business &
Technology, Salem (VA)
National Inst of Technology
(WV)
National School of
Technology, Inc., North
Miami Beach (FL)
New England Inst of Tech &
Florida Culinary Inst (FL)
Newport Business Inst,
Lower Burrell (PA)
Niagara County Comm Coll
(NY)
Northeast Mississippi Comm
Coll (MS)
Northeast State Tech Comm
Coll (TN)
Northeast Wisconsin Tech
Coll (WI)
North Iowa Area Comm Coll
(IA)
North Seattle Comm Coll
(WA)
Northwestern Connecticut
Comm-Tech Coll (CT)
Northwestern Michigan Coll
(MI)
Oakland Comm Coll (MI)
Ocean County Coll (NJ)
Ohio Inst of Photography and
Technology (OH)
Ohio Valley Coll of
Technology (OH)
Olympic Coll (WA)
Orange Coast Coll (CA)
Palomar Coll (CA)
Pasadena City Coll (CA)
Phoenix Coll (AZ)
Pioneer Pacific Coll (OR)
Pitt Comm Coll (NC)
Portland Comm Coll (OR)
Quinebaug Valley Comm
Coll (CT)
Rasmussen Coll Mankato
(MN)
Remington Coll–Lafayette
Campus (LA)
RETS Tech Center (OH)
Richmond Comm Coll (NC)
Rockingham Comm Coll
(NC)
St. Vincent's Coll (CT)
Shelton State Comm Coll
(AL)
Sinclair Comm Coll (OH)
Somerset Comm Coll (KY)
South Coll (TN)
South Coll-Asheville (NC)
Southern Maine Comm Coll
(ME)
Southern State Comm Coll
(OH)
South Puget Sound Comm
Coll (WA)
South U (FL)
South U (SC)
Southwestern Illinois Coll (IL)

Southwestern Oregon Comm
Coll (OR)
Springfield Tech Comm Coll
(MA)
Stanly Comm Coll (NC)
Stark State Coll of
Technology (OH)
State U of NY Coll of
Technology at Alfred (NY)
Stautzenberger Coll (OH)
Thompson Inst (PA)
Trenholm State Tech Coll,
Montgomery (AL)
Tri-County Comm Coll (NC)
Union Comm Coll (NJ)
U of Northwestern Ohio (OH)
Utah Career Coll (UT)
Vance-Granville Comm Coll
(NC)
Vatterott Coll, St. Joseph
(MO)
Vatterott Coll, Springfield
(MO)
Vatterott Coll, Omaha (NE)
Ventura Coll (CA)
Vincennes U (IN)
Virginia Coll at Jackson (MS)
Waubonsee Comm Coll (IL)
Western Wyoming Comm
Coll (WY)
Westwood Coll–Denver
North (CO)

**Medical/Health Management
and Clinical Assistant**
Oklahoma State U,
Oklahoma City (OK)

Medical Insurance Coding
Alexandria Tech Coll (MN)
Columbus State Comm Coll
(OH)
Dakota County Tech Coll
(MN)
Goodwin Coll (CT)
Herzing Coll, Minneapolis
Drafting School Division
(MN)
Kent State U, Salem
Campus (OH)
Kilian Comm Coll (SD)
LDS Business Coll (UT)
National School of
Technology, Inc., North
Miami Beach (FL)
Paris Jr Coll (TX)
Springfield Tech Comm Coll
(MA)

**Medical Insurance/Medical
Billing**
Jackson Comm Coll (MI)
Kent State U, Salem
Campus (OH)

**Medical Laboratory
Technology**
Camden County Coll (NJ)
Cecil Comm Coll (MD)
Fayetteville Tech Comm Coll
(NC)
Frederick Comm Coll (MD)
Harford Comm Coll (MD)
Iowa Lakes Comm Coll (IA)
Jefferson Comm Coll (NY)
Minnesota State Comm and
Tech Coll–Fergus Falls
(MN)
Mohawk Valley Comm Coll
(NY)
Northwest-Shoals Comm
Coll (AL)
Ohio State U Ag Tech Inst
(OH)
Phoenix Coll (AZ)
Portland Comm Coll (OR)
Reading Area Comm Coll
(PA)
Rowan-Cabarrus Comm Coll
(NC)
Schoolcraft Coll (MI)
Vincennes U (IN)

**Medical Microbiology and
Bacteriology**
Riverside Comm Coll (CA)

Medical Office Assistant
Alpena Comm Coll (MI)
Clovis Comm Coll (NM)
Daymar Coll, Louisville (KY)
Harrisburg Area Comm Coll
(PA)
Indiana Business Coll,
Muncie (IN)
Iowa Lakes Comm Coll (IA)
Keiser Coll, Miami (FL)
LDS Business Coll (UT)
MTI Coll of Business and
Technology, Houston (TX)
MTI Coll of Business and
Technology, Houston (TX)
Sauk Valley Comm Coll (IL)
Sawyer Coll, Hammond (IN)
Silicon Valley Coll, Walnut
Creek (CA)
Stautzenberger Coll (OH)
Vatterott Coll, St. Ann (MO)
Vatterott Coll, Oklahoma City
(OK)
Western Wyoming Comm
Coll (WY)

**Medical Office Computer
Specialist**
Iowa Lakes Comm Coll (IA)
Western Wyoming Comm
Coll (WY)

Medical Office Management
Academy of Medical Arts and
Business (PA)
Beaufort County Comm Coll
(NC)
Briarwood Coll (CT)
Coll of Lake County (IL)
Fayetteville Tech Comm Coll
(NC)
Gaston Coll (NC)
Kilian Comm Coll (SD)
Minnesota School of
Business-Richfield (MN)
Minot State U–Bottineau
Campus (ND)
Newport Business Inst,
Lower Burrell (PA)
Northeast Wisconsin Tech
Coll (WI)
Patricia Stevens Coll (MO)
Pennsylvania Inst of
Technology (PA)
Pikes Peak Comm Coll (CO)
Prince George's Comm Coll
(MD)
St. Cloud Tech Coll (MN)
Schuylkill Inst of Business
and Technology (PA)
Spencerian Coll (KY)
The U of Akron–Wayne Coll
(OH)
U of Arkansas Comm Coll at
Batesville (AR)
Virginia Coll at Jackson (MS)

Medical Physiology
Comm Coll of the Air Force
(AL)

**Medical Radiologic
Technology**
Allegany Coll of Maryland
(MD)
Asheville-Buncombe Tech
Comm Coll (NC)
Broome Comm Coll (NY)
Bunker Hill Comm Coll (MA)
Burlington County Coll (NJ)
Caldwell Comm Coll and
Tech Inst (NC)
Camden County Coll (NJ)
Cape Fear Comm Coll (NC)
Capital Comm Coll (CT)
Carolinas Coll of Health
Sciences (NC)
Century Coll (MN)
Chesapeake Coll (MD)
City Colls of Chicago,
Malcolm X Coll (IL)
City Colls of Chicago, Wilbur
Wright Coll (IL)
Cleveland Comm Coll (NC)
Clovis Comm Coll (NM)

Coastal Georgia Comm Coll
(GA)
Coll of DuPage (IL)
Coll of Lake County (IL)
Coll of Southern Idaho (ID)
Comm Coll of Allegheny
County (PA)
Comm Coll of Rhode Island
(RI)
Comm Coll of the Air Force
(AL)
Delgado Comm Coll (LA)
Del Mar Coll (TX)
El Centro Coll (TX)
Erie Comm Coll (NY)
Essex County Coll (NJ)
Eugenio María de Hostos
Comm Coll of City U of NY
(NY)
Foothill Coll (CA)
Gadsden State Comm Coll
(AL)
Galveston Coll (TX)
Hagerstown Comm Coll
(MD)
Harrisburg Area Comm Coll
(PA)
Houston Comm Coll System
(TX)
Hutchinson Comm Coll and
Area Vocational School
(KS)
Illinois Eastern Comm Colls,
Olney Central Coll (IL)
Ivy Tech State Coll–Central
Indiana (IN)
Ivy Tech State Coll–
Columbus (IN)
Ivy Tech State Coll–
Eastcentral (IN)
Ivy Tech State Coll–Wabash
Valley (IN)
Jackson Comm Coll (MI)
Jackson State Comm Coll
(TN)
Jefferson Comm Coll (KY)
Jefferson State Comm Coll
(AL)
Johnston Comm Coll (NC)
John Wood Comm Coll (IL)
Kaskaskia Coll (IL)
Kellogg Comm Coll (MI)
Kent State U, Salem
Campus (OH)
Keystone Coll (PA)
Kishwaukee Coll (IL)
Lake Superior Coll (MN)
Lansing Comm Coll (MI)
Lincoln Land Comm Coll (IL)
Manatee Comm Coll (FL)
Mercy Coll of Northwest Ohio
(OH)
Meridian Comm Coll (MS)
Midland Coll (TX)
Midlands Tech Coll (SC)
Mineral Area Coll (MO)
Mohawk Valley Comm Coll
(NY)
Montcalm Comm Coll (MI)
Montgomery Coll (MD)
Montgomery County Comm
Coll (PA)
Moraine Valley Comm Coll
(IL)
Mott Comm Coll (MI)
Nassau Comm Coll (NY)
Normandale Comm Coll
(MN)
Northampton County Area
Comm Coll (PA)
North Arkansas Coll (AR)
North Country Comm Coll
(NY)
North Hennepin Comm Coll
(MN)
North Shore Comm Coll
(MA)
Oakland Comm Coll (MI)
Orangeburg-Calhoun Tech
Coll (SC)
Owensboro Comm and Tech
Coll (KY)
Parkland Coll (IL)

Pennsylvania Coll of Technology (PA)
Penn State U New Kensington Campus of the Commonwealth Coll (PA)
Pima Comm Coll (AZ)
Pitt Comm Coll (NC)
Quinsigamond Comm Coll (MA)
Riverland Comm Coll (MN)
St. Philip's Coll (TX)
St. Vincent's Coll (CT)
Santa Barbara City Coll (CA)
South Arkansas Comm Coll (AR)
Southeast Comm Coll (KY)
Southeast Comm Coll, Lincoln Campus (NE)
Southwestern Comm Coll (NC)
Spartanburg Tech Coll (SC)
Springfield Tech Comm Coll (MA)
Union County Coll (NJ)
U of Kentucky, Lexington Comm Coll (KY)
Volunteer State Comm Coll (TN)
Waycross Coll (GA)
Wor-Wic Comm Coll (MD)
York Tech Coll (SC)

Medical Reception
Alexandria Tech Coll (MN)
Iowa Lakes Comm Coll (IA)
Lower Columbia Coll (WA)

Medical Staff Services Technology
Beckfield Coll (KY)

Medical Transcription
Alexandria Tech Coll (MN)
Central Arizona Coll (AZ)
Dakota County Tech Coll (MN)
El Centro Coll (TX)
Elgin Comm Coll (IL)
International Inst of the Americas, Phoenix (AZ)
Iowa Lakes Comm Coll (IA)
Jackson Comm Coll (MI)
Kaplan Coll (IA)
Kilian Comm Coll (SD)
LDS Business Coll (UT)
Lehigh Carbon Comm Coll (PA)
Lower Columbia Coll (WA)
Mid Michigan Comm Coll (MI)
Montana State U Coll of Tech-Great Falls (MT)
Mountain State Coll (WV)
Northern Essex Comm Coll (MA)
Northland Pioneer Coll (AZ)
Oakland Comm Coll (MI)
Saint Charles Comm Coll (MO)
Western Dakota Tech Inst (SD)
Westwood Coll–Denver North (CO)
Williston State Coll (ND)

Medium/Heavy Vehicle and Truck Technology
Dakota County Tech Coll (MN)

Mental and Social Health Services And Allied Professions Related
Broome Comm Coll (NY)
Oakland Comm Coll (MI)
Pitt Comm Coll (NC)

Mental Health/Rehabilitation
Alvin Comm Coll (TX)
Anne Arundel Comm Coll (MD)
Columbus State Comm Coll (OH)
Comm Coll of the Air Force (AL)
Del Mar Coll (TX)
Dutchess Comm Coll (NY)

Elgin Comm Coll (IL)
Fiorello H LaGuardia Comm Coll of City U of NY (NY)
Hopkinsville Comm Coll (KY)
Houston Comm Coll System (TX)
Kingsborough Comm Coll of City U of NY (NY)
Lackawanna Coll (PA)
Lenoir Comm Coll (NC)
Macomb Comm Coll (MI)
Marshalltown Comm Coll (IA)
McLennan Comm Coll (TX)
Metropolitan Comm Coll (NE)
Middlesex Comm Coll (CT)
Mohawk Valley Comm Coll (NY)
Mt. San Antonio Coll (CA)
Naugatuck Valley Comm Coll (CT)
New Hampshire Tech Inst (NH)
North Country Comm Coll (NY)
Northern Essex Comm Coll (MA)
North Shore Comm Coll (MA)
Orange County Comm Coll (NY)
Oxnard Coll (CA)
Reading Area Comm Coll (PA)
St. Clair County Comm Coll (MI)
Sinclair Comm Coll (OH)
South Plains Coll (TX)
South Suburban Coll (IL)
Southwestern Comm Coll (NC)
Virginia Western Comm Coll (VA)

Merchandising
Coll of DuPage (IL)
Cuyahoga Comm Coll (OH)

Merchandising, Sales, and Marketing Operations Related (General)
Broome Comm Coll (NY)
Iowa Lakes Comm Coll (IA)
Northeast Wisconsin Tech Coll (WI)
Southwestern Michigan Coll (MI)
Wisconsin Indianhead Tech Coll (WI)

Metal and Jewelry Arts
Garden City Comm Coll (KS)
Gem City Coll (IL)
Mesalands Comm Coll (NM)
Mohave Comm Coll (AZ)
Palomar Coll (CA)
Paris Jr Coll (TX)
Pasadena City Coll (CA)

Metallurgical Technology
Arkansas Northeastern Coll (AR)
Comm Coll of the Air Force (AL)
Elgin Comm Coll (IL)
Linn-Benton Comm Coll (OR)
Macomb Comm Coll (MI)
Penn State U DuBois Campus of the Commonwealth Coll (PA)
Penn State U Fayette Campus of the Commonwealth Coll (PA)
Penn State U Hazleton Campus of the Commonwealth Coll (PA)
Penn State U New Kensington Campus of the Commonwealth Coll (PA)
Penn State U Shenango Campus of the Commonwealth Coll (PA)

Penn State U Wilkes-Barre Campus of the Commonwealth Coll (PA)
Penn State U York Campus of the Commonwealth Coll (PA)
Schoolcraft Coll (MI)
Sierra Coll (CA)
Southwestern Illinois Coll (IL)

Middle School Education
Arkansas Northeastern Coll (AR)
Arkansas State U–Mountain Home (AR)
Eastern Wyoming Coll (WY)
Lincoln Coll, Lincoln (IL)
Miami Dade Coll (FL)
Northeast Texas Comm Coll (TX)
Ozarka Coll (AR)
Vincennes U (IN)

Military Studies
Barton County Comm Coll (KS)

Military Technologies
Calhoun Comm Coll (AL)
Comm Coll of the Air Force (AL)

Mining Technology
Casper Coll (WY)
Coll of Eastern Utah (UT)
Eastern Arizona Coll (AZ)
Illinois Eastern Comm Colls, Wabash Valley Coll (IL)
Mountain Empire Comm Coll (VA)
Sierra Coll (CA)
Trinidad State Jr Coll (CO)
Western Wyoming Comm Coll (WY)

Modern Languages
Amarillo Coll (TX)
Barton County Comm Coll (KS)
Brookdale Comm Coll (NJ)
Cape Cod Comm Coll (MA)
City Colls of Chicago, Wilbur Wright Coll (IL)
Coll of the Sequoias (CA)
Everett Comm Coll (WA)
Galveston Coll (TX)
Lon Morris Coll (TX)
Middlesex County Coll (NJ)
Midland Coll (TX)
Northwest Coll (WY)
Odessa Coll (TX)
Oklahoma City Comm Coll (OK)
Otero Jr Coll (CO)
Palo Alto Coll (TX)
Pasadena City Coll (CA)
San Diego City Coll (CA)

Mortuary Science and Embalming
Delta Coll (MI)

Motorcycle Maintenance and Repair Technology
Iowa Lakes Comm Coll (IA)

Multi-/Interdisciplinary Studies Related
Brookdale Comm Coll (NJ)
Central Carolina Tech Coll (SC)
Harford Comm Coll (MD)
Kaplan Coll (IA)
Laramie County Comm Coll (WY)
Linn-Benton Comm Coll (OR)
Midlands Tech Coll (SC)
Mid-South Comm Coll (AR)
Northwest-Shoals Comm Coll (AL)
Pennsylvania Coll of Technology (PA)
Snead State Comm Coll (AL)
Williston State Coll (ND)

Museum Studies
Northland Pioneer Coll (AZ)

Music
Abraham Baldwin Ag Coll (GA)
Alvin Comm Coll (TX)
Amarillo Coll (TX)
American River Coll (CA)
Andrew Coll (GA)
Anne Arundel Comm Coll (MD)
Arizona Western Coll (AZ)
Atlanta Metropolitan Coll (GA)
Austin Comm Coll (TX)
Barton County Comm Coll (KS)
Bergen Comm Coll (NJ)
Bronx Comm Coll of City U of NY (NY)
Brookdale Comm Coll (NJ)
Bucks County Comm Coll (PA)
Burlington County Coll (NJ)
Butler County Comm Coll (KS)
Butte Coll (CA)
Caldwell Comm Coll and Tech Inst (NC)
Calhoun Comm Coll (AL)
Cañada Coll (CA)
Cape Cod Comm Coll (MA)
Casper Coll (WY)
Cedar Valley Coll (TX)
Centralia Coll (WA)
Central Piedmont Comm Coll (NC)
Central Wyoming Coll (WY)
Chabot Coll (CA)
Chesapeake Coll (MD)
City Colls of Chicago, Malcolm X Coll (IL)
City Colls of Chicago, Wilbur Wright Coll (IL)
Clarendon Coll (TX)
Coastal Bend Coll (TX)
Coffeyville Comm Coll (KS)
Colby Comm Coll (KS)
Coll of Lake County (IL)
Coll of Southern Idaho (ID)
Coll of the Desert (CA)
Coll of the Sequoias (CA)
Colorado Northwestern Comm Coll (CO)
Columbia Coll (CA)
Columbia State Comm Coll (TN)
Comm Coll of Allegheny County (PA)
Comm Coll of Rhode Island (RI)
Contra Costa Coll (CA)
Crowder Coll (MO)
Darton Coll (GA)
Daytona Beach Comm Coll (FL)
Delgado Comm Coll (LA)
Del Mar Coll (TX)
Delta Coll (MI)
Eastern Arizona Coll (AZ)
Eastern Oklahoma State Coll (OK)
Eastern Wyoming Coll (WY)
East Los Angeles Coll (CA)
East Mississippi Comm Coll (MS)
Edison Comm Coll (FL)
El Camino Coll (CA)
Essex County Coll (NJ)
Everett Comm Coll (WA)
Finger Lakes Comm Coll (NY)
Foothill Coll (CA)
Fort Scott Comm Coll (KS)
Galveston Coll (TX)
Garden City Comm Coll (KS)
Garrett Coll (MD)
Gavilan Coll (CA)
Georgia Perimeter Coll (GA)
Grand Rapids Comm Coll (MI)
Gulf Coast Comm Coll (FL)
Harrisburg Area Comm Coll (PA)
Hill Coll of the Hill Jr College District (TX)

Hillsborough Comm Coll (FL)
Hinds Comm Coll (MS)
Hiwassee Coll (TN)
Holyoke Comm Coll (MA)
Howard Comm Coll (MD)
Illinois Eastern Comm Colls, Lincoln Trail Coll (IL)
Illinois Eastern Comm Colls, Olney Central Coll (IL)
Iowa Lakes Comm Coll (IA)
Isothermal Comm Coll (NC)
Jefferson Coll (MO)
Jefferson Davis Comm Coll (AL)
J. Sargeant Reynolds Comm Coll (VA)
Kellogg Comm Coll (MI)
Kingsborough Comm Coll of City U of NY (NY)
Kirkwood Comm Coll (IA)
Lansing Comm Coll (MI)
Laramie County Comm Coll (WY)
Lawson State Comm Coll (AL)
Lewis and Clark Comm Coll (IL)
Lincoln Coll, Lincoln (IL)
Lincoln Land Comm Coll (IL)
Lon Morris Coll (TX)
Lorain County Comm Coll (OH)
Los Angeles Pierce Coll (CA)
Los Angeles Valley Coll (CA)
Lower Columbia Coll (WA)
Manatee Comm Coll (FL)
Manchester Comm Coll (CT)
McHenry County Coll (IL)
McLennan Comm Coll (TX)
Miami Dade Coll (FL)
Middlesex County Coll (NJ)
Midland Coll (TX)
Milwaukee Area Tech Coll (WI)
MiraCosta Coll (CA)
Modesto Jr Coll (CA)
Mohave Comm Coll (AZ)
Morton Coll (IL)
Mt. San Jacinto Coll (CA)
Napa Valley Coll (CA)
Naugatuck Valley Comm Coll (CT)
Niagara County Comm Coll (NY)
Northeast Comm Coll (NE)
Northeastern Oklahoma A&M Coll (OK)
Northeast Mississippi Comm Coll (MS)
Northern Essex Comm Coll (MA)
North Harris Coll (TX)
North Idaho Coll (ID)
North Seattle Comm Coll (WA)
Northwest Coll (WY)
Northwestern Michigan Coll (MI)
Northwest-Shoals Comm Coll (AL)
Oakton Comm Coll (IL)
Odessa Coll (TX)
Oklahoma City Comm Coll (OK)
Orange Coast Coll (CA)
Palm Beach Comm Coll (FL)
Palo Alto Coll (TX)
Palomar Coll (CA)
Pasadena City Coll (CA)
Pensacola Jr Coll (FL)
Pima Comm Coll (AZ)
Pratt Comm Coll and Area Vocational Sch (KS)
Raritan Valley Comm Coll (NJ)
Riverside Comm Coll (CA)
St. Louis Comm Coll at Florissant Valley (MO)
St. Philip's Coll (TX)
San Diego City Coll (CA)
San Joaquin Delta Coll (CA)
San Juan Coll (NM)
Santa Barbara City Coll (CA)
Santa Monica Coll (CA)

Sauk Valley Comm Coll (IL)
Schenectady County Comm Coll (NY)
Seward County Comm Coll (KS)
Shelton State Comm Coll (AL)
Sheridan Coll (WY)
Sinclair Comm Coll (OH)
Snow Coll (UT)
Southeastern Comm Coll (NC)
South Plains Coll (TX)
Southwestern Coll (CA)
Southwestern Oregon Comm Coll (OR)
Southwest Mississippi Comm Coll (MS)
Spokane Falls Comm Coll (WA)
Three Rivers Comm Coll (MO)
Tidewater Comm Coll (VA)
Trinidad State Jr Coll (CO)
Triton Coll (IL)
Truett-McConnell Coll (GA)
Umpqua Comm Coll (OR)
Utah Valley State Coll (UT)
Ventura Coll (CA)
Vermilion Comm Coll (MN)
Victor Valley Coll (CA)
Villa Maria Coll of Buffalo (NY)
Vincennes U (IN)
Waubonsee Comm Coll (IL)
Western Wyoming Comm Coll (WY)
Yuba Coll (CA)

Musical Instrument Fabrication and Repair
Minnesota State Coll–Southeast Tech (MN)
Orange Coast Coll (CA)
Queensborough Comm Coll of City U of NY (NY)

Music History, Literature, and Theory
Hill Coll of the Hill Jr College District (TX)
Lincoln Coll, Lincoln (IL)
Snow Coll (UT)

Music Management and Merchandising
American River Coll (CA)
Century Coll (MN)
Collin County Comm Coll District (TX)
Full Sail Real World Education (FL)
Houston Comm Coll System (TX)
Lincoln Coll, Lincoln (IL)
Musictech Coll (MN)
Northeast Comm Coll (NE)
Orange Coast Coll (CA)
Schenectady County Comm Coll (NY)
Villa Maria Coll of Buffalo (NY)

Music Performance
Butler County Comm Coll (KS)
Comm Coll of the Air Force (AL)
Jamestown Comm Coll (NY)
Macomb Comm Coll (MI)
Manatee Comm Coll (FL)
Miami Dade Coll (FL)
Nassau Comm Coll (NY)
Northeast Comm Coll (NE)
Parkland Coll (IL)
Schenectady County Comm Coll (NY)

Music Related
Globe Coll (MN)
Minnesota School of Business–Brooklyn Center (MN)
Minnesota School of Business-Plymouth (MN)
Minnesota School of Business-Richfield (MN)

Music Teacher Education

Amarillo Coll (TX)
Casper Coll (WY)
Coastal Bend Coll (TX)
Coffeyville Comm Coll (KS)
Colby Comm Coll (KS)
Coll of Lake County (IL)
Copiah-Lincoln Comm Coll (MS)
Del Mar Coll (TX)
Delta Coll (MI)
Eastern Wyoming Coll (WY)
Frederick Comm Coll (MD)
Hill Coll of the Hill Jr College District (TX)
Holmes Comm Coll (MS)
Howard Coll (TX)
Illinois Eastern Comm Colls, Lincoln Trail Coll (IL)
Illinois Eastern Comm Colls, Olney Central Coll (IL)
Iowa Lakes Comm Coll (IA)
Lon Morris Coll (TX)
Manatee Comm Coll (FL)
Miami Dade Coll (FL)
Midland Coll (TX)
Northeast Comm Coll (NE)
Northeast Mississippi Comm Coll (MS)
North Idaho Coll (ID)
Northwest Coll (WY)
Parkland Coll (IL)
Pensacola Jr Coll (FL)
Roane State Comm Coll (TN)
Schoolcraft Coll (MI)
Shelton State Comm Coll (AL)
Snow Coll (UT)
Southwest Mississippi Comm Coll (MS)
Umpqua Comm Coll (OR)
Vincennes U (IN)
Walters State Comm Coll (TN)
Waubonsee Comm Coll (IL)

Music Theory and Composition

Hill Coll of the Hill Jr College District (TX)
Houston Comm Coll System (TX)
Manatee Comm Coll (FL)

Music Therapy

Pasadena City Coll (CA)

Nail Technician and Manicurist

Clovis Comm Coll (NM)
Colorado Northwestern Comm Coll (CO)
Olympic Coll (WA)
Somerset Comm Coll (KY)

Natural Resources/ Conservation

Colorado Northwestern Comm Coll (CO)
Delta Coll (MI)
Finger Lakes Comm Coll (NY)
Fulton-Montgomery Comm Coll (NY)
Iowa Lakes Comm Coll (IA)
Itasca Comm Coll (MN)
Kirkwood Comm Coll (IA)
Minot State U–Bottineau Campus (ND)
Nebraska Indian Comm Coll (NE)
Niagara County Comm Coll (NY)
Pensacola Jr Coll (FL)
Rochester Comm and Tech Coll (MN)
State U of NY Coll of A&T at Morrisville (NY)
Vermilion Comm Coll (MN)
Vincennes U (IN)

Natural Resources Management

Feather River Comm Coll District (CA)

Finger Lakes Comm Coll (NY)
Ohio State U Ag Tech Inst (OH)
St. Petersburg Coll (FL)
Santa Fe Comm Coll (NM)

Natural Resources Management and Policy

American River Coll (CA)
Blackfeet Comm Coll (MT)
Butte Coll (CA)
Central Carolina Tech Coll (SC)
Coll of Lake County (IL)
Coll of the Desert (CA)
Columbia Coll (CA)
Delta Coll (MI)
Finger Lakes Comm Coll (NY)
Garrett Coll (MD)
Greenfield Comm Coll (MA)
Hawkeye Comm Coll (IA)
Itasca Comm Coll (MN)
Lac Courte Oreilles Ojibwa Comm Coll (WI)
Lord Fairfax Comm Coll (VA)
Northwest Coll (WY)
Ohio State U Ag Tech Inst (OH)
Pikes Peak Comm Coll (CO)
San Joaquin Delta Coll (CA)
Snow Coll (UT)
Spokane Comm Coll (WA)
State U of NY Coll of A&T at Morrisville (NY)
Trinidad State Jr Coll (CO)
Ventura Coll (CA)
Vermilion Comm Coll (MN)
Vincennes U (IN)

Natural Sciences

Amarillo Coll (TX)
Andrew Coll (GA)
Cabrillo Coll (CA)
Casper Coll (WY)
Centralia Coll (WA)
Chabot Coll (CA)
Coll of Southern Idaho (ID)
Coll of the Canyons (CA)
Colorado Mountn Coll (CO)
Galveston Coll (TX)
Gavilan Coll (CA)
Iowa Lakes Comm Coll (IA)
Jefferson Comm Coll (NY)
Miami Dade Coll (FL)
Naugatuck Valley Comm Coll (CT)
Northwest Coll (WY)
Orange Coast Coll (CA)
San Joaquin Delta Coll (CA)
Seward County Comm Coll (KS)
Sisseton-Wahpeton Comm Coll (SD)
Snow Coll (UT)
Umpqua Comm Coll (OR)
U of Pittsburgh at Titusville (PA)
Victor Valley Coll (CA)

Non-Profit Management

Goodwin Coll (CT)
Miami Dade Coll (FL)

Nuclear and Industrial Radiologic Technologies Related

Linn State Tech Coll (MO)

Nuclear Engineering

Itasca Comm Coll (MN)

Nuclear Medical Technology

Amarillo Coll (TX)
Bronx Comm Coll of City U of NY (NY)
Caldwell Comm Coll and Tech Inst (NC)
Coll of DuPage (IL)
Comm Coll of Allegheny County (PA)
Comm Coll of the Air Force (AL)
Darton Coll (GA)
Florida Hospital Coll of Health Sciences (FL)

Forsyth Tech Comm Coll (NC)
Galveston Coll (TX)
Gloucester County Coll (NJ)
Harrisburg Area Comm Coll (PA)
Hillsborough Comm Coll (FL)
Houston Comm Coll System (TX)
Howard Comm Coll (MD)
Jefferson Comm Coll (KY)
Kettering Coll of Medical Arts (OH)
Lorain County Comm Coll (OH)
Miami Dade Coll (FL)
Midlands Tech Coll (SC)
Oakland Comm Coll (MI)
Orange Coast Coll (CA)
Pitt Comm Coll (NC)
Prince George's Comm Coll (MD)
Springfield Tech Comm Coll (MA)
Triton Coll (IL)
Union County Coll (NJ)
U of Kentucky, Lexington Comm Coll (KY)
Vincennes U (IN)

Nuclear/Nuclear Power Technology

Central Florida Comm Coll (FL)
Texas State Tech Coll–Waco/Marshall Campus (TX)
Westmoreland County Comm Coll (PA)

Nursing Assistant/Aide and Patient Care Assistant

Alexandria Tech Coll (MN)
Cabarrus Coll of Health Sciences (NC)
Colorado Northwestern Comm Coll (CO)
Comm Coll of Allegheny County (PA)
Glendale Comm Coll (AZ)
Jefferson Coll (MO)
Johnson County Comm Coll (KS)
Lake Region State Coll (ND)
Laramie County Comm Coll (WY)
Louisiana Tech Coll–Mansfield Campus (LA)
Lower Columbia Coll (WA)
Midlands Tech Coll (SC)
Mineral Area Coll (MO)
Modesto Jr Coll (CA)
Northeast Wisconsin Tech Coll (WI)
North Iowa Area Comm Coll (IA)
Trinidad State Jr Coll (CO)
Waubonsee Comm Coll (IL)
Western Iowa Tech Comm Coll (IA)
Western Wyoming Comm Coll (WY)

Nursing (Licensed Practical/ Vocational Nurse Training)

Alexandria Tech Coll (MN)
Alpena Comm Coll (MI)
Amarillo Coll (TX)
Arizona Western Coll (AZ)
Atlanta Metropolitan Coll (GA)
Bainbridge Coll (GA)
Bates Tech Coll (WA)
Big Bend Comm Coll (WA)
Bismarck State Coll (ND)
Butte Coll (CA)
Carl Sandburg Coll (IL)
Carteret Comm Coll (NC)
Casper Coll (WY)
Central Arizona Coll (AZ)
Central Comm Coll–Columbus Campus (NE)
Central Comm Coll–Grand Island Campus (NE)
Centralia Coll (WA)

Central Oregon Comm Coll (OR)
Central Piedmont Comm Coll (NC)
Chemeketa Comm Coll (OR)
Clark State Comm Coll (OH)
Coastal Bend Coll (TX)
Coffeyville Comm Coll (KS)
Colby Comm Coll (KS)
Coll of Southern Maryland (MD)
Coll of the Canyons (CA)
Colorado Mountn Coll (CO)
Columbus State Comm Coll (OH)
Comm Coll of Allegheny County (PA)
Contra Costa Coll (CA)
Dakota County Tech Coll (MN)
Darton Coll (GA)
Daytona Beach Comm Coll (FL)
Delaware Tech & Comm Coll, Terry Cmps (DE)
Delta Coll (MI)
Delta Coll of Arts and Technology (LA)
Des Moines Area Comm Coll (IA)
Durham Tech Comm Coll (NC)
East Arkansas Comm Coll (AR)
Eastern Maine Comm Coll (ME)
Edgecombe Comm Coll (NC)
Elaine P. Nunez Comm Coll (LA)
El Camino Coll (CA)
El Centro Coll (TX)
Elgin Comm Coll (IL)
Eugenio María de Hostos Comm Coll of City U of NY (NY)
Everett Comm Coll (WA)
Fayetteville Tech Comm Coll (NC)
Feather River Comm Coll District (CA)
Galveston Coll (TX)
Gavilan Coll (CA)
Gogebic Comm Coll (MI)
Gordon Coll (GA)
Grand Rapids Comm Coll (MI)
Green River Comm Coll (WA)
Hawaii Comm Coll (HI)
Hawkeye Comm Coll (IA)
Heartland Comm Coll (IL)
Hill Coll of the Hill Jr College District (TX)
Hinds Comm Coll (MS)
Hopkinsville Comm Coll (KY)
Howard Coll (TX)
Howard Comm Coll (MD)
Illinois Eastern Comm Colls, Olney Central Coll (IL)
Indian Hills Comm Coll (IA)
Isothermal Comm Coll (NC)
Itasca Comm Coll (MN)
Jackson Comm Coll (MI)
James H. Faulkner State Comm Coll (AL)
Jefferson Coll (MO)
Jefferson Comm Coll (OH)
John A. Logan Coll (IL)
Johnson County Comm Coll (KS)
Kellogg Comm Coll (MI)
Kingwood Coll (TX)
Kirkwood Comm Coll (IA)
Kirtland Comm Coll (MI)
Lake Area Tech Inst (SD)
Lake Region State Coll (ND)
Lamar State Coll–Port Arthur (TX)
Lansing Comm Coll (MI)
Lehigh Carbon Comm Coll (PA)
Lincoln Coll, Lincoln (IL)
Los Angeles Valley Coll (CA)

Louisiana Tech Coll–Florida Parishes Campus (LA)
Louisiana Tech Coll–Mansfield Campus (LA)
Lower Columbia Coll (WA)
Luna Comm Coll (NM)
Manhattan Area Tech Coll (KS)
Marshalltown Comm Coll (IA)
Merritt Coll (CA)
Metropolitan Comm Coll (NE)
Midlands Tech Coll (SC)
Mid Michigan Comm Coll (MI)
Mid-Plains Comm Coll, North Platte (NE)
Milwaukee Area Tech Coll (WI)
Mineral Area Coll (MO)
Minnesota State Coll–Southeast Tech (MN)
Minnesota State Comm and Tech Coll–Fergus Falls (MN)
MiraCosta Coll (CA)
Montana State U Coll of Tech-Great Falls (MT)
Mott Comm Coll (MI)
New River Comm Coll (VA)
Northcentral Tech Coll (WI)
North Dakota State Coll of Science (ND)
Northeast Comm Coll (NE)
Northeast Wisconsin Tech Coll (WI)
Northern Maine Comm Coll (ME)
North Idaho Coll (ID)
North Iowa Area Comm Coll (IA)
Northland Pioneer Coll (AZ)
North Seattle Comm Coll (WA)
Northwest Coll (WY)
Northwest Iowa Comm Coll (IA)
Northwest-Shoals Comm Coll (AL)
Oakland Comm Coll (MI)
Oakton Comm Coll (IL)
Olympic Coll (WA)
Ouachita Tech Coll (AR)
Pasadena City Coll (CA)
Pennsylvania Coll of Technology (PA)
Reading Area Comm Coll (PA)
Rockingham Comm Coll (NC)
St. Cloud Tech Coll (MN)
St. Philip's Coll (TX)
San Diego City Coll (CA)
San Joaquin Delta Coll (CA)
Santa Barbara City Coll (CA)
Seward County Comm Coll (KS)
Shelton State Comm Coll (AL)
Sierra Coll (CA)
Southeast Comm Coll, Beatrice Campus (NE)
Southern Maine Comm Coll (ME)
South Plains Coll (TX)
South Puget Sound Comm Coll (WA)
Southwestern Comm Coll (NC)
Spokane Comm Coll (WA)
Temple Coll (TX)
Trinidad State Jr Coll (CO)
Triton Coll (IL)
Union County Coll (NJ)
United Tribes Tech Coll (ND)
Vance-Granville Comm Coll (NC)
Vincennes U (IN)
Western Wyoming Comm Coll (WY)
Westmoreland County Comm Coll (PA)
Wichita Area Tech Coll (KS)

Williston State Coll (ND)
Yuba Coll (CA)

Nursing Midwifery

The Florida School of Midwifery (FL)
Miami Dade Coll (FL)

Nursing (Registered Nurse Training)

Abraham Baldwin Ag Coll (GA)
Alamance Comm Coll (NC)
Albuquerque Tech Vocational Inst (NM)
Allegany Coll of Maryland (MD)
Alpena Comm Coll (MI)
Alvin Comm Coll (TX)
Amarillo Coll (TX)
American River Coll (CA)
Andrew Coll (GA)
Anne Arundel Comm Coll (MD)
Arapahoe Comm Coll (CO)
Arizona Western Coll (AZ)
Arkansas Northeastern Coll (AR)
Arkansas State U–Beebe (AR)
Asheville-Buncombe Tech Comm Coll (NC)
Atlantic Cape Comm Coll (NJ)
Austin Comm Coll (TX)
Bainbridge Coll (GA)
Barton County Comm Coll (KS)
Beaufort County Comm Coll (NC)
Bellevue Comm Coll (WA)
Bergen Comm Coll (NJ)
Berkshire Comm Coll (MA)
Big Bend Comm Coll (WA)
Big Sandy Comm and Tech Coll (KY)
Blackhawk Tech Coll (WI)
Bladen Comm Coll (NC)
Blue Ridge Comm Coll (NC)
Borough of Manhattan Comm Coll of City U of NY (NY)
Bowling Green State U-Firelands Coll (OH)
Brevard Comm Coll (FL)
Bristol Comm Coll (MA)
Bronx Comm Coll of City U of NY (NY)
Brookdale Comm Coll (NJ)
Broome Comm Coll (NY)
Brunswick Comm Coll (NC)
Bucks County Comm Coll (PA)
Bunker Hill Comm Coll (MA)
Burlington County Coll (NJ)
Butler County Comm Coll (KS)
Butte Coll (CA)
Cabarrus Coll of Health Sciences (NC)
Cabrillo Coll (CA)
Caldwell Comm Coll and Tech Inst (NC)
Calhoun Comm Coll (AL)
Camden County Coll (NJ)
Cape Cod Comm Coll (MA)
Cape Fear Comm Coll (NC)
Capital Comm Coll (CT)
Carl Sandburg Coll (IL)
Carolinas Coll of Health Sciences (NC)
Casper Coll (WY)
Cecil Comm Coll (MD)
Central Alabama Comm Coll (AL)
Central Arizona Coll (AZ)
Central Carolina Tech Coll (SC)
Central Comm Coll–Grand Island Campus (NE)
Central Florida Comm Coll (FL)
Centralia Coll (WA)
Central Lakes Coll (MN)

Central Maine Medical Center School of Nursing (ME)
Central Oregon Comm Coll (OR)
Central Piedmont Comm Coll (NC)
Central Wyoming Coll (WY)
Century Coll (MN)
Chabot Coll (CA)
Chemeketa Comm Coll (OR)
Chipola Coll (FL)
Cincinnati State Tech and Comm Coll (OH)
City Colls of Chicago, Malcolm X Coll (IL)
Clarendon Coll (TX)
Clark Coll (WA)
Clark State Comm Coll (OH)
Cleveland Comm Coll (NC)
Cleveland State Comm Coll (TN)
Clinton Comm Coll (NY)
Clovis Comm Coll (NM)
Coastal Bend Coll (TX)
Coastal Carolina Comm Coll (NC)
Coastal Georgia Comm Coll (GA)
Cochran School of Nursing (NY)
Coffeyville Comm Coll (KS)
Colby Comm Coll (KS)
Coll of DuPage (IL)
Coll of Eastern Utah (UT)
Coll of Lake County (IL)
Coll of Southern Idaho (ID)
Coll of Southern Maryland (MD)
Coll of the Canyons (CA)
Coll of the Desert (CA)
Coll of the Sequoias (CA)
Collin County Comm Coll District (TX)
Colorado Mountn Coll (CO)
Colorado Northwestern Comm Coll (CO)
Columbia-Greene Comm Coll (NY)
Columbia State Comm Coll (TN)
Columbus State Comm Coll (OH)
Comm Coll of Allegheny County (PA)
Comm Coll of Denver (CO)
Comm Coll of Rhode Island (RI)
Connors State Coll (OK)
Contra Costa Coll (CA)
Copiah-Lincoln Comm Coll (MS)
Corning Comm Coll (NY)
County Coll of Morris (NJ)
Crouse Hospital School of Nursing (NY)
Crowder Coll (MO)
Cuesta Coll (CA)
Cumberland County Coll (NJ)
Cuyahoga Comm Coll (OH)
Darton Coll (GA)
Daytona Beach Comm Coll (FL)
Delaware County Comm Coll (PA)
Delaware Tech & Comm Coll, Terry Cmps (DE)
Delgado Comm Coll (LA)
Del Mar Coll (TX)
Delta Coll (MI)
Des Moines Area Comm Coll (IA)
Doña Ana Branch Comm Coll (NM)
Donnelly Coll (KS)
Durham Tech Comm Coll (NC)
Dutchess Comm Coll (NY)
Eastern Arizona Coll (AZ)
Eastern Maine Comm Coll (ME)
Eastern Oklahoma State Coll (OK)

Eastern Shore Comm Coll (VA)
East Los Angeles Coll (CA)
Edgecombe Comm Coll (NC)
Edison Comm Coll (FL)
Edison State Comm Coll (OH)
El Camino Coll (CA)
El Centro Coll (TX)
Elgin Comm Coll (IL)
Elizabethtown Comm Coll (KY)
Erie Comm Coll (NY)
Essex County Coll (NJ)
Eugenio María de Hostos Comm Coll of City U of NY (NY)
Everett Comm Coll (WA)
Fairmont State Comm & Tech Coll (WV)
Fayetteville Tech Comm Coll (NC)
Finger Lakes Comm Coll (NY)
Fiorello H LaGuardia Comm Coll of City U of NY (NY)
Florida Hospital Coll of Health Sciences (FL)
Forsyth Tech Comm Coll (NC)
Fort Scott Comm Coll (KS)
Frederick Comm Coll (MD)
Front Range Comm Coll (CO)
Fulton-Montgomery Comm Coll (NY)
Gadsden State Comm Coll (AL)
Galveston Coll (TX)
Garden City Comm Coll (KS)
Gaston Coll (NC)
Gavilan Coll (CA)
Georgia Perimeter Coll (GA)
Germanna Comm Coll (VA)
Glendale Comm Coll (AZ)
Glen Oaks Comm Coll (MI)
Gloucester County Coll (NJ)
Gogebic Comm Coll (MI)
Goodwin Coll (CT)
Gordon Coll (GA)
Grand Rapids Comm Coll (MI)
Great Basin Coll (NV)
Greenfield Comm Coll (MA)
Guilford Tech Comm Coll (NC)
Gulf Coast Comm Coll (FL)
Hagerstown Comm Coll (MD)
Harcum Coll (PA)
Harford Comm Coll (MD)
Harrisburg Area Comm Coll (PA)
Hawaii Comm Coll (HI)
Hawkeye Comm Coll (IA)
Heartland Comm Coll (IL)
Henderson Comm Coll (KY)
Hesston Coll (KS)
Hibbing Comm Coll (MN)
Hillsborough Comm Coll (FL)
Hinds Comm Coll (MS)
Hiwassee Coll (TN)
Holmes Comm Coll (MS)
Holyoke Comm Coll (MA)
Hopkinsville Comm Coll (KY)
Houston Comm Coll System (TX)
Howard Coll (TX)
Howard Comm Coll (MD)
Hudson County Comm Coll (NJ)
Hutchinson Comm Coll and Area Vocational School (KS)
Illinois Eastern Comm Colls, Frontier Comm Coll (IL)
Illinois Eastern Comm Colls, Olney Central Coll (IL)
Indian Hills Comm Coll (IA)
Iowa Lakes Comm Coll (IA)
Ivy Tech State Coll–Bloomington (IN)
Ivy Tech State Coll–Central Indiana (IN)

Ivy Tech State Coll–Eastcentral (IN)
Ivy Tech State Coll–Lafayette (IN)
Ivy Tech State Coll–North Central (IN)
Ivy Tech State Coll–Northwest (IN)
Ivy Tech State Coll–Southcentral (IN)
Ivy Tech State Coll–Southeast (IN)
Ivy Tech State Coll–Southwest (IN)
Ivy Tech State Coll–Wabash Valley (IN)
Ivy Tech State Coll–Whitewater (IN)
Jackson Comm Coll (MI)
Jackson State Comm Coll (TN)
James A. Rhodes State Coll (OH)
James H. Faulkner State Comm Coll (AL)
James Sprunt Comm Coll (NC)
Jamestown Comm Coll (NY)
Jefferson Coll (MO)
Jefferson Comm Coll (KY)
Jefferson Comm Coll (NY)
Jefferson Davis Comm Coll (AL)
Jefferson State Comm Coll (AL)
John A. Logan Coll (IL)
Johnson County Comm Coll (KS)
Johnston Comm Coll (NC)
John Tyler Comm Coll (VA)
John Wood Comm Coll (IL)
J. Sargeant Reynolds Comm Coll (VA)
Kalamazoo Valley Comm Coll (MI)
Kansas City Kansas Comm Coll (KS)
Kapiolani Comm Coll (HI)
Kaskaskia Coll (IL)
Kauai Comm Coll (HI)
Keiser Coll, Miami (FL)
Kellogg Comm Coll (MI)
Kent State U, Tuscarawas Campus (OH)
Kettering Coll of Medical Arts (OH)
Kingsborough Comm Coll of City U of NY (NY)
Kirkwood Comm Coll (IA)
Kirtland Comm Coll (MI)
Kishwaukee Coll (IL)
Labouré Coll (MA)
Lac Courte Oreilles Ojibwa Comm Coll (WI)
Lake City Comm Coll (FL)
Lake Land Coll (IL)
Lakeland Comm Coll (OH)
Lakeshore Tech Coll (WI)
Lake-Sumter Comm Coll (FL)
Lake Superior Coll (MN)
Lamar State Coll–Orange (TX)
Lamar State Coll–Port Arthur (TX)
Lansing Comm Coll (MI)
Laramie County Comm Coll (WY)
Laredo Comm Coll (TX)
Lawson State Comm Coll (AL)
Lehigh Carbon Comm Coll (PA)
Lenoir Comm Coll (NC)
Lewis and Clark Comm Coll (IL)
Lincoln Coll, Lincoln (IL)
Lincoln Land Comm Coll (IL)
Linn-Benton Comm Coll (OR)
Lorain County Comm Coll (OH)
Lord Fairfax Comm Coll (VA)

Los Angeles Harbor Coll (CA)
Los Angeles Pierce Coll (CA)
Los Angeles Trade-Tech Coll (CA)
Los Angeles Valley Coll (CA)
Lower Columbia Coll (WA)
Luzerne County Comm Coll (PA)
Macomb Comm Coll (MI)
Manatee Comm Coll (FL)
Manhattan Area Tech Coll (KS)
Maric Coll, San Diego (CA)
Marion Tech Coll (OH)
Marshalltown Comm Coll (IA)
Massasoit Comm Coll (MA)
Mayland Comm Coll (NC)
Maysville Comm Coll (KY)
McLennan Comm Coll (TX)
Mercy Coll of Northwest Ohio (OH)
Meridian Comm Coll (MS)
Merritt Coll (CA)
Metropolitan Comm Coll (NE)
Miami Dade Coll (FL)
Middle Georgia Coll (GA)
Middlesex Comm Coll (MA)
Middlesex County Coll (NJ)
Midland Coll (TX)
Midlands Tech Coll (SC)
Mid Michigan Comm Coll (MI)
Mid-Plains Comm Coll, North Platte (NE)
Miles Comm Coll (MT)
Milwaukee Area Tech Coll (WI)
Mineral Area Coll (MO)
Minneapolis Comm and Tech Coll (MN)
Minnesota State Coll–Southeast Tech (MN)
Minnesota State Comm and Tech Coll–Fergus Falls (MN)
Mississippi Gulf Coast Comm Coll (MS)
Mitchell Comm Coll (NC)
Moberly Area Comm Coll (MO)
Modesto Jr Coll (CA)
Mohave Comm Coll (AZ)
Mohawk Valley Comm Coll (NY)
Monroe County Comm Coll (MI)
Montcalm Comm Coll (MI)
Montgomery Coll (MD)
Montgomery County Comm Coll (PA)
Moraine Park Tech Coll (WI)
Moraine Valley Comm Coll (IL)
Morton Coll (IL)
Motlow State Comm Coll (TN)
Mott Comm Coll (MI)
Mountain Empire Comm Coll (VA)
Mt. San Antonio Coll (CA)
Mt. San Jacinto Coll (CA)
Mount Wachusett Comm Coll (MA)
Napa Valley Coll (CA)
Nash Comm Coll (NC)
Nassau Comm Coll (NY)
Naugatuck Valley Comm Coll (CT)
New Hampshire Comm Tech Coll, Berlin/Laconia (NH)
New Hampshire Comm Tech Coll, Manchester/Stratham (NH)
New Hampshire Tech Inst (NH)
New Mexico State U–Carlsbad (NM)
Niagara County Comm Coll (NY)
Normandale Comm Coll (MN)

Northampton County Area Comm Coll (PA)
North Arkansas Coll (AR)
North Central Missouri Coll (MO)
North Central State Coll (OH)
Northcentral Tech Coll (WI)
North Country Comm Coll (NY)
Northeast Alabama Comm Coll (AL)
Northeast Comm Coll (NE)
Northeastern Oklahoma A&M Coll (OK)
Northeast Iowa Comm Coll (IA)
Northeast Mississippi Comm Coll (MS)
Northeast Texas Comm Coll (TX)
Northeast Wisconsin Tech Coll (WI)
Northern Essex Comm Coll (MA)
Northern Maine Comm Coll (ME)
North Harris Coll (TX)
North Hennepin Comm Coll (MN)
North Idaho Coll (ID)
North Iowa Area Comm Coll (IA)
Northland Pioneer Coll (AZ)
North Seattle Comm Coll (WA)
North Shore Comm Coll (MA)
Northwest Coll (WY)
Northwestern Michigan Coll (MI)
Northwest Iowa Comm Coll (IA)
Northwest-Shoals Comm Coll (AL)
Northwest State Comm Coll (OH)
Oakland Comm Coll (MI)
Oakton Comm Coll (IL)
Ocean County Coll (NJ)
Odessa Coll (TX)
Oklahoma City Comm Coll (OK)
Oklahoma State U, Oklahoma City (OK)
Olympic Coll (WA)
Orangeburg-Calhoun Tech Coll (SC)
Orange County Comm Coll (NY)
Otero Jr Coll (CO)
Owensboro Comm and Tech Coll (KY)
Owens Comm Coll, Findlay (OH)
Owens Comm Coll, Toledo (OH)
Palm Beach Comm Coll (FL)
Palomar Coll (CA)
Panola Coll (TX)
Paris Jr Coll (TX)
Parkland Coll (IL)
Pasadena City Coll (CA)
Pasco-Hernando Comm Coll (FL)
Peninsula Coll (WA)
Pennsylvania Coll of Technology (PA)
Penn State U Fayette Campus of the Commonwealth Coll (PA)
Penn State U Mont Alto Campus of the Commonwealth Coll (PA)
Penn State U Worthington Scranton Cmps Commonwealth Coll (PA)
Penn Valley Comm Coll (MO)
Pensacola Jr Coll (FL)
Phillips Beth Israel School of Nursing (NY)
Phoenix Coll (AZ)
Piedmont Virginia Comm Coll (VA)

Pikes Peak Comm Coll (CO)
Pima Comm Coll (AZ)
Pitt Comm Coll (NC)
Polk Comm Coll (FL)
Portland Comm Coll (OR)
Pratt Comm Coll and Area Vocational School (KS)
Prince George's Comm Coll (MD)
Queensborough Comm Coll of City U of NY (NY)
Quinsigamond Comm Coll (MA)
Raritan Valley Comm Coll (NJ)
Reading Area Comm Coll (PA)
Rend Lake Coll (IL)
Richmond Comm Coll (NC)
Riverland Comm Coll (MN)
Riverside Comm Coll (CA)
Roane State Comm Coll (TN)
Roanoke-Chowan Comm Coll (NC)
Rochester Comm and Tech Coll (MN)
Rockingham Comm Coll (NC)
Rogue Comm Coll (OR)
Rowan-Cabarrus Comm Coll (NC)
Saint Charles Comm Coll (MO)
St. Clair County Comm Coll (MI)
St. Johns River Comm Coll (FL)
Saint Joseph's Hospital Health Center School of Nursing (NY)
St. Louis Comm Coll at Florissant Valley (MO)
St. Luke's Coll (IA)
St. Petersburg Coll (FL)
Cath Med Ctr of Brooklyn & Queens Sch of Nursing (NY)
St. Vincent's Coll (CT)
San Diego City Coll (CA)
San Joaquin Delta Coll (CA)
San Juan Coll (NM)
Santa Barbara City Coll (CA)
Santa Fe Comm Coll (NM)
Santa Monica Coll (CA)
Sauk Valley Comm Coll (IL)
Schoolcraft Coll (MI)
Scottsdale Comm Coll (AZ)
Seminole Comm Coll (FL)
Seward County Comm Coll (KS)
Shelton State Comm Coll (AL)
Sheridan Coll (WY)
Sierra Coll (CA)
Sinclair Comm Coll (OH)
Sisseton-Wahpeton Comm Coll (SD)
Somerset Comm Coll (KY)
South Central Tech Coll (MN)
South Coll (TN)
Southeast Comm Coll (KY)
Southeast Comm Coll, Lincoln Campus (NE)
Southeastern Comm Coll (NC)
Southern Maine Comm Coll (ME)
Southern State Comm Coll (OH)
Southern West Virginia Comm and Tech Coll (WV)
South Plains Coll (TX)
South Puget Sound Comm Coll (WA)
Southside Virginia Comm Coll (VA)
South Suburban Coll (IL)
South Texas Comm Coll (TX)
Southwestern Coll (CA)
Southwestern Comm Coll (NC)
Southwestern Illinois Coll (IL)

Southwestern Michigan Coll (MI)
Southwestern Oregon Comm Coll (OR)
Southwest Mississippi Comm Coll (MS)
Southwest Missouri State U–West Plains (MO)
Spokane Comm Coll (WA)
Spoon River Coll (IL)
Springfield Tech Comm Coll (MA)
Stanly Comm Coll (NC)
Stark State Coll of Technology (OH)
State U of NY Coll of A&T at Morrisville (NY)
State U of NY Coll of Technology at Alfred (NY)
State U of NY Coll of Technology at Canton (NY)
State U of NY Coll of Technology at Delhi (NY)
Sullivan County Comm Coll (NY)
Temple Coll (TX)
Thomas Nelson Comm Coll (VA)
Three Rivers Comm Coll (MO)
Tidewater Comm Coll (VA)
Tompkins Cortland Comm Coll (NY)
Tri-County Comm Coll (NC)
Trident Tech Coll (SC)
Trinidad State Jr Coll (CO)
Triton Coll (IL)
Umpqua Comm Coll (OR)
Union County Coll (NJ)
United Tribes Tech Coll (ND)
U of Arkansas Comm Coll at Batesville (AR)
U of Kentucky, Lexington Comm Coll (KY)
Utah Valley State Coll (UT)
Vance-Granville Comm Coll (NC)
Ventura Coll (CA)
Victor Valley Coll (CA)
Vincennes U (IN)
Virginia Western Comm Coll (VA)
Walters State Comm Coll (TN)
Washtenaw Comm Coll (MI)
Waubonsee Comm Coll (IL)
Waycross Coll (GA)
Weatherford Coll (TX)
Western Iowa Tech Comm Coll (IA)
Western Nevada Comm Coll (NV)
Western Wisconsin Tech Coll (WI)
West Kentucky Comm and Tech Coll (KY)
Westmoreland County Comm Coll (PA)
West Virginia Northern Comm Coll (WV)
Wilson Tech Comm Coll (NC)
Wor-Wic Comm Coll (MD)
Yakima Valley Comm Coll (WA)
Yavapai Coll (AZ)
York Tech Coll (SC)
Yuba Coll (CA)

Nursing Related
Big Sandy Comm and Tech Coll (KY)
Cincinnati State Tech and Comm Coll (OH)
Lamar State Coll–Port Arthur (TX)
Somerset Comm Coll (KY)
Tillamook Bay Comm Coll (OR)

Nutrition Sciences
Mohawk Valley Comm Coll (NY)
Sisseton-Wahpeton Comm Coll (SD)

Occupational Health and Industrial Hygiene
Niagara County Comm Coll (NY)
Northampton County Area Comm Coll (PA)

Occupational Safety and Health Technology
Bates Tech Coll (WA)
Camden County Coll (NJ)
Comm Coll of the Air Force (AL)
Cossatot Comm Coll of the U of Arkansas (AR)
Cuyamaca Coll (CA)
Delgado Comm Coll (LA)
Del Mar Coll (TX)
Durham Tech Comm Coll (NC)
Honolulu Comm Coll (HI)
Houston Comm Coll System (TX)
Ivy Tech State Coll–Central Indiana (IN)
Ivy Tech State Coll–Northeast (IN)
Ivy Tech State Coll–Northwest (IN)
Ivy Tech State Coll–Wabash Valley (IN)
Lanier Tech Coll (GA)
Mineral Area Coll (MO)
Mt. San Antonio Coll (CA)
Okefenokee Tech Coll (GA)
Oklahoma State U, Oklahoma City (OK)
San Diego City Coll (CA)
Texas State Tech Coll–Waco/Marshall Campus (TX)
Trinidad State Jr Coll (CO)
The U of Akron–Wayne Coll (OH)

Occupational Therapist Assistant
Allegany Coll of Maryland (MD)
Anoka Tech Coll (MN)
Briarwood Coll (CT)
Bristol Comm Coll (MA)
Cabarrus Coll of Health Sciences (NC)
Cape Fear Comm Coll (NC)
Cincinnati State Tech and Comm Coll (OH)
Coll of DuPage (IL)
Comm Coll of Allegheny County (PA)
Comm Coll of Rhode Island (RI)
Darton Coll (GA)
Delgado Comm Coll (LA)
Del Mar Coll (TX)
Florida Hospital Coll of Health Sciences (FL)
Green River Comm Coll (WA)
Guilford Tech Comm Coll (NC)
Harcum Coll (PA)
Houston Comm Coll System (TX)
Ivy Tech State Coll–Central Indiana (IN)
Jamestown Comm Coll (NY)
Johnson County Comm Coll (KS)
J. Sargeant Reynolds Comm Coll (VA)
Lake Area Tech Inst (SD)
Lake Superior Coll (MN)
Lehigh Carbon Comm Coll (PA)
Lewis and Clark Comm Coll (IL)
Lincoln Land Comm Coll (IL)
Macomb Comm Coll (MI)
Manatee Comm Coll (FL)
Manchester Comm Coll (CT)
Michiana Coll, South Bend (IN)
Middle Georgia Coll (GA)
Midlands Tech Coll (SC)

Mott Comm Coll (MI)
North Dakota State Coll of Science (ND)
Owens Comm Coll, Toledo (OH)
Parkland Coll (IL)
Pennsylvania Coll of Technology (PA)
Penn State U DuBois Campus of the Commonwealth Coll (PA)
Penn State U Mont Alto Campus of the Commonwealth Coll (PA)
Penn State U Worthington Scranton Cmps Commonwealth Coll (PA)
Pitt Comm Coll (NC)
Polk Comm Coll (FL)
Quinsigamond Comm Coll (MA)
Rend Lake Coll (IL)
Rockingham Comm Coll (NC)
St. Philip's Coll (TX)
Schoolcraft Coll (MI)
South Suburban Coll (IL)
Springfield Tech Comm Coll (MA)
Stanly Comm Coll (NC)
State U of NY Coll of Technology at Canton (NY)
Union County Coll (NJ)
Western Iowa Tech Comm Coll (IA)

Occupational Therapy
Allegany Coll of Maryland (MD)
Amarillo Coll (TX)
Andrew Coll (GA)
Austin Comm Coll (TX)
Barton County Comm Coll (KS)
Bay State Coll (MA)
Bristol Comm Coll (MA)
Casper Coll (WY)
City Colls of Chicago, Wilbur Wright Coll (IL)
Coastal Georgia Comm Coll (GA)
Coffeyville Comm Coll (KS)
Coll of DuPage (IL)
Coll of Southern Idaho (ID)
Daytona Beach Comm Coll (FL)
Durham Tech Comm Coll (NC)
Everett Comm Coll (WA)
Fiorello H LaGuardia Comm Coll of City U of NY (NY)
Hillsborough Comm Coll (FL)
John A. Logan Coll (IL)
Kapiolani Comm Coll (HI)
Keystone Coll (PA)
Kingwood Coll (TX)
Kirkwood Comm Coll (IA)
Manatee Comm Coll (FL)
Milwaukee Area Tech Coll (WI)
Morgan Comm Coll (CO)
Nashville State Tech Comm Coll (TN)
Northeast Mississippi Comm Coll (MS)
North Shore Comm Coll (MA)
Oklahoma City Comm Coll (OK)
Orange County Comm Coll (NY)
Palm Beach Comm Coll (FL)
Pasadena City Coll (CA)
Penn Valley Comm Coll (MO)
Quinsigamond Comm Coll (MA)
Roane State Comm Coll (TN)
Saint Charles Comm Coll (MO)
Sauk Valley Comm Coll (IL)
Sinclair Comm Coll (OH)
South Texas Comm Coll (TX)

Stark State Coll of Technology (OH)
Trident Tech Coll (SC)
Vincennes U (IN)
Western Wisconsin Tech Coll (WI)
Wisconsin Indianhead Tech Coll (WI)
Yakima Valley Comm Coll (WA)

Oceanography (Chemical and Physical)
Arizona Western Coll (AZ)
Everett Comm Coll (WA)
Northeast Mississippi Comm Coll (MS)
Riverside Comm Coll (CA)
Southern Maine Comm Coll (ME)

Office Management
Academy Coll (MN)
Alexandria Tech Coll (MN)
Alpena Comm Coll (MI)
Berkeley Coll-New York City Campus (NY)
Berkeley Coll-Westchester Campus (NY)
Big Bend Comm Coll (WA)
Calhoun Comm Coll (AL)
Cincinnati State Tech and Comm Coll (OH)
Clover Park Tech Coll (WA)
Coll of DuPage (IL)
Comm Coll of Allegheny County (PA)
Comm Coll of the Air Force (AL)
Consolidated School of Business, York (PA)
Cuyamaca Coll (CA)
Delaware County Comm Coll (PA)
Delta Coll (MI)
Edmonds Comm Coll (WA)
Erie Comm Coll (NY)
Fisher Coll (MA)
Gogebic Comm Coll (MI)
Great Basin Coll (NV)
Green River Comm Coll (WA)
Howard Comm Coll (MD)
Iowa Lakes Comm Coll (IA)
Lake Land Coll (IL)
Lake Region State Coll (ND)
Lake-Sumter Comm Coll (FL)
Lord Fairfax Comm Coll (VA)
Lower Columbia Coll (WA)
McIntosh Coll (NH)
Middlesex Comm Coll (MA)
Modesto Jr Coll (CA)
Mott Comm Coll (MI)
National Coll of Business & Technology, Salem (VA)
New England Inst of Tech & Florida Culinary Inst (FL)
North Seattle Comm Coll (WA)
Oakland Comm Coll (MI)
Olympic Coll (WA)
Peninsula Coll (WA)
Saint Charles Comm Coll (MO)
St. Cloud Tech Coll (MN)
South Coll-Asheville (NC)
Southern Arkansas U Tech (AR)
South Hills School of Business & Technology, State College (PA)
Southwestern Oregon Comm Coll (OR)
State U of NY Coll of Technology at Canton (NY)
Tillamook Bay Comm Coll (OR)
The U of Akron–Wayne Coll (OH)
Vista Comm Coll (CA)
Western Wisconsin Tech Coll (WI)

Office Occupations and Clerical Services
Alamance Comm Coll (NC)
Alexandria Tech Coll (MN)
Big Sandy Comm and Tech Coll (KY)
Darton Coll (GA)
Del Mar Coll (TX)
Delta Coll (MI)
East Mississippi Comm Coll (MS)
El Centro Coll (TX)
Hillsborough Comm Coll (FL)
Inst of Business & Medical Careers (CO)
Iowa Lakes Comm Coll (IA)
Lake Region State Coll (ND)
Lanier Tech Coll (GA)
Lehigh Carbon Comm Coll (PA)
Minot State U–Bottineau Campus (ND)
Modesto Jr Coll (CA)
North Country Comm Coll (NY)
Northeast Wisconsin Tech Coll (WI)
Okefenokee Tech Coll (GA)
Pennsylvania Coll of Technology (PA)
Pennsylvania Inst of Technology (PA)
Spokane Falls Comm Coll (WA)
Terra State Comm Coll (OH)
United Tribes Tech Coll (ND)

Operations Management
Alamance Comm Coll (NC)
Alexandria Tech Coll (MN)
Alpena Comm Coll (MI)
Asheville-Buncombe Tech Comm Coll (NC)
Atlanta Metropolitan Coll (GA)
Bowling Green State U-Firelands Coll (OH)
Bunker Hill Comm Coll (MA)
Cleveland Comm Coll (NC)
DeKalb Tech Coll (GA)
Durham Tech Comm Coll (NC)
Gaston Coll (NC)
Goodwin Coll (CT)
Great Basin Coll (NV)
Johnston Comm Coll (NC)
Kishwaukee Coll (IL)
Lehigh Carbon Comm Coll (PA)
Macomb Comm Coll (MI)
Massasoit Comm Coll (MA)
McHenry County Coll (IL)
Mineral Area Coll (MO)
North Central State Coll (OH)
Oakland Comm Coll (MI)
Owens Comm Coll, Findlay (OH)
Pitt Comm Coll (NC)
Remington Coll–Mobile Campus (AL)
Stark State Coll of Technology (OH)
Waubonsee Comm Coll (IL)

Ophthalmic and Optometric Support Services And Allied Professions Related
Mid Michigan Comm Coll (MI)

Ophthalmic Laboratory Technology
Central Pennsylvania Coll (PA)
Comm Coll of Aurora (CO)
Comm Coll of the Air Force (AL)
DeKalb Tech Coll (GA)
Durham Tech Comm Coll (NC)
East Mississippi Comm Coll (MS)
Everett Comm Coll (WA)
Hillsborough Comm Coll (FL)
Lakeland Comm Coll (OH)
Middlesex Comm Coll (CT)

Portland Comm Coll (OR)
Raritan Valley Comm Coll (NJ)
St. Cloud Tech Coll (MN)
Spokane Comm Coll (WA)
Thomas Nelson Comm Coll (VA)
Triton Coll (IL)
Westmoreland County Comm Coll (PA)

Ophthalmic/Optometric Services
Howard Comm Coll (MD)
Luzerne County Comm Coll (PA)

Ophthalmic Technology
Miami Dade Coll (FL)
Penn Valley Comm Coll (MO)
Triton Coll (IL)
Volunteer State Comm Coll (TN)

Optical Sciences
Corning Comm Coll (NY)

Opticianry
Arkansas State U–Mountain Home (AR)
Cuyahoga Comm Coll (OH)
Essex County Coll (NJ)
Harrisburg Area Comm Coll (PA)
J. Sargeant Reynolds Comm Coll (VA)
Milwaukee Area Tech Coll (WI)
Triton Coll (IL)

Optometric Technician
Barton County Comm Coll (KS)
Darton Coll (GA)
Hiwassee Coll (TN)
Sauk Valley Comm Coll (IL)

Ornamental Horticulture
Abraham Baldwin Ag Coll (GA)
Bergen Comm Coll (NJ)
Bronx Comm Coll of City U of NY (NY)
Butte Coll (CA)
Central Florida Comm Coll (FL)
Chabot Coll (CA)
Coll of DuPage (IL)
Coll of Lake County (IL)
Coll of the Desert (CA)
Coll of the Sequoias (CA)
Comm Coll of Allegheny County (PA)
Cumberland County Coll (NJ)
Cuyamaca Coll (CA)
El Camino Coll (CA)
Finger Lakes Comm Coll (NY)
Foothill Coll (CA)
Forsyth Tech Comm Coll (NC)
Gwinnett Tech Coll (GA)
Hawkeye Comm Coll (IA)
Hillsborough Comm Coll (FL)
Howard Coll (TX)
J. Sargeant Reynolds Comm Coll (VA)
Kent State U, Salem Campus (OH)
Kirkwood Comm Coll (IA)
Kishwaukee Coll (IL)
Lenoir Comm Coll (NC)
Los Angeles Pierce Coll (CA)
Metropolitan Comm Coll (NE)
Miami Dade Coll (FL)
Minot State U–Bottineau Campus (ND)
MiraCosta Coll (CA)
Mississippi Gulf Coast Comm Coll (MS)
Modesto Jr Coll (CA)
Mt. San Antonio Coll (CA)
Oakland Comm Coll (MI)
Orange Coast Coll (CA)

Pennsylvania Coll of
Technology (PA)
Pensacola Jr Coll (FL)
San Joaquin Delta Coll (CA)
Santa Barbara City Coll (CA)
Sierra Coll (CA)
Spokane Comm Coll (WA)
Texas State Tech Coll–
Waco/Marshall Campus
(TX)
Triton Coll (IL)
Ventura Coll (CA)
Victor Valley Coll (CA)

Orthoptics
Oklahoma City Comm Coll
(OK)

Orthotics/Prosthetics
Century Coll (MN)
Spokane Falls Comm Coll
(WA)

Painting
The Art Inst of Pittsburgh
(PA)
Cuyamaca Coll (CA)
Keystone Coll (PA)
Lincoln Coll, Lincoln (IL)
Luzerne County Comm Coll
(PA)

Painting and Wall Covering
Ivy Tech State Coll–Central
Indiana (IN)
Ivy Tech State Coll–
Eastcentral (IN)
Ivy Tech State Coll–Lafayette
(IN)
Ivy Tech State Coll–North
Central (IN)
Ivy Tech State Coll–
Northeast (IN)
Ivy Tech State Coll–
Northwest (IN)
Ivy Tech State Coll–
Southwest (IN)
Ivy Tech State Coll–Wabash
Valley (IN)

Paleontology
Mesalands Comm Coll (NM)

Paralegal/Legal Assistant
Globe Coll (MN)
Minnesota School of
Business–Brooklyn Center
(MN)
Minnesota School of
Business–Plymouth (MN)

**Parks, Recreation and
Leisure**
American River Coll (CA)
Bellevue Comm Coll (WA)
Bergen Comm Coll (NJ)
Cabrillo Coll (CA)
Camden County Coll (NJ)
Cape Cod Comm Coll (MA)
Centralia Coll (WA)
Chabot Coll (CA)
Chesapeake Coll (MD)
Coastal Bend Coll (TX)
Coll of the Desert (CA)
Colorado Mountn Coll,
Timberline Cmps (CO)
Colorado Northwestern
Comm Coll (CO)
Comm Coll of Denver (CO)
Comm Coll of the Air Force
(AL)
Del Mar Coll (TX)
Dutchess Comm Coll (NY)
Fayetteville Tech Comm Coll
(NC)
Frederick Comm Coll (MD)
Garrett Coll (MD)
Gordon Coll (GA)
Greenfield Comm Coll (MA)
Iowa Lakes Comm Coll (IA)
Jefferson Davis Comm Coll
(AL)
Kingsborough Comm Coll of
City U of NY (NY)
Kirkwood Comm Coll (IA)
Lawson State Comm Coll
(AL)

Merritt Coll (CA)
Miami Dade Coll (FL)
Mineral Area Coll (MO)
Minneapolis Comm and Tech
Coll (MN)
Mt. San Antonio Coll (CA)
Northeast Mississippi Comm
Coll (MS)
Northern Essex Comm Coll
(MA)
Northwest Coll (WY)
Northwestern Connecticut
Comm-Tech Coll (CT)
Orange County Comm Coll
(NY)
Palomar Coll (CA)
Pasadena City Coll (CA)
Rend Lake Coll (IL)
San Diego City Coll (CA)
San Juan Coll (NM)
Santa Barbara City Coll (CA)
Santa Fe Comm Coll (NM)
Santa Monica Coll (CA)
Southeastern Comm Coll
(NC)
State U of NY Coll of
Technology at Delhi (NY)
Tompkins Cortland Comm
Coll (NY)
Vance-Granville Comm Coll
(NC)
Ventura Coll (CA)
Vermilion Comm Coll (MN)
Vincennes U (IN)

**Parks, Recreation and
Leisure Facilities
Management**
Abraham Baldwin Ag Coll
(GA)
Andrew Coll (GA)
Butte Coll (CA)
Coastal Georgia Comm Coll
(GA)
Coll of the Desert (CA)
Colorado Mountn Coll, Alpine
Cmps (CO)
Colorado Mountn Coll,
Timberline Cmps (CO)
County Coll of Morris (NJ)
Cuesta Coll (CA)
Feather River Comm Coll
District (CA)
Finger Lakes Comm Coll
(NY)
Frederick Comm Coll (MD)
Garrett Coll (MD)
Hawkeye Comm Coll (IA)
James H. Faulkner State
Comm Coll (AL)
Keystone Coll (PA)
Kirkwood Comm Coll (IA)
Modesto Jr Coll (CA)
Mohawk Valley Comm Coll
(NY)
Moraine Valley Comm Coll
(IL)
Mt. San Antonio Coll (CA)
North Country Comm Coll
(NY)
Northland Pioneer Coll (AZ)
Northwest Coll (WY)
Northwestern Connecticut
Comm-Tech Coll (CT)
Palomar Coll (CA)
Southeastern Comm Coll
(NC)
Southwestern Coll (CA)
Spokane Comm Coll (WA)
State U of NY Coll of A&T at
Morrisville (NY)
State U of NY Coll of
Technology at Delhi (NY)
Vermilion Comm Coll (MN)
Western Nevada Comm Coll
(NV)

**Parks, Recreation, and
Leisure Related**
Albuquerque Tech Vocational
Inst (NM)
Cincinnati State Tech and
Comm Coll (OH)

Feather River Comm Coll
District (CA)
Southwestern Comm Coll
(NC)

**Parts, Warehousing, and
Inventory Management**
Central Wyoming Coll (WY)

Pastoral Studies/Counseling
Hesston Coll (KS)

**Perioperative/Operating
Room and Surgical Nursing**
Comm Coll of Allegheny
County (PA)

**Personal and Culinary
Services Related**
Arizona Western Coll (AZ)
The Art Inst of Pittsburgh
(PA)

**Personal/Miscellaneous
Services**
Lorain County Comm Coll
(OH)

Petroleum Technology
Coastal Bend Coll (TX)
Northeast Wisconsin Tech
Coll (WI)
Odessa Coll (TX)
South Plains Coll (TX)
U of Alaska Anchorage,
Kenai Peninsula Coll (AK)

**Pharmacology and
Toxicology**
Silicon Valley Coll, Walnut
Creek (CA)

**Pharmacology and
Toxicology Related**
Silicon Valley Coll, Walnut
Creek (CA)

Pharmacy
Abraham Baldwin Ag Coll
(GA)
Arapahoe Comm Coll (CO)
Barton County Comm Coll
(KS)
Casper Coll (WY)
Coastal Bend Coll (TX)
Colby Comm Coll (KS)
Columbia State Comm Coll
(TN)
Durham Tech Comm Coll
(NC)
Holmes Comm Coll (MS)
Iowa Lakes Comm Coll (IA)
Isothermal Comm Coll (NC)
Lorain County Comm Coll
(OH)
Mid Michigan Comm Coll
(MI)
Northeast Mississippi Comm
Coll (MS)
Northwest-Shoals Comm
Coll (AL)
Pasadena City Coll (CA)
Riverside Comm Coll (CA)
St. Clair County Comm Coll
(MI)
Shelton State Comm Coll
(AL)
Vincennes U (IN)

Pharmacy Technician
Albany Tech Coll (GA)
Casper Coll (WY)
Century Coll (MN)
Comm Coll of Allegheny
County (PA)
Comm Coll of the Air Force
(AL)
Darton Coll (GA)
Everett Comm Coll (WA)
Fayetteville Tech Comm Coll
(NC)
Harrisburg Area Comm Coll
(PA)
Hillsborough Comm Coll (FL)
Inst of Business & Medical
Careers (CO)
Midlands Tech Coll (SC)
North Central State Coll (OH)

North Dakota State Coll of
Science (ND)
North Seattle Comm Coll
(WA)
Oakland Comm Coll (MI)
Pima Comm Coll (AZ)
Roane State Comm Coll
(TN)
Silicon Valley Coll, Walnut
Creek (CA)
U of Northwestern Ohio (OH)
Vatterott Coll, Springfield
(MO)
Washtenaw Comm Coll (MI)
Weatherford Coll (TX)
Wichita Area Tech Coll (KS)

Philosophy
Andrew Coll (GA)
Barton County Comm Coll
(KS)
Bergen Comm Coll (NJ)
Burlington County Coll (NJ)
Cañada Coll (CA)
Cape Cod Comm Coll (MA)
Coastal Georgia Comm Coll
(GA)
Coll of the Desert (CA)
Contra Costa Coll (CA)
Darton Coll (GA)
Daytona Beach Comm Coll
(FL)
Donnelly Coll (KS)
East Los Angeles Coll (CA)
El Camino Coll (CA)
Everett Comm Coll (WA)
Foothill Coll (CA)
Georgia Perimeter Coll (GA)
Harford Comm Coll (MD)
Iowa Lakes Comm Coll (IA)
Kellogg Comm Coll (MI)
Lansing Comm Coll (MI)
Laramie County Comm Coll
(WY)
Lincoln Coll, Lincoln (IL)
Lon Morris Coll (TX)
Lord Fairfax Comm Coll (VA)
Lower Columbia Coll (WA)
Manatee Comm Coll (FL)
Miami Dade Coll (FL)
MiraCosta Coll (CA)
Northeastern Oklahoma
A&M Coll (OK)
Orange Coast Coll (CA)
Oxnard Coll (CA)
Palm Beach Comm Coll (FL)
Palo Alto Coll (TX)
Pasadena City Coll (CA)
Pensacola Jr Coll (FL)
Riverside Comm Coll (CA)
St. Philip's Coll (TX)
San Joaquin Delta Coll (CA)
San Juan Coll (NM)
Santa Barbara City Coll (CA)
Santa Monica Coll (CA)
Snow Coll (UT)
Southwestern Coll (CA)
Triton Coll (IL)
Utah Valley State Coll (UT)
Yuba Coll (CA)

Phlebotomy
Alexandria Tech Coll (MN)
Columbus State Comm Coll
(OH)

**Photographic and Film/
Video Technology**
Calhoun Comm Coll (AL)
County Coll of Morris (NJ)
Dakota County Tech Coll
(MN)
Miami Dade Coll (FL)
Olympic Coll (WA)
Platt Coll San Diego (CA)
Texas State Tech Coll–
Waco/Marshall Campus
(TX)

Photography
Amarillo Coll (TX)
Anne Arundel Comm Coll
(MD)
Antonelli Coll (OH)
Antonelli Inst (PA)

The Art Inst of Philadelphia
(PA)
The Art Inst of Pittsburgh
(PA)
The Art Inst of Seattle (WA)
Austin Comm Coll (TX)
Bergen Comm Coll (NJ)
Brookdale Comm Coll (NJ)
Butte Coll (CA)
Carteret Comm Coll (NC)
Casper Coll (WY)
Cecil Comm Coll (MD)
Chabot Coll (CA)
Coll of DuPage (IL)
Coll of Southern Idaho (ID)
Colorado Mountn Coll (CO)
Columbia Coll (CA)
Comm Coll of Denver (CO)
Cuyahoga Comm Coll (OH)
Dakota County Tech Coll
(MN)
Daytona Beach Comm Coll
(FL)
East Los Angeles Coll (CA)
El Camino Coll (CA)
Everett Comm Coll (WA)
Fiorello H LaGuardia Comm
Coll of City U of NY (NY)
Foothill Coll (CA)
Fort Scott Comm Coll (KS)
Greenfield Comm Coll (MA)
Gwinnett Tech Coll (GA)
Harrisburg Area Comm Coll
(PA)
Hawkeye Comm Coll (IA)
Hill Coll of the Hill Jr College
District (TX)
Holyoke Comm Coll (MA)
Howard Comm Coll (MD)
Iowa Lakes Comm Coll (IA)
Keystone Coll (PA)
Lansing Comm Coll (MI)
Lincoln Coll, Lincoln (IL)
Linn-Benton Comm Coll
(OR)
Los Angeles Pierce Coll (CA)
Los Angeles Trade-Tech Coll
(CA)
Los Angeles Valley Coll (CA)
Lower Columbia Coll (WA)
Luzerne County Comm Coll
(PA)
Metropolitan Comm Coll
(NE)
Miami Dade Coll (FL)
Middlesex County Coll (NJ)
Milwaukee Area Tech Coll
(WI)
Modesto Jr Coll (CA)
Mott Comm Coll (MI)
Mt. San Antonio Coll (CA)
Mt. San Jacinto Coll (CA)
Napa Valley Coll (CA)
Nashville State Tech Comm
Coll (TN)
Nassau Comm Coll (NY)
Northeastern Oklahoma
A&M Coll (OK)
Northeast Mississippi Comm
Coll (MS)
North Harris Coll (TX)
Northland Pioneer Coll (AZ)
Northwest Coll (WY)
Oakland Comm Coll (MI)
Odessa Coll (TX)
Ohio Inst of Photography and
Technology (OH)
Orange Coast Coll (CA)
Palm Beach Comm Coll (FL)
Palomar Coll (CA)
Pasadena City Coll (CA)
St. Louis Comm Coll at
Florissant Valley (MO)
San Diego City Coll (CA)
San Joaquin Delta Coll (CA)
Santa Monica Coll (CA)
Scottsdale Comm Coll (AZ)
Sierra Coll (CA)
Southwestern Coll (CA)
Sullivan County Comm Coll
(NY)
Thomas Nelson Comm Coll
(VA)
Ventura Coll (CA)

Villa Maria Coll of Buffalo
(NY)
Washtenaw Comm Coll (MI)
Western Wyoming Comm
Coll (WY)
Westmoreland County
Comm Coll (PA)
Yuba Coll (CA)

Physical Anthropology
Northwest Coll (WY)

**Physical Education
Teaching and Coaching**
Abraham Baldwin Ag Coll
(GA)
Alvin Comm Coll (TX)
Amarillo Coll (TX)
Andrew Coll (GA)
Anne Arundel Comm Coll
(MD)
Arizona Western Coll (AZ)
Barton County Comm Coll
(KS)
Bucks County Comm Coll
(PA)
Butler County Comm Coll
(KS)
Butte Coll (CA)
Cabrillo Coll (CA)
Cañada Coll (CA)
Cape Cod Comm Coll (MA)
Casper Coll (WY)
Chabot Coll (CA)
Chemeketa Comm Coll (OR)
Chesapeake Coll (MD)
City Colls of Chicago,
Malcolm X Coll (IL)
Clarendon Coll (TX)
Clinton Comm Coll (NY)
Coastal Bend Coll (TX)
Coffeyville Comm Coll (KS)
Colby Comm Coll (KS)
Coll of Southern Idaho (ID)
Coll of the Canyons (CA)
Coll of the Desert (CA)
Coll of the Sequoias (CA)
Columbia Coll (CA)
Columbia State Comm Coll
(TN)
Copiah-Lincoln Comm Coll
(MS)
Crowder Coll (MO)
Cuesta Coll (CA)
Daytona Beach Comm Coll
(FL)
Dean Coll (MA)
Del Mar Coll (TX)
Eastern Oklahoma State Coll
(OK)
Eastern Wyoming Coll (WY)
East Los Angeles Coll (CA)
El Camino Coll (CA)
Essex County Coll (NJ)
Everett Comm Coll (WA)
Finger Lakes Comm Coll
(NY)
Foothill Coll (CA)
Frederick Comm Coll (MD)
Fulton-Montgomery Comm
Coll (NY)
Gadsden State Comm Coll
(AL)
Galveston Coll (TX)
Garden City Comm Coll (KS)
Garrett Coll (MD)
Gavilan Coll (CA)
Georgia Perimeter Coll (GA)
Harrisburg Area Comm Coll
(PA)
Hill Coll of the Hill Jr College
District (TX)
Hillsborough Comm Coll (FL)
Howard Coll (TX)
Iowa Lakes Comm Coll (IA)
Jefferson Coll (MO)
Jefferson Davis Comm Coll
(AL)
John A. Logan Coll (IL)
Kellogg Comm Coll (MI)
Kirkwood Comm Coll (IA)
Lansing Comm Coll (MI)
Laramie County Comm Coll
(WY)
Lincoln Coll, Lincoln (IL)

Linn-Benton Comm Coll (OR)
Lon Morris Coll (TX)
Lorain County Comm Coll (OH)
Los Angeles Valley Coll (CA)
Lower Columbia Coll (WA)
Luzerne County Comm Coll (PA)
Manatee Comm Coll (FL)
McLennan Comm Coll (TX)
Miami Dade Coll (FL)
Middlesex County Coll (NJ)
Midland Coll (TX)
Mitchell Comm Coll (NC)
Modesto Jr Coll (CA)
Montgomery County Comm Coll (PA)
Mt. San Jacinto Coll (CA)
Niagara County Comm Coll (NY)
Northeast Comm Coll (NE)
Northeastern Oklahoma A&M Coll (OK)
Northeast Mississippi Comm Coll (MS)
Northern Essex Comm Coll (MA)
North Harris Coll (TX)
Northwest Coll (WY)
Odessa Coll (TX)
Orange Coast Coll (CA)
Oxnard Coll (CA)
Palm Beach Comm Coll (FL)
Palo Alto Coll (TX)
Palomar Coll (CA)
Pasadena City Coll (CA)
Pratt Comm Coll and Area Vocational School (KS)
Prince George's Comm Coll (MD)
Roane State Comm Coll (TN)
San Diego City Coll (CA)
San Joaquin Delta Coll (CA)
Santa Barbara City Coll (CA)
Santa Monica Coll (CA)
Sauk Valley Comm Coll (IL)
Seward County Comm Coll (KS)
Shelton State Comm Coll (AL)
Sinclair Comm Coll (OH)
Snow Coll (UT)
South Plains Coll (TX)
Southwestern Illinois Coll (IL)
Southwest Mississippi Comm Coll (MS)
Spoon River Coll (IL)
State U of NY Coll of Technology at Delhi (NY)
Trinidad State Jr Coll (CO)
Umpqua Comm Coll (OR)
Vermilion Comm Coll (MN)
Vincennes U (IN)
Walters State Comm Coll (TN)
Waycross Coll (GA)
West Hills Comm Coll (CA)
Yuba Coll (CA)

Physical Sciences
Abraham Baldwin Ag Coll (GA)
Alvin Comm Coll (TX)
Amarillo Coll (TX)
American River Coll (CA)
Arkansas State U–Beebe (AR)
Austin Comm Coll (TX)
Barton County Comm Coll (KS)
Butte Coll (CA)
Casper Coll (WY)
Cecil Comm Coll (MD)
Centralia Coll (WA)
Central Oregon Comm Coll (OR)
Central Wyoming Coll (WY)
Chesapeake Coll (MD)
City Colls of Chicago, Wilbur Wright Coll (IL)
Clovis Comm Coll (NM)
Coastal Bend Coll (TX)
Coll of the Canyons (CA)

Colorado Mountn Coll, Alpine Cmps (CO)
Colorado Northwestern Comm Coll (CO)
Columbia Coll (CA)
Crowder Coll (MO)
Eastern Oklahoma State Coll (OK)
El Camino Coll (CA)
Feather River Comm Coll District (CA)
Fort Scott Comm Coll (KS)
Frederick Comm Coll (MD)
Fulton-Montgomery Comm Coll (NY)
Galveston Coll (TX)
Gordon Coll (GA)
Harrisburg Area Comm Coll (PA)
Hill Coll of the Hill Jr College District (TX)
Howard Comm Coll (MD)
Hutchinson Comm Coll and Area Vocational School (KS)
Iowa Lakes Comm Coll (IA)
Jefferson Coll (MO)
Lawson State Comm Coll (AL)
Lehigh Carbon Comm Coll (PA)
Lincoln Coll, Lincoln (IL)
Linn-Benton Comm Coll (OR)
Miami Dade Coll (FL)
Middlesex County Coll (NJ)
MiraCosta Coll (CA)
Montgomery County Comm Coll (PA)
Naugatuck Valley Comm Coll (CT)
Northeastern Oklahoma A&M Coll (OK)
North Idaho Coll (ID)
Northwest Coll (WY)
Northwestern Connecticut Comm-Tech Coll (CT)
Northwestern Michigan Coll (MI)
Orange County Comm Coll (NY)
Otero Jr Coll (CO)
Palm Beach Comm Coll (FL)
Pasadena City Coll (CA)
Pennsylvania Coll of Technology (PA)
Portland Comm Coll (OR)
Pratt Comm Coll and Area Vocational School (KS)
Riverside Comm Coll (CA)
Roane State Comm Coll (TN)
San Diego City Coll (CA)
San Joaquin Delta Coll (CA)
San Juan Coll (NM)
Santa Fe Comm Coll (NM)
Seward County Comm Coll (KS)
Snow Coll (UT)
Southeast Comm Coll, Beatrice Campus (NE)
Southwestern Coll (CA)
Southwest Mississippi Comm Coll (MS)
Spoon River Coll (IL)
Umpqua Comm Coll (OR)
Union County Coll (NJ)
Utah Valley State Coll (UT)
Ventura Coll (CA)
Vermilion Comm Coll (MN)
Victor Valley Coll (CA)
Western Nevada Comm Coll (NV)

Physical Sciences Related
Mt. San Antonio Coll (CA)
Schoolcraft Coll (MI)

Physical Therapist Assistant
Allegany Coll of Maryland (MD)
Atlantic Cape Comm Coll (NJ)
Barton County Comm Coll (KS)

Berkshire Comm Coll (MA)
Broome Comm Coll (NY)
Cape Cod Comm Coll (MA)
Capital Comm Coll (CT)
Central Florida Comm Coll (FL)
Central Pennsylvania Coll (PA)
Colby Comm Coll (KS)
Coll of DuPage (IL)
Comm Coll of Allegheny County (PA)
Comm Coll of Rhode Island (RI)
Comm Coll of the Air Force (AL)
Darton Coll (GA)
Delgado Comm Coll (LA)
Delta Coll (MI)
Dutchess Comm Coll (NY)
Essex County Coll (NJ)
Everett Comm Coll (WA)
Fayetteville Tech Comm Coll (NC)
Green River Comm Coll (WA)
Guilford Tech Comm Coll (NC)
Gulf Coast Comm Coll (FL)
Harcum Coll (PA)
Hesser Coll (NH)
Houston Comm Coll System (TX)
Ivy Tech State Coll–Eastcentral (IN)
Jackson State Comm Coll (TN)
Jefferson State Comm Coll (AL)
Johnson County Comm Coll (KS)
Kansas City Kansas Comm Coll (KS)
Kaskaskia Coll (IL)
Kellogg Comm Coll (MI)
Kingsborough Comm Coll of City U of NY (NY)
Lake Area Tech Inst (SD)
Lake City Comm Coll (FL)
Lake Land Coll (IL)
Lake Superior Coll (MN)
Lehigh Carbon Comm Coll (PA)
Lincoln Land Comm Coll (IL)
Linn State Tech Coll (MO)
Lorain County Comm Coll (OH)
Macomb Comm Coll (MI)
Manatee Comm Coll (FL)
Manchester Comm Coll (CT)
Marion Tech Coll (OH)
Miami Dade Coll (FL)
Michiana Coll, South Bend (IN)
Middle Georgia Coll (GA)
Midlands Tech Coll (SC)
Montana State U Coll of Tech-Great Falls (MT)
Montgomery Coll (MD)
Mott Comm Coll (MI)
Nassau Comm Coll (NY)
Naugatuck Valley Comm Coll (CT)
Niagara County Comm Coll (NY)
North Central State Coll (OH)
Northeast Wisconsin Tech Coll (WI)
North Iowa Area Comm Coll (IA)
North Shore Comm Coll (MA)
Oakton Comm Coll (IL)
Owens Comm Coll, Toledo (OH)
Pasco-Hernando Comm Coll (FL)
Penn State U DuBois Campus of the Commonwealth Coll (PA)
Penn State U Hazleton Campus of the Commonwealth Coll (PA)

Penn State U Mont Alto Campus of the Commonwealth Coll (PA)
Penn State U Shenango Campus of the Commonwealth Coll (PA)
Pensacola Jr Coll (FL)
Polk Comm Coll (FL)
Rockingham Comm Coll (NC)
St. Petersburg Coll (FL)
St. Philip's Coll (TX)
San Juan Coll (NM)
South Arkansas Comm Coll (AR)
South Coll (TN)
Southeast Comm Coll (KY)
South U (FL)
Southwestern Comm Coll (NC)
Southwestern Illinois Coll (IL)
Spokane Falls Comm Coll (WA)
Springfield Tech Comm Coll (MA)
Stanly Comm Coll (NC)
State U of NY Coll of Technology at Canton (NY)
Union County Coll (NJ)
U of Pittsburgh at Titusville (PA)
Villa Maria Coll of Buffalo (NY)
Volunteer State Comm Coll (TN)
Western Iowa Tech Comm Coll (IA)
Western Wisconsin Tech Coll (WI)
Williston State Coll (ND)

Physical Therapy
Amarillo Coll (TX)
Andrew Coll (GA)
Arapahoe Comm Coll (CO)
Barton County Comm Coll (KS)
Bay State Coll (MA)
Blackhawk Tech Coll (WI)
Butler County Comm Coll (KS)
Caldwell Comm Coll and Tech Inst (NC)
Casper Coll (WY)
Central Piedmont Comm Coll (NC)
Clarendon Coll (TX)
Clark State Comm Coll (OH)
Coastal Georgia Comm Coll (GA)
Colby Comm Coll (KS)
Coll of Southern Idaho (ID)
Columbia State Comm Coll (TN)
Daytona Beach Comm Coll (FL)
Delta Coll (MI)
Donnelly Coll (KS)
Essex County Coll (NJ)
Fiorello H LaGuardia Comm Coll of City U of NY (NY)
Gwinnett Tech Coll (GA)
Hillsborough Comm Coll (FL)
Hiwassee Coll (TN)
Holmes Comm Coll (MS)
Indian Hills Comm Coll (IA)
James A. Rhodes State Coll (OH)
Jefferson Comm Coll (KY)
John Tyler Comm Coll (VA)
Kapiolani Comm Coll (HI)
Keystone Coll (PA)
Kingsborough Comm Coll of City U of NY (NY)
Laredo Comm Coll (TX)
Lawson State Comm Coll (AL)
Luna Comm Coll (NM)
Manatee Comm Coll (FL)
McLennan Comm Coll (TX)
Meridian Comm Coll (MS)
Miami Dade Coll (FL)
Mid Michigan Comm Coll (MI)

Milwaukee Area Tech Coll (WI)
Monroe County Comm Coll (MI)
Morgan Comm Coll (CO)
Morton Coll (IL)
Mount Wachusett Comm Coll (MA)
Nash Comm Coll (NC)
New Hampshire Comm Tech Coll, Manchester/Stratham (NH)
Northeast Comm Coll (NE)
Northeastern Oklahoma A&M Coll (OK)
Northeast Mississippi Comm Coll (MS)
Northeast Wisconsin Tech Coll (WI)
Oakton Comm Coll (IL)
Odessa Coll (TX)
Oklahoma City Comm Coll (OK)
Orange County Comm Coll (NY)
Palm Beach Comm Coll (FL)
Penn Valley Comm Coll (MO)
Pensacola Jr Coll (FL)
Riverside Comm Coll (CA)
Roane State Comm Coll (TN)
Sanford-Brown Coll, Hazelwood (MO)
Sauk Valley Comm Coll (IL)
Seminole Comm Coll (FL)
Sinclair Comm Coll (OH)
Somerset Comm Coll (KY)
South Plains Coll (TX)
Southwestern Comm Coll (NC)
Stark State Coll of Technology (OH)
Trident Tech Coll (SC)
Vincennes U (IN)
Waycross Coll (GA)
West Kentucky Comm and Tech Coll (KY)

Physician Assistant
Barton County Comm Coll (KS)
Barton County Comm Coll (KS)
City Colls of Chicago, Malcolm X Coll (IL)
Coastal Georgia Comm Coll (GA)
Coll of Southern Idaho (ID)
Cuyahoga Comm Coll (OH)
Darton Coll (GA)
Delta Coll (MI)
Fairmont State Comm & Tech Coll (WV)
Foothill Coll (CA)
Globe Coll (MN)
Kettering Coll of Medical Arts (OH)
Keystone Coll (PA)
Manatee Comm Coll (FL)
Minnesota School of Business–Brooklyn Center (MN)
Minnesota School of Business-Plymouth (MN)

Physics
Amarillo Coll (TX)
Andrew Coll (GA)
Arizona Western Coll (AZ)
Atlanta Metropolitan Coll (GA)
Austin Comm Coll (TX)
Barton County Comm Coll (KS)
Bergen Comm Coll (NJ)
Brookdale Comm Coll (NJ)
Bunker Hill Comm Coll (MA)
Burlington County Coll (NJ)
Butler County Comm Coll (KS)
Casper Coll (WY)
Cecil Comm Coll (MD)
Chabot Coll (CA)
Coastal Bend Coll (TX)

Coastal Georgia Comm Coll (GA)
Coll of Southern Idaho (ID)
Coll of the Desert (CA)
Columbia Coll (CA)
Columbia State Comm Coll (TN)
Comm Coll of Allegheny County (PA)
Contra Costa Coll (CA)
Cuesta Coll (CA)
Cuyamaca Coll (CA)
Darton Coll (GA)
Daytona Beach Comm Coll (FL)
Del Mar Coll (TX)
Eastern Arizona Coll (AZ)
El Camino Coll (CA)
Everett Comm Coll (WA)
Finger Lakes Comm Coll (NY)
Foothill Coll (CA)
Georgia Perimeter Coll (GA)
Great Basin Coll (NV)
Hill Coll of the Hill Jr College District (TX)
Holyoke Comm Coll (MA)
John A. Logan Coll (IL)
Kellogg Comm Coll (MI)
Kingsborough Comm Coll of City U of NY (NY)
Linn-Benton Comm Coll (OR)
Lon Morris Coll (TX)
Lorain County Comm Coll (OH)
Los Angeles Harbor Coll (CA)
Lower Columbia Coll (WA)
Manatee Comm Coll (FL)
Miami Dade Coll (FL)
Middlesex County Coll (NJ)
Midland Coll (TX)
MiraCosta Coll (CA)
Northampton County Area Comm Coll (PA)
Northeast Comm Coll (NE)
North Idaho Coll (ID)
Northwest Coll (WY)
Odessa Coll (TX)
Oklahoma City Comm Coll (OK)
Orange Coast Coll (CA)
Palo Alto Coll (TX)
Pasadena City Coll (CA)
Pensacola Jr Coll (FL)
Red Rocks Comm Coll (CO)
Salem Comm Coll (NJ)
San Juan Coll (NM)
Santa Barbara City Coll (CA)
Santa Monica Coll (CA)
Sauk Valley Comm Coll (IL)
Snow Coll (UT)
Southwestern Coll (CA)
Spoon River Coll (IL)
State U of NY Coll of A&T at Morrisville (NY)
Triton Coll (IL)
Utah Valley State Coll (UT)
Vermilion Comm Coll (MN)
Vincennes U (IN)
West Hills Comm Coll (CA)

Physics Teacher Education
Manatee Comm Coll (FL)

Piano and Organ
Hill Coll of the Hill Jr College District (TX)
Iowa Lakes Comm Coll (IA)
Lincoln Coll, Lincoln (IL)
Lon Morris Coll (TX)
Northeastern Oklahoma A&M Coll (OK)

Pipefitting and Sprinkler Fitting
Cecil Comm Coll (MD)
Delta Coll (MI)
Fayetteville Tech Comm Coll (NC)
Forsyth Tech Comm Coll (NC)
Ivy Tech State Coll–Bloomington (IN)

Ivy Tech State Coll–Central Indiana (IN)
Ivy Tech State Coll–Columbus (IN)
Ivy Tech State Coll–Eastcentral (IN)
Ivy Tech State Coll–Kokomo (IN)
Ivy Tech State Coll–Lafayette (IN)
Ivy Tech State Coll–North Central (IN)
Ivy Tech State Coll–Northeast (IN)
Ivy Tech State Coll–Northwest (IN)
Ivy Tech State Coll–Southcentral (IN)
Ivy Tech State Coll–Southwest (IN)
Ivy Tech State Coll–Wabash Valley (IN)
Ivy Tech State Coll–Whitewater (IN)
Kellogg Comm Coll (MI)
Los Angeles Trade-Tech Coll (CA)
Northern Maine Comm Coll (ME)
Palomar Coll (CA)
Ranken Tech Coll (MO)
St. Cloud Tech Coll (MN)
Southern Maine Comm Coll (ME)
State U of NY Coll of Technology at Alfred (NY)
State U of NY Coll of Technology at Canton (NY)
State U of NY Coll of Technology at Delhi (NY)
Trenholm State Tech Coll, Montgomery (AL)
Western Nevada Comm Coll (NV)

Plant Nursery Management
Comm Coll of Allegheny County (PA)
Cuyamaca Coll (CA)
Dakota County Tech Coll (MN)
Edmonds Comm Coll (WA)
Foothill Coll (CA)
Miami Dade Coll (FL)
Modesto Jr Coll (CA)
Ohio State U Ag Tech Inst (OH)
Pennsylvania Coll of Technology (PA)

Plant Protection and Integrated Pest Management
Los Angeles Pierce Coll (CA)

Plant Sciences
Rend Lake Coll (IL)

Plastics Engineering Technology
Cincinnati State Tech and Comm Coll (OH)
Coll of DuPage (IL)
Cumberland County Coll (NJ)
Edgecombe Comm Coll (NC)
Elaine P. Nunez Comm Coll (LA)
Grand Rapids Comm Coll (MI)
Isothermal Comm Coll (NC)
Kalamazoo Valley Comm Coll (MI)
Kellogg Comm Coll (MI)
Kent State U, Tuscarawas Campus (OH)
Lorain County Comm Coll (OH)
Macomb Comm Coll (MI)
Mount Wachusett Comm Coll (MA)
Northeastern Oklahoma A&M Coll (OK)
Northwest State Comm Coll (OH)
Pennsylvania Coll of Technology (PA)

Quinebaug Valley Comm Coll (CT)
St. Clair County Comm Coll (MI)
St. Petersburg Coll (FL)
Sinclair Comm Coll (OH)
South Texas Comm Coll (TX)
State U of NY Coll of A&T at Morrisville (NY)
Terra State Comm Coll (OH)

Platemaking/Imaging
Pennsylvania Coll of Technology (PA)

Plumbing Technology
Luzerne County Comm Coll (PA)
Macomb Comm Coll (MI)
Mayland Comm Coll (NC)
Pennsylvania Coll of Technology (PA)
Vatterott Coll, St. Ann (MO)

Political Science and Government
Abraham Baldwin Ag Coll (GA)
Atlanta Metropolitan Coll (GA)
Austin Comm Coll (TX)
Bainbridge Coll (GA)
Barton County Comm Coll (KS)
Bergen Comm Coll (NJ)
Brookdale Comm Coll (NJ)
Burlington County Coll (NJ)
Butler County Comm Coll (KS)
Butte Coll (CA)
Cañada Coll (CA)
Casper Coll (WY)
Centralia Coll (WA)
Chabot Coll (CA)
Chemeketa Comm Coll (OR)
Coastal Bend Coll (TX)
Coastal Georgia Comm Coll (GA)
Coffeyville Comm Coll (KS)
Colby Comm Coll (KS)
Coll of Southern Idaho (ID)
Coll of the Canyons (CA)
Coll of the Desert (CA)
Colorado Northwestern Comm Coll (CO)
Columbia State Comm Coll (TN)
Contra Costa Coll (CA)
Copiah-Lincoln Comm Coll–Natchez Campus (MS)
Darton Coll (GA)
Del Mar Coll (TX)
Donnelly Coll (KS)
Eastern Arizona Coll (AZ)
Eastern Oklahoma State Coll (OK)
Eastern Wyoming Coll (WY)
East Los Angeles Coll (CA)
El Camino Coll (CA)
Everett Comm Coll (WA)
Finger Lakes Comm Coll (NY)
Foothill Coll (CA)
Gavilan Coll (CA)
Gloucester County Coll (NJ)
Gordon Coll (GA)
Gulf Coast Comm Coll (FL)
Harford Comm Coll (MD)
Hill Coll of the Hill Jr College District (TX)
Hinds Comm Coll (MS)
Iowa Lakes Comm Coll (IA)
Jefferson Coll (MO)
Jefferson Davis Comm Coll (AL)
John A. Logan Coll (IL)
Kellogg Comm Coll (MI)
Kirkwood Comm Coll (IA)
Laramie County Comm Coll (WY)
Lawson State Comm Coll (AL)
Lincoln Coll, Lincoln (IL)
Lon Morris Coll (TX)

Lorain County Comm Coll (OH)
Lower Columbia Coll (WA)
Marshalltown Comm Coll (IA)
Miami Dade Coll (FL)
Middlesex County Coll (NJ)
Midland Coll (TX)
MiraCosta Coll (CA)
Northeastern Oklahoma A&M Coll (OK)
Northeast Mississippi Comm Coll (MS)
Northern Essex Comm Coll (MA)
North Harris Coll (TX)
North Idaho Coll (ID)
Northwest Coll (WY)
Odessa Coll (TX)
Oklahoma City Comm Coll (OK)
Orange Coast Coll (CA)
Otero Jr Coll (CO)
Palm Beach Comm Coll (FL)
Pasadena City Coll (CA)
Pima Comm Coll (AZ)
Reading Area Comm Coll (PA)
Red Rocks Comm Coll (CO)
Rend Lake Coll (IL)
Riverside Comm Coll (CA)
St. Philip's Coll (TX)
Salem Comm Coll (NJ)
San Diego City Coll (CA)
San Joaquin Delta Coll (CA)
San Juan Coll (NM)
Santa Barbara City Coll (CA)
Santa Monica Coll (CA)
Sauk Valley Comm Coll (IL)
Snow Coll (UT)
Southwestern Coll (CA)
Spoon River Coll (IL)
Triton Coll (IL)
Umpqua Comm Coll (OR)
Vermilion Comm Coll (MN)
Vincennes U (IN)
Waycross Coll (GA)
Western Wyoming Comm Coll (WY)

Political Science and Government Related
Clarendon Coll (TX)
Georgia Perimeter Coll (GA)

Portuguese
Miami Dade Coll (FL)

Postal Management
Central Piedmont Comm Coll (NC)
Comm Coll of Denver (CO)
Daytona Beach Comm Coll (FL)
Fayetteville Tech Comm Coll (NC)
Hinds Comm Coll (MS)
Lenoir Comm Coll (NC)
Longview Comm Coll (MO)
Mississippi Gulf Coast Comm Coll (MS)
San Diego City Coll (CA)
South Plains Coll (TX)

Poultry Science
Abraham Baldwin Ag Coll (GA)
Crowder Coll (MO)
Modesto Jr Coll (CA)
Northeast Texas Comm Coll (TX)

Precision Metal Working Related
Jefferson Coll (MO)
Northeast Wisconsin Tech Coll (WI)
Northwest State Comm Coll (OH)
Oakland Comm Coll (MI)

Precision Production Related
Jefferson Coll (MO)
Midlands Tech Coll (SC)
Mott Comm Coll (MI)

Northeast Wisconsin Tech Coll (WI)
Southwestern Michigan Coll (MI)
Western Wisconsin Tech Coll (WI)

Precision Production Trades
Coll of DuPage (IL)

Precision Systems Maintenance and Repair Technologies Related
Northeast Wisconsin Tech Coll (WI)
Southwestern Michigan Coll (MI)

Pre-Dentistry Studies
Barton County Comm Coll (KS)
Calhoun Comm Coll (AL)
Centralia Coll (WA)
Clarendon Coll (TX)
Coastal Georgia Comm Coll (GA)
Darton Coll (GA)
Eastern Wyoming Coll (WY)
Georgia Perimeter Coll (GA)
Hiwassee Coll (TN)
Howard Comm Coll (MD)
Iowa Lakes Comm Coll (IA)
Laramie County Comm Coll (WY)
Miami Dade Coll (FL)
Rend Lake Coll (IL)
St. Philip's Coll (TX)
Sauk Valley Comm Coll (IL)
Western Wyoming Comm Coll (WY)

Pre-Engineering
Abraham Baldwin Ag Coll (GA)
Alpena Comm Coll (MI)
Amarillo Coll (TX)
American River Coll (CA)
Andrew Coll (GA)
Arizona Western Coll (AZ)
Austin Comm Coll (TX)
Barton County Comm Coll (KS)
Bowling Green State U-Firelands Coll (OH)
Bronx Comm Coll of City U of NY (NY)
Butler County Comm Coll (KS)
Cabrillo Coll (CA)
Caldwell Comm Coll and Tech Inst (NC)
Cape Cod Comm Coll (MA)
Casper Coll (WY)
Centralia Coll (WA)
Central Oregon Comm Coll (OR)
Chabot Coll (CA)
Chipola Coll (FL)
City Colls of Chicago, Wilbur Wright Coll (IL)
Coastal Georgia Comm Coll (GA)
Coffeyville Comm Coll (KS)
Colby Comm Coll (KS)
Coll of Eastern Utah (UT)
Coll of the Canyons (CA)
Coll of the Desert (CA)
Coll of the Sequoias (CA)
Columbia State Comm Coll (TN)
Corning Comm Coll (NY)
Crowder Coll (MO)
Cuesta Coll (CA)
Cumberland County Coll (NJ)
Darton Coll (GA)
Del Mar Coll (TX)
Delta Coll (MI)
Eastern Oklahoma State Coll (OK)
East Los Angeles Coll (CA)
East Mississippi Comm Coll (MS)
Edison State Comm Coll (OH)
Elgin Comm Coll (IL)

Essex County Coll (NJ)
Everett Comm Coll (WA)
Finger Lakes Comm Coll (NY)
Garden City Comm Coll (KS)
Gavilan Coll (CA)
Georgia Perimeter Coll (GA)
Greenfield Comm Coll (MA)
Hibbing Comm Coll (MN)
Hill Coll of the Hill Jr College District (TX)
Hinds Comm Coll (MS)
Hiwassee Coll (TN)
Holyoke Comm Coll (MA)
Iowa Lakes Comm Coll (IA)
Isothermal Comm Coll (NC)
Itasca Comm Coll (MN)
Jefferson Coll (MO)
Jefferson Comm Coll (NY)
John A. Logan Coll (IL)
Kalamazoo Valley Comm Coll (MI)
Kirkwood Comm Coll (IA)
Lansing Comm Coll (MI)
Laramie County Comm Coll (WY)
Lawson State Comm Coll (AL)
Lenoir Comm Coll (NC)
Lewis and Clark Comm Coll (IL)
Lincoln Land Comm Coll (IL)
Linn-Benton Comm Coll (OR)
Longview Comm Coll (MO)
Lon Morris Coll (TX)
Lorain County Comm Coll (OH)
Los Angeles Harbor Coll (CA)
Los Angeles Pierce Coll (CA)
Los Angeles Valley Coll (CA)
Lower Columbia Coll (WA)
Macomb Comm Coll (MI)
Maple Woods Comm Coll (MO)
Marshalltown Comm Coll (IA)
Mesabi Range Comm and Tech Coll (MN)
Metropolitan Comm Coll (NE)
Miami Dade Coll (FL)
Middlesex Comm Coll (CT)
Middlesex Comm Coll (MA)
Midland Coll (TX)
Mid Michigan Comm Coll (MI)
Milwaukee Area Tech Coll (WI)
Minnesota State Comm and Tech Coll–Fergus Falls (MN)
Mississippi Gulf Coast Comm Coll (MS)
Moberly Area Comm Coll (MO)
Mohawk Valley Comm Coll (NY)
Monroe County Comm Coll (MI)
Mountain Empire Comm Coll (VA)
Mt. San Antonio Coll (CA)
Naugatuck Valley Comm Coll (CT)
Northeast Alabama Comm Coll (AL)
Northeastern Oklahoma A&M Coll (OK)
Northeast Mississippi Comm Coll (MS)
North Harris Coll (TX)
North Hennepin Comm Coll (MN)
North Shore Comm Coll (MA)
Northwest Coll (WY)
Northwestern Connecticut Comm-Tech Coll (CT)
Northwest-Shoals Comm Coll (AL)
Oakland Comm Coll (MI)
Oakton Comm Coll (IL)

Odessa Coll (TX)
Oklahoma City Comm Coll (OK)
Otero Jr Coll (CO)
Palm Beach Comm Coll (FL)
Pensacola Jr Coll (FL)
Piedmont Virginia Comm Coll (VA)
Polk Comm Coll (FL)
Portland Comm Coll (OR)
Pratt Comm Coll and Area Vocational School (KS)
Quinebaug Valley Comm Coll (CT)
Quinsigamond Comm Coll (MA)
Rainy River Comm Coll (MN)
Reading Area Comm Coll (PA)
Roane State Comm Coll (TN)
Rochester Comm and Tech Coll (MN)
Saint Charles Comm Coll (MO)
St. Louis Comm Coll at Florissant Valley (MO)
St. Philip's Coll (TX)
Salem Comm Coll (NJ)
San Diego City Coll (CA)
Santa Monica Coll (CA)
Seward County Comm Coll (KS)
Snow Coll (UT)
South Plains Coll (TX)
South Suburban Coll (IL)
Southwestern Coll (CA)
Spoon River Coll (IL)
State U of NY Coll of A&T at Morrisville (NY)
Trinidad State Jr Coll (CO)
Umpqua Comm Coll (OR)
Vermilion Comm Coll (MN)
Vincennes U (IN)
Virginia Western Comm Coll (VA)
Walters State Comm Coll (TN)
Washtenaw Comm Coll (MI)
Western Wyoming Comm Coll (WY)
West Hills Comm Coll (CA)
Yakima Valley Comm Coll (WA)
Yuba Coll (CA)

Pre-Law
Barton County Comm Coll (KS)
Darton Coll (GA)
Hiwassee Coll (TN)
St. Philip's Coll (TX)

Pre-Law Studies
Calhoun Comm Coll (AL)
Centralia Coll (WA)
Central Wyoming Coll (WY)
Eastern Arizona Coll (AZ)
Gulf Coast Comm Coll (FL)
Iowa Lakes Comm Coll (IA)
Kellogg Comm Coll (MI)
Laramie County Comm Coll (WY)
Lawson State Comm Coll (AL)
Lower Columbia Coll (WA)
Northeast Comm Coll (NE)
Rend Lake Coll (IL)
Riverside Comm Coll (CA)
Western Wyoming Comm Coll (WY)

Pre-Medical Studies
Barton County Comm Coll (KS)
Calhoun Comm Coll (AL)
Centralia Coll (WA)
City Colls of Chicago, Malcolm X Coll (IL)
Clarendon Coll (TX)
Coastal Georgia Comm Coll (GA)
Darton Coll (GA)
Eastern Arizona Coll (AZ)
Eastern Wyoming Coll (WY)

Georgia Perimeter Coll (GA)
Hiwassee Coll (TN)
Howard Comm Coll (MD)
Iowa Lakes Comm Coll (IA)
Kellogg Comm Coll (MI)
Laramie County Comm Coll (WY)
Miami Dade Coll (FL)
Rend Lake Coll (IL)
St. Philip's Coll (TX)
San Juan Coll (NM)
Sauk Valley Comm Coll (IL)
Western Wyoming Comm Coll (WY)

Pre-Nursing Studies
Connors State Coll (OK)
Hiwassee Coll (TN)
Iowa Lakes Comm Coll (IA)
Keystone Coll (PA)
Miami Dade Coll (FL)
St. Philip's Coll (TX)
South U (FL)
Western Wyoming Comm Coll (WY)

Pre-Pharmacy Studies
Amarillo Coll (TX)
Andrew Coll (GA)
Calhoun Comm Coll (AL)
Centralia Coll (WA)
City Colls of Chicago, Malcolm X Coll (IL)
Coastal Georgia Comm Coll (GA)
Coll of Southern Idaho (ID)
Darton Coll (GA)
Delta Coll (MI)
Eastern Arizona Coll (AZ)
Eastern Wyoming Coll (WY)
Georgia Perimeter Coll (GA)
Hiwassee Coll (TN)
Howard Comm Coll (MD)
Iowa Lakes Comm Coll (IA)
Kellogg Comm Coll (MI)
Laramie County Comm Coll (WY)
Luzerne County Comm Coll (PA)
Manatee Comm Coll (FL)
Miami Dade Coll (FL)
Reading Area Comm Coll (PA)
Rend Lake Coll (IL)
St. Philip's Coll (TX)
Sauk Valley Comm Coll (IL)
Southwestern Illinois Coll (IL)
Western Wyoming Comm Coll (WY)

Pre-Theology/Pre-Ministerial Studies
Hiwassee Coll (TN)
Kellogg Comm Coll (MI)

Pre-Veterinary Studies
Barton County Comm Coll (KS)
Calhoun Comm Coll (AL)
Centralia Coll (WA)
Coastal Georgia Comm Coll (GA)
Darton Coll (GA)
Eastern Wyoming Coll (WY)
Hiwassee Coll (TN)
Howard Comm Coll (MD)
Iowa Lakes Comm Coll (IA)
Kellogg Comm Coll (MI)
Laramie County Comm Coll (WY)
Miami Dade Coll (FL)
Ohio State U Ag Tech Inst (OH)
Rend Lake Coll (IL)
Sauk Valley Comm Coll (IL)
Western Wyoming Comm Coll (WY)

Printing Press Operation
Iowa Lakes Comm Coll (IA)
Lake Land Coll (IL)

Printmaking
Keystone Coll (PA)

Professional Studies
Pratt Comm Coll and Area Vocational School (KS)

Psychiatric/Mental Health Services Technology
Allegany Coll of Maryland (MD)
Central Florida Comm Coll (FL)
Comm Coll of Allegheny County (PA)
Comm Coll of Rhode Island (RI)
Darton Coll (GA)
Dutchess Comm Coll (NY)
Eastfield Coll (TX)
Hagerstown Comm Coll (MD)
Houston Comm Coll System (TX)
Ivy Tech State Coll–Bloomington (IN)
Ivy Tech State Coll–Central Indiana (IN)
Ivy Tech State Coll–Columbus (IN)
Ivy Tech State Coll–Eastcentral (IN)
Ivy Tech State Coll–Kokomo (IN)
Ivy Tech State Coll–Lafayette (IN)
Ivy Tech State Coll–Northeast (IN)
Ivy Tech State Coll–Northwest (IN)
Ivy Tech State Coll–Southcentral (IN)
Ivy Tech State Coll–Southeast (IN)
Ivy Tech State Coll–Southwest (IN)
Ivy Tech State Coll–Wabash Valley (IN)
Ivy Tech State Coll–Whitewater (IN)
Kingsborough Comm Coll of City U of NY (NY)
Montgomery Coll (MD)
Montgomery County Comm Coll (PA)
North Dakota State Coll of Science (ND)
Pennsylvania Coll of Technology (PA)
Pikes Peak Comm Coll (CO)
Pitt Comm Coll (NC)
San Joaquin Delta Coll (CA)
Yuba Coll (CA)

Psychology
Abraham Baldwin Ag Coll (GA)
Amarillo Coll (TX)
Andrew Coll (GA)
Atlanta Metropolitan Coll (GA)
Atlantic Cape Comm Coll (NJ)
Austin Comm Coll (TX)
Bainbridge Coll (GA)
Barton County Comm Coll (KS)
Bergen Comm Coll (NJ)
Bronx Comm Coll of City U of NY (NY)
Brookdale Comm Coll (NJ)
Bucks County Comm Coll (PA)
Bunker Hill Comm Coll (MA)
Burlington County Coll (NJ)
Butler County Comm Coll (KS)
Butte Coll (CA)
Cañada Coll (CA)
Cape Cod Comm Coll (MA)
Casper Coll (WY)
Centralia Coll (WA)
Central Wyoming Coll (WY)
Chabot Coll (CA)
Clarendon Coll (TX)
Clovis Comm Coll (NM)
Coastal Bend Coll (TX)

Coastal Georgia Comm Coll (GA)
Coffeyville Comm Coll (KS)
Colby Comm Coll (KS)
Coll of Southern Idaho (ID)
Coll of the Canyons (CA)
Coll of the Desert (CA)
Colorado Mountn Coll (CO)
Colorado Mountn Coll, Timberline Cmps (CO)
Colorado Northwestern Comm Coll (CO)
Columbia Coll (CA)
Columbia State Comm Coll (TN)
Comm Coll of Allegheny County (PA)
Connors State Coll (OK)
Crowder Coll (MO)
Cuesta Coll (CA)
Darton Coll (GA)
Daytona Beach Comm Coll (FL)
Delaware County Comm Coll (PA)
Del Mar Coll (TX)
Delta Coll (MI)
Donnelly Coll (KS)
Eastern Arizona Coll (AZ)
Eastern Oklahoma State Coll (OK)
Eastern Wyoming Coll (WY)
East Los Angeles Coll (CA)
East Mississippi Comm Coll (MS)
El Camino Coll (CA)
Everett Comm Coll (WA)
Finger Lakes Comm Coll (NY)
Fisher Coll (MA)
Foothill Coll (CA)
Frederick Comm Coll (MD)
Fulton-Montgomery Comm Coll (NY)
Garrett Coll (MD)
Gavilan Coll (CA)
Georgia Perimeter Coll (GA)
Gloucester County Coll (NJ)
Gogebic Comm Coll (MI)
Gordon Coll (GA)
Great Basin Coll (NV)
Gulf Coast Comm Coll (FL)
Harcum Coll (PA)
Harford Comm Coll (MD)
Harrisburg Area Comm Coll (PA)
Hesser Coll (NH)
Hill Coll of the Hill Jr College District (TX)
Hinds Comm Coll (MS)
Hiwassee Coll (TN)
Howard Comm Coll (MD)
Hutchinson Comm Coll and Area Vocational School (KS)
Iowa Lakes Comm Coll (IA)
Itasca Comm Coll (MN)
Jefferson Coll (MO)
John A. Logan Coll (IL)
John Wood Comm Coll (IL)
Kellogg Comm Coll (MI)
Kingwood Coll (TX)
Kirkwood Comm Coll (IA)
Laramie County Comm Coll (WY)
Lawson State Comm Coll (AL)
Lincoln Coll, Lincoln (IL)
Lon Morris Coll (TX)
Lorain County Comm Coll (OH)
Los Angeles Valley Coll (CA)
Lower Columbia Coll (WA)
Manatee Comm Coll (FL)
Miami Dade Coll (FL)
Middlesex County Coll (NJ)
Midland Coll (TX)
Mid Michigan Comm Coll (MI)
MiraCosta Coll (CA)
Mitchell Comm Coll (NC)
Mohave Comm Coll (AZ)
Monroe County Comm Coll (MI)

Coastal Georgia Comm Coll (GA)
Northeastern Oklahoma A&M Coll (OK)
Northeast Mississippi Comm Coll (MS)
North Idaho Coll (ID)
Northwest Coll (WY)
Odessa Coll (TX)
Oklahoma City Comm Coll (OK)
Otero Jr Coll (CO)
Palm Beach Comm Coll (FL)
Palo Alto Coll (TX)
Pasadena City Coll (CA)
Pensacola Jr Coll (FL)
Pratt Comm Coll and Area Vocational School (KS)
Reading Area Comm Coll (PA)
Red Rocks Comm Coll (CO)
Rend Lake Coll (IL)
Riverside Comm Coll (CA)
St. Philip's Coll (TX)
Salem Comm Coll (NJ)
San Diego City Coll (CA)
San Joaquin Delta Coll (CA)
San Juan Coll (NM)
Santa Barbara City Coll (CA)
Santa Monica Coll (CA)
Sauk Valley Comm Coll (IL)
Seward County Comm Coll (KS)
Southwestern Coll (CA)
Spoon River Coll (IL)
Terra State Comm Coll (OH)
Trinidad State Jr Coll (CO)
Triton Coll (IL)
Umpqua Comm Coll (OR)
Utah Valley State Coll (UT)
Vermilion Comm Coll (MN)
Vincennes U (IN)
Waycross Coll (GA)
Western Wyoming Comm Coll (WY)
West Hills Comm Coll (CA)
Yuba Coll (CA)

Public Administration
Anne Arundel Comm Coll (MD)
Barton County Comm Coll (KS)
County Coll of Morris (NJ)
Del Mar Coll (TX)
East Los Angeles Coll (CA)
Eugenio María de Hostos Comm Coll of City U of NY (NY)
Fayetteville Tech Comm Coll (NC)
Hinds Comm Coll (MS)
Jefferson Coll (MO)
Lansing Comm Coll (MI)
Laramie County Comm Coll (WY)
Manatee Comm Coll (FL)
Mesalands Comm Coll (NM)
Miami Dade Coll (FL)
Middle Georgia Coll (GA)
Mohawk Valley Comm Coll (NY)
Mountain Empire Comm Coll (VA)
Mt. San Jacinto Coll (CA)
Northeast Mississippi Comm Coll (MS)
Palomar Coll (CA)
Reading Area Comm Coll (PA)
Red Rocks Comm Coll (CO)
Salem Comm Coll (NJ)
San Joaquin Delta Coll (CA)
San Jose City Coll (CA)
San Juan Coll (NM)
Scottsdale Comm Coll (AZ)
Sinclair Comm Coll (OH)
Southwestern Coll (CA)
Thomas Nelson Comm Coll (VA)
Vincennes U (IN)
Westmoreland County Comm Coll (PA)

Public Administration and Social Service Professions Related
Cleveland State Comm Coll (TN)
Sauk Valley Comm Coll (IL)

Public Health
Hill Coll of the Hill Jr College District (TX)

Public Health Education and Promotion
Coll of Southern Idaho (ID)

Public Health Related
Western Wisconsin Tech Coll (WI)

Public Policy Analysis
Anne Arundel Comm Coll (MD)
Del Mar Coll (TX)
Fort Scott Comm Coll (KS)
Hill Coll of the Hill Jr College District (TX)

Public Relations, Advertising, and Applied Communication Related
Keystone Coll (PA)

Public Relations/Image Management
Amarillo Coll (TX)
Brookdale Comm Coll (NJ)
Coastal Bend Coll (TX)
Comm Coll of the Air Force (AL)
Crowder Coll (MO)
Glendale Comm Coll (AZ)
Kellogg Comm Coll (MI)
Kirkwood Comm Coll (IA)
Lansing Comm Coll (MI)
Northeast Mississippi Comm Coll (MS)
Vincennes U (IN)

Publishing
Milwaukee Area Tech Coll (WI)
Westmoreland County Comm Coll (PA)

Purchasing, Procurement/Acquisitions and Contracts Management
Cincinnati State Tech and Comm Coll (OH)
Columbus State Comm Coll (OH)
Comm Coll of the Air Force (AL)
Miami U Hamilton (OH)
South Puget Sound Comm Coll (WA)

Quality Control and Safety Technologies Related
Lake Superior Coll (MN)

Quality Control Technology
Arkansas State U–Beebe (AR)
Austin Comm Coll (TX)
Broome Comm Coll (NY)
Central Comm Coll–Columbus Campus (NE)
Century Coll (MN)
Coll of the Canyons (CA)
Columbus State Comm Coll (OH)
Comm Coll of Allegheny County (PA)
Contra Costa Coll (CA)
Delta Coll (MI)
Des Moines Area Comm Coll (IA)
Edison State Comm Coll (OH)
Elizabethtown Comm Coll (KY)
Fort Scott Comm Coll (KS)
Grand Rapids Comm Coll (MI)
Heartland Comm Coll (IL)
Illinois Eastern Comm Colls, Frontier Comm Coll (IL)

Illinois Eastern Comm Colls, Lincoln Trail Coll (IL)
Ivy Tech State Coll–Lafayette (IN)
James A. Rhodes State Coll (OH)
Kishwaukee Coll (IL)
Lakeshore Tech Coll (WI)
Lansing Comm Coll (MI)
Longview Comm Coll (MO)
Lorain County Comm Coll (OH)
Los Angeles Pierce Coll (CA)
Macomb Comm Coll (MI)
Metropolitan Comm Coll–Business & Technology College (MO)
Mott Comm Coll (MI)
Mountain View Coll (TX)
Mt. San Antonio Coll (CA)
Naugatuck Valley Comm Coll (CT)
Northampton County Area Comm Coll (PA)
North Central State Coll (OH)
Northeast Wisconsin Tech Coll (WI)
Northwest State Comm Coll (OH)
Oklahoma State U, Oklahoma City (OK)
Pennsylvania Coll of Technology (PA)
St. Clair County Comm Coll (MI)
St. Petersburg Coll (FL)
Sinclair Comm Coll (OH)
Springfield Tech Comm Coll (MA)
Terra State Comm Coll (OH)
Texas State Tech Coll–Waco/Marshall Campus (TX)
Washtenaw Comm Coll (MI)
Waubonsee Comm Coll (IL)
Wisconsin Indianhead Tech Coll (WI)

Radio and Television
Alvin Comm Coll (TX)
Amarillo Coll (TX)
The Art Inst of Pittsburgh (PA)
Austin Comm Coll (TX)
Brevard Comm Coll (FL)
Bucks County Comm Coll (PA)
Centralia Coll (WA)
Chabot Coll (CA)
Coffeyville Comm Coll (KS)
Colby Comm Coll (KS)
Cuesta Coll (CA)
Daytona Beach Comm Coll (FL)
Del Mar Coll (TX)
Delta Coll (MI)
Foothill Coll (CA)
Gulf Coast Comm Coll (FL)
Hesser Coll (NH)
Hillsborough Comm Coll (FL)
Holmes Comm Coll (MS)
Illinois Eastern Comm Colls, Wabash Valley Coll (IL)
International Coll of Broadcasting (OH)
Iowa Lakes Comm Coll (IA)
Isothermal Comm Coll (NC)
Keystone Coll (PA)
Kirkwood Comm Coll (IA)
Lake Land Coll (IL)
Lansing Comm Coll (MI)
Lawson State Comm Coll (AL)
Lewis and Clark Comm Coll (IL)
Lincoln Coll, Lincoln (IL)
Los Angeles Valley Coll (CA)
Manatee Comm Coll (FL)
Miami Dade Coll (FL)
Middlesex Comm Coll (CT)
Modesto Jr Coll (CA)
Mt. San Antonio Coll (CA)
Napa Valley Coll (CA)
National Coll of Business & Technology, Lexington (KY)

Northeast Comm Coll (NE)
Northeast Mississippi Comm Coll (MS)
Odessa Coll (TX)
Oxnard Coll (CA)
Palomar Coll (CA)
Parkland Coll (IL)
Pasadena City Coll (CA)
Pima Comm Coll (AZ)
St. Louis Comm Coll at Florissant Valley (MO)
San Diego City Coll (CA)
Santa Monica Coll (CA)
Sullivan County Comm Coll (NY)
Tompkins Cortland Comm Coll (NY)
Vincennes U (IN)
Virginia Western Comm Coll (VA)

Radio and Television Broadcasting Technology
Bates Tech Coll (WA)
Briarwood Coll (CT)
Brookdale Comm Coll (NJ)
Cedar Valley Coll (TX)
Central Comm Coll–Hastings Campus (NE)
Central Wyoming Coll (WY)
Clover Park Tech Coll (WA)
County Coll of Morris (NJ)
Gadsden State Comm Coll (AL)
Hillsborough Comm Coll (FL)
Houston Comm Coll System (TX)
Iowa Lakes Comm Coll (IA)
Jefferson State Comm Coll (AL)
Kellogg Comm Coll (MI)
Luzerne County Comm Coll (PA)
Manatee Comm Coll (FL)
Miami Dade Coll (FL)
Milwaukee Area Tech Coll (WI)
Mineral Area Coll (MO)
Northampton County Area Comm Coll (PA)
Oakland Comm Coll (MI)
Parkland Coll (IL)
Santa Fe Comm Coll (NM)
Schoolcraft Coll (MI)

Radiologic Technology/ Science
Amarillo Coll (TX)
Barton County Comm Coll (KS)
Blackhawk Tech Coll (WI)
Brevard Comm Coll (FL)
Brookdale Comm Coll (NJ)
Carolinas Coll of Health Sciences (NC)
Columbus State Comm Coll (OH)
Comm Coll of Denver (CO)
Delta Coll (MI)
Eastern Maine Comm Coll (ME)
Edgecombe Comm Coll (NC)
Edison Comm Coll (FL)
El Centro Coll (TX)
Fayetteville Tech Comm Coll (NC)
Florida Hospital Coll of Health Sciences (FL)
Florida National Coll (FL)
Foothill Coll (CA)
Hillsborough Comm Coll (FL)
Holyoke Comm Coll (MA)
Keiser Coll, Miami (FL)
Kettering Coll of Medical Arts (OH)
Keystone Coll (PA)
Lakeland Comm Coll (OH)
Lakeshore Tech Coll (WI)
Laramie County Comm Coll (WY)
Laredo Comm Coll (TX)
Manatee Comm Coll (FL)
Marion Tech Coll (OH)
Massasoit Comm Coll (MA)
Miami Dade Coll (FL)

Middlesex Comm Coll (MA)
Middlesex County Coll (NJ)
Midland Coll (TX)
Mitchell Tech Inst (SD)
Montgomery County Comm Coll (PA)
Niagara County Comm Coll (NY)
North Central State Coll (OH)
Northcentral Tech Coll (WI)
Northern Essex Comm Coll (MA)
Pasco-Hernando Comm Coll (FL)
Pensacola Jr Coll (FL)
Pima Medical Inst, Mesa (AZ)
Pima Medical Inst, Tucson (AZ)
Pima Medical Inst (WA)
Polk Comm Coll (FL)
Prince George's Comm Coll (MD)
Rowan-Cabarrus Comm Coll (NC)
St. Luke's Coll (IA)
St. Petersburg Coll (FL)
Sinclair Comm Coll (OH)
Somerset Comm Coll (KY)
South Coll (TN)
Southeast Arkansas Coll (AR)
Southern Maine Comm Coll (ME)
Triton Coll (IL)
Virginia Western Comm Coll (VA)
Washtenaw Comm Coll (MI)
Waycross Coll (GA)
Western Wisconsin Tech Coll (WI)

Radio, Television, and Digital Communication Related
Hillsborough Comm Coll (FL)
Keystone Coll (PA)

Range Science and Management
Central Wyoming Coll (WY)
Colby Comm Coll (KS)
Coll of Southern Idaho (ID)
Eastern Oklahoma State Coll (OK)
Northeast Texas Comm Coll (TX)
Northwest Coll (WY)
Snow Coll (UT)
Vermilion Comm Coll (MN)

Reading Teacher Education
East Mississippi Comm Coll (MS)
Merritt Coll (CA)

Real Estate
Alamance Comm Coll (NC)
Amarillo Coll (TX)
American River Coll (CA)
Anne Arundel Comm Coll (MD)
Austin Comm Coll (TX)
Bellevue Comm Coll (WA)
Bergen Comm Coll (NJ)
Big Sandy Comm and Tech Coll (KY)
Bristol Comm Coll (MA)
Butte Coll (CA)
Cabrillo Coll (CA)
Calhoun Comm Coll (AL)
Camden County Coll (NJ)
Carl Sandburg Coll (IL)
Cedar Valley Coll (TX)
Central Piedmont Comm Coll (NC)
Chabot Coll (CA)
Chemeketa Comm Coll (OR)
Cincinnati State Tech and Comm Coll (OH)
Coll of DuPage (IL)
Coll of Southern Idaho (ID)
Coll of the Canyons (CA)
Coll of the Desert (CA)
Coll of the Sequoias (CA)

Collin County Comm Coll District (TX)
Columbia-Greene Comm Coll (NY)
Columbus State Comm Coll (OH)
Comm Coll of Allegheny County (PA)
Contra Costa Coll (CA)
Cuesta Coll (CA)
Cuyahoga Comm Coll (OH)
Cuyamaca Coll (CA)
Del Mar Coll (TX)
Delta Coll (MI)
Durham Tech Comm Coll (NC)
East Los Angeles Coll (CA)
East Mississippi Comm Coll (MS)
Edison State Comm Coll (OH)
El Camino Coll (CA)
Elizabethtown Comm Coll (KY)
Foothill Coll (CA)
Forsyth Tech Comm Coll (NC)
Glendale Comm Coll (AZ)
Harrisburg Area Comm Coll (PA)
Hill Coll of the Hill Jr College District (TX)
Hinds Comm Coll (MS)
Houston Comm Coll System (TX)
Iowa Lakes Comm Coll (IA)
Isothermal Comm Coll (NC)
Jefferson Comm Coll (KY)
Jefferson Comm Coll (OH)
Kent State U, Trumbull Campus (OH)
Lamar State Coll–Orange (TX)
Lansing Comm Coll (MI)
Laredo Comm Coll (TX)
Lehigh Carbon Comm Coll (PA)
Lorain County Comm Coll (OH)
Los Angeles Harbor Coll (CA)
Los Angeles Pierce Coll (CA)
Los Angeles Trade-Tech Coll (CA)
Los Angeles Valley Coll (CA)
Luzerne County Comm Coll (PA)
McHenry County Coll (IL)
McLennan Comm Coll (TX)
Merritt Coll (CA)
Miami U Hamilton (OH)
Milwaukee Area Tech Coll (WI)
MiraCosta Coll (CA)
Modesto Jr Coll (CA)
Montgomery County Comm Coll (PA)
Morton Coll (IL)
Mt. San Antonio Coll (CA)
Mt. San Jacinto Coll (CA)
Napa Valley Coll (CA)
Nassau Comm Coll (NY)
New Hampshire Tech Inst (NH)
Northeast Alabama Comm Coll (AL)
Northeast Comm Coll (NE)
Northern Essex Comm Coll (MA)
Oakton Comm Coll (IL)
Ocean County Coll (NJ)
Orange County Comm Coll (NY)
Oxnard Coll (CA)
Palomar Coll (CA)
Paris Jr Coll (TX)
Pasadena City Coll (CA)
Phoenix Coll (AZ)
Pima Comm Coll (AZ)
Portland Comm Coll (OR)
Rainy River Comm Coll (MN)
Raritan Valley Comm Coll (NJ)
Red Rocks Comm Coll (CO)

St. Louis Comm Coll at Florissant Valley (MO)
San Diego City Coll (CA)
San Jose City Coll (CA)
San Juan Coll (NM)
Santa Barbara City Coll (CA)
Santa Monica Coll (CA)
Scottsdale Comm Coll (AZ)
Sierra Coll (CA)
Sinclair Comm Coll (OH)
Southern State Comm Coll (OH)
South Plains Coll (TX)
Southwestern Coll (CA)
Southwestern Illinois Coll (IL)
Spokane Falls Comm Coll (WA)
Tidewater Comm Coll (VA)
Triton Coll (IL)
Ventura Coll (CA)
Victor Valley Coll (CA)
Western Nevada Comm Coll (NV)
Westmoreland County Comm Coll (PA)

Receptionist
Alexandria Tech Coll (MN)
Bristol Comm Coll (MA)
Centralia Coll (WA)
Iowa Lakes Comm Coll (IA)
Lower Columbia Coll (WA)
Minot State U–Bottineau Campus (ND)

Recording Arts Technology
Kansas City Kansas Comm Coll (KS)
Miami Dade Coll (FL)
Olympic Coll (WA)

Rehabilitation and Therapeutic Professions Related
Clover Park Tech Coll (WA)
Comm Coll of Rhode Island (RI)
Springfield Tech Comm Coll (MA)
Union County Coll (NJ)

Rehabilitation Therapy
Iowa Lakes Comm Coll (IA)
Nassau Comm Coll (NY)

Religious Education
Lincoln Coll, Lincoln (IL)
Lon Morris Coll (TX)
Northeast Mississippi Comm Coll (MS)

Religious Studies
Amarillo Coll (TX)
Andrew Coll (GA)
Barton County Comm Coll (KS)
Lansing Comm Coll (MI)
Laramie County Comm Coll (WY)
Lon Morris Coll (TX)
Manatee Comm Coll (FL)
Orange Coast Coll (CA)
Palm Beach Comm Coll (FL)
Pasadena City Coll (CA)
Pensacola Jr Coll (FL)
San Joaquin Delta Coll (CA)

Resort Management
The Art Inst of Pittsburgh (PA)

Respiratory Care Therapy
Albuquerque Tech Vocational Inst (NM)
Allegany Coll of Maryland (MD)
Alvin Comm Coll (TX)
Amarillo Coll (TX)
American River Coll (CA)
Andrew Coll (GA)
Atlantic Cape Comm Coll (NJ)
Augusta Tech Coll (GA)
Barton County Comm Coll (KS)
Bergen Comm Coll (NJ)
Berkshire Comm Coll (MA)

Borough of Manhattan Comm Coll of City U of NY (NY)
Bowling Green State U–Firelands Coll (OH)
Brookdale Comm Coll (NJ)
Butte Coll (CA)
Camden County Coll (NJ)
Carteret Comm Coll (NC)
Central Piedmont Comm Coll (NC)
Cincinnati State Tech and Comm Coll (OH)
City Colls of Chicago, Malcolm X Coll (IL)
Coastal Georgia Comm Coll (GA)
Coll of DuPage (IL)
Coll of Southern Idaho (ID)
Coll of the Desert (CA)
Collin County Comm Coll District (TX)
Columbia State Comm Coll (TN)
Columbus State Comm Coll (OH)
Comm Coll of Allegheny County (PA)
Comm Coll of Rhode Island (RI)
Copiah-Lincoln Comm Coll–Natchez Campus (MS)
County Coll of Morris (NJ)
Cuyahoga Comm Coll (OH)
Darton Coll (GA)
Daytona Beach Comm Coll (FL)
Delaware County Comm Coll (PA)
Delgado Comm Coll (LA)
Del Mar Coll (TX)
Delta Coll (MI)
Des Moines Area Comm Coll (IA)
Doña Ana Branch Comm Coll (NM)
Durham Tech Comm Coll (NC)
East Los Angeles Coll (CA)
Edgecombe Comm Coll (NC)
Edison Comm Coll (FL)
El Camino Coll (CA)
El Centro Coll (TX)
Essex County Coll (NJ)
Fayetteville Tech Comm Coll (NC)
Foothill Coll (CA)
Forsyth Tech Comm Coll (NC)
Frederick Comm Coll (MD)
Front Range Comm Coll (CO)
Gloucester County Coll (NJ)
Guilford Tech Comm Coll (NC)
Gulf Coast Comm Coll (FL)
Gwinnett Tech Coll (GA)
Harrisburg Area Comm Coll (PA)
Hawkeye Comm Coll (IA)
Hillsborough Comm Coll (FL)
Hinds Comm Coll (MS)
Holmes Comm Coll (MS)
Houston Comm Coll System (TX)
Howard Coll (TX)
Ivy Tech State Coll–Central Indiana (IN)
Ivy Tech State Coll–Lafayette (IN)
Ivy Tech State Coll–Northeast (IN)
Ivy Tech State Coll–Northwest (IN)
Ivy Tech State Coll–Southcentral (IN)
Jackson State Comm Coll (TN)
James A. Rhodes State Coll (OH)
Jefferson Comm Coll (KY)
Jefferson Comm Coll (OH)

Johnson County Comm Coll (KS)
J. Sargeant Reynolds Comm Coll (VA)
Kalamazoo Valley Comm Coll (MI)
Kansas City Kansas Comm Coll (KS)
Kapiolani Comm Coll (HI)
Kaskaskia Coll (IL)
Kettering Coll of Medical Arts (OH)
Kirkwood Comm Coll (IA)
Lakeland Comm Coll (OH)
Lake Superior Coll (MN)
Lansing Comm Coll (MI)
Lehigh Carbon Comm Coll (PA)
Lincoln Land Comm Coll (IL)
Los Angeles Valley Coll (CA)
Luzerne County Comm Coll (PA)
Macomb Comm Coll (MI)
Manatee Comm Coll (FL)
Manchester Comm Coll (CT)
Massasoit Comm Coll (MA)
Maysville Comm Coll (KY)
McLennan Comm Coll (TX)
Meridian Comm Coll (MS)
Metropolitan Comm Coll (NE)
Miami Dade Coll (FL)
Middlesex County Coll (NJ)
Midland Coll (TX)
Midlands Tech Coll (SC)
Milwaukee Area Tech Coll (WI)
Mississippi Gulf Coast Comm Coll (MS)
Modesto Jr Coll (CA)
Mohawk Valley Comm Coll (NY)
Monroe County Comm Coll (MI)
Montana State U Coll of Tech-Great Falls (MT)
Montgomery County Comm Coll (PA)
Moraine Valley Comm Coll (IL)
Mott Comm Coll (MI)
Mt. San Antonio Coll (CA)
Napa Valley Coll (CA)
Nassau Comm Coll (NY)
North Central State Coll (OH)
Northeast Mississippi Comm Coll (MS)
Northeast Wisconsin Tech Coll (WI)
Northern Essex Comm Coll (MA)
North Harris Coll (TX)
North Shore Comm Coll (MA)
Oakland Comm Coll (MI)
Odessa Coll (TX)
Oklahoma City Comm Coll (OK)
Orangeburg-Calhoun Tech Coll (SC)
Orange Coast Coll (CA)
Parkland Coll (IL)
Penn Valley Comm Coll (MO)
Pensacola Jr Coll (FL)
Pima Comm Coll (AZ)
Pima Medical Inst, Mesa (AZ)
Pima Medical Inst, Tucson (AZ)
Pitt Comm Coll (NC)
Prince George's Comm Coll (MD)
Quinsigamond Comm Coll (MA)
Raritan Valley Comm Coll (NJ)
Reading Area Comm Coll (PA)
Roane State Comm Coll (TN)
Rochester Comm and Tech Coll (MN)

Rockingham Comm Coll (NC)
Rogue Comm Coll (OR)
St. Luke's Coll (IA)
Saint Paul Coll–A Comm & Tech College (MN)
St. Petersburg Coll (FL)
St. Philip's Coll (TX)
Santa Monica Coll (CA)
Seminole Comm Coll (FL)
Seward County Comm Coll (KS)
Shelton State Comm Coll (AL)
Sheridan Coll (WY)
Sinclair Comm Coll (OH)
Somerset Comm Coll (KY)
Southeast Comm Coll (KY)
Southeast Comm Coll, Lincoln Campus (NE)
Southern Maine Comm Coll (ME)
South Plains Coll (TX)
Southside Virginia Comm Coll (VA)
Southwestern Comm Coll (NC)
Spartanburg Tech Coll (SC)
Spokane Comm Coll (WA)
Springfield Tech Comm Coll (MA)
Stanly Comm Coll (NC)
Stark State Coll of Technology (OH)
Sussex County Comm Coll (NJ)
Temple Coll (TX)
Trident Tech Coll (SC)
Triton Coll (IL)
Union County Coll (NJ)
U of Arkansas Comm Coll at Hope (AR)
U of Kentucky, Lexington Comm Coll (KY)
Victor Valley Coll (CA)
Vincennes U (IN)
Volunteer State Comm Coll (TN)
Washtenaw Comm Coll (MI)
Waycross Coll (GA)
Weatherford Coll (TX)
Western Wisconsin Tech Coll (WI)

Respiratory Therapy Technician
Columbus State Comm Coll (OH)
Edgecombe Comm Coll (NC)
Harrisburg Area Comm Coll (PA)
Heart of Georgia Tech Coll (GA)
Kansas City Kansas Comm Coll (KS)
Massasoit Comm Coll (MA)
Miami Dade Coll (FL)
Northern Essex Comm Coll (MA)
Okefenokee Tech Coll (GA)

Restaurant, Culinary, and Catering Management
The Art Inst of New York City (NY)
California Culinary Academy (CA)
Central Florida Comm Coll (FL)
Cincinnati State Tech and Comm Coll (OH)
City Colls of Chicago, Malcolm X Coll (IL)
Coll of DuPage (IL)
Coll of Lake County (IL)
Comm Coll of Allegheny County (PA)
Cuyahoga Comm Coll (OH)
Florida Culinary Inst (FL)
Hillsborough Comm Coll (FL)
Iowa Lakes Comm Coll (IA)
John Wood Comm Coll (IL)
Keystone Coll (PA)
Linn-Benton Comm Coll (OR)

Mohawk Valley Comm Coll (NY)
Moraine Valley Comm Coll (IL)
New England Culinary Inst (VT)
Northland Pioneer Coll (AZ)
Orange Coast Coll (CA)
Pima Comm Coll (AZ)
Rasmussen Coll Mankato (MN)
State U of NY Coll of Technology at Alfred (NY)
State U of NY Coll of Technology at Delhi (NY)
Vincennes U (IN)

Restaurant/Food Services Management
The Art Inst of Pittsburgh (PA)
Columbus State Comm Coll (OH)
Iowa Lakes Comm Coll (IA)
Keystone Coll (PA)
Lehigh Carbon Comm Coll (PA)
Massasoit Comm Coll (MA)
Oakland Comm Coll (MI)
St. Philip's Coll (TX)

Retailing
Bates Tech Coll (WA)
Centralia Coll (WA)
Coll of DuPage (IL)
Comm Coll of Allegheny County (PA)
Comm Coll of Rhode Island (RI)
Edmonds Comm Coll (WA)
Garden City Comm Coll (KS)
Hutchinson Comm Coll and Area Vocational School (KS)
Iowa Lakes Comm Coll (IA)
Johnson County Comm Coll (KS)
Moraine Valley Comm Coll (IL)
Northeast Comm Coll (NE)
Orange Coast Coll (CA)
Patricia Stevens Coll (MO)
Pitt Comm Coll (NC)
Waubonsee Comm Coll (IL)
Western Wisconsin Tech Coll (WI)
Wisconsin Indianhead Tech Coll (WI)

Robotics Technology
Coll of DuPage (IL)
Comm Coll of Allegheny County (PA)
Delaware County Comm Coll (PA)
Ivy Tech State Coll–Columbus (IN)
Ivy Tech State Coll–Southwest (IN)
Ivy Tech State Coll–Wabash Valley (IN)
Ivy Tech State Coll–Whitewater (IN)
Jefferson Coll (MO)
Jefferson State Comm Coll (AL)
Kellogg Comm Coll (MI)
Louisville Tech Inst (KY)
Macomb Comm Coll (MI)
Oakland Comm Coll (MI)
Pikes Peak Comm Coll (CO)
Schoolcraft Coll (MI)
Spartanburg Tech Coll (SC)
Terra State Comm Coll (OH)
Waubonsee Comm Coll (IL)
Yuba Coll (CA)

Romance Languages
Coll of the Desert (CA)
Lon Morris Coll (TX)

Russian
Austin Comm Coll (TX)
El Camino Coll (CA)
Everett Comm Coll (WA)

Russian Studies
Manatee Comm Coll (FL)

Safety/Security Technology
Cuyahoga Comm Coll (OH)
Des Moines Area Comm Coll (IA)
John Tyler Comm Coll (VA)
Lakeland Comm Coll (OH)
Macomb Comm Coll (MI)

Sales and Marketing/Marketing And Distribution Teacher Education
Parkland Coll (IL)

Sales, Distribution and Marketing
Academy Coll (MN)
Burlington County Coll (NJ)
Central Carolina Tech Coll (SC)
Centralia Coll (WA)
Central Pennsylvania Coll (PA)
Coll of DuPage (IL)
Collin County Comm Coll District (TX)
Cuyahoga Comm Coll (OH)
Dakota County Tech Coll (MN)
Fayetteville Tech Comm Coll (NC)
Hesser Coll (NH)
Iowa Lakes Comm Coll (IA)
Johnson County Comm Coll (KS)
John Wood Comm Coll (IL)
Lake Region State Coll (ND)
LDS Business Coll (UT)
McIntosh Coll (NH)
Montgomery County Comm Coll (PA)
Pioneer Pacific Coll (OR)
Santa Barbara City Coll (CA)
South Suburban Coll (IL)
State U of NY Coll of Technology at Alfred (NY)
Vincennes U (IN)
Western Dakota Tech Inst (SD)
Western Wisconsin Tech Coll (WI)

Sales Operations
Coll of Lake County (IL)

Salon/Beauty Salon Management
Oakland Comm Coll (MI)

Sanitation Technology
Kirkwood Comm Coll (IA)
Palomar Coll (CA)
Red Rocks Comm Coll (CO)

Science Teacher Education
Chemeketa Comm Coll (OR)
Colby Comm Coll (KS)
Dutchess Comm Coll (NY)
Eastern Oklahoma State Coll (OK)
Harrisburg Area Comm Coll (PA)
Holmes Comm Coll (MS)
Iowa Lakes Comm Coll (IA)
Manatee Comm Coll (FL)
Miami Dade Coll (FL)
Northeast Mississippi Comm Coll (MS)
Northwest Coll (WY)
Snow Coll (UT)
Vermilion Comm Coll (MN)
Vincennes U (IN)

Science Technologies Related
Cascadia Comm Coll (WA)
Cincinnati State Tech and Comm Coll (OH)
Comm Coll of Allegheny County (PA)
Delaware County Comm Coll (PA)
Front Range Comm Coll (CO)
Harford Comm Coll (MD)
Victor Valley Coll (CA)

Science, Technology and Society
Southeast Arkansas Coll (AR)

Sculpture
Keystone Coll (PA)

Secondary Education
Alpena Comm Coll (MI)
Barton County Comm Coll (KS)
Calhoun Comm Coll (AL)
Central Wyoming Coll (WY)
City Colls of Chicago, Malcolm X Coll (IL)
Clarendon Coll (TX)
Eastern Arizona Coll (AZ)
Eastern Wyoming Coll (WY)
Essex County Coll (NJ)
Gulf Coast Comm Coll (FL)
Hiwassee Coll (TN)
Howard Comm Coll (MD)
Kellogg Comm Coll (MI)
Mid Michigan Comm Coll (MI)
Montgomery County Comm Coll (PA)
Northeast Texas Comm Coll (TX)
Northwest-Shoals Comm Coll (AL)
Rend Lake Coll (IL)
Sauk Valley Comm Coll (IL)
Utah Valley State Coll (UT)
Western Wyoming Comm Coll (WY)

Securities Services Administration
Schenectady County Comm Coll (NY)

Security and Loss Prevention
Cincinnati State Tech and Comm Coll (OH)
Comm Coll of the Air Force (AL)
Harford Comm Coll (MD)
Hesser Coll (NH)
Nassau Comm Coll (NY)

Security and Protective Services Related
Clover Park Tech Coll (WA)
Pima Comm Coll (AZ)

Selling Skills and Sales
Alexandria Tech Coll (MN)
Century Coll (MN)
Coll of DuPage (IL)
Cuyahoga Comm Coll (OH)
Hibbing Comm Coll (MN)
Iowa Lakes Comm Coll (IA)
Lake Superior Coll (MN)
Lincoln Land Comm Coll (IL)
McHenry County Coll (IL)
Moraine Valley Comm Coll (IL)
Orange Coast Coll (CA)
Santa Barbara City Coll (CA)

Sheet Metal Technology
Comm Coll of Allegheny County (PA)
Ivy Tech State Coll–Central Indiana (IN)
Ivy Tech State Coll–Lafayette (IN)
Ivy Tech State Coll–North Central (IN)
Ivy Tech State Coll–Northeast (IN)
Ivy Tech State Coll–Northwest (IN)
Ivy Tech State Coll–Southcentral (IN)
Ivy Tech State Coll–Southwest (IN)
Ivy Tech State Coll–Wabash Valley (IN)
Kellogg Comm Coll (MI)
Macomb Comm Coll (MI)
Northwest State Comm Coll (OH)
Western Nevada Comm Coll (NV)

Sign Language Interpretation and Translation
American River Coll (CA)
Austin Comm Coll (TX)
Blue Ridge Comm Coll (NC)
Burlington County Coll (NJ)
Central Piedmont Comm Coll (NC)
Cincinnati State Tech and Comm Coll (OH)
Clovis Comm Coll (NM)
Coll of the Sequoias (CA)
Collin County Comm Coll District (TX)
Columbus State Comm Coll (OH)
Comm Coll of Allegheny County (PA)
Delgado Comm Coll (LA)
Del Mar Coll (TX)
Eastfield Coll (TX)
Front Range Comm Coll (CO)
Georgia Perimeter Coll (GA)
Hillsborough Comm Coll (FL)
Houston Comm Coll System (TX)
John A. Logan Coll (IL)
Johnson County Comm Coll (KS)
Lake Region State Coll (ND)
Lansing Comm Coll (MI)
Los Angeles Pierce Coll (CA)
McLennan Comm Coll (TX)
Miami Dade Coll (FL)
Mott Comm Coll (MI)
Mt. San Antonio Coll (CA)
Mount Wachusett Comm Coll (MA)
Nashville State Tech Comm Coll (TN)
New River Comm Coll (VA)
Northcentral Tech Coll (WI)
Northern Essex Comm Coll (MA)
Northwestern Connecticut Comm-Tech Coll (CT)
Oklahoma State U, Oklahoma City (OK)
Palomar Coll (CA)
Pasadena City Coll (CA)
Pikes Peak Comm Coll (CO)
Pima Comm Coll (AZ)
Portland Comm Coll (OR)
Riverside Comm Coll (CA)
St. Louis Comm Coll at Florissant Valley (MO)
Saint Paul Coll–A Comm & Tech College (MN)
St. Petersburg Coll (FL)
Santa Fe Comm Coll (NM)
Sheridan Coll (WY)
Sinclair Comm Coll (OH)
South Puget Sound Comm Coll (WA)
Southwestern Illinois Coll (IL)
Spartanburg Tech Coll (SC)
Spokane Falls Comm Coll (WA)
Terra State Comm Coll (OH)
Union County Coll (NJ)
Vincennes U (IN)
Waubonsee Comm Coll (IL)
Wilson Tech Comm Coll (NC)

Small Business Administration
Alexandria Tech Coll (MN)
Iowa Lakes Comm Coll (IA)
Lake Region State Coll (ND)
Northland Pioneer Coll (AZ)

Small Engine Mechanics and Repair Technology
Alexandria Tech Coll (MN)
Bates Tech Coll (WA)
Century Coll (MN)
Iowa Lakes Comm Coll (IA)
Louisville Tech Inst (KY)
North Dakota State Coll of Science (ND)
Southwestern Coll (CA)

Social Psychology
Macomb Comm Coll (MI)
Manatee Comm Coll (FL)

Social Sciences
Abraham Baldwin Ag Coll (GA)
Amarillo Coll (TX)
American River Coll (CA)
Ancilla Coll (IN)
Andrew Coll (GA)
Anne Arundel Comm Coll (MD)
Arizona Western Coll (AZ)
Arkansas State U–Beebe (AR)
Atlantic Cape Comm Coll (NJ)
Bowling Green State U–Firelands Coll (OH)
Bristol Comm Coll (MA)
Brookdale Comm Coll (NJ)
Bucks County Comm Coll (PA)
Butte Coll (CA)
Casper Coll (WY)
Centralia Coll (WA)
Central Oregon Comm Coll (OR)
Central Wyoming Coll (WY)
Chabot Coll (CA)
Chemeketa Comm Coll (OR)
Chesapeake Coll (MD)
Clarendon Coll (TX)
Clinton Comm Coll (NY)
Coffeyville Comm Coll (KS)
Coll of the Canyons (CA)
Coll of the Desert (CA)
Coll of the Sequoias (CA)
Colorado Mountn Coll, Alpine Cmps (CO)
Colorado Mountn Coll (CO)
Colorado Mountn Coll, Timberline Cmps (CO)
Columbia-Greene Comm Coll (NY)
Comm Coll of Allegheny County (PA)
Corning Comm Coll (NY)
Daytona Beach Comm Coll (FL)
Dean Coll (MA)
Dutchess Comm Coll (NY)
East Mississippi Comm Coll (MS)
Edison Comm Coll (FL)
Essex County Coll (NJ)
Feather River Comm Coll District (CA)
Finger Lakes Comm Coll (NY)
Foothill Coll (CA)
Fulton-Montgomery Comm Coll (NY)
Galveston Coll (TX)
Garden City Comm Coll (KS)
Garrett Coll (MD)
Gavilan Coll (CA)
Gloucester County Coll (NJ)
Gogebic Comm Coll (MI)
Harrisburg Area Comm Coll (PA)
Hill Coll of the Hill Jr College District (TX)
Hinds Comm Coll (MS)
Houston Comm Coll System (TX)
Howard Coll (TX)
Howard Comm Coll (MD)
Hutchinson Comm Coll and Area Vocational School (KS)
Iowa Lakes Comm Coll (IA)
Jamestown Comm Coll (NY)
J. Sargeant Reynolds Comm Coll (VA)
Kingwood Coll (TX)
Kirkwood Comm Coll (IA)
Lamar State Coll–Orange (TX)
Laramie County Comm Coll (WY)
Laredo Comm Coll (TX)
Lawson State Comm Coll (AL)

Lehigh Carbon Comm Coll (PA)
Lon Morris Coll (TX)
Lorain County Comm Coll (OH)
Lower Columbia Coll (WA)
Luzerne County Comm Coll (PA)
Manatee Comm Coll (FL)
Merritt Coll (CA)
Miami Dade Coll (FL)
Middlesex County Coll (NJ)
MiraCosta Coll (CA)
Modesto Jr Coll (CA)
Montgomery County Comm Coll (PA)
Mt. San Jacinto Coll (CA)
Niagara County Comm Coll (NY)
Northeast Comm Coll (NE)
Northeastern Oklahoma A&T Coll (OK)
Northeast Mississippi Comm Coll (MS)
North Idaho Coll (ID)
Northwest Coll (WY)
Northwestern Connecticut Comm-Tech Coll (CT)
Northwestern Michigan Coll (MI)
Odessa Coll (TX)
Orange Coast Coll (CA)
Otero Jr Coll (CO)
Palm Beach Comm Coll (FL)
Pasadena City Coll (CA)
Pratt Comm Coll and Area Vocational School (KS)
Raritan Valley Comm Coll (NJ)
Reading Area Comm Coll (PA)
Riverside Comm Coll (CA)
Roane State Comm Coll (TN)
Rogue Comm Coll (OR)
Salem Comm Coll (NJ)
San Diego City Coll (CA)
San Joaquin Delta Coll (CA)
Sheridan Coll (WY)
Southwest Mississippi Comm Coll (MS)
Spoon River Coll (IL)
State U of NY Coll of A&T at Morrisville (NY)
State U of NY Coll of Technology at Alfred (NY)
State U of NY Coll of Technology at Canton (NY)
State U of NY Coll of Technology at Delhi (NY)
Thomas Nelson Comm Coll (VA)
Tompkins Cortland Comm Coll (NY)
Triton Coll (IL)
Umpqua Comm Coll (OR)
Utah Valley State Coll (UT)
Victor Valley Coll (CA)
Vincennes U (IN)
Western Wyoming Comm Coll (WY)
West Hills Comm Coll (CA)
Yuba Coll (CA)

Social Studies Teacher Education
Manatee Comm Coll (FL)

Social Work
Abraham Baldwin Ag Coll (GA)
Alamance Comm Coll (NC)
Amarillo Coll (TX)
Andrew Coll (GA)
Asheville-Buncombe Tech Comm Coll (NC)
Atlanta Metropolitan Coll (GA)
Atlantic Cape Comm Coll (NJ)
Austin Comm Coll (TX)
Barton County Comm Coll (KS)
Beaufort County Comm Coll (NC)

Bristol Comm Coll (MA)
Brookdale Comm Coll (NJ)
Bucks County Comm Coll (PA)
Capital Comm Coll (CT)
Casper Coll (WY)
Central Piedmont Comm Coll (NC)
Century Coll (MN)
Chipola Coll (FL)
Clark State Comm Coll (OH)
Coffeyville Comm Coll (KS)
Colby Comm Coll (KS)
Coll of Lake County (IL)
Comm Coll of Allegheny County (PA)
Comm Coll of Rhode Island (RI)
Comm Coll of the Air Force (AL)
Connors State Coll (OK)
Cumberland County Coll (NJ)
Darton Coll (GA)
Del Mar Coll (TX)
Delta Coll (MI)
Des Moines Area Comm Coll (IA)
Eastfield Coll (TX)
East Los Angeles Coll (CA)
Edgecombe Comm Coll (NC)
Edmonds Comm Coll (WA)
El Camino Coll (CA)
Elgin Comm Coll (IL)
Essex County Coll (NJ)
Galveston Coll (TX)
Gogebic Comm Coll (MI)
Harrisburg Area Comm Coll (PA)
Hesser Coll (NH)
Hill Coll of the Hill Jr College District (TX)
Holmes Comm Coll (MS)
Illinois Eastern Comm Colls, Wabash Valley Coll (IL)
Iowa Lakes Comm Coll (IA)
Jefferson Coll (MO)
Jefferson Comm Coll (KY)
John A. Logan Coll (IL)
Kellogg Comm Coll (MI)
Kilian Comm Coll (SD)
Kirkwood Comm Coll (IA)
Lac Courte Oreilles Ojibwa Comm Coll (WI)
Lake Land Coll (IL)
Lansing Comm Coll (MI)
Lawson State Comm Coll (AL)
Lehigh Carbon Comm Coll (PA)
Lorain County Comm Coll (OH)
Manatee Comm Coll (FL)
Manchester Comm Coll (CT)
Marion Tech Coll (OH)
Mesalands Comm Coll (NM)
Miami Dade Coll (FL)
Mitchell Comm Coll (NC)
Monroe County Comm Coll (MI)
Naugatuck Valley Comm Coll (CT)
Nebraska Indian Comm Coll (NE)
New Mexico State U–Carlsbad (NM)
Northampton County Area Comm Coll (PA)
Northeastern Oklahoma A&M Coll (OK)
Northeast Mississippi Comm Coll (MS)
Northwest State Comm Coll (OH)
Ocean County Coll (NJ)
Owensboro Comm and Tech Coll (KY)
Palm Beach Comm Coll (FL)
Pratt Comm Coll and Area Vocational School (KS)
Reading Area Comm Coll (PA)
Rend Lake Coll (IL)
St. Philip's Coll (TX)

San Diego City Coll (CA)
San Juan Coll (NM)
Santa Fe Comm Coll (NM)
Sauk Valley Comm Coll (IL)
Seward County Comm Coll (KS)
South Plains Coll (TX)
Southwestern Coll (CA)
Southwestern Oregon Comm Coll (OR)
Spokane Falls Comm Coll (WA)
Terra State Comm Coll (OH)
Umpqua Comm Coll (OR)
The U of Akron–Wayne Coll (OH)
Vincennes U (IN)
Waubonsee Comm Coll (IL)
Western Wyoming Comm Coll (WY)
West Virginia Northern Comm Coll (WV)

Social Work Related
Clarendon Coll (TX)
Northeast Comm Coll (NE)

Sociology
Abraham Baldwin Ag Coll (GA)
Andrew Coll (GA)
Atlantic Cape Comm Coll (NJ)
Austin Comm Coll (TX)
Bainbridge Coll (GA)
Barton County Comm Coll (KS)
Bergen Comm Coll (NJ)
Brookdale Comm Coll (NJ)
Bunker Hill Comm Coll (MA)
Burlington County Coll (NJ)
Butler County Comm Coll (KS)
Cañada Coll (CA)
Casper Coll (WY)
Centralia Coll (WA)
Chabot Coll (CA)
Chesapeake Coll (MD)
Clarendon Coll (TX)
Coastal Bend Coll (TX)
Coastal Georgia Comm Coll (GA)
Coffeyville Comm Coll (KS)
Colby Comm Coll (KS)
Coll of Southern Idaho (ID)
Coll of the Desert (CA)
Coll of the Sequoias (CA)
Columbia Coll (CA)
Columbia State Comm Coll (TN)
Comm Coll of Allegheny County (PA)
Connors State Coll (OK)
Contra Costa Coll (CA)
Darton Coll (GA)
Daytona Beach Comm Coll (FL)
Delaware County Comm Coll (PA)
Del Mar Coll (TX)
Eastern Arizona Coll (AZ)
Eastern Oklahoma State Coll (OK)
Eastern Wyoming Coll (WY)
East Los Angeles Coll (CA)
East Mississippi Comm Coll (MS)
El Camino Coll (CA)
Everett Comm Coll (WA)
Finger Lakes Comm Coll (NY)
Foothill Coll (CA)
Garden City Comm Coll (KS)
Garrett Coll (MD)
Gavilan Coll (CA)
Georgia Perimeter Coll (GA)
Gloucester County Coll (NJ)
Gogebic Comm Coll (MI)
Gordon Coll (GA)
Great Basin Coll (NV)
Gulf Coast Comm Coll (FL)
Hill Coll of the Hill Jr College District (TX)
Hinds Comm Coll (MS)
Hiwassee Coll (TN)

Iowa Lakes Comm Coll (IA)
Jefferson Coll (MO)
John Wood Comm Coll (IL)
Kellogg Comm Coll (MI)
Kirkwood Comm Coll (IA)
Laramie County Comm Coll (WY)
Lawson State Comm Coll (AL)
Lincoln Coll, Lincoln (IL)
Lon Morris Coll (TX)
Lorain County Comm Coll (OH)
Los Angeles Valley Coll (CA)
Lower Columbia Coll (WA)
Miami Dade Coll (FL)
Middlesex County Coll (NJ)
Midland Coll (TX)
Mid Michigan Comm Coll (MI)
MiraCosta Coll (CA)
Mohave Comm Coll (AZ)
Northeastern Oklahoma A&M Coll (OK)
North Harris Coll (TX)
North Idaho Coll (ID)
Northwest Coll (WY)
Odessa Coll (TX)
Oklahoma City Comm Coll (OK)
Orange Coast Coll (CA)
Oxnard Coll (CA)
Palo Alto Coll (TX)
Pasadena City Coll (CA)
Pima Comm Coll (AZ)
Pratt Comm Coll and Area Vocational School (KS)
Red Rocks Comm Coll (CO)
Rend Lake Coll (IL)
St. Philip's Coll (TX)
Salem Comm Coll (NJ)
San Diego City Coll (CA)
San Joaquin Delta Coll (CA)
San Juan Coll (NM)
Santa Barbara City Coll (CA)
Santa Monica Coll (CA)
Sauk Valley Comm Coll (IL)
Seward County Comm Coll (KS)
Snow Coll (UT)
Southwestern Coll (CA)
Spoon River Coll (IL)
Umpqua Comm Coll (OR)
Vermilion Comm Coll (MN)
Vincennes U (IN)
Waycross Coll (GA)
Western Wyoming Comm Coll (WY)

Soil Conservation
Ohio State U Ag Tech Inst (OH)
Snow Coll (UT)
Southeast Comm Coll, Beatrice Campus (NE)
Trinidad State Jr Coll (CO)
Vermilion Comm Coll (MN)

Soil Science and Agronomy
Iowa Lakes Comm Coll (IA)

Solar Energy Technology
Cabrillo Coll (CA)
Chabot Coll (CA)
Comm Coll of Allegheny County (PA)
Pennsylvania Coll of Technology (PA)
Red Rocks Comm Coll (CO)
San Jose City Coll (CA)

Spanish
Arizona Western Coll (AZ)
Austin Comm Coll (TX)
Cabrillo Coll (CA)
Cañada Coll (CA)
Casper Coll (WY)
Centralia Coll (WA)
Chabot Coll (CA)
Cleveland Comm Coll (NC)
Coll of the Canyons (CA)
Coll of the Sequoias (CA)
Contra Costa Coll (CA)
East Los Angeles Coll (CA)
El Camino Coll (CA)
Everett Comm Coll (WA)

Foothill Coll (CA)
Gavilan Coll (CA)
Gordon Coll (GA)
Hill Coll of the Hill Jr College District (TX)
Iowa Lakes Comm Coll (IA)
Jefferson Coll (MO)
Kirkwood Comm Coll (IA)
Laramie County Comm Coll (WY)
Lincoln Coll, Lincoln (IL)
Lon Morris Coll (TX)
Los Angeles Valley Coll (CA)
Manatee Comm Coll (FL)
Merritt Coll (CA)
Miami Dade Coll (FL)
Midland Coll (TX)
MiraCosta Coll (CA)
North Idaho Coll (ID)
Orange Coast Coll (CA)
Oxnard Coll (CA)
Pasadena City Coll (CA)
Red Rocks Comm Coll (CO)
Riverside Comm Coll (CA)
St. Philip's Coll (TX)
San Joaquin Delta Coll (CA)
Santa Barbara City Coll (CA)
Santa Fe Comm Coll (NM)
Sauk Valley Comm Coll (IL)
Snow Coll (UT)
Southwestern Coll (CA)
Triton Coll (IL)
Vincennes U (IN)
Vista Comm Coll (CA)
Western Wyoming Comm Coll (WY)

Special Education
Cleveland Comm Coll (NC)
Comm Coll of Rhode Island (RI)
Eastern Wyoming Coll (WY)
Kellogg Comm Coll (MI)
Lehigh Carbon Comm Coll (PA)
Northampton County Area Comm Coll (PA)
Rend Lake Coll (IL)
Sauk Valley Comm Coll (IL)
Western Wyoming Comm Coll (WY)

Special Education (Early Childhood)
Calhoun Comm Coll (AL)
Motlow State Comm Coll (TN)
Northeast Texas Comm Coll (TX)
Northland Pioneer Coll (AZ)
Olympic Coll (WA)

Special Education (Hearing Impaired)
North Florida Comm Coll (FL)

Special Products Marketing
American River Coll (CA)
The Art Inst of Houston (TX)
Asnuntuck Comm Coll (CT)
Bergen Comm Coll (NJ)
Brookdale Comm Coll (NJ)
Burlington County Coll (NJ)
Cabrillo Coll (CA)
Camden County Coll (NJ)
Central Piedmont Comm Coll (NC)
Columbia Coll (CA)
Copiah-Lincoln Comm Coll (MS)
Cuyamaca Coll (CA)
Daytona Beach Comm Coll (FL)
Del Mar Coll (TX)
Des Moines Area Comm Coll (IA)
Dutchess Comm Coll (NY)
El Camino Coll (CA)
El Centro Coll (TX)
Fiorello H LaGuardia Comm Coll of City U of NY (NY)
Hinds Comm Coll (MS)
Jefferson Comm Coll (OH)
Kapiolani Comm Coll (HI)
Kirkwood Comm Coll (IA)

Lansing Comm Coll (MI)
Modesto Jr Coll (CA)
Naugatuck Valley Comm Coll (CT)
Northeast Mississippi Comm Coll (MS)
Oakton Comm Coll (IL)
Orange Coast Coll (CA)
Palm Beach Comm Coll (FL)
Palomar Coll (CA)
Penn Valley Comm Coll (MO)
Phoenix Coll (AZ)
St. Louis Comm Coll at Florissant Valley (MO)
San Diego City Coll (CA)
San Joaquin Delta Coll (CA)
Scottsdale Comm Coll (AZ)
Sinclair Comm Coll (OH)
Southern Maine Comm Coll (ME)
South Plains Coll (TX)
South Puget Sound Comm Coll (WA)
State U of NY Coll of A&T at Morrisville (NY)
Vermilion Comm Coll (MN)
Westmoreland County Comm Coll (PA)
Yakima Valley Comm Coll (WA)

Speech and Rhetoric
Abraham Baldwin Ag Coll (GA)
Amarillo Coll (TX)
Andrew Coll (GA)
Arkansas State U–Beebe (AR)
Atlanta Metropolitan Coll (GA)
Austin Comm Coll (TX)
Bainbridge Coll (GA)
Brookdale Comm Coll (NJ)
Cañada Coll (CA)
Casper Coll (WY)
City Colls of Chicago, Wilbur Wright Coll (IL)
Clarendon Coll (TX)
Coastal Bend Coll (TX)
Coll of the Desert (CA)
Coll of the Sequoias (CA)
Columbia State Comm Coll (TN)
Cuyamaca Coll (CA)
Darton Coll (GA)
Del Mar Coll (TX)
Eastern Oklahoma State Coll (OK)
East Los Angeles Coll (CA)
El Camino Coll (CA)
Everett Comm Coll (WA)
Foothill Coll (CA)
Garden City Comm Coll (KS)
Hill Coll of the Hill Jr College District (TX)
Howard Coll (TX)
Iowa Lakes Comm Coll (IA)
Jefferson Coll (MO)
Lansing Comm Coll (MI)
Linn-Benton Comm Coll (OR)
Lon Morris Coll (TX)
Los Angeles Valley Coll (CA)
Lower Columbia Coll (WA)
Manatee Comm Coll (FL)
Midland Coll (TX)
Mid Michigan Comm Coll (MI)
MiraCosta Coll (CA)
Modesto Jr Coll (CA)
Monroe County Comm Coll (MI)
Northeast Comm Coll (NE)
North Harris Coll (TX)
Northwest Coll (WY)
Odessa Coll (TX)
Palo Alto Coll (TX)
Palomar Coll (CA)
Pasadena City Coll (CA)
Pima Comm Coll (AZ)
Pratt Comm Coll and Area Vocational School (KS)
Rend Lake Coll (IL)
Riverside Comm Coll (CA)

St. Philip's Coll (TX)
San Diego City Coll (CA)
San Joaquin Delta Coll (CA)
Sauk Valley Comm Coll (IL)
Seward County Comm Coll (KS)
Spoon River Coll (IL)
Triton Coll (IL)
Vermilion Comm Coll (MN)

Speech-Language Pathology
Coll of DuPage (IL)
Fayetteville Tech Comm Coll (NC)
Guilford Tech Comm Coll (NC)
Parkland Coll (IL)

Speech/Theater Education
Mid Michigan Comm Coll (MI)
Pratt Comm Coll and Area Vocational School (KS)
Vincennes U (IN)

Speech Therapy
Mount Wachusett Comm Coll (MA)
Northeast Mississippi Comm Coll (MS)

Sport and Fitness Administration
Barton County Comm Coll (KS)
Bucks County Comm Coll (PA)
Central Oregon Comm Coll (OR)
Columbus State Comm Coll (OH)
Dean Coll (MA)
Hesser Coll (NH)
Holyoke Comm Coll (MA)
Howard Comm Coll (MD)
Iowa Lakes Comm Coll (IA)
Keystone Coll (PA)
Kingsborough Comm Coll of City U of NY (NY)
Lake-Sumter Comm Coll (FL)
Lehigh Carbon Comm Coll (PA)
Lorain County Comm Coll (OH)
New Hampshire Tech Inst (NH)
Northampton County Area Comm Coll (PA)
North Iowa Area Comm Coll (IA)
Oakland Comm Coll (MI)
Spokane Falls Comm Coll (WA)
State U of NY Coll of Technology at Alfred (NY)
Sullivan County Comm Coll (NY)
Tompkins Cortland Comm Coll (NY)
Vincennes U (IN)

Statistics
Chabot Coll (CA)
Daytona Beach Comm Coll (FL)
Eastern Wyoming Coll (WY)
Lincoln Coll, Lincoln (IL)
Manatee Comm Coll (FL)
Pasadena City Coll (CA)

Structural Engineering
Bristol Comm Coll (MA)

Substance Abuse/Addiction Counseling
Alvin Comm Coll (TX)
Amarillo Coll (TX)
Asnuntuck Comm Coll (CT)
Broome Comm Coll (NY)
Butler County Comm Coll (KS)
Century Coll (MN)
Clark Coll (WA)
Coll of DuPage (IL)
Coll of Lake County (IL)

Columbus State Comm Coll (OH)
Comm Coll of Allegheny County (PA)
Comm Coll of Rhode Island (RI)
Corning Comm Coll (NY)
Dawson Comm Coll (MT)
Eastfield Coll (TX)
Edmonds Comm Coll (WA)
Elgin Comm Coll (IL)
Erie Comm Coll (NY)
Finger Lakes Comm Coll (NY)
Gadsden State Comm Coll (AL)
Howard Coll (TX)
Howard Comm Coll (MD)
Kansas City Kansas Comm Coll (KS)
Lac Courte Oreilles Ojibwa Comm Coll (WI)
Lamar State Coll–Port Arthur (TX)
Lower Columbia Coll (WA)
Mesabi Range Comm and Tech Coll (MN)
Miami Dade Coll (FL)
Middlesex Comm Coll (CT)
Midland Coll (TX)
Milwaukee Area Tech Coll (WI)
Minneapolis Comm and Tech Coll (MN)
Mohawk Valley Comm Coll (NY)
Moraine Park Tech Coll (WI)
Mt. San Jacinto Coll (CA)
Naugatuck Valley Comm Coll (CT)
New Hampshire Tech Inst (NH)
North Shore Comm Coll (MA)
Northwestern Connecticut Comm-Tech Coll (CT)
Odessa Coll (TX)
Oklahoma State U, Oklahoma City (OK)
Peninsula Coll (WA)
Quinebaug Valley Comm Coll (CT)
Rogue Comm Coll (OR)
St. Petersburg Coll (FL)
Sisseton-Wahpeton Comm Coll (SD)
Southwestern Comm Coll (NC)
Southwestern Oregon Comm Coll (OR)
Spokane Falls Comm Coll (WA)
Sullivan County Comm Coll (NY)
Tillamook Bay Comm Coll (OR)
Tompkins Cortland Comm Coll (NY)
Triton Coll (IL)
Vincennes U (IN)
Washtenaw Comm Coll (MI)
Wor-Wic Comm Coll (MD)
Yakima Valley Comm Coll (WA)
Yuba Coll (CA)

Surgical Technology
Austin Comm Coll (TX)
Bismarck State Coll (ND)
Blue Ridge Comm Coll (NC)
Brevard Comm Coll (FL)
Cabarrus Coll of Health Sciences (NC)
Central Carolina Tech Coll (SC)
Central Wyoming Coll (WY)
Cincinnati State Tech and Comm Coll (OH)
City Colls of Chicago, Malcolm X Coll (IL)
Coastal Carolina Comm Coll (NC)
Coll of DuPage (IL)
Coll of Southern Idaho (ID)

Columbus State Comm Coll (OH)
Comm Coll of Allegheny County (PA)
Comm Coll of the Air Force (AL)
Cuyahoga Comm Coll (OH)
DeKalb Tech Coll (GA)
Delaware County Comm Coll (PA)
Delta Coll (MI)
Durham Tech Comm Coll (NC)
Eastern Idaho Tech Coll (ID)
Edgecombe Comm Coll (NC)
El Centro Coll (TX)
Fayetteville Tech Comm Coll (NC)
Guilford Tech Comm Coll (NC)
Hinds Comm Coll (MS)
Iowa Lakes Comm Coll (IA)
Ivy Tech State Coll–Central Indiana (IN)
Ivy Tech State Coll–Columbus (IN)
Ivy Tech State Coll–Eastcentral (IN)
Ivy Tech State Coll–Kokomo (IN)
Ivy Tech State Coll–Lafayette (IN)
Ivy Tech State Coll–Northwest (IN)
Ivy Tech State Coll–Southwest (IN)
Ivy Tech State Coll–Wabash Valley (IN)
James H. Faulkner State Comm Coll (AL)
Lake Superior Coll (MN)
Lamar State Coll–Port Arthur (TX)
Lanier Tech Coll (GA)
Lansing Comm Coll (MI)
Lorain County Comm Coll (OH)
Luzerne County Comm Coll (PA)
Macomb Comm Coll (MI)
Manchester Comm Coll (CT)
Metropolitan Comm Coll (NE)
Midlands Tech Coll (SC)
Montgomery County Comm Coll (PA)
Nassau Comm Coll (NY)
National School of Technology, Inc., North Miami Beach (FL)
Niagara County Comm Coll (NY)
North Arkansas Coll (AR)
Northeast Comm Coll (NE)
Northeast State Tech Comm Coll (TN)
Northeast Wisconsin Tech Coll (WI)
Oakland Comm Coll (MI)
Odessa Coll (TX)
Okefenokee Tech Coll (GA)
Oklahoma City Comm Coll (OK)
Paris Jr Coll (TX)
Polk Comm Coll (FL)
Rochester Comm and Tech Coll (MN)
St. Cloud Tech Coll (MN)
Seward County Comm Coll (KS)
Sinclair Comm Coll (OH)
Somerset Comm Coll (KY)
Southeast Arkansas Coll (AR)
Southern Maine Comm Coll (ME)
South Plains Coll (TX)
Southwestern Coll (CA)
Spokane Comm Coll (WA)
Springfield Tech Comm Coll (MA)
Texas State Tech Coll–Harlingen (TX)
Washtenaw Comm Coll (MI)

Waycross Coll (GA)
Western Wisconsin Tech Coll (WI)
Wichita Area Tech Coll (KS)

Surveying Engineering
Minot State U–Bottineau Campus (ND)

Survey Technology
Asheville-Buncombe Tech Comm Coll (NC)
Austin Comm Coll (TX)
Bates Tech Coll (WA)
Burlington County Coll (NJ)
Centralia Coll (WA)
Central Piedmont Comm Coll (NC)
Chabot Coll (CA)
Cincinnati State Tech and Comm Coll (OH)
Cuyamaca Coll (CA)
Delaware Tech & Comm Coll, Terry Cmps (DE)
Eastern Oklahoma State Coll (OK)
Fayetteville Tech Comm Coll (NC)
Guilford Tech Comm Coll (NC)
Hawkeye Comm Coll (IA)
Lansing Comm Coll (MI)
Macomb Comm Coll (MI)
Middle Georgia Coll (GA)
Middlesex County Coll (NJ)
Milwaukee Area Tech Coll (WI)
Mohawk Valley Comm Coll (NY)
Morrison Inst of Technology (IL)
Mott Comm Coll (MI)
Mt. San Antonio Coll (CA)
New Hampshire Comm Tech Coll, Berlin/Laconia (NH)
Oklahoma State U, Oklahoma City (OK)
Owens Comm Coll, Toledo (OH)
Palm Beach Comm Coll (FL)
Palomar Coll (CA)
Pennsylvania Coll of Technology (PA)
Penn State U Wilkes-Barre Campus of the Commonwealth Coll (PA)
Red Rocks Comm Coll (CO)
Rend Lake Coll (IL)
Santa Fe Comm Coll (NM)
Sierra Coll (CA)
Sinclair Comm Coll (OH)
Stark State Coll of Technology (OH)
State U of NY Coll of Environ Sci & For Ranger Sch (NY)
State U of NY Coll of Technology at Alfred (NY)
Sullivan County Comm Coll (NY)
Vincennes U (IN)
Westwood Coll–Denver North (CO)

System Administration
Academy Coll (MN)
AIB Coll of Business (IA)
American River Coll (CA)
Andover Coll (ME)
Anne Arundel Comm Coll (MD)
Austin Comm Coll (TX)
Berkeley Coll (NJ)
Blue Ridge Comm Coll (NC)
Brevard Comm Coll (FL)
The Brown Mackie Coll–Lenexa Campus (KS)
Cambria County Area Comm Coll (PA)
Camden County Coll (NJ)
Cape Cod Comm Coll (MA)
Central Comm Coll–Columbus Campus (NE)
Central Comm Coll–Grand Island Campus (NE)

Central Comm Coll–Hastings Campus (NE)
Centralia Coll (WA)
CHI Inst (PA)
Cleveland Comm Coll (NC)
Coastal Bend Coll (TX)
The Coll of Westchester (NY)
Cuesta Coll (CA)
Cumberland County Coll (NJ)
Dakota County Tech Coll (MN)
Davis Coll (OH)
Del Mar Coll (TX)
Durham Tech Comm Coll (NC)
Eastfield Coll (TX)
Edgecombe Comm Coll (NC)
Edison Comm Coll (FL)
Fayetteville Tech Comm Coll (NC)
Fiorello H LaGuardia Comm Coll of City U of NY (NY)
Florida National Coll (FL)
Gogebic Comm Coll (MI)
Hawkeye Comm Coll (IA)
Heartland Comm Coll (IL)
Hinds Comm Coll (MS)
Holmes Comm Coll (MS)
IntelliTec Coll, Grand Junction (CO)
Iowa Lakes Comm Coll (IA)
Island Drafting and Tech Inst (NY)
Lake Area Tech Inst (SD)
Lakeland Comm Coll (OH)
Linn-Benton Comm Coll (OR)
Louisville Tech Inst (KY)
Metropolitan Comm Coll-Business & Technology College (MO)
Midland Coll (TX)
Milwaukee Area Tech Coll (WI)
Mineral Area Coll (MO)
Minot State U–Bottineau Campus (ND)
MTI Coll of Business and Technology, Houston (TX)
Naugatuck Valley Comm Coll (CT)
Olympic Coll (WA)
Owensboro Comm and Tech Coll (KY)
Palm Beach Comm Coll (FL)
Parkland Coll (IL)
Quinebaug Valley Comm Coll (CT)
Rasmussen Coll Mankato (MN)
Santa Barbara City Coll (CA)
Seminole Comm Coll (FL)
Sheridan Coll (WY)
Silicon Valley Coll, Walnut Creek (CA)
Sinclair Comm Coll (OH)
Southwest Mississippi Comm Coll (MS)
Stanly Comm Coll (NC)
Texas State Tech Coll–Harlingen (TX)
Tompkins Cortland Comm Coll (NY)
Triton Coll (IL)
U of Arkansas Comm Coll at Batesville (AR)
Vincennes U (IN)
Washtenaw Comm Coll (MI)
Western Wisconsin Tech Coll (WI)
York Tech Inst (PA)

System, Networking, and Lan/Wan Management
Academy Coll (MN)
Brevard Comm Coll (FL)
Iowa Lakes Comm Coll (IA)
LDS Business Coll (UT)
Metropolitan Comm Coll-Business & Technology College (MO)
Midland Coll (TX)
Mitchell Tech Inst (SD)

MTI Coll of Business and Technology, Houston (TX)
Olympic Coll (WA)
Pikes Peak Comm Coll (CO)
St. Philip's Coll (TX)
Sawyer Coll, Hammond (IN)
Silicon Valley Coll, Walnut Creek (CA)
Southeastern Tech Coll (GA)
Southwestern Comm Coll (NC)
Vatterott Coll, Springfield (MO)

Systems Science and Theory
Northeast Wisconsin Tech Coll (WI)

Taxation
Globe Coll (MN)
Minnesota School of Business–Brooklyn Center (MN)
Minnesota School of Business-Plymouth (MN)
Minnesota School of Business-Richfield (MN)

Teacher Assistant/Aide
Alamance Comm Coll (NC)
Big Bend Comm Coll (WA)
Blackfeet Comm Coll (MT)
Brunswick Comm Coll (NC)
Bucks County Comm Coll (PA)
Carteret Comm Coll (NC)
Centralia Coll (WA)
Chabot Coll (CA)
Chemeketa Comm Coll (OR)
City Colls of Chicago, Malcolm X Coll (IL)
Cleveland Comm Coll (NC)
Clover Park Tech Coll (WA)
Clovis Comm Coll (NM)
Coll of the Desert (CA)
Colorado Northwestern Comm Coll (CO)
Delaware County Comm Coll (PA)
Delta Coll (MI)
Des Moines Area Comm Coll (IA)
Durham Tech Comm Coll (NC)
El Centro Coll (TX)
Fort Scott Comm Coll (KS)
Fulton-Montgomery Comm Coll (NY)
Garden City Comm Coll (KS)
Illinois Eastern Comm Colls, Lincoln Trail Coll (IL)
Isothermal Comm Coll (NC)
John A. Logan Coll (IL)
Kingsborough Comm Coll of City U of NY (NY)
Kirkwood Comm Coll (IA)
Lansing Comm Coll (MI)
Lewis and Clark Comm Coll (IL)
Linn-Benton Comm Coll (OR)
Lower Columbia Coll (WA)
Manchester Comm Coll (CT)
Miami Dade Coll (FL)
Middlesex County Coll (NJ)
MiraCosta Coll (CA)
Montgomery County Comm Coll (PA)
Nash Comm Coll (NC)
New Hampshire Tech Inst (NH)
Northeast Mississippi Comm Coll (MS)
Northland Pioneer Coll (AZ)
Ocean County Coll (NJ)
Odessa Coll (TX)
Pasadena City Coll (CA)
Rockingham Comm Coll (NC)
St. Cloud Tech Coll (MN)
St. Philip's Coll (TX)
San Diego City Coll (CA)
San Jose City Coll (CA)
Sierra Coll (CA)

Southeastern Comm Coll (NC)
South Suburban Coll (IL)
Vance-Granville Comm Coll (NC)
Victor Valley Coll (CA)

Teaching Assistants/Aides Related
Louisiana Tech Coll–Florida Parishes Campus (LA)
Northland Pioneer Coll (AZ)

Technical and Business Writing
Austin Comm Coll (TX)
Cincinnati State Tech and Comm Coll (OH)
Clovis Comm Coll (NM)
Coll of Lake County (IL)
Columbus State Comm Coll (OH)
El Camino Coll (CA)
Florida National Coll (FL)
Houston Comm Coll System (TX)
Linn-Benton Comm Coll (OR)
State U of NY Coll of A&T at Morrisville (NY)
Terra State Comm Coll (OH)
Washtenaw Comm Coll (MI)

Technical Teacher Education
Lake Region State Coll (ND)
North Dakota State Coll of Science (ND)

Technology/Industrial Arts Teacher Education
Eastern Arizona Coll (AZ)
Iowa Lakes Comm Coll (IA)
Kellogg Comm Coll (MI)
Manatee Comm Coll (FL)
Roane State Comm Coll (TN)

Telecommunications
Amarillo Coll (TX)
Anne Arundel Comm Coll (MD)
Brookdale Comm Coll (NJ)
Butte Coll (CA)
CHI Inst (PA)
Cincinnati State Tech and Comm Coll (OH)
Coffeyville Comm Coll (KS)
Cuesta Coll (CA)
Daytona Beach Comm Coll (FL)
DeKalb Tech Coll (GA)
Des Moines Area Comm Coll (IA)
Dutchess Comm Coll (NY)
ECPI Coll of Technology, Newport News (VA)
ECPI Coll of Technology, Virginia Beach (VA)
ECPI Tech Coll, Richmond (VA)
ECPI Tech Coll, Roanoke (VA)
Gadsden State Comm Coll (AL)
Gwinnett Tech Coll (GA)
Hinds Comm Coll (MS)
Howard Comm Coll (MD)
Illinois Eastern Comm Colls, Lincoln Trail Coll (IL)
Jefferson Comm Coll (MO)
Kirkwood Comm Coll (IA)
Lake Land Coll (IL)
Lansing Comm Coll (MI)
McIntosh Coll (NH)
Meridian Comm Coll (MS)
Middlesex Comm Coll (MA)
Miles Comm Coll (MT)
Mitchell Tech Inst (SD)
Mohawk Valley Comm Coll (NY)
Mount Wachusett Comm Coll (MA)
Napa Valley Coll (CA)
Niagara County Comm Coll (NY)

Northeast Wisconsin Tech Coll (WI)
Owens Comm Coll, Toledo (OH)
Oxnard Coll (CA)
Palomar Coll (CA)
Pasadena City Coll (CA)
Queensborough Comm Coll of City U of NY (NY)
Reading Area Comm Coll (PA)
St. Louis Comm Coll at Florissant Valley (MO)
St. Petersburg Coll (FL)
San Diego City Coll (CA)
Schenectady County Comm Coll (NY)
Seminole Comm Coll (FL)
South Plains Coll (TX)
South Puget Sound Comm Coll (WA)
Southwestern Coll (CA)
Trident Tech Coll (SC)

Telecommunications Technology
Alexandria Tech Coll (MN)
Clark Coll (WA)
Collin County Comm Coll District (TX)
ECPI Tech Coll, Glen Allen (VA)
ECPI Tech Coll, Richmond (VA)
ECPI Tech Coll, Roanoke (VA)
Marion Tech Coll (OH)
Miami Dade Coll (FL)
Mitchell Tech Inst (SD)
Northern Essex Comm Coll (MA)
Penn State U Beaver Campus of the Commonwealth Coll (PA)
Penn State U DuBois Campus of the Commonwealth Coll (PA)
Penn State U Fayette Campus of the Commonwealth Coll (PA)
Penn State U Hazleton Campus of the Commonwealth Coll (PA)
Penn State U New Kensington Campus of the Commonwealth Coll (PA)
Penn State U Shenango Campus of the Commonwealth Coll (PA)
Penn State U Wilkes-Barre Campus of the Commonwealth Coll (PA)
Penn State U York Campus of the Commonwealth Coll (PA)

Theatre Design and Technology
Comm Coll of Rhode Island (RI)
Howard Comm Coll (MD)
Lake-Sumter Comm Coll (FL)
Nassau Comm Coll (NY)
Santa Barbara City Coll (CA)
Western Wyoming Comm Coll (WY)

Theatre/Theatre Arts Management
Gulf Coast Comm Coll (FL)

Theology
Assumption Coll for Sisters (NJ)
Lon Morris Coll (TX)
Mid-America Baptist Theological Seminary (TN)
Northeast Mississippi Comm Coll (MS)
Riverside Comm Coll (CA)

Therapeutic Recreation
Carteret Comm Coll (NC)
Colorado Mountn Coll (CO)
Comm Coll of Allegheny County (PA)

Cuesta Coll (CA)
Edmonds Comm Coll (WA)
Keystone Coll (PA)
Moraine Valley Comm Coll (IL)
North Central State Coll (OH)
Northwestern Connecticut Comm-Tech Coll (CT)
Santa Barbara City Coll (CA)
Vincennes U (IN)

Tool and Die Technology
Asheville-Buncombe Tech Comm Coll (NC)
Dunwoody Coll of Technology (MN)
Fayetteville Tech Comm Coll (NC)
Gadsden State Comm Coll (AL)
Hawkeye Comm Coll (IA)
Ivy Tech State Coll–Bloomington (IN)
Ivy Tech State Coll–Central Indiana (IN)
Ivy Tech State Coll–Columbus (IN)
Ivy Tech State Coll–Eastcentral (IN)
Ivy Tech State Coll–Kokomo (IN)
Ivy Tech State Coll–Lafayette (IN)
Ivy Tech State Coll–North Central (IN)
Ivy Tech State Coll–Northeast (IN)
Ivy Tech State Coll–Northwest (IN)
Ivy Tech State Coll–Southcentral (IN)
Ivy Tech State Coll–Southwest (IN)
Ivy Tech State Coll–Wabash Valley (IN)
Ivy Tech State Coll–Whitewater (IN)
Jackson State Comm Coll (TN)
Kishwaukee Coll (IL)
Macomb Comm Coll (MI)
Milwaukee Area Tech Coll (WI)
North Iowa Area Comm Coll (IA)
Northwest Iowa Comm Coll (IA)
Northwest State Comm Coll (OH)
Oakland Comm Coll (MI)
Pennsylvania Coll of Technology (PA)
Terra State Comm Coll (OH)
Trenholm State Tech Coll, Montgomery (AL)
Western Iowa Tech Comm Coll (IA)
Wilson Tech Comm Coll (NC)

Tourism and Travel Services Management
AIB Coll of Business (IA)
Allentown Business School (PA)
Amarillo Coll (TX)
Arapahoe Comm Coll (CO)
Bay State Coll (MA)
Bergen Comm Coll (NJ)
Blue Ridge Comm Coll (NC)
Bradford School (OH)
Briarwood Coll (CT)
Bryant & Stratton Business Inst, Syracuse (NY)
Bunker Hill Comm Coll (MA)
Butte Coll (CA)
Cañada Coll (CA)
Central Pennsylvania Coll (PA)
Central Piedmont Comm Coll (NC)
Chabot Coll (CA)
Coll of DuPage (IL)
Columbus State Comm Coll (OH)
Comm Coll of Denver (CO)

Consolidated School of Business, York (PA)
Corning Comm Coll (NY)
Dakota County Tech Coll (MN)
Daytona Beach Comm Coll (FL)
Dutchess Comm Coll (NY)
Elgin Comm Coll (IL)
Elmira Business Inst (NY)
Erie Business Center South (PA)
Finger Lakes Comm Coll (NY)
Fiorello H LaGuardia Comm Coll of City U of NY (NY)
Fisher Coll (MA)
Florida National Coll (FL)
Foothill Coll (CA)
Gwinnett Tech Coll (GA)
Harrisburg Area Comm Coll (PA)
Holyoke Comm Coll (MA)
Houston Comm Coll System (TX)
Iowa Lakes Comm Coll (IA)
Jefferson Comm Coll (NY)
John A. Logan Coll (IL)
Johnson County Comm Coll (KS)
Kapiolani Comm Coll (HI)
Kaplan Coll (IA)
Kent State U, Trumbull Campus (OH)
Kingsborough Comm Coll of City U of NY (NY)
Lakeland Comm Coll (OH)
Lansing Comm Coll (MI)
Lincoln Coll, Lincoln (IL)
Lorain County Comm Coll (OH)
Luzerne County Comm Coll (PA)
MacCormac Coll (IL)
Maple Woods Comm Coll (MO)
Massasoit Comm Coll (MA)
McIntosh Coll (NH)
Miami Dade Coll (FL)
Mineral Area Coll (MO)
Minneapolis Business Coll (MN)
MiraCosta Coll (CA)
Mountain West Coll (UT)
New Hampshire Tech Inst (NH)
Newport Business Inst, Lower Burrell (PA)
Northeast Wisconsin Tech Coll (WI)
Northern Essex Comm Coll (MA)
North Harris Coll (TX)
North Shore Comm Coll (MA)
Northwest Coll (WY)
Palomar Coll (CA)
Pasadena City Coll (CA)
Patricia Stevens Coll (MO)
Pennsylvania Coll of Technology (PA)
Phoenix Coll (AZ)
Pima Comm Coll (AZ)
Quinsigamond Comm Coll (MA)
Raritan Valley Comm Coll (NJ)
Rasmussen Coll Mankato (MN)
Rasmussen Coll St. Cloud (MN)
Reading Area Comm Coll (PA)
Rockingham Comm Coll (NC)
St. Petersburg Coll (FL)
St. Philip's Coll (TX)
San Diego City Coll (CA)
Schenectady County Comm Coll (NY)
Schiller International USwitzerland)
Shelton State Comm Coll (AL)

Sinclair Comm Coll (OH)
Southwestern Coll (CA)
State U of NY Coll of A&T at Morrisville (NY)
State U of NY Coll of Technology at Delhi (NY)
Sullivan County Comm Coll (NY)
Tompkins Cortland Comm Coll (NY)
U of Alaska Southeast, Ketchikan Campus (AK)
U of Northwestern Ohio (OH)
Westmoreland County Comm Coll (PA)
Yakima Valley Comm Coll (WA)

Tourism and Travel Services Marketing
AIB Coll of Business (IA)
Coll of DuPage (IL)
Dakota County Tech Coll (MN)
Edmonds Comm Coll (WA)
Harrisburg Area Comm Coll (PA)
Iowa Lakes Comm Coll (IA)
Luzerne County Comm Coll (PA)
Milwaukee Area Tech Coll (WI)
Moraine Valley Comm Coll (IL)
Rasmussen Coll Mankato (MN)
Tompkins Cortland Comm Coll (NY)
Waubonsee Comm Coll (IL)

Tourism Promotion
AIB Coll of Business (IA)
Central Oregon Comm Coll (OR)
Coll of DuPage (IL)
Comm Coll of Allegheny County (PA)
Florida National Coll (FL)
Iowa Lakes Comm Coll (IA)
Lehigh Carbon Comm Coll (PA)
Rasmussen Coll Mankato (MN)

Tourism/Travel Marketing
Edmonds Comm Coll (WA)
Harrisburg Area Comm Coll (PA)
Lehigh Carbon Comm Coll (PA)
National Coll of Business & Technology, Salem (VA)

Trade and Industrial Teacher Education
Copiah-Lincoln Comm Coll (MS)
Del Mar Coll (TX)
East Los Angeles Coll (CA)
ECPI Coll of Technology, Newport News (VA)
ECPI Tech Coll, Richmond (VA)
Garden City Comm Coll (KS)
Iowa Lakes Comm Coll (IA)
Isothermal Comm Coll (NC)
Lenoir Comm Coll (NC)
Manatee Comm Coll (FL)
Northeastern Oklahoma A&M Coll (OK)
Northeast Iowa Comm Coll (IA)
Northeast Mississippi Comm Coll (MS)
Northwest Coll (WY)
Palo Alto Coll (TX)
Portland Comm Coll (OR)
Pratt Comm Coll and Area Vocational School (KS)
Snow Coll (UT)
Southwestern Comm Coll (NC)
Spartanburg Tech Coll (SC)
U of Arkansas Comm Coll at Hope (AR)
Victor Valley Coll (CA)

Transportation and Materials Moving Related
Cecil Comm Coll (MD)
Mid-Plains Comm Coll, North Platte (NE)

Transportation Management
Calhoun Comm Coll (AL)
Del Mar Coll (TX)
Milwaukee Area Tech Coll (WI)
Northwest State Comm Coll (OH)

Transportation Technology
Central Piedmont Comm Coll (NC)
Coll of DuPage (IL)
Fort Scott Comm Coll (KS)
Houston Comm Coll System (TX)
Los Angeles Trade-Tech Coll (CA)
Milwaukee Area Tech Coll (WI)
Mt. San Antonio Coll (CA)
Nassau Comm Coll (NY)
Northeast Wisconsin Tech Coll (WI)
North Hennepin Comm Coll (MN)
Oxnard Coll (CA)
San Diego City Coll (CA)
Sinclair Comm Coll (OH)
Triton Coll (IL)
West Hills Comm Coll (CA)

Truck and Bus Driver/Commercial Vehicle Operation
Alexandria Tech Coll (MN)
Dakota County Tech Coll (MN)
Wichita Area Tech Coll (KS)

Turf and Turfgrass Management
Anoka Tech Coll (MN)
Brunswick Comm Coll (NC)
Cincinnati State Tech and Comm Coll (OH)
Coll of Lake County (IL)
Comm Coll of Allegheny County (PA)
Cuyamaca Coll (CA)
Guilford Tech Comm Coll (NC)
Iowa Lakes Comm Coll (IA)
Kent State U, Salem Campus (OH)
Kishwaukee Coll (IL)
Lake City Comm Coll (FL)
Linn State Tech Coll (MO)
Minot State U–Bottineau Campus (ND)
Northland Pioneer Coll (AZ)
Northwestern Michigan Coll (MI)
Ohio State U Ag Tech Inst (OH)
Oklahoma State U, Oklahoma City (OK)
Pennsylvania Coll of Technology (PA)
Rochester Comm and Tech Coll (MN)
Southwestern Oregon Comm Coll (OR)
State U of NY Coll of Technology at Delhi (NY)
Texas State Tech Coll–Waco/Marshall Campus (TX)
Western Iowa Tech Comm Coll (IA)
The Williamson Free School of Mecha Trades (PA)

Urban Studies/Affairs
Comm Coll of Rhode Island (RI)
Lawson State Comm Coll (AL)
Lorain County Comm Coll (OH)
Riverside Comm Coll (CA)

St. Philip's Coll (TX)
Santa Monica Coll (CA)

Vehicle and Vehicle Parts And Accessories Marketing
Dakota County Tech Coll (MN)
Northeast Wisconsin Tech Coll (WI)
Pennsylvania Coll of Technology (PA)

Vehicle/Equipment Operation
Comm Coll of the Air Force (AL)
Western Nevada Comm Coll (NV)

Vehicle Maintenance and Repair Technologies Related
Albuquerque Tech Vocational Inst (NM)
Massasoit Comm Coll (MA)
North Dakota State Coll of Science (ND)
Pennsylvania Coll of Technology (PA)
Victor Valley Coll (CA)

Vehicle/Petroleum Products Marketing
Central Comm Coll–Hastings Campus (NE)

Veterinary/Animal Health Technology
Cedar Valley Coll (TX)
Central Florida Comm Coll (FL)
Columbus State Comm Coll (OH)
County Coll of Morris (NJ)
Duluth Business U (MN)
Eastern Wyoming Coll (WY)
Education Direct Center for Degree Studies (PA)
Everett Comm Coll (WA)
Jefferson Coll (MO)
Lehigh Carbon Comm Coll (PA)
Macomb Comm Coll (MI)
Midland Coll (TX)
Minnesota School of Business-Richfield (MN)
Northampton County Area Comm Coll (PA)
Parkland Coll (IL)
Pima Comm Coll (AZ)
Snead State Comm Coll (AL)
Sussex County Comm Coll (NJ)
Utah Career Coll (UT)

Veterinary Sciences
Casper Coll (WY)
Colby Comm Coll (KS)
Del Mar Coll (TX)
Eastern Oklahoma State Coll (OK)
Hinds Comm Coll (MS)
Holmes Comm Coll (MS)
Holyoke Comm Coll (MA)
Isothermal Comm Coll (NC)
Kirkwood Comm Coll (IA)
Lorain County Comm Coll (OH)
Macomb Comm Coll (MI)
Miami Dade Coll (FL)
Monroe County Comm Coll (MI)
Northeastern Oklahoma A&M Coll (OK)
North Harris Coll (TX)
Northwest-Shoals Comm Coll (AL)
Palo Alto Coll (TX)
Pasadena City Coll (CA)
Reading Area Comm Coll (PA)
Snow Coll (UT)
State U of NY Coll of Technology at Alfred (NY)
Vincennes U (IN)

Veterinary Technology
Bergen Comm Coll (NJ)
Brevard Comm Coll (FL)
Colby Comm Coll (KS)
Coll of Southern Idaho (ID)
Colorado Mountn Coll (CO)
Columbia State Comm Coll (TN)
Columbus State Comm Coll (OH)
Comm Coll of Denver (CO)
Cuyahoga Comm Coll (OH)
Fiorello H LaGuardia Comm Coll of City U of NY (NY)
Foothill Coll (CA)
Gaston Coll (NC)
Globe Coll (MN)
Harcum Coll (PA)
Hinds Comm Coll (MS)
Holyoke Comm Coll (MA)
Jefferson Coll (MO)
Johnson County Comm Coll (KS)
Kirkwood Comm Coll (IA)
Lansing Comm Coll (MI)
Los Angeles Pierce Coll (CA)
Maple Woods Comm Coll (MO)
Midland Coll (TX)
Minnesota School of Business–Brooklyn Center (MN)
Minnesota School of Business-Plymouth (MN)
Northeast Comm Coll (NE)
North Shore Comm Coll (MA)
Northwestern Connecticut Comm-Tech Coll (CT)
Oklahoma State U, Oklahoma City (OK)
St. Petersburg Coll (FL)
State U of NY Coll of Technology at Canton (NY)
State U of NY Coll of Technology at Delhi (NY)
Stautzenberger Coll (OH)
Trident Tech Coll (SC)
Vatterott Coll, Omaha (NE)
Yakima Valley Comm Coll (WA)
Yuba Coll (CA)

Violin, Viola, Guitar and Other Stringed Instruments
Minnesota State Coll–Southeast Tech (MN)

Visual and Performing Arts
Amarillo Coll (TX)
Atlantic Cape Comm Coll (NJ)
Berkshire Comm Coll (MA)
Bristol Comm Coll (MA)
Brookdale Comm Coll (NJ)
Bucks County Comm Coll (PA)
Calhoun Comm Coll (AL)
Holyoke Comm Coll (MA)
Hutchinson Comm Coll and Area Vocational School (KS)
Kingwood Coll (TX)
Laramie County Comm Coll (WY)
Moraine Valley Comm Coll (IL)
Mt. San Jacinto Coll (CA)
Nassau Comm Coll (NY)
Queensborough Comm Coll of City U of NY (NY)
Raritan Valley Comm Coll (NJ)
Western Wyoming Comm Coll (WY)

Visual and Performing Arts Related
The Art Inst of Philadelphia (PA)
Comm Coll of Allegheny County (PA)
Santa Fe Comm Coll (NM)

Vocational Rehabilitation Counseling
Edmonds Comm Coll (WA)
Manatee Comm Coll (FL)
Spokane Falls Comm Coll (WA)

Voice and Opera
Alvin Comm Coll (TX)
Coastal Bend Coll (TX)
Coffeyville Comm Coll (KS)
Del Mar Coll (TX)
Hill Coll of the Hill Jr College District (TX)
Iowa Lakes Comm Coll (IA)
Kirkwood Comm Coll (IA)
Lansing Comm Coll (MI)
Lincoln Coll, Lincoln (IL)
Lon Morris Coll (TX)
Snow Coll (UT)

Watchmaking and Jewelrymaking
Northeast Wisconsin Tech Coll (WI)
North Seattle Comm Coll (WA)

Water Quality and Wastewater Treatment Management And Recycling Technology
Bristol Comm Coll (MA)
Collin County Comm Coll District (TX)
Delta Coll (MI)
Green River Comm Coll (WA)
Linn-Benton Comm Coll (OR)
Minot State U–Bottineau Campus (ND)
New Hampshire Comm Tech Coll, Berlin/Laconia (NH)
Northwest-Shoals Comm Coll (AL)
St. Cloud Tech Coll (MN)
San Juan Coll (NM)
Trinidad State Jr Coll (CO)
Vermilion Comm Coll (MN)

Water Resources Engineering
Bristol Comm Coll (MA)

Water, Wetlands, and Marine Resources Management
Iowa Lakes Comm Coll (IA)
Keystone Coll (PA)

Web/Multimedia Management and Webmaster
Academy Coll (MN)
American River Coll (CA)
Andover Coll (ME)
Antonelli Coll (OH)
The Art Inst of Pittsburgh (PA)
Atlantic Cape Comm Coll (NJ)
Bates Tech Coll (WA)
Cambria County Area Comm Coll (PA)
Camden County Coll (NJ)
Cape Cod Comm Coll (MA)
Central Comm Coll–Columbus Campus (NE)
Central Comm Coll–Grand Island Campus (NE)
Central Comm Coll–Hastings Campus (NE)
Central Pennsylvania Coll (PA)
Clovis Comm Coll (NM)
The Coll of Westchester (NY)
Columbia-Greene Comm Coll (NY)
Dakota County Tech Coll (MN)
Del Mar Coll (TX)
Delta Coll (MI)
Fayetteville Tech Comm Coll (NC)
Florida Career Coll (FL)
Harrisburg Area Comm Coll (PA)

Hawkeye Comm Coll (IA)
Lake Area Tech Inst (SD)
Lakeland Comm Coll (OH)
Laramie County Comm Coll (WY)
Metropolitan Comm Coll-Business & Technology College (MO)
Mid-South Comm Coll (AR)
Milwaukee Area Tech Coll (WI)
Minneapolis Comm and Tech Coll (MN)
Minot State U–Bottineau Campus (ND)
Monroe County Comm Coll (MI)
Northern Essex Comm Coll (MA)
North Seattle Comm Coll (WA)
Olympic Coll (WA)
Pioneer Pacific Coll (OR)
Platt Coll San Diego (CA)
Remington Coll–Mobile Campus (AL)
Riverland Comm Coll (MN)
Saint Charles Comm Coll (MO)
St. Petersburg Coll (FL)
St. Philip's Coll (TX)
Salem Comm Coll (NJ)
Sawyer Coll, Hammond (IN)
Seminole Comm Coll (FL)
Sheridan Coll (WY)
Sinclair Comm Coll (OH)
Southwestern Coll (CA)
Springfield Tech Comm Coll (MA)
Stanly Comm Coll (NC)
Stark State Coll of Technology (OH)
Sullivan County Comm Coll (NY)
Texas State Tech Coll–Harlingen (TX)
Trident Tech Coll (SC)
Triton Coll (IL)
Vincennes U (IN)
Washtenaw Comm Coll (MI)
Western Wyoming Comm Coll (WY)

Web Page, Digital/ Multimedia and Information Resources Design
Academy Coll (MN)
Alexandria Tech Coll (MN)
American River Coll (CA)
Arapahoe Comm Coll (CO)
The Art Inst of Houston (TX)
The Art Inst of Pittsburgh (PA)
The Art Insts International Minnesota (MN)
Berkeley Coll (NJ)
Brevard Comm Coll (FL)
Bunker Hill Comm Coll (MA)
Camden County Coll (NJ)
Cape Cod Comm Coll (MA)
Capital Comm Coll (CT)
Central Wyoming Coll (WY)
Clover Park Tech Coll (WA)
Clovis Comm Coll (NM)
CollAmerica–Fort Collins (CO)
Coll of the Sequoias (CA)
The Coll of Westchester (NY)
Collin County Comm Coll District (TX)
Cuesta Coll (CA)
Dakota County Tech Coll (MN)
Davis Coll (OH)
Delaware County Comm Coll (PA)
Del Mar Coll (TX)
Delta Coll (MI)
Duluth Business U (MN)
ECPI Tech Coll, Glen Allen (VA)
ECPI Tech Coll, Richmond (VA)
El Centro Coll (TX)

Fayetteville Tech Comm Coll (NC)
Florida National Coll (FL)
Galveston Coll (TX)
Globe Coll (MN)
Guilford Tech Comm Coll (NC)
Hawkeye Comm Coll (IA)
Heartland Comm Coll (IL)
Hibbing Comm Coll (MN)
Kansas City Kansas Comm Coll (KS)
Lake City Comm Coll (FL)
Lakeland Comm Coll (OH)
Laramie County Comm Coll (WY)
LDS Business Coll (UT)
Louisville Tech Inst (KY)
Mesabi Range Comm and Tech Coll (MN)
Metropolitan Comm Coll-Business & Technology College (MO)
Minneapolis Comm and Tech Coll (MN)
Minnesota School of Business–Brooklyn Center (MN)
Minnesota School of Business-Plymouth (MN)
Minnesota School of Business-Richfield (MN)
Minot State U–Bottineau Campus (ND)
Monroe County Comm Coll (MI)
Montana State U Coll of Tech-Great Falls (MT)
Northern Essex Comm Coll (MA)
North Seattle Comm Coll (WA)
Palm Beach Comm Coll (FL)
Parkland Coll (IL)
Pasco-Hernando Comm Coll (FL)
Peninsula Coll (WA)
Pennsylvania Coll of Technology (PA)
Pennsylvania Inst of Technology (PA)
Platt Coll San Diego (CA)
Rasmussen Coll Mankato (MN)
Remington Coll–Lafayette Campus (LA)
Richmond Comm Coll (NC)
Riverland Comm Coll (MN)
Seminole Comm Coll (FL)
Sheridan Coll (WY)
Southeastern Tech Coll (GA)
Southwestern Coll (CA)
Stanly Comm Coll (NC)
Stark State Coll of Technology (OH)
Stautzenberger Coll (OH)
Texas State Tech Coll–Harlingen (TX)
Tompkins Cortland Comm Coll (NY)
Trident Tech Coll (SC)
Triton Coll (IL)
U of Arkansas Comm Coll at Batesville (AR)
Utah Valley State Coll (UT)
Vincennes U (IN)
Vista Comm Coll (CA)
Washtenaw Comm Coll (MI)
Western Wyoming Comm Coll (WY)
York County Comm Coll (ME)
York Tech Inst (PA)

Welding Technology
Alamance Comm Coll (NC)
Alexandria Tech Coll (MN)
American River Coll (CA)
Anoka Tech Coll (MN)
Arizona Western Coll (AZ)
Arkansas Northeastern Coll (AR)
Austin Comm Coll (TX)
Bainbridge Coll (GA)

Beaufort County Comm Coll (NC)
Big Bend Comm Coll (WA)
Bismarck State Coll (ND)
Bladen Comm Coll (NC)
Butler County Comm Coll (KS)
Butte Coll (CA)
Cabrillo Coll (CA)
Casper Coll (WY)
Cecil Comm Coll (MD)
Central Comm Coll–Columbus Campus (NE)
Central Comm Coll–Grand Island Campus (NE)
Central Comm Coll–Hastings Campus (NE)
Centralia Coll (WA)
Central Oregon Comm Coll (OR)
Central Piedmont Comm Coll (NC)
Central Wyoming Coll (WY)
Chabot Coll (CA)
Chemeketa Comm Coll (OR)
Clark Coll (WA)
Coastal Bend Coll (TX)
Coffeyville Comm Coll (KS)
Coll of DuPage (IL)
Coll of Eastern Utah (UT)
Coll of Oceaneering (CA)
Coll of Southern Idaho (ID)
Coll of the Canyons (CA)
Coll of the Desert (CA)
Coll of the Sequoias (CA)
Comm Coll of Allegheny County (PA)
Contra Costa Coll (CA)
Cossatot Comm Coll of the U of Arkansas (AR)
Cuesta Coll (CA)
Del Mar Coll (TX)
Delta Coll (MI)
Des Moines Area Comm Coll (IA)
Doña Ana Branch Comm Coll (NM)
Dunwoody Coll of Technology (MN)
Eastern Arizona Coll (AZ)
Eastern Idaho Tech Coll (ID)
Eastern Maine Comm Coll (ME)
Eastern Wyoming Coll (WY)
El Camino Coll (CA)
Elgin Comm Coll (IL)
Everett Comm Coll (WA)
Fayetteville Tech Comm Coll (NC)
Forsyth Tech Comm Coll (NC)
Fort Scott Comm Coll (KS)
Front Range Comm Coll (CO)
Garden City Comm Coll (KS)
Grand Rapids Comm Coll (MI)
Great Basin Coll (NV)
Green River Comm Coll (WA)
Hawaii Comm Coll (HI)
Hawkeye Comm Coll (IA)
Heartland Comm Coll (IL)
Hill Coll of the Hill Jr College District (TX)
Hinds Comm Coll (MS)
Honolulu Comm Coll (HI)
Hutchinson Comm Coll and Area Vocational School (KS)
Iowa Lakes Comm Coll (IA)
Isothermal Comm Coll (NC)
Jefferson Coll (MO)
John A. Logan Coll (IL)
Kalamazoo Valley Comm Coll (MI)
Kellogg Comm Coll (MI)
Kirkwood Comm Coll (IA)
Kirtland Comm Coll (MI)
Lake Area Tech Inst (SD)
Lamar State Coll–Port Arthur (TX)
Lansing Comm Coll (MI)
Lenoir Comm Coll (NC)

Linn-Benton Comm Coll (OR)
Los Angeles Pierce Coll (CA)
Los Angeles Trade-Tech Coll (CA)
Louisiana Tech Coll–Delta Ouachita Campus (LA)
Louisiana Tech Coll–Mansfield Campus (LA)
Lower Columbia Coll (WA)
Macomb Comm Coll (MI)
Manhattan Area Tech Coll (KS)
Metropolitan Comm Coll (NE)
Midland Coll (TX)
Mid-Plains Comm Coll, North Platte (NE)
Milwaukee Area Tech Coll (WI)
Minnesota State Coll–Southeast Tech (MN)
Mississippi Gulf Coast Comm Coll (MS)
Moberly Area Comm Coll (MO)
Modesto Jr Coll (CA)
Monroe County Comm Coll (MI)
Mountain View Coll (TX)
Mt. San Antonio Coll (CA)
Napa Valley Coll (CA)
New Hampshire Comm Tech Coll, Manchester/Stratham (NH)
New Mexico State U–Carlsbad (NM)
New River Comm Coll (VA)
North Central State Coll (OH)
North Dakota State Coll of Science (ND)
Northeast Comm Coll (NE)
Northeastern Oklahoma A&M Coll (OK)
Northeast State Tech Comm Coll (TN)
Northeast Wisconsin Tech Coll (WI)
North Harris Coll (TX)
North Idaho Coll (ID)
North Iowa Area Comm Coll (IA)
Northland Pioneer Coll (AZ)
Northwest Coll (WY)
Northwest Iowa Comm Coll (IA)
Oakland Comm Coll (MI)
Odessa Coll (TX)
Olympic Coll (WA)
Orange Coast Coll (CA)

Oxnard Coll (CA)
Palomar Coll (CA)
Paris Jr Coll (TX)
Pasadena City Coll (CA)
Pennsylvania Coll of Technology (PA)
Pikes Peak Comm Coll (CO)
Pima Comm Coll (AZ)
Portland Comm Coll (OR)
Pratt Comm Coll and Area Vocational School (KS)
Red Rocks Comm Coll (CO)
Rend Lake Coll (IL)
Roanoke-Chowan Comm Coll (NC)
Rogue Comm Coll (OR)
St. Clair County Comm Coll (MI)
St. Cloud Tech Coll (MN)
St. Philip's Coll (TX)
San Diego City Coll (CA)
San Juan Coll (NM)
Santa Monica Coll (CA)
Schoolcraft Coll (MI)
Shelton State Comm Coll (AL)
Sheridan Coll (WY)
Sierra Coll (CA)
Somerset Comm Coll (KY)
Southeast Comm Coll, Lincoln Campus (NE)
Southeastern Comm Coll (NC)
Southern West Virginia Comm and Tech Coll (WV)
South Plains Coll (TX)
South Puget Sound Comm Coll (WA)
Southwestern Illinois Coll (IL)
Southwestern Michigan Coll (MI)
Southwestern Oregon Comm Coll (OR)
Southwest Mississippi Comm Coll (MS)
Spokane Comm Coll (WA)
Spokane Falls Comm Coll (WA)
State U of NY Coll of Technology at Alfred (NY)
State U of NY Coll of Technology at Delhi (NY)
Terra State Comm Coll (OH)
Texas State Tech Coll–Harlingen (TX)
Texas State Tech Coll–Waco/Marshall Campus (TX)
Trenholm State Tech Coll, Montgomery (AL)

Triangle Tech, Inc.–DuBois School (PA)
Tri-County Comm Coll (NC)
Triton Coll (IL)
Tulsa Welding School (OK)
United Tribes Tech Coll (ND)
Utah Valley State Coll (UT)
Vance-Granville Comm Coll (NC)
Vatterott Coll, St. Ann (MO)
Ventura Coll (CA)
Victor Valley Coll (CA)
Vincennes U (IN)
Washtenaw Comm Coll (MI)
Waycross Coll (GA)
Western Nevada Comm Coll (NV)
Western Wyoming Comm Coll (WY)
West Hills Comm Coll (CA)
Westmoreland County Comm Coll (PA)
Wichita Area Tech Coll (KS)
Yuba Coll (CA)

Western Civilization
Lincoln Coll, Lincoln (IL)
Lon Morris Coll (TX)

Wildlife and Wildlands Science And Management
Abraham Baldwin Ag Coll (GA)
Barton County Comm Coll (KS)
Cabrillo Coll (CA)
Casper Coll (WY)
Eastern Oklahoma State Coll (OK)
Eastern Wyoming Coll (WY)
Frederick Comm Coll (MD)
Front Range Comm Coll (CO)
Garrett Coll (MD)
Hiwassee Coll (TN)
Iowa Lakes Comm Coll (IA)
Itasca Comm Coll (MN)
Keystone Coll (PA)
Kirkwood Comm Coll (IA)
Laramie County Comm Coll (WY)
Minot State U–Bottineau Campus (ND)
Mt. San Antonio Coll (CA)
Northeastern Oklahoma A&M Coll (OK)
Northeast Mississippi Comm Coll (MS)
North Idaho Coll (ID)
Northwest Coll (WY)

Penn State U DuBois Campus of the Commonwealth Coll (PA)
Pratt Comm Coll and Area Vocational School (KS)
Seward County Comm Coll (KS)
Snow Coll (UT)
Spokane Comm Coll (WA)
State U of NY Coll of A&T at Morrisville (NY)
Vermilion Comm Coll (MN)
Western Wyoming Comm Coll (WY)

Wildlife Biology
Colby Comm Coll (KS)
Colorado Northwestern Comm Coll (CO)
Eastern Arizona Coll (AZ)
Everett Comm Coll (WA)
Garrett Coll (MD)
Holmes Comm Coll (MS)
Iowa Lakes Comm Coll (IA)
Keystone Coll (PA)
Kirkwood Comm Coll (IA)
Northeastern Oklahoma A&M Coll (OK)
Northeast Mississippi Comm Coll (MS)
North Idaho Coll (ID)
Pratt Comm Coll and Area Vocational School (KS)
Vermilion Comm Coll (MN)

Wind/Percussion Instruments
Coffeyville Comm Coll (KS)
Iowa Lakes Comm Coll (IA)
Kirkwood Comm Coll (IA)

Women'S Studies
Bergen Comm Coll (NJ)
Cabrillo Coll (CA)
Chabot Coll (CA)
Foothill Coll (CA)
Manatee Comm Coll (FL)
Northern Essex Comm Coll (MA)
Palomar Coll (CA)
Southwestern Coll (CA)
Tompkins Cortland Comm Coll (NY)
Yuba Coll (CA)

Wood Science and Wood Products/Pulp And Paper Technology
Copiah-Lincoln Comm Coll (MS)
Cossatot Comm Coll of the U of Arkansas (AR)

Lower Columbia Coll (WA)
State U of NY Coll of A&T at Morrisville (NY)

Woodworking
Bucks County Comm Coll (PA)
Coll of Southern Idaho (ID)
State U of NY Coll of Technology at Delhi (NY)

Woodworking Related
Oakland Comm Coll (MI)
Pennsylvania Coll of Technology (PA)

Word Processing
Academy of Medical Arts and Business (PA)
Camden County Coll (NJ)
Coastal Bend Coll (TX)
Coll of the Desert (CA)
Coll of the Sequoias (CA)
The Coll of Westchester (NY)
Corning Comm Coll (NY)
Dakota County Tech Coll (MN)
Del Mar Coll (TX)
Delta Coll (MI)
Eastfield Coll (TX)
Edgecombe Comm Coll (NC)
Fayetteville Tech Comm Coll (NC)
Florida National Coll (FL)
Galveston Coll (TX)
Gogebic Comm Coll (MI)
Hawkeye Comm Coll (IA)
Henderson Comm Coll (KY)
Iowa Lakes Comm Coll (IA)
Kellogg Comm Coll (MI)
Kishwaukee Coll (IL)
Lorain County Comm Coll (OH)
Los Angeles Valley Coll (CA)
Louisiana Tech Coll–Florida Parishes Campus (LA)
Lower Columbia Coll (WA)
Metropolitan Comm Coll-Business & Technology College (MO)
Milwaukee Area Tech Coll (WI)
Mississippi Gulf Coast Comm Coll (MS)
Modesto Jr Coll (CA)
Mohave Comm Coll (AZ)
Monroe County Comm Coll (MI)
Naugatuck Valley Comm Coll (CT)

Newport Business Inst, Lower Burrell (PA)
Northern Essex Comm Coll (MA)
Orange Coast Coll (CA)
Orange County Comm Coll (NY)
Owensboro Comm and Tech Coll (KY)
Palm Beach Comm Coll (FL)
Pratt Comm Coll and Area Vocational School (KS)
Quinebaug Valley Comm Coll (CT)
Rasmussen Coll Mankato (MN)
Riverland Comm Coll (MN)
Riverside Comm Coll (CA)
St. Cloud Tech Coll (MN)
Schenectady County Comm Coll (NY)
Seminole Comm Coll (FL)
Sinclair Comm Coll (OH)
Stanly Comm Coll (NC)
Stark State Coll of Technology (OH)
Texas State Tech Coll–Harlingen (TX)
Three Rivers Comm Coll (MO)
Trumbull Business Coll (OH)
Vincennes U (IN)
Washtenaw Comm Coll (MI)
Western Wyoming Comm Coll (WY)
West Virginia Northern Comm Coll (WV)
Yuba Coll (CA)

Zoology/Animal Biology
Casper Coll (WY)
Centralia Coll (WA)
Chabot Coll (CA)
Colby Comm Coll (KS)
Coll of Southern Idaho (ID)
Daytona Beach Comm Coll (FL)
El Camino Coll (CA)
Everett Comm Coll (WA)
Hill Coll of the Hill Jr College District (TX)
Lincoln Coll, Lincoln (IL)
Northeast Mississippi Comm Coll (MS)
North Idaho Coll (ID)
Palm Beach Comm Coll (FL)
Palomar Coll (CA)
Pensacola Jr Coll (FL)
Snow Coll (UT)
Spoon River Coll (IL)

Associate Degree Programs at Four-Year Colleges

Accounting
Alvernia Coll (PA)
American U of Puerto Rico (PR)
Bacone Coll (OK)
Baker Coll of Allen Park (MI)
Baker Coll of Auburn Hills (MI)
Baker Coll of Cadillac (MI)
Baker Coll of Clinton Township (MI)
Baker Coll of Flint (MI)
Baker Coll of Jackson (MI)
Baker Coll of Muskegon (MI)
Baker Coll of Owosso (MI)
Baker Coll of Port Huron (MI)
Becker Coll (MA)
Bluefield State Coll (WV)
Briarcliffe Coll (NY)
Brigham Young U–Hawaii (HI)
British Columbia Inst of Technology (BC, Canada)
California U of Pennsylvania (PA)
Calumet Coll of Saint Joseph (IN)
Central Christian Coll of Kansas (KS)
Champlain Coll (VT)
Chestnut Hill Coll (PA)
Clayton Coll & State U (GA)
Coll of Mount St. Joseph (OH)
Coll of St. Joseph (VT)
Coll of Saint Mary (NE)
Colorado Tech U Sioux Falls Campus (SD)
Columbia Union Coll (MD)
Davenport U, Dearborn (MI)
Davenport U, Grand Rapids (MI)
Davenport U, Kalamazoo (MI)
Davenport U, Lansing (MI)
Davenport U, Lapeer (MI)
Davenport U, Warren (MI)
Davis & Elkins Coll (WV)
DeVry U, Westminster (CO)
Evangel U (MO)
Fairmont State U (WV)
Faulkner U (AL)
Ferris State U (MI)
Florida Metropolitan U-Tampa Coll, Brandon (FL)
Florida Metropolitan U-Fort Lauderdale Coll (FL)
Florida Metropolitan U-Tampa Coll, Lakeland (FL)
Florida Metropolitan U-Tampa Coll (FL)
Franciscan U of Steubenville (OH)
Franklin U (OH)
Goldey-Beacom Coll (DE)
Gwynedd-Mercy Coll (PA)
Hawai'i Pacific U (HI)
Husson Coll (ME)
Immaculata U (PA)
Indiana Inst of Technology (IN)
Inter American U of PR, Aguadilla Campus (PR)

Inter Amer U of PR, Barranquitas Campus (PR)
Inter American U of PR, Bayamón Campus (PR)
Inter American U of PR, Fajardo Campus (PR)
Inter American U of PR, Metropolitan Campus (PR)
Inter American U of PR, Ponce Campus (PR)
Inter American U of PR, San Germán Campus (PR)
International Coll (FL)
International Coll of the Cayman IslandsCayman Islands)
Johnson & Wales U (FL)
Johnson & Wales U (RI)
Johnson State Coll (VT)
Jones Coll, Jacksonville (FL)
Kansas State U (KS)
King's Coll (PA)
Lake Superior State U (MI)
Macon State Coll (GA)
Manchester Coll (IN)
Marian Coll (IN)
Marygrove Coll (MI)
Merrimack Coll (MA)
Methodist Coll (NC)
Missouri Southern State U (MO)
Mitchell Coll (CT)
Morrison U (NV)
Mount Aloysius Coll (PA)
Mount Marty Coll (SD)
Mount Olive Coll (NC)
National American U, Colorado Springs (CO)
National American U, Denver (CO)
National American U (NM)
National American U (SD)
National American U–Sioux Falls Branch (SD)
Newbury Coll (MA)
Northwood U (MI)
Northwood U, Florida Campus (FL)
Northwood U, Texas Campus (TX)
Oakland City U (IN)
Peirce Coll (PA)
Point Park U (PA)
Purdue U North Central (IN)
Sacred Heart U (CT)
Saint Francis U (PA)
St. John's U (NY)
Saint Joseph's U (PA)
Shawnee State U (OH)
Siena Heights U (MI)
Southern Adventist U (TN)
Southern Alberta Inst of Technology (AB, Canada)
Southern New Hampshire U (NH)
South U (AL)
South U (GA)
Southwest Baptist U (MO)
State U of NY Coll of A&T at Cobleskill (NY)
Strayer U (DC)
Sullivan U (KY)
Teikyo Post U (CT)
Thiel Coll (PA)
Thomas Coll (ME)

Thomas Edison State Coll (NJ)
Thomas More Coll (KY)
Tiffin U (OH)
Tri-State U (IN)
Union Coll (NE)
U of Alaska Anchorage (AK)
U of Charleston (WV)
U of Cincinnati (OH)
U of Dubuque (IA)
The U of Findlay (OH)
U of Mary (ND)
U of Minnesota, Crookston (MN)
U of Rio Grande (OH)
U of the District of Columbia (DC)
U of the Virgin Islands (VI)
U of Toledo (OH)
The U of West Alabama (AL)
Urbana U (OH)
Villa Julie Coll (MD)
Walsh U (OH)
Washington & Jefferson Coll (PA)
Webber International U (FL)
West Virginia State Coll (WV)
West Virginia U Inst of Technology (WV)
Wilson Coll (PA)
Youngstown State U (OH)

Accounting and Business/Management
Central Christian Coll of Kansas (KS)
Chestnut Hill Coll (PA)
Mount Aloysius Coll (PA)
National American U, Colorado Springs (CO)
Ohio U–Southern Campus (OH)
Peirce Coll (PA)

Accounting and Finance
Central Christian Coll of Kansas (KS)
Southern Alberta Inst of Technology (AB, Canada)

Accounting Related
Montana State U–Billings (MT)
Park U (MO)
Peirce Coll (PA)

Accounting Technology and Bookkeeping
Baker Coll of Flint (MI)
British Columbia Inst of Technology (BC, Canada)
Cleary U (MI)
Davenport U, Dearborn (MI)
Davenport U, Holland (MI)
Davenport U, Kalamazoo (MI)
Davenport U, Lapeer (MI)
Davenport U, Warren (MI)
Georgia Southwestern State U (GA)
Kent State U (OH)
Lake Superior State U (MI)
Lewis-Clark State Coll (ID)
New York Inst of Technology (NY)
Ohio U (OH)

Ohio U–Southern Campus (OH)
Peirce Coll (PA)
Robert Morris Coll (IL)
St. Augustine Coll (IL)
The U of Akron (OH)
U of Alaska Fairbanks (AK)
The U of Montana–Missoula (MT)
U of Rio Grande (OH)
Valdosta State U (GA)
Virginia Coll at Birmingham (AL)
Wright State U (OH)
Youngstown State U (OH)

Acting
Central Christian Coll of Kansas (KS)
New World School of the Arts (FL)

Administrative Assistant and Secretarial Science
Alabama State U (AL)
American U of Puerto Rico (PR)
Arkansas State U (AR)
Atlantic Union Coll (MA)
Bacone Coll (OK)
Baker Coll of Auburn Hills (MI)
Baker Coll of Cadillac (MI)
Baker Coll of Clinton Township (MI)
Baker Coll of Flint (MI)
Baker Coll of Jackson (MI)
Baker Coll of Muskegon (MI)
Baker Coll of Owosso (MI)
Baker Coll of Port Huron (MI)
Ball State U (IN)
Baptist Bible Coll (MO)
Black Hills State U (SD)
Bluefield State Coll (WV)
Briarcliffe Coll (NY)
British Columbia Inst of Technology (BC, Canada)
Campbellsville U (KY)
Central Missouri State U (MO)
Clayton Coll & State U (GA)
Clearwater Christian Coll (FL)
Columbia Coll, Caguas (PR)
Concordia Coll (NY)
Dakota State U (SD)
Davenport U, Dearborn (MI)
Dickinson State U (ND)
Dordt Coll (IA)
Eastern Kentucky U (KY)
Eastern Oregon U (OR)
Evangel U (MO)
Fairmont State U (WV)
Faith Baptist Bible Coll and Theological Seminary (IA)
Faulkner U (AL)
Fort Hays State U (KS)
Fort Valley State U (GA)
Georgia Southwestern State U (GA)
God's Bible School and Coll (OH)
Grace Coll (IN)
Henderson State U (AR)
Idaho State U (ID)
Indiana State U (IN)

Inter American U of PR, Aguadilla Campus (PR)
Inter Amer U of PR, Barranquitas Campus (PR)
Inter American U of PR, Bayamón Campus (PR)
Inter American U of PR, Fajardo Campus (PR)
Inter American U of PR, Metropolitan Campus (PR)
Inter American U of PR, Ponce Campus (PR)
Inter American U of PR, San Germán Campus (PR)
Johnson & Wales U (RI)
Jones Coll, Jacksonville (FL)
Kent State U (OH)
Kentucky Christian Coll (KY)
Lake Superior State U (MI)
Lamar U (TX)
Lancaster Bible Coll (PA)
Lewis-Clark State Coll (ID)
Lincoln U (MO)
Macon State Coll (GA)
Mayville State U (ND)
Mercyhurst Coll (PA)
Montana State U–Billings (MT)
Montana Tech of The U of Montana (MT)
Morrison U (NV)
Mountain State U (WV)
Mount Vernon Nazarene U (OH)
Murray State U (KY)
New York Inst of Technology (NY)
North Central U (MN)
Northern Michigan U (MI)
Northern State U (SD)
Northwestern Coll (IA)
Northwestern State U of Louisiana (LA)
Oakland City U (IN)
Ohio U (OH)
Ohio U–Chillicothe (OH)
Pillsbury Baptist Bible Coll (MN)
Pontifical Catholic U of Puerto Rico (PR)
Reformed Bible Coll (MI)
Robert Morris Coll (IL)
St. Augustine Coll (IL)
Southeastern Louisiana U (LA)
Southern Arkansas U–Magnolia (AR)
Southwest Baptist U (MO)
Sullivan U (KY)
Tabor Coll (KS)
Tennessee State U (TN)
Thomas Coll (ME)
Trinity Baptist Coll (FL)
Trinity Bible Coll (ND)
Universidad Adventista de las Antillas (PR)
The U of Akron (OH)
U of Alaska Fairbanks (AK)
U of Alaska Southeast (AK)
U of Arkansas at Fort Smith (AR)
U of Cincinnati (OH)
The U of Findlay (OH)
The U of Montana–Western (MT)

U of Puerto Rico, Cayey U Coll (PR)
U of Rio Grande (OH)
U of Sioux Falls (SD)
U of the District of Columbia (DC)
U of the Virgin Islands (VI)
U of Toledo (OH)
Utah State U (UT)
Valdosta State U (GA)
Vermont Tech Coll (VT)
Virginia Coll at Birmingham (AL)
Washburn U (KS)
Weber State U (UT)
West Virginia State Coll (WV)
West Virginia U Inst of Technology (WV)
Williams Baptist Coll (AR)
Winona State U (MN)
Wright State U (OH)
Youngstown State U (OH)

Adult and Continuing Education Administration
Saint Joseph's Coll of Maine (ME)

Adult Development and Aging
Chestnut Hill Coll (PA)
Madonna U (MI)
Saint Mary-of-the-Woods Coll (IN)
U of Toledo (OH)

Advertising
Academy of Art U (CA)
The Art Inst of California–San Diego (CA)
Fashion Inst of Technology (NY)
Johnson & Wales U (FL)
Johnson & Wales U (RI)
New England School of Communications (ME)
Northwood U (MI)
Northwood U, Florida Campus (FL)
Northwood U, Texas Campus (TX)
Pacific Union Coll (CA)
U of the District of Columbia (DC)
West Virginia State Coll (WV)
Xavier U (OH)

Aeronautical/Aerospace Engineering Technology
British Columbia Inst of Technology (BC, Canada)
Central Missouri State U (MO)
Purdue U (IN)
Southern Alberta Inst of Technology (AB, Canada)
U of New Haven (CT)

Aeronautics/Aviation/Aerospace Science and Technology
Daniel Webster Coll (NH)
Embry-Riddle Aeronautical U, Extended Campus (FL)
Indiana State U (IN)
Purdue U (IN)

Agribusiness
Morehead State U (KY)
Vermont Tech Coll (VT)

Agricultural and Domestic Animals Services Related
Sterling Coll (VT)

Agricultural and Food Products Processing
North Carolina State U (NC)

Agricultural and Horticultural Plant Breeding
Sterling Coll (VT)

Agricultural Animal Breeding
Sterling Coll (VT)

Agricultural/Biological Engineering and Bioengineering
State U of NY Coll of A&T at Cobleskill (NY)

Agricultural Business and Management
Andrews U (MI)
Central Christian Coll of Kansas (KS)
Clayton Coll & State U (GA)
Dickinson State U (ND)
Dordt Coll (IA)
MidAmerica Nazarene U (KS)
North Carolina State U (NC)
State U of NY Coll of A&T at Cobleskill (NY)
U of Minnesota, Crookston (MN)
U of New Hampshire (NH)

Agricultural Business and Management Related
Penn State U Abington Coll (PA)
Penn State U Altoona Coll (PA)
Penn State U at Erie, The Behrend Coll (PA)
Penn State U Berks Cmps of Berks-Lehigh Valley Coll (PA)
Penn State U Lehigh Valley Cmps of Berks-Lehigh Valley Coll (PA)
Penn State U Schuylkill Campus of the Capital Coll (PA)
Penn State U Univ Park Campus (PA)

Agricultural Business Technology
U of Alaska Fairbanks (AK)

Agricultural Economics
The U of British Columbia (BC, Canada)

Agricultural Mechanization
Andrews U (MI)
Clayton Coll & State U (GA)
State U of NY Coll of A&T at Cobleskill (NY)
Virginia Polytechnic Inst and State U (VA)

Agricultural Production
U of Arkansas at Monticello (AR)
Western Kentucky U (KY)

Agricultural Production Related
Sterling Coll (VT)

Agricultural Public Services Related
Sterling Coll (VT)

Agriculture
Andrews U (MI)
Clayton Coll & State U (GA)
Dalton State Coll (GA)
Lincoln U (MO)
Lubbock Christian U (TX)
Macon State Coll (GA)
Murray State U (KY)
North Carolina State U (NC)

Oklahoma Panhandle State U (OK)
Purdue U (IN)
South Dakota State U (SD)
Southern Utah U (UT)
State U of NY Coll of A&T at Cobleskill (NY)
Sterling Coll (VT)
U of Delaware (DE)
U of Minnesota, Crookston (MN)

Agriculture and Agriculture Operations Related
Eastern Kentucky U (KY)
Sterling Coll (VT)

Agronomy and Crop Science
Andrews U (MI)
State U of NY Coll of A&T at Cobleskill (NY)
U of Minnesota, Crookston (MN)

Aircraft Powerplant Technology
British Columbia Inst of Technology (BC, Canada)
Embry-Riddle Aeronautical U (FL)
Embry-Riddle Aeronautical U, Extended Campus (FL)
Georgia Southwestern State U (GA)
Idaho State U (ID)
Kansas State U (KS)
Northern Michigan U (MI)
Thomas Edison State Coll (NJ)

Airframe Mechanics and Aircraft Maintenance Technology
British Columbia Inst of Technology (BC, Canada)
Clayton Coll & State U (GA)
Georgia Southwestern State U (GA)
Kansas State U (KS)
Lewis U (IL)
U of Alaska Anchorage (AK)
U of Alaska Fairbanks (AK)
Utah State U (UT)
Wentworth Inst of Technology (MA)

Airline Flight Attendant
The U of Akron (OH)

Airline Pilot and Flight Crew
Andrews U (MI)
Baker Coll of Flint (MI)
Baker Coll of Muskegon (MI)
Central Christian Coll of Kansas (KS)
Daniel Webster Coll (NH)
Embry-Riddle Aeronautical U (FL)
Kansas State U (KS)
Southern Illinois U Carbondale (IL)
Thomas Edison State Coll (NJ)
U of Alaska Anchorage (AK)
U of Dubuque (IA)
Winona State U (MN)

Air Traffic Control
Thomas Edison State Coll (NJ)
U of Alaska Anchorage (AK)
Valdosta State U (GA)

Allied Health and Medical Assisting Services Related
Bloomsburg U of Pennsylvania (PA)
National American U, Colorado Springs (CO)

Allied Health Diagnostic, Intervention, and Treatment Professions Related
British Columbia Inst of Technology (BC, Canada)
Cameron U (OK)
Gwynedd-Mercy Coll (PA)

Kent State U (OH)
The U of Akron (OH)

American History
Central Christian Coll of Kansas (KS)
Emmanuel Coll (GA)

American Indian/Native American Studies
Bacone Coll (OK)

American Literature
Haskell Indian Nations U (KS)
Huron U USA in London United Kingdom)

American Native/Native American Languages
Idaho State U (ID)

American Sign Language (Asl)
Bethel Coll (IN)
Idaho State U (ID)
Madonna U (MI)
North Central U (MN)
Rochester Inst of Technology (NY)

American Studies
Paul Smith's Coll of Arts and Sciences (NY)

Ancient Near Eastern and Biblical Languages
Bethel Coll (IN)
North Central U (MN)

Anesthesiologist Assistant
U Coll of the Cariboo (BC, Canada)

Animal Health
Sterling Coll (VT)

Animal/Livestock Husbandry and Production
Saint Mary-of-the-Woods Coll (IN)
Sterling Coll (VT)
U Coll of the Cariboo (BC, Canada)
U of Connecticut (CT)
U of New Hampshire (NH)

Animal Nutrition
Sterling Coll (VT)

Animal Sciences
Andrews U (MI)
Becker Coll (MA)
State U of NY Coll of A&T at Cobleskill (NY)
Sterling Coll (VT)
U of Connecticut (CT)
U of Minnesota, Crookston (MN)
U of New Hampshire (NH)

Animal Sciences Related
Sterling Coll (VT)

Animal Training
Becker Coll (MA)

Animation, Interactive Technology, Video Graphics and Special Effects
Academy of Art U (CA)
Champlain Coll (VT)
Kent State U (OH)
New England School of Communications (ME)

Anthropology
Kwantlen U Coll (BC, Canada)
Richmond, The American International U in London United Kingdom)
Université Laval (QC, Canada)

Apparel and Accessories Marketing
Clayton Coll & State U (GA)
The U of Montana–Missoula (MT)

Apparel and Textiles
Academy of Art U (CA)
Fashion Inst of Technology (NY)

Applied Art
Academy of Art U (CA)
The Art Inst of Fort Lauderdale (FL)
National American U (NM)
New World School of the Arts (FL)
Rochester Inst of Technology (NY)
U of Maine at Presque Isle (ME)
The U of Montana–Western (MT)
Villa Julie Coll (MD)

Applied Horticulture
Georgia Southwestern State U (GA)
Kent State U (OH)
Oakland City U (IN)
Sterling Coll (VT)
Temple U (PA)
U of Connecticut (CT)
The U of Maine at Augusta (ME)
Valdosta State U (GA)

Applied Horticulture/ Horticultural Business Services Related
U of Massachusetts Amherst (MA)

Applied Mathematics
Central Methodist Coll (MO)
Hawai'i Pacific U (HI)
Rochester Inst of Technology (NY)

Aquaculture
The U of British Columbia (BC, Canada)

Archeology
Weber State U (UT)

Architectural Drafting and Cad/Cadd
Baker Coll of Flint (MI)
Baker Coll of Muskegon (MI)
British Columbia Inst of Technology (BC, Canada)
Indiana State U (IN)
Indiana U–Purdue U Indianapolis (IN)
Montana Tech of The U of Montana (MT)
U of Toledo (OH)
Western Kentucky U (KY)

Architectural Engineering Technology
Baker Coll of Cadillac (MI)
Baker Coll of Clinton Township (MI)
Baker Coll of Owosso (MI)
Baker Coll of Port Huron (MI)
Bluefield State Coll (WV)
British Columbia Inst of Technology (BC, Canada)
Central Christian Coll of Kansas (KS)
Clayton Coll & State U (GA)
DeVry U, Westminster (CO)
Ferris State U (MI)
Indiana U–Purdue U Fort Wayne (IN)
Norfolk State U (VA)
Northern Kentucky U (KY)
Northern Michigan U (MI)
Purdue U (IN)
Purdue U Calumet (IN)
Purdue U North Central (IN)
Southern Alberta Inst of Technology (AB, Canada)
Thomas Edison State Coll (NJ)
U of Alaska Anchorage (AK)
U of Cincinnati (OH)
U of the District of Columbia (DC)
Vermont Tech Coll (VT)

Wentworth Inst of Technology (MA)
West Virginia State Coll (WV)

Architectural Technology
Southern Alberta Inst of Technology (AB, Canada)
The U of Maine at Augusta (ME)

Architecture
Central Christian Coll of Kansas (KS)
Coll of Staten Island of the City U of NY (NY)
New York Inst of Technology (NY)

Architecture Related
Abilene Christian U (TX)

Army R.O.T.C./Military Science
Methodist Coll (NC)

Art
Academy of Art U (CA)
Adrian Coll (MI)
The Art Inst of Colorado (CO)
Ashland U (OH)
Bacone Coll (OK)
Burlington Coll (VT)
Carroll Coll (MT)
Central Christian Coll of Kansas (KS)
Clayton Coll & State U (GA)
Coll of Saint Mary (NE)
Defiance Coll (OH)
Eastern New Mexico U (NM)
Fashion Inst of Technology (NY)
Felician Coll (NJ)
Huron U USA in London United Kingdom)
Idaho State U (ID)
Immaculata U (PA)
John Brown U (AR)
Lindsey Wilson Coll (KY)
Lourdes Coll (OH)
Macon State Coll (GA)
Madonna U (MI)
Manchester Coll (IN)
Marian Coll (IN)
Methodist Coll (NC)
Miami International U of Art & Design (FL)
Mount Olive Coll (NC)
North Greenville Coll (SC)
Parsons School of Design, New School U (NY)
Pontifical Catholic U of Puerto Rico (PR)
Reinhardt Coll (GA)
Richmond, The American International U in London United Kingdom)
Rivier Coll (NH)
Rochester Inst of Technology (NY)
Sacred Heart U (CT)
St. Gregory's U (OK)
Shawnee State U (OH)
Siena Heights U (MI)
State U of NY Empire State Coll (NY)
Suffolk U (MA)
Union Coll (NE)
U of Rio Grande (OH)
U of Toledo (OH)
U of Wisconsin–Green Bay (WI)
Villa Julie Coll (MD)
West Virginia State Coll (WV)

Art History, Criticism and Conservation
Lourdes Coll (OH)
Thomas More Coll (KY)
Université Laval (QC, Canada)

Artificial Intelligence and Robotics
Clayton Coll & State U (GA)
Huron U USA in London United Kingdom)
Lamar U (TX)

Pacific Union Coll (CA)
Southern Alberta Inst of Technology (AB, Canada)
U of Cincinnati (OH)

Art Teacher Education
Central Christian Coll of Kansas (KS)
Clayton Coll & State U (GA)
Immaculata U (PA)

Athletic Training
Central Christian Coll of Kansas (KS)
Mitchell Coll (CT)

Audio Engineering
Five Towns Coll (NY)
New England School of Communications (ME)

Audiology and Hearing Sciences
Ohio U (OH)

Autobody/Collision and Repair Technology
British Columbia Inst of Technology (BC, Canada)
Georgia Southwestern State U (GA)
Idaho State U (ID)
Lewis-Clark State Coll (ID)
Montana State U–Billings (MT)
Montana Tech of The U of Montana (MT)
Northern Michigan U (MI)
Valdosta State U (GA)
Weber State U (UT)

Automobile/Automotive Mechanics Technology
Andrews U (MI)
Arkansas State U (AR)
Baker Coll of Flint (MI)
Boise State U (ID)
British Columbia Inst of Technology (BC, Canada)
Central Missouri State U (MO)
Ferris State U (MI)
Georgia Southwestern State U (GA)
Idaho State U (ID)
Lamar U (TX)
Lewis-Clark State Coll (ID)
McPherson Coll (KS)
Montana State U–Billings (MT)
Montana Tech of The U of Montana (MT)
Northern Michigan U (MI)
Oakland City U (IN)
Pittsburg State U (KS)
Southern Adventist U (TN)
Southern Alberta Inst of Technology (AB, Canada)
Southern Utah U (UT)
U of Alaska Anchorage (AK)
U of Alaska Southeast (AK)
Valdosta State U (GA)
Walla Walla Coll (WA)
Weber State U (UT)
West Virginia U Inst of Technology (WV)

Automotive Engineering Technology
State U of NY at Farmingdale (NY)
The U of Akron (OH)
Vermont Tech Coll (VT)
West Virginia U Inst of Technology (WV)

Aviation/Airway Management
Clayton Coll & State U (GA)
Daniel Webster Coll (NH)
Everglades U, Boca Raton (FL)
Fairmont State U (WV)
Mountain State U (WV)
Northern Kentucky U (KY)
Park U (MO)
The U of Akron (OH)
U of Alaska Anchorage (AK)

U of Alaska Fairbanks (AK)
U of Dubuque (IA)
U of Minnesota, Crookston (MN)
U of the District of Columbia (DC)

Avionics Maintenance Technology
Andrews U (MI)
Baker Coll of Flint (MI)
British Columbia Inst of Technology (BC, Canada)
Clayton Coll & State U (GA)
Fairmont State U (WV)
Georgia Southwestern State U (GA)
Hampton U (VA)
Lewis U (IL)
Mountain State U (WV)
Northern Michigan U (MI)
Southern Alberta Inst of Technology (AB, Canada)
U of Alaska Anchorage (AK)
U of Minnesota, Crookston (MN)
U of the District of Columbia (DC)
Walla Walla Coll (WA)
Wentworth Inst of Technology (MA)

Baking and Pastry Arts
The Art Inst of California–San Diego (CA)
The Culinary Inst of America (NY)
Johnson & Wales U (RI)
Kendall Coll (IL)
Southern New Hampshire U (NH)
Virginia Coll at Birmingham (AL)

Banking and Financial Support Services
Globe Inst of Technology (NY)
Hilbert Coll (NY)
International Coll of the Cayman IslandsCayman Islands)
Mountain State U (WV)
Northwood U (MI)
Northwood U, Florida Campus (FL)
Northwood U, Texas Campus (TX)
The U of Akron (OH)
U of Indianapolis (IN)

Behavioral Sciences
Central Christian Coll of Kansas (KS)
Coll for Lifelong Learning (NH)
Felician Coll (NJ)
Lewis-Clark State Coll (ID)
Methodist Coll (NC)
Mount Aloysius Coll (PA)

Biblical Studies
Alaska Bible Coll (AK)
American Baptist Coll of American Baptist Theol Sem (TN)
Appalachian Bible Coll (WV)
Barclay Coll (KS)
Beacon Coll and Graduate School (GA)
Bethel Coll (IN)
California Christian Coll (CA)
Calvary Bible Coll and Theological Seminary (MO)
Central Christian Coll of Kansas (KS)
Clear Creek Baptist Bible Coll (KY)
Coll of Biblical Studies–Houston (TX)
Columbia International U (SC)
Covenant Coll (GA)
Crown Coll (MN)
Dallas Baptist U (TX)
Eastern Mennonite U (VA)

Faith Baptist Bible Coll and Theological Seminary (IA)
Faulkner U (AL)
Fresno Pacific U (CA)
Geneva Coll (PA)
God's Bible School and Coll (OH)
Grace Coll (IN)
Grace U (NE)
Heritage Christian U (AL)
Hillsdale Free Will Baptist Coll (OK)
Houghton Coll (NY)
Howard Payne U (TX)
John Brown U (AR)
Lancaster Bible Coll (PA)
Life Pacific Coll (CA)
Manhattan Christian Coll (KS)
North Central U (MN)
Oak Hills Christian Coll (MN)
Ohio Valley Coll (WV)
Ouachita Baptist U (AR)
Pacific Union Coll (CA)
Practical Bible Coll (NY)
Prairie Bible Coll (AB, Canada)
Reformed Bible Coll (MI)
Shasta Bible Coll (CA)
Simpson Coll and Graduate School (CA)
Southeastern Bible Coll (AL)
Tabor Coll (KS)
Trinity Bible Coll (ND)
Trinity Coll of Florida (FL)
Universidad Adventista de las Antillas (PR)
Warner Pacific Coll (OR)
Washington Bible Coll (MD)
Western Baptist Coll (OR)
William Tyndale Coll (MI)

Biochemistry
Saint Joseph's Coll (IN)

Biological and Biomedical Sciences Related
Gwynedd-Mercy Coll (PA)

Biological and Physical Sciences
Bluefield State Coll (WV)
Central Christian Coll of Kansas (KS)
Clayton Coll & State U (GA)
Crown Coll (MN)
Dalton State Coll (GA)
Indiana U East (IN)
Madonna U (MI)
Medgar Evers Coll of the City U of NY (NY)
Mitchell Coll (CT)
Montana Tech of The U of Montana (MT)
Mount Olive Coll (NC)
Ohio U (OH)
Ohio U–Chillicothe (OH)
Ohio U–Southern Campus (OH)
Ohio U–Zanesville (OH)
Penn State U Altoona Coll (PA)
Penn State U Schuylkill Campus of the Capital Coll (PA)
Rochester Coll (MI)
Sacred Heart U (CT)
State U of NY Coll of A&T at Cobleskill (NY)
State U of NY Empire State Coll (NY)
Sterling Coll (VT)
Tri-State U (IN)
U of Cincinnati (OH)
Valparaiso U (IN)
Villa Julie Coll (MD)
Washburn U (KS)

Biological Specializations Related
Kent State U (OH)

Biology/Biological Sciences
Adrian Coll (MI)
Brewton-Parker Coll (GA)
Canadian Mennonite U (MB, Canada)

Central Christian Coll of Kansas (KS)
Chestnut Hill Coll (PA)
Cleveland Chiropractic Coll-Kansas City Campus (MO)
Cleveland Chiropractic Coll-Los Angeles Campus (CA)
Crown Coll (MN)
Cumberland U (TN)
Dalton State Coll (GA)
Felician Coll (NJ)
Fresno Pacific U (CA)
Idaho State U (ID)
Indiana U–Purdue U Fort Wayne (IN)
Indiana U South Bend (IN)
Inter Amer U of PR, Barranquitas Campus (PR)
Lourdes Coll (OH)
Macon State Coll (GA)
Methodist Coll (NC)
Montana Tech of The U of Montana (MT)
Mount Olive Coll (NC)
Pine Manor Coll (MA)
Presentation Coll (SD)
Reinhardt Coll (GA)
Rochester Inst of Technology (NY)
Sacred Heart U (CT)
Saint Joseph's U (PA)
Shawnee State U (OH)
Thomas Edison State Coll (NJ)
Thomas More Coll (KY)
U of Dubuque (IA)
The U of Maine at Augusta (ME)
U of New Hampshire at Manchester (NH)
U of Rio Grande (OH)
The U of Tampa (FL)
U of Toledo (OH)
U of Wisconsin–Green Bay (WI)
Villa Julie Coll (MD)
Wright State U (OH)
York Coll of Pennsylvania (PA)

Biology/Biotechnology Laboratory Technician
British Columbia Inst of Technology (BC, Canada)
Ferris State U (MI)
State U of NY Coll of A&T at Cobleskill (NY)
U of the District of Columbia (DC)
Villa Julie Coll (MD)
Weber State U (UT)

Biology Teacher Education
Central Christian Coll of Kansas (KS)

Biomedical/Medical Engineering
Vermont Tech Coll (VT)

Biomedical Technology
Baker Coll of Flint (MI)
Faulkner U (AL)
Indiana U–Purdue U Indianapolis (IN)
Penn State U Altoona Coll (PA)
Penn State U at Erie, The Behrend Coll (PA)
Penn State U Berks Cmps of Berks-Lehigh Valley Coll (PA)
Penn State U Schuylkill Campus of the Capital Coll (PA)
Thomas Edison State Coll (NJ)
Wentworth Inst of Technology (MA)

Biotechnology
British Columbia Inst of Technology (BC, Canada)
Vermont Tech Coll (VT)

Broadcast Journalism
Cornerstone U (MI)
Evangel U (MO)
Five Towns Coll (NY)
International Coll of the Cayman IslandsCayman Islands)
John Brown U (AR)
Manchester Coll (IN)
New England School of Communications (ME)
North Central U (MN)
Ohio U–Zanesville (OH)
Southern Alberta Inst of Technology (AB, Canada)
Trevecca Nazarene U (TN)

Buddhist Studies
Heritage Bible Coll (NC)

Building/Property Maintenance and Management
Park U (MO)
Valdosta State U (GA)

Business Administration and Management
Adrian Coll (MI)
Alabama State U (AL)
Alaska Pacific U (AK)
Alderson-Broaddus Coll (WV)
Alvernia Coll (PA)
American Indian Coll of the Assemblies of God, Inc (AZ)
American InterContinental U (CA)
American InterContinental U-LondonUnited Kingdom)
American International Coll (MA)
The American U in DubaiUnited Arab Emirates)
American U of Puerto Rico (PR)
The American U of RomeItaly)
Andrews U (MI)
Anna Maria Coll (MA)
Austin Peay State U (TN)
Averett U (VA)
Bacone Coll (OK)
Baker Coll of Allen Park (MI)
Baker Coll of Auburn Hills (MI)
Baker Coll of Cadillac (MI)
Baker Coll of Clinton Township (MI)
Baker Coll of Flint (MI)
Baker Coll of Jackson (MI)
Baker Coll of Muskegon (MI)
Baker Coll of Owosso (MI)
Baker Coll of Port Huron (MI)
Ball State U (IN)
Baptist Bible Coll (MO)
Becker Coll (MA)
Benedictine U (IL)
Bentley Coll (MA)
Bethel Coll (IN)
Briarcliffe Coll (NY)
British Columbia Inst of Technology (BC, Canada)
Bryan Coll (TN)
California U of Pennsylvania (PA)
Calumet Coll of Saint Joseph (IN)
Cameron U (OK)
Campbellsville U (KY)
Cardinal Stritch U (WI)
Carroll Coll (MT)
Central Baptist Coll (AR)
Central Christian Coll of Kansas (KS)
Chaminade U of Honolulu (HI)
Champlain Coll (VT)
Charleston Southern U (SC)
Chestnut Hill Coll (PA)
Clarion U of Pennsylvania (PA)
Clayton Coll & State U (GA)
Cleary U (MI)

Coll for Lifelong Learning (NH)
Coll of Mount St. Joseph (OH)
Coll of Mount Saint Vincent (NY)
Coll of St. Joseph (VT)
Coll of Saint Mary (NE)
Coll of Santa Fe (NM)
Colorado Tech U Sioux Falls Campus (SD)
Columbia Coll (MO)
Columbia Coll, Caguas (PR)
Concord Coll (WV)
Concordia Coll (NY)
Concordia U (OR)
Covenant Coll (GA)
Crown Coll (MN)
Dakota State U (SD)
Dakota Wesleyan U (SD)
Dallas Baptist U (TX)
Dalton State Coll (GA)
Daniel Webster Coll (NH)
Davenport U, Dearborn (MI)
Davenport U, Grand Rapids (MI)
Davenport U, Kalamazoo (MI)
Davenport U, Lansing (MI)
Davenport U, Lapeer (MI)
Davenport U, Warren (MI)
Davis & Elkins Coll (WV)
Defiance Coll (OH)
Edinboro U of Pennsylvania (PA)
Emmanuel Coll (GA)
Excelsior Coll (NY)
Fairmont State U (WV)
State U of NY at Farmingdale (NY)
Faulkner U (AL)
Felician Coll (NJ)
Five Towns Coll (NY)
Florida Metropolitan U-Tampa Coll, Brandon (FL)
Florida Metropolitan U-Fort Lauderdale Coll (FL)
Florida Metropolitan U-Tampa Coll, Lakeland (FL)
Florida Metropolitan U-Tampa Coll (FL)
Franciscan U of Steubenville (OH)
Franklin U (OH)
Fresno Pacific U (CA)
Gannon U (PA)
Geneva Coll (PA)
Globe Inst of Technology (NY)
Goldey-Beacom Coll (DE)
Grace Bible Coll (MI)
Grantham U (LA)
Gwynedd-Mercy Coll (PA)
Haskell Indian Nations U (KS)
Hawai'i Pacific U (HI)
Hilbert Coll (NY)
Huron U USA in LondonUnited Kingdom)
Husson Coll (ME)
Immaculata U (PA)
Indiana Inst of Technology (IN)
Indiana State U (IN)
Indiana U Northwest (IN)
Indiana U of Pennsylvania (PA)
Indiana U–Purdue U Fort Wayne (IN)
Inter American U of PR, Aguadilla Campus (PR)
Inter Amer U of PR, Barranquitas Campus (PR)
Inter American U of PR, Bayamón Campus (PR)
Inter American U of PR, Fajardo Campus (PR)
Inter American U of PR, Metropolitan Campus (PR)
Inter American U of PR, Ponce Campus (PR)

Inter American U of PR, San Germán Campus (PR)
International Coll (FL)
International Coll of the Cayman IslandsCayman Islands)
Johnson & Wales U (CO)
Johnson & Wales U (RI)
Johnson State Coll (VT)
Jones Coll, Jacksonville (FL)
Jones Coll, Miami (FL)
Kansas Wesleyan U (KS)
Kent State U (OH)
King's Coll (PA)
Lake Superior State U (MI)
Limestone Coll (SC)
Lincoln Memorial U (TN)
Lindsey Wilson Coll (KY)
Long Island U, Brooklyn Campus (NY)
Lourdes Coll (OH)
Lyndon State Coll (VT)
MacMurray Coll (IL)
Macon State Coll (GA)
Madonna U (MI)
Maine Maritime Academy (ME)
Manchester Coll (IN)
Marian Coll (IN)
Marietta Coll (OH)
Mayville State U (ND)
Medaille Coll (NY)
Medgar Evers Coll of the City U of NY (NY)
Mercyhurst Coll (PA)
Merrimack Coll (MA)
Methodist Coll (NC)
MidAmerica Nazarene U (KS)
Midway Coll (KY)
Missouri Baptist U (MO)
Missouri Southern State U (MO)
Missouri Valley Coll (MO)
Missouri Western State Coll (MO)
Mitchell Coll (CT)
Montana State U–Billings (MT)
Montreat Coll (NC)
Morrison U (NV)
Mountain State U (WV)
Mount Aloysius Coll (PA)
Mount Ida Coll (MA)
Mount Marty Coll (SD)
Mount Olive Coll (NC)
Mount St. Mary's Coll (CA)
National American U, Colorado Springs (CO)
National American U, Denver (CO)
National American U (NM)
National American U (SD)
National American U–Sioux Falls Branch (SD)
Newbury Coll (MA)
Newman U (KS)
New Mexico Inst of Mining and Technology (NM)
New York Inst of Technology (NY)
Niagara U (NY)
Nichols Coll (MA)
North Central U (MN)
Northern Kentucky U (KY)
Northern Michigan U (MI)
Northern State U (SD)
Northwest Coll (WA)
Northwestern State U of Louisiana (LA)
Northwood U (MI)
Northwood U, Florida Campus (FL)
Northwood U, Texas Campus (TX)
Notre Dame Coll (OH)
Nyack Coll (NY)
Oakland City U (IN)
Ohio Dominican U (OH)
Ohio U (OH)
Ohio U–Chillicothe (OH)
Oklahoma Panhandle State U (OK)
Park U (MO)

Paul Smith's Coll of Arts and Sciences (NY)
Peirce Coll (PA)
Pikeville Coll (KY)
Pine Manor Coll (MA)
Point Park U (PA)
Pontifical Catholic U of Puerto Rico (PR)
Presentation Coll (SD)
Providence Coll (RI)
Purdue U North Central (IN)
Reinhardt Coll (GA)
Richmond, The American International U in LondonUnited Kingdom)
Rider U (NJ)
Rivier Coll (NH)
Robert Morris Coll (IL)
Rochester Inst of Technology (NY)
Roger Williams U (RI)
Rust Coll (MS)
Sacred Heart U (CT)
Sage Coll of Albany (NY)
St. Augustine Coll (IL)
St. Francis Coll (NY)
Saint Francis U (PA)
St. Gregory's U (OK)
Saint Joseph's U (PA)
Saint Peter's Coll (NJ)
Salve Regina U (RI)
Schiller International UFrance)
Schiller International USpain)
Shawnee State U (OH)
Shaw U (NC)
Sheldon Jackson Coll (AK)
Shepherd U (WV)
Siena Heights U (MI)
Southeastern U (DC)
Southern Alberta Inst of Technology (AB, Canada)
Southern New Hampshire U (NH)
Southern Vermont Coll (VT)
Southern Wesleyan U (SC)
South U (AL)
South U (GA)
Southwest Baptist U (MO)
Spring Hill Coll (AL)
State U of NY Coll of A&T at Cobleskill (NY)
State U of NY Empire State Coll (NY)
Stratford U (VA)
Strayer U (DC)
Sullivan U (KY)
Taylor U (IN)
Taylor U Fort Wayne (IN)
Teikyo Post U (CT)
Thomas Coll (ME)
Thomas Edison State Coll (NJ)
Tiffin U (OH)
Trinity Bible Coll (ND)
Tri-State U (IN)
Troy State U Dothan (AL)
Tulane U (LA)
Union Coll (NE)
Universidad Adventista de las Antillas (PR)
The U of Akron (OH)
U of Alaska Anchorage (AK)
U of Alaska Fairbanks (AK)
U of Alaska Southeast (AK)
U of Bridgeport (CT)
U of Charleston (WV)
U of Cincinnati (OH)
U of Dubuque (IA)
The U of Findlay (OH)
U of Indianapolis (IN)
The U of Maine at Augusta (ME)
U of Maine at Fort Kent (ME)
U of Management and Technology (VA)
U of Mary (ND)
U of Minnesota, Crookston (MN)
The U of Montana-Western (MT)
U of New Hampshire (NH)
U of New Hampshire at Manchester (NH)

U of New Haven (CT)
U of Regina (SK, Canada)
U of Rio Grande (OH)
U of Saint Francis (IN)
The U of Scranton (PA)
U of Sioux Falls (SD)
U of the Virgin Islands (VI)
U of Toledo (OH)
U of Wisconsin–Green Bay (WI)
Upper Iowa U (IA)
Urbana U (OH)
Valdosta State U (GA)
Vermont Tech Coll (VT)
Villa Julie Coll (MD)
Walla Walla Coll (WA)
Walsh U (OH)
Washington & Jefferson Coll (PA)
Wayland Baptist U (TX)
Waynesburg Coll (PA)
Webber International U (FL)
Wentworth Inst of Technology (MA)
Wesley Coll (DE)
Western Baptist Coll (OR)
Western Kentucky U (KY)
West Virginia State Coll (WV)
West Virginia U Inst of Technology (WV)
Williams Baptist Coll (AR)
Williamson Christian Coll (TN)
Wilson Coll (PA)
York Coll of Pennsylvania (PA)
Youngstown State U (OH)

Business Administration, Management and Operations Related
American InterContinental U Online (IL)
Briarcliffe Coll (NY)
Coleman Coll, La Mesa (CA)
DeVry U (NJ)
Embry-Riddle Aeronautical U (FL)
Embry-Riddle Aeronautical U, Extended Campus (FL)
Mountain State U (WV)
Peirce Coll (PA)
St. Augustine Coll (IL)
Southern Alberta Inst of Technology (AB, Canada)
U of Management and Technology (VA)

Business and Personal/Financial Services Marketing
Southern New Hampshire U (NH)

Business Automation/Technology/Data Entry
Austin Peay State U (TN)
Baker Coll of Clinton Township (MI)
Central Christian Coll of Kansas (KS)
Kent State U (OH)
Montana State U–Billings (MT)
Montana Tech of The U of Montana (MT)
Pace U (NY)
The U of Akron (OH)
The U of Montana–Western (MT)
U of Rio Grande (OH)
U of Toledo (OH)
Youngstown State U (OH)

Business/Commerce
Atlanta Christian Coll (GA)
Baker Coll of Flint (MI)
Bluefield State Coll (WV)
Brescia U (KY)
California U of Pennsylvania (PA)
Castleton State Coll (VT)
Central Christian Coll of Kansas (KS)
Champlain Coll (VT)

Coll of Staten Island of the City U of NY (NY)
Crown Coll (MN)
Cumberland U (TN)
Dalton State Coll (GA)
Delaware Valley Coll (PA)
DeVry U, Westminster (CO)
Eastern Nazarene Coll (MA)
Gannon U (PA)
Glenville State Coll (WV)
God's Bible School and Coll (OH)
Hillsdale Free Will Baptist Coll (OK)
Idaho State U (ID)
Indiana U East (IN)
Indiana U Kokomo (IN)
Indiana U South Bend (IN)
Indiana U Southeast (IN)
Kent State U (OH)
Limestone Coll (SC)
Macon State Coll (GA)
Marygrove Coll (MI)
Marymount Coll of Fordham U (NY)
Montana State U–Billings (MT)
Mount Vernon Nazarene U (OH)
New Mexico State U (NM)
Nicholls State U (LA)
Northern Kentucky U (KY)
Peirce Coll (PA)
Penn State U Abington Coll (PA)
Penn State U Altoona Coll (PA)
Penn State U at Erie, The Behrend Coll (PA)
Penn State U Berks Cmps of Berks-Lehigh Valley Coll (PA)
Penn State U Harrisburg Campus of the Capital Coll (PA)
Penn State U Lehigh Valley Cmps of Berks-Lehigh Valley Coll (PA)
Penn State U Schuylkill Campus of the Capital Coll (PA)
Penn State U Univ Park Campus (PA)
Southern Nazarene U (OK)
Southern Wesleyan U (SC)
Southwest Baptist U (MO)
Thomas More Coll (KY)
Thomas U (GA)
Troy State U Montgomery (AL)
Tulane U (LA)
U of Management and Technology (VA)
The U of Montana–Western (MT)
U of Toledo (OH)
Webber International U (FL)
Xavier U (OH)

Business/Corporate Communications
Central Christian Coll of Kansas (KS)
Chestnut Hill Coll (PA)

Business Machine Repair
Boise State U (ID)
Idaho State U (ID)
Lamar U (TX)
U of Alaska Anchorage (AK)

Business, Management, and Marketing Related
The Art Inst of California–San Francisco (CA)
The U of Akron (OH)
U of Southern Indiana (IN)

Business/Managerial Economics
Central Christian Coll of Kansas (KS)
Hawai'i Pacific U (HI)
Northwood U (MI)
Saint Peter's Coll (NJ)
Urbana U (OH)

Business Operations Support and Secretarial Services Related
The U of Akron (OH)

Business Teacher Education
Central Christian Coll of Kansas (KS)
Clayton Coll & State U (GA)
Faulkner U (AL)
Inter American U of PR, Fajardo Campus (PR)
Macon State Coll (GA)
U of the District of Columbia (DC)

Cabinetmaking and Millwork
British Columbia Inst of Technology (BC, Canada)
Valdosta State U (GA)

Cad/Cadd Drafting/Design Technology
Kent State U (OH)
Shawnee State U (OH)
Southern Alberta Inst of Technology (AB, Canada)

Cardiopulmonary Technology
Bacone Coll (OK)

Cardiovascular Technology
Argosy U/Twin Cities, Eagan (MN)
Argosy U/Twin Cities, Eagan (MN)
British Columbia Inst of Technology (BC, Canada)
Gwynedd-Mercy Coll (PA)
Molloy Coll (NY)
Nebraska Methodist Coll (NE)
U Coll of the Cariboo (BC, Canada)
U of Toledo (OH)

Carpentry
British Columbia Inst of Technology (BC, Canada)
Idaho State U (ID)
Northern Michigan U (MI)
Southern Utah U (UT)
U Coll of the Cariboo (BC, Canada)
Valdosta State U (GA)

Cartography
Northern Michigan U (MI)
Southern Alberta Inst of Technology (AB, Canada)
U of Arkansas at Fort Smith (AR)

Celtic Languages
Sacred Heart U (CT)

Ceramic Arts and Ceramics
Rochester Inst of Technology (NY)

Chemical Engineering
Ball State U (IN)
Excelsior Coll (NY)
Ferris State U (MI)
U of New Haven (CT)
U of the District of Columbia (DC)
West Virginia State Coll (WV)

Chemical Technology
British Columbia Inst of Technology (BC, Canada)
Indiana U–Purdue U Fort Wayne (IN)
Lawrence Technological U (MI)
Millersville U of Pennsylvania (PA)
Nicholls State U (LA)
Southern Alberta Inst of Technology (AB, Canada)
State U of NY Coll of A&T at Cobleskill (NY)
The U of Akron (OH)
U of Toledo (OH)
Weber State U (UT)

Chemistry
Adrian Coll (MI)
Bethel Coll (IN)
Castleton State Coll (VT)
Central Christian Coll of Kansas (KS)
Central Methodist Coll (MO)
Chestnut Hill Coll (PA)
Clayton Coll & State U (GA)
Dalton State Coll (GA)
Hannibal-LaGrange Coll (MO)
Idaho State U (ID)
Indiana U South Bend (IN)
Keene State Coll (NH)
Lake Superior State U (MI)
Lindsey Wilson Coll (KY)
Lourdes Coll (OH)
Macon State Coll (GA)
Madonna U (MI)
Methodist Coll (NC)
Ohio Dominican U (OH)
Rochester Inst of Technology (NY)
Sacred Heart U (CT)
Saint Joseph's U (PA)
Siena Heights U (MI)
Thomas Edison State Coll (NJ)
Thomas More Coll (KY)
U of Indianapolis (IN)
U of New Haven (CT)
U of Rio Grande (OH)
The U of Tampa (FL)
U of Wisconsin–Green Bay (WI)
Villa Julie Coll (MD)
Wright State U (OH)
York Coll of Pennsylvania (PA)

Chemistry Related
U of the Incarnate Word (TX)

Chemistry Teacher Education
Central Christian Coll of Kansas (KS)

Child Care and Support Services Management
The Baptist Coll of Florida (FL)
Central Missouri State U (MO)
Chestnut Hill Coll (PA)
Eastern New Mexico U (NM)
Henderson State U (AR)
Idaho State U (ID)
Mount Aloysius Coll (PA)
Mount Vernon Nazarene U (OH)
Nicholls State U (LA)
St. Augustine Coll (IL)
Southeast Missouri State U (MO)
U Coll of the Cariboo (BC, Canada)
U of Central Arkansas (AR)
Weber State U (UT)
Youngstown State U (OH)

Child Care/Guidance
Eastern Kentucky U (KY)

Child Care Provision
Eastern Kentucky U (KY)
Mayville State U (ND)
Mercy Coll (NY)
Murray State U (KY)
Pacific Union Coll (CA)
Saint Mary-of-the-Woods Coll (IN)
U of Alaska Fairbanks (AK)

Child Care Services Management
Cameron U (OK)
U of Louisiana at Monroe (LA)

Child Development
Alabama State U (AL)
Boise State U (ID)
Eastern Kentucky U (KY)
Evangel U (MO)

Fairmont State U (WV)
Ferris State U (MI)
Franciscan U of Steubenville (OH)
Grambling State U (LA)
Lewis-Clark State Coll (ID)
Madonna U (MI)
Mitchell Coll (CT)
Northern Michigan U (MI)
Ohio U (OH)
Purdue U Calumet (IN)
Reformed Bible Coll (MI)
Southern Utah U (UT)
Southern Vermont Coll (VT)
Trevecca Nazarene U (TN)
U of Cincinnati (OH)
U of the District of Columbia (DC)
Villa Julie Coll (MD)
Washburn U (KS)
Weber State U (UT)
Youngstown State U (OH)

Child Guidance
Siena Heights U (MI)
Thomas Edison State Coll (NJ)
Tougaloo Coll (MS)

Christian Studies
Coll of Biblical Studies–Houston (TX)
God's Bible School and Coll (OH)
Heritage Bible Coll (NC)
Vennard Coll (IA)
Wayland Baptist U (TX)

Cinematography and Film/Video Production
Academy of Art U (CA)
American InterContinental U, Atlanta (GA)
American InterContinental U-LondonUnited Kingdom)
The Art Inst of Atlanta (GA)
The Art Inst of Colorado (CO)
The Art Inst of Fort Lauderdale (FL)
Burlington Coll (VT)
Five Towns Coll (NY)
Miami International U of Art & Design (FL)
New England School of Communications (ME)
Rochester Inst of Technology (NY)
Southern Adventist U (TN)

City/Urban, Community and Regional Planning
U of the District of Columbia (DC)

Civil Drafting and Cad/Cadd
British Columbia Inst of Technology (BC, Canada)
Montana Tech of The U of Montana (MT)
Southern Alberta Inst of Technology (AB, Canada)

Civil Engineering
Macon State Coll (GA)
U of New Haven (CT)

Civil Engineering Technology
Bluefield State Coll (WV)
British Columbia Inst of Technology (BC, Canada)
Fairmont State U (WV)
Ferris State U (MI)
Idaho State U (ID)
Indiana U–Purdue U Fort Wayne (IN)
Indiana U–Purdue U Indianapolis (IN)
Kansas State U (KS)
Michigan Technological U (MI)
Missouri Western State Coll (MO)
Murray State U (KY)
Point Park U (PA)
Purdue U Calumet (IN)

Purdue U North Central (IN)
Southern Alberta Inst of
Technology (AB, Canada)
Thomas Edison State Coll
(NJ)
U of Cincinnati (OH)
U of Massachusetts Lowell
(MA)
U of New Hampshire (NH)
U of the District of Columbia
(DC)
U of Toledo (OH)
Vermont Tech Coll (VT)
Wentworth Inst of
Technology (MA)
West Virginia U Inst of
Technology (WV)
Youngstown State U (OH)

**Clinical Laboratory Science/
Medical Technology**
Arkansas State U (AR)
Clayton Coll & State U (GA)
Coll of St. Catherine–
Minneapolis (MN)
Dalton State Coll (GA)
Faulkner U (AL)
Indiana U East (IN)
Northern Michigan U (MI)
U of Toledo (OH)
Villa Julie Coll (MD)
Weber State U (UT)

**Clinical/Medical Laboratory
Assistant**
Jones Coll, Miami (FL)
Northern Michigan U (MI)
The U of Maine at Augusta
(ME)
Youngstown State U (OH)

**Clinical/Medical Laboratory
Science and Allied
Professions Related**
The U of Akron (OH)

**Clinical/Medical Laboratory
Technology**
Argosy U/Twin Cities, Eagan
(MN)
Baker Coll of Owosso (MI)
British Columbia Inst of
Technology (BC, Canada)
City U (WA)
Clayton Coll & State U (GA)
Coll of Staten Island of the
City U of NY (NY)
Dakota State U (SD)
Dalton State Coll (GA)
Eastern Kentucky U (KY)
Fairmont State U (WV)
State U of NY at Farmingdale
(NY)
Faulkner U (AL)
Felician Coll (NJ)
Ferris State U (MI)
The George Washington U
(DC)
Indiana U Northwest (IN)
Macon State Coll (GA)
Madonna U (MI)
Marshall U (WV)
Northern Michigan U (MI)
Our Lady of the Lake Coll
(LA)
Penn State U Schuylkill
Campus of the Capital Coll
(PA)
Presentation Coll (SD)
Shawnee State U (OH)
Southern Alberta Inst of
Technology (AB, Canada)
State U of NY Coll of A&T at
Cobleskill (NY)
U of Alaska Anchorage (AK)
U of Cincinnati (OH)
U of Maine at Presque Isle
(ME)
U of Rio Grande (OH)
U of the District of Columbia
(DC)
Villa Julie Coll (MD)
Weber State U (UT)
Youngstown State U (OH)

Clothing/Textiles
The Art Inst of Fort
Lauderdale (FL)
Indiana U Bloomington (IN)

**Commercial and Advertising
Art**
Academy of Art U (CA)
American InterContinental U
(CA)
Andrews U (MI)
The Art Inst of Atlanta (GA)
The Art Inst of California–
San Diego (CA)
The Art Inst of California–
San Francisco (CA)
The Art Inst of Colorado (CO)
The Art Inst of Fort
Lauderdale (FL)
The Art Inst of Washington
(VA)
Baker Coll of Auburn Hills
(MI)
Baker Coll of Clinton
Township (MI)
Baker Coll of Flint (MI)
Baker Coll of Muskegon (MI)
Baker Coll of Owosso (MI)
Becker Coll (MA)
Briarcliffe Coll (NY)
British Columbia Inst of
Technology (BC, Canada)
Champlain Coll (VT)
Fairmont State U (WV)
Fashion Inst of Technology
(NY)
Felician Coll (NJ)
Ferris State U (MI)
Florida Metropolitan
U-Tampa Coll (FL)
The Illinois Inst of Art (IL)
Indiana U–Purdue U Fort
Wayne (IN)
International Academy of
Design & Technology (FL)
International Acad of
Merchandising & Design,
Ltd (IL)
Miami International U of Art &
Design (FL)
Mitchell Coll (CT)
Mount Ida Coll (MA)
Newbury Coll (MA)
Northern Michigan U (MI)
Northern State U (SD)
Pace U (NY)
Parsons School of Design,
New School U (NY)
Pratt Inst (NY)
Robert Morris Coll (IL)
Sacred Heart U (CT)
Sage Coll of Albany (NY)
Silver Lake Coll (WI)
Suffolk U (MA)
U of Arkansas at Fort Smith
(AR)
U of New Haven (CT)
U of Saint Francis (IN)
U of the District of Columbia
(DC)
Villa Julie Coll (MD)
Virginia Intermont Coll (VA)
Walla Walla Coll (WA)

Commercial Photography
The Art Inst of Atlanta (GA)
Harrington Coll of Design (IL)
Paier Coll of Art, Inc. (CT)
The U of Akron (OH)

**Communication and
Journalism Related**
Champlain Coll (VT)
New England School of
Communications (ME)
Tulane U (LA)

**Communication and Media
Related**
Champlain Coll (VT)

**Communication/Speech
Communication and
Rhetoric**
Baker Coll of Jackson (MI)

Brigham Young U–Hawaii
(HI)
Cameron U (OK)
Central Christian Coll of
Kansas (KS)
Clearwater Christian Coll
(FL)
Coll of Mount St. Joseph
(OH)
Idaho State U (ID)
Lyndon State Coll (VT)
The New England Inst of Art
(MA)
Presentation Coll (SD)
Sage Coll of Albany (NY)
Southern Nazarene U (OK)
Thomas More Coll (KY)
Tri-State U (IN)
Tulane U (LA)
The U of Montana–Missoula
(MT)
U of Rio Grande (OH)
West Virginia State Coll (WV)
Wright State U (OH)

**Communications Systems
Installation and Repair
Technology**
Idaho State U (ID)
U Coll of the Cariboo (BC,
Canada)

**Communications
Technologies and Support
Services Related**
New England School of
Communications (ME)

**Communications
Technology**
Bluefield State Coll (WV)
East Stroudsburg U of
Pennsylvania (PA)
Ferris State U (MI)
Vennard Coll (IA)

**Community Organization
and Advocacy**
Alabama State U (AL)
Cazenovia Coll (NY)
Fairmont State U (WV)
Samford U (AL)
State U of NY Empire State
Coll (NY)
Thomas Edison State Coll
(NJ)
The U of Akron (OH)
The U of Findlay (OH)
U of New Hampshire (NH)
U of New Mexico (NM)

Community Psychology
Kwantlen U Coll (BC,
Canada)

**Computer and Information
Sciences**
Alderson-Broaddus Coll
(WV)
Baker Coll of Allen Park (MI)
Black Hills State U (SD)
Bluefield State Coll (WV)
Central Christian Coll of
Kansas (KS)
Chaminade U of Honolulu
(HI)
Champlain Coll (VT)
Coleman Coll, La Mesa (CA)
Columbia Coll (MO)
Dalton State Coll (GA)
Delaware Valley Coll (PA)
Edinboro U of Pennsylvania
(PA)
Florida Metropolitan
U-Tampa Coll, Brandon
(FL)
Franklin U (OH)
Georgia Southwestern State
U (GA)
Globe Inst of Technology
(NY)
Haskell Indian Nations U
(KS)
Huron U USA in
LondonUnited Kingdom)
Inter Amer U of PR,
Barranquitas Campus (PR)

Jones Coll, Miami (FL)
Kentucky State U (KY)
King's Coll (PA)
Lewis-Clark State Coll (ID)
Lyndon State Coll (VT)
Madonna U (MI)
Midway Coll (KY)
Millersville U of Pennsylvania
(PA)
Montana State U–Billings
(MT)
National American U, Denver
(CO)
Oklahoma Panhandle State
U (OK)
Pacific Union Coll (CA)
Penn State U Schuylkill
Campus of the Capital Coll
(PA)
Sacred Heart U (CT)
Sage Coll of Albany (NY)
St. Augustine Coll (IL)
Southern New Hampshire U
(NH)
Spring Hill Coll (AL)
Thomas Coll (ME)
Thomas Edison State Coll
(NJ)
Thomas More Coll (KY)
Tri-State U (IN)
Troy State U Montgomery
(AL)
Tulane U (LA)
U of Alaska Anchorage (AK)
U of Arkansas at Fort Smith
(AR)
U of Charleston (WV)
U of Cincinnati (OH)
The U of Maine at Augusta
(ME)
The U of Montana–Western
(MT)
U of New Haven (CT)
Villa Julie Coll (MD)
Weber State U (UT)
Youngstown State U (OH)

**Computer and Information
Sciences And Support
Services Related**
Becker Coll (MA)
Cleary U (MI)
Florida Metropolitan
U-Tampa Coll, Brandon
(FL)
Huron U USA in
LondonUnited Kingdom)
Montana State U–Billings
(MT)
Mountain State U (WV)
Strayer U (DC)
U of Arkansas at Fort Smith
(AR)

**Computer and Information
Sciences Related**
Huron U USA in
LondonUnited Kingdom)
Lindsey Wilson Coll (KY)
Madonna U (MI)
National American U, Denver
(CO)

**Computer and Information
Systems Security**
Champlain Coll (VT)
Huron U USA in
LondonUnited Kingdom)

Computer Engineering
The U of Scranton (PA)

**Computer Engineering
Related**
U Coll of the Cariboo (BC,
Canada)

**Computer Engineering
Technologies Related**
Southern Alberta Inst of
Technology (AB, Canada)

**Computer Engineering
Technology**
Andrews U (MI)
Baker Coll of Owosso (MI)
Capitol Coll (MD)
Clayton Coll & State U (GA)

Dalton State Coll (GA)
Eastern Kentucky U (KY)
Excelsior Coll (NY)
Grantham U (LA)
Johnson & Wales U (RI)
Kansas State U (KS)
Lake Superior State U (MI)
Madonna U (MI)
Missouri Tech (MO)
National American U (SD)
Oakland City U (IN)
Oregon Inst of Technology
(OR)
Peirce Coll (PA)
Purdue U Calumet (IN)
Purdue U North Central (IN)
U of Cincinnati (OH)
U of the District of Columbia
(DC)
Vermont Tech Coll (VT)
Weber State U (UT)
Wentworth Inst of
Technology (MA)

Computer Graphics
Academy of Art U (CA)
The Art Inst of California–
San Francisco (CA)
The Art Inst of Colorado (CO)
The Art Inst of Washington
(VA)
Baker Coll of Cadillac (MI)
Champlain Coll (VT)
Coleman Coll, La Mesa (CA)
Huron U USA in
LondonUnited Kingdom)
The Illinois Inst of Art (IL)
International Academy of
Design & Technology (FL)
International Acad of
Merchandising & Design,
Ltd (IL)
Kent State U (OH)
Miami International U of Art &
Design (FL)
New England School of
Communications (ME)
Southern Alberta Inst of
Technology (AB, Canada)
U Coll of the Cariboo (BC,
Canada)
U of Advancing Technology
(AZ)
Villa Julie Coll (MD)

**Computer Hardware
Technology**
Inter American U of PR,
Aguadilla Campus (PR)

**Computer/Information
Technology Services
Administration Related**
Champlain Coll (VT)
Dalton State Coll (GA)
Huron U USA in
LondonUnited Kingdom)
Medgar Evers Coll of the City
U of NY (NY)
National American U, Denver
(CO)
Southern Alberta Inst of
Technology (AB, Canada)
The U of Akron (OH)
Vennard Coll (IA)

**Computer Installation and
Repair Technology**
Dalton State Coll (GA)
Inter American U of PR,
Bayamón Campus (PR)
U Coll of the Cariboo (BC,
Canada)

**Computer Maintenance
Technology**
Eastern Kentucky U (KY)

Computer Management
Champlain Coll (VT)
Coll for Lifelong Learning
(NH)
Daniel Webster Coll (NH)
Davenport U, Lansing (MI)
Faulkner U (AL)
Five Towns Coll (NY)

International Coll of the
Cayman IslandsCayman
Islands)
Life U (GA)
Northwood U (MI)
Northwood U, Florida
Campus (FL)
Oakland City U (IN)
Thomas Coll (ME)

Computer Programming
Atlantic Union Coll (MA)
Baker Coll of Flint (MI)
Baker Coll of Muskegon (MI)
Baker Coll of Owosso (MI)
Baker Coll of Port Huron (MI)
Black Hills State U (SD)
Briarcliffe Coll (NY)
California U of Pennsylvania
(PA)
Castleton State Coll (VT)
Charleston Southern U (SC)
Coll of Staten Island of the
City U of NY (NY)
Dakota State U (SD)
Daniel Webster Coll (NH)
Delaware Valley Coll (PA)
DeVry U, Westminster (CO)
State U of NY at Farmingdale
(NY)
Florida Metropolitan U-Fort
Lauderdale Coll (FL)
Florida Metropolitan
U-Tampa Coll, Lakeland
(FL)
Florida Metropolitan
U-Tampa Coll (FL)
Gwynedd-Mercy Coll (PA)
Huron U USA in
LondonUnited Kingdom)
Indiana U East (IN)
Johnson & Wales U (RI)
Kansas State U (KS)
Kent State U (OH)
Limestone Coll (SC)
Lindsey Wilson Coll (KY)
Macon State Coll (GA)
National American U, Denver
(CO)
National American U (SD)
National American U–Sioux
Falls Branch (SD)
Newbury Coll (MA)
New York U (NY)
Oakland City U (IN)
Oregon Inst of Technology
(OR)
Pontifical Catholic U of
Puerto Rico (PR)
Purdue U Calumet (IN)
Purdue U North Central (IN)
Richmond, The American
International U in
LondonUnited Kingdom)
Saint Francis U (PA)
State U of NY Coll of A&T at
Cobleskill (NY)
Stratford U (VA)
Tiffin U (OH)
U of Advancing Technology
(AZ)
U of Arkansas at Little Rock
(AR)
U of Cincinnati (OH)
U of Indianapolis (IN)
U of Toledo (OH)
Villa Julie Coll (MD)
Walla Walla Coll (WA)
West Virginia State Coll (WV)
York Coll of Pennsylvania
(PA)
Youngstown State U (OH)

**Computer Programming
Related**
Huron U USA in
LondonUnited Kingdom)
Inter Amer U of PR,
Barranquitas Campus (PR)
National American U, Denver
(CO)
Stratford U (VA)

Computer Programming (Specific Applications)
Georgia Southwestern State U (GA)
Huron U USA in LondonUnited Kingdom)
Idaho State U (ID)
Kent State U (OH)
Macon State Coll (GA)
National American U, Denver (CO)
Peirce Coll (PA)
Robert Morris Coll (IL)
U of Toledo (OH)

Computer Programming (Vendor/Product Certification)
Huron U USA in LondonUnited Kingdom)

Computer Science
Arkansas Baptist Coll (AR)
Bacone Coll (OK)
Baker Coll of Allen Park (MI)
Baker Coll of Owosso (MI)
Bethel Coll (IN)
Black Hills State U (SD)
British Columbia Inst of Technology (BC, Canada)
Calumet Coll of Saint Joseph (IN)
Carroll Coll (MT)
Central Christian Coll of Kansas (KS)
Central Methodist Coll (MO)
Chestnut Hill Coll (PA)
Clayton Coll & State U (GA)
Columbia Union Coll (MD)
Columbus State U (GA)
Creighton U (NE)
Dalton State Coll (GA)
Davis & Elkins Coll (WV)
Defiance Coll (OH)
Excelsior Coll (NY)
State U of NY at Farmingdale (NY)
Felician Coll (NJ)
Florida Metropolitan U–Tampa Coll, Lakeland (FL)
Florida Metropolitan U–Tampa Coll (FL)
Grantham U (LA)
Huron U USA in LondonUnited Kingdom)
Indiana U–Purdue U Fort Wayne (IN)
Indiana U South Bend (IN)
Indiana U Southeast (IN)
Inter American U of PR, Aguadilla Campus (PR)
Inter Amer U of PR, Barranquitas Campus (PR)
Inter American U of PR, Bayamón Campus (PR)
Inter American U of PR, Fajardo Campus (PR)
Inter American U of PR, Ponce Campus (PR)
Johnson & Wales U (RI)
Kansas Wesleyan U (KS)
Keene State Coll (NH)
Limestone Coll (SC)
Lincoln U (MO)
Lyndon State Coll (VT)
Macon State Coll (GA)
Madonna U (MI)
Manchester Coll (IN)
Medgar Evers Coll of the City U of NY (NY)
Merrimack Coll (MA)
Methodist Coll (NC)
Millersville U of Pennsylvania (PA)
Missouri Southern State U (MO)
Montana Tech of The U of Montana (MT)
Morrison U (NV)
Mountain State U (WV)
Mount Aloysius Coll (PA)
Newbury Coll (MA)
Oakland City U (IN)

Ohio U–Southern Campus (OH)
Park U (MO)
Richmond, The American International U in LondonUnited Kingdom)
Rivier Coll (NH)
Rochester Inst of Technology (NY)
Sacred Heart U (CT)
Saint Joseph's U (PA)
Southeastern U (DC)
Southern Adventist U (TN)
Southwest Baptist U (MO)
State U of NY Coll of A&T at Cobleskill (NY)
Sullivan U (KY)
Tabor Coll (KS)
Thomas Edison State Coll (NJ)
Universidad Adventista de las Antillas (PR)
U of Dubuque (IA)
The U of Findlay (OH)
U of Maine at Fort Kent (ME)
U of Rio Grande (OH)
U of the Virgin Islands (VI)
Weber State U (UT)
Wentworth Inst of Technology (MA)
West Virginia State Coll (WV)

Computer Software and Media Applications Related
Huron U USA in LondonUnited Kingdom)
Indiana U–Purdue U Fort Wayne (IN)
New England School of Communications (ME)

Computer Software Engineering
Grantham U (LA)

Computer Software Technology
U of New Hampshire (NH)

Computer Systems Analysis
Baker Coll of Flint (MI)
British Columbia Inst of Technology (BC, Canada)
Davenport U, Dearborn (MI)
Davenport U, Gaylord (MI)
Davenport U, Grand Rapids (MI)
Davenport U, Holland (MI)
Davenport U, Kalamazoo (MI)
Davenport U, Lansing (MI)
Davenport U, Warren (MI)
Huron U USA in LondonUnited Kingdom)
Kansas State U (KS)
The U of Akron (OH)
U of Toledo (OH)

Computer Systems Networking and Telecommunications
Baker Coll of Allen Park (MI)
Baker Coll of Flint (MI)
Champlain Coll (VT)
Coleman Coll, La Mesa (CA)
Davenport U, Dearborn (MI)
Davenport U, Gaylord (MI)
Davenport U, Grand Rapids (MI)
Davenport U, Holland (MI)
Davenport U, Kalamazoo (MI)
Davenport U, Lansing (MI)
Davenport U, Warren (MI)
DeVry U (NJ)
Huron U USA in LondonUnited Kingdom)
National American U, Denver (CO)
Remington Coll–Colorado Springs Campus (CO)
Robert Morris Coll (IL)
Sage Coll of Albany (NY)
Stratford U (VA)
Strayer U (DC)
Vermont Tech Coll (VT)

Computer Teacher Education
Baker Coll of Flint (MI)
Central Christian Coll of Kansas (KS)

Computer Technology/ Computer Systems Technology
Dalton State Coll (GA)
DeVry U, Westminster (CO)
Eastern Kentucky U (KY)
Kent State U (OH)
Peirce Coll (PA)
Southeast Missouri State U (MO)
State U of NY Coll of A&T at Cobleskill (NY)
U Coll of the Cariboo (BC, Canada)

Computer Typography and Composition Equipment Operation
Baker Coll of Auburn Hills (MI)
Baker Coll of Cadillac (MI)
Baker Coll of Clinton Township (MI)
Baker Coll of Flint (MI)
Baker Coll of Jackson (MI)
Calumet Coll of Saint Joseph (IN)
Davis & Elkins Coll (WV)
Faulkner U (AL)
McNeese State U (LA)
Northern Michigan U (MI)
U of Toledo (OH)

Conducting
Central Christian Coll of Kansas (KS)

Construction Engineering Technology
Baker Coll of Owosso (MI)
British Columbia Inst of Technology (BC, Canada)
Central Missouri State U (MO)
Coll of Staten Island of the City U of NY (NY)
Fairmont State U (WV)
Ferris State U (MI)
Lake Superior State U (MI)
Lawrence Technological U (MI)
Northern Michigan U (MI)
Purdue U Calumet (IN)
Purdue U North Central (IN)
The U of Akron (OH)
U of Alaska Southeast (AK)
U of Cincinnati (OH)
U of New Hampshire (NH)
U of Toledo (OH)
Vermont Tech Coll (VT)
Wentworth Inst of Technology (MA)
Wright State U (OH)

Construction Management
Baker Coll of Flint (MI)
British Columbia Inst of Technology (BC, Canada)
John Brown U (AR)
Pratt Inst (NY)
U of New Hampshire (NH)
Wentworth Inst of Technology (MA)

Construction Trades Related
British Columbia Inst of Technology (BC, Canada)

Consumer Merchandising/ Retailing Management
Baker Coll of Owosso (MI)
Fairmont State U (WV)
Johnson & Wales U (RI)
Madonna U (MI)
Mount Ida Coll (MA)
Newbury Coll (MA)
Sullivan U (KY)
Thomas Edison State Coll (NJ)
U of Toledo (OH)

Cooking and Related Culinary Arts
The Art Inst of California–San Diego (CA)
Kendall Coll (IL)
Lexington Coll (IL)
Virginia Coll at Birmingham (AL)

Corrections
Baker Coll of Muskegon (MI)
Bluefield State Coll (WV)
Eastern Kentucky U (KY)
John Jay Coll of Criminal Justice, the City U of NY (NY)
Lake Superior State U (MI)
Lamar U (TX)
Macon State Coll (GA)
Marygrove Coll (MI)
U of Indianapolis (IN)
U of New Haven (CT)
U of the District of Columbia (DC)
U of Toledo (OH)
Washburn U (KS)
Weber State U (UT)
West Virginia U Inst of Technology (WV)
Xavier U (OH)
York Coll of Pennsylvania (PA)
Youngstown State U (OH)

Cosmetology
Lamar U (TX)
Valdosta State U (GA)

Counseling Psychology
Central Christian Coll of Kansas (KS)

Counselor Education/ School Counseling and Guidance
Central Christian Coll of Kansas (KS)
Our Lady of Holy Cross Coll (LA)

Court Reporting
Johnson & Wales U (RI)
Metropolitan Coll, Tulsa (OK)
U of Cincinnati (OH)
Villa Julie Coll (MD)

Creative Writing
Bethel Coll (IN)
Haskell Indian Nations U (KS)
Huron U USA in LondonUnited Kingdom)
Manchester Coll (IN)
U of Maine at Presque Isle (ME)
The U of Tampa (FL)

Criminalistics and Criminal Science
U of New Haven (CT)

Criminal Justice/Law Enforcement Administration
Adrian Coll (MI)
American InterContinental U (CA)
Arkansas State U (AR)
Ashland U (OH)
Ball State U (IN)
Becker Coll (MA)
Bemidji State U (MN)
Boise State U (ID)
Calumet Coll of Saint Joseph (IN)
Campbellsville U (KY)
Castleton State Coll (VT)
Central Christian Coll of Kansas (KS)
Champlain Coll (VT)
Chestnut Hill Coll (PA)
Clayton Coll & State U (GA)
Columbia Coll (MO)
Columbus State U (GA)
Dakota Wesleyan U (SD)
Dalton State Coll (GA)
Defiance Coll (OH)
Eastern Kentucky U (KY)

State U of NY at Farmingdale (NY)
Faulkner U (AL)
Florida Metropolitan U–Tampa Coll (FL)
Fort Valley State U (GA)
Glenville State Coll (WV)
Grambling State U (LA)
Hannibal-LaGrange Coll (MO)
Hilbert Coll (NY)
Indiana U Northwest (IN)
Indiana U South Bend (IN)
Johnson & Wales U (FL)
Johnson & Wales U (RI)
Kansas Wesleyan U (KS)
Lake Superior State U (MI)
Lincoln U (MO)
Louisiana Coll (LA)
Lourdes Coll (OH)
MacMurray Coll (IL)
Macon State Coll (GA)
Mansfield U of Pennsylvania (PA)
Mercyhurst Coll (PA)
Methodist Coll (NC)
Mitchell Coll (CT)
Mount Ida Coll (MA)
Newbury Coll (MA)
Northern Michigan U (MI)
Ohio U–Southern Campus (OH)
Park U (MO)
Remington Coll–Colorado Springs Campus (CO)
Roger Williams U (RI)
St. John's U (NY)
Saint Joseph's U (PA)
Salve Regina U (RI)
Siena Heights U (MI)
Southern Utah U (UT)
Southern Vermont Coll (VT)
Suffolk U (MA)
Thomas Edison State Coll (NJ)
Thomas More Coll (KY)
Thomas U (GA)
Tri-State U (IN)
U of Arkansas at Fort Smith (AR)
U of Cincinnati (OH)
The U of Findlay (OH)
U of Indianapolis (IN)
U of Maine at Fort Kent (ME)
U of Maine at Presque Isle (ME)
U of New Haven (CT)
U of the District of Columbia (DC)
Urbana U (OH)
Washburn U (KS)
West Virginia State Coll (WV)
Youngstown State U (OH)

Criminal Justice/Police Science
Arkansas State U (AR)
Armstrong Atlantic State U (GA)
Becker Coll (MA)
Bluefield State Coll (WV)
Cameron U (OK)
Dalton State Coll (GA)
Defiance Coll (OH)
Eastern Kentucky U (KY)
Edinboro U of Pennsylvania (PA)
Fairmont State U (WV)
Husson Coll (ME)
Idaho State U (ID)
Inter American U of PR, Fajardo Campus (PR)
Inter American U of PR, Ponce Campus (PR)
John Jay Coll of Criminal Justice, the City U of NY (NY)
Lake Superior State U (MI)
MacMurray Coll (IL)
Macon State Coll (GA)
Mercyhurst Coll (PA)
Middle Tennessee State U (TN)
Missouri Southern State U (MO)

Nicholls State U (LA)
Northern Kentucky U (KY)
Northern Michigan U (MI)
Northwestern State U of Louisiana (LA)
Ohio U (OH)
Ohio U–Chillicothe (OH)
Southeastern Louisiana U (LA)
Southern U and A&M Coll (LA)
Tiffin U (OH)
The U of Akron (OH)
U of Arkansas at Little Rock (AR)
U of Arkansas at Pine Bluff (AR)
U of Cincinnati (OH)
U of Louisiana at Monroe (LA)
U of New Haven (CT)
U of the District of Columbia (DC)
U of the Virgin Islands (VI)
U of Toledo (OH)
U of Wisconsin–Superior (WI)
Washburn U (KS)
Weber State U (UT)
York Coll of Pennsylvania (PA)
Youngstown State U (OH)

Criminal Justice/Safety
Augusta State U (GA)
Bethel Coll (IN)
Cazenovia Coll (NY)
Central Christian Coll of Kansas (KS)
Champlain Coll (VT)
Colorado Tech U Sioux Falls Campus (SD)
Florida Metropolitan U–Tampa Coll, Brandon (FL)
Florida Metropolitan U–Tampa Coll, Lakeland (FL)
Georgia Southwestern State U (GA)
Husson Coll (ME)
Idaho State U (ID)
Indiana U East (IN)
Indiana U Kokomo (IN)
Indiana U–Purdue U Fort Wayne (IN)
Indiana U–Purdue U Indianapolis (IN)
International Coll (FL)
Kent State U (OH)
King's Coll (PA)
Madonna U (MI)
Manchester Coll (IN)
Missouri Western State Coll (MO)
Mountain State U (WV)
Mount Aloysius Coll (PA)
Murray State U (KY)
New Mexico State U (NM)
Penn State U Altoona Coll (PA)
Pikeville Coll (KY)
St. Francis Coll (NY)
St. Gregory's U (OK)
Saint Joseph's Coll of Maine (ME)
Shaw U (NC)
Shepherd U (WV)
The U of Maine at Augusta (ME)
U of New Haven (CT)
The U of Scranton (PA)
Weber State U (UT)
Xavier U (OH)

Criminology
Ball State U (IN)
Chaminade U of Honolulu (HI)
Dalton State Coll (GA)
Faulkner U (AL)
Indiana State U (IN)
Indiana U of Pennsylvania (PA)

Kwantlen U Coll (BC, Canada)
Marquette U (WI)
U of the District of Columbia (DC)

Crop Production
Sterling Coll (VT)
U of Massachusetts Amherst (MA)

Culinary Arts
The Art Inst of Atlanta (GA)
The Art Inst of California–San Diego (CA)
The Art Inst of Colorado (CO)
The Art Inst of Fort Lauderdale (FL)
The Art Inst of Phoenix (AZ)
Baker Coll of Muskegon (MI)
Boise State U (ID)
The Culinary Inst of America (NY)
Idaho State U (ID)
Johnson & Wales U (CO)
Johnson & Wales U (FL)
Johnson & Wales U (RI)
Kendall Coll (IL)
Lexington Coll (IL)
Mercyhurst Coll (PA)
Newbury Coll (MA)
Nicholls State U (LA)
Oakland City U (IN)
Paul Smith's Coll of Arts and Sciences (NY)
Purdue U Calumet (IN)
Robert Morris Coll (IL)
St. Augustine Coll (IL)
Saint Francis U (PA)
Southern New Hampshire U (NH)
State U of NY Coll of A&T at Cobleskill (NY)
Stratford U (VA)
Sullivan U (KY)
The U of Akron (OH)
U of Alaska Anchorage (AK)
U of Alaska Fairbanks (AK)
The U of Montana–Missoula (MT)
U of New Hampshire (NH)
Virginia Coll at Birmingham (AL)
Virginia Intermont Coll (VA)
West Virginia U Inst of Technology (WV)

Culinary Arts Related
The Culinary Inst of America (NY)
Delaware Valley Coll (PA)
Lexington Coll (IL)
New York Inst of Technology (NY)
Shepherd U (WV)

Customer Service Support/Call Center/Teleservice Operation
Davenport U, Dearborn (MI)
Davenport U, Grand Rapids (MI)
Davenport U, Holland (MI)
Davenport U, Kalamazoo (MI)
Davenport U, Lansing (MI)
Davenport U, Warren (MI)
National American U–Sioux Falls Branch (SD)

Cytotechnology
Indiana U–Purdue U Indianapolis (IN)
Indiana U Southeast (IN)

Dairy Husbandry and Production
Sterling Coll (VT)

Dairy Science
State U of NY Coll of A&T at Cobleskill (NY)
U of New Hampshire (NH)
Vermont Tech Coll (VT)

Dance
New World School of the Arts (FL)

Dance Related
New World School of the Arts (FL)

Data Entry/Microcomputer Applications
Baker Coll of Allen Park (MI)
Huron U USA in London United Kingdom)
National American U, Denver (CO)

Data Entry/Microcomputer Applications Related
Baker Coll of Allen Park (MI)
Huron U USA in London United Kingdom)

Data Modeling/Warehousing and Database Administration
Huron U USA in London United Kingdom)

Data Processing and Data Processing Technology
American InterContinental U Online (IL)
Baker Coll of Auburn Hills (MI)
Baker Coll of Cadillac (MI)
Baker Coll of Clinton Township (MI)
Baker Coll of Flint (MI)
Baker Coll of Jackson (MI)
Baker Coll of Muskegon (MI)
Baker Coll of Owosso (MI)
Baker Coll of Port Huron (MI)
British Columbia Inst of Technology (BC, Canada)
Campbellsville U (KY)
Clayton Coll & State U (GA)
Davenport U, Kalamazoo (MI)
Dordt Coll (IA)
State U of NY at Farmingdale (NY)
Five Towns Coll (NY)
Florida Metropolitan U–Tampa Coll, Lakeland (FL)
Florida Metropolitan U–Tampa Coll (FL)
Hawai'i Pacific U (HI)
Huron U USA in London United Kingdom)
Lake Superior State U (MI)
Lamar U (TX)
Lincoln U (MO)
Macon State Coll (GA)
Midway Coll (KY)
Missouri Southern State U (MO)
Montana State U–Billings (MT)
Montana Tech of The U of Montana (MT)
New York Inst of Technology (NY)
Northern Michigan U (MI)
Northern State U (SD)
Sacred Heart U (CT)
St. Francis Coll (NY)
Saint Francis U (PA)
St. John's U (NY)
Saint Peter's Coll (NJ)
State U of NY Coll of A&T at Cobleskill (NY)
Thomas More Coll (KY)
The U of Akron (OH)
U of Cincinnati (OH)
The U of Montana–Western (MT)
U of the Virgin Islands (VI)
U of Toledo (OH)
Western Kentucky U (KY)
West Virginia U Inst of Technology (WV)
Wright State U (OH)
Youngstown State U (OH)

Dental Assisting
Louisiana State U Health Sciences Center (LA)
U of Alaska Anchorage (AK)
The U of Maine at Augusta (ME)

U of Southern Indiana (IN)
Valdosta State U (GA)

Dental Hygiene
Argosy U/Twin Cities, Eagan (MN)
Armstrong Atlantic State U (GA)
Baker Coll of Port Huron (MI)
Clayton Coll & State U (GA)
Dalton State Coll (GA)
East Tennessee State U (TN)
State U of NY at Farmingdale (NY)
Ferris State U (MI)
Indiana U Northwest (IN)
Indiana U–Purdue U Fort Wayne (IN)
Indiana U–Purdue U Indianapolis (IN)
Indiana U South Bend (IN)
Lamar U (TX)
Louisiana State U Health Sciences Center (LA)
Mass Coll of Pharmacy and Allied Health Sciences (MA)
Minnesota State U Mankato (MN)
Missouri Southern State U (MO)
Montana State U–Billings (MT)
Mount Ida Coll (MA)
New York U (NY)
Shawnee State U (OH)
Southern Adventist U (TN)
Tennessee State U (TN)
U of Alaska Anchorage (AK)
U of Arkansas at Fort Smith (AR)
U of Bridgeport (CT)
U of Louisville (KY)
The U of Maine at Augusta (ME)
U of New England (ME)
U of New Haven (CT)
U of New Mexico (NM)
The U of South Dakota (SD)
U of Southern Indiana (IN)
Valdosta State U (GA)
Vermont Tech Coll (VT)
Weber State U (UT)
Western Kentucky U (KY)
West Liberty State Coll (WV)
West Virginia U Inst of Technology (WV)
Wichita State U (KS)
Youngstown State U (OH)

Dental Laboratory Technology
Idaho State U (ID)
Indiana U–Purdue U Fort Wayne (IN)
Louisiana State U Health Sciences Center (LA)
Southern Illinois U Carbondale (IL)

Design and Visual Communications
The American U in Dubai United Arab Emirates)
Champlain Coll (VT)
International Academy of Design & Technology (FL)
Pace U (NY)
Shepherd U (WV)
Wilmington Coll (DE)

Desktop Publishing and Digital Imaging Design
Davenport U, Dearborn (MI)
Davenport U, Holland (MI)
Davenport U, Kalamazoo (MI)
Davenport U, Lansing (MI)
Davenport U, Lapeer (MI)
Davenport U, Warren (MI)
U Coll of the Cariboo (BC, Canada)

Developmental and Child Psychology
Central Christian Coll of Kansas (KS)
Fresno Pacific U (CA)
Mitchell Coll (CT)
U of Sioux Falls (SD)
Villa Julie Coll (MD)

Diagnostic Medical Sonography and Ultrasound Technology
Argosy U/Twin Cities, Eagan (MN)
Baker Coll of Auburn Hills (MI)
Baker Coll of Owosso (MI)
Baker Coll of Port Huron (MI)
Coll of St. Catherine (MN)
Coll of St. Catherine–Minneapolis (MN)
Mountain State U (WV)
Nebraska Methodist Coll (NE)
New York U (NY)
Southern Alberta Inst of Technology (AB, Canada)
Virginia Coll at Birmingham (AL)

Diesel Mechanics Technology
British Columbia Inst of Technology (BC, Canada)
Georgia Southwestern State U (GA)
Idaho State U (ID)
Lewis-Clark State Coll (ID)
Montana State U–Billings (MT)
U of Alaska Anchorage (AK)
Valdosta State U (GA)
Weber State U (UT)

Dietetics
Ball State U (IN)
Faulkner U (AL)
Loma Linda U (CA)
Purdue U Calumet (IN)
Rochester Inst of Technology (NY)
U of Minnesota, Crookston (MN)
U of New Hampshire (NH)
U of Ottawa (ON, Canada)
Youngstown State U (OH)

Dietetic Technician
U of New Hampshire (NH)

Dietician Assistant
Eastern Kentucky U (KY)

Dietitian Assistant
Pacific Union Coll (CA)
Penn State U Univ Park Campus (PA)
Youngstown State U (OH)

Digital Communication and Media/Multimedia
Academy of Art U (CA)
Champlain Coll (VT)

Divinity/Ministry
Atlantic Union Coll (MA)
Carson-Newman Coll (TN)
Central Christian Coll of Kansas (KS)
Clear Creek Baptist Bible Coll (KY)
Coll of Biblical Studies–Houston (TX)
Faith Baptist Bible Coll and Theological Seminary (IA)
Faulkner U (AL)
Manhattan Christian Coll (KS)
MidAmerica Nazarene U (KS)
Mount Olive Coll (NC)
North Central U (MN)
Pacific Union Coll (CA)
St. Louis Christian Coll (MO)
Warner Pacific Coll (OR)

Dog/Pet/Animal Grooming
Becker Coll (MA)

Drafting
Eastern Kentucky U (KY)
U of Arkansas at Fort Smith (AR)

Drafting and Design Technology
Baker Coll of Auburn Hills (MI)
Baker Coll of Cadillac (MI)
Baker Coll of Clinton Township (MI)
Baker Coll of Flint (MI)
Baker Coll of Muskegon (MI)
Baker Coll of Owosso (MI)
Baker Coll of Port Huron (MI)
Black Hills State U (SD)
Boise State U (ID)
British Columbia Inst of Technology (BC, Canada)
California U of Pennsylvania (PA)
Central Christian Coll of Kansas (KS)
Central Missouri State U (MO)
Clayton Coll & State U (GA)
Dalton State Coll (GA)
Eastern Kentucky U (KY)
Fairmont State U (WV)
Ferris State U (MI)
Georgia Southwestern State U (GA)
Hamilton Tech Coll (IA)
Idaho State U (ID)
Keene State Coll (NH)
Kentucky State U (KY)
Lake Superior State U (MI)
Lamar U (TX)
LeTourneau U (TX)
Lewis-Clark State Coll (ID)
Lincoln U (MO)
Missouri Southern State U (MO)
Montana State U–Billings (MT)
Montana Tech of The U of Montana (MT)
Murray State U (KY)
Northern Michigan U (MI)
Northern State U (SD)
Saint Francis U (PA)
Southern Utah U (UT)
Thomas Edison State Coll (NJ)
Tri-State U (IN)
U Coll of the Cariboo (BC, Canada)
The U of Akron (OH)
U of Alaska Anchorage (AK)
U of Cincinnati (OH)
U of Rio Grande (OH)
U of Toledo (OH)
Utah State U (UT)
Virginia Coll at Birmingham (AL)
Weber State U (UT)
West Virginia State Coll (WV)
West Virginia U Inst of Technology (WV)
Wright State U (OH)
Youngstown State U (OH)

Drafting/Design Engineering Technologies Related
Idaho State U (ID)
The U of Akron (OH)

Drama and Dance Teacher Education
Central Christian Coll of Kansas (KS)

Dramatic/Theatre Arts
Adrian Coll (MI)
Bacone Coll (OK)
Brigham Young U–Hawaii (HI)
Central Christian Coll of Kansas (KS)
Clayton Coll & State U (GA)
Five Towns Coll (NY)
Indiana U Bloomington (IN)
Macon State Coll (GA)
Methodist Coll (NC)
Murray State U (KY)

North Central U (MN)
North Greenville Coll (SC)
Prairie Bible Coll (AB, Canada)
Thomas More Coll (KY)
Université Laval (QC, Canada)
U Coll of the Fraser Valley (BC, Canada)
U of Sioux Falls (SD)
U of Wisconsin–Green Bay (WI)
Villa Julie Coll (MD)

Drawing
Academy of Art U (CA)
Central Christian Coll of Kansas (KS)
New World School of the Arts (FL)
Northern Michigan U (MI)
Parsons School of Design, New School U (NY)
Pratt Inst (NY)
Sacred Heart U (CT)

Early Childhood Education
Baker Coll of Allen Park (MI)
Baker Coll of Jackson (MI)
Bethel Coll (IN)
Champlain Coll (VT)
Coll for Lifelong Learning (NH)
Coll of Saint Mary (NE)
Columbia Union Coll (MD)
Crown Coll (MN)
Indiana U–Purdue U Fort Wayne (IN)
Lancaster Bible Coll (PA)
Lindsey Wilson Coll (KY)
Mercyhurst Coll (PA)
Montana State U–Billings (MT)
Oakland City U (IN)
Ohio U–Southern Campus (OH)
Point Park U (PA)
St. Augustine Coll (IL)
U Coll of the Cariboo (BC, Canada)
U of Great Falls (MT)
Wheelock Coll (MA)
Wilmington Coll (DE)
Wilson Coll (PA)

Ecology
Paul Smith's Coll of Arts and Sciences (NY)
Sterling Coll (VT)

E-Commerce
Champlain Coll (VT)

Economics
Adrian Coll (MI)
Central Christian Coll of Kansas (KS)
Clayton Coll & State U (GA)
Dalton State Coll (GA)
Macon State Coll (GA)
Methodist Coll (NC)
Richmond, The American International U in London United Kingdom)
Sacred Heart U (CT)
State U of NY Empire State Coll (NY)
Strayer U (DC)
Thomas More Coll (KY)
U of Sioux Falls (SD)
The U of Tampa (FL)
U of Wisconsin–Green Bay (WI)
Washington & Jefferson Coll (PA)

Education
Alabama State U (AL)
Bacone Coll (OK)
Baker Coll of Auburn Hills (MI)
Baker Coll of Cadillac (MI)
Central Baptist Coll (AR)
Central Christian Coll of Kansas (KS)

Clayton Coll & State U (GA)
Cumberland U (TN)
Dalton State Coll (GA)
Evangel U (MO)
Inter Amer U of PR,
 Barranquitas Campus (PR)
Kent State U (OH)
Lamar U (TX)
Lindsey Wilson Coll (KY)
Macon State Coll (GA)
Medgar Evers Coll of the City
 U of NY (NY)
Montreat Coll (NC)
Mountain State U (WV)
Pontifical Catholic U of
 Puerto Rico (PR)
Reinhardt Coll (GA)
Saint Francis U (PA)
Spring Hill Coll (AL)
State U of NY Empire State
 Coll (NY)
U of Southern Indiana (IN)

Educational/Instructional Media Design
Ferris State U (MI)
U of Wisconsin–Superior
 (WI)

Educational Leadership and Administration
Shasta Bible Coll (CA)

Education Related
Kent State U (OH)
The U of Akron (OH)
Wayland Baptist U (TX)

Education (Specific Levels and Methods) Related
Sheldon Jackson Coll (AK)

Electrical and Electronic Engineering Technologies Related
Boise State U (ID)
Kent State U (OH)
Lawrence Technological U
 (MI)
New York Inst of Technology
 (NY)
Southern Alberta Inst of
 Technology (AB, Canada)

Electrical and Power Transmission Installation
British Columbia Inst of
 Technology (BC, Canada)

Electrical, Electronic and Communications Engineering Technology
Andrews U (MI)
Arkansas State U (AR)
Arkansas Tech U (AR)
Baker Coll of Cadillac (MI)
Baker Coll of Muskegon (MI)
Baker Coll of Owosso (MI)
Bluefield State Coll (WV)
Boise State U (ID)
Briarcliffe Coll (NY)
British Columbia Inst of
 Technology (BC, Canada)
Cameron U (OK)
Capitol Coll (MD)
Clayton Coll & State U (GA)
Columbia Coll, Caguas (PR)
Dalton State Coll (GA)
DeVry Inst of Technology
 (NY)
DeVry U, Phoenix (AZ)
DeVry U, Fremont (CA)
DeVry U, Long Beach (CA)
DeVry U, Pomona (CA)
DeVry U, West Hills (CA)
DeVry U, Colorado Springs
 (CO)
DeVry U, Westminster (CO)
DeVry U, Orlando (FL)
DeVry U, Alpharetta (GA)
DeVry U, Decatur (GA)
DeVry U, Addison (IL)
DeVry U, Chicago (IL)
DeVry U, Tinley Park (IL)
DeVry U, Kansas City (MO)
DeVry U (NJ)
DeVry U, Columbus (OH)
DeVry U, Irving (TX)

DeVry U, Arlington (VA)
DeVry U, Federal Way (WA)
Eastern Kentucky U (KY)
Excelsior Coll (NY)
Fairmont State U (WV)
Fort Valley State U (GA)
Grantham U (LA)
Hamilton Tech Coll (IA)
Idaho State U (ID)
Indiana State U (IN)
Indiana U–Purdue U Fort
 Wayne (IN)
Indiana U–Purdue U
 Indianapolis (IN)
Johnson & Wales U (RI)
Kansas State U (KS)
Keene State Coll (NH)
Kentucky State U (KY)
Lake Superior State U (MI)
Lamar U (TX)
Lawrence Technological U
 (MI)
Lincoln U (MO)
McNeese State U (LA)
Merrimack Coll (MA)
Michigan Technological U
 (MI)
Missouri Tech (MO)
Missouri Western State Coll
 (MO)
Murray State U (KY)
Northern Michigan U (MI)
Northern State U (SD)
Northwestern State U of
 Louisiana (LA)
Ohio U (OH)
Oregon Inst of Technology
 (OR)
Penn State U Altoona Coll
 (PA)
Penn State U at Erie, The
 Behrend Coll (PA)
Penn State U Berks Cmps of
 Berks-Lehigh Valley Coll
 (PA)
Penn State U Schuylkill
 Campus of the Capital Coll
 (PA)
Pittsburg State U (KS)
Point Park U (PA)
Purdue U (IN)
Purdue U Calumet (IN)
Purdue U North Central (IN)
Rochester Inst of Technology
 (NY)
Shepherd U (WV)
Southern Utah U (UT)
Thomas Edison State Coll
 (NJ)
The U of Akron (OH)
U of Alaska Anchorage (AK)
U of Arkansas at Little Rock
 (AR)
U of Cincinnati (OH)
U of Massachusetts Lowell
 (MA)
The U of Montana–Missoula
 (MT)
U of the District of Columbia
 (DC)
U of Toledo (OH)
Vermont Tech Coll (VT)
Washburn U (KS)
Weber State U (UT)
Wentworth Inst of
 Technology (MA)
West Virginia State Coll (WV)
West Virginia U Inst of
 Technology (WV)
Wichita State U (KS)
Wright State U (OH)
Youngstown State U (OH)

Electrical, Electronics and Communications Engineering
Fairfield U (CT)
Macon State Coll (GA)
Missouri Tech (MO)
U Coll of the Cariboo (BC,
 Canada)
U of New Haven (CT)

Electrical/Electronics Drafting and Cad/Cadd
Johnson & Wales U (RI)

Electrical/Electronics Equipment Installation and Repair
Georgia Southwestern State
 U (GA)
Idaho State U (ID)
Lewis-Clark State Coll (ID)
U Coll of the Cariboo (BC,
 Canada)
U of Arkansas at Fort Smith
 (AR)
Valdosta State U (GA)

Electrician
Georgia Southwestern State
 U (GA)
U Coll of the Cariboo (BC,
 Canada)
Valdosta State U (GA)

Electrocardiograph Technology
DeVry U, Westminster (CO)

Electromechanical and Instrumentation And Maintenance Technologies Related
Georgia Southwestern State
 U (GA)
Southern Alberta Inst of
 Technology (AB, Canada)

Electromechanical Technology
Clayton Coll & State U (GA)
Excelsior Coll (NY)
Idaho State U (ID)
Michigan Technological U
 (MI)
Northern Michigan U (MI)
Shawnee State U (OH)
Shepherd U (WV)
The U of Akron (OH)
U of the District of Columbia
 (DC)
Walla Walla Coll (WA)
Wright State U (OH)

Elementary and Middle School Administration/ Principalship
Inter Amer U of PR,
 Barranquitas Campus (PR)

Elementary Education
Alaska Pacific U (AK)
Central Christian Coll of
 Kansas (KS)
Clayton Coll & State U (GA)
Dalton State Coll (GA)
God's Bible School and Coll
 (OH)
Hillsdale Free Will Baptist
 Coll (OK)
Inter Amer U of PR,
 Barranquitas Campus (PR)
Inter American U of PR,
 Fajardo Campus (PR)
Macon State Coll (GA)
Mountain State U (WV)
New Mexico Highlands U
 (NM)
Vennard Coll (IA)
Villa Julie Coll (MD)
Wilson Coll (PA)

Emergency Care Attendant (Emt Ambulance)
Kent State U (OH)
Southern Alberta Inst of
 Technology (AB, Canada)
Trinity Coll of Nursing and
 Health Sciences (IL)

Emergency Medical Technology (Emt Paramedic)
Arkansas State U (AR)
Baker Coll of Cadillac (MI)
Baker Coll of Clinton
 Township (MI)
Baker Coll of Muskegon (MI)
Ball State U (IN)
Clayton Coll & State U (GA)

Creighton U (NE)
Eastern Kentucky U (KY)
Faulkner U (AL)
Hannibal-LaGrange Coll
 (MO)
Idaho State U (ID)
Indiana U–Purdue U
 Indianapolis (IN)
Inter American U of PR,
 Metropolitan Campus (PR)
Kent State U (OH)
Montana State U–Billings
 (MT)
Mountain State U (WV)
Nebraska Methodist Coll
 (NE)
Nicholls State U (LA)
Our Lady of the Lake Coll
 (LA)
Saint Francis U (PA)
Shawnee State U (OH)
Shepherd U (WV)
Southwest Baptist U (MO)
U of Alaska Anchorage (AK)
U of Arkansas at Fort Smith
 (AR)
U of Pittsburgh at Johnstown
 (PA)
U of Saint Francis (IN)
U of the District of Columbia
 (DC)
U of Toledo (OH)
Valdosta State U (GA)
Weber State U (UT)
Western Kentucky U (KY)
Youngstown State U (OH)

Energy Management and Systems Technology
Baker Coll of Flint (MI)
U of Cincinnati (OH)

Engineering
Brescia U (KY)
Briar Cliff U (IA)
Campbell U (NC)
Central Christian Coll of
 Kansas (KS)
Clayton Coll & State U (GA)
Coll of Staten Island of the
 City U of NY (NY)
Columbia Union Coll (MD)
Columbus State U (GA)
Daniel Webster Coll (NH)
Faulkner U (AL)
Geneva Coll (PA)
Lake Superior State U (MI)
Macon State Coll (GA)
Mitchell Coll (CT)
Montana Tech of The U of
 Montana (MT)
Mountain State U (WV)
Palm Beach Atlantic U (FL)
Robert Morris U (PA)
Southern Adventist U (TN)
Union Coll (NE)
U Coll of the Cariboo (BC,
 Canada)
U of New Haven (CT)
York Coll of Pennsylvania
 (PA)
Youngstown State U (OH)

Engineering Related
British Columbia Inst of
 Technology (BC, Canada)
Eastern Kentucky U (KY)
Montana State U–Billings
 (MT)

Engineering-Related Technologies
Southern Alberta Inst of
 Technology (AB, Canada)

Engineering Science
Daniel Webster Coll (NH)
Merrimack Coll (MA)
Rochester Inst of Technology
 (NY)
U of Cincinnati (OH)

Engineering Technologies Related
Cameron U (OK)
Kent State U (OH)
McNeese State U (LA)

Shepherd U (WV)
The U of Akron (OH)
Western Kentucky U (KY)

Engineering Technology
Andrews U (MI)
Arkansas State U (AR)
Clayton Coll & State U (GA)
Fairmont State U (WV)
John Brown U (AR)
Lake Superior State U (MI)
Macon State Coll (GA)
McNeese State U (LA)
Missouri Tech (MO)
Montana Tech of The U of
 Montana (MT)
New Mexico State U (NM)
New Mexico State U (NM)
Pacific Union Coll (CA)
Rochester Inst of Technology
 (NY)
State U of NY Coll of A&T at
 Cobleskill (NY)
Tri-State U (IN)
U of Alaska Anchorage (AK)
U of the District of Columbia
 (DC)
Valdosta State U (GA)
Vermont Tech Coll (VT)
Wentworth Inst of
 Technology (MA)
Youngstown State U (OH)

English
Adrian Coll (MI)
Calumet Coll of Saint Joseph
 (IN)
Carroll Coll (MT)
Central Christian Coll of
 Kansas (KS)
Central Methodist Coll (MO)
Clayton Coll & State U (GA)
Clearwater Christian Coll
 (FL)
Coll of Santa Fe (NM)
Dalton State Coll (GA)
Felician Coll (NJ)
Fresno Pacific U (CA)
Hannibal-LaGrange Coll
 (MO)
Hillsdale Free Will Baptist
 Coll (OK)
Huron U USA in
 LondonUnited Kingdom)
Idaho State U (ID)
Indiana U–Purdue U Fort
 Wayne (IN)
Kwantlen U Coll (BC,
 Canada)
Lourdes Coll (OH)
Macon State Coll (GA)
Madonna U (MI)
Manchester Coll (IN)
Methodist Coll (NC)
Pine Manor Coll (MA)
Presentation Coll (SD)
Richmond, The American
 International U in
 LondonUnited Kingdom)
Sacred Heart U (CT)
Siena Heights U (MI)
Thomas More Coll (KY)
Université Laval (QC,
 Canada)
U of Dubuque (IA)
U of Rio Grande (OH)
The U of Tampa (FL)
U of the District of Columbia
 (DC)
U of Wisconsin–Green Bay
 (WI)
Xavier U (OH)

English Composition
Central Christian Coll of
 Kansas (KS)
Huron U USA in
 LondonUnited Kingdom)
Kwantlen U Coll (BC,
 Canada)

English/Language Arts Teacher Education
Central Christian Coll of
 Kansas (KS)
Lyndon State Coll (VT)

English Literature (British and Commonwealth)
Huron U USA in
 LondonUnited Kingdom)

Entrepreneurial and Small Business Related
Haskell Indian Nations U
 (KS)

Entrepreneurship
Baker Coll of Flint (MI)
British Columbia Inst of
 Technology (BC, Canada)
Davenport U, Dearborn (MI)
Davenport U, Gaylord (MI)
Davenport U, Grand Rapids
 (MI)
Davenport U, Warren (MI)
Lyndon State Coll (VT)
Northwood U (MI)
The U of Akron (OH)
U of the District of Columbia
 (DC)

Environmental Control Technologies Related
Kent State U (OH)

Environmental Design/ Architecture
Northern Michigan U (MI)

Environmental Engineering Technology
Baker Coll of Flint (MI)
Baker Coll of Owosso (MI)
Baker Coll of Port Huron (MI)
Kansas State U (KS)
New York Inst of Technology
 (NY)
Ohio U (OH)
Southern Alberta Inst of
 Technology (AB, Canada)
U of Cincinnati (OH)
U of the District of Columbia
 (DC)
U of Toledo (OH)
Vermont Tech Coll (VT)
Wentworth Inst of
 Technology (MA)

Environmental/ Environmental Health Engineering
British Columbia Inst of
 Technology (BC, Canada)
Ohio U (OH)
Ohio U–Chillicothe (OH)

Environmental Health
British Columbia Inst of
 Technology (BC, Canada)
The U of Akron (OH)

Environmental Science
Central Christian Coll of
 Kansas (KS)
U of Wisconsin–Green Bay
 (WI)

Environmental Studies
Central Christian Coll of
 Kansas (KS)
Defiance Coll (OH)
Dickinson State U (ND)
Kent State U (OH)
Macon State Coll (GA)
Mountain State U (WV)
Ohio U–Chillicothe (OH)
Paul Smith's Coll of Arts and
 Sciences (NY)
Samford U (AL)
Southern Vermont Coll (VT)
State U of NY Coll of A&T at
 Cobleskill (NY)
Sterling Coll (VT)
Thomas Edison State Coll
 (NJ)
U of Cincinnati (OH)
U of Dubuque (IA)
The U of Findlay (OH)
U of Ottawa (ON, Canada)
U of Toledo (OH)
U of Wisconsin–Green Bay
 (WI)

Equestrian Studies
Centenary Coll (NJ)
Johnson & Wales U (RI)
Midway Coll (KY)
Murray State U (KY)
Ohio U (OH)
Saint Mary-of-the-Woods Coll (IN)
State U of NY Coll of A&T at Cobleskill (NY)
Teikyo Post U (CT)
The U of Findlay (OH)
U of Massachusetts Amherst (MA)
U of Minnesota, Crookston (MN)
The U of Montana–Western (MT)
U of New Hampshire (NH)

European History
Emmanuel Coll (GA)

European Studies
Richmond, The American International U in LondonUnited Kingdom)
Sacred Heart U (CT)

Executive Assistant/ Executive Secretary
Baker Coll of Allen Park (MI)
Baker Coll of Flint (MI)
Davenport U, Dearborn (MI)
Davenport U, Holland (MI)
Davenport U, Kalamazoo (MI)
Davenport U, Lansing (MI)
Davenport U, Lapeer (MI)
Davenport U, Warren (MI)
Kentucky State U (KY)
Montana Tech of The U of Montana (MT)
Murray State U (KY)
Robert Morris Coll (IL)
U Coll of the Cariboo (BC, Canada)
The U of Akron (OH)
The U of Montana–Missoula (MT)
Western Kentucky U (KY)
Youngstown State U (OH)

Family and Community Services
Baker Coll of Flint (MI)
Central Christian Coll of Kansas (KS)
State U of NY Coll of A&T at Cobleskill (NY)

Family and Consumer Economics Related
Dalton State Coll (GA)
Fairmont State U (WV)

Family and Consumer Sciences/Human Sciences
Clayton Coll & State U (GA)
Mount Vernon Nazarene U (OH)
U of Alaska Anchorage (AK)

Family and Consumer Sciences/Human Sciences Related
Morehead State U (KY)

Farm and Ranch Management
Idaho State U (ID)
Johnson & Wales U (RI)
Midway Coll (KY)
Oklahoma Panhandle State U (OK)

Fashion/Apparel Design
Academy of Art U (CA)
American InterContinental U (CA)
American InterContinental U, Atlanta (GA)
American InterContinental U-LondonUnited Kingdom)
The Art Inst of California–San Francisco (CA)
The Art Inst of Fort Lauderdale (FL)
The Art Inst of Portland (OR)

Cazenovia Coll (NY)
Fashion Inst of Technology (NY)
The Illinois Inst of Art (IL)
Indiana U Bloomington (IN)
International Academy of Design & Technology (FL)
International Acad of Merchandising & Design, Ltd (IL)
Miami International U of Art & Design (FL)
Mount Ida Coll (MA)
Parsons School of Design, New School U (NY)
U of the Incarnate Word (TX)

Fashion Merchandising
Academy of Art U (CA)
American InterContinental U (CA)
American InterContinental U, Atlanta (GA)
American InterContinental U-LondonUnited Kingdom)
Clayton Coll & State U (GA)
Fairmont State U (WV)
International Acad of Merchandising & Design, Ltd (IL)
Johnson & Wales U (FL)
Johnson & Wales U (RI)
Laboratory Inst of Merchandising (NY)
Lynn U (FL)
Miami International U of Art & Design (FL)
Mount Ida Coll (MA)
Newbury Coll (MA)
Northwood U (MI)
Northwood U, Texas Campus (TX)
Parsons School of Design, New School U (NY)
Shepherd U (WV)
Southern New Hampshire U (NH)
Thomas Coll (ME)
The U of Akron (OH)
U of Bridgeport (CT)
U of the District of Columbia (DC)
U of the Incarnate Word (TX)
Weber State U (UT)
West Virginia State Coll (WV)

Fiber, Textile and Weaving Arts
Academy of Art U (CA)

Film/Cinema Studies
Academy of Art U (CA)
Burlington Coll (VT)
Indiana U South Bend (IN)

Film/Video and Photographic Arts Related
Haskell Indian Nations U (KS)
New England School of Communications (ME)

Finance
British Columbia Inst of Technology (BC, Canada)
Central Christian Coll of Kansas (KS)
Chestnut Hill Coll (PA)
Clayton Coll & State U (GA)
Davenport U, Dearborn (MI)
Davenport U, Grand Rapids (MI)
Davenport U, Warren (MI)
Fairmont State U (WV)
Hawai'i Pacific U (HI)
Indiana U South Bend (IN)
International Coll of the Cayman IslandsCayman Islands)
Johnson & Wales U (RI)
Marian Coll (IN)
Methodist Coll (NC)
Newbury Coll (MA)
Sacred Heart U (CT)
Saint Joseph's U (PA)
Saint Peter's Coll (NJ)

Southern Alberta Inst of Technology (AB, Canada)
Thomas Edison State Coll (NJ)
U of Cincinnati (OH)
Walsh U (OH)
Webber International U (FL)
West Virginia State Coll (WV)
Youngstown State U (OH)

Finance and Financial Management Services Related
British Columbia Inst of Technology (BC, Canada)

Financial Planning and Services
British Columbia Inst of Technology (BC, Canada)
The U of Maine at Augusta (ME)

Fine Arts Related
Saint Francis U (PA)
York Coll of Pennsylvania (PA)

Fine/Studio Arts
Academy of Art U (CA)
Corcoran Coll of Art and Design (DC)
Manchester Coll (IN)
Pace U (NY)
Pine Manor Coll (MA)
Pratt Inst (NY)
Richmond, The American International U in LondonUnited Kingdom)
Rochester Inst of Technology (NY)
Sage Coll of Albany (NY)
St. Gregory's U (OK)
Thomas More Coll (KY)
The U of Maine at Augusta (ME)
U of New Hampshire at Manchester (NH)

Fire Protection and Safety Technology
British Columbia Inst of Technology (BC, Canada)
Eastern Kentucky U (KY)
Montana State U–Billings (MT)
Thomas Edison State Coll (NJ)
The U of Akron (OH)
U of Nebraska–Lincoln (NE)
U of New Haven (CT)
U of Toledo (OH)

Fire Science
Idaho State U (ID)
Lake Superior State U (MI)
Lamar U (TX)
Lewis-Clark State Coll (ID)
Madonna U (MI)
Mountain State U (WV)
Providence Coll (RI)
U of Alaska Anchorage (AK)
U of Alaska Fairbanks (AK)
U of Cincinnati (OH)
U of New Haven (CT)
U of the District of Columbia (DC)

Fire Services Administration
U of New Haven (CT)

Fish/Game Management
State U of NY Coll of A&T at Cobleskill (NY)
Winona State U (MN)

Fishing and Fisheries Sciences And Management
Sterling Coll (VT)

Floriculture/Floristry Management
Inter Amer U of PR, Barranquitas Campus (PR)

Folklore
Université Laval (QC, Canada)

Food Preparation
Lexington Coll (IL)

Food Science
Lamar U (TX)
Macon State Coll (GA)

Food Service and Dining Room Management
Lexington Coll (IL)

Food Services Technology
Purdue U Calumet (IN)
State U of NY Coll of A&T at Cobleskill (NY)
U of the District of Columbia (DC)

Foodservice Systems Administration
Murray State U (KY)

Foods, Nutrition, and Wellness
Cedar Crest Coll (PA)
Eastern Kentucky U (KY)
Madonna U (MI)
Southern Adventist U (TN)
U of Maine at Presque Isle (ME)
U of New Hampshire (NH)
U of Ottawa (ON, Canada)

Foreign Languages and Literatures
Dalton State Coll (GA)

Foreign Languages Related
U of Alaska Fairbanks (AK)

Forensic Science and Technology
Arkansas State U (AR)
British Columbia Inst of Technology (BC, Canada)
U of Arkansas at Fort Smith (AR)

Forest Engineering
Columbus State U (GA)

Forest/Forest Resources Management
British Columbia Inst of Technology (BC, Canada)
Sterling Coll (VT)
U of Maine at Presque Isle (ME)

Forest Resources Production and Management
Sterling Coll (VT)

Forestry
Clayton Coll & State U (GA)
Columbus State U (GA)
Dalton State Coll (GA)
Paul Smith's Coll of Arts and Sciences (NY)
Sterling Coll (VT)
Thomas Edison State Coll (NJ)
U of Maine at Fort Kent (ME)
Winona State U (MN)

Forestry Related
Sterling Coll (VT)

Forestry Technology
British Columbia Inst of Technology (BC, Canada)
Glenville State Coll (WV)
Michigan Technological U (MI)
Paul Smith's Coll of Arts and Sciences (NY)
The U of British Columbia (BC, Canada)
U of Maine at Fort Kent (ME)
U of New Hampshire (NH)

Forest Sciences and Biology
Sterling Coll (VT)

French
Adrian Coll (MI)
Chestnut Hill Coll (PA)
Clayton Coll & State U (GA)
Idaho State U (ID)

Indiana U–Purdue U Fort Wayne (IN)
Methodist Coll (NC)
Université Laval (QC, Canada)
U of Wisconsin–Green Bay (WI)
Xavier U (OH)

Funeral Service and Mortuary Science
Lynn U (FL)
Mount Ida Coll (MA)
Point Park U (PA)

Furniture Design and Manufacturing
Rochester Inst of Technology (NY)

General Studies
American Public U System (WV)
Arkansas State U (AR)
Arkansas Tech U (AR)
Austin Peay State U (TN)
Averett U (VA)
Avila U (MO)
Bacone Coll (OK)
Black Hills State U (SD)
Brewton-Parker Coll (GA)
Calumet Coll of Saint Joseph (IN)
Cameron U (OK)
Castleton State Coll (VT)
Central Baptist Coll (AR)
Chaminade U of Honolulu (HI)
City U (WA)
Clearwater Christian Coll (FL)
Coll for Lifelong Learning (NH)
Coll of Saint Mary (NE)
Columbia Union Coll (MD)
Concordia Coll (AL)
Concordia U (MI)
Concordia U at Austin (TX)
Concordia U, St. Paul (MN)
Crown Coll (MN)
Dalton State Coll (GA)
Eastern Connecticut State U (CT)
Eastern Mennonite U (VA)
Eastern Nazarene Coll (MA)
Eastern New Mexico U (NM)
Franciscan U of Steubenville (OH)
Hillsdale Free Will Baptist Coll (OK)
Huron U USA in LondonUnited Kingdom)
Idaho State U (ID)
Indiana State U (IN)
Indiana U Bloomington (IN)
Indiana U East (IN)
Indiana U Kokomo (IN)
Indiana U Northwest (IN)
Indiana U of Pennsylvania (PA)
Indiana–Purdue U Fort Wayne (IN)
Indiana U–Purdue U Indianapolis (IN)
Indiana U South Bend (IN)
Indiana U Southeast (IN)
Johnson State Coll (VT)
Lawrence Technological U (MI)
Lebanon Valley Coll (PA)
Liberty U (VA)
Louisiana Tech U (LA)
Macon State Coll (GA)
McNeese State U (LA)
Messenger Coll (MO)
Monmouth U (NJ)
Morehead State U (KY)
Mount Aloysius Coll (PA)
Mount Marty Coll (SD)
Mount Vernon Nazarene U (OH)
New Mexico State U (NM)
New York U (NY)
Nicholls State U (LA)
Northwestern State U of Louisiana (LA)

Nyack Coll (NY)
Oakland City U (IN)
Ohio Dominican U (OH)
Okanagan U Coll (BC, Canada)
Oklahoma Panhandle State U (OK)
Our Lady of the Lake Coll (LA)
Palm Beach Atlantic U (FL)
Rider U (NJ)
Rochester Inst of Technology (NY)
St. Augustine Coll (IL)
Saint Joseph's Coll of Maine (ME)
Shawnee State U (OH)
Sheldon Jackson Coll (AK)
Shepherd U (WV)
Siena Heights U (MI)
Silver Lake Coll (WI)
Simpson Coll and Graduate School (CA)
South Dakota School of Mines and Technology (SD)
Southeastern Louisiana U (LA)
Southern Adventist U (TN)
Southern Arkansas U–Magnolia (AR)
Southwest Baptist U (MO)
Temple U (PA)
Toccoa Falls Coll (GA)
Trevecca Nazarene U (TN)
U of Arkansas at Fort Smith (AR)
U of Arkansas at Little Rock (AR)
U of Central Arkansas (AR)
U of Louisiana at Monroe (LA)
U of Maine at Fort Kent (ME)
U of Mobile (AL)
U of New Haven (CT)
U of North Florida (FL)
U of Phoenix–Hawaii Campus (HI)
U of Phoenix–Louisiana Campus (LA)
U of Phoenix–Phoenix Campus (AZ)
U of Rio Grande (OH)
The U of South Dakota (SD)
U of Toledo (OH)
Utah State U (UT)
Vennard Coll (IA)
Virginia Intermont Coll (VA)
Warner Southern Coll (FL)
Western Kentucky U (KY)
Wilmington Coll (DE)

Geography
Dalton State Coll (GA)
Kwantlen U Coll (BC, Canada)
Université Laval (QC, Canada)
The U of Tampa (FL)
Wright State U (OH)

Geological and Earth Sciences/Geosciences Related
Kwantlen U Coll (BC, Canada)

Geology/Earth Science
Adrian Coll (MI)
Clayton Coll & State U (GA)
Dalton State Coll (GA)
Idaho State U (ID)
Indiana U East (IN)
U of Wisconsin–Green Bay (WI)

Geophysics and Seismology
U of Ottawa (ON, Canada)

German
Adrian Coll (MI)
Idaho State U (ID)
Indiana U–Purdue U Fort Wayne (IN)
Methodist Coll (NC)
Xavier U (OH)

Germanic Languages
U of Wisconsin–Green Bay (WI)

Gerontology
Coll of Mount St. Joseph (OH)
King's Coll (PA)
Madonna U (MI)
Manchester Coll (IN)
Millersville U of Pennsylvania (PA)
Ohio Dominican U (OH)
Pontifical Catholic U of Puerto Rico (PR)
Siena Heights U (MI)
Thomas More Coll (KY)
U of Toledo (OH)
West Virginia State Coll (WV)
Winona State U (MN)

Graphic and Printing Equipment Operation/ Production
Ball State U (IN)
Chowan Coll (NC)
Fairmont State U (WV)
Ferris State U (MI)
Idaho State U (ID)
Lewis-Clark State Coll (ID)
Murray State U (KY)
Pacific Union Coll (CA)
U of the District of Columbia (DC)
West Virginia U Inst of Technology (WV)

Graphic Communications
Academy of Art U (CA)
New England School of Communications (ME)

Graphic Design
Academy of Art U (CA)
Art Academy of Cincinnati (OH)
The Art Inst of California–San Diego (CA)
The Art Inst of Portland (OR)
Becker Coll (MA)
Champlain Coll (VT)
Coll of Mount St. Joseph (OH)
Corcoran Coll of Art and Design (DC)
New World School of the Arts (FL)
Pratt Inst (NY)
Rochester Inst of Technology (NY)
Union Coll (NE)
U Coll of the Cariboo (BC, Canada)

Graphic/Printing Equipment
Eastern Kentucky U (KY)

Greenhouse Management
Sterling Coll (VT)

Hazardous Materials Information Systems Technology
Ohio U (OH)

Hazardous Materials Management and Waste Technology
Ohio U (OH)

Health and Medical Administrative Services Related
British Columbia Inst of Technology (BC, Canada)
Kent State U (OH)
The U of Akron (OH)

Health and Physical Education
Bethel Coll (IN)
Central Christian Coll of Kansas (KS)
Haskell Indian Nations U (KS)
Mount Vernon Nazarene U (OH)
Robert Morris Coll (IL)

Health/Health Care Administration
Baker Coll of Auburn Hills (MI)
Baker Coll of Flint (MI)
Baker Coll of Muskegon (MI)
British Columbia Inst of Technology (BC, Canada)
Chestnut Hill Coll (PA)
Madonna U (MI)
Methodist Coll (NC)
National American U, Denver (CO)
New York U (NY)
Point Park U (PA)
Saint Joseph's U (PA)
Southeastern U (DC)
The U of Scranton (PA)
West Virginia U Inst of Technology (WV)

Health Information/Medical Records Administration
Baker Coll of Auburn Hills (MI)
Baker Coll of Cadillac (MI)
Baker Coll of Clinton Township (MI)
Baker Coll of Flint (MI)
Baker Coll of Jackson (MI)
Baker Coll of Port Huron (MI)
Boise State U (ID)
Clayton Coll & State U (GA)
Coll of St. Catherine–Minneapolis (MN)
Coll of Saint Mary (NE)
Dakota State U (SD)
Dalton State Coll (GA)
Davenport U, Kalamazoo (MI)
Davenport U, Warren (MI)
Eastern Kentucky U (KY)
Fairmont State U (WV)
Faulkner U (AL)
Ferris State U (MI)
Gwynedd-Mercy Coll (PA)
Indiana U Northwest (IN)
Inter American U of PR, San Germán Campus (PR)
Montana State U–Billings (MT)
Park U (MO)
Southern Alberta Inst of Technology (AB, Canada)
Universidad Adventista de las Antillas (PR)
Washburn U (KS)

Health Information/Medical Records Technology
Baker Coll of Flint (MI)
Baker Coll of Jackson (MI)
Coll of St. Catherine (MN)
Davenport U, Dearborn (MI)
Davenport U, Holland (MI)
Davenport U, Lapeer (MI)
Davenport U, Warren (MI)
Eastern Kentucky U (KY)
Gwynedd-Mercy Coll (PA)
Idaho State U (ID)
International Coll (FL)
Louisiana Tech U (LA)
Macon State Coll (GA)
Missouri Western State Coll (MO)
Molloy Coll (NY)
New York U (NY)
Weber State U (UT)
Western Kentucky U (KY)

Health/Medical Preparatory Programs Related
Emmanuel Coll (GA)
Union Coll (NE)

Health Professions Related
British Columbia Inst of Technology (BC, Canada)
East Tennessee State U (TN)
Howard Payne U (TX)
Lock Haven U of Pennsylvania (PA)

Health Science
Covenant Coll (GA)
Howard Payne U (TX)
Macon State Coll (GA)

Newman U (KS)
Northwest Coll (WA)
South U (AL)
Union Coll (NE)

Health Services/Allied Health/Health Sciences
Central Christian Coll of Kansas (KS)
Lindsey Wilson Coll (KY)
National American U, Denver (CO)

Health Teacher Education
Central Christian Coll of Kansas (KS)
Clayton Coll & State U (GA)

Heating, Air Conditioning and Refrigeration Technology
Central Missouri State U (MO)

Heating, Air Conditioning, Ventilation and Refrigeration Maintenance Technology
Boise State U (ID)
British Columbia Inst of Technology (BC, Canada)
Ferris State U (MI)
Georgia Southwestern State U (GA)
Lamar U (TX)
Lewis-Clark State Coll (ID)
Montana State U–Billings (MT)
Northern Michigan U (MI)
Oakland City U (IN)
U of Alaska Anchorage (AK)
U of Cincinnati (OH)
Valdosta State U (GA)

Heavy Equipment Maintenance Technology
British Columbia Inst of Technology (BC, Canada)
Ferris State U (MI)
Georgia Southwestern State U (GA)
U of Alaska Anchorage (AK)
The U of Montana–Missoula (MT)
Valdosta State U (GA)

Hebrew
North Central U (MN)

Histologic Technician
Argosy U/Twin Cities, Eagan (MN)

Histologic Technology/ Histotechnologist
Argosy U/Twin Cities, Eagan (MN)

History
Adrian Coll (MI)
Bacone Coll (OK)
Central Christian Coll of Kansas (KS)
Dalton State Coll (GA)
Felician Coll (NJ)
Fresno Pacific U (CA)
Idaho State U (ID)
Indiana U East (IN)
Indiana U–Purdue U Fort Wayne (IN)
Kwantlen U Coll (BC, Canada)
Lindsey Wilson Coll (KY)
Lourdes Coll (OH)
Macon State Coll (GA)
Marian Coll (IN)
Methodist Coll (NC)
Millersville U of Pennsylvania (PA)
North Central U (MN)
Pine Manor Coll (MA)
Richmond, The American International U in London United Kingdom)
Sacred Heart U (CT)
Saint Joseph's Coll of Maine (ME)
State U of NY Empire State Coll (NY)
Thomas More Coll (KY)

U of Rio Grande (OH)
The U of Tampa (FL)
U of the District of Columbia (DC)
U of Wisconsin–Green Bay (WI)
Villa Julie Coll (MD)
Wright State U (OH)
Xavier U (OH)

History Teacher Education
Central Christian Coll of Kansas (KS)

Home Furnishings
Eastern Kentucky U (KY)

Home Furnishings and Equipment Installation
Eastern Kentucky U (KY)

Horticultural Science
Andrews U (MI)
Bacone Coll (OK)
Boise State U (ID)
Eastern Kentucky U (KY)
Murray State U (KY)
State U of NY Coll of A&T at Cobleskill (NY)
Thomas Edison State Coll (NJ)
U of Connecticut (CT)
U of Minnesota, Crookston (MN)
U of New Hampshire (NH)
Vermont Tech Coll (VT)

Hospital and Health Care Facilities Administration
DeVry U, Westminster (CO)

Hospitality Administration
Baker Coll of Flint (MI)
Baker Coll of Owosso (MI)
Champlain Coll (VT)
Indiana U–Purdue U Fort Wayne (IN)
Johnson & Wales U (FL)
Kendall Coll (IL)
Lewis-Clark State Coll (ID)
Lexington Coll (IL)
National American U (NM)
Paul Smith's Coll of Arts and Sciences (NY)
Siena Heights U (MI)
The U of Akron (OH)
U of Alaska Southeast (AK)
U of Minnesota, Crookston (MN)
U of the District of Columbia (DC)
Washburn U (KS)
Youngstown State U (OH)

Hospitality Administration Related
Champlain Coll (VT)
Lexington Coll (IL)
Mountain State U (WV)
Penn State U Berks Cmps of Berks-Lehigh Valley Coll (PA)
Penn State U Univ Park Campus (PA)
Purdue U (IN)

Hospitality and Recreation Marketing
Champlain Coll (VT)
U Coll of the Cariboo (BC, Canada)
The U of Akron (OH)

Hotel/Motel Administration
Baker Coll of Muskegon (MI)
Baker Coll of Owosso (MI)
Baker Coll of Port Huron (MI)
Bluefield State Coll (WV)
Champlain Coll (VT)
Florida Metropolitan U–Fort Lauderdale Coll (FL)
Indiana U–Purdue U Indianapolis (IN)
International Coll of the Cayman Islands Cayman Islands)
Johnson & Wales U (FL)
Johnson & Wales U (RI)

Kendall Coll (IL)
Lexington Coll (IL)
Mercyhurst Coll (PA)
Mount Ida Coll (MA)
National American U, Colorado Springs (CO)
National American U (NM)
Newbury Coll (MA)
Northwood U (MI)
Northwood U, Florida Campus (FL)
Northwood U, Texas Campus (TX)
Paul Smith's Coll of Arts and Sciences (NY)
Purdue U Calumet (IN)
Rochester Inst of Technology (NY)
Southern Alberta Inst of Technology (AB, Canada)
State U of NY Coll of A&T at Cobleskill (NY)
Stratford U (VA)
Sullivan U (KY)
Thomas Edison State Coll (NJ)
U Coll of the Cariboo (BC, Canada)
The U of Akron (OH)
U of Minnesota, Crookston (MN)
U of New Haven (CT)
U of the Virgin Islands (VI)
Webber International U (FL)
West Virginia State Coll (WV)
Youngstown State U (OH)

Human Development and Family Studies
Mitchell Coll (CT)
Penn State U Altoona Coll (PA)
Penn State U Schuylkill Campus of the Capital Coll (PA)
Penn State U Univ Park Campus (PA)
State U of NY Empire State Coll (NY)

Human Development and Family Studies Related
U of Toledo (OH)
Utah State U (UT)

Human Ecology
Sterling Coll (VT)

Humanities
Bacone Coll (OK)
Burlington Coll (VT)
Central Christian Coll of Kansas (KS)
Faulkner U (AL)
Felician Coll (NJ)
Huron U USA in London United Kingdom)
Immaculata U (PA)
Macon State Coll (GA)
Michigan Technological U (MI)
Newbury Coll (MA)
Ohio U (OH)
Sage Coll of Albany (NY)
St. Gregory's U (OK)
Saint Peter's Coll (NJ)
Shawnee State U (OH)
State U of NY Empire State Coll (NY)
U of Cincinnati (OH)
The U of Findlay (OH)
U of Sioux Falls (SD)
U of Wisconsin–Green Bay (WI)
Villa Julie Coll (MD)
Washburn U (KS)
Wichita State U (KS)

Human Resources Management
Baker Coll of Owosso (MI)
British Columbia Inst of Technology (BC, Canada)
Central Christian Coll of Kansas (KS)
Chestnut Hill Coll (PA)
King's Coll (PA)

Montana State U–Billings (MT)
Montana Tech of The U of Montana (MT)
Thomas Edison State Coll (NJ)
The U of Findlay (OH)
The U of Montana–Western (MT)
U of Richmond (VA)
Urbana U (OH)

Human Resources Management and Services Related
Becker Coll (MA)
Concordia U Coll of Alberta (AB, Canada)

Human Services
Adrian Coll (MI)
Baker Coll of Clinton Township (MI)
Baker Coll of Flint (MI)
Baker Coll of Muskegon (MI)
Beacon Coll (FL)
Burlington Coll (VT)
Champlain Coll (VT)
Chestnut Hill Coll (PA)
Coll of Saint Mary (NE)
Grace Bible Coll (MI)
Hilbert Coll (NY)
Indiana U East (IN)
Indiana U–Purdue U Fort Wayne (IN)
Kendall Coll (IL)
Kent State U (OH)
Kent State U (OH)
Mercy Coll (NY)
Merrimack Coll (MA)
Metropolitan Coll of New York (NY)
Mitchell Coll (CT)
Mount Vernon Nazarene U (OH)
Mount Vernon Nazarene U (OH)
New York U (NY)
Northern Kentucky U (KY)
Ohio U (OH)
Ohio U–Chillicothe (OH)
Ohio U–Southern Campus (OH)
Sheldon Jackson Coll (AK)
Southern Vermont Coll (VT)
State U of NY Empire State Coll (NY)
U of Alaska Anchorage (AK)
U of Cincinnati (OH)
U of Great Falls (MT)
The U of Maine at Augusta (ME)
U of Maine at Fort Kent (ME)
U of Saint Francis (IN)
The U of Scranton (PA)
Walsh U (OH)

Hydrology and Water Resources Science
Lake Superior State U (MI)
U of the District of Columbia (DC)

Illustration
Academy of Art U (CA)
Becker Coll (MA)
Pratt Inst (NY)

Industrial Arts
Austin Peay State U (TN)
Dalton State Coll (GA)
Eastern Kentucky U (KY)
U of Cincinnati (OH)
The U of Montana–Missoula (MT)
Weber State U (UT)

Industrial Design
Academy of Art U (CA)
Ferris State U (MI)
Northern Michigan U (MI)
Oakland City U (IN)
Rochester Inst of Technology (NY)
Wentworth Inst of Technology (MA)

Industrial Electronics Technology
Dalton State Coll (GA)
Lewis-Clark State Coll (ID)
U Coll of the Cariboo (BC, Canada)

Industrial Engineering
U of New Haven (CT)
U of Toledo (OH)

Industrial Mechanics and Maintenance Technology
Arkansas Tech U (AR)
British Columbia Inst of Technology (BC, Canada)
Dalton State Coll (GA)
Valdosta State U (GA)

Industrial Production Technologies Related
Fashion Inst of Technology (NY)
Kent State U (OH)
U of Nebraska–Lincoln (NE)

Industrial Radiologic Technology
Baker Coll of Owosso (MI)
Ball State U (IN)
Boise State U (ID)
Faulkner U (AL)
Ferris State U (MI)
Fort Hays State U (KS)
The George Washington U (DC)
Inter American U of PR, San Germán Campus (PR)
Lamar (TX)
Northern Kentucky U (KY)
Our Lady of the Lake Coll (LA)
U of Cincinnati (OH)
U of the District of Columbia (DC)
Washburn U (KS)
Widener U (PA)

Industrial Technology
Baker Coll of Muskegon (MI)
Ball State U (IN)
British Columbia Inst of Technology (BC, Canada)
Cameron U (OK)
Central Missouri State U (MO)
Dalton State Coll (GA)
Eastern Kentucky U (KY)
Edinboro U of Pennsylvania (PA)
Excelsior Coll (NY)
Fairmont State U (WV)
Ferris State U (MI)
Indiana U–Purdue U Fort Wayne (IN)
Kansas State U (KS)
Keene State Coll (NH)
Kent State U (OH)
Millersville U of Pennsylvania (PA)
Morehead State U (KY)
Murray State U (KY)
Northern Michigan U (MI)
Oklahoma Panhandle State U (OK)
Purdue U Calumet (IN)
Purdue U North Central (IN)
Southeastern Louisiana U (LA)
Southern Alberta Inst of Technology (AB, Canada)
Southern Arkansas U–Magnolia (AR)
Thomas Edison State Coll (NJ)
Tri-State U (IN)
The U of Akron (OH)
U of Alaska Fairbanks (AK)
U of Arkansas at Pine Bluff (AR)
U of Cincinnati (OH)
U of New Haven (CT)
U of Rio Grande (OH)
U of Toledo (OH)
Weber State U (UT)

Wentworth Inst of Technology (MA)
Wright State U (OH)

Information Science/Studies
Albertus Magnus Coll (CT)
Alvernia Coll (PA)
Arkansas Tech U (AR)
Baker Coll of Cadillac (MI)
Baker Coll of Clinton Township (MI)
Baker Coll of Flint (MI)
Baker Coll of Jackson (MI)
Baker Coll of Muskegon (MI)
Baker Coll of Owosso (MI)
Baker Coll of Port Huron (MI)
Ball State U (IN)
Briarcliffe Coll (NY)
British Columbia Inst of Technology (BC, Canada)
Calumet Coll of Saint Joseph (IN)
Campbellsville U (KY)
Champlain Coll (VT)
Clayton Coll & State U (GA)
Coll of St. Joseph (VT)
Colorado Tech U Sioux Falls Campus (SD)
Dakota State U (SD)
Dalton State Coll (GA)
Daniel Webster Coll (NH)
DeVry U, Colorado Springs (CO)
DeVry U (NJ)
Fairmont State U (WV)
State U of NY at Farmingdale (NY)
Faulkner U (AL)
Goldey-Beacom Coll (DE)
Grantham U (LA)
Huron U USA in LondonUnited Kingdom)
Husson Coll (ME)
Indiana Inst of Technology (IN)
Johnson State Coll (VT)
Jones Coll, Jacksonville (FL)
Limestone Coll (SC)
Macon State Coll (GA)
Mansfield U of Pennsylvania (PA)
Missouri Southern State U (MO)
Morrison U (NV)
Mountain State U (WV)
Mount Olive Coll (NC)
Murray State U (KY)
National American U, Colorado Springs (CO)
National American U, Denver (CO)
National American U (NM)
National American U (SD)
National American U–Sioux Falls Branch (SD)
Newman U (KS)
Oakland City U (IN)
Oklahoma Panhandle State U (OK)
Pacific Union Coll (CA)
Penn State U Altoona Coll (PA)
Penn State U Berks Cmps of Berks-Lehigh Valley Coll (PA)
Penn State U Lehigh Valley Cmps of Berks-Lehigh Valley Coll (PA)
Penn State U Schuylkill Campus of the Capital Coll (PA)
Purdue U North Central (IN)
Richmond, The American International U in LondonUnited Kingdom)
Rivier Coll (NH)
Saint Peter's Coll (NJ)
Shepherd U (WV)
Siena Heights U (MI)
Southeastern U (DC)
Southern New Hampshire U (NH)
Southern Utah U (UT)
South U (AL)
South U (GA)

State U of NY Coll of A&T at Cobleskill (NY)
Strayer U (DC)
Trevecca Nazarene U (TN)
Tulane U (LA)
Union Coll (NE)
U of Alaska Anchorage (AK)
U of Cincinnati (OH)
U of Indianapolis (IN)
U of Minnesota, Crookston (MN)
The U of Montana–Western (MT)
U of Pittsburgh at Bradford (PA)
The U of Scranton (PA)
The U of Tampa (FL)
U of Toledo (OH)
U of Wisconsin–Green Bay (WI)
Villa Julie Coll (MD)
Washburn U (KS)
Weber State U (UT)
Youngstown State U (OH)

Information Technology
American InterContinental U–LondonUnited Kingdom)
Huron U USA in LondonUnited Kingdom)
Indiana Inst of Technology (IN)
International Acad of Merchandising & Design, Ltd (IL)
International Coll (FL)
McNeese State U (LA)
National American U, Denver (CO)
National American U–Sioux Falls Branch (SD)
Point Park U (PA)
South U (GA)
U of Massachusetts Lowell (MA)

Institutional Food Workers
Fairmont State U (WV)
Kendall Coll (IL)
Lexington Coll (IL)
State U of NY Coll of A&T at Cobleskill (NY)

Instrumentation Technology
Clayton Coll & State U (GA)
Idaho State U (ID)
McNeese State U (LA)

Insurance
Mercyhurst Coll (PA)
Thomas Edison State Coll (NJ)
Université Laval (QC, Canada)
U of Cincinnati (OH)

Interdisciplinary Studies
Bluefield State Coll (WV)
Burlington Coll (VT)
Cardinal Stritch U (WI)
Central Methodist Coll (MO)
Coll of Mount Saint Vincent (NY)
Hillsdale Free Will Baptist Coll (OK)
Kansas State U (KS)
Mountain State U (WV)
North Central U (MN)
Northwest Coll (WA)
Ohio Dominican U (OH)
Ohio U–Southern Campus (OH)
State U of NY Empire State Coll (NY)
Suffolk U (MA)
Tabor Coll (KS)
Unity Coll (ME)
The U of Akron (OH)
U of Sioux Falls (SD)
U of Wisconsin–Green Bay (WI)
Villa Julie Coll (MD)

Interior Architecture
Fashion Inst of Technology (NY)

U of New Haven (CT)
Watkins Coll of Art and Design (TN)

Interior Design
Academy of Art U (CA)
American InterContinental U (CA)
American InterContinental U, Atlanta (GA)
American InterContinental U–LondonUnited Kingdom)
The American U in DubaiUnited Arab Emirates)
The Art Inst of Portland (OR)
Baker Coll of Allen Park (MI)
Baker Coll of Auburn Hills (MI)
Baker Coll of Clinton Township (MI)
Baker Coll of Flint (MI)
Baker Coll of Muskegon (MI)
Baker Coll of Owosso (MI)
Baker Coll of Port Huron (MI)
Becker Coll (MA)
British Columbia Inst of Technology (BC, Canada)
Chaminade U of Honolulu (HI)
Coll of Mount St. Joseph (OH)
Corcoran Coll of Art and Design (DC)
Eastern Kentucky U (KY)
Fairmont State U (WV)
Harrington Coll of Design (IL)
The Illinois Inst of Art (IL)
Indiana U–Purdue U Fort Wayne (IN)
International Academy of Design & Technology (FL)
International Acad of Merchandising & Design, Ltd (IL)
Marian Coll (IN)
Miami International U of Art & Design (FL)
Newbury Coll (MA)
New York School of Interior Design (NY)
Parsons School of Design, New School U (NY)
Robert Morris Coll (IL)
Rochester Inst of Technology (NY)
Sage Coll of Albany (NY)
Southern Utah U (UT)
U of the Incarnate Word (TX)
Virginia Coll at Birmingham (AL)
Watkins Coll of Art and Design (TN)
Weber State U (UT)
Wentworth Inst of Technology (MA)

Intermedia/Multimedia
The Art Inst of Atlanta (GA)
The Art Inst of Colorado (CO)
The Art Inst of Portland (OR)
Champlain Coll (VT)
International Academy of Design & Technology (FL)
International Acad of Merchandising & Design, Ltd (IL)
New England School of Communications (ME)
New World School of the Arts (FL)
Robert Morris Coll (IL)

International Business/Trade/Commerce
The American U of RomeItaly)
British Columbia Inst of Technology (BC, Canada)
Champlain Coll (VT)
Florida Metropolitan U-Fort Lauderdale Coll (FL)
Northwood U (MI)
Northwood U, Florida Campus (FL)

Richmond, The American International U in LondonUnited Kingdom)
Saint Peter's Coll (NJ)
Schiller International U (FL)
Schiller International UFrance)
Schiller International UGermany)
Schiller International USpain)
Schiller International UUnited Kingdom)
Southern New Hampshire U (NH)
State U of NY Coll of A&T at Cobleskill (NY)
Thomas Edison State Coll (NJ)
U of Saint Francis (IN)
Webber International U (FL)

International Relations and Affairs
Richmond, The American International U in LondonUnited Kingdom)
Thomas More Coll (KY)

Italian
Immaculata U (PA)

Italian Studies
John Cabot Ultaly)

Japanese
Winona State U (MN)

Jazz/Jazz Studies
Five Towns Coll (NY)
Indiana U South Bend (IN)
Southern U and A&M Coll (LA)
Université Laval (QC, Canada)

Journalism
Bacone Coll (OK)
Ball State U (IN)
Bethel Coll (IN)
Central Christian Coll of Kansas (KS)
Clayton Coll & State U (GA)
Creighton U (NE)
Dalton State Coll (GA)
Evangel U (MO)
Indiana U Southeast (IN)
John Brown U (AR)
Macon State Coll (GA)
Madonna U (MI)
Manchester Coll (IN)
North Central U (MN)
Villa Julie Coll (MD)

Juvenile Corrections
U of New Haven (CT)

Kindergarten/Preschool Education
Atlantic Union Coll (MA)
Baker Coll of Clinton Township (MI)
Baker Coll of Muskegon (MI)
Baker Coll of Owosso (MI)
Becker Coll (MA)
Bethel Coll (IN)
California U of Pennsylvania (PA)
Central Christian Coll of Kansas (KS)
Champlain Coll (VT)
Clayton Coll & State U (GA)
Coll of Mount St. Joseph (OH)
Crown Coll (MN)
Eastern Nazarene Coll (MA)
Edinboro U of Pennsylvania (PA)
Indiana U–Purdue U Indianapolis (IN)
Indiana U South Bend (IN)
Johnson Bible Coll (TN)
Kansas Wesleyan U (KS)
Keene State Coll (NH)
Kendall Coll (IL)
Lake Superior State U (MI)
Lourdes Coll (OH)
Lynn U (FL)
Manchester Coll (IN)

Marian Coll (IN)
Marygrove Coll (MI)
McNeese State U (LA)
Mitchell Coll (CT)
Mount Aloysius Coll (PA)
Mount Ida Coll (MA)
Mount St. Mary's Coll (CA)
Nova Southeastern U (FL)
Ohio U–Southern Campus (OH)
Pacific Union Coll (CA)
Purdue U Calumet (IN)
Rivier Coll (NH)
Rust Coll (MS)
State U of NY Coll of A&T at Cobleskill (NY)
Taylor U (IN)
Tennessee State U (TN)
Tougaloo Coll (MS)
U of Alaska Fairbanks (AK)
U of Alaska Southeast (AK)
U of Arkansas at Pine Bluff (AR)
U of Great Falls (MT)
The U of Montana–Western (MT)
U of Rio Grande (OH)
U of Sioux Falls (SD)
Villa Julie Coll (MD)
Washburn U (KS)
Western Kentucky U (KY)
William Tyndale Coll (MI)
Wilmington Coll (DE)

Kinesiology and Exercise Science
Atlantic Union Coll (MA)
Manchester Coll (IN)
Thomas More Coll (KY)

Labor and Industrial Relations
Indiana U Bloomington (IN)
Indiana U Kokomo (IN)
Indiana U Northwest (IN)
Indiana U–Purdue U Indianapolis (IN)
Indiana U South Bend (IN)
Indiana U Southeast (IN)
Providence Coll (RI)
State U of NY Empire State Coll (NY)
Université Laval (QC, Canada)
The U of Akron (OH)
Youngstown State U (OH)

Labor Studies
Indiana U–Purdue U Fort Wayne (IN)

Landscape Architecture
Eastern Kentucky U (KY)
State U of NY Coll of A&T at Cobleskill (NY)
U of Arkansas at Little Rock (AR)
U of New Hampshire (NH)

Landscaping and Groundskeeping
State U of NY at Farmingdale (NY)
North Carolina State U (NC)
State U of NY Coll of A&T at Cobleskill (NY)
U of Massachusetts Amherst (MA)
U of New Hampshire (NH)
Vermont Tech Coll (VT)

Laser and Optical Technology
Capitol Coll (MD)
Excelsior Coll (NY)
Idaho State U (ID)
Indiana U Bloomington (IN)
Pacific Union Coll (CA)

Latin
Idaho State U (ID)

Latin American Studies
U Coll of the Fraser Valley (BC, Canada)

Legal Administrative Assistant/Secretary
Baker Coll of Auburn Hills (MI)
Baker Coll of Clinton Township (MI)
Baker Coll of Flint (MI)
Baker Coll of Jackson (MI)
Baker Coll of Muskegon (MI)
Baker Coll of Owosso (MI)
Baker Coll of Port Huron (MI)
Ball State U (IN)
Clarion U of Pennsylvania (PA)
Clayton Coll & State U (GA)
Davenport U, Dearborn (MI)
Davenport U, Kalamazoo (MI)
Dordt Coll (IA)
Ferris State U (MI)
Johnson & Wales U (RI)
Lamar U (TX)
Lewis-Clark State Coll (ID)
Montana State U–Billings (MT)
Montana Tech of The U of Montana (MT)
Morrison U (NV)
Mountain State U (WV)
Northern Michigan U (MI)
Pacific Union Coll (CA)
Peirce Coll (PA)
Robert Morris Coll (IL)
Shawnee State U (OH)
Southern Alberta Inst of Technology (AB, Canada)
Sullivan U (KY)
Thomas Coll (ME)
The U of Akron (OH)
U of Cincinnati (OH)
U of Detroit Mercy (MI)
The U of Montana–Missoula (MT)
U of Richmond (VA)
U of Rio Grande (OH)
U of the District of Columbia (DC)
U of Toledo (OH)
Washburn U (KS)
West Virginia U Inst of Technology (WV)
Wright State U (OH)
Youngstown State U (OH)

Legal Assistant/Paralegal
Anna Maria Coll (MA)
Atlantic Union Coll (MA)
Ball State U (IN)
Becker Coll (MA)
Bluefield State Coll (WV)
Boise State U (ID)
Briarcliffe Coll (NY)
Burlington Coll (VT)
Champlain Coll (VT)
Clayton Coll & State U (GA)
Coll of Mount St. Joseph (OH)
Coll of Saint Mary (NE)
Davenport U, Grand Rapids (MI)
Davenport U, Kalamazoo (MI)
Eastern Kentucky U (KY)
Faulkner U (AL)
Ferris State U (MI)
Florida Metropolitan U–Tampa Coll, Brandon (FL)
Florida Metropolitan U-Fort Lauderdale Coll (FL)
Florida Metropolitan U–Tampa Coll, Lakeland (FL)
Florida Metropolitan U–Tampa Coll (FL)
Gannon U (PA)
Grambling State U (LA)
Hilbert Coll (NY)
Husson Coll (ME)
Indiana U South Bend (IN)
International Coll (FL)
Johnson & Wales U (RI)
Jones Coll, Jacksonville (FL)
Jones Coll, Miami (FL)
Kent State U (OH)

Lake Superior State U (MI)
Lewis-Clark State Coll (ID)
Madonna U (MI)
Marywood U (PA)
McNeese State U (LA)
Merrimack Coll (MA)
Metropolitan Coll, Tulsa (OK)
Missouri Western State Coll (MO)
Morrison U (NV)
Mountain State U (WV)
Mount Aloysius Coll (PA)
National American U (SD)
National American U–Sioux Falls Branch (SD)
Newbury Coll (MA)
Nicholls State U (LA)
Ohio U–Chillicothe (OH)
Peirce Coll (PA)
Robert Morris Coll (IL)
Sage Coll of Albany (NY)
St. John's U (NY)
Saint Mary-of-the-Woods Coll (IN)
Shawnee State U (OH)
Shepherd U (WV)
South U (AL)
South U (GA)
Suffolk U (MA)
Sullivan U (KY)
Teikyo Post U (CT)
Thomas Coll (ME)
Thomas Edison State Coll (NJ)
Tulane U (LA)
The U of Akron (OH)
U of Alaska Anchorage (AK)
U of Alaska Fairbanks (AK)
U of Alaska Southeast (AK)
U of Arkansas at Fort Smith (AR)
U of Cincinnati (OH)
U of Great Falls (MT)
U of Hartford (CT)
U of Indianapolis (IN)
U of Louisville (KY)
The U of Montana–Missoula (MT)
U of Toledo (OH)
U of West Florida (FL)
Villa Julie Coll (MD)
Virginia Coll at Birmingham (AL)
Washburn U (KS)
Wesley Coll (DE)
Western Kentucky U (KY)
Wichita State U (KS)
Widener U (PA)
William Woods U (MO)

Legal Professions and Studies Related
Peirce Coll (PA)

Legal Studies
Becker Coll (MA)
Central Christian Coll of Kansas (KS)
Central Christian Coll of Kansas (KS)
Clayton Coll & State U (GA)
Hilbert Coll (NY)
Lake Superior State U (MI)
Mountain State U (WV)
Ohio Dominican U (OH)
Sage Coll of Albany (NY)
Southeastern U (DC)
U of Detroit Mercy (MI)
The U of Montana–Missoula (MT)
U of New Haven (CT)

Legal Support Services Related
Central Missouri State U (MO)

Liberal Arts and Sciences And Humanities Related
Beacon Coll (FL)
Huron U USA in LondonUnited Kingdom)
Troy State U Dothan (AL)
Troy State U Montgomery (AL)

The U of Akron (OH)
U of Hartford (CT)

Liberal Arts and Sciences/ Liberal Studies
Adams State Coll (CO)
Adelphi U (NY)
Alabama State U (AL)
Albertus Magnus Coll (CT)
Alderson-Broaddus Coll (WV)
Alvernia Coll (PA)
Alverno Coll (WI)
American International Coll (MA)
American U of Puerto Rico (PR)
The American U of RomeItaly)
Anderson Coll (SC)
Andrews U (MI)
Aquinas Coll (MI)
Armstrong Atlantic State U (GA)
Ashland U (OH)
Augusta State U (GA)
Averett U (VA)
Bacone Coll (OK)
Ball State U (IN)
Beacon Coll (FL)
Becker Coll (MA)
Bemidji State U (MN)
Bethany Lutheran Coll (MN)
Bethel Coll (IN)
Bethel U (MN)
Bluefield State Coll (WV)
Brescia U (KY)
Briar Cliff U (IA)
Bryan Coll (TN)
Bryn Athyn Coll of the New Church (PA)
Burlington Coll (VT)
Butler U (IN)
Calumet Coll of Saint Joseph (IN)
Campbell U (NC)
Cardinal Stritch U (WI)
Cazenovia Coll (NY)
Centenary Coll (NJ)
Champlain Coll (VT)
Charleston Southern U (SC)
Charter Oak State Coll (CT)
Chester Coll of New England (NH)
Christendom Coll (VA)
Clarion U of Pennsylvania (PA)
Clarke Coll (IA)
Colby-Sawyer Coll (NH)
Coll for Lifelong Learning (NH)
Coll of St. Catherine (MN)
Coll of St. Catherine–Minneapolis (MN)
Coll of St. Joseph (VT)
Coll of Staten Island of the City U of NY (NY)
Colorado Christian U (CO)
Columbia Coll (MO)
Columbus State U (GA)
Concordia Coll (NY)
Concordia U (OR)
Concordia U at Austin (TX)
Crossroads Coll (MN)
Crown Coll (MN)
Cumberland U (TN)
Dakota State U (SD)
Dakota Wesleyan U (SD)
Dallas Baptist U (TX)
Daniel Webster Coll (NH)
Dickinson State U (ND)
Dominican Coll (NY)
Eastern Connecticut State U (CT)
Eastern U (PA)
East Texas Baptist U (TX)
Edgewood Coll (WI)
Edinboro U of Pennsylvania (PA)
Emmanuel Coll (GA)
Endicott Coll (MA)
Excelsior Coll (NY)
Fairleigh Dickinson U, Teaneck-Metro Campus (NJ)

Fairmont State U (WV)
State U of NY at Farmingdale (NY)
Faulkner U (AL)
Felician Coll (NJ)
Ferris State U (MI)
Five Towns Coll (NY)
Florida A&M U (FL)
Florida Atlantic U (FL)
Florida Coll (FL)
Florida State U (FL)
The Franciscan U (IA)
Franklin Coll SwitzerlandSwitzerland)
Fresno Pacific U (CA)
Gannon U (PA)
Glenville State Coll (WV)
Grace Bible Coll (MI)
Grace U (NE)
Grand View Coll (IA)
Gwynedd-Mercy Coll (PA)
Haskell Indian Nations U (KS)
Hilbert Coll (NY)
Hillsdale Free Will Baptist Coll (OK)
Huron U USA in LondonUnited Kingdom)
Immaculata U (PA)
Indiana State U (IN)
International Coll of the Cayman IslandsCayman Islands)
John Brown U (AR)
Johnson State Coll (VT)
John Wesley Coll (NC)
Keene State Coll (NH)
Kent State U (OH)
Kentucky State U (KY)
LaGrange Coll (GA)
Lake Superior State U (MI)
La Salle U (PA)
Lebanon Valley Coll (PA)
Lewis-Clark State Coll (ID)
Limestone Coll (SC)
Long Island U, Brooklyn Campus (NY)
Loras Coll (IA)
Lourdes Coll (OH)
Lyndon State Coll (VT)
Macon State Coll (GA)
Marian Coll (IN)
Marietta Coll (OH)
Marygrove Coll (MI)
Marymount Coll of Fordham U (NY)
Marymount U (VA)
Medaille Coll (NY)
Medgar Evers Coll of the City U of NY (NY)
Mercy Coll (NY)
Mercyhurst Coll (PA)
Merrimack Coll (MA)
Methodist Coll (NC)
MidAmerica Nazarene U (KS)
Millersville U of Pennsylvania (PA)
Minnesota State U Mankato (MN)
Minnesota State U Moorhead (MN)
Missouri Valley Coll (MO)
Mitchell Coll (CT)
Molloy Coll (NY)
Montana State U–Billings (MT)
Montana Tech of The U of Montana (MT)
Mountain State U (WV)
Mount Aloysius Coll (PA)
Mount Marty Coll (SD)
Mount Olive Coll (NC)
Mount St. Mary's Coll (CA)
Murray State U (KY)
National American U (SD)
National U (CA)
Neumann Coll (PA)
Newman U (KS)
New Mexico Inst of Mining and Technology (NM)
New York U (NY)
Niagara U (NY)
North Central U (MN)

Northern Michigan U (MI)
Northern State U (SD)
North Greenville Coll (SC)
Northwest Coll (WA)
Northwestern Coll (MN)
Nyack Coll (NY)
Oak Hills Christian Coll (MN)
Oakland City U (IN)
The Ohio State U at Lima (OH)
The Ohio State U at Marion (OH)
The Ohio State U–Mansfield Campus (OH)
The Ohio State U–Newark Campus (OH)
Ohio U (OH)
Ohio U–Chillicothe (OH)
Ohio U–Southern Campus (OH)
Ohio U–Zanesville (OH)
Ohio Valley Coll (WV)
Okanagan U Coll (BC, Canada)
Oregon Inst of Technology (OR)
Pace U (NY)
Pacific Union Coll (CA)
Park U (MO)
Paul Smith's Coll of Arts and Sciences (NY)
Peace Coll (NC)
Penn State U Abington Coll (PA)
Penn State U Altoona Coll (PA)
Penn State U at Erie, The Behrend Coll (PA)
Penn State U Berks Cmps of Berks-Lehigh Valley Coll (PA)
Penn State U Harrisburg Campus of the Capital Coll (PA)
Penn State U Lehigh Valley Cmps of Berks-Lehigh Valley Coll (PA)
Penn State U Schuylkill Campus of the Capital Coll (PA)
Penn State U Univ Park Campus (PA)
Pine Manor Coll (MA)
Presentation Coll (SD)
Providence Coll (RI)
Reformed Bible Coll (MI)
Reinhardt Coll (GA)
Richmond, The American International U in LondonUnited Kingdom)
Rivier Coll (NH)
Rochester Coll (MI)
Rocky Mountain Coll (MT)
Roger Williams U (RI)
Sacred Heart U (CT)
Sage Coll of Albany (NY)
St. Augustine Coll (IL)
St. Cloud State U (MN)
St. Francis Coll (NY)
St. Gregory's U (OK)
St. John's U (NY)
Saint Joseph's U (PA)
Saint Leo U (FL)
St. Louis Christian Coll (MO)
Saint Mary-of-the-Woods Coll (IN)
Salve Regina U (RI)
Schiller International U (FL)
Schiller International UFrance)
Schiller International UGermany)
Schiller International USpain)
Schiller International UUnited Kingdom)
Schiller International U, American Coll of SwitzerlandSwitzerland)
Schreiner U (TX)
Simon's Rock Coll of Bard (MA)
Southern Connecticut State U (CT)

Southern New Hampshire U (NH)
Southern Polytechnic State U (GA)
Southern Vermont Coll (VT)
Spring Arbor U (MI)
State U of NY Coll of A&T at Cobleskill (NY)
Stephens Coll (MO)
Sterling Coll (VT)
Strayer U (DC)
Taylor U Fort Wayne (IN)
Teikyo Post U (CT)
Thiel Coll (PA)
Thomas Edison State Coll (NJ)
Thomas More Coll (KY)
Thomas U (GA)
Trinity Bible Coll (ND)
Tri-State U (IN)
The U of Akron (OH)
U of Alaska Fairbanks (AK)
U of Alaska Southeast (AK)
U of Arkansas at Fort Smith (AR)
U of Arkansas at Monticello (AR)
U of Bridgeport (CT)
U of Central Florida (FL)
U of Cincinnati (OH)
U of Delaware (DE)
U of Hartford (CT)
U of Indianapolis (IN)
U of La Verne (CA)
The U of Maine at Augusta (ME)
U of Maine at Fort Kent (ME)
U of Maine at Presque Isle (ME)
U of New Hampshire (NH)
U of New Hampshire at Manchester (NH)
U of Saint Francis (IN)
U of Saint Mary (KS)
U of South Florida (FL)
U of Toledo (OH)
U of Wisconsin–Eau Claire (WI)
U of Wisconsin–La Crosse (WI)
U of Wisconsin–Oshkosh (WI)
U of Wisconsin–Platteville (WI)
U of Wisconsin–Stevens Point (WI)
U of Wisconsin–Superior (WI)
U of Wisconsin–Whitewater (WI)
Upper Iowa U (IA)
Urbana U (OH)
Valdosta State U (GA)
Villa Julie Coll (MD)
Villanova U (PA)
Virginia Intermont Coll (VA)
Walsh U (OH)
Washburn U (KS)
Waynesburg Coll (PA)
Weber State U (UT)
Wesley Coll (DE)
Western Connecticut State U (CT)
Western New England Coll (MA)
Western Oregon U (OR)
West Virginia State Coll (WV)
West Virginia U Inst of Technology (WV)
Wichita State U (KS)
Williams Baptist Coll (AR)
William Tyndale Coll (MI)
Wilson Coll (PA)
Winona State U (MN)
Xavier U (OH)
York Coll (NE)
York Coll of Pennsylvania (PA)

Library Assistant
Ohio Dominican U (OH)
Southern Alberta Inst of Technology (AB, Canada)
The U of Maine at Augusta (ME)

Library Science
U of the District of Columbia (DC)

Literature
Manchester Coll (IN)
North Central U (MN)
Sacred Heart U (CT)
Université Laval (QC, Canada)

Livestock Management
Sterling Coll (VT)

Logistics and Materials Management
Park U (MO)
The U of Akron (OH)
U of Toledo (OH)

Machine Shop Technology
Dalton State Coll (GA)
Georgia Southwestern State U (GA)
Valdosta State U (GA)

Machine Tool Technology
Boise State U (ID)
British Columbia Inst of Technology (BC, Canada)
Fashion Inst of Technology (NY)
Ferris State U (MI)
Georgia Southwestern State U (GA)
Idaho State U (ID)
Lake Superior State U (MI)
Lamar U (TX)
Missouri Southern State U (MO)
Weber State U (UT)

Management Information Systems
Arkansas State U (AR)
Cameron U (OK)
Coll of Saint Mary (NE)
Colorado Christian U (CO)
Colorado Tech U Sioux Falls Campus (SD)
Columbia Coll, Caguas (PR)
Daniel Webster Coll (NH)
Davenport U, Dearborn (MI)
Davenport U, Warren (MI)
Florida Metropolitan U-Fort Lauderdale Coll (FL)
Globe Inst of Technology (NY)
Hilbert Coll (NY)
Husson Coll (ME)
Inter American U of PR, Bayamón Campus (PR)
Johnson State Coll (VT)
Lake Superior State U (MI)
Lindsey Wilson Coll (KY)
Lock Haven U of Pennsylvania (PA)
Morehead State U (KY)
National American U (NM)
National American U–Sioux Falls Branch (SD)
Northern Michigan U (MI)
Northwood U (MI)
Northwood U, Texas Campus (TX)
Peirce Coll (PA)
Robert Morris Coll (IL)
St. Augustine Coll (IL)
Saint Joseph's Coll (IN)
Saint Joseph's U (PA)
Shawnee State U (OH)
Southeastern U (DC)
Southern Alberta Inst of Technology (AB, Canada)
Taylor U (IN)
Thiel Coll (PA)
The U of Akron (OH)
U of Management and Technology (VA)
U of Wisconsin–Green Bay (WI)
Weber State U (UT)
Wilson Coll (PA)
Wright State U (OH)

Management Information Systems and Services Related
Coll of Mount St. Joseph (OH)
Davis & Elkins Coll (WV)
Purdue U (IN)
U of Southern Indiana (IN)

Management Science
British Columbia Inst of Technology (BC, Canada)

Manufacturing Technology
Kent State U (OH)
Lawrence Technological U (MI)
Lewis-Clark State Coll (ID)
Missouri Western State Coll (MO)
Penn State U at Erie, The Behrend Coll (PA)
U Coll of the Cariboo (BC, Canada)

Marine Biology and Biological Oceanography
Mitchell Coll (CT)

Marine Science/Merchant Marine Officer
State U of NY Maritime Coll (NY)
U of the District of Columbia (DC)

Marine Technology
Thomas Edison State Coll (NJ)
U of Alaska Southeast (AK)

Maritime Science
Maine Maritime Academy (ME)

Marketing/Marketing Management
Baker Coll of Allen Park (MI)
Baker Coll of Auburn Hills (MI)
Baker Coll of Cadillac (MI)
Baker Coll of Clinton Township (MI)
Baker Coll of Flint (MI)
Baker Coll of Jackson (MI)
Baker Coll of Muskegon (MI)
Baker Coll of Owosso (MI)
Baker Coll of Port Huron (MI)
Ball State U (IN)
Bluefield State Coll (WV)
Boise State U (ID)
British Columbia Inst of Technology (BC, Canada)
Central Christian Coll of Kansas (KS)
Champlain Coll (VT)
Chestnut Hill Coll (PA)
Clayton Coll & State U (GA)
Dalton State Coll (GA)
Daniel Webster Coll (NH)
Davenport U, Dearborn (MI)
Davenport U, Grand Rapids (MI)
Davenport U, Kalamazoo (MI)
Davenport U, Lansing (MI)
Davenport U, Warren (MI)
Five Towns Coll (NY)
Florida Metropolitan U-Tampa Coll, Brandon (FL)
Florida Metropolitan U-Fort Lauderdale Coll (FL)
Florida Metropolitan U-Tampa Coll, Lakeland (FL)
Florida Metropolitan U-Tampa Coll (FL)
Hawai'i Pacific U (HI)
Idaho State U (ID)
Inter American U of PR, Fajardo Campus (PR)
Johnson & Wales U (CO)
Johnson & Wales U (FL)
Johnson & Wales U (RI)
King's Coll (PA)
Newbury Coll (MA)

New England School of Communications (ME)
Peirce Coll (PA)
Purdue U North Central (IN)
Sage Coll of Albany (NY)
Saint Joseph's U (PA)
Saint Peter's Coll (NJ)
Siena Heights U (MI)
Southeastern U (DC)
Southern New Hampshire U (NH)
Strayer U (DC)
Sullivan U (KY)
Teikyo Post U (CT)
Thomas Edison State Coll (NJ)
Tulane U (LA)
U of Bridgeport (CT)
U of Cincinnati (OH)
U of Management and Technology (VA)
U of Sioux Falls (SD)
U of the District of Columbia (DC)
Urbana U (OH)
Walsh U (OH)
Webber International U (FL)
Weber State U (UT)
West Virginia State Coll (WV)
Wilson Coll (PA)
Wright State U (OH)
Youngstown State U (OH)

Marketing Related
Southern Alberta Inst of Technology (AB, Canada)

Marriage and Family Therapy/Counseling
Central Christian Coll of Kansas (KS)

Masonry
Valdosta State U (GA)

Massage Therapy
National American U–Sioux Falls Branch (SD)
Virginia Coll at Birmingham (AL)

Mass Communication/Media
Adrian Coll (MI)
Bacone Coll (OK)
Becker Coll (MA)
Black Hills State U (SD)
Central Christian Coll of Kansas (KS)
Champlain Coll (VT)
Clayton Coll & State U (GA)
Cornerstone U (MI)
Evangel U (MO)
Five Towns Coll (NY)
Fresno Pacific U (CA)
Inter American U of PR, Bayamón Campus (PR)
Macon State Coll (GA)
Madonna U (MI)
Methodist Coll (NC)
Newbury Coll (MA)
North Central U (MN)
Reinhardt Coll (GA)
Richmond, The American International U in LondonUnited Kingdom)
Sacred Heart U (CT)
U Coll of the Fraser Valley (BC, Canada)
U of Dubuque (IA)
U of Rio Grande (OH)
Villa Julie Coll (MD)
Wilson Coll (PA)

Materials Science
U of New Hampshire (NH)

Mathematics
Bacone Coll (OK)
Central Baptist Coll (AR)
Central Christian Coll of Kansas (KS)
Clayton Coll & State U (GA)
Creighton U (NE)
Dalton State Coll (GA)
Felician Coll (NJ)
Fresno Pacific U (CA)

Hillsdale Free Will Baptist Coll (OK)
Huron U USA in LondonUnited Kingdom)
Idaho State U (ID)
Indiana U East (IN)
Indiana U–Purdue U Fort Wayne (IN)
Lindsey Wilson Coll (KY)
Macon State Coll (GA)
Methodist Coll (NC)
Richmond, The American International U in LondonUnited Kingdom)
Sacred Heart U (CT)
State U of NY Empire State Coll (NY)
Thomas Edison State Coll (NJ)
Thomas More Coll (KY)
Thomas U (GA)
Tri-State U (IN)
U of Great Falls (MT)
U of Rio Grande (OH)
The U of Tampa (FL)
U of Wisconsin–Green Bay (WI)
York Coll of Pennsylvania (PA)

Mathematics Teacher Education
Central Christian Coll of Kansas (KS)

Mechanical Design Technology
Clayton Coll & State U (GA)
Ferris State U (MI)
Lincoln U (MO)

Mechanical Drafting
Cameron U (OK)

Mechanical Drafting and Cad/Cadd
Baker Coll of Flint (MI)
British Columbia Inst of Technology (BC, Canada)
Indiana U–Purdue U Indianapolis (IN)
Montana Tech of The U of Montana (MT)
Purdue U (IN)

Mechanical Engineering
Fairfield U (CT)
Macon State Coll (GA)
U of New Haven (CT)

Mechanical Engineering/ Mechanical Technology
Andrews U (MI)
Baker Coll of Flint (MI)
Bluefield State Coll (WV)
British Columbia Inst of Technology (BC, Canada)
Excelsior Coll (NY)
Fairmont State U (WV)
State U of NY at Farmingdale (NY)
Ferris State U (MI)
Indiana U–Purdue U Fort Wayne (IN)
Indiana U–Purdue U Indianapolis (IN)
Johnson & Wales U (RI)
Kansas State U (KS)
Kent State U (OH)
Lake Superior State U (MI)
Lawrence Technological U (MI)
Michigan Technological U (MI)
Murray State U (KY)
New York Inst of Technology (NY)
Penn State U Altoona Coll (PA)
Penn State U at Erie, The Behrend Coll (PA)
Penn State U Berks Cmps of Berks-Lehigh Valley Coll (PA)
Point Park U (PA)
Purdue U Calumet (IN)
Purdue U North Central (IN)

Rochester Inst of Technology (NY)
Southern Alberta Inst of Technology (AB, Canada)
Thomas Edison State Coll (NJ)
The U of Akron (OH)
U of Arkansas at Little Rock (AR)
U of Cincinnati (OH)
U of Massachusetts Lowell (MA)
U of New Haven (CT)
U of Rio Grande (OH)
U of the District of Columbia (DC)
U of Toledo (OH)
Vermont Tech Coll (VT)
Weber State U (UT)
Wentworth Inst of Technology (MA)
West Virginia U Inst of Technology (WV)
Youngstown State U (OH)

Mechanical Engineering Technologies Related
Purdue U (IN)

Mechanics and Repair
Idaho State U (ID)
Lewis-Clark State Coll (ID)

Medical Administrative Assistant and Medical Secretary
Baker Coll of Auburn Hills (MI)
Baker Coll of Cadillac (MI)
Baker Coll of Clinton Township (MI)
Baker Coll of Flint (MI)
Baker Coll of Jackson (MI)
Baker Coll of Muskegon (MI)
Baker Coll of Owosso (MI)
Baker Coll of Port Huron (MI)
Boise State U (ID)
British Columbia Inst of Technology (BC, Canada)
Davenport U, Dearborn (MI)
Davenport U, Lansing (MI)
Davenport U, Lapeer (MI)
Davenport U, Warren (MI)
Dickinson State U (ND)
Hannibal-LaGrange Coll (MO)
Lamar U (TX)
Montana State U–Billings (MT)
Montana Tech of The U of Montana (MT)
Morrison U (NV)
Northern Michigan U (MI)
Pacific Union Coll (CA)
Sullivan U (KY)
Thomas Coll (ME)
Universidad Adventista de las Antillas (PR)
The U of Akron (OH)
U of Cincinnati (OH)
The U of Montana–Missoula (MT)
U of Rio Grande (OH)
Washburn U (KS)
West Virginia U Inst of Technology (WV)
Wright State U (OH)
Youngstown State U (OH)

Medical/Clinical Assistant
Argosy U/Twin Cities, Eagan (MN)
Arkansas Tech U (AR)
Baker Coll of Allen Park (MI)
Baker Coll of Auburn Hills (MI)
Baker Coll of Cadillac (MI)
Baker Coll of Clinton Township (MI)
Baker Coll of Flint (MI)
Baker Coll of Jackson (MI)
Baker Coll of Muskegon (MI)
Baker Coll of Owosso (MI)
Baker Coll of Port Huron (MI)
Bluefield State Coll (WV)
Clayton Coll & State U (GA)

Colorado Tech U Sioux Falls Campus (SD)
Davenport U, Lansing (MI)
Eastern Kentucky U (KY)
Faulkner U (AL)
Florida Metropolitan U-Tampa Coll, Brandon (FL)
Florida Metropolitan U-Tampa Coll (FL)
Georgia Southwestern State U (GA)
Idaho State U (ID)
International Coll (FL)
Jones Coll, Jacksonville (FL)
Montana State U–Billings (MT)
Mountain State U (WV)
Mount Aloysius Coll (PA)
National American U, Colorado Springs (CO)
National American U, Denver (CO)
National American U–Sioux Falls Branch (SD)
Ohio U (OH)
Palmer Coll of Chiropractic (IA)
Presentation Coll (SD)
Robert Morris Coll (IL)
South U (AL)
South U (GA)
The U of Akron (OH)
U of Alaska Anchorage (AK)
U of Alaska Fairbanks (AK)
U of Toledo (OH)
Valdosta State U (GA)
Virginia Coll at Birmingham (AL)
West Virginia State Coll (WV)
Youngstown State U (OH)

Medical/Health Management and Clinical Assistant
Lewis-Clark State Coll (ID)
National American U, Denver (CO)

Medical Illustration
Clayton Coll & State U (GA)

Medical Insurance Coding
Baker Coll of Allen Park (MI)
Davenport U, Dearborn (MI)
Davenport U, Holland (MI)
Davenport U, Kalamazoo (MI)
Davenport U, Lansing (MI)
Davenport U, Lapeer (MI)
Davenport U, Warren (MI)
Virginia Coll at Birmingham (AL)

Medical Insurance/Medical Billing
Baker Coll of Allen Park (MI)
Davenport U, Dearborn (MI)
Davenport U, Holland (MI)
Davenport U, Kalamazoo (MI)
Davenport U, Lansing (MI)
Davenport U, Warren (MI)
Virginia Coll at Birmingham (AL)

Medical Laboratory Technology
Argosy U/Twin Cities, Eagan (MN)
British Columbia Inst of Technology (BC, Canada)
Evangel U (MO)
Villa Julie Coll (MD)

Medical Office Assistant
Lewis-Clark State Coll (ID)
Mercy Coll of Health Sciences (IA)
Virginia Coll at Birmingham (AL)

Medical Office Computer Specialist
Baker Coll of Allen Park (MI)
Virginia Coll at Birmingham (AL)

Medical Office Management
Dalton State Coll (GA)
DeVry U, Westminster (CO)
National American U,
Colorado Springs (CO)
The U of Akron (OH)
Youngstown State U (OH)

Medical Radiologic Technology
Argosy U/Twin Cities, Eagan (MN)
Arkansas State U (AR)
Bacone Coll (OK)
Bluefield State Coll (WV)
British Columbia Inst of Technology (BC, Canada)
Coll of St. Catherine (MN)
Coll of St. Catherine–Minneapolis (MN)
Fairleigh Dickinson U, Florham (NJ)
Fairleigh Dickinson U, Teaneck-Metro Campus (NJ)
Gannon U (PA)
Idaho State U (ID)
Indiana U Northwest (IN)
Indiana U–Purdue U Indianapolis (IN)
Indiana U South Bend (IN)
Kent State U (OH)
La Roche Coll (PA)
Loma Linda U (CA)
Mercy Coll of Health Sciences (IA)
Missouri Southern State U (MO)
Morehead State U (KY)
Northern Kentucky U (KY)
Penn State U Schuylkill Campus of the Capital Coll (PA)
Presentation Coll (SD)
Saint Joseph's Coll of Maine (ME)
Shawnee State U (OH)
Southern Adventist U (TN)
Southern Alberta Inst of Technology (AB, Canada)
Thomas Edison State Coll (NJ)
Trinity Coll of Nursing and Health Sciences (IL)
The U of Akron (OH)
U of Arkansas at Fort Smith (AR)
U of New Mexico (NM)
U of Saint Francis (IN)
U of Southern Indiana (IN)
Valdosta State U (GA)
Weber State U (UT)

Medical Transcription
Baker Coll of Flint (MI)
Baker Coll of Jackson (MI)
Dalton State Coll (GA)
Davenport U, Holland (MI)
Davenport U, Lansing (MI)
DeVry U, Westminster (CO)

Mental and Social Health Services And Allied Professions Related
U of Alaska Fairbanks (AK)
The U of Maine at Augusta (ME)

Mental Health/Rehabilitation
Evangel U (MO)
Felician Coll (NJ)
Lake Superior State U (MI)
St. Augustine Coll (IL)
U of Toledo (OH)
Washburn U (KS)

Merchandising
Clayton Coll & State U (GA)
The U of Akron (OH)

Merchandising, Sales, and Marketing Operations Related (General)
Clayton Coll & State U (GA)

Merchandising, Sales, and Marketing Operations Related (Specialized)
Central Missouri State U (MO)
Clayton Coll & State U (GA)

Metal and Jewelry Arts
Academy of Art U (CA)
Rochester Inst of Technology (NY)

Metallurgical Technology
Penn State U Altoona Coll (PA)
Penn State U at Erie, The Behrend Coll (PA)
Penn State U Berks Cmps of Berks-Lehigh Valley Coll (PA)
Penn State U Schuylkill Campus of the Capital Coll (PA)
Purdue U Calumet (IN)

Microbiology
Canadian Mennonite U (MB, Canada)
Inter Amer U of PR, Barranquitas Campus (PR)

Middle School Education
Central Christian Coll of Kansas (KS)
Dalton State Coll (GA)
U of Arkansas at Fort Smith (AR)

Military Studies
Hawai'i Pacific U (HI)

Mining Technology
British Columbia Inst of Technology (BC, Canada)

Missionary Studies and Missiology
Central Christian Coll of Kansas (KS)
Faith Baptist Bible Coll and Theological Seminary (IA)
God's Bible School and Coll (OH)
Hillsdale Free Will Baptist Coll (OK)
Manhattan Christian Coll (KS)
North Central U (MN)
Prairie Bible Coll (AB, Canada)

Modern Greek
North Central U (MN)

Modern Languages
Macon State Coll (GA)
North Central U (MN)
Sacred Heart U (CT)
York Coll of Pennsylvania (PA)

Molecular Biochemistry
Sacred Heart U (CT)

Multi-/Interdisciplinary Studies Related
International Coll (FL)
Mountain State U (WV)
Ohio U (OH)
Shepherd U (WV)
Sterling Coll (VT)
The U of Akron (OH)
U of Alaska Fairbanks (AK)
U of Arkansas at Fort Smith (AR)
U of Toledo (OH)

Music
Bethel Coll (IN)
Brigham Young U–Hawaii (HI)
Central Baptist Coll (AR)
Central Christian Coll of Kansas (KS)
Chowan Coll (NC)
Clayton Coll & State U (GA)
Crown Coll (MN)
Dallas Baptist U (TX)
Emmanuel Coll (GA)
Five Towns Coll (NY)
Fresno Pacific U (CA)
Grace Bible Coll (MI)
Grace U (NE)
Hillsdale Free Will Baptist Coll (OK)
John Brown U (AR)
Kwantlen U Coll (BC, Canada)
Lourdes Coll (OH)
Macon State Coll (GA)
Marian Coll (IN)
Methodist Coll (NC)
Mount Olive Coll (NC)
Mount Vernon Nazarene U (OH)
Musicians Inst (CA)
North Central U (MN)
Peace Coll (NC)
Reinhardt Coll (GA)
Sacred Heart U (CT)
Shawnee State U (OH)
Thomas More Coll (KY)
Trinity Bible Coll (ND)
The U of Maine at Augusta (ME)
U of Rio Grande (OH)
The U of Tampa (FL)
U of the District of Columbia (DC)
Williams Baptist Coll (AR)
York Coll of Pennsylvania (PA)

Musical Instrument Fabrication and Repair
Indiana U Bloomington (IN)

Music History, Literature, and Theory
Central Christian Coll of Kansas (KS)

Music Management and Merchandising
Central Christian Coll of Kansas (KS)
Chowan Coll (NC)
Five Towns Coll (NY)
The New England Inst of Art (MA)

Music Performance
Central Christian Coll of Kansas (KS)
New World School of the Arts (FL)

Music Related
Alverno Coll (WI)

Music Teacher Education
Central Christian Coll of Kansas (KS)
Union Coll (NE)

Music Theory and Composition
Central Christian Coll of Kansas (KS)
Kwantlen U Coll (BC, Canada)
New World School of the Arts (FL)
North Central U (MN)

Natural Resources and Conservation Related
Sterling Coll (VT)

Natural Resources/ Conservation
Sterling Coll (VT)
U of Minnesota, Crookston (MN)

Natural Resources/ Conservation Related
Sterling Coll (VT)

Natural Resources Management
Sterling Coll (VT)

Natural Resources Management and Policy
Bacone Coll (OK)
Lake Superior State U (MI)
Sterling Coll (VT)

U of Alaska Fairbanks (AK)
U of Minnesota, Crookston (MN)

Natural Sciences
Alderson-Broaddus Coll (WV)
Central Christian Coll of Kansas (KS)
Charleston Southern U (SC)
Felician Coll (NJ)
Fresno Pacific U (CA)
Haskell Indian Nations U (KS)
Lourdes Coll (OH)
Madonna U (MI)
Medgar Evers Coll of the City U of NY (NY)
Roberts Wesleyan Coll (NY)
Shawnee State U (OH)
Sterling Coll (VT)
Thomas Edison State Coll (NJ)
U of Cincinnati (OH)
U of Toledo (OH)
Villanova U (PA)

Naval Architecture and Marine Engineering
British Columbia Inst of Technology (BC, Canada)

Non-Profit Management
Davenport U, Dearborn (MI)

Nuclear Engineering
Arkansas Tech U (AR)

Nuclear Engineering Technology
Excelsior Coll (NY)

Nuclear Medical Technology
Ball State U (IN)
British Columbia Inst of Technology (BC, Canada)
Dalton State Coll (GA)
Ferris State U (MI)
The George Washington U (DC)
Kent State U (OH)
Molloy Coll (NY)
Southern Alberta Inst of Technology (AB, Canada)
Thomas Edison State Coll (NJ)
The U of Findlay (OH)
Valdosta State U (GA)
West Virginia State Coll (WV)

Nuclear/Nuclear Power Technology
Thomas Edison State Coll (NJ)

Nursing Administration
British Columbia Inst of Technology (BC, Canada)

Nursing Assistant/Aide and Patient Care Assistant
Central Christian Coll of Kansas (KS)
Montana Tech of The U of Montana (MT)

Nursing (Licensed Practical/ Vocational Nurse Training)
Central Christian Coll of Kansas (KS)
Davenport U, Dearborn (MI)
Dickinson State U (ND)
Georgia Southwestern State U (GA)
Grace U (NE)
Kent State U (OH)
Lamar U (TX)
Lewis-Clark State Coll (ID)
Medgar Evers Coll of the City U of NY (NY)
Montana State U–Billings (MT)
Northern Michigan U (MI)
U Coll of the Cariboo (BC, Canada)
The U of Montana–Missoula (MT)

U of the District of Columbia (DC)
Vermont Tech Coll (VT)

Nursing (Registered Nurse Training)
Alcorn State U (MS)
Alvernia Coll (PA)
Angelo State U (TX)
Arkansas State U (AR)
Atlantic Union Coll (MA)
Augusta State U (GA)
Bacone Coll (OK)
Baker Coll of Clinton Township (MI)
Baker Coll of Flint (MI)
Baker Coll of Muskegon (MI)
Baker Coll of Owosso (MI)
Ball State U (IN)
Becker Coll (MA)
Bethel Coll (IN)
Bluefield State Coll (WV)
Boise State U (ID)
British Columbia Inst of Technology (BC, Canada)
Cardinal Stritch U (WI)
Castleton State Coll (VT)
Central Christian Coll of Kansas (KS)
Clarion U of Pennsylvania (PA)
Coll of St. Catherine–Minneapolis (MN)
Coll of Saint Mary (NE)
Coll of Staten Island of the City U of NY (NY)
Columbia Coll (MO)
Columbia Coll, Caguas (PR)
Covenant U (GA)
Dakota Wesleyan U (SD)
Dalton State Coll (GA)
Davenport U, Dearborn (MI)
Davis & Elkins Coll (WV)
Eastern Kentucky U (KY)
Excelsior Coll (NY)
Fairmont State U (WV)
State U of NY at Farmingdale (NY)
Felician Coll (NJ)
Ferris State U (MI)
Gardner-Webb U (NC)
Gwynedd-Mercy Coll (PA)
Hannibal-LaGrange Coll (MO)
Hillsdale Free Will Baptist Coll (OK)
Houston Baptist U (TX)
Indiana State U (IN)
Indiana U East (IN)
Indiana U Kokomo (IN)
Indiana U Northwest (IN)
Indiana U–Purdue U Fort Wayne (IN)
Indiana U–Purdue U Indianapolis (IN)
Indiana U South Bend (IN)
Inter Amer U of PR, Barranquitas Campus (PR)
Inter American U of PR, Fajardo Campus (PR)
Inter American U of PR, Metropolitan Campus (PR)
Inter American U of PR, Ponce Campus (PR)
Jewish Hospital Coll of Nursing and Allied Health (MO)
Kansas Wesleyan U (KS)
Kent State U (OH)
Kentucky State U (KY)
Lamar U (TX)
Lester L. Cox Coll of Nursing and Health Sciences (MO)
Lincoln Memorial U (TN)
Lincoln U (MO)
Lock Haven U of Pennsylvania (PA)
Loma Linda U (CA)
Louisiana Tech U (LA)
Macon State Coll (GA)
Marshall U (WV)
Marymount U (VA)
McNeese State U (LA)
Mercy Coll of Health Sciences (IA)

Mercyhurst Coll (PA)
Midway Coll (KY)
Montana Tech of The U of Montana (MT)
Morehead State U (KY)
Mount Aloysius Coll (PA)
Mount St. Mary's Coll (CA)
Nebraska Methodist Coll (NE)
Newman U (KS)
Nicholls State U (LA)
Norfolk State U (VA)
North Central U (MN)
Northern Kentucky U (KY)
North Georgia Coll & State U (GA)
Northwestern State U of Louisiana (LA)
Ohio U (OH)
Ohio U–Chillicothe (OH)
Ohio U–Southern Campus (OH)
Ohio U–Zanesville (OH)
Oklahoma Panhandle State U (OK)
Our Lady of the Lake Coll (LA)
Pacific Union Coll (CA)
Park U (MO)
Penn State U Altoona Coll (PA)
Pikeville Coll (KY)
Presentation Coll (SD)
Purdue U Calumet (IN)
Purdue U North Central (IN)
Regis Coll (MA)
Reinhardt Coll (GA)
Rivier Coll (NH)
Shawnee State U (OH)
Shepherd U (WV)
Southern Adventist U (TN)
Southern Arkansas U–Magnolia (AR)
Southern Vermont Coll (VT)
Southwest Baptist U (MO)
Tennessee State U (TN)
Thomas U (GA)
Trinity Coll of Nursing and Health Sciences (IL)
Troy State U (AL)
Universidad Adventista de las Antillas (PR)
U of Alaska Anchorage (AK)
U of Arkansas at Fort Smith (AR)
U of Arkansas at Little Rock (AR)
U of Charleston (WV)
U of Cincinnati (OH)
U of Indianapolis (IN)
The U of Maine at Augusta (ME)
U of Mobile (AL)
U of New England (ME)
U of Pittsburgh at Bradford (PA)
U of Rio Grande (OH)
U of Saint Francis (IN)
U of South Carolina Spartanburg (SC)
The U of South Dakota (SD)
U of Southern Indiana (IN)
U of the District of Columbia (DC)
U of the Sacred Heart (PR)
U of the Virgin Islands (VI)
U of Toledo (OH)
The U of West Alabama (AL)
Vermont Tech Coll (VT)
Walsh U (OH)
Warner Pacific Coll (OR)
Weber State U (UT)
Western Kentucky U (KY)

Nursing Related
British Columbia Inst of Technology (BC, Canada)
Inter American U of PR, Aguadilla Campus (PR)
Madonna U (MI)

Nursing Science
La Roche Coll (PA)
Trinity Coll of Nursing and Health Sciences (IL)

Occupational Health and Industrial Hygiene
British Columbia Inst of Technology (BC, Canada)

Occupational Safety and Health Technology
Ferris State U (MI)
Indiana U Bloomington (IN)
Lamar U (TX)
Montana Tech of The U of Montana (MT)
Murray State U (KY)
Shepherd U (WV)
Southwest Baptist U (MO)
U of Cincinnati (OH)
U of New Haven (CT)
Washburn U (KS)
Wright State U (OH)

Occupational Therapist Assistant
Baker Coll of Muskegon (MI)
California U of Pennsylvania (PA)
Clarion U of Pennsylvania (PA)
Coll of St. Catherine (MN)
Coll of St. Catherine–Minneapolis (MN)
Idaho State U (ID)
Kent State U (OH)
Loma Linda U (CA)
Mountain State U (WV)
Mount Aloysius Coll (PA)
Mount St. Mary's Coll (CA)
U of Louisiana at Monroe (LA)
U of Saint Francis (IN)
U of Southern Indiana (IN)
Wichita State U (KS)

Occupational Therapy
Clayton Coll & State U (GA)
Dalton State Coll (GA)
Faulkner U (AL)
Newman U (KS)
Shawnee State U (OH)
Southern Adventist U (TN)

Office Management
Baker Coll of Flint (MI)
Baker Coll of Jackson (MI)
Dalton State Coll (GA)
Emmanuel Coll (GA)
Georgia Southwestern State U (GA)
God's Bible School and Coll (OH)
International Coll of the Cayman IslandsCayman Islands)
Lake Superior State U (MI)
Mercyhurst Coll (PA)
Park U (MO)
Peirce Coll (PA)
Shawnee State U (OH)
U Coll of the Cariboo (BC, Canada)
Virginia Coll at Birmingham (AL)
Youngstown State U (OH)

Office Occupations and Clerical Services
Georgia Southwestern State U (GA)
Ohio U–Southern Campus (OH)
U of Alaska Fairbanks (AK)
Valdosta State U (GA)
Wright State U (OH)
Youngstown State U (OH)

Operations Management
Baker Coll of Flint (MI)
British Columbia Inst of Technology (BC, Canada)
Indiana State U (IN)
Indiana U–Purdue U Fort Wayne (IN)
Indiana U–Purdue U Indianapolis (IN)
Northern Kentucky U (KY)
Purdue U (IN)
Thomas Edison State Coll (NJ)

Ophthalmic Laboratory Technology
Indiana U Bloomington (IN)
Rochester Inst of Technology (NY)

Opticianry
The U of Akron (OH)

Optometric Technician
Indiana U Bloomington (IN)

Organizational Communication
Creighton U (NE)

Ornamental Horticulture
State U of NY at Farmingdale (NY)
Ferris State U (MI)
State U of NY Coll of A&T at Cobleskill (NY)
U of Massachusetts Amherst (MA)
U of New Hampshire (NH)
Utah State U (UT)
Vermont Tech Coll (VT)

Orthotics/Prosthetics
Baker Coll of Flint (MI)

Painting
Academy of Art U (CA)
Central Christian Coll of Kansas (KS)
New World School of the Arts (FL)
Pratt Inst (NY)

Parks, Recreation and Leisure
Central Christian Coll of Kansas (KS)
Clayton Coll & State U (GA)
Johnson & Wales U (RI)
Mitchell Coll (CT)
Mount Olive Coll (NC)
Oklahoma Panhandle State U (OK)
Thomas Edison State Coll (NJ)
U of Maine at Presque Isle (ME)
U of the District of Columbia (DC)

Parks, Recreation and Leisure Facilities Management
Eastern Kentucky U (KY)
Indiana Inst of Technology (IN)
Johnson & Wales U (RI)
Paul Smith's Coll of Arts and Sciences (NY)
State U of NY Coll of A&T at Cobleskill (NY)

Pastoral Studies/Counseling
Central Christian Coll of Kansas (KS)
North Central U (MN)
Notre Dame Coll (OH)
Providence Coll (RI)

Pediatric Nursing
British Columbia Inst of Technology (BC, Canada)

Perfusion Technology
Boise State U (ID)
U Coll of the Cariboo (BC, Canada)

Perioperative/Operating Room and Surgical Nursing
British Columbia Inst of Technology (BC, Canada)

Personal and Culinary Services Related
Lexington Coll (IL)

Petroleum Technology
British Columbia Inst of Technology (BC, Canada)
McNeese State U (LA)
Montana State U–Billings (MT)
Montana Tech of The U of Montana (MT)

Pharmacy
Clayton Coll & State U (GA)

Pharmacy, Pharmaceutical Sciences, and Administration Related
Vermont Tech Coll (VT)

Pharmacy Technician
Baker Coll of Flint (MI)
Baker Coll of Jackson (MI)
Baker Coll of Muskegon (MI)
DeVry U, Westminster (CO)
Florida Metropolitan U–Tampa Coll, Brandon (FL)
Idaho State U (ID)
Mount Aloysius Coll (PA)
Valdosta State U (GA)

Philosophy
Clayton Coll & State U (GA)
Dalton State Coll (GA)
Felician Coll (NJ)
Kwantlen U Coll (BC, Canada)
Methodist Coll (NC)
Sacred Heart U (CT)
Thomas More Coll (KY)
Université Laval (QC, Canada)
The U of Tampa (FL)
U of the District of Columbia (DC)
U of Wisconsin–Green Bay (WI)
York Coll of Pennsylvania (PA)

Photographic and Film/Video Technology
Burlington Coll (VT)
New England School of Communications (ME)

Photography
Academy of Art U (CA)
Andrews U (MI)
The Art Inst of Colorado (CO)
The Art Inst of Fort Lauderdale (FL)
Cazenovia Coll (NY)
Central Christian Coll of Kansas (KS)
Corcoran Coll of Art and Design (DC)
New World School of the Arts (FL)
Pacific Union Coll (CA)
Paier Coll of Art, Inc. (CT)
Pillsbury Baptist Bible Coll (MN)
Rochester Inst of Technology (NY)
Sage Coll of Albany (NY)
The U of Maine at Augusta (ME)
Villa Julie Coll (MD)

Photojournalism
Southern Alberta Inst of Technology (AB, Canada)

Physical Education Teaching and Coaching
Adrian Coll (MI)
Central Christian Coll of Kansas (KS)
Clayton Coll & State U (GA)
Fresno Pacific U (CA)
Hillsdale Free Will Baptist Coll (OK)
Macon State Coll (GA)
Methodist Coll (NC)
Mitchell Coll (CT)
U of Rio Grande (OH)

Physical Sciences
Bacone Coll (OK)
Central Christian Coll of Kansas (KS)
Faulkner U (AL)
Mitchell Coll (CT)
Roberts Wesleyan Coll (NY)

Nicholls State U (LA)
U of Alaska Anchorage (AK)

Pharmacy
Clayton Coll & State U (GA)

Physical Science Technologies Related
The U of Akron (OH)
Western Kentucky U (KY)

Physical Therapist Assistant
Arkansas State U (AR)
Baker Coll of Flint (MI)
Baker Coll of Muskegon (MI)
Becker Coll (MA)
Central Christian Coll of Kansas (KS)
Coll of St. Catherine (MN)
Coll of St. Catherine–Minneapolis (MN)
Fairleigh Dickinson U, Florham (NJ)
Idaho State U (ID)
Kent State U (OH)
Loma Linda U (CA)
Missouri Western State Coll (MO)
Mountain State U (WV)
Mount Aloysius Coll (PA)
Mount St. Mary's Coll (CA)
New York U (NY)
Our Lady of the Lake Coll (LA)
Southern Illinois U Carbondale (IL)
South U (AL)
South U (GA)
U of Central Arkansas (AR)
U of Evansville (IN)
U of Indianapolis (IN)
U of Saint Francis (IN)
Wichita State U (KS)

Physical Therapy
Alvernia Coll (PA)
Briar Cliff U (IA)
Central Christian Coll of Kansas (KS)
Clayton Coll & State U (GA)
Dalton State Coll (GA)
Davenport U, Lansing (MI)
Fairmont State U (WV)
Faulkner U (AL)
Lynn U (FL)
Macon State Coll (GA)
Mercyhurst Coll (PA)
Shawnee State U (OH)
Southern Adventist U (TN)
U of Central Arkansas (AR)
U of Cincinnati (OH)
U of Evansville (IN)
Washburn U (KS)

Physician Assistant
Central Christian Coll of Kansas (KS)
Dalton State Coll (GA)
Southern Adventist U (TN)

Physics
Adrian Coll (MI)
Clayton Coll & State U (GA)
Dalton State Coll (GA)
Idaho State U (ID)
Macon State Coll (GA)
Rochester Inst of Technology (NY)
Thomas Edison State Coll (NJ)
Thomas More Coll (KY)
U of the Virgin Islands (VI)
York Coll of Pennsylvania (PA)

Piano and Organ
Bethel Coll (IN)
Central Christian Coll of Kansas (KS)
John Brown U (AR)
Kwantlen U Coll (BC, Canada)
New World School of the Arts (FL)
Pacific Union Coll (CA)

Pipefitting and Sprinkler Fitting
British Columbia Inst of Technology (BC, Canada)
U Coll of the Cariboo (BC, Canada)

Plant Nursery Management
Inter Amer U of PR, Barranquitas Campus (PR)
State U of NY Coll of A&T at Cobleskill (NY)

Plant Protection and Integrated Pest Management
North Carolina State U (NC)
Sterling Coll (VT)

Plant Sciences
State U of NY Coll of A&T at Cobleskill (NY)

Plant Sciences Related
Sterling Coll (VT)

Plastics Engineering Technology
British Columbia Inst of Technology (BC, Canada)
Ferris State U (MI)
Kent State U (OH)
Penn State U at Erie, The Behrend Coll (PA)
Shawnee State U (OH)

Plumbing Technology
U Coll of the Cariboo (BC, Canada)
Valdosta State U (GA)

Political Science and Government
Adrian Coll (MI)
Bacone Coll (OK)
Clayton Coll & State U (GA)
Dalton State Coll (GA)
Fresno Pacific U (CA)
Idaho State U (ID)
Indiana U–Purdue U Fort Wayne (IN)
Kwantlen U Coll (BC, Canada)
Macon State Coll (GA)
Methodist Coll (NC)
Richmond, The American International U in LondonUnited Kingdom)
Sacred Heart U (CT)
Thomas More Coll (KY)
Université Laval (QC, Canada)
The U of Scranton (PA)
The U of Tampa (FL)
U of Toledo (OH)
U of Wisconsin–Green Bay (WI)
Villa Julie Coll (MD)
Xavier U (OH)
York Coll of Pennsylvania (PA)

Postal Management
Macon State Coll (GA)
Washburn U (KS)

Precision Production Trades
Valdosta State U (GA)

Precision Systems Maintenance and Repair Technologies Related
Arkansas Tech U (AR)
British Columbia Inst of Technology (BC, Canada)

Pre-Dentistry Studies
Central Christian Coll of Kansas (KS)
Concordia U Wisconsin (WI)
Newman U (KS)

Pre-Engineering
Atlantic Union Coll (MA)
Boise State U (ID)
Brescia U (KY)
Briar Cliff U (IA)
Campbell U (NC)
Charleston Southern U (SC)
Clayton Coll & State U (GA)
Columbus State U (GA)

Covenant Coll (GA)
Eastern Kentucky U (KY)
Edgewood Coll (WI)
Faulkner U (AL)
Ferris State U (MI)
Fort Valley State U (GA)
Hannibal-LaGrange Coll (MO)
Keene State Coll (NH)
LaGrange Coll (GA)
Macon State Coll (GA)
Marian Coll (IN)
Medgar Evers Coll of the City U of NY (NY)
Methodist Coll (NC)
Minnesota State U Mankato (MN)
Missouri Southern State U (MO)
Montana State U–Billings (MT)
Newman U (KS)
Niagara U (NY)
Northern State U (SD)
Pacific Union Coll (CA)
Purdue U North Central (IN)
Richmond, The American International U in LondonUnited Kingdom)
St. Gregory's U (OK)
Schreiner U (TX)
Shawnee State U (OH)
Siena Heights U (MI)
Southern Utah U (UT)
U of New Hampshire (NH)
U of Sioux Falls (SD)
Washburn U (KS)
West Virginia State Coll (WV)
Winona State U (MN)

Pre-Law Studies
Calumet Coll of Saint Joseph (IN)
Newman U (KS)
Northwest Coll (WA)
Peirce Coll (PA)
Thomas More Coll (KY)

Pre-Medical Studies
Central Christian Coll of Kansas (KS)
Concordia U Wisconsin (WI)
Newman U (KS)
Schiller International USpain)
Schiller International UUnited Kingdom)
State U of NY Coll of A&T at Cobleskill (NY)
U of Ottawa (ON, Canada)

Pre-Nursing Studies
Central Christian Coll of Kansas (KS)
Concordia U Wisconsin (WI)
Trinity International U (IL)

Pre-Pharmacy Studies
Central Christian Coll of Kansas (KS)
Dalton State Coll (GA)
Emmanuel Coll (GA)
Macon State Coll (GA)
U Coll of the Cariboo (BC, Canada)

Pre-Theology/Pre-Ministerial Studies
Manchester Coll (IN)
St. Gregory's U (OK)

Pre-Veterinary Studies
Central Christian Coll of Kansas (KS)
Newman U (KS)
Schiller International USpain)
Schiller International UUnited Kingdom)
Shawnee State U (OH)

Printing Management
Central Missouri State U (MO)
Southern Alberta Inst of Technology (AB, Canada)

Printmaking
Academy of Art U (CA)
New World School of the Arts (FL)

Professional Studies
Ohio Valley Coll (WV)
Thomas Coll (ME)

Psychiatric/Mental Health Services Technology
Lake Superior State U (MI)
Northern Kentucky U (KY)
U of Toledo (OH)

Psychology
Adrian Coll (MI)
Argosy U/Twin Cities, Eagan (MN)
Bluefield State Coll (WV)
Calumet Coll of Saint Joseph (IN)
Central Christian Coll of Kansas (KS)
Central Methodist Coll (MO)
Chestnut Hill Coll (PA)
Crown Coll (MN)
Dalton State Coll (GA)
Davis & Elkins Coll (WV)
Eastern New Mexico U (NM)
Felician Coll (NJ)
Fresno Pacific U (CA)
Hillsdale Free Will Baptist Coll (OK)
Indiana U–Purdue U Fort Wayne (IN)
Kwantlen U Coll (BC, Canada)
Lourdes Coll (OH)
Macon State Coll (GA)
Marian Coll (IN)
Methodist Coll (NC)
Mitchell Coll (CT)
Montana State U–Billings (MT)
Mount Olive Coll (NC)
Newbury Coll (MA)
North Central U (MN)
Richmond, The American International U in LondonUnited Kingdom)
Sacred Heart U (CT)
Siena Heights U (MI)
Thomas More Coll (KY)
U of Rio Grande (OH)
The U of Tampa (FL)
U of Wisconsin–Green Bay (WI)
Villa Julie Coll (MD)
Wright State U (OH)
Xavier U (OH)

Psychology Teacher Education
Central Christian Coll of Kansas (KS)

Public Administration
Central Methodist Coll (MO)
Indiana U Bloomington (IN)
Indiana U Northwest (IN)
Indiana U–Purdue U Fort Wayne (IN)
Indiana U–Purdue U Indianapolis (IN)
Indiana U South Bend (IN)
Macon State Coll (GA)
Medgar Evers Coll of the City U of NY (NY)
Point Park U (PA)
Thomas Edison State Coll (NJ)
The U of Maine at Augusta (ME)
U of Regina (SK, Canada)
U of the District of Columbia (DC)

Public Administration and Social Service Professions Related
Indiana U–Purdue U Fort Wayne (IN)
The U of Akron (OH)
U of Saint Francis (IN)

Public Health
U of Alaska Fairbanks (AK)

Public Policy Analysis
Indiana U Bloomington (IN)
Saint Peter's Coll (NJ)

Public Relations, Advertising, and Applied Communication Related
Champlain Coll (VT)
Madonna U (MI)

Public Relations/Image Management
Champlain Coll (VT)
John Brown U (AR)
Johnson & Wales U (RI)
Madonna U (MI)
New England School of Communications (ME)
Xavier U (OH)

Purchasing, Procurement/ Acquisitions and Contracts Management
Mercyhurst Coll (PA)
Saint Joseph's U (PA)
Strayer U (DC)
Thomas Edison State Coll (NJ)
U of Management and Technology (VA)

Quality Control and Safety Technologies Related
Madonna U (MI)

Quality Control Technology
Baker Coll of Cadillac (MI)
Baker Coll of Flint (MI)
Baker Coll of Muskegon (MI)
Eastern Kentucky U (KY)
U of Cincinnati (OH)

Rabbinical Studies
Université Laval (QC, Canada)

Radiation Biology
Inter Amer U of PR, Barranquitas Campus (PR)

Radiation Protection/Health Physics Technology
Argosy U/Twin Cities, Eagan (MN)

Radio and Television
Academy of Art U (CA)
The Art Inst of Fort Lauderdale (FL)
Ashland U (OH)
Newbury Coll (MA)
New England School of Communications (ME)
Northwestern Coll (MN)
Ohio U (OH)
Ohio U–Zanesville (OH)
Southern Alberta Inst of Technology (AB, Canada)
Xavier U (OH)
York Coll of Pennsylvania (PA)

Radio and Television Broadcasting Technology
British Columbia Inst of Technology (BC, Canada)
Lyndon State Coll (VT)
Mountain State U (WV)
The New England Inst of Art (MA)
New England School of Communications (ME)
New York Inst of Technology (NY)
Ohio U–Southern Campus (OH)
Southern Adventist U (TN)

Radiologic Technology/ Science
Allen Coll (IA)
Argosy U/Twin Cities, Eagan (MN)
Baker Coll of Clinton Township (MI)
Baker Coll of Muskegon (MI)
Boise State U (ID)
Champlain Coll (VT)
Clayton Coll & State U (GA)
Dalton State Coll (GA)

Radio, Television, and Digital Communication Related
Southern Alberta Inst of Technology (AB, Canada)

Range Science and Management
Sterling Coll (VT)

Real Estate
British Columbia Inst of Technology (BC, Canada)
Fairmont State U (WV)
Ferris State U (MI)
Kent State U (OH)
Lamar U (TX)
Saint Francis U (PA)
Thomas Edison State Coll (NJ)
U of Cincinnati (OH)

Receptionist
Baker Coll of Allen Park (MI)
The U of Montana–Missoula (MT)

Recording Arts Technology
New England School of Communications (ME)

Religious Education
Aquinas Coll (MI)
The Baptist Coll of Florida (FL)
Calvary Bible Coll and Theological Seminary (MO)
Central Baptist Coll (AR)
Cornerstone U (MI)
Dallas Baptist U (TX)
Eastern Nazarene Coll (MA)
Hillsdale Free Will Baptist Coll (OK)
Houghton Coll (NY)
Manhattan Christian Coll (KS)
Mercyhurst Coll (PA)
Methodist Coll (NC)
MidAmerica Nazarene U (KS)
Reformed Bible Coll (MI)
Warner Pacific Coll (OR)
Washington Bible Coll (MD)

Religious/Sacred Music
Aquinas Coll (MI)
The Baptist Coll of Florida (FL)
Clearwater Christian Coll (FL)
Hillsdale Free Will Baptist Coll (OK)
Immaculata U (PA)
Manhattan Christian Coll (KS)
MidAmerica Nazarene U (KS)
Mount Vernon Nazarene U (OH)
North Central U (MN)
Saint Joseph's Coll (IN)
Vennard Coll (IA)

Religious Studies
Adrian Coll (MI)
Aquinas Coll (MI)
Atlantic Union Coll (MA)
Brescia U (KY)
Brewton-Parker Coll (GA)
Calumet Coll of Saint Joseph (IN)
Central Christian Coll of Kansas (KS)
Felician Coll (NJ)

Indiana U Northwest (IN)
Indiana U–Purdue U Fort Wayne (IN)
Lewis-Clark State Coll (ID)
Mansfield U of Pennsylvania (PA)
Midwestern State U (TX)
Mountain State U (WV)
Mount Aloysius Coll (PA)
Nebraska Methodist Coll (NE)
Newman U (KS)
Washburn U (KS)

Global U of the Assemblies of God (MO)
Grace Bible Coll (MI)
Griggs U (MD)
Holy Apostles Coll and Seminary (CT)
Howard Payne U (TX)
Kentucky Mountain Bible Coll (KY)
Liberty U (VA)
Lourdes Coll (OH)
Madonna U (MI)
Manchester Coll (IN)
MidAmerica Nazarene U (KS)
Missouri Baptist U (MO)
Mount Marty Coll (SD)
Mount Olive Coll (NC)
Presentation Coll (SD)
Sacred Heart U (CT)
Shaw U (NC)
Tabor Coll (KS)
Thomas More Coll (KY)
The U of Findlay (OH)
U of Sioux Falls (SD)
Vennard Coll (IA)
Washington Bible Coll (MD)

Religious Studies Related
Lindsey Wilson Coll (KY)

Resort Management
Rochester Inst of Technology (NY)
U Coll of the Cariboo (BC, Canada)

Respiratory Care Therapy
Ball State U (IN)
Columbia Union Coll (MD)
Dakota State U (SD)
Dalton State Coll (GA)
Faulkner U (AL)
Ferris State U (MI)
Gannon U (PA)
Gwynedd-Mercy Coll (PA)
Indiana U Northwest (IN)
Indiana U–Purdue U Indianapolis (IN)
Lamar U (TX)
Loma Linda U (CA)
Macon State Coll (GA)
Mansfield U of Pennsylvania (PA)
Missouri Southern State U (MO)
Molloy Coll (NY)
Morehead State U (KY)
Mountain State U (WV)
Nebraska Methodist Coll (NE)
Newman U (KS)
Nicholls State U (LA)
Northern Kentucky U (KY)
Our Lady of Holy Cross Coll (LA)
Point Park U (PA)
St. Augustine Coll (IL)
Shawnee State U (OH)
Shenandoah U (VA)
Southern Adventist U (TN)
Southern Illinois U Carbondale (IL)
Thomas Edison State Coll (NJ)
Universidad Adventista de las Antillas (PR)
The U of Akron (OH)
U of Arkansas at Fort Smith (AR)
The U of Montana–Missoula (MT)
U of Pittsburgh at Johnstown (PA)
U of Southern Indiana (IN)
U of the District of Columbia (DC)
U of Toledo (OH)
Vermont Tech Coll (VT)
Weber State U (UT)
Western Kentucky U (KY)
West Virginia U Inst of Technology (WV)

York Coll of Pennsylvania (PA)
Youngstown State U (OH)

Respiratory Therapy Technician
U Coll of the Cariboo (BC, Canada)

Restaurant, Culinary, and Catering Management
Johnson & Wales U (RI)
Lexington Coll (IL)
The U of Akron (OH)
U of New Hampshire (NH)

Restaurant/Food Services Management
Lexington Coll (IL)
Rochester Inst of Technology (NY)
U of New Hampshire (NH)

Retailing
Johnson & Wales U (RI)

Robotics Technology
British Columbia Inst of Technology (BC, Canada)
Indiana U–Purdue U Indianapolis (IN)
Purdue U (IN)
U of Rio Grande (OH)

Safety/Security Technology
John Jay Coll of Criminal Justice, the City U of NY (NY)
Keene State Coll (NH)
Lamar U (TX)
Madonna U (MI)
Ohio U (OH)
Ohio U–Chillicothe (OH)
U of Cincinnati (OH)

Sales and Marketing/ Marketing And Distribution Teacher Education
Central Christian Coll of Kansas (KS)

Sales, Distribution and Marketing
Baker Coll of Flint (MI)
Baker Coll of Jackson (MI)
Champlain Coll (VT)
Dalton State Coll (GA)
Johnson & Wales U (RI)
Purdue U North Central (IN)
Thomas Edison State Coll (NJ)
U Coll of the Cariboo (BC, Canada)
The U of Findlay (OH)

Science Teacher Education
Central Christian Coll of Kansas (KS)
U of Cincinnati (OH)

Science Technologies Related
British Columbia Inst of Technology (BC, Canada)
Madonna U (MI)
Ohio Valley Coll (WV)

Science, Technology and Society
Samford U (AL)

Sculpture
Academy of Art U (CA)
New World School of the Arts (FL)

Secondary Education
Central Christian Coll of Kansas (KS)
Dalton State Coll (GA)
Mountain State U (WV)
Vennard Coll (IA)

Security and Loss Prevention
John Jay Coll of Criminal Justice, the City U of NY (NY)
U of New Haven (CT)

York Coll of Pennsylvania (PA)
Youngstown State U (OH)

Security and Protective Services Related
Ohio U (OH)

Selling Skills and Sales
The U of Akron (OH)

Sheet Metal Technology
British Columbia Inst of Technology (BC, Canada)
Montana State U–Billings (MT)

Sign Language Interpretation and Translation
Bethel Coll (IN)
Coll of St. Catherine (MN)
Fairmont State U (WV)
Gardner-Webb U (NC)
Mount Aloysius Coll (PA)
North Central U (MN)
Rochester Inst of Technology (NY)
U of Arkansas at Little Rock (AR)
U of Louisville (KY)

Slavic Languages
U of Ottawa (ON, Canada)

Small Business Administration
Central Christian Coll of Kansas (KS)
Lewis-Clark State Coll (ID)

Small Engine Mechanics and Repair Technology
British Columbia Inst of Technology (BC, Canada)
The U of Montana–Missoula (MT)

Social Psychology
Central Christian Coll of Kansas (KS)
Kwantlen U Coll (BC, Canada)
Park U (MO)

Social Sciences
Adrian Coll (MI)
Campbellsville U (KY)
Central Christian Coll of Kansas (KS)
Clayton Coll & State U (GA)
Crown Coll (MN)
Evangel U (MO)
Faulkner U (AL)
Felician Coll (NJ)
Kwantlen U Coll (BC, Canada)
Lindsey Wilson Coll (KY)
Long Island U, Brooklyn Campus (NY)
Newbury Coll (MA)
Ohio U (OH)
Ohio U–Zanesville (OH)
Richmond, The American International U in LondonUnited Kingdom)
Sage Coll of Albany (NY)
Saint Peter's Coll (NJ)
Samford U (AL)
Shawnee State U (OH)
State U of NY Empire State Coll (NY)
Tri-State U (IN)
U of Cincinnati (OH)
The U of Findlay (OH)
The U of Maine at Augusta (ME)
U of Sioux Falls (SD)
U of Southern Indiana (IN)
U of Toledo (OH)
Valparaiso U (IN)
Villa Julie Coll (MD)
Warner Pacific Coll (OR)
Wayland Baptist U (TX)

Social Sciences Related
Concordia U at Austin (TX)

Social Science Teacher Education
Central Christian Coll of Kansas (KS)

Social Studies Teacher Education
Central Christian Coll of Kansas (KS)

Social Work
Central Christian Coll of Kansas (KS)
Champlain Coll (VT)
Dalton State Coll (GA)
Edinboro U of Pennsylvania (PA)
Haskell Indian Nations U (KS)
Indiana U East (IN)
Methodist Coll (NC)
Northern State U (SD)
Siena Heights U (MI)
Suffolk U (MA)
U of Cincinnati (OH)
U of Rio Grande (OH)
U of Toledo (OH)
U of Wisconsin–Green Bay (WI)
Wright State U (OH)
Youngstown State U (OH)

Sociology
Adrian Coll (MI)
Bacone Coll (OK)
Central Christian Coll of Kansas (KS)
Clayton Coll & State U (GA)
Dalton State Coll (GA)
Felician Coll (NJ)
Fresno Pacific U (CA)
Grand View Coll (IA)
Kwantlen U Coll (BC, Canada)
Lourdes Coll (OH)
Macon State Coll (GA)
Methodist Coll (NC)
Montana State U–Billings (MT)
Newbury Coll (MA)
Penn State U Univ Park Campus (PA)
Richmond, The American International U in LondonUnited Kingdom)
Sacred Heart U (CT)
Thomas More Coll (KY)
U of Dubuque (IA)
U of Rio Grande (OH)
The U of Scranton (PA)
The U of Tampa (FL)
Villa Julie Coll (MD)
Wright State U (OH)
Xavier U (OH)

Soil Conservation
U of Minnesota, Crookston (MN)

Soil Science and Agronomy
Sterling Coll (VT)

Soil Sciences Related
Sterling Coll (VT)

Spanish
Adrian Coll (MI)
Central Christian Coll of Kansas (KS)
Chestnut Hill Coll (PA)
Clayton Coll & State U (GA)
Fresno Pacific U (CA)
Idaho State U (ID)
Indiana U–Purdue U Fort Wayne (IN)
Methodist Coll (NC)
Sacred Heart U (CT)
Thomas More Coll (KY)
The U of Tampa (FL)
U of Wisconsin–Green Bay (WI)
Xavier U (OH)

Spanish Language Teacher Education
Central Christian Coll of Kansas (KS)

Special Education
Edinboro U of Pennsylvania (PA)
Montana State U–Billings (MT)
St. Augustine Coll (IL)

Special Education (Hearing Impaired)
Ohio U–Chillicothe (OH)

Special Education (Mentally Retarded)
Valdosta State U (GA)

Special Education (Multiply Disabled)
Inter Amer U of PR, Barranquitas Campus (PR)

Special Education Related
Minot State U (ND)

Special Education (Speech Or Language Impaired)
U of Nebraska at Omaha (NE)

Special Products Marketing
Ball State U (IN)
Ferris State U (MI)
Johnson & Wales U (FL)
Johnson & Wales U (RI)
Lamar U (TX)
Newbury Coll (MA)
Northern Michigan U (MI)
Purdue U Calumet (IN)
U of Minnesota, Crookston (MN)

Speech and Rhetoric
Clayton Coll & State U (GA)
Dalton State Coll (GA)
Ferris State U (MI)
Macon State Coll (GA)
Madonna U (MI)

Speech-Language Pathology
Baker Coll of Muskegon (MI)
Indiana State U (IN)
Southern Adventist U (TN)

Speech Teacher Education
Central Christian Coll of Kansas (KS)

Sport and Fitness Administration
Central Christian Coll of Kansas (KS)
Lake Superior State U (MI)
Mitchell Coll (CT)
Northwood U (MI)
Northwood U, Texas Campus (TX)
U Coll of the Cariboo (BC, Canada)
Webber International U (FL)

Statistics
Huron U USA in LondonUnited Kingdom)

Substance Abuse/Addiction Counseling
Bacone Coll (OK)
Calumet Coll of Saint Joseph (IN)
Keene State Coll (NH)
Newman U (KS)
St. Augustine Coll (IL)
The U of Akron (OH)
U of Great Falls (MT)
U of Toledo (OH)

Surgical Technology
Baker Coll of Clinton Township (MI)
Baker Coll of Flint (MI)
Baker Coll of Jackson (MI)
Baker Coll of Muskegon (MI)
Boise State U (ID)
Florida Metropolitan U-Tampa Coll, Brandon (FL)
Loma Linda U (CA)
Mercy Coll of Health Sciences (IA)

Montana State U–Billings (MT)
Mountain State U (WV)
Mount Aloysius Coll (PA)
Our Lady of the Lake Coll (LA)
Presentation Coll (SD)
Trinity Coll of Nursing and Health Sciences (IL)
The U of Akron (OH)
U of Arkansas at Fort Smith (AR)
The U of Montana–Missoula (MT)
U of Pittsburgh at Johnstown (PA)
U of Saint Francis (IN)
Valdosta State U (GA)
Virginia Coll at Birmingham (AL)
West Virginia U Inst of Technology (WV)

Survey Technology
British Columbia Inst of Technology (BC, Canada)
Ferris State U (MI)
Glenville State Coll (WV)
Kansas State U (KS)
Paul Smith's Coll of Arts and Sciences (NY)
Thomas Edison State Coll (NJ)
The U of Akron (OH)
U of Alaska Anchorage (AK)
U of New Hampshire (NH)

System Administration
Coleman Coll, La Mesa (CA)
DeVry U, Colorado Springs (CO)
Huron U USA in LondonUnited Kingdom)
National American U, Denver (CO)
U Coll of the Cariboo (BC, Canada)

System, Networking, and Lan/Wan Management
Baker Coll of Auburn Hills (MI)
Champlain Coll (VT)
Huron U USA in LondonUnited Kingdom)
National American U, Denver (CO)
Peirce Coll (PA)
U Coll of the Cariboo (BC, Canada)

Systems Engineering
Missouri Tech (MO)

Taxation
British Columbia Inst of Technology (BC, Canada)

Teacher Assistant/Aide
Alabama State U (AL)
Alverno Coll (WI)
Boise State U (ID)
Dordt Coll (IA)
Johnson Bible Coll (TN)
Lamar U (TX)
Mount Ida Coll (MA)
New Mexico Highlands U (NM)
New Mexico State U (NM)
Our Lady of Holy Cross Coll (LA)
The U of Akron (OH)
U of New Mexico (NM)

Technical and Business Writing
Ferris State U (MI)
Murray State U (KY)
Paul Smith's Coll of Arts and Sciences (NY)

Technical Teacher Education
Eastern Kentucky U (KY)
New York Inst of Technology (NY)
Northern Kentucky U (KY)
Western Kentucky U (KY)

Technology/Industrial Arts Teacher Education
Arkansas State U (AR)

Telecommunications
Briarcliffe Coll (NY)
Capitol Coll (MD)
Champlain Coll (VT)
Clayton Coll & State U (GA)
Coll of Saint Mary (NE)
Columbia Coll Hollywood (CA)
Inter American U of PR, Bayamón Campus (PR)
State U of NY Coll of A&T at Cobleskill (NY)
Vermont Tech Coll (VT)

Telecommunications Technology
Penn State U Altoona Coll (PA)
Penn State U at Erie, The Behrend Coll (PA)
Penn State U Berks Cmps of Berks-Lehigh Valley Coll (PA)
Penn State U Schuylkill Campus of the Capital Coll (PA)
Southern Alberta Inst of Technology (AB, Canada)

Theatre Design and Technology
Indiana U Bloomington (IN)
Johnson State Coll (VT)
U of Rio Grande (OH)

Theatre/Theatre Arts Management
Haskell Indian Nations U (KS)

Theological and Ministerial Studies Related
Bacone Coll (OK)
Brescia U (KY)
Central Baptist Coll (AR)
Pillsbury Baptist Bible Coll (MN)
U of Saint Francis (IN)

Theology
Appalachian Bible Coll (WV)
The Baptist Coll of Florida (FL)
Briar Cliff U (IA)
Central Christian Coll of Kansas (KS)
Creighton U (NE)
Franciscan U of Steubenville (OH)
Griggs U (MD)
Heritage Bible Coll (NC)
Marian Coll (IN)
Ohio Dominican U (OH)
Sacred Heart Major Seminary (MI)
Université Laval (QC, Canada)
Warner Southern Coll (FL)
Washington Bible Coll (MD)
William Jessup U (CA)
Williams Baptist Coll (AR)
William Tyndale Coll (MI)
Xavier U (OH)

Therapeutic Recreation
Indiana Inst of Technology (IN)
Johnson & Wales U (RI)
Mitchell Coll (CT)
U of Southern Maine (ME)

Tourism and Travel Services Management
Baker Coll of Flint (MI)
Baker Coll of Muskegon (MI)
Black Hills State U (SD)
Brigham Young U–Hawaii (HI)
British Columbia Inst of Technology (BC, Canada)
Champlain Coll (VT)
Inter American U of PR, Ponce Campus (PR)

International Coll of the Cayman IslandsCayman Islands)
Johnson & Wales U (FL)
Johnson & Wales U (RI)
Morrison U (NV)
Mountain State U (WV)
National American U, Colorado Springs (CO)
Newbury Coll (MA)
Ohio U (OH)
Paul Smith's Coll of Arts and Sciences (NY)
Robert Morris Coll (IL)
Rochester Inst of Technology (NY)
Schiller International U (FL)
Southern Alberta Inst of Technology (AB, Canada)
Sullivan U (KY)
The U of Akron (OH)
U of Alaska Southeast (AK)
The U of Montana–Western (MT)
U of New Haven (CT)
Webber International U (FL)

Tourism and Travel Services Marketing
Champlain Coll (VT)
Ohio U–Southern Campus (OH)

Tourism Promotion
Champlain Coll (VT)
U Coll of the Cariboo (BC, Canada)

Tourism/Travel Marketing
Johnson & Wales U (RI)
Ohio U (OH)
Pontifical Catholic U of Puerto Rico (PR)
State U of NY Coll of A&T at Cobleskill (NY)
The U of Montana–Western (MT)

Trade and Industrial Teacher Education
British Columbia Inst of Technology (BC, Canada)
Indiana State U (IN)
Murray State U (KY)
Purdue U (IN)
Valdosta State U (GA)

Transportation and Highway Engineering
British Columbia Inst of Technology (BC, Canada)

Transportation and Materials Moving Related
Southern Alberta Inst of Technology (AB, Canada)

Transportation Technology
Baker Coll of Flint (MI)
Maine Maritime Academy (ME)
U of Cincinnati (OH)
U of Toledo (OH)

Turf and Turfgrass Management
North Carolina State U (NC)
State U of NY Coll of A&T at Cobleskill (NY)
U of Massachusetts Amherst (MA)

Urban Studies/Affairs
Clayton Coll & State U (GA)
Mount St. Mary's Coll (CA)
Saint Peter's Coll (NJ)
U of the District of Columbia (DC)
U of Wisconsin–Green Bay (WI)

Vehicle and Vehicle Parts And Accessories Marketing
Northwood U (MI)
Northwood U, Florida Campus (FL)
Northwood U, Texas Campus (TX)

Vehicle/Equipment Operation
Baker Coll of Flint (MI)
The U of Montana–Missoula (MT)

Vehicle Maintenance and Repair Technologies Related
British Columbia Inst of Technology (BC, Canada)
U of Alaska Fairbanks (AK)

Veterinary/Animal Health Technology
Argosy U/Twin Cities, Eagan (MN)
Baker Coll of Cadillac (MI)
Baker Coll of Jackson (MI)
Baker Coll of Muskegon (MI)
Becker Coll (MA)
Medaille Coll (NY)
Morehead State U (KY)
Northwestern State U of Louisiana (LA)
Purdue U (IN)
U Coll of the Cariboo (BC, Canada)
The U of Maine at Augusta (ME)
Wilson Coll (PA)

Veterinary Sciences
Clayton Coll & State U (GA)
Fort Valley State U (GA)

Veterinary Technology
Argosy U/Twin Cities, Eagan (MN)
Becker Coll (MA)
Fairmont State U (WV)
Fort Valley State U (GA)
Lincoln Memorial U (TN)
Medaille Coll (NY)
Mount Ida Coll (MA)
National American U (SD)
Vermont Tech Coll (VT)

Violin, Viola, Guitar and Other Stringed Instruments
Five Towns Coll (NY)
Kwantlen U Coll (BC, Canada)
New World School of the Arts (FL)

Visual and Performing Arts
Briarcliffe Coll (NY)
Indiana U East (IN)
Miami International U of Art & Design (FL)
Thomas More Coll (KY)
U of Arkansas at Fort Smith (AR)

Voice and Opera
Central Christian Coll of Kansas (KS)
Five Towns Coll (NY)
Kwantlen U Coll (BC, Canada)
New World School of the Arts (FL)

Watchmaking and Jewelrymaking
Fashion Inst of Technology (NY)

Water Quality and Wastewater Treatment Management And Recycling Technology
Lake Superior State U (MI)
Murray State U (KY)
U of the District of Columbia (DC)
Wright State U (OH)

Web/Multimedia Management and Webmaster
Academy of Art U (CA)
Champlain Coll (VT)
Davenport U, Dearborn (MI)
Davenport U, Grand Rapids (MI)
Davenport U, Holland (MI)

Associate Degree Programs at Four-Year Colleges

Web/Multimedia Management and Webmaster

Davenport U, Kalamazoo (MI)
Davenport U, Warren (MI)
Huron U USA in LondonUnited Kingdom)
Lewis-Clark State Coll (ID)
Limestone Coll (SC)
New England School of Communications (ME)

Web Page, Digital/ Multimedia and Information Resources Design
The Art Inst of Atlanta (GA)
The Art Inst of Portland (OR)
Baker Coll of Allen Park (MI)
Champlain Coll (VT)

Huron U USA in LondonUnited Kingdom)
National American U, Denver (CO)
New England School of Communications (ME)
Robert Morris Coll (IL)
Strayer U (DC)
U Coll of the Cariboo (BC, Canada)

Welding Technology
Boise State U (ID)
British Columbia Inst of Technology (BC, Canada)
Excelsior Coll (NY)
Ferris State U (MI)

Georgia Southwestern State U (GA)
Idaho State U (ID)
Lamar U (TX)
Lewis-Clark State Coll (ID)
Oakland City U (IN)
Southern Alberta Inst of Technology (AB, Canada)
U of Alaska Anchorage (AK)
The U of Montana–Missoula (MT)
U of Toledo (OH)
Valdosta State U (GA)

Western Civilization
Central Christian Coll of Kansas (KS)

Wildlife and Wildlands Science And Management
British Columbia Inst of Technology (BC, Canada)
State U of NY Coll of A&T at Cobleskill (NY)
Sterling Coll (VT)
U of Minnesota, Crookston (MN)
Winona State U (MN)

Wildlife Biology
Central Christian Coll of Kansas (KS)

Wind/Percussion Instruments
Five Towns Coll (NY)
New World School of the Arts (FL)

Women'S Studies
Indiana U–Purdue U Fort Wayne (IN)

Wood Science and Wood Products/Pulp And Paper Technology
U of Arkansas at Monticello (AR)

Word Processing
Baker Coll of Allen Park (MI)
Huron U USA in LondonUnited Kingdom)

Youth Ministry
Central Christian Coll of Kansas (KS)
Prairie Bible Coll (AB, Canada)

Zoology/Animal Biology
Central Christian Coll of Kansas (KS)

Alphabetical Listing of Two-Year Colleges

In this index, the page locations of profiles are printed in regular type, **Special Messages** in *italics,* and **In-Depth Descriptions** in **bold type.** When there is more than one number in **bold type,** it indicates that the institution has more than one **In-Depth Description;** in most such cases, the first of the series is a general institutional description.

Cambria County Area Community College (PA)	384
Cambria-Rowe Business College, Indiana (PA)	384
Cambria-Rowe Business College, Johnstown (PA)	384
Cambridge College (CO)	122
Camden County College (NJ)	*297*
Camelot College (LA)	218
Cameron College (LA)	218
Cankdeska Cikana Community College (ND)	350
Cañada College (CA)	88
Cape Cod Community College (MA)	237
Cape Fear Community College (NC)	335
Capital Community College (CT)	130
Career College of Northern Nevada (NV)	291
Career Colleges of Chicago (IL)	164
Career Technical College (LA)	218
Career Training Academy, Monroeville (PA)	385
Career Training Academy, New Kensington (PA)	385
Career Training Academy, Pittsburgh (PA)	385
Carl Albert State College (OK)	372
Carl Sandburg College (IL)	164
Carolinas College of Health Sciences (NC)	335
Carroll Community College (MD)	230
Carteret Community College (NC)	336
Cascadia Community College (WA)	466
Casper College (WY)	486
Catawba Valley Community College (NC)	336
Cayuga County Community College (NY)	312
Cecil Community College (MD)	230
Cedar Valley College (TX)	429
Center for Advanced Legal Studies (TX)	429
Center for Advanced Manufacturing & Technology (PA)	385
Central Alabama Community College (AL)	62
Central Arizona College (AZ)	71
Central Carolina Community College (NC)	336
Central Carolina Technical College (SC)	411
Central Community College–Columbus Campus (NE)	286
Central Community College–Grand Island Campus (NE)	286
Central Community College–Hastings Campus (NE)	287
Central Florida College (FL)	136
Central Florida Community College (FL)	136
Central Florida Institute (FL)	136
Central Georgia Technical College (GA)	152
Centralia College (WA)	466
Central Kentucky Technical College (KY)	210
Central Lakes College (MN)	257
Central Maine Community College (ME)	226
Central Maine Medical Center School of Nursing (ME)	226
Central Ohio Technical College (OH)	354
Central Oregon Community College (OR)	*376*
Central Pennsylvania College (PA)	*385*
Central Piedmont Community College (NC)	336
Central Texas College (TX)	429, **526**
Central Virginia Community College (VA)	454
Central Wyoming College (WY)	486
Centro de Estudios Multidisciplinarios (PR)	490
Century College (MN)	257
Cerritos College (CA)	88
Cerro Coso Community College (CA)	88
Chabot College (CA)	88
Chaffey College (CA)	89
Chandler-Gilbert Community College (AZ)	72
Chaparral College (AZ)	72
Charter College (AK)	69
Chatfield College (OH)	355
Chattahoochee Technical College (GA)	153
Chattahoochee Valley Community College (AL)	63
Chattanooga State Technical Community College (TN)	419
Chemeketa Community College (OR)	377
Chesapeake College (MD)	230
Chief Dull Knife College (MT)	284
CHI Institute (PA)	385
CHI Institute, RETS Campus (PA)	385
Chipola College (FL)	136
Chippewa Valley Technical College (WI)	478
Churchman Business School (PA)	385
Cincinnati College of Mortuary Science (OH)	355
Cincinnati State Technical and Community College (OH)	355
Cisco Junior College (TX)	430
Citrus College (CA)	89
City College, Casselberry (FL)	137
City College, Fort Lauderdale (FL)	137
City College, Gainesville (FL)	137
City College, Miami (FL)	137
City College of San Francisco (CA)	89
City Colleges of Chicago, Harold Washington College (IL)	165

City Colleges of Chicago, Harry S. Truman College (IL)	165
City Colleges of Chicago, Kennedy-King College (IL)	165
City Colleges of Chicago, Malcolm X College (IL)	165
City Colleges of Chicago, Olive-Harvey College (IL)	166
City Colleges of Chicago, Richard J. Daley College (IL)	166
City Colleges of Chicago, Wilbur Wright College (IL)	166
Clackamas Community College (OR)	377
Clarendon College (TX)	430
Clark College (WA)	466
Clark State Community College (OH)	356
Clatsop Community College (OR)	377
Cleveland Community College (NC)	337
Cleveland Institute of Electronics (OH)	356
Cleveland State Community College (TN)	419
Clinton Community College (IA)	194
Clinton Community College (NY)	312
Clinton Junior College (SC)	411
Cloud County Community College (KS)	203
Clover Park Technical College (WA)	467
Clovis Community College (NM)	303
Coahoma Community College (MS)	269
Coastal Bend College (TX)	430
Coastal Carolina Community College (NC)	337
Coastal Georgia Community College (GA)	153
Coastline Community College (CA)	89
Cochise College, Douglas (AZ)	72
Cochise College, Sierra Vista (AZ)	72
Cochran School of Nursing (NY)	312
Coconino Community College (AZ)	72
Coffeyville Community College (KS)	203
Colby Community College (KS)	*203*
Coleman College, San Marcos (CA)	89
CollegeAmerica–Colorado Springs (CO)	122
CollegeAmerica–Denver (CO)	122
CollegeAmerica–Flagstaff (AZ)	73
CollegeAmerica–Fort Collins (CO)	122
College of Alameda (CA)	90
College of Art Advertising (OH)	356
College of Business and Technology (FL)	137
College of Court Reporting (IN)	183
College of DuPage (IL)	166
College of Eastern Utah (UT)	450
College of Lake County (IL)	167
College of Marin (CA)	90
College of Menominee Nation (WI)	478
College of Micronesia–FSM (FM)	490
College of Oceaneering (CA)	90
The College of Office Technology (IL)	167
College of San Mateo (CA)	90
College of Southern Idaho (ID)	163
College of Southern Maryland (MD)	231
College of The Albemarle (NC)	337
College of the Canyons (CA)	90
College of the Desert (CA)	90
College of the Mainland (TX)	431
College of the Marshall Islands (Marshall Islands)	491
College of the Redwoods (CA)	91
College of the Sequoias (CA)	91
College of the Siskiyous (CA)	*91*
The College of Westchester (NY)	313, **528**
Collin County Community College District (TX)	431
Colorado Mountain College, Alpine Campus (CO)	122
Colorado Mountain College, Spring Valley Campus (CO)	*122*, **530**
Colorado Mountain College, Timberline Campus (CO)	123
Colorado Northwestern Community College (CO)	*123*
Colorado School of Healing Arts (CO)	124
Colorado School of Trades (CO)	124
Columbia Basin College (WA)	467
Columbia College (CA)	92
Columbia College, Yauco (PR)	490
Columbia Gorge Community College (OR)	378
Columbia-Greene Community College (NY)	313
Columbia State Community College (TN)	419
Columbus State Community College (OH)	356
Columbus Technical College (GA)	153
Commonwealth Business College, Merrillville (IN)	183
Commonwealth Business College, Michigan City (IN)	184
Commonwealth Institute of Funeral Service (TX)	431
Commonwealth Technical Institute (PA)	386
Community College of Allegheny County (PA)	386, **532**
Community College of Aurora (CO)	124
The Community College of Baltimore County (MD)	231
Community College of Beaver County (PA)	386
Community College of Denver (CO)	124
Community College of Philadelphia (PA)	386
Community College of Rhode Island (RI)	410

Community College of Southern Nevada (NV)	291
Community College of the Air Force (AL)	63
Community College of Vermont (VT)	453
Compton Community College (CA)	92
Computer Career Center (TX)	431
ConCorde Career College (TN)	420
Concorde Career Institute (CA)	92
Concorde Career Institute (MO)	274
Connors State College (OK)	372
Consolidated School of Business, Lancaster (PA)	386
Consolidated School of Business, York (PA)	387
Contra Costa College (CA)	92
The Cooking and Hospitality Institute of Chicago (IL)	167, **534**
Cooper Career Institute (FL)	137
Coosa Valley Technical College (GA)	153
Copiah-Lincoln Community College (MS)	269
Copiah-Lincoln Community College–Natchez Campus (MS)	269
Copper Mountain College (CA)	93
Corning Community College (NY)	313
Cossatot Community College of the University of Arkansas (AR)	80
Cosumnes River College (CA)	93
Cottey College (MO)	274
County College of Morris (NJ)	297
Court Reporting Institute of Dallas (TX)	432
Court Reporting Institute of Houston (TX)	432
Cowley County Community College and Area Vocational–Technical School (KS)	204
Crafton Hills College (CA)	93
Craven Community College (NC)	338
The Creative Center (NE)	287
Crestmont College (CA)	93
Crouse Hospital School of Nursing (NY)	314
Crowder College (MO)	274
Crowley's Ridge College (AR)	80
Crown College (WA)	467
Crownpoint Institute of Technology (NM)	303
Cuesta College (CA)	93
Cumberland County College (NJ)	298
Cuyahoga Community College (OH)	357
Cuyamaca College (CA)	94
Cy-Fair College (TX)	432
Cypress College (CA)	94
Dabney S. Lancaster Community College (VA)	454
Dakota County Technical College (MN)	257
Dallas Institute of Funeral Service (TX)	432
Danville Area Community College (IL)	168
Danville Community College (VA)	454
Darton College (GA)	153
Davenport University, Granger (IN)	184
Davenport University, Hammond (IN)	184
Davenport University, Merrillville (IN)	184
Davenport University, Alma (MI)	244
Davenport University, Bad Axe (MI)	244
Davenport University, Bay City (MI)	244
Davenport University, Caro (MI)	244
Davenport University, Midland (MI)	244
Davenport University, Romeo (MI)	244
Davenport University, Saginaw (MI)	244
Davidson County Community College (NC)	338
Davis College (OH)	357
Dawson Community College (MT)	284
Daymar College, Louisville (KY)	210
Daymar College, Owensboro (KY)	210
Daytona Beach Community College (FL)	137
Dean College (MA)	*237*, **536**
Dean Institute of Technology (PA)	387
De Anza College (CA)	94
Deep Springs College (CA)	94
DeKalb Technical College (GA)	154
Delaware College of Art and Design (DE)	134
Delaware County Community College (PA)	387
Delaware Technical & Community College, Jack F. Owens Campus (DE)	134
Delaware Technical & Community College, Stanton/Wilmington Campus (DE)	134
Delaware Technical & Community College, Terry Campus (DE)	135
Delgado Community College (LA)	218
Del Mar College (TX)	432
Delta College (MI)	244
Delta College of Arts and Technology (LA)	219
Delta School of Business & Technology (LA)	219
Denmark Technical College (SC)	411
Denver Academy of Court Reporting (CO)	125
Denver Automotive and Diesel College (CO)	125
Des Moines Area Community College (IA)	194
Diablo Valley College (CA)	94
DigiPen Institute of Technology (WA)	467
Diné College (AZ)	73
Dixie State College of Utah (UT)	450
Dodge City Community College (KS)	204

Don Bosco College of Science and Technology (CA)	95
Doña Ana Branch Community College (NM)	303
Donnelly College (KS)	204
Dorothea Hopfer School of Nursing at The Mount Vernon Hospital (NY)	314
Douglas Education Center (PA)	388
D-Q University (CA)	95
Draughons Junior College (KY)	211
Draughons Junior College, Clarksville (TN)	420
Draughons Junior College, Nashville (TN)	420
DuBois Business College (PA)	388
Duff's Business Institute (PA)	388
Duluth Business University (MN)	258
Dunwoody College of Technology (MN)	258
Durham Technical Community College (NC)	338
Dutchess Community College (NY)	314
Dyersburg State Community College (TN)	420
East Arkansas Community College (AR)	81
East Central College (MO)	275
East Central Community College (MS)	270
East Central Technical Institute (GA)	154
Eastern Arizona College (AZ)	73
Eastern Idaho Technical College (ID)	163
Eastern Maine Community College (ME)	227
Eastern New Mexico University–Roswell (NM)	304
Eastern Oklahoma State College (OK)	373
Eastern Shore Community College (VA)	454
Eastern West Virginia Community and Technical College (WV)	475
Eastern Wyoming College (WY)	487
Eastfield College (TX)	433
East Georgia College (GA)	154
East Los Angeles College (CA)	95
East Mississippi Community College (MS)	270
ECPI College of Technology, Newport News (VA)	455
ECPI College of Technology, Virginia Beach (VA)	455
ECPI Technical College (NC)	338
ECPI Technical College, Glen Allen (VA)	455
ECPI Technical College, Richmond (VA)	455
ECPI Technical College, Roanoke (VA)	456
Edgecombe Community College (NC)	338
Edison Community College (FL)	137
Edison State Community College (OH)	357
Edmonds Community College (WA)	467
Education Direct Center for Degree Studies (PA)	388, **538**
Elaine P. Nunez Community College (LA)	219
El Camino College (CA)	95
El Centro College (TX)	433
Electronic Computer Programming College (TN)	420
Electronic Data Processing College of Puerto Rico–San Sebastian (PR)	490
Electronic Institute, Middletown (PA)	388
Elgin Community College (IL)	168
Elizabethtown Community College (KY)	211
Elizabethtown Technical College (KY)	211
Ellis Hospital School of Nursing (NY)	315
Ellsworth Community College (IA)	195
Elmira Business Institute (NY)	315
El Paso Community College (TX)	434
Emory University, Oxford College (GA)	155
Empire College (CA)	95
Enterprise-Ozark Community College (AL)	63
Erie Business Center, Main (PA)	388
Erie Business Center South (PA)	388
Erie Community College (NY)	315
Erie Institute of Technology (PA)	389
Essex County College (NJ)	298
Estrella Mountain Community College (AZ)	73
ETI Technical College of Niles (OH)	358
Eugenio María de Hostos Community College of the City University of New York (NY)	315
Everest College (AZ)	73
Everest College (CA)	96
Everest College, Arlington (TX)	434
Everest College, Dallas (TX)	434
Everett Community College (WA)	468
Evergreen Valley College (CA)	96
Fairmont State Community & Technical College (WV)	475, **540**
Fashion Careers of California College (CA)	96
Fashion Institute of Design and Merchandising, Los Angeles Campus (CA)	96, **542**
Fashion Institute of Design and Merchandising, Orange County (CA)	96
Fashion Institute of Design and Merchandising, San Diego Campus (CA)	96
Fashion Institute of Design and Merchandising, San Francisco Campus (CA)	97
Fayetteville Technical Community College (NC)	338
Feather River Community College District (CA)	97
FINE Mortuary College (MA)	238
Finger Lakes Community College (NY)	316

Fiorello H. LaGuardia Community College of the City University of New York (NY)	*316*
Fisher College (MA)	238, **544**
Flathead Valley Community College (MT)	*284*
Flint Hills Technical College (KS)	205
Flint River Technical College (GA)	155
Florence-Darlington Technical College (SC)	411
Florida Career College (FL)	138
Florida College of Natural Health, Altamonte Springs (FL)	138
Florida College of Natural Health, Miami (FL)	138
Florida College of Natural Health, Pompano Beach (FL)	138
Florida College of Natural Health, Sarasota (FL)	138
Florida Community College at Jacksonville (FL)	138
Florida Culinary Institute (FL)	138
Florida Hospital College of Health Sciences (FL)	138
Florida Keys Community College (FL)	139
Florida Metropolitan University–Orange Park Campus (FL)	139
Florida National College (FL)	139, **546**
The Florida School of Midwifery (FL)	139
Florida Technical College, Auburndale (FL)	139
Florida Technical College, DeLand (FL)	139
Florida Technical College, Jacksonville (FL)	139
Florida Technical College, Orlando (FL)	139
Floyd College (GA)	155
Fond du Lac Tribal and Community College (MN)	258
Foothill College (CA)	97
Forrest Junior College (SC)	411
Forsyth Technical Community College (NC)	339
Fort Belknap College (MT)	284
Fort Berthold Community College (ND)	350
Fort Peck Community College (MT)	285
Fort Scott Community College (KS)	205
Foundation College, San Diego (CA)	98
Fountainhead College of Technology (TN)	420
Fox College (IL)	168
Fox Valley Technical College (WI)	478
Frank Phillips College (TX)	434
Frederick Community College (MD)	231
Fresno City College (CA)	98
Front Range Community College (CO)	125
Fullerton College (CA)	98
Full Sail Real World Education (FL)	139
Fulton-Montgomery Community College (NY)	317
Gadsden State Community College (AL)	63
Gadsden State Community College-Ayers Campus (AL)	64
Gainesville College (GA)	155
Gallipolis Career College (OH)	358
Galveston College (TX)	434
Gamla College (NY)	317
Garden City Community College (KS)	205
Garrett College (MD)	232
Gaston College (NC)	339
Gateway Community and Technical College (KY)	211
GateWay Community College (AZ)	74
Gateway Community College (CT)	130
Gateway Technical College (WI)	478
Gavilan College (CA)	98
Gem City College (IL)	168
Genesee Community College (NY)	317
George Corley Wallace State Community College (AL)	64
George C. Wallace Community College (AL)	64
Georgia Aviation & Technical College (GA)	155
Georgia Medical Institute–DeKalb (GA)	155
Georgia Military College (GA)	155
Georgia Perimeter College (GA)	155
Germanna Community College (VA)	456
Gibbs College (CT)	131
Gibbs College (MA)	238
Gibbs College (NJ)	299
Glendale Community College (AZ)	74
Glendale Community College (CA)	99
Glen Oaks Community College (MI)	245
Globe College (MN)	258
Gloucester County College (NJ)	299
Gogebic Community College (MI)	245
Golden West College (CA)	99
Goodwin College (CT)	131
Gordon College (GA)	156
Grand Rapids Community College (MI)	245
Grays Harbor College (WA)	468
Grayson County College (TX)	434
Great Basin College (NV)	291
Greenfield Community College (MA)	238
Green River Community College (WA)	468
Greenville Technical College (SC)	412
Gretna Career College (LA)	219
Griffin Technical College (GA)	156
Grossmont College (CA)	99
Guam Community College (GU)	490

Guilford Technical Community College (NC)	340
Gulf Coast Community College (FL)	140
Gupton-Jones College of Funeral Service (GA)	156
Gwinnett Technical College (GA)	156
Hagerstown Business College (MD)	232
Hagerstown Community College (MD)	232
Halifax Community College (NC)	340
Hallmark Institute of Aeronautics (TX)	434
Hallmark Institute of Technology (TX)	434
Hamilton College (IA)	195
Hamilton College (NE)	287
Hamilton College-Lincoln (NE)	287
Harcum College (PA)	389, **548**
Harford Community College (MD)	233
Harrisburg Area Community College (PA)	389
Hartnell College (CA)	99
Hawaii Business College (HI)	160
Hawaii Community College (HI)	161
Hawaii Tokai International College (HI)	161
Hawkeye Community College (IA)	195
Haywood Community College (NC)	340
Hazard Community and Technical College (KY)	211
Heald College-Concord (CA)	99
Heald College-Fresno (CA)	99
Heald College-Hayward (CA)	99
Heald College-Honolulu (HI)	161
Heald College-Portland (OR)	378
Heald College-Rancho Cordova (CA)	99
Heald College-Roseville (CA)	100
Heald College-Salinas (CA)	100
Heald College-San Francisco (CA)	100
Heald College-San Jose (CA)	100
Heald College-Stockton (CA)	100
Heartland Community College (IL)	168
Heart of Georgia Technical College (GA)	157
Helene Fuld College of Nursing of North General Hospital (NY)	317
Henderson Community College (KY)	212
Hennepin Technical College (MN)	259
Henry Ford Community College (MI)	246
Heritage College (CO)	125
Heritage College (MO)	275
Heritage College (NV)	292
Heritage College of Hair Design (OK)	373
Herkimer County Community College (NY)	317
Herzing College (AL)	64
Herzing College, Winter Park (FL)	140
Herzing College (GA)	157
Herzing College (LA)	219
Herzing College (WI)	479
Herzing College, Lakeland Medical–Dental Division (MN)	259
Herzing College, Minneapolis Drafting School Division (MN)	259
Hesser College (NH)	293, **550**
Hesston College (KS)	206
Hibbing Community College (MN)	259
Hickey College (MO)	*275*
Highland Community College (IL)	169
Highland Community College (KS)	206
Highline Community College (WA)	*469*
High-Tech Institute (AZ)	74
High-Tech Institute (CA)	100
High-Tech Institute (GA)	157
High-Tech Institute (MN)	259
High-Tech Institute (MO)	275
High-Tech Institute (NV)	292
High-Tech Institute, Memphis (TN)	420
High-Tech Institute, Nashville (TN)	420
High-Tech Institute (TX)	434
Hill College of the Hill Junior College District (TX)	434
Hillsborough Community College (FL)	140
Hinds Community College (MS)	270
Hiwassee College (TN)	421
Hocking College (OH)	358
Holmes Community College (MS)	271
Holy Cross College (IN)	184, **552**
Holyoke Community College (MA)	238
Hondros College (OH)	358
Honolulu Community College (HI)	161
Hopkinsville Community College (KY)	212
Horry-Georgetown Technical College (SC)	412
Housatonic Community College (CT)	131
Houston Community College System (TX)	435
Howard College (TX)	435
Howard Community College (MD)	233
Hudson County Community College (NJ)	299
Hudson Valley Community College (NY)	318
Huertas Junior College (PR)	490
Humacao Community College (PR)	490
Huntington Junior College (WV)	475
Hussian School of Art (PA)	390
Hutchinson Community College and Area Vocational School (KS)	206

Quinsigamond Community College (MA)	242
Rainy River Community College (MN)	265
Ramírez College of Business and Technology (PR)	491
Randolph Community College (NC)	344
Ranger College (TX)	443
Ranken Technical College (MO)	280
Rappahannock Community College (VA)	462
Raritan Valley Community College (NJ)	301
Rasmussen College Eagan (MN)	265
Rasmussen College Mankato (MN)	265
Rasmussen College Minnetonka (MN)	266
Rasmussen College St. Cloud (MN)	266
Reading Area Community College (PA)	405
Redlands Community College (OK)	375
Red Rocks Community College (CO)	128
Reedley College (CA)	111
The Refrigeration School (AZ)	77
Reid State Technical College (AL)	67
Remington College–Baton Rouge Campus (LA)	225
Remington College–Cleveland Campus (OH)	368
Remington College–Cleveland West Campus (OH)	368
Remington College–Dallas Campus (TX)	443
Remington College–Fort Worth Campus (TX)	444
Remington College–Houston Campus (TX)	444
Remington College–Jacksonville Campus (FL)	147
Remington College–Lafayette Campus (LA)	225
Remington College–Little Rock Campus (AR)	83
Remington College–Memphis Campus (TN)	425
Remington College–Mobile Campus (AL)	67
Remington College–Nashville Campus (TN)	425
Remington College–New Orleans Campus (LA)	225
Remington College–Pinellas Campus (FL)	147
Remington College–Tampa Campus (FL)	147
Rend Lake College (IL)	178
Renton Technical College (WA)	472
The Restaurant School at Walnut Hill College (PA)	405, **598**
RETS Institute of Technology (KY)	216
RETS Institute of Technology (PA)	406
RETS Medical and Business Institute (KY)	216
RETS Tech Center (OH)	368
Richard Bland College of The College of William and Mary (VA)	462
Richland College (TX)	444
Richland Community College (IL)	178
Richmond Community College (NC)	344
Rich Mountain Community College (AR)	83
Ridgewater College (MN)	266
Rio Hondo College (CA)	111
Rio Salado College (AZ)	78
Riverland Community College (MN)	267
River Parishes Community College (LA)	225
Riverside Community College (CA)	112
Roane State Community College (TN)	425
Roanoke-Chowan Community College (NC)	345
Robeson Community College (NC)	345
Rochester Business Institute (NY)	325
Rochester Community and Technical College (MN)	267
Rockford Business College (IL)	178
Rockingham Community College (NC)	345
Rockland Community College (NY)	326
Rock Valley College (IL)	179
Rogue Community College (OR)	379
Rosedale Bible College (OH)	368
Rosedale Technical Institute (PA)	406
Rose State College (OK)	375
Rowan-Cabarrus Community College (NC)	345
Rowan Technical College (KY)	216
Roxbury Community College (MA)	242
Sacramento City College (CA)	112
Saddleback College (CA)	112
Sage College (CA)	112
Saginaw Chippewa Tribal College (MI)	252
St. Catharine College (KY)	216
Saint Charles Community College (MO)	280
St. Clair County Community College (MI)	252
St. Cloud Technical College (MN)	267
St. Elizabeth College of Nursing (NY)	326
St. Johns River Community College (FL)	147
Saint Joseph's Hospital Health Center School of Nursing (NY)	326
St. Louis Community College at Florissant Valley (MO)	281
St. Louis Community College at Forest Park (MO)	281
St. Louis Community College at Meramec (MO)	281
St. Luke's College (IA)	200
Saint Paul College–A Community & Technical College (MN)	268
St. Petersburg College (FL)	148
St. Philip's College (TX)	444
Saint Vincent Catholic Medical Centers School of Nursing (NY)	326
St. Vincent's College (CT)	133
Salem Community College (NJ)	301

Salish Kootenai College (MT)	285
Salt Lake Community College (UT)	451
Samaritan Hospital School of Nursing (NY)	326
Sampson Community College (NC)	346
San Antonio College (TX)	444
San Bernardino Valley College (CA)	112
Sandersville Technical College (GA)	158
Sandhills Community College (NC)	346
San Diego City College (CA)	112
San Diego Golf Academy (CA)	113
San Diego Mesa College (CA)	113
San Diego Miramar College (CA)	113
Sanford-Brown College, Fenton (MO)	281
Sanford-Brown College, Hazelwood (MO)	281
Sanford-Brown College, North Kansas City (MO)	282
Sanford-Brown College, St. Charles (MO)	282
San Joaquin Delta College (CA)	113
San Joaquin Valley College (CA)	113
San Jose City College (CA)	114
San Juan College (NM)	306
Santa Ana College (CA)	114
Santa Barbara City College (CA)	114
Santa Fe Community College (FL)	148
Santa Fe Community College (NM)	306
Santa Monica College (CA)	115, **600**
Santa Rosa Junior College (CA)	115
Santiago Canyon College (CA)	115
Sauk Valley Community College (IL)	179
Savannah Technical College (GA)	158
Sawyer College, Hammond (IN)	193
Sawyer College, Merrillville (IN)	193
Schenectady County Community College (NY)	326
Schiller International University (Switzerland)	491
Schoolcraft College (MI)	253
School of Advertising Art (OH)	368
School of Communication Arts (NC)	346
School of Urban Missions–New Orleans (LA)	225
Schuylkill Institute of Business and Technology (PA)	406
Scott Community College (IA)	200
Scottsdale Community College (AZ)	78
Scottsdale Culinary Institute (AZ)	78
Seattle Central Community College (WA)	472
Seminole Community College (FL)	148
Seminole State College (OK)	375
Sequoia Institute (CA)	115
Seward County Community College (KS)	209
Shasta College (CA)	115
Shawnee Community College (IL)	179
Shelton State Community College (AL)	68
Sheridan College (WY)	488
Shoreline Community College (WA)	472
Sierra College (CA)	116
Silicon Valley College, Emeryville (CA)	116
Silicon Valley College, Fremont (CA)	116
Silicon Valley College, San Jose (CA)	116
Silicon Valley College, Walnut Creek (CA)	116
Simmons Institute of Funeral Service (NY)	327
Sinclair Community College (OH)	368
Sisseton-Wahpeton Community College (SD)	418
Sitting Bull College (ND)	351
Skagit Valley College (WA)	472
Skyline College (CA)	117
Snead State Community College (AL)	68
Snow College (UT)	451
Solano Community College (CA)	117
Somerset Christian College (NJ)	301
Somerset Community College (KY)	216
Sonoma College, Petaluma (CA)	117
Sonoma College, San Francisco (CA)	117
South Arkansas Community College (AR)	83
South Central Technical College (MN)	268
South Coast College (CA)	117
South College (TN)	425
South College-Asheville (NC)	346
Southeast Arkansas College (AR)	84
Southeast Community College (KY)	216
Southeast Community College, Beatrice Campus (NE)	290
Southeast Community College, Lincoln Campus (NE)	290
Southeast Community College, Milford Campus (NE)	290
Southeastern Business College, Chillicothe (OH)	369
Southeastern Business College, Jackson (OH)	369
Southeastern Business College, Lancaster (OH)	369
Southeastern Career College (TN)	425
Southeastern Career Institute (TX)	444
Southeastern Community College (NC)	346
Southeastern Community College, North Campus (IA)	200
Southeastern Community College, South Campus (IA)	200
Southeastern Illinois College (IL)	179

Southeastern Technical College (GA)	158
Southeast Missouri Hospital College of Nursing and Health Sciences (MO)	282
Southeast Technical Institute (SD)	418
Southern Arkansas University Tech (AR)	84
Southern California Institute of Technology (CA)	117
Southern Maine Community College (ME)	228
Southern State Community College (OH)	369
Southern Union State Community College (AL)	69
Southern University at Shreveport (LA)	226
Southern West Virginia Community and Technical College (WV)	476
South Florida Community College (FL)	149
South Georgia College (GA)	159
South Georgia Technical College (GA)	159
South Hills School of Business & Technology, Altoona (PA)	406
South Hills School of Business & Technology, State College (PA)	406
South Mountain Community College (AZ)	78
South Piedmont Community College (NC)	347
South Plains College (TX)	444
South Puget Sound Community College (WA)	472
South Seattle Community College (WA)	473
Southside Virginia Community College (VA)	462
South Suburban College (IL)	179
South Texas Community College (TX)	445
South University (FL)	149
South University (SC)	413
Southwestern College (CA)	117
Southwestern College of Business (KY)	217
Southwestern College of Business, Cincinnati (OH)	369
Southwestern College of Business, Cincinnati (OH)	369
Southwestern College of Business, Dayton (OH)	369
Southwestern College of Business, Middletown (OH)	370
Southwestern Community College (IA)	200
Southwestern Community College (NC)	347
Southwestern Illinois College (IL)	180
Southwestern Indian Polytechnic Institute (NM)	307
Southwestern Michigan College (MI)	253
Southwestern Oklahoma State University at Sayre (OK)	375
Southwestern Oregon Community College (OR)	380
Southwest Florida College (FL)	149
Southwest Georgia Technical College (GA)	159
Southwest Institute of Healing Arts (AZ)	78
Southwest Institute of Technology (TX)	445
Southwest Mississippi Community College (MS)	273
Southwest Missouri State University–West Plains (MO)	282
Southwest Tennessee Community College (TN)	425
Southwest Texas Junior College (TX)	445
Southwest Virginia Community College (VA)	463
Southwest Wisconsin Technical College (WI)	482
Spartanburg Methodist College (SC)	414, **602**
Spartanburg Technical College (SC)	414
Spartan School of Aeronautics (OK)	375
Spencerian College (KY)	217
Spencerian College–Lexington (KY)	217
Spokane Community College (WA)	473
Spokane Falls Community College (WA)	473
Spoon River College (IL)	180
Springfield College (MO)	282
Springfield College in Illinois (IL)	181
Springfield Technical Community College (MA)	242
Stanly Community College (NC)	347
Stark State College of Technology (OH)	370
State Fair Community College (MO)	282
State University of New York College of Agriculture and Technology at Morrisville (NY)	327
State University of New York College of Environmental Science & Forestry, Ranger School (NY)	328, **604**
State University of New York College of Technology at Alfred (NY)	328
State University of New York College of Technology at Canton (NY)	329
State University of New York College of Technology at Delhi (NY)	329
Stautzenberger College (OH)	370
Stevens-Henager College (UT)	452
Stone Child College (MT)	286
Suffolk County Community College (NY)	329
Sullivan County Community College (NY)	330
Summit Institute (FL)	149
Surry Community College (NC)	347
Sussex County Community College (NJ)	302
Swainsboro Technical College (GA)	159
Tacoma Community College (WA)	474
Taft College (CA)	118
Tallahassee Community College (FL)	149